An essential Textbook for UG students in Engineering Colleges, Institutes and Universities in Electrical Engg., Electronics and Telecommunication Engg., Computer Science Engg., M.Sc. (Electronics), Applied Physics and Instrumentation Engg. Also suitable for AMIE, Grad IETE syllabus and GATE, UPSC, and other competitive examinations.

Circuit Theory

(Analysis And Synthesis)

8th Revised Edition

DR. ABHIJIT CHAKRABARTI

B.E. (Electrical), M.Tech., (Power Apparatus & Systems),
Ph.D. (Tech.), C. Eng., F.I.E. (I), M.I.E.T. (UK)
***Former** Vice Chancellor, Jadavpur University, Kolkata*
***Former** Vice Chairman and Chairman (actg.)*
West Bengal State Council of Higher Education, W.B.
Professor(HAG) Retd. and Ex. Head, Deptt. of Electrical Engineering
Indian Institute of Engineering Science and Technology, Shibpur
Howrah-711103 (W.B.)

DHANPAT RAI & CO. (Pvt.) Ltd.
EDUCATIONAL & TECHNICAL PUBLISHERS

Published by : GAGAN KAPUR
Dhanpat Rai & Co. (P) Ltd., Delhi

Regd. Office : 4576/15, Agarwal Road
Darya Ganj, New Delhi-110002
Phone : 2324 7736, 37, 38, dhanpatrai@gmail.com

Proof reading, referencing and editing assistance : *P. Bandyopadhyay* and *Paramita Seal*

Technical Assistance and computing : *Agnimitro Chakrabarti*

Disclaimer

Every effort has been made to avoid errors or omissions in this publication. In spite of this, some errors might have crept in. Any mistake, error or discrepancy noted may be brought to our notice which shall be taken care of in the next edition. It is notified that neither the publisher nor the author or seller will be responsible for any damage or loss of action to any one, of any kind, in any manner, therefrom.

EDITIONS : 1999, 2001, 2003, 2004, 2006, 2010, 2015

REPRINT EDITION : 2000, 02, 03, 05, 07-09, 2011, 2012, 2013, 2016, 2017, 2018, 2019

EIGHTH EDITION : 2023

REPRINT : 2025

PRICE : ₹ 725/-

Typesetting by : North Delhi Computer Convention, Delhi–110009,
ndcc.in@gmail.com

Printed at : Natraj Offset, Delhi

Preface To The Eighth Edition

This book is once again thoroughly revised and reoriented as per latest revised syllabi of different Universities, Institutes and AICTE. A new chapter containing quality MCQ problems has been added in order to provoke the interest of the students for self learning and paying in-depth thoughts to analyse the problems in circuit (network) theory.

The text and the worked out problems, including harder and thought proving problems, are redistributed to suit the need of students preparing for semester examinations as well as for professional and competitive examinations.

The author acknowledges the assistance of his family members for supporting the revision exercise of the author. The author expects that the new edition will be more helpful and encouraging. Any suggestion in this regard will be highly appreciated.

Kolkata, October, 2022 **AUTHOR**

Preface To The First Edition

The subject of "Circuit Theory" can be divided into two broad categories — Analysis and Synthesis. In analysis, the network being given, the object is to determine the aspects (*i.e.*, circuit variables and or parameters). On the other hand, in synthesis, some operating characteristics are specified and the problem is to find such a network. For most of the linear network problems, a formal solution does exists, the tools of solution being the network theorems and other performance analysis techniques. However, there is nothing resembling a formal solution applicable to each and every problem for circuit synthesis and limited number of tools available in order to realise a given function in terms of practical networks.

In this book attempts have been made to present an unique self-study format for both circuit analysis and synthesis parts. The subject-matter is divided into chapters covering duly recognised areas of theory and study. The chapters begin with statements of pertinent definitions, principles and theorems together with illustrative examples. This is followed by sets of additional solved examples matching the theory presented and amplifying the presented theoretical concepts. The illustrative examples as well as the supplementary problems give the reader an opportunity to have a wider exposure and to develop problem-solving skills. At the end of each chapter numerical sums similar to the solved examples have been included alongwith short hints.

The topics covered in this book include fundamental circuit responses, application of Kirchhoff's laws including node voltage and mesh current methods in circuit analysis, sinusoidal steady state analysis, polyphase circuits, network theorems both in d.c. and a.c. circuits, analysis of signal waveforms, circuit transients, Laplace transformation and its application in electric circuits, mutually coupled circuits, two port networks, network functions, graph thoery, Fourier analysis, network synthesis etc.

Though this book is primarily prepared for the syllabi of circuit theory or network analysis in Engineering degree colleges and Universities, it would be highly suitable for IETE and AMIE courses as well as for GATE, UPSC and other competitive examinations.

In this context I want to express my gratitude towards the Vice Chancellor of BE College (Deemed University) for granting me permission in publishing the book and to the editorial staff of M/s Dhanpat Rai and Company Pvt. Ltd, Delhi, particularly to Sh. Gagan Kapur, and O.P Choudhary. I must acknowledge the support and encouragement of Sh. J.C. Kapur in preparation of the manuscript and coordinating the entire job of editing, proof reading, drafting etc. in a short span of time. I must acknowledge the overall guidance of my respected teacher Prof. (Dr.) A.K. Mukhopadhyay, Dean, Calcutta University.

My sinceremost thanks go to Ms. P. Bandyopadhyay who has put her hard labour in checking each and individual circuit diagram alongwith the final proof of this book, including the preparation of the index.

Any suggestion and constructive criticism in the development of this book will be appreciated.

A. CHAKRABARTI

Dedicated to
my Mother
Late Anjali Chakrabarti

– AUTHOR

Contents

7 Laplace Transformation and its Application in Electric Circuit Analysis 369 – 422

8 Analysis of Special Signal Waveforms 423 – 446

9 Analysis of Coupled Circuits 447 – 476

13 Network Topology (Graph Theory) 657 – 696

14 Fourier Analysis 697 – 720

CHAPTER

1

DC Network Analysis

1.1 CIRCUIT ELEMENTS

1.1.1 Resistance

Electrical *resistance* is the property of a material by virtue of which it opposes the flow of electrons through the material. Thus, resistance restricts the flow of electric current through the material. The unit of resistance (R) being "ohm" (Ω), quantitatively it is obtained from Ohm's law*. The resistance offered by a material when a current of I ampere flows through it with V volt potential difference across the material is obtained as

$$R = \frac{V}{I} \qquad ...(1.1)$$

When an electric current flows through any conductor, heat is generated due to collision of free electrons with atoms. If I amps be the strength of current for a potential difference of V volts across the conductor, the *power* absorbed by the resistor is given by

$$P = VI = (IR)\, I = I^2 R \text{ watts} \qquad ...(1.2)$$

The *energy* lost in the resistance in form of heat is then expressed as

$$W = \int_0^t P . dt = Pt = I^2\ Rt = \frac{V^2}{R} \times t \qquad ...(1.3)$$

1.1.2 Inductance

Inductance is the property of a material by virtue of which it opposes any change of magnitude or direction of electric current passing through the conductor. The unit of inductance being "henry" (L), it is given by Faraday's laws of Electromagnetic Induction. Inductance is said to be one henry when current through a coil of conductor changes at the rate of one ampere per second inducing one volt across the coil.

A wire of finite length, when twisted into a coil, it becomes a simplest *inductor*. As soon as current will flow through the coil, an electromagnetic field is formed. However, with any change of flow or direction of current, the electromagnetic field

* *Ohm's Law*. Physical condition being unchanged, the current through any conductor is directly proportional to the applied potential difference across it.

i.e. $V \propto I$ or $V = R \cdot I$ [R being the constant of proportionality termed as *resistance*]

$\therefore\ R = \frac{V}{I}$

Ohm's law is applied for any "bilateral conductor".

changes. This change of field induces a voltage (v_L) across the coil, given by (Lenz's Law)

$$v_L = -L\frac{di}{dt} \quad ...(1.4)$$

where i is the current through the inductor in ampere.

Thus, in a pure inductive circuit with applied voltage v, we can write

$$v + v_L = 0$$

or,
$$v = -v_L = L\frac{di}{dt}$$

It may be noted from equation (1.4) that the *voltage across the inductor would be zero if the current through it remains constant*. This means that an inductor behaves as a *short circuited coil* in steady state, when direct steady current flows through it. However, for any small change in current strength or change in direction, inductance will appear. It may also be observed from equation (1.4) that for a minute change in current within zero time ($dt = 0$) it gives an infinite voltage across the inductor which is physically not at all feasible. Thus in an inductor, *the current cannot change abruptly*. An inductor thus behaves as *open circuit* just after switching across d.c. voltage but as short circuit at steady state.

Also, the *power* absorbed by the inductor is given by

$$P = v \times i = Li.\frac{di}{dt} \text{ watts} \quad ...(1.5)$$

Energy absorbed by the inductor will thus be given by

$$W = \int_o^t P\,dt = \int_o^t Li\frac{di}{dt}\,dt = \frac{1}{2}Li^2 \quad ...(1.6)$$

Thus from equations (1.5) and (1.6) it is evident that the inductor can *store* finite amount of energy, even the *voltage across it may be nil. A pure inductor does not dissipate energy, but only stores it.*

1.1.3 Capacitance

It is the *capability* of an element to *store electric charge* within it. A capacitor stores electric energy in the form of electric field being established by the two polarities of charges on the two electrodes of a capacitor. Quantitatively capacitance is a measure of *charge per unit voltage* that can be stored in an element. The unit of capacitance (C) is Farad (F). The capacitance is said to be one Farad provided one coulomb of charge can be stored with one volt across the two electrodes of the element. The element, which has capacitance, is called *capacitor*.

q being the amount of charge that can be stored in a capacitor of capacitance C against a potential difference of v volts, we can write

$$C = \frac{q}{v} \quad ...(1.7)$$

i.e.,
$$i = C\frac{dv}{dt} \quad \left[\because\ i = \frac{dq}{dt}\right] \quad ...(1.8)$$

where lower case letters represent the *instantaneous* values of the respective parameters ;

or
$$dv = \frac{1}{C}\,i\,dt$$

or
$$\int_{v_o}^{v_t} dv = \frac{1}{C}\int_o^t i\,dt$$

[v_o = Initial voltage of capacitor,
v_t = Final voltage of capacitor]

or
$$v_t - v_o = \frac{1}{C}\int_o^t i\,dt$$

i.e.,
$$v_t = \frac{1}{C}\int_o^t i\,dt + v_o \quad ...(1.9)$$

The *power* absorbed by the capacitor is given by

$$p = vi = vC\frac{dv}{dt}$$

and the *energy* stored by the capacitor is

$$W = \int_o^t P\,dt = \int_o^t vC\frac{dv}{dt}\,dt = \frac{1}{2}Cv^2 \quad ...(1.10)$$

Thus, we observe that *the voltage across the capacitor being constant, current through it is zero*. This means that the capacitor, on application of d.c. voltage and with no initial charge first acts as *short circuit* but as soon as the full charge it retains, the capacitor behaves an *open circuit*. Also, a capacitor *never dissipates energy* and only stores it. It can store finite amount energy, even if the current through it is zero.

Table 1.1 exhibits the voltage current relations of the three circuit elements *R, L* and C.

Table 1.1 *Voltage-Current Relationship of Circuit Elements*

Circuit Element	Voltage (volts)	Current (amps)	Power (watts)
R (Ω)	$v = Ri$	$i = \frac{v}{R}$	$p = i^2 R$
L (H)	$v = L\frac{di}{dt}$	$i = \frac{1}{L}\int v\,dt + i_o$ [i_o being the initial current]	$p = Li\frac{di}{dt}$
C (F)	$v = \frac{1}{C}\int i dt + v_o$ [v_o being the initial voltage]	$i = C\frac{dv}{dt}$	$p = Cv\frac{dv}{dt}$

Since at steady state i in the inductor and v in capacitor are zero hence energy consumed (W) is zero for both inductor and capacitor in steady state.

EXAMPLE 1.1 *A 100 Ω resistance is directly switched on across a 10 V battery. What is the current through the resistor ? How much is the power loss ? Also find the energy consumed in 5 secs.*

SOLUTION. From the given data

$$V = 10\text{ V}, \quad R = 100\,\Omega;$$

$$\therefore \quad I = \frac{V}{R} = \frac{10}{100} = \mathbf{0.1\ A}$$

Power loss $= I^2 R = (0.1)^2 \times 100 = \mathbf{1\ W.}$

$$\left[\text{Also Power loss} = \frac{V^2}{R} = \frac{10^2}{100} = 1\text{ W}\right]$$

Energy consumed

$$= I^2 Rt = 1 \times 5 \text{ watts sec.}$$

$$= \mathbf{5\ joules.}$$

EXAMPLE 1.2 *The strength of current in 1 Henry inductor changes at a rate of 1 A/sec. Find the voltage across it and determine the magnitude of energy stored in the inductor after 2 secs.*

SOLUTION. From the given data

$$L = 1\text{ H}; \quad \frac{di}{dt} = 1\text{ A/sec.}$$

$$\therefore \quad v = L\frac{di}{dt} = 1 \times 1 = \mathbf{1\ V.}$$

The energy stored is given as

$$W = \frac{1}{2}Li^2 = \frac{1}{2} \times 1 \times 2^2$$

$$= \mathbf{2\ joules.}$$

EXAMPLE 1.3 *A capacitor has a capacitance of 5 μF. Calculate the stored energy in it if a d.c. voltage of 100 V is applied across it.*

SOLUTION. When the capacitor will be full charged, the voltage across it would be 100 V.

Then we get $V = 100\text{ V}, \ C = 5 \times 10^{-6}\text{ F}$

Stored energy is thus given as

$$W = \frac{1}{2}CV^2 = \frac{1}{2} \times 5 \times 10^{-6} \times (100)^2$$

$$= \mathbf{2.5 \times 10^{-2}\ joules.}$$

EXAMPLE 1.4 *The current and voltage profile of an element vs time has been shown in Fig. E1.1. Determine the element and find its value.*

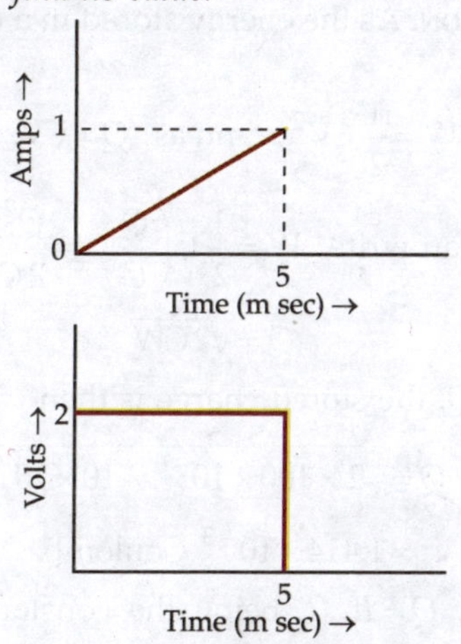

Fig. E1.1

SOLUTION. By observation, it is revealed that since V and I are not proportional, hence the element cannot be resistor. Also at end of 5 ms, even if $i \neq 0$, the voltage across the element becomes suddenly zero (*i.e.*, the element behaves as a short circuit). Then the element cannot be a capacitor too. On the other hand, the current through it is zero at $t = 0$ and the voltage is zero across the element at $t = 5$ m sec. Thus the element must be an **inductor**.

It may also be observed from the profiles that

$$\frac{di}{dt} = \frac{1}{5 \times 10^{-3}} = 0.2 \times 10^3 \text{ A/sec}$$

and v (initial) $= 2$ V

$$\therefore \quad L = \frac{v}{di/dt} = \frac{2}{0.2 \times 10^3} = \mathbf{10\ mH.}$$

EXAMPLE 1.5 *A 50 μF capacitor is charged to retain 10 mJ of energy by a constant charging current of 1 A. Determine the voltage across the capacitor.*

CHAPTER 1

Solution. The energy stored in a capacitor is given by

$$W = \frac{1}{2} CV^2 \text{ i.e., } V = \sqrt{\frac{2W}{C}};$$

V being the voltage developed across the capacitor of capacitance C.

Here, $$V = \sqrt{\frac{2 \times 100 \times 10^{-4}}{50 \times 10^{-6}}} = \mathbf{20\ V.}$$

Example 1.6 *A capacitor of 100 μF stores 10 mJ of energy. Obtain the amount of charge stored in it. How much time does it take to build up this charge if the charging current is 0.1 A ?*

Solution. As the energy stored in a capacitor is given by

$$W = \frac{1}{2} CV^2, \text{ and as } Q = CV.$$

$$\therefore \text{We can write, } W = \frac{1}{2} C\left(\frac{Q}{C}\right)^2 = \frac{Q^2}{2C}$$

i.e., $$Q = \sqrt{2CW}$$

Here Q, the stored charge is then

$$Q = \sqrt{2 \times 100 \times 10^{-6} \times 10 \times 10^{-3}}$$
$$= 1.414 \times 10^{-3} \text{ Coulomb.}$$

Again, $Q = It$, 'I' being the constant charging current and 't' the charging time.

$$\therefore \quad t = \frac{Q}{I} = \frac{1.414 \times 10^{-3}}{0.1} = \mathbf{14.14\ ms.}$$

Example 1.7 *Figure E1.2 exhibits the voltage-time profile of a source to charge a capacitor of 50 μF. What is the charging current ?*

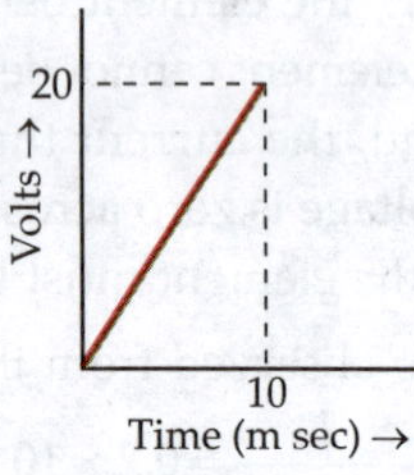

Fig. E1.2

Solution. Here,

$$\frac{dv}{dt} = \frac{20}{10} = 2 \text{ V/m sec} = 2 \times 10^3 \text{ V/sec}$$

$$\therefore \quad i_{\text{charging}} = C\frac{dv}{dt} = 50 \times 10^{-6} \times 2 \times 10^3$$
$$= \mathbf{0.1\ A.}$$

1.2 SERIES AND PARALLEL COMBINATION OF RESISTANCES

Let the three pure resistances R_1, R_2 and R_3 be connected in series against a d.c. voltage source V as shown in Fig. 1.1. Then, by inspection, it can be written that

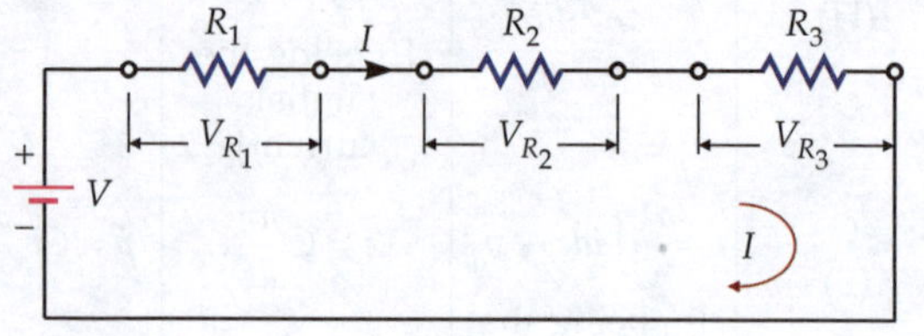

Fig. 1.1 Series connection of pure resistance in d.c. circuit

$$V = V_{R_1} + V_{R_2} + V_{R_3} \quad \text{...(1.11)}$$

[V_{R_1}, V_{R_2} and V_{R_3} being the voltage drops against individual resistances]

Assuming I to be the circuit current, and R being the equivalent of all the series resistances, equation (1.11) can be written as

$$IR = IR_1 + IR_2 + IR_3$$

i.e., $$R = (R_1 + R_2 + R_3) \quad \text{...(1.12)}$$

This proves that *the equivalent resistance in the d.c. circuit is the simple sum of individual resistances.*

Also, $$I = \frac{V}{R_1 + R_2 + R_3} \text{ amps} \quad \text{...(1.13)}$$

and P, the *total power loss* is given by

$$P = I^2 R_1 + I^2 R_2 + I^2 R_3$$
$$= I^2 (R_1 + R_2 + R_3) \quad \text{...(1.14)}$$

i.e., $$P = I(V_{R_1} + V_{R_2} + V_{R_3}) \quad \text{...(1.15)}$$

Figure 1.2 shows the connection of three resistors in parallel across a d.c. voltage source V. Let the source current be I while the branch currents

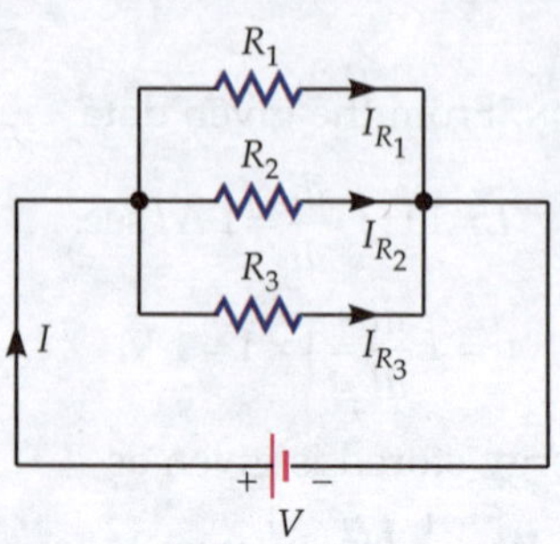

Fig. 1.2 Parallel connection of pure resistance across a d.c. source

are I_{R_1}, I_{R_2} and I_{R_3} respectively. The voltage drop in each branch being same, we can write,

$$V = I_{R_1}\ R_1 = I_{R_2}\ R_2 = I_{R_3}\ R_3 \quad ...(1.16)$$

Also, by inspection,

$$I = I_{R_1} + I_{R_2} + I_{R_3}$$

or,

$$\frac{V}{R} = \frac{V}{R_1} + \frac{V}{R_2} + \frac{V}{R_3}$$

(R being the equivalent of three resistances in parallel)

$$\therefore \quad \frac{1}{R} = \frac{1}{R_1} + \frac{1}{R_2} + \frac{1}{R_3} \quad ...(1.17)$$

[It may be noted that for a two branch circuit,

$$\frac{1}{R} = \frac{1}{R_1} + \frac{1}{R_2} \ \textit{i.e.,}\ R = \frac{R_1\ R_2}{R_1 + R_2} \quad ...(1.18)$$

Also, for the two branch circuit,

$$I = I_{R_1} + I_{R_2} = V\left(\frac{1}{R_1} + \frac{1}{R_2}\right)$$

$$= I_{R_1}\ R_1\left(\frac{R_1 + R_2}{R_1\ R_2}\right) = I_{R_1}\ \frac{R_1 + R_2}{R_2}$$

i.e.,

$$I_{R_1} = I \times \frac{R_2}{R_1 + R_2} \quad ...(1.19)$$

Similarly,

$$I_{R_2} = I\ \frac{R_1}{R_1 + R_2} \quad ...(1.20)$$

Equations (1.19) and (1.20) are popularly called as "shunt formulae".]

The power loss in circuit shown in Fig. 1.2 is given by

$$P = P_{R_1} + P_{R_2} + P_{R_3}$$

(P_{R_1}, P_{R_2} and P_{R_3} being the individual power losses in the resistors R_1, R_2 and R_3 respectively)

or,

$$P = (I_{R_1}^2 \cdot R_1 + I_{R_2}^2 \cdot R_2 + I_{R_3}^2 \cdot R_3)$$

$$= \left(\frac{V^2}{R_1} + \frac{V^2}{R_2} + \frac{V^2}{R_3}\right) \quad ...(1.21)$$

$$= V^2\left[\frac{1}{R_1} + \frac{1}{R_2} + \frac{1}{R_3}\right] \text{ watts} \quad ...(1.22)$$

EXAMPLE 1.8 *Find the equivalent resistance of the circuit shown in Fig. E1.3. Given, $R_1 = R_4 = 5\,\Omega$ and $R_2 = R_3 = 2\,\Omega$.*

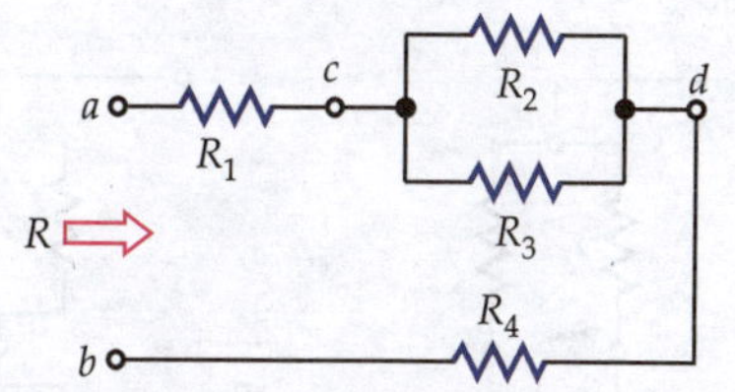

Fig. E1.3 Series connection of pure resistance in d.c. circuit

SOLUTION. Equivalent resistance across *c-d* is given by

$$R_{cd} = \frac{R_2\ R_3}{R_2 + R_3} = \frac{2 \times 2}{2 + 2} = 1\,\Omega$$

$$\therefore \quad R = R_1 + R_{cd} + R_4 = \mathbf{11\,\Omega}.$$

EXAMPLE 1.9 *Determine equivalent resistance R across x-y in Figs. E1.4 (a), (b) and (c).*

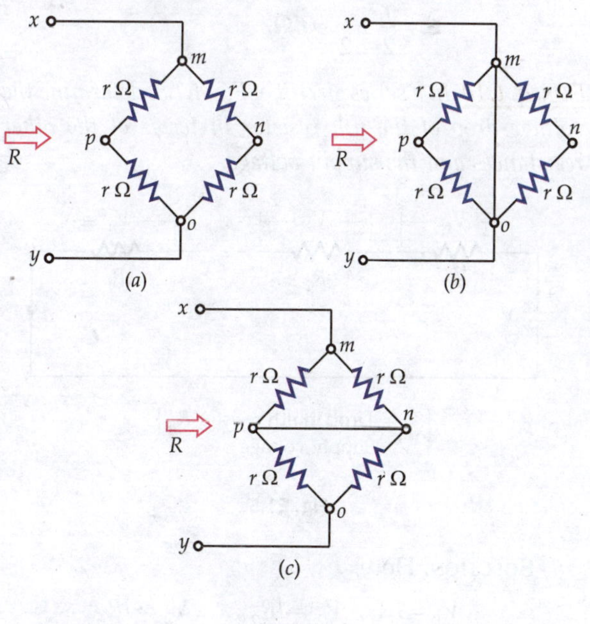

Fig. E1.4

SOLUTION. Figure E1.4(*a*) can be reduced as Fig. E1.4(*d*).

Here R = (resistance in branch mn + resistance in branch no) in parallel to (resistance in branch mp + resistance in branch po)

$$= (r + r) \,||\, (r + r) = 2r \,||\, 2r = \boldsymbol{r\,\Omega}.$$

Inspection of Fig. E1.4(*b*) reveals that the equivalent resistance of the combination is zero as out of three parallel branches (*i.e.*, branch *mno*, branch *mo* and branch *mpo*) one of the branch (branch *mo*) is a short circuit and does not have any resistance.

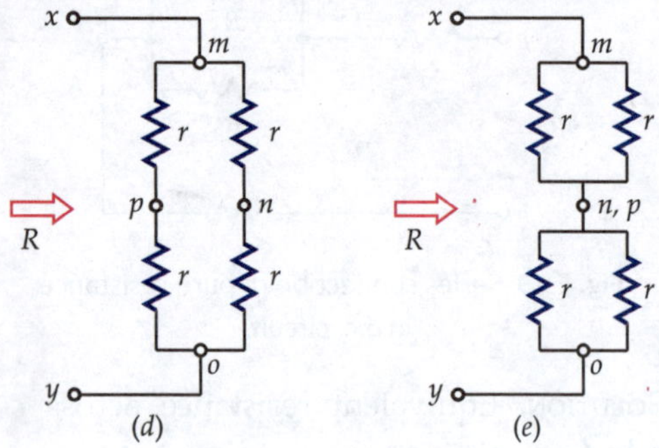

Fig. E1.4

Again, Fig. E1.4(*c*) can be reduced as shown in Fig. E1.4(*e*). It may be noted that *n-p* being shorted, the equivalent resistance is given by

$$R = [r \,||\, r] + [r \,||\, r]$$
$$= \frac{r}{2} + \frac{r}{2} = \boldsymbol{r\,\Omega}.$$

EXAMPLE 1.10 *In a series circuit of Fig. E1.5, determine the voltage drop of the nth resistor in terms of the other resistances and the supply voltage.*

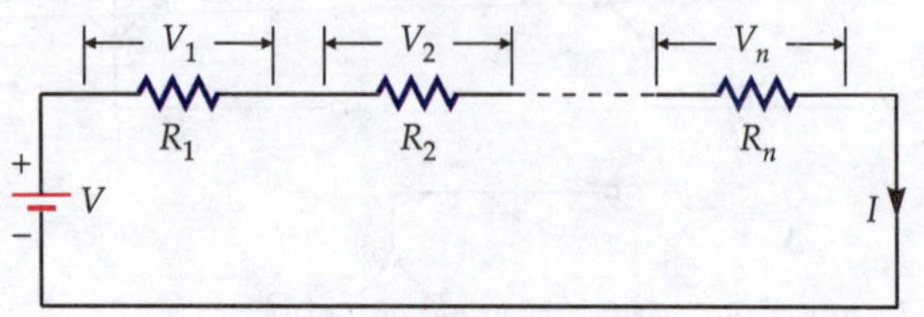

$\begin{bmatrix} V_n = \text{Drop in } n\text{th resistor } R_n \\ V = \text{Supply voltage} \end{bmatrix}$

Fig. E1.5

SOLUTION. Here,

$$V_1 = IR_1,\ V_2 = IR_2, \ldots\ V_n = IR_n$$

$$\therefore \quad V_n = \frac{V}{R_1 + R_2 + \ldots.\ R_n} . R_n$$

$$\left[\because I = \frac{V}{R_1 + R_2 + \ldots. + R_n}\right]$$

i.e., $$V_n = \frac{\boldsymbol{R_n}}{\boldsymbol{R}} . \boldsymbol{V}$$

[Assuming the equivalent resistance of $R_1, R_2, \ldots, R_n$ to be R]

EXAMPLE 1.11 *Find the equivalent resistance of the circuit shown in Fig. E1.6.*

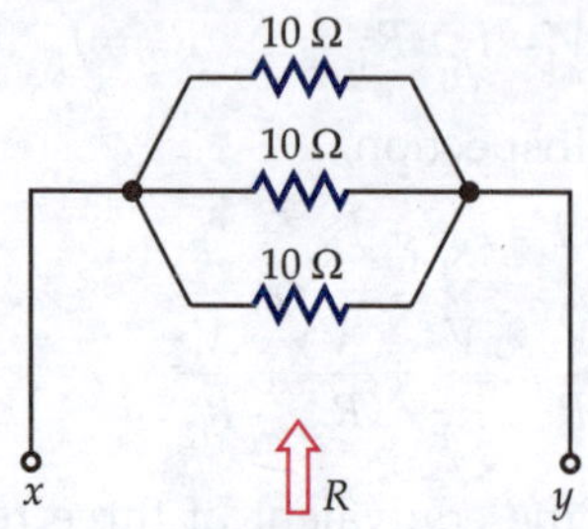

Fig. E1.6

SOLUTION. Here, three resistances each of 10 Ω are connected in parallel.

$$\therefore \quad \frac{1}{R} = \frac{1}{10} + \frac{1}{10} + \frac{1}{10} = \frac{3}{10}$$

(R being the equivalent resistance)

$$\therefore \quad R = \frac{10}{3} = \mathbf{3.33\,\Omega}. \qquad \text{(across } xy)$$

EXAMPLE 1.12 *A current of 10 A flows into a circuit consisting of 2, 4, 10 and 20 Ω resistances respectively in parallel. Determine the current in each resistance.*

SOLUTION. Let R being the equivalent resistance of the parallel circuit.

$$\therefore \quad \frac{1}{R} = \frac{1}{2} + \frac{1}{4} + \frac{1}{10} + \frac{1}{20} = \frac{18}{20} \text{ mho}$$

$$\therefore \quad R = \frac{20}{18}\,\Omega$$

The potential difference, V, across the circuit (also across each branch of it), is given by

$$V = RI, \ I \text{ being the total current}$$
$$= \frac{20}{18} \times 10 = 11.11 \text{ V}.$$

$$\therefore \quad I_1 = V / R_1 = \frac{11.11}{2} = \mathbf{5.55\ A}$$

$$I_2 = V / R_2 = \frac{11.11}{4} = \mathbf{2.78\ A}$$

$$I_3 = V / R_3 = \frac{11.11}{10} = \mathbf{1.11\ A}$$

$$I_4 = V / R_4 = \frac{11.11}{20} = \mathbf{0.55\ A.}$$

Check

It may be seen that

$$I = I_1 + I_2 + I_3 + I_4 = 10 \text{ A}$$

EXAMPLE 1.13 *Find the equivalent resistance across x-y of the circuit drawn in Fig. E1.7.*

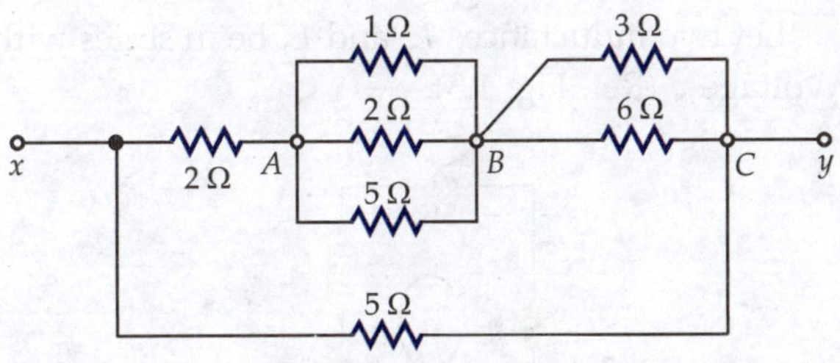

Fig. E1.7

SOLUTION. The circuit is to be reduced to a simple one by solving for resistance between AB and BC. The reduction has been shown in Fig. E1.7(a)

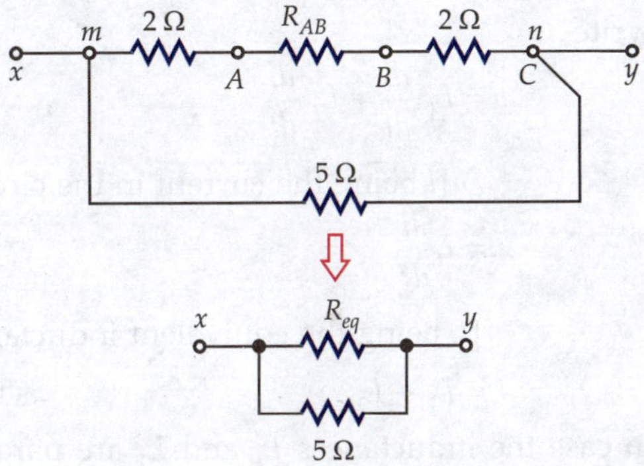

Fig. E1.7(a)

Here $\quad \dfrac{1}{R_{AB}} = 1 + \dfrac{1}{2} + \dfrac{1}{5} = \dfrac{17}{10} \quad$ *i.e.,* $R_{AB} = \dfrac{10}{17}\,\Omega$

Also, $\quad \dfrac{1}{R_{BC}} = \dfrac{1}{3} + \dfrac{1}{6} = \dfrac{1}{2}$

or, $\quad R_{BC} = 2\,\Omega.$

Assuming $R_{eq.}$ to be the equivalent series resistance of path $m-n$ in Fig. E1.7(a),

$$R_{eq.} = 2 + \frac{10}{17} + 2 = 4.59\,\Omega$$

$\therefore$ The resistance across x-y becomes

$$R = \frac{5 \times R_{eq.}}{5 + R_{eq.}} = \frac{5 \times 4.59}{5 + 4.59} = \mathbf{2.39\,\Omega}.$$

EXAMPLE 1.14 *In Fig. E1.8, find R across x-y terminals.*

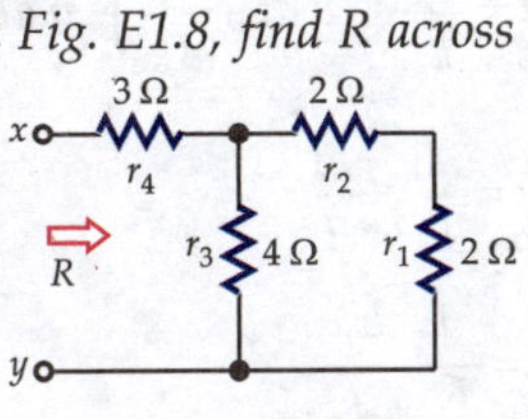

Fig. E1.8

SOLUTION. Let the resistances be named as r_1, r_2, r_3 and r_4 as shown in Fig. E1.8.

It may be observed that r_1 and r_2 are in series and the combination is in parallel with r_3. This combination is then in series with r_4.

i.e., $\quad R = [(r_1 + r_2) \,||\, r_3] + r_4 = \mathbf{5\,\Omega}.$

EXAMPLE 1.15 *A resistive network is shown in Fig. E1.9. Find the equivalent resistance looking from terminal x-y.*

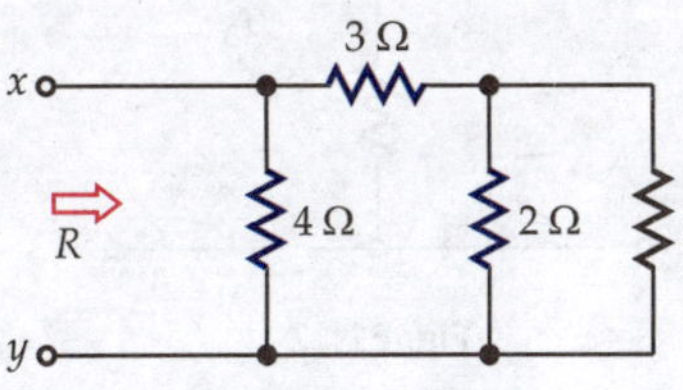

Fig. E1.9

SOLUTION. Let R be the equivalent resistance of the network looking from terminal x-y towards the network.

$$R = [(2\,||\,2) + 3\,]\,||\,4 = \mathbf{2\,\Omega}.$$

EXAMPLE 1.16 *Find the equivalent resistance of the circuit shown in Fig. E1.10 across x-y.*

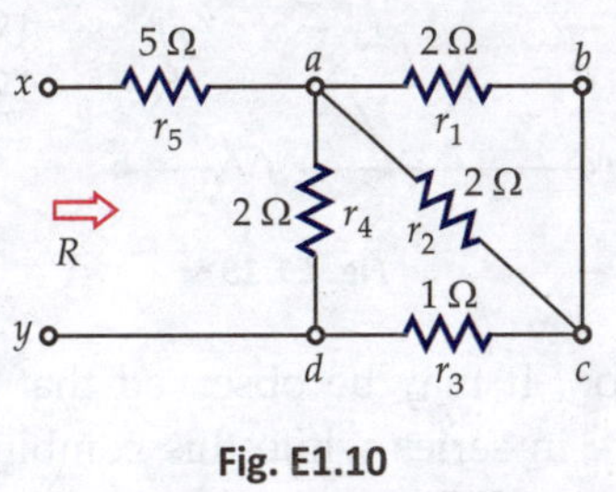

Fig. E1.10

SOLUTION. r_1 and r_2 are in parallel and the equivalent resistance of r_1 and r_2 is in series with r_3. This combination is again in parallel to a-b in parallel to r_4.

$\therefore$ The net resistance across a-b terminals is

$$r_{ab} = [(r_1 \,||\, r_2) + r_3] \,||\, r_4 = 1\,\Omega$$

$$\therefore \quad R = r_5 + r_{ab} = 5 + 1 = \mathbf{6\,\Omega}.$$

EXAMPLE 1.17 *Find R across terminal x-y in Fig. E1.11.*

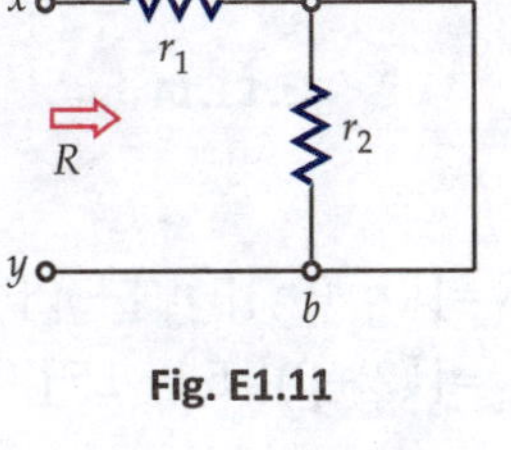

Fig. E1.11

Solution. As *a-b* terminal is shorted in Fig. E1.11, hence r_2 is of no use. Hence R is equivalent to only r_1.

i.e., $R = r_1$.

Example 1.18 *Figure E1.12 represents a resistance circuited, open circuited at terminal y-z. Find the equivalent resistance of the network looking towards it from the terminals a-b.*

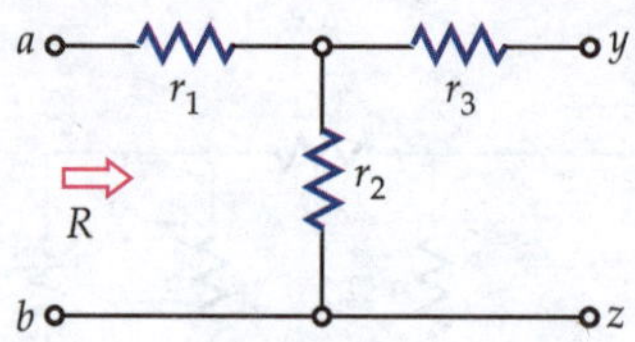

Fig. E1.12

Solution. Let R be the resistance of the network of Fig. E1.12 looking from terminal *a-b* when terminal *y-z* is open circuited.

$$\therefore \quad R = (r_1 + r_2).$$

[$\because$ *y* is open, r_3 is of no use]

Example 1.19 *Find R across x-y in Fig. E1.13.*

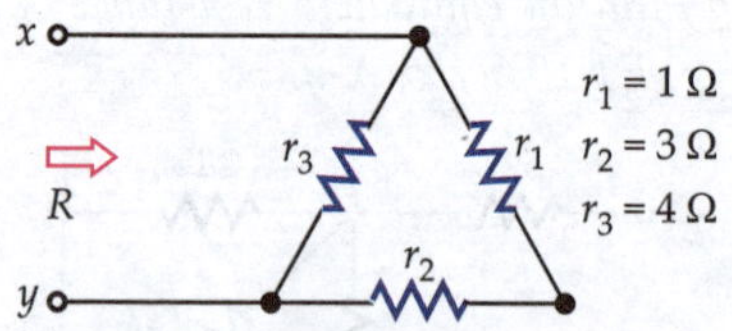

Fig. E1.13

Solution. It may be observed that across *x-y*, r_1 and r_2 are in series while this combination of r_1 and r_2 is in parallel to r_3.

$$\therefore \quad R = (r_1 + r_2) \,||\, r_3 = \mathbf{2\,\Omega}.$$

Example 1.20 *Find the resistance R across x-y in the network in Fig. E1.14.*

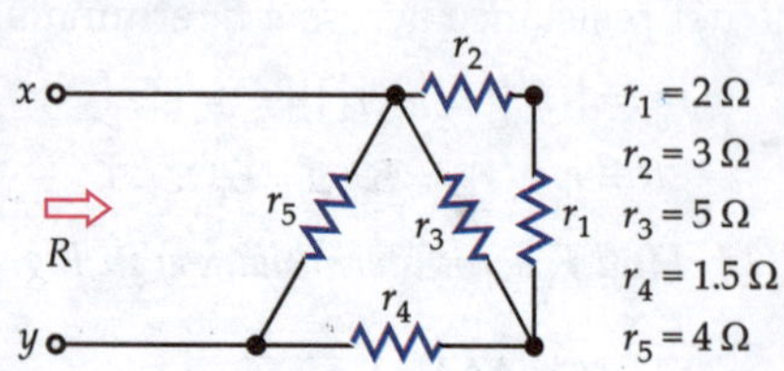

Fig. E1.14

Solution.

$$R = [\{(r_1 + r_2) \,||\, r_3\} + r_4] \,||\, r_5$$
$$= [\{(2+3) \,||\, 5\} + 1.5] \,||\, 4 = \mathbf{2\,\Omega}.$$

1.3 SERIES AND PARALLEL COMBINATION OF INDUCTANCES

Let two inductances L_1 and L_2 be in series with a voltage v (Ref. Fig. 1.3).

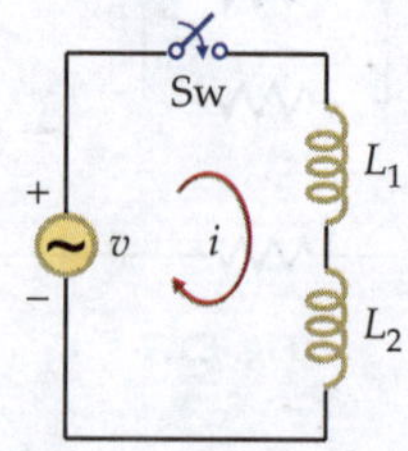

Fig. 1.3 Series connection of inductances

Here, the supply voltage being equal to the summation of voltage drops across L_1 and L_2, we can write

$$v = L_1 \frac{di}{dt} + L_2 \frac{di}{dt}$$

[*i* being the current in the circuit]

$$= L\frac{di}{dt}$$

[*L* being the equivalent inductance]

i.e., $$L = L_1 + L_2 \quad ...(1.23)$$

In case the inductances L_1 and L_2 are parallel, the supply voltage being v, the branch currents i_1 and i_2, for the parallel circuit, from Fig. 1.4.

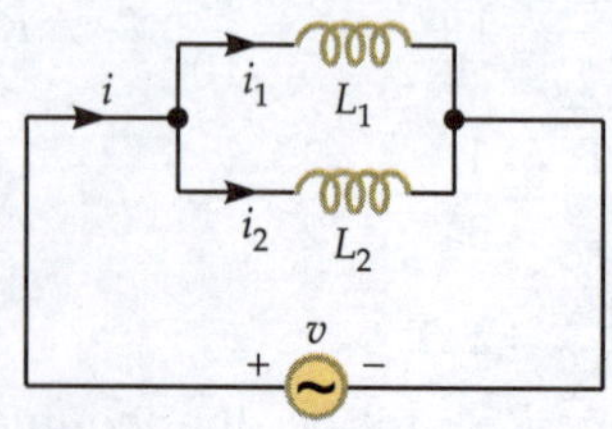

Fig. 1.4 Parallel connection of inductances

$$v = L_1 \frac{di_1}{dt} = L_2 \frac{di_2}{dt} \quad ...(1.24)$$

and $$i = i_1 + i_2 \quad ...(1.25)$$

From equation (1.24) we can write,

$$\frac{1}{L}\int v\,dt = \frac{1}{L_1}\int v\,dt + \frac{1}{L_2}\int v\,dt$$

i.e., $$\frac{1}{L} = \frac{1}{L_1} + \frac{1}{L_2}$$

or, $$L = \frac{L_1 L_2}{L_1 + L_2} \quad ...(1.26)$$

1.4 SERIES AND PARALLEL COMBINATION OF CAPACITANCES

Let us assume a voltage v being applied in a circuit containing two capacitances C_1 and C_2 in series. Let C be their equivalent capacitance and i be the series current.

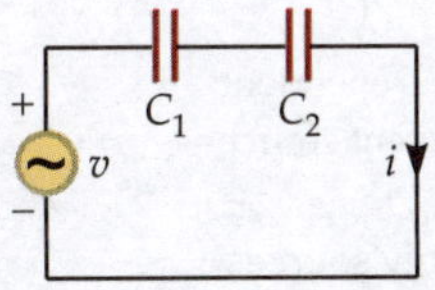

Fig. 1.5 Series connection of capacitances

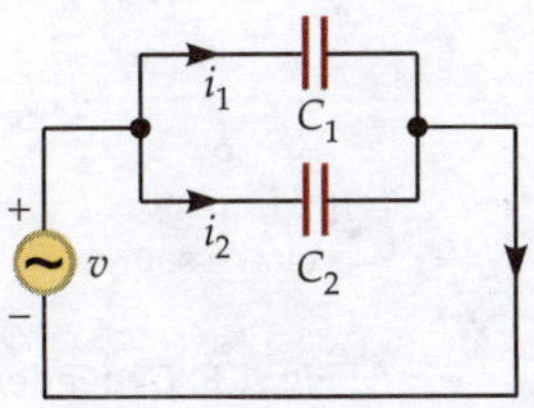

Fig. 1.6 Parallel connection of capacitances

Here, the applied voltage in the summation of the individual voltage drops across C_1 and C_2.

i.e., $v = \text{drop across } C_1 + \text{drop across } C_2$

or, $$\frac{1}{C}\int i\,dt = \frac{1}{C_1}\int i\,dt + \frac{1}{C_2}\int i\,dt$$

or, $$\frac{1}{C} = \frac{1}{C_1} + \frac{1}{C_2}$$

i.e., $$C = \frac{C_1 C_2}{C_1 + C_2} \quad \text{...(1.27)}$$

On the other hand, if the capacitances C_1 and C_2 are in parallel, i_1 and i_2 being the branch currents, the total current i is given by

$$i = i_1 + i_2$$

or $$C\frac{dv}{dt} = C_1\frac{dv}{dt} + C_2\frac{dv}{dt}$$

i.e., $$C = C_1 + C_2 \quad \text{...(1.28)}$$

EXAMPLE 1.21 *Three inductances of 4 H each are connected in series. What is the equivalent inductance ?*

SOLUTION. The equivalent inductance L is given by

$$L = L_1 + L_2 + L_3 = 4 + 4 + 4 = \mathbf{12\ H.}$$

EXAMPLE 1.22 *Three pure inductances, as shown in Fig. E1.15, are connected. Find the equivalent inductance.*

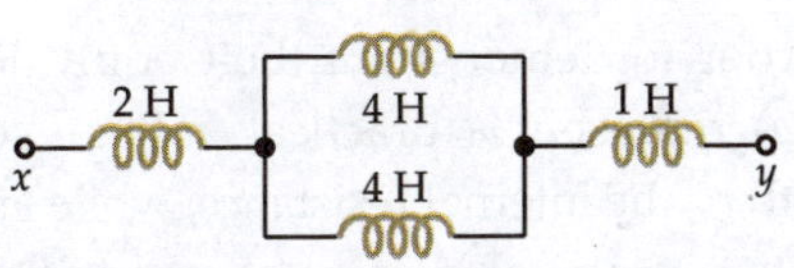

Fig. E1.15

SOLUTION. The equivalent inductance of the parallel connection is

$$L = \frac{4 \times 4}{4 + 4} = 2\ \text{H}$$

∴ The net inductance of the circuit across x-y is

$$L_{x-y} = 2 + 2 + 1 = \mathbf{5\ H.}$$

EXAMPLE 1.23 *Find the equivalent capacitance of the combination shown in Fig. E1.16 across x-y.*

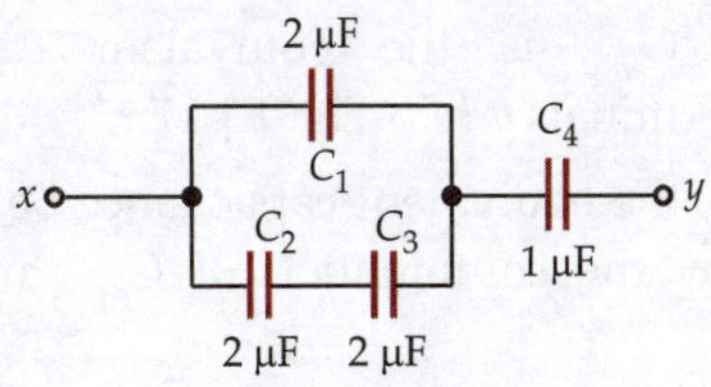

Fig. E1.16

SOLUTION. The equivalent combination of C_1 and C_2 is $\left(\frac{2 \times 2}{2 + 2}\right)$ μF, *i.e.,* 1 μF.

The equivalent combination of this 1 μF and C_1 is $(C_1 + 1)$ μF, 3 μF.

∴ The net capacitance across x-y is

$$\frac{3 \times C_4}{3 + C_4} \quad \textit{i.e.,} \quad \mathbf{\frac{3}{4}\ \mu F.}$$

EXAMPLE 1.24 *Find the equivalent capacitance across x-y (Fig. E1.17).*

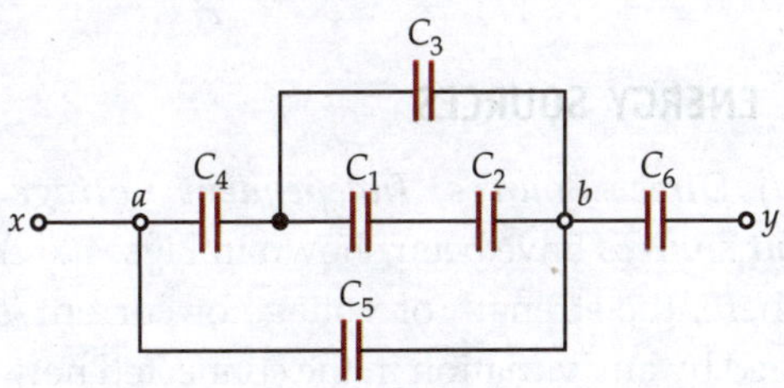

Fig. E1.17

SOLUTION. The equivalent capacitance of C_1, C_2 and C_3 is

$$C_{eq_1} = \left[\frac{C_1 C_2}{C_1 + C_2} + C_3\right]$$

C_{eq_1} is in series with C_4. The equivalent combination is

$$C_{eq_2} = \frac{C_4 \times C_{eq_1}}{C_4 + C_{eq_1}}$$

Again C_{eq_2} is in parallel with C_5.

$$\therefore \quad C_{eq_3} = C_5 + C_{eq_2}$$

$$= C_5 + \frac{C_4\, C_{eq_1}}{C_4 + C_{eq_1}}$$

$$= C_5 + \frac{C_4\left[\dfrac{C_1 C_2}{C_1 + C_2} + C_3\right]}{C_4 + \dfrac{C_1 C_2}{C_1 + C_2} + C_3}$$

Then, C_{eq_3} is the equivalent capacitance between terminals *a-b* in Fig. E1.17.

Hence, the equivalent capacitance between *x-y* is given by the combination of C_{eq_3} and C_6 (in series)

i.e., $$C_{x-y} = \frac{C_{eq_3} \times C_6}{C_{eq_3} + C_6}$$

$$= \frac{\left(C_5 + \dfrac{C_4\left[\dfrac{C_1 C_2}{C_1 + C_2} + C_3\right]}{C_4 + \dfrac{C_1 C_2}{C_1 + C_2} + C_3}\right) \times C_6}{\left(C_5 + \dfrac{C_4\left[\dfrac{C_1 C_2}{C_1 + C_2} + C_3\right]}{C_4 + \dfrac{C_1 C_2}{C_1 + C_2} + C_3}\right) + C_6}$$

1.5 ENERGY SOURCES

(*a*) ***Direct Sources. Independent voltage and current sources*** have been shown in Figs. 1.7(*a*) and (*b*) where, the strength of voltage or current is not changed by any variation in the connected network.

(*a*) Independent voltage source (*b*) Independent current source

Fig. 1.7 Independent energy sources

On the other hand, when the strength of voltage or current changes in the source for any change in the connected network, they are called *dependent sources*. Dependent voltage and current sources have been shown in Figs. 1.8(*a*) and (*b*) respectively.

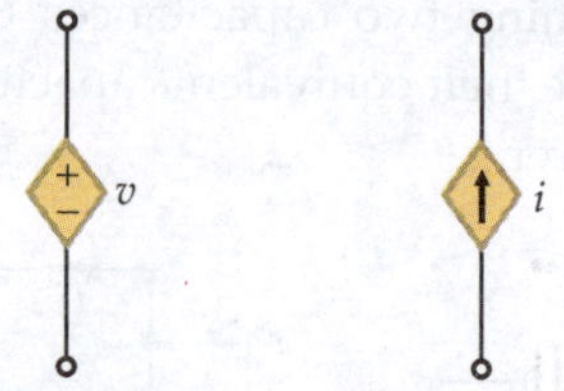

(*a*) Dependent voltage source (*b*) Dependent current source

Fig. 1.8 Dependent energy sources

(*b*) ***Alternating Sources.*** In network application one may encounter other type of sources where the voltage or current may vary with time *sinusoidally, exponentially* etc. In the latter part of this chapter we will come across these type of sources while we could discuss about "Sources with Periodic Waveforms".

1.6 SOURCE TRANSFORMATION

Any *practical voltage source* (or simply, a *voltage source*) consists of an *ideal* voltage source in series with an internal impedance (for ideal source, this impedance being zero, the output voltage becomes independent of the load current) while any *practical current source* (or, *a current source*) is an *ideal* current source in parallel with air internal impedance (for ideal current source, this parallel impedance is infinity such that the source current does not face any branching through this internal impedance path).

Examples of voltage sources. Batteries and generators are normally used as voltage sources.

Examples of current sources. Most of the semiconductor devices like transistor etc. are treated as current sources.

The voltage and current sources are mutually transferable.

In order to demonstrate their equivalence, let Fig. 1.9(*a*) represent a practical voltage source in series with r_v, the internal resistance, while Fig. 1.9 (*b*) represents a practical current source with parallel internal resistance r_i.

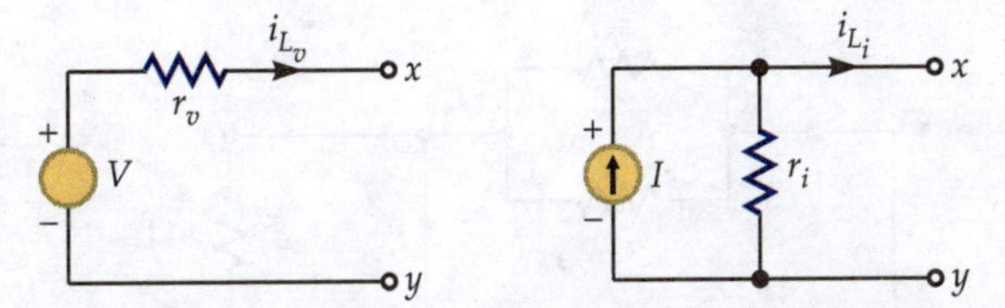

(a) A practical voltage source (b) A practical current source

Fig. 1.9

In the first case the load current will be given by

$$i_{L_v} = \frac{V}{r_v + r_L} \quad \text{[assuming a load resistance } r_L \text{ connected at terminal } x\text{-}y]$$

and in the second case, the load current is

$$i_{Li} = I \frac{r_i}{r_i + r_L} \quad \text{[assuming the same load resistance connected across the load terminals } x\text{-}y \text{ of the current source]}$$

Two sources to become identical,

$$\frac{V}{r_v + r_L} = I \frac{r_i}{r_i + r_L}$$

However, for the current source, the terminal voltage at x-y would be Ir_i, x-y being open.

i.e., $$V = I \cdot r_i$$

With this, we finally get

$$r_v + r_L = r_i + r_L$$

i.e., $$r_v = r_i$$

∴ *For any practical voltage source, if the ideal voltage be V and internal resistance be r_v, the voltage source can be replaced by a current source I with the internal resistance in parallel to the current source.*

Example 1.25 *A battery has an internal resistance of 0.5 ohm and open circuit voltage of 12 V. What is the power lost within the battery and the terminal voltage on full load if a resistance of 3 ohms is connected across the terminals of the battery ?*

Solution. The internal resistance will be in series with the load. Hence the circuit current will be

$$I = \frac{12}{3.5} = 3.43 \text{ A}$$

Terminal voltage

$$= IR_L = 3.43 \times 3 = \mathbf{10.3\ V}$$

Power loss in the battery

$$= I^2 R_{int} = (3.43)^2 \times 0.5 = \mathbf{5.88\ W.}$$

Example 1.26 *Three resistances of 3, 4 and 5 Ω are connected in parallel and this combination is put in series with 2 Ω resistor.*

(a) Find the equivalent resistance of the combination (at terminals P-Q) [Ref. Fig. E1.18]

(b) Obtain current in each circuit when a battery of 10 V with internal resistance of 0.1 Ω is connected across P-Q.

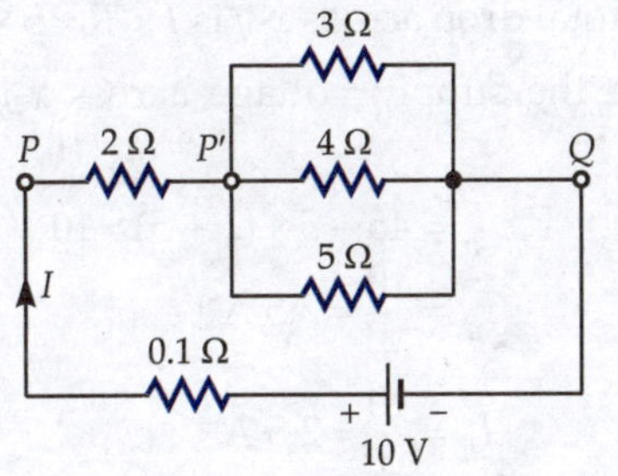

Fig. E1.18

Solution. (a)

$$R_{\text{equiv.}} = \frac{1}{\frac{1}{3} + \frac{1}{4} + \frac{1}{5}} + 2 = \mathbf{3.28\,\Omega} \text{ [across } P\text{-}Q]$$

(b) $$I \text{ (in Fig. E1.18)} = \frac{10}{3.28 + 0.1} = 2.96 \text{ A}$$

∴ Voltage across

$$P\text{-}Q = 10 - 2.96 \times 0.1 = 9.704 \text{ V}$$

Drop in $$P'Q = 9.704 - 2.96 \times 2 = 3.784 \text{ V}$$

∴ $$I_{3\Omega} = \frac{3.784}{3} = \mathbf{1.26\ A}$$

$$I_{4\Omega} = \frac{3.784}{4} = \mathbf{0.946\ A}$$

$$I_{5\Omega} = \frac{3.784}{5} = \mathbf{0.7568\ A}$$

[Check : $I = 1.26 + 0.946 + 0.7568 = 2.96$ A]

Example 1.27 *Calculate the voltage that is to be connected across terminals x-y in Fig. E1.19 such that the voltage across the 2 Ω resistor is 10 V. Also find I_a and I_b. What is the total power loss in the circuit ?*

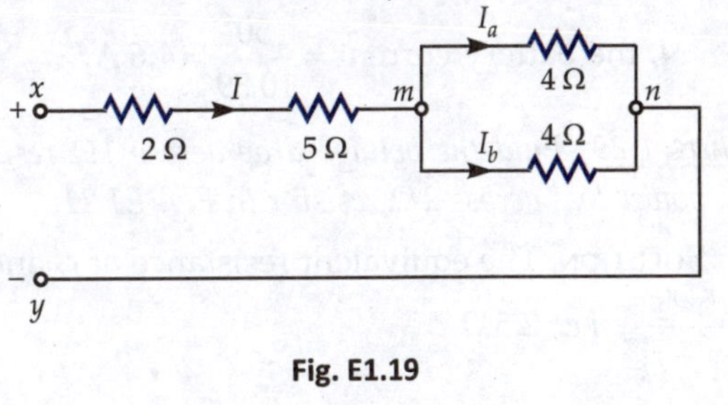

Fig. E1.19

CHAPTER 1

Solution. The equivalent resistance across the terminals x-y is

$$R = \frac{4 \times 4}{4+4} + 5 + 2 = 9\,\Omega$$

However if the drop across 2 Ω resistor is to be 10 V, the current through it (I) should be $I = \frac{10}{2} = 5$ A.

$\therefore$The total drop across x-y is $I \times R = 5 \times 9 = 45$ V

Hence the supply voltage across x-y must be **45 V.**

Again $V_{m-n} = 45 - 5 \times (2+5) = 10$ V

$$\therefore \quad I_a = \frac{10}{4} = 2.5 \text{ A}$$

and $$I_b = \frac{10}{4} = 2.5 \text{ A.}$$

The total power loss in the circuit is $I^2 R$

i.e., $5^2 \times 9 = \mathbf{225\ W.}$

Example 1.28 Determine the current drawn from the battery of Fig. E1.20.

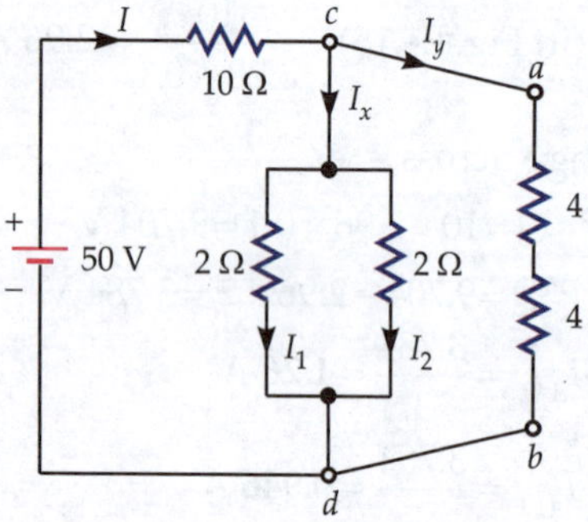

Fig. E1.20

Solution. The equivalent resistance in a-b path is 8 Ω and that of c-d is 1Ω.

Hence, the net resistance of the circuit across the battery is

$$\left(\frac{1 \times 8}{1+8} + 10\right)\Omega = 10.89\,\Omega$$

$\therefore$ I, the battery current $= \frac{50}{10.89} = \mathbf{4.6\ A.}$

Example 1.29 Find the voltage drop across 1Ω resistor and power loss across 2 Ω resistor in Fig. E1.21.

Solution. The equivalent resistance of r_1 and r_2 is $\frac{r_1 r_2}{r_1 + r_2}$, *i.e.*, 2.5 Ω.

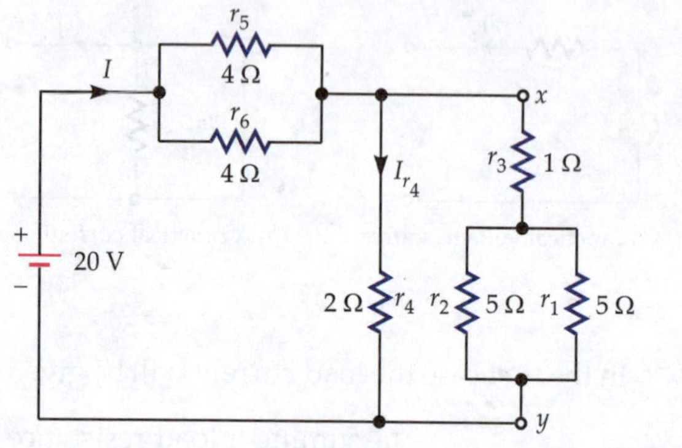

Fig. E1.21

Hence $R_{x-y} = 2.5 + 1 = 3.5\,\Omega$

Equivalent resistance of r_4 and R_{x-y} is

$$\frac{3.5 \times 2}{3.5+2} \quad \text{or, } 1.27\,\Omega.$$

Again, the equivalent resistance of r_5 and r_6 is

$$\frac{r_5 \times r_6}{r_5 + r_6} \quad \text{or, } 2\,\Omega.$$

Hence, the net circuit resistance becomes

$$R_{eq} = 2 + 1.27 = 3.27\,\Omega$$

$$\therefore \quad I = \frac{20}{3.27} = 6.12 \text{ A.}$$

The current through r_4 is then given by

$$I_{r_4} = I \frac{R_{x-y}}{R_{x-y} + r_4} = 6.12 \times \frac{3.5}{3.5+2} \simeq 3.9 \text{ A.}$$

Hence, power loss in r_4 is

$$P_{r_4\,(\text{loss})} = I_{r_4}^2 \times r_4 = 3.9^2 \times 2 = \mathbf{30.4\ W.}$$

Also

$$V_{x-y} = [20 - I\,(\text{combination of } r_5 \text{ and } r_6)] \text{ volts}$$
$$= 20 - 6.12 \times 2 = 7.76 \text{ V.}$$

$\therefore$ Drop across $r_3 = V_{x-y}$ − drop across combination of r_1 and r_2

$$= 7.76 - I_{xy} \times 2.5$$
$$= 7.76 - (I - I_{r_4})2.5$$
$$= 7.76 - (6.12 - 3.9)2.5 = \mathbf{2.21\ V.}$$

Example 1.30 A 20 μF capacitor is connected in parallel with a 40 μF capacitor and the combination is connected across a time-varying voltage source. At a particular time, the current supplied by the source is 5 A. Obtain the magnitudes of instantaneous currents through the individual capacitors.

Solution. As the capacitors are in parallel, the voltage v across them is given by

$$v = \frac{1}{C_1}\int i_1\,dt = \frac{1}{C_2}\int i_2\,dt$$

$$\therefore \quad i_1 = C_1\frac{dv}{dt} \text{ and } i_2 = C_2\frac{dv}{dt}$$

i.e., $$\frac{i_1}{i_2} = \frac{C_1}{C_2} = \frac{20}{40} = \frac{1}{2} \qquad ...(i)$$

Also, $i_1 + i_2 = 5$ A ...(ii)

Solving (i) and (ii),

$$i_1 = \mathbf{1.67\ A} \text{ and } i_2 = \mathbf{3.33\ A.}$$

Example 1.31 *A 50 μF capacitor is initially charged to accumulate 100 μC. One uncharged capacitor of 200 μF is connected across it in parallel. How much charge will be transferred ?*

Solution. Let C_1 and C_2 be the capacitances in μF of two capacitors connected in parallel. Let the voltage across their terminal, at steady state, be V.

$$\therefore \quad V = \frac{Q_1}{C_1} = \frac{Q_2}{C_2}$$

i.e., $$\frac{C_1}{C_2} = \frac{Q_1}{Q_2} \text{ or } \frac{Q_1}{Q_2} = \frac{50}{200} = \frac{1}{4}$$

[$C_1 = 50\,\mu$F, $C_2 = 200\,\mu$F; Q_1 and Q_2 are the charges shared by C_1 and C_2]

Also, $$Q_1 + Q_2 = 100\,\mu\text{ C} (= 100 \times 10^{-6}\text{ C})$$

$$\therefore \quad Q_1 = 20\,\mu\text{C}$$

i.e., $$Q_2 = 80\,\mu\text{C}$$

Thus in steady state, C_1 will have **20 μC** charge while Q_2 will retain **80 μC** charge.

Example 1.32 *A voltage of 100 V d.c. is applied across two capacitors in series having capacitances 100 μF and 25 μF. Find the voltage drop across each capacitor.*

Solution. Let V_{C_1} and V_{C_2} be the voltage drops across C_1 and C_2. Since the capacitors are in series hence the charge through each of the capacitor will be same

i.e., $$C_1 V_{C_1} = C_2 V_{C_2} \qquad ...(i)$$

and $$V_{C_1} + V_{C_2} = 100 \qquad ...(ii)$$

Solving (i) and (ii) when $C_1 = 100\,\mu$F and $C_2 = 25\,\mu$F,

$$V_{C_1} = \mathbf{20\ V} \text{ and } V_{C_2} = \mathbf{80\ V.}$$

1.7 STAR-DELTA CONNECTION

Like series and parallel connections, the resistances may be connected in 'star' (or Y) and 'delta' (Δ) connection as shown in Figs. 1.10(*a*) and 1.10(*b*).

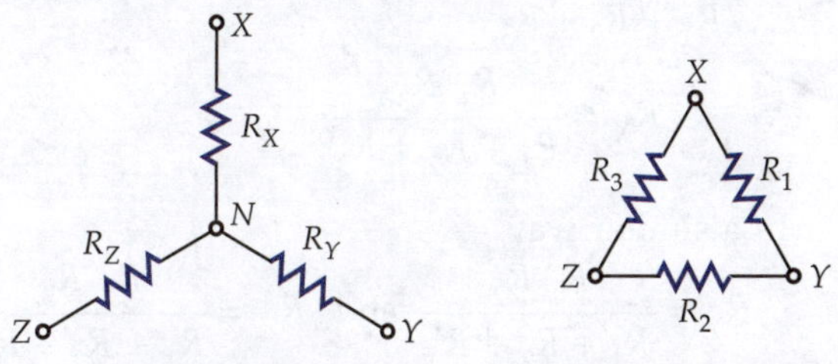

(*a*) Star connection (*b*) Delta connection

Fig. 1.10 Connection of resistance in star and delta connection

Circuits shown in Figs. 1.10(*a*) and (*b*) are identical provided their respective resistances from the terminals *XY*, *YZ* and *ZX* are equal.

In the star connection,

$$R_{X-Y} = R_X + R_Y$$
$$R_{Y-Z} = R_Y + R_Z \qquad ...(1.29)$$
and $$R_{Z-X} = R_Z + R_X$$

Similarly, in delta connection, the resistance seen from the terminals *XY*, *YZ* and *ZX* are respectively

$$R_{X-Y} = R_1 \,||\, (R_2 + R_3) = \frac{R_1(R_2 + R_3)}{R_1 + R_2 + R_3}$$

$$R_{Y-Z} = R_2 \,||\, (R_1 + R_3) = \frac{R_2(R_1 + R_3)}{R_1 + R_2 + R_3} \qquad ...(1.30)$$

$$R_{Z-X} = R_3 \,||\, (R_1 + R_2) = \frac{R_3(R_1 + R_2)}{R_1 + R_2 + R_3}$$

Next, we equate the resistances in star and delta across appropriate terminals. We get

$$R_X + R_Y = \frac{R_1(R_2 + R_3)}{R_1 + R_2 + R_3} \qquad ...(1.31)$$

$$R_Y + R_Z = \frac{R_2(R_1 + R_3)}{R_1 + R_2 + R_3} \qquad ...(1.32)$$

$$R_Z + R_X = \frac{R_3(R_1 + R_2)}{R_1 + R_2 + R_3} \qquad ...(1.33)$$

Subtracting equation (1.32) from equation (1.31), we get

$$R_X - R_Z = \frac{R_1 R_2 + R_1 R_3}{R_1 + R_2 + R_3} - \frac{R_2 R_1 + R_2 R_3}{R_1 + R_2 + R_3} \qquad ...(1.34)$$

Then, adding equation (1.33) to equation (1.34)

$$2R_X = \frac{R_1 R_2 + R_1 R_3 - R_2 R_1 - R_2 R_3 + R_3 R_1 + R_3 R_2}{(R_1 + R_2 + R_3)}$$

$$= \frac{2(R_1 R_3)}{R_1 + R_2 + R_3}$$

$$\therefore \quad R_X = \frac{R_1 R_3}{R_1 + R_2 + R_3}$$

In a similar way,

$$R_Y = \frac{R_1 R_2}{R_1 + R_2 + R_3} \quad \text{and} \quad R_Z = \frac{R_2 R_3}{R_1 + R_2 + R_3}$$

Thus, we see, if the resistances in Δ connected resistive network are known, we can find the equivalent star network when

$$\left.\begin{aligned} R_X &= \frac{R_1 R_3}{R_1 + R_2 + R_3} \\ R_Y &= \frac{R_1 R_2}{R_1 + R_2 + R_3} \\ R_Z &= \frac{R_2 R_3}{R_1 + R_2 + R_3} \end{aligned}\right\} \quad \text{...(1.35)}$$

R_X, R_Y and R_Z being the equivalent resistances in the star network of the resistances connected in delta network and designated as R_1, R_2 and R_3.

Let us now multiply each two equations of (1.35) and add the three. We get

$$R_X R_Y + R_Y R_Z + R_Z R_X = \frac{R_1^2 R_2 R_3 + R_2^2 R_1 R_3 + R_3^2 R_1 R_2}{(R_1 + R_2 + R_3)^2} \quad \text{...(1.36)}$$

Let the equation (1.36) be divided by R_X. Then we get

$$R_Y + R_Z + \frac{R_Y R_Z}{R_X} = \frac{R_1 R_2 R_3 (R_1 + R_2 + R_3)}{R_X (R_1 + R_2 + R_3)^2}$$

$$= \frac{R_1 R_2 R_3}{(R_1 + R_2 + R_3) R_X}$$

or, $$R_Y + R_Z + \frac{R_Y R_Z}{R_X} = \frac{R_1 R_2 R_3}{(R_1 + R_2 + R_3)} \times \frac{(R_1 + R_2 + R_3)}{R_1 R_3}$$

$= R_2$ [Substituting the value of R_X from equation (1.35)]

In a similar way, dividing equation (1.36) by R_Y, we get

$$R_X + R_Z + \frac{R_Z R_X}{R_Y} = R_3$$

and dividing equation (1.37) by R_Z, we get

$$R_Y + R_X + \frac{R_X R_Y}{R_Z} = R_1$$

Thus we can find R_1, R_2 and R_3 *i.e.*, the equivalent Δ network provided R_X, R_Y and R_Z are known in a given star network.

The equations are given as

$$\left.\begin{aligned} R_1 &= R_X + R_Y + \frac{R_X R_Y}{R_Z} \\ R_2 &= R_Y + R_Z + \frac{R_Y R_Z}{R_X} \\ R_3 &= R_X + R_Z + \frac{R_X R_Z}{R_Y} \end{aligned}\right\} \quad \text{...(1.37)}$$

EXAMPLE 1.33 *With reference to Fig. E1.22, convert Π connected resistors to equivalent T connection.*

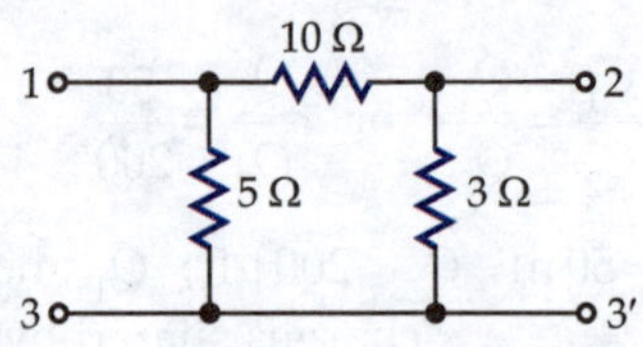

Fig. E1.22

SOLUTION. Figure E1.22 represents the Π connection of three resistors. The component resistors of equivalent *T* connection (Fig. E1.23) are shown below following the principle of Δ to star conversion.

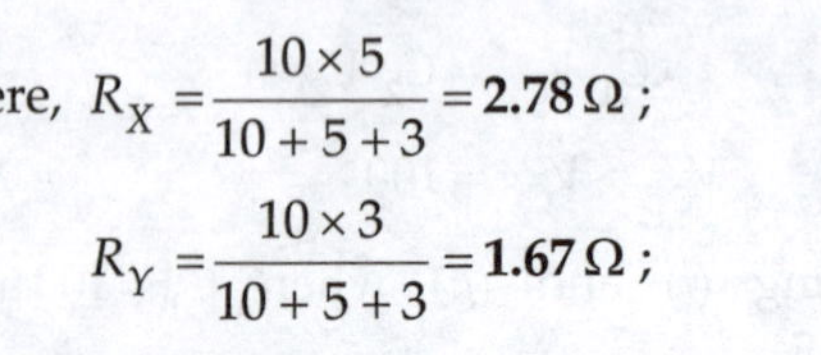

Fig. E1.23

Here, $$R_X = \frac{10 \times 5}{10 + 5 + 3} = \mathbf{2.78\,\Omega};$$

$$R_Y = \frac{10 \times 3}{10 + 5 + 3} = \mathbf{1.67\,\Omega};$$

$$R_Z = \frac{5 \times 3}{10 + 5 + 3} = \mathbf{0.83\,\Omega}.$$

Example 1.34 *Find the equivalent resistance between terminals x-y in the resistive network of Fig. E1.24.*

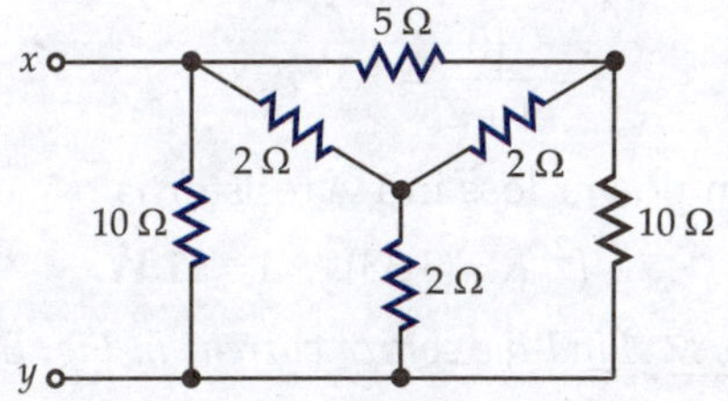

Fig. E1.24

Solution. Here for the network of Fig. E1.24, the inside Y resistances is first converted to equivalent Δ. Fig. E1.25 represents the equivalent network.

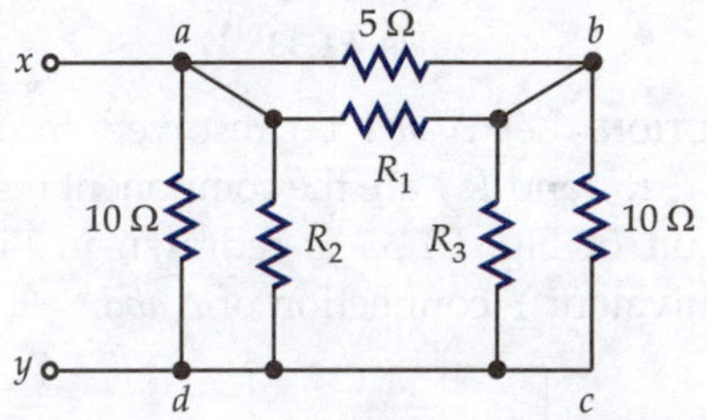

Fig. E1.25

Here, $R_1 = 2 + 2 + \dfrac{2 \times 2}{2} = 6\,\Omega$

Due to symmetry of the inside star network of Fig. E1.24, in Fig. E1.25,

$$R_1 = R_2 = R_3 = 6\,\Omega$$

Hence, $R_{ab} = \dfrac{5 \times R_1}{5 + R_1} = 2.73\,\Omega$

$$R_{bc} = \frac{10 \times R_3}{10 + R_3} = 3.75\,\Omega$$

$$R_{ad} = \frac{10 \times R_2}{10 + R_2} = 3.75\,\Omega$$

Fig. E1.26 represents the equivalent network of Fig. E1.25.

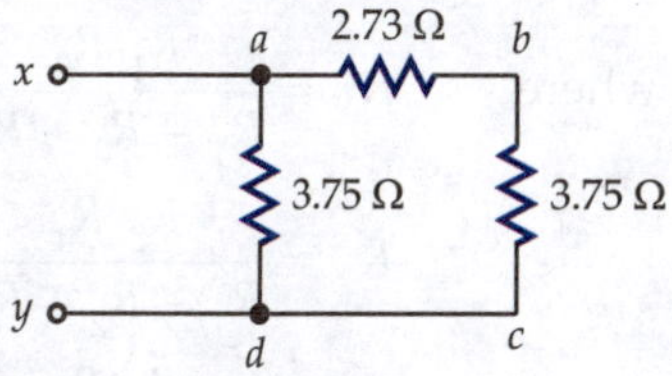

Fig. E1.26

Here,

$$R_{x-y} = R_{ad} \,||\, (R_{ab} + R_{bc})$$

$$= \mathbf{2.375\ \Omega.}$$

Example 1.35 *In Fig. E1.27, find the equivalent star network.*

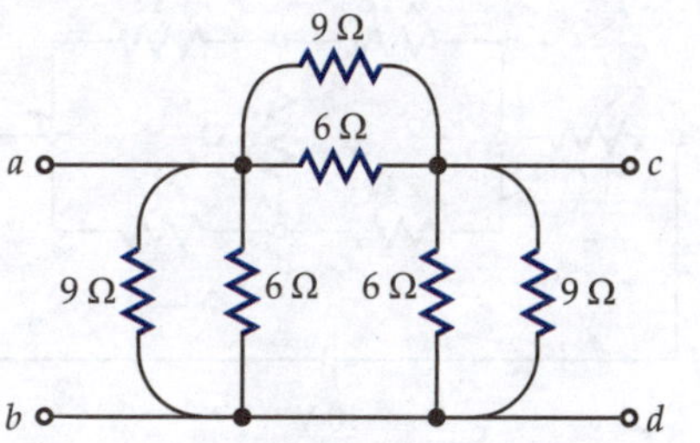

Fig. E1.27

Solution. Figure E1.28 represents the equivalent network of Fig. E1.27

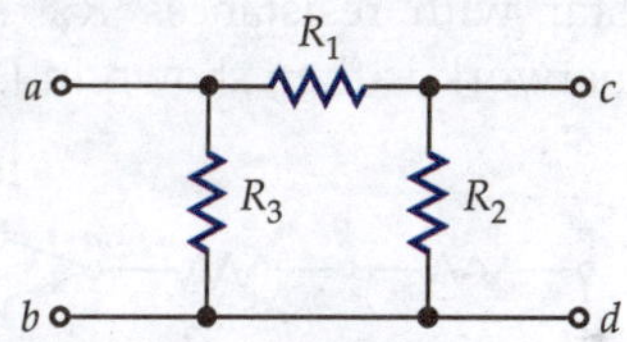

Fig. E1.28

Here,

$$R_1 = \frac{9 \times 6}{9 + 6} = 3.6\,\Omega$$

$$= R_2 = R_3.$$

Figure E1.29 represents the equivalent star network of Fig. E1.28

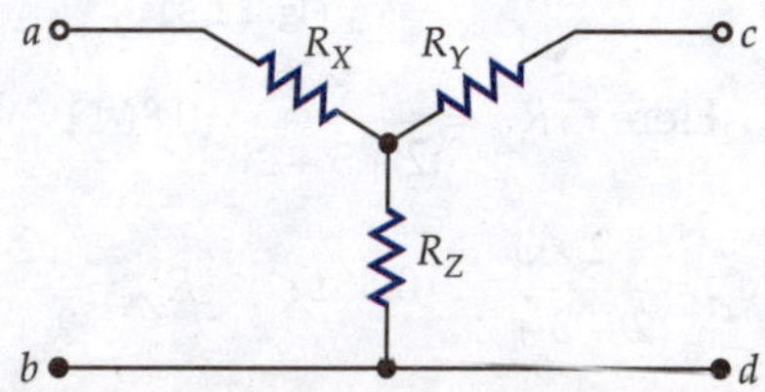

Fig. E1.29

It may be noted that star connection is frequently called as $Y\,(Y_{ye})$ connection while delta connection is also called as mesh connection. In case, the resistances are replaced by impedances, the result remains the same *i.e.*, only the resistances in the equations (1.35) and (1.37) are to be replaced by respective impedances.

Also, observing Figs. 1.11 (*a*) and (*b*), it may be indicated in this context that the star connection may also be termed as T connection while the delta connection can be termed as Π (pi) connection.

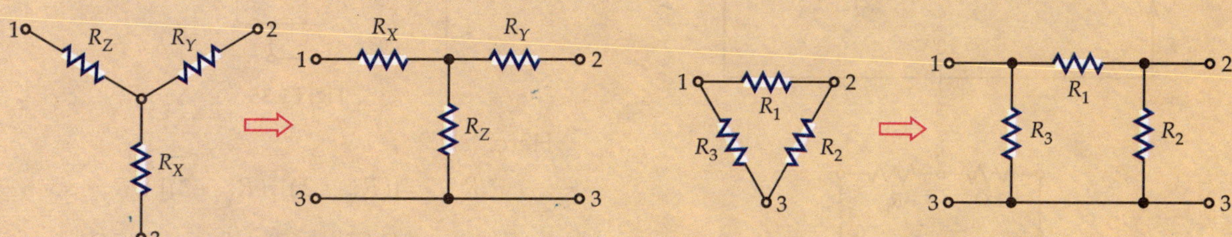

(*a*) T connection (*b*) Pie connection

Fig. 1.11

C H A P T E R 1

where, $R_X = \dfrac{R_1\,R_3}{R_1 + R_2 + R_3} = \dfrac{3.6 \times 3.6}{3 \times 3.6} = \mathbf{1.2\,\Omega}$

$$R_Y = \frac{R_2\,R_1}{R_1 + R_2 + R_3} = \mathbf{1.2\,\Omega}$$

and $R_Z = \dfrac{R_3\,R_2}{R_1 + R_2 + R_3} = \mathbf{1.2\,\Omega.}$

EXAMPLE 1.36 *Find the power loss in 1Ω resistor of Fig. E1.30.*

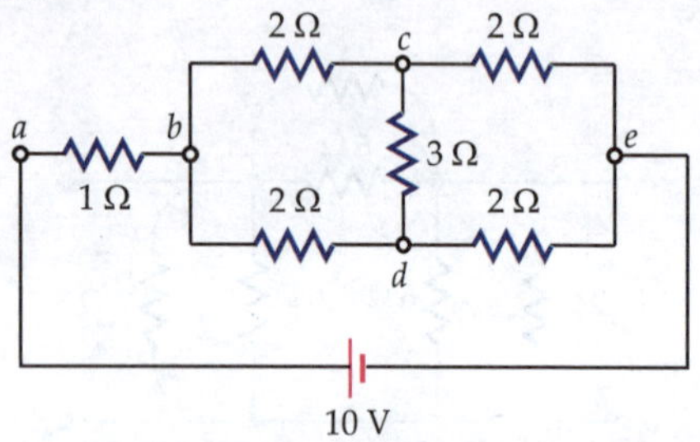

Fig. E1.30

SOLUTION. Let $\Delta\, bcd$ be reduced to equivalent star with resistances R_X, R_Y, R_Z and the whole network is then shown in Fig. E1.31.

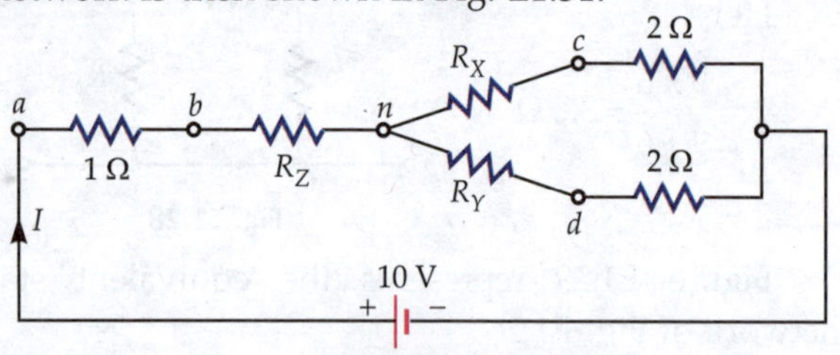

Fig. E1.31

Here, $R_X = \dfrac{2 \times 3}{2 + 3 + 2} = 0.86\,\Omega$

$$R_Y = \frac{2 \times 3}{2 + 3 + 2} = 0.86\,\Omega \;;\quad R_Z = \frac{2 \times 2}{2 + 3 + 2} = 0.57\,\Omega.$$

Figure E1.32 represents the equivalent circuit of Fig. E1.31.

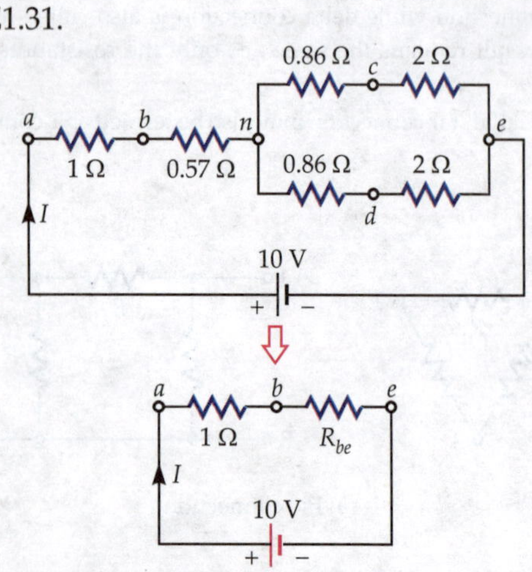

Fig. E1.32

Here,

$$R_{b-e} = [(0.86 + 2) \,||\, (0.86 + 2)] + 0.57 = 2\,\Omega$$

$$\therefore \quad I = \frac{10}{1 + 2} = 3.33\text{ A.}$$

Then power loss in 1Ω resistor is

$$I^2\,R = (3.33)^2 \times 1 = \mathbf{11\ W.}$$

EXAMPLE 1.37 *Find the source current in Fig. E1.33.*

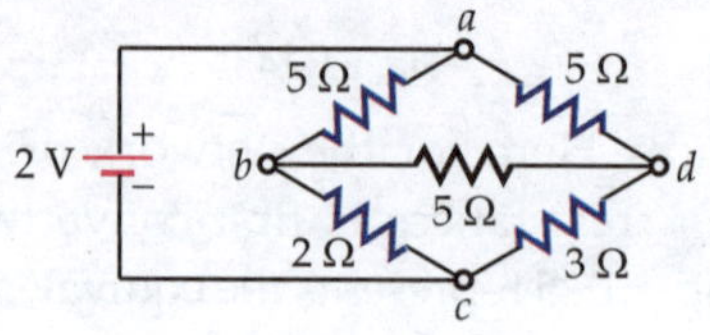

Fig. E1.33

SOLUTION. Let $\Delta\, abd$ be resolved in Y circuit when R_X, R_Y and R_Z are the component resistances. The circuit of Fig. E1.33 is redrawn in Fig. E1.34 with equivalent Y connection of $\Delta\, abd$.

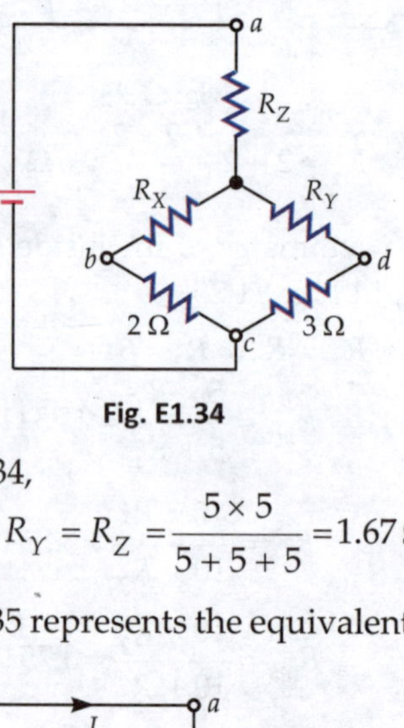

Fig. E1.34

In Fig. E1.34,

$$R_X = R_Y = R_Z = \frac{5 \times 5}{5 + 5 + 5} = 1.67\,\Omega$$

Figure E1.35 represents the equivalent circuit of Fig. E1.34.

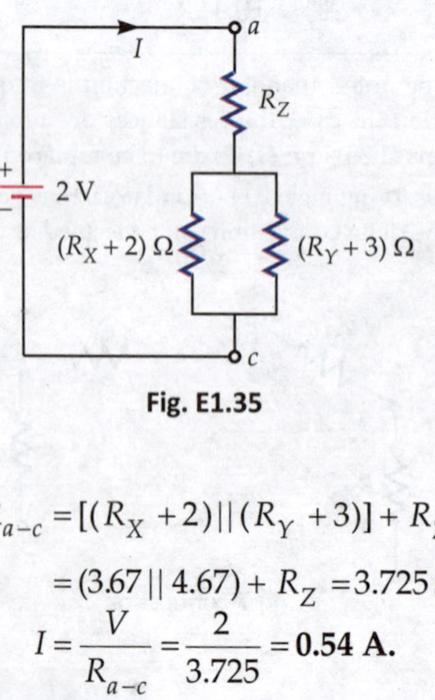

Fig. E1.35

Here,

$$R_{a-c} = [(R_X + 2) \,||\, (R_Y + 3)] + R_Z$$

$$= (3.67 \,||\, 4.67) + R_Z = 3.725\,\Omega$$

$$\therefore \quad I = \frac{V}{R_{a-c}} = \frac{2}{3.725} = \mathbf{0.54\ A.}$$

EXAMPLE 1.38 *Find the equivalent resistance across x-y in Fig. E1.36.*

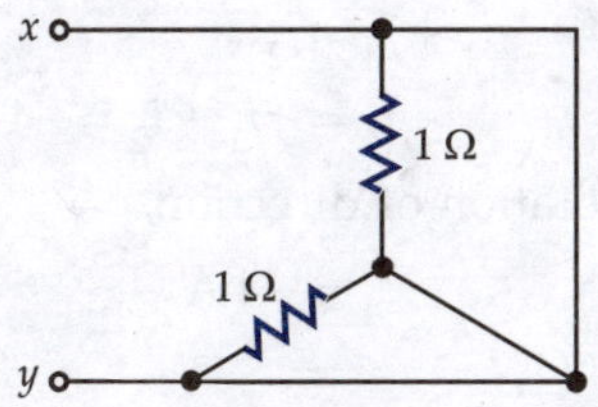

Fig. E1.36

SOLUTION. Figure E1.37 represents the circuit with equivalent Δ connection of the internal star network of Fig. E1.36.

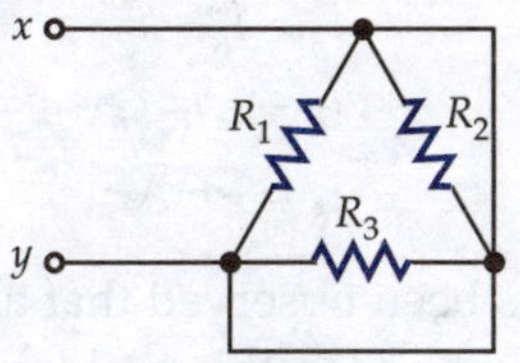

Fig. E1.37

$$\text{Here,}\quad R_1 = 1 + 1 + \frac{1\times 1}{0} = \infty$$

$$R_2 = 1 + 0 + \frac{1\times 0}{1} = 1\Omega$$

$$R_3 = 1 + 0 + \frac{1\times 0}{1} = 1\Omega$$

Figure E1.38 represents the equivalent circuit of Fig. E1.37.

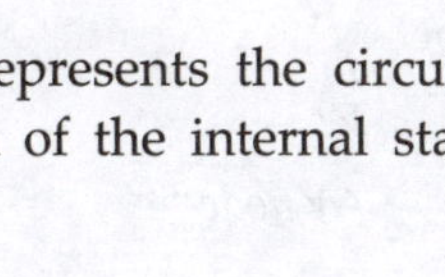

Fig. E1.38

$$\text{Here,}\quad R'_2 = \frac{R_2\times 0}{R_2 + 0} = 0$$

$$\text{and}\quad R'_3 = \frac{R_3\times 0}{R_3 + 0} = 0$$

[∵ R_2 and R_3 are shunted by short circuits]

Figure E1.39 represents the final equivalent circuit when R_{x-y} **=0.**

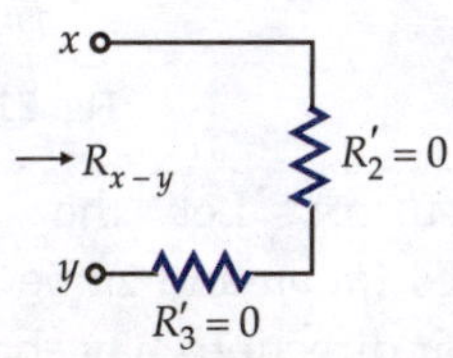

Fig. E1.39

1.8 KIRCHHOF'S LAWS

A German physicist Gustav Kirchhoff developed two laws enabling easier analysis of an interconnection of any number of circuit elements. The first law deals with flow of current and is popularly known as *Kirchhoff's Current Laws* (KCL) while the second one deals with voltage drop in a closed network and is known as *Kirchhoff's voltage laws* (KVL).

KCL : The algebraic sum of currents at any node* of a circuit is zero.

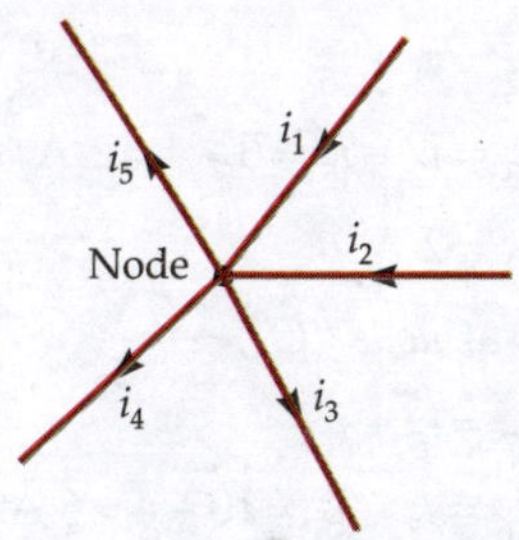

Fig. 1.12 Currents meeting at a point in a network

In Fig. 1.12, as per KCL,

$$i_1 + i_2 - i_3 - i_4 - i_5 = 0 \,.....$$

(the direction of incoming currents to a node being +ve, the outgoing currents should be taken –ve. The reverse sense of directions can also be taken).

$$\text{Thus}\quad i_1 + i_2 = i_3 + i_4 + i_5 \qquad ...(1.38)$$

i.e., the algebraic sum of currents entering a node must be equal to the algebraic sum of the currents leaving a node**.

EXAMPLE 1.39 *Find the magnitude and direction of the unknown currents in Fig. E1.40.*

Given

$$i_1 = 10\ A,\ i_2 = 6\ A,\ i_5 = 4\ A.$$

SOLUTION. By observation, it is evident that

$$i_1 = i_7$$

$$\therefore\quad i_7 = 10\text{ A}$$

At *node "a"*, from KCL,

$$i_1 = i_2 + i_4$$

$$\text{or,}\quad 10 = 6 + i_4 \quad \text{or,}\ i_4 = 4\text{ A}$$

* A node is a junction of two or more branches of an electrical network.

** KCL also indicates the law of conservation of charges and can also be stated as at any node of a circuit, at every instant of time, *the sum of incoming currents is equal to the sum of outgoing currents.*

CHAPTER 1

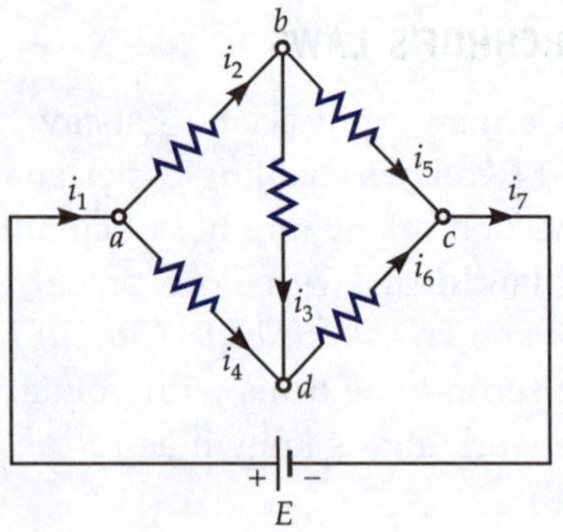

Fig. E1.40*

At *node "b"*, utilising KCL,

$$i_2 = i_3 + i_5$$

or, $$i_3 = i_2 - i_5 = 6 - 4 = 2 \text{ A}$$

i.e., $$i_3 = 2 \text{ A}$$

Similarly, at *node "C"*,

$$i_7 = i_5 + i_6$$

giving $$i_6 = i_7 - i_5 = 10 - 4 = 6 \text{ A.}$$

∴ $$i_6 = 6 \text{ A}$$

Then, all the unknown currents of the problem being determined, the branch currents become

$$i_1 = i_7 = \mathbf{10\ A}$$
$$i_2 = \mathbf{6\ A}$$
$$i_3 = \mathbf{2\ A}$$
$$i_4 = \mathbf{4\ A}$$
$$i_5 = \mathbf{4\ A}$$
$$i_6 = \mathbf{6\ A.}$$

It may be noted that the assumed directions of unknown currents are arbitrary and any direction can be taken. Let us repeat the same problem with the assumed direction of currents reversed. The given values are bracketed in the respective places in Fig. E1.41.

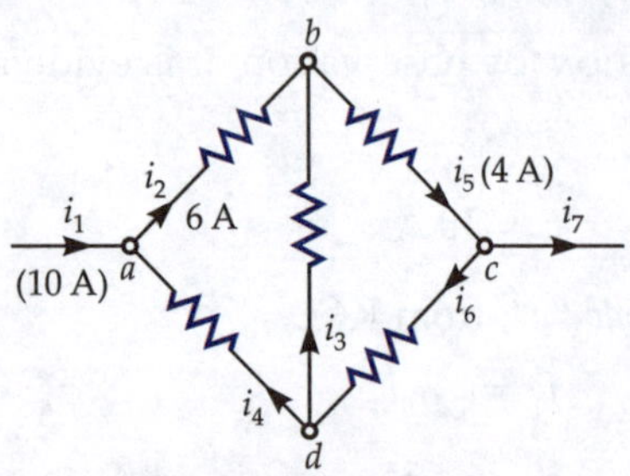

Fig. E1.41

Let the direction of unknown currents i_3, i_4 and i_6 be reversed in Fig. E1.41. Applying KCL at *node "a"*,

$$i_1 + i_4 = i_2$$

or, $$i_4 = -i_1 + i_2 = -4 \text{ A}$$

i.e., in this notation of direction,

$$i_4 = -4 \text{ A}$$

At *node "b"*,

$$i_2 + i_3 = i_5$$

or, $$i_3 = i_5 - i_2 = -2 \text{ A}$$

∴ $$i_3 = -2 \text{ A}$$

At *node "c"*,

$$i_5 = i_6 + i_7$$

or, $$i_6 = i_5 - i_7 = 4 - 10 = -6 \text{ A.}$$

∴ $$i_6 = -6 \text{ A}$$

It has thus been observed that all the unknown currents, determined in this problem assumed with reversed sense of sign have come out as –ve. This clearly indicates that the assumed signs of unknown currents could not influence the final magnitude and direction of currents *i.e.*, say i_3 *in loop "abd"* of Fig. E1.41 has come out to be + 4 A when assumed to be flowing downwards from "*b*" to "*d*". In Fig. E1.41, *in loop "abd"*, i_3 has been assumed to be flowing upwards from "*d*" to "*b*" but has come out to be (– 4 A) indicating the versatility of KCL where the assumed direction of currents in solving the problems does not have any implication on the final value and direction of the current determined.

EXAMPLE 1.40 *In Fig. E1.42, find "v" and the magnitude and direction of the unknown currents in the branches xn, yn and zn.*

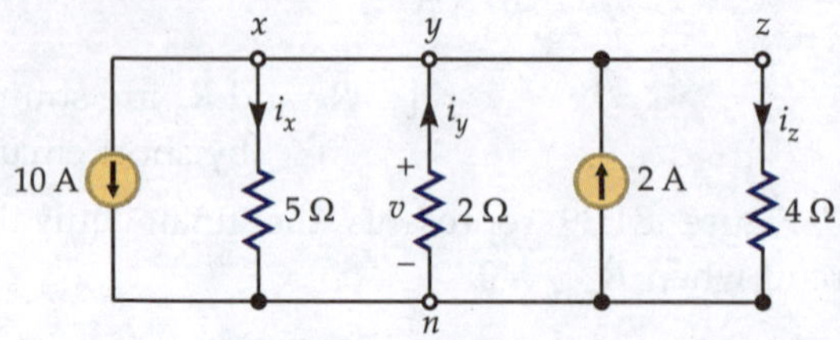

Fig. E1.42

SOLUTION. Let the unknown currents in branches *xn*, *yn* and *zn* be i_x, i_y and i_z respectively and their directions have been shown in Fig. E1.42.

* Numerical values of resistances in the circuits of Fig. E1.40 and E1.41 are not required in solving the given problems and hence not indicated in the respective figures.

At *node "y"* form KCL,

$$10 + i_x + i_z = i_y + 2$$

or, $$i_x - i_y + i_z = -8 \qquad \text{...}(i)$$

Again, from Ohm's law,

$$i_x = \frac{v}{5}\text{ A},\ i_y = -\frac{v}{2}\text{ A and } i_z = \frac{v}{4}\text{ A}$$

Then, from (*i*),

$$\frac{v}{5} + \frac{v}{2} + \frac{v}{4} = -8$$

or, $$v = -8 \times \frac{20}{19} = -8.42\text{ V}$$

[–ve sign of v indicates node n to be +ve and at higher potential]

$$v = -8.42\text{ V}$$

$$\therefore \quad i_x = -\frac{8.42}{5} = -\mathbf{1.684\ A}$$

[*i.e.*, current flows from "*n*" to "*x*"]

$$i_y = -\frac{(-8.42)}{2} = \mathbf{4.21\ A}$$

[*i.e.*, current flows from "*n*" to "*y*"]

$$i_z = -\frac{8.42}{4} = -\mathbf{2.1\ A}$$

[*i.e.*, current flows from "*n*" to "*z*"]

Figure E1.43 represents actual direction of currents in the redrawn circuit.

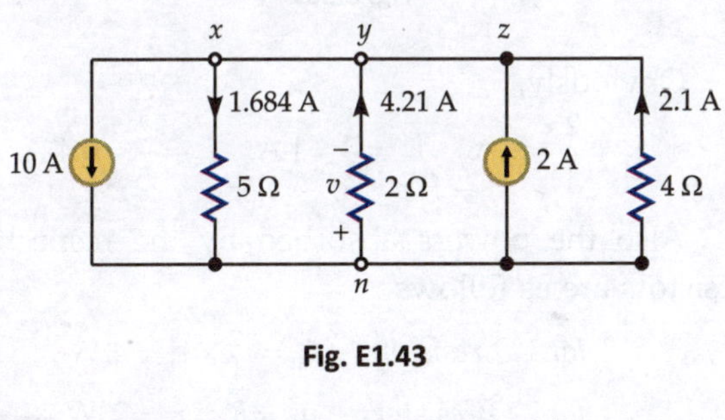

Fig. E1.43

EXAMPLE 1.41 *Find i_1 and i_2 in Fig. E1.44.*

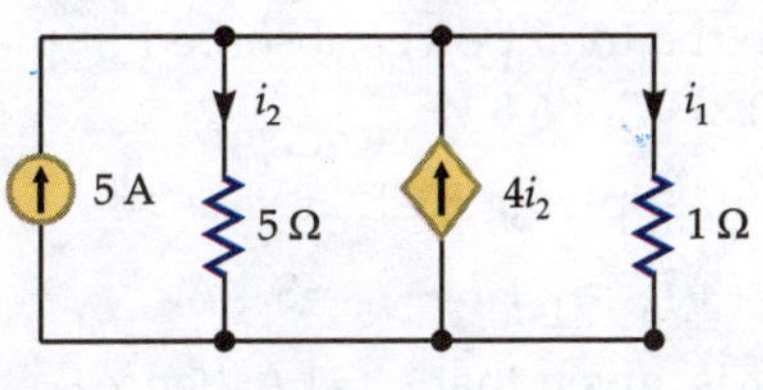

Fig. E1.44

SOLUTION. Let us assume that the voltage drop across 5 Ω or 1 Ω resistor be v volts (Fig. E1.45 where v is shown with assumed polarity)

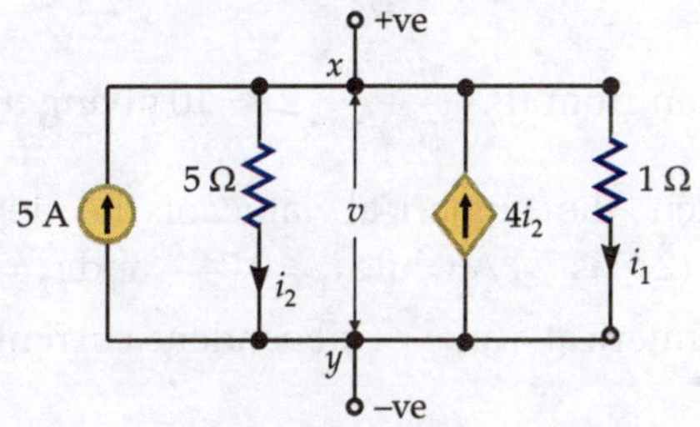

Fig. E1.45

Applying KCL at *node x*,

$$i_2 + i_1 = 5 + 4i_2$$

or, $$i_1 - 3i_2 = 5 \qquad \text{...}(i)$$

However,

$$i_1 = \frac{v}{1} = v\text{ A} \quad \text{and} \quad i_2 = \frac{v}{5}\text{ A}$$

Then from (*i*),

$$v - \frac{3}{5}v = 5 \quad \text{or} \quad v = 12.5\text{ V}$$

This gives $i_1 = \mathbf{12.5\ A}$ and $i_2 = \mathbf{2.5\ A}$.

Check

As at *node x*, $i_1 + i_2 = 5 + 4\,i_2$, hence, with the obtained values of i_1 and i_2, this equation is satisfied.

EXAMPLE 1.42 *Obtain the numerical value of the voltage dependent current source in Fig. E1.46.*

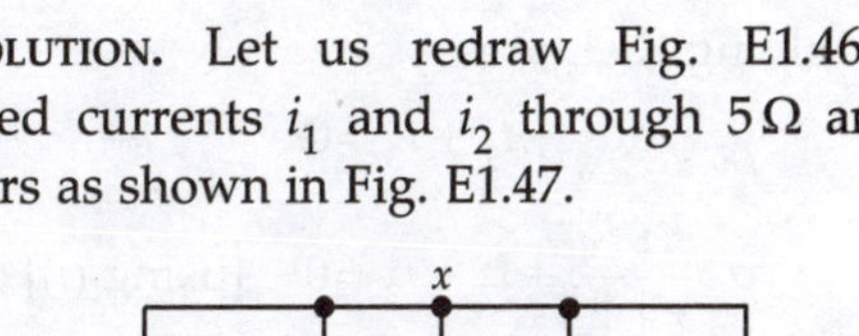

Fig. E1.46

SOLUTION. Let us redraw Fig. E1.46 with assumed currents i_1 and i_2 through 5 Ω and 2 Ω resistors as shown in Fig. E1.47.

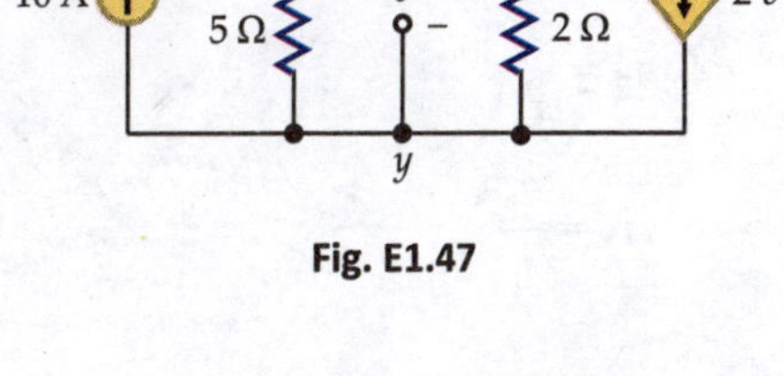

Fig. E1.47

Applying KCL at *node x*,

$$i_1 + i_2 + 2v = 10 \quad ...(i)$$

But $\quad i_1 = \frac{v}{5}$ A and $i_2 = \frac{v}{2}$ A

Then from (*i*), $\frac{v}{5} + \frac{v}{2} + 2v = 10$ giving $v = 3.7$ V.

Then, the numerical value of the dependent source ($2v$) is 7.4 A while $i_1 = 0.74$ A and $i_2 = 1.85$ A.

Numerical value of dependent current source = **7.4 A.**

Example 1.43 *Figure E1.48 represents an approximate equivalent circuit of a field effect transistor amplifier. Using KCL find the output voltage v_2 in terms of input voltage v_1.*

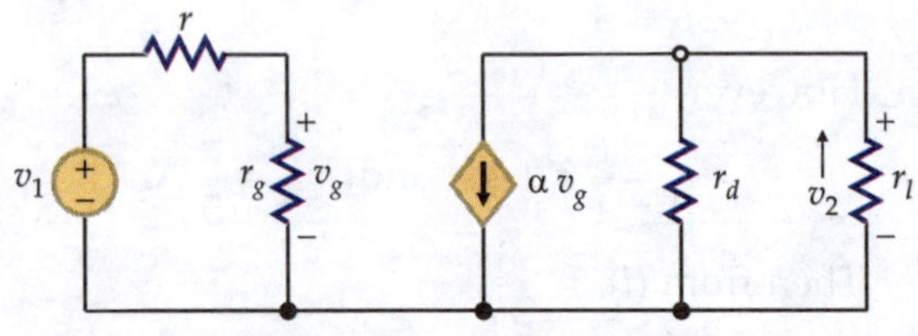

Fig. E1.48

Solution. The circuit of Fig. E1.48 is redrawn as shown in Fig. E1.49.

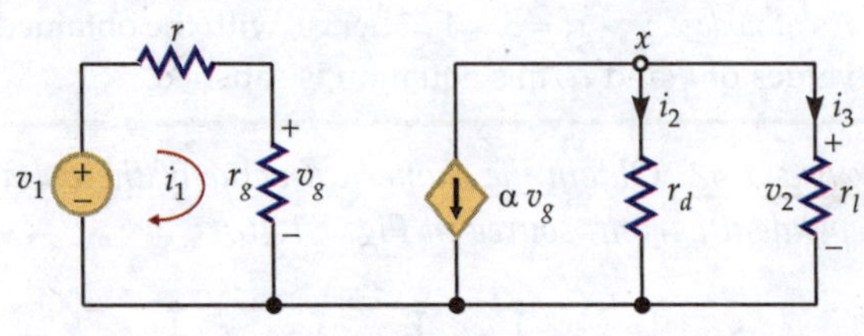

Fig. E1.49

Here, $\quad i_1 = \frac{v_1}{r + r_g}$ A

$$v_g = \frac{v_1}{r + r_g} . r_g \text{ volts} \quad ...(i)$$

Applying KCL at *x*,

$$\alpha v_g + i_2 + i_3 = 0.$$

or, $\quad \alpha . \frac{v_1 r_g}{r + r_g} + i_2 + i_3 = 0 \quad$ [using (*i*)] $\quad ...(ii)$

However,

$$i_2 = \frac{v_2}{r_d}$$

and $\quad i_3 = \frac{v_2}{r_l}.$

Thus from (*ii*),

$$\alpha \frac{v_1 r_g}{r + r_g} + \frac{v_2}{r_d} + \frac{v_2}{r_l} = 0$$

or, $\quad v_2 \left(\frac{1}{r_d} + \frac{1}{r_l} \right) = -\frac{\alpha r_g v_1}{r_g + r}$

or $\quad v_2 = \frac{-\alpha r_g v_1 r_d r_l}{(r_g + r)(r_d + r_l)}.$

Example 1.44 *What is the power absorbed in the resistors of Fig. E1.50 ? Assume $i_0 = 1$ A.*

Also find the current from 2 V source.

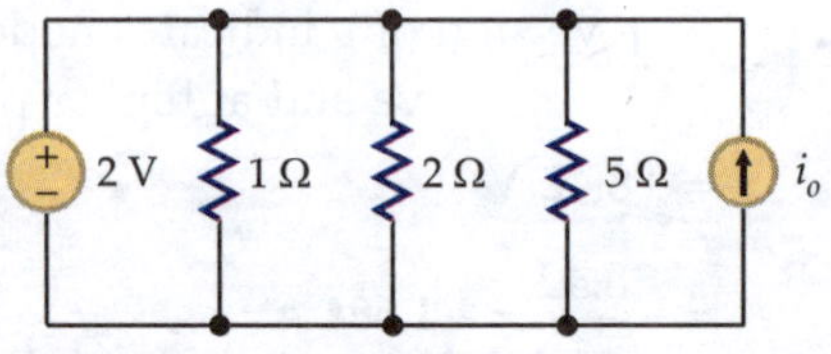

Fig. E1.50

Solution. Let us redraw the circuit as shown in Fig. E1.51 with the currents i_1, i_2 and i_5 as assumed through the respective resistances.

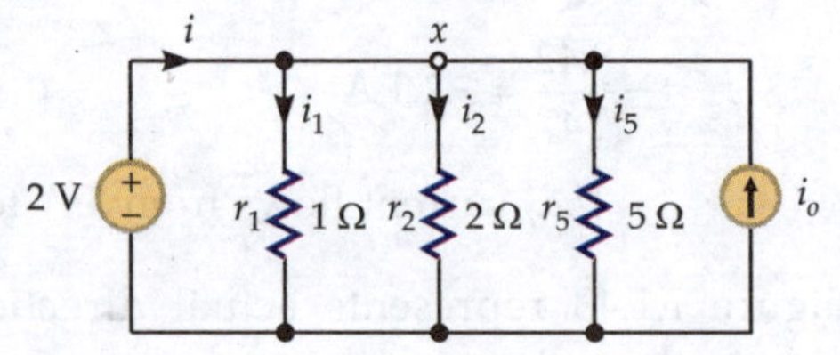

Fig. E1.51

Obviously,

$$i_1 = \frac{2}{1} = 2 \text{ A}; \quad i_2 = \frac{2}{2} = 1 \text{ A}; \quad i_5 = \frac{2}{5} = 0.4 \text{ A}.$$

Also the powers absorbed by the respective resistors are as follows :

for 1Ω *resistor* : $p_1 = i_1^2 \times r_1 = 4$ W

for 2 Ω *resistor* : $p_2 = i_2^2 \times r_2 = 2$ W

for 5 Ω *resistor* : $p_5 = i_5^2 \times r_5 = 0.8$ W

Then the total power absorbed in the circuit is $(4 + 2 + 0.8)$ W or 6.8 W.

Again, applying KCL at *node "x"*,

$$i + i_0 = i_1 + i_2 + i_5 = 3.4 \text{ A}.$$

As it is, given that $i_0 = 1$ A, hence,

$$i = 3.4 - i_0 = 2.4 \text{ A}.$$

∴ We finally obtain the power absorbed in resistors as follows :

$p_1 = 4$ **W**, $p_2 = 2$ **W** and $p_5 = 0.8$ **W** while the voltage source current is **2.4 A.**

Check

The power delivered by the voltage source is (vi) *i.e.,* 4.8 W. The power delivered by the current source is vi_0 *i.e.,* 2 W. The total source power is then $4.8 + 2.0 = 6.8$ W while the net power consumed has been obtained as 6.8 W. This shows conservation of power.

EXAMPLE 1.45 *Obtain the value of i in Fig. E1.52 if* $i_1 = 3$ *A,* $i_2 = -2$ *A in the dependent current sources.*

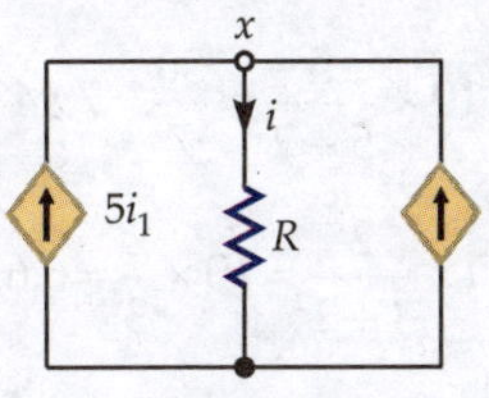

Fig. E1.52

SOLUTION. Utilising KCL at *node "x"*,

$$5i_1 + 3i_2 = i$$

or, $$5 \times 3 + 3(-2) = i$$

or, $$\mathbf{i = 9\ A.}$$

EXAMPLE 1.46 *Obtain the value of R in the circuit of Fig. E1.53.*

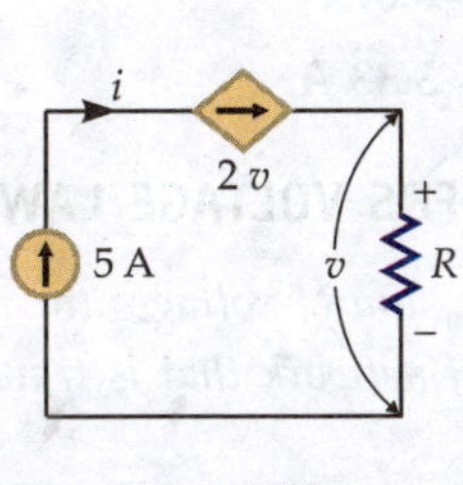

Fig. E1.53

SOLUTION. In the circuit of Fig. E1.53.

$$i = 5 = 2v.$$

∴ $$v = 5/2 = 2.5\ \text{V}.$$

However,

$$v = iR$$

or, $$2.5 = 5 \,.\, R$$

i.e., $$\mathbf{R = 0.5\ \Omega.}$$

EXAMPLE 1.47 *Obtain the value of i in the circuit of Fig. E1.54 if :*

(a) $v = 1$ *V* *(b)* $v = +2$ *V.*

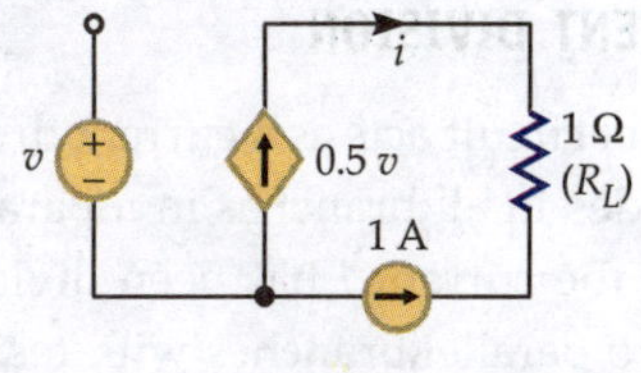

Fig. E1.54

SOLUTION. In the right hand *loop*, by KCL,

$$i = 0.5\,v - 1$$

for $v = 1$ V, $i = -$ **0.5 A,**

i.e., *i* is flowing in the anticlockwise direction.

For $v = +2$ V,

$\mathbf{i = 0}$; *i.e.* no current in the loop.

EXAMPLE 1.48 *Find v in Fig. E1.55 if* $v_1 = 20$ *V.*

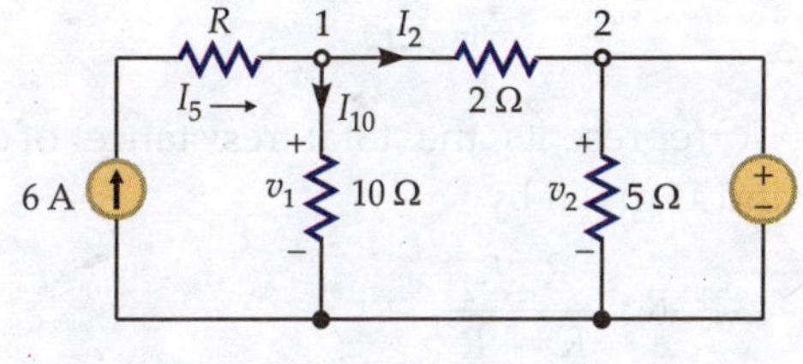

Fig. E1.55

SOLUTION. Current through the 10 Ω resistor is $\frac{v_1}{10}$ *i.e.,* 2 A(I_{10}).

Applying KCL at *node* 1 in the network,

$$I_5 = I_{10} + I_2$$

or, $$I_2 = I_5 - I_{10} = 6 - 2 = 4\ \text{A}$$

[∵ I_5 is the source current (6 A)]

This gives drop v_{12} in the 2 Ω resistor as $4 \times 2 = 8$ V.

However, $v_1 = 20$ V;

hence, $$v_2 = 20 - v_{12} = 12\ \text{V}.$$

By inspection it is evident that $v_2 = v$.

∴ $$\mathbf{v = 12\ V}$$

The current entering the voltage source v can also be found by applying KCL at *node* 2.

Here, I_2 = current through 5 Ω resistor + current entering v (the voltage source).

or, current entering $v = I_2 -$ current through 5 Ω resistor

$$= 4 - \frac{v_2}{5} = 4 - \frac{12}{5} = \mathbf{1.6\ A.}$$

CHAPTER 1

1.9 CURRENT DIVISION

A parallel circuit acts as a current divider as the current divides in all branches in a parallel circuit. In Fig. 1.13, the current I has been divided into I_1 and I_2 in two parallel branches with resistances R_1 and R_2 while V represents the drop across R_1 or R_2.

Obviously, $I_1 = \dfrac{V}{R_1}$ and $I_2 = \dfrac{V}{R_2}$.

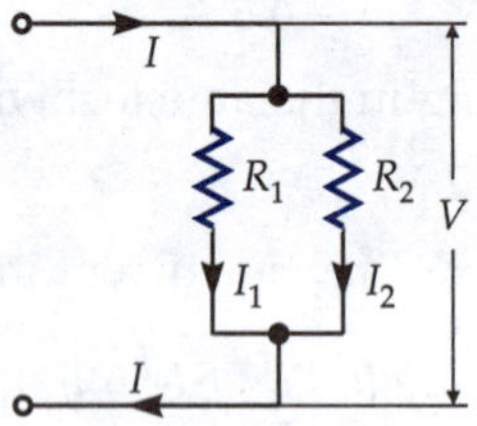

Fig. 1.13

Let R represents the total resistance of the circuit and is given by

$$R = \frac{R_1\, R_2}{R_1 + R_2}$$

Also, $$I = \frac{V}{R} = \frac{V\,(R_1 + R_2)}{R_1\, R_2}$$

But $V = I_1\, R_1 = I_2\, R_2$.

$\therefore$ We finally get,

$$I = \frac{I_1\, R_1\,(R_1 + R_2)}{R_1\, R_2} = \frac{I_1}{R_2}(R_1 + R_2) \quad ...(1.39)$$

and also, $$I = \frac{I_2\, R_2}{R_1\, R_2}(R_1 + R_2) = \frac{I_2}{R_1}(R_1 + R_2) \quad ...(1.40)$$

Thus, from (1.39),

$$I_1 = I\frac{R_2}{R_1 + R_2} \quad ...(1.41)$$

while from (1.40),

$$I_2 = I\frac{R_1}{R_1 + R_2} \quad ...(1.42)$$

To conclude, it may be said that *the current in any of the parallel branches is equal to the ratio of opposite branch resistance to the total resistance, multiplied by the total current.*

EXAMPLE 1.49 *Find i_1, i_2, i_3 and i_4 in Fig. E1.56.*

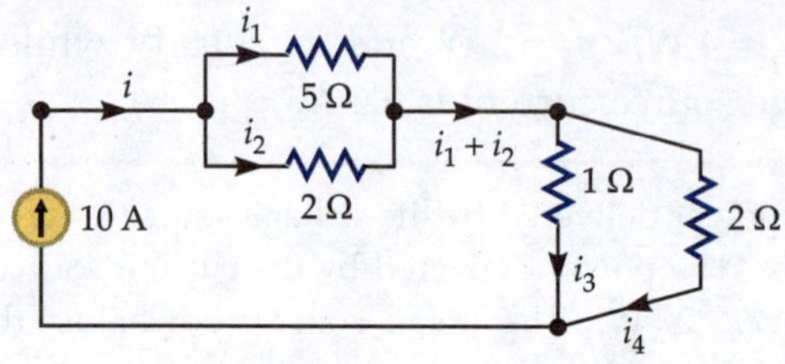

Fig. E1.56

SOLUTION. Using the current division method,

$$i_1 = i \times \frac{2}{5+2} = 10 \times \frac{2}{7} = 2.857 \text{ A}$$

$$i_2 = 10 \times \frac{5}{5+2} = \frac{50}{7} = 7.143 \text{ A}$$

$$i_3 = i \times \frac{2}{1+2} = 10 \times \frac{2}{3} = 6.67 \text{ A}$$

$$i_4 = i \times \frac{1}{1+2} = 10 \times \frac{1}{3} = 3.33 \text{ A}$$

It may be noted that in every case $i_1 + i_2 = 10$ A and $i_3 + i_4 = 10$ A. Then the obtained branch currents are

i_1 = **2.857 A**
i_2 = **7.143 A**
i_3 = **6.67 A**
i_4 = **3.33 A.**

1.10 KIRCHHOFF'S VOLTAGE LAW (KVL)

The algebraic sum of voltages (or voltage drops) in any closed path of network that is traversed in a single direction is zero.

Both the Figures (Fig. 1.14 and Fig. 1.15) show closed circuits (also termed as mesh). As per KVL, in Fig. 1.14,

$$-V_1 + (-V_2) + iR_1 + iR_2 = 0 \quad ...(1.43)$$

[Here, the assumed current i causes a +ve drop of voltage when flowing from +ve to –ve potential while –ve drop while the current flowing from –ve to +ve potential]

or, $$i\,(R_1 + R_2) = V_1 + V_2$$

giving $$i = \frac{V_1 + V_2}{(R_1 + R_2)}.$$

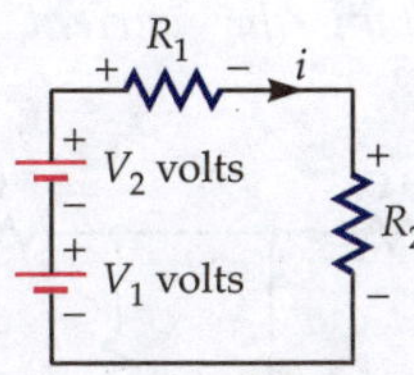

Fig. 1.14 Application of KVL with series connected voltage sources

On the other hand, in Fig. 1.15, from KVL, with assumed direction of the circuit current i,

$$-V_1 + iR_1 + V_2 + iR_2 + iR_3 = 0 \qquad ...(1.44)$$

or, $$i(R_1 + R_2 + R_3) = V_1 - V_2$$

giving $$i = \frac{V_1 - V_2}{R_1 + R_2 + R_3}$$

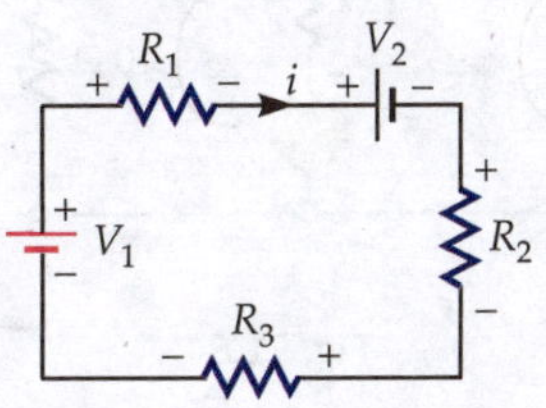

Fig. 1.15 Application of KVL while voltage sources are connected in opposite polarity

It may be noted that the voltage V_1 is –ve in both the equations (1.43) and (1.44) while V_2 is –ve in Eqn. (1.43) but +ve in Eqn. (1.44). This is because of the fact that in Fig. 1.14 and in Fig. 1.15, with assumed directions of current, the current within the source (V_1) flows from –ve to +ve polarity while for V_2, the current flows from –ve to +ve polarity within V_2 (Fig. 1.14) and from +ve to –ve polarity in Fig. 1.15.

In this context it may be noted that for dependent sources in the circuit, KVL can also be applied. *In case of calculation of power of any source, when the current enters the source, the power is absorbed by the source while the source delivers the power if the current is coming out of the source.*

EXAMPLE 1.50 *In Fig. E1.57, find v_s using Kirchhoff's laws.*

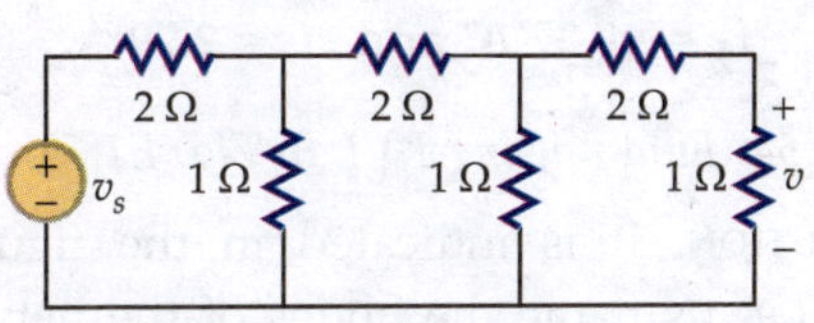

Fig. E1.57

SOLUTION. Figure E1.57 is redrawn as shown in Fig. E1.58.

In branch "*de*",

$$i_{de} = \frac{v}{1} = v \text{ A.}$$

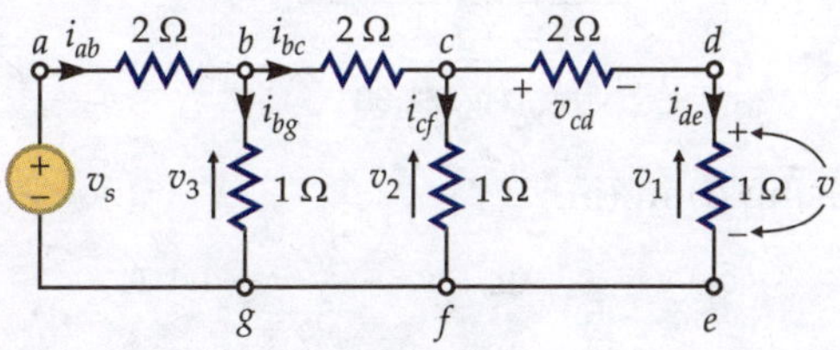

Fig. E1.58

However,

$$v_2\,(= v_{cf}) = v_{cd} + v_{de}$$
$$= i_{de}.2 + v = 2v + v = 3v.$$
$$\left[\because\ i_{de} = \frac{v}{1} \text{ (in branch } de)\right]$$

$$\therefore \quad i_{cf} = \frac{v_{cf}}{1} = 3v \text{ A.}$$

Also, $$v_3 = v_{bc} + v_{cf} = (i_{cf} + i_{de})2 + 3v$$
$$= (3v + v)2 + 3v = 11\,v$$

Again

$$i_{ab} = i_{bg} + i_{bc} = \frac{v_3}{1} + (i_{cf} + i_{de})$$
$$= 11\,v + 4\,v = 15\,v$$

However,

$$v_s = v_{ab} + v_3 = i_{ab} \times 2 + 11\,v$$
$$= 30\,v + 11\,v = 41\,v$$

$$\therefore \quad \mathbf{v_s = 41\,v.}$$

EXAMPLE 1.51 *Find the current i in Fig. E1.59.*

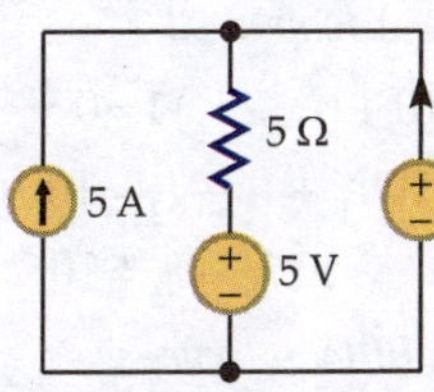

Fig. E1.59

SOLUTION. The circuit is redrawn as shown in Fig. E1.60. Here, utilising KCL,

$$i_2 = i_1 + i = 5 + i \qquad ...(i)$$

Using KVL *in loop abcd*,

$$5i_2 + 5 = 8 \quad \text{or,} \quad i_2 = \frac{3}{5} \text{ A} \qquad ...(ii)$$

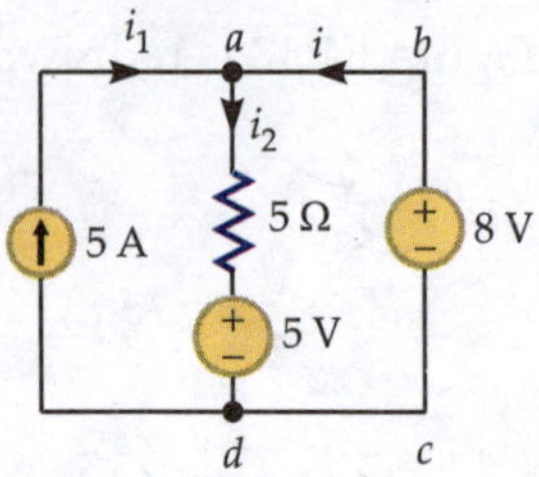

Fig. E1.60

Using (*i*) in (*ii*),

$$5 + i = \frac{3}{5} \quad \text{or,} \quad i = -\frac{22}{5} = -4.4 \text{ A}$$

$$\boldsymbol{i = -4.4 \text{ A.}}$$

[the –ve sign indicates that the actual current in branch *bc* enters 8 V source]

EXAMPLE 1.52 *Find the current and power dissipated in the 5 Ω resistor in the circuit shown in Fig. E1.61.*

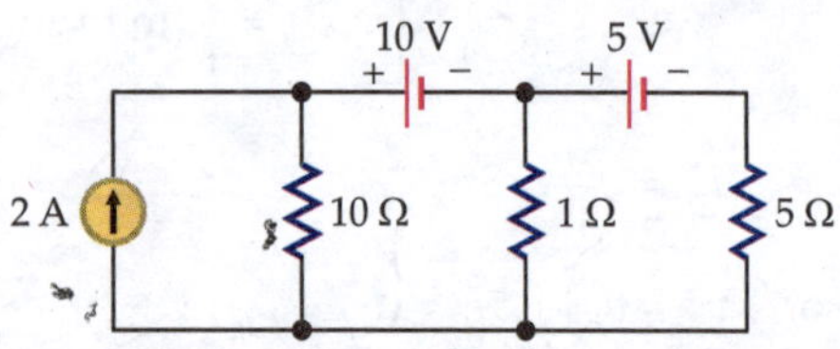

Fig. E1.61

SOLUTION. At first step, the 2 A current source is transformed to an equivalent voltage source and the circuit is redrawn in Fig. E1.62.

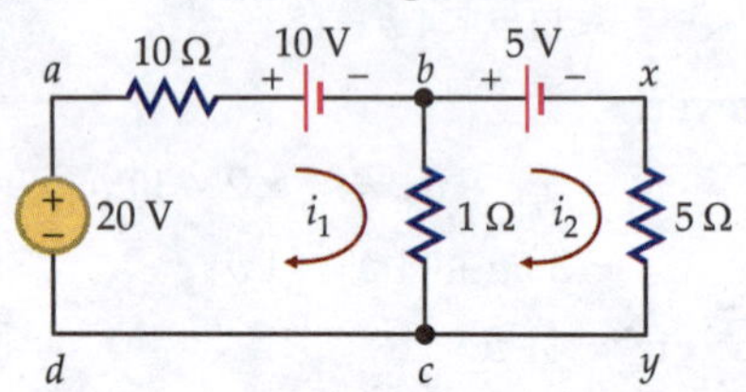

Fig. E1.62

Applying KVL at *loop abcd*,

$$-20 + 10\,i_1 + 10 + (i_1 - i_2)1 = 0$$

or, $$10\,i_1 + i_1 - i_2 = 10$$

or, $$11\,i_1 - i_2 = 10 \qquad \text{...}(i)$$

Applying KVL *in loop bxyc*,

$$(i_2 - i_1)1 + 5 + 5i_2 = 0$$

or, $$i_1 - 6i_2 = 5 \qquad \text{...}(ii)$$

Solving (*i*) and (*ii*), $i_2 = -\frac{9}{13}$ A *i.e.*, the current through 5 Ω resistor is $\frac{9}{13}$ A flowing from *y* to *x*. The power loss p_5 in the 5 Ω resistor is $(i_2^2 \times 5)$ *i.e.*, **2.4 W (approx.).**

EXAMPLE 1.53 *Obtain the current i_1 using KVL (Fig. E1.63).*

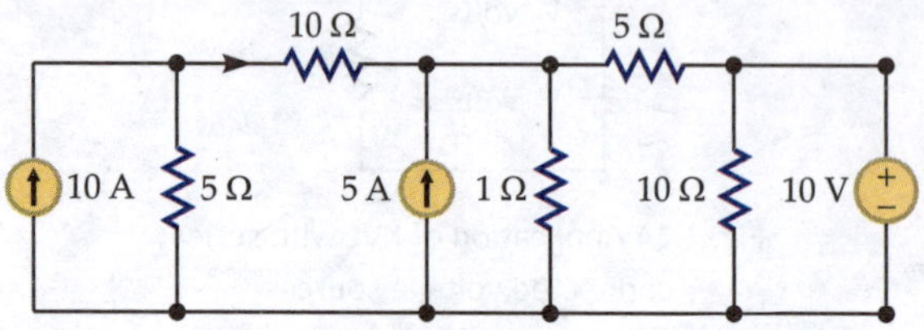

Fig. E1.63

SOLUTION. The current sources of Fig. E1.63 are transformed to the voltage sources as shown in Fig. E1.64.

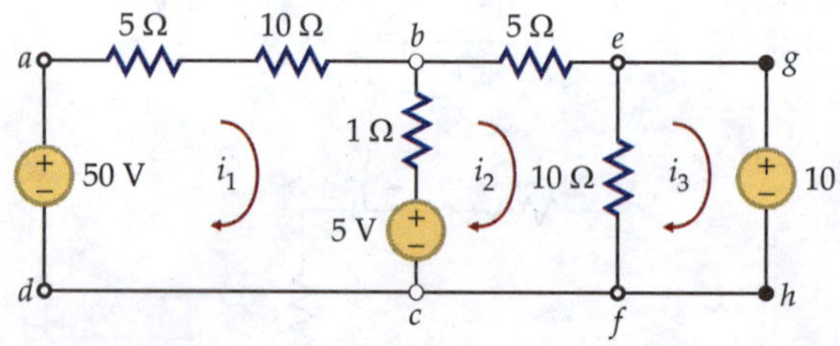

Fig. E1.64

In *loop abcd*,

$$-50 + 15\,i_1 + (i_1 - i_2)1 + 5 = 0$$

or, $$16\,i_1 - i_2 = 45 \qquad \text{...}(i)$$

In loop befc,

$$-5 + (i_2 - i_1)1 + 5i_2 + (i_2 - i_3)10 = 0$$

or, $$16\,i_2 - i_1 - 10\,i_3 = 5 \qquad \text{...}(ii)$$

In loop eghf, $$(i_3 - i_2)10 + 10 = 0$$

or, $$10\,i_3 - 10\,i_2 = -10 \qquad \text{...}(iii)$$

From (*iii*),

$$i_3 - i_2 = -1 \quad \text{or} \quad i_3 = (i_2 - 1) \qquad \text{...}(iv)$$

Using (*iv*) in (*ii*),

$$16\,i_2 - i_1 - 10\,(i_2 - 1) = 5$$

or, $$16\,i_2 - i_1 - 10\,i_2 + 10 = 5$$

or, $$6i_2 - i_1 = -5$$

or, $$i_1 - 6\,i_2 = 5 \qquad \text{...}(v)$$

Solving (*i*) and (*v*),

$$\boldsymbol{i_2 = -0.37 \text{ A} \quad \text{and} \quad i_1 = 2.79 \text{ A.}}$$

EXAMPLE 1.54 *Find v using KVL in Fig. E1.65.*

SOLUTION. It is indicated in the figure that $i_L = 1$ A. Let us name the nodes of the network of Fig. E1.65 as shown.

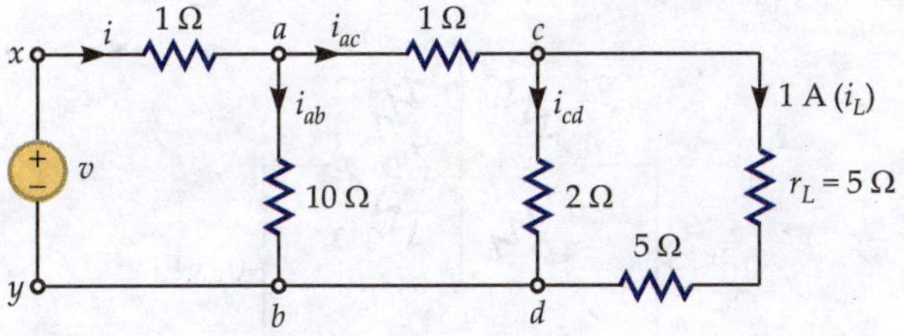

Fig. E1.65

$$\therefore \quad v_{cd} = i_L\,(5+5) = 10\,i_L = 10 \text{ V and thus}$$

$$i_{cd} = \frac{10}{2} = 5 \text{ A.}$$

This gives,

$$i_{ac} = i_{cd} + i_L = 6 \text{ A}$$

(using KCL at node *c*)

Then $v_{ac} = i_{ac} \times 1 = 6$ V

and $v_{ab} = v_{ac} + v_{cd} = 6 + 10 = 16$ V.

$$\therefore\ i_{ab} = \frac{v_{ab}}{10} = 1.6 \text{ A and for KCL at node } a,$$

$$i = i_{ab} + i_{ac} \text{ giving } i = 7.6 \text{ A.}$$

Using KVL at the leftmost loop of Fig. E1.65,

$$v = v_{xa} + v_{ab} = 7.6 \times 1 + 16 + 7.6 \times 5$$

$$\mathbf{v = 61.6\ V.}$$

Example 1.55 *In Fig. E1.66 find voltage drop across x-y terminals.*

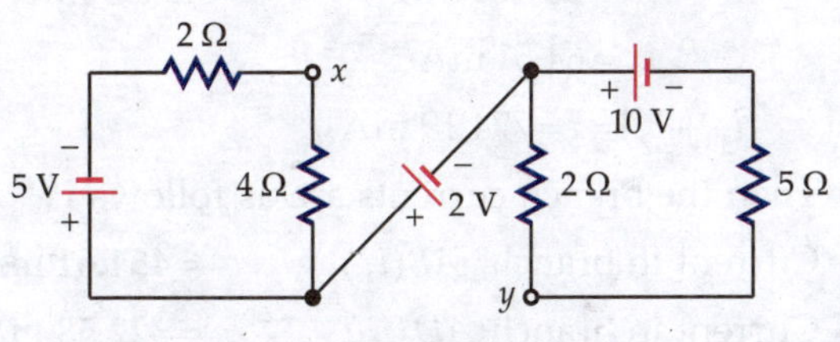

Fig. E1.66

Solution. Let us redraw the circuit with designated loop currents (Fig. E1.67).

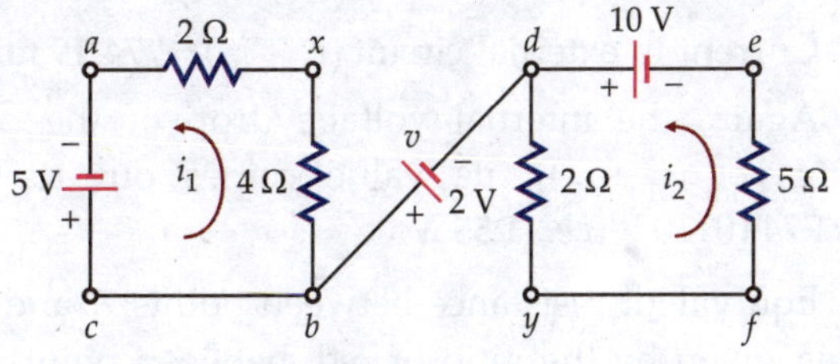

Fig. E1.67

In loop axbc, KVL gives

$$-5 + 4i_1 + 2i_1 = 0 \qquad \text{or,} \quad i_1 = \frac{5}{6} \text{ A.}$$

$$\therefore \qquad v_{bx} = -v_{xb} = 4i_1$$

(drop across 4 Ω resistor)

$$= 3.33 \text{ V}$$

(*x* terminal –ve as the current i_1 flows from *b* to *x*)

Similarly, *in loop defy,*

$$-10 + 2i_2 + 5i_2 = 0 \quad \text{or,} \quad i_2 = \frac{10}{7} \text{ A.}$$

and $\quad v_{dy} = \dfrac{10}{7} \times 2 = 2.857$ V. (*d* terminal +ve)

The voltage between terminals *x* and *y* is then

$$v_{xb} + v + v_{dy} = (-3.333 + 2 + 2.857) \text{ V} = 1.524 \text{ V;}$$

$$\mathbf{v_{xy} = 1.524\ V.}$$

v_{xb} is –ve because polarity of terminal *x* is – *ve* and the equivalent circuit of the network for the part *x-y* of the circuit is as follows : (Fig. E1.67(*a*))

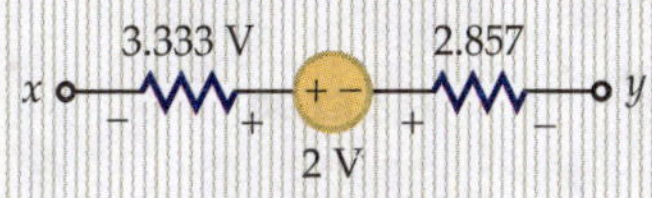

Fig. E1.67(*a*)

Example 1.56 *Determine the power loss across the 5 Ω resistor in Fig. E1.68.*

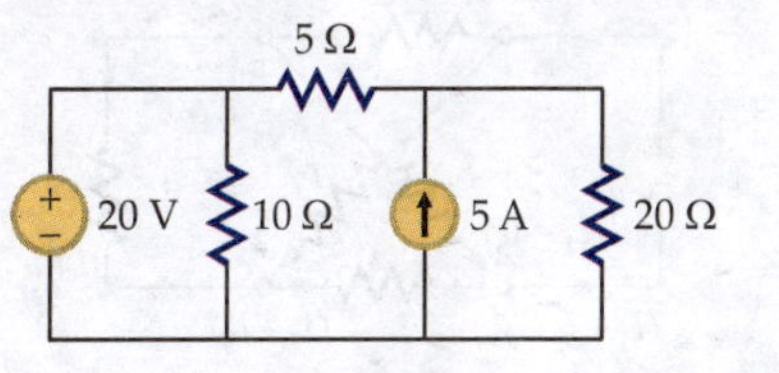

Fig. E1.68

Solution. In the first step, the current source of 5 A is converted to an equivalent voltage source (Fig. E1.69).

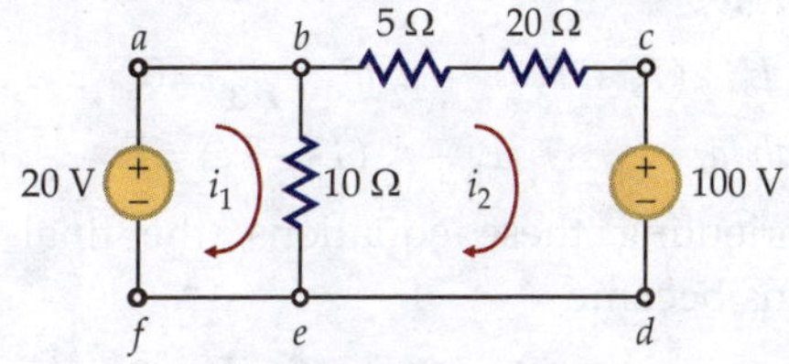

Fig. E1.69

In loop abef, using KVL,

$$20 = (i_1 - i_2)\,10 \quad \text{or,} \quad i_1 - i_2 = 2 \qquad \text{...(}i\text{)}$$

In loop bcde, using KVL,

$$25\,i_2 + 100 + (i_2 - i_1)\,10 = 0.$$

or, $$35\,i_2 - 10\,i_1 = -100 \qquad \text{...(}ii\text{)}$$

Using (*i*) in (*ii*),

$$35\, i_2 - 10\,(2 + i_2) = -100$$

or, $$25\, i_2 - 20 = -100$$

or, $$i_2 = -3.2 \text{ A}$$

(*i.e.*, actually i_2 flows from terminal *c* to terminal *b*)

∴ the power loss in the 5 Ω resistor is $(i_2^2 \times 5)$ W

i.e., $$p = (3.2)^2 \times 5 \text{ W}$$

or, $$\mathbf{p = 51.2\ W.}$$

EXAMPLE 1.57 *Obtain the mesh equations of the circuit shown in Fig. E1.70.*

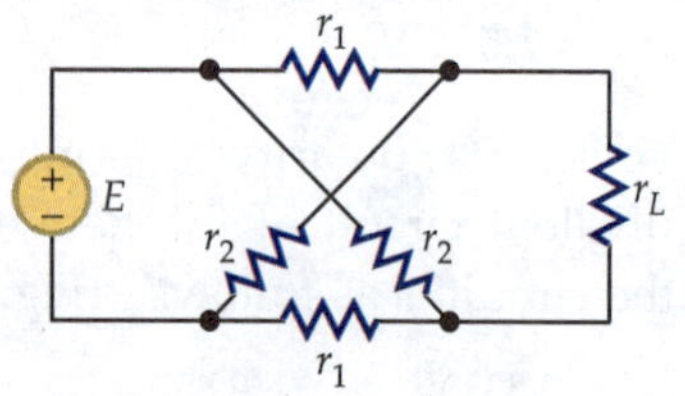

Fig. E1.70

SOLUTION. The circuit of Fig. E1.70 is redrawn (Fig. E1.71) to show the current distribution within the loops.

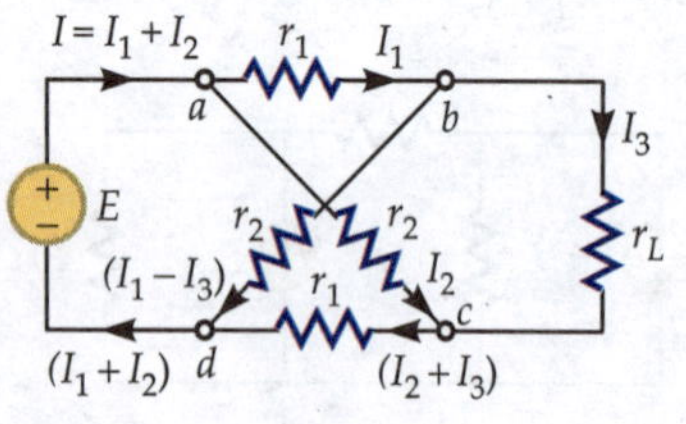

Fig. E1.71

Using KVL,

In loop abca, $$r_1 I_1 + r_L I_3 - r_2 I_2 = 0 \qquad ...(i)$$

In loop bcdb,

$$r_L I_3 + (I_2 + I_3)\, r_1 - r_2\,(I_1 - I_3) = 0 \qquad ...(ii)$$

In loop abda, $$r_1 I_1 + r_2\,(I_1 - I_3) = E \qquad ...(iii)$$

Reorienting these equations, the final mesh equations become

$$\mathbf{r_1 I_1 - r_2 I_2 + r_L I_3 = 0}$$

$$\mathbf{-r_2 I_1 + r_1 I_2 + I_3\,(r_1 + r_2 + r_L) = 0}$$

$$\mathbf{(r_1 + r_2)\, I_1 - r_2 I_3 = E}$$

EXAMPLE 1.58 *Obtain the branch currents in the unbalanced bridge circuit of Fig. E1.72. Also determine the voltage drop across AC and the equivalent resistance between terminals A and C in the bridge.*

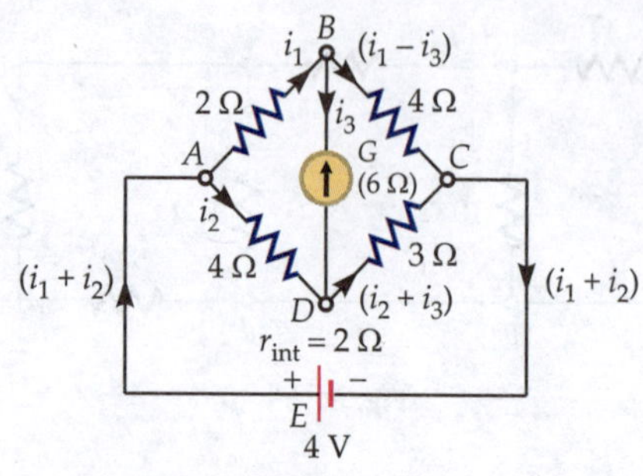

Fig. E1.72

SOLUTION. The assumed directions of currents have been shown in the figure (Fig. E1.72).

Applying KVL *in loop ABDA,*

$$2i_1 + 6i_3 - 4i_2 = 0$$

or, $$i_1 + 3i_3 - 2i_2 = 0$$

i.e., $$i_1 - 2i_2 + 3i_3 = 0 \qquad ...(i)$$

From *loop BCDB*, application of KVL yields

$$4\,(i_1 - i_3) - 3\,(i_2 + i_3) - 6i_3 = 0$$

or, $$4\, i_1 - 3\, i_2 - 13\, i_3 = 0 \qquad ...(ii)$$

Also, using KVL, from *loop ABCEA,*

$$2i_1 + 4\,(i_1 - i_3) + 2\,(i_1 + i_2) - 4 = 0$$

or, $$8\, i_1 + 2\, i_2 - 4\, i_3 = 4$$

i.e., $$4\, i_1 + i_2 - 2\, i_3 = 2 \qquad ...(iii)$$

Solving these equations (*i*), (*ii*) and (*iii*), we get

$$i_1 = 451.61 \text{ mA} \; ; \quad i_2 = 322.58 \text{ mA}$$

$$i_3 = 64.51 \text{ mA}$$

and $$(i_1 + i_2) = i = 774.19 \text{ mA}$$

Then the branch currents are as follows :

Current in branch $AB(i_1)$ **= 451.61 mA**

Current in branch $AD(i_2)$ **= 322.58 mA**

Current in branch $BD(i_3)$ **= 64.51 mA**

Current in branch $BC(i_1 - i_3)$ **= 387.1 mA**

Current in branch $DC(i_2 + i_3)$ **= 387.09 mA**

Current in external circuit $(i_1 + i_2)$ **= 774.19 mA.**

Again, the internal voltage drop of the cell being $[r_{int}\,(i_1 + i_2)]$, its value comes out to be $(2 \times 774.10)\, 10^{-3}$ *i.e.*, **1.55 V.**

Equivalent resistance between points *A* and *C* being given by the ratio of p.d. between points *A* and *C* to the current between these two points, the numerical value of the equivalent resistance becomes

$$r_{\text{equiv. (AC)}} = \frac{2.452}{0.77419} = \mathbf{3.17\ \Omega.}$$

EXAMPLE 1.59 *In Fig. E1.73 obtain the voltage output across r_L.*

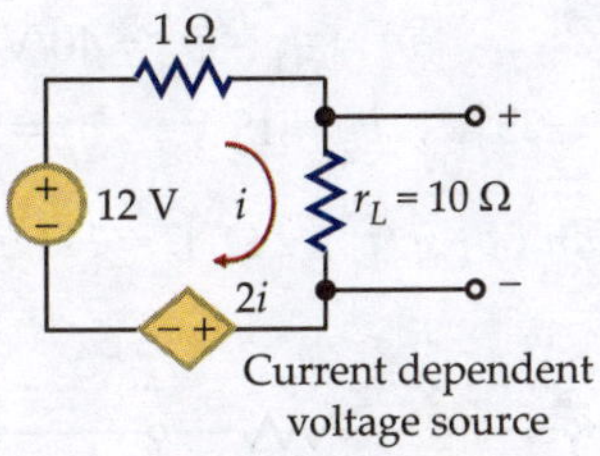

Fig. E1.73

SOLUTION. Using KVL in the loop of Fig. E1.73,

$$-12 + i \times 1 + i \times 10 + 2\,i = 0$$

or, $$13\,i = 12$$

$$i = 0.92 \text{ A}$$

Thus, the drop across r_L is $(0.92 \times r_L)$ or **9.2 V.**

EXAMPLE 1.60 *Obtain i_R in terms of i_S (Fig. E1.74)*

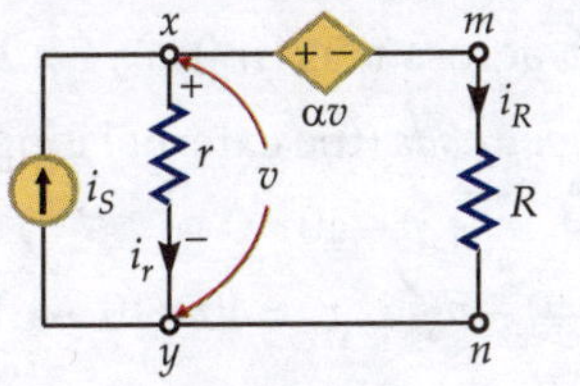

Fig. E1.74

SOLUTION. Using KCL at *node x*,

$$i_S = i_r + i_R$$

or, $$i_S = \frac{v}{r} + i_R \qquad \text{...}(i)$$

[since the drop v_{xy} across r to be v volts]

In loop xmny,

$$-v + \alpha v + i_R\, R = 0$$

or, $$-v(1-\alpha) = -i_R \,.\, R$$

i.e., $$v = \frac{i_R \,.\, R}{1-\alpha} \qquad \text{...}(ii)$$

Substitution of equation (*ii*) in (*i*),

$$i_S = \frac{i_R \,.\, R}{1-\alpha} \cdot \frac{1}{r} + i_R = i_R \left(\frac{R}{r(1-\alpha)} + 1 \right)$$

which gives

$$i_R = \frac{i_S}{\dfrac{R}{r(1-\alpha)} + 1} = i_S \frac{r(1-\alpha)}{R + r(1-\alpha)}$$

$$\therefore \quad \boldsymbol{i_R = i_S \frac{r\,(1-\alpha)}{R + r\,(1-\alpha)}}.$$

EXAMPLE 1.61 *Find the voltage drop and power loss in R_L if $i_1 = 1$ A in the dependent current source (Fig. E1.75).*

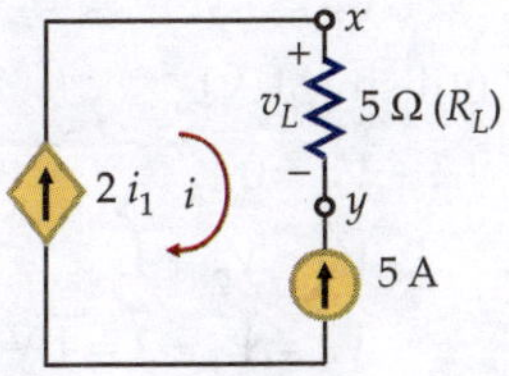

Fig. E1.75

SOLUTION. Using KVL *in loop* of Fig. E1.75,

$$i\,.\,5 = v_L$$

or, $$v_L = (2i_1 - 5)\,5 = (2-5)\,5 = -15 \text{ V}.$$

This indicates that the drop across R_L is **15 V** with +**ve polarity at *y*.**

However, the current (i) through 5 Ω resistor being $(2i_1 - 5)$ *i.e.*, −3 A (when $i_1 = 1$ A), flowing from y to x terminal, the power dissipated in R_L is $i^2 R_L$ *i.e.*, **45 watts.**

EXAMPLE 1.62 *In Fig. E1.76 find i by KVL. Assume $v_2 = 10$ in the dependent voltage source.*

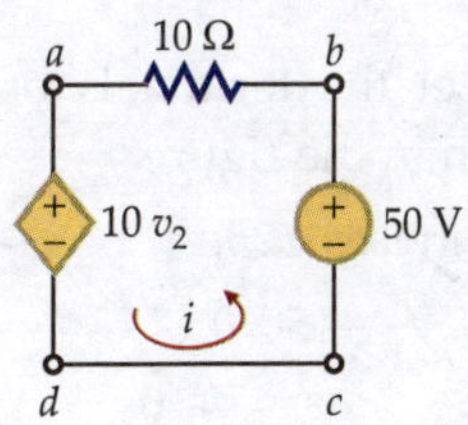

Fig. E1.76

SOLUTION. Using KVL in the loop of Fig. E1.76,

$$10\,v_2 - 50 + 10\,i = 0$$

or, $$10 \times 10 + 10\,i = 50$$

or $$i = -5 \text{ A}.$$

i.e., actual current in the loop flows from terminal *a* to terminal *b* in 10 Ω resistor.

i.e., $\;$ ***i* = 5 A** flowing from *a* to *b*.

EXAMPLE 1.63 *A network is shown in Fig. E1.77 where, some of the drops across a few resistors are shown. Find V_1 and V_2 using KVL.*

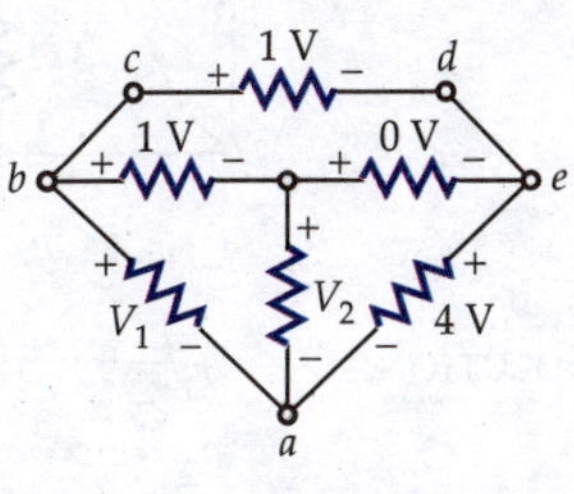

Fig. E1.77

CHAPTER 1

Solution. *In loop abcdea*, by KVL,

$$-V_1 + 1 + 4 = 0$$

or, $$V_1 = 5 \text{ V}.$$

In loop abo, utilising KVL,

$$-V_1 + 1 + V_2 = 0$$

or $$V_1 = V_2 + 1$$

i.e., $$V_2 = V_1 - 1 = 4 \text{ V}$$

Thus the value of V_2 is given by

$$\mathbf{V_2 = 4 \text{ V}.}$$

Example 1.64 *In Fig. E1.78 find the magnitudes of V_1 and V_2 using KVL.*

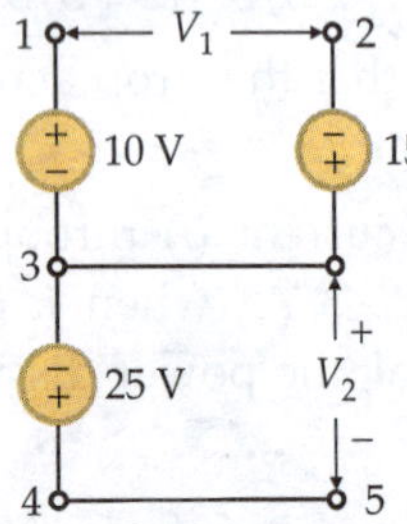

Fig. E1.78

Solution. Let the terminals of Fig. E1.78 be named as shown in the figure.

Using KVL in *loop-123*,

$$-10 + V_1 - 15 = 0$$

or $$V_1 = 25 \text{ V}.$$

Similarly, using KVL *in loop-345*,

$$25 + V_2 = 0$$

or $$V_2 = -25 \text{ V}$$

i.e., $$\mathbf{V_1 = 25 \text{ V}}$$

$$\mathbf{V_2 = -25 \text{ V}.}$$

Example 1.65 *Obtain v_1, v_2 and v_s in the circuit of Fig. E1.79.*

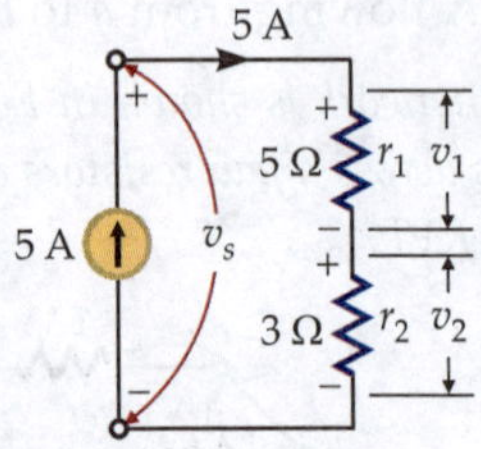

Fig. E1.79

Solution. $$v_1 = 5 \times 5 = 25 \text{ V}$$

$$v_2 = 5 \times 3 = 15 \text{ V}$$

Applying KVL in the loop,

$$-v_s + v_1 + v_2 = 0$$

or, $$v_s = v_1 + v_2 = 40 \text{ V}.$$

Then $\mathbf{v_1 = 25 \text{ V}}$; $\mathbf{v_2 = 15 \text{ V}}$; $\mathbf{v_s = 40 \text{ V}}$.

Example 1.66 *Find v_s if $r_1 = 2\,\Omega$; $r_2 = 1\,\Omega$; $r_3 = 5\,\Omega$. (Ref. Fig. E1.80).*

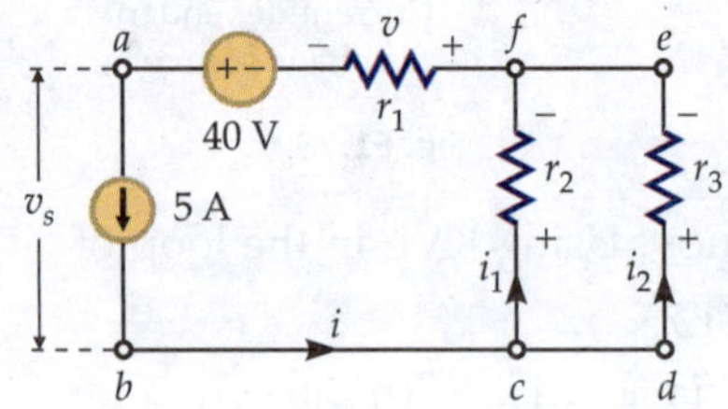

Fig. E1.80

Solution. $$i_2 = i\frac{r_2}{r_2 + r_3} = 5 \cdot \frac{1}{6} = \frac{5}{6} \text{ A}.$$

The drop across r_3 is thus $\frac{5}{6} \times 5 = \frac{25}{6} = 4.16$ V

The drop across r_1 is (ir_1) *i.e.*, $5 \times 2 = 10$ V $(= v)$

Thus, *in loop abde* (the external loop) using KVL,

$$v_s + i_2\, r_3 + v - 40 = 0$$

or, $$v_s = 40 - v - i_2\, r_3 = 40 - 10 - 4.16 \simeq \mathbf{25.84 \text{ V}.}$$

Example 1.67 *Find i, the numerical value of the current dependent source and the drop across the resistances using KVL (Fig. E1.81).*

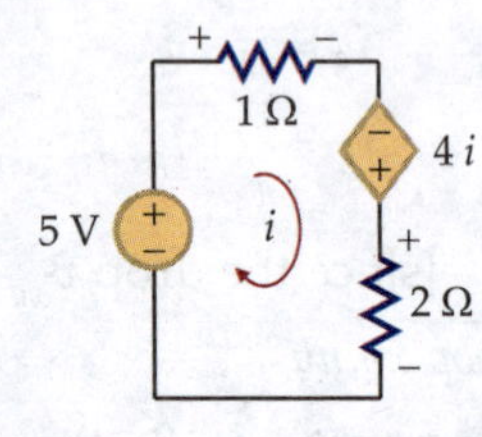

Fig. E1.81

Solution. Using KVL,

$$-5 + i \times 1 - 4i + 2i = 0$$

or, $$\mathbf{i = -5 \text{ A}}$$

(actual current direction is anticlockwise).

$\therefore$ Drop across $1\,\Omega$ resistor $= 5 \times 1 = \mathbf{5 \text{ V}}$

Drop across $2\,\Omega$ resistor $= 5 \times 2 = \mathbf{10 \text{ V}}$

Numerical value of current dependent source

$$= 4i = 4 \times 5 = \mathbf{20 \text{ V}.}$$

It may be noted here that actually the polarity of the dependent source would be the opposite to that given in Fig. E1.81 causing i to flow anticlockwise.

EXAMPLE 1.68 *In the network of Fig. E1.82, (a) find V_{X-Y} (open circuit voltage) (b) if X-Y is short circuited, what is the current through the short circuited terminals ? (c) Also find drop across 2 A current source when X-Y is open circuited. (d) What will be the polarities of voltages in Fig. E1.82 if the direction of current in 2 A source is reversed ?*

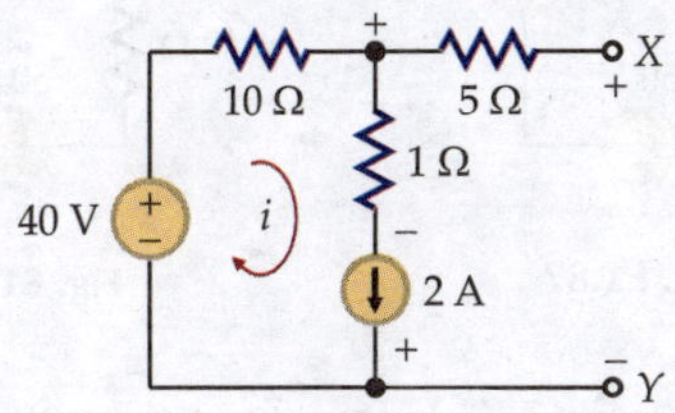

Fig. E1.82

SOLUTION. (*a*) Let i be the current flowing through the left loop of Fig. E1.82 while X-Y remains open circuited.

Obviously, by inspection $i = 2$ A.

$\therefore$ Drop across 10 Ω resistor $= 2 \times 10 = 20$ V

Then $V_{X-Y} = 40 -$ drop across 10 Ω resistor $= 20$ V

V_{X-Y} (open circuit) $=$ **20 V.**

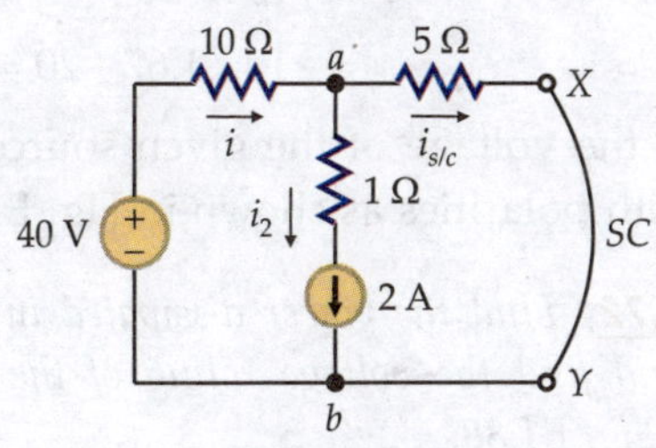

Fig. E1.83

(*b*) Let X-Y terminal be short circuited (Ref. Fig. E1.83). Using KCL at *node "a"*, we can write

$$i = i_2 + i_{s/c}$$

But $\quad i = \dfrac{40 - v_{ab}}{10}$ A $\quad$ [$\because$ assumed voltage against terminals *a-b* is v_{ab}]

$\therefore \quad i_2 = 2$ A;

$$i_{s/c} = \frac{v_{ab}}{5} \text{ A}$$

Thus, $\quad \dfrac{40 - v_{ab}}{10} = 2 + \dfrac{v_{ab}}{5}$

or, $\quad \dfrac{v_{ab}}{5} + \dfrac{v_{ab}}{10} = 2 \quad$ or $\quad v_{ab} = \dfrac{20}{3} = 6.66$ V

This gives the short circuit current through *x-y* as

$$i_{s/c}\,(x\text{-}y \text{ shorted}) = \frac{6.66}{5} = \mathbf{1.34\ A.}$$

(*c*) Again with X-Y terminals open, the current is 2 A in the left loop (Fig. E1.82).

Applying KVL in the *loop* gives

$$-40 + 10\,i + i \times 1 - v_{2A} = 0$$

[assuming the drop across 2 A sources as v_{2A}]

As $\quad i = 2$ A,

we get $\quad v_{2A} = \mathbf{-18\ V.}$

(*d*) The actual polarity of the 2 A source is reversed. The circuit is redrawn for the sake of better undestanding (Fig. E1.84) with polarities marked.

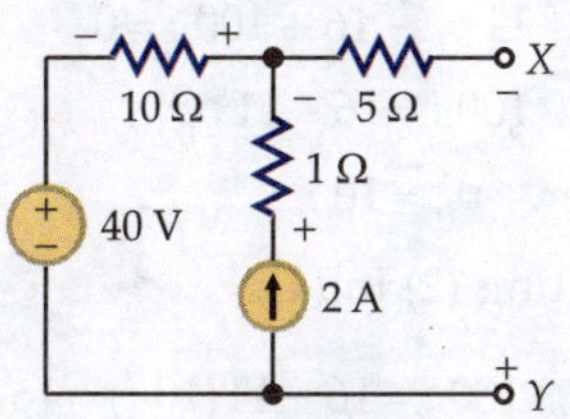

Fig. E1.84

EXAMPLE 1.69 *Find v_r in terms of v_s (Fig. E1.85).*

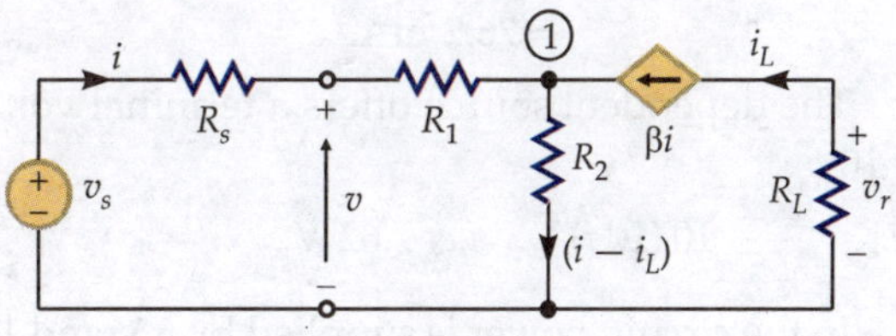

Fig. E1.85

SOLUTION. Using KVL in the *left loop*,

$$v_s = i\,R_s + iR_1 + (i - i_L)\,R_2 \qquad \text{...}(i)$$

Using KCL at node (1),

$$(i - i_L) = i + \beta . i = i\,(1 + \beta) \qquad \text{...}(ii)$$

Using (*ii*) in (*i*),

$$v_s = iR_s + iR_1 + i\,(1 + \beta)\,R_2$$
$$= i\,[R_s + R_1 + R_2\,(1 + \beta)]$$

i.e., $\quad i = \dfrac{v_s}{R_s + R_1 + R_2\,(1 + \beta)}$

As the current flowing through R_L is i_L, hence

$$v_r = i_L\,R_L = (-\beta i)\,R_L = -\frac{v_s\,\beta\,R_L}{R_s + R_1 + R_2\,(1 + \beta)}$$

[$\because i_L \equiv -\beta . i$]

$$\therefore \quad v_r = \frac{-R_L\,\beta\,v_s}{R_s + R_1 + R_2\,(1 + \beta)}.$$

CHAPTER 1

EXAMPLE 1.70 *Find i in the circuit of Fig. E1.86. Check the power balance condition.*

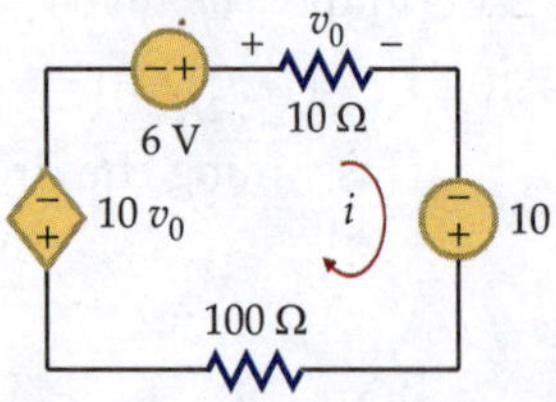

Fig. E1.86

SOLUTION. Applying KVL in the given loop,

$$10\,v_0 - 6 + v_0 - 10 + 100\,i = 0$$

or, $$11\,v_0 - 16 + 100\,i = 0$$

or, $$100\,i = 16 - 11\,v_0 \qquad ...(1)$$

However, $$v_0 = 10\,i \qquad ...(2)$$

Substituting (2) in (1),

$$100\,i = 16 - 11\,(10\,i) = 16 - 110\,i$$

$\therefore$ $$210\,i = 16$$

i.e., $$i = \frac{16}{210}$$

$$= \mathbf{76.2\ mA.}$$

The dependent source offers a terminal voltage of 10 v_0

i.e., 10 (10 i) V *i.e*, 7.62 V.

In the circuit, power is supplied by 6 V and 10 V source while power is absorbed by 100 Ω resistor (dissipating heat) and the dependent source.

Thus power supplied by 6 V source

$$= 6 \times 0.0762 = 0.4572\ \text{W}$$

power supplied by 10 V source

$$= 10 \times 0.0762 = 0.762\ \text{W}$$

$\therefore$ Total power supplied

$$= 0.4572 + 0.762$$

$$= 1.219\ \text{W} \simeq \mathbf{1.22\ W.}$$

Again, power absorbed by the dependent source is $(7.62 \times 0.0762) = 0.5806$ W while that by the 110 Ω resistance is $110 \times (0.0762)^2 = 0.6387$ W.

$\therefore$ Total power absorbed

$$= 0.5806 + 0.6387$$

$$\simeq \mathbf{1.22\ W.}$$

Thus, the total power balance is maintained.

EXAMPLE 1.71 *Find V such that 100 C charge is injected to the 50 V source in 1 min in the circuit of Fig. E1.87.*

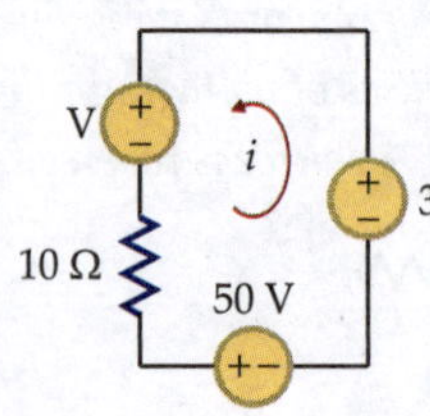

Fig. E1.87

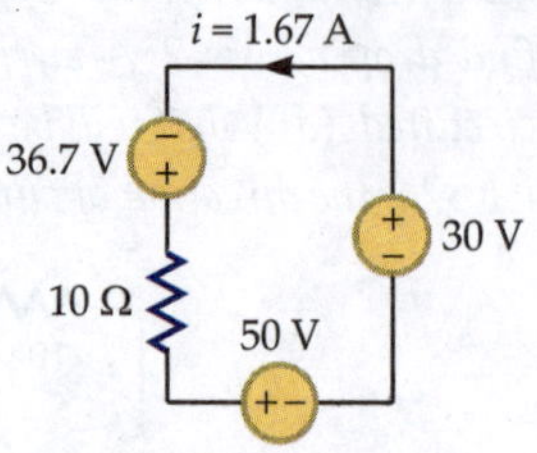

Fig. E1.87(*a*)

SOLUTION. In order to inject the 100 C charge to the 50 V source, the current in the *loop* of Fig. E1.87 must be anticlockwise.

But $$i = \frac{Q}{t} = \frac{100}{60} = 1.67\ \text{A}$$

$$[\because Q = 100\ \text{C};\ t = 1\ \text{min} = 60\ \text{sec.}]$$

Applying KVL in the *loop*,

$$V + 10\,i + 50 - 30 = 0$$

or, $$V = -10\,i - 20$$

$$= -10 \times 1.67 - 20 = -36.7\ \text{V}.$$

Thus the voltage of the given source must be **36.7 V** with polarities as shown in Fig. E1.87(*a*).

EXAMPLE 1.72 *Find the power dissipated in the 100 Ω resistor and find the voltage rating of the dependent source in Fig. E1.88.*

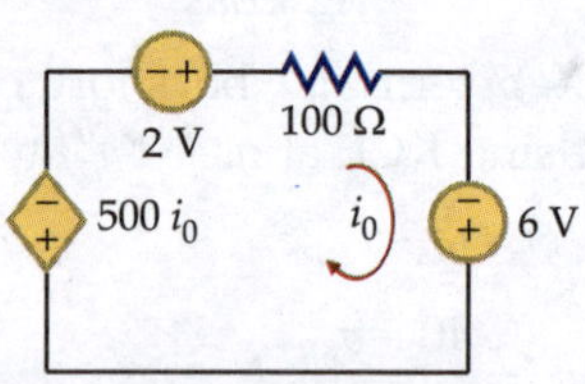

Fig. E1.88

SOLUTION. Applying KVL in the given figure,

$$-6 + 500\,i_0 - 2 + 100\,i_0 = 0$$

or, $$600\,i_0 = 8$$

$\therefore$ $$i_0 = 13.33\ \text{mA}$$

Then, the power dissipated in 100 Ω resistor is

$$i_0^2 \times 100 = \mathbf{17.8\ mW.}$$

The voltage rating of the dependent source is 500 i_0.

i.e., $$500 \times 0.01333 = \mathbf{6.67\ V.}$$

1.11 VOLTAGE DIVISION IN SERIES CIRCUITS

Let us consider a voltage source E with resistors r_1 and r_2 in series across it (Fig. 1.16).

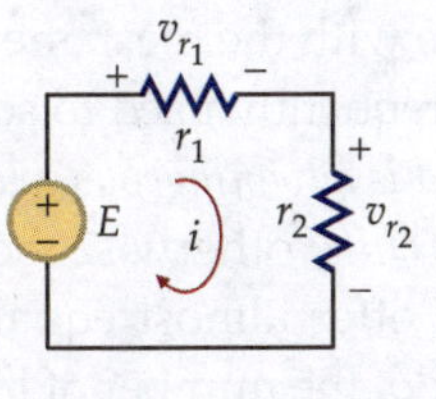

Fig. 1.16

Obviously, the current in the loop will be

$$i = \frac{E}{r_1 + r_2}$$

and voltage across r_1 is $\quad v_{r_1} = ir_1 = \dfrac{Er_1}{r_1 + r_2}$

while voltage across r_2 is $\quad v_{r_2} = ir_2 = \dfrac{Er_2}{r_1 + r_2}$

...(1.45)

Thus, the voltage across a resistor in series circuit is equal to the value of that resistor times the total impressed voltage across the series elements divided by the total resistance of the series elements.

EXAMPLE 1.73 *Design a voltage divider circuit with two resistances r_1 and r_2 such that the drop v_1 (drop across r_1) is twice the drop v_2 (drop across r_2) in the circuit of Fig. E1.89.*

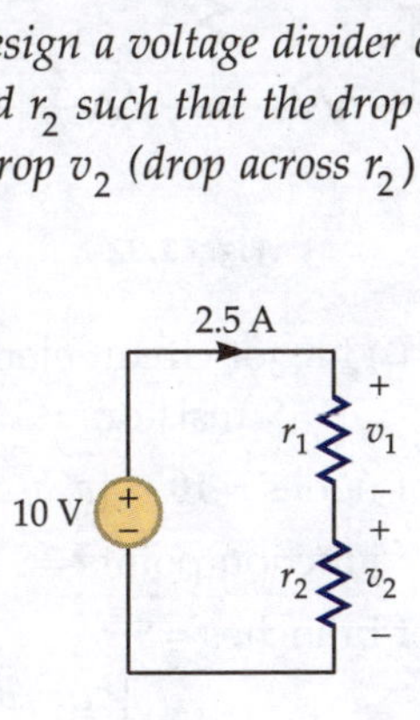

Fig. E1.89

SOLUTION. Using Ohm's law,

$$(r_1 + r_2) = r_t = \frac{10}{2.5} = 4\,\Omega$$

$$[\because v = 10 \text{ volts}, \ i = 2.5 \text{ Amps.}]$$

Since $\quad v_1 = 2v_2, \quad r_1 = 2r_2$

Hence $\quad r_t = r_1 + r_2$

$$= 2r_2 + r_2 = 3r_2$$

However, r_t being $4\,\Omega$,

$$r_2 = \frac{4}{3} = 1.33\,\Omega$$

and $\quad r_1 = 2r_2 = 2.66\,\Omega$

$\therefore \quad r_1 = \mathbf{2.66\,\Omega}$

while $\quad r_2 = \mathbf{1.33\,\Omega}$

Check

With $r_1 = 2.66\,\Omega$,

$v_1 = 2.5 \times 2.66 = 6.65$ V

and $\quad v_2 = 1.33 \times 2.5 = 3.325$ V.

It is then evident that $v_1 = 2v_2$

EXAMPLE 1.74 *Find the voltage needed across a-b terminal so that drop across the $10\,\Omega$ resistor is 45 V. Also find the corresponding drop across the $5\,\Omega$ resistor (Fig. E1.90).*

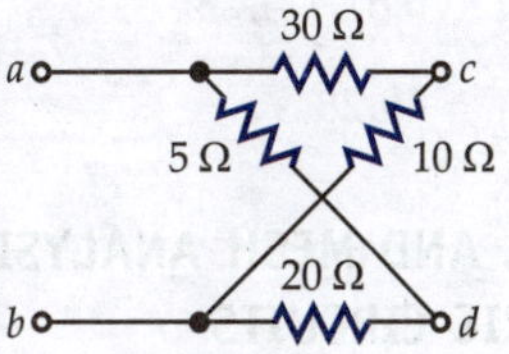

Fig. E1.90

SOLUTION. *In loop acb*, following voltage division rule, the drop across $10\,\Omega$ resistor being 45 V ($= v_{10}$, say) we can write

$$v_{10} = 45 = V_{ab}\,\frac{10}{10 + 30} = \frac{V_{ab}}{4}$$

$\therefore \quad V_{ab} = 180$ V.

Then, the supply voltage

$$V_{ab} = \mathbf{180\ V}$$

The corresponding drop across $5\,\Omega$ resistor is

$$V_5 = \frac{5}{5 + 20}\,.\,V_{ab} = 180 \times \frac{1}{5} = 36 \text{ V}$$

i.e., $\quad V_5 = \mathbf{36\ V.}$

EXAMPLE 1.75 *Find the voltage needed across a-b terminal of Fig. E1.91 so that the drop across the $10\,\Omega$ resistor is 30 V.*

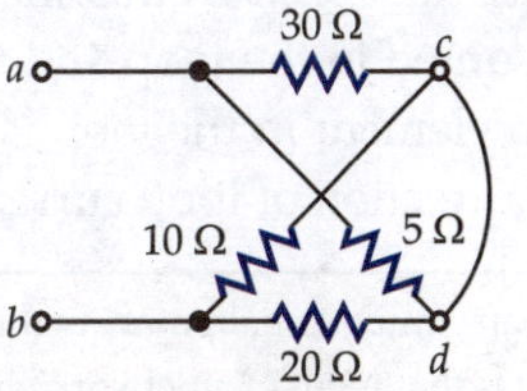

Fig. E1.91

Solution. With *c-d* terminal shorted (Fig. E1.91), 10 Ω resistance is in parallel to the 20 Ω resistance.

∴ Equivalent resistance of this parallel combination is

$$\frac{10 \times 20}{10+20} = 6.67\ \Omega$$

Similarly, the equivalent resistance of 5 Ω and 30 Ω resistances is

$$\frac{30 \times 5}{30+5} = 4.286\ \Omega.$$

Then, the drop across the 10 Ω resistor being 30 V (v_{10}, say), we can write, following voltage division principle,

$$30 = \frac{6.67}{6.67+4.286} V_{ab}$$

or, V_{ab} = **49.28 V.**

1.12 NODAL AND MESH ANALYSIS OF ELECTRIC CIRCUITS

There is another method of solution of the network *i.e.*, by *nodal analysis* where it is essential to compute all branch currents. In writing the current expression the assumption is made that the *node potential* is always higher than the other voltages appearing in the equation. In case it turns out *not* to be so, a negative value for the current would result.

In the nodal method the number of independent node-pair equations needed is one less than the number of junctions in the network. That is, if "n" denotes the number of independent node equations and "j" the number of junctions,

$$n = j - 1$$

There is one more method of analysing an electrical network—the *mesh analysis*, the name being derived from the similarities in appearance between the closed loops of a network and a physical "*fence*" or *mesh*. In this method, a distinct current is assumed in the loop and the polarities of drops in each element in the loop is determined by the assumed direction of loop current for that loop. KVL is then applied around each closed loop and by solving these loop equations (linear simultaneous equations), the branch currents are determined.

To compare with the mesh method (where KVL equations are frequently used to solve the network), the *nodal method is advantageous when the network has many parallel circuits;* otherwise, both the nodal and mesh methods offer almost equal advantages [for the mesh method, the number of independent mesh equations needed is $m = b - (j-1)$, where b is the number of branches].

If $m < n$, the mesh method offers advantages while for $m > n$ i.e., when the number of parallel paths in the network is more, nodal method is preferred.

Example 1.76 *In the circuit configuration of Fig. E1.92 obtain the number of (i) circuit elements (ii) nodes* (iii) junction points** (iv) branches*** and (v) meshes.*

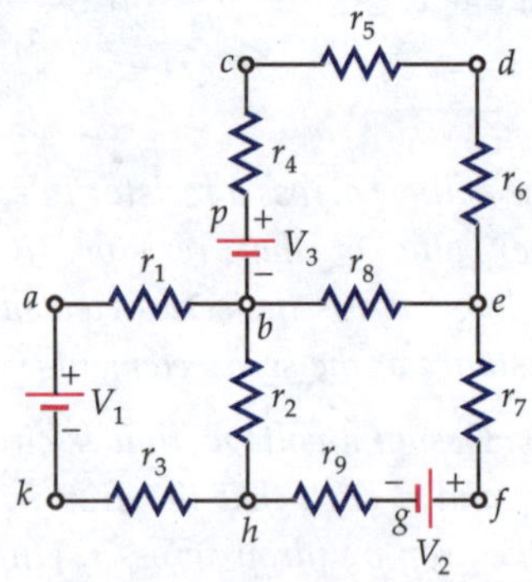

Fig. E1.92

Solution. (*i*) No. of circuit elements = **12**
[9 resistors + 3 voltage sources]

(*ii*) No. of nodes = **10** [*a, b, c, d, e, f, g, h, k, p*]

(*iii*) No. of junction points = **3** [*b, e, h*]

(*iv*) No. of branches = **5**
[*bcde, be, bh, befgh, bakh*]

(*v*) No. of meshes = **3.** [*abhk, bcde, befh*]

Example 1.77 *In the circuit configuration of Fig. E1.93, determine, the number of*

(*i*) *circuit elements* (*ii*) *nodes*

(*iii*) *junction points* (*iv*) *branches and*

(*v*) *meshes.*

* **Node.** It is an equipotential point at which two or more circuit elements are joined.

** **Junction.** It is that point of a network where three or more circuit elements are joined.

*** **Branch.** It is a part of a network which lies between junction points.

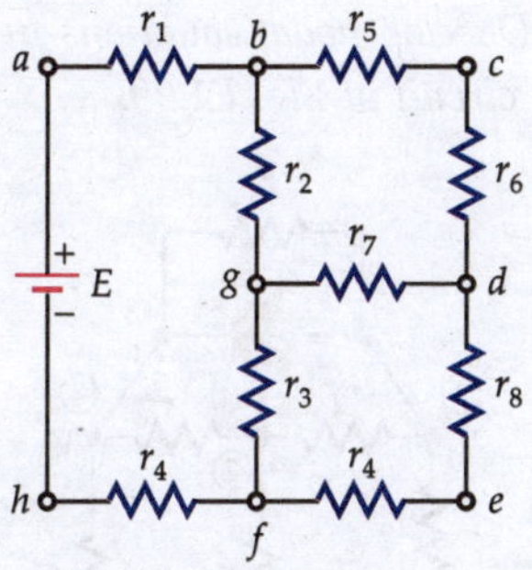

Fig. E1.93

Solution. (*i*) No. of circuit elements = **10**

(9 resistors + 1 voltage source)

(*ii*) No. of nodes

$= \mathbf{8}\ (a, b, c, d, e, f, g, h)$

(*iii*) No. of junction points

$= \mathbf{4}\ (b, g, d, f)$

(*iv*) No. of branches

$= \mathbf{6}\ [r_2 \text{ and } (r_5 + r_6), r_7, r_3 \text{ and } (r_7 + r_8), (r_1 + r_4)]$

(*v*) No. of meshes

= **3** [*abfh, bcdg, gdef*].

Example 1.78 *Using nodal method, find the current through r_2 (Fig. E1.94).*

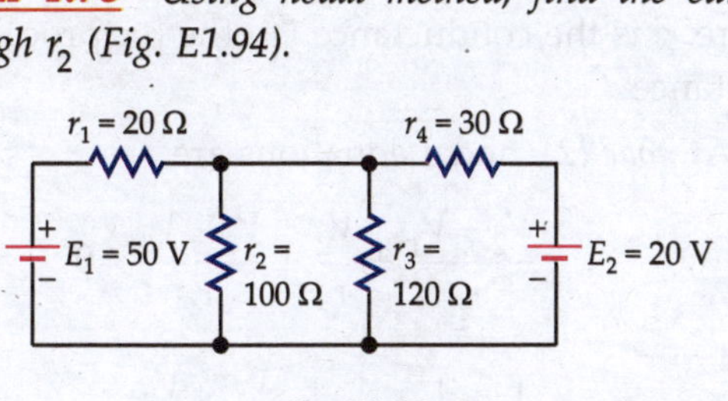

Fig. E1.94

Solution. Let us redraw the circuit with naming of the nodes and branch currents (Fig. E1.95).

at *node "b"*, $i = i_1 + i_2 + i_3$.

(electrically *nodes b* and *c* are same)

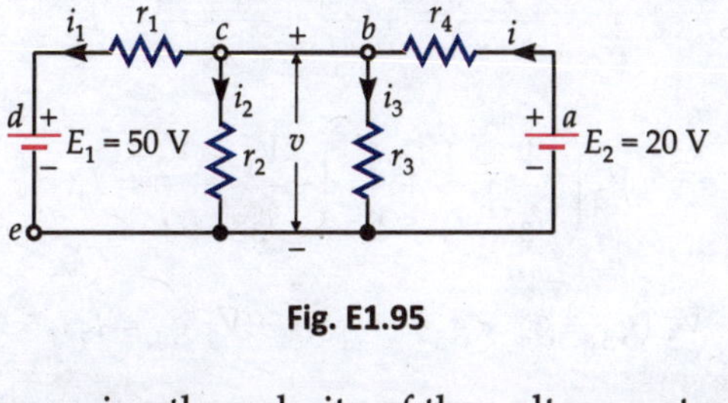

Fig. E1.95

Assuming the polarity of the voltage v at *node c* or *b*, we thus get

$$\frac{20 - v}{r_4} = \frac{v - 50}{r_1} + \frac{v}{r_2} + \frac{v}{r_3}$$

$$\text{or,} \quad \frac{v - 20}{30} + \frac{v - 50}{20} + \frac{v}{100} + \frac{v}{120} = 0.$$

$$\therefore \quad v = 31.18 \text{ V}$$

$$\therefore \quad i_2 = \frac{v}{r_2} = \frac{31.18}{100} \text{ A} = 0.3118 \text{ A}$$

i.e., current through $r_2 = \mathbf{311.8\ mA.}$

Example 1.79 *Develop nodal equations in the circuit shown in Fig. E1.96.*

Solution. At *node (1)*, let the potential be v_1 (+ve). The nodal equations are as follows :

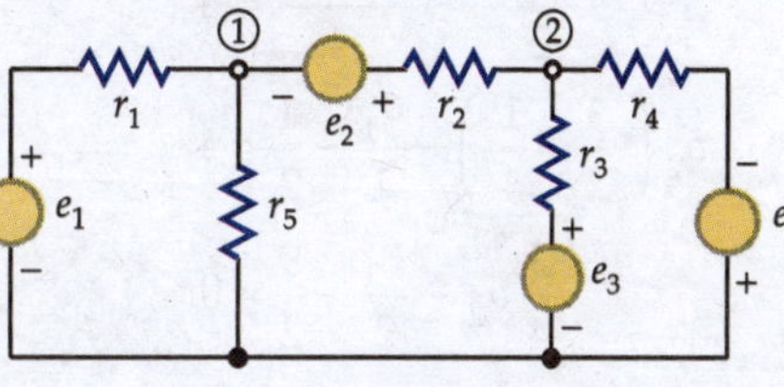

Fig. E1.96

$$\frac{v_1 - e_1}{r_1} + \frac{v_1}{r_5} + \frac{v_1}{r_2} - \frac{v_2 - e_2}{r_2} = 0$$

$$\text{or} \quad v_1\left(\frac{1}{r_1} + \frac{1}{r_2} + \frac{1}{r_5}\right) - \frac{v_2}{r_2} = \frac{e_1}{r_1} - \frac{e_2}{r_2} \quad \text{...}(i)$$

At *node (2)*, let the potential be v_2 (+ve). The nodal equations are then

$$\frac{v_2 - e_2}{r_2} + \frac{v_2 - e_3}{r_3} + \frac{v_2 + e_4}{r_4} - \frac{v_1}{r_2} = 0$$

$$\text{or,} \quad v_2\left(\frac{1}{r_2} + \frac{1}{r_3} + \frac{1}{r_4}\right) - \frac{v_1}{r_2} = \frac{e_2}{r_2} + \frac{e_3}{r_3} - \frac{e_4}{r_4} \quad \text{...}(ii)$$

(*i*) and (*ii*) give the nodal equations of the given network.

Example 1.80 *Using nodal method find the current through the resistors in the circuit configuration of Fig. E1.97.*

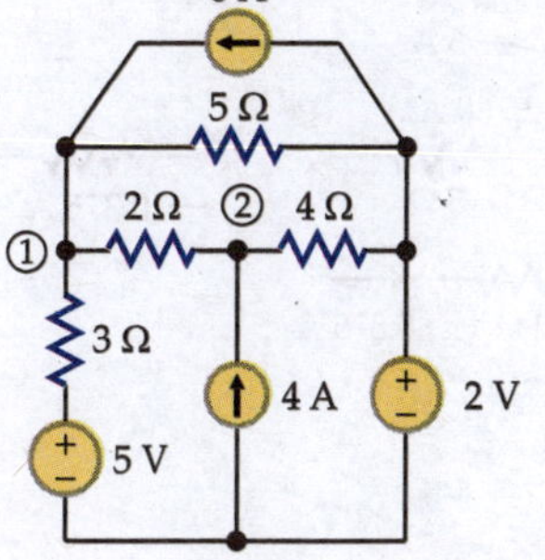

Fig. E1.97

Solution. Naming the respective *nodes* of the circuit as (1) and (2) and assuming the voltages to be v_1 (+ve) and v_2 (+ve) respectively at these nodes, nodal equations at *nodes (1)* and *(2)* are as follows :

For node (1),

$$\frac{v_1-5}{3}+\frac{v_1-v_2}{2}+\frac{v_1-2}{5}=6$$

or, $$v_1\left(\frac{1}{3}+\frac{1}{2}+\frac{1}{5}\right)-\frac{v_2}{2}-\frac{2}{5}-\frac{5}{3}-6=0$$

or, $$\frac{31}{30}v_1-\frac{v_2}{2}-\frac{121}{15}=0 \quad \text{...(a)}$$

For node (2),

$$\frac{v_2-v_1}{2}+\frac{v_2-2}{4}=4$$

or, $$v_2\left(\frac{1}{2}+\frac{1}{4}\right)-\frac{v_1}{2}-\frac{1}{2}=4$$

or, $$\frac{3}{4}v_2-\frac{v_1}{2}-\frac{9}{2}=0 \quad \text{...(b)}$$

Solving (*a*) and (*b*),

$$v_1=15.76 \text{ V while } v_2=16.51 \text{ V}$$

∴ Current through 3 Ω resistor

$$=\frac{v_1-5}{3}=\frac{15.76-5}{3}\simeq \mathbf{3.6\ A}$$

Current through 2 Ω resistor

$$=\frac{v_1-v_2}{2}=\frac{15.76-16.51}{2}=\mathbf{-0.375\ A}$$

[*i.e*, flowing from *node* (2) to *node* (1)].

Current through 5 Ω resistor

$$=\frac{v_1-2}{5}=\frac{15.76-2}{5}=\mathbf{2.76\ A},$$

current through 4 Ω resistor

$$=\frac{v_2-2}{4}=\frac{16.51-2}{4}=\mathbf{3.63\ A.}$$

Figure E1.98 confirms the KCL both at nodes (1) and (2) as a check.

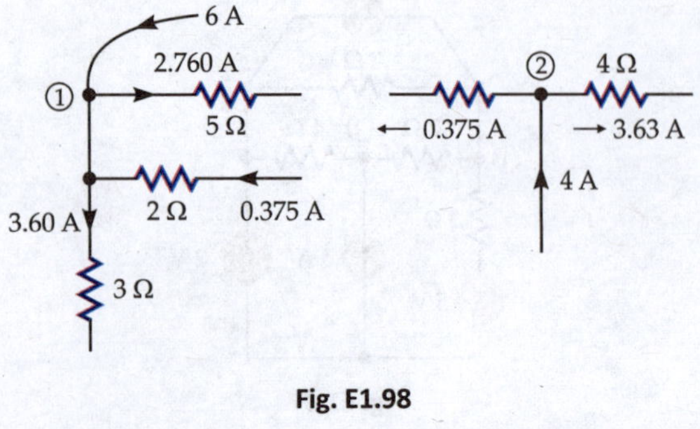

Fig. E1.98

Example 1.81 *Develop nodal equations in nodes (1), (2) and (3) in the circuit of Fig. E1.99.*

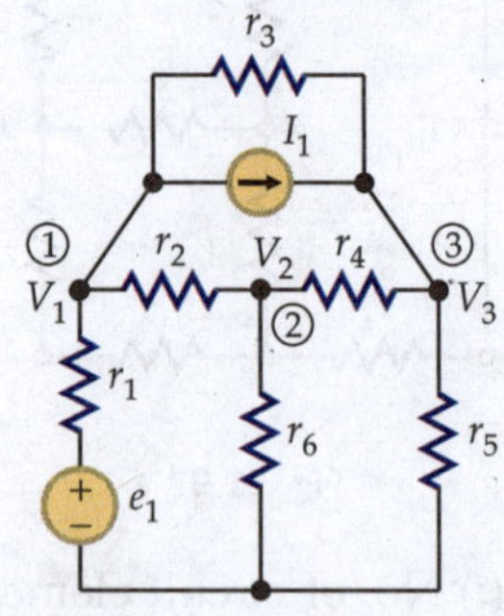

Fig. E1.99

Solution. At *node (1)*, using nodal method,

$$\frac{V_1-V_2}{r_2}+\frac{V_1-e_1}{r_1}+\frac{V_1-V_3}{r_3}+I_1=0$$

or, $$V_1\left(\frac{1}{r_1}+\frac{1}{r_2}+\frac{1}{r_3}\right)-\frac{V_2}{r_2}-\frac{V_3}{r_3}=\frac{e_1}{r_1}-I_1$$

or, $$V_1(g_1+g_2+g_3)-V_2g_2-V_3g_3=\frac{e_1}{r_1}-I_1 \quad \text{...(A)}$$

where, g is the conductance *i.e.*, the reciprocal of resistance.

At *node (2)*, nodal equations are

$$\frac{V_2-V_1}{r_2}+\frac{V_2}{r_6}+\frac{V_2-V_3}{r_4}=0$$

or, $$V_2\left(\frac{1}{r_2}+\frac{1}{r_4}+\frac{1}{r_6}\right)-\frac{V_1}{r_2}-\frac{V_3}{r_4}=0$$

or, $$V_2(g_2+g_4+g_6)-V_1g_2-V_3g_4=0 \quad \text{...(B)}$$

At *node (3)*, the nodal analysis gives,

$$\frac{V_3-V_2}{r_4}+\frac{V_3}{r_5}+\frac{V_3-V_1}{r_3}=I_1$$

or, $$V_3\left(\frac{1}{r_3}+\frac{1}{r_4}+\frac{1}{r_5}\right)-\frac{V_1}{r_3}-\frac{V_2}{r_4}=I_1$$

or, $$V_3(g_3+g_4+g_5)-V_1g_3-V_2g_4=I_1 \quad \text{...(C)}$$

(*A*), (*B*), (*C*) give the nodal equations.

EXAMPLE 1.82 *Using nodal method, find the battery currents in the circuit of Fig. E1.100.*

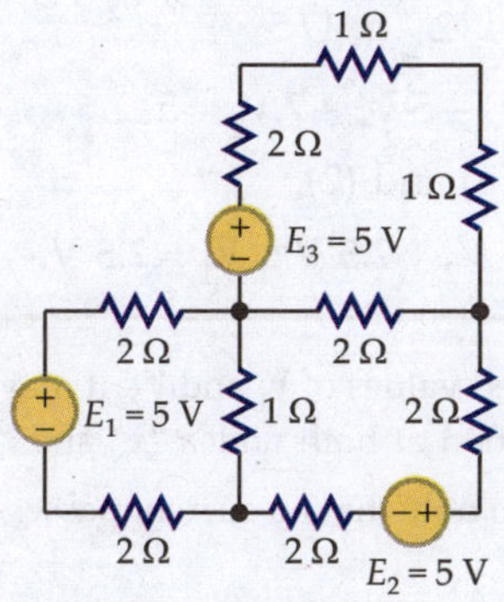

Fig. E1.100

SOLUTION. Let us redesignate the given circuit with nodal names and respective potentials (Fig. E1.101).

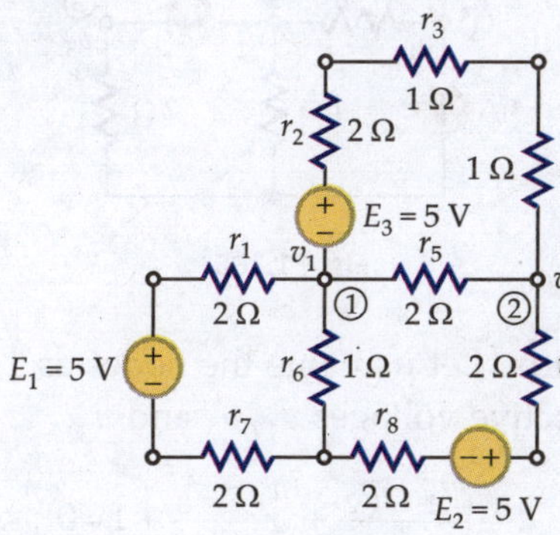

Fig. E1.101

At *node (1)*,

$$\frac{v_1 - E_1}{r_1 + r_7} + \frac{v_1}{r_6} + \frac{v_1 + E_3 - v_2}{r_2 + r_3 + r_4} + \frac{v_1 - v_2}{r_5} = 0$$

or, $$\frac{v_1 - 5}{4} + \frac{v_1}{1} + \frac{v_1 - v_2 + 5}{4} + \frac{v_1 - v_2}{2} = 0$$

or, $$2\,v_1 - 0.75\,v_2 = 0 \quad \text{...(A)}$$

At *node (2)*,

$$\frac{v_2 - E_2}{r_8 + r_9} + \frac{v_2 - v_1}{r_5} + \frac{v_2 - E_3 - v_1}{r_2 + r_3 + r_4} = 0$$

or, $$\frac{v_2 - 5}{4} + \frac{v_2 - v_1}{2} + \frac{v_2 + v_1 - 5}{4} = 0$$

or, $0.25\,v_2 + 0.5\,v_2 + 0.25\,v_2 - 0.5\,v_1 - 0.25\,v_1 = 2.5$

or, $$v_2 - 0.75\,v_1 = 2.5 \quad \text{...(B)}$$

Solving (*A*) in (*B*),

$$v_1 = 1.3 \quad \text{and} \quad v_2 = 3.47$$

$\therefore$ Current of $E_1 = \dfrac{v_1 - E_1}{r_1 + r_7} = \mathbf{-0.925\ A}$

(coming out from E_1)

Current of $E_2 = \dfrac{v_2 - E_2}{r_8 + r_9} = \mathbf{2.225\ A}$

(coming out from E_2)

Current of $E_3 = \dfrac{v_1 - v_2 + E_3}{r_2 + r_3 + r_4} = \mathbf{0.706\ A}$

(flowing from v_1 to v_2 via r_2, r_3 and r_4).

EXAMPLE 1.83 *In the circuit of Fig. E1.102, find the current in 1Ω resistor.*

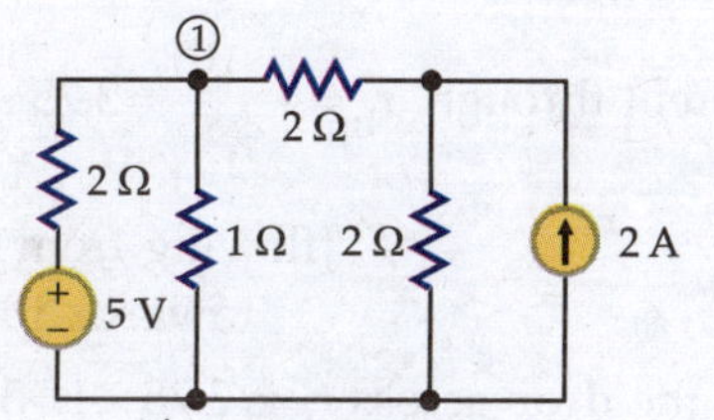

Fig. E1.102

SOLUTION. Let us first convert the current source of Fig. E1.102 to voltage source and draw the equivalent network (Fig. E1.103). Let the +ve voltage at *node (1)* be v_1 V.

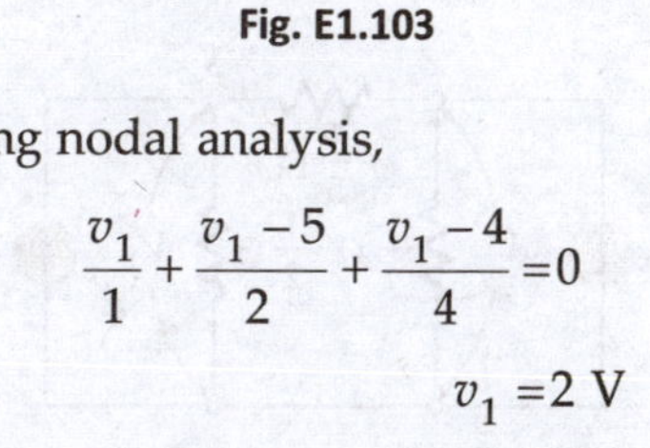

Fig. E1.103

$\therefore$ Using nodal analysis,

$$\frac{v_1}{1} + \frac{v_1 - 5}{2} + \frac{v_1 - 4}{4} = 0$$

or, $$v_1 = 2\ \text{V}$$

Hence, the current through the 1Ω resistor is

$$\frac{v_1}{1} = \mathbf{2\ A.}$$

EXAMPLE 1.84 *In Fig. E1.104, find $V_{o/c}$ by nodal analysis.*

SOLUTION. At *node "x"*, let the potential be v.

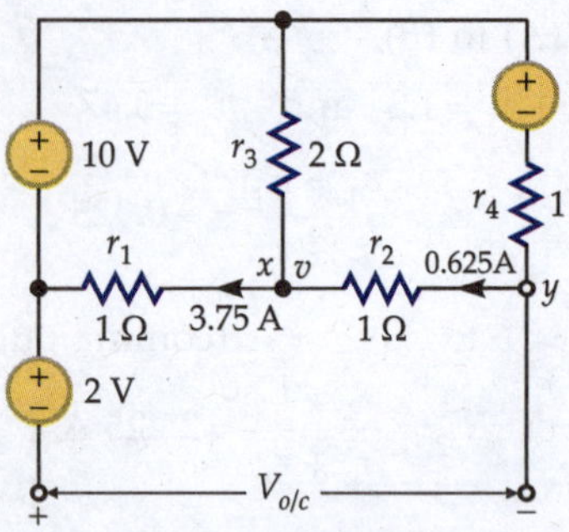

Fig. E1.104

∴ Nodal equations give,

$$\frac{v+5}{1+1}+\frac{v}{2}+\frac{v+10}{1}=0$$

or, $\quad 0.5\,v+2.5+0.5\,v+v+10=0$

or, $\quad v=-6.25$ V.

∴Current through $r_1=\dfrac{v+10}{r_1}=3.75$ A

[flowing from x terminal towards 10 V source]

Then the drop across r_1 is $3.75\times 1=3.75$ V with +ve polarity at side from which the current enters r_1.

Again, the current through r_2 is $\dfrac{v+5}{r_2+r_4}=-0.625$ A; the drop in 1Ω being

$1\times(-0.625)=-0.625$ V

(the polarity of drop across r_2 is +ve towards terminal y).

Thus

$$V_{o/c}=-2\text{ V}+\text{drop across } r_1+\text{drop across } r_2$$
$$=-2-3.75-0.625=-\mathbf{6.375\ V.}$$

EXAMPLE 1.85 *Find V_1 and V_2 in Fig. E1.105.*

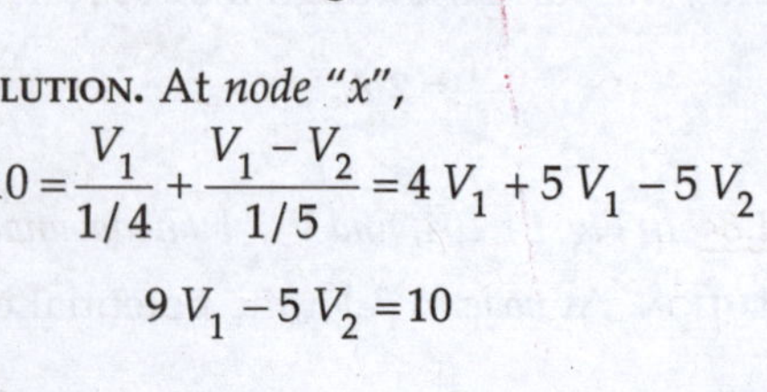

Fig. E1.105

SOLUTION. At *node "x"*,

$$10=\frac{V_1}{1/4}+\frac{V_1-V_2}{1/5}=4\,V_1+5\,V_1-5\,V_2$$

or, $\quad 9\,V_1-5\,V_2=10 \qquad$ ...(1)

At *node "y"*,

$$5=\frac{V_2}{1/2}+\frac{V_2-V_1}{1/5}=2\,V_2+5\,V_2-5\,V_1$$

or, $\quad -5\,V_1+7\,V_2=5 \qquad$ ...(2)

Solving (1) and (2),

$$V_2=\mathbf{2.5\ V};\ V_1=\mathbf{2.5\ V.}$$

Check

With obtained values of V_1 and V_2, it may be seen that KCL is satisfied at both nodes "x" and "y"; it is also interesting to note that no current passes through $\frac{1}{5}$ Ω resistor.

EXAMPLE 1.86 *In the network configuration of Fig. E1.106 find the current and voltage drops through 5 Ω resistor.*

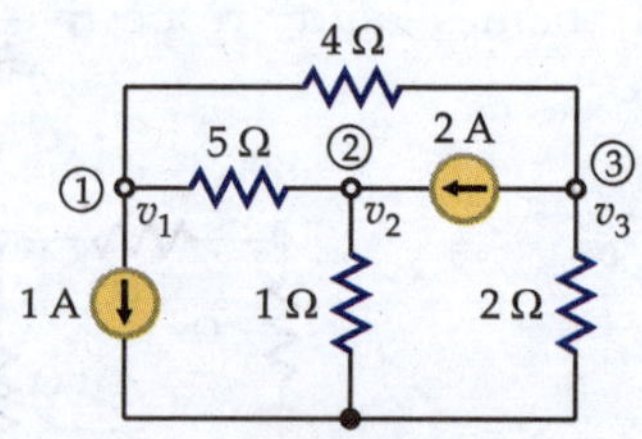

Fig. E1.106

SOLUTION. Let us name the nodes as 1, 2 and 3 with respective voltages v_1, v_2 and v_3.

Here, $\quad \dfrac{v_1-v_2}{5}+\dfrac{v_1-v_3}{4}+1=0$

For *node (1)*,

i.e., $\quad v_1\times 0.45-0.2\,v_2-0.25\,v_3=-1$

or, $\quad 0.45\,v_1-0.2\,v_2-0.25\,v_3=-1 \qquad$ ...(*A*)

Similarly, for *node (2)*,

$$\frac{v_2-v_1}{5}+\frac{v_2}{1}=2$$

or, $\quad 1.2\,v_2-0.2\,v_1=2 \qquad$ ...(*B*)

and for *node (3)*,

$$2+(v_3-v_1)/4+\frac{v_3}{2}=0$$

or, $\quad 0.75\,v_3-0.25\,v_1=-2 \qquad$ ...(*C*)

Thus the equations are

$$0.45\,v_1-0.2\,v_2-0.25\,v_3=-1$$
$$-0.2\,v_1+1.2\,v_2=2$$
$$-0.25\,v_1+0.75\,v_3=-2$$

In Matrix form,

$$\begin{bmatrix} 0.45 & -0.2 & -0.25 \\ -0.2 & 1.2 & 0 \\ -0.25 & 0 & 0.75 \end{bmatrix}\begin{bmatrix} v_1 \\ v_2 \\ v_3 \end{bmatrix} = \begin{bmatrix} -1 \\ 2 \\ -2 \end{bmatrix}$$

$$\therefore \quad \Delta = \begin{bmatrix} 0.45 & -0.2 & -0.25 \\ -0.2 & 1.2 & 0 \\ -0.25 & 0 & 0.75 \end{bmatrix}$$

$$= 0.45\,(1.2 \times 0.75) - (-0.2)(-0.2 \times 0.75) + (-0.25)(0.25 \times 1.2) = 0.3\,;$$

$$\Delta_1 = \begin{bmatrix} -1 & -0.2 & -0.25 \\ 2 & 1.2 & 0 \\ -2 & 0 & 0.75 \end{bmatrix}$$

$$= -1\,(1.2 \times 0.75) + 0.2\,(2 \times 0.75) - 0.25\,(2 \times 1.2)$$

$$= -1.2\,;$$

$$\Delta_2 = \begin{bmatrix} 0.45 & -1 & -0.25 \\ -0.2 & 2 & 0 \\ -0.25 & -2 & 0.75 \end{bmatrix}$$

$$= 0.45\,(2 \times 0.75) + 1\,(-0.2 \times 0.75) - 0.25\,(+0.2 \times 2 + 2 \times 0.25)$$

$$= 0.3\,;$$

$$\therefore \quad v_1 = \frac{\Delta_1}{\Delta} = -\frac{1.2}{0.3} = -4\text{ V}\,;$$

$$v_2 = \frac{\Delta_2}{\Delta} = \frac{0.3}{0.3} = 1\text{ V}$$

The current through 5 Ω resistor is then

$$\frac{v_1 - v_2}{5} = \frac{-4-1}{5} = \mathbf{-1\ A}\,;$$

i.e., flowing terminal (2) to terminal (1).

The voltage drop in 5Ω resistor is $(v_1 - v_2) = $ **– 5 V** having +ve polarity at the side of *node (2).*

Example 1.87 *What is the value of R such that the powers supplied by both the sources are equal to each other (Fig. E1.107) ?*

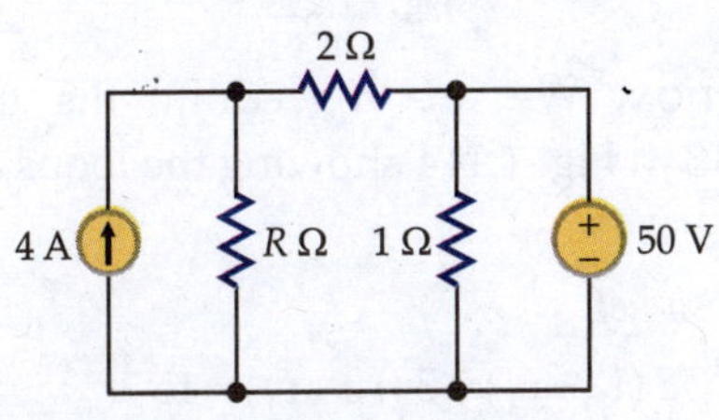

Fig. E1.107

Solution. The circuit of Fig. E1.107 is redrawn with nodes and currents named (Fig. E1.108) ;

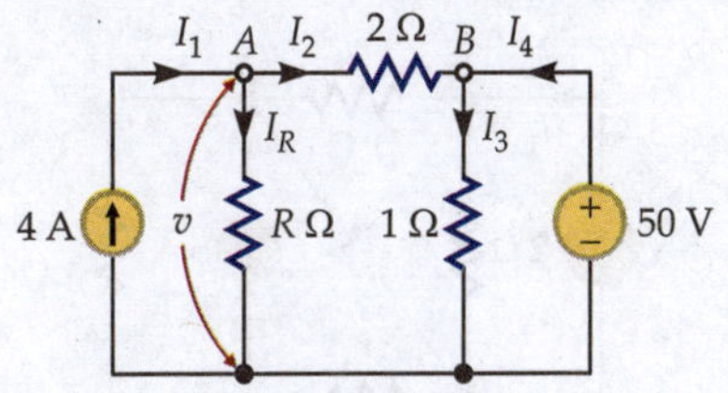

Fig. E1.108

At *node (A)*,

$$I_1 = I_R + I_2$$

or, $$4 = \frac{v}{R} + \frac{v-50}{2} = \frac{v}{R} + 0.5\,v - 25$$

$$\therefore \quad 4 + 25 = 29 = \frac{v}{R} + 0.5\,v \qquad ...(i)$$

At *node (B)*,

$$I_2 + I_4 = I_3$$

or, $$\frac{v-50}{2} + I_4 = \frac{50}{1} = 50$$

or, $$0.5\,v + I_4 = 75 \qquad ...(ii)$$

Solving for (*i*) and (*ii*),

$$\frac{v}{R} - I_4 = -46$$

$$\therefore \quad I_4 = \frac{v}{R} + 46 \qquad ...(iii)$$

Again power flow from both sources being equal,

$$50\,I_4 = 4v \qquad ...(iv)$$

Utilising (*iv*) in (*iii*),

$$\frac{v}{R} = \frac{1}{12.5}\,v - 46 \qquad ...(v)$$

Comparing (*i*) and (*v*), $v = 129.3$ volts

∴From (*i*), R becomes – ve which is not possible.

Thus there can not be any value of *R* for which powers drawn from both the sources are equal.

Example 1.88 *Find current through the resistor r_2 by nodal method (Fig. E1.109).*

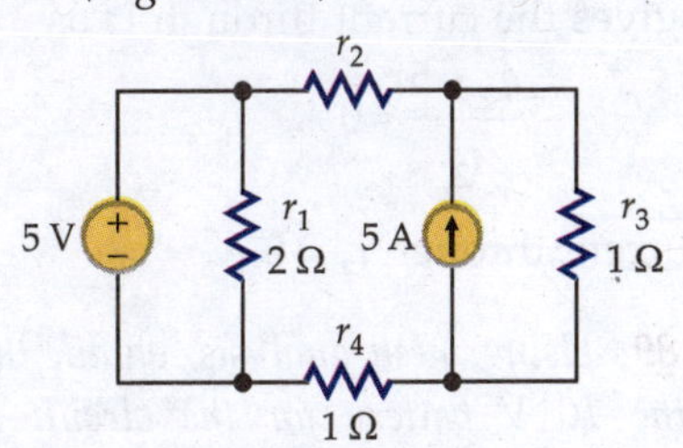

Fig. E1.109

Solution. Let us redraw the circuit using the nodal voltage and *node* names (Fig. E1.110)

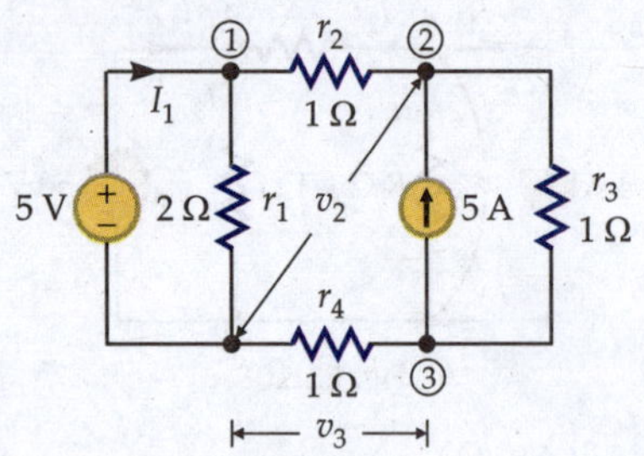

Fig. E1.110

At *node (1)*,

$$I_1 = \frac{5}{r_1} + \frac{5 - v_2}{r_2} = 2.5 + \frac{5 - v_2}{1}$$

$$\therefore \quad v_2 + I_1 = 7.5 \qquad ...(i)$$

At *node (2)*,

$$\frac{v_2 - 5}{r_2} + \frac{v_2 - v_3}{r_3} = 5$$

or, $$v_2 - 5 + v_2 - v_3 = 5$$

or, $$2v_2 - v_3 = 10 \qquad ...(ii)$$

At *node (3)*,

$$\frac{v_3 - v_2}{r_3} + \frac{v_3}{r_4} + 5 = 0$$

or, $$v_3 - v_2 + v_3 = -5$$

or, $$2v_3 - v_2 = -5 \qquad ...(iii)$$

From (*iii*),

$$v_3 = \frac{v_2 - 5}{2} \qquad ...(iv)$$

Utilising (*iv*) in (*ii*),

$$2v_2 - \frac{v_2 - 5}{2} = 10$$

or, $$2\,v_2 - 0.5\,v_2 + 2.5 = 10$$

or, $$1.5\,v_2 = 7.5$$

$$\therefore \quad v_2 = 5 \text{ V}$$

This gives the current through r_2 as

$$\frac{v_2 - 5}{r_2} = 0 \text{ A.}$$

$\therefore$ Current through r_2 = **0 A.**

Example 1.89 *Using mesh analysis, obtain the current through the 10 V battery for the circuit shown in Fig. E1.111.*

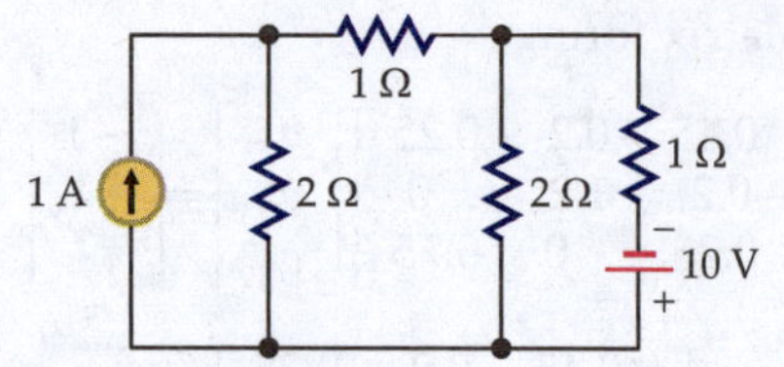

Fig. E1.111

Solution. The current source is first converted to an equivalent voltage source and the *loop* currents are named (Fig. E1.112).

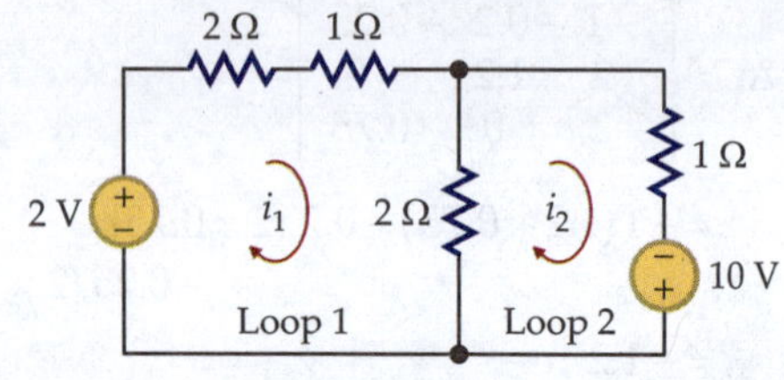

Fig. E1.112

Applying KVL *in loop-1*,

$$-2 + 3i_1 + (i_1 - i_2)2 = 0$$

or, $$5i_1 - 2i_2 = 2 \qquad ...(1)$$

and *in loop-2*,

$$2\,(i_2 - i_1) + i_2 - 10 = 0$$

or, $$-2i_1 + 3i_2 - 10 = 0 \qquad ...(2)$$

Solving equations (1) & (2),

$$i_2 = \mathbf{4.91\ A} \text{ and } i_1 = \mathbf{2.36\ A.}$$

$\therefore$ Current of the 10 V battery is 4.91 A which enters the battery through –ve terminal as shown.

Example 1.90 *What is the power loss in the 10 Ω resistor in the network shown in Fig. E1.113 ? Use mesh method.*

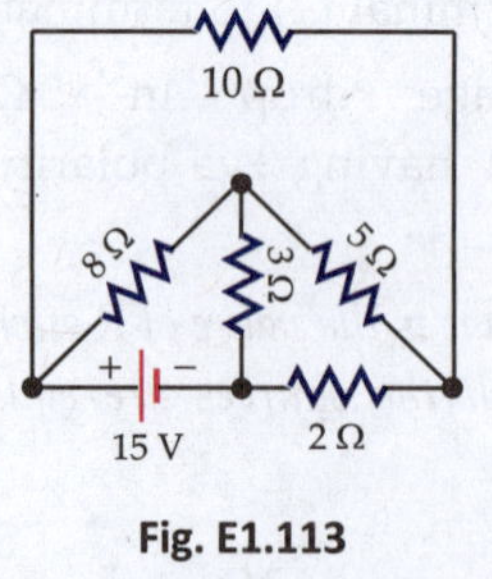

Fig. E1.113

Solution. We are to redraw the circuit of Fig. E1.113 in Fig. 1.114 showing the loops and loop currents.

In *mesh aef*,

$$8\,(i_1 - i_3) + 3\,(i_1 - i_2) = 15$$

or, $$11\,i_1 - 3\,i_2 - 8\,i_3 = 15 \qquad ...(i)$$

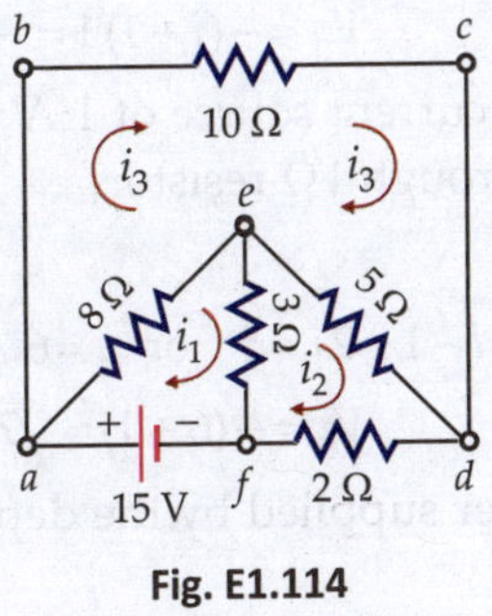

Fig. E1.114

In *mesh efd*,

$$5(i_2 - i_3) + 2i_2 + 3(i_2 - i_1) = 0$$

or, $$-3i_1 + 10i_2 - 5i_3 = 0 \quad ...(ii)$$

In *mesh abcde*,

$$10i_3 + (i_3 - i_2)5 + (i_3 - i_1)8 = 0$$

or, $$-8i_1 - 5i_2 + 23i_3 = 0 \quad ...(iii)$$

Thus the *loop* equations are

$$11i_1 - 3i_2 - 8i_3 = 15$$
$$-3i_1 + 10i_2 - 5i_3 = 0$$
$$-8i_1 - 5i_2 + 23i_3 = 0$$

Solving by Cramer's rule,

i_3 = current through the 10 Ω resistor

$$= \frac{\begin{vmatrix} 11 & -3 & 15 \\ -3 & 10 & 0 \\ -8 & -5 & 0 \end{vmatrix}}{\begin{vmatrix} 11 & -3 & -8 \\ -3 & 10 & -5 \\ -8 & -5 & 23 \end{vmatrix}} \simeq 1.23 \text{ A}$$

∴ Current through 10 Ω resistor = **1.23 A.**

Power loss $(p) = i_3^2\, r = (1.23)^2 \times 10 =$ **15.13 W.**

EXAMPLE 1.91 *Determine the node voltages and the current through the resistors using mesh method for the network shown in Fig. E1.115.*

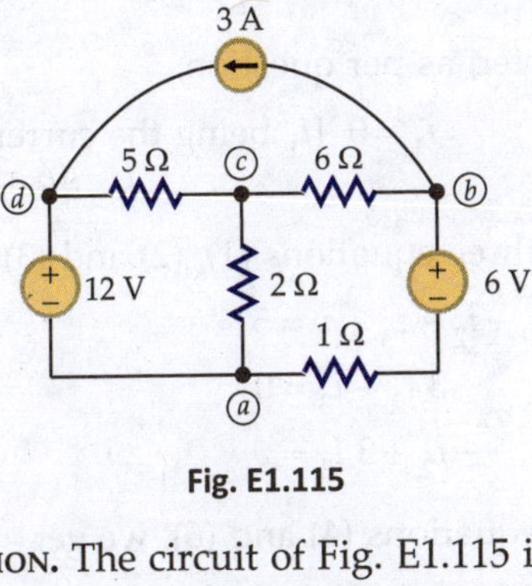

Fig. E1.115

SOLUTION. The circuit of Fig. E1.115 is redrawn with the loop currents in the three loops (Fig. E1.116).

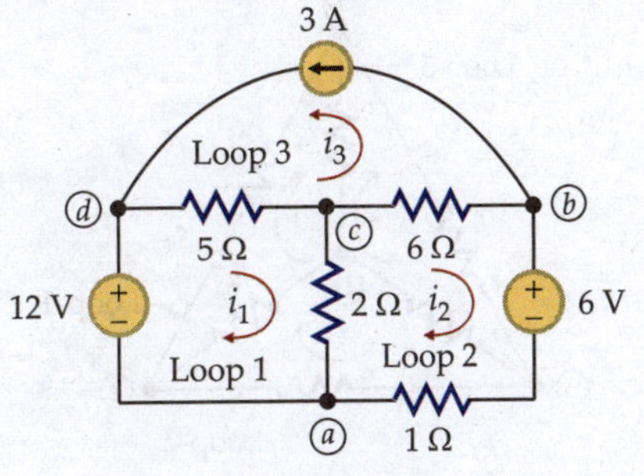

Fig. E1.116

For loop-1,

$$(i_1 + i_3)5 + (i_1 - i_2)2 = 12$$

or, $$(i_1 + 3)5 + (i_1 - i_2)2 = 12$$

or, $$7i_1 - 2i_2 = -3 \quad ...(i)$$

For loop-2,

$$(i_2 - i_1)2 + (i_2 + i_3)6 + i_2 .1 = -6$$

or, $$(i_2 - i_1)2 + (i_2 + 3)6 + i_2 = -6$$

or, $$-2i_1 + 9i_2 = -24 \quad ...(ii)$$

Solving equations (*i*) and (*ii*),

$$i_1 = -1.27 \text{ A}; \quad i_2 = -2.95 \text{ A}.$$

∴ Current through 5 Ω resistor

$$= (i_1 + i_3) = -1.27 + 3 = 1.73 \text{ A}$$

Current through 2 Ω resistor

$$= (i_1 - i_2) = -1.27 - (-2.95) = 1.68 \text{ A}$$

Current through 6 Ω resistor

$$= (i_2 + i_3) = -2.95 + 3 = 0.05 \text{ A}$$

Current through 1 Ω resistor

$$= i_2 = -2.95 \text{ A}$$

Also,

voltage at *node "a"*

$$= \mathbf{0\ V}$$

voltage at *node "b"*

$$= i_2 \times 1 + 6 = -2.95 \times 1 + 6 = \mathbf{3.05\ V}$$

voltage at *node "c"*

$$= (i_1 - i_2)2 = 1.68 \times 2 = \mathbf{3.36\ V}$$

voltage at *node "d"*

$$= \mathbf{12\ V.}$$

EXAMPLE 1.92 *In Fig. E1.117, obtain the mesh equations. If $e_1 = e_2 = e_3 = 1$ V and all the resistances are equal to each other, being 1 Ω each, what would be the loop currents ?*

CHAPTER 1

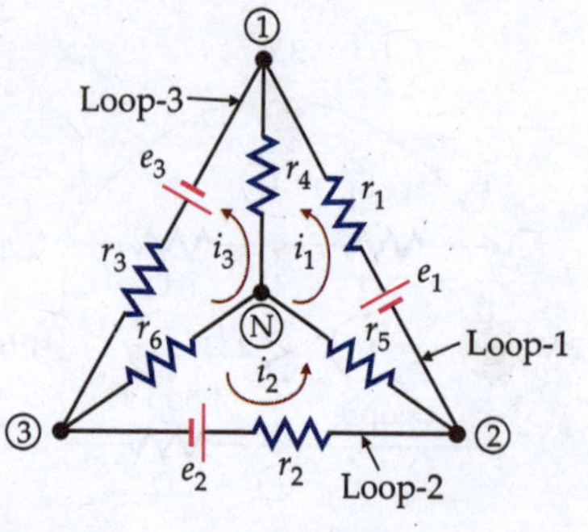

Fig. E1.117

Solution. Let the loop currents be i_1, i_2 and i_3. The loop equations are given below :

For loop-1

$$i_1 r_1 + (i_1 - i_3) r_4 + (i_1 - i_2) r_5 = e_1$$

or, $$i_1 (r_1 + r_4 + r_5) - i_2 r_5 - i_3 r_4 = e_1 \quad ...(i)$$

For loop-2

$$(i_2 - i_1) r_5 + (i_2 - i_3) r_6 + i_2 r_2 = e_2$$

or, $$-i_1 r_5 + i_2 (r_2 + r_5 + r_6) - r_6 i_3 = e_2 \quad ...(ii)$$

For loop-3

$$i_3 r_3 + (i_3 - i_2) r_6 + (i_3 - i_1) r_4 = e_3$$

or, $$-i_1 r_4 - i_2 r_6 + i_3 (r_3 + r_4 + r_6) = e_3 \quad ...(iii)$$

If $e_1 = e_2 = e_3 = 1$ V, and all the resistances are equal, from symmetry it is evident that

$$i_1 = i_2 = i_3 = i \text{ (say)}$$

Thus for *loop-1*,

$$e_1 = 1 = ir = 1 \times i$$

$\therefore$ $$i = \mathbf{1\ A.}$$

The loop currents in all the loops will be identical and equal to 1 A for each loop.

Example 1.93 *What is the power supplied by the dependent source in Fig. E1.118 ?*

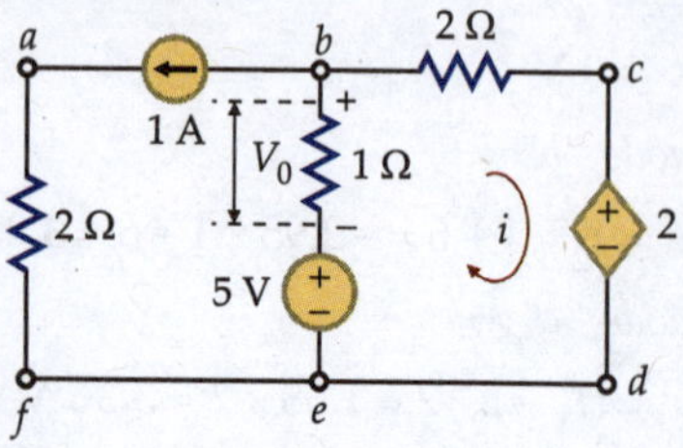

Fig. E1.118

Solution. *In loop bcde,*

$$-5 - V_0 + 2\,i + 2\,V_0 = 0$$

or, $$V_0 + 2i = 5 \quad ...(i)$$

But $$V_0 = -(i+1)1 = -i - 1 \quad ...(ii)$$

[Since the current source of 1 A with also force 1 A current through 1 Ω resistor]

Using *(ii)*,

$$-i - 1 + 2i = 5 \quad \text{or} \quad i = 6 \text{ A}$$

$\therefore$ $$V_0 = -(6+1) = -7 \text{ V} \quad \text{[from } (ii)\text{]}$$

Thus power supplied by the dependent source is

$$2V_0\, i = 2 \times (-7) \times 6$$
$$= \mathbf{-84\ W} \text{ (power being absorbed).}$$

Example 1.94 *Find v by mesh method such that the current through the 5 V source is zero (Fig. E1.119).*

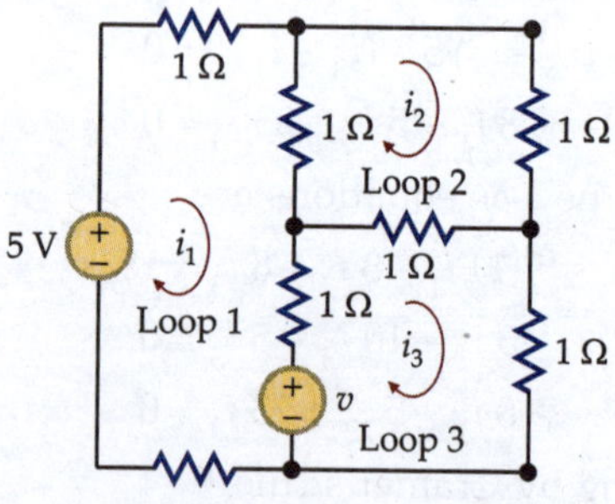

Fig. E1.119

Solution. *In loop-1,*

$$-5 + i_1 \times 1 + (i_1 - i_2)1 + (i_1 - i_3)1 + v = 0$$

or, $$3i_1 - i_2 - i_3 = -v + 5 \quad ...(1)$$

In loop-2,

$$i_2 \times 1 + (i_2 - i_3)1 + (i_2 - i_1)1 = 0$$

or, $$3\,i_2 - i_1 - i_3 = 0$$

or, $$-i_1 + 3\,i_2 - i_3 = 0 \quad ...(2)$$

In loop-3,

$$(i_3 - i_2)1 + i_3 \times 1 - v + (i_3 - i_1)1 = 0$$

or, $$-i_1 - i_2 + 3\,i_3 = v \quad ...(3)$$

However, as per question,

$i_1 = 0$ [i_1 being the current through the 5 V source]

$\therefore$ The three equations (1), (2) and (3) become

$$-i_2 - i_3 + v = 5 \quad ...(4)$$
$$3\,i_2 - i_3 = 0 \quad ...(5)$$
$$-i_2 + 3\,i_3 = v \quad ...(6)$$

From equations (4) and (6), we get

$$-4i_3 = 5 - 2v \quad ...(7)$$

However, from equations (5) and (6),

$$i_3 = \frac{3}{8} v \qquad \text{...(8)}$$

Using (8) in (7),

$$-4 \times \left(\frac{3}{8} v \right) = 5 - 2v$$

or, $$-\frac{3}{2} v = 5 - 2v \text{ or } v = 10 \text{ V}$$

$\therefore$ The voltage v should be **10 V.**

EXAMPLE 1.95 *Using mesh analysis, find the current flow through the 50 V source in the network of Fig. E1.120.*

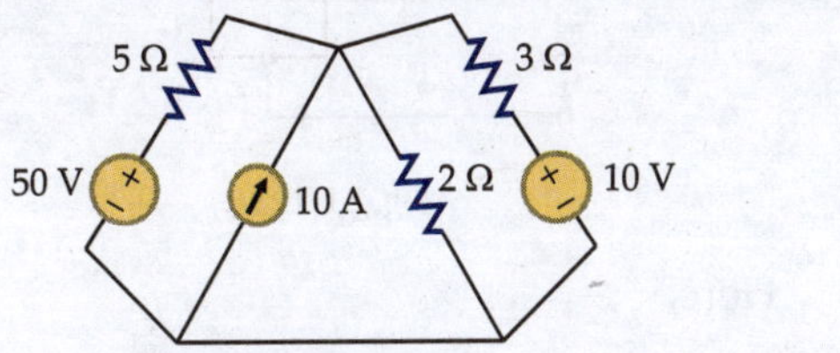

Fig. E1.120

SOLUTION. The current source is first transferred to the voltage source and the network is redrawn in Fig. E1.121.

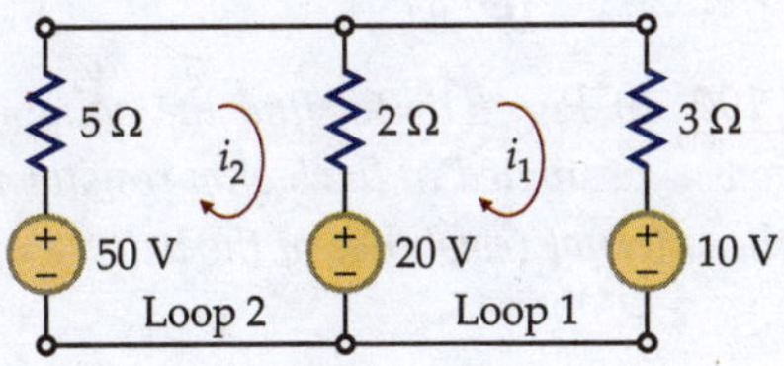

Fig. E1.121

In loop-1,

$$3 i_1 + 10 - 20 + (i_1 - i_2) 2 = 0$$

or, $$5 i_1 - 2 i_2 = 10 \qquad \text{...(i)}$$

In loop-2,

$$5 i_2 + (i_2 - i_1) 2 + 20 - 50 = 0$$

or, $$-2 i_1 + 7 i_2 = 30 \qquad \text{...(ii)}$$

Solving equations (*i*) and (*ii*),

i_2 = current through 50 V source = **5.48 A**

EXAMPLE 1.96 *In the circuit of Fig. E1.122, find* (V_2 / V_1) *using mesh method.*

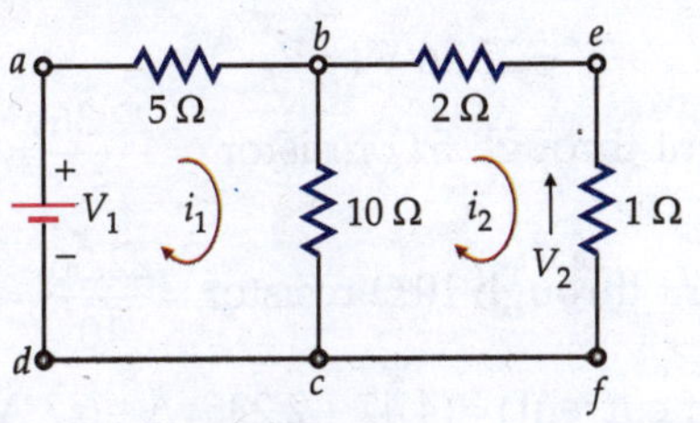

Fig. E1.122

SOLUTION. In the *loop abcd,* let the loop current be i_1 and *in loop befc* it is i_2.

$\therefore$ *In loop abcd,*

$$5 i_1 + (i_1 - i_2) 10 = V_1$$

i.e., $$15 i_1 - 10 i_2 = V_1 \qquad \text{...(1)}$$

while, *in loop befc,*

$$2 i_2 + i_2 \times 1 + (i_2 - i_1) 10 = 0$$

or, $$-10 i_1 + 13 i_2 = 0 \qquad \text{...(2)}$$

Solving (1) and (2),

$$i_2 = \frac{10}{95} V_1 \qquad \text{...(3)}$$

But, $$V_2 = i_2 \times 1 = i_2 = \frac{10}{95} V_1 \qquad \text{[using (3)]}$$

$$\therefore \quad \frac{V_2}{V_1} = \frac{10}{95} = \mathbf{\frac{2}{19}}.$$

EXAMPLE 1.97 *Write down the mesh equations for the network shown in Fig. E1.123.*

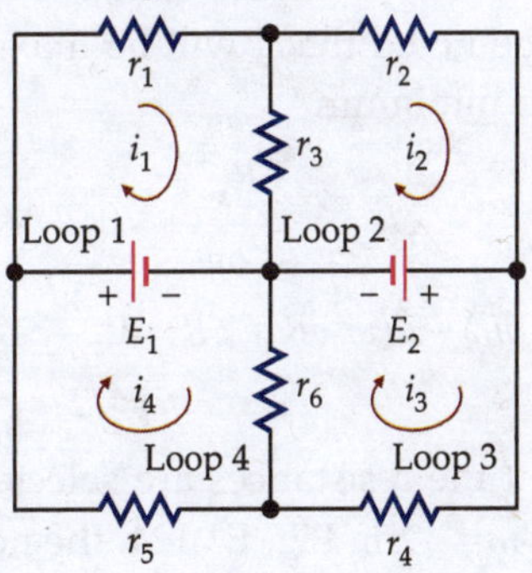

Fig. E1.123

SOLUTION. *In loop-1,*

$$i_1 r_1 + (i_1 - i_2) r_2 - E_1 = 0$$

or, $$i_1 (r_1 + r_2) - i_2 r_2 = E_1 \qquad \text{...(i)}$$

In loop-2,

$$i_2 r_3 + E_2 + (i_2 - i_1) r_2 = 0$$

or, $$-i_1 r_2 + i_2 (r_2 + r_3) = -E_2 \qquad \text{...(ii)}$$

In loop-3,

$$i_3 r_4 + (i_3 - i_4) r_6 - E_2 = 0$$

or, $$i_3 (r_4 + r_6) - i_4 r_6 = E_2 \qquad \text{...(iii)}$$

In loop-4,

$$i_4 r_5 + (i_4 - i_3) r_6 + E_1 = 0$$

or, $$i_4 (r_5 + r_6) - i_3 r_6 = -E_1 \qquad \text{...(iv)}$$

Thus the loop equations are

$$\mathbf{i_1 (r_1 + r_2) - i_2 r_2 = E_1}$$
$$\mathbf{-i_1 r_2 + i_2 (r_2 + r_3) = -E_2}$$
$$\mathbf{i_3 (r_4 + r_6) - i_4 r_6 = E_2}$$
$$\mathbf{i_4 (r_5 + r_6) - i_3 r_6 = -E_1}$$

ADDITIONAL PROBLEMS

EXAMPLE 1.98 *Find the condition when the circuit current is maximum (Fig. E1.124)*

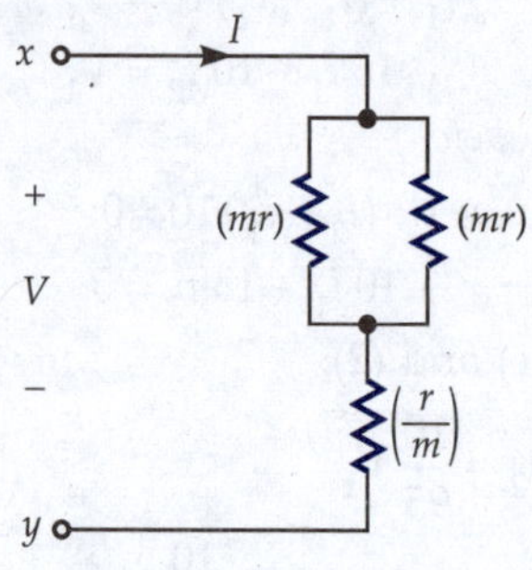

Fig. E1.124

SOLUTION. The equivalent resistance across x-y is

$$R_{x-y} = \frac{mr}{2} + \frac{r}{m} = \frac{m^2 r + 2r}{2m}.$$

It may be noted that I will be maximum when R_{x-y} will be minimum

i.e., $$\frac{\delta R_{x-y}}{\delta m} = 0.$$

i.e., $$2m(2mr) - 2(m^2 R + 2R) = 0.$$

i.e., $$m = \sqrt{2}.$$

Hence, if the resistances are selected in such a way so that $m = \sqrt{2}$ in Fig. E1.124, the net resistance of the circuit (R_{x-y}) will be minimum giving the circuit current to be maximum.

The current in the circuit is

$$I = \frac{V}{\frac{\sqrt{2}\,r}{2} + \frac{r}{\sqrt{2}}} = \frac{V}{\frac{2r + 2r}{2\sqrt{2}}} = \frac{V}{\sqrt{2}\,r}$$

when $$R_{x-y} = \frac{\sqrt{2}\,r}{2} + \frac{r}{\sqrt{2}} = \frac{2r+2r}{2\sqrt{2}} = \sqrt{2}\,r.$$

∴ Power consumed across x-y terminals is

$$I^2 R_{x-y} = \left(\frac{V}{\sqrt{2}\,r}\right)^2 \times \sqrt{2}\,r = \frac{V^2}{\sqrt{2}\,r} \text{ watts.}$$

EXAMPLE 1.99 *Two 100 W, 220 V bulbs are required to be connected across a 400 volts supply. Find the value of the resistance to be inserted in the line so that the voltage across the bulbs does not exceed 220 V.*

SOLUTION. Total power drawn from the circuit is (2 × 100) *i.e.,* 200 W.

Hence supply current I is given by

$$I = \frac{200 \text{ W}}{220 \text{ V}} = 0.91 \text{ A}$$

Hence the current of 0.91 A (= I) is to be flown in the circuit (Fig. E1.125). Let r be the series resistance to be inserted in the circuit such that the voltage across the bulbs is 220 V.

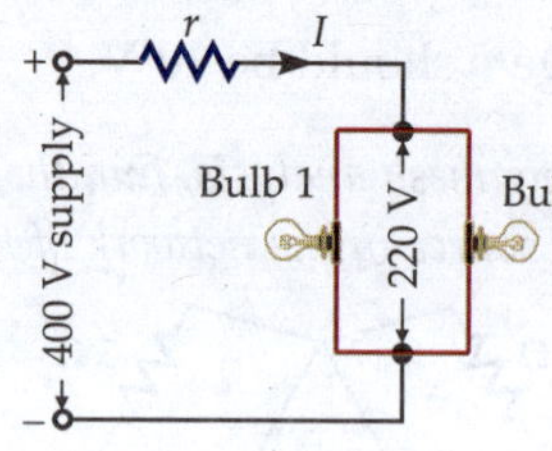

Fig. E1.125

Here,

Supply voltage = drop across r + bulb voltage

i.e., $$400 = v_r + 220$$

∴ $$v_r = 400 - 220 = Ir = 0.91\,r$$

or, $$180 = 0.91\,r$$

∴ $$r = \mathbf{197.8\ \Omega}.$$

EXAMPLE 1.100 *In Fig. E1.126, find the value of R such that the power dissipated in the 5 ohm resistor is 100 W. Assume the internal resistance of the battery of 50 volts to be 1 Ω.*

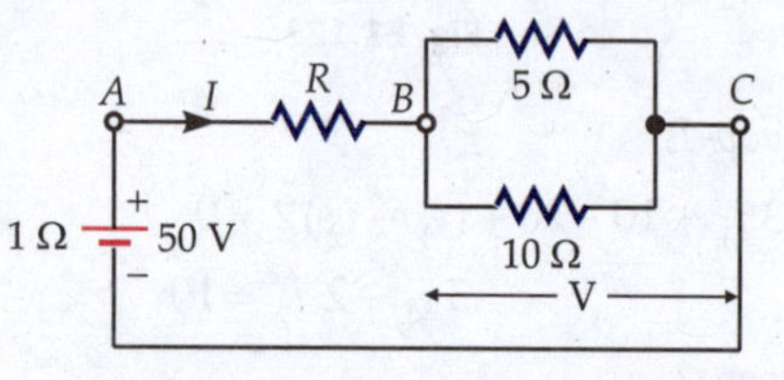

Fig. E1.126

SOLUTION. Power loss in 5 Ω resistor is

$$P = \frac{V^2}{R}$$

or, $$100 = \frac{V^2}{5}$$

i.e., $$V = 22.36 \text{ V } (= V_{BC})$$

∴ Current through 5 Ω resistor $= \dfrac{22.36}{5} = 4.47$ A

Current through 10 Ω resistor $= \dfrac{22.36}{10} = 2.236$ A

∴ I (net current) = (4.47 + 2.236) A ≃ 6.7 A

However, $I = \dfrac{V}{\text{int. resistance} + R + 5 \| 10}$

or, $6.7 = \dfrac{50}{1 + 3.33 + R}$

or, $6.7 + 22.31 + 6.7\,R = 50$

or, $R = \mathbf{3.134\,\Omega}$.

Hence R should be $3.134\,\Omega$ such that the power loss in $5\,\Omega$ resistor is 100 W.

EXAMPLE 1.101 *With reference to Fig. E1.127, determine the voltage drop across the pure resistance R_L if the control current in the dependent current source is 1 Amp. Assume $R_L = 2\,\Omega$.*

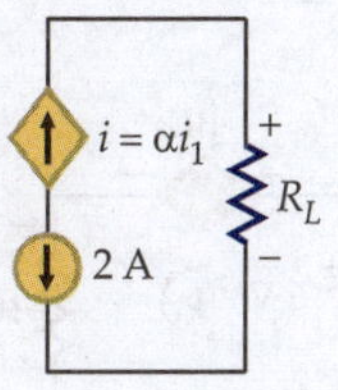

Fig. E1.127

SOLUTION. Let the voltage drop across R_L be V_L. Applying KVL in the circuit,

V_L = drop across R_L due to i-drop across R_L due to 2 A source

[It is assumed that the direction of drop due to flow of current i from dependent source is +ve while that due to flow of 2 A in R_L is –ve.]

i.e., $V_L = iR_L - 2\,.\,R_L = 2i - 4$ $[\because R_L = 2\,\Omega]$

$= 2\,\alpha\, i_1 - 4 = \mathbf{2\,(\alpha - 2)\ V}.$

$[\because\ i_1$, the control current in the dependent source is 1 A]

EXAMPLE 1.102 *Find the power loss in the resistors and the power delivered by the two d.c. constant voltage sources as shown in Fig. E1.128.*

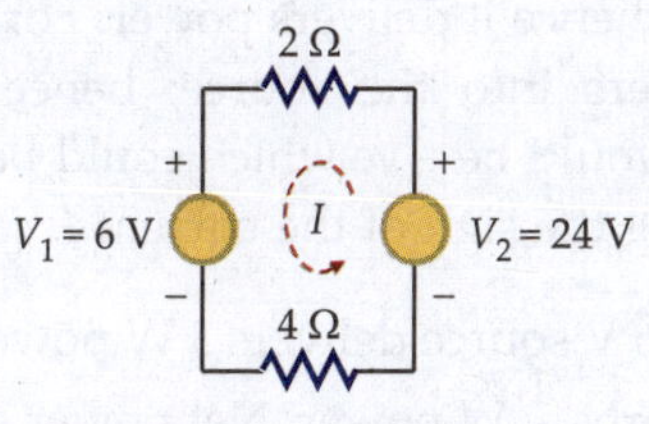

Fig. E1.128

SOLUTION. As $V_2 > V_1$, current flow (I) in the circuit is from V_2 to V_1 as shown by dotted line in Fig. E1.128.

$$I = \frac{V_2 - V_1}{2 + 4} = 3\text{ A}$$

$\therefore$ Power consumed in $2\,\Omega$ resistor is $(3)^2 \times 2\,(=18\text{ W})$ and that in $4\,\Omega$ resistor is $(3)^2 \times 4\,(=36\text{ W})$.

Power given by source V_2 is $V_2 \times I$ *i.e.,* (24×3) W or 72 W ; power absorbed by 6 V source (as the current enters into the 6 V source hence it absorbs power) is given by $V_1 \times I$ *i.e.,* (6×3) W or 18 W.

Hence, we see that the only source of power in this circuit is V_2 which gives 72 W. This power is being absorbed by (*i*) $2\,\Omega$ resistor (**18 W**), (*ii*) V_1 source (**18 W**) and (*iii*) $4\,\Omega$ resistor (**36 W**).

EXAMPLE 1.103 *What is the magnitude of current drained from the 10 V source in Fig. E1.129(a) ?*

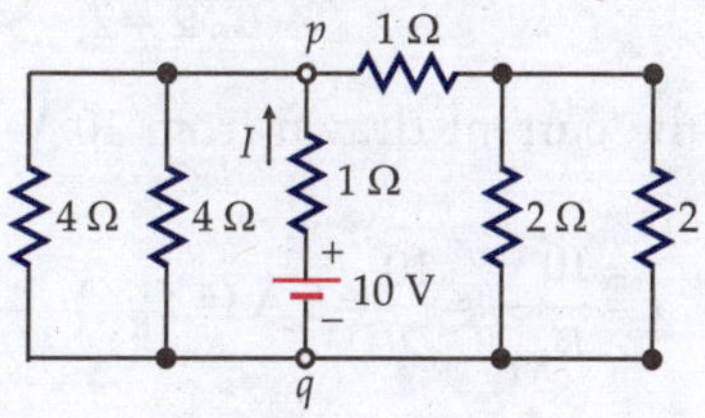

Fig. E1.129 (*a*)

SOLUTION. First step is to obtain the equivalent circuit of the network shown in Fig. E1.129(*a*). We redraw the circuit in Fig. E1.129(*b*) removing the voltage source 100 V. We observe that R_1 and R_2 as well as R_5 and R_6 are in parallel while R_3 is in series with the parallel combination of R_1 and R_2.

This gives the reduced network shown in Fig. E1.129(*b*).

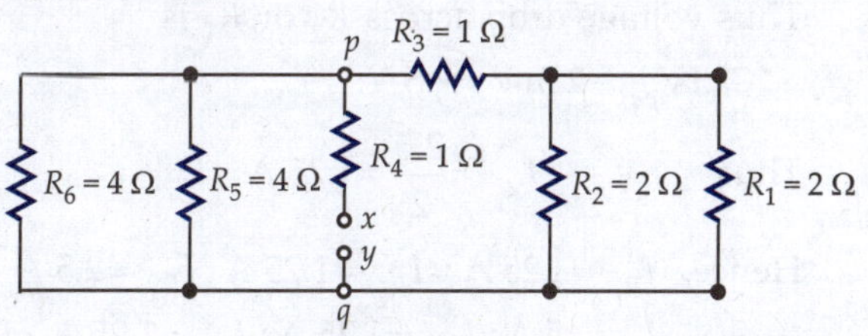

Fig. E1.129 (*b*)

Further network reduction is possible and shown in Fig. E1.129(*c*).

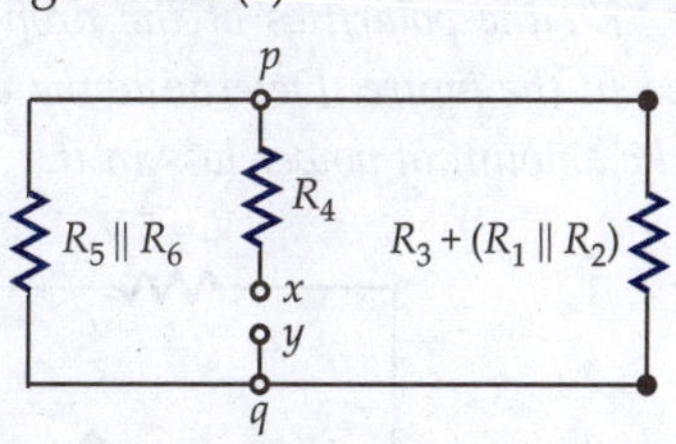

Fig. E1.129 (*c*)

Finally, R_{XY}, the net equivalent resistance is given by (Fig. E1.129(*d*))

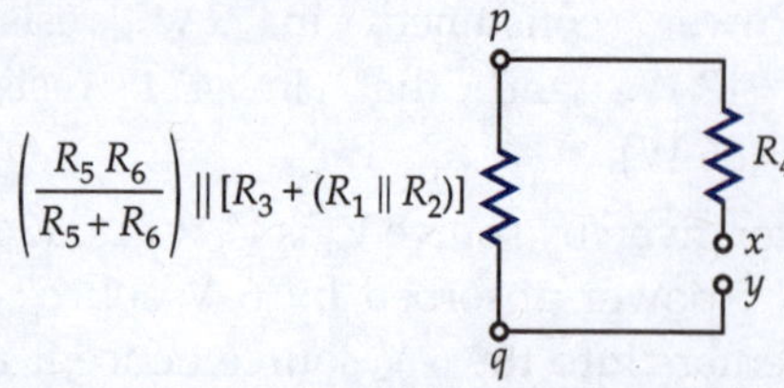

Fig. E1.129 (*d*)

$$R_{XY} = R_4 + \{(R_5 \| R_6) \| [R_3 + (R_1 \| R_2)]\} = 2\,\Omega$$

$$\left[\because R_{XY} = 1 + \left\{\left(\frac{4\times 4}{4+4}\right) \| \left[1+\frac{2\times 2}{2+2}\right]\right\}\right.$$

$$\left. = 1 + \{2 \| 2\} = 1 + \frac{2\times 2}{2+2} = 1 + 1 = 2\,\Omega\right]$$

Hence the current drawn from 10 V source is given by

$$I = \frac{10\text{ V}}{R_{XY}} = \frac{10}{2} = \mathbf{5\ A\ (= I_{R_4})}$$

The currents through individual resistors can be calculated as follows :

Drop across $R_4 = 5\text{ A} \times 1\,\Omega = 5\text{ V}$

$\therefore \quad V_{pq} = 10 - 5 = 5\text{ V}$

$\therefore \quad I_{R_5} = I_{R_6} = \frac{5}{4} = 1.25\text{ A}$

i.e., $\quad I_{R_3} = 5\text{ A} - (2\times 1.25)\text{ A} = 2.5\text{ A}$

$\therefore \quad V_{\text{drop}}$ across $R_3 = 2.5 \times 1 = 2.5$ V.

Thus voltage drop across R_2 or R_1 is

$(V_{pq} - 2.5)\ V = 2.5$ V.

Thus $\quad I_{R_2} = \frac{2.5}{2} = 1.25\text{ A} = I_{R_1}$.

Hence, $I_{R_1} = 1.25\text{ A}$; $I_{R_2} = 1.25\text{ A}$; $I_{R_3} = 2.5\text{ A}$

$I_{R_4} = 5\text{ A}$; $I_{R_5} = 1.25\text{ A}$; $I_{R_6} = 1.25\text{ A}$

EXAMPLE 1.104 *Fig. E1.130 represents a constant current source in series with a dependent current source feeding a resistance "r", the polarities of the drop across "r" being marked in the figure. Determine the value of "r" and obtain the amount of power loss in it.*

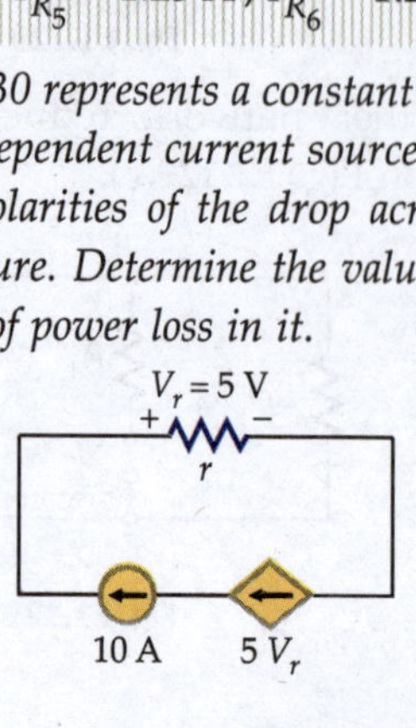

Fig. E1.130

SOLUTION. Obviously, for Ohm's law, the drop across r (*i.e.*, V_r) is the product of the circuit current and resistance.

$\therefore \quad (10 + 5\,V_r)\,r = V_r$

With $\quad V_r = 5$ Volts (given),

$\mathbf{r = 1/7\ ohm.}$

$\therefore$ Power loss in r is given by

$$P_r = (35)^2\,\frac{1}{7} = \mathbf{175\ watts.}$$

EXAMPLE 1.105 *Fig. E1.131 represents a series connection of a battery with a dependent voltage source feeding a resistor. Find I. Also obtain the power delivered by the sources if* $\beta = 2$.

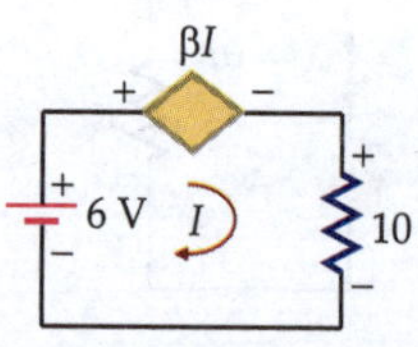

Fig. E1.131

SOLUTION. Using KVL,

$$\beta I + 10 \times I - 6 = 0$$

or, $\quad I = \frac{6}{(10+\beta)}\text{ A}$

If $\beta = 2$, $\quad I = \mathbf{\frac{1}{2}\ A.}$

$\therefore$ Power delivered by 6 V source is $6 \times \frac{1}{2} = 3$ W

while the power delivered by (βI) dependent voltage source is the product of voltage βI with the current

i.e., $\quad \left(-1/2 \times \beta \times \frac{1}{2}\right)$ or $\left(-\frac{1}{2}\right)$ W.

For 6 V source, current is coming out from the source and hence it delivers power. For (βI) source, correct enters into the source; hence its power delivered would be – ve which could be simulated by reversing the sign of the current I.

Hence 6 V source delivers 3 W power while (βI) source absorbs $\frac{1}{2}$ W power. Net power given to the resistance is then

2.5 W $\left[\text{also } P_{\text{loss}} \text{ in "r" is } \left(\frac{1}{2}\right)^2 \times 10\ \textit{i.e.}, 2.5\text{ W}\right]$.

EXAMPLE 1.106 *In the circuit shown in Fig. E1.132 find I, I_L and voltage drop across R_L.*

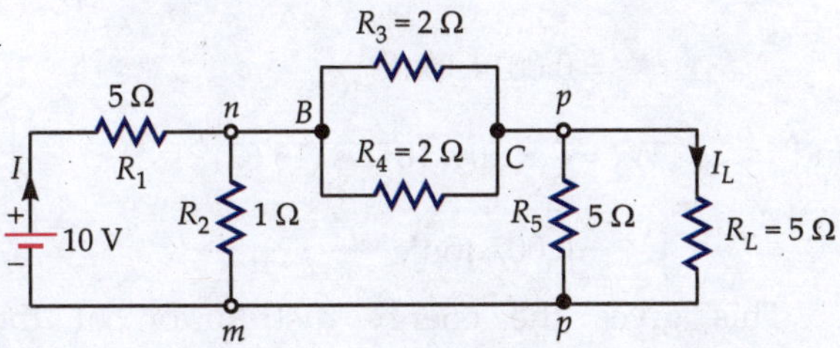

Fig. E1.132

SOLUTION. The first step is the network reduction. Equivalent of R_5 and R_L is $\dfrac{R_5 \times R_L}{R_5 + R_L}$ *i.e.,* $2.5\,\Omega$. This $2.5\,\Omega$ is in series with the parallel combination of R_3 and R_4 *i.e.,* with $\dfrac{R_3\,R_4}{R_3 + R_4}$ *i.e.,* with 1Ω resistance. Thus resistance across *n-m* terminal is given by

$$R_{n-m} = (2.5 + 1) \,||\, R_2$$

i.e.,
$$\frac{3.5 \times 1.0}{3.5 \times 1.0} = 0.78\,\Omega$$

$\therefore$ The net resistance of the circuit becomes $(R_1 + 0.78)\,\Omega$

i.e., $5.78\,\Omega\,(R_{eq})$.

Hence $I = \dfrac{10\text{ V}}{R_{eq}} = \mathbf{1.73\ A}$

This gives drop across R_1 as (1.73×5) V or 8.65 V.

$$\therefore \quad V_{m-n} = 10 - 8.65 = 1.35\text{ V}.$$

This gives

$$I_{R_2} = \frac{1.35}{1.0} = 1.35\text{ A}$$

Again parallel combination of R_3 and R_4 gives the net resistance as

$$\frac{2 \times 2}{2 + 2} = 1\Omega.$$

$\therefore$ Drop across this parallel combination is

$$(I - I_{R_2}) \times 1 = 0.38\text{ A} \times 1 \quad i.e.,\ 0.38\text{ V}$$

$$\therefore \quad V_{pq} = 1.35\text{ V} - 0.38\text{ V} = \mathbf{0.97\ V.}$$

This gives the drop across R_L.

The current across R_L is given by

$$I_{R_L} = \frac{V_{pq}}{R_L} = \frac{0.97}{5}\text{ A}$$

i.e., $I_L = \mathbf{0.194\ amps.}$

EXAMPLE 1.107 *With reference to Fig. E1.133, determine the voltage appearing across terminals y-z if a d.c. voltage of 100 V is applied across x-y terminals.*

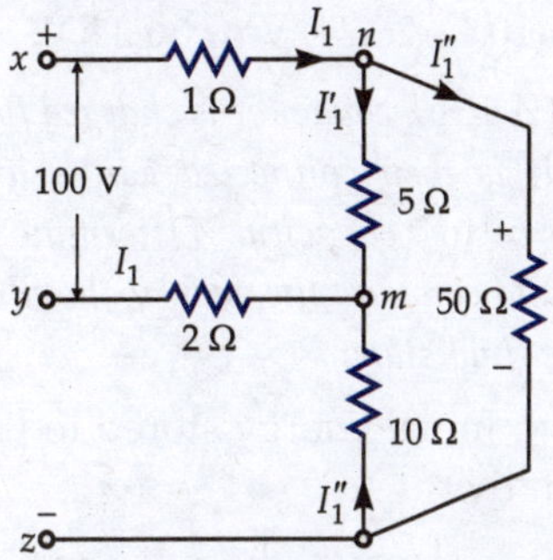

Fig. E1.133

SOLUTION. Let the current through 1Ω resistor be I_1 amps. while that through $5\,\Omega$ and $50\,\Omega$ resistor are I_1' and I_1'' respectively.

Obviously equivalent resistance across the terminal *n-m* is given by

$$R_{n-m} = \frac{5\,(50 + 10)}{5 + 50 + 10}\text{ ohms} = 4.62\,\Omega$$

$\therefore R_{x-y}$ (net resistance across *x-y*)

$$= 1 + 4.62 + 2 = 7.62\,\Omega$$

Hence $I_1 = \dfrac{100}{7.62} = 13.12\text{ A}$

By current division,

$$I_1' = I_1 \times \frac{60}{50 + 10 + 5}$$

$$= 13.12 \times \frac{60}{65} = 12.11\text{ A}$$

[Also, $V_{nm} = 100\text{ V} -$ drop across 1Ω resistor − drop across 2 ohm resistor

or, $V_{nm} = 100 - 13.12 \times 1 - 13.12 \times 2$
$= 60.64$ V

$\therefore \quad I_1' = \dfrac{60.64\text{ V}}{5\Omega} = 12.12\text{ A.}$]

CHAPTER 1

Similarly, $I_1'' = I_1 \times \frac{5}{5+10+50} = 1.01$ A

$$[\text{Also, } I_1'' = I_1 - I_1' = 13.12 - 12.11 = 1.01 \text{ A}]$$

This gives voltage across $10\,\Omega$ resistor as

$$v_{10\Omega} = I_1'' \times 10\,\Omega = 1.01 \times 10 = 10.1 \text{ V}.$$

The voltage drop across $2\,\Omega$ resistor is obviously $(I_1 \times 2)$ V *i.e.*, (13.12×2) V *i.e.*, 26.24 V.

Hence voltage across *y-z* terminals is

$$(10.1 + 26.24) \text{ V or } \mathbf{36.34\ V}.$$

EXAMPLE 1.108 *A 10 μF capacitor is charged full by a 100 V d.c. source. It is then connected across an uncharged capacitor of 50 μF capacity. Determine the energy distribution and compare the energy stored in the initial as well as the final state.*

SOLUTION. Initial energy stored in the capacitor is then given by

$$W_{in} = \frac{1}{2} CV^2 = \frac{1}{2} \times 10 \times 10^{-6} \times (100)^2$$

[∵ The capacitance of the charged capacitor is 10 μF]

i.e., $W_{in} = 0.05$ Joule

The initial charge

$$Q_{in} = CV = 10 \times 10^{-6} \times 100 = 0.001 \text{ coloumb.}$$

When this charged capacitor is connected across the uncharged capacitor, this charge is redistributed. Let W_1 be the charge of the initially charged capacitor of capacitance C and W_2 be that of the initially uncharged capacitor of capacitance C', now being charged.

∴ $W_1 = \frac{1}{2} CV'^2$ [V' being the final voltage]

and $W_2 = \frac{1}{2} C' V'^2$

Again $V' = \frac{Q}{C}$, Q being the final charge of the capacitors and C being their final capacitance.

Obviously, Q will be same to the value of Q_{in} and C_{eq} is given by the combination of C and C' in parallel.

i.e., $Q = 0.001$ Coulomb

and $C_{eq} = C + C' = (10 + 50)\,\mu\text{F} = 60\,\mu\text{F}$

∴ $V' = \frac{0.001}{60 \times 10^{-6}} = 16.67$ V

This gives,

$$W_1 = \frac{1}{2} \times 10 \times (16.67)^2 \times 10^{-6}$$
$$= 0.0014 \text{ Joule.}$$

and $W_2 = \frac{1}{2} \times 50 \times 10^{-6} \times (16.67)^2$

$$= 0.007 \text{ Joule}$$

This gives the energy distribution of the capacitor *i.e.*, C will have **0.0014** Joule while C′will have **0.007** Joule.

Final energy $W_f = W_1 + W_2 =$ **0.0084** Joule. Here we see that the initial energy being 0.05 Joule, the final energy comes to be 0.0084 Joule. Then the energy dissipated through the lead wires is (0.05 − 0.0084) Joule or **0.0416** Joule.

EXAMPLE 1.109 *Obtain the equivalent inductance at terminal "1-2" for the circuit shown in Fig. E1.134.*

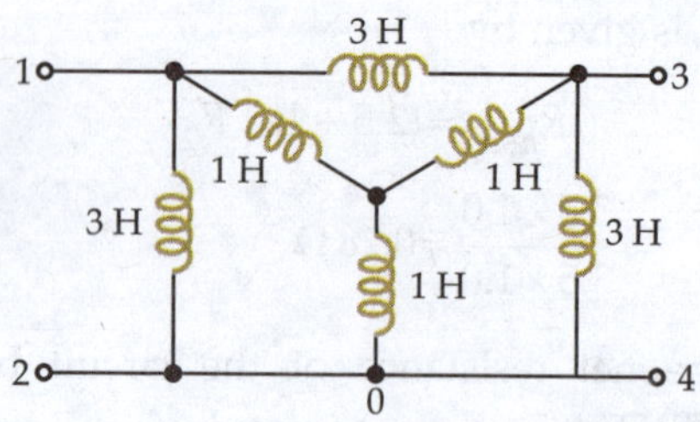

Fig. E1.134

SOLUTION. This problem can be best solved utilising star-delta transformation. Let us first convert the internal star connected inductances to an equivalent delta. This is shown in Fig. E1.135(*a*).

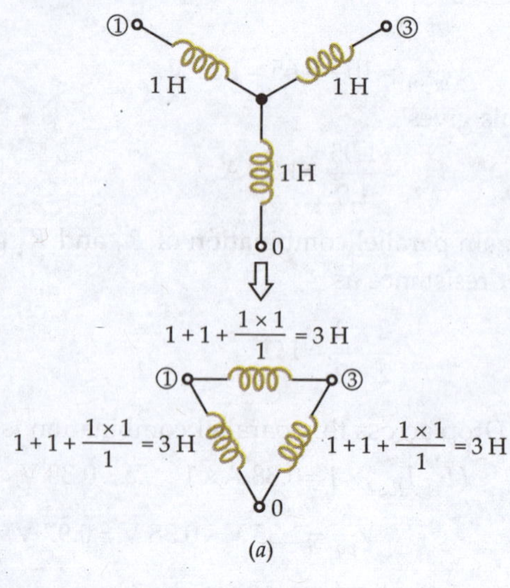

(*a*)

Fig. E1.135

Hence the equivalent circuit configuration of Fig. E1.134 becomes that shown in Fig. E1.135(*b*). Further circuit reduction gives Fig. E1.135(*c*) where each arm inductance is $\frac{3 \times 3}{3+3}$

i.e., 1.5 H

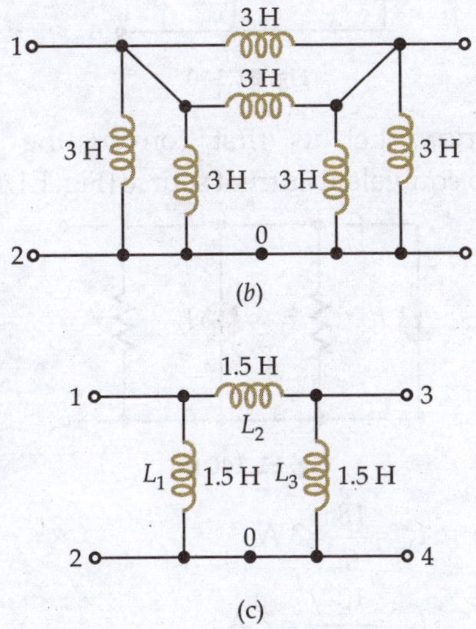

Fig. E1.135

Thus the equivalent inductance across 1-2 is given by

$$L_{1-2} = L_1 \,||\, (L_2 + L_3) = 1.5 \,||\, 3 = \frac{1.5 \times 3}{1.5+3} = \mathbf{1\ H.}$$

Example 1.110 *Three inductances, 1 H, 2 H and L H are in parallel. Find the value of L such that the equivalent inductance is maximum. At this value of L, what is the value of equivalent inductance ?*

Solution. The equivalent inductance of 1 H and 2 H is given by

$$L_{eq} = \frac{1 \times 2}{1+2} = \frac{2}{3}\ \text{H}$$

Again, the net inductance of L_{eq} and L in parallel is given by

$$L'_{eq} = \frac{L_{eq} \cdot L}{L_{eq} + L} = \frac{\frac{2}{3} L}{L + \frac{2}{3}} = \frac{\frac{2}{3}}{1 + \frac{2}{3\,L}}$$

L'_{eq} is to be max. This is possible if $L \to \infty$ and if $L \to \infty$,

$$L'_{eq} = \frac{\frac{2}{3}}{1} = \mathbf{\frac{2}{3}\ H.}$$

Example 1.111 *In Fig. E1.136, a parallel combination of 10 mH and 20 mH is in parallel. A time varying voltage is applied across the inductances and at any time instant and the total current supplied by the time varying source is 25 amps. Obtain the value of instantaneous currents through each of the inductances.*

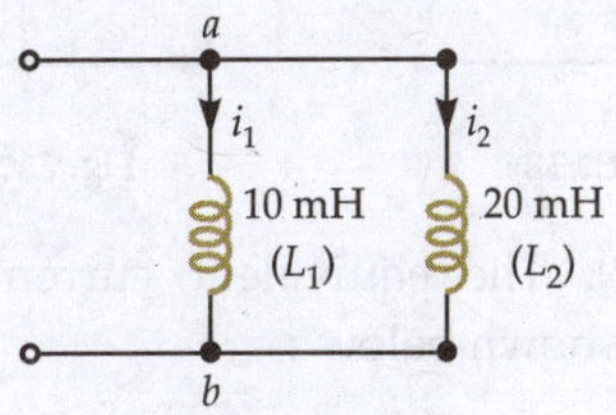

Fig. E1.136

Solution. Let the voltage, across terminal *a-b* be *v*.

$$\therefore \quad v = L_1 \frac{di_1}{dt} \quad \text{and} \quad v = L_2 \frac{di_2}{dt}.$$

This gives, $i_1 = \frac{1}{L_1} \int v\, dt\ ;\ i_2 = \frac{1}{L_2} \int v\, dt$

i.e., $$\frac{i_1}{i_2} = \frac{L_2}{L_1} = \frac{20}{10} = 2 \qquad ...(i)$$

Also, $i_1 + i_2 = 25$

Thus we get two equations,

$$i_1 = 2i_2\ ;\ i_1 + i_2 = 25.$$

These equations give,

$$i_1 = \mathbf{16.67\ A},\ i_2 = \mathbf{8.33\ A.}$$

Example 1.112 *Convert the following current source (Fig. E1.137) to equivalent voltage source.*

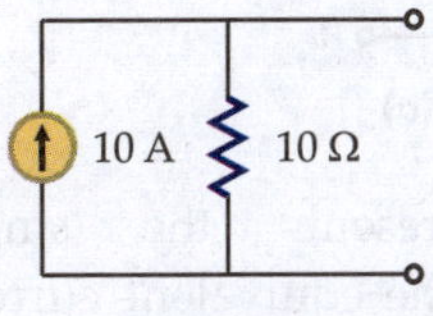

Fig. E1.137

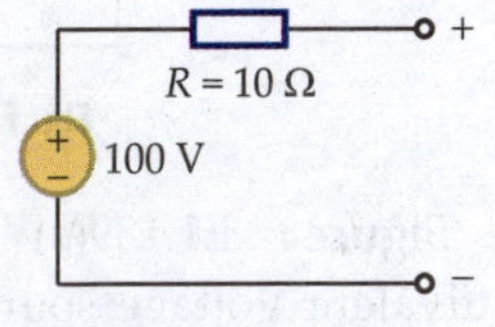

Fig. E1.137 (*a*)

Solution. Equivalent voltage source $V_{eq.}$ is given by,

$$V_{eq} = 10\ \text{A} \times 10\ \Omega = \mathbf{100\ V},\ R \text{ being } 10\ \Omega.$$

Figure E1.137(*a*) represents the equivalent voltage source.

<u>Example 1.113</u> Obtain an equivalent current source of the given voltage source as given in Fig. E1.38.

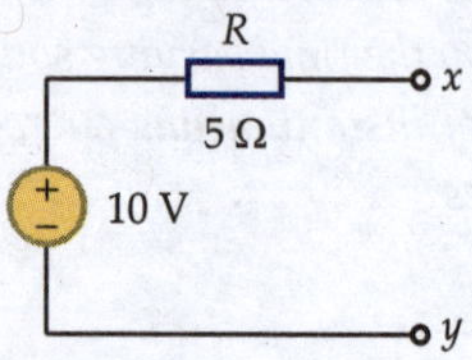

Fig. E1.138

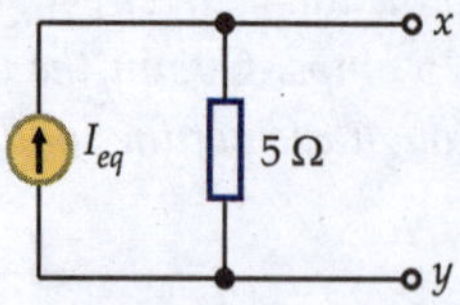

Fig. E1.138 (*a*)

Solution. The equivalent current source is obtained as shown below :

$$I_{eq.} = \frac{V}{R} = \frac{10}{5} = \mathbf{2\ A},\ R \text{ being } 5\,\Omega.$$

The equivalent current source is shown in Fig. E1.138(*a*).

<u>Example 1.114</u> Find equivalent current source for the circuit shown in Fig. E1.139.

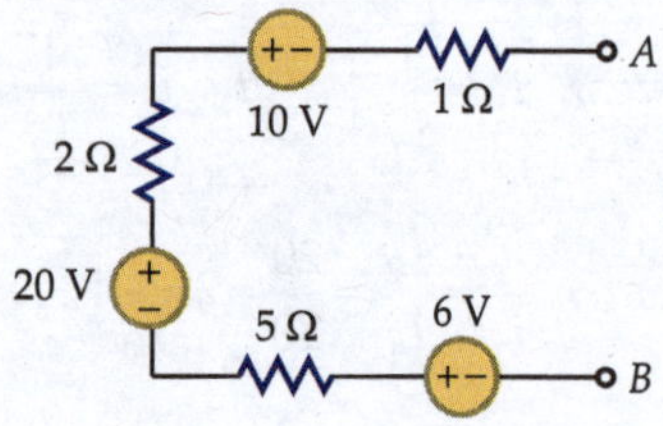

Fig. E1.139

Solution. The equivalent voltage source is obtained as follows :

$$V_{eq.} = 6 + 20 - 10 = 16\ \text{V}$$
$$R_{eq} = 5 + 2 + 1 = 8\,\Omega$$

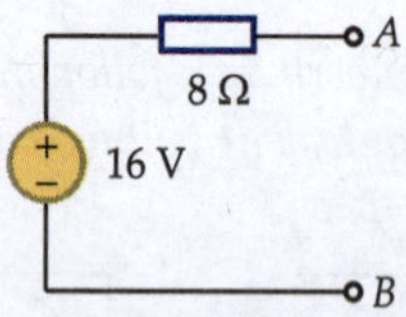

Fig. E1.139 (*a*)

Figure E1.139(*a*) represents the single equivalent voltage source. The equivalent current source can be obtained as

$$I_{eq} = \frac{16}{8} = \mathbf{2\ A};\ R = 8\,\Omega$$

Figure E1.139(*b*) represents the required equivalent current source.

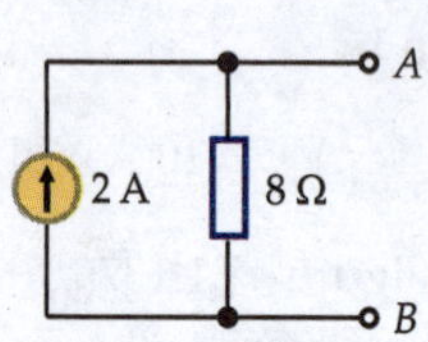

Fig. E1.139 (*b*)

<u>Example 1.115</u> Obtain a single current source for the network shown in Fig. E1.140.

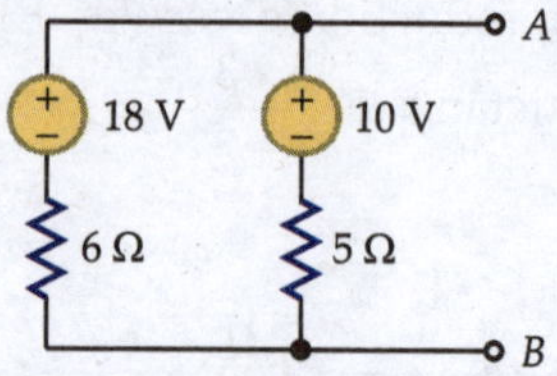

Fig. E1.140

Solution. Let us first convert the voltage sources to equivalent current source (Fig. E1.140(*a*)).

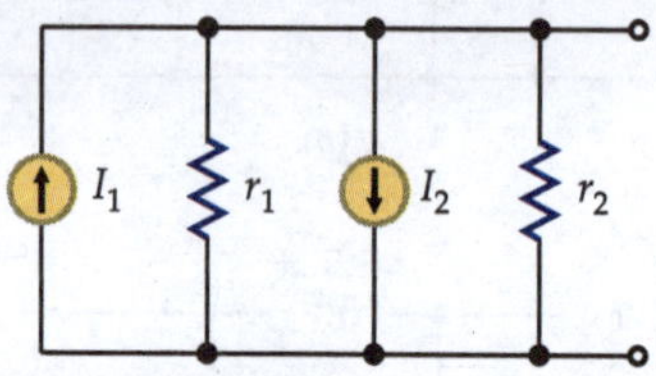

Fig. E1.140 (*a*)

$$\text{Here,}\quad I_1 = \frac{18}{6} = 3\ \text{A}$$
$$I_2 = \frac{10\ \text{V}}{5\,\Omega} = 2\ \text{A};$$

while $r_1 = 6\,\Omega,\ r_2 = 5\,\Omega$

The equivalent current source is obtained as

$$I_{eq} = I_1 - I_2 = \mathbf{1\ A}$$
$$R = \frac{r_1\, r_2}{r_1 + r_2} = \frac{6 \times 5}{6 + 5} = \mathbf{2.73\,\Omega}.$$

Figure E1.140(*b*) represents the equivalent current source.

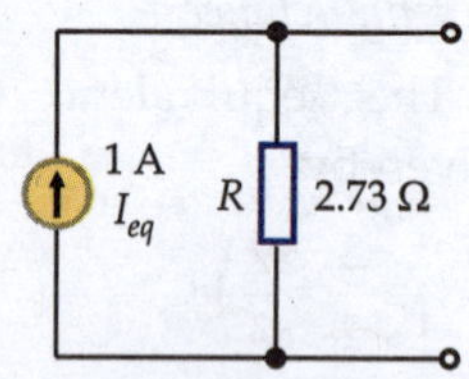

Fig. E1.140 (*b*)

<u>Example 1.116</u> Convert the following circuit (Fig. E1.141) into a single voltage source.

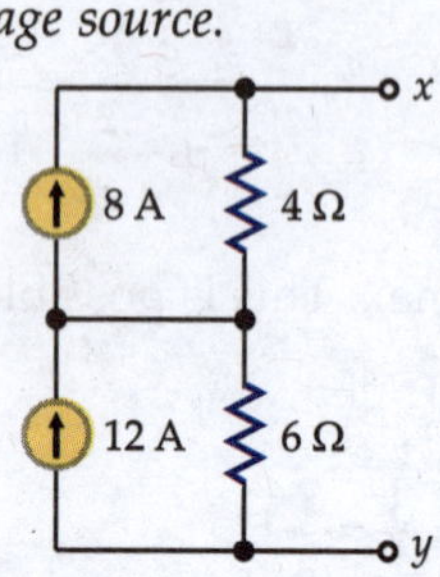

Fig. E1.141

Solution. Let us first convert the multiple current sources to equivalent voltage sources as shown in

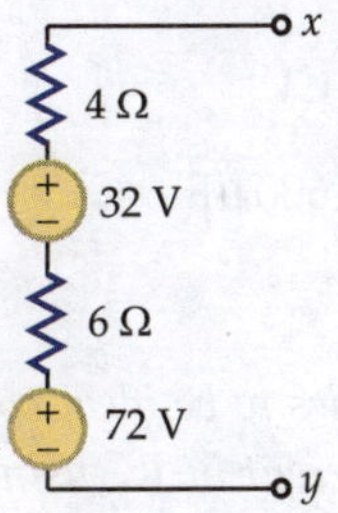

Fig. E1.141 (*a*)

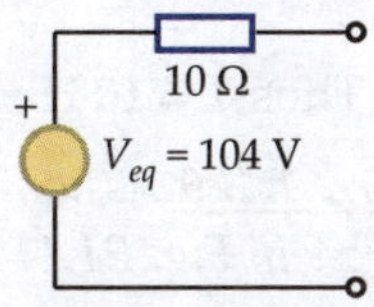

Fig. E1.141 (*b*)

Fig. E1.141(*a*). Next, these voltage sources are transformed into single voltage source (Fig. E1.141(*b*)), where

$$V_{eq} = 32 + 72 = \mathbf{104\ V}$$

and $$R = 4 + 6 = \mathbf{10\ \Omega}.$$

Example 1.117 Find the equivalent capacitance between terminals x-y in Fig. E1.142.

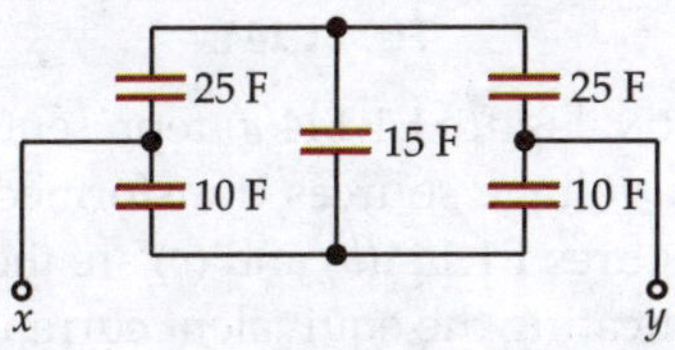

Fig. E1.142

Solution. Figure E1.142 is redrawn as Fig. E1.142(*a*).

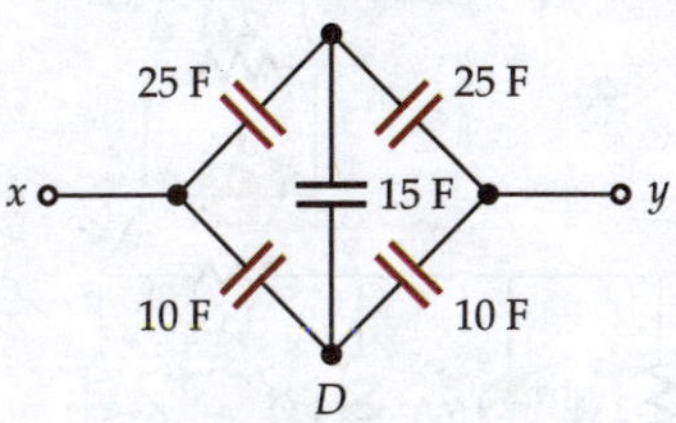

Fig. E1.142 (*a*)

Here star at point *D* of Fig. 1.142(*a*) has been replaced by equivalent delta having delta branch capacitances C_1, C_2, C_3.

Subsequent network reductions are shown in Figs. 1.142(*b*)-(*d*) where in Fig. 1.142(*b*),

$$C_1 = \frac{10 \times 15}{10 + 15 + 10} = 4.28\ \text{F}$$

$$C_2 = \frac{15 \times 10}{15 + 10 + 10} = 4.28\ \text{F}$$

$$C_3 = \frac{10 \times 10}{10 + 10 + 15} = 2.86\ \text{F}.$$

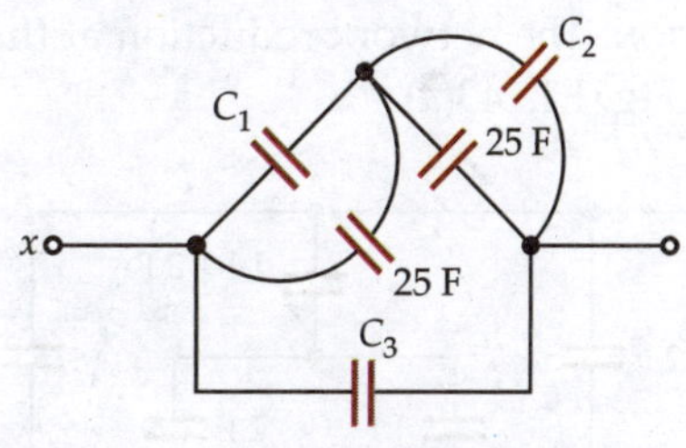

Fig. E1.142 (*b*)

Figure E1.142(*c*) combines C_1 and 25 F and also C_2 and 25 F of Fig. E1.142(*b*) to give equivalent capacitances C_4 and C_5 respectively.

$$C_4 = C_1 + 25 = 29.28\ \text{F}$$

$$C_5 = C_2 + 25 = 29.28\ \text{F}.$$

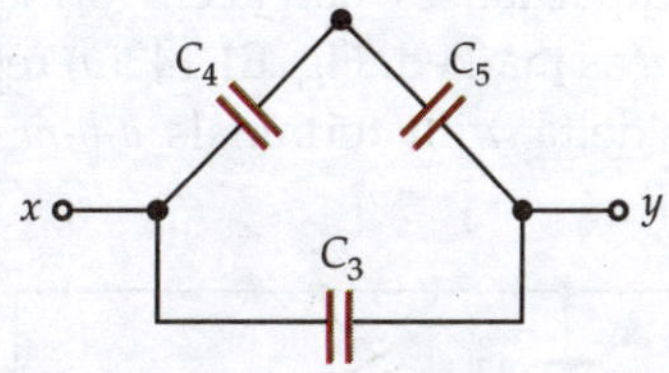

Fig. E1.142 (*c*)

In Fig. 1.142(*d*), C_6 is formed by series combination of C_4 and C_5.

$$\therefore \quad C_6 = \frac{29.14 \times 29.28}{29.14 + 29.28} = 14.64\ \text{F}.$$

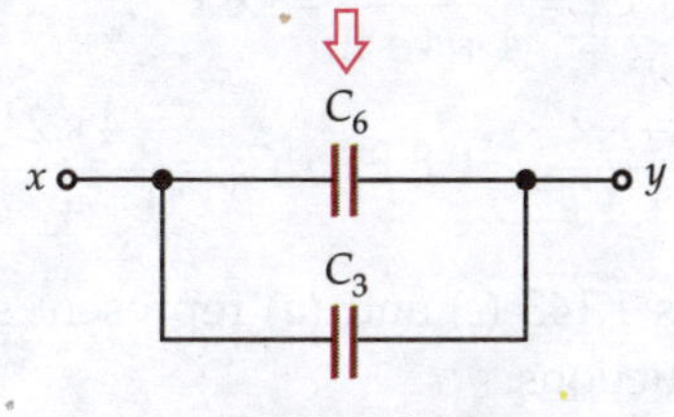

Fig. E1.142 (*d*)

Thus, the equivalent capacitance between *x*-*y* is given by

$$C_{x-y} = C_6 + C_3 = 14.64 + 2.86 = 17.5\ \text{F}$$

$$\therefore \quad \mathbf{C_{x-y} = 17.5\ F.}$$

Example 1.118 What should be the value of C such that equivalent capacitance across x-y is 5 F (Fig. E1.143).

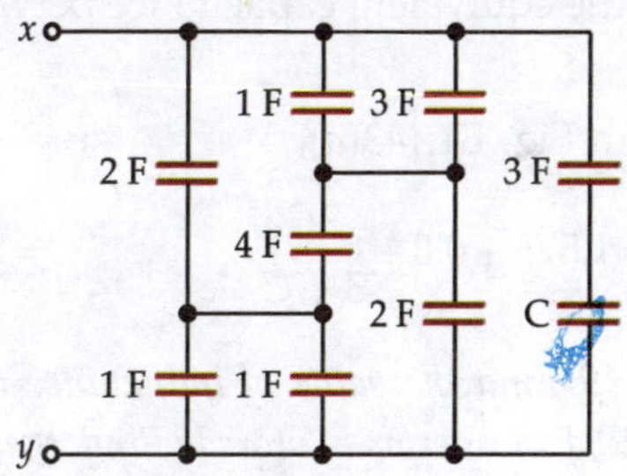

Fig. E1.143

C H A P T E R 1

Solution. The network reduction at first step is shown in Fig. E1.143(*a*).

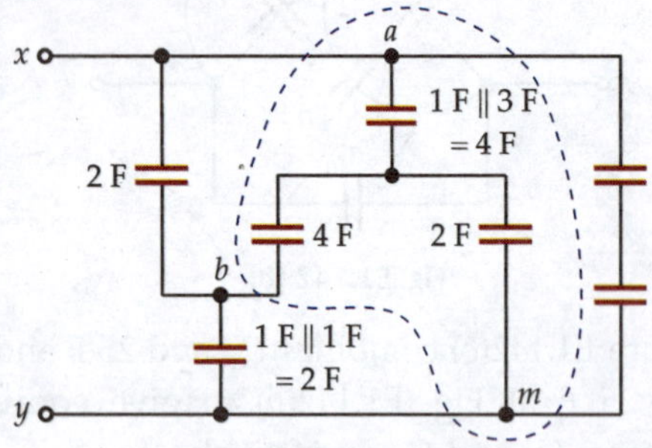

Fig. E1.143 (*a*)

Observation of Fig. E1.143(*a*) reveals a star circuit of capacitances has been formed between points *a-b-m* as marked. Fig. E1.143(*b*) represents an equivalent delta with terminals *a-b-m* within the main circuit.

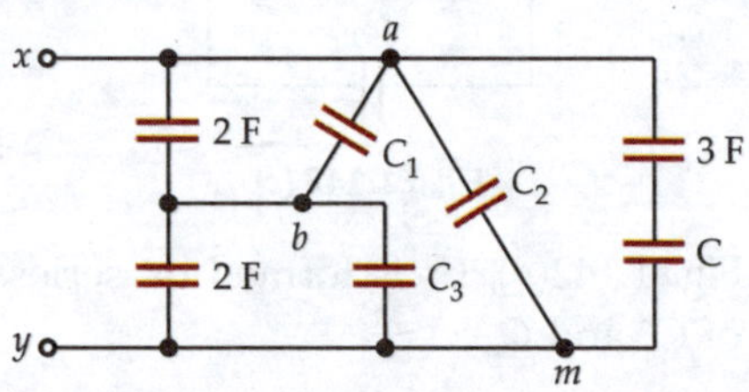

Fig. E1.143 (*b*)

Here, $C_1 = \dfrac{4 \times 4}{4+4+2} = 1.6 \text{ F}$;

$$C_2 = \frac{4 \times 2}{4+4+2} = 0.8 \text{ F}; \quad C_3 = \frac{4 \times 2}{4+4+2} = 0.8 \text{ F}.$$

Figures 1.143 (*c*) and (*d*) represent subsequent circuit reductions.

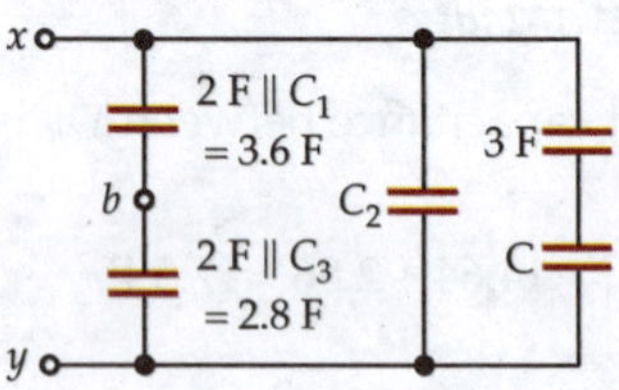

Fig. E1.143 (*c*)

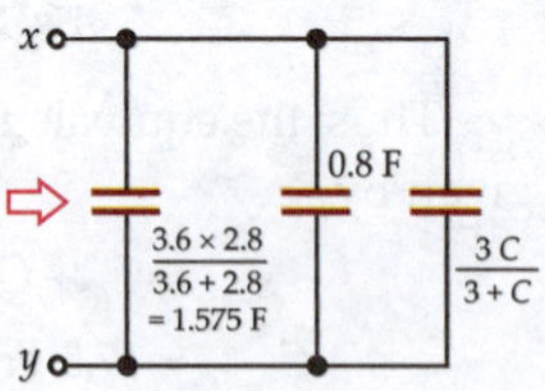

Fig. E1.143 (*d*)

Since the equivalent capacitance between $x - y$ is to be 5 F.

∴ From Fig. E1.143(*d*),

$$5 = 1.575 + 0.8 + \frac{3C}{3+C} \qquad \therefore \quad C = \mathbf{21 \text{ F}}.$$

Example 1.119 *Find the value of inductance that carries 2 A and 20 J of energy is stored. Find the value of a capacitor with 500 V across it, in which 20 J is stored.*

Solution. Inductive energy $(E_L) = \frac{1}{2} Li^2$

$$\therefore \quad L = \frac{2E_L}{i^2} = \frac{40}{4} = 10 \text{ H}.$$

Capacitive energy $(E_C) = \frac{1}{2} CV^2$

$$\therefore \quad C = \frac{2E_C}{V^2} = \frac{40}{500^2} = 1600 \ \mu\text{F}$$

Thus $\mathbf{L = 10 \text{ H}; C = 1600 \ \mu F}$.

Example 1.120 *Assuming the batteries to be ideal voltage sources in Fig. E1.144, find the current in R_L using the concept of source transformations.*

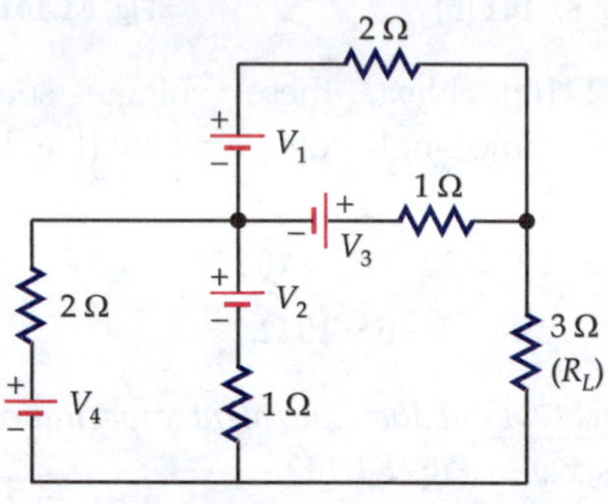

Fig. E1.144

Solution. Figure E1.144(*a*) represents the circuit with given voltage sources transformed to current sources. Figures E1.144(*b*) and (*c*) are the respective circuits indicating the equivalent current sources of Fig. E1.144(*a*) and then its equivalent voltage sources.

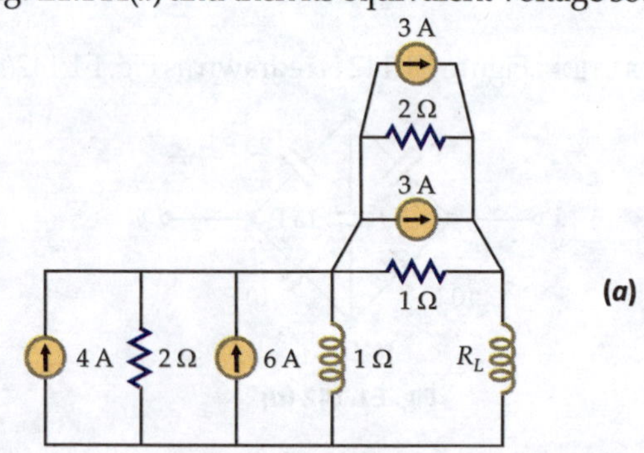

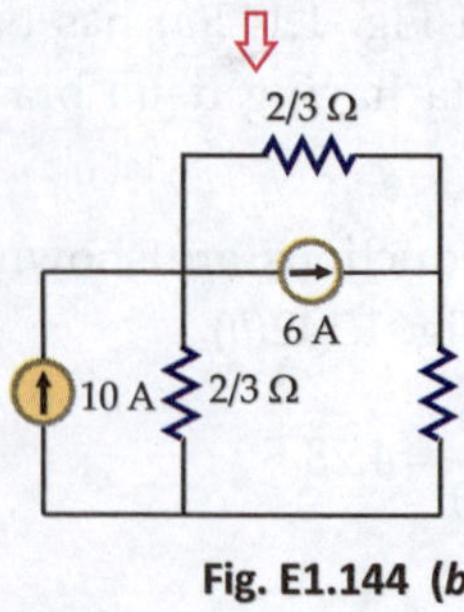

Fig. E1.144 (*b*)

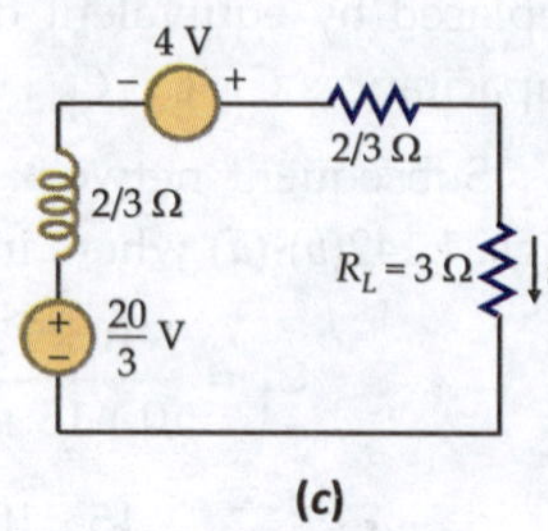

(*c*)

Here, $$i = \frac{\dfrac{20}{3} + 4}{\dfrac{2}{3} + \dfrac{2}{3} + 3} = \frac{(32/3)}{(13/3)} = \mathbf{2.46 \text{ A}}.$$

EXAMPLE 1.121 *Find the drop across the 2 Ω resistor (Fig. E1.145).*

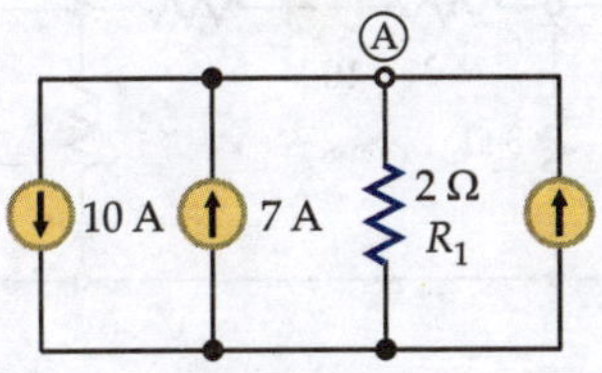

Fig. E1.145

SOLUTION. Applying KCL at *node (A)*,

$$-10+7+5-I_{r_1}=0$$

or, I_{r_1} (current through R_1)

$$=2\text{ A(direction-away from } node\text{ (A))}$$

$\therefore$ Drop across $R_1 = 2\times 2 = \mathbf{4\ V}$.

EXAMPLE 1.122 *In the circuit of Fig. E1.146 find the current through r_L.*

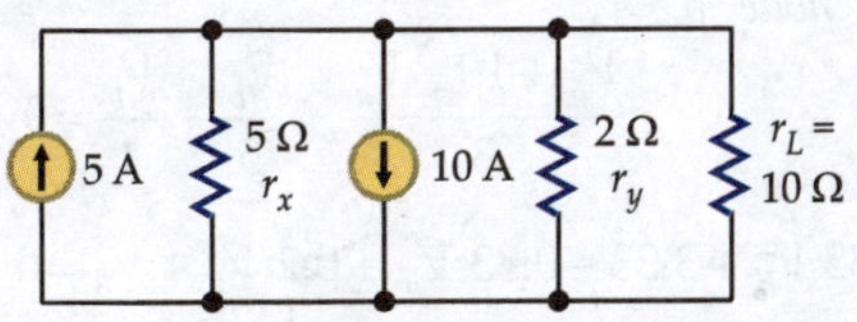

Fig. E1.146

SOLUTION. The circuit of Fig. E1.146 is reduced to that of Fig. E1.147.

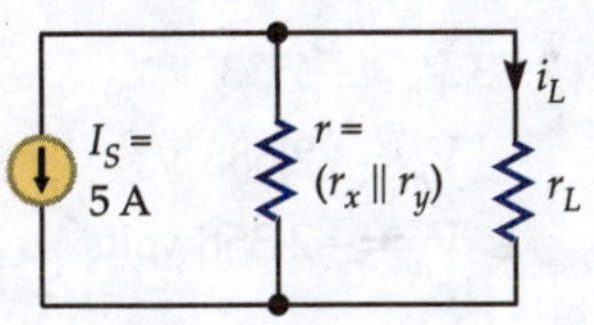

Fig. E1.147

The equivalent current source I_S would be (10 A − 5 A) = 5 A directed downwards; the net resistance of r_x and r_y would be $\frac{5\times 2}{5+2}=\frac{10}{7}\,\Omega$.

By current division method

$$i_L = I_S \times \frac{r}{r+r_L} = 5\,\frac{10/7}{\frac{10}{7}+10}$$

$$=5\times\frac{10/7}{80/7}=5\times\frac{10}{7}\times\frac{7}{80}=\frac{5}{8}\text{ A}$$

i.e. $\qquad i_L = \mathbf{\frac{5}{8}\ A.}$

EXAMPLE 1.123 *Find v in the circuit of Fig. E1.148. Also obtain the numerical value of the dependent source.*

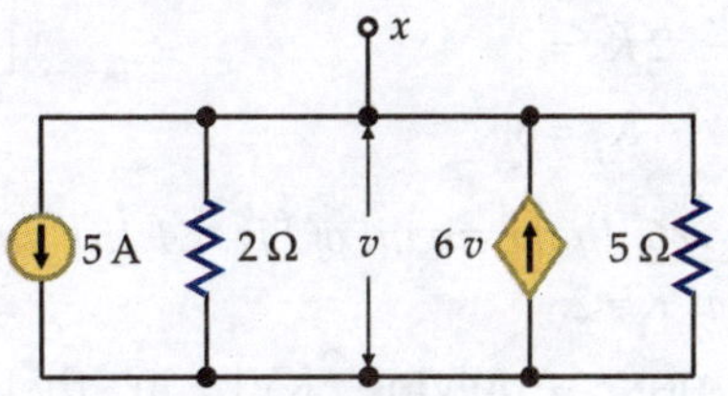

Fig. E1.148

SOLUTION. Applying KCL at *node "x"*,

$$-5+6v-\frac{v}{2}-\frac{v}{5}=0$$

or, $$\frac{53}{10}v=5$$

$\therefore$ $$v=\frac{50}{53}=\mathbf{0.943\ V.}$$

$\therefore$ The numerical value of the dependent source is then $6\times 0.943 = 5.66$ A.

i.e., dependent source is **5.66 A.**

EXAMPLE 1.124 *Find the value of the dependent source in Fig. E1.149.*

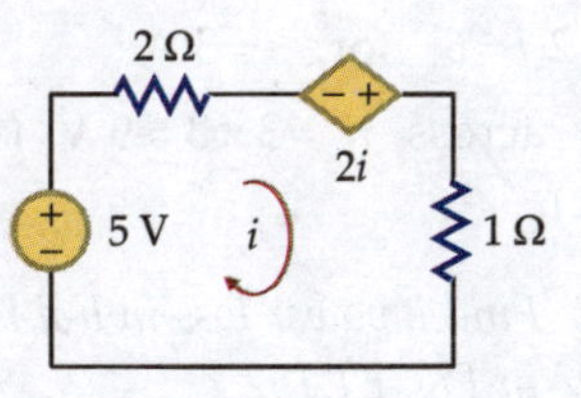

Fig. E1.149

SOLUTION. Applying KVL in the *loop*,

$$-5+2\,i-2\,i+i=0$$

or, $$i=5\text{ A.}$$

$\therefore$ Value of the dependent source = **10 V.**

EXAMPLE 1.125 *Find the value of K_i in Fig. E1.150.*

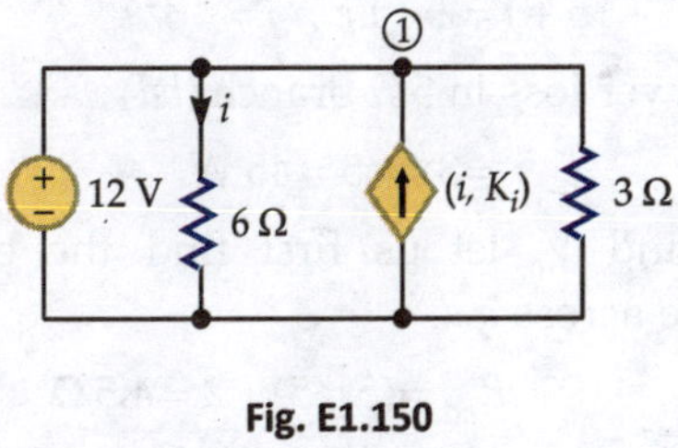

Fig. E1.150

SOLUTION. By inspection, $i=\frac{12}{6}=2$ A and current through 3 Ω resistor is $\frac{12}{3}=4\text{ A}\,(i_{3\Omega})$.

Applying KCL at *node (1)*,

$$i \cdot K_i = i + i_{3\Omega}$$

or, $2K_i = 2 + 4$ $[\because i = 2 \text{ A}]$

$\therefore$ $\mathbf{K_i = 3.}$

EXAMPLE 1.126 *In the circuit of Fig. E1.151 find the drop across r_L if K = 2.*

SOLUTION. Applying KVL in the loop of Fig. E1.151,

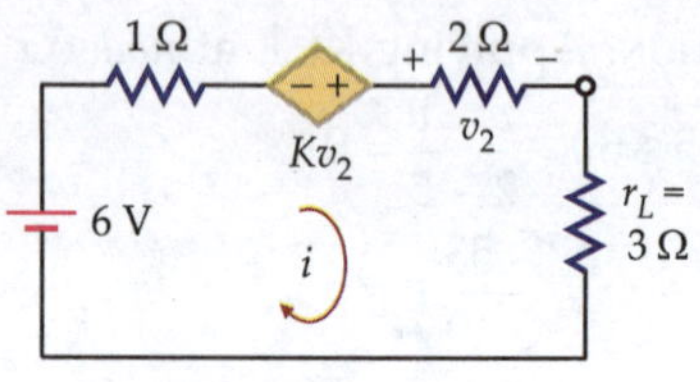

Fig. E1.151

$$-6 + i \times 1 - Kv_2 + v_2 + ir_L = 0$$

or, $-6 + i - 2v_2 + v_2 + 3i = 0.$

or, $-v_2 + 4i = 6$ ...(*i*)

But $v_2 = i \times 2 = 2i$ ...(*ii*)

Utilising (*ii*) in (*i*),

$$2i = 6 \quad \text{or,} \quad i = 3 \text{ A}$$

$\therefore$ Drop across $r_L = 3 \times 3 = \mathbf{9\ V}$ (with positive polarity at *x*).

EXAMPLE 1.127 *Find i, power loss in b-d branch. What is the value of V in Fig. E1.152 ?*

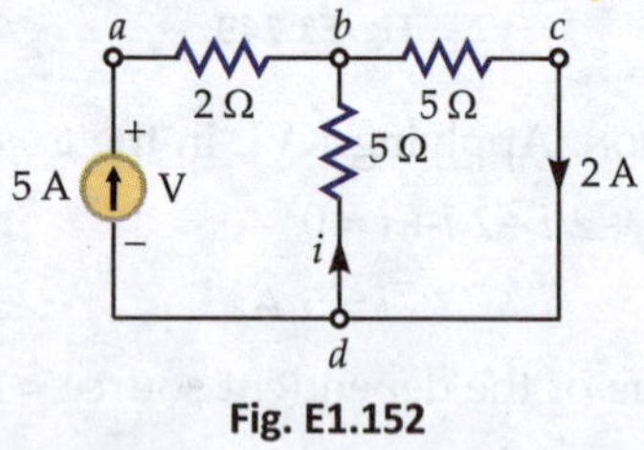

Fig. E1.152

SOLUTION. Applying KCL at *node b*,

$$5 + i = 2 \quad i.e., \quad i = -3 \text{ A}$$

$\therefore$ Power loss in 5 Ω branch (*bd*)

$$= 3^2 \times 5 = 45 \text{ W}$$

To find *V*, let us first find the equivalent resistance across *a-d*.

$$R_{ad} = (5 \,||\, 5) + 2 = 4.5\,\Omega$$

$\therefore$ $V_{ad} (\equiv V) = 5 \text{ A} \times 4.5\,\Omega = 22.5 \text{ V}.$

Then current in branch *b-d* = **3 A** from *b* to *d*, power loss **45 W** and voltage across the current source = **22.5 V.**

EXAMPLE 1.128 *Find i and V_x in Fig. E1.153.*

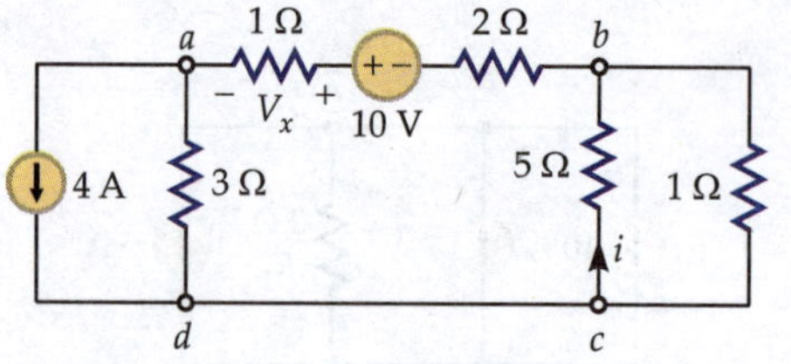

Fig. E1.153

SOLUTION. Let the potential at *node a* be V_a and at *b* be V_b.

Applying nodal analysis at *node a*,

$$4 + \frac{V_a}{3} + \frac{V_a - 10 - V_b}{3} = 0$$

or, $4 + 0.33\,V_a + 0.33\,V_a - 3.33 - 0.33\,V_b = 0$

or, $0.66\,V_a - 0.33\,V_b = -0.67$ ...(1)

At *node b*,

$$\frac{V_b + 10 - V_a}{3} + \frac{V_b}{5} + \frac{V_b}{1} = 0$$

or, $0.33\,V_b + 3.33 - 0.33\,V_a + 0.2\,V_b + V_b = 0$

or, $1.53\,V_b - 0.33\,V_a = -3.33$

or, $3.06\,V_b - 0.66\,V_a = -6.66$ ...(2)

From (1) and (2),

$$2.73\,V_b = -7.33$$

$\therefore$ $V_b = -2.685$ V;

$V_a = -2.358$ volts

Again, $i = -\left(\frac{V_b}{5}\right)$

[$\because$ *i* shown in Fig. E1.153 is against the direction of the assumed respective branch current]

i.e., $i = -\frac{-2.685}{5} = \mathbf{0.537\ A.}$ **(upwards)**

Current in branch *a-b* is $\frac{V_a - 10 - V_b}{3}$ A

i.e., $\frac{-2.358 - 10 + 2.685}{3}$ A

i.e., -3.22 A (actual direction will be then *b* to *a*)

$\therefore$ $V_x = 3.22 \times 1 = \mathbf{3.22\ V.}$

EXAMPLE 1.129 *Find V_0 in Fig. E1.154.*

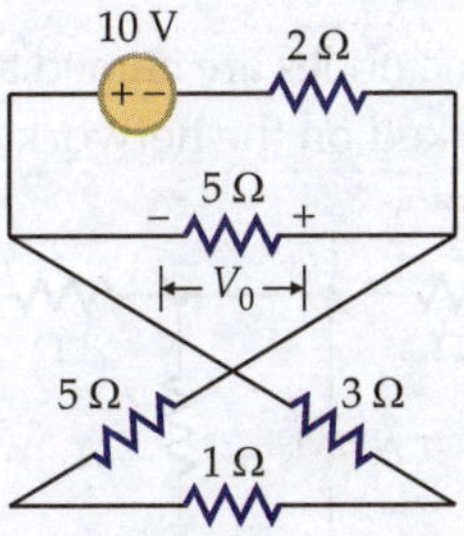

Fig. E1.154

SOLUTION. The network of Fig. E1.154 is reduced as shown in Fig. E1.154(*a*).

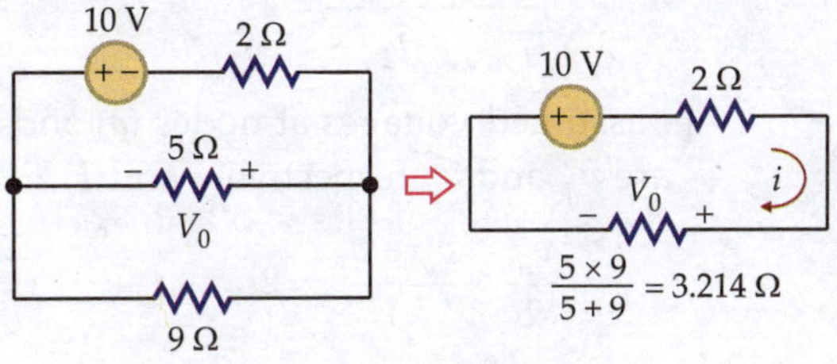

Fig. E1.154(*a*)

Here, applying KVL we get,

$$10 + 2\,i + V_0 = 0$$

or, $$2\,i = (-V_0 - 10) \qquad ...(1)$$

But $$V_0 = 3.214\,i$$

$\therefore$ $$i = \frac{V_0}{3.214}\ \text{A.}$$

Thus from (1),

$$2\frac{V_0}{3.214} = -V_0 - 10$$

or, $$0.622\,V_0 = -V_0 - 10$$

or, $$V_0 = \mathbf{-6.165\ V.}$$

i.e., the actual polarity of V_0 would be just the reverse shown in Fig. E1.154(*a*).

EXAMPLE 1.130 *Find V_0 in Fig. E1.155.*

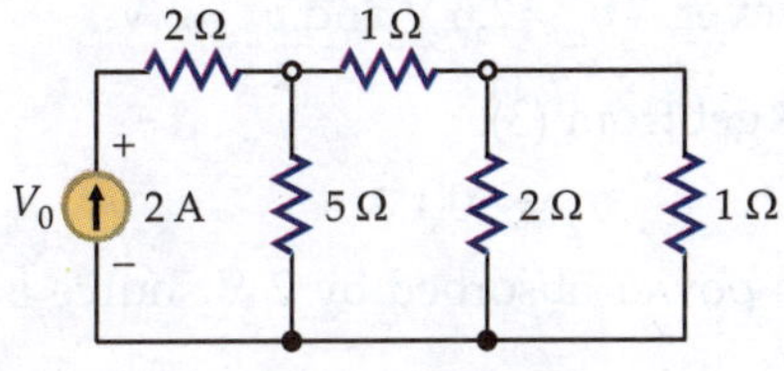

Fig. E1.155

SOLUTION. The equivalent resistance across 2 A source is $[\{1 \| 2+1\} \| 5] + 2\ \Omega$ *i.e.*, $\frac{13}{4}\ \Omega$. Thus the equivalent conductance is $\frac{4}{13}\ \Omega$.

However, $I = V_0 \times$ equivalent conductance

$\therefore$ $$V_0 = \frac{I}{\text{equivalent conductance}}$$

$$= \frac{2}{\frac{4}{13}} = 6.5\ \text{V.}$$

$\therefore$ Voltage across the current source is **6.5 V.**

EXAMPLE 1.131 *Find current through the 5 Ω resistor in Fig. E1.156.*

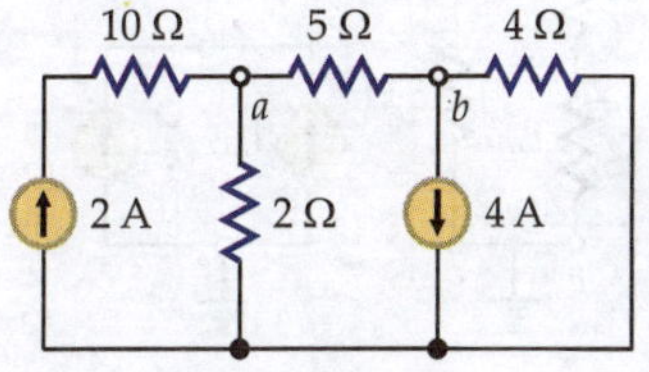

Fig. E1.156

SOLUTION. Let v_a and v_b the nodal voltages at nodes *a* and *b* respectively. Following nodal analysis at *node a*,

$$\frac{v_a}{2} + \frac{v_a - v_b}{5} = 2$$

or, $$0.5\,v_a + 0.2\,v_a - 0.2\,v_b = 2$$

or, $$0.7\,v_a - 0.2\,v_b = 2 \qquad ...(1)$$

At *node b*, nodal analysis gives

$$\frac{v_b - v_a}{5} + \frac{v_b}{4} + 4 = 0$$

or, $$0.45\,v_b - 0.2\,v_a + 4 = 0$$

or, $$-0.2\,v_a + 0.45\,v_b = -4 \qquad ...(2)$$

From (1),

$$v_b = 3.5\,v_a - 10 \qquad ...(3)$$

Substitution of (3) in (2),

$$-0.2\,v_a + 0.45(3.5\,v_a - 10) = -4$$

or, $$v_a = 0.4\ \text{V}$$

and $$v_b = -8.7\ \text{V}$$

Thus current through the 5 Ω resistor is

$$\frac{v_a - v_b}{5} = \frac{0.4 - (-8.7)}{5} = \mathbf{1.78\ A.}$$

CHAPTER 1

EXAMPLE 1.132 *Find v_0 in the network of Fig. E1.157. Also find the p.d. between node x and earth*.*

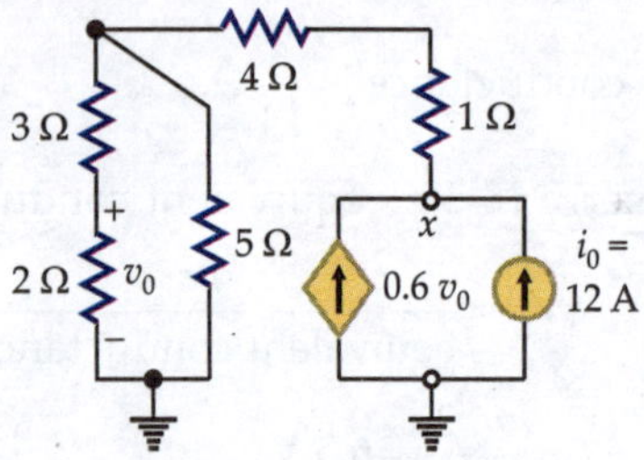

Fig. E1.157

SOLUTION. Let us designate the currents in the given network as shown in Fig. E1.157(*a*).

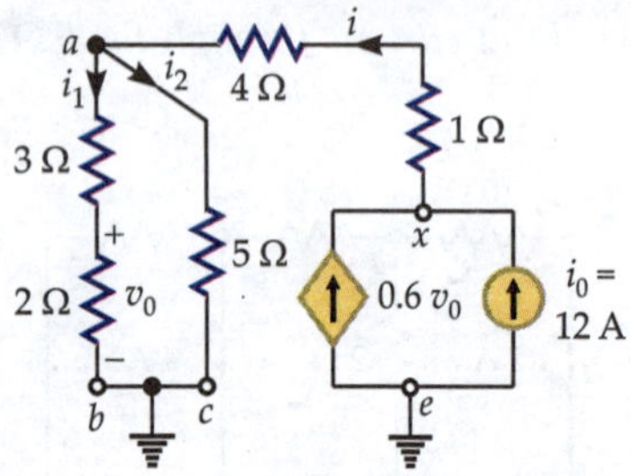

Fig. E1.157(*a*)

Here, $\quad i = 0.6\, v_0 + 12$

also, $\quad i = i_1 + i_2$

Since branches *ab* and *ac* have identical resistances hence

$$i_1 = i_2 \text{ and } i = 12 + 0.6\, v_0 = 2\, i_1 = 2\, i_2$$

Now, $\quad v_0 = (i_1 \times 2)$ V.

Since $\quad i = 2\, i_1$, we write

$$i_1 = \frac{i}{2} = \frac{1}{2}(12 + 0.6\, v_0)$$

and $\quad v_0 = i_1 \times 2 = 12 + 0.6\, v_0$

$\therefore \quad 0.4\, v_0 = 12$ giving $v_0 = \dfrac{12}{0.4} = 30$ V

In order to find the p.d. between *node x* and earth, let us find the equivalent resistance across *x-e node* in Fig. E1.157(*a*).

$$R_{xe} = (5 \,||\, 5) + 4 + 1 = 7.5\,\Omega$$

$\therefore v_{x-e}$ (p.d. across x and e) drop across 7.5 Ω resistance due to ($0.6\, v_0$) current source + drop across 7.5 Ω resistance due to 12 A source

$$= 0.6\, v_0 \times 7.5 + 12 \times 7.5$$

$$= 18 \times 7.5 + 12 \times 7.5 = 225 \text{ V}.$$

i.e., p.d. across *node x* and earth **= 225 V.**

EXAMPLE 1.133 *Find the power delivered by each of the energy source in Fig. E1.158.*

SOLUTION. The nodes are named and the arbitrary currents are marked on the network of Fig. E1.158.

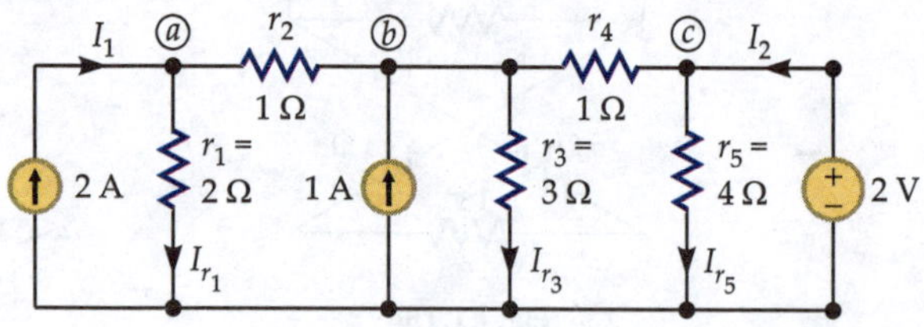

Fig. E1.158

At *node* (*a*), using the nodal analysis technique,

$$\frac{v_a}{r_1} + \frac{v_a - v_b}{r_2} = 2$$

[$\because$ assumed voltages at nodes (*a*) and (*b*) are v_a and v_b respectively and $I_1 = 2$ A]

or, $$\frac{v_a}{2} + \frac{v_a - v_b}{1} = 2$$

or, $$1.5\, v_a - v_b = 2 \qquad ...(1)$$

At *node* (*b*), the nodal analysis yields,

$$\frac{v_b - v_a}{r_2} + \frac{v_b}{r_3} + \frac{v_b - v_c}{r_4} = 1$$

[$\because$ mode voltage at (2) is v_c]

or $$\frac{v_b - v_a}{1} + \frac{v_b}{3} + \frac{v_b - 2}{1} = 1$$

or, $$-v_a + 2.33\, v_b = 3 \qquad ...(2)$$

Solving for (1) and (2),

$$v_b = 2.6 \text{ V and } v_a = 3.07 \text{ V};$$

$\therefore$Power delivered by 2 A source is (2 × 3.07) or, **6.14** watt and power delivered by 1 A source is (1 × 2.6) or, **2.6** W (*i.e.*, total of 8.74 W).

On the other hand, at *node* (*c*), using nodal analysis,

$$\frac{v_c}{r_5} + \frac{v_c - v_b}{1} = I_2 \qquad ...(3)$$

However, $\quad v_b = 2.6$ V and $v_c = 2$ V.

$\therefore$We get from (3),

$$I_2 = -0.1 \text{ A}$$

Thus power absorbed by 2 V source is (0.1 × 2) or, **0.2 W.**

* 'p.d.' stands for 'potential difference' and 'earth' in electrical engineering is synonymous to ground.

Check

Total power loss in the circuit is given by

$$I_{r_1}^2 \times r_1 + \left(\frac{v_a - v_b}{r_2}\right)^2 \times r_2 + I_{r_3}^2 \times r_3 + \left(\frac{v_b - v_c}{r_4}\right)^2 r_4 + I_{r_5}^2 \times r_5$$

$$= 1.535^2 \times 2 + (0.47)^2 \times 1 + (0.87)^2 \times 3 + (0.6)^2 \times 1 + (0.5)^2 \times 4 = 8.56 \text{ W}$$

$\therefore$ Total power absorbed $= 8.56 + 0.2 = 8.76$ W

EXAMPLE 1.134 *Obtain the currents through each of the sources and their respective power dissipation in the network of Fig. E1.159.*

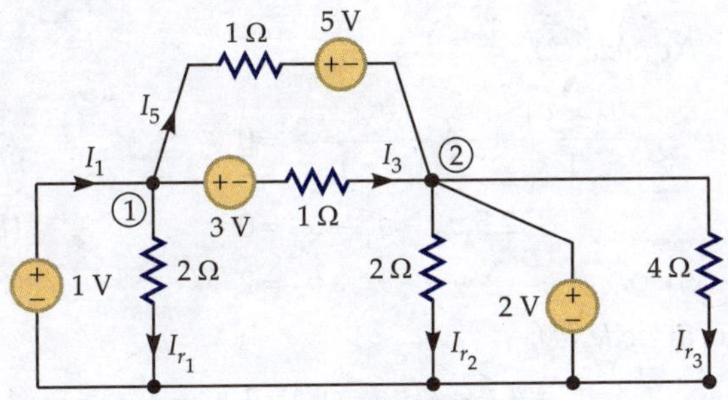

Fig. E1.159

SOLUTION. At *node "1"*, from KCL,

$$I_1 = I_{r_1} + I_5 + I_3 \qquad ...(1)$$

However,

$$I_{r_1} = \frac{1 \text{ V}}{2\ \Omega} = 0.5 \text{ A}$$

$$I_3 = \frac{\text{Voltage at } node\,(1) - 3 - \text{voltage at } node\,(2)}{1\Omega}$$

$$= \frac{1-3-2}{1} = \mathbf{-4\ A}$$

$$I_5 = \frac{\text{Voltage at } node\,(1) - 5 - \text{voltage at } node\,(2)}{1\Omega}$$

$$= \frac{1-5-2}{1} = \mathbf{-6\ A}$$

$\therefore$ From equation (*i*), $I_1 = 0.5 - 4 - 6 = \mathbf{-9.5\ A.}$

As I_1 and I_5 have come to be in opposite directions of the assumed currents, hence, in the circuit actual current I_1 enters the source 1 V and actual current I_5 comes out of the source 5 V.

$\therefore$ Power absorbed by 1 V source $= 9.5 \times 1 = 9.5$ W

Power delivered by 5 V source $= 6 \times 5 = 30$ W

Again applying KCL at *node (2)*,

$$I_2 + I_3 + I_5 = I_{r_2} + I_{r_3}$$

or,
$$I_2 = I_{r_2} + I_{r_3} - I_3 - I_5$$

$$= \frac{2}{2} + \frac{2}{4} - (-4) - (-6)$$

$$= 1 + 0.5 + 4 + 6 = \mathbf{11.5\ A}$$

i.e., current coming that from 2 V source is 10.5 A.

$\therefore$ Power delivered by 2 V source

$$= 11.5 \times 2 = 23 \text{ W}.$$

Also, I_3 has been obtained to be flowing in reverse direction than that assumed in Fig. E1.159.

$\therefore$ 3 V source is delivering power which is $3 \times 4 = 12$ W.

Thus,

Power absorbed by 1 V source = **9.5 W**

Power delivered by 2 V source = **21 W**

Power delivered by 3 V source = **12 W**

Power delivered by 5 V source = **30 W.**

EXAMPLE 1.135 *Develop the nodal equation of the circuit shown in Fig. E1.160 in matrix form.*

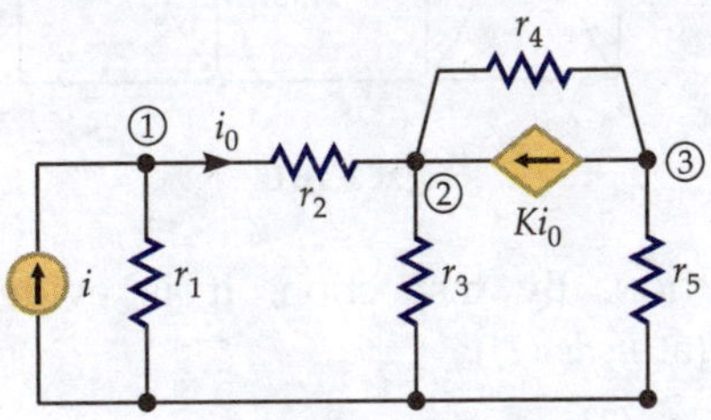

Fig. E1.160

SOLUTION. At *node (1)*, the voltage being v_1

$$i = \frac{v_1}{r_1} + \frac{v_1 - v_2}{r_2}$$

[voltage at *node (2)* is assumed v_2]

or,
$$v_1\left(\frac{1}{r_1} + \frac{1}{r_2}\right) - v_2 \cdot \frac{1}{r_2} = i \qquad ...(A)$$

At *node (2)*,

$$Ki_0 = \frac{v_2}{r_3} + \frac{v_2 - v_3}{r_4} + \frac{v_2 - v_1}{r_2}$$

[Voltage at *node (3)* being v_3]

or,
$$-\frac{v_1}{r_2} + v_2\left(\frac{1}{r_3} + \frac{1}{r_4} + \frac{1}{r_2}\right) - v_3\,\frac{1}{r_4} = Ki_0 \qquad ...(B)$$

CHAPTER 1

At *node (3)*,

$$Ki_0 + \frac{v_3}{r_5} + \frac{v_3 - v_2}{r_4} = 0$$

or, $$v_3\left(\frac{1}{r_4} + \frac{1}{r_5}\right) - v_2 \cdot \frac{1}{r_4} + Ki_0 = 0$$

or, $$-v_2 \cdot \frac{1}{r_4} + v_3\left(\frac{1}{r_4} + \frac{1}{r_5}\right) = -Ki_0 \qquad ...(C)$$

These equations in matrix form are shown below :

$$\begin{bmatrix} (1/r_1 + 1/r_2) & \left(-\frac{1}{r_2}\right) & 0 \\ -\frac{1}{r_2} & \left(\frac{1}{r_3} + \frac{1}{r_4} + \frac{1}{r_2}\right) & \left(-\frac{1}{r_4}\right) \\ 0 & -\frac{1}{r_4} & \left(\frac{1}{r_4} + \frac{1}{r_5}\right) \end{bmatrix} \begin{bmatrix} v_1 \\ v_2 \\ v_3 \end{bmatrix} = \begin{bmatrix} i \\ K i_0 \\ -K i_0 \end{bmatrix}$$

EXAMPLE 1.136 *In the network of Fig. E1.161, find v_1, v_2 and v_3 by nodal analysis.*

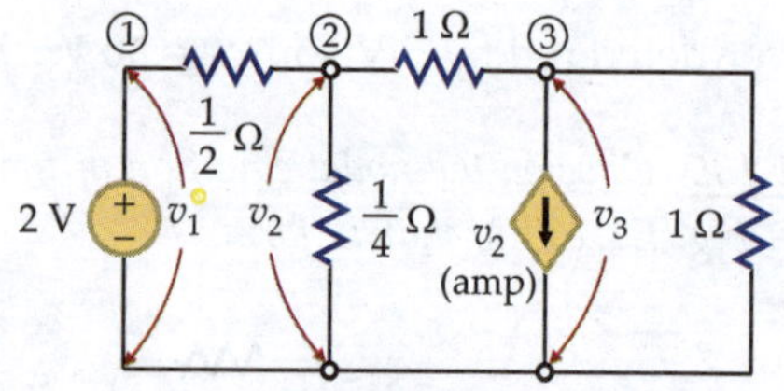

Fig. E1.161

SOLUTION. By inspection, it is evident that $v_1 = 2$ V (at *node (1)*).

At *node (2)*,

$$\frac{v_2 - v_1}{1/2} + \frac{v_2}{1/4} + \frac{v_2 - v_3}{1} = 0$$

or, $$2v_2 + 4v_2 + v_2 - 2v_1 - v_3 = 0$$

or, $$7v_2 - 2v_1 - v_3 = 0$$

or, $$7v_2 - v_3 = 4 \qquad ...(A)$$

$[\because v_1 = 2 \text{ V}]$

At *node (3)*,

$$\frac{v_3 - v_2}{1} + v_2 + \frac{v_3}{1} = 0$$

or, $$2v_3 = 0 \quad \therefore v_3 = 0 \qquad ...(B)$$

This gives $v_2 = \frac{4}{7}$ V [from [*A*)]

Thus **$v_1 = 2$ V; $v_2 = \frac{4}{7}$ V; $v_3 = 0$ V.**

EXAMPLE 1.137 *In the network of Fig. E1.162 find the nodal voltages by node voltage analysis method.*

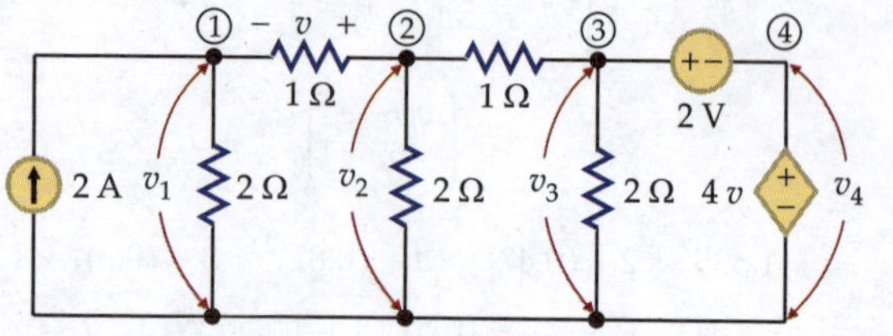

Fig. E1.162

SOLUTION. At *node (1)*,

$$2 = \frac{v_1}{2} + \frac{v_1 - v_2}{1}$$

or, $$1.5\,v_1 - v_2 = 2 \qquad ...(A)$$

At *node (2)*,

$$\frac{v_2 - v_1}{1} + \frac{v_2}{2} + \frac{v_2 - v_3}{1} = 0$$

or, $$2.5\,v_2 - v_1 - v_3 = 0 \qquad ...(B)$$

Also, $$v_3 - v_4 = 2 \qquad ...(C)$$

and at *node (4)*,

$$v_4 = 4\,v = 4\,(v_2 - v_1) = 4\,v_2 - 4\,v_1 \qquad ...(D)$$

Thus, substituting the value of v_4 from (*D*) in (*C*),

$$v_3 - (4\,v_2 - 4\,v_1) = 2$$

or, $$4\,v_1 - 4\,v_2 + v_3 = 2 \qquad ...(E)$$

We thus finally arrived at the three equations

$$1.5\,v_1 - v_2 = 2 \qquad ...(a)$$
$$-v_1 + 2.5\,v_2 - v_3 = 0 \qquad ...(b)$$
$$4\,v_1 - 4\,v_2 + v_3 = 2 \qquad ...(c)$$

Solving for (*b*) and (*c*),

$$3v_1 - 1.5\,v_2 = 2 \qquad ...(F)$$

Multiplying (*a*) by 2, we get

$$3v_1 - 2v_2 = 4 \qquad ...(G)$$

Now, solving for (*F*) and (*G*),

$$0.5\,v_2 = -2$$

$$\therefore \quad v_2 = -4 \text{ V}$$

$$\therefore \quad v_1 = -1.33 \text{ V}$$

$$v_3 = -8.68 \text{ V}$$

$$v_4 = v_3 - 2 = -10.68 \text{ V} = 4\,v$$

$$\therefore \quad v = -\frac{10.68}{4} = \mathbf{-2.67\ V.}$$

EXAMPLE 1.138 *Form the nodal equations for the network shown in Fig. E1.163.*

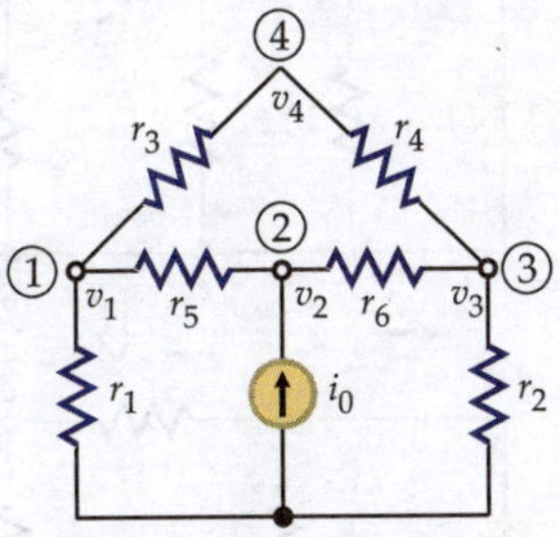

Fig. E1.163

SOLUTION. Let the nodes are named alongwith their voltages on the figure itself.

At *node-1*,

$$\frac{v_1}{r_1}+\frac{v_1-v_2}{r_5}+\frac{v_1-v_4}{r_3}=0$$

$$\text{or, } v_1\left(\frac{1}{r_1}+\frac{1}{r_3}+\frac{1}{r_5}\right)-\frac{v_2}{r_5}-\frac{v_4}{r_3}=0 \qquad ...(1)$$

$$\text{At } \textit{node-2},\quad i_0=\frac{v_2-v_1}{r_5}+\frac{v_2-v_3}{r_6}$$

$$\text{or,}\quad -v_1/r_5+v_2\left(\frac{1}{r_5}+\frac{1}{r_6}\right)-\frac{v_3}{r_6}=i_0 \qquad ...(2)$$

At *node-3*,

$$\frac{v_3-v_2}{r_6}+\frac{v_3}{r_2}+\frac{v_3-v_4}{r_4}=0$$

$$\text{or,}\quad -\frac{v_2}{r_6}+v_3\left(\frac{1}{r_2}+\frac{1}{r_4}+\frac{1}{r_6}\right)-\frac{v_4}{v_4}=0 \qquad ...(3)$$

$$\text{At } \textit{node-4},\quad \frac{v_4-v_1}{r_3}+\frac{v_4-v_3}{r_4}=0$$

$$\text{or,}\quad -\frac{v_1}{r_3}-\frac{v_3}{r_4}+v_4\left(\frac{1}{r_3}+\frac{1}{r_4}\right)=0 \qquad ...(4)$$

The nodal equations are thus (1) to (4) and in matrix form,

$$\begin{bmatrix} v_1 \\ v_2 \\ v_3 \\ v_4 \end{bmatrix}\begin{bmatrix} \left(\frac{1}{r_1}+\frac{1}{r_3}+\frac{1}{r_5}\right) & -\frac{1}{r_5} & 0 & -\frac{1}{r_3} \\ -\frac{1}{r_5} & \left(\frac{1}{r_5}+\frac{1}{r_6}\right) & -\frac{1}{r_6} & 0 \\ 0 & -\frac{1}{r_6} & \left(\frac{1}{r_2}+\frac{1}{r_4}+\frac{1}{r_6}\right) & -\frac{1}{r_4} \\ -\frac{1}{r_3} & 0 & -\frac{1}{r_4} & \left(\frac{1}{r_3}+\frac{1}{r_4}\right) \end{bmatrix}$$

$$=\begin{bmatrix} 0 \\ i_0 \\ 0 \\ 0 \end{bmatrix}.$$

EXAMPLE 1.139 *Find I in Fig. E1.164.*

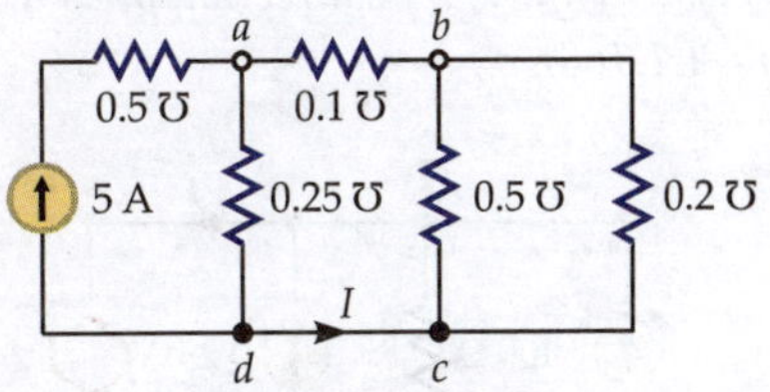

Fig. E1.164

SOLUTION. The circuit constants are given in terms of mho *i.e.*, conductances.

∴ Equivalent conductance across *b-c* is 0.5 + 0.2 = 0.7 mho.

Then equivalent conductance across *a-d* is obtained in addition to 0.25 mho by adding the conductance 0.1 mho with 0.7 mho parallelly. Fig. E1.164(*a*) represents the equivalent circuit. Finally, this equivalent conductance is combined with the parallel conductance as shown in Fig. E1.164(*b*).

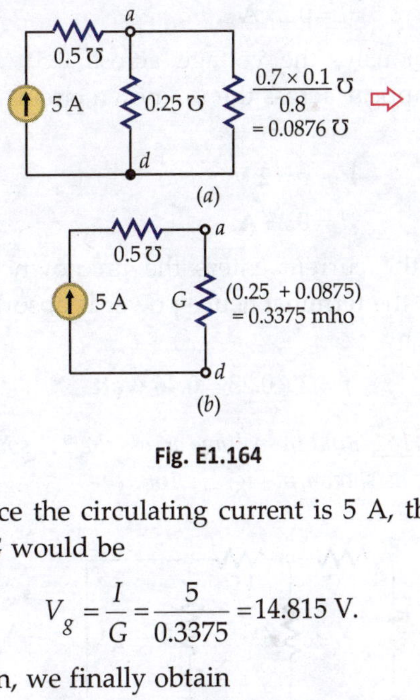

Fig. E1.164

Since the circulating current is 5 A, the drop across *G* would be

$$V_g=\frac{I}{G}=\frac{5}{0.3375}=14.815 \text{ V}.$$

Then, we finally obtain

$$V_g=V_{ad}=14.815 \text{ V}.$$

However, the current direction (I) wanted for is shown in Fig. E1.164. Since the direction of I is opposite to that of 5 A source hence

$$I=-(14.815)\times 0.7=-10.37 \text{ A}$$

[∵ equivalent conductance across *b-c* is 0.7 mho]

Thus the current, asked for, is **– 10.37 A.**

CHAPTER 1

EXAMPLE 1.140 *Find V, I and the power absorbed by the unknown element if 0.5 A source supplies 1 W to the circuit (Fig. E1.165).*

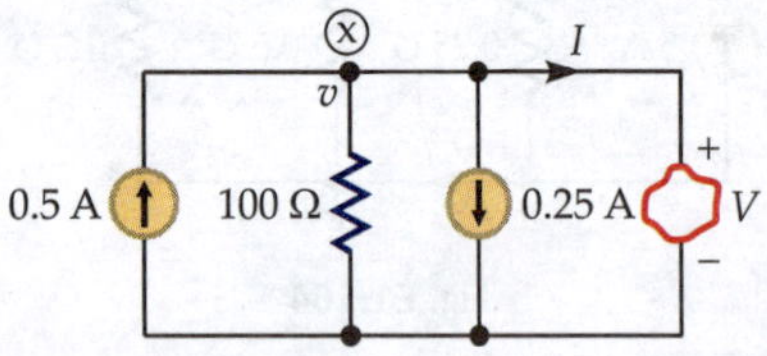

Fig. E1.165

SOLUTION. Voltage across 0.5 A current source is

$$v = \frac{\text{Power}}{\text{Current}} = \frac{1\text{ W}}{0.5\text{ A}} = 2\text{ V}$$

Applying nodal analysis at *node x*,

$$0.5 = \frac{v}{100} + 0.25 + I$$

or, $$0.5 = \frac{2}{100} + 0.25 + I \qquad [\because v = 2\text{ V}]$$

$\therefore$ $$I = 0.23\text{ A}$$

Obviously, the voltage across 0.5 A source would appear across the unknown circuit element too.

$\therefore$ $$V \equiv v = \mathbf{2\ V}$$

while $$I = \mathbf{0.23\ A.}$$

As the current enters the unknown element through the terminal hence power is absorbed and is given by

$$p = 2 \times 0.23 = \mathbf{0.46\ watt.}$$

EXAMPLE 1.141 *Find the voltage across the 2 A source with polarities as shown in Fig. E1.166.*

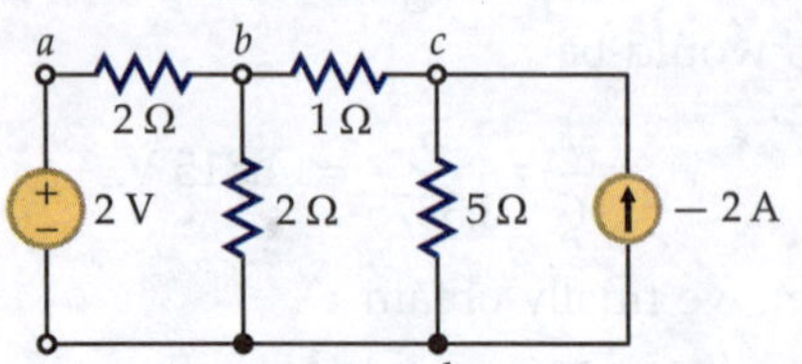

Fig. E1.166

SOLUTION. Let us first transform the 2 V source to current source and draw the network (Fig. E1.166(*a*)) where v be the drop across −2 A source.

Next the current source is again converted to the equivalent voltage source (Fig. E1.166(*b*)).

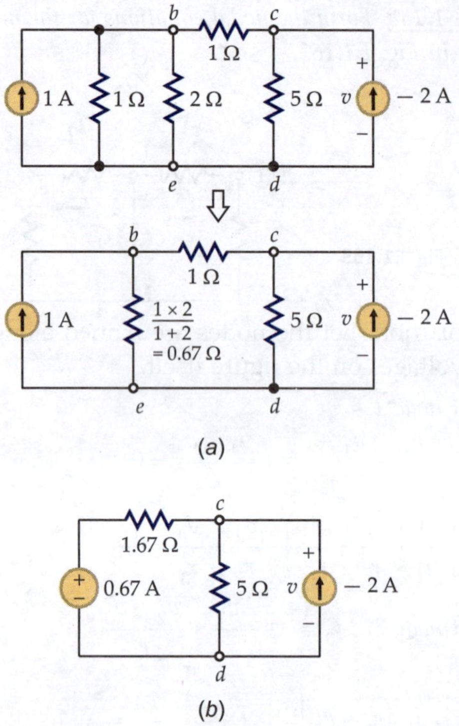

Fig. E1.166

Applying KCL at *node C*,

$$\frac{v - 0.67}{1.67} + \frac{v}{5} = -2$$

or, $$0.6\,v - 0.4 + 0.2\,v = -2$$

or, $$0.8\,v = -1.6$$

$\therefore$ $$v = \mathbf{-2\ V.}$$

EXAMPLE 1.142 *Find r in the circuit of Fig. E1.167.*

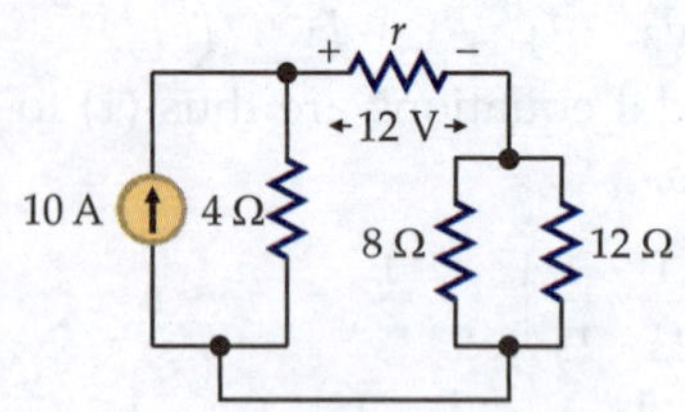

Fig. E1.167

SOLUTION. Parallel combination of 8 Ω and 12 Ω resistances gives

$$\frac{8 \times 12}{12 + 8} = 4.8\,\Omega.$$

Let i be the current through r.

$\therefore$ $$i = \frac{12}{r}$$

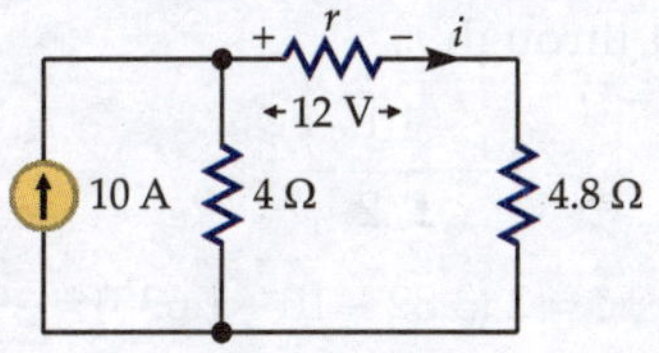

Fig. E1.167 (*a*)

and also from Fig. E1.167(*a*),

$$i = 10\frac{4}{4+r+4.8}$$

[from the current division formulae]

or, $$\frac{12}{r} = \frac{40}{4+r+4.8}$$

or, $$r + 8.8 = 3.33\,r$$

∴ $$r = \mathbf{3.78\,\Omega.}$$

EXAMPLE 1.143 Find the current through 1Ω resistor (Fig. E1.168).

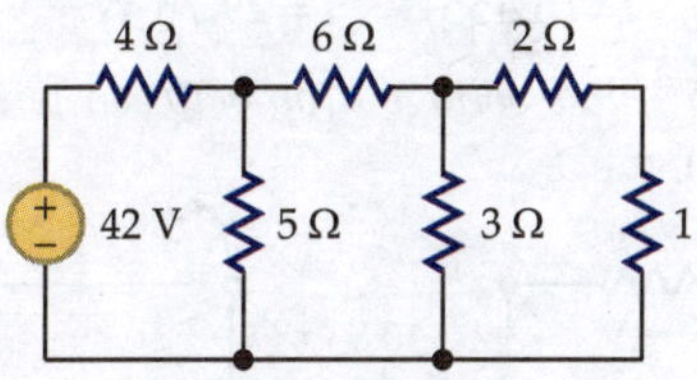

Fig. E1.168

SOLUTION. Equivalent resistance across the 42 V source is

$$R_{eq} = ([\{(1+2)||3\}+6]||5)+4$$

$$= \frac{7.5\times 5}{7.5+5} + 4 = 7\,\Omega$$

∴In Fig. E1.168,

$$I_{4\Omega} = \frac{42}{7} = 6\text{ A};$$

drop across 4 Ω resistor = 24 V.

∴Potential across 5 Ω resistor = 42 − 24 = 18 V.

Current through 5 Ω resistor is $I_{5\Omega} = \frac{18}{5} = 3.6$ A.

Thus current through 6Ω resistor ($I_{6\Omega}$) is 6 − 3.6 = 2.4 A

∴Drop across 6 Ω resistor is 6 × 2.4 = 14.4 V.

Finally, the potential across 3Ω resistor is 18 − 14.4 = 3.6 V

Thus current in 1Ω resistor is $\frac{3.6}{(2+1)} = \mathbf{1.2\ A.}$

EXAMPLE 1.144 By nodal analysis, find the current through 2 V source (Fig. E1.169).

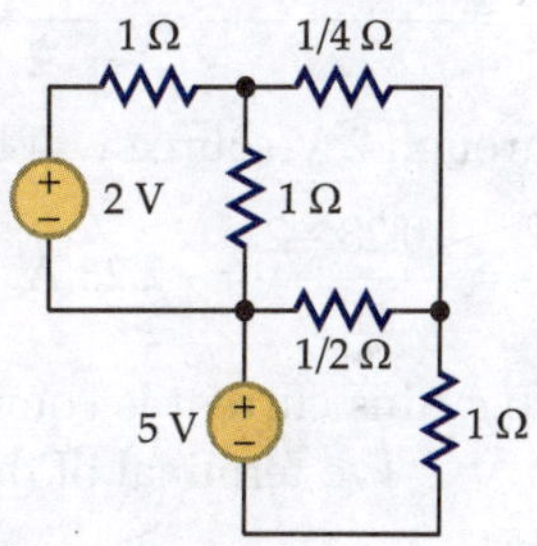

Fig. E1.169

SOLUTION. Naming the nodes and assigning the voltage in the nodes, the circuit is redrawn as shown in Fig. E1.170.

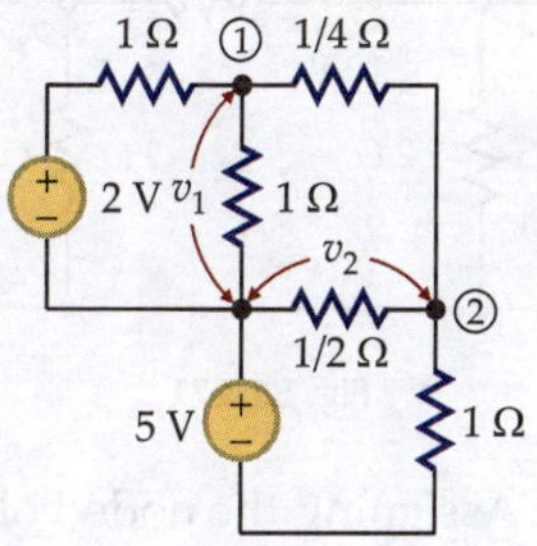

Fig. E1.170

At *node-1*,

$$\frac{v_1-2}{1} + \frac{v_1-v_2}{1/4} + \frac{v_1}{1} = 0$$

or, $$6\,v_1 - 4\,v_2 = 2$$

or, $$3\,v_1 - 2\,v_2 = 1 \quad ...(A)$$

At *node-2*,

$$\frac{v_2}{1/2} + \frac{v_2+5}{1} + \frac{v_2-v_1}{1/4} = 0$$

or, $$2\,v_2 + v_2 + 5 + 4v_2 - 4v_1 = 0$$

or, $$-4\,v_1 + 7\,v_2 = -5 \quad ...(B)$$

From (*A*)

$$v_2 = \frac{3\,v_1 - 1}{2} \quad ...(C)$$

Utilising the value of v_2 from (C) in (*B*),

$$-4\,v_1 + 7.\frac{3\,v_1-1}{2} = -5$$

or, $$-4\,v_1 + 10.5\,v_1 - 3.5 = -5$$

or, $$6.5\,v_1 - 3.5 = -5$$

or, $$v_1 = -\frac{1.5}{6.5} = -0.23 \text{ V}.$$

i.e, $$v_2 = \frac{3(-0.23)-1}{2} = \frac{-0.69-1}{2} = -0.845$$

Current through 2 V source will be

$$\frac{v_1 - 2}{1} = \frac{-0.23-2}{1} = \mathbf{-2.23 \text{ A.}}$$

[*i.e.*, this current is coming out of the +ve terminal of the 2 V source]

EXAMPLE 1.145 *Find the power loss in the resistors of the network of Fig. E1.171. Use node analysis.*

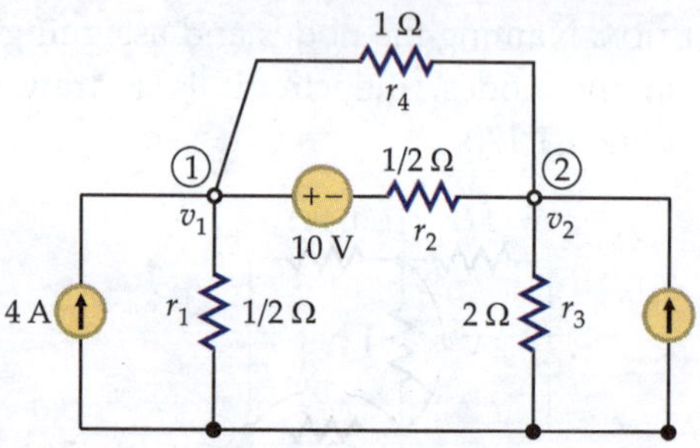

Fig. E1.171

SOLUTION. Assigning the node voltages to be v_1 and v_2 at the *nodes (1)* and *(2)* respectively, from Fig. E1.171, using nodal methods,

For *node-1*,

$$4 = \frac{v_1}{1/2} + \frac{v_1 - v_2}{1} + \frac{v_1 - 10 - v_2}{1/2}$$

or, $$4 = 2\,v_1 + v_1 + 2\,v_1 - v_2 - 2\,v_2 - 20$$

$$\therefore \quad 5\,v_1 - 3\,v_2 = 24 \qquad \text{...(1)}$$

For *node-2*,

$$\frac{v_2}{1} + \frac{v_2 + 10 - v_1}{1/2} + \frac{v_2 - v_1}{1} = 2$$

or, $$v_2 + 2\,v_2 + v_2 - 2\,v_1 - v_1 = -18$$

or, $$4\,v_2 - 3\,v_1 = -18 \qquad \text{...(2)}$$

Solving (1) and (2),

$$v_1 = 3.82 \text{ V}$$
$$v_2 = -1.635 \text{ V}$$

Current through r_1

$$= \frac{v_1}{1/2} = \frac{3.82}{1/2} = 7.64 \text{ A}$$

Power loss in r_1

$$= (7.64)^2 \times \frac{1}{2} = \mathbf{29.18 \text{ W}}$$

Current through r_2

$$= \frac{v_1 - 10 - v_2}{1/2}$$

$$= 2\,(3.82 - 10 + 1.635) = -9.09 \text{ A}$$

Power loss in r_2

$$= (-9.09)^2 \times \frac{1}{2} = \mathbf{41.31 \text{ W}}$$

Current through r_3

$$= \frac{v_2}{1} = -\frac{1.635}{1} = -1.635 \text{ A}$$

Power loss in r_3

$$= (1.635)^2 \times 1 = \mathbf{2.67 \text{ W}}$$

Current through r_4

$$= \frac{v_1 - v_2}{r_4} = \frac{3.82 + 1.635}{1} = 5.455 \text{ A}$$

Power loss in r_4

$$= (5.455)^2 \times 1 = \mathbf{29.76 \text{ W.}}$$

EXAMPLE 1.146 *Find voltage drop between terminals a-e (Fig. E1.172).*

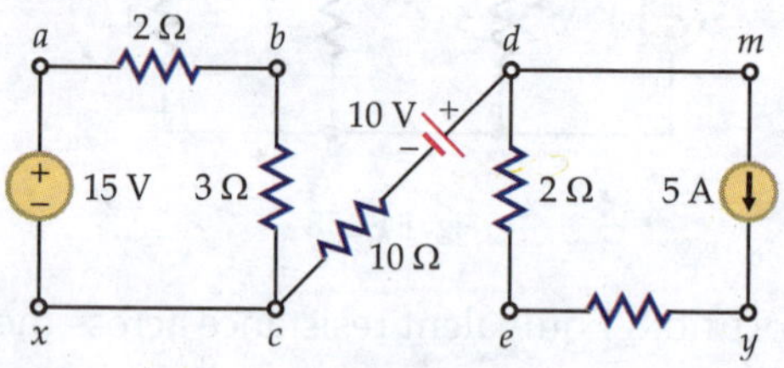

Fig. E1.172

SOLUTION. The circulating current in the *loop a-b-c-x* is

$$I_1 = \frac{15}{2+3} = 3 \text{ A.}$$

However, the circulating current in the *loop d-e-y-m* is 5 A. Thus the drops across 2 Ω and 3 Ω resistors *in loop a−b−c−x* are $3 \times 2 = 6$ V (V_{ab}) and $3 \times 3 = 9$ V (V_{bc}) respectively. The drop across 2 Ω (V_{d-c}) resistor *in loop d-e-y-m* is $5 \times 2 = 10$ V (V_{d-e}). The respective polarities of the drops are shown in Fig. E1.172(*a*).

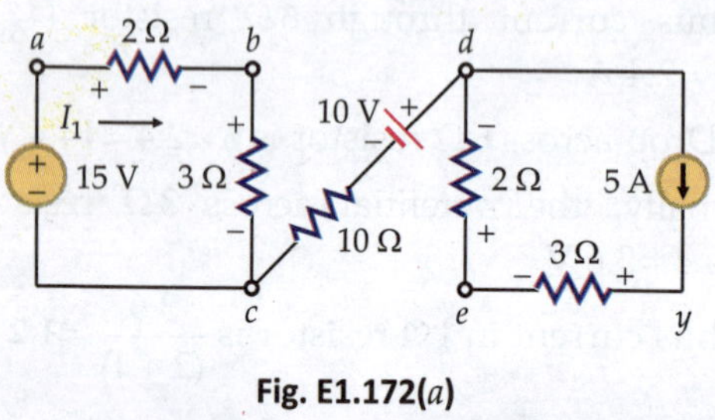

Fig. E1.172(*a*)

Thus the drop across terminals *a-e* is given by

$$V_{a-e} = V_{ab} + V_{bc} + V_{cd} + V_{de}$$

Taking into account the respective polarities,

$$V_{a-e} = 6 + 9 - 10 - 10 = -5 \text{ V}.$$

Then the drop across terminal *a-e* is **– 5 V.**

[*i.e.*, actually terminal *a* is of –ve polarity and *e* is +ve polarity]

EXAMPLE 1.147 *Find the drop between the terminals y and d in the network of Fig. E1.173.*

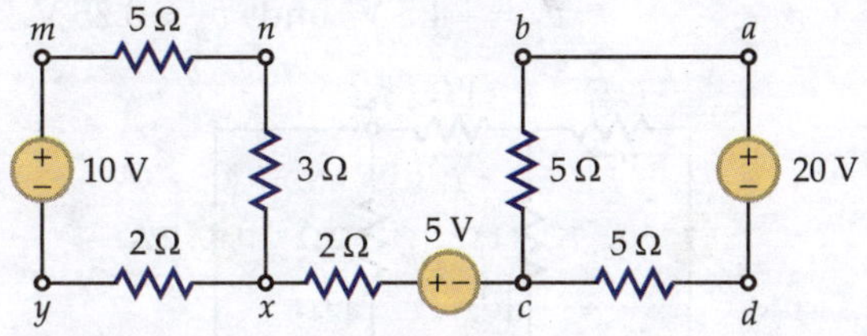

Fig. E1.173

SOLUTION. The current *in loop m-n-x-y* is given by

$$I_1 = \frac{10}{5+3+2} = 1 \text{ A} \quad [\text{Fig. 1.173}(a)]$$

∴ drop in *m-n* branch

$$V_{m-n} = 5 \times 1 = 5 \text{ V},$$

drop in *n-x* branch

$$V_{n-x} = 3 \times 1 = 3 \text{ V},$$

drop in *x-y* branch

$$v_{x-y} = 2 \times 1 = 2 \text{ V}.$$

Similarly, the current *in loop a-b-c-d*,

$$I_2 = \frac{20}{5+5} = 2 \text{ A}$$

and drop in branch *b-c*,

$$V_{b-c} = 5 \times 2 = 10 \text{ V},$$

drop in branch *c-d*,

$$V_{c-d} = 5 \times 2 = 10 \text{ V}$$

The respective polarities of the respectively voltage drops are shown in Fig. E1.173(*a*).

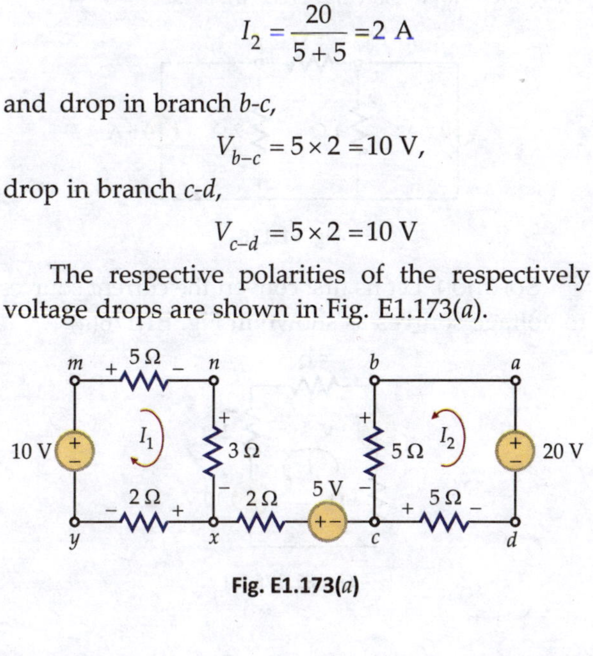

Fig. E1.173(*a*)

Inspecting the respective polarities,

$$V_{y-d} = V_{y-x} + V_{x-c} + V_{c-d}$$

$$= -2 + 5 + 10 = \mathbf{13 \text{ V}}.$$

EXAMPLE 1.148 *In Fig. E1.174, find V_0. Also find the current through a-b if the terminals a-b are shorted.*

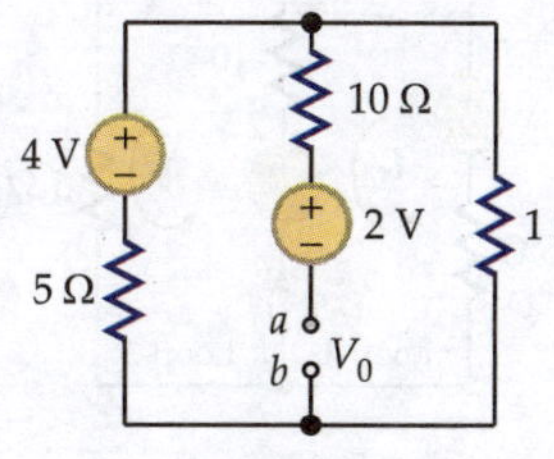

Fig. E1.174

SOLUTION. The given circuit is redrawn in Fig. E1.174(*a*). Let us assume that terminal *x* is +ve. As *y-z* branch is open hence no current would flow through r_2 till *a-b* is open; however voltage V_0 will appear across *a-b*. The circulating current through the closed *loop x-y-p-q-z-x* is

$$I = \frac{4}{5+1} = \frac{2}{3} \text{ A}$$

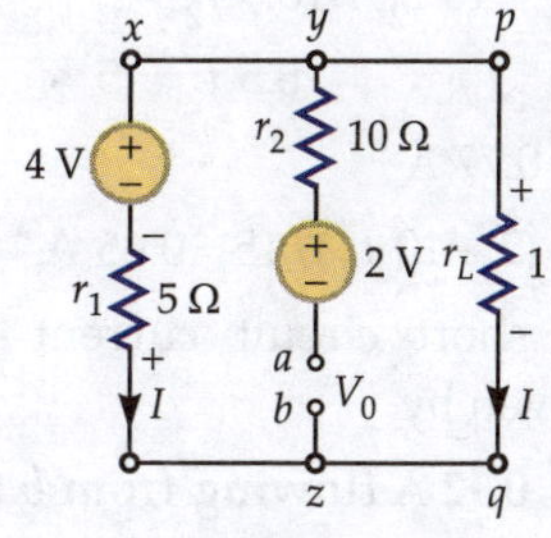

Fig. E1.174(*a*)

Thus the drop across r_1 is $5 \times \frac{2}{3} = \frac{10}{3}$ V (V_{r_L}), polarities being marked in Fig. E1.174(*a*). Also, the drop across 1Ω resistor is $\frac{2}{3} \times 1 = \frac{2}{3}$ V, polarities being marked in the same figure.

Thus, *in loop x-y-z-x*, adding the voltage drops, we get

$$V_{r_1} - 4 + 2 + V_0 = 0$$

[∵ drop across r_2 is zero and we assume the polarity of terminal *a* to be +ve]

or, $$V_0 = 2 - V_{r_L} = 2 - \frac{10}{3} = -\frac{4}{3} = \mathbf{-1.33 \text{ V}}.$$

(*i.e.*, actually terminal *b* is +ve)

CHAPTER 1

Next we short the terminals *a-b*. Using mesh analysis (Fig. E1.174(*b*)). We can write the loop equations as

$$5\,I_1 - 4 + 10\,(I_1 - I_2) + 2 = 0 \quad \text{for } \textit{loop-1} \quad ...(1)$$

and $$-2 + 10\,(I_2 - I_1) + I_2 \times 1 = 0 \quad \text{for } \textit{loop-2} \quad ...(2)$$

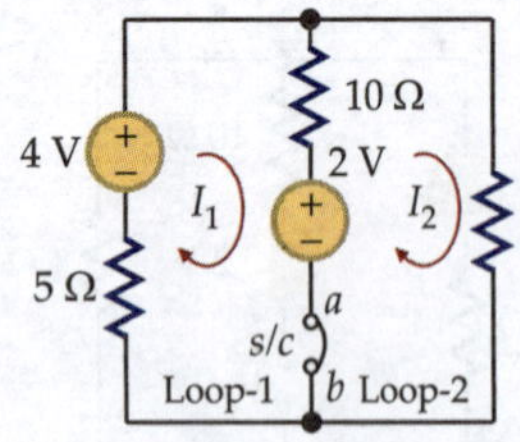

Fig. E1.174(*b*)

Simplification of (1) and (2) yields

$$15\,I_1 - 10\,I_2 = 2 \quad ...(1(a))$$

and $$-10\,I_1 + 11\,I_2 = 2 \quad ...(2(a))$$

Multiplying (2(*a*)) by 1.5, we get

$$-15\,I_1 + 16.5\,I_2 = 3 \quad ...(2(b))$$

Adding (1(*a*)) and (2(*b*)), we get

$$-10\,I_2 + 16.5\,I_2 = 2 + 3$$

or, $$6.5\,I_2 = 5$$

$\therefore$ $$I_2 = 0.77 \text{ A}$$

and $$I_1 = (2 + 10\,I_2)/15 = 0.65 \text{ A}$$

Thus the short circuit current through *a-b* terminals is given by

$$\boldsymbol{I_2 - I_1 = 0.12 \textbf{ A flowing from } b \textbf{ to } a.}$$

EXAMPLE 1.149 *In Fig. E1.175, using node analysis, find the current in the resistors.*

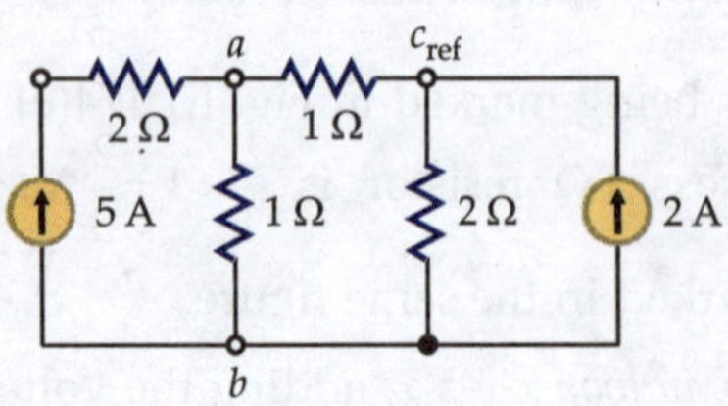

Fig. E1.175

SOLUTION. At *node a*, nodal analysis gives,

$$5 = \frac{v_a - v_b}{1} + \frac{v_a}{1}$$

[$\because$ *node* C is a reference node and the node voltages at *node* (*a*) and (*b*) are v_a and v_b respectively]

$\therefore$ $$2v_a - v_b = 5 \quad ...(1)$$

Similarly, at *node b*, nodal analysis gives

$$\frac{v_b - v_a}{1} + \frac{v_b}{2} + 5 + 2 = 0$$

or, $$1.5\,v_b - v_a = -7$$

Multiplying the above equation by 2, we get

$$3\,v_b - 2v_a = -14 \quad ...(2)$$

Adding equations (1) and (2), we get,

$$-v_b + 3\,v_b = 5 - 14$$

or, $$2\,v_b = -9$$

$\therefore$ $$v_b = -4.5 \text{ V} \quad \text{and} \quad v_a = 0.25 \text{ V}.$$

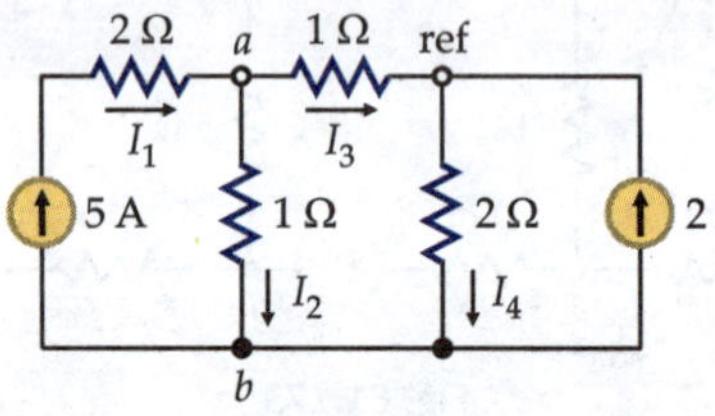

Fig. E1.175 (*a*)

Then, looking at Fig. E1.175(*a*),

$$I_1 = 5 \text{ A}, \; I_2 = \frac{v_a - v_b}{1} = 4.75 \text{ A}$$

$$I_3 = \frac{v_a}{1} = 0.25 \text{ A}$$

$$I_4 = \frac{v_b}{2} = \mathbf{-2.25 \text{ A}.}$$

[$\therefore v_b$ being –ve, the ref. is +ve w.r.t. *b* thus, actually, I_4 flows downwards in Fig. E1.175(*a*)].

EXAMPLE 1.150 *Find the current through the 5 Ω resistor using mesh analysis (Fig. E1.176).*

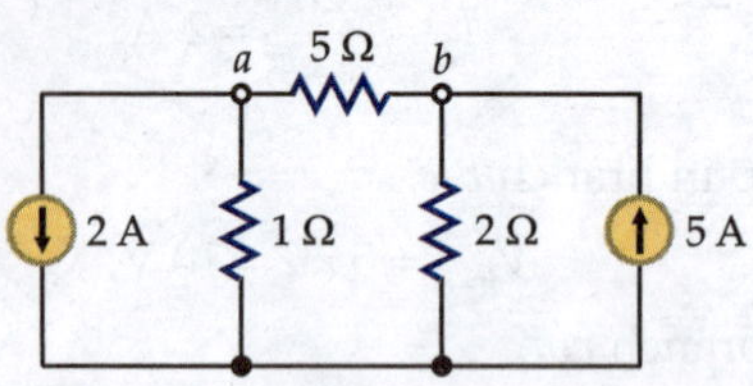

Fig. E1.176

SOLUTION. Let us first convert the current sources to voltage sources as shown in Fig. E1.176(*a*).

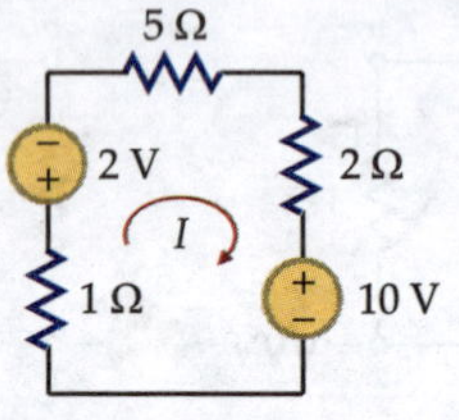

Fig. E1.176 (*a*)

Let I be the current through the $5\,\Omega$ resistor. Using mesh equations, we find

$$I \times 1 + 2 + 5 \times I + 2 \times I + 10 = 0$$

or, $$8\,I = -12$$

$\therefore$ $$I = -\frac{3}{2}\text{ A} = \mathbf{-1.5\ A.}$$

i.e., the current flows from 10 V source to 2 V source in anticlockwise direction in Fig. E1.176(*a*). This gives that the current flows from *node b* to *node a* in Fig. E1.176.

Example 1.151 *In Fig. E1.177, find v, i and the power absorbed by the unknown circuit element.*

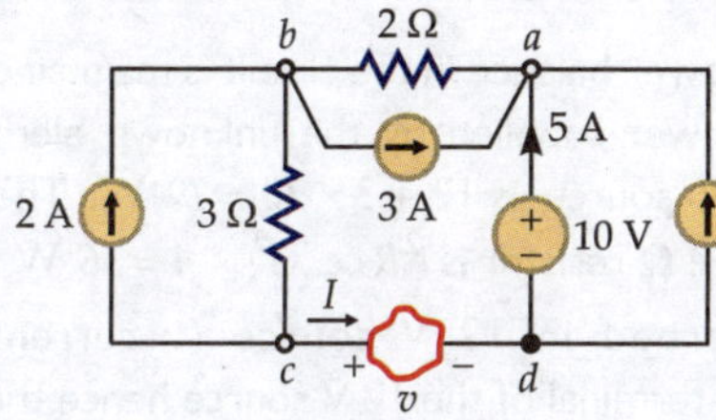

Fig. E1.177

Solution. Using nodal analysis at *node a*,

$$3 + 5 + 4 = i_{ab} = 12\text{ A.}$$

$\therefore$ The voltage across the $2\,\Omega$ resistor is

$$12 \times 2 = 24\text{ V}$$

For *node b*, nodal analysis gives

$$12 + 2 = 3 + i_{bc} \quad \therefore \quad i_{bc} = 11\text{ A}$$

Thus, the voltage across $3\,\Omega$ resistor is

$$11 \times 3 = 33\text{ V.}$$

i can now be obtained by using KCL for *node C*.

Here, $i_{bc} = i + 2$ or, $i = i_{bc} - 2 = 11 - 2 = \mathbf{9\ A.}$

Figure E1.177(*a*) represents the equivalent circuit of Fig. E1.177 with corresponding voltage drops across resistances.

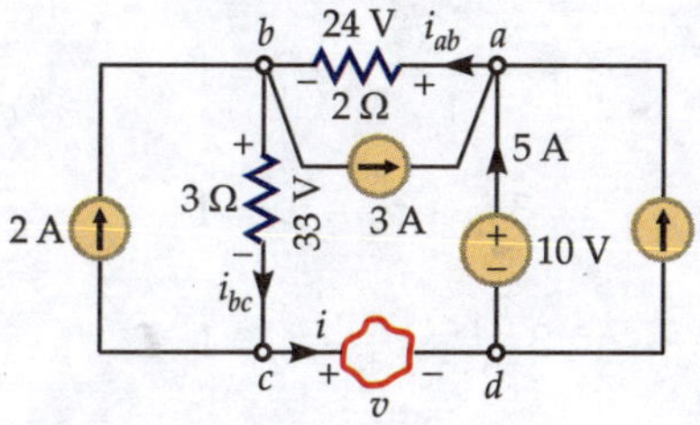

Fig. E1.177 (*a*)

Applying KVL at the *loop abcd*,

$$-10 + 24 + 33 + v = 0$$

or, $$v = \mathbf{-47\ V.}$$

Thus the power absorbed by unknown element is

$$-47 \times i = (-47 \times 9) = \mathbf{-423\ W.}$$

[Since current enters through +ve terminal of the unknown element while v is –ve, power absorbed is –ve].

Example 1.152 *Find V_1 in Fig. E1.178.*

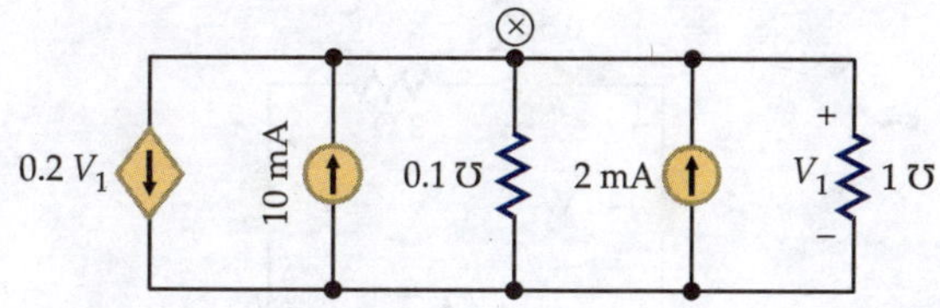

Fig. E1.178

Solution. It is evident from the figure that V_1 is the voltage at *node* (*x*), marked on the figure.

Thus, current in 0.1 mho resistor is $(V_1 \times 0.1)$ A while that in 1 mho resistor is $(V_1 \times 1)$ A.

Then, the application of *node* analysis at *node* (*x*) yields,

$$10 \times 10^{-3} + 2 \times 10^{-3} = 0.2\,V_1 + V_1 \times 0.1 + V_1 \times 1$$

or, $$1.3\,V_1 = 12 \times 10^{-3}$$

or, $$V_1 = \mathbf{9.23\ mV.}$$

Example 1.153 *Find v_x in Fig. E1.179 and find r_2 and r_3.*

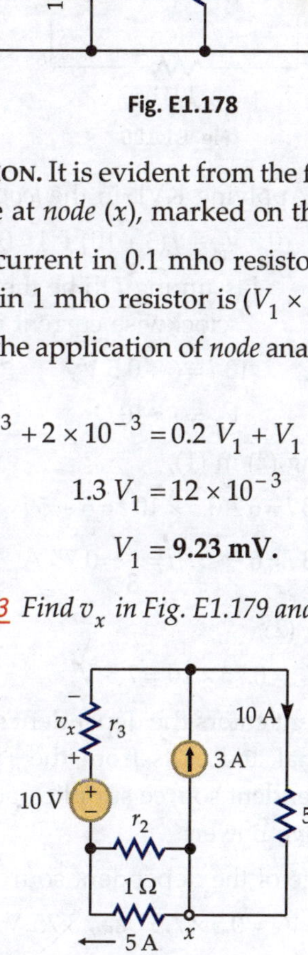

Fig. E1.179

Solution. Applying KVL in the external loop,

$$-10 + v_x + 10 \times 5 + 5 \times 1 = 0$$

or, $$v_x = \mathbf{-45\ V}$$

$\therefore$ $$r_3 = \frac{v_x}{7} = \frac{45}{7} = \mathbf{6.93\,\Omega}$$

[$\because$ current entering at x is 10 A, current through r_2 being $10 - (3 + 5) = 2$ A and through 10 V source is $(5 + 2) = 7$ A]

Again, drop across 1Ω resistor is $5\ A \times 1\Omega$ *i.e.*, 5 V.

$$\therefore \quad r_2 = \frac{5}{2} = \mathbf{2.5\,\Omega}$$

[$\because$ current through r_2 is 2 A]

EXAMPLE 1.154 *Find V_x in Fig. E1.180 at the polarities marked. What is the power absorbed by the dependent source ?*

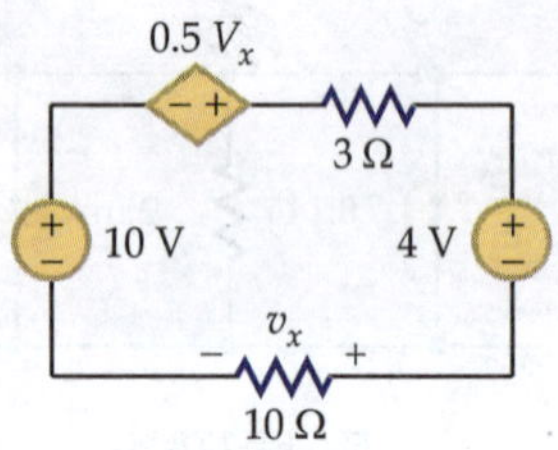

Fig. E1.180

SOLUTION. Applying KVL in the *loop*,

$$-10 - 0.5\,V_x + i\,(3 + 10) + 4 = 0$$

[assuming i to be the circulating clockwise current in the loop]

or, $\quad 13\,i = 6 + 0.5\,V_x$ ...(1)

However, $\quad V_x = i \times 10\,\Omega$ ...(2)

Substituting (2) in (1),

$$13\,i = 6 + 0.5 \times 10\,i = 6 + 5\,i$$

or, $\quad 8\,i = 6 \quad \therefore\ i = \frac{6}{8} = 0.75\ A$

Then from (2),

$$V_x = 0.75 \times 10 = \mathbf{7.5\ V.}$$

Since current enters the dependent source from the –ve terminal and exits from the +ve terminal hence the dependent source supplies power (*i.e.*, it absorbs negative power).

The voltage of the dependent source is

$$0.5\,V_x = 0.5 \times 7.5 \quad i.e.,\ 3.75\ V.$$

$$\therefore \quad p_{\text{dep. source}} = 3.75\ V \times 0.75\ A = 2.81\ W$$

i.e., the power absorbed by the dependent source is **(– 2.81) W.**

EXAMPLE 1.155 *Find the power absorbed by the unknown circuit element in Fig. E1.181 if the 20 V source supplies 60 W power.*

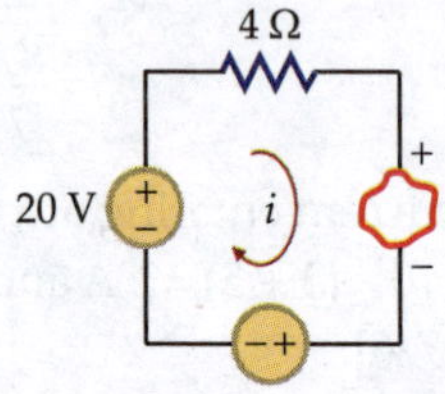

Fig. E1.181

SOLUTION. $\quad i = \frac{P}{V}$

[i = current through 20 V source, P = power rating of 20 V source, V = voltage of 20 V source]

or, $\quad \frac{60}{20} = 3\ A$

Then, applying KVL in the loop,

$$-20 + 4 \times 3 + v + 12 = 0$$

or, $\quad v = -4\ V.$

i.e., the unknown element will absorb -4×3 *i.e.*, -12 W power which means that it would supply **12 W power.**

note Power balance in the circuit is maintained as the power supplied by the unknown element and that by 20 V source is $12 + 3 \times 20 = 72$ W. The power dissipated by 4 Ω resistor is i^2R *i.e.*, $3^2 \times 4 = 36$ W and the power absorbed in 12 V source ($\because$ current enters through +ve terminal of the 12 V source hence the source absorbs power) is $12 \times 3 = 36$ W. Thus the total power consumed in the circuit is $36 + 36 = 72$ W.

EXAMPLE 1.156 *For the circuit shown in Fig. E1.182, find the power loss in the $1/2\,\Omega$ resistor and 1Ω resistor. Also find the value of the dependent source.*

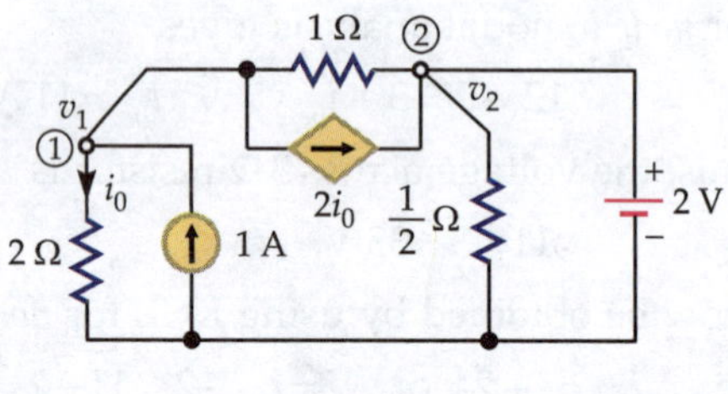

Fig. E1.182

SOLUTION. At *node-1*,

$$i_0 + \frac{v_1 - v_2}{1} + 2i_0 = 1$$

or $\quad 3\,i_0 + v_1 - v_2 = 1$

or, $\quad 3\frac{v_1}{2} + v_1 - v_2 = 1$

or, $\quad 2.5\,v_1 - v_2 = 1$

or, $\quad 2.5\,v_1 - 2 = 1 \quad [\because v_2 = 2\ V]$

or, $\quad v_1 = \frac{3}{2.5} = 1.2$ volt.

Thus, $i_0 = \frac{v_1}{2} = 0.6$ A

and the value of the dependent source $= 2\,i_0 = 1.2$ A

Current through $1/2\,\Omega$ resistor $= \frac{v_2}{1/2} = 4$ A.

Power loss in it $= 4^2 \times \frac{1}{2} = 8$ W

Current through 1Ω resistor

$$= \frac{v_1 - v_2}{1} = \frac{1.2 - 2}{1} = -0.8 \text{ A}$$

Power loss in the 1Ω resistor $= 0.8^2 \times 1 = 0.64$ W.

Thus,

Power loss in $\frac{1}{2}\Omega$ resistor = **8 W.**

Power loss in 1Ω resistor = **0.64 W.**

The values of the dependent source = **1.2 A.**

Check

Power produced

$$= 1\text{A} \times v_1 + 2i_0 \times (v_2 - v_1) + 2\text{V} \times 3.6 \text{ A}$$
$$= 1.2 + 0.96 + 7.2 = 9.36 \text{ W};$$

and power absorbed

$$= 8\text{W} + 0.64 \text{ W} + i_0^2 \times 2$$
$$= 8 + 0.64 + 0.72 = 9.36 \text{ W}.$$

Example 1.157 *Using node analysis, find the value of α for the circuit shown in Fig. E1.183 when the power loss in the 1Ω resistor is 9 W.*

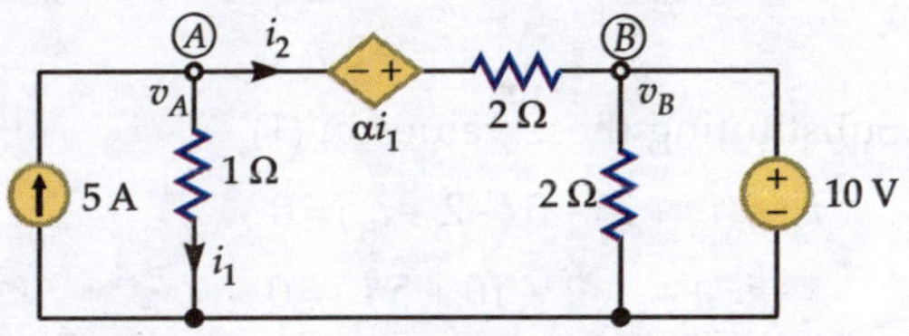

Fig. E1.183

Solution. As per the question,

$$i_1^2 \times 1 = 9 \quad \text{or,} \quad i_1 = 3 \text{ A.}$$

$$\therefore \quad v_A = 3 \times 1 = 3 \text{ V}$$

At *node (A)*,

$$5 = i_1 + i_2$$

However, $i_1 = 3$ A,

$$i_2 = \frac{v_A + \alpha\, i_1 - v_B}{2} = \frac{3 + 3\alpha - 10}{2}$$

$[\because v_B = 10 \text{ V}]$

Thus, we can write,

$$5 = 3 + \frac{3\alpha - 7}{2} = -0.5 + 1.5\,\alpha$$

$$\therefore \quad \alpha = \frac{5.5}{1.5} = \mathbf{3.67.}$$

Example 1.158 *Using Nodal analysis, find the voltage at node y in Fig. E1.184.*

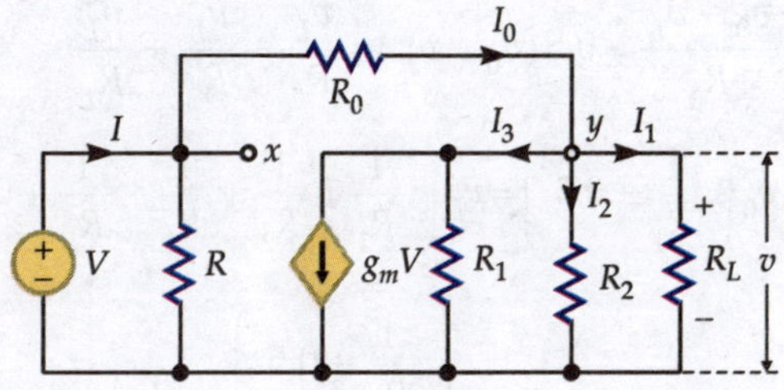

Fig. E1.184

Solution. At *node y*, the nodal analysis gives

$$I_0 = I_1 + I_2 + I_3 \qquad ...(1)$$

where, $I_1 = \frac{v}{R_L}$; $I_2 = \frac{v}{R_2}$

$$I_3 = \frac{v}{R_1} + g_m V \quad \text{and} \quad I_0 = \frac{V - v}{R_0}$$

[assuming node voltage at y to be v]

Thus from (1),

$$\frac{V - v}{R_0} = \frac{v}{R_L} + \frac{v}{R_2} + \frac{v}{R_1} + g_m V$$

or, $$v\left(\frac{1}{R_1} + \frac{1}{R_2} + \frac{1}{R_L} + \frac{1}{R_0}\right) = V\left(\frac{1}{R_0} - g_m\right)$$

$$\therefore \quad \mathbf{v = V \frac{\left(\frac{1}{R_0} - g_m\right)}{\left(\frac{1}{R_1} + \frac{1}{R_2} + \frac{1}{R_L} + \frac{1}{R_0}\right)}}.$$

Example 1.159 *It is given that in the network of Fig. E1.185, $R_1 = R_2 = 100\,\Omega$, $R_3 = 40\,\Omega$, $R_L = 10\,\Omega$, $v_0 = 5$ V. Find v_L using nodal analysis.*

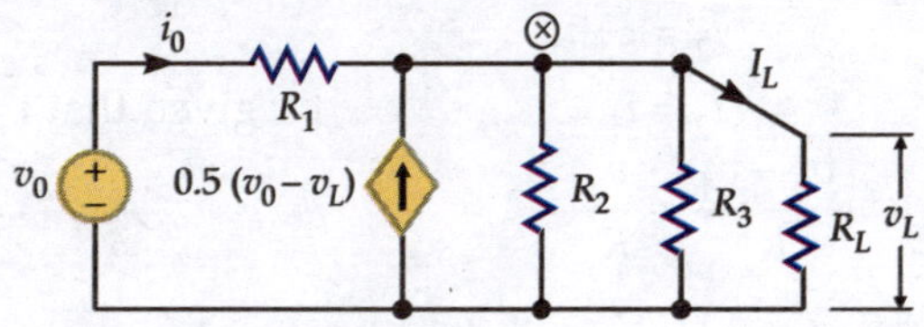

Fig. E1.185

CHAPTER 1

SOLUTION. At *node x*, nodal analysis gives

$$i_0 + 0.5(v_0 - v_L) = \frac{v_L}{R_2} + \frac{v_L}{R_3} + \frac{v_L}{R_L}$$

However, $$i_0 = \frac{v_0 - v_L}{R_1}$$

Then we get

$$\frac{v_0 - v_L}{R_1} + 0.5(v_0 - v_L) = \frac{v_L}{R_2} + \frac{v_L}{R_3} + \frac{v_L}{R_L}$$

or, $$v_0\left(\frac{1}{R_1} + 0.5\right) = v_L\left(\frac{1}{R_1} + \frac{1}{R_2} + \frac{1}{R_3} + \frac{1}{R_L} + 0.5\right).$$

$$\therefore\ v_L = v_0 \frac{\left(\frac{1}{R_1} + 0.5\right)}{\left(\frac{1}{R_1} + \frac{1}{R_2} + \frac{1}{R_L} + 0.5 + \frac{1}{R_3}\right)}$$

$$= 5 \frac{\left(\frac{1}{100} + 0.5\right)}{\left(\frac{1}{100} + \frac{1}{100} + \frac{1}{10} + 0.5 + \frac{1}{40}\right)}$$

$$= 5 \frac{0.51}{(0.02 + 0.1 + 0.5 + 0.025)} = \mathbf{3.95\ V.}$$

EXAMPLE 1.160 *Assuming $v_d = 0$ and $i = 0$, for the case of ideal op. amp. ; prove that $\frac{v_0}{v_s} = 1 + \frac{R_2}{R_1}$ [Fig. E1.186].*

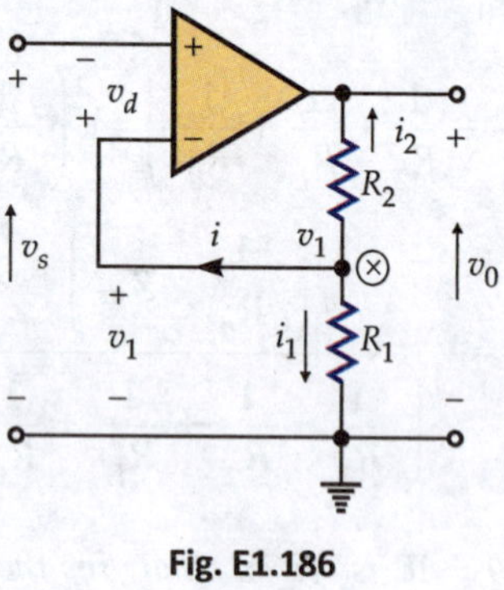

Fig. E1.186

SOLUTION. Assuming a current i_2 through R_2 downwards in Fig. E1.186,

$$i_2 = i + i_1$$

or, $$i_2 = i_1 \qquad [\because \text{given that } i = 0]$$

or, $$\frac{v_0 - v_1}{R_2} = \frac{v_1}{R_1} \qquad ...(1)$$

However, by observation,

$$v_s = v_d + v_1 = v_1 \qquad [\because \text{given that } v_d = 0]$$

Thus equation (1) *i.e.,*

$$\frac{v_0 - v_1}{R_2} = \frac{v_1}{R_1} \text{ becomes } \frac{v_0 - v_s}{R_2} = \frac{v_s}{R_1}$$

or, $$\frac{v_0}{R_2} = v_S\left(\frac{1}{R_2} + \frac{1}{R_1}\right)$$

$$\therefore\ \frac{v_0}{v_S} = R_2\left(\frac{1}{R_1} + \frac{1}{R_2}\right) = \left(\mathbf{1 + \frac{R_2}{R_1}}\right).$$

EXAMPLE 1.161 *Using mesh analysis, find the magnitude of the current dependent source (Fig. E1.187) and the current through the 2 Ω resistor.*

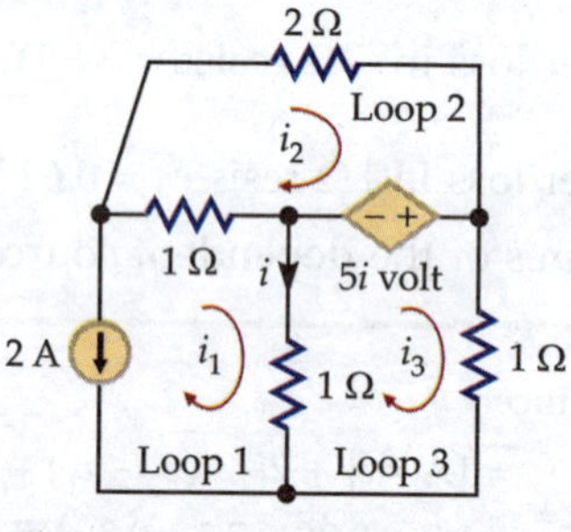

Fig. E1.187

SOLUTION. It is evident that *in loop-1,*

$$i_1 = -2\text{ A}$$

In loop-3,

$$i_3 \times 1 + (i_3 - i_1)1 - 5i = 0 \qquad ...(1)$$

However, $$i = i_1 - i_3$$

and $$i_1 = -2\text{ A}$$

Substituting these values in (1),

$$i_3 + (i_3 + 2) - 5(-2 - i_3) = 0$$

or, $$i_3 + i_3 + 2 + 10 + 5i_3 = 0$$

or, $$7i_3 + 12 = 0$$

or, $$i_3 = -\frac{12}{7} = -1.71\text{ A}$$

In loop-2,

$$i_2 \times 2 + 5i + (i_2 - i_1) = 0$$

or, $$2i_2 + 5(i_1 - i_3) + i_2 - i_1 = 0.$$

or, $$3i_2 + 4i_1 - 5(-1.71) = 0$$

or, $$4i_1 + 3i_2 = -8.55$$

or, $$4(-2) + 3i_2 = -8.55$$

$$\therefore\ 3i_2 = -8.55 + 8 = -0.55$$

$$\therefore\ i_2 = \mathbf{-0.183\ A.}$$

Also, $i = i_1 - i_3 = -2 - (-1.71)$
$= -2 + 1.71 = -0.29$ A.

Value of dependent source
$= 5\,i = -5 \times 0.29 = -1.45$ volt.

Thus, the magnitude of the dependent source $=$ **1.45 V.**

The magnitude of the actual current i which, as found out, is upwards in the circuit, the actual polarity of dependent source is opposite to that shown.

The current through 2 Ω resistor is i_2 *i.e.,* 0.183 A flowing anticlockwise in *loop-2*.

EXAMPLE 1.162 *Find the loop currents i_1, i_2 and i_3 in the network of Fig. E1.188 by mesh method.*

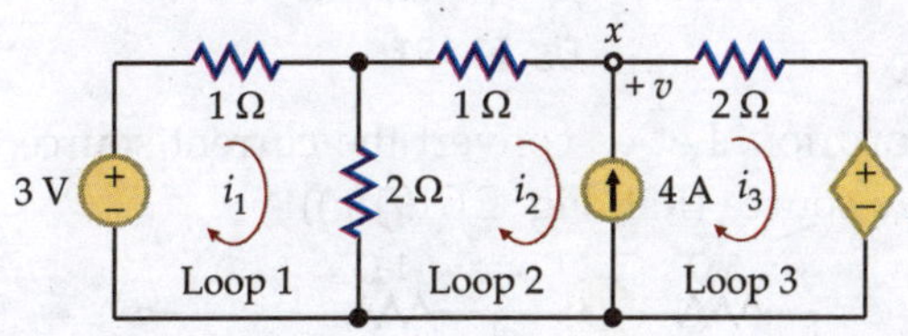

Fig. E1.188

SOLUTION. *In loop-1,* mesh analysis gives,

$$i_1 \times 1 + (i_1 - i_2)2 - 3 = 0$$

or, $$3\,i_1 - 2\,i_2 = 3 \qquad ...(1)$$

In loop 2,

$$2\,(i_2 - i_1) + i_2 \times 1 + v = 0$$

[where v is the assumed voltage at mode "x"]

or, $$3\,i_2 - i_1 + v = 0 \qquad ...(2)$$

But using KVL *in loop 3,*

$$v = 2\,i_3 + 2\,i_1 \qquad ...(3)$$

Using the value of v from (3) in (2),

$$3\,i_2 - i_1 + 2\,i_3 + 2\,i_1 = 0$$

or, $$i_1 + 3\,i_2 + 2\,i_3 = 0 \qquad ...(4)$$

Also, the inspection of the *loop 3* reveals,

$$i_3 - i_2 = 4 \qquad ...(5)$$

Thus finally, we get

$$3\,i_1 - 2\,i_2 = 3 \qquad \text{[eqn. (1)]}$$
$$i_1 + 3\,i_2 + 2\,i_3 = 0 \qquad \text{[eqn. (4)]}$$
$$i_3 - i_2 = 4 \qquad \text{[eqn. (5)]}$$

Solving these equations,

$$i_2 = -\frac{\mathbf{27}}{\mathbf{17}}\ \mathbf{A}$$

$$i_1 = -\frac{\mathbf{1}}{\mathbf{17}}\ \mathbf{A}$$

$$i_3 = \frac{\mathbf{41}}{\mathbf{17}}\ \mathbf{A}$$

EXAMPLE 1.163 *In Fig. E1.189, find the magnitude of V_0 and the current supplied by it. Assume power loss in 2 Ω resistor as 18 watts.*

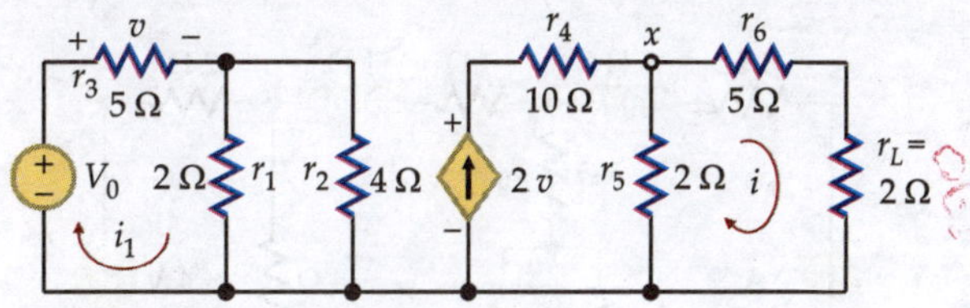

Fig. E1.189

SOLUTION. As the power loss in the 2 Ω (r_L) resistor is 18 W,

$$\therefore \quad i^2\,r_L = 18 \quad \text{or} \quad i = \sqrt{\frac{18}{2}} = 3 \text{ A}$$

[$\because i$ = current through r_L and $r_L = 2\,\Omega$]

Let the loop current in the left-most loop in Fig. E1.189 be i_1. Mesh equation for this loop is given by

$$V_0 = \left(5 + \frac{2 \times 4}{2+4}\right) i_1 = \left(5 + \frac{4}{3}\right) i_1$$

$$\therefore \quad i_1 = \frac{3\,V_0}{19} \qquad ...(i)$$

$$\therefore \quad v = 5\,i_1 = \frac{3}{19} V_0 \times 5 = \frac{15}{19} V_0 \qquad ...(ii)$$

Now, at *node x,*

$$2\,v = \frac{V_x}{2} + 3$$

or, $$2 \times \frac{15}{19} V_0 = \frac{V_x}{2} + 3$$

$$\therefore \quad \left(\frac{30}{19} V_0 - 3\right) 2 = V_x \qquad ...(iii)$$

But in the rightmost *loop*, V_x (drop across r_5) is given by

$$V_x = i\,(5+2) = 7\,i = 21 \text{ V}$$

Utilising the value of V_x in (*iii*),

$$\left(\frac{30}{19} V_0 - 3\right) 2 = 21$$

CHAPTER 1

or, $\frac{60}{19} V_0 = 21 + 6 = 27$

$\therefore \quad V_0 = \frac{27 \times 19}{60} = 8.55 \text{ V}$

Thus $\quad V_0 = \mathbf{8.55\ V}.$

The current supplied by V_0 is i_1 and given by

$$i_1 = \frac{3\,V_0}{19} = \frac{25.65}{19} = 13.5 \text{ A}$$

$\therefore$ Current supplied by voltage source = **13.5 A.**

EXAMPLE 1.164 *Find v_0 in Fig. E1.190 at steady state.*

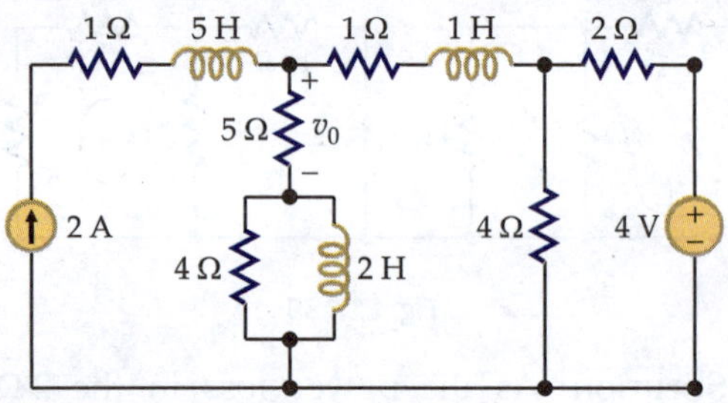

Fig. E1.190

SOLUTION. At steady state, the drops across the inductances are zero as the inductance would offer short circuit against d.c. excitation at $t = \infty$. The circuit then reduces to that as shown in Fig. E1.190(*a*). The 4 V source is then transformed to equivalent current source and the network is redrawn as shown in Fig. E1.190(*b*). Next, the right hand current source is again converted to equivalent voltage source and the network is drawn again in Fig. E1.190(*c*).

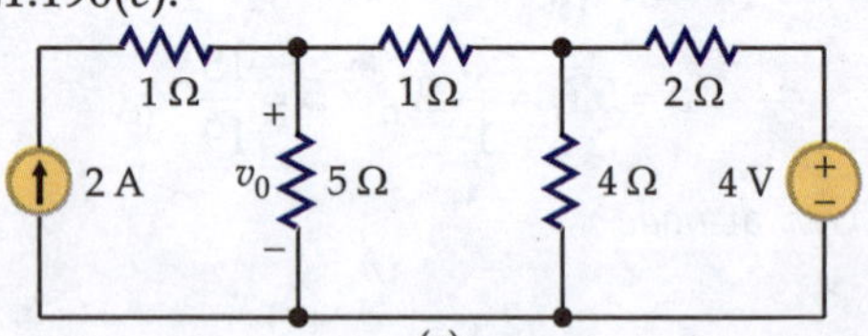

(*a*)

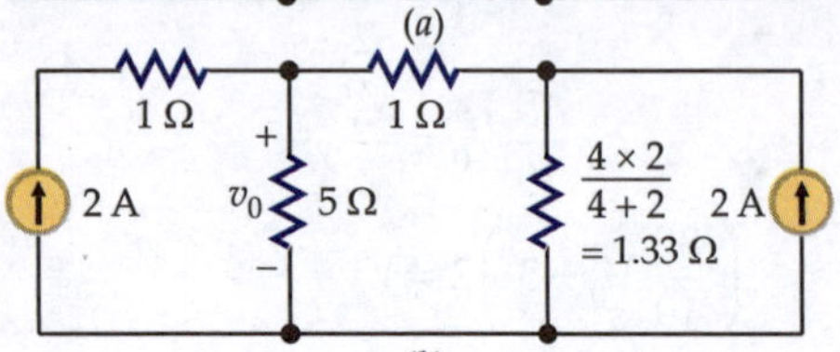

(*b*)

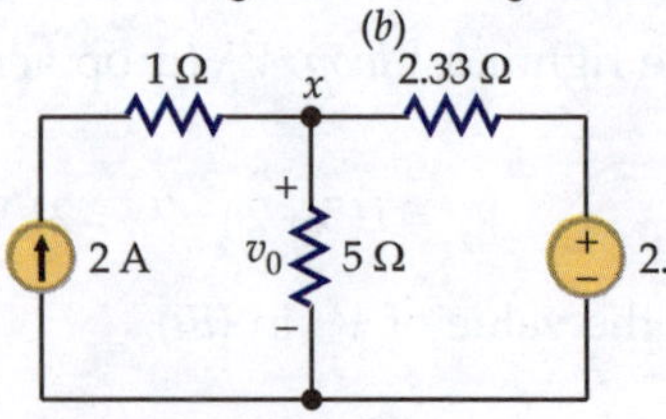

(*c*)

Fig. E1.190

Next, applying KCL at *node x*,

$$2 = \frac{v_0}{5} + \frac{v_0 - 2.66}{2.33}$$

$$= 0.2\,v_0 + 0.43\,v_0 - 1.142$$

$$= 0.63\,v_0 - 1.142$$

$\therefore \quad v_0 = \mathbf{4.99\ V.}$

EXAMPLE 1.165 *Find V_0 in Fig. E1.191 and obtain the magnitude of the current through 3 Ω resistor.*

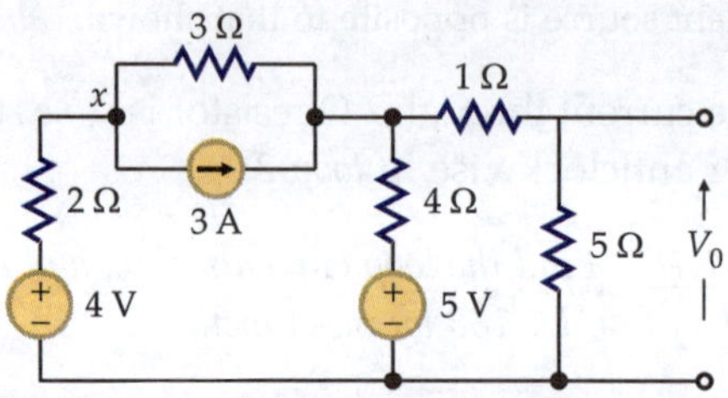

Fig. E1.191

SOLUTION. Let us convert the current source to voltage source (Ref. Fig. E1.191(*a*))

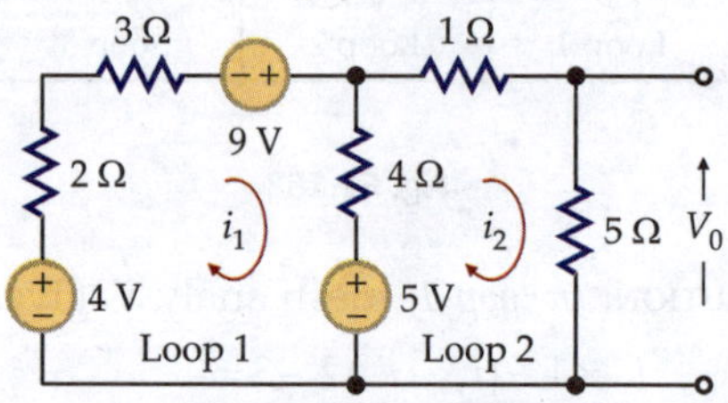

Fig. E1.191(*a*)

In loop-1, mesh analysis yields

$$i_1 (2 + 3 + 4) - i_2 \times 4 - 4 - 9 + 5 = 0$$

or, $\quad 9\,i_1 - 4\,i_2 = 8 \quad$ ...(1)

In loop-2, the mesh analysis yields

$$i_2 (4 + 1 + 5) - 4\,i_1 - 5 = 0$$

or, $\quad -4\,i_1 + 10\,i_2 = 5 \quad$ ...(2)

From (1), $\quad i_1 = \frac{8}{9} + \frac{4}{9} i_2 \quad$ or, $\quad i_1 = 0.89 + 0.444\,i_2$

Substitution of i_1 into (2) reveals

$$-4\,(0.89 + 0.444\,i_2) + 10\,i_2 = 5$$

or, $\quad 8.222\,i_2 = 5 + 3.56 = 8.56$

$\therefore \quad i_2 = 1.041 \text{ A}$

Thus, $\quad V_0 = i_2 \times 5 = \mathbf{5.21\ V.}$

Again i_2 being 1.041 A, $i_1 = 1.352$ A.

Referring Fig. E1.191, current through 3 Ω resistor is $(i_1 - 3 \text{ A})$ (applying KCL at *node x*) *i.e.*, **– 1.698 A** (the current is flowing from right to left terminal of 3 Ω resistor).

Example 1.166 *Find i_0, i_2 and the value of the dependent source [Ref. Fig. E1.192].*

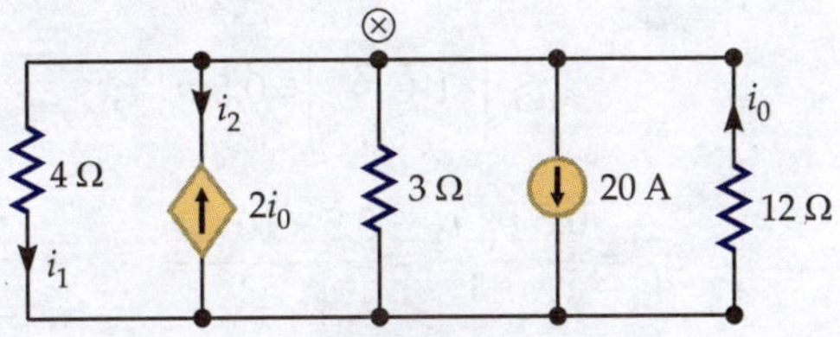

Fig. E1.192

Solution. Let v be the node voltage at *node x*. Applying nodal analysis at (x) *node*,

$$\frac{v}{4}+\frac{v}{3}+\frac{v}{12}+20=2\,i_0$$

However, by inspection, $-i_0=\dfrac{v}{12}$ A

∴We get

$$\frac{v}{4}+\frac{v}{3}+\frac{v}{12}+20=-2\,\frac{v}{12}=-\frac{v}{6}$$

or, $$\frac{3\,v+4\,v+v+2\,v}{12}=-20$$

or, $$\frac{10\,v}{12}=-20$$

or, $$v=-24\text{ V.}$$

Thus, $i_1=\dfrac{v}{4}=-6$ A, $i_0=-\dfrac{v}{12}=\mathbf{2\ A}$.

$2\,i_0$ (value of dependent source) = **4 A**.

$$i_2=-2\,i_0=\mathbf{-4\ A.}$$

Example 1.167 *Find the current through the 5 m ohm resistor [Fig. E1.193].*

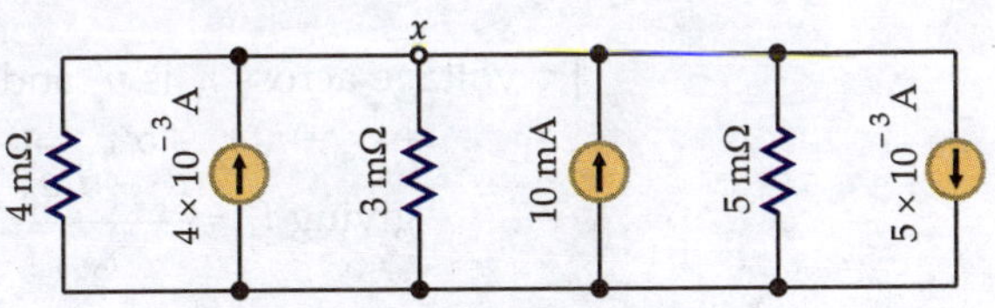

Fig. E1.193

Solution. Applying nodal analysis at *node x*,

$$4\times10^{-3}+10\times10^{-3}=\frac{V}{4\times10^{-3}}+\frac{V}{3\times10^{-3}}+\frac{V}{5\times10^{-3}}+5\times10^{-3}$$

$$14\times10^{-3}-5\times10^{-3}=V\,[\,0.25+0.33+0.2\,]10^{3}$$

or, $$9\times10^{-3}=V\times10^{3}\times0.78$$

or, $$V=\frac{9\times10^{-3}}{0.78\times10^{3}}=11.54\times10^{-6}\text{ volts}$$

∴ Current through 5 m ohm resistor is

$$I_5=\frac{11.54\times10^{-6}}{5\times10^{-3}}=\mathbf{2.31\times10^{-3}\ A}\text{ (downwards).}$$

Example 1.168 *Find v in Fig. E1.194. Also find the power loss in r_1.*

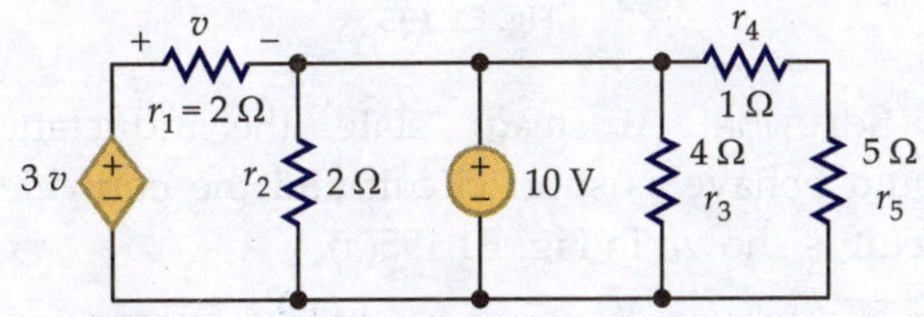

Fig. E1.194

Solution. The given circuit is reduced as shown in Fig. E1.194(*a*). [$R_{eq.}$ is the equivalent resistance of r_5, r_4, r_3 and r_2]

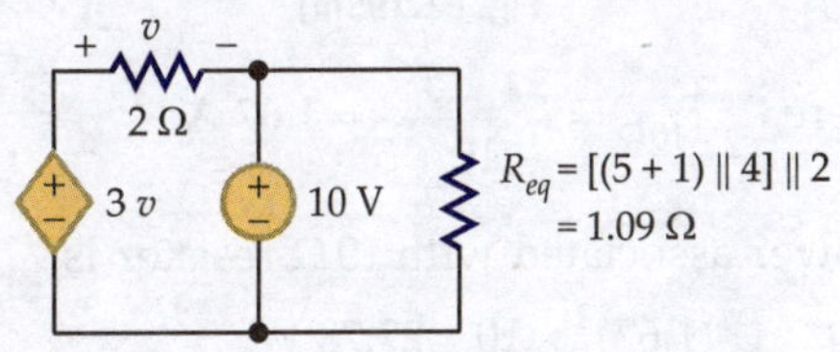

Fig. E1.194(*a*)

Obviously, as shown in Fig. E1.194(*a*),

$$R_{eq.}=1.09\,\Omega.$$

Figure E1.194(*b*) represents the further equivalent of the given circuit.

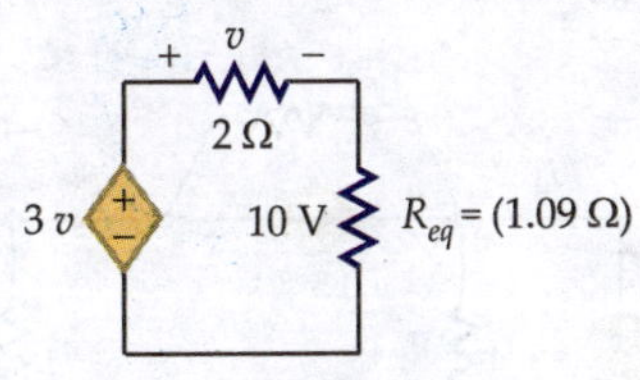

Fig. E1.194(*b*)

Applying KVL in this final equivalent circuit,

$$-3\,v+v+10=0$$

or, $$v=\mathbf{5\ V.}$$

But $$v=2\,i$$

∴ $$i=2.5\text{ A.}$$

Thus, the power loss in the 2 Ω resistance is given by

$$(2.5)^2\times2=\mathbf{12.5\ W.}$$

Example 1.169 *If $I_0=5$ A, find the current, voltage and power associated with 10 Ω resistor of Fig. E1.195. (Assume steady state operation).*

CHAPTER 1

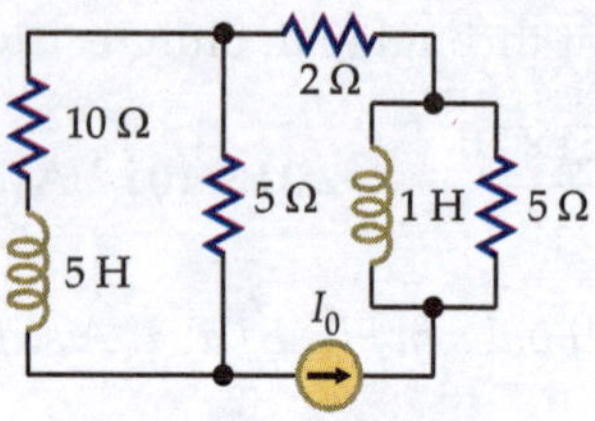

Fig. E1.195

Solution. At steady state, the inductances would behave as short circuit and the equivalent circuit is shown in Fig. E1.195(*a*).

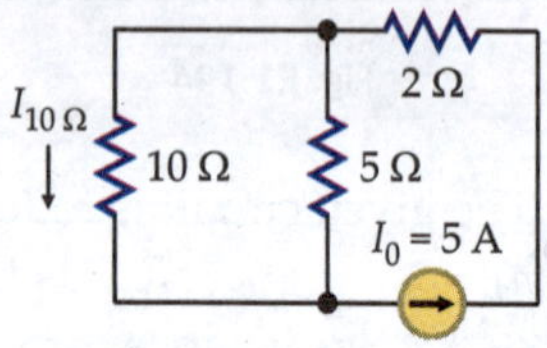

Fig. E1.195(*a*)

Here, $I_{10\Omega} = I_0 \dfrac{5}{10+5} = \mathbf{1.67\ A}$

Power associated with 10 Ω resistor is

$$(1.67)^2 \times 10 = \mathbf{27.78\ W}.$$

Voltage across 10 Ω resistor is

$$I_{10\Omega} \times 10 = \mathbf{16.70\ V}.$$

Example 1.170 *Find v_L using Kirchhoff's laws in Fig. E1.196.*

[$r_L = 10\,\Omega$, $v_0 = 10$ V, $r_1 = r_2 = 1\Omega$]

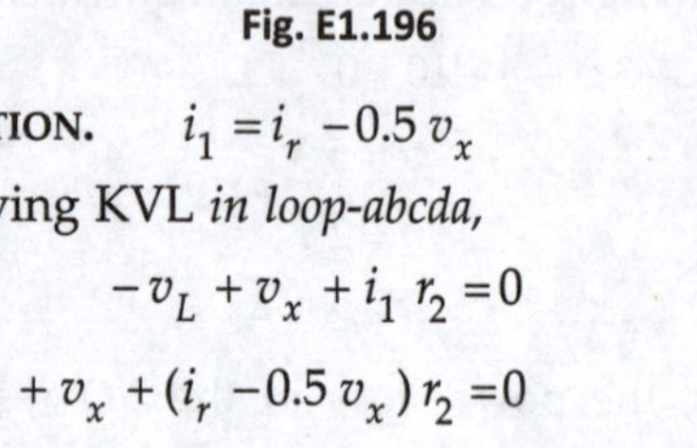

Fig. E1.196

Solution. $i_1 = i_r - 0.5\, v_x$ ...(1)

Applying KVL *in loop-abcda,*

$$-v_L + v_x + i_1 r_2 = 0$$

or, $-v_L + v_x + (i_r - 0.5\, v_x) r_2 = 0$

or, $-v_L + v_0 + \left[\left(-\dfrac{v_L}{r_L}\right) - 0.5\, v_0\right] r_2 = 0$

$$\left[\text{taking into account that } i_r = -\frac{v_L}{r_L}, v_x \equiv v_0\right]$$

or, $v_L = v_0 - \left(\dfrac{v_2}{r_L} + 0.5\, v_0\right) r_2 = \left(0.5\, v_0 - \dfrac{v_L}{r_L}\right) r_2$

or, $v_L \left(1 + \dfrac{r_2}{r_L}\right) = 0.5\, v_0\, r_2$

$\therefore$ $v_L = \dfrac{0.5\, v_0\, r_2}{1 + \dfrac{1}{r_L}} = \dfrac{0.5 \times 10 \times 1}{1 + \dfrac{1}{10}}$

or $v_L = \dfrac{50}{11} = \mathbf{4.55\ V}.$

Example 1.171 *Find v_0 using Kirchhoff's laws in the circuit of Fig. E1.197. Assume $r_4 = 5$ ohms.*

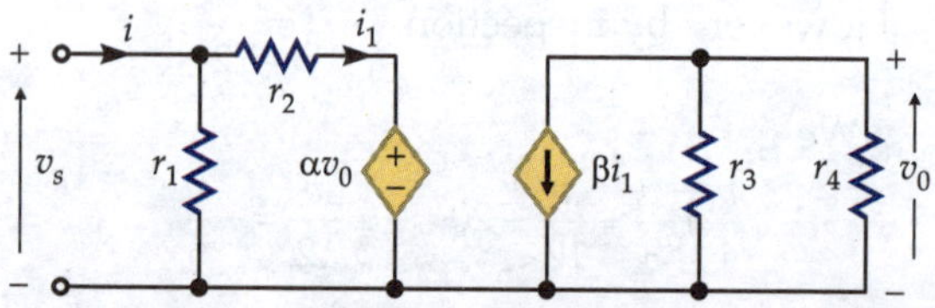

[$r_1 = 1000\,\Omega$, $r_2 = 500\,\Omega$, $r_3 = 50\,\Omega$, $\alpha = 0.5$, $\beta = 2$, $v_s = 10$ V]

Fig. E1.197

Solution. Here applying KVL at the *output loop,*

$$v_0 = -\beta\, i_1\, (r_3 \,||\, r_4) = -\frac{\beta\, r_3\, r_4}{r_3 + r_4}\, i_1 \qquad \text{...(1)}$$

But in the *input loop,*

$$i_1 = \frac{v_s - \alpha v_0}{r_2} \qquad \text{...(2)}$$

[$\because$ voltage across r_1 is v_s and $-v_s + i_1 r_2 + \alpha\, v_0 = 0$ giving $i_1 = \dfrac{v_s - \alpha\, v_0}{r_2}$]

Using (2) in (1), we get,

$$v_0 = -\frac{\beta\, r_3\, r_4}{r_3 + r_4}\left(\frac{v_s - \alpha\, v_0}{r_2}\right)$$

or, $v_0 \left(1 - \dfrac{\beta\, r_3\, r_4\, \alpha}{r_2\,(r_3 + r_4)}\right) = -\dfrac{\beta\, r_3\, r_4\, v_s}{(r_3 + r_4)\, r_2}$

$\therefore$ $v_0 = -\left(\dfrac{\beta\, r_3\, r_4\, v_s}{r_2\,(r_3 + r_4)}\right) \Big/ \left(1 - \dfrac{\beta\, r_3\, r_4\, \alpha}{r_2\,(r_3 + r_4)}\right)$

$= \mathbf{-183.48\ mV}.$

EXAMPLE 1.172 *Find* $\frac{V_L}{V_s}$ *in the circuit shown in Fig. E1.198 using KVL.*

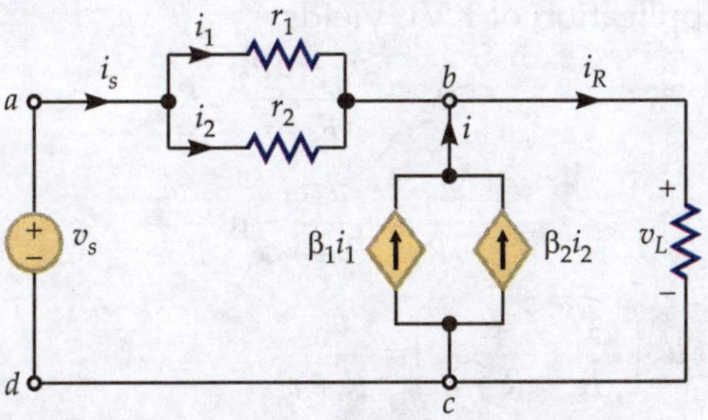

$[r_1 = r_2 = 2\,\Omega, V_s = 10\text{ V}, r_L = 5\,\Omega, \beta_1 = \beta_2 = 2]$

Fig. E1.198

SOLUTION. Applying KVL *in loop a-b-c-d*,

$$V_L = V_s - \left(\frac{r_1 r_2}{r_1 + r_2}\right) i_s = 10 - \frac{2 \times 2}{2+2} i_s$$

or, $\quad V_L = 10 - i_s \quad$ ...(1)

Again, $\quad \beta_1 i_1 + \beta_2 i_2 = i$

since $\quad \beta_1 = \beta_2 = \beta \text{ (say)},$

hence $\quad i = \beta(i_1 + i_2) = \beta i_s \quad$ ...(2)

However in Fig. E1.198,

$$V_s = \frac{r_1 r_2}{r_1 + r_2} . i_s + (i_s + i) r_L$$

[applying KVL in outer loop],

or, $\quad V_s = i_s + i_s r_L + \beta i_s r_L \quad$ [using (2)]

$\therefore$ R_{in} (net resistance of the original circuit across *a-d*)

$$= \frac{V_s}{i_s} = (1 + r_L + \beta r_L)\,\Omega$$

$$= (1 + 5 + 2 \times 5) = 16\,\Omega$$

$$\therefore \quad i_s = \frac{V_s}{R_{in}} = \frac{10}{16} = 0.625 \text{ A}$$

Then from (1),

$$V_L = 10 - i_s = 10 - 0.625 = 9.375 \text{ V.}$$

Then

$$\frac{V_L}{V_s} = \frac{9.375}{10} = \mathbf{0.9375.}$$

EXAMPLE 1.173 *In the network shown in Fig. E1.199, find* V_{out} *provided the given values of the conductances are marked in the figure.*

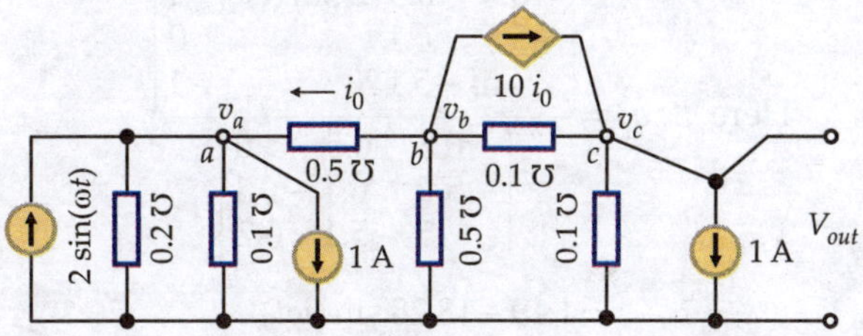

Fig. E1.199

SOLUTION. $i_0 = \frac{v_b - v_a}{1/0.5} = 0.5\, v_b - 0.5\, v_a$

[$\because$ "*g*", the conductance between the nodes, having nodal voltages v_a and v_b, is 0.5 mho]

Using nodal analysis at *node a,*

$$v_a\,[0.2 + 0.1 + 0.5] - v_b\,(0.5) = 2 \sin(\omega t) - 1 \quad \text{...(1)}$$

Nodal analysis at *node b* gives

$$-0.5\, v_a + v_b\,(0.5 + 0.5 + 0.1) - 0.1\, v_c = -10\, i_0$$

[assuming v_c to be the potential at *node c*]

or, $$-0.5\, v_a + 1.1\, v_b - 0.1\, v_c = -10\, i_0 \quad \text{...(2)}$$

Nodal analysis at *node* (*c*) gives

$$-0.1\, v_b + 0.2\, v_c = 10\, i_0 - 1 \quad \text{...(3)}$$

$\therefore$ In matrix form, rearrangement provides

$$\begin{bmatrix} 0.8 & -0.5 & 0 \\ -0.5 & 1.1 & -0.1 \\ 0 & -0.1 & 0.2 \end{bmatrix} \begin{bmatrix} v_a \\ v_b \\ v_c \end{bmatrix} = \begin{bmatrix} 2 \sin(\omega t) - 1 \\ -10\, i_0 \\ 10\, i_0 - 1 \end{bmatrix}$$

But as shown above, $\quad i_0 = 0.5\, v_b - 0.5\, v_a,$

the matrix becomes

$$\begin{bmatrix} 0.8 & -0.5 & 0 \\ -0.5 & 1.1 & -0.1 \\ 0 & -0.1 & 0.2 \end{bmatrix} \begin{bmatrix} v_a \\ v_b \\ v_c \end{bmatrix} = \begin{bmatrix} 2 \sin(\omega t) - 1 \\ -5\, v_b + 5\, v_a \\ 5\, v_b - 5\, v_a - 1 \end{bmatrix}$$

The terms in the forcing function that contain v_a and v_b are moved across the equal sign. They stay in the same row and combined with the appropriate coefficients.

$$\begin{bmatrix} 0.8 & -0.5 & 0 \\ -0.5 & 1.1 & -0.1 \\ 0 & -0.1 & 0.2 \end{bmatrix} \begin{bmatrix} v_a \\ v_b \\ v_c \end{bmatrix} = \begin{bmatrix} 2 \sin(\omega t) - 1 \\ 0 \\ -1 \end{bmatrix}$$

CHAPTER 1

Here $v_c = \dfrac{\begin{vmatrix} 0.8 & -0.5 & 2\sin(\omega t)-1 \\ -5.5 & 6.1 & 0 \\ 5 & -5.1 & -1 \end{vmatrix}}{\begin{vmatrix} 0.8 & -0.5 & 0 \\ -5.5 & 6.1 & -0.1 \\ 5 & -5.1 & 0.2 \end{vmatrix}}$

$= 1.19 - 18.28 \sin(\omega t)$

By inspection, it is evident that

$v_c \equiv v_{out}$ and hence

$v_{out} = \mathbf{1.19 - 18.28 \sin (\omega t)}$.

Example 1.174 *In the circuit of Fig. E1.200, find v_0.*

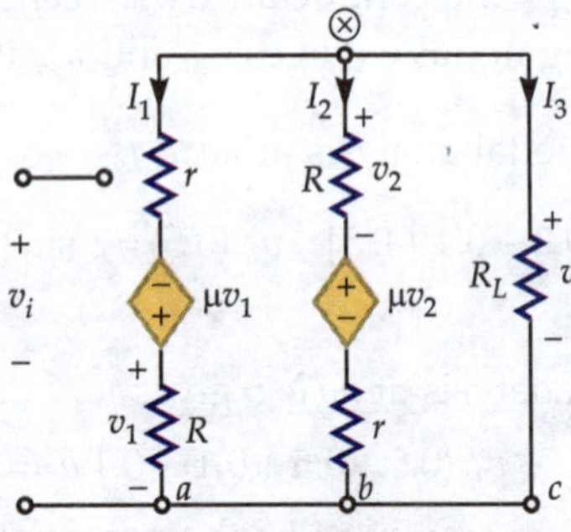

Fig. E1.200

Solution. Nodal analysis at *node* (*x*) gives

$$\frac{v_0 + \mu v_1}{r+R} + \frac{v_0 - \mu v_2}{R+r} + \frac{v_0}{R_L} = 0 \qquad ...(1)$$

$$\left[I_1 = \frac{v_0 - (-\mu v_1)}{r+R};\ I_2 = \frac{v_0 - \mu v_2}{R+r};\ I_3 = \frac{v_0}{R_L} \text{ and } I_1 + I_2 + I_3 = 0 \text{ at node } (x) \right]$$

Again, drop in R in branch x-a is $\left(\dfrac{v_0 + \mu v_1}{R+r}\right) R$ since the current I_1 is $\dfrac{v_0 + \mu v_1}{r+R}$ and flowing through branch x-a.

Then, by KVL, $v_1 = v_i - \left(\dfrac{v_0 + \mu v_1}{R+r}\right) R$

or, $$v_1 = v_i - \frac{v_0 R}{R+r} - \frac{\mu v_1 R}{R+r}$$

or, $$v_1 \left(1 + \frac{\mu R}{R+r}\right) = \frac{v_i (R+r) - v_0 R}{R+r}$$

or, $$v_1 \left(\frac{R+r+\mu R}{R+r}\right) = \frac{v_i (R+r) - v_0 R}{R+r}$$

or, $$v_1 = \frac{v_i (R+r) - v_0 R}{r + R(1+\mu)} \qquad ...(2)$$

Again, the drop in R of branch x-b is $I_2 R$

i.e., drop in R is $\dfrac{v_0 - \mu v_2}{R+r} . R.$

Application of KVL yields

$$v_2 = \frac{v_0 - \mu v_2}{R+r} . R$$

or, $$\frac{v_2}{R} = \frac{v_0}{R+r} - \mu \frac{v_2}{R+r}$$

or, $$v_2 \left(\frac{1}{R} + \frac{\mu}{R+r}\right) = \frac{v_0}{R+r}$$

or, $$v_2 \left(\frac{R+r+\mu R}{R(R+r)}\right) = \frac{v_0}{R+r}$$

or, $$v_2 \left[\frac{r + R(1+\mu)}{R(r+R)}\right] = \frac{v_0}{R+r}$$

or, $$v_2 \left[\frac{r + R(1+\mu)}{R(r+R)}\right] = \frac{v_0}{R+r}$$

or, $$v_2 = \frac{v_0 R}{r + R(1+\mu)} \qquad ...(3)$$

Substitution of (2) and (3) in (1) yields

$$\frac{v_0 + \mu . \dfrac{v_i (R+r) - v_0 R}{r + R(1+\mu)}}{r+R} + \frac{v_0 - \mu . \dfrac{v_0 R}{r + R(1+\mu)}}{R+r} + \frac{v_0}{R_L} = 0$$

or, $$v_0 + \mu \frac{v_i (R+r) - v_0 R}{r + R(1+\mu)} + v_0 - \mu \frac{v_0 R}{r + R(1+\mu)} + \frac{v_0 (R+r)}{R_L} = 0$$

or, $$2v_0 + \frac{\mu v_i (R+r)}{r + R(1+\mu)} - \frac{v_0 R \mu}{r + R(1+\mu)} - \frac{\mu v_0 R}{r + R(1+\mu)} + \frac{v_0 (R+r)}{R_L} = 0$$

or, $$2v_0 - \frac{2 v_0 R \mu}{r + R(1+\mu)} + \frac{\mu v_i (R+r)}{r + R(1+\mu)} + \frac{v_0 (R+r)}{R_L} = 0$$

or, $$v_0 \left[2 - \frac{2\mu R}{r + R(1+\mu)} + \frac{(R+r)}{R_L}\right] + \frac{\mu v_i (R+r)}{r + R(1+\mu)} = 0$$

or, $$v_0 \left[\frac{2 R_L \{r + R(1+\mu)\} - 2\mu R + (R+r)}{\{r + R(1+\mu)\} R_L}\right] = -\frac{\mu v_i (R+r)}{r + R(1+\mu)}$$

$$\therefore \quad \mathbf{v_0 = -\frac{\mu v_i (R+r) R_L}{2R_L \{r + R(1+\mu)\} - 2\mu R + (R+r)}}.$$

EXERCISES

1. A 2 V battery supplies current of 1 A to a circuit having a load resistance R only. Determine the value of R and obtain the amount of power loss across R. Also find the energy consumed in the resistor in 10 secs.

$$\left[\textbf{Hint. } R = \frac{V}{I}\,\Omega\,;\; P_{loss} = I^2 R \left(= \frac{V^2}{R}\right) \text{ watts}\,;\; W_{loss} = P.t \text{ joule}\right]$$

2. In an inductor of 50 mH, the induced voltage is 10 volts when a varying current is flown through it. Determine the value of the rate of change of current and obtain the magnitude of energy stored after 2 secs.

$$\left[\textbf{Hint. } \text{Obtain } \frac{di}{dt} \text{ form the formulae } v = L\frac{di}{dt}\,.\; W_{stored} = \frac{1}{2}Li^2,\ i \text{ being } \left(\frac{di}{dt}\right) \text{ times the time of charging}\right]$$

3. A 100 µF capacitor is charged to have 50 mJ of energy by a constant charging current of 0.5 A. Find the value of the voltage across the capacitor and determine the time to charge the capacitor upto this level by the charging current.

$$\left[\textbf{Hint. } V = \sqrt{\frac{2W}{C}} \text{ volts; } Q = \sqrt{2\,CW} \text{ coulomb and } t = \frac{Q}{I} \text{ sec.}\right]$$

4. Find the equivalent resistance of the circuit between a-b as shown in Fig. P1.1(a) and P1.1(b).

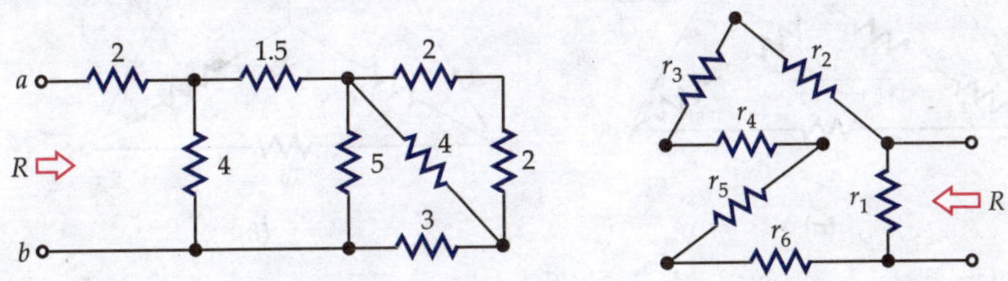

Fig. P1.1 (a) (b)

[**Hints.** In Fig. P1.1 (a), $R = [\{(2 + 2) \,||\, 4) + 3\} \,||\, 5) + 1.5] \,||\, 4]$

and this combination is in series with 2 Ω. In Fig. P1.1(b).

$$R = (r_1) \,||\, (r_2 + r_3 + r_4 + r_5 + r_6)\,]$$

5. Find the equivalent capacitance of the circuit across $x - y$ shown in Fig. P1.2.

[**Hints.** Equivalent capacitance between $a - b$ is 6 F. This capacitance is in series with 12 F. The equivalent capacitance then becomes $\frac{6 \times 12}{6 + 12}$ F *i.e.*, 4 F.

Hence $C_{xy} = 4 + 10 = 14$ F]

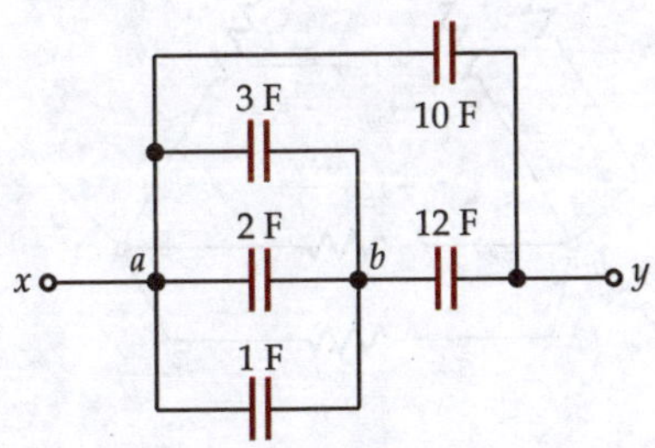

Fig. P1.2

6. Find the equivalent capacitance of the system of capacitances shown in Fig. P1.3.

$$\left[\textbf{Hints. } C_{mn} = 2 + 2 = 4 \text{ F}\,;\right.$$

$$C_{mno} = \left(\frac{4 \times 4}{4 + 4}\right) || \, 2 = 4 \text{ F}$$

$$\left.\therefore \quad C_{a-b} = \frac{4 \times 6}{4 + 6} = 2.4 \text{ F}\right]$$

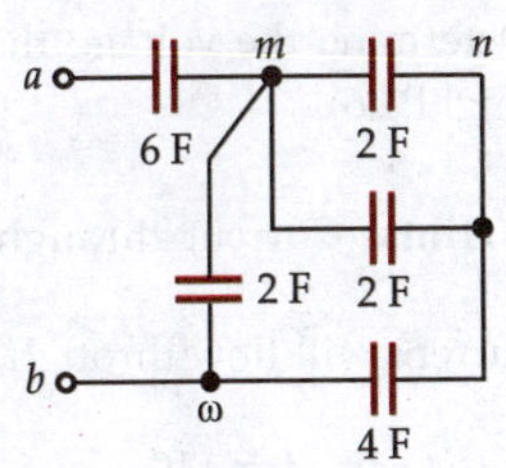

Fig. P1.3

7. Find equivalent pi circuit of the following network (Fig. P1.4) and find R_{a-b} (all the resistances being 1Ω).

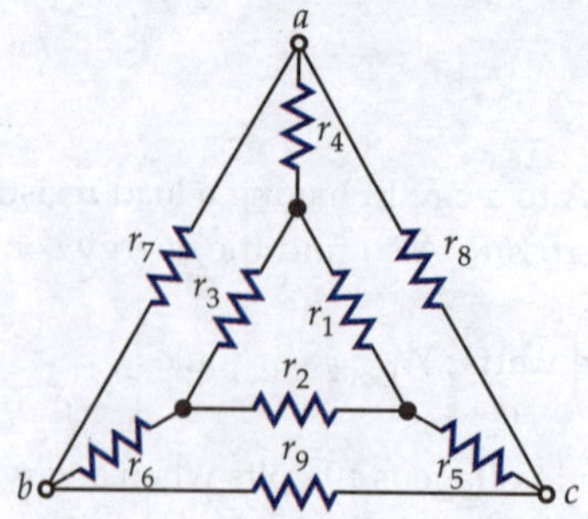

Fig. P1.4

[**Hint.** The resistances in Fig. P1.4 are named first. The internal Δ is to be resolved in Y as shown in Figs. P1.4(*a*) & (*b*).

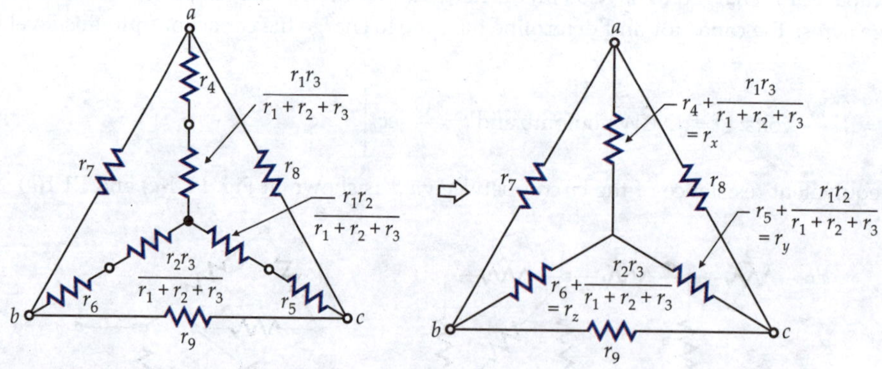

Fig. 1.4 (*a*) (*b*)

Finally, the internal star is resolved into Δ and the network reduction is shown in Fig. P1.5.

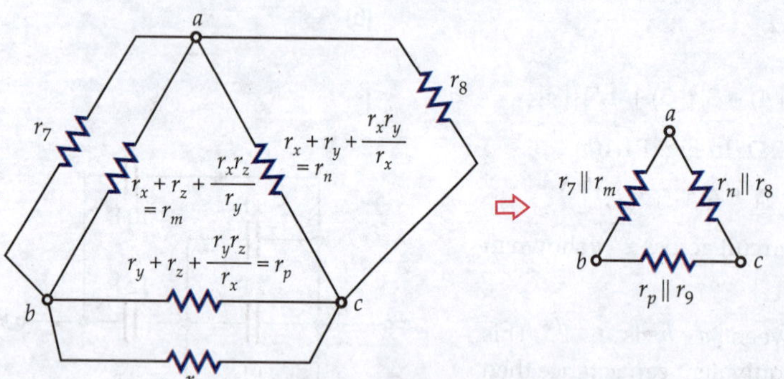

Fig. P1.5

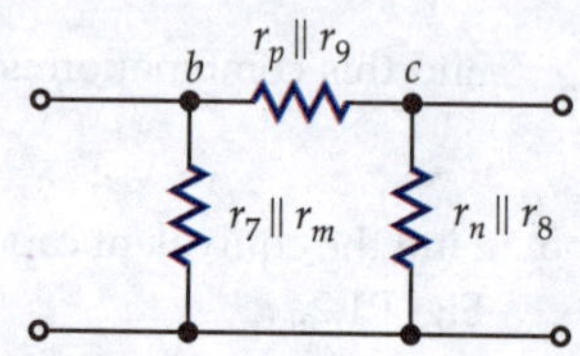

Fig. P1.5 (*a*)

Here, $R_{ab} = r_{ab} \,||\, (r_{ac} + r_{bc})$

Fig. P1.5 can be redrawn in Fig. P1.5(*a*) to show the π circuit.]

8. Determine the voltage that must be applied at *x-y* terminal such that the voltage across 4Ω resistor is 5 V (Fig. P1.6)

[**Hints.** Current through 4Ω resistor $= \dfrac{5\text{ V}}{4\,\Omega}$ A. This current will flow through the circuit as I.

$$R_{x-y} = \left(\frac{5 \times 10}{5 + 10} + 1 + 4\right)\Omega \quad \therefore \quad V = I \,.\, R_{x-y}$$]

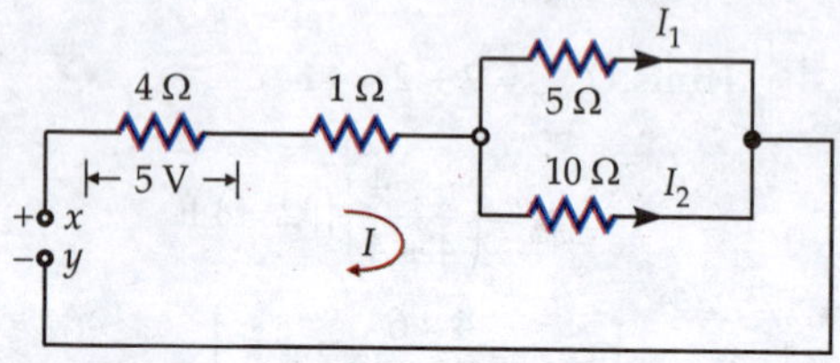

Fig. P1.6

9. Obtain the drop across the 1 ohm resistor in the circuit shown in Fig. P1.7 when the control current i_c in the dependent current source is – 1 A. Assume α = 4 and the magnitude of current in the constant current source as 1 A.

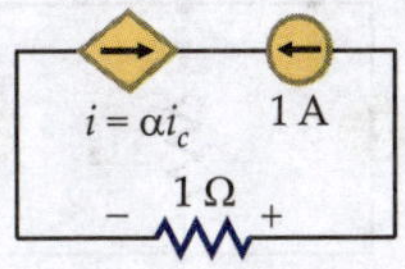

Fig. P1.7

[**Hints.** Assuming drop across 1Ω resistor as V_R, V_R = (drop in 1Ω resistor due to i – drop in 1Ω resistor due to 1 A.)

$$= \alpha\, i_C \times 1 - 1 \times 1 = 4(-1) - 1 = -5\text{ V}$$

i.e., the actual +ve polarity of the drop is opposite to that shown in Fig. P1.6]

10. What is the power loss in 5 Ω resistor of Fig. P1.8 ?

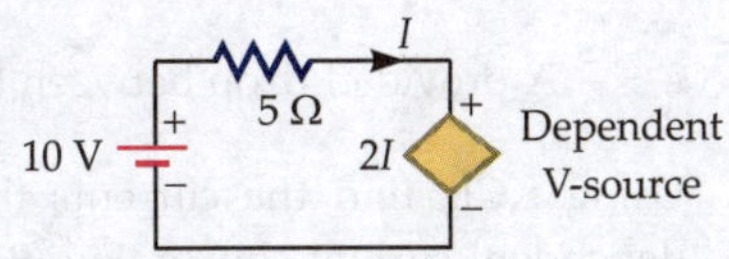

Fig. P1.8

[**Hint.** Using KVL,

$$10 = 5\,I + 2\,I \qquad \therefore \qquad I = 1.43\text{ A}$$

$$\therefore \qquad P_{5\,\Omega} = (1.43)^2 \times 5 = 10.23\text{ W}.$$

Also $P_{5\,\Omega}$ = Power delivered by 10 V source minus power absorbed by 2 I voltage source

$$= 10 \times 1.43 - 2 \times I \times 1.43 = 10.22\text{ W}]$$

11. Find equivalent capacitance of the combination shown in Fig. P1.9 and Fig. P1.10.

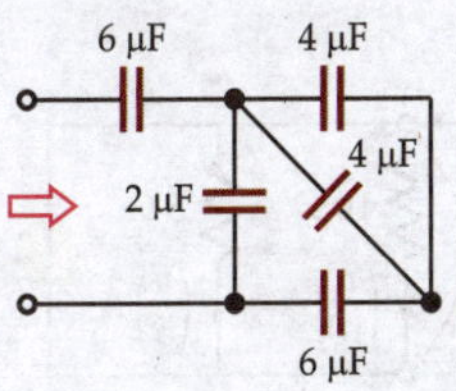

Fig. P1.9

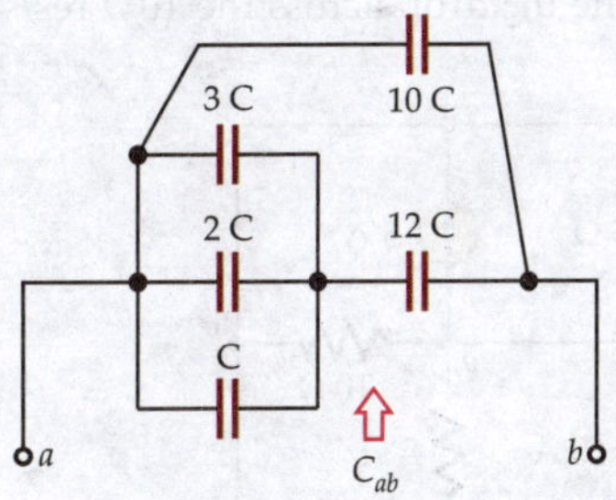

Fig. P1.10

[**Hint.** (Fig. P1.9), $C = \dfrac{\left\{\left(\dfrac{(4+4)\times 6}{8+6}\right) + 2\right\} \times 6}{\left(\dfrac{(4+4)\,6}{8+6}\right) + 2 + 6} = 2.85\ \mu\text{F}$. In Fig. P1.10, $C_{ab} = 14\,C$]

12. Using KCL, obtain the values of unknown currents in Fig. P1.11.

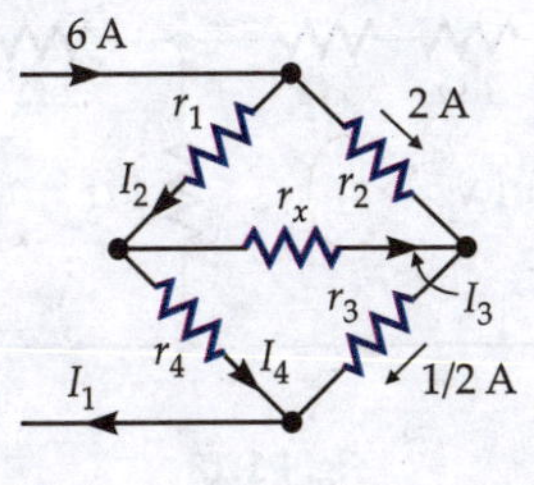

Fig. P1.11

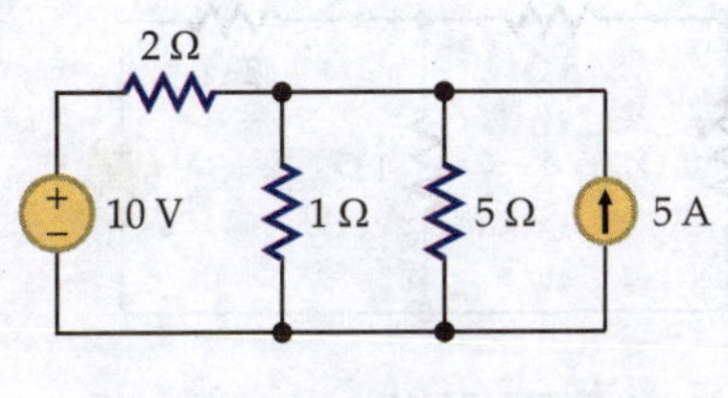

Fig. P1.12

[**Hint.** Solve in the same way as done in Example 1.39]

13. Using KCL, find the currents through 1 Ω and 5 Ω resistors in Fig. P1.12.

[**Hint.** First convert the voltage source to 5 A constant current source in parallel to a 2 Ω resistor and then refer Example 1.40]

14. Obtain i_x, i_y and the numerical value of the current dependent current source (Fig. P1.13)

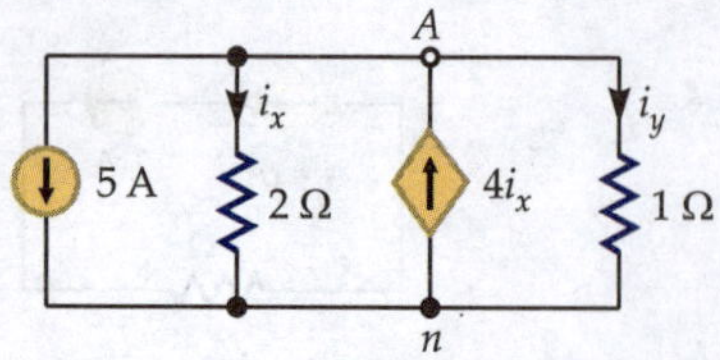

Fig. P1.13

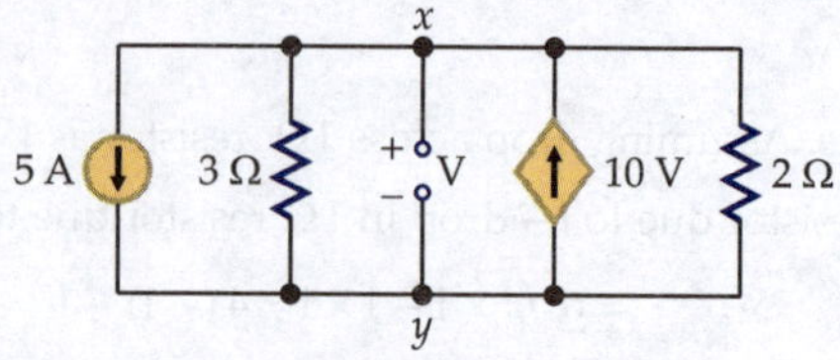

Fig. P1.14

[**Hint.** Solve as shown in Example 1.41 but here at terminal "A", $i_x + i_y + 5 = 4\,i_x$ and obviously $i_x = \frac{v}{2}$ A and $i_y = \frac{v}{1}$ A provided drop between terminals "A" and "n" is assumed to be v with terminal "A" as +ve.]

15. Using KCL, find the currents through the resistors 3 Ω and 2 Ω and the numerical value of the voltage dependent current source (Fig. P1.14).

[**Hint.** Assuming flow of currents through 3 Ω and 2 Ω resistors to be downward and assuming them to be i_3 and i_2 respectively, $i_3 + i_2 + 5 = 10$ V (applying KCL at *node x*). However with $i_3 = \frac{V}{3}$ and $i_2 = \frac{V}{2}$, V can be obtained which will give the values of i_3 and i_2 as well as the numerical value of the voltage dependent current source.]

16. Determine the drop across the 10 Ω resistor in Fig. P1.15 by KCL.

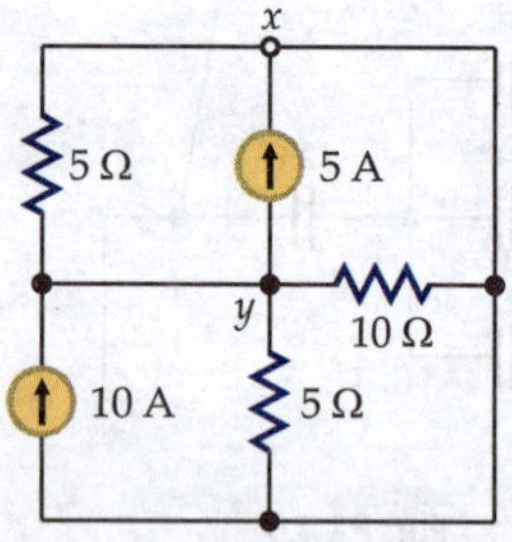

Fig. P1.15

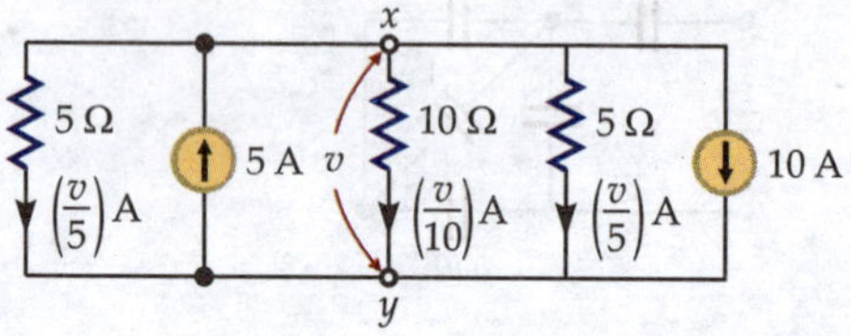

Fig. P1.16

[**Hint.** The circuit is redrawn as shown in Fig. P1.16. Here by KCL, $\frac{v}{5} + \frac{v}{10} + \frac{v}{5} + 10 = 5$; v can be obtained from the above equation and then the current $\left(\frac{v}{10}\right)$ through 10 Ω resistor can be determined]

17. Find i_1 and i_2 in Fig. P1.17.

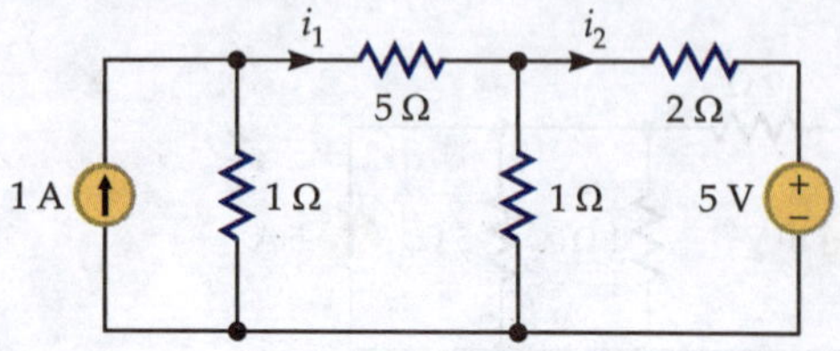

Fig. P1.17

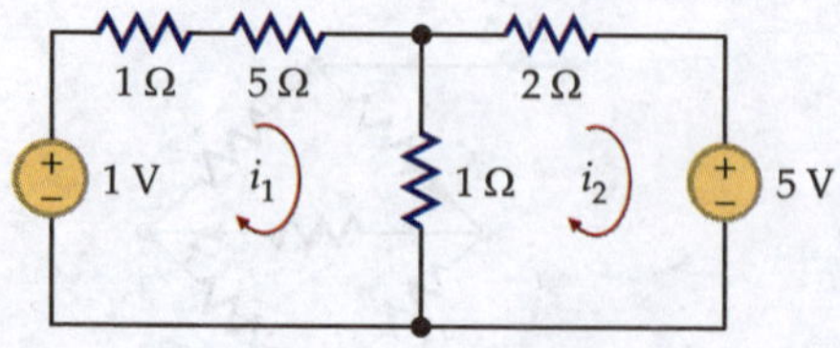

Fig. P1.18

[**Hint.** With reference to the solved example Ex. 1.53, the current source of 1 A is turned to voltage source of 1 V. The circuit is then redrawn as shown in Fig. P1.18.

Applying KVL in the two loops separately,

$$6\,i_1 + (i_1 - i_2) - 1 = 0 \text{ and } 2\,i_2 + 5 + (i_2 - i_1) = 0.$$

Solving these two equations, i_1 and i_2 can be obtained].

18. In Fig. P1.19, find the voltage drop between terminals *x*-*y*.

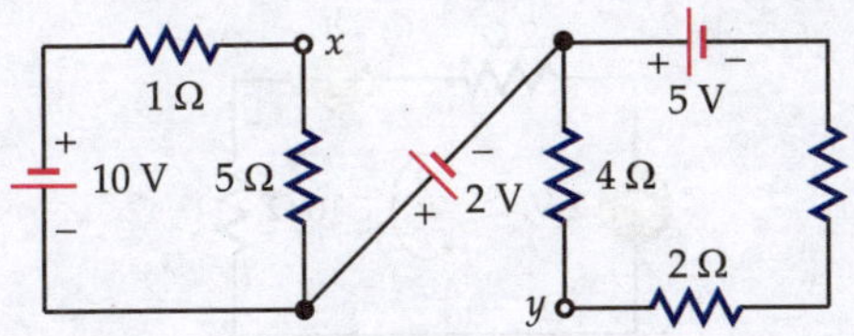

Fig. P1.19

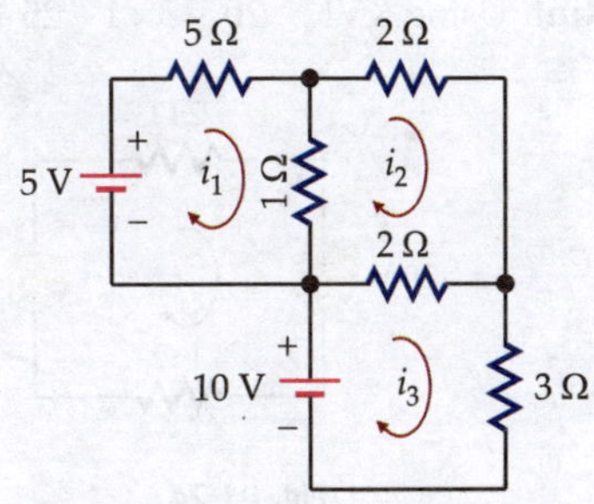

Fig. P1.20

[**Hint.** Do in the same way as done in Example 1.55. However, take care of the respective polarities of the drop across 5 Ω and 4 Ω resistances]

19. In Fig. P1.20, find the power loss in the 3 Ω resistor.

[**Hint.** Assuming the loop currents i_1, i_2 and i_3, KVL yields

$$5\,i_1 + (i_1 - i_2)\,1 = 5$$

$$2\,i_2 + (i_2 - i_1)\,1 + (i_2 - i_3)\,2 = 0$$

$$(i_3 - i_2)\,2 + 3\,i_3 = 10$$

Find i_1, i_2, i_3 by solving these equations while $p_3 = i_3^2 \times 3$ W]

20. In Fig. P1.21, find the current through the 3 Ω resistance using Kirchhoff's laws.

[**Hint.** Refer Example 1.58]

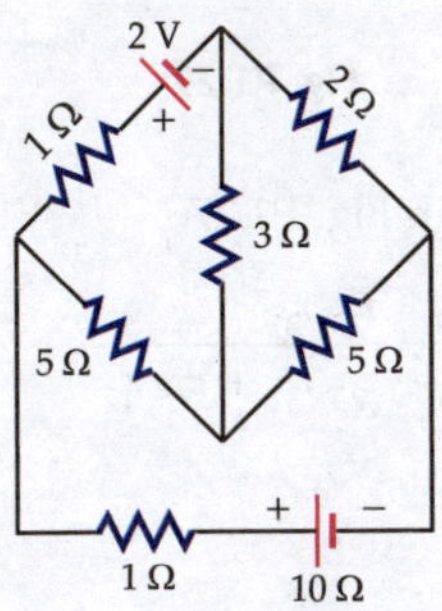

Fig. P1.21

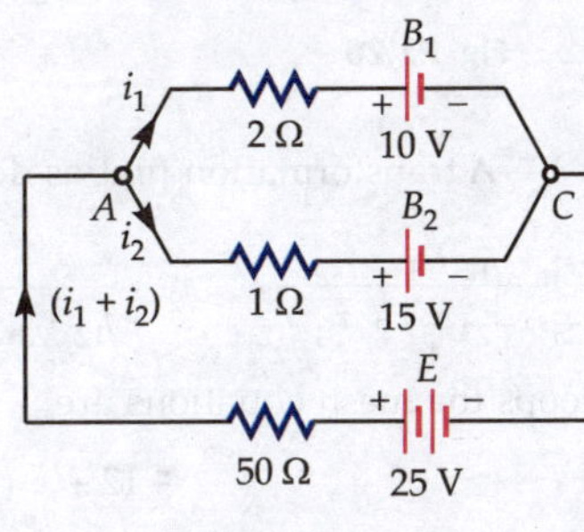

Fig. P1.22

21. Find the current taken from the 25 V battery in Fig. P1.22.

[**Hint.** *In loop* AB_1CEA, $2\,i_1 + 10 - 25 + 50\,(i_1 + i_2) = 0$ and *in loop* $AB_2\;CB_1\;A$, $2\,i_1 + 10 - 15 - i_2 = 0$. Solving these two equations, i_1 and i_2 can be obtained and the net current from the 25 V battery is given by $(i_1 + i_2)$; note the direction of i_2 finally and check KCL at *node* A.]

22. Find the drop across the 5 Ω resistor in Fig. P1.23 if the value of *I* in the dependent source is (*a*) 2A, (*b*) – 2 A.

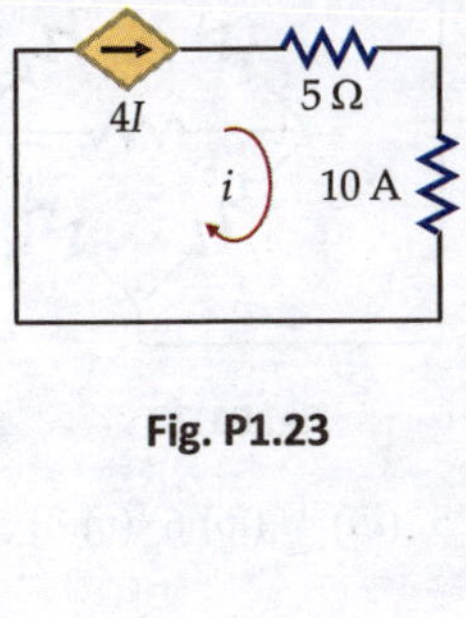

Fig. P1.23

[**Hint.** Ref. Example 1.61]

23. Find the power loss in the 2 Ω resistance using KVL (Fig. P1.24).
[**Hint.** Using KVL, $20 + i \times 1 - 25 + 2\,i = 0$; then find i and $p_2 = (i^2 \times 2)$ watts]

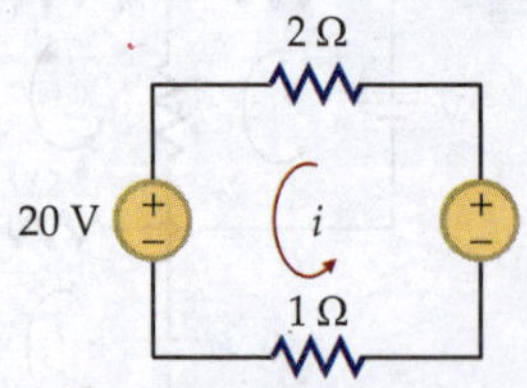

Fig. P1.24

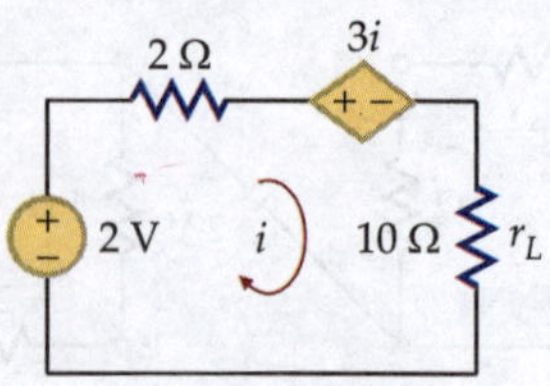

Fig. P1.25

24. Find the voltage drop across r_L. Also obtain the value of the current dependent source of Fig. P1.25.
[**Hint.** Ref. Example 1.67]

25. In Fig. P1.26 find the power loss in the 5 Ω resistor.

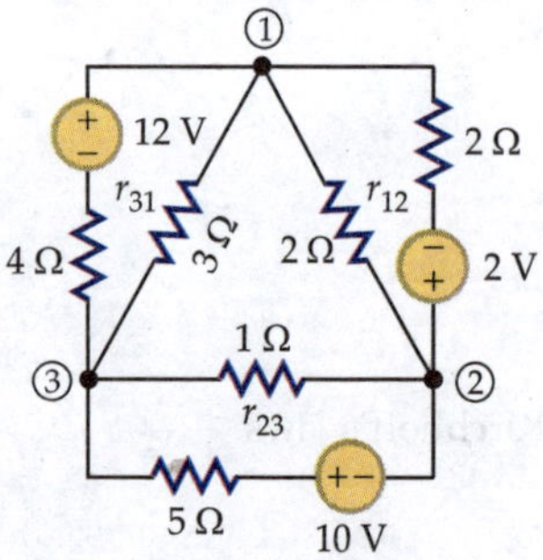

Fig. P1.26

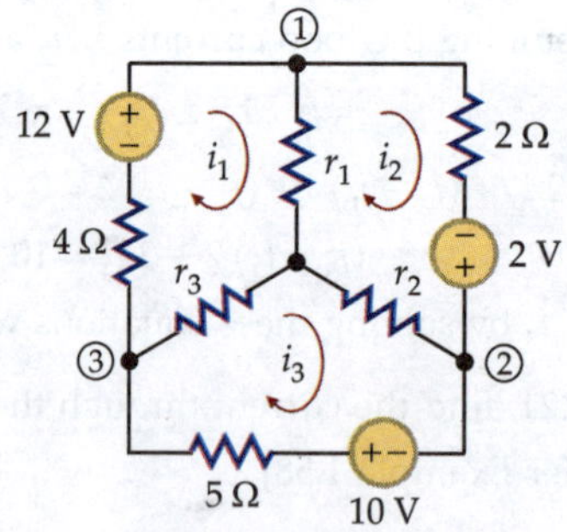

Fig. P1.27

[**Hint.** Go for $Y - \Delta$ transformation first as done for the network shown in Fig. P1.27.

$$r_1 = \frac{r_{12}\,r_{31}}{r_{12}\,r_{23} + r_{23}\,r_{31} + r_{31}\,r_{12}}\;;\quad r_2 = \frac{r_{12}\,r_{23}}{r_{12}\,r_{23} + r_{23}\,r_{31} + r_{31}\,r_{12}}\;;\quad r_3 = \frac{r_{23}\,r_{31}}{r_{12}\,r_{23} + r_{23}\,r_{31} + r_{31}\,r_{12}}$$

In the three loops the mesh equations are

$$-12 + r_1\,(i_1 - i_2) + (i_1 - i_3)\,r_3 = 0 \quad ...(1)$$

$$(i_2 - i_1)\,r_1 + 2\,i_2 - 2 + (i_2 - i_3)\,r_2 = 0 \quad ...(2)$$

$$-10 + 5\,i_3 + (i_3 - i_1)\,r_3 + (i_3 - i_2)\,r_2 = 0 \quad ...(3)$$

Solving these equations, i_3 can be obtained and the power loss p_5 against the 5 Ω resistor is $(i_3^2\,.\,5)$ W.]

26. Find the number of (*i*) circuit elements, (*ii*) nodes (*iii*) junction points (*iv*) branches and (*v*) meshes in the circuit configuration shown in Fig. P1.28.

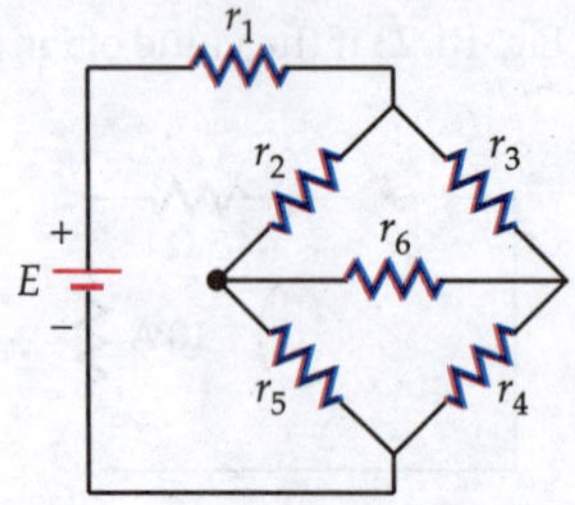

Fig. P1.28

[**Hint.** Ref. Example 1.76. Here, (*i*) 7 (*ii*) 5 (*iii*) 4 (*iv*) 6 (*v*) 3]

27. Solve the network configuration in Fig. P1.29 to find the current through the 3 Ω and 4 Ω resistors.

[**Hint.** Ref. Example 1.78

Here, $i_{4\,\Omega} = \dfrac{10}{4}$ A ; to find $i_{3\,\Omega}$, assume *node x*'' having potential v (+ve).

$$\therefore \quad \frac{v-10}{2} + \frac{v-10}{5} + \frac{v-10}{3} = 0;$$

then obtaining v, current through 3 Ω resistor is $\dfrac{v-10}{3}$ A.]

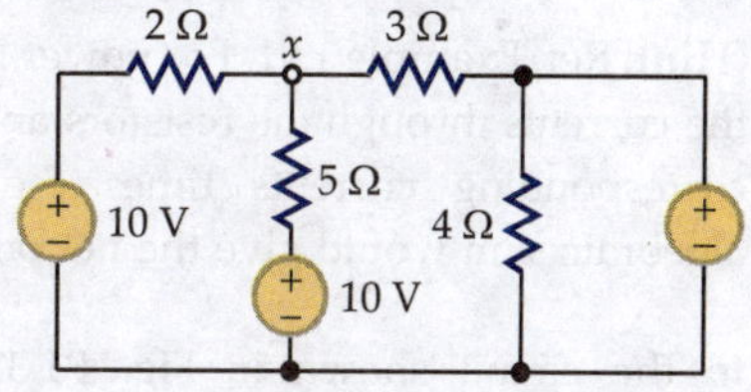

Fig. P1.29

28. Solve the network shown in Fig. P1.30.

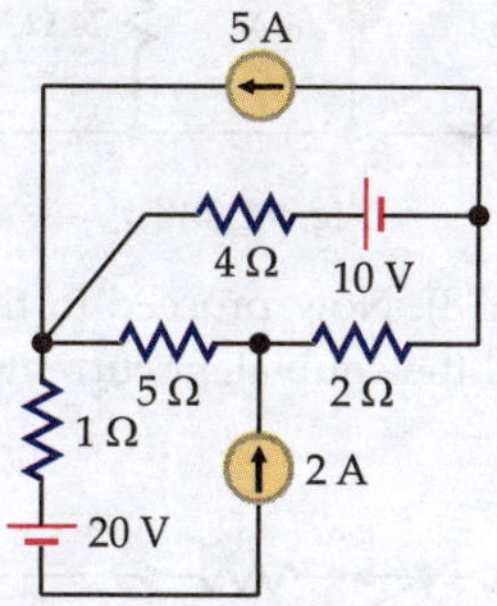

Fig. P1.30

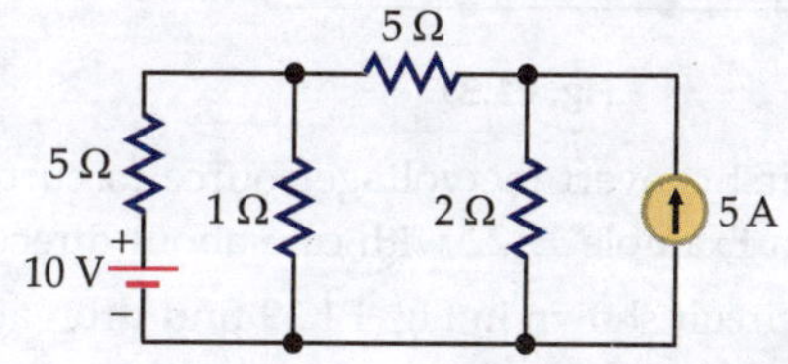

Fig. P1.31

[**Hint.** Do in same way as done in Example 1.80]

29. Find the power loss in 1Ω resistor in the circuit of Fig. P1.31.

[**Hint.** Ref. Example 1.83]

30. Find the potential at *nodes (1)* and *(2)* in Fig. P1.32.

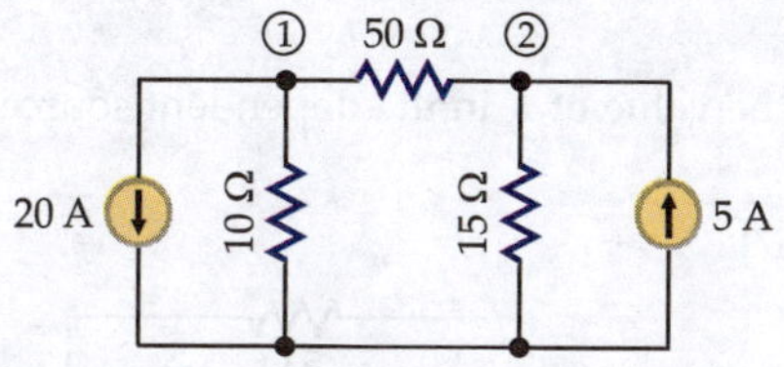

Fig. P1.32

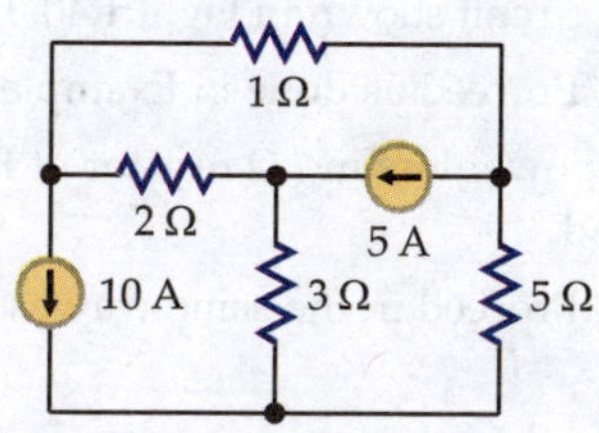

Fig. P1.33

[**Hint.** Do in the same way as done in Example 1.85]

31. In the circuit of Fig. P1.33, find the current in 1Ω resistor.

[**Hint.** Solve in the same way as shown in Example 1.86]

32. Find the value of R in Fig. P1.34 when the power supplied by both the sources is equal to each other.

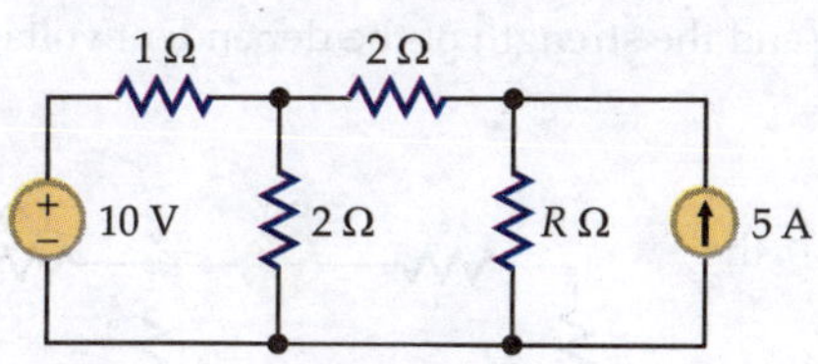

Fig. P1.34

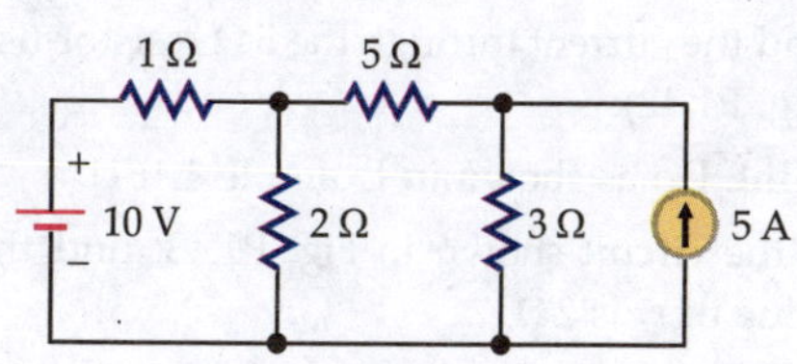

Fig. P1.35

[**Hint.** Do in the same way as shown in Example 1.87]

33. Using mesh method, obtain the current through 1Ω resistor in the network of Fig. P1.35.

[**Hint.** Do in the same way as Example 1.89 with a care in taking the polarities of sources]

CHAPTER 1

34. Using mesh method, obtain the loop currents in the network of Fig. P1.36. What is the total power loss ?

[**Hint.** Ref. Example 1.91. For power loss calculation, find the currents through the resistors and find the square of corresponding currents times the resistances. Their algebraic sum would give the net power loss]

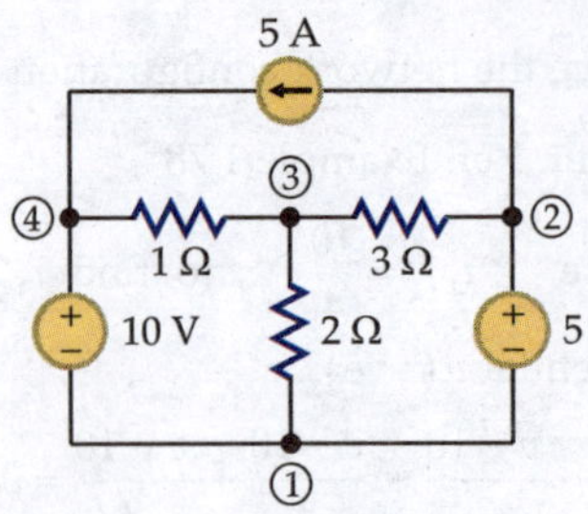

Fig. P1.36

35. In the circuit shown in Fig. P1.37, find the current through r_L.

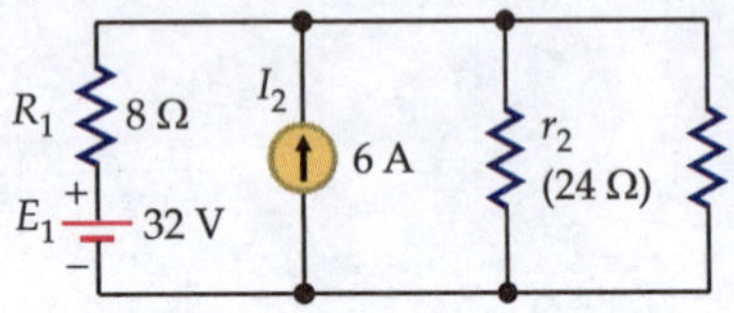

Fig. P1.37

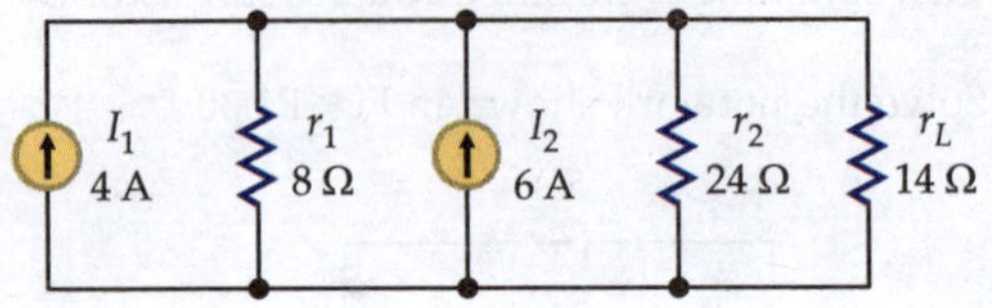

Fig. P1.38

[**Hint.** First convert the voltage source to current source (ref. Fig. P1.38). Now proceed in the same way as shown in Example 1.122 with care about directions of I_1 and I_2 to find the equivalent current source I_s].

36. For the circuit shown in Fig. P1.39 find drop across r_L if $K = 4$.

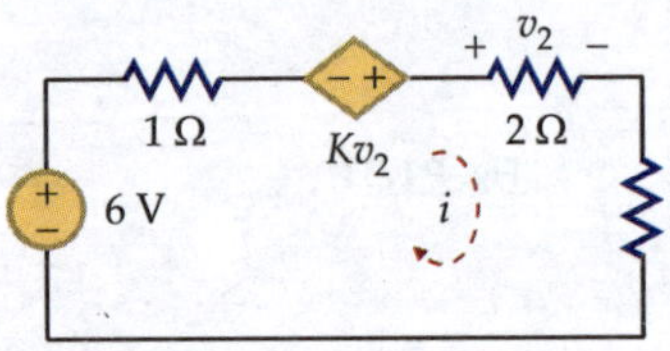

Fig. P1.39

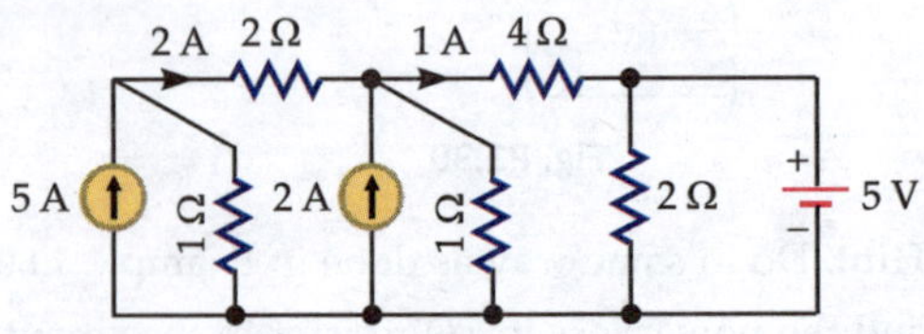

Fig. P1.40

[**Hint.** Ref. Example 1.126, where the loop equation is now $-6 + i - Kv_2 + v_2 + ir_L = 0$ and $v_2 = i \times 2$]

37. In the circuit shown in Fig. P1.40, find the power delivered/absorbed by each of the energy sources.

[**Hint.** Proceed as done in Example 1.133]

38. If the power loss in 1 Ω resistor of Fig. P1.41 is 25 W, find the value of K in the dependent source using nodal method.

[**Hint.** Proceed in the same way as shown in Example 1.157]

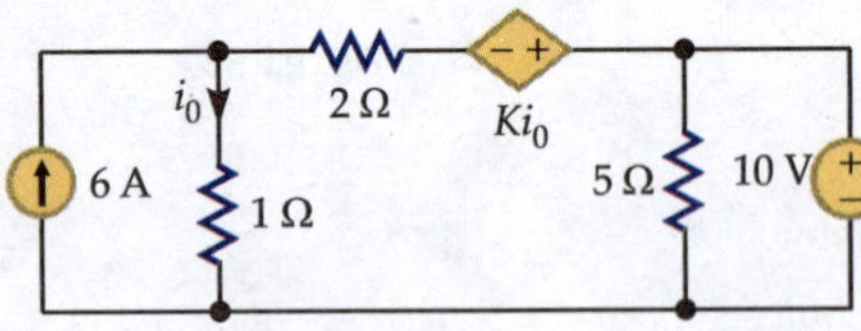

Fig. P1.41

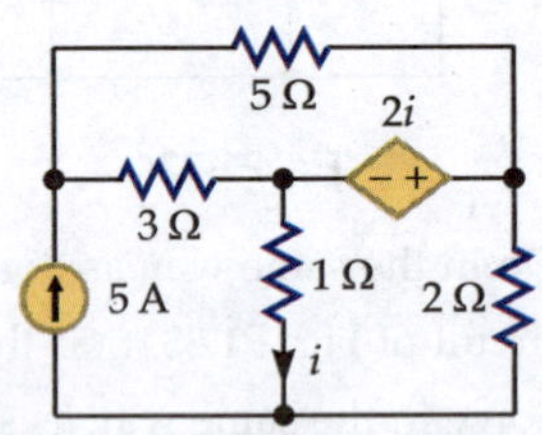

Fig. P1.42

39. Find the current through the 5 Ω resistor using mesh method and the strength of the dependent voltage source (Fig. P1.42).

[**Hint.** Do as shown in Example 1.161]

40. In the circuit shown in Fig. P1.43, find the drop across r_L if the value of r_L is 2 Ω.

[**Hint.** Apply mesh equations in both the loops assuming clockwise loop currents as i_1 and i_2 as shown by dotted in the figure.

$$9\,i_1 - 4\,i_2 = 2\cos\omega t + 6 - 5 = 2\cos\omega t + 1 \text{ and } -4\,i_1 + 8\,i_2 = 5$$

Solving, $i_2 = 0.14\cos\omega t + 0.875$ and drop across r_L is $(i_2 \times r_L)$ V]

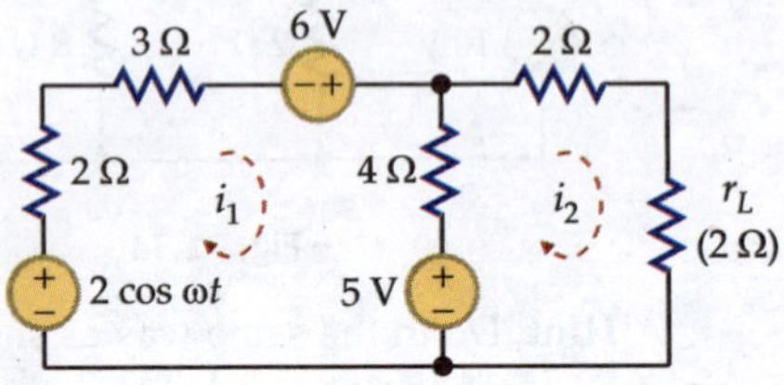

Fig. P1.43

CHAPTER

2

Sinusoidal Steady State Analysis

2.1 SOURCES WITH PERIODIC WAVEFORMS

The pictorial representation of different types of periodic waveforms have been shown in Fig. 2.1. These waveforms can be represented by

$$f(t) = f(t + nT)$$

where n is an integer and T is the time period.

Out of these periodic functions, the sinusoidal function being the most common and being used extensively, we will discuss here the different representative values and expansions of the sinusoidal functions only.

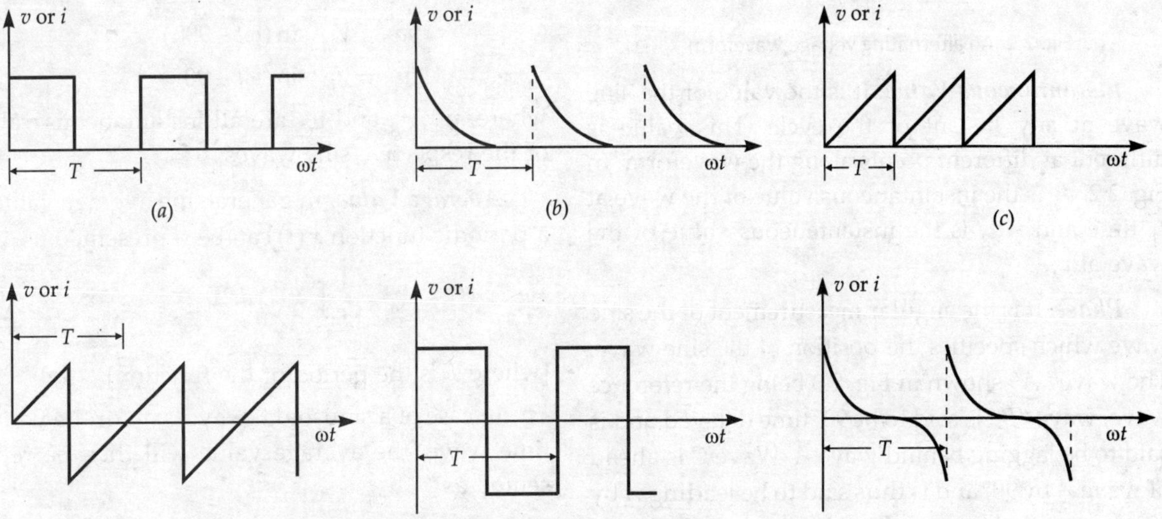

Fig. 2.1 Different periodic functions (*a-f*)

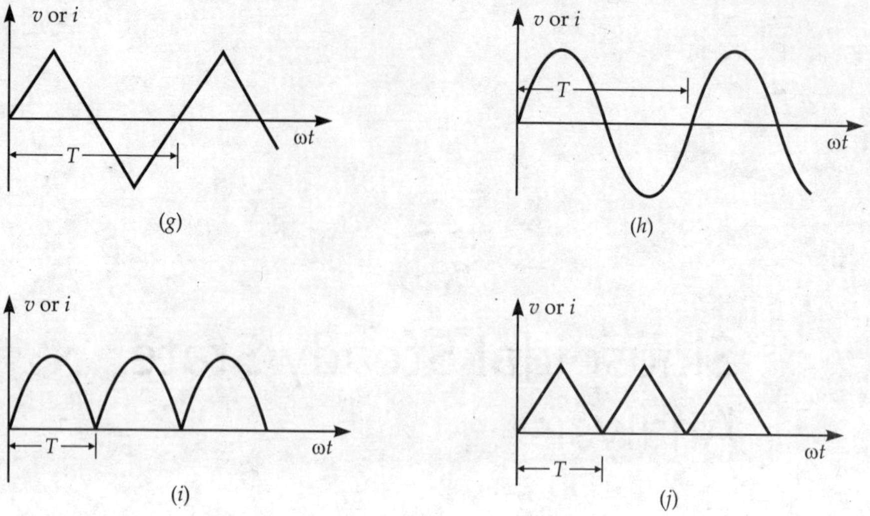

Fig. 2.1 Different periodic functions (*g-h*)

Sinusoidal periodic fraction (Fig. 2.1*h*) being an alternating quantity, it is characterised by the following values :

Peak Value (Amplitude). It is the maximum value of the wave during either positive or negative half cycle. In Fig. 2.2, V_m is the peak value of sinusoidal voltage wave.

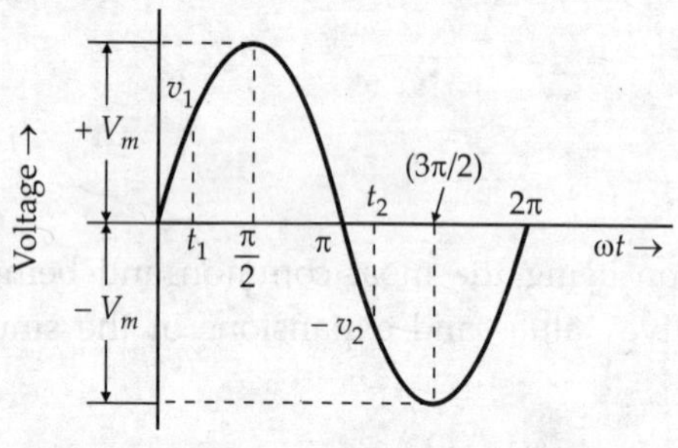

Fig. 2.2 An alternating voltage waveform

Instantaneous Value. It is the value of the sine wave at any instant of the cycle. This value is different at different points along the waveform. In Fig. 2.2, v_1 is the instantaneous value of the wave at t_1 time and $-v_2$ is the instantaneous value of the wave at t_2.

Phase. It is the angular measurement of the sine wave which specifies the position of the sine wave. The wave "*A*" shown in Fig. 2.3 being the reference wave, wave "*B*" is said to be 90° time delayed and is said to be lagging behind wave *A*. Wave *C* is ahead of wave *A* by 90° and is thus said to be leading *A* by 90°. Lag angle is represented by "$-\phi$" while lead is represented by "$+\phi$".

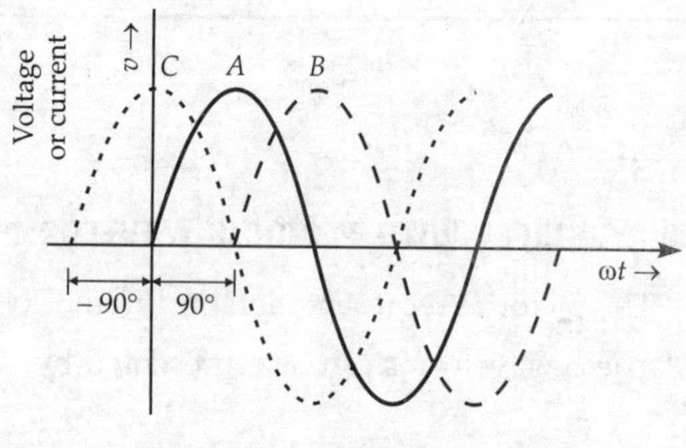

Fig. 2.3 Illustration of "Phase" concept

The reference sine wave may be represented as

$$v_A = V_m \sin \omega t, \text{ (assuming a voltage wave)}$$

the lagging sine wave *B* and leading sine wave *C* can be expressed as

$$v_B = V_m \sin(\omega t - 90°)$$

$$v_C = V_m \sin(\omega t + 90°)$$

where, v_A, v_B and v_C are all instantaneous values of the respective sine waves.

Average Value. In general, the average value of a periodic function $x(t)$ can be represented as

$$x_{av} = \frac{1}{T}\int_0^T x(t)\,dt \qquad \text{...(2.1)}$$

[where *T* is the period of the function]

In case of a sinusoidal wave, say for the voltage time wave, the average value will then be represented as

$$v_{av} = \frac{1}{\pi}\int_0^{\pi} V_m \sin \omega t \, d(\omega t)$$

It may be noted that the average value of the sinusoidal voltage wave is computed for $\frac{1}{2}$ cycle as the average value of the sine wave would be zero for a complete cycle.

i.e.,
$$v_{av} = \frac{1}{\pi}[-V_m \cos \omega t]_o^\pi$$
$$= \frac{2V_m}{\pi} = 0.637\ V_m \qquad ...(2.2)$$

RMS Value (Root Mean Square Value)

As the effective value of a sine wave is zero for the entire cycle hence in order to get the effective value, we compute the capability of the sine wave in terms of its heating power. This is represented by the *root mean square* value (also known as *effective* value) and can be represented by

$$x_{\text{rms}} = \sqrt{\frac{1}{T}\int_0^T x(t)^2\, dt}\,, \qquad ...(2.3)$$

for a periodic function, T being the time period.

Hence for a sinusoidal voltage waves,

$$V_{rms} = \sqrt{\frac{1}{2\pi}\int_0^{2\pi}(V_n \sin \omega t)^2\, d(\omega t)}$$
$$= \sqrt{\frac{1}{2\pi}\int_0^{2\pi} V_m^2\left[\frac{1-\cos 2\omega t}{2}\right] d(\omega t)}$$
$$= \sqrt{\frac{V_m^2}{2}} = \frac{V_m}{\sqrt{2}} = 0.707\ V_m \qquad ...(2.4)$$

Form Factor

Two alternating waves of same peak values and same frequency may look different, *i.e.,* their configurations are different. *Form factor* represents this change in configuration of periodic waves where the frequencies and amplitudes are same. Form Factor* is defined by the ratio of r.m.s. and average values. The Form Factor of a sinusoidal voltage wave is then given by,

$$\text{Form Factor (FF)} = \frac{V_{rms}}{V_{av}} = \frac{0.707\ V_m}{0.637\ V_m} = 1.11$$

In representation of a.c. quantities, it may be noted that usually, the instantaneous values are represented by lower case letters with no suffix while the average values are represented by lower case letters with "*av*" suffix. The r.m.s. values are usually expressed by capital letters with 'rms' suffix or simply by capital letters.

EXAMPLE 2.1 *A voltage wave is represented by*

$v = 200 \sin 314\, t$.

Find (a) Maximum value (b) RMS value (c) Average value (d) Frequency (e) Time period (f) Instantaneous value after 0.05 sec.

SOLUTION. Here (*a*) by inspection, the peak or maximum value is **200 V** (V_m).

(*b*) RMS value is $V = \frac{V_m}{\sqrt{2}} = \mathbf{141.4\ V.}$

(*c*) Average value is
$$v_{av} = \frac{2V_m}{\pi} = 0.637\ V_m = \mathbf{127.4\ V.}$$

(*d*) Frequency $(f) = \frac{\omega}{2\pi} = \frac{314}{2\pi} = \mathbf{50\ Hz}$.

(*e*) Time period $(T) = \frac{1}{f} = \mathbf{0.02\ sec.}$

(*f*) The instantaneous value of the given wave, after 0.05 sec is
$$v = 200 \sin(314 \times 0.05) = \mathbf{0\ V.}$$

EXAMPLE 2.2 *A voltage wave is represented by a cosine function with 2π time period in Fig. E2.1 as $v = V_m \cos\theta$. Find its average value.*

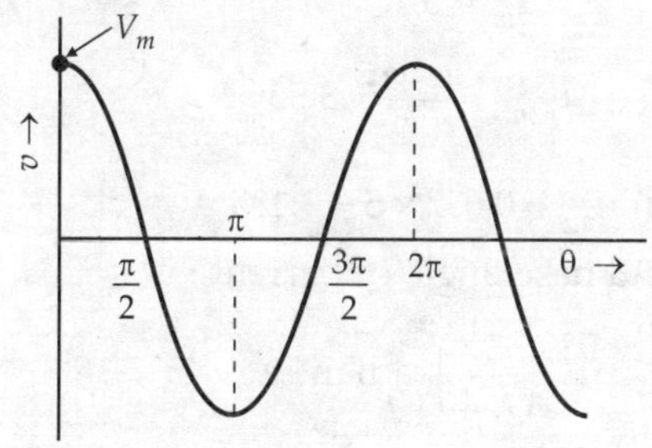

Fig. E.2.1

SOLUTION.
$$v_{av} = \frac{1}{\pi}\int_{\pi/2}^{3\pi/2} V_m \cos\theta\, d\theta = \frac{V_m}{\pi}[-\sin\theta]_{\pi/2}^{3\pi/2}$$
$$= -\frac{V_m}{\pi}[-1-1] = \frac{2V_m}{\pi} = \mathbf{0.637\ V_m}.$$

[A cosine wave is identical to a sine wave except that the function is shifted 90° in time axis].

* In any alternating wave, the frequency f is given by $f = \frac{\omega}{2\pi}$, ω being the angular displacement in per unit time. The time period T is then $T = \frac{1}{f}$. (f is represented in Hz while T is in second).

CHAPTER 2

EXAMPLE 2.3 *A voltage of v volts is applied in a circuit containing only resistance of 10 Ω. If the voltage wave be represented by v = 10 sin (314 t), find the peak current, r.m.s. current and average current.*

SOLUTION

$$v = 10 \sin (314\, t) \text{ and } R = 10\,\Omega$$

$$\therefore \qquad i = \frac{10}{R} \sin (314\, t) = 1.0 \sin (314\, t)$$

Hence, by observation, $I_m = \mathbf{1.0\ A}$ while the r.m.s. and average values are given as

$$I_{r.m.s.} = \frac{I_m}{\sqrt{2}} = \mathbf{0.707\ A}$$

and $\qquad I_{av} = \mathbf{0.637},\ I_m = \mathbf{0.637\ A.}$

EXAMPLE 2.4 *Find the r.m.s. value of power loss in the resistor described in Example 2.3.*

SOLUTION. Power loss in r.m.s. values would be

$$P_{r.m.s.} = P = V_{r.m.s.}\, I_{r.m.s.} = \frac{10}{\sqrt{2}} \times \frac{1}{\sqrt{2}} = \mathbf{5\ W.}$$

EXAMPLE 2.5 *In a circuit, the current wave is represented as* $i = 5\sin\left(314t - \frac{\pi}{4}\right)$.

Find (i) r.m.s. value of current (ii) average value of current (iii) phase angle of current.

SOLUTION. (*i*) By inspection,

$$I_m = 5\text{ A}$$

$$\therefore \qquad I_{r.m.s.} = \frac{5}{\sqrt{2}} = \mathbf{3.536\ A.}$$

(*ii*) $i_{av.} = 0.637 \times 5 = \mathbf{3.185\ A.}$

(*iii*) Phase angle of current *i* is

$\left(-\frac{\pi}{4}\right)$ radian *i.e.*, **– 45°.**

This means that the current lags the source voltage by 45°.

EXAMPLE 2.6 *In a circuit, the voltage and current waves are represented as*

$$v = 10 \sin (\omega t + 45°) \text{ and } i = 10 \sin (\omega t + 60°)$$

Find out their phase relationships.

SOLUTION. By inspection it is revealed that ***i* leads *v* by 15°** as

$$i = 10 \sin [(\omega t + 45°) + 15°]$$

while $\qquad v = 10 \sin (\omega t + 45°).$

EXAMPLE 2.7 *A voltage is represented by v = 10 sin ωt, while the corresponding current is represented by i = 5 sin (ωt – ϕ). What is the phase relationship between the two waves ?*

SOLUTION. As the sign of ϕ, the phase difference between *v* and *i*, is –ve, hence it can be concluded that in this circuit ***i* lags *v*** by an angle of ϕ.

EXAMPLE 2.8 *Obtain the expression of the instantaneous and average powers dissipated in a resistance R connected across a sinusoidal alternating voltage source represented as* $v = V_m \sin \omega t$.

SOLUTION. Average power,

$$p_{av} = \left[\frac{1}{T}\int_0^T i^2\, dt\right] R = I_{r.m.s.}^2\, R$$

$$= \left(\frac{V_m/\sqrt{2}}{R}\right)^2 R = \frac{\mathbf{V_m^2}}{\mathbf{2R}}$$

Instantaneous power*

$$p = v_i = V_m \sin \omega t \cdot \frac{V_m}{R} \sin \omega t$$

$$= \frac{V_m^2}{R} \sin^2 \omega t = \frac{\mathbf{V_m^2}}{\mathbf{2R}} \boldsymbol{(1 - \cos 2\,\omega t)}$$

EXAMPLE 2.9 *The voltage and current in an a.c. circuit are given as v = 100 sin (314 t) ; i = 10 sin (314 t).*

Determine the average power and r.m.s. power.

SOLUTION.

$$V = \frac{V_m}{\sqrt{2}} = 70.7\text{ V};\quad I = \frac{I_m}{\sqrt{2}} = 7.07\text{ A};$$

$$\therefore \qquad P_{r.m.s.} = V \times I \simeq \mathbf{500\ W} = P_{av}$$

Also, $\quad P_{av} = I_{r.m.s.}^2\, R = (7.07)^2 \times 10$

$$\left[\because\ R = \frac{V_m}{I_m} = \frac{100}{10} = 10\,\Omega\right]$$

$$\simeq \mathbf{500\ W.}$$

EXAMPLE 2.10 *A periodic voltage waveform has been shown in Fig. E2.2. Determine :*

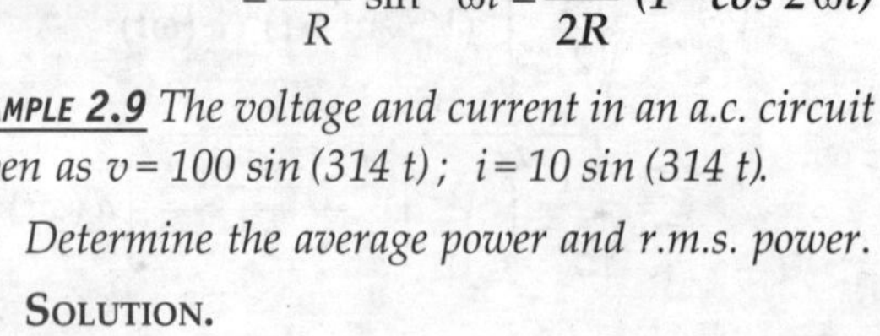

Fig. E2.2

* Normally we express instantaneous value with small letters and r.m.s. value with capital letters.

(i) frequency of the waveform

(ii) wave equation for $0 < t < 100$ m sec.

(iii) r.m.s. value

(iv) average value

(v) form factor

Solution. (*i*) Since it is a periodic but non-alternating waveform hence here the time period $T = 100$ m sec.

$$\therefore \quad f = \frac{1}{T} = \frac{1}{100 \times 10^{-3}} = \mathbf{10\ Hz.}$$

(*ii*) The wave is a linear function at $0 < t < T$.

$$\therefore \quad v = \frac{10}{100 \times 10^{-3}} t = \mathbf{100\ t.}$$

[this is in form of $y = mx$]

(*iii*) r.m.s. value

$$= \sqrt{\frac{1}{T}\int_0^T v^2\, dt}$$

$$= \sqrt{\frac{1}{100 \times 10^{-3}} \int_0^{100 \times 10^{-3}} (100\, t)^2\, dt}$$

$$= \sqrt{\frac{(100)^2}{100 \times 10^{-3}} \left[\frac{t^3}{3}\right]_0^{100 \times 10^{-3}}}$$

$$= 316.22 \times 0.0183 = \mathbf{5.78\ V.}$$

(*iv*) Since the wave is a linear function,

$$v_{av} = \frac{10}{2} = \mathbf{5\ V}$$

(*v*) Form Factor $= \dfrac{\text{rms value}}{\text{av. value}} = \dfrac{5.78}{5} = \mathbf{1.156.}$

Example 2.11 *A non-alternating periodic waveform has been shown in Fig. E2.3. Find its form factor.*

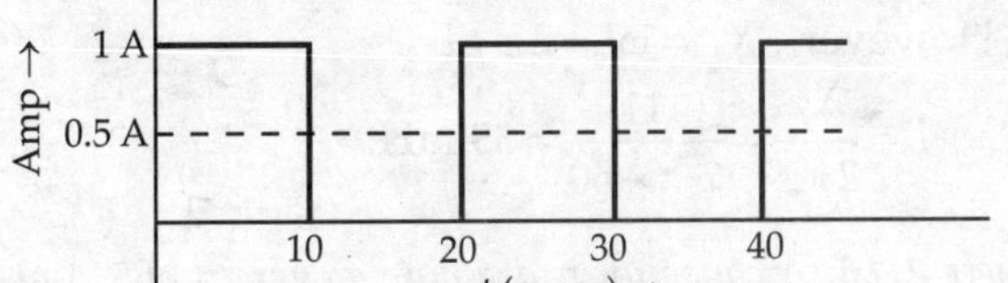

Fig. E2.3

Solution. Here, for the non-alternating periodic waveform, $T = 20$ m sec

$$I = \sqrt{\frac{1}{T}\int i^2\, dt}$$

$$= \sqrt{\frac{1}{20 \times 10^{-3}} \int_0^{10 \times 10^{-3}} 1^2\, dt}$$

[$i = 1$ A for $0 < t < 10$ m sec and $i = 0$ A for $10 < t < 20$ m sec]

$$= 7.07 \sqrt{t \Big|_0^{10 \times 10^{-3}}} = 7.07 \times 0.1 = 0.707 \text{ A.}$$

$$i_{av} = \frac{1}{T}\int_0^{10 \times 10^{-3}} 1\, dt$$

$$= \frac{1}{20 \times 10^{-3}} \times t \Big|_0^{10 \times 10^{-3}} = 50 \times 0.01 = 0.5 \text{ A.}$$

$$\therefore \text{ Form Factor} = \frac{0.707}{0.5} = \mathbf{1.414.}$$

Example 2.12 *Solve Example 2.11 without integration.*

Solution. In this problem, $T = 20$ m sec

$I_{r.m.s.}$ can also be obtained as follows (Ref. Fig. E2.4) :

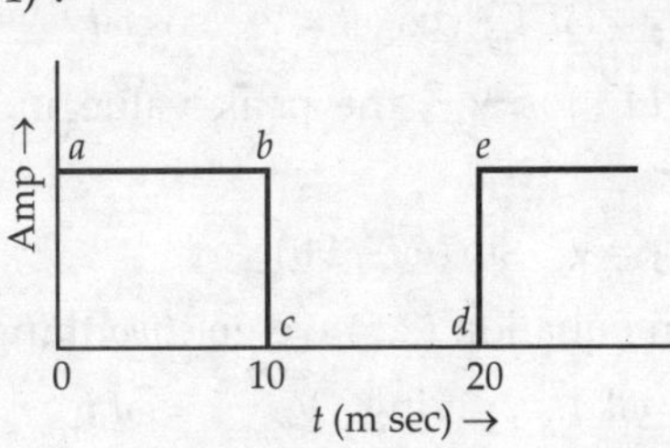

Fig. E2.4

$$I_{r.m.s.} = \sqrt{\frac{(\text{Current during 0 to 10 m sec})^2 \times (oc\ \text{period}) + (\text{Current during 10 to 20 m sec})^2 \times (cd\ \text{period})}{\text{Time period}}}$$

$$= \sqrt{\frac{1^2 \times 10 \text{ m sec} + 0^2 \times 10 \text{ m sec}}{20 \text{ m sec}}} = 0.707 \text{ A}$$

Similarly,

$$I_{av} = \frac{\text{Current during 0 to 10 m sec} \times oc + \text{Current during 10 to 20 m sec} \times cd}{20 \text{ m sec}} = 0.5 \text{ A.}$$

$$\therefore \text{ Form Factor} = (I_{r.m.s.} / I_{av}) = \mathbf{1.414.}$$

EXAMPLE 2.13 *Obtain the average power p in a pure resistive circuit of 10 ohms when the current flowing through it is $i = 10 \cos \omega t$. A.*

SOLUTION.

$$p = i^2 R = 10^2 \cos^2 \omega t \times 10 = 1000 \cos^2 \omega t$$

Hence average power for the period 0 to π,

$$p_{av} = \frac{1}{\pi}\int_0^{\pi} p \, d(\omega t) = \frac{1}{\pi}\int_0^{\pi} 1000 \cos^2 \omega t \, d(\omega t) = \mathbf{500\ W}.$$

2.2 A.C. IN INDUCTANCE AND CAPACITANCE

Let an a.c. source of voltage v volt be applied to a pure inductor of inductance L henry such that the instantaneous current is i amps. (Fig. 2.4).

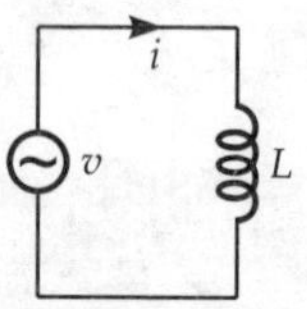

Fig. 2.4 Inductance energized by a.c. source

Obviously

$$i = I_m \sin \omega t.$$

Hence, the induced voltage e is given by

$$e = L\frac{di}{dt}$$

i.e., $$e = L\frac{d}{dt}(I_m \sin \omega t)$$

$$= \omega L I_m \cos \omega t = V_m \cos \omega t$$

When $(\omega L I_m)$ is V_m, the peak value induced voltage.

i.e., $$e = V_m \sin(\omega t + 90) \qquad ...(2.5)$$

Thus from equation (2.5) we get *two* things—

(*i*) $V_m = \omega L I_m$ giving $V_{r.m.s.} = \omega L I_{r.m.s.}$ i.e., $X_L I$ where X_L $(= \omega L)$ is termed as *inductive reactance* and is measured in ohms.

(*ii*) the current through the inductor lags the voltage across the inductor by 90° (Fig. 2.5)

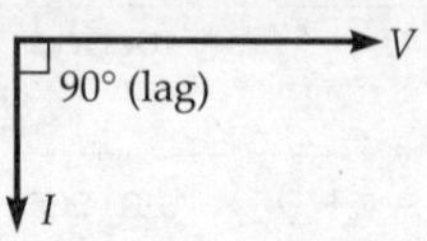

Fig. 2.5 Phasor diagram of pure inductive circuit

In case the inductor is replaced by a pure capacitance (C), the voltage source being represented by $v (= V_m \sin \omega t)$ [Fig. 2.6], the instantaneous current in the capacitor is given by

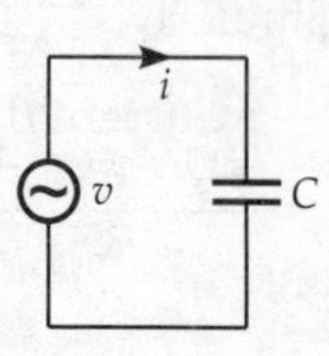

Fig. 2.6 Capacitance fed by a.c. source.

$$i = C\frac{dv}{dt} = C\frac{d}{dt}(V_m \sin \omega t) = \omega C V_m \cos \omega t$$

$$= I_m \cos \omega t = I_m \sin(\omega t + 90°)$$

Here also we observe two other things :

(*i*) $I_m = \omega C V_m$ gives $I_{r.m.s.} = \omega C V_{r.m.s.}$

i.e., $(\omega C) = \frac{I}{V}$;

Thus, $\frac{V}{I} = X_C = \frac{1}{\omega C}$ where X_C can be termed as *capacitive reactance* (in ohms).

(*ii*) The current through the capacitor leads the voltage across it by 90°.

EXAMPLE 2.14 *An a.c. voltage of 220 V is applied to a pure inductance at 50 Hz. If the current is 5 A, find the instantaneous voltage and current.*

SOLUTION.

$$I_m = \sqrt{2}\, I = \sqrt{2} \times 5 = 7.07 \text{ A}$$

$$\omega = 2\pi f = 2\pi \times 50 = 314 \text{ rad/sec.}$$

$$\therefore \quad i = I_m \sin \omega t = 7.07 \sin 314\, t \text{ amps.}$$

[assuming the current to be the reference]

Again $V_m = \sqrt{2}\, V = \sqrt{2} \times 220 = 311$ V.

In inductor, the current lags the voltage by 90°.

$$\therefore \quad v = 311 \sin(314\, t + 90°) \text{ V}$$

[If the voltage is taken as reference,

$$\mathbf{v = 311 \sin 314\, t \text{ V}}$$

and $$\mathbf{i = 7.07 \sin(314\, t - 90°) \text{ amps.}}]$$

EXAMPLE 2.15 *In an a.c. circuit, containing pure inductance, the voltage applied is 110 V, 50 Hz while the current is 10 A. Find the value of inductive reactance and inductance.*

SOLUTION. Here, inductive reactance X_L is given by

$$X_L = \frac{V}{I} = \frac{110}{10} = \mathbf{11\ ohms.}$$

However, $X_L = \omega L = 2\pi f L$

$$\therefore \quad L = \frac{X_L}{2\pi f} = \frac{11}{2\pi \times 50} = \mathbf{35\ mH.}$$

EXAMPLE 2.16 *A capacitor is drawing a current of 5 A at 230 V, 50 Hz. Determine the instantaneous voltage and current.*

SOLUTION. $I_m = \sqrt{2} \times I = \sqrt{2} \times 5 = 7.07$ A

$$\omega = 2\pi \times 50 = 314 \text{ rad/sec.}$$

$\therefore \quad i = 7.07 \sin 314\, t$ amp.

[assuming the current to be the reference phasor]

Again, $V_m = \sqrt{2} \times V = \sqrt{2} \times 230 = 325.22$ V.

$\therefore \quad v = 325.22 \sin (314\, t - 90°)$

since the voltage in the capacitor lags the current in the capacitor by 90°.

[If the voltage is taken to be the reference phasor,

$$v = \mathbf{325.22 \sin 314\, t \ V}$$

and $\quad i = \mathbf{7.07 \sin (314\, t + 90°)\ amps}$]

EXAMPLE 2.17 *Find the capacitance from the data given in Example 2.16.*

SOLUTION. Here,

$$X_C = \frac{V}{I} = \frac{230}{5} = 46\,\Omega$$

But $\quad X_C = \dfrac{1}{\omega C}$

$$\therefore \quad C = \frac{1}{\omega \times X_C} = \frac{1}{314 \times 46} \simeq \mathbf{69.2\,\mu F.}$$

EXAMPLE 2.18 *An a.c. voltage v (= 100 sin 314 t volts) is applied across a 0.5 H inductor. What is the instantaneous current ?*

SOLUTION. $X_L = 2\pi\, fL = 314 \times 0.5 = 157\,\Omega$

Also, $\quad I_m = \dfrac{V_m}{X_L} = \dfrac{100}{157} = 0.637$ A

Since the current in inductor lags the voltage by 90°

$$\therefore \quad i = I_m \sin (\omega t - 90°)$$

$$= \mathbf{0.637 \sin (314\, t - 90°)\ A.}$$

EXAMPLE 2.19 *What is the reactance of a 1 Henry inductor at (i) d.c. and (ii) 50 Hz ?*

SOLUTION. *(i)* At d.c.,

$$X_L = 2\pi f L = 2\pi \times 0 \times 1 = 0\,\Omega$$

(ii) At 50 Hz,

$$X_L = 2\pi f L = 2\pi \times 50 \times 1 = \mathbf{314\,\Omega.}$$

EXAMPLE 2.20 *What is the inductance of a coil having 10 Ω reactance at 50 Hz ?*

SOLUTION. Here,

$$L = \frac{X_L}{2\pi f} = \frac{10}{2\pi \times 50} = \mathbf{31.8\ mH.}$$

EXAMPLE 2.21 *An inductor of 20 mH offers a reactance of 100 Ω. Determine the supply frequency.*

SOLUTION. As $X_L = 2\pi f L$

$$\therefore \quad f = \frac{X_L}{2\pi L} = \frac{100}{2\pi \times 20 \times 10^{-3}}$$

$$= \mathbf{796\ Hz.}$$

EXAMPLE 2.22 *Determine the reactance of a 50 μF capacitor in a d.c. supply and also in an a.c. supply of 100 Hz.*

SOLUTION. In d.c., $f = 0$

$$X_C = \frac{1}{2\pi f C} = \frac{1}{2\pi \times 0 \times 50 \times 10^{-6}}$$

or, $\quad X_C = \infty\,\Omega$

at 100 Hz,

$$X_C = \frac{1}{2\pi \times 100 \times 50 \times 10^{-6}}$$

$$= \mathbf{31.8\,\Omega.}$$

EXAMPLE 2.23 *A capacitor of 50 μF offers a reactance of 50 Ω against an a.c. supply of 100 V. Find the capacitor current and frequency of the supply.*

SOLUTION. $\quad I = \dfrac{V}{X_C} = \dfrac{100}{50} = \mathbf{2\ A}$

as $\quad X_C = \dfrac{1}{2\pi f C}$

$$\therefore \quad f = \frac{1}{2\pi (X_C)\, C} = \mathbf{63.6\ Hz.}$$

EXAMPLE 2.24 *The voltage and current through an a.c. circuit are given by*

$$v = V_m \sin \omega t, \quad i = I_m \cos \omega t$$

What is the phase difference between these two variables ?

SOLUTION. $\quad v = V_m \sin \omega t$

$$i = I_m \cos \omega t = I_m \sin (\omega t + 90)$$

Hence the phase difference between v and i is **90°** and the current is leading the voltage.

EXAMPLE 2.25 *In an inductive circuit the applied voltage is $v = V_m \sin \omega t$. Obtain the expression for instantaneous power.*

SOLUTION. $v = V_m \sin \omega t$

$\therefore \quad i = I_m \sin (\omega t - \phi) \quad$ [where ϕ is assumed to be the angle of lag]

CHAPTER 2

$$\therefore \ p = vi = [V_m \sin \omega t][I_m \sin(\omega t - \phi)]$$

$$= V_m I_m \times \frac{1}{2}[\cos(\omega t - \omega t + \phi) - \cos(\omega t + \omega t - \phi)]$$

$$= \frac{1}{2} V_m I_m [\cos\phi - \cos(2\omega t - \phi)]$$

$$= |\mathbf{V}||\mathbf{I}|\cos\phi - |\mathbf{V}||\mathbf{I}|\cos(2\omega t - \phi)$$

[In this case $\phi = 90°$

$$\therefore \ p = \frac{1}{2} V_m I_m [\cos 90° - \cos(2\omega t - 90°)]$$

$$= -|V||I|\sin 2\omega t \,]$$

EXAMPLE 2.26 *The voltage and current through a circuit element is* $v = 100 \sin(314\,t + 45°)$ *volts and* $i = 10 \sin(314\,t - 45°)$ *amps. Identify the circuit element and find its value.*

SOLUTION. In Fig. E2.5, the phasors v and i are drawn with reference to x axis. The lead and lag angles have been shown by +ve or –ve signs respectively.

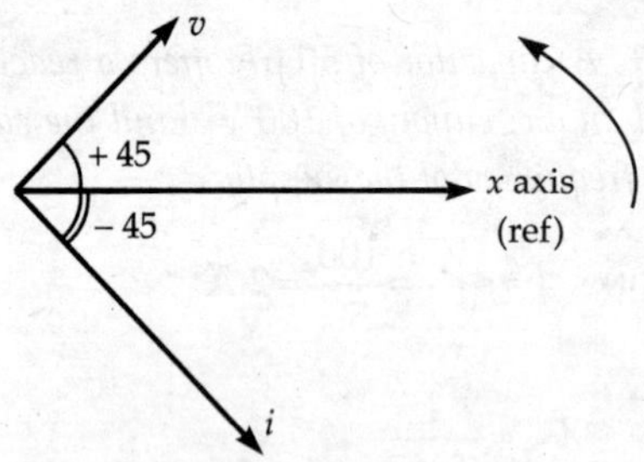

Fig. E2.5

The phase difference between v and i is

$$(45° + 45°) = 90°.$$

However, it is seen that the v leads i (Fig. E2.5). Hence the circuit is an *inductor*.

Here, $X_L = \dfrac{V_m}{I_m}$

$$= \frac{100}{10} = 10\,\Omega = 2\pi f L$$

$$\therefore \quad L = \frac{X_L}{2\pi f} = \frac{10}{2\pi \times 50}\ \text{H}$$

$$\left[\because \omega t = 314\,t \ \therefore \ \omega = 314 \text{ rad/sec} \quad i.e., f = \frac{\omega}{2\pi} = 50 \text{ Hz}\right]$$

Thus $L = \mathbf{31.8\ mH}$.

2.3 INTRODUCTION TO SINUSOIDAL STEADY STATE ANALYSIS OF SERIES AND PARALLEL AC CIRCUITS

This chapter deals with the *sinusoidal steady state analysis* of networks involving *R, L* and *C* in different configurations (*series* and or *parallel*). This chapter also leads to the concept of *complex impedance* and *power factor*.

At first, the analytical concept of series and parallely *a.c.* circuits being introduced, the performance of different combinations of *R, L* and *C* circuits will be analysed.

Series and parallel *a.c.* circuits are extensively used in electrical and electronics engineering and hence their analysis is very important. It may be noticed that all the *a.c.* quantities being vector quantities, they have both *magnitudes* and *directions* (or *angles*). Either *polar* or *rectangular*, both forms of representations are extensively used in analysing *a.c.* circuits.

The common symbols used throughout the chapter are as follows :

R = Pure resistance element (ohm),

L = Pure inductance element (H),

C = Pure capacitance element (F or μF),

Z = Impedance (ohms),

X_L = Inductive reactance (ohms) $= 2\pi f L$,

X_C = Capacitive reactance (ohms) $= \dfrac{1}{2\pi f C}$,

f = Supply frequency (Hz),

ω = Angular frequency (rad./sec),

$\phi°$ or $\theta°$ = angle between voltage and current or reactance and resistance.

note In this chapter as well as in this book, the capital letters like *I, V* etc. represent *r.m.s. quantities,* capital letters with suffix "max" represent maximum values and small alphabets like *v, i* represent *instantaneous* values, unless mentioned otherwise.

In a *series* circuit (Fig. 2.7), the current being same through each of the impedances, the voltage phasors are related to the current by the respective drops across each impedance vectorially added together.

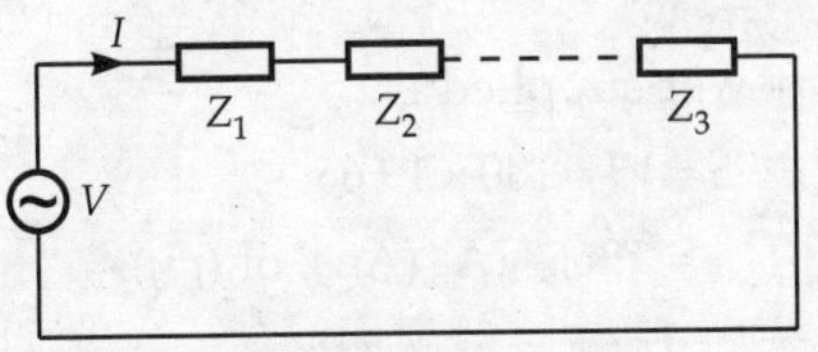

Fig. 2.7 Series a.c. circuit.

i.e., $$V = IZ_1 + IZ_2 + IZ_3 + ... + Z_n = IZ_{eq} \quad ...(2.6)$$

where $$Z_{eq} = \text{equivalent impedance}$$
$$= Z_1 + Z_2 + ... + Z_n \quad ...(2.6(a))$$

On the other hand, in a *parallel* circuit (Fig. 2.8), the voltage drop across each element being same,

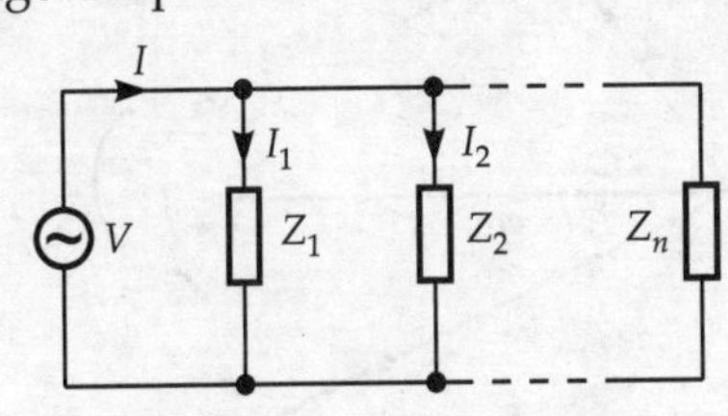

Fig. 2.8 Parallel a.c. circuit.

the currents through each branch are different. The branch currents are to be vectorially added to give the total current.

i.e., $$I_1 = \frac{V}{Z_1} = VY_1$$

$$I_2 = \frac{V}{Z_2} = VY_2 \text{ and so on.}$$

i.e., $$I = I_1 + I_2 + ... + I_n$$

or, $$VY_{eq.} = VY_1 + VY_2 + ... + VY_n + V$$
$$= V(Y_1 + Y_2 + Y_3 + ... + Y_n)$$

i.e., $$Y_{eq} = Y_1 + Y_2 + ... + Y_n \quad ...(2.6(b))$$

2.4 CURRENTS AND VOLTAGE DIVISION IN A.C. CIRCUITS

In an *a.c.* parallel circuit (Fig. 2.9),

$$I_a\, Z_a = I_b\, Z_b$$

i.e., $$\frac{I_a}{I_b} = \frac{Z_b}{Z_a}$$

or $$\frac{I_a + I_b}{I_b} = \frac{Z_b + Z_a}{Z_a}$$

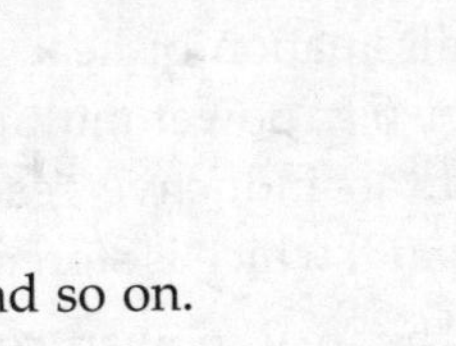

Fig. 2.9

or, $$I_b = \frac{Z_a}{Z_a + Z_b}(I_a + I_b) = I_0\frac{Z_a}{Z_a + Z_b} \quad ...(2.7)$$

Similarly,

$$I_a = I_0\frac{Z_b}{Z_a + Z_b} \quad ...(2.7(a))$$

Again, in *a.c.* series circuit (Fig. 2.10),

$$I_0 = \frac{V_0}{Z_a + Z_b}$$

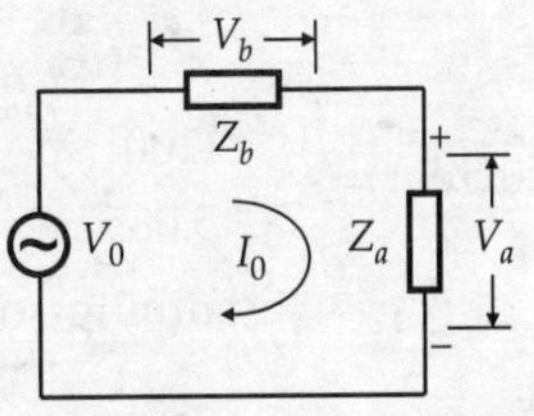

Fig. 2.10

But $$V_a = I_0\, Z_a = \frac{Z_a}{Z_a + Z_b}V_0 \quad ...(2.8)$$

Similarly,

$$V_b = I_0\, Z_b = \frac{Z_b}{Z_a + Z_a}V_0 \quad ...(2.8(a))$$

[Also, for current division,

$$I_a = \frac{Y_a}{Y_a + Y_b}I_0\,;\; I_b = \frac{Y_b}{Y_a + Y_b}I_0$$

and for voltage division

$$V_a = \frac{Y_b}{Y_a + Y_b}V_0 \text{ and } V_b = \frac{Y_a}{Y_a + Y_b}\cdot V_0\Bigg].$$

EXAMPLE 2.27 *A 4 ohm resistor is connected to a 10 mH inductor across a 100 V, 50 Hz voltage source. Find*

(*i*) *Impedance of the circuit.*
(*ii*) *Input current.*
(*iii*) *Drop across the resistor and inductance.*
(*iv*) *Power factor of the circuit.*
(*v*) *Real power consumed in the circuit.*
(*vi*) *Total power supplied.*

SOLUTION. In this circuit (Fig. E2.6),

$$X_L = 2\,\pi\, f\, L$$
$$= 2\,\pi \times 50 \times 10 \times 10^{-3} = 3.14\,\Omega,$$

and it is given that $R = 4\,\Omega$

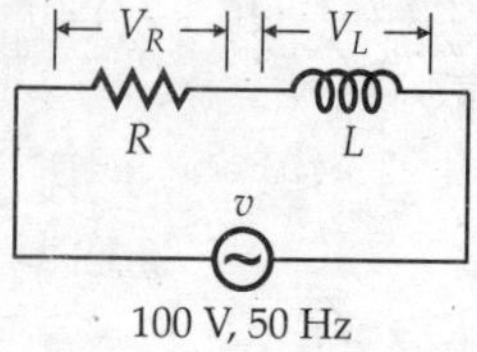

Fig. E2.6

$$\therefore \quad Z = R + j\,X_L = 4 + j\,3.14$$
$$= 5.085\,\Omega\ \angle 38.13° \text{ ohms}$$

i.e., impedance of the circuit is **5.085 Ω ∠38.13°**.

(Ans. of (*i*))

$$\therefore\ I\,(\text{input current}) = \frac{V}{Z} = \frac{100}{5.085}\angle -38.13°\ \text{A}$$

[assuming source voltage as $v = 100\ \angle 0°$ V]

i.e., magnitude input current = **19.66 A**

(Ans. of (*ii*))

Drop across the resistance

$$(= V_R) = IR = 19.66\ \angle -38.13° \times 4$$
$$= 78.64\ \angle -38.13°\ \text{V}$$

while the drop across the reactance

$$(= V_L) = j\,I\,X_L = j\,19.66\ \angle -38.13° \times 3.14$$
$$= (19.66 \times 3.14)\ \angle 90° - 38.13°$$
$$= 61.73\ \angle 51.87\ \text{V}$$

Thus, $V_R = \mathbf{78.64\ \angle -38.13°\ V}$, $V_L = \mathbf{61.73\ \angle 51.87°\ V}$ (Ans. of (*iii*))

Since the power factor of the circuit is the cosine of angle between the voltage and current, here, power factor (p.f.) would be cos (−38.13°) *i.e.*, **0.787 lag** (the p.f. is lagging as the sign of angle between *V* and *I* is *–ve*, *i.e.*, current is lagging the voltage. Also it may be noted that in *R-L* series circuit, the p.f. is lagging) (Ans. of (*iv*))

The real power consumed by the circuit is *VI* cos ϕ

i.e.,
$$P = 100 \times 19.66 \times 0.787$$
$$= \mathbf{1547\ W}\ \text{(Ans. of } (v)\text{)}.$$

Check

Also, power consumed is $I^2\,R$ *i.e.*, here $(19.66)^2 \times 4 = 1546$ W.

Total power supplied is

$$S = VI = 100 \times 19.66$$
$$= \mathbf{1966\ VA}\ \text{(Ans. of } (vi)\text{)}.$$

Check

Also $S = \sqrt{(VI\cos\phi)^2 + (VI\sin\phi)^2}$

$$= [(100 \times 19.66 \times 0.787)^2 + (100 \times 19.66 \times 0.617)^2]^{1/2}$$
$$= 1966\ \text{VA}.$$

The phasor diagram of the parameters of the given problem is shown in Fig. E2.7.

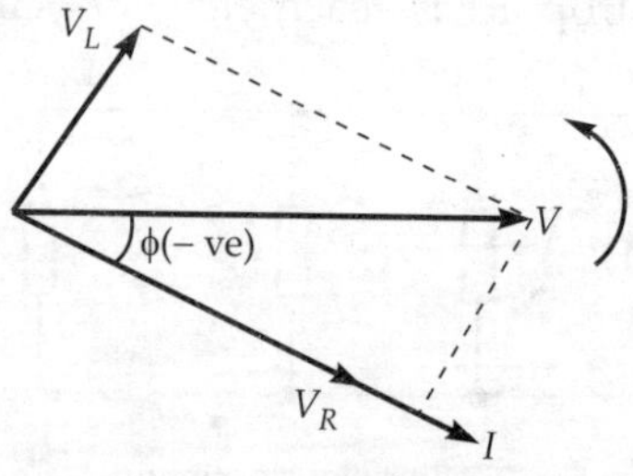

Fig. E2.7

It may be noted here, that the real power (*P*) is only *consumed* in *resistive part* of the circuit. This is the dissipation of heat in the resistance in form of *energy* (*i.e.*, power multiplied by time). On the other hand, an inductive reactance draws only *reactive power* (Q) which is stored in form of *magnetic energy*.

The real power consumed is either I^2R or *VI* cos ϕ while the reactive power is *VI* sin ϕ Obviously S (total power) is given by

$$S = P + j\,Q = \sqrt{P^2 + Q^2}\ \angle \tan^{-1}\frac{Q}{P}$$

where $|S| = |VI|$]

EXAMPLE 2.28 *In a series R-L circuit, R = 20 ohms while L = 60 mH. The input current lags the supply voltage by 60°. Obtain the value of applied frequency.*

SOLUTION. $\tan\phi = \dfrac{\omega L}{R}$

[where ϕ is the angle of lag and $\omega = 2\pi f$]

or,
$$\tan 60° = \frac{\omega \times 0.06}{20}$$

[$\because\ R = 20\,\Omega,\ L = 60\ \text{mH} = 0.06\ \text{H}$]

$$\therefore \quad \omega = \frac{20 \times 1.732}{0.06} = 577.33\ \text{rad/sec.}$$

This gives $f = \dfrac{\omega}{2\pi} = \dfrac{577.33}{2\pi} = \mathbf{91.93\ Hz.}$

2.5 SINUSOIDAL RESPONSE OF SERIES *RL* CIRCUIT

Let the applied current in the series *R-L* circuit (Fig. 2.11) be *i* while

$$i = I_m \sin \omega t \quad ...(2.9)$$

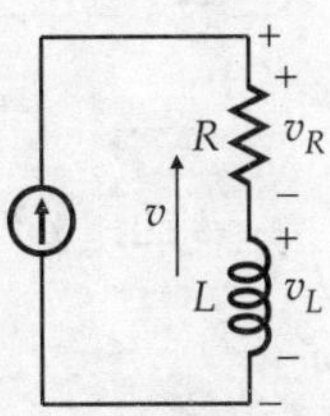

Fig. 2.11 *R-L* series circuit being energized by a current source.

Let v_R and v_L be the voltage drops at steady state across *R* and *L* elements respectively such that the net voltage drop *v* across the circuit is the vectorial summation of v_R and v_L.

$$\text{Thus} \quad v_R = i\,R = R\,I_m \sin \omega t \quad ...(2.10)$$

$$v_L = L\frac{di}{dt} = L\frac{d}{dt}(I_m \sin \omega\, t)$$

$$= \omega\, L\, I_m \cos \omega t$$

$$\text{or,} \quad v_L = \omega\, L\, I_m \sin(\omega t + 90) \quad ...(2.11)$$

$$\text{and} \quad v = v_R + v_L = R\, I_m \sin \omega t + \omega L\, I_m \sin(\omega t + 90°)$$

$$= R\, I_m \sin \omega t + \omega L\, I_m \sin \omega t \cos 90° + \omega L\, I_m \cos \omega t \sin 90°$$

$$\text{or,} \quad V_m \sin(\omega t + \theta) = R\, I_m \sin \omega t + \omega\, L\, I_m \sin \omega t \cos 90° + \omega L\, I_m \cos \omega t \sin 90°$$

$$\text{or,} \quad V_m \sin \omega t \cos\theta + V_m \cos \omega t \sin\theta = R\, I_m \sin \omega t + \omega\, L\, I_m \sin \omega t \cos 90° + \omega\, L\, I_m \cos \omega t \sin 90° \quad ...(2.12)$$

Equating coefficients of like terms, from equation (2.12),

$$V_m \sin \omega t \cos\theta = R\, I_m \sin \omega t$$

$$[\because \omega L\, I_m \sin \omega t \cos 90° = 0]$$

$$\text{and} \quad V_m \cos \omega t \sin\theta = \omega L\, I_m \cos \omega t \sin 90°$$

$$= \omega L\, I_m \cos \omega t$$

Then we finally obtain,

$$V_m \cos\theta = R\, I_m$$

$$\text{and} \quad V_m \sin\theta = \omega\, L\, I_m \quad ...(2.13)$$

$$\therefore \quad V_m = \sqrt{(R\, I_m)^2 + (\omega L\, I_m)^2}$$

$$= I_m \sqrt{R^2 + (\omega L)^2} = (I_m\, Z) \quad ...(2.14)$$

$$\text{and} \quad \theta = \tan^{-1}\frac{\omega L}{R} \quad ...(2.15)$$

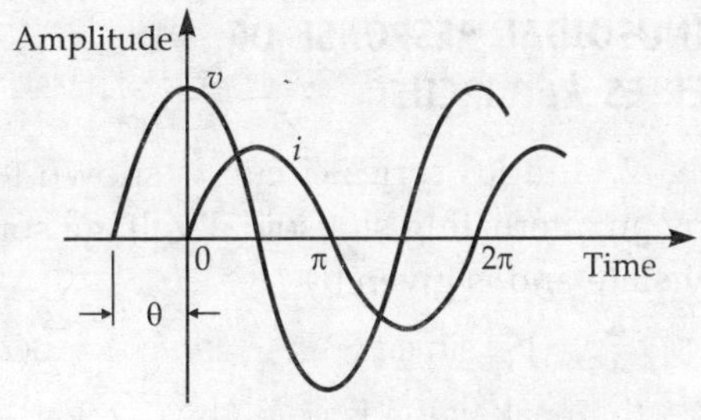

Fig. 2.12 Sketch of *i* and *v*

The functions *v* and *i* have been shown in Fig. (2.12). The current *i* lags the voltage *v* by an angle θ. The *impedance* of this circuit (*RL* series circuit) is complex and is given by

$$Z = R + j\,\omega\, L[\text{Eq. (2.14)}]$$

$$= \sqrt{R^2 + (\omega L)^2}\,\angle \tan^{-1}\frac{\omega L}{R}. \quad ...(2.16)$$

[Ref. Fig. 2.13]

Also, from equation (2.14),

$$I_m = \frac{V_m}{Z} = \frac{V_m}{(R + j\omega L)\angle \tan^{-1}\frac{\omega L}{R}}$$

$$= \frac{V_m}{R + j\omega L}\angle -\tan^{-1}\frac{\omega L}{R} \quad ...(2.17)$$

and in r.m.s. values also,

$$I = \frac{V}{R + j\,\omega L}\angle -\tan^{-1}\frac{\omega L}{R} \quad ...(2.18)$$

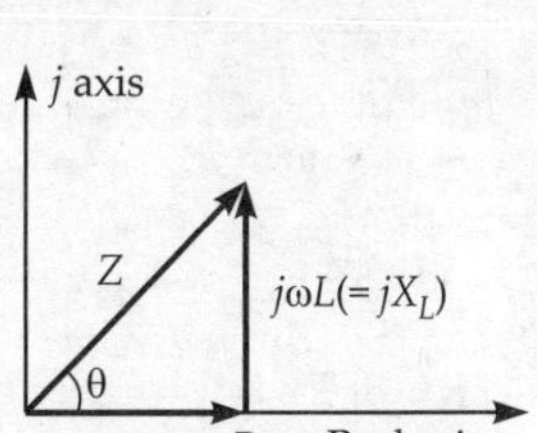

Fig. 2.13 Complex impedance triangle.

Assuming the voltage phasor to the reference $[V = V\angle 0°]$, equations (2.17) and (2.18) clearly show the current *lagging* the voltage by an angle θ given by $\theta = -\tan^{-1}\frac{\omega L}{R}$ (the presence of negative sign indicates the *angle of lag*). The instantaneous current, with voltage as reference phasor, is then given as

$$i = \frac{V_m}{\sqrt{R^2 + \omega^2 L^2}} \sin\left(\omega t - \tan^{-1}\frac{\omega L}{R}\right) \quad ...(2.19)$$

2.6 SINUSOIDAL RESPONSE OF SERIES *RC* CIRCUIT

In Fig. 2.14, a *RC* series circuit is shown to be excited by an alternating sinusoidal voltage source in steady state and is given by

$$v = V_m \sin \omega t \quad ...(2.20)$$

where V_m, the peak value is given by ($\sqrt{2}\, V$).

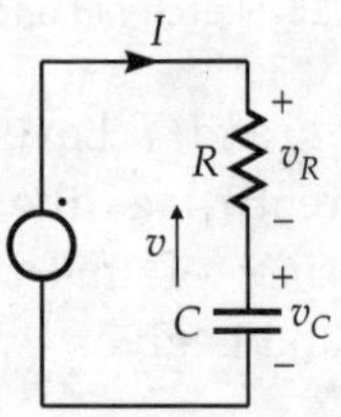

Fig. 2.14 R.C. series circuit excited by voltage sinusoid.

Obviously, in the series circuit of Fig. 2.14,

$$V = I\left(R + \frac{1}{j\,\omega C}\right) \quad ...(2.21)$$

$$= I\left(R - j\frac{1}{\omega C}\right) = IZ \quad ...(2.22)$$

where, $$Z = R - \frac{j}{\omega C}$$

$$= \sqrt{R^2 + \left(\frac{1}{\omega C}\right)^2} \angle -\tan^{-1}\frac{1}{\omega RC}$$

...(2.23)

i.e., $$I = \frac{V}{Z} = \frac{V}{\sqrt{R^2 + \left(\frac{1}{\omega C}\right)^2} \angle -\tan^{-1}\frac{1}{\omega RC}}$$

$$= \frac{V}{\sqrt{R^2 + \left(\frac{1}{\omega C}\right)^2}} \angle \tan^{-1}\frac{1}{\omega RC}$$

...(2.24)

Expression (2.24) shows that the current in the *RC* series circuit leads the voltage reference by an angle θ given by $\theta = \angle \tan^{-1}\frac{1}{\omega RC}$ [+ ve sign of angle represents angle of lead].

The corresponding instantaneous current is then given by

$$i = I_m \sin(\omega t + \theta)$$

$$= \frac{V_m}{\sqrt{R^2 + \frac{1}{\omega^2 C^2}}} \sin\left(\omega t + \tan^{-1}\frac{1}{\omega RC}\right)$$

...(2.25)

The phasor diagram of the *RC* series circuit, being energized by sinusoidal voltage source, at steady state, has been shown in Fig. 2.15 while the waveform sketch is given in Fig. 2.16.

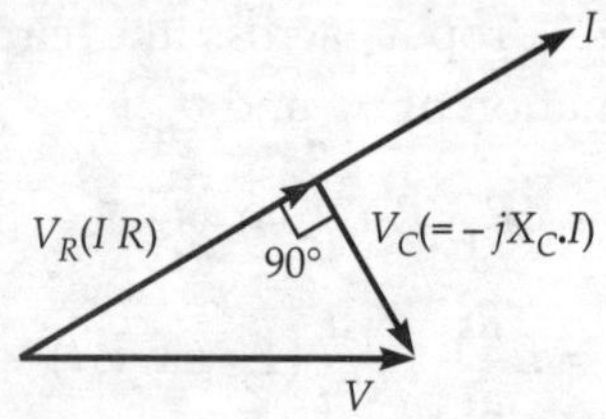

Fig. 2.15 Phasor diagram of *RC* series circuit.

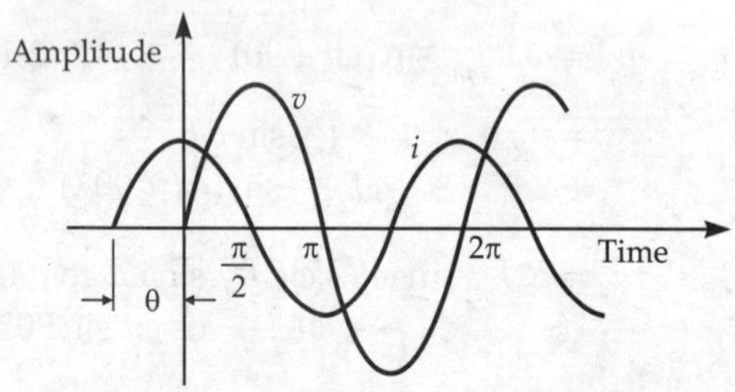

Fig. 2.16 Sketch of current and voltage in series *RC* circuit.

2.7 SINUSOIDAL RESPONSE OF SERIES *RLC* CIRCUIT

With reference to Fig. 2.17, the application of Kirchhoff's law results

$$V = IR + j\,I X_L + I\frac{1}{j\omega . C}$$

$$\left[\text{where } v_R = IR;\ v_L = j\,I\,X_L;\ v_C = I\frac{1}{j\,\omega C}\right]$$

or, $$V = I\left[R + j\,\omega L + \frac{1}{j\,\omega C}\right] \quad ...(2.26)$$

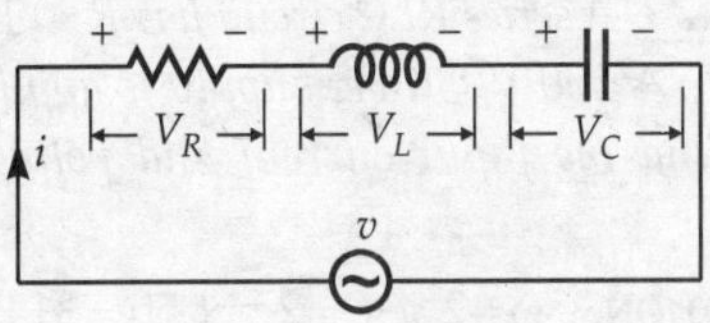

Fig. 2.17 Voltage sinusoid applied at *RLC* series circuit.

Let Z be the net impedance of the circuit. This gives, from equation (2.26),

$$V = IZ = I\left[R + j\,\omega L + \frac{1}{j\,\omega C}\right]$$

or, $$Z = R + j\left(\omega L - \frac{1}{\omega C}\right)$$

$$= \sqrt{R^2 + \left(\omega L - \frac{1}{\omega C}\right)^2} \angle \tan^{-1}\frac{(\omega L) - \left(\frac{1}{\omega C}\right)}{R}. \quad ...(2.27)$$

Expression (2.27) also gives the expression of the *complex impedance* (Z) which indicates that the circuit will become *inductive* if $\omega L > \frac{1}{\omega C}$ and then the sign of the angle of Z is +ve. On the other hand, for $\omega L < \frac{1}{\omega C}$, the circuit will become *capacitive* and the sign of the angle of the impedance will then be negative.

The instantaneous current expression then becomes (with voltage as reference phasor)

$$i = \frac{V}{Z} = \frac{V}{\sqrt{R^2 + \left(\omega L - \frac{1}{\omega C}\right)^2}} \angle -\tan^{-1}\frac{\omega L - 1/\omega C}{R} \quad ...(2.28)$$

Expression (2.28) shows that the current lags the voltage by an angle θ given by

$$\theta = -\tan^{-1}\frac{\omega L - \frac{1}{\omega C}}{R}$$

provided $\omega L > \frac{1}{\omega C}$ and the current leads the voltage by an angle θ given by $\theta = \tan^{-1}\frac{\omega L - \frac{1}{\omega C}}{R}$ provided $\omega L < \frac{1}{\omega C}$.

Figs. 2.18 and 2.19 exhibit the phasor diagrams of *RLC* series circuit.

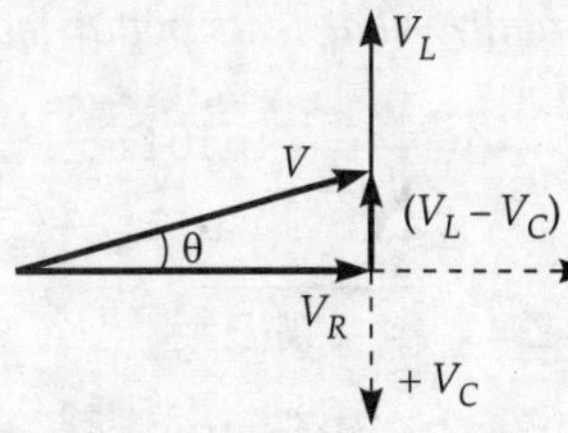

Fig. 2.18 Phasor diagram of series *RLC* circuit when $\omega L > \frac{1}{\omega C}$ *i.e.*, $V_L > V_C$. Here *I* lags *V* (θ is –ve)

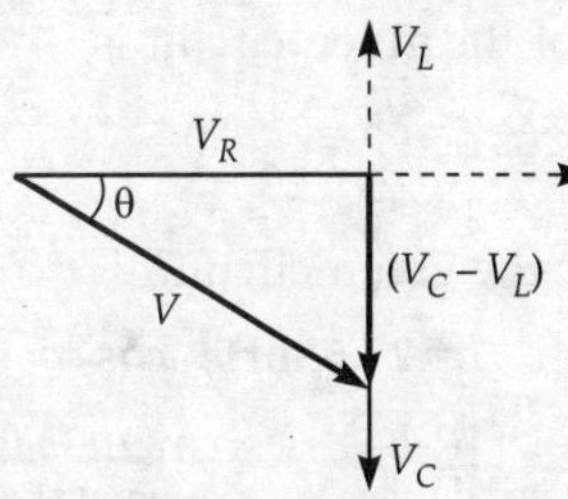

Fig. 2.19 Phasor diagram of series *RLC* circuit when $\omega L < \frac{1}{\omega C}$ *i.e.*, $V_L < V_C$. Here *I* leads *V* (θ is +ve)

EXAMPLE 2.29 *In a series R-L circuit, the inductance being 20 mH, the impedance is 17.85 Ω. The angle of lag of the input current from the applied voltage being 63.5°, find the values of angular frequency and the resistance of the circuit.*

SOLUTION.

$$\tan\phi = \frac{\omega L}{R}$$

or, $$\tan 63.5° = \frac{0.02\,\omega}{R} \quad [\because \phi = 63.5°;\ L = 20\text{ mH}]$$

or, $$2\,R = 0.02\,\omega \quad i.e.,\ R = 0.01\,\omega \quad ...(1)$$

But $$Z = \sqrt{R^2 + (\omega L)^2}$$

$$= \sqrt{(0.01\,\omega)^2 + (0.02\,\omega)^2}$$

[∵ in (1) we have obtained $R = 0.01\,\omega$ and $L = 0.02$ H]

$$\therefore \quad Z = 0.0224\,\omega \text{ or } 17.85 = 0.0224\,\omega$$

$$\therefore \quad \omega = 796.875\text{ rad/sec.}$$

and $$R = 0.01\,\omega = 7.98\,\Omega \simeq 8\,\Omega$$

Thus we have obtained,

$R = 8\,\Omega$; ω = **796.875 rad / sec.**

EXAMPLE 2.30 *A R-L series circuit draws a current of 1 A when connected across a 10 V, 50 Hz a.c. supply. Assuming the resistance to be 5 ohms, find the inductance of the circuit. What is its power factor ?*

SOLUTION. $Z = \frac{V}{I} = \frac{10}{1} = 10\,\Omega$

$[\because V = 10\text{ V},\ I = 1\text{ A}]$

But $\quad Z = \sqrt{R^2 + (\omega L)^2}$

$\therefore \quad (\omega L)^2 = Z^2 - R^2 = 10^2 - 5^2 = 75$

Thus $\quad L = \sqrt{\frac{75}{\omega^2}} = 0.0276$ H *i.e.,* 27.6 mH

The inductance of the circuit is 27.6 mH.

The p.f. of the given circuit is,

$$\cos\phi = \frac{R}{Z} = \frac{5}{10} = 0.5.$$

Then, for the given circuit,

$$\mathbf{L = 27.6\ mH;\ \cos\phi = 0.5\ (lag).}$$

EXAMPLE 2.31 *A R-L series circuit has resistance of 20 ohms and inductance of 0.02 Henry. If the net impedance of the given circuit be $40\angle\phi°$ ohm, find ϕ and the frequency of the circuit.*

SOLUTION. $Z\angle\theta = R + j\,X_L = 20 + j\,0.02\,(2\,\pi\,f)$

or, $\quad 40\angle\phi = 20 + j\,0.1256\,f \quad$ ...(1)

Again, $\quad \phi = \cos^{-1}\frac{R}{Z} = \cos^{-1}\frac{20}{40} = 60°$

Also, $\quad X_L = Z\sin\phi = 40\sin 60° = 34.64\,\Omega$

But from (1),

$$X_L = 0.1256\,f$$

$\therefore \quad f = \frac{34.64}{0.1256} = 276$ Hz

Thus we find $\quad \mathbf{\phi = 60°\ (lag)\ ;\ f = 276\ Hz.}$

EXAMPLE 2.32 *A series circuit has $R = 4\,\Omega$ and $L = 0.01$ H. Find the impedance at 100 Hz and 500 Hz.*

SOLUTION. $Z = R + j\,X_L$ while $X_L = 2\,\pi\,f\,L.$

for $f = 100$ Hz, $X_{L_{100}} = 2\,\pi \times 100 \times 0.01 = 6.28\,\Omega$

for $f = 500$ Hz, $X_{L_{500}} = 2\,\pi \times 500 \times 0.01 = 31.4\,\Omega$

$\therefore \quad Z_{\text{for 100 Hz}} = \sqrt{(4)^2 + (6.28)^2}$

$$= 7.45\,\Omega\angle\tan^{-1}\frac{6.28}{4} = \mathbf{7.45\angle 57.5°\,\Omega}$$

$$Z_{\text{for 500 Hz}} = \sqrt{(4)^2 + (31.4)^2} = \mathbf{31.65\angle 82.75°\,\Omega.}$$

[It may be noted that Z, the impedance changes with system frequency]

EXAMPLE 2.33 *A series RLC circuit has $R = 10\,\Omega$, $L = 1$ H, $C = 20\,\mu$F. A 100 V, 50 Hz supply is applied across the circuit. Find the input current and voltage across the elements.*

SOLUTION. $\omega = 2\,\pi\,f = 2\,\pi \times 50 = 314$ rad/sec.

$$X_L = \omega L = 314 \times 1 = 314\,\Omega$$

$$X_C = \frac{1}{\omega C}$$

$$= \frac{1}{314 \times 20 \times 10^{-6}} = \frac{10^6}{6280} = 159.24\,\Omega$$

$$Z = R + j\,(X_L - X_C)$$

$$= 10 + j\,(314 - 159.24)$$

$$= (10 + j\,155)\,\Omega = 155.33\,\Omega\angle 86°$$

$\therefore \quad I = \frac{V}{Z} = \frac{100\angle 0°}{155.33\angle 86°} = \mathbf{0.644\angle -86°\ A.}$

Also, $\quad V_R = IR = 0.644\angle -86° \times 10$

$$= \mathbf{6.44\angle -86°\ V.}$$

$$V_L = j\,X_L\,I = 314\angle 90° \times 0.644\angle -86°$$

$$= \mathbf{202.15\angle 4°\ V}$$

$$V_C = -j\,X_C\,I$$

$$= 159.24\angle -90° \times 0.644\angle -86°$$

$$= \mathbf{102.55\angle -176°\ V.}$$

EXAMPLE 2.34 *In a series RLC circuit, an AC voltage of $120\angle 0°$ V is applied at a frequency of 400 rad/sec. The input current leads the voltage by 63.5°. Find the value of R if L = 25 mH and C = 50 μF. What are the drops across L and C ?*

SOLUTION.

$$X_L = j\omega L = j\,400 \times 25 \times 10^{-3} = j\,10\,\Omega.$$

$$X_C = \frac{1}{j\omega C} = -\frac{j}{400 \times 50 \times 10^{-6}} = -j\,50\,\Omega.$$

However, $\quad Z = R + j\,(X_L - X_C) = (R - j\,40)\,\Omega.$

Also, $\quad \tan^{-1}\frac{X_L - X_C}{R} = \phi$

(where ϕ is the angle between V and I in the circuit)

or, $\quad \tan(-63.5°) = \frac{10 - 50}{R}$

or, $\quad -40 = R \times (-2) \quad \therefore \quad R = 20\,\Omega$

[Here, ϕ is leading hence the sign of ϕ is –ve]

Also, $I = \frac{V}{Z} = \frac{120 \angle 0°}{20 - j\,40}$

$= \frac{120 \angle 0°}{44.7 \angle -63.5°} = 2.68 \angle 63.5°$ A.

However,

$V_L = j\,IX_L = j \times 2.68 \angle 63.5° \times 10$

$= 26.8 \angle (90° + 63.5°)$ V

or, $\mathbf{V_L = 26.8 \angle 153.5° \ V}$

and $V_C = -j\,I\,X_c = (2.68 \angle 63.5° - 90°)(50)$

$= \mathbf{134 \angle -26.5° \ V}$.

EXAMPLE 2.35 *In a series RLC circuit, $R = 8\,\Omega$, $X_C = 5\,\Omega$, $X_L = 10\,\Omega$. A voltage V is applied across the combination such that the series current is 2 A and it lags the system voltage by 10°. Assuming the system frequency to be 50 Hz, find the drops across each of the units. What is the supply voltage ?*

SOLUTION.

V_R = drop across $R = IR = 2 \angle -10° \times 8$

$= 16 \angle -10° = (15.76 - j\,2.78)$ V

V_L = drop across $L = j\,I\,X_L$

$= (2 \angle -10° + 90°) \times 10$

$= 20 \angle 80° = (3.47 + j\,19.7)$ V

V_C = drop across $C = I(-j\,X_C)$

$= 2 \angle -10° (5 \angle -90°) = 10 \angle -100°$

$= (-0.347 - j\,1.969)$ V

$\therefore$ Supply voltage = vector sum of $(V_R + V_L + V_C)$

$= 15.76 - j\,2.78 + 3.47 + j\,19.7 - 0.347 - j\,1.969$

$= 18.883 + j\,14.951$

$\simeq \mathbf{24.08 \angle 38.37° \ volts.}$

EXAMPLE 2.36 *In the circuit shown in Fig. E2.8, $r_1 = 8\,\Omega$, $r_2 = 3.5\,\Omega$, $C_1 = 800\,\mu F$, $C_2 = 250\,\mu F$. If the supply frequency is 60 Hz, find*

(i) drop across each circuit element

(ii) total resistive and total capacitive drop

(iii) supply voltage

(iv) impedance angle of each branch

(v) power factor of the circuit

Draw the vector diagram.

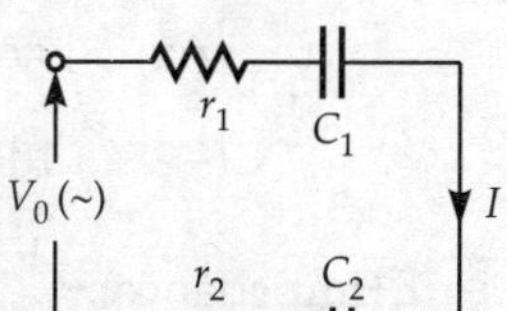

Fig. E2.8

SOLUTION. (*i*) Drop across $r_1 = V_{r_1} = Ir_1 = \mathbf{80\ V}$

Drop across

$C_1 = V_{C_1} = I\,X_{C_1}$

$= I(2\pi f C_1)^{-1} = \frac{10}{2\pi \times 60 \times 800 \times 10^{-6}}$

$= \mathbf{33.2\ V}$

Drop across

$r_2 = V_{r_2} = Ir_2 = \mathbf{35\ V}$

Drop across

$C_2 = \frac{I}{2\pi f C_2} = \frac{10}{2\pi \times 60 \times 250 \times 10^{-6}} = \mathbf{106\ V}.$

(*ii*) Total resistive drop

$V_{r_1} + V_{r_2} = \mathbf{115\ V} \ (= V_r)$

Total capacitive drop

$= 33.2 + 106 = \mathbf{139.2\ V} \ (= V_c)$.

(*iii*) Drop in branch 1 (comprising of r_1 and C_1)

$V_1 = I(r_1 - j\,X_{C_1})$

$= V_{r_1} - j\,V_{c_1} = (80 - j\,33.2)$ V

Similarly, drop in branch 2 (comprising of r_2 and C_2)

$V_2 = I(r_2 - j\,X_{C_2})$

$= V_{r_2} - j\,V_{c_2} = (35 - j\,106)$ V

$\therefore$ Supply voltage

$V_0 = I[(r_1 + r_2) - j(X_{C_1} + X_{C_2})]$

$= \mathbf{115 - j\,139.3\ V.}$

(*iv*) Impedance angle of

$Br_1 = \theta_1 = \tan^{-1} \frac{X_{C_1}}{r_1} = \mathbf{22°33'\ (-\,ve).}$

Impedance angle of

$Br_2 = \theta_2 = \tan^{-1} \frac{X_{C_2}}{r_2} = \mathbf{71°45'\ (-\,ve).}$

(*v*) PF angle $= \tan^{-1} \frac{X_{C_1} + X_{C_2}}{r_1 + r_2} = \mathbf{50°20'}.$

The phasor diagram is shown in Fig. E2.9.

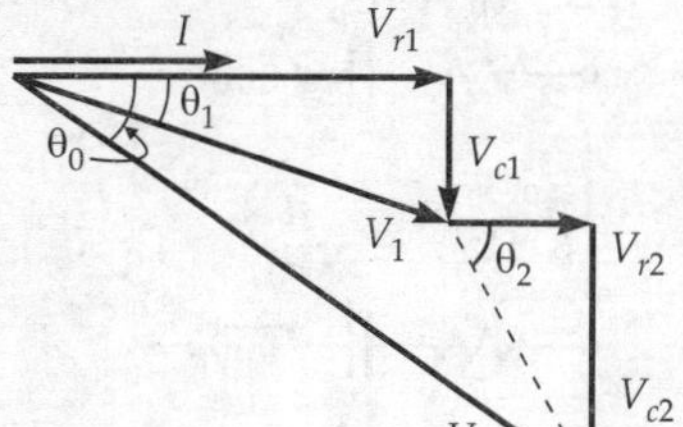

Fig. E2.9

C H A P T E R 2

EXAMPLE 2.37 *In the series RLC circuit of Fig. E2.10 $R = 4.2\,\Omega$, $L = 0.03$ H, $C = 450\,\mu$F. If $I = 10$ A, find the drop across each element, supply voltage and power factor angle. Also draw the vector diagram. Assume $f = 50$ Hz.*

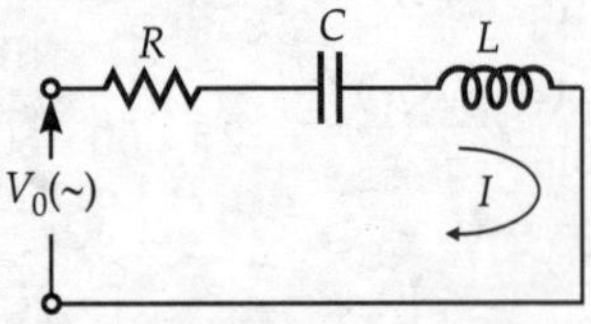

Fig. E2.10

SOLUTION.

Drop across $R\,(V_R) = IR = \mathbf{42\ V}$

Drop across $L(V_L) = I\,X_L = I\,(2\,\pi\,f\,L) = \mathbf{94.2\ V}$

Drop across $C\,(V_C) = I\,X_C = \dfrac{I}{2\,\pi\,f\,C} = \mathbf{70.7\ V}$

$$V_0 = I\,[R + j\,(X_L - X_C)]$$

$$= V_R + j\,(V_L - V_C) = \mathbf{42 + j\,23.5\ V}$$

and $\quad$ PF angle $= \tan^{-1} \dfrac{X_L - X_C}{R} = \mathbf{29°22'}$

Figure E2.11 represents the vector diagram.

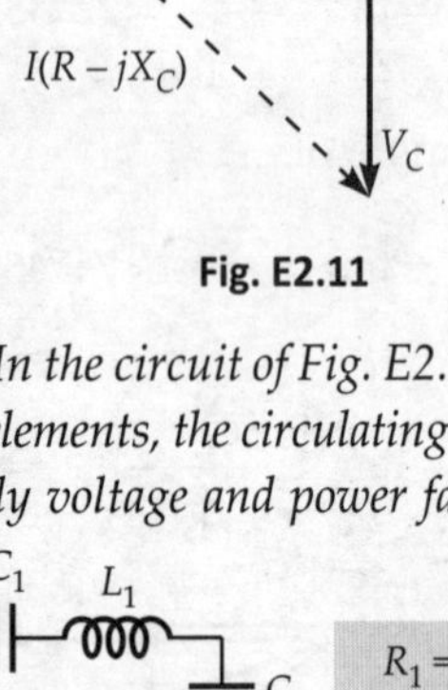

Fig. E2.11

EXAMPLE 2.38 *In the circuit of Fig. E2.12, given the values of each of the elements, the circulating current being 10 A, find the supply voltage and power factor.*

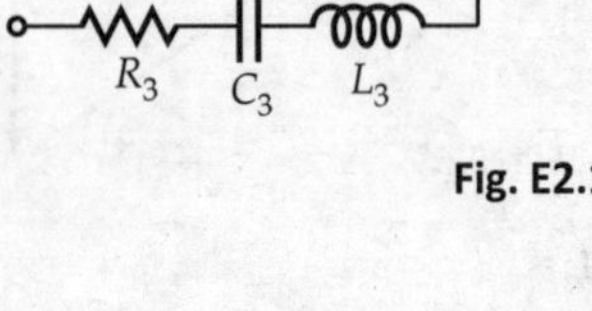

$R_1 = 5\,\Omega$, $R_2 = 2.5\,\Omega$,
$R_3 = 8.8\,\Omega$, $X_{C1} = 12\,\Omega$
$X_{C2} = 5.5\,\Omega$, $X_{L1} = 6.6\,\Omega$,
$X_{L2} = 10\,\Omega$, $X_{C2} = 7.4\,\Omega$

Fig. E2.12

SOLUTION. By inspection,

$$V_0 = I\,[(R_1 + R_2 + R_3) + j\,(X_{L_1} + X_{L_2}) - j\,(X_{C_1} + X_{C_2} + X_{C_3})]$$

$$= 10\,[16.3 + j\,(16.6 - 25)] = (163 - j\,83)$$

$$= 182.9\,\angle \tan^{-1}\left(-\frac{83}{163}\right) = 182.9\,\angle -26.9°\ \text{V}$$

The P.F. is then cos (26.9°) lead = **0.89 (lead)** and the supply voltage is $\mathbf{182.9\angle -26.9°\ V}$.

EXAMPLE 2.39 *An iron cored coil draws 2 A at 0.5 p.f. lag against a 50 Hz 100 V supply. Iron core being then removed, the voltage applied being 50 V, the current rises to 5 A to a p.f. of 0.78 lag. Find the inductance in each case.*

SOLUTION. *1st Case (core within the coil)*

$$Z\,(\text{impedance}) = \frac{V}{I} = \frac{100}{2} = 50\,\Omega$$

$$R\,(\text{resistance}) = \frac{\text{watt}}{I^2} = \frac{VI\cos\phi}{I^2}$$

$$= \frac{100 \times 2 \times 0.5}{2^2} = \mathbf{25\,\Omega}$$

$$\therefore \quad X = \sqrt{Z^2 - R^2} = \sqrt{50^2 - 25^2} = \mathbf{43.3\,\Omega}$$

and $\quad L(\text{inductance}) = \dfrac{X}{2\,\pi\,f} = \dfrac{43.3}{314} = \mathbf{138\ mH.}$

2nd case (Coil without the core)

$$Z = \frac{50\,(V)}{5\,(A)} = 10\,\Omega$$

$$R = \frac{VI\cos\phi}{I^2} = \frac{50 \times 5 \times 0.78}{5^2} = 7.8\,\Omega\,;$$

$$\therefore \quad X = \sqrt{Z^2 - R^2} = \sqrt{10^2 - 7.8^2} = 6.25\,\Omega$$

$$\therefore \quad L(\text{inductance}) = \frac{6.25}{2\pi f} = \frac{6.25}{314} = \mathbf{20\ mH.}$$

EXAMPLE 2.40 *An impedance of Z Ω draws a current of (– 2 + j 10) A from a 50 Hz (100 + j 50) supply. What is the value of impedance, power factor and real power consumed ?*

SOLUTION. Given,

$$V = (100 + j\,50)\ \text{V} \simeq 112\ \angle 26.55°\ \text{V}$$

$$I = (-2 + j\,10)\ A = 10.2\ \angle +103.3°\ \text{A}$$

$$\therefore \quad Z\,(\text{impedance}) = \frac{V}{I} = \frac{112\ \angle 26.55°}{10.2\ \angle +103.3°}$$

$$= \mathbf{10.98\angle -74.75°\Omega}$$

Thus, ϕ, the p.f. angle $= 74.75° \simeq 75°$.

and $\cos\phi = \text{p.f.} = \mathbf{0.263}$.

Thus, $W = VI\cos\phi = 112 \times 10.2 \times 0.263$

$= \mathbf{300\ W}$. $[\because P = VI\cos\phi]$

EXAMPLE 2.41 *An impedance Z, when connected to 100 V, 25 Hz supply, produces 1 A while the same circuit produces 0.5 A when the applied voltage is 100 V but the frequency is 50 Hz. What will be the frequency at which the circuit impedance will be half to that when 25 Hz voltage was applied to it in the first case ?*

SOLUTION. Let R be the resistance and x the reactance at 25 Hz. Obviously, the reactance at 50 Hz would be $2x$. Following the concept of $Z^2 = R^2 + X^2$, in the first case, when the applied voltage is 100 V, 25 Hz,

$$\left(\frac{100}{1}\right)^2 = R^2 + x^2 \quad \text{...(1)}$$

On the other hand, in the second case, when the voltage is 100 V, 50 Hz,

$$\left(\frac{100}{0.5}\right)^2 = R^2 + (2x)^2$$

or, $$(200)^2 = R^2 + 4x^2 \quad \text{...(2)}$$

Solving (1) and (2),

$$(100)^2 - (200)^2 = -3x^2$$

or, $x = 100\,\Omega$ [when 25 Hz was applied]

and $R = 0\,\Omega$

Also, $Z = \sqrt{R^2 + x^2} = 100\,\Omega$

To have $Z = 50\,\Omega$, $x^2 = 50^2$ or, $x = 50\,\Omega$

$[\because R = 0]$

This indicates that the applied frequency must be half to that of 25 Hz *i.e.*, **12.5 Hz.**

EXAMPLE 2.42 *In the circuit of Fig. E2.13, $r_1 = 8.2\,\Omega$, $r_2 = 2.7\,\Omega$, $L_1 = 0.01$ H, $L_2 = 0.03$ H, $f = 25$ cycles and the circulating current $I = 10$ A. Find—*

(i) Drop across each element.

(ii) Total resistive and inductive drop.

(iii) Supply voltage.

(iv) Impedance angle of each of the R-L branch and power factor of the circuit.

Also draw the phasor diagram.

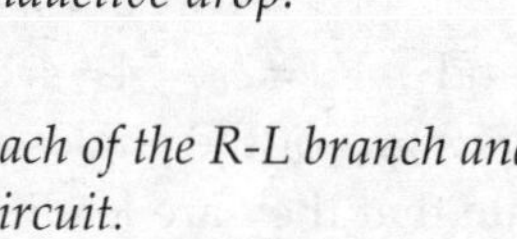

Fig. E2.13

SOLUTION. (*i*) The drop across r_1 is given by

$$V_{r_1} = Ir_1 = 10 \times 8.2 = \mathbf{82\ V.}$$

Drop across L_1 is given by

$$V_{L_1} = Ix_{l_1} = 10 \times 2\pi \times 25 \times 0.01 = \mathbf{15.7\ V.}$$

Drop across r_2 is given by

$$V_{r_2} = Ir_2 = 10 \times 2.7 = \mathbf{27\ V.}$$

Drop across

$$L_2 = Ix_{l_2} = 10 \times 2\pi \times 25 \times 0.03$$

$$= \mathbf{47.1\ V}\,(V_{L_2}).$$

$\therefore$ Drop across R_1 and L_1 (branch-1)

$$= V_1 = I\sqrt{r_1^2 + x_{L_1}^2}$$

$$= 10\sqrt{8.2^2 + (2\pi \times 25 \times 0.01)^2}$$

$$= \mathbf{83.5\ V.}$$

Similarly, Drop across R_2 and L_2 (branch-2) $= V_2$

$$= I\sqrt{r_2^2 + x_{L_2}^2} = \mathbf{54.2\ V.}$$

(*ii*) Total resistive drop

$$(V_r) = V_{r_1} + V_{r_2} = 82 + 27 = \mathbf{109\ V.}$$

Total inductive drop

$$(V_L) = V_{L_1} + V_{L_2} = 15.7 + 47.1 = \mathbf{62.8\ V.}$$

(*iii*) Supply voltage, $V_0 = \sqrt{V_R^2 + V_L^2} = \mathbf{125.7\ V.}$

(*iv*) θ_1 = imp. angle of branch-1

$$= \tan^{-1}\frac{x_{L_1}}{r_1} = \mathbf{10°50'}.$$

θ_2 = imp. angle of branch-2

$$= \tan^{-1}\frac{x_{L_2}}{r_2} = \mathbf{60°10'}.$$

and P.F. angle $= \theta_0 = \tan^{-1}\dfrac{x_{L_1} + x_{L_2}}{r_1 + r_2} = 30°$;

$$\text{P.F.} = \cos 30° = \mathbf{0.866.}$$

Figure E2.13(*a*) represents the phasor diagram.

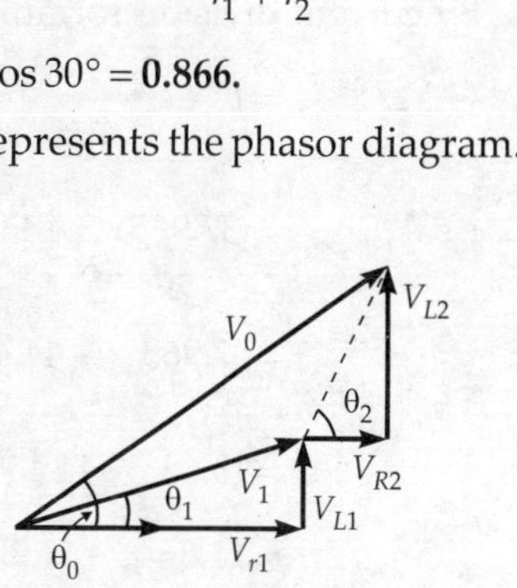

Fig. E2.13 (*a*)

EXAMPLE 2.43 *In the network shown in Fig. E2.14, find I_1, I_2 and I when a 200 V AC 50 Hz voltage is applied at the input.*

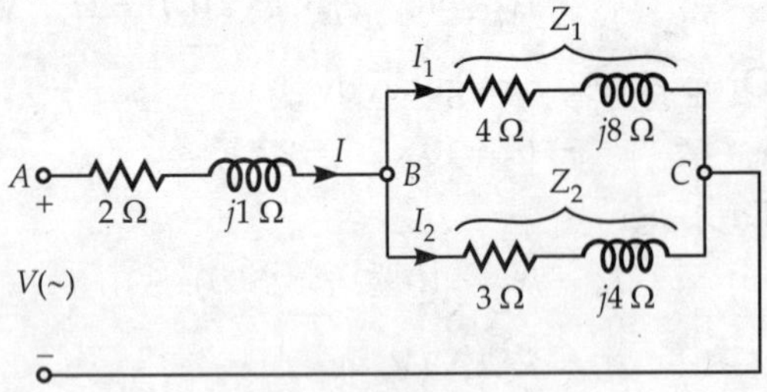

Fig. E2.14

SOLUTION. From Fig. E2.14,

$$Z_{BC} = \frac{Z_1 Z_2}{Z_1 + Z_2}$$

However,

$$Z_1 = (4 + j\,8)\,\Omega = 8.95\ \angle 63.45°\,\Omega$$

and

$$Z_2 = (3 + j\,4)\,\Omega = 5\ \angle 53°\,\Omega$$

Thus,

$$Z_{BC} = \frac{8.95\ \angle 63.45° \times 5\angle 53°}{8.95\angle 63.45° + 5\angle 53°}$$

$$= \frac{44.7\ \angle 116.45°}{13.9\ \angle 59.75°}$$

$$= 3.216\ \angle 56.7° = (1.76 + j\,2.69)\,\Omega$$

However, $Z_{AB} + Z_{BC} = Z_{AC}$

Thus,

$$Z_{AC} = (2 + j\,1) + (1.76 + j\,2.69)$$

$$= (3.76 + j\,3.69)\,\Omega$$

$$= 5.268\ \angle 44.45°$$

This gives

$$I = \frac{V}{Z_{AC}} = \frac{200\ \angle 0°}{5.268\angle 44.45°}$$

$$= 37.965\ \angle -44.45°\ \text{A}$$

$$= \mathbf{(27.1 - j\,26.59)\ A}$$

By current division formula,

$$I_1 = I\frac{Z_2}{Z_1 + Z_2}$$

$$= (37.965)\ \angle -44.45°\ \frac{5\ \angle 53°}{4 + j\,8 + 3 + j\,9}$$

$$= 37.965\ \angle -44.45°\ \frac{5\angle 53°}{13.9\ \angle 59.75°}$$

$$= 13.66\ \underline{/ -44.45° + 53° - 59.75°}$$

$$= \mathbf{13.66\ \angle -51.2°\ A}$$

and

$$I_2 = I\frac{Z_1}{Z_1 + Z_2}$$

$$= 37.965\ \angle -44.75°\ \frac{8.95\ \angle 63.45°}{13.9\ \angle 59.75°}$$

$$= 24.45\ \underline{/ -44.75° + 63.45° - 59.75°}$$

$$= 24.45\ \angle -41°\ \text{A}$$

Thus,

$$\mathbf{I_1 = 13.66\angle -51.2°\ A}$$

$$\mathbf{I_2 = 24.45\ \angle -41°\ A}$$

$$\mathbf{I = 37.965\ \angle -44.45°\ A.}$$

EXAMPLE 2.44 *In the RL series circuit of Fig. E2.15, find the supply voltage V provided V_R (= drop across R) = (4 + j 2) V and V_L (=drop across L) = (2 + j 4) V. Draw the phasor diagram.*

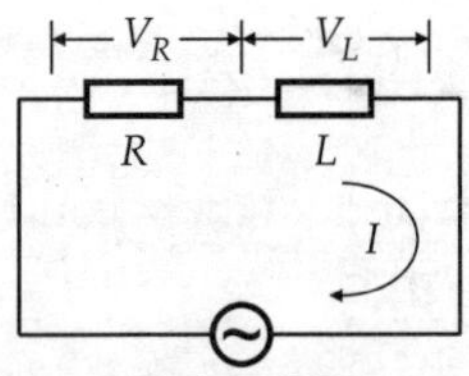

Fig. E2.15

SOLUTION. $V = V_R + V_L$ (vectorial)

$$= (4 + j\,2) + (2 + j\,4) = 6 + j\,6$$

$$= \mathbf{8.485\ \angle 45°\ V.}$$

The phasor diagram is shown in Fig. E2.16

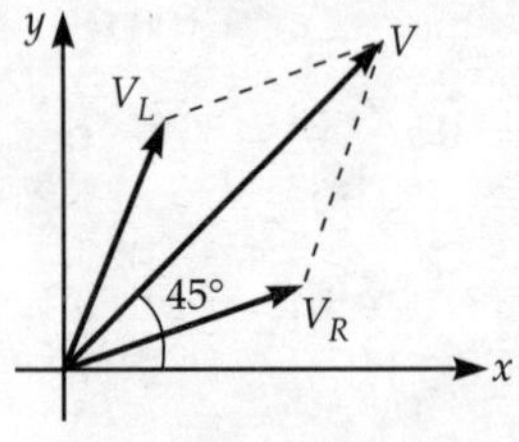

Fig. E2.16

where, V_R is 26.6° leading the x-axis and V_L is 63.44° leading the x-axis.

[∵ $V_R = 4 + j\,2 = 4.47\ \angle 26.56° \simeq 4.47\ \angle 26.6°$ V

and $V_L = 2 + j\,4 = 4.47\ \angle 63.44°$ V

+ve signs of the angles of both the voltages indicate that they are leading the x-axis.]

EXAMPLE 2.45 *100 V, 50 Hz is applied across a series RLC circuit having R = 10 Ω, L = 100 mH and C = 1000 μF. Find the current and drop across each element.*

SOLUTION. $R = 10\,\Omega$; $L = 100$ mH $= 0.1$ H

$\therefore \quad X_L = 2\pi f L = 314 \times 0.1 = 31.4\,\Omega,$

$C = 1000\,\mu F,$

$$X_C = \frac{1}{2\pi f \times C}$$

$$= \frac{1}{314 \times 1000} \times 10^6 = 3.18\,\Omega,$$

and $\quad Z = R + j(X_L - X_C)$

$= 10 + j(31.4 - 3.18)$

$= (10 + j\,28.22)\,\Omega$

$= 30\angle 70.49° \simeq 30\angle 70.5°\,\Omega$

It gives $I = \frac{V}{Z} = \frac{100\angle 0°}{30\angle 70.5°} = \mathbf{3.33\angle -70.5°\ A.}$

Thus, $V_R = IR = 3.33\angle -70.5° \times 10$

$= \mathbf{33.3\angle -70.5°\ V.}$

$V_L = IX_L = 3.33\angle -70.5° \times 31.4\angle 90°$

$= \mathbf{104.56\angle 19.5°\ V}$

$V_C = IX_C = 3.33\angle -70.5° \times 3.18\angle -90°$

$= \mathbf{10.59\angle -160.5°\ V.}$

EXAMPLE 2.46 *Two impedances Z_1 and Z_2 are connected in parallel across an a.c. 50 Hz supply and taking currents I_{Z_1} and I_{Z_2} respectively. The supply current being I_S, find the value of r.m.s. and instantaneous current in Z_2 provided*

$$I_S = 6\angle 30°\ A;\ I_{Z_1} = 2\angle 20°\ A.$$

SOLUTION. Since $I_S = I_{Z_1} + I_{Z_2}$,

[in parallel branch circuit, main current is vector sum of branch currents]

$I_{Z_2} = I_S - I_{Z_1} = 6\angle 30° - 2\angle 20°$

$= 6(\cos 30 + j\sin 30°) - 2(\cos 20° + j\sin 20°)$

$= 5.2 + j3 - 1.88 - j0.69$

$= 3.32 + j2.31 = 4.045\angle 35°.$

Thus r.m.s. value of the current in Z_2 is

$$I_{Z_2} = \mathbf{4.045\angle 35°\ A.}$$

In order to find the instantaneous value, let us first obtain the peak current *i.e.*, $I_{Z_{2(max)}}$ which is actually $(\sqrt{2} \times 4.045)$ A *i.e.*, 5.72 A.

At system frequency of 50 Hz, the expression for instantaneous current is then given by

$$i_{Z_2} = \mathbf{5.72\sin(314\,t + 35°).}\quad [\because \phi = 35°]$$

EXAMPLE 2.47 *In Fig. E2.17,*

$I_1 = (1 - j2)$, $I_1' = (3 + j3)$. Find I_1''.

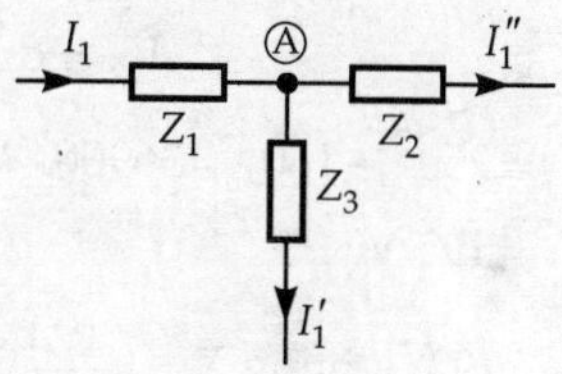

Fig. E2.17

SOLUTION. Applying KCL at node (A),

$I_1 = I_1' + I_1''$

or, $\quad I_1'' = I_1 - I_1' = (1 - j2) - (3 + j3)$

$= (-2 - j5)$ A

$= \mathbf{5.39\angle -111.80°\ A.}$

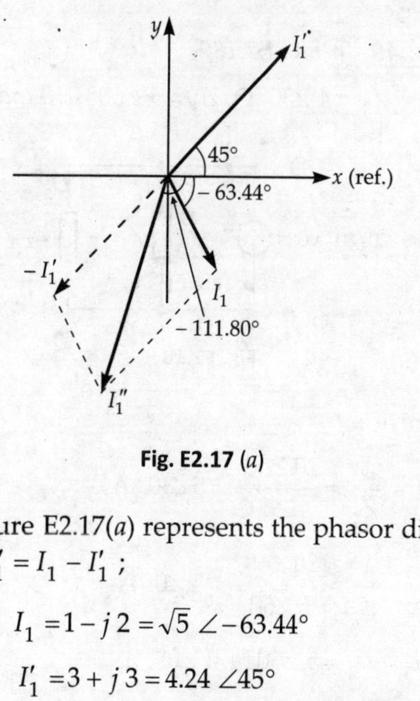

Fig. E2.17 (*a*)

[Figure E2.17(*a*) represents the phasor diagram where $I_1'' = I_1 - I_1'$;

$I_1 = 1 - j2 = \sqrt{5}\angle -63.44°$

and $\quad I_1' = 3 + j3 = 4.24\angle 45°$

–ve angle indicates lag and +ve angle indicates lead]

EXAMPLE 2.48 *A supply of 250 V, 50 Hz is applied to a series RC circuit. Find the value of C if the power absorbed by the resistor be 400 W at 160 V. What is the energy stored in the capacitor ?*

SOLUTION. Let I be the circulating current in the series RC circuit.

$$I = \frac{\text{watt}}{\text{V (across } R)} = \frac{400}{160} = 2.5\ A$$

CHAPTER 2

Let the voltage across the capacitor be V_C volts.

Then, $V_C^2 = V_S^2 - V_R^2$

[where, V_S = supply voltage
V_R = drop across R]

$= 250^2 - 160^2 = 36900.$

$\therefore \quad V_C = 192$ V

or $\quad I X_C = 192$, giving $X_C = \dfrac{192}{I} = 76.84$ A

But $\quad X_C = \dfrac{1}{2\pi f C}$

$\therefore \quad C = \dfrac{1}{2\pi f X_C} = \dfrac{1}{76.84 \times 314} = 41.45\,\mu$F

Energy stored in capacitor $= \dfrac{1}{2} C V_C^2$

$= \dfrac{1}{2}(41.45) \times 10^{-6} \times (192)^2 = \mathbf{0.765}$ **J.**

EXAMPLE 2.49 *In Fig. E2.18,*

$Z_1 = 4\angle 30°\,\Omega$, $Z_2 = 5\angle 60°\,\Omega$. Find I.

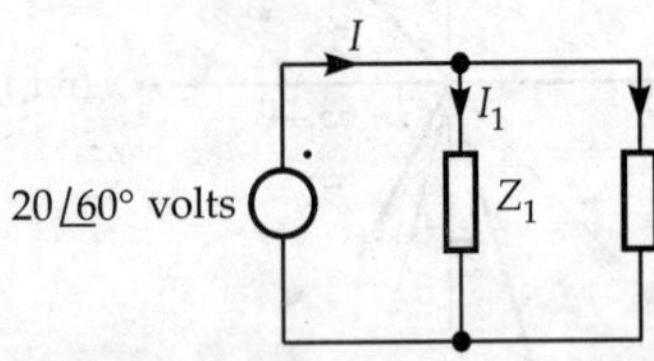

Fig. E2.18

SOLUTION.

$$I_1 = \frac{V}{Z_1} = \frac{20\angle 60°}{4\angle 30°} = 5\angle 30° \text{ A}$$

$$I_2 = \frac{V}{Z_2} = \frac{20\angle 60°}{5\angle 60°} = 4\angle 0° \text{ A}$$

$\therefore \quad I_1 + I_2 = 5\angle 30° + 4\angle 0°$

$= 5(\cos 30 + j\sin 30°) + 4(\cos 0 + j \sin 0)$

$= 5 \times 0.866 + j\,5 \times 0.5 + 4$

$= 4.33 + j\,2.5 + 4$

or, $\quad I = \mathbf{8.7\angle 16.7°}$ **A.**

EXAMPLE 2.50 *An impedance Z_1 $(2 - j\,5)$ is connected in parallel with another impedance Z_2 $(1 + j\,1)$ ohm. If the applied voltage is $17\angle 0°$ V, find the branch currents as well as the total current.*

SOLUTION. $Z_1 = 2 - j\,5 = 5.38\angle -68.2°\,\Omega$

$Z_2 = 1 + j\,1 = \sqrt{2}\angle 45°\,\Omega$

$\therefore \quad I_1$ (current through Z_1) $= \dfrac{17\angle 0°}{5.38\angle -68.2}$

$= 3.16\angle 68.2°$ A

and $\quad I_2$ (current through Z_2) $= \dfrac{17\angle 0°}{\sqrt{2}\angle 45°}$

$= 12.02\angle -45°$ A

$\therefore$ Total current,

$I = I_1 + I_2 = 3.16\angle 68.2° + 12.02\angle -45°$

$= \mathbf{11.1\angle -29.8°}$ **A.**

EXAMPLE 2.51 *In Fig. E2.19, $R_1 = 3\,\Omega$, $R_2 = 10\,\Omega$ and $-j\,X_C = -j\,8\,\Omega$. Find I_1, I_2 and I. Also obtain Z_{eq} across a-b.*

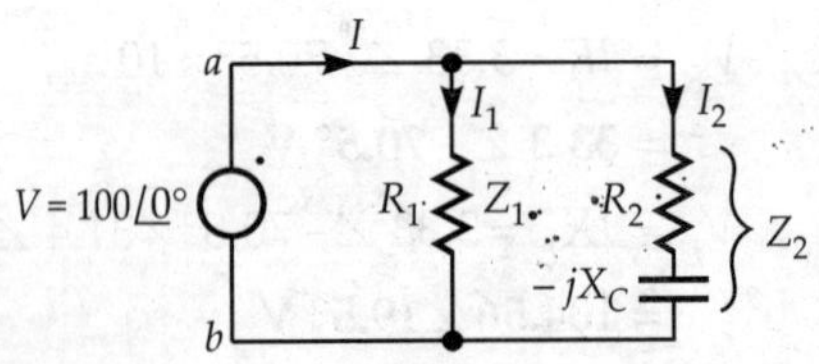

Fig. E2.19

SOLUTION. $Z_1 = R_1 = 3\,\Omega = 3\angle 0°\,\Omega$

$Z_2 = R_2 - j\,X_2 = (10 - j\,8)\,\Omega$

$= 12.8\angle -38.66°\,\Omega$

and $\quad \dfrac{Z_1 Z_2}{Z_1 + Z_2}$ [*i.e.*, Z_{eq} across *a-b*]

$= \dfrac{3\angle 0° \times 12.8\angle -38.66°}{3\angle 0° + 12.8\angle -38.66°}$

$= \mathbf{2.52\angle -7.05°\,\Omega}$

Now, $\quad I_1 = \dfrac{V}{Z_1} = \dfrac{100\angle 0°}{3\angle 0°} = \mathbf{33.33\angle 0°}$ **A**

$I_2 = \dfrac{V}{Z_2} = \dfrac{100}{12.8\angle -38.66}$

$= \mathbf{7.81\angle 38.66°}$ **A**

$\therefore \quad I_1 + I_2 = 33.33 + 7.81(\cos 38.66 + j\sin 38.66)$

$= \mathbf{(39.43 + j\,4.88)}$ **A** $(= I)$.

Check

Also,

$$Z_{eq} = \frac{V}{(I_1 + I_2)} = \frac{V}{39.43 + j\,4.88} = \frac{100\angle 0°}{39.73\angle 7.05°}$$

$= 2.52\angle -7.05\,\Omega.$

EXAMPLE 2.52 *A series RL circuit has $R = 25\,\Omega$ and $X_L = 32\,\Omega$. It is connected in parallel to a capacitor of $100\,\mu$F and the combination is connected across a 200 V, 50 Hz supply. Find the current in each branch. Draw the vector diagram showing the total current.*

SOLUTION. $R = 25\,\Omega,\ X_L = 32\,\Omega$

[Ref. Fig. E2.20]

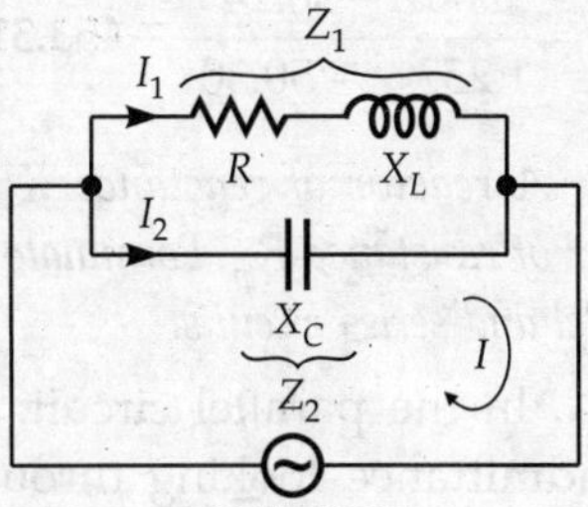

Fig. E2.20

$$\therefore \quad Z_1 = \sqrt{R^2 + X_L^2} = 40.6\,\Omega$$

and
$$\phi_1 = \tan^{-1}\frac{32}{25} = 52°$$

$$I_1 = \frac{200\angle 0°\text{ V}}{40.6\angle 52°} = \mathbf{4.93\angle -52°\ A}$$

$$I_2 = \frac{|V|}{|X_C|}$$

But
$$X_C = \frac{1}{j2\pi fC} = \frac{1}{j\,2\times 50\times 3.14\times 100\times 10^{-6}}$$

$$= -j\,31.85\,\Omega$$

$$\therefore \quad I_2 = \frac{200\angle 0°}{-j\,31.85} = 6.279\angle 90°\text{ A}$$

Figure E2.21 represents the corresponding phasor diagram

$$I_T\ (\text{total current}) = I_1 + I_2\ (\text{vectorial})$$
$$= 4.93\,(\cos 52° - j\sin 52°)$$
$$+ 6.279\,(\cos 90° + j\sin 90°)$$
$$= 3.04 + j\,2.39$$
$$= 3.86\angle 38.17°\quad [+38.1° \text{ indicates lead}]$$

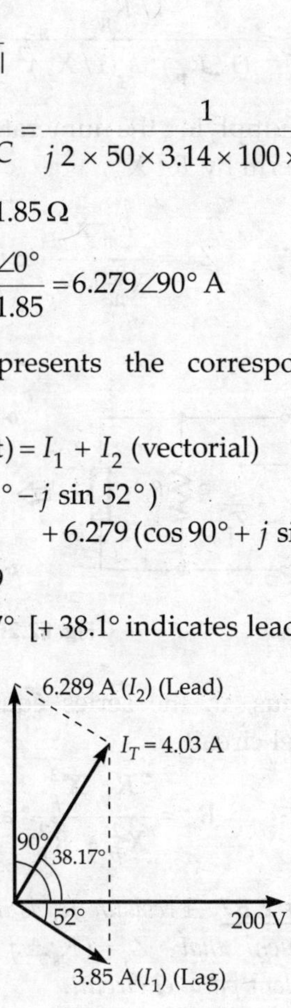

Fig. E2.21

EXAMPLE 2.53 *A series R-L circuit has resistance and reactance of $15\,\Omega$ and $10\,\Omega$ respectively. Calculate the value of a capacitor which when connected across the series combination in parallel, the system attains unity p.f.*

SOLUTION. $R = 15\,\Omega,\ X_L = 10\,\Omega$

$$\therefore\ Z = \sqrt{R^2 + X_L^2} = 18.03\,\Omega\ \angle 33.7°\,\Omega$$

Let X_C be the capacitance connected across R-L combination such that p.f. of the combination becomes unity. Assuming the current through the capacitance to be I_C,

$$I_C = I_L \sin\phi \quad \text{[Ref. Fig. E2.22]}$$

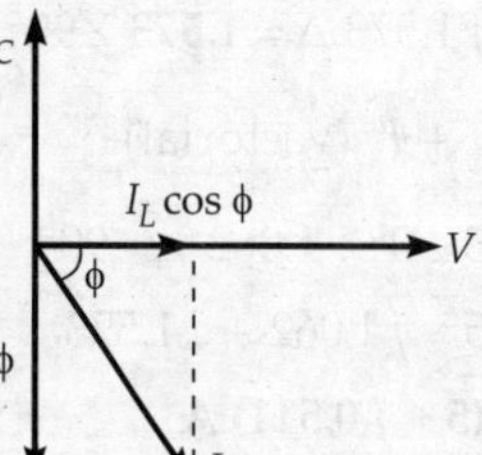

Fig. E2.22

[I_C being the capacitor current, it must balance $I_L \sin\phi$, the reactive part of I_L (the current through Z) such that the net current is $I_L \cos\phi$],

or,
$$\frac{V}{X_C} = \frac{V}{Z}\cdot\frac{X_L}{Z}$$

or,
$$X_C = \frac{Z^2}{X_L} = \frac{R^2 + X_L^2}{X_L} = \frac{325}{10} = 32.5\,\Omega$$
$$= \frac{1}{2\pi fC}$$

$$\therefore \quad C = \frac{1}{2\pi f X_C}$$
$$= \frac{1}{2\times\pi\times 50\times 32.5} = \mathbf{98\,\mu F.}$$

EXAMPLE 2.54 *A resistance of $10\,\Omega$, an inductance of 150 mH and a capacitor of $100\,\mu$ F are connected across a 50 V, 50 Hz source. Find the branch currents and total current. Draw the phasor diagram.*

SOLUTION. Referring Fig. E2.23,

$$I_1 = \frac{50\angle 0°}{10\angle 0°} = \mathbf{5\angle 0°\ A}$$

$$I_2 = \frac{50\angle 0°}{(2\pi f\times 0.15)\angle 90°} = \mathbf{1.062\angle -90°\ A.}$$

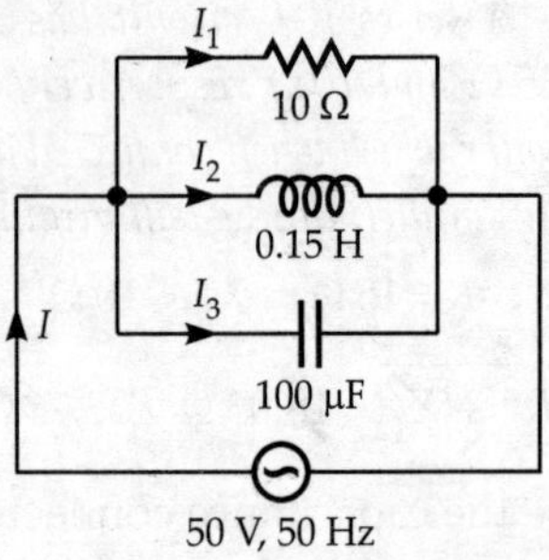

Fig. E2.23

$$I_3 = j\,\omega CV$$
$$= j \times 2 \times \pi \times 50 \times 100 \times 10^{-6} \times 50$$
$$= j\,1.573 \text{ A} = \mathbf{1.573 \angle 90° \text{ A}}.$$

$\therefore\ I_1 + I_2 + I_3$ (vectorial)

$$= 5\angle 0° + 1.062\angle -90° + 1.573\angle 90°$$
$$= 5 - j\,1.062 + j\,1.573$$

or, $I_{\text{Total}} = \mathbf{(5 + j\,0.511)\ A}$

$$= \mathbf{5.026 \angle 5.84°\ A.}$$

Figure E2.24 represents the phasor diagram.

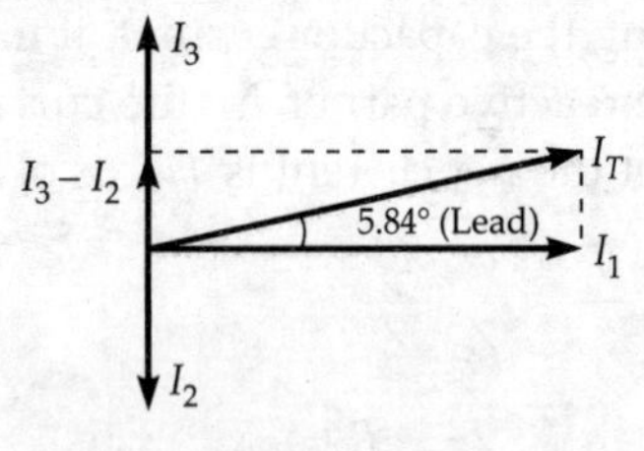

Fig. E2.24

EXAMPLE 2.55 *In the network of Fig. E2.25,*

$$I_1 = 216\angle -49°,\ \ Y_1 = 0.31 - j\,0.354 \text{ mho};$$
$$I_2 = 352\angle -51°;\ \ Y_2 = 0.49 - j\,0.61$$

Find I and V.

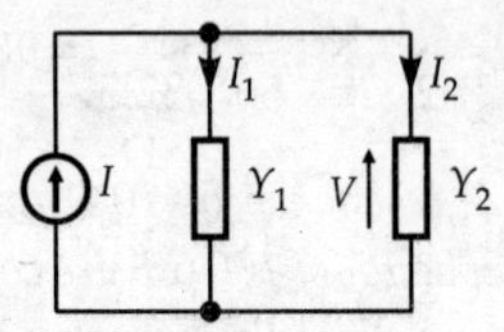

Fig. E2.25

SOLUTION. $I = I_1 + I_2$ (vectorial)

$$= 216\angle -49° + 352\angle -51°$$
$$= 363.23 - j\,436.6$$
$$= \mathbf{568} \angle -50.24° \text{ A}.$$

Also, $Y = Y_1 + Y_2$

$$= 0.31 - j\,0.359 + 0.49 - j\,0.61$$

[Y represents equivalent admittance of Y_1 and Y_2]

$$= (0.8 - j\,0.964) \text{ mho}$$
$$= 1.253\angle -50.3° \text{ mho}.$$

Thus,

$$V = \frac{I}{Y} = \frac{568\angle -50.24°}{1.253\angle -50.30°} \simeq \mathbf{453.31} \angle 0° \text{ V}.$$

EXAMPLE 2.56 *A reactor of reactance X_p is in parallel with a resistor of resistance R_p. Formulate the equivalence between parallel and series circuits.*

SOLUTION. In the parallel circuit, Y_p being the equivalent admittance looking through the input terminals,

$$Y_p = \frac{1}{R_p} + \frac{1}{\pm j\,X_p}$$

$$\text{and } Z_p = \frac{1}{Y_p} = \frac{1}{\dfrac{1}{R_p} \mp j\dfrac{1}{X_p}}.$$

$$= \frac{1/R_p}{(1/R_p)^2 + (1/X_p)^2} \pm j\,\frac{1/X_p}{(1/R_p)^2 + (1/X_p)^2}$$

Multiplying the numerator and denominator of each term by $R_p^2\,X_p^2$,

$$Z_p = \frac{R_p\,X_p^2}{X_p^2 + R_p^2} \pm j\,\frac{R_p^2\,X_p}{X_p^2 + R_p^2} = R_s \pm j\,X_s$$

(Fig. E2.26)

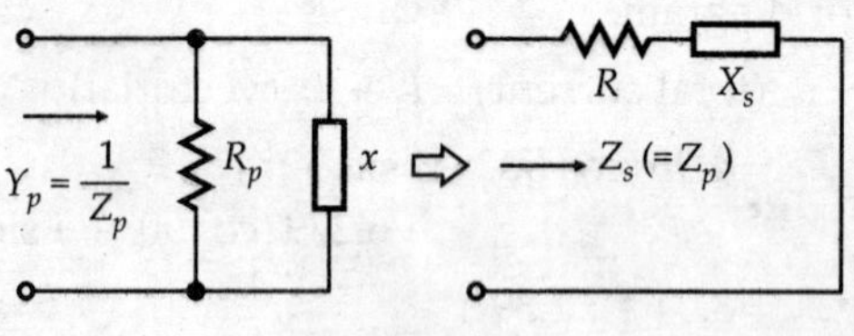

Fig. E2.26

Thus, in the series equivalent circuit of the parallel circuit,

$$\boldsymbol{R_s = \frac{R_p\,X_p^2}{X_p^2 + R_p^2}} \text{ and } \boldsymbol{X_s = \frac{R_p^2\,X_p}{X_p^2 + R_p^2}}.$$

EXAMPLE 2.57 *A resistor R_s is in series with a reactance X_s such that $Z_s = (R_s \pm j\,X_s)$ ohms. Obtain its equivalent parallel circuit.*

SOLUTION.

$$Z_s = R_s \pm j X_s$$

or, $$Y_s = \frac{1}{Z_s} = \frac{1}{R_s \pm j X_s}$$

$$= \frac{R_s}{R_s^2 + X_s^2} \mp j \frac{X_s}{R_s^2 + X_s^2}$$

$$= G_p \mp j B_p$$

where $G_p = \frac{R_s}{R_s^2 + X_s^2}$ and $B_p = \frac{X_s}{R_s^2 + X_s^2}$

Obviously

$$Y_s = G_p \mp j B_p = \frac{1}{R_p} \mp \frac{1}{j X_p}$$

This gives $\boldsymbol{R_p = \frac{R_s^2 + X_s^2}{R_s}}$; $\boldsymbol{X_p = \frac{R_s^2 + X_s^2}{X_s}}$

R_p and X_p give the parallel equivalent of the given series circuit.

EXAMPLE 2.58 *Fig. E2.27 represents a d.c. 10 V voltage source as well as 10 V a.c. 50 Hz voltage source while Z_1 and Z_2 are two unknown impedances. When Z_1 is connected across 10 V d.c. source, it draws a current of 10 A while it draws a current of 8 A if connected across 10 V a.c. source. On the other hand, if Z_2 is connected across 10 V d.c. source, it does not draw any current and draws only 5 A current if connected across 10 V a.c. source. Find the elements in Z_1 and Z_2.*

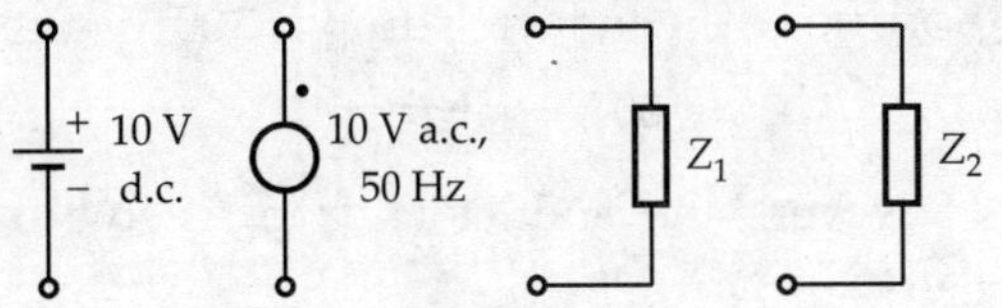

Fig. E2.27

SOLUTION. When Z_1 is connected across *a.c.* source, it draws 10 A current.

$$\therefore \quad R_1 = \frac{10 \text{ V}}{10 \text{ A}} = 1 \Omega$$

Again, when Z_1 is connected across *a.c.* source, it draws 8 A current.

$$\therefore \quad Z_1 = \frac{10}{8} = 1.25 \Omega$$

Thus, the inductive reactance in Z_1 is given by

$$X_1 = \sqrt{Z_1^2 - R_1^2} = \sqrt{1.25^2 - 1^2} = 0.75 \Omega$$

Thus, $Z_1 = (1 + j\,0.75)\,\Omega$

On the other hand, Z_2, when connected across 10 V *d.c.* source, does not draw any current at steady state.

$\therefore$ Z_2 is a capacitor.

It draws a current of 5 A when connected across 10 V *a.c.*

i.e., $$I = \frac{V}{X_c} \text{ or } X_C = \frac{V}{I} = \frac{10}{5} = 2 \text{ giving}$$

$$Z_2 = -j\,2\,\Omega.$$

EXAMPLE 2.59 *A 50 Hz sinusoidal voltage $v = 311 \sin \omega t$ is applied to a RL series circuit. If the magnitude of resistance is 5 Ω and that of inductance is 0.02 H,*

(a) Calculate the r.m.s. or effective value of steady state current and relative phase angle

(b) Obtain the expression for the instantaneous current

(c) Compute the effective magnitude and phase of voltage drops appearing across each circuit element.

SOLUTION. (*a*) Let V represent the r.m.s. value and be taken as reference

$$\therefore \quad V = \frac{V_m}{\sqrt{2}} = \frac{311}{\sqrt{2}} = 220 \text{ V}$$

i.e., $$V = 220 + j\,0 = 220 \angle 0° \text{ V}$$

But $$Z = R + j\,\omega L$$

$$= 5 + j\,.2\,\pi\,.\,50\,.\,0.02 = (5 + j\,6.28)\,\Omega$$

$$= \sqrt{5^2 + 6.28^2} \angle \tan^{-1} \frac{6.28}{5.0}$$

$$= 8.03 \angle 51.47° \Omega$$

$$\therefore \quad I = \frac{V}{Z} = \frac{220 \angle 0°}{8.03 \angle 51.47°} = \mathbf{27.39 \angle -51.47° \text{ A.}}$$

Thus, the effective value of the circuit current is 27.39 A while the angle of lag of the current from the voltage is 51.47°.

(*b*) The instantaneous current is then given by

$$i = I_m \sin(\omega t + \theta)$$

$$= (27.39) \times \sqrt{2} \sin(\omega t - 51.47°)$$

$$= \mathbf{38.73 \sin(\omega t - 51.47°) \text{ A.}}$$

(*c*) The voltage drop across the resistor is given by

$$V_R = IR = (27.39 \angle -51.47) \times 5$$

$$= \mathbf{136.95 \angle -51.47° \text{ V.}}$$

CHAPTER 2

The voltage drop across the inductance is

$$V_L = j\, I X_L$$
$$= (j\,27.39 \angle -51.47°)(2\,\pi\,.\,50\,.\,0.02)$$
$$= 1 \angle 90°\,.\,27.39 \angle -51.47°\,.\,6.28$$
$$= 172 \angle 90° - 51.47° = \mathbf{172 \angle 38.43° \ V.}$$

Check

$V = V_R + V_L$ (vectorially)

$= 136.95 \angle -51.47° + 172 \angle 38.53° = 220 + j\,0$ V]

EXAMPLE 2.60 *In a series R-L circuit, $R = 10\,\Omega$, $L = 20$ mH. The circuit current being 10 sin 314 t A, find the total voltage drop (v) across the elements R and L. Also obtain the phase angle between i and v.*

SOLUTION. The phase angle θ between v and i is given by

$$\theta = \tan^{-1}\frac{\omega L}{R}$$
$$= \tan^{-1}\frac{2\,\pi \times 50 \times 20 \times 10^{-3}}{10} = \mathbf{32.13°.}$$

[$\because$ $i = 10 \sin 314\,t$ $\therefore$ $\omega = 314 = 2\,\pi\,f$ *i.e.,* $f = 50$ Hz]

$$v = I_m \sqrt{R^2 + (\omega L)^2}\ \sin(\omega t + \theta)$$
$$= 10\sqrt{10^2 + (314 \times 20 \times 10^{-3})^2}\ \sin(314\,t + \theta)$$
$$= \mathbf{118.08 \sin(314\,t + 32.13°)\ V.}$$

[here, i lags v by 32.13°]

EXAMPLE 2.61 *In a series R-L circuit, the current and voltage are given as*

$$i = 1 \cos(314\,t - 20°),\ v = 10 \cos(314\,t + 10°).$$

Find the values of R and L.

SOLUTION. Let v be the reference vector, i lags v by $(20 + 10) = 30°$.

Also, $\dfrac{V_m}{I_m} = \dfrac{10}{1} = 10.$

Hence, $\dfrac{10}{1} = \sqrt{R^2 + (314.\,L)^2}$

or, $R^2 + (314.\,L)^2 = 100$ ...(1)

and $\tan 30° = 0.577 = \dfrac{314\,L}{R}$ ...(2)

Solving (1) and (2), $L = \mathbf{15.9\ mH}$; $R = \mathbf{8.66\,\Omega}$.

EXAMPLE 2.62 *In a series RC circuit, the values of $R = 10\,\Omega$ and $C = 25$ nF. A sinusoidal voltage of 50 MHz is applied and the maximum voltage across the capacitance is 2.5 V. Find the maximum voltage across the series combination.*

SOLUTION. $\omega = 2\,\pi\,f$

$$= 2\,.\,\pi\,.\,50 \times 10^6 \text{ rad/sec}$$
$$= 314 \times 10^6 \text{ rad/sec.}$$

The current through the capacitor being given by $I = \omega C V$, in this problem,

$$I_{max} = \omega C\, V_{max}$$
$$= 314 \times 10^6 \times 25 \times 10^{-9} \times 2.5$$
$$= 19.625 \text{ A}$$

Again,

$$V_{max} = I_{max}\ Z = I_{max}\sqrt{R^2 + \left(\frac{1}{\omega C}\right)^2}$$
$$= 19.625\sqrt{10^2 + \left(\frac{1}{2\,.\,\pi\,.\,50 \times 10^6 \times 25 \times 10^{-9}}\right)^2}$$
$$= \mathbf{196.59\ V.}$$

EXAMPLE 2.63 *In a series LCR circuit, the maximum inductor voltage is twice the capacitor voltage maximum. However, the circuit current lags the applied voltage by 30° and the instantaneous drop across the inductance is given by $v_L = 100 \sin 377\,t$ V. Assuming the resistance being $20\,\Omega$, find the values of the inductance and capacitance.*

SOLUTION. The inductor drop is 100 V (max),

i.e., $v_{L(max)} = 100 \text{ V} = \omega L\, I_{max}$

However, the inductor drop is twice the capacitor drop.

$\therefore$ $\dfrac{1}{2}.100 = I_{max}\ X_C = \dfrac{I_{max}}{\omega C}$

Thus,

$50\,\omega = \dfrac{I_{max}}{C}$ ...(1)

and $\dfrac{100}{\omega} = I_{max}\,.\,L$ ...(2)

Also,

$$\tan\theta = \frac{\omega L - \dfrac{1}{\omega C}}{R}$$

or, $\tan 30° = \dfrac{\omega L - \dfrac{1}{\omega C}}{20} = 0.577$

i.e., $0.577 = \dfrac{\omega^2\,LC - 1}{20\,\omega C}$ ...(3)

Solving for (1) and (2),

$\omega^2\,LC = 2$ ...(4)

Substituting the value of $\omega^2 LC$ in (3), we get,

$$0.577 = \frac{1}{20\,\omega C}$$

or, $$C = \frac{1}{20 \times 0.577 \times \omega}$$

$$= \frac{1}{20 \times 0.577 \times 377} = \mathbf{230\,\mu F.}$$

Thus from (4),

$$L = \frac{2}{\omega^2 C} = \frac{2}{(377)^2 \times 230 \times 10^{-6}}$$

$$= \mathbf{61.18\ mH.}$$

2.8 SINUSOIDAL RESPONSE OF PARALLEL *R-L* CIRCUIT

Figure 2.20 represents a parallel *R-L* circuit excited by a sinusoid.

At steady state,

$$I_R = \frac{V}{R} \qquad \text{...(2.29)}$$

and $$I_L = \frac{V}{j X_L} = \frac{V}{j\omega L} \qquad \text{...(2.30)}$$

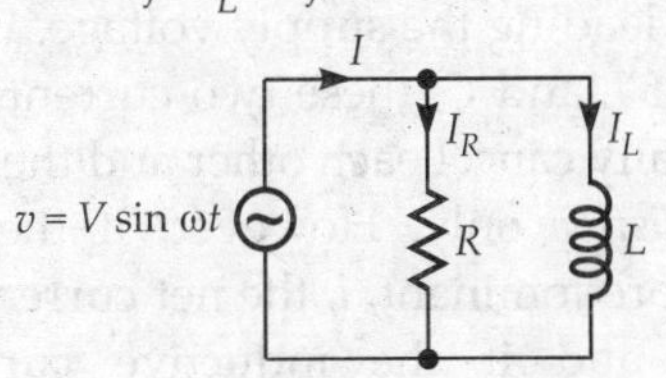

Fig. 2.20 A parallel *R-L* circuit being energized by sinusoid

However, applying Kirchhoff's Current Law,

$$I = I_R + I_L$$

$$= V\left(\frac{1}{R} + \frac{1}{j\omega L}\right) = VY \qquad \text{...(2.31)}$$

[$\because$ Y = admittance = $G + jB$;

where, G = conductance = $1/R$ mho

B = inductive susceptance = $1/X_L$ mho].

Here, $$Y = \frac{1}{R} + \frac{1}{j\omega L} = \frac{1}{R} - j\frac{1}{\omega L} \qquad \text{...(2.32)}$$

[it may be noted that, actual sign of B is –ve].

Also, the total current supplied by the source in steady state *lags* the voltage by impedance angle given by

$$\theta = \tan^{-1}\frac{-1/\omega L}{1/R} = \tan^{-1}\left(-\frac{R}{\omega L}\right) \qquad \text{...(2.33)}$$

Again, as $i = i_R + i_L$, we can further write,

$$i = \frac{v}{R} + \frac{1}{L}\int v\,dt = \frac{V_m}{R}\cos\omega t + \frac{V_m}{\omega L}\sin\omega t$$

[assuming $v = V_m \cos\omega t$]

$$\therefore\ i = \sqrt{\left(\frac{1}{R}\right)^2 + \left(\frac{1}{\omega L}\right)^2}\ V_m \cos(\omega t - \theta), \qquad \text{...(2.34)}$$

when θ is given by equation (2.33)

If $R >> \omega L$, $\theta \to 90°$ and $i = \frac{V_m}{\omega L}\cos(\omega t - 90°)$.

With this relatively high resistance, the *current drawn by the resistance branch is low* and then $i \simeq i_L$.

If, on the other hand,

$R << \omega L$, $\theta \to 0°$ and $i = \frac{V_m}{R}\cos\omega t$.

Here, the *current drawn by the inductive branch is negligible* and then $i \simeq i_R$.

2.9 SINUSOIDAL RESPONSE OF PARALLEL *RC* CIRCUIT

Figure 2.21 represents a parallel *RC* circuit at steady state and excited by sinusoidal voltage source $v = V_m \sin\omega t$.

Here, $$I_R = \frac{V}{R};$$

$$I_C = \frac{V}{1/j\omega C}$$

$$\left[\because |X_C| = \frac{1}{\omega C}\right]$$

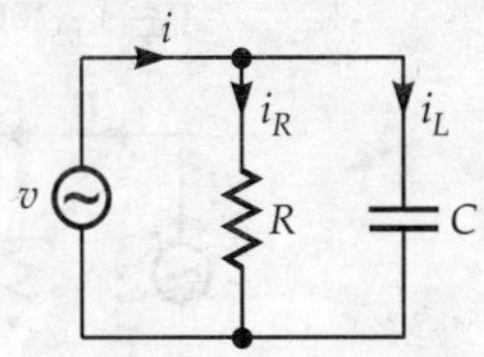

Fig. 2.21 Sinusoid applied to parallel *RC* circuit.

However, vectorially,

$$I = I_R + I_C$$

which gives, $$I = V\left[\frac{1}{R} + \frac{1}{1/j\omega C}\right]$$

or, $$I = V\left[\frac{1}{R} + j\,\omega C\right] = V[G + jB] \qquad \text{...(2.35)}$$

where, $G = 1/R$ mho and $B = +\,\omega C$ mho

and $$\theta = \tan^{-1}\frac{\omega C}{1/R} = \tan^{-1}(\omega RC) \qquad \text{...(2.36)}$$

Thus, it is evident that the *current leads the voltage* by an angle given by expression (2.36).

Also, $i = i_R + i_C$

$$= \frac{v}{R} + C\frac{dv}{dt}$$

$$= \frac{V_m}{R}\sin\omega t + \omega CV_m \cos\omega t$$

Then, $$i = \sqrt{\left(\frac{1}{R}\right)^2 + (\omega C)^2}\, V_m \sin(\omega t + \theta), \qquad \text{...(2.37)}$$

θ being given by expression (2.37).

If $R >> \frac{1}{\omega C}$, $\theta \to 90°$

and $i \simeq i_c = \omega C V_m \sin(\omega t + 90°)$

and if $R << \frac{1}{\omega C}$, $\theta \to 0°$

and $i \simeq i_R = \frac{V_m}{R}\sin\omega t.$

2.10 SINUSOIDAL RESPONSE OF PARALLEL *RLC* CIRCUIT

Figure 2.22 represents a steady state parallel *RLC* circuit being energized by a voltage sinusoid

$$v = V_m \sin\omega t.$$

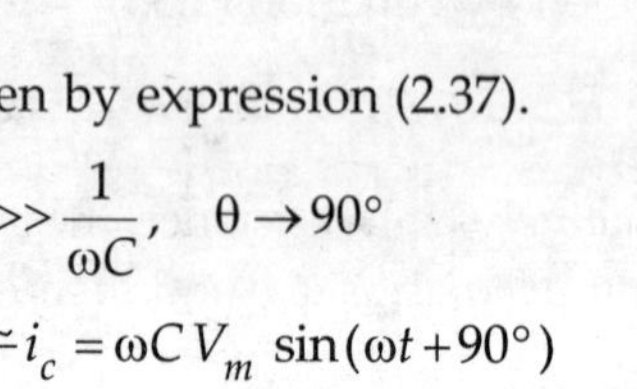

Fig. 2.22 Parallel *RLC* circuit.

Here, $i = i_R = i_L + i_C = \frac{v}{R} + \frac{1}{L}\int v\,dt + C\frac{dv}{dt}$

$$= \frac{V_m}{R}\sin\omega t - \frac{V_m}{\omega L}\cos\omega t + \omega C\, V_m \cos\omega t \qquad \text{...(2.38)}$$

Let $i = A\sin(\omega t + \theta)$

$$= A\sin\omega t\cos\theta + A\cos\omega t\sin\theta \qquad \text{...(2.39)}$$

Equating the coefficients of sin ωt and cos ωt in (2.38) and (2.39), we get

$$\frac{V_m}{R} = A\cos\theta$$

and $$\left(\omega C - \frac{1}{\omega L}\right)V_m = A\sin\theta$$

Then $$\tan\theta = \frac{\omega C - \frac{1}{\omega L}}{1/R} \qquad \text{...(2.40)}$$

$$\cos\theta = \frac{1/R}{\sqrt{\left(\frac{1}{R}\right)^2 + \left(\omega C - \frac{1}{\omega L}\right)^2}} \qquad \text{...(2.40(a))}$$

$$A = \sqrt{\left(\frac{1}{R}\right)^2 + \left(\omega C - \frac{1}{\omega L}\right)^2}\,.\,V_m \qquad \text{...(2.41)}$$

and $$i = \sqrt{\left(\frac{1}{R}\right)^2 - \left(\omega C - \frac{1}{\omega L}\right)^2}$$
$$\times V_m \sin\left[\omega t + \tan^{-1}\left(\omega C - \frac{1}{\omega L}\right)R\right] \qquad \text{...(2.42)}$$

Obviously, the sign of the phase angle θ depends on the relative values of ωC and $\frac{1}{\omega L}$.

In this context it may be noted that the inductive branch current I_L is at 90° lagging the supply voltage while the capacitive branch current I_C is at 90° leading the supply voltage. With proper selection of *L* and *C*, these two currents I_L and I_C may mutually cancel each other and the net current can be *resistive* only. However, if the capacitive current is predominant, *i*, the net current would be capacitive and if the inductive current I_L is predominant, the net current *i* would be inductive.

EXAMPLE 2.64 *The current in the resistive branch of a parallel RC circuit is given by i_r = 10 cos (1000 t – 10°) amp. What is the current in the capacitance ? Assume R = 10 Ω, C = 10 μF.*

SOLUTION. In the parallel *RC* circuit,

$$v_c = v_r \qquad \text{...(A)}$$

However,

$$v_r = Ri_R = 10 \times 10\cos(1000\,t - 10°)\,\text{V}$$
$$= 100\cos(1000\,t - 10°) \qquad \text{...(B)}$$

The capacitive current i_c will obviously lead the voltage v_r (and thus v_c) by 90°.

$$\therefore\ i_c = \omega CV\cos(1000\,t - 10° + 90°) \qquad \text{...(C)}$$
$$= 1000 \times 10 \times 10^{-6} \times 100\cos(1000\,t + 80°)\,\text{A}$$
$$= \mathbf{1\cos(1000\,t + 80°)\,A.}$$

[Here *V* in eqn. (*C*) has been shown to be equivalent to the r.m.s. value of the expression of v_r in eqn. (*B*)].

EXAMPLE 2.65 *Fig. E2.28 represents a parallel RL circuit being energized by a sinusoidal a.c. voltage of*

$$v = 100 \sin (1000\, t + 36°)\ V.$$

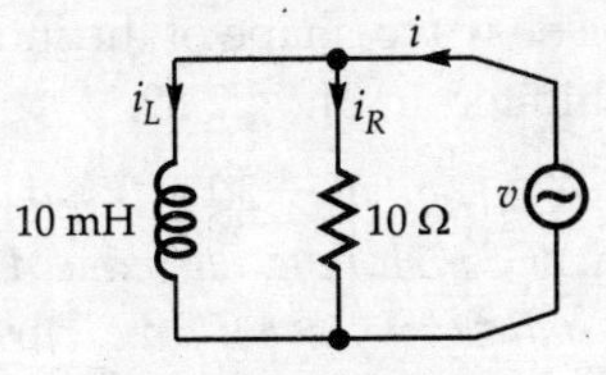

Fig. E2.28

Obtain the instantaneous value of currents through R and L. Hence obtain the total current in term of R.M.S. values.

SOLUTION.

$$i_R = \frac{V_m}{R} \sin (1000\, t + 36°)$$

$$= 10 \sin (1000\, t + 36°) \text{ A}$$

$$= 10 \cos (1000\, t - 54°) \quad ...(A)$$

$$i_L = \frac{V_m}{\omega L} \sin (1000\, t + 36° - 90°)$$

$$[\because i_L \text{ would lag } v \text{ by } 90°]$$

$$= 10 \sin (1000\, t - 54°)$$

$$\left[\because \frac{V_m}{\omega L} = \frac{100}{1000 . 10 \times 10^{-3}} = 10\right]$$

$$= 10 \cos (1000\, t - 144°) \quad ...(B)$$

From (A) and (B) we get,

$I_R = 10\angle -54°$ [Please note that there are the r.m.s. values]

and $I_L = 10\angle -144°$

$\therefore$ net r.m.s. current

$$I = I_R + I_L = 10\angle -54° + 10\angle -144°$$

$$= 10 (\cos 54° - j \sin 54°) + 10 [\cos (-144°) + j \sin (-144°)]$$

$$= 5.88 - j\, 8.1 - 8.1 - j\, 5.88 = (-2.22 - j\, 13.97) \text{ A}$$

i.e., $\mathbf{I = 14.14 \angle -99° \ A}$

EXAMPLE 2.66 *The applied voltage in a parallel RLC circuit is given by*

$$v = \left[50 \sin\left(5000\, t + \frac{\pi}{4}\right)\right] V$$

If the values of R, L and C be given as 20 Ω, 1.6×10^{-3} H and 20 μF, find the total current supplied by the source.

SOLUTION. In the parallel *RLC* circuit, the net current from the source will be vector sum of the branch currents I_R, I_L and I_C.

Now, $$I_R = \frac{V}{R} = \frac{(50/\sqrt{2})\angle 45°}{20}$$

$$= 1.768 \angle 45° \text{ A}$$

$$\left[\text{from } v = 50 \sin\left(5000\, t + \frac{\pi}{4}\right),\ V = \frac{50}{\sqrt{2}} \angle \frac{\pi}{4} \text{ volts}\right]$$

$$I_L = \frac{V}{X_L}$$

$$= \frac{(50/\sqrt{2})\angle 45°}{5000 \times 1.6 \times 10^{-3} \angle 90°}$$

$$= 4.421 \angle -45° \text{ A}$$

$$[\because X_L = j\omega L = j \times 5000 \times 1.6 \times 10^{-3} \text{ ohms}]$$

$$I_C = \frac{V}{X} = j\, V\omega C$$

$$= \left(\frac{50}{\sqrt{2}}\right) \angle 45° \times 5000 \times 20 \times 10^{-6} \angle 90°$$

$$= 3.54 \angle 135° \text{ A}$$

$$\therefore\ I = I_R + I_L + I_C$$

$$= (1.768 \angle 45° + 4.421\angle -45° + 3.54\angle 135°)$$

$$= 1.768 (\cos 45° + j \sin 45°) + 4.421 (\cos 45° - j \sin 45°) + 3.54 (\cos 135° + j \sin 135°)$$

$$= 1.768 \times 0.707 + j\, 1.768 \times 0.707 + 4.421 \times 0.707 - j\, 4.421 \times 0.707 + 3.54 \times (-0.707) + j\, 3.54 \times 0.707$$

$$= (1.873 + j\, 0.627) \text{ A}$$

$\therefore$ $\mathbf{I = 1.975 \angle 18.5° \ A}$ **(lead).**

[*I* is the net current from source]

ADDITIONAL EXAMPLES

EXAMPLE 2.67 *A repeating function current of $i = 10^3\, t$ is applied in a resistor of 5 Ω. Find the power expression and its magnitude between O to T m sec. Assume T = 2 m sec.*

SOLUTION.

$$v = Ri = (5\times 10^3\ t)\ \text{V}$$

$$\therefore\quad p = vi = 5\times 10^3\ t\times 10^3\ t$$

$$= (5\times 10^6\ t^2)\ \text{W}.\qquad [p, i, v \text{ are all instantaneous values}]$$

$$\therefore\quad P = \frac{1}{T}\int_0^T p\,dt$$

$$= \frac{1}{2\times 10^{-3}}\int_0^{2\times 10^{-3}} 5\times 10^6\ t^2\,dt$$

$$= \mathbf{6.67\ W.}$$

EXAMPLE 2.68 *A current waveform of 2 m sec duration is applied across a pure inductance. Waveform of current through it at $t \le 0.25$ m sec, 0.25 m sec $\le t \le 0.75$ m sec, 0.75 m sec $\le t \le 1$ m sec, 1 m sec $< t < 1.25$ m sec is shown in Fig. E2.29. Find the induced voltage waveform.*

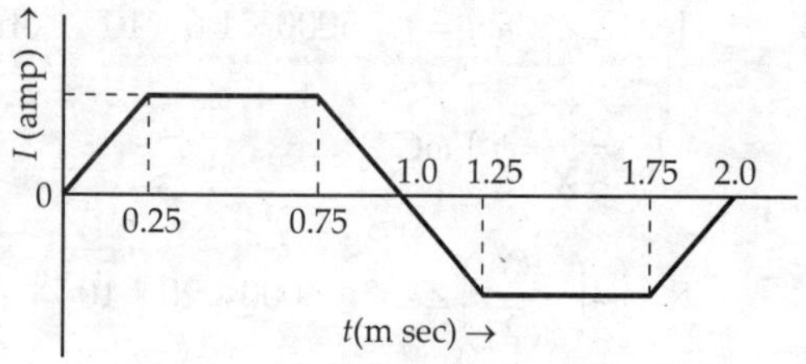

Fig. E2.29

SOLUTION. Within the time interval $0 \le t \le 0.25$ m sec, the current wave is linearly rising. This gives the voltage induced in the inductance constant ;

$$\left[\because e = L\frac{di}{dt}, \text{ and } i \text{ is linearly varying, hence } \frac{di}{dt} \text{ will be constant}\right]$$

During the period 0.25 m sec $\le t \le 0.75$ m sec, the current wave has constant amplitude. Thus di/dt is zero and hence the voltage induced will be zero. Between 0.75 m sec $\le t \le 1.0$ m sec, the current wave is linearly decreasing. This gives the voltage induced in the inductance is constant. This wave shape will be maintained till 1.25 m sec as the current continuously goes on decreasing linearly till 1.25 sec. The wave-shape of the induced voltage has been exhibited in Fig. E2.30.

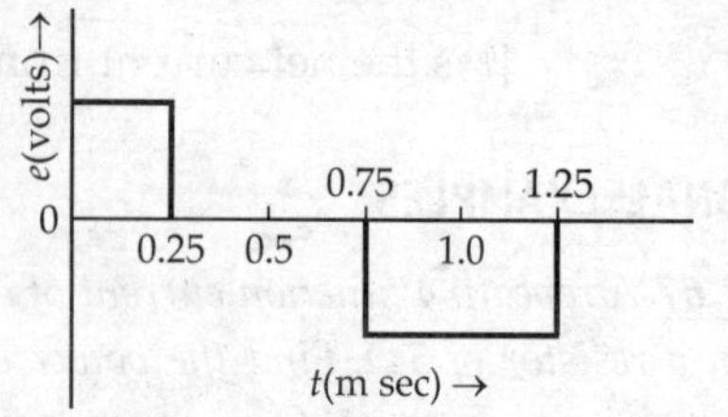

Fig. E2.30

EXAMPLE 2.69 *A current of $i = 300\ t$ is suddenly applied to an inductance of 1 mH. Find the induced voltage. What would be the induced voltage if a d.c. current of 10 A is applied suddenly ?*

SOLUTION. The induced voltage in the first case, V_L, is given by

$$V_L = L\frac{di}{dt}$$

$$= 1\times 10^{-3}\times\frac{d}{dt}(300\ t)\ \text{V} = \mathbf{0.3\ V.}$$

If the applied current is a constant of 10 amp, the induced voltage is

$$V_L = L\frac{di}{dt} = 1\times 10^{-3}\ \frac{d}{dt}(10) = \mathbf{0\ V.}$$

[The corresponding powers will be

$$p_1 = V_L\cdot i$$

$$= 0.3\times 300\ t = 90\ t \text{ watts } \textit{in the first case}$$

and

$$p_2 = V_L\cdot i$$

$$= 0\times 300\ t = 0\ \text{W } \textit{in the second case.}\ ]$$

EXAMPLE 2.70 *A voltage wave is shown in Fig. E2.31 where $v = 100\ (1 - e^{-10t})$ for $0 < t < 1$ and $v = 100\ e^{-10t}$ for $1 < t < 2$. Find the r.m.s. value of the voltage wave upto $t = 2$.*

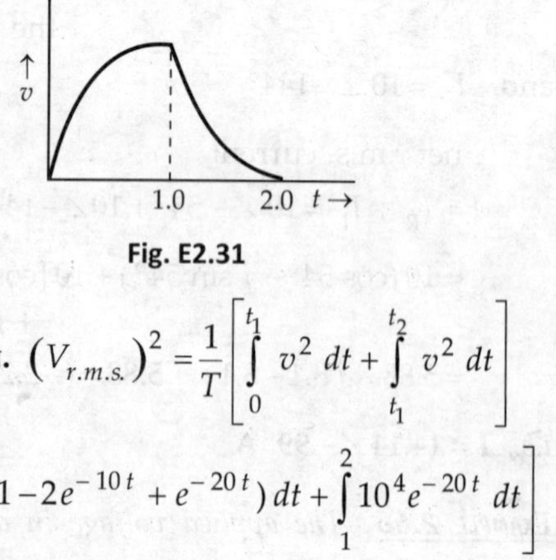

Fig. E2.31

SOLUTION. $$(V_{r.m.s.})^2 = \frac{1}{T}\left[\int_0^{t_1} v^2\,dt + \int_{t_1}^{t_2} v^2\,dt\right]$$

$$= \frac{1}{2}\left[\int_0^1 10^4(1 - 2e^{-10t} + e^{-20t})\,dt + \int_1^2 10^4 e^{-20t}\,dt\right]$$

$$= 5000\left[\left(t + 0.2e^{-10t} - 0.05\,e^{-20t}\right)\Big|_0^1 - (1/20)e^{-20t}\Big|_1^2\right]$$

$$\therefore\quad V_{rms} = \mathbf{65.25\ V.}$$

Example 2.71 *A current wave is given by*

$$i = 50 + 30 \sin \omega t.$$

Obtain the value of $I_{r.m.s.}$.

Solution. $I^2_{r.m.s.} = \dfrac{1}{2\pi}\int_0^{2\pi} (50 + 30 \sin \omega t)^2 \, d(\omega t)$

[as $\omega = 2\pi f$, hence, time period is 2π]

$$= \frac{1}{2\pi}\int_0^{2\pi} (2500 + 3000 \sin \omega t + 900 \sin^2 \omega t)\, d(\omega t)$$

$$= \frac{1}{2\pi}[2500\,(2\pi) + 0 + 900\,\pi] = 2950.$$

$\therefore$ $I_{r.m.s.} = \sqrt{2950} = \mathbf{54.31\ A.}$

Also, $I_{r.m.s.} = \sqrt{(50)^2 + \dfrac{1}{2}(30)^2} = 54.30$ A

$\because$ If a function $x(t)$ is expressed as

$$x(t) = a_0 + (a_1 \cos \omega t + a_2 \cos 2\,\omega t + \ldots) + (b_1 \sin \omega t + b_2 \sin 2\,\omega t + \ldots),$$

$$x_{\text{r.m.s.}} = \sqrt{a_0^2 + \frac{1}{2}(a_1^2 + a_2^2 + \ldots) + \frac{1}{2}(b_1^2 + b_2^2 + \ldots)}.$$

Example 2.72 *The voltage across an inductor is given by* $v(t) = te^{-t}$ *volts at* $t \geq 0$. *Obtain the expression for current. Assume inductance of the inductor to be 10 mH.*

Solution. The current in any inductor is given by

$$i = \frac{1}{L}\int_0^t v(t)\,dt$$

$$= \frac{1}{10 \times 10^{-3}}\int te^{-t} dt = 100\,[-e^{-t}(t+1)]_0^t$$

$$= 100\,[-e^{-t}(t+1) + 1]$$

$$= \mathbf{100\,(1 - e^{-t} - te^{-t})\ A.}$$

Example 2.73 *The current i (t) in a 10 Ω resistor is shown in Fig. E2.32. Draw the profile of v (t) and show the peak voltage magnitude. What is peak power ?*

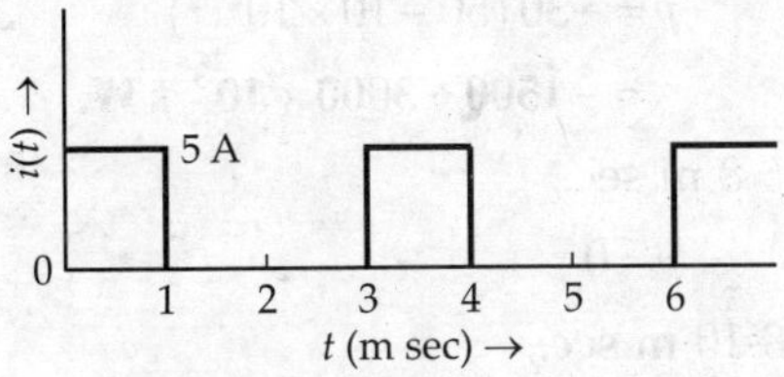

Fig. E2.32

Solution. In the resistor, the instantaneous voltage drop is given by

$$v(t) = Ri(t)$$

when $v_{max} = Ri_{max} = 10 \times 5 = 50$ V

[Ref. Fig. E2.32(*a*) for profile of $v(t)$].

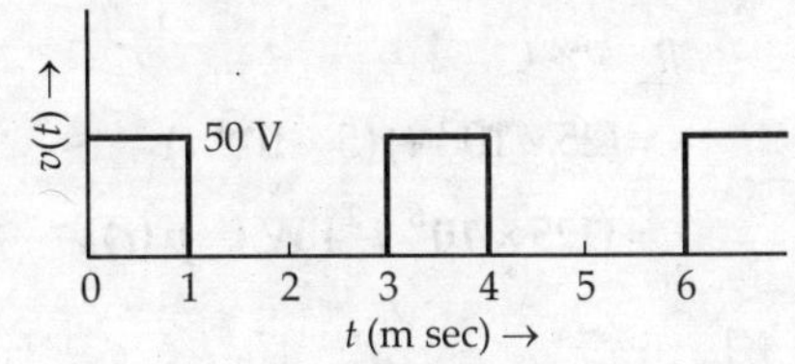

Fig. E2.32 (*a*)

Peak power is

$$p_{max} = i_{max} \times v_{max}$$

$$= 5 \times 50 = \mathbf{250\ watts.}$$

Notice Fig. E2.32(*b*) for $p(t)$ profile.

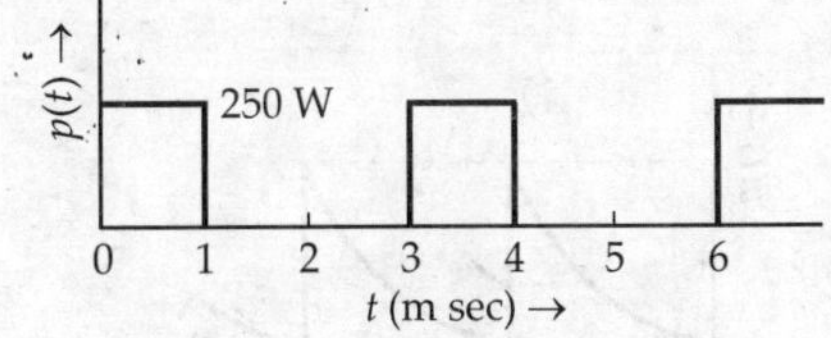

Fig. E2.32 (*b*)

Thus, $v(t)$ being shown in **Fig. E2.32(*a*),**

$$v_{max} = \mathbf{50\ V}$$

and $p_{max} = \mathbf{250\ watts.}$

Example 2.74 *A current as shown in Fig. E2.33 is applied across a 5 Ω resistor. Find v (t) and p (t) and draw the respective profiles.*

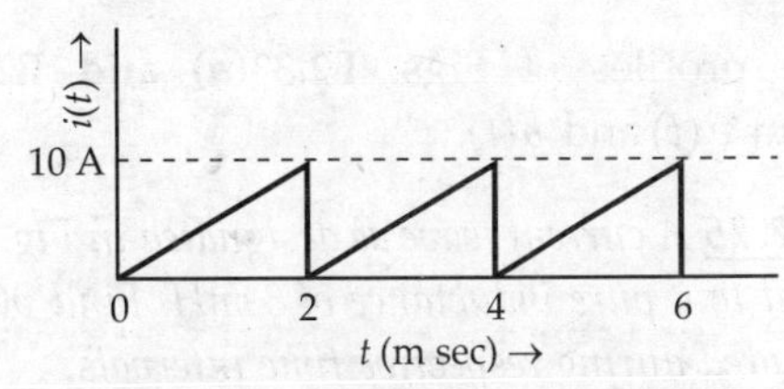

Fig. E2.33

Solution. $v(t) = Ri(t)$;

$$v_{max} = Ri_{max} = 5 \times 10 = 50 \text{ V}.$$

From Fig. E2.33, slope of graph is given by

$$m = \frac{10 \text{ A}}{2 \times 10^{-3} \text{ sec}} = 5 \times 10^3 \text{ A/sec}.$$

From the concept of co-ordinate geometry, the straight line equation for i is as follows :

$$i(t) = mt = 5 \times 10^3\ t \text{ amps}$$

$$\therefore \quad v(t) = 5 \times 10^3\ t \times R = \mathbf{25 \times 10^3\ t\ volts}$$

$$[\because R = 5\,\Omega]$$

$v(t)$ is shown in Fig. E2.33(a)

$$p = v \times i$$

$$= (25 \times 10^3\ t)(5 \times 10^3\ t)$$

$$= \mathbf{(125 \times 10^6\ t^2)\ W\ (\equiv p(t))}.$$

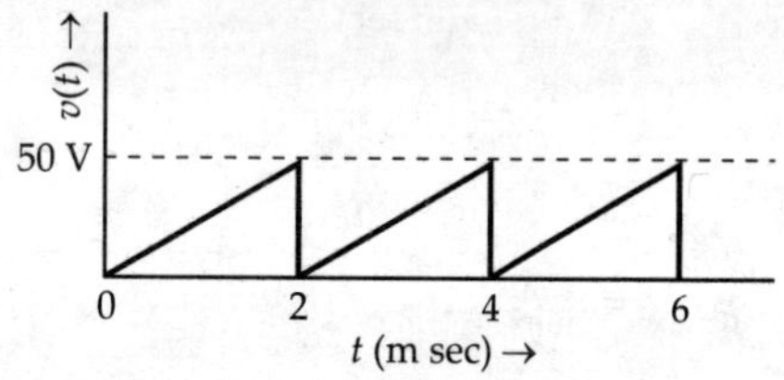

Fig. E2.33 (a)

Figure E2.33(b) represents the profile of $p(t)$.

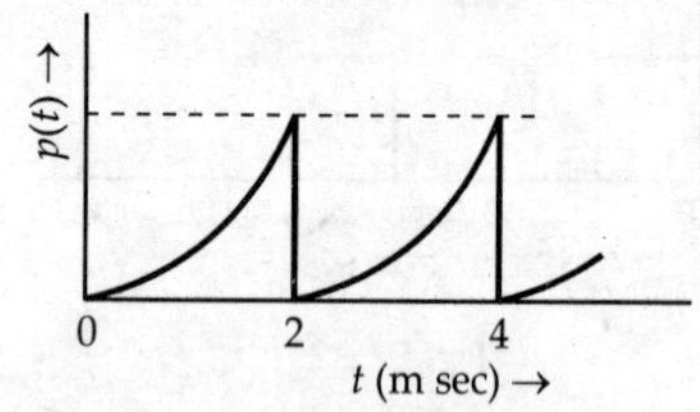

Fig. E2.33 (b)

$$\left[\text{Av. power } P = \frac{1}{T}\int_0^T vi\,dt \right.$$

$$\left. = \frac{1}{2 \times 10^{-3}} \int_0^T 125 \times 10^6\ t^2\,dt = 167\text{ W.} \right]$$

The profiles of **Figs. E2.33(a) and E2.33(b)** represent $v(t)$ and $p(t)$.

EXAMPLE 2.75 *A current wave as designated in Fig. E2.34 is applied to a pure inductance of 3 mH. Find v(t) and power stored during respective time intervals.*

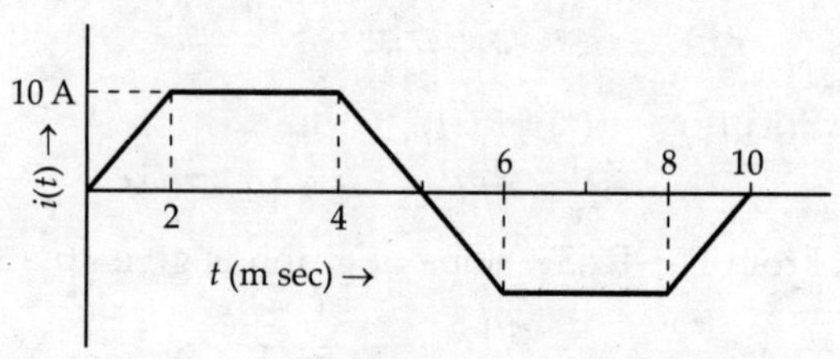

Fig. E2.34

SOLUTION. The current equations are shown below for respective time intervals :

0-2 m sec, $\quad i = \dfrac{10}{2 \times 10^{-3}}\, t = 5 \times 10^3\ t$ amps.

2-4 m sec, $\quad i = 10$ A (const.)

4-6 m sec, $\quad i = 10 - \dfrac{10}{1 \times 10^{-3}}(t - 4 \times 10^{-3})$

$$= (50 - 10 \times 10^3\ t) \text{ amps.}$$

6-8 m sec, $\quad i = -10$ A (const)

8-10 m sec, $i = 5 \times 10^3\ t$ amps.

Since voltage across the inductor is given by $v_L = L\dfrac{di}{dt}$ hence the voltage drops across the inductor for respective time intervals would be

0-2 m sec.,

$$v_L = L\frac{di}{dt} = 3 \times 10^{-3}\,\frac{d}{dt}(5 \times 10^3\ t) = \mathbf{15\ V}$$

2-4 m sec.,

$$v_L = L\frac{di}{dt} = 3 \times 10^{-3}\,\frac{d}{dt}(10\text{ A}) = \mathbf{0}.$$

4-6 m sec.,

$$v_L = L\frac{di}{dt} = 3 \times 10^{-3}\,\frac{d}{dt}(50 - 10 \times 10^3\ t)$$

$$= \mathbf{-30\ V}.$$

6-8 m sec.,

$$v_L = L\frac{di}{dt} = 3 \times 10^{-3}\,\frac{d}{dt}(-10\text{ A}) = \mathbf{0}.$$

8-10 m sec.,

$$v = 3 \times 10^{-3}\,\frac{d}{dt}(+5 \times 10^3\ t) = \mathbf{15\ V}.$$

Also, power stored

for 0-2 m sec.,

$$= vi = 15 \times 5 \times 10^3\ t = \mathbf{75 \times 10^3\ t\ W}.$$

for 2-4 m sec.,

$$p = 0 \times 10 = \mathbf{0\ W}.$$

for 4-6 m sec.,

$$p = -30\,(50 - 10 \times 10^3\ t)$$

$$= \mathbf{-1500 + 3000 \times 10^3\ t\ W}.$$

for 6-8 m sec.,

$$p = 0$$

for 8-10 m sec.,

$$p = \mathbf{75 \times 10^3\ t\ W}.$$

EXAMPLE 2.76 *A voltage source v(t) is connected across a capacitor of 2F. Find the energy stored in the capacitor from t = 0 to 10 sec, if $v(t) = t^2 e^{-2t}$.*

SOLUTION.

$$\text{Energy} = \int_{t_0}^{t} v(t)\, i(t)\, dt = \int_{t_0}^{t} v_c \frac{dv}{dt}\, dt$$

$$= C\int_{t_0}^{t} v\, dv = c.\frac{1}{2}[v(t)^2 - v(t_0)^2]$$

Since $v(t) = t^2 e^{-2t}$,

$$v(10) = 10^2 e^{-20} = 2.06 \times 10^{-7} \text{ volts.}$$

$$\therefore \quad \text{Energy} = 2 \times \frac{1}{2}[(2.06 \times 10^{-7})^2 = 0^2]$$

$$= 4.3 \times 10^{-4} \text{ J.}$$

Thus, Energy stored for 10 sec. = $\mathbf{4.3 \times 10^{-4}}$ **J.**

EXAMPLE 2.77 *A current wave i(t) (Fig. E2.35) is applied to an inductance of 10 H. Find v (t).*

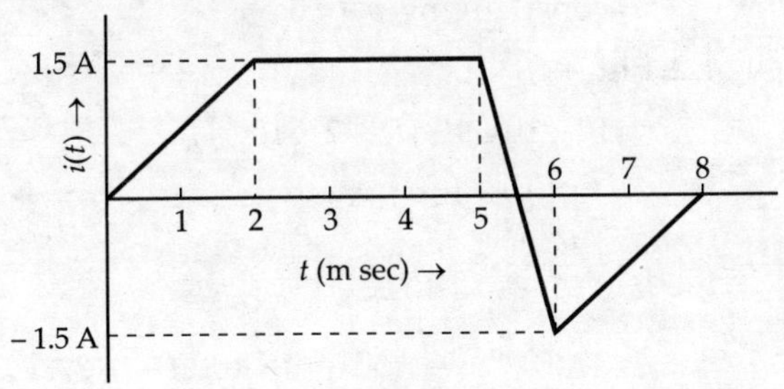

Fig. E2.35

SOLUTION. Let us find the slopes first corresponding to different time intervals :

$0 < t < 2$ Slope $= \dfrac{1.5}{2} = 0.75$ A/sec. $\left(\dfrac{di}{dt}\right)$

$2 < t < 5$ Slope = 0 A/sec. (Const. current)

$5 < t < 6$ Slope $= -\dfrac{1.5 + 1.5}{1} = -3$ A/sec $\left(\dfrac{di}{dt}\right)$

[Slope is +ve for ascending wave and – ve for descending wave]

$6 < t < 8$ Slope $= \dfrac{1.5}{2} = 0.75$ A/sec $\left(\dfrac{di}{dt}\right)$

The drop across inductance $v_2(t)$ can now be obtained as follows :

for $0 < t < 2$ s,

$$v_L(t) = L\frac{di}{dt} = 10 \times 0.75 = \mathbf{7.5\ V.}$$

for $2 < t < 5$ s,

$$v_L(t) = L\frac{di}{dt} = 10 \times 0 = \mathbf{0\ V.}$$

for $5 < t < 6$ s,

$$v_L(t) = L\frac{di}{dt} = 10 \times (-3) = \mathbf{-30\ V.}$$

for $6 < t < 8$ s,

$$v_L(t) = L\frac{di}{dt} = 10 \times 0.75 = \mathbf{7.5\ V.}$$

Fig. E2.35(*a*) shows the profile of $v(t)$.

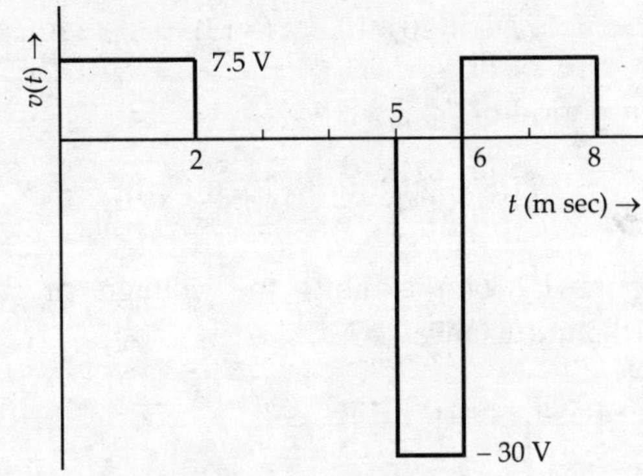

Fig. E2.35 (*a*)

EXAMPLE 2.78 *A current i(t) has been shown in Fig. E2.36. If it is applied across a pure inductance of 20 mH, find the profile of v (t).*

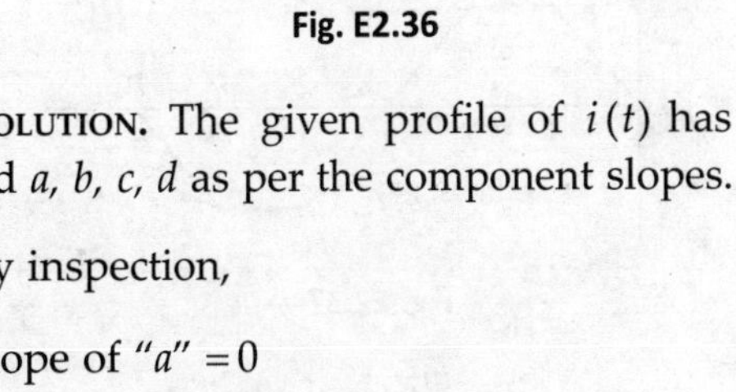

Fig. E2.36

SOLUTION. The given profile of $i(t)$ has been named *a*, *b*, *c*, *d* as per the component slopes.

By inspection,

Slope of "*a*" = 0

Slope of "*b*" $= \dfrac{20 - 10}{1} = 10$ A/S

Slope of "*c*" $= -\dfrac{20 - (-10)}{2} = 15$ A/S

Slope of "*d*" $= \dfrac{10}{2} = 5$ A/S.

Now,

for period of "*a*",

$$v_L = L\frac{di}{dt} = 20 \times 10^{-3} \times 0 = \mathbf{0\ volt},$$

for period of "*b*",

$$v_L = L\frac{di}{dt} = 20 \times 10^{-3} \times 10 = \mathbf{0.2\ volt},$$

for period of "*c*",

$$v_L = L\frac{di}{dt} = 20 \times 10^{-3} \times (-15) = \mathbf{-0.3\ volt},$$

and for period of "*d*",

$$v_L = L\frac{di}{dt} = 20 \times 10^{-3} \times 5 = \mathbf{0.1\ volt.}$$

Figure E2.36(*a*) exhibits the voltage profile across the inductance.

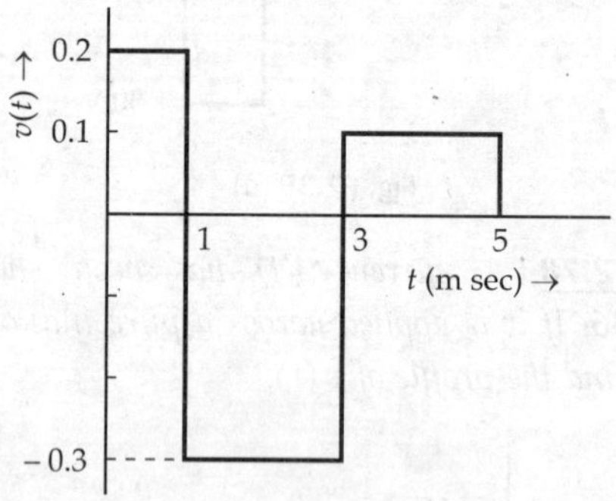

Fig. E2.36 (*a*)

EXAMPLE 2.79 *A current source i (t) is applied to a series LCR circuit (Figs. E2.37 and E2.37(a)). Find voltage across each element.*

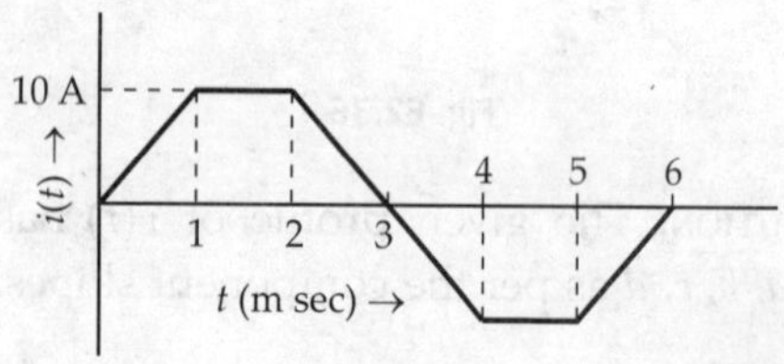

Fig. E2.37

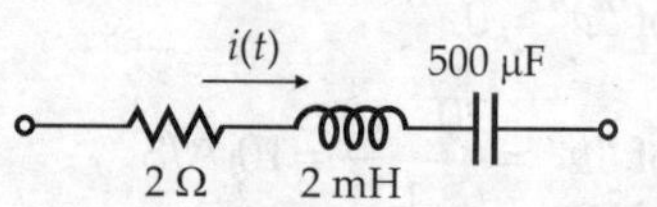

Fig. E2.37 (*a*)

SOLUTION. The drop across resistance $v_R\,(t)$ is shown in Fig. E2.37(*b*) where

$$v_{R(\max)} = i_{\max} \times R = 10 \times 2 = 20\ \text{V}.$$

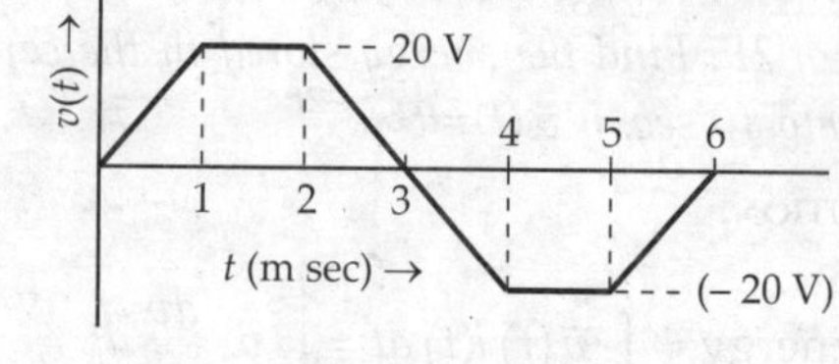

Fig. E2.37 (*b*)

In order to find $v_L\,(t)$ [drop across inductance] the expression for i is obtained first for different time intervals; the voltages are then calculated using $v_L = L\frac{di}{dt}$.

For 0-1 m sec,

$$i = \frac{10}{1 \times 10^{-3}}\, t \text{ amp}$$

$$= 10 \times 10^3\ t \text{ Amp.}$$

$$v_L\,(0-1\text{ m sec}) = 2 \times 10^{-3} \times 10 \times 10^3 = \mathbf{20\ V.}$$

$$[\because i = 10 \times 10^3\ t,\ di/dt = 10 \times 10^3\ \text{A/sec.}]$$

For 1-2 m sec,

$$i = \text{const. giving } v_L = 0.$$

For 2-4 m sec,

$$i = 10 - 10 \times 10^3\,(t - 2 \times 10^{-3})$$

$$= 30 - 10 \times 10^3\ t \text{ A}$$

$$\therefore \quad v_L = L\frac{di}{dt}$$

$$= 3 \times 10^{-3} \times \frac{d}{dt}(30 - 10 \times 10^3\ t) = \mathbf{-30\ V.}$$

For 4-5 m sec.,

$$v_L = 0 \text{ since } i = \text{const.}$$

For 5-6 m sec.,

$$i = +10 \times 10^3\ t \text{ amp.}$$

$$\therefore\ v_L\,(5-6\text{ m sec}) = L\frac{di}{dt}$$

$$= 3 \times 10^{-3} \times 10 \times 10^3$$

$$= \mathbf{30\ V.}$$

Figure. E2.37(*c*) represents $v_L\,(t)$.

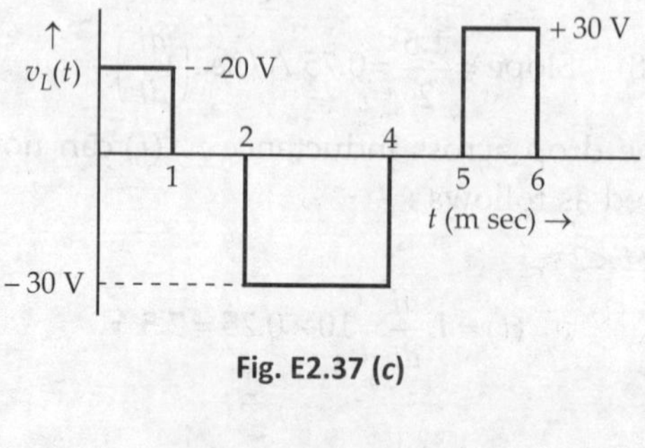

Fig. E2.37 (*c*)

Next $v_c(t)$ [drop across the capacitor] is obtained

$v_c(t)$ [for $0 < t < 1 \times 10^{-3}$ sec]

$$= \frac{1}{C}\int i\,dt$$

$$= \frac{1}{500 \times 10^{-6}} \int_0^t 10 \times 10^3\, t\,dt$$

$$= 10 \times 10^6\, t^2 \text{ volts.}$$

$$= 10 \times 10^6 (1 \times 10^{-3})^2 = \mathbf{10\ volts.}$$

$v_c(t)$ [for $1 \times 10^{-3} < t < 2 \times 10^{-3}$ sec]

$$= 10 + \frac{1}{C}\int_{10^{-3}}^{t} dt$$

$$= 10 + \frac{1}{500 \times 10^{-6}} \int_{10^{-3}}^{2 \times 10^{-3}} (10)\,dt$$

$$= 10 + 20 \times 10^{+3} (2 \times 10^{-3} - 10^{-3})$$

$$= \mathbf{30\ volts.}$$

Exactly in a similar way, $v_c(t)$ for $2 \times 10^{-3} < t < 4 \times 10^{-3}$ sec and other intervals 4 to 5 m sec and 5 to 6 m sec can be determined as is left for the reader as an exercise.

EXAMPLE 2.80 *A voltage is defined by*

$$v(t) = \begin{cases} 0 & \text{for } t < 0 \\ 2t & \text{for } 0 < t < 2 \text{ sec} \\ 4e^{-(t-2)} & \text{for } 2 < t \text{ sec} \end{cases}$$

and is applied to a 10 μF capacitor. Find i (t).

SOLUTION. $i(t) = c\dfrac{dv(t)}{dt}$.

At $t < 0$, $v(t) = 0$; this $i(t) = \mathbf{0}$.

At $0 < t < 2$ sec, $v = 2t$

$$\therefore\ i = c\frac{dv(t)}{dt} = 10 \times 10^{-6}\frac{d(2t)}{dt} = \mathbf{20\ \mu\ A.}$$

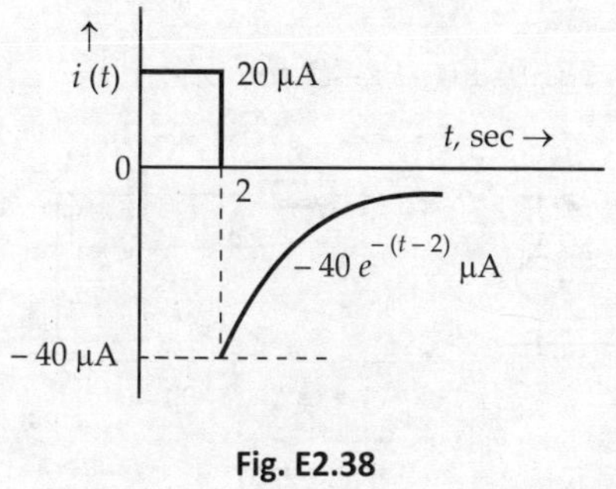

Fig. E2.38

for $2 < t$ sec,

$$i = 10 \times 10^{-6}\frac{d}{dt}(4e^{-(t-2)})$$

$$= 10 \times 10^{-6} [-4e^{-(t-2)}]$$

$$i = \mathbf{-40\, e^{-(t-2)}\ \mu A.}$$

[To obtain power in $t < 0$, it is evident that since

$v = 0,\ i = 0,\ p = 0;$

for $0 < t < 2$ sec,

$$p = vi = 2t \times 20 = 40\,t\ \mu W$$

for $2 < t$,

$$p = 4e^{-(t-2)} \times (-40\, e^{-(t-2)})$$

$$= -160\, e^{-2(t-2)}\ \mu\ W.]$$

EXAMPLE 2.81 *The current through an inductor of inductance 0.1 mH is given by*

$i_L(t) = 0.1 \sin 10^4\, t$ amps. Find $v_L(t)$.

SOLUTION.

$$v_L(t) = L\frac{di_L(t)}{dt} = L\frac{d}{dt}(0.1 \sin 10^4\, t)$$

$$= 0.1 \times 0.1 \times 10^{-3} \times 10^4 \cos 10^4\, t$$

$$= 0.1 \cos 10^4\, t \text{ volts.}$$

or $v_L(t) = \mathbf{(0.1 \cos 10^4\, t)\ volts.}$

EXAMPLE 2.82 *A current $i(t) = \sin \omega t$ passes through an inductance whose inductance is given by*

$$L(t) = 1 + te^{-t}\ H.$$

Find $v_L(t)$.

SOLUTION. The voltage across an inductance is given by

$$v_L(t) = \frac{d\phi}{dt} \text{ when } \phi = Li(t).$$

Here $\phi(t) = L(t)\, i(t) = (te^{-t} + 1) \sin \omega t$

$$\therefore\ V_L(t) = \frac{d}{dt}[(te^{-t} + 1) \sin \omega t]$$

$$= (1 + te^{-t})(\omega \cos \omega t) + (\sin \omega t)(e^{-t} - te^{-t})$$

$$= \omega \cos \omega t + te^{-t}\, \omega \cos \omega t + e^{-t} \sin \omega t - te^{-t} \sin \omega t$$

$$= \omega \cos \omega t (1 + te^{-t}) + e^{-t} \sin \omega t (1 - t)$$

$$\therefore\ \mathbf{v_L(t) = \omega \cos \omega t\, (1 + te^{-t}) + e^{-t} \sin \omega t\, (1 - t).}$$

CHAPTER 2

EXAMPLE 2.83 *A voltage $v(t) = 2\sin\omega t$ is applied across a capacitor having time varying capacitance given by $c(t) = (1 + 0.1\sin t)$ F. Find $i(t)$.*

SOLUTION. Since

$$q(t) = c(t)\,v(t), \text{ here,}$$

$$q(t) = (1 + 0.1\sin t)(2\sin\omega t)$$

But $$i(t) = \frac{dq(t)}{dt}.$$

$\therefore$ here,

$$i(t) = \frac{d}{dt}[(1 + 0.1\sin t)(2\sin\omega t)]$$

$$= (2\sin\omega t)(0.1\cos t) + (1 + 0.1\sin t)(2\,\omega\cos\omega t)$$

or $\mathbf{i(t) = 0.2\sin\omega t\cos t + 2\omega\cos\omega t\,(1 + 0.1\sin t).}$

EXAMPLE 2.84 *A current $i(t) = \sin 2\pi t$ is applied to a capacitance of $c = 1\,\mu$F. Find $v_c(t)$ at $t = \frac{1}{4}$ sec.*

SOLUTION.

$$v_c(t) = \frac{1}{C}\int_{t_0}^{t} i\,dt = \frac{1}{10^{-6}}\int_{0}^{1/4}\sin 2\pi t$$

$$= \frac{1}{2\pi \times 10^{-6}}[-\cos 2\pi t]_0^{1/4}$$

$$= 15.9 \times 10^4 \text{ volts}$$

$$\therefore\ v_c\left(\frac{1}{4}\text{ sec}\right) = \mathbf{15.9 \times 10^4\ volts.}$$

EXAMPLE 2.85 *A voltage $v(t)$ is connected to a capacitance $c = 2$F. Find the energy stored in the capacitor for $t = 0$ to 10 sec. Assume $v(t) = e^{-t}(\sin t)$.*

Solution. Capacitive energy

$$= \frac{1}{2}c[v(t)^2 - v(t_0)^2]$$

Here, $v(t) = (\sin t)\,e^{-t}$

$$\therefore\quad v(10) = (\sin 10)\,e^{-10}$$

$$= (-0.544)(4.54 \times 10^{-5})$$

$$v(0) = 0$$

$$\therefore\ \text{Energy} = \frac{1}{2} \times 2\,[\{-0.544 \times 4.54 \times 10^{-5}\}^2 - 0^2]$$

$$v(0) = 0.$$

$$\therefore\ \text{Energy} = \frac{1}{2} \times 2\,[\{-0.544 \times 4.54 \times 10^{-5}\}^2 - 0^2]$$

$$= \mathbf{6.1 \times 10^{-10}\ J.}$$

EXAMPLE 2.86 *In a series RLC circuit $R = 3\,\Omega$, $X_L = j\,6\,\Omega$, $X_C = -j\,2\,\Omega$. What is the voltage applied across the combination if the series current is $10\angle -143°$ A?*

SOLUTION.

$$Z = R + j(X_L - X_C)$$

$$= 3 + j(6 - 2) = 3 + j\,4$$

$$= 5\angle 53°\,\Omega.$$

Let the supply voltage be $V\angle\phi°$.

Here

$$V\angle\phi° = (Z)(I) = 5\angle 53° \times 10\angle -143°.$$

$$= \mathbf{50\angle -90°\ V}$$

i.e., the voltage leads the current by

$$\mathbf{(143° - 90°) = 53°.}$$

EXAMPLE 2.87 *Find the magnitude and direction of current through Z if $Z = (2 + j\,1 - j\,0.5)\,\Omega$ [Fig. E2.39].*

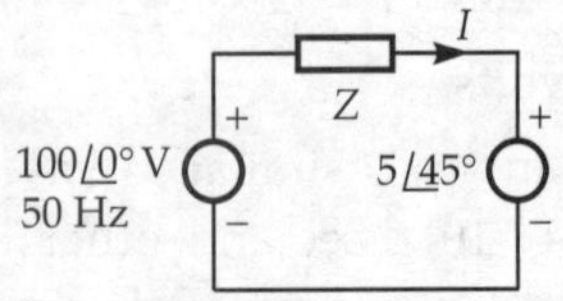

Fig. E2.39

SOLUTION.

$$Z = 2 + j(1 - 0.5) = (2 + j\,0.5)\,\Omega$$

$$= 2.06\angle 14°\,\Omega.$$

$\therefore$ *I*, the current through Z is given by

$$I = \frac{10\angle 0° - 5\angle 45°}{2.06\angle 14°}\ \text{A}$$

$$= \frac{7.37\angle -28.7°}{2.06\angle 14°}$$

$$= 3.58\angle -42.7°\ \text{A}$$

Here, it is seen that the current lags the voltage by **42.7°** while the magnitude of current is **3.58 A.**

EXAMPLE 2.88 *In Fig. E2.40, find Z.*

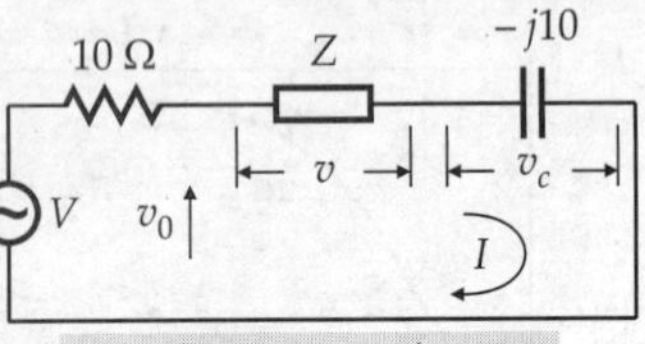

$v_0 = 5\angle 60°$ V, $v_C = 2\angle -30°$V

Fig. E2.40

SOLUTION.

$$v_0 = 5\angle 60° = (2.5 + j\,4.33)\text{ V}$$

$$v_C = 2\angle -30° = (1.732 - j\,1)\text{ V}$$

$$v = v_0 - v_C \text{ (vectorial subtraction)}$$

also $$I = \frac{v_C}{X_C} = \frac{v_C}{-j\,10} = \frac{2\angle -30°}{10\angle -90°} = 0.2\angle 60° \text{ A}$$

$$Z = \frac{v}{I} = \frac{5\angle 60° - 2\angle -30°}{0.2\angle 60°} = \frac{0.768 + j\,5.33}{0.2\angle 60°}$$

$$= \mathbf{26.92\angle 21.8°\,\Omega.}$$

EXAMPLE 2.89 *A voltage of 230 V ∠45°, 50 Hz is applied across an RLC series circuit where the input current is 10 ∠–30° A. If $R = 5\,\Omega$, $X_L = j\,8\,\Omega$, find the value of capacitive reactance.*

SOLUTION.

$$Z_{\text{total}} = \frac{V}{I} = \frac{230\angle 45°}{10\angle -30°}$$

$$= 23\angle 75°\,\Omega = (5.95 + j\,22.21)\,\Omega$$

However,

$$Z = R + j\,(X_L - X_C) = 5 + j\,(8 - X_C)$$

or, $$23^2 = 5^2 + (8 - X_C)^2 \qquad [\because Z = 23\,\Omega \text{ and } Z^2 = \sqrt{R^2 + (X_L - X_C)^2}\,]$$

or, $$23^2 - 5^2 = 64 - 16\,X_C + X_C^2$$

or, $$X_C^2 - 16\,X_C + 64 - 23^2 + 5^2 = 0$$

or, $$X_C^2 - 16\,X_C - 440 = 0$$

$$\therefore\ X_C = \frac{16 \pm \sqrt{16^2 + 4 \times 440}}{2}$$

$$= 8 \pm 22.45 = \text{either } 30.45 \text{ or } -14.45$$

Taking the +ve root only

$$X_C = \frac{1}{2\,\pi\,fC}$$

or, $$C = \frac{1}{2\,\pi\,f\,X_C} = \frac{1}{2\,\pi \times 50 \times 30.45}$$

$$= 1.05 \times 10^{-4}\text{ F} = 105\,\mu\text{F}.$$

Thus $\mathbf{X_C = 30.45\,\Omega}$ [or $C = 105\,\mu$F]

EXAMPLE 2.90 *An unknown impedance of Z Ω is connected in series with $(5 + j\,8)\,\Omega$ coil (Fig. E2.41). If $I = 2.5\angle -15°$ A, find the value of Z.*

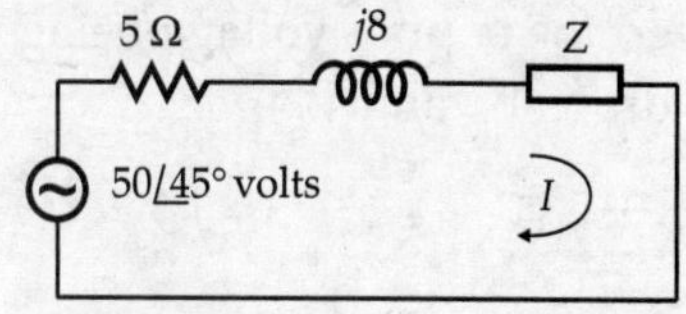

Fig. E2.41

SOLUTION. Let Z_0 be the net impedance of the circuit.

Obviously

$$Z_0 = \frac{V}{I} = \frac{50\angle 45°}{2.5\angle -15°}$$

or, $$Z_0 = 20\angle 60° = (10 + 17.3)\,\Omega$$

However, $$Z_0 = (5 + j\,8)\,\Omega + Z$$

or, $$10 + j\,17.3 = 5 + j\,8 + Z.$$

$$\therefore\ Z = (5 + j\,9.3)\,\Omega$$

$$= \mathbf{10.56\angle 61.74°\,\Omega.}$$

EXAMPLE 2.91 *A heater takes 10 A at 50 V. Calculate the impedance of a choke of 5 Ω resistance to be placed in series with it in order that it may work at 200 V, 50 Hz supply. Find the power factor of the circuit.*

SOLUTION. In Fig. E2.42, it is given that $I = 10$ A, V_H (drop across heater) $= 50$ V, R_C (resistance of choke) $= 5\,\Omega$, $V_S = 200$ V.

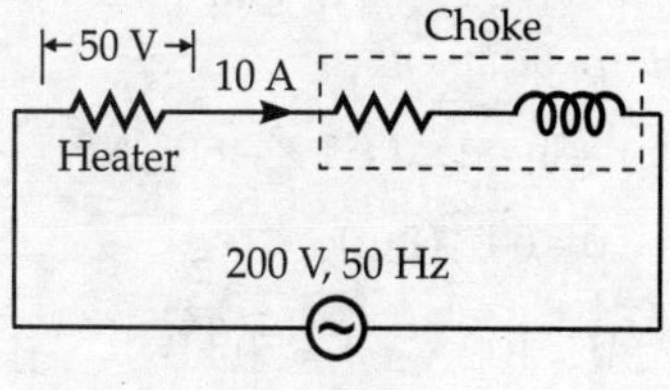

Fig. E2.42

$$\therefore\ R_H \text{ (Resistance of heater)} = \frac{50}{10} = 5\,\Omega$$

Hence, net resistance of the circuit is

$$R = R_H + R_C = 5 + 5 = 10\,\Omega$$

Obviously, V_{R_H} (drop across R_H)

$$= R_H \times I = 5 \times 10 = 50\text{ V}$$

and $$V_{R_C} = R_C \times I = 50\text{ V}$$

CHAPTER 2

Also, V_{R_L} (drop across X_L, the inductive reactance of the choke)

$$= IX_L = 10\,X_L \text{ V}$$

However, the supply voltage being the vector sum of the drops V_R and V_L,

$$V = (V_{R_C} + V_{R_H}) + j\,V_L$$

$$(200)^2 = (50+50)^2 + V_L^2$$

$$\therefore \quad V_L^2 = 200^2 - 100^2$$

or, $$V_L = 173.21 \text{ V}$$

or, $$X_L = \frac{173.21}{I} = \frac{173.21}{10} = 17.32\,\Omega$$

This gives the impedance of the choke as

$$Z = \sqrt{R_C^2 + X_L^2} = \sqrt{5^2 + (17.32)^2} = 18\,\Omega$$

Thus the impedance of the coil = **18 Ω.**

∴ The impedance of the whole circuit

$$= \sqrt{(R_C + R_H)^2 + X_L^2)}$$

$$= \sqrt{10^2 + (17.32)^2} = 20\,\Omega.$$

$$\text{Power factor} = \frac{R}{Z} = \frac{10}{20} = 0.5$$

Thus for the given problem,

Z (coil) = 18 Ω, P. F. = 0.5.

EXAMPLE 2.92 *A coil takes a current of 1 ∠60° A (lag) from 100 V, 60 Hz supply. Calculate its inductance, resistance and impedance.*

SOLUTION. Given, $I = 1\angle -60°$ A

$$\therefore \quad \phi = 60° \text{ (lag)}$$

$$V = 100 \text{ V}, \; f = 50 \text{ Hz}$$

$$\therefore \quad Z = \frac{V}{I} = \frac{100}{1\angle -60°} = 100\angle 60°\,\Omega$$

However, $$\cos\phi (\text{p.f.}) = \frac{R}{Z}$$

$$\therefore \quad R = Z\cos\phi = 100\cos 60° = 50\,\Omega$$

Again, $$Z = \sqrt{R^2 + X_L^2}$$

$$\therefore \quad X_L^2 = Z^2 - R^2 = (100)^2 - (50)^2$$

$$\therefore \quad X_L = 86.6\,\Omega$$

and $$L = \frac{X_L}{2\pi f} = \frac{86.6}{2\times 3.14\times 60} = 0.23 \text{ H}$$

Thus, for the given problem,

$R = 50\,\Omega$; $L = 230$ mH; $Z = 100\,\Omega$.

EXAMPLE 2.93 *In Fig. E2.43, "r" is a pure resistance and "CH" the choke coil, connected in series. Power dissipated in r being 250 W and that in choke being 50 W, find the value of the reactance in the choke and the value of the supply voltage.*

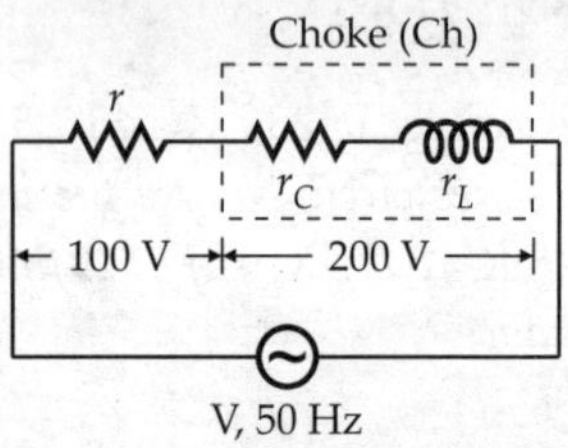

Fig. E2.43

SOLUTION. Power dissipated $= \dfrac{V^2}{R}$

∴ For the non inductive resistor,

$$r = \frac{V^2}{W} = \frac{100^2}{250} = 40\,\Omega$$

and current through r,

$$I = \frac{\text{drop across } r}{r}$$

i.e., $$I = \frac{100}{40} = 2.5 \text{ A}$$

Obviously, the current flowing through the choke would also be 2.5 A.

As the power loss in choke can only take place in the resistive part of the choke, hence,

$$I^2 r_C = 50$$

or, $$r_C = \frac{50}{(2.5)^2} = 8\,\Omega$$

But the drop across the coil is 200 V, while through current is 2.5 A.

$$\therefore \quad Z_{Ch} = \frac{V}{I} = \frac{200}{2.5} = 80\,\Omega$$

and $$X_L = \sqrt{(Z_{Ch})^2 - r_C^2}$$

$$= \sqrt{(80)^2 - (8)^2} = 79.6\,\Omega$$

Again, the total resistive drop = drop across r + drop across r_C

or, resistive drop $= 2.5 \times 40 + 2.5 \times 8 = 120$ V

Drop across inductance in coil

$$= IX_L = 2.5 \times 79.6 = 199 \text{ V}$$

$\therefore$ Supply voltage $|V| = \sqrt{120^2 + 199^2} = 232.38$ V

Hence we obtain

$$\mathbf{X_L \text{ (Ch)} = 79.6\,\Omega \quad \text{and} \quad V = 232.38 \text{ V}.}$$

EXAMPLE 2.94 *It is given that in Fig. E2.44,*

$R_1 = 6.4\,\Omega$, $R_2 = 2.4\,\Omega$, $X_{L_1} = 4.8\,\Omega$, $X_{L_2} = 8\,\Omega$, $V_0 = 100$ V, 60 cps.

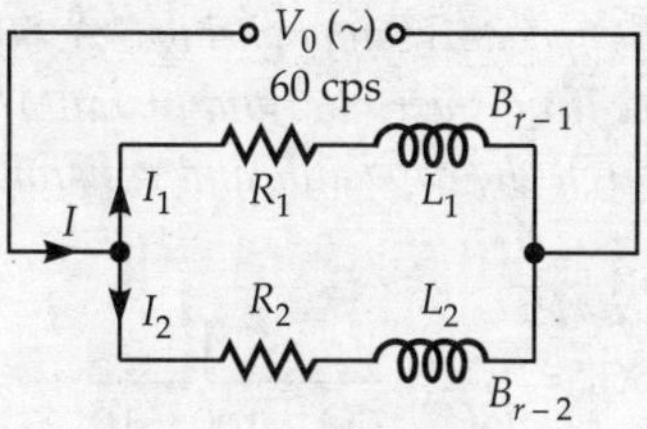

Fig. E2.44

Find :

(*i*) *Conductances, susceptances of each element.*

(*ii*) *Net conductance and net susceptance of the circuit.*

(*iii*) *Admittance of each branch and that of the entire circuit.*

(*iv*) *Branch currents.*

(*v*) *Supply current.*

(*vi*) *P.F. angle of the circuit.*

SOLUTION. (*i*) Z_1 (imp. of Br. - 1) $= R_1 + j\,X_{L_1}$

$$\therefore \quad Y_1 = \frac{1}{Z_1} = \frac{1}{R_1 + j\,X_{L_1}} = \frac{R_1 - j\,X_{L_1}}{R_1^2 + X_{L_1}^2}$$

$$= \frac{R_1}{R_1^2 + X_{L_1}^2} - j\,\frac{X_{L_1}}{R_1^2 + X_{L_1}^2} = g_1 - jb_1$$

where g_1 = conductance of 1st branch

and b_1 = susceptance of 1st branch.

Similarly,

$$Y_2 = \frac{1}{Z_2} = \frac{1}{R_2 + j\,X_{L_2}}$$

$$= \frac{R_2}{R_2^2 + X_{L_2}^2} - j\,\frac{X_{L_2}}{R_2^2 + X_{L_2}^2} = g_2 - jb_2$$

Here $\quad g_1 = \dfrac{R_1}{R_1^2 + X_{L_1}^2} = \mathbf{0.1 \text{ mho}},$

$$g_2 = \frac{R_2}{R_2^2 + X_{L_2}^2} = \mathbf{0.035 \text{ mho}}$$

$$b_1 = \frac{X_{L_1}}{R_1^2 + X_{L_1}^2} = \mathbf{0.075 \text{ mho}}$$

$$b_2 = \frac{X_{L_2}}{R_2^2 + X_{L_2}^2} = \mathbf{0.115 \text{ mho}.}$$

(*ii*) Net conductance

$$g_0 = g_1 + g_2 = \mathbf{0.135 \text{ mho}}$$

Net susceptance

$$b_0 = b_1 + b_2 = \mathbf{0.19 \text{ mho}.}$$

(*iii*) $Y_1 = g_1 - jb_1 = \mathbf{(0.1 - j\,0.075) \text{ mho}}$

$Y_2 = g_2 - j\,b_2 = \mathbf{(0.035 - j\,0.115) \text{ mho}}$

$Y = g_0 - j\,b_0 = \mathbf{(0.135 - j\,0.19) \text{ mho}.}$

(*iv*) $I_1 = V_0\,Y_1 = \mathbf{(10 - j\,7.5) \text{ A}}$

$I_2 = V_0\,Y_2 = \mathbf{3.5 - j\,11.5 \text{ A}.}$

(*v*) $I = I_1 + I_2 = V_0\,Y = \mathbf{(13.5 - j\,19) \text{ A}.}$

(*vi*) $\phi = \tan^{-1}\dfrac{b_0}{g_0} = -54.64°$

$\therefore \quad$ PF = **0.58 (lag).**

Figure E2.45 represents the phasor diagram.

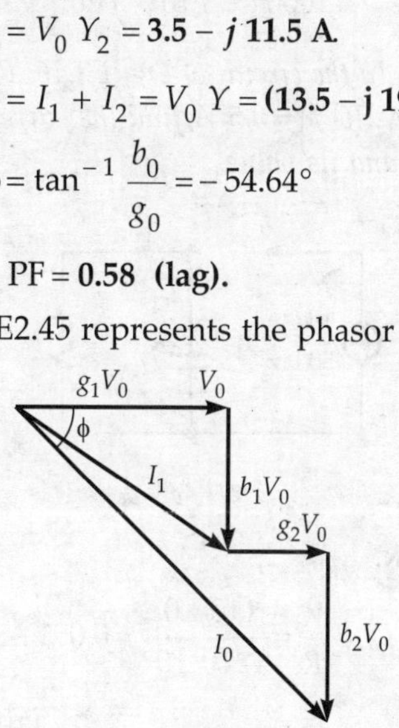

Fig. E2.45

EXAMPLE 2.95 *A 10 Ω resistance is connected in series with a parallel combination of a capacitor (C Farad) and a 20 mH pure inductor. At angular frequency of 1000 rad/sec, find the value of C such that the line current is 45° out of phase with the line voltage.*

SOLUTION. It is evident that since the voltage and currents are 45° out of phase, hence the net reactance of the parallel *LC* combination must be $(\pm\,j\,10)\,\Omega$ since $R = 10\,\Omega$, i.e., $$\frac{1}{\pm j\,10} = \frac{1}{j\,\omega L} + \frac{1}{1/j\,\omega C}$$

$$\left[\because \text{ in parallel combination, } Y = j\,B, G \text{ being zero ; } \frac{1}{Z} = \left(\frac{1}{X_L} + \frac{1}{X_C}\right)\right].$$

$$= \frac{1}{j \times 1000 \times 20 \times 10^{-3}} + j \times 1000 \times C$$

$$\therefore \quad C = \frac{1}{j\,1000}\left(\frac{1}{\pm j\,10} - \frac{1}{j\,20}\right)$$

i.e., either $$C = \frac{1}{j\,1000}\left(\frac{1}{j\,10} - \frac{1}{j\,20}\right)$$

or $$C = \frac{1}{j\,1000}\left(-\frac{1}{j\,10} - \frac{1}{j\,20}\right)$$

∴ either C is –ve or C is +ve. Since C can not be –ve, hence

$$C = \frac{1}{1000}\left(-\frac{1}{j\,10} - \frac{1}{j\,20}\right) = \mathbf{150\ \mu F.}$$

EXAMPLE 2.96 *In the circuit of Fig. E2.46, R dissipates a power of 10 W. If $|I| = 0.5$ A, find the current drawn by the capacitor and its value.*

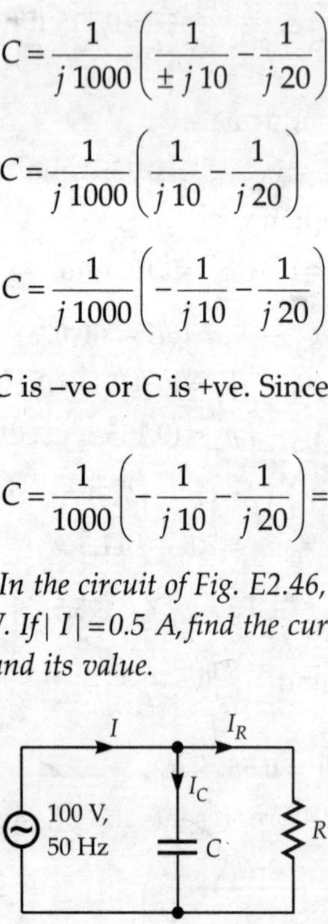

Fig. E2.46

SOLUTION.

$$I_R = \frac{V}{R} = \frac{110\,\angle 0°}{1210\,\angle 0°} = 0.091\text{ A.}$$

$$\left[\because R = \frac{V^2}{P} = \frac{110^2}{10} = 1210\,\Omega\right]$$

Also, $$I = \sqrt{I_R^2 + I_C^2}$$

$$\therefore \quad I_C = \sqrt{I^2 - I_R^2}$$

$$= \sqrt{(0.5)^2 - (0.091)^2} = 0.492\text{ A.}$$

Also, $$C = \frac{I_C}{2\,\pi\,fV} = \frac{0.492}{314 \times 110} = \mathbf{14.2\ \mu F.}$$

EXAMPLE 2.97 *Three circuit elements, $R = 2\,\Omega$, $X_L = 5\,\Omega$, $X_C = 10\,\Omega$ are connected in parallel supply frequency being 50 Hz, find the input admittance.*

SOLUTION. From the theory of parallel circuit,

$$Y = G + j\,(B_C - B_L)\,;$$

where, $$G = \frac{1}{R},\ B_L = \frac{1}{X_L}\,;\ B_C = \frac{1}{X_C}$$

$$= \frac{1}{2} + j\left(\frac{1}{10}\right) - j\,\frac{1}{5} = 0.5 + j\,(0.1 - 0.2)$$

$$= \mathbf{(0.5 - j\,0.1)\ mho.}$$

Y represents the input admittance of the given circuit.

EXAMPLE 2.98 *A 10 Ω resistor is connected in parallel with a 100 μF capacitor. Supply being 5 A, 50 Hz constant current source, find the r.m.s. and instantaneous branch currents through the capacitor and resistor.*

SOLUTION.

$$X_C = \frac{1}{\omega C} = \frac{1}{314 \times 100 \times 10^{-6}} = 31.8\,\Omega$$

∴ Z (the equivalent impedance of R and X_C)

$$= \frac{(R)(-jX_C)}{R + (-j\,X_C)}$$

$$= \frac{10\,(-j\,31.8)}{10 - j\,31.8} = \frac{318\,\angle -90°}{33.33\,\angle -72.54°}$$

$$= 9.54\,\angle -17.46°\,\Omega$$

This gives,

$$V = IZ = 5\,\angle 0° \times 9.54\,\angle -17.46°$$

$$= 47.7\,\angle -17.46°\text{ V}$$

Thus, $$I_R = \frac{V}{R} = \frac{47.7\,\angle -17.46°}{10\,\angle 0°}$$

$$= \mathbf{4.77\,\angle -17.46°\ A.}$$

and $$I_C = \frac{V}{-j\,X_C}$$

$$= \frac{47.7\,\angle -17.46°}{31.8\,\angle -90°} = \mathbf{1.5\,\angle 72.54°\ A.}$$

The instantaneous values are then

$$i_R = I_{\max(R)}\sin(\omega t + \phi_R)$$

$$= \sqrt{2} \times 4.77\sin(314\,t - 17.46°)$$

$$= \mathbf{6.744\sin(314\,t - 17.46°)}$$

and $$i_C = \sqrt{2}\,I_C\sin(314\,t + 72.54°)$$

$$= \mathbf{2.12\sin(314\,t + 72.54°)\ A.}$$

EXAMPLE 2.99 *A R-L series circuit is in parallel with a pure resistance* (R_2) *as shown in Fig. E2.47 and the combination is connected across a 10 Hz a.c. source. The power delivered to the resistances is 100 W. Find the value of inductance.*

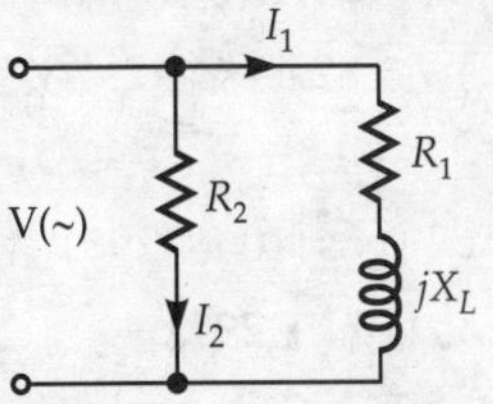

[$V = 50\angle 0°$, $R_1 = 10\ \Omega$
$R_2 = 50\ \Omega$, $f = 10$ Hz]

Fig. E2.47

SOLUTION. The power loss in R_2 is given by

$$\frac{V^2}{R_2} = \frac{(50)^2}{50} = 50 \text{ W}$$

$\therefore$ Power loss in R_1 becomes (100 – 50) W *i.e.,* 50 W

However, assuming the current through $(R_1 + jX_L)$ to be I_1 amps,

$$I_1^2\ R_1 = 50 \text{ W}$$

$$\therefore \quad I_1 = \sqrt{\frac{50}{10}} = 2.236 \text{ A.}$$

Also, $V^2 = (\text{drop across } R_1)^2 + (\text{drop across } X_L)^2$

or, $50^2 = (2.236 \times 10)^2 + V_L^2$

[$\because$ V_L is the drop across X_L]

$\therefore$ $V_L^2 = (50^2 - 497.3)$ or $V_L = 44.75$ V

However,

$$V_L = I_1\ X_L$$

or,
$$X_L = \frac{V_L}{I_1} = \frac{44.75}{2.236} = 20\ \Omega$$

Thus
$$L = \frac{X_L}{2\pi f} = \frac{20}{2 \times 3.14 \times 10} \quad [\because f = 10 \text{ Hz}]$$

$$= \mathbf{318.7\ mH.}$$

EXAMPLE 2.100 *In the circuit of Fig. E2.48, the current flowing through the unknown reactance (X) is 5 A when a supply of 100 V is applied at the input. The power dissipated in (R) is 100 W. On the other hand, if a capacitor of reactance* (X_C) *is inserted in series with (X), the current remains the same. Obtain the values of X and* X_C.

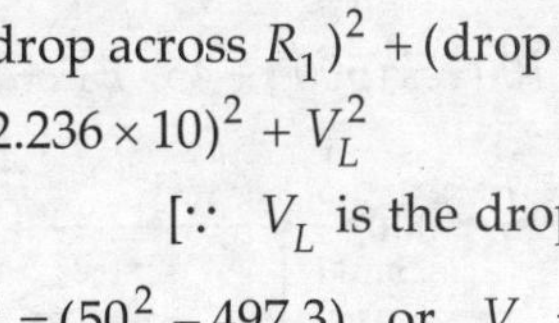

Fig. E2.48

SOLUTION. Power loss in the resistor being 100 W, X_C not being in the circuit,

$$R = \frac{P}{I^2} = \frac{100}{5^2} = 4\ \Omega$$

This time, $Z = \frac{V}{I} = \frac{100}{5} = 20\ \Omega$

Also, $X = \sqrt{Z^2 - R^2} = \sqrt{20^2 - 4^2}$

$= \pm 19.6\ \Omega$ (purely reactive)

When a capacitor of X_C is inserted,

$$Z = \frac{V}{I} = \frac{100}{5} = 20\ \Omega = \sqrt{4^2 + (X - X_C)^2}$$

$$= \sqrt{4^2 + (\pm 19.6 - X_C)^2}$$

$$\therefore \quad 400 = 4^2 + (\pm 19.6 - X_C)^2$$

or, $(\pm 19.6 - X_C)^2 = 384$

i.e., $\pm 19.6 - X_C = \sqrt{384} = 19.6$

This gives X_C = **either 0 or, – 39.2 Ω** and X is correspondingly either **19.6 Ω or – 19.6 Ω.**

i.e., if X is purely inductive having +ve value of 19.6 Ω, X_C should be zero value, but if is of +ve value of 19.6, X_C becomes +ve value of 39.2 Ω *i.e.,* X_C becomes a capacitor instead of a inductor.

EXAMPLE 2.101 *An industrial load takes 100 kW of load at 0.8 p.f. (lag) while operating at 220 V, 50 Hz. If the p.f. of the bus is to be improved to unity, what should be the rating of a capacitor connected in parallel with the load ?*

SOLUTION. Industrial load

$$(I_L) = \frac{100 \times 10^3}{220 \times 0.8} \quad [\because P = VI \cos \phi]$$

or, $I_L = 568.18$ A

and p.f. $= \cos \phi = 0.8$ giving $\phi = -37°$

This gives

$$I_L = 568.18 \angle -37°$$

$$= I_{LR} - j\ I_{LI} = 453.77 - j\ 342$$

Once the capacitor is connected in shunt to the load bus, letting I_C being the capacitor current,

$$I_{\text{input}} = I_{LR} + j\ (I_C - I_{LI})$$

The input current to be resistive ($\cos\phi$ = unity), I_C must be equal to I_{LI}

i.e., $I_C = j\, I_{LI} = j\, \omega CV.$

Thus, $$C = \frac{I_{LI}}{\omega V} = \frac{342}{314 \times 220} = \mathbf{0.005\ F.}$$

EXAMPLE 2.102 *In a parallel R-L circuit, $R = 2\,\Omega$ while $X_L = 4\Omega$. A current source of $10\angle 0°$ A feeds the combination. Find the branch currents.*

SOLUTION. Let main current be

$$I = 10 + j0 = 10\angle 0°\ \text{A},$$

resistive branch current be I_R and the inductive branch current be I_L.

By current division rule,

$$I_R = I\frac{j\,X_L}{R + j\,X_L} = 10\angle 0° \frac{4\angle 90°}{2 + j\,4}$$

or, $$I_R = \frac{40\angle 90°}{4.47\angle 63.44°} = \mathbf{8.95\angle 26.56°\ A}$$

and $$I_L = I\frac{R}{R + j\,X_L}$$

$$= 10\angle 0° \frac{2\angle 0°}{2 + j\,4} = \frac{20\angle 0°}{4.47\angle 63.44°}$$

$$= \mathbf{4.474\angle -63.44°\ A.}$$

EXAMPLE 2.103 *In Fig. E2.49, $v_L = 100\cos(10\,t + 30°)$. If $R = 10\,\Omega$, $X_C = -j\,4\Omega$ and $X_L = 10\,\Omega$, find v_s.*

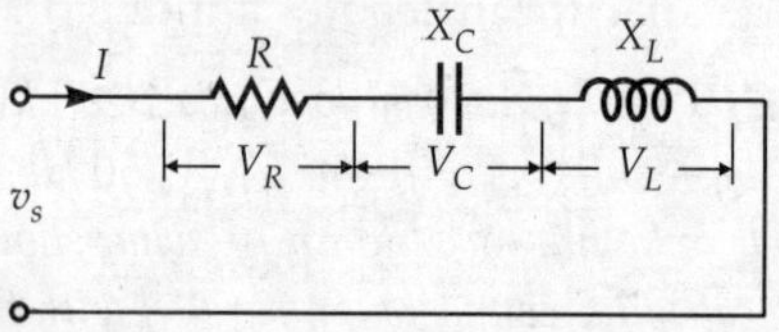

Fig. E2.49

SOLUTION.

$$V_L = \frac{100}{\sqrt{2}}\angle 30° = 70.7\angle 30°\ \text{V}$$

$$Z_L = j\omega L = j\,10\,\Omega\ (\textit{i.e.},\ j\,X_L)$$

$$\therefore\quad I = \frac{V_L}{Z_L} = \frac{70.7\angle 30°}{10\angle 90°} = 7.07\angle -60°\ \text{A}$$

This gives

$$V_R = IR = 7.07\angle -60° \times 10 = 70.7\angle -60°\ \text{V}$$

$$V_C = IZ_C = 7.07\angle -60°(-j\,4)$$

$$= 7.07 \times 4\angle -60° - 90° = 28.28\angle -150°\ \text{V}$$

Thus

$$V_S = V_R + V_L + V_C$$

$$= 70.7\angle -60° + 70.7\angle 30° + 28.28\angle -150°$$

$$= 35.35 - j\,61.23 + 61.23 + j\,35.35$$
$$-24.49 - j\,14.14$$

$$= (72.09 - j\,40.02)\ \text{V} = 82.44\angle -29°\ \text{V}$$

This gives

$$v_S = (82.44 \times \sqrt{2})\cos(10\,t - 29°)$$

$$= \mathbf{116.57\cos(10\,t - 29°).}$$

Figure E2.50 gives the phasor diagram.

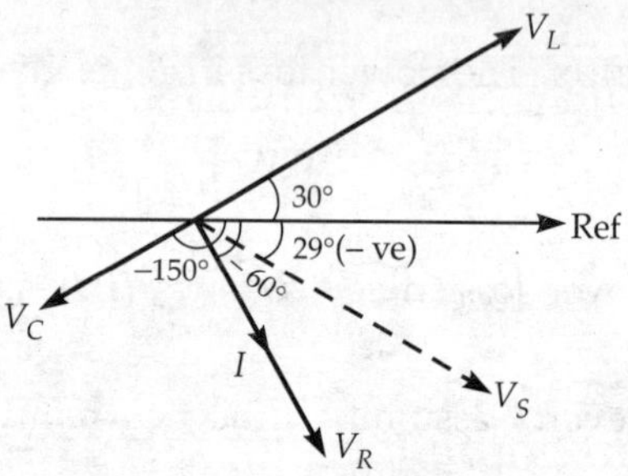

Fig. E2.50

EXAMPLE 2.104 *In the circuit of Fig. E2.51, the voltage across the capacitor is given by*

$v_C(t) = 100\cos(500\,t + 45°)$. Find $v_s(t)$ and i.

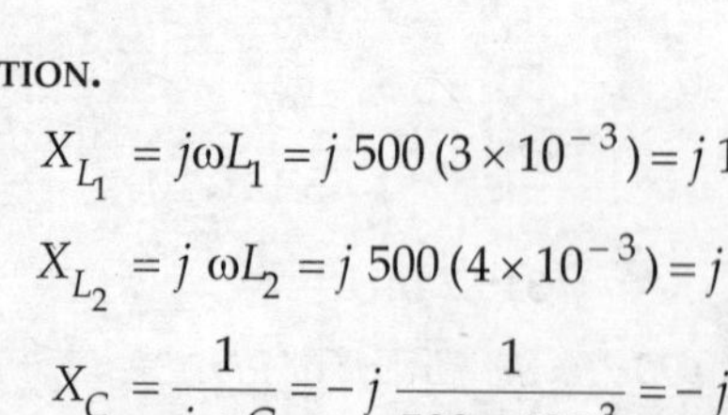

Fig. E2.51

SOLUTION.

$$X_{L_1} = j\omega L_1 = j\,500\,(3 \times 10^{-3}) = j\,1.5\,\Omega$$

$$X_{L_2} = j\,\omega L_2 = j\,500\,(4 \times 10^{-3}) = j\,2\,\Omega$$

$$X_C = \frac{1}{j\,\omega C} = -j\frac{1}{500 \times 10^{-3}} = -j\,2\,\Omega$$

Thus, the admittance of $R - L_2$ circuit branch is given by

$$Y_{R-L_2} = \frac{1}{2 + j\,2} = 0.354\angle -45°$$

$$= (0.25 - j\,0.25)\ \text{mho}$$

Again Y_C being $\frac{1}{X_C} = j\,0.5$, the equivalent admittance of Y_C and Y_{R-L_2} is given by

$$Y = Y_C + Y_{R-L_2}$$
$$= j\,0.5 + 0.25 - j\,0.25 = 0.25 + j\,0.25$$
$$= 0.354\ \angle 45°\ \text{mho}$$

From this

$$I = YV_C = 0.354\ \angle 45° \times \frac{100}{\sqrt{2}}\ \angle 45°$$
$$= 25\ \angle 90°\ \text{V}$$

Then, $\quad i = 25\sqrt{2}\cos(500\,t + 90°)$

$$= -\mathbf{35.4\ sin\ (500\ \mathit{t})\ A}$$

Now, drop across L_1 is obtained as

$$V_{\text{drop}(L_1)} = I\,X_{L_1} = 25\ \angle 90° \times 1.5\ \angle 90°$$
$$= 37.5\ \angle 180°\ \text{V}$$

Finally, the supply voltage is obtained as

$$V_S = IX_{L_1} + V_C = 37.5\ \angle 180° + \frac{100}{\sqrt{2}}\ \angle 45°$$
$$= -37.5 + j\,0 + 70.72 \times \frac{1}{\sqrt{2}} + j\,70.72 \times \frac{1}{\sqrt{2}}$$
$$= -37.5 + 50 + j\,50 = 12.5 + j\,50$$
$$= 51.54\ \angle 76°\ \text{V}$$

This gives

$$v_S(t) = \sqrt{2} \times 51.54\cos(500\,t + 76°)$$
$$= \mathbf{72.88\ cos\ (500\ \mathit{t} + 76°)\ V.}$$

Example 2.105 *What capacitance is to be inserted in series in the circuit of Fig. E2.52, such that the input current is in phase with the voltage ?*

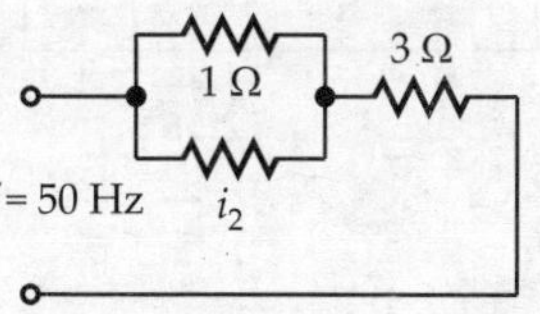

Fig. E2.52

Solution. The input impedance of the given circuit is given by

$$Z_{in} = 3 + \frac{1(j\,2)}{1 + j\,2} = 3 + \frac{j\,2}{1 + j\,2}$$
$$= 3 + \frac{j\,2\,(1 - j\,2)}{5} = 3 + j\,0.4 + 0.8$$

The input current will be in phase with the supply voltage provided the reactive part of the impedance does not exist after inserting the capacitor in series. It is *possible* provided

$$\frac{j}{\omega C} = j\,0.4 \qquad \text{[assuming the capacitance of the inserted capacitor to be } C]$$

or, $\quad C = \frac{1}{\omega \times 0.4} = \frac{1}{314 \times 0.4} \qquad [\because\ \omega = 2\pi f = 314]$

$$= \mathbf{7.96 \times 10^{-3}\ F.}$$

Example 2.106 *In the network shown in Fig. E2.53, $V = 29\ \angle -23°\ V$, $V_1 = 10\ \angle 0°\ V$. Find I_3 if $Z_3 = 10.81\ \angle -33.67°\ \Omega$.*

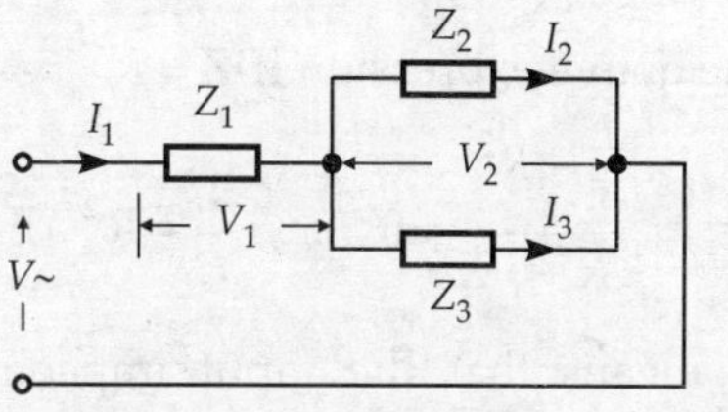

Fig. E2.53

Solution. Vectorially, $V = V_1 + V_2$

$$\therefore\quad V_2 = V - V_1 = 29\ \angle -23° - 10\ \angle 0°$$
$$= 26.69 - j\,11.33 - 10 - j\,0$$
$$= 16.69 - j\,11.33 = 20.17\ \angle -34.17°\ \text{V}$$

$$\therefore\quad I_3 = \frac{V_2}{Z_3}$$
$$= \frac{16.69 - j\,11.33}{10.81\ \angle -33.67} = \mathbf{1.86\ \angle -0.5°\ A.}$$

Example 2.107 *Under which condition, the input impedance Z of the circuit shown in Fig. E2.54 will be purely resistive ?*

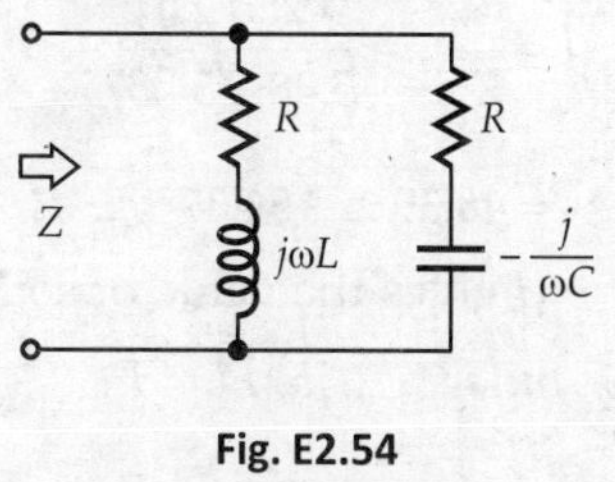

Fig. E2.54

Solution. By observation,

$$Z = \frac{Z_1\,Z_2}{Z_1 + Z_2}$$

when $Z_1 = R + j\,\omega L$ and $Z_2 = R - \frac{j}{\omega C}$

$$\therefore\ Z = \frac{(R + j\,\omega L)\left(R - \frac{j}{\omega C}\right)}{(R + j\,\omega L) + \left(R - \frac{j}{\omega C}\right)} = \frac{R^2 + \frac{L}{C} + j\,RX}{2R + jX}$$

where, $$X = \left(\omega L - \frac{1}{\omega C}\right)$$

or, $$Z - R = \frac{R^2 + \frac{L}{C} + j\,RX}{2R + j\,X} - R$$

or, $$Z - R = \frac{\frac{L}{C} - R^2}{2R + jX}$$

In the above expression if $Z = R$,

$$\frac{\frac{L}{C} - R^2}{2R + j\,X} = 0 \quad i.e., \quad \boldsymbol{\frac{L}{C} = R^2}.$$

This means that the input impedance $Z = R$ gives the necessary criterion of input impedance to be purely resistive.

EXAMPLE 2.108 *An impedance of 10 ∠37° ohm is in parallel with another impedance 18 ∠56.3° ohm and a voltage of 250 ∠0° V is applied across the combination. Find the source current.*

SOLUTION. $Z_1 = 10\ \angle 37°\,\Omega,\ Z_2 = 18\ \angle 56.3°\,\Omega$

$$\therefore\ Z_{\text{equiv.}} = \frac{Z_1\,Z_2}{Z_1 + Z_2} = \frac{10\ \angle 37° \times 18\ \angle 56.3°}{10\ \angle 37° + 18\ \angle 56.3°}$$

$$= \frac{180\ \angle 93.31°}{25.98 + j\,20.99}$$

$$= \frac{180\ \angle 93.31°}{33.4\ \angle 38.93°} \simeq 5.38\ \angle 54.37°\,\Omega$$

This gives

$$I = \frac{V}{Z_{eq.}} = \frac{250\ \angle 0°}{5.38\ \angle 54.37°}$$

$$= \mathbf{46.39\ \angle -54.37°\ A.}$$

[I gives the value of source current]

EXAMPLE 2.109 *In Fig. E2.55, Find I.*

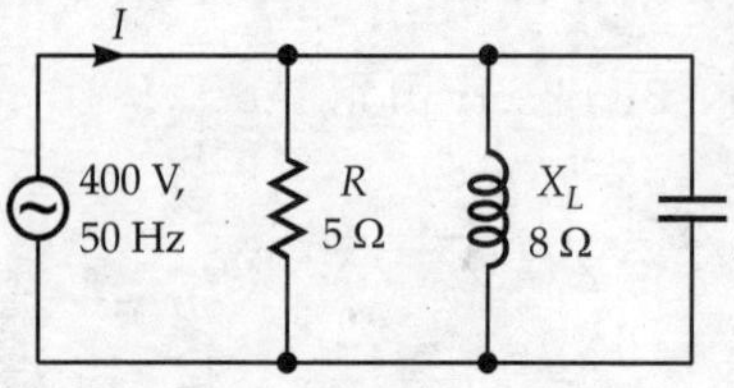

Fig. E2.55

SOLUTION.

$$Y_R = G = \frac{1}{R}\ \angle 0°$$

$$= 0.2\ \angle 0° = 0.2\ \angle 0°\ \text{mho}$$

$$Y_{X_L} = B_L\ \angle -90°$$

$$= \frac{1}{X_L}\ \angle -90° = 0.125\ \angle -90°\ \text{mho}$$

$$Y_{X_C} = B_C\ \angle 90° = \frac{1}{X_C}\ \angle 90°$$

$$= 0.05\ \angle 90°\ \text{mho}$$

$$\therefore\ Y_{\text{equiv.}} = Y_R + Y_{X_L} + Y_{X_C}$$

$$= 0.2\ \angle 0° + 0.125\ \angle -90° + 0.05\ \angle 90°$$

$$= (0.2 + j\,0) + (0 - j\,0.125) + (0 + j\,0.05)$$

$$= (0.2 - j\,0.075)\ \text{mho} = 0.214\ \angle -20.6°\ \text{mho}$$

This gives

$$Z_{\text{equiv.}} = \frac{1}{Y_{\text{equiv.}}} = \frac{1}{0.214\ \angle -20.6°}$$

$$= 4.67\ \angle 20.6°\,\Omega$$

Thus, $$I = \frac{V}{Z} = \frac{400\angle 0°}{4.67\angle 20.6°} = \mathbf{85.60\ \angle -20.6°\ A.}$$

[Here I is lagging the voltage by 20.6°]

EXAMPLE 2.110 *In Fig. E2.56, $R = 2$ ohm while $X_C = 1.25\,\Omega$. Find E.*

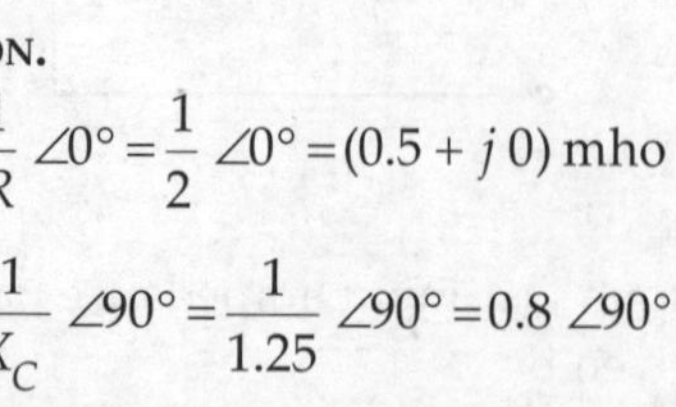

Fig. E2.56

SOLUTION.

$$Y_R = \frac{1}{R}\ \angle 0° = \frac{1}{2}\ \angle 0° = (0.5 + j\,0)\ \text{mho}$$

$$Y_C = \frac{1}{X_C}\ \angle 90° = \frac{1}{1.25}\ \angle 90° = 0.8\ \angle 90° = j\,0.8.$$

∴ Net admittance

$$Y = Y_R + Y_C = 0.5 + j\,0 + j\,0.8$$

$$= 0.5 + j\,0.8 = 0.94\ \angle 58°\ \text{mho}$$

Obviously,

$$E = IY = 5\ \angle 0° \times 0.94\ \angle 58° = \mathbf{4.7\ \angle 58°\ V}$$

EXAMPLE 2.111 *Find V in the circuit of Fig. E2.57.*

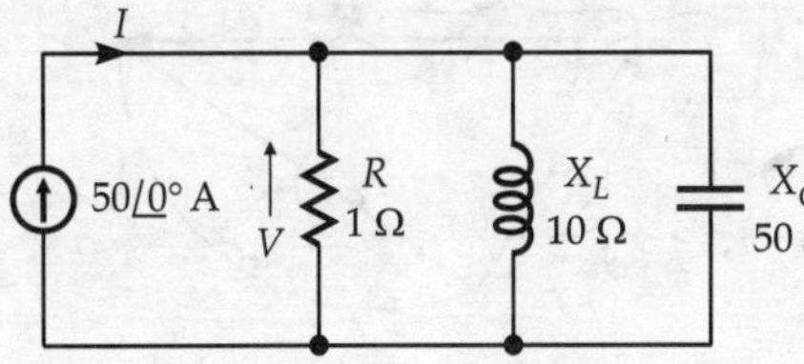

Fig. E2.57

SOLUTION.

$$Y_1 = \frac{1}{R}\angle 0° = 1\angle 0° \text{ mho}$$

$$Y_2 = \frac{1}{X_L}\angle -90° = 0.1\angle -90° \text{ mho}$$

$$Y_3 = \frac{1}{X_C}\angle 90° = 0.02\angle 90° \text{ mho}$$

$$\therefore \quad Y_{\text{equiv.}} = Y_1 + Y_2 + Y_3$$

$$= 1(\cos 0° + j\sin 0°) + 0.1(\cos 90° - j\sin 90°) + 0.02(\cos 90° + j\sin 90°)$$

$$= 1 - j\,0.1 + j\,0.02 = (1 - j\,0.08) \text{ mho}$$

Then,

$$V = I\,Y_{\text{equiv.}} = 50\angle 0° \times (1 - j\,0.08)$$

$$= 50\angle 0° \times 1.003\angle -4.57° \simeq \mathbf{50\angle -4.57\ V}$$

Here, voltage would lag the current by 4.57°.

EXAMPLE 2.112 *A choke coil is connected across a 250 V, 50 Hz supply. If the input current be 10 A and power loss in the choke be 1 kW, find the impedance, resistance and inductance of the choke. What is the power factor of the circuit ? What would be the value of the input current if a capacitor of C Farad is connected in series with the coil such that the power factor of the entire circuit becomes unity ?*

SOLUTION. Given,

$$V_S \text{ (Supply voltage)} = 250 \text{ V, 50 Hz.}$$

$I = 10$ A, Power loss in choke $= 1$ kW $= 10^3$ W.

$\therefore$ Impedance of the coil

$$|(Z_{\text{coil}})| = \frac{|V_S|}{|I|} = \frac{250}{10} = 25\,\Omega$$

But loss in watts in coil $= I^2R = 1000$ W.

$$\therefore \quad R = \frac{1000}{I^2} = \frac{1000}{10^2} = 10\,\Omega.$$

Then, from $Z = \sqrt{R^2 + X_L^2}$, we get

$$X_L = \sqrt{Z^2 - R^2}$$

or,

$$X_L = \sqrt{25^2 - 10^2} \simeq 23\,\Omega$$

$$\text{Power factor} = \frac{R}{Z} = \frac{10}{25} = 0.4 \text{ (lag)}$$

Hence, for the given coil,

$$R = 10\,\Omega,\ X_L = 23\,\Omega,\ Z = 25\,\Omega$$

and **P. F. = 0.4 (lag).**

Let us assume that a capacitor "C" be connected in series with the coil such that the net p.f. becomes unity. This is only possible if

$$X_L = X_C$$

or, $X_C = 23\,\Omega$ $\quad [\because X_L = 23\,\Omega]$

$$\frac{1}{2\,\pi\,f\,C} = 23$$

$$\therefore \quad C = \frac{1}{2\pi \times 50 \times 23} = 138.5\,\mu\text{F}$$

Thus it is observed that a capacitor of 138.5 μF is to be placed in series with the choke such that p.f. of the circuit is unity.

Then, the current taken by the circuit

$$= \frac{250}{Z} = \frac{250}{R} = \mathbf{25\ A}$$

$[\because$ at *upf*, $X_L = X_C$, $Z = R + j(X_L - X_C) = R]$

EXAMPLE 2.113 *In a R-L series circuit, the inductance is variable. If an a.c. voltage of V volts is applied at 50 Hz, find the maximum power transfer from source to load.*

SOLUTION. With reference to Fig. E2.58,

$$I = \frac{V}{Z} = \frac{V}{\sqrt{R^2 + X_L^2}} = \frac{V}{R} \times \frac{R}{\sqrt{R^2 + X_L^2}} = K\cos\phi$$

$$[\because \frac{V}{R} \text{ is a constant} = K \text{ and } \cos\phi = p.f. = \frac{R}{Z}]$$

$I = K\cos\phi$ represent a circle of I in polar form

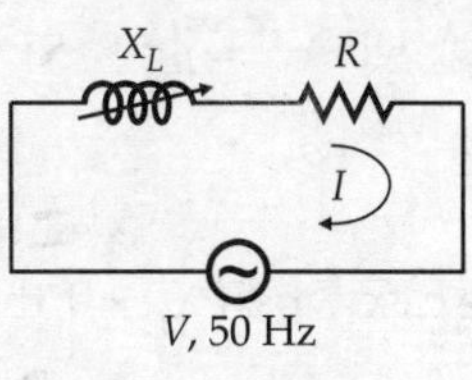

Fig. E2.58

CHAPTER 2

Let $x = I\cos\phi,\ y = -I\sin\phi$

[y is –ve as the current lags the voltage in inductive circuit]

$$\therefore\ x = \frac{V}{Z}\cos\phi = \frac{V}{Z}\cdot\frac{R}{Z}$$

$$= \frac{V}{\sqrt{R^2+X_L^2}}\cdot\frac{R}{\sqrt{R^2+X_L^2}} = \frac{VR}{R^2+X_L^2}$$

$$y = -\frac{V}{Z}\sin\phi$$

$$= -\frac{V}{\sqrt{R^2+X_L^2}}\cdot\frac{X_L}{\sqrt{R^2+X_L^2}} = -\frac{VX_L}{R^2+X_L^2}$$

Thus,

$$x^2+y^2 = \frac{V^2R^2}{(R^2+X_L^2)^2}+\frac{V^2X_L^2}{(R^2+X_L^2)^2}$$

$$= \frac{V^2R^2+V^2X_L^2}{(R^2+X_L^2)^2}$$

$$= \frac{V^2(R^2+X_L^2)}{(R^2+X_L^2)^2} = \frac{V^2}{R^2+X_L^2}$$

$$= \left(\frac{R}{R^2+X_L^2}\right)\frac{V^2}{R}$$

$$= \frac{V}{R}\times\frac{V}{R^2+X_L^2}\times R = \frac{V}{R}\times x$$

$$\therefore\ x^2+y^2 = \frac{V}{R}x$$

or, $$\left(x-\frac{V}{2R}\right)^2+(y-0)^2 = \left(\frac{V}{2R}\right)^2$$

The above equation represents a circle with centre at $\left(\frac{V}{2R}, 0\right)$ and of radius $\left(\frac{V}{2R}\right)$.

Figure E2.58(a) represents the circle diagram. If we study two extreme conditions, we find that for $X_L = 0$,

$$I = \frac{V}{R} \qquad \text{[\textit{i.e.}, current is maximum]}$$

On the other hand, if $X_L = \infty$ or very large,

$$I = \frac{V}{\infty} = 0 \qquad \text{[\textit{i.e.}, no current]}$$

Also, for the case when $X_L = 0$, the $p.f.$, $\frac{R}{Z} = \frac{R}{R} = 1$

i.e. the p.f. is unity.

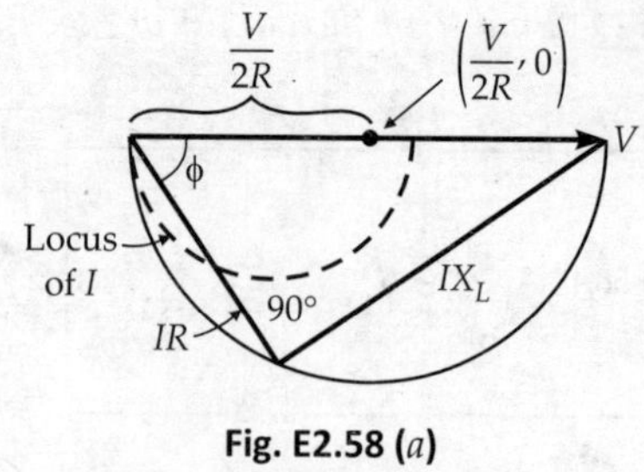

Fig. E2.58 (*a*)

When X_L is very large,

$$I = \frac{V}{Z} \simeq \frac{V}{X_L}$$

i.e., $$|I| = \frac{V}{X_L} \quad\text{and}\quad \angle I = -90°$$

i.e., p.f. is zero lagging.

Again, Power (real) $= VI\cos\phi$

If V is held constant, power would be maximum if $I\cos\phi$ = maximum *i.e.,* $\cos\phi = 1$.

At this time, Power (max) $= VI = V\times\frac{V}{R} = \frac{\mathbf{V^2}}{\mathbf{R}}$.

Then, maximum power becomes $\frac{\mathbf{V^2}}{\mathbf{R}}$.

Example 2.114 *In the above problem, instead of varying X_L from 0 to ∞, if R is varied keeping X_L constant, what could be the maximum power ?*

Solution. We have seen in the previous problem that

$$x = \frac{VR}{R^2+X_L^2} \quad\text{and}\quad y = -\frac{VX_L}{R^2+X_L^2}$$

This gives $$x^2+y^2 = \frac{V^2}{R^2+X_L^2}$$

However, $$x^2+y^2 = \frac{V^2}{R^2+X_L^2}$$

$$= \left(-\frac{V}{X_L}\right)\left(-\frac{VX_L}{R^2+X_L^2}\right) = -\frac{Vy}{X_L}$$

i.e., $$(x-0)^2+\left(y+\frac{V}{2X_L}\right)^2 = \left(\frac{V}{2X_L}\right)^2$$

The equation just derived shows the equation of a circle whose radius is $\left(\frac{V}{2X_L}\right)$ and centre is at $\left(0, -\frac{V}{2X_L}\right)$.

Two extreme conditions of current give

$$I = \frac{V}{Z} = \frac{V}{X_L} \quad [\text{when } R = 0, Z \equiv X_L]$$

i.e., the power factor becomes zero lag;

and $$I = \frac{V}{\infty} = 0 \quad [\text{when } R = \infty].$$

In case R is very large (but not infinity), $I = \frac{V}{R}$ and is of very low magnitude.

Then in this case, the current is of zero p.f. lag when $R = 0$ and becomes fully inductive. When R is very high, the current value is lower but the p.f. is unity (Fig. E2.59).

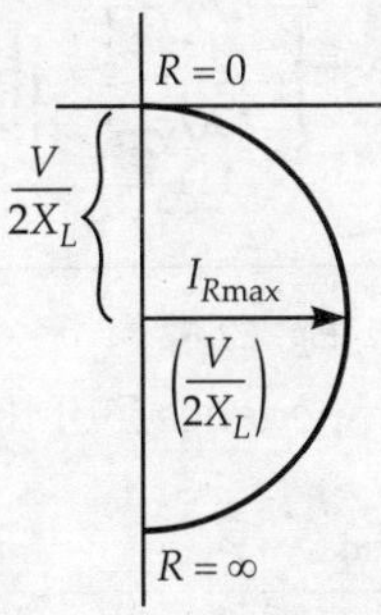

Fig. E2.59

Again power is given by $P = VI\cos\phi$.

Since V is constant, thus power would be maximum when $I\cos\phi$ is maximum.

Maximum value of $I\cos\phi = \frac{V}{2X_L}$

Thus, the amount of maximum power is given by

$$P_{max} = VI\cos\phi = \frac{V^2}{2X_L}.$$

EXAMPLE 2.115 *Two impedances Z_1 and Z_2 are in parallel across a 25 Hz, 100 V source. If $Z_1 = 9 - j\,15$; $Z_2 = 12 - j\,10$ ohms, find the currents through Z_1 and Z_2. Also find the total current, power factor angle of each branch and the entire circuit.*

SOLUTION. $$Y_1 = \frac{1}{Z_1} = \frac{1}{R_1 - j X_{C_1}}$$

$$= \frac{R_1 + j X_{C_1}}{R_1^2 + X_{C_1}^2} = g_1 + j\, b_1$$

where $$g_1 = \frac{R_1}{R_1^2 + X_{C_1}^2};\; b_1 = \frac{X_{C_1}}{R_1^2 + X_{C_1}^2}$$

Similarly,

$$Y_2 = \frac{1}{Z_2}$$

$$= \frac{R_2}{R_2^2 + X_{C_1}^2} + j\frac{X_{C_2}}{R_2^2 + X_{C_2}^2} = g_2 + jb_2$$

Here, $Z_1 = 9 - j\,15$ and $Z_2 = 12 - j\,10$

i.e., $R_1 = 9\,\Omega,\; X_{C_1} = 15\,\Omega,\; R_2 = 12\,\Omega,\; X_{C_2} = 10\,\Omega$

Thus, $$g_1 = \frac{9}{9^2 + 15^2} = 0.0294 \text{ mho}$$

$$g_2 = \frac{12}{12^2 + 10^2} = 0.0492 \text{ mho}$$

$$b_1 = \frac{15}{9^2 + 15^2} = 0.049 \text{ mho}$$

$$b_2 = \frac{10}{9^2 + 15^2} = 0.041 \text{ mho}$$

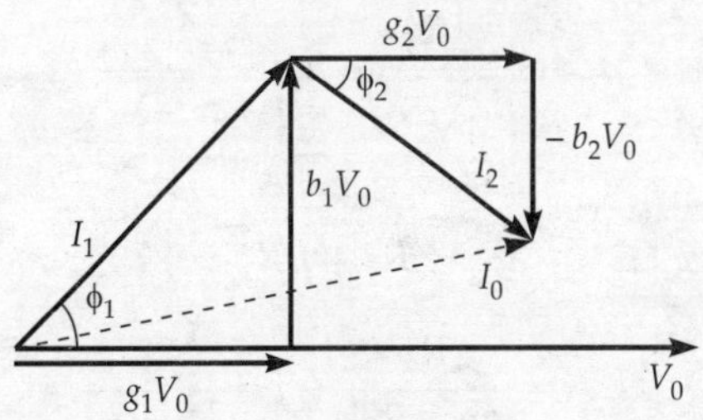

Fig. E2.60

Thus equivalent conductance

$$= g_1 + g_2 = 0.0786 \text{ mho}\,(g_0)$$

and equivalent susceptance (capacitive)

$$= b_1 + b_2 = 0.09 \text{ mho}\,(b_0)$$

Now, $I_1 =$ (current through Z_1)

$$= V_0\,(Y_1) = V_0\,(g_1 + jb_1)$$

$$= 100\,(0.0294 + j0.049) = (2.94 + j4.9)\text{ V},$$

$$I_2 = V_0\,(g_2 + j\,b_2) = (4.92 + j\,4.1)\text{ V}$$

and $$I = I_1 + I_2 = (7.86 + j\,9.0)\text{ A}$$

$$\phi_1 = \angle\tan^{-1}\frac{b_1}{g_1} = \mathbf{59°};\; \phi_2 = \angle\tan^{-1}\frac{b_2}{g_2} = \mathbf{39.80°}$$

and PF angle $\phi_0 = \tan^{-1}\frac{b_0}{g_0} = \mathbf{48.8°\ (lead)}$.

EXAMPLE 2.116 *(Fig. E2.61)*

Given $Z_1 = (4.4 - j\,6.6)\,\Omega$;

$Z_2 = (8.5 + j\,4.1)\,\Omega$; $V_0 = 10\ V$

$f = 50$ Hz.

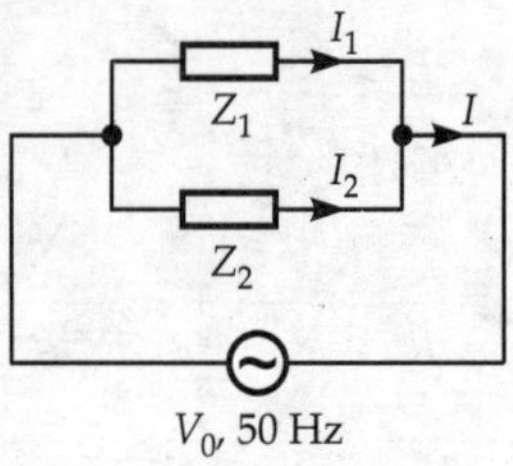

Fig. E2.61

Find (i) net admittance of the circuit

(ii) branch currents and total currents

(iii) P.F. of the given circuit.

Solution. (*i*) Let equivalent admittance of the given parallel circuit be

$$Y = Y_1 + Y_2$$

where $$Y_1 = \frac{1}{Z_1} = \frac{1}{R_1 - j X_{C_1}}$$

$$= \frac{R_1}{R_1^2 + X_{C_1}^2} + j \frac{X_{C_1}}{R_1^2 + X_{C_1}^2}$$

and $$Y_2 = \frac{1}{Z_2} = \frac{1}{R_2 + j X_{L_2}}$$

$$= \frac{R_2}{R_2^2 + X_{L_2}^2} - j \frac{X_{L_2}}{R_2^2 + X_{L_2}^2}$$

Here, $R_1 = 3.4\,\Omega$; $R_2 = 8.5\,\Omega$,

$X_{C_1} = 6.6\,\Omega$, $X_{L_2} = 4.1\,\Omega$

$$\therefore \quad g_1 = \frac{R_1}{R_1^2 + X_{C_1}^2} = 0.062 \text{ mho};$$

$$g_2 = \frac{R_2}{R_2^2 + X_{L_2}^2} = 0.096 \text{ mho}$$

$\therefore$ Net Conductance $= g_0 = g_1 + g_2 = 0.158$ mho

$$\text{Again} \quad b_1 = \frac{X_{C_1}}{R_1^2 + X_{C_1}^2} = 0.12 \text{ mho};$$

$$b_2 = \frac{X_{L_2}}{R_2^2 + X_{L_2}^2} = 0.045 \text{ mho}$$

Thus, the equivalent susceptance (capacitive)

$$= b_1 - b_2 = 0.12 - 0.045 = 0.075 \text{ mho}$$

(*i*) Thus equivalent admittance $= Y = Y_1 + Y_2$

$$= (g_1 + g_2) + j(b_1 - b_2)$$

$$= \mathbf{(0.158 + \textit{j}\ 0.075)\ mho.}$$

(*ii*) Branch currents are given by

$$I_1 = (g_1 + jb_1) V_0 = (0.62 + j\,1.2) \text{ A}$$

and $$I_2 = (g_2 - j\,b_2) V_0 = (0.96 - j\,0.46 \text{ A})$$

$$\therefore \quad I = I_1 + I_2 (= V_0 Y) = \mathbf{(1.58 + j\,0.75)\ A.}$$

$$(iii) \cos\phi_0 = \cos\left(\tan^{-1}\frac{b_1 - b_2}{g_1 + g_2}\right)$$

$$= \cos 25.39° = \mathbf{0.9.}$$

Example 2.117 *(Fig. E2.62) What should be the value of C such that the input power factor is unity for any frequency f of the source ?*

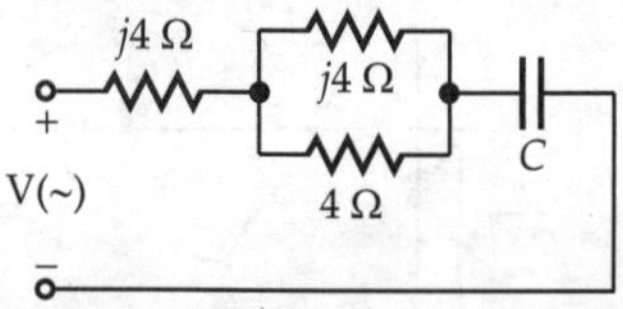

Fig. E2.62

Solution. The impedance Z of the given circuit is given as

$$Z = j\,4 + \frac{4 \times j\,4}{4 + j\,4} - \frac{j}{\omega C}$$

$$= -\frac{j}{\omega C} + j\,4 + \frac{j\,16(4 - j\,4)}{32}$$

$$= -\frac{j}{\omega C} + j\,4 + j\,2 + 2 = -\frac{j}{\omega C} + j\,6 + 2$$

The power factor will be unity (*i.e.*, the phase angle between the input voltage and current will be zero) only if the reactive part of the impedance is zero

i.e., if $\frac{1}{\omega C} = 6$

or, $$C = \frac{1}{6\,\omega} = \frac{1}{6 \times 314} = 796\ \mu\text{F}.$$

$[\because\ \omega = 2\pi f$ and $f = 50$ Hz (assumed)$]$

Thus, the required capacitance would be **796 μF only.**

Example 2.118 *An a.c. bridge is shown in Fig. E2.63. Obtain the condition of bridge balance.*

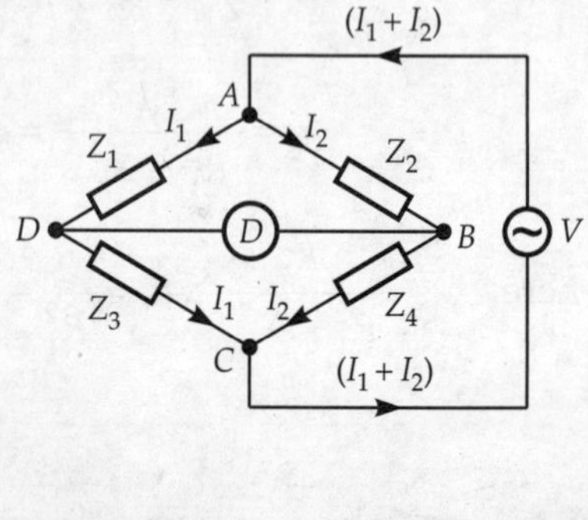

Fig. E2.63

SOLUTION. Condition of bridge balance gives no current through detector D, *i.e.*, drop across AB is equal to the drop across AD arm and drop across BC arm is equal to drop across CD arm.

i.e., $$I_1 Z_1 = I_2 Z_2$$

and $$I_1 Z_3 = I_2 Z_4$$

Combining these two equations,

$$\frac{Z_1}{Z_3} = \frac{Z_2}{Z_4} \text{ or, } Z_1 Z_4 = Z_2 Z_3 \quad ...(i)$$

As *a.c.* quantities are used, equation (*i*) means

$$Z_1 Z_4 \angle(\phi_1 + \phi_4) = Z_2 Z_3 \angle(\phi_2 + \phi_3)$$

The above condition gives the necessary condition of bridge balance.

EXAMPLE 2.119 *In the a.c. bridge of Fig. E2.64, at balance $Z_1 Z_4 = Z_2 Z_3$. Find R_X and L_X in terms of other arm parameter.*

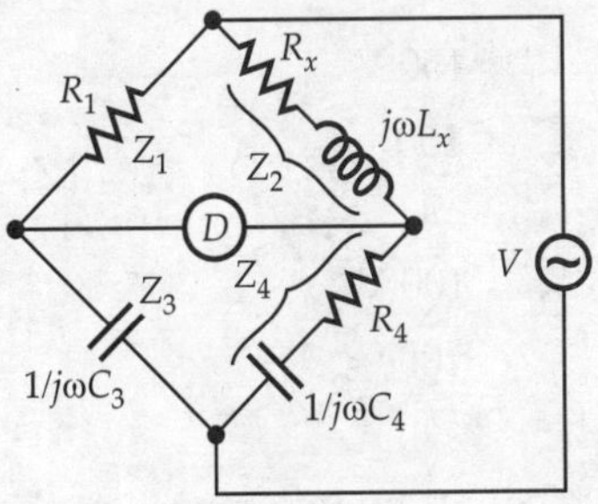

Fig. E2.64

SOLUTION.

$$Z_1 = R_1;$$

$$Z_2 = R_X + j\,\omega L_X;$$

$$Z_3 = \frac{1}{j\,\omega C_3};$$

$$Z_4 = R_4 + \frac{1}{j\,\omega C_4}$$

Following, $Z_1 Z_4 = Z_2 Z_3$,

$$R_1\left(R_4 + \frac{1}{j\,\omega C_4}\right) = \frac{1}{j\,\omega C_3}(R_X + j\omega L_X)$$

or, $$R_1 R_4 - j\frac{R_1}{\omega C_4} = \frac{L_X}{C_3} - j\frac{R_X}{\omega C_3}$$

Equating real and imaginary parts,

$$L_X = R_1 R_4 C_3;\ R_X = R_1 \frac{C_3}{C_4}.$$

EXAMPLE 2.120 *In Fig. E2.65, find the current locus of series RC circuit and find maximum power.*

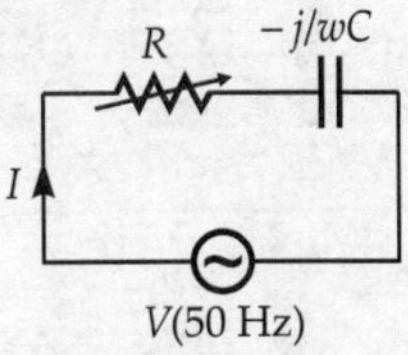

Fig. E2.65

SOLUTION. Drops across R and C are given as

$$V_R = IR \text{ and } V_C = IX_C$$

and supply voltage V is then obtained as

$$V^2 = V_R^2 + V_C^2$$

or, $$V = I\sqrt{R^2 + X_C^2} \text{ giving } I = \frac{V}{\sqrt{R^2 + X_C^2}}$$

Again, $$I = \frac{V}{\sqrt{R^2 + X_C^2}} = \frac{V}{X_C} \cdot \frac{X_C}{\sqrt{R^2 + X_C^2}}$$

$$= \frac{V}{X_C} \sin\phi$$

$$\left[\because \sin\phi = \frac{X_C}{Z} \text{ in } RC \text{ series circuit, } \phi \text{ being the p.f. angle}\right]$$

or, $$I = K \sin\phi$$

$$\left[\because \frac{V}{X_C} = \text{constant} = K\,(\text{say})\right]$$

The above equation represents a circle in polar coordinates. To represent the circle in rectangular co-ordinates, let $I\cos\phi = x$; $I\sin\phi = y$

$$\therefore x = \frac{V}{\sqrt{R^2 + X_C^2}} \cdot \frac{R}{\sqrt{R^2 + X_C^2}} = \frac{VR}{R^2 + X_C^2}$$

$$\left[\because \text{in } RC \text{ series circuit, } I = \frac{V}{Z} = \frac{V}{\sqrt{R^2 + X_C^2}};\ \cos\phi = \frac{R}{Z}\right]$$

Similarly,

$$y = I\sin\phi = \frac{V}{\sqrt{R^2 + X_C^2}} \cdot \frac{X_C}{\sqrt{R^2 + X_C^2}}$$

$$= \frac{VX_C}{R^2 + X_C^2}$$

Squaring and adding,

$$x^2 + y^2 = \frac{V^2 R^2}{(R^2 + X_C^2)^2} + \frac{V^2 X_C^2}{(R^2 + X_C^2)^2}$$

$$= \frac{V^2 R^2 + V^2 X_C^2}{(R^2 + X_C^2)^2} = V^2 \frac{(R^2 + X_C^2)}{(R^2 + X_C^2)^2}$$

$$= \frac{V^2}{R^2 + X_C^2} = \frac{V^2 . X_c}{X_C (R^2 + X_C^2)}$$

$$= \frac{V}{X_C} . \frac{VX_C}{(R^2 + X_C^2)} = \frac{V}{X_C} . y$$

or, $$x^2 + y^2 = \frac{V}{X_C} . y$$

or, $$(x - 0)^2 + \left(y - \frac{V}{2X_C} \right)^2 = \left(\frac{V}{2X_C} \right)^2$$

The above equation represents a circle whose radius is $\frac{V}{2X_C}$ and centre is at $\left(0, \frac{V}{2X_C}\right)$.

The current locus diagram is shown in **Fig. E2.66** ; when $R=0$, the current is $I = \frac{V}{X_C}$ and leading the voltage by 90° (O-Y) in Fig. E2.66).

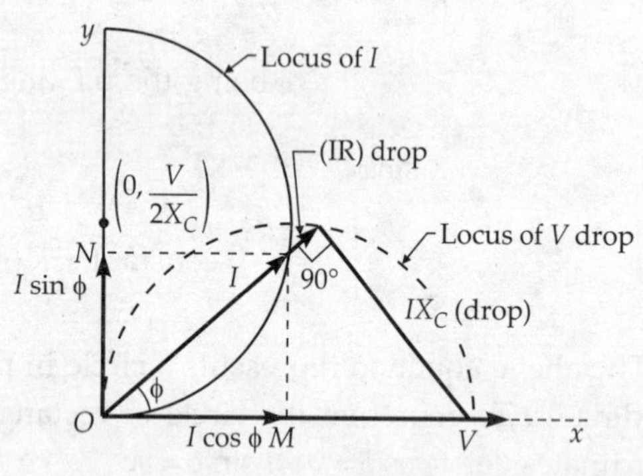

Fig. E2.66

In Fig. E2.66, $OM = I \cos \phi$ and $ON = I \sin \phi$.

Maximum power will flow when OM is maximum

i.e., when the value of OM is $\frac{V}{2X_C}$; *p.f.* being cos 45° (0.707).

[Maximum power becomes

$$VI_{max} = V \times \frac{V}{2X_C} = \mathbf{V^2 / 2X_C \text{ W.}}$$]

EXAMPLE 2.121 *A voltage of 200 V, 50 Hz is applied to a RLC series circuit (Fig. E2.67) where*

$$V_R = 170 \text{ V}, V_L = 150 \text{ V and } V_C = 100 \text{ V}.$$

The circulating current being 4 A, find the power factor of the circuit and power loss provided inductance has an inherent resistance part in it.

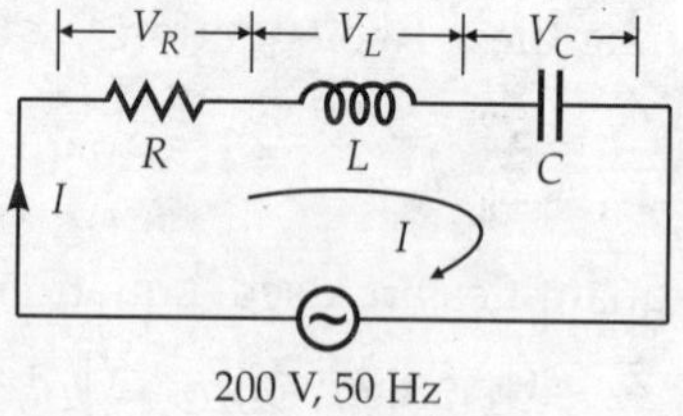

Fig. E2.67

SOLUTION.

$$V_R = 170 \text{ V}, I = 4 \text{ A}$$

$$\therefore \quad R = \frac{170}{4} = 42.5 \, \Omega$$

Also, $$V_L = 150 \text{ V}$$

$$\therefore \quad Z_1 = \frac{150}{4} = 37.5 \, \Omega \qquad [Z_L = r_L + j\,x_L]$$

and $$V_C = 100 \text{ V}$$

$$\therefore \quad X_C = \frac{100}{4} = 25 \, \Omega$$

Again Z being the impedance of the circuit,

$$Z = \frac{V}{I} = \frac{200}{4} = 50 \, \Omega$$

Thus, from the theory of *a.c.* series circuit,

$$R + (r_l + j\,x_l) - \frac{j}{\omega C} = Z$$

or, $$(R + r_l) + j\,(x_l - 25) = 50$$

or, $$(r_l + 42.5)^2 + (x_l - 25)^2 = 50^2 \qquad ...(1)$$

Again, $Z_l = r_l + jx_l = 37.5$ (as shown above)

or, $$r_l^2 + x_l^2 = 37.5^2 \qquad ...(2)$$

Solving (1) and (2),

$$r_l = 0.526\,x_l - 14.08 \qquad ...(3)$$

i.e., $$(0.526\,x_l - 14.08)^2 + x_l^2 = 37.5^2$$

or, $$x_l = 37.25 \, \Omega \text{ and } r_l = 5.50 \, \Omega$$

P.F. of the circuit $= \frac{r_l + R}{Z} = \frac{42.5 + 5.5}{50} = \mathbf{0.96}$

Power loss

$$= I^2 (r_l + R) = (5.5 + 42.5) \times 4^2 = \mathbf{768 \text{ W.}}$$

EXAMPLE 2.122 *A current of 2 A flows through a resistor in series with a coil while 200 V is applied across the combination at 50 Hz. If the voltage across the resistor be 100 V while that across the coil be 150 V, calculate (a) the impedance, resistance and reactance of the coil, (b) the power absorbed by coil, (c) the total power.*

SOLUTION. Let r_1 = resistance of the unknown resistor,

$$Z_l = r_l + j\,x_l = \text{impedance of the coil.}$$

Now, drop across r_1 being 100 V, the current through it 2 A,

$$r_1 = \frac{100}{2} = 50\,\Omega.$$

Net impedance (Z) of the series combination is $\frac{200}{2} = 100\,\Omega$

$$\therefore \quad r_1 + (r_l + jx_l) = 100$$

or, $(r_1 + r_l) + j\,x_l = 100$

or, $r^2 + x_l^2 = 100^2$ (where $r = r_1 + r_l$) ...(1)

Again drop across the coil only being 150 V,

$$Z_l = r_l + j\,x_l = \frac{150}{2} = 75$$

or $r_l^2 + x_l^2 = 75^2$ ...(2)

Subtracting (2) from (1),

$$(r_1 + r_l)^2 - r_l^2 = 100^2 - 75^2$$

or, $r_1^2 + 2\,r_1\,r_l = 4375$

or, $50^2 + 100\,r_l = 4375$

Thus $r_l = 18.75\,\Omega$

From (2), $x_l^2 = 75^2 - (18.75)^2$

$\therefore$ $x_l = 72.62\,\Omega$

Thus, (*i*) $Z_l = 75\,\Omega$, $r_l = 18.75\,\Omega$, $x_l = 72.62$

and (*ii*) P_l (power absorbed by coil)

$$= I^2\,r_l = 2^2 \times 18.75 = \mathbf{75\ W}$$

and total power $= I^2\,(r_1 + r_l) = \mathbf{275\ W.}$

EXAMPLE 2.123 *In the network of Fig. E2.68, if $I = 5\angle 60°$, find Z.*

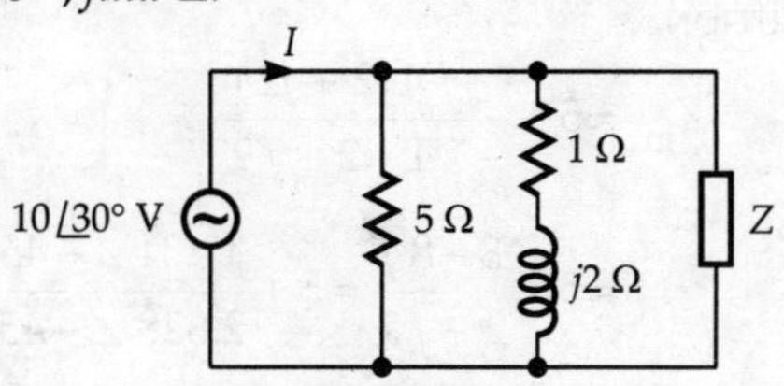

Fig. E2.68

SOLUTION. The admittance of the given network would be given by

$$Y = \frac{I}{V} = \frac{5\angle 60°}{10\angle 30°} = 0.5\angle 30°\text{ mho}$$

However,

$$Y = Y_1 + Y_2 + Y_3$$

where $Y_3 = \frac{1}{Z}$, $Y_2 = \frac{1}{1 + j\,2} = (0.2 - j\,0.4)$ mho

and $Y_1 = \frac{1}{5} = 0.2$ mho.

i.e., $0.5\angle 30° = 0.2 + 0.2 - j\,0.4 + Y_3$

or, $Y_3 = 0.433 + j\,0.1 - 0.2 - 0.2 + j\,0.4$

$$= -0.033 + j\,0.5$$

$$= 0.5\angle 86.22°\text{ mho.}$$

Thus $Z = \frac{1}{Y_3} = \frac{1}{0.5\angle 86.22°}$

$$= \mathbf{(0.033 + j\,0.499)\,\Omega.}$$

[*i.e.*, Z is consisting of a resistor of 0.033 Ω and a inductive reactance 0.499 Ω in series]

EXAMPLE 2.124 *In Fig. E2.69, $R = 10\,\Omega$, $X_L = j\,8\,\Omega$. Find Z.*

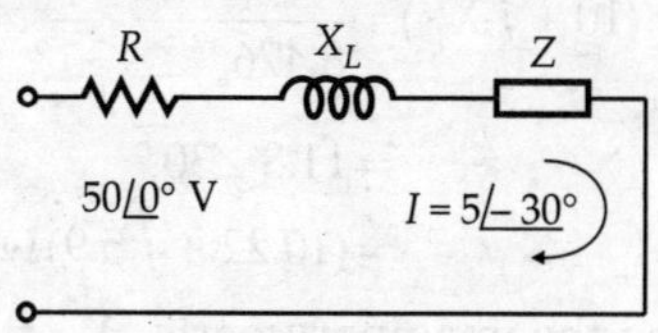

Fig. E2.69

SOLUTION.

$$Z_{eq} = \frac{V}{I} = \frac{50\angle 0°}{5\angle -30°} = 10\angle 30°\,\Omega$$

However,

$$Z_{eq} = R + j\,X_L + Z$$

$$\therefore \quad Z = R + j\,X_L - Z_{eq}$$

$$= 10 + j\,8 - 10\angle 30°$$

or, $Z = 10 + j\,8 - 8.66 - j\,5$

$$= (1.34 + j\,3) = \mathbf{3.29\angle 66°\,\Omega}$$

Thus Z is 3.29 ∠66° *i.e.*, a series combination of resistance of **1.34 Ω** and inductive reactance of **3 ohms.**

EXAMPLE 2.125 *In the network of Fig. E2.70, find X_L.*

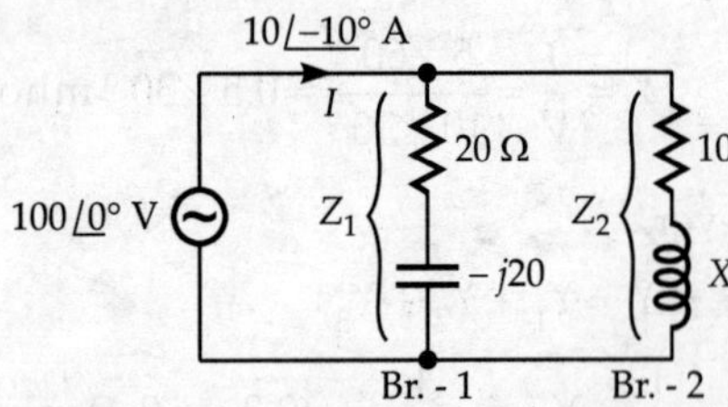

Fig. E2.70

SOLUTION. Current through branch-1 is given by

$$I_1 = \frac{V}{Z_1} = \frac{100\angle 0°}{20 - j\,20} = \frac{100\angle 0°}{28.28\angle -45°}$$

$$= 3.54\angle +45° \text{ A.}$$

∴ Current in branch-2 is given by

$$I_2 = I - I_1$$
$$= 10\angle -10° - 3.54\angle +45°$$
$$= (9.84 - j\,1.74) - (2.503 + j\,2.503)$$
$$= (7.337 - j\,4.243) \text{ A}$$
$$= 8.476\angle -30° \text{ A}$$

However, $$I_2 = \frac{V}{Z_2} = \frac{100 + j\,0}{10 + j\,X_L}$$

∴ $$(10 + j\,X_L) = \frac{100\angle 0°}{8.476°\angle -30°}$$

$$= 11.8\angle 30°$$
$$= (10.22 + j\,5.9)\,\Omega$$

Equating the imaginary parts, X_L **= 5.9 Ω.**

EXAMPLE 2.126 *Find r in the circuit of Fig. E2.71, such that the input power factor is 0.9 lag.*

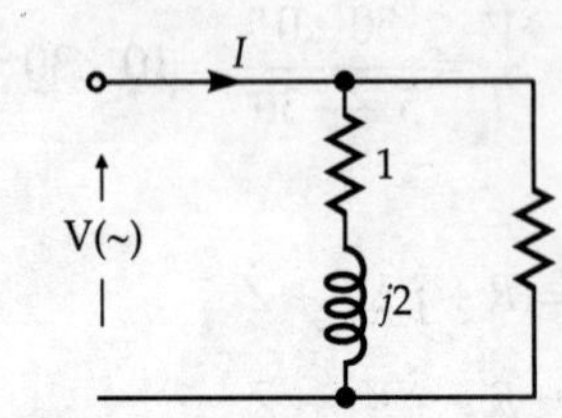

Fig. E2.71

SOLUTION. The equivalent admittance of the given network is

$$Y = \frac{1}{1 + j\,2} + \frac{1}{r} = 0.2 - j\,0.4 + \frac{1}{r}$$

$$= \left[\left(0.2 + \frac{1}{r}\right) - j\,0.4\right] \text{ mho.}$$

For the lagging p.f. operation of 0.9, the angle of admittance is $\cos^{-1}\ 0.9 = -25.85°$.

i.e., $$\frac{0.4}{0.2 + \frac{1}{r}} = \tan 25.85° = 0.484$$

or, $$0.2 + \frac{1}{r} = 0.826$$

or, $$\frac{1}{r} = 0.826 - 0.2 = 0.626$$

i.e., r = **1.6 ohm.**

EXAMPLE 2.127 *Obtain input p.f. of the given circuit (Fig. E2.72). Values shown are in ohms.*

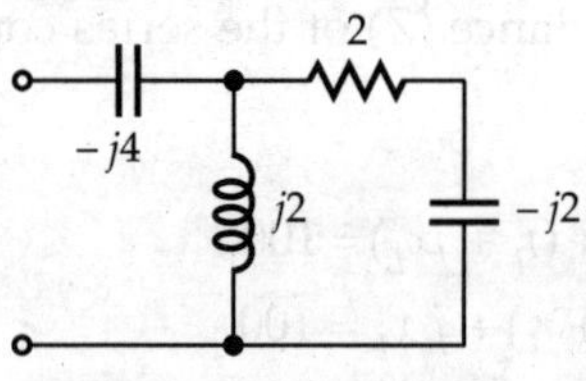

Fig. E2.72

SOLUTION.

$$Z_{input} = -j\,4 + \frac{j\,2\,(2 - j\,2)}{j\,2 + 2 - j\,2}$$

$$= -j\,4 + \frac{j\,4 + 4}{2} = -j\,4 + 2 + j\,2$$

$$= (2 - j\,2) = 2.828\angle -45°\,\Omega$$

∴ Input p.f. is cos 45° = **0.707 (lead).**

It may be noted that the equivalent of this circuit is a resistor of 2 ohms in series with a capacitor of $-j\,2$ ohm reactance.

EXAMPLE 2.128 *In the network of Fig. E2.73, find input admittance and power factor.*

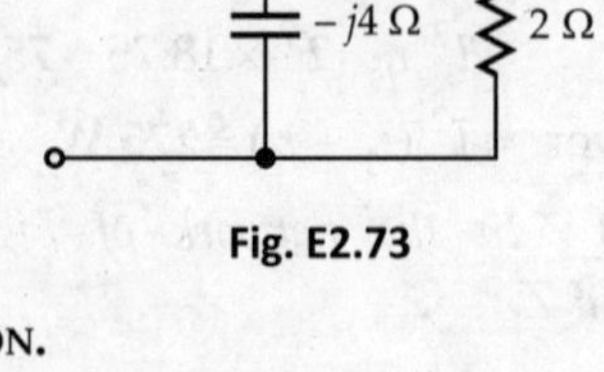

Fig. E2.73

SOLUTION.

$$Z_{in} = 5 + \frac{-j\,4\,(2 + j2)}{-j\,4 + 2 + j\,2}$$

$$= 5 + \frac{8 - 8\,j}{2 - j\,2} = 5 + \frac{11.31\angle -45°}{2.828\angle -45°}$$

∴ $$Z_{in} = 5 + 4 = 9\,\Omega$$

The input impedance is thus purely resistive of 9 Ω. Input admittance is given by **1/9 mho** *i.e.*, **0.111 mho.** As the input impedance is purely resistive, the input p.f. would be unity.

EXAMPLE 2.129 *In the circuit of Fig. E2.74, find I.*

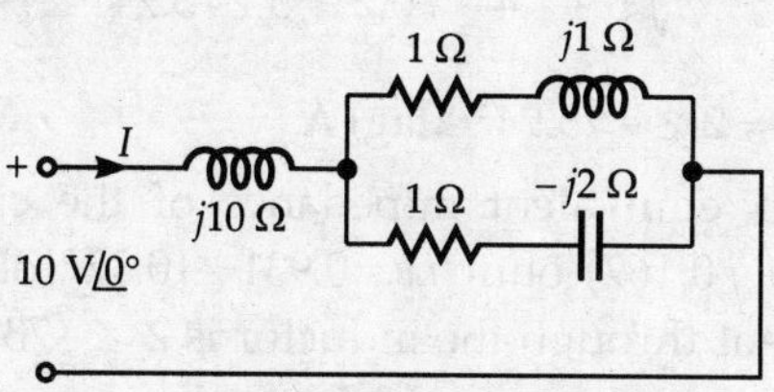

Fig. E2.74

SOLUTION.

$$Z_{in} = j\,10 + \frac{(1+j\,1)(1-j\,2)}{1+j\,1+1-j\,2}$$

$$= j\,10 + \frac{1+j\,1-j\,2+2}{2-j\,1} = j\,10 + \frac{3-j\,1}{2-j\,1}$$

$$= j\,10 + \frac{(3-j\,1)(2+j\,1)}{2^2+1^2}$$

$$= j\,10 + \frac{6+j\,3-j\,2+1}{5} = j\,10 + 1.4 + j\,0.2$$

$$= 1.4 + j\,10.2 = 10.3\,\angle 82.18°\,\Omega$$

$$\therefore\; I = \frac{V}{Z_{in}} = \frac{10\,\angle 0°}{10.3\,\angle 82.18}$$

$$= \mathbf{0.97\,\angle -82.18°\ A.} \qquad \text{[lagging current]}$$

EXAMPLE 2.130 *A voltage of $v = 200 \sin \omega t + 50 \sin 3\,\omega t$ is applied across a parallel circuit as shown in Fig. E2.75. If the supply voltage has a frequency of 50 Hz, obtain the rms values of current in each branch, the total current and power input.*

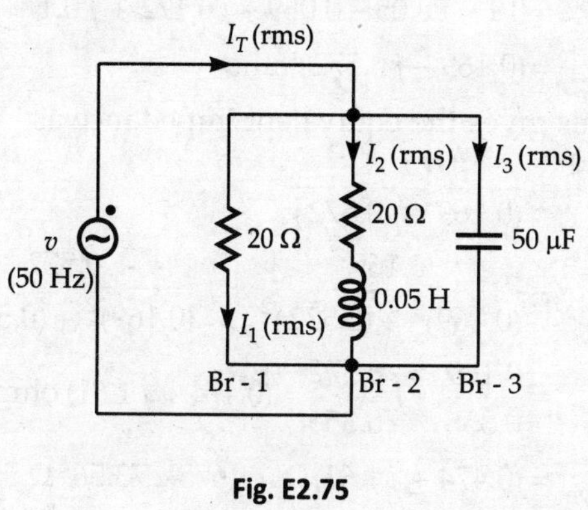

Fig. E2.75

SOLUTION. Let us designate the branches first like Br-1, Br-2 and Br-3 as shown in the figure. It may be noted that as

$$f = 50 \text{ Hz},$$

$$\omega = 2 \times \pi \times 50 = 314 \text{ rad/sec}.$$

Let Z_{11} = impedance of branch-1 at freq. 50 Hz.

Then $Z_{11} = 20\,\Omega$

Obviously Z_{12}, the impedance of branch-1 at frequency (3 × 50) Hz would be $Z_{12} = 20\,\Omega$.

[∵ resistance is independent of frequency]

For branch-2, at 50 Hz,

$$Z_{21} = 20 + j\,0.05 \times 314$$

$$= 20 + j\,15.7 = 25.4\,\angle 38.15° \text{ ohm}$$

and at (50 × 3) Hz,

$$Z_{22} = 20 + 3\,j \times 0.05 \times 314$$

$$= 20 + j\,47.1 = 51.2° 67° \text{ ohm}$$

For branch-3, at 50 Hz,

$$Z_{31} = -j\frac{1}{314 \times 50 \times 10^{-6}} = j\,63.7$$

$$= 63.7\,\angle -90° \text{ ohm}$$

and at (3 × 50) Hz,

$$Z_{32} = -j\frac{1}{3 \times 314 \times 50 \times 10^{-6}}$$

$$= -j\,21.23 = 21.23\,\angle -90° \text{ ohm}.$$

Thus, $I_{1\,rms} = \sqrt{I_{11(rms)}^2 + I_{12\,rms}^2}$

[where $I_{11\,rms}$ = current in branch-1 due to ω freq.

$I_{12\,rms}$ = current in branch-1 due to 3 ω freq.]

$$= \sqrt{\left(\frac{200}{\sqrt{2}}/20\right)^2 + \left(\frac{50}{\sqrt{2}}/20\right)^2} = \mathbf{7.31\ A.}$$

[∵ current in Br-1 due to ω is (V_{rms}/Z_{11}) and that in Br-1 due to 3 ω is (V_{rms}/Z_{12})]

Similarly,

$$I_{2(rms)} = \sqrt{I_{21(rms)}^2 + I_{22(rms)}^2}$$

$$= \sqrt{\left[\left(\frac{200}{\sqrt{2}}\right)\Big/25.4\right]^2 + \left[\left(\frac{50}{\sqrt{2}}\right)\Big/51.2\right]^2}$$

$$= \mathbf{5.62\ A.}$$

CHAPTER 2

and

$$I_{3(\text{rms})} = \sqrt{\left[\left(\frac{200}{\sqrt{2}}\right)\Big/63.7\right]^2 + \left[\left(\frac{50}{\sqrt{2}}\right)\Big/21.23\right]^2}.$$

$$= 2.78 \text{ A.}$$

It may be noted that in every case, the r.m.s. current in each branch is the vector sum of r.m.s. current in the same branch for each of frequency components.

Total r.m.s. current is given by

$$I_{T(\text{r.m.s.})} = I_{1(\text{r.m.s.})} + I_{2(\text{r.m.s.})} + I_{3(\text{r.m.s.})}$$

$$= \mathbf{15.7\ A}$$

and Power input = Summation of power in each branch

$$= I_1^2 \times 20 + I_2^2 \times 20 + 0$$

[$\because$ there is no power consumed in branch-3]

i.e., Power input $= 7.31^2 \times 20 + 5.62^2 \times 20 = \mathbf{1700\ W}$.

EXAMPLE 2.131 *In the circuit of Fig. E2.76, find the current through the inductor. What is the equivalent impedance ?*

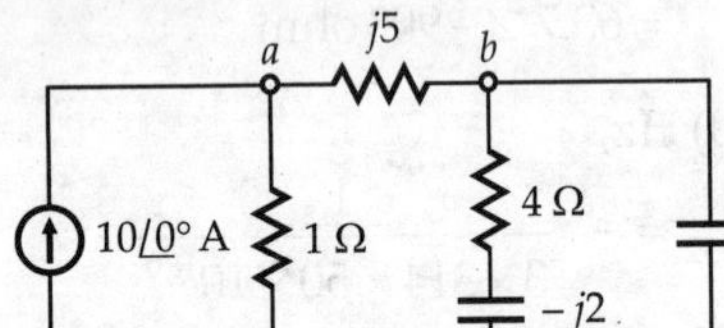

Fig. E2.76

SOLUTION. Impedance across *b-c* is given by

$$Z_{bc} = \frac{2(4-j2)}{2+4-j2} = \frac{(4-j2)}{(3-j1)} = \frac{(4-j2)(3+j1)}{3^2+1^2}$$

$$= \frac{12+j4-j6+2}{10} = (1.4 - j0.2)\Omega$$

Next, equivalent impedance across *a-d* is given by

$$Z_{ad} = \frac{1(j5+Z_{bc})}{1+j5+Z_{bc}} = \frac{j5+1.4-j0.2}{1+j5+1.4-j0.2}$$

$$= \frac{1.4+j4.8}{2.4+j4.8} = \frac{3.36-j6.72+j11.52+23.04}{28.8}$$

$$= \frac{+26.4+j4.8}{28.8} = \mathbf{+0.917 + j0.167\,\Omega}.$$

$\therefore$ Current through $(j5)\Omega$ inductor is given by (using current division formula),

$$I_{j5\Omega} = 10\,\frac{1\angle 0°}{j5+Z_{bc}}$$

$$= 10\,\frac{1\angle 0°}{j5+1.4-j0.2} = \frac{10\angle 0°}{5\angle 73.74°}$$

$$= \mathbf{2\angle -73.74°\ (lag)\ A.}$$

Thus, equivalent impedance of the circuit is $(-0.917 + j0.167)$ ohm *i.e.*, $0.931\angle 10.32°$ ohm and the current through the inductor is $2\angle -73.74°$ A.

EXAMPLE 2.132 *Find the equivalent impedance of the given network in Fig. E2.77. What is the current through the capacitor ?*

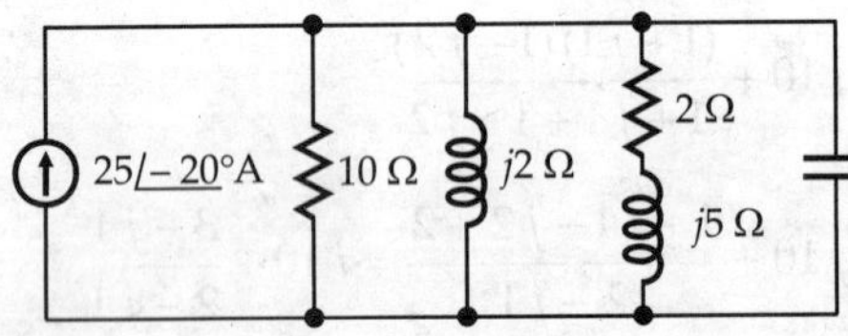

Fig. E2.77

SOLUTION. As four branches are in parallel, the admittance in each branch can be obtained as

$$Y_1 = \frac{1}{Z_1} = \frac{1}{10} = 0.1 \text{ mho}$$

$$Y_2 = \frac{1}{j2} = -j0.5 \text{ mho}$$

$$Y_3 = \frac{1}{2+j5} = \frac{2}{2^2+5^2} - j\frac{5}{2^2+5^2}$$

$$= (0.069 - j0.172) \text{ mho}$$

$$Y_4 = \frac{1}{-j10} = j0.1 \text{ mho.}$$

Thus net admittance

$$Y = Y_1 + Y_2 + Y_3 + Y_4$$

$$= 0.1 - j0.05 + 0.069 - j0.172 + j0.1$$

$$= (0.169 - j0.572) \text{ mho}$$

This gives the equivalent impedance as

$$\frac{1}{Y} = \frac{1}{(0.169 - j0.572)}$$

$$= \frac{0.169}{(0.169)^2 + (0.572)^2} + j\frac{0.572}{(0.169)^2+(0.572)^2}$$

$$= \frac{0.169}{0.356} + j\frac{0.572}{0.356} = (0.474 + j1.61) \text{ ohm}$$

i.e., $Z_{eq} = (0.474 + j1.61)\Omega = 1.675\angle 73.56°\,\Omega$

Again the drop across the parallel connected elements is given by

$$V = IZ = 25\angle -20 \times 1.675\angle 73.56°$$

$$= 41.87\angle 53.56° \text{ V}$$

Thus current through the capacitor is given by

$$I_4 = \frac{V}{X_C} = \frac{41.87\angle 53.56°}{10\angle -90°} = \mathbf{4.187\angle 143.56\ A.}$$

EXAMPLE 2.133 *In the circuit of Fig. E2.78, $R_1 = 1.5\,\Omega$, $R_2 = 5.6\,\Omega$, $R_3 = 7\,\Omega$; $x_{L_1} = 3.4\,\Omega$, $x_{C_1} = 6.5\,\Omega$, $x_{C_2} = 4.7\,\Omega$, $x_{L_3} = 8.2\,\Omega$..*

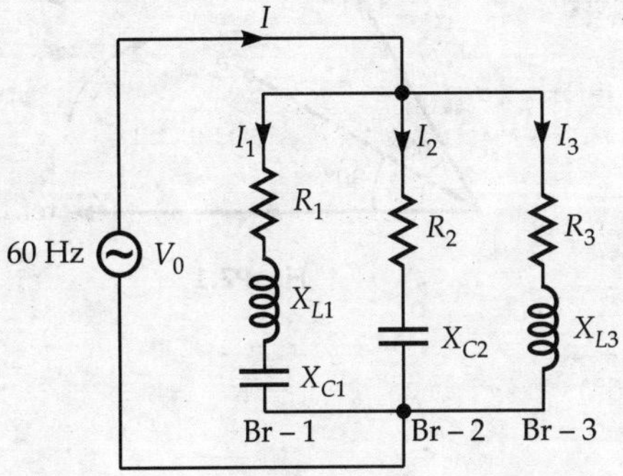

Fig. E2.78

Assuming $V_0 = 100$ V, $f = 60$ Hz, find the equivalent conductance, susceptance and admittance of the given circuit. What is supply current and power factor ?

SOLUTION.

g_1 = conductance of branch-1

$$= \frac{R_1}{R_1 + (x_{L_1} - x_{C_1})^2}$$

$$= \frac{1.5}{1.5 + (3.4 - 6.5)^2} = 0.1264 \text{ mho}$$

$$g_2 = \text{conductance of branch-2} = \frac{R_2}{R_2^2 + x_{C_2}^2}$$

$$= \frac{5.6}{(5.6)^2 + (4.7)^2} = 0.1047 \text{ mho}$$

$$g_3 = \text{conductance of branch-3} = \frac{R_3}{R_3^2 + x_{L_3}^2}$$

$$= \frac{7}{7^2 + 8.2^2} = 0.06 \text{ mho}$$

Thus equivalent conductance

$$(g_0) = g_1 + g_2 + g_3$$

$$= 0.1264 + 0.1047 + 0.06 = 0.2911 \text{ mho.}$$

Similarly,

b_1 = susceptance of branch-1

$$= \frac{-(x_{L_1} - x_{C_1})}{R_1^2 + (x_{L_1} - x_{C_1})^2} = 0.26 \text{ mho,}$$

b_2 = susceptance of branch-2

$$= \frac{x_{C_2}}{R_2^2 + x_{C_2}^2} = 0.088 \text{ mho}$$

and b_3 = susceptance of branch-3

$$= -\frac{x\,L_3}{R_3^2 + x_{L_3}^2} = -0.0705 \text{ mho}$$

Thus, equivalent (b_0) susceptance

$$= b_1 + b_2 + b_3$$

$$= 0.26 + 0.088 - 0.0705$$

$$= 0.2775 \text{ mho.}$$

$\therefore$ Equivalent admittance of the given circuit is

$$Y_0 = g_0 + j\,b_0$$

$$= (0.2911 + j\,0.2775).$$

and input current I

$$= V_0\,Y_0 = 100\,(0.2911 + j\,0.2775)$$

$$= \mathbf{(29.11 + j\,27.75)\ A.}$$

Supply power factor is

$$\cos\phi_0 = \cos\angle\tan^{-1}\frac{b_0}{g_0} = \mathbf{0.725\ (lead)}$$

The vector diagram is shown in Fig. E2.79.

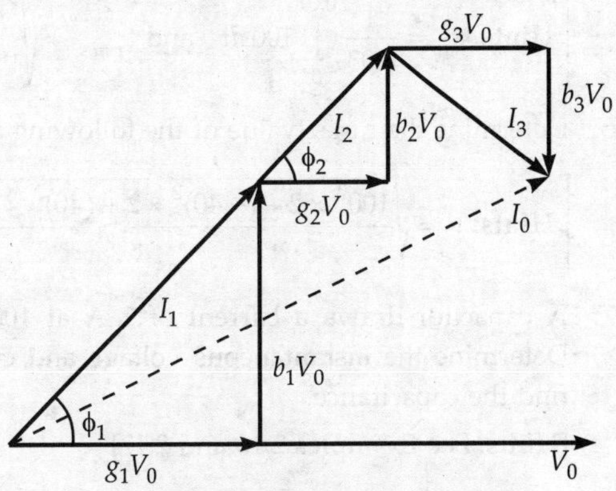

$$\left[\phi_1 = \tan^{-1}\frac{b_1}{g_1}\ ;\ \phi_2 = \tan^{-1}\frac{b_2}{g_2}\right]$$

Fig. E2.79

CHAPTER 2

EXERCISES

1. A current wave is represented by : $i = 10 \sin 377t$.
   Find (*a*) frequency (*b*) Time period (*c*) Maximum value (*d*) R.M.S. value (*e*) Average value and (*f*) Instantaneous value when $t = 0.03$ sec.
   [Hints. Ref. Example 2.1]
2. In a circuit, the voltage wave is represented by
   $$v = 100 \sin\left(314t + \frac{\pi}{4}\right)$$
   Determine (*i*) r.m.s. value of the wave (*ii*) average value of it and (*iii*) phase angle of it.
   [Hints. See Example 2.5]
3. A voltage is represented by, $v = 10 \sin(\omega t + 30°)$ while the circuit current is represented by
   $$i = 10 \sin(\omega t + 60°)$$
   Determine the phase-angle relationship between the waveforms.
   [Hints. i leads v, Angle of lead is 30° (Fig. P2.1)]

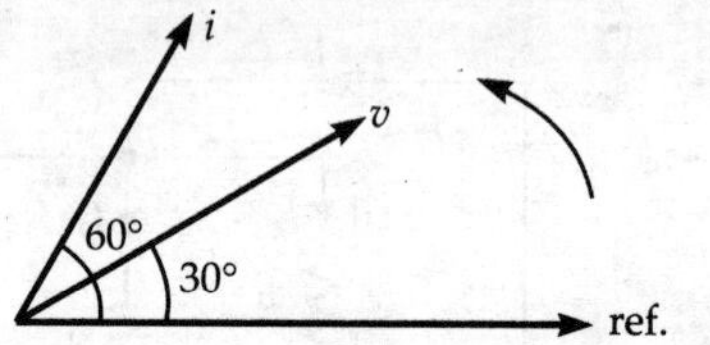

Fig. P2.1

4. Two waves A and B are given as
   $$A = A_m \sin(\omega t + 30°)\,; \quad B = B_m \sin(\omega t - 45°)$$
   What is the phase relationship between A and B ?
   [Hints. Ref. to the vector diagram (Fig. P2.2) and find ϕ]

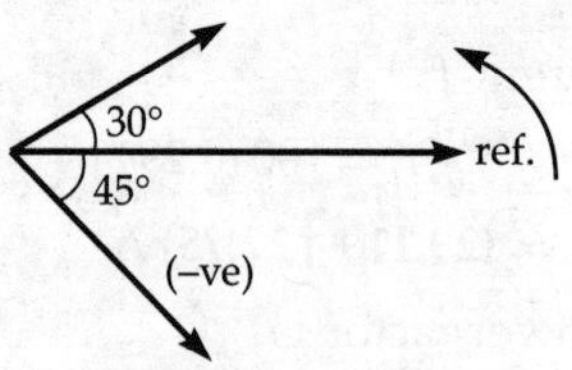

Fig. P2.2

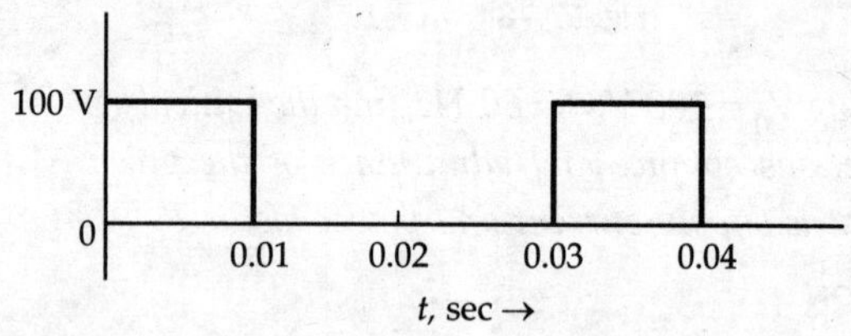

Fig. P2.3

5. Obtain average and effective values of the waveform shown in Fig. P2.3.
   $$\left[\textbf{Hints. } v_{av} = \frac{1}{0.03}\int_0^{0.01} 100\,dt \text{ and } v_{r.m.s.} = \sqrt{\frac{1}{0.03}\int_0^{0.01} (100)^2\,dt}\right]$$
6. Determine the r.m.s. value of the following waveform (Fig. P2.4)
   $$\left[\textbf{Hints. } V = \sqrt{\frac{100^2 \times 2 + (-40)^2 \times 2 + (40)^2 \times 2 + 0^2 \times 2}{8}}\right]$$

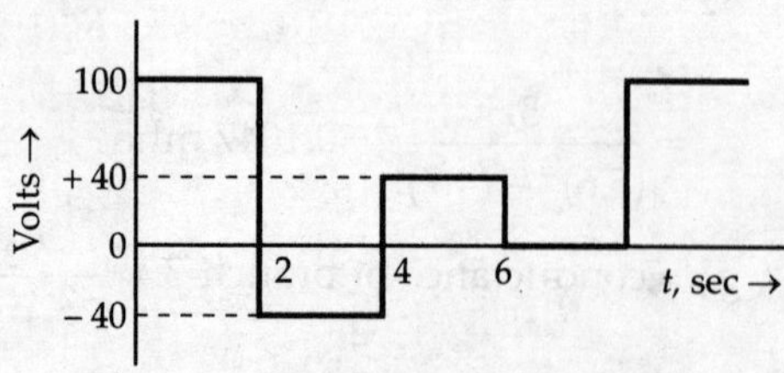

Fig. P2.4

7. A capacitor draws a current of 1 A at 100 V, 25 Hz. Determine the instantaneous voltage and current. Also find the capacitance.
   [Hints. See Examples 2.16 and 2.17]
8. An inductor of 50 μH offers a reactance of 25 Ω. If the supply voltage has an r.m.s. value of 100 volts, find the current through the inductor and find the frequency.
   $$\left[\textbf{Hints. } I = \frac{V}{X_L} = \frac{100}{25} = 4\text{ A}\,; \; f = \frac{X_L}{2\pi L} = \frac{25}{2 \times \pi \times 50 \times 10^{-6}}\text{ Hz}\right]$$

9. An a.c. voltage of 100 V (rms) is applied on a pure inductor of 1 H. If the supply (*f*) is 50 Hz, find the current through the inductor and the instantaneous expression for current.

$$\left[\textbf{Hints. } I = \frac{V}{X_L} = \frac{100}{2\pi \times 50 \times 1} \text{ A}; \; i = (\sqrt{2}\, I)\sin(314t - 90°)\right]$$

10. The voltage and current in a circuit element is $v = 100\cos(377t - 80°)$; $i = 10\cos(377t + 10°)$. Identify the element and obtain its value.

[**Hints.** With ref. to Fig. P2.5, $\phi = 90°$ while i leads v.

$\therefore$ the element is a capacitor.

$$X_C = \frac{V_m}{I_m} = \frac{100}{10} = 10\,\Omega$$

$$\therefore \quad C = \frac{1}{2\pi (X_c) f} = \frac{1}{2\pi \times 10 \times 60} \text{ F}\Big]$$

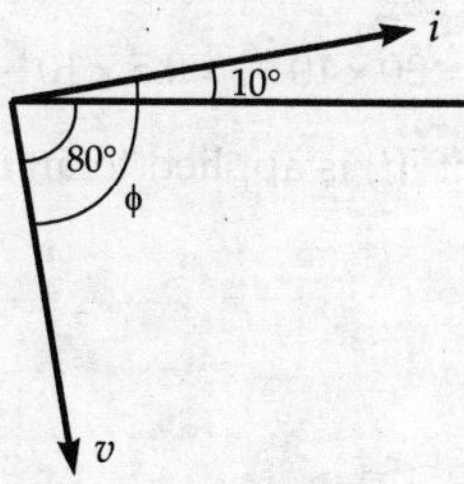

Fig. P2.5

11. The voltage and current in a circuit element is

$$v = 400\sin(314t - 20°); \quad i = 40\sin(314t - 20°)$$

Identify the element and find its value.

[**Hints.** Since $\phi = 0°$, in this case, the circuit element is a resistor. $R = V_m / I_m = 400/40 = 10\,\Omega$]

12. A 10 V (rms) as source having 50 Hz frequency is applied over a 60 mH pure inductance. Find the circuit current.

$$\left[\textbf{Hints. } I = \frac{V}{X_L} = \frac{V}{2\pi f L} \text{ A}\right]$$

13. A sinusoidal voltage of 100 V (rms) is applied to a pure capacitor of 0.1 μF. If the supply frequency is 100 Hz, find the capacitive reactance and circuit current.

$$\left[\textbf{Hints. } X_C = \frac{1}{2\pi f C} = \frac{1}{2\pi \times 100 \times 0.1 \times 10^{-6}}\,\Omega \quad \therefore \quad I = \frac{V}{X_C} \text{ amp.}\right]$$

14. Draw the voltage waveform across the inductance for the following types of wave shapes of current applied through a pure inductance. (Fig. P2.6 and Fig. P2.7)

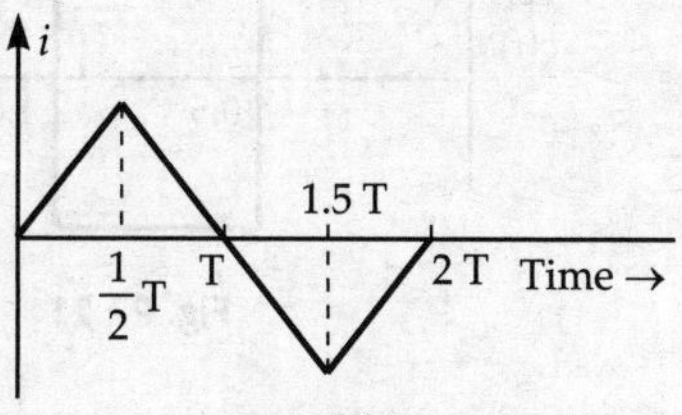

Fig. P2.6

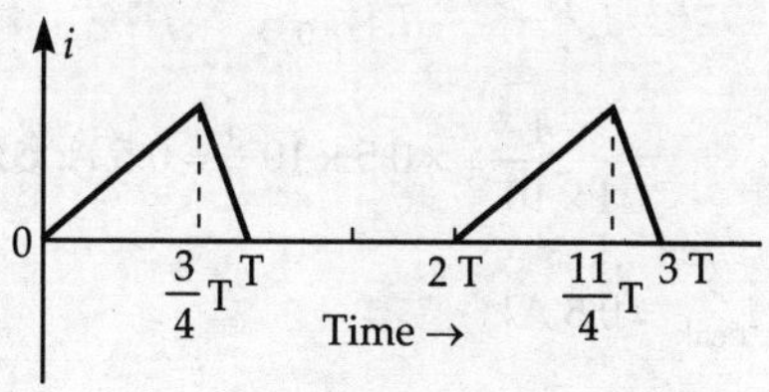

Fig. P2.7

[**Hint.** Following Fig. P2.6,

$L\dfrac{di}{dt}$ is constant upto $t = \dfrac{1}{2}T$ in +ve side and for $t = \dfrac{1}{2}T$ to $t = 1.5\,T$ it is again constant at –ve side of voltage axis.

Following Fig. P2.7,

$L\dfrac{di}{dt}$ is constant upto $t = \dfrac{3}{4}T$ and goes to –ve side. It remains constant at –ve side till $t = T$. Between T and $2T$, there will be no voltage induced and the waveshape of voltage similar to time between O and T will be repeated.]

15. The voltage across an inductor is given by : $v(t) = 0$ for $t \le 0$; $v(t) = 20\,te^{-2t}$ for $t \ge 0$.
Obtain the expression for current in the inductor.
[**Hint.** Solve this problem in the same way as shown in Example 2.72.]

16. A saw tooth voltage as shown in Fig. P2.8 is applied to a capacitor of $C = 30\,\mu F$. Find the capacitor current.

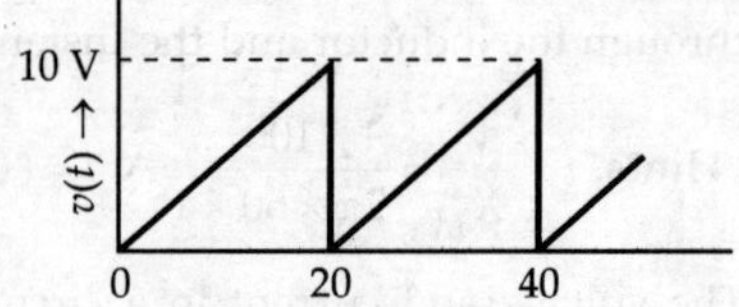

Fig. P2.8

[**Hint.** $i = c\dfrac{dv}{dt}$ while $\dfrac{dv}{dt}$

$$= \frac{10}{20 \times 10^{-3}} = 0.5 \times 10^3 \text{ V/sec}$$

$$\therefore \quad i = 30 \times 10^{-6} \times 0.5 \times 10^3 = 15 \text{ mA}]$$

17. A current *i*(*t*) is applied to an inductance (*L*) of 2 H (Fig. P2.9). Find $v_L(t)$.

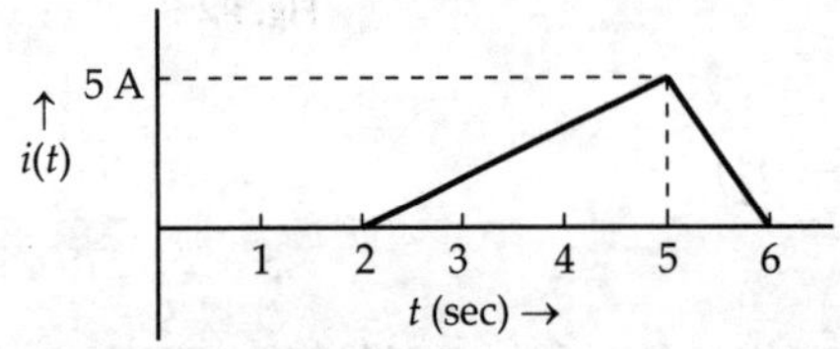

Fig. P2.9

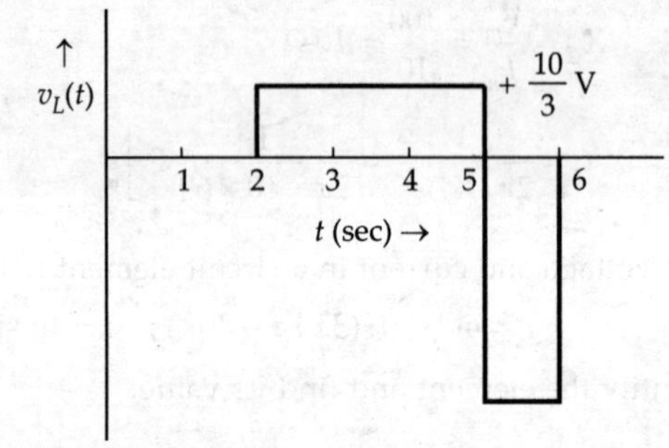

Fig. P2.10

[**Hint.** For $0 < t < 2\text{s}, \quad i = 0; \; v_L = 0$

$$2 < t < 5\text{s}, \quad \frac{di}{dt} = \frac{5}{3}; \; v_L = 2 \times \frac{5}{3} = \frac{10}{3}$$

$$5 < t < 6\text{s}, \quad \frac{di}{dt} = -\frac{5}{1} \text{ A/s}; \; v_L = 2 \times (-5) = -10 \text{ V}$$ Ref. Fig. P2.10.

18. A square voltage wave (Fig. P2.11) is applied across a 1 mH inductor. What is the type of current ? What is the peak current ?

[**Hint.** $i_L = \dfrac{1}{L}\displaystyle\int v\,dt = \dfrac{v}{L}.t\Big|_0^{0.5\times10^{-3}}$

$$= \frac{1}{1 \times 10^{-3}} \times 0.5 \times 10^{-3} = 0.5 \text{ A, constant current}$$

Also, $i_{peak} = 0.5$ A]

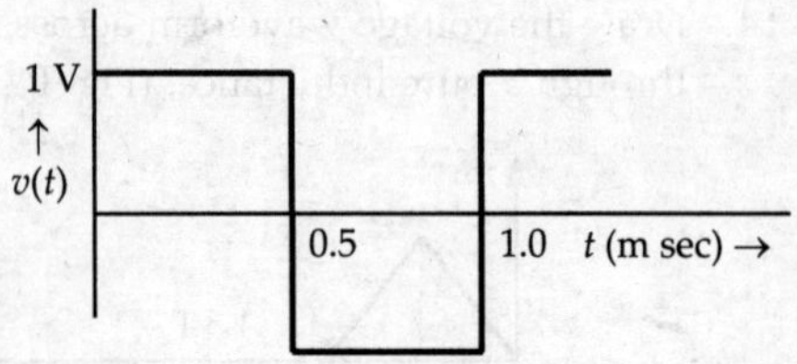

Fig. P2.11

19. A voltage of $v_c(t) = \sin 2\pi T$ is applied across a capacitor of 10^{-5} F. Find *i* at *T* = 0 and 0.25 s.

[**Hint.** $v_c(t) = \sin 2\pi T \quad \therefore \; i = C \,.\, 2\pi \cos 2\pi T$

at $T = 0$, $\quad i = 10^{-5} \times 2\pi \times 1 = 2\pi \times 10^{-5}$ A

at $T = 0.25$ s, $\quad i = 10^{-5} \times 2\pi \times \cos\dfrac{2\pi}{4} = 0$ A]

20. A 60 Hz sinusoidal voltage $v = 100 \sin \omega t$ is applied to a series *RL* circuit. Assuming $R = 10\,\Omega$, $L = 0.01$ H, find the steady state current and relative phase angle. Also compute the effective magnitude and phase of voltage drops appearing across each circuit element.

[**Hint.** Ref. Example 2.27]

21. A current of $i = \sin 500t$ flows through a series *RL* circuit having $R = 10\,\Omega$ and $L = 0.02$ H. Calculate the total applied voltage *v*.

[**Hint.** $v = \sqrt{R^2 + (\omega L)^2}\, I_{max} \sin(\omega t + \theta);\ \theta = \tan^{-1}\frac{\omega L}{R}$;

$$I_m = \frac{1}{\sqrt{2}} = 0.707 \text{ A. Hence } v \text{ can be calculated.]}$$

22. In a series *R-L* circuit, $R = 20\,\Omega$, $L = 60$ mH. If the current lags the voltage by 60°, obtain the value of ω in rad/sec.

[**Hint.** $\tan\theta = \frac{\omega L}{R}$; $\theta = 60°$,

$$L = 0.06\,H, R = 20\Omega. \text{ Now find out } \omega. \text{]}$$

23. In a series *RC* circuits, if $R = 20\,\Omega$, $C = 2.5$ pF, the applied voltage sinusoid be at 25 MHz, find the maximum voltage across the series combination if the maximum voltage drop across the capacitance be 2 V.

[**Hint.** See Example 2.30]

24. In a series RC circuit, the source current is given by $i = 2\cos 5000\,t$ A. Find the total applied voltage.

[**Hint.** Use the formula $v = \sqrt{R^2 + \left(\frac{1}{\omega C}\right)^2}\, I_m \cos\left(\omega t - \tan^{-1}\frac{1}{\omega C R}\right)$.]

25. A series circuit consists of *R*, *L* and *C* while the circuit current is $i = I_m \sin\omega t$. Obtain the voltage across each element and draw the current, voltage *vs* time wave forms.

[**Hint.** $v_R = iR = R\,I_m \sin\omega t$; $v_L = L\frac{d}{dt}(I_m \sin\omega t) = \omega L\, I_m \cos\omega t$

$$v_C = \frac{1}{C}\int I_m \sin\omega t\, dt = \frac{I_m}{\omega C}(-\cos\omega t). \text{]}$$

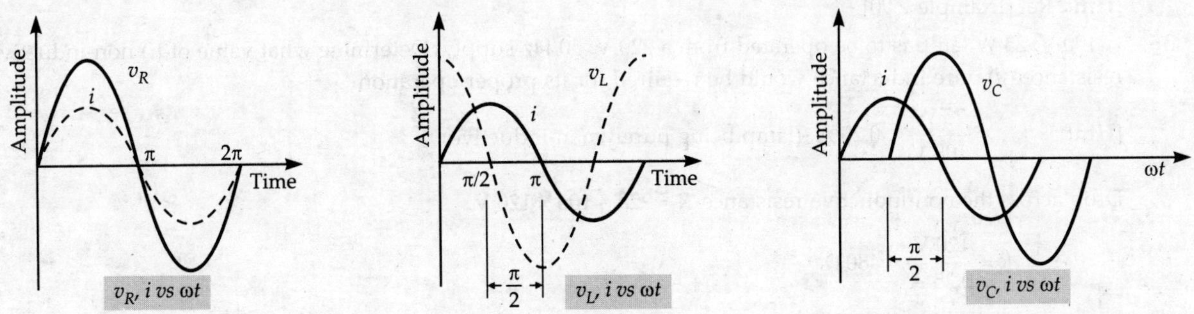

Fig. P2.12

26. In a series *RLC* circuit, $L = 10$ mH, *R* and *C* are unknown. The instantaneous total voltage and currents are given as $v = 100\cos(314\,t - 5°)$ V ; $i = 10\cos(314\,t - 50°)$ V. Find *R* and *C*.

[**Hint.** The current lags the voltage by 50° − 5° = 45°.

$$\therefore \quad \omega L > \frac{1}{\omega C};\ \tan 45° = 1 = \left[\left(\omega L - \frac{1}{\omega C}\right)\Big/ R\right]$$

$$\text{and} \quad \frac{V_m}{I_m} = \sqrt{R^2 + \left(\omega L - \frac{1}{\omega C}\right)^2} = \sqrt{2R^2}$$

$$\text{or,} \quad \frac{100}{10} = \sqrt{2}\,R \quad \therefore\ R = \frac{10}{\sqrt{2}} = 7.07\,\Omega.$$

Then, from the formula $\left(\omega L - \frac{1}{\omega C}\right) = R$, find *C* for $\omega = 314$ rad / sec.]

27. The current in the resistive branch of a parallel *RC* circuit is given by $i_R = 1.0\cos(1000\,t - 30°)$ A. What is the current in the capacitive branch if $R = 5\,\Omega$, $C = 10\,\mu$F ?

[**Hint.** Refer Example 2.32]

28. In a parallel *R-L* circuit, $R = 5\,\Omega$, $L = 0.02$ H. The circuit is connected across a sinusoidal *a.c.* voltage of peak value 100 V, frequency 1000 rad/sec. If the voltage is delayed by an angle of 50° from an arbitrary reference, find the source current r.m.s. value.

[**Hint.** Refer Example 2.33]

29. A coil has a resistance of 25 ohm and an inductance of 1 Henry. Determine the inductance of the coil. If an A.C. voltage of 200 V (rms), 50 Hz is applied across the coil, find the input current, power factor, real power and reactive power flow in the coil.

[**Hint.** Ref. Example 2.35]

30. In a coil, the inductance being 50 mH, the impedance is $20\,\Omega$. If the power factor of the circuit be 0.5 lag, find the values of angular frequency and resistance of the coil.

[**Hint.** Ref. Example 2.37]

31. A *R-L* series circuit draws a circuit current of 5 A when connected across a 50 V, 50 Hz *a.c.* supply. Assuming the resistance to be 7.5 ohm, find the inductive reactance of the circuit. What is its power factor ?

[**Hint.** Ref. Example 2.38]

32. A series *RLC* circuit has $R = 5\,\Omega$, $L = 0.5$ H, $C = 10\,\mu$F. A 200 V, 50 Hz supply is applied across the circuit. Find the input current and voltage across each element.

[**Hint.** Ref. Example 2.41]

33. In the above problem, if the series current is $1\text{ A}\ \angle 0°$, what would be the supply voltage at $f = 50$ Hz ?

[**Hint.** Ref. Example 2.43]

34. An unknown impedance of $Z_x\ \Omega$ is connected to an *a.c.* supply of $100\ \angle 30°$ in series with a $(2 + j\,4)\,\Omega$ choke. Assuming the through current to be $I = 4\ \angle -10°$, find the value of Z_x.

[**Hint.** Ref. Example 2.90]

35. A 100 V, 25 W lamp is to be operated from a 220 V, 50 Hz supply. Determine what value of (*i*) non-inductive resistance (*ii*) pure inductance would be required for its proper operation.

[**Hint.** $I_{1\text{ A}} = \dfrac{25\text{ W}}{100\text{ V}} = 0.25\text{ A}$ (lamp being purely non-inductive)

Drop across the non-inductive resistance $R = 220 - 100 = 120$ V.

$$\therefore \quad R = \frac{120\text{ V}}{0.25\text{ A}} = 480\,\Omega.$$

If instead of *R*, X_L is to be connected in series with lamp,

$$V^2 = V_R^2 + V_L^2\,; \quad \text{or} \quad V_L^2 = (220)^2 - (100)^2 \quad \therefore\ V_L = 196\text{ V}.$$

$$\therefore \quad X_L = (196/I)\,\Omega \quad \text{and} \quad L = \frac{X_L}{2\pi f},$$

f being the frequency ; *L* is expressed in Henry].

36. Two coils Ch_1 and Ch_2 are connected in series and a current of 1 A is passing through them. Drop across Ch_1 being 15 V and that across Ch_2 being 10 V in d.c. and 18 V across Ch_1 and 15 V across Ch_2 in a.c., calculate for each coil, (*i*) resistance and inductances at 50 Hz and (*ii*) power factor. Also find the p.f. of the whole circuit.

[**Hint.** for Ch_1: $r_{ch_1} = \dfrac{15}{1} = 15\,\Omega$ (since in d.c., inductance is inactive hence, the ratio of *d.c.* drop to the through current gives the resistance of the choke.) But when *a.c.* is applied, $Z_{Ch_1} = \dfrac{18}{1} = 18\,\Omega$

$$\therefore \quad X_{Ch_1} = \sqrt{(Z_{Ch_1})^2 - (r_{Ch_1})^2} = 9.95\,\Omega$$

Then, $r_{Ch_1} = 15\,\Omega$, $X_{Ch_1} = 9.95\,\Omega$, $Z_{Ch_1} = 18\,\Omega$; $\quad \text{PF}_{Ch_1} = \dfrac{r_{Ch_1}}{Z_{Ch_1}} = \dfrac{15}{18} = 0.833.$

Similarly for Ch_2, $r_{Ch_2} = \frac{10}{1} = 10\,\Omega$, $Z_{Ch_2} = \frac{15}{1} = 15\,\Omega$

$$X_{Ch_2} = \sqrt{15^2 - 10^2} = 11.18\,\Omega\,; \qquad \text{PF} = \frac{r_{Ch_2}}{Z_{Ch_2}} = \frac{10}{15} = 0.67.$$

Then, $r_{Ch_2} = 10\,\Omega\,;\ X_{Ch_2} = 11.18\,\Omega.$

37. In the circuit of Fig. P2.13, $I_1 = (10 + j\,5)$ A while $Z = (500 + 100)\,\Omega$. What is the value of supply voltage, power factor and real power ?
[**Hint.** Ref. Ex. 2.48]

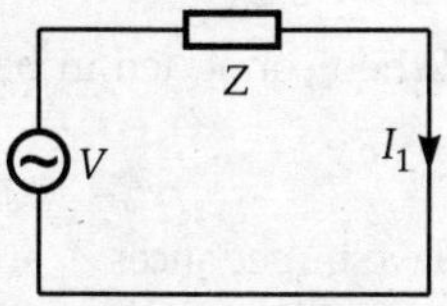

Fig. P2.13

38. A supply of 400 V, 50 Hz is applied to a series *RC* circuit. Find the value of *C* if the power absorbed by the resistor be 500 W at 150 V. What is the energy stored in capacitor ?

[**Hint.** Ref. Ex. 2.56]

39. In Ex. 2.57 in the text, find *I* provided, $Z_1 = 6\angle -20°$ and $Z_2 = 10\angle 45°$. Assume input voltage to be $100\angle 0°$.
[**Hint.** Ref. Ex. 2.57]

40. An impedance of $(6 - j\,6)$ is connected in parallel with another impedance $(4 + j\,4)$ ohm. If the applied voltage be $20\angle 10°$ V, find the branch currents and the total current.

[**Hint.** Ref. Ex. 2.58]

41. A series *RC* circuit has $R = 15\,\Omega$ and $C = 100\,\mu$F. It is connected in parallel to an inductor of 500 mH and the combination is connected across a 100 V, 50 Hz source. Find the current in each branch. Draw the vector diagram showing the total current.
[**Hint.** Ref. Ex. 2.60]

42. A 100 Ω resistor, an 200 mH inductor and a 500 μF capacitor are connected in parallel across a 100 V, 50 Hz source. Find the branch currents and total current and draw the phasor diagram.

[**Hint.** Ref. Ex. 2.62]

43. Ref. Fig. P2.14. What is current through Z ?
[**Hint.** Ref. Example 2.87]

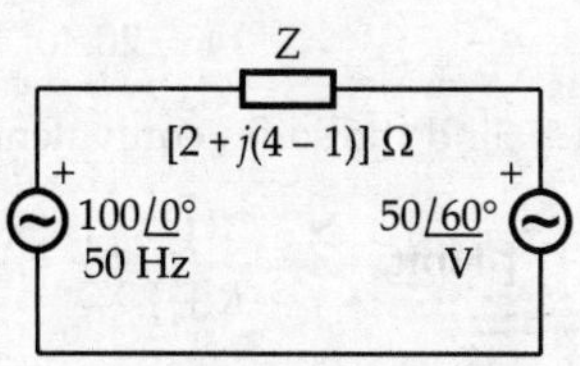

Fig. P2.14

44. A 10 Ω resistor is in series with a 80 mH inductor and the combination is connected across a 110 V, 50 Hz source. Obtain the values of (*i*) total impedance of the circuit, (*b*) input current (*c*) the voltage across the resistor and the inductor.
[**Hint.** Find X_L (= ω*L*) and obtain $Z (= R + j\,X_L)$ in polar form.

$$I = \frac{V}{Z} \text{ (vectorial); } V_R = IR \text{ (vectorial) and } V_L = j\,I\,X_L\,.\ ]$$

45. An inductive coil consumes 5×10^2 W of power across a 110 V, 50 Hz *a.c.* source while the current through it is 25 A. Determine the resistance and inductance of the coil.
[**Hint.** $I^2R = 500$ while $I = 25$ A. Find *R*.

$$Z = V / I = 110/25)\,\Omega = \sqrt{R^2 + X_L^2}\,.\ \text{Then obtain } X_L \text{ from where } L = \frac{X_L}{2\pi f} \text{ H]}$$

46. In the circuit of Fig. P2.15, $X_L = 12\,\Omega$, $X_C = 18\,\Omega$, $R = 10\,\Omega$. Find the drop across each element if the current *I* flowing through the series circuit is $10\angle 0°$ A.

[**Hint.** $V_R = IR = (10\angle 0° \times 10)$ V ;

$V_L = I\,(jX_L) = 10\angle 0° \times 12\angle 90°$ V

$V_C = I\,(-jX_C) = 10\angle 0° \times (18)\angle -90°$ V

Obviously $V = V_R + V_L + V_C$ (Vectorial).]

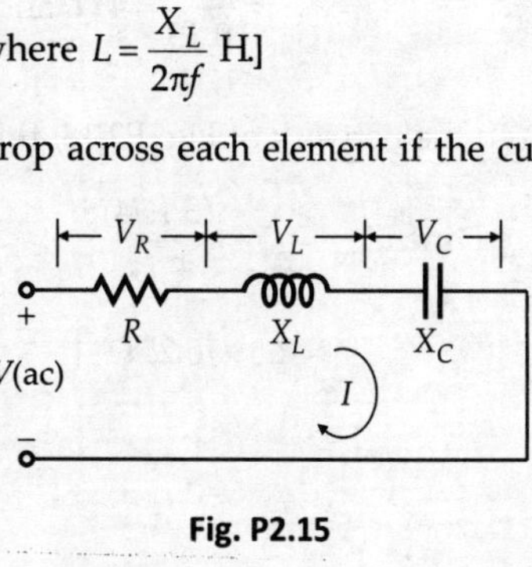

Fig. P2.15

47. Two impedances Z_A and Z_B are connected in series once and then in parallel. Assuming $Z_A = 4 + j\,2$ and $Z_B = 2 - j\,3$ ohms, find the equivalent impedance in each case.

[**Hint.** When connected in series, $Z_{eq} = Z_A + Z_B$

When connected in parallel, $Z_{eq} = \dfrac{1}{Y_{eq}} = \dfrac{1}{Y_{eq}} = \dfrac{1}{Y_A + Y_B} = \dfrac{1}{\dfrac{1}{Z_A} + \dfrac{1}{Z_B}}$.]

48. Two impedances Z_1 and Z_2 are connected in parallel across 10 V, 50 Hz source and taking currents of $2\angle 30°$ and $4\angle -10°$ A respectively. Find the input admittance of the circuit and total current from the source.

[**Hint.** $I_1 = 2\angle 30°$; $I_2 = 4\angle -10°$ I (total) $= I_1 + I_2$ (vectorial) ;

$Y_1 = \dfrac{I_1}{V}$; $Y_2 = \dfrac{I_2}{V}$ $\quad \therefore \; Y = Y_1 + Y_2$.]

49. A *RLC* circuit is shown in Fig. P2.16. Calculate C such that the input current is 45° out of phase with the input voltage at a frequency of 2000 rad/sec.

[**Hint.** For the input current to be 45° out of phase, with the input voltage, the net reactance of the parallel branches of the circuit must be ± 20 Ω.

$\therefore \; \pm \dfrac{j}{20} = -\dfrac{j}{\omega L} + j\,\omega C$. From here, C can be found out.]

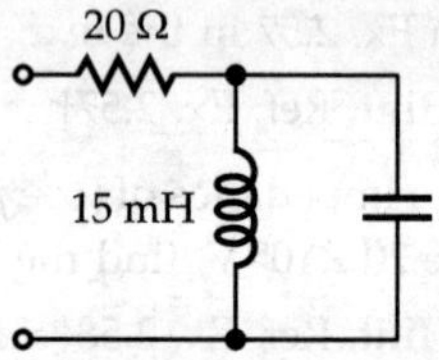

Fig. P2.16

50. Z_1 and Z_2 are in parallel while $Z_1 = 10\angle -53°\,\Omega$ and $Z_2 = 20\angle 37°\,\Omega$. The combination draws a current of $(2 + j)$A from an *a.c.* voltage sources. Obtain I_1 and I_2.

[**Hint.** $Y = Y_1 + Y_2 = \dfrac{1}{10}\angle 53° + \dfrac{1}{20}\angle -37° = 0.1118\angle 26.5°$ mho

$I = 2 + j\,1 = 2.236\angle 26.5°$ mho

$V = I/Y = 20\angle 0°\ V;\ I_1 = VY_1 = 2\angle 53°$ A; $I_2 = VY_2 = 1\angle -37°$ A.]

51. Find the series equivalent of the parallel circuit shown in Fig. P2.17.

[**Hint.** $Z = \dfrac{R\,(jX_L)}{R + j\,X_L} = \dfrac{(4\angle 0°)(3\angle 90°)}{4 + j\,3} = 2.4\angle 53°$

$= 1.44 + j\,1.92\,\Omega$

$\therefore \quad Z_S = 1.44 + j\,1.92$ ohm.]

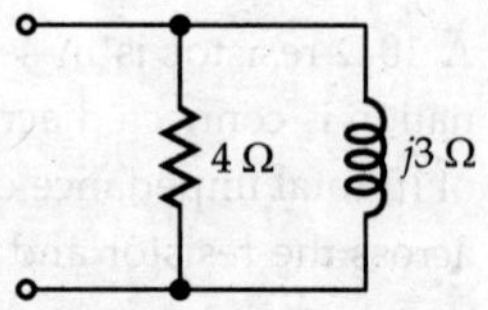

Fig. P2.17

52. Assume, for a series circuit, $R_S = 1.44\,\Omega$ while $X_S = j\,1.92\,\Omega$. Find its parallel equivalent.

[**Hint.** $Y_S = \dfrac{1}{Z_S} = G_p - jB_p = \dfrac{1}{1.44 + j\,1.92} = 0.25 - j\,0.333 = 3\,\Omega$

$\therefore \quad R_p = \dfrac{1}{G_p} = \dfrac{1}{0.25} = 4\,\Omega$ and $X_p = \dfrac{1}{B_p} = \dfrac{1}{0.333} = 3\,\Omega$

53. In the network of Fig. P2.18, find Z_{int}.

[**Hint.** $Z_{int} = j5 + \dfrac{(3 + j4)5}{3 + j4 + 5}$

$= 2.5 + j6.25\,\Omega$]

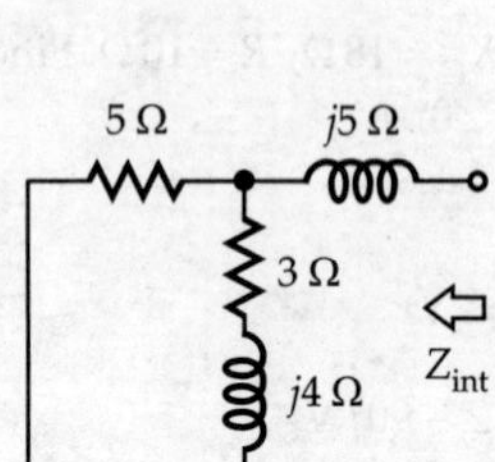

Fig. P2.18

54. Find Z in the circuit given in Fig. P2.19.

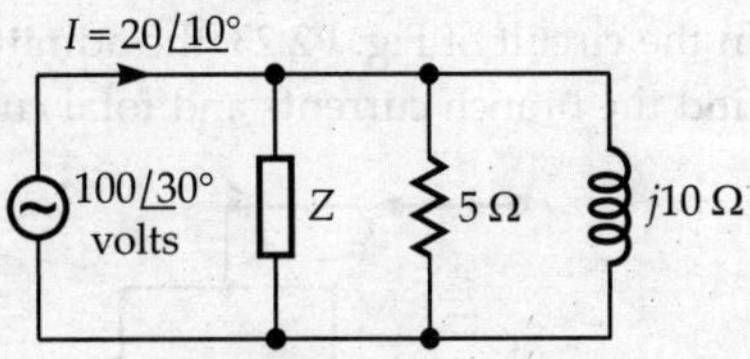

Fig. P2.19

[**Hint.** $Y = \dfrac{I}{V} = \dfrac{20\ \angle 10°}{100\ \angle 30°}$

However, $Y = Y_1 + Y_2 + Y_3$ ...(1)

where, $Y_1 = \dfrac{1}{Z},\ Y_2 = \dfrac{1}{5}$ and $Y_3 = \dfrac{1}{j\ 10}$

Thus Y_1 is obtained from (1) giving Z.]

55. In the network of Fig. P2.20, find the drop in *AD* branch.

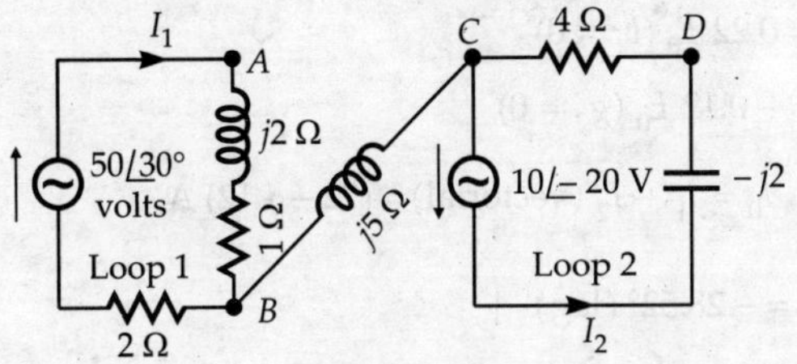

Fig. P2.20

[**Hint.** Since loops 1 and 2 are independent, no current will flow through $j\ 5\,\Omega$ *i.e.*, *BC* branch giving $V_{BC} = 0$.

Here, $I_1 = \dfrac{50\ \angle 30°}{[(1 + j\ 2) + 2]}$ A and $V_{AB} = I_1 \times (1 + j\ 2)$ V

Similarly, $I_2 = \dfrac{10\ \angle -20°}{(4 - j\ 2)}$ A and $V_{CD} = (I_2 \times 4)$ V

$\therefore \quad V_{AD} = V_{AB} + V_{BC} + (-\ V_{CD})$

[$\because$ I_2 is anticlockwise, for V_{CD} drop, *D* is at higher potential (+ ve)] .]

56. In Fig. P2.21, Z_X is unknown, $Z_2 = 10\,\Omega$, $Z_3 = (5 - j\ 4)\,\Omega$. Find Z_X.

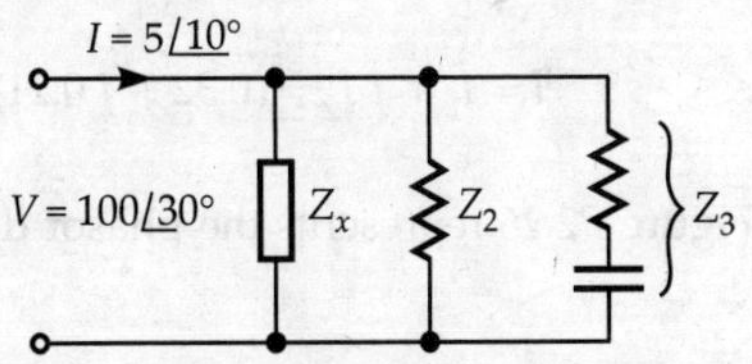

Fig. P2.21

[**Hint.** $Y_{eq.} = \dfrac{I}{V}$; $Y_{eq} = Y_X + Y_2 + Y_3$

when $Y_X = \dfrac{1}{Z_X}$; $Y_2 = \dfrac{1}{Z_2}$; $Y_3 = \dfrac{1}{Z_3}$; then find Y_X.

$\therefore \quad Z_X = \dfrac{1}{Y_X}$.]

57. In the circuit of Fig. P2.22, if $r = 6.3\,\Omega$, $C = 440\,\mu$F, $I = 10$ A, find the drops across *r* and C and find the input voltage and power factor provided the input voltage has a frequency of 50 Hz.

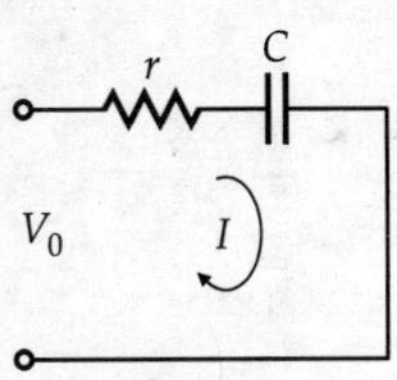

Fig. P2.22

[**Hint.** $V_r = r\ I = 63$ V ; $V_C = x_c\ I = 72.4$ V;

$V_0 = V_r - j\ V_C = 95.9\ \text{V}\ \angle -49°$,

current leading ;

PF = cos 49°.]

58. In the circuit of Fig. P2.23, the admittance of branch-1 is 0.22 mho, that of branch-2 is 0.12 mho. If $E_0 = 100$ V, find the branch currents and total currents.

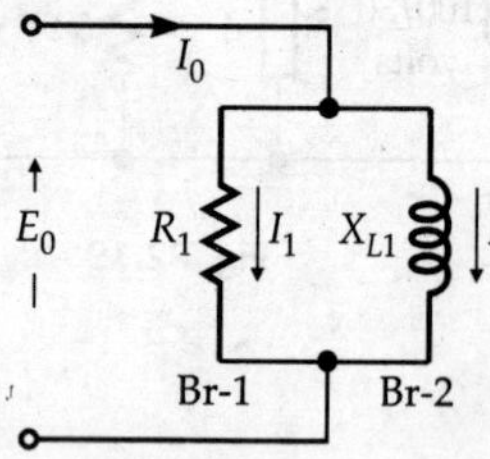

Fig. P2.23

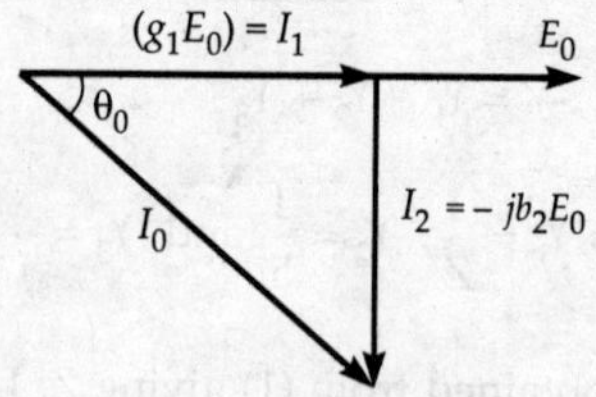

Fig. P2.24

[**Hint.** $I_1 = (g_1 - j\,b_1)\,E_0 = 0.22\,E_0\;(b_1 = 0)$

$I_2 = (g_2 - j\,b_2)\,E_0 = -\,0.12\,E_0\;(g_2 = 0)$

$|\,I_0\,| = \sqrt{I_1^2 + I_2^2}$ and $I_0 = I_1 + I_2$ (vectorial) $= (22 - j\,12)$ A.

$$\theta = \tan^{-1}\frac{b_1 + b_2}{g_1 + g_2} = -\,28.52°\text{ (lag).}$$]

59. In the circuit of Fig. P2.25, find I_1, I_2, I_0 and input p.f. provided $g_1 = 0.32$, $b_1 = 0$; $g_2 = 0$, $b_2 = 0.21$ mho. Assume $f = 50$ Hz, $E = 100$ V.

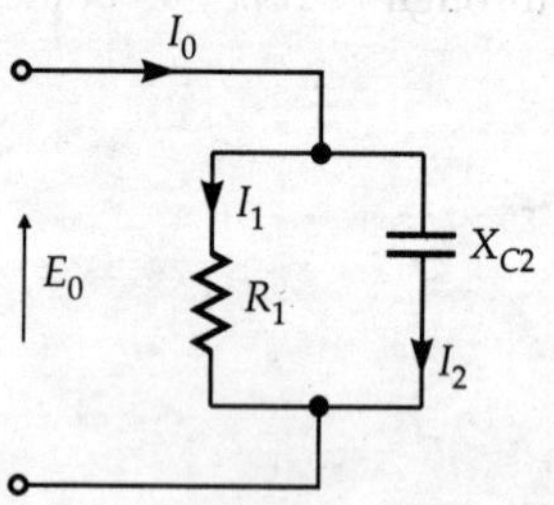

Fig. P2.25

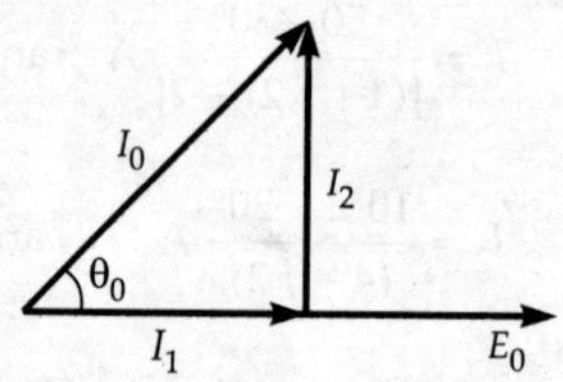

Fig. P2.26

[**Hint.** $I_1 = (g_1 + j\,b_1)\,E_0 = 0.32\,E_0$ A; $I_2 = (g_2 + j\,b_2)\,E_0 = j\,0.21\,E_0$ A

$$\therefore \quad I = I_1 + j\,I_2 = (0.32 + j\,0.21)\,E_0\text{ A};\ \theta_0 = \tan^{-1}\left(\frac{b_1 + b_2}{g_1 + g_2}\right) = 33.3°\text{ (lead)}$$

Figure P2.26 represents the phasor diagram.]

CHAPTER

3

Resonance, Selectivity and Power Relations in AC Circuits

3.1 RESONANCE

Resonance in electrical circuits consisting of passive and active elements represents a particular state of the circuit when the current or voltage in the circuit is *maximum* or *minimum* with respect to the magnitude of excitation at a particular frequency, the circuit impedance being either *minimum* or *maximum* at the power factor unity.

The phenomenon of resonance is observed in both series or parallel *a.c.* circuits comprising of *R*, *L* and *C* and excited by an a.c. source.

3.2 SERIES RESONANCE

In the series *RLC* circuit of Fig. 3.1, the circuit current *I* is given by

$$I = \frac{V}{Z}\ \text{A}$$

where *Z* represents the equivalent impedance of the circuit.

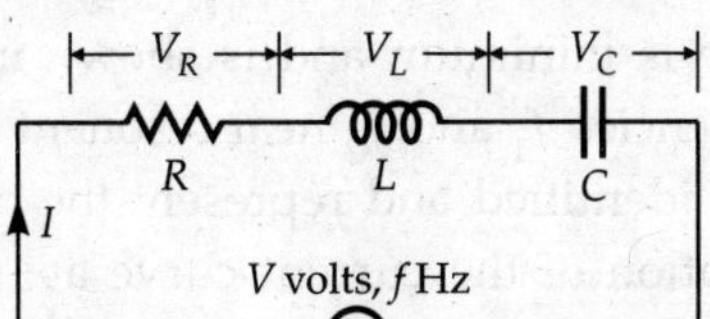

Fig. 3.1 Series Resonance Circuit.

$$Z = R + j\,\omega L + \frac{1}{j\,\omega C}$$

$$= R + j\,\omega L - \frac{j}{\omega C}$$

or,
$$Z = R + j\,(X_L - X_C) \qquad \text{...(3.1)}$$

where $X_L = \omega L$ and $X_C = \dfrac{1}{\omega C}$

$$= R + j\,X \qquad \text{...(3.1(a))}$$

where $(X_L - X_C)$ is X, the net reactance

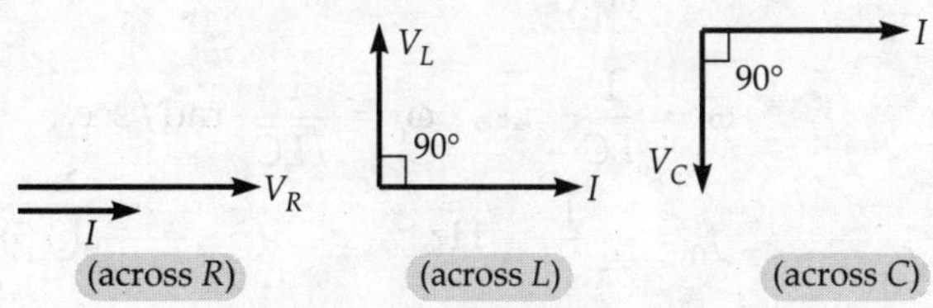

Fig. 3.2 Voltage and current phasor.

$$\text{Thus } I = \frac{V}{R + j\,(X_L - X_C)} = \frac{V}{R + j\,X}\ \text{A} \qquad \text{...(3.2)}$$

and voltage drop across resistance *R* is

$$V_R = IR \text{ (in phase with } I)$$

voltage drop across inductance *L* is

$$V_L = I\,X_L \text{ (leading } I \text{ by } 90^\circ)$$

voltage drop across capacitance *C* is

$$V_C = I\,X_C \text{ (lagging } I \text{ by } 90^\circ)$$

The phasor diagram of the variables of the entire circuit has been shown in Fig. 3.3.

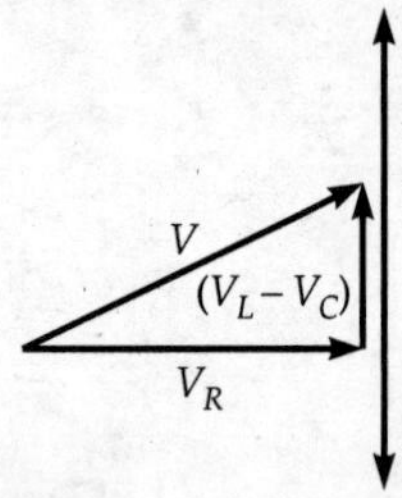

Fig. 3.3 Voltage vector diagram of RLC series circuit.

Resonance condition is obtained when $X_L = X_C$ *in the series circuit* [this is obtained by either decreasing the supply frequency when X_L would decrease and X_C would increase or by increasing the supply frequency making X_L to increase and X_C to decrease]

When $X_L = X_C$, $Z = R + j\,0 = R$

Also, $I_0 = \dfrac{V}{Z} = \dfrac{V}{R}$ A

[I_0 = current at resonance]

The p.f. (power factor) of the circuit becomes

$$\cos\phi = \frac{R}{Z} = \frac{R}{R} = 1.$$

The expression of frequency of resonance can be obtained as follows :

Let ω_0 or f_0 be the frequency at which

$$X_L = X_C$$

i.e., $\omega_0 L = \dfrac{1}{\omega_0 C}$

or, $\omega_0^2 = \dfrac{1}{LC}$ *i.e.,* $\omega_0 = \dfrac{1}{\sqrt{LC}}$ rad/sec.

i.e., $f_0 = \dfrac{1}{2\pi\sqrt{LC}}$ Hz. ...(3.3)

Voltage vector diagram at resonance is shown in Fig. 3.4.

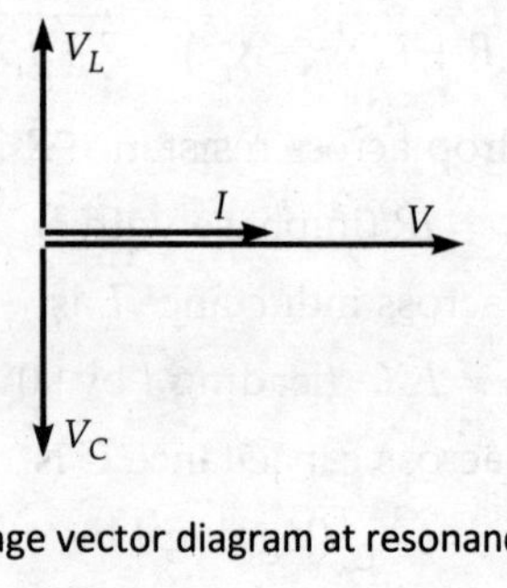

Fig. 3.4 Voltage vector diagram at resonance ($V_L = V_C$).

3.2.1 Properties of Resonance of *RLC* Series Circuit

1. The applied voltage and the resulting current are in phase which also mean that the p.f. of the *RLC* series resonant circuit is unity.
2. The net reactance is zero at resonance and the impedance does have the resistive part only.
3. The current in the circuit is maximum and is (V/R) A. [Since at resonance, the line current in the series *LCR* circuit is maximum hence it is called *acceptor circuit*].
4. At resonance, the circuit has got minimum impedance and maximum admittance.
5. Frequency of resonance is given by

$$f_0 = \frac{1}{2\,\pi\sqrt{LC}}\ \text{Hz}$$

3.2.2 Variation of Resistance, Inductive and Capacitive Reactance with Frequency

Figure 3.5 represents the variation of circuit parameters with frequency. Also, the current is

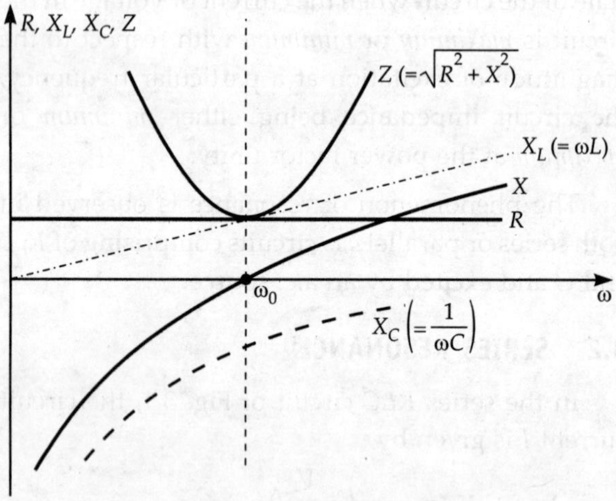

Fig. 3.5 Variation of circuit parameters with frequency.

maximum at resonance frequency while the impedance is minimum and is shown in Fig. 3.6. Two frequencies f_1 and f_2 near resonant frequency have been identified and represent the two points of interception of the current curve at $1/\sqrt{2}\, I_0$, I_0 being the current at resonance. As the product of $I_0/\sqrt{2}$ and $V/\sqrt{2}$ represent r.m.s. power which becomes $P_0/2$ hence the points f_1 and f_2 are also called *half power points; f_1 being the lower half power frequency* and f_2 being the *upper half power frequency*.

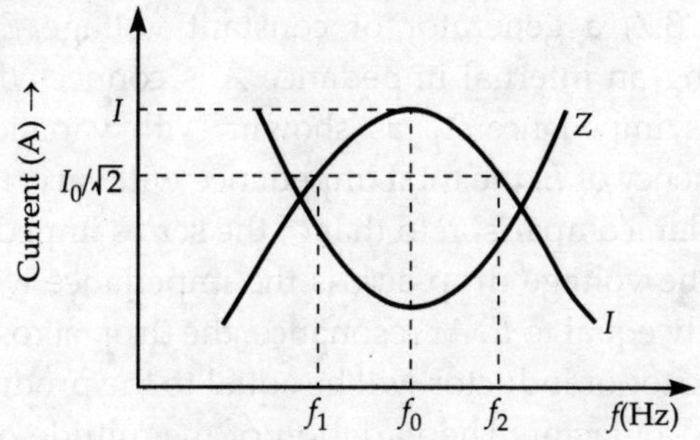

Fig. 3.6 Variation of current and impedance in a series resonating circuit.

3.2.3 *Q* Factor of Series Resonating Circuit

In a series resonating circuit, Q factor (*quality factor*) is defined as the ratio of the voltage across the inductor or capacitor to the applied voltage. It is also the voltage magnification in the circuit at resonance.

$$Q = \frac{V_L}{V} = \frac{V_C}{V}$$

where V_L is the voltage across the inductor, V_C the voltage across the capacitor at resonance and V the applied voltage.

$$\therefore\ Q = \frac{V_L}{V} = \frac{I_0 X_L}{I_0 R} = \frac{X_L}{R} = \frac{\omega_0 L}{R} \quad \text{[for the coil]} \qquad ...(3.4)$$

$$\text{also}\quad Q = \frac{V_C}{V} = \frac{I X_C}{I_0 R} = \frac{X_C}{R} = \frac{1}{\omega_0 CR} \quad \text{[for the capacitor]} \qquad ...(3.5)$$

Again

$$V_L = I_0 X_L = \frac{V}{R} X_L = \frac{V}{R}.\omega_0 L = \frac{\omega_0 L}{R} V$$

$$= Q \text{ factor} \times V \text{ volts} \qquad ...(3.5(a))$$

$$\text{and}\quad V_C = I_0 X_C = \frac{V}{R}.\frac{1}{\omega_0 C} = \frac{1}{\omega_0 RC}.V$$

$$= Q \text{ factor} \times V \text{ volts} \qquad ...(3.6)$$

Also,

$$Q = \frac{\omega_0 L}{R} = \frac{1}{\sqrt{LC}}.\frac{L}{R} = \frac{1}{R}\sqrt{\frac{L}{C}}, \quad \left[\because \omega_0 = \frac{1}{\sqrt{LC}}\right] \qquad ...(3.6(a))$$

$$\text{and also}\quad Q = \frac{1}{\omega_0 RC} = \frac{1}{\frac{1}{\sqrt{LC}} RC} = \frac{1}{R}\sqrt{\frac{L}{C}}$$

3.2.4 Bandwidth of Series Resonating Circuit and its Relation with *Q* Factor

The frequency band within the limits of lower and upper half power frequency is called the *bandwidth* of the resonant circuit. The response of the resonating circuit within the bandwidth is assumed to be flat.

At half power frequencies, the net reactance of the series resonant circuit is R and given by

$$X = \pm(X_L - X_C) = R$$

[± sign indicates the predominance of either X_L or X_C depending on the lower or upper frequency range]

$$\text{i.e.,}\quad R = \pm\left(\omega L - \frac{1}{\omega C}\right) = \pm X$$

Let f_1 be the frequency when the net circuit reactance be – ve and f_2 be frequency when the net circuit reactance is + ve.

$$\text{Thus,}\quad \left(\omega_2 L - \frac{1}{\omega_2 C}\right) = R \qquad ...(3.7)$$

$$\text{and}\quad \left(\omega_1 L - \frac{1}{\omega_1 C}\right) = -R \qquad ...(3.8)$$

Adding equations (3.7) and (3.8)

$$(\omega_2 + \omega_1) L - \frac{1}{C}\left(\frac{1}{\omega_2} + \frac{1}{\omega_1}\right) = 0$$

$$\text{or,}\quad (\omega_2 + \omega_1) L - \frac{1}{C}\left(\frac{\omega_1 + \omega_2}{\omega_2 \omega_1}\right) = 0$$

Thus either

$$L = \frac{1}{C}.\frac{1}{\omega_2 \omega_1} \quad \text{or} \quad \omega_2 \omega_1 = \frac{1}{LC} \qquad ...(3.9)$$

Again subtracting equation (3.8) from equation (3.7),

$$(\omega_2 - \omega_1) L + \frac{1}{C}\left(\frac{1}{\omega_1} - \frac{1}{\omega_2}\right) = 2R$$

$$\text{or,}\quad (\omega_2 - \omega_1) L + \frac{1}{C}\left(\frac{\omega_2 - \omega_1}{\omega_2 \omega_1}\right) = 2R \qquad ...(3.10)$$

Dividing equation (3.10) by L,

$$(\omega_2 - \omega_1) + \frac{1}{LC}\left(\frac{\omega_2 - \omega_1}{\omega_2 \omega_1}\right) = \frac{2R}{L}$$

$$\text{or,}\quad (\omega_2 - \omega_1) + \frac{1}{LC}\frac{(\omega_2 - \omega_1)}{\frac{1}{LC}} = \frac{2R}{L}\left[\because \omega_2\,\omega_1 = \frac{1}{LC}\right]$$

$$\text{or,}\quad 2(\omega_2 - \omega_1) = \frac{2R}{L}$$

$$\text{or,}\quad (\omega_2 - \omega_1) = \frac{R}{L} \qquad ...(3.11)$$

However, from (3.4),

$$Q = \omega_0 \frac{L}{R} \quad i.e., \quad \frac{R}{L} = \frac{\omega_0}{Q}$$

∴ Thus comparing with (3.11),

$$\frac{\omega_0}{Q} = (\omega_2 - \omega_1)$$

$$\therefore \quad Q = \frac{\omega_0}{\omega_2 - \omega_1} = \frac{f_0}{f_2 - f_1} \qquad ...(3.12)$$

$$i.e., \quad Q = \frac{f_0}{\text{Bandwidth}} = \frac{\text{Resonant frequency}}{\text{Bandwidth}^*} \qquad ...(3.12(a))$$

3.3 SELECTIVITY **

The *selectivity* of a resonating circuit is defined by the ratio of f_0 (the frequency of resonance) to the bandwidth of the circuit.

$$i.e., \quad \text{Selectivity} = \frac{f_0}{f_2 - f_1} \qquad ...(3.13)$$

note f_1 and f_2 are also called 3 dB points as the current ratio (I_1/I_0, where I_1 is the current at frequency f_1 and I_0 the current at frequency f_0) in dB can be expressed as

$$\text{dB (ratio)} = 20\log_{10}\frac{I_1}{I_0} = 20\log_{10}\left(\frac{1}{\sqrt{2}}\right), \qquad ...(3.13(a))$$

since I_1 is $\frac{1}{\sqrt{2}}$ times I_0, by definition.

$$i.e., \quad \text{dB} = -3$$

i.e., I_1 is lower than I_0 by 3 dB and similarly, f_1 is also lower than f_0 by 3 dB. The power dissipation at f_1 or f_2 would be half of that of power dissipation at f_0.

$$\left[P_{f_1} = I_1^2\,R = \left(\frac{I_0}{\sqrt{2}}\right)^2 R = \frac{I_0^2\,R}{2} = \frac{P_0}{2} = P_{f_2}\right].$$

3.3.1 Physical Interpretation of Selectivity in Resonance Circuits

Series and parallel *AC* circuits are used to pick up resonant frequency signals. In series circuit (Fig. 3.7) a generator of constant voltage E and having an internal impedance Z is connected to a series impedance Z_L as shown. With variation of frequency of E, the total impedance will vary. If Z is small in comparison to that of the series impedance Z_L, the voltage drop across the impedance will be mostly equal to E. At resonance, the drop across the capacitor or inductor will be equal to the product of E and Q factor. The variation of magnitude of the

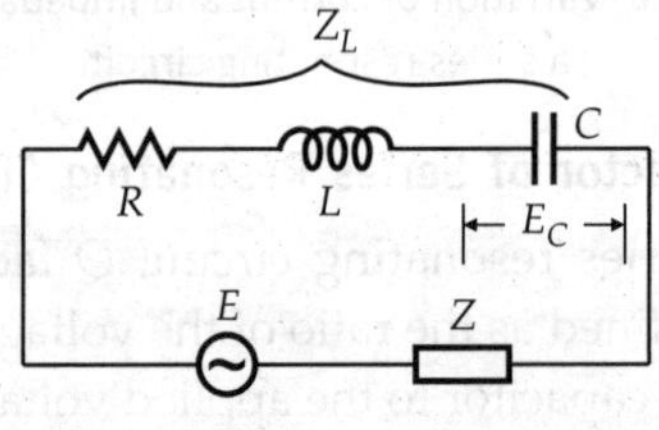

Fig. 3.7 Series resonating circuit

voltage across the capacitor (say E_C) with frequency indicates that the voltage (E_C) reaches a sharp peak just below the resonance frequency. This property of this circuit is called "selectivity."

On the other hand, if Z is large in the same circuit, the impedance Z_L will be small compared to Z and the current in this circuit is approximately E/Z at all frequencies. The circuit is not selective. Then a series circuit is only *selective* if supplied from a voltage source having a low internal impedance.

In a parallel resonating circuit let E_C be the voltage across the capacitor (*i.e.*, across the parallel combination). If Z is small at all frequencies in comparison to the impedance of the parallel circuit Z_L, E_C will be almost same to E and the circuit is not selective. If, however, Z is large compared to the impedance Z_L of the parallel circuit, the current flow will be equal to $\frac{E}{Z}$.

Here E_C is proportional to the impedance of the parallel circuit and hence the circuit becomes selective.

Thus a parallel circuit attains *selectivity* provided Z is large.

* The bandwidth of a series resonance circuit thus becomes $\frac{R}{L}$ from equation 3.11.

** Also, selectivity is inversely proportional to Bandwidth. Bandwidth being narrow, the element has greater selectivity.

3.4 RELATION BETWEEN FRACTIONAL DETUNING FACTOR (δ) AND Q_0 (Q FACTOR AT RESONANCE)

The circuit impedance of a resonating circuit is given by

$$Z = R + j\left(\omega L - \frac{1}{\omega C}\right)$$

$$= R\left[1 + j\left(\frac{\omega L}{R} - \frac{1}{\omega CR}\right)\right]$$

$$= R\left[1 + j\left(\frac{\omega_0 L}{R}\cdot\frac{\omega}{\omega_0} - \frac{1}{\omega_0 RC}\cdot\frac{\omega_0}{\omega}\right)\right]$$

$$= R\left[1 + j\left(Q_0\cdot\frac{\omega}{\omega_0} - Q_0\frac{\omega_0}{\omega}\right)\right]$$

$$\left[\because Q_0 = \frac{1}{\omega_0 RC} = \frac{\omega_0 L}{R}\right]$$

$$= R\left[1 + j\,Q_0\left(\frac{\omega}{\omega_0} - \frac{\omega_0}{\omega}\right)\right] \qquad ...(3.14)$$

The *fractional detuning factor* (δ) is defined as

$$\delta = \frac{f - f_0}{f_0} = \frac{\omega - \omega_0}{\omega_0}$$

or,
$$(1 + \delta) = \frac{\omega}{\omega_0} \qquad ...(3.15)$$

Thus, utilising (3.15) in (3.14),

$$Z = R\left[1 + j\,Q_0\left\{(1+\delta) - \frac{1}{1+\delta}\right\}\right]$$

$$= R\left[1 + j\,Q_0\,\delta\left(\frac{2+\delta}{1+\delta}\right)\right] \qquad ...(3.16)$$

$$\simeq R\,[1 + j\,Q_0\,\delta] \qquad ...(3.16(a))$$

Since δ is usually small.

At resonance, $\omega = \omega_0$ giving $\delta = 0$.

Thus at resonance $Z = R$.

3.5 EXPRESSION OF HALF POWER FREQUENCIES IN *RLC* SERIES RESONATING CIRCUIT AND RELATIONSHIP BETWEEN f_0, f_1 AND f_2

From equation (3.9),

$$\omega_2\,\omega_1 = \frac{1}{LC} \qquad ...(3.17)$$

Also, at resonance,

$$\omega_0 = \frac{1}{\sqrt{LC}} \qquad ...(3.18)$$

Thus, comparing (3.17) and (3.18),

$$\omega_0^2 = \omega_1\,\omega_2 \quad i.e.,\quad \omega_0 = \sqrt{\omega_1\,\omega_2}$$

Thus, the *resonant frequency is the geometric mean of the two half power frequencies.*

Again, from equation (3.9),

$$\omega_1\omega_2 = \frac{1}{LC}$$

and from equation (3.11),

$$(\omega_2 - \omega_1) = \frac{R}{L}$$

Substituting the value of ω_2 from (3.9) in (3.11),

$$\frac{1}{\omega_1\,LC} - \omega_1 = \frac{R}{L}$$

or,
$$\frac{1 - \omega_1^2 LC}{\omega_1\,LC} = \frac{R}{L}$$

or
$$1 - \omega_1^2\,LC = \omega_1\,RC$$

or,
$$\omega_1^2\,LC + \omega_1 RC - 1 = 0$$

or,
$$\omega_1 = \frac{-RC \pm \sqrt{R^2C^2 - 4LC}}{2LC}$$

$$= \frac{-R \pm \sqrt{R^2 - 4\dfrac{L}{C}}}{2L} \qquad ...(3.18(a))$$

Taking the +ve sign of the radical,

$$\omega_1 = \frac{-R + \sqrt{R^2 - 4\dfrac{L}{C}}}{2L}$$

$$= -\frac{R}{2L} + \sqrt{\left(\frac{R}{2L}\right)^2 - \frac{1}{LC}}$$

Similarly, substituting the value of ω_1 from (3.9) in (3.11), simplification yields

$$\omega_2 = \frac{R}{2L} + \sqrt{\left(\frac{R}{2L}\right)^2 - \frac{1}{LC}} \qquad ...(3.18(b))$$

3.6 FREQUENCIES AT WHICH V_C AND V_L ARE MAXIMUM

It may be noted that V_C and V_L are not maximum at resonant frequency in case of series resonance

CHAPTER 3

but at some other frequency value. This can be obtained as follows :

$$V_C = \frac{V}{\sqrt{R^2 + \left(\omega L - \frac{1}{\omega C}\right)^2}} \frac{1}{\omega C}$$

$$\left[\because V_C = IX_C \text{ and } I = \frac{V}{Z},\ X_C = \frac{1}{\omega C}, Z = \sqrt{R^2 + (X_L - X_C)^2}\ \right]$$

or, $$V_C^2 = \frac{V^2}{\omega^2 C^2 \left[R^2 + \left(\omega L - \frac{1}{\omega C}\right)^2\right]}$$

$$= \frac{V^2}{\omega^2 C^2 \left[R^2 + \frac{(\omega^2 LC - 1)^2}{\omega^2 C^2}\right]}$$

$$= \frac{V^2}{\omega^2 C^2 R^2 + (\omega^2 LC - 1)^2}$$

The frequency at which V_C is maximum can be obtained by differentiating V_C and equating the first derivative to zero. We would differentiate V_C^2 here and proceed as follows :

$$\frac{dV_C^2}{d\omega} = 0$$

$$= -\frac{V^2 [2\,\omega_0 C^2 R^2 + 2\,(\omega_0^2 LC - 1)\, 2\,\omega_0 LC]}{[\omega_0^2 C^2 R^2 + (\omega_0^2 LC - 1)^2]^2}$$

or, $$2\,\omega_0 C^2 R^2 + 2\,(\omega_0^2 LC - 1)\,2\,\omega_0 LC = 0 \qquad [\because V \neq 0]$$

or, $$2\,\omega_0^2 L^2 C + CR^2 - 2L = 0$$

or, $$\omega_0^2 = \frac{1}{LC} - \frac{R^2}{2L^2}$$

i.e., $$\omega_0 = \sqrt{\frac{1}{LC} - \frac{R^2}{2L^2}}$$

giving $$f_0 = \frac{1}{2\pi}\sqrt{\frac{1}{LC} - \frac{R^2}{2L^2}} \qquad \ldots(3.19)$$

Expression (3.19) gives the expression of the frequency at which the voltage across the capacitor is maximum.

To find the frequency at which V_L is maximum, we proceed in the same manner.

Here, $$V_L = IX_L = \frac{V\omega L}{\sqrt{R^2 + \left(\omega L - \frac{1}{\omega C}\right)^2}}$$

or, $$V_L^2 = \frac{V^2 \omega^2 L^2}{R^2 + \left(\omega L - \frac{1}{\omega C}\right)^2}$$

$$= \frac{V^2 \omega^4 L^2 C^2}{\omega^2 C^2 R^2 + (\omega^2 LC - 1)^2}$$

By differentiating V_L^2 with respect to ω and setting $\frac{dV_L^2}{d\omega} = 0$, we have

$$2\,\omega^2 LC - \omega^2 C^2 R^2 - 2 = 0$$

or, $$\omega^2 [2\,LC - C^2 R^2] = 2$$

i.e., $$\omega^2 = \frac{2}{2LC - C^2 R^2}$$

$$\therefore \quad \omega = \frac{1}{\sqrt{LC - \frac{C^2 R^2}{2}}}$$

or, $$f_0 = \frac{1}{2\pi\sqrt{LC - \frac{C^2 R^2}{2}}} \qquad \ldots(3.20)$$

Expression (3.20) gives the expression of the frequency at which the voltage across the inductor is maximum.

It can be seen from Eq. (3.19) that the maximum value of V_C occurs at f_C below $f_0 = 1/2\pi\sqrt{LC}$. This can be explained physically also. Current I increases from zero frequency upto resonant frequency f_0, while X_C $(= 1/2\,\pi f C)$ decreases continuously with an increase in frequency. At frequencies below f_C, the increase of I is greater than the decrease of $1/2\,\pi f C$, with the net result that V_C $(= IX_C)$ increases. Since I is maximum at resonance and decreases with frequencies above f_C it is obvious that the maximum value of V_C cannot be at a frequency above f_C because both I and $1/2\,\pi f C$ will be decreasing for any increase in frequency. In the frequency range between f_C and f_0, the decrease in $1/2\,\pi f C$ is greater than the increase in I with a net decrease in V_C.

Similarly, from Eq. (3.20) it can be seen that the maximum value of V_L occurs at f_L which is above

f_0. Both ωL and I are increasing as the frequency is varied from zero upto resonant frequency f_0. Consequently their product is increasing over this range of frequencies. At resonance the current reaches its maximum value but ωL is still increasing. Clearly f_L will be greater than f_0.

It is interesting to note that if R is vanishingly small; f_L, f_C and f_0 correspond to a single value equal to $1/2\pi\sqrt{LC}$.

3.7 EFFECT OF RESISTANCE ON THE FREQUENCY RESPONSE CURVE

Figure 3.8 shows the variation of current with frequency for two series *RLC* circuits having the same *L* and *C* but different values of *R*. These curves are referred to as *frequency response curves*.

As can be seen the curve with small resistance rises steeply and has a tall narrow peak while the curve with large resistance rises less steeply and has a low broad peak. Thus the effect of large resistance is to flatten the curve.

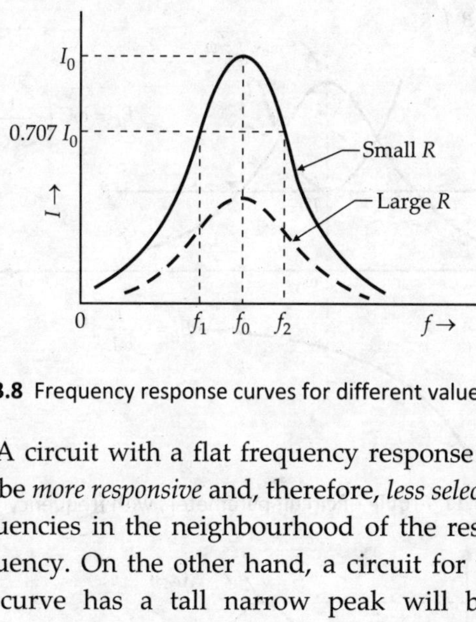

Fig. 3.8 Frequency response curves for different values of *R*.

A circuit with a flat frequency response curve will be *more responsive* and, therefore, *less selective* at frequencies in the neighbourhood of the resonant frequency. On the other hand, a circuit for which the curve has a tall narrow peak will be *less responsive* and, therefore, *more selective* at frequencies in the neighbourhood of resonant frequency.

3.8 PARALLEL RESONANCE

Figure 3.9 represents a parallel resonating circuit where a coil is connected in parallel with a capacitor *C* and the combination is connected across a *a.c.* voltage source of variable frequency. Fig. 3.10 represents the vector diagram of the given circuit.

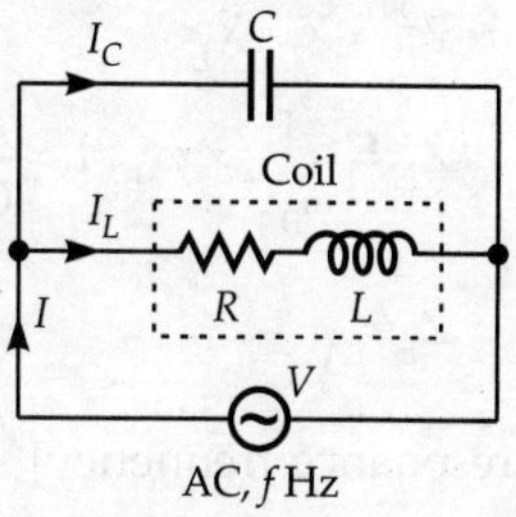

Fig. 3.9 A typical parallel resonating circuit.

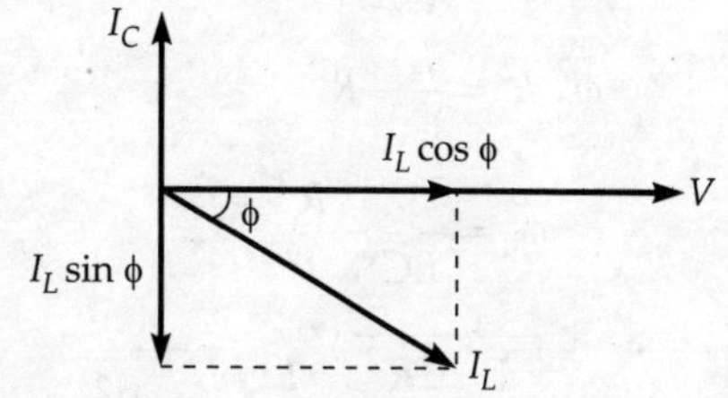

Fig. 3.10 Vector diagram of the parallel a.c. circuit.

Let I_C = the current through the capacitor,
I_L = the current through the coil,
I = vector sum of I_L and I_C *i.e.*, the source current,
V = supply voltage,
V_R = drop across R,
V_L = drop across L,
V_C = drop across C,
ϕ = p.f. angle of the coil (*i.e.*, the angle of lag of I_L then V),
Z_L = coil impedance,
X_C = capacitor impedance (or simple capacitor reactance).

Here $$I_C = \frac{V}{X_C}$$

and $$I_L = \frac{V}{Z_L} = \frac{V}{\sqrt{R^2 + X_L^2}} = \frac{V}{\sqrt{R^2 + (\omega L)^2}}$$

$$\cos\phi = \frac{R}{Z}.$$

At resonance, the capacitive current must be equal to the inductive part of the coil current *i.e.*, the imaginary components of I_L and I_C must cancel each other at resonance.

i.e., $$I_C = I_L \sin\phi$$

or, $$\frac{V}{X_C} = \frac{V}{Z_L} \times \frac{X_L}{Z_L}$$

where $$\sin\phi = \frac{X_L}{Z_L},$$

or, $$Z_L^2 = X_C\, X_L \qquad ...(3.21)$$

Also, $$Z_L^2 = \frac{1}{\omega_0 C} \times \omega_0 \, . \, L = \frac{L}{C}$$

i.e., $$Z_L = \sqrt{\frac{L}{C}} \qquad ...(3.21(a))$$

[ω_0 represents resonance frequency]

or, $$\sqrt{R^2 + \omega_0^2\, L^2} = \sqrt{\frac{L}{C}}$$

or, $$\omega_0^2\, L^2 = \frac{L}{C} - R^2$$

i.e., $$\omega_0^2 = \frac{1}{LC} - \frac{R^2}{L^2}$$

$\therefore$ $$\omega_0 = \sqrt{\frac{1}{LC} - \frac{R^2}{L^2}} = \frac{1}{L}\sqrt{\frac{L}{C} - R^2} \qquad ...(3.22)$$

i.e., $$f_0 = \frac{1}{2\,\pi L}\sqrt{\frac{L}{C} - R^2} \qquad ...(3.22(a))$$

If the resistance of the coil be neglected,

$$f_0 = \frac{1}{2\pi L}\sqrt{\frac{L}{C}} = \frac{1}{2\,\pi\sqrt{LC}}$$

[*i.e.*, the frequency of resonances of series circuit]

Again, at resonance, since the reactive components of I_L and I_C balances each other, the only remaining part of the current is $I_L\ \cos\phi (= I)$

$$I = I_L\ \cos\phi$$

or, $$\frac{V}{Z_\Omega} = \frac{V}{Z_L} \cdot \frac{R}{Z_L}$$

[Z_Ω = equivalent impedance of parallel circuit.]

or, $$Z_\Omega = \frac{Z_L^2}{R} = \frac{L/C}{R} = \frac{L}{CR} \qquad ...(3.23)$$

[$\because$ From eqn. (3.21(*a*)), $Z_L = \sqrt{L/C}$]

Then, the equivalent impedance of the parallel resonating circuit is L/CR at resonance. This impedance is called *dynamic resistance* of the parallel circuit. Normally R being less, this impedance is *very high* at resonance and then the current is *much lower* in the parallel circuit. Then, this circuit is also called *rejector circuit*.

The current at resonance is then $\frac{V}{Z_\Omega}$ *i.e.*, $\frac{V}{L/CR}$

and as $I_L\ \sin\phi$ and I_C cancels each other in Fig. 3.10, hence the power factor of this parallel resonance circuit at resonance is *unity*.

Properties of Resonance of Parallel LRC Circuit

1. Power factor is unity.
2. Current at resonance is $[V/(L/CR)]$ and is in phase with the applied voltage. The value of current at resonance is minimum.
3. Net impedance at resonance of the parallel circuit is maximum and equal to $(L/CR)\,\Omega$.
4. The admittance is minimum and the net susceptance is zero at resonance.
5. The resonance frequency of this circuit is given by

$$f_0 = \frac{1}{2\,\pi}\sqrt{\frac{1}{LC} - \frac{R^2}{L^2}}$$

3.8.1 Variation of Capacitive and Inductive Susceptance, Impedance and Current with Frequency

The profile of Z, I, R, B (susceptance) are drawn with respect to frequency in Fig. 3.11. Half power frequency points as shown on the impedance curve are shown in Fig. 3.12.

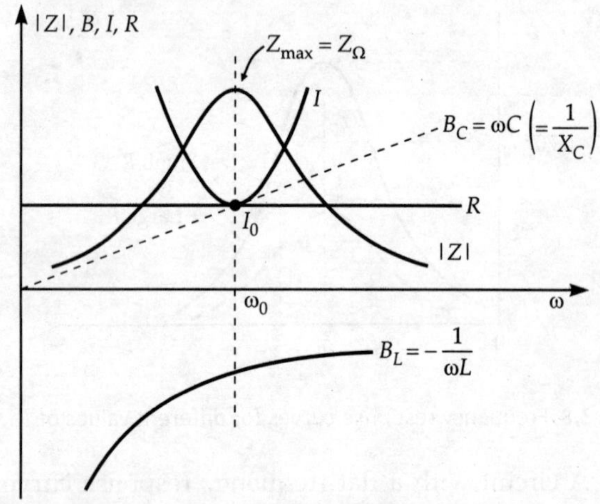

Fig. 3.11 Profile of circuit parameters with frequency.

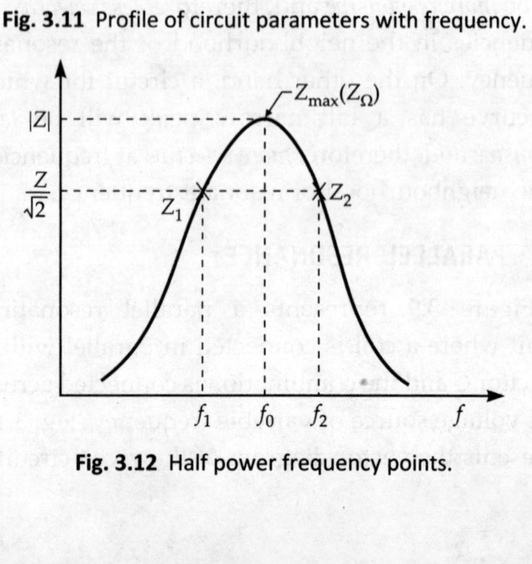

Fig. 3.12 Half power frequency points.

[In Fig. 3.12, Bandwidth = $f_1 \rightarrow f_2$ frequency of resonance $= f_0$ Z_{max} $(= Z_\Omega) \rightarrow$ impedance of resonating circuit at f_0; Z_1 and Z_2 are the impedances at half power frequencies]

3.8.2 *Q* Factor of Parallel Resonating Circuit

Q factor of a parallel circuit is the current magnification of the circuit at resonance. It represents the ratio of the current circulating between the two parallel branches.

i.e., $Q = \dfrac{I_C}{I} = \dfrac{V/X_C}{V/Z_\Omega} = \dfrac{Z_\Omega}{X_C} = \dfrac{L}{CR} \times \dfrac{1}{\dfrac{1}{\omega_0 C}}$

or $Q = \dfrac{L}{CR} \times \omega_0 C = \dfrac{\omega_0 L}{R} = Q$ factor of series circuit.

But $\omega_0 = \dfrac{1}{\sqrt{LC}}$

$$\therefore \quad Q = \frac{1}{R}\sqrt{\frac{L}{C}} \quad ...(3.24)$$

A parallel resonating circuit is also frequently called *rejector circuit* or *anti-resonant circuit.* Another common name of this circuit is *tuned circuit.*

3.8.3 Relationship between Bandwidth, Detuning Factor, Quality Factor, Impedance and Selectivity of a Parallel Resonant Circuit

The impedance of a parallel resonance circuit at any angular frequency ω is given by (Ref. Fig. 3.9)

$$Z = \frac{(R + j\,\omega L)\dfrac{1}{j\omega C}}{R + j\,\omega L + \dfrac{1}{j\,\omega C}}$$

$$= \frac{R\left(1 + j\dfrac{\omega L}{R}\right)\left(\dfrac{1}{j\,\omega C}\right)}{R\left[1 + j\dfrac{\omega L}{R}\left(1 - \dfrac{1}{\omega^2 LC}\right)\right]}$$

$$= \frac{\dfrac{1}{j\,\omega C} + \dfrac{L}{CR}}{1 + j\dfrac{\omega L}{R}\left(1 - \dfrac{1}{\omega^2 LC}\right)} \quad ...(3.25)$$

Next bringing in the concept of fractional detuning factor δ, it is given by

$$\delta = \frac{\omega - \omega_0}{\omega_0}$$

[ω_0 = frequency of resonance]

or, $$1 + \delta = \frac{\omega}{\omega_0} \quad ...(3.26)$$

Also, $\dfrac{\omega L}{R} = \dfrac{\omega_0 L}{R} \times \dfrac{\omega}{\omega_0} = Q_0(1 + \delta)$

$$\left[\because Q_0 = \frac{\omega_0 L}{R}\right] \quad ...(3.27)$$

Also,

$$\frac{1}{\omega^2 LC} = \frac{\omega_0^2}{\omega^2} \times \frac{1}{\omega_0^2 LC} = \frac{\omega_0^2}{\omega^2} \times \frac{1}{\dfrac{1}{LC} \times LC}$$

$$\left[\because \omega_0 = \frac{1}{\sqrt{LC}}\right]$$

or, $$\frac{1}{\omega^2 LC} = \frac{\omega_0^2}{\omega^2} \quad ...(3.28)$$

Using equations (3.28) and (3.27) in equation (3.25),

$$Z = \frac{\dfrac{L}{CR}\left[1 + \dfrac{R}{j\,\omega L}\right]}{1 + j\,Q_0(1+\delta)\left[1 - \dfrac{\omega_0^2}{\omega^2}\right]}$$

$$= \frac{\dfrac{L}{CR}\left[1 - j\dfrac{R}{\omega L}\right]}{1 + j\,Q_0(1+\delta)\left(1 - \dfrac{\omega_0^2}{\omega^2}\right)}$$

$$= \frac{\dfrac{L}{CR}\left[1 - j\dfrac{1}{\omega L/R}\right]}{1 + j\,Q_0(1+\delta)\left(1 - \dfrac{\omega_0^2}{\omega^2}\right)}$$

$$= \frac{\dfrac{L}{CR}\left[1 - j\dfrac{1}{Q_0(1+\delta)}\right]}{1 + j\,Q_0(1+\delta)\left[1 - \dfrac{1}{(1+\delta)^2}\right]}$$

CHAPTER 3

$$= \frac{\left\{\frac{L}{CR}\right\}\left\{1 - j\frac{1}{Q_0\,(1+\delta)}\right\}}{1 + j\,Q_0\left[(1+\delta) - \frac{1}{1+\delta}\right]}$$

$$= \frac{\frac{L}{CR}\left[1 - j\frac{1}{Q_0\,(1+\delta)}\right]}{1 + j\,Q_0\left[\frac{(1+\delta)^2 - 1}{1+\delta}\right]}$$

$$= \frac{\frac{L}{CR}\left[1 - j\frac{1}{Q_0\,(1+\delta)}\right]}{1 + j\,Q_0\left[\frac{1 + 2\delta + \delta^2 - 1}{1+\delta}\right]}$$

$$= \frac{\frac{L}{CR}\left[1 - j\frac{1}{Q_0\,(1+\delta)}\right]}{1 + j\,Q_0\,\delta\frac{(2+\delta)}{1+\delta}} \quad ...(3.29)$$

At resonance, $\omega = \omega_0$ and hence $\delta = 0$.

$$\therefore \quad Z_\Omega = \frac{L}{CR}\left[1 - j\frac{1}{Q_0}\right] \quad ...(3.30)$$

For higher Q_0, $\frac{1}{Q_0}$ is small and may be neglected.

$\therefore\ Z_\Omega \to \frac{L}{CR}$ [as derived earlier].

Again for $\delta < 1$, the equation (3.29) can be written as

$$Z = \frac{\frac{L}{CR}\left[1 - j\frac{1}{Q_0}\right]}{1 + j\,Q_0\,\delta \times (2)} \quad ...(3.31)$$

But Q_0 being high, $1/Q_0$ may be neglected.

Thus equation (3.31) becomes

$$Z = \frac{\frac{L}{CR}}{1 + j\,Q_0\,2\delta} = \frac{Z_\Omega}{1 + j\,2\delta\,Q_0}$$

$$\left[\because \frac{L}{CR} = Z_\Omega\right]$$

or, $$\frac{Z}{Z_\Omega} = \frac{1}{1 + j\,2\,\delta\,Q_0} \quad ...(3.32)$$

However, from the concept of half power frequency, following to the graph of Fig. 3.12, for the parallel resonating circuit,

$$\frac{Z}{Z_\Omega} = \frac{1}{\sqrt{2}} \quad ...(3.32(a))$$

[Z is either Z_1 or Z_2]

Comparing equations (3.32) and (3.32(*a*)),

$$\frac{1}{1 + j\,2\,\delta\,Q_0} = \frac{1}{\sqrt{2}}$$

or, $$1 + j\,2\,\delta\,Q_0 = \sqrt{2}$$

or, $$1^2 + (2\,\delta\,Q_0)^2 = (\sqrt{2})^2$$

or, $$(2\,\delta\,Q_0)^2 = 2 - 1 = 1$$

$$\therefore \quad 2\,\delta\,Q_0 = \sqrt{1} = \pm 1$$

This gives $$\delta = \pm\frac{1}{2\,Q_0} \quad ...(3.33)$$

However, $$\delta = \frac{f_2 - f_0}{f_0}, \quad ...(3.33(a))$$

$$\therefore \quad \frac{f_2 - f_0}{f_0} = \frac{1}{2\,Q_0} \quad ...(3.34)$$

[following equations 3.33 and 3.33(*a*)]

Similarly, for lower half power frequency,

$$\frac{f_1 - f_0}{f_0} = -\frac{1}{2Q_0} \quad ...(3.35)$$

Combining equations (3.34) and (3.35),

$$(f_2 - f_0) - (f_1 - f_0) = f_0\left[\frac{1}{2\,Q_0} + \frac{1}{2\,Q_0}\right]$$

or, $$f_2 - f_1 = \frac{f_0}{Q_0}$$

i.e., $$\text{Bandwidth} = \frac{f_0}{Q_0} \quad ...(3.36)$$

and $$\text{selectivity} = \frac{f_0}{f_2 - f_1} = Q_0 \quad ...(3.37)$$

The relationship between impedance, detuning factor and quality factor being represented by equation (3.29), equations (3.36) and (3.37) represent the relationship between bandwidth, selectivity and quality factor.

3.9 RESONANCE BETWEEN PARALLEL *RC* AND *RL* CIRCUIT

Figure 3.13 represents a parallel combination of *R-C* and *R-L* circuit.

Let Y_1 = admittance of R_1-C circuit

Y_2 = admittance of R_2-L circuit.

Y = net admittance $= Y_1 + Y_2$

$$= \frac{1}{R_1 - jX_C} + \frac{1}{R_2 + jX_L}$$

$$= \frac{R_1 + jX_C}{R_1^2 + X_C^2} + \frac{R_2 - jX_L}{R_2^2 + X_L^2}$$

$$= \left[\frac{R_1}{R_1^2 + X_C^2} + \frac{R_2}{R_2^2 + X_L^2}\right] + j\left[\frac{X_C}{R_1^2 + X_C^2} - \frac{X_L}{R_2^2 + X_L^2}\right]$$

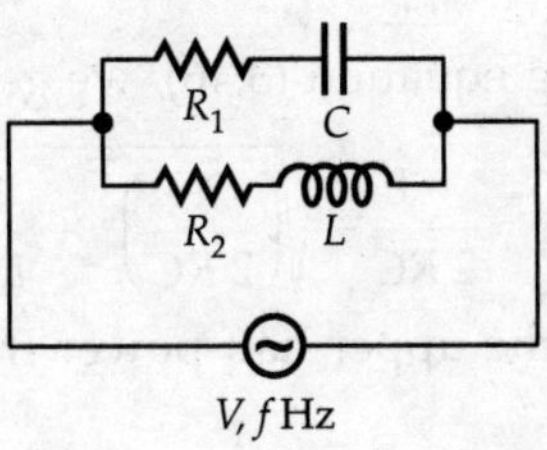

Fig. 3.13 Resonance between *R-C* and *R-L* circuit.

The circuit will be at resonance when the imaginary parts of capacitive and inductive admittances are cancelled.

i.e., $$\frac{X_C}{R_1^2 + X_C^2} = \frac{X_L}{R_2^2 + X_L^2}$$

or, $$X_C(R_2^2 + X_L^2) = X_L(R_1^2 + X_C^2)$$

or, $$\frac{1}{\omega_0 C}(R_2^2 + \omega_0^2 L^2) = \omega_0 L\left(R_1^2 + \frac{1}{\omega_0^2 C^2}\right)$$

if $R_2^2 = R_1^2 = \frac{L}{C}$, above equation becomes

$$\frac{1}{\omega_0 C}\left(\frac{L}{C} + \omega_0^2 L^2\right) = \omega_0 L\left(\frac{L}{C} + \frac{1}{\omega_0^2 C^2}\right)$$

i.e., $$\frac{L}{\omega_0 C^2} + \frac{\omega_0 L^2}{C} = \frac{\omega_0 L^2}{C} + \frac{L}{\omega_0 C^2}$$

i.e., RHS = LHS provided

$$R_2 = R_1 = \sqrt{L/C} \qquad ...(3.38)$$

This indicates that the circuit will be at resonance for any frequency provided

$$R_1 = R_2 = \sqrt{L/C}.$$

Again, in this circuit,

$$I_C \sin\phi_1 = I_L \sin\phi_2$$

[assuming I_C = current in R_1 C circuit while I_L = current in R_2 L circuit and ϕ_1 and ϕ_2 are the respective p.f.]

$$\therefore \quad \frac{V}{\sqrt{R_1^2 + \frac{1}{\omega_0^2 C^2}}} \cdot \frac{(1/\omega_0 C)}{\sqrt{R_1^2 + \frac{1}{\omega_0^2 C^2}}} = \frac{V}{\sqrt{R_2^2 + \omega_0^2 L^2}} \times \frac{\omega_0 L}{\sqrt{R_2^2 + \omega_0^2 L^2}}$$

$$\left[\because I_C = \frac{V}{Z_{(RC\ \text{circuit})}} \text{ and } I_L = \frac{V}{Z_{(RL\ \text{circuit})}}\right.$$

$$\left.\sin\phi_1 = \frac{X_C}{Z_{(RC\ \text{circuit})}} \text{ and } \sin\phi_2 = \frac{X_L}{Z_{(RL\ \text{circuit})}}\right]$$

or, $$\frac{(1/\omega_0 C)}{\left(\sqrt{R_1^2 + \frac{1}{\omega_0^2 C^2}}\right)^2} = \frac{\omega_0 L}{\left(\sqrt{R_2^2 + \omega_0^2 L^2}\right)^2}$$

or, $$\frac{1}{\omega_0 C\left(R_1^2 + \frac{1}{\omega_0^2 C^2}\right)} = \frac{\omega_0 L}{R_2^2 + \omega_0^2 L^2}$$

or, $$\frac{1}{R_1^2 \omega_0 C + \frac{1}{\omega_0 C}} = \frac{\omega_0 L}{R_2^2 + \omega_0^2 L^2}$$

or, $$\frac{\omega_0 C}{R_1^2 \omega_0^2 C^2 + 1} = \frac{\omega_0 L}{R_2^2 + \omega_0^2 L^2}$$

or, $$R_2^2 + \omega_0^2 L^2 = \frac{L}{C}(R_1^2 \omega_0^2 C^2 + 1)$$

$$= R_1^2 \omega_0^2 LC + \frac{L}{C}$$

or, $$\omega_0^2 [L^2 - R_1^2 LC] = \frac{L}{C} - R_2^2$$

or, $$\omega_0^2 LC\left[\frac{L}{C} - R_1^2\right] = \frac{L}{C} - R_2^2$$

CHAPTER 3

$$\therefore \quad \omega_0 = \frac{1}{\sqrt{LC}}\left[\frac{\frac{L}{C} - R_2^2}{\frac{L}{C} - R_1^2}\right]^{1/2} \qquad \text{...(3.39)}$$

$$\text{or,} \quad f = \frac{1}{2\,\pi\sqrt{LC}}\left[\frac{\frac{L}{C} - R_2^2}{\frac{L}{C} - R_1^2}\right] \qquad \text{...(3.40)}$$

Expressions (3.39) and (3.40) give the expression of resonance of parallel *R-C* and *R-L* circuit.

3.10 PARALLEL RESONANCE OF *RLC* CIRCUITS

In the circuit (parallel *RLC* circuit) shown in Fig. 3.14, the condition for resonance occurs when the *susceptance part is zero.*

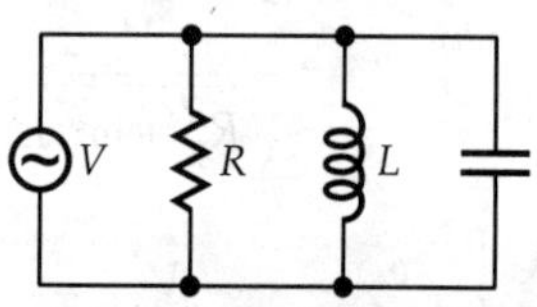

Fig. 3.14 Parallel *RLC* circuit.

However, admittance

$$Y = G + jB \qquad \text{...(3.41)}$$

$$= \frac{1}{R} + j\omega C + \frac{1}{j\omega L} \qquad \text{...(3.42)}$$

$$= \frac{1}{R} + j\left(\omega C - \frac{1}{\omega L}\right) \qquad \text{...(3.43)}$$

The frequency at which resonance occurs is

$$\omega_0\, C - \frac{1}{\omega_0\, L} = 0$$

$$\omega_0 = \frac{1}{\sqrt{LC}} \qquad \text{...(3.44)}$$

The voltage and current with frequency has been shown in Fig. 3.15. At resonant frequency, the current becomes minimum.

The bandwidth is given by : $\text{BW} = f_2 - f_1$

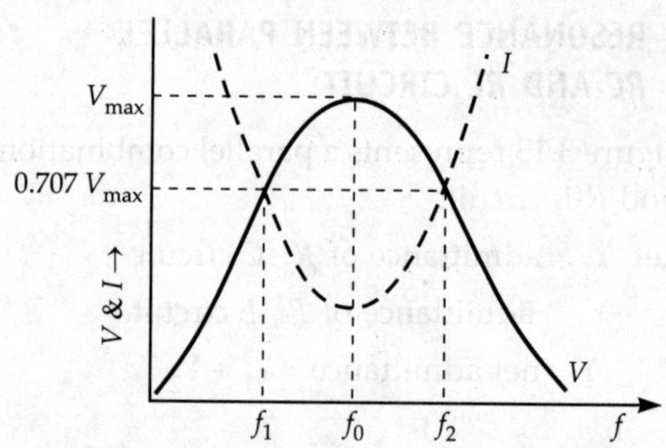

Fig. 3.15 Voltage and current variation with frequency.

In such a parallel circuit, to obtain the lower half-power frequency,

$$\omega_1\, C - \frac{1}{\omega_1\, L} = -\frac{1}{R} \qquad \text{...(3.45)}$$

From equation (3.45),

$$\omega_1^2 + \frac{\omega_1}{RC} - \frac{1}{LC} = 0 \qquad \text{...(3.46)}$$

Simplifying equation (3.46), we get

$$\omega_1 = \frac{-1}{2\,RC} + \sqrt{\left(\frac{1}{2\,RC}\right)^2 + \frac{1}{LC}} \qquad \text{...(3.47)}$$

Similarly, the upper half-power frequency can be obtained as

$$\omega_2\, C - \frac{1}{\omega_2\, L} = \frac{1}{R} \qquad \text{...(3.48)}$$

From equation (3.48),

$$\omega_2 = \frac{1}{2\,RC} + \sqrt{\left(\frac{1}{2\,RC}\right)^2 + \frac{1}{LC}} \qquad \text{...(3.49)}$$

and bandwidth $\text{BW} = \omega_2 - \omega_1 = \dfrac{1}{RC}$

The *Quality factor** is defined as

$$Q_r = \frac{\omega_0}{\omega_2 - \omega_1}$$

$$\text{or,} \quad Q_0 = \frac{\omega_0}{1/RC} = \omega_0\, RC \qquad \text{...(3.50)}$$

* Also, $\quad Q = 2\pi \times \dfrac{\text{maximum energy stored}}{\text{energy dissipated / cycle}}$

In case of an Inductor, the maximum energy stored $= \frac{1}{2} LI_L^2$ and energy dissipated per cycle $= \left(\frac{I}{\sqrt{2}}\right)^2 \times R \times T$ [*T* being the time period]

$$\therefore \quad Q_{\text{factor}}\,(Q) = 2\pi \times \frac{(1/2)(I_L^2) \times L}{\frac{I^2}{2} R \times \frac{1}{f}} \qquad \therefore \quad Q = 2\pi\,\frac{\frac{1}{2} L\left(\frac{V}{\omega L}\right)^2 R}{\frac{V^2}{2} \times \frac{1}{f}} = \frac{2\pi\, fLR}{\omega^2\, L^2} = \frac{R}{\omega L}$$

On the other hand, for a capacitor, maximum energy stored $= 1/2(CV^2)$ and energy dissipated per cycle $= P \times T = \dfrac{V^2}{2 \times R} \times \dfrac{1}{f}$

$$\therefore \quad \text{Quality factor } (Q) = 2\pi \times \frac{1/2(CV^2)}{\frac{V^2}{2\,R} \times \frac{1}{f}} = 2\pi\, f\,CR = \omega\, CR.$$

EXAMPLE 3.1 *A RLC tank circuit is composed of components having values as $R=0.2\,\Omega$; $L=100$ mH and $C=50\,\mu F$. Determine the resonance frequency and the corresponding input current at 24 V.*

SOLUTION. $$f_0 = \frac{1}{2\pi\sqrt{100\times10^{-3}\times50\times10^{-6}}}\text{ Hz}$$

$$=71.21\text{ Hz}$$

At resonance $I=\dfrac{V}{R}=\dfrac{24}{0.2}=\mathbf{120\ A.}$

EXAMPLE 3.2 *A series LCR circuit has inductance of 10 mH and resistance of 2 ohms. What is the value of capacitance that will produce resonance. Also find the current at resonance frequency and the maximum instantaneous energy stored in the inductance at resonance. Assume the supply as 230 V, 10000 Hz.*

SOLUTION. As $f_0=\dfrac{1}{2\pi\sqrt{LC}}$

[f being the resonance frequency]

$$\therefore\ C=\frac{1}{f_0^2\times4\pi^2\times L}$$

$$=\frac{1}{(10{,}000)^2\times4\pi^2\times10\times10^{-3}}=\mathbf{0.025\ \mu F}$$

Again, $I_0=\dfrac{V}{R}$

[$\because I_0$ being the circuit current during series resonance *i.e.*, when $Z=R$]

$$=\frac{230\angle0^\circ}{2}=\mathbf{115\angle0^\circ\ A}$$

Energy in inductor (instantaneous, maximum)

$$=\frac{1}{2}LI_{max}^2=\frac{1}{2}L\times(\sqrt{2}\,I_{rms})^2$$

$$=LI_{rms}^2=10\times10^{-3}\times(115)^2=\mathbf{132.25\ J.}$$

EXAMPLE 3.3 *What is the resonance frequency of a series RLC circuit where $R=10\,\Omega$, $L=25$ mH and $C=100\,\mu F$? Evaluate the Q factor also.*

SOLUTION. $$f_0=\frac{1}{2\pi\sqrt{LC}}$$

$$=\frac{1}{2\pi\sqrt{25\times10^{-3}\times100\times10^{-6}}}\text{ Hz}\simeq\mathbf{100.71\ Hz.}$$

We know, Q factor of a series *LRC* circuit can be expressed as any of the two following relations

$$Q=\frac{\omega_0 L}{R}\text{ or }\frac{1}{\omega_0 RC}$$

Using $Q=\dfrac{\omega_0 L}{R}$,

$$Q=\frac{2\pi\times100.71\times25\times10^{-3}}{10}=\mathbf{1.58}$$

[Using $Q=\dfrac{1}{\omega_0 RC}$

$$Q=\frac{1}{2\pi\times100.71\times10\times100\times10^{-6}}=1.58\Big]$$

i.e., both the formulae yield same result.

EXAMPLE 3.4 *A coil is at resonance at 10 kHz with a capacitor. If the resistance and inductance of the coil are $200\,\Omega$ and 5 H, find the Q factor of the coil.*

SOLUTION. $f_0=10000$ Hz; $L=5$ H; $R=200\,\Omega$

$$Q=\frac{2\pi f_0 L}{R}=\frac{2\pi\times10000\times5}{200}=\mathbf{1570}\text{ (very high).}$$

EXAMPLE 3.5 *A coil has a resistance of $20\,\Omega$ and inductance of 80 mH and is connected in series with a 100 pF capacitor. Determine, at resonance, the circuit impedance and also find the resonant frequency. If the supply to the circuit is a 50 V source having an internal impedance of 2 ohms, find also the circuit current and the voltage across the capacitor.*

SOLUTION.

$$f_0=\frac{1}{2\pi\sqrt{80\times10^{-3}\times100\times10^{-12}}}$$

[f_0 = frequency of resonance]

$$=56.298\text{ kHz}$$

$Z=R=20\,\Omega$ [at resonance, $Z=R$]

$$I_0=\frac{V}{R}=\frac{50\ V}{20\,\Omega}=2.5\text{ A}$$

[I_0 = current at resonance]

$$V_C=I\,X_C=2.5\times\frac{1}{2\pi f_0 C}$$

[V_C = voltage across the capacitor]

$$=\frac{2.5}{2\pi\times56.298\times10^3\times100\times10^{-12}}$$

$$=\mathbf{70.71\ kV.}$$

EXAMPLE 3.6 *A coil having an inductance and resistance of 50 mH and 100 ohms is connected in series with a capacitor and a 100 V, 1 kHz source. Obtain the value of capacitance that will cause resonance in the circuit. Find the circuit current at resonance frequency.*

SOLUTION.

$$f_0 = \frac{1}{2\pi\sqrt{LC}} \quad \text{or,} \quad 1000 = \frac{1}{2\pi\sqrt{50\times10^{-3}\times C}}$$

$$\therefore \quad C = \frac{1}{4\pi^2\times50\times10^{-3}\times(1000)^2} = 0.5\,\mu\text{F}$$

$$|I_0| = \frac{|V|}{|Z|}$$

[Z_0 being the circuit impedance at resonance and is equal to the value of resistance]

$$= \frac{100}{10} = \mathbf{10\ A.}$$

EXAMPLE 3.7 *A 5 μF condenser is connected in series with a coil having inductance of 50 mH. Determine the frequency of resonance, the resistance of the coil if a 50 V source operating at resonance frequency causes a circuit current of 10 mA. What is the Q factor of the coil ?*

SOLUTION.

$$f_0 = \frac{1}{2\pi\sqrt{LC}}$$

$$= \frac{1}{2\pi\sqrt{50\times10^{-3}\times5\times10^{-6}}}$$

$$= 318.47\ \text{Hz}$$

$$\text{Also,} \quad I_0 = \frac{V}{R} \qquad [\text{at resonance } |Z| = |R|]$$

$$\text{or,} \quad 10\times10^{-3} = \frac{50}{R} \qquad [\because I_0 = 10\text{ mA, given}]$$

$$\therefore \quad R = \frac{50}{10\times10^{-3}} = 5000\,\Omega$$

$$Q_{\text{factor}} = \frac{\omega_0 L}{R} = \frac{2\pi\times318.47\times50\times10^{-3}}{5000}$$

$$= \mathbf{0.02} \quad [\text{very low}].$$

EXAMPLE 3.8 *A 50 μF capacitor, when connected in series with a coil having 40 Ω resistance, resonates at 1000 Hz. Find the inductance of the coil. Also obtain the circuit current if the applied voltage is 100 V. Also calculate the voltage across the capacitor and the coil at resonance.*

SOLUTION. At resonance,

$$X_L = X_C \quad \text{or,} \quad 2\pi f_0 L = \frac{1}{2\pi f_0 C}$$

$$\therefore \quad L = \frac{1}{4\pi^2 f_0^2 C}\ \text{H}$$

$$= \frac{1}{4\pi^2\times(1000)^2\times50\times10^{-6}} = \mathbf{0.5\ mH}$$

$$|I_0| = \frac{V}{Z} = \frac{V}{R} \text{ at resonance } = \frac{100}{40} = \mathbf{2.5\ A}$$

[Power loss of the coil

$$= I_0^2 R = (2.5)^2\times40 = 250 \text{ watts}]$$

$$\text{Again,} \quad V_C = I_0 X_C = 2.5\times\frac{1}{2\pi f_0 C}$$

$$= 2.5\times\frac{1}{2\pi\times1000\times50\times10^{-6}} = \mathbf{7.96\ V}$$

Again,

$$X_L = \omega L = 2\pi\times1000\times0.5\times10^{-3}$$

$$= 3.14\,\Omega$$

$$\therefore \quad V_{\text{coil}} = I_0 Z \text{ coil (at resonance)}$$

$$= 2.5\sqrt{(40)^2+(3.14)^2} = \mathbf{100.31\ V.}$$

EXAMPLE 3.9 *A series RLC circuit has $R = 1.5\,\Omega$, $X_C = 5\,\Omega$ and the inductance is impure having its resistance of 3 Ω and inductive reactance of 1 Ω. Find the input impedance and the circuit current. Calculate the frequency of resonance. The supply is 100 V, 50 Hz.*

SOLUTION. $Z_{\text{input}} = (R_L + jX_L) + R - jX_C$

[R_L and X_L are the resistance and inductive reactance of the coil, R is the circuit resistance and X_C the capacitive reactance]

$$= (3+j1) + 1.5 - j5$$

$$= (4.5 - j4)\,\Omega = \mathbf{6.02\angle -41.63°\,\Omega}$$

$$I = \frac{100\angle 0°}{6.02\angle 41.63°} = 16.6\angle 41.63°\ \text{A}$$

$$\text{Again,} \quad L = \frac{X_L}{2\pi f} = \frac{1}{2\pi\times50} = 3.18\times10^{-3}\ \text{H}$$

$$\text{and} \quad C = \frac{1}{X_C\times2\pi f} = 6.37\times10^{-4}\ \text{F}$$

At resonance frequency,

$$X_L = X_C$$

$$\text{or,} \quad 2\pi f_0 L = \frac{1}{2\pi f_0 C}$$

$$\text{i.e.,} \quad f_0 = \frac{1}{2\pi\sqrt{LC}}$$

$$= \frac{1}{2\pi\sqrt{3.18\times10^{-3}\times6.37\times10^{-4}}}$$

$$= \mathbf{111.82\ Hz \simeq 112\ Hz.}$$

EXAMPLE 3.10 *Determine the relationship between the resonance frequency f_0 and the half-power frequency f_1 and f_2 in a series resonating circuit.*

SOLUTION. At f_1 or f_2, the circuit current drops to $(1/\sqrt{2})$ of its resonant value. This means that the impedance must have been $\sqrt{2}$ times the resonant value.

$$\therefore \quad Z \equiv \sqrt{R^2 + (X_L - X_C)^2} = \sqrt{2}\, R$$

i.e., $$(X_L - X_C) = \pm R$$

or, $$\omega L - \frac{1}{\omega C} = \pm R \qquad ...(a)$$

When $\omega L > \frac{1}{\omega C}$ R is +ve.

The frequency at which $\omega L > \frac{1}{\omega C}$ is termed as f_2 (or ω_2). On the other hand, when $\omega L < \frac{1}{\omega C}$, R is –ve *i.e.,* the frequency at which this occurs, gives f_1 (or ω_1).

Equation (*a*) can be rewritten as

$$\omega^2 LC \mp R\omega C - 1 = 0$$

Here, $$\omega_1 = \frac{-RC + \sqrt{R^2C^2 + 4LC}}{2LC}$$

$$= -\frac{RC}{2LC} + \frac{1}{2}\sqrt{\left(\frac{RC}{LC}\right)^2 + \frac{4LC}{L^2C^2}}$$

$$= -\frac{R}{2L} + \frac{1}{2}\sqrt{\left(\frac{R}{L}\right)^2 + \frac{4}{LC}} \qquad ...(b)$$

and $$\omega_2 = \frac{R}{2L} + \frac{1}{2}\sqrt{\left(\frac{R}{L}\right)^2 + \frac{4}{LC}} \qquad ...(c)$$

Multiplying equations (*b*) and (*c*)

$$\omega_1 \omega_2 = \frac{1}{4}\left[\left(\frac{R}{L}\right)^2 + \frac{4}{LC}\right] - \frac{1}{4}\left(\frac{R}{L}\right)^2 = \frac{1}{LC} = \omega_0^2$$

$$\therefore \quad \omega_0 = \sqrt{\omega_1 \omega_2} \qquad \textbf{[or, } f_0 = \sqrt{f_1 f_2}\textbf{]}$$

Also, $$\omega_2 - \omega_1 = \left[\frac{R}{2L} + \frac{1}{2}\sqrt{\left(\frac{R}{L}\right)^2 + \frac{4}{LC}} + \frac{R}{2L} - \frac{1}{2}\sqrt{\left(\frac{R}{L}\right)^2 + \frac{4}{LC}} = \frac{R}{L}\right]$$

$$\therefore \quad f_2 - f_1 \text{ (i.e., bandwidth, BW)} = \frac{R}{2\pi L} \qquad ...(d)$$

Also,

$$\left[\text{BW} = \frac{R}{2\pi L} = \frac{\frac{\omega_0 L}{Q}}{2\pi L} = \frac{2\pi f_0 L}{Q} \times \frac{1}{2\pi L} = \frac{f_0}{Q}\right] \qquad ...(e)$$

EXAMPLE 3.11 *Find the relation between f_1, f_2 and BW in terms of f_r.*

SOLUTION. We have seen in Example 3.10,

$$f_2 - f_1 = \text{BW}\left(= \frac{R}{2\pi L}\right) \qquad ...(f)$$

and $\sqrt{f_1 f_2} = f_r$ (f_r being the frequency of resonance) ...(*g*)

Squaring equation (*g*), we get,

$$f_1 f_2 = fr^2 \quad \text{or,} \quad f_2 = \frac{fr^2}{f_1} \qquad ...(i)$$

Substitution of equation (*i*) in (*f*), we get

$$\frac{fr^2}{f_1} - f_1 = \text{BW} \quad \text{or} \quad f_1^2 + f_1\,\text{BW} - fr^2 = 0$$

$$\therefore \quad f_1 = \frac{-\text{BW} \pm \sqrt{(\text{BW})^2 + 4 f_r^2}}{2}$$

$$= -\frac{\text{BW}}{2} + \sqrt{\frac{(\text{BW})^2}{4} + fr^2}$$

[–ve sign has not been taken into account]

However, as $\frac{(\text{BW})^2}{4}$ is so small, it can be neglected. This gives

$$f_1 \simeq f_r - \frac{\text{BW}}{2} \qquad ...(j)$$

In a similar way,

$$f_2 \simeq f_r + \frac{\text{BW}}{2}. \qquad ...(k)$$

EXAMPLE 3.12 *Calculate half-power frequencies of a series resonant circuit where the resonance frequency is 150×10^3 Hz and the bandwidth is 75 kHz.*

SOLUTION. We know $f_2 - f_1 = \text{BW}$

and $\sqrt{f_1 f_2} = fr$

(fr being the frequency of resonance)

Here, $f_2 - f_1 = 75$, $\sqrt{f_1 f_2} = f_r = 150$

Solving these two equations,

$$\mathbf{f_1 = 117\ kHz\ ; \quad f_2 = 192\ kHz.}$$

EXAMPLE 3.13 *A 220 V, 100 Hz ac source supplies a series LCR circuit with a capacitor and a coil. If the coil has 50 mΩ resistance and 5 mH inductance, find, at a resonance frequency of 100 Hz what is the value of capacitor? Also calculate the Q factor and half power frequencies of the circuit.*

C H A P T E R 3

Solution. We know,

$$f_0 = \frac{1}{2\pi\sqrt{LC}}$$

or, $$100 = \frac{1}{2\pi\sqrt{5\times10^{-3}\times C}}$$

or, $$C = \frac{1}{4\pi^2\times100^2\times5\times10^{-3}} = \mathbf{507\,\mu F}$$

$$Q = \frac{\omega_0 L}{R} = \frac{2\pi\times100\times5\times10^{-3}}{50\times10^{-3}} = 62.83$$

$$\text{BW(bandwidth)} = \frac{f_0}{Q} = \frac{100}{62.83} = 1.59\text{ Hz}$$

f_2, higher half power frequency

$$= f_0 + \frac{\text{BW}}{2} = 100 + \frac{1.59}{2} = \mathbf{100.795\ Hz}$$

f_1, lower half power frequency

$$= f_0 - \frac{\text{BW}}{2} = 100 - \frac{1.59}{2} = \mathbf{99.205\ Hz.}$$

Example 3.14 *A current source, having internal resistance as 50 kΩ feeds a tank circuit. If the constituents of the tank circuits are a 500 nF capacitor and a coil of resistance 50 ohms and inductance 250 mH, find the frequency of resonance and Q factor.*

Solution. $$f_0 = \frac{1}{2\pi}\sqrt{\frac{1}{LC} - \frac{R^2}{L^2}}$$

[for the tank circuit]

$$= \frac{1}{2\pi}\sqrt{\frac{1}{0.25\times500\times10^{-9}} - \left(\frac{50}{0.25}\right)^2} = \mathbf{449.26\ Hz}$$

$$Q = \frac{\omega_0 L}{R} = \frac{2\pi\times449.26\times0.25}{50} = \mathbf{14.16.}$$

Example 3.15 *A coil with resistance of 10 ohms and inductance of 0.5 H is connected in parallel with a 400μF capacitor. Calculate the frequency at which the circuit will act as a non-inductive resistance. Find its value.*

Solution. For a *R-L* and *C* parallel combination, at resonance, the resonance frequency is given by

$$f_0 = \frac{1}{2\pi}\sqrt{\frac{1}{LC} - \left(\frac{R}{L}\right)^2}$$

or, $$\omega_0^2 = \frac{1}{LC} - \left(\frac{R}{L}\right)^2$$

$$= \frac{1}{0.5\times400\times10^{-6}} - \left(\frac{10}{0.5}\right)^2$$

or, $$\omega_0 = 67.82\text{ rad/sec}$$

[ω_0 being the frequency of resonance]

$$\therefore\quad f_0 = \frac{67.82}{2\pi} = \mathbf{10.80\ Hz.}$$

We have also seen in the text that in parallel circuit, at resonance, the circuit offers only a resistance (known as dynamic resistance) the value of which is given by $\frac{L}{CR}$ ohms

$$= \frac{0.5}{400\times10^{-6}\times10} = \mathbf{125\,\Omega.}$$

Example 3.16 *A 50 Hz, 220 V is applied to a series RLC circuit where R = 10 ohms, L = 500 mH. The through current is found to be maximum. What is the value of the capacitive reactance ? Next, a capacitor is connected in parallel with the series combination. What would be the value of the capacitance such that the combination is at resonance at 100 Hz ? Calculate the total supply current in each case.*

Solution. ***Case a*** : at 50 Hz [*Series Circuit*]

As per the question, the current is maximum. Hence, the capacitive reactance is equal to the inductive reactance ;

i.e., $$X_C = \omega_0 L = 100\pi\times500\times10^{-3} = \mathbf{157\,\Omega}$$

[Here, $\omega_0 = 2\pi\times50 = 100\pi$ Hz]

Case b : at 100 Hz, Z_{series} branch

$$= 10 + j\left(157\times2 - \frac{157}{2}\right)$$

[$\because$ X_L at 100 Hz is twice X_L at 50 Hz and X_C at 100 Hz is half of X_C at 50 Hz]

$$\therefore\quad Z_{\text{series branch}} = 10 + j\,(314 - 78.5)$$

$$= 235.7\angle 87.56°\text{ ohm}$$

$$\therefore\quad Y_{\text{series branch}} = \frac{1}{235.7}\angle -87.56°$$

$$= 4.2\times10^{-3}\angle -87.56°$$

$$= 10^{-3}\,[0.179 - j\,4.196]\text{ mho}$$

$$= G_S + jB_S$$

A capacitor now is connected in parallel to Z_{series} branch having admitance (Y-series branch). Since resonance occurs hence the susceptance of (Y-series branch) must be equal to the susceptance *B* of the parallely connected capacitor.

$\therefore$ *B*, the capacitive susceptance of the capacitor is

$$= \omega C = 4.19\times10^{-3}\text{ mho}$$

[at $\omega = 2\pi\times100 = 200\pi$ rad/sec]

This gives

$$C = \frac{4.19 \times 10^{-3}}{200\,\pi}\ \text{F}$$

$$= 6.68 \times 10^{-6}\ \text{F} = \mathbf{6.68\ \mu\ F}$$

At 50 Hz, $I = \frac{V}{R} = \frac{220}{10} = \mathbf{22\ A}$

At 100 Hz (parallel resonance)

$$I = 220 \times \text{Real part of } Y$$

$$= 220 \times 10^{-3} \times 0.179 = \mathbf{39.38\ mA.}$$

EXAMPLE 3.17 *Show that the condition for resonance in a parallel RCL circuit is same to that of a series RLC circuit.*

SOLUTION. For resonance, the circuit impedance in a series circuit and the circuit admittance in a parallel circuit must be resistive.

In the series connection case,

$$Z_{\text{series}} = R + j\,(X_L - X_C) \qquad ...(a)$$

in the parallel connection case,

$$Y = \frac{1}{R} + j\left(X_C - \frac{1}{X_L}\right) \qquad ...(b)$$

in (*a*), at resonance, for the series circuit

$$X_L = X_C \text{ giving } f_0 = \frac{1}{2\pi\sqrt{LC}}$$

in (*b*), at resonance, for the parallel circuit,

$$X_C = \frac{1}{X_L} \text{ giving } f_0 = \frac{1}{2\pi\sqrt{LC}}.$$

EXAMPLE 3.18 *Determine all the currents in the circuit shown in Fig. E3.1.*

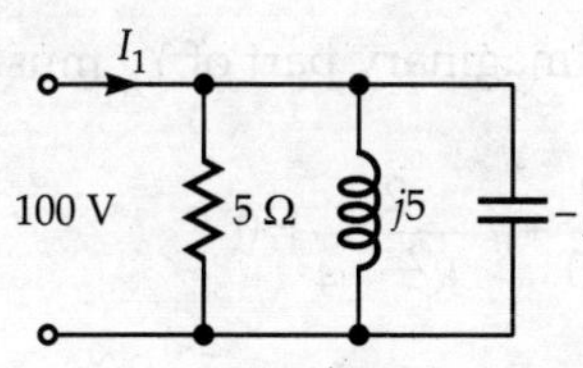

Fig. E3.1

SOLUTION. Let the currents through the *R*, *L* and *C* be I_R, I_L and I_C. The circuit is at resonance since $X_L = X_C$.

$$I_R = \frac{100\angle 0^\circ}{5} = \mathbf{20\angle 0^\circ\ A}\,;$$

$$I_L = \frac{100\ \angle 0^\circ}{5\ \angle 90^\circ} = \mathbf{20\angle{-90^\circ}\ A}$$

$$I_C = \frac{100\angle 0^\circ}{5\angle{-90^\circ}} = \mathbf{20\angle 90^\circ\ A.}$$

Let $I_X = I_L + I_C$

$$= 20\ \angle{-90^\circ} + 20\ \angle 90^\circ$$

$$= 0\ \text{A}$$

[at resonance this obviously happens]

∴ $I = \text{Supply current} = \boldsymbol{I_R = 20\ \angle 0^\circ}.$

EXAMPLE 3.19 *In a tank circuit show that the circulating current at resonance is given by* $I = V\left[\frac{C}{L}\right]^{1/2}$ *for a supply voltage of V volts (a.c.). Neglect any resistance of the circuit.*

SOLUTION. A tank circuit has been shown in Fig. E3.2.

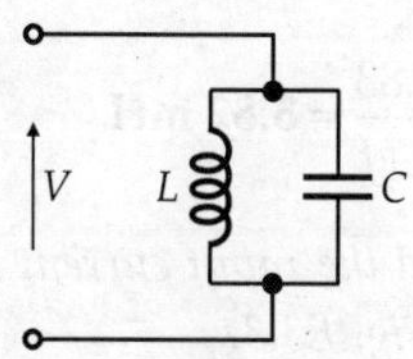

Fig. E3.2

Here, at resonance, $X_L = X_C$

∴ Current through *L* is identical to current through *C*.

Now, current through *L* (or *C*) is given by

$$I = \frac{V}{X_L} = \frac{V}{2\,\pi\, f_n\, L}$$

[f_n = frequency of resonance]

$$= \frac{V}{2\,\pi\,\frac{1}{2\pi\sqrt{LC}}\,.\,L} = V\sqrt{\frac{C}{L}} = V\left[\frac{C}{L}\right]^{1/2}\ \textbf{A.}$$

EXAMPLE 3.20. *A 400 V, 50 Hz supply feeds energy to a parallel circuit consisting of a 10 ∠30° ohm branch and a 10 ∠–60° ohm branch. Determine the impedance of a circuit element such that, if connected in series with the source, the system comes at resonance.*

SOLUTION. *abcd* is the parallel circuit as shown in Fig. E3.3.

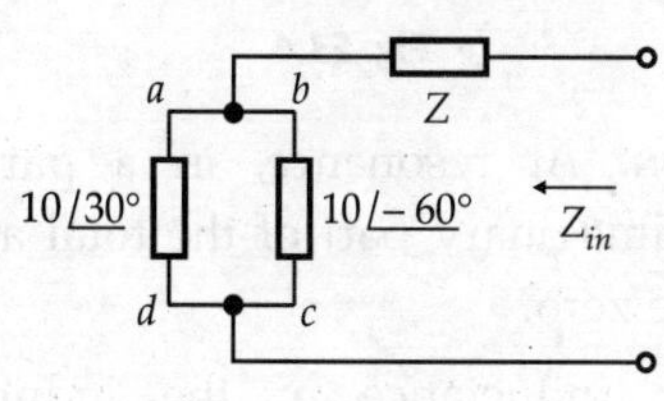

Fig. E3.3

$$Z_{abcd} = \frac{10\angle 30° \times 10\angle -60°}{10\angle 30° + 10\angle -60°} = \frac{100\angle -30°}{13.6 - j\,3.66}$$

$$= \frac{100\angle -30°}{14.15\angle -15°} = (6.83 - j\,1.83)\text{ ohm}$$

$$\therefore\ Z_{in} = Z + Z_{abcd}$$

[assuming Z to be the series circuit element]

$$= Z + (6.83 - j\,1.83)\text{ ohm}$$

for the system to be in resonance, there must be no imaginary part. Hence Z must be equal to $(+\,j\,1.83)$ *i.e.*, (jX_L)

i.e., $X_L = 2\,\pi f L$

gives $L = \dfrac{1.83}{2\,\pi f} = \mathbf{5.82\ mH}$.

EXAMPLE 3.21 *Find the input current and power for the circuit shown in Fig. E3.3.*

SOLUTION. Z_{in}

[as given in the previous example]

$$= 6.83\,\Omega$$

[$\because$ we had found that Z is cancelling out with imaginary part of the parallel circuit hence, $Z_{in} = 6.83$ as evident from the previous example]

$$\therefore\quad I = \frac{400}{6.83} = 58.56\text{ A}\,[V = 400\text{ V}]$$

Power $= V.I$ [at resonance $\cos\phi = 1$]

$$= 400 \times 58.56 = \mathbf{23.42\ kW}.$$

EXAMPLE 3.22 *Show that no value of R_L in the circuit shown in Fig. E3.4 will make it resonant.*

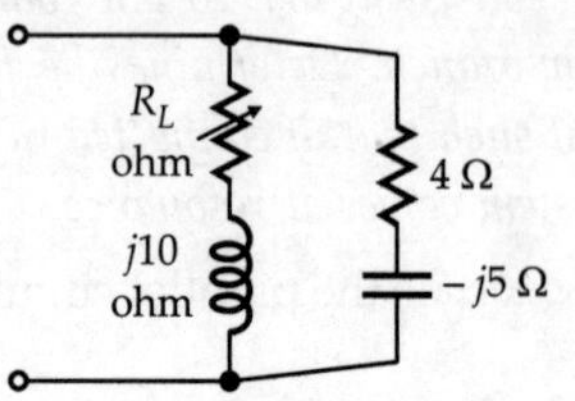

Fig. E3.4

SOLUTION. At resonance, in a parallel *RLC* circuit, the imaginary part of the total admittance (Y_T) must be zero.

Let the inductance of the inductive and capacitive circuits be given as Y_L and Y_C.

$$\therefore\quad Y_L = \frac{1}{R_L + j\,10} = \frac{R_L - j\,10}{R_L^2 + 100}\text{ mho}$$

$$Y_C = \frac{1}{4 - j\,5} = \frac{4 + j\,5}{4^2 + 5^2}\text{ mho}$$

Thus imaginary part of Y_T is

$$\left(\frac{-10}{R_L^2 + 100} + \frac{5}{41}\right)\text{ mho at resonance,}$$

$$\therefore\quad \frac{10}{R_L^2 + 100} = \frac{5}{41}\quad\text{or}\quad R_L^2 = -18$$

Thus, $\mathbf{R_L = j4.24}$

This value of R_L is physically impossible.

EXAMPLE 3.23 *Calculate the value of R_C in the circuit shown in Fig. E3.5 to yield resonance.*

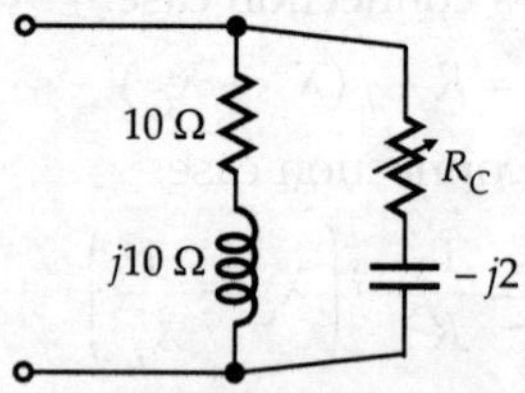

Fig. E3.5

SOLUTION. In circuit of Fig. E3.5,

$$Y_L = \frac{1}{10 + j\,10}\text{ mho}$$

$$= \frac{10 - j\,10}{100 + 100} = \frac{10}{200} - j\,\frac{10}{200}$$

and $$Y_C = \frac{1}{R_C - j\,2} = \frac{R_C + j\,2}{R_C^2 + 4}\text{ mho}$$

at resonance, imaginary part of Y_L must be equal to that of Y_C

i.e., $$-j\,\frac{10}{200} + j\,\frac{2}{R_C^2 + 4} = 0$$

This gives $\mathbf{R_C = 6\ ohm}$.

EXAMPLE 3.24 *A circuit has been shown in Fig. E3.6. Find the frequency at which this circuit will be at resonance. If the capacitor and inductors are interchanged, what would be the value of the resonance frequency ?*

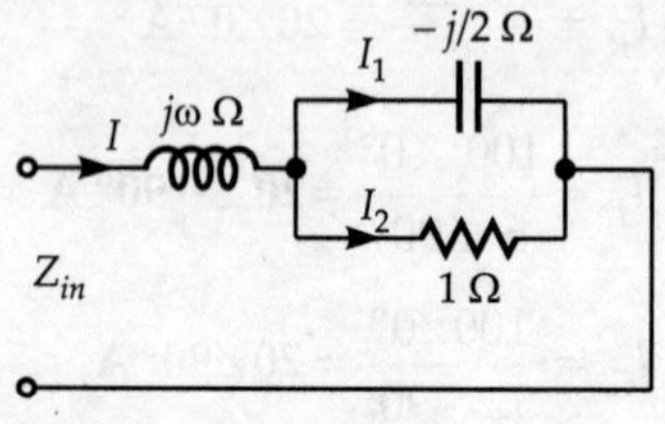

Fig. E3.6

SOLUTION. At resonance, imaginary part of input impedance must be zero.

However,

$$Z_{in} = j\omega + \frac{(-j/2\omega)\times 1}{-j/2\,\omega + 1}$$

$$\therefore \quad Z_{in} = j\,\omega - \frac{j}{2\,\omega - j} = j\,\omega - \frac{j\,(2\omega + j)}{1 + 4\,\omega^2}$$

Thus the imaginary part of Z_{in} is

$$\left(\omega - \frac{2\,\omega}{1 + 4\,\omega^2}\right)\Omega$$

At resonance, $\omega - \dfrac{2\,\omega}{1 + 4\,\omega^2} = 0.$

This gives, $\omega = \mathbf{0.5\ rad/sec.}$

If the capacitor and the inductor of the circuit are interchanged,

$$Z_{in} = -\frac{j}{2\,\omega} + \frac{j\,\omega}{1 + j\,\omega}$$

$$= -\frac{j}{2\,\omega} + \frac{j\,\omega(1 - j\,\omega)}{1 + \omega^2}$$

$$= -\frac{j}{2\,\omega} + \frac{j\,\omega}{1 + \omega^2} + \frac{\omega^2}{1 + \omega^2}$$

Thus $\quad -\dfrac{1}{2\,\omega} + \dfrac{\omega}{1 + \omega^2} = 0.$

[Since at resonance, imaginary part of the input impedance is zero.]

This gives $\omega = \mathbf{1\ rad/sec.}$

3.11 INSTANTANEOUS POWER IN A.C. CIRCUIT

In a passive a.c. circuit, let the *instantaneous voltage* be

$$v = V_m \sin \omega t$$

while the current is given by

$$i = I_m \sin(\omega t - \phi),$$

ϕ being the *phase difference* between the voltage and current at any instant (ϕ is negative when *voltage leads* and ϕ is positive when *voltage lags* the current; $\phi = 0$ when the current and voltage are in same phase voltage being the reference phasor).

$\therefore$ The instantaneous power p is thus given by

$$p = vi = V_m I_m \sin \omega t \sin(\omega t - \phi)$$

$$= \frac{1}{2} \times 2\, V_m I_m \sin \omega t \sin(\omega t - \phi)$$

$$= \frac{1}{2} V_m I_m \left[\cos(\omega t - \omega t + \phi) - \cos(\omega t + \omega t - \phi)\right]$$

$$= \frac{1}{2} V_m I_m \left[\cos\phi - \cos(2\,\omega t - \phi)\right]$$

$$= \frac{1}{2} V_m I_m \cos\phi - \frac{1}{2} V_m I_m \cos(2\,\omega t - \phi) \quad \text{...(3.51)}$$

The second term in the right hand side of equation (3.51) contains a double frequency term and it is evident that the magnitude of the average value of this term is zero since the average of a sinusoidal quantity of double frequency over a complete cycle is zero. Thus the instantaneous power consists only the term $\left(\frac{1}{2} V_m I_m \cos\phi\right)$ which is the *average power in the passive circuit.*

Thus the average power in the passive circuit is given by

$$P_{av} \text{ (or simply } P) = \tfrac{1}{2} V_m\, I_m \cos\phi$$

$$= \frac{V_m}{\sqrt{2}} \times \frac{I_m}{\sqrt{2}} \cos\phi$$

$$= V \times I \times \cos\phi \quad \text{...(3.52)}$$

In a purely resistive circuit $\phi = 0$ [since the current and voltage are in same phase]. Thus the average power in a.c. circuit having a pure resistance is

$$P_R = VI \cos 0° = VI \text{ watts} \quad \text{...(3.53)}$$

On the other hand, in a pure capacitive circuit, $\phi = 90°$ and in a pure inductive circuit $\phi = -90°$, the current in capacitive circuit being leading the voltage by 90° while that in a pure inductive circuit lags the voltage by 90°.

$\therefore$ In a pure capacitive circuit, the average power

$$P = VI \cos(+90°) = 0$$

while the same in a pure inductive circuit is given by (equation 3.54)

$$P = VI \cos(-90°) = 0 \quad \text{...(3.54)}$$

Thus the average power consumed by the pure inductance or capacitance is zero.

CHAPTER 3

In the pure inductive circuit it can also be shown that over a complete cycle,

$$P_{av} = \frac{1}{2\pi}\int_0^{2\pi} v \times i\, d\theta \; [\theta = \omega t]$$

$$= \frac{1}{2\pi}\int_0^{2\pi} V_m \sin\theta \times I_m \sin\left(\theta - \frac{\pi}{2}\right) d\theta$$

[∵ i lags v by $\pi/2$]

$$= \frac{1}{2\pi}\int_0^{2\pi} -\frac{V_m I_m}{2} \times 2\sin\theta\cos\theta\, d\theta$$

$$= -\frac{1}{2\pi}\int_0^{2\pi} \frac{V_m I_m}{2}\sin 2\theta\, d\theta$$

$$= -\frac{1}{2\pi}\int_0^{2\pi} \frac{V_m}{\sqrt{2}} \times \frac{I_m}{\sqrt{2}}\sin 2\theta\, d\theta$$

$$= -\frac{1}{2\pi}\int_0^{2\pi} V \times I \sin 2\theta\, d\theta$$

$$= -\frac{VI}{2\pi}\int_0^{2\pi} \sin 2\theta\, d\theta = -\frac{VI}{2\pi}\left[-\frac{\cos 2\theta}{2}\right]_0^{2\pi}$$

$$= -\frac{VI}{2\pi}\left[-\left(\frac{\cos 4\pi}{2} - \frac{\cos 0}{2}\right)\right]$$

$$= -\frac{VI}{4\pi}[-(1-1)] = -\frac{VI}{4\pi} \times 0 = 0.$$

The average power in a pure inductive circuit is thus zero. Similarly, the average value of the power in a capacitive circuit is zero.

On the other hand, in a resistive circuit,

$$P = \frac{1}{2\pi}\int_0^{2\pi} v \times i\, d\theta$$

[the average power over a complete cycle]

or,

$$P = \frac{1}{2\pi}\int_0^{2\pi} V_m \sin\theta \times I_m \sin\theta\, d\theta$$

$$= \frac{V_m I_m}{2\pi}\int_0^{2\pi} \sin^2\theta\, d\theta$$

$$= \frac{V_m I_m}{2\pi}\int_0^{2\pi} \frac{1}{2}(1 - \cos 2\theta)\, d\theta$$

$$= \left(\frac{V_m}{\sqrt{2}}\right)\left(\frac{I_m}{\sqrt{2}}\right) \times \frac{1}{2\pi}\int_0^{2\pi} (1 - \cos 2\theta)\, d\theta$$

$$= \frac{VI}{2\pi}\left[\theta - \frac{\sin 2\theta}{2}\right]_0^{2\pi}$$

$$= \frac{VI}{2\pi}\left[(2\pi - 0) - \left(\frac{\sin 4\pi}{2} - \frac{\sin 2 \times 0}{2}\right)\right]$$

$$= \frac{VI}{2\pi}\,(2\pi - 0) - (0 - 0)\,] = \frac{VI}{2\pi} \times 2\pi = VI \text{ watts}$$

Thus the average power in a resistive circuit is then given by (VI) watts.

The average power in an a.c. circuit is also termed as a *true power, real power, active power* or simply, the *power.*

Obviously in a resistive circuit,

$$VI = (IR)\, I = I^2 R \text{ watts}$$

or

$$VI = V \times \frac{V}{R} = \frac{V^2}{R} \text{ watts.} \qquad ...(3.55)$$

3.12 POWER FACTOR

The term ($\cos\phi$) in the term ($VI \cos\phi$ *i.e.,* in the average power) is called *power factor*. It is the cosine of the angle between the voltage and current in any a.c. circuit. Power factor (p.f.) is unity in resistive circuit (the angle between voltage and current

It may be noted that $\cos\phi$ in the expression $P = VI\cos\phi$ is called *power factor* and is expressed either as

$$\cos\phi = \frac{R}{Z} \quad \text{or} \quad \cos\phi = \frac{P}{S} = \frac{VI\cos\phi}{VI}\left(= \frac{\text{Watt}}{\text{VA}}\right).$$

$\sin\phi$ in the expression $Q = VI\sin\phi$ is called *reactive factor* and is expressed either as

$$\sin\phi = \frac{X}{Z} \quad \text{or} \quad \sin\phi = \frac{Q}{S} = \frac{VI\sin\phi}{VI}\left(= \frac{\text{VAR}}{\text{VA}}\right).$$

With reduction of magnitude of ϕ, the phase angle between the voltage and current, power factor improves and reactive factor decreases. Improvement of power factor in any a.c. system is highly desired. The following table represents the power factor of different loads.

Loads	R	L	C	R-L	R-C
Power Factor	Unity [$\cos\phi = 1$]	Zero lag [$\cos\phi = \cos(-90°) = 0$	Zero lead [$\cos\phi = \cos(+90°) = 0$	Lagging [$\cos\phi$]	Leading [$\cos\phi$]

being zero), leading in capacitive circuit (current being leading the voltage), lagging in inductive circuit (current being lagging the voltage).

3.13 APPARENT POWER

The product VI is called the *apparent power* and is usually indicated by the symbol "S". It is expressed in (VA).

3.14 REACTIVE POWER

The product of r.m.s. values of voltage and current with the sine of the angle between them is called the *reactive power* in a.c. circuit and is denoted by Q, the unit being VAR (Volt-ampere reactive)

$$Q = VI \sin \phi \qquad \text{...(3.56)}$$

The other names of reactive power are *wattless power* and *quadrature power*.

The following table represents the different expressions of power in a.c. circuits :

Table 3.1

Circuit	Real Power | (P) |	Reactive Power | (Q) |	Apparent Power (or Total Power) | S |
R	$VI \cos \phi$ $= VI\,[\phi = 0°]$	$VI \sin \phi$ $= 0\,[\phi = 0°]$	$S = \sqrt{P^2 + Q^2}$ $= VI$
L	$VI \cos \phi$ $= VI \cos 90°$ $= 0$	$VI \sin \phi$ $= VI \sin 90°$ $= VI$ (lag)	$S = \sqrt{P^2 + Q^2}$ $= VI$
C	$VI \cos \phi$ $= VI \cos(90°)$ $= 0$	$VI \sin \phi$ $= VI \sin(90°)$ $= VI$ (lead)	$S = \sqrt{P^2 + Q^2}$ $= VI$
R-L circuit	$VI \cos \phi$ $[0° < \phi < 90°]$	$VI \sin \phi$ $[0° < \phi < 90°]$	$S = \sqrt{P^2 + Q^2}$ $= VI$
R-C circuit	$VI \cos \phi$ $[0° < \phi < 90°]$	$VI \sin \phi$ $[0° < \phi < 90°]$	$S = \sqrt{P^2 + Q^2}$ $= VI$

3.15 POWER TRIANGLE

It is the geometrical representation of the apparent power, average power and reactive power. In an inductive load the V-I phasors are shown in Fig. 3.16(a) while the real reactive components of the current are shown in Fig. 3.16(b). Fig. 3.16(c) then represents the power triangle for the inductive load.

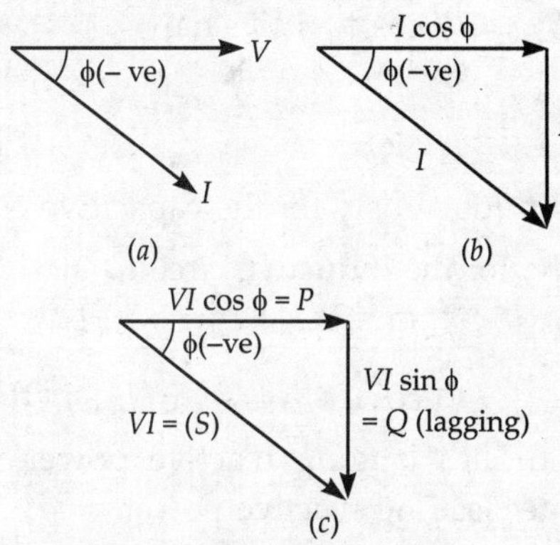

Fig. 3.16 Development of concept of power triangle for inductive load.

Similarly, for the capacitive circuit, the phasors and the power triangle are also shown in Fig. 3.17.

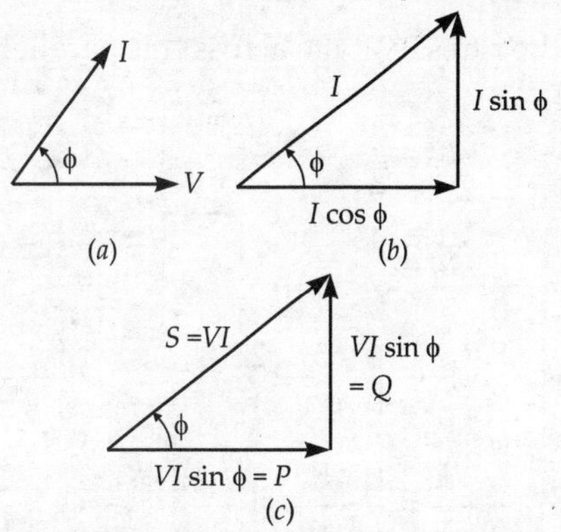

Fig. 3.17 Development power triangle for capacitive load.

CHAPTER 3

Also, $P = VI \cos \phi = (IZ)\,I \cdot \dfrac{R}{Z} = I^2 R$ and $Q = VI \sin \phi = (IZ)\,I \dfrac{X}{Z} = I^2 X.$

It may be observed that P is always + ve for any values of V and I till $0 < \phi < 90°$. Thus even if V and I are a.c. quantities, P, the real power in R, R-L or R-C circuit is always positive. On the other hand, it is also true that I^2R is the power loss in the resistor (Joule's law) and for any value of I, the magnitude of I^2R must be positive. However, Q may be either + ve or – ve depending on whether X is positive or negative. It may be noted that for the inductive circuit, X is equivalent to $(j\,X_L)$; on the other hand, for capacitor circuit, X is equivalent to $(-\,j\,X_C)$ making the sign of Q to be negative. Thus, the reactive power of inductance is positive while that of capacitance is negative. We thus say that an inductance absorbs reactive power while a capacitance injects reactive power. Again, for a pure inductance or a pure capacitance, θ being 90°, $P = 0$ and thus a pure inductance or a pure capacitance does not consume any real power. In inductance, reactive power is utilized to develop the flux while in the capacitance, the reactive power's function is to store the charge. The total power S is the vector sum of P and Q $(= P \pm jQ = \sqrt{P^2 + Q^2} \angle \tan^{-1} \dfrac{\pm Q}{P})$

3.16 COMPLEX POWER

The three sides (S, P, Q) of a power triangle are shown in Figs. 3.16 and 3.17. Complex power(s) can be obtained from the product VI^*. *Complex power* (Frequently denoted by S) is given by

$$VI^* = Ve^{j\theta} \cdot Ie^{-j(\theta+\phi)} = VI e^{-j\phi}$$

$$\because \quad V = Ve^{j\theta} \text{ and } I = Ie^{j(\theta+\phi)}$$

$$\therefore \quad VI^* = VI\cos\phi - j\,VI\sin\phi$$

$$= P - jQ$$

or $$S = P - jQ \qquad ...(3.57)$$

(obviously for the capacitive circuit)

Similarly, for the inductive circuit,

$$VI^* = Ve^{j\theta} \cdot Ie^{-j(\theta-\phi)} = VI e^{j\phi}$$

$$= VI\cos\phi + jVI\sin\phi = P + j\,Q(=S)$$

$(+Q)$ indicates lagging reactive power while $(-Q)$ indicates leading reactive power.

Example 3.25 *An impedance of $(3 + j4)\,\Omega$ is connected in parallel with a resistance of $10\,\Omega$. Find the ratio of power loss in these parallel circuits.*

Solution. Let $Z_1 = 3 + j4 = 5\angle 53°\,\Omega$

and $Z_2 = 10\,\Omega$

Let the r.m.s. voltage across this parallel combination be V.

$$\therefore \quad I_1 = \frac{V}{Z_1} = \frac{V}{5\angle 53°}$$

and $$I_2 = \frac{V}{Z_2} = \frac{V}{10}\,\Omega$$

Thus, $$\frac{|I_1|}{|I_2|} = \frac{V/5}{V/10} = \frac{2}{1}.$$

$$\therefore \quad \frac{P_1}{P_2} = \frac{I_1^2 R_1}{I_2^2 R_2} = \left(\frac{I_1}{I_2}\right)^2 \frac{R_1}{R_2} = 4 \times \frac{3}{10} = \frac{6}{5}.$$

i.e., The ratio of power loss = **6/5**.

Example 3.26 *A $\frac{1}{5}$ HP induction motor runs at an efficiency of 85%. If the operating p.f. is 0.8 lag, find the reactive power taken by the motor.*

Solution. $\frac{1}{5}$ HP $= \frac{746}{5} = 149.2$ W

$$P_{input} = \frac{P_{out}}{\eta} \quad [\eta = \text{efficiency}]$$

$$= \frac{149.2}{0.85} = 175.53 \text{ W}$$

However,

$$\text{p.f.} = 0.8 = \cos\phi$$

$$\therefore \quad \sin\phi = 0.6.$$

Then $$Q = VI\sin\phi = \frac{P_{input}}{\cos\phi} \times \sin\phi$$

$$= \frac{149.2}{0.85} \times \frac{1}{0.8} \times 0.6 = 131.65 \text{ VAR}.$$

$\therefore$ Reactive power taken = **131.65 VAR**.

Example 3.27 *On a power destruction system, three loads run in parallel.*

Load A : 100 VA, 0.5 pf (lag)

Load B : 150 W, 0.8 pf (lead)

Load C : 200 VA, 100 VAR (lag)

Find the net power position.

Solution.

For load A,

$$S_A = 100 \text{ VA}, \cos\phi = 0.5$$

$$\therefore \quad P_A = S_A \times \text{p.f.} = 100 \times 0.5 = 50 \text{ W}$$

Also, $\sin\phi = 0.866$

$$\therefore \quad Q_A = 100 \times 0.866 = \mathbf{86.6\ VAR}$$

For load B,

$$P_B = 150 \text{ W}, \cos\phi = 0.8 \text{ (lead)}$$

$$\therefore \quad \sin\phi = 0.6$$

$$S_B = \frac{P_B}{\cos\phi} = \frac{150}{0.8} = 187.5 \text{ VA}$$

$$Q_B = -S_B \sin\phi$$

[– ve sign is due to leading p.f.]

$$= -187.5 \times 0.6 = \mathbf{-112.5\ VAR}$$

For load C,

$$S_C = 200 \text{ VA}; \quad Q_C = 100 \text{ VAR}$$

$$\sin\phi = \frac{Q_C}{S_C} = \frac{100}{200} = 0.5$$

$$\therefore \quad \phi = 30° \text{ and } \cos\phi = 0.866 \text{ (lag)}.$$

$$\therefore \quad P_C = S_C \times \text{p.f.} = 200 \times 0.866 = 173.2 \text{ W}$$

Hence,

$$\text{Net } P = P_A + P_B + P_C$$

$$= 50 + 150 + 173.2 = \mathbf{373.2\ W}$$

$$\text{Net } Q = Q_A + Q_B + Q_C$$

$$= 86.6 - 112.5 + 100 = \mathbf{74.1\ VAR}$$

$$\text{Net } S = \sqrt{P^2 + Q^2} = \mathbf{380.46\ VA}.$$

EXAMPLE 3.28 *Two parallel branches Z_1 and Z_2 take the currents I_1 and I_2 as follows :*

$$I_1 = 3.15\ \angle 68°\ A;\ I_2 = 12\ \angle{-45°}\ A$$

Find the complex power drawn from the supply if the supply voltage is $17\angle 0°$ V.

SOLUTION. $I_1 = 3.15\ \angle 68°\ \text{A}\ ;\ I_2 = 12\ \angle{-45°}\ \text{A}$

$\therefore\ I = I_1 + I_2$ (vectorial addition)

$$= 3.15\ \angle 68° + 12\ \angle{-45°} = 11.1\ \angle{-29.8°}\ \text{A}.$$

Thus the complex power

$$S = VI^* = 17\angle 0° \times 11.1\angle{+29.8°}$$

$$= 189\ \angle 29.8° = (164 + j\,94)\ \text{VA}.$$

i.e., the complex power = **164 (W) + *j* 94 (VAR).**

EXAMPLE 3.29 *The current in a circuit lag the voltage by 30°. If the input power be 400 W and the supply voltage be $v = 100 \sin (377\,t + 10°)$, find the complex power.*

SOLUTION. Given that

$$\phi = 30°\ \text{lag},\quad \cos\phi = \cos 30° = 0.866\ \text{lag}$$

$$\therefore\quad I = \frac{\text{Power}}{V\cos\phi} = \frac{400}{\frac{100}{\sqrt{2}} \times 0.866}$$

$$= 6.53\ \text{A at}\ \angle{-30°}.$$

Again S (complex power)

$$= VI^* = \frac{100}{\sqrt{2}} \times 6.53\ \angle{+30°}$$

$$= 461.74\,(\cos 30° + j\sin 30°)$$

$$= \mathbf{10\,(40 + j\,23.1)\ VA}.$$

EXAMPLE 3.30 *The voltages across two series connected circuit elements are :*

$$v_1 = 100 \sin\omega t\ V \text{ and } v_2 = 50 \sin(\omega t - 30°)\ V.$$

If the circuit current is (4 + j2) A, find the complex power of the circuit.

SOLUTION. $V_1 = \frac{100}{\sqrt{2}} \sin\omega t \equiv \frac{100}{\sqrt{2}} \angle 0°$

$$= (70.72 + j\,0)\ \text{V}$$

$$V_2 = \frac{50}{\sqrt{2}} \angle{-30°}$$

$$= 35.36\,(\cos 30° - j\sin 30°)$$

$$= (30.62 - j\,17.68)\ \text{V}$$

Net voltage

$$= (70.72) + (30.62 - j\,17.68)$$

$$= (101.34 - j\,17.68)\ \text{V}.$$

$$= 102.87\ \angle{-9.9°}\ \text{V}.$$

The current being $(4 + j2)$ A *i.e.*, $4.47\ \angle 26.565°$ A, the complex power is given by

$$S = 102.87\ \angle{-9.9°} \times 4.47\ \angle{-26.565°}$$

$$= 459.8°\ \angle{-36.46°}\ \text{VA}$$

$$\simeq \mathbf{(370 - j\,273)\ VA}.$$

EXAMPLE 3.31 *A 10 kW single phase motor is supplied by an a.c. source of 50 Hz. If the terminal voltage of the motor is $230\angle 0°$ volts, the p.f. of the motor be 0.5 lag, the interconnecting cable of the voltage source and the motor be having 0.1 Ω resistance, find the source power.*

SOLUTION.

$$I_{\text{source}} = \frac{\text{Active power}}{\text{Voltage} \times \text{P.f.}} = \frac{10 \times 10^3}{230 \times 0.5} = 87\ \text{A}.$$

It may be noticed here that the terminal voltage at the motor being 230 V, the drop of voltage in the cable connecting the source and motor would be $(87\ \text{A} \times 0.1\,\Omega)$ *i.e.*, 8.7 V at angle $(\cos^{-1} 0.5)$ *i.e.*, 60°.

$\therefore$ Supply voltage

$$= \text{Vector sum of}\left(\begin{array}{c}\text{terminal voltage}\\ \text{of motor}\end{array} + \begin{array}{c}\text{drop in}\\ \text{cable}\end{array}\right)$$

$$= 230\ \angle 0° + 8.7\ \angle{-60°}$$

$$= 237.65\ \angle{-1.8°}\ \text{V}$$

Thus the source power is given by $VI \cos\theta$

$$= 237.65 \times 87 \times \cos(60 - 1.8°)$$

$$= 10895\ \text{W}$$

Thus P_{source} = **10.895 kW.**

EXAMPLE 3.32 *In the network of Fig. E3.7, find the power delivered by the source.*

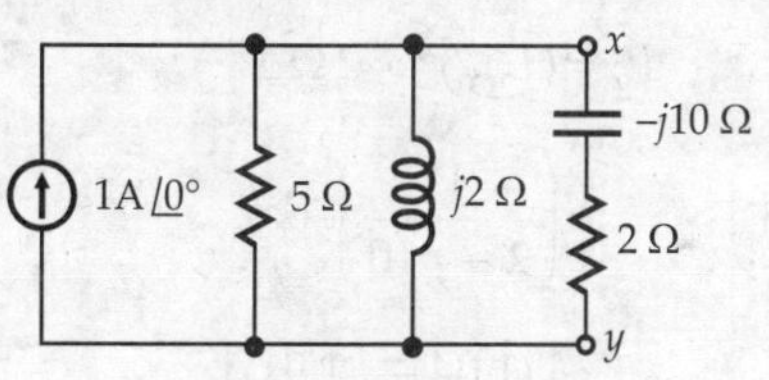

Fig. E3.7

SOLUTION. Using nodal analysis at node "x" (also assuming the voltage at "x" to be V),

$$\frac{V}{5} + \frac{V}{j\,.2} + \frac{V}{2 - j\,10} = 1 + j\,0$$

or $$\frac{V}{5} - j\frac{2V}{2^2} + \frac{V\,(2 + j\,10)}{2^2 + 10^2} = 1$$

or $$\frac{V}{5} - j\frac{V}{2} + \frac{V}{52} + j\frac{5V}{52} = 1$$

or $(0.2 + 0.0192)\,V + j\,V(-0.5 + 0.096) = 1$

or, $(0.2192 - j\,0.404)\,V = 1$

$$\therefore \quad V = \frac{1}{0.2192 - j\,0.404}$$

$$= 2.176 \angle 61.52°\text{ Volt}$$

$\therefore \quad |V|(\equiv V_{x-y}) = 2.176$ V,

the supply current being 1 A.

The current being the reference phasor in this problem, the obtained voltage leads the current by 61.52° (this makes the whole circuit inductive).

$\therefore$ Active Power supplied (P)

$$= V\,.\,I\cos\phi$$

$$= 2.176 \times 1 \times \cos 61.52° = \mathbf{1.04\ W}.$$

Reactive Power supplied (Q)

$$= VI\sin\phi$$

$$= 2.176 \times 1 \times \sin 61.52° = \mathbf{1.913\ W}.$$

Total Power

$$= \sqrt{P^2 + Q^2} = \mathbf{2.177\ VA.}$$

EXAMPLE 3.33 *How much real power is dissipated in the 5 Ω and 2 Ω resistors of Example 3.32 ?*

SOLUTION. Power dissipated in the 5 Ω resistor

$$P_5 = (I_{5\Omega}^2 \times 5\Omega) = \left(\frac{V}{5}\right)^2 \times 5$$

$$= \left(\frac{2.176}{5}\right)^2 \times 5 = \mathbf{0.947\ W}$$

Power dissipated in the 2 Ω resistor

$$P_2 = (I_{2\Omega})^2 \times 2\Omega$$

$$= \left(\frac{V}{2 - j\,10}\right)^2 \times 2$$

$$= \left|\frac{(1.04 - j\,1.91)}{2 - j\,10}\right|^2 \times 2 = \mathbf{0.09\ W.}$$

Check

> Net power is thus $P_5 + P_2 = 0.947 + 0.09 = 1.037$ W. The minor difference between the obtained result of net power values in Ex. 3.32 and in Ex. 3.33 is due to tolerances in calculation.

EXAMPLE 3.34 *In an a.c. circuit, $v = 100\sin(\omega t + 30°)$ V, $i = 5\sin(\omega t - 30°)$ A. Find apparent power and reactive power.*

SOLUTION. $V_{r.m.s.} = \dfrac{100}{\sqrt{2}} = 70.72$ V

$$I_{r.m.s.} = \frac{5}{\sqrt{2}} = 3.54\text{ A}$$

$\therefore$ Apparent power $= (70.72 \times 3.54) \simeq$ **250 VA.**

Reactive power (Q) $= VI\sin\phi$

But, $\phi = 30° - (-30°) = 60°$

$\therefore \quad Q = 70.72 \times 3.54 \times \sin 60° = 217$ VAR

i.e., Reactive power = **217 VAR.**

EXAMPLE 3.35 *Two impedances Z_1 and Z_2 are connected in parallel. The current through Z_1 is I_1 having instantaneous expression as $3\sin(\omega t - 60°)$ A, while the line current I_L is having instantaneous expression as $10\sin(\omega t + 90°)$ A. Find the current through Z_2 and obtain the value of complex power if the voltage across the parallel combination is $100\angle 0°$ V.*

SOLUTION. $I_1 = \dfrac{3}{\sqrt{2}}\angle -60° = 1.06 - j\,1.832$ A

$$I_L = \frac{10}{\sqrt{2}}\angle +90° = 0 + j\,7.07\text{ A}$$

$\therefore \quad I_2 = I_L - I_1$ (vector difference)

$$= j\,7.07 - 1.06 + j\,1.832$$

$$= (-1.06 + j\,8.904)\text{ A}$$

i.e., $\quad |\boldsymbol{I_2}| = \mathbf{8.97 \angle 96.79°\ A.}$

Thus $\quad S_2$ = Complex power in Z_2

$$= 100\angle 0° \times 8.97\angle -96.79°$$

$$= 897\angle -96.79°$$

$$= \mathbf{(-106.2 + j\,890.7)\ VA.}$$

EXAMPLE 3.36 *Two parallel impedances draw currents I_1 and I_2 when $I_1 = 40\angle 20°$ A, $I_2 = 30\angle -65°$ A. If the supply voltage be $100\angle 0°$ V, obtain the values of line current and power factor. What is the input power ?*

SOLUTION. I, the line current

$= I_1 + I_2$ (vectorial sum)

$$= 40\angle 20° + 30\angle -65°$$

$$= 40(\cos 20° + j\sin 20°) + 30(\cos 65° - j\sin 65°)$$

$$= 37.6 + j\,13.68 + 12.68 - j\,27.19$$

$$= (50.28 - j\,13.51)\text{ A.}$$

$$\therefore \quad |I| = \sqrt{50.28^2 + 13.51^2} = 52\text{ A}$$

i.e., $\quad I_{line} = \mathbf{52\ A}$

and $\quad \tan\phi = -\dfrac{13.51}{50.28} = -0.27$

Thus $\cos\phi = \cos(\tan^{-1} 0.27) = 0.965$ (lag)

$\therefore$ **p. f. = 0.965 lag**

The input power is

$$P = VI\cos\phi = 100 \times 52 \times \cos(\tan^{-1}\phi)$$
$$= 5018 \text{ W}$$

i.e, Input power = **5.018 kW.**

EXAMPLE 3.37 *A 10 Ω is in series with a 2Ω capacitive reactance and the combination is connected across a 5Ω resistor. If the input current to this combination is 10∠0° A, find the power factor of the circuit.*

SOLUTION. $Z_1 = (10 - j2)\,\Omega$ and $Z_2 = 5\,\Omega$.

Z_1 is in parallel to Z_2.

$$\therefore Z_{\text{equiv.}} = \frac{Z_1 Z_2}{Z_1 + Z_2} = \frac{5(10 - j2)}{10 - j2 + 5} = \frac{50 - j10}{15 - j2}$$
$$= \frac{(50 - j10)(15 + j2)}{229}$$
$$= \frac{750 + j100 - j150 + 20}{229}$$
$$= \frac{770}{229} - j\frac{50}{229} = (3.36 - j0.218)\,\Omega$$
$$= 3.37\,\angle -3.72°\,\Omega.$$

The power factor of the circuit is thus

cos 3.37° (lead) *i.e.,* **0.998 lead.**

EXAMPLE 3.38 *An impedance of $Z_1 = (2 + j3)\,\Omega$ is connected in parallel with another impedance $Z_2 = (1 - j2)\,\Omega$. If the input reactive power is 100 VAR (lag), what is the total active power ?*

SOLUTION. $Y = Y_1 + Y_2$

$$= \frac{1}{2 + j3} + \frac{1}{1 - j2} = \frac{2 - j3}{13} + \frac{1 + j2}{5}$$
$$= (0.154 - j0.231) + 0.2 + j0.4$$
$$= (0.354 + j0.169) \text{ mho} = 0.392\,\angle 25.5° \text{ mho}.$$

Then real power $P = 100 \cot 25.5° \simeq$ **210 W.**

$[\because Q = P\tan\phi \;\; \therefore P = Q\cot\phi]$.

EXAMPLE 3.39 *Find the amount of reactive power drawn by the circuit shown in Fig. E3.8.*

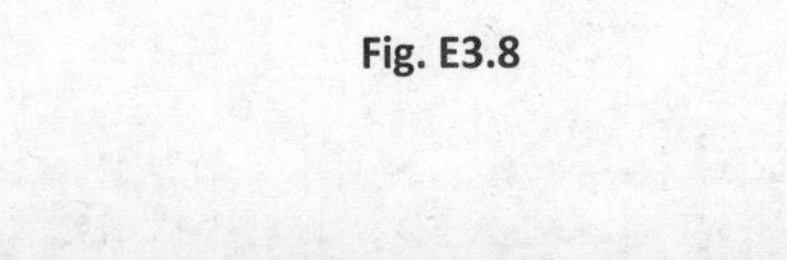

Fig. E3.8

SOLUTION.

$$Y_{a-b} = \frac{1}{2} + \frac{1}{j5} + \frac{1}{-j1} = 0.5 - j0.2 + j1$$
$$= (0.5 + j0.8) \text{ mho}.$$
$$\therefore Z_{ab} = \frac{(0.5 - j0.8)}{(0.5)^2 + (0.8)^2}\,\Omega \qquad \left[\because Z_{ab} = \frac{1}{Y_{ab}}\right]$$
$$= (0.56 - j0.899)\,\Omega$$

Thus $Z_{c-d} = (2 + j1) + (0.56 - j0.899)$

$$= (2.56 + j0.101)\,\Omega$$
$$\therefore I = \frac{V}{Z_{c-d}} = \frac{100\,\angle 0°}{2.56 + j0.101} = \frac{100\,\angle 0°}{2.56\,\angle 2.26°}$$
$$= 39\,\angle -2.26° \text{ A}$$

[*i.e.,* current is lagging the voltage by 2.26°]

This gives Q (reactive power) = $VI\sin\phi$

$$= 100 \times 39 \times \sin 2.26°$$
$$= 3900 \times 0.04 = \textbf{153.79 VAR.}$$

[The reactive power is inductive]

EXAMPLE 3.40 *How much energy is consumed during one cycle by an impedance of $(2 + j4)\,\Omega$ when connected against a 12 V 50 Hz source ?*

SOLUTION. As $V = 12\,\angle 0°$, $Z = (2 + j4)\,\Omega$,

$$\therefore I = \frac{V}{Z} = \frac{12\,\angle 0°}{(2 + j4)} = \frac{12\,\angle 0°}{4.47\,\angle 63.44°}$$
$$= 2.68\,\angle -63.44° \text{ A}$$

$\therefore$ Power consumed by the impedance

$$P = 12 \times 2.68 \cos 63.44 = 14.38 \text{ W}$$

Energy consumed in one cycle (0.02 sec)

$$\left[\because T = \frac{1}{f} = \frac{1}{50} = 0.02 \text{ s}\right]$$
$$= (14.38 \text{ Joule/sec})(0.02) \text{ sec} = \textbf{0.29 J.}$$

EXAMPLE 3.41 *A two element series circuit draws 100 W power and 5 A current from a 50 Hz 100 V source. Obtain the values of the series elements.*

SOLUTION. $Z = \dfrac{V}{I} = \dfrac{100}{5} = 20\,\Omega$

and $\cos\phi = \dfrac{P}{VI} = \dfrac{100}{100 \times 20} = 0.05$

As $\cos\phi = 0.05 \quad \therefore \cos^{-1} 0.05 \simeq \pm 87°$.

Hence $Z = 20\,[\cos 87° \pm j\sin 87°]$

$$= (1 \pm j19.97)\,\Omega$$

CHAPTER 3

This means that the series elements are resistance in series with either inductive reactance or capacitive reactance. Obviously,

$$R = 1\,\Omega$$

$$X_L = j\,19.97\,\Omega \qquad \left[L = \frac{19.97}{2\pi \times 50} = \mathbf{0.0635\ H}\right]$$

or $\quad X_C = -j\,19.97\,\Omega$

$$\left[C = \frac{1}{2\pi \times 50 \times 19.97} = \mathbf{1.59 \times 10^{-4}\ F}\right].$$

EXAMPLE 3.42 *Find the real power delivered by the source in Fig. E3.9.*

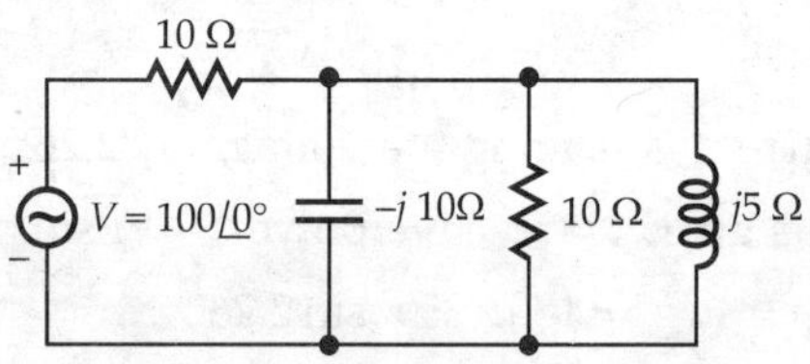

Fig. E3.9

SOLUTION. Here the admittance of each branch is to be calculated first.

$$Y_1 = \frac{1}{-j\,10} = +j\,0.1\text{ mho}$$

$$Y_2 = \frac{1}{10} = 0.1\text{ mho}$$

$$Y_3 = \frac{1}{j\,5} = -j\,0.2\text{ mho}$$

∴ The impedance seen by the voltage source is

$$Z_1 = 10 + \frac{1}{Y_1 + Y_2 + Y_3} = 10 + \frac{1}{j\,0.1 + 0.1 - j\,0.2}$$

$$= 10 + \frac{1}{0.1 - j\,0.1} = 10 + 5 + j\,5$$

$$= 15.8\angle 18.43°\,\Omega \qquad [Z_i \text{ is inductive circuit}]$$

$$\therefore \quad I_{source} = \frac{V_{source}}{Z_i} = \frac{100\,\angle 0°\,(\text{r.m.s.})}{15.8\,\angle -18.43°}$$

$$= 6.32\,\angle -18.43°$$

$$P = V_S\,I_S \cos\phi = 100 \times 6.32 \times \cos 18.43°$$

$$= 599.60\text{ W}$$

$$\therefore \quad P = \mathbf{599.60\ W.}$$

EXAMPLE 3.43 *The inductive reactance in series with Z in the circuit of Fig. E3.10 has a value of 25 Ω. If the voltage drop across Z is 179 volts, the power dissipated in the circuit is 320 W. Find (a) the p.f. of circuit (b) circuit resistance (c) find the inductive part of Z. (d) what is the value of net reactive power drain ?*

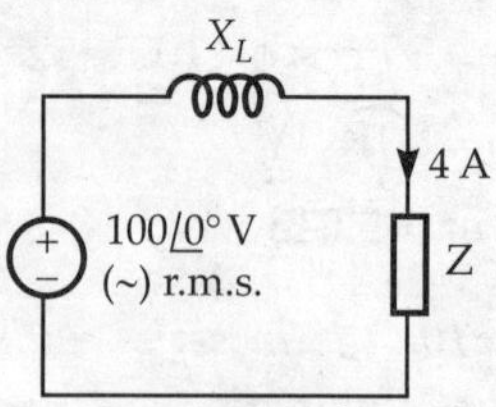

Fig. E3.10

SOLUTION. $\text{p.f.} = \frac{\text{Active power}}{\text{VA power}} = \frac{320}{4 \times 100} = 0.8$

i.e. p.f. of the circuit = **0.8**

Circuit resistance

$$R = \frac{\text{Active power}}{(\text{Current})^2} = \frac{320}{4^2} = 20\,\Omega$$

i.e., circuit resistance = **20 Ω**

However,

$$IZ = 179$$

$$\therefore \quad |Z| = \frac{179}{4} = 44.75\,\Omega$$

However, the resistive part of the impedance = 20 Ω

i.e., $\quad |20 + j\,x_l| = 44.75$

or, $\quad \sqrt{20^2 + x_l^2} = 44.75\,\Omega$

$$\therefore \quad x_l = \mathbf{40\ \Omega}$$

(x_l is the inductive part of Z)

i.e., inductive part of $Z = \mathbf{40\ \Omega}$

Net reactive power drain

$$= I^2\,(X_L + x_l) = 4^2\,(25 + 40)$$

$$= 1040\text{ VAR}$$

i.e., $\quad$ net Q_{ind} = **1040 VAR**

EXAMPLE 3.44 *Find the power dissipated in the circuit shown in Fig. E3.11.*

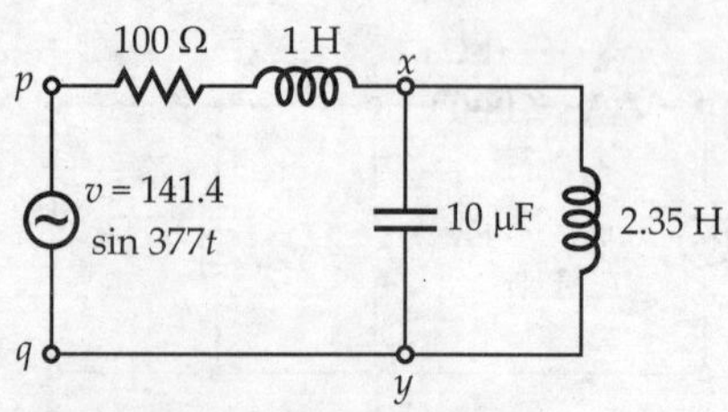

Fig. E3.11

Solution. The net impedance between x-y terminals (Fig. E3.11) is

$$Z_{xy} = \frac{j\omega L\left(\frac{1}{j\omega C}\right)}{j\omega L + \frac{1}{j\omega C}} = \frac{\frac{L}{C}}{j\left(\omega L - \frac{1}{\omega C}\right)}$$

$$= \frac{\frac{2.35}{10 \times 10^{-6}}}{j\left(377 \times 2.35 - \frac{1}{377 \times 10 \times 10^{-6}}\right)}$$

$$= -377\, j\, \Omega$$

It may be observed that Z_{x-y} is purely capacitive.

The source current $= I = \frac{(141.4)/\sqrt{2}}{Z_{pq}}$

But $Z_{pq} = (100 + j\,377) - j\,377$

$= 100\,\Omega$ (purely resistive)

Thus $I = \frac{100}{100} = 1$ A (purely resistive)

The power factor is evidently unity.

The power dissipated

$= I^2 \times R = 1^2 \times 100 = 100$ W.

$\therefore$ P_{loss} **= 100 W.**

Example 3.45 *A voltage $v(t) = 150 \sin 10^3\, t$ is applied a series RLC circuit where, $R = 40\,\Omega$, $L = 0.13$ H, $C = 10\,\mu F$.*

Find (i) the power supplied by the source

(ii) the reactive power supplied by the source

(iii) the reactive power of the capacitor

(iv) the reactive power of the inductor

(v) the power factor of the circuit.

Solution. $I = \frac{V}{Z} = \frac{\left(\frac{150}{\sqrt{2}}\right)}{50\,\angle 36.82°}$

$$\left[\because Z = R + j(X_L - X_C) = R + j\left(\omega L - \frac{1}{\omega C}\right) = 40 + j\,(130 - 100) = 50\,\angle 36.82°\right]$$

$= 2.12\,\angle -36.82°$ A

$\therefore$ P = real power supplied

$= VI \cos\phi = \left(\frac{150}{\sqrt{2}}\right)(2.12) \cos 36.82° = 180$ W.

[Also $P = I^2 R = 2.12^2 \times 40 = 180$ W]

i.e., the power supplied by the source = **180 W**

The reactive power supplied by the source

$= VI \sin\phi = \frac{150}{\sqrt{2}} \times 2.12 \times \sin 36.82°$

$= 135$ VAR (lag)

i.e., reactive power supplied = **135 VAR**

The reactive power of the capacitor

$= I^2 X_C = 2.12^2 \times \frac{1}{\omega C} = 2.12^2 \times \frac{1}{10^{-2}}$

i.e., reactive power supplied to the capacitor

= **450 VAR**

(Truly speaking, the capacitor supplies reactive power)

Similarly, the reactive power supplied to the inductor

$= I^2 X_L = 2.12^2 \times 130$

i.e., reactive power of the inductor = **585 VAR**

(inductor absorbs reactive power)

The power factor of the circuit is

$\cos\phi = \cos 36.82° = 0.8$ (lag)

P.F. = **0.8 lag.**

Example 3.46 *With reference to Fig. E3.12, find the power consumed in the 5 Ω resistor when*

$I_1 = (0.8 + j\,0.2)$ A and $I_2 = -(1 - j\,0.5)$ A.

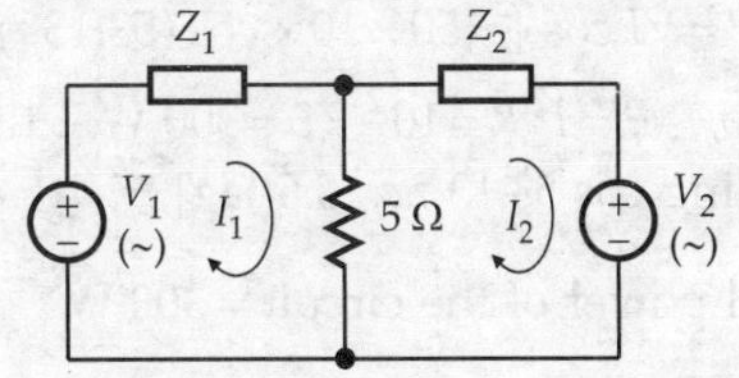

Fig. E3.12

Solution. Power dissipated in $5\,\Omega$ resistor is given by

$$P_{5\Omega} = Re\,\{(I_1 - I_2)^2\}\,5$$
$$= Re\,[(0.8 + j\,0.2 + 1 - j\,0.5)^2 \times 5]$$
$$= Re\,[(1.8 - j\,0.3)^2\, 5]$$
$$= Re\,[15.75 - j\,5.4] = \mathbf{15.75\ W.}$$

Example 3.47 *A current is given by $3 \angle -120°$ A through an impedance of $(1 + j\,2)\,\Omega$. Find the complex power.*

Solution. Complex power $(S) = VI^* = (ZI)\,I^*$

$$= I^2\,Z$$

[it may be recalled that product of I and I^* is I^2]

$$= 3^2\,(1 + j2) = \mathbf{(9 + j\,18)\ VA}$$

[This is an inductive circuit with real power demand of 9 W and reactive demand of 18 VAR]

Example 3.48 *In the circuit of Fig. E3.13, find the total power of the circuit.*

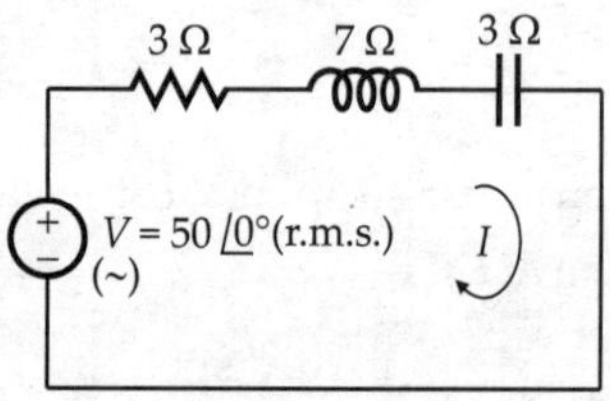

Fig. E3.13

Solution. The total impedance of the circuit is given by

$$Z_{net} = 3 + j\,7 + (-\,j\,3) = (3 + j\,4)\,\Omega$$

$$= 5 \angle 53.13°\,\Omega$$

$$\therefore \quad I = \frac{50 \angle 0°}{5 \angle 53.13°} \left(i.e., \frac{V}{Z}\right)$$

$$= 10 \angle -53.13°\ \text{A}$$

[$\angle$ of Z is +ve while $\angle$ of I is –ve. It gives us that the net circuit effect is inductive]

The total power is then

$$P = VI \cos\phi = 50 \times 10 \times \cos(53.13°) = \mathbf{300\ W}$$

[Also, $P = I^2 R = 10^2 \times 3 = 300$ W, the power factor being cos 53.13 *i.e.*, **0.6 lag**]

Total power of the circuit = **300 W.**

Example 3.49 *Find the average power consumed by the circuit in Fig. E3.14.*

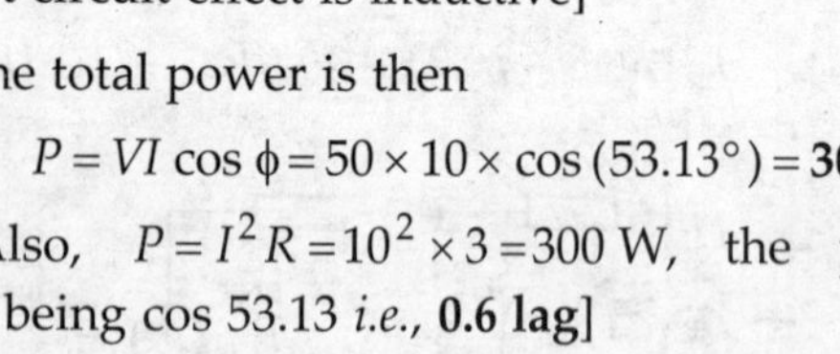

Fig. E3.14

Solution. $Y_1 = \dfrac{1}{3.33 \angle 0°} = 0.3 \angle 0°$ mho

$$Y_2 = \frac{1}{2.5} \angle -90° = 0.4 \angle -90°\ \text{mho.}$$

Net admittance

$$Y = Y_1 + Y_2 = 0.3\angle 0° + 0.4\angle -90°$$

$$= (0.3 - j0.4) = 0.5\angle -53.13°\ \text{mho}$$

$\therefore$ Net impedance

$$(Z) = \frac{1}{Y} = \frac{1}{0.5 \angle -53.13°} = 2 \angle 53.13°\,\Omega$$

Thus $\quad I$ = current drawn from input

$$= \frac{V}{Z} = \frac{20 \angle 53.13°}{2 \angle 53.13°} = 10 \angle 0°\ \text{A}$$

The net circuit current is thus resistive.

The total power delivered to the circuit is

$$P = VI \cos\phi$$

[ϕ being the angle between V and I which is in this case is 53.13°]

$$= 20 \times 10 \times \cos 53.13° = 120\ \text{W}$$

Also, it can be seen

$$P = I^2 R = 20^2 \times 0.3 = 120\ \text{W}$$

The average power drawn by the circuit = **120 W.**

Example 3.50 *In the network of Fig. E3.15, $V = 100 \angle 53.13°$ V (r.m.s.); $R = 3.33\,\Omega$; $X_L = 1.43\,\Omega$; $X_C = 3.33\,\Omega$.*

Find the true power consumed by the circuit.

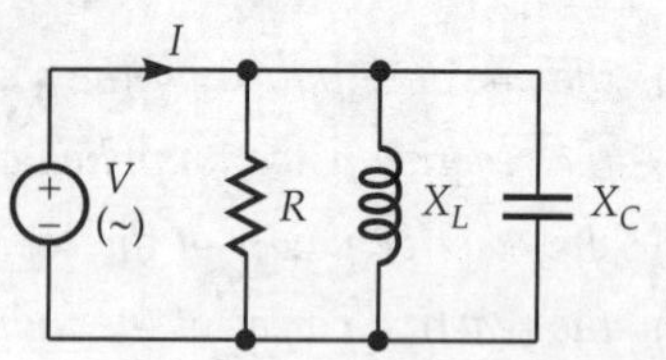

Fig. E3.15

Solution. In Fig. E3.15,

$$Y_1 = \frac{1}{3.33 \angle 0°} = 0.3 \angle 0°\ \text{mho}$$

$$Y_2 = \frac{1}{1.43 \angle 90°} = 0.7 \angle -90°\ \text{mho}$$

$$Y_2 = \frac{1}{3.33 \angle -90°} = 0.3 \angle +90°\ \text{mho}$$

$\therefore$ Y = net admittance

$$= 0.3 \angle 0° + 0.7 \angle -90° + 0.3 \angle +90$$
$$= 0.3 - j\,0.7 + j\,0.3 = 0.3 - j\,0.4$$
$$= 0.5 \angle -53.13° \text{ mho.}$$

$$\therefore Z \text{ (net impedance)} = \frac{1}{Y} = \frac{1}{0.5 \angle -53.13°}$$
$$= 2 \angle 53.13° \,\Omega$$

Thus the input current (I)

$$= \frac{V}{2} = \frac{100 \angle 53.13}{2 \angle 53.13} = 50 \angle 0° \text{ A}$$

[The input circuit current is found to be resistive]

Total power delivered to the circuit is

$$P = VI \cos\phi = 100 \times 50 \times \cos 53.13° = 3000 \text{ W}$$

[Angle between I and V is 53.13°]

$\therefore$ P = **3000 W** (true power)

Also, $\cos\phi = \cos 53.13°$ = **0.6 lag.**

EXAMPLE 3.51 *Find the magnitude of the reactive powers in the inductors in Fig. E3.16.*

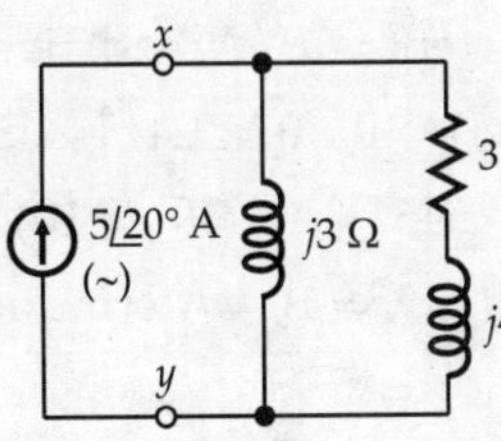

Fig. E3.16

SOLUTION.

$$Z_{x-y} = \frac{j\,3\,(3 + j\,4)}{j\,3 + 3 + j\,4} = \frac{j\,9 - 12}{3 + 7\,j}$$
$$= \frac{15 \angle 143.13°}{7.61 \angle 66.8°} = 1.97 \angle 76.33° \,\Omega$$

$$\therefore \quad V_{xy} = I_{\text{source}} \times Z_{x-y}$$
$$= 5 \angle 20° \text{ A} \times 1.97 \angle 76.33° \,\Omega$$
$$= 9.85 \angle 96.33° \text{ V}$$

Thus $S = V_{x-y}\, I^*_{\text{source}}$

$$= 9.85 \angle 96.33° \times 5 \angle -20°$$
$$= 49.25 \angle 76.33° \text{ VA}$$
$$= (11.63 + j\,47.84) \text{ VA}$$

$\therefore$ The magnitude of the reactive power in the reactors is **47.84 VAR**.

EXAMPLE 3.52 *In the circuit of Fig. E3.17, find the real power loss in Z. Given that*

$$v_1 = 100 \sin(\omega t + 60°)\ V$$
$$v_2 = 50 \sin(\omega t - 45°)\ V,\ Z = 5 \angle 45°\ A.$$

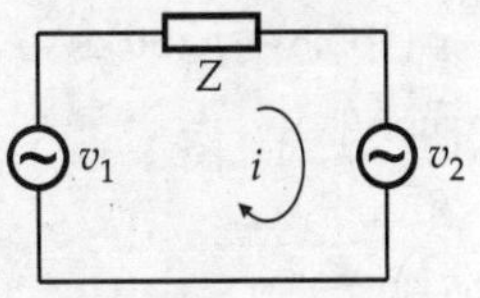

Fig. E3.17

SOLUTION. $v_1 = 100 \sin(\omega t + 60°)$ V

$$\therefore \quad v_1 = \frac{100 \angle 60°}{\sqrt{2}} = 70.72 \text{ V} \angle 60°$$

$$v_2 = 50 \sin(\omega t - 45°) \text{ V}$$

$$\therefore \quad v_2 = \frac{50 \angle -45°}{\sqrt{2}} = 35.36 \text{ V} \angle -45°$$

However,

$$I = \frac{V_1 - V_2}{Z}$$

or

$$Z = \frac{70.72 \angle 60° - 35.36 \angle -45°}{5 \angle 45°}$$
$$= 14.144 \angle 15° - 7.07 \angle -90°$$
$$= 13.66 + j\,3.66 + j\,7.07$$
$$= (13.66 + j\,10.73)\,\Omega$$

$\therefore$ The resistance part of Z is 13.66 Ω and obviously the real power loss in 13.66 Ω = $(5^2 \times 13.66)$ W

i.e., Power loss in Z = **341.5 W.**

EXAMPLE 3.53 *A 100 kVA 0.8 p.f. (lag) load runs in parallel to a 150 kW 0.95 lead power factor load and the combination runs in parallel with 300 kVA, 250 kVAR inductive load. Determine the complex power of the three loads.*

SOLUTION. $S_1 = 100 \angle \cos^{-1} 0.8 = 100 \angle 36.87°$

$$= 100\,(\cos 36.87° + j \sin 36.87°)$$
$$= (80 + j\,60) \text{ kVA.}$$

To obtain S_2 we observe that $S_2 = P_2 - j\,Q_2$, the –ve sign indicates the leading VAR as per the question. However,

$$P_2 = 150 \text{ kW (given)}$$
$$Q_2 = P_2 \tan\phi_2 = P_2 \tan(\cos^{-1}\phi_2)$$
$$= 150 \tan(\cos^{-1} 0.95) = 49.30 \text{ kVAR.}$$

$$\therefore \quad S_2 = (150 - j\,49.30) \text{ kVA}$$

Similarly,

$$S_3 = P_3 + j\,Q_3 \text{ [+ sign with } Q \text{ indicates inductive load]}$$

$$= \sqrt{300^2 - 250^2} + j\,250$$

$$= (165.8 + j\,250)\,\text{kVA}$$

$\therefore$ Net complex power

$$= S_1 + S_2 + S_3$$

$$= 80 + j\,60 + 150 - j\,49.3 + 165.8 + j\,250$$

$$= \mathbf{(395.8 + j\,260.7)\,kVA.}$$

EXAMPLE 3.54 *Find the power supplied by each source (Fig. E3.18).*

SOLUTION. Let the loop currents be I_1 and I_2 as shown in Fig. E3.18.

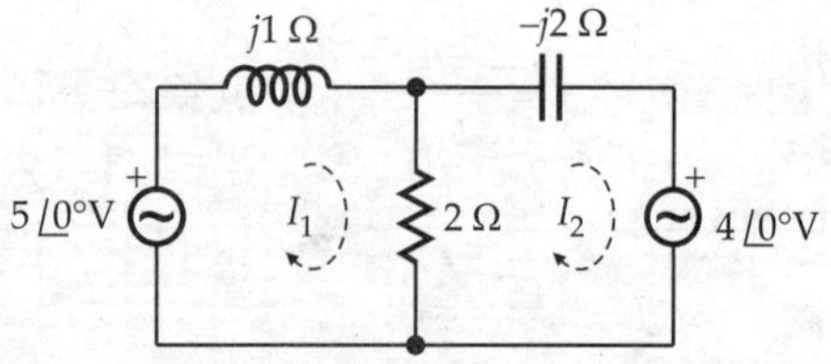

Fig. E3.18

The loop equations give

$$(2 + j1)\,I_1 - 2I_2 = 5\,\angle 0° = 5 + j\,0$$

and $$-2I_1 + (2 - j2)I_2 = -4\,\angle 0° = -4 - j\,0$$

In matrix form,

$$\begin{bmatrix} 2 + j1 & -2 \\ -2 & 2 - j2 \end{bmatrix} \begin{bmatrix} I_1 \\ I_2 \end{bmatrix} = \begin{bmatrix} 5 + j\,0 \\ -4 - j\,0 \end{bmatrix}$$

By Cramer's Rule,

$$I_1 = \frac{\begin{vmatrix} 5 + j\,0 & -2 \\ -4 - j\,0 & 2 - j\,2 \end{vmatrix}}{\begin{vmatrix} 2 + j\,1 & -2 \\ -2 & 2 - j\,2 \end{vmatrix}} = \frac{2 - j\,10}{2 - j\,2}$$

$$= \frac{(2 - j\,10)(2 + j\,2)}{2^2 + 2^2}$$

$$= \frac{24 - j\,16}{8} = 3 - j\,2 = 3.61\,\angle -33.69°\text{ A}$$

and $$I_2 = \frac{\begin{vmatrix} 2 + j\,1 & 5 + j\,0 \\ -2 & -4 - j\,0 \end{vmatrix}}{\begin{vmatrix} 2 + j\,1 & -2 \\ -2 & 2 - j\,2 \end{vmatrix}} = \frac{2 - j\,4}{2 - j\,2}$$

$$= \frac{(2 - j\,4)(2 + j\,2)}{4 + 4} = \frac{12 - j\,4}{8}$$

$$= 1.58\,\angle -18.43°\text{ A}$$

$$\therefore \quad P_1 = V_1\,I_1 \cos\phi_1$$

$$= 5 \times 3.61 \cos 33.69° = 15.02\text{ W}$$

$$P_2 = V_2\,I_2 \cos\phi_2$$

$$= 4 \times 1.58 \cos 18.43° = 6\text{ W}$$

[It may be noted as I_2 enters the source 4 V, hence here the source absorbs power]

$\therefore$ Power supplied by 5 V source = **15.02 W**

Power absorbed by 4 V source = **6 W.**

EXAMPLE 3.55 *Two impedances, $(1 + j1)\,\Omega$ and $(1 - j\,1)\,\Omega$ are connected in parallel across a 10 V source. Find the power supplied by the source.*

SOLUTION. $Z_1 = (1 + j\,1)\,\Omega$; $Z_2 = (1 - j\,1)\,\Omega$.

As $Z_1 \parallel Z_2$

$$\therefore \quad Z = \frac{Z_1\,Z_2}{Z_1 + Z_2} = \frac{(1 + j\,1)(1 - j\,1)}{1 + j\,1 + 1 - j\,1}$$

$$= \frac{1 - j\,1 + j\,1 + 1}{2} = 1\,\Omega$$

$$\therefore \quad I_{\text{source}} = \frac{V_{\text{source}}}{Z} = \frac{10\,\angle 0°}{1\,\angle 0°}\text{ A} = 10\text{ A}$$

[The net current is 10 A, resistive]

$$S_1 = (1 + j\,1) \times 10\,\angle 0° = 1.414\,\angle 45° \times 10\,\angle 0°$$

$$= 14.14\,\angle 45°\text{ VA} = (10 + j\,10)\text{ VA}$$

i.e., $P_1 = \mathbf{10\ W}$; $Q_1 = \mathbf{10\ VAR}$ (inductive)

Similarly,

$$S_2 = (1 - j\,1) \times 10\,\angle 0° = 1.414\,\angle -45° \times 10\,\angle 0°$$

$$= 14.14\,\angle -45° = (10 - j\,10)\text{ VA.}$$

i.e., $P_2 = \mathbf{10\ W}$; $Q_2 = \mathbf{10\ VAR}$ (capacitive).

In this problem since the magnitude of inductance VAR is equal to the magnitude of the capacitive VAR, hence, there would be no net VAR flow from the source and the current is purely resistive. Also, the net power flow is only real power.

EXAMPLE 3.56 *Determine the complex power drawn from the current source in Fig. E3.19.*

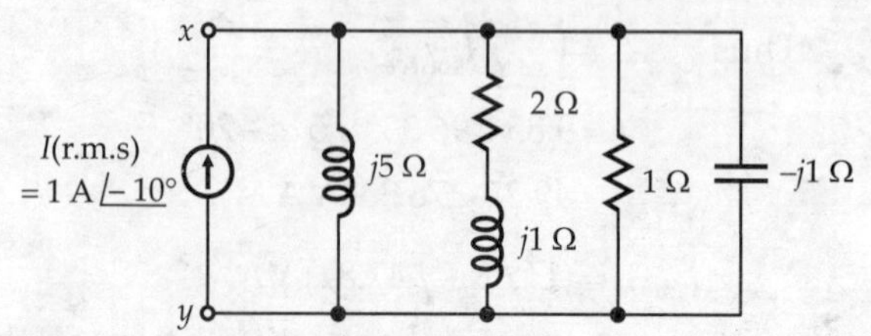

Fig. E3.19

SOLUTION. Let us first obtain the value of input admittance of the circuit at terminal *x-y*

$$\therefore\; Y = Y_1 + Y_2 + Y_3 + Y_4$$

$$= \frac{1}{j5} + \frac{1}{2+j1} + \frac{1}{1} + \frac{1}{-j1}$$

$$= -0.2\,j + \frac{2}{5} - \frac{1}{5}j + 1.j + 1 = \frac{7}{5} + 0.6\,j$$

$$= (1.4 + 0.6\,j)\text{ mho}$$

Once Y, the net admittance at *x-y* is known, we then find Z.

$$Z = \frac{1}{Y} = \frac{1}{1.4 + j\,0.6} = \frac{1.4 - j\,0.66}{(1.4)^2 + (0.6)^2}$$

$$= 0.6 - j\,0.26$$

$$= 0.654\,\angle -23.43°\,\Omega \qquad [\textit{i.e., } Z \text{ is capacitive}]$$

$$\therefore\; V_{x-y} = ZI = 0.654\,\angle -23.43° \times 1\,\angle -10°$$

$$= 0.654\,\angle -33.43°\text{ V}$$

[*i.e.,* voltage lags behind current]

$\therefore$ Complex power drawn is

$$S = V_{x-y}\,I^* = 0.654 \times 1\underline{/-33.43 + 10°}$$

$$= 0.654\,\angle -23.43° = (0.6 - j\,0.26)\text{ VA.}$$

i.e., $\quad S = \mathbf{(0.6 - j\,0.26)\ VA.}$

EXAMPLE 3.57 *A current source is given by $i(t) = 4\sin(\omega t - 10°)$ A and feeds a series R-L circuit of $(1 + j\,2)\,\Omega$. Find the real power supplied by the source.*

SOLUTION. Real power

$$= (I_{r.m.s.})^2 \times R = \left(\frac{4}{\sqrt{2}}\right)^2 \times 1 = \mathbf{8\ W.}$$

EXAMPLE 3.58 *Find the real power loss in the impedance Z (Fig. E3.20).*

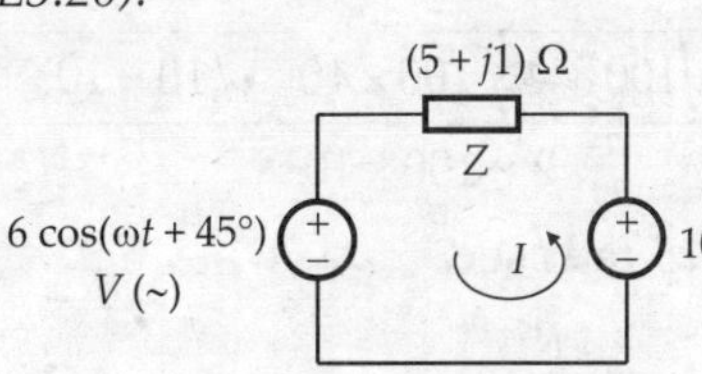

Fig. E3.20

SOLUTION. Let I be the circuit current given by

$$I = \frac{10\,\angle 0° - 6\,\angle +45°}{5 + j1} = \frac{10 - 4.24 - j\,4.24}{5 + j1}$$

$$= \frac{5.76 - j\,4.24}{5 + j1}$$

$$= \frac{7.15\,\angle -36.36'}{5.1\,\angle 11.31°} = 1.4\,\angle -47.67°\text{ A}$$

However, this current is the peak current while the r.m.s. current is $\frac{1.4}{\sqrt{2}} = 0.99$ A.

$\therefore$ Power loss in $Z = (0.99)^2 \times 5 = \mathbf{4.9\ W.}$

EXAMPLE 3.59 *Find the real and reactive power supplied by the voltage source (Fig. E3.21).*

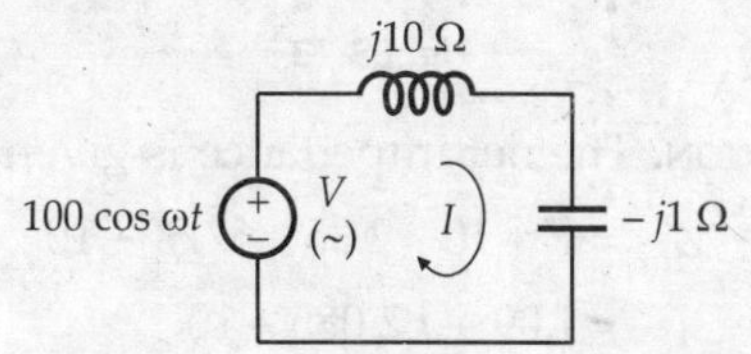

Fig. E3.21

SOLUTION. Let the circuit current be I (Fig. E3.21)

$$\therefore\; I = \frac{100\,\angle 0°}{j10 - j\,1} = \frac{100\,\angle 0°}{j9} = 11.11\,\angle -90°\text{ A}$$

However,

$$I_{\text{r.m.s.}} = 11.11/\sqrt{2} = 7.86\text{ A}$$

Complex power supplied

$$= \frac{100}{\sqrt{2}}\,\angle 0° \times 7.86\,\angle +90°$$

$$= (0 + j\,555.50)\text{ A}$$

$\therefore$ Real power supplied = **0 W;**

Reactive power = **555.5 VAR.**

EXAMPLE 3.60 *What is the power factor of the circuit shown in Fig. E3.22 ? Assume $\omega = 1$ rad / sec.*

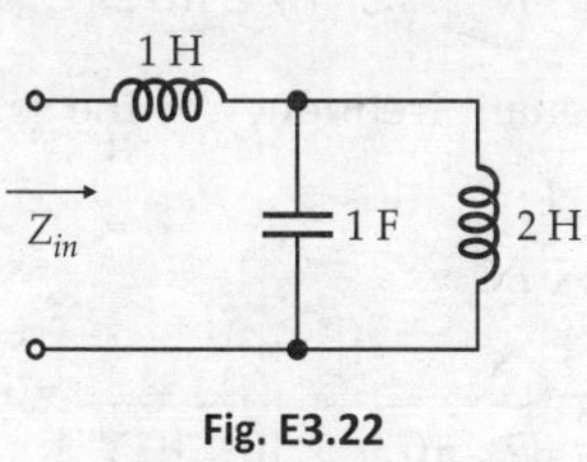

Fig. E3.22

SOLUTION. In Fig. E3.22,

$$Z_{in} = j\omega \times 1 + \frac{\dfrac{1}{j\omega \times 1} \times j\omega 2}{\dfrac{1}{j\omega \times 1} + j\omega \times 2}$$

$$= j\omega + \frac{2}{\dfrac{1}{j\omega} + 2\,j\omega} = j + \frac{2}{-j + 2\,j} = j + \frac{2}{j}$$

$$= j - 2j = -j = 1\,\angle -90°$$

$\therefore$ Power factor of the circuit = **cos 90° = 0**

[This circuit is thus called ZPF circuit]

EXAMPLE 3.61 *In the circuit of Fig. E3.23, if* $Z = 2.35\ \angle 62.5°\ \Omega$, *find the complex power of the source.*

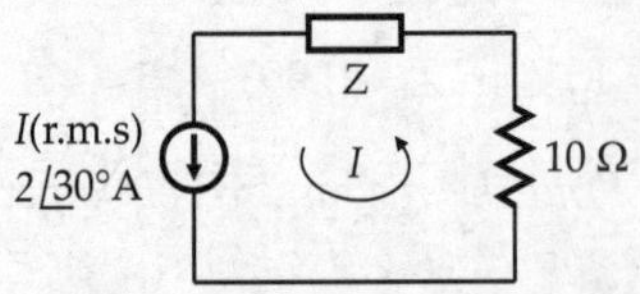

Fig. E3.23

SOLUTION. The net impedance is given by

$$Z_{in} = Z + 10 = 2.35\ \angle 62.5° + 10$$
$$= 1.09 + j\,2.085 + 10$$
$$= 11.09 + j\,2.085 = 11.28\ \angle 10.65°\ \Omega$$

∴ Voltage across the source is then

$$V = Z_{in}\ I = 11.28\ \angle 10.65° \times 2\ \angle 30°$$
$$= 22.57\ \angle 40.65°\ \text{V}$$

∴ Complex power delivered

$$= VI^* = 22.57\ \angle 40.65 \times 2\ \angle -30°$$
$$= 45.14\ \angle 10.65°\ \text{VA}$$
$$= \mathbf{(44.36 + j\,8.34)\ VA}.$$

ADDITIONAL EXAMPLES

EXAMPLE 3.62 *A series RLC circuit has* $R = 2\,\Omega$, $L = 2.0$ *mH,* $C = 10\,\mu$*F. Calculate (i) Q factor of the circuit, (ii) the bandwidth, (iii) the resonant frequency and (iv) the half power frequency* f_1 *and* f_2.

SOLUTION. $R = 2\,\Omega,\ L = 2\text{ mH},\ C = 10\,\mu\text{F}.$

∴ f_0 (resonant frequency of the series circuit)

$$= \frac{1}{2\pi\sqrt{LC}}$$
$$= \frac{1}{2\,\pi\sqrt{2\times10^{-3}\times10\times10^{-6}}} = \mathbf{1126.13\ Hz}.$$

(**Ans.** of (*iii*))

Q factor of the circuit

$$= \frac{\omega_0\,L}{R} = \frac{2\,\pi\times1126.13\times2\times10^{-3}}{2} = \mathbf{7.07}.$$

(**Ans.** of (*i*))

The Bandwidth

$$= f_2 - f_1$$
$$= \frac{R}{2\,\pi\,L} = \frac{2}{2\times3.14\times2\times10^{-3}} = \mathbf{159.23\ Hz}$$

(**Ans.** of (*ii*))

The half power frequencies are given by

$$f_1 = \frac{-R + \sqrt{R^2 + 4\,L/C}}{4\,\pi\,L}$$
$$= \frac{-2 + \sqrt{4 + 4\times2\times10^{-3}/10\times10^{-6}}}{4\pi\times2\times10^{-3}}$$
$$= \mathbf{1049.16\ Hz}$$

$$f_2 = \frac{R + \sqrt{R^2 + 4\,L/C}}{4\,\pi\,L}$$
$$= \frac{2 + \sqrt{4 + 4\times10^{-3}\times2/10\times10^{-6}}}{4\,\pi\times2\times10^{-3}}$$
$$= \mathbf{1208.4\ Hz}.$$

(**Ans.** of (*iv*))

EXAMPLE 3.63 *In a RLC series circuit, the resistance, inductance and capacitance are* $10\,\Omega$, *100 mH and 10 microfarad. Calculate* ω_0, ω_1 *and* ω_2. *Also find BW and selectivity.*

SOLUTION.

$$\omega_0 = \frac{1}{\sqrt{LC}} = \frac{1}{\sqrt{100\times10^{-3}\times10\times10^{-6}}}$$
$$= \mathbf{1000\ rad/sec.}$$

$$\omega_1 = \frac{-R + \sqrt{R^2 + 4\,L/C}}{2\,L}$$
$$= \frac{-10 + \sqrt{100 + 4\times100\times10^{-3}/10\times10^{-6}}}{2\times100\times10^{-3}}$$
$$= \mathbf{951.25\ rad/sec.}$$

$$\omega_2 = \frac{+R + \sqrt{R^2 + 4\,L/C}}{2\,L}$$
$$= \frac{10 + \sqrt{100 + 4\times100\times10^{-3}/10\times10^{-6}}}{2\times100\times10^{-3}}$$
$$= \mathbf{1051.25\ rad/sec.}$$

$$\text{BW} = f_2 - f_1 = \frac{R}{2\,\pi\,L}$$
$$= \frac{10}{2\pi\times100\times10^{-3}} = 15.92\text{ Hz}$$

$$\text{Selectivity} = \frac{1}{Q},$$

But $$Q = \frac{\omega_0\,L}{R} = \frac{1000\times100\times10^{-3}}{10} = 10$$

$$\therefore \text{Selectivity} = \mathbf{\frac{1}{10} = 0.1.}$$

EXAMPLE 3.64 *Obtain the values of R, L, C in a series RLC circuit that resonates at 1.5 kHz and consumes 50 W from a 50 V a.c. source operating at the resonance frequency. The bandwidth is 0.75 kHz.*

SOLUTION. For the series circuit, gat resonance,

$$V_R = V_{supply} = 50 \text{ V}$$

But $P_{loss} = V_R^2 / R$ or, $\dfrac{50^2}{R}$

$$\therefore \quad R = \mathbf{50\,\Omega}. \qquad [\because P_{loss} = 50 \text{ W}]$$

The Q factor is $\dfrac{f_0}{BW} = \dfrac{1.5}{0.75} = 2.$

Again,

$$Q = \frac{\omega_0 L}{R} = \frac{2\pi f_0 L}{R} = \frac{2\pi \times 1.5 \times 10^3 L}{50}$$

or,
$$L = \frac{50 \times 2}{2\pi \times 1.5 \times 10^3} = \mathbf{0.0106 \text{ H}.}$$

Again,

$$f_0 = \frac{1}{2\pi\sqrt{LC}} \text{ in series resonating circuit.}$$

$$\therefore \; C = \frac{1}{4\pi^2 f_0^2 L}$$

$$= \frac{1}{4 \times 3.14^2 \times (1.5 \times 10^3)^2 \times 0.0106}$$

$$= 1.06 \times 10^{-6} \text{ F.}$$

Thus $R = \mathbf{50\,\Omega}$; $L = \mathbf{0.0106 \text{ H}}$; $C = \mathbf{1.06\,\mu \text{ F}}$.

EXAMPLE 3.65 *A series resonating circuit has $R = 1\,k\Omega$, half power frequencies of 10 and 90 kHz. Determine the bandwidth and the resonant frequency. Calculate the inductance and capacitance of the circuit.*

SOLUTION. Bandwidth (= BW) = $f_2 - f_1$

$$= 90 - 10 = 80 \text{ kHz}$$

In series circuit,

$$f_0 = \sqrt{f_2 f_1} = \sqrt{90 \times 10} = 30 \text{ kHz}$$

The Q factor of the coil is given by

$$Q = \frac{f_0}{BW} = \frac{30}{80} = \frac{3}{8} \text{ only.}$$

Also, $$Q = \frac{2\pi f_0 L}{R}$$

or $$\frac{3}{8} = \frac{2\pi \times 30 \times 10^3 \times L}{1000}$$

$$\therefore \quad L = \frac{3 \times 1000}{8 \times 2 \times \pi \times 30 \times 10^3} = 2 \text{ mH}$$

At series resonance,

$$X_L = X_C$$

i.e., $$\omega_0 L = \frac{1}{\omega_0 C}$$

i.e., $$C = \frac{1}{(2\pi f_0)^2 L}$$

$$= \frac{1}{4\pi^2 \times (30 \times 10^3)^2 \times 0.002}$$

$$= 0.014\,\mu\text{F.}$$

Thus, BW = **80 kHz**; f_0 = **30 kHz**;

L = **2 mH**; C = **0.014 μF.**

EXAMPLE 3.66 *Find the magnitude of the frequency when the drop across the capacitor in series RLC circuit is maximum.*

SOLUTION. Circuit impedance

$$Z = \sqrt{R^2 + (X_L - X_C)^2}.$$

Circuit current, $I = \dfrac{V}{Z}$ and drop across C is

$$V_C = IX_C = \frac{V}{Z} . X_C$$

i.e., $$V_C^2 = \frac{V^2 \times X_C^2}{Z^2}$$

or, $$V_C^2 = \frac{V^2}{(\omega C)^2 \left[R^2 + \left(\omega L - \dfrac{1}{\omega C} \right)^2 \right]}$$

To find $V_{C_{max}}$, the above expression is to be differentiated w.r.t. ω and the result is to be equated to zero. [*the reader may do this as an exercise*]. The solution gives

$$\omega_C = \sqrt{\frac{1}{LC} - \frac{R^2}{2L^2}} \textbf{ rad/sec.}$$

EXAMPLE 3.67 *Find the value of R_1 such that the circuit given in Fig. E3.24 is resonant.*

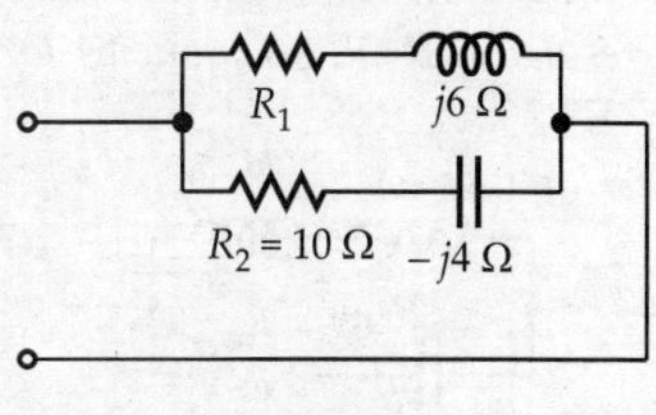

Fig. E3.24

Solution. The equivalent admittance of the given circuit is

$$Y = \frac{1}{R_1 + j6} + \frac{1}{10 - j4} = \frac{R_1 - j6}{R_1^2 + 36} + \frac{10 + j4}{10^2 + 16}$$

$$= \frac{R_1}{R_1^2 + 36} - j\frac{6}{R_1^2 + 36} + \frac{10}{10^2 + 16} + j\frac{4}{10^2 + 16}$$

$$= \frac{R_1}{R_1^2 + 36} + \frac{10}{10^2 + 16} + j\left(\frac{4}{10^2 + 16} - \frac{6}{R_1^2 + 36}\right)$$

During resonance, the imaginary part of Y must be zero.

i.e., $$\frac{4}{10^2 + 16} = \frac{6}{R_1^2 + 36}$$

or, $$R_1^2 + 36 = 6 \times 116/4 = 174$$

$\therefore$ $$\mathbf{R_1 = 11.75\ \Omega.}$$

Example 3.68 *A series RLC circuit has 10 Ω resistance, 60 mH inductance and C farad capacitance. At a frequency of 25 Hz, the p.f. of the circuit is 45° lead. At what frequency will the circuit be resonant ?*

Solution. $f = 25$ Hz

$\therefore$ $$\omega = 2\pi \times 25 = 157 \text{ rad/sec.}$$

Again, since $\tan\phi = \dfrac{X_C - X_L}{R}$

$\therefore$ $$\tan\phi = \frac{(1/\omega C) - \omega L}{R}$$

or $$\tan 45° = \frac{1 - \omega^2 LC}{R\omega C} = 1$$

$\therefore$ $$1 - \omega^2 LC = R\omega C$$

or, $$1 - (157)^2 \times 60 \times 10^{-3} \times C = 10 \times 157 \times C$$

or, $$1 = C[1570 + 157^2 \times 60 \times 10^{-3}] = C \times 3049$$

$\therefore$ $$C = 328\ \mu\text{F}$$

Thus, the resonant frequency is

$$\omega_0 = \frac{1}{\sqrt{LC}} = \frac{1}{\sqrt{60 \times 10^{-3} \times 328 \times 10^{-6}}}$$

$$= \mathbf{225.43\ rad/sec.}$$

Example 3.69 *Determine R_L and R_C that causes the circuit to be resonant at all frequencies for the circuit shown in Fig. E3.25.*

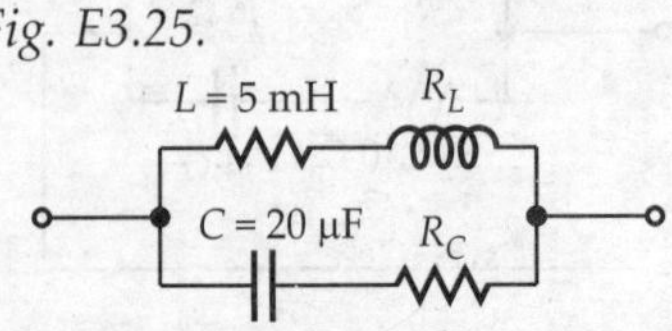

Fig. E3.25

Solution. It has been shown in the text that for a R_L-L are R_C-C parallel circuit, the condition of all time resonance is that

$$R_L^2 = R_C^2 = \frac{L}{C}$$

i.e., $$R_L = R_C = \sqrt{\frac{L}{C}} = \sqrt{\frac{5 \times 10^{-3}}{20 \times 10^{-6}}} = \mathbf{15.8\ \Omega.}$$

Example 3.70 *A series resonating circuit has a source frequency of 5 kHz and source impedance of $(2 + j4)\Omega$. The load impedance being $(10 - jX_C)\Omega$, find the value of C provided the power consumed by the resistor is maximum.*

Solution. $f_0 = 5000$ Hz

The total impedance of the given circuit is

$$Z_T = Z_{\text{source}} + Z_{\text{load}} = 2 + j4 + 10 - jX_C$$

$$= [12 + j(4 - X_C)]\Omega$$

At resonance the imaginary part of Z_T is zero *i.e.,* at resonance, $X_L = X_C$

$\therefore$ $$X_C = 4\ \Omega = \frac{1}{\omega_0 C}$$

$\therefore$ $$C = \frac{1}{\omega_0 X_C} = \frac{1}{2\pi \times 5000 \times 4} = \mathbf{8\ \mu F.}$$

At resonance, $Z_T = 12\ \Omega$ (resistive)

i.e., $$I = \frac{V}{Z_T} = \frac{100}{12} = 8.33 \text{ A}$$

Power in the resistor

$$= I^2 R = (8.33)^2 \times 10 = \mathbf{694.44\ W.}$$

[It may be noted that as at resonance I is maximum, hence, the power transfer is maximum].

Example 3.71 *For a series resonant circuit, $R = 5\ \Omega$, $L = 1$ H and $C = 0.25\ \mu F$. Find the resonance frequency and Bandwidth.*

Solution. ω_0 (resonance frequency of *RLC* circuit)

$$= \frac{1}{\sqrt{LC}}$$

$$= \frac{1}{\sqrt{1 \times 0.25 \times 10^{-6}}} = 2000 \text{ rad/sec}$$

i.e., $$f_0 = \frac{\omega_0}{2\pi} = \mathbf{318.47\ Hz.}$$

BW (Bandwidth) $= \dfrac{R}{L} = \dfrac{5}{1} = 5$ rad/sec. $=$ **0.8 Hz.**

EXAMPLE 3.72 *The Q factor of a RLC circuit is 5 at its resonance frequency of 1 kHz. Assuming the power dissipation of 250 W when the current drawn is 1 A, find the circuit parameters. Determine the BW of the circuit.*

SOLUTION.

$$W = I^2 R$$

or, $$R = \frac{W}{I^2} = \frac{250}{1^2} = 250 \text{ ohm}$$

Also, $$Q \text{ factor} = \frac{\omega_0 L}{R} = \frac{2\pi \times 1000 \times L}{250} = 5$$

[$\because$ $Q = 5$, as given]

$\therefore$ $$L = \frac{250 \times 5}{2\pi \times 1000} = 0.2 \text{ H.}$$

However, f_0 (resonant frequency) $= \dfrac{1}{2\pi\sqrt{LC}}$

$\therefore$ $$1000 = \frac{1}{2\pi\sqrt{0.2 \times C}}$$

or, $$10^6 = \frac{1}{4\pi^2 \times 0.2 \times C}$$

$\therefore$ $$C = \frac{1}{4\pi^2 \times 0.2} \times 10^{-6} = 0.127\,\mu\text{F.}$$

Thus, the parameters of *LRC* circuit are

$$R = \mathbf{250\,\Omega}\,;\; L = \mathbf{0.2\,H}\,;\; C = \mathbf{0.127\,\mu F}$$

Again, $$Q = \frac{f_0}{\text{BW}} = \frac{1000}{\text{BW}} = 5$$

$\therefore$ BW = **200 Hz.**

EXAMPLE 3.73 *In Fig. E3.26, $R = R_L = 1\Omega$, $L = 1$ H, $C = 0.5$ F. Find the resonance frequency and the admittance at the resonant frequency.*

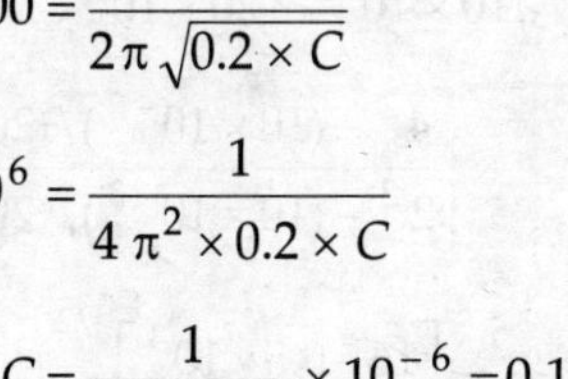

Fig. E3.26

SOLUTION. The circuit admittance seen by the current source is

$$Y = \frac{1}{R} + j\omega C + \frac{1}{R_L + j\,\omega L}$$

$$= \frac{1}{R} + j\omega C + \frac{R_L - j\omega L}{R_L^2 + \omega^2 L^2}$$

$$= \frac{1}{R} + \frac{R_L}{R_L^2 + \omega^2 L^2} + j\left(\omega C - \frac{\omega L}{R_L^2 + \omega^2 L^2}\right)$$

At resonance, the imaginary part of *Y* must be zero.

$\therefore$ $$\omega_0 C - \frac{\omega_0 L}{R_L^2 + \omega_0^2 L^2} = 0$$

or $$R_L^2 + \omega_0^2 L^2 = \frac{L}{C}$$

or, $$\omega_0^2 L^2 = \frac{L}{C} - R_L^2$$

$\therefore$ $$\omega_0 = \left[\frac{1}{LC} - \frac{R_L^2}{L^2}\right]^{1/2}$$

Here substituting the values of *L*, *R* and *C*,

$$\omega_0 = \left[\frac{1}{1 \times 0.5} - \frac{1^2}{1^2}\right]^{1/2} = \mathbf{1\ rad/sec.}$$

The admittance at resonance is

$$Y = \frac{1}{R} + \frac{R_L}{R_L^2 + \omega_0^2 L^2}$$

[$\because$ imaginary part is zero]

$$= 1 + \frac{1}{1 + 1^2 \,.\, 1^2} = \mathbf{1.5\ mho.}$$

EXAMPLE 3.74 *A variable frequency constant voltage signal generator supplies a RLC circuit at sinusoidal mode. Find the frequency at which maximum voltage across the inductor would appear.*

SOLUTION. $$Z = \sqrt{R^2 + \left(\omega L - \frac{1}{\omega C}\right)^2}$$

for the series *RLC* circuit.

$$\therefore\; I = \frac{V}{Z} = \frac{V}{\sqrt{R^2 + \left(\omega L - \frac{1}{\omega C}\right)^2}} \quad \text{[at resonance]}$$

The magnitude of the voltage across *L* is

$$V_L = \omega L\, I = \omega L . \frac{V}{\sqrt{R^2 + \left(\omega L - \frac{1}{\omega C}\right)^2}} \qquad ...(1)$$

The frequency at which V_L is maximum can be obtained by setting the derivative of (1) equal to zero,

or, $$\frac{dV_L}{d\omega} = \frac{d}{d\omega}\,\omega LV\,[\,R^2 + \omega^2 L^2 - 2\,(L/C) + 1/(\omega^2 C^2)\,]^{-1/2} = 0$$

or,

$$0 = \frac{\left[R^2 + \omega^2 L^2 - 2\left(\frac{L}{C}\right) + \frac{1}{(\omega^2 C^2)}\right]^{1/2} . LV - \omega L V \times \frac{1}{2}\left[R^2 + \omega^2 L^2 - 2\left(\frac{L}{C}\right) + \frac{1}{(\omega^2 C^2)}\right]^{-1/2} \times \left(2\,\omega L^2 - \frac{2}{\omega^3 C^2}\right)}{\left[R^2 + \omega^2 L^2 - 2\frac{L}{C} + \frac{1}{(\omega^2 C^2)}\right]}$$

or, $$\left(R^2 + \omega^2 L^2 - 2\frac{L}{C} + \frac{1}{\omega^2 C^2}\right)^{1/2}$$

$$= \frac{1}{2}\omega\left(R^2 + \omega^2 L^2 - 2\frac{L}{C} = \frac{1}{\omega^2 C^2}\right)^{-1/2}\left(2\,\omega L^2 - \frac{2}{\omega^3 C^2}\right)$$

or, $$\left(R^2 + \omega^2 L^2 - 2\frac{L}{C} + \frac{1}{\omega^2 C^2}\right) = L^2\omega^2 - \frac{1}{\omega^2 C^2}$$

or, $$R^2 - 2\frac{L}{C} + \frac{2}{\omega^2 C^2} = 0$$

$$\therefore\ \omega = \sqrt{\frac{2}{2\,LC - R^2 C^2}}$$

$$= \frac{1}{\sqrt{LC}}\left[\frac{2}{2 - \frac{R^2 C}{L}}\right]^{1/2}$$

$$= \frac{1}{\sqrt{LC}}\left[\frac{2L}{2L - R^2 C}\right]^{1/2}$$

$$= \frac{1}{\sqrt{LC}}\sqrt{\frac{2\frac{\omega_0 L}{R}}{2\frac{\omega_0 L}{R} - \omega_0 RC}}$$

$$= \frac{1}{\sqrt{LC}}\sqrt{\frac{2Q_0}{2Q_0 - \frac{1}{Q_0}}}$$

$$\left(\text{Since } Q_0 = \frac{\omega_0 L}{R} = \frac{1}{\omega_0 CR}\right)$$

$$\therefore\quad \omega = \frac{\mathbf{1}}{\sqrt{\mathbf{LC}}}\sqrt{\frac{\mathbf{2\,Q_0^2}}{\mathbf{2Q_0^2 - 1}}}.$$

Example 3.75 *Find the resonant frequency for the parallel circuit shown in Fig. E3.27.*

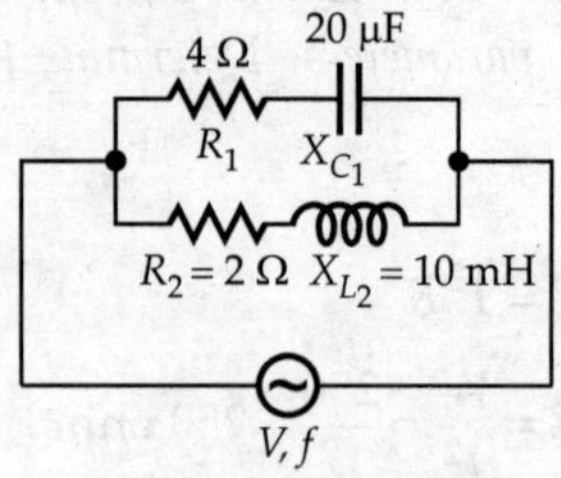

Fig. E3.27

Solution. Given that $R_1 = 4\Omega,\ C_1 = 20\,\mu F,\ R_2 = 2\,\Omega,\ L_2 = 10\,mH$

$$\therefore\quad \omega_0 = \frac{1}{\sqrt{L_2 C_1}}\left[\frac{R_1^2 - L_2/C_1}{R_2^2 - L_2/C_1}\right]^{1/2}$$

$$= \frac{1}{\sqrt{10\times 10^{-3} \times 20 \times 10^{-6}}} \times \left[\frac{4^2 - (10\times 10^{-3})/(20\times 10^{-6})}{2^2 - (10\times 10^{-3})/(20\times 10^{-6})}\right]^{1/2}$$

$$= 2236\left[\frac{16 - 0.5\times 10^3}{4 - 0.5\times 10^3}\right]^{1/2}$$

$$= 2209 \text{ rad/sec.}$$

$$\therefore\quad f_0 = \frac{2209}{2\pi} = \mathbf{351.75\ Hz.}$$

Example 3.76 *In a series RLC circuit, instantaneous voltage and currents are $v = 100\sin(314\,t + 30°)$ V and $i = 4\sin(314\,t + 30°)$. Find the values of R and C provided L=0.5 H.*

Solution. We observe that in the series *RLC* circuit, the instantaneous voltage and currents are in phase. This indicates that the circuit is at resonance, the net circuit impedance being *R*.

$$\therefore\quad R = \frac{V_m}{I_m} = \frac{100}{4} = 25\,\Omega$$

At resonance,

$$X_L = X_C$$

or, $$\omega_0\, L = \frac{1}{\omega_0 C}$$

i.e., $$C = \frac{1}{\omega^2 L} = 20.2\times 10^{-6}\ F = \mathbf{20.2\,\mu F.}$$

EXAMPLE 3.77 *A resonating series circuit has 10 Ω resistance. If the supply is 10 V, obtain the power at half power frequency.*

SOLUTION. I_0 (= current at resonance)

$$= \frac{V}{R} = \frac{10}{10} = 1\text{ A}.$$

We know, power at half power frequency is 1/2 P_{max};

$$\therefore \quad P_{1/2\,power} = \frac{1}{2} P_{max} \quad [P_{max} = \text{power at the time of resonance}]$$

$$= \frac{1}{2}(I)^2 \times R = \frac{1}{2} \times 1^2 \times 10 = \mathbf{5\ W}.$$

EXAMPLE 3.78 *A RLC circuit operates at a frequency of ω and the ratio of ω to the resonant frequency is α. Obtain an expression of admittance of the circuit in terms of R, Q and α.*

SOLUTION. $Z = R + j(X_L - X_C)$ in the series circuit.

$$\therefore Y = \frac{1}{R + j\left(\omega L - \frac{1}{\omega C}\right)}$$

$$= \frac{1/R}{1 + j\left(\alpha\omega_0 L/R - \frac{1}{\alpha\,\omega_0\,RC}\right)} \quad \left[\because \text{ given that } \frac{\omega}{\omega_0} = \alpha\right]$$

$$= \frac{1}{R\left[1 + j\left(\alpha Q - \frac{Q}{\alpha}\right)\right]} \quad \left[\because Q = \frac{\omega_0 L}{R} = \frac{1}{\omega_0 RC}\right]$$

$$\text{or,} \quad Y = \frac{1}{R\left[1 + jQ\left(\alpha - \frac{1}{\alpha}\right)\right]}$$

Thus, the admittance is given by

$$\mathbf{Y = \frac{1}{R\left[1 + jQ\left(\alpha - \frac{1}{\alpha}\right)\right]}\ \text{mho.}}$$

EXAMPLE 3.79. *Show that the given circuit is resonant at supply frequency [Fig. E.3.28].*

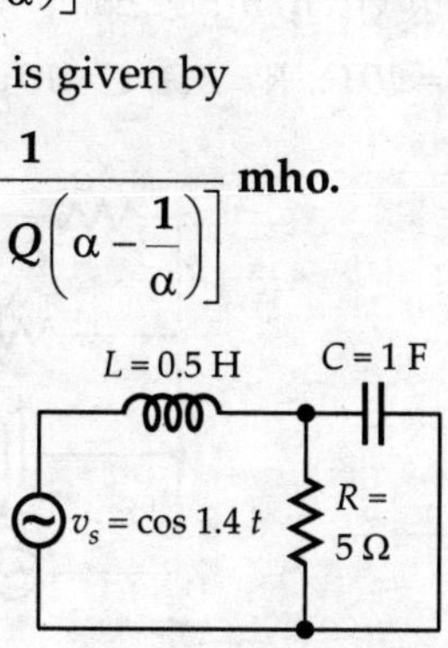

Fig. E3.28

SOLUTION. The impedance of the given circuit seen by the source is

$$Z_{eq} = j\omega L + \frac{R(1/j\omega C)}{R + \frac{1}{j\omega C}}$$

$$= j\omega L + \frac{R}{j\,\omega RC + 1}$$

$$= j\omega \times 0.5 + \frac{5}{1 + j\omega \times 5 \times 1}$$

$$= 0.5\,j\omega + \frac{5}{1 + j\omega 5}$$

$$= 0.5\,j\omega + \frac{5(1 - j\,\omega 5)}{1 + (5\,\omega)^2} = j\,0.5\,\omega + \frac{5 - j\,\omega 25}{1 + 25\,\omega^2}$$

$$\text{or,} \quad Z_{eq} = 5 + j\,0.5\,\omega - j\,25\,\omega/(1 + 25\,\omega^2)$$

$$= 5 + j\left[0.5\,\omega - \frac{25\,\omega}{1 + 25\,\omega^2}\right]$$

At resonance, the imaginary part is of Z_{eq} zero.

$$\text{i.e.,} \quad 0.5\,\omega_0 - \frac{25\,\omega_0}{1 + 25\,\omega_0^2} = 0$$

[assuming resonance frequency to be ω_0]

$$\text{or,} \quad 0.5\,\omega_0 = \frac{25\,\omega_0}{1 + 25\,\omega_0^2}$$

$$\text{or,} \quad 1 + 25\,\omega_0^2 = \frac{25}{0.5} = 50$$

$$\text{or,} \quad 25\,\omega_0^2 = 49$$

$$\therefore \quad \omega_0 = \mathbf{1.4\ rad/sec.}$$

Since the frequency of source is 1.4 rad/sec., the circuit in Fig. E3.28 is in resonance.

EXAMPLE 3.80 *Find the Q factor and frequency of resonance of the circuit shown in Fig. E3.29.*

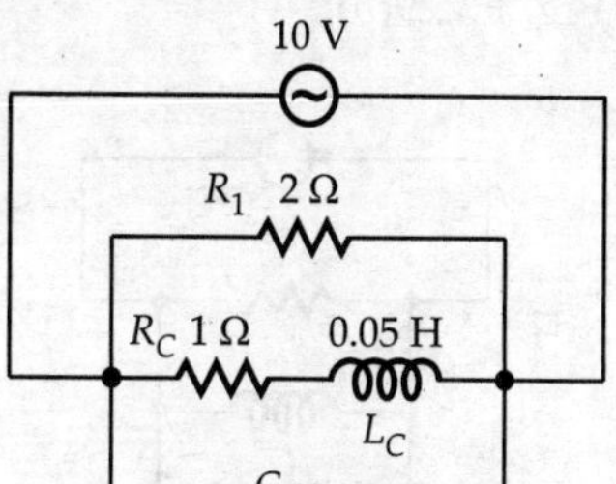

Fig. E3.29

Solution. The circuit shown in Fig. E3.29 is first reduced as shown in Fig. E3.29(*a*) using the concept of series parallel equivalent.

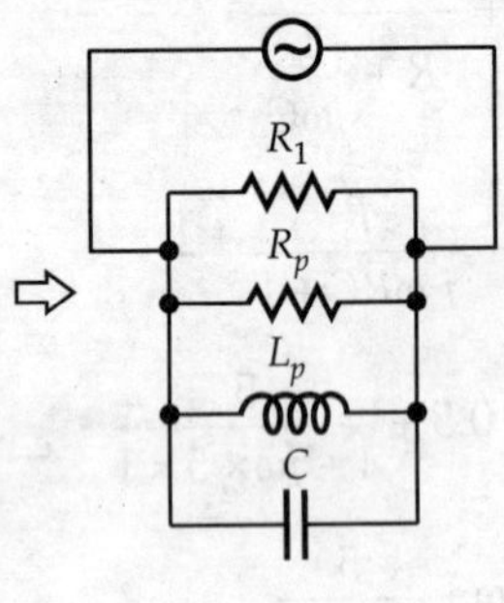

Fig. E3.29 (*a*)

Here, in Fig. E3.29(*a*),

$$R_p = \frac{R_C^2 + X_{LC}^2}{R_C}$$

$$= R_C + R_C \frac{X_{LC}^2}{R_C^2} = R_C\,(1 + Q_C^2)$$

$\left[\because Q_C = \dfrac{X_{LC}}{R_C}\right.$ at resonance; Q_C being the Q factor of the coil $\left.\right]$

Also,

$$X_p = \frac{R_C^2 + X_{LC}^2}{X_{LC}} = X_{LC} + X_{LC}\,\frac{R_C^2}{X_{LC}^2}$$

$$= X_{LC}\,[1 + 1/(X_{LC}^2 / R_C^2] = X_{LC}\left[1 + \frac{1}{Q_C^2}\right]$$

Finally, following Fig. E3.29(*b*),

$$R_{eq} = \frac{R_1 R_p}{R_1 + R_p}$$

Also, in Fig. E3.29(*b*),

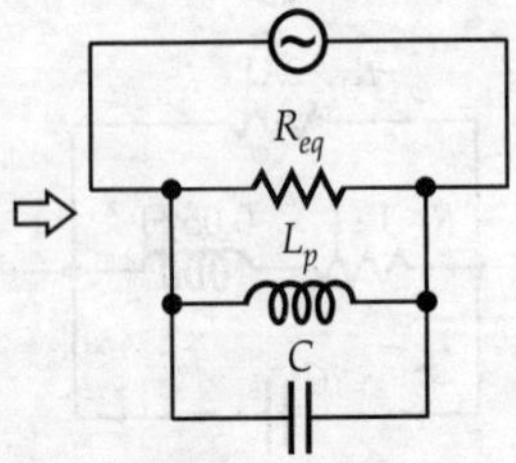

Fig. E3.29 (*b*)

The current magnification [*i.e.*, the net Q factor (Q_p)] is given by

$$\frac{I_C}{I_{R_{eq}}} = \frac{V / X_C}{V / R_{eq}} = \frac{R_{eq}}{X_C} = \omega_0\, C\, R_{eq}$$

[ω_0 being the frequency of resonance]

Thus, for the given circuit,

$$R_{eq} = \frac{R_1\, R_p}{R_1 + R_p}\,;\; R_p = R_C\left(1 + Q_{coil}^2\right)$$

$$X_p = X_{LC}\left(1 + \frac{1}{Q_{coil}^2}\right)$$

Q_p, quality factor of the parallel circuit $= \omega_0 CR_{eq}$

The frequency of resonance $\omega_0 = \dfrac{1}{L_C}\sqrt{\dfrac{L_C}{C} - R_C^2}$

[Ref. Figs. E3.29 and E3.26 derived in Ex. 3.73]

Here, $Q_{coil} = \dfrac{\omega_0 L_C}{R_C} = \dfrac{1414 \times 0.05}{1} = 70.7$

$$\left[\because \omega_0 = \frac{1}{0.05}\sqrt{\frac{0.05}{10 \times 10^{-6}} - 1^2} = \mathbf{1414\ rad/sec.}\right]$$

$$\therefore \quad R_p = 1(1 + 70.7^2) = 5000\,\Omega$$

This gives $R_{eq} = \dfrac{5000 \times 2}{5000 + 2} = 2\,\Omega$

Then Q_p, the Q factor of the parallel circuit is

$$Q_p = \omega_0 CR_{eq}$$

$$= 1414 \times 10 \times 10^{-6} \times 2 = \mathbf{0.03}.$$

Thus for the given circuit, the Q factor is **0.03** and ω_0 (the frequency of resonance) = **1414 rad/sec.**

Example 3.81. *Obtain the resonant frequency of the circuit given in Fig. E3.30.*

[$R_C = 10\,\Omega$, $R = 2\,\Omega$, $C = 10\,\mu F$, $L_C = 0.1\,H$]

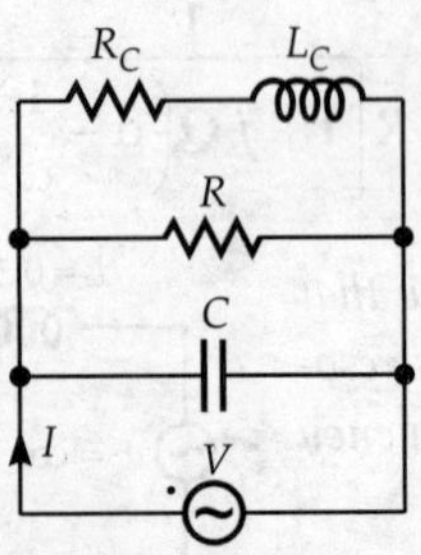

Fig. E3.30

SOLUTION. Since the circuit is a parallel combination of resistance, inductance and capacitance,

$$Y\,(\text{admittance}) = \frac{1}{R} + j\omega C + \frac{1}{R_C + j\omega L_C}$$

$$= \frac{1}{R} + \frac{R_c - j\,\omega L_C}{(R_C)^2 + (\omega L_C)^2} + j\,\omega C$$

$$= \frac{1}{R} + \frac{R_C}{R_C^2 + \omega^2 L_C^2} + j\left[\omega C - \frac{\omega L_C}{R_C^2 + \omega^2 L_C^2}\right] \qquad \text{...(1)}$$

The circuit will be at resonance when the imaginary part of (1) will be zero.

i.e., when $\omega_0 C - \dfrac{\omega_0 L_C}{R_C^2 + \omega_0^2 L_C^2} = 0$

[ω_0 = frequency of resonance]

or, $$\frac{L_C}{R_C^2 + \omega_0^2 L_C^2} = C$$

or, $$\omega_0^2 L_C^2 = \frac{L}{C} - R_C^2$$

$\therefore$ $$\omega_0^2 = \frac{1}{L_C^2}\left[\frac{L}{C} - R_C^2\right]$$

or, $$\omega_0 = \frac{1}{L_C}\sqrt{\frac{L}{C} - R_C^2}\ \text{rad/sec.}$$

or, $$f_0 = \frac{1}{2\pi L_C}\sqrt{\frac{L}{C} - R_C^2}\ \text{Hz}$$

(Pl. ref. to Ex. 3.80 also)

The above expression gives the frequency of resonance of *LCR* circuit as shown in Fig. E3.30.

In this problem,

$$f_0 = \frac{1}{2\pi \times 0.1}\sqrt{\frac{0.1}{10 \times 10^{-6}} - 10^2}$$

$$= \mathbf{158.44\ Hz.}$$

EXAMPLE 3.82. *A coil of inductance 9 H and resistance 50 Ω is in series with a capacitor and is supplied from a constant voltage variable frequency source. The circuit is at resonance at 75 Hz and the circuit current is 1 A. Find the frequency when the current is 0.5 A.*

SOLUTION. For the series *RLC* circuit,

$$Z = R\,[1 + 2\,j\,Q_0\,\delta] \qquad \text{...(1)}$$

where $Q_0 = \dfrac{\omega_0 L}{R} = Q$ factor at resonance.

$$\delta = \frac{\omega - \omega_0}{\omega_0} = \frac{f - f_0}{f_0}$$

At resonance $Z \equiv R$ and $I_0 = \dfrac{V}{R}$.

However, at the required frequency, $I = 0.5\,I_0$,

$$|Z| = 2\,R.$$

or, from (1), $(2\,R)^2 = R^2\,(1 + 4\,\delta^2\,Q_0^2)$

[using rectangular representation of the vectors]

or, $$R^2 . 4\,\delta^2\,Q_0^2 = 4\,R^2 - R^2 = 3\,R^2$$

or, $$4\delta^2\,Q_0^2 = 3$$

or, $$2\,\delta\,Q_0 = \pm\sqrt{3}$$

or, $$\delta = \frac{\pm\sqrt{3}}{2\,Q_0}$$

But $$Q_0 = \frac{\omega_0\,L}{R} = \frac{2\pi \times 75 \times 9}{50} \simeq 85$$

$\therefore$ $$\delta = \frac{\pm\sqrt{3}}{2 \times 85}$$

$$= \pm 0.0102$$

However,

$$\delta = \frac{f - f_0}{f}$$

$\therefore$ $$f = f_0 \pm \delta\,f_0$$

$$= 75 \pm 0.0102 \times 75$$

$$\simeq \mathbf{75.765\ Hz}\ \text{or}\ \mathbf{74.24\ Hz.}$$

EXAMPLE 3.83 *Show that the circuit shown in Fig. E3.31 can have more than one resonant condition. Assume C to be variable.*

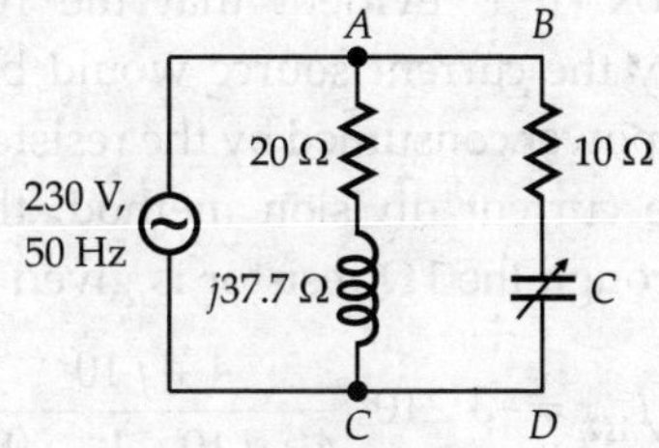

Fig. E3.31

SOLUTION. Let the admittance of branch *AC* be Y_1 and that of branch *BD* be Y_2

$$\therefore \quad Y_1 = \frac{1}{20 + j\,37.7}$$

and $$Y_2 = \frac{1}{10 - j\,X_C}$$

i.e., $$Y_1 = 0.011 - j\,0.0207$$

and $$Y_2 = \frac{10 + j\,X_C}{100 + X_C^2}$$

At resonance, the imaginary parts of Y_1 and Y_2 must balance each other.

$$\therefore \quad 0.0207 = \frac{X_C}{100 + X_C^2}$$

or, $$0.0207\,X_C^2 - X_C + 2.07 = 0.$$

or, $$X_C = 46.14 \text{ or } 2.17$$

At 50 Hz, $$C = \frac{1}{314\,X_C}$$

$$= \text{either } 69\,\mu\text{F or } \mathbf{1.46\,\mu F.}$$

As C can be either 69 μF or 1.46 μF to have resonance, it is evident that the given circuit is *resonant under both the conditions.*

EXAMPLE 3.84 *Find the real power supplied by the current source E3.32.*

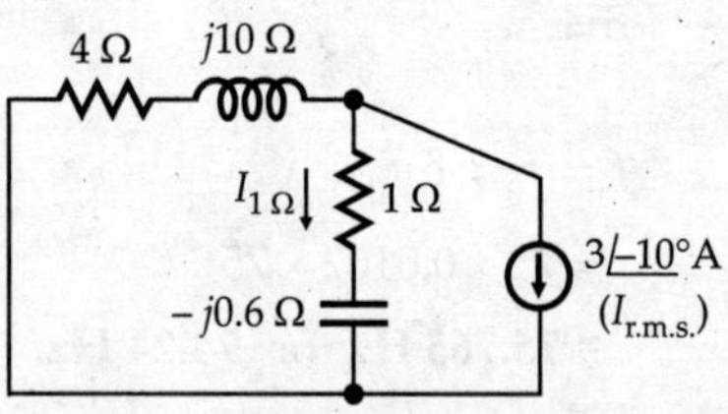

Fig. E3.32

SOLUTION. It is evident that the real power supplied by the current source would be equal to the sum of power consumed by the resistors 1 Ω and 4 Ω. By the current division method, the current passing through the 1 Ω resistor is given by

$$I_{1\Omega} = -3\,\angle 10° \frac{4 + j\,10}{4 + j\,10 + 1 - j\,0.6}$$

$$= 3.03 - j\,0.2$$

$$= 3.03\,\angle -3.8° \text{ A.}$$

Again

$$I_{4\Omega} = I - I_{1\Omega}$$

$$= 3\,(\cos 10 - j\,\sin 10) - 3.03 + j\,0.2$$

$$= -0.08 - j\,0.32$$

$$= 0.32\,\angle -103.74° \text{ A}$$

This loss in 1 Ω resistor $= (3.03)^2 \times 1 = 9.18$ W

and loss in 4 Ω resistor $= (0.32)^2 \times 4 = 0.43$ W

Hence the net power supplied by the sources

$$= 9.18 \text{ W} + 0.43 \text{ W} \simeq \mathbf{9.61\ W.}$$

EXAMPLE 3.85 *In Fig. E3.33, obtain the values of the complex power of the sources.*

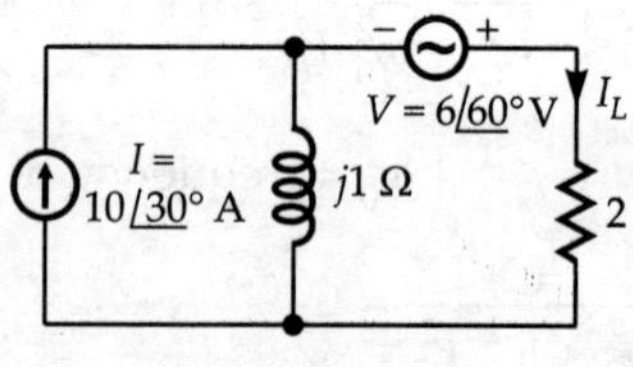

Fig. E3.33

SOLUTION. Let us first convert the current source to the voltage source and redraw the circuit (Fig. E3.34).

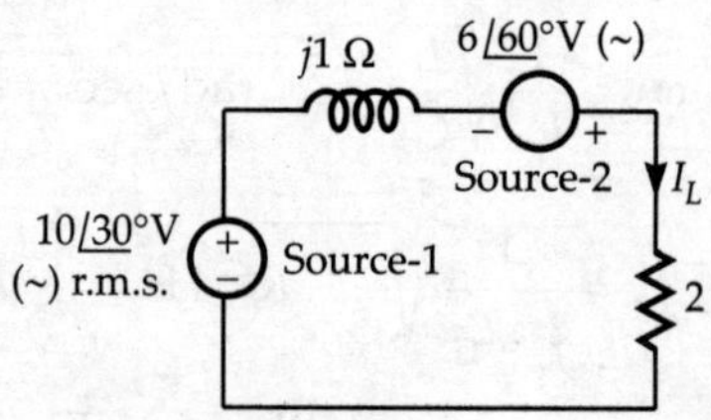

Fig. E3.34

In the circuit,

$$I_L = \frac{10\,\angle 30° + 6\,\angle 60°}{2 + j1}$$

$$= \frac{10(\cos 30° + j\,\sin 30°) + 6(\cos 60° + j\,\sin 60°)}{2 + j\,1}$$

$$= \frac{(8.66 + j\,5) + (3 + j\,5.2)}{2 + j\,1}$$

$$= \frac{11.66 + j\,10.2}{2 + j\,1} = \frac{15.5\,\angle 41.18°}{2.24\,\angle 26.56°}$$

$$= 6.92\,\angle 14.62° \text{ A}$$

$\therefore\ S_{L_1}$ (complex power of source-1)

$= 10\angle 30° \times 6.92\angle -14.62 = 69.2\ \angle 15.38°$ VA

$= \mathbf{(66.72 + j\,18.35)\ VA.}$

S_{L_2} (complex power of source-2)

$= 6\ \angle 60° \times 6.92\ \angle -14.62°$

$= 41.52\ \angle 45.38°\ \text{VA} = \mathbf{(29.16 + j\,29.55)\ VA.}$

Check

The power consumed in the 2Ω resistor is $(6.92)^2 \times 2 \simeq 96$ W. This power is supplied by the real parts of S_{L_1} and S_{L_2}. It can be seen that the sum of real parts of S_{L_1} and S_{L_2} is $66.72 + 29.16 \simeq 96$ W.

EXAMPLE 3.86 *In the circuit of Fig. E3.35, if $Z_L = 5 + j\,8.66$, find the power factor as well as the power dissipated. What is the value of the capacitance that will make the p.f. to be unity when placed in series with Z ?*

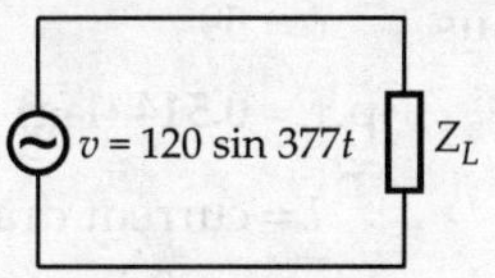

Fig. E3.35

SOLUTION. $Z_L = (5 + j\,8.66)\Omega = 10\ \angle 60° \Omega$

$\therefore$ p.f. $= \cos 60° = 0.5$

Power dissipated

$$= I^2 R = \left(\frac{V}{Z}\right)^2 R$$

$$= \left[\frac{(120/\sqrt{2})}{10}\right]^2 \times 5 = \mathbf{360\ W}$$

The p.f. of the circuit will only be unity if the capacitive reactance connected across Z_L can balance the inductive reactive of Z_L.

Then $X_C = -j\,8.66\,\Omega$

i.e., $C = \dfrac{1}{8.66 \times 377} = \mathbf{306\ \mu F.}$

EXAMPLE 3.87 *In a certain RC circuit, the real power flow being 500 W, the reactive power 300 VAR. What is the apparent power ?*

SOLUTION. $P = VI \cos\phi = 500$ W,

$Q = VI \sin\phi = 300$ W

$$\therefore \frac{Q}{P} = \tan\phi = \frac{300}{500} = 0.6 \quad \therefore \phi = 31°$$

Thus apparent power $= \dfrac{P}{\cos\phi} = \dfrac{500}{0.857} = \mathbf{583\ VA.}$

EXAMPLE 3.88 *Find P and Q in the network of Fig. E3.36.*

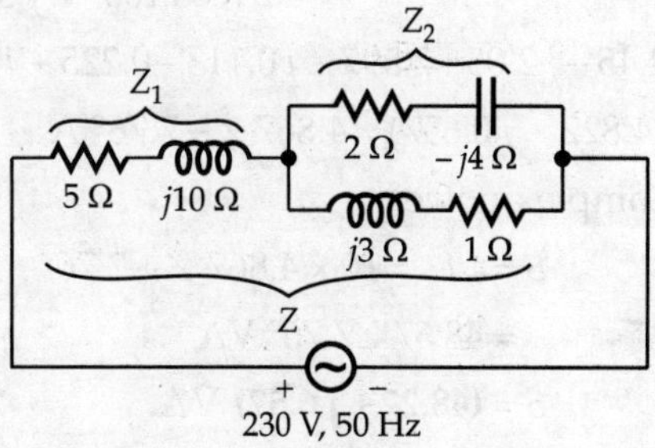

Fig. E3.36

SOLUTION. $Z_1 = (5 + j\,10)\Omega$,

$Z_2 = (2 - j4)\Omega$,

$Z_3 = (1 + j3)\Omega$

Total impedance

$$Z = Z_1 + \frac{Z_2\,Z_3}{Z_2 + Z_3}$$

$$= (5 + j\,10) + \frac{(2 - j4)(1 + j\,3)}{(2 - j4) + (1 + j3)}$$

$$= (5 + j\,10) + \frac{2 + j6 - j\,4 + 12}{3 - j\,1}$$

$$= (5 + j\,10) + \frac{(14 + j\,2)}{3 - j\,1}$$

$$= (5 + j\,10) + \frac{14.12\ \angle 8.1°}{3.16\ \angle -18°}$$

$= 5 + j\,10 + 4.46\ \angle 26.1°$

$= 5 + j\,10 + 4 + j\,1.95 = (9 + j\,11.95)\Omega$

$$\therefore\ I = \frac{V}{Z} = \frac{230}{9 + j\,11.95} = \frac{230}{14.95\ \angle 53°}$$

$= 15.385\ \angle -53°$ A [*i.e.,* $\phi = 53°$ lag]

$\therefore\ P = VI \cos\phi = 230 \times 15.385 \cos° = \mathbf{2130\ W}$

and $Q = VI \sin\phi = 230 \times 15.385 \sin 53° = \mathbf{2826\ VAR}$

EXAMPLE 3.89 *The currents through three parallel impedances are given by $I_1 = 3.2\ \angle -40°\ A$; $I_2 = 2.6\ \angle 2.5°$; $I_3 = 1.3\ \angle 100°\ A$.*

Find the net complex power supplied to these impedances. [Assume $V_{r.m.s} = 10\ \angle 0°\ V$]

SOLUTION. Net current $I = I_1 + I_2 + I_3$ (vectorial addition)

$= 3.2\ \angle -40° + 2.6\ \angle 2.5° + 1.3\ \angle 100°$

$$= 3.2\,(\cos 40 - j\sin 40°) + 2.6\,(\cos 2.5° + j\sin 2.5°) + 1.3\,(\cos 100° + j\sin 100°)$$

$$= 2.45 - j\,2.05 + 2.597 + j\,0.113 - 0.225 + j1.28$$

$$= (4.822 - j\,0.657) = 4.867\,\angle -7.76°\text{ A}$$

∴ Complex power

$$S = VI^* = 10 \times 4.867\,\angle +7.76°$$

$$= 48.67\,\angle 7.76°\text{ VA}$$

i.e., $S = \mathbf{(48.22 + j\,6.57)\ VA.}$

EXAMPLE 3.90 *In the network of Fig. E3.37, if $V_1 = 100\,\angle 0°$ V; $V_2 = 100\,\angle -60°$ V; $Z_1 = (6 + j\,8)\,\Omega$; $Z_2\ (6 - j\,8)\,\Omega$, find the power absorbed by Z_3.*

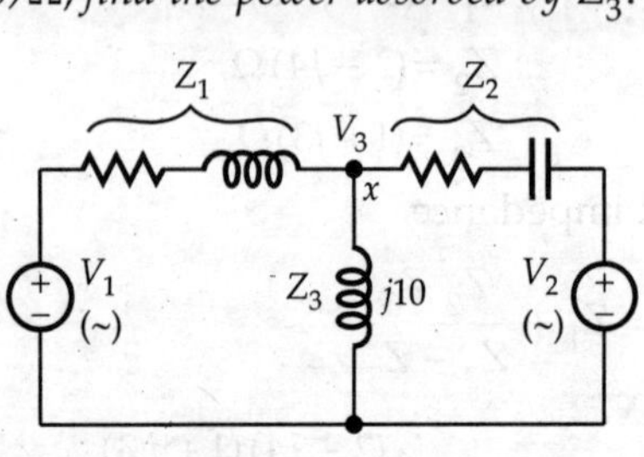

Fig. E3.37

SOLUTION. Applying nodal analysis in the network of Fig. E3.37,

$$\frac{V_3 - V_1}{Z_1} + \frac{V_3}{Z_3} + \frac{V_3 - V_2}{Z_2} = 0$$

[by naming the node x as V_3]

or
$$V_3\left[\frac{1}{Z_1} + \frac{1}{Z_2} + \frac{1}{Z_3}\right] = \frac{V_1}{Z_1} + \frac{V_2}{Z_2}$$

$$= \frac{100\,\angle 0°}{6 + j\,8} + \frac{100\,\angle -60°}{6 - j\,8} \quad ...(1)$$

However,

$$\frac{1}{Z_1} + \frac{1}{Z_2} + \frac{1}{Z_3} = \frac{1}{6 + j\,8} + \frac{1}{6 - j\,8} + \frac{1}{j\,10}$$

$$= \frac{1}{10\,\angle -53.2°} + \frac{1}{10\,\angle -53.2°} + \frac{1}{10\,\angle 90°}$$

$$= 0.06 - j\,0.08 - j\,0.1 + 0.06 + j\,0.08$$

$$= 0.12 - j\,0.1 = 0.156\,\angle -39.82°$$

Thus from (1),

$$V_3 \times 0.156\,\angle -39.82° = \frac{100\,\angle -0°}{10\,\angle 53.2} + \frac{100\,\angle -60°}{10\,\angle -53.2°}$$

$$= (10\,\angle -53.2° + 10\,\angle -6.8°)$$

$$= 6 - j\,8 + 9.9 - j\,1.18$$

$$= (15.9 - j\,9.18) = 18.4\,\angle -30°.$$

$$\therefore\quad V_3 = \frac{18.4\,\angle -30°}{0.156\,\angle -39.82°} = 118\,\angle 9.8°\text{ V}$$

and
$$I_3 = \frac{V_3}{Z_3} = \frac{118\,\angle 9.8°}{10\,\angle 90°} = 11.8\,\angle -80.2°\text{ A}$$

∴ Power of the inductor

$$= I^2 X_L = 11.8^2 \times 10 = 1.392\text{ kVAR}$$

i.e., Q(inductor) = **1.392 kVAR** (absorbed).

EXAMPLE 3.91 *An impedance of $(3 + j5)\,\Omega$ is connected across a 10 V, 50 Hz source. Find (i) power factor (ii) real and reactive power (iii) current drawn by the impedance.*

SOLUTION. $Z = 3 + j\,5 \equiv R + j\,X_L$

[the + sign indicates inductive circuit]

$$\therefore\quad \cos\phi = \frac{R}{Z} = \frac{3}{3 + j\,5} = \frac{3}{5.83} = 0.514$$

Thus $\phi = 59°$

p.f. = **0.514 (lag)**

$$I = \text{current drawn} = \frac{V}{Z} = \frac{10\,\angle 0°}{3 + j\,5}$$

$$= 1.715\,\angle -59°\text{ A}$$

i.e., $I = \mathbf{1.715\,\angle -59°\ A}$

Real power $(P) = VI\cos\phi$

$$= 10 \times 1.715 \times \cos 59° = 8.833\text{ W}$$

Reactive power $(Q) = VI\sin\phi$

$$= 10 \times 1.715\sin 59° = 14.7\text{ VAR}$$

i.e., $P = \mathbf{8.833\ W}$

$Q = \mathbf{14.7\ VAR}$ **inductive.**

EXAMPLE 3.92 *Two impedances $Z_1 = 5\,\angle -30°\,\Omega$ and $Z_2 = 10\,\angle +45°\,\Omega$ are connected in parallel. The combination draws $(2 + j\,4)$ A current from a voltage source. Determine the voltage source and the complex power for each branch.*

SOLUTION.
$$Y_1 = \frac{1}{5\,\angle -30°} = 0.2\,\angle 30°\text{ mho.}$$

$$Y_2 = \frac{1}{10\,\angle 45°} = 0.1\,\angle -45°\text{ mho.}$$

$$\therefore\quad Y = Y_1 + Y_2 = 0.2\,\angle 30° + 0.1\,\angle -45°$$

$$= 0.2(\cos 30° + j\sin 30°) + 0.1(\cos 45° - j\sin 45°)$$

$$= 0.173 + j\,0.1 + 0.071 - j\,0.071$$

$$= 0.244 + j\,0.029 = 0.246\,\angle 6.8°\text{ mho.}$$

$$I = (2 + j\,4)\text{ A} = 4.47\,\angle 63.43°$$

$$\therefore \quad V = \frac{I}{Y} = \frac{4.47 \angle 63.43°}{0.246 \angle 6.8°} = 18.17 \angle 56.63° \text{ V}$$

$$V = 18.17 \angle 56.63° \text{ V}$$

$$I_1 = VY_1 = 18.17 \angle 56.63° \times 0.2 \angle 30°$$
$$= 3.634 \angle 86.63° \text{ A}$$

$$I_2 = VY_2 = 18.17 \angle 56.63° \times 0.1 \angle -45°$$
$$= 1.817 \angle 11.63° \text{ A}$$

$\therefore$ S_1 (Complex power in branch-1)

$$= VI_1^* = 18.17 \angle 56.63° \times 3.634 \angle -86.63°$$
$$= 66 \angle -30° \text{ VA}$$
$$= (57.16 - j\,33) \text{ VA}$$

S_2 (Complex power in branch-2)

$$= VI_2^* = 18.17 \angle 56.63° \times 1.817 \angle -56.63°$$
$$= 33 \angle 45° \text{ VA} = (23.33 + j\,23.33) \text{ VA}$$

Thus, complex power in branch-1

= **(56.63 – *j* 33) VA**

and complex power in branch-2

= **(23.33 + *j* 23.33) VA.**

EXAMPLE 3.93 *A voltage of 100 ∠0° volts is applied across p-q terminals of the circuit shown in Fig. E3.38 to produce current of 40 ∠ 10° A. Find the value of Z when r = 5 Ω. What would be the active power consumed in Z ?*

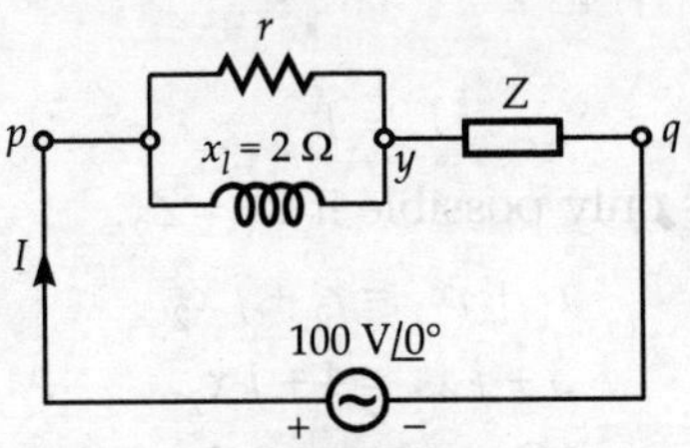

Fig. E3.38

SOLUTION. The impedance across *x-y* is

$$Z_{p-y} = \frac{r \times j2}{r + j2} = \frac{5 \times j2}{5 + j2} = \frac{j10}{5 + j2}$$

$$= \frac{10 \angle 90°}{5.38 \angle 21.8°}$$

$$= 1.86 \angle 68.2° \,\Omega.$$

$$\therefore \quad Z_{p-q} = Z + Z_{x-y} = Z + 0.69 + j\,1.73$$
$$= [(Z + 0.69) + j\,1.73]\,\Omega$$

The supply voltage being 100 V, the circuit current of 40 ∠10° A is obtained as

$$I = \frac{V}{Z_{pq}}$$

$$\text{or,} \quad 40 \angle 10° = \frac{100 \angle 0°}{(Z + 0.69) + j\,1{-}73}$$

$$\text{or,} \quad (Z + 0.69) + j\,1.73 = 2.5 \angle -10°$$
$$= 2.46 - j\,0.434.$$

$$\text{or,} \quad Z = 2.46 - 0.69 - j\,0.434 - j\,1.73$$
$$= \mathbf{(1.77 - j\,2.164)\,\Omega}$$

Thus, the real part of Z is 1.77 Ω. The reactive part of Z is 2.164 (capacitive) Ω.

As the circuit current is 40 A, hence the amount of active power consumed (P_z) is given by

$$P_z = 40^2 \times 1.77 = 2832 \text{ W}.$$

i.e., Active power consumed in Z = **2832 W.**

EXAMPLE 3.94 *Obtain the average power consumed by the circuit given in Fig. E3.39.*

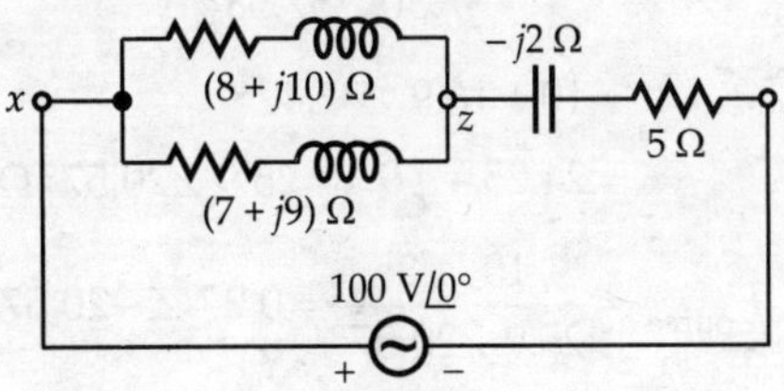

Fig. E3.39

SOLUTION. In the circuit of Fig. E3.39, the impedance between points *x-z* is

$$Z_{x-z} = \frac{(8 + j\,10)(7 + j\,9)}{8 + j\,10 + 7 + j\,9}$$

$$= \frac{56 - 90 + j\,70 + j\,72}{15 + j\,19} = \frac{-34 + j\,142}{15 + j\,19}\,\Omega$$

However,

$$Z_{zy} = (5 - j\,2)\,\Omega,$$

$$\therefore \quad Z_{xy} = Z_{x-z} + Z_{z-y}$$

$$= \frac{-34 + j\,142}{15 + j\,19} + 5 - j\,2$$

$$= \frac{146 \angle 180° - 76.53°}{24.2 \angle 51.7°} + 5 - j\,2$$

$$= 6.033 \angle 51.77° + 5 - j\,2$$

$$= 8.75 + j\,2.74 = 9.17 \angle 17.38°\,\Omega$$

$$\therefore \quad I = \frac{V}{Z} = \frac{100 \angle 0°}{9.17 \angle 17.38} = 10.9 \angle -17.38° \text{ A}$$

Thus average power

$$(P) = VI \cos \phi = 100 \times 10.9 \times \cos 17.38° = 1040 \text{ W}.$$

i.e., P_{av} = **1040 W.**

CHAPTER 3

EXAMPLE 3.95 *Find the power dissipated in the circuit given in Fig. E3.40.*

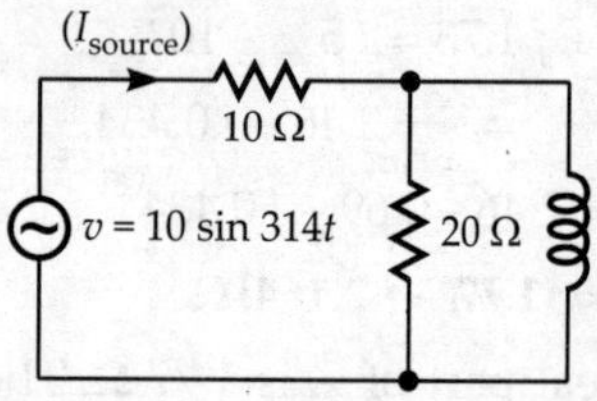

Fig. E3.40

SOLUTION. The net impedance of the given circuit across the voltage source is given by

$$Z_{net} = 10 + \frac{(20)(j\,31.5)}{20 + j\,31.5}$$

$$= 10 + \frac{630\,\angle 90°}{37.30\,\angle 57.58°}$$

$$= 10 + 16.9\,\angle 32.42°$$

$$= 24.25 + j\,9.1 = 25.9\,\angle 20.57°\,\Omega$$

$$\therefore \quad I_{source} = \frac{10/\sqrt{2}}{25.9\,\angle 20.57°} = 0.27\,\angle -20.57°\text{ A}$$

Thus power dissipated

$$= \left(\frac{10}{\sqrt{2}}\right) \times 0.27 \times \cos(20.57°)$$

$$= 7.07 \times 0.27 \times 0.936 = \mathbf{1.79\ W.}$$

Also the power dissipated can be obtained as

$$10 \times (I_{source})^2 + \left[I_{source} \times \frac{j\,31.5}{20 + j\,31.5}\right]^2 \times 20$$

$$= 10 \times 0.27^2 + \left[0.27 \times \frac{31.5}{37.30}\right]^2 \times 20$$

$$= 0.74 + 1.039 \simeq \mathbf{1.78\ W.}$$

EXAMPLE 3.96 *Find the reactive power of the inductor (Fig. E3.41).*

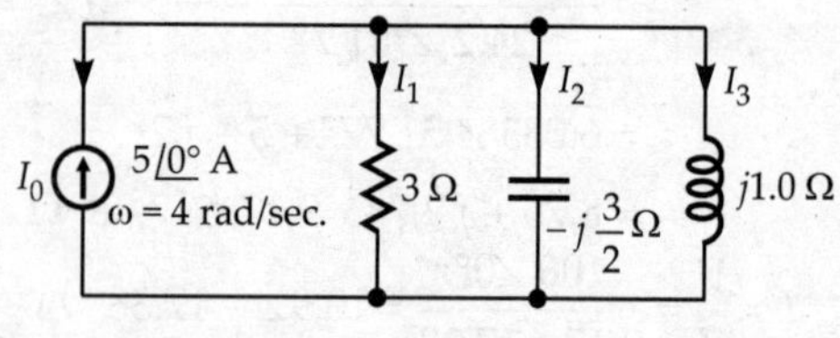

Fig. E3.41

SOLUTION. The equivalent impedance of the resistive and capacitive circuit is given by

$$Z_1 = \frac{3\left(-j\frac{3}{2}\right)}{3 - j\frac{3}{2}}\,\Omega = \frac{-j\,9}{6 - j\,3} = \left(\frac{-j\,3}{2 - j}\right)\,\Omega.$$

We can then write $I_3 = I_0 \dfrac{Z_1}{Z_1 + j\,1.0}$

[using current division formulae]

$$\text{or} \quad I_3 = 5\,\angle 0° \frac{\frac{-j\,3}{2-j}}{\frac{-j\,3}{2-j} + j\,1.0} = \frac{-j\,3}{-j\,3 + j\,(2-j)} \times 5$$

$$= \frac{-j\,15}{1 - j} = \frac{15\,\angle -90°}{1.414\,\angle -45°} = 10.6\,\angle -45°\text{ A}$$

∴ Q (reactive power) of inductance

$$= I_3^2 \times j\,1.0 = 112.4\text{ VAR (inductive)}$$

i.e., Reactive power of inductance = **112.4 VAR**

EXAMPLE 3.97 *A r.m.s. voltage of 100 V is applied to a parallel combination of two impedances $Z_1 = r_1 + j\,x_1$ and $Z_2 = r_2 + j\,x_2$. If $r_1 = 3\,\Omega$ and $r_2 = 4\,\Omega$, and the magnitude of two branch currents be same, determine the source current and the complex power supplied by the source.*

SOLUTION. It is said that the branch currents are same

i.e. $\quad I_1 = I_2$

This is only possible if $Z_1 = Z_2$.

or, $\quad r_1 + jx_1 = r_2 + j\,x_2$

or $\quad 3 + j\,x_1 = 4 + j\,x_2$

i.e., when $x_1 = 4\Omega$ and $x_2 = 3\,\Omega$.

$$\therefore \quad I_1 = \frac{100\,\angle 0°}{Z_1} = \frac{100\,\angle 0°}{3 + j\,4} = \frac{100\,\angle 0°}{5\,\angle 53.2°}$$

$$= 20\,\angle -53.2° = (12 - j\,16)\text{ A}$$

$$\text{and} \quad I_2 = \frac{100\,\angle 0°}{Z_2} = \frac{100\,\angle 0°}{4 + j\,3} = \frac{100\,\angle 0°}{5\,\angle 36.8°}$$

$$= 20\,\angle -36.8° = (16 - j\,12)\text{ A}$$

∴ Net current

$$I = I_1 + I_2 = (12 - j\,16 + 16 - j\,12)\text{ A}$$

or, $\quad I = 28 - j\,28 = \mathbf{39.6\,\angle -45°\ A}$

Complex power S (supplied) $= VI^*$

$$= 100\,\angle 0° \times 39.6\,\angle 45°$$

$$= 3960\,\angle 45° = \mathbf{(2800 + j\,2800)\ VA.}$$

EXAMPLE 3.98 *In the network of Fig. E3.42, find the complex power supplied by each source.*

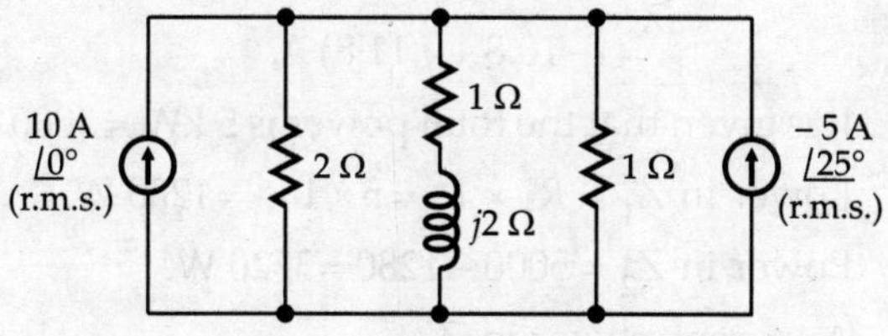

Fig. E3.42

SOLUTION. Let us first convert the current sources into voltage sources and the circuit is redrawn (Fig. E3.43).

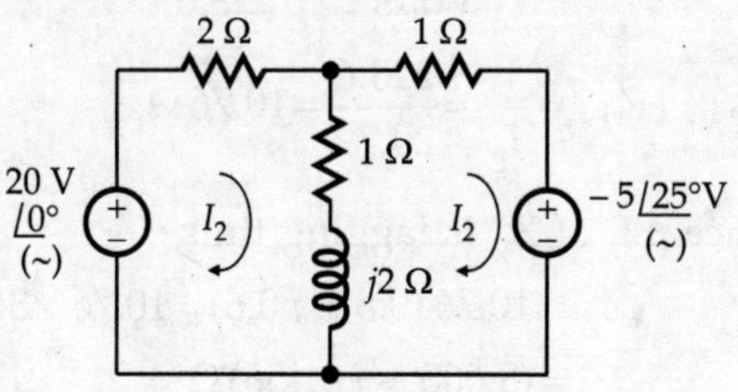

Fig. E3.43

Let the loop currents be I_1 and I_2. Application of KVL yields,

$$2I_1 + (1+j2)(I_1 - I_2) = 20\angle 0° = 20 + j0$$

or $\quad I_1(3+j2) - I_2(1+j2) = 20 + j0 \quad$ ...(1)

and $\quad 1\times I_2 + (1+j2)(I_2 - I_1) = 5\angle 25°$

$$= 4.53 + j2.11$$

or $\quad -(1+j2)I_1 + (2+j2)I_2 = 4.53 + j2.11 \quad$ ...(2)

In matrix form,

$$\begin{bmatrix}(3+j2) & -(1+j2)\\ -(1+j2) & (2+j2)\end{bmatrix}\begin{bmatrix}I_1\\ I_2\end{bmatrix} = \begin{bmatrix}20+j0\\ 4.53+j2.11\end{bmatrix}$$

$$\therefore I_1 = \frac{\begin{vmatrix}20+j0 & -1-j2\\ 4.53+j2.11 & 2+j2\end{vmatrix}}{\begin{vmatrix}3+j2 & -1-j2\\ -1-j2 & 2+j2\end{vmatrix}}$$

$$= \frac{40+j40+4.53+j9.06+j2.11-4.22}{6+j6+j4-4-1-j2-j2+4}$$

$$= \frac{40.31+j51.17}{5+j6}$$

$$= \frac{(40.31+j51.17)(5-j6)}{25+36}$$

$$= \frac{508.57+j14}{61}$$

$$= 8.34 + j0.229 = 8.34\angle 1.57 \text{ A}$$

$$I_2 = \frac{\begin{vmatrix}3+j2 & 20+j0\\ -1-j2 & 4.53+j2.11\end{vmatrix}}{\begin{vmatrix}3+j2 & -1-j2\\ -1-j2 & 2+j2\end{vmatrix}}$$

$$= \frac{13.59+j6.33+j9.06-4.22+20+j40}{5+j6}$$

$$= \frac{29.37+j55.40}{5+j6} = \frac{(29.37+j55.40)(5-j6)}{61}$$

$$= \frac{145.85-j176.22+j277+332.4}{61}$$

$$= \frac{479.25+j100.78}{61} = 8.03\angle 11.88° \text{ A}$$

$$\therefore S_1 = V_1 I_1^* = 20\angle 0° \times 8.34\angle -1.57°$$

$$= \mathbf{(166.74 - j4.57)\ VA};$$

$$S_2 = V_2 I_2^* = 5\angle 25° \times 8.03\angle -11.86°$$

$$= 40.15\angle 13.12° \text{ VA} = \mathbf{(39.1 + j9.11)\ VA}$$

Here as I_1 comes out of the source but I_2 enters the source hence S_1 is the power supplied by the source and S_2 is the power injected to the source.

EXAMPLE 3.99 *In the network of Fig. E3.44, $Z_A = (10+j8)\Omega$ $\quad Z_B = (9-j6)\Omega$, $\quad Z_C = (3+j2)\Omega$. Voltage across Z_C is $100\angle 0°$ V. Find the complex power of Z_A and Z_B.*

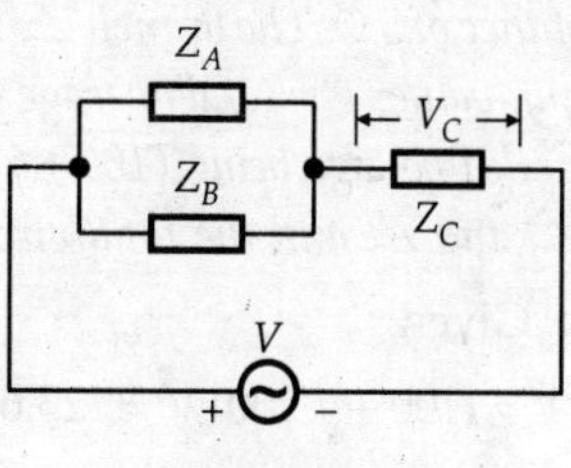

Fig. E3.44

SOLUTION. $Z_A = (10+j8)\Omega = 12.8\angle 38.5°\Omega$

$$\therefore \quad Y_A = \frac{1}{12.8\angle 38.5°}$$

$$= 0.078\angle -38.5° \text{ mho.}$$

$$= (0.061 - j0.049) \text{ mho.}$$

Similarly,

$$Z_B = (9-j6)\Omega = 10.8\angle -33.7°\Omega \text{ giving}$$

$$Y_B = \frac{1}{10.8\angle -33.7°}$$

$$= (0.078 + j0.051) \text{ mho.}$$

Net admittance of the parallel branch

$$(Y) = Y_A + Y_B.$$

i.e., $Y = 0.061 - j\,0.049 + 0.078 + j\,0.051$

$$= (0.139 + j\,0.002) \text{ mho.}$$

Again $Z_C = (3 + j\,2)\Omega = 3.61\,\angle 33.7°\,\Omega.$

$$\therefore \quad I_C = \frac{V_C}{Z_C} = \frac{100\,\angle 0°}{3.61\,\angle 33.7°} = 27.7\,\angle -33.7° \text{ A.}$$

Using the current division formulae,

$$I_A = I_C\,\frac{Y_A}{Y} = 27.7\,\angle -33.7 \times \frac{0.078\,\angle -38.5°}{0.139\,\angle 0.82°}$$

$$= 27.7\,\angle -33.7 \times 0.561\,\angle -39.32°$$

$$= 15.54\,\angle -73.02° \text{ A.}$$

Similarly,

$$I_B = I_C \times \frac{Y_B}{Y} = 27.7\,\angle -33.7° \times \frac{0.078 + j\,0.051}{0.139 + j\,0.002}$$

$$= 18.6\,\angle -1.35° = 18.6 - j0.44$$

$$= 18.6\angle -1.35° \text{ A}$$

Thus, $I_A = \mathbf{15.54\,\angle -73.02°\ A}$

$I_B = \mathbf{18.5\,\angle -1.35°\ A.}$

EXAMPLE 3.100 *Two impedances Z_1 and Z_2 are connected in parallel. The branch Z_1 takes a leading current of 16 A and has a resistance of 5 Ω. The branch Z_2 takes a lagging current of 0.8 p.f. value. The total average power supplied being 5 kW, applied voltage being (100 + j 200) V, obtain the values of Z_2 and Z_2 and the total circuit current.*

SOLUTION. Given,

$$V = (100 + j\,200)\,V = 223.6\,\angle 63.4°\text{ V}$$

$$\therefore \quad |Z_1| = \frac{V}{I_1} = \frac{223.6}{16} = 13.98\,\Omega$$

[∵ branch-1 takes 16 A leading current]

From the given theory, Z_1 is capacitive as the current Z_1 is leading.

$$\therefore \quad Z_1 = 5 - j\,x_c$$

or $\quad 5^2 + x_C^2 = z_1^2 = 13.98^2.$

$$\therefore \quad x_C^2 = 13.98^2 - 5^2$$

or $\quad |x_C| = 13.1\,\Omega$

This gives,

$$Z_1 = (5 - j\,13.1)\,\Omega = 14\,\angle -69°\,\Omega.$$

and $\quad I_1 = \dfrac{V}{Z_1} = \dfrac{223.6\,\angle 63.4°}{14\,\angle -69°} = 16\,\angle 132.4°\text{ A}$

$$= (-10.8 + j\,11.8)\text{ A.}$$

It is given that the total power is 5 kW = 5000 W.

Power in $Z_1 = R_1 \times I_1^2 = 5 \times 16^2 = 1280$ W.

Power in $Z_2 = 5000 - 1280 = 3720$ W.

Apparent power in Z_2

$$= \frac{\text{Power in } Z_2}{\text{p.f.}} = \frac{3720}{0.8} = 4650 \text{ VA}$$

and $\quad I_2 = \dfrac{\text{VA power}}{\text{Volts}} = \dfrac{4650}{223.6} = 20.79$ A

$$\therefore \quad |Z_2| = \frac{V}{I_2} = \frac{223.6}{20.79} = 10.76\,\Omega$$

Since p.f. of Z_2 is lagging thus

$$Z_2 = 10.76\,(0.8 + j\,0.6) = 10.76\,\angle 36.87°\,\Omega$$

$$= (8.608 + j\,6.456)\,\Omega$$

$$I_2 = \frac{V}{Z_2} = \frac{223.6\,\angle 63.4}{10.76\,\angle 36.87°}$$

$$= 26.78\,\angle 26.53° \text{ A.}$$

∴ Net current $I = I_1 + I_2$

$$= 16\,\angle 132.4° + 20.78\,\angle 26.53°$$

$$= 22.5\,\angle 69.7° \text{ A.}$$

Thus finally we obtain,

circuit current = **22.5 ∠69.7° A** (Capacitive)

$Z_1 = \mathbf{14\,\angle -69\,\Omega}$ (Capacitive)

$Z_2 = \mathbf{10.76\,\angle 36.87°\,\Omega}$ (Inductive).

EXAMPLE 3.101 *Two impedances 14.89 ∠20° Ω and 20.60 ∠29° Ω are connected in parallel across a voltage source of 200 ∠0° V. Determine the power and power factor of the circuit.*

SOLUTION. $Z_1 = 14.89\,\angle 20°\,\Omega$

$$\therefore \quad Y_1 = \frac{1}{Z_1} = \frac{1}{14.89}\,\angle -20°$$

$$= (0.06 - j\,0.023) \text{ mho.}$$

$$Z_2 = 20.60\,\angle 29°\,\Omega$$

$$\therefore \quad Y_2 = \frac{1}{20.60}\,\angle -29° = 0.0485\,\angle -29°$$

$$= (0.04 - j\,0.024) \text{ mho.}$$

The net circuit admittance is then $Y_1 + Y_2$

i.e., $\quad Y = Y_1 + Y_2 = (0.1 - j\,0.047)$ mho

The input current

$$= I = VY = 200\,(0.1 - j\,0.047)$$

$$= 20 - j\,9.4 = 22.10\,\angle -25.17°\text{ A.}$$

$\therefore$ p.f. of the circuit = cos 25.17 = **0.905 (lag.)**

The input power

$$= VI\cos\phi = 200 \times 22.1 \times \cos 25.17$$

$$= 4000\text{ W.}$$

i.e., Input power to the circuit = **4 kW.**

EXAMPLE 3.102 *Find the average power drawn by the circuit of Fig. E3.45.*

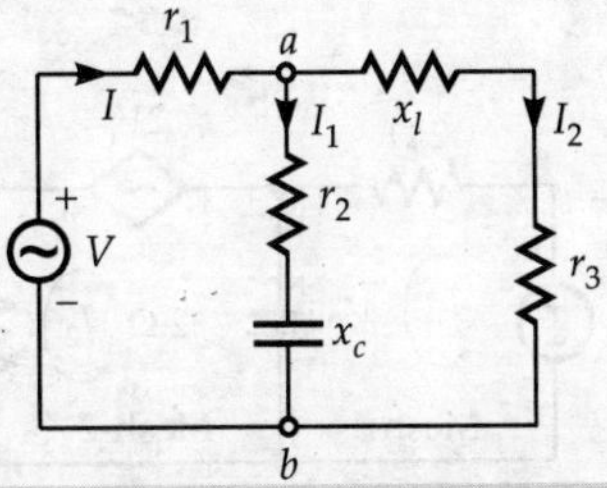

[Given : $V = 100\angle 0°$ V ; $r_1 = 4\,\Omega$; $r_2 = 9\,\Omega$; $r_3 = 8\,\Omega$; $x_c = -j7\,\Omega$; $x_l = j6\,\Omega$]

Fig. E3.45

SOLUTION. The net impedance across the terminals *a-b* is

$$Z_{ab} = (r_2 - j\,x_c) \,||\, (r_3 + j\,x_l)$$

$$= \frac{(9 - j\,7) \times (8 + j\,6)}{9 - j\,7 + 8 + j\,6}$$

$$= \frac{11.4\,\angle -37.8° \times 10\,\angle 36.87°}{17.03\,\angle -3.37°}$$

$$= 6.7\,\angle 2.44°$$

$$= 6.68 + j\,0.28\text{ ohm.}$$

[Given : $V = 100\,\angle 0°$ V; $r_1 = 4\,\Omega$, $r_2 = 9\,\Omega$, $r_3 = 8\,\Omega$, $x_c = -j\,7\,\Omega$, $x_l = j\,6\,\Omega$]

Hence, the net impedance of the circuit becomes

$$Z = (r_1 + 6.68 + j\,0.28)\,\Omega = (4 + 6.68 + j\,0.28)\,\Omega$$

$$= 10.68 + j\,0.28 = 10.68\,\angle 1.5°\text{ ohm.}$$

This gives I (= Source current)

$$= \frac{V}{Z} = \frac{100\,\angle 0°}{10.68\,\angle 1.5°} = 9.36\,\angle -1.5°\text{ A}$$

The average power drawn by the circuit is thus,

$$P = VI\cos\phi = 100 \times 9.36 \times \cos 1.5° = 936\text{ W.}$$

i.e., Average power drawn = **936 W.**

EXAMPLE 3.103 *In the network of Fig. E3.46, find the complex power absorbed by the inductive branch and determine the net reactive powers supplied by the two sources. Obtain the value of C_1 if the capacitor takes 10 VAR. Assume $v_1 = 10\,\angle 0°$ volts, 50 Hz and $v_2 = 20\,\angle 0°$ volts, 50 Hz.*

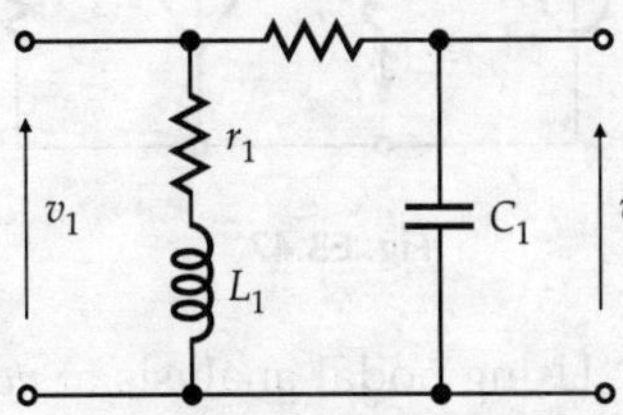

[$r_1 = 1\,\Omega$, $L = 1$ mH, $r_2 = 2\,\Omega$]

Fig. E3.46

SOLUTION. $L_1 = 1$ mH

$$\therefore \quad X_{L_1} = 2\pi \times 50 \times 1 \times 10^{-3} = 0.314\,\Omega.$$

Let the current through the inductive branch be I_{L_1}.

$$\therefore \quad I_{L_1} = \frac{10\,\angle 0°}{r_1 + j\,X_{L_1}} = \frac{10\,\angle 0°}{1 + j\,0.314}$$

$$= \frac{10\,\angle 0°}{1.048\,\angle 17.43} = 9.54\,\angle -17.43°\text{ A.}$$

Given that the voltage (V_{L_1}) across the inductive branch is $10\,\angle 0°$ V.

$\therefore$ S_{L_1} (power in the inductive branch)

$$= V_{L_1} \times I^*_{L_1} = 10\,\angle 0° \times 9.54\,\angle 17.93°$$

$$= 95.4\,\angle 17.93°$$

$$= (90.77 + j\,29.37)\text{ VA.}$$

i.e., Complex power absorbed by the inductive circuit

$$= \mathbf{(90.77 + j\,29.37)\ VA}$$

It is given that C_1 takes 10 VAR.

$$\therefore \quad X_C = \frac{(V_C)^2}{Q_C} = \frac{(\text{voltage across } C_1)^2}{10}$$

$$= \frac{20^2}{10}$$

or

$$C = \frac{1}{2\pi \times 50 \times 40} = \mathbf{79.58\ \mu F}$$

The net reactive power supplied by the sources is the same as the power absorbed by the inductor and supplied by the capacitor.

$$\therefore \quad Q = 29.37 - 10 = \mathbf{19.37\ VAR.}$$

Example 3.104 *How much power is delivered by the current source in the circuit of Fig. E3.47 ?*

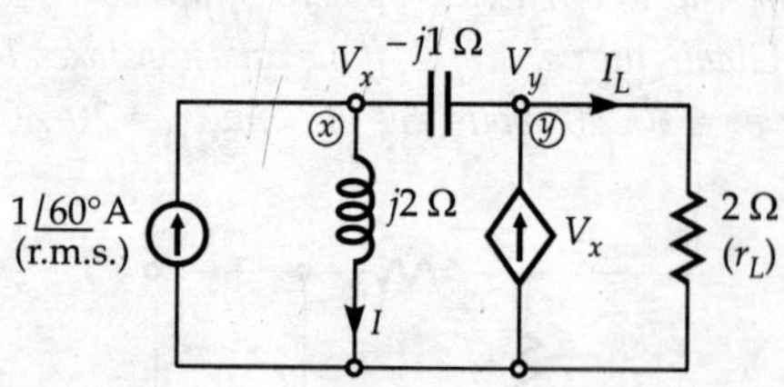

Fig. E3.47

Solution. Using nodal analysis at *node* (*x*),

$$\frac{V_x}{j2} + \frac{V_x - V_y}{-j1} = 1\angle 60°$$

or $$V_x\left[\frac{1}{j2} - \frac{1}{j1}\right] + \frac{V_y}{j1} = 1\angle 60°$$

or $$V_x\,[-j0.5 + j1] + V_y\,(-j1) = 1\angle 60°$$

or, $$j0.5\,V_x - j\,V_y = 1\angle 60 \qquad ...(A)$$

Nodal analysis at *node* (*y*) yields

$$\frac{V_y}{2} + \frac{V_y - V_x}{-j1} - V_x = 0$$

or $$\frac{V_x}{j1} + V_y\left(\frac{1}{2} - \frac{1}{j1}\right) - V_x = 0$$

or $$V_x\left(1 - \frac{1}{j1}\right) = V_y\left(\frac{1}{2} - \frac{1}{j1}\right)$$

or $$V_x\,(1 + j) = V_y\,(0.5 + j)$$

$$\therefore \quad V_y = V_x\left(\frac{1+j}{0.5+j}\right) \qquad ...(B)$$

Utilising (*B*) in (*A*),

$$j0.5\,V_x - j\,V_x\left(\frac{1+j}{0.5+j}\right) = 1\angle 60°$$

or $$j0.5\,V_x - j\,V_x\left(\frac{1.414\angle +45°}{1.12\angle +63.43°}\right) = 1\angle 60°$$

or $$j0.5\,V_x - j1.263\angle -18.43°\,V_x = 1\angle 60°$$

or $$(0.5\angle 90° - 1.263\angle 71.57°)\,V_x = 1\angle 60°$$

$$\therefore \quad V_x = \frac{1\angle 60°}{0.5\angle 90° - 1.263\angle 71.57°}$$

$$= \frac{1\angle 60°}{0.804\angle -119.76°} = 1.244\angle 179.76°\text{ V}$$

$\therefore$ Complex power delivered by the source is given by

$$S_1 = V_x \times 1\angle -60°$$
$$= \mathbf{1.244\angle 119.36°\ VA.}$$

It may be noted that the complex power supplied by the dependent source can also be found out as follows :

$S_x = V_y \times V_x^*$; V_y can be obtained from above and V_x has been found out.

Example 3.105 *What is the power loss in the 5 Ω resistor (Fig. E3.48) ?*

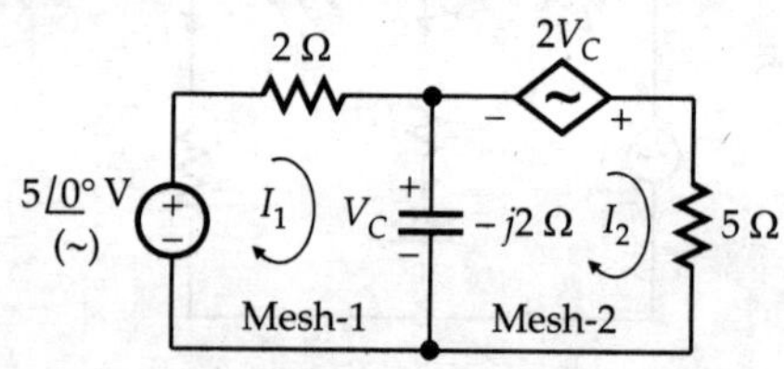

Fig. E3.48

Solution. Let the currents in the loops be I_1 and I_2.

Using loop analysis in mesh (1),

$$2I_1 - j2\,(I_1 - I_2) = 5\angle 0°$$

or $$2I_1 - j2I_1 + j2I_2 = 5\angle 0°$$

or $$I_1\,(1 - j) + j\,I_2 = 2.5\angle 0° \qquad ...(A)$$

In mesh (2),

$$-V_C - 2V_C + 5I_2 = 0$$

or $$3V_C = 5I_2 \qquad ...(B)$$

Also, $$V_C = -j2\,(I_1 - I_2) \qquad ...(C)$$

Using (*C*) in (*B*),

$$3(-j2)(I_1 - I_2) = 5I_2$$

or $$-j6I_1 + j6I_2 = 5I_2$$

or $$I_2\,(5 - j6) = -j6I_1$$

or $$I_1 = I_2\frac{5 - j6}{-j6} = I_2\frac{(5 - j6)(j6)}{36}$$

$$= j\,I_2\left(\frac{5}{6} - j1\right) = I_2\left(1 + j\frac{5}{6}\right) \qquad ...(D)$$

Next solving for (*A*) and (*D*),

$$I_2 = 1.13 - j0.51 = 1.24\angle -24.44°$$

$\therefore$ Power loss (P_l) in 5 Ω resistor

$$= (1.24)^2 \times 5 = \mathbf{7.69\ W.}$$

EXAMPLE 3.106 *Find the power loss in the 10 Ω resistor for the circuit in Fig. E3.49. What is the voltage across the load resistor r_L ?*

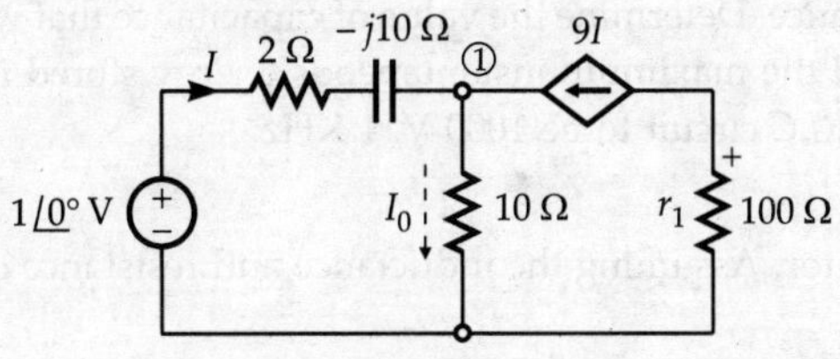

Fig. E3.49

SOLUTION. Let the current through the 10 Ω resistor be I_0.

Applying KCL at *node* (1),

$$I + 9\,I = I_0$$

or, $$I_0 = 10\,I = 10\,\frac{1\angle 0° - V_1}{5 - j\,10}$$

[assuming node voltage at node (1) to be V_1]

$$= \frac{10}{11.18\angle -63.43°}(1\angle 0° - V_1)$$

$$= 0.895\angle 63.43° - 0.895\,V_1\angle 63.43°$$

But $$V_1 = 10\,I_0$$

$\therefore$ $$I_0 = 0.895\angle 63.43° - 0.895 \times 10 I_0 \angle 63.43°$$

$$= 0.895\angle 63.43° - 8.95\,I_0\,(\cos 63.43° + j\sin 63.4°)$$

$$= 0.895\angle 63.43° - I_0\,(4 + j\,8)$$

or $$I_0\,(5 + j\,8) = 0.895\angle 63.43°$$

or $$I_0 = \frac{0.895\angle 63.43°}{5 + j\,8} = \frac{0.895\angle 63.43°}{9.43\angle 58°}$$

i.e., $$I_0 = 0.095\angle 5.43° \text{ A}$$

Thus power loss in 10 Ω resistor

$$= I_0^2 \times 10 = (0.095)^2 \times 10 \text{ W}$$

or $$P_{loss}\,(10\,\Omega) = 0.09 \text{ W}$$

Let the voltage drop in r_L be V_{r_L} volts.

We notice,

$$V_{r_L} = -9\,I \times 100$$

$$= -9 \times \frac{I_0}{10} \times 100 = -90\,I_0.$$

$$= -90 \times 0.095\angle 5.43°$$

$$= 90\angle 180° \times 0.095\angle 5.43°$$

$$= 8.55\angle 185.43° \text{ V}$$

i.e., drop in 100 Ω resistor = **8.55 ∠185.43° V.**

EXAMPLE 3.107 *A single phase 240 V induction motor runs in parallel with a 160 Ω resistor. If the motor takes 2 A and the total current be 3 A, find the power and power factor of the motor.*

SOLUTION. $|I_m|$ (motor current) = 2 A

$$|I_r| \text{ (current in resistor)} = \frac{240}{160} = 1.5 \text{ A.}$$

Let the motor current in phasor form be $(I_\omega - j\,I_\mu)$ such that

$$I_m = (I_\omega - jI_\mu)$$

$\therefore$ $$\sqrt{I_\omega^2 + I_\mu^2} = I_m = 2$$

i.e. $$I_\omega^2 + I_\mu^2 = 4 \qquad ...(a)$$

Again, the total current being 3 A,

$$I_r + I_m = 3 \text{ A}$$

or $$I_r\angle 0° + (I_\omega - j\,I_\mu) = 3$$

[I_r, the resistor current being at unity p.f.]

or $$(I_r + I_\omega) - jI_\mu = 3$$

or $$(I_\omega + 1.5)^2 + (I_\mu)^2 = 9 \qquad ...(b)$$

Subtracting equation (*b*) from equation (*a*),

$$I_\omega^2 - (I_\omega + 1.5)^2 = 4 - 9$$

or $$(I_\omega + 1.5)^2 - I_\omega^2 = 5$$

or $$I_\omega^2 + 3I_\omega + 2.25 - I_\omega^2 = 5$$

or $$I_\omega = \frac{5 - 2.25}{3} = 0.917 \text{ A}$$

And from (*a*),

$$I_\mu = 1.78 \text{ A.}$$

Thus the motor current is

$$I_m = (0.917 - j\,1.78) \text{ A} = 2\angle -62.74°$$

The total current

$$I = 0.917 - j\,1.78 + 1.5$$

$$= (2.477 - j\,1.78) \text{ A}$$

Power of the motor

$$= VI_m \cos\phi = 240 \times 2 \times \cos 62.74°$$

$$= 219.8 \simeq 220 \text{ W.}$$

Thus the p.f. of the motor = cos 62.74° = **0.458** and the power of the motor = **220 W.**

CHAPTER 3

EXERCISES

1. A series *RLC* circuit has 50 mH inductance and 5 ohm resistance. Determine the value of capacitance that would produce resonance. Also find the current at resonance and the maximum instantaneous energy stored in the inductance at resonance. Assume the supply to the series *RLC* circuit to be 1000 V, 1 KHz.

   [**Hint.** Ref. Ex. 3.2]

2. A coil produces resonance at 20 kHz in series with a capacitor. Assuming the inductance and resistance of the coil to be 10 H and 100 Ω, find the *Q* factor of the coil.

   [**Hint.** Ref Ex. 3.4]

3. A 80 pF capacitor is in series with a coil having 10 Ω resistance and 50 mH inductance. At resonance, obtain the circuit impedance and also find the resonant frequency. If the supply to the *RLC* circuit is 25 V having an internal impedance of 1 ohm, find also the circuit current and the voltage across the capacitor.

   [**Hint.** Ref. Ex. 3.5]

4. A series circuit with $R = 3\,\Omega$, $L = 10$ mH and a variable capacitance *C* has an applied voltage with a frequency $f = 1$ kHz. Find C for series resonance.

   [**Hint.** At resonance the reactances are equal *i.e.*, $X_L = X_C$ or, $C = \dfrac{1}{L(2\pi f)^2}$.]

5. A 10 μF condenser is connected in series with a coil having $L = 10$ mH. Determine the frequency of resonance, the resistance of the coil if a 100 V source is applied creating resonance, the circuit current being 50 mA. What is the *Q* factor of the coil ?

   [**Hint.** Ref. Ex. 3.7]

6. Calculate half-power frequencies of a series resonating circuit where the resonance frequency is 100 kHz. Assume the bandwidth to be 50 kHz.

   [**Hint.** Ref. Ex. 3.12]

7. A coil having 100 milli ohm resistance and 50 mH inductance is connected to a capacitor in series, the applied voltage being 230 V, 100 Hz *a.c.* source. Find, at the resonance frequency of 100 Hz, what is the value of the capacitor. Also calculate the *Q* factor and half power frequencies of the circuit.

   [**Hint.** Ref. Ex. 3.13]

8. A current source, having an internal resistance of 10 kΩ feeds a tank circuit containing a coil (having $L_C = 200$ mH, $R_C = 10\,\Omega$) in parallel to capacitor of 100 μF. Find the frequency of resonance and *Q* factor.

   [**Hint.** Ref. Ex. 3.14]

9. A 230 V, 50 Hz supply feeds energy to a parallel AC circuit consisting of a $5\angle 60°$ ohm branch and a $10\angle -30$ ohm branch. Determine the impedance of a circuit element such that if connected in series with the source, the system is at resonance.

   [**Hint.** Ref. Ex. 3.20]

10. A $-j\,5\Omega$ capacitor reactance is in series with a resistance *R* and the combination is in parallel with another series *R-L* circuit where $R_L = 5\,\Omega$, $L = 100$ mH. Find the value of *R* to produce resonance.

    [**Hint.** Ref. Ex. 3.23]

11. A series *RLC* circuit has $R = 5\,\Omega$, $L = 10$ mH and $C = 15\,\mu$F. Calculate (*i*) *Q* factor of the circuit, (*ii*) the band width (*iii*) the resonant frequency and (*iv*) the half power frequency f_1 and f_2.

    [**Hint.** Ref. Ex. 3.62]

12. Obtain the values of *R*, *L* and C in a series circuit that makes resonance at 2 kHz and consume 100 W from a 100 V *a.c.* source operating at resonant frequency. The bandwidth is 0.8 kHz.

    [**Hint.** Ref. Ex. 3.64]

13. A resistance of r_1 is in series with $j\,2\,\Omega$ inductive reactance and the combination is in parallel with a *R-C* series circuit having resistance of 5 Ω and capacitive reactance of $-j\,\Omega$. Find the value of r_1 to create resonance.

    [**Hint.** Ref. Ex. 3.67]

14. A series resonating circuit has a source frequency of 10 kHz and source impedance of $(1 + j\,2)\,\Omega$. The load impedance being $(5 - j\,X_C)\,\Omega$, find the value of C provided the power consumed by the resistor is maximum.

[**Hint.** Ref. Ex. 3.70]

15. On a power distribution system, three loads run in parallel :

Load A : 50 VA, 0.7 p.f. (lag)

Load B : 175 W, 0.5 p.f. (lead)

Load C : 400 VA, 225 VAR (lag)

Find the net power position.

[**Hint.** Solve as done in Ex. 3.27]

16. Two impedances Z_A and Z_B take the following currents : $I_A = 10\angle 65°$ A ; $I_B = 8\angle -25°$ A. Supply voltage being 24 V, taking it to be the reference phasor, find the amount of complex power drawn from the supply.

[**Hint.** Solve as done in Ex. 3.28]

17. The voltages across two series connected circuit elements are $v_1 = 50 \sin \omega t$ and $v_2 = 20 \sin(\omega t - 45°)$ V. If the circuit current is $(2 + j4)$ A, find the complex power of the circuit.

[**Hint.** Solve as done in Ex. 3.30]

18. A 5 kW single phase induction motor is supplied by an a.c. source of 50 Hz. Terminal voltage being $220\angle 0°$ V, the power factor of the motor is 0.8 lag. If the connecting cable between the source and motor has 0.2 ohm resistance, find the source power.

[**Hint.** Solve in the same way as done in Ex. 3.31]

19. In the network of Fig. P3.1, find the power delivered by the source.

[**Hint.** Ref. Ex. 3.32]

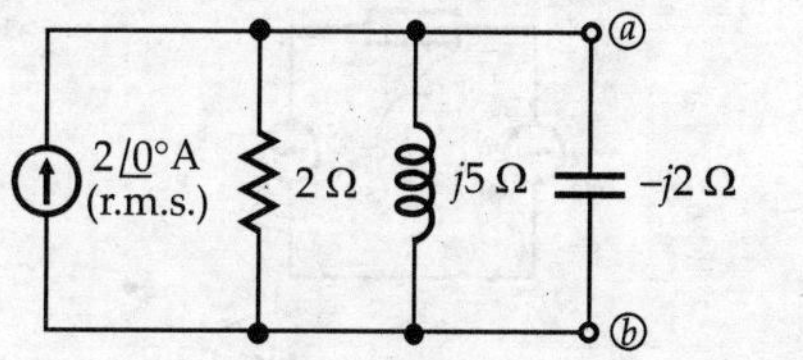

Fig. P3.1

20. In an a.c. circuit, $v = 220 \sin(\omega t + 45°)$ while $i = 2 \sin(\omega t - 45°)$. Find the true power.

[**Hint.** Ref. Ex. 3.34]

21. A $8\,\Omega$ resistance is in series with a $5\,\Omega$ capacitive reactance. The combination is connected across a $2\,\Omega$ resistor. If the input current to this combination is $5\angle 0°$ A, find the p.f. of the circuit.

[**Hint.** Solve as done in Ex. 3.37]

22. An impedance $Z_1 = (4 + j\,3)\,\Omega$ is connected in parallel with another impedance $Z_2 = (2 - j\,4)\,\Omega$. If the input reactive power is 125 VAR, lagging, what is the total active power ?

[**Hint.** Solve in the same way as done in Ex. 3.38]

23. How much energy is consumed during one cycle by an impedance of $(5 + j\,4)\,\Omega$ when connected against a 10 V, 60 Hz source ?

[**Hint.** Ref. Ex. 3.40]

24. In Fig. P3.2, find the true power delivered by the source.

[**Hint.** Ref. Ex. 3.42]

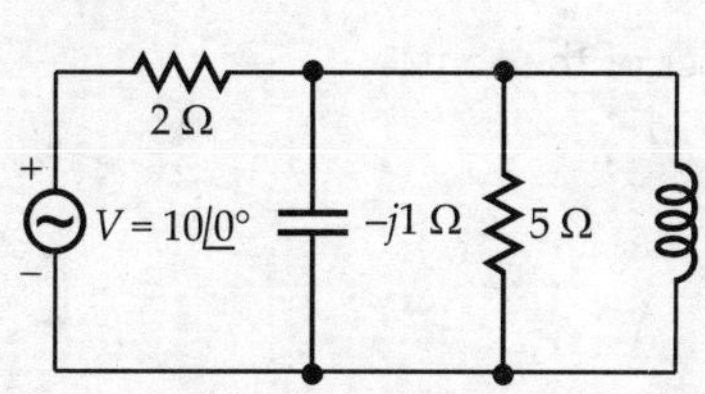

Fig. P3.2

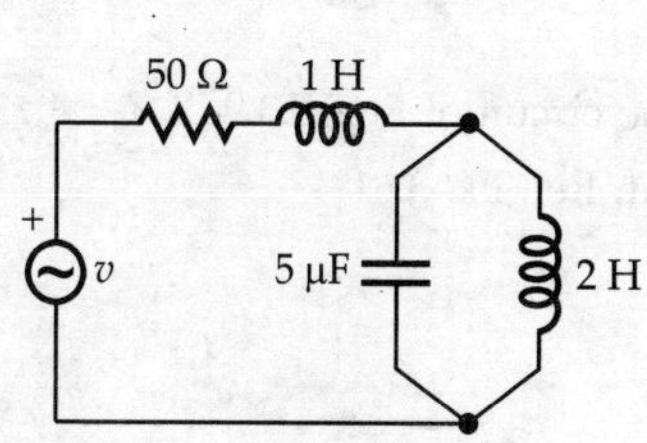

Fig. P3.3

25. In Fig. P3.3, if $v = 70 \sin 314\,t$, find the power dissipated in the resistor.

[**Hint.** Ref. Ex. 3.44]

26. A current is given by $5 \angle -60°$ A through an impedance of $(2 + j\,3)\,\Omega$. Find the complex power.
[Hint. Ref. Ex. 3.47]

27. In Fig. P3.4, if $v = 24 \angle 50°$ V, find the average power consumed in the circuit.
[Hint. Ref. Ex. 3.49]

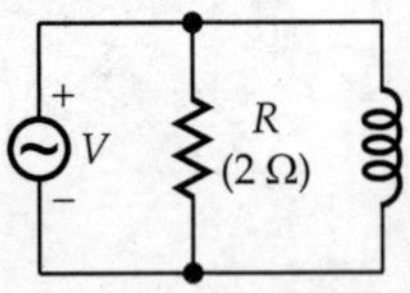

Fig. P3.4

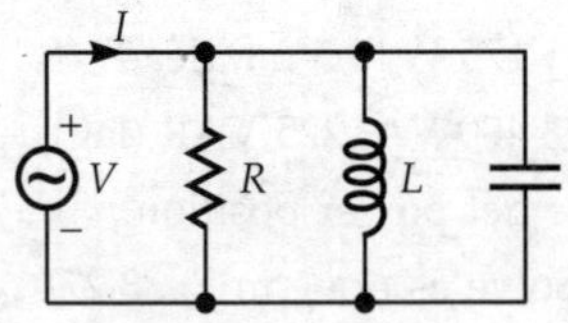

Fig. P3.5

28. In the network of Fig. P3.5, $V = 50 \angle 36°$, $R = 5\,\Omega$, $L = 1$ H, $C = 0.5$ F, $\omega = 100$ rad / sec. Find the true power consumed by the circuit.
[Hint. Ref. Ex. 3.50]

29. In the circuit of Fig. P3.6, find the real power loss in Z. Given that $v_1 = 220 \sin(\omega t + 36°)$ V; $v_2 = 400 \sin(\omega t - 45°)$ V. Assume $I = 10 \angle 45°$ A.
[Hint. Ref. Ex. 3.52]

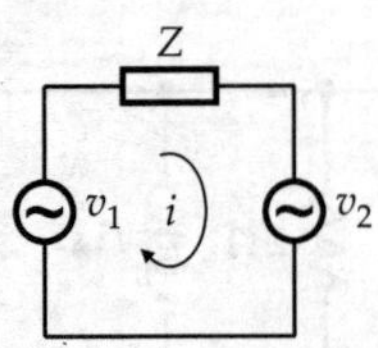

Fig. P3.6

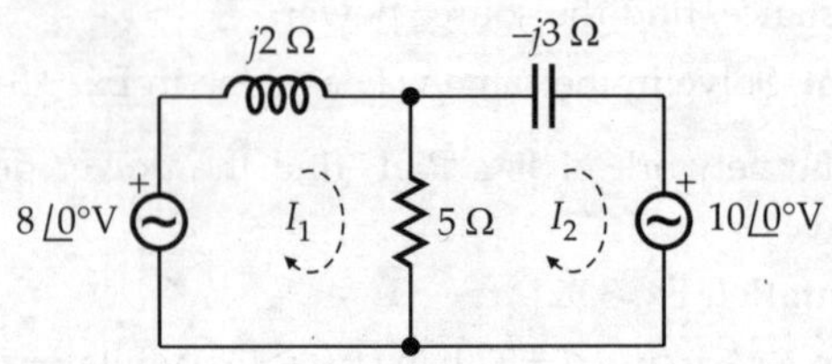

Fig. P3.7

30. In the circuit of Fig. P3.7, find the power supplied by each source.
[Hint. Ref. Ex. 3.54]

31. In the network of Fig. P3.8, find complex power drawn from the current source.
[Hint. Ref. Ex. 3.56]

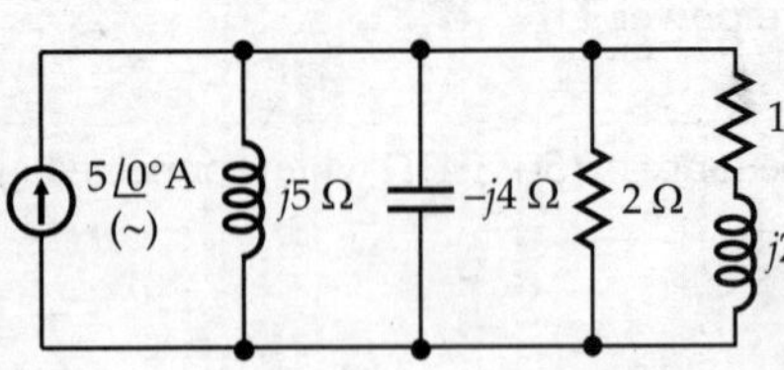

Fig. P3.8

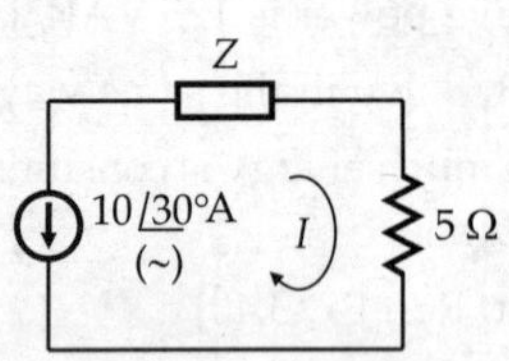

Fig. P3.9

32. In the circuit of Fig. P.3.9, if $Z = 4 \angle 50°\,\Omega$, find the complex power of the source.
[Hint. Ref. Ex. 3.61]

CHAPTER

4

Analysis of Three Phase Circuits

4.1 INTRODUCTION

A *three phase electric system* may be considered as three separate single phase systems *phase displaced* from each other by 120° or $2\pi/3$ radians and the peaks of the respective voltages do not occur *simultaneously*. Fig. 4.1 represents the graphical pattern of voltages in a three phase system.

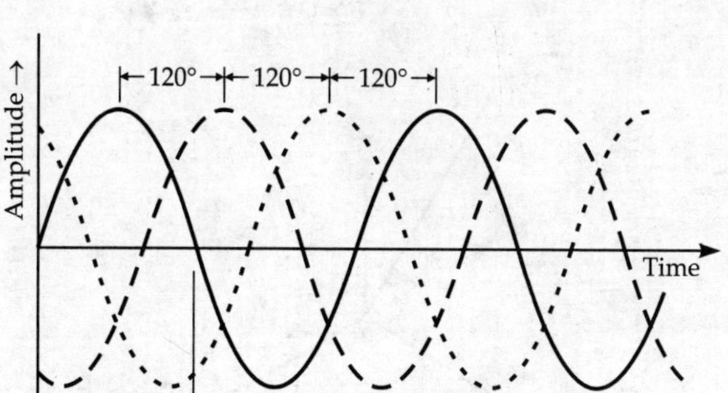

Fig. 4.1 Graphical representation of three phase system.

The common configurations of inter-connections in a three phase system are either *star* or *delta* connections (Fig. 4.2 and Fig. 4.3).

The star connection shown in the figure represents the phasors connected in star, *n* being the *star* or *neutral* point. V_{nR}, V_{nY} and V_{nB} represent the *phase voltages* and may simply be termed as V_R, V_Y, V_B. The voltages between lines *i.e.*, V_{YR}, V_{RB} and V_{BY} are termed as *line voltages*. In a balanced three phase system,

$$V_R = V\angle 0° \text{ V}$$

$$V_Y = V\angle -120° \text{ V}$$

$$V_B = V\angle +120° \text{ or } V\angle -240° \text{ V}.$$

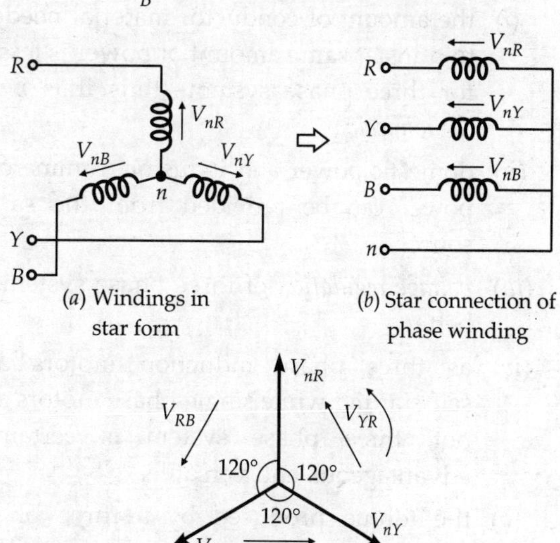

(*a*) Windings in star form

(*b*) Star connection of phase winding

(c) Vector representation of phase voltage

Fig. 4.2 Star connection of phases and generating voltages.

It may be noted that the voltages between the neutral and line are called phase voltage while the voltages between two lines are called line voltages.

In delta connection (Fig. 4.3), the neutral point being not available directly, the line voltages and the corresponding plan voltages are identical. The line voltages in delta connection are designated as

$$V_{RY} = V \angle 0° \text{ V}$$

$$V_{YB} = V \angle -120° \text{ V}$$

$$V_{BR} = V \angle -240° \text{ V} \quad \text{or} \quad V \angle +120° \text{ V}.$$

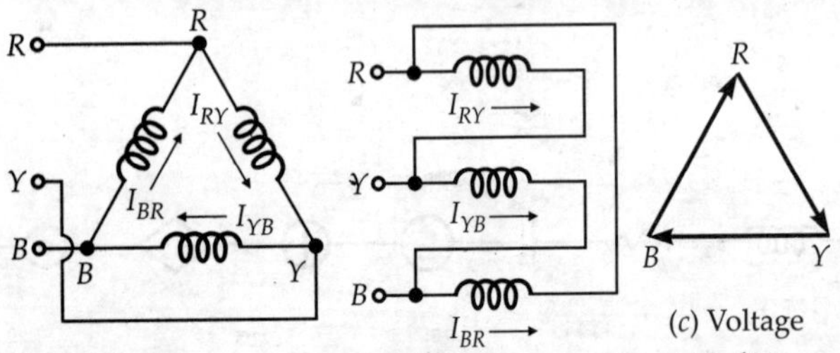

(*a*) Windings connected in delta form (*b*) Delta connection of phase winding (*c*) Voltage vector diagram of Δ winding

Fig. 4.3 Delta connection of phases generating voltages / currents.

4.2 ADVANTAGES OF THREE PHASE SYSTEM

The advantages of a three phase system over a single phase system are as under :

(*i*) the amount of conductor material needed to transfer same amount of power is lesser for three phase system—thus it is *more economical,*

(*ii*) domestic power and industrial/commercial power can be provided from the same source,

(*iii*) *voltage regulation* of three phase system is better,*

(*iv*) as three phase induction motors are self-starting while single phase motors are not, three phase system is certainly advantageous and versatile,

(*v*) the torque produced by a three phase motor is more,

(*vi*) for a given size of the frame, three phase generator provides more output.

4.3 RELATIONSHIP BETWEEN LINE AND PHASE VOLTAGES AND CURRENTS IN A STAR CONNECTION

Let V_R, V_Y and V_B represent the phase voltages in Fig. 4.4 while the line voltages are given by V_{RY}, V_{YB} and V_{BR}.

Let $|V_R| = |V_Y| = |V_B| = V_{ph}$

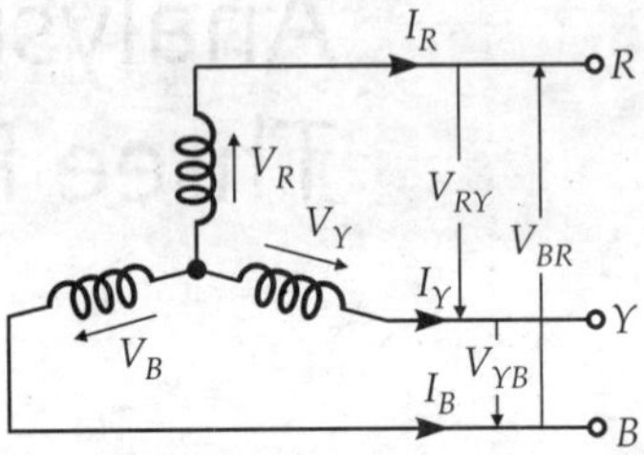

Fig. 4.4 Diagrammatic view of connection

It may be observed that the line voltage V_{RY} is the vector difference of V_R and V_Y or the vector sum V_R and V_Y (reversed).

i.e., $V_{RY} = V_R - V_Y$ (Refer to Fig. 4.5)

i.e., $V_{RY} = \sqrt{V_R^2 + V_Y^2 + 2\,V_R\,V_Y \cos 60°}$

[∵ angle between V_R and $-V_Y$ is 60°]

$$= \sqrt{V_{ph}^2 + V_{ph}^2 + 2\,V_{ph}^2 \cos 60°}$$

$$= \sqrt{2\,V_{ph}^2 + 2\,V_{ph}^2 \times \frac{1}{2}} = \sqrt{3}\,V_{ph}$$

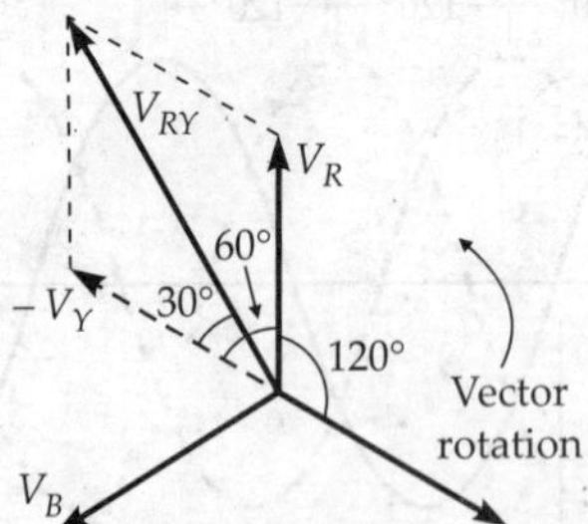

Fig. 4.5 Vectorial addition of phase voltage.

Similarly,

$$V_{YB} = V_Y - V_B \text{ (vector difference)}$$
$$= \sqrt{3}\,V_{ph}$$

and $$V_{BR} = V_B - V_R \text{ (vector difference)}$$
$$= \sqrt{3}\,V_{ph}$$

* Also refer to *"An introduction to Network, Filters and Transmission Lines"* by the same author.

However,

$$V_{RY} = V_{YB} = V_{BR} = V_L \text{ (line voltage)}$$

Thus it is proved that in star (or Y) connection,

$$V_L = \sqrt{3}\, V_{ph}$$

On the other hand, observation revealed that each line is in series with its individual phase winding. Hence in star connection, the *line current in each line is the same as the current in the phase winding* to which the line is connected.

Let current in line R be I_R, current in line Y be I_Y and the current in line B be I_B.

Since $I_R = I_Y = I_B = I_{ph}$ (say), in star connection it is generalised as

$$I_L = I_{ph}$$

i.e., line currents = phase currents.

For any balanced star connection, $I_R + I_Y + I_B = 0$ (vectorial sum)

To summarise, in star connection,

(*a*) the line voltages are 120° apart from each other (phase voltages are also 120° apart from each other);

(*b*) line voltages are 30° ahead of their respective phase voltage (refer to Fig. 4.6) ;

(*c*) the angle between the line currents and the corresponding line voltage is 30° + φ) with current lagging by an angle φ (for lagging loads). This is evident from Fig. 4.6 ;

(*d*) line voltage magnitude is $\sqrt{3}$ times the phase voltage magnitude;

(*e*) the current in line and phase are same.

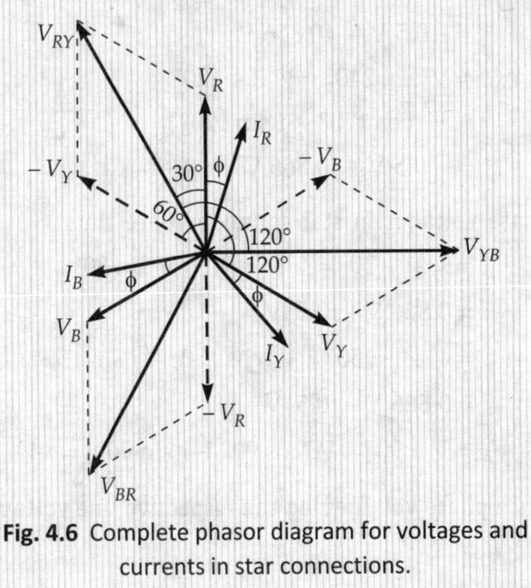

Fig. 4.6 Complete phasor diagram for voltages and currents in star connections.

Power in Star Connection

The *total active* or *real power* in the circuit is the sum of the individual three phase powers.

∴ Total active power = 3 × individual phase power

$$= 3 \times V_{ph}\, I_{ph} \cos\phi$$

$$= \sqrt{3} \times (\sqrt{3}\, V_{ph})\, I_{ph} \cos\phi$$

$$= \sqrt{3}\, V_L\, I_L \cos\phi \times 10^{-3} \text{ kW}$$

[∵ in star connection, $I_{ph} = I_L$ and $V_L = \sqrt{3}\, V_{ph}$ and ϕ = angle between phase voltage and phase current]

Similarly, total reactive power Q is then

$$Q = \sqrt{3}\, V_L\, I_L \sin\phi \times 10^{-3} \text{ kVAR}$$

S, the total *apparent power* or *complex power* of the 3 phase circuit is obviously

$$S = \sqrt{P^2 + Q^2} = \sqrt{3}\, V_L\, I_L \text{ volt-amp.}$$

4.4 RELATIONSHIP BETWEEN LINE AND PHASE VOLTAGES AND CURRENTS IN DELTA CONNECTION

It may be observed from Fig. 4.7 of the delta that currents in each line is the vector difference of two phase currents flowing through the line (*i.e.*, the vector difference of corresponding phase currents).

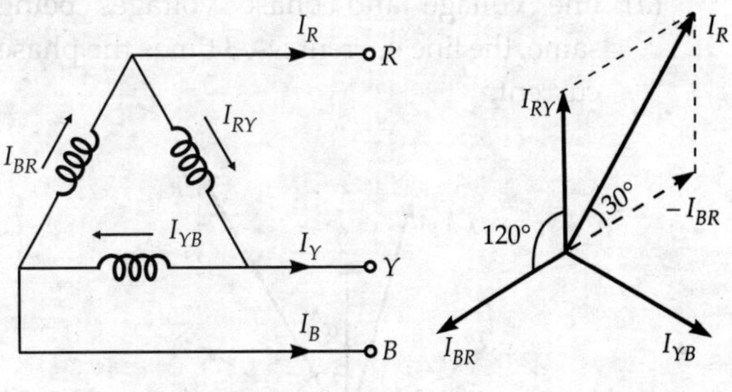

Fig. 4.7 Vector resolution of currents in Δ connection

Assuming the phase currents in Δ be I_{RY}, I_{YB}, I_{BR}, the line currents I_R, I_Y and I_B are given as

$$\left.\begin{aligned} I_R &= I_{BR} - I_{RY} \\ I_Y &= I_{RY} - I_{YB} \\ I_B &= I_{YB} - I_{BR} \end{aligned}\right\} \text{ (vectorial difference)}$$

CHAPTER 4

Current I_R can be obtained by compounding I_{RY} and I_{YB} (reversed) and its value is given by (Fig. 4.7)

$$I_R = \sqrt{I_{BR}^2 + I_{RY}^2 + 2\, I_{BR}\, I_{RY}\, \cos(60°)}$$

However, assuming

$$|I_{BR}| = |I_{RY}| = |I_{YB}| = |I_{ph}|,$$

$$I_R = \sqrt{2 I_{ph}^2 + 2 I_{ph}^2 \cos 60°} = \sqrt{3}\, I_{ph}.$$

Similarly, $I_Y = \sqrt{3}\, I_{ph}$; $I_B = \sqrt{3}\, I_{ph}$

Assuming all the line currents having equal magnitude,

$$I_L = \sqrt{3}\, I_{ph}$$

On the other hand, since the *neutral* does not exist in the delta connection, *phase voltage is same to that of line voltage,*

i.e., $$V_{RY} = V_{YB} = V_{BR} = V_L = V_{ph}$$

To summarise, in a delta connection,

(*a*) line currents are 120° apart from each other as well as phase currents ;

(*b*) line currents are 30° behind the respective phase currents (Refer to Fig. 4.8) ;

(*c*) the angle between the line currents and corresponding line voltages is (30° + ϕ) with the current lagging by an angle ϕ(Fig. 4.8) ;

(*d*) line voltage and phase voltages being same, the line current is √3 times the phase current.

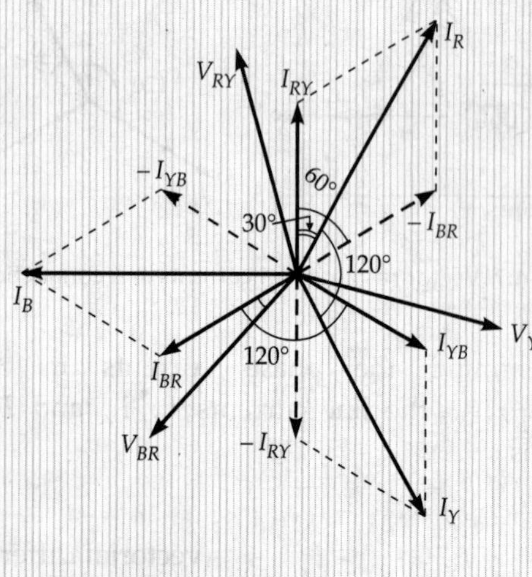

Fig. 4.8 Vector resolution of voltages and currents in Δ connection

Power in Delta Connection

The power/phase in delta connection

$$= V_{ph}\, I_p \cos\phi$$

Total power $= 3\, V_{ph}\, I_{ph} \cos\phi$

However, in a delta connection,

$$V_{ph} = V_L \quad \text{and} \quad I_{ph} = \frac{I_L}{\sqrt{3}}.$$

Hence, in terms of line values, the above expression for real power becomes

$$P = 3\, V_{ph}\, I_{ph} \cos\phi$$

$$= \sqrt{3}\, V_L\, (\sqrt{3}\, I_{ph}) \cos\phi = \sqrt{3}\, V_L\, I_L \cos\phi\,(\text{W})$$

$$= \sqrt{3}\, V_L\, I_L \cos\phi \times 10^{-3}\ \text{kW}$$

$$[\because \text{in delta connection, } I_L = \sqrt{3}\, I_{ph}]$$

Similarly, the total *reactive power* in three phase balanced delta connection is given by

$$Q = \sqrt{3}\, V_L\, I_L \sin\phi\ \text{VAR}$$

$$= \sqrt{3}\, V_L\, I_L \sin\phi \times 10^{-3}\ \text{kVAR}$$

and the *apparent power (or complex power)* of the same circuit becomes

$$S = \sqrt{P^2 + Q^2} = \sqrt{3}\, V_L\, I_L\ \text{V A}$$

$$= \sqrt{3}\, V_L I \times 10^{-3}\ \text{kVA}$$

note **1.** Line voltage in star connection can be represented by (rms values)

$$V_{RY} = V \angle 0° = V + j\,0 \,.\, V = V + j\,0$$

$$V_{YB} = V \angle -120° = V(\cos 120° - j \sin 120°)$$

$$= -0.5\ \text{V} + j0.866\ \text{V}$$

$$V_{BR} = V \angle -240° = V \angle +120°$$

$$= V(\cos 120° + j \sin 120°)$$

$$= -0.5\ \text{V} + j0.866\ \text{V}$$

Phase voltages in star connection are thus

$$V_R = V \angle -30° = V(\cos 30° - j \sin 30°)$$

$$= 0.866\ \text{V} - j0.5\ \text{V}$$

$$V_Y = V \angle -150° = V(\cos 150° - j \sin 150°)$$

$$= 0.866\ \text{V} - j0.5\ \text{V}$$

$$V_B = V \angle 90° = V(\cos 90° + j \sin 90°) = j\,V$$

since phase voltages lag the respective line voltages by 30°.

The instantaneous values of the line voltage in the star connection are thus

$$v_{ry} = V_m \sin \omega t, \; v_{yb} = V_m \sin(\omega t - 120°)$$

$$v_{br} = V_m \sin(\omega t + 120°) \equiv V_m \sin(\omega t - 240°)$$

and the instantaneous values of the phase voltages are

$$v_r = \frac{V_m}{\sqrt{3}} \sin(\omega t - 30°)$$

$$v_y = \frac{V_m}{\sqrt{3}} \sin(\omega t - 120° - 30°)$$

$$= \frac{V_m}{\sqrt{3}} \sin(\omega t - 150°)$$

$$v_b = \frac{V_m}{\sqrt{3}} \sin(\omega t + 120° - 30°)$$

$$= \frac{V_m}{\sqrt{3}} \sin(\omega t + 90°)$$

2. If the line voltages are taken as reference, in delta connection, as in star connection, for r.m.s. values,

$$V_{RY} = V \angle 0°, V_{YB} = V \angle -120°,$$

$$V_{BR} = V \angle +120°$$

As the phase voltages in Δ connection are identical to line voltages, hence the phase voltages can also be represented as done in line voltages.

For the currents, the line currents are represented as

$$I_R = I \angle -(30 + \phi),$$

$$I_Y = I \angle -(30 + \phi) - 120°$$

$$= I \angle -(150° + \phi)$$

and $$I_B = I \angle -(30° + \phi) + 120°$$

$$= I \angle 90 - \phi$$

The instantaneous voltages (line voltages) being represented in the same manner as done in star connection, the instantaneous values for line currents are expressed as

$$i_r = \frac{I_m}{\sqrt{3}} \sin[\omega t - (30 + \phi)],$$

$$i_y = \frac{I_m}{\sqrt{3}} \sin[\omega t - (30 + \phi) - 120°]$$

and $$i_b = \frac{I_m}{\sqrt{3}} \sin[\omega t - (30 + \phi) + 120°]$$

4.5 MEASUREMENT OF POWER AND POWER FACTOR OF A BALANCED THREE PHASE LOAD

A three phase balanced voltage is applied on a balanced three phase load when the current in each of the phases lags by an angle ϕ behind the corresponding phase voltages. From Fig. 4.9, current through current coil of $W_1 = I_R$, current through current coil of $W_2 = I_B$, while potential difference across voltage coil of

$$W_1 = V_{RN} - V_{YN} = V_{RY} \text{ (line voltage)},$$

and the potential difference across voltage coil of

$$W_2 = V_{RN} - V_{YN} = V_{BY}$$

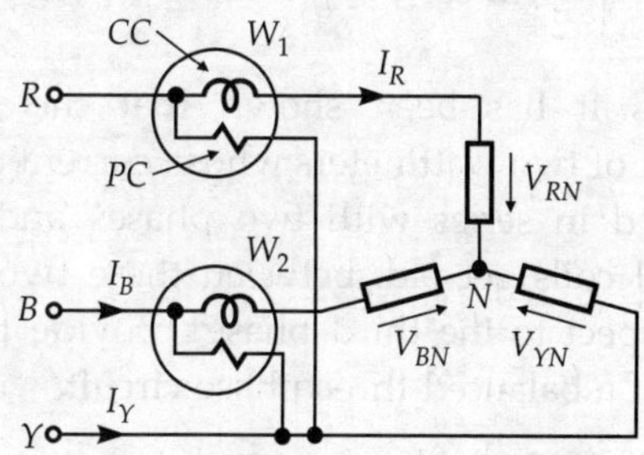

Fig. 4.9 Two wattmeter connection to measure power in three phase balanced load.

Also, phase difference between I_R and V_{RY} is $(30° + \phi)$ while that between I_B and V_{BY} is $(30° - \phi)$ [Refer to Fig. 4.10].

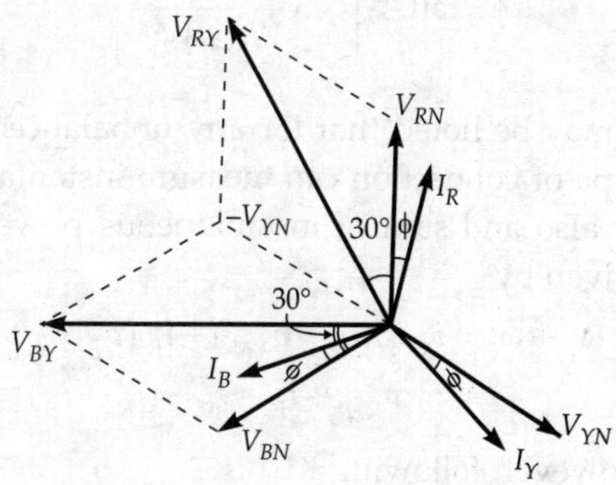

Fig. 4.10 Phasor diagram of the circuit.

Thus reading on wattmeter W_1 is given by

$$W_1 = V_{RY} I_R \cos(30° + \phi)$$

while reading on wattmeter W_2 is given by

$$W_2 = V_{BY} I_B \cos(30° - \phi)$$

CHAPTER 4

Since the load is balanced,

$$|I_R|=|I_Y|=|I_B|=I \text{ (say) and}$$

$$|V_{RY}|=|V_{BY}|=V_L \text{ (say)}$$

$$\therefore \quad W_1 = V_L\ I\cos(30+\phi) \text{ while}$$

$$W_2 = V_L\ I\cos(30°-\phi)$$

Thus, the total power P is given by

$$\begin{aligned} W &= W_1 + W_2 \\ &= V_L\ I\cos(30°+\phi) + V_L\ I\cos(30°-\phi) \\ &= V_L\ I[\cos(30°+\phi)+\cos(30°-\phi)] \\ &= V_L\ I[\cos 30°\cos\phi - \sin 30°\sin\phi \\ &\qquad + \cos 30°\cos\phi + \sin 30°\sin\phi] \\ &= \left(\frac{\sqrt{3}}{2}.2\cos\phi\right)V_L\ I = \sqrt{3}\ V_L\ I\cos\phi \end{aligned}$$

Thus it has been shown that the sum of readings of two wattmeters whose current coils are connected in series with two phases and whose potential coils get p.d. between these two phases with respect to the third phase, provide the total power of a balanced three phase circuit.

Also, from above,

$$W_2 - W_1 = V_L\ I\sin\phi$$

and
$$\tan\phi = \sqrt{3}\left(\frac{W_2-W_1}{W_2+W_1}\right)$$

Thus p.f. angle can also be obtained as

$$\phi = \tan^{-1}\left[\sqrt{3}\ \frac{W_2-W_1}{W_2+W_1}\right]$$

It may be noted that for any unbalanced load this type of connection can measure instantaneous power also and sum of instantaneous powers are then given by

$$\begin{aligned} \omega_1 + \omega_2 &= i_R\ (v_{RN} - v_{YN}) + i_B\ (v_{BN} - v_{YN}) \\ &= i_R\ v_{RN} + i_B\ v_{BN} - (i_R + i_B)\ v_{YN} \end{aligned}$$

However, following KCL,

$$i_R + i_b = -i_y$$

$$\therefore \quad \omega_1 + \omega_2 = i_R\ v_{RN} + i_B\ v_{BN} + i_y\ v_{YN}$$

= total instantaneous power of the circuit.

4.5.1 Variation in Wattmeter Readings

We have seen above that for a lagging p.f. load, $W_1 = V_L\ I_L\ \cos(30°+\phi)$ and $W_2 = V_L\ I_L\ \cos(30°-\phi)$, ϕ being the power factor angle. Thus, *the wattmeter readings vary not only on load but on p.f. too.* Let us observe a few typical case to clarify the above facts.

When $\phi = 0$, P.F. is unity

Load is resistive and it may be observed $W_1 = W_2 = V_L I_L\ \cos 30° = 0.866\ V_L I_L$. Hence both the meters will read +ve and equal readings.

When $\phi = 60°$ *i.e.,* p.f. is 0.5 lag

Then, $W_1 = V_L\ I_L\ \cos(30+60°) = 0$

and $W_2 = V_L\ I_L\ \cos(30-60°) = 0.866\ V_L\ I_L$.

$$[\because \cos(-\theta) = \cos\theta]$$

Hence in case the p.f. is 0.5 lag, W_1 will read zero but W_2 will read +ve.

When $\phi = 90°$ *i.e.,* p.f. is 0 (zero) :

Then,

$$\begin{aligned} W_1 &= V_L I_L\ \cos(30°+90°) \\ &= -0.5\ V_L\ I_L \quad \textit{i.e.,}\ (-)\text{ ve reading.} \end{aligned}$$

and
$$\begin{aligned} W_2 &= V_L I_L\ \cos(30-90°) \\ &= +0.5\ V_L\ I_L \quad \textit{i.e.,}\ (+)\text{ ve reading.} \end{aligned}$$

Under this condition, W_1 would read –ve. To obtain a reading on W_1, it is necessary to *interchange the leads* of either the pressure coil or current coil. The readings taken after reversal of pressure coil are to be taken as –ve.

It may be noted that for $\phi = 90°$, $W_2 = -W_1$ *i.e.,* $W_1 + W_2 = 0$ while for $90° > \phi > 60°$, W_2 will be +ve and W_1 will be –ve.

Two wattmeter method can be applied to measure the *reactive power also.* This can be obtained as follows :

We have seen that

$$\tan\phi = \frac{\sqrt{3}\,(W_2 - W_1)}{W_2 + W_1}.$$

$$\begin{aligned} \text{Again } \sqrt{3}\,(W_2 - W_1) &= \sqrt{3}\,[V_L\ I_L\ \cos(30°-\phi) \\ &\qquad - V_L\ I_L\ \cos(30°+\phi)] \\ &= \sqrt{3}\ V_L\ I_L\ (\cos 30°\cos\phi + \sin 30°\sin\phi \\ &\qquad - \cos 30°\cos\phi + \sin 30°\sin\phi) \\ &= \sqrt{3}\ V_L\ I_L\ \sin\phi. \end{aligned}$$

Thus the value $\sqrt{3}\,(W_2 - W_1)$ in the two wattmeter method gives the reactive power of the load.

It may be noted that, for any leading p.f. load,

$$\tan\phi = -\frac{\sqrt{3}(W_2 - W_1)}{(W_2 + W_1)}$$

and reactive volt ampere

$$= -\sqrt{3}(W_2 - W_1).$$

The reactive power for leading p.f. is –ve *i.e.*, reactive power is supplied to the system. On the other hand, reactive power for lagging p.f. load is +ve *i.e.*, the load then demands the reactive power.

4.6 UNBALANCED LOADS

When the loads in all the three phases of either star or delta connection are not identical to each other in all respects, they are called unbalanced loading (Fig. 4.11). The phase currents in delta and phase or line current in star connection differ in unbalanced loading giving rise to flow of neutral current. Obviously, at star point in any star connection,

$$I_R + I_Y + I_B = I_N \text{ (neutral current)}$$

and for three phase balanced loads,

$I_N = 0$ while for three phase unbalanced loading I_N is a finite quantity.

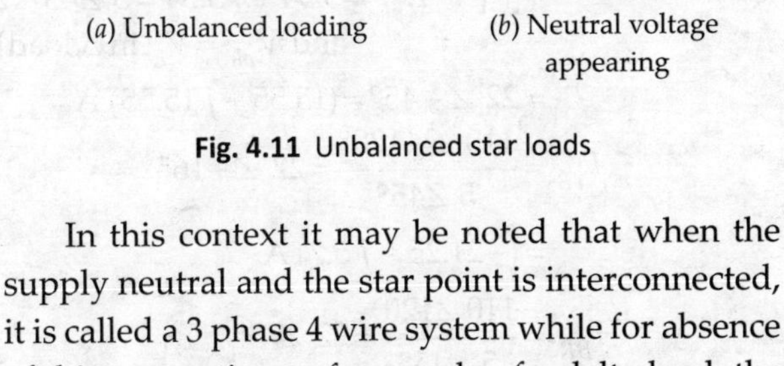

(*a*) Unbalanced loading (*b*) Neutral voltage appearing

Fig. 4.11 Unbalanced star loads

In this context it may be noted that when the supply neutral and the star point is interconnected, it is called a 3 phase 4 wire system while for absence of this connection or for supply of a delta load, the system is called a three phase 3 wire system. In unbalanced loading, due to flow of unequal currents in each of the phases, a voltage appears at the neutral and its value can be determined as follows :

The current in each phase (or line) being I_R, I_Y, I_B at 0,

$$I_R + I_Y + I_B = V_{RO}\,Y_R + V_{YO}\,Y_Y + V_{BO}\,Y_B$$

$$= (V_{RN} - V_{ON})Y_R + (V_{YN} - V_{ON})Y_Y + (V_{BN} - V_{ON})Y_B$$

$$= (V_{RN}\,Y_R + V_{YN}\,Y_Y + Y_{BN}\,Y_B) - V_{ON}\,(Y_R + Y_Y + Y_B)$$

However, as per KCL,

$$I_R + I_Y + I_B = 0$$

Thus, $$V_{RN}\,Y_R + V_{YN}\,Y_Y + V_{BN}\,Y_B - V_{ON}\,(Y_R + Y_Y + Y_B) = 0$$

or, $$V_{ON} = \frac{V_{RN}\,Y_R + V_{YN}\,Y_Y + V_{BN}\,Y_B}{Y_R + Y_Y + Y_B}$$

[V_{ON} represents the neutral shift]

EXAMPLE 4.1 *A star connected load has impedance of (3 + j 4) ohm in each phase and is connected across a balanced three phase delta connected alternator having line voltage of 120 V. Obtain the line currents of both the load and generator.*

SOLUTION. For the load :

$$Z_{ph} = 3 + j\,4 = 5\angle 53.13°\,\Omega$$

$$V_{ph} = \frac{120}{\sqrt{3}}$$

$$[\because \text{ in } Y \text{ connection, } V_{ph} = \frac{V_L}{\sqrt{3}}]$$

$$\therefore\quad I_{ph_R} = \frac{120\angle 0°}{\sqrt{3}\times 5\angle 53.15} = 13.86\angle -53.13°\text{ A}$$

$$I_{ph_Y} = \frac{120\angle -120°}{\sqrt{3}\times 5\angle 53.13°} = 13.86\angle -173.13°\text{ A}$$

$$I_{ph_B} = \frac{120\angle +120°}{\sqrt{3}\times 5\angle 53.13°} = 13.86\angle 66.87°$$

where I_{ph_R}, I_{phy} and I_{ph_B} represent the phase current of phases, *R*, *Y* and *B* of the load. Since the load is star connected, hence line currents being equal to phase current in this case,

$$I_{ph_R} = I_{L_R} = \mathbf{13.86\angle -53.13°\ A}$$

Similarly,

$$I_{L_Y} = \mathbf{13.86\angle -173.13°\ A}$$

$$I_{L_B} = \mathbf{13.86\angle 66.87°\ A}$$

C H A P T E R 4

Again, for the Δ connected alternator, the supply current being the line currents of the load, the phase currents would be $(1/\sqrt{3})$ times the corresponding line currents. Thus, for the alternator,

$$\boldsymbol{I_{L_R}} = \mathbf{13.86\angle -53.13° \ A}$$

$$[\text{while } I_{ph_R} = 8\angle -53.15° \text{ A}]$$

$$\boldsymbol{I_{L_Y}} = \mathbf{13.86\angle -173.13° \ A}$$

$$[\text{while } I_{ph_Y} = 8\angle -173.13° \text{ A}]$$

$$\boldsymbol{I_{L_B}} = \mathbf{13.86\angle 66.87° \ A}$$

$$[\text{while } I_{ph_B} = 8\angle -66.87° \text{ A}]$$

EXAMPLE 4.2 *In Fig. E4.1, find the line currents provided the supply is balanced 100 V, 50 Hz three phase supply.*

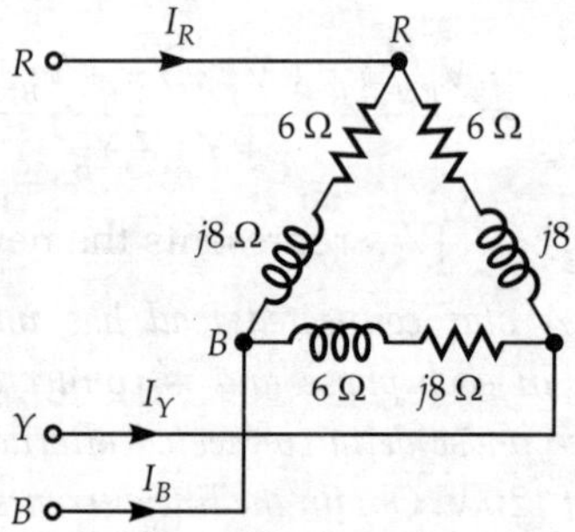

Fig. E4.1

SOLUTION. I_{ph} (phase current) $= \dfrac{V_{ph}}{Z_{ph}}$

Since in Δ connection,

$$V_{ph} \equiv V_{L-L} \quad \text{and} \quad I_L = \sqrt{3}\, I_{ph}$$

here, $$I_{ph\,(RY)} = \frac{100\angle 0°}{6+j8}$$

$$= \frac{100\angle 0°}{10\angle 53.13°} = 10\angle -53.13° \text{ A}$$

Similarly,

$$I_{ph\,(YB)} = \frac{100\angle -120°}{10\angle 53.13°} = 10\angle -173.13° \text{ A}$$

and $$I_{ph\,(BR)} = \frac{100\angle +120°}{10\angle 53.13°} = 10\angle 66.87° \text{ A.}$$

The line currents in each line would be same and are given by

$$|I_L| = \sqrt{3}\,|I_{ph}| = \mathbf{17.32\ A}\,[\boldsymbol{I_R = I_Y = I_B}].$$

EXAMPLE 4.3 *A r.m.s. voltage in a three phase star circuit is given by 231 V (ph. – N). Write the instantaneous voltage expression. If the current in each phase lag the corresponding phase voltages by 30°, what are the expressions of instantaneous currents ?*

SOLUTION. In Y connection,

$$V_{L-L} = \sqrt{3}\,V_{ph} = 1.732 \times 231 = 400 \text{ V}$$

$$\therefore \quad V_{R(L-L)} = \sqrt{2}\,(400)\sin\omega t = 566\sin\omega t \text{ V}$$

$$V_{Y(L-L)} = 566\sin(\omega t - 120°) \text{ V}$$

$$V_{B(L-L)} = 566\sin(\omega t - 240°)$$

$$= 566\sin(\omega t + 120°) \text{ V}$$

As the phase currents would lag the corresponding phase voltages by 30°,

hence, $$I_{R(ph)} = \left(\frac{231}{Z}\right) \times \sqrt{2}\sin(\omega t - 30°)$$

$$= \mathbf{327\sin(\omega t - 30°)\ A}\,[Z = 1 \text{ ohm}]$$

$$I_{Y(ph)} = 327\sin(\omega t - 120° - 30°)$$

$$= \mathbf{327\sin(\omega t - 150°)\ A}$$

$$I_{B(ph)} = 327\sin(\omega t + 120° - 30°)$$

$$= \mathbf{327\sin(\omega t + 90°)\ A.}$$

EXAMPLE 4.4 *A three phase balanced system supplies 110 V to a delta connected load whose phase impedances are equal to (3.54 + j 3.54) ohm. Determine the line currents and draw the phasor diagram.*

SOLUTION. Refer to Fig. E4.2,

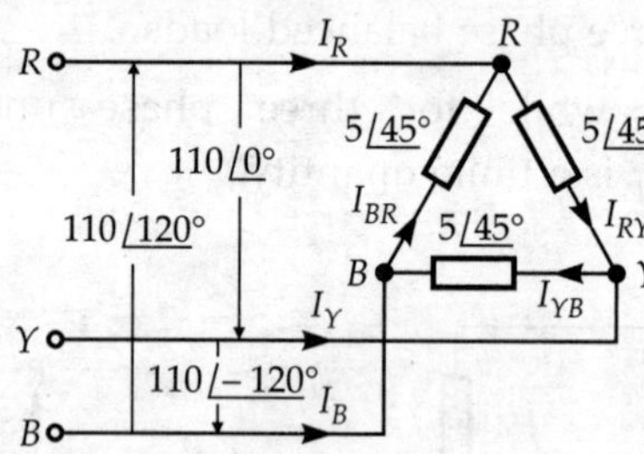

Fig. E4.2

$$I_{RY} = \frac{110\angle 0°}{5\angle 45°}$$

$$[\because Z_{ph} = 3.54 + j\,3.54 = 5\angle 45° \Omega \text{ and } V_{ph} = V_L \text{ in } \Delta \text{ load}]$$

$$= 22\angle -45° = (15.55 - j\,15.55) \text{ A}$$

$$I_{YB} = \frac{110\angle -120°}{5\angle 45°} = 22\angle -165°$$

$$= (-21.25 - j\,5.7) \text{ A}$$

$$I_{BR} = \frac{110\angle 120}{5\angle 45°} = 22\angle 75°$$

$$= (5.7 + j\,21.2) \text{ A}$$

Line currents are obtained as follows :

$$I_R = I_{RY} - I_{BR} = 15.55 - j\,15.55 - 5.7 - j\,21.2$$

$$= (9.85 - j\,36.75) \text{ A} = 38.05\angle -75° \text{ A}$$

$$I_Y = I_{YB} - I_{RY} = (-21.25 - j\,5.7) - 15.55 + j\,15.55$$

$$= 38.05 \angle 165° \text{ A}$$

and $I_B = I_{BR} - I_{YB} = 5.7 + j\,21.2 + 21.25 + j\,5.7$

$$= 26.95 + j\,26.9 = 38.05 \angle 45° \text{ A}$$

i.e., Line currents are

$$\boldsymbol{I_R = 38.05 \angle -75° \text{ A}}$$

$$\boldsymbol{I_Y = 38.05 \angle 165° \text{ A}}$$

$$\boldsymbol{I_B = 38.05 \angle 45° \text{ A}.}$$

The phasor diagram is shown in Fig. E4.3.

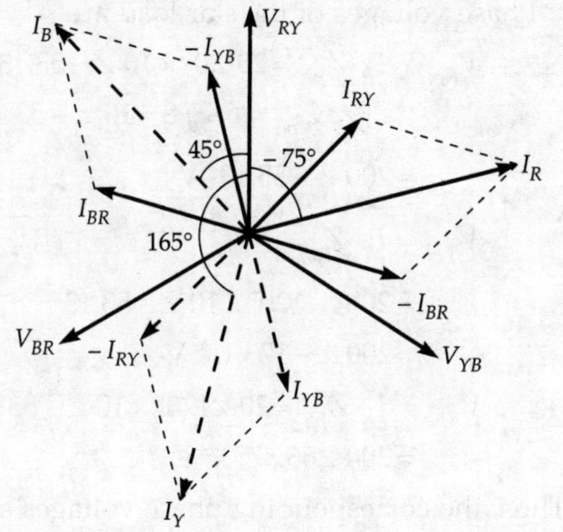

Fig. E4.3

EXAMPLE 4.5 *A three phase 4 wire 100 V (L-L) system supplied a balanced Y connected load having impedances of 10 ∠–30°Ω in each phase. Find line currents and draw the phasor diagram. How much current is flowing through the neutral ?*

SOLUTION. Refer to Fig. E4.4.

$$I_R = \frac{V_{RN}}{Z_R} = \frac{100 \angle 0°}{10 \angle -30°} = 10 \angle 30° \text{ A}$$

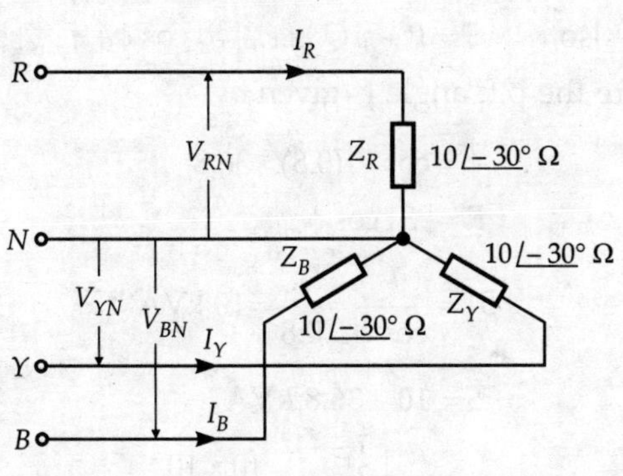

Fig. E4.4

$$I_Y = \frac{V_{YN}}{Z_Y} = \frac{100 \angle -120°}{10 \angle -30°} = 10 \angle -90° \text{ A}$$

$$I_B = \frac{V_{BN}}{Z_B} = \frac{100 \angle 120°}{10 \angle -30°} = 10 \angle 150° \text{ A}$$

Thus, the line currents are

$$\boldsymbol{I_R = 10 \angle 30° \text{ A}; \quad I_Y = 10 \angle -90° \text{ A};}$$

$$\boldsymbol{I_B = 10 \angle 150° \text{ A}}$$

and I_N (current through neutral)

$$= -(I_R + I_Y + I_B)$$

$$= -(10 \angle 30° + 10 \angle -90° + 10 \angle 150°)$$

$$= -10\,[\cos 30° + j \sin 30° + \cos 90° - j \sin 90° + \cos 150° + j \sin 150°]$$

$$= -10\,[0.866 + j\,0.5 + 0 - j\,1 - 0.866 + j\,0.5] = \mathbf{0.}$$

The phasor diagram is shown in Fig. E4.5.

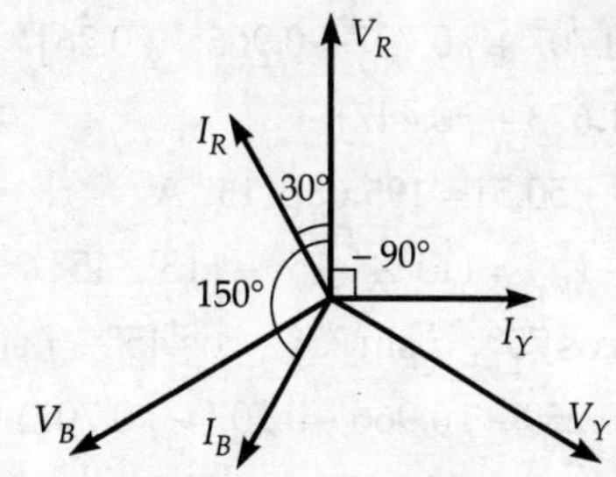

Fig. E4.5

EXAMPLE 4.6 *A Δ connected load has a parallel combination of resistance (5 Ω) and capacitive reactance (– j 5 Ω) in each phase. If a balanced 3 phase 400 V supply is applied between lines, find the phase currents and line currents and draw the phasor diagram.*

SOLUTION. (Refer to Fig. E4.6)

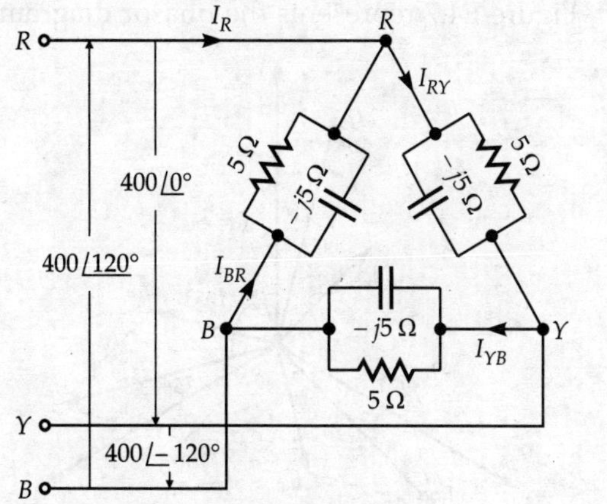

Fig. E4.6

Z_{ph} (phase impedance) $= [5 \,||\, (-j\,5)]\,\Omega$

$$= \frac{25\angle -90^\circ}{5 - j\,5} = \frac{25\angle -90^\circ}{7.07\angle -45^\circ} = 3.54\angle -45^\circ\,\Omega$$

$$\therefore \quad I_{RY} = \frac{V_{RY}}{Z_{ph}} = \frac{400\angle 0^\circ}{3.54\angle -45^\circ} = \mathbf{113\angle 45^\circ\ A}$$

$$I_{YB} = \frac{V_{YB}}{Z_{ph}} = \frac{400\angle -120^\circ}{3.54\angle -45^\circ} = \mathbf{113\angle -75^\circ\ A}$$

$$I_{BR} = \frac{V_{BR}}{Z_{ph}} = \frac{400\angle 120^\circ}{3.54\angle -45^\circ} = \mathbf{113\angle 165^\circ\ A}$$

[It may be noted here, for Δ load,

$$|V_L| = |V_{ph}| = 400\text{ V}]$$

Now,

$$I_R = I_{RY} - I_{BR} = 113\angle 45^\circ - 113\angle 165^\circ$$
$$= 113\,[\cos 45^\circ + j\sin 45^\circ - \cos 165^\circ - j\sin 165^\circ]$$
$$= 113\,[0.707 + j\,0.707 + 0.966 - j\,0.26]$$
$$= 113\,[1.673 + j\,0.447]$$
$$= 189 + j\,50.51 = \mathbf{195.68\angle 15^\circ\ A}$$

$$I_Y = I_{YB} - I_{RY} = 113\angle -75^\circ - 113\angle 45^\circ$$
$$= 113\,(\cos 75^\circ - j\sin 75^\circ - \cos 45^\circ - j\sin 45^\circ)$$
$$= 113\,(0.259 - j\,0.966 - 0.707 - j\,0.707)$$
$$= 113\,(-0.448 - j\,1.673) = -50.51 - j\,189$$
$$= 195.65\angle +75^\circ\text{ A} = \mathbf{195.65\angle -105^\circ\ A}$$

$$I_B = I_{BR} - I_{YB} = 113\angle 165^\circ - 113\angle -75^\circ$$
$$= 113\,(\cos 165^\circ + j\sin 165^\circ - \cos 75^\circ + j\sin 75^\circ)$$
$$= 113\,(-0.966 + j\,0.26 - 0.259 + j\,0.966)$$
$$= 113\,(-1.225 + j\,1.226)$$
$$= -138.43 + j\,138.43$$
$$= \mathbf{195.72\angle -45^\circ\ A}\ (= 195.72\angle 135^\circ\text{ A})$$

Figure E4.7 represents the phasor diagram.

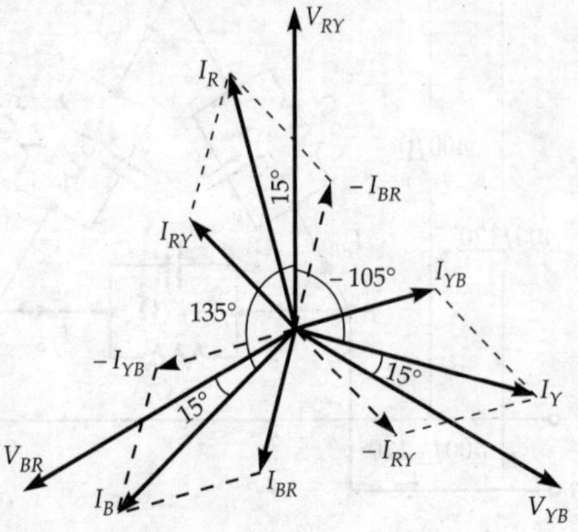

Fig. E4.7

Example 4.7 *The line currents of a delta connected generator being 20 A (3 ph. system), a star connected load is applied across the terminals of the generator. If the load has impedances of $(6 - j\,8)\,\Omega$ per phase, find the phase voltage of the generator.*

Solution. For the generator, the line currents are (Δ connection)

$$I_R = 20\angle 0^\circ\text{ A};\ I_Y = 20\angle -120^\circ\text{ A}$$
$$I_B = 20\angle 120^\circ\text{ A}.$$

As the load is star connected, the line currents will be the phase currents too of the load.

∴ Phase voltages of the star load are

$$V_{RN} = I_R\,Z_{ph} = 20\angle 0^\circ \times 10\angle -53.13^\circ$$
$$[\because Z_{ph} = 6 - j\,8 = 10\angle -53.13^\circ\,\Omega]$$
$$= 200\angle -53.13^\circ\text{ V};$$
$$V_{YN} = I_Y\,Z_{ph}$$
$$= 20\angle -120^\circ \times 10\angle -53.13^\circ$$
$$= 200\angle -173.13^\circ\text{ V};$$
$$V_{BN} = I_B\,Z_{ph} = 20\angle 120^\circ \times 10\angle -53.13^\circ$$
$$= 200\angle 66.87^\circ\text{ V}$$

Thus, the corresponding phase voltages are

$$V_{RN} = \mathbf{200\angle -53.13^\circ\ V}$$
$$V_{YN} = \mathbf{200\angle -173.13^\circ\ V}$$
$$V_{BN} = \mathbf{200\angle 66.87^\circ\ V.}$$

Example 4.8 *A balanced 3 phase load draws 8 kW at a lagging p.f. of 0.8. If the line voltage applied is 440 V, find the complex power and line current.*

Solution. Complex power (3 ph.)

$$S = \sqrt{3}\,V_L\,I_L$$

However, $\quad V_L = 440$ V

Also, $\quad S = P + j\,Q$ *i.e.*, $|S|\cos\phi + j\,|S|\sin\phi$

where the p.f. angle is given by

$$\phi = \cos^{-1}(0.8) = 36.8^\circ$$

$$\because \quad P = |S|\cos\phi;$$

hence $$|S| = \frac{P}{\cos\phi} = \frac{8}{0.8} = 10\text{ kVA}$$

i.e., $$S = \mathbf{10\angle 36.8\ kVA}$$

and $$I_L = \frac{|S|}{\sqrt{3} \times 440} = \frac{10 \times 10^3}{\sqrt{3} \times 440} = \mathbf{13.12\ A.}$$

EXAMPLE 4.9 *In the system given in Example 4.8, another load is connected such that it draws 4.5 kVA at p.f. 0.6 lead. What is the total line current ?*

SOLUTION. In Example 4.8, we have seen

$$S_1 = 10\angle 36.87° \text{ kVA},$$
$$\phi_1 = 36.8° \text{ (lag)}$$

Also, $S_2 = 7.5\angle -53.13°$

$[\because \cos\phi = 0.6 \text{ lead means } \phi = -53.13°]$

$\therefore$ Total power

$$S = S_1 + S_2 = 10\angle 36.87° + 7.5\angle -53.13°$$
$$= 8 + j6 + 4.5 - j6$$
$$= 12.5 + j0 = 12.5\angle 0° \text{ kVA}$$
$$I_L = \frac{|S|}{\sqrt{3}V_L} = \frac{12.5\times 10^3}{\sqrt{3}\times 440} = \mathbf{16.4\ A.}$$

EXAMPLE 4.10 *A three phase 220 V supply is applied to a balanced Δ connected three phase load. The phase current being $I_{ab} = 10\angle -30°$ A, find I_a. Compute the total power received by the Δ load. Find the value of the resistance portion of the phase impedance.*

SOLUTION. (Refer to Fig. E4.8). Given,

$$I_{ab} = 10\angle -30° \text{ A}$$
$$\therefore \quad I_{bc} = 10\angle -150° \text{ A}$$
and $$I_{ca} = 10\angle -270° \text{ A}$$

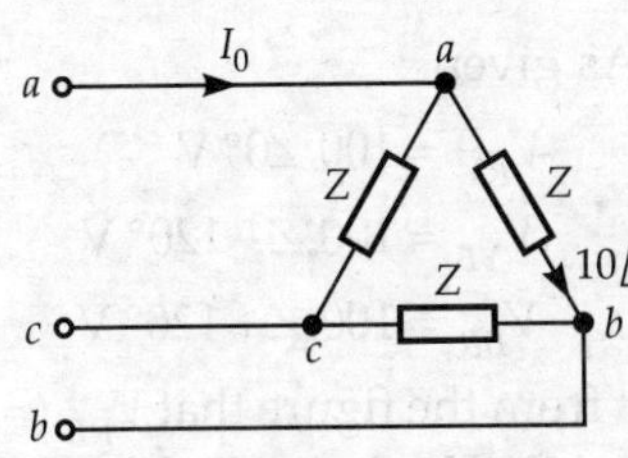

Fig. E4.8

Obviously,

$$I_a = I_{ab} - I_{ca} = 10\angle -30° - 10\angle -270°$$
$$= 10[\cos 30° - j\sin 30° - \cos 270° + j\sin 270°]$$
$$= 10[0.866 - j0.5 - 0 - j1.0]$$
$$= 8.66 - j15 = 17.32\angle -60°$$
$$\therefore I_a = 17.32\angle -60° \text{ A.}$$

Total power received

$$= \sqrt{3}V_L I_L \cos\phi_L = 3V_{ph} I_{ph} \cos\phi_{ph}$$
$$= 3\times 220\times 10\times \cos 30° = 5710 \text{ W.}$$
$$\therefore \text{Power in each phase} = \frac{5710}{3} = 1903.3 \text{ W.}$$

However, power is consumed in the resistive part only

$$\therefore \quad I_{ph}^2 R_{ph} = W_{ph}$$
or, $$1903.3 = 10^2 \times R_{ph}$$
$$\therefore \quad R_{ph} = \mathbf{19.033\ \Omega.}$$

Thus, the resistive part of each impedance is **19.033 Ω.**

EXAMPLE 4.11 *The phase impedance of a delta connected load is $(15 + j20)\Omega$. What is the line current if the applied line voltage is 220 V ? Obtain the amount of power consumed per phase. What is the phasor sum of the three line currents ?*

SOLUTION. In Fig. E4.9,

$$|V_{ab}| = ||V_{bc}| = |V_{ca}| = 220 \text{ V}$$

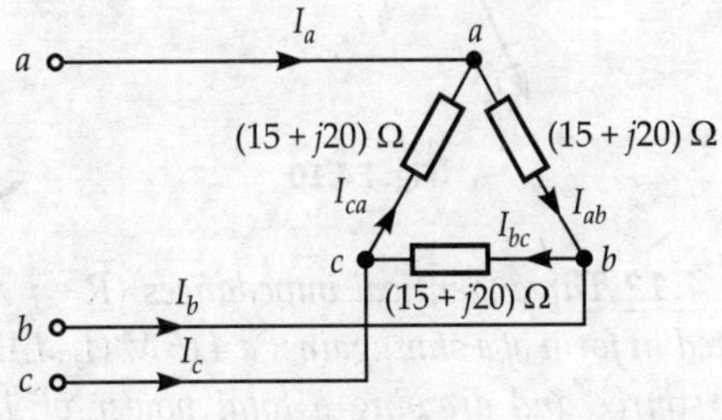

Fig. E4.9

While each voltage is displaced from the other by 120°,

$$\therefore \quad I_{ab} = \frac{V_{ab}}{Z} = \frac{220\angle 0°}{25\angle 53.2°}$$
$$[\because Z_{ph} = (15 + j20)\Omega = 25\angle 53.2°\Omega]$$
$$= 8.8\angle -53.2° \text{ A.}$$

Similarly,

$$I_{bc} = 8.8\angle -53.2° - 120° = 8.8\angle -173.2° \text{ A}$$
and $$I_{ca} = 8.8\angle -53.2° - 240°$$
$$= 8.8\angle -293.2° = 88\angle 66.8° \text{ A}$$

Now,

$$I_a = I_{ab} - I_{ca} = (8.8\angle -53.2° - 8.8\angle 66.8°) \text{ A}$$
$$= 5.28 - j7.04 - 3.46 - j8.08 = 1.82 - j15.12$$
$$= \mathbf{15.21\angle -83.14°\ A.}$$
$$\therefore \quad I_b = 15.21\angle -83.14° - 120°$$
$$= \mathbf{15.21\angle -203.14°\ A}$$
$$I_c = 15.21\angle -83.14° + 120°$$
$$= \mathbf{15.21\angle 36.7°\ A}$$

Power consumed

$$= I_{ph}^2 R = 8.8^2 \times 15 = \mathbf{1160\ W.}$$

CHAPTER 4

Now,

$$I_a + I_b + I_c = 15.21 \angle -83.14° + 15.21 \angle 203.14° + 15.21 \angle 36.7°$$

$$= 0°$$

[Also, by KCL, the sum of currents flowing into a node must be zero].

The phasor diagram is shown in Fig. E4.10.

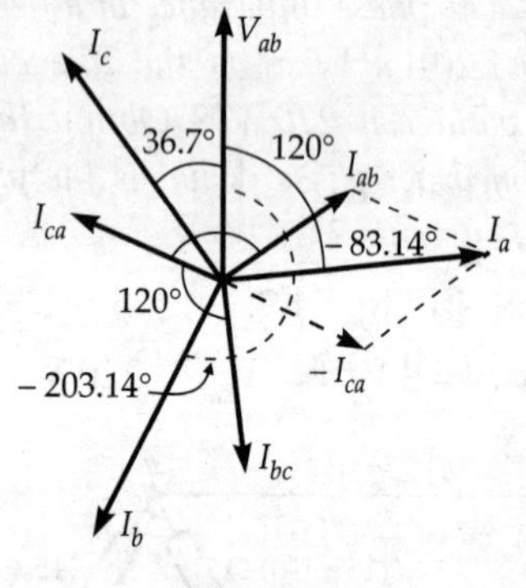

Fig. E4.10

Example 4.12 *Three identical impedances $(R + j X_L)$ are connected in form of a star against a 415 V (L-L) 3 phase voltage source and drawing a total power of 1.8 kW. Obtain the resistive and reactive components of each phase impedance. Assume the line current to be 10 A.*

Solution.

$$V_{ph} = \frac{V_{L-L}}{\sqrt{3}} = \frac{415}{\sqrt{3}} = 240 \text{ V}$$

$$\therefore \quad Z_{ph} = \frac{V_{ph}}{I_{ph}} = \frac{240}{10} = 24\,\Omega$$

However per phase power $= \frac{1.8}{3} \times 10^3 = 600$ W.

Thus, $I_{ph}^2 R = 600$

$$\therefore \quad R_{ph} = \frac{600}{I_{ph}^2} = \frac{600}{10^2} = 6\,\Omega$$

Thus $X_{ph} = \sqrt{Z_{ph}^2 - R_{ph}^2}$

$$= \sqrt{24^2 - 6^2} = 23.23\,\Omega$$

$$\therefore \quad Z_{ph} = R_{ph} + j X_{ph} = \mathbf{(6 + j\,23.23)\,\Omega}.$$

Example 4.13 *A balanced Y connected load has an impedance of $(2 + j\,3.46)\,\Omega$ between line and neutral. If the voltage across phase R be $20 \angle 30°$ V, find current in phases Y and B. What is the voltage from line Y to neutral ? Also obtain V_{RB}.*

Solution.

$$I_{RN} = \frac{V_{RN}}{Z_R} = \frac{20 \angle 30°}{4 \angle 60°}$$

$$[\because (2 + j\,3.46) = 4 \angle 60°\,\Omega]$$

$$= 5 \angle -30° \text{ A.}$$

$$\therefore \quad I_{YN} = 5 \angle -30 - 120° = 5 \angle -150° \text{ A}$$

$$I_{BN} = 5 \angle -30 + 120° = 5 \angle 90° \text{ A}$$

i.e., $I_{ph\,(Y)} = 5 \angle -150°$ A ; $I_{ph\,(B)} = 5 \angle 90°$ A

$$V_{YN} = 20 \angle 30° - 120° = \mathbf{20 \angle -90° \text{ V}}$$

$[\because V_{YN}$ is displaced from V_{RN} by $-120°]$

Now, $V_{RB} = V_{RN} + V_{NB} = 20 \angle 30° - 20 \angle 150°$

$$[\because V_{BN} = 20 \underline{/30° + 120°} = 20 \angle 150° \, V]$$

$$= \mathbf{34.65 \angle 0° \text{ V}}.$$

Example 4.14 *Find I_B in the three phase circuit of Fig. E4.11. Assume $Z_R = 5 \angle 30°$; $Z_Y = 2 \angle 60°$ ohm, the applied line voltage is 100 V. Assuming the supply to be 50 Hz, write the expressions for i_R, i_Y, i_B.*

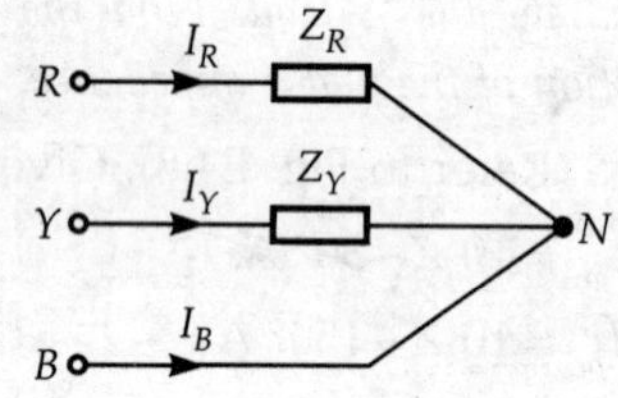

Fig. E4.11

Solution. As given,

$$V_{RY} = 100 \angle 0° \text{ V}$$

$$V_{YB} = 100 \angle -120° \text{ V}$$

$$V_{BR} = 100 \angle +120° \text{ V}$$

It is evident from the figure that $V_{RB}\ (= -V_{BR})$ is applied on Z_R while V_{YB} is applied on Z_Y.

Thus,

$$I_R = \frac{-V_{BR}}{Z_R} = \frac{-100 \angle 120°}{5 \angle 30°} = -20 \angle 90° \text{ A}$$

and $I_Y = \frac{V_{YB}}{Z_Y} = \frac{100 \angle -120°}{2 \angle 60°} = 50 \angle -180°$ A

Since at N, $I_R + I_Y + I_B = 0$ [using KCL],

$$I_B = -(I_R + I_Y) = +20 \angle 90° - 50 \angle -180°$$

$$= j\,20 + 50 = \mathbf{53.85 \angle + 21.8° \text{ A}}.$$

Since $\omega = 2\pi f = 314$ rad / sec,

$$i_R = \mathbf{-20\sqrt{2} \sin (314\,t + 90°) \text{ A}}$$

$$i_Y = \mathbf{50\sqrt{2} \sin (314\,t - 180°) \text{ A}}$$

$$i_B = \mathbf{53.85\,\sqrt{2} \sin (314\,t + 21.8°) \text{ A}}.$$

EXAMPLE 4.15 *A 3 phase 400 V, 50 Hz source supplies power to a 3 phase balanced motor load. If the line current be 25 A, power factor being 0.85, obtain the values of real and reactive power consumed.*

SOLUTION.

$$P = \sqrt{3}\, V_L I_L \cos\phi$$
$$= \sqrt{3} \times 400 \times 25 \times 0.85 = \mathbf{14.72\ kW}$$
$$Q = \sqrt{3}\, V_L\, I_L \sin\phi = \sqrt{3} \times 400 \times 25 \times 0.53$$
$$[\because \sin\phi = \sin(\cos^{-1} 0.85) = 0.53]$$
$$= \mathbf{9.123\ kVAR}$$
$$[S = \text{total power} = \sqrt{P^2 + Q^2} = \mathbf{17.32\ kVA}].$$

EXAMPLE 4.16 *A 20 HP induction motor is supplied from a 400 V, 3 phase, 50 Hz power system. The efficiency being 90%, the p.f. of operation is 0.8. Obtain (i) the active power consumed (ii) the apparent power (iii) the reactive power, (iv) the line current.*

SOLUTION.

(*i*) $P_{\text{input}} = \dfrac{\text{Output Power}}{\text{efficiency}}$

$$= \frac{20 \times 746}{0.9} = 16578\ \text{W} = \mathbf{16.578\ kW}.$$

(*ii*) Also, $\text{PF (power factor)} = \dfrac{P}{S}$

[S = total or apparent power]

$$\therefore \quad S = \frac{P}{(\text{PF})} = \frac{16.578}{0.8} = \mathbf{20.72\ kVAR}$$

(*iii*) $Q = \sqrt{S^2 - P_{in}^2}$

$$= \sqrt{20.72^2 - 16.578^2} = \mathbf{12.43\ kVAR}$$

(*iv*) Line current

$$= \frac{P}{\sqrt{3} \times V_L \times \cos\phi} = \frac{16.578 \times 10^3}{\sqrt{3} \times 400 \times 0.8} \simeq \mathbf{30\ A}$$

EXAMPLE 4.17 *Three impedances of* $(4 - j\,3)\,\Omega$ *are connected in star against a 440 V 3 ph voltage source. Find the power consumed. Also obtain the reactive power of the load.*

SOLUTION.

$$|V_L| = 440\ \text{V}; \quad \therefore V_{ph} = \frac{440}{\sqrt{3}} = 254\ \text{V}.$$
$$Z_{ph} = 4 - j\,3 = 5\,\angle{-36.88°}\,\Omega$$
$$\therefore \quad |I_L| = \frac{|V_{ph}|}{|Z_{ph}|} = \frac{254}{5} \simeq 51\ \text{A}$$

[in Y load $I_L = I_{ph}$]

Power factor of the load

$$= \frac{R_{ph}}{Z_{ph}} = \frac{4}{\sqrt{4^2 + 3^2}} = \frac{4}{5} = 0.8\ \text{(lead)}$$
$$\therefore \quad I_L = 51\,\angle\cos^{-1} 0.8$$
$$= 51\,\angle 36.88°\ \text{A (leading)}$$

Thus, $P = \sqrt{3} \times V_L\, I_L \cos\phi$

$$= \sqrt{3} \times 440 \times 51 \times \cos 36.88°$$
$$= \mathbf{31.09\ kW}$$
$$Q = \sqrt{3}\, V_L\, I_L \sin\phi$$
$$= \sqrt{3} \times 440 \times 51 \times \sin 36.88°$$
$$= \mathbf{23.325\ kVAR\ (leading)}.$$

EXAMPLE 4.18 *A 3 ph load has a resistance of 10 Ω in each phase and is connected in (i) star and (ii) delta against a 400 V 3 ph supply. Compare the power consumed in both the cases.*

SOLUTION. $V_L = 400$ V

$$\therefore \quad V_{ph} = 231\ \text{V};\ Z_{ph} = R_{ph} = 10\,\Omega.$$
$$\therefore \quad I_{ph} = \left(\frac{400}{\sqrt{3}}\right) \Big/ 10 = 23.1\ \text{A}$$

(for star connection)

and $\quad I_{ph} = \dfrac{400}{10} = 40\ \text{A} \quad$ (for Δ connection)

However, V_{ph} for Y connection is 231 V

and $\quad V_{ph}$ for Δ connection is 400 V

$$\therefore \quad P_{\text{star}} = 3\, V_{ph}\, I_{ph} \cos\phi = 3 \times 231 \times 23.1$$

[$\cos\phi = 1$, resistive load]

$$= \mathbf{16\ kW}$$
$$P_{\text{delta}} = 3\, V_{ph}\, I_{ph} \cos\phi = 3 \times 400 \times 40 = \mathbf{48\ kW}$$

As $\phi = 0°$, the reactive power is zero.

Note that the power consumed in Δ connection is three times the power consumed in Y connection.

EXAMPLE 4.19 *In Fig. E4.12,* $Z_A = Z_B = 10\,\angle 0°\,\Omega$ *while the supply is a three phase 50 Hz, 100 V between lines (balanced). Find the power consumed by the load.*

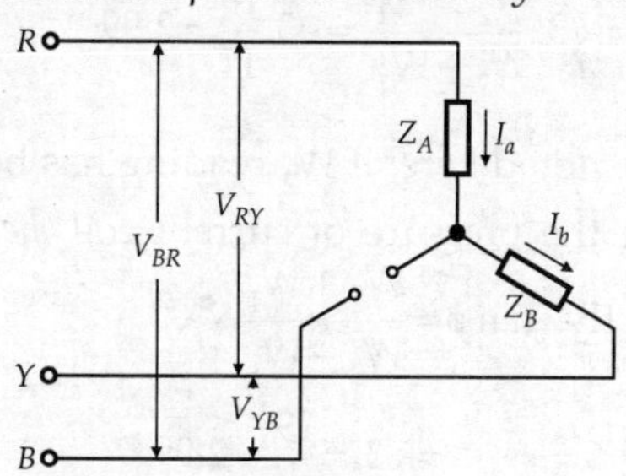

Fig. E4.12

CHAPTER 4

SOLUTION. $V_{ph} = \frac{V_L}{\sqrt{3}} = \frac{100}{\sqrt{3}} = 57.74 \text{ V}$

$$Z_{ph} = 10 \angle 0° \Omega.$$

$$\therefore \quad I_a = \frac{V_{R(ph)} \angle 0°}{10 \angle 0°} = \frac{57.74 \angle 0°}{10 \angle 0°}$$

$$= 5.774 \angle 0° \text{ A}$$

$$I_b = \frac{V_{Y(ph)}}{Z_B} = \frac{57.74 \angle -120°}{10 \angle 0°}$$

$$= 5.774 \angle -120° \text{ A}$$

It may be observed that in phase R,

$$V_{R(ph)} = 57.74 \angle 0° \text{ V}$$

and $I_R (= I_a) = 5.774 \angle 0°$ A

i.e., ϕ (angle between $V_{R(ph)}$ and I_R) is 0°

This gives

$$P_R = V_{R(ph)} \, I_{R(ph)} \cos \phi$$

$$= 57.74 \times 5.774 = 333.40 \text{ W7}$$

In phase, Y,

$$V_{Y(ph)} = 57.74 \angle -120° \text{ V}$$

and $I_Y (= I_b) = 5.774 \angle -120°$ A

Hence ϕ between $V_{Y(ph)}$ and I_Y is 0°.

Thus $P_Y = V_{Y(ph)} \, I_Y \cos \phi$

$$= 57.74 \times 5.774 = 333.40 \text{ W}$$

Total power consumed by the load is thus

$333.4 \times 2 = 666.8$ W.

EXAMPLE 4.20 *The power readings of two watt meters are + 15 kW and – 4 kW for a three phase load. If the supply voltage is balanced 440 V, find the true power drawn by the load, the power factor and line current.*

SOLUTION. True power drawn = 15 – 4 = **11 kW**

$$\tan \phi = \sqrt{3} \cdot \frac{W_2 - W_1}{W_2 + W_1} = \sqrt{3} \frac{W_2 - (-W_1)}{W_2 + (-W_1)}$$

$$= \sqrt{3} \frac{W_2 + W_1}{W_2 - W_1} = \sqrt{3} \frac{19}{11} = 2.99$$

It may be noted here, if W_2 reading has been taken reversing the pressure or current coil, *i.e.*, if W_1 is –ve, directly $\tan \phi = \frac{W_2 + W_1}{W_2 - W_1} \times \sqrt{3}$

$$= \sqrt{3} = \frac{19}{11} = 2.99$$

$$\therefore \phi = 71.52° \, [W_2 = 15 \text{ kW} ; W_1 = -4 \text{ kW}]$$

Thus,

$$\cos \phi = \cos 71.52° = \mathbf{0.317 \text{ (lag)}}$$

Again power $= \sqrt{3} \, V_L \, I_L \cos \phi$

$$\therefore I_L = \frac{\text{Power}}{\sqrt{3} \, V_L \cos \phi} = \frac{11 \times 10^3}{\sqrt{3} \times 440 \times 0.317} = 45.53 \text{ A}$$

$\therefore$ True power = **11 kW**

P.F. = **0.317 (lag)**

Line current = **45.53 A**

EXAMPLE 4.21 *A three phase 400 V load has a power factor of 0.4. Two wattmeters are connected to measure the power. If the input power be 10 kW, find the reading of each instrument.*

SOLUTION. $\tan \phi = \frac{\sqrt{3} (W_2 - W_1)}{W_2 + W_1}$

But $\cos \phi = 0.4 \quad \therefore \quad \phi = 66.42°$

i.e., $\sqrt{3} \frac{W_2 - W_1}{W_2 + W_1} = \tan 66.42° = 2.292$ ...(1)

Also, $W_1 + W_2 = \text{input power} = 10$ ...(2)

Substituting (2) in (1),

$$\sqrt{3} (W_2 - W_1) = 2.292 \times 10$$

$\therefore \quad W_2 - W_1 = 13.23$ ...(3)

From (2) and (3),

$$W_2 = \mathbf{11.615 \text{ W}}$$

$$W_1 = \mathbf{-1.615 \text{ W.}}$$

ADDITIONAL EXAMPLES

EXAMPLE 4.22 *A 3 phase, star connected system with 400 V (L-L) is connected to three loads : 25 ∠0°, 11 ∠–20° and 15 ∠10° ohm (also connected in star). Find the line current, power and the current in the neutral of the system.*

SOLUTION.

$$Z_1 = 25 \angle 0° \Omega ; Z_2 = 11 \angle -20° \Omega$$

and $Z_3 = 15 \angle 10° \Omega$

$$V_{ph} = \frac{V_L}{\sqrt{3}} = 231 \text{ V}$$

$$\therefore \quad I_1 = \frac{V_{ph}}{Z_1} = \frac{231}{25 \angle 0°} = 9.24 \angle 0° \text{ A}$$

Similarly,

$$I_2 = \frac{V_{ph}}{Z_2} = \frac{231\angle -120°}{11\angle -20°} = 21\angle -100°\text{ A}$$

and
$$I_3 = \frac{V_{ph}}{Z_3} = \frac{231\angle 120°}{15\angle 10°} = 15.4\angle 110°\text{ A}$$

where, I_1, I_2 and I_3 are phase currents at the load. Obviously, due to star connection, the line currents must be equal to phase currents.

$$\therefore \quad I_{L_1} = I_1 = \mathbf{9.24\angle 0°\text{ A}}$$
$$I_{L_2} = I_2 = \mathbf{21\angle -100°\text{ A}}$$
$$I_{L_3} = I_3 = \mathbf{15.4\angle 110°\text{ A}}$$

Power in the phases would be

$$P_1 = V_{ph}\ I_1\ \cos 0° \simeq 2134\text{ W}$$
$$P_2 = V_{ph}\ I_2\ \cos 20° = 4558.45\text{ W}$$
$$P_3 = V_{ph}\ I_3\ \cos 10° = 3503.36\text{ W.}$$

$\therefore$ Total power $= 10195.81\text{ W} = \mathbf{10.2\text{ kW}}$

Current in neutral

$$I_N = 9.24\angle 0° + 21\angle -100° + 15.4\angle 110°$$
$$= 9.24 - 3.65 - j\,20.68 - 5.27 + j\,14.47$$
$$= (0.33 - j\,6.21) = \mathbf{6.22\angle -87°\text{ A.}}$$

EXAMPLE 4.23 *In the phase sequence of 1-2-3 find the phase current and the line currents of the Δ connected load provided the supply is a balanced 100 V, 50 Hz 3 ph supply [Fig. E4.13].*

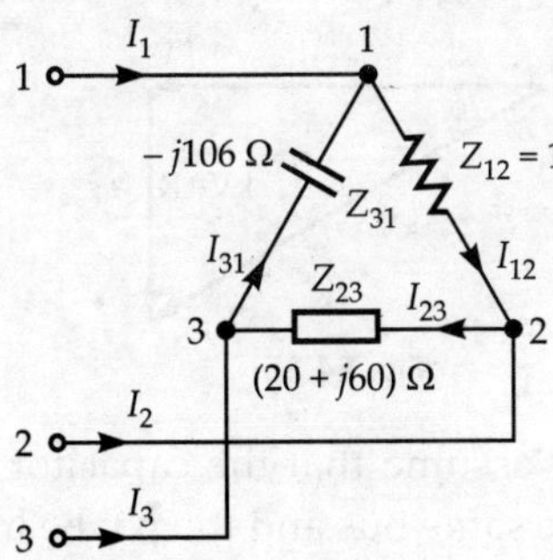

Fig. E4.13

SOLUTION. Given :

$$V_{1-2} = 100\angle 0°\text{ V,}$$
$$V_{2-3} = 100\angle -120°\text{ V}$$
$$V_{3-1} = 100\angle +120°\text{ V}$$

and
$$Z_{12} = 100\angle 0° = 100 + j\,0$$
$$Z_{23} = 20 + j\,60 = 63.25\angle 71.6°\,\Omega$$
$$Z_{31} = -j\,106 = 106\angle -90°\,\Omega$$

As in Δ connection, $V_{ph} = V_L$

$\therefore$ Phase currents are detailed as :

$$I_{12} = \frac{V_{1-2}}{Z_{12}} = \frac{100\angle 0°}{100\angle 0°} = \mathbf{1\angle 0°\text{ A}}$$

$$I_{23} = \frac{V_{2-3}}{Z_{23}} = \frac{100\angle -120°}{63.25\angle 71.6°} = \mathbf{1.58\angle 191.6°\text{ A}}$$

$$I_{31} = \frac{V_{3-1}}{Z_{31}} = \frac{100\angle 120°}{106\angle -90°} = \mathbf{0.943\angle 210°\text{ A}}$$

Line currents are given as

$$I_1 = I_{12} - I_{31} = 1\angle 0° - 0.943\angle 210°$$
$$= 1 - (-0.817 - j\,0.4715)$$
$$= 0.183 - j\,0.4715 = \mathbf{0.506\angle -68.79°\text{ A}}$$
$$I_2 = I_{23} - I_{12} = 1.58\angle -191.6° - 1\angle 0°$$
$$= -1.55 + j\,0.318 - 1$$
$$= -2.55 + j\,0.318 = \mathbf{2.57\angle 173°\text{ A}}$$
$$I_3 = I_{31} - I_{23} = 0.943\angle 210° - 1.58\angle -191.6°$$
$$= (-0.817 - j\,0.4715) + 1.55 - j\,0.318$$
$$= (0.733 - j\,0.7895)$$
$$= \mathbf{1.08\angle -47.13°\text{ A.}}$$

EXAMPLE 4.24 *If a balanced 50 V, 50 Hz 3 phase voltage be applied across a two phase load as shown in Fig. E4.14, find the power reading in the wattmeters.*

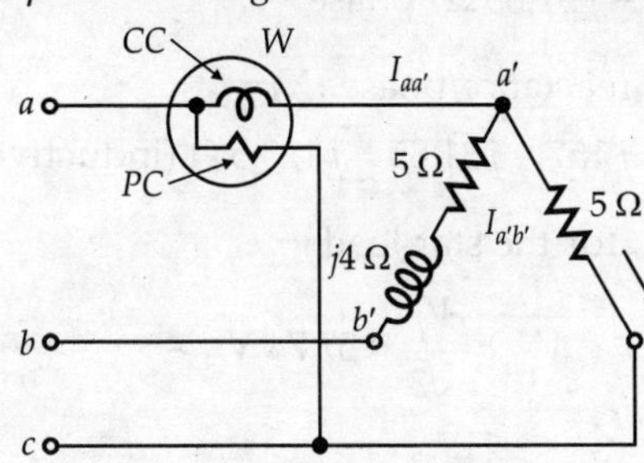

Fig. E4.14

SOLUTION. Given,

$$V_{a-b} = 50\angle 0°\text{ V},\ V_{b-c} = 50\angle -120°\text{ V},$$
$$V_{c-a} = 50\angle 120°\text{ V}$$

Also,

$$Z_{a'b'} = 5 + j\,4 = 6.4\angle 38.7°\text{ ohm.}$$

and
$$Z_{a'c'} = 5\,\Omega\text{ (resistive)}$$

Then,

$$I_{a'b'} = V_{a-b} / Z_{a'b'} = \frac{50\angle 0°}{6.4\angle 38.7°} = 7.8\angle -38.7°\text{ A}$$

$$I_{a'c'} = \frac{V_{ac}}{5} = \frac{-50\angle 120°}{5} = -10\angle 120°\text{ A.}$$

C H A P T E R 4

Therefore,

$$I_{aa'} = I_{a'b'} + I_{a'c'} = 7.8 \angle -38.7 - 10 \angle 120°$$
$$= 6.087 - j\,4.88 + 5 - j\,8.66$$
$$= 11.087 - j\,13.54 = 17.5 \angle -50.69° \text{ A}$$

Thus the current through CC (current coil) of the wattmeter is 17.5 A.

The voltage across the wattmeter is $V_{ab} = 50 \angle 0° \text{ V}$

$\therefore$ Reading of wattmeter $= I_{aa'} \times V_{ab}$

$$= 17.5 \times 50 \times \cos[0° - (-50.69°)] = \mathbf{554.4\ W.}$$

[In case the PC (potential coil) of wattmeter is connected between $b'c'$,

$$W = 17.5 \times 50 \times \cos[-120° + 50.69°] = \mathbf{309\ W.}]$$

EXAMPLE 4.25 *A three phase Y connected load has an inductor of 500 mH and capacitance of 100 μF in each phase. The load is connected across a 100 V, 50 Hz three phase balanced system. Find the line currents for the load.*

SOLUTION.

$$X_L = 2\pi fL = 314 \times 500 \times 10^{-3} = j\,157\,\Omega/\text{phase}$$

$$X_C = \frac{1}{2\pi f C} = \frac{1}{314 \times 100 \times 10^{-6}}$$

$$= -j\,31.85\,\Omega/\text{phase}$$

$\therefore$ Net reactance/phase (X)

$$= j\,157 - j\,31.85 = j\,125.5\,\Omega \text{ (inductive)}$$

Again, for the star load,

$$V_{ph} = \frac{V_L}{\sqrt{3}} = 57.74 \text{ V}$$

Thus,

$$I_{ph_1}\ (= I_{L_1}) = \frac{V_{ph}}{X} = \frac{57.74 \angle 0°}{j\,125.15} = 0.46 \angle -90° \text{ A}$$

$$[\because j\,125.15 \equiv 125.15 \angle 90°]$$

It may be noted that as the given load is star connected hence line current and phase currents could be identical.

Also, $I_{ph_2}\ (= I_{L_2}) = 0.46 \angle -90° - 120° = 0.46 \angle 210° \text{ A}$

and $I_{ph_3}\ (= I_{L_3}) = 0.46 \angle -90° + 120° = 0.46 \angle 30° \text{ A}$

Thus, the required line currents in ampere are

$I_{L_1} = \mathbf{0.46 \angle -90°\ (lag)}$, $I_{L_2} = \mathbf{0.46 \angle -210°\ (lag)}$

$I_{L_3} = \mathbf{0.46 \angle 30°\ (lead)}$

EXAMPLE 4.26 *Three inductive coils, having per phase resistance of 40 Ω and inductive reactance of 30 Ω are connected in star across a 415 V 3 ph 50 Hz supply. Calculate the rating of the three capacitors which must be connected in star to the supply in order to bring the overall p.f. to unity.*

SOLUTION. Here, $R = 40\,\Omega,\ X_L = 30\,\Omega$

$\therefore$ $Z = (40 + j\,30)\,\Omega$

i.e., $|Z| = \sqrt{40^2 + 30^2} = 50\,\Omega$ (*i.e.,* Z_{ph})

and $\cos\phi = \dfrac{R}{Z} = \dfrac{40}{50} = 0.8$ lag.

$$V_{ph} = \frac{V_L}{\sqrt{3}} = \frac{415}{\sqrt{3}} = 240 \text{ V.}$$

$$I_L = I_{ph} \text{ (due to star connection)}$$

$$= \frac{V_{ph}}{Z_{ph}} = \frac{240}{50} = 4.8 \text{ A}$$

$\therefore$ $\text{kVA} = \sqrt{3}\,V_L I_L$

$$= \sqrt{3} \times 415 \times 4.8 = 3.45 \text{ kVA}$$

and $\text{kW} = \sqrt{3}\,V_L\,I_L \cos\phi$

$$= \sqrt{3} \times 415 \times 4.8 \times 0.8 = 2.76 \text{ kW}$$

With reference to Fig. E4.15, let ϕ be p.f. angle when the total load supplied be 3.45 kVA. The reactive power demand is now

$$3.45 \times \sin\phi = 3.45 \times 0.6 = 2.07 \text{ kVAR}$$

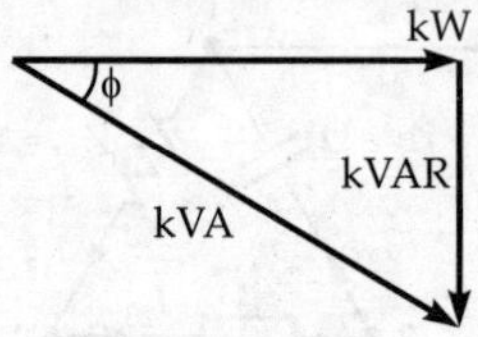

Fig. E4.15

Let us now assume that the capacitor bank be connected at the same bus and the p.f. be improved to unity.

$\therefore$ New kVA input

$$= \frac{\text{kW}}{\cos\phi} = \frac{2.76}{1} = 2.76 \text{ kVA}$$

New kVAR $= 2.76 \sin\phi = 2.76 \times 0 = 0$

[for *upf*, $\sin\phi = 0$]

i.e., the kVAR demand 2.07 kVAR has been supplied by the capacitor bank (the kVAR supplied by the bank would be leading).

Let us now assume that I_C be the line current of the bank and hence

$$\sqrt{3}\, V_L I_C = 2.07$$

or, $$I_C = \frac{2.07 \times 10^3}{\sqrt{3} \times V_L} = 2.87 \text{ A.}$$

Since the capacitor bank is star connected, current drawn by each capacitor is

$$I_{ph\,(c)} = I_L = 2.87 \text{ A.}$$

then, $$X_C / ph = \frac{240}{2.87}\left[i.e., \frac{V_{ph}}{I_{ph}} \right] = 83.48\,\Omega$$

But $$X_C = \frac{1}{2\pi f C}$$

i.e., here, $$C = \frac{1}{314 \times 83.48} = 38.2\ \mu\text{F.}$$

Thus, the rating of the capacitor in each phase would be **38.2 μF, 240 V, 0.69 kVAR**

$$[\because 3 \text{ ph kVAR} = 2.07, \text{ per phase kVAR} = \frac{2.07}{3} = \mathbf{0.69}]$$

EXAMPLE 4.27 *A delta connected load (Fig. E4.16) has following impedances : $Z_{RY} = j\,10\,\Omega$; $Z_{YB} = 10\,\angle 0°\,\Omega$, $Z_{BR} = -j\,10\,\Omega$. If the load be connected across a three phase 100 V supply (balanced), obtain the line currents.*

SOLUTION. Refer to Fig. E4.16

$$V_{RY} = 100\,\angle 0°\text{ V}$$
$$V_{YB} = 100\,\angle -120°\text{ V}$$
$$V_{BR} = 100\,\angle +120°\text{ V}$$

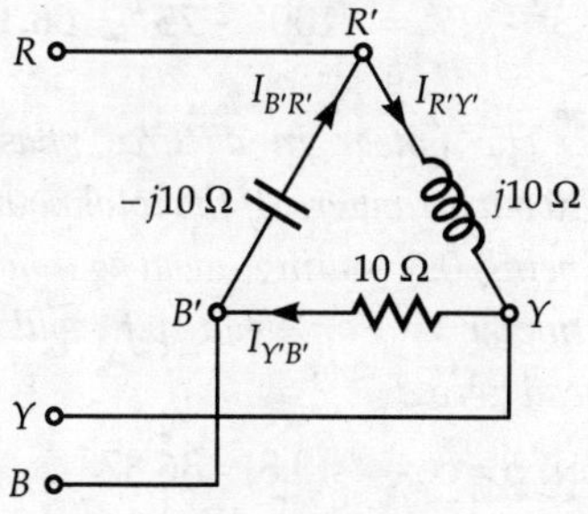

Fig. E4.16

Again, $$Z_{R'Y'} = j\,10\,\Omega$$
$$Z_{Y'B'} = 10\,\Omega$$
$$Z_{B'R'} = -j\,10\,\Omega$$

Thus $$I_{R'Y'} = \frac{V_{RY}}{Z_{R'Y'}} = \frac{100\,\angle 0°}{j\,10}$$
$$= 10\,\angle -90°\text{ A}$$

$$I_{Y'B'} = \frac{V_{YB}}{Z_{Y'B'}} = \frac{100\,\angle -120°}{10}$$
$$= 10\,\angle -120°\text{ A}$$

$$I_{B'R'} = \frac{V_{BR}}{Z_{B'R'}} = \frac{100\,\angle +120°}{-j\,10}$$
$$= 10\,\angle 210°\text{ A}$$

Applying KCL at each node, line currents

$$I_{RR'} = I_{R'Y'} - I_{B'R'} = 10\,\angle -90° - 10\,\angle 210°$$
$$= -j\,10 + 8.66 + j\,5 = \mathbf{(8.66 - j\,5)\ A}$$

$$I_{YY'} = I_{Y'B'} - I_{R'Y'} = 10\,\angle -120° - 10\,\angle -90°$$
$$= -5 - j\,8.66 + j\,10 = \mathbf{(-5 + j\,1.34)\ A}$$

and $$I_{BB'} = I_{B'R'} - I_{Y'B'}$$
$$= 10\,\angle 210° - 10\,\angle -120°$$
$$= -8.66 - j\,5 + 5 + j\,8.66$$
$$= \mathbf{(-3.66 + j\,3.6)\ A.}$$

EXAMPLE 4.28 *A balanced 3 ph star connected load is connected across a 11 kV, 50 Hz, 3 ph supply. If the load consumes 150 kW and takes a leading current of 100 A, find the circuit constants of the load on per phase basis.*

SOLUTION.

$$|Z_{ph}|_{\text{load}} = \frac{|V_{ph}|}{|I_{ph}|} = \frac{(11000/\sqrt{3})}{100} = 63.51\,\Omega$$

However, the power consumed $= I_{ph}^2\, R$ (Watts)

$\therefore$ In this case $10^3 \times 150 = (100)^2 \times R_{ph} \times 3$

Thus $R = 5\,\Omega$

This gives

$$X_{ph} = \sqrt{Z_{ph}^2 - R_{ph}^2} = \sqrt{(63.51)^2 - (5)^2} = 63.31\,\Omega$$

As the input current is leading, hence X_{ph} must be capacitive.

$$\therefore \quad \frac{1}{2\pi f C} = 63.31, \text{ giving } C = 50.28\ \mu\text{F.}$$

The circuit constants are

$$R = \mathbf{5\,\Omega / ph}$$
$$C = \mathbf{50.28\ \mu F / ph.}$$

EXAMPLE 4.29 *Given in Fig. E4.17, $Z_a = 5\,\angle 30°\,\Omega$, $Z_b = 10\,\angle 0°\,\Omega$, $Z_c = 5\,\angle 60°\,\Omega$; find I_a provided the given load is supplied from a 3 ph 50 Hz 25 V source.*

SOLUTION. In the given Δ connected load,

$$|V_{L-L}| = |V_{ph}| = 25\text{ V.}$$

CHAPTER 4

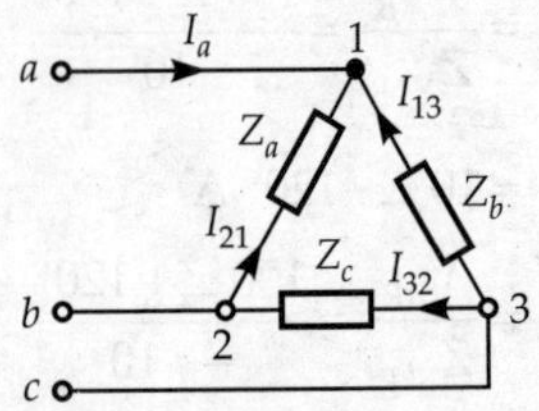

Fig. E4.17

However, $V_{ab} = 25\angle 0°$ V,

$V_{bc} = 25\angle -120°$ V

and $V_{ca} = 25\angle 120°$ V

Also, $I_{13} = \dfrac{V_{ac}}{Z_b} = \dfrac{-25\angle 120°}{10\angle 0°}$

$= -2.5\angle 120°$ A

and $I_{21} = \dfrac{V_{ba}}{Z_a} = \dfrac{-25\angle 0°}{5\angle 30°}$

$= -5\angle -30°$ A.

However,

$I_a = I_{13} - I_{21} = -2.5\angle 120° + 5\angle -30°$

$= 1.25 - j\,2.165 + 4.33 - j\,2.5$

$= (5.58 - j\,4.665) = \mathbf{7.273\angle -40°\ A.}$

Example 4.30 *In Fig. E4.18, phase B is open. Input currents of phase R and Y being given, find the neutral wire current. Draw the phasor diagram.*

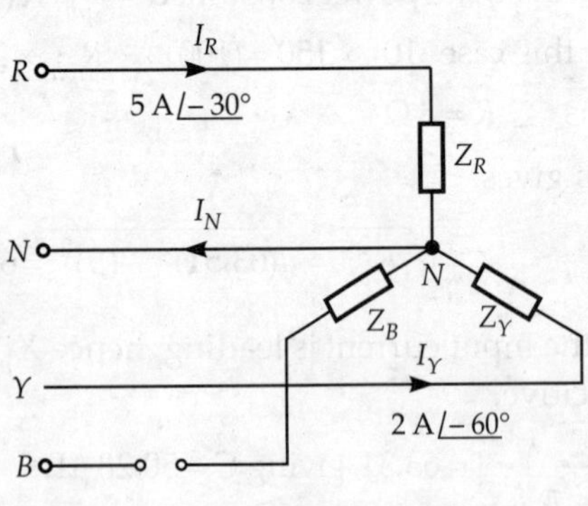

Fig. E4.18

Solution. $I_R = 5\angle -30°$ A ; $I_Y = 2\angle -60°$ A ; $I_B = 0$

Applying KCL at N, $I_R + I_Y + I_B = I_N$

or, $I_N = I_R + I_Y = 5(\cos 30° - j\sin 30°)$

$+ 2(\cos 60° - j\sin 60°)$

$= 4.33 - j\,2.5 + 1 - j\,1.732$

$= (5.33 - j\,4.232)$ A

$= \mathbf{6.81\angle -38.45°\ A.}$

The phasor diagram is shown in Fig. E4.19.

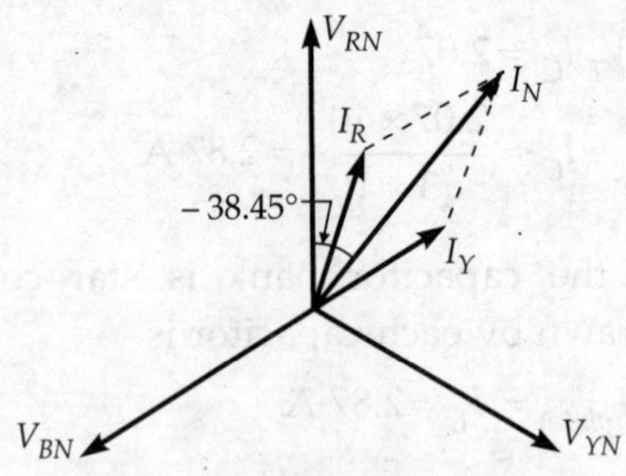

Fig. E4.19

Example 4.31 *The apparent power input to a 3 ph balanced Y connected load is 100 kVA while the corresponding true power is 75 kW at 100 A. Calculate the power factor, phase and line voltage.*

Solution. $\cos\phi = \dfrac{P}{S} = \dfrac{75\times 10^3}{100\times 10^3} = \mathbf{0.75\ (p.f.)}$

As $P = 75\times 10^3$ W

$\therefore$ We can write $75000 = \sqrt{3}\times V_L\times I_L\times\cos\phi$

Here $I_L = 100$ A, $\cos\phi = 0.75$.

$\therefore$ $V_L = \dfrac{75000}{\sqrt{3}\times 100\times 0.75} = \mathbf{577.37\ V}$

and because of Y connection,

$V_{ph} = \dfrac{1}{\sqrt{3}}\times 577.37$ *i.e.*, $V_{ph} = \mathbf{333.35\ V.}$

[The reactive power drawn is

$Q = \sqrt{S^2 - P^2} = \sqrt{100^2 - 75^2} = \mathbf{66.14\ kVAR}$]

Example 4.32 *The power in a three phase circuit is measured by two wattmeters. If the total power is 50 kW, power factor being 0.8 leading, what will be the reading of each wattmeter ? For what p.f. will one of the wattmeters read zero ?*

Solution. $\phi = \cos^{-1}(0.8) = 36.87°$

$\therefore$ $\tan\phi = 0.75.$

As the p.f. is leading,

$\tan\phi = \dfrac{\sqrt{3}(W_2 - W_1)}{W_1 + W_2}$

or, $0.75 = \dfrac{\sqrt{3}(W_2 - W_1)}{50}$

or, $W_2 - W_1 = 21.65.$

Again $W_1 + W_2 = 50$

$\therefore \quad W_2 = \mathbf{35.825\ W}$

and $\quad W_1 = \mathbf{-14.175\ W}$

One of the wattmeters would read zero when the p.f. **would be 0.5.**

Example 4.33 *A resistance of 300 Ω and a capacitor of 398 Ω are connected in series across R phase and Y phase of a 3 phase 50 Hz, 400 V system. Obtain the value of the voltage between the junction point of the resistor and capacitor and phase B.*

Solution. Refer to Fig. E4.20

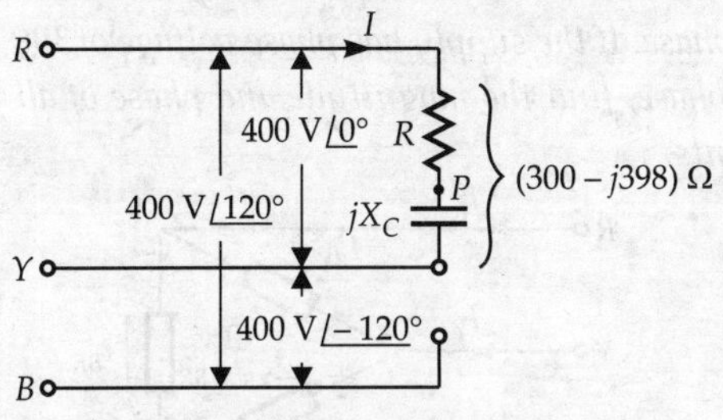

Fig. E4.20

Here, $\quad R = 300\,\Omega$ and $-j\,X_C = 398\,\Omega$

$$\therefore\ I_{RY}\ (=I) = \frac{400\angle 0^\circ}{300 - j398} = \frac{400}{498\angle -53^\circ}$$

or, $\quad I = 0.8\ \angle 53^\circ$ A.

Let the junction point of R and X_C be denoted by p.

$$\therefore \begin{pmatrix}\text{Drop}\\ \text{across } R\end{pmatrix} + \begin{pmatrix}\text{Drop across point } P\\ \text{and terminal } B\end{pmatrix} + (V_{BR}) = 0$$

or, $\quad 300 \times I + V_{PB} + V_{BR} = 0$

or, $\quad V_{PB} = -V_{BR} - 0.8\ \angle 53 \times 300 = -V_{BR} - 240\ \angle 53^\circ$

$$= -400\ \angle +120^\circ - 240\ \angle 53^\circ$$

$$= 200 - j\,346 - 144 - j\,192$$

$$= 56 - j\,538 = 541\ \angle -84^\circ \text{ V}.$$

Thus, the voltage between the junction of the R and X_C and the line B is **541 ∠ – 84° V.**

Example 4.34 *Three identical resistances are connected in a star fashion against a balanced three phase voltage supply. If one of the resistances be removed, by how much the power be reduced ?*

Solution. When all the resistances are present :

$$P = 3\,V_{ph}^2 / R = 3\left(\frac{V_L}{\sqrt{3}}\right)^2 \times \frac{1}{R} = \frac{V_L^2}{R}.$$

When one of the phase resistances is abolished,

$$P = 2\left(\frac{V_L}{2}\right)^2 \times \frac{1}{R} = \frac{V_L^2}{2R}$$

[∵ When one phase resistance is removed voltage across each resistance is $(V_L/2)$ Ref. Fig. E4.21].

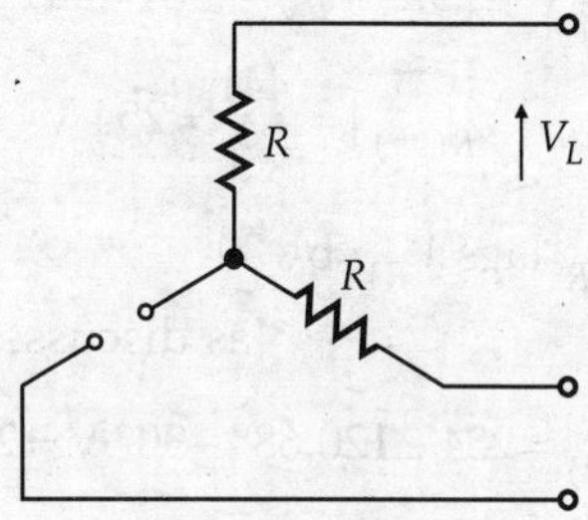

Fig. E4.21

$$\therefore \text{Reduction in power} = \frac{\dfrac{V_L^2}{R} - \dfrac{V_L^2}{2R}}{V_L^2/R} \times 100 = \mathbf{50\%}$$

[The reader may check the same problem for Δ where the power reduction would be

$$3\frac{V_L^2}{R} - 2\frac{V_L^2}{R} = \frac{V_L^2}{R} \text{ i.e., } 33.33\%$$].

Example 4.35 *A three phase 400 V, 50 Hz, 25 HP motor is delta connected and is operating at 0.85 lag and efficiency of 80%. What is the line current ?*

Solution. Output of motor

$$= 25 \times 746 = 18.65 \text{ kW}$$

Motor input

$$= \frac{\text{output of motor}}{\eta\,(\text{efficiency})} = \frac{18650}{0.8} = 23312.5 \text{ W}$$

$$V_L = 400 \text{ V} ; \text{P.F.} = 0.85 \text{ lag}$$

Line current

$$(I_L) = \frac{\text{Motor input}}{\sqrt{3}\,V_L \cos\phi} = \frac{23312.5}{\sqrt{3} \times 400 \times 0.85} = \mathbf{39.59\ A.}$$

Example 4.36 *Three impedances Z_1, Z_2 and Z_3 are connected in star and is fed from a balanced three phase system. It is given that the drops across Z_1 and Z_2 are 295 ∠97.5° and 206 ∠ – 25° V respectively. What is the voltage drop between the star point of the load and supply neutral ?*

Solution. Let V_R, V_Y and V_B be the phase voltages of the supply. Let V_N be the neutral potential *i.e.*, the voltage between the star point and load neutral.

$$\therefore \quad V_{drop(R\,ph)} = V_R - V_N = 295 \angle 97.5° \quad ...(1)$$

and $$V_{drop(Y\,ph)} = V_Y - V_N = 206 \angle -25° \quad ...(2)$$

$$\therefore \; V_{RY} = 295 \angle 97.5° - 206 \angle -25°$$
$$= (-38.5 + j\,292.5 - 186.7 + j\,87.06)$$
$$= (-225.2 + j\,379.56) = 441 \angle 120.68° \text{ V}$$

Then $$|V_{R(ph)}| = \frac{441}{\sqrt{3}} = 254 \text{ V}$$

while V_R lags V_{RY} by 30°

[as discussed in the text]

$$\therefore \; V_{R(ph)} = 254 \angle 120.68° - 30° \text{ V} = 254 \angle 90.68° \text{ V}$$

Again from (1),

$$V_N = V_R - V_{drop(R\,ph)}$$
$$= 254 \angle -90.68° - 295 \angle 97.5°$$
$$= -3.01 + j\,254 + 38.5 - j\,292.48$$
$$= 35.49 - j\,38.48 = \mathbf{52.35 \angle -47.31° \text{ V}}.$$

EXAMPLE 4.37 *A balanced 440 V, 3 ph voltage is applied on an unbalanced star connected load. It is given that the supply voltage R is 254 ∠–30° V and the drop across the load connected in R phase is 200 ∠– 15° V. Calculate the voltage between the star point of the load and the supply neutral. Also find the voltage across the loads in Y and B phases.*

SOLUTION. $$V_R = \frac{V_L}{\sqrt{3}} = \frac{440}{1.732} = 254 \angle -30° \text{ V}$$

(given)

[∵ star connection, V_{ph} lags the V_{L-L} by 30°]

and $$V_{drop(R)} = 200 \angle -15° \text{ V}.$$

Thus neutral voltage

$$(E_N) = 254 \angle -30° - 200 \angle -15°$$
$$= 220 - j\,127 - 193.19 + j\,51.76$$
$$= 26.81 - j\,75.24 = 79.87 \angle -70.39° \text{ V}.$$

Thus the drop across the star neutral and the star point of the load = 79.87 ∠–70.39° V

To find V_Y and V_B,

$$V_Y = 254 \angle -30° - 120° - E_N$$
$$= 254 \angle -150° - E_N$$
$$= -220 - j\,127 - 26.81 + j\,75.25$$
$$= (-246.81 - j\,51.75) \text{ V}$$
$$= 252.18 \angle -168.16° \text{ V}$$

and $$V_B = 254 \angle -30° + 120° - E_N$$
$$= 254 \angle 90° - 26.81 + j\,75.25$$
$$= j\,254 - 26.81 + j\,75.25$$
$$= j\,329.25 - 26.81 = 330 \angle 94.65° \text{ V}$$

∴ Voltage between star point of the load and star neutral

$$= \mathbf{79.87 \angle -70.39° \text{ V}}$$

and voltages $V_Y = \mathbf{252.18 \angle -168.16° \text{ V}}$

and $V_B = \mathbf{330 \angle 94.65° \text{ V}}$.

EXAMPLE 4.38 *A delta connected load is shown in Fig. E4.22 when each phase has an impedance of 130 ∠–67.5° Ω in each phase. If the supply has phase voltage of 390 ∠30° V in R phase, find the magnitude and phase of all the line currents.*

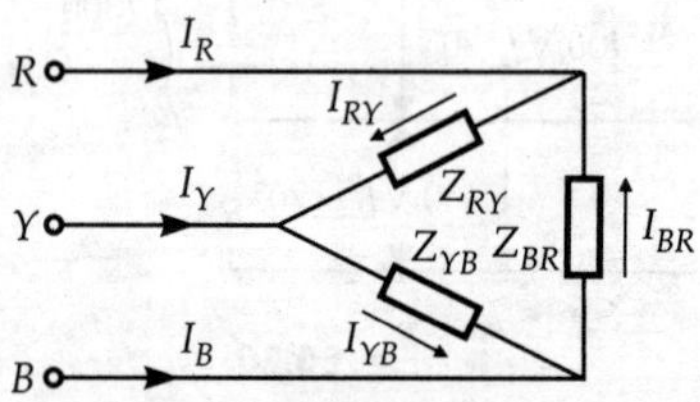

Fig. E4.22

SOLUTION. It is given that V_{R-n} (supply side phase voltage, not shown in the figure) is 390 ∠30° V.

$$\therefore \quad V_{Y-n} = 390 \angle 30° - 120° = 390 \angle -90° \text{ V}$$

and $$V_{B-n} = 390 \angle 30° + 120° = 390 \angle 150° \text{ V}$$

Thus, the supply side line voltages are

$$V_{RY} = V_{R-n} - V_{Y-n} = 390 \angle 30° - 390 \angle -90°$$
$$= 675.5 \angle 60° \text{ V},$$

$$V_{YB} = V_{Y-n} - V_{B-n} = 390 \angle -90° - 390 \angle 150°$$
$$= 675.5 \angle -60° \text{ V}$$

$$V_{BR} = V_{B-n} - V_{R-n} = 390 \angle 150° - 390 \angle 30°$$
$$= 675.5 \angle 180° \text{ V}$$

For the delta load, the phase currents are

$$I_{RY} = \frac{V_{RY}}{Z_{RY}} = \frac{675.5 \angle 60°}{130 \angle -67.5°}$$

$$[\because Z_{ph(\Delta)} = 130 \angle -67.5° \text{ ohm}]$$

$$= 5.2 \angle 127.5° \text{ A}$$

$$I_{YB} = \frac{V_{YB}}{Z_{YB}} = \frac{675.5 \angle -60°}{130 \angle -67.5°} = 5.2 \angle 7.5° \text{ A}$$

$$I_{BR} = \frac{V_{BR}}{Z_{BR}} = \frac{675.5 \angle 180°}{130 \angle -67.5°} = 5.2 \angle 247.5° \text{ A}$$

[∵ cos 37.47° is + ve]

Thus the line currents are (for Δ load)

$$I_R = I_{RY} - I_{BR} = 5.2 \angle 127.5 - 5.2 \angle 247.5$$
$$= -3.17 + j\,4.13 + 1.99 + j\,4.8 = -1.18 + j\,8.93$$
$$= 9 \angle 97.53° \text{ A.}$$

$$I_Y = I_{YB} - I_{RY} = 5.2 \angle 7.5 - 5.2 \angle 127.5$$
$$= 5.16 + j\,0.68 + 3.17 - j\,4.13$$
$$= 8.33 - j\,3.45 = 9.02 \angle -22.5° \text{ A}$$

$$I_B = I_{BR} - I_{YB} = 5.2 \angle 297.5 - 5.2 \angle 7.5°$$
$$= -1.99 - j\,4.8 - 5.16 - j\,0.68$$
$$= -7.15 - j\,5.48 = 9 \angle(-142.53°) \text{ A}$$

$$\therefore I_R = \mathbf{9 \angle 97.53° \text{ A}}$$
$$I_Y = 9.02 \angle -22.6° \text{ A} \simeq \mathbf{9 \angle -22.6° \text{ A}}$$
$$I_B = \mathbf{9 \angle 37.47° \text{ A.}}$$

EXAMPLE 4.39 *A balanced delta connected load contains $(4 + j\,2)\,\Omega/ph$, while a balanced Y connected load consists of $(1 - j\,2)\,\Omega/ph$. Both the loads are connected in parallel to a three phase three wire system having line voltage of 220 V. The supply has a resistance of 0.1 ohm/ph. Find the total power delivered to the individual loads and the loss of power in the lines.*

SOLUTION. For the balanced Δ load,

$$V_{ph} = V_L = 220 \text{ V}$$
$$Z_{ph} = (4 + j\,2)\,\Omega = 4.472\,\Omega \angle 26.56°$$

$$\therefore \quad |I_{ph}| = \frac{|V_{ph}|}{|Z_{ph}|} = \frac{220}{4.472} = 49.2 \text{ A}$$

Thus $|I_L| = \sqrt{3}\, I_{ph} = 85.21$ A.

Thus power consumed in Δ load

$$= \sqrt{3}\, V_L\, I_L \cos\phi$$
$$= \sqrt{3} \times 220 \times 85.21 \times \cos 26.56°$$
$$= \mathbf{29.04 \text{ kW.}}$$

Next, for the balanced Y load,

$$V_{ph} = \frac{1}{\sqrt{3}} \times V_L = 127 \text{ V.}$$

But $\quad Z_{ph} = (1 - j\,2)\,\Omega = 2.24 \angle -63.44°\,\Omega$

$$\therefore \quad |I_{ph}| = \frac{127}{2.24} = 56.7 \text{ A};$$

for star load, $\quad |I_L| = 56.7$ A.

∴ The power consumed in Y load,

$$\sqrt{3}\, V_L\, I_L \cos\phi = \sqrt{3} \times 220 \times 56.7 \times \cos 63.44°$$
$$= \mathbf{9.66 \text{ kW.}}$$

∴ Total load supplied = 29.04 + 9.66 = 38.7 kW.

Again the total line current from the supply

$$I_{L_{\text{total}}} = I_{L_{\Delta\,(\text{loud})}} + I_{L_{\lambda\,(\text{loud})}}$$
$$= 85.21 + 56.7 \simeq 142 \text{ A}$$

This gives the line loss

$$= (I_{L_{tot}})^2 \times R_{\text{line}} = (142)^2 \times 0.1$$

[∵ supply line has 0.1 Ω resistance]

$$= \mathbf{2.016 \text{ kW.}}$$

EXAMPLE 4.40 *A balanced Y connected load is supplied from a balanced 3 phase 400 V system. If the current in each phase is 15 A and lags the phase voltage by 30°, find the phase voltage and the total power.*

SOLUTION. $V_{ph} = \dfrac{V_L}{\sqrt{3}} = \dfrac{400}{\sqrt{3}} = 231 \text{ V}$

As the current lags the corresponding phase voltage by 30°, hence, the p.f. is cos 30° (lag) *i.e.*, 0.866.

The power $\quad P = \sqrt{3}\, V_L\, I_L \cos\phi$

$$= \sqrt{3} \times 400 \times 15$$
$$= 0.866 \times 10^{-3} = \mathbf{9 \text{ kW.}}$$

EXAMPLE 4.41 *In the given circuit of Fig. E4.23, find the value of the unknown impedance provided no current flows in branch y.*

SOLUTION. Let

$$V_{r-y} = V \angle 0° \text{ V}$$
$$V_{y-b} = V \angle -120° \text{ V}$$

and $\quad V_{b-r} = V \angle 120° \text{ V}$

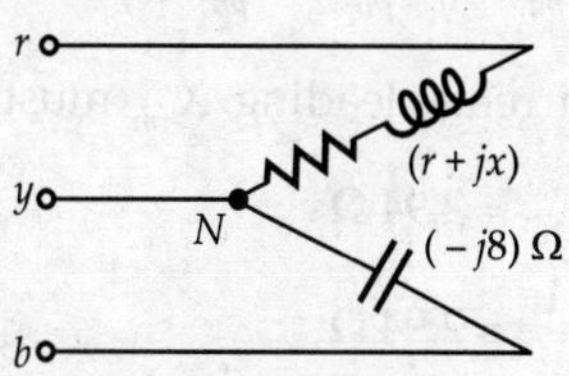

Fig. E4.23

Let the current through the capacitor be I_C

$$\therefore \quad I_C = \frac{V \angle -120°}{X_C} \qquad \left[\because I_C = \frac{V_{y-b}}{X_C}\right]$$

$$= \frac{V}{8} \angle -120° + 90°$$

[∵ $X_C = -j\,8 = 8 \angle -90°$]

$$= \frac{V}{8} \angle -30° \text{ A}$$

Let current through phase y be I_y. Redrawing Fig. E4.24 with current directions taken into account [Fig. E4.24], application of KCL at N yields

$$I_y = I_C - I_L = 0 \quad [\because \text{No current would flow through } y]$$

$$\therefore \quad I_C = I_L$$

i.e., $$\frac{V}{r+jx} = \frac{V}{8}\angle -30^\circ$$

or, $$r + jx = 8\angle 30^\circ$$
$$= 8\cos 30^\circ + j(\sin 30^\circ).8$$
$$= (6.93 + j4)\Omega$$

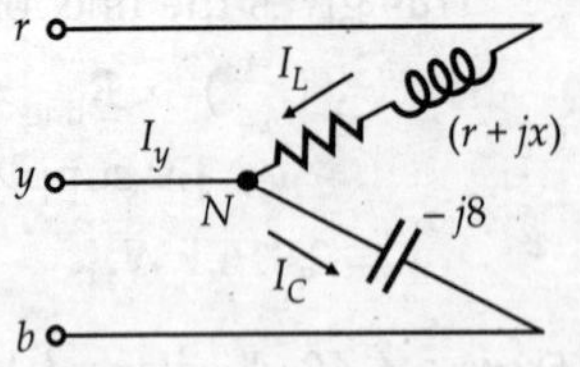

Fig. E4.24

Thus, for I_y to be zero, $r = \mathbf{6.93\,\Omega}$; $x = \mathbf{4\,\Omega}$.

EXAMPLE 4.42 *A balanced 3 phase star connected load draws 10 kW from a three phase balanced systems of 400 V, 50 Hz while the line current is 75 A (leading p.f.). Find the circuit element of the load.*

SOLUTION.

$$Z_{ph}\text{ (phase impedance)} = \frac{V_{ph}}{I_{ph}} = \frac{400}{75\sqrt{3}} = 3\,\Omega$$

$$\left[\text{in star load, } I_{ph} = I_{\text{Line}}\ ;\ V_{ph} = \frac{V_L}{\sqrt{3}}\right]$$

$$\text{Power/phase} = I_{ph}^2 R_{ph} \quad \text{or,} \quad \frac{10\times 10^3}{3} = 75^2 R_{ph}$$

$$\therefore \quad R_{ph} = \frac{10\times 1000}{3\times 75\times 75} = 0.6\,\Omega$$

$$\therefore \quad X_{ph} = \sqrt{Z_{ph}^2 - R_{ph}^2} = \sqrt{3^2 - (0.6)^2} = 2.94\,\Omega$$

As the current is leading, X_{ph} must be capacitive.

$$\therefore \quad X_C = 2.94\,\Omega$$

or, $$\frac{1}{\omega C} = 2.94\,\Omega$$

$$\therefore \quad C = \frac{1}{2.94\times 2\pi f} = \frac{1}{2.94\times 2\times\pi\times 50}$$
$$= \mathbf{1083\,\mu F.}$$

EXAMPLE 4.43 *A three phase induction motor takes 100 kVA at 0.6 p.f. (lag) from a 440 V three phase 50 Hz source (balanced). There is another load on the same line and the load is connected in form of a Δ having 8 Ω resistance and – j 24 Ω reactance in series in each phase. Find the total VA power, average power, reactive power, line current and the p.f. of the combination.*

SOLUTION. For the motor, $\cos\phi$(p.f.) = 0.6 lag

$$\therefore \quad \phi = 53.13^\circ(-\text{ve}).$$

This gives P_m (real power taken by the motor)
$$= S\cos\phi = 100\times 0.6 = 60\text{ kW}$$

and Q_m (reactive power taken by the motor)
$$= S\sin\phi = 100\times 0.8 = 80\text{ kVAR}$$

Again, for the Δ connected load,
$$V_{ph} = V_{L-L} = 440\text{ V};$$

the phase impedances
$$(Z_{ph}) = 8 - j\,24 = 25.3\angle -71.56^\circ\,\Omega$$

∴ for the Δ load,
$$|I_{ph}| = \frac{V_{ph}}{Z_{ph}} = \frac{440}{25.3} = 17.4\text{ A}$$

This gives $I_{L(\text{load})} = \sqrt{3}\,I_{ph} = 30.13$ A

where $I_{L(\text{load})}$ is the line current for Δ load.

∴ For the Δ load,
$$P_\Delta = \sqrt{3}\times V_L\times I_L\cos\phi$$
$$= \sqrt{3}\times 440\times 30.13\times\cos 71.56^\circ$$
$$= 7.263\text{ kW}$$

and $$Q_\Delta = \sqrt{3}\,V_L I_L\sin\phi$$
$$= \sqrt{3}\times 440\times 30.13\times\sin 71.56^\circ$$
$$= 21.783\text{ kVAR},$$

and $$S_\Delta = \sqrt{P_\Delta^2 + Q_\Delta^2} \simeq 23\text{ kVA}$$

∴ Total VA power
$$(S_T) = S + S_\Delta + 100 + 23 = \mathbf{123\ kVA}$$

Total real power
$$= P_T + P_M + P_\Delta = 60 + 7.263 = \mathbf{67.263\ kW}$$

and total reactive power
$$= Q_T = Q_M + Q_\Delta = 80 + 21.783 = \mathbf{101.783\ kVAR}$$

$$\text{Net power factor} = \frac{P_T}{S_T} = \frac{67.263}{123} = \mathbf{0.546\ lag}$$

$$\text{Also, total line current} = I_{m\,(\text{line})} = I_{\Delta\,(\text{line})}$$
$$= \frac{S_T}{\sqrt{3}\,V_{L-L}} = \frac{123\times 10^3}{\sqrt{3}\times 440} = \mathbf{161.4\ A.}$$

EXAMPLE 4.44 *A star connected alternator supplies a delta connected load. The impedance of each branch is $(6 + j\,8)\Omega$. The line voltage is 400 V. Obtain the current in phase of the load. Also find the current in each phase of the alternator. What is the power drawn by the load and its power factor ? Determine the reactive power of the load.*

SOLUTION.

$$Z_{ph} = (6 + j\,8)\Omega = 10\,\angle 53.13°\Omega$$
$$V_L = 400 \text{ V}$$

The load being delta connected,

$$V_L = V_{ph} = 400 \text{ V}$$

$$\therefore\ I_{ph\,(load)} = \frac{V_{ph}}{Z_{ph}} = \frac{400}{10} = 40 \text{ A (magnitude)}.$$

Thus, the phase current in load is 40 A. Thus the line current of the alternator is $(\sqrt{3} \times 40)$ A; phase current of the alternator is also $(40\sqrt{3})$ A.

$$\text{Load power} = 3\, I_{ph}^2\, R_{ph} \text{ (load)}$$
$$= 3 \times 40^2 \times 6 = 28.8 \text{ kW}.$$

P.F. of load,

$$\cos\phi_L = \frac{R_{ph}}{Z_{ph}} = \frac{6}{\sqrt{6^2 + 8^2}} = 0.6 \text{ lag}$$

$$\text{Reactive power of load} = \sqrt{3}\, V_L\, I_L \sin\phi$$
$$= \sqrt{3} \times 400 \times (\sqrt{3} \times 40) \times 0.8 = 38.39 \text{ kVAR}.$$

Thus, I_{ph} (load) = **40 A**, I_{ph} (alt) = **40 $\sqrt{3}$ A**

P_{load} = **28.8 kW**, Q_{load} = **38.39 kVAR**

EXAMPLE 4.45 *A 440 V (L-L) 3 phase 5 wire 50 Hz source system feeds two balanced star connected loads having impedance (10 + j 5)Ω per phase and 15 Ω per phase respectively. Find the power delivered to each load and the total power delivered by the source in each phase.*

SOLUTION. For each of the loads (connected in parallel),

$$V_{ph} = \frac{V_L}{\sqrt{3}} = 254 \text{ V}$$

Then, $|I_{ph_1}|$ [the load current of first load]

$$= \frac{254}{\sqrt{5^2 + 10^2}} = 22.72 \text{ A}$$

[∵ Z (impedance) of first load]

and $$\theta = \tan^{-1}\frac{5}{10} = 26.57°.$$

i.e., $$I_{ph_1} = I_{L_1} = 22.72\,\angle -26.57° \text{ (lag)}$$

∴ Power delivered by the source to this load

$$= P_1 = \sqrt{3} \times 440 \times 22.72 \times \cos 26.57° = \mathbf{15.48\ kW}$$

Similarly, $$|I_{ph_2}| = \frac{254}{15} = 17 \text{ A}.$$

[∵ impedance of 2nd load is purely resistive and is 15 Ω only]

Obviously, the power delivered to this load is

$$P_2 = \sqrt{3} \times 440 \times 17 \times \cos 0° = \mathbf{12.9\ kW}.$$

[∵ resistor load, p.f. = 1]

Thus, the total load supplied to the loads is

$$P_1 + P_2 = 15.48 + 12.9 = \mathbf{28.38\ kW} \text{ (3 phase)}$$

Thus per phase power supplied is

$$P_{S(ph)} = \frac{28.38}{3} = \mathbf{9.46\ kW}.$$

EXAMPLE 4.46 *A balanced Y connected 3 phase load has an impedance of Z_{ph} (= 5 − j 4) ohms in each phase. Find the line currents if a balanced 3 ph source of 100 V is applied across it. Draw the phasor diagram.*

SOLUTION. $$V_{ph} = \frac{100}{\sqrt{3}} = 57.74 \text{ V};$$

$$Z_{ph} = 5 - j\,4 = 6.4\,\angle -38.66°\,\Omega$$

$$\therefore\ I_{L_1} = I_{ph_1} = \frac{57.74\,\angle 0°}{6.4\,\angle -38.66°} = \mathbf{9.02\,\angle 38.66°\ A}$$

$$I_{L_2} = I_{ph_2} = 9.02\,\angle +38.66° - 120°$$
$$= \mathbf{9.02\,\angle -81.34°\ A}$$

$$I_{L_3} = I_{ph_3} = 9.02\,\angle 38.66° + 120°$$
$$= \mathbf{9.02\,\angle 158.66°\ A}.$$

The phasor diagram is shown in Fig. E4.25.

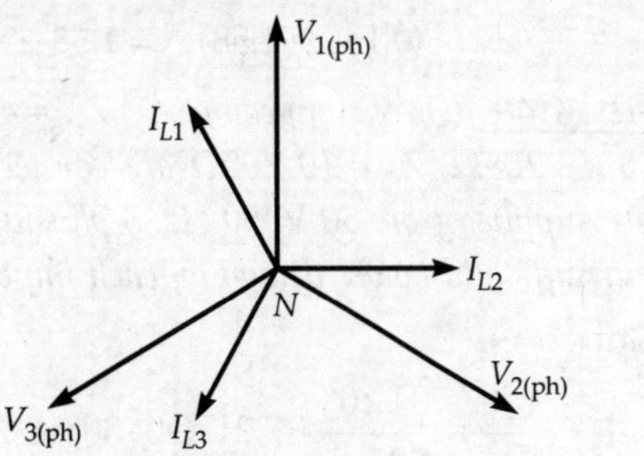

Fig. E4.25

EXAMPLE 4.47 *Find I_X and I_Z in the network of Fig. E4.26 provided the input voltage is 10 V (L-L).*

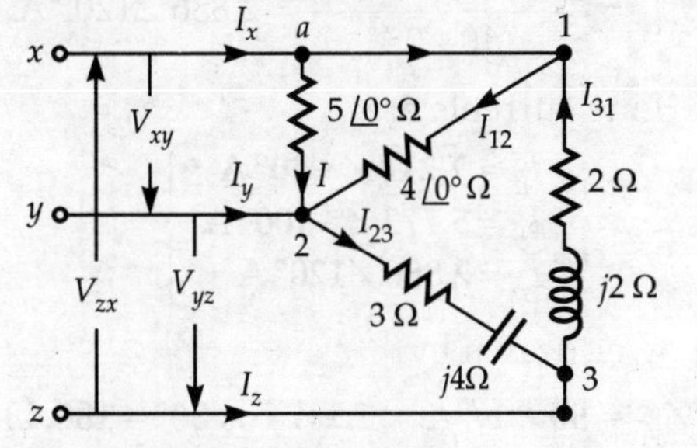

Fig. E4.26

CHAPTER 4

SOLUTION. Given,

$$V_{xy} = 10\angle 0^\circ \text{ V};\quad V_{yz} = 10\angle -120^\circ \text{ V}$$
$$V_{zx} = 10\angle +120^\circ \text{ V}$$

Applying KCL at node 1,

[it may be noted that terminals *a* and 1 are actually same terminals]

$$I_X = I + I_{12} - I_{31}$$

or, $$I_X = \frac{V_{xy}}{5\angle 0^\circ} + \frac{V_{xy}}{4\angle 0^\circ} - \frac{V_{zx}}{2+j2}$$
$$= \frac{10\angle 0^\circ}{5\angle 0^\circ} + \frac{10\angle 0^\circ}{4\angle 0^\circ} - \frac{10\angle 120^\circ}{2.828\angle 45^\circ}$$
$$= 2 + j0 + 2.5 + j0 - 3.535\angle 75^\circ$$
$$= 4.5 - 3.535\times 0.259 - j\,3.535\times 0.966$$
$$= (3.584 - j\,3.415)\text{ A}$$

i.e., $I_X = \mathbf{4.95\angle -43.62^\circ\ A.}$

Again, $I_Z = I_{31} - I_{23}$

$$= \frac{V_{zx}}{(2+j2)} - \frac{V_{yz}}{3-j4}$$
$$= \frac{10\angle 120^\circ}{2.828\angle 45^\circ} - \frac{10\angle -120^\circ}{5\angle -53.13^\circ}$$
$$= 3.54\angle 75^\circ - 2\angle -66.87^\circ$$
$$= 0.916 - j\,3.42 - 0.786 + j\,1.84$$
$$= (0.13 - j\,1.58)\text{ A} = \mathbf{1.58\angle -85.30^\circ\ A.}$$

EXAMPLE 4.48 *Three impedances, $Z_A = 4\angle 30^\circ\Omega$, $Z_B = 5\angle -20^\circ\Omega$, $Z_C = 10\angle 0^\circ\Omega$ are connected in star and are supplied from 50 V, 50 Hz, 3 ph source. Obtain line currents and power drawn by each impedance.*

SOLUTION.

$$I_a = \frac{(50/\sqrt{3})\angle 0^\circ}{4\angle 30^\circ} = 7.217\angle -30^\circ \text{ A}$$
$$I_b = \frac{(50/\sqrt{3})\angle -120^\circ}{5\angle -20^\circ} = 5.772\angle -100^\circ \text{ A}$$
$$I_c = \frac{(50/\sqrt{3})\angle +120^\circ}{10\angle 0^\circ} = 2.886\angle 120^\circ \text{ A.}$$

∴ Line currents are

$$\left.\begin{aligned} I_a &= \mathbf{7.217\angle -30^\circ\ A} \\ I_b &= \mathbf{5.772\angle -100^\circ\ A} \\ I_c &= \mathbf{2.886\angle 120^\circ\ A} \end{aligned}\right\}$$

Power drawn by

$$Z_A = \mathbf{50\times 1/\sqrt{3}\times 7.217\cos 30^\circ = 180.43\ W.}$$
$$[V_a\, I_a \cos\phi_a]$$

Power drawn by

$$Z_B = \mathbf{50\times 1/\sqrt{3}\times 5.772\times\cos 20^\circ = 156.57\ W.}$$

Power drawn by

$$Z_C = \mathbf{50\times 1/\sqrt{3}\times 2.886\times\cos 0^\circ = 83.31\ W.}$$

EXAMPLE 4.49 *In Fig. E4.27, find the current through the loads.*

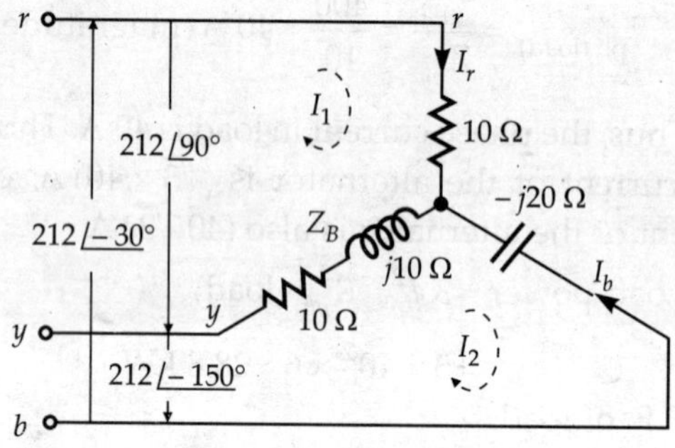

Fig. E4.27

SOLUTION. Let the loop currents be designated as shown in Fig. E4.27 by dotted lines.

Applying KVL in loop *r-o-y*,

$$10\,I_1 + (10+j\,10)[I_1 - I_2] = 212\angle 90^\circ$$

or, $$I_1\,[10+10+j\,10] - (10+j\,10)\,I_2 = 212\angle 90^\circ$$

or, $$I_1\,[20+j\,10] - [10+j\,10]\,I_2 = 212\angle 90^\circ \qquad ...(1)$$

Similarly, in loop *y-o-b*,

$$-j\,20\,I_2 + I_2\,(10+j\,10) - I_1\,(10+j\,10) = 212\angle -150^\circ$$

or, $$I_2\,[10+j\,10-j\,20] - I_1\,(10+j\,10) = 212\angle -150^\circ$$

or, $$-I_1\,(10+j\,10) + I_2\,[10-j\,10] = 212\angle -150^\circ \qquad ...(2)$$

Solving for (1) and (2),

$$I_1 = 3.66\angle 15^\circ \text{ A}$$
$$I_2 = 11.96\angle -114^\circ \text{ A}$$

Thus, $I_r = I_1 = \mathbf{3.66\angle 15^\circ\ A}$

$$I_b = -I_2 = \mathbf{11.96\angle 66^\circ\ A}$$
$$I_y = I_2 - I_1 = 11.96\angle -114^\circ - 3.66\angle 15^\circ$$
$$= -4.86 - j\,10.93 - 3.535 - j\,0.947$$
$$= -8.395 - j\,11.877$$
$$= \mathbf{14.544\angle 125.75^\circ\ A.}$$

[where I_y is the current through $(10+j\,10)\Omega$ load]

EXAMPLE 4.50 *A 3 phase balanced 400 V supply feeds two parallel connected three phase loads L_1 and L_2. L_1 is a star connected lighting load having $(20+j\,37.75)\Omega$/ph while L_2 is a delta connected RC load of $(30 - j\,159.31)\Omega$/ph. Find the line current, power factor, real and reactive power taken by the combination.*

SOLUTION. $V_{ph} = \frac{V_L}{\sqrt{3}} = \frac{400}{\sqrt{3}} = 231$ V

(applicable for Y load)

$$Z_{L_{1(ph)}} = 20 + j\,37.75 = 42.5\,\angle 62°\,\Omega$$

$$Z_{L_{2(ph)}} = 30 - j\,159.31 = 162\,\angle -79.3°\Omega$$

$$\therefore \quad I_{\text{Load 1}(ph)} = \frac{V_{ph}}{42.5} = \frac{231}{42.5} = 5.4\text{ A}\,\angle -62°\text{ A}$$

$$I_{\text{Load 2}(ph)} = \frac{V_{ph}}{Z_{ph}} = \frac{V_L}{Z_{ph}}$$

$$= \frac{400}{162} = 2.47\text{ A}\,\angle 79.3°\text{ A}$$

For Load-1,

$$I_{\text{Line}} = I_{ph}\ (Y\text{ connection}) = 5.4\,\angle -62°\text{ A}$$

For Load-2,

$$I_{\text{Line}} = \sqrt{3}\,I_{ph} = \sqrt{3} \times 2.47 = 4.28\,\angle 79.3°\text{ A}$$

$\therefore$ Total line current

$$= 5.4\,\angle -62° + 4.28\,\angle 79.3°$$

$$= 2.535 - j\,4.77 + 0.795 + j\,4.2$$

$$= 3.33 - j\,0.57 = 3.37\,\angle -9.7°\text{ A}$$

The total real power

$$= P_T = \sqrt{3} \times 400 \times 3.37 \times \cos 9.7 = 2.3\text{ kW}$$

Total reactive power

$$Q_T = \sqrt{3} \times 400 \times 3.37 \times \sin 9.7 = 0.393\text{ kVAR}$$

Thus,

I_{Line} = 3.37 A

P. F. = cos 9.7° = 0.985 (lag)

Power (real) = 2.3 kW

$\therefore$ Power (reactive) = 393 VAR.

EXAMPLE 4.51 *A Y-connected alternator has 231 V/ph. It supplies a set of lighting loads at phase R, having phase impedance of 40 ∠0° Ω, a capacitive load of 10 ∠–60° Ω at phase Y and an inductive load of 5 ∠45° Ω at phase B. The loads are connected in delta. Obtain the phase currents, line currents and line voltages.*

SOLUTION. For the source,

$$V_{ph} = 231\text{ V}$$

$$\therefore \quad V_L = \sqrt{3}\,V_{ph} = 400\text{ V}$$

But for the load, due to Δ connection,

$V_L = V_{ph}$, obviously this being 400 V

i.e., $V_{RY} = 400\,\angle 0°\text{ V}$; $V_{YB} = 400\,\angle -120°\text{ V}$,

$$V_{BR} = 400\,\angle +120°\text{ V}$$

Thus,

$$I_{RY} = \frac{V_{RY}}{Z_{RY}} = \frac{400\,\angle 0°}{40\,\angle 0°} = 10\,\angle 0°\text{ A}$$

[∵ given that Z (imp.) between R and Y = 40 ∠0° ohms]

$$I_{YB} = \frac{400\,\angle -120°\,(i.e.,\ V_{YB})}{Z_{YB}}$$

$$= \frac{400\,\angle -120°}{10\,\angle -60°} = 40\,\angle -60°\text{ A}$$

$$I_{BR} = \frac{V_{BR}}{Z_{BR}} = \frac{400\,\angle 120°}{5\,\angle 45°} = 80\,\angle 75°\text{ A}$$

[∵ connected load between YB and BR are 10 ∠–60° and 5 ∠45° ohms respectively]

∴ The phase currents of the load are

10 ∠0° A, 40 ∠– 60° A, 80 ∠75° A.

Line currents are obtained as follows (Fig. E4.28)

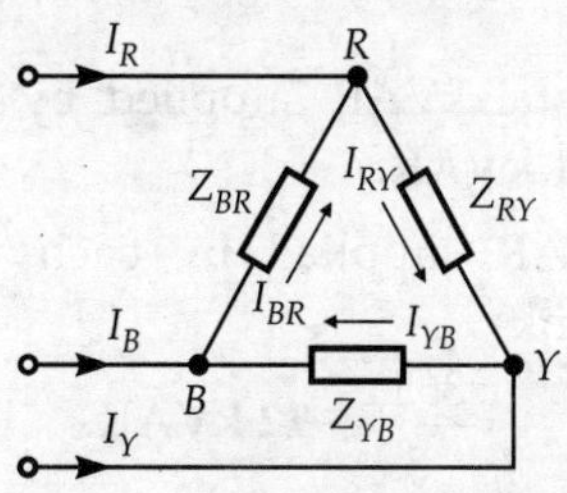

Fig. E4.28

$$I_R = I_{RY} - I_{BR} = 10\,\angle 0° - 80\,\angle 75°$$

$$= 10 - 20.7 - j\,77.27$$

$$= -10.7 - j\,77.27 = 78\,\angle -97.88°\text{ A}$$

$$I_Y = I_{YB} - I_{RY} = 40\,\angle -60° - 10\,\angle 0°$$

$$= 20 - j\,34.64 - 10$$

$$= 10 - j\,34.64 = 36.05\,\angle -74°\text{ A}$$

and $$I_B = I_{BR} - I_{YB} = 80\,\angle 75° - 40\,\angle -60°$$

$$= 20.7 + j\,77.27 - 20 + j\,34.64$$

$$= 0.7 + j\,112 = 112\,\angle 89.65°\text{ A}$$

Then the line currents of the load are

78 ∠–97.88° A, 36.05∠–74° A, 112∠89.65° A

Line voltages have already been obtained as

400 ∠0° V, 400 ∠– 120° V, 400 ∠+ 120° V

EXAMPLE 4.52 *A 3 phase 415 V, 50 Hz induction motor bus draws 20 kW at a lagging p.f. of 0.4. Calculate the total kVAR rating of three shunt capacitors which, when connected in Δ fashion, would raise the p.f. of the bus to 0.9 lag. What is the value of each phase capacitance ?*

CHAPTER 4

SOLUTION. P_L (load power)

$$=20 \text{ kW at } 0.4 \text{ p.f. lag}$$

$$\therefore \quad \phi_l = \cos^{-1} 0.4 = 66.4°$$

Q_L (reactive demand of load)

$$= P_L \tan \phi_l = 45.78 \text{ kVAR}$$

When the capacitances are in parallel, the real power status for the system being remaining the same, the net Q changes.

As the new p.f. becomes 0.9.

$$\therefore \quad \phi_{new} = \cos^{-1} 0.9 = 25.8°.$$

The reactive power is now

$$Q_{new} = P_L \tan 25.8° = 20 \times 0.4834 = 9.67 \text{ kVAR}$$

Thus the reactive power supplied by the capacitors

$$Q_C = Q_L - Q_{new} = 45.78 - 9.67 \simeq 36.11 \text{ kVAR}$$

$\therefore$ The total kVAR supplied by the capacitor bank is **36.11 kVAR.**

i.e., the kVAR supplied by each phase of the capacitor bank

$$= \frac{36.11}{3} \simeq \mathbf{12\ kVAR.}$$

Let us first assume the capacitor bank is in Δ.

$$I_{c(ph)} = \frac{Q_{ph}}{V_{ph}} = \frac{12000}{415} \simeq 29 \text{ A.}$$

$$\text{But } Z_{c_{ph}} (= X_{c_{ph}}) = \frac{V_{ph}}{I_{c_{ph}}} = \frac{415}{29} = 14.31 \Omega$$

$$\therefore \quad C_{ph} = \frac{1}{\omega X_c} \qquad \left[\because X_C = \frac{1}{\omega C}\right]$$

$$= \frac{1}{314 \times 14.31} = \mathbf{222\ \mu F.}$$

On the other hand, if the capacitor bank is connected in Y,

$$I_{c_{ph}} = \frac{Q_{ph}}{V_{ph}} = \frac{12000}{\frac{415}{\sqrt{3}}} = 50 \text{ A}$$

$$\text{But } Z_{c_{ph}} (X_{c_{ph}}) = \frac{V_{ph}}{I_{ph}} = \frac{415}{\sqrt{3}} \times \frac{1}{50} = 4.8 \Omega$$

$$\therefore \quad C_{ph} = \frac{1}{\omega X_c} = \frac{1}{314 \times 4.8} = \mathbf{664\ \mu F.}$$

EXAMPLE 4.53 *Three coils are arranged in star connection in such a way so that the mutual inductance between each pair of coil is 300 mH. The self inductance of the coil being 800 mH, the resistance 100 Ω, find the current taken by each coil when a balanced three phase 50 Hz voltage of 100 V (L-L) is applied between each two lines of the star connected load. What is the power factor of the load ?*

SOLUTION. The phase voltage of R phase would be

$$V_R = (R + j\,\omega L)\, I_R + j\,\omega M\, I_Y + j\,\omega M\, I_B$$

[where, R and L are the resistance and inductance of R phase (obviously of each phase), M, the mutual inductance and I_R, I_Y and I_B the phase (or lie) currents]

But $\quad R = 100\,\Omega,\ \omega L = 314 \times 0.8 = 251.2\,\Omega,$

$$\omega M = 314 \times 0.3 = 94.2\,\Omega$$

$$\therefore \quad \frac{100 \angle 0°}{\sqrt{3}} = (100 + j\,251.2)\, I_R + j\,94.2\, I_Y + j\,94.2\, I_B$$

$$= (100 + j\,251.2)\, I \angle 0° + j\,94.2 \times I \angle -120° + j\,94.2 \times I \angle -120°$$

$$= (100 + j\,251.2)\, I - j\,94.2\, I$$

$$= 186\, I \angle 57.5°$$

$$\therefore \quad |I| = \frac{57.74}{186} = \mathbf{0.31\ A}$$

and $\quad \text{PF} = \cos 57.5° = \mathbf{0.537}.$

EXAMPLE 4.54 *Three impedances, Z_A, Z_B and Z_C are connected in star across a 100 V, 50 Hz balanced three phase supply. Assuming $Z_A = 50 \angle 0°\,\Omega$, $Z_B = j\,10\,\Omega$, $Z_C = -j\,10\,\Omega$, find the drop across each impedance and the potential of the neutral.*

SOLUTION. Let

$$V_{AB} = 100 \angle 0° \text{ V},\ V_{BC} = 100 \angle -120° \text{ V}$$

$$V_{CA} = 100 \angle 120° \text{ V}$$

$$\therefore \quad V_{AN} = \frac{100}{\sqrt{3}} \angle -30° \text{ V} = 57.74 \angle -30° \text{ V}$$

[$\because$ Phase voltage leads the corresponding reference line voltage by 30° as shown in the text of star connection]

Similarly,

$$V_{BN} = 57.74 \angle -30° - 120° = 57.74 \angle -150° \text{ V}$$

and $\quad V_{CN} = 57.74 \angle -30° + 120° = 57.74 \angle 90° \text{ V}.$

Again $Y_A = \frac{1}{Z_A} = \frac{1}{50\angle 0°} = (0.02 + j\,0)$ mho

$$Y_B = \frac{1}{Z_B} = \frac{1}{j\,10} = 0.1\angle -90° \text{ mho}$$

$$Y_C = \frac{1}{Z_C} = \frac{1}{-j\,10} = 0.1\angle +90° \text{ mho}$$

$$\therefore V_{AN}\,Y_A = 57.74\angle -30° \times (0.02)$$
$$= 1.155\angle -30° \text{ A} (= I_A),$$

$$V_{BN}\,Y_B = 57.74\angle -150° \times 0.1\angle -90°$$
$$= 5.774\angle -240° \text{ A} (= I_B)$$

and $V_{CN}\,Y_C = 57.74\angle 90° \times 0.1\angle 90°$

$$= 5.774\angle 180° \text{ A} (= I_C)$$

$\therefore$ The current in neutral is $(I_A + I_B + I_C)$

$$= 1.155\angle -30° + 5.774\angle -240° + 5.774\angle 180°$$
$$= 1 - j\,0.578 - 2.887 + j\,5 - 5.774$$
$$= (-7.661 + j\,4.422) \text{ A}$$

Again net Y is given by

$$Y_A + Y_B + Y_C = 0.02 + j\,0 - j\,0.1 + j\,0.1$$
$$= 0.02\ (Y) \text{ mho}$$

Then, the neutral potential is

$$V_N = \frac{I_N}{Y} = \frac{-7.661 + j\,4.422}{0.02}$$

or, $V_N = -383.05 + j\,221.1 = \mathbf{442\angle 150°\ V}$

Thus, voltage drop across Z_A is given by

$$V_{drop(A)} = V_{AN} - V_N$$
$$= 57.74\angle -30° - 442\angle 150°$$
$$= 50 - j\,28.87 + 383.05 - j\,221.1$$
$$= 500\angle -30° \text{ V}$$

Voltage drop across Z_B is

$$V_{drop(B)} = V_{BN} - V_N$$
$$= 57.74\angle -150° - 442\angle 150°$$
$$= -50 - j\,28.87 + 383.05 - j\,221.1$$
$$= 416.42\angle -36.8° \text{ V}$$

Voltage drop across Z_C is

$$V_{drop(C)} = V_{CN} - V_N$$
$$= 57.74\angle 90° - 442\angle 150°$$
$$= +j\,57.74 + 383.1 - j\,221.1$$
$$= 416.42\angle -23.09° \text{ V}$$

$\therefore$ The potential across the neutral is

$$V_N = 442\angle 150° \text{ V}$$

and drop across each impedances are

$$V_{drop(A)} = \mathbf{500\angle -30°\ V}$$
$$V_{drop(B)} = \mathbf{416.42\angle -36.88°\ V}$$
$$V_{drop(C)} = \mathbf{416.42\angle -23.09°\ V.}$$

EXERCISES

1. A star connected load has impedance of $(5 + j\,8)\,\Omega$ in each phase and is connected across a balanced 400 V three phase delta connected alternator having line voltage as specified. Obtain the line currents of both the load and generator.
   [Hint. Ref. Ex. 4.1]
2. Find the line currents of a 100 V, 50 Hz supply feeding a delta connected $(4 + j\,3)\,\Omega$ impedances/ph.
   [Hint. Ref. Ex 4.2]
3. A three phase 4 wire 400 *V* (*L–L*) system supplies a balanced star load having impedances of $20\angle -60°\,\Omega$ in each phase. Find the line currents and draw the phasor diagram. What is the current flow through the neutral ?
   [Hint. Ref. Ex 4.5]
4. A delta connected load has a parallel combination of $5\,\Omega$ and $-j\,8\,\Omega$ impedance in each phase. If a balanced 100 V *(L-L)* 3 ph 50 Hz supply is applied between lines, find the phase currents and line currents. Also draw the phasor diagram.
   [Hint. Ref. Ex. 4.6]
5. The line currents of a delta connected generator being 100 A, 3 ph system, a star connected load is applied across the terminals of the generator. If the load has impedance of $(8 + j\,4)\,\Omega$/ph, find the phase voltage of the generator.
   [Hint. Ref. Ex. 4.7]

6. A 3 ph 220 V supply is applied to a balanced delta connected 3 phase load. The phase current being $I_{RY} = 5 \angle -20°$ A, find I_R. Compute the total power received by the load. Find the value of the resistive portion of the phase impedance.

   [**Hint.** Ref. Ex 4.10]

7. A delta connected load has phase impedance of $(10 + j\,12)$ ohm/ph. What is the line current if the applied line voltage is 250 V, 3 ph ? Obtain the amount of power consumed/ph. What is the phasor sum of the three line currents ?

   [**Hint.** Ref. Ex. 4.11]

8. A balanced star load has an impedance of $(4 + j\,3)\,\Omega$ between line and neutral. If the voltage across phase R be $50 \angle 10°$, find current in phases Y and B. What is the voltage from line Y to neutral ? Also obtain V_{RB}.

   [**Hint.** Ref. Ex. 4.13]

9. If $Z_A = Z_B = 10 \angle 10°\,\Omega$, $Z_C = \infty$, a three phase balanced 50 Hz, 100 V is applied between lines, find the power consumed by the load.

   [**Hint.** Ref. Ex. 4.18]

10. Calculate the magnitude of line current in the circuit shown in Fig. P4.1.

    [**Hint.** Imp./ph. $= 1 + j\,1 + 3 + j\,5 = (4 + j\,6)\,\Omega$

    $\therefore \; |I_{\text{Line}}| = \dfrac{100}{\sqrt{4^2 + 6^2}}$ A.]

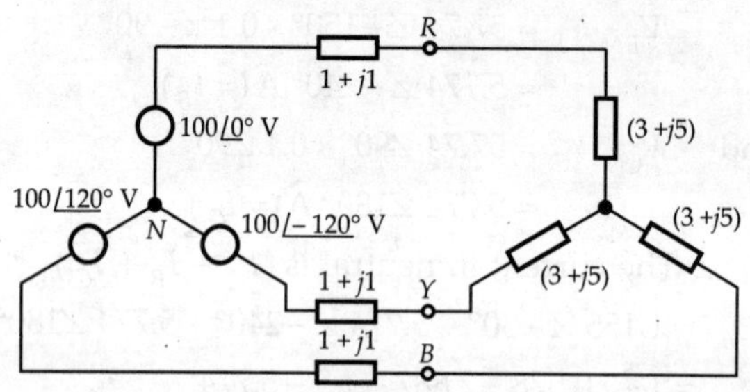

Fig. P4.1

11. Find the line currents in Fig. P4.2.

    [**Hint.** Find Z / ph. $I_1 = \dfrac{400 \angle 0}{Z}$;

    $$I_2 = \frac{400 \angle -120°}{Z} \text{ A}, \; I_3 = \frac{400 \angle -240°}{Z} \text{ A.]}$$

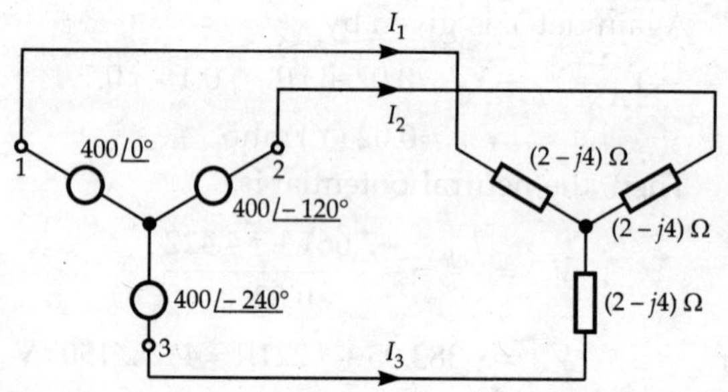

Fig. P4.2

12. A balanced 3 ph. 3 wire system supplies two balanced Y connected loads. The first load draws 8 kW at 0.8 pf lagging while the other requires 10 kW at 0.6 pf leading. Find the individual load currents and total current. Assume $V_{L-L} = 400$ V.

    [**Hint.** $I_1 = \dfrac{P_1}{V \cos \phi_1}$; $P_1 = 8 \times 10^3$ W, $\phi_1 = \cos^{-1}(0.8)$ [–ve]

    $V_{L-L} = V = 400$ V ; $I_2 = \dfrac{P_2}{V \cos \phi_2}$; $P_2 = 10 \times 10^3$ W ; $V = V_{L-L}$, $\phi_2 = \cos^{-1}(0.6)$ [+ve]

    Then obtain $I_1 + I_2$ (vectorially).]

13. A delta load has $45 \angle 0°\,\Omega$, $10 \angle -60°\,\Omega$, $20 \angle 45°\,\Omega$ load between 1-2, 2-3 and 3-1 phases. If the supply is 100 V, 3 ph, 50 Hz, find the phase currents, line currents and line voltages. Show that the line currents add up to zero.

    [**Hint.** $I_{ph_1} = \dfrac{V_{L_1}}{Z_1} = \dfrac{100 \angle 0°}{45 \angle 0°}$ A, $I_{ph_2} = \dfrac{100 \angle -120°}{10 \angle -60°}$ A, $I_{ph_3} = \dfrac{100 \angle +120°}{20 \angle 45°}$ A.

    Then $I_1 = I_{ph_1} - I_{ph_3}$; $I_2 = I_{ph_2} - I_{ph_1}$; $I_3 = I_{ph_3} - I_{ph_2}$

    (all vectorial operations). See $I_{L_1} + I_{L_2} + I_{L_3} = 0$.]

14. An induction motor draws a three phase power. Two wattmeter measurement is applied to find the total power. If $W_1 = 10$ kW, $W_2 = 5$ kW, find the total three phase power (real), reactive power and power factor.

    [**Hint.** $P_{\text{total}} = W_1 + W_2$; $Q_{\text{total}} = \sqrt{3}\,(W_1 - W_2)$; $\phi = \tan^{-1} \dfrac{W_1 - W_2}{W_1 + W_2}$.]

CHAPTER 5

Analysis of Transient Response in Passive Circuits (*Differential Equation Approach*)

5.1 INTRODUCTION

Analysis of behaviour of electric circuit reveals that as soon as a circuit is switched from one condition to another either by change of source or by alteration of circuit elements, branch currents and voltage drops change from their initial values to new values. These changes take a short spell of time to settle to permanent values (steady state) till further switching or circuit alteration is attempted. This brief spell of time is called *transient time* and the value of the variables (current and voltage drop) during this period is called *transient value.* This chapter deals with transient analysis of *passive* electric circuits using initial conditions and differential equation approach.

5.2 PREAMBLE OF DIFFERENTIAL EQUATION APPROACH

The *first order circuit*, during its transient state of operation, is governed by a first order linear differential equation and in reality the first order circuit contains resistance(s) and one inductor or capacitor *i.e.*, the resistance and one energy storing component. On the other hand, a *second order circuit* contains two independent energy storage elements with or without addition to resistance(s).

The first order circuit equation is given by

$$\frac{dy}{dt} + ay = bx$$

where x is the input, y the output and a and b are the constants. Superposition and linearity, both are applicable in first order passive circuits. The *natural response* of the first order circuit is obtained when the governing equation of the circuit, at its transient state, is given by

$$\frac{dy}{dt} + ay = 0$$

[*i.e.*, by a *homogeneous differential equation*]

The solution for such a equation is given by

$$y = Ke^{-\alpha t},$$

where K is a constant and if evaluated using initial conditions, the solution y becomes a *particular solution.* At $t = 0$, if $y = y_0$, then the natural response of the circuit is given by the following equation :

$$y_n = y_0 \, e^{-\alpha t} \quad \text{for } t > 0.$$

[for $t = 0$, y at t_0 $(= y_0)$ becomes K in the general solution $y = Ke^{-\alpha t}$].

When x (input) is specified, it is called *forcing function* and the solution y is called the *forced response* (or the *particular integral* y_p). The complete solution is given by

$$y = y_p + y_n$$
$$= y_p + Ke^{-\alpha t} \quad \text{for } t > 0.$$

K is determined with given initial conditions.

Elaborating further we can say that if the first order circuit is governed by a *non-homogeneous* differential equation

$$\frac{dy}{dt} + ay = bx = Q(\text{say}),$$

where Q is either a function of independent variable or a constant, the solution is then given by

$$y = e^{-\alpha t} \int Qe^{\alpha t}\, dt + Ke^{-\alpha t} = y_p + y_c$$

Here $y_p \left(= e^{-\alpha t} \int Qe^{\alpha t}\, dt\right)$ is known as *particular integral* and $y_c \left(= Ke^{-\alpha t}\right)$ is known as *complementary function.* It may be noted here that y_p does not contain the arbitrary constant K and the complementary function does not depend on the forcing function Q.

If Q is constant, we can write

$$y = e^{-\alpha t} \cdot Q \cdot \frac{e^{\alpha t}}{a} + Ke^{-\alpha t}$$
$$= \frac{Q}{a} + Ke^{-\alpha t}$$

A second order differential equation may be expressed as

$$A\frac{d^2y}{dt^2} + B\frac{dy}{dt} + Cy = 0$$

[A, B, C being constants]

The general solution of this second order differential equation is given by

$$y = K_1 e^{\alpha_1 t} + K_2 e^{\alpha_2 t},$$

where K_1 and K_2 are the constants and α_1 and α_2 are the roots of the *characteristic equation.*

$$Ap^2 + Bp + C = 0$$

α_1 and α_2 are given by

$$\alpha_1, \alpha_2 = -\frac{B}{2A} \pm \frac{1}{2A}\sqrt{B^2 - 4AC}$$

If $\alpha_1 = \alpha_2$, the roots are said to be repetitive type and the general solution is given by

$$y = K_1 e^{-\frac{B}{2A} \cdot t} + K_2 e^{-\frac{B}{2A} \cdot t}$$

Let us now explore applications of the discussions we have in the preceeding paragraphs. A series RC or RL circuit energized by a voltage source or a parallel RC or RL circuit energized by a current source are the examples of linear first order circuits. When the voltage in such a series circuit or current in such a parallel circuit is applied by switching at $t = 0$, the governing differential equation is given by

$$\frac{dy}{dt} + ay = bx \,(= Q)$$

where the forcing function is either voltage or current. The forced response is obtained at $t > 0$ as $y = y_p + y_c$ (as discussed earlier). Next, we suppose that this series or parallel circuit attains steady state and the voltage or current source is suddenly shorted at $t = 0$. The differential equation of the circuit at $t = 0+$ is obtained as $\frac{dy}{dt} + ay = 0$ as there is no forcing function (*i.e.*, voltage or current source).

The natural response of circuit is obtained as

$$y = Ke^{-\alpha t} \quad \text{for } t > 0.$$

We now explore another possibility ; let a first order circuit be at steady state with a constant source and at $t = 0$, switching takes place and the circuit now jumps to another constant source supply. Obviously, the solution will have the form

$$y = Y_s + Ke^{-\alpha t}, \quad t > 0$$

where Y_s is the new steady state value.

Let us assume that at $t = 0^+$,

$$y = Y_0.$$

$$\therefore \quad y\,(\text{at } t = 0^+) = Y_s + Ke^{-\alpha \cdot 0} = Y_s + K$$

or $$Y_0 = Y_s + K$$

[$\because$ we assumed $y = Y_0$ at $t = 0^+$]

$$\therefore \quad K = (Y_0 - Y_s)$$

Then finally,

$$y = Y_s + (Y_0 - Y_s)\,e^{-\alpha t}, \quad t > 0.$$

If the switching takes place at $t \neq 0$ but at $t = t_0$, we can write

$$y = Y_s + (Y_0 - Y_s)\,e^{-\alpha(t - t_0)}$$

In reality, a first order circuit may face this situation when switching takes place from one d.c. source to another d.c. source.

$t = 0^+$ indicates the instant just after $t = 0$th instant of time. Similarly, $t = 0^-$ indicates the instant just before the $t = 0$th instant of time.

The second order circuit being containing R, L and C elements; for convenience we assume the constants A, B and C of the second order differential equation as

$$A=1,\ \ B=2\alpha \ \text{ and } \ C=\omega_0^2$$

[α is the *damping factor* and ω_0 the *frequency of oscillation*]

$\therefore$ The homogeneous second order differential equation becomes

$$\frac{d^2y}{dt^2}+2\alpha\frac{dy}{dt}+\omega_0^2\, y=0$$

and the characteristic equation becomes

$$p^2+2\alpha p+\omega_0^2=0$$

or $$(p+\alpha)^2+\omega_0^2-\alpha^2=0$$

The roots of the above equation are p_1 and p_2 and are called *natural frequencies*. Depending on the relative values of α and ω_0 there are *three* different cases for the roots :

(*i*) $\alpha>\omega_0$ **[overdamped condition]**

$$p_1=-\alpha+(\alpha^2-\omega_0^2)^{1/2}=-s_1$$

$$p_2=-\alpha-(\alpha^2-\omega_0^2)^{1/2}=-s_2$$

s_1 and s_2 being real and positive.

The natural response is then given by

$$y_n=K_1e^{-s_1t}+K_2e^{-s_2t},\ \ t>0.$$

(*ii*) $\alpha<\omega_0$ **[underdamped condition]**

Let $\omega_0^2-\alpha^2=\omega_d^2$

The roots are complex conjugate with negative real part.

$$p_1=-\alpha+j\omega_d\ ;\ p_2=-\alpha-j\omega_d$$

The natural response is given by

$$y_n=e^{-\alpha t}\,(K_1\cos\omega_d t+K_2\sin\omega_d t)$$

(*iii*) $\alpha=\omega_0$ **[critically damped condition]**

$$(p+\alpha)^2=0\ ;\ p=-\alpha=-\omega_0$$

and two roots p_1 and p_2 coincide.

The natural response is given by

$$y_n=(K_1+K_2t)\,e^{-\alpha t},\ \ t>0.$$

In all the above cases, K_1 and K_2 are determined from initial conditions, usually the values of y and (dy/dt) at $t=0^+$.

5.3 TRANSIENT RESPONSE OF SERIES *R-L* CIRCUIT HAVING D.C. EXCITATION (FIRST ORDER CIRCUIT)

Let a d.c. voltage V be applied suddenly (*i.e.*, at $t=0$) by closing a switch K in a series *R-L* circuit as shown in Fig. 5.1

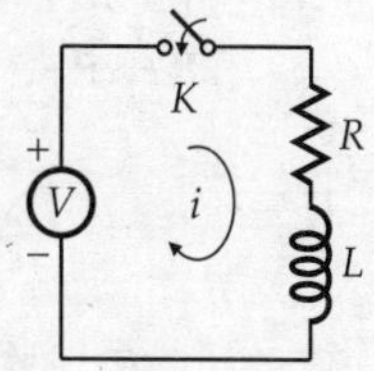

Fig. 5.1 Series *RL* circuit.

Applying Kirchhoff's voltage law (KVL) yields

$$Ri+L\frac{di}{dt}=V \qquad \text{...(5.1)}$$

or, $$\frac{di}{dt}+i\frac{R}{L}=\frac{V}{L}$$

or, $$\left(p+\frac{R}{L}\right)i=\frac{V}{L}\ \left[\text{where } p=\frac{d}{dt}\right] \qquad \text{...(5.2)}$$

Equation (5.2) is a *non-homogeneous differential equation* and the forced response is obtained from its solution ; the solution is given by

$$i=i_C+i_p\ ;$$

where i_C is the *complementary function* that always goes to zero value in a relatively short time (transient solution) and is given by

$$i_C=c\,e^{-(R/L)t}\ ;$$

c being a constant ; i_p is the particular solution of i that provides the steady state response.

$$i_p=e^{(-R/L)t}\int e^{(R/L)t}\left(\frac{V}{L}\right)dt=\frac{V}{R}.$$

Hence the net solution i is given by

$$i=ce^{-(R/L).\,t}+\frac{V}{R} \qquad \text{...(5.3)}$$

An inductance, due to its "electrical inertia" does not allow sudden change of current through it following the rules of electromagnetic induction and hence at current though it just before switching is same to the current just after the switching. This is represented as

$$i(0^-)\equiv i(0^+)$$

CHAPTER 5

However, before switching, there was no current through the inductor and hence at time $t=0^+$ (*i.e.*, just after the switching) the current through the inductor will also be zero.

i.e., $$i(0^+)=0$$

With the initial condition, equation (5.3) at $t=0^+$ becomes

$$0=c\,e^{-(R/L).0}+\frac{V}{R}$$

i.e., $$c=-\frac{V}{R}$$

This gives,

$$i=-\frac{V}{R}e^{-(R/L).t}+\frac{V}{R}$$

or, $$i=\frac{V}{R}(1-e^{-(R/L).t})\text{ A} \qquad ...(5.4)$$

Expression (5.4) clearly shows the exponential rise of current *i* charging the inductor. The profile of *i* vs *t* has been shown in Fig. 5.2.

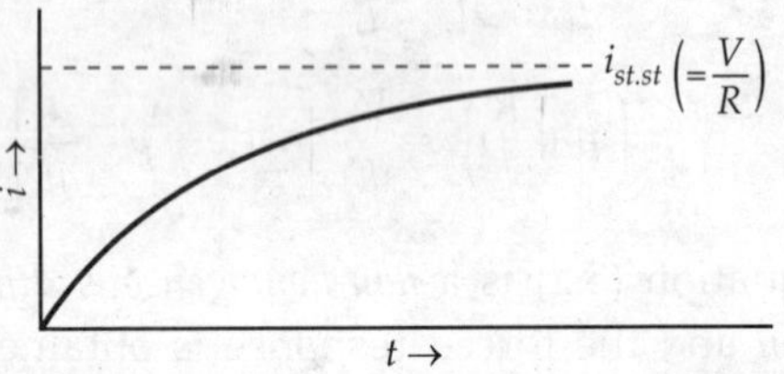

Fig. 5.2 Charging current profile in *R-L* circuit.

It may be noted that once the transient dies out within the short spell of time (which can be observed by substituting large values of *t*) the *steady state current* (final current) remains in the circuit given by (*V/R*).

It may also be observed that if we put $t=\frac{L}{R}$, expression (5.4) becomes

$$i=\frac{V}{R}(1-e^{-1})=\frac{V}{R}(1-0.368)=0.632\,I_S \qquad ...(5.5)$$

[I_S being the steady state current $=V/R$]

Expression (5.5) means that at time $t=\frac{L}{R}$, the current through the *R-L* circuit rises to 63.2% of the final value. Conventionally, this time is known as "time constant" (TC) and is the ratio of *L* and *R* in the *L-R* circuit. (*R/L*) is the inverse of TC and is called "damping ratio".

The voltage drops across the resistance and inductance during the transient period is given by

$$v_R=iR=V(1-e^{-(R/L).t})$$

and $$v_L=L\frac{di}{dt}=L\frac{d}{dt}\left[\frac{V}{R}(1-e^{-(R/L).t})\right]$$

$$=V\,e^{-(R/L).t}.$$

It may now be observed that the voltage transient across the resistor is an *exponential rise* while that across the inductance is *exponentially decaying*.

Obviously

$$v_R+v_L=V(1-e^{-(R/L).t})+V\,e^{-(R/L).t}=V.$$

The instantaneous powers in the resistor and inductor are given as

$$p_R=v_R\,i=V(1-e^{-(R/L).t}).\frac{V}{R}(1-e^{-(R/L).t})$$

$$=\frac{V^2}{R}(1-2\,e^{-(R/L).t}+e^{-2(R/L).t}) \qquad ...(5.6)$$

and $$p_L=v_L\,i=V\,e^{-(R/L).t}.\frac{V}{R}(1-e^{-(R/L).t})$$

$$=\frac{V^2}{R}(e^{-(R/L).t}-e^{-2(R/L).t}) \qquad ...(5.6(a))$$

The total power (p) being

$$p_R+p_L=\frac{V^2}{R}(1-2e^{-(R/L).t}+e^{-2(R/L).t})$$

$$+\frac{V^2}{R}(e^{-(R/L).t}-e^{-2(R/L).t})$$

$$=(V^2/R)(1-e^{-(R/L).t})\text{ VA}$$

Let us now analyse another transient condition (natural response) of the *R-L* circuit assuming that following the closing of the switch, the circuit reaches at steady state (at $t=\infty$) and suddenly the voltage is withdrawn by opening the switch *K* and throwing it to *K*′. Application of KVL yields (Fig. 5.3)

$$Ri+L\frac{di}{dt}=0$$

[Voltage source is withdrawn by opening the switch *K*]

or, $$(p+R/L)\,i=0 \qquad ...(5.7)$$

Equation (5.7) is a *homogeneous differential* equation having only complementary function in the solution of *i*, particular function is zero.

$$\therefore\ i=i_C+0=i_C=c\,e^{-(R/L).t} \qquad ...(5.8)$$

However, at $t = 0^+$, the inductor will keep the steady state current (V/R) even the switch is thrown to position K' (Fig. 5.3) short circuiting the charged R-L circuit and withdrawing the voltage source.

$$\therefore \quad i(0^+) = i_{st.st}(0^-) = \frac{V}{R}.$$

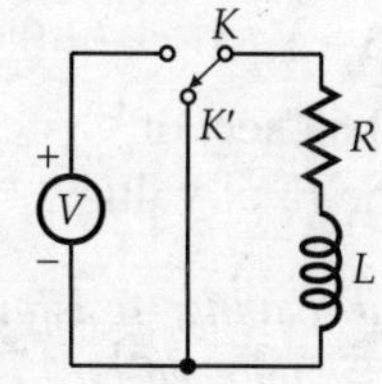

Fig. 5.3 *R-L* discharging circuit.

This gives from equation (5.8)

$$\frac{V}{R} = c' e^{-(R/L).0} = c'$$

Hence the final solution becomes

$$i = \frac{V}{R} e^{-(R/L).t} = I_0 e^{-(R/L).t} \text{ A} \quad ...(5.9)$$

[I_0 being (V/R)]

The decaying current i is thus a exponentially decaying function, the profile being shown in Fig. 5.4.

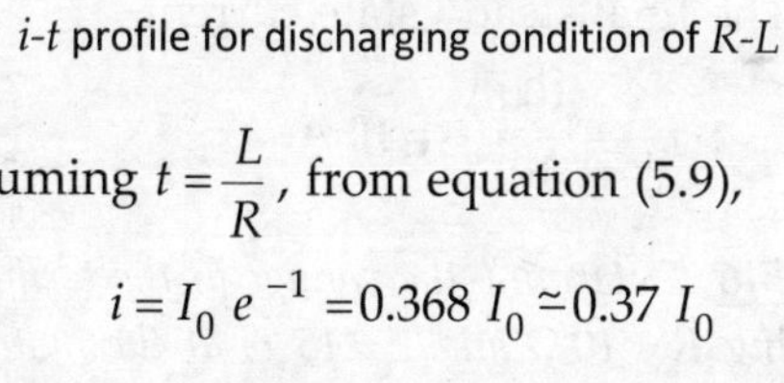

Fig. 5.4 *i-t* profile for discharging condition of *R-L* circuit.

Assuming $t = \frac{L}{R}$, from equation (5.9),

$$i = I_0 e^{-1} = 0.368\, I_0 \simeq 0.37\, I_0$$

$\frac{L}{R}$ being called "time constant" it is observed that the decaying current will reach to 37% of the initial steady state current at one time constant.

The corresponding voltages across the resistance and inductance are then given as

$$v_R = iR = V e^{-(R/L).t}$$

and $$v_L = L\frac{di}{dt} = -V e^{-(R/L).t}$$

The instantaneous powers are given by

$$p_R = v_R\, i = \frac{V^2}{R} e^{-2(R/L).t} \text{ W}$$

and $$p_L = v_L\, i = -\frac{V^2}{R} e^{-2(R/L).t} \text{ VA.}$$

EXAMPLE 5.1 *In a series R-L circuit, the application of a direct voltage results a steady state current of 0.632 I in 1 second. I being the final steady state value of the current. However, after the current has reached its final value, a sudden short circuit is applied against the source. What would be the value of the current after one second ?*

SOLUTION. The charging current in the R-L circuit is given by

$$i = I(1 - e^{-t/T});$$

T being the time constant.

Here, in the first case,

$$0.632\, I = I(1 - e^{-t/T})$$

or, $$0.632 = (1 - e^{-t/T}) \qquad [\because t = 1 \text{ sec., given}]$$

or, $$e^{-1/t} = 1 - 0.632 = 0.368.$$

As soon as short circuit is applied in steady state, current will start decaying from I. The decay current i' is given by

$$i' = I e^{-t/T}$$

After a decay for 1 sec,

$$i = I e^{-t/T} = I \times 0.368 = 0.368\, I.$$

$\therefore$ The value of the decay current after 1 sec. of application of short circuit is **0.368 *I*.**

EXAMPLE 5.2 *Find the current in a series R-L circuit having R = 2 Ω and L = 10 H while a d.c. voltage of 100 V is applied. What is the value of this current after 5 sec. of switching on ?*

SOLUTION. Time constant $= \frac{L}{R} = \frac{10}{2} = 5$ sec.

Charging constant is given by

$$i = I(1 - e^{-t/T});$$

I being the steady state current.

Here, $$i = \frac{100}{2}(1 - e^{-t/5}) = 50(1 - e^{-t/5})$$

$$\left[\because I = \frac{100 \text{ V}}{2\,\Omega}\right]$$

$\therefore \quad i_{\text{steady state}} = 50 \text{ A}; \; i_{\text{transient}} = -50\, e^{-t/5} \text{ A}$

After $\quad t = 5$ sec., $i_{\text{transient}} = -50\, e^{-t/5}$

$$= -50 \times \frac{1}{e} = -18.518 \text{ A}$$

Thus i (after 5 sec.)

$$= i_{\text{st. state}} + i_{\text{transient}}$$

$$= 50 - 18.518 = \mathbf{31.482\ A.}$$

EXAMPLE 5.3 *A series R-L circuit has R = 25 ohm and L = 5 Henry. A d.c. voltage of 100 V is applied at t = 0. Find (a) the equations for charging current, voltage across R and L and (b) the current in the circuit 0.5 second later and (c) the time at which the drops across R and L are same.*

SOLUTION. (*a*) $\frac{L}{R}$ = time constant $(T) = \frac{5}{25} = \frac{1}{5}$ sec.

The charging current is given by

$$i = I(1 - e^{-t/T});$$

T being the final steady state current.

Here, $\quad i = \frac{100}{25}(1 - e^{-t/(1/5)})$ or $\mathbf{4\,(1 - e^{-5t})\ A}$

Voltage drop across R is

$$v_R = iR = 4 \times 25\,(1 - e^{-5t})$$

$$= \mathbf{100\,(1 - e^{-5t})\ V}$$

Voltage drop across L is,

$$v_L = L\frac{di}{dt}$$

or $\quad v_L = 5 \times \frac{d}{dt}[4\,(1 - e^{-5t})] = \mathbf{100\, e^{-5t}\ V}$

(*b*) At $t = 0.5$ sec.,

$$i = 4\,(1 - e^{-5(0.5)}) = 4\,(1 - e^{-2.5}) = \mathbf{3.67\ A.}$$

(*c*) To satisfy the condition of $v_R \equiv v_L$, $v_R = v_L = 50$ V, since applied voltage is 100 V.

$\therefore \quad 50 = L\frac{di}{dt} = 100\, e^{-5t}$

or, $\quad 0.5 = e^{-5t}$ or $t = \mathbf{0.139\ sec.}$

EXAMPLE 5.4 *A d.c. voltage of 100 V is applied to a coil having R = 100 Ω and L = 10 H. What is the value of the current 0.1 sec later the switching on ? What is the time taken by the current to reach half of its final value ?*

SOLUTION. Final current $I = \frac{V}{R} = \frac{100}{10} = 10$ A.

$$T \text{ (time constant)} = \frac{L}{R} = \frac{10}{10} = 1 \text{ sec.}$$

The charging current is given by

$$i = I\,(1 - e^{-t/T}) \text{ or } i = 10\,(1 - e^{-t})$$

The value of current 0.1 sec. later is

$$i = 10\,(1 - e^{-0.1}) = \mathbf{0.95\ A.}$$

Again, when the current will be half of final value,

$$5 = 10\,(1 - e^{-t})$$

or, $\quad 0.5 = (1 - e^{-t}) \;\therefore\; t = 0.69$ sec.

Hence, after **0.69 sec.** of switching, the current will be just half the final value.

EXAMPLE 5.5 *A coil having resistance of 10 Ω and inductance of 1 H is switched on to a direct voltage of 100 V. Calculate the rate of change of the current (a) at the instant of closing the switch and (b) when t = L/ R (c) Also find the steady state value of the current.*

SOLUTION. The charging current,

$$i = \frac{V}{R}(1 - e^{-t/T})$$

where$T$ is the time constant $= \frac{1}{10} = 0.1$ sec.

$\therefore \quad i = \frac{100}{10}(1 - e^{-t/0.1})$ or $i = 10\,(1 - e^{-10t})$

$\therefore \quad \frac{di}{dt} = 100\, e^{-10t}$

Thus the rate of change of current at the instant of closing the switch ($t = 0$) is

$$\frac{di}{dt} = 100\, e^{-10 \times 0} = \mathbf{100\ A/sec.}$$

(*b*) When $t = \frac{L}{R} = 0.1$ sec.,

$$\frac{di}{dt} = 100\, e^{-10 \times 0.1} = \mathbf{36.8\ A/sec.}$$

(*c*) The final steady state current

$$i_{\text{st.}} = \frac{100 \text{ V}}{10\,\Omega} = \mathbf{10\ A.}$$

EXAMPLE 5.6 *Determine the voltage at the terminals of a coil having R = 10 Ω and L = 15 H at the instant when the current is 10 A and increasing @ 5 A/sec. Also find the stored energy in the inductor. Compute the same exercise for the case when the current decreases @ 5 A/sec.*

SOLUTION. In the L-R circuit,

$$E = iR + L\frac{di}{dt}$$

[i = current, E = voltage at coil terminals]

$$= 10i + 15\frac{di}{dt} = 10 \times 10 + 15 \times 5 = \mathbf{175\ V.}$$

$$\text{Energy stored} = \frac{1}{2}LI^2 = \frac{1}{2}\times 15\times 10^2 = \mathbf{750\ J}$$

When the current is decaying,

$$E = iR - L\frac{di}{dt} = 10\times 10 - 15\times 5 = \mathbf{25\ V.}$$

$$\text{Energy stored} = \frac{1}{2}LI^2 = \frac{1}{2}15\times 10^2 = \mathbf{750\ J.}$$

EXAMPLE 5.7 *In Fig. E5.1 the switch K is kept first at position 1 and steady state condition is reached. At t = 0, the switch is moved to position 2. Find the current in both the cases.*

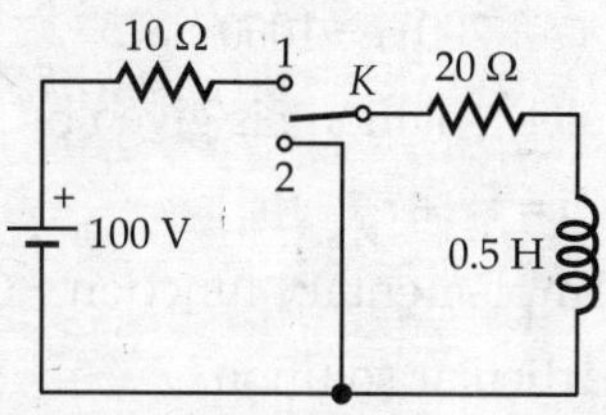

Fig. E5.1

SOLUTION. When the switch is at 1, the steady state current becomes

$$i = \frac{100}{10+20} = \mathbf{3.33\ A}$$

As soon as the switch is moved to position 2 at $t = 0$, the *LR* circuit starts decaying and the decay current is given by

$$i = I\,e^{-t/T}$$

where *I* is the initial steady state current and *T* is time constant (*L*/*R*)

or, $$i = 3.33\,e^{-t/0.025} = \mathbf{3.33\,e^{-40t}\ A.}$$

EXAMPLE 5.8 *In Fig. E5.2 steady state condition is reached with 100 V d.c. source. At t = 0, switch K is suddenly opened. Find the expression of current through the inductor after t = 1/2 sec.*

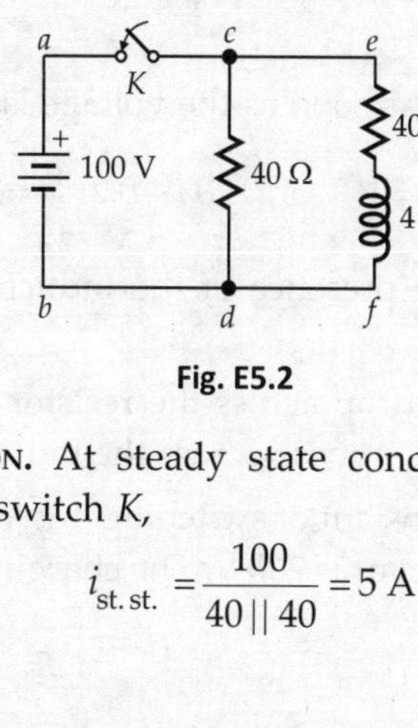

Fig. E5.2

SOLUTION. At steady state condition of close position of switch *K*,

$$i_{st.\,st.} = \frac{100}{40\,||\,40} = 5\ \text{A}$$

Thus $i_{st.\,st.}$, the current from 100 V d.c. source is 5 A when *K* is closed. As the circuit paths *cd* and *ef*, both have same resistance, hence, the current in each branch is 2.5 A.

As soon as *K* is opened, the source is removed and the *LR* circuit starts discharging. The decay current is given by

$$i = 2.5\,e^{-t/T} \quad \text{where } T = \frac{L}{R}$$

or, $$i = 2.5\,e^{-t/0.05} = 2.5\,e^{-20t}\ \text{A.}$$

at $t = 1/2$ sec.,

$$= 2.5\,e^{-20\times 1/2} = \mathbf{1.14\times 10^{-4}\ A.}$$

EXAMPLE 5.9 *In Fig. E5.3, the switch is closed at position 1 at t = 0. At t = 0.5 m sec. the switch is moved to position 2. Find the expression for the current in both the conditions and sketch the transient.*

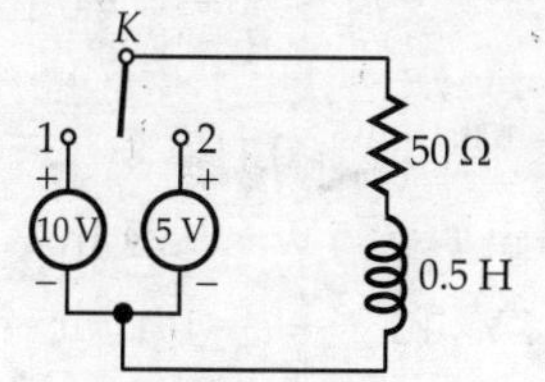

Fig. E5.3

SOLUTION. At position 1 of the switch,

$$50i + 0.5\frac{di}{dt} = 10$$

or, $$500\,i + 5\frac{di}{dt} = 100$$

$$(p+100)\,i = 20 \qquad \text{...(a)}$$

The complete solution of equation (*a*) consists of the complementary function (i_C) and the particular solution (i_p)

$$\therefore \quad i = i_C + i_p$$

But $$i_C = c\,e^{-100t}$$

$$i_p = e^{-(R/L).t}\int e^{(R/L).t}\left(\frac{V}{L}\right)dt = \frac{V}{R}.$$

$$\therefore \quad i = ce^{-100t} + \frac{V}{R} = ce^{-100t} + 0.2$$

However, at $t = 0$, $i = 0$ (Due to presence of inductor)

Using this initial condition,

$$i = c + 0.2 \text{ or } 0 = c + 0.2$$

$$\therefore \quad c = -0.2$$

CHAPTER 5

Hence $i = -0.2\, e^{-100t} + 0.2$

$$= \mathbf{0.2\,(1 - e^{-100\,t})\ A}$$

After time interval of $t = 0.5$ m sec.,

$$i = 0.2\,(1 - e^{-100 \times 0.5 \times 10^{-3}})$$

$$= 9.754 \times 10^{-3}\ \text{A} \simeq 9.75\ \text{mA}$$

With the switch in position 2, the applied voltage is 5 V, polarity being the same to that of the earlier condition.

Here $50i + 0.5\dfrac{di}{dt} = 5$ or $100\,i + \dfrac{di}{dt} = 10$

or, $(p + 100)\,i = 10$ ...(*b*)

Here also $i = i_C + i_p$

where $i_C = c'\,e^{-100(t - t')}$

and $i_p = \dfrac{V}{R} = \dfrac{5}{50} = 0.1$ A.

$\therefore\ i = c'\,e^{-100(t-t')} + 0.1$

However, at $t = t'$, i was 9.75 mA.

Hence $9.75 \times 10^{-3} = c' + 0.1$ or $c' = -0.09$

Thus $\mathbf{i = -0.09\, e^{-100\,(t - t')} + 0.1\ A.}$

It may be noted that had the switch been at position 1, the steady state current would have been 0.2 A. However at $t = t'$ (*i.e.*, at 0.5 m sec.), the switch is shifted to position 2 and the current is heading for the final value of 0.1 A.

The graph is shown in Fig. E5.4. This problem is a typical example of the transient analysis when the circuit is switched from one d.c. source to another d.c. source.

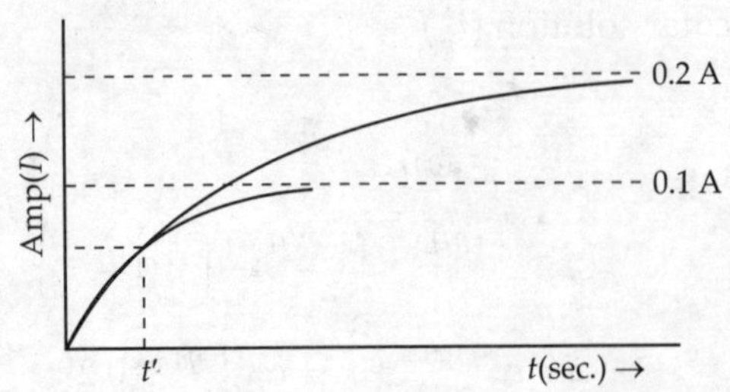

Fig. E5.4

EXAMPLE 5.10 *A d.c. voltage of 100 V is applied in the circuit (Fig. E5.5) and the switch K is open. The switch K is closed at t = 0. Find the complete expression for the current.*

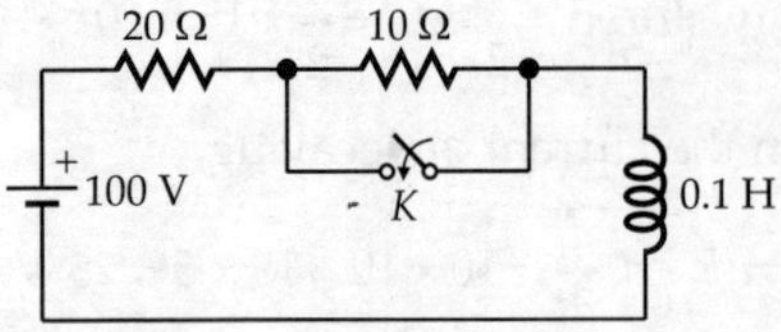

Fig. E5.5

SOLUTION. As soon as the switch is closed at $t = 0$, the mesh equation becomes

$$100 = 20i + 0.1\frac{di}{dt}$$

or $(p + 200)\,i = 1000$

The complete solution i is given by

$$i = i_C + i_p$$

where i_C = complementary function $= C\,e^{-200\,t}$

and i_p = particular solution

$$= e^{-(R/L).\,t} \int \left(\frac{V}{L}\right) e^{+(R/L).\,t}\, dt$$

or $i_p = \dfrac{V}{R} = \dfrac{100}{20} = 5$ A.

$\therefore\ i = C\,e^{-200\,t} + 5$

However, before switching operation, the steady state current in the circuit is $[V/(20 + 10)\,\Omega]$ *i.e.*, 3.33 A.

Due to the presence of inductor,

at $t = 0$, $i = 3.33$ A

Thus $i = C + 5$ or $3.33 = C + 5$ or $C = -1.67$

Hence the complete solution is

$$\mathbf{i = -1.67\, e^{-200\,t} + 5\ A.}$$

EXAMPLE 5.11 *A direct voltage of 200 V is suddenly applied to a series L-R circuit having $R = 20\,\Omega$ and inductance 0.2 H. Determine the voltage drop across the inductor at the instant of switching on and at 0.02 sec later.*

SOLUTION. As soon as the voltage is applied

$$Ri + L\frac{di}{dt} = V \quad \text{or,} \quad 20\,i + 0.2\frac{di}{dt} = 200$$

Due to the presence of the inductor at $t = 0^+$, $i = 0$.

Hence the drop across the resistor being zero, 200 V drop will appear across the inductor.

Hence, at instant of switching, the voltage drop across the inductor is 200 V. The charging current is given by

$$i = \frac{V}{R}(1 - e^{-t/T})$$

or, $$i = \frac{200}{20}(1 - e^{-t/(L/R)}) = 10\,(1 - e^{-100\,t})$$

at $t = 0.02$ sec.,

$$i = 10\,(1 - e^{-100 \times 0.02}) = 8.646 \text{ A.}$$

The voltage across the inductor after lapse of 0.02 sec from switching is

$$L\frac{di}{dt} = 200 - iR = 200 - 8.646 \times 20 = \mathbf{27\ V.}$$

The rate of change of current at $t = 0.01$ sec. is then

$$\frac{di}{dt} = \frac{27\text{ V}}{L} = \frac{27}{0.2} = \mathbf{135\ A/sec.}$$

EXAMPLE 5.12 *A d.c. source of V volts supplies a steady current of I A to a series L-R circuit having resistance of R ohms and inductance of L Henry. A part of total resistance is suddenly shorted. Derive an expression for the current flowing from the d.c. source subsequent to this operation.*

SOLUTION. Let R_x be the part of the resistance that is shorted at $t = 0$. If i be current after t sec. in the circuit, we can write by KVL

$$(R - R_X)\,i + L\frac{di}{dt} = V$$

or, $$i = c\,e^{-\left(\frac{R - R_X}{L}\right)t} + \frac{V}{R - R_X}$$

$$\left[\, i \text{ being equal to } i_C + i_p,\ i_C = c\,e^{-\left(\frac{R - R_X}{L}\right)t},\quad i_p = \frac{V}{R - R_X} \right]$$

However, at $t = 0$, $i = \dfrac{V}{R}$

$$\therefore\quad c = \frac{V}{R} - \frac{V}{R - R_X}$$

$$= V\left[\frac{R - R_X - R}{R(R - R_X)}\right] = -\frac{V R_X}{R(R - R_X)}$$

Hence $$i = \frac{V}{R - R_X} - \frac{V R_X}{R(R - R_X)}\,e^{-\left(\frac{R - R_X}{L}\right).t}$$

$$= \frac{V}{R - R_X}\left[1 - \frac{R_X}{R}\,e^{-\left(\frac{R - R_X}{L}\right)t}\right]$$

Thus the expression for the current at t sec. later then the switching of s.c to a part of R has been derived.

5.4 TRANSIENT RESPONSE IN SERIES *RC* CIRCUIT HAVING D.C. EXCITATION (FIRST ORDER CIRCUIT)

Let a d.c. voltage V be applied (at $t = 0$) by closing a switch S in a series R-C circuit (Fig. 5.5). The current at $t > 0$ being i, application of KVL leads to

$$Ri + \frac{1}{C}\int i\,dt = V \qquad \text{...(5.10)}$$

Differentiation of equation (5.10) results,

$$R\frac{di}{dt} + \frac{i}{C} = 0 \quad \text{or} \quad \left(p + \frac{1}{RC}\right)i = 0 \qquad \text{...(5.11)}$$

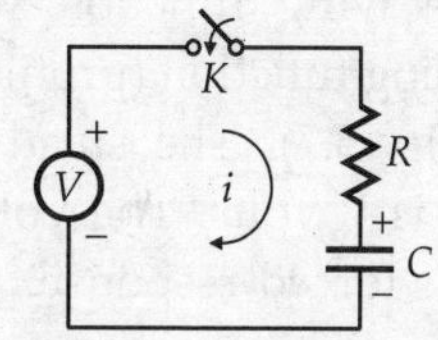

Fig. 5.5 Series *RC* circuit.

Equation (5.11) is a *homogeneous differential equation* whose solution will contain only complementary function, the particular function being zero. The solution will give natural response.

$$\therefore\quad i = i_C = K\,e^{-t/RC} \qquad \text{...(5.12)}$$

With application of voltage and assuming no initial charge across the capacitor, the capacitor will not produce any voltage across it but acts as a short circuit causing the circuit current to be (V/R).

i.e., at $t = 0^+$, $\quad i(0^+) = \dfrac{V}{R}$

Hence, from equation (5.12),

$$\text{at } t = 0^+ \quad \frac{V}{R} = K$$

Finally, we then obtain,

$$i = \frac{V}{R}e^{-t/RC}\ \text{A} \qquad \text{...(5.13)}$$

It may be observed that the charging current is a decaying function, the plot being shown in Fig. 5.6. As the capacitor is getting charged, the charging current dies out.

The corresponding voltage drops across the resistor and capacitor can be obtained as follows :

$$v_R = iR = Ve^{-t/RC} \qquad \text{...(5.14)}$$

CHAPTER 5

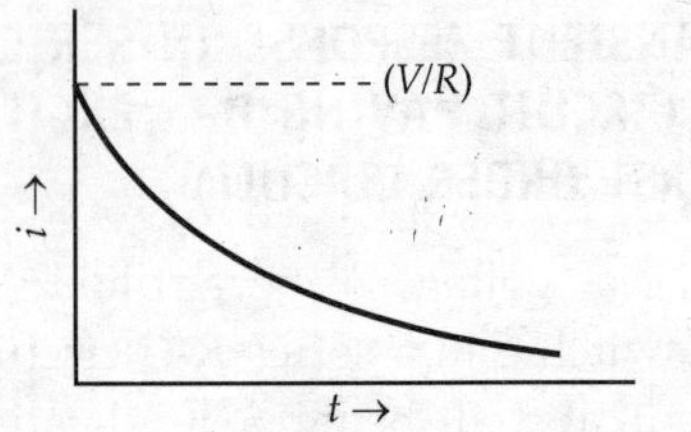

Fig. 5.6 Profile of current in RC charging circuit.

and $$v_C = \frac{1}{C}\int i\,dt = \frac{1}{C}\int_0^t \frac{V}{R} e^{-t/RC}\,dt$$

$$= V\left(1 - e^{-t/RC}\right). \qquad ..(5.15)$$

Observing equations (5.14) and (5.15) it reveals that v_R is a decaying function while v_C is an exponentially rising function (profiles of v_R and v_C are shown in Fig. 5.7). The steady state voltage across capacitor is V volts. The voltage across the capacitor exhibits forced response.

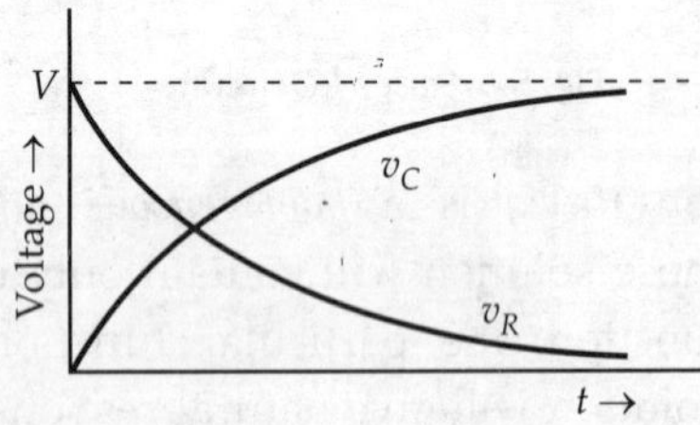

Fig. 5.7 Profiles of v_R and v_C in RC charging circuit.

Time constant is obtained by putting $t = RC$ which gives $v_C = V(1 - 0.368) = 0.632$ V *i.e.*, the time by which the capacitor attains 63.2% of steady state voltage.

The instantaneous powers are given by

$$p_R = i\,v_R = \frac{V^2}{R} e^{-2\frac{t}{RC}} \text{ W}$$

and $$p_C = i\,v_C = \frac{V^2}{R}\left(e^{-t/RC} - e^{-2t/RC}\right) \text{W}$$

Let us now study the discharging case when the switch S is thrown to a contact S' such that the R-C circuit is shorted and the voltage source is withdrawn (Fig. 5.8.)

Application of KVL yields

$$Ri + \frac{1}{C}\int i\,dt = 0 \qquad ...(5.16)$$

Differentiating (5.16), we get

$$R\frac{di}{dt} + \frac{i}{C} = 0 \quad \text{or} \quad \left(p + \frac{1}{RC}\right) i = 0 \qquad ...(5.17)$$

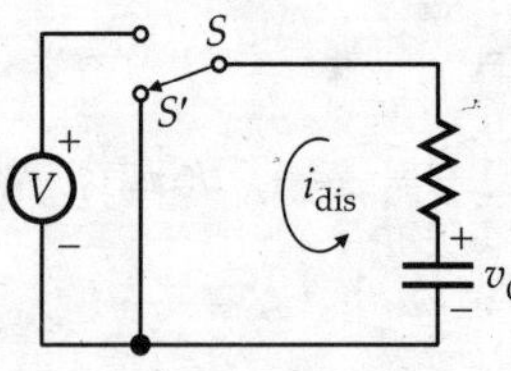

Fig. 5.8 Discharging in RC series circuit.

Equation (5.17) being a homogeneous differential equation, its solution reveals

$$i = i_c \text{ (complementary function)}$$

$$= K' e^{-t/RC} \qquad ...(5.18)$$

However at $t = 0^+$, the voltage across the capacitor will start discharging current through the resistor in *opposite* to the original current direction (shown by i_{dis} in Fig. 5.8). Hence the *direction of i during discharge is negative* and its *magnitude is given by (V/R).*

Thus $$i(0^+) = -\frac{V}{R}$$

Hence, from equation (5.18), we get

$$-\frac{V}{R} = K' \text{ (at } t = 0^+)$$

The complete solution is then

$$i = -\frac{V}{R} e^{-t/RC} \text{ A.}$$

The decay transient is plotted in Fig. 5.9 (natural response of the circuit).

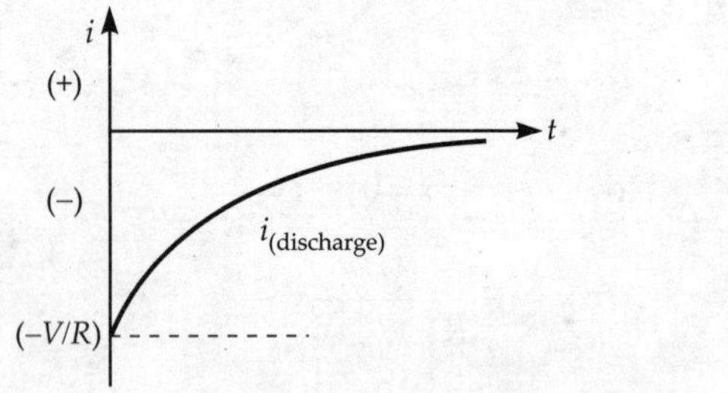

Fig. 5.9 Current decay transient in RC discharging circuit.

The corresponding transient voltages are given by

v_R (voltage drop across R)

$$= iR = -V e^{-t/RC}$$

and v_C (voltage drop across C)

$$= \frac{1}{C}\int i\,dt = Ve^{-t/RC}$$

Obviously, $v_R + v_C = 0$

Figure 5.10 represents the profiles of v_R and v_C with t.

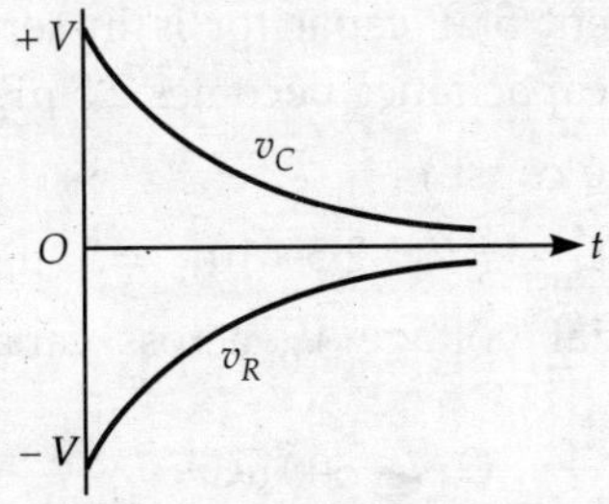

Fig. 5.10 v_R and v_C in RC discharging circuit.

In the discharging circuit, the time constant is given by the product of R and C such that

$$v_C = V e^{-1} = 0.369 \text{ V} \simeq 0.37 \text{ V}$$

i.e., the time by which the capacitor discharges to 37% of its initial voltage.

The instantaneous powers are given by

$$p_R = v_R\, i = \frac{V^2}{R} e^{-2t/RC} \text{ W.}$$

and $$p_C = v_C\, i = -\frac{V^2}{R} e^{-2t/RC} \text{ W.}$$

The charge stored in the capacitor during charging is given by

$$q = C v_C = CV(1 - e^{-t/RC}) \text{ or } q = Q(1 - e^{-t/RC})$$

while that during discharging is given by

$$q = C v_C = C V e^{-t/RC} \text{ columbs.}$$

or, $$q = Q e^{-t/RC} \text{ columbs.}$$

EXAMPLE 5.13 *Calculate the time taken by a capacitor of 1 μF and in series with a 1 MΩ resistance to be charged upto 80% of the final value.*

SOLUTION. The time constant T is given by

$$T = RC = 1 \times 10^6 \times 1 \times 10^{-6} = 1 \text{ sec.}$$

The charging of capacitor is expressed by the following equation

$$q = Q_0 (1 - e^{-t/RC})$$

Here, $q = 0.8\, Q_0$; $R = 1$ sec.

$\therefore$ $0.8 = 1 - e^{-t}$

$0.2 = e^{-t}$

$\therefore$ $t =$ **1.61 sec.**

EXAMPLE 5.14 *A d.c. constant voltage source feeds a resistance of 2000 kΩ in series with a 5 μF capacitor. Find the time taken for the capacitor when the charge retained will be decayed to 50% of the initial value, the voltage source being short circuited.*

SOLUTION. Time constant

$$T = RC = 2 \times 10^6 \times 5 \times 10^{-6} = 10 \text{ sec.}$$

The decaying condition is represented by the following expression

$$q = Q_0\, e^{-t/T}$$

However, $q = 0.5\, Q_0$

$\therefore$ $0.5\, Q_0 = Q_0\, e^{-t/T}$

or, $0.5 = e^{-t/T} = e^{-t/10}$

or, $-t/10 = \log_e (0.5)$

$\therefore$ $t =$ **6.94 sec.**

EXAMPLE 5.15 *In Fig. E5.6, the switch K is closed. Find the time when the current from the battery reaches to 500 mA.*

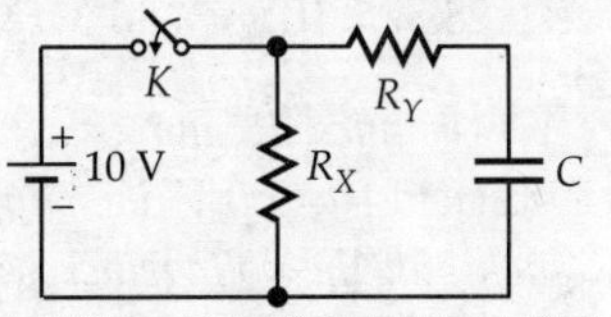

[$R_X = 50\ \Omega$; $R_Y = 70\ \Omega$, $C = 100\ \mu$F]

Fig. E5.6

SOLUTION. Let current through R_X be I_X and through C by I_Y after the switch K is closed.

$$I_X = \frac{10}{50} = 0.2 \text{ A} = 200 \text{ mA.}$$

However,

$$I = I_X + I_Y \qquad [I \text{ being the current from the supply}]$$

or, $500 = 200 + I_Y$

[$\because$ Supply current is 500 mA]

$\therefore$ $I_Y = 300$ mA

But $$I_Y = \frac{V}{R_Y} e^{-t/T}$$

[$T = RC = 70 \times 100 \times 10^{-6} = 0.007$ sec.]

or, $$0.3 = \frac{10}{70} e^{-\frac{t}{0.007}}$$

or, $$-\frac{t}{0.007} = \log_e (2.1)$$

$\therefore$ $t =$ **5.2 m sec.**

This is the time required when the d.c. source current flow will be 500 mA.

EXAMPLE 5.16 *A 10 μF capacitor is initially charged to 100 volts d.c. It is then discharged through a resistance of R ohms for 20 seconds when the p.d. across the capacitor is 50 V. Calculate the value of R.*

SOLUTION. In the discharging condition of the capacitor,

$$q = Q_0\, e^{-t/RC} \quad \text{or} \quad v = V_0\, e^{-t/RC}$$

As per the question, capacitor p.d. gets discharged to 50 V from the initial p.d. of 100 V.

$\therefore \quad v = 0.5\, V_0$

Hence we obtain,

$$0.5 = e^{-t/R \times 10 \times 10^{-6}}$$

or, $\quad \log_e 0.5 = -\dfrac{t}{R \times 10^{-5}} = -\dfrac{20}{R \times 10^{-5}}$

or, $\quad -0.7 = -\dfrac{20}{R \times 10^{-5}}$

$\therefore \quad R = 28.57 \times 10^5 = \mathbf{2.86\ M\Omega}.$

EXAMPLE 5.17 *A resistance R and 5 μF capacitor are connected in series across a 100 V d.c. supply. Calculate the value of R such that the voltage across the capacitor becomes 50 V in 5 sec after the circuit is switched on.*

SOLUTION. In case of charging

$$q = Q_0\,(1 - e^{-t/T})$$

$$[T = RC = (5 \times 10^{-6}\ R)\ \text{sec.}]$$

or, $\quad v = V_0\,(1 - e^{-t/T})$

As per the question, the p.d. across the capacitor is 50 V within 5 sec.

$\therefore \quad v = 0.5\, V_0 \qquad [V_0 = \text{final p.d. in steady state} = 100\ \text{V}]$

and $\quad t = 5$ sec.

$\therefore \quad 0.5 = 1 - e^{-5/5 \times 10^{-6} R}$

or, $\quad -0.5\, v = -e^{-10^6/R}$

$\therefore \quad R = \mathbf{1.45\ Mohm.}$

EXAMPLE 5.18 *A 5 μF capacitor is initially charged with 500 μC. At t = 0, the switch K is closed (Fig. E5.7). Determine the voltage drop across the resistor at t < T and at t = ∞.*

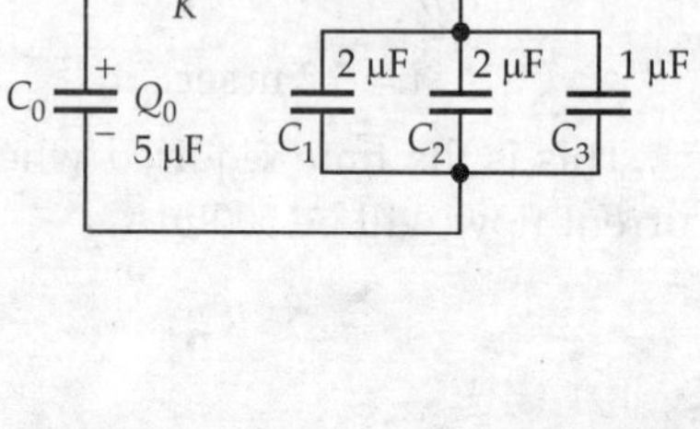

Fig. E5.7

SOLUTION. The equivalent capacitance of bank of parallel capacitors is 5 μF. As soon as *K* is closed, this equivalent 5 μF capacitor is in series with C_0 and the net capacitance becomes 2.5 μF.

$\therefore$ *T* (time const.)

$$= RC_{net} = 10 \times 2.5 \times 10^{-6} = 25\ \mu\ \text{sec.}$$

The initial voltage V_0 across capacitor C_0 is given by

$$V_0 = \frac{Q_0}{C_0} = \frac{500\ \mu\text{C}}{5 \times 10^{-6}} = 100\ \text{V}$$

With closing of *K*, the capacitor C_0 will start discharging, however at $t = 0^+$, there will be no voltage across C_1, C_2 or C_3.

Thus the entire voltage drop will be across *R* only (v_R) at $t = 0^+$ time.

i.e., $\quad v_R = V_0$ (decaying)

$$= V_0\, e^{-t/RC} = 100\, e^{-t/25 \times 10^{-6}}$$

$$= \mathbf{100\, e^{-40 \times 10^4 t}\ V}$$

At $t = \infty$, v_R becomes zero.

It is also evident that in steady state ($t = \infty$), the charge of C_0 will be distributed through C_1, C_2 and C_3 and no current will flow through the circuit. Hence $i = 0$, $v_R = iR = 0$.

EXAMPLE 5.19 *In Fig. E5.8, a capacitor of capacitance C is charged to a voltage V_0 (d.c.) and is allowed to discharge through a resistance R while charging another capacitor of capacitance αC. Determine the final voltage at terminal "a-b" under steady state condition.*

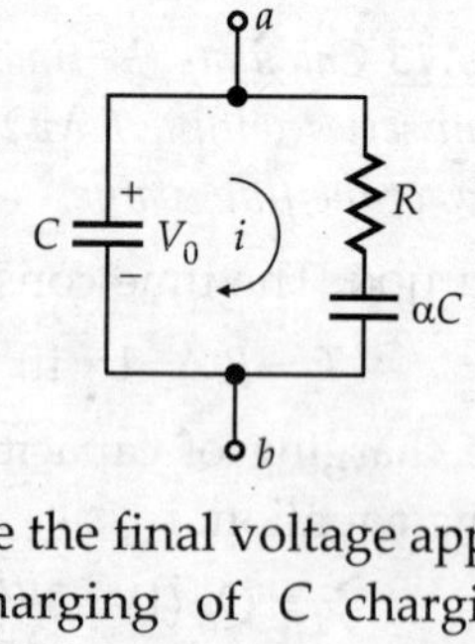

Fig. E5.8

SOLUTION. Let V_f be the final voltage appearing across *a-b* after discharging of C charging αC through *R*.

Equating the charge of the two capacitors

$$V_f\,(\alpha C) = V_0 C - V_f C$$

or, $\quad V_f\,(1 + \alpha) = V_0$

$\therefore \quad \mathbf{V_f = V_0 / (1 + \alpha).}$

[It may be noted that the final voltage across *a-b* is independent of *R*]

EXAMPLE 5.20 *In example 5.19, what fraction of energy originally stored is lost ?*

SOLUTION. Initial energy $= \frac{1}{2} CV_0^2$

Final energy

$$= \frac{1}{2} (\alpha C) V_f^2 + \frac{1}{2} CV_f^2 = \frac{1}{2} CV_f^2 [1+\alpha]$$

$$= \frac{1}{2}(1+\alpha) C \left(\frac{V_0}{1+\alpha}\right)^2 = \frac{1}{2} \frac{V_0^2 C}{(1+\alpha)}$$

$$\left[\because V_f = \frac{V_0}{1+\alpha}, \text{ as derived in Ex. 5.19}\right]$$

Hence,

$$\text{loss in energy} = \text{initial energy} - \text{final energy}$$

$$= \frac{1}{2} CV_0^2 - \frac{1}{2} CV_0^2 \cdot \frac{1}{\alpha+1}$$

$$= \frac{1}{2} CV_0^2 \left[1 - \frac{1}{1+\alpha}\right]$$

$$= \frac{1}{2} CV_0^2 \cdot \frac{\alpha}{1+\alpha}.$$

It may be noted that this loss of energy is due to presence of resistance R. However, the loss expression is independent of R.

EXAMPLE 5.21 *The 10 μF capacitor in RC circuit of Fig. E5.9 has initial charge of 100 μC with polarities as shown in the Fig. E5.9. At t = 0, the switch being closed, a d.c. voltage of 100 V is applied. Find the expression for the current.*

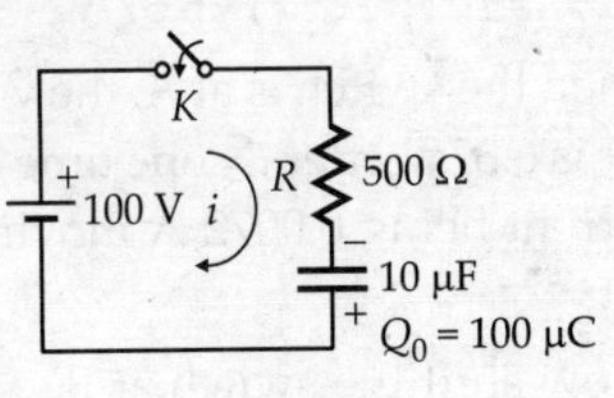

Fig. E5.9

SOLUTION. In the charging case,

$$100 = 500 \times i + \frac{1}{10 \times 10^{-6}} \int i\, dt$$

or, $$0 = 500 \frac{di}{dt} + \frac{i}{C}$$

or, $(p+200)\, i = 0$

or, $$i = K e^{-200t}$$

However, due to initial charge of 100 μC in the polarity shown, the equivalent voltage becomes

$$V_0 = q_0 / C = \frac{100 \times 10^{-6}}{10 \times 10^{-6}} = 10 \text{ V}.$$

This 10 V sends also current in the direction of i. Hence at $t = 0$,

$$i_0 = (V + V_0)/R = \frac{110}{500} = 0.22 \text{ A}.$$

Thus at $t = 0$, $0.22 = K e^{-200 \times 0}$

or, $$K = 0.22.$$

Thus the expression for current becomes

$$\mathbf{i = 0.22\, e^{-200t} \text{ A}.}$$

EXAMPLE 5.22 *Steady state is reached in the circuit shown in Fig. E5.10 when the switch is at 1 ; at t = 0, the switch is moved to 2. Find the drop across the capacitor as well as across the resistor. Also find the energy stored across the capacitor after t = 0.1 m sec.*

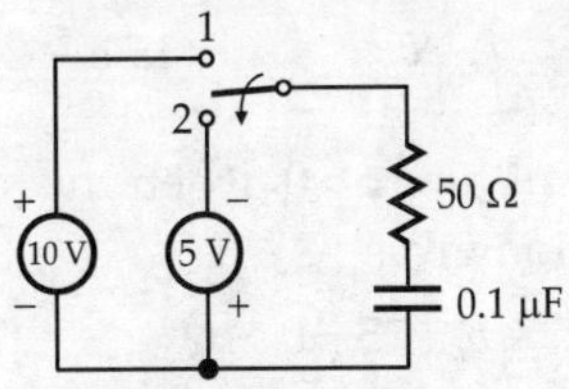

Fig. E5.10

SOLUTION When the switch is at 1, steady state is reached and the capacitor acquires 10 V potential, current being zero.

$\therefore$ $v_C(0) = 10$ V ; $i(0^-) = 0$ [ref. Fig. E5.10(*a*)]

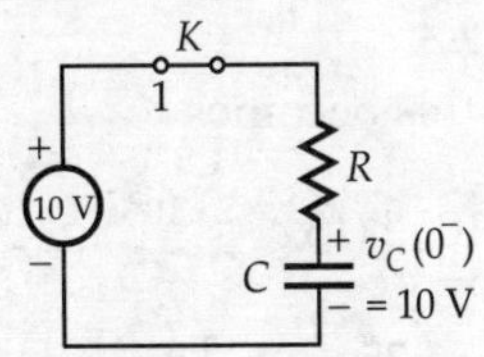

Fig. E5.10 (*a*) Circuit just before switching and when the switch is at 1

However, just after the switching the potential current will increase but the capacitor voltage will not change initially.

$$\therefore \quad v_C(0^+) = 10 \text{ V}.$$

Also, the polarity of the capacitor is such that the 5 V source becomes additive with $v_C(0^+)$ but drives the current in opposite direction refer to Fig. E5.10(*b*)]

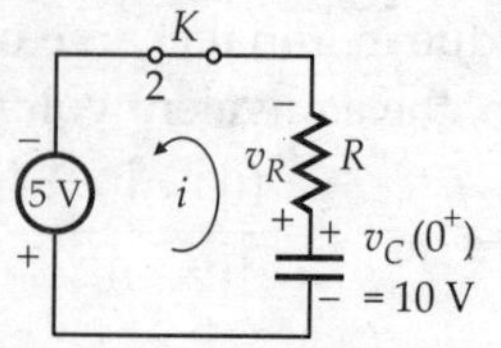

Fig. E5.10 (*b*) Circuit just after switching to 2 ($t = 0^+$).

The total voltage in the circuit is thus

$$v_C(0^+) + 5\text{ V} = 15\text{ V}$$

RC being equal to $50 \times 0.1 \times 10^{-6} = 5 \times 10^{-6}$ sec., the transient part of v_C is given by

$$v_{C_{\text{transient}}} = 15\, e^{-\frac{t}{5\times 10^{-6}}} = 15\, e^{-2\times 10^{5}\, t}\text{ V}$$

However, the steady state voltage will be (– 5 V) as this opposite current i will now charge the capacitor in the opposite direction and will raise the potential to –ve value in time $t = \infty$. Hence the total solution becomes

$$v_C = v_{C_{\text{transient}}} + v_{C_{\text{st. state}}} = \mathbf{(15\, e^{-2\times 10^5\, t} - 5)\ V.}$$

However at time $t > 0$, when the switch is at 2, KVL application gives

$$v_R - v_C - 5 = 0$$

[v_R being the resistive drop]

$$\therefore \quad v_R = 5 + v_C = -5 + 15\, e^{-2\times 10^5 t} + 5$$

$$= \mathbf{15\, e^{-2\times 10^5\, t}\ V.}$$

Energy stored in the capacitor is given by

$$\frac{1}{2} C v_C^2 = \frac{1}{2} \times 0.1 \times 10^{-6} \times (15\, e^{-2\times 10^5 t} - 5)^2$$

at $t = 0.1$ m sec, this becomes

$$\frac{1}{2} \times 0.1 \times 10^{-6}\, (15\, e^{-2\times 10^5 \times 1 \times 10^{-4}} - 5)^2$$

$$= \mathbf{1.25 \times 10^{-6}\ J.}$$

Example 5.23 *In Fig. E5.11, the switch K is closed at position A at t = 0. After the lapse of time equivalent to one time constant, the switch is moved to position B. Determine the complete current.*

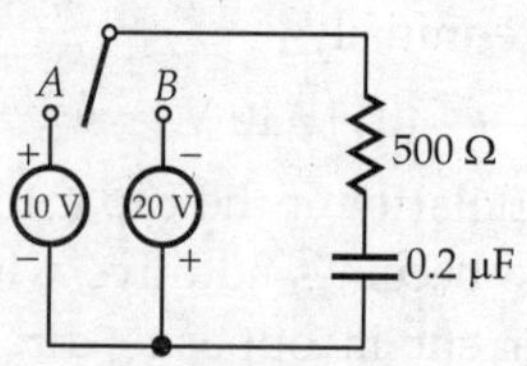

Fig. E5.11

Solution. Let us first assume that the switch is at A.

For the time interval

$$0 < t < \text{Time Const } (T),$$

$$V = R\, i + \frac{1}{C}\int i\, dt$$

or,
$$10 = 500\, i + \frac{1}{0.2 \times 10^{-6}} \int i\, dt$$

or,
$$0 = 500 \frac{di}{dt} + \frac{1}{0.2 \times 10^{-6}}$$

i.e. $(p + 10^4)\, i = 0$

$$\therefore \quad i = K\, e^{-10000\, t}\text{ A.}$$

However, at $t = 0$,

$$i_0 = \frac{V}{R} = \frac{10}{500} = 0.02\text{ A}$$

Hence, $0.02 = K\, e^{-10000 \times 0}$

or, $K = 0.02$

Thus the charging current is given by

$$i = 0.020\, e^{-10000\, t}\text{ A}$$

[the switch being at A]

This current will continue till one time constant when the switch is moved to position B.

However,

$$T = RC = 500 \times 0.2 \times 10^{-6} = 10^{-4}\text{ sec.}$$

Also at one time constant,

$$i = 0.02\, e^{-1} = 0.0072\text{ A.}$$

At this time the capacitor voltage is given by

$$v_C = 10\,(1 - e^{-1}) = 6.37\text{ V.}$$

Thus when the switch is at A, the voltage across the capacitor is 6.37 V after t = one time constant, the transient current being 0.0072 A moving clockwise in the circuit.

Let us now shift the switch at B.

The circuit configuration is drawn in Fig. E5.12. It can be observed that the stored voltage of 6.31 V is now additive to supply voltage of 20 V. Both these voltages drive the current now in the direction shown (anticlockwise) and is opposite to the case when the switch was at A.

The current equation in this case is given by

$$i = K'\, e^{-10000\,(t - t')}$$

assuming t' = one time constant.

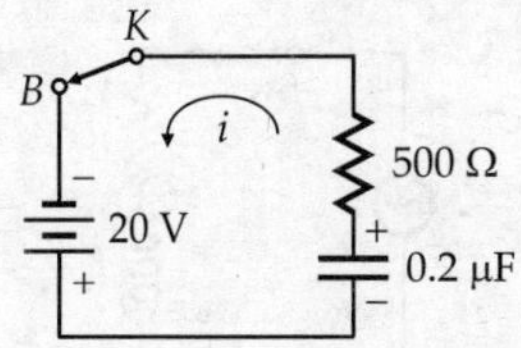

Fig. E5.12

However, at $t = t'$,

$$i = -(20 + 6.37)/500 = -0.052 \text{ A}$$

Then at $t = t'$

$$-0.052 = K' e^{-10000 \times 0} \quad \text{or} \quad K' = -0.052.$$

Thus the complete current expression becomes

$$\mathbf{i = -0.052\, e^{-10000\,(t - t')}\ A.}$$

at $t = t'$, the current has a negative peak value of 0.052 A which then starts decreasing while the capacitor is getting charged with time. This current will finally become zero when t' will be very high *i.e.*, the capacitor will be completely charged in the reverse side (Fig. E5.13)

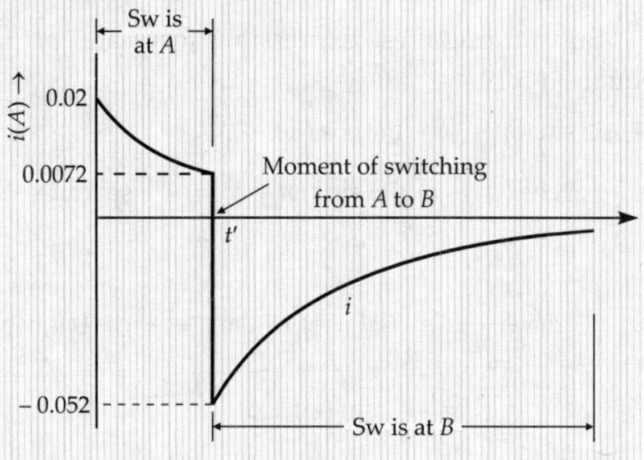

Fig. E5.13

EXAMPLE 5.24 *A capacitor C has initial charge of 10 μC. It is connected in series with R (polarity being indicated) and a switch K is closed at t = 0. Draw a sketch of graph for the charge with time in the capacitor.*

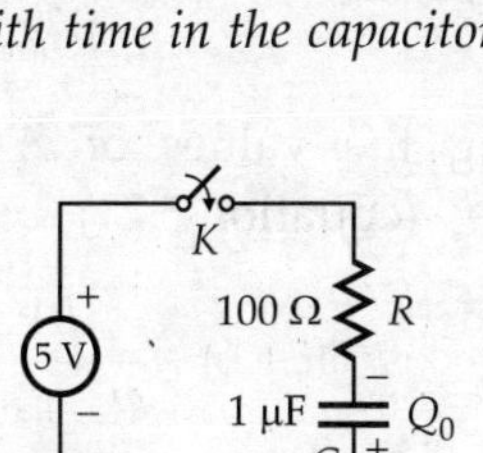

Fig. E5.14

SOLUTION. Given : Q_0 (initial charge) = 100 μC.

$\therefore V_0$ (initial voltage across the capacitor)

$$= Q_0 / C = 10\,\mu\,C/1\,\mu F$$

$$= 10 \text{ V} \quad [\ i.e.,\ v_C\ (0^-)]$$

We designate this voltage as a negative potential as per polarities shown in the figure.

$$\therefore \quad v_C\ (0^-) = -10 \text{ V}$$

As soon as the circuit is switched on, the supply voltage (5 V) will be additive with V_0 (*i.e.*, $v_C\ (0^-)$) and the net current flow in the circuit will be clockwise.

The net voltage of the circuit is then $(-5 \text{ V} - 10 \text{ V})$ *i.e.*, (-15 V)

Hence $v_C = -15\, e^{-t/RC} + 5$

[$\because$ at $t = \infty$, the transient will die out and the steady state part will remain. The capacitor voltage will become equal to the supply voltage].

$$= -15\, e^{-t/10^2 \times 10^{-6}} + 5$$

$$= (-15\, e^{-10^4 t} + 5) \text{ V}$$

v_C can also be determined in the following way :

$$v_C = K e^{-t/RC} + V_0$$

at $t = 0^+$, $\quad v_C\ (0^+) = v_C\ (0^-) = -10$ V

Also V_0, the steady state voltage = Supply voltage = 5 V

$\therefore$ at $t = 0^+$, $\quad -10 = K(1) + 5$

$\therefore \quad K = -15.$

This gives $\quad v_C = (-15\, e^{-t/RC} + 5).$

The current will charge the capacitor in reverse polarity and this will result in decay of initial charge of the capacitor to zero value and then due to the charging current, the capacity will be charged with +ve potential at the top plate. This mean that v_C will become zero at one moment (when the 5 V supply voltage will be equal and opposite to the potential stored in the capacitor due to initial charge.)

Let that time be t'.

Hence we can write at t'

$$v_C = -15\, e^{-10^4 t} + 5 = 0.$$

This is only possible if

i.e. $\quad -15\, e^{-10^4 t} = -5.$

$$e^{-10^4 t} = \frac{1}{3} \quad \text{or} \quad -10^4 t = -1.0986$$

$$\therefore \quad t = 1.0986 \times 10^{-4} \text{ sec} \simeq 0.11 \text{ m sec.}$$

Again, the final charge Q being (CV) the magnitude of this charge becomes, at steady state, $(1 \times 10^{-6} \times 5)$ *i.e.*, 5 μ C.

$$\text{Also} \quad q = K' e^{-t/RC} + 5$$

$$\text{at} \quad t = 0^+, \quad q \equiv q(0^+) \equiv q(0^-) = -10 \, \mu \, C$$

$$\therefore \quad -10 = K' \times 1 + 5$$

$$\therefore \quad K' = -15 \, \mu \, C$$

$$\text{i.e.,} \quad \mathbf{q = (-15e^{-t/T} + 5) \, \mu C.}$$

$$\text{and} \quad i = \frac{dq}{dt} = 15 \times \frac{1}{RC} e^{-t/T}$$

$$= 15 \times 10^{-4} \, e^{-10^4 t}$$

$$= \mathbf{1.5 \, e^{-10^4 t} \, mA.}$$

Profile of Q is drawn in **Fig. E5.15.**

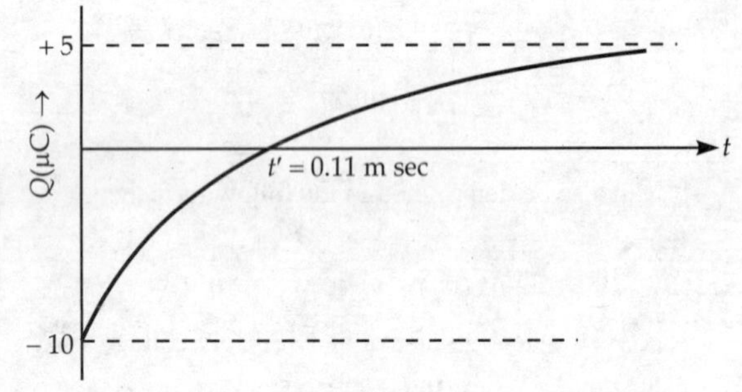

Fig. E5.15

5.5 TRANSIENT RESPONSE IN SERIES *RL* CIRCUIT WITH SINUSOIDAL EXCITATION (FIRST ORDER CIRCUIT)

Let $v = V_m \sin(\omega t + \phi)$ where ϕ varies from $0 - 2\pi$ depending on the switching instant. Application of KVL at $t = 0^+$ in Fig. 5.11 after the switch is closed, gives

$$Ri + L\frac{di}{dt} = V_m \sin(\omega t + \phi)$$

$$\text{or,} \quad \frac{R}{L} i + \frac{di}{dt} = \frac{V_m}{L} \sin(\omega t + \phi)$$

$$\text{or,} \quad \left(p + \frac{R}{L}\right) i = \frac{V_m}{L} \sin(\omega t + \phi) \qquad ...(5.19)$$

where "p" represents first derivative of i.

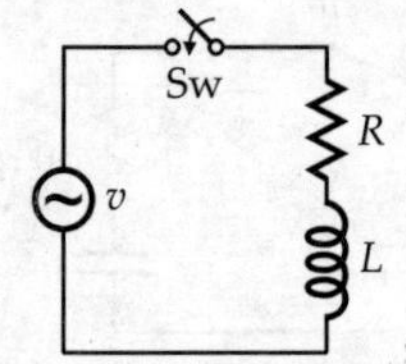

Fig. 5.11 Series *RL* circuit.

The complementary function of equation 5.19 is

$$i_C = C \, e^{-(R/L)t} \qquad ...(5.20)$$

Next we are to obtain the particular solution of current (i_p) such that the net current solution i is given by

$$i = i_C + i_p \text{ (forced response)}$$

$$\text{Let} \quad i_p = A \cos(\omega t + \phi) + B \sin(\omega t + \phi) \qquad ...(5.21)$$

where A and B are unknown constants.

$\therefore$ The first derivative of i_p becomes

$$pi_p = -A\omega \sin(\omega t + \phi) + B\omega \cos(\omega t + \phi)$$

Substituting these expressions for i_p and pi_p in equation 5.19,

$$[-A\omega \sin(\omega t + \phi) + B\omega \cos(\omega t + \phi)]$$

$$+ \frac{R}{L}[A \cos(\omega t + \phi) + B \sin(\omega t + \phi)] = \frac{V_m}{L} \sin(\omega t + \phi) \qquad ...(5.22)$$

$$\text{or,} \quad \left(-A\omega + \frac{BR}{L}\right) \sin(\omega t + \phi) + \left(B\omega + \frac{AR}{L}\right) \cos(\omega t + \phi) = \frac{V_m}{L} \sin(\omega t + \phi)$$

Equating coefficients of like terms,

$$\left[-A\omega + \frac{BR}{L}\right] = \frac{V_m}{L}; \quad A = \frac{-\omega L V_m}{R^2 + \omega^2 L^2}$$

$$\left[B\omega + \frac{AR}{L}\right] = 0; \quad B = \frac{RV_m}{R^2 + \omega^2 L^2}$$

Substituting the values of A and B in the expression for i_p (equation 5.21)

$$i_p = \frac{-\omega L V_m}{R^2 + \omega^2 L^2} \cos(\omega t + \phi) + \frac{RV_m}{R^2 + \omega^2 L^2} \sin(\omega t + \phi)$$

$$= \frac{V_m}{\sqrt{R^2 + \omega^2 L^2}} [-\omega L \cos(\omega t + \phi) + R \sin(\omega t + \phi)]$$

Let $R = \cos\theta$ and $\omega L = \sin\theta$; θ being $\tan^{-1}\dfrac{\omega L}{R}$.

Thus,

$$i = \frac{V_m}{\sqrt{R^2+\omega^2 L^2}}\left[\sin(\omega t+\phi)\cos\theta - \cos(\omega t+\phi)\sin\theta\right]$$

or, $$i_p = \frac{V_m}{\sqrt{R^2+\omega^2 L^2}}\sin(\omega t+\phi-\theta)]$$

$$= \frac{V_m}{\sqrt{R^2+\omega^2 L^2}}\left[\sin\left(\omega t+\phi-\tan^{-1}\frac{\omega L}{R}\right)\right]$$

This gives the net current solution as

$$i = i_C + i_p$$

or, $$i = Ce^{-\left(\frac{R}{L}\right).t} + \frac{V_m}{\sqrt{R^2+\omega^2 L^2}}\sin\left(\omega t+\phi-\tan^{-1}\frac{\omega L}{R}\right) \quad ...(5.23)$$

However, the inductance will oppose any sudden change of current though it.

As there was no current in the circuit before the switch was closed, hence $i_0 = 0$.

Then at $t = 0$,

$$i_0 = 0 = C + \frac{V_m}{\sqrt{R^2+\omega^2 L^2}}\sin\left(\phi-\tan^{-1}\frac{\omega L}{R}\right).$$

or, $$C = -\frac{V_m}{\sqrt{R^2+\omega^2 L^2}}\sin\left(\phi-\tan^{-1}\frac{\omega L}{R}\right)$$

Substituting of value of C, in equation (5.23),

$$i = e^{-(R/L)t}\left[-\frac{V_m}{\sqrt{R^2+\omega^2 L^2}}\sin\left(\phi-\tan^{-1}\frac{\omega L}{R}\right)\right] + \frac{V_m}{\sqrt{R^2+\omega^2 L^2}}\sin\left(\omega t+\phi-\tan^{-1}\frac{\omega L}{R}\right) \quad ...(5.24)$$

The final part of equation (5.24) contains the exponential factor $e^{-(R/L)t}$ which becomes zero at relatively short time as with increasing t, $e^{-(R/L)t}$ decreases. The expression within the bracket depends on the value of ϕ *i.e.*, the instant when the switch is closed.

The second part of equation (5.24) is the steady state current which lags the applied voltage by an angle given by $\tan^{-1}\dfrac{\omega L}{R}$.

EXAMPLE 5.25 *A 50 Hz 400 V (peak value) sinusoidal voltage is applied at t = 0 to a series R-L circuit having resistance 5 Ω and inductance 0.2 H. Obtain an expression of current at any instant "t". Calculate the value of the transient current 0.01 sec after switching on.*

SOLUTION. Z (impedance of L-R circuit)

$$= 5 + j\times 2\pi\times 50\times 0.2 = 63\angle 85.44°\,\Omega$$

Applying KVL in the R-L circuit,

$$Ri + L\frac{di}{dt} = 400\sin 314\,t$$

or, $$i\frac{R}{L} + \frac{di}{dt} = \frac{400}{L}\sin 314\,t$$

or, $$\left(p+\frac{R}{L}\right)i = \frac{400}{0.2}\sin 314\,t$$

$$= 2000\sin 314\,t$$

The complementary function i_C is given by

$$i_C = Ce^{-(R/L)t} = Ce^{-25t}$$

and the particular solution is

$$i_p = \frac{400}{Z}\sin\left(\omega t+\phi-\tan^{-1}\frac{\omega L}{R}\right)$$

$$= 6.35\sin(314\,t - 85.44°)$$

$$= 6.35\sin(314\,t - 1.49)$$

$$[\therefore 85.44° \equiv 1.49 \text{ rad.}]$$

$\therefore$ The complete solution is,

$$i = i_C + i_p$$

i.e., $$\mathbf{i = Ce^{-25t} + 6.35\sin(314\,t} - 1.49)$$

at $t = 0$, $\quad i = 0 \quad \therefore\ 0 = C + 6.35\sin(-1.49)$

$\therefore \quad C = 6.33$

The current becomes

$$i = 6.33e^{-25t} + 6.35\sin(314\,t - 1.49)$$

at $t = 0.01$ sec.

$$i_C = 6.33\,e^{-25\times 0.01} = \mathbf{4.93\ A.}$$

[Since i_C is the transient part that is only wanted in the problem, hence we need not calculate i_p which is a steady state part.]

EXAMPLE 5.26 *An a.c. voltage of $v = V\sin 100\pi t$ is applied to a series R-L circuit. If the L-R circuit has R = 10 Ω and L = 0.1 H, calculate the ratio of maximum value to which the current rise to the steady state maximum value when the voltage is applied at an instant t = 0.002 sec.*

Solution. The complementary function for the current in this *R-L* circuit where a.c. voltage is applied at *t* time is given by

$$i_C = Ce^{-(R/L)t}$$

and particular solution is given by

$$i_p = \frac{V_m}{\sqrt{R^2+\omega^2 L^2}} \sin\left(\omega t + \phi - \tan^{-1}\frac{\omega L}{R}\right)$$

where ϕ is the phase angle voltage at time $t = 0$.

In this problem $\phi = 0$.

$$\therefore \quad i = i_C + i_p$$

$$= Ce^{-(R/L)t} + \frac{V_m}{\sqrt{R^2+\omega^2 L^2}} \sin\left(\omega t + \phi - \tan^{-1}\frac{\omega L}{R}\right)$$

or, $$i = Ce^{-100t} + \frac{V}{32.95}\sin(500\pi t - 1.26)$$

$$\left[\because R/L = 100\,;\ |Z| = \sqrt{R^2+\omega^2 L^2} = 32.95 \text{ and } \phi = 0\,;\ \tan^{-1}\frac{\omega L}{R} = 1.26\right]$$

at $t = 0.002$ sec.

$$i = Ce^{-100\times 0.002} + \frac{V}{32.95}\sin(500\times\pi\times 0002 - 1.26)$$

$$= 0.82\,C + \frac{V}{32.95}\sin(\pi - 1.26)$$

But at $t = 0.002$ sec., $i = 0$

$$\therefore \quad 0 = 0.82\,C + \frac{V}{32.95}\sin(\pi - 1.26)$$

$$\therefore \quad 0.82\,C = -\frac{V}{32.95}\sin(\pi - 1.26)$$

$$\therefore \quad C = -\frac{V}{32.95\times 0.82}\sin(\pi - 1.26)$$

$$= -0.037\times 0.952\text{ V} = (-0.0352\text{ V}).$$

Thus

$$\boldsymbol{i = V\left[-0.0352\,e^{-100t} + 0.03\sin(500\pi t - 1.26)\right]\text{ A}}$$

It may be observed that *i* will be maximum if the 2nd term in the bracketed portion is maximum with –ve sign. This is possible if

$$\sin(500\pi t - 1.26) = -1$$

i.e., $$500\pi t - 1.26 = \frac{3\pi}{2}$$

$$\therefore \quad t = \frac{1.5\pi + 1.26}{500\pi} = 0.0038\text{ sec.}$$

With $t = 0.0038$ sec.

$$i_c = -0.0352\,e^{-100t}\text{ V}$$

$$= -0.0352\,e^{-100\times 0.0038}\text{ V}$$

$$= (-0.024\text{ V})\text{ A.}$$

and $$i = V.0.03\sin(500\pi\times 0.0038 - 1.26)$$

$$= (-0.02999\text{ V})$$

$\therefore$Max. value of current is

$$i = [(-0.024) + (-0.0299)]\text{ V} = (-0.054\text{ V})$$

Thus, the ratio of maximum value to which the current rises to the steady state maximum value is given by

$$\text{Ratio} = \frac{(0.054\text{ V})}{(0.0299\text{ V})} = \mathbf{1.8.}$$

Example 5.27 *Obtain the current at $t > 0$, if a.c. voltage v is applied when the switch K is moved to 2 from 1 at $t = 0$ (Fig. E5.16). Assume a steady state current of 1 A in the LR circuit when the switch was at position 1.*

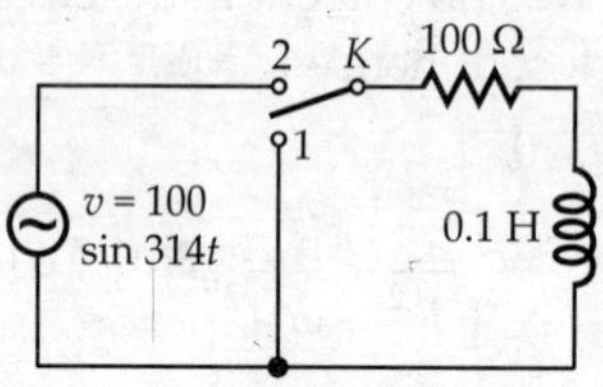

Fig. E5.16

Solution. At position 1 of the switch *K*, the steady state current in the circuit is 1 A, *i.e.*, $i(0^-) = 1$ A. As soon as the switch is moved to position 2, at $t = 0$, the a.c. voltage *v* appears across the *LR* series circuit. Due to presence of inductance,

$$i(0^-) = i(0^+) = 1\text{ A.}$$

$$Z = R + jX_L = 100 + j\,2\pi\times 50\times 0.1$$

$$= 104.8\angle 17.47°\,\Omega$$

Applying KVL in the *RL* circuit,

$$R.i + L\frac{di}{dt} = v$$

or, $$100\,i + 0.1\frac{di}{dt} = 100\sin 314\,t$$

or, $$10^3\,i + \frac{di}{dt} = 10^3\sin 314\,t$$

i.e., $$(p + 10^3)\,i = 10^3\sin 314\,t$$

$$\therefore \quad i_C = Ce^{-R/L.t}$$

$$= Ce^{-\frac{100}{0.1}t} = Ce^{-1000t}$$

$$i_p = \frac{V_m}{Z}\sin\left(\omega t + \phi - \tan^{-1}\frac{\omega L}{R}\right)$$

$$= \frac{100\sqrt{2}}{104.8}\sin(314\,t - 17.47°)$$

$$[\because \phi = 0°]$$

$$= 1.345\sin(314\,t - 0.304)$$

Then the complete current is given by

$$i = i_C + i_p$$

$$= Ce^{-1000t} + 1.345\sin(314\,t - 0.304)$$

However, at $t = 0^+$,

$$i(0^+) = 1\text{ A}$$

$$\therefore \quad 1 = C + 1.345\sin(-0.304) = C + (-0.3)$$

or, $\quad C = 1.3$

Hence $\boldsymbol{i = 1.3\,e^{-1000t} + 1.345\sin(314\,t - 0.304)}$.

5.6 TRANSIENT RESPONSE IN *RLC* CIRCUIT WITH D.C. EXCITATION (SECOND ORDER CIRCUIT)

Application of KVL in the series *RLC* circuit $t = 0^+$ after the switch is closed, leads to the following differential equation

$$iR + L\frac{di}{dt} + \frac{1}{C}\int idt = V_0 \text{ (Fig. 5.12)}$$

By differentiation,

$$L\frac{d^2 i}{dt^2} + R\frac{di}{dt} + \frac{i}{C} = 0$$

or, $$\left(p^2 + \frac{R}{L}p + \frac{1}{LC}\right)i = 0 \qquad ...(5.25)$$

Equation (5.25) is a second order, linear, homogenous differential equation. The characteristic equation then becomes

$$p^2 + \frac{R}{L}p + \frac{1}{LC} = 0$$

where the coefficients are constant. The roots of the characteristic equation then become

$$p_1, p_2 = \frac{-R/L \pm \sqrt{(R/L)^2 - 4/LC}}{2}.$$

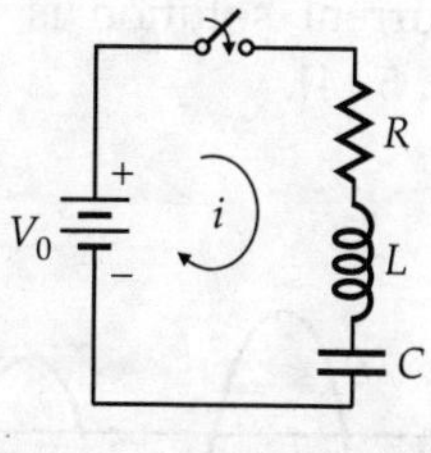

Fig. 5.12 Series *RLC* circuit.

Let $\quad \alpha = (-R/2L)$

and $\quad \beta = \sqrt{(R/2L)^2 - \frac{1}{LC}}$

Hence, $p_1 = \alpha + \beta$

$$p_2 = \alpha - \beta$$

Also, the solution of differential equation (5.25) becomes

$$i = C_1\,e^{p_1 t} + c_2\,C^{p_2 t} \qquad ...(5.26)$$

C_1 and C_2 being the constants.

Case 1. When $\left(\frac{R}{2L}\right)^2 > \frac{1}{LC}$

This time β is positive real quantity. Hence, the roots p_1 and p_2 are real but unequal.

$$\therefore \quad p_1 = \alpha + \beta\,;\ p_2 = \alpha - \beta$$

and $$i = C_1\,e^{(\alpha+\beta)t} + C_2\,e^{(\alpha-\beta)t}$$

$$= e^{\alpha t}(C_1\,e^{\beta t} + C_2\,e^{-\beta t}) \qquad ...(5.27)$$

The current response is *over-damped* (Fig. 5.13).

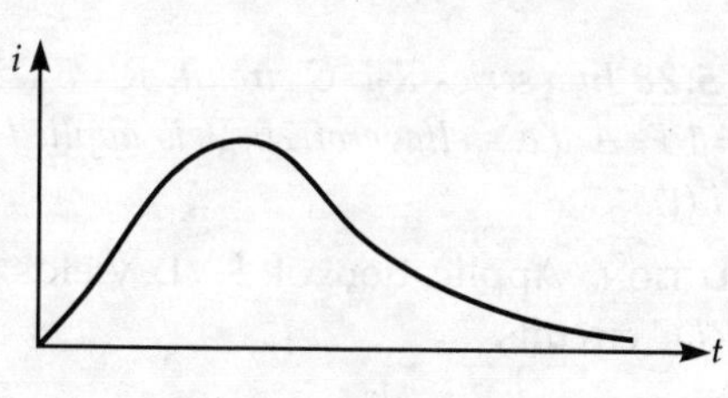

Fig. 5.13 Current over-damping.

Case 2. When $\left(\frac{R}{2L}\right)^2 < \frac{1}{LC}$

This time β is imaginary and then the roots p_1 and p_2 are complex conjugates.

$$p_1 = \alpha + j\beta; \qquad p_2 = \alpha - j\beta$$

and $$i = C_1\,e^{(\alpha + j\beta)t} + C_2\,e^{(\alpha - j\beta)t}$$

$$= e^{\alpha t}(C_1\,e^{j\beta t} + C_2\,e^{-j\beta t})$$

$$= e^{\alpha t}[C_1\cos(\beta t) + C_2\sin(\beta t)]$$

$$...(5.28)$$

Thus the current solution is *underdamped* (or oscillatory) [Fig. 5.14].

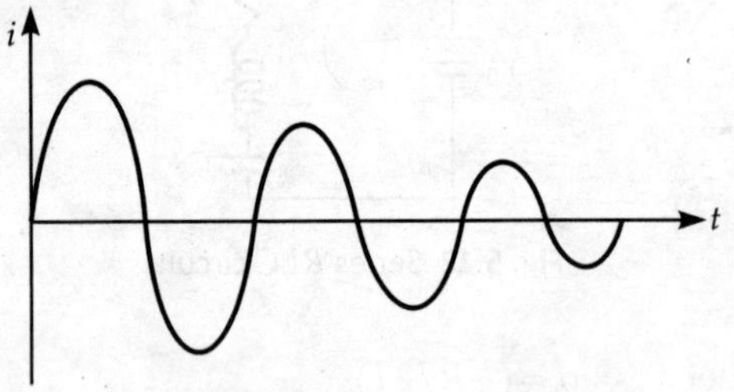

Fig. 5.14 Current oscillation.

Case 3. When $\left(\frac{R}{2L}\right)^2 = \frac{1}{LC}$

This time β is zero.

Hence, roots p_1 and p_2 are real and equal.

$$p_1 = p_2 = \alpha \quad \text{and} \quad i = C_1\, e^{\alpha t} + C_2\, te^{\alpha t}$$

$$= e^{\alpha t}\,(C_1 + C_2\, t) \qquad \text{...(5.29)}$$

The current response is then a *critically* damped one (Fig. 5.15).

Fig. 5.15 Critical damping of current.

Example 5.28 *In a series R-L-C circuit,* $R = 5\,\Omega$, $L = 1\,H$ *and* $C = 1\,F$. *A d.c. voltage of 20 V is applied at* $t = 0$. *Obtain i (t).*

Solution. Application of KVL yields, in the series *RLC* circuits

$$iR + L\frac{di}{dt} + \frac{1}{C}\int i\,dt = V \qquad \text{...(1)}$$

On differentiation,

$$L\frac{d^2 i}{dt^2} + R\frac{di}{dt} + \frac{i}{C} = 0$$

or,
$$\left(Lp^2 + Rp + \frac{1}{C}\right)i = 0 \qquad \text{...(2)}$$

Thus the characteristic equation is

$$Lp^2 + Rp + \frac{1}{C} = 0,$$

or,
$$p^2 + 5p + 1 = 0 \qquad \text{...(3)}$$

$$\therefore \quad p_1, p_2 = \frac{-5 \pm \sqrt{25-4}}{2} = \frac{-5 \pm 4.58}{2}$$

$$= -0.21, -4.79.$$

$\therefore$ The solution becomes

$$i(t) = K_1\, e^{-0.21\,t} + K_2\, e^{-4.79\,t} \qquad \text{...(4)}$$

As current in inductance cannot change instantaneously and also the voltage across the capacitor does not change instantaneously,

hence, $i(0^+) = 0$ and $\frac{1}{C}\int i\,dt = 0$

Thus from (1),

$$L\frac{di}{dt} = V \text{ (at } t = 0^+).$$

or,
$$\frac{di}{dt}(0^+) = \frac{V}{L} = \frac{20}{1} = 20 \text{ A/sec.}$$

Again, substituting $i = 0$ at $t = 0^+$ in (4),

$$0 = K_1\, e^{-0.21\times 0} + K_2\, e^{-4.79\times 0}$$

$$= K_1 + K_2 \qquad \text{...(5)}$$

Again, differentiating equation (4),

$$\frac{di}{dt} = -0.21\,\text{K}_1\, e^{-0.21\,t} - 4.79\, e^{-4.79\,t}$$

or, at $t = 0^+$,

$$20 = -0.21\,\text{K}_1\, e^{-0.21\times 0} - 4.79\,\text{K}_2\, e^{-4.7\times 0}$$

$$= -0.21\,K_1 - 4.79\,\text{K}_2$$

or,
$$20 = 0.21\,K_2 - 4.79\,K_2 = -4.58\,K_2$$

$$[\because K_1 + K_2 = 0]$$

$$\therefore \quad K_2 = -4.37\,; \quad \text{Hence } K_1 = 4.37$$

$$\therefore \quad \mathbf{i\,(t) = (4.37\, e^{-0.21t} - 4.37\, e^{-4.79t})\ A.}$$

5.7 TRANSIENT RESPONSE IN SERIES *RC* CIRCUIT WITH SINUSOIDAL EXCITATION (FIRST ORDER CIRCUIT)

$$v = V_m \sin(\omega t + \phi)$$

Application of KVL in the series *R-C* circuit of Fig. 5.16 yields

$$R\,.\,i + \frac{1}{C}\int i\,dt = V_m \sin(\omega t + \phi) \qquad \text{...(5.30)}$$

Differentiation of equation (5.29) gives,

$$\left(p + \frac{1}{RC}\right)i = \frac{\omega V_m}{R}\cos(\omega t + \phi)$$

...(5.31)

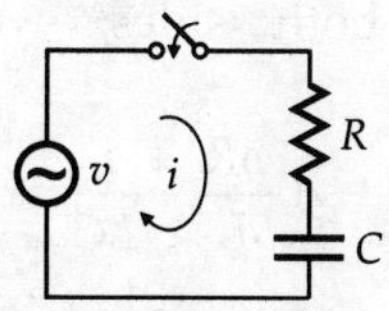

Fig. 5.16 AC voltage application in RC series.

The complementary function being i_C, the current solutions (forced response) of the differential equation (5.31) is given by

$$i = i_C + i_p$$

where $\quad i_C = C' e^{-t/RC},$ C' being a constant

and $i_p = \dfrac{V_m}{\sqrt{(R^2 + (1/\omega C)^2)}} \sin\left(\omega t + \phi + \tan^{-1}\dfrac{1}{\omega CR}\right)$

[The particular function i_p has been obtained in a similar way as has been done for the case with $R-L$ circuit under sinusoidal response].

$$\therefore \quad i = C' e^{-t/2C} + \frac{V_m}{\sqrt{R^2 + \left(\dfrac{1}{\omega C}\right)^2}} \sin\left(\omega t + \phi + \tan^{-1}\frac{1}{\omega CR}\right) \quad ...(5.32)$$

In order to determine the constant C', the circuit condition at $t = 0$ is considered.

At $t = 0$, the capacitor acts as short circuit.

$\therefore\ i_0$ (initial current) $= \dfrac{V_m}{R} \sin\phi$

Hence setting $t = 0$, the complete solution becomes

$$i_0 \left(= \frac{V_m}{R}\sin\phi\right) = C' + \frac{V_m}{\sqrt{R^2 + (1/\omega C)^2}} \sin\left(\phi + \tan^{-1}\frac{1}{\omega CR}\right)$$

or, $$C' = \frac{V_m}{R}\sin\phi - \frac{V_m}{\sqrt{R^2 + \left(\dfrac{1}{\omega C}\right)^2}} \sin\left(\phi + \tan^{-1}\frac{1}{\omega CR}\right)$$

Substitution of C' in equation (5.32),

$$i = e^{-t/RC}\left[\frac{V_m}{R}\sin\phi - \frac{V_m}{\sqrt{R^2 + \left(\dfrac{1}{\omega C}\right)^2}} \sin\left(\phi + \tan^{-1}\frac{1}{\omega CR}\right)\right] + \frac{V_m}{\sqrt{R^2 + (1/\omega C)^2}} \sin\left(\omega t + \phi + \tan^{-1}\frac{1}{\omega CR}\right) \quad ...(5.33)$$

The first term being the transient with *decay factor* $e^{-t/RC}$, the second term of equation (5.33) is the *steady state* current which *leads* the applied voltage by $\angle \tan^{-1}(1/\omega CR)$.

EXAMPLE 5.29 *A series R-C circuit has $R = 20\,\Omega$ and $C = 100\,\mu F$. A voltage $v = 200 \sin 314\,t$ is applied at $t = 2.14$ m sec. Obtain an expression for i. Also, find the value of current after time 1 m sec from the switching instant.*

SOLUTION. It may be noted that the voltage is applied **not** at $t = 0$ but at ϕ where

$$t \equiv 2.14 \text{ m sec.} = 314 \times 0.00214 = 0.672 \text{ rad.}$$

$\therefore$ As soon as the switch is closed, the application of KVL leads to

$$iR + \frac{1}{C}\int i\,dt = 200 \sin(314\,t + 0.672)$$

This leads to the solution

$$i = i_C + i_p$$

where i_C = complementary function

$$= Ke^{-t/RC} = Ke^{-500\,t}$$

$$[RC = 100 \times 10^{-6} \times 20 = 2 \times 10^{-3} \text{ sec.}]$$

and i_p = particular solution

$$= \frac{V_m}{Z}\sin\left(314\,t + 0.672 + \tan^{-1}\left(\frac{1}{R\omega C}\right)\right)$$

$$= \frac{200}{37.6}\sin(314\,t + 0.672 + 1.01)$$

$$\left[\text{Here } Z = R - j\frac{1}{\omega C} = 20 - j\frac{10^6}{314 \times 100} = 20 - j\,31.8 = 37.6 \ \ -1.01\,\Omega\right]$$

Hence the complete solution i is given by

$$i = i_C + i_p$$

$$= Ke^{-500\,t} + 5.32 \sin(314\,t + 0.672 + 1.01) \text{ A}$$

However, at $t = 0^+$, i will be given by the ratio of voltage at $t = 2.14$ m sec to the resistance only as $t = 0^+$ indicates the moment just after the switching, but the switching is performed at $t = 2.14$ m sec and not $t = 0$. Hence $t = 0^+$ here means $t = (2.14 \text{ m sec.})^+$.

$$\therefore \quad i(0^+) = \frac{200 \sin 314 \times 0.00214}{20} = 6.22 \text{ A}$$

Hence we get

$$6.22 = K(1) + 5.32 \sin(1.682) = K + 5.29$$

$$\therefore \quad K = 0.93$$

CHAPTER 5

$$\therefore \quad i = 0.93\, e^{-500\,t} + 5.32 \sin(314\,t + 0.672 + 1.01)$$

$$= \mathbf{0.93\, e^{-500\,t} + 5.32 \sin(314\,t + 1.682)\ A}$$

After 1 m sec. the current becomes

$$i = 0.93\, e^{-500 \times 10^{-3}} + 5.32 \sin(314 \times 10^{-3} + 1.682)$$

$$= 0.564 + 4.85 = \mathbf{5.414\ A.}$$

5.8 TRANSIENT RESPONSE IN SERIES *RLC* CIRCUIT WITH SINUSOIDAL EXCITATION (SECOND ORDER CIRCUIT)

$$v = V_m \sin(\omega t + \phi)$$

As soon as the switch is closed, the mesh equation becomes

$$R.i + L\frac{di}{dt} + \frac{1}{C}\int i\,dt = V_m \sin(\omega t + \phi) \qquad ...(5.34)$$

Differentiation leads

$$\left(p^2 + \frac{R}{L}p + \frac{1}{LC}\right) i = \frac{\omega V_m}{L} \cos(\omega t + \phi) \qquad ...(5.35)$$

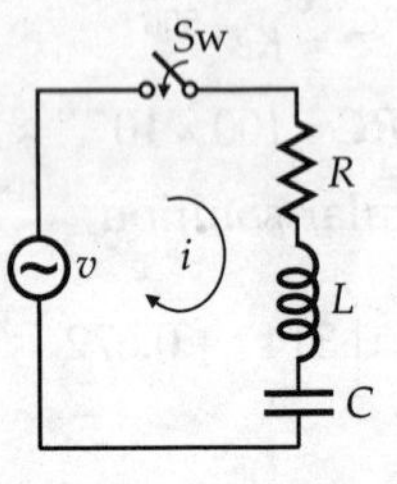

Fig. 5.17 *AC* application in *RLC* series circuit.

The particular solution can be obtained as follows :

Let

$$i_p = A\cos(\omega t + \phi) + B\sin(\omega t + \phi)$$

$$i'_p = -A\,\omega \sin(\omega t + \phi) + B\,\omega \cos(\omega t + \phi)$$

$$i''_p = -A\omega^2 \cos(\omega t + \phi) - B\,\omega^2 \sin(\omega t + \phi)$$

Substitution of values of i'_p and i''_p in (5.35)

$$[-A\,\omega^2 \cos(\omega\, t + \phi) - B\,\omega^2 \sin(\omega\, t + \phi)]$$

$$+ \frac{R}{L}[-A\,\omega \sin(\omega\, t + \phi) + B\,\omega \cos(\omega\, t + \phi)]$$

$$+ \frac{1}{LC}[A\cos(\omega t + \phi) + B\sin(\omega t + \phi)]$$

$$= \frac{\omega V_m}{L}\cos(\omega t + \phi)$$

Comparing both sides, we get for sine coefficients,

$$-B\omega^2 - A\frac{\omega R}{L} + \frac{B}{LC} = 0$$

or
$$A\left(\frac{\omega R}{L}\right) + B\left(\omega^2 - \frac{1}{LC}\right) = 0 \qquad ...(5.36)$$

and for cosine coefficients,

$$-A\omega^2 + B\frac{\omega R}{L} + A\frac{1}{LC} = \frac{\omega V_m}{L}$$

or,
$$A\left(-\omega^2 + \frac{1}{LC}\right) + B\left(\frac{\omega R}{L}\right) = \frac{\omega V_m}{L} \qquad ...(5.37)$$

From equation (5.36),

$$A = -B\frac{\left(\omega^2 - \frac{1}{LC}\right)}{\frac{\omega R}{L}} = B\frac{\left(\frac{1}{LC} - \omega^2\right)}{\frac{\omega R}{L}}$$

Substitution of A in equation (5.37) yields.

$$B\left[\left(-\omega^2 + \frac{1}{LC}\right)^2 + \frac{\omega^2 R^2}{L^2}\right] = \frac{\omega^2 R V_m}{L^2}$$

$$\therefore \quad B = \frac{V_m \frac{\omega^2 R}{L^2}}{\left[\left(-\omega^2 + \frac{1}{LC}\right)^2 + \frac{\omega^2 R^2}{L^2}\right]}$$

$$= \frac{V_m \frac{\omega^2 R}{L^2}}{\left[\left(\frac{1}{LC} - \omega^2\right)^2 + \frac{\omega^2 R^2}{L^2}\right]}$$

Thus

$$A = +B\frac{\left(-\omega^2 + \frac{1}{LC}\right)}{\frac{\omega R}{L}} = \frac{V_m\,\omega\left(\frac{1}{LC} - \omega^2\right)}{L\left[\left(\frac{1}{LC} - \omega^2\right)^2 + \frac{\omega^2 R^2}{L^2}\right]}$$

Hence with the values of A and B

$$i_p = + \frac{V_m\,\omega\left(-\omega^2 + \frac{1}{LC}\right)}{L\left[\left(\omega^2 + \frac{1}{LC}\right)^2 + \frac{\omega^2 R^2}{L^2}\right]}\cos(\omega t + \phi)$$

$$+ \frac{V_m \frac{\omega^2 R}{L^2}}{\left[\left(-\omega^2 + \frac{1}{LC}\right)^2 + \frac{\omega^2 R^2}{L^2}\right]}\sin(\omega t + \phi)$$

Let $$M\sin\theta = \frac{V_m\,\omega\left(-\omega^2+\dfrac{1}{LC}\right)}{L\left[\left(-\omega^2+\dfrac{1}{LC}\right)^2+\dfrac{\omega^2R^2}{L^2}\right]}$$

and $$M\cos\theta = \frac{V_m\dfrac{\omega^2 R}{L^2}}{\left[\left(-\omega^2+\dfrac{1}{LC}\right)^2+\dfrac{\omega^2R^2}{L^2}\right]}$$

Also $$\frac{M\sin\theta}{M\cos\theta} = \tan\theta$$

$$= \frac{\dfrac{V_m\,\omega}{L}\left(-\omega^2+\dfrac{1}{LC}\right)}{V_m\dfrac{\omega^2R}{L^2}} = \frac{L}{\omega R}\left(-\omega^2+\frac{1}{LC}\right)$$

$$= \frac{1}{R}\left(-\omega L+\frac{1}{\omega C}\right)$$

$$\therefore\ \theta = \tan^{-1}\left[\frac{1}{R}\left(-\omega L+\frac{1}{\omega C}\right)\right]$$

Thus,

$$i_p = M\sin\theta\cos(\omega t+\phi)+M\cos\theta\sin(\omega t+\phi)$$
$$= [\sin(\omega t+\phi)\cos\theta+\cos(\omega t+\phi)\sin\theta]\,M$$
$$= M\sin(\omega t+\phi+\theta)$$

$$\therefore\ i_p = M\left[\sin\left\{\omega t+\phi+\tan^{-1}\frac{1}{R}\left(\frac{1}{\omega C}-\omega L\right)\right\}\right]$$

However,

$$M = \sqrt{M^2\cos^2\theta+M^2\sin^2\theta}$$
$$= \frac{V_m}{\sqrt{R^2+\left(\dfrac{1}{\omega C}-\omega L\right)^2}}$$

Thus

$$i_p = \frac{V_m}{\sqrt{R^2+\left(\dfrac{1}{\omega C}-\omega L\right)^2}}\sin\left(\omega t+\phi+\tan^{-1}\frac{\dfrac{1}{\omega C}-\omega L}{R}\right)$$

the complementary function i_C being equal to the d.c. response of RLC circuit.

Then, for overdamped case, when $\left(\dfrac{R}{2L}\right)^2 > \dfrac{1}{LC}$,

$$i = e^{\alpha t}\left(C_1e^{\beta t}+C_2e^{-\beta t}\right)+\frac{V_m}{\sqrt{R^2+\left(\dfrac{1}{\omega C}-\omega L\right)^2}}\sin\left(\omega t+\phi+\tan^{-1}\frac{\dfrac{1}{\omega C}-\omega L}{R}\right),$$

for underdamped case, when $\left(\dfrac{R}{2L}\right)^2 < \dfrac{1}{LC}$,

$$i = e^{\alpha t}(C_1\cos\beta t+C_2\sin\beta t)+\frac{V_m}{\sqrt{R^2+\left(\dfrac{1}{\omega C}-\omega L\right)^2}}\sin\left(\omega t+\phi+\tan^{-1}\frac{\left(\dfrac{1}{\omega C}-\omega L\right)}{R}\right).$$

and for the critically damped case, when

$$\left(\frac{R}{2L}\right)^2 = \frac{1}{LC},$$

$$i = e^{\alpha t}(C_1+C_2 t)+\frac{V_m}{\sqrt{R^2+\left(\dfrac{1}{\omega C}-\omega L\right)^2}}\sin\left(\omega t+\phi+\tan^{-1}\frac{\left(\dfrac{1}{\omega C}-\omega L\right)}{R}\right).$$

EXAMPLE 5.30 *In Fig. E5.17 with switch open, steady state is reached with $v = 100\sin 314\,t$ volts. The switch is closed at $t = 0$. The circuit is allowed to come to steady state again. Determine the steady state current and complete solution of transient current.*

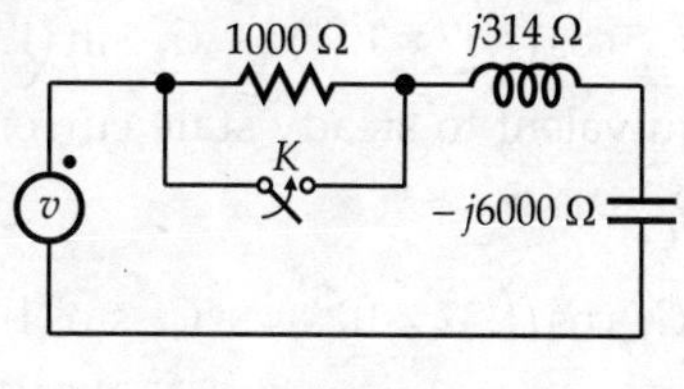

Fig. E5.17

SOLUTION. Before the switch is operated, *i.e.*, at $t < 0$,

$$Z = 1000 + j(314-6000)$$
$$= 5773.27\angle(-1.39\text{ rad})\,\Omega$$

$$\therefore \quad |I_{max}| = \frac{100\text{ V}}{5773.27} = 0.0173\text{ A}$$

at an angle of $\angle 1.39$ rad $(= 79.64°)$

[It may be observed that V is taken as reference]

$$\therefore \quad I_{max} = 0.0173\ \angle 79.64° = (0.003 + j\,0.017)\text{ A}$$

This is the steady state peak current before switching *i.e.*, when $t < 0$.

After K is closed, the resistance is by passed and hence

$$I'_{max} = \frac{100}{j\,(314 - 6000)} = -0.0176\text{ A at } \angle 90°$$

i.e., $|I'_{max}| = 0.0176$ A and $\phi = 90°$ (lag)

i.e. $i_{st.\,state} = 0.0176 \sin(314\,t - 90°)$

$= \mathbf{0.0176 \cos 314\,t\,.\ (t > 0).}$

Next task is to find i during the transient period.

It may be noted that due to pressure of inductance, the reactive part of component of I_{max} at $t < 0$ must be same at $t = 0^+$.

Hence $\quad i(0^-) \equiv i(0^+) = 0.017$ A.

Again in RLC circuit the roots of the characteristic equation

$$p^2 + \frac{R}{L}p + \frac{1}{LC} = 0 \text{ is given by}$$

$$p_1, p_2 = \frac{-R/L \pm \sqrt{\left(\frac{R}{L}\right)^2 - 4.\frac{1}{LC}}}{2}$$

in this problem at $t = 0^+$, $R = 0$.

$$\therefore \quad p_1, p_2 = \pm j\,1.37 \times 10^3$$

$$\left[\because L = \frac{X_L}{2\pi f} = \frac{314}{314} = 1\text{ H};\ C = \frac{1}{2\pi f\,X_C} = 5.3 \times 10^{-7}\right]$$

$$\therefore i_C = C_1\,e^{p_1 t} + C_2\,e^{p_2 t}$$

$$= C_1 \cos(1.37 \times 10^3)\,t + C_2 \sin(1.37 \times 10^3)\,t$$

i_p being equivalent to steady state current,

$$i = i_C + i_p$$

$$= C_1 \cos(1.37 \times 10^3)\,t + C_2 \sin(1.37 \times 10^3)\,t + 0.0176 \cos 314\,t.$$

$\therefore$ Again, when the steady state current was flowing,

$$v_C(0^-)_{max} = 0.0173 \times 6000\ \angle 79.64 - 90°$$

$$= 103.8\ \angle -10.36° = (102 - j\,18.66)\text{ V}.$$

Across the capacitor, the reactive part of the voltage will remain the same at $t = (0^-)$ and $t = (0^+)$ time;

then $\quad v_C(0^-) = v_C(0^+) = -18.66\text{ V.}\ \left(= -\frac{di}{dt}(0^+)\right)$

Thus the initial conditions are

$$i(0^+) = 0.017\text{ A}$$

$$v_C(0^+) = -18.66\text{ V}$$

Also

$$i = 0.0176 \cos 314\,t + C_1 \cos(1.37 \times 10^3)\,t + C_2 \sin(1.37 \times 10^3)\,t$$

and

$$\frac{di}{dt} = -0.0176 \times 314 \sin 314\,t - C_1 \times 1.37 \times 10^3 \sin(1.37 \times 10^3)\,t + C_2 \times 1.37 \times 10^3 \cos(1.37 \times 10^3)\,t$$

With initial condition,

$$0.017 = 0.0176 + C_1$$

and $\quad 18.66 = C_2 \times 1.37 \times 10^3$;

i.e., $\quad C_1 = -6 \times 10^{-4}$

and $\quad C_2 = 13.7 \times 10^{-3}$.

Finally, therefore,

$$i = 0.0176 \cos 314\,t + (-6 \times 10^{-4} \cos 1.37 \times 10^3\,t) + (13.7 \times 10^{-3}) \sin 1.37 \times 10^3\,t$$

$$= (17.6 \times 10^{-3} \cos 314\,t - 0.6 \times 10^{-3} \cos 1.37 \times 10^3\,t + 13.7 \times 10^{-3} \sin 1.37 \times 10^3\,t)\text{ A}$$

or, $\quad \mathbf{i = (17.6 \cos 314\,t - 0.6 \cos 1.37 \times 10^3\,t + 13.7 \sin 1.37 \times 10^3\,t)\text{ mA.}}$

EXAMPLE 5.31 *Figure E5.18 represents a parallel RLC circuit where R = 0.1 Ω, L = 0.5 H and C is 1 F. Capacitor C has an initial voltage of 10 V (polarity being shown in the figure). The switch K is closed at time t = 0. Obtain v (t).*

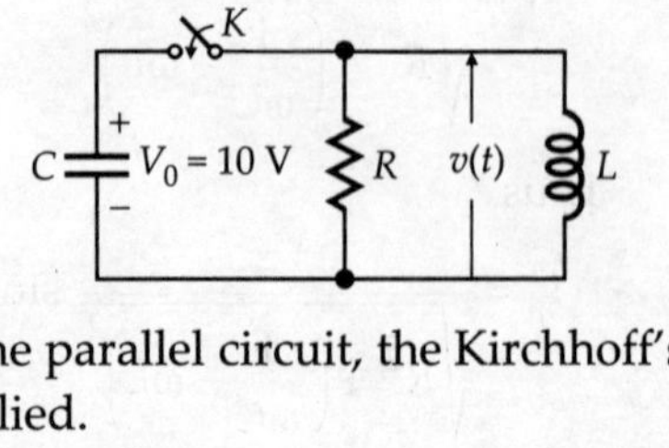

Fig. E5.18

SOLUTION. In the parallel circuit, the Kirchhoff's current law is applied.

$$\frac{1}{L}\int v\,dt + Gv + C\frac{dv}{dt} = 0 \qquad \text{...(1)}$$

$$\left[\because i_L = \frac{1}{L}\int v\,dt;\ i_R = Gv,\ G \text{ being the conductance and } i_C = C\frac{dv}{dt}.\right]$$

Differentiating equation (1)

$$\frac{v}{L}+G\frac{dv}{dt}+C\frac{d^2v}{dt^2}=0.$$

or, $$\left(Cp^2+Gp+\frac{1}{L}\right)v=0 \qquad ...(2)$$

The characteristic equation is then

$$Cp^2+Gp+\frac{1}{L}=0 \text{ or } p^2+10\,p+2=0.$$

i.e., $$p_1, p_2=\frac{-1\pm\sqrt{100-8}}{2}=\frac{-1\pm 9.6}{2}$$

or, $$p_1=4.3 \text{ and } p_2=-5.3$$

The general solution is then

$$v(t)=K_1\,e^{+4.3\,t}+K_2\,e^{-5.3\,t} \qquad ...(3)$$

At $t=0^+, v(0^+)=10$ V

(due to presence of initial charge across C)

and $$\frac{1}{L}\int v\,dt=i_L=0.$$

$\therefore$ From equation (1), at $t=0^+$,

$$C\frac{dv}{dt}+10\times 10=0 \text{ or } \frac{dv}{dt}=-\frac{100}{C}=-100 \text{ V/sec.}$$

Substituting $v(0^+)=10$ in equation (3), at $t=0^+$

$$10=K_1+K_2 \qquad ...(4)$$

Again, differentiating equation (3),

$$\frac{dv(t)}{dt}=4.3\,K_1\,e^{4.3\,t}-5.3\,K_2\,e^{-5.3\,t}$$

But, at $t=0^+$, $\dfrac{dv(t)}{dt}=-100.$

$\therefore$ $$-100=4.3\,K_1-5.3\,K_2$$

i.e., $$4.3\,K_1-5.3\,K_2=-100$$

or, $$4.3\,K_1-5.3\,(10-K_1)=-100 \qquad \text{[from (4)]}$$

or, $$4.3\,K_1-53+5.3\,K_1=-100$$

or, $$9.6\,K_1=-47$$

i.e., $$K_1=-4.896$$

This gives $K_2=14.896$.

Finally, therefore,

$$v(t)=\mathbf{-4.896\,e^{+4.3\,t}+14.896\,e^{-5.3\,t}\ V.}$$

ADDITIONAL EXAMPLES

EXAMPLE 5.32 *In Fig E5.19, determine the current expressions i_1 and i_2 at $t>0$ if the switch is closed at $t=0$.*

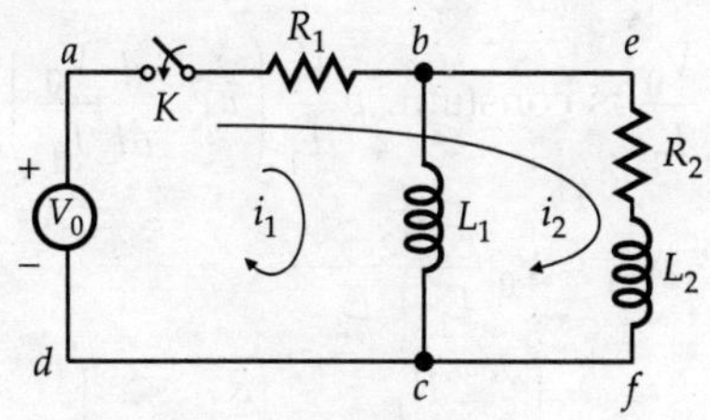

Fig. E5.19

SOLUTION. At $t=0$, the switch being closed, in loop *abcd*,

$$V_0=i_1\,R_1+L_1\frac{di_1}{dt}+i_2\,R_1$$

or, $$i_1\frac{R_1}{L_1}+\frac{di_1}{dt}+i_2\frac{R_1}{L_1}=\frac{V_0}{L_1}$$

or, $$(p+R_1/L_1)\,i_1+(R_1/L_1)\,i_2=V_0/L_1 \qquad ...(1)$$

Similarly, in loop *aefd*,

$$V_0=(i_1+i_2)\,R_1+i_2\,R_2+L_2\frac{di_2}{dt}$$

$$=i_1\,R_1+(R_1+R_2)\,i_2+L_2\frac{di_2}{dt}$$

or, $$i_1\frac{R_1}{L_2}+i_2\frac{R_1+R_2}{L_2}+\frac{di_2}{dt}=\frac{V_0}{L_2}$$

or, $$\left(p+\frac{R_1+R_2}{L_2}\right)i_2+i_1\frac{R_1}{L_2}=\frac{V_0}{L_2}$$

or, $$i_1\frac{R_1}{L_2}+\left(p+\frac{R_1+R_2}{L_2}\right)i_2=\frac{V_0}{L_2} \qquad ...(2)$$

Rearranging equations (1) and (2) in matrix form,

$$\begin{bmatrix} p+\dfrac{R_1}{L_1} & \dfrac{R_1}{L_1} \\ \dfrac{R_1}{L_2} & p+\dfrac{R_1+R_2}{L_2}\end{bmatrix}\begin{bmatrix} i_1 \\ i_2\end{bmatrix}=\begin{bmatrix} V_0/L_1 \\ V_0/L_2\end{bmatrix}$$

Using Cramer's rule,

$$i_1=\frac{\begin{vmatrix} V_0/L_1 & R_1/L_1 \\ V_0/L_2 & p+\dfrac{R_1+R_2}{L_2}\end{vmatrix}}{\Delta}.$$

However,

$$\begin{vmatrix} V_0/L_1 & R_1/L_1 \\ V_0/L_2 & p+\dfrac{R_1+R_2}{L_2} \end{vmatrix} = p\frac{V_0}{L_1} + V_0\frac{R_1+R_2}{L_1 L_2} - \frac{V_0 R_1}{L_1 L_2},$$

Since $\frac{V_0}{L_1}$ is constant, $p\frac{V_0}{L_1}\left(i.e., \frac{d}{dt}\frac{V_0}{L_1}\right)$ is zero.

Thus, $\Delta i_1 = V_0 \dfrac{R_2}{L_1+L_2}$

where $$\Delta = \begin{bmatrix} p+\dfrac{R_1}{L_1} & \dfrac{R_1}{L_1} \\ \dfrac{R_1}{L_2} & p+\dfrac{R_1+R_2}{L_2} \end{bmatrix}$$

$$= \left(p^2 + p\frac{R_1+R_2}{L_2} + p\frac{R_1}{L_1} + \frac{R_1(R_1+R_2)}{L_1 L_2} - \frac{R_1^2}{L_1 L_2}\right)$$

$$= p^2 + \left(\frac{R_1 L_1 + R_2 L_1 + R_1 L_2}{L_1 L_2}\right)p + \frac{R_1 R_2}{L_1 L_2}$$

$$= p^2 + Mp + N.$$

where $$M = \frac{R_1 L_1 + R_2 L_1 + R_1 L_2}{L_1 L_2}$$

$$N = \frac{R_1 R_2}{L_1 L_2}.$$

Hence we finally obtain,

$$(p^2 + Mp + N)\, i_1 = V_0 \frac{R_2}{L_1 + L_2}.$$

The characteristic equation is of the form

$$p^2 + M.p + N = 0.$$

Here, $$p_1, p_2 = \frac{-M \pm \sqrt{M^2 - 4N}}{2},$$

i.e., $$p_1 = \left(-\frac{M}{2} + \frac{\sqrt{M^2-4N}}{2}\right)$$

and $$p_2 = -\frac{M}{2} - \frac{\sqrt{M^2-4N}}{2}$$

Observation reveals the quantity $M^2 - 4N > 0$.

Hence p_1 and p_2 are *real* and *unequal* and the complementary function is given by

$$i_{c_1} = e^{-M/2.t}\left(C_1 e^{\frac{\sqrt{M^2-4N}}{2}t} + C_2 e^{-\frac{\sqrt{M^2-4N}}{2}t}\right)$$

the particular solution being

$$i_{p_1} = \frac{V_0}{R_1}$$

$$\therefore \quad i_1 = i_{c_1} + i_{p_1}$$

$$= e^{-(M/2)t}\left(C_1 e^{\frac{\sqrt{M^2-4N}}{2}.t} + C_2 e^{-\frac{\sqrt{M^2-4N}}{2}.t}\right) + \frac{V_0}{R_1}$$

C_1 and C_2 can be obtained for initial condition.

In a similar way

$$i_2 = \frac{\begin{vmatrix} p+R_1/L_1 & V_0/L_1 \\ R_1/L_2 & V_0/L_2 \end{vmatrix}}{\Delta};$$

Δ being the determinant

or, $$\Delta i_2 = p\frac{V_0}{L_2} + \frac{R_1 V_0}{L_1 L_2} - V_0\frac{R_1}{L_1 L_2} = 0$$

$$\left[\because p\frac{V_0}{L_2} = 0\right]$$

or, $$\left[p^2 + \left(\frac{R_1 L_1 + R_2 L_1 + R_1 L_2}{L_1 L_2}\right)p + \frac{R_1 R_2}{L_1 L_2}\right] i_2 = 0.$$

or, $$(p^2 + Mp + N)\, i_2 = 0.$$

The complementary function i_{c_2} being same as i_{c_1} in this part i_{p_2} is zero since the differential equation with i_2 is of homogeneous nature.

$$\therefore\ i_2 = i_{c_2} + 0 = e^{(-M/2)t}\left(C_1' e^{\frac{\sqrt{M^2-4N}}{2}t} + C_2' e^{-\frac{\sqrt{M^2-4N}}{2}t}\right)$$

It may be observed that at steady state, L_1 acts as short circuit, the transient being vanished within this time, the current i_1 is given by (V_0/R_1) only. Steady state i_2 will be obviously zero as the entire source current will pass as i_1 getting a short circuited path though *b-c* [Ref. Fig. E5.19(*a*)]

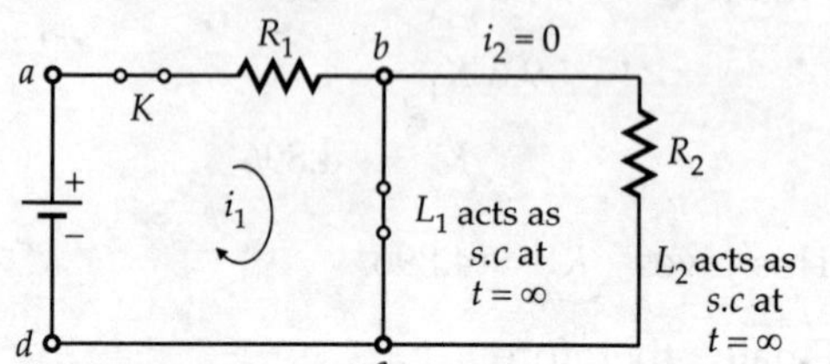

Fig. E5.19(*a*)

EXAMPLE 5.33 *A d.c. voltage of 100 V is suddenly applied in the network shown in Fig. E5.20. Find the transient currents in both the loops and obtain the transient voltage across the capacitor.*

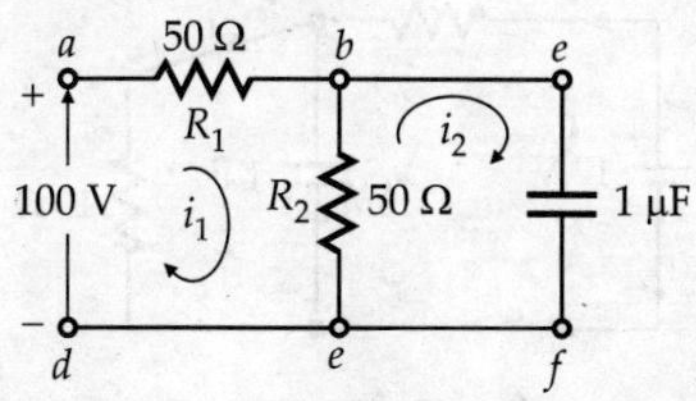

Fig. E5.20

SOLUTION. Applying KVL in loop *abcd*,

$$50\,i_1 + (i_1 - i_2)\,50 = 100$$

or, $$100\,i_1 - 50\,i_2 = 100$$

or, $$2i_1 - i_2 = 2$$

or, $$2\frac{di_1}{dt} - \frac{di_2}{dt} = 0$$

i.e., $$2\,pi_1 - pi_2 = 0$$

or, $$pi_2 = 2\,pi_1 \qquad ...(a)$$

Next, applying KVL in loop *befc*,

$$(i_2 - i_1)\,50 + \frac{1}{C}\int i_2\,dt = 0 \qquad ...(b)$$

or, $$-50\,i_1 + 50\,i_2 + \frac{1}{1\times 10^{-6}}\int i_2\,dt = 0$$

or, $$-50\frac{di_1}{dt} + 50\frac{di_2}{dt} + \frac{i_2}{1\times 10^{-6}} = 0$$

or, $$-50\,pi_1 + 50\,pi_2 + i_2 \times 10^6 = 0 \qquad ...(c)$$

However, $pi_1 = \frac{1}{2}\,pi_2$ (from (*a*))

Thus equation (*c*) becomes

$$-25\,pi_2 + 50\,pi_2 + i_2 \times 10^6 = 0$$

or, $$(25\,p + 10^6)\,i_2 = 0$$

i.e., $$(p + 4\times 10^4)\,i_2 = 0 \qquad ...(d)$$

Since equation (*d*) is a homogeneous differential equation hence the particular solution is zero and the complementary function i_{C_2} is given by

$$i_2 = i_{C_2} = Ke^{-4\times 10^4\,t} \qquad ...(e)$$

At $t = 0$, equation (*b*) becomes

$$(i_2 - i_1)\,50 = 0 \quad \text{or} \quad i_1 = i_2$$

Using $i_1 = i_2$ in the original loop equation of loop *abcd*,

$$50\,i_1 = 100 \quad \text{or} \quad i_1 = 2\text{ A}$$

This gives

$$i_2 = 2\text{ A} \qquad [\because i_1 = i_2]$$

Thus from equation (*e*), at $t = 0$,

$$K = 2$$

Thus $$\mathbf{i_2 = 2e^{-4\times 10^4\,t}\ A.}$$

Again in loop *abcd*, we have already obtained

$$2i_1 - i_2 = 2 \quad \text{or} \quad 2i_1 - (2e^{-4\times 10^4 t}) = 2$$

$$i_1 - e^{-4\times 10^4\,t} = 1$$

or, $$\mathbf{i_1 = 1 + e^{-4\times 10^4\,t}\ A.}$$

The transient voltage across the capacitor is given by

$$v_c = \frac{1}{C}\int i_2\,dt = \frac{1}{1\times 10^{-6}}\int 2\,e^{-4\times 10^4\,t}\,dt$$

$$\mathbf{= 50\,(1 - e^{-4\times 10^4\,t})\ V.}$$

Also $v_c = V(1 - e^{-t/RC})$

where V is the steady state voltage across the capacitor.

V = Supply voltage – drop across R_1

(refer to Fig. E5.20(*a*)).

$= 100 - i_1 \times R_1 = 100 - 1 \times 50 = 50$ V

[$\because$ Steady state $i_1 = 1$ A]

$\therefore\ v_c = 50\,(1 - e^{-4\times 10^4\,t})$

$$\left[\because \frac{1}{RC} = \frac{1}{(R_1 \,||\, R_2)\,C} = \frac{1}{25\times 10^{-6}} = 4\times 10^4\right]$$

EXAMPLE 5.34 *In a RC series circuit $R = 1\,\Omega$ and $C = 0.5$ F. An exponential voltage $v = 10\,e^{-t}$ is suddenly applied at $t = 0$. Obtain $i\,(t)$. Assume no initial charge in the capacitor.*

SOLUTION. Application of KVL in the series *RC* circuit,

$$iR + \frac{1}{C}\int i\,dt = v = 10\,e^{-t} \qquad ...(1)$$

Differentiating (1),

$$R\frac{di}{dt} + \frac{1}{C}.\,i = -10\,e^{-t}$$

or, $$\frac{di}{dt} + \frac{i}{RC} = -10\,e^{-t}$$

or, $$\frac{di}{dt} + \frac{i}{1 \times 0.5} = -10\, e^{-t}$$

or, $$\frac{di}{dt} + 2i = -10\, e^{-t}$$

i.e., $$(p+2)\, i = -10\, e^{-t} \qquad ...(2)$$

The characteristic equation being $(p+2)=0$, the complementary function is given by

$$i_C = K_1\, e^{-2t}$$

and the trail solution of particular function is

$$i_p = A e^{-t}.$$

where A is undetermined coefficient.

Substituting the value of i_p in equation (2),

$$-Ae^{-t} + 2\,Ae^{-t} = -10\, e^{-t}$$

$$\therefore \quad Ae^{-t} = -10\, e^{-t}$$

i.e., $$A = -10$$

Particular function then becomes

$$i_p = -10\, e^{-t}$$

However, at $t=0^+$, the capacitor would behave as short circuit and

$$i(0^+) = \frac{V}{R} = \frac{10}{1} = 10 \text{ A}$$

[But the voltage drop across the capacitor is zero i.e., $\frac{1}{C}\int i\, dt = 0$]

As $$i = i_C + i_p = K_1\, e^{-2t} - 10\, e^{-t}$$

hence at $t=0^+$, $i(0^+)$ being 10 A,

$$10 = K - 10.$$

$$\therefore \quad K = 20.$$

Finally, therefore,

$$\boldsymbol{i(t) = (20\, e^{-2t} - 10\, e^{-t})\ \text{A}.}$$

EXAMPLE 5.35 *In the circuit of Fig. E5.21, find i (t) at $t = 0^+$ following switching of S from (1) to (2). Assume steady state of the circuit while S was at (1).*

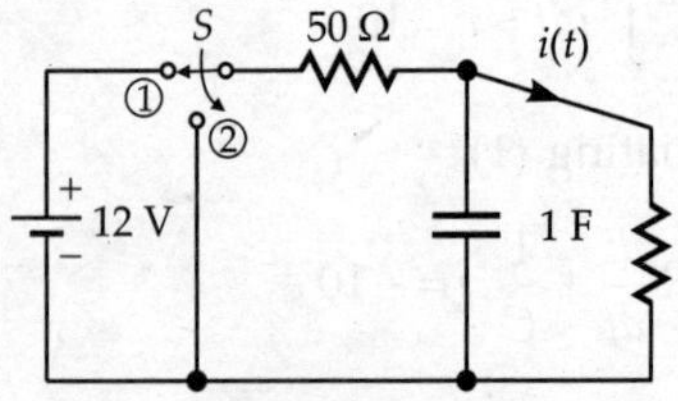

Fig. E5.21

SOLUTION. When the switch was at (1), following Fig. E5.22, at steady state, capacitor being fully charged, $i_0 = i$.

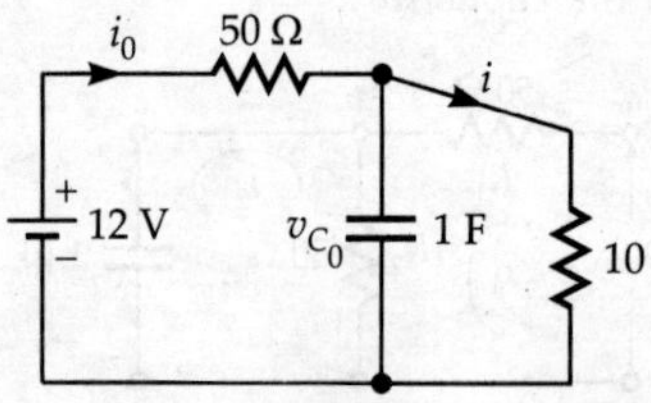

Fig. E5.22

Also, $$i = \frac{12}{50+10} = \frac{1}{5} \text{ A}$$

The drop in 50 Ω resistor being $\left(50 \times \frac{1}{5}\right)$ or 10 V, the voltage across the capacitor is 12 – 10 *i.e.,* 2 V.

Hence $i(t)$ at $t = 0(-) = \frac{1}{5}$ A,

$$v_{C_0}\ (i.e.,\ v_C \text{ at } t=0) = 2 \text{ V}.$$

Following switching of S from (1) to (2), the voltage source is removed and the capacitor will start discharging through 10 Ω in parallel to 50 Ω resistor.

$i(t)$ at $t = 0^+$ (current through 10 Ω resistor at $t=0$)

$$= \frac{2\text{V}}{10\,\Omega} = \frac{1}{5} \text{ A}$$

However,

$$i(t) = C_1 + C_2\, e^{-t/RC} \qquad ...(a)$$

But $$RC = 1 \times \frac{10 \times 50}{10+50} = 8.33 \text{ sec.}$$

Also at $t=0$, $i = \frac{1}{5}$ A;

thus at $t=0$, $C_1 + C_2 = \frac{1}{5}$ A

Also, for $i(t)$ at $t = \infty$,

$i(t) = 0$ [∵ the capacitor discharges completely]

i.e., $C_1 + C_2\, e^{-\infty} = 0$ or $C_1 = 0$

This gives $C_2 = \frac{1}{5}$.

Thus the complete response from (*a*) is obtained as –0.12

$$\boldsymbol{i(t) = \frac{1}{5}\, e^{-0.12\,t}.}$$

Example 5.36 *Given : v_C at time $(t_0) = 10$ V; v_C at time (t) = 25 V $(t > t_0)$. Obtain the expression for v_C (t) (Fig. E5.23).*

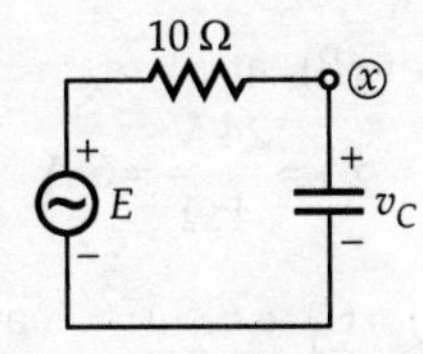

Fig. E5.23

Solution. The capacitance voltage being unable to change suddenly,

$$v_C(t_0^+) = v_C(t_0) = v_c(t_0^-) = 10 \text{ V}$$

Application of KCL at node x in the circuit of Fig. E5.23 yields

$$\frac{v_C - E}{10} + \frac{1}{C}\frac{dv_C}{dt} = 0$$

or,
$$\frac{v_C - E}{10} + \frac{dv_C}{dt} = 0$$

giving
$$0.1\, v_C + \frac{dv_C}{dt} = 0.1 \text{ E}$$

or,
$$v_C\,(p + 0.1) = 0.1 \text{ E},$$

p being the operator.

The characteristic equation being $S + 0.1 = 0$, the single root of this equation is $S_1 = -0.1$. The complementary solution is thus given by

$$v_{C_{\text{comp}}} = C_1\, e^{-0.1\,t} \qquad ...(1)$$

The particular solution is

$$v_C = \frac{0.1}{0 + 0.1}(25) = 25 \text{ V}$$

$$[\because v_C\,(t) \text{ at } t > t_0 = 25 \text{ V}]$$

∴ The complete solution is

$$v_C = v_{C_{\text{comp}}} + v_{C_{\text{part}}} = C_1\, e^{-0.1\,t} + 25$$

Using initial condition,

$$v_C(t_0^+) = 10 = 25 + C_1\, e^{-0.1\,t_0}$$

or,
$$C_1\, e^{-0.1\,t_0} = -15$$

∴
$$C_1 = -15\, e^{0.1\,t_0}$$

Thus,
$$v_C\,(t) = \mathbf{25 - 15\, e^{-0.1\,(t - t_0)}}.$$

Example 5.37 *With application of a step input signal across an inductor, the current in the inductor is $(1 - e^{-0.5\,t})$ at $t = 0^+$, the initial current through the inductor being zero. If there is also an additional current of $0.75\, e^{-0.5\,t}$ through the inductor at $t = 0^+$, what would be value of net transient current at $t = 0^+$?*

Solution. As, with zero initial current and applying step signal $i_L = 1 - e^{-0.5\,t}$ A, hence, the transient current would be $e^{-0.5\,t}$ A through the inductor. Also, another transient current of $0.75\, e^{-0.5\,t}$ A flows through the inductor at same time due to another parallel source.

$$\therefore\ I_{\text{transient}}\,(\text{net}) = e^{-0.5\,t} + 0.75\, e^{-0.5\,t}$$

[Superposition theorem]

or, Net transient current = $\mathbf{1.75\, e^{-0.5\,t}}$ **A**.

Example 5.38 *Find the expression of discharging voltage of the capacitor at $t = 0+$ following switching at $t = 0$ (Fig. E5.24).*

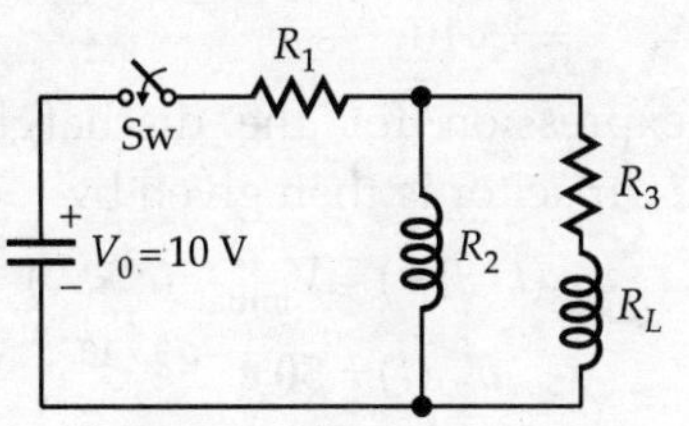

[V_0 = initial voltage across the capacitor]

Fig. E5.24

Solution. The capacitor is removed. The net impedance of the circuit through the open circuited terminals will then be

$$R_{th} = [(R_3 + R_L) \,||\, R_2] + R_1$$
$$= [6 \,||\, 6] + 1 = 4\,\Omega$$

The initial voltage across the capacitor being 10 V (V_0), the expression for the discharge voltage would be

$$v_C\,(t) = V_0\, e^{-t/RC} = 10\, e^{-t/4\times 1}$$
$$= \mathbf{10\, e^{-t/4}\ V.}$$

Example 5.39 *Find the expression of voltage across the capacitor following switching at $t = 0$ if the stored initial voltage (v_C (0)) is 50 V. What would be the time constant of the discharging circuit (Fig. E5.25)?*

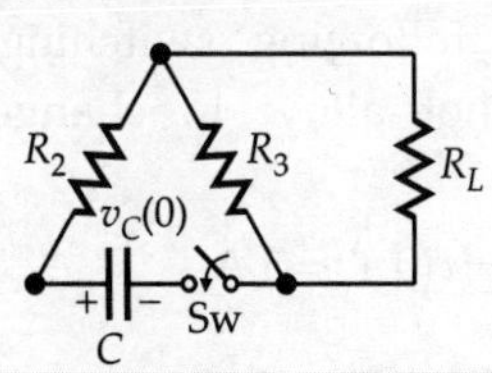

[$R_3 = R_L = 4\,\Omega$, $R_2 = 1\,\Omega$, C = 100 μF]

Fig. E5.25

Solution. At $t=0^+$, the circuit is redrawn in Fig. E5.26. The net resistance of the discharging circuit would be

$$(R_3 \,||\, R_L)+R_2=3\,\Omega$$

i.e., $R_{net}=3\,\Omega$

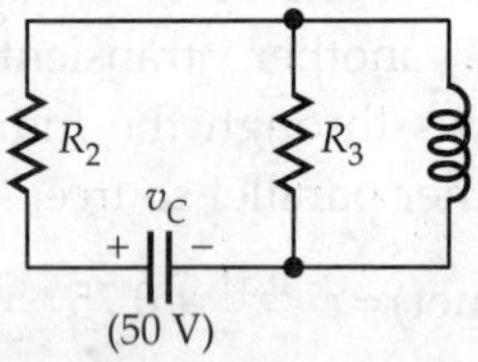

Fig. E5.26

Time constant being given by τ,

$$\tau = RC = 3\times 100\times 10^{-6} = \mathbf{3\times 10^{-4}\ sec.};$$

i.e., time constant of the discharging circuit

$$=3\times 10^{-4}\text{ sec.}$$

The expression for the discharging voltage across the capacitor is then given by

$$v_C\,(t=0+)=V_{initial}\,(e^{-t/\tau})$$

or, $$v_C\,(t)=\mathbf{50\,e^{-t/3\times 10^{-9}}\ V.}$$

Example 5.40 *Find i (t) following switching of K at t = 0 in the circuit of Fig. E5.27 from (A) to (B).*

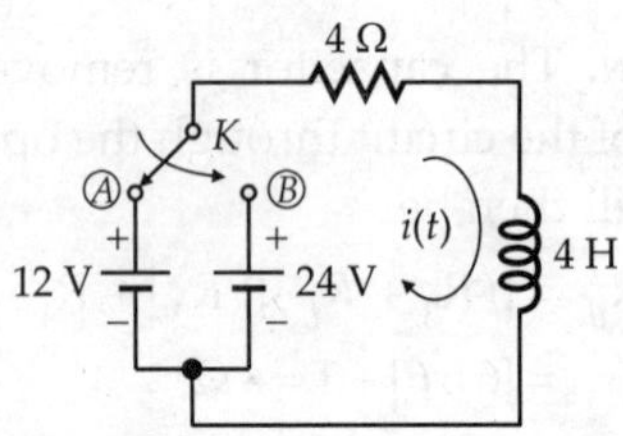

Fig. E5.27

Solution. In Fig. E5.27, *K* is at (*A*) for steady state condition.

$\therefore$ Current through the inductor is given by

$$i_{st.\,state}=\frac{12}{4}=3\text{ A}$$

[Inductor acts as s.c. at steady state]

i.e., $i\,(0-)=3$ A.

Obviously, following switching at $t=0$, the inductor will not allow to change the current through it.

$$\therefore\quad i\,(0-)=i\,(0+)=3\text{ A}$$

Also, $i\,(t)=C_1+C_2\,e^{-\lambda t}$

when $$\lambda=\frac{R}{L}=\frac{4}{4}=1\text{ sec.}$$

At $t=0$, $i=3$ A.

$$\therefore\quad C_1+C_2\,e^0=3$$

or $$C_1+C_2=3 \qquad ...(1)$$

Following *K* at (*B*), at $t=\infty$,

$$i\,(t=\infty)=\frac{24\text{ V}}{4\,\Omega}=6\text{ A}$$

$\therefore$ From $i\,(t)=C_1+C_2\,e^{-\lambda t}$, at $t=\infty$,

$$C_1+C_2\,.0=6 \quad\text{or,}\quad C_1=6 \qquad ...(2)$$

This gives $C_2=-3$.

Thus the complete response is

$$i\,(t)=6+(-3)\,e^{-1.t} \quad\text{or}\quad \mathbf{i\,(t)=6-3e^{-t}\ A.}$$

Example 5.41 *Find the current through C at t = 0 + following switching of S at t = 0 [Fig. E5.28].*

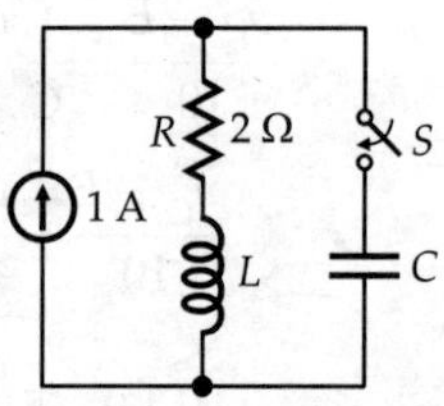

Fig. E5.28

Solution. When the switch was open, the current source drives the current of 1 A through *R-L* circuit, *i.e.,* $i\,(0-)=1$ A. (Fig. E5.28(*a*)).

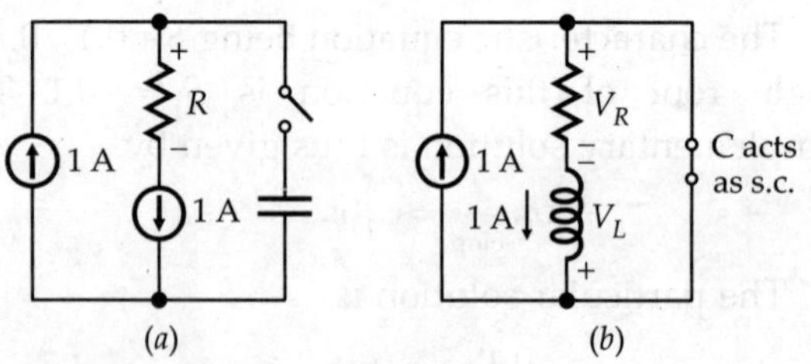

Fig. E5.28

Following switching at $t=0$, the capacitor acts as short circuit; however, inductor current would remain at 1 A as the inductor does not allow the current to change at $t=0^+$ (Fig. E5.28(*b*)).

Obviously

$$V_R+V_L=0$$

or, $$V_L=-V_R=-1\times 2=-2\text{ V.}$$

i.e., the voltage developed across the inductor due to switching is 2 V but in the polarity as shown in Fig. E5.28(*b*). It is thus evident that the current through the capacitor is zero as the current driven by the V_L source through C is opposite to that of the current source.

i.e., $i\,(0+)=\mathbf{0}$ **(through the capacitor).**

EXAMPLE 5.42 *If a step signal u(t) is applied across a RC circuit, the expression of voltage is given by*

$$v_C(t) = (1 - e^{-t})\,V,$$

the RC circuit being initially at rest.

If there is an initial voltage of 1 V on the capacitor and the input signal is 3u(t), find the expression for $v_C(t)$.

SOLUTION. Following a step signal input,

$$v_C(t) = 1 - e^{-t}.$$

Now as V_0, the initial voltage, is 1 Volt on the capacitor,

$$v_C(t)_1 = 1.e^{-t} = e^{-t}\ \text{V}.$$

If the step signal of $3u(t)$ is now applied,

$$v_C(t)_2 = (3 - 3e^{-t})\ \text{V}.$$

Thus following the theorem of superposition, the net voltage is given by

$$v_C(t) = e^{-t} + 3 - 3e^{-t} = \mathbf{(3 - 2e^{-t})\ V}.$$

EXAMPLE 5.43 *In Fig. E5.29, find the expression for currents and voltages through the inductor L and resistances R_1 and R_2 after the switch is opened. Assume steady state initial condition with the switch closed at t = 0(−). [L= 1 H, $R_1 = R_2 = 10\,\Omega$]*

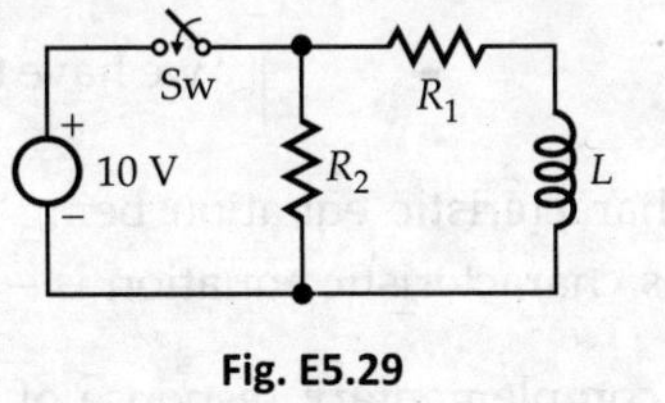

Fig. E5.29

SOLUTION. As soon as the switch is opened at $t = 0$, the inductor would start to discharge the energy it stored through $(R_1 + R_2)$.

Thus, the time constant of the discharging circuit is given by

$$\tau = \frac{L}{R_1 + R_2} = \frac{1}{20} = 0.05\ \text{sec.}$$

i_L being the discharging current, the discharging circuit is shown in Fig. E5.29(*a*).

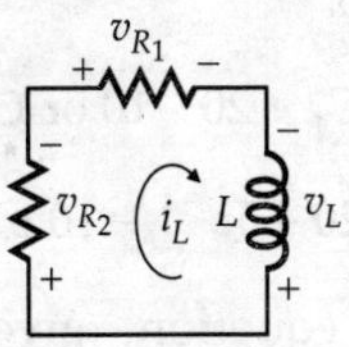

Fig. E5.29 (*a*)

Here applying KVL in the discharging loop,

$$v_L = v_{R_1} + v_{R_2} = i_L(R_1 + R_2)$$

As the current through the inductor cannot be changed instantly hence i_L will be maintained same to $i_L(0-)$ *i.e.*, the same on the current in the inductor before switching.

Obviously,

$$i_L(0^-) = \frac{10}{R_1} = \frac{10}{10} = 1\,\text{A}\,(= i_L(0^+))$$

Thus we get

$$v_L = 1(R_1 + R_2) = 20\ \text{V}\ (t = 0)$$

In the discharging circuit, this 20 V is the initial voltage.

$$\therefore \quad v_L(t) = 20\,e^{-t/\tau} = 20\,e^{-t/0.05} = \mathbf{20\,e^{-20t}\ V}$$

$$\text{and} \quad i_L(t) = i_{L(t=0)}\,e^{-t/\tau} = e^{-20t}\ \text{A}$$

$$v_{R_1} = i_L(t) \times R_1 = \mathbf{10\,e^{-20t}\ V}$$

$$v_{R_2} = i_L(t) \times R_2 = \mathbf{10\,e^{-20t}\ V.}$$

EXAMPLE 5.44 *In Fig. E5.30, $L_1 = L_2 = 1$ H; $R_1 = R_2 = 5\,\Omega$; $I_0 = 10$ A. If $R_L = 1\Omega$, find the drop across R_L at $t = 0+$ following open switching of the "S" at $t = 0$. Assume steady state before switching.*

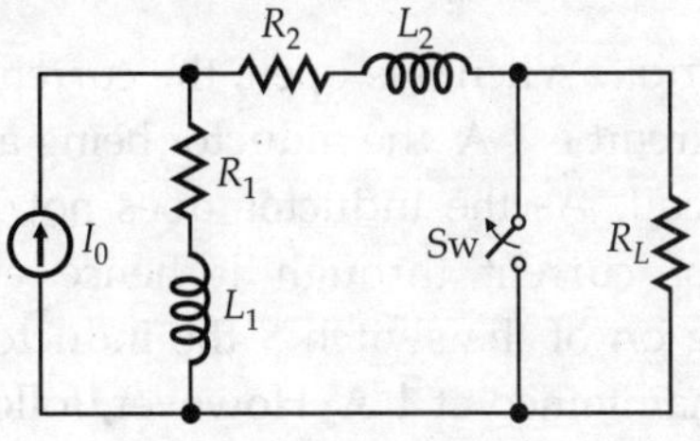

Fig. E5.30

SOLUTION. When the switch was closed, steady state is achieved and if switch is opened at $t = 0$, the steady state current that was flowing through L_2 is given by

$$i_{L_2}(0^-) = I_0 \times \frac{R_2}{R_1 + R_2}$$

[Note that L_1 and L_2 both act as *s.c.* at steady state. Also, the switch bypasses R_L]

$$= 10 \times \frac{5}{10} = 5\ \text{A.}$$

Fig. E5.31 represents the circuit at $t = 0^+$.

CHAPTER 5

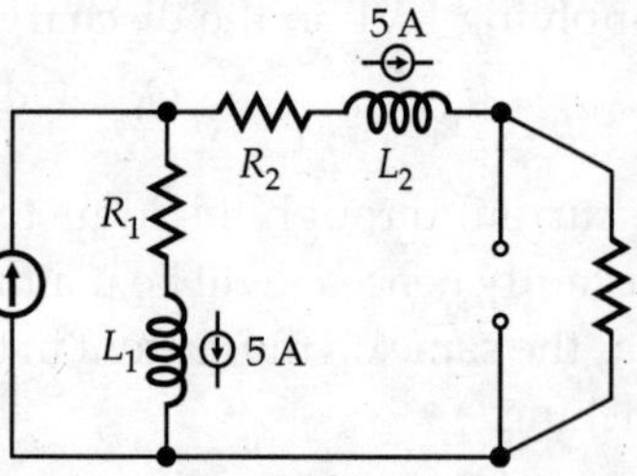

Fig. E5.31 Represents the current.

As the current through L_1 and L_2 cannot charge instantly, hence current $i_{L_2}(0^+)$ will be same as $i_{L_2}(0^-)$. Thus current through R_L will now be $i_L(0^+)$ *i.e.*, 5 A.

$\therefore\ v_{R_L}$ (drop across R_L) $= 5 \times R_L = 5 \times 1 = 5$ V.

$\therefore$ Drop in $R_L = \mathbf{5\ V}$.

EXAMPLE 5.45 *In Fig. E5.32, S is switched on at t = 0. Find $\frac{di}{dt}$ in the inductor following switching.*

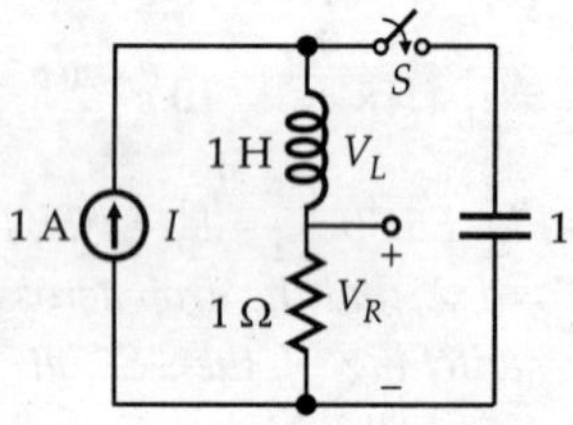

Fig. E5.32

SOLUTION. When *S* is open, the current through the *R-L* circuit is 1 A, the inductor being acting as a short circuit. As the inductor does not allow the change of current through it hence even after switching on of the switch *S* the inductor current will be maintained at 1 A. However, following the switching, the capacitor will act as short circuit. At $t = 0^+$, the configuration of the circuit is shown in Fig. E5.32(*a*).

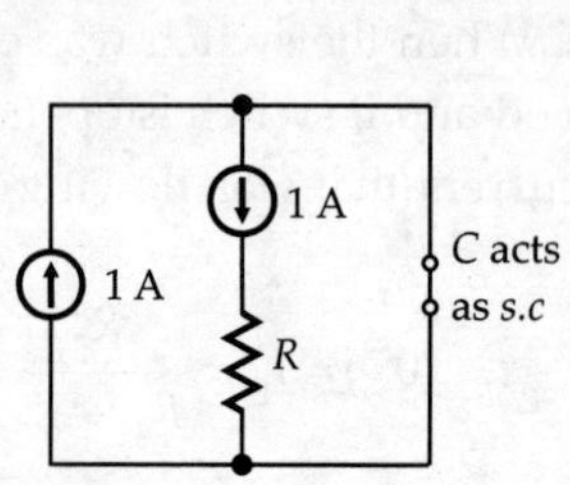

Fig. E5.32 (*a*)

At $t = 0^+$, $\quad V_R + V_L = 0$

But $\quad V_R = 1\,A \times 1\,\Omega = 1\,V$

$\therefore \quad V_L = -V_R = -1$ V.

But $\quad V_L = L\dfrac{di}{dt}$

or $\quad \dfrac{di}{dt} = \dfrac{V_L}{L} = -\dfrac{1}{1} = \mathbf{-1\ A/sec.}$

EXAMPLE 5.46 *In the circuit of Fig. E5.33, the initial voltage stored being 5 V at the polarities shown, find $v_C(t)$ [Fig. E5.33 is the circuit at $t = 0^+$].*

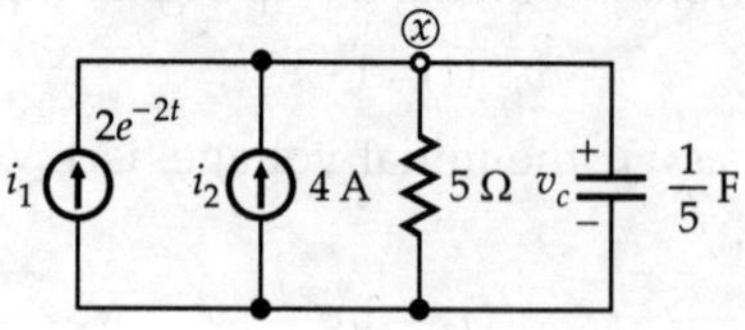

Fig. E5.33

SOLUTION. Applying KCL at $t = 0^+$ at the node (*x*), we get

$$-2e^{-2t} - 4 + \frac{1}{5}v_c + \frac{1}{5}\frac{dv_C}{dt} = 0$$

$$\left[\because C = \frac{1}{5}\text{ F and current through resistance} = \frac{v_C}{5}\right]$$

or, $\quad 0.2\,v_C + 0.2\dfrac{dv_C}{dt} = 4 + 2\,e^{-2t}$

or, $\quad v_C\,(p+1) = 20 + 10\,e^{-2t}$

$$\left[\because \text{we have taken } p \equiv \frac{d}{dt}\right]$$

The characteristic equation being $S + 1 = 0$, the root of this characteristic equation is -1.

$\therefore$ The complementary response of the solution is

$$v_{C(c)} = C_1\,e^{-t} \qquad ...(1)$$

The particular response is obtained as follows :

$$v_p = \frac{20}{0+1} + \frac{10\,e^{-2t}}{-2+1} = 20 - 10\,e^{-2t}$$

$\therefore$ The complete response is

$$v_c = C_1\,e^{-t} + 20 - 10\,e^{-2t}$$

At $t = 0$, $v_c = 5$.

$\therefore \quad 5 = C_1 + 20 - 10$ or $C_1 = -5$

Thus $v_c(t) = \mathbf{20 - 5e^{-t} - 10\,e^{-2t}}$ **V.**

The above equation gives the complete response of the capacitor voltage at $t = 0(+)$.

EXAMPLE 5.47 *Find the steady state voltage across the capacitor as well as R_L (Fig. E5.34). If the current source is removed at $t=0$, find the current through R_L and the drop across it at $t=0+$.*

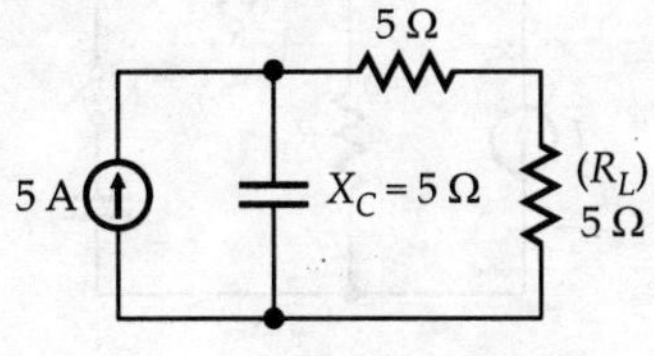

Fig. E5.34

SOLUTION. With 5 A d.c. source, X_C will be charged at $t=\infty$ (steady state).

$$\therefore \quad v_C\ (t=\infty)=5\left(\frac{1}{X_C}\right)=1\text{ V}$$

i.e., Steady state voltage drop across X_C is **1 Volt.**

At steady state, no current will pass through X_C (which would have 1 V p.d. across it with +ve polarity at the upper plate)

Thus the capacitor would act as open circuit (Fig. E5.34(*a*)).

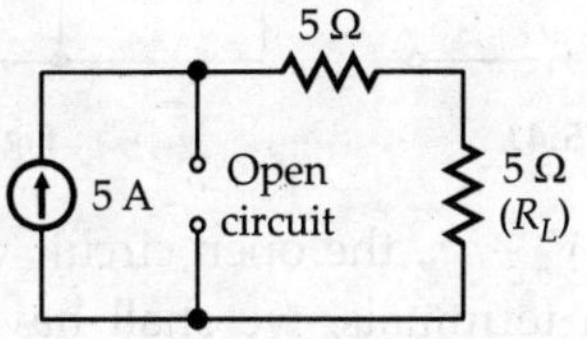

Fig. E5.34 (*a*)

Thus, steady state voltage across R_L is given by

$$v_{R_L}=i_{R_L}\times R_L=5\times 5=25\text{ V}$$

[$\because$ current through $R_L=5$ A]

As soon as the current source is removed, the capacitor would start discharging through the right hand loop of Fig. E5.34(*a*)

The discharge current at $t=0^+$ will be given by

$$i_{\text{dis.}}\ (t=0^+)=\frac{v_C(0^+)}{5+5}=0.1\text{ A}$$

[$\because v_C\ (0^+)$ would be same at $v_C\ (0^-)$]

Thus, the current through $R_L=0.1$ A while the drop across R_L due to discharge current is given by

$$v_{R_L}\ (0^+)=0.1\times 5=\mathbf{0.5\ V.}$$

EXAMPLE 5.48 *In Fig. E5.35, find the current through inductor at $t=0^+$ as well as the voltage after closing "S" at $t=0$.*

$V_S=10$ V ; $R_1=10\,\Omega$
$R_2=5\,\Omega$, $R_L=1\,\Omega$;
$L=0.5$ H

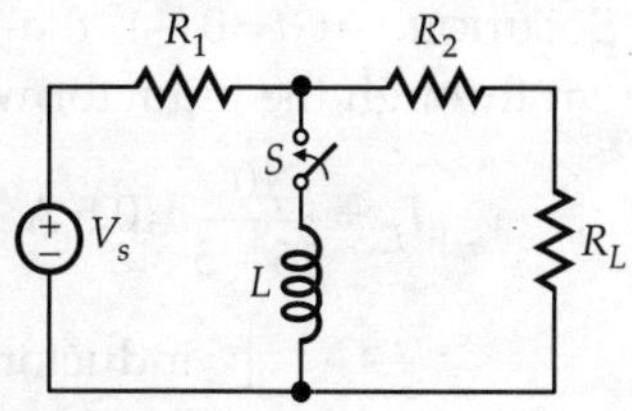

Fig. E5.35

SOLUTION. The inductor L is removed first. Fig. E5.35(*a*) represents the circuit to find R_{th}.

$$\text{Here,}\quad R_{th}=R_1\,||\,(R_2+R_L)=\frac{10\times 6}{10+6}=3.75\,\Omega$$

$$\therefore \quad \tau\text{ (time constant)}=\frac{L}{R_{th}}=\frac{0.5}{3.75}=0.133\text{ sec.}$$

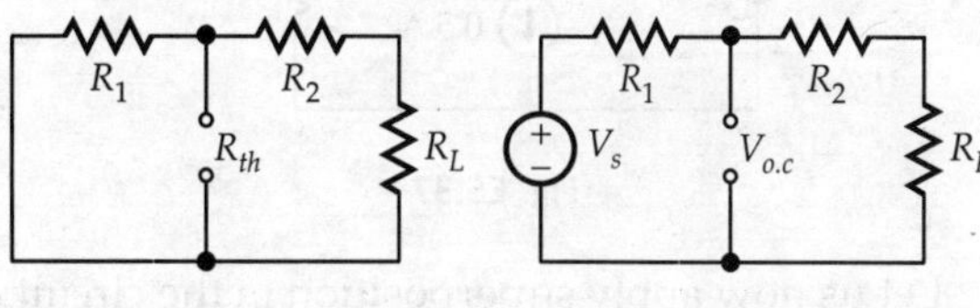

Fig. E5.35

Figure E5.35(*b*) represents the circuit to find $V_{o.c}$ across the open circuited terminal.

$$V_{o.c}=V_s-\frac{V_s}{R_1+R_2+R_L}\,.\,R_1$$

$$=10-\frac{10}{16}=9.375\text{ V.}$$

$\therefore$ Current through the inductor is given by

$$i_L\ (t)=\frac{V_{o.c}}{R_{th}}(1-e^{-t/\tau})=\frac{9.375}{3.75}(1-e^{-t/0.133})$$

or, $\quad i_L\ (t)=2.5\,(1-e^{-7.52\,t})$ A.

and $\quad v_L\ (t)=V_{o.c}\ e^{-t/\tau}=9.375\,e^{-t/0.133}$

or, $\quad v_L\ (t)=\mathbf{9.375\ e^{-7.52\,t}\ V.}$

EXAMPLE 5.49 *With switch open in the circuit of Fig. E5.36, steady state is reached. Find the net current in the 10 Ω resistor after switching of K.*

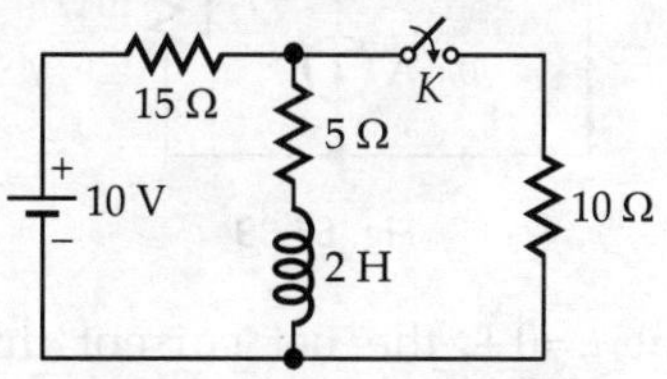

Fig. E5.36

CHAPTER 5

Solution. At $t = 0\,(-)$, the switch being open, current through the inductor was

$$I_L = \frac{10}{15+5} = 0.5\text{ A}$$

[∵ inductor acts at short circuit at steady state with d.c. excitation]

Thus the inductor will retain this current of 0.5 A at $t = 0\,(+)$ following switching of K and then act as an independent current source of 0.5 A at $t = 0\,(+)$. The circuit at $t = 0^+$ would then be like that shown in Fig. E5.37.

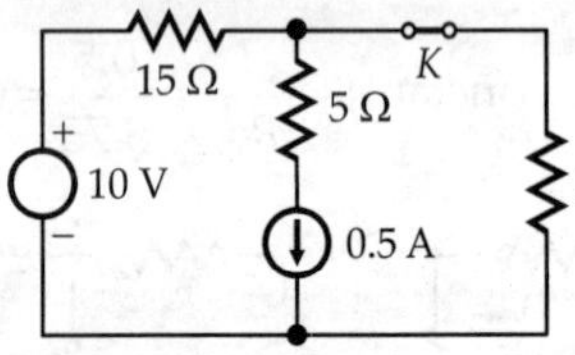

Fig. E5.37

Let us now apply superposition in the circuit of Fig. E5.37.

With 10 V source alone, the source current I_1 (Fig. E5.38) is given by

$$I_1 = \frac{10}{25} = 0.4\text{ A}$$

[*i.e.*, the current through 10 Ω resistor]

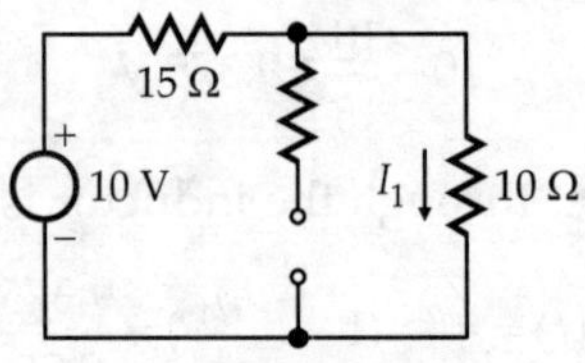

Fig. E5.38

Again, with 0.5 A current source (Fig. E5.39), the current in the 10 Ω resistor is

$$I_2 = 0.5 \times \frac{15}{10+15} = 0.5 \times 0.6 = 0.3\text{ A.}$$

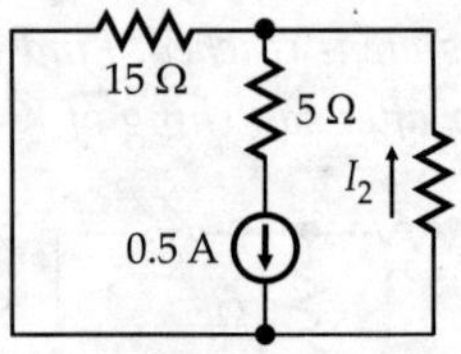

Fig. E5.39

Thus at $t = 0+$, the net current through 10 Ω resistor is given by $I_1 - I_2 = 0.4 - 0.3 = $ **0.1 A going downwards.**

Example 5.50 *Find the expression of voltage across the capacitor C in Fig. E5.40.*

[$R_1 = 10\,\Omega$, $R_2 = 5\,\Omega$, $C = 50\,\mu F$]

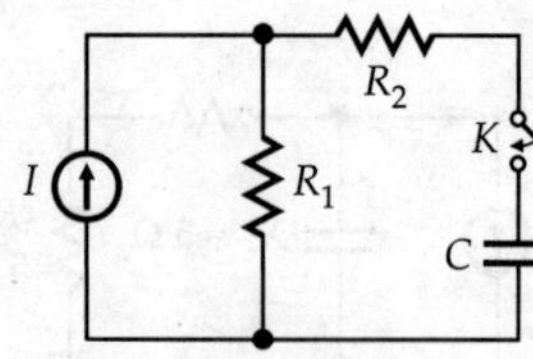

Fig. E5.40

Solution. Keeping K open, effect of C being nil, if we look back through the open circuited terminals of the network after removing C, the net internal resistance (or in general term impedance) is $R_1 + R_2$ which is actually Thevenin's impedance (it may be recalled that to find Thevenin's impedance, the current source is to be removed (ref. Fig. E5.41).

$$\therefore \quad Z_{th} = R_1 + R_2 = 15\,\Omega\,(\equiv R_{th})$$

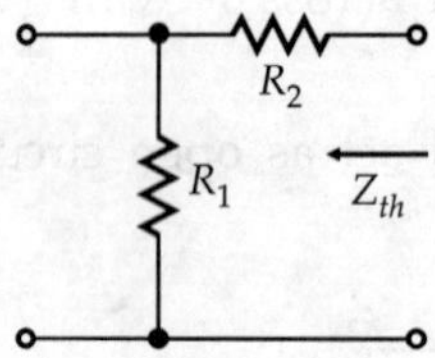

Fig. E5.41

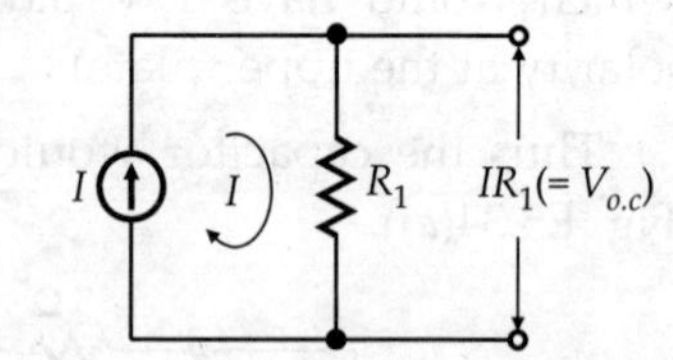

Fig. E5.42

To find $V_{o.c}$ *i.e.*, the open circuit voltage at the open switch terminals, we shall have to find the drop across R_1 (Fig. E5.42).

i.e., $\quad V_{o.c} = IR_1 = 1 \times 10 = 10\text{ V}$

This $V_{o.c}$ is the steady state voltage across as C after switching of K (for the d.c. source I).

$$\therefore \quad v_C(t) = V_{o.c}\,(1 - e^{-t/R_{Th}\cdot C})$$

$$= 10\,(1 - e^{-t/15 \times 50 \times 10^{-6}})$$

or, $\quad$ $\mathbf{v_C(t) = 10\,(1 - e^{-t/75 \times 10^{-5}})\text{ V.}}$

where $v_C(t)$ is the expression of voltage across the capacitor being charged by the source I.

Example 5.51 *In Fig. E5.43, find the expression for current at $t = 0+$, following switching (opening of S). Assume steady state when S was closed.*

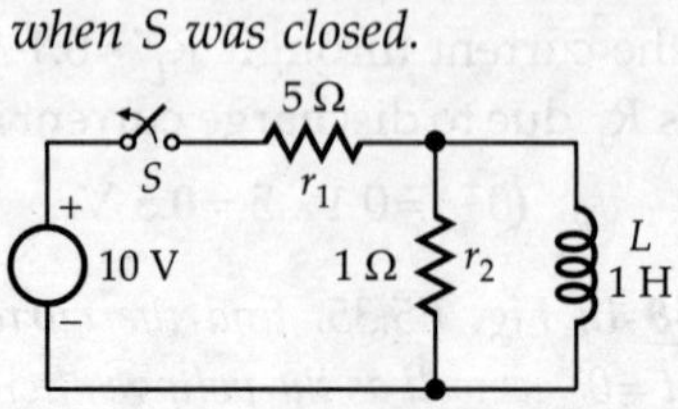

Fig. E5.43

Solution. At steady state, the switch being closed, L acts as short circuit.

$$\therefore \quad i(0^-) = \frac{10}{r_1} = 2 \text{ A.}$$

Also, the current through the inductor is 2 A at $t = 0^-$. Following opening of the switch, the voltage source is removed and the inductor would start discharging through r_2. The initial current I_0 being 2 A, the decaying current through L would be

$$i(t) = I_0\, e^{-\frac{r_2}{L}.t} = 2e^{-1.t} \quad [\text{at } t = 0+]$$

or, $$i(t) = \mathbf{2e^{-t}\ A}$$

[the direction of $i(t)$ would be clockwise in the $L - r_2$ loop].

***Example 5.52** In the circuit of Fig. E5.44, find $v_c(t)$ and $i_c(t)$ following switching on the capacitor at $t = 0$. [$R_1 = R_2 = 10\,\Omega$, $R_3 = 5\,\Omega$, $C = 100\,\mu$F, $V = 20$ volts]*

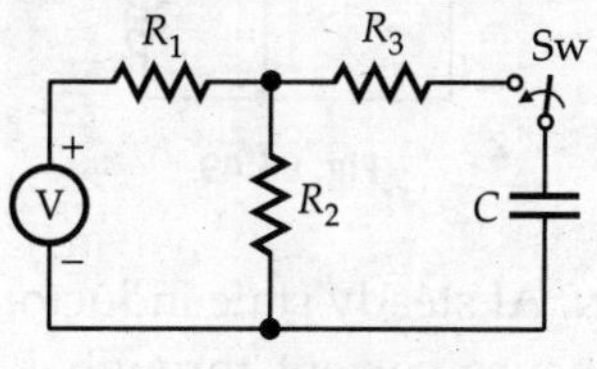

Fig. E5.44

Solution. Let us first remove the capacitor and try to find the net impedance (*i.e.*, the Thevenin resistance) of the circuit (Fig. E5.45).

$$R_{th} = (R_1 \,||\, R_2) + R_3 = \frac{10 \times 10}{10 + 10} + 5 = 10\,\Omega$$

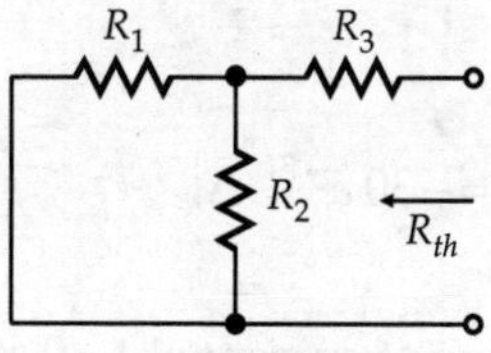

Fig. E5.45

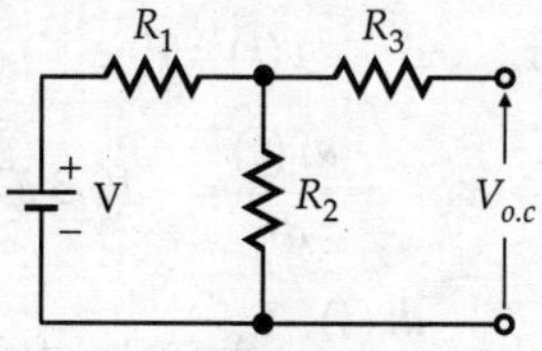

Fig. E5.46

To find $V_{o.c}$ across the removed capacitor terminal, we draw the circuit again as shown in Fig. E5.46.

$$\text{Here,}\quad V_{o.c} = \frac{VR_2}{R_1 + R_2}$$

$$= \frac{20}{10 + 10}.10 = 10 \text{ V.}$$

Obviously, $V_{o.c}$ would be the final voltage across C.

$$\therefore \quad v_C(t) = V_{o.c}(1 - e^{-t/\tau})$$

where $$V_{o.c} = 10 \text{ V}; \tau = R_{th} C$$

$$= 10 \times 100 \times 10^{-6} = 10^{-3} \text{ sec.}$$

This gives

$$v_C(t)\Big|_{t=0^+} = \mathbf{10\,(1 - e^{-10^3\,t})\ V}$$

and obviously

$$i_C(t) = \frac{V_{o.c}}{R_{th}} e^{-t/RC} = \frac{10}{10} e^{-t/10^{-3}} = e^{-10^3\,t}$$

i.e., $$i_C(t)\Big|_{t=0^+} = \mathbf{e^{-10^3\,t}\ A.}$$

***Example 5.53** Fig. E5.47 represents a RC circuit at $t = 0+$; $v_C(0) = 10$ V. Find $v_C(t)$, $i_C(t)$ and $v(t)$.*

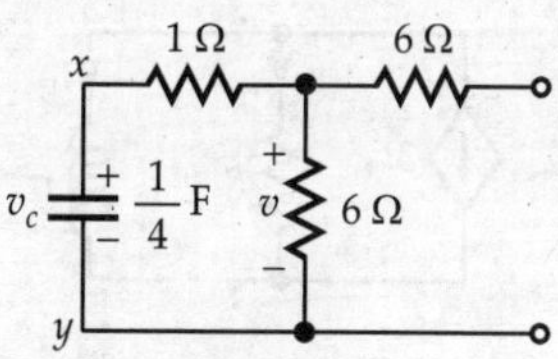

Fig. E5.47

Solution. The equivalent resistance across $x - y$ is

$$1 + \frac{6 \times 6}{6 + 6} = 4\,\Omega.$$

$\therefore$ Nodal equation at x at $t = 0+$ gives

$$\frac{v_C}{4} + C\frac{dv_C}{dt} = 0$$

or $$\frac{v_C}{4} + \frac{1}{4}\frac{dv_C}{dt} = 0$$

or, $$\frac{dv_C}{dt} + v_C = 0$$

or, $$v_C(p + 1) = 0 \qquad \text{...(1)}$$

(1) Gives the complementary solution as $v_{c_{comp}} = C_1 e^{-t}$ V. As the source is not a constant source, the differential equation relating v_C will not have any particular integral solution. Putting the initial condition [at $t = 0$, $v_C(0)$ being 10 V],

$$10 = C_1 \cdot e^{-0} \quad i.e., \; C_1 = 10$$

[C_1 being the constant]

$$\therefore \quad v_C(t) = \mathbf{10\,e^{-t}\ V.}$$

Obviously,

$$i_C(t) = C\frac{dv_C}{dt} = \frac{1}{4}[10(-1)e^{-t}] = \mathbf{-2.5\,e^{-t}\ A.}$$

[$-i_C(t)$ indicates discharging current and flows from the capacitor +ve plate towards the resistance network]

$$i_C(t) = -2.5\,e^{-t}\ \text{A}$$

$$v(t) = \left[i_C(t) \times \frac{6}{6+6}\right]6$$

$$= 3i_C(t) = (+7.50\,e^{-t})\ \text{V}$$

$$\boldsymbol{v(t) = 7.50\,e^{-t}\ \text{V}.}$$

[discharging current taken as +ve direction makes $i_c(t)$ +ve]

EXAMPLE 5.54 *If the initial current through the inductor be 1 A, find $i_L(t)$ at $t = 0+$ in the circuit of Fig. E5.48.*

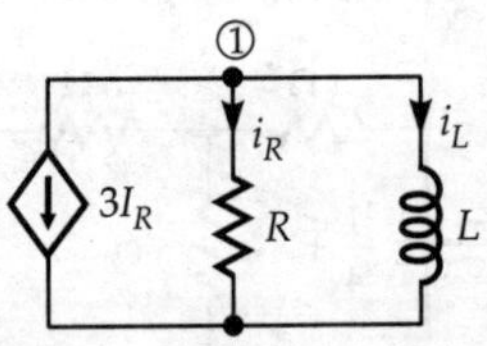

Fig. E5.48

SOLUTION. Using KCL at node (1),

$$3i_R + i_R + i_L = 0$$

or, $$4i_R + i_L = 0$$

But $i_R = \dfrac{v_1}{R}$ [actually directed upwards]

[let the voltage at node (1) be v_1]

$$\therefore \quad \frac{4v_1}{R} + i_L = 0 \qquad \text{...(1)}$$

However, v_1 is also the e.m.f induced in the inductor at $t = 0^+$

i.e., $$v_1 = L\frac{di_L}{dt} \qquad \left[\because v_1 = -L\frac{d(-i_L)}{dt}\right]$$

$$\therefore \text{ From (1)} \quad \frac{4L}{R}\frac{di_L}{dt} + i_L = 0.$$

i.e., $$\frac{di_L}{dt} + \frac{R}{4L}i_L = 0$$

or, $$i_L\left(p + \frac{R}{4L}\right) = 0 \qquad \text{...(2)}$$

Since the dependent source does not have any particular solution hence the differential equation given by (2) will not have any particular integral and will be containing only complementary solution.

$$\therefore \quad i_L = C_1\,e^{-R/4L\,.\,t}$$

Substitution of initial condition of i_L at $t = 0$ gives

$$\therefore \quad \boldsymbol{C_1 = 1\; i_L = e^{-R/4L\,.\,t}\ \text{A}.}$$

EXAMPLE 5.55 *An inductor of 10 H is suddenly disconnected from 100 V d.c. supply (Fig. E5.49). Find*

(a) the initial rate of change of current just after switching.

(b) initial voltage across R_0.

(c) the voltage across the switch at the instant of separation of contacts.

(d) the rate at which the coil loses energy 1 sec after switching.

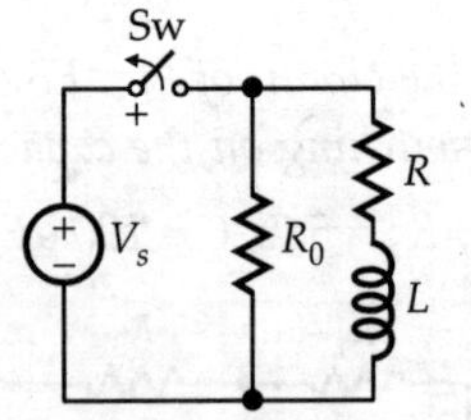

Fig. E5.49

SOLUTION. At steady state inductor acts as short circuit and hence current through L at $t = 0(-)$ is given by

$$I_0 = \frac{V_s}{R} = \frac{100}{10} = 10\ \text{A}$$

Following switching, at $t = 0^+$,

$$i(t) = I_0\,e^{-\frac{R+R_0}{L}\,.\,t} = 10\,e^{-\frac{10+20}{10}t}$$

or, $$i(t) = 10\,e^{-3t}\ \text{A}$$

$$\therefore \quad \frac{di(t)}{dt} = -10.3\,e^{-3t} = -30\,e^{-3t}\ \text{A},$$

when $\dfrac{di(t)}{dt}$ is the rate of change of current at $t = 0+$.

$\therefore$ Initial rate of change of current is **– 30 A/sec** and the –ve sign indicates that it is a discharging current (Fig. E5.50).

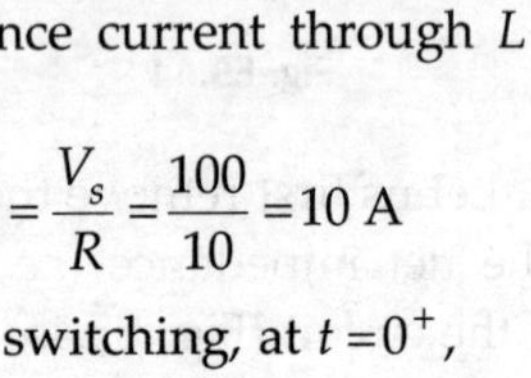

Fig. E5.50

$$\therefore \quad \left.\frac{di(t)}{dt}\right|_{\text{initial}} = -30 \text{ A/sec.}$$

Again, initial current being 10 A, the drop across R_0 is given by

$$v_{\text{drop}(R_0)} = R_0 \cdot I_0 = 20 \times 10 = \mathbf{200\ V.}$$

Due to property of inductance, the current through the inductor at $t = 0+$ would not change instantly and would remain 10 A. Let the voltage across the separated switch contacts be V. The circuit being shown in Fig. E5.51, KVL in the left loop yields

$$-V_S + V - (I_0) R_0 = 0$$

or, $\quad -100 + V - 10 \times 20 = 0$

or, $\quad V = 300$ V

$\therefore$ **Voltage across switch at $t = 0^+$ is 300 V.**

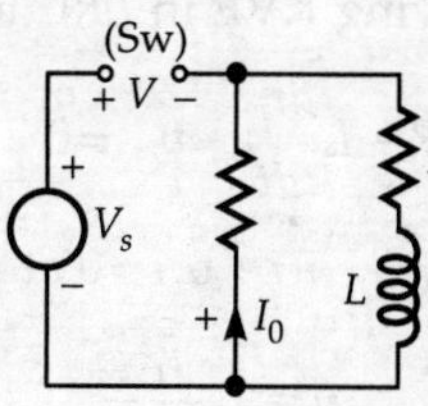

Fig. E5.51

Rate of energy in the inductance = power loss in inductance

$$= L\frac{di(t)}{dt} \times i_{\text{at 1 sec.}}$$

But $\quad \dfrac{di(t)}{dt} = -30\, e^{-3t}$

$\therefore$ at $t = 1$ sec,

$$\frac{di(t)}{dt} = -30\, e^{-3} = -1.5 \text{ A/sec.}$$

$\therefore$ Rate of energy loss

$$= 10 \times (-1.5) \times 0.5 = -7.47 \text{ J/sec.}$$

[i at $t = 1$ sec is given by

$$i(1 \text{ sec.}) = 10\, e^{-3.1} = 10\, e^{-3} \simeq 0.5 \text{ A}]$$

i.e., Rate of energy loss = **–7.47 W.**

[The –ve sign here indicates the reduction in energy storage]

EXAMPLE 5.56 *Find the voltage drop (V_L) across L at $t = 0(+)$ following switching in the circuit of Fig. E5.52.*

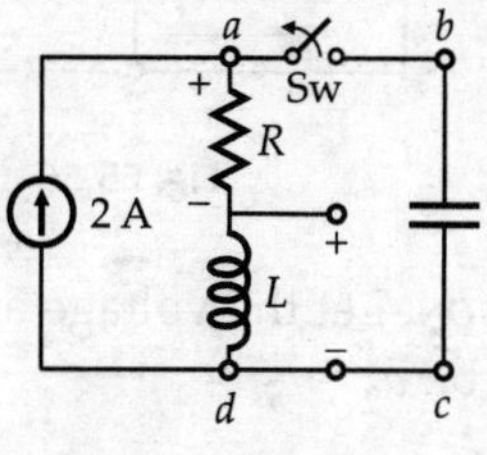

Fig. E5.52

SOLUTION. At $t = 0^+$, the capacitor 10 μF will act as short circuited. Thus the voltage across the capacitor at $t = 0+$ is given by $V_C(0^+) = 0$.

$\therefore$ In loop *abcd*, at $t = 0^+$, applying KVL, we can write,

$$V_R + V_L = 0 \qquad [\because V_R + V_L + V_C = 0 \text{ and } V_C = 0 \text{ at time } t = 0^+]$$

i.e., $\quad V_L = -V_R \qquad$ ...(1)

Again, before switching *i.e.,* at $t = 0(-)$, the current through the *R-L* circuit was $I(0-) = 2$ A. The source being a direct current source, the inductor was acting as a short circuit at $t = 0(-)$ when 2 A current was flowing through it. The voltage drop across the resistance at $t = 0(-)$ was $V_R = (2\text{A}) \times (1)\Omega$ *i.e.,* 2 V.

It may be noted here that the inductor would not allow the current at $t = 0(-)$ to die down at $t = 0(+)$ as it opposes any change of current through it by developing a back emf across itself. Obviously this back emf being V_L, we get from equation (1),

$$V_L = -V_R = \mathbf{-2\ V.}$$

$\therefore$ The drop across L at $t = (0+)$ would be –2 V which simply means a 2V drop with +ve polarity at "*d*".

EXAMPLE 5.57 *Given that current in the circuit at t = 0 is 5 A. Obtain i (t) at $t = 0^+$ (Fig. E5.53).*

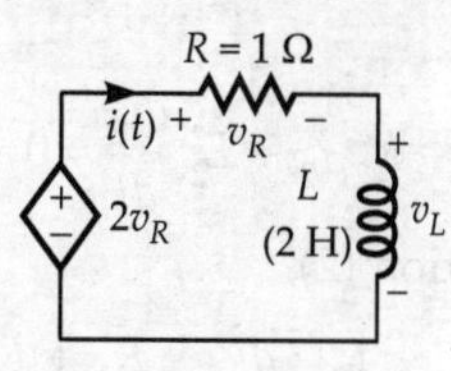

Fig. E5.53

SOLUTION. At $t = 0+$, the loop equation is given by

$$L\frac{di(t)}{dt} + i(t)\, R = 2v_R \qquad ...(i)$$

But $L = 2$ H; $R = 1\Omega$;

$$v_R = i(t)\, R = 1 \times i(t) = i(t).$$

$\therefore$ Equation (1) becomes,

$$2\,\frac{di(t)}{dt} + i(t) = 2\, i(t)$$

or, $$2\,\frac{d}{dt}[i(t)] - i(t) = 0$$

or, $$\frac{d}{dt}\, i(t) - 0.5\, i(t) = 0$$

CHAPTER 5

The characteristic equation of this differential equation being $(p-0.5)=0$, the equation has a single root given by

$$p_1 = 0.5.$$

The solution is thus given by

$$i(t) = Ce^{0.5t} \text{ A}, \quad C \text{ being the constant.}$$

Putting the initial condition,

i.e., at $t=0$, $\quad i(0) = 5$ A,

we get $\quad C = 5$.

The final solution thus becomes

$$i(t) = 5e^{+0.5t} \text{ A} \, [t > 0].$$

EXAMPLE 5.58 *Write down the differential equation for the circuit shown in Fig. E5.54 at $t = 0^+$.*

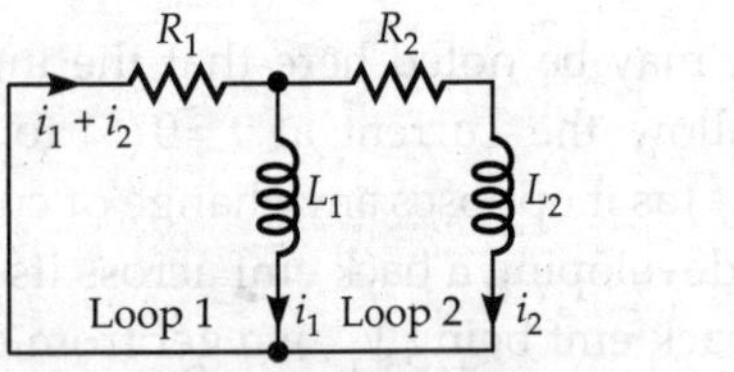

Fig. E5.54

SOLUTION. Application of KVL in loop-1, yields $(t = 0+)$

$$R_1(i_1 + i_2) + L_1 \frac{di_1}{dt} = 0 \quad \text{...(1)}$$

Application of KVL involving loop-1 and loop-2 yields

$$R_1(i_1 + i_2) + R_2 i_2 + L_2 \frac{di_2}{dt} = 0 \quad \text{...(2)}$$

From equation (2),

$$i_1 = -\frac{L_2}{R_1} \cdot \frac{di_2}{dt} - \frac{R_1 + R_2}{R_1} i_2 \quad \text{...(3)}$$

Substituting of (3) in (1), simplification yields

$$\frac{d^2 i_2}{dt^2} + \left(\frac{R_1 + R_2}{L_2} + \frac{R_1}{L_1} \right) \frac{di_2}{dt} + \frac{R_1 R_2}{L_1 L_2} i_2 = 0$$

...(4)

Equation (4) represents the second order differential equation describing the given circuit.

EXAMPLE 5.59 *Find* $\left.\frac{di_L}{dt}\right|_{t=0^+}$ *and* $\left.\frac{dv_C}{dt}\right|_{t=0^+}$ *in Fig. E5.55.*

SOLUTION. Using KCL at *node* (1),

$$i_L + i + \alpha i = 0 \quad \text{or} \quad i_L + i(1+\alpha) = 0$$

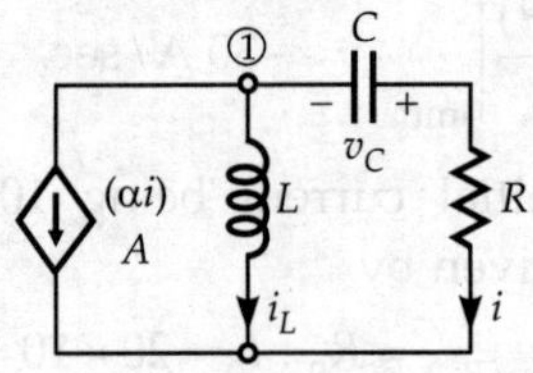

Fig. E5.55

But here $\quad -i = C \dfrac{dv_C}{dt}$

[assuming voltage in the capacitor as v_C]

or, $\quad (1+\alpha) C \dfrac{dv_C}{dt} = i_L$

$$\therefore \quad \frac{dv_C}{dt} = \frac{i_L}{(1+\alpha) C} \quad \text{...(1)}$$

Applying KVL in *LRC* loop,

$$iR - L\frac{di_L}{dt} - v_C = 0 \quad \text{...(2)}$$

But $\because$ $i_L + i + \alpha i = 0$ at node (1)

$$\therefore \quad i = -\frac{i_L}{1+\alpha}.$$

Using this expression of *i* in (2),

$$\frac{-i_L}{1+\alpha} R - L\frac{di_L}{dt} - v_C = 0$$

or, $$\frac{di_L}{dt} = -\frac{R}{L(1+\alpha)} i_L - \frac{1}{L} v_C \quad \text{...(3)}$$

Equations (1) and (3) give us the required values of

$$\frac{dv_C}{dt} \text{ and } \frac{di_L}{dt} \text{ at } t = 0^+.$$

EXAMPLE 5.60 *Find the voltage of the capacitor at $t = 0^+$ assuming no charge stored in the capacitor at $t = 0$].*

[Fig. E5.56 represents the circuit at $t = (0+)$]

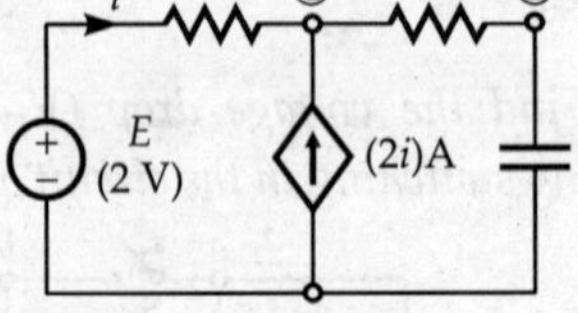

Fig. E5.56

SOLUTION. Let the voltage at node (1) be v_1 and that at (2) be v_2.

Applying KCL at node (1),

$$\frac{v_1 - v_2}{1} = 2i + i = 3i = 3\left(\frac{E - v_1}{3}\right)$$

or, $$v_1 - v_2 = E - v_1$$

or, $$2v_1 = E + v_2$$

$$\therefore \quad v_1 = \frac{E + v_2}{2} \qquad \text{...(1)}$$

Using KCL at node (2),

$$\frac{v_2 - v_1}{1} + C\frac{dv_2}{dt} = 0$$

or, $$v_2 - v_1 + \frac{dv_2}{dt} = 0$$

or, $$v_2 - \frac{E + v_2}{2} + \frac{dv_2}{dt} = 0$$

$$\left[\because v_1 = \frac{E + v_2}{2} \text{ from (1)}\right]$$

or, $$\frac{v_2}{2} + \frac{dv_2}{dt} = \frac{E}{2}$$

$$v_2\,(p + 0.5) = \frac{E}{2} \qquad \text{...(2)}$$

This differential equation would have a complementary as well as particular solution.

The complementary solution is

$$v_2\,(t)_{\text{comp.}} = C_1\, e^{-0.5t}$$

while the particular solution is

$$v_2\,(t)_{\text{part}} = \frac{E/2}{0.5} = 2\text{ V} \qquad [\because E = 2V]$$

$\therefore$ Complete solution is $v_2\,(t) = 2 + C_1\, e^{-0.5t}$

Application of initial condition $(v_2\,(0) = 0)$ yields,

$$C_1 = -2.$$

$$\therefore \quad \mathbf{v_2\,(t) = 2 - 2\,C_1 e^{-0.5\,t}\ V.}$$

EXAMPLE 5.61 *In the network of Fig. E5.57, find the current through the inductor for all values of t.*

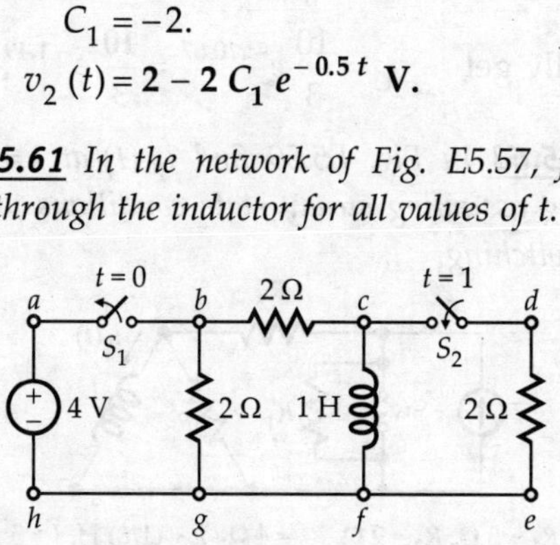

Fig. E5.57

SOLUTION. Case 1 : $(t < 0)$

At $t = 0\,(-)$ *i.e.*, when $t < 0$, the inductor would behave like a short circuit and as S_2 remained open while S_1 is closed, the current through 1 H inductor will be wholly determined by two 2 Ω resistances (Fig. E5.57(*a*)).

$$I = \frac{4}{\dfrac{2 \times 2}{2 + 2}} = 4\text{ A}$$

and $$I_L = 4\,\frac{2}{2 + 2} = \mathbf{2\ A.\ [i\,(0-)]}$$

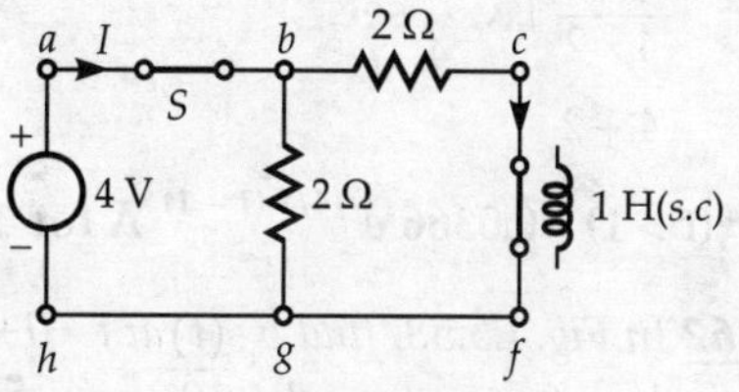

Fig. E5.57 (*a*)

Case 2 : $(0 < t < 1)$

The switch S_1 is now opened and S_2 too is open. The circuit configuration is shown in Fig. E5.57(*b*). As the inductance would try to retain its current of 2 A hence $i\,(0+) = i\,(0-) = 2$ A. The decaying current $I_L\ (0 < t < 1)$ is then given by

$$I_L = 2 \times e^{-\frac{4}{1}t} = \mathbf{2\,e^{-4t}\ A}$$

$$[\because L/R = 4/1 = 4 \text{ sec in Fig. E5.57}(b)]$$

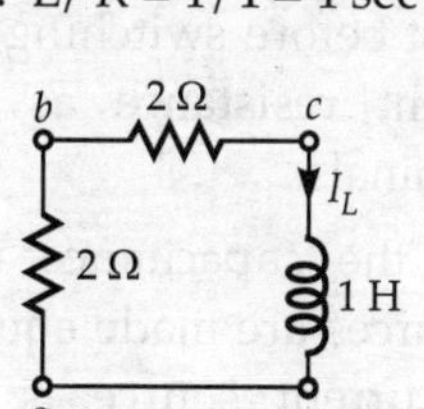

Fig. E5.57 (*b*)

Case 3 : $[t = 1\,(-)]$

Just before $t = 1$, $I_L = 2\,e^{-4.1} = 2\,e^{-4}$ A

i.e., $$I_L = \mathbf{0.0366\ A.}$$

Case 4 : $[t = 1+]$

Just after switching on S_2, the inductor current will remain same as I_L at $t = 1\,(-)$.

Hence at $t = 1+$, $I_L = \mathbf{0.0366\ A.}$

Case 5 : ($t > 1$)

The condition of the circuit is shown in Fig. 5.57(c).

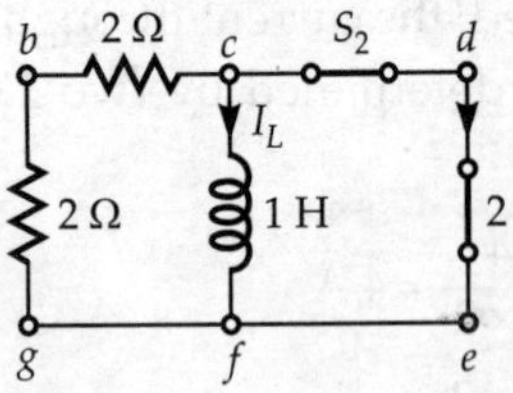

Fig. E5.57 (c)

Now, the time constant is L/R *i.e.,*

$$\frac{1}{\dfrac{4\times 2}{4+2}} \text{ i.e., } \frac{3}{4} \text{ sec.}$$

$\therefore$ $\mathbf{I_L\ (t > 1) = 0.0366\, e^{-4/3\,(t-1)}}$ **A for $1 < t$.**

EXAMPLE 5.62 *In Fig. E5.58, find $v_c\,(t)$ at $t = 0+$ while the switching is done from x to y at $t = 0$.*

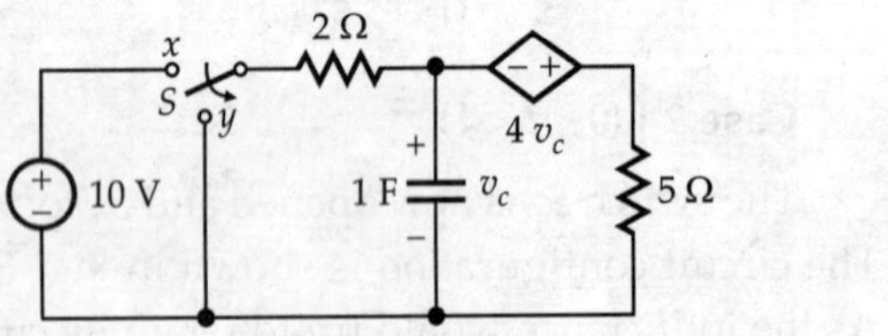

Fig. E5.58

SOLUTION. The voltage across the capacitor at $t > 0$ following switching at $t = 0$ from x to y is given by (discharging condition) $v_C = V_0\, e^{-t/\lambda}$ $(t > 0)$ where, V_0 is actually $v_C\,(0-)$ *i.e.,* the voltage across the capacitor just before switching; $\lambda = RC$ while R is the equivalent resistance as seen from the capacitance terminals.

To find R, the capacitance is removed, all independent sources are made equal to zero and a driving point current source is applied at the capacitor terminals (Fig. E5.58(a)).

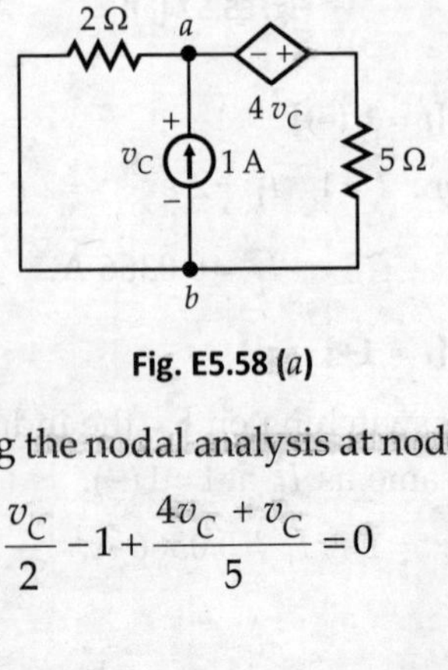

Fig. E5.58 (a)

Applying the nodal analysis at node (a), we get

$$\frac{v_C}{2} - 1 + \frac{4v_C + v_C}{5} = 0$$

or, $$\frac{v_C}{2} + \frac{4}{5}v_C + \frac{v_C}{5} = 1$$

or, $$1.5\, v_C = 1$$

i.e., $$v_C = \frac{1}{1.5} = 0.67 \text{ V} \qquad ...(1)$$

$\therefore$ R (net resistance across a-b in Fig. E5.58(a))

$$= \frac{v_C \text{ Volt}}{1\,A} = 0.67\,\Omega$$

This gives

$$\lambda = (0.67 \times 1) = 0.67 \text{ sec} \quad [\because R = 0.67\,\Omega, C = 1\text{ F}]$$

To find $v_C\,(0^-)$, let the circuit E5.58 be redrawn as shown in Fig. E5.58(b). Applying KVL around the outer loop,

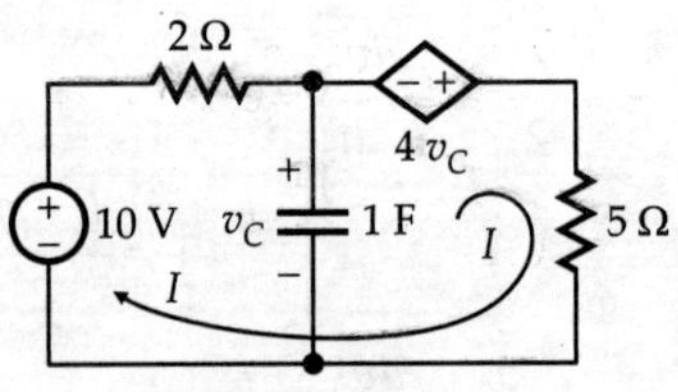

Fig. E5.58 (b)

$$5\,I - 10 + 2\,I - 4\,v_C = 0$$

[$\because$ Current through capacitor is zero as the capacitor behaves open circuit at $t = 0^-$]

or, $$7I - 10 - 4v_C = 0 \qquad ...(2)$$

Also in the rightmost loop,

$$-v_C - 4v_C + 5I = 0$$

or, $$I = v_C \qquad ...(3)$$

Substitution of (3) in (2) gives

$$7v_C - 10 - 4v_C = 0$$

or, $$v_C = \frac{10}{3} \text{ V (at } t = 0-) = V_0$$

Thus from $v_C = V_0\, e^{-t/\lambda}$,

we finally get $$v_C = \frac{10}{3} e^{-t/0.67} = \mathbf{\frac{10}{3} e^{-1.49\,t}} \textbf{ V.}$$

EXAMPLE 5.63 *In Fig. E5.59 find $i_L\,(t)$ at $t = 0^+$ after switching assuming steady state conditions prevailing before switching.*

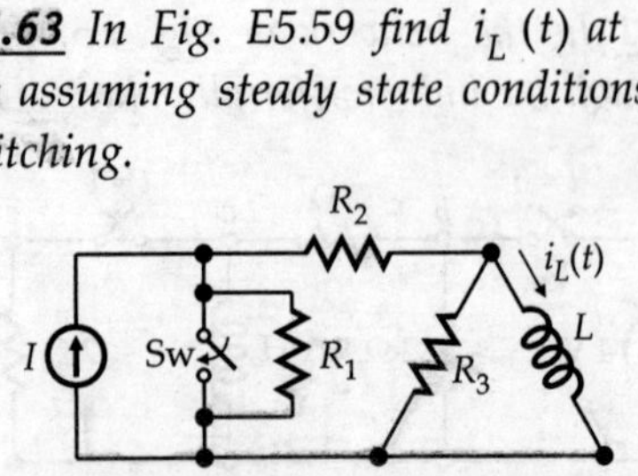

[$R_1 = 3\,\Omega$, $R_2 = 2\,\Omega$, $R_3 = 4\,\Omega$; $L = (1/6)$ H, $I = 5$ A

Fig. E5.59

SOLUTION. With switch open, L acts as short circuit and the circuit is displayed in Fig. E5.59(a).

$$i_L(0^-) = I\frac{R_1}{R_1 + R_2}$$

$$= 5 . \frac{3}{3+2} = 3 \text{ A}$$

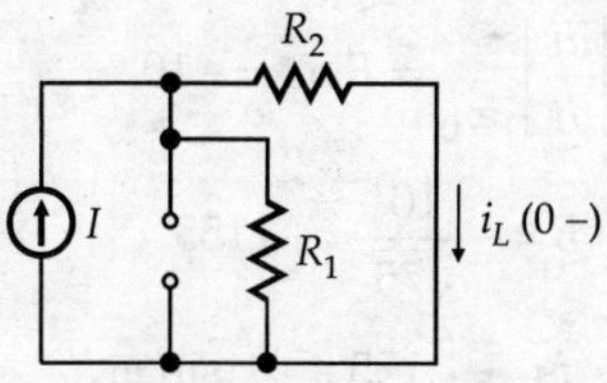

Fig. E5.59 (a)

Since inductance does not allow the current passing through it to change abruptly, hence we can write $i_L(0+) = 3$ A

At $t = 0+$, the circuit is redrawn in two parts as shown in Figs. E5.60(a) and E5.60(b).

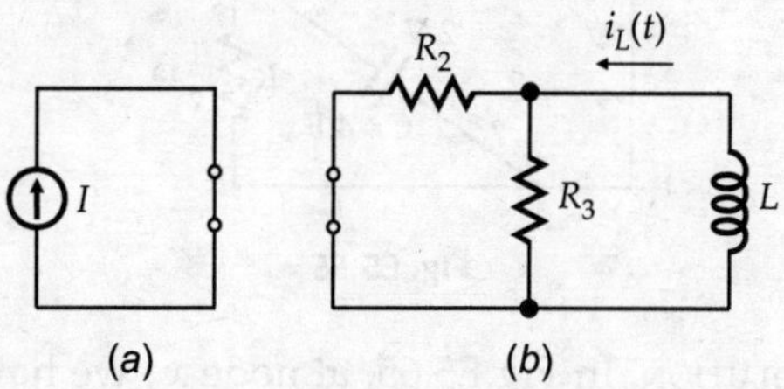

Fig. E5.60

Since R_2 and R_3 are parallel across L and since the original current source is shorted at $t = 0+$, we can take into account Fig. E5.60(b). With the current $i_L(0-)$ as the decaying source current through L and parallel contribution of R_2 and R_3. Since at steady state i_L approaches zero, we now can write

$$i_L(t) = 0 + (3 - 0)\, e^{-t/T}$$

where T is time const $= L/R$

$$\text{Hence} \quad T = \frac{1/6}{\dfrac{R_2 \times R_3}{R_2 + R_3}} = \frac{1/6}{\dfrac{2 \times 4}{4+2}} = \frac{1}{8}.$$

$$\therefore \quad \boldsymbol{i_L(t) = 3e^{-8t}} \textbf{ amp.}$$

EXAMPLE 5.64 *In Fig. E5.61 the circuit is at steady state with switch open for long time. Obtain $v(t)$ at $t = 0+$ following closing of switch.*

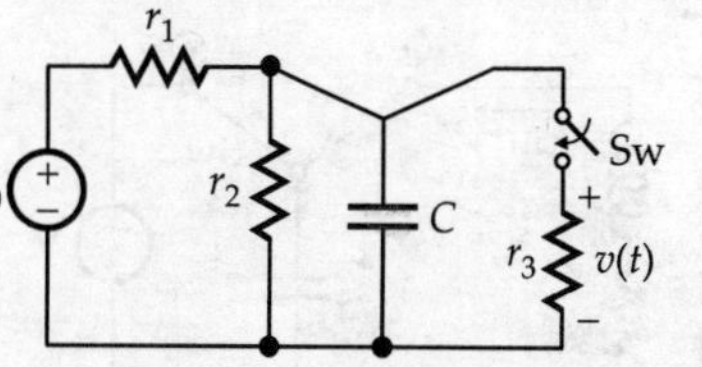

[$r_1 = r_2 = 5\ \Omega$, $r_3 = 10\ \Omega$, $C = 0.5$ F, $V_0 = 10$ V]

Fig. E5.61

SOLUTION. At steady state and before closing of switch, C acts as open circuit and the voltage across it is same to that across r_2. Voltage across r_2 is given by

$$V_{R_2} = \frac{V_0}{r_1 + r_2} \times r_2 = \frac{10}{5+5} \times 5 = 5 \text{ V}$$

$$\therefore \quad V_C(0-) = 5 \text{ V}$$

$$\text{Also,} \quad V_C(0+) = 5 \text{ V}$$

As the switch is closed at $t = 0$, steady will again reach and C will again act as open circuit. The circuit at $t = \infty$ is redrawn in Fig. E5.62.

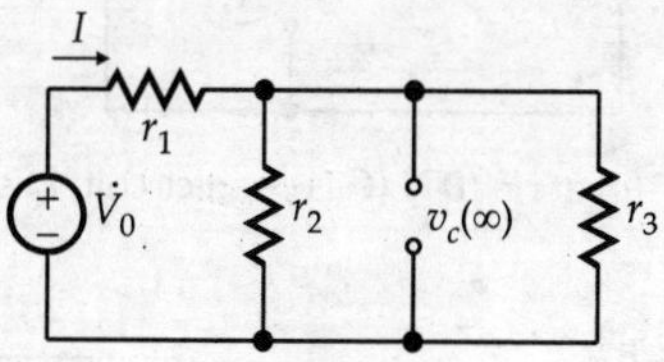

Fig. E5.62

$$\text{Here} \quad I = \frac{V_0}{r_1 + (r_2 \,||\, r_3)}$$

$$= \frac{10}{5 + (5\,||\,10)} = 1.2 \text{ A}$$

$$\therefore \quad v_c(\infty) = 1.2 \times (r_2 \,||\, r_3)$$

$$= 1.2 \times 3.33 \simeq 4 \text{ V}.$$

To find the time constant of the circuit we find that r_1, r_2 and r_3 are in parallel across C.

$$\therefore \quad RC = [(r_1 \,||\, r_2) \,||\, r_3] \times C$$

$$= \frac{2.5 \times 10}{2.5 + 10} \times \frac{1}{2} = 1 \text{ sec}$$

Now we can write $v(t)$ as

$$v(t) = v_c(\infty) + [(v_c(0-) - v_c(\infty)]\, e^{-(RC)t}$$

$$\left[\begin{array}{ccc} v_c(\infty) = \text{final steady state value of voltage across } r_3 & ; & v_c(0-) = \text{initial value of voltage across } r_3 \end{array}\right]$$

$$\text{or} \quad v(t) = 4 + (5 - 4)\, e^{-t}$$

$$= \boldsymbol{(4 + e^{-t})} \textbf{ volts.}$$

EXAMPLE 5.65 *Switch (Sw) is at position "a" for a long time when, at $t = 0$, it is switched to "b" position. Find $i(t)$ for $t > 0$. [Fig. E5.63]*

C H A P T E R 5

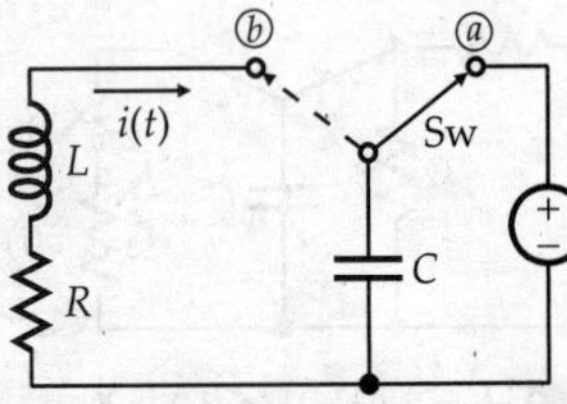

[$L = 1$ H; $R = 10\ \Omega$; $C = 0.1$ F; $V = 10$ volts]

Fig. E5.63

SOLUTION. We draw the circuit at $t = 0^-$ as well as at $t = 0^+$ and $t = (\infty)$ in Fig. E5.64(*a*), E5.64(*b*) and E5.64(*c*).

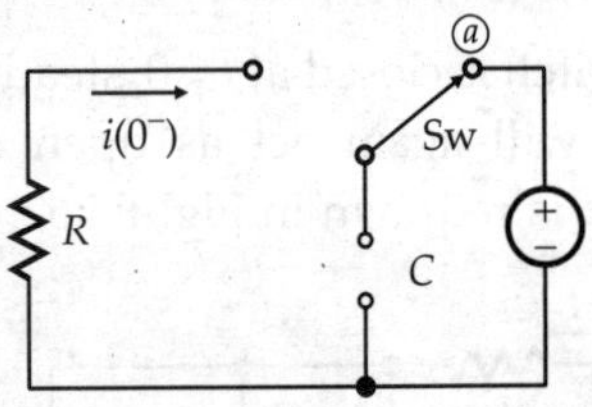

Fig. E5.64 (*a*) at $t = (0^-)$ (*C* is open circuit, *L* is shorted).

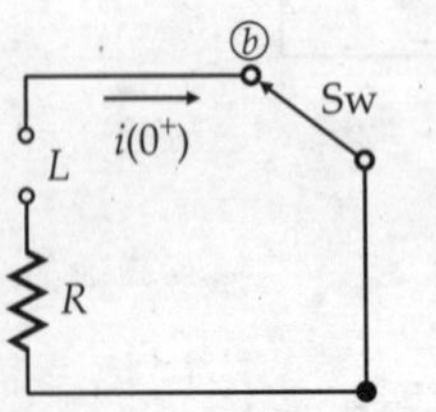

Fig. E5.64 (*b*) at $t = (0^+)$ (*C* is shorted, *L* is open circuit).

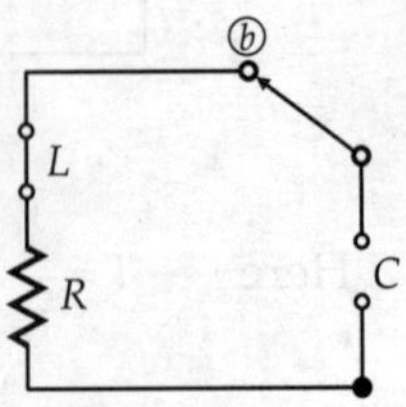

Fig. E5.64 (*c*) at $t = \infty$.

At $t = (0^-)$, L is short circuited while C is open. Thus $i(0^-) = 0$. At $t = (0^+)$, C is short circuited and L is open circuited. Also $i(0^+) = 0$.

At $t = (0^+)$,

$$L\frac{di}{dt} = v_L = -10 \text{ volts.}$$

$$\therefore \quad \frac{di}{dt}(0+) = -\frac{10}{L} = -10 \text{ A/sec.} \qquad [\because L = 1 \text{ H}]$$

Also, at $t \to \infty$,

$$i = 0 \qquad [\because C \text{ acts as open circuit}]$$

$$\therefore \quad \frac{R}{L}(=2\alpha) = \frac{10}{1} = 10$$

$$\therefore \quad \alpha = 5.$$

Also, $\omega_0^2 = \dfrac{1}{LC} = \dfrac{1}{1 \times 0.1} = 10.$

$$[\because L = 1 \text{ H}; C = 0.1 \text{ F}]$$

$$\therefore \quad \omega_d^2 = \omega_0^2 - \alpha^2 = 10^2 - 5^2 = 75$$

$$i(t) = K + Ae^{-\alpha t}\cos\omega_d t + Be^{-\alpha t}\sin\omega_d t$$

At $t = \infty$, $\quad i = 0 \quad \therefore K = 0$

At $t = (0+)$, $\quad i = 0 \quad \therefore \quad A = 0$

$$\therefore \quad i(t) = Be^{-\alpha t}\sin\omega_d t$$

Also, $\left.\dfrac{di}{dt}\right|_{t=0} = B\omega_d = -10$

$$\therefore \quad B = -\frac{10}{\sqrt{75}} = -1.155.$$

$$\therefore \quad i = -1.155\, e^{-\alpha t}\sin\omega_d t$$

$$= \mathbf{-1.155\, e^{-5t}\sin 8.66\, t.}$$

EXAMPLE 5.66 *If $I = 10$ A, and the switching is done at $t = 0$, find $v(t)$ for $t > 0$ if the initial capacitor voltage be 2 V.*

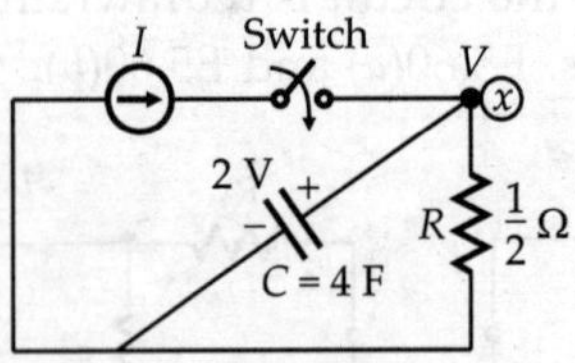

Fig. E5.65

SOLUTION. In Fig.E5.65, at node x, we have

$$\frac{V}{R} + C\frac{dV}{dt} = 10 \qquad \ldots(i)$$

At $t = 0$, capacitor has initial voltage of 2 V.

i.e., $V(0^-) = V(0^+) = 2$ V, as capacitor does not change its voltage immediately after switching.

Hence from (*i*)

$$\frac{dV}{dt} + \frac{V}{RC} = \frac{10}{C}.$$

or

$$\frac{dV}{dt} + \frac{1}{2}V = \frac{10}{C} = 2.5 \qquad \ldots(ii)$$

(*ii*) Being a first order homogeneous equation,

$$v(t) = e^{-0.5t}\int 2.5\, e^{0.5t}\, dt + C_1 e^{-0.5t}$$

$$= \frac{2.5}{0.5} + C_1 e^{-0.5t}$$

[C_1 being the integration constant]

i.e., $\quad v(t) = 5 + C_1 e^{-0.5t}$

at $t = 0$, $\quad v(t) = 2.5$ V.

This gives, $2 = 5 + C_1$ or $C_1 = -3$.

Hence finally we have, $\mathbf{v(t) = 5 - 3e^{-0.5t}}$ **volts.**

EXERCISES

1. The values of R and L in a series R-L circuit are $10\,\Omega$ and 40 H respectively. At the instant of closing the switch, the supply current rises at the rate of 5 A/sec. Calculate the value of applied voltage, rate of growth of current when 6 A flows in the circuit. Also find the stored energy in the inductor.

[**Hint.** $iR + L\dfrac{di}{dt} = V$ at $t = 0$, $i = 0$. $\therefore \quad \dfrac{di}{dt} = \dfrac{V}{L} = 5$ (given)

$\therefore \quad V = 5L = 5 \times 40 = 200$ V.

Initial stored energy $= \dfrac{1}{2} LI^2 = 0$ [$\because I = 0$]

If $i = 6$ A, $\quad L\dfrac{di}{dt} = 200 - iR = 200 - 6 \times 10 = 140$

$\therefore \quad \dfrac{di}{dt} = \dfrac{140}{40} = 3.5$ A / sec.

Stored energy $= \dfrac{1}{2} LI^2$; calculate.]

2. A d.c. voltage of 20 V is applied in a RL circuit where $R = 5\,\Omega$ and $L = 10$ H. Find (*a*) the time constant (T) (*b*) the maximum value of stored energy.

[**Hint.** First find T and steady state current I. The max. value of stored energy will become $(1/2)\, LI^2$.]

3. A 100 V d.c. source is applied in a coil where $R = 10\,\Omega$ and $L = 10$ H. Find the energy supplied to the coil in the first 5 sec. If the coil is then disconnected and immediately short circuited, find the energy dissipated.

[**Hint.** $I = \dfrac{V}{R}$; $i = \dfrac{V}{R}(1 - e^{-t/T})$; Energy $= \displaystyle\int_0^5 ei\,dt$

Current at the instant of short circuit is $i = \dfrac{V}{R}(1 - e^{-5/T})$ A. Energy dissipated $= \dfrac{1}{2} Li^2$ J]

4. A 5 μF condenser is connected through a 1000 K Ω resistor to a d.c. source (10 V). After being charged for half minute, the condenser is disconnected and discharged through a resistor (R). Determine the energy dissipated in R.

[**Hint.** $v = V_0\,(1 - e^{-t/T})$.

$V_0 = 10$ V; $T = RC = (1 \times 10^6 \times 5 \times 10^{-6})$ sec.

$t = 30$ sec.

The energy dissipated in R is the energy stored when disconnected from the d.c. source ($= (1/2)\, Cv^2$ J).]

5. A constant voltage of 100 V is applied at $t = 0$ to a series RC circuit having $R = 5$ M Ω and $C = 20$ μF. Assuming no initial charge to the capacitor, find expression for i, voltage across R and C.

[**Hint.** $v_C = V_0\,(1 - e^{-t/T})$ while $T = RC$; $V_0 = 100$ V, $R = 5 \times 10^6\,\Omega$,

$C = 20 \times 10^{-6}$ F; $i = C\dfrac{dv_C}{dt} = C\dfrac{d}{dt}[V_0\,(1 - e^{-t/T})]$ and $v_R = iR$]

6. A 220 V, 50 Hz sinusoidal voltage is applied to a coil having $R = 1\,\Omega$ and $X_L = 5\,\Omega$. Find the energy stored in the coil 5 m sec. later the voltage has passed through the zero and is in the increasing slope.

[**Hint.**

$$i_C = e^{-\frac{R}{L}.t}\left[-\frac{V_m}{Z}\sin\left(\phi - \tan^{-1}\frac{\omega L}{R}\right)\right]$$

$$i_p = \frac{V_m}{Z}\sin\left(\omega t + \phi - \tan^{-1}\frac{\omega L}{R}\right.$$

CHAPTER 5

But $\quad V_m = 220\sqrt{2}$ V

$$Z = 1 + j\,5,\ L \text{ being } \left(\frac{5}{2\pi f}\right),\ \phi = 0°$$

$$t = 0.005 \text{ sec.}$$

Thus $i\,(= i_C + i_p)$ can be obtained. Energy stored $= \frac{1}{2} LI^2$ J]

7. In Fig. P5.1 switch K is closed at position 1 at $t = 0$. After one time constant, the switch is moved to position 2. Obtain the current expression for $0 < t < T$ and $t > T$, T being the time constant.

[**Hint.** Solve as done in Ex. 5.22]

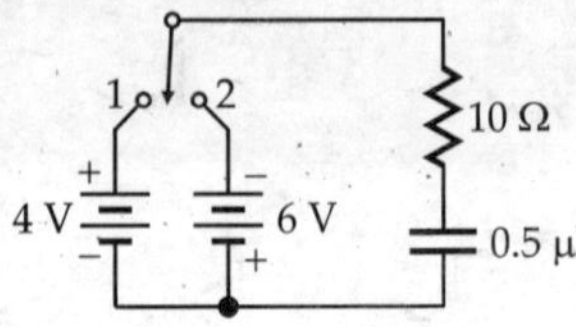

Fig. P5.1

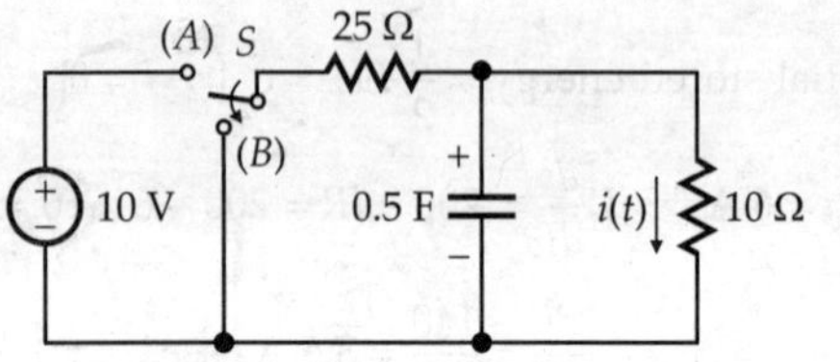

Fig. P5.2

8. Find $i\,(t)$ at $t = 0+$ in Fig. P5.2 following switching of the switch "S" at $t = 0$ from (A) to (B). Assume steady state of the circuit while "S" was at (A).

[**Hint.** Solve the problem as shown in Ex. 5.35]

9. The circuit in Fig. P5.3 at steady state has no initial voltage across the capacitor. Find $v_C\,(t)$ and $i_C\,(t)$ at $t = 0+$ following the application of the source voltage at $t = 0$.

[**Hint.** $\quad v_C\,(t) = V_S\,(1 - e^{-t/RC})$ –see the text.

$$\therefore \quad i_C(t) = \frac{dv_C}{dt}(t)\,.\,C = C\left[\frac{d}{dt}\,V_S\,(1 - e^{-t/RC})\right]$$

$$= \frac{1}{R}\,e^{-t/RC}\,.\,V_S = \frac{V_S}{R}\,(e^{-t/RC})\text{ A}$$

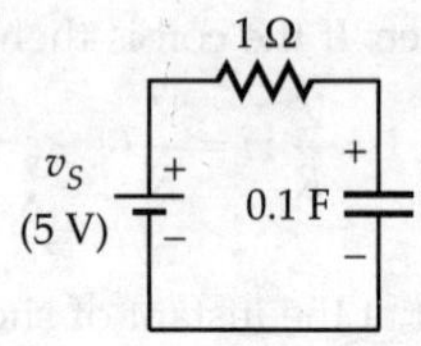

Fig. P5.3

10. In the above problem, what is the value of $v_R\,(t)$?

[**Hint.** $v_R\,(t) =$ drop across $R\,(1\Omega) = i_C\,(t) \times R = V_S\,(e^{-t/RC})$]

11. In the network of Fig. P5.4, find the expression of discharging voltage of the capacitor at $t = 0+$ following switching at $t = 0$.

[**Hint.** Ref. Ex. 5.38]

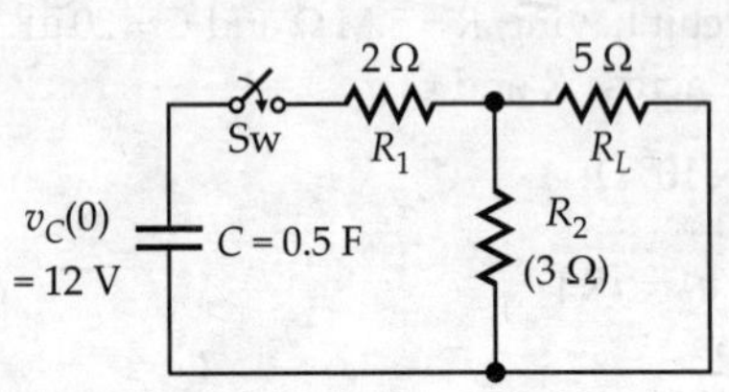

Fig. P5.4

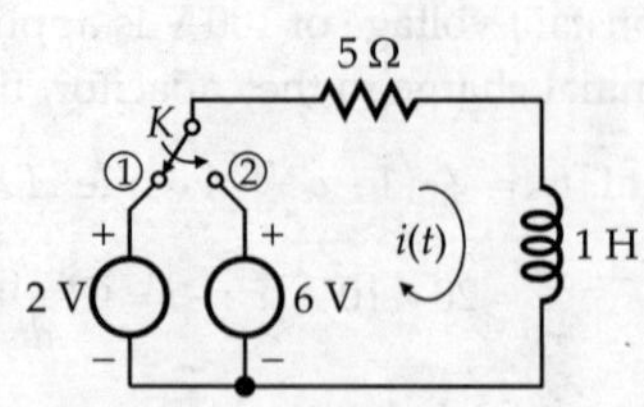

Fig. P5.5

12. In Fig. P5.5, the switch is at (1) and steady state condition is reached. Following switching of K at $t = 0$ from (A) to (B), find the expression for $i\,(t)$ at $t = (0+)$

[**Hint.** Follow Ex. 5.40]

13. In the *RL* circuit of Fig. P5.6, find $v_L(t)$, $v_R(t)$.

Hint. With reference to text, following switching

$$i(t) = \frac{E}{R}(1 - e^{-\frac{R}{L}.t})$$

$$\therefore \quad v_L(t) = L\frac{di}{dt} = L\frac{d}{dt}\left(\frac{E}{R}\left(1 - e^{-\frac{R}{L}t}\right)\right)$$

$$= \frac{L \times E \times R}{R \times L} e^{-\frac{R}{L}t} = Ee^{-\frac{R}{L}t} \text{ V};$$

$$\therefore \quad v_R(t) = i_L(t) \times R = E(1 - e^{-\frac{R}{L}t}) \text{ V}$$

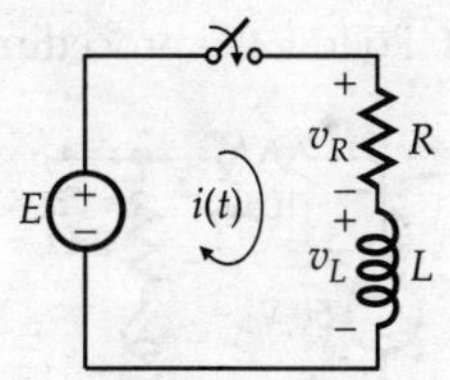

Fig. P5.6

14. In the circuit of Fig. P5.7, show that following switching, the capacitor across the voltage is given by $v_C(t) = u(t)(1 - e^{-t/RC})R$.

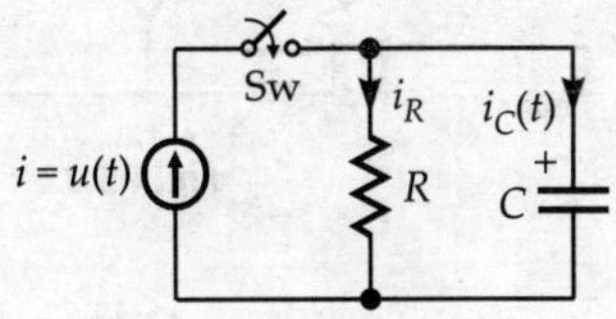

Fig. P5.7

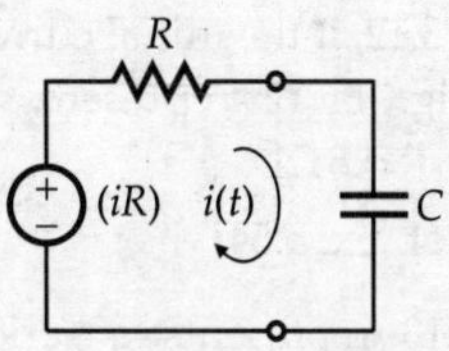

Fig. P5.7 (*a*)

[**Hint.** ∵ The conversion of current source *i* gives a voltage source in series with the resistance *R* hence the circuit can be shown to be that as shown in Fig. P5.7(*a*).

Obviously from the text, here

$$v_C(t) = iR(1 - e^{-t/RC}) = u(t)(1 - e^{-t/RC})R\ ]$$

15. Show that in the above problem,

$$i(t) = e^{-t/RC}u(t) \quad \text{and } i_R(t) = (1 - e^{-t/RC})u(t).$$

[**Hint.** $i(t) = C\dfrac{dv_C}{dt} = u(t)e^{-t/RC}$

and $i_R(t) = \dfrac{v_C(t)}{R} = \dfrac{u(t)(1 - e^{-t/RC})R}{R} = u(t)(1 - e^{-t/RC})$]

16. In the network of Fig. P5.8, $L_1 = L_2 = 50 \times 10^{-3}$ H; $R_1 = R_2 = 10\,\Omega$; $R_L = 5\,\Omega$

If $I = 5$ A (*dc*), find the drop across R_L at $t = 0^+$ following the switching of *S* from (1) to (2) at $t = 0$. Assume steady state before switching.

[**Hint.** Ref. Ex. 5.44]

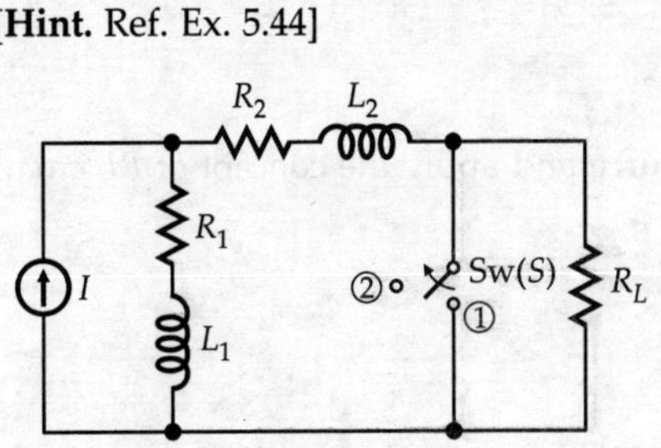

Fig. P5.8

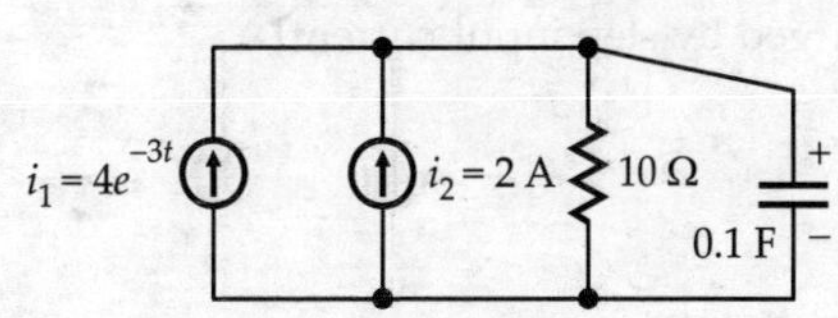

Fig. P5.9

17. If the initial voltage stored in the capacitor is zero volts, find $v_c(t)$ in the circuit of Fig. P5.9. This figure represents the circuit condition at $t = 0^+$.

[**Hint.** Ref. Ex. 5.46]

18. Steady state is achieved in the circuit of Fig. P5.10, following switching; find the current in the 5 Ω resistor at 't' time.

[**Hint.** Follow the procedure as shown in Ex. 5.49]

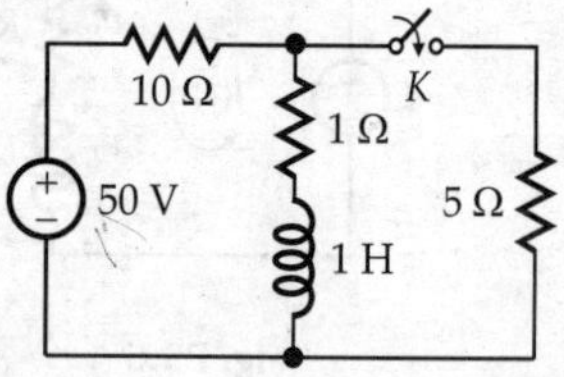

Fig. P5.10

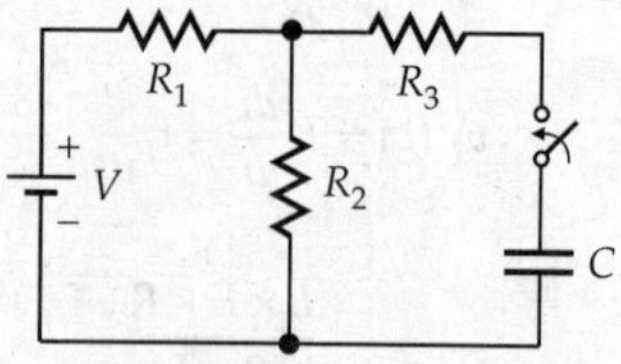

Fig. P5.11

19. In the circuit of Fig. P5.11, $C = 10\ \mu F$, $V = 10$ V, $R_1 = R_2 = 10\,\Omega$ $R_3 = 5\,\Omega$. Find $i_C(t)$ following switching on of the capacitor at $t = 0$.

[**Hint.** Refer to Ex. 5.52]

20. In Fig. P5.12, if the initial current through the inductor is 1 A, find $i_L(t)$. Fig. P5.12 represents the circuit condition at $t = 0+$. [$L = 1$ H, $R = 5\,\Omega$]

[**Hint.** Ref. Ex. 5.54]

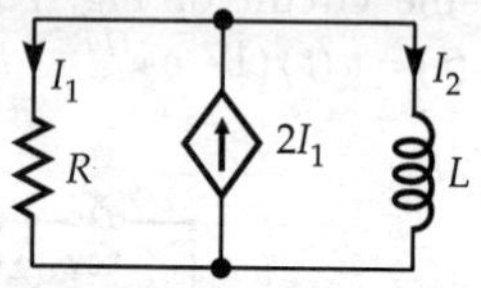

Fig. P5.12

21. Fig. P5.13 represents a series *RL* circuit at $t = 0+$ following switching of a dependent voltage source. If the initial current in the circuit is 2 A, find $i(t)$ at $t = 0+$.

[**Hint.** Do in the same way as shown in Ex. 5.57]

22. Find the voltage developed across the capacitor at $t = 0+$ following switching at $t = 0$. Assume no initial charge stored in the capacitor (Fig. P5.14).

[**Hint.** Ref. Ex. 5.60]

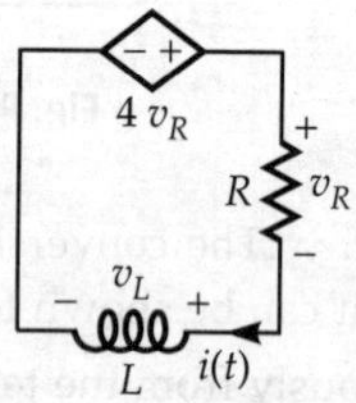

Fig. P5.13

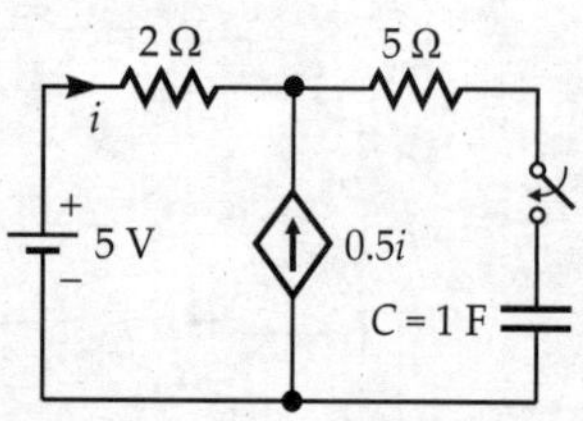

Fig. P5.14

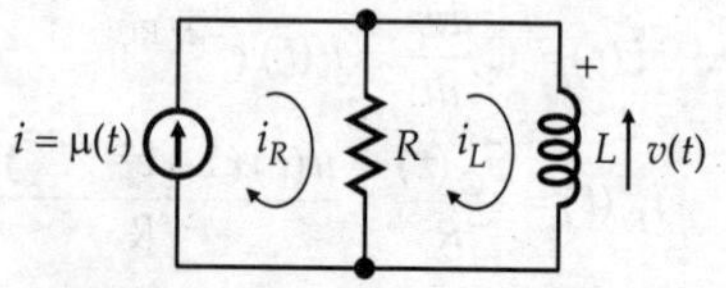

Fig. P5.15

23. If Fig. P5.15 represents the circuit at $t = 0+$, show that

$$i_L(t) = (1 - e^{-Rt/L})\,u(t),\ i_R(t) = e^{-Rt/L}\,u(t)$$

$$v(t) = Re^{-Rt/L}\,u(t)$$

[**Hint.** Convert the current source to the equivalent voltage source and apply the concept of *RL* circuit being charged by step input current]

CHAPTER

6

Application of Network Theorems in D.C. Circuits

(*With and Without Controlled Sources*)

6.1 INTRODUCTION

Important and fundamental theorems of circuit theory have been introduced in this chapter. Illustrative examples have also been provided to explain the applicability of these theorems in different types of d.c. networks (with independent sources as well as with controlled sources). A thorough understanding of each theorem is important because analysing of electrical and electronic circuits needs these theorems very much.

6.2 THEVENIN'S THEOREM

This theorem is possibly the most extensively used network theorem. It is applicable where it is desired to determine the current through or voltage across any one element in a network without going through the rigorous method of solving a set of network equations.

6.2.1 Statement of Thevenin's Theorem*

Any two terminal bilateral linear d.c. circuits can be replaced by an equivalent circuit consisting of a voltage source and a series resistor.

6.2.2 Explanation

Let us consider a simple d.c. circuit as shown in Fig. 6.1(*a*). We are to find I_L by Thevenin's Theorem.

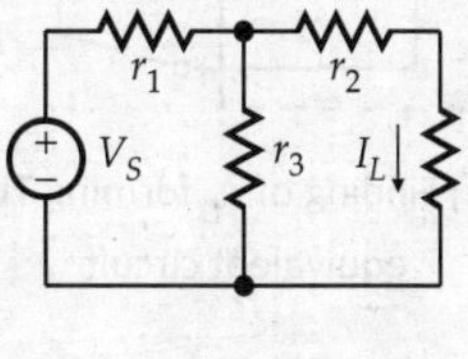

Fig. 6.1 (*a*) A Simple d.c. circuit

In order to find the equivalent voltage source, r_L is removed (Fig. 6.1(*b*)) and $V_{o.c}$ is calculated.

$$V_{o.c} = I\,r_3 = \frac{V_S}{r_1 + r_3} \cdot r_3.$$

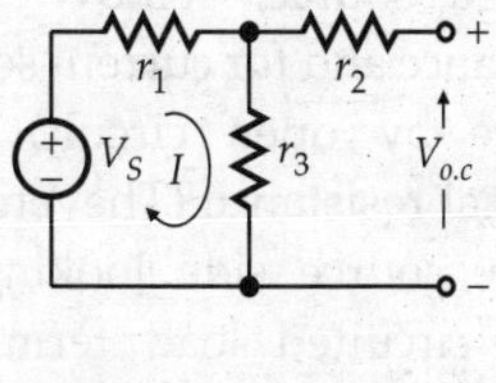

Fig. 6.1 (*b*) Finding of V_{oc}

* A more general statement of Thevenin's Theorem is that any linear active network consisting of independent and or dependent voltage and current sources and linear bilateral network elements can be replaced by an equivalent circuit consisting of a voltage source in series with a resistance, the voltage source being the open circuited voltage across the open circuited load terminals and the resistance being the internal resistance of the source network looking through the open circuited load terminals.

Next, to find the internal resistance of the network (*Thevenin's resistance* or *equivalent resistance*) in series with $V_{o.c}$, the voltage source is removed (deactivated) by a short circuit (as the source does not have any internal resistance) as shown in Fig. 6.1(*c*).

$$R_{Th} = r_2 + \frac{r_1 \, r_3}{r_1 + r_3}.$$

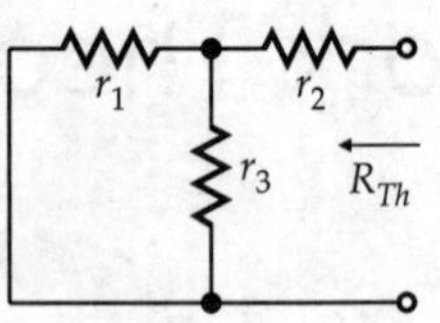

Fig. 6.1 (*c*) Finding of R_{Th}

As per Thevenin's theorem, the equivalent circuit being Fig. 6.1(*d*),

$$I_L = \frac{V_{o.c}}{R_{Th} + r_L} \text{ A.}$$

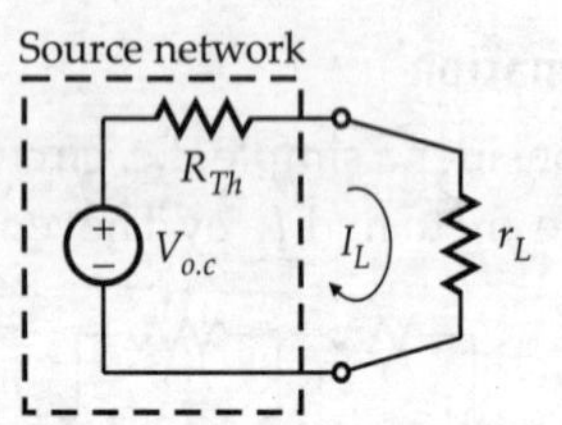

Fig. 6.1 (*d*) Finding of I_L forming Thevenin's equivalent circuit

6.2.3 Steps for Solution of a Network Utilizing Thevenin's Theorem

Step 1 Remove the load resistor (R_L) and find the open circuit voltage ($V_{o.c}$) across the open circuited load terminals.

Step 2 Deactivate the constant sources (for voltage source, remove it by internal resistance and for current source delete the source by open circuit) and find the internal resistance (Thevenin's resistance) of the source side looking through the open circuited load terminals. Let this resistance be R_{Th}.

Step 3 Obtain Thevenin's equivalent circuit (Fig. 6.2) by placing R_{Th} in series with $V_{o.c}$.

Step 4 Reconnect R_L across the load terminals as shown in Fig. 6.2.

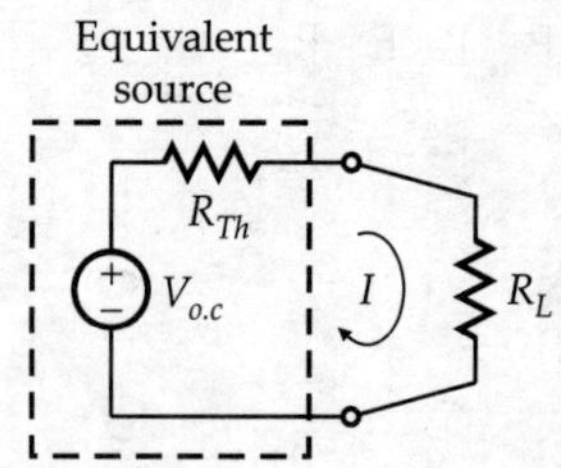

Fig. 6.2 Thevenin's Equivalent network.

Obviously I (the load current)

$$= \frac{V_{o.c}}{R_{Th} + R_L}.$$

6.2.4 Different Methods of Finding R_{Th}

(*Thevenin's equivalent resistance or Internal impedance*)

(*a*) ***For independent sources.*** The most common method of finding R_{Th}, the internal resistance of any linear, bilateral network containing independent current or voltage sources is to deactivate the source by internal resistance *i.e.*, for independent current source, deactivate it by removing the source and for voltage source, deactivate it by shorting it (assuming the internal resistance of the voltage source being zero). Then find the internal resistance of the network looking through the load terminals kept open circuited. This method is illustrated in the following examples.

(*b*) ***For the circuits containing dependent sources in addition to or in absence of independent source***

1st method. Find $V_{o.c}$ across the open circuited load terminals by conventional network analysis. Next, short the load terminals and find the short circuit current ($I_{s.c}$) through the shorted terminals.

The internal resistance of the source network is then obtained as

$$R_{Th} = \frac{V_{o.c}}{I_{s.c}}.$$

2nd method. Remove the load resistance and apply a d.c. driving voltage v_{dc} at the open circuited load terminals. Keep the other independent sources deactivated during this time (*i.e.*, short the voltage source terminals and open the current source terminals). A d.c. driving current i_{dc} will flow in the circuit from the load terminals due to application of v_{dc}.

The internal resistance of the source network is then obtained as

$$R_{Th} = \frac{v_{dc}}{i_{dc}}.$$

Both the two methods highlighted above have been illustrated in the following examples.

EXAMPLE 6.1 *In the network of Fig. E6.1, find the current through the 10 Ω resistor utilising Thevenin's Theorem.*

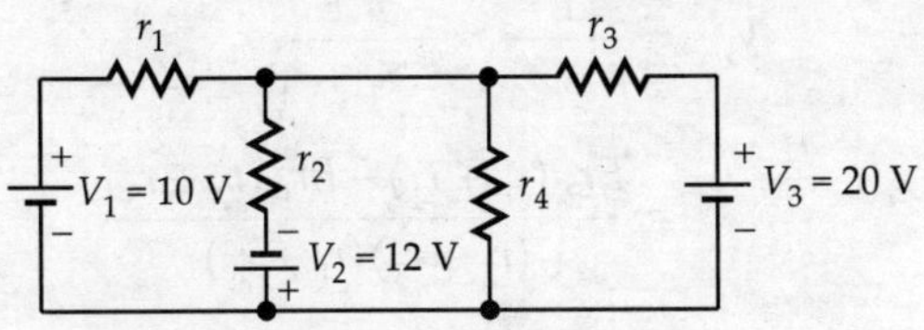

$[r_1 = 2\,\Omega, r_2 = 5\,\Omega, r_3 = 1\,\Omega, r_4 = 10\,\Omega]$

Fig. E6.1

SOLUTION. Let the resistance r_4 (10 Ω) be removed and the circuit is exhibited in Fig. E6.1(*a*).

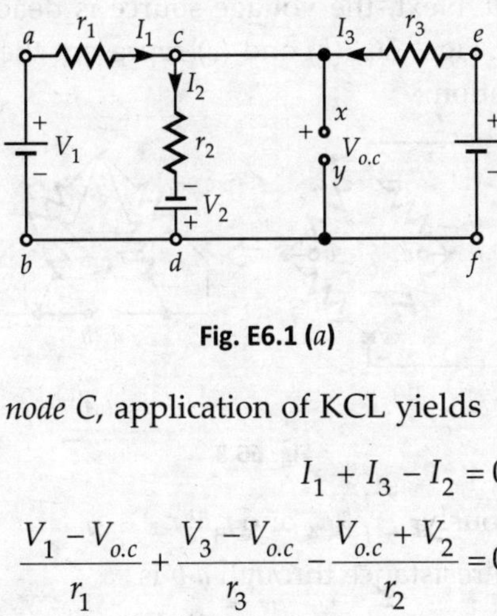

Fig. E6.1 (*a*)

At node C, application of KCL yields

$$I_1 + I_3 - I_2 = 0$$

or, $$\frac{V_1 - V_{o.c}}{r_1} + \frac{V_3 - V_{o.c}}{r_3} - \frac{V_{o.c} + V_2}{r_2} = 0$$

[Assuming the open circuit voltage across the terminals x-y in Fig. E6.1(*a*) to be $V_{o.c}$; obviously, the potential at *C* node is $V_{o.c}$]

i.e., $$\frac{10 - V_{o.c}}{2} + \frac{20 - V_{o.c}}{1} - \frac{V_{o.c} + 12}{5} = 0$$

or, $$-0.5\,V_{o.c} - V_{o.c} - 0.2\,V_{o.c} = 2.4 - 20 - 5$$

or, $$1.7\,V_{o.c} = +22.6 \text{ V}$$

∴ $$V_{o.c} = 13.29 \text{ V}$$

Next, the independent voltage sources are removed by short circuits (Fig. E6.1(*b*))

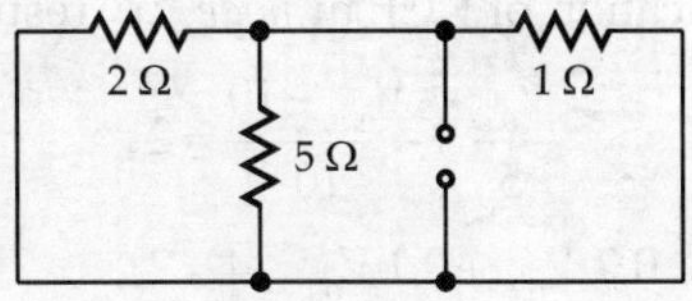

Fig. E6.1 (*b*)

Here, $$\frac{1}{R_{Th}} = \frac{1}{2} + \frac{1}{5} + \frac{1}{1}$$

or, $$R_{Th} = \frac{10}{17}\,\Omega$$

Thevenin's equivalent circuit being shown in Fig. E6.1(*c*),

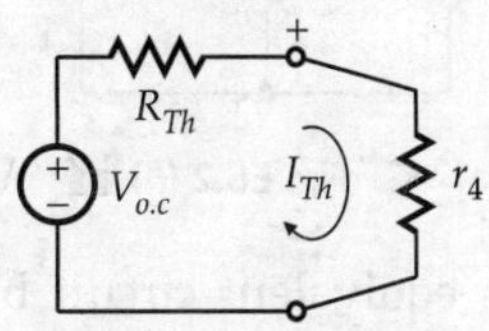

Fig. E6.1 (c)

$$I_4 \text{ (current through } r_4) \equiv I_{Th} = \frac{V_{o.c}}{R_{Th} + r_4}$$

i.e., $$I_4 = \frac{13.29}{\frac{10}{17} + 10} = 1.26 \text{ A}$$

Thus current through r_4 **is 1.26 A.**

EXAMPLE 6.2 *In the circuit of Fig. E6.2, find the power loss in the 1 Ω resistor by Thevenin's Theorem.*

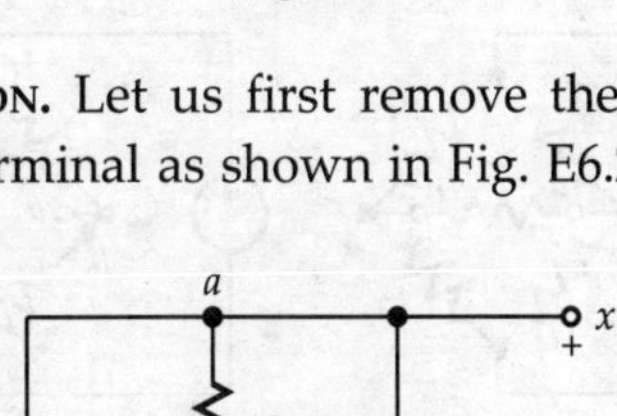

Fig. E6.2

SOLUTION. Let us first remove the 1Ω resistor from *x-y* terminal as shown in Fig. E6.2(*a*).

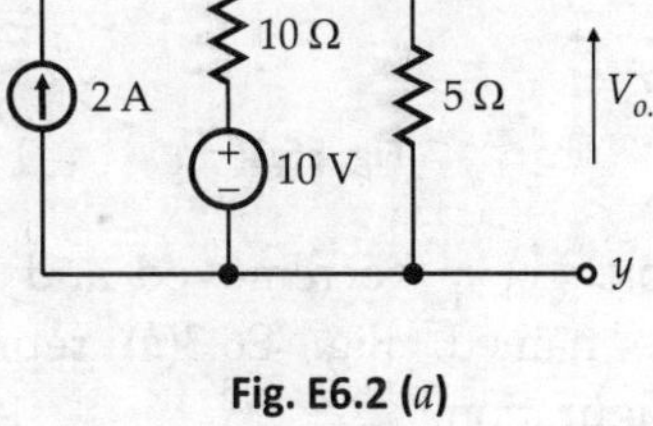

Fig. E6.2 (*a*)

Application of KCL at *node "a"* results

$$\frac{V_{o.c}}{5}+\frac{V_{o.c}-10}{10}=2$$

or, $\quad 0.2\,V_{o.c}+0.1\,V_{o.c}-1=2$

or, $\quad V_{o.c}=10\text{ V}$

Figure E6.2(*b*) represents the circuit with independent sources deactivated.

$$R_{Th}=\frac{5\times 10}{5+10}=3.33\,\Omega$$

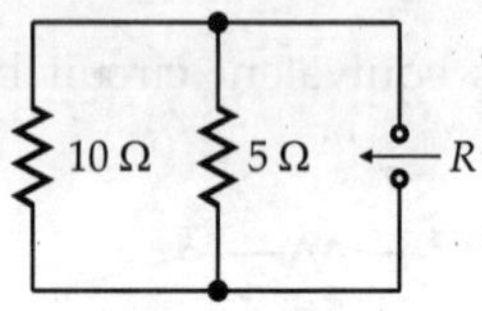

Fig. E6.2 (*b*)

Thevenin's equivalent circuit being shown in Fig. E6.2(*c*).

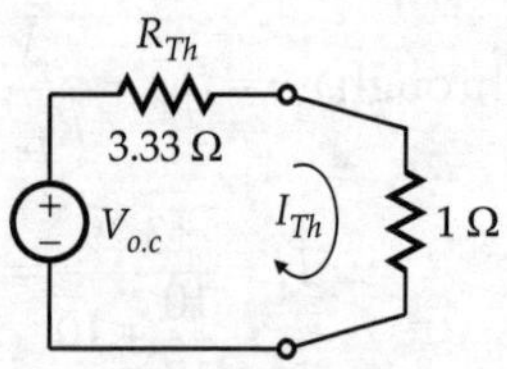

Fig. E6.2 (c)

Here, current through 1Ω resistor is then given by

$$I_{Th}=\frac{V_{o.c}}{R_{Th}+1}=\frac{10}{3.33+1}=2.31\text{ A.}$$

$\therefore$ Power loss in 1Ω resistor

$$=(2.31)^2\times 1=\mathbf{5.33\ W.}$$

EXAMPLE 6.3 *Thevenize the bridge circuit across a-b in Fig. E6.3.*

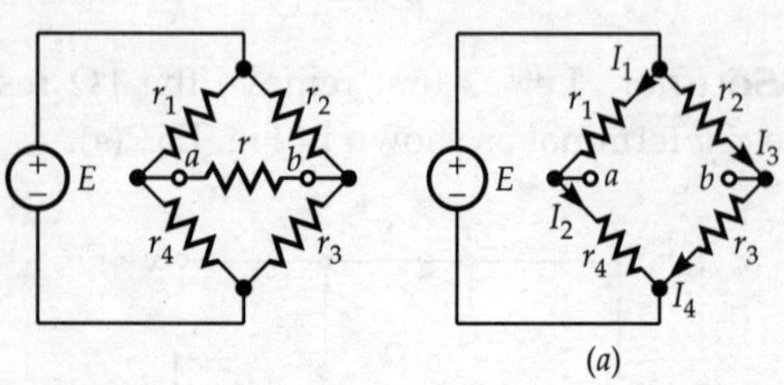

Fig. E6.3

SOLUTION. Let r_L be removed and the branch currents be named. Fig. E6.3(*a*) represents the circuit configuration.

With terminals *a-b* open circuited,

$$I_1=I_2 \quad \text{and} \quad I_3=I_4$$

Also, $\quad I_1=\dfrac{E}{r_1+r_4}\,;$ ...(1)

and $\quad I_3=\dfrac{E}{r_2+r_3}$ ...(2)

Again, $\quad V_{a-b}\,(=V_{o.c})=I_3\,r_2-I_1\,r_1$ ...(3)

Substitution of (1) and (2) in (3) yields

$$V_{o.c}=\frac{E}{r_2+r_3}\,r_2-\frac{E}{r_1+r_4}\,r_1$$

$$=\frac{Er_2\,(r_1+r_4)-Er_1\,(r_2+r_3)}{(r_2+r_3)(r_1+r_4)}$$

$$=\frac{E\,[r_1\,r_2+r_4\,r_2-r_1\,r_2-r_1\,r_3]}{(r_2+r_3)(r_1+r_4)}$$

or, $\quad V_{o.c}=\dfrac{E\,(r_4\,r_2-r_1\,r_3)}{(r_2+r_3)(r_1+r_4)}$ ...(4)

$V_{o.c}$ in (4) represents the Thevenin voltage across *a-b*. Next, the voltage source is deactivated such that Figs. E6.3(*b*) and (*c*) represent the circuit configuration.

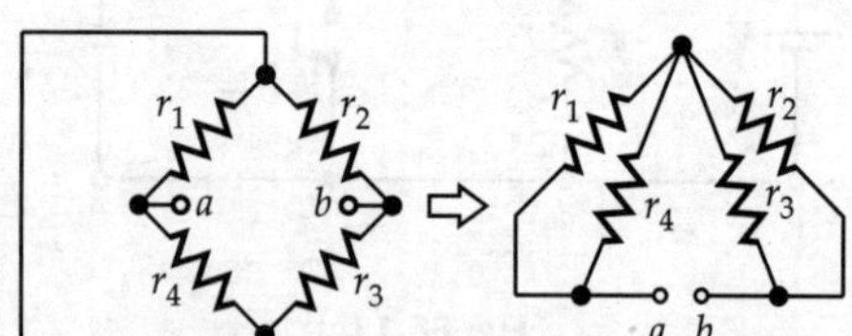

(*b*) (*c*)

Fig. E6.3

Obviously, $\quad r_1\,||\,r_4$ and $r_3\,||\,r_2$

$\therefore$ The resistance through *a-b* is

$$R_{ab}=(r_1\,||\,r_4)+(r_3\,||\,r_2)=\frac{r_1\,r_4}{r_1+r_4}+\frac{r_3\,r_2}{r_3+r_2}$$

$$=\frac{r_1\,r_4\,(r_3+r_2)+r_2\,r_3\,(r_1+r_4)}{(r_1+r_4)(r_2+r_3)}$$

$$=\frac{r_1\,r_2\,r_3+r_1\,r_2\,r_4+r_3\,r_4\,r_1+r_3\,r_4\,r_2}{(r_1+r_4)(r_3+r_2)}$$

$\therefore$ In the given bridge circuit,

$$V_{o.c}=\frac{\mathbf{E\,(r_4\,r_2-r_1\,r_3)}}{\mathbf{(r_2+r_3)\,(r_1+r_4)}}$$

and $\quad R_{\text{int}}=\dfrac{\mathbf{r_1\,r_2\,r_3+r_1\,r_2\,r_4+r_3\,r_4\,r_1+r_3\,r_4\,r_2}}{\mathbf{(r_1+r_4)\,(r_3+r_2)}}.$

EXAMPLE 6.4 *In the circuit of Fig. E6.4, find the power loss in r_L utilising Thevenin's Theorem.*

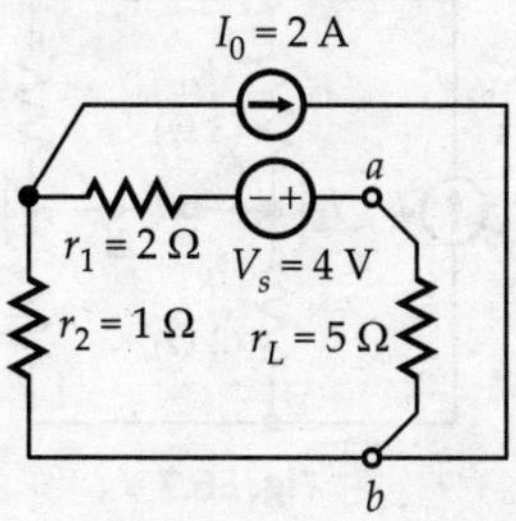

Fig. E6.4

SOLUTION. Let r_L be removed and let us first find the open circuit voltage V_{Th} across the open circuited *a-b* terminals (Fig. E6.4(*a*)).

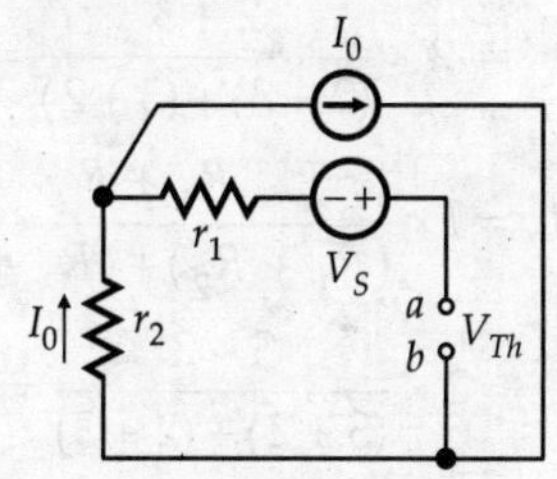

Fig. E6.4 (*a*)

Here, $V_{Th} = V_S - I_0 r_2$

[$\because$ no current flows through r_1 hence [no voltage drop will occur across r_1]

or, $V_{Th} = 4 - 2 \times 1 = 2$ V

To find R_{int} (*i.e.*, the internal resistance of the circuit across *a-b*), all the constant sources are deactivated *i.e.*, $V_S = 0$ and $I_0 = 0$. Fig. E6.4(*b*) represents the required circuit.

Obviously, $R_{Th} = r_1 + r_2 = 3\,\Omega$

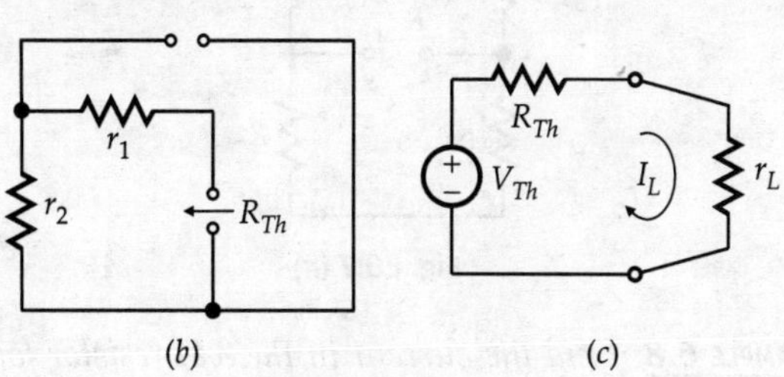

Fig. E6.4

Thus we have obtained the equivalent Thevenin's circuit (Fig. E6.4(*c*)) where

$V_{o.c.} = V_{Th} = 2$ V,

$R_{Th} = R_{int} = 3\,\Omega$

$\therefore$ I_L (load current through r_L) $= \dfrac{2}{3 + r_L}$

$= \dfrac{2}{8} = \dfrac{1}{4}$ A $= \mathbf{0.25\ A}$

$\therefore$ Power loss P_L in

$r_L = I_L^2 \times r_L = (0.25)^2 \times 5 = \mathbf{0.3125\ W.}$

EXAMPLE 6.5 *Determine the current through the 5 Ω resistor in the circuit of Fig. E6.5.*

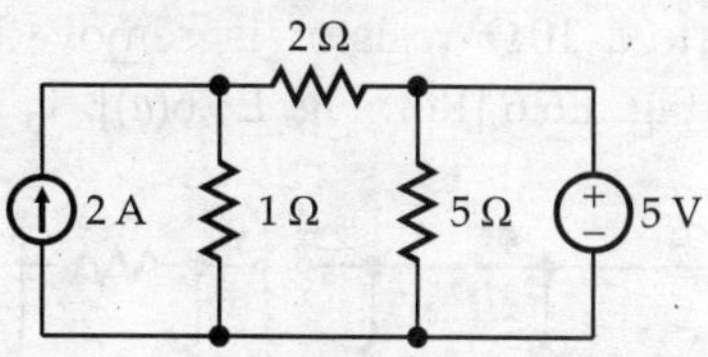

Fig. E6.5

SOLUTION. 5 Ω resistor is removed from the circuit of Fig. E6.5 and obviously, the open circuit voltage across *x-y* is 5 V (Fig. E6.5(*a*))

i.e., $V_{o.c} = 5$ V

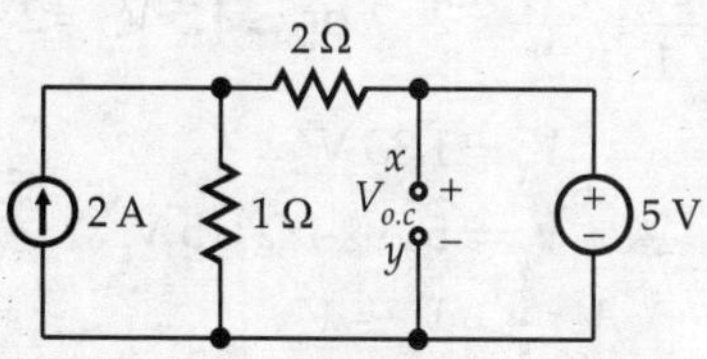

Fig. E6.5 (*a*)

To obtain the Thevenin resistance of the given circuit across the open circuited terminal *x-y*, the independent sources are deactivated and shown in Fig. E6.5(*b*).

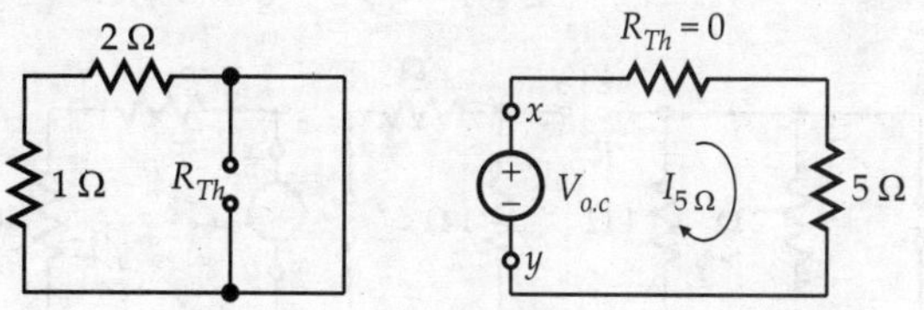

Fig. E6.5 (*b*)

It is evident from Fig. E6.5(*b*) that

$R_{Th} = 0.$

Thus, the Thevenin current *i.e.*, the current through the 5 Ω resistor is given by

$I_{5\Omega} = \dfrac{V_{o.c}}{R_{Th} + 5} = \dfrac{5}{5} = \mathbf{1\ A.}$ (Fig. E6.5(*c*))

EXAMPLE 6.6 *What is the power loss in the* $10\,\Omega$ *resistor ? Use Thevenin's Theorem in Fig. E6.6.*

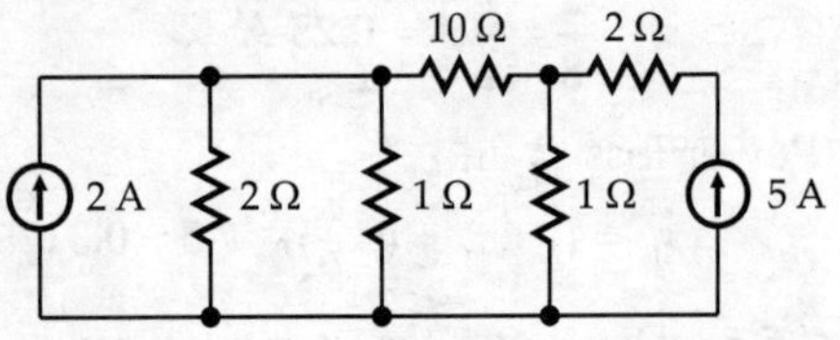

Fig. E6.6

SOLUTION. $10\,\Omega$ resistor is removed from the circuit of Fig. E6.6 [Ref. Fig. E6.6(*a*)].

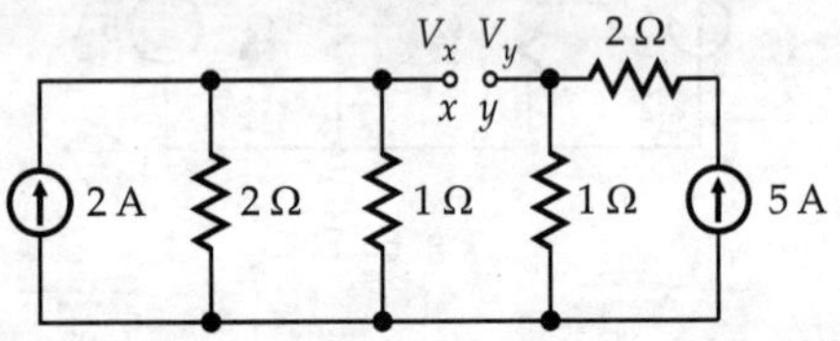

Fig. E6.6 (*a*)

Application of KCL at *node 'x'* yields

$$\frac{V_x}{1}+\frac{V_x}{2}=2 \quad \text{or,} \quad 1.5\,V_x=2$$

$\therefore \quad V_x = 1.33\text{ V}$

Also, $\quad V_y = 5\text{ A}\times 1\,\Omega = 5\text{ V}$

$$\therefore \quad V_{x-y} = V_x - V_y$$
$$= 1.33 - 5 = -3.67\text{ V}$$

[*i.e.*, y terminal is $-$ve]

Obviously, V_{x-y} is identical to V_{Th}.

With reference to Fig. E6.6(*b*),

$$R_{Th} = 1+\frac{2\times 1}{2+1} = 1+\frac{2}{3}=\frac{5}{3}\,\Omega$$

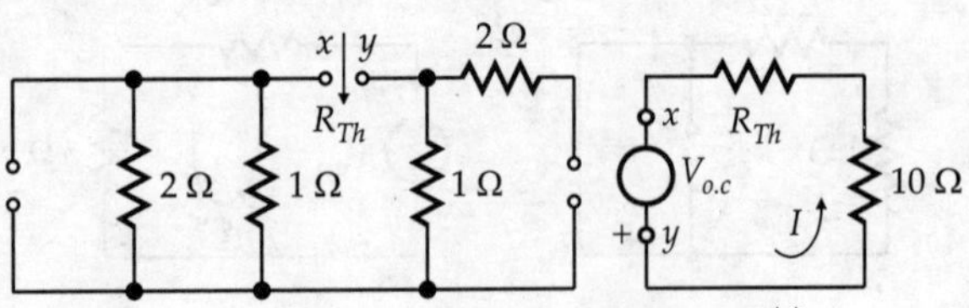

(*b*) (*c*)

Fig. E6.6

Thevenin's equivalent circuit being drawn in Fig. E6.6(*c*),

$$I_{10\Omega} \equiv I = \frac{V_{o.c}}{R_{Th}+10} = \frac{3.67}{\frac{5}{3}+10} = 0.315\text{ A}$$

(anticlockwise)

$\therefore$ Current through $10\,\Omega$ resistor = **0.315 A.**

EXAMPLE 6.7 *In the network of Fig. E6.7, find* V_{x-y} *and* R_{int} *(across x - y) using Thevenin's Theorem.*

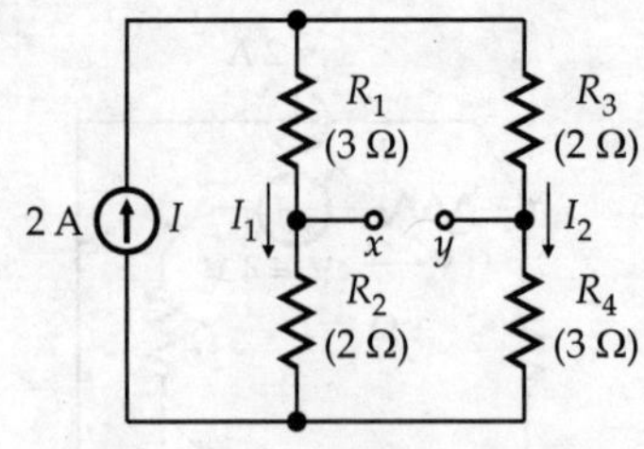

Fig. E6.7

SOLUTION. In Fig. E6.7,

$$I_1 = I\,\frac{R_3+R_4}{(R_1+R_2)+(R_3+R_4)}$$

[by current division formula]

$$= 2\times\frac{2+3}{(2+3)+(3+2)} = 1\text{ A}$$

and
$$I_2 = I\times\frac{R_1+R_2}{(R_1+R_2)+(R_3+R_4)}$$
$$= 2\times\frac{3+2}{(3+2)+(2+3)} = 1\text{ A}$$

Thus, the voltage drop across $R_2 = 1\times 2 = 2$ V

and voltage drop across $R_4 = 1\times 3 = 3$ V

$$\therefore \quad V_{x-y} = V_x - V_y = 2\text{V} - 3\text{V} = -\mathbf{1\ V}$$

i.e., Y is at higher potential.

To find R_{int}, across x - y, current source is removed and $(R_1 + R_2)$ is in parallel to $(R_3 + R_4)$

$$\therefore \quad R_{int} = (R_1+R_2)\,||\,(R_3+R_4) \text{ [Fig. E6.7(a)]}$$
$$= 5\,||\,5 = \mathbf{2.5\,\Omega}.$$

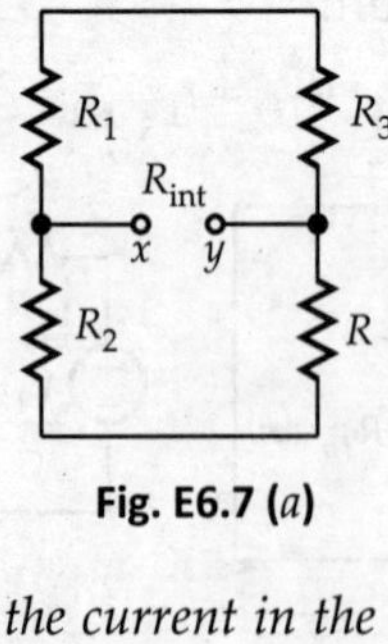

Fig. E6.7 (*a*)

EXAMPLE 6.8 *Find the current in the* $3\,\Omega$ *resistor for the circuit shown in Fig. E6.8.*

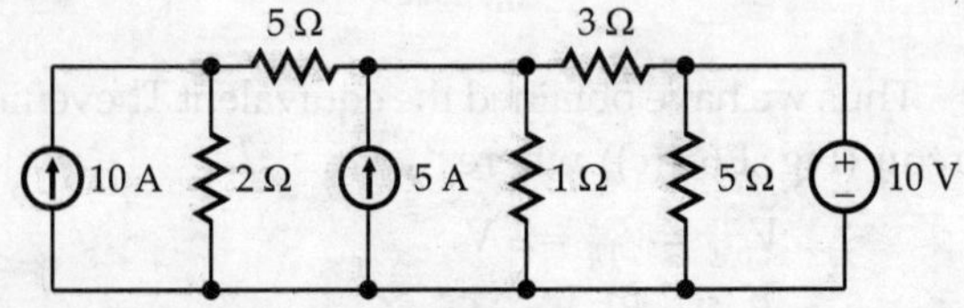

Fig. E6.8

Solution. The current sources are transformed to voltage sources first (Ref. Fig. E6.8(*a*)).

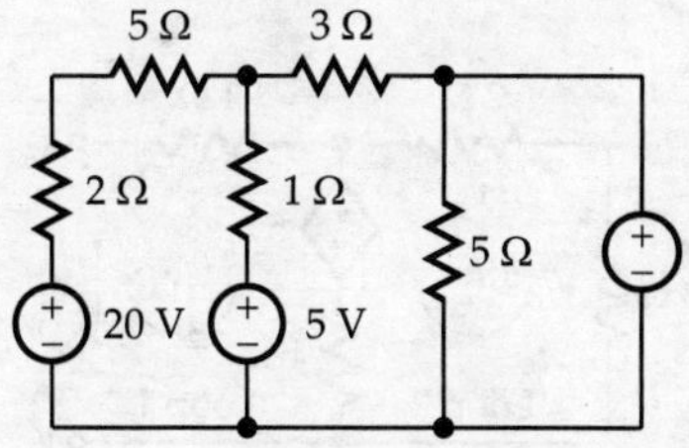

Fig. E6.8 (*a*)

Next, the 3 Ω resistor is removed (Fig. E6.8(*b*))

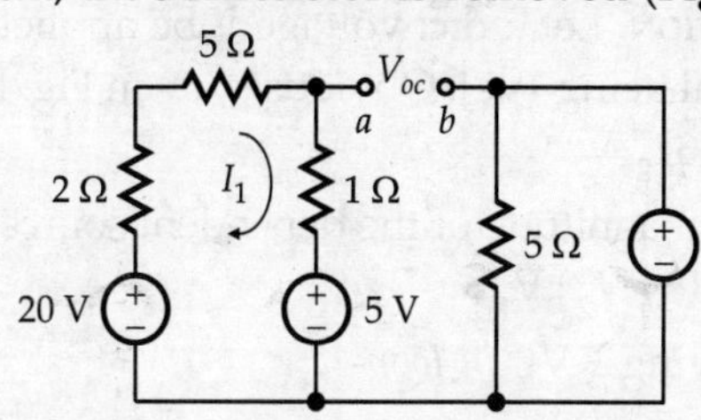

Fig. E6.8 (*b*)

The circulating current (I_1) in the left-most loop is then given by

$$I_1 = \frac{20-5}{2+5+1} = \frac{15}{8}\text{ A}$$

$$\therefore \quad V_{o.c} = 20 - \frac{15}{8}(2+5) - 10$$

$$= -3.125\text{ V} \qquad [\textit{i.e.}, \text{'b' terminal is +ve}]$$

To find the Thevenin's resistance of the given circuit, the sources are deactivated as shown in Fig. E6.8(*c*).

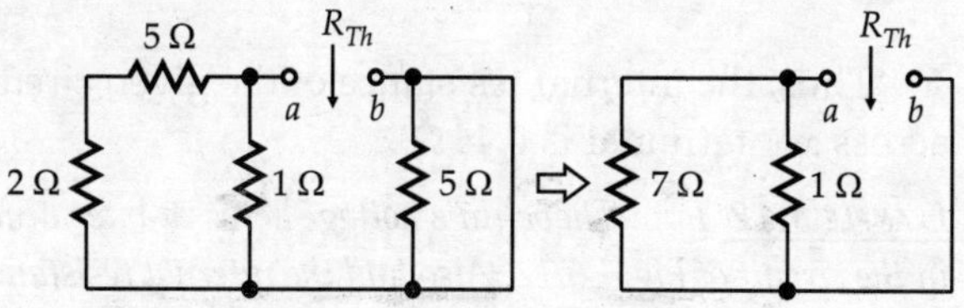

Fig. E6.8 (*c*)

Here $R_{Th} = \frac{7 \times 1}{7+1} = \frac{7}{8}\,\Omega$

The Thevenin's equivalent circuit being given in Fig. E6.8(*d*), the current through 3 Ω resistor is given by

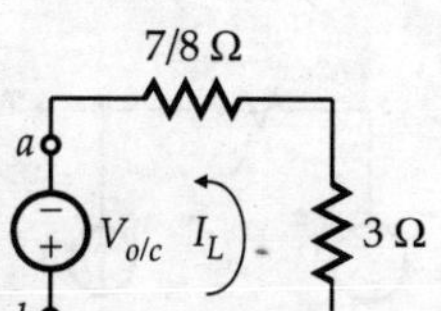

Fig. E6.8 (*d*)

$$I_L = \frac{V_{o.c}}{\frac{7}{8}+3} = \frac{3.125}{\frac{7}{8}+3} = 0.806\text{ A (anticlockwise)}$$

Thus, the current through the 3 Ω resistor is **0.806 A.**

Example 6.9 *Find the Thevenin's equivalent circuit for the network shown in Fig. E6.9 at the right of terminal a-b.*

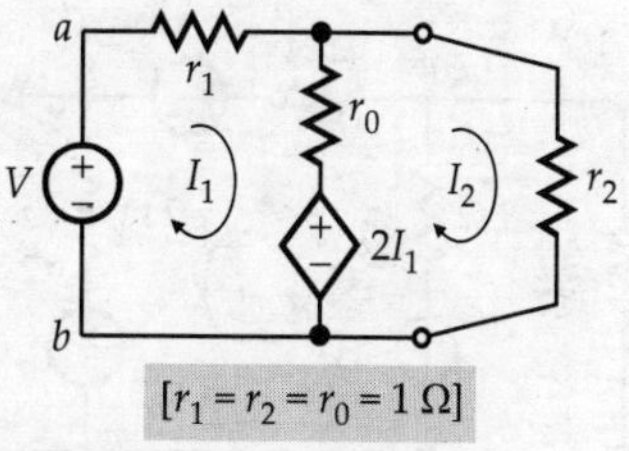

Fig. E6.9

Solution. Let the terminals *a-b* be open circuited. This leads to $I_1 = 0$ and the depending voltage source $2I_1$ is also zero. Also, $I_2 = 0$. Obviously $V_{o.c}$ (*i.e.*, the open circuit voltage across *a-b*) is zero.

Next, a dc voltage supply v_{dc} be applied across *a-b* such that the input current be I_1 at terminal *a*.

Applying KVL at the left loop under this condition,

$$v_{dc} = I_1 r_1 + I_1 r_0 - I_2 r_0 + 2I_1$$

or, $$v_{dc} = r_1 I_1 + r_0 (I_1 - I_2) + 2I_1 \qquad ...(a)$$

Applying KVL at the outer loop,

$$v_{dc} = r_1 I_1 + r_2 I_2 \qquad ...(b)$$

However,

$$r_1 = r_2 = r_0 = 1\,\Omega$$

∴ (*a*) becomes

$$v_{dc} = I_1 + I_1 - I_2 + 2I_1 = 4I_1 - I_2 \qquad ...(c)$$

and (*b*) becomes

$$v_{dc} = I_1 + I_2 \qquad ...(d)$$

From (*d*),

$$I_2 = v_{dc} - I_1.$$

Using this value of I_2 in (*c*),

$$v_{dc} = 4I_1 - (v_{d.c.} - I_1)$$

or, $$2v_{dc} = 5I_1$$

$$\therefore \quad \frac{v_{dc}}{I_1} = \frac{5}{2} = 2.5\,\Omega$$

Thus, the internal resistance of the circuit across *a-b* is 2.5 Ω.

The given circuit is thus Thevenised to give

$$\mathbf{V_{o.c} = 0\ V}$$

$$\mathbf{R_{int} = 2.5\,\Omega.}$$

EXAMPLE 6.10 *Obtain Thevenin's equivalent circuit across x-y terminals (Fig. E6.10).*

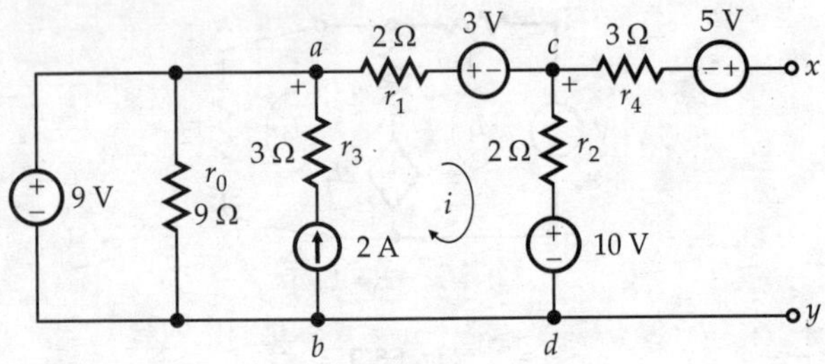

Fig. E6.10

SOLUTION. Application of KVL at loop *acdb*,

$$-V_{ab} + ir_1 + 3 + ir_2 + 10 = 0$$

or, $\quad -9 + 2\,i + 3 + 2\,i + 10 = 0 \quad [\because V_{a-b} = 9\text{ V}]$

or, $\quad 4\,i = -4 \;\; i.e.,\; i = -1\text{ A}$

$\therefore$ Drop in r_2 is $\quad 2 \times (-1) = -2$ V

This gives $\quad V_{c-d} = 10 - 2 = 8$ V

$\therefore \quad V_{o.c} = V_{c-d} + 5 = 8 + 5 = \mathbf{13\ V.}$

To find R_{int} $(= R_{Th})$ the independent sources are removed (Fig. E6.10(*a*)).

$$R_{Th} = \frac{2 \times 2}{2+2} + 3 = 4\,\Omega\,.$$

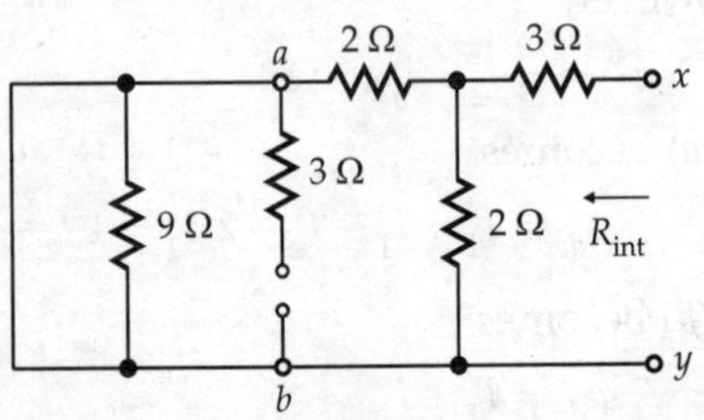

Fig. E6.10 (*a*)

9 Ω resistance has no effectivity as it is shorted. Also, 3 Ω resistance in branch *a-b* is not effective as the branch itself is open circuited.

Thevenin's equivalent circuit has been shown in Fig. 6.10(*b*).

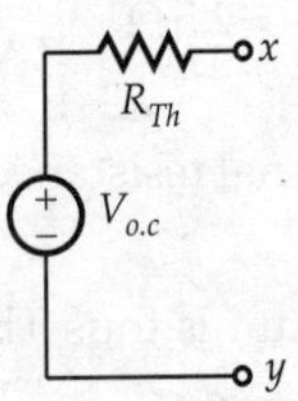

Fig. E6.10 (*b*)

EXAMPLE 6.11 *Find the internal resistance of the network given in Fig. E6.11 looking through open circuited x-y terminal.*

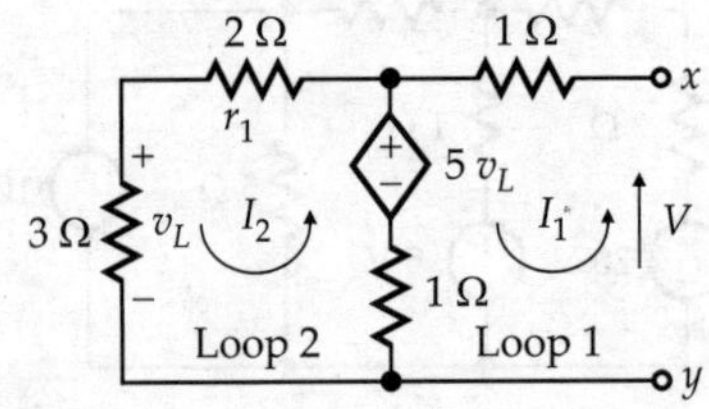

Fig. E6.11

SOLUTION. Let a d.c. voltage *V* be applied at *x-y* [*x* terminal being +ve]. Obviously, v_L in Fig. E6.11 is $(I_2 \times 3)$ or $3I_2$ V.

$\therefore$ The magnitude of the dependent source is then $(5v_L)$ or, $(15 \times I_2)$ V.

Applying KVL *in loop-1,*

$$V = (1+1)\,I_1 + 5v_L - 1 \times I_2$$

or, $\quad V = 2I_1 + 15I_2 - I_2 = 2I_1 + 14I_2 \qquad \text{...(1)}$

Application of KVL *in loop-2* yields

$$0 = (1+3+2)\,I_2 - 5v_L - 1 \times I_1$$

or, $\quad 0 = 6I_2 - 15I_2 - I_1 = -9I_2 - I_1 \qquad \text{...(2)}$

Thus, from (2), $\quad I_2 = -\dfrac{1}{9}\,I_1$

Utilising this in (1), $\quad V = 2I_1 - 1.56\,I_1 \qquad \text{...(3)}$

Obviously, from (3),

$$\frac{V}{I_1} = R_{int} = \mathbf{0.44\,\Omega.}$$

Thus, the internal resistance of the given circuit across *x-y* terminal is **0.44 Ω.**

EXAMPLE 6.12 *Find Thevenin's voltage across a-b terminal in the circuit of Fig. E6.12. Also find the internal resistance across the open circuited a-b terminal.*

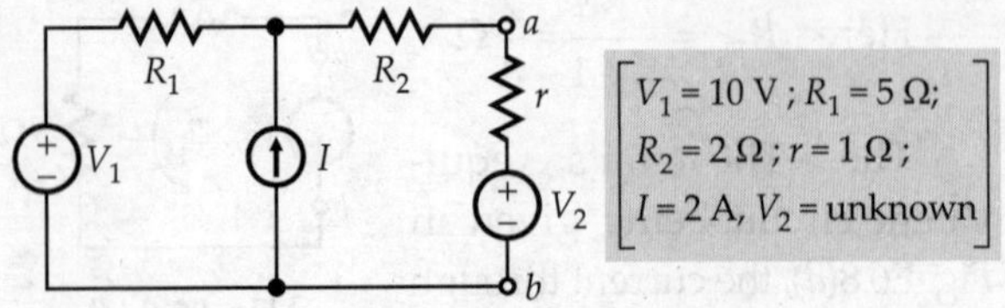

Fig. E6.12

SOLUTION. Let the terminals *a-b* be open circuited. No current flows through *r*. The circuit is shown in Fig. E6.12(*a*).

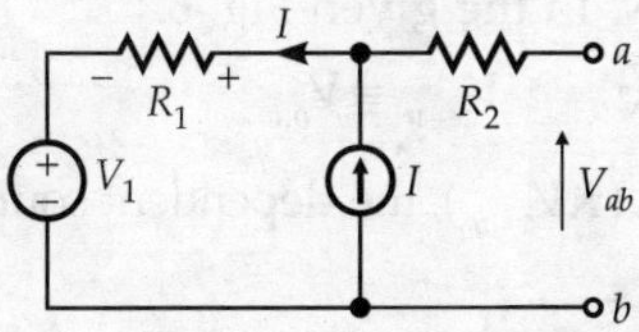

Fig. E6.12 (a)

Using KVL at left hand loop,

$$V_{a-b}\,(=V_{Th}) = V_1 + IR_1 = 10 + 2 \times 5 = 20 \text{ V}.$$

Next, all the independent sources of the given circuit are replaced by their internal resistances in order to find the Thevenin's resistance across *a-b*. [The circuit configuration is shown in Fig. E6.12(*b*)].

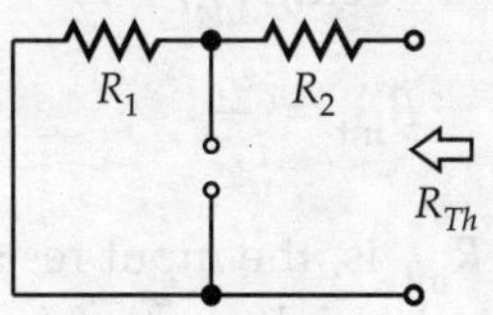

Fig. E6.12 (b)

The voltage source V_1 is short circuited and the current source is open circuited.

$$\therefore \qquad R_{Th} = R_1 + R_2 = 5 + 2 = 7\,\Omega.$$

Thus we obtain V_{Th} **= 20 V ;** R_{Th} **= 7 Ω.**

EXAMPLE 6.13 *In the circuit of Fig. E6.13, find the internal resistance of the circuit looking through terminals x-y. Also find* $V_{o.c}$ *across x-y.*

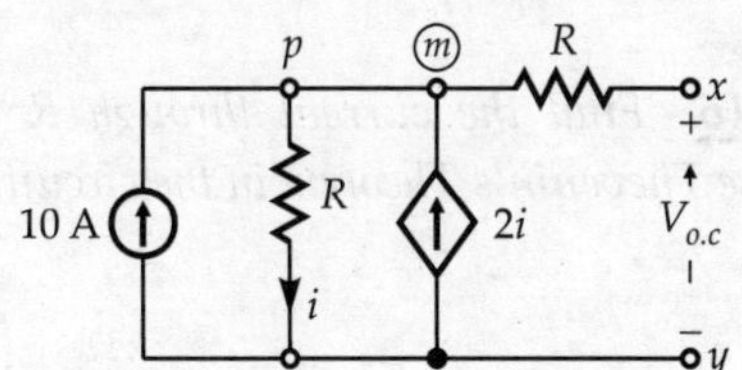

Fig. E6.13

SOLUTION. Let us first find R_{int} (internal resistance of the circuit through *x-y*). For this purpose, we remove the constant current source 10 A by open circuit and apply a voltage source v_0 across *x-y*.

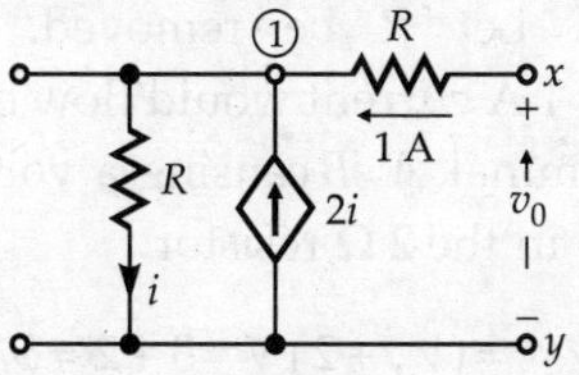

Fig. E6.13 (a)

Fig. E6.13(*a*) exhibits this circuit. Let us assume that the current entering through terminals *x-y* be 1 A.

Application of KCL *at node 1* in Fig. E6.13(*a*) reveals,

$$2i - i + 1 = 0 \quad i.e., \quad i = -1 \text{ A}$$

Figure E6.13(*b*) represents the circuit configuration and the respective voltage drops across the resistances. (1 A current through *R* is replaced by *i* directed opposite).

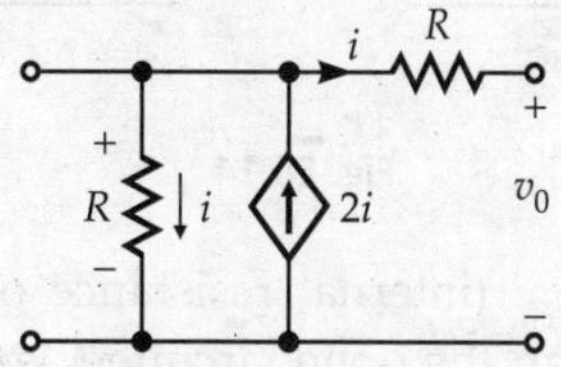

Fig. E6.13 (b)

Here, application of KVL in the outer loop yields

$$iR - v_0 - iR = 0 \quad i.e., \quad v_0 = 0.$$

$$\text{Thus,} \qquad R_{\text{int}} = \frac{v_0}{i} = \frac{0}{-1} = 0\,\Omega.$$

Application of KCL *at node "m"* in Fig. E6.13 yields

$$10 + 2i - i = 0 \quad i.e., \quad i = -10 \text{ A}$$

However, $V_{o.c}$ is the drop across branch $p-q$ in Fig. E6.13 which is very much evident.

$$\therefore \qquad V_{o.c} = V_{p-q} = i \times R = (-10\ R) \text{ V}.$$

[Ref. Fig. E6.13(*c*) also]

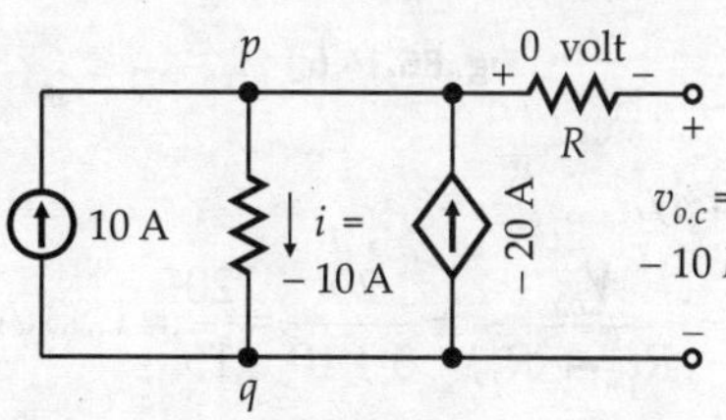

Fig. E6.13 (c)

EXAMPLE 6.14 *In the circuit of Fig. E6.14, if* $r = 5\,\Omega$, $R_L = 10\,\Omega$, $v_0 = 10$ *V,* $i_0 = 2$ *A, find the current through* R_L *using Thevenin's theorem.*

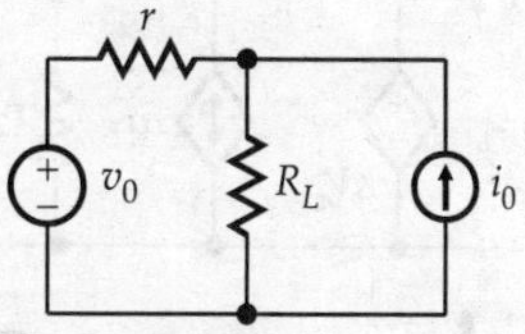

Fig. E6.14

Solution. Let R_L be removed, the circuit configuration being shown in Fig. E6.14(*a*).

Here $V_{o.c}$ (*i.e.*, V_{Th}) $= i_0 r + v_0$

or, $$V_{o.c} = 2 \times 5 + 10 = 20 \text{ V}$$

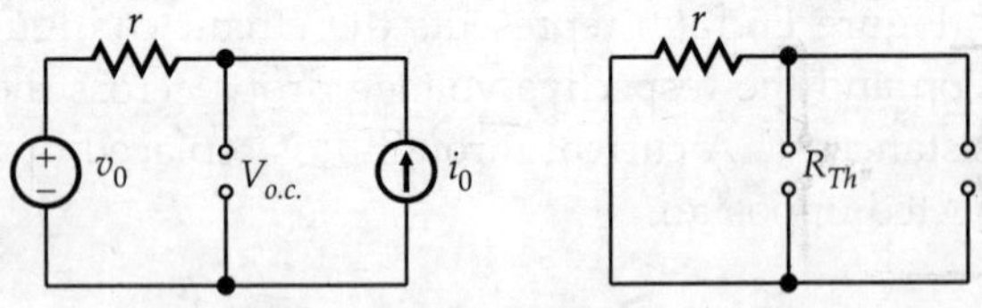

(*a*) (*b*)

Fig. E6.14

To find R_{Th} (internal resistance of the circuit looking through the open circuited terminals), the constant sources are deactivated [Fig. E6.14(*b*)].

Here $R_{Th} = r = 5\,\Omega.$

Thus, the given circuit has been Thevenised across the open circuited terminals *x-y*

where $V_{o.c} = 20$ V and $R_{Th} = 5\,\Omega$

Thus, the Thevenin's current (*I*) through R_L can be obtained from the Thevenin's equivalent circuit (Fig. E6.14(*c*)).

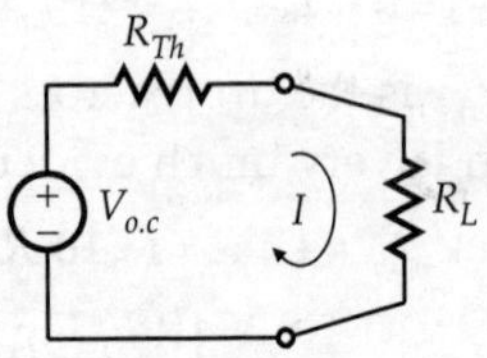

Fig. E6.14 (*c*)

Obviously,

$$I = \frac{V_{o.c}}{R_{Th} + R_L} = \frac{20}{5+10} = \frac{20}{15} = 1.33 \text{ A.}$$

Then, the current through R_L is **1.33 A.**

Example 6.15 *Thevenise the circuit to the left of terminal x-y in the network shown in Fig. E6.15. Assume K = 0.*

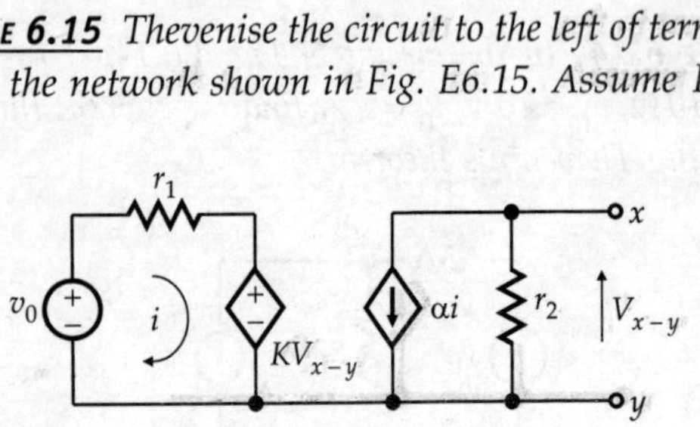

Fig. E6.15

Solution. In the given Fig. 6.15,

$$V_{x-y} \equiv V_{o.c}.$$

As $K = 0, (KV_{x-y})$, the dependent source becomes zero. Thus

$$i = (V_0 / r_1) \text{ A}$$

Also, $V_{x-y} (= V_{o.c}) = -(\alpha\, i) \times r_2$

or, $$V_{x-y} = -\alpha\left(\frac{V_0}{r_1}\right) r_2 = -\frac{\alpha\, V_0\, r_2}{r_1} \text{ V}$$

Let us now deactivate the constant sources. Then $i = 0$ and $\alpha\, i = 0$. If a driving voltage v is now applied at *x-y* terminals, the input current entering through *x* terminal being i_{dc},

$$R_{\text{int}} = \frac{v}{i_{dc}}$$

[when R_{int} is, the input resistance looking back through *x-y* terminal while $\alpha i = 0$]

But obviously, $i_{dc} = \dfrac{v}{r_2}$

$$\therefore \quad R_{\text{int}} = \frac{v}{\dfrac{v}{r_2}} = r_2\,\Omega$$

Thus, with $K = 0$ the given circuit has been thevenised where,

$$V_{o.c} (= V_{Th}) = -\frac{\alpha\, \boldsymbol{V_0 r_2}}{\boldsymbol{r_1}} \textbf{ V and } R_{\text{int}} = \boldsymbol{r_2}\,\boldsymbol{\Omega}.$$

Example 6.16 *Find the current through R assuming R = 3 Ω. Use Thevenin's Theorem in the circuit shown in Fig. E6.16.*

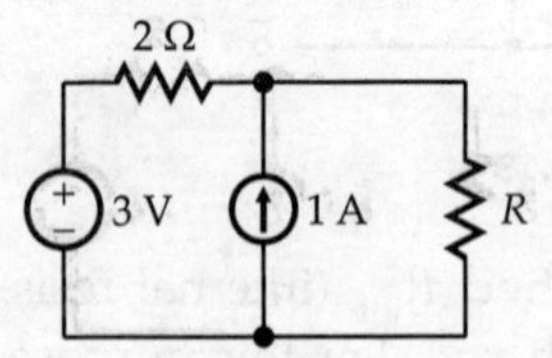

Fig. E6.16

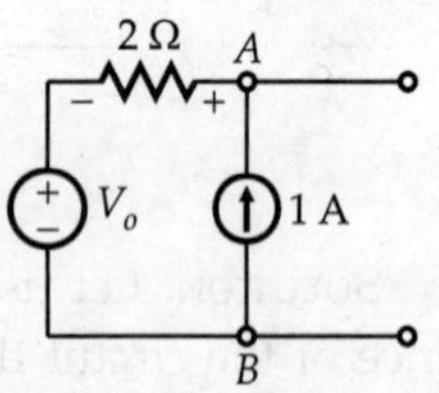

Fig. E6.16 (*a*)

Solution. Let *R* be removed. It may be observed that 1 A current would flow only towards the left of terminal *A - B* causing a voltage drop of 2 × 1 (*i.e.*, 2 V) in the 2 Ω resistor.

Also, $V_{o.c} = (V_0 + 2)\text{ V} = 3 + 2 = 5 \text{ V}$

[Fig. E6.16(*a*))

To find R_{int} (= R_{Th}), all the constant sources are deactivated and the circuit configuration is shown in Fig. E6.16(*b*). Obviously $R_{int} = 2\,\Omega$.

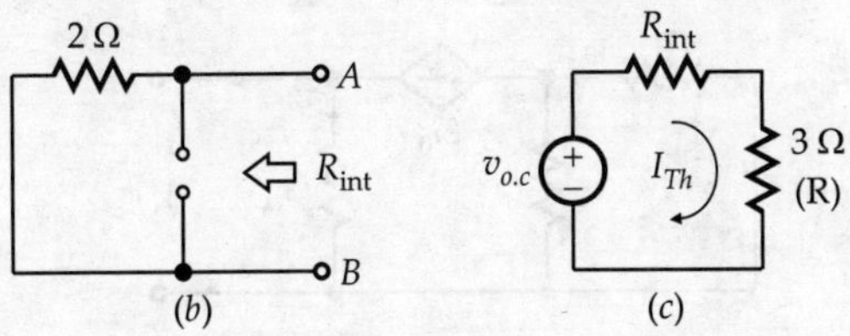

Fig. E6.16

Thevenin's equivalent circuit being drawn in Fig. E6.16(*c*), the current through $R\,(=3\,\Omega)$ is given by

$$I_{Th} = \frac{V_{o.c}}{R_{int} + R} = \frac{5}{3+2} = \mathbf{1\ A.}$$

EXAMPLE 6.17 *In Fig. E6.17, a resistance "r" is shown to be connected across an active network. It is given that when*

(i) $r = \infty$, $V = 5\ V$

(ii) $r = 0$, *current output of the active source is 2.5 A. What would be the current through r when the value of r is 5 Ω ?*

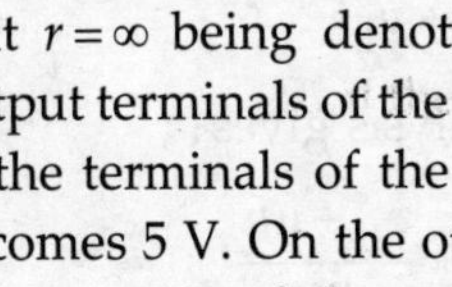

Fig. E6.17

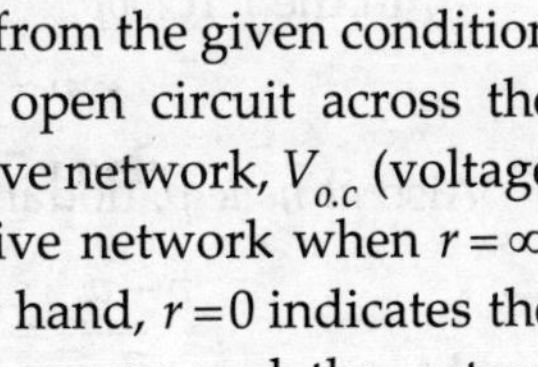

Fig. E6.17 (*a*)

SOLUTION. It is evident from the given condition that $r = \infty$ being denoting open circuit across the output terminals of the active network, $V_{o.c}$ (voltage at the terminals of the active network when $r = \infty$) becomes 5 V. On the other hand, $r = 0$ indicates the short circuit of the active source and the output current being $I_{s.c}$, it is given that

$$I_{s.c} = 2.5\ A.$$

Thus, R_{int} (internal resistance of the given source)

$$= \frac{V_{o.c}}{I_{s.c}} = \frac{5}{2.5} = 2\,\Omega$$

Figure E6.17(*a*) being representing the Thevenin's equivalent circuit, the current through 5 Ω resistor is

$$I_{5\Omega} = \frac{V_{o.c}}{R_{int} + 5} = \frac{5}{2+5} = \frac{5}{7} = \mathbf{0.71\ A}$$

EXAMPLE 6.18 *Obtain Thevenin's equivalent to the left of terminal a-b in the circuit of Fig. E6.18.*

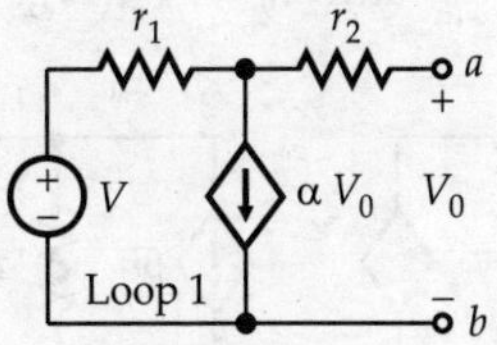

Fig. E6.18

SOLUTION. In Fig. E6.18, the loop current being αV_0, it would create a drop of $(r_1\,\alpha\,V_0)$ across r_1.

Assuming $V_0 \equiv V_{o.c}$,

Application of KVL *in loop-1* gives

$$-V + r_1\,\alpha\,V_{o.c} + V_{o.c} = 0$$

or, $$V_{o.c} = V - r_1\,\alpha\,V_{o.c}$$

i.e., $$V_{o.c}\,(1 + r_1\,\alpha) = V$$

$\therefore$ $$V_{o.c} = \frac{V}{1 + \alpha\,r_1}$$

To determine R_{int}, $a-b$ terminals are shorted, V_0 becomes zero. Since $V_0 = 0$, the voltage control current source $\alpha\,V_0$ is also equal to zero. Thus, r_1, r_2 are in series with *V*. The circulating current being $I_{s.c}$

$I_{s.c} = \dfrac{V}{r_1 + r_2}$ and hence, the internal resistance of the given network is given by

$$R_{int} = \frac{V_{o.c}}{I_{s.c}} = \frac{V}{1 + \alpha\,r_1} \cdot \frac{r_1 + r_2}{V} = \frac{r_1 + r_2}{1 + \alpha\,r_1}.$$

This gives the Thevenin's equivalent circuit as

$$\mathbf{V_{o.c} = \frac{V}{1 + \alpha\,r_1};\ R_{int} = \frac{r_1 + r_2}{1 + \alpha\,r_1}.}$$

EXAMPLE 6.19 *Find Thevenin's equivalent impedance of the given circuit in Fig. E6.19 looking from x-y terminals.*

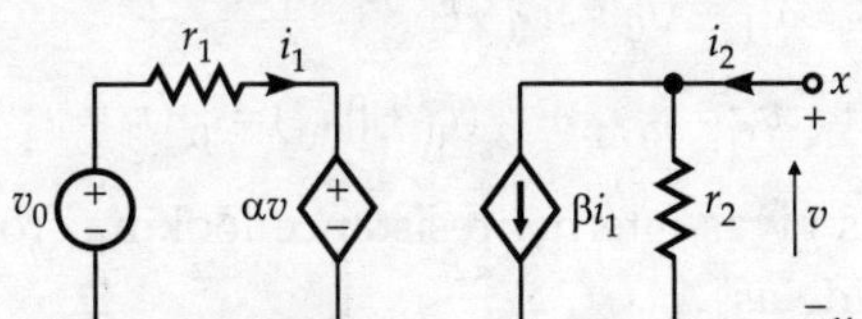

Fig. E6.19

SOLUTION. Let v_0 be deactivated and v be replaced by v_{dc}, the driving point voltage at *x-y* such that $v \equiv v_{dc}$ and $i_2 \equiv i_{dc}$ (Fig. E6.19(*a*))

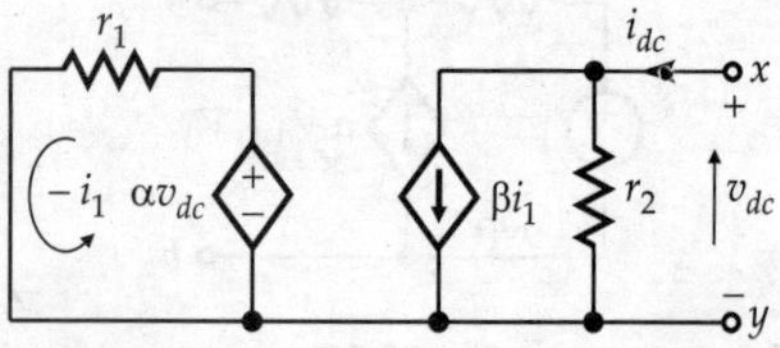

Fig. E6.19 (*a*)

$$\text{Here, } -i_1 = \frac{\alpha\, v_{dc}}{r_1} \quad ...(i)$$

At node x, KCL yields

$$i_{dc} = \beta i_1 + \frac{v_{dc}}{r_2} = \beta\left(-\frac{\alpha\, v_{dc}}{r_1}\right) + \frac{v_{dc}}{r_2}$$

$$\text{or,} \quad i_{dc} = v_{dc}\left(\frac{1}{r_2} - \frac{\alpha\beta}{r_1}\right)$$

$$\therefore \quad \frac{v_{dc}}{i_{dc}} = Z_{\text{int}\,(x-y)} = \frac{1}{\dfrac{1}{r_2} - \dfrac{\alpha\beta}{r_1}} = \frac{r_1\, r_2}{r_1 - r_2\,\alpha\beta}\,\Omega$$

$$\text{i.e.,} \quad Z_{\text{int}} = \frac{r_1\, r_2}{r_1 - r_2\,\alpha\beta}\,\Omega.$$

EXAMPLE 6.20 *(a) Find Thevenin's impedance of the circuit given in Fig. E6.20 looking from (i) input (ii) output.*

(b) Find Z_{input} at terminals a-b and x-y respectively (Fig. E6.20(b))

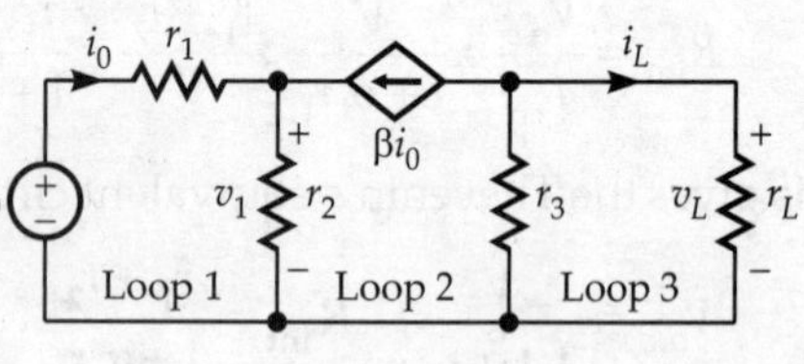

Fig. E6.20

SOLUTION. (*a*) *In loop-1,* $v_0 = i_0\, r_1 + v_1$ [Fig. E6.20]

$$\text{But} \quad v_1 = (i_0 + \beta\, i_0)\, r_2$$

$$\therefore \quad v_0 = i_0\, r_1 + r_2\,(i_0 + \beta\, i_0) = i_0\,(r_1 + r_2 + \beta r_2)$$

This gives internal resistance looking from the input side as

$$Z_{\text{int (input)}} = \frac{v_0}{i_0} = \mathbf{(r_1 + r_2 + \beta r_2)\,\Omega}$$

To find the output impedance, let R_L be removed by a driving point *dc* voltage $v_{dc}\ (= v_L)$ such that $i_{dc} = -i_L$. (Fig. E6.20(*a*)).

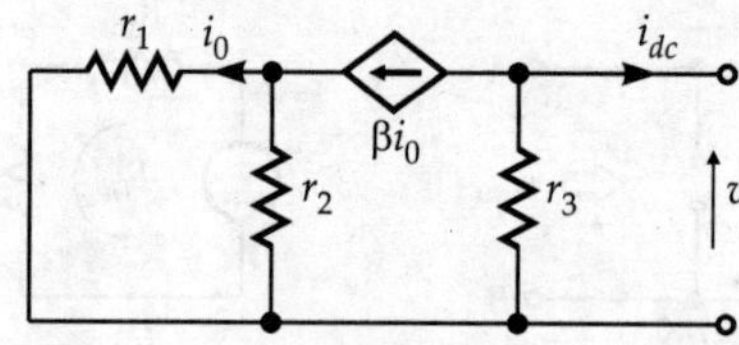

Fig. E6.20 (*a*)

$$\text{Here,} \quad i_{dc} = \frac{v_{dc}}{r_3} + \beta i_0 \quad ...(1)$$

$$\text{But} \quad i_0 = -\beta i_0\,\frac{r_2}{r_1 + r_2} \quad ...(2)$$

Equation (2) can only hold for $i_0 = 0$.

$$\text{Thus,} \quad i_{dc} = \frac{v_{dc}}{r_3} \quad \text{[from (1)]}$$

$$\text{Thus} \quad \frac{v_{dc}}{i_{dc}} = \mathbf{r_3 = Z_{\text{int (output)}}}$$

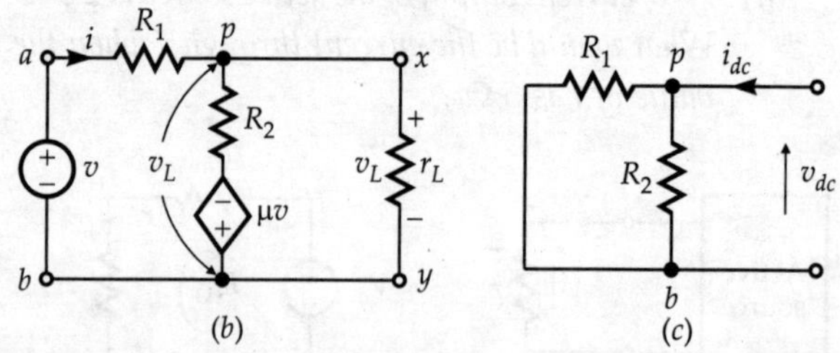

Fig. E6.20

(*b*) In the left *loop*,

$$v = iR_1 + v_L \quad ...(3)$$

Also *at node p*, nodal analysis gives

$$\frac{v - v_L}{R_1} = \frac{v_L}{r_L} + \frac{v_L + \mu v}{R_2}$$

$$\text{or} \quad \frac{v}{R_1} - \frac{v_L}{R_1} = \frac{v_L}{r_L} + \frac{v_L}{R_2} + \frac{\mu v}{R_2}$$

$$\text{or,} \quad v\left(\frac{1}{R_1} - \frac{\mu}{R_2}\right) = v_L\left(\frac{1}{r_L} + \frac{1}{R_2} + \frac{1}{R_1}\right)$$

$$\therefore \quad v_L = v\,\frac{\left(\dfrac{1}{R_1} - \dfrac{\mu}{R_2}\right)}{\left(\dfrac{1}{r_L} + \dfrac{1}{R_2} + \dfrac{1}{R_1}\right)} \quad ...(4)$$

Using (4) in (3),

$$v = iR_1 + v\frac{\left(\frac{1}{R_1}-\frac{\mu}{R_2}\right)}{\left(\frac{1}{r_L}+\frac{1}{R_2}+\frac{1}{R_1}\right)}$$

or $\quad v(1-m) = iR_1$

$$\therefore \quad \frac{v}{i} = \mathbf{Z_{input\,(from\;a-b)}} = \frac{\mathbf{R_1}}{\mathbf{1-m}}$$

$$\left[\text{where } m = \frac{\frac{1}{R_1}-\frac{\mu}{R_2}}{\frac{1}{r_L}+\frac{1}{R_2}+\frac{1}{R_1}}\right]$$

$Z_{input\,(from\;x-y)}$ can be obtained from the same circuit by deactivating the source v and applying v_{dc} at x-y such that $v_{dc} \equiv v_L$ and input current being i_{dc}. Obviously, v being zero, $\mu v = 0$.

Thus $\quad v_{dc} = i_{dc} \times$ equiv. resistance between $p = b$

[ref. Fig. E6.20]

$$= i_{dc} \times \frac{R_1\,R_2}{R_1+R_2}$$

$$\therefore \quad Z_{input\,(x-y)} = v_{dc}/i_{dc} = \mathbf{(R_1\,R_2)/(R_1+R_2)}.$$

6.3 NORTON'S THEOREM

Norton theorem is converse of Thevenin's theorem. It consists of equivalent current source instead of equivalent voltage source as done in Thevenin's theorem. The determination of internal resistance of the source network is identical in both the theorems. However, in final stage, *i.e.*, in the Norton equivalent circuit, the current generator is placed in parallel to the internal resistance unlike to that in Thevenin's theorem where the equivalent voltage source was placed in series with the internal resistance.

6.3.1 Statement of Norton's Theorem

A linear active network consisting of independent and or dependant voltage and current sources and linear bilateral network elements can be replaced by an equivalent circuit consisting of a current source in parallel with a resistance, the current source being the short circuited current across the load terminal and the resistance being the internal resistance of the source network looking through the open circuited load terminals.

6.3.2 Explanation

In order to find the current through r_L, the load resistance (Fig. 6.3), by Norton's theorem, let us replace r_L by short circuit (Fig. 6.3(a)).

$$\text{Obviously,}\quad i = \frac{V_S}{r_1 + \frac{r_2\,r_3}{r_2+r_3}} \quad \text{and}\quad i_{s.c} = i\frac{r_3}{r_3+r_2}$$

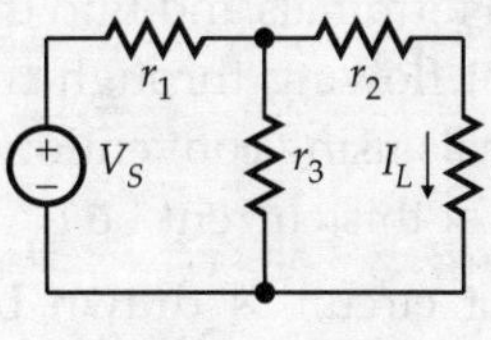

Fig. 6.3 A simple dc network

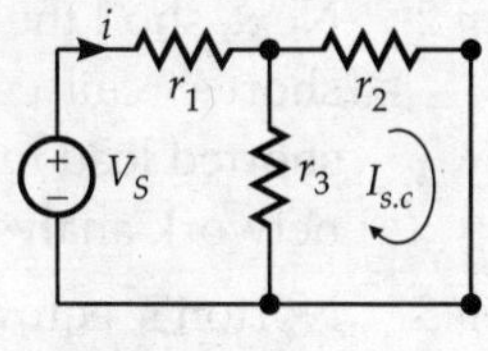

Fig. 6.3 (a) Finding of i_{sc}

Next, the short circuit is removed and the independent source is deactivated as done in Thevenin's theorem (Fig. 6.3(b)).

$$\text{Here,}\quad R_{int} = r_2 + \frac{r_1\,r_3}{r_1+r_3}.$$

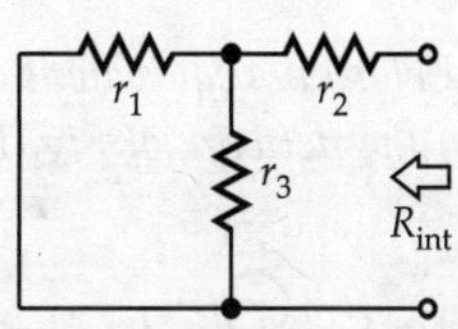

Fig. 6.3 (b) Finding of R_{Th} (or R_{int})

As per Norton's theorem, the equivalent source circuit would contain a current source in parallel to the internal resistance, the current source being the short circuited current across the shorted terminals of the load resistor (Fig. 6.3(c)).

$$\text{Obviously,}\quad I_L = i_{s.c}\frac{R_{int}}{R_{int}+r_L}$$

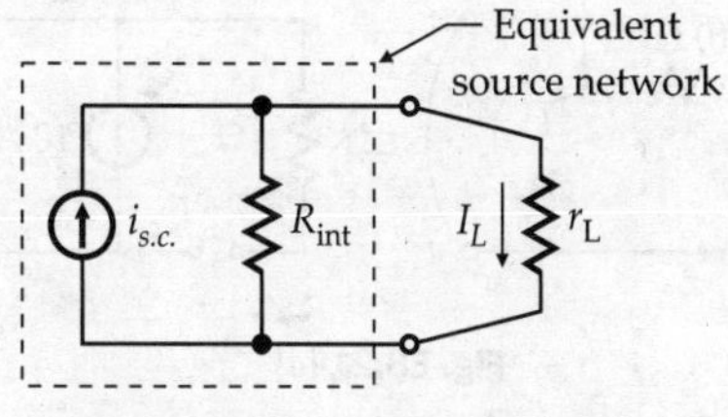

Fig. 6.3 (c) Norton's equivalent circuit

It may be noted here that determination of R_{int} for the source system in Norton Theorem is identical to that of Thevenin's theorem already described.

CHAPTER 6

6.3.3 Steps for Solution of a Network Utilizing Norton's Theorem

Step 1 Remove the load resistor and find the internal resistance of the source network by deactivating the constant sources. This procedure is exactly same as described for Thevenin's theorem. Let this resistance be R_{int}.

Step 2 Next, short the load terminals and find the short circuit current flowing through the shorted load terminals using conventional network analysis. Let this current be $i_{s.c}$.

Step 3 Norton's equivalent circuit is drawn by keeping R_{int} in parallel to $i_{s.c}$ as shown in Fig. 6.3(*c*).

Step 4 Reconnect the load resistor (R_L) across the load terminals and the current through it (I_L) is then given by

$$I_L = i_{s.c} \frac{R_{int}}{R_{int} + R_L}$$

Example 6.21 *Find Norton's equivalent circuit to the left of terminals x-y in the network of Fig. E6.21.*

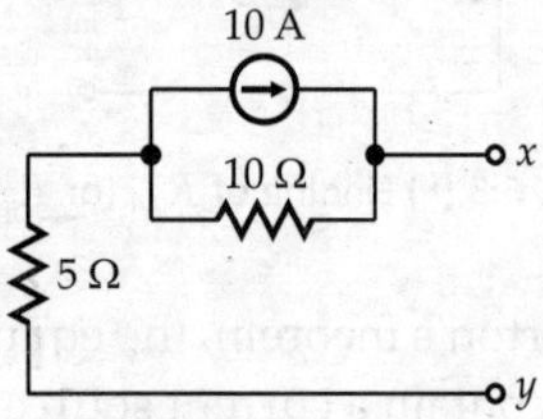

Fig. E6.21

Solution. Let us first short the terminals *x-y* (Fig. E6.21(*a*)).

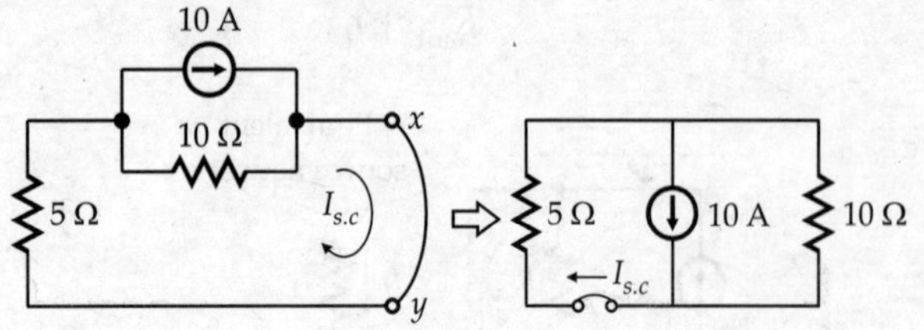

Fig. E6.21 (*a*)

Here, $I_{s.c}$ is the current through the 5 Ω resistor.

$$\therefore \quad I_{s.c} = 10 \times \frac{10}{10+5} = 6.67 \text{ A}$$

[by current divider rule]

To determine the equivalent resistance of the circuit of Fig. E6.21, looking through $x-y$, the constant source is deactivated as shown in Fig. E6.21(*b*).

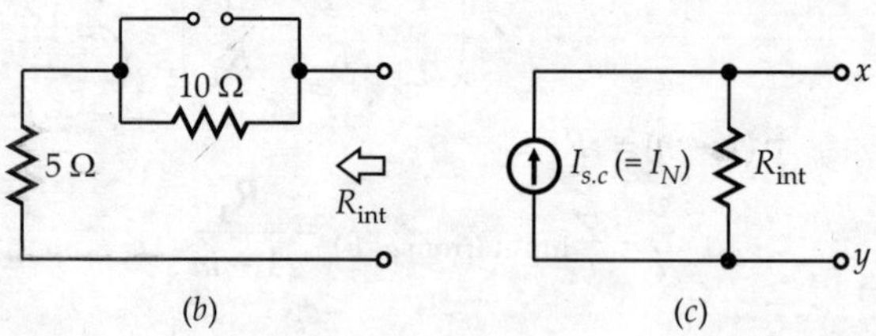

Fig. E6.21

Here, $R_{int} = 10 + 5 = 15\,\Omega$

Norton's equivalent circuit has been shown in Fig. E6.21(*c*),

Here, I_N **= 6.67 A;** R_{int} **= 15 Ω.**

Example 6.22 *Find the current in the 5 Ω resistor for the circuit shown in Fig. E6.22.*

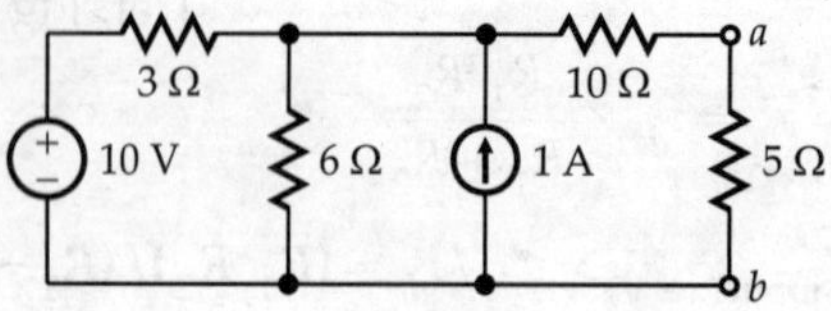

Fig. E6.22

Solution. Let us first remove the 5 Ω resistor and short the *a-b* terminals (Fig. E6.22(*a*)).

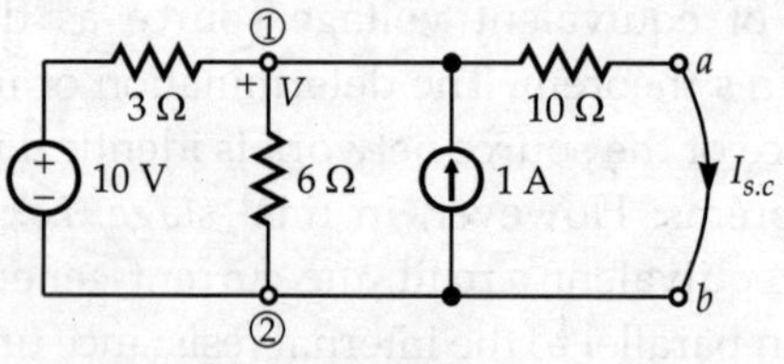

Fig. E6.22 (*a*)

Assuming the voltage to be +ve *at node 1* in Fig. E6.22(*a*), nodal analysis gives

$$\frac{V-10}{3} + \frac{V}{6} - 1 + \frac{V}{10} = 0$$

or, $\quad 0.33\text{ V} + 0.17\text{ V} + 0.1\text{ V} = 4.33$

or, $\quad V = 7.22\text{ V}$

Applying KVL at the right most loop (1-*a*-*b*-2),

$$-V + I_{s.c} \times 10 = 0$$

or, $\quad -7.22 + 10\,I_{s.c} = 0$

$\therefore \quad I_{s.c} = 0.722\text{ A} (= I_N)$.

To find Norton's equivalent resistance through *a-b*, 5 Ω resistor is removed and all the constant sources are deactivated (Fig. E6.22(*b*)).

Here, $R_{int} = \dfrac{3 \times 6}{3+6} + 10 = 12\ \Omega$.

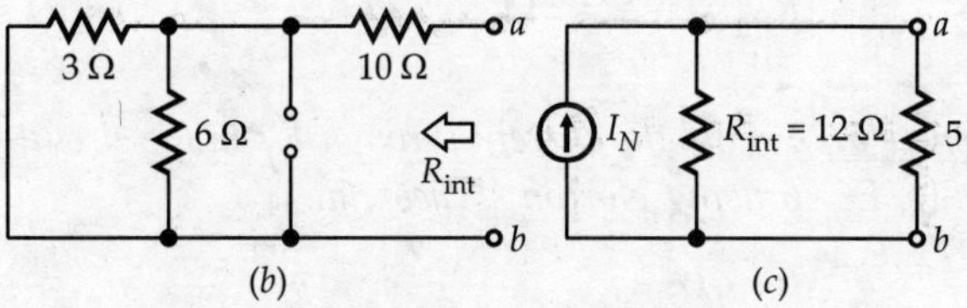

Fig. E6.22

Norton's equivalent circuit being shown in Fig. E6.22(*c*), current through 5 Ω resistor ($I_{5\Omega}$) is given by

$$I_{5\Omega} = I_N \frac{R_{int}}{R_{int}+5} = 0.722 \times \frac{12}{12+5}$$

$$= 0.5096\ \text{A} (\simeq 509.6\ \text{mA})$$

i.e., the current through 5 Ω resistance is **509.6 mA.**

Example 6.23 *Find the Norton's equivalent circuit across a-b for the network shown in Fig. E6.23.*

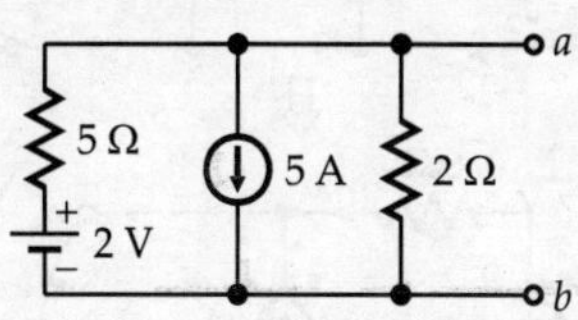

Fig. E6.23

Solution. Let us first apply short circuit across *a-b* . 2 Ω resistor is then by-passed as shown in Fig. E6.23(*a*).

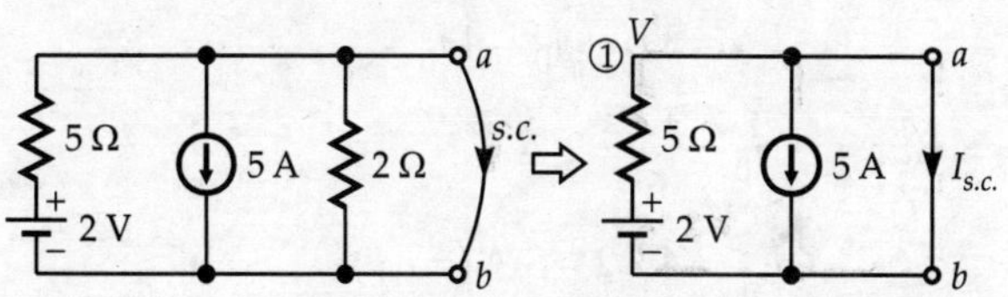

Fig. E6.23 (*a*)

Taking first the 2 V source (Fig. E6.23(*b*)),

$$2 = 5 \times I'_{s.c}$$

$$\therefore \quad I'_{s.c} = \frac{2}{5} = 0.4\ \text{A}$$

Next, taking 5 A source only (Fig. E6.23(*c*)),

$$I''_{s.c} = -5\ \text{A}$$

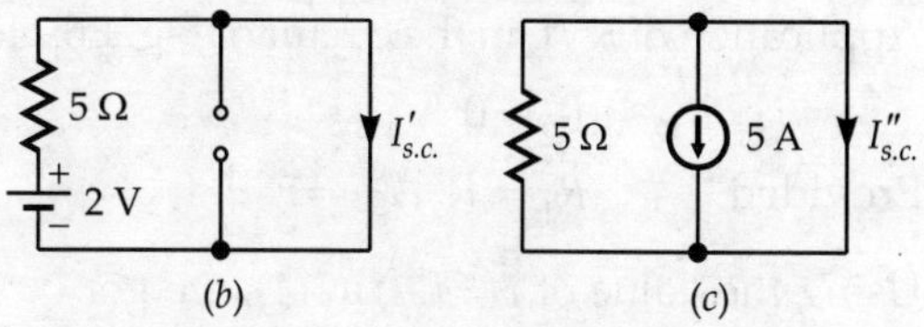

Fig. E6.23

∴ Using the principle of superposition,

$$I_{s.c} = I'_{s.c} + I''_{s.c} = -4.6\ \text{A}$$

To find R_{int}, the constant sources are deactivated (Fig. E6.23(*d*)).

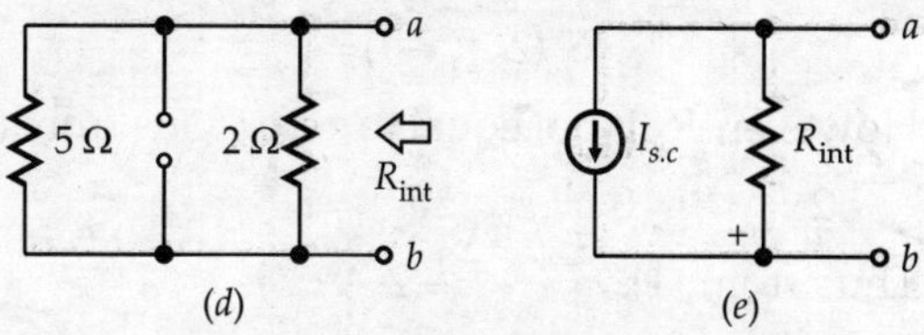

Fig. E6.23

Here, $R_{int} = \dfrac{5 \times 2}{5+2} = 1.43\ \Omega$.

Norton's equivalent circuit is shown in **Fig. E6.23(*e*)**.

Example 6.24 *In the circuit of Fig. E6.24, if $R_1 = R_2 = 4\ \Omega$, find the short circuit current through x-y (use Norton's theorem). What will happen if $R_1 = 2\ R_2$?*

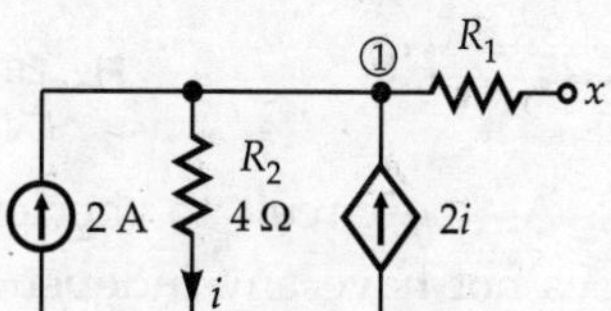

Fig. E6.24

Solution. Let us throw a short circuit across *x-y* as shown in Fig. E6.24(*a*).

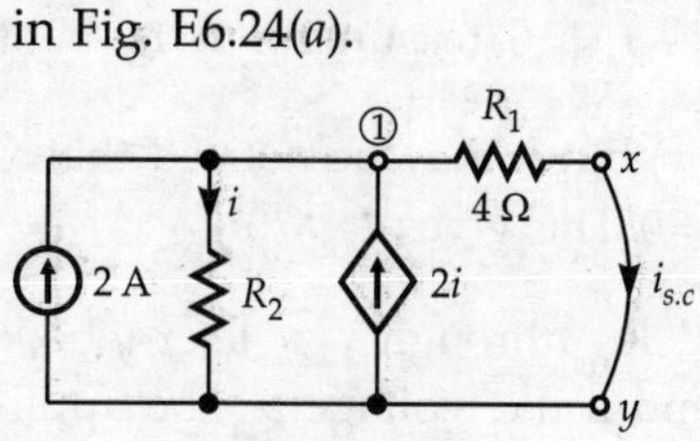

Fig. E6.24 (*a*)

Application of KCL *at node* 1, yields

$$2 + 2i - i - i_{s.c} = 0$$

i.e., $$i + 2 = i_{s.c} \quad \text{...(1)}$$

CHAPTER 6

Application of KVL in the circuit of Fig. E6.24(a),

$$i_{s.c}\ R_1 - i\ R_2 = 0$$

Provided $\quad R_1 = R_2,\ i_{s.c} = i \quad$ ...(2)

Using the value of $i\,(= i_{s.c})$ in (1), we get

$$\boldsymbol{i_{s.c} = \infty}\ \textbf{A.}$$

This shows that Norton equivalent circuit can not be drawn for the given figure]

In case $R_1 = 2R_2$, we find from

$$i_{s.c}\ R_1 - iR_2 = 0,$$

$$2\ i_{s.c}\ R_2 - i\ R_2 = 0$$

or, $\quad R_2\,(2\ i_{s.c} - i) = 0 \quad$ ...(3)

However, R_2 is not equal to zero. Thus from (3),

$2\ i_{s.c} - i = 0 \quad$ *i.e.*, $\ 2\ i_{s.c} = i$.

Thus from (1), $\quad i_{s.c} = -2$ A

Norton Theorem is then applicable in the given problem provided $R_1 \neq R_2$.

EXAMPLE 6.25 *Find Norton's equivalent circuit to the left of terminal x-y in Fig. E6.25.*

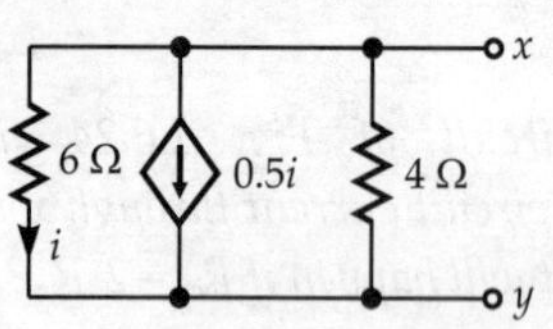

Fig. E6.25

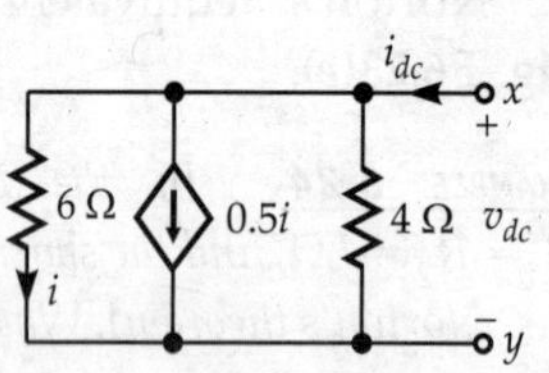

Fig. E6.25 (a)

SOLUTION. As the circuit to the left of x-y in Fig. E6.25 does not have any independent source hence $\boldsymbol{I_{s.c}\ (= I_N) = 0}$.

This can be shown as shorting x-y, 4 Ω resistor being defunct, nodal analysis gives $\frac{v}{6} + 0.5\left(\frac{v}{6}\right) + I_{s.c} = 0$ (assuming v to be the node voltage at x) but it may be noticed that x-y being shorted, $v = 0$. This gives $I_{s.c} = 0$

To find R_{int} through x-y, let x-y be kept open circuited and a d.c. voltage v_{dc} be applied, input current being i_{dc} (Fig. E6.25(a)).

Here, $\quad i_{dc} = \dfrac{v_{dc}}{4} + 0.5\,i + \dfrac{v_{dc}}{6}$

But $\quad i = \dfrac{v_{dc}}{6}$

$$\therefore \quad i_{dc} = \frac{v_{dc}}{4} + 0.5 \times \frac{v_{dc}}{6} + \frac{v_{dc}}{6}$$

$$= \frac{v_{dc}}{4} + \frac{1}{12}\,v_{dc} + \frac{v_{dc}}{6} = \frac{v_{dc}}{2}.$$

i.e., $\quad R_{int} = \dfrac{v_{dc}}{i_{dc}} = 2\,\Omega.$

EXAMPLE 6.26 *Find the current through R_L in the circuit of Fig. E6.26 using Norton's Theorem.*

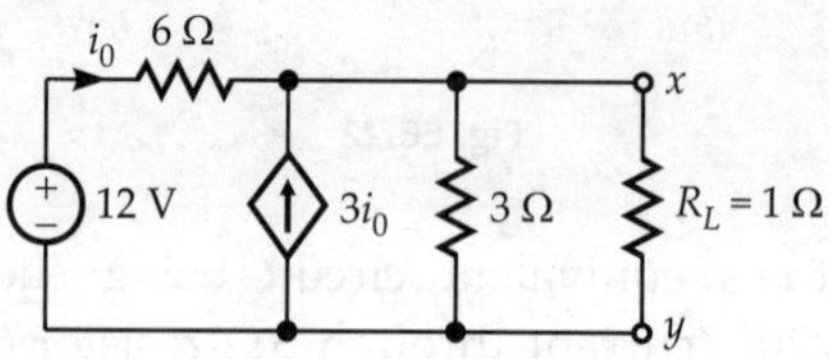

Fig. E6.26

SOLUTION. Let us first remove R_L from x-y terminals and short x-y (Fig. E6.26(a)).

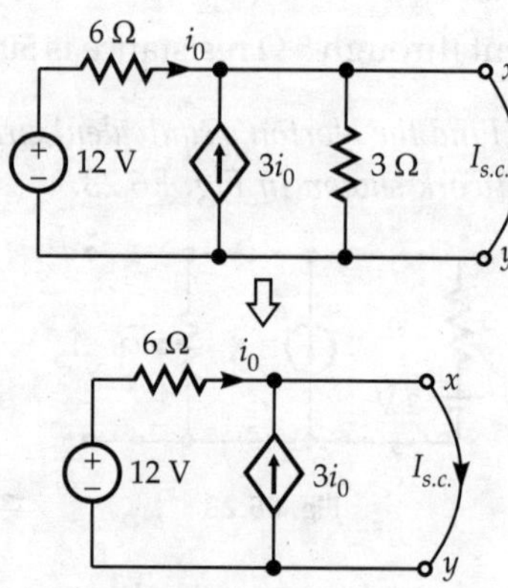

Fig. E6.26 (a)

It is evident from the figure that

$$I_{s.c} = 3\,i_0 + i_0 = 4\,i_0$$

But $\quad i_0 = \dfrac{12}{6} = 2$ A

$$\therefore \quad I_{s.c} = 4 \times 2 = 8\ \text{A}\ (= I_N)$$

Let us now remove the short circuit and the circuit is open circuited at x-y (Fig. E6.26(b)).

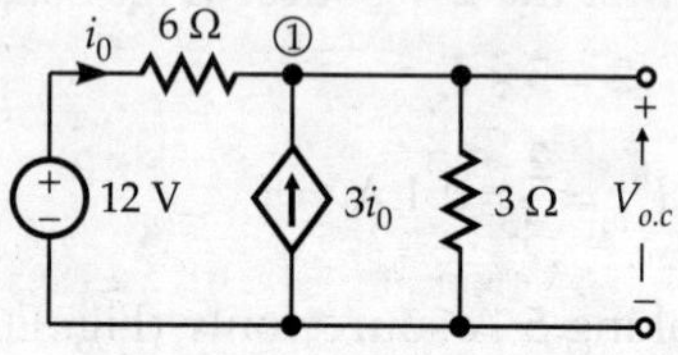

Fig. E6.26 (b)

Nodal analysis *at node* 1 gives

$$i_0 + 3i_0 - \frac{v_{o.c}}{3} = 0 \quad \text{or} \quad 4i_0 - \frac{v_{o.c}}{3} = 0$$

or, $$4\left(\frac{12 - v_{o.c}}{6}\right) - \frac{v_{o.c}}{3} = 0$$

or, $$8 - \frac{2\,v_{o.c}}{3} - \frac{v_{o.c}}{3} = 0$$

or, $$v_{o.c} = 8 \text{ V}$$

This gives $$R_{int} = \frac{v_{o.c}}{I_{s.c}} = \frac{8}{8} = 1\,\Omega.$$

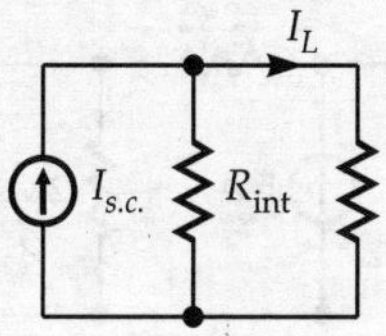

Fig. E6.26 (*c*)

Norton's equivalent circuit being shown in Fig. E6.26(*c*).

I_L (current through 1 Ω resistor)

$$= I_{s.c}\frac{R_{int}}{R_{int} + R_L} = 8\frac{1}{1+1} = \mathbf{4\ A.}$$

Example 6.27 *Find Norton's equivalent to the right of a-b terminal (Fig. E6.27).*

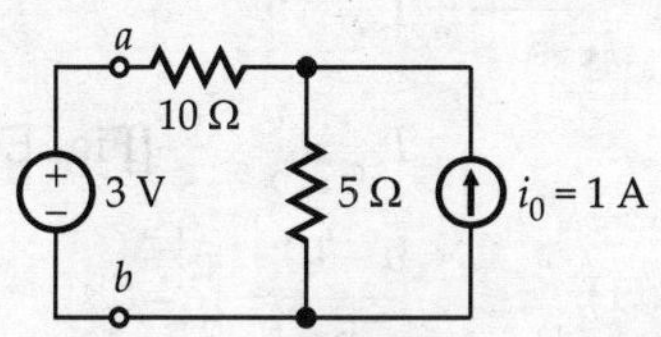

Fig. E6.27

Solution. Let us first remove the voltage source and short *a-b* terminals (Fig. E6.27(*a*)).

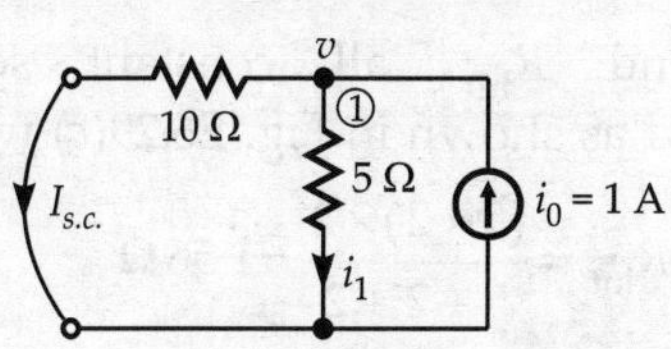

Fig. E6.27 (*a*)

Assuming v to be node voltage *at node* 1, KCL *at node* (1) yields

$$\frac{v}{10} + \frac{v}{5} = 1$$

or, $$\frac{3v}{10} = 1 \quad i.e., \quad v = \frac{10}{3} = 3.33 \text{ V}$$

This gives $$I_{s.c} = \frac{v}{10} = \frac{3.33}{10} \text{ A} = 0.333 \text{ A}$$

Next, *a-b* terminal is kept open circuited (Fig. E6.27(*b*)) deactivating the sources.

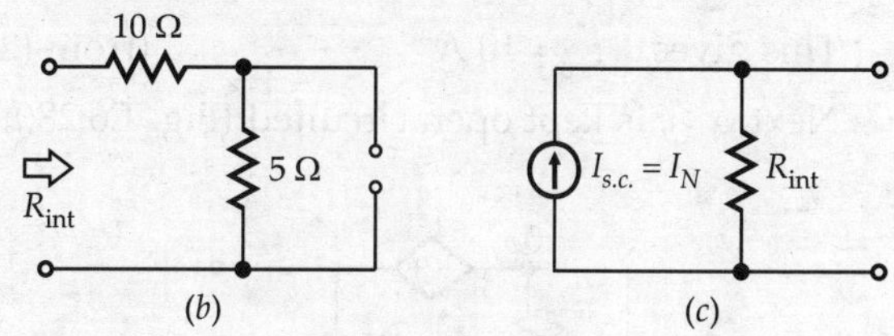

Fig. E6.27

Here $$R_{int} = 10 + 5 = 15\,\Omega.$$

Thus, The Norton equivalent circuit is determined where

$$\mathbf{R_{int} = 15\,\Omega}$$

$$\mathbf{I_{s.c} = 0.333\ A} \text{ (Fig. E6.27(}c\text{)).}$$

Example 6.28 *Find the current through 1.6 Ω resistor in the circuit of Fig. E6.28.*

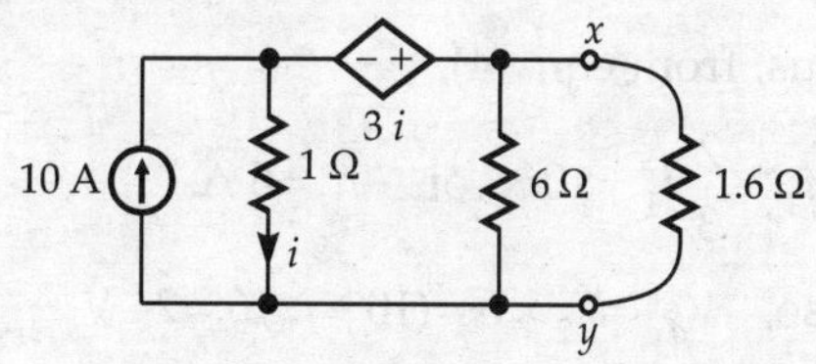

Fig. E6.28

Solution. Let us first remove the 1.6 Ω resistor and short *x-y* terminal (Fig. E6.28(*a*)).

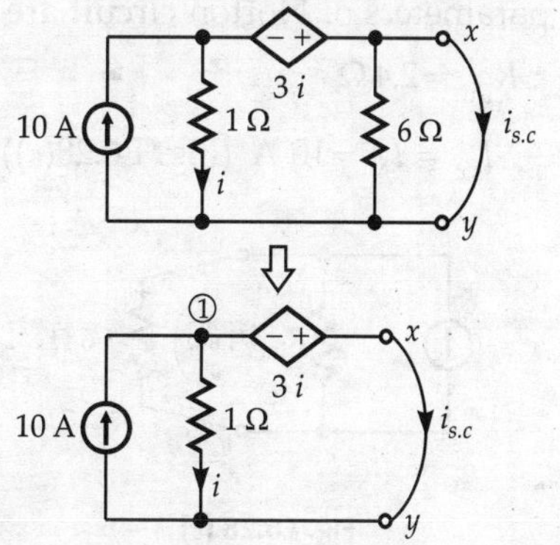

Fig. E6.28 (*a*)

Let the node voltage at (1) be v volts.

$$\therefore \quad i = \frac{v}{1} = v \text{ A} \qquad ...(1)$$

Application of KCL *at node* 1 yields

$$10 = i + i_{s.c} \qquad ...(2)$$

Also, KVL at *right loop* yields

$$-v-3i=0 \quad \text{or} \quad v=-3i \qquad ...(3)$$

Comparison of (1) and (3) yields that these equations are only valid if $v=i=0$.

This gives, $i_{s.c}=10$ A (from (2))

Next, x - y is kept open circuited (Fig. E6.28(b))

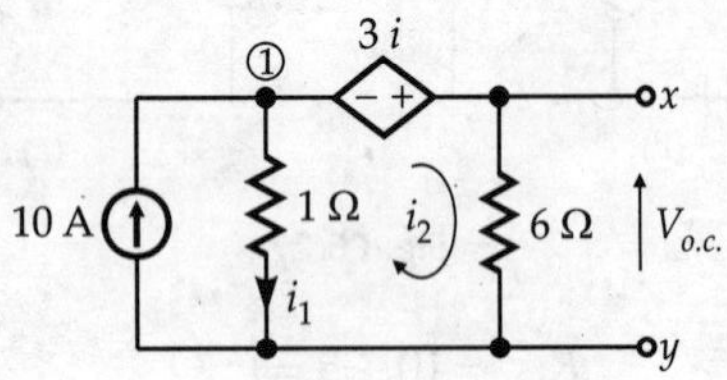

Fig. E6.28 (b)

At node 1, $\quad 10=i_1+i_2 \qquad ...(4)$

But $\quad i_2=\dfrac{v+3i_1}{6}$ [by Ohm's law in the middle loop]

i.e., $\quad i_2=\dfrac{i_1\times 1+3i_1}{6}=\dfrac{2}{3}i_1$

Thus, from eqn. (4),

$$i_1+\frac{2}{3}i_1=10 \quad \text{or} \quad i_1=6 \text{ A}$$

Also, $V_{o.c}=i_2\times 6=(10-i_1)6=24$ V

Hence

$$R_{int}=\frac{V_{o.c}}{I_{s.c}}=\frac{24}{10}=2.4\,\Omega$$

The parameters of Norton circuit are thus

$$R_{int}=2.4\,\Omega$$

$$I_{s.c}=I_N=10 \text{ A} \quad \text{(Fig. E6.28}(c))$$

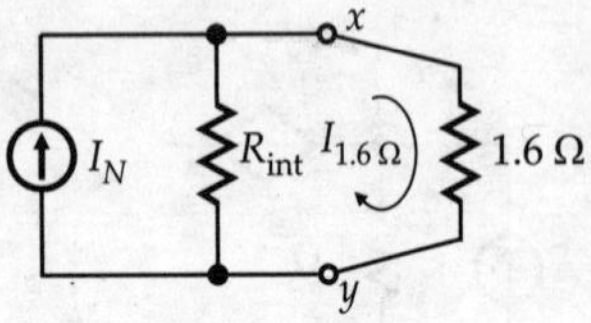

Fig. E6.28 (c)

$\therefore$ Current through 1.6 Ω resistor is

$$I_{(1.6\Omega)}=I_{s.c}\frac{R_{int}}{R_{int}+1.6}$$

$$=10\frac{2.4}{2.4+1.6}=\mathbf{6\ A.}$$

EXAMPLE 6.29 *In Fig. E6.29, find the power loss in 1 Ω resistor (R_L) using Norton's Theorem.*

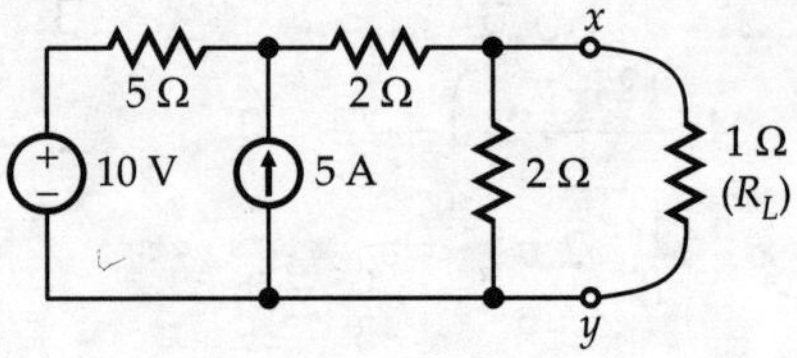

Fig. E6.29

SOLUTION. Let us remove the 1Ω resistor and short x - y (Fig. E6.29(a))

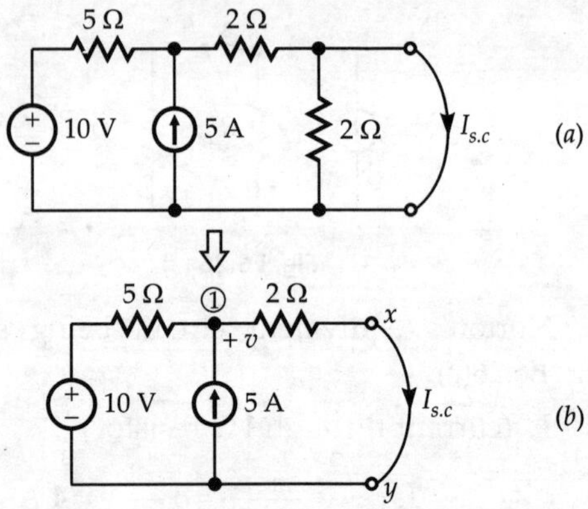

Fig. E6.29

At node 1, assuming node potential to be v,

$$\frac{v-10}{5}+I_{s.c}=5 \qquad ...(1)$$

But $\quad I_{s.c}=\dfrac{v}{2}$ [Fig. E6.29(b)]

$\therefore$ from (1), $\quad \dfrac{v-10}{5}+\dfrac{v}{2}=5$

$$0.7\,v=7$$

i.e., $\quad v=10$ V

$\therefore \quad I_{s.c}=v/2=5$ A

To find R_{int}, all constant sources are deactivated as shown in Fig. E6.29(c) where

$$R_{int}=\frac{(5\times 2)\times 2}{5+2+2}=1.56\,\Omega$$

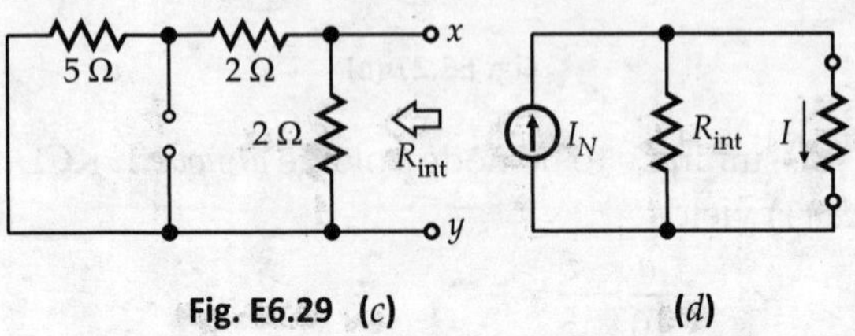

Fig. E6.29 (c) (d)

Norton's equivalent circuit has been drawn in Fig. E6.29(d) where

$$R_{\text{int}} = 1.56\,\Omega$$

$$I_{s.c} = I_N = 5\text{ A}$$

Here, $I = I_N \dfrac{R_{\text{int}}}{R_{\text{int}}+1} = 5 \times \dfrac{1.56}{1.56+1} = 3.04\text{ A}.$

$\therefore$Power loss in $1\,\Omega$ resistor $= (3.04)^2 \times 1 = \mathbf{9.26\ W.}$

EXAMPLE 6.30 *Find Norton equivalent to the left of x-y terminals in Fig. E6.30.*

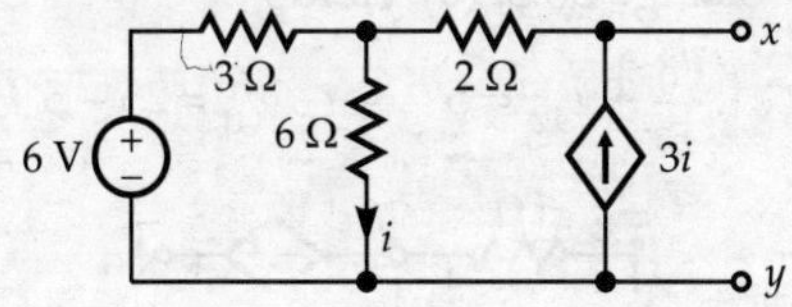

Fig. E6.30

SOLUTION. x-y be shorted first (Fig. E6.30(*a*))

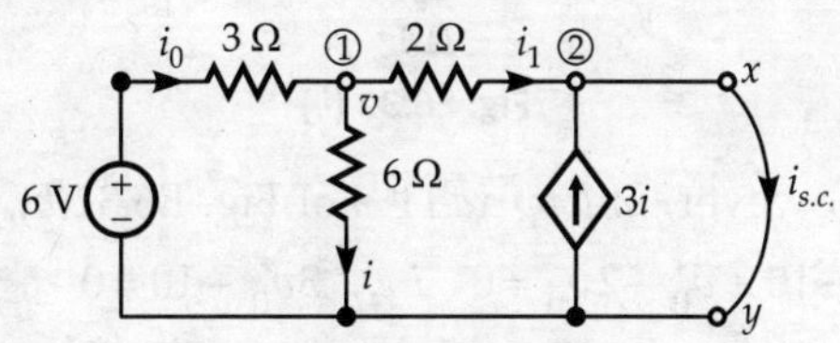

Fig. E6.30 (*a*)

At node 1, $\dfrac{v-6}{3} + \dfrac{v}{6} + \dfrac{v}{2} = 0$

[assuming voltage *at node* 1 to be v]

or, $v = 2\text{ V}$

This gives $i = \dfrac{v}{6} = \dfrac{2}{6} = \dfrac{1}{3}\text{ A}$

$$i_0 = -\frac{v-6}{3} = -\frac{2-6}{3} = \frac{4}{3}\text{ A}$$

$$i_1 = i_0 - i = \frac{4}{3} - \frac{1}{3} = 1\text{ A}$$

At node 2, $i_1 + 3i = I_{s.c}$

$\therefore \quad I_{s.c} = 1 + 3 \times \dfrac{1}{3} = 2\text{ A}$

To find R_{int}, x-y is open circuited (Fig. E6.30(*b*)) and the constant source is deactivated. A d.c. voltage v_{dc} is applied such that the input current is i_{dc}.

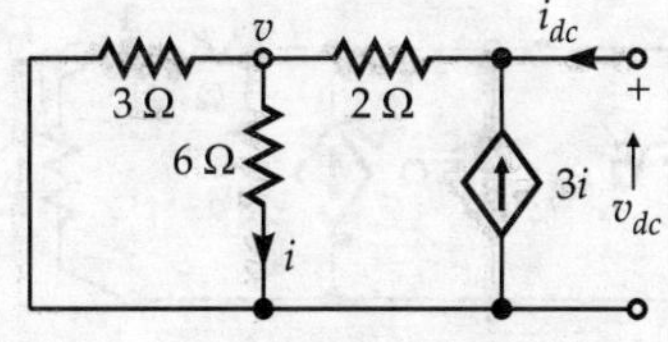

Fig. E6.30 (*b*)

Here, $\dfrac{v_{dc}-v}{2} = i_{dc} + 3i$;

also $i = \dfrac{v}{6}$ and $\dfrac{v_{dc}-v}{2} = \dfrac{v}{6} + \dfrac{v}{3}$ *i.e.* $v = 0.5\, v_{dc}$

Thus, $i = \dfrac{v}{6} = \dfrac{0.5\, v_{dc}}{6}$

and then $\dfrac{v_{dc}-v}{2} = i_{dc} + 3 . \dfrac{0.5\, v_{dc}}{6}$

$$= i_{dc} + \frac{0.5\, v_{dc}}{2}$$

or, $\dfrac{v_{dc} - 0.5\, v_{dc}}{2} = i_{dc} + \dfrac{0.5\, v_{dc}}{2}$ or $i_{dc} = 0$

$\therefore \quad R_{\text{int}} = \dfrac{v_{dc}}{i_{dc}} = \dfrac{v_{dc}}{0} = \infty\,\Omega.$

The given circuit has thus been Nortonised with

$$\boldsymbol{R_{int} = \infty\,\Omega}$$

$$\boldsymbol{I_{s.c} = I_N = 2\text{ A.}}$$

EXAMPLE 6.31 *Find Norton's equivalent circuit across x-y for the circuit shown in Fig. E6.31.*

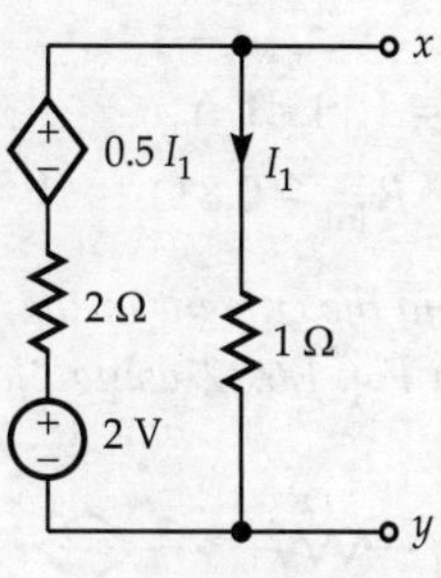

Fig. E6.31

SOLUTION. It is evident from Fig. E6.31,

$$V_{x-y} = V_{o.c} = 1 \times I_1 = I_1$$

Application of KVL in the *left loop,*

$$I_1 - 2 + 2I_1 - 0.5\, I_1 = 0$$

or, $2.5\, I_1 = 2$ or $I_1 = 0.8\text{ A}$

This gives $V_{o.c}\,(= V_{x-y}) = 0.8\text{ V}$

Next, short circuiting the x-y terminals, Fig. E6.31(*a*) gives

$$I_{s.c} = \frac{2\text{ V}}{2\,\Omega} = 1\text{ A}$$

[$\because 1\,\Omega$ resistor is defunct due to shorting of $x-y$ terminal, hence $I_1 = 0$ making the dependent source $0.5\, I_1$ to be zero]

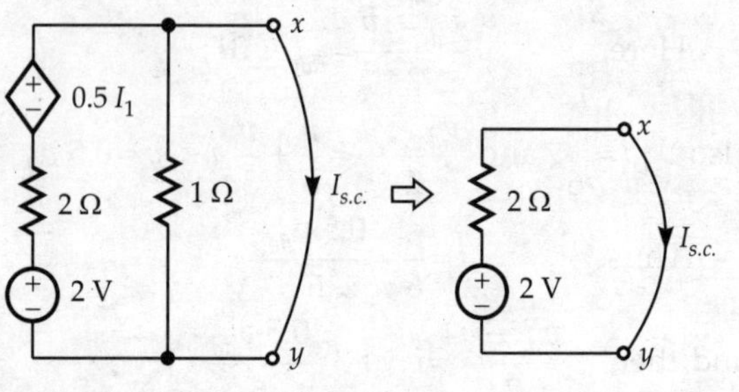

Fig. E6.31 (*a*)

The internal resistance of the given circuit is thus obtained as

$$R_{\text{int}} = \frac{V_{o.c}}{I_{s.c}} = \frac{0.8}{1} = 0.8\,\Omega$$

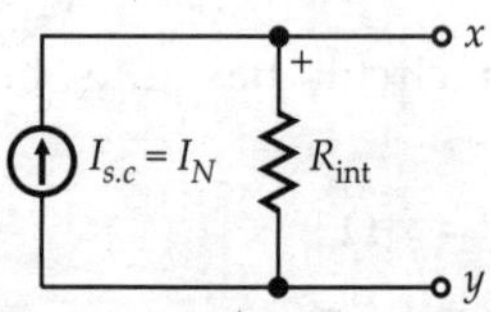

Fig. E6.31 (*b*)

Norton's equivalent circuit is shown in Fig. E6.31(*b*)

where, $\quad \boldsymbol{I_{s.c}\ (= I_N) = 1\ \text{A}}$

$\qquad\qquad \boldsymbol{R_{\text{int}} = 0.8\,\Omega.}$

EXAMPLE 6.32 *Find the current in the* 1 Ω *resistor across terminals 1-1′ in Fig. E6.32 using Norton's theorem.*

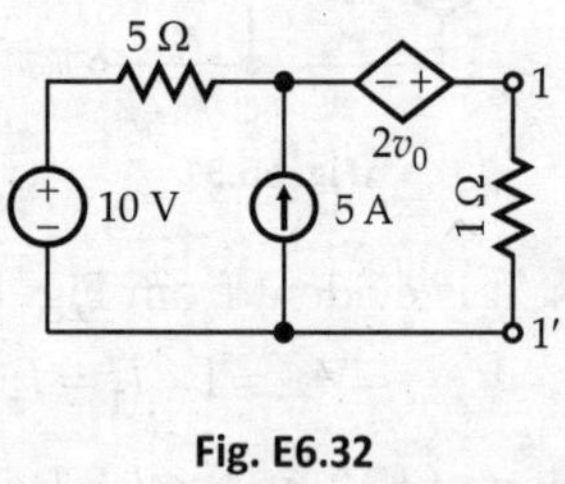

Fig. E6.32

SOLUTION. Let the 1 Ω resistor be removed from 1 – 1′ terminals of the circuit shown in Fig. E6.32. The new circuit configuration is shown in Fig. E6.32(*a*).

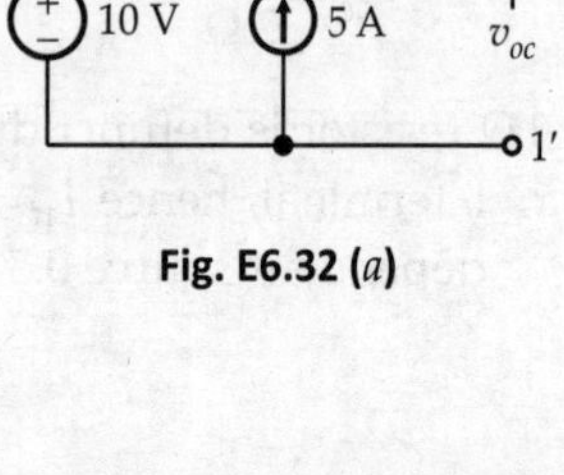

Fig. E6.32 (*a*)

Here $\quad v_{o.c} = 10 + v_0 + 2v_0 = 10 + 3v_0$

But $\quad v_0 = 5\,\text{A} \times 5\,\Omega = 25\ \text{V}$

[∵ loop current in the leftmost loop of Fig. E6.32(*a*) is 5 A causing a drop of $5 \times 5 = 25$ V in the polarities shown];

$\therefore \quad v_{o.c} = 10 + 3 \times 25 = 85\ \text{V}$

In order to find R_{int}, let us first short the output terminals 1 – 1′ of Fig. E6.32 and application of KCL at *node a* of Fig. E6.32(*b*) yields

$$\frac{v_0}{5} + I_{s.c} = 5 \quad \text{or} \quad v_0 = 25 - 5\,I_{s.c} \qquad \text{...(A)}$$

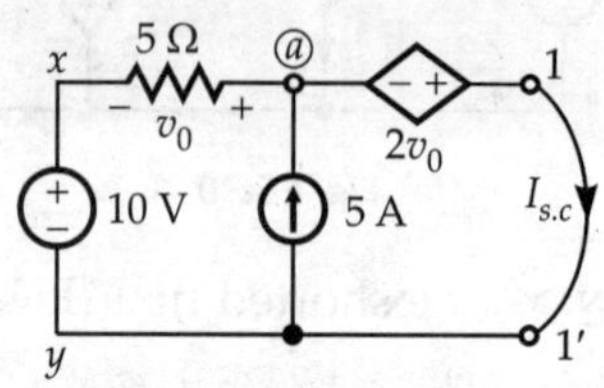

Fig. E6.32 (*b*)

However, *in loop xa* 11′ *y* of Fig. E6.32(*b*),

$$-10 - v_0 - 2v_0 = 0 \quad i.e., \quad 3v_0 + 10 = 0 \qquad \text{...(B)}$$

Using (A) in (B), we get

$$3\,(25 - 5\,I_{s.c}) + 10 = 0$$

i.e., $\qquad I_{s.c} = 5.67$ A.

This gives $\quad R_{\text{int}} = \dfrac{v_{o.c}}{I_{s.c}} = \dfrac{85}{5.67} \simeq 15\,\Omega.$

Norton's equivalent circuit thus gives $\boldsymbol{I_{s.c} = 5.67\ \text{A}}$ and $\boldsymbol{R_{\text{int}} = 15\,\Omega}$ as shown in Fig. E6.32(*c*).

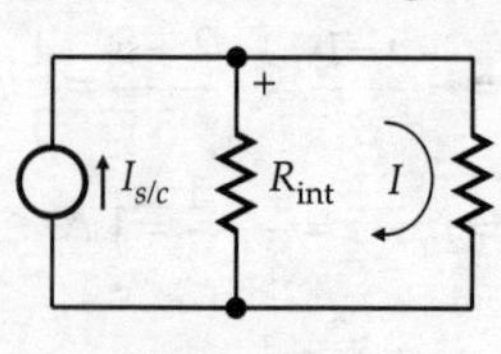

Fig. E6.32 (*c*)

Here *I* (current through 1 Ω resistor)

$$= I_{s.c} \frac{R_{\text{int}}}{R_{\text{int}} + 1} = \mathbf{5.315\ A.}$$

EXAMPLE 6.33 *Find the power loss in the* 10 Ω *resistor in the circuit of Fig. E6.33 using Norton's theorem.*

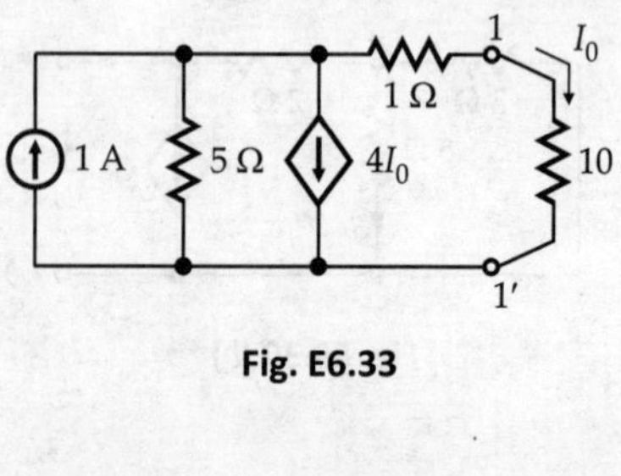

Fig. E6.33

Solution. Removing the 10 Ω resistor,

$$V_{o.c} = (V_{1-1'}) = 1 \times 5 = 5 \text{ V} \quad \text{(Fig. E6.33(}a\text{))}.$$

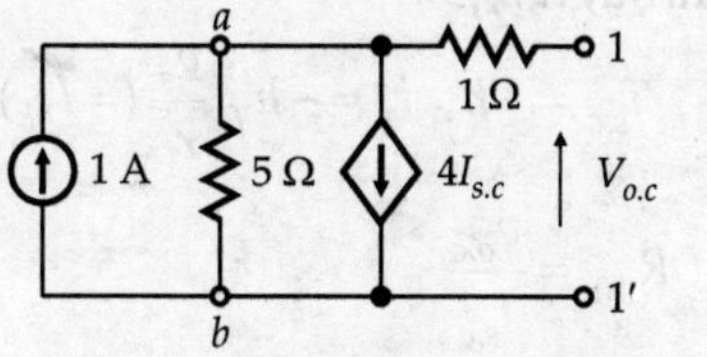

Fig. E6.33 (*a*)

Next, short circuiting *x*-*y* terminals in Fig. E6.33(*b*), and assuming the node voltage at "*a*" being *v*, nodal analysis at this node yields

$$1 = \frac{v}{5} + 4\,I_{s.c} + I_{s.c}$$

or, $$5\,I_{s.c} + \frac{v}{5} = 1 \qquad ...(1)$$

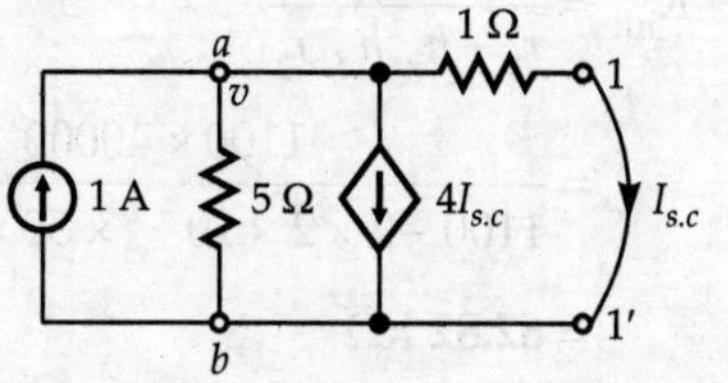

Fig. E6.33 (*b*)

Also, $I_{s.c} = \frac{v}{1} = v$ A

From (1), $5I_{s.c} + \frac{I_{s.c}}{5} = 1$

or, $I_{s.c} = 0.1923$ A

This gives

$$R_{\text{int}} = \frac{V_{o.c}}{I_{s.c}} = \frac{5}{0.1923} = 26\,\Omega$$

Thus, Norton's equivalent circuit is given by

$I_{s.c} = 0.1923$ A,

$R_{\text{int}} = 26\,\Omega$.

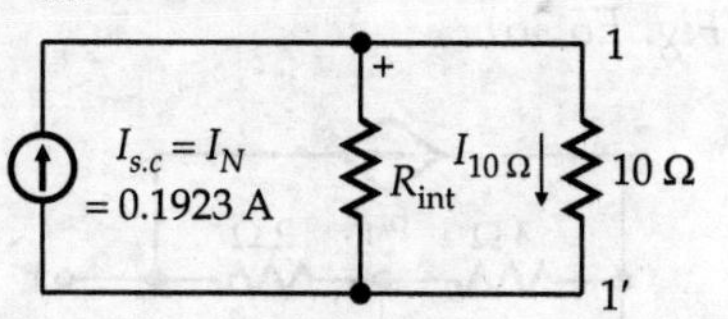

Fig. E6.33 (*c*)

Referring to Fig. E6.33(*c*),

$$I_{10\Omega} = I_{s.c}\,\frac{R_{\text{int}}}{R_{\text{int}} + 10} = 0.14 \text{ A}$$

∴ Power loss in the 10 Ω resistor

$$= (I_{10\Omega})^2 \times 10 = \mathbf{0.195\ W}.$$

Example 6.34 *Find the current in 1Ω resistor using Norton's theorem (Fig. E6.34).*

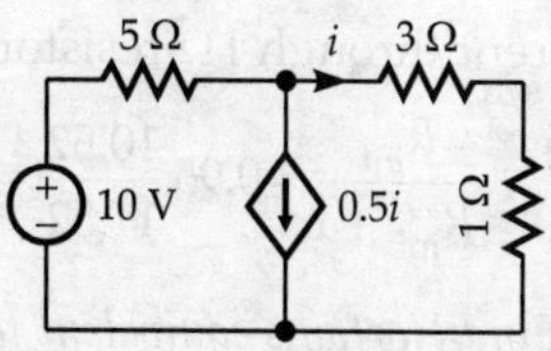

Fig. E6.34

Solution. Removing 1 Ω resistor, with reference to Fig. E6.34(*a*), $i = 0$ and hence $v_{o.c} = 10$ V (0.5 *i* source gets eliminated as $i = 0$).

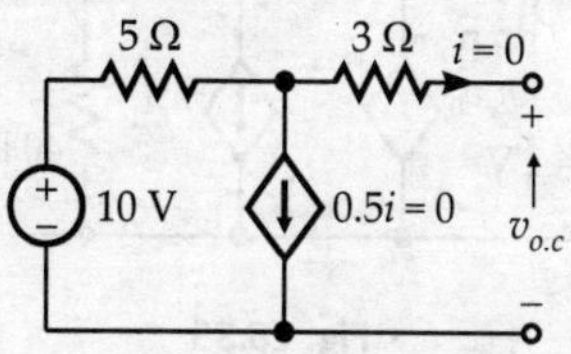

Fig. E6.34 (*a*)

Next, short circuiting the output terminals (Fig. E6.34(*b*)), nodal analysis *at node* (1) gives

$$\frac{v - 10}{5} + 0.5\,i_{s.c} + i_{s.c} = 0 \qquad ...(1)$$

[assuming *node* (1) voltage to be *v*]

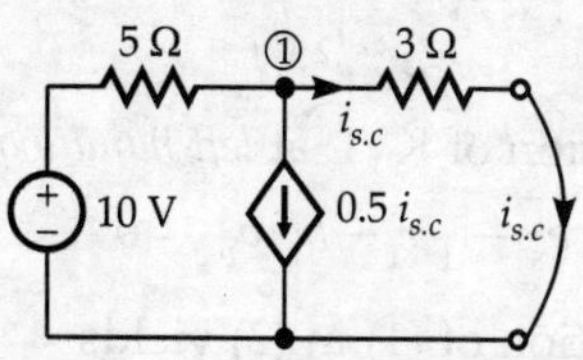

Fig. E6.34 (*b*)

But $v = 3i_{s.c}$

Thus from (1),

$$\frac{3\,i_{s.c} - 10}{5} + 1.5\,i_{s.c} = 0$$

or, $2.1\,i_{s.c} = 2$ or $i_{s.c} = 0.95$ A.

This gives $R_{\text{int}} = \frac{v_{o.c}}{i_{s.c}} = \frac{10}{0.95} = 10.52\,\Omega.$

Norton's equivalent circuit is then obtained in Fig. E6.34(*c*)

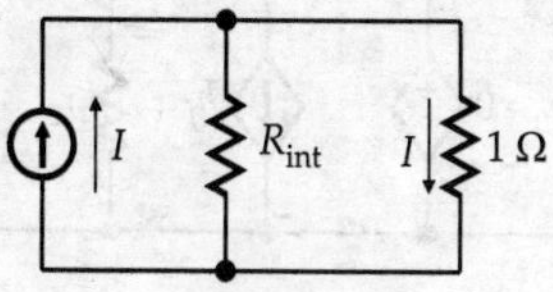

Fig. E6.34 (*c*)

where $I_{s.c}\,(=I_N)=0.95$ A

and $R_{int}=10.52\ \Omega$.

Here, current through 1Ω resistor is given by

$$I = I_{s.c}\frac{R_{int}}{R_{int}+1} = 0.95\frac{10.52}{11.52} = \mathbf{0.86\ A.}$$

EXAMPLE 6.35 *Find Norton's equivalent to the left of x-y terminals for the CE configuration of transistor equivalent circuit shown in Fig. E6.35. Assume $h_r = 2\times 10^{-4}$; $h_f = 50$.*

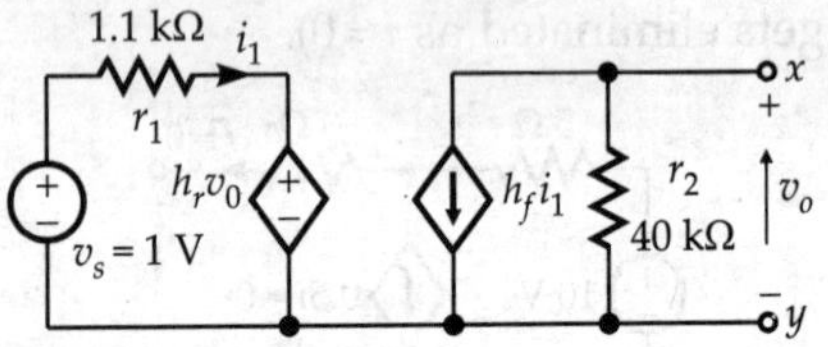

Fig. E6.35

SOLUTION. Let us find the open circuit voltage $v_{o.c}\,(=v_0$ in Fig. E6.35) across *x-y*.

At node x, nodal analysis gives

$$-h_f\, i_1 - \frac{v_{o.c}}{r_2} = 0$$

or, $$i_1 = -\frac{v_{o.c}}{r_2\, h_f} \qquad ...(1)$$

Application of KVL at *left hand loop* yields

$$v_s - i_1\, r_1 - h_r\, v_{o.c} = 0 \qquad ...(2)$$

Substitution of (1) in (2) yields

$$v_s + \frac{v_{o.c}}{r_2\, h_f}\, r_1 - h_r\, v_{o.c} = 0$$

or, $$v_s = v_{o.c}\left(h_r - \frac{r_1}{r_2\, h_f}\right)$$

i.e., $$v_{o.c} = v_s\left(\frac{r_2\, h_f}{h_r\, h_f\, r_2 - r_1}\right) \qquad ...(3)$$

Next, short circuit is applied at *x-y* terminals such that v_0 becomes zero (Fig. E6.35(*a*)).

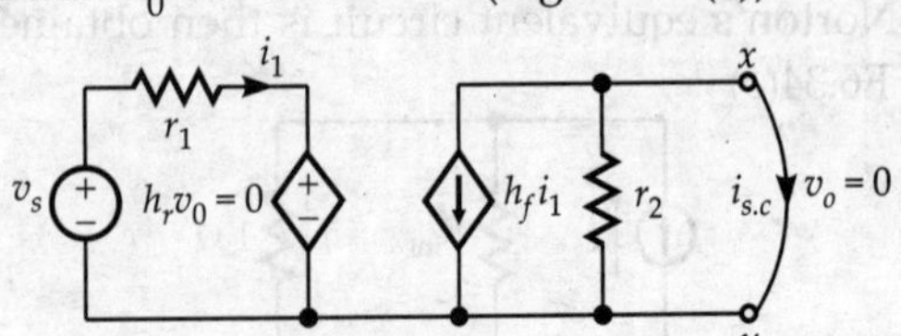

Fig. E6.35 (*a*)

Obviously, in the left loop, $v_s = i_1\, r_1$ and in the right loop, $-h_f\, i_1 - i_{s.c} = 0$ [no current being flowing through r_2]

or, $$i_{s.c} = -h_f\, i_1 = -h_f\frac{v_s}{r_1}\,(=I_N) \qquad ...(4)$$

$$\therefore \quad R_{int} = \frac{v_{o.c}}{i_{s.c}}$$

$$= v_s\left(\frac{r_2\, h_f}{h_r\, h_f\, r_2 - r_1}\right)\times\frac{r_1}{(-h_f\, v_s)}$$

$$= \frac{r_1\, r_2}{r_1 - h_r\, h_f\, r_2}$$

Thus, Norton's equivalent circuit is formed with

$$R_{int} = \frac{r_1\, r_2}{r_1 - h_r\, h_f\, r_2}$$

$$= \frac{1100\times 40000}{1100 - 2\times 2\times 10^{-4}\times 50\times 40\times 10^3}$$

$$= \mathbf{62.82\ k\Omega}$$

and $$I_N\,(=i_{s.c}) = -h_f\frac{v_s}{r_1}$$

$$= -50\times\frac{1}{1100} = \mathbf{-45.45\ mA.}$$

Figure E6.35(*b*) represents Norton's equivalent circuit.

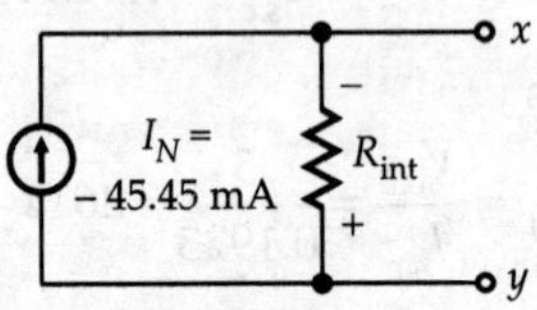

Fig. E6.35 (*b*)

EXAMPLE 6.36 *Find Norton's equivalent to the left of x-y terminal (Fig. E6.36).*

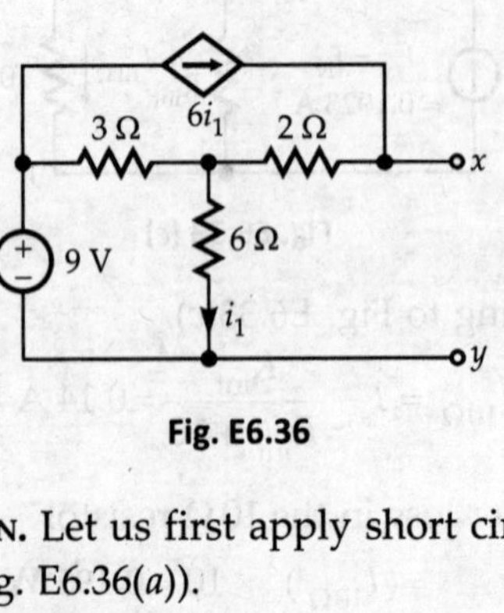

Fig. E6.36

SOLUTION. Let us first apply short circuit at *x-y* terminal (Fig. E6.36(*a*)).

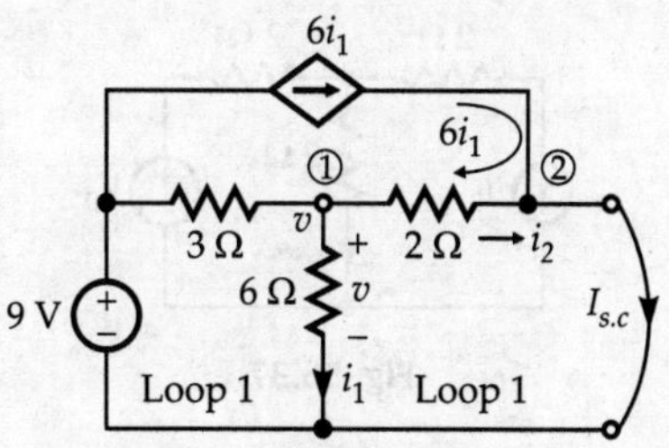

Fig. E6.36 (*a*)

Here, $\quad i_1 = \frac{v}{6}$

[assuming voltage at node (1) to be v]

At node (2), KCL yields,

$$i_2 + 6i_1 = I_{s.c}$$

or, $\quad \frac{v}{2} + 6 \cdot \frac{v}{6} = I_{s.c} \qquad [\because i_2 = \frac{v}{2}]$

or, $\quad \frac{3}{2} v = I_{s.c} \quad$ *i.e.*, $\; I_{s.c} = 1.5\text{ V}$

Again at *node* (1), nodal analysis gives

$$\frac{v-9}{3} + \frac{v}{6} + \frac{v}{2} = 0$$

or, $\quad v = 3\text{ V}$

Thus $\quad I_{s.c} = 1.5 \times 3 = 4.5\text{ A} (= I_N)$

Let us now keep *x-y* open circuited such that potential at *x-y* terminal becomes $v_{o.c}$ (Fig. E6.36(*b*)).

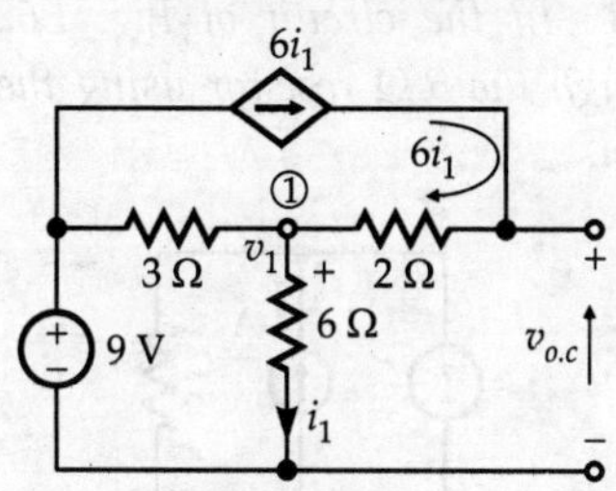

Fig. E6.36 (*b*)

At node (1), nodal analysis gives

$$\frac{v_1 - 9}{3} + i_1 = 6i_1 \qquad \text{[assuming nodal voltage at (1) to be } v_1\text{]}$$

$\therefore \quad \frac{v_1}{3} - 3 - 5i_1 = 0$

But $\quad i_1 = \frac{v_1}{6}$ A.

Thus we get

$$\frac{v_1}{3} - 3 - \frac{5}{6} v_1 = 0$$

or, $\quad -\frac{3v_1}{6} = 3 \quad$ or $\quad v_1 = -6\text{ V}$

However,

$$v_{o.c} = +v_1 + (2\,\Omega \times 6i_1\text{ A}) = v_1 + 12\,i_1$$

$$= v_1 + 12 \cdot \frac{v_1}{6} = 3v_1 = -18\text{ V}$$

$[\because v_1 = -6\text{ V}]$

Thus $\quad R_{\text{int}} = \frac{v_{o.c}}{I_{s.c}} = \frac{-18}{4.5} = 4\,\Omega$

[neglecting – ve sign]

This gives Norton equivalent as

$$I_N = \mathbf{4.5\ A}, \quad R_{\text{int}} = \mathbf{4\,\Omega}.$$

6.4 SUPERPOSITION THEOREM

This theorem finds use in solving a network where two or more sources are present and connected not in series or in parallel.

6.4.1 Statement of Superposition Theorem

If a number of voltage or current sources are acting simultaneously in a linear network, the resultant current in any branch is the algebraic sum of the currents that would be produced in it, when each source acts alone replacing all other independent sources by their internal resistances.

6.4.2 Explanation

In Fig. 6.4, to apply superposition theorem, let us first take the source V_1 alone at first replacing V_2 by short circuit (Fig. 6.4(*a*)).

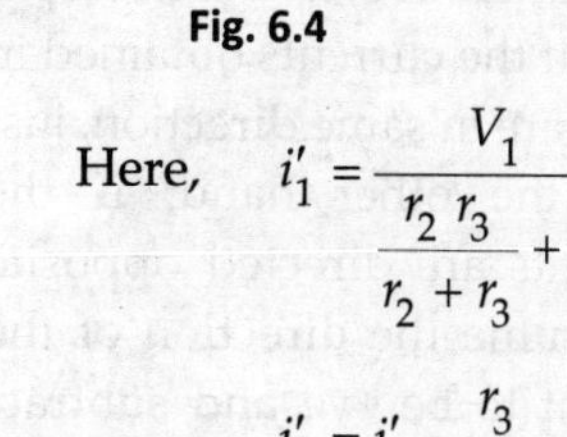

Fig. 6.4

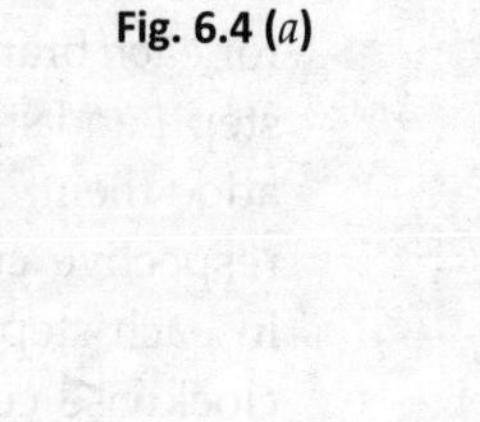

Fig. 6.4 (*a*)

Here, $\quad i_1' = \dfrac{V_1}{\dfrac{r_2 r_3}{r_2 + r_3} + r_1}$

$$i_2' = i_1' \frac{r_3}{r_2 + r_3}$$

and $\quad i_3' = i_1' - i_2'$

Next, removing V_1 by short circuit, let the circuit be energized by V_2 only (Fig. 6.4(*b*)).

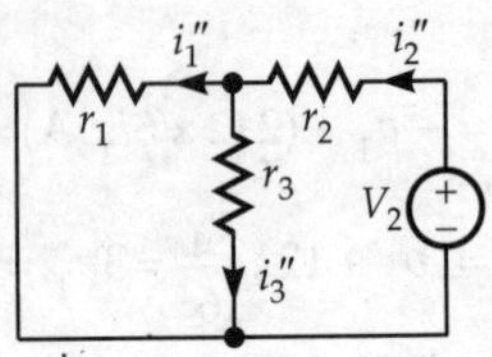

Fig. 6.4 (*b*)

Here, $i_2'' = \dfrac{V_2}{\dfrac{r_1 r_3}{r_1 + r_3} + r_2}$ and $i_1'' = i_2'' \dfrac{r_3}{r_1 + r_3}$

Also, $i_3'' = i_2'' - i_1''$.

As per Superposition theorem,

$$i_3 = i_3' + i_3''$$
$$i_2 = i_2' - i_2''$$
$$i_1 = i_1' - i_1''$$

[It may be noted that during application of Superposition, the direction of currents calculated for each source should be taken care of.]

6.4.3 Steps for Solution of a Network Utilizing the Principle of Superposition

Step 1 Take only one independent source of voltage/current and deactivate the other independent voltage/current sources. (For voltage sources, remove the source and short circuit the respective circuit terminals and for current sources, just delete the source keeping the respective circuit terminals open). Obtain branch currents.

Step 2 Repeat the above step for each of the independent sources.

Step 3 To determine the net branch current utilising Superposition theorem, just add the currents obtained in step 1 and step 2 for each branch. If the currents obtained in step 1 and step 2 are in same direction, just add them; on the other hand, if the respective currents are directed opposite in each step, assume the direction of the clockwise current to be +ve and subtract the current obtained in the next step from the original current. The net current in each branch is then obtained.

Example 6.37 *In Fig. E6.37 when $V_0 = 0, I = 2$ A; find I when $V_0 = 10$ V.*

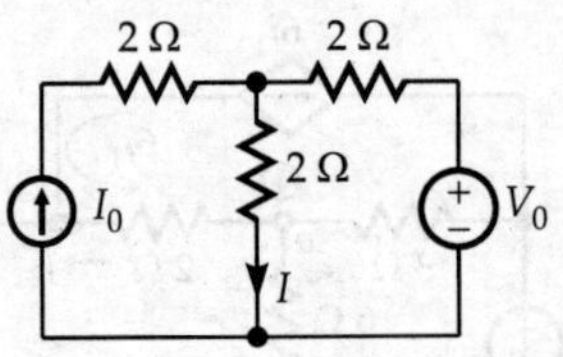

Fig. E6.37

Solution. When $V_0 = 0$, the circuit will look like that shown in Fig. E6.37(*a*). This time it is evident that $I = 2$ A.

Next, $V_0 = 10$ V is applied.

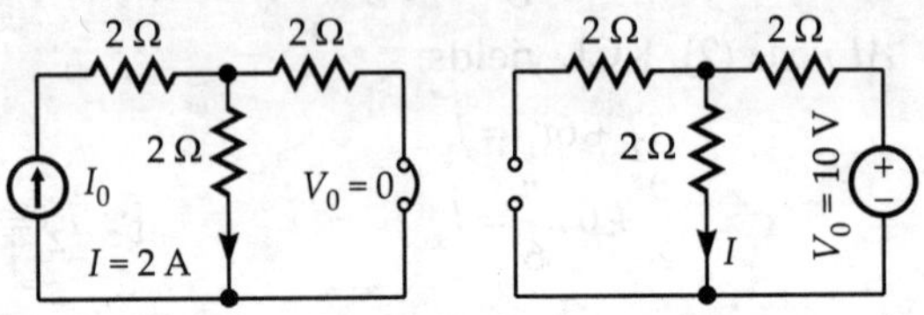

(*a*) (*b*)

Fig. E6.37

Utilising the concept Superposition, the circuit diagram is shown in Fig. E6.37(*b*) for the voltage source alone. This time $I = \dfrac{10}{2+2} = 2.5$ A.

$\therefore$ Net current through the required resistor *i.e.*, $I = 2 + 2.5 =$ **4.5 A** as per Superposition theorem.

Example 6.38 *In the circuit of Fig. E6.38, find the current through the 5 Ω resistor using the principle of Superposition.*

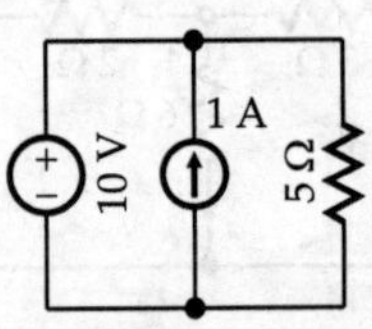

Fig. E6.38

Solution. Setting the voltage source deactivated first, current through 5 Ω resistor is zero.

[$\because$ With referene to Fig. E6.38(*a*), the current source will pass the entire current through the shorted path *i.e.*, the deactivated voltage source path and no current would flow through 5 Ω resistor]

i.e., $I' = 0$

Next, deactivating the current source, the current through the 5 Ω resistor is only $\dfrac{10}{5}$ (=2) A (= I'')

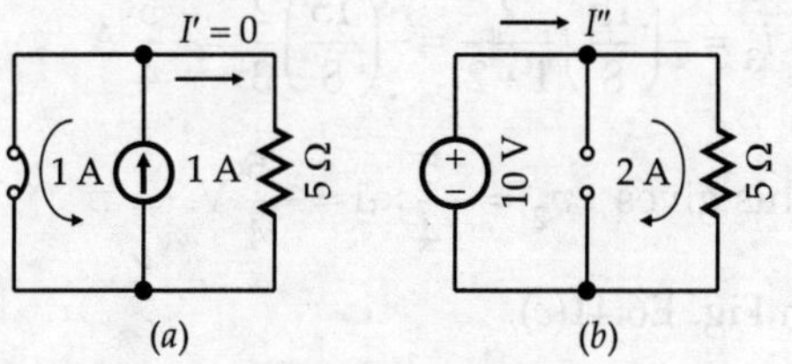

Fig. E6.38

Using the principle of Superposition,

I, the current through the 5 Ω resistor is

$$I' + I'' = 0 + 2 = \mathbf{2\ A}.$$

EXAMPLE 6.39 *Find I in the circuit shown in Fig. E6.39.*

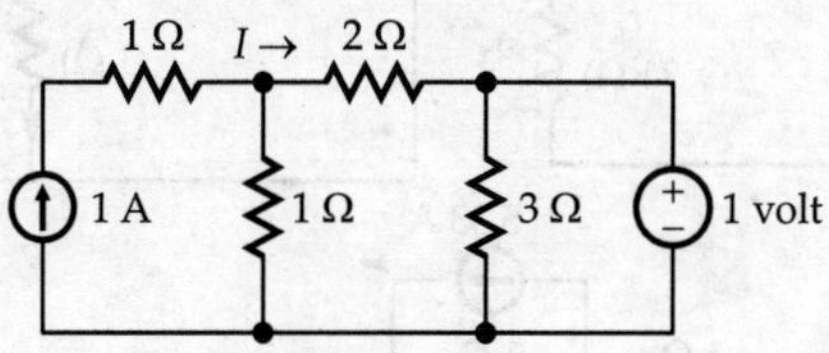

Fig. E6.39

SOLUTION. Principle of Superposition is applied by taking 1 V source only at first (Fig. E6.39(*a*)).

$$I_s = \frac{1\ \text{V}}{[(1+2)||3]\ \Omega} = (1/1.5)\ \text{A}$$

$$I_1 = I_s\,\frac{3}{3+2+1} = \frac{1}{1.5}\times\frac{3}{6} = \frac{1}{3}\ \text{A}$$

[by current division formula]

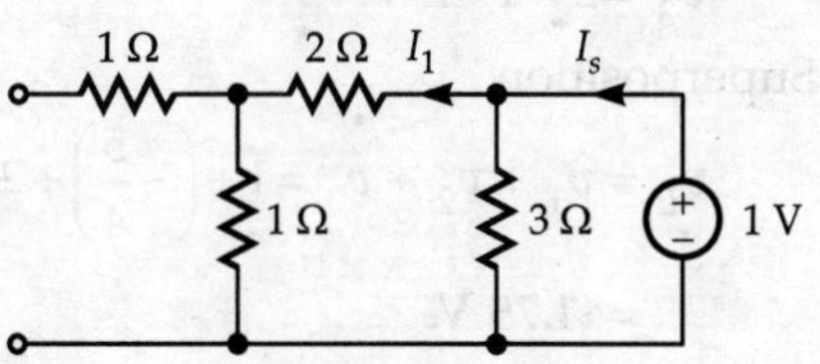

Fig. E6.39 (*a*)

Next, let us assume the current source only (Fig. E6.39(*b*)).

$$I_2 = 1 \times \frac{1}{1+2} = \frac{1}{3}\ \text{A}$$

[by current division formula]

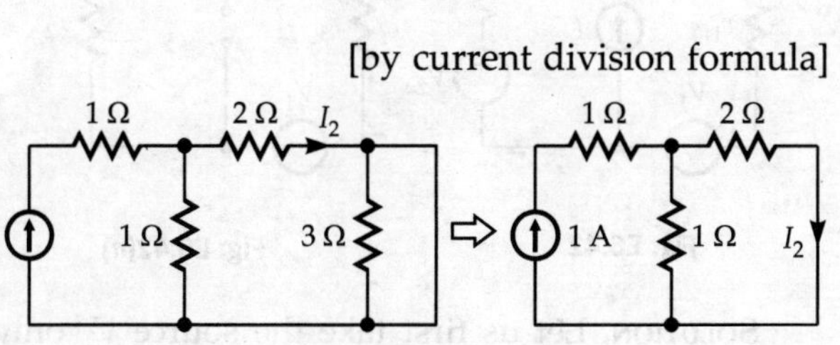

Fig. E6.39 (*b*)

It may be observed that utilising the principle of Superposition, the net response can be obtained when both the sources (1 A and 1 V) are present. The current through 2 Ω resistor is obtained as

$$I = (I_1 - I_2) = \frac{1}{3} - \frac{1}{3} = 0$$

[I_1 and I_2 being directed reverse].

EXAMPLE 6.40 *Using Superposition theorem, find the current through a link that is to be connected between terminals a-b. Assume the link resistance to be zero [Fig. E6.40].*

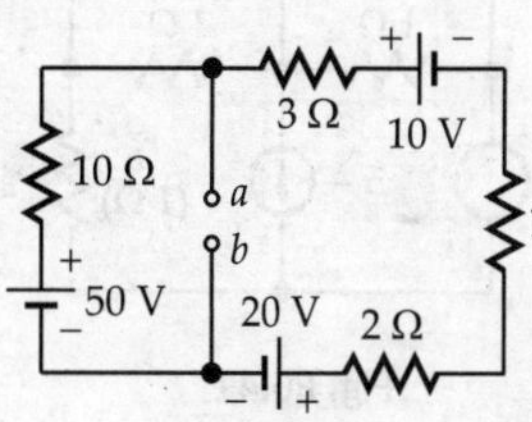

Fig. E6.40

SOLUTION. As the link resistance between terminals *a-b* is zero, hence, the link is practically a short circuiting link and the current through the link is assumed to be $I_{s.c}$.

Let us now first take the 50 V source. The circuit configuration for this case is shown in Fig. E6.40(*a*).

Here $\quad I_{s.c_1} = \frac{50}{10} = 5\ \text{A}$

[As *a-b* is short circuited, no current will flow through loop-2 in Fig. E6.40(*a*)].

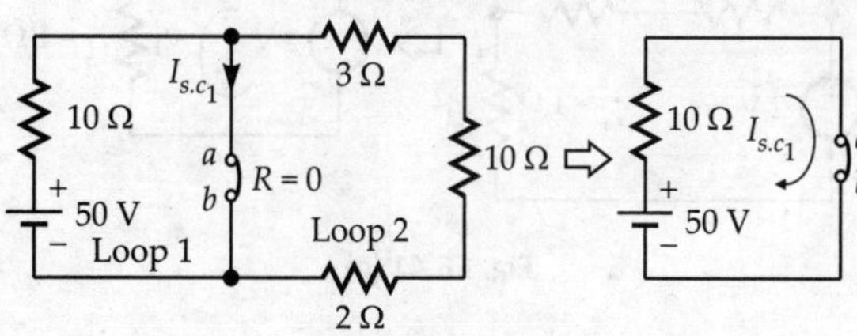

Fig. E6.40 (*a*)

Next, the sources 10 V and 20 V are considered and the circuit configuration is shown in Fig. E6.40(*b*).

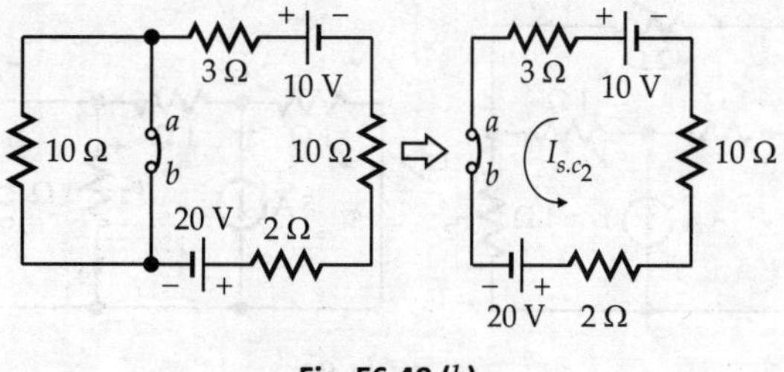

Fig. E6.40 (*b*)

Here, $I_{s.c_2} = \dfrac{20+10}{3+2+10} = 2 \text{ A}$

Following Superposition theorem,

$$I_{s.c} = I_{s.c_1} + I_{s.c_2} = 5 + 2 = 7 \text{ A}$$

i.e., the current through the short circuit link is **7 A.**

EXAMPLE 6.41 *Find v_L in the circuit of Fig. E6.41 using Superposition theorem.*

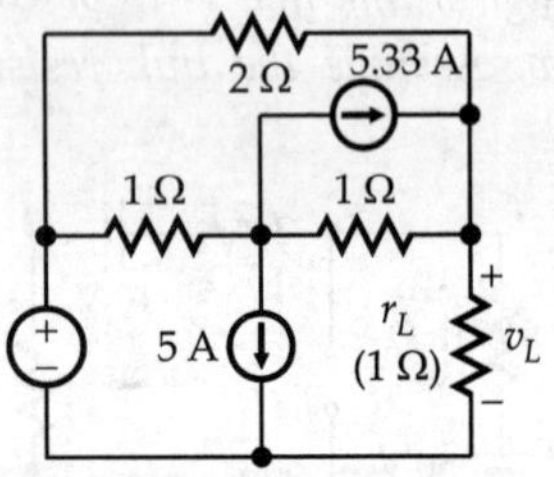

Fig. E6.41

SOLUTION. Let us first take the 2 V source deactivating the current sources (Fig. E6.41(*a*)).

$$i_1 = \frac{2}{\dfrac{2\times 2}{2+2}+1} = 1 \text{ A}$$

$\therefore$ v_1 (drop across r_L due to 2 V source)

$$= 1 \times 1 = 1 \text{ V}$$

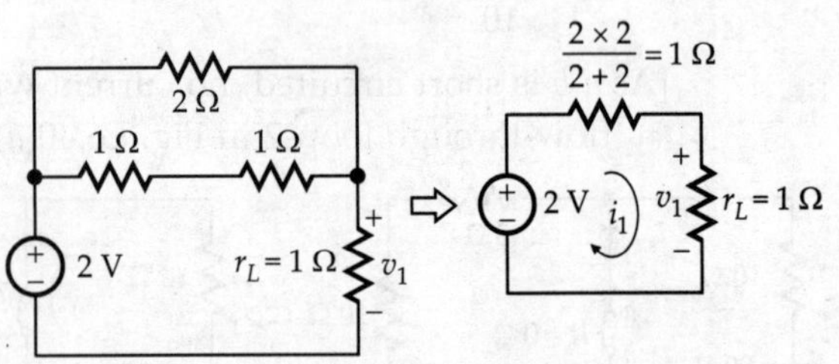

Fig. E6.41 (*a*)

Next, taking the lower current source only (Fig. E6.41(*b*)).

$$i_2 = (-5)\frac{1}{1+1+\dfrac{2}{3}} = (-5)\frac{3}{8} = -\frac{15}{8} \text{ A.}$$

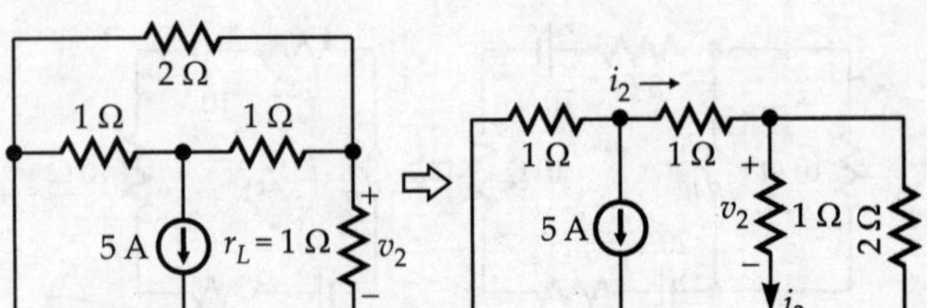

Fig. E6.41 (*b*)

$$\therefore\ i_3 = -\left(\frac{15}{8}\right)\frac{2}{1+2} = -\left(\frac{15}{8}\right)\frac{2}{3} = -\frac{5}{4} \text{ A}$$

This gives $v_2 = -\dfrac{5}{4} \times 1 = -\dfrac{5}{4}$ V.

In Fig. E6.41(*c*),

$$i_4 = 5.33\frac{1}{\dfrac{2}{3}+2} = 3 \text{ A} \qquad \text{[with 5.33 A source]}$$

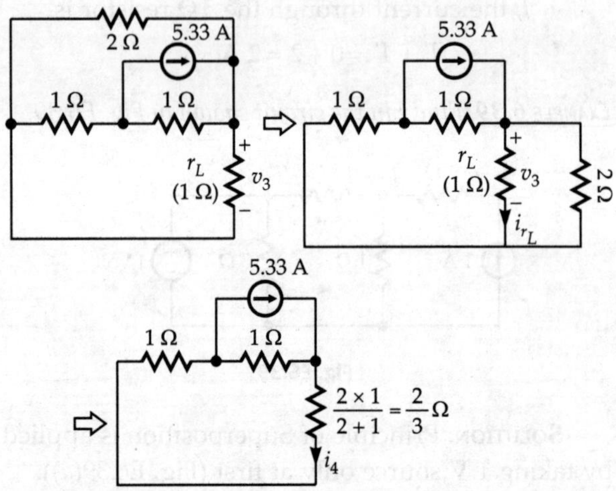

Fig. E6.41 (*c*)

This gives

$$i_{r_L} = 3\frac{2}{2+1} = 2 \text{ A.}$$

$$\therefore \qquad v_3 = 2 \times 1 = 2 \text{ V.}$$

By Superposition,

$$v_L = v_1 + v_2 + v_3 = 1 + \left(-\frac{5}{4}\right) + 2 = \frac{7}{4} \text{ V}$$

$$= \mathbf{1.75\ V.}$$

EXAMPLE 6.42 *For the circuit shown in Fig. E6.42, find the current through r_1. [$V_1 = 12$ V, $r_1 = 4\,\Omega$, $I = 3$ A, $r_2 = 2\,\Omega$, $V_2 = 24$ V].*

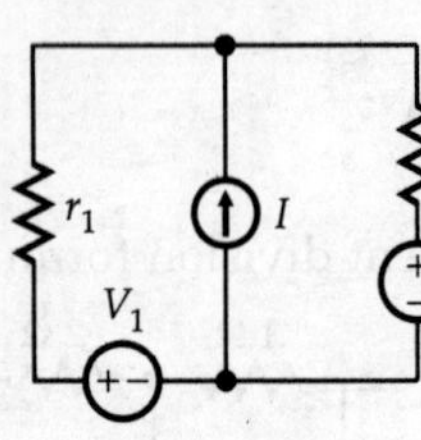

Fig. E6.42

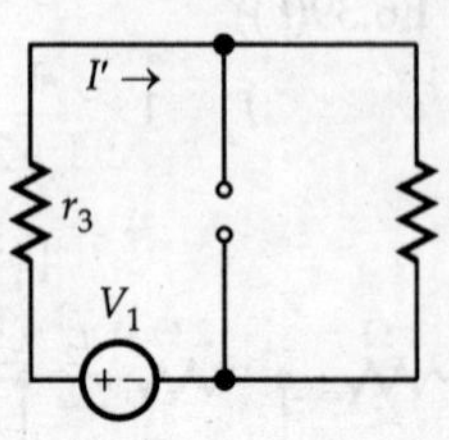

Fig. E6.42(*a*)

SOLUTION. Let us first take the source V_1 only deactivating the other source (Fig. E6.42(*a*)).

Here, $$I' = \frac{V_1}{r_1 + r_2} = \frac{12}{4+2} = 2\ \text{A}$$

Next, deactivating I and V_1, taking only V_2 (Fig. E6.42(b)).

$$I'' = \frac{V_2}{r_1 + r_2} = \frac{24}{4+2} = 4\ \text{A}$$

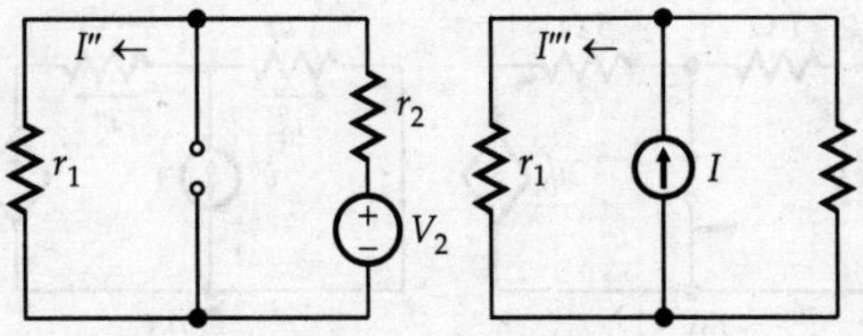

(b) (c)

Fig. E6.42

Then we take only the current source and deactivate V_1 and V_2 (Fig. E6.42(c)).

Here, $$I''' = I\frac{r_2}{r_1 + r_2} = 3\frac{2}{2+4} = 1\ \text{A}$$

Taking note that I'' and I''' are in reverse directions in comparison to I', using the principle of Superposition, the current through r_1 is given by

$$I_{r_1} = I' - I'' - I'''$$
$$= 2 - 4 - 1 = -3\ \text{A}$$

i.e., the net current through r_1 will flow **downward** and its magnitude will be **3 A.**

EXAMPLE 6.43 *Find the current in the 10 Ω resistor. (Fig. E6.43).*

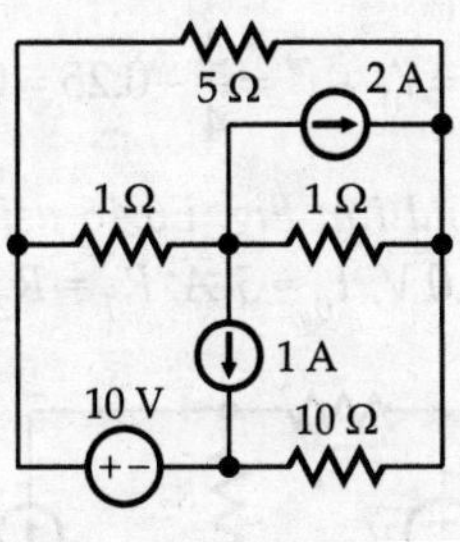

Fig. E6.43

SOLUTION. Referring to Fig. E6.43(a), for the 10 V source only,

$$I' = \frac{10}{\frac{5\times 2}{5+2} + 10} = \frac{10}{\frac{10}{7} + 10} = \frac{10\times 7}{80} = \frac{7}{8}\ \text{A}$$

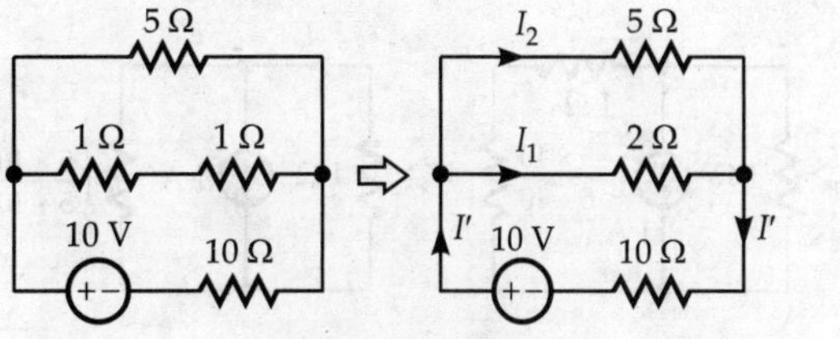

Fig. E6.43 (a)

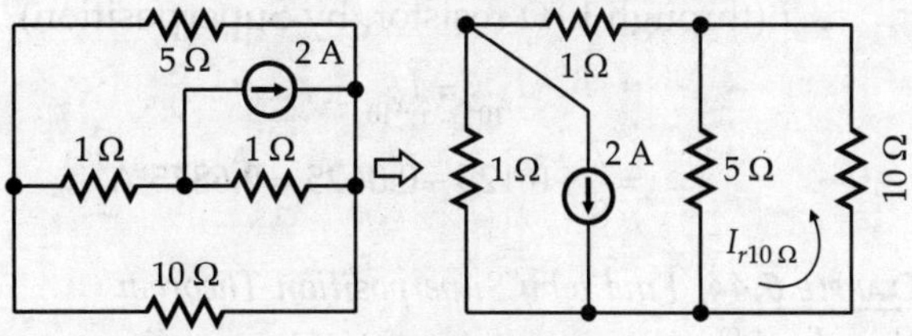

Fig. E6.43 (b)

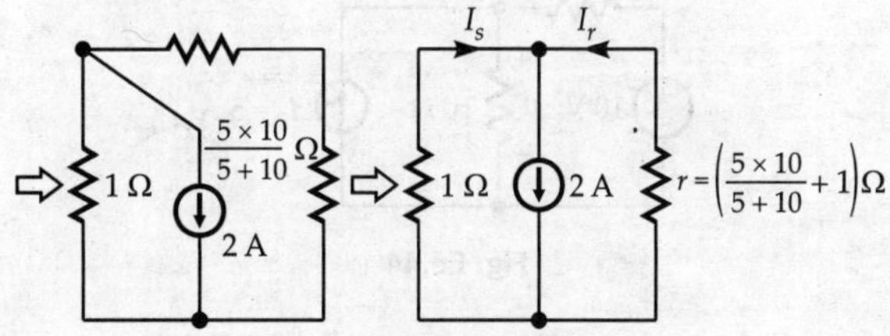

Fig. E6.43 (c)

Assuming 2 A current source only, referring to Figs. E6.43(b) & (c),

$$I_r = 2\frac{1}{1+r}$$

where $$r = \frac{5\times 10}{5+10} + 1 = 4.33\ \Omega$$

$$\therefore \quad I_r = 0.375\ \text{A}$$

Thus $$I_{r_{10\,\Omega}} = 0.375 \times \frac{5}{5+10} = 0.125\ \text{A.}$$

Next let us assume only 1 A source (Figs. E6.43(d) and (e)).

$$I_x = 1\frac{1}{1+1+\frac{5\times 10}{5+10}} = 0.1875\ \Omega$$

and $$I_{x_{10}} = 0.1875\frac{5}{10+5} = 0.0625\ \text{A}$$

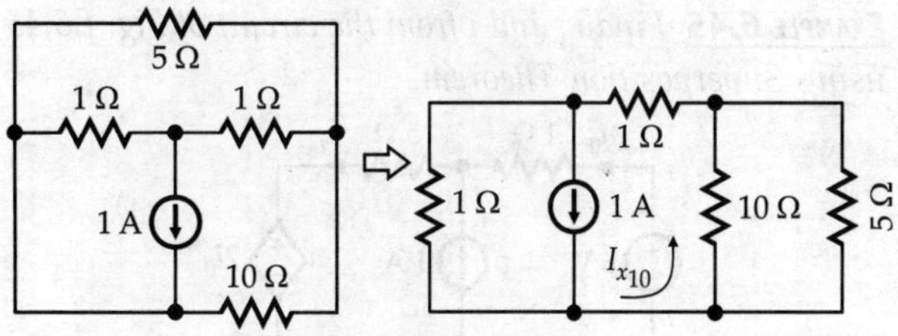

Fig. E6.43 (d)

CHAPTER 6

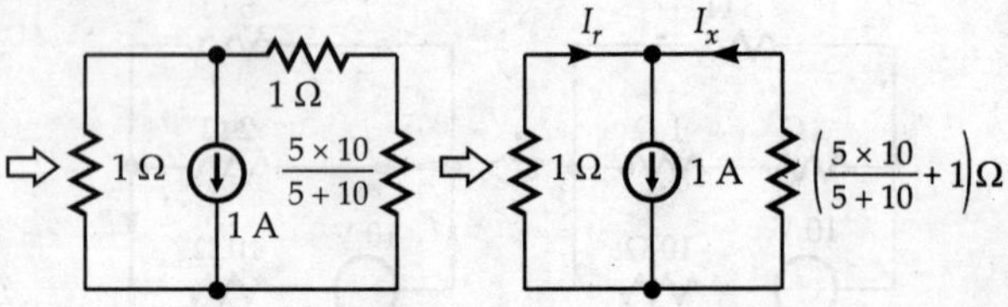

Fig. E6.43 (*e*)

$\therefore$ I (through 10 Ω resistor, by Superposition)

$$= I' - I_{r_{10}} - I_{x_{10}}$$

$$= \frac{7}{8} - 0.125 - 0.0625 = \mathbf{0.6875\ A.}$$

EXAMPLE 6.44 *Find v by Superposition Theorem (Fig. E6.44).*

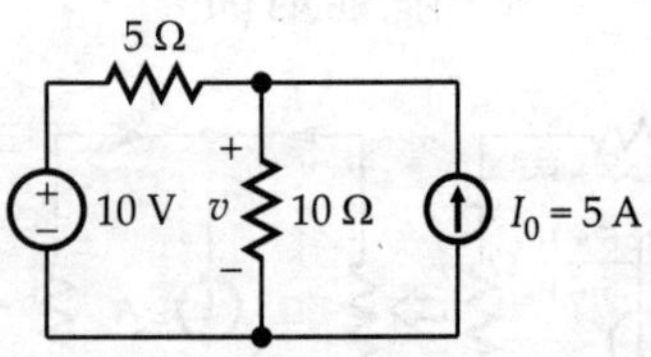

Fig. E6.44

SOLUTION. Taking the 10 V source only, with reference to Fig. E6.44(*a*),

$$v_1 = 10 \times i = 10\,\frac{10}{5+10} = 6.67\ \text{V}$$

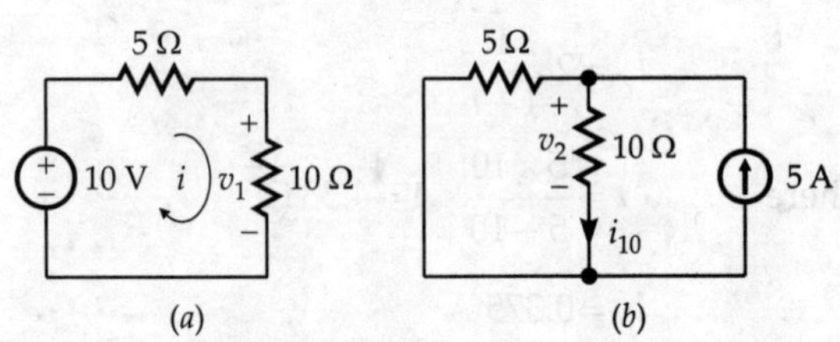

(*a*) (*b*)

Fig. E6.44

Taking the 5 A source only, with reference to Fig. E6.44(*b*),

$$i_{10} = 5\,\frac{5}{5+10} = 1.67\ \text{A}$$

$$\therefore \quad v_2 = 1.67 \times 10 = 16.70\ \text{V}$$

By Superposition theorem,

$$v = v_1 + v_2 = 6.67 + 16.70 = \mathbf{23.37\ V.}$$

EXAMPLE 6.45 *Find i_0 and i from the circuit of Fig. E6.45 using Superposition Theorem.*

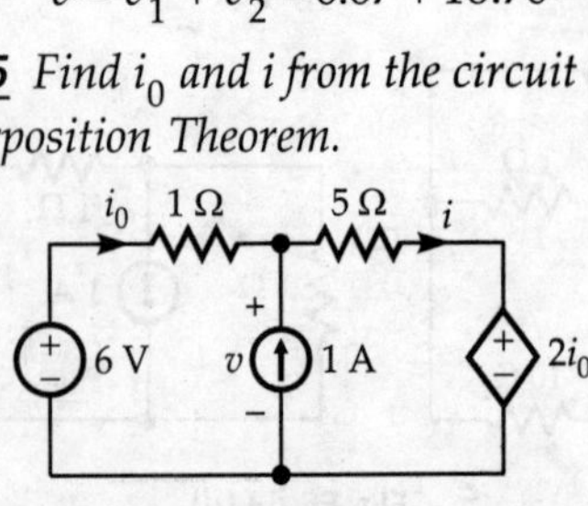

Fig. E6.45

SOLUTION. Assuming only 6 V source to be active, with reference to Fig. E6.45(*a*),

$$-6 + (1+5)\,i_0' + 2i_0' = 0$$

or $$8i_0' = 6 \quad \therefore \quad i_0' = \frac{3}{4}\ \text{A}$$

$$\therefore \quad i_0' = i' = \frac{3}{4}\ \text{A}$$

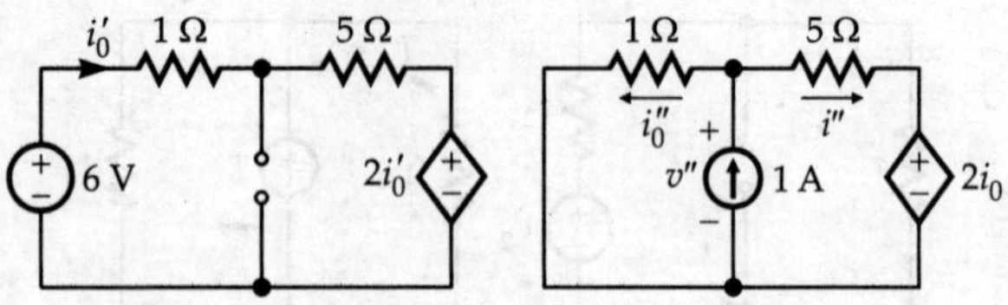

(*a*) (*b*)

Fig. E6.45

Next, assuming 1 A source active only, with reference to

$$1 = i_0'' + i''$$

$$= \frac{v''}{1} + \frac{v'' - 2i_0''}{5} = 1.2\,v'' - 0.4\,i_0''$$

But $$i_0'' = \frac{v''}{1}$$

$\therefore$ We finally get,

$$1 = 1.2\,i_0'' - 0.4\,i_0'' = 0.8\,i_0''$$

i.e., $$i_0'' = 1.25\ \text{A} \quad \text{and} \quad i'' = \frac{v'' - 2i_0''}{5}$$

$$= -i_0''/5 = -0.25\ \text{A}$$

Using the principle of Superposition,

$$i_0 = i_0' - i_0'' = \frac{3}{4} - 1.25 = \mathbf{-0.5\ A}$$

and $$i = i_0' + i'' = \frac{3}{4} - 0.25 = \mathbf{0.5\ A.}$$

EXAMPLE 6.46 *Find i in Fig. E6.46 using Superposition theorem if V_s = 10 V, I_0 = 5 A, $R_1 = R_2$ = 10 Ω.*

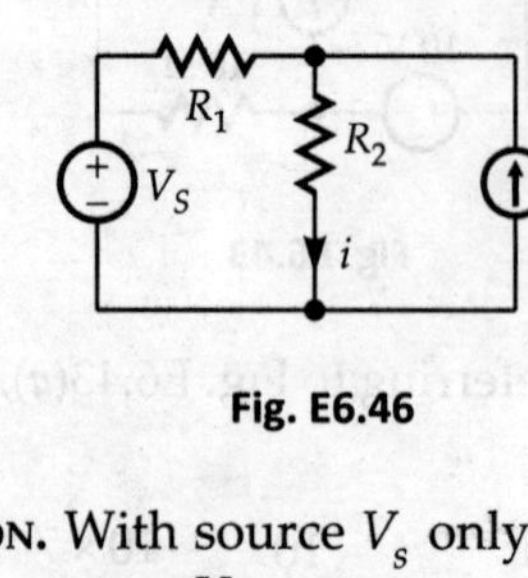

Fig. E6.46

SOLUTION. With source V_s only,

$$i' = \frac{V_s}{R_1 + R_2} = 0.5\ \text{A}$$

With source I_0 only, current i'' through

$$R_2 = I_0 \frac{R_1}{R_1 + R_2} = 2.5 \text{ A}$$

Thus, by Superposition principles,

$$i = i' + i'' = 0.5 + 2.5 = 3 \text{ A}$$

6.5 MAXIMUM POWER TRANSFER THEOREM

This theorem is used to find the value of load resistance for which there would be maximum amount of power transfer from source to load.

6.5.1 Statement of Maximum Power Transfer Theorem

A resistance load, being connected to a dc network, receives maximum power when the load resistance is equal to the internal resistance (Thevenin's equivalent resistance) of the source network as seen from the load terminals.

6.5.2 Explanation

A variable resistance R_L is connected to a dc source network as shown in Fig. 6.5(*a*) while Fig. 6.5(*b*) represents the Thevenin voltage V_0 and Thevenin resistance R_{Th} of the source network. The aim is to determine the value of R_L such that it receives maximum power from the dc source.

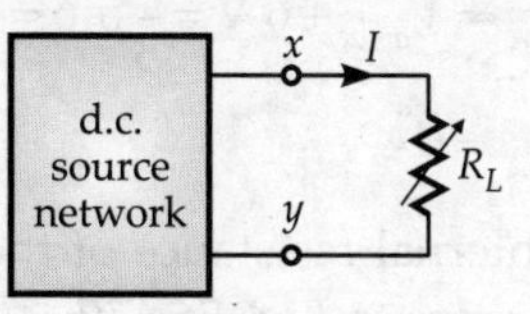

Fig. 6.5 (*a*) Load connected to the dc source network.

With reference to Fig. 6.5(*b*),

$$I = \frac{V_0}{R_{Th} + R_L}$$

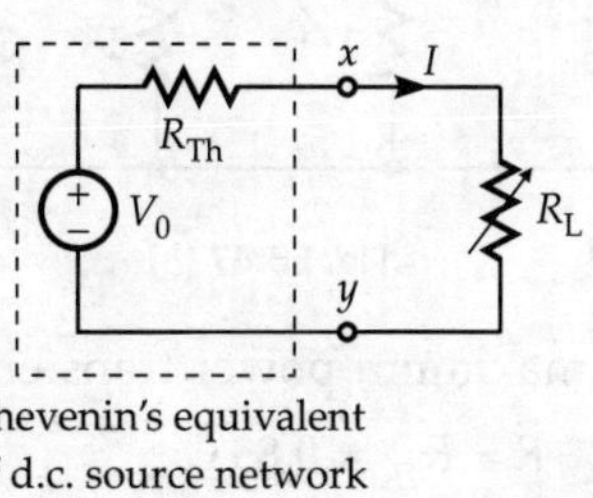

Fig. 6.5 (*b*) Equivalent source network and load.

while the power delivered to the resistive load is

$$P_L = I^2 R_L = \left(\frac{V_0}{R_{Th} + R_L} \right)^2 \times R_L.$$

P_L can be maximised by varying R_L and hence, maximum power can be delivered when $(dP_L / dR_L) = 0$.

However,

$$\frac{dP_L}{dR_L} = \frac{1}{[(R_{Th} + R_L)^2]^2} \left[(R_{Th} + R_L)^2 \frac{d}{dR_L}(V_0^2 R_L) - V_0^2 R_L \frac{d}{dR_L}(R_{Th} + R_L)^2 \right]$$

$$= \frac{1}{(R_{Th} + R_L)^4} [(R_{Th} + R_L)^2 V_0^2 - V_0^2 R_L \times 2 (R_{Th} + R_L)]$$

$$= \frac{V_0^2 (R_{Th} + R_L - 2 R_L)}{(R_{Th} + R_L)^3} = \frac{V_0^2 (R_{Th} - R_L)}{(R_{Th} + R_L)^3}$$

But $\dfrac{dP_L}{dR_L} = 0$

$\therefore$ Finally, $\dfrac{V_0^2 (R_{Th} - R_L)}{(R_{Th} + R_L)^3} = 0$

which gives $(R_{Th} - R_L) = 0$ or, $R_{Th} = R_L$

Hence, it has been proved that power transfer from a dc source network to a resistive network is maximum when the internal resistance of the dc source network is equal to the load resistance.

Again, with $R_L = R_{Th}$, the system being perfectly *matched* for load and source, the power transfer becomes maximum and this amount of power (P_{max}) can be obtained as

$$P_{max} = \frac{V_0^2 R_{Th}}{(R_{Th} + R_{Th})^2} = \frac{V_0^2}{4 R_{Th}}$$

(it may be noted that this is the power consumed by the load).

Obviously, the power transfer by the source would be also $\dfrac{V_0^2}{4 R_{Th}}$, the load power and source power being the same.

The total power supplied is thus

$$P = 2 \frac{V_0^2}{4 R_{Th}} = \frac{V_0^2}{2 R_{Th}}$$

During maximum power transfer the efficiency η becomes

$$\eta = \frac{P_{max}}{P} \times 100 = 50\%$$

The concept of maximum power transfer by making the source resistance equal to the load resistance has wide application in communication circuits where the magnitude of power transfer is sufficiently small. To achieve maximum power transfer, then the source and load resistances are matched and with flow of maximum power from source to load, low efficiency of 50% is tolerated. On the other hand, in electric power transmission systems, the load resistance being sufficiently greater than the source resistance, it is difficult to achieve the condition of maximum power transfer ordinarily. Moreover, in power system, emphasis is given to keep voltage drops and line losses to a minimum value and hence operation of the power system, operating with bulk power transmission capability, becomes uneconomical if it be operated with only 50% efficiency just for the sake of maximum power transfer. Hence in power transmission systems this criterion of maximum power transfer is seldom realised.

6.5.3 Steps for Solution of a Network Utilizing Maximum Power Transfer Theorem

Following steps may be executed to solve the problems relating to maximum power transfer theorem :

Step 1 Remove the load resistance and find Thevenin's resistance (R_{Th}) of the source network looking through the open circuited load terminals.

Step 2 As per maximum power transfer theorem, this R_{Th} is the load resistance of the network *i.e.*, $R_L = R_{Th}$ that allows maximum power transfer.

Step 3 Find the Thevenin's voltage (V_0) across the open circuited load terminals.

Step 4 Maximum power transfer is given by :

$$\frac{V_0^2}{4\,R_{Th}}$$

EXAMPLE 6.47 *Find the value of R in the circuit of Fig. E6.47 such that maximum power transfer takes place. What is the amount of this power ?*

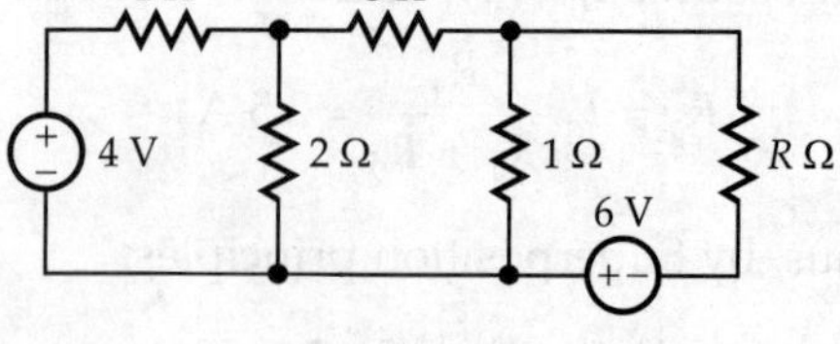

Fig. E6.47

SOLUTION. Let R be replaced first and the open circuit voltage be $V_{o.c}$ (Fig. E6.47(*a*))

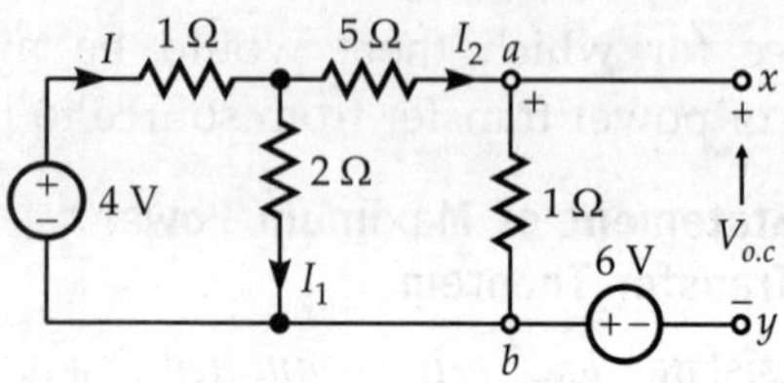

Fig. E6.47 (*a*)

Here $I = \dfrac{4\text{ V}}{[\{(5+1)\,||\,2\} + 1]\,\Omega} = \dfrac{4}{\frac{5}{2}} = \dfrac{8}{5}$ A

$\therefore \quad I_2 = I\dfrac{2}{2+5+1} = \dfrac{8}{5} \times \dfrac{1}{4} = \dfrac{2}{5}$ A

The drop across *a-b* branch is then

$$V_{a-b} = \frac{2}{5} \times 1 = \frac{2}{5}\text{ V}$$

Obviously,

$$V_{o.c} = V_{a-b} + 6\text{ V} = \frac{2}{5} + 6 = \frac{32}{5}\text{ V}$$

or, $\quad V_{o.c} = 6.4$ V

To find internal resistance of the circuit across *x-y*, with reference to Fig. E6.47(*b*),

$$R_{Th} = \{1\,||\,2+5\}\,||\,1 = \frac{17}{3}\,||\,1 = \frac{17}{20}\,\Omega$$

$$= 0.85\,\Omega$$

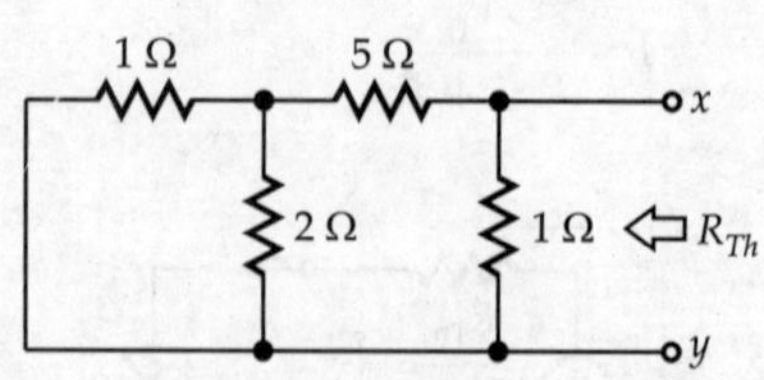

Fig. E6.47 (*b*)

As per maximum power transfer theorem,

$$R = R_{Th} = \mathbf{0.85\,\Omega}$$

and P_{max} (max. power) $= \dfrac{V_{o.c}^2}{4\,R} = \dfrac{(6.4)^2}{4 \times 0.85} \simeq$ **12 W.**

EXAMPLE 6.48 *What should be the value of R such that maximum power transfer can take place from the rest of the network to R in Fig. E6.48 ? Obtain the amount of this power.*

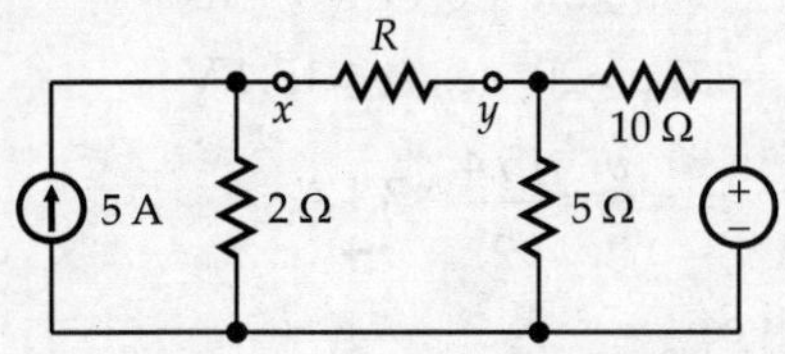

Fig. E6.48

SOLUTION. Let us first convert the "I" source to "V" source and remove R from x-y terminal, the voltage at these terminals being $V_{o.c}$.

With reference to Fig. E6.48(*a*),

$$i = \frac{24}{15} = 1.6 \text{ A}$$

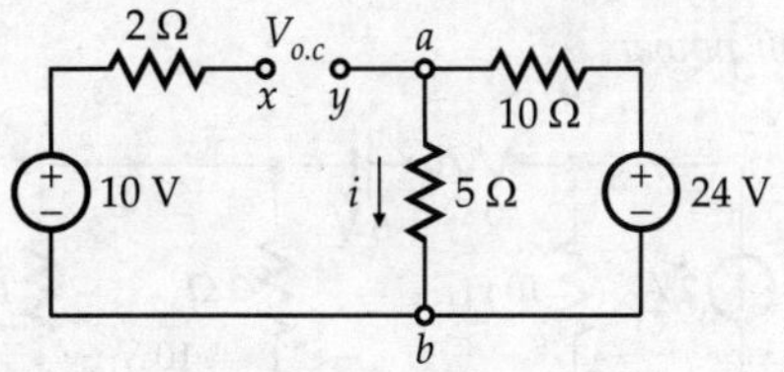

Fig. E6.48 (*a*)

$\therefore \quad V_{a-b}$ = drop across 5 Ω = 1.6 × 5 = 8 V

Thus in the left loop,

$$-10 + V_{o.c} + 8 = 0$$

or, $\quad V_{o.c} = 2$ V

Again, with reference to Fig. E6.48(*b*), R_{Th} (internal resistance of the circuit looking through x - y) is obtained as

$$R_{Th} = \frac{10 \times 5}{10 + 5} + 2 = 5.33\,\Omega$$

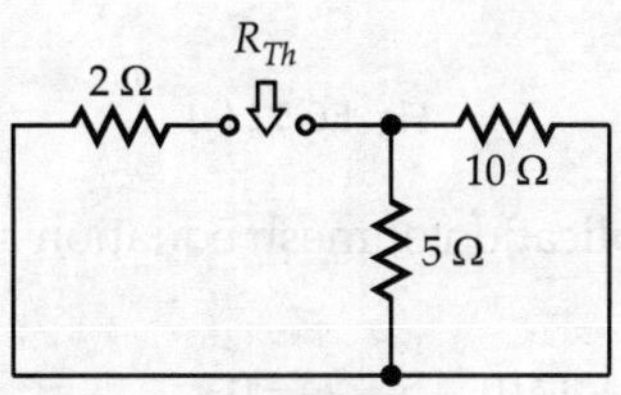

Fig. E6.48 (*b*)

As per maximum power transfer theorem,

$$R = R_{Th} = \mathbf{5.33\,\Omega}.$$

and $\quad P_{max} = \frac{V_{o.c}^2}{4R} = \frac{2^2}{4 \times 5.33} = \mathbf{188\ mW.}$

EXAMPLE 6.49 *Assuming maximum power transfer from the source to R, find the value of this amount of power in the circuit of Fig. E6.49.*

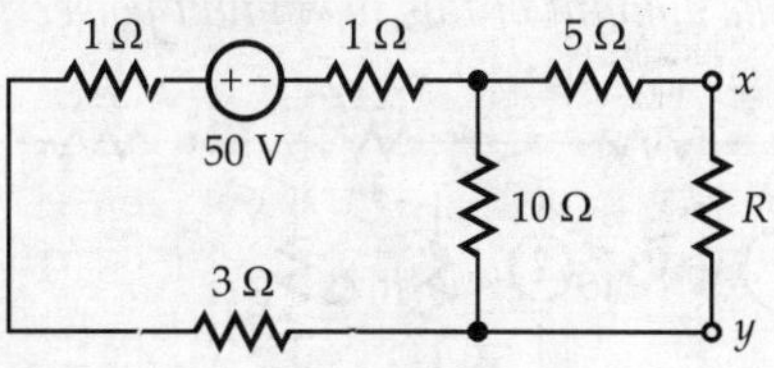

Fig. E6.49

SOLUTION. R is removed by open circuit. With reference to Fig. E6.49(*a*),

$$I = \frac{50}{15} = 3.333\,\Omega$$

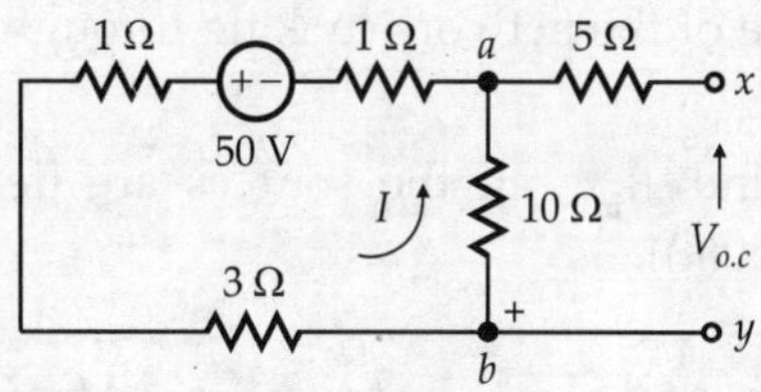

Fig. E6.49 (*a*)

$$\therefore \quad V_{o.c} = V_{10\Omega} = 3.333 \times 10 = 33.33 \text{ V}$$

[It may be noted that *b* will be having +ve polarity as the current in 10 Ω resistor flows from *b* to *a*]

$\therefore \quad V_{x-y} = -33.33$ V $\quad$ [*y* terminal being +ve]

$(= V_{o.c})$

With reference to Fig. E6.49(*b*),

$$R_{Th} = \frac{5 \times 10}{5 + 10} + 5 = 8.33\,\Omega$$

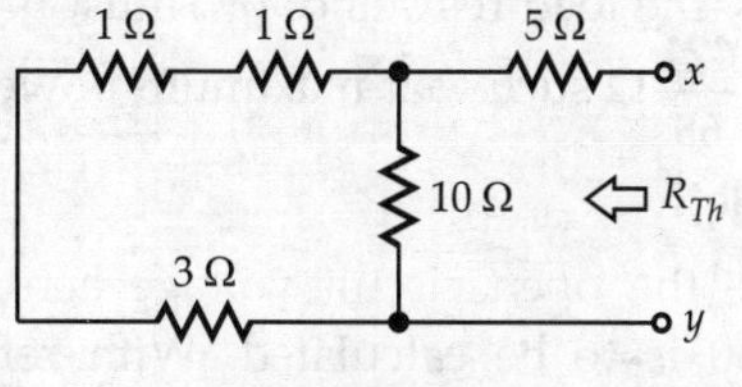

Fig. E6.49 (*b*)

As per maximum power transfer theorem,

$$R = R_{Th} = \mathbf{8.33\,\Omega}$$

and $\quad P_{max} = \frac{V_{o.c}^2}{4\,R}$

$$= \frac{(-33.33)^2}{4 \times 8.33} = \mathbf{33.34\ W.}$$

EXAMPLE 6.50 *What resistance should be connected across x - y in the circuit shown in Fig. E6.50 such that maximum power is developed across this load resistance ? What is the amount of this maximum power ?*

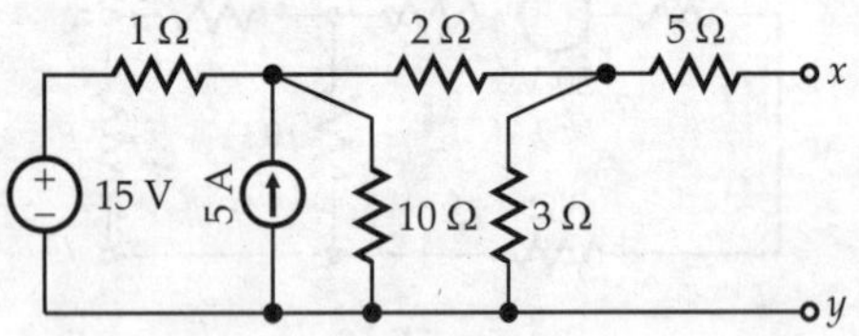

Fig. E6.50

SOLUTION. Let r_L be the resistance that is to be connected across x - y for maximum power transfer from source to load. As per maximum power transfer theorem, r_L should be equal to the internal resistance of the network looking through $x-y$. Let this be R_{int}.

To find R_{int}, all the sources are deactivated (Fig. E6.50(*a*)).

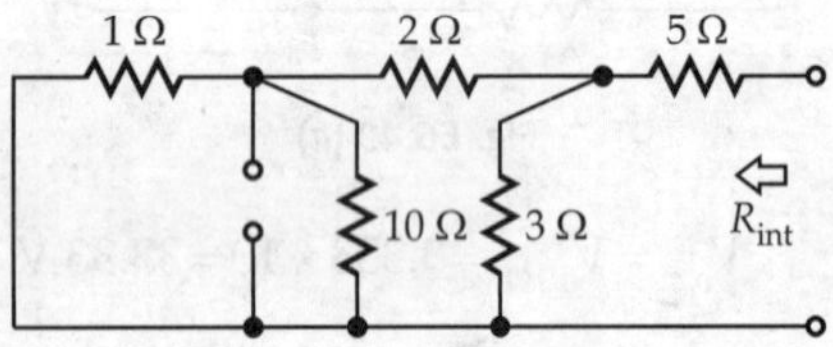

Fig. E6.50 (*a*)

Here, $R_{int} = [\{(1 || 10) + 2\} || 3] + 5$

$$= \frac{\left(\frac{1\times 10}{1+10}+2\right)3}{\left(\frac{1\times 10}{1+10}+2\right)+3} + 5 = \frac{421}{65}\ \Omega$$

Thus, the load resistance (r_L) must be having a value of $\mathbf{\frac{421}{65}}$ Ω such that maximum power transfer is possible.

Next, the open circuit voltage across x - y in Fig. E6.50 is to be calculated. With reference to Fig. E6.50(*b*), *at node* (1), KCL gives

$$i_1 + i_2 + i_3 = 5$$

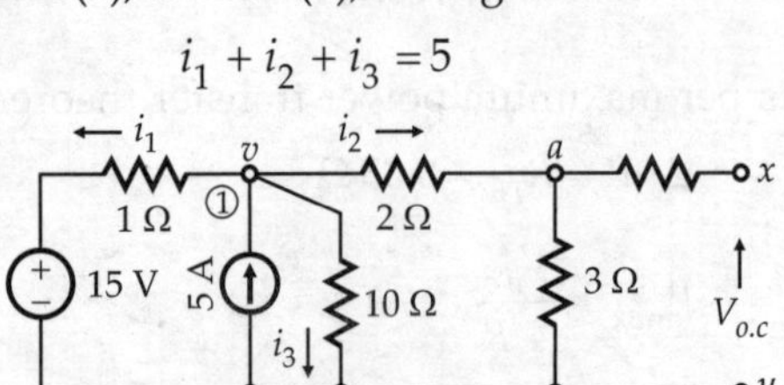

Fig. E6.50 (*b*)

or, $$\frac{v-15}{1} + \frac{v}{5} + \frac{v}{10} = 5$$

[assuming the voltage at *node (1)* to be v]

or, $$v + 0.2\,v + 0.1\,v = 5 + 15$$

or, $$1.3\,v = 20 \text{ i.e., } v = 15.4 \text{ V}$$

$$\therefore \quad i_2 = \frac{v}{5} = \frac{15.4}{5} \simeq 3.1 \text{ A.}$$

This gives

$$V_{o.c} = i_2 \times 3 = 3.1 \times 3 = 9.3 \text{ V}$$

Amount of maximum power transfer is given by

$$P_{max} = \frac{V_{o.c}^2}{4\ R_{Th}} = \frac{(9.3)^2}{4 \times \frac{421}{65}} = \mathbf{3.34\ W.}$$

EXAMPLE 6.51 *Find R to have maximum power transfer in the circuit of Fig. E6.51. Also obtain the amount of maximum power.*

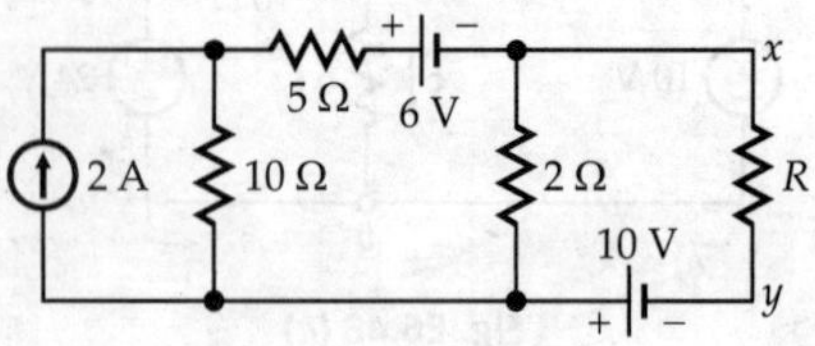

Fig. E6.51

SOLUTION. Let us first convert the current source to voltage source first as shown in Fig. E6.51(*a*). R is also replaced by open circuit. Here $V_{o.c}$ is the open circuit voltage at the output terminal x - y.

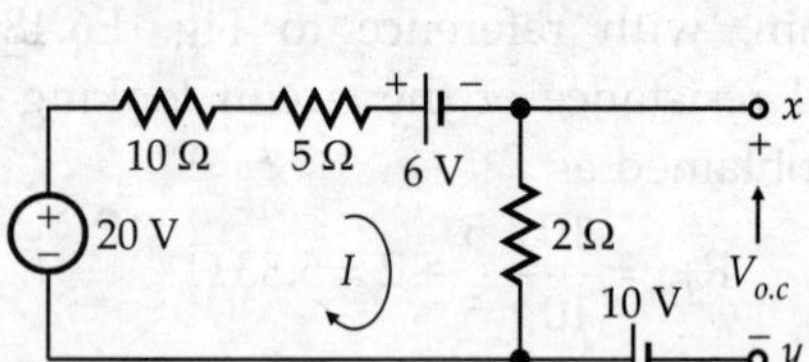

Fig. E6.51 (*a*)

The application of mesh equation at the *left loop* yields

$$-20 + 6 + I(10 + 5 + 2) = 0$$

or, $$I = \frac{14}{17} \text{ A.}$$

This gives $$V_{o.c} = 10 + \frac{14}{17} \times 2 = 11.65 \text{ V}$$

[$\because V_{o.c}$ = drop across 2 Ω + potential of 10 V battery]

The internal resistance of the circuit looking from x - y terminals is obtained by deactivating all sources as shown in Fig. E6.51(b).

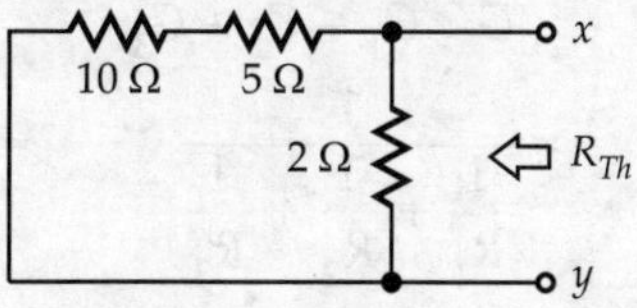

Fig. E6.51 (b)

Here $R_{Th} = \frac{15 \times 2}{15+2} = \frac{30}{17} = 1.765\,\Omega$

As per the theorem of maximum power transfer,

$$R = \mathbf{1.765\,\Omega} \; (= R_{Th})$$

and P_{max} (amount of maximum power transfer)

$$= \frac{V_{Th}^2}{4\,R} = \frac{11.65^2}{4 \times 1.765} = \mathbf{19.22\ W.}$$

6.6 MILLMAN'S THEOREM

The utility of this theorem is that, any number of parallel voltage sources can be reduced to one equivalent one.

6.6.1 Statement of Millman's Theorem

When a number of voltage sources ($V_1, V_2, \ldots, V_n$) *are in parallel having internal resistances* ($R_1, R_2, \ldots, R_n$) *respectively, the arrangement can be replaced by a single equivalent voltage source V in series with an equivalent series resistance R as given below (Refer Figs. 6.6(a) and (b)).*

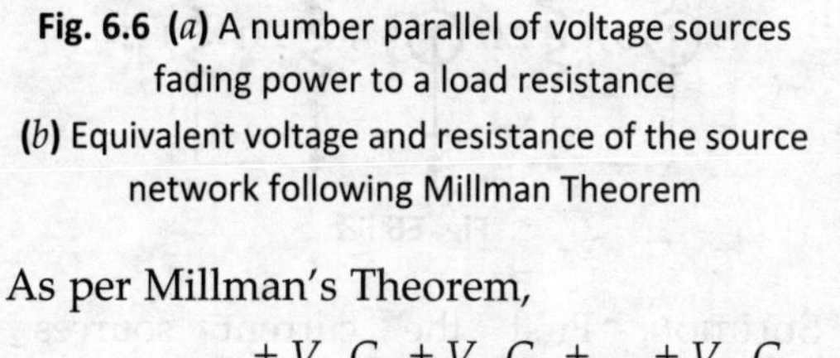

Fig. 6.6 (a) A number parallel of voltage sources fading power to a load resistance
(b) Equivalent voltage and resistance of the source network following Millman Theorem

As per Millman's Theorem,

$$V = \frac{\pm V_1\,G_1 \pm V_2\,G_2 \pm \ldots \pm V_n\,G_n}{G_1 + G_2 + \ldots + G_n};$$

$$R = \frac{1}{G} = \frac{1}{G_1 + G_2 + \ldots + G_n}$$

6.6.2 Explanation

Assuming a dc network of numerous parallel voltage sources with internal resistances supplying power to a load resistance R_L (Fig. 6.7), all voltage sources are converted to current sources as shown in Fig. 6.8.

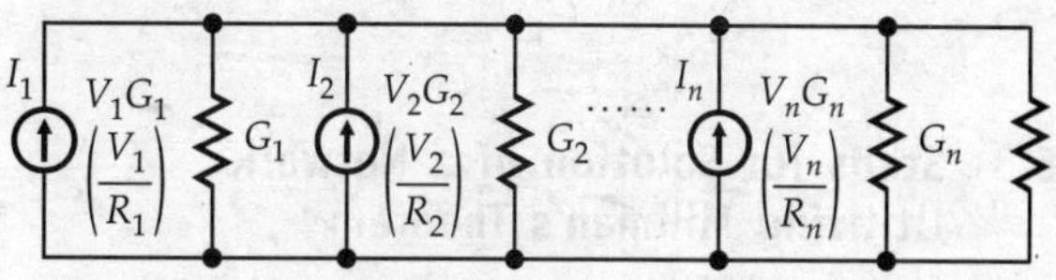

Fig. 6.7 Conversion of parallel voltage sources to current sources

Let I represent the resultant current of the parallel current sources while G the equivalent conductance (Fig. 6.8) such that

$$I = I_1 + I_2 + I_3 + \ldots;\ G = G_1 + G_2 + G_3 + \ldots$$

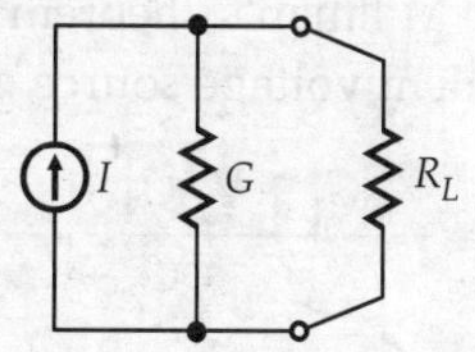

Fig. 6.8 Eqivalent current sources and conductance

Next, the resulting current source is converted to an equivalent voltage source as depicted in Fig. 6.9.

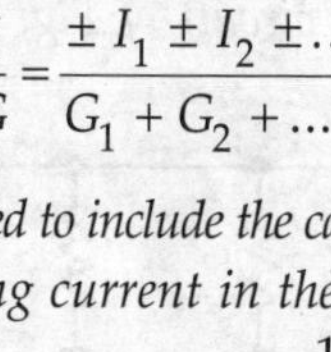

Fig. 6.9 Equivalent voltage source of the current source

Thus $V = \frac{I}{G} = \frac{\pm I_1 \pm I_2 \pm \ldots \pm I_n}{G_1 + G_2 + \ldots + G_n}$

[*+ and – signs appeared to include the cases where the sources may not be supplying current in the same direction.*]

Also $R = \frac{1}{G} = \frac{1}{G_1 + G_2 + G_3 + \ldots + G_n}$

and $V = \dfrac{\pm \frac{V_1}{R_1} \pm \frac{V_2}{R_2} \pm \ldots \pm \frac{V_n}{R_n}}{\frac{1}{R_1} + \frac{1}{R_2} + \ldots + \frac{1}{R_n}}$

where R is the equivalent resistance connected with the equivalent voltage source in series.

Thus finally,

$$V = \frac{\pm V_1 G_1 \pm V_2 G_2 \pm .... \pm V_n G_n}{G_1 + G_2 + ... + G_n}$$

$$= \frac{\sum_{K=1}^{n} V_K G_K}{\sum_{K=1}^{n} G_K} \text{ and } G_K = \frac{1}{R_K}.$$

6.6.3 Steps for Solution of a Network Utilizing Millman's Theorem

Following steps can be executed to get a direct solution of the problems relating Millman's theorem :

Step 1 Obtain the conductance $(G_1, G_2, ...)$ of each voltage source $(V_1, V_2, ...)$ and find G, the equivalent conductance removing the load.

Step 2 Apply Millman's theorem to find V, the equivalent voltage source given by

$$V = \frac{V_1 G_1 + V_2 G_2 + ... + V_n G_n}{G_1 + G_2 + ... G_n}$$

Step 3 Determine (R), the equivalent series resistance with the equivalent voltage source (V).

$$R = \frac{1}{G}$$

Step 4 The current through the load is then given by

$$I_L = \frac{V}{R + R_L};$$

R_L being the load resistance.

EXAMPLE 6.52 *Using Millman's theorem, find the current through R_L in the circuit of Fig. E6.52 and find the voltage drop.*

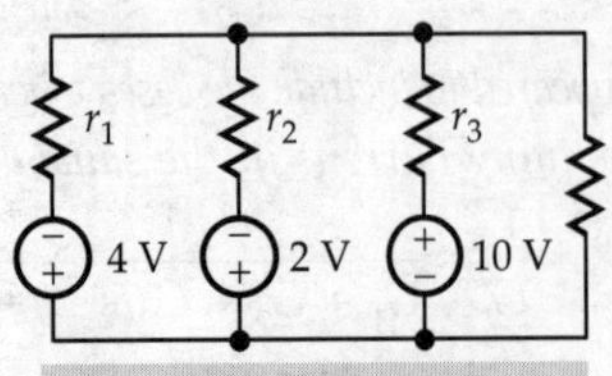

$[r_1 = r_2 = r_3 = 4\,\Omega;\ R_L = 10\,\Omega]$

Fig. E6.52

SOLUTION. Let V be the equivalent voltage source while R the equivalent resistance to be inserted in series with the voltage source of the Millman's equivalent source network.

Here, $$V = \frac{-V_1 G_1 - V_2 G_2 + V_3 G_3}{G_1 + G_2 + G_3}$$

and $$R = \frac{1}{G} = \frac{1}{G_1 + G_2 + G_3}$$

$$= \frac{1}{\frac{1}{R_1} + \frac{1}{R_2} + \frac{1}{R_3}}$$

Substituting the numerical values,

$$V = \frac{-4 \times \frac{1}{4} - 2 \times \frac{1}{4} + 10 \times \frac{1}{4}}{\frac{1}{4} + \frac{1}{4} + \frac{1}{4}}$$

$$= \frac{-1 - \frac{1}{2} + \frac{5}{2}}{\frac{3}{4}} = \frac{4}{3}\text{ V}$$

and $$R = \frac{1}{\frac{1}{4} + \frac{1}{4} + \frac{1}{4}} = \frac{4}{3}\,\Omega$$

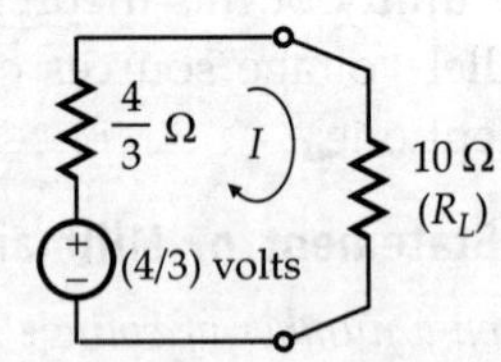

Fig. E6.52 *(a)*

From Fig. E6.52(*a*), the equivalent circuit, (Millman's network),

$$I = \frac{4/3}{\frac{4}{3} + 10} = \frac{4}{3} \times \frac{3}{34} = 0.12\text{ A}$$

The current through $10\,\Omega$ resistor is thus **0.12 A** while the drop across it is $10 \times 0.12 = $ **1.2 V.**

EXAMPLE 6.53 *Find the current through the $1\,\Omega$ resistor using Millman's Theorem (Fig. E6.53).*

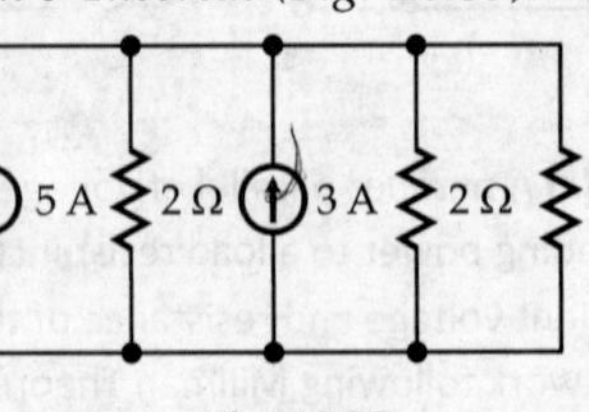

Fig. E6.53

SOLUTION. First the current sources are combined such that the total current is obtained as

$$I = I_1 + I_2 = 5 + 3 = 8\text{ A.}$$

$$G = G_1 + G_2 = \frac{1}{2} + \frac{1}{2} = 1\text{ mho}$$

Converting current source to an equivalent voltage source

$$V = \frac{I}{G} = \frac{8}{1} = 8 \text{ V}$$

and $$R = \frac{1}{G} = \frac{1}{1} = 1\Omega$$

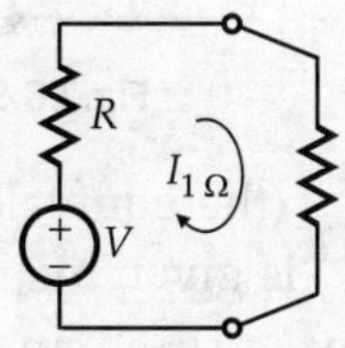

Fig. E6.53 (*a*)

Figure E6.53(*a*) being representing the Millman's equivalent network, the current through 1 Ω resistor is

$$I_{1\Omega} = \frac{V}{R+1} = \frac{8}{1+1} = \mathbf{4\ A.}$$

Example 6.54 *Find Millman's equivalent for the left of the terminals x-y in Fig. E6.54.*

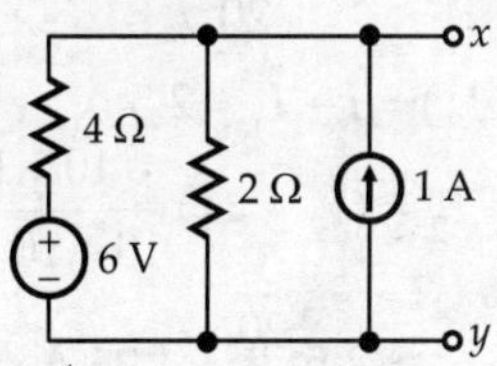

Fig. E6.54

Solution. Let us first convert the current source of 1 A to voltage source (Fig. E6.54(*a*)).

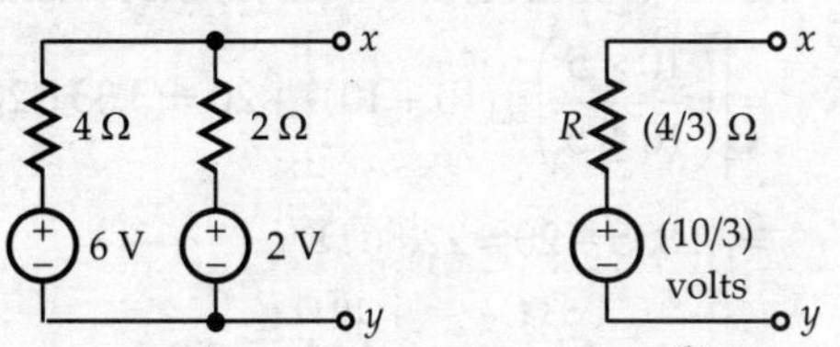

(*a*) (*b*)

Fig. E6.54

Millman's equivalent voltage is then given by

$$V = \frac{V_1 G_1 + V_2 G_2}{G_1 + G_2} = \frac{6 \times \frac{1}{4} + 2 \times \frac{1}{2}}{\frac{1}{4} + \frac{1}{2}}$$

$$= \frac{\frac{3}{2}+1}{\frac{3}{4}} = \frac{5}{2} \times \frac{4}{3} = \mathbf{\frac{10}{3}\ V};$$

$$R = \frac{1}{\frac{1}{4}+\frac{1}{2}} = \frac{1}{\frac{3}{4}} = \mathbf{\frac{4}{3}\ \Omega}.$$

Millman's equivalent circuit is thus obtained and shown in Fig. E6.54(*b*).

6.7 RECIPROCITY THEOREM

6.7.1 Statement of Reciprocity Theorem

In any branch of a network, the current (I) due to a single source of voltage (V) elsewhere in the network is equal to the current through the branch in which the source was originally placed when the source is placed in the branch in which the current (I) was originally obtained.

6.7.2 Explanation

In simple sense, the location of the voltage source and the through current may be interchanged without a change in current. However, the polarity of the voltage source should have the identicality with the direction of branch current in each position.

The limitation of this theorem is that it is applicable only to single-source networks and not in multisource network. Moreover, the network where reciprocity theorem is applied should be a linear one and containing of resistors, inductors, capacitors and coupled circuits. The network should not have any time varying element.

6.7.3 Steps for Solution of a Network Utilizing Reciprocity Theorem

Step 1 The branches between which reciprocity is to be established are to be selected first.

Step 2 The current in the branch is obtained using conventional network analysis.

Step 3 The voltage source is interchanged between the branches concerned.

Step 4 The current in the branch where the voltage source was existing earlier is calculated.

It may be observed that the currents obtained in step 2 and step 4 are identical to each other.

Example 6.55 *Show the application of reciprocity theorem in the network of Fig. E6.55.*

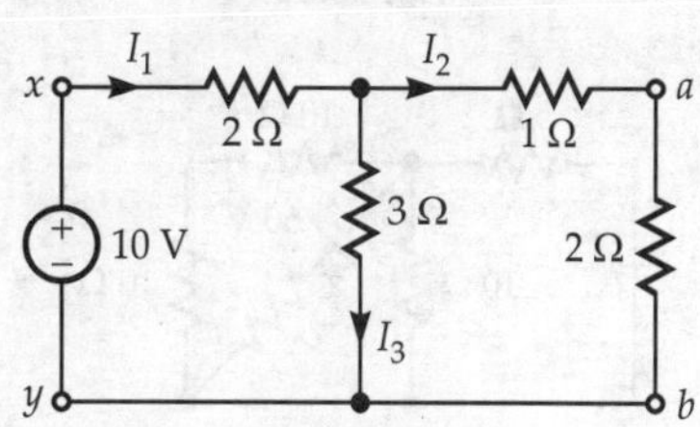

Fig. E6.55

Solution. With reference to Fig. E6.55, the equivalent resistance across *x-y* is given by

$$R_{eq} = [(2+1)||3]+2 = 3.5\,\Omega$$

$$\therefore \quad I_1 = \frac{10}{3.5} = 2.86 \text{ A}$$

$$I_2 = 2.86 \times \frac{3}{3+3} = 1.43 \text{ A}$$

$$I_3 = 2.86 - 1.43 = \mathbf{1.43\ A.}$$

With reference to Fig. E6.55(*a*),

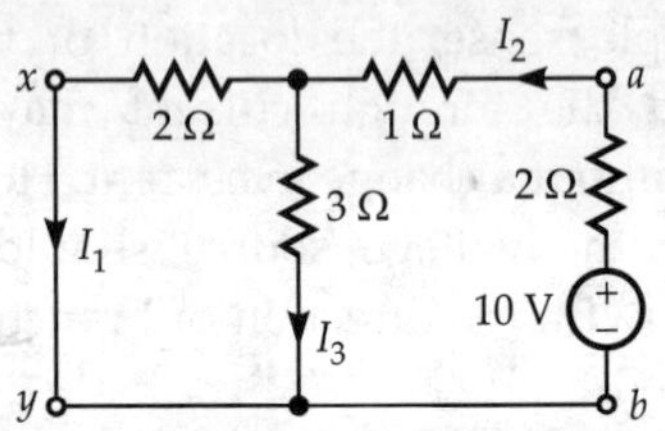

Fig. E6.55 (*a*)

$$R_{eq} = (2||3)+1+2 = \frac{6}{5}+3 = \frac{21}{5} = 4.2\,\Omega$$

$$\therefore \quad I_2 = \frac{10\text{ V}}{4.2\,\Omega} = 2.381 \text{ A}$$

This gives

$$I_1 = I_2 \frac{3}{3+2} = 2.381 \times \frac{3}{5} = \mathbf{1.43\ A.}$$

Hence we observe that when the source was in branch *x-y* as in Fig. E6.55, the *a-b* branch current is 1.43 A ; again when the source is in branch *a-b*, (Fig. E6.55(*a*)) the $x-y$ branch current becomes 1.43 A. This proves the *reciprocity theorem.*

Example 6.56 *Show the validity of reciprocity theorem in Figs. E6.56 and 6.56(a).*

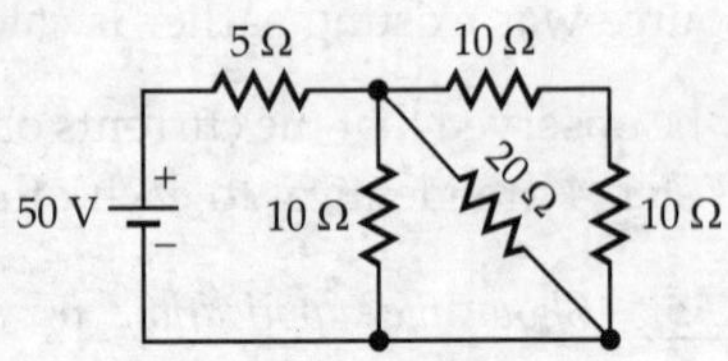

Fig. E6.56

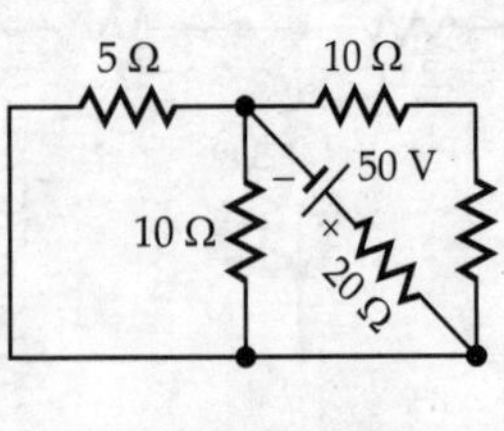

Fig. E6.56 (*a*)

Solution. Let Fig. E6.56 be redrawn as shown in Fig. E6.56(*b*)

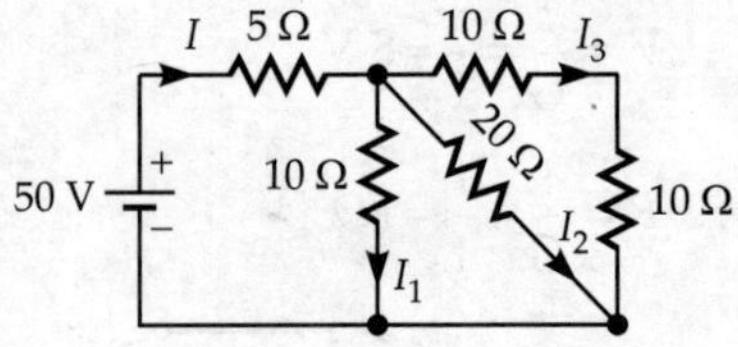

Fig. E6.56 (*b*)

Here R_{eq} (the equivalent resistance across the 50 V battery) is given by

$$R_{eq} = [\{(10+10)||20\}||10]+5 = 10\,\Omega$$

$$\therefore \quad I = \frac{50}{10} = 5 \text{ A.}$$

This gives

$$I_1 = I\frac{(10+10)||20}{[(10+10)||20]+10}$$

$$= 5 \times \frac{10}{20} = 2.5 \text{ A}$$

$$\therefore \quad (I_2 + I_3) = I - I_1 = 2.5 \text{ A.}$$

while $$I_2 = (I_2 + I_3)\frac{10+10}{10+10+20}$$

$$= 2.5\frac{20}{40} = \mathbf{1.25\ A}$$

and obviously $I_3 = 1.25$ A

Again redrawing Fig. E6.56(*a*) in Fig. 6.56(*c*), across the 50 V source, the equivalent resistance is

$$R_{eq} = \left[\left(\frac{10\times 5}{10+5}\right)||(10+10)\right]+20 = (3.33||20)+20$$

$$= 2.855 + 20 = 22.86\,\Omega$$

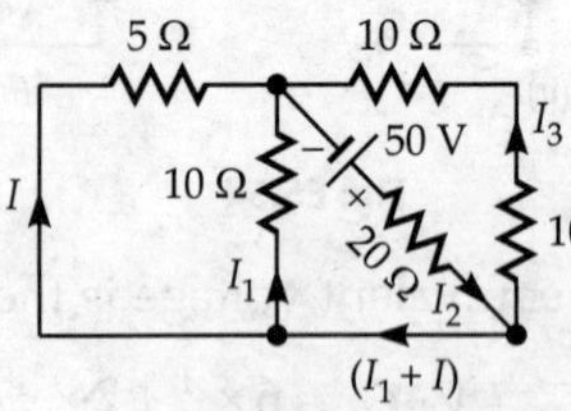

Fig. E6.56 (*c*)

$$\therefore \quad I_2 = \frac{50}{22.86} = 2.187 \text{ A.}$$

This gives

$$(I_1 + I) = I_2 \frac{20}{20+\frac{10\times 5}{10+5}} = 1.875 \text{ A}$$

and $$I = (I_1 + I)\frac{10}{10+5} = 1.25 \text{ A.}$$

Thus we see that in Fig. E6.56,

$$I_2 = \mathbf{1.25\ A.}$$

On the other hand, in Fig. E6.56(*a*) with placement of 50 V source in I_2 branch, now, $I = 1.25$ A. Thus the reciprocity theorem is proved.

6.8 SUBSTITUTION THEOREM

6.8.1 Statement of Substitution Theorem

The voltage across the current through any branch of a dc bilateral network being known, this branch can be replaced by any combination of elements that will make the same voltage across and current through the chosen branch.

In other words, the theorem, in its simplest form tells that for branch equivalence, the terminal voltage and current must be same.

6.8.2 Explanation

Let us take a simple network (Fig. 6.10) where we take to see the branch equivalence of the load resistance R_L.

Obviously, $\quad I = \dfrac{24}{3+5} = 3\text{ A}$

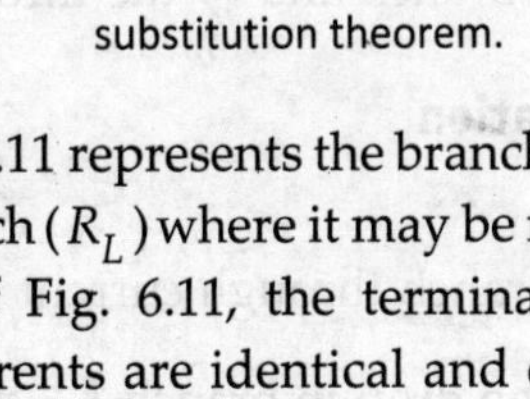

Fig. 6.10 A simple dc circuit to explain substitution theorem.

Figure 6.11 represents the branch equivalents of the *x-y* branch (R_L) where it may be noted that in all the cases of Fig. 6.11, the terminal voltages and through currents are identical and equal to that of the branch *x-y* (R_L).

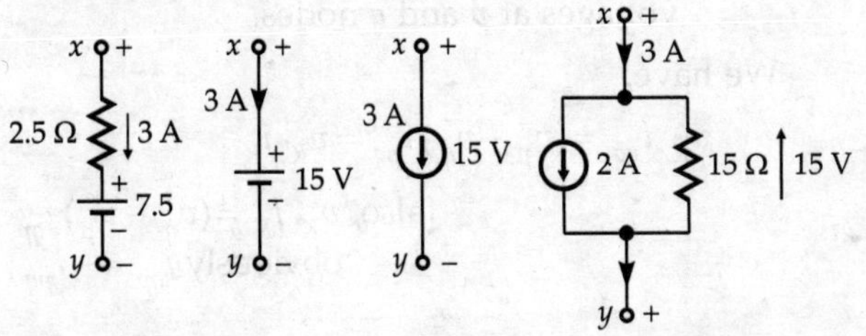

Fig. 6.11 Equivalent of branch *x-y* of Fig. 6.10.

It may also be observed that a known potential difference and current in a branch can be replaced by an ideal voltage and current source respectively.

The limitation of this theorem is that the theorem cannot be used to solve the network containing two or more sources that are not in series or in parallel.

6.8.3 Steps for Solution of a Network Utilizing Substitution Theorem

Step 1 First obtain the concerned branch voltage and through current, given by V_{xy} and $I_{x\text{-}y}$.

Step 2 The branch may be substituted by an independent voltage source as shown below (Figs. 6.12 and 6.13).

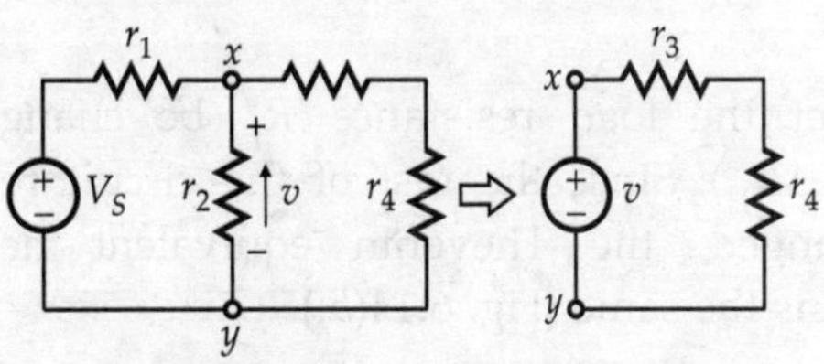

Fig. 6.12 Substitution by voltage source.

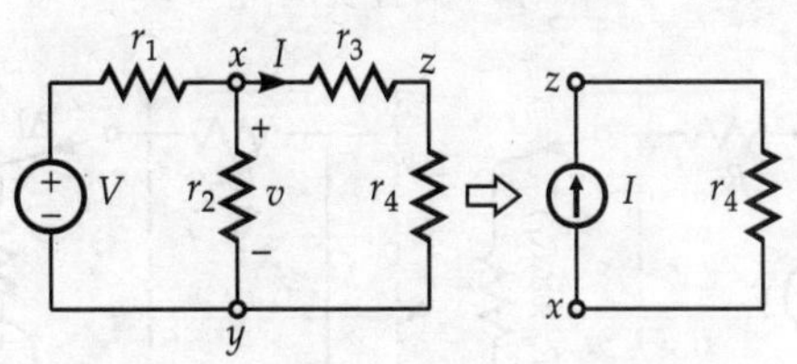

Fig. 6.13 Substitution by current source.

6.9 COMPENSATION THEOREM

6.9.1 Statement of Compensation Theorem

In a linear time-invariant network when the resistance (R) of an uncoupled branch carrying a current (I) is changed by (ΔR), the currents in all the branches would change and can be obtained by assuming that an ideal voltage source of (V_c) has been connected [such that $V_c = I(\Delta R)$] in series with ($R + \Delta R$) when all other sources in the network are replaced by their internal resistances.

[The source voltage (V_c) opposes the flow of original current].

6.9.2 Explanation

Let us assume a load R_L be connected to a dc source network whose Thevenin's equivalent gives

V_0 as the Thevenin voltage and R_{Th} as Thevenin resistance (internal resistance of the network) as evident from Fig. 6.14(a).

Here, $$I = \frac{V_0}{R_{Th} + R_L}$$

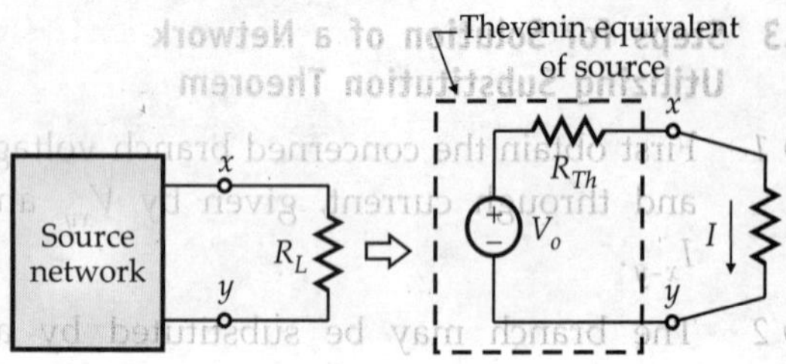

Fig. 6.14 (a) Load connected to dc source and its Thevenin's equivalent.

Let the load resistance R_L be changed to $(R_L + \Delta R_L)$. Since the rest of the circuit remains unchanged, the Thevenin equivalent network remains the same (Fig. 6.14(b)).

Here $$I' = \frac{V_0}{R_{Th} + (R_L + \Delta R_L)}$$

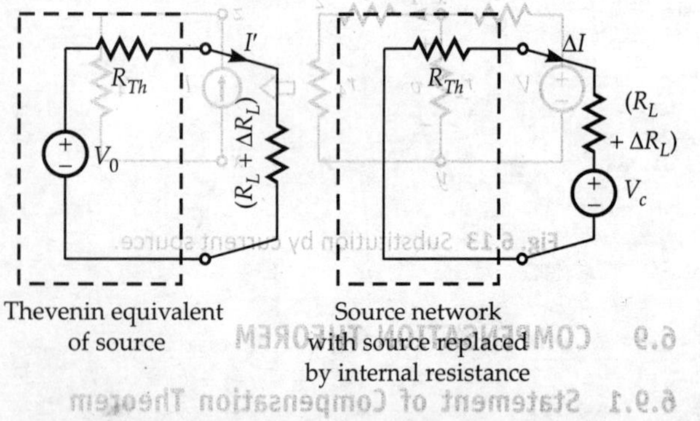

Fig. 6.14 (b) Explanation of Compensation theorem.

The change of current being termed as ΔI, we find

$$\Delta I = I' - I$$

$$= \frac{V_0}{R_{Th} + (R_L + \Delta R_L)} - \frac{V_0}{R_{Th} + R_L}$$

$$= \frac{V_0\,\{R_{Th} + R_L - (R_{Th} + R_L + \Delta R_L)\}}{(R_{Th} + R_L + \Delta R_L)(R_{Th} + R_L)}$$

$$= -\left(\frac{V_0}{R_{Th} + R_L}\right)\frac{\Delta R_L}{R_{Th} + R_L + \Delta R_L}$$

$$= -\frac{I\,\Delta R_L}{R_{Th} + R_L + \Delta R_L}$$

$$= \frac{(-V_c)}{R_{Th} + R_L + \Delta R_L}$$

[V_c being equal to $I(\Delta R_L)$ and is termed as compensating voltage]

Thus it has been proved that with change of branch resistance, branch current(s) is/are changed and the change is equivalent to an ideal compensating voltage source in series with the branch opposing the original current, all other sources in the network being replaced by their internal resistances.

6.10 TELLEGEN'S THEOREM

This theorem is one of the most general theorems in network analysis. Regardless to the type and nature*, Tellegen's theorem is applicable to any network made up of lumped two terminal elements.

6.10.1 Statement of Tellegen's Theorem

For any given time, the sum of power delivered to each branch of any electric network is zero.

Thus for K^{th} branch, this theorem states that $\sum_{K=1}^{n} v_K\, i_K = 0$; n being the number of branches, v_K the drop in the branch and i_K the through current.

6.10.2 Explanation

Let

$i_{pq (= i_K)}$ = Kth branch through current

v_K = voltage drop in branch $K = v_p - v_q$ while v_p and v_q are the respective node voltages at p and q nodes.

We have,

$$v_K\, i_{pq} = (v_p - v_q)\, i_{pq} = v_K\, i_K$$

[also, $v_K\, i_K = (v_q - v_p)\, i_{qp}$, obviously $i_{qp} = -i_{pq}$]

* The circuits and or circuit elements may be linear/non linear, passive/active, time invariant/time varying and the circuit may contain dependent/ independent sources.

Summing these two relations,

$$2\,v_K\,i_K = (v_p - v_q)\,i_{pq} + (v_q - v_p)\,i_{qp}$$

or, $$v_K\,i_K = \frac{1}{2}[(v_p - v_q)\,i_{pq} + (v_q - v_p)\,i_{qp}]$$

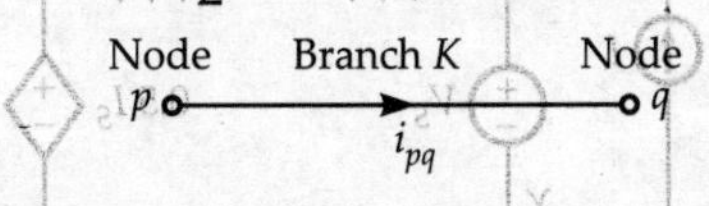

Fig. 6.15 Branch of a circuit being connected between nodes p and q.

Such an equation can be written for every branch of the network. Assuming n branches, generalisation yields

$$\sum_{K=1}^{n} v_K\,i_K = \frac{1}{2}\sum_{p=1}^{n}\sum_{q=1}^{n}(v_p - v_q)\,i_{pq}$$

$$= \frac{1}{2}\sum_{p=1}^{n} v_p\left(\sum_{q=1}^{n} i_{pq}\right) - \frac{1}{2}\sum_{q=1}^{n} v_q\left(\sum_{p=1}^{n} i_{pq}\right)$$

However, following Kirchhoff's current law, the algebraic sum of currents at each node is equal to zero.

i.e., $$\sum_{p=1}^{n} i_{pq} = 0\,;\ \sum_{q=1}^{n} i_{qp} = 0$$

With this, finally we obtain

$$\sum_{K=1}^{n} v_K\,i_K = 0.$$

Thus it has been observed that the *sum of power delivered to a closed network is zero.* This proves the Tellegen's theorem and also validity the conservation of power in any electrical network. It is also evident that the sum of power delivered to the network (obviously by independent sources) is equal to the sum of power absorbed by all passive elements of the network.

6.10.3 Steps for Solution of a Network Utilizing Tellegen's Theorem

In order to justify this theorem in electric network the first step is to find the branch voltage drops and the corresponding branch currents using conventional analysis. Tellgen's theorem can then be justified by summing all products of branch voltage and currents.

Tellegen's theorem can also be stated as follows :

In any linear, non-linear, passive, active, time variant or time invariant network the summation of power (instantaneous or complex power for ac source) is zero;

i.e., for a network having number of branches "b",

$$\sum_{b=1}^{b} v_b\,i_b = 0$$

If the set of voltages and currents is taken corresponding to two different instants of time, t_1 and t_2, Tellegen's theorem is also applicable where we get

$$\sum_{b=1}^{b} v_b(t_1)\,i_b(t_2) = \sum_{b=1}^{b} v_b(t_2)\,i_b(t_1) = 0$$

EXAMPLE 6.57 *In the network of Fig. E6.57, check the validity of Tellegen's theorem provided*

$$V_1 = 8\ V,\ V_2 = 4\ V,\ V_4 = 2\ V,$$
$$I_1 = 4\ A,\ I_2 = 2\ A,\ I_3 = 1\ A.$$

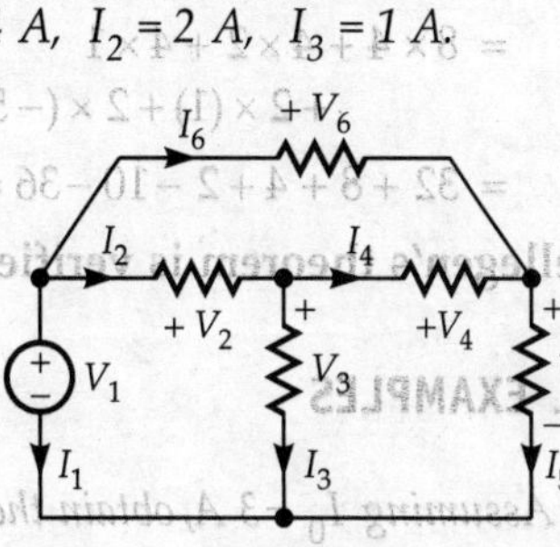

Fig. E6.57

SOLUTION. Let us redraw the given figure with designated loops and nodes (Fig. E6.57(a)).

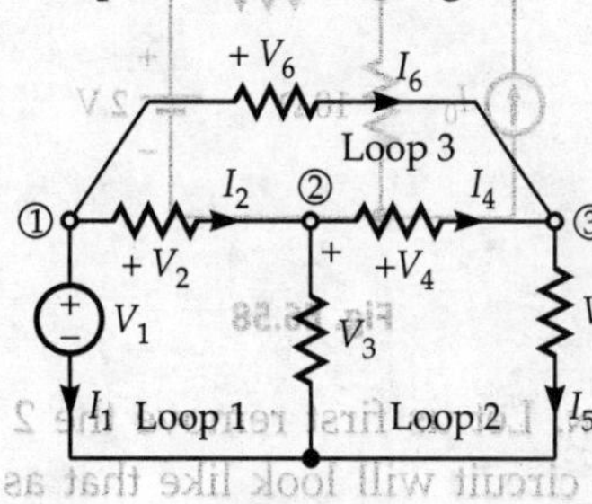

Fig. E6.57 (a)

In loop-1, KVL yields

$$-V_1 + V_2 + V_3 = 0$$

or, $$V_3 = V_1 - V_2 = 8 - 4 = 4\ \text{V}$$

Similarly, *in loop-2,* KVL yields

$$-V_3 + V_4 + V_5 = 0$$

or, $$V_5 = V_3 - V_4$$

or, $$V_5 = 4 - 2 = 2\ \text{V}$$

and in *loop-3,* KVL yields

$$-V_2 + V_6 - V_4 = 0$$

or, $$V_6 = V_2 + V_4 = 4 + 2 = 6\ \text{V}$$

On the other hand *at node* (1), KCL yields

$$I_1 + I_2 + I_6 = 0$$

or, $$I_6 = -I_1 - I_2 = -4 - 2 = -6\ \text{A.}$$

Similarly, application of KCL *at node* (2) results

$$I_2 = I_3 + I_4, I_4 = I_2 - I_3 = 2 - I = 1 \text{ A},$$

and *at node* (3),

$$I_4 + I_6 = I_5$$

or, $$I_5 = 1 + (-6) = -5 \text{ A}$$

∴ Summation of powers in the branches gives

$$\sum_{b=1}^{b} V_b I_b = V_1 I_1 + V_2 I_2 + V_3 I_3$$

$$+ V_4 I_4 + V_5 I_5 + V_6 I_6$$

$$= 8 \times 4 + 4 \times 2 + 4 \times 1$$

$$+ 2 \times (1) + 2 \times (-5) + 6 \times (-6)$$

$$= 32 + 8 + 4 + 2 - 10 - 36 = 0$$

Thus, **Tellegen's theorem is verified.**

ADDITIONAL EXAMPLES

EXAMPLE 6.58 *Assuming $I_0 = 3$ A, obtain the Thevenin's equivalent circuit looking across 2 V voltage source in Fig. E6.58.*

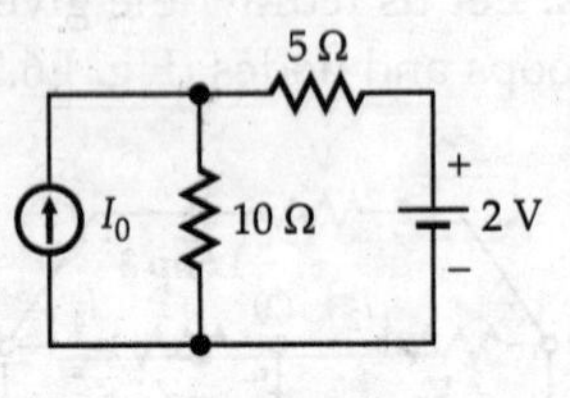

Fig. E6.58

SOLUTION. Let us first remove the 2 V voltage source. The circuit will look like that as shown in Fig. E6.58(*a*).

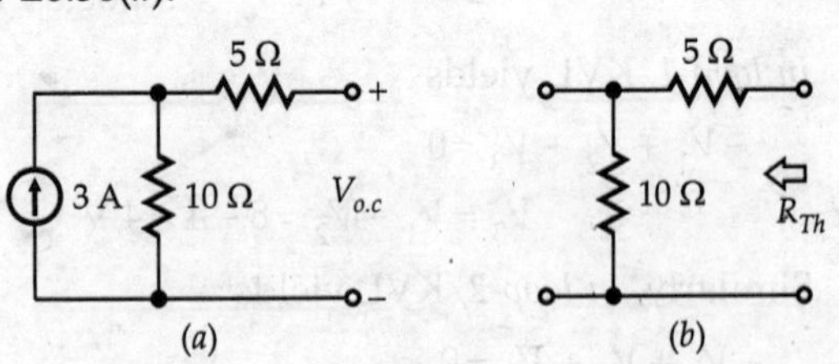

Fig. E6.58

Here, $V_{o.c} (= V_{Th}) = 3 \text{ A} \times 10\,\Omega = 30$ V.

To find the internal resistance of the given circuit across the 2 V source, let us deactivate the current source and find the internal resistance (Refer Fig. E6.58(*b*)).

Here, $R_{Th} = 5 + 10 = 15\,\Omega$

∴ For the given circuit, $V_{Th} = \mathbf{30\ V}$

$R_{Th} = \mathbf{15\,\Omega}$.

EXAMPLE 6.59 *Find Thevenin's equivalent circuit across X-Y in Fig. E6.59.*

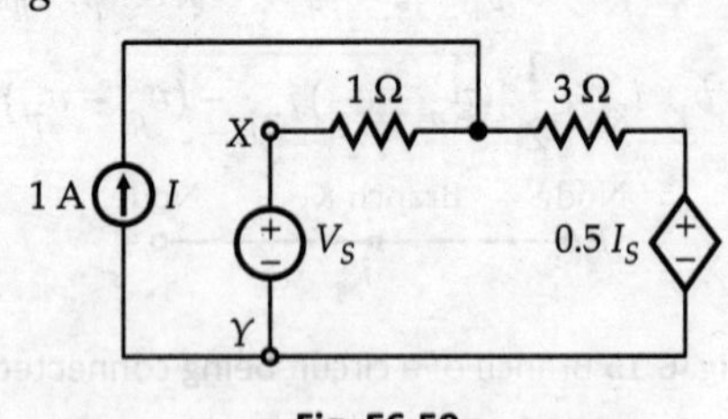

Fig. E6.59

SOLUTION. With terminal *X-Y* open circuited, the circuit configuration is shown in Fig. E6.59(*a*). Obviously, due to removal of V_S, $I_S = 0$ and this makes the controlled source 0.5 I_S to be zero.

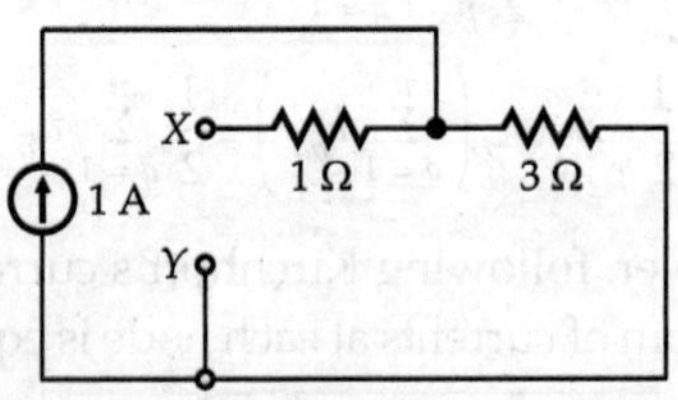

Fig. E6.59 (*a*)

∴ $V_{Th} = V_{o.c}$ (across X - Y) $= 1 \times 3 = \mathbf{3\ V}$ with +ve polarity at X.

To find R_{Th} across *X-Y*, the current source of 1 A is first deactivated by open circuiting it while the controlled source exists (Fig. E6.59(*b*)); a voltage source V_0 is applied at X - Y.

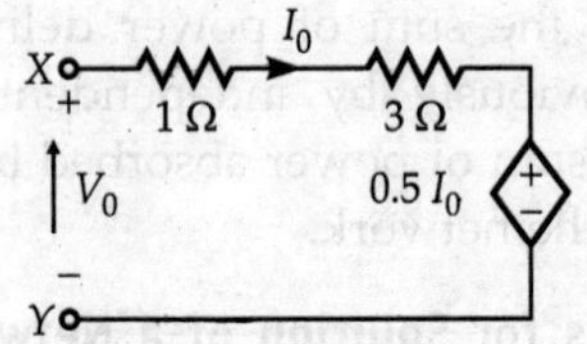

Fig. E6.59 (*b*)

Here, $V_0 = I_0 (1 + 3) + 0.5\, I_0 = 4.5\, I_0$

∴ $(V_0 / I_0) = \mathbf{4.5\,\Omega} (= R_{Th})$.

EXAMPLE 6.60 *Obtain Thevenin's equivalent resistance of the circuit given in Fig. E6.60 from input terminals 1-1′.*

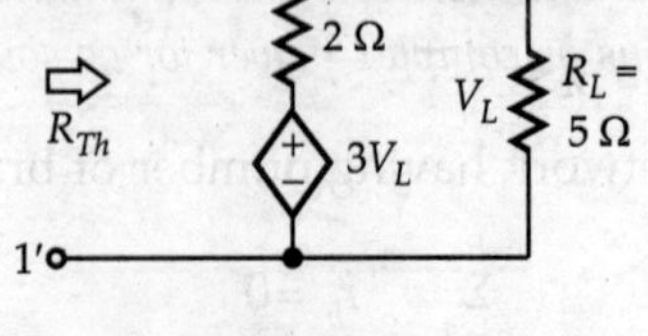

Fig. E6.60

Solution. Let us apply a voltage V_0 at the input terminals such that the current in the loops be I_1 and I_2 as shown in Fig. E6.60(*a*).

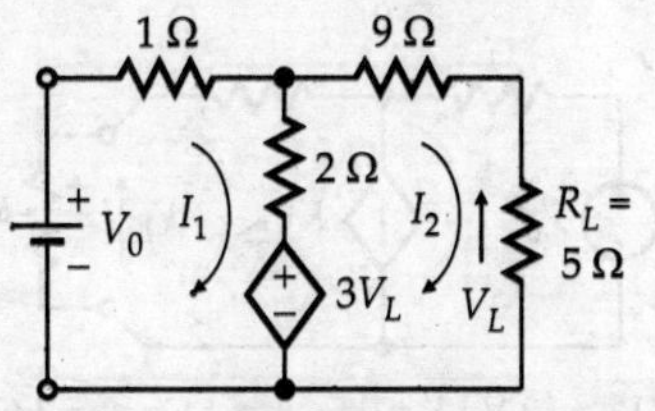

Fig. E6.60 (*a*)

Obviously,

$$V_L = I_2 \, R_L = 5 \, I_2$$

$\therefore$ The dependent voltage source is $3 \, V_L = 15 \, I_2$

Again, application of KVL *in loop-1* yields

$$V_0 = (1+2) \, I_1 + 3V_L - 2 I_2$$

or, $$V_0 = 3 \, I_1 + 15 \, I_2 - 2 \, I_2 = 3 \, I_1 + 13 \, I_2 \quad ...(1)$$

In loop-2 KVL yields,

$$0 = -2 \, I_1 + (2+9+5) \, I_2 - 3 \, V_L$$

or, $$0 = -2 \, I_1 + 16 \, I_2 - 15 \, I_2$$

or, $$0 = -2 \, I_1 + I_2 \quad ...(2)$$

$$\therefore \quad I_1 = \frac{\begin{vmatrix} V_0 & 13 \\ 0 & +1 \end{vmatrix}}{\begin{vmatrix} 3 & 13 \\ -2 & +1 \end{vmatrix}} = \frac{+V_0}{29}$$

$$\therefore \quad \frac{V_0}{I_1} = R_{int} = \mathbf{29 \, \Omega.}$$

Example 6.61 *For the circuit shown in Fig. E6.61, determine Thevenin equivalent circuit with respect to terminals x-y. Use the result to obtain the value of a resistance R to be connected between x-y so that R receives maximum power.*

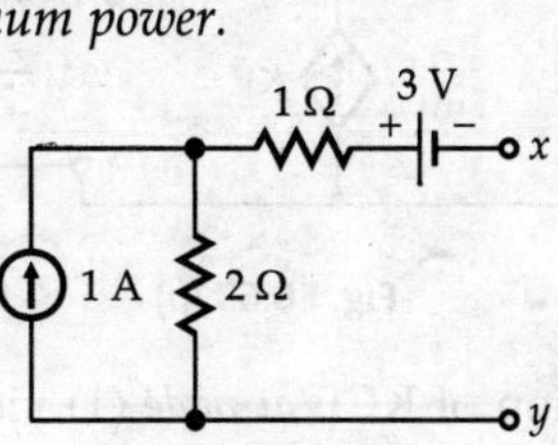

Fig. E6.61

Solution. Current through 2 Ω resistor being 1 A, the drop across it is 2 V (refer to Fig. E6.61(*a*)).

However, in *loop axyb*, KVL yields,

$$-2 + 3 + V_{o.c} = 0$$

or, $$V_{o.c} = \mathbf{-1 \, V.}$$

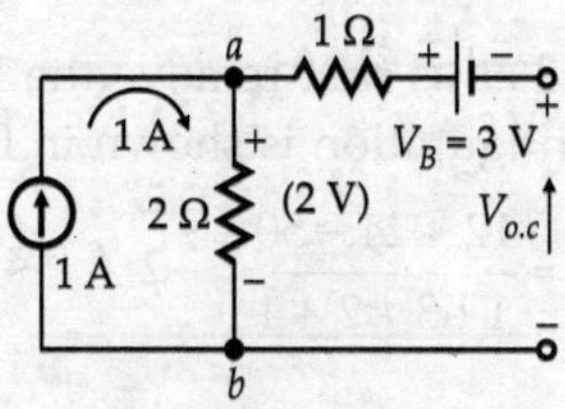

Fig. E6.61 (*a*)

The internal resistance (or Thevenin resistance is obtained by deactivating the sources as shown in Fig. E6.61(*b*).

$$R_{Th} = 1 + 2 = 3 \, \Omega$$

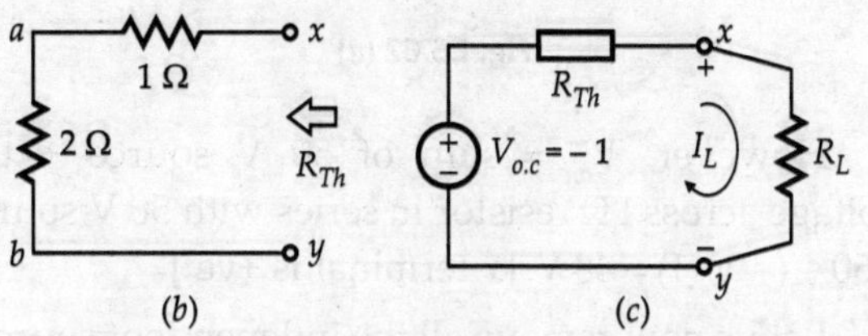

Fig. E6.61

Thus Thevenin's equivalent circuit is drawn in Fig. E6.61(*c*) where R_L be the required unknown load resistance that extracts maximum power.

$$I_L = \frac{V_{o.c}}{R_{Th} + R_L} = \frac{-1}{3 + R_L} \text{ A}$$

The power consumed in R_L is then $I_L^2 \, R_L$

i.e., $$R_L = \left(-\frac{1}{3 + R_L} \right)^2 \times R_L = \frac{R_L}{R_L^2 + 6 \, R_L + 9}$$

Obviously P_L would be maximum when the denominator of the above equation is zero.

i.e., $$R_L^2 + 6 \, R_L + 9 = 0$$

or, $$R_L = \frac{-6 \pm \sqrt{36 - 36}}{2} = -3 \, \Omega \; i.e. \; 3 \, \Omega$$

[–ve *R* does not have any meaning]

Thus, the resistance that can be connected across *x-y* in Thevenin's equivalent circuit is 3 Ω only.

Example 6.62 *Find the current in the 10 Ω resistor in the circuit of Fig. E6.62 using Thevenin's Theorem. What is the power loss in that resistor ?*

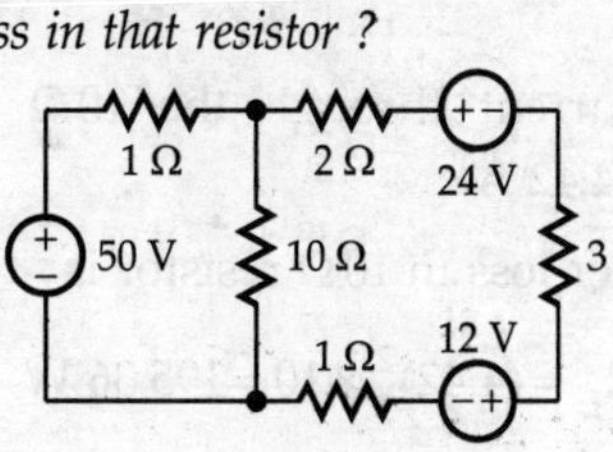

Fig. E6.62

Solution. Let us first remove the 10 Ω resistor. The circuit configuration is shown in Fig. E6.62(*a*).

Here, $i_1 = \dfrac{12 + 24 - 50}{1+3+2+1} = -2 \text{ A}$

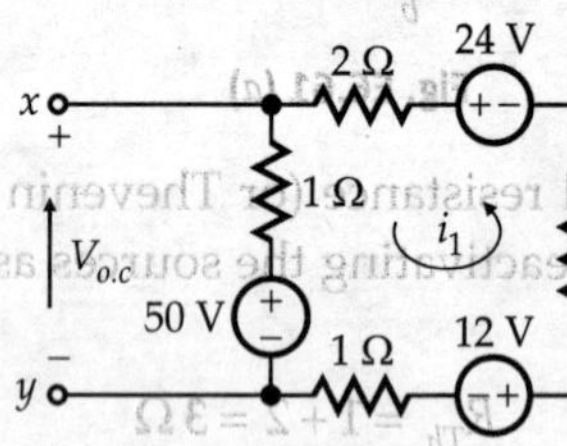

Fig. E6.62 (*a*)

However, $V_{o.c}$ = sum of 50 V source + the voltage across 1 Ω resistor in series with 50 V source $= 50 + (-2)(1) = 48$ V. [*x* terminal is +ve].

Let us now remove all the independent sources from the original network keeping their internal resistances. The circuit configuration, as looked from *x*-*y* terminals, is shown in Fig. E6.62(*b*).

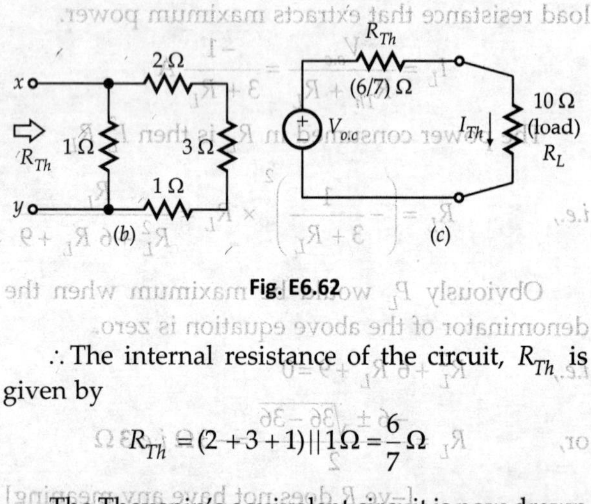

Fig. E6.62

∴ The internal resistance of the circuit, R_{Th} is given by

$$R_{Th} = (2+3+1) \,||\, 1\,\Omega = \frac{6}{7}\,\Omega$$

The Thevenin's equivalent circuit is now drawn in Fig. E6.62(*c*).

Here, I_{Th} (Thevenin's current)

$$= \frac{V_{o.c}}{R_{Th} + R_L} = \frac{48}{\frac{6}{7} + 10} = 4.42 \text{ A}$$

∴ The current through the 10 Ω resistor of Fig. E6.62 is **4.42 A.**

The power loss in 10 Ω resistor is

$$I_{Th}^2 \times R_L = (4.42)^2 \times 10 = 195.36 \text{ W}$$

i.e., $\quad P_{\text{loss}} = \mathbf{195.36\ W.}$

Example 6.63 *Find Thevenin's equivalent voltage and resistance for the network to the left of terminal x-y shown in Fig. E6.63.*

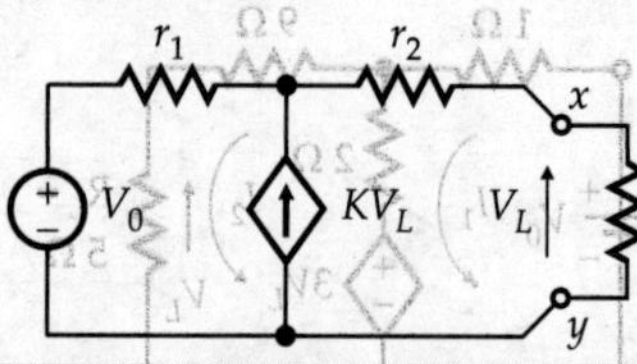

[$V_0 = 10$ V ; $K = 0.5$; $r_1 = 1$ Ω ; $r_2 = 2$ Ω]

Fig. E6.63

Solution. Let R_L be removed. No current will flow through r_2 (Refer to Fig. E6.63(*a*)).

Here, $\quad V_{Th} = V_0 + (KV_L)\,r_1 \quad$ ...(1)

However, $\quad V_{Th} \equiv V_L$

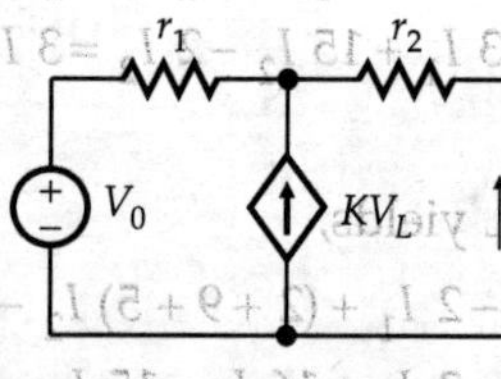

Fig. E6.63 (*a*)

∴ (1) becomes

$$V_{Th} = V_0 + (KV_{Th})\,r_1$$

or, $$V_{Th} = \frac{V_0}{1 - Kr_1} = \frac{10}{1 - 0.5 \times 1} = 20 \text{ V.}$$

Let us now apply a voltage *V* across terminals *x*-*y* deactivating V_0 such that a current *I* flows within the circuit through the terminal *x* (Refer to Fig. E6.63(*b*)).

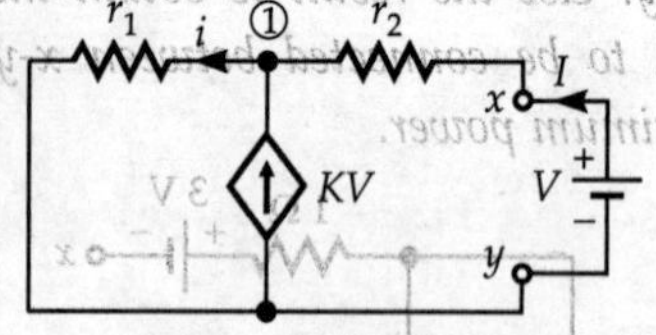

Fig. E6.63 (*b*)

Application of KCL *at node* (1) yields

$$i = KV + I \qquad ...(2)$$

while, application of KVL at the *outer loop* yields

$$V = Ir_2 + iR_1 \qquad ...(3)$$

Substitution of the value of *i* from (2) in (3) gives

$$V = Ir_2 + (KV + I)\,r_1 = I\,(r_1 + r_2) + KVr_1$$

or, $V(1-Kr_1) = I(r_1 + r_2)$

or, $\dfrac{V}{I} = Z_{Th} = \dfrac{r_1 + r_2}{1 - Kr_1} = \dfrac{1+2}{1-0.5\times 1} = 6\,\Omega$

Thus, for the given problem,

$$V_{Th} = 20\text{ V};\ Z_{Th} = 6\,\Omega.$$

EXAMPLE 6.64 *Find the Thevenin's equivalent to the left of terminals x-y in the network of Fig. E6.64.*

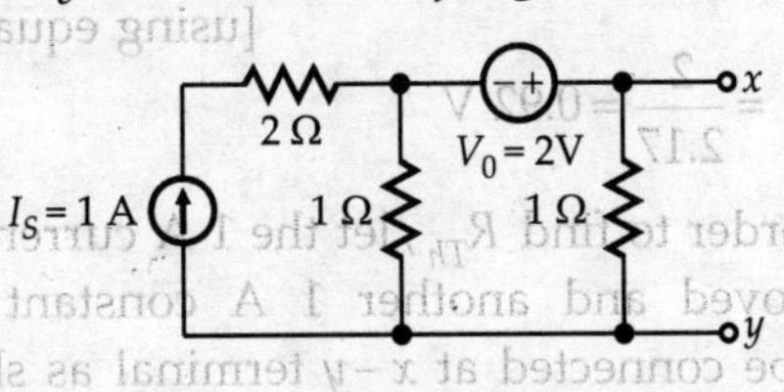

Fig. E6.64

SOLUTION. The currents have been designated in Fig. E6.64(*a*)

where $V_{o.c} = (I_2 \times 1)$ V

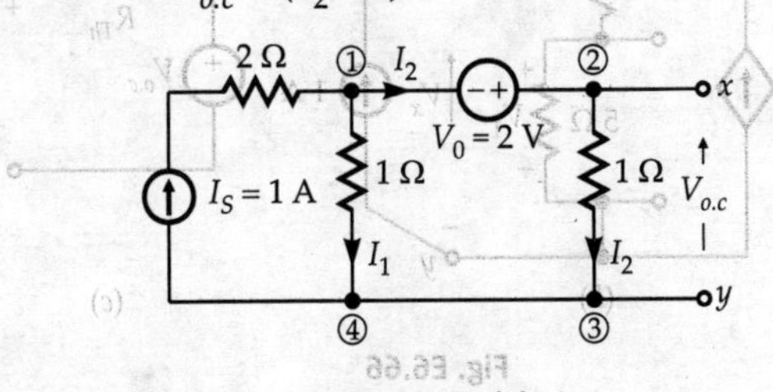

Fig. E6.64 (*a*)

At node (1), KCL yields

$$I_S = I_1 + I_2$$

or, $I_1 + I_2 = 1$ ...(1)

In loop 1-2-3-4, KVL yields

$$-2 + I_2 \times 1 + I_2 \times 1 - I_1 \times 1 = 0$$

or, $2I_2 - I_1 = +2$ ...(2)

Solving (1) and (2),

$$I_2 = 1\text{ A}$$

This gives $V_{o.c} = 1$ V

In order to find R_{Th}, the constant sources have been deactivated as shown in Fig. E6.64(*b*) and then

$$R_{Th} = (1\,||\,1) = \frac{1}{2}\,\Omega.$$

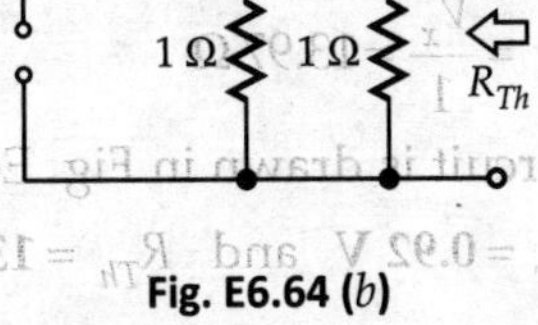

Fig. E6.64 (*b*)

$\therefore$ The given circuit has been Thevenised as

$$V_{o.c} = 1\text{ V}$$

$$R_{Th} = \frac{1}{2}\,\Omega.$$

EXAMPLE 6.65 *What is the power loss in the 10 Ω resistor of the circuit in Fig. E6.65?*

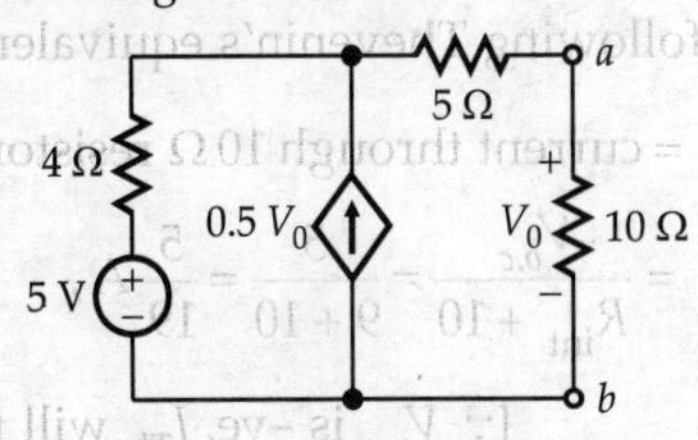

Fig. E6.65

SOLUTION. Let us first remove the 10 Ω resistor from *a-b* terminals (Fig. E6.65(*a*)). In the *left most loop*, the circulating current will obviously be $(0.5\,V_0)$ A.

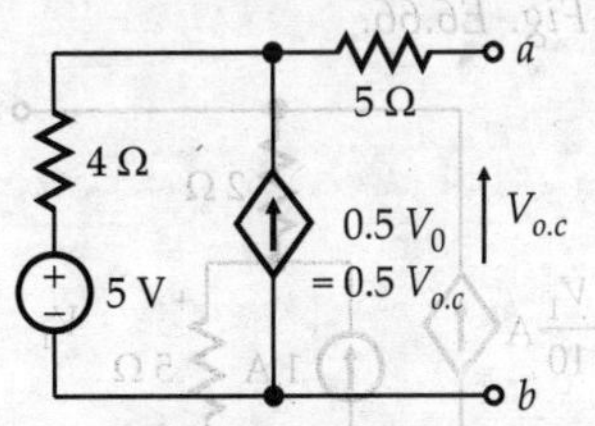

Fig. E6.65 (*a*)

Applying KVL in the leftmost loop,

$$5 - (-0.5\,V_0) \times 4 = V_{o.c}$$

[$\because$ The current $(0.5\,V_0)$ A is anticlockwise causing voltage drop additive to the 5 V source; also, current through 5 Ω resistor being nil, $V_{o.c}$ is the voltage drop across *x-y* terminal].

$\therefore$ $V_{o.c} = 5 + 2\,V_0$ ...(1)

But with reference to Fig. E6.65(*a*),

$$V_0 \equiv V_{o.c}$$

$\therefore$ From (1),

$V_{o.c} = -5$ V [*i.e.*, *b* terminal is +ve].

From Fig. E6.65(*b*), where *a-b* terminal is shorted, it is evident that $0.5\,V_0 = 0$ as there is no drop across short path.

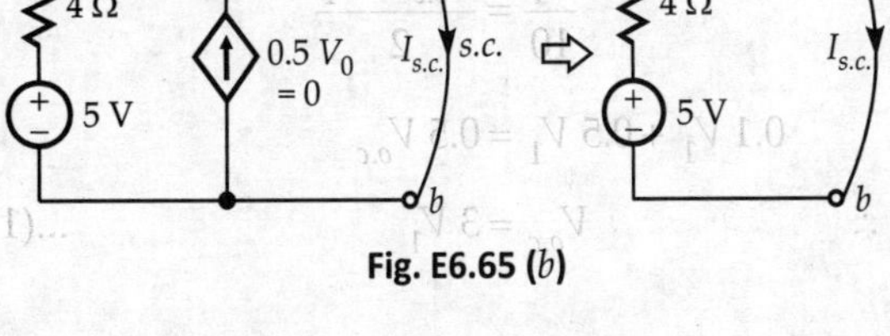

Fig. E6.65 (*b*)

$$\therefore \quad I_{s.c} = \frac{5\text{ V}}{(4+5)\,\Omega} = \frac{5}{9}\text{ A}$$

Thus, $R_{\text{int}}\ (= R_{Th}) = \dfrac{V_{o.c}}{I_{s.c}} = \dfrac{5}{\frac{5}{9}} = 9\,\Omega$

[–ve sign of $V_{o.c}$ is neglected]

Thus, following Thevenin's equivalent circuit,

I_{Th} = current through 10 Ω resistor

$$= \frac{V_{o.c}}{R_{\text{int}} + 10} = \frac{5}{9+10} = \frac{5}{19}\text{ A},$$

[∵ $V_{o.c}$ is –ve, I_{Th} will flow from terminal b to a]

∴ P_{loss} in 10 Ω resistor is $(5/19)^2 \times 10$ *i.e.*, **692.5 mW.**

EXAMPLE 6.66 *Find Thevenin's equivalent across x-y in the circuit of Fig. E6.66.*

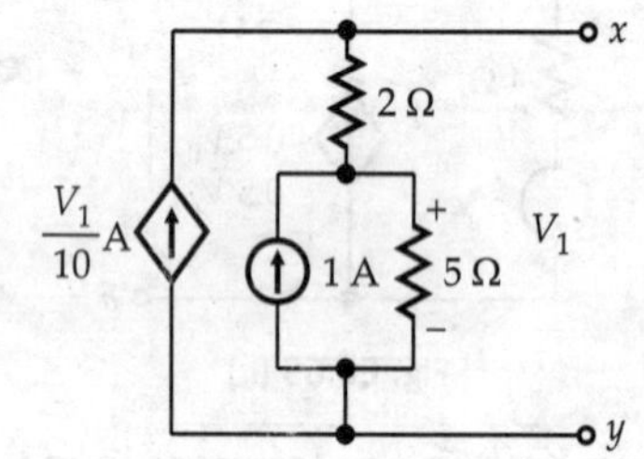

Fig. E6.66

SOLUTION. Let the open circuit voltage across *x-y* be $V_{o.c}$. Let us select two nodes m_1 and m_2 as shown in Fig. E6.66(*a*) and apply nodal analysis.

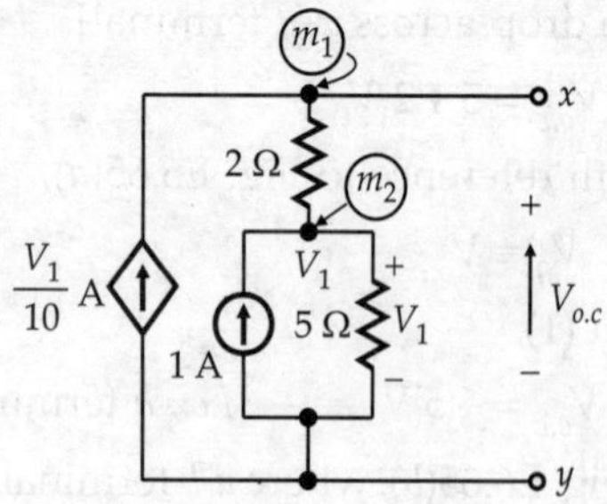

Fig. E6.66 (*a*)

At node m_1,

$$\frac{V_1}{10} = \frac{V_{o.c} - V_1}{2}$$

or, $\quad 0.1\,V_1 + 0.5\,V_1 = 0.5\,V_{o.c}$

$$\therefore \quad V_{o.c} = 3\,V_1 \qquad \ldots(1)$$

At node m_2,

$$1 = \frac{V_1 - V_{o.c}}{2} + \frac{V_1}{5} = 0.5\,V_1 + 0.2\,V_1 - 0.5\,V_{o.c}$$

or, $\quad V_{o.c} = \dfrac{1 - 0.7\,V_1}{0.5}$

$$= \frac{1 - 0.7\dfrac{V_{o.c}}{1.2}}{0.5} = 2 - 1.17\,V_{o.c}$$

[using equation (1)]

or, $\quad V_{o.c} = \dfrac{2}{2.17} = 0.92\text{ V}$

In order to find R_{Th}, let the 1 A current source be removed and another 1 A constant current source be connected at $x-y$ terminal as shown in Fig. E6.66(*b*). Let potential at (x) be V_x.

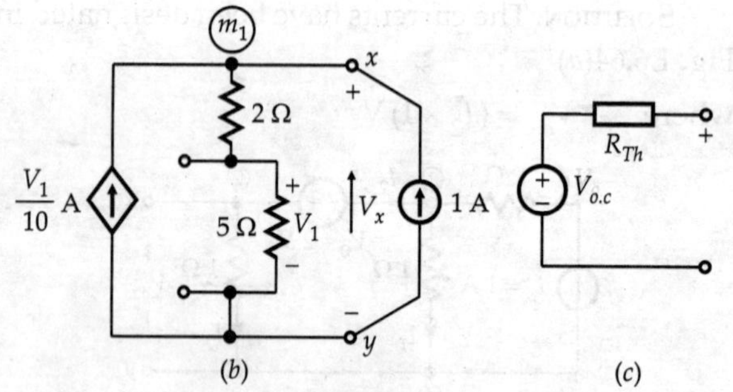

Fig. E6.66

At node m_1, nodal analysis reveals,

$$\frac{V_1}{10} + 1 = \frac{V_x}{7} \qquad \ldots(2)$$

But drop across 2 Ω resistor is $\left(\dfrac{V_x}{7} \times 2\right)$ V

Thus in the central branch of the circuit of Fig. E6.66(*b*),

$$V_1 = \left(V_x - \frac{V_x}{7} \times 2\right) = (V_x - 0.286\,V_x) = 0.714\,V_x \qquad \ldots(3)$$

Using equation (3) in (2)

$$\frac{0.714\,V_x}{10} + 1 = \frac{V_x}{7}$$

or, $\quad 0.0714\,V_x + 1 = 0.143\,V_x$

or $\quad V_x = \dfrac{1}{0.0716} = 13.97\text{ V};$

$$R_{Th} = \frac{V_x}{1} = 13.97\,\Omega$$

Thevenin's circuit is drawn in Fig. E6.66(*c*) where

$$V_{o.c} = \mathbf{0.92\ V} \text{ and } R_{Th} = \mathbf{13.97\,\Omega}.$$

EXAMPLE 6.67 *Find the value of the current I flowing through the 50 Ω resistor in the bridge network shown in Fig. E6.67 using Thevenin's theorem.*

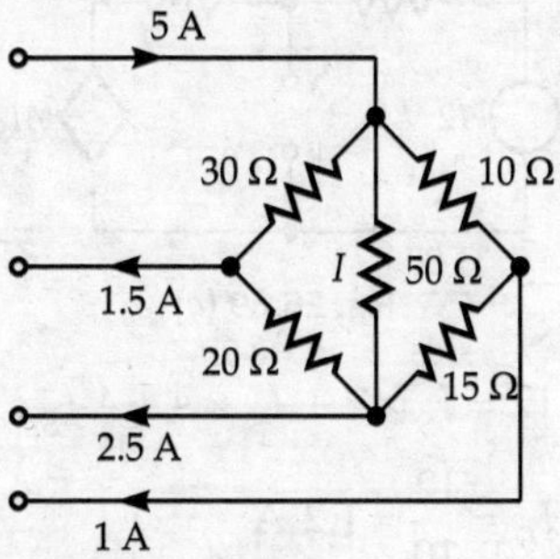

Fig. E6.67

SOLUTION. 50 Ω resistor is removed and the circuit is redrawn in Fig. E6.67(*a*).

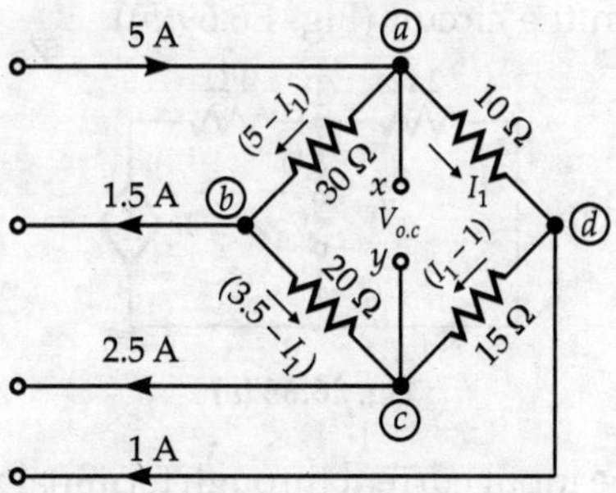

Fig. E6.67 (*a*)

Applying KCL *at nodes* (*a*), (*b*), (*c*) and (*d*), the branch currents are designated.

In loop a-d-c-b-a,

$$10\,I_1 + (I_1 - 1)\,15 - (3.5 - I_1)\,20 - (5 - I_1)\,30 = 0$$

or $$10\,I_1 + 15\,I_1 + 20\,I_1 + 30\,I_1 = 15 + 70 + 150$$

or $$75\,I_1 = 235$$

or $$I_1 = 3.13 \text{ A}$$

∴ Drop in *a-d* branch (v_{ad}) is given by

$$v_{ad} = 10\,I_1 = 31.33 \text{ V}$$

and drop in dc branch (v_{dc}) is given by

$$v_{dc} = (I_1 - 1)\,15 = 2.13 \times 15 = 32 \text{ V}$$

As for v_{ad}, *node a* is +ve and for v_{dc}, *node d* is +ve, hence

$$v_{xy} = v_{ad} + v_{dc} = 63.33 \text{ V}$$

Obviously

$$V_{o.c} = v_{xy} = 63.33 \text{ V}$$

With reference to Fig. E6.67(*b*), the internal resistance is given by

$$R_{Th} = (30 + 20)\,||\,(10 + 15)$$

$$= 50\,||\,25 = \frac{50 \times 25}{50 + 25} = \frac{50}{3}\,\Omega$$

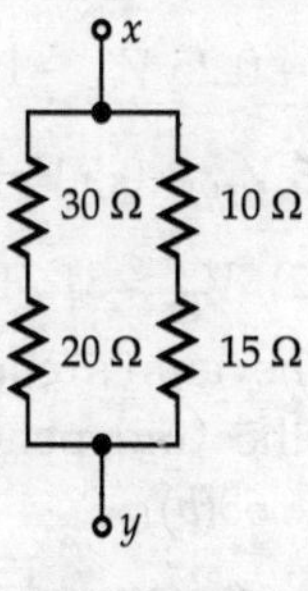

Fig. E6.67 (*b*)

From Thevenin's equivalent circuit, thus the current through the 50 Ω resistor is

$$I_{50\Omega} = \frac{V_{o.c}}{R_{Th} + 50} = \frac{63.33}{\dfrac{50}{3} + 50} = \mathbf{0.95\ A.}$$

EXAMPLE 6.68 *Utilising Thevenin's Theorem, find the current in 5 Ω resistance in the circuit of Fig. E6.68, connected between terminals 1-1′.*

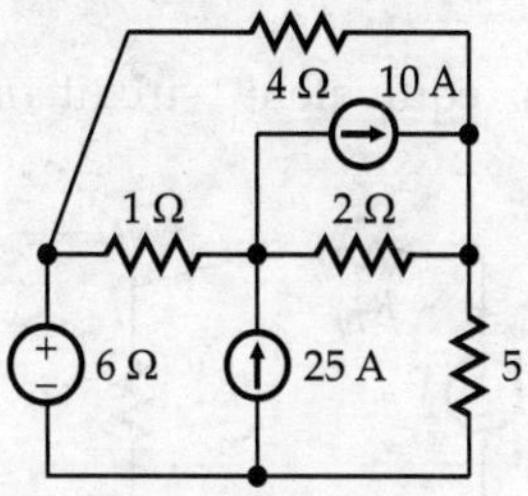

Fig. E6.68

SOLUTION. Let the 5 Ω resistor be removed (Refer to Fig. E6.68(*a*)). Let the potential *at node* (*x*) be *V*.

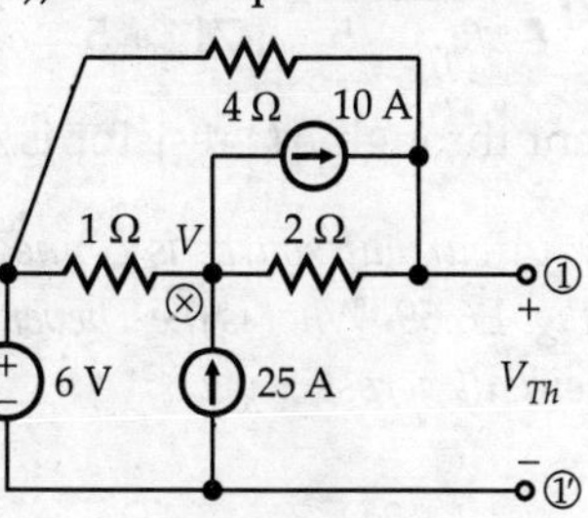

Fig. E6.68 (*a*)

Application of KCL *at node* (*x*) yields

$$\frac{V - 6}{1} + \frac{V - V_{Th}}{2} + 10 = 25$$

[V_{Th} = open circuit voltage at 1 – 1′]

or, $\quad V - 6 + 0.5\,V - 0.5\,V_{Th} = 15$

or, $\quad 1.5\,V - 0.5\,V_{Th} = 21 \qquad ...(1)$

Again, *at node* (1), KCL yields

$$\frac{V_{Th} - V}{2} + \frac{V_{Th} - 6}{4} = 10$$

or, $\quad 0.5\,V_{Th} - 0.5\,V + 0.25\,V_{Th} - 1.5 = 10$

or, $\quad 0.75\,V_{Th} - 0.5\,V = 11.5 \qquad ...(2)$

From (1) and (2), $V_{Th} = 31.71$ V

To find the Thevenin's equivalent resistance across 1-1′, all the independent sources are deactivated (Fig. E6.68(*b*)).

Here, $R_{Th} = (2+1)\,||\,4\,\Omega = \frac{12}{7} = 1.714\,\Omega$

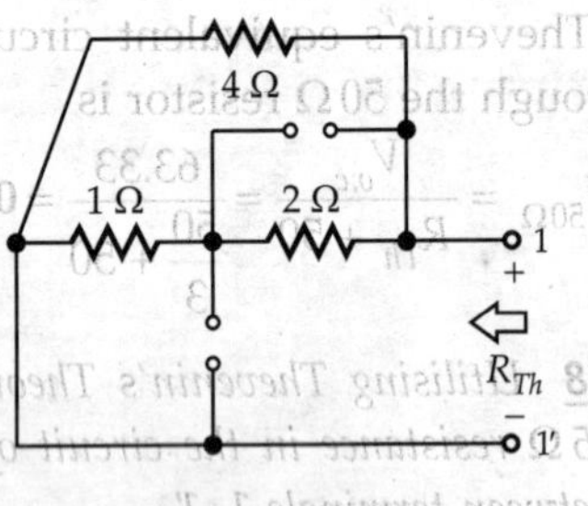

Fig. E6.68 (*b*)

Thevenin's equivalent circuit is drawn in Fig. E6.68(*c*).

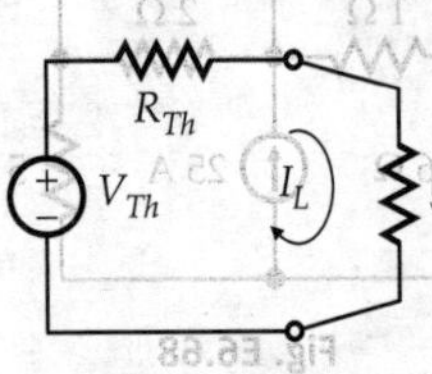

Fig. E6.68 (*c*)

Here, $I_L = \frac{V_{Th}}{R_{Th} + 5} = \frac{31.71}{1.714 + 5} = \frac{31.71}{6.714} = 4.73$ A

∴ Current through 5 Ω resistor is **4.73 A.**

EXAMPLE 6.69 *A current source is connected across x-y terminals of Fig. E6.69. What is the Thevenin's equivalent of the given circuit across x-y ?*

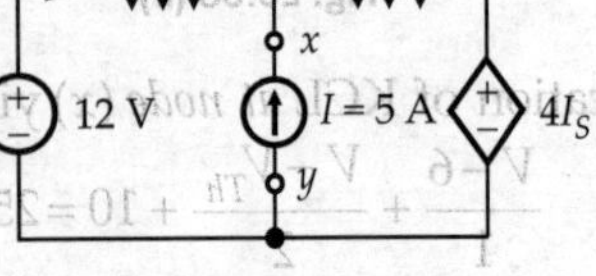

Fig. E6.69

SOLUTION. Let the current source across *x-y* be removed (Fig. E6.69(*a*)).

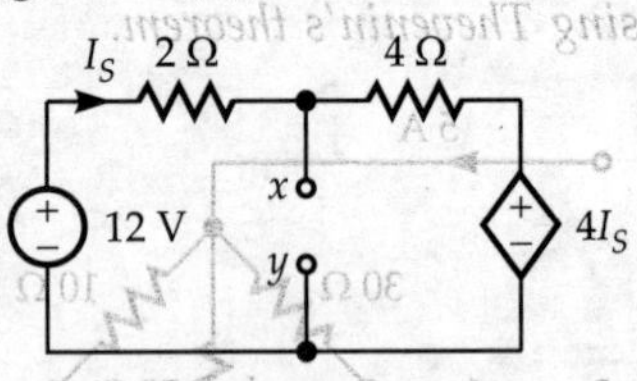

Fig. E6.69 (*a*)

Here, $\quad 12 = I_S \times 2 + I_S \times 4 + 4\,I_S$

or, $\quad I_S = \frac{12}{10} = 1.2$ A

∴ $\quad V_{Th} = V_{x-y} = 12\text{ V} - 2 \times 1.2 = 9.6$ V.

Let us now make the voltage source deactivated and a voltage of V_0 be applied across *x - y*. The current controlled dependent voltage source remains in the circuit (Fig. E6.69(*b*)).

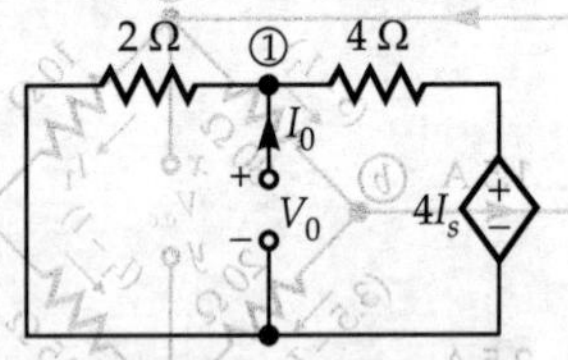

Fig. E6.69 (*b*)

Let the input current through terminal *x-y* be I_0. Application of node analysis *at node* (1) gives

$$I_0 = \frac{V_0}{2} + \frac{V_0 - 4\,I_S}{4} \qquad ...(1)$$

However it is evident that $I_S = -\frac{V_0}{2}$, comparing Figs. E6.69(*a*) and (*b*).

From (1),

$$I_0 = \frac{V_0}{2} + \frac{V_0 - 4\left(-\frac{V_0}{2}\right)}{4}$$

$$= \frac{V_0}{2} + \frac{V_0}{4} + \frac{V_0}{2} = \frac{5}{4}V_0$$

∴ $\quad \frac{V_0}{I_0} = R_{Th}$ (internal resistance of the circuit across *x - y*)

$$= \frac{4}{5}\,\Omega$$

∴The Thevenin's equivalent of the given circuit is as follows :

$$V_{Th} = \mathbf{9.6\ V},\ R_{Th} = \frac{\mathbf{4}}{\mathbf{5}}\,\Omega.$$

EXAMPLE 6.70 *Find the power loss in the 2 Ω resistor using Thevenin's theorem (Fig. E6.70).*

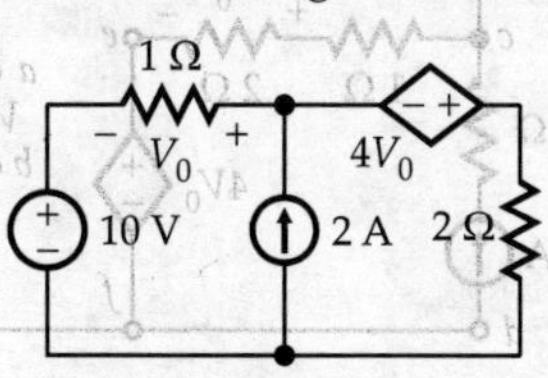

Fig. E6.70

SOLUTION. Let the 2 Ω resistor be removed and the circuit is shown in Fig. E6.70(*a*).

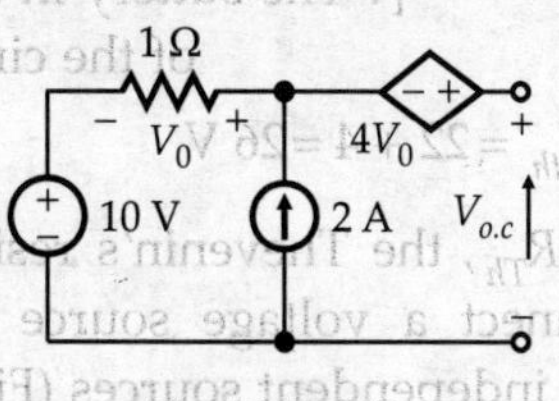

Fig. E6.70 (*a*)

Here, $V_{o.c} = 10 + V_0 + 4\,V_0 = 10 + 5\,V_0$

But $V_0 = 2 \times 1\text{ V} = 2\text{ V}$;

It may be noticed here that 2 A current flows in the left loop in the anticlockwise direction but the polarity of the drop V_0 is such that $V_0 = (2 \times 1)$ V.

$\therefore \quad V_{o.c} = 10 + 5 \times 2 = 20$ V

To find R_{Th}, let us first short the output terminals of the given circuit and KVL yields (Fig. E6.70(*b*)) ;

$$10 + V_0 + 4\,V_0 = 0$$

or, $$10 + 5\,V_0 = 0 \qquad \text{...(A)}$$

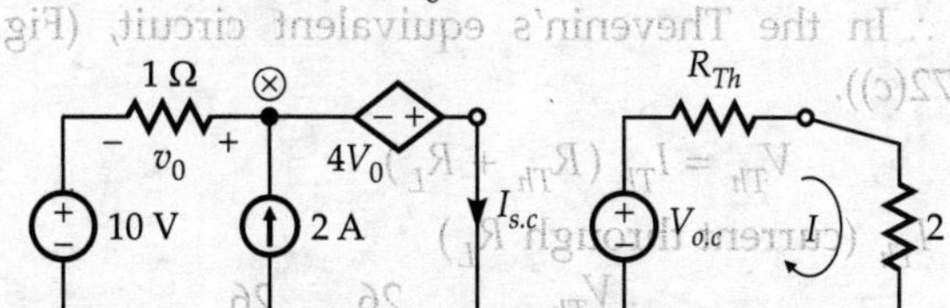

Fig. E6.70 (*b*)

However, application of KCL *at node* (*x*) in Fig. E6.70(*b*),

$$\frac{V_0}{1} + I_{s.c} = 2 \quad \text{or} \quad V_0 = 2 - I_{s.c}$$

Thus from (A),

$$10 + 5\,(2 - I_{s.c}) = 0 \quad \text{or} \quad I_{s.c} = 4\text{ A}$$

Hence, $$R_{Th} = \frac{V_{o.c}}{I_{s.c}} = \frac{20}{4} = 5\,\Omega$$

Thus, from the Thevenin's equivalent circuit (Fig. E6.70(*c*)).

I (the current through 2 Ω resistor)

$$= \frac{V_{o.c}}{R_{Th} + 2} = \frac{20}{5 + 2} = 2.86\text{ A}$$

and the power loss $= (2.86)^2 \times 2 = \mathbf{16.36\ W}$.

EXAMPLE 6.71 *Find the current through R_L in the circuit shown in Fig. E6.71 using Thevenin's theorem.*

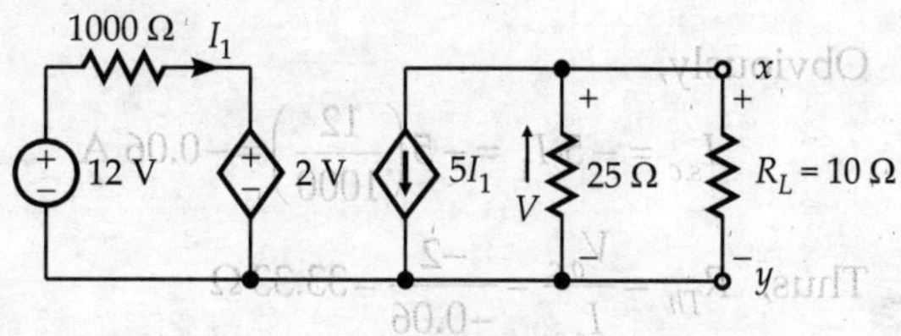

Fig. E6.71

SOLUTION. Let us first remove R_L (Fig. E6.71(*a*)).

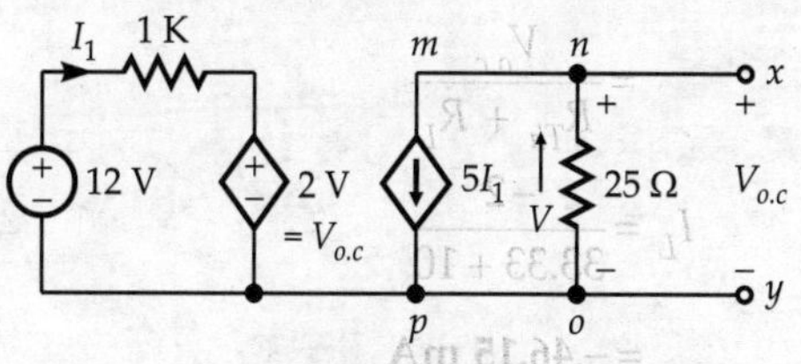

Fig. E6.71 (*a*)

Here $V_{o.c} \equiv V \equiv V_{xy} = (-5\,I_1) \times 25$

[∵ The direction of 5 I_1, the current in the *loop m-n-o-p*, is opposite to the polarity of assumed voltage drop *V* in 25 Ω resistor]

i.e., $$V_{o.c} = -125\,I_1.$$

But $$I_1 = \frac{12 - 2\,V}{1000} = \frac{12 - 2\,V_{o.c}}{1000} \qquad [\because V_{o.c} \equiv V]$$

Thus finally,

$$V_{o.c} = -125\left(\frac{12 - 2\,V_{o.c}}{1000}\right)$$

or, $\quad 0.75\,V_{o.c} = -1.5 \quad$ *i.e.,* $V_{o.c} = -2$ V

To determine R_{Th}, let us short the terminals *x*-*y* (Fig. E6.71(*b*)). Due to short circuit between

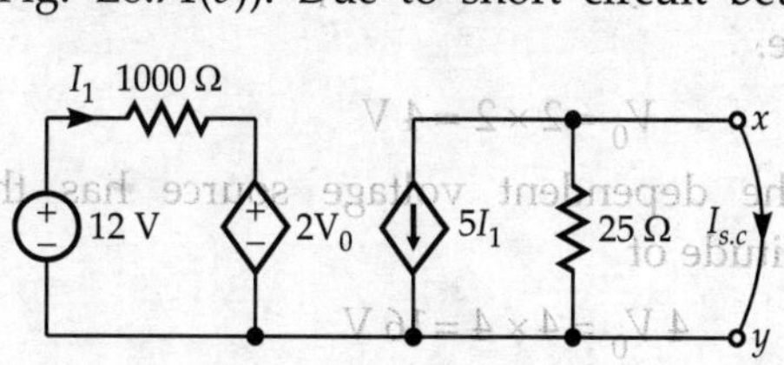

Fig. E6.71 (*b*)

$x - y$, the voltage V diminishes to zero. Thus the dependent source (2V) in the left loop vanishes (Fig. E6.71(c)).

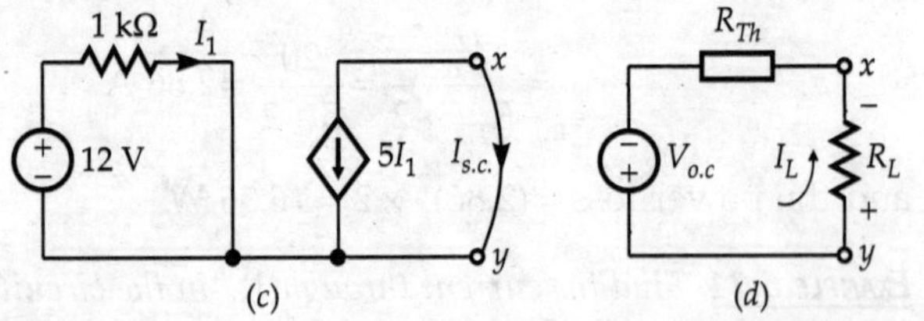

Fig. E6.71

Obviously,

$$I_{s.c} = -5\,I_1 = -5\left(\frac{12}{1000}\right) = -0.06 \text{ A}$$

Thus, $$R_{Th} = \frac{V_{o.c}}{I_{s.c}} = \frac{-2}{-0.06} = 33.33\,\Omega$$

Figure E6.71(*d*) being representing the Thevenin's equivalent circuit, I_L (current through R_L)

$$= \frac{V_{o.c}}{R_{Th} + R_L}$$

or, $$I_L = \frac{-2}{33.33 + 10}$$

$$= -\mathbf{46.15\ mA}$$

(*i.e.,* 46.15 mA anticlockwise).

EXAMPLE 6.72 *In the circuit of Fig. E6.72, find the current through R_L using Thevenin's theorem.*

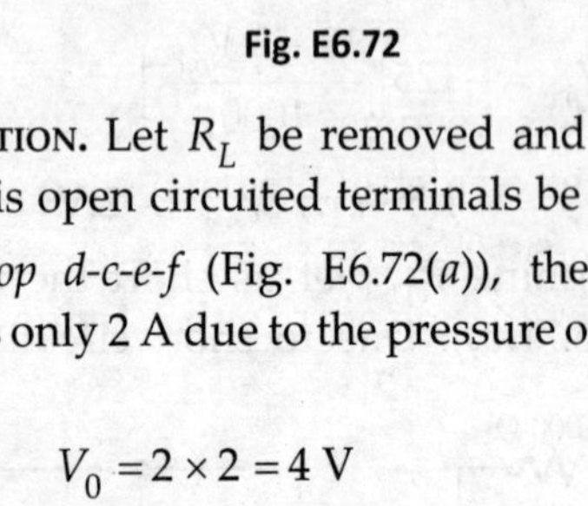

Fig. E6.72

SOLUTION. Let R_L be removed and the voltage across this open circuited terminals be V_{Th}.

In loop d-c-e-f (Fig. E6.72(*a*)), the circulating current is only 2 A due to the pressure of the current source.

$\therefore \quad V_0 = 2 \times 2 = 4$ V

The dependent voltage source has thus a magnitude of

$$4\,V_0 = 4 \times 4 = 16 \text{ V}$$

$\therefore \quad V_{c.d} = 2 \times 1 + V_0 + 4V_0 = 22$ V

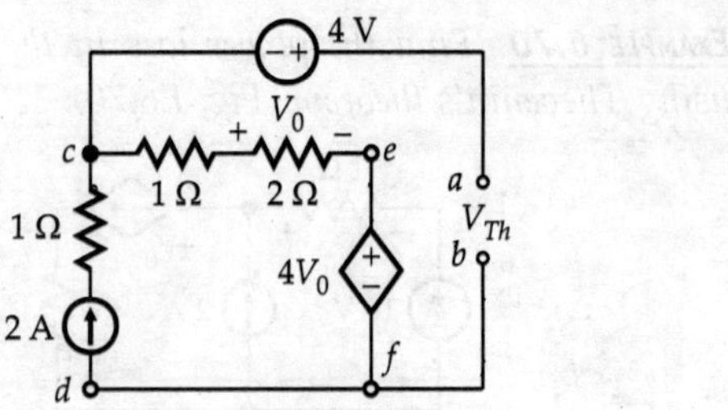

Fig. E6.72 (*a*)

Thus $V_{Th} = V_{c-d} + 4$ V

[$\because$ The battery in the *a-c* branch of the circuit has 4 V],

i.e., $\quad V_{th} = 22 + 4 = 26$ V

To find R_{Th}, the Thevenin's resistance across $a-b$, we connect a voltage source V across *a-b* removing all independent sources (Fig. E6.72(*b*)).

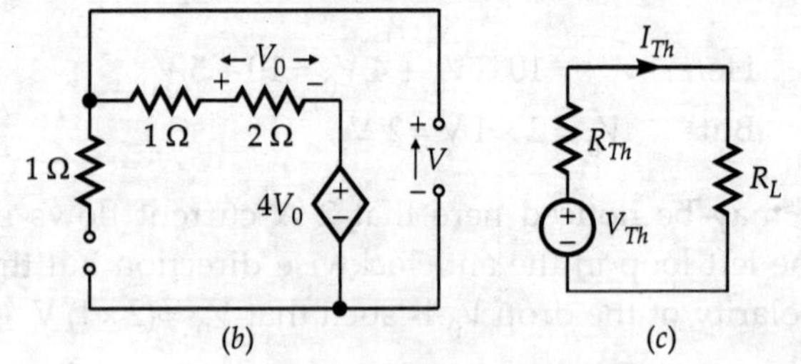

Fig. E6.72

Here, $\quad V = I\,(2+1) + 4\,V_0$ where $V_0 = 2\,I$

$\therefore \quad V = 3\,I + 4 \times 2\,I = 11\,I.$

Thus $\quad \dfrac{V}{I} = R_{\text{int}}\ (= R_{th}) = 11\,\Omega.$

$\therefore$ In the Thevenin's equivalent circuit, (Fig. E6.72(*c*)).

$$V_{Th} = I_{Th}\,(R_{Th} + R_L)$$

or, I_{Th} (current through R_L)

$$= \frac{V_{Th}}{R_{Th} + R_L} = \frac{26}{11+5} = \frac{26}{16} = \mathbf{1.625\ A.}$$

EXAMPLE 6.73 *A d.c. voltage is applied at X-Y terminals of the network shown in Fig. E6.73. Find the internal impedance of the given circuit when looking through X-Y terminals.*

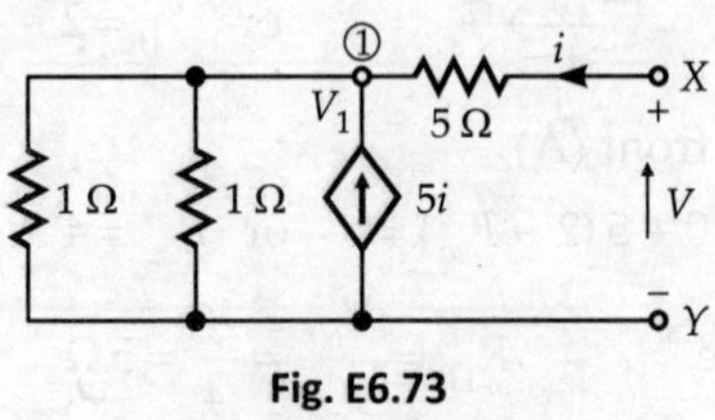

Fig. E6.73

Solution. Applying KCL *at node* (1) in Fig. E6.73,

$$\frac{V_{X-Y}-V_1}{5}+5\,i=\frac{V_1}{1}+\frac{V_1}{1}$$

[Assuming V_1 to be the node voltage *at node* 1 and V_{X-Y} to be the voltage equal to V at $X-Y$ such that input current is i through X]

or, $$\frac{V_{X-Y}}{5}-\frac{V_1}{5}+5\left(\frac{V_{X-Y}-V_1}{5}\right)=2\,V_1 \qquad \left[\because\ i=\frac{V_{X-Y}-V_1}{5}\right]$$

or, $$\frac{V_{X-Y}}{5}-\frac{V_1}{5}+V_{X-Y}-V_1=2V_1$$

or, $$1.2\,V_{X-Y}-1.2\,V_1=2V_1$$

i.e., $$1.2\,V_{X-Y}=3.2\,V_1\,;$$

$$\therefore\quad V_{X-Y}=2.67\,V_1$$

Again $$i=\frac{V_{X-Y}-V_1}{5}$$

$$=\frac{V_{X-Y}-\frac{1}{2.67}V_{X-Y}}{5}=0.125\,V_{X-Y}$$

$\therefore$ R_{int} (internal impedance looking from X-Y)

$$=\frac{V_{X-Y}}{i}$$

$$=\frac{V_{X-Y}}{0.125\,V_{X-Y}}=8\,\Omega$$

Thus the internal impedance of the given network looking through $X-Y$ is $8\,\Omega$.

Example 6.74 *Find the Thevenin's equivalent of the circuit across X–Y.(Fig. E6.74).*

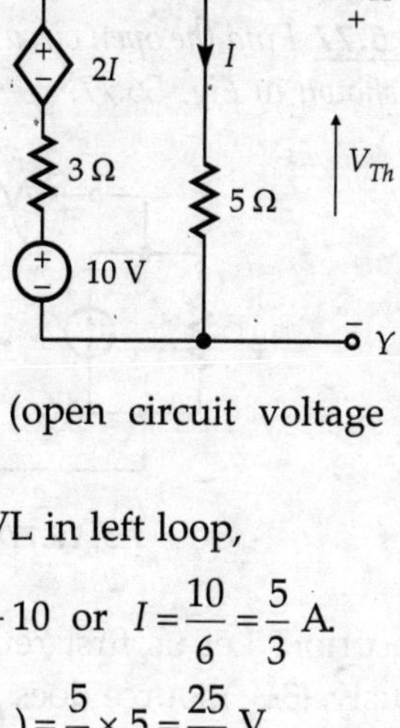

Fig. E6.74

Solution. V_{X-Y} (open circuit voltage across $X-Y$) $=5\,I$

But following KVL in left loop,

$$3\,I+5\,I=2\,I+10\ \text{ or }\ I=\frac{10}{6}=\frac{5}{3}\text{ A}$$

$$\therefore\quad V_{X-Y}\,(=V_{Th})=\frac{5}{3}\times 5=\frac{25}{3}\text{ V}$$

Let us now short circuit $X-Y$ terminals (Refer Fig. E6.74(*a*)).

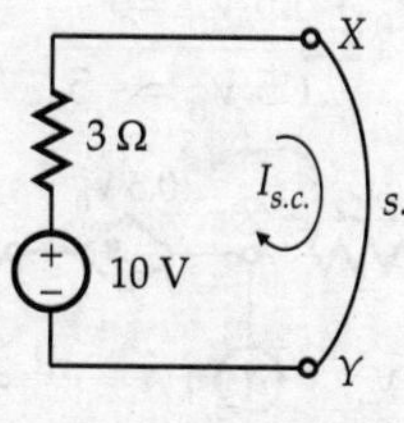

Fig. E6.74 (*a*)

It may be noted here that since $X-Y$ is now shorted, no current would pass through $5\,\Omega$ resistor and hence I, the current through $5\,\Omega$ resistor is zero. This will make the dependent source too to be zero. Thus from Fig. E6.74(*a*),

$$I_{s.c}=\frac{10}{3}\text{ A}$$

Hence the Thevenin's resistance R_{Th} looking from terminals $X-Y$ would be

$$R_{Th}=\frac{V_{X-Y}}{I_{s.c}}=\frac{25}{3}\times\frac{3}{10}=2.5\,\Omega$$

Thus the given circuit has been Thevenised as

$$V_{X-Y}(=V_{o.c})=\frac{25}{3}\text{ V}$$

and $$R_{Th}=2.5\,\Omega.$$

Example 6.75 *Find the Thevenin's equivalent circuit for the circuit shown in Fig. E6.75 at left of a-b terminals.*

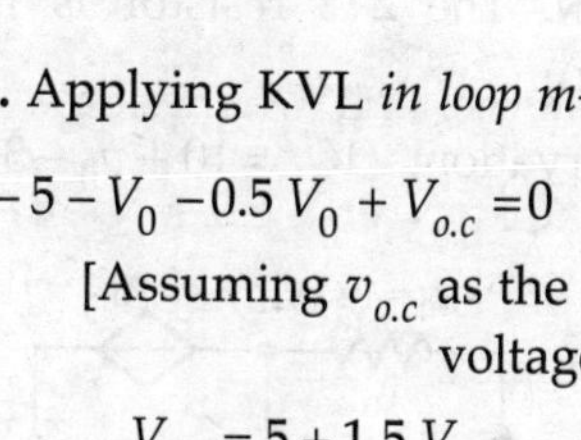

Fig. E6.75

Solution. Applying KVL *in loop m-a-b-n,*

$$-5-V_0-0.5\,V_0+V_{o.c}=0$$

[Assuming $v_{o.c}$ as the open circuit voltage across *a-b*]

or, $$V_{o.c}=5+1.5\,V_0.$$

But due to 1 A current source in the *left loop,*

$$V_0=1\times 2=2\text{ V}$$

Thus $$V_{o.c}=5+1.5\times 2=8\text{ V}$$

Again applying short circuit at *a-b* and applying KVL in Fig. E6.75(*a*),

$$5 + V_0 + 0.5\, V_0 = 0$$

or,
$$1.5\, V_0 = -5$$

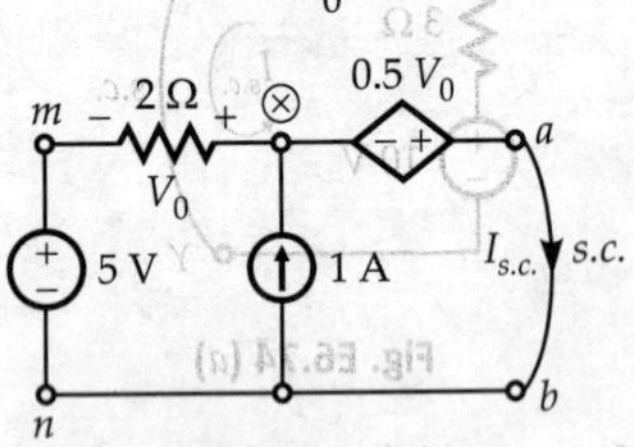

Fig. E6.75 (*a*)

$$\therefore \quad V_0 = -\frac{5}{1.5}\ \text{V}$$

However, $\frac{V_0}{2} = 1 - I_{s.c}$

[Applying KCL *at node x*]

or,
$$-1.67 = 1 - I_{s.c} \quad \left[\because V_0 = -\frac{5}{1.5}\ \text{V}\right]$$

$$\therefore \quad I_{s.c} = 1 + 1.67 = 2.67\ \text{A}$$

Thus $R_{Th} = \frac{V_{o.c}}{I_{s.c}} = \frac{8}{2.67} \simeq 3$ Ohm

Thus the given circuit has been Thevenised as

$V_{o.c}$ = **8 V** and R_{Th} = **3 Ω.**

EXAMPLE 6.76 *Obtain current in 2 Ω resistor in the circuit of Fig. E6.76 by Thevenin's theorem.*

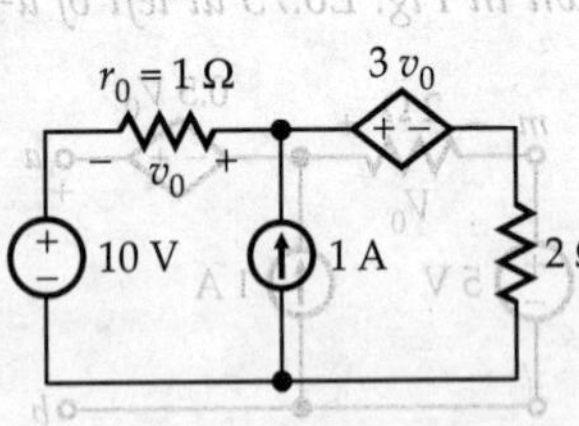

Fig. E6.76

SOLUTION. The 2 Ω resistor is first removed (Fig. E6.76(*a*)).

By observation, $V_{o.c} = 10 + v_0 - 3v_0$

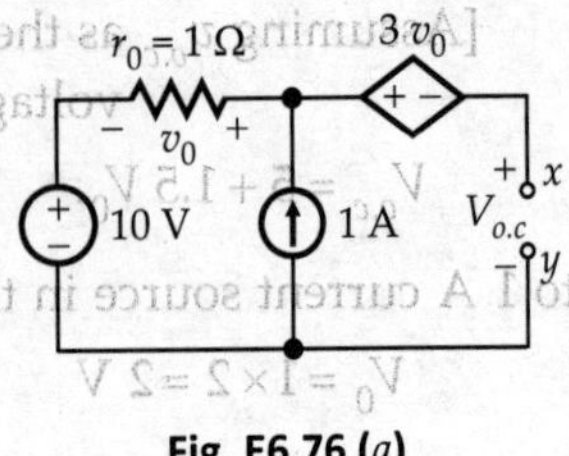

Fig. E6.76 (*a*)

But due to open circuit of *x-y* terminal, 1 A source will circulate through r_0.

$$\therefore \quad v_0\ (\text{drop across } r_0) = 1\ \text{A} \times r_0 = 1 \times 1 = 1\ \text{V}$$

Thus $V_{o.c} = 10 + 1 - 3 = 8$ V

Let us now short the terminals *x-y* (Fig. E6.76(*b*)).

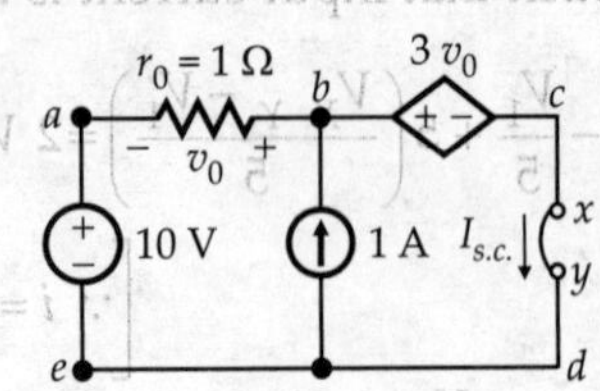

Fig. E6.76 (*b*)

In loop abcde, KVL yields

$$10 + v_0 - 3v_0 = 0 \qquad \text{...(1)}$$

Applying KCL *at node b*,

$$\frac{v_0}{1} = 1 - I_{s.c} \quad \text{or} \quad v_0 = 1 - I_{s.c}$$

Thus, from (1), the substitution of v_0 gives

$$10 + (1 - I_{s.c}) - 3\,(1 - I_{s.c}) = 0$$

or,
$$I_{s.c} = -4\ \text{A}$$

[*i.e.*, $I_{s.c}$ is directed from *y* to *x*]

Thus the internal resistance of the given circuit looking through *x-y* terminal,

$$R_{Th} = \frac{V_{o.c}}{I_{s.c}} = \frac{8}{4} = 2\ \Omega$$

Thus the current through 2 Ω resistor would be

$$\frac{V_{o.c}}{R_{Th} + 2} = \frac{8}{2+2} = 2\ \text{A}$$

∴Current through 2 Ω resistor is **2 A.**

EXAMPLE 6.77 *Find the open circuit voltage across r in the circuit shown in Fig. E6.77.*

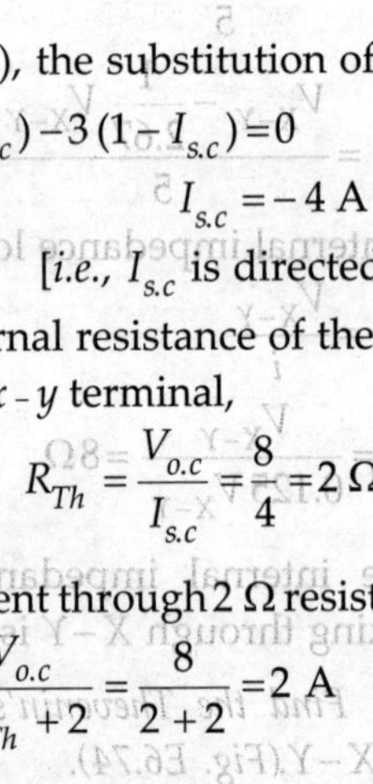

Fig. E6.77

SOLUTION. Let us first remove the *r*Ω resistor. Obviously, ($3V_r$) source does not then exist as with removal of the resistor *r*Ω, the current through *r*Ω resistor is zero. Fig. E6.77(*a*) exhibits the circuit configuration. 2 A current will flow only through 10 Ω resistor. Drop across 10 Ω resistor is then $V_{10\Omega} = 2 \times 10$ V.

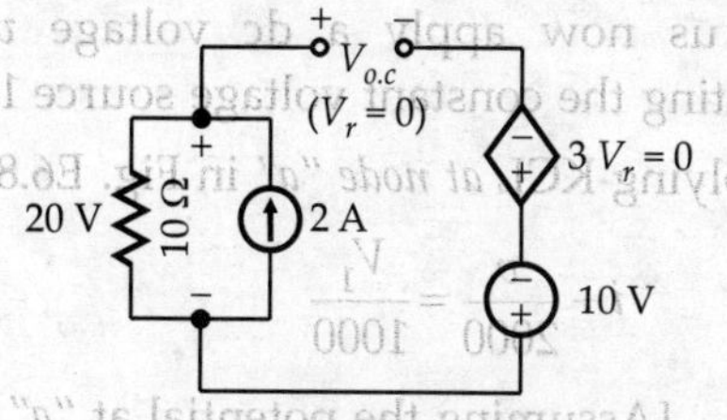

Fig. E6.77 (*a*)

Applying KVL in the given circuit of Fig. E6.77(*a*),

$$V_{o.c} = 20 + 10 = \mathbf{30\ V.}$$

EXAMPLE 6.78 *Thevenise the circuit shown in Fig. E6.78 against terminals a-b. Assume $V_0 = 12$ volts.*

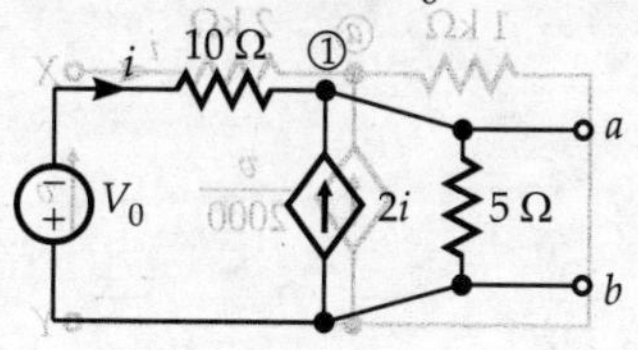

Fig. E6.78

SOLUTION. Since *a-b* is open circuited, the voltage across the 5 Ω resistor would appear across *a - b* and let it be termed as $V_{o.c}$.

Application of KCL *at node* (1) yields

$$\frac{V_{o.c} - V_0}{10} - 2i + \frac{V_{o.c}}{5} = 0 \quad ...(i)$$

However,

$$V_0 = 12 \text{ V}$$

and
$$i = \frac{V_0 - V_{o.c}}{10} = \frac{12 - V_{o.c}}{10} \text{ A}$$

∴ From (1) we get

$$\frac{V_{o.c} - 12}{10} - 2\left(\frac{12 - V_{o.c}}{10}\right) + \frac{V_{o.c}}{5} = 0$$

or, $\quad 0.1\,V_{o.c} - 1.2 - 2.4 + 0.2\,V_{o.c} + 0.2\,V_{o.c} = 0$

or, $\quad 0.5\,V_{o.c} = 3.6 \quad \therefore \quad V_{o.c} = \dfrac{3.6}{0.5} = 7.2$ V

Thus the Thevenin's voltage across *a - b* is 7.2 V.

To find internal resistance of the circuit looking through *a-b*, let us first deactivate the source V_0; then let us apply a dc source *v* at *a-b* terminal such that the input current is i_{in} (Refer to Fig. E6.78(*a*))

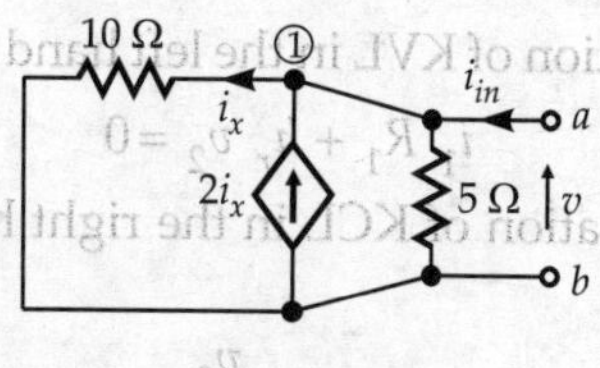

Fig. E6.78 (*a*)

Applying KCL *at node* (1),

$$\frac{v}{10} + \frac{v}{5} - 2i_x - i_{in} = 0$$

or,
$$\frac{v}{10} + \frac{v}{5} + 2\frac{v}{10} - i_{in} = 0$$

[∵ $i_x = -\dfrac{v}{10}$; note that i_x in Fig. E6.78(*a*) is directed opposite to *i* in Fig. E6.78]

or,
$$i_{in} = \frac{v}{2} \text{ V}$$

∴
$$R_{\text{int}} = \frac{v}{i_{in}} = 2\ \Omega$$

Then the given circuit has been Thevenised having

$$V_{o.c} = \mathbf{7.2\ V},\ R_{\text{int}} = \mathbf{2\ \Omega}.$$

EXAMPLE 6.79 *In Fig. E6.79, find the open circuit voltage across R utilising Thevenin's theorem. Also find the internal resistance of the circuit looking within the circuit from the open circuited terminals.*

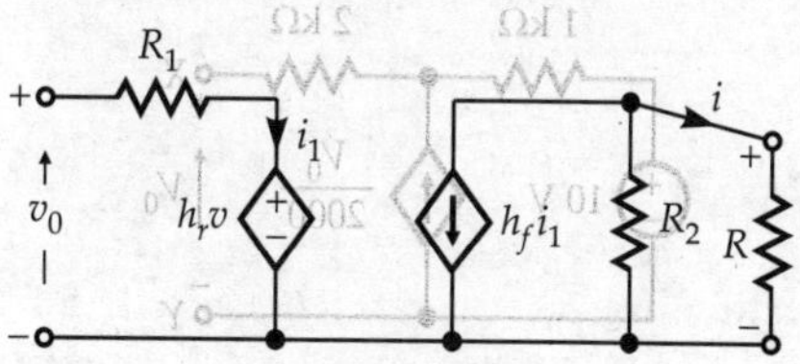

Fig. E6.79

SOLUTION. Let us remove the independent sources alongwith the load resistance *R* (Refer to Fig. E6.79(*a*)). We also assume that a voltage v_2 is applied ($= V_{o.c}$) across the open circuited terminals and the input current is 1 A.

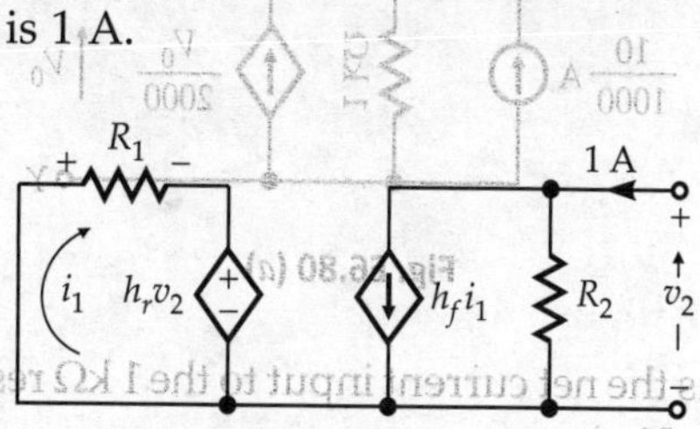

Fig. E6.79 (*a*)

CHAPTER 6

Application of KVL in the left hand loop yields

$$i_1 R_1 + h_r v_2 = 0 \quad ...(1)$$

while application of KCL in the right handed loop yields

$$h_f i_1 + \frac{v_2}{R_2} = 1 \quad ...(2)$$

From (1), $$i_1 = -\frac{h_r v_2}{R_1} \quad ...(3)$$

Utilising (3) in (2),

$$h_f \left(-\frac{h_r v_2}{R_1} \right) + \frac{v_2}{R_2} = 1$$

or, $$-h_f h_r \frac{v_2}{R_1} + \frac{v_2}{R_2} = 1$$

or, $$v_2 = \frac{R_1 R_2}{R_1 - h_f h_r R_2} (= V_{o.c})$$

i.e., $$\mathbf{V_{o.c} = \frac{R_1 R_2}{R_1 - h_f h_r R_2}}.$$

$$\therefore \quad R_{int} = \frac{V_{o.c}}{1\text{ A}} = \frac{R_1 R_2}{R_1 - h_f h_r R_2}.$$

EXAMPLE 6.80 *Obtain Thevenin's equivalent circuit across X - Y (Fig. E6.80).*

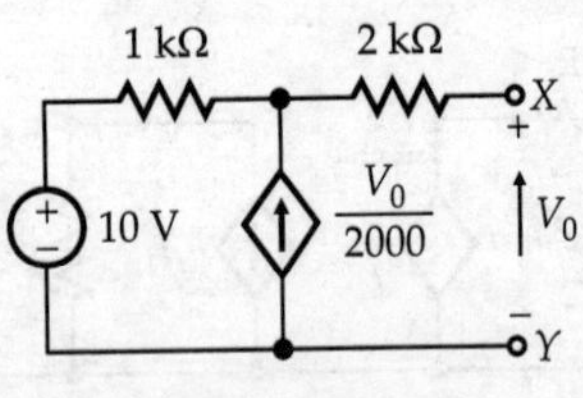

Fig. E6.80

SOLUTION. Let us convert the constant voltage source (10 V) to current source (Refer to Fig. E6.80(*a*)).

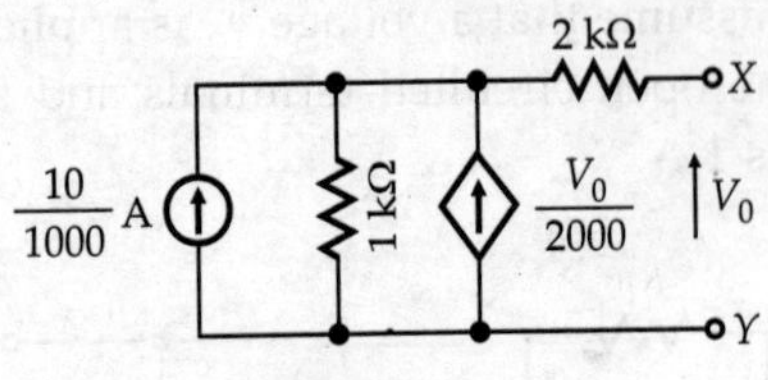

Fig. E6.80 (*a*)

Thus the net current input to the 1 kΩ resistor is

$$\left(\frac{10}{1000} + \frac{V_0}{2000} \right) \text{A}$$

$\therefore$ $V_{o.c}$ (open circuit voltage across $X - Y$)

$$= \left(\frac{10}{1000} + \frac{V_0}{2000} \right) \times 1000 = (10 + 0.5 V_0)$$

Let us now apply a dc voltage v at X-Y deactivating the constant voltage source 10 V.

Applying KCL *at node "a"* in Fig. E6.80(*b*),

$$i + \frac{v}{2000} = \frac{V_1}{1000}.$$

[Assuming the potential at "a" to be V_1]

or, $$\frac{v - V_1}{2000} + \frac{v}{2000} = \frac{V_1}{1000}$$

or, $$\frac{v}{1000} = \frac{3V_1}{2000}$$

$$\therefore \quad v = 1.5\, V_1$$

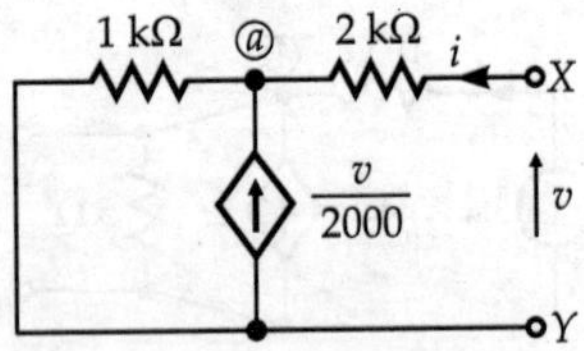

Fig. E6.80 (*b*)

However,

$$i = \frac{v - V_1}{2000} = \frac{v - \frac{v}{1.5}}{2000} = \frac{0.5\, v}{2000 \times 1.5} = \frac{v}{6000}.$$

$\therefore$ R_{int} (*at X - Y terminal*)

$$= \frac{v}{i} = \frac{v}{\frac{v}{6000}} = 6000\, \Omega.$$

Thus the given circuit has been Thevenised with

$$V_{o.c} = \mathbf{(10 + 0.5\, V_0)} \text{ and } R_{int} = \mathbf{6\text{ k}\Omega}.$$

EXAMPLE 6.81 *Thevenise the network shown in Fig. E6.81.*

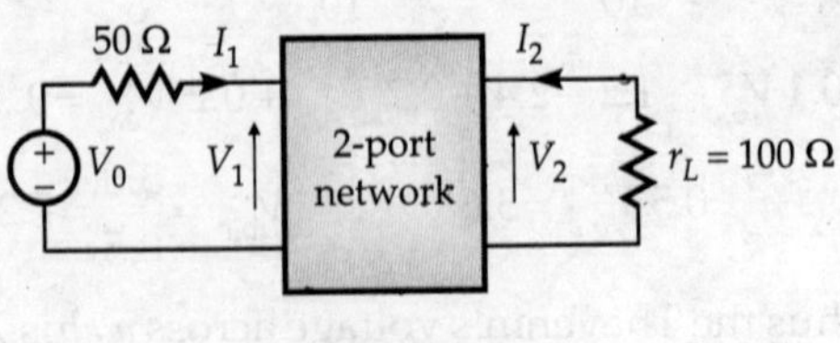

Fig. E6.81

SOLUTION. Let the input voltage be removed and input port be left open.

$$\therefore \quad I_1 = 0 \text{ and } V_{o.c} \equiv V_1.$$

However, from the concept of two port network,

$$V_1 = Z_{11}\, I_1 + Z_{12}\, I_2 = Z_{12}\, I_2 \qquad [\because I_1 = 0] \quad ...(1)$$

However, in the output port, the current being $-I_2$ (directed inwards), the output voltage V_2 is given by

$$V_2 = -r_L \times I_2 \quad ...(2)$$

However, with $I_1 = 0$,

$$V_2 = Z_{21}\, I_1 + Z_{22}\, I_2 = Z_{22}\, I_2 \qquad [\because I_1 = 0] \quad ...(3)$$

Subtraction of (2) from (3) yields

$$(Z_{22} + r_L)\, I_2 = 0.$$

Z_{22} and r_L being two +ve quantities, the sum of Z_{22} and r_L cannot be zero.

$\therefore$ From (3), $\quad I_2 = 0.$

This gives, from (1),

$$V_1 = 0 = V_{Th} \quad ...(4)$$

Again, since $V_1 = z_{11}\, I_1 + Z_{12}\, I_2$, hence using

$$I_2 = -\frac{V_2}{r_L},$$

$$V_1 = z_{11}\, I_1 - \frac{Z_{12}}{r_L} V_2 \quad ...(5)$$

and since $V_2 = Z_{21}\, I_1 + Z_{22}\, I_2$, hence with same value of I_2 we get

$$V_2 = z_{21}\, I_1 - Z_{22} \frac{V_2}{r_L}$$

$$\therefore \quad V_2 = \frac{Z_{21}\, r_L}{r_L + Z_{22}} I_1 \quad ...(6)$$

Using (6) in (5),

$$V_1 = Z_{11}\, I_1 - Z_{12} \frac{Z_{21}}{r_L + Z_{22}} I_1$$

$\therefore R_{int}$ (Thevenin's resistance looking from input terminals) $= \dfrac{V_1}{I_1}$

$$= Z_{11} - \frac{Z_{12}\, Z_{21}}{r_L + Z_{22}}$$

Thus, the given network has been Thevenised with

$$V_{Th} = \mathbf{0\ V} \text{ and } R_{int} = \mathbf{Z_{11}} - \frac{\mathbf{Z_{12}\, Z_{21}}}{\mathbf{r_L + Z_{22}}}.$$

EXAMPLE 6.82 *A two port network has been shown in Fig. E6.82, where the block represents a network of resistors. A resistance R is connected at the output. The given conditions of the network are*

(i) When $R = \infty$, $V = 10$ V

(ii) When $R = 0$, $I = 5$ A

Find the value of V when $R = 8\,\Omega$.

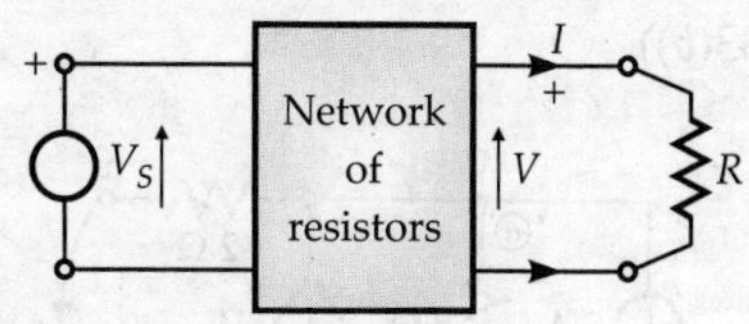

Fig. E6.82

SOLUTION. When $R = \infty$, $V = 10$ V *i.e.*, $V_{o.c} = 10$ V

When $\quad R = 0, I = 5$ A *i.e.*, $I_{s.c} = 5$ A

$\therefore \quad R_{int}$ (equivalent R of the block)

$$= \frac{V_{o.c}}{I_{s.c}} = \frac{10}{5} = 2\,\Omega$$

The equivalent network is shown below (Fig. E6.82(*a*)).

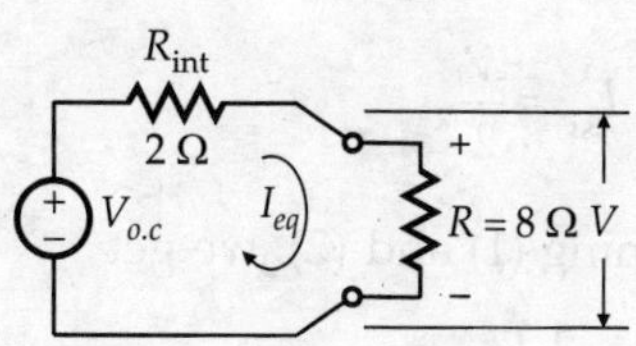

Fig. E6.82 (*a*)

Here $\quad I_{eq} = \dfrac{V_{o.c}}{R_{int} + R} = \dfrac{10}{2 + 8} = 1$ A $\quad [\because R = 8\,\Omega]$

Hence under this condition,

$$V = I_{eq.} \times R = 1 \times 8 = \mathbf{8\ V}.$$

EXAMPLE 6.83 *In the circuit of Fig. E6.83, find the Thevenin's equivalent circuit left to x-y terminals.*

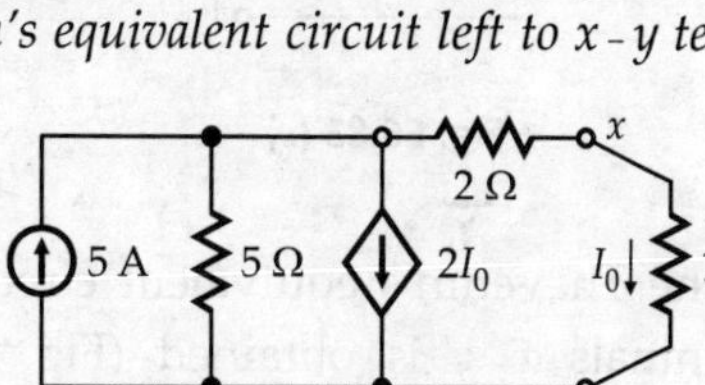

Fig. E6.83

SOLUTION. Removing the $10\,\Omega$ resistor,

$$V_{o.c} = 5\text{ A} \times 5\,\Omega = 25\text{ V} (= V)$$

[Refer to Fig. E6.83(*a*)]

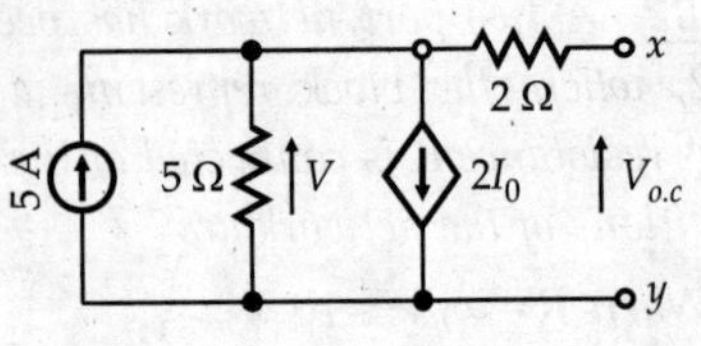

Fig. E6.83 (*a*)

Let us now short circuit the terminals $x-y$ (Fig. E6.83(*b*)).

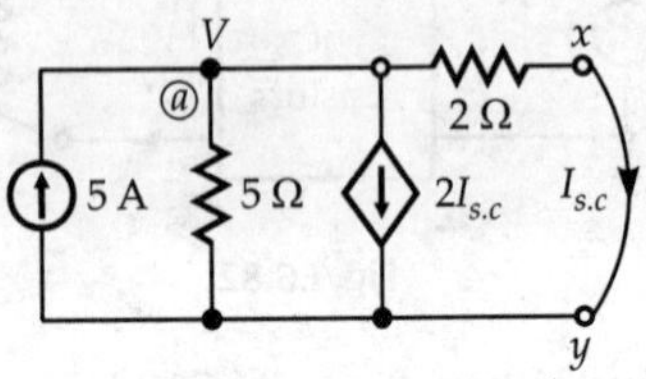

Fig. E6.83 (*b*)

At node (*a*), the application of KCL yields

$$5 = \frac{V}{5} + 2\, I_{s.c} + I_{s.c}$$

or, $$3\, I_{s.c} + \frac{V}{5} = 5 \qquad \text{...(1)}$$

Also $$I_{s.c} = \frac{V}{2} \qquad \text{...(2)}$$

Combining (1) and (2), we get

$$3\, I_{s.c} + \frac{2\, I_{s.c}}{5} = 5 \quad \text{or} \quad I_{s.c} = 1.47 \text{ A}$$

Hence, $$R_{Th} = \frac{V_{o.c}}{I_{s.c}} = \frac{25}{1.47} = 17\,\Omega$$

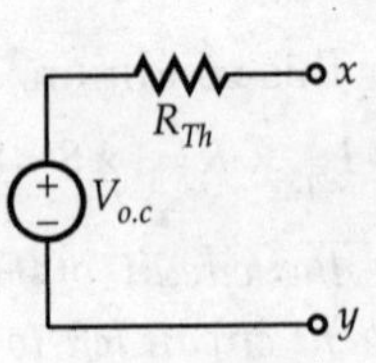

Fig. E6.83 (*c*)

Then, the Thevenin's equivalent circuit to the left of terminals $x-y$ is obtained (Fig. E6.83(*c*)) where

$$V_{o.c} = \mathbf{25\ V}$$

$$I_{s.c} = \mathbf{1.47\ A.}$$

Example 6.84 *Obtain Thevenin's equivalent circuit to the left of a-b in the circuit of Fig. E6.84. Also find* (V_0 / V_1).

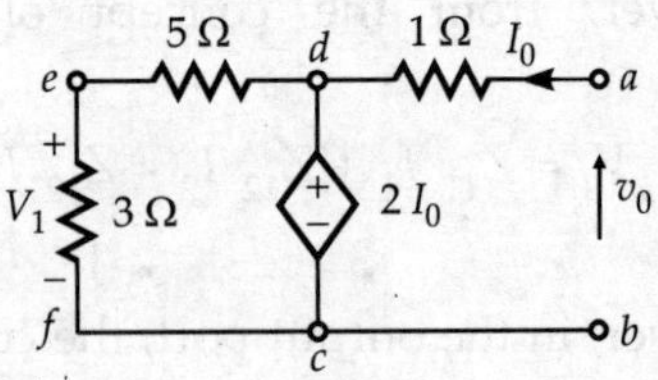

Fig. E6.84

Solution. As the given circuit does not have any independent source hence a dc voltage of 1 V (= say V_0) is applied at $a-b$ terminal. Let the input current be I_0.

Applying KVL *in loop abcd*, (Fig. E6.84(*a*)).

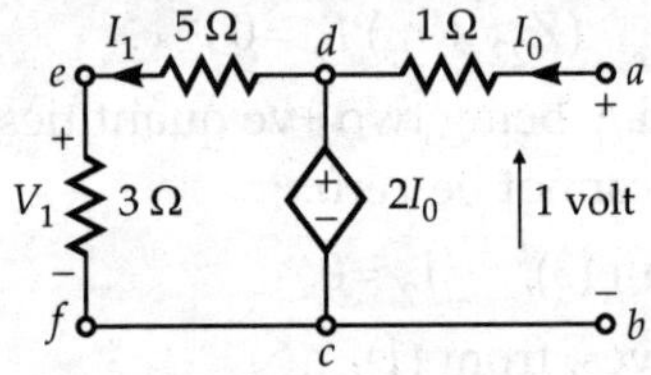

Fig. E6.84 (*a*)

$$1 = I_0 \times 1 + 2\, I_0$$

or, $$3\, I_0 = 1 \quad \therefore \quad I_0 = \frac{1}{3} \text{ A.}$$

This gives

$$R_{Th} = \frac{V_0}{I_0} = \frac{1}{\frac{1}{3}} = 3\,\Omega.$$

Also, KVL *in loop a-d-e-f-c-b* gives

$$1 = I_0 \times 1 + I_1 \times 5 + I_1 \times 3$$

or, $$8\, I_1 = 1 - I_0 = 1 - \frac{1}{3}$$

$$\therefore \quad I_1 = \frac{2}{3} \times \frac{1}{8} = \frac{1}{12} \text{ A}$$

This gives,

$$V_1 = 3 \times \frac{1}{12} = \frac{1}{4} \text{ V}$$

Thus, $$V_0 / V_1 = \frac{1}{\frac{1}{4}} = 4.$$

Thus, the given circuit has been Thevenised and the internal resistance to the left of *a-b* is given by

$$R_{Th} = \mathbf{3\,\Omega}$$

Also $$(V_0 / V_1) = \mathbf{4.}$$

EXAMPLE 6.85 *Obtain the current through 1 Ω resistor by Thevenin's Theorem (Fig. E6.85).*

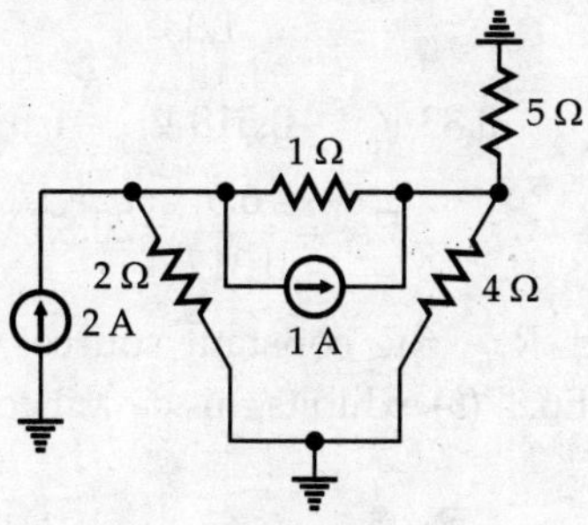

Fig. E6.85

SOLUTION. 1 Ω resistor is removed from Fig. E6.85 and the circuit configuration is shown in Fig. E6.85(*a*).

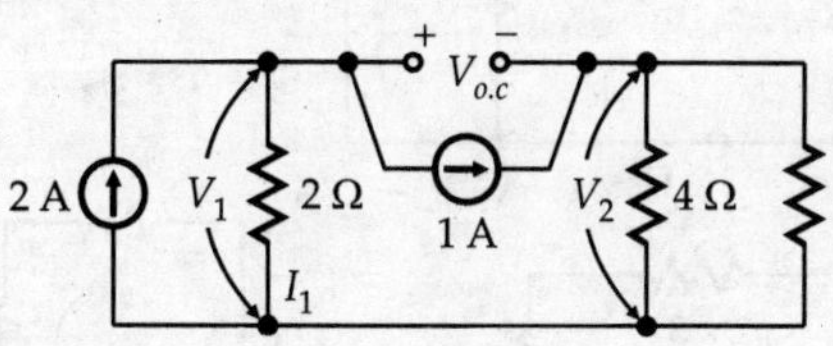

Fig. E6.85 (*a*)

Here $I_1 = 2 - 1 = 1\text{ A}$

$\therefore$ $V_1 = 1\text{ A} \times 2\,\Omega = 2\text{ V}$

Also, $V_2 = 1\text{ A} \times \dfrac{4 \times 5}{4+5} = \dfrac{20}{9}\text{ V}$

$\therefore$ $V_{o.c} = V_1 - V_2 = 2 - \dfrac{20}{9} = -\dfrac{2}{9}\text{ V}$

Deactivating the constant sources, R_{Th} from Fig. E6.85(*b*) is obtained as

$$R_{Th} = 2 + \frac{4 \times 5}{4+5} = 2 + \frac{20}{9} = \frac{38}{9}\,\Omega.$$

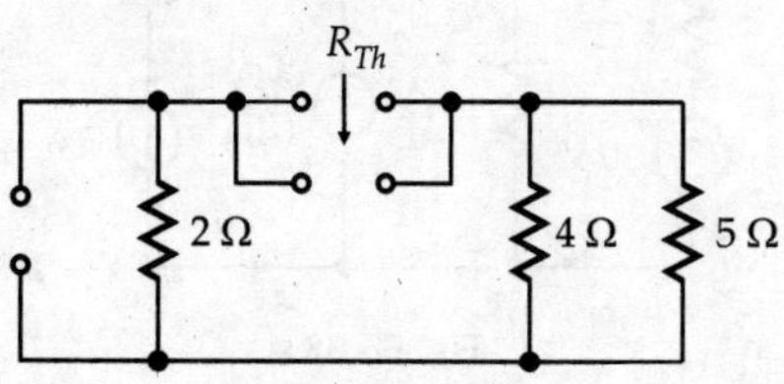

Fig. E6.85 (*b*)

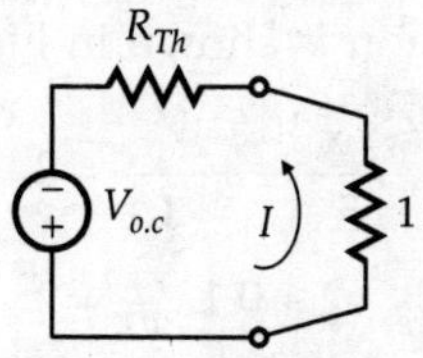

Fig. E6.85 (*c*)

Figure E6.85(*c*) being representing the equivalent circuit (Thevnin's equivalent),

$$I = \frac{V_{o.c}}{R_{Th} + 1} = \frac{2/9}{\frac{38}{9} + 1}$$

$$= \frac{2}{47}\text{ A} = 43\text{ mA (anticlockwise)}$$

Thus the current through 1 Ω resistor = **43 mA.**

EXAMPLE 6.86 *Find the ammeter reading in Fig. E6.86 using Thevenin's theorem.*

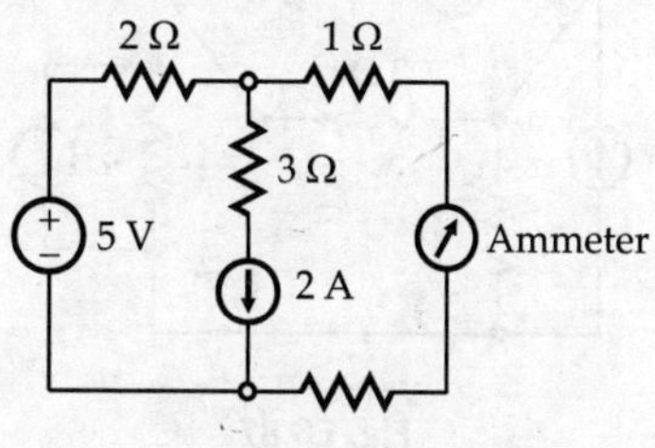

Fig. E6.86

SOLUTION. Let the ammeter be removed [Fig. E6.86(*a*)],

$$V_{o.c} = 5 - 2 \times 2 = 1\text{ V}$$

[$\because$ Circulating current in the leftmost loop is 2 A and $V_{o.c} \equiv V_{x-y}$]

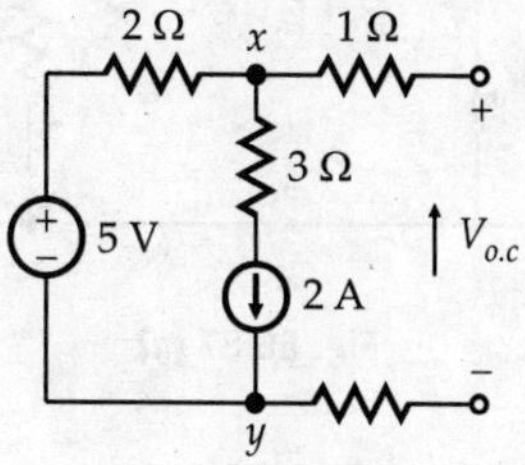

Fig. E6.86 (*a*)

With reference to Fig. E6.86(*b*),

$$R_{int}\ (= R_{Th}) = 2 + 1 = 3\,\Omega$$

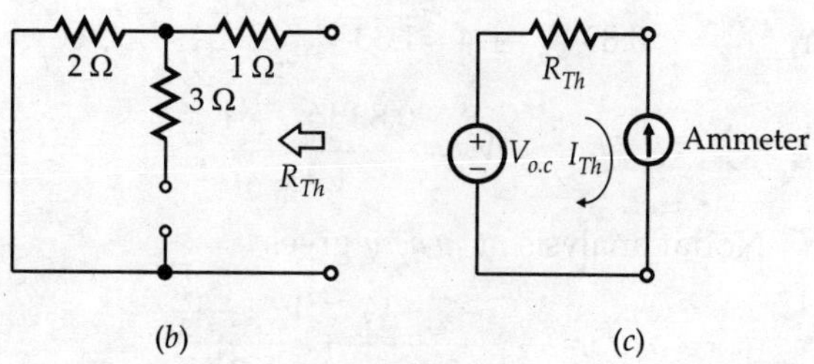

(*b*) (*c*)

Fig. E6.86

Figure E6.86(*c*) being representing the Thevenin's equivalent circuit,

$$I_{Th} = \frac{V_{o.c}}{R_{Th} + 0} \quad [\because \text{ Ammeter resistance is usually negligibly small}]$$

$$= \frac{1}{3} \text{ A} = 0.33 \text{ A}.$$

Thus, the current through the ammeter is **0.33 A.**

Example 6.87 *Using Thevenin's theorem, find the current through 1 Ω resistor in the circuit shown in Fig. E6.87.*

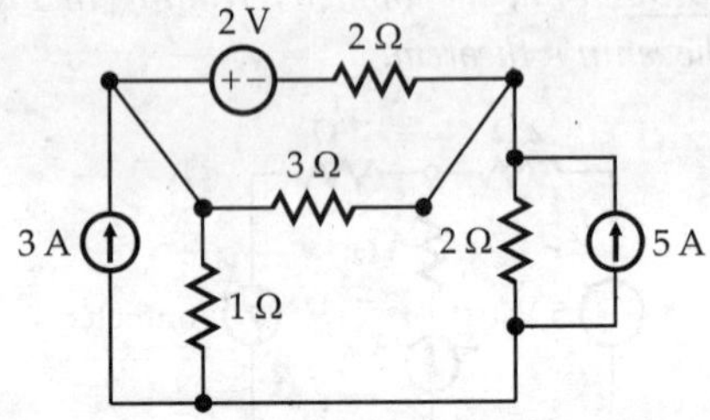

Fig. E6.87

Solution. Let the 1 Ω resistor be removed (Fig. E6.87(*a*)) and the potential across the open circuited terminal be $V_{o.c}$ while the potential at *node 'x'* be V_0.

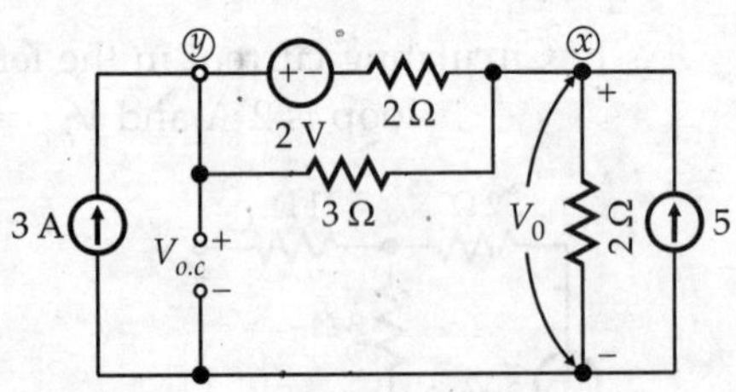

Fig. E6.87 (*a*)

At *node x*, nodal analysis gives,

$$\frac{V_0}{2} = 5 + \frac{V_{o.c} - V_0}{3} + \frac{V_{o.c} - 2 - V_0}{2}$$

or, $0.5\,V_0 + 0.33\,V_0 + 0.5\,V_0 = 0.33\,V_{o.c} + 0.5\,V_{o.c} - 1 + 5$

or, $0.83\,V_{o.c} + 4 = 1.33\,V_0$

or, $$V_0 = \frac{0.83\,V_{o.c} + 4}{1.33}$$

Nodal analysis *at node y* gives,

$$3 = \frac{V_{o.c} - 2 - V_0}{2} + \frac{V_{o.c} - V_0}{3}$$

or, $0.5\,V_0 + 0.33\,V_0 = 0.5\,V_{o.c} + 0.33\,V_{o.c} - 4$

or, $0.83\,V_{o.c} - 0.83\,V_{o.c} - 4 = 0$

Using the value of V_0 in the above equation

$$0.83\,V_{o.c} - 0.83\,\frac{0.83\,V_{o.c} + 4}{1.33} - 4 = 0$$

or, $0.83\,V_{o.c} - 0.518\,V_{o.c} - 6.5 = 0$

or, $$V_{o.c} = \frac{6.5}{0.312} = 20.83 \text{ V}$$

To find R_{Th}, the constant sources are deactivated. Fig. E6.87(*b*) exhibits this circuit configuration where,

$$R_{Th} = \frac{2 \times 3}{2 + 3} + 2 = \frac{6}{5} + 2 = 3.2\ \Omega$$

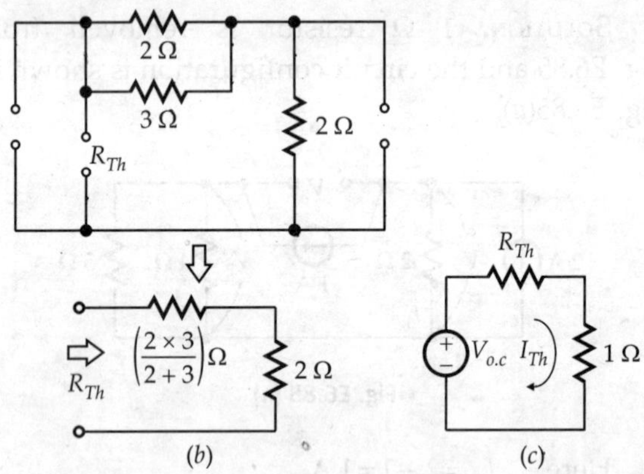

Fig. E6.87

∴ Current in 1 Ω resistance is obtained from the Thevenin's equivalent circuit (Fig. E6.87(*c*)) where

$$I_{Th} = \frac{V_{o.c}}{R_{Th} + 1} = \frac{20.83}{3.2 + 1} = 4.96 \text{ A}$$

Thus the current through 1 Ω resistor is **4.96 A.**

Example 6.88 *Find current through R_L in Fig. E6.88.*

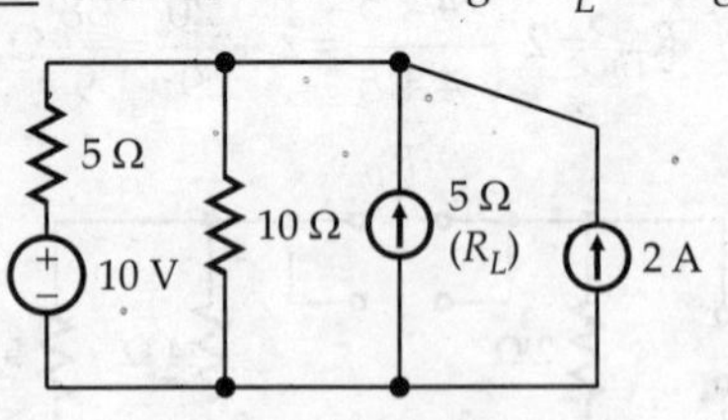

Fig. E6.88

Solution. 5 Ω (R_L) resistor being removed, the circuit configuration is shown in Fig. E6.88(*a*).

At node x, $$\frac{V_{o.c} - 10}{5} + \frac{V_{o.c}}{10} = 2$$

or, $0.2\,V_{o.c} - 2 + 0.1\,V_{o.c} = 2$

or, $0.3\,V_{o.c} = 4$

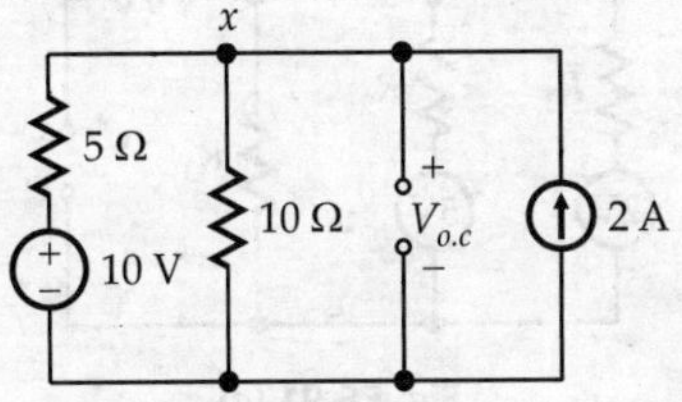

Fig. E6.88 (*a*)

$$\therefore \quad V_{o.c} = \frac{4}{0.3} = 13.33 \text{ V}$$

To find R_{Th}, the constant sources are deactivated (Fig. E6.88(*b*))

$$\text{Here } R_{Th} = \frac{10 \times 5}{10 + 5} = \frac{50}{15} = 3.33\,\Omega$$

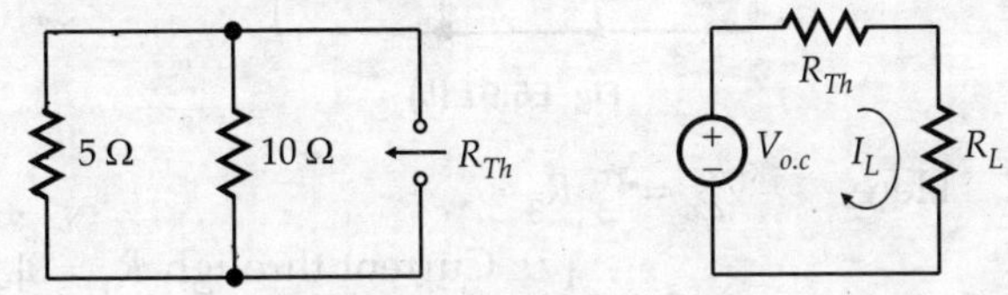

(*b*) (*c*)

Fig. E6.88

Thevenin's equivalent circuit being shown in Fig. E6.88(*c*),

$$I_L = \frac{V_{o.c}}{R_{Th} + R_L} = \frac{13.33}{3.33 + 5} = \mathbf{1.6\ A.}$$

Thus, the current through R_L is 1.6 A.

EXAMPLE 6.89 *If V_L represents the drop across R_L in Fig. E6.89, find the current across R_L utilising Thevenin's Theorem. Assume $R_L = 10\,\Omega$ and α factor in the dependent current source as 0.5.*

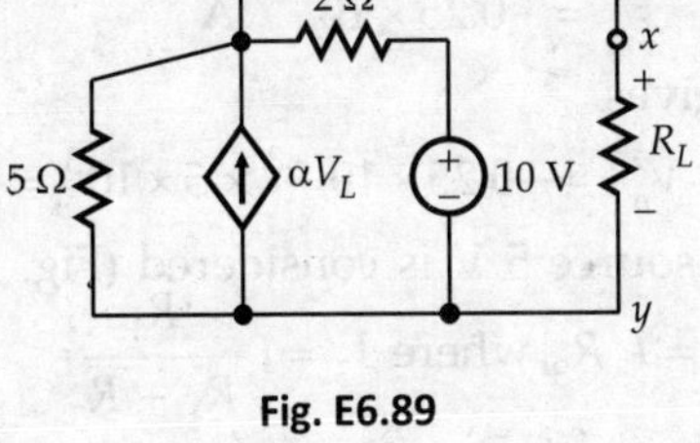

Fig. E6.89

SOLUTION. Let R_L be removed. Circuit configuration is shown in Fig. E6.89(*a*). Let the open circuit voltage across *x-y* (*i.e.*, the Thevenin's voltage) be $V_{o.c}$.

Obviously the polarity of *node 1* would be +ve having magnitude $V_{o.c}$.

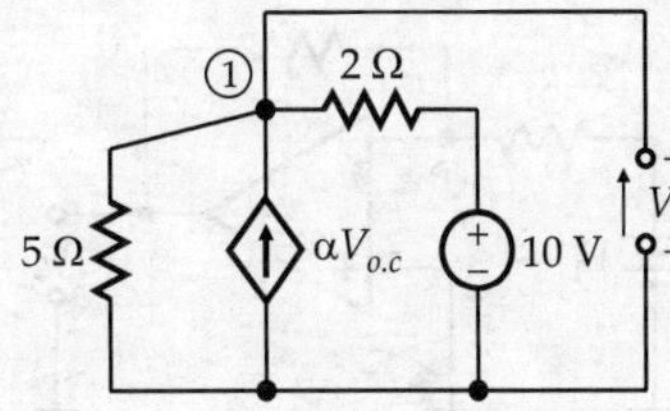

Fig. E6.89 (*a*)

∴Nodal analysis with respect to *node 1* reveals

$$\frac{V_{o.c} - 10}{2} - \alpha V_{o.c} + \frac{V_{o.c}}{5} = 0$$

[αV_L has been replaced by $\alpha V_{o.c}$]

$$\text{or, } 0.5\,V_{o.c} - 5 - 0.5\,V_{o.c} + 0.2\,V_{o.c} = 0$$

$$0.2\,V_{o.c} = 5$$

$$\therefore \quad V_{o.c} = 25 \text{ V}$$

To find the internal resistance of the given circuit across *x-y*, the independent voltage source is shorted (or deactivated) and a d.c. voltage V_0 is applied between *x-y* terminals. Let the input current be I_0 through terminal *x*. (Ref. to Fig. E6.89(*b*)).

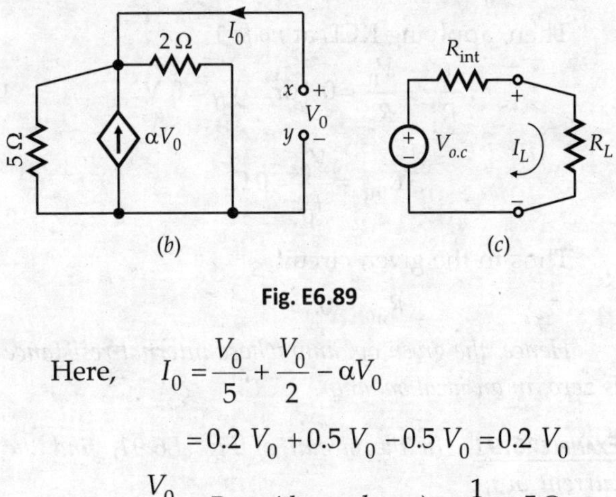

(*b*) (*c*)

Fig. E6.89

$$\text{Here,} \quad I_0 = \frac{V_0}{5} + \frac{V_0}{2} - \alpha V_0$$

$$= 0.2\,V_0 + 0.5\,V_0 - 0.5\,V_0 = 0.2\,V_0$$

$$\therefore \quad \frac{V_0}{I_0} = R_{int} \text{ (through } x\text{-}y) = \frac{1}{0.2} = 5\,\Omega.$$

The Thevenin's equivalent circuit being shown in Fig. E6.89(*c*) ;

I_L (load current through R_L)

$$= \frac{V_{o.c}}{R_{int} + R_L} = \frac{25}{5 + 10} = \mathbf{1.67\ A.}$$

EXAMPLE 6.90 *In the op. amp. circuit of Fig. E6.90, $\frac{V_2}{V_1} = -\frac{R_2}{R_1}$. If the output is at no load, Thevenise the given circuit.*

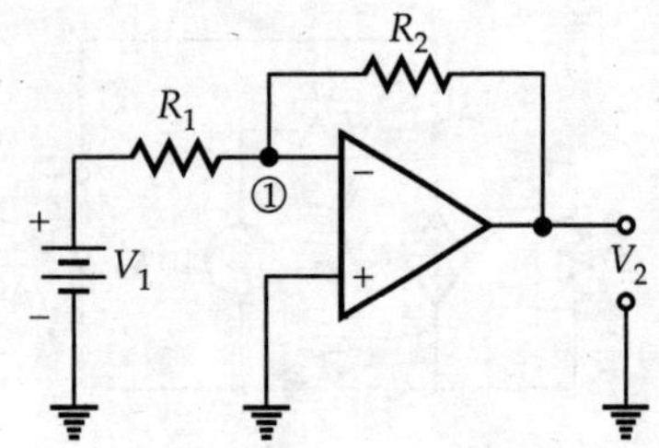

Fig. E6.90

Solution. As the output of the op. amp is unloaded hence,

$$V_2 \equiv V_{o.c} \equiv V_{Th}.$$

$$\text{Thus } \mathbf{V_{Th} = V_1\left(-\frac{R_2}{R_1}\right)}$$

[from the given condition]

In order to find the internal resistance through the open circuited terminals, let us first deactivate the constant source voltage V_1 and apply another d.c. voltage V_0 at the output so that the current entering through the output terminal within the circuit is I_0.

Then, applying KCL at *node* 1

$$\frac{0}{R_1} - \frac{V_0}{R_2} = 0 \quad \text{or,} \quad V_0 = \mathbf{0\ V}.$$

$$\therefore \qquad R_{\text{int}} = \frac{V_0}{I_0} = \mathbf{0\ \Omega}.$$

Thus in the given circuit,

$$R_{\text{int}} = 0.$$

Hence, the given op. amp whose internal resistance is zero, in an ideal op. amp.

Example 6.91 *In the circuit of Fig. E6.91, find the current in r_L.*

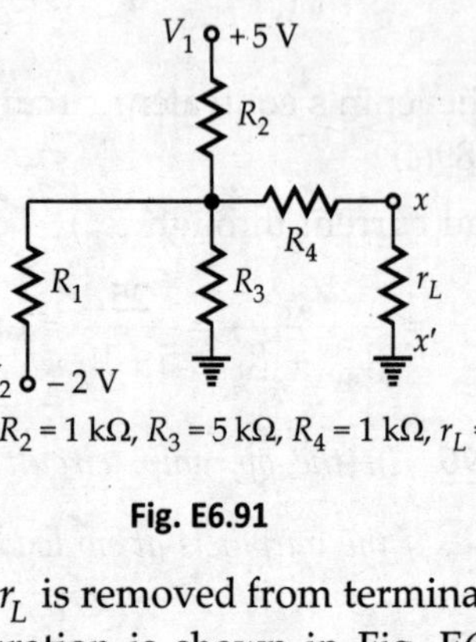

$[R_1 = 500\ \Omega,\ R_2 = 1\ \text{k}\Omega,\ R_3 = 5\ \text{k}\Omega,\ R_4 = 1\ \text{k}\Omega,\ r_L = 2\ \text{k}\Omega]$

Fig. E6.91

Solution. r_L is removed from terminal *x-x′*. The circuit configuration is shown in Fig. E6.91(*a*). To

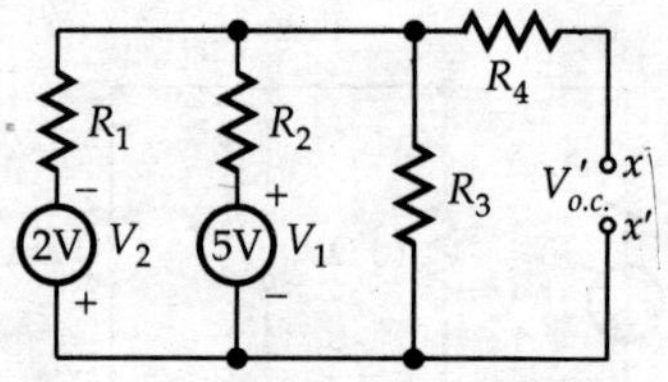

Fig. E6.91 (*a*)

find $V_{o.c}$ across *x-x′*, let us first apply V_2 first following the principle of Superposition removing V_1. Fig. E6.91(*b*) represents this condition.

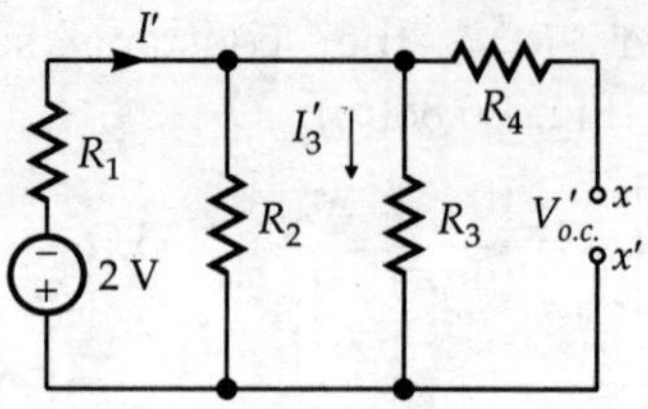

Fig. E6.91 (*b*)

$$\text{Here} \qquad V'_{o.c} = I'_3\, R_3$$

[∵ Current through R_1 = 0].

$$\text{However,} \quad I'_3 = I'\,\frac{R_2}{R_2 + R_3}$$

$$\text{But} \qquad I' = -\frac{2}{R_1 + (R_2 \,||\, R_3)}$$

$$= -\frac{2}{\left(0.5 + \dfrac{1 \times 5}{6}\right)\text{k}\Omega}$$

$$= -\frac{2}{\dfrac{8}{6}\,\text{k}\Omega} = -\left(2 \times \frac{6}{8 \times 10^3}\right)$$

$$= -1.5 \times 10^{-3}\ \text{A}$$

$$\therefore \qquad I_3 = -1.5 \times 10^{-3}\,\frac{1000}{6000}$$

$$= -0.25 \times 10^{-3}\ \text{A}$$

This gives

$$V'_{o.c} = -0.25 \times 10^{-3} \times 5 \times 10^3 = -1.25\ \text{V}.$$

Next, source 5 V is considered (Fig. E6.91(*c*)) ;

$$\text{Here } V''_{o.c} = I_3 R_3 \text{ where } I_3 = I\,\frac{R_1}{R_1 + R_3}$$

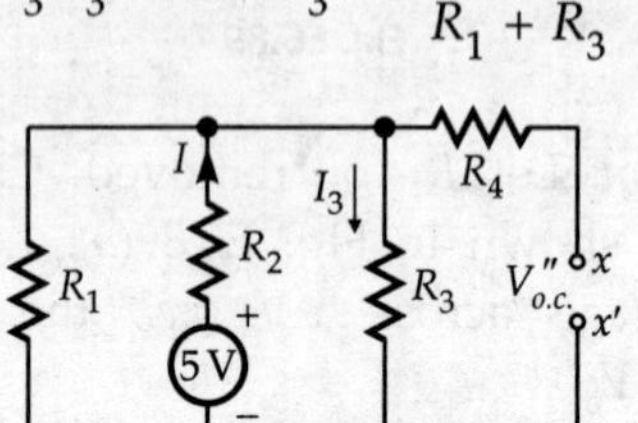

Fig. E6.91 (*c*)

But $$I = \frac{5}{R_2 + \dfrac{R_1 R_3}{R_1 + R_3}}$$

$$= \frac{5}{\left(1 + \dfrac{0.5 \times 5}{5.5}\right) \text{k}\Omega} = 3.44 \times 10^{-3} \text{ A.}$$

This gives

$$I_3 = 3.44 \times 10^{-3} \frac{0.5 \times 10^3}{(0.5 + 5)10^3}$$

$$= 0.3127 \times 10^{-3} \text{ A,}$$

$$\therefore \quad V''_{o.c} = 0.3127 \times 10^{-3} \times 5 \times 10^3 = 1.564 \text{ V.}$$

$$\therefore \quad V_{o.c} = V'_{o.c} + V''_{o.c}$$

$$= -1.25 + 1.564 = 0.314 \text{ V}$$

(with x terminal +ve)

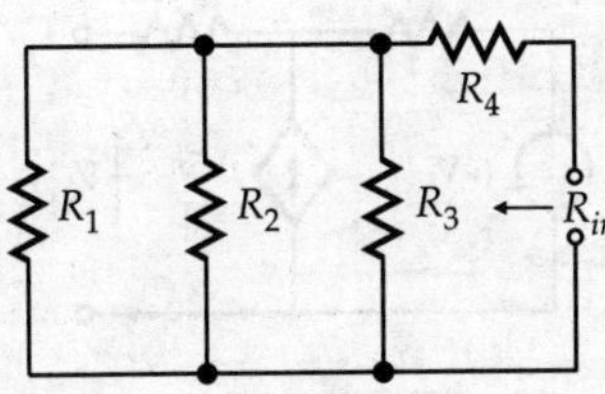

Fig. E6.91 (d)

R_{int} (= R_{Th}) is given by (Refer to Fig. E6.91(c))

$$R_{Th} = \left[\left(\frac{R_1 R_2}{R_1 + R_2}\right) \Big\| R_3\right] + R_4$$

$$= \left[\left\{\frac{(0.5 \times 1)}{1.5}\right\} \| 5\right] + 1$$

$$= \frac{0.33 \times 5}{5.33} + 1 = \frac{1.65 + 5.33}{5.33} = 1.31 \text{ k}\Omega$$

$\therefore$ From Thevenin's equivalent circuit, i_L (current through r_L)

$$= \frac{V_{Th}}{R_{Th} + r_L} = \frac{0.314}{(1.31 + 2) \times 10^3} = \mathbf{0.095 \text{ mA.}}$$

EXAMPLE 6.92 *Thevenise the given circuit of Fig. E6.92 across the diode D.*

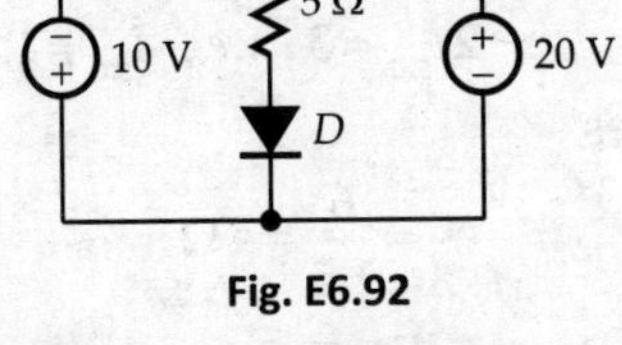

Fig. E6.92

SOLUTION. Let the diode D be removed (Fig. E6.92(a)).

At node x, nodal analysis gives

$$\frac{V_{o.c} + 10}{10} + \frac{V_{o.c} - 20}{10} = 0$$

[$\because$ No current flows through 5 Ω resistor]

or, $$0.1 V_{o.c} + 1 + 0.1 V_{o.c} - 2 = 0$$

or, $$0.2 V_{o.c} = 1 \text{ i.e., } V_{o.c} = 5 \text{ V.}$$

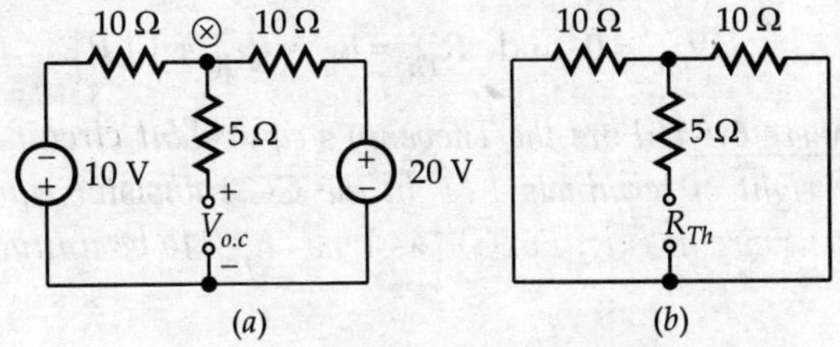

Fig. E6.92

Again to find Thevenin's resistance, the constant sources are deactivated (Fig. E6.92(b))

Here $$R_{Th} = \frac{10 \times 10}{10 + 10} + 5 = 10\,\Omega$$

Then the given circuit has been Thevenised as

$$V_{o.c} = \mathbf{5\ V}, \ R_{Th} = \mathbf{10\,\Omega}. \quad \text{[across diode } D]$$

EXAMPLE 6.93 *A small signal model of CC amplifier is shown in Fig. E6.93. Find its Thevenin equivalent for the right of 1-1′.*

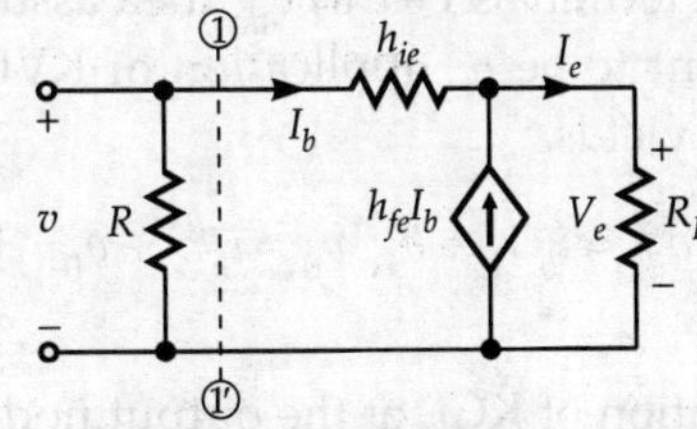

Fig. E6.93

SOLUTION. In order to find the Thevenin's equivalent to the right of 1-1′, let the supply (v) be removed. As there is no independent source in the right portion of Fig. E6.93, hence it is evident that with removal of the supply, $I_b = 0$ and $h_{fe} I_b$ subsequently becomes zero. This gives

$$V_{Th} = V_{o.c} = 0.$$

Let us now apply a d.c. source v_0 at the supply terminal 1-1′ such that input current be I_b.

CHAPTER 6

Obviously, $I_e = I_b + h_{fe} I_b$

and $v_0 = h_{ie} I_b + I_e R_E$

$= h_{ie} I_b + (I_b + h_{fe} I_b) R_E$

or, $v_0 = h_{ie} I_b + (h_{fe} + 1) I_b R_E$

This gives,

$$R_{Th} = \frac{v_0}{I_b} = h_{ie} + (h_{fe} + 1) R_E.$$

The given circuit has then been Thevenised to the right of 1-1′ with

$$\mathbf{V_{o.c} = 0 \text{ and } R_{Th} = h_{ie} + (h_{fe} + 1) R_E.}$$

EXAMPLE 6.94 *Find the Thevenin's equivalent circuit of the right of terminals 1-1′ in the CC transistor equivalent circuit (Fig. E6.94). Assume "h_{rc}" to be unity.*

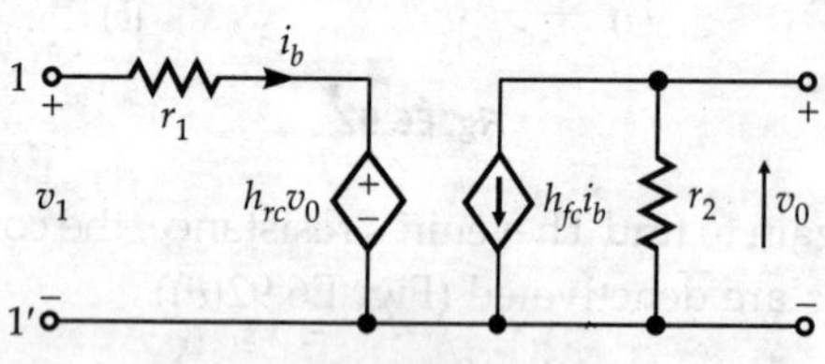

Fig. E6.94

SOLUTION. Let us first remove the supply voltage. As there is no independent voltage source at the right of terminals 1–1′ hence the Thevenin's voltage would be zero and the Thevenin's equivalent circuit would only consist of R_{Th}.

If we now consider a driving dc voltage source at the input terminals 1–1′ as v_{dc} then assuming the input current to be i_b, application of KVL around the *left loop* yields

$$v_{dc} = i_b r_1 + h_{rc} v_0 = i_b r_1 + v_0 \quad [\because h_{rc} = 1] \qquad ...(1)$$

Application of KCL at the output node gives

$$v_0 = -\mathbf{h_{fc}\, i_b\, r_2} \qquad ...(2)$$

Using the value of v_0 from (2) in (1), we get

$$v_{dc} = i_b r_1 + (-h_{fc} i_b r_2)$$

$$\therefore \quad R_{Th} = \frac{v_{dc}}{i_b} = r_1 - h_{fc} r_2$$

The Thevenin's equivalent circuit of the given circuit at the right of terminals 1–1′ is then given by

$$\mathbf{R_{Th} = (r_1 - h_{fc} r_2).}$$

EXAMPLE 6.95 *Determine the current through the 5Ω resistor in Fig. E6.95.*

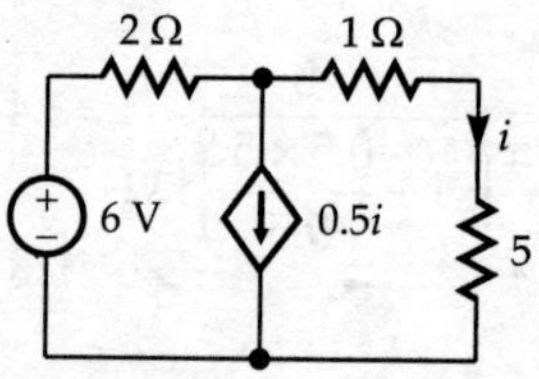

Fig. E6.95

SOLUTION. Let the 5Ω resistor be removed (Fig. E6.95(*a*)). No current would flow through the 1Ω resistor (*i.e.*, $i = 0$) and the 2 Ω resistor will only have a drop of 6 V across it,

i.e., $V_{o.c} (= V_{Th}) = 6$ V

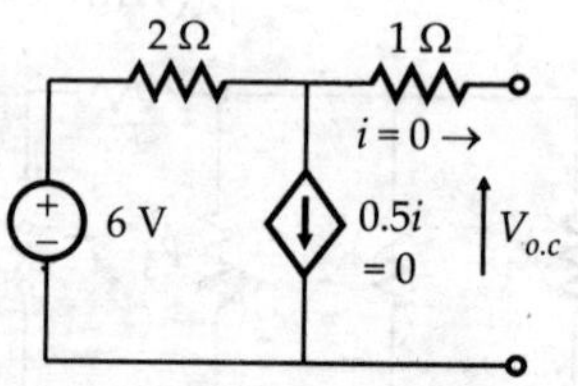

Fig. E6.95 (*a*)

Next the open circuited terminals be shorted (Fig. E6.95(*b*)).

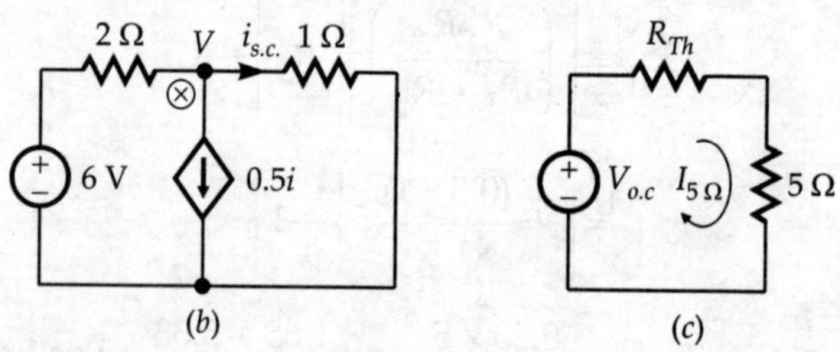

Fig. E6.95

Here, $$i_{s.c} + 0.5\, i_{s.c} = \frac{6 - V}{2} \qquad ...(a)$$

[Assuming the potential at (*x*) *node* to be + *V* volts]

But $V = i_{s.c} \times 1$ V

∴ From (*a*),

$$i_{s.c} + 0.5\, i_{s.c} = \frac{6 - i_{s.c}}{2}$$

or, $2 i_{s.c} = 3$ *i.e.*, $i_{s.c} = 1.5$ A.

This gives

$$R_{Th} = \frac{V_{o.c}}{i_{s.c}} = \frac{6}{1.5} = 4\,\Omega$$

Obviously, from the Thevenin's equivalent circuit of Fig. E6.95(*c*),

$$I_{5\Omega} = \frac{V_{o.c}}{R_{Th}+5} = \frac{6}{4+5} = \frac{2}{3} \textbf{ A.}$$

EXAMPLE 6.96 *Find the internal resistance of the circuit given in Fig. E6.96 looking back to the circuit removing r_L.*

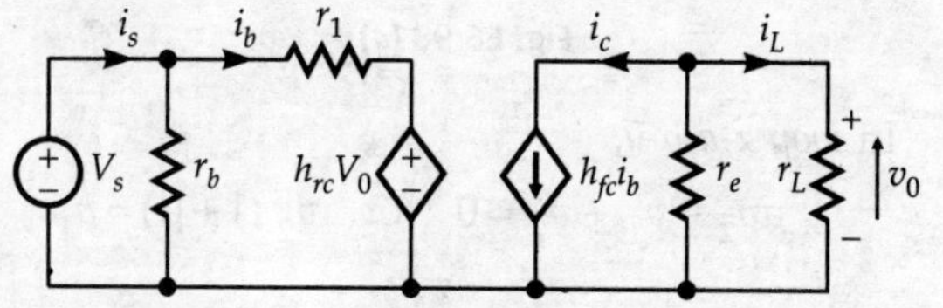

Fig. E6.96

SOLUTION. Let r_L be replaced by a dc driving voltage source v_{dc} while the source V_s is deactivated (Fig. E6.96(*a*)).

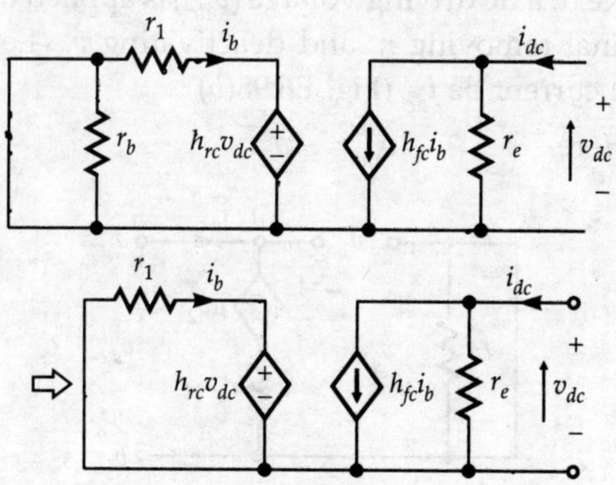

Fig. E6.96 (*a*)

Here, $\quad i_b = -\dfrac{h_{rc}\,v_{dc}}{r_1}$ (in the *left loop*)

Applying KCL at *node* (*x*),

$$i_{dc} = \frac{V_{dc}}{r_e} + h_{fc}\,i_b$$

or, $$i_{dc} = \frac{v_{dc}}{r_e} + h_{fc}\left(-\frac{h_{rc}\,v_{dc}}{r_1}\right)$$

$$= \frac{v_{dc}}{r_e} - \frac{h_{fc}\,h_{rc}\,v_{dc}}{r_1}$$

$$= v_{dc}\left[\frac{1}{r_e} - \frac{h_{fc}\,h_{rc}}{r_1}\right]$$

$$\therefore \quad R_{Th} = \frac{v_{dc}}{i_{dc}} = \frac{\mathbf{1}}{\dfrac{\mathbf{1}}{r_e} - \dfrac{h_{fc}\,h_{rc}}{r_1}}.$$

EXAMPLE 6.97 *Using Thevenin's Theorem, find the power loss in R_L if R_L is 10 Ω (Fig. E6.97).*

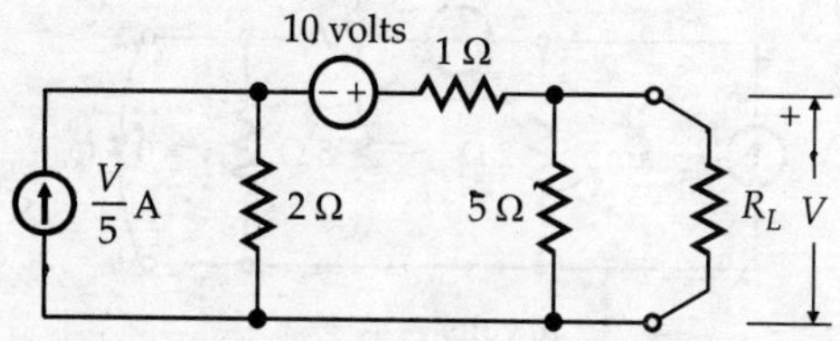

Fig. E6.97

SOLUTION. Let us replace R_L by open circuit and nodes are identified as shown in Fig. E6.97(*a*).

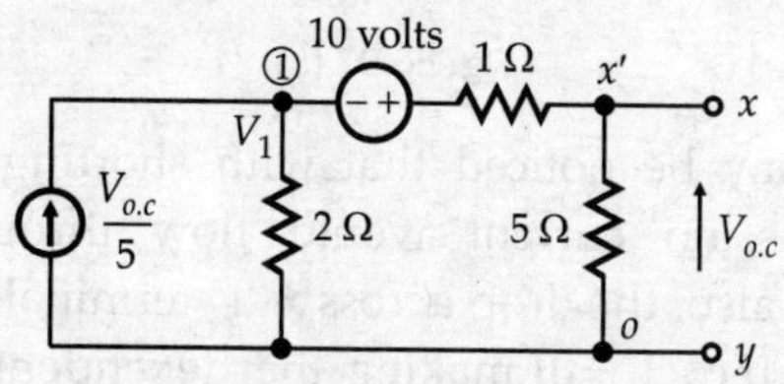

Fig. E6.97 (*a*)

At *node (1)*, nodal analysis gives

$$-\frac{V_{o.c}}{5} + \frac{V_1}{2} + \frac{V_1+10}{1+5} = 0$$

or, $\quad -0.2\,V_{o.c} + 0.5\,V_1 + 0.17\,V_1 + 1.67 = 0$

or, $\quad V_{o.c} = 2.5\,V_1 + 0.85\,V_1 + 8.35$

or, $\quad V_{o.c} = (3.35\,V_1 + 8.35) \qquad$ ...(1)

However, observation reveals that

$$V_{o.c} = \frac{V_1+10}{1+5} \times 5$$

[∵ in branch (1) – *x*′ – 0, current being $\left(\dfrac{V_1+10}{1+5}\right)$ A, the drop across 5 Ω resistor is $\left(\dfrac{V_1+10}{1+5} \times 5\right)$ volts which is $V_{o.c}$]

or, $\quad V_{o.c} = 0.833\,(V_1 + 10)$

or, $\quad 0.833\,V_1 = V_{o.c} - 8.33$

or, $\quad V_1 = \dfrac{V_{o.c} - 8.33}{0.833} \qquad$ ...(2)

Using (2) in (1),

$$V_{o.c} = 3.35 \,.\, \frac{V_{o.c} - 8.33}{0.833} + 8.35$$

$$= 4.02\,V_{o.c} - 33.5 + 8.35$$

or, $\quad V_{o.c} = 6.26$ V

CHAPTER 6

To find R_{int} [$= R_{Th}$], the output terminals are shorted (Fig. E6.97(*b*)).

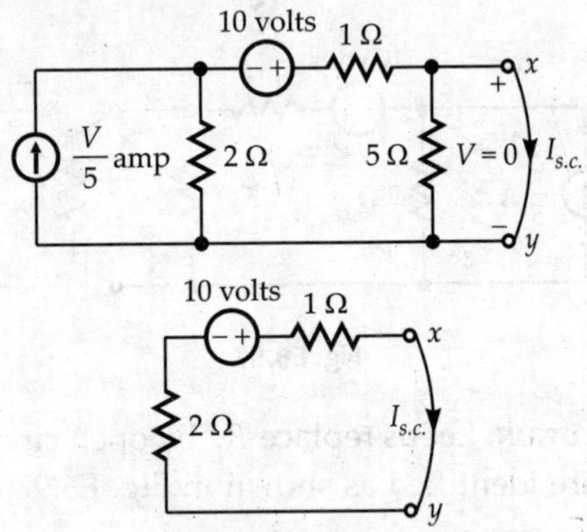

Fig. E6.97 (*b*)

It may be noticed that with shorting of x-y terminals no current would flow through 5Ω resistor; also, the drop across x-y terminals would be zero [*i.e.*, $V = 0$] making the dependent source strength $\left(\frac{V}{5}\right)$ A to be zero (Fig. E6.97(*b*)).

$$\therefore \quad I_{s.c} = \frac{10}{3} = 3.33 \text{ A.}$$

Then, the internal resistance would be

$$R_{int} = \frac{V_{o.c}}{I_{s.c}} = \frac{6.26}{3.33} = 1.88\,\Omega$$

Figure E6.97(*c*) represents the Thevenin's equivalent circuit.

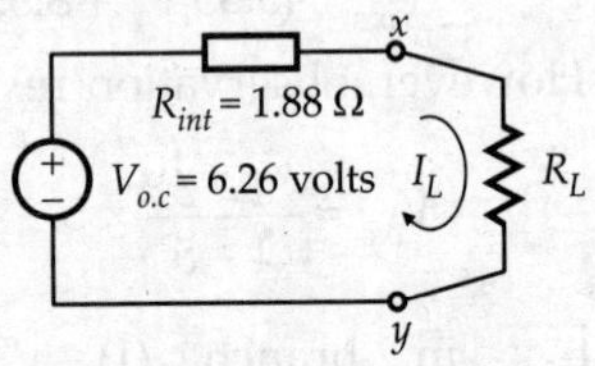

Fig. E6.97 (*c*)

Here I_L, the current through R_L is given by

$$I_L = \frac{V_{o.c}}{R_{int} + R_L} = \frac{6.26}{1.88 + 10} = 0.53 \text{ A}$$

$$\therefore \; P_L \text{ (power loss in } R_L) = I_L^2 \, R_L = (0.53)^2 \times 10$$

$$= \mathbf{2.78\ W.}$$

EXAMPLE 6.98 *Find the current through r_L in the circuit of Fig. E6.98 using Thevenin's theorem.*

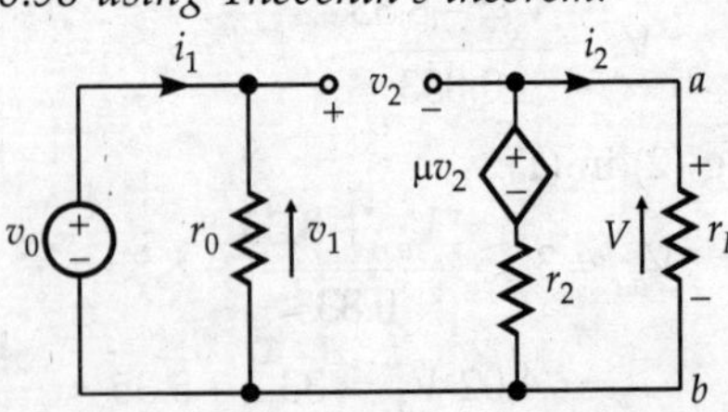

Fig. E6.98

SOLUTION. Let r_L be removed. The open circuit voltage across a-b is then μv_2 (Fig. E6.98(*a*)).

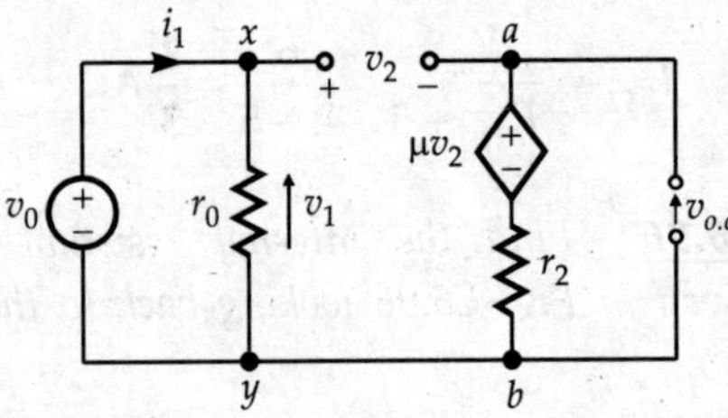

Fig. E6.98 (*a*)

In *loop x-a-b-y*,

$$\mu v_2 - v_1 + v_2 = 0 \quad \text{or} \quad v_2\,(1 + \mu) = v_1$$

$$\therefore \qquad v_2 = \frac{v_1}{1 + \mu}$$

$$\text{Thus} \qquad v_{o.c} = \mu v_2 = \frac{\mu v_1}{1 + \mu}$$

Next, a dc driving voltage (v_{dc}) is applied at a-b terminal removing r_L and deactivating v_0. Let the input current be i_{dc} (Fig. E6.98(*b*)).

$$\text{Here,} \qquad v_{dc} = -v_2.$$

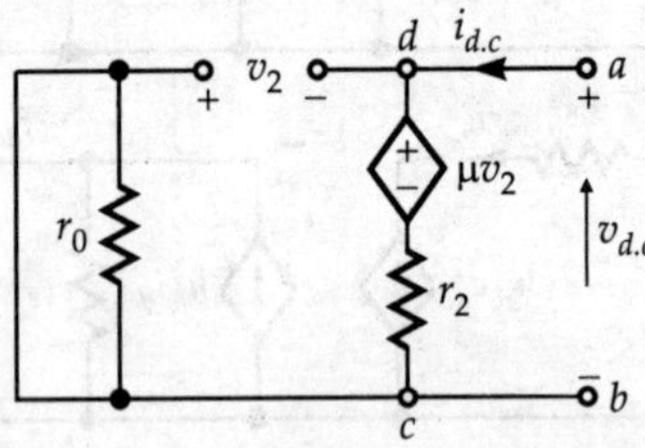

Fig. E6.98 (*b*)

In *loop a-d-c-b*,

$$v_{dc} = \mu v_2 + i_{dc}\, r_2 = -\mu v_{dc} + i_{dc}\, r_2$$

i.e.,
$$v_{dc}\,(1 + \mu) = i_{dc}\, r_2$$

or
$$\frac{v_{dc}}{i_{dc}} = R_{int} = \frac{r_2}{1 + \mu}.$$

Thevenin's equivalent circuit is then drawn in Fig. E6.98(*c*),

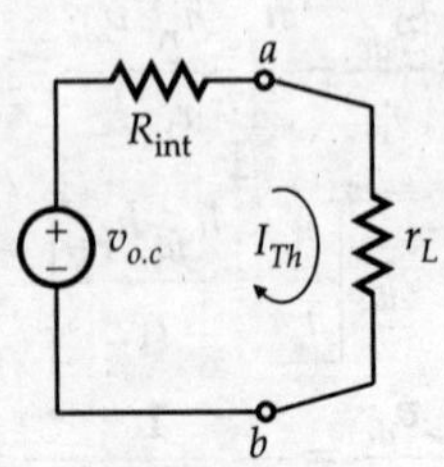

Fig. E6.98 (*c*)

where, $R_{\text{int}} = \dfrac{r_2}{1+\mu}$

$$v_{o.c} = v_{Th} = \mu \frac{v_1}{1+\mu}.$$

Obviously,

$$I_{Th} = \frac{v_{o.c}}{R_{\text{int}} + r_L} = \frac{\dfrac{\mu v_1}{1+\mu}}{\dfrac{r_2}{1+\mu} + r_L} = \frac{\mu v_1}{r_2 + r_L\,(1+\mu)}.$$

Example 6.99 *Assuming the op-amp to be ideal, find the input impedance of the op-amp shown in Fig. E6.99.*

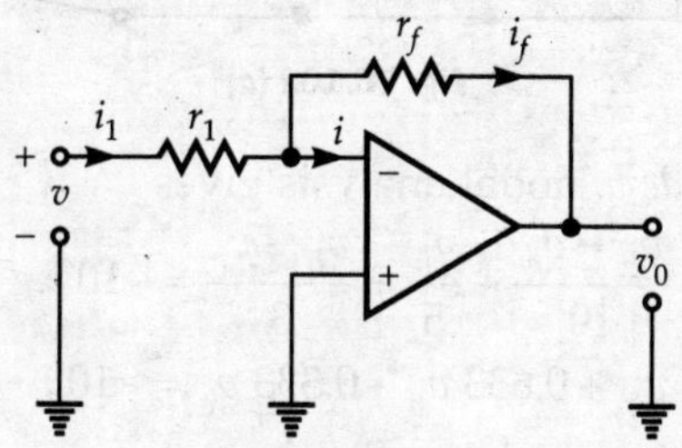

Fig. E6.99

Solution. Since the op-amp is ideal, the inverting terminal is a virtual ground and hence,

$$v = i_1\, r_1 + 0$$

Hence $\quad Z_{in} = \dfrac{v}{i_1} = \boldsymbol{r_1}.$

Example 6.100 *Find Z_{input} of the unity follower circuit shown in Fig. E6.100 (Assume the input resistance across the input terminals to be r_{in} and $|v_0 / v_1| = A_v$).*

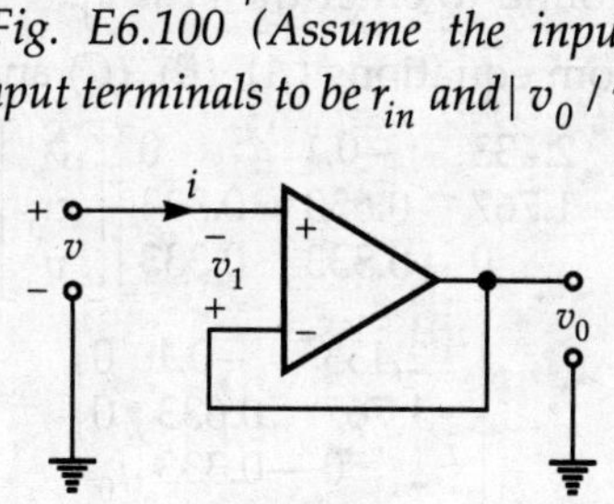

Fig. E6.100

Solution. Here

$$v = ir_{in} + v_0$$

or, $\quad v = ir_{in} - v_1 A_v$

[$\because$ polarity of v_1 is reverse]

or, $\quad v = ir_{in} - (ir_{in}) A_v$

$$= ir_{in}\,(1 - A_v)$$

$\therefore \quad Z_{in} = \dfrac{v}{i} = \boldsymbol{r_{in}\,(1 - A_v)}.$

Example 6.101 *Find Thevenin's equivalent circuit for the network shown in Fig. E6.101 at the left of terminals x-y.*

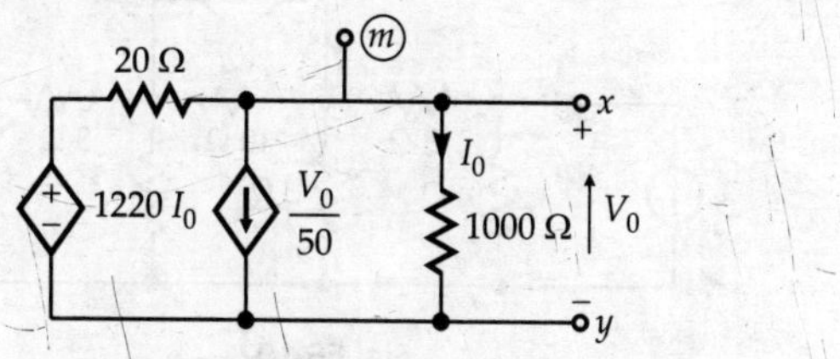

Fig. E6.101

Solution. Since the given circuit does not have any independent source, to find R_{Th} (the internal resistance of the network looking back through x-y), 1 A source is connected across x-y as shown in Fig. E6.101(a).

At *node* (m), nodal analysis reveals

$$1 = \frac{V_0 - 1220\, I_0}{20} + \frac{V_0}{50} + \frac{V_0}{1000} \qquad \text{...(1)}$$

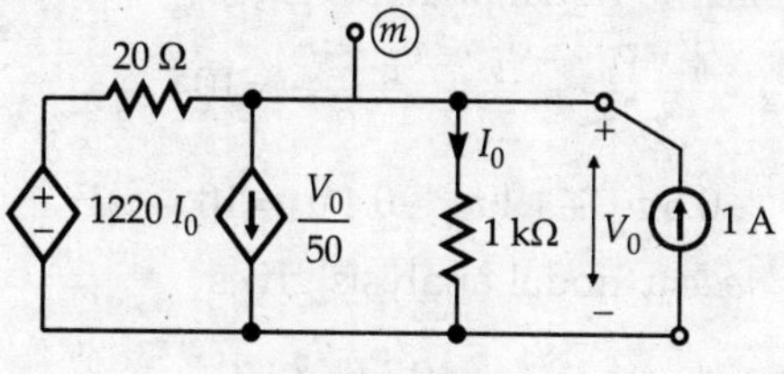

Fig. E6.101 (a)

However,

$$I_0 = \frac{V_0}{1000} \qquad \text{...(2)}$$

Thus, utilising (2) in (1),

$$1 - \frac{V_0}{50} = \frac{V_0}{1000} + \frac{V_0 - 1.22\, V_0}{20}$$

or, $\quad 1 - 0.02\, V_0 = 0.001\, V_0 - 0.011\, V_0$

$\therefore \quad V_0 = \dfrac{1}{0.01} = 100\ \text{V}$

and $\quad R_{Th} = \dfrac{V_0}{1} = \dfrac{100}{1} = 100\,\Omega$

Figure E6.101(b) represents the Thevenin's equivalent circuit with

$$V_{o.c} = V_0 = \mathbf{100\ V} \text{ and } R_{Th} = \mathbf{100\,\Omega}.$$

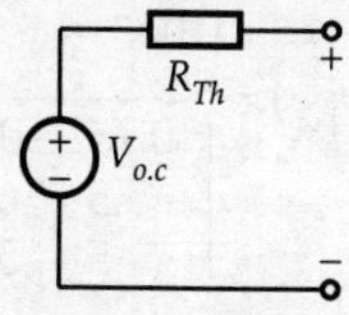

Fig. E6.101 (b)

CHAPTER 6

EXAMPLE 6.102 *Find the Thevenin's equivalent of the network shown in Fig. E6.102.*

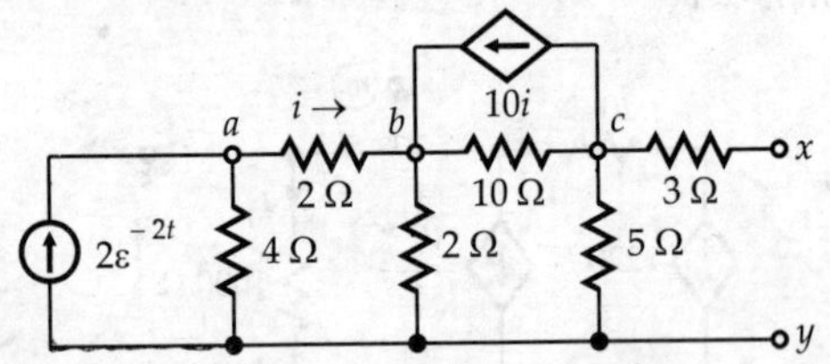

Fig. E6.102

SOLUTION. Let the open circuit voltage across $x-y$ terminals be $V_{o.c}$ (*i.e.*, the Thevenin's voltage). Let us designate the nodes as *a*, *b*, *c* in the given figure and the nodal voltages be v_a, v_b and v_c. Obviously $v_c \equiv V_{o.c}$ *i.e.*, the Thevenin's voltage.

$$\frac{v_a}{4}+\frac{v_a-v_b}{2}=2\varepsilon^{-2t}$$

or, $$0.75\,v_a-0.5\,v_b=2\varepsilon^{-2t} \quad ...(1)$$

At *node b*, nodal analysis gives

$$\frac{v_b-v_a}{2}+\frac{v_b}{2}+\frac{v_b-v_c}{10}=10\,i$$

or, $$-0.5\,v_a+1.1\,v_b-0.1\,v_c=10\,i \quad ...(2)$$

At *node c*, nodal analysis gives

$$\frac{v_c-v_b}{10}+10\,i+\frac{v_c}{5}=0$$

or, $$-0.1\,v_b+0.3\,v_c=-10\,i \quad ...(3)$$

Putting these equations in matrix form,

$$\begin{bmatrix}0.75 & -0.5 & 0\\ -0.5 & 1.1 & -0.1\\ 0 & -0.1 & 0.3\end{bmatrix}\begin{bmatrix}v_a\\ v_b\\ v_c\end{bmatrix}=\begin{bmatrix}2\varepsilon^{-2t}\\ 10\,i\\ -10\,i\end{bmatrix} \quad ...(4)$$

However, inspection reveals that

$$i=\frac{v_a-v_b}{2}=0.5\,v_a-0.5\,v_b \quad ...(5)$$

Utilising (5) in (4), we get

$$\begin{bmatrix}0.75 & -0.5 & 0\\ -5.5 & 6.1 & -0.1\\ +5 & -5.1 & 0.3\end{bmatrix}\begin{bmatrix}v_a\\ v_b\\ v_c\end{bmatrix}=\begin{bmatrix}2\varepsilon^{-2t}\\ 0\\ 0\end{bmatrix}$$

Thus, $$v_c\,(=v_{o.c})=\frac{\begin{vmatrix}0.75 & -0.5 & 2\varepsilon^{-2t}\\ 5.5 & 6.1 & 0\\ 5 & -5.1 & 0\end{vmatrix}}{\begin{vmatrix}0.75 & -0.5 & 0\\ -5.5 & 6.1 & -0.1\\ 5 & -5.1 & 0.3\end{vmatrix}}$$

$$=-\mathbf{282.1\,\varepsilon^{-2t}\ V.}$$

To find the internal resistance, a current source of i_0 is applied at the $x-y$ terminals of the given network (Fig. E6.102(*a*)) deactivating the fixed sources. At *node* a, nodal analysis reveals,

$$\frac{v_a}{6}+\frac{v_a}{2}+\frac{v_a-v_b}{10}=10\,i$$

or, $$0.767\,v_a-0.1\,v_b=10\,i \quad ...(A)$$

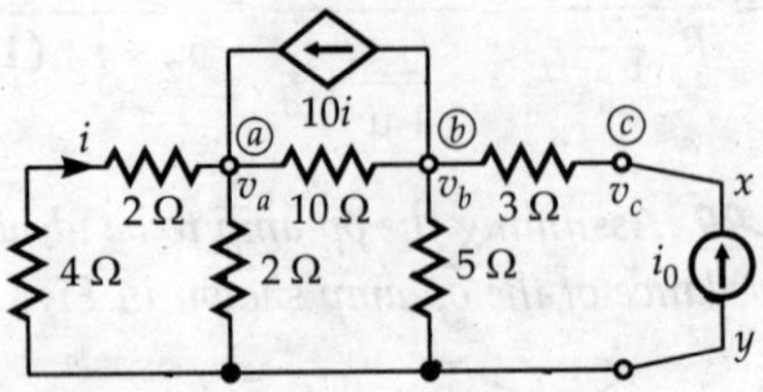

Fig. E6.102 (*a*)

At *node b*, nodal analysis gives

$$\frac{v_b-v_a}{10}+\frac{v_b}{5}+\frac{v_b-v_c}{3}=-10\,i$$

or, $$-0.1\,v_a+0.633\,v_b-0.333\,v_c=-10\,i \quad ...(B)$$

At *node c*, nodal analysis gives,

$$\frac{v_c-v_b}{3}=i_0$$

or, $$-0.333\,v_b-0.333\,v_c=i_0 \quad ...(C)$$

But $$i=-\frac{v_a}{4+2}$$

or, $$i=-0.167\,v_a \quad ...(D)$$

[as seen from the *left loop* of Fig. 6.102(*a*), current is –ve as it is found to enter the *node a*].

Thus from equations (*A*), (*B*), (*C*) and (*D*),

we get $$\begin{bmatrix}2.433 & -0.1 & 0\\ -1.767 & 0.633 & -0.333\\ 0 & -0.333 & 0.333\end{bmatrix}\begin{bmatrix}v_a\\ v_b\\ v_c\end{bmatrix}=\begin{bmatrix}0\\ 0\\ i_0\end{bmatrix}$$

$$\therefore\quad v_c=\frac{\begin{vmatrix}2.433 & -0.1 & 0\\ -1.767 & 0.633 & 0\\ 0 & -0.333 & i_0\end{vmatrix}}{\begin{vmatrix}2.433 & -0.1 & 0\\ -1.767 & 0.633 & -0.333\\ 0 & -0.333 & 0.333\end{vmatrix}}=7.4\,i_0$$

$$\therefore\quad R_{\text{int}}\ (=\text{Thevenin's resistance})=\frac{v_c}{i_0}=\mathbf{7.4\,\Omega.}$$

Thevenin's equivalent circuit is drawn in Fig. E6.102(*b*).

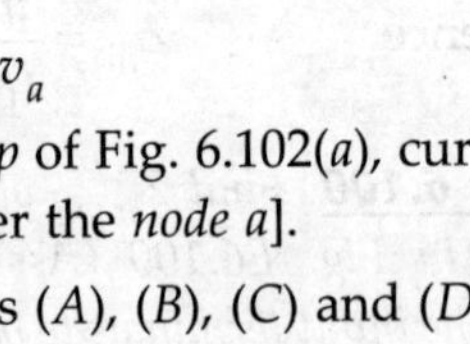

Fig. E6.102 (*b*)

EXAMPLE 6.103 *In the circuit shown in Fig E6.103, find the Norton's equivalent circuit at the left of terminals x-y.*

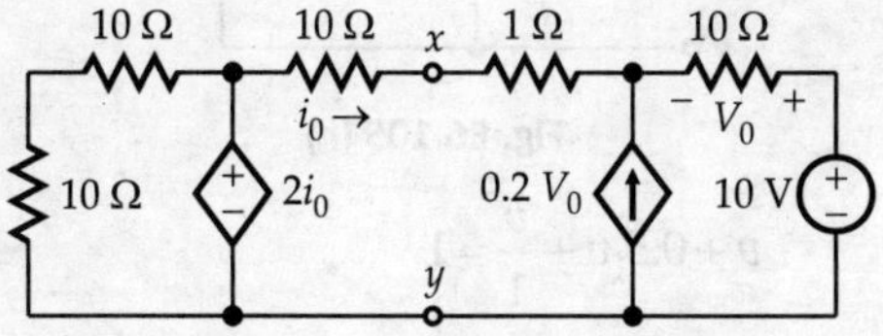

Fig. E6.103

SOLUTION. Since Norton's equivalent of the left of terminals $x-y$ of Fig. E6.103 is wanted, the right part of the given circuit does not have any significance. Let us now delete the right part of the given circuit and a 1 A current source is applied across $x-y$ as shown in Fig. E6.103(*a*).

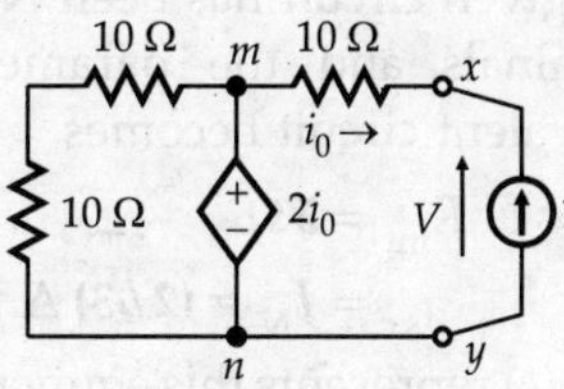

Fig. E6.103 (*a*)

Applying KVL at the *loop m-x-y-n*

$$-2i_0 + 10\,i_0 + V = 0$$

[Assuming the potential across $x-y$ to be V volts]

or, $\quad V = -8i_0 \qquad$ ...(*i*)

Since in branch *mx*,

$$i_0 = -1\text{ A}$$

[1 A source being fed back to the circuit at *x*]

$\therefore \quad V = +8\text{ V}$

Thus, internal resistance $R_{\text{int}} = \dfrac{V}{1} = 8$ ohms.

Also, with no independent source at the left of terminal of $x-y$, shorting of terminal $x-y$ to find $I_{s.c}$ will lead to the fact that

$$I_{s.c} = 0.$$

Thus the Norton's equivalent circuit at the left of $x-y$ exhibits that

$$\boldsymbol{I_{s.c.} = 0 \text{ and } R_{int} = 8\,\Omega.}$$

EXAMPLE 6.104 *Find Norton's equivalent circuit at the left of terminals a-b for the circuit given in Fig. E6.104.*

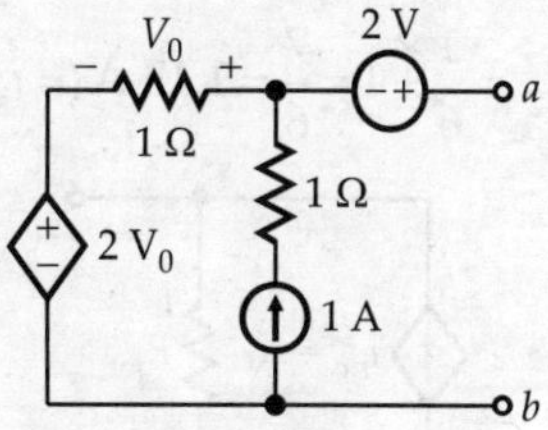

Fig. E6.104

SOLUTION. Let us first apply a d.c. voltage source v_{dc} at $a-b$ deactivating constant sources (Fig. E6.104(*a*)).

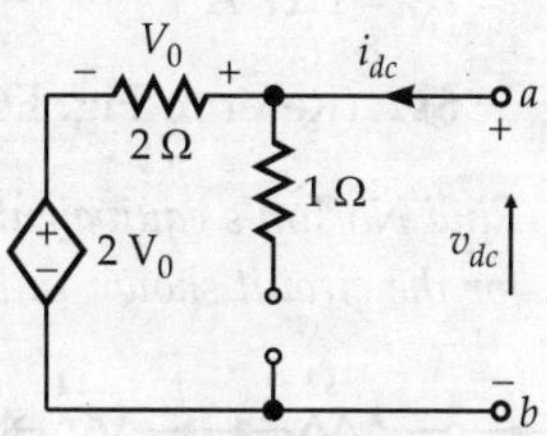

Fig. E6.104 (*a*)

Here, $\quad v_{dc} = 2i_{dc} - 2V_0$

But $\quad V_0 = 2i_{dc}$

Thus we get $\quad v_{dc} = 2i_{dc} + 2\times 2\, i_{dc} = 6\, i_{dc}$

This gives $\quad R_{\text{int}} = \dfrac{v_{dc}}{i_{dc}} = 6\,\Omega.$

Let us now apply a short circuit at $a-b$ (Fig. E6.104(*b*)).

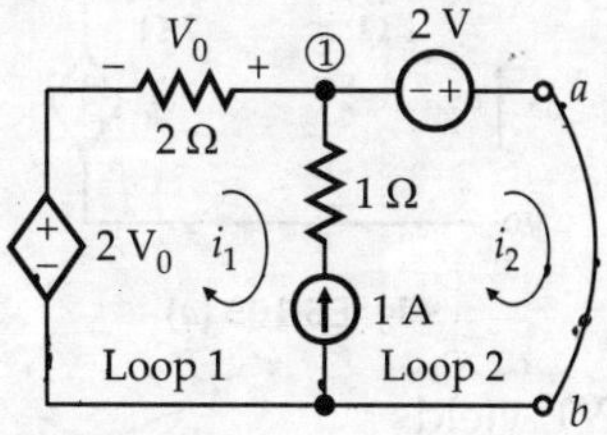

Fig. E6.104 (*b*)

Application of KVL at *loop-1* yields,

$$-2V_0 - V_0 + 1(i_1 - i_2) = 0 \qquad ...(1)$$

But observation yields $\quad i_1 - i_2 = -1$ A.

$\therefore$ From (1), $\quad -3V_0 - 1 = 0 \;$ *i.e.* $\; V_0 = -\dfrac{1}{3}$ V

However, *in loop-1*, $\quad V_0 = -(i_1)\times 2$

This gives $\quad i_1 = \dfrac{1}{6}$ A.

Again, at *node (1)*,

$$i_1 + 1 = i_2\ ;$$

i.e., $$i_2 = \frac{1}{6} + 1 = \frac{7}{6} = 1.17\ \text{A}\,(= i_{s.c})$$

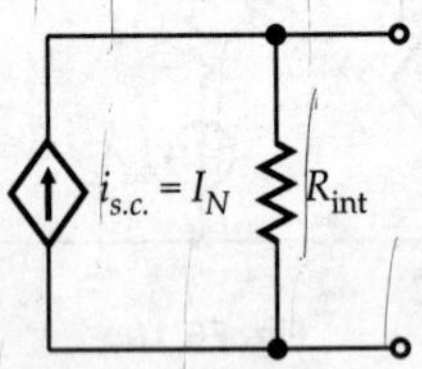

Fig. E6.104 (c)

Norton's equivalent is thus obtained with

$$i_{s.c} = I_N = \mathbf{1.17\ A}$$

$$R_{int} = \mathbf{6\,\Omega}\ \text{(Refer to Fig. E6.104(}c\text{)).}$$

EXAMPLE 6.105 *Find Norton's equivalent to the right of terminals $x-y$ for the circuit shown in Fig. E6.105.*

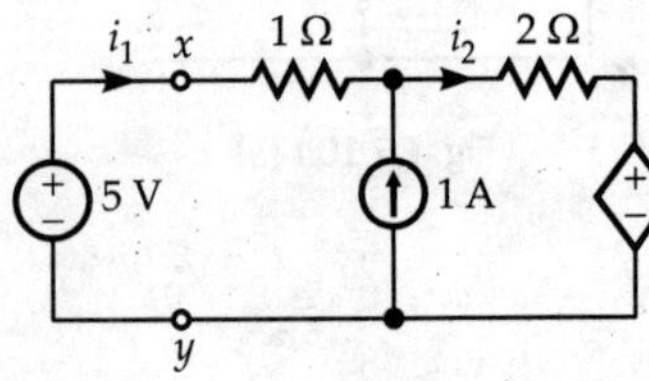

Fig. E6.105

SOLUTION. Let us first remove the source (5 V) from $x-y$ terminal and a driving voltage v_{dc} is applied, 1 A constant current source being deactivated (Fig. E6.105(*a*)).

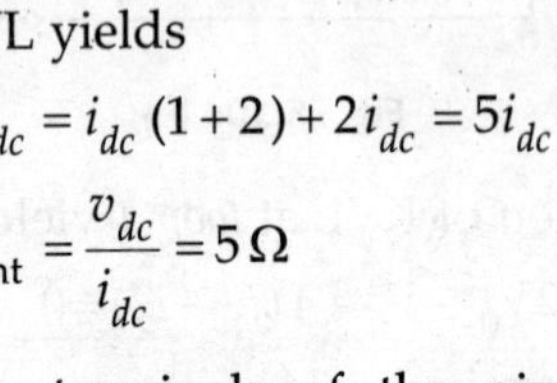

Fig. E6.105 (a)

Here, KVL yields

$$v_{dc} = i_{dc}(1+2) + 2i_{dc} = 5i_{dc}$$

$$\therefore\quad R_{int} = \frac{v_{dc}}{i_{dc}} = 5\,\Omega$$

Next, *x-y* terminals of the given circuit is shorted (Fig. E6.105(*b*)). Assuming *node voltage at (1)* to be $+\,v$, nodal analysis at (1) gives

$$i_{s.c} + i_2 = 1\ \text{A}$$

or, $$\frac{v}{1} + \frac{v - 2i_{s.c}}{2} = 1$$

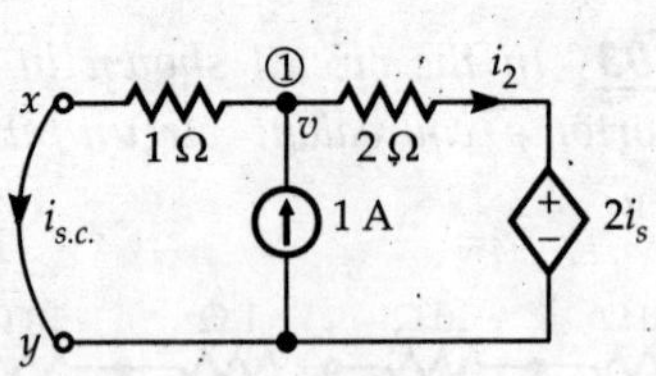

Fig. E6.105 (b)

or, $$v + 0.5\,v + \frac{v}{1} = 1$$

[$\because$ in Fig. E6.105(*b*), $i_{s.c} = -\frac{v}{1}$ and noting that the direction of $i_{s.c}$ in Fig. E6.105(*b*) is opposite to that (i_1) in Fig. E6.105]

or, $$v = \frac{2}{3}\ \text{V}.$$

This gives $$|i_{s.c}| = \frac{v}{1} = \frac{2}{3}\ \text{A}$$

Thus, the given circuit has been Nortonised at the said terminals and the parameters of the Norton's equivalent circuit becomes

$$R_{int} = \mathbf{5\,\Omega}$$

$$i_{s.c} = I_N = \mathbf{(2/3)\ A.}$$

Fig. E6.105(*c*) represents this equivalent circuit.

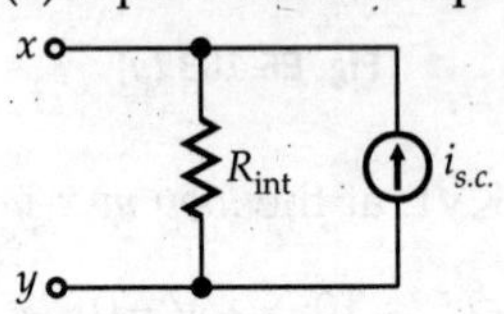

Fig. E6.105 (c)

EXAMPLE 6.106 *Find Norton's equivalent across x-y for the circuit shown in Fig. E6.106.*

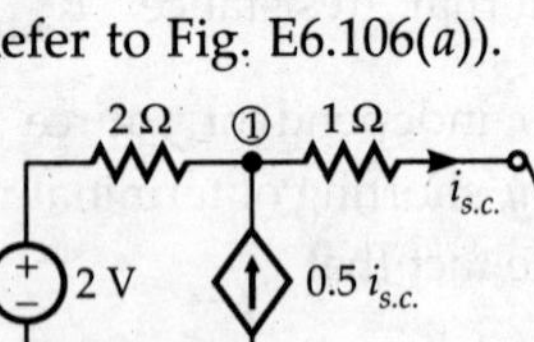

Fig. E6.106

SOLUTION. Let us first short circuit across $x-y$ in Fig. E6.106 (Refer to Fig. E6.106(*a*)).

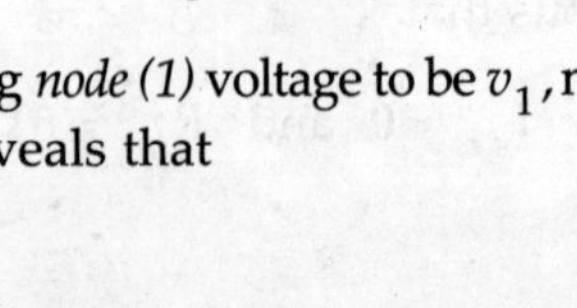

Fig. E6.106 (a)

Assuming *node (1)* voltage to be v_1, nodal analysis at *node (1)* reveals that

$$\frac{v_1 - 2}{2} + i_{s.c} = 0.5\, i_{s.c}$$

or, $\quad 0.5\, v_1 - 1 + 0.5\, i_{s.c} = 0 \qquad \ldots(1)$

But $\quad i_{s.c} = \frac{v_1}{1} = v_1$ A

$\therefore$ From (1),

$$0.5\, i_{s.c} - 1 + 0.5\, i_{s.c} = 0$$

or, $\quad i_{s.c} = 1$ A

Let us now open x-y (Fig. E6.106(b)) $i_x = 0$ giving the value of the dependent source ($0.5\, i_x$) to be zero too.

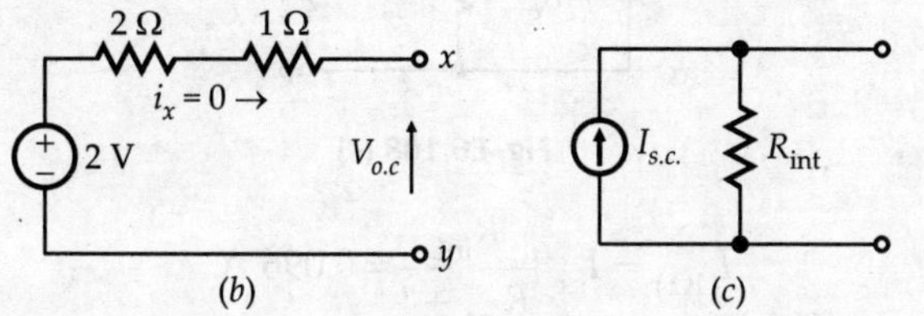

Fig. E6.106

$\therefore \quad v_{o.c} = 2$ V

Hence $\quad R_{int} = \frac{v_{o.c}}{i_{s.c}} = \frac{2}{1} = 2\,\Omega$

We have thus obtained Norton's equivalent circuit where,

$$i_{s.c} = \mathbf{I_N = 1\,A}; \; R_{int} = \mathbf{2\,\Omega}.$$

Figure E6.106(c) represents the Norton's equivalent circuit.

EXAMPLE 6.107 *Find Norton's equivalent of the circuit shown in Fig. E6.107 at the left of x-y terminals.*

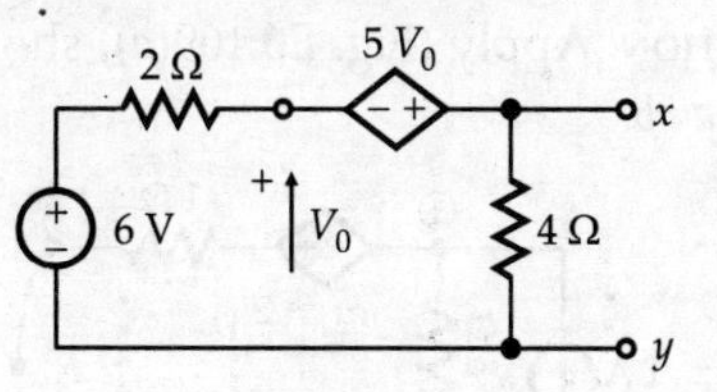

Fig. E6.107

SOLUTION. Let x-y be shorted (Fig. E6.107(a)). $I_{s.c}$ being the circulating current through the *loop*,

$$V_0 = 6 - 2\, I_{s.c} \qquad \ldots(1)$$

Applying KVL in the same *loop*,

$$-6 + 2\, I_{s.c} - 5\, V_0 = 0$$

or, $\quad -6 + 2\, I_{s.c} - 5(6 - 2 I_{s.c}) = 0 \qquad$ [using (1)]

or, $\quad 12\, I_{s.c} = 36 \;\therefore\; I_{s.c} (= I_N) = 3$ A.

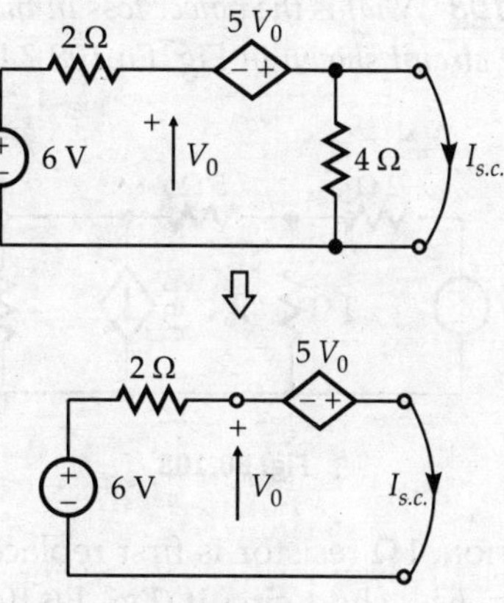

Fig. E6.107 (a)

Let us now remove the short circuit and keep x-y open (Refer to Fig. E6.107(b)). Applying KVL in *loop a-b-c-d*.

$$4\, i + 5\, V_0 + V_0 = 0$$

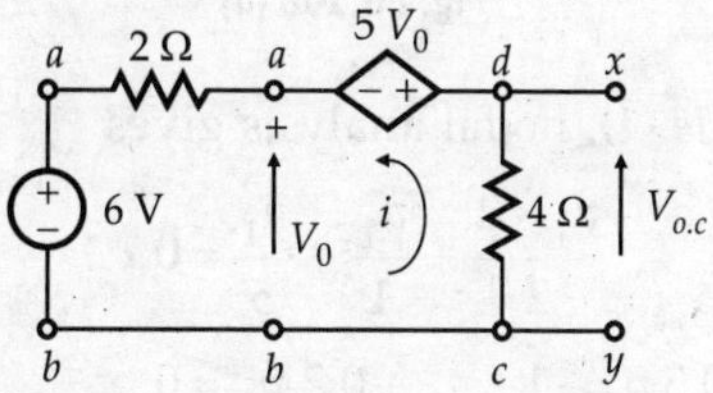

Fig. E6.107 (b)

But $\quad V_0 = 2i + 6 \qquad \left[\because\; i = \frac{V_0 - 6}{2}\text{ A}\right]$

Thus finally, we get

$$4i + 5(2i + 6) + 2i + 6 = 0$$

or $\quad 16\, i = -36 \;$ *i.e.*, $\; i = -\frac{36}{16}$ A

This gives $\quad V_{o.c} = -4i = 4 \times \frac{36}{16} = 9$ V

Hence, $\quad R_{int} = \frac{V_{o.c}}{I_{s.c}} = \frac{9}{3} = 3\,\Omega$

The given circuit has thus been Nortonised with

$$R_{int} = \mathbf{3\,\Omega};\; I_{s.c} = \mathbf{I_N = 3\,A} \;\text{ [Fig. E6.107(}c\text{)].}$$

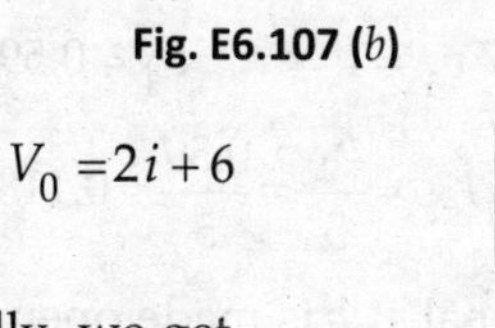

Fig. E6.107 (c)

CHAPTER 6

EXAMPLE 6.108 *What is the power loss in the 1 Ω resistor (R_L) of the circuit shown in Fig. E6.108 ? Use Norton's Theorem.*

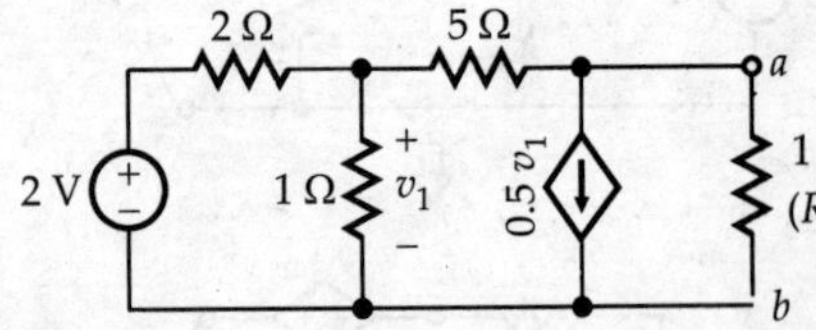

Fig. E6.108

SOLUTION. 1 Ω resistor is first replaced from the terminal $a-b$ by short circuit (Fig. E6.108(*a*)).

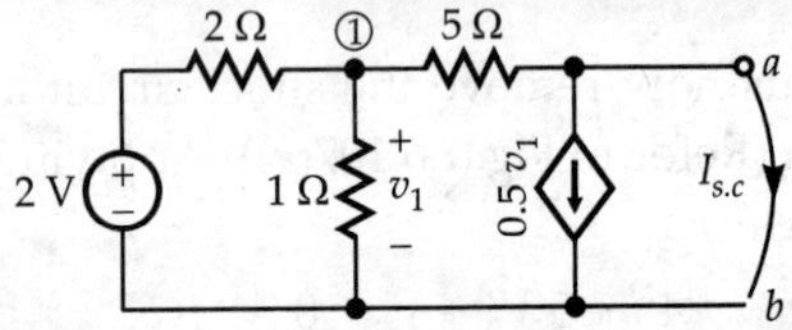

Fig. E6.108 (*a*)

At *node (1)*, nodal analysis gives

$$\frac{v_1-2}{2}+\frac{v_1}{1}+\frac{v_1}{5}=0$$

or, $$0.5\,v_1-1+v_1+0.2\,v_1=0$$

or, $$1.7\,v_1=1 \quad \therefore \quad v_1=0.59\text{ V}$$

Hence, $$I_{s.c}=\frac{v_1}{5}=\frac{0.59}{5}=0.118\text{ A}$$

Next, terminal $a-b$ is made open circuited (Fig. E6.108(*b*)) and a dc voltage v_{dc} is applied at $a-b$ terminal deactivating the independent sources.

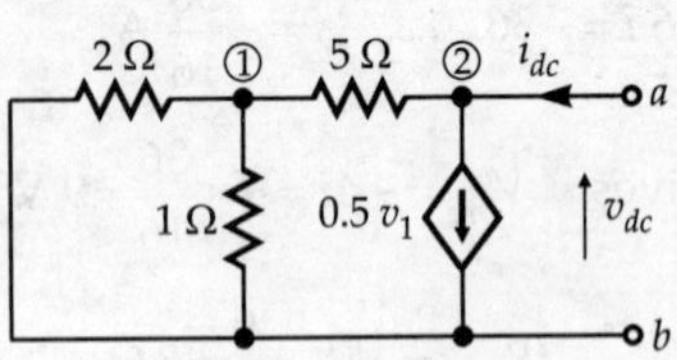

Fig. E6.108 (*b*)

Here, $$\frac{v_1}{2}+\frac{v_1}{1}+\frac{v_1-v_{dc}}{5}=0$$

or, $$0.5\,v_1+v_1+0.2\,v_1-0.2\,v_{dc}=0$$

or, $$1.7\,v_1=0.2\,v_{dc} \quad \therefore \quad v_1=0.1176\,v_{dc}$$

However, at *node (2)*,

$$i_{dc}=0.5\,v_1+\frac{v_{dc}-v_1}{5}$$

or, $$i_{dc}=0.5\,(0.1176\,v_{dc})+\frac{v_{dc}-0.1176\,v_{dc}}{5}$$

or, $$i_{dc}=0.059\,v_{dc}+0.2\,v_{dc}-0.024\,v_{dc}$$
$$=0.235\,v_{dc}$$

i.e., $$R_{\text{int}}=\frac{v_{dc}}{i_{dc}}=\frac{1}{0.235}=4.25\,\Omega$$

Norton's equivalent circuit being shown in Fig. E6.108(*c*),

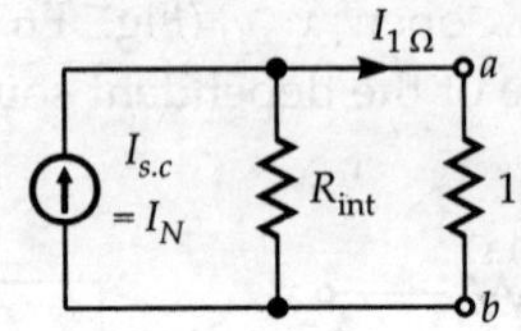

Fig. E6.108 (*c*)

$$I_{(1\Omega)}=I_{s.c}\,\frac{R_{\text{int}}}{R_{\text{int}}+1}=0.096\text{ A.}$$

$\therefore$ Power loss in 1 Ω resistor

$$=1\times(0.096)^2=\mathbf{0.00912\ W.}$$

EXAMPLE 6.109 *Find the Norton equivalent of the circuit shown in Fig. E6.109 at the left of terminals $a-b$. [$i_S=1\,A$, $r_1=5\,\Omega$, $\alpha=2$, $r_2=1\,\Omega$].*

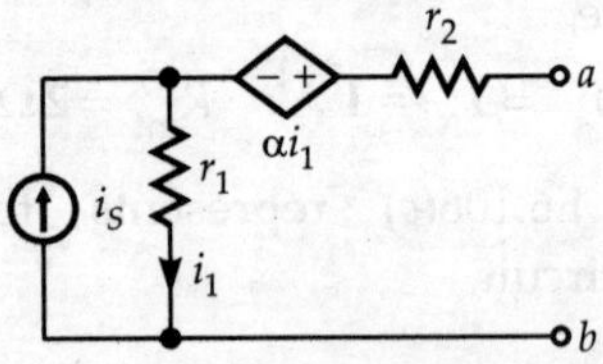

Fig. E6.109

SOLUTION. Apply (Fig. E6.109(*a*)) short circuit at terminal $a-b$.

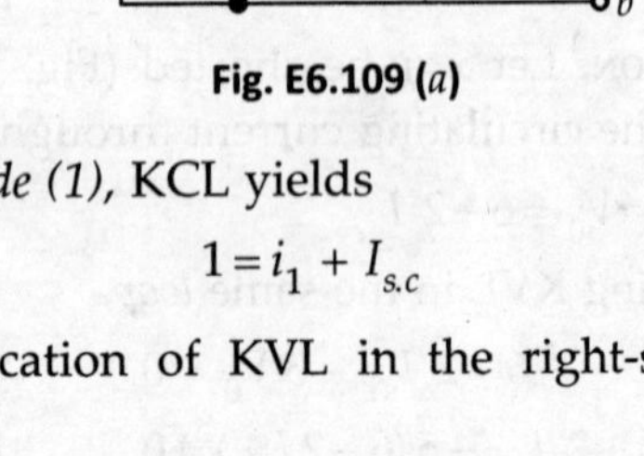

Fig. E6.109 (*a*)

At *node (1)*, KCL yields

$$1=i_1+I_{s.c} \qquad \text{...(1)}$$

Application of KVL in the right-sided loop yields

$$-2i_1+I_{s.c}\times 1-5i_1=0$$

or, $-2(1-I_{s.c.})+I_{s.c}-5(1-I_{s.c.})=0$

[using equation (1)]

or, $-2+2\,I_{s.c.}+I_{s.c.}-5+5\,I_{s.c.}=0$ ...(2)

or, $8\,I_{s.c.}=7$ *i.e.*, $I_{s.c.}=\dfrac{7}{8}$ A

Let us now keep $a-b$ open circuited such that $V_{o.c}$ is the open circuit voltage across $a-b$ (Fig. E6.109(*b*)).

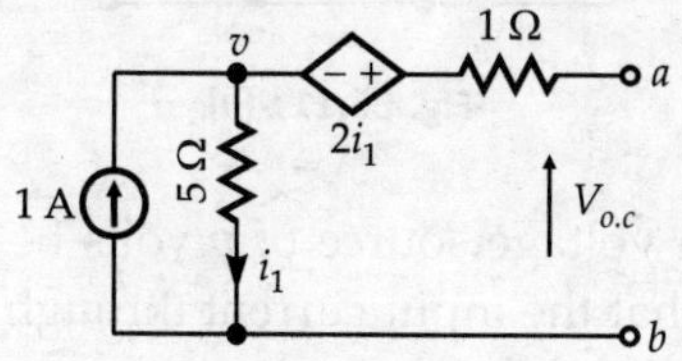

Fig. E6.109 (*b*)

Obviously,

$$v=i_1\times 5=5i_1=5\times 1=5\text{ V}$$

$$\therefore \quad V_{o.c}=v+2\,i_1=5+2\times 1=7\text{ V}$$

This gives $R_{\text{int}}=\dfrac{V_{o.c}}{I_{s.c}}=\dfrac{7}{\frac{7}{8}}=8\,\Omega.$

Norton's equivalent circuit is thus obtained where

$$I_N=\frac{7}{8}\text{ A};\quad R_{\text{int}}=8\,\Omega.$$

EXAMPLE 6.110 *Find Norton's equivalent for the network at the left of terminals 1-2 in Fig. E6.110.*

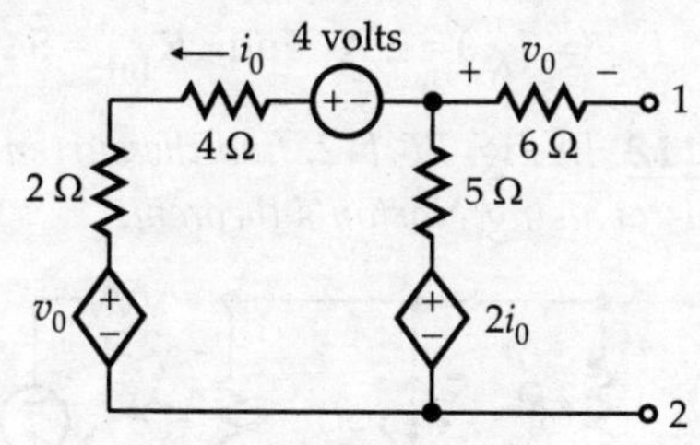

Fig. E6.110

SOLUTION. Let the loop currents be i and $i_{s.c.}$ as shown in Fig. E6.110(*a*) after short circuiting the contacts 1–2.

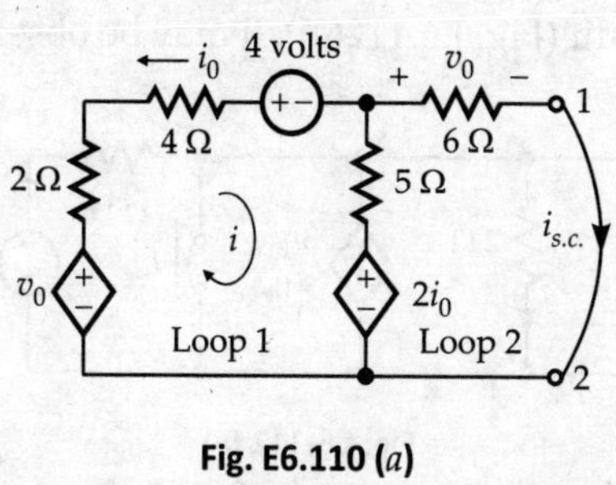

Fig. E6.110 (*a*)

In loop-1,

$$(4+2+5)\,i-5\,i_{s.c}=(v_0-2i_0-4)$$

or, $11\,i-5\,i_{s.c}=v_0-2i_0-4$ ...(1)

In loop-2, $11\,i_{s.c}-5\,i=2i_0$ ...(2)

But observation reveals

$$i_0=-\,i \quad ...(3)$$

and $v_0=6i_{s.c}$ ...(4)

Using (3) in (2),

$$11\,i_{s.c}-5(-i_0)=2i_0$$

or, $11\,i_{s.c}=-3\,i_0 \quad \therefore\ i_0=-\dfrac{11}{3}\,i_{s.c}$ ...(5)

Using (5), (4) and (3) in (1),

$$-11\left(-\frac{11}{3}\,i_{s.c}\right)-5\,i_{s.c}=6\,i_{s.c}-2\left(-\frac{11}{3}\,i_{s.c}\right)-4$$

or $\dfrac{121}{3}\,i_{s.c}-5\,i_{s.c}-6\,i_{s.c}-\dfrac{22}{3}\,i_{s.c}+4=0$

or, $22\,i_{s.c}=-4$

$$\therefore \quad i_{s.c}=-0.182\text{ A}$$

Thus, $i_{s.c}$ *i.e.*, Norton's equivalent current becomes −0.182 A. In order to find Norton's equivalent resistance of the network (*i.e.*, the internal resistance), let a voltage v be applied at 1–2 terminals removing the short circuit link (Fig. E6.110(*b*)). The 4 volts source is deactivated. Let the loop currents be i_1 and i_2.

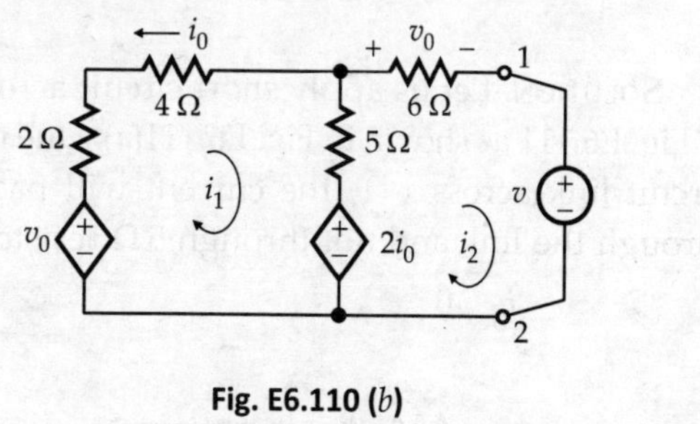

Fig. E6.110 (*b*)

Obviously for *left loop*,

$$11\,i_1-5\,i_2=v_0-2\,i_0 \quad ...(A)$$

and for the *right loop*,

$$11\,i_2-5\,i_1=2i_0-v \quad ...(B)$$

Also, $i_0=-\,i_1$ and $v_0=6i_2$

Thus we see for (A) and (B),

$$-11\,i_0-5i_2=v_0-2i_0=6i_2-2i_0$$

or, $-9i_0-11\,i_2=0$ ...(C)

Also from (B) we get

$$11\,i_2 - 5(-i_0) = 2\,i_0 - v$$

or, $\quad 11\,i_2 + 5i_0 - 2i_0 = -v$

or, $\quad 3i_0 + 11\,i_2 = -v \qquad$ ...(D)

However from (C), $\quad i_0 = -\dfrac{11}{9} i_2 \qquad$ ...(E)

Using (E) in (D), $\quad 3\left(-\dfrac{11}{9} i_2\right) + 11\,i_2 = -v$

or, $\quad -\dfrac{11}{3} i_2 + 11\,i_2 = -v \quad$ or $\quad v / i_2 = -7.4\,\Omega$

i.e., $\quad R_{int} = 7.4\,\Omega$

[Neglecting –ve sign; it may be noted that –ve sign implies that the current is opposite to the assumed +ve direction]

Thus, Norton's equivalent circuit is obtained where

$$\boldsymbol{I_N\ (= i_{s.c}) = -\,0.182\ A}$$

and $\quad \boldsymbol{R_N\ (= R_{int}) = 7.4\,\Omega}$.

EXAMPLE 6.111 *Obtain Norton's equivalent circuit across x - y in Fig. E6.111.*

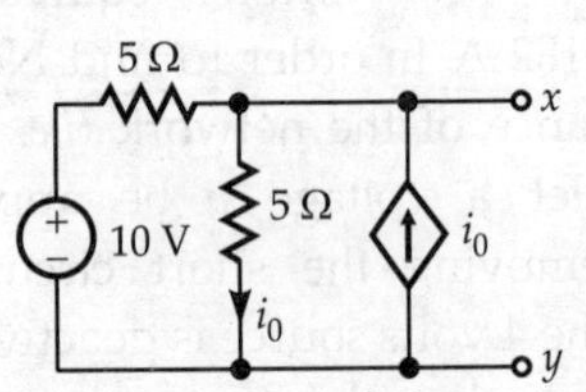

Fig. E6.111

SOLUTION. Let us apply short circuit across $x-y$ in Fig. E6.111 as shown in Fig. E6.111(*a*). Due to short circuit link across x - y, the current will pass only through the link and not through 5 Ω resistor (r_2).

$$\therefore \quad i_0 = 0$$

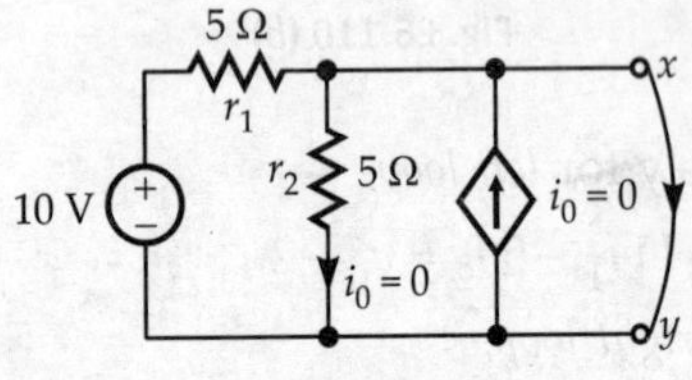

Fig. E6.111 (*a*)

This makes the dependent source to be zero.

$$\therefore \quad I_{s.c} = \frac{10\ \text{V}}{r_1\ \Omega} = 2\ \text{A}.$$

To find R_{int}, let us remove the short circuit link across x - y deactivating the 10 V source (Fig. E6.111(*b*)).

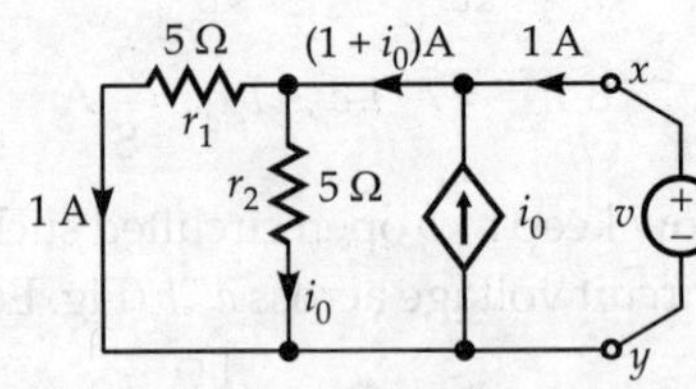

Fig. E6.111 (*b*)

Also, a voltage source of v volts be applied at x - y such that the input current through x terminal is 1 A into the circuit.

$$\therefore \quad v = 1\ \text{A} \times r_1 = 5\ \text{V}$$

[$\because$ i_0 flows only through r_2]

i.e., $\quad \dfrac{v\ \text{volts}}{1\ \text{A}} = R_{int} = 5\,\Omega$

Thus, it has been obtained that $R_{int} = 5\,\Omega$.

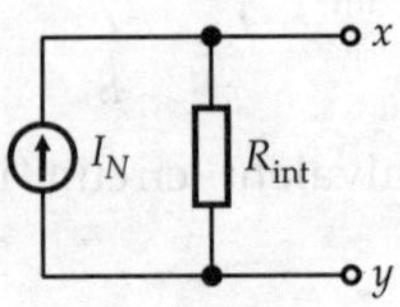

Fig. E6.111 (*c*)

Figure E6.111(*c*) represents the Norton's equivalent circuit where

$$\boldsymbol{I_{s.c}\ (= I_N) = 2\ A \quad \text{and} \quad R_{int} = 5\,\Omega.}$$

EXAMPLE 6.112 *In Fig. E6.112, find the current through the 1 Ω resistor using Norton's theorem.*

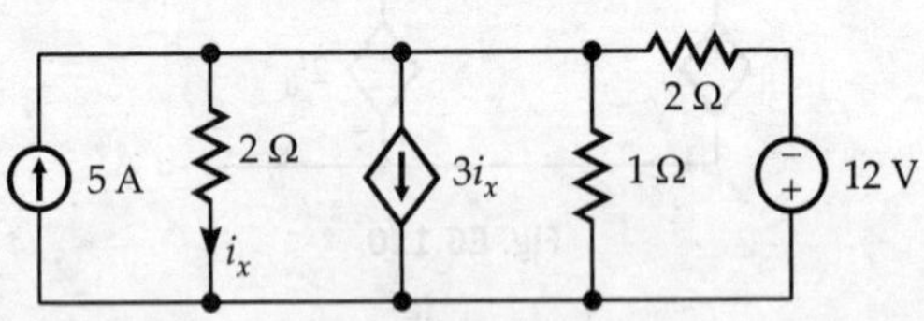

Fig. E6.112

SOLUTION. Let us first replace the 1 Ω resistor by short circuit (Fig. E6.112(*a*)). It may be observed that

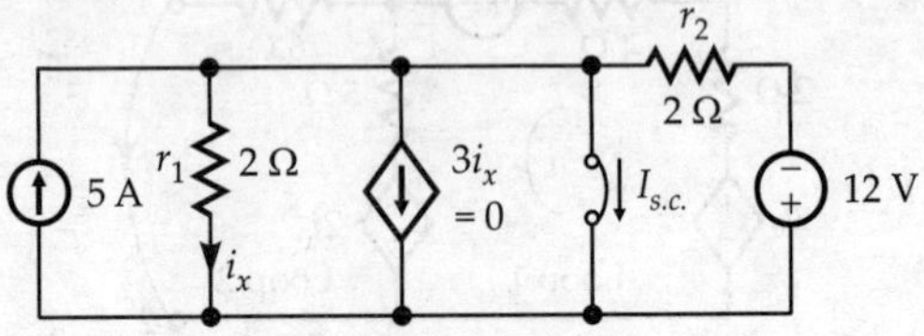

Fig. E6.112 (*a*)

due to the shorting link, there will be no current through the resistor r_1 in Fig. E6.112(*a*); *i.e.*, $i_x = 0$ making the magnitude of the dependent source zero. Thus the current through the shorting link ($I_{s.c}$) is given by

$$I_{s.c} = 5\text{ A} - \frac{12\text{ V}}{2\,\Omega} = -1\text{ A}$$

To obtain the value of R_{int} (*i.e.* the Norton's equivalent resistance), the shorting link is removed, the constant sources are deactivated and a supply v_0 is applied at the open circuited portion that leads to input current i_0 (Fig. E6.112(*b*)).

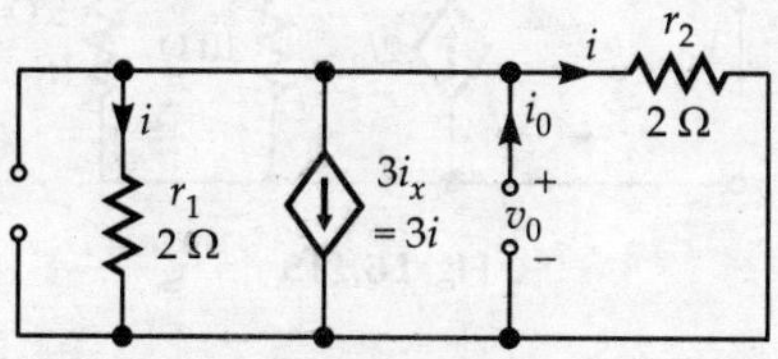

Fig. E6.112 (*b*)

From Fig. E6.112(*b*),

$$i_0 = 3i + i + i = 5\,i, \text{ while } v_0 = i \times 2 = 2i$$

$$\therefore \quad R_{int} = \frac{v_0}{i_0} = \frac{2i}{5i} = \frac{2}{5}\,\Omega$$

Figure E6.112(*c*) represents the Norton's equivalent circuit where

$$I_{s.c} = -1\text{ A};\ R_{int} = \frac{2}{5}\,\Omega$$

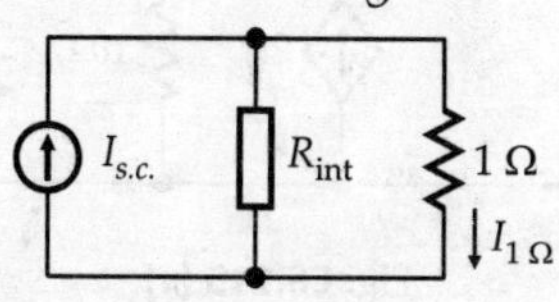

Fig. E6.112 (*c*)

$\therefore$ Current through $1\,\Omega$ resistor is obtained as

$$I_{1\Omega} = I_{s.c} \times \frac{R_{int}}{R_{int}+1} = (-1)\frac{2/5}{2/5+1}$$

$$= -\frac{2/5}{7/5} = \mathbf{-0.286\ A.}$$

EXAMPLE 6.113 *Obtain Norton's equivalent of the circuit shown in Fig. E6.113.*

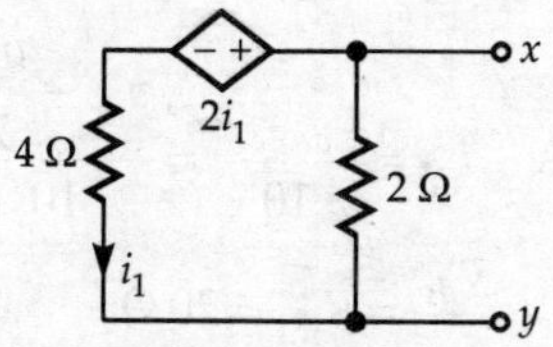

Fig. E6.113

SOLUTION. x - y terminals are shorted first (Fig. E6.113(*a*)).

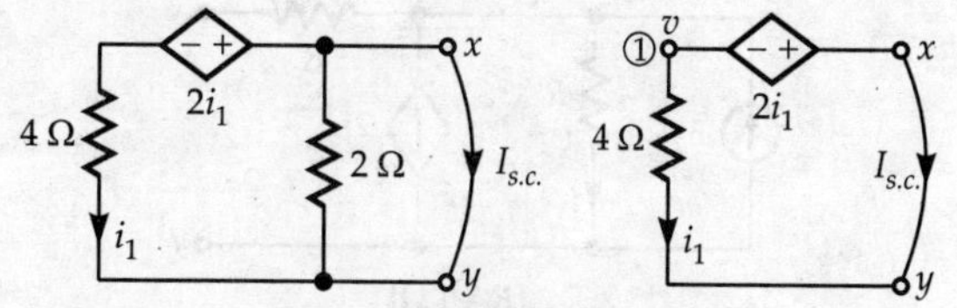

Fig. E6.113 (*a*)

Here, $\quad v = -4i_1 = -4 \cdot \frac{v}{4} = -v$

[Assuming node voltage at (1) being v]

i.e., $\quad 2v = 0$ *i.e.*, $v = 0$.

As $v = 0$, i_1 becomes zero giving the magnitude of the dependent source becoming zero.

Thus, $\quad I_{s.c} = 0$.

This leads to the conclusion that in absence of any independent source, Norton's equivalent current source does not exist.

To obtain R_{int}, x - y terminal is made open circuited and a dc voltage v_{dc} is applied such that input current is i_{dc} (Fig. E6.113(*b*)).

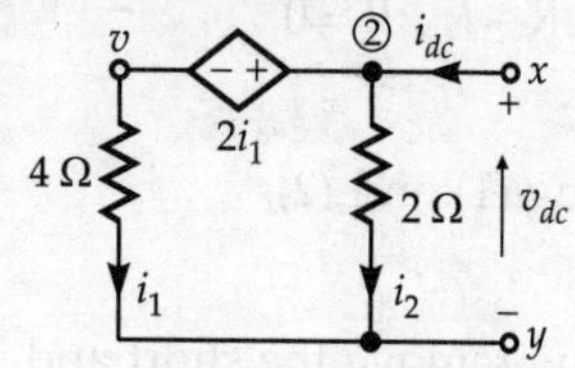

Fig. E6.113 (*b*)

Obviously,

$$v_{dc} - v = 2i_1 = 2 \cdot \frac{v}{4} = \frac{v}{2}$$

$$\therefore \quad v_{dc} = \frac{3}{2}\,v$$

Using KCL at *node* (2),

$$i_{dc} = i_1 + i_2 = \frac{v}{4} + \frac{v_{dc}}{2} = \frac{\frac{2v_{dc}}{3}}{4} + \frac{v_{dc}}{2}$$

or, $$i_{dc} = \frac{v_{dc}}{6} + \frac{v_{dc}}{2} = \frac{2}{3}\,v_{dc}$$

i.e., $$R_{int} = \frac{v_{dc}}{i_{dc}} = \frac{3}{2}\,\Omega$$

Norton's equivalent of the given circuit is thus obtained

where, $\quad R_{int} = \frac{3}{2}\,\Omega$ and $I_{s.c}\ (= \boldsymbol{I_N}) = \mathbf{0}$.

EXAMPLE 6.114 *In the circuit of Fig. E6.114, find Norton's equivalent at the left of terminal x - y.*

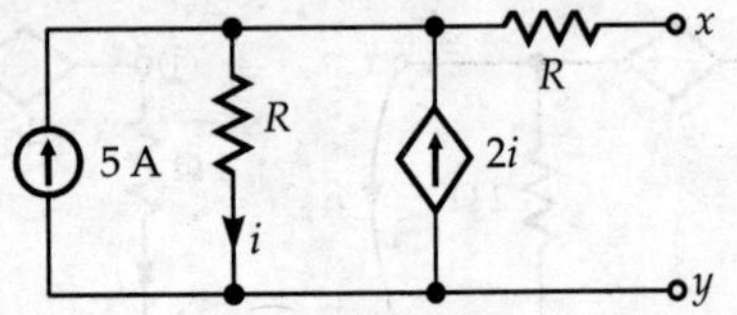

$[R = 1\,\Omega]$

Fig. E6.114

SOLUTION. Let us apply short circuit across $x - y$ [Fig. E6.114(*a*)].

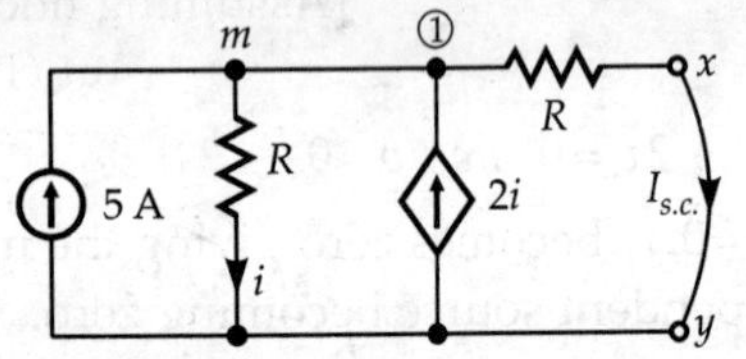

Fig. E6.114 (*a*)

At *node (1)*, KCL yields

$$5 + 2i = i + I_{s.c}$$

or, $$5 + i = I_{s.c} \quad ...(1)$$

In *loop m-x-y-n*, KVL yields

$$iR - I_{s.c}\,R = 0$$

or, $$i = I_{s.c} \quad ...(2)$$

Comparing (1) and (2),

$$I_{s.c} = \infty.$$

Let us now remove the short and $x - y$ terminal be open circuited (Fig. E6.114(*b*)).

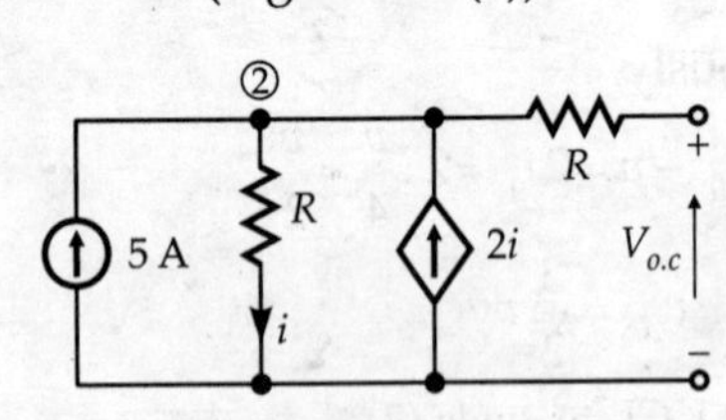

Fig. E6.114 (*b*)

At node (2), $5 = i - 2i$ or, $i = -5$ A

Assuming voltage at *node (2)* to be v volts,

$$\frac{v}{R} = i$$

i.e., $$v = -5\,R.$$

Observation at Fig. E6.114(*b*) reveals that

$$v \equiv V_{o.c}$$

$$\therefore \quad V_{o.c} = -5R = -5 \times 1 = -5\text{ V}$$

This gives

$$R_{\text{int}} = \frac{V_{o.c}}{I_{s.c}} = \frac{-5}{\infty} = 0\,\Omega$$

Hence, we finally obtain $R_{\text{int}} = \mathbf{0\,\Omega}$ and $I_{s.c} = \boldsymbol{I_N} = \infty.$

This means that Norton's equivalent of the given circuit does not exist.

EXAMPLE 6.115 *Find the Norton's equivalent of the circuit shown in Fig. E6.115.*

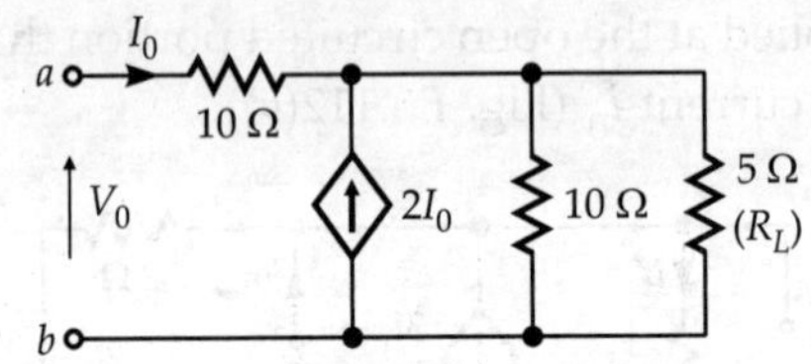

Fig. E6.115

SOLUTION. Let short circuit be applied at $(a - b)$ terminal (V_0 being removed). Thus I_0 being zero, the dependent source vanishes and obviously I_N (Norton current) $= 0$.

In order to find the input resistance R_{int} through $a - b$, let a voltage v_{dc} be applied at $a - b$ such that the input current becomes i_{dc} (Fig. E6.115(*a*)). Let the node voltage at *node (1)* be v.

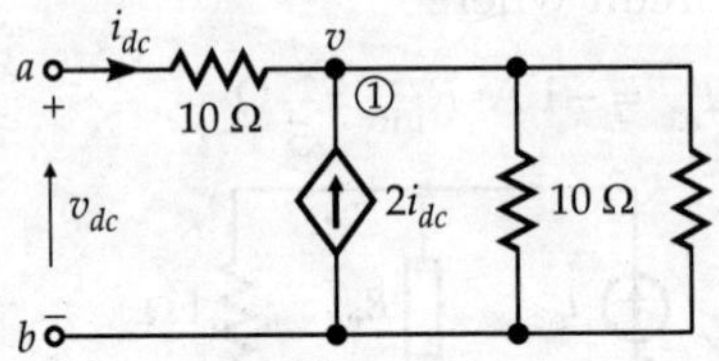

Fig. E6.115 (*a*)

Nodal analysis gives

$$\frac{v_{dc} - v}{10} + 2\left(\frac{v_{dc} - v}{10}\right) - \frac{v}{10} - \frac{v}{5} = 0 \qquad \left[\because i_{dc} = \frac{v_{dc} - v}{10}\right]$$

or, $$0.1\,v_{dc} + 0.2\,v_{dc} - 0.1\,v - 0.2\,v - 0.1\,v - 0.2\,v = 0$$

or, $$0.3\,v_{dc} - 0.6\,v = 0$$

$$\therefore \quad v_{dc} = 2v$$

This gives $$i_{dc} = \frac{v_{dc} - v}{10} = \frac{v_{dc} - \frac{v_{dc}}{2}}{10} = \frac{0.5\,v_{dc}}{10}$$

$$\therefore \quad \frac{v_{dc}}{i_{dc}} = R_{\text{int}} = 20\,\Omega.$$

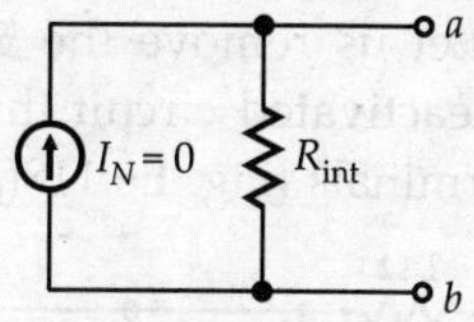

Fig. E6.115 (b)

Thus the Norton equivalent of the given circuit becomes

$$I_N = \mathbf{0}$$

$$R_{int} = \mathbf{20\,\Omega} \text{ (Fig. E6.115(}b\text{))}.$$

Example 6.116 *Find the Norton's equivalent circuit at the left of terminal x - y in Fig. E6.116.*

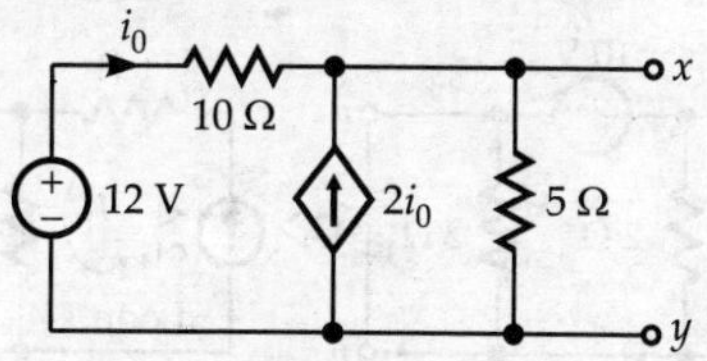

Fig. E6.116

Solution. In order to find R_{int}, let us apply first v_{dc} at terminals $x - y$ in Fig. E6.116(a).

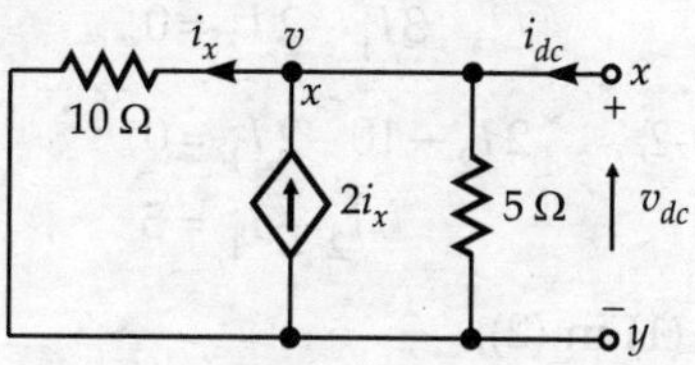

Fig. E6.116 (a)

Assuming the node x voltage to be v, application of KCL at *node x* yields

$$\frac{v_{dc}}{5} + \frac{v_{dc}}{10} - 2i_x - i_{dc} = 0 \qquad \text{...(1)}$$

However, in Fig. E6.116, the direction of the current in the dependent current source being upwards, the primary current i_0 is rightwards. To make the analogous source, $(2i_x)$ current in Fig. E6.116(a) is also made upwards but i_x is taken as opposite to i_0.

Thus in Fig. E6.116(a),

$$i_x = -\frac{v_{dc}}{10}$$

From (1) we thus get

$$\frac{v_{dc}}{5} + \frac{v_{dc}}{10} - 2\left(-\frac{v_{dc}}{10}\right) - i_{dc} = 0$$

or, $$\frac{v_{dc}}{5} + \frac{v_{dc}}{10} + \frac{v_{dc}}{5} = i_{dc}$$

or, $$\frac{v_{dc}}{i_{dc}} = 2\,\Omega\,(= R_{int})$$

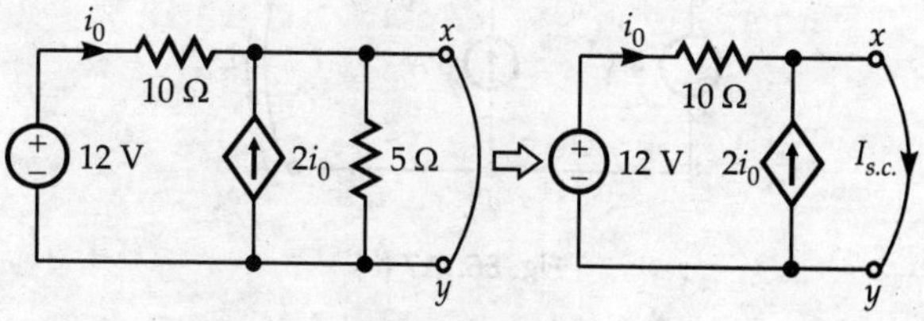

Fig. E6.116 (b)

Next, $x - y$ terminals are shorted and at *node (1)* in Fig. E6.116(b),

$$I_{s.c} = 2i_0 + i_0 = 3i_0;$$

but $$i_0 = \frac{12}{10} = 1.2 \text{ A.}$$

$$\therefore \qquad I_{s.c} = 3 \times 1.2 = 3.6 \text{ A.}$$

Norton's equivalent circuit is thus obtained as

$$I_{s.c} = \mathbf{3.6\ A}, \quad R_{int} = \mathbf{2\,\Omega}.$$

Example 6.117 *Determine the power loss in 1Ω resistor using Norton's theorem. (Fig. E6.117).*

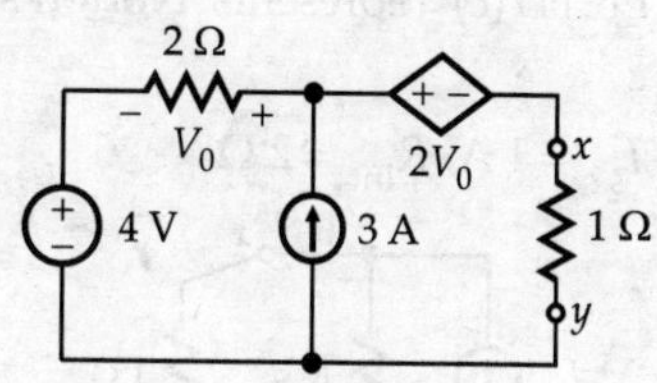

Fig. E6.117

Solution. Removing the 1Ω resistor first (Fig. E6.117(a)).

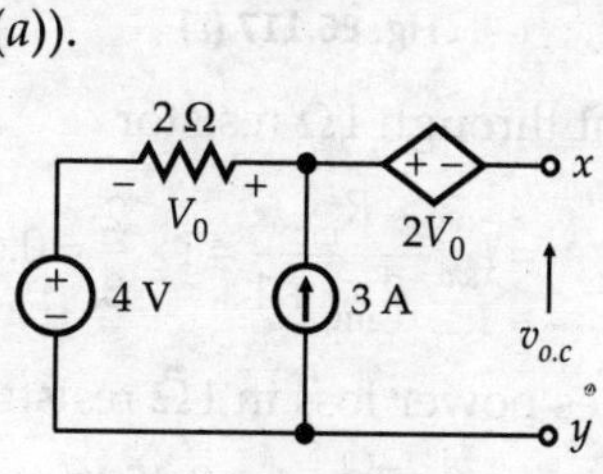

Fig. E6.117 (a)

Here, application of KVL yields,

$$-4 - V_0 + 2V_0 + v_{o.c} = 0$$

or, $$v_{o.c} = (4 - V_0) \qquad \text{...(1)}$$

However,

$$V_0 = 3\text{ A} \times 2\,\Omega = 6\text{ V}$$

[∵ loop current in the *left loop* = 3 A]

Hence from (1), $v_{o.c} = 4 - 6 = -2$ V.

Let us now short the terminals $x-y$ (Fig. E6.117(*b*)).

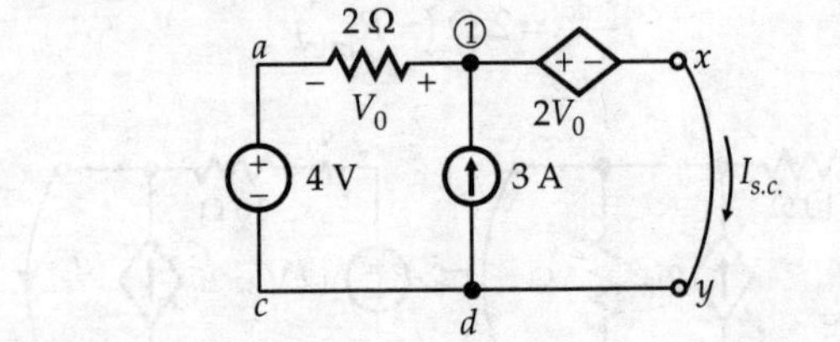

Fig. E6.117 (*b*)

In *loop axydc*, KVL yields

$$-4 - V_0 + 2V_0 = 0$$

or, $$V_0 = 4\text{ V} \quad ...(2)$$

Application of KCL in *node (1)* yields

$$\frac{V_0}{2} + I_{s.c} = 3$$

or, $$I_{s.c} = 3 - \frac{V_0}{2} = 3 - 2 = 1\text{ A}$$

This gives $$R_{int} = \frac{v_{o.c}}{I_{s.c}} = \frac{2}{1} = 2\,\Omega$$

[– ve sign of R_{int} is neglected].

Figure E6.117(*c*) represents Norton's equivalent circuit

where $I_{s.c} = 1\text{ A}$, $R_{int} = 2\,\Omega$.

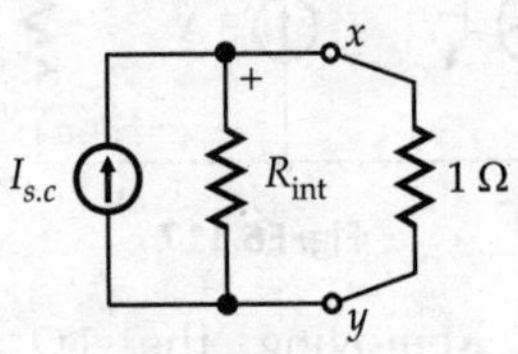

Fig. E6.117 (*c*)

∴ Current through $1\,\Omega$ resistor

$$= I_{s.c}\frac{R_{int}}{R_{int}+1} = 1 \times \frac{2}{3} = 0.67\text{ A}.$$

This gives power loss in $1\,\Omega$ resistor as

$$(0.67)^2 \times 1 \simeq \mathbf{0.45\ W}.$$

Example 6.118 *What is the current in the* $5\,\Omega$ *resistor across a-b terminals of the network shown in Fig. E6.118 ? Use Norton's theorem.*

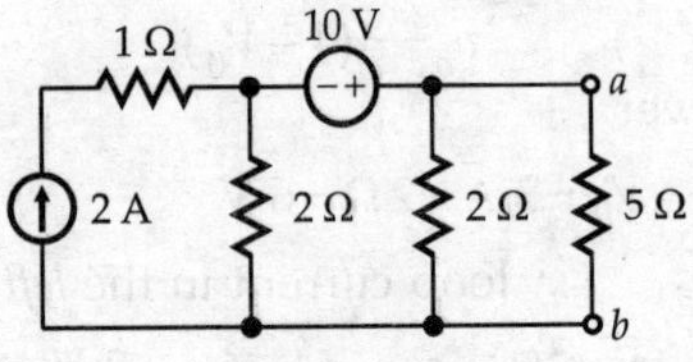

Fig. E6.118

Solution. Let us remove the $5\,\Omega$ resistor and look into the deactivated circuit through the open circuited *a-b* terminals (Fig. E6.118(*a*)).

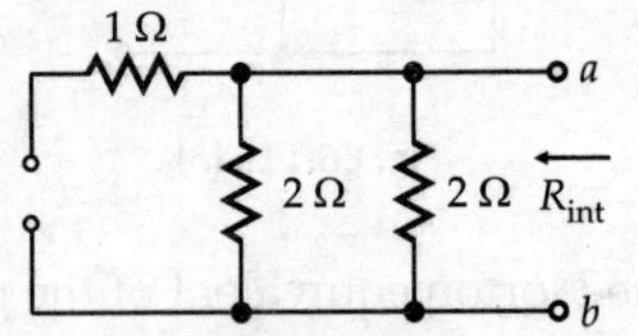

Fig. E6.118 (*a*)

Here $R_{int} = 2 \| 2 = 1\,\Omega$.

Let us now short *a-b* of the circuit shown in Fig. E6.118. The circuit configuration is shown in Fig. E6.118(*b*).

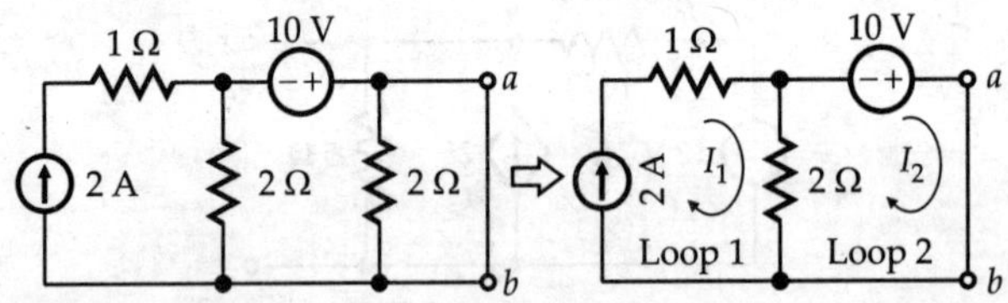

Fig. E6.118 (*b*)

In *loop-1*,

$$I_1 \times 1 + I_1 \times 2 - I_2 \times 2 = 0$$

or, $$3I_1 - 2I_2 = 0 \quad ...(1)$$

In loop-2, $$2I_2 - 10 - 2I_1 = 0$$

or, $$I_2 - I_1 = 5 \quad ...(2)$$

Using (1) in (2),

$$I_2 - \left(\frac{2I_2}{3}\right) = 5$$

$$\therefore \quad I_2 = 15\text{ A}, \text{ and } I_1 = 10\text{ A}.$$

It is evident from Fig. E6.118(*b*), $I_2 \equiv I_{s.c}$ *i.e.*, the short circuit current. Then Norton's equivalent circuit is given by

$$I_{s.c} = 15\text{ A}, \quad R_{int} = 1\,\Omega.$$

Norton's equivalent circuit is shown in Fig. E6.118(*c*).

∴ Current in $5\,\Omega$ resistor

$$= I_{5\Omega} = I_{s.c}\frac{R_{int}}{R_{int}+5} = \mathbf{2.5\ A.}$$

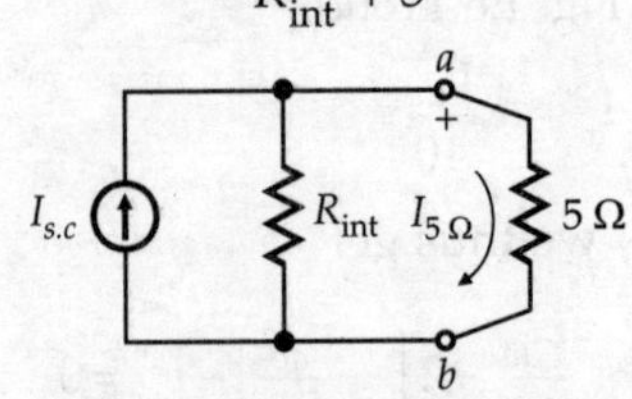

Fig. E6.118 (*c*)

EXAMPLE 6.119 *In the circuit of Fig. E6.119, find Norton's equivalent circuit at the left of terminal x-y.*

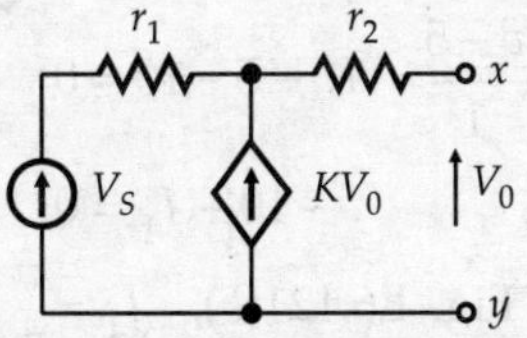

$[V_S = 10\text{ V}; K = -0.15, r_1 = r_2 = 5\,\Omega]$

Fig. E6.119

SOLUTION. It is obvious that the loop current in the *loop-1* of Fig. E6.119 being KV_0, the drop across r_1 is $(KV_0\, r_1)$.

Application of KVL *in loop-1* yields

$$-V_S - KV_0 r_1 + V_0 = 0$$

$$\therefore \quad V_0(1 - Kr_1) = V_S$$

or $$V_0\,(= V_{o.c}) = \frac{V_S}{1 - Kr_1}$$

In order to apply Norton's theorem, *x-y* terminals are shorted (Fig. E6.119(*a*)). As V_0 becomes zero with shorting of *x-y*, the magnitude of dependent source vanishes and then in the circuit of Fig. E6.119(*a*),

$$I_{s.c} = \frac{V_S}{r_1 + r_2}$$

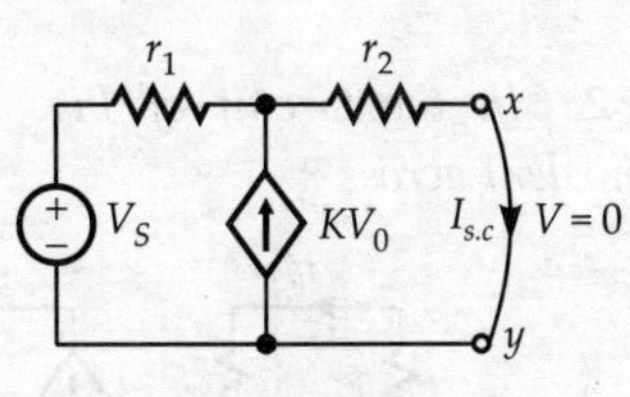

Fig. E6.119 (*a*)

Thus, the internal resistance of the circuit across *x-y* becomes

$$R_{\text{int}} = \frac{V_0}{I_{s.c}} = \frac{V_S}{1 - Kr_1} \times \frac{r_1 + r_2}{V_S} = \frac{r_1 + r_2}{1 - Kr_1}$$

$$= \frac{10}{1 - 0.15 \times 5} = 40\,\Omega$$

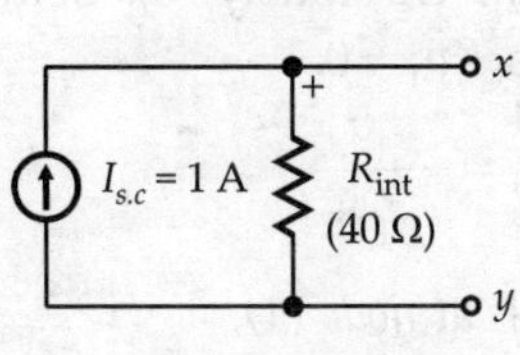

Fig. E6.119 (*b*)

$$\therefore \quad I_{s.c} = \frac{V_S}{r_1 + r_2} = \frac{10}{5 + 5} = 1\text{ A}$$

Norton's equivalent circuit has been shown in Fig. E6.119(*b*),

where $I_{s.c.} = \mathbf{1\ A}$ and $R_{\text{int}} = \mathbf{40\,\Omega}$.

EXAMPLE 6.120 *Using Norton's theorem find the current in the 5 Ω resistor in the network shown in Fig. E6.120.*

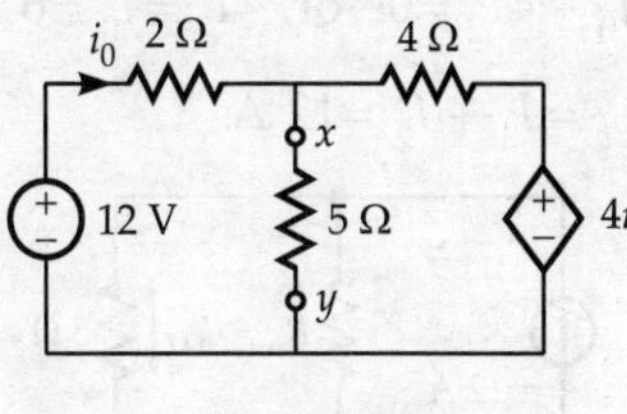

Fig. E6.120

SOLUTION. Let us first remove the 5 Ω resistor from x-y terminals and apply a dc driving voltage V_{dc} deactivating the constant source of 10 V such that the input current through x be i_{dc} (Fig. E6.120(*a*)).

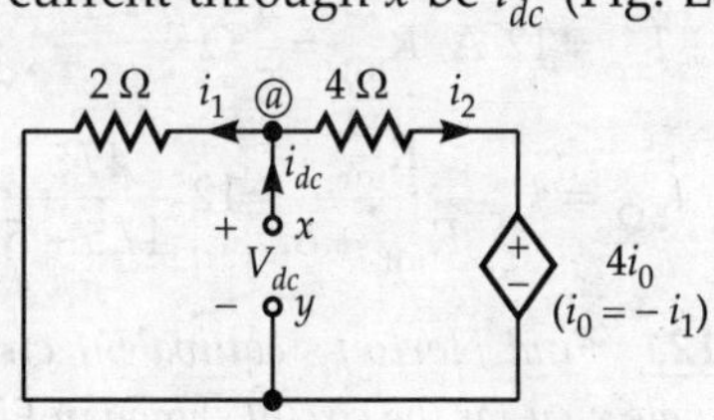

Fig. E6.120 (*a*)

Here, at node (*a*), $i_{dc} = i_1 + i_2$.

Assuming the potential at (*a*) being $+v$,

$$|i_1| = \frac{V_{dc}}{2};\ i_2 = \frac{V_{dc} - 4i_0}{4}.$$

$$\text{Thus, } i_{dc} = +\frac{V_{dc}}{2} + \frac{V_{dc} - 4i_0}{4}$$

$$= +\frac{V_{dc}}{2} + \frac{V_{dc}}{4} + \frac{V_{dc}}{2}$$

$$\left[\because i_0 = -i_1 = -\frac{V_{dc}}{2}\right]$$

i.e., $$\frac{V_{dc}}{i_{dc}} (= R_{\text{int}}) = \frac{4}{5}\,\Omega$$

To find Norton's current source, let x-y terminals in Fig. E6.120 be shorted [Fig. E6.120(*b*)].

Loop currents being shown, *in loop 1*,

$$-12 + 2I_1 = 0 \text{ or, } I_1 = 6\text{ A}\,(= i_0)$$

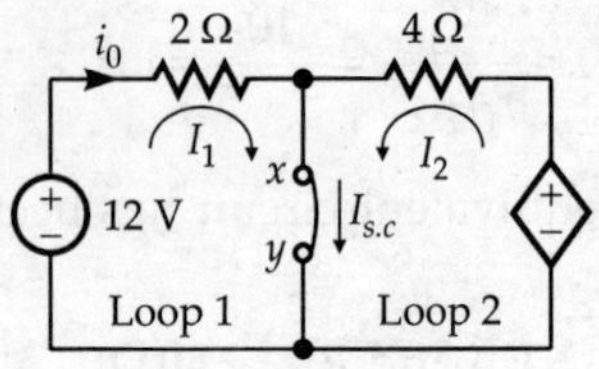

Fig. E6.120 (*b*)

In loop-2,

$$-4i_0 + 4I_2 = 0 \quad \text{or,} \quad I_2 = i_0 = 6 \text{ A.}$$

Thus, $\quad I_{s.c} = I_1 + I_2 = 12 \text{ A.}$

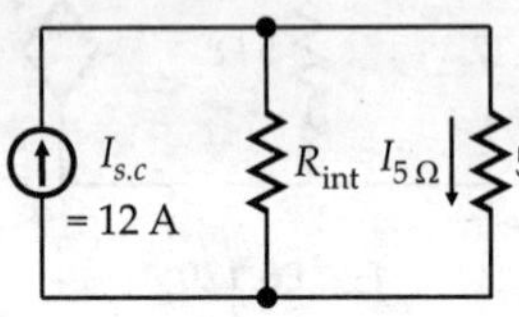

Fig. E6.120 (*c*)

Norton's equivalent circuit being shown in Fig. E6.120(*c*),

$$I_{s.c} = 12 \text{ A}, R_{int} = \frac{4}{5} \Omega$$

$$\therefore \quad I_{5\Omega} = I_{s.c} \frac{R_{int}}{R_{int} + 5} = 12 \frac{4/5}{4/5 + 5} = \mathbf{1.66 \text{ A.}}$$

EXAMPLE 6.121 *Find Norton's equivalent circuit at the left of terminals x - y for the circuit shown in Fig. E6.121.*

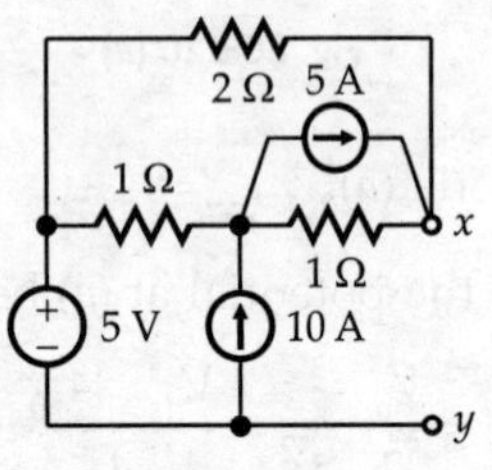

Fig. E6.121

SOLUTION. To find the internal resistance of the network looking through x - y, the constant sources are deactivated (Fig. E6.121(*a*))

Here, $\quad R_{int} = (1+1) \,||\, 2 = 1 \Omega.$

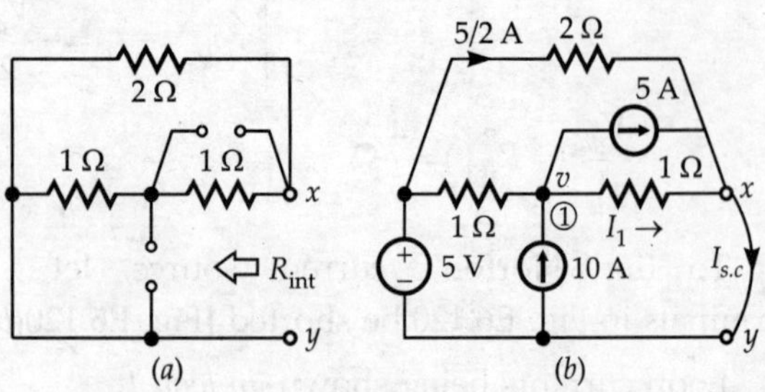

Fig. E6.121

Let us now short circuit x - y (Fig. E6.121(*b*)). Assuming *node (1)* potential to be v, nodal analysis at *node (1)* gives

$$\frac{v-5}{1} + I_1 + 5 - 10 = 0$$

or, $\quad v - 10 + I_1 = 0 \qquad$ ...(1)

But from Fig. E6.121(*b*), $I_1 = \frac{v}{1}$ and hence (1) becomes,

$$2v - 10 = 0 \quad i.e., \quad v = 5 \text{ V}$$

i.e., $\quad I_1 = 5 \text{ A.}$

Next, at *node (x)*,

$$I_{s.c} = I_1 + 5 + \frac{5}{2} = 12.5 \text{ A.}$$

[$\because$ It is evident from Fig. E6.121(*b*) that current through 2 Ω resistor is (5/2) A]

This gives in Norton's equivalent circuit as

$$I_{s.c} = \mathbf{12.5 \text{ A}}; \; R_{int} = \mathbf{1 \Omega.}$$

Figure E6.121(*c*) represents the Norton's equivalent circuit.

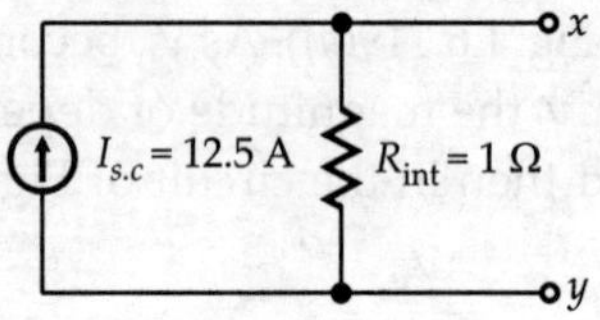

Fig. E6.121 (*c*)

EXAMPLE 6.122 *In the circuit of Fig. E6.122, find Norton's equivalent across r_L.*

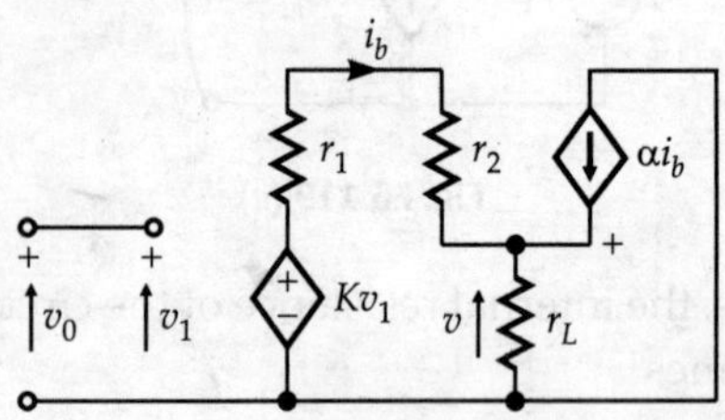

Fig. E6.122

SOLUTION. Let us first replace r_L with a dc driving source voltage v_{dc} $(= v)$ such that input current is i_{dc} [Fig. E6.122(*a*)]. Obviously, v_0 being deactivated, $v_1 = 0$ and also $Kv_1 = 0$.

Here, $\quad i_b = -\frac{v_{dc}}{r_1 + r_2} \qquad$ ...(1)

Using KCL at *node (1)*,

$$i_{dc} = -i_b - \alpha i_b = -i_b(1 + \alpha) \qquad \text{...(2)}$$

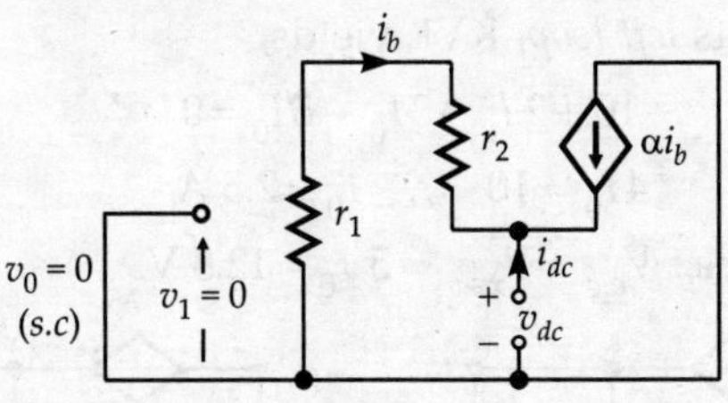

Fig. E6.122 (a)

Using (1) in (2),

$$i_{dc} = + \frac{v_{dc}}{r_1 + r_2}(1+\alpha)$$

or $$R_{\text{int}} = \frac{v_{dc}}{i_{dc}} = \frac{r_1 + r_2}{1+\alpha}$$

Next, v_{dc} being removed, the original sources being activated, s.c is applied across r_L (Fig. E6.122(b)).

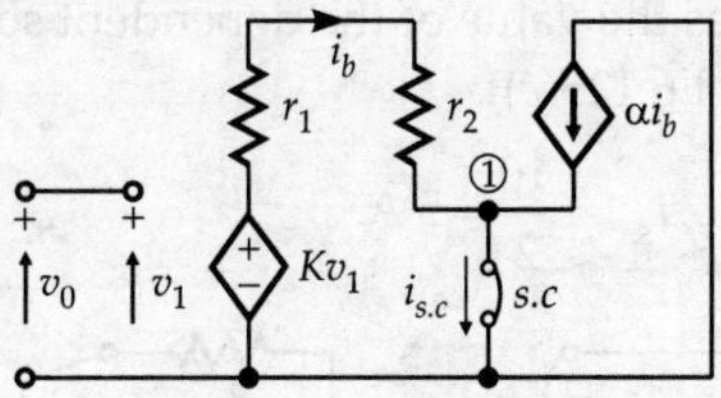

Fig. E6.122 (b)

Here, $i_{s.c} = i_b + \alpha\, i_b = i_b\,(1+\alpha)$.

However, $$i_b = \frac{Kv_1}{r_1 + r_2}$$

Thus, $$i_{s.c} = \frac{Kv_1}{r_1 + r_2}(1+\alpha).$$

Norton's equivalent circuit is thus obtained where

$$i_{s.c}\,(=I_N) = \frac{Kv_1}{r_1 + r_2}(1+\alpha)$$

and $$R_{\text{int}} = \frac{r_1 + r_2}{1+\alpha}.$$

EXAMPLE 6.123 *Find Norton's equivalent circuit across R_L in the circuit of Fig. E6.123.*

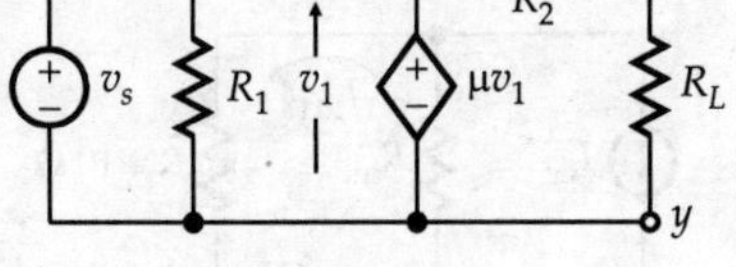

Fig. E6.123

SOLUTION. Let R_L be removed [Fig. E6.123(a)]

Obviously, $$v_{o.c} = \mu v_1 \quad \text{...(1)}$$

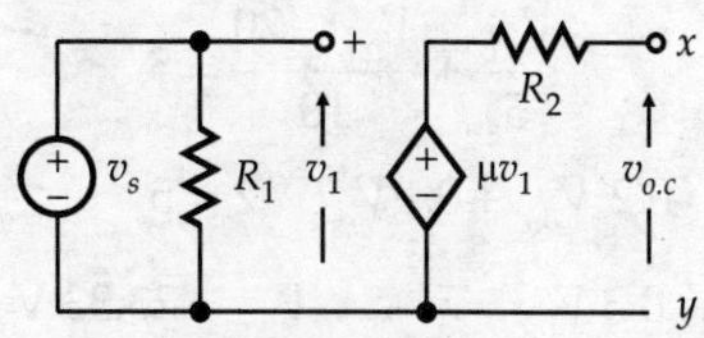

Fig. E6.123 (a)

Next, short circuit is applied across R_L (Fig. E6.123(b)).

Obviously, $$i_{s.c} = \frac{\mu v_1}{R_2}.$$

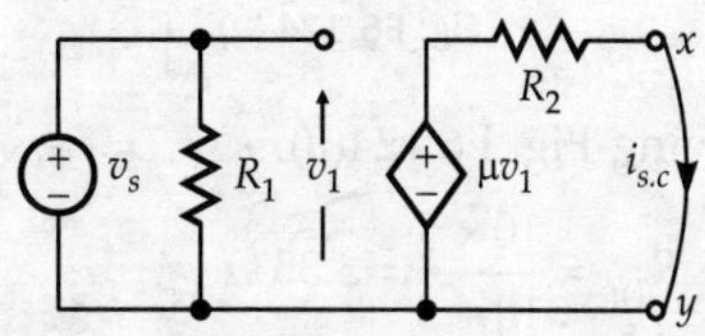

Fig. E6.123 (b)

The internal resistance of the circuit across R_L then can be found out as

$$R_{\text{int}} = \frac{v_{o.c}}{i_{s.c}} = \frac{\mu v_1}{\dfrac{\mu v_1}{R_2}} = R_2$$

Norton's equivalent circuit thus can be drawn (Fig. E6.123(c)), where

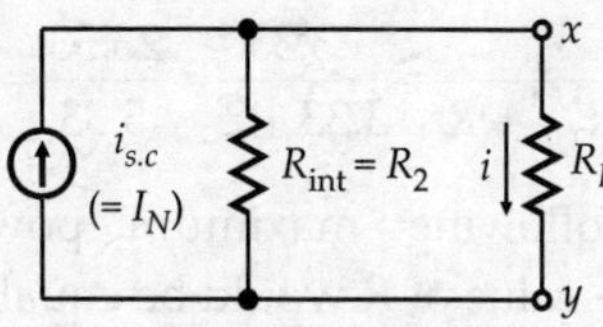

Fig. E6.123 (c)

$$R_{\text{int}} = R_2 \quad \text{and} \quad i_{s.c} = \frac{\mu v_1}{R_2} = \frac{\mu v_s}{R_2}$$

$$\left[\text{Here, } i = i_{s.c}\,\frac{R_2}{R_2 + R_L}\ \text{A}\right]$$

EXAMPLE 6.124 *Find the current through R using Thevenin's theorem. Also, find the value of R such that maximum power transfer takes place from the source to R in the network of Fig. E6.124.*

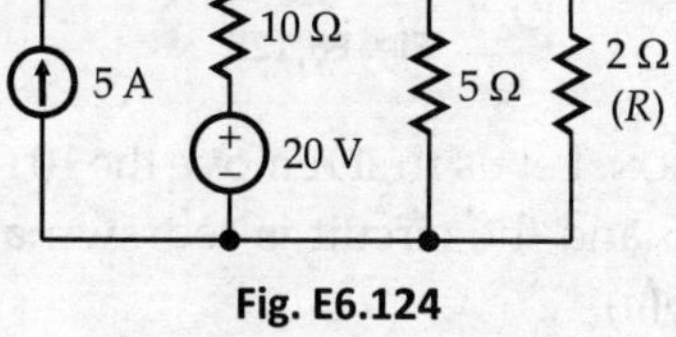

Fig. E6.124

Solution. Let R be removed (Fig. E6.124(a)). Nodal analysis gives

$$\frac{V_{o.c}}{5}+\frac{V_{o.c}-20}{10}=5$$

or, $\quad 0.2\,V_{o.c}+0.1\,V_{o.c}-2=5$

or, $\quad 0.3\,V_{o.c}=7 \quad \therefore \quad V_{o.c}=23.33\text{ V}$

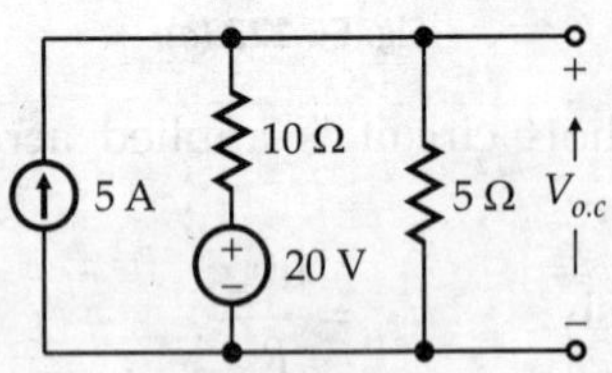

Fig. E6.124 (a)

Following Fig. E6.124(b),

$$R_{Th}=\frac{10\times 5}{10+5}=3.33\,\Omega$$

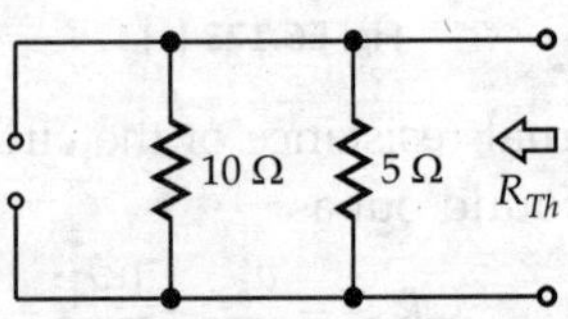

Fig. E6.124 (b)

Thus, from Thevenin's equivalent circuit,
$I_{2\Omega}$ (current through 2 Ω resistor, R)

$$=\frac{V_{o.c}}{R_{Th}+R}=\frac{23.33}{3.33+2}=\frac{23.33}{5.33}=\mathbf{4.38\ A.}$$

Then, following maximum power transfer theorem, the value of R would be equal to the value of R_{Th} such that maximum power transfer takes place between the source and load.

i.e., $R=R_{Th}=$ **3.33 Ω** for maximum power transfer.

Example 6.125 *Find the current through the 10 Ω resistor in Fig. E6.125 using (i) Thevenin's Theorem (ii) Norton's Theorem.*

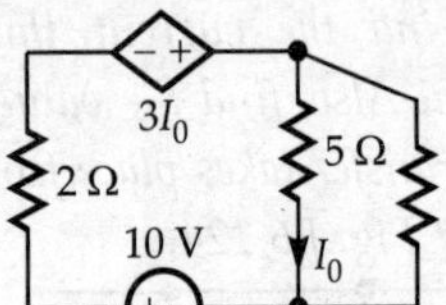

Fig. E6.125

Solution. Let us first remove the 10 Ω resistor in Fig. E6.125 and the circuit is redrawn as shown in Fig. E6.125(a).

In its *left loop*, KVL yields,

$$-10+2I_0-3I_0+5I_0=0$$

or, $\quad 4I_0=10 \quad \therefore \quad I_0=2.5\text{ A}$

Thus, $V_{o.c}=V_{x-y}=5\,I_0=12.5\text{ V}.$

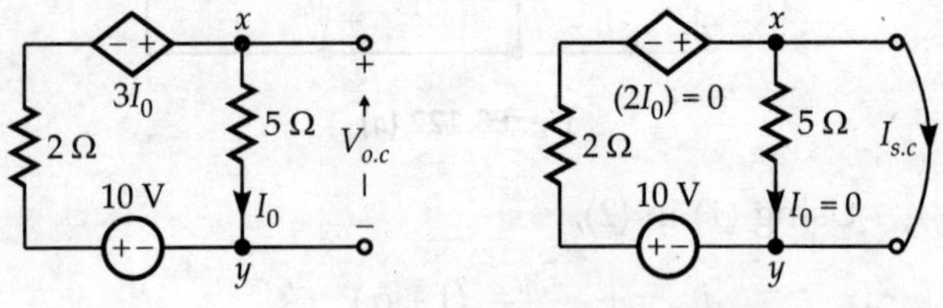

(a) (b)

Fig. E6.125

Next, short circuit is applied across the open circuited terminals (Fig. E6.125(b)) and it becomes evident that due to short circuit across $x-y$, no current would pass through 5 Ω resistor and $I_0=0$. This makes the value of the dependent source to be zero (Fig. E6.125(c)).

$$\therefore \quad I_{s.c}=\frac{10}{2}=5\text{ A}.$$

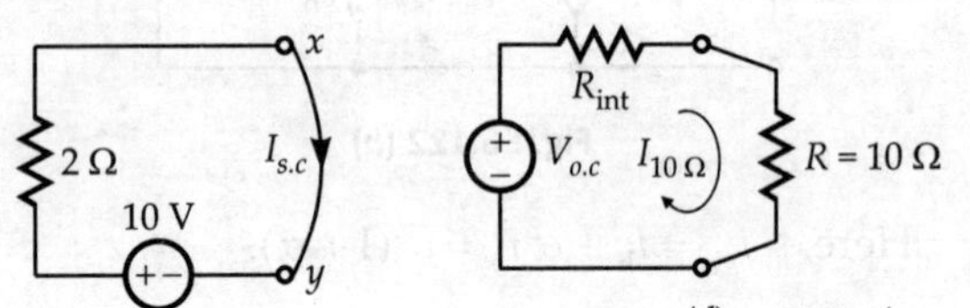

(c) (d)

Fig. E6.125

This gives

$$R_{\text{int}}=\frac{V_{o.c}}{I_{s.c}}=\frac{12.5}{5}=2.5\text{ ohm}.$$

Then, following Thevenin's theorem, (Fig. E6.125(d)), the current through the 10 Ω resistor is

$$I_{10\Omega}=\frac{V_{o.c}}{R_{\text{int}}+R}=\frac{12.5}{2.5+10}=\mathbf{1\ A.}$$

On the other hand, following Norton's theorem (Fig. E6.125(e)),

$$I_{10\Omega}=5\,\frac{R_{\text{int}}}{R_{\text{int}}+R}=5\,.\,\frac{2.5}{2.5+10}=\mathbf{1\ A.}$$

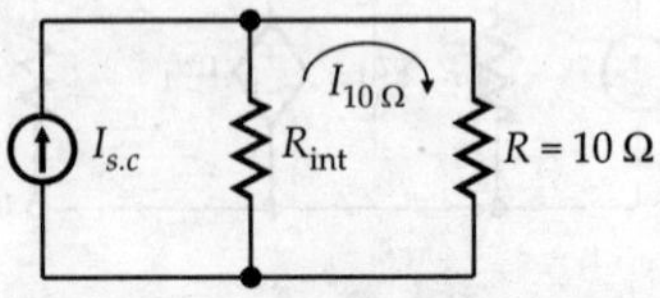

Fig. E6.125 (e)

EXAMPLE 6.126 *Find current in the 2 Ω resistance in the circuit of Fig. E6.126 using both Thevenin's theorem and Norton's theorem.*

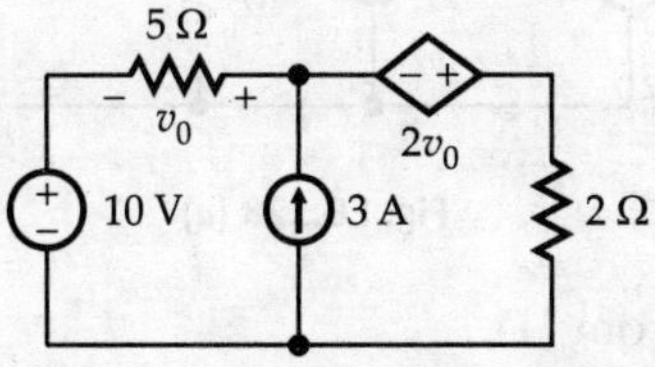

Fig. E6.126

SOLUTION. Referring Fig. E6.126(*a*) where 2Ω resistor is replaced by open circuit,

$$-10 - v_0 - 2v_0 + V_{o.c} = 0$$

or, $$V_{o.c} = (3v_0 + 10)\text{ V} \quad ...(1)$$

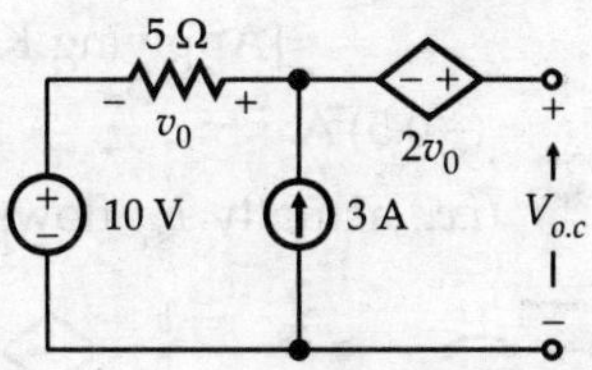

Fig. E6.126 (*a*)

But $v_0 = 3\text{ A} \times 5\,\Omega = 15\text{ V}$

Then from (1),

$$V_{o.c} = 3 \times 15 + 10 = 55\text{ V}.$$

Next, the open circuited terminals being shorted in Fig. E6.126(*b*), we find

$$-10 - v_0 - 2v_0 = 0 \quad \text{or,} \quad v_0 = -\frac{10}{3}\text{ V}$$

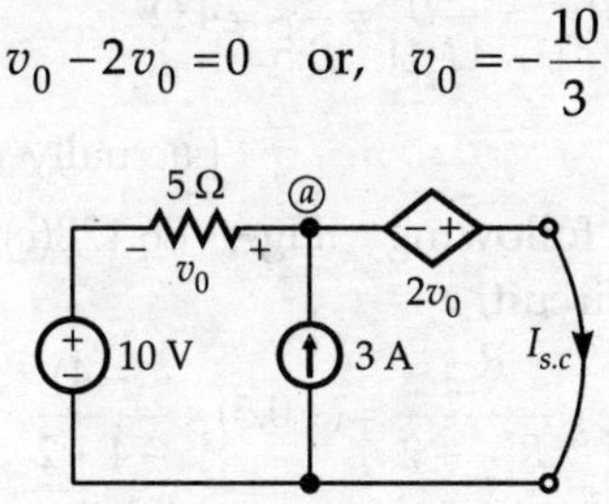

Fig. E6.126 (*b*)

Again at *node a*, nodal analysis gives

$$\frac{v_0}{5} = 3 - I_{s.c}$$

or, $$I_{s.c} = 3 - \frac{v_0}{5} = 3 - \frac{\left(-\frac{10}{3}\right)}{5} = \frac{11}{3}\text{ A}$$

$$\therefore \quad R_{int} = \frac{V_{o.c}}{I_{s.c}} = \frac{55}{\frac{11}{3}} = 15\,\Omega$$

Thus, following Thevenin's equivalent circuit (Fig. E6.126(*c*)),

$$I = \frac{V_{o.c}}{R_{int} + 2} = \frac{55}{15 + 2} = \mathbf{3.235\text{ A}}.$$

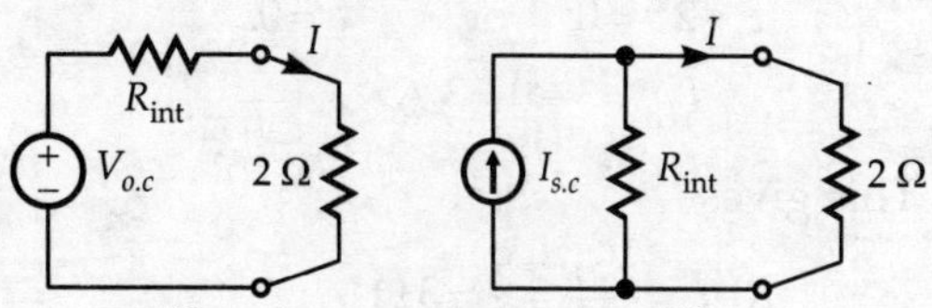

(*c*) (*d*)

Fig. E6.126

On the other hand, from Norton's equivalent circuit (Fig. E6.126(*d*)),

$$I = I_{s.c}\frac{R_{int}}{R_{int} + 2} = \frac{11}{3} \times \frac{15}{17} = \mathbf{3.235\text{ A}}.$$

EXAMPLE 6.127 *Find the current in the 6 Ω resistor in Fig. E6.127 using Thevenin's theorem. Verify your result using Norton's theorem.*

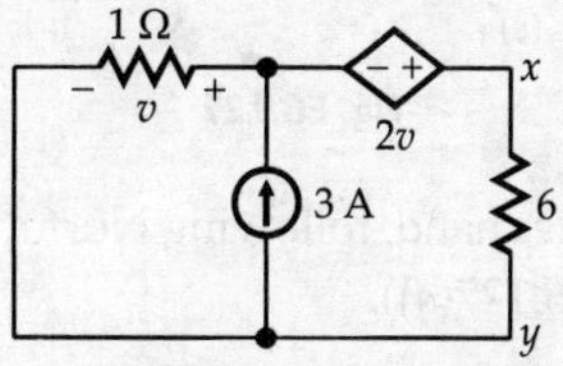

Fig. E6.127

SOLUTION. Let the 6Ω resistor be removed (Fig. E6.127(*a*)).

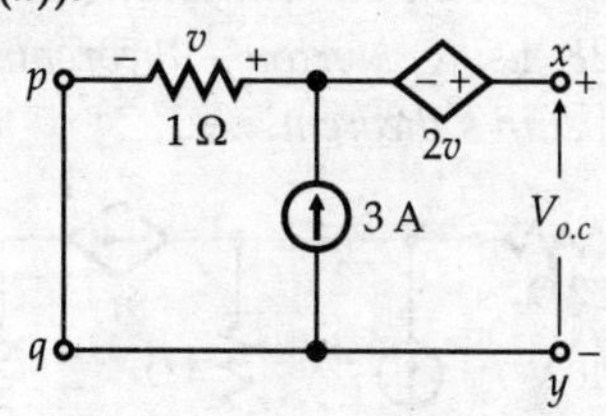

Fig. E6.127 (*a*)

Obviously, $v = 3\text{ A} \times 1\Omega = 3\text{ V}$.

Thus in *loop p-x-y-q*,

$$-v - 2v + V_{o.c} = 0.$$

or, $$V_{o.c} = 3v = 9\text{ V}.$$

Next, x - y is short circuited (Fig. E6.127(*b*)).

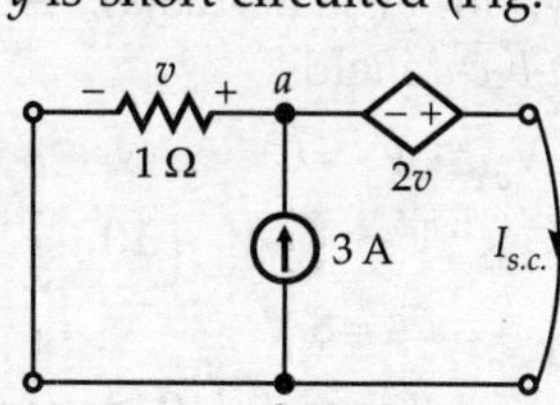

Fig. E6.127 (*b*)

Nodal analysis at *node a* gives

$$\frac{v}{1} - 3 + I_{s.c} = 0 \quad \text{or,} \quad I_{s.c} = 3 - v$$

However, *loop* analysis gives

$$-v - 2v = 0 \quad \text{or,} \quad v = 0.$$

$$\therefore \quad I_{s.c} = 3 - 0 = 3\text{ A.}$$

This gives

$$R_{\text{int}} = \frac{V_{o.c}}{I_{s.c}} = \frac{9}{3} = 3\,\Omega$$

Then following Thevenin's equivalent circuit (Fig. E6.127(*c*)).

$$I = \frac{V_{o.c}}{R_{\text{int}} + 6} = \frac{9}{3+6} = \mathbf{1\ A}$$

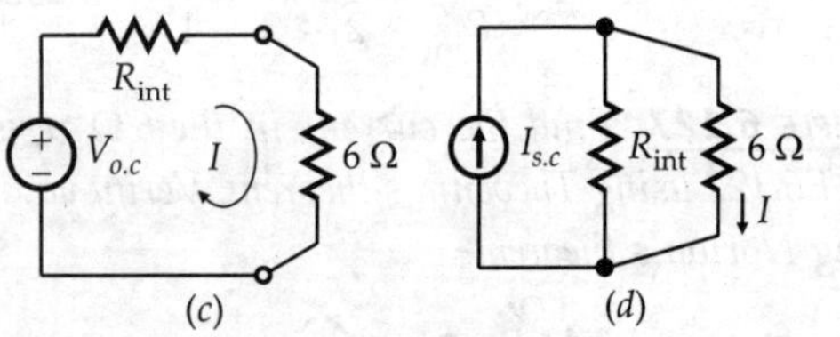

Fig. E6.127

On the other hand, following Norton's equivalent circuit (Fig. E6.127(*d*)),

$$I = I_{s.c}\,\frac{R_{\text{int}}}{R_{\text{int}} + 6} = 3 \cdot \frac{3}{3+6} = \mathbf{1\ A.}$$

EXAMPLE 6.128 *Find the current through the 2 Ω resistor in Fig. E6.128 using Norton's theorem. Verify your result by Thevenin's theorem.*

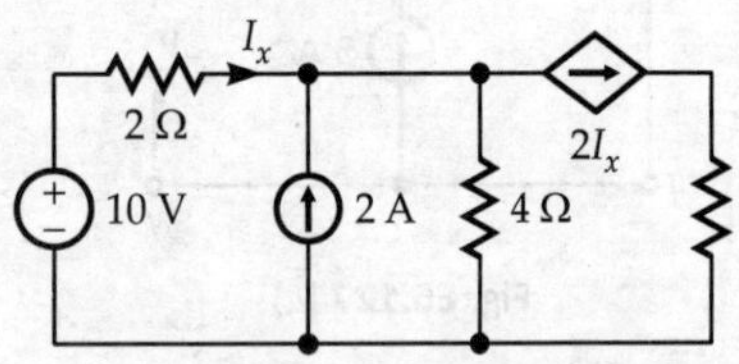

Fig. E6.128

SOLUTION. Let the 2 Ω resistor be removed (Fig. E6.128(*a*)) first. Let the drop across the 4 Ω resistor be V_1.

Obviously, in Fig. E6.128(*a*), Application of KVL in loop *a-b-c-d* yields

$$-10 + V_{o.c} + V_1 = 0$$

or, $$V_{o.c} = -V_1 + 10 \qquad \ldots(1)$$

But $$V_1 = 2 \times 4 = 8\text{ V}$$

[Since $I_x = 0$, dependent current source $(2I_x)$ does not exist]

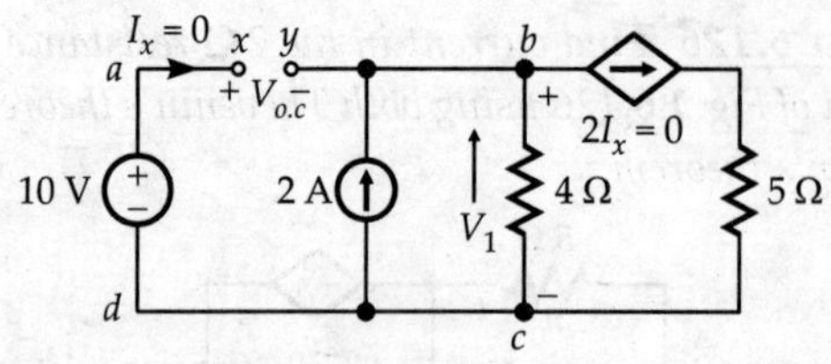

Fig. E6.128 (*a*)

Thus from (1),

$$V_{o.c} = -8 + 10 = +2\text{ V}$$

Again, shorting the terminals x-y in Fig. E6.128(*b*),

$$V_1' = 10\text{ V (by inspection)},$$

and $$I_{s.c} + 2 = 2\,I_{s.c} + \frac{10}{4} = 2\,I_{s.c} + 2.5$$

[Applying KCL at *node b*]

or, $$I_{s.c} = (-0.5)\text{ A.}$$

(*i.e.*, actually $I_{s.c}$ flows from y to x)

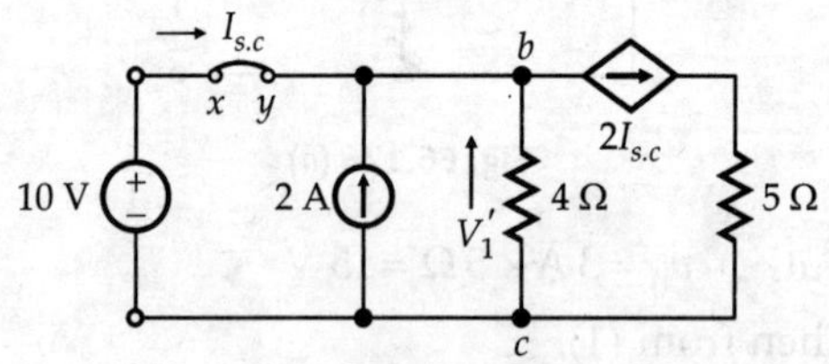

Fig. E6.128 (*b*)

Thus, the internal resistance R_{eq} is obtained as

$$R_{eq} = \frac{|V_{o.c}|}{|I_{s.c}|} = \frac{2}{0.5} = 4\,\Omega$$

[actually $R_{eq} = -4\,\Omega$]

Then, following Fig. E6.128(*c*); Norton's equivalent circuit,

$$I = I_{s.c}\,\frac{R_{eq}}{R_{eq} + 2} = (-0.5) \times \frac{(-4)}{-4+2} = \mathbf{-1.0\ A.}$$

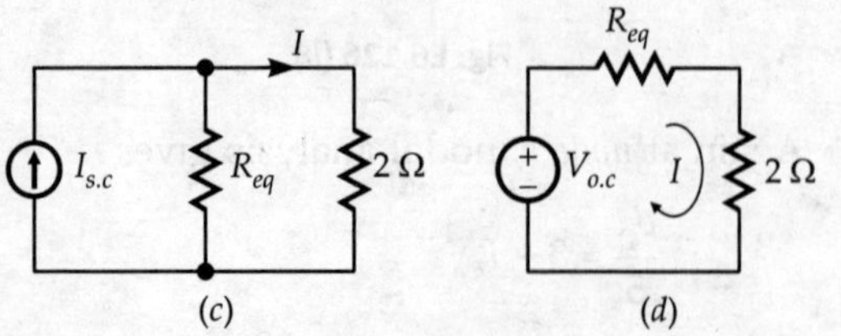

Fig. E6.128

Using Thevenin's equivalent circuit (Fig. E6.128(*d*)),

$$I = \frac{V_{o.c}}{R_{eq} + 2} = \frac{+2}{-4+2} = \mathbf{-1.0\ A.}$$

EXAMPLE 6.129 *Find the current through 3 Ω resistor in the circuit of Fig. E6.129 using Norton's theorem. Verify the result using Thevenin's theorem.*

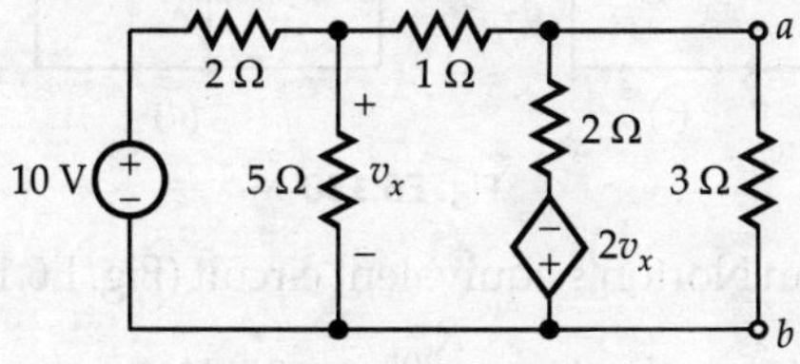

Fig. E6.129

SOLUTION. Let us remove the 3 Ω resistor first and short terminals *a-b* (Fig. E6.129(*a*)).

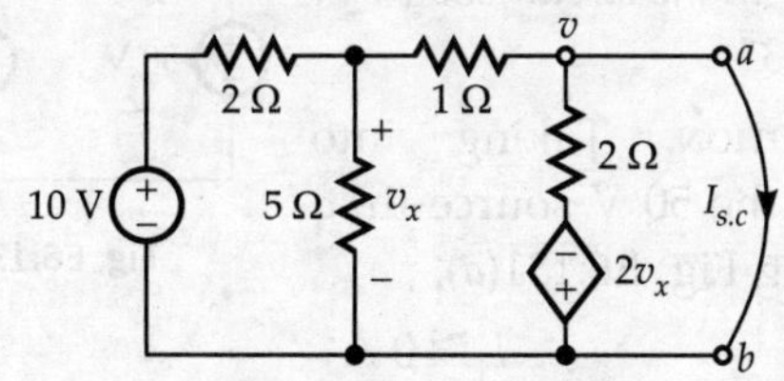

Fig. E6.129 (*a*)

At *node a*, nodal analysis gives

$$\frac{v-v_x}{1}+\frac{v+2v_x}{2}+I_{s.c}=0$$

[Assuming *node a* voltage to be v]

But $v=0$, since *a-b* terminals are shorted. Thus, the nodal equation finally becomes

$$-v_x+v_x+I_{s.c}=0 \quad i.e. \quad I_{s.c}=0$$

Next, terminal *a-b* is open circuited (Fig. E6.129(*b*))

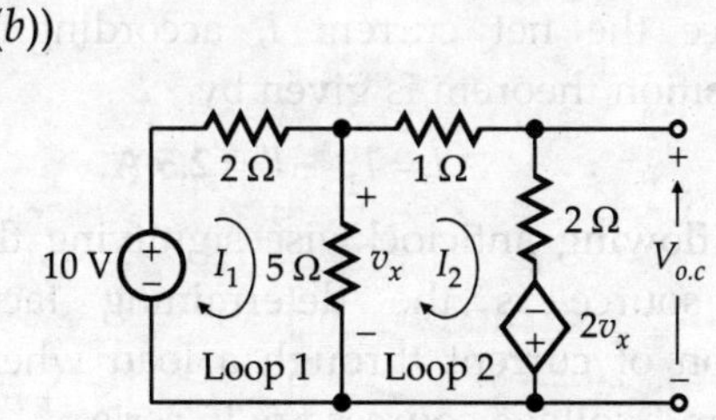

Fig. E6.129 (*b*)

In loop-1, KVL yields

$$-10+2I_1+5(I_1-I_2)=0$$

or, $$7I_1-5I_2=10 \qquad ...(1)$$

In loop-2, KVL yields

$$-v_x+I_2\times 1+2I_2-2v_x=0$$

or, $$-3v_x+3I_2=0 \quad \text{or} \quad v_x=I_2 \qquad ...(2)$$

But $$v_x=(I_1-I_2)5 \qquad ...(3)$$

Substituting (2) in (3), we get

$$I_2=5I_1-5I_2 \quad \text{or} \quad 5I_1-6I_2=0 \quad \text{or} \quad I_1=\frac{6}{5}I_2$$

Then from (1),

$$7\left(\frac{6}{5}I_2\right)-5I_2=10$$

or, $$3.4\,I_2=10 \quad \text{or} \quad I_2=2.94\text{ A}$$

and $$I_1=3.528\text{ A.}$$

This gives $v_x=2.94$ V and $2v_x$ (the dependent source) as 5.88 V.

$$\therefore \quad V_{o.c}=\text{drop across } 2\Omega \text{ in } loop\ 2-2v_x$$
$$=I_2\times 2-5.88=0$$

Thus from Norton's equivalent circuit (Fig. E6.129(*c*)),

$$I=I_{s.c}\frac{R_{int}}{R_{int}+3}=0 \qquad [\because I_{s.c}=0]$$

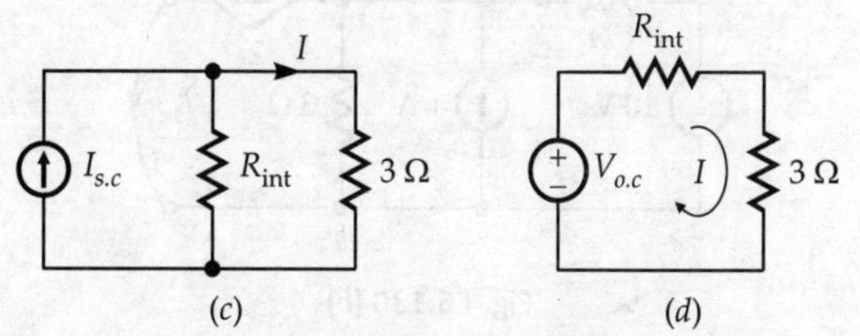

Fig. E6.129

While from Thevenin's equivalent circuit (Fig. E6.129(*d*)),

$$I=\frac{V_{o.c}}{R_{int}+3}=0 \qquad [\because V_{o.c}=0]$$

EXAMPLE 6.130 *Find the current in 2Ω resistor using Thevenin's theorem in Fig. E6.130. Verify the result by Norton's theorem.*

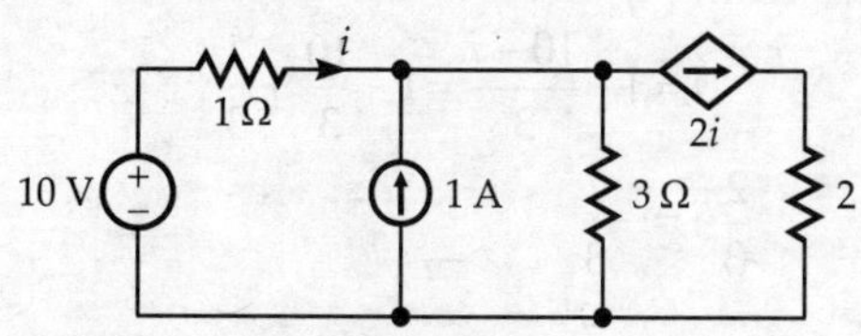

Fig. E6.130

SOLUTION. Let the 2 Ω resistor be removed (Fig. E6.130(*a*)).

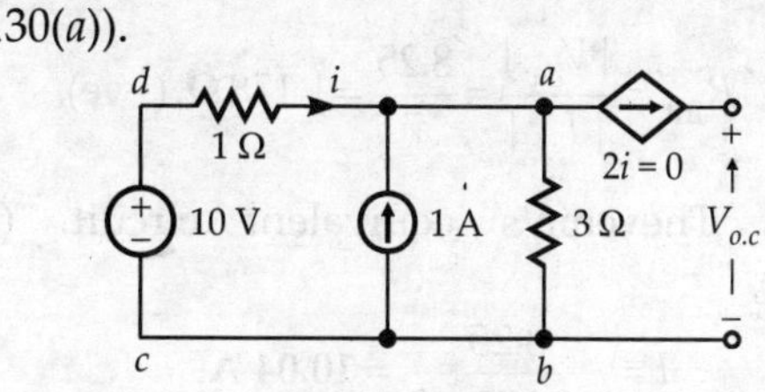

Fig. E6.130 (*a*)

C H A P T E R 6

Obviously $2i = 0$ as no current can flow through open circuit.

Also, $V_{o.c} = V_{3\Omega}$

At *node a*, $$\frac{V_{o.c}}{3} = i + 1 \quad ...(1)$$

or, $$V_{o.c} = 3i + 3$$

Also, in *loop abcd*,

$$-10 + i \times 1 + V_{o.c} = 0$$

or, $$V_{o.c} = 10 - i \quad ...(2)$$

Comparing (1) and (2),

$$3i + 3 = 10 - i$$

or, $$4i = 7 \text{ i.e., } i = 1.75 \text{ A}$$

$$\therefore \quad V_{o.c} = 3 \times 1.75 + 3 = 8.25 \text{ V.}$$

Next, the output terminals are shorted (Fig. E6.130(*b*)).

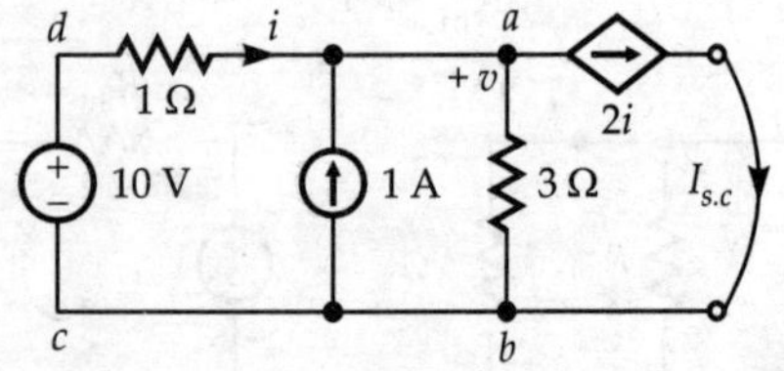

Fig. E6.130 (*b*)

Obviously, $$I_{s.c} = 2i \quad ...(3)$$

At *node a*

or, $$(i+1) = \frac{v}{3} + 2i \text{ or } i = 1 - \frac{v}{3} \quad ...(4)$$

Again in *loop a-b-c-d*,

$$-10 + i \times 1 + v = 0$$

or, $$v = 10 - i \quad ...(5)$$

Thus from (4)

$$i = 1 - \frac{10-i}{3} = 1 - \frac{10}{3} + \frac{i}{3}$$

or, $$\frac{2}{3} i = -\frac{7}{3}$$

$$\therefore \quad i = -\frac{7}{2} \text{ A} = -3.5 \text{ A.}$$

$$\therefore \quad I_{s.c} = -7 \text{ A.}$$

$$R_{int} = \frac{|V_{o.c}|}{|I_{s.c}|} = \frac{8.25}{7} = 1.178\,\Omega.\,(-ve)$$

From Thevenin's equivalent circuit, (Fig. E6.130(*c*)),

$$I = \frac{8.25}{-1.178 + 2} = \mathbf{10.04\ A.}$$

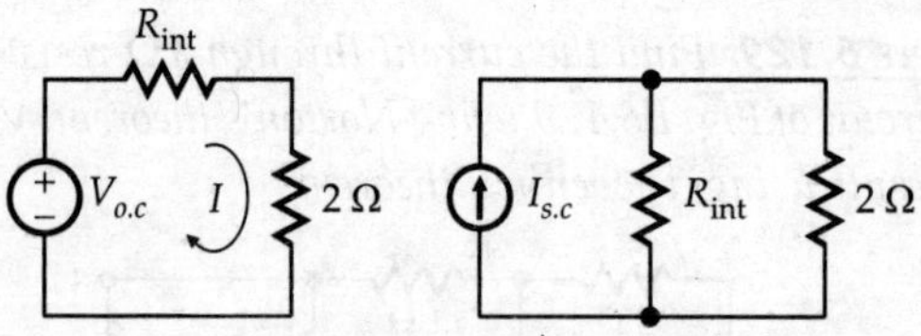

(*c*) (*d*)

Fig. E6.130

From Norton's equivalent circuit (Fig. E6.130(*d*)),

$$I = I_{s.c} \frac{R_{int}}{R_{int} + 2} = \mathbf{10.04\ A.}$$

Example 6.131 *Applying Superposition theorem, find the current through r in the circuit shown in Fig. E6.131.*

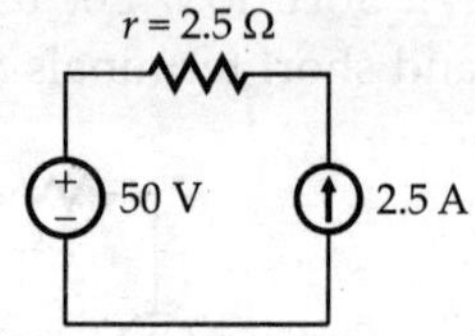

Fig. E6.131

Solution. Taking into account the 50 V source first, following Fig. E6.131(*a*),

$$I_1 = 0 \text{ A}$$

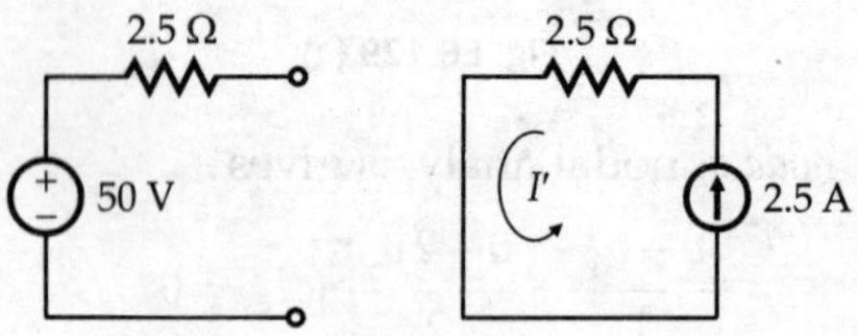

(*a*) (*b*)

Fig. E6.131

On the other hand, taking the 2.5 A source alone, following Fig. E6.131(*b*),

$$I' = 2.5 \text{ A.}$$

Hence the net current *I*, according to the superposition theorem is given by

$$I = I_1 + I' = \mathbf{2.5\ A.}$$

Current flowing anticlockwise signifying that the current source is the determining factor in circulation of current through a load when both current and voltage sources are in series.

Example 6.132 *In the circuit of Fig. E6.132, find R if $i = 0.1$ A (Use Superposition theorem).*

Solution. Let us take the +10 V supply first,

$$i_1 = \frac{10}{10 + R}$$

$$\left[\begin{array}{c}\text{Assuming the current through}\\ R \text{ is } i_1 \text{ for 10 V source only}\end{array}\right]$$

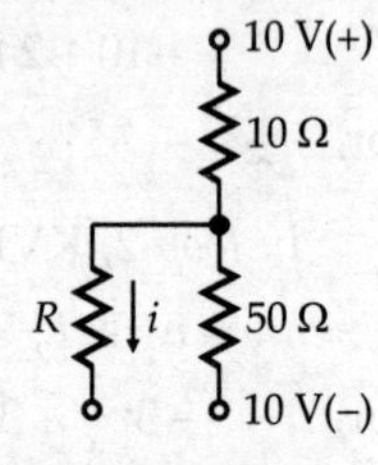

Fig. E6.132

Next, taking the -10 V source only, for the current i_2 due to -10 V source, we can write

$$i_2 = -\frac{10}{50+R}$$

As per Superposition theorem,

$$i = i_1 + i_2 = \frac{10}{10+R} - \frac{10}{50+R}$$

$$0.1 = 10\left[\frac{1}{10+R} - \frac{1}{50+R}\right]$$

or $\quad 0.01 = \dfrac{50+R-10-R}{500+60\,R+R^2} = \dfrac{40}{500+60\,R+R^2}$

or, $\quad 5 + 0.6\,R + 0.01\,R^2 = 40$

or, $\quad 0.01\,R^2 + 0.6\,R - 35 = 0$

$\therefore \quad R = \dfrac{-0.6 \pm \sqrt{0.36+1.4}}{0.02} = (-30 \pm 66.33)\,\Omega$

The feasible value of R is thus

$$(-30 + 66.33)\,\Omega = \mathbf{36.33\,\Omega}.$$

EXAMPLE 6.133 *In the π circuit shown in Fig. E6.133, find the current in the 2 Ω resistor.*

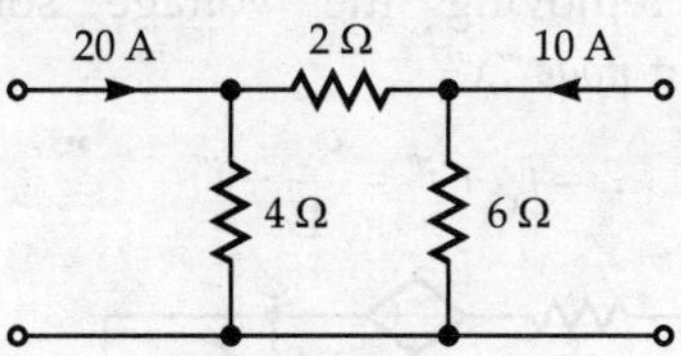

Fig. E6.133

SOLUTION. Taking the 20 A source only,

$$I'_{2\Omega} = 20 \cdot \frac{4}{2+6+4} = 6.67\text{ A.}$$

On the other hand, taking 10 A source only

$$I''_{2\Omega} = 10 \cdot \frac{6}{6+2+4} = 5\text{ A}$$

Thus, using the principle of Superposition,

$$I_{2\Omega} = 6.67 - 5 = \mathbf{1.67\text{ A.}}$$

EXAMPLE 6.134 *Find v_0 in the network of Fig. E6.134 using Superposition theorem.*

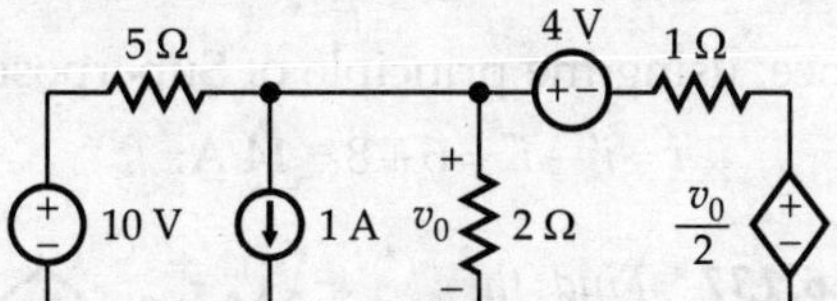

Fig. E6.134

SOLUTION. Let us take the 10 V source only (Fig. E6.134(*a*)).

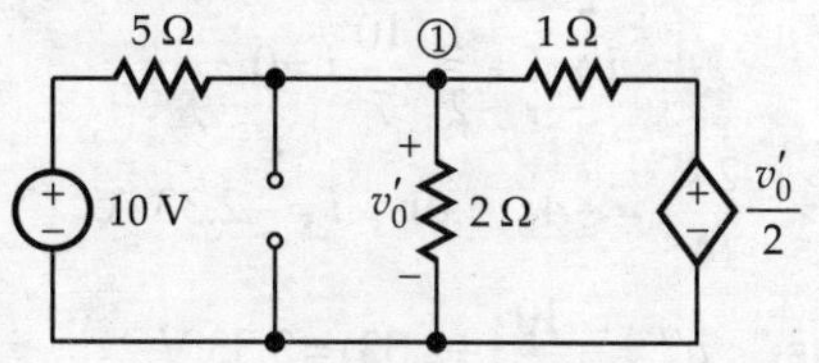

Fig. E6.134 (*a*)

At *node* (1), $\quad \dfrac{v'_0}{2} + \dfrac{v'_0 - v'_0/2}{1} + \dfrac{v'_0 - 10}{5} = 0$

or, $\quad 0.5\,v'_0 + v'_0 - 0.5\,v'_0 + 0.2\,v'_0 - 2 = 0$

or, $\quad 1.2\,v'_0 = 2$

or, $\quad v'_0 = 1.67$ V.

Next, taking the current source only (Fig. E6.134(*b*) at *node* (1),

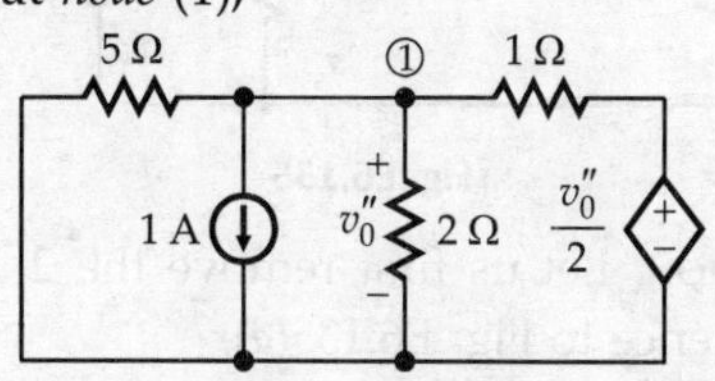

Fig. E6.134 (*b*)

$$\frac{v''_0}{2} + 1 + \frac{v''_0}{5} + \frac{v''_0 - \frac{v''_0}{2}}{1} = 0$$

or, $\quad 0.5\,v''_0 + 0.2\,v''_0 + v''_0 - 0.5\,v''_0 + 1 = 0$

or, $\quad 1.2\,v''_0 = -1$

$\therefore \quad v''_0 = -0.833$ V

Next, taking the 4 V source only, with reference to Fig. E6.134(*c*),

$$i \times \frac{10}{7} + 4 + 1 \times i + \frac{v'''_0}{2} = 0 \qquad \text{...(1)}$$

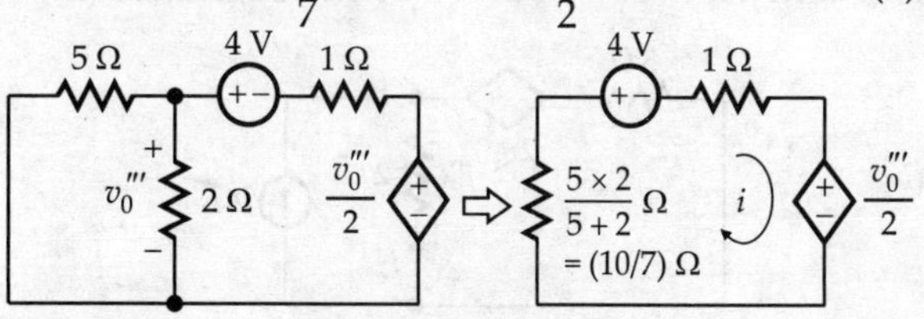

Fig. E6.134 (*c*)

However,

$$v'''_0 = -i_{2\Omega} \times 2\,\Omega$$

and $\quad i_{2\Omega} = i\dfrac{5}{5+2} = \dfrac{5}{7}\,i$

$\therefore \quad v'''_0 = -\dfrac{5}{7}\,i \times 2 = -\dfrac{10}{7}\,i \qquad \text{...(2)}$

Using (2) in (1),

$$\frac{10\,i}{7} + 4 + i + \frac{1}{2}\left(-\frac{10}{7}\,i\right) = 0$$

$$i + 4 + \frac{1}{2} \cdot \frac{10}{7} i = 0$$

or, $\frac{24}{14} i = -4$ or, $i = -2.33$ A

Thus $v_0''' = -\frac{10}{7}(-2.33) = 3.33$ V

Using the principle of Superposition,

$$v_0 = v_0' + v_0'' + v_0''' = 1.67 + (-0.833) + 3.33 = \mathbf{4.167\ V.}$$

EXAMPLE 6.135 *Find i in the circuit of Fig. E6.135 using Superposition principle.*

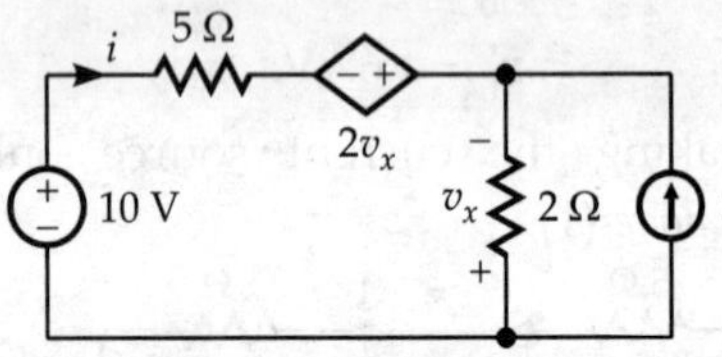

Fig. E6.135

SOLUTION. Let us first remove the 2 A source. With reference to Fig. E6.135(*a*),

$$-10 + 5i' - 2v_x - 2i' = 0$$

or, $3i' - 2v_x = 10$ ...(1)

Also, $v_x = -2i'$ ...(2)

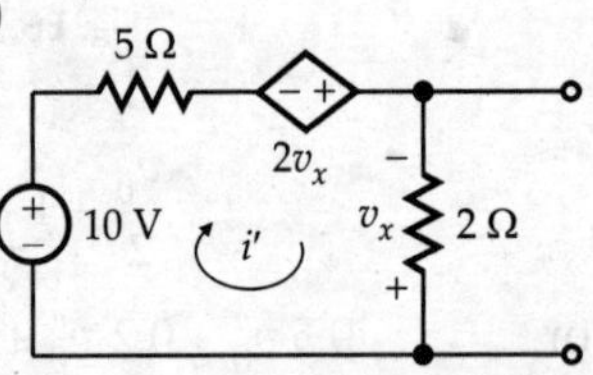

Fig. E6.135 (*a*)

Thus, from (1),

$$3i' - 2(-2i') = 10$$

or, $i' = \frac{10}{7} = 1.43$ A.

Next, referring Fig. E6.135(*b*) where 2 A source is retained and 10 V source is removed, at *node* (*x*),

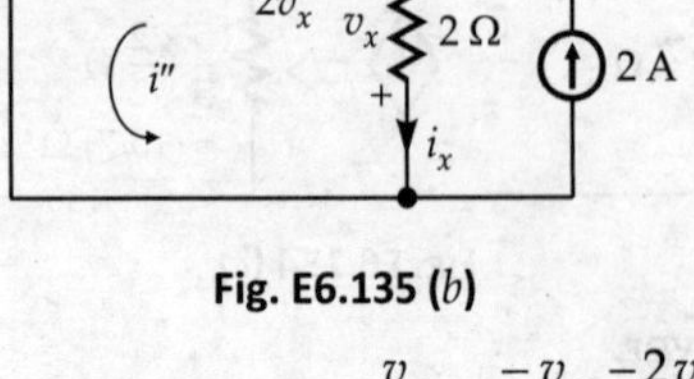

Fig. E6.135 (*b*)

$$2 = i_x + i'' = -\frac{v_x}{2} + \frac{-v_x - 2v_x}{5}$$

$$= -0.5\,v_x - 0.2\,v_x - 0.4\,v_x$$

or, $v_x = -1.82$ V

Thus $i'' = \frac{-v_x - 2v_x}{5} = -\frac{3v_x}{5} \simeq 1.1$ A

Using the principle of Superposition,

$$i = i' - i'' = 1.43 - 1.1 = \mathbf{0.33\ A.}$$

EXAMPLE 6.136 *Find i using Superposition theorem (Fig. E6.136).*

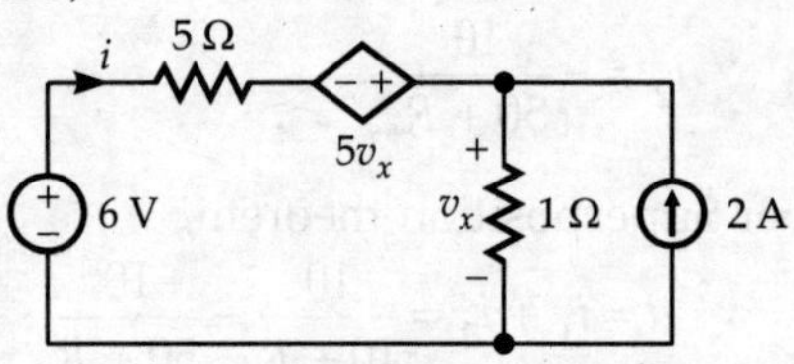

Fig. E6.136

SOLUTION. Removing the current source (Fig. E6.136(*a*)),

$$6 = 5i' - 5v_x + i' = 6i' - 5v_x \quad \text{...(1)}$$

Also, $v_x = 1 \times i' = i'$ ...(2)

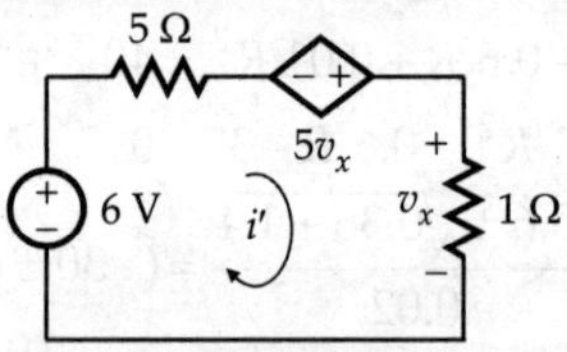

Fig. E6.136 (*a*)

Using (2) in (1),

$$6 = 6i' - 5i' = i' \quad \textit{i.e.,}\ i' = 6\ \text{A.}$$

Next, removing the voltage source (Fig. E6.136(*b*)), at *node "x"*,

$$2 = i_x + i'' = \frac{v_x}{1} + i'' \quad \text{...(3)}$$

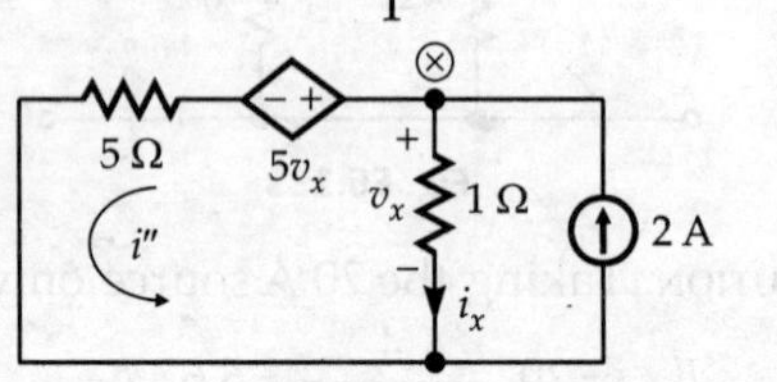

Fig. E6.136 (*b*)

But loop analysis in the *left loop* gives

$$-v_x + 5v_x + 5i'' = 0$$

or, $4v_x = -5i''$

or, $i'' = -\frac{4}{5} v_x$ ...(4)

Using (4) in (3),

$$2 = -\frac{5i''}{4} + i'' = -\frac{1}{4} i'' \qquad \therefore \quad i'' = -8\ \text{A.}$$

Hence, using the principle of Superposition,

$$i = i' - i'' = 6 + 8 = \mathbf{14\ A.}$$

EXAMPLE 6.137 *Find the power loss in 5 Ω resistor by Superposition theorem in Fig. E6.137.*

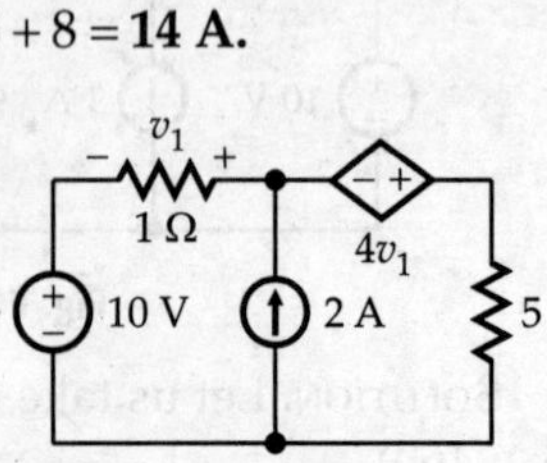

Fig. E6.137

Solution. Assuming the 10 V source first (Fig. E6.137(*a*)), KVL yields

$$-10 - v_1 - 4v_1 + 5I_1 = 0$$

or, $$5I_1 = 5v_1 + 10 \quad ...(1)$$

But $$v_1 = -1 \times I_1 \quad ...(2)$$

Using (2) in (1),

$$10\ I_1 = 10$$

i.e., $$I_1 = \frac{10}{10} = 1$$

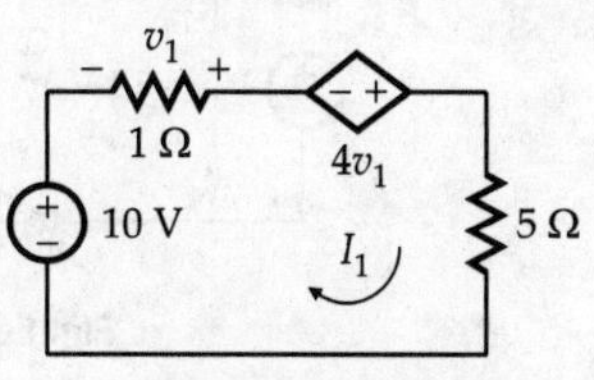

Fig. E6.137 (*a*)

Next, taking the current source only, referring Fig. E6.137(*b*), at *node* (1),

$$2 = \frac{v_1}{1} + \frac{v_1 + 4v_1}{5}$$

$$= v_1 + 0.2\ v_1 + 0.8\ v_1$$

or $v_1 = 1$ V.

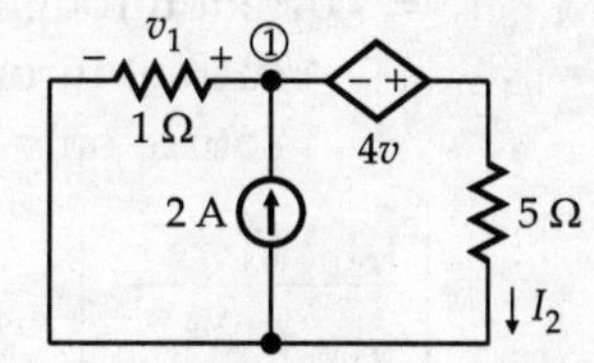

Fig. E6.137 (*b*)

$$\therefore \quad I_2 \text{ (Fig. E6.137 (}b\text{))} = \frac{v_1 + 4v_1}{5} = 1 \text{ A.}$$

Hence, the current through 5Ω resistor is

$$I = I_1 + I_2 = 2 \text{ A.}$$

∴ Power loss in 5Ω resistor is $(2)^2 \times 5 = $ **20 W.**

Example 6.138 *Using Superposition theorem, find I_1 and I_2 in the circuit shown in Fig. E6.138.*

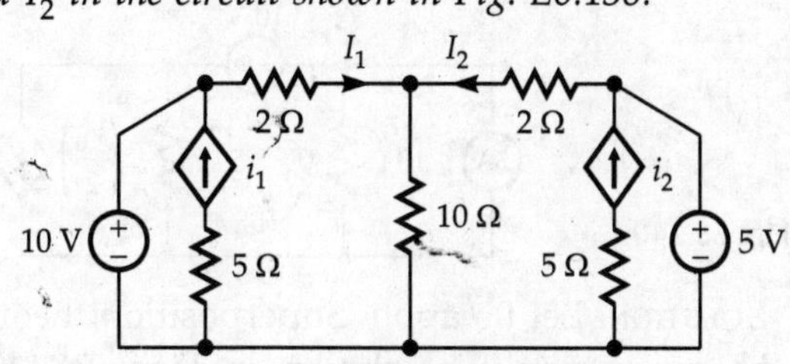

Fig. E6.138

Solution. Taking 10 V source first (Fig. E6.138(*a*)), *nodal analysis* at (*x*) yields

$$\frac{V_x - 10}{2} + \frac{V_x}{10} + \frac{V_x}{2} = 0$$

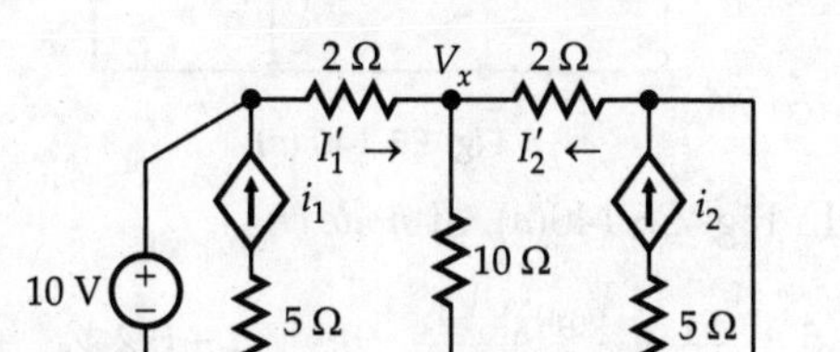

Fig. E6.138 (*a*)

or, $$1.1\ V_x = 5 \quad \text{or,} \quad V_x = \frac{5}{1.1} = 4.545 \text{ V}$$

$$\therefore \quad I_1' = -\frac{V_x - 10}{2} = -\frac{4.545 - 10}{2} = 2.727 \text{ A}$$

$$I_2' = -\frac{V_x}{2} = -2.272 \text{ A}$$

Next, assuming only 5 V source, with reference to Fig. E6.138(*b*),

$$\frac{V_x}{2} + \frac{V_x - 5}{2} + \frac{V_x}{10} = 0 \quad \text{or,} \quad 1.1\ V_x = 2.5$$

$$\therefore \quad V_x = 2.273 \text{ V}$$

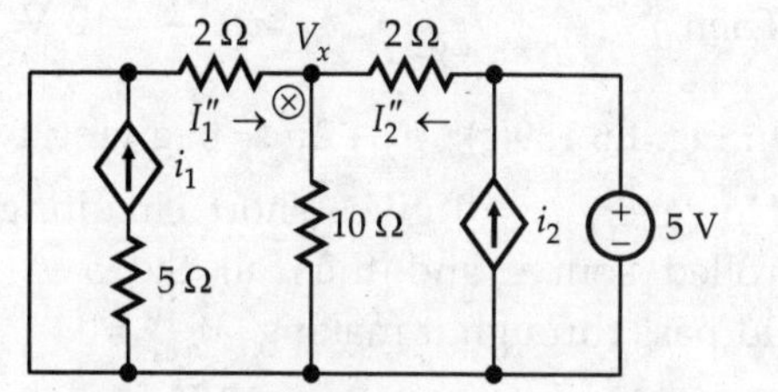

Fig. E6.138 (*b*)

This gives

$$I_1'' = -\frac{V_x}{2} = -1.136 \text{ A}$$

and $$I_2' = -\frac{V_x - 5}{2} = 0.227 \text{ A}$$

Using the principle of Superposition,

$$I_1 = I_1' + I_1'' = 2.727 - 1.136 \simeq \mathbf{1.6\ A}$$

$$I_2 = I_2' + I_2'' = -2.272 + 0.227 = \mathbf{-2.045\ A.}$$

Example 6.139 *Using Superposition theorem, find the Thevenin equivalent circuit of the portion of the network at the left of terminal x - y (Fig. E6.139). Also determine the current through the 1Ω resistor (R_L) at the right hand side of x - y.*

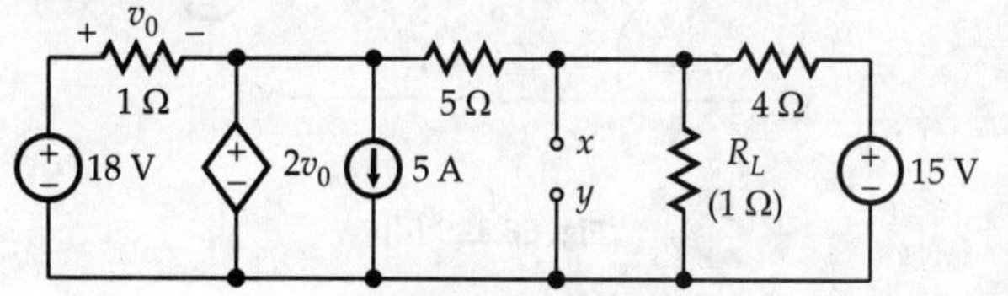

Fig. E6.139

Solution. The portion of the network at the left of *x* - *y* terminals is kept only (Fig. E6.139(*a*)) to find $V_{o.c}$ across *x* - *y*.

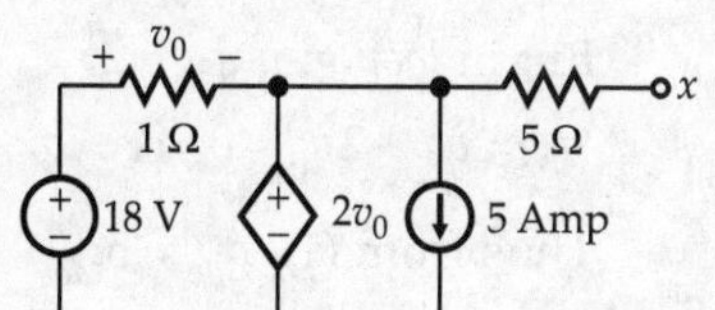

Fig. E6.139 (*a*)

Next, Superposition is applied as shown in Figs. E6.139(*b*) and (*c*). In Fig. E6.139(*b*),

$$-18+v_1+2v_1=0,$$

or, $$v_1=+\frac{18}{3}=6\text{ V}$$

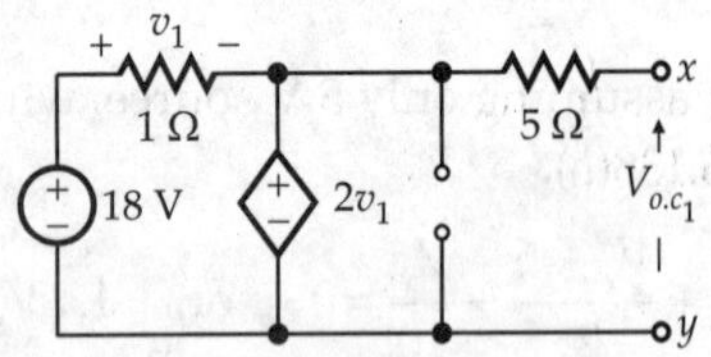

Fig. E6.139 (*b*)

Then, $$V_{o.c_1}=2v_1=2\,.\,\frac{18}{3}=12\text{ V.}$$

In Fig. E6.139(*c*), $v_2+2v_2=0$ giving $v_2=0.$

However, $v_2=0$ gives short circuiting of the controlled source and thus all the 5 A current would pass through it making $V_{o.c_2}=0.$

Thus, $V_{o.c}=V_{o.c_1}+V_{o.c_2}=12$ V.

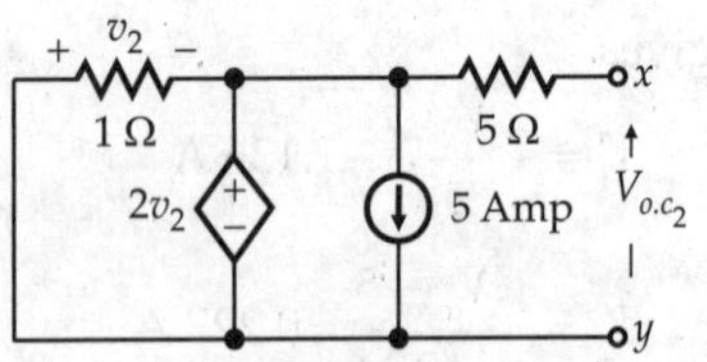

Fig. E6.139 (*c*)

Thevenin's equivalent resistance (*i.e.*, the internal resistance) is obtained by deactivating the sources in the original circuit (Fig. E6.139(*d*)). A dc voltage v_{dc} is applied at x - y, current input being i_{dc}.

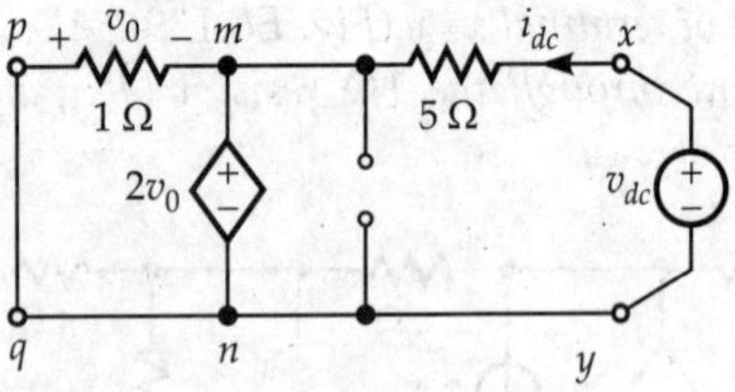

Fig. E6.139 (*d*)

Using KVL in *loop x-m-n-y*,

$$-v_{dc}+5i_{dc}+2v_0=0 \qquad \text{...(1)}$$

But in *loop m-n-q-p*,

$$v_0+2v_0=0,\ i.e.,\ v_0=0.$$

Thus from (1), $v_{dc}=5i_{dc}$

or, $$\frac{v_{dc}}{i_{dc}}=5\,\Omega=R_{Th}\ \text{(Thevenin resistance)}$$

Figure E6.139(*e*) represents Thevenin's equivalent circuit. The right hand portion of the original network (Fig. E6.139) is reconnected with this equivalent network.

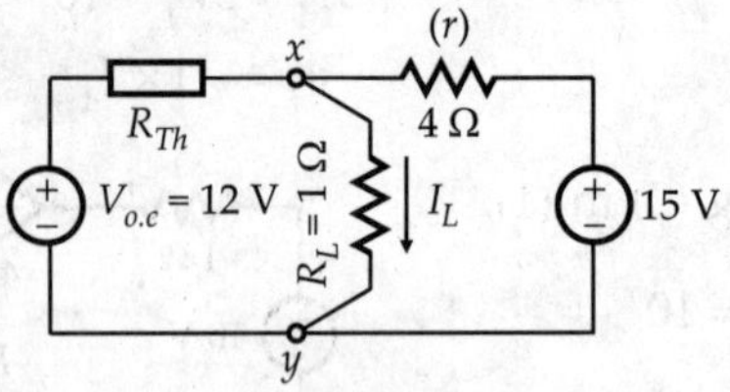

Fig. E6.139 (*e*)

Using Superposition principle, the current through 1Ω resistance is obtained as

I_L = current through R_L due to $V_{o.c}$ only + current through R_L due to 15 V source only

$$=\left[\frac{V_{o.c}}{R_{Th}+\dfrac{R_L\times r}{R_L+r}}\right]\times\frac{r}{R_L+r}+\left[\frac{15}{4+\dfrac{R_{Th}\times R_L}{R_{Th}+R_L}}\right]\times\frac{R_{Th}}{R_{Th}+R_L}$$

$$=\frac{123}{29}=4.24\text{ A}$$

Thus the current though R_L is **4.24 A.**

EXAMPLE 6.140 *Figure E6.140 represents a mixed circuit. Find the magnitude of V_0 by Superposition theorem and find the power produced by each of the sources.*

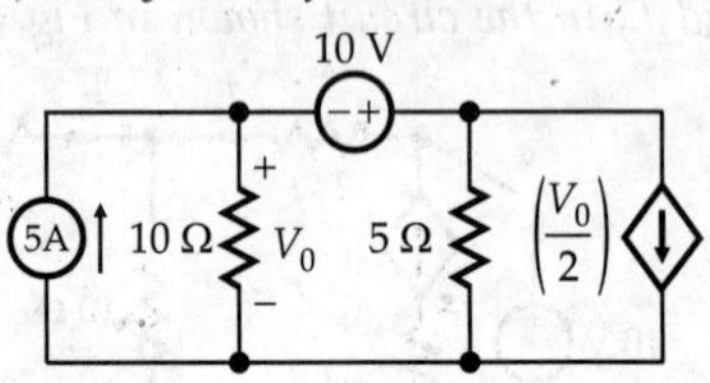

Fig. E6.140

SOLUTION. Let us apply Superposition theorem in the given circuit as shown in Figs. E6.140(*a*) and (*b*).

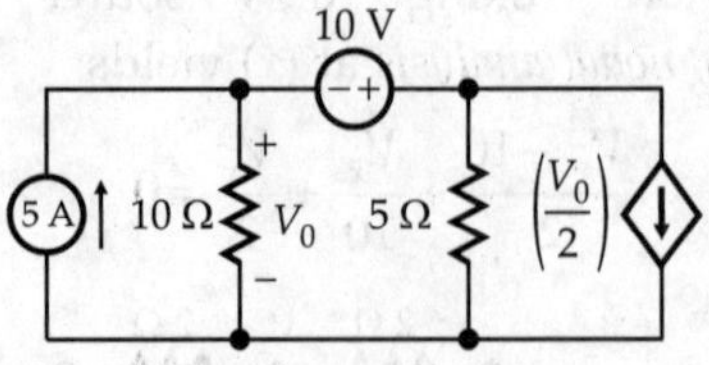

Fig. E6.140 (*a*)

In Fig. E6.140(*a*), at *node* (n_a),

$$5=\frac{V_{01}}{10}+\frac{V_{01}}{5}+\frac{V_{01}}{2}=0.1\,V_{01}+0.2\,V_{01}+0.5\,V_{01}$$

$$\therefore\quad V_{01}=6.25\text{ V} \qquad \text{...(1)}$$

In Fig. E6.140(*b*), let at *node* (n_b) the voltage be V_{n_2}. Then, nodal analysis at *node* (n_b) gives

$$\frac{V_{02}}{10}+\frac{V_{02}}{2}+\frac{V_{n_2}}{5}=0 \quad ...(2)$$

But $\quad V_{n_2}=(V_{02}+10) \quad ...(3)$

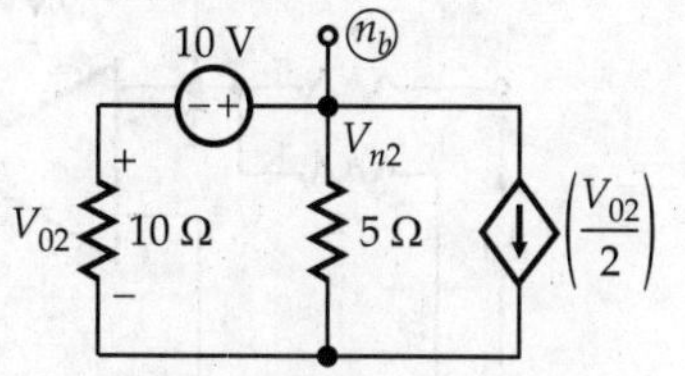

Fig. E6.140 (*b*)

Using equation (3) in (2), we get

$$0.6\,V_{02}+\frac{V_{02}+10}{5}=0$$

or, $\quad 0.8\,V_{02}=-2 \quad$ or $\quad V_{02}=-2.5$ V $\quad ...(4)$

Since $V_0=V_{01}+V_{02}$, we get

$$V_0=6.25+(-2.5)=3.75 \text{ V}$$

Thus, using Superposition theorem, V_0 **= 3.75 V.**
Next, we are to find the powers generated by the sources as follows :

(*i*) Power generated by 5 A source = Voltage across 5 A source × 5 A current $=3.75\times 5=18.75$ W [this power is fed to the circuit]

(*ii*) To find power generated by 10 V source, let us draw the final circuit (Fig. E6.140(*c*)).

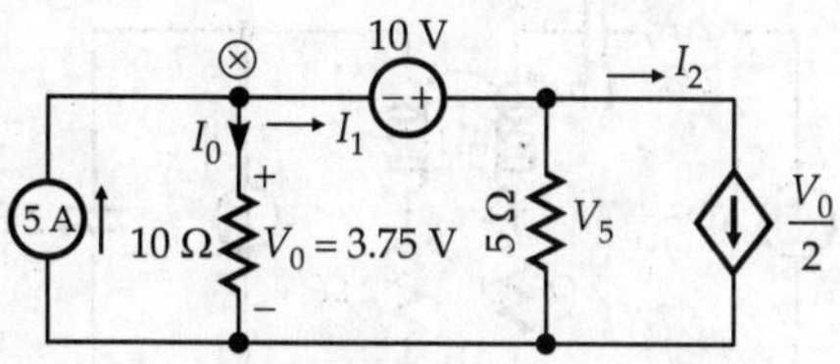

Fig. E6.140 (*c*)

At *node* (*x*),

$$5=I_0+I_1$$

But $\quad I_0=\frac{V_0}{10}=\frac{3.75}{10}=0.375 \text{ A}$

$\therefore \quad I_1=5-I_0=5-0.375=4.625$ A

Since I_1 flows though 10 V source

$\therefore$ Power given by 10 V source

$$=10\times 4.625=46.25 \text{ W}$$

[This power is fed to the circuit]

(*iii*) Let the drop across 5 Ω resistor be V_5 volts. Application of KVL in the central loop,

$$-V_0-10+V_5=0$$

or, $\quad V_5=V_0+10=3.75+10=13.75$ V

Thus power of the dependent source is then

$$(13.75 \text{ V}\times I_2)\text{ W}=13.75\times\frac{V_0}{2} \qquad \left[\because I_2\equiv\frac{V_0}{2}\text{ A}\right]$$

i.e., power of dependent source

$$=13.75\times\frac{3.75}{2}=25.78 \text{ W. (intake)}$$

Since the current enters the dependent source through the +ve terminal hence, this power is supplied to the dependent source.

Thus finally,

Power given by 5 A source = **18.75 W**

Power given by 10 A source = **46.25 W**

Power given by $\frac{V_0}{2}$ source = **– 25.78 W.**

EXAMPLE 6.141 *Find v using the principle of Superposition in Fig. E6.141.*

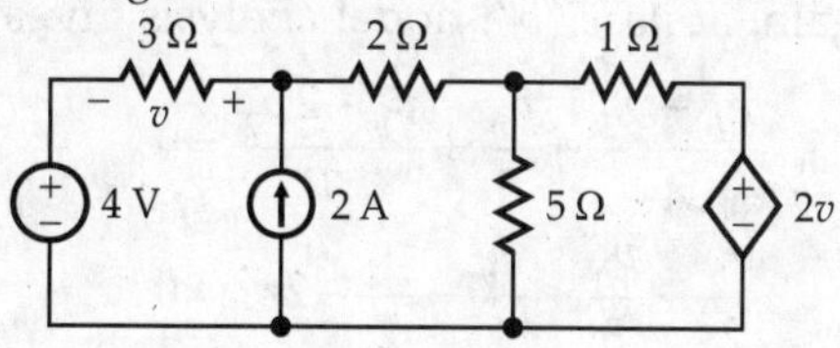

Fig. E6.141

SOLUTION. Taking the voltage source only and referring Fig. E6.141(*a*).

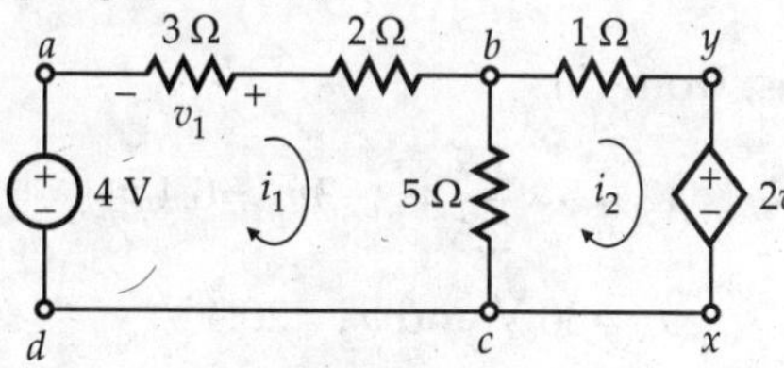

Fig. E6.141 (*a*)

In *loop a-b-c-d*,

$$-4+3i_1+2i_1+5(i_1-i_2)=0$$

or, $\quad 10\,i_1-5i_2=4 \quad ...(1)$

In *loop b-c-x-y*,

$$5(i_2-i_1)+1\times i_2+2v_1=0 \quad ...(2)$$

But $\quad v_1=-3i_1$ (in *loop a-b-c-d*)

Thus, (2) reduces to,

$$5(i_2-i_1)+i_2-6i_1=0$$

or, $\quad -11\,i_1+6i_2=0 \quad ...(3)$

From (3), $\quad i_2=\frac{11}{6}i_1 \quad ...(4)$

Using (4) in (1),

$$10\,i_1 - \frac{55}{6} i_1 = 4$$

or, $$\frac{5}{6} i_1 = 4 \text{ i.e., } i_1 = \frac{24}{5}\text{ A}$$

$\therefore$ $$v_1 = -3i_1 = -\frac{72}{5} = -14.4\text{ V.}$$

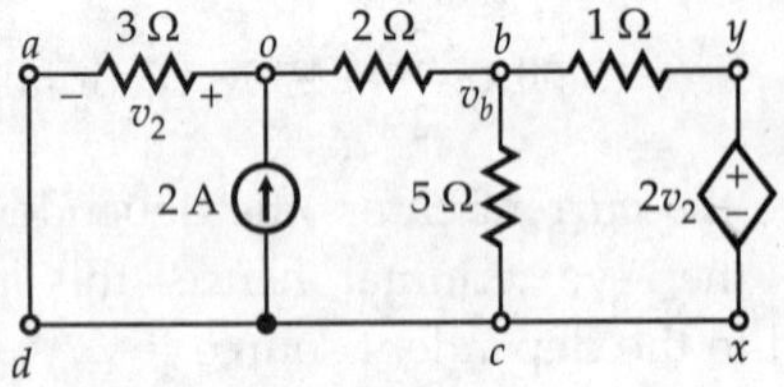

Fig. E6.141 (*b*)

Referring Fig. E6.141(*b*), nodal analysis at *node* "o" reveals

$$2 = \frac{v_2}{3} + \frac{v_2 - v_b}{2} \quad \text{or} \quad 2 = \frac{5}{6} v_2 - \frac{1}{2} v_b$$

or, $$12 = 5v_2 - 3v_b \qquad ...(5)$$

Again, at *node* "*b*", nodal analysis gives

$$\frac{v_b - v_2}{2} + \frac{v_b}{5} + \frac{v_b - 2v_2}{1} = 0$$

or, $$\frac{v_b}{2} + \frac{v_b}{5} + \frac{v_b}{1} - \frac{v_2}{2} - 2v_2 = 0$$

or, $$1.7\,v_b - 2.5\,v_2 = 0$$

or, $$v_2 = \frac{1.7}{2.5} v_b \qquad ...(6)$$

Thus, from (5),

$$12 = 5 \times \frac{1.7}{2.5} v_b - 3v_b = 0.4\,v_b$$

$\therefore$ $v_b = 30$ V and $v_2 = 20.4$ V.

From the principle of Superposition,

$$v = v_1 + v_2 = -14.4 + 20.4 = \mathbf{6\ V.}$$

EXAMPLE 6.142 *In the op-amp. circuit shown in Fig. E6.142, find V_0 by Superposition.*

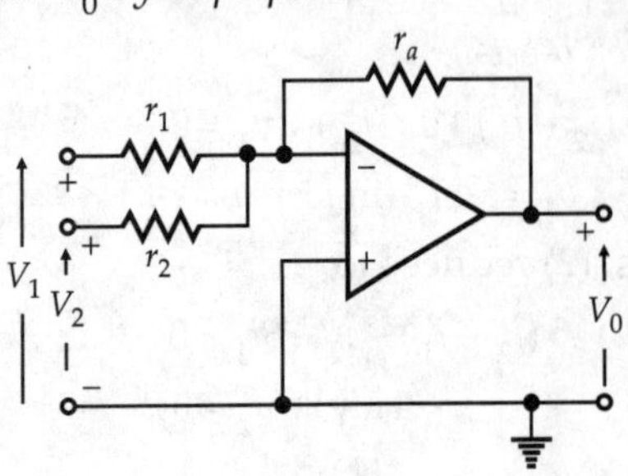

Fig. E6.142

SOLUTION. Let us take V_1 only at first deactivating V_2 (Fig. E6.142(*a*)), at *node* (1), assuming *node* (1) voltage to be v,

$$\frac{v - v_1}{r_1} + \frac{v}{r_2} + \frac{v - v_0'}{r_a} = 0 \qquad ...(1)$$

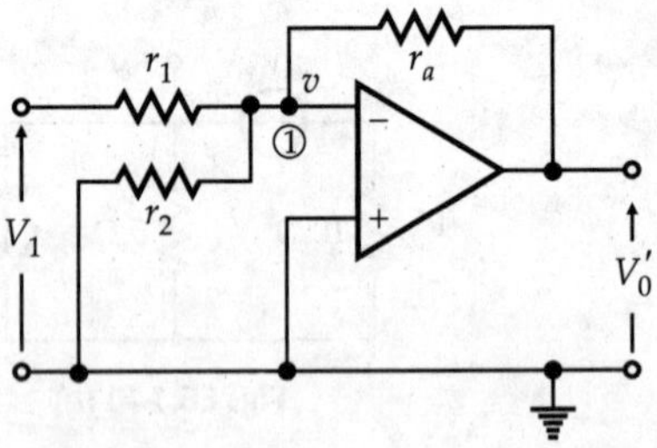

Fig. E6.142 (*a*)

But, in an ideal op-amp, *node (1)* is virtual ground, being at the same voltage as the ground. Hence $v = 0$. Thus we obtain from (1),

$$-\frac{v_1}{r_1} - \frac{v_0'}{r_a} = 0 \quad \text{or} \quad V_0' = -\frac{r_a}{r_1} v_1.$$

Similarly, deactivating v_1, applying v_2 only,

$$V_0'' = -\frac{r_a}{r_2} v_2.$$

Thus, using the principle of Superposition

$$V_0 = V_0' + V_0'' = -\left(\frac{r_a}{r_1} v_1 + \frac{r_a}{r_2} v_2\right).$$

EXAMPLE 6.143 *In Fig. E6.143, by Superposition, find v_x and i_x in the coupled coil circuit.*

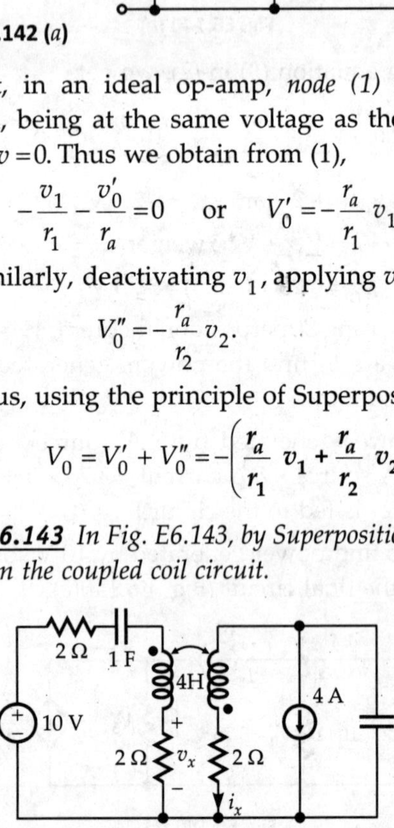

Fig. E6.143

SOLUTION. Because each source is dc, the inductors can be replaced by short circuits in steady state while the capacitors are represented by open circuits. Mutual inductance does not play any role since its effects appear only when the currents through the coils are changing with time. Fig. E6.143(*a*) represents the circuit with voltage source only while Fig. E6.143(*b*) represents the circuit with current source only. Obviously, in Fig. E6.143(*a*), due to pressure of open circuit (that appears due to presence of capacitor in steady state),

$$v_x' = 0, i_x' = 0.$$

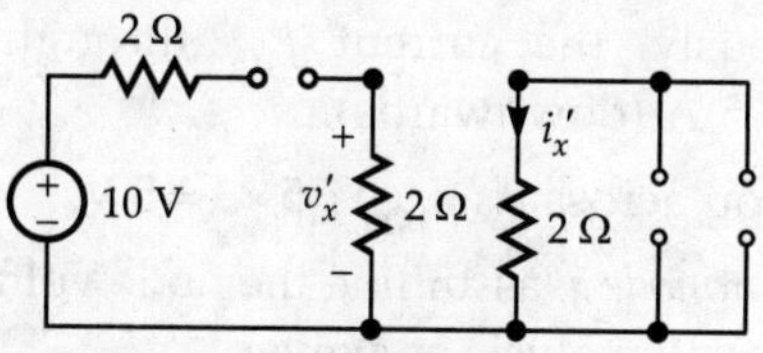

Fig. E6.143 (*a*)

However, in Fig. E6.143(*b*), by simple current division formulae, we see that

$$i''_x = -4 \text{ A}.$$

This makes $\quad v''_x = 0 \text{ V}.$

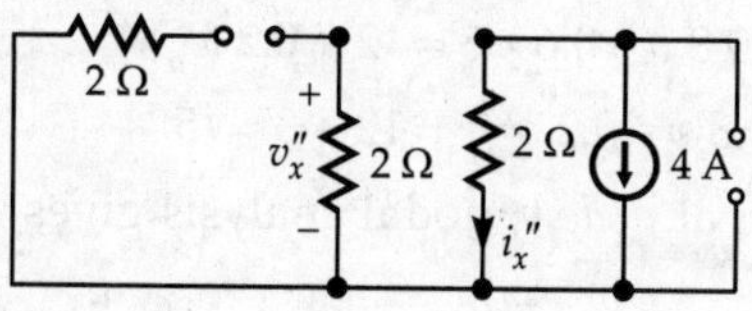

Fig. E6.143 (*b*)

Thus, application of Superposition principle yields

$$v_x = v'_x + v''_x = \mathbf{0\ V}$$

while $\quad i_x = i'_x + i''_x = \mathbf{-4\ A.}$

Example 6.144 *Find the value of R such that maximum power transfer takes place from the current sources to the load R in Fig. E6.144. Obtain the amount of power transfer.*

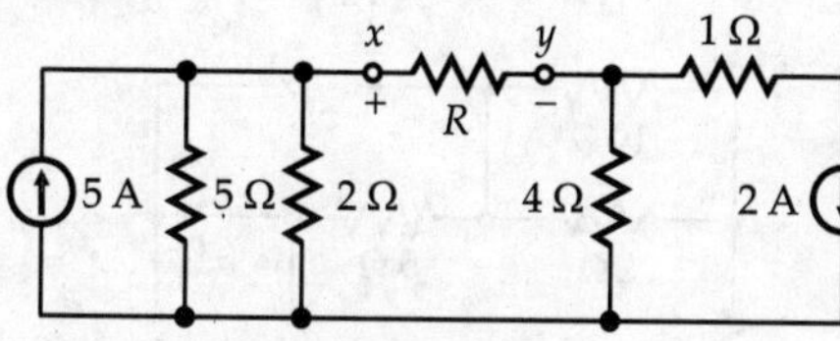

Fig. E6.144

Solution. Replacing R by open circuit and designating the nodal voltages as V_x and V_y we get from Fig. E6.144(*a*),

$$5 = \frac{V_x}{5} + \frac{V_x}{2} \quad \text{or} \quad \frac{7}{10} V_x = 5$$

or, $\quad V_x = \frac{50}{7} = 7.143 \text{ V}$

and $\quad V_y = -V_{ab} = -4 \times 2 = -8 \text{ V}$

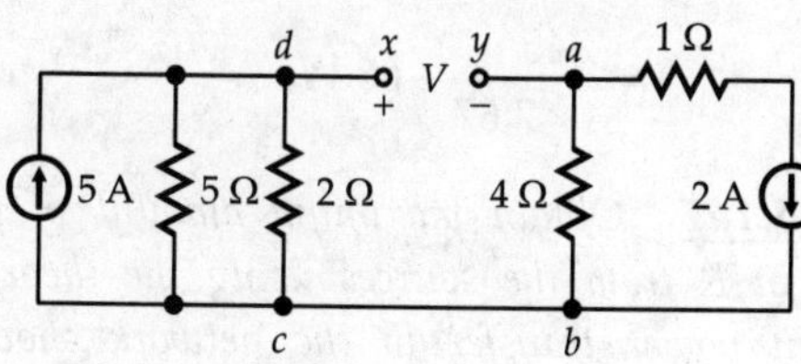

Fig. E6.144 (*a*)

∴ In loop *a-b-c-d*,

$$-V_x + V_{o.c} + V_y = 0$$

or, $\quad V_{o.c} = V_x - V_y = 7.143 - (-8) = 15.143 \text{ V}$

With reference to Fig. E6.144(*b*),

$$R_{Th} = \frac{2 \times 5}{2+5} + 4 = \frac{10}{7} + 4 = \frac{38}{7} = 5.43\ \Omega.$$

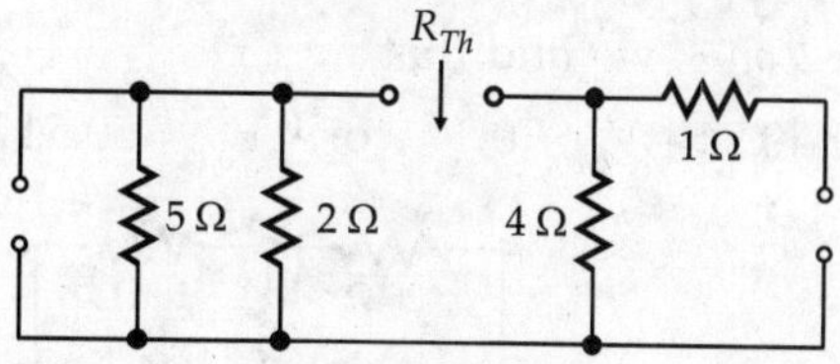

Fig. E6.144 (*b*)

∴ From maximum power transfer theorem,

$$R = R_{Th} = \mathbf{5.43\ \Omega}$$

and $\quad P_{max} = \frac{V^2_{o.c}}{4R} = \frac{(15.143)^2}{4 \times 5.43} = \mathbf{10.96\ W.}$

Example 6.145 *What is the value of R such that maximum power transfer takes place from the sources to R in the circuit of Fig. E6.145 ? Determine the amount of maximum power.*

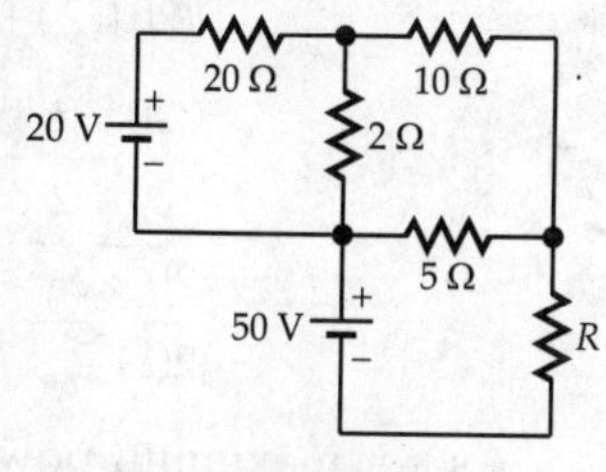

Fig. E6.145

Solution. Replacing R and naming the loop currents, with reference to Fig. E6.145(*a*), at *loop-1*,

$$-20 + I_1 (20 + 2) - 2 I_2 = 0$$

or, $\quad 22 I_1 - 2 I_2 = 20$

or, $\quad 11 I_1 - I_2 = 10 \quad$ ...(1)

At *loop-2*,

$$(10 + 5 + 2) I_2 - 2 I_1 = 0$$

or, $\quad 17 I_2 - 2 I_1 = 0$

or, $\quad I_1 = \frac{17}{2} I_2 = 8.5 I_2 \quad$ ...(2)

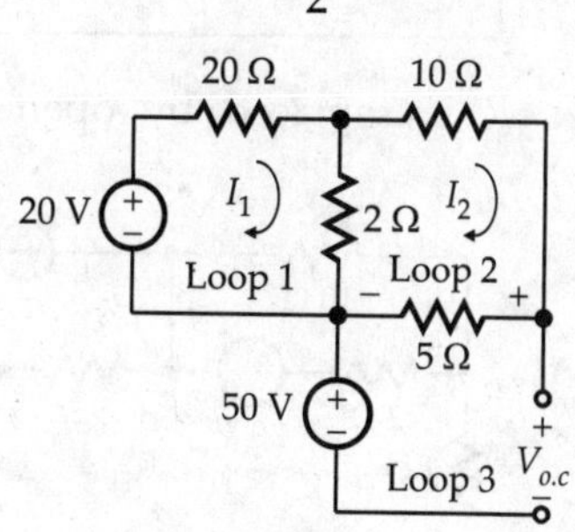

Fig. E6.145 (*a*)

Using (2) in (1),

$$11(8.5\,I_2) - I_2 = 10 \quad \text{or} \quad 92.5\,I_2 = 10$$

i.e.,
$$I_2 = \frac{10}{92.5} = 0.108 \text{ A}$$

Thus, drop across $5\,\Omega$,

i.e.,
$$V_{5\Omega} = 0.108 \times 5 = 0.54 \text{ V}$$

∴ *In loop-3*, we find that

$$-50 - 0.54 + V_{o.c} = 0 \qquad \text{or,} \quad V_{o.c} = 50.54 \text{ V}$$

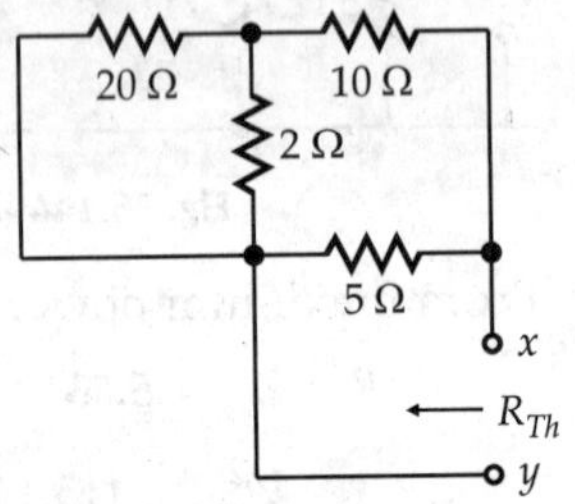

Fig. E6.145 (*b*)

To find internal resistance across x - y we find

$$R_{Th} = [\{(20\,||\,2) + 10\}\,||\,5]\,\Omega$$

$$= \frac{\left(\frac{20\times 2}{20+2}+10\right)5}{\frac{20\times 2}{20+2}+10+5} = \frac{11.82\times 5}{16.82} \simeq 3.5\,\Omega$$

As per maximum power transfer theorem,

$$R = R_{Th} = \mathbf{3.5\,\Omega}$$

and
$$P_{max} = \frac{V_{o.c}^2}{4\,R} = \frac{(50.54)^2}{4\times 3.5} = \mathbf{182.44\ W.}$$

EXAMPLE 6.146 *What is amount of maximum power transfer to R in the circuit of Fig. E6.146 ?*

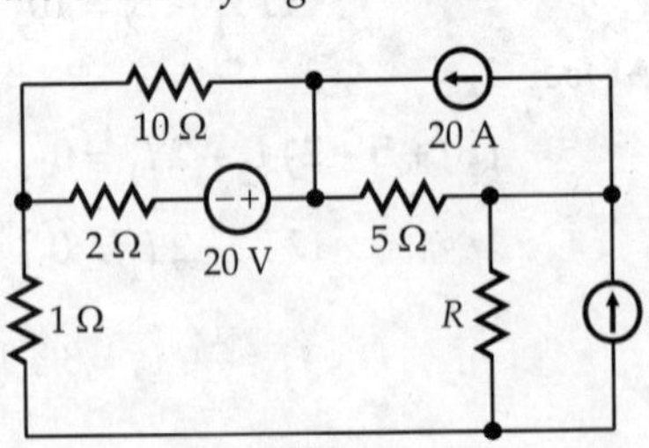

Fig. E6.146

SOLUTION. R is replaced by open circuit in Fig. E6.146(*a*).

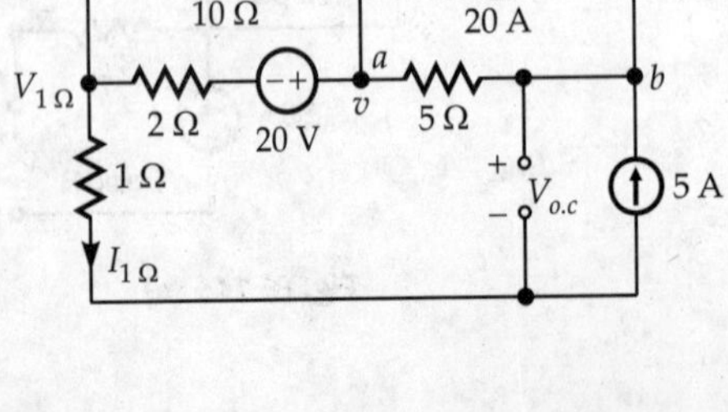

Fig. E6.146 (*a*)

Obviously, the current $I_{1\Omega}$ through the 1Ω resistor is 5 A (downwards).

∴ Drop across it $(V_{1\Omega}) = 5 \times 1 = 5$ V.

Also, at *node a*, assuming the node voltage to be v volts, nodal analysis at a gives

$$\frac{v - V_{1\Omega}}{10} + \frac{v - 20 - V_{1\Omega}}{2} + \frac{v - V_{o.c}}{5} = 2$$

or, $$0.1\,v - 0.1\,V_{1\Omega} + 0.5\,v - 10 - 0.5\,V_{1\Omega} + 0.2\,v - 0.2\,V_{o.c} = 2$$

or, $$0.8\,v - 0.6\,V_{1\Omega} = 12 + 0.2\,V_{o.c}$$

or, $$0.8\,v - 0.6\times 5 = 12 + 0.2\,V_{o.c}$$

i.e., $$0.8\,v - 0.2\,V_{o.c} = 12 + 3 = 15 \qquad \text{...(1)}$$

Again, at *node b*, nodal analysis gives

$$\frac{V_{o.c} - v}{5} + 2 = 5$$

or, $$0.2\,V_{o.c} - 0.2\,v = 3 \qquad \text{...(2)}$$

Solving for (1) and (2),

$$0.6\,v = 18 \text{ as } v = 30 \text{ V}$$

∴ $$V_{o.c} = 45 \text{ V} \qquad \text{[from (2)]}$$

Again, with reference to Fig. E6.146(*b*),

$$R_{Th} = \{(10\,||\,2) + 1\} + 5 = \left(\frac{20}{12}+1\right) + 5 = 7.67\,\Omega$$

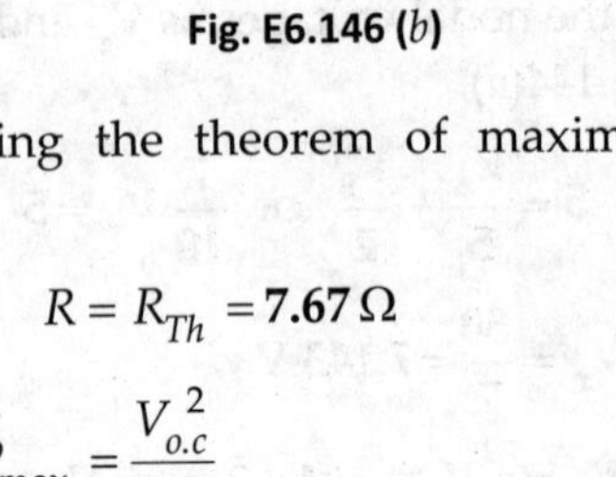

Fig. E6.146 (*b*)

Following the theorem of maximum power transfer

$$R = R_{Th} = \mathbf{7.67\,\Omega}$$

and
$$P_{max} = \frac{V_{o.c}^{\,2}}{4\,R} = \frac{45^2}{4\times 7.67} \simeq \mathbf{66\ W.}$$

EXAMPLE 6.147 *Obtain maximum amount of power transfer in R from the sources using the theorem of maximum power transfer in the network shown in Fig. E6.147.*

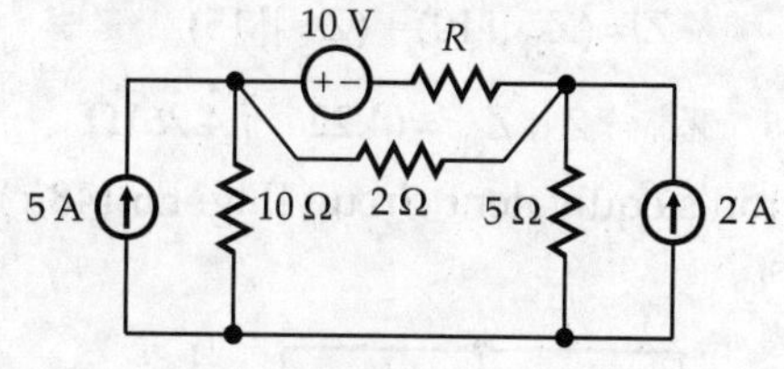

Fig. E6.147

Solution. Replacing R by open and naming the *node* voltages as V_a and V_b, from Fig. E6.147(*a*) we get, for *node a*,

$$5 = \frac{V_a}{10} + \frac{V_a - V_b}{2}$$

or, $$5 = \frac{6V_a - 5V_b}{10} \quad \text{or} \quad 6V_a - 5V_b = 50 \qquad ...(1)$$

and for *node b*, $$2 = \frac{V_b}{5} + \frac{V_b - V_a}{2}$$

or, $$2 = \frac{7V_b - 5V_a}{10}$$

or, $$-5V_a + 7V_b = 20 \qquad ...(2)$$

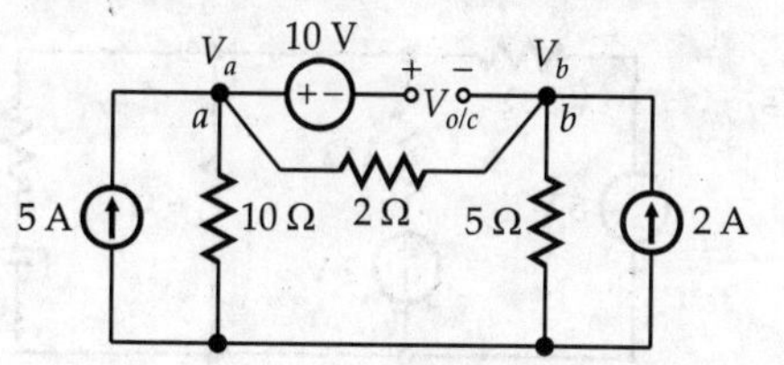

Fig. E6.147 (*a*)

Solving for (1) and (2),

$$V_a = 26.47 \text{ V}$$

and $$V_b = 21.76 \text{ V}$$

Thus, in the *central loop* of Fig. E6.147(*a*)

$$-V_a + 10 + V_{o.c} + V_b = 0$$

or, $$V_{o.c} = V_a - 10 - V_b = -5.3 \text{ V}$$

With reference to Fig. E6.147(*b*),

$$R_{Th} = (10+5)||2 = \frac{15 \times 2}{15+2} = 1.765\,\Omega$$

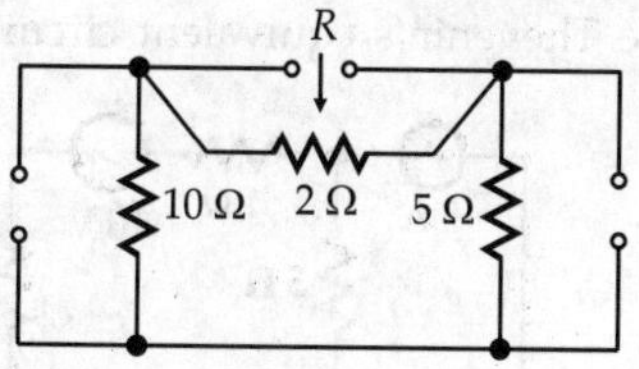

Fig. E6.147 (*b*)

∴ As per maximum power transfer theorem,

$$R = R_{Th} = 1.765\,\Omega$$

and $$P_{max} = \frac{V_{o.c}^2}{4R} = \frac{(-5.3)^2}{4 \times 1.765} \simeq \mathbf{4\ W.}$$

Example 6.148 *In Fig. E6.148, find i using Norton's theorem.*

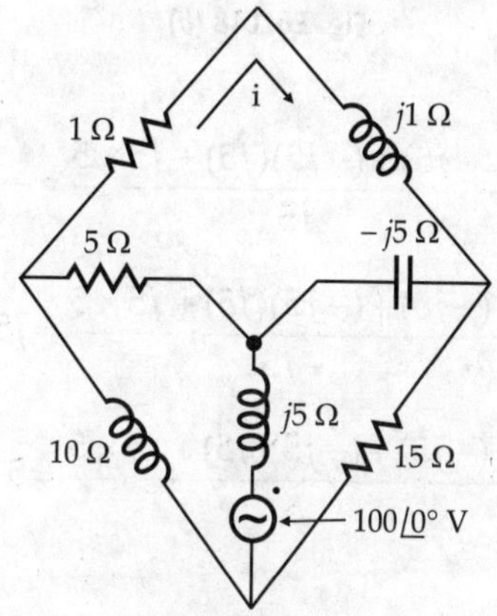

Fig. E6.148

Solution. Since i flows though $(1 + j1)\,\Omega$ impedance let us remove $(1 + j1)\,\Omega$ first and apply short circuit across the open circuited terminals [Fig. E6.148(*a*)].

$$i_N = \frac{\begin{vmatrix} 0 & -5 & j5 \\ -100\angle 0° & 15+j5 & -j5 \\ 100\angle 0° & -j5 & 15 \end{vmatrix}}{\begin{vmatrix} 5-j5 & -5 & j5 \\ -5 & 15+j5 & -j5 \\ j5 & -j5 & 15 \end{vmatrix}} = -(2.675 + j5 - 1)\text{ A}$$

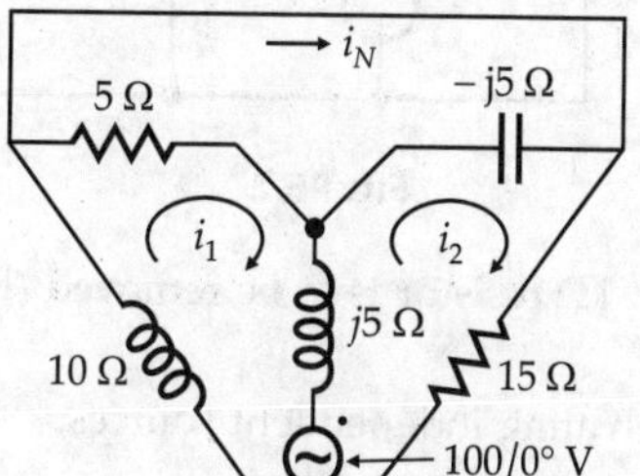

Fig. E6.148 (*a*)

To find internal impedance through the terminals where $(1 + j1)\,\Omega$ were connected we are to take help of star delta transformation [Fig. E6.148(*b*)].

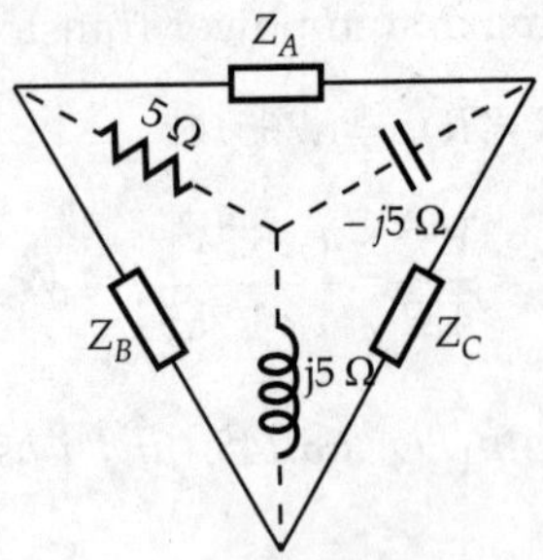

Fig. E6.148 (*b*)

Here

$$Z_A = \frac{5(-j5)+(-j5)(j5)+j5\times 5}{j5} = -j5\,\Omega$$

$$Z_B = \frac{5(-j5)+(-j5)(j5)+j5\times 5}{-j5} = j5$$

$$Z_C = \frac{5(-j5)+(-j5)(j5)+j5\times 5}{5} = 5$$

$$Z = (Z_B \,||\, 10) + (Z_C \,||\, 15)$$

$$\therefore \quad Z_N = Z \,||\, Z_A = (4.22 - j\,4.26)\,\Omega$$

Norton's equivalent circuit [Fig. E6.148(*c*)] then becomes,

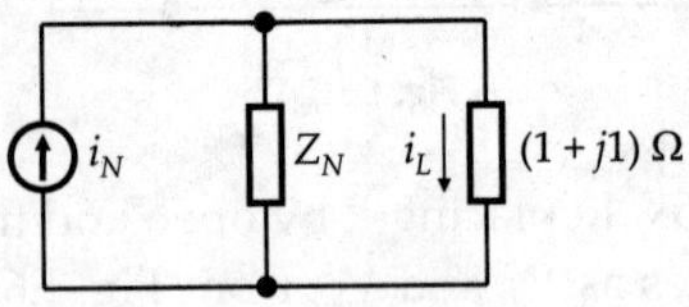

Fig. E6.148 (*c*)

Here $\quad i_L = i_N \times \dfrac{Z_N}{Z_N + (1+j1)}$

$$= \frac{(-2.675 - j\,5.89)\times(4.22 - j4.26)}{(4.22 - j4.26 + 1 + j1)}$$

$$= \mathbf{(-3.675 - j4.22)\ A.}$$

EXERCISES

1. Find the current through the 6Ω resistor using Thevenin's theorem in the circuit shown in Fig. P6.1.
[**Hint.** Ref. Ex. 6.1]

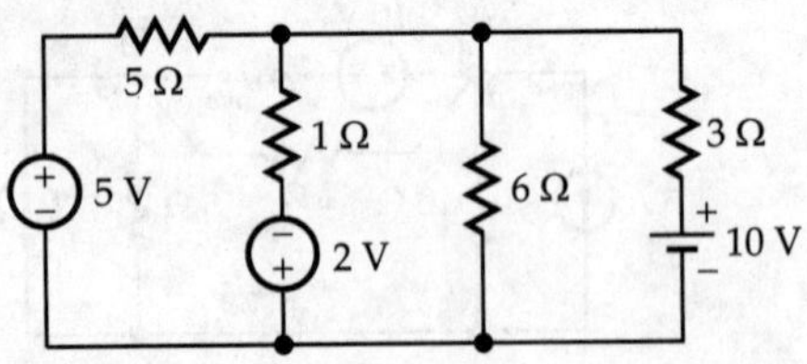

Fig. P6.1

2. Using Thevenin's theorem, find the current in the 1Ω resistor in the network of Fig. P6.2.

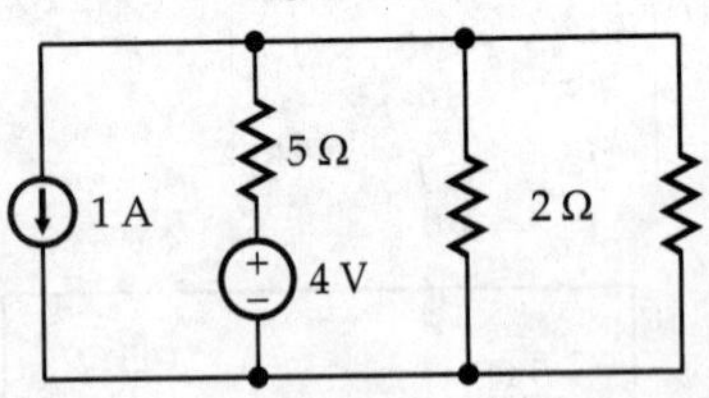

Fig. P6.2

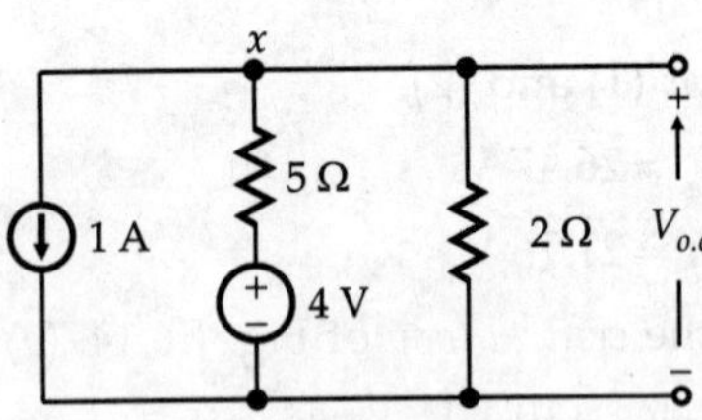

Fig. P6.3

[**Hint.** 1Ω resistor is to be removed (Fig. P6.3). At node "*x*", $\dfrac{V_{o.c} - 4}{5} + \dfrac{V_{o.c}}{2} + 1 = 0$. Then obtain $V_{o.c}$

Deactivating independent sources, $\quad R_{Th} = \dfrac{2\times 5}{2+5}\,\Omega$ and $\quad I_{Th} = \dfrac{V_{o.c}}{R_{Th}+1}$;

Notice the direction of I_{Th}, the current through 1Ω resistor in the Thevenin's equivalent circuit. Also refer Ex. 6.2]

3. Using Thevenin's theorem, find the power loss in R_L in the circuit shown in Fig. P6.4.
[**Hint.** Ref. Ex. 6.4]

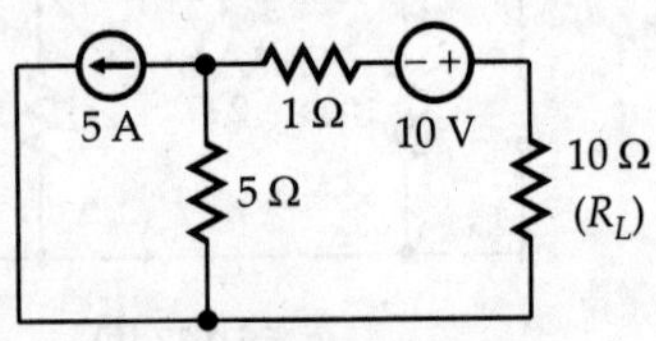

Fig. P6.4

4. What is the power loss in the 5 Ω resistor ? (Fig. P6.5)

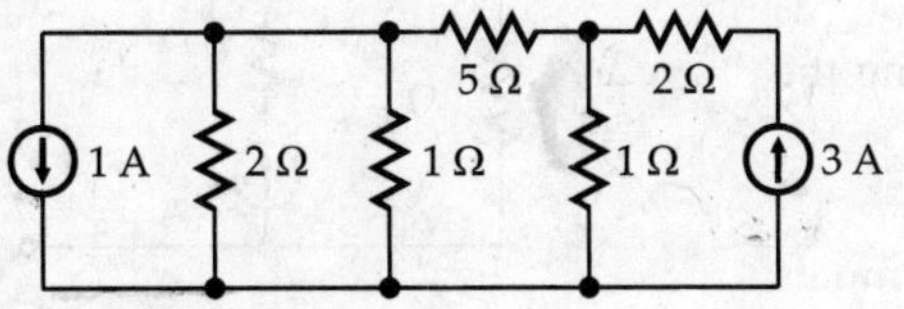

Fig. P6.5

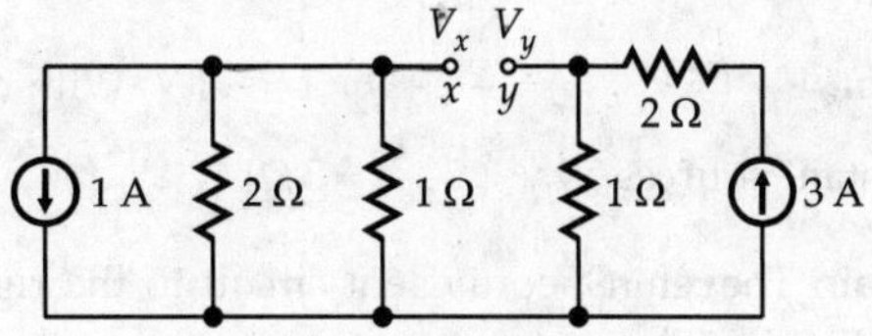

Fig. P6.6

[**Hint.** 5 Ω resistor is removed (Fig. P6.6).

Here, $\frac{V_x}{1} + \frac{V_x}{2} + 1 = 0$; find V_x and $V_y = 1 \times 3 = 3$ V

$$\therefore \quad V_{x-y} = V_x - V_y = V_{o.c}$$

Deactivating constant sources, $R_{Th} = \left(1 + \frac{1 \times 2}{1 + 2}\right) \Omega$. Thus, $I_{Th} = \frac{V_{o.c}}{R_{Th} + 5}$ A.]

5. What is the power loss in the 6 Ω resistor in the circuit shown in Fig. P6.7 ?

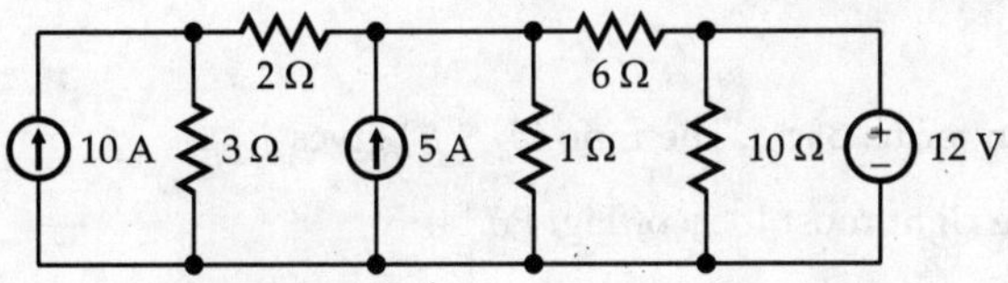

Fig. P6.7

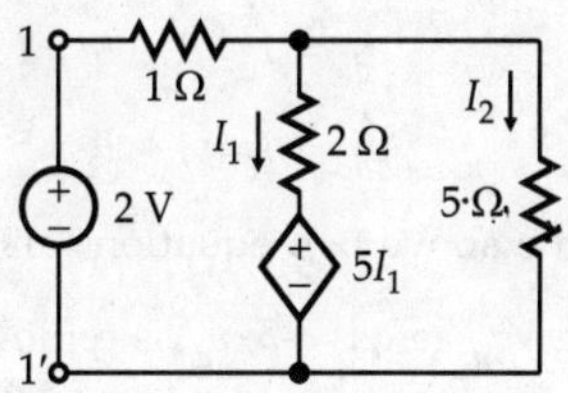

Fig. P6.8

[**Hint.** Refer Ex. 6.8]

6. Find the Thevenin's equivalent circuit for the network to the right of terminals 1 – 1′ in Fig. P6.8.
[**Hint.** Ref. Ex. 6.9]

7. Find $V_{o.c}$ and R_{Th} in Figs. P6.9(*a*) and (*b*).

[**Hint.** In Fig. 6.9(*a*), *i* flows anticlockwise in the left loop causing polarities additive to v_0 while in Fig. 6.96(*b*), *i* flows clockwise developing a drop across r_1 such that it opposes v_0.

$\therefore$ In Fig. P6.9(*a*), $V_{o.c} = v_0 + ir_1$,

While in Fig. P6.9(*b*), $V_{o.c} = v_0 - ir_1$.

Deactivating constant sources, in both the cases, $R_{Th} = r_1 + r_2$.]

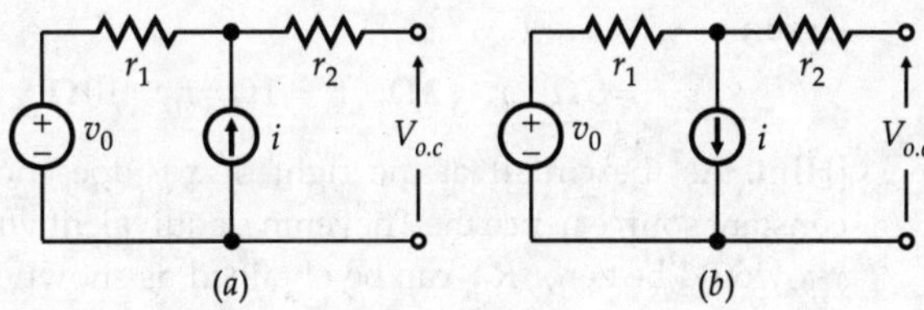

Fig. P6.9

8. Thevenise the circuit shown in Fig. P6.10 to the left of terminal *a-b*
[**Hint.** Ref. Ex. 6.13]

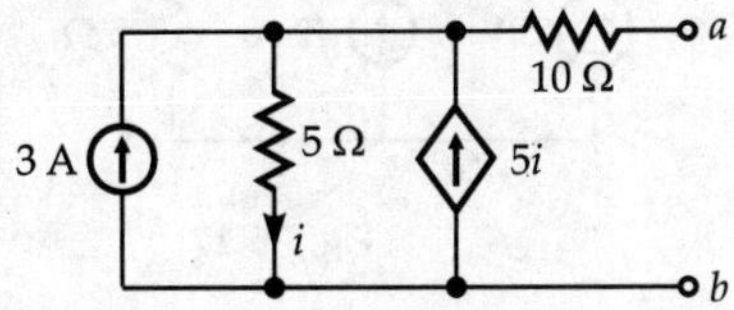

Fig. P6.10

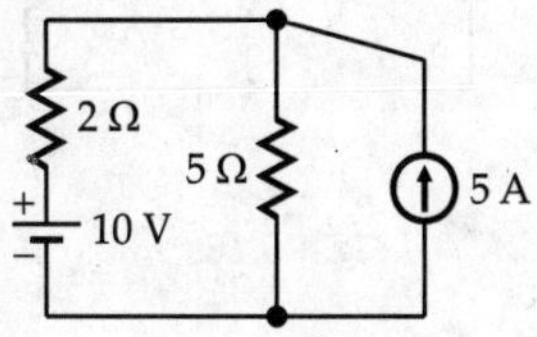

Fig. P6.11

9. Find the current through the 5Ω resistor in the circuit shown in Fig. P6.11.
[**Hint.** Ref. Ex. 6.14]

CHAPTER 6

10. Thevenise the circuit shown in Fig. P6.12 at the left of terminal 2-2′.

[**Hint.** $V_{Th}\,(=V_{2-2'}) = -2 + 1\times 1 = -1\,\text{V}$. With deactivating the constant sources, $R_{Th} = 2 + 1 = 3\,\Omega$]

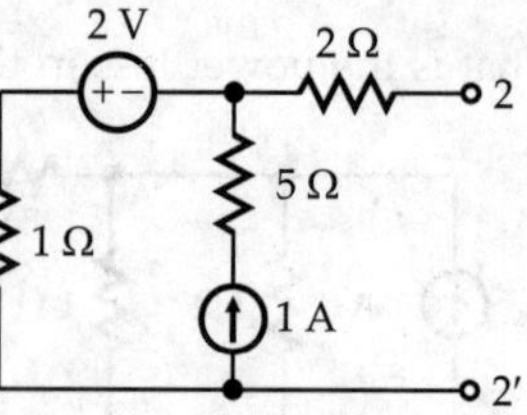

Fig. P6.12

11. Obtain Thevenin's equivalent circuit to the right of terminals *a-b* (Fig. P6.13).

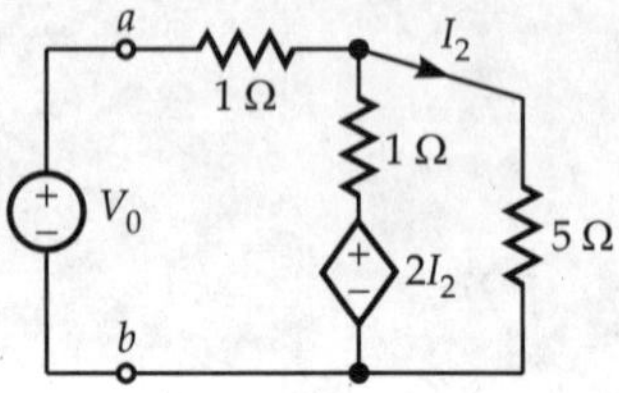

Fig. P6.13

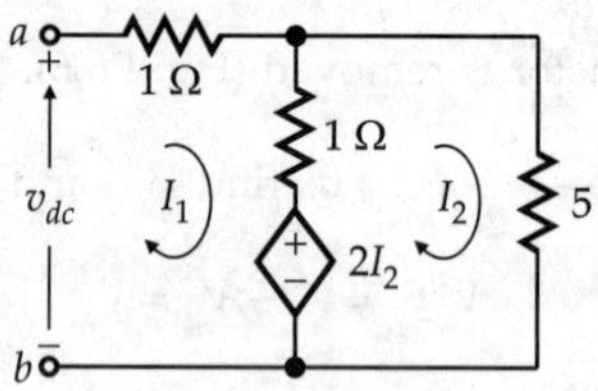

Fig. P6.14

[**Hint.** Remove V_0 and apply a dc voltage v_{dc} as shown in Fig. P6.14.

Here $\qquad v_{dc} = I_1\times 1 + I_1\times 1 + 2I_2 - I_2\times 1 = I_1 - 2I_2$

Also, $\qquad v_{dc} = I_1\times 1 + I_2\times 5 = I_1 + 5I_2$

Solve the above two equations and find I_1 in terms of v_{dc}. The ratio (v_{dc}/I_1) gives R_{Th}.

To find V_{Th} across *a-b*, v_{dc} is removed. In the right most loop of Fig. P6.14,

$$-2\,I_2 + (I_2 - I_1)1 + 5\,I_2 = 0 \qquad \text{...}(a)$$

Also, $$V_{Th} = 5I_2 \qquad \text{...}(b)$$

$\therefore\; I_1 = 0,\; I_2 = 0$ from (*a*) giving $V_{Th} = 0$ from (*b*).]

12. Thevenise the circuit shown in Fig. P6.15 across x-y terminals. Assume

$$r_1 = 5\,\Omega,\; r_2 = 2\,\Omega,\; r_0 = 1\,\Omega,\; r_L = 10\,\Omega.$$

[**Hint.** As the circuit at the right of *x-y* does not have any constant source hence the Thevenin's equivalent voltage across *x-y* would be zero. R_{Th} can be obtained as shown in Ex. 6.60]

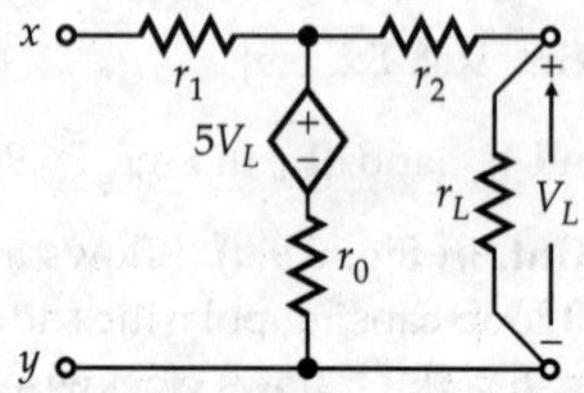

Fig. P6.15

13. In the circuit of Fig. P6.16, find the current through 10 Ω resistor using Thevenin's Theorem.

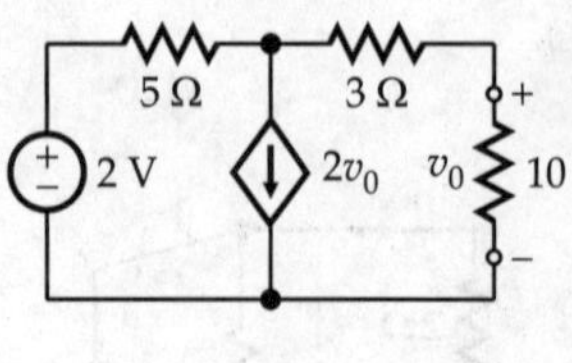

Fig. P6.16

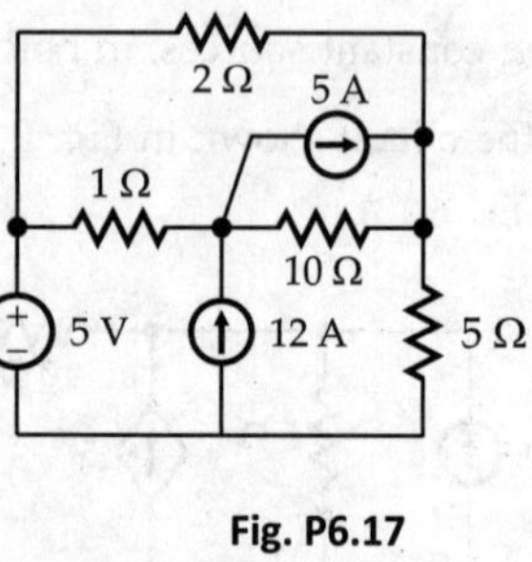

Fig. P6.17

[**Hint.** Ref. Ex. 6.63, take care that in this problem $2v_0$ current is downwards and opposite to that shown in Ex. 6.63]

14. Find the power loss in the 5 Ω resistor for the circuit shown in Fig. P6.17. Using Thevenin's theorem. [**Hint.** Ref. Ex 6.68]

15. For the circuit shown in Fig. P6.18, find the current in r_L using Thevenin's theorem.

[**Hint.** Ref. Ex. 6.69]

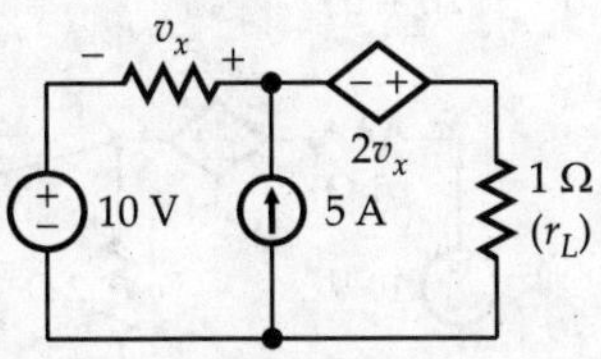

Fig. P6.18

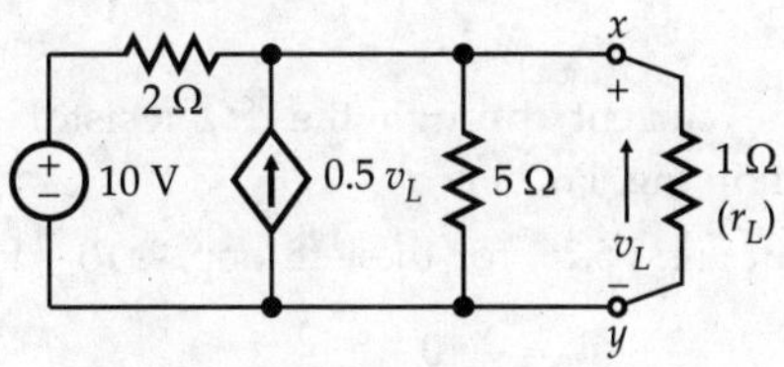

Fig. P6.19

16. Thevenise the circuit shown in Fig. P6.19 to the left of r_L.

[**Hint.** Let r_L be removed; voltage across $x - y$ is $V_{o.c}$.

At node "x", $\dfrac{10 - V_{o.c}}{2} + 0.5\,v_{o.c} - \dfrac{V_{o.c}}{5} = 0.$ Then find $V_{o.c}$

Deactivating the 10 V source, a dc voltage v_{dc} is connected across $x - y$. Input current through x is then say i_{dc}. KCL at x yields

$$i_{dc} = \frac{v_{dc}}{5} - 0.5\,v_{dc} + \frac{v_{dc}}{2}\,;\ \text{Obviously } \frac{v_{dc}}{i_{dc}} \text{ gives } R_{Th}\ .]$$

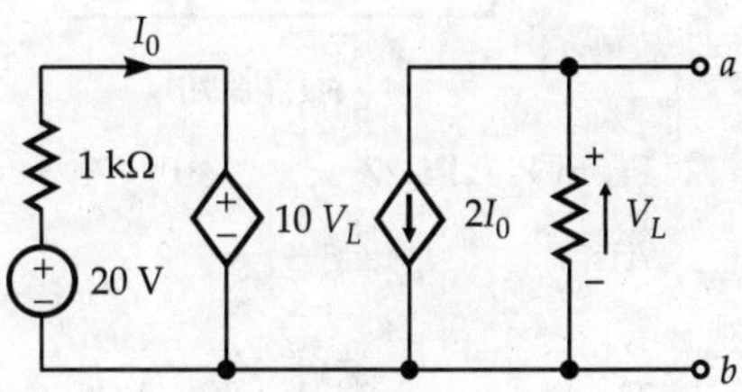

Fig. P6.20

17. For the circuit shown in Fig. P6.20, find the equivalent Thevenin voltage and resistance left to terminal *a-b*

[**Hint.** Ref. Ex. 6.71]

18. Find the current in 5Ω resistor for the circuit shown in Fig. P6.21.

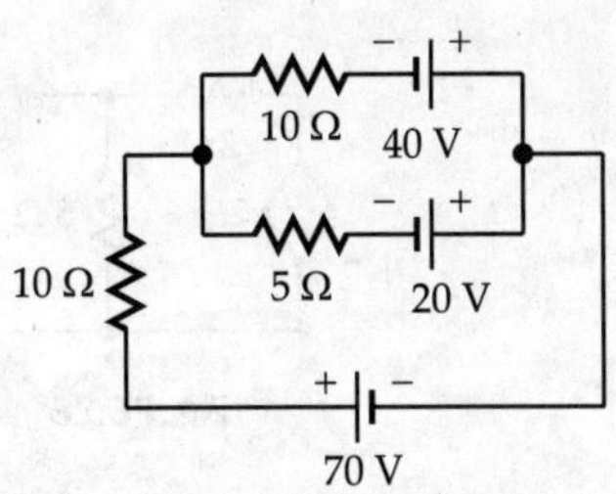

Fig. P6.21

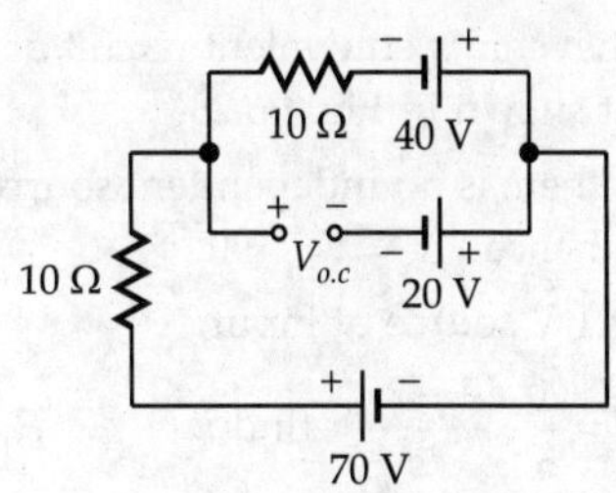

Fig. P6.22

[**Hint.** 5 Ω resistor is removed and obviously $V_{o.c}$ across the open circuited terminals would be (ref. to Fig. P6.22)

$$V_{o.c} = 70 - 20 - 40 = 10\ \text{V}.$$

Deactivating the constant sources, $R_{Th} = \left(\dfrac{10 \times 10}{10 + 10}\right)\Omega \quad \therefore \quad I_{Th}\ (\text{through } 5\,\Omega) = \dfrac{V_{o.c}}{R_{Th} + 5}$.]

19. Obtain the value of current through the 5 Ω resistor in Fig. P6.23.

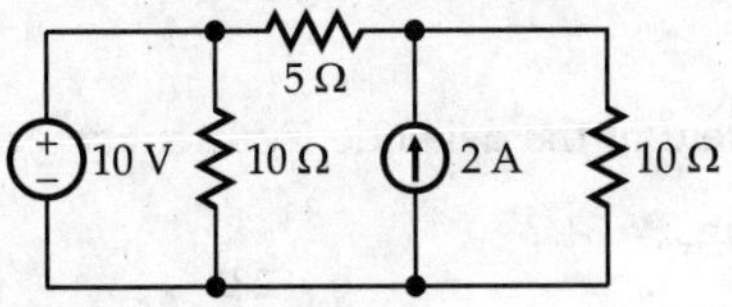

Fig. P6.23

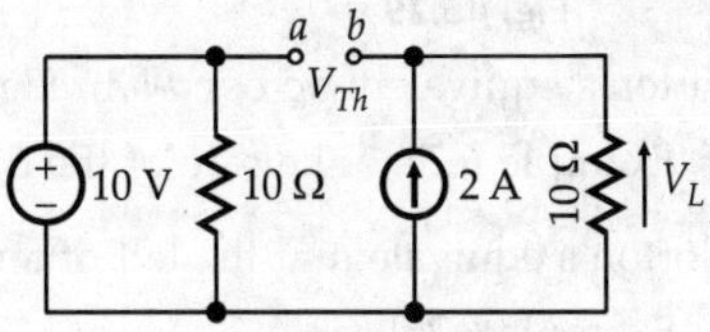

Fig. P6.24

[**Hint.** 5 Ω resistor is removed (Fig. P6.24)

$$V_L = 2 \times 10 = 20\ \text{V}$$

$\therefore \quad V_{Th} = 10\ \text{V} - V_L = 10 - 20 = -10\ \text{V};\quad$ *i.e.,* b terminal should have +ve polarity.

Deactivating the constant sources,

$$R_{Th} = 10 + 10 = 20\,\Omega \quad \therefore \; I_{Th}\,(5\,\Omega) = \frac{V_{o.c}}{R_{Th}+5} = -\frac{10}{20+5}\text{ A }].$$

20. Find the current through the 1Ω resistor using Thevenin's theorem in Fig. P6.25.

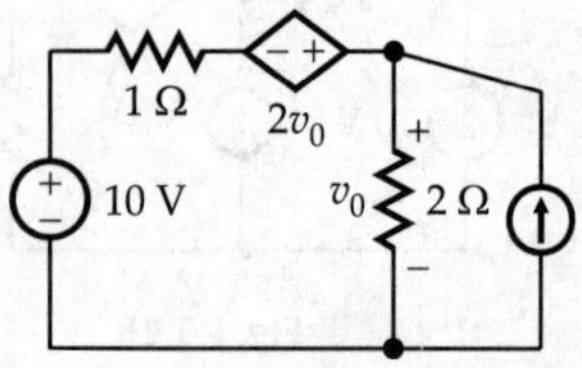

Fig. P6.25

[**Hint.** In Fig. P6.26, for the left loop, $-10 - V_{o.c} - 2v_0 + v_0 = 0$

or, $\quad v_0 = -10 - v_{o.c}$

But $\quad v_0 = 5 \times 2 = 10$ V

$\therefore \quad V_{o.c} = -20$ V

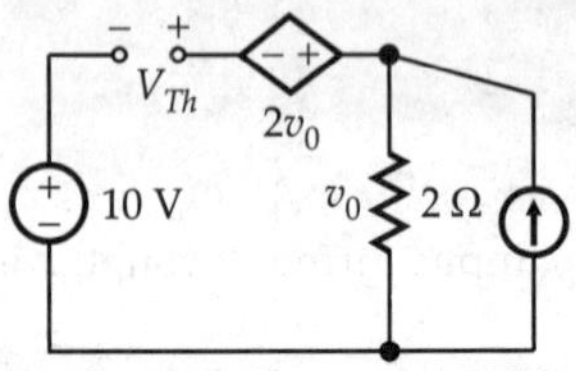

Fig. P6.26

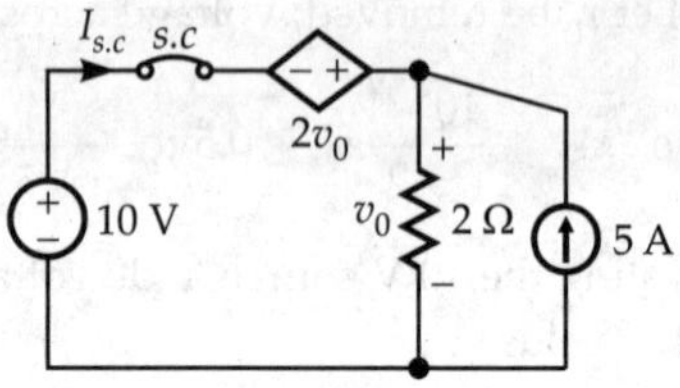

Fig. P6.27

From Fig. P6.27, $\quad -10 - 2v_0 + v_0 = 0$ or $v_0 = -10$ V

Also, $\quad I_{s.c} + 5 = \frac{v_0}{2} = -5 \quad \therefore \quad I_{s.c} = -10$ A.

Thus $\quad R_{Th} = \frac{V_{o.c}}{I_{s.c}} = 2\,\Omega.$ $\quad$ This gives $\quad I_{Th} = \frac{V_{o.c}}{R_{Th}+1} = -\frac{20}{2+1} = -6.67$ A .

21. Obtain Thevenin's equivalent circuit at the input terminals for the circuit shown in Fig. P6.28.

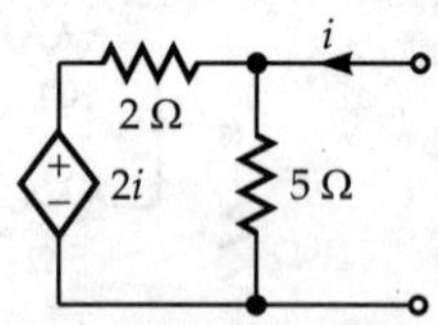

Fig. P6.28

[**Hint.** As there is no independent source to the left of the input terminals hence $V_{o.c} = V_{Th} = 0$.

Applying 1 V source at input,

$$i = \frac{1}{5} + \frac{1-2i}{2}, \text{ find } i. \quad \therefore \quad R_{Th} = \frac{1\text{ V}}{i\text{ A}}.$$

22. Find the Norton's equivalent circuit across *x-y* for the network shown in Fig. P6.29.

[**Hint.** Ref. Example 6.23]

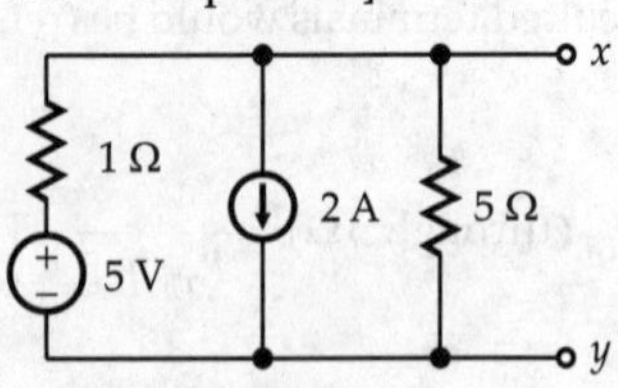

Fig. P6.29

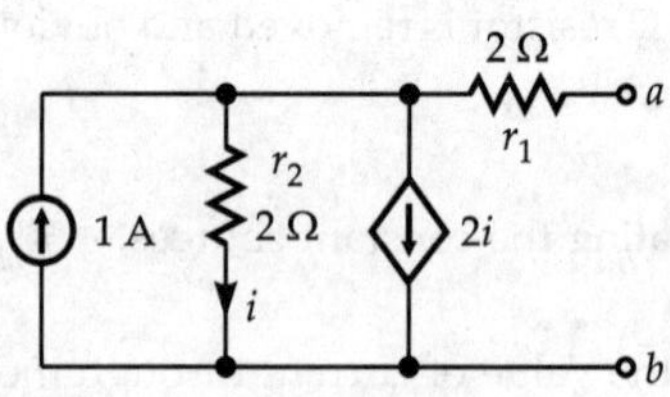

Fig. P6.30

23. Obtain Norton's equivalent across *a-b* in Fig. P6.30.

[**Hint.** Ref. Example 6.24. Take care of the direction of current in the dependent current source]

24. What is Norton's equivalent at the left of terminal *a-b* in Fig. P6.31 ?

[**Hint.** Ref. Example 6.25]

25. Find the current through r_L in the circuit of Fig. P6.32 using Norton's Theorem.

[**Hint.** Ref. Example 6.26]

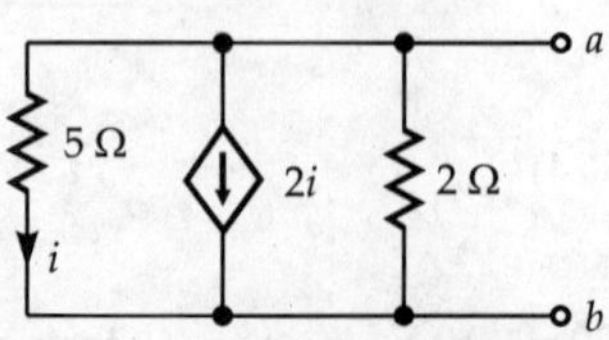

Fig. P6.31

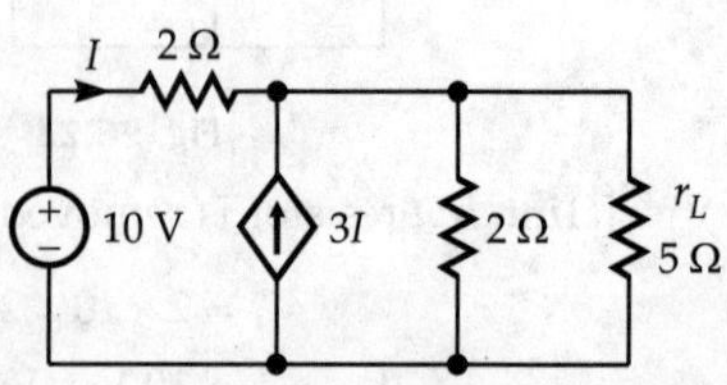

Fig. P6.32

26. What is the power loss in 2 Ω resistor in the circuit of Fig. P6.33 ? Use Norton's theorem.
[**Hint.** Ref. Example 6.28]

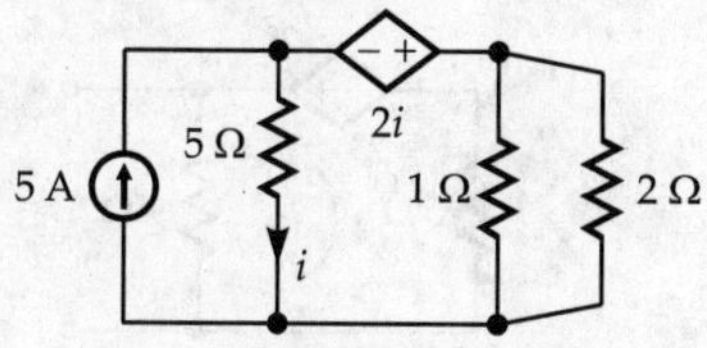

Fig. P6.33

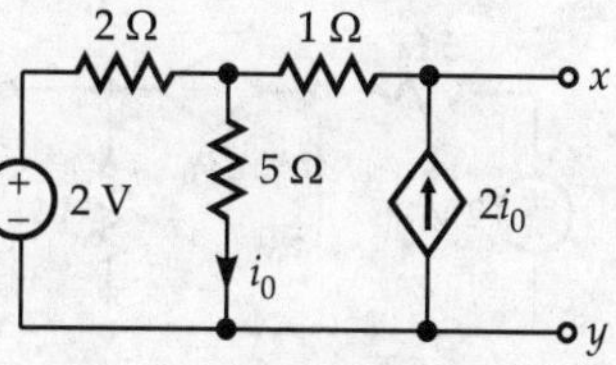

Fig. P6.34

27. Obtain Norton's equivalent to the left to $x - y$ terminals in Fig. P6.34.
[**Hint.** Ref. Example 6.30]

28. What is the current through 10 Ω resistor across $x - y$ terminal of the circuit shown in Fig. P6.35 ? Use Norton's theorem.
[**Hint.** Ref. Example 6.31]

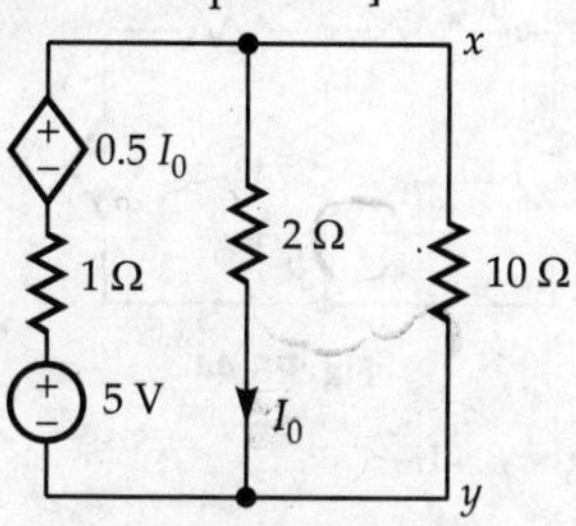

Fig. P6.35

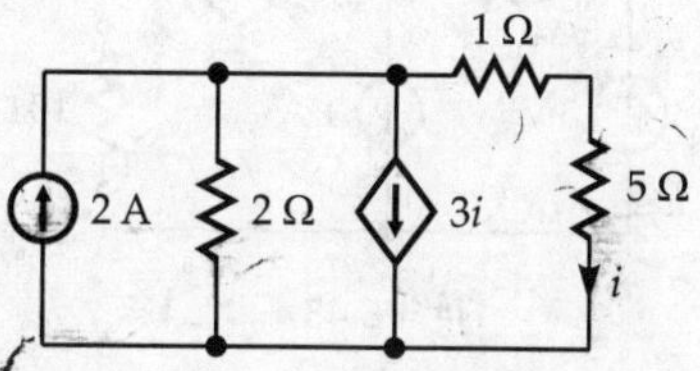

Fig. P6.36

29. What is the power loss in the 5 Ω resistor for the circuit shown in Fig. P6.36 ? Use Norton's theorem.
[**Hint.** Ref. Example 6.33]

30. Using Norton's theorem, find the current in the 5Ω resistor in Fig. P6.37.
[**Hint.** Ref. Example 6.34]

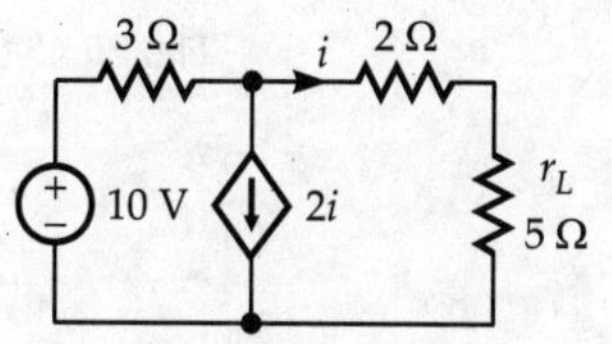

Fig. P6.37

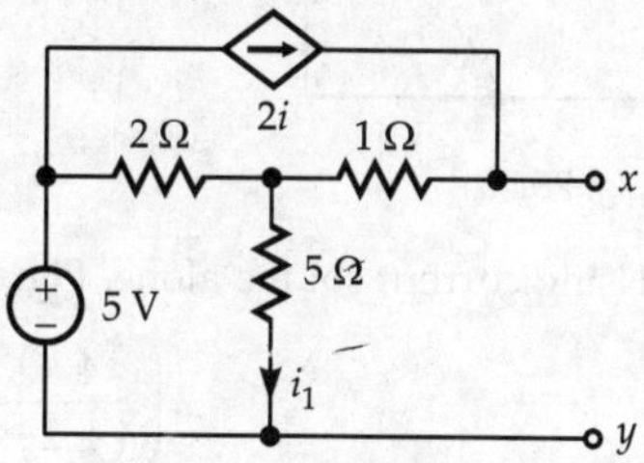

Fig. P6.38

31. Use Norton's theorem to find the Norton's equivalent of the circuit to the left of $x - y$ in Fig. P6.38.
[**Hint.** Ref. Example 6.36]

32. Find Norton's equivalent at the left of 1-1′ in Fig. P6.39 using Norton's equivalent.
[**Hint.** Refer Example 6.104]

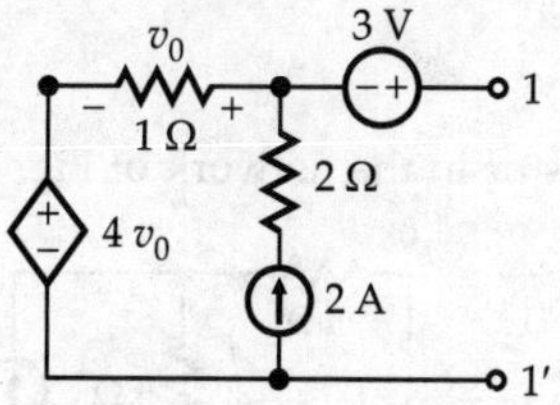

Fig. P6.39

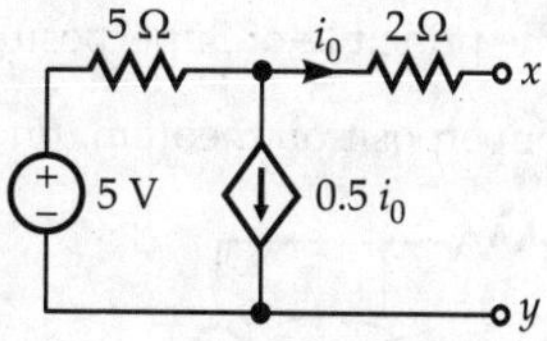

Fig. P6.40

33. Determine Norton's equivalent at the left of x-y using Norton's theorem in Fig. P6.40.
[**Hint.** Refer Example 6.106]

34. Obtain Norton's equivalent of the network shown in Fig. P6.41 at the left of terminals *a-b*.
[**Hint.** Ref. Example 6.107]

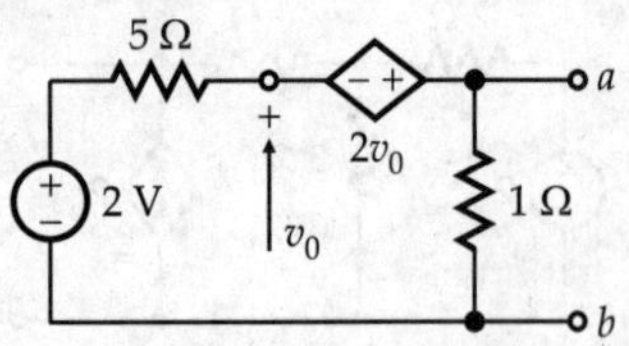

Fig. P6.41

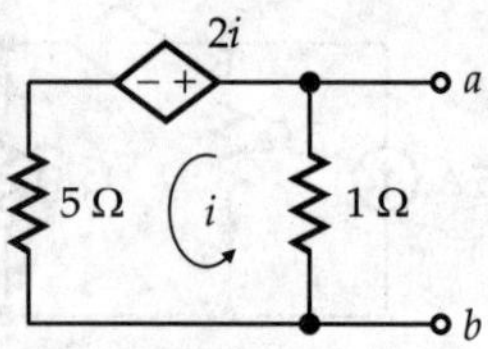

Fig. P6.42

35. Determine Norton's equivalent circuit to the left of terminal *a-b* in Fig. P6.42.
[**Hint.** Ref. Example 6.113]

36. Obtain the magnitude of power loss in 10 Ω resistor using Norton's theorem in Fig. P6.43.
[**Hint.** Ref. Example 6.117]

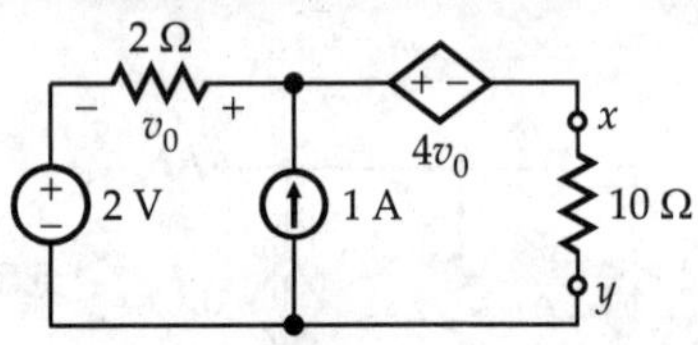

Fig. P6.43

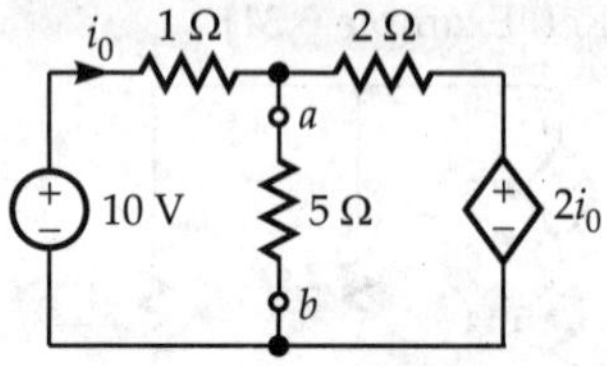

Fig. P6.44

37. What is the current in the 5Ω resistor? Use Norton's theorem in Fig. P6.44.
[**Hint.** Ref. Example 6.120]

38. Using Superposition theorem, find the current *i* and voltage at node (1) in the circuit of Fig. P6.45.

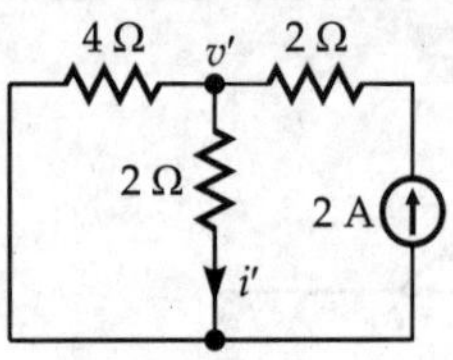

Fig. P6.45

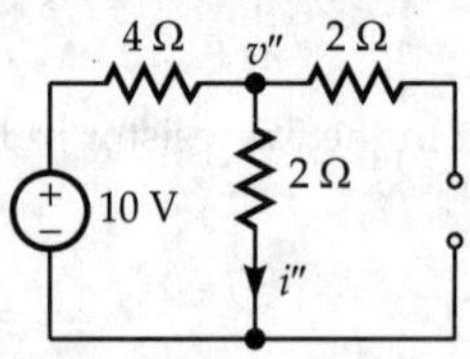

Fig. P6.45 (*a*)

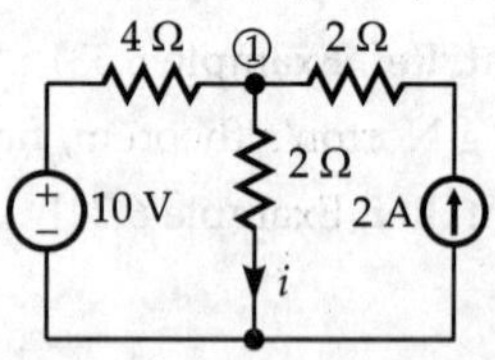

Fig. P6.45 (*b*)

[**Hint.** Using current source alone, Fig. P6.45(*a*),

$$i' = 2\left(\frac{4}{4+2}\right) = 1.33 \text{ A}$$

$$v' = i' \times 2 = 2.66 \text{ V}$$

Using voltage source alone, Fig. P6.45(*b*),

$$i'' = \frac{v''}{2}. \text{ But } v'' = 10 . \frac{2}{2+4} = 3.33 \text{ V}$$

$\therefore$
$$i'' = 1.667 \text{ A}$$

Using the principle of Superposition, $v_1 = v' + v''$ and $i = i' + i''$]

39. Using Superposition theorem, find the current through the 5 Ω resistor in the network of Fig. P6.46.

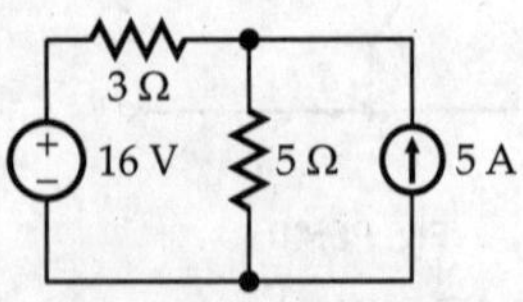

Fig. P6.46

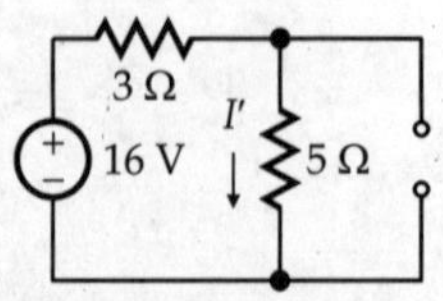

Fig. P6.46 (*a*)

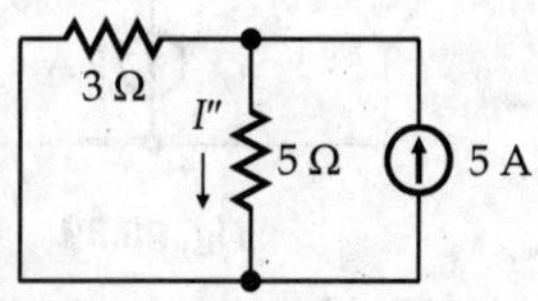

Fig. P6.46 (*b*)

[**Hint.** Using voltage source alone, Fig. P6.46(*a*)

$$I' = \frac{16}{3+5} = 2 \text{ A}$$

Using current source alone, Fig. P6.46(*b*),

$$I'' = 5\frac{3}{3+5} = \frac{15}{8} \text{ A}$$

$$\therefore \quad I = I' + I'']$$

40. Find the currents through the resistance r_1 in the circuit of Fig. P6.47.

[**Hint.** Taking 24 V source alone, $I' = \dfrac{24}{4+4} = 3 \text{ A}$

Taking 16 V source alone, $I'' = \dfrac{16}{4+4} = 2 \text{ A}$

Assuming 2 A source alone, $I''' = 2 . \dfrac{4}{4+4} = 1 \text{ A}$

$\therefore \quad I \text{ (through } r_1) = I' - I'' - I''' = 0 \text{ A}]$

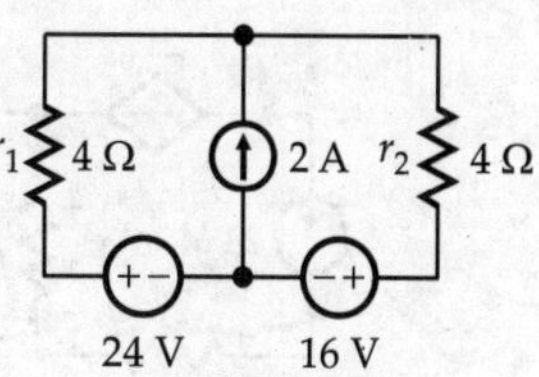

Fig. P6.47

41. Find i in the circuit shown in Fig. P6.48 using Superposition theorem.

[**Hint.** Taking the voltage source only

$10 = 10\, i_1 - 5v_x + 2i_1 ;\ v_x = 2i_1$; then find i_1.

Next, removing the voltage source, nodal analysis gives

$5 = \dfrac{v_x}{2} + i_2 ;\ - v_x + 5v_x - 10\, i_2 = 0,$

thus i_2 can be obtained.

$\therefore \quad i = i_1 - i_2]$

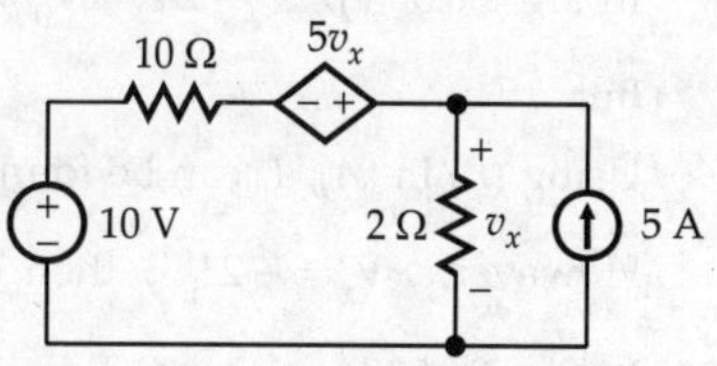

Fig. P6.48

42. Find the value of the dependent current source in the circuit of Fig. P6.49.

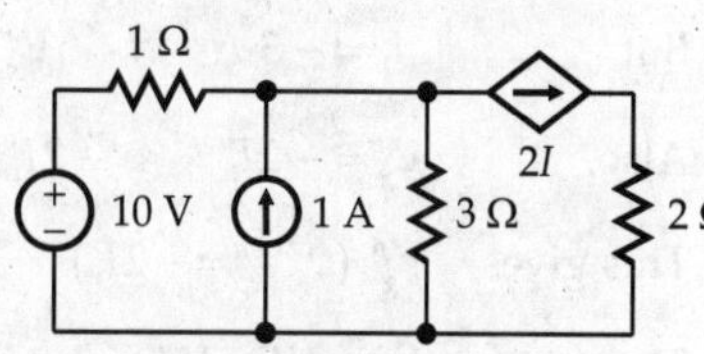

Fig. P6.49

[**Hint.** With reference. to Fig. P6.49(*a*),

$$\frac{10-v}{1} = \frac{v}{3} + 2\left(\frac{10-v}{1}\right).$$

Obtain v. Then find I_1 and $2I_1$.

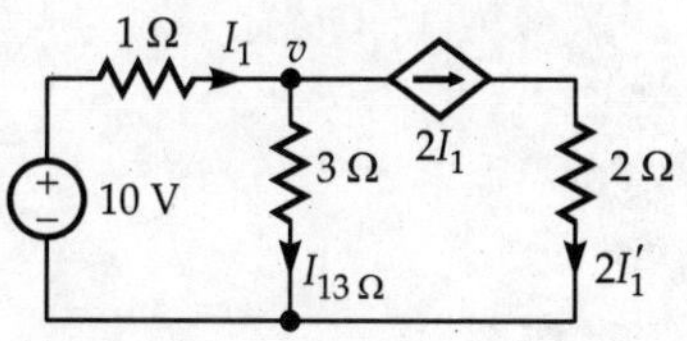

Fig. P6.49 (*a*)

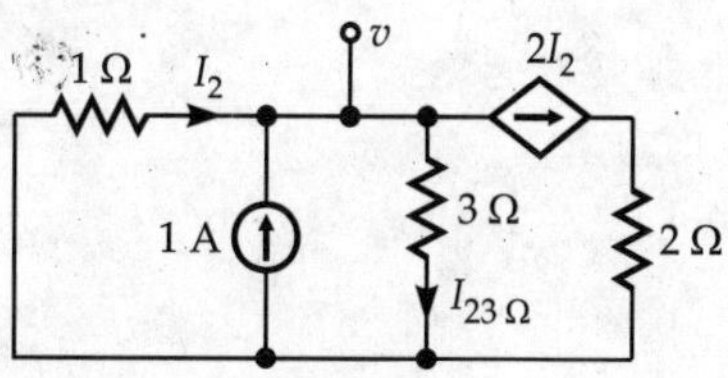

Fig. P6.49 (*b*)

Again, with reference to Fig. P6.49(*b*),

$$1 + I_2 = 2I_2 + \frac{v}{3} \quad \text{or,} \quad \frac{v}{3} + I_2 = 1$$

However, $\quad I_2 = -\dfrac{v}{1}$

Obtaining I_2, $2I_2$ can be found out. Obviously, $\quad 2I = 2I_1 + 2I_2$]

CHAPTER 6

43. Find V_x in the circuit of Fig. P6.50 using Superposition theorem.

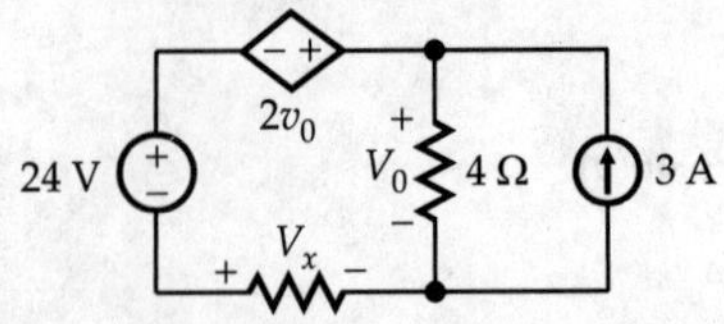

Fig. P6.50

[**Hint.** Refer to Fig. P6.50(*a*) and (*b*)

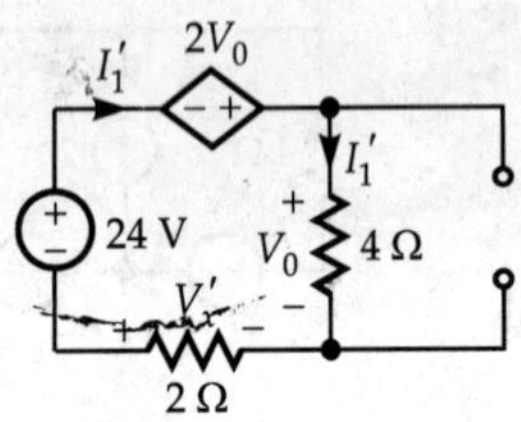

Fig. P6.50 (*a*)

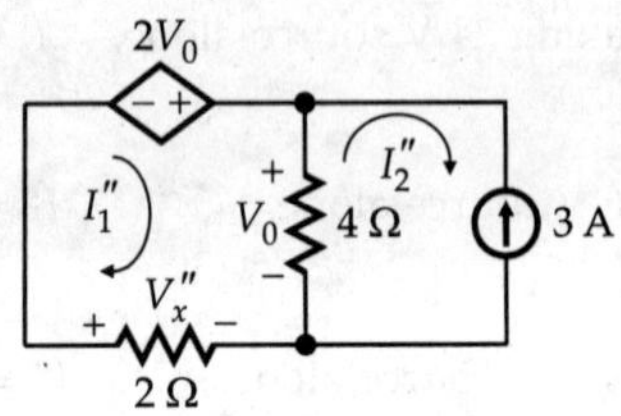

Fig. P6.50 (*b*)

In Fig. P6.50(*a*), $\quad -24 - 2V_0 + (4 + 2)\, I_1' = 0$ ...(A)

But $\quad V_0 = -4I_1'$ ...(B)

Using (*B*) in (*A*), I_1' can be found out.

However, $V_x' = -2I_1'$; then V_x' due to 24 V source can be obtained.

In Fig. P6.50(*b*), using KVL, $\quad -2V_0 + V_0 - V_x'' = 0$

$\therefore \quad V_x'' = -V_0 = -4(I_1'' - I_2'')$

But $\quad I_2'' = -3 \text{ A} \quad \therefore \quad V_x'' = -4I_1'' - 12$

Also, $\quad V_x'' = -2I_1'' \quad \therefore \quad -2I_1'' = -4I_1'' - 12 \quad$ or, $I_1'' = 6$ A.

This gives $\quad V_x''$ ($\because V_x'' = -2I_1''$).

Then $\quad V_x = V_x' + V_x''$.]

CHAPTER

7

Laplace Transformation and Its Application in Electric Circuit Analysis

7.1 INTRODUCTION

Laplace transformation is a very powerful method of solving linear differential equations. As the transient response of an electrical circuit can best be described by a linear differential equation hence, Laplace transformation finds its application in solving the transient behaviour of the electric circuits. Solution of a linear differential equation by Laplace transformation consists essentially *three* steps ; *in the first step the differential is transformed into an algebraic equation. This algebraic equation is then solved conventionally in the next step and in the last step the solution is transformed back in such a way that it becomes the required solution of the differential equation.*

The Laplace transform is also advantageous because this method automatically takes care of *initial conditions* without the necessity of first determining the general solution and then obtain from it a particular solution. Laplace transformation also provides the *direct solution of non-homogeneous differential equations.*

7.2 LAPLACE TRANSFORMATION

The time function being usually designated by *lowercase letter* and the Laplace transformation by *capital letter,* the Laplace transformation of a function $f(t)$ is defined as

$$F(s) = \pounds\, f(t) = \int_0^{\infty} f(t)\, e^{-st}\, dt \qquad ...(7.1)$$

s being the *intermediate or transformed variable.* s is a part of the exponential function and it is described in equation (7.1) that to have Laplace transformation of $f(t)$, the original time function $f(t)$ must be multiplied by (e^{-st}) and then integrated from $t = 0$ to $t = \infty$. Also, $f(t)$ is to be defined for $t > 0$ and $f(t) = 0$ for $t \le 0$.

The operation of $\pounds\, f(t)\, [= F(s)]$ is in the *complex frequency domain* or simply in the s-domain* where s is the complex variable $(\sigma + j\omega)$. In electrical engineering, for most of the function convergence can be assumed provided the real part of the function is positive which, in this context provides $Re[s] > 0$.

* In the time function, *t* represents time; s in the Laplace transform that must represent the dimension inverse of time *i.e.,* frequency. It is this reason that the transformed variable is described as a complex frequency.

Inverse Laplace Transform permits going back in the reverse direction, *i.e.*, from *s* domain to time domain

i.e., $£^{-1}[F(s)] = f(t) = \frac{1}{2\pi j}\int_{\sigma_0 - j\omega}^{\sigma_0 + j\omega} F(s)\, e^{st}\, ds$ ...(7.2)

7.3 (A) LAPLACE TRANSFORM OF A DERIVATIVE $\left[\frac{df(t)}{dt}\right]$

From relation it is evident that

$$\int u\, dv = uv - \int v\, du \quad ...(7.3)$$

Let $u = f(t),\ dv = e^{-st}\, dt$

$\therefore$ $du = f'(t),\ v = -\frac{1}{s} e^{-st}$

Thus integration of equation (7.3) by parts yields

$$F(s) = f(t)\left[-\frac{1}{s} e^{-st}\right]_0^\infty - \int_0^\infty -\frac{1}{s} e^{-st} f'(t)\, dt$$

$$= -\frac{f(t)}{s} e^{-st}\Big|_0^\infty + \frac{1}{s}\int_0^\infty f'(t) e^{-st} dt$$

$$= \frac{f(0+)}{s} + \frac{1}{s}\int_0^\infty f'(t)\, e^{-st}\, dt$$

or, $s\,F(s) = f(0+) + \int_0^\infty f'(t) e^{-st}\, dt$

$$\therefore \int_0^\infty f'(t) e^{-st}\, dt = s\,F(s) - f(0+) \quad ...(7.4)$$

Observation of equation (7.4) reveals that this expression gives the expression for the Laplace transformation of the derivative $f(t)$

$$\therefore \quad £\frac{df(t)}{dt} = £\, f'(t) e^{-st}\, dt \quad ...(7.5)$$

Thus equation (7.4) can be written as

$$£ f'(t) = s\,F(s) - f(0+) \quad ...(7.6)$$

7.3 (B) LAPLACE TRANSFORM OF AN INTEGRAL $\int f(t)\, dt$

$$£\left[\int f(t)\, dt\right] = \int_0^\infty \int f(t)\, dt\, e^{-st}\, dt$$

Let $u = \int f(t)\, dt$

and $dv = e^{-st}\, dt.$

The integration by parts gives us

$$£\left[\int f(t)\, dt\right] = \left[\int f(t)\, dt\left(-\frac{1}{s} e^{-st}\right)\right]_0^\infty - \int_0^\infty \left(-\frac{1}{s} e^{-st}\right) f(t)\, dt$$

$$= \frac{1}{s}\int f(t)\, dt\Big|_{0+} + \frac{1}{s} F(s) \quad ...(7.7)$$

$\left[\int f(t)\Big|_{0+}\right.$ gives the value of the integral at $t = 0+\left.\right]$

7.4 LAPLACE TRANSFORM OF COMMON FORCING FUNCTIONS

(*i*) Unit Step function

The most common *driving function* in electrical engineering is the *unit step function* and is denoted as

$$u(t) = \begin{cases} 0 & t \le 0 \\ 1 & t > 0 \end{cases}$$

i.e., the function has no magnitude for the time $t \le 0$ and has a positive unit magnitude at time $t > 0$ (Fig. 7.1)

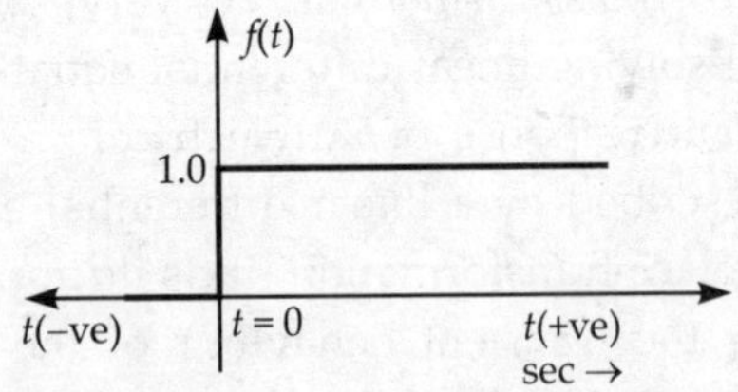

Fig. 7.1 Unit step function occurring at $t = 0$.

The Laplace transformation can be obtained as

$$F(s) = £\, u(t) = \int_0^\infty e^{-st}\, dt$$

$$\therefore \quad F(s) = \frac{1}{s} \quad ...(7.8)$$

The unit step function in electric circuits represents the closing of a switch applying a constant voltage V (say) to the circuit. Obviously, its *Laplace transform would be* (V/s).

(*ii*) Exponential function

Exponential function being also very common in electric circuits, it is described by

$$f(t) = e^{-\alpha t} \quad ...(7.9)$$

and is shown in Fig. 7.2.

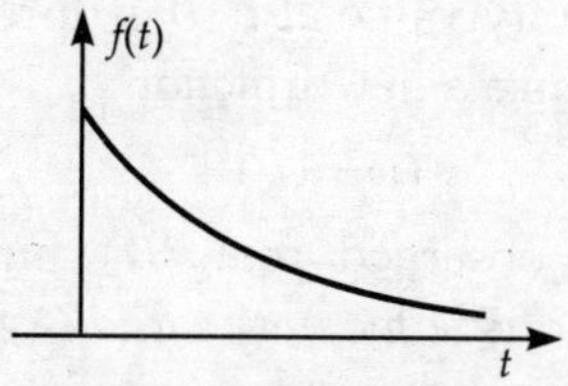

Fig. 7.2 An Exponential function.

Direct application of Laplace transform method gives

$$F(s) = £\, f(t) = £\, e^{-\alpha t}$$

$$= \int_0^\infty e^{-\alpha t}\, e^{-st}\, dt = \frac{1}{s+\alpha} \qquad ...(7.10)$$

[it may be noticed that the time '*t*' is kept restricted at +ve values only]

(*iii*) Sinusoidal function

The function being extremely common for circuits encountering a.c. source, the *sinusoidal function* (diagrammatically represented in Fig. 7.3) in time domain is given by

$$f(t) = \sin \omega t = \frac{e^{j\omega t} - e^{-j\omega t}}{2j} \qquad ...(7.11)$$

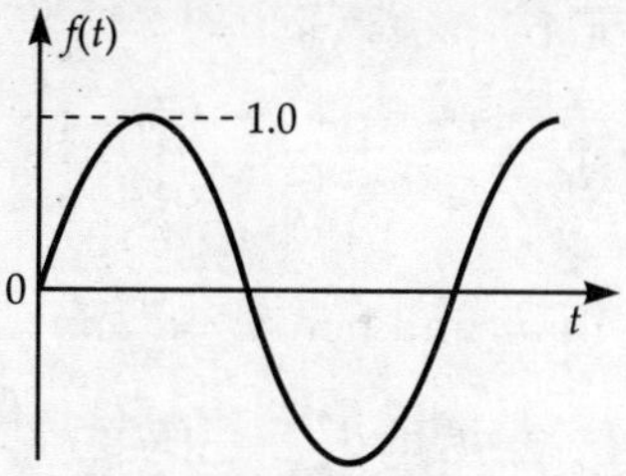

Fig. 7.3 A Sinusoidal function.

Hence, Laplace transformation

$$F(s) = £\, f(t) = £\, \sin \omega t$$

or, $$£\, \sin \omega t = \frac{1}{2j} \int_0^\infty e^{-(s-j\omega)t} - e^{-(s+j\omega)t}$$

$$= \frac{1}{2j}\left[\frac{1}{s-j\omega} - \frac{1}{s+j\omega}\right] = \frac{\omega}{s^2+\omega^2}$$

...(7.12)

(*iv*) Cosinusoidal function

This function is given by

$$f(t) = \cos \omega t \qquad ...(7.13)$$

and obviously

$$\cos \omega t = \frac{1}{\omega}\frac{d}{dt}(\sin \omega t) \qquad ...(7.14)$$

The *cosine function* being shown in Fig. 7.4, its Laplace transformation is given by

$$F(s)_{\cos} = £\, f(t) = £\, (\cos \omega t)$$

$$= \frac{1}{\omega}[s\, F(s) - f(0+)]$$

(Refer to equation 7.4)

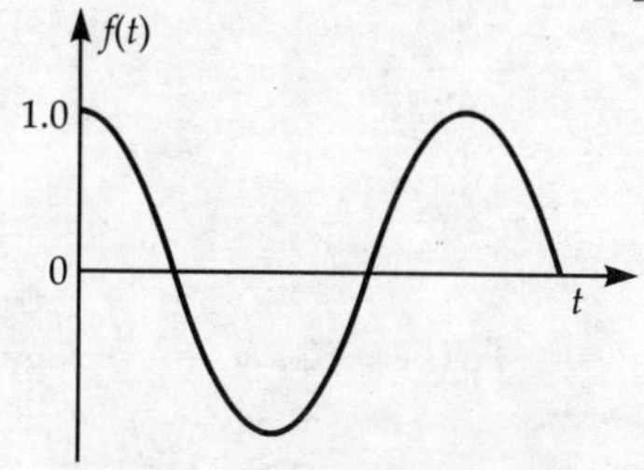

Fig. 7.4 Cosine function.

However, $F(s)$ for sine function is $(\omega / s^2 + \omega^2)$, as has just been derived in equation 7.12.

$$\therefore \quad F(s)_{\cos} = £\, (\cos \omega t)$$

$$= \frac{1}{\omega}\left[s\frac{\omega}{s^2+\omega^2} - 0\right] = \frac{s}{s^2+\omega^2} \qquad ...(7.15)$$

(*v*) Ramp function

A *ramp function* is given by

$$f(t) = t \qquad ...(7.16)$$

Applying directly the Laplace transform method to the ramp function (Fig. 7.5),

$$F(s) = \int_0^\infty te^{-st}\, dt$$

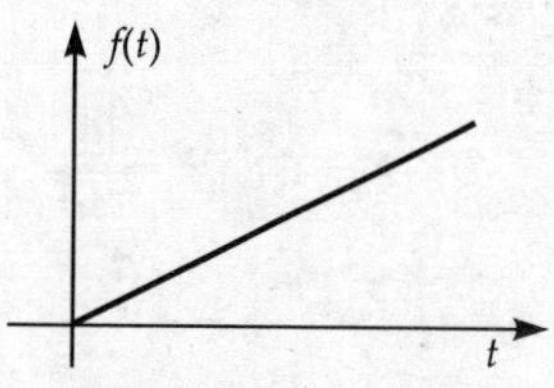

Fig. 7.5 Ramp function.

Integration by parts gives

$$F(s) = -\frac{t\, e^{-st}}{s}\Bigg|_0^\infty + \int_0^\infty \frac{1}{s} e^{-st}\, dt = \frac{1}{s^2}$$

$$\therefore \quad F(s) = \frac{1}{s^2} \qquad ...(7.16(a))$$

(*vi*) Parabolic function

The *parabolic function* being given by $f(t) = t$, the Laplace transform of this can be achieved as follows :

$$F(s) = \pounds\, f(t) = \pounds\, t^2 = \pounds \int 2t\, dt$$

$\left[\because \int 2t\, dt \text{ in the form of } t^2 \text{ in terms of an integral}\right]$

$$\therefore \quad F(s) = \pounds \int 2t\, dt$$

$$= \frac{F_1(s)}{s} + \frac{f^{-1}(0+)}{s} = \frac{F_1(s)}{s} + 0 \qquad ..(7.17)$$

However,

$$F_1(s) = \pounds\, 2t = \frac{2}{s^2} \qquad ...(7.18)$$

∴ Utilising equations (7.18) in equation (7.17),

$$F(s) = \frac{2}{s^3}$$

Hence the Laplace transform of a parabolic function (Fig. 7.6) is given by

$$F(s) = \frac{2}{s^3} \qquad ...(7.19)$$

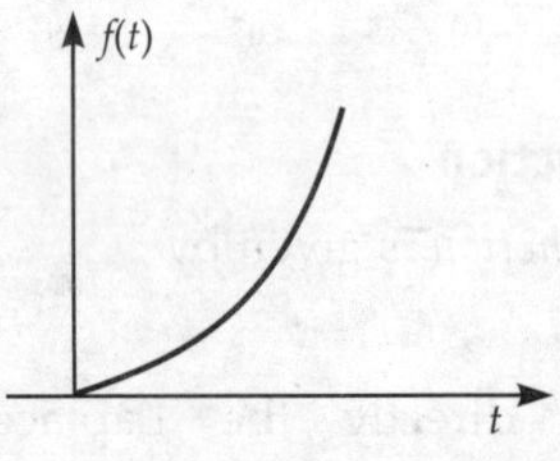

Fig. 7.6 Parabolic function

It may be noted that the Laplace transform of a square function involves a cubic inverse function of *s*. This can be generated as

$$\pounds f(t) = \pounds\, t^n = \frac{\underline{|n}}{s^{n+1}}$$

where $f(t) = t^n$.

(*vii*) Unit impulse function

The *unit impulse function* given by

$$\delta(t) = \lim_{\Delta t \to 0} \frac{u(t) - u(t - \Delta t)}{\Delta t} \qquad ...(7.20)$$

which is obviously a derivative of the unit step functions *i.e.*,

$$\delta(t) = \frac{d}{dt} u(t) \qquad ...(7.21)$$

$\delta(t)$ has the value zero for $t > 0$ and ∞ at $t = 0$. However, infinity value at $t = 0$ is unrealisable. Let us now introduce a new function

$$g(t) = 1 - e^{-\alpha t} \qquad ...(7.22)$$

It may be observed, that $g(t)$ could approach $\delta(t)$ provided α is alone very large. Again,

$$g'(t) = \frac{d}{dt} g(t) = \alpha\, e^{-\alpha t}$$

and $$\int_0^{\omega} g'(t)\, dt = \int_0^{\omega} \alpha\, e^{-\alpha t} = 1.$$

If we now apply Laplace transform directly,

$$F(\delta) = \pounds\, \delta(t) = \lim_{\alpha \to \omega} \pounds\, g'(t)$$

$$= \lim_{\alpha \to \infty} \pounds\, \alpha\, e^{-\alpha t}$$

$$= \lim_{\alpha \to \infty} \frac{\alpha}{s + \alpha} = 1.$$

This gives that Laplace transform of an unit impulse function is unity.

(*viii*) Laplace transform of t^n

From definition,

$$F(s) = \int_{0(-)}^{\infty} t^n\, e^{-st}\, dt$$

Integration by parts yields

$$F(s) = -\frac{t^n}{s} e^{-st} \Bigg|_{0(-)}^{\infty} - \int_{0(-)}^{\infty} -\frac{1}{s} e^{-st}\, n t^{n-1} dt$$

$\int u\, dv = uv - \int v\, du$ and here $u = t^n$, $dv = e^{st}\, dt$

giving $du = nt^{n-1}\, dt$ and $v = -(1/s)\, e^{-st}$

or, $$F(s) = 0 + \frac{n}{s} \pounds \{t^{n-1}\}$$

$$= \frac{n}{s} \cdot \frac{n-1}{s} \cdot \frac{n-1}{s} \cdots\cdots \frac{3}{2} \cdot \frac{2}{5} \cdot \frac{1}{5} \cdot \pounds \{t^0\}$$

However,

$$\pounds \{t^0\} = \frac{1}{s}$$

$$\therefore \quad \pounds \{t'\} = \frac{1}{s^2}, \pounds \{t^2\} = \frac{2}{s^3}, \pounds \{t^3\} = \frac{6}{s^4} \text{ \& so on.}$$

$$\therefore\ \pounds \{t^n u(t)\} = F(s) = \frac{\underline{|n}}{s^{n+1}}$$

$$\left[\text{Also, } \pounds [e^{-\alpha t}\, t^n] = \frac{\underline{|n}}{(s + \alpha)^{n+1}}\right]$$

(ix) Laplace transform of $e^{-\alpha t}$ sin ωt

Let $f(t) = e^{-\alpha t} \sin \omega t = e^{-\alpha t} \dfrac{e^{j\omega t} - e^{-j\omega t}}{2j}$

$$= \frac{1}{2j}[e^{-(\alpha - j\omega)t} - e^{-(\alpha + j\omega)t}]$$

$$\therefore \quad F(s) = \frac{1}{2j}\left[\frac{1}{s+(\alpha - j\omega)} - \frac{1}{s+(\alpha + j\omega)}\right]$$

$$= \frac{\omega}{(s+\alpha)^2 + \omega^2}$$

[for £$(e^{-\alpha t} \cos \omega t)$, refer to Example 7.1]

(x) Laplace transform of $\delta(t)$

From definition, $F(s) = \int_{0(-)}^{\infty} \delta(t) e^{-st}\, dt = 1.$

(xi) Laplace transform of sinh θt

Let $f(t) = \sinh \theta t = \dfrac{e^{\theta t} - e^{-\theta t}}{2}$

$$\therefore \quad F(s) = \frac{1}{2}\left(\frac{1}{s-\theta} - \frac{1}{s+\theta}\right) = \frac{\theta}{s^2 - \theta^2}*$$

(xii) Laplace transform of cosh θt

Let $f(t) = \cosh \theta t = \dfrac{e^{\theta t} + e^{-\theta t}}{2}$

$$\therefore \quad F(s) = \frac{1}{2}\left(\frac{1}{s-\theta} + \frac{1}{s+\theta}\right) = \frac{s}{s^2 - \theta^2}.$$

Table 7.1 Laplace Transform of Some Useful Functions

$f(t)$	$F(s)$	$f(t)$	$F(s)$
$u(t)$	$\frac{1}{s}$	$e^{-\alpha t} t^n$	$\frac{\lfloor n}{(s+\alpha)^{n+1}}$
$e^{-\alpha t}$	$\frac{1}{s+\alpha}$	$e^{-\alpha t} \sin \omega t$	$\frac{\omega}{(s+\alpha)^2 + \omega^2}$
$\sin \omega t$	$\frac{\omega}{s^2 + \omega^2}$	$e^{-\alpha t} \cos \omega t$	$\frac{s+\alpha}{(s+\alpha)^2 + \omega^2}$
$\cos \omega t$	$\frac{s}{s^2 + \omega^2}$	$\delta(t)$	1
t	$\frac{1}{s^2}$	$\sinh \theta t$	$\frac{\theta}{s^2 - \theta^2}$
t^2	$\frac{2}{s^3}$	$\cosh \theta t$	$\frac{s}{s^2 - \theta^2}$
t^n	$\frac{\lfloor n}{s^{n+1}}$		

* θ is a constant term.

7.5 INITIAL VALUE AND FINAL VALUE THEOREM

The direct Laplace transform of the derivative of $(df(t)/dt)$ with limit $s \to \infty$ gives

$$\lim_{s\to\infty} £\left[\frac{df(t)}{dt}\right] = \lim_{s\to\infty} \int_0^{\infty} \frac{df(t)}{dt} e^{-\alpha t}\, dt$$

$$= \lim_{s\to\infty} \{sF(s) - f(0+)\} \quad ...(7.23)$$

However, with $s \to \infty$, $e^{-st} \to 0$.

$$\therefore \quad \lim_{s\to\infty} \{sF(s) - f(0+)\} = 0$$

Since, $f(0+)$ is a constant,

$$\therefore \quad f(0+) = \lim_{s\to\infty} [sF(s)] \quad ...(7.24)$$

Equation (7.24) permits the evaluation of the initial value of the time domain solution $f(t)$. It is then possible to work directly with the transform version of the solution to obtain *initial values* by performing the operation called for on the right hand side of equation (7.24). Equation (7.24) can be stated as *Initial value theorem.*

In the same way the final value theorem can also be developed from the direct Laplace transform of the derivative, however, the limit is now taken as $s \to 0$.

$$\lim_{s\to 0} £\left[\frac{d\,f(t)}{dt}\right] = \lim_{s\to 0} \int_0^{\infty} \frac{d\,f(t)}{dt} e^{-st}\, dt$$

$$= \lim_{s\to 0} \{s\,F(s) - f(0+)\}, \quad ...(7.25)$$

But $\displaystyle \lim_{s\to 0} \int_0^{\infty} \frac{d\,f(t)}{dt} e^{-st} dt = \int_0^{\infty} df(t)$

$$= f(\infty) - f(0+) \quad ...(7.26)$$

However, $f(0+)$ being a constant,

$$f(\infty) - f(0+) = -f(0+) + \lim_{s\to 0} [sF(s)],$$

$$\therefore \quad f(\infty) = \lim_{s\to 0} [s\,F(s)]$$

i.e., $$\lim_{s\to 0} [s\,F(s)] = \lim_{t\to\infty} f(t) \quad ...(7.27)$$

Expression (7.27) is the *final value theorem* and is useful where the transform solution of problem is available and the needed information is about the *final* or *steady state* solution.

7.6 TIME DISPLACEMENT THEOREM

This theorem states that if a function $f(t)$ be Laplace transformable, and if $\pounds f(t) = F(s)$, then

$$\pounds f(t-T) = e^{-sT} F(s), \quad ...(7.28)$$

where, the function $f(t-T)$ is the function $f(t)$ displaced by T. By this theorem, the *displacement in the time domain* becomes multiplication by e^{-sT} in the s-domain.

EXAMPLE 7.1 *Obtain the Laplace transform of $e^{-\theta t}\cos \omega t$, θ being a constant.*

SOLUTION. By definition, $\pounds f(t) = \int_0^{\infty} f(t) e^{-st}\, dt$

In this case,

$$f(t) = e^{-\theta t} \cos \omega t$$

$$\pounds f(t) = \pounds [e^{-\theta t} \cos \omega t]$$

$$= \int_0^{\infty} \cos \omega t \, e^{-(s+\theta)t}\, dt$$

$$= \left[\frac{-(s+\theta)\cos \omega t \, e^{-(s+\theta)t} + e^{-(s+\theta)t} \omega \sin \omega t}{(s+\theta)^2 + \omega^2}\right]_0^{\infty}$$

$$= \frac{s+\theta}{(s+\theta)^2 + \omega^2}.$$

EXAMPLE 7.2 *Obtain the Laplace transformation of $f(t) = 1 - e^{-at}$, a being a constant.*

SOLUTION.

$$\pounds f(t) = \pounds(1 - e^{-at}) = \int_0^{\infty} (1 - e^{-at}) e^{-st}\, dt$$

$$= \int_0^{\infty} e^{-st}\, dt - \int_0^{\infty} e^{-(s+a)t}\, dt$$

$$= \left[-\frac{1}{s} e^{-st} + \frac{1}{s+a} e^{-(s+a)t}\right]_0^{\infty}$$

$$= \frac{1}{s} - \frac{1}{s+a} = \frac{a}{s(s+a)}.$$

EXAMPLE 7.3 *Obtain the Laplace transform of the pulse shown in Fig. E7.1. (The function is known as gate function).*

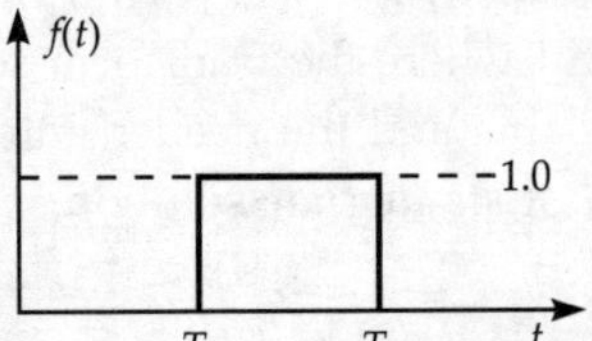

Fig. E7.1

SOLUTION. Here, we utilise the time displacement theorem. The pulse may be considered to have delayed unit step functions as its constituents and as shown in Fig. E7.1(*a*)

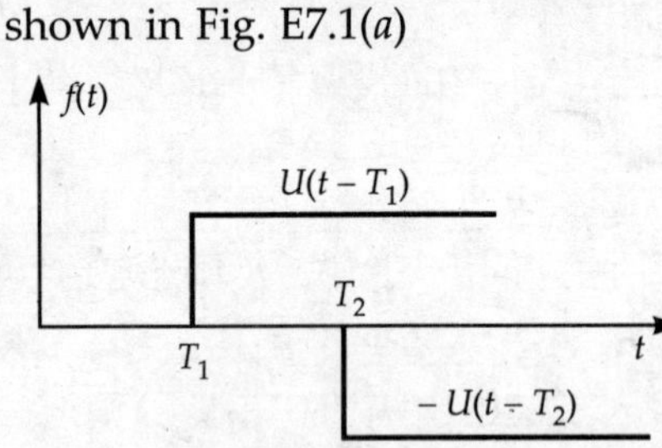

Fig. E7.1 (*a*)

Hence $\quad f(t-T) \equiv u(t-T_1) - u(t-T_2)$

and $\quad \pounds f(t-T) = \pounds u(t-T_1) - \pounds u(t-T_2).$

This gives $\pounds(\text{pulse}) = \dfrac{e^{-sT_1}}{s} - \dfrac{e^{-sT_2}}{s}.$

EXAMPLE 7.4 *A function is given by*

$$f(t) = Ae^{-\alpha t} \sin(\beta t + \psi).$$

Evaluate : $\lim_{t \to 0} f(t)$

SOLUTION. The given function is

$$f(t) = Ae^{-\alpha t} \sin(\beta t + \psi)$$

as $\quad t \to 0, \ \lim_{t \to 0} f(t) = A \sin \psi.$

EXAMPLE 7.5 *In the Laplace domain, a function is given by*

$$F(s) = M\left[\frac{(s+\alpha)\sin\theta}{(s+\alpha)^2 + \beta^2} + \frac{\beta\cos\theta}{(s+\alpha)^2 + \beta^2}\right]$$

Show, by initial value theorem, $\lim_{t \to 0} f(t) = M \sin\theta.$

SOLUTION. As per initial value theorem,

$$\lim_{t \to 0} f(t) = \lim_{s \to \infty} sF(s).$$

However,

$$sF(s) = sM\left[\frac{(s+\alpha)\sin\theta}{(s+\alpha)^2 + \beta^2} + \frac{\beta\cos\theta}{(s+\alpha)^2 + \beta^2}\right]$$

$$= M\left[\frac{s(s+\alpha)\sin\theta}{(s+\alpha)^2 + \beta^2} + \frac{s\beta\cos\theta}{(s+\alpha)^2 + \beta^2)}\right]$$

$$= M\left[\frac{\left(1+\frac{\alpha}{s}\right)\sin\theta}{\left(1+\frac{\alpha}{s}\right)^2 + \left(\frac{\beta}{s}\right)^2} + \frac{\frac{\beta}{s}\cos\theta}{\left(1+\frac{\alpha}{s}\right)^2 + \left(\frac{\beta}{s}\right)^2}\right],$$

(dividing the numerator and denominator by s^2)

$$\therefore \quad \lim_{s \to \infty} sF(s) = M \sin\theta = \lim_{t \to 0} f(t)$$

EXAMPLE 7.6 *A function, in Laplace domain is given by*

$$F(s)=\frac{2}{s}-\frac{1}{s+3}.$$

Obtain its value by Final value theorem in t domain.

SOLUTION. As per final value theorem,

$$\lim_{t\to\infty} f(t)=\lim_{s\to 0} s\,F(s).$$

However, $s\,F(s)=2-\dfrac{s}{s+3}.$

$\therefore$ $\lim_{s\to 0} s\,F(s)=2$

Hence, $\lim_{t\to\infty} f(t)=\mathbf{2}.$

EXAMPLE 7.7 *A shifted unit step function is expressed as $f(t)=u(t-a)$. Obtain its Laplace transform.*

SOLUTION. $F(s)=\int_a^{\infty} f(t)\,e^{-st}\,dt=\int_a^{\infty} 1.e^{-st}\,dt$

$$=-\frac{1}{s}e^{-st}\Big|_a^{\infty}$$

$$\therefore \quad \pounds\,u(t-a)=e^{-as}\left(\frac{1}{s}\right).$$

EXAMPLE 7.8 *A scale change is performed to a time-variable function f (t) by introducing t_0 in the time domain where t_0 is a + ve constant. The new function being $f(t/t_0)$, obtain its Laplace transform.*

SOLUTION.

$$\pounds[f(t/t_0)]=\int_0^{\infty} f(t/t_0)\,e^{-st}\,dt$$

$$=t_0\int_0^{\infty} f(t/t_0)\,e^{-(t_0\,.\,s)\,t/t_0}\,d(t/t_0)$$

Let $t/t_0=T.$

$$\therefore \quad \pounds[f(t/t_0)]=\pounds[f(T)]$$

$$=t_0\int_0^{\infty} f(T)\,e^{-t_0 sT}\,dT$$

$$\therefore \quad \pounds[f(t/t_0)]=\mathbf{t_0 F(t_0 s).}$$

The result obtained here has been termed as *'Scaling Theorem'*.

EXAMPLE 7.9 *A ramp function occurs at $t=a$. Find its Laplace Transform.*

SOLUTION. Ramp function occurring at $t=0$ is denoted by $r(t)$ and is the integration of step function. Hence, the ramp function occurring at $t=a$ will be denoted by $r(t-a)$ and will obviously be the integration of shifted step function, *i.e.*,

$$r(t-a)\equiv\int_0^t u(t-a)\,dt.$$

$$\therefore\ \pounds[r(t-a)]=\pounds\int_0^t u(t-a)\,dt$$

$$=\frac{1}{s}\pounds\,u(t-a)=\frac{1}{s}.\frac{1}{s}e^{-as}=\frac{e^{-as}}{s^2}.$$

EXAMPLE 7.10 *An impulse function is given by $\delta(t-t_1)$. Obtain its Laplace transform.*

SOLUTION. With reference to equation (7.2) in the text,

$$\delta(t)=\frac{d}{dt}u(t)$$

$$\therefore \quad \delta(t-t_1)=\frac{d}{dt}u(t-t_1)$$

Hence $\pounds[\delta(t-t_1)]=\pounds\left[\dfrac{d}{dt}u(t-t_1)\right]$

$$=s\,\pounds[u(t-t_1)]$$

$$=s\,\frac{e^{-t_1 s}}{s}=e^{-t_1 s}.$$

$$\therefore \quad \pounds[\delta(t-t_1)]=\mathbf{e^{-t_1 s}}.$$

EXAMPLE 7.11 *A half cycle sine wave function is given by $v(t)=\sin\omega t$. Determine its Laplace transform.*

SOLUTION. $v(t)=\sin\omega t=\sin\dfrac{2\pi t}{T}$

$$\left[\because\ \omega=2\pi f=\frac{2\pi}{T}\right]$$

This function will be positive for $0\le t\le\dfrac{T}{2}$, T being the time period. Also it is observed that the half cycle sine wave has unity amplitude.

Observing Figs. E7.2(*b*) and (*c*), it is noticed that the half cycle sine wave shown in Fig. E7.2 is the combination of two sin waves given by the relations

$$v_1=\left[\sin 2\pi\frac{t}{T}\right]u(t)$$

and $$v_2=\left[\sin\frac{2\pi}{T}\left(t-\frac{T}{2}\right)\right]u\left(t-\frac{T}{2}\right)$$

when v_2 is shifted by $\dfrac{T}{2}$ from v_1.

CHAPTER 7

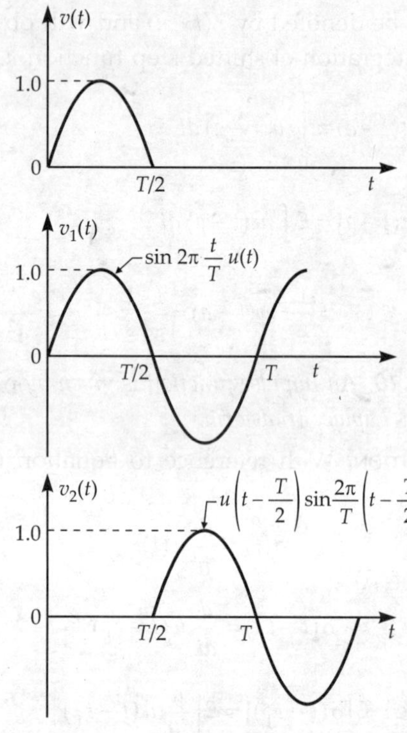

Fig. E7.2

Addition of v_1 and v_2 graphically gives the desired half cycle of the sine wave

$$\therefore\ v(t) = \sin\frac{2\pi t}{T}\,.\,u(t) + \sin\frac{2\pi}{T}\left(t-\frac{T}{2}\right).\,u\left(t-\frac{T}{2}\right)$$

Utilising Laplace transform methods,

$$V(s) = \frac{\frac{2\pi}{T}}{s^2+\left(\frac{2\pi}{T}\right)^2}\left[1+e^{-\frac{T}{2}.s}\right].$$

Example 7.12 *Obtain the Laplace transform of the square wave train shown in Fig. E7.3(a).*

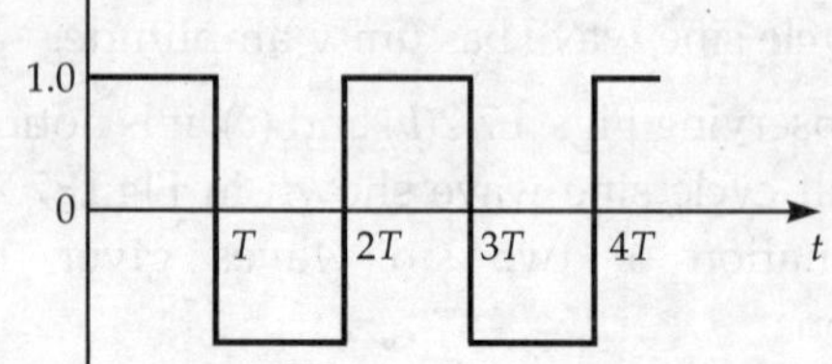

(*a*)

Fig. E7.3

Solution. Observing the original wave shape (square wave pulse train), it may be seen that this wave shape can be formed by adding different unit step functions and shifted step functions [Fig. E7.3(*b*)].

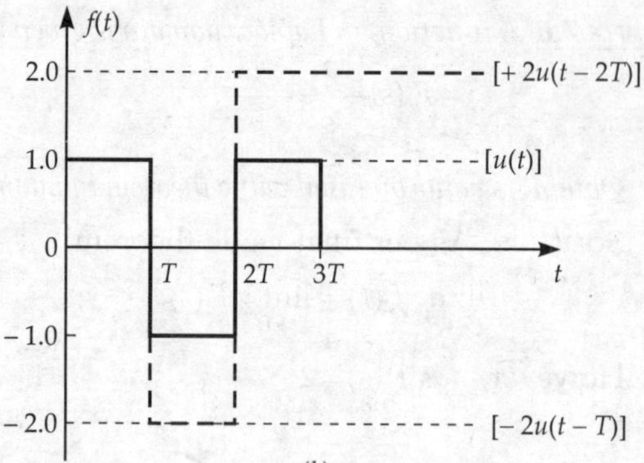

(*b*)

Fig. E7.3

i.e., $\quad f(t) = u(t) - 2\,u(t-T) + 2\,u(t-2T) - 2\,u(t-3T) + \ldots\ldots$

$$\therefore\ F(s) = \text{£}[u(t) - 2\,u(t-T) + 2\,u(t-2T) - 2\,u(t-3T) + \ldots\ldots]$$

$$= \frac{1}{s} - \frac{2e^{-Ts}}{s} + \frac{2e^{-2Ts}}{s} - \frac{2e^{-3T}}{s} + \ldots\ldots$$

$$= \frac{\mathbf{1}}{\boldsymbol{s}}\,[\mathbf{1} - \mathbf{2}e^{-Ts}\,(\mathbf{1} - e^{-Ts} + e^{-2Ts} - e^{-3Ts} + \ldots..)]$$

7.7 CONVOLUTION

Convolution of two real functions corresponds to multiplication of their respective functions.

Thus if, £ $f_1(t) = F_1(s)$ and £ $f_2(t) = F_2(s)$, Convolution is defined by

$$\text{£}[f_1(t) * f_2(t)] = F_1(s)\,F_2(s) \qquad \ldots(7.29)$$

(the word "convolve" means to revolve continuously). The two functions $f_1(t)$ and $f_2(t)$ are multiplied in such a manner that one is continually moving with time τ (say) relative to the other

$$\textit{i.e.,}\quad f_1(t) * f_2(t) = \int_0^t f_1(t-\tau)\,f_2(\tau)\,d\tau \qquad \ldots(7.30)$$

The statement of the mathematical expression given in expression (7.29) is called *Convolution Theorem.*

Let $\text{£}[f_1(t) * f_2(t)] = F(s) \qquad \ldots(7.30(a))$

$$\textit{i.e.,}\quad F(s) = \int_0^\infty [f_1(t) * f_2(t)]\,e^{-st}\,dt$$

$$= \int_{t=0}^\infty \left[\int_{\tau=0}^t f_1(t-\tau)\,f_2(\tau)\,d\tau\right] e^{-st}\,dt \quad \ldots(7.31)$$

Again, an unit step function $u(t-\tau)=0$ if $t<\tau$ *i.e.* if $\tau > t$. Thus if we multiply the r.h.s. of expression (7.31) by $u(t-\tau)$, the product will be zero for values of $\tau > t$. The upper limit of integration of the inner integral *i.e.*, of $\int_{\tau=0}^{t}$ can then be changed to $\int_{\tau=0}^{\infty}$ if the inner integral is multiplied by $u(t-\tau)$.

Thus the expression (7.30) can be written as

$$F(s)=\int_{t=0}^{\infty}\left[\int_{\tau=0}^{\infty} f_1(t-\tau)\, f_2(\tau)\, u(t-\tau)\, e^{-st}\, d\tau\right] dt$$

As the functions are Laplace transformable,

$$F(s)=\int_{\tau=0}^{\infty}\left[\int_{t=0}^{\infty} f_1(t-\tau)\, f_2(\tau)\, u(t-\tau)\, e^{-st}\, dt\right] d\tau$$

However, $f_2(\tau)$ is not a function of t.

$$\therefore\ F(s)=\int_{\tau=0}^{\infty} f_2(\tau)\left[\int_{t=0}^{\infty} f_1(t-\tau)\, u(t-\tau) e^{-st}\, dt\right] d\tau$$

But the inner integral is the transform of the displaced time function and this can be expressed as $e^{-st}\,F_1(s)$.

$$\therefore\quad F(s)=\int_{\tau=0}^{\infty} f_2(\tau)\, e^{-s\tau}\, F_1(s)\, d\tau$$

$$=F_1(s)\int_{0}^{\infty} f_2(\tau)\, e^{-s\tau}\, d\tau$$

$$=F_1(s)\, F_2(s) \qquad ...(7.32)$$

$\therefore$ From equation (7.30),

$$£[f_1(t) * f_2(t)] = F(s)$$

$$= F_1(s)\, F_2(s) \qquad ...(7.33)$$

Thus the convolution theorem is proved.

7.8 APPLICATION OF LAPLACE TRANSFORMATION TECHNIQUE IN ELECTRIC CIRCUIT ANALYSIS

Figure 7.7 represents a series *R-L* circuit with imposed voltage being $v(t)$ and circulating current

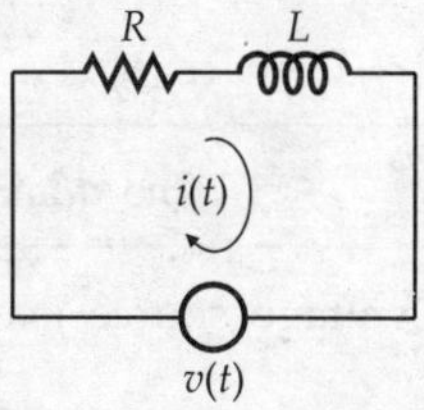

Fig. 7.7 *R-L* series circuit.

being $i(t)$ at any finite value of t after switching. Kirchhoff's law gives

$$Ri(t) + L\frac{di(t)}{dt} = v(t) \qquad ...(7.34)$$

Expression (7.34) gives the loop equation in time domain. Here, we observe that if this time domain equation is converted to Laplace domain,

$$i(t) \to I(s)$$

[$\because$ we have seen earlier that $£\, f(t) = F(s)$],

$$\frac{di(t)}{dt} \to [sI(s) - i(0^+)],$$

since, $£\left[\dfrac{df(t)}{dt}\right] = sF(s) - f(0^+)$ and $v(t) \to V(s)$.

Hence, Laplace transformation of equation (7.34) gives

$$RI(s) + L[sI(s) - i(0^+)] = V(s) \qquad ...(7.35)$$

The circuit representation of expression in (7.35) is shown in Fig. 7.8. The initial current appears in the circuit shown in *s*-domain as a voltage source $[Li(0^+)]$. Kirchhoff's voltage law remains valid in *s*-domain.

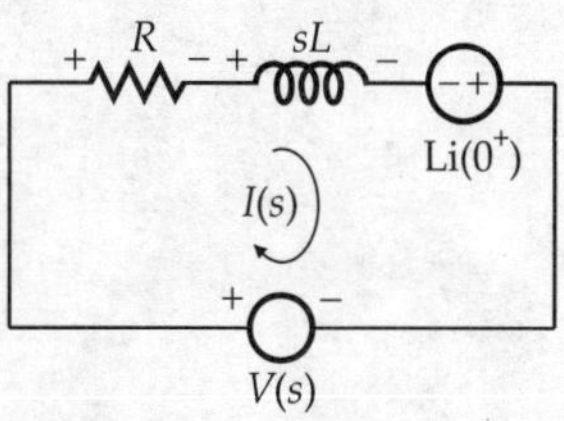

Fig. 7.8 *R-L* circuit in s-doman

Following Table 7.2 exhibits transformation of some conventional time domain and complex frequency (*s*) domain sources and circuits for ready reference.

CHAPTER 7

Table 7.2

	Time domain	*s-domain*
1.	Constant voltage source (say a battery terminal voltage) V,	$\frac{V}{s}$
2.	Time dependent voltage source, $V = f(t)$.	$V(s)$
3.	Constant current source I,	$\frac{I}{s}$
4.	Time dependent current source, $I = f(t)$.	$I(s)$
5.	(*a*) Resistance element (R)	R
	(*b*) current is $i(t)$ through R causing drop $v = Ri(t)$.	$V(s) = RI(s)$
6.	(*a*) Inductance element (L).	Ls
	(*b*) Initial current is $i(0^+)$, clockwise, circuit current being $i(t)$; $v(t) = L\frac{di(t)}{dt}$.	$V(s) = [sLI(s) - Li(0^+)]$ (Fig. 7.9) 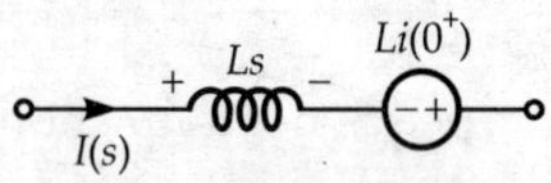 **Fig. 7.9** [If the initial current is $-i(0^+)$, the voltage equation becomes $V(s) = [sLI(s) + Li(0^+)]$ and the equivalent circuit in Laplace domain is [Fig. 7.9(*a*)]. 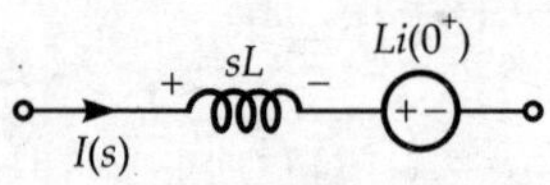 **Fig. 7.9(a)**
	(*c*) Current in the inductor is given by $i(t) = \frac{1}{L}\int_0^t v(t)\,dt + i(0^+)$.	$I(s) = \frac{1}{L}\cdot\frac{V(s)}{s} + \frac{i(0^+)}{s} = I_L(s) + I_0(s)$ which gives the following circuit configuration in s-domain (Fig. 7.10) $\frac{i(0^+)}{s} = I_0(s)$. 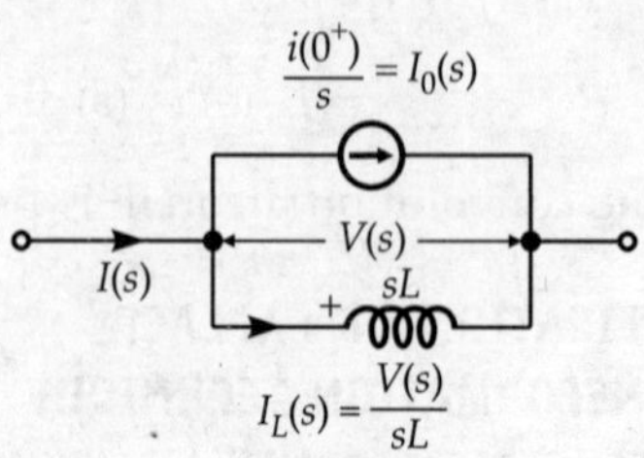 **Fig. 7.10**

	Time domain	*s-domain*
7.	(*a*) Capacitance element (C)	$1/Cs$
	(*b*) Initial voltage is V_0, with +ve polarity at the side of the capacitor that opposes charging current $i(t)$ though it. $$v(t) = V_0 + \frac{1}{C}\int_0^t i(t)\,dt$$	$$V(s) = \frac{V_0}{s} + \frac{1}{C}\frac{I(s)}{s} = \frac{V_0}{s} + \frac{I(s)}{Cs}.$$ The equivalent circuit [Fig. 7.11(*a*)] would be, in s domain, 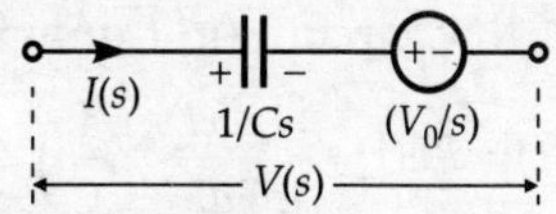 **Fig. 7.11(*a*)**
	(*c*) If the polarity of the initial voltage be $-V_0$ *i.e.*, it assists charging current $i(t)$, $$v(t) = -V_0 + \frac{1}{C}\int_0^t i(t)dt$$	$$V(s) = -\frac{V_0}{s} + \frac{I(s)}{Cs}$$ which gives the equivalent circuit [Fig. 7.11(*b*)] as 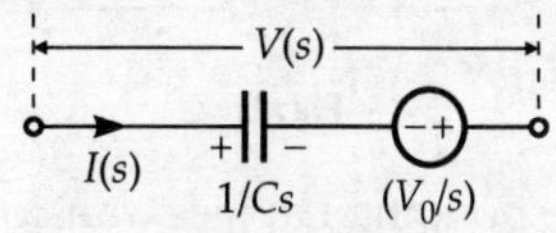 **Fig. 7.11(*b*)**
	(*d*) Current in the capacitor is given by $$i(t) = C\frac{dv(t)}{dt}$$	$$I(s) = C[V(s)s - V(0^+)] = I_C(s) - I_C(0^+)$$ which gives the equivalent circuit [Fig. 7.11(*c*)] as 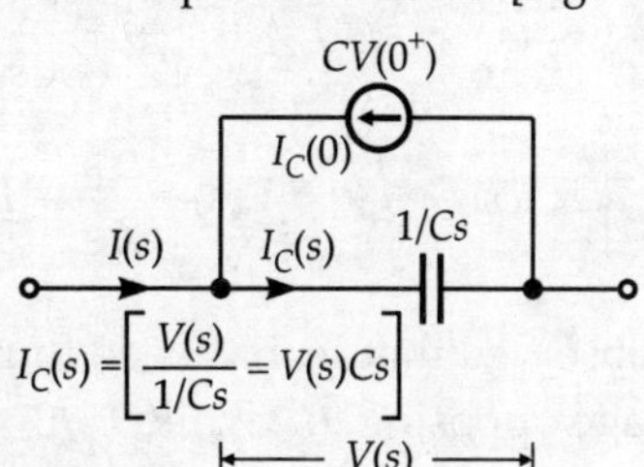 **Fig. 7.11 (*c*)**
8.	Mutual inductance between two coils being M, currents being i_1 and i_2, self-inductances being L_1 and L_2, the voltage drops in each the linked coil is given by $$v_1(t) = L_1\frac{di_1(t)}{dt} + M\frac{di_2(t)}{dt}$$ and $$v_2(t) = L_2\frac{di_2(t)}{dt} + M\frac{di_1(t)}{dt}$$	$$V_1(s) = L_1 sI_1(s) - Li_1(0^+) + MsI_2(s) - Mi_2(0^+) \quad ...(a)$$ $$V_2(s) = L_2 sI_2(s) - Li_2(0^+) + MsI_1(s) - Mi_1(0^+) \quad ...(b)$$ The circuit configuration corresponding to equation (*a*), 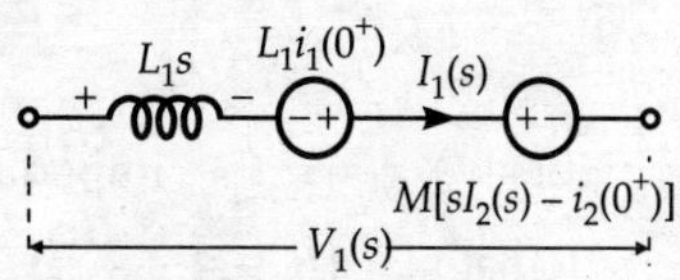 **Fig. 7.12 (*a*)** and corresponding to equation (*b*), 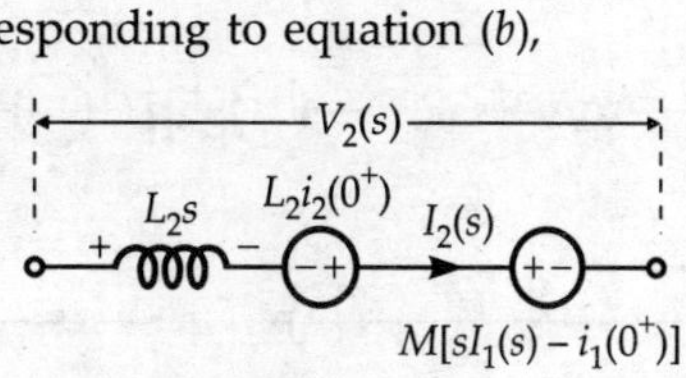 **Fig. 7.12 (*b*)**

CHAPTER 7

EXAMPLE 7.13 *A time dependent voltage $V(t)$ is applied to a series connection of RLC network. Find s-domain impedance and current. Assume initial condition of the voltage in inductor to be assisting the input current and that in capacitor opposing the input current. Draw the t-domain and s domain circuits.*

SOLUTION. Using KVL in Fig. E7.4 of the series connection of *RLC* circuit, (in *t*-domain),

$$v(t) = Ri(t) + L\frac{di(t)}{dt} + \frac{1}{C}\int i(t)\,dt$$

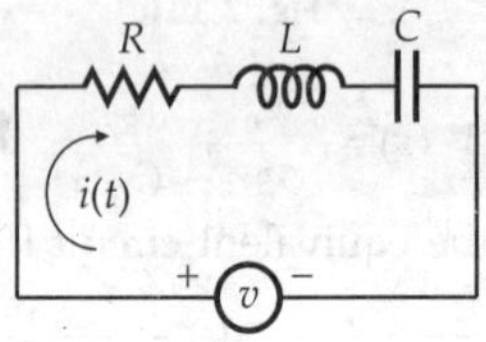

Fig. E7.4

The corresponding Laplace transform is given by,

$$RI(s) + sLI(s) - Li(0^+) + \frac{1}{sC}I(s) + \frac{V_0}{s} = V(s)$$

or,
$$RI(s) + sLI(s) - Li(0^+) + \frac{I(s)}{Cs} + \frac{Q_0}{Cs} = V(s)$$

$$\therefore \quad I(s)\left[R + sL + \frac{1}{Cs}\right] = V(s) - \frac{Q_0}{Cs} + Li(0^+) \quad \text{...}(i)$$

it may be observed that V_0 has been found to be the initial voltage opposing $i(t)$, while $Li(0^+)$ is the drop due to initial current in inductor. Obviously, $V_0 = \dfrac{Q_0}{C}$ where, Q_0 is the initial charge stored in capacitor of capacitance C. Also, in equation (*i*), all the quantities in r.h.s. indicate voltages.

$$\therefore \quad I(s) = \frac{V(s) - \dfrac{Q_0}{Cs} + Li(0^+)}{\left[R + sL + \dfrac{1}{Cs}\right]} \quad \text{...}(ii)$$

Here obviously, $Z(s) \equiv$ the impedance of the circuit in s-domain $= (R + sL + \frac{1}{Cs})$ while the

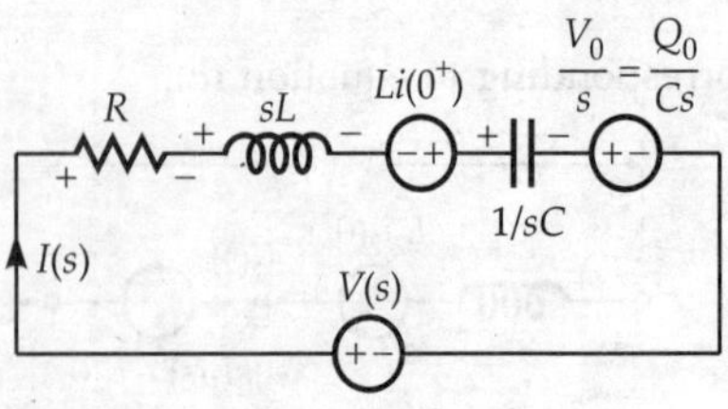

Fig. E7.5

expression of current in *s-domain is given by expression (ii)*. The *s*-domain circuit has been shown in Fig. E7.5.

[Z(s) has also been termed as *operational impedance*]

EXAMPLE 7.14 *A two mesh network is shown in Fig. E7.6. Obtain the expression for $I_1(s)$ and $I_2(s)$ when the switch is closed.*

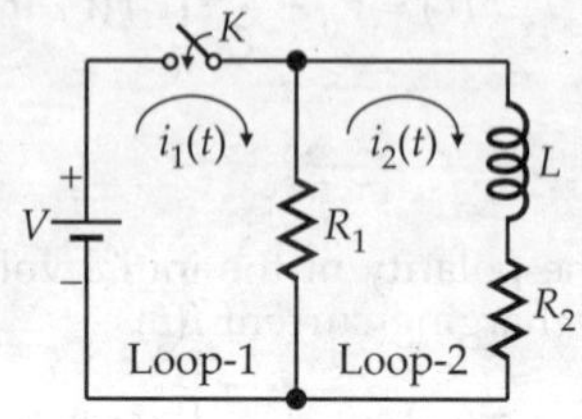

Fig. E7.6

SOLUTION. Utilising KVL *in Loop 1* and *Loop 2*, we get

$$R_1[i_1(t) - i_2(t)] = V \quad \text{...}(i)$$

and
$$R_2 i_2(t) + R_1 i_2(t) - R_1 i_1(t) + L\frac{di_2(t)}{dt} = 0 \quad \text{...}(ii)$$

Utilising Laplace Transform of equations (*i*) and (*ii*),

$$R_1[I_1(s) - I_2(s)] = \frac{V}{s} \quad \text{...}(iii)$$

$$I_2(s)[R_2 + R_1 + sL] - R_1 I_1(s) = Li(0^+) = 0 \quad \text{...}(iv)$$

Expressions (*iii*) & (*iv*) give the Laplace transform of equations (*i*) & (*ii*). Let us show these equations in matrix form,

$$\begin{bmatrix} (R_1) & (-R_1) \\ (-R_1) & (R_1 + R_2 + sL) \end{bmatrix} \begin{bmatrix} I_1(s) \\ I_2(s) \end{bmatrix} = \begin{bmatrix} \frac{V}{s} \\ 0 \end{bmatrix}$$

assuming the initial current $i(0^+)$ to be zero through the inductance

$$\therefore \quad I_1(s) = \frac{V}{s}\left[\frac{R_1 + R_2 + sL}{R_1(R_2 + sL)}\right]$$

$$I_2(s) = \frac{V}{s}\frac{1}{(R_2 + sL)}.$$

EXAMPLE 7.15 *Find the loop currents in Laplace domain in matrix form.*

SOLUTION. For loop 1 (Fig. E7.7), using of KVL gives

$$V = i_1(t)[R_1 + R_2] - i_2(t).R$$

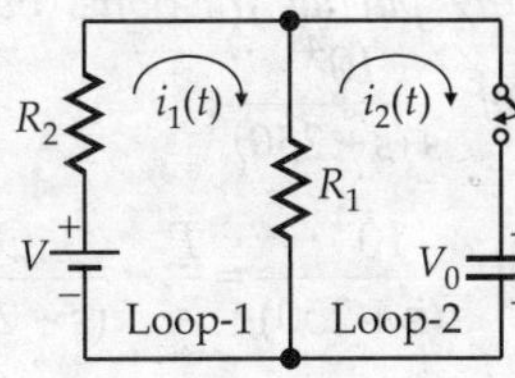

Fig. E7.7

Its Laplace transform gives,

$$\frac{V}{s} = I_1(s)[R_1 + R_2] - I_2(s).R_1 \quad \text{...(i)}$$

For loop-2, using KVL,

$$0 = i_2(t).R_1 - i_1(t)R_1 + \frac{1}{C}\int i_2(t)\,dt$$

The Laplace transform of this equation is

$$0 = -I_1(s)R_1 + I_2(s)\left[R_1 + \frac{1}{Cs}\right] + \frac{V_0}{s}$$

$$\therefore \quad -\frac{V_0}{s} = -R_1 I_1(s) + I_2(s)\left[R_1 + \frac{1}{Cs}\right] \quad \text{...(ii)}$$

This gives,

$$\begin{bmatrix} \frac{V}{s} \\ -\frac{V_0}{s} \end{bmatrix} = \begin{bmatrix} R_1 + R_2 & -R_1 \\ -R_1 & R_1 + \frac{1}{Cs} \end{bmatrix} \begin{bmatrix} I_1(s) \\ I_2(s) \end{bmatrix}$$

or, $$\begin{bmatrix} I_1(s) \\ I_2(s) \end{bmatrix} = \begin{bmatrix} R_1 + R_2 & -R_1 \\ -R_1 & R_1 + \frac{1}{Cs} \end{bmatrix}^{-1} \begin{bmatrix} \frac{V}{s} \\ -\frac{V_0}{s} \end{bmatrix}.$$

7.9 PARTIAL FRACTION EXPANSION METHOD

Let us consider that a Laplace transform in s-domain is expressed as the ratio of two polynomials in s-domain ; *i.e.*,

$$F(s) = \frac{M(s)}{N(s)}$$

where $M(s)$ is of higher degree than $N(s)$. The following example shows how the partial fraction is applicable, in solving problems dealing Laplace transformation.

When $F(s) = \dfrac{M(s)}{N(s)} = \dfrac{s+2}{s^2 - 5s + 6}$,

we assume $\dfrac{s+2}{s^2 - 5s + 6} = \dfrac{s+2}{(s-2)(s-3)}$

or, $$\frac{s+2}{(s-2)(s-3)} = \frac{p}{s-2} + \frac{Q}{s-3} \quad \text{...(7.36)}$$

when P & Q are two coefficients.

The value of P and Q can be determined as follows : In order to determine P and Q let us first multiply both sides of equation (7.36) by $(s-2)$. We then get

$$\frac{s+2}{(s-2)(s-3)}(s-2) = \frac{P}{(s-2)}.(s-2) + \frac{Q(s-2)}{(s-3)}$$

$$= P + \frac{Q(s-2)}{(s-3)}$$

$$\therefore \quad P + \frac{Q(s-2)}{(s-3)} = \frac{(s+2)}{(s-3)} \quad \text{...(7.37)}$$

Substituting $s = 2$, (7.37) becomes, $P = -4$

Again, multiplying both the sides of (7.36) by $(s-3)$,

$$\frac{(s+2)}{(s-2)(s-3)}(s-3) = P\frac{(s-3)}{(s-2)} + Q\frac{(s-3)}{(s-3)}$$

or, $$\frac{(s+2)}{(s-2)} = P\frac{(s-3)}{(s-2)} + Q$$

Substituting $s = 3$, in (7.38) we get, $Q = 5$

Thus, from (7.36),

$$\frac{(s+2)}{(s-2)(s-3)} = -\frac{4}{s-2} + \frac{5}{s-3}$$

$$\therefore \quad F(s) = \frac{(s+2)}{s^2 - 5s + 6} = -\frac{4}{s-2} + \frac{5}{s-3}$$

i.e., $$f(t) = -4e^{2t} + 5e^{3t} \quad \text{...(7.37(a))}$$

Heaviside Expansion Formulae

If $$F(s) = \frac{M(s)}{N(s)},$$

$$£^{-1}\left[\frac{M(s)}{N(s)}\right] = \sum_{K=1}^{n} \frac{M(a_k)}{N'(a_k)} e^{a_k t} \quad \text{...(7.38)}$$

Here, a_k are n nos. of distinct roots of $N(s)$

Application of Heaviside Expansion Formulae

Let $$F(s) = \frac{(s+2)}{s^2 - 5s + 6} = \frac{(s+2)}{(s-2)(s-3)} = \frac{M(s)}{N(s)}$$

$$\therefore \quad M(s) = (s+2)$$

$$N(s) = s^2 - 5s + 6$$

$$N'(s) = 2s - 5$$

The roots of $N(s)$ are $s=2,3$ *i.e.*, $a_1=2, a_2=3$

Thus from (7.38),

$$£^{-1}\left[\frac{M(s)}{N(s)}\right]=\frac{M(2)}{N'(2)}e^{2t}+\frac{M(3)}{N'(3)}e^{3t}$$

$$=\frac{(s+2)\big|_2}{2s-5\big|_2}e^{2t}+\frac{s+2\big|_3}{2s-5\big|_3}e^{3t}$$

i.e., $$f(t)=-4e^{2t}+5e^{3t} \qquad ...(7.38(a))$$

Thus we see that equations [7.37(*a*)] and [7.38(*a*)], both, give the same result.

EXAMPLE 7.16 *Find the inverse Laplace transform of* $\dfrac{1}{s(s^2-\theta^2)}$.

SOLUTION. $$\frac{1}{s(s^2-\theta^2)}=\frac{1}{s(s+\theta)(s-\theta)}$$

∴ Using partial fraction,

$$\frac{1}{s(s^2-\theta^2)}=\frac{A}{s}+\frac{B}{(s+\theta)}+\frac{C}{(s-\theta)} \qquad ...(A)$$

Multiplying both sides of (*A*) by *s*,

$$\frac{1}{(s^2-\theta^2)}=A+\frac{B.s}{(s+\theta)}+\frac{C.s}{(s-\theta)}.$$

With $s=0$, $$A=\frac{1}{s^2-\theta^2}\bigg|_{s=0}=-\frac{1}{\theta^2}$$

Again, multiplying (*A*) by $(s+\theta)$,

$$\frac{1}{s(s-\theta)}=A\frac{s+\theta}{s}+B+\frac{C(s+\theta)}{(s-\theta)}$$

with $s=-\theta$, $B=\dfrac{1}{2\theta^2}$.

Also, multiplying (*A*) by $(s-\theta)$,

$$\frac{1}{s(s+\theta)}=A\left(\frac{s-\theta}{s}\right)+B\frac{(s-\theta)}{(s+\theta)}+C$$

with $s=\theta$, $C=\dfrac{1}{2\theta^2}$.

$$\therefore\quad £^{-1}\left[\frac{1}{s(s^2-\theta^2)}\right]=£^{-1}\left[\frac{-1/\theta^2}{s}+\frac{1/2\theta^2}{s+\theta}+\frac{1/2\theta^2}{s-\theta}\right]$$

$$\therefore\quad f(t)=-\frac{1}{\theta^2}+\frac{1}{2\theta^2}e^{-\theta t}+\frac{1}{2\theta^2}e^{\theta t}.$$

$$=-\frac{1}{\theta^2}+\frac{1}{\theta^2}\left[\frac{e^{\theta t}+e^{-\theta t}}{2}\right]$$

$$=\frac{\mathbf{1}}{\theta^2}\,\mathbf{(\cos h\,\theta t-1).}$$

EXAMPLE 7.17 *Using partial fractions, obtain inverse Laplace transform of* $\dfrac{10^4}{s(s+250)}$.

SOLUTION. Let $$\frac{10^4}{s(s+250)}=\frac{P}{s}+\frac{Q}{(s+250)} \qquad ...(i)$$

Multiplying both sides of (*i*) by *s*, with $s=0$,

$$P=\frac{10^4}{250}=40$$

and multiplying (*i*) by $(s+250)$, with $s=-250$,

$$Q=\frac{10^4}{-250}=-40$$

$$\therefore\ £^{-1}\left[\frac{10^4}{s(s+250)}\right]=£^{-1}\left[\frac{40}{s}-\frac{40}{s+250}\right]$$

$$=\mathbf{40-40\,e^{-250\,t}}.$$

EXAMPLE 7.18 *A function in s-domain is given by* $F(s)=\dfrac{50}{s^2+2s+2}$. *Find the inverse Laplace transform.*

SOLUTION. $$F(s)=\frac{50}{s^2+2s+2}=\frac{50}{(s+1)^2+1}$$

$$=50\times\frac{1}{(s+1)^2+1}$$

$$\therefore\quad f(t)=£^{-1}[F(s)]=\mathbf{50\,e^{-t}\sin t.}$$

EXAMPLE 7.19 *A function in Laplace domain is given by* $I(s)=\dfrac{s+1}{s(s^2+4s+4)}$. *Obtain its inverse form.*

SOLUTION. $$I(s)=\frac{s+1}{s(s^2+4s+4)}=\frac{s+1}{s(s+2)^2}$$

$$=\frac{P}{s}+\frac{Q}{(s+2)}+\frac{R}{(s+2)^2} \qquad ...(i)$$

where *P*, *Q* and *R* are coefficients.

Multiplying (*i*) by *s*, with $s=0$,

$$P=\frac{s+1}{(s+2)^2}\bigg|_{s=0}=\frac{1}{4}$$

Multiplying (*i*) by $(s+2)^2$,

$$R=\frac{s+1}{s}-Q(s+2)-\frac{P(s+2)^2}{s}$$

$$s=-2,\ R=\frac{s+1}{s}\bigg|_{-2}=\frac{1}{2}.$$

To find *Q* coefficient, we are to take the coefficient of the quadratic term of $I(s)$ and then that is to be differentiated.

$$\therefore\ Q=\frac{d}{ds}\left[\frac{s+1}{s}\right]=-\frac{1}{s^2};\ \text{at}\ s=-2,\ Q=-\frac{1}{4}.$$

This gives,

$$I(s)=\frac{1/4}{s}-\frac{1/4}{s+2}+\frac{1/2}{(s+2)^2}$$

or,
$$f(t)=\frac{1}{4}-\frac{1}{4}e^{-2t}+\frac{1}{2}te^{-2t}.$$

EXAMPLE 7.20 *A function is given by* $F(s)=\frac{250}{(s+100)(s+50)}$ *in the s-domain. Find f(t) using Heaviside formula.*

SOLUTION. $F(s)=\frac{250}{(s+100)(s+50)}=\frac{M(s)}{N(s)}.$

$$\therefore\quad M(s)=250,\ N(s)=(s+100)(s+50)$$
$$=s^2+150s+5000$$

i.e., $N'(s)=2s+150$

also, the roots a_1 & a_2 of $N(s)$ are given by

$$a_1=-100,\ a_2=-50.$$

$$\therefore\ f(t)=\pounds^{-1}[F(s)]$$
$$=\frac{250}{2s+150}\bigg|_{-100}e^{-100t}+\frac{250}{2s+150}\bigg|_{-50}e^{-50t}$$
$$=\frac{250}{-50}e^{-100t}+\frac{250}{50}e^{-50t}$$
$$=\mathbf{-5\,e^{-100t}+5\,e^{-50t}}.$$

EXAMPLE 7.21 *Obtain inverse Laplace transform of I (s) when* $I(s)=\frac{250}{(s^2+625)(s+2)}$.

SOLUTION. $I(s)=\frac{250}{(s^2+625)(s+2)}$

$$=\frac{250}{(s+2)(s+j25)(s-j25)}=\frac{A}{s+2}+\frac{B}{s+j25}+\frac{C}{s-j25}$$

where A, B and C are coefficients.

$$A=\frac{250}{s^2+625}\bigg|_{s=-2}=\frac{250}{629}\simeq 0.4$$

$$B=\frac{250}{(s+2)(s-j25)}\bigg|_{s=-j25}$$
$$=\frac{250}{(2-j25)(-j50)}=-\frac{5}{(25+j2)}$$

$$C=\frac{250}{(s+2)(s+j25)}\bigg|_{s=j25}$$
$$=\frac{250}{(2+j25)(j50)}=-\frac{5}{(25-j2)}$$

Thus, $I(s)=0.4\big|_{(s+2)}-\frac{5}{(25+j2)(s+j25)}-\frac{5}{(25-j2)(s-j25)}$

$$\therefore\ i(t)=\mathbf{0.4\,e^{-2t}-\frac{5}{(25+j2)}e^{-j25t}-\frac{5}{(25-j2)}e^{j25t}}$$

CHAPTER 7

The following is the ready guide for solving problems with partial fractions :

(*i*) When $F(s)=\frac{M(s)}{N(s)}$ and $N(s)=(s-x)(s-y)(s-z)$, the roots being real and simple

$$F(s)=\frac{A}{s-x}+\frac{B}{s-y}+\frac{C}{s-z}$$

Here, $A=F(s)(s-x)\big|_{s=x}$; $B=F(s)(s-y)\big|_{s=y}$; $C=F(s)(s-z)\big|_{s=z}$

(*ii*) When $F(s)=\frac{M(s)}{N(s)}$, $N(s)=(s-x)^n N_1(s)$, the roots being real and multiple

$$F(s)=\frac{A_0}{(s-x)^n}+\frac{A_1}{(s-x)^{n-1}}+\ldots.+\frac{A_{n-1}}{(s-x)}+\frac{M_1(s)}{N_1(s)}$$

When $\frac{M_1(s)}{N_1(s)}$ represent the other terms of expansion,

$$A_0=(s-x)^n F(s)\big|_{s=x}\quad A_1=\frac{d}{ds}F_1(s)\bigg|_{s=x}\quad A_2=\frac{1}{\underline{|2}}\frac{d^2}{ds^2}F_1(s)\bigg|_{s=x}\quad\ldots..\quad A_n=\frac{1}{\underline{|n}}\frac{d^n}{ds^n}F_1(s)\bigg|_{s=x}$$

(*iii*) When $F(s)=\frac{M(s)}{N_1(s)[s-a+jb][s-a-jb]}$, roots being complex,

$$F(s)=\frac{A}{s-a-jb}+\frac{B}{s-a+jb}+\frac{M_1(s)}{N_1(s)}\quad\text{where, }\frac{M_1(s)}{N_1(s)}\text{ represent other terms}$$

Here, $A=\frac{M(a+jb)}{N_1(a+j\beta)(+2jb)}$; $B=\frac{M(a-jb)}{N_1(a-j\beta)(-2jb)}$

[Ordinarily, $B=A^*$, where A^* is the complex conjugate of A]

7.10(A) STEP RESPONSE OF *RL* SERIES CIRCUIT

In this article, the step response of a *R-L* circuit, initially de-energized, has been considered [Fig. 7.13(*a*)]. The governing equation is given by

$$Eu(t) = Ri(t) + L\frac{di}{dt} \quad ...(7.39)$$

[∵ E exists only when s is closed *i.e.*, the voltage is $E\,u(t)$ *i.e.*, the unit step function.]

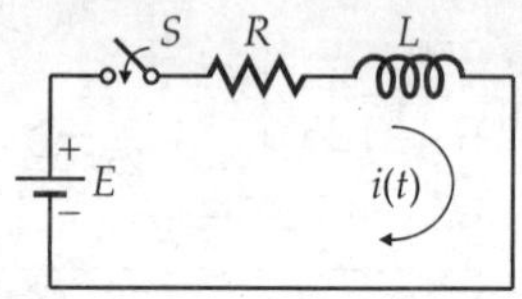

Fig. 7.13 (*a*) Circuit of with step response.

The Laplace transform of equation (7.39) is given by

$$\frac{E}{s} = RI(s) + L[sI(s) - i(0)] \quad ...[7.39(a)]$$

It may be noted that $i(0)$ indicates the information regarding the initial value of the current which is zero here as the circuit has been assumed to be in the de-energized condition.

∴ Equation [7.39(*a*)] becomes

$$\frac{E}{s} = I(s)[R + sL]$$

or, $$I(s) = \frac{E/L}{s\left(s+\frac{R}{L}\right)} = \frac{A}{s} + \frac{B}{s+\frac{R}{L}}$$

[expressing in the form of partial fraction]

where $$A = \left[\frac{E/L}{s+\frac{R}{L}}\right]_{s=0} = \frac{E}{R}$$

$$B = \left[\frac{E/L}{s}\right]_{s=-\frac{R}{L}} = -\frac{E}{R}$$

Thus, $$I(s) = \frac{E/R}{s} + \frac{(-E/R)}{s+\frac{R}{L}}$$

∴ $$i(t) = \frac{E}{R} - \frac{E}{R}e^{-\frac{R}{L}.t}.$$

[taking inverse Laplace transform]

7.10(B) STEP RESPONSE OF *RC* SERIES CIRCUIT

Let us assume that the capacitance of the circuit is initially having a charge Q_0 owing to the flow of some previously applied current. Let the switch K be now closed. The governing equation of the circuit [Fig. 7.13(*b*)] is then given by

$$Eu(t) = Ri(t) + \frac{1}{C}\int i(t)\,dt \quad ...(7.40)$$

[Supply voltage being applied at the moment of switching and is a step response voltage with magnitude E (d.c.)]

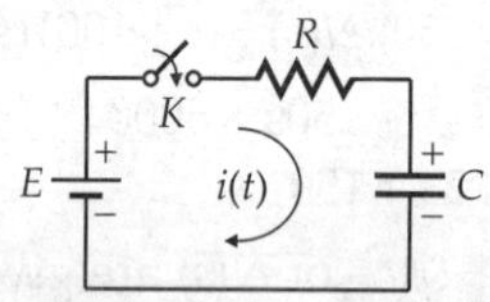

Fig. 7.13 (*b*) Step response of the *RC* circuit.

The Laplace equation is then given by

$$\frac{E}{s} = RI(s) + \frac{1}{C}\left[\frac{I(s)}{s} + \frac{i(0)}{s}\right] \quad ...[7.40(a)]$$

In the above equation, the term $i(0)$ indicates the current in the circuit in initial condition when $i(0) \equiv \int_{-\infty}^{0} i\,dt = Q_0$.

∴ $$\frac{E}{s} = RI(s) + \frac{1}{C}\left[\frac{I(s)}{s} + \frac{Q_0}{s}\right]$$

i.e., $$\frac{E}{s} - \frac{Q_0}{C.s} = I(s)\left[R + \frac{1}{C.s}\right]$$

$$I(s) = \frac{\frac{1}{s}\left(E - \frac{Q_0}{c}\right)}{R + \frac{1}{Cs}} = \frac{E - \frac{Q_0}{C}}{s\left(R + \frac{1}{Cs}\right)}$$

or, $$I(s) = \frac{E - \frac{Q_0}{C}}{R\left(s + \frac{1}{Rc}\right)} = \frac{E - \frac{Q_0}{C}}{R}\left[\frac{1}{s + \frac{1}{RC}}\right] \quad ...[7.40(b)]$$

$$= \left(\frac{E}{R} - \frac{Q_0}{R_C}\right)\left[\frac{1}{s + \frac{1}{RC}}\right]$$

∴ $$i(t) = \left(\frac{E}{R} - \frac{Q_0}{RC}\right)e^{-\frac{1}{RC}.t}$$

[taking inverse Laplace transforms]

Also, we can write $I(s) = \dfrac{E - V_{in}}{s\left(\dfrac{1}{sC} + R\right)}$ from [7.40(b)] since V_{in} is the initial voltage stored in the capacitor given by (Q_0 / C)

$$\therefore \quad V_c(s) = \frac{V_{in}}{s} + \frac{I(s)}{Cs} = \frac{V_{in}}{s} + \frac{E - V_{in}}{s^2 C\left[\dfrac{1}{sC} + R\right]}$$

$$\therefore \quad V_c(t) = V_{in} + E - V_{in} - (E - V_{in})\, e^{-t/RC}$$

$$= E - (E - V_{in})\, e^{-t/RC} \text{ volt.}$$

7.11(A) STEP CURRENT RESPONSE OF A *RL* PARALLEL CIRCUIT

In Fig. 7.14(*a*), the constant current source of magnitude *I* is applied across parallel contribution of *R* and *L*. Obviously,

$$RI_R = L\frac{dI_L}{dt} \quad \text{...(7.41)}$$

and $$I = I_R + I_L \quad \text{...[7.41(a)]}$$

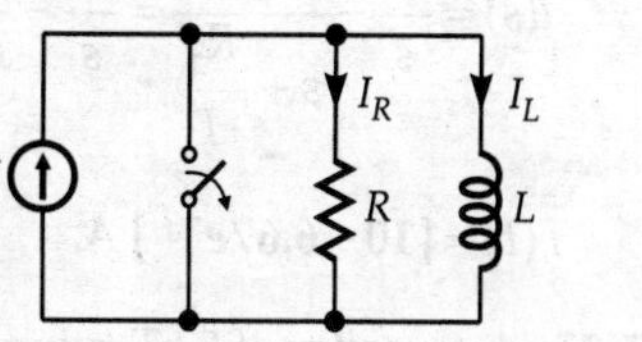

Fig. 7.14 (*a*) Step input to parallel *R-L* circuit.

Multiplying [7.41(*a*)] by *R*, we can write

$$RI = RI_R + RI_L$$

Using (7.41) we find

$$RI = L\frac{dI_L}{dt} + RI_L \quad \text{...[7.41(b)]}$$

This expression represents the governing differential equation of the circuit shown in Fig. 7.14(*a*) just after switching of current source. The solution* is given by

$$i_L = i\,(1 - e^{(-R/L)t})$$

and $$i_R = i - i_L = ie^{(-R/L)t}$$

7.11(B) STEP CURRENT RESPONSE OF *RC* PARALLEL CIRCUIT

Following application of constant current source *I* to the parallel *RC* circuit by opening the switch in the circuit of Fig. 7.14(*b*), we can write, (at $t = 0+$)

$$I = i_R + i_C \quad \text{...(7.42)}$$

and $$Ri_R = \frac{1}{C}\int_0^t i_c\, dt \quad \text{...[7.42(a)]}$$

(We assume the switch is opened at $t = 0$ while the circuit was in steady state at $t = 0-$)

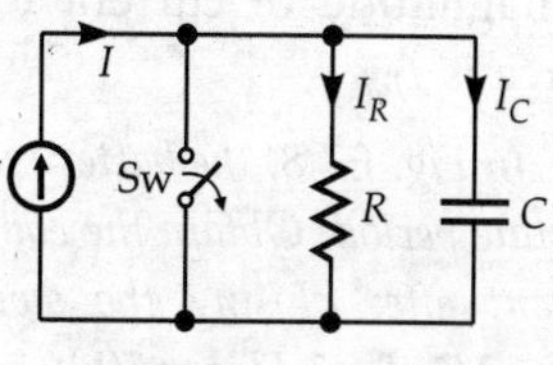

Fig. 7.14 (*b*) Step current input to prallel *R-C* circuit.

Multiplying equation (7.42) by *R*, we get

$$RI = Ri_R + Ri_C$$

$$= \frac{1}{C}\int_0^t i_C\, dt + Ri_C$$

[using equation 7.42(*a*)]

* We can write equation [7.41(*b*)] as

$$\frac{I(s)}{s} \cdot R = I_L(s)(R + Ls)$$

or $$I_L(s) = I(s)\frac{R}{s(R + Ls)} = I(s)\frac{(R/L)}{s\left(\dfrac{R}{L} + s\right)} = I(s)\left[\frac{A_0}{s} + \frac{B_0}{s + \dfrac{R}{L}}\right]$$

Here, $$A_0 = \left.\frac{(R/L)}{\left(s + \dfrac{R}{L}\right)}\right|_{s=0} = 1 \; ; \qquad B_0 = \left.\frac{R/L}{s}\right|_{s = -\frac{R}{L}} = -1$$

$$\therefore \quad I_L(s) = I(s)\left[\frac{1}{s} - \frac{1}{s + R/L}\right]$$

$$\therefore \quad i_L(t) = i(t)\,[1 - e^{-(R/L).t}] \quad \text{...[7.41(c)]}$$

CHAPTER 7

Taking Laplace transformation, we can write

$$R\frac{I(s)}{s} = R\,I_C(s) + \frac{1}{Cs}I_C(s)$$

$$= I_C(s)\left[R + \frac{1}{Cs}\right]$$

or $$I_C(s) = \frac{I(s).R}{\left(R+\frac{1}{Cs}\right)s} = I(s)\left[\frac{1}{s+\frac{1}{RC}}\right]$$

Taking Laplace inverse we can write

$$\therefore \quad i_C(t) = i(t)[e^{-1/RC.t}] \qquad ...[7.42(b)]$$

Expression [7.42(*b*)] represents the capacitor current at $t = 0+$ while the resistor current at $t = 0+$ is given by

$$i_R(t) = i(t) - i_C(t)$$

$$= i(t)(1 - e^{-t/RC})$$

$$= I(1 - e^{-1/RC.t}) \qquad ...[7.42(c)]$$

(Since the magnitude of current for the constant current source is *I*).

EXAMPLE 7.22 *In Fig. E7.8, the battery voltage is applied for a steady state period. Obtain the complete expression for the current after closing the switch K. Assume* $R_1 = 1\Omega$, $R_2 = 2\Omega$, $L = 1\,H$, $E = 10\,V$.

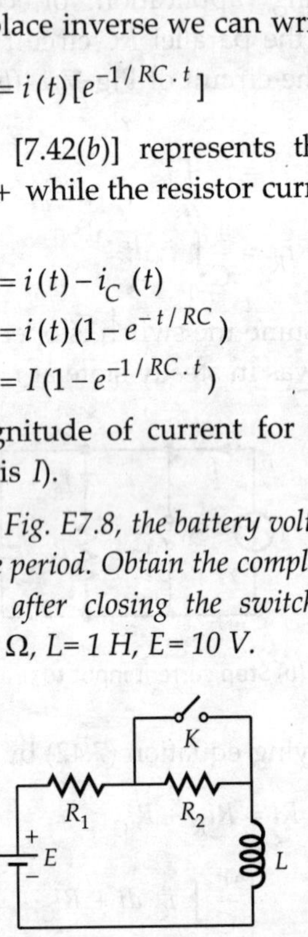

Fig. E7.8

SOLUTION. As soon as the switch is closed, the current $i(t)$ is given by (KVL),

$$Eu(t) = R_1\,i(t) + L\frac{di(t)}{dt} \qquad ...(i)$$

Laplace transformation yields,

$$\frac{E}{s} = R_1 I(s) + sLI(s) - Li(0+)$$

$$\therefore \quad \frac{E}{s} + Li(0+) = I(s)[R_1 + sL]$$

$$\therefore \quad I(s) = \frac{E + sLi(0+)}{s(R_1 + sL)} = \frac{\frac{E}{L} + si(0+)}{s\left(s + \frac{R_1}{L}\right)} \qquad ...(ii)$$

However, partial fraction gives,

$$I(s) = \frac{A}{s} + \frac{B}{s + \frac{R_1}{L}}$$

$$\therefore \quad A = \left.\frac{\frac{E}{L} + si(0+)}{s + \frac{R_1}{L}}\right|_{s=0} = \frac{E}{R_1} = \frac{10}{1} = 10\text{ A}$$

$$B = \left.\frac{\frac{E}{L} + si(0+)}{s}\right|_{s=-\frac{R_1}{L}} = -\frac{E}{R_1} + i(0+)$$

However, the current just before the switching is

$$i(0-) = i(0+) = \frac{E}{R_1 + R_2} = \frac{10}{3} = 3.33\text{ A}$$

$$\therefore \quad B = \frac{E}{R_1} + i(0+) = -\frac{10}{1} + 3.33 = -6.67\text{ A}$$

$$\therefore \quad I(s) = \frac{10}{s} - \frac{6.67}{s + \frac{R_1}{L}} = \frac{10}{s} - \frac{6.67}{s+1}$$

$$\therefore \quad i(t) = [\mathbf{10 - 6.67}e^{-t}]\textbf{ A}$$

EXAMPLE 7.23 *A capacitor of 5 μF being charged initially to 10 V is connected to a resistance of 10 kΩ and is allowed to discharge through it by switching of a switch K. Find the expression of discharging current.*

SOLUTION. The circuit is drawn as shown in Fig. E7.9. As soon as the switch *K* is closed, the

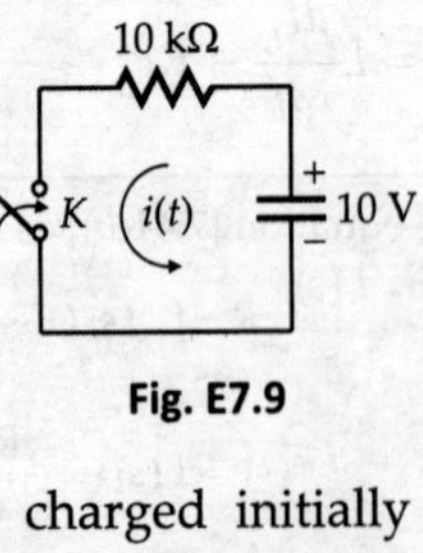

Fig. E7.9

capacitor, being charged initially to 10 V, starts discharging. Let the discharge current be $i(t)$. Application of KVL in the discharging loop gives

$$0 = Ri(t) + \frac{1}{C}\int i(t)\,dt$$

Laplace transformation gives,

$$0 = RI(s) + \frac{1}{C}\left[\frac{I(s)}{s} + \frac{Q_0}{s}\right]$$

or $$-\frac{Q_0}{Cs} = I(s)\left[R+\frac{1}{Cs}\right]$$

or, $$I(s) = -\frac{Q_0/Cs}{\left(R+\frac{1}{Cs}\right)}$$

$$= -\frac{Q_0}{CR\left(s+\frac{1}{RC}\right)} = -\frac{10}{R\left(s+\frac{1}{RC}\right)}$$

$$\left[\because \frac{Q_0}{C} = 10\text{ V}\right]$$

$$\therefore \quad i(t) = -\frac{10}{R}(e^{-t/RC})$$

$$= -\frac{10}{10\times 10^3}e^{-t/10\times 10^3\times 5\times 10^{-6}}$$

$$= -10^3 e^{-20t}\text{ A.}$$

7.12 IMPULSE RESPONSE OF SERIES *RC* NETWORK

Figure 7.15 represents a series *RC* network excited at $t=0$ by an *impulse function* of magnitude *E*.

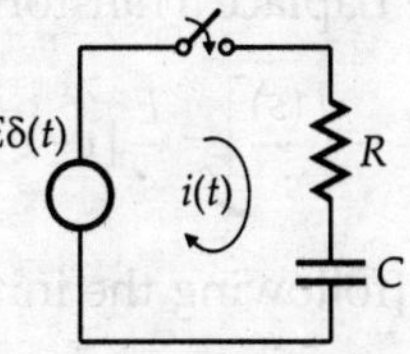

Fig. 7.15 Series *RC* network under the influence of impulse function

Applying KVL,

$$E\delta(t) = Ri(t) + \frac{1}{C}\int i(t)\,dt \qquad \text{...(7.43)}$$

Taking Laplace transform of eqn. (7.43),

$$E = RI(s) + \frac{1}{C}\left[\frac{I(s)}{s}+\frac{Q_0}{s}\right] \qquad \text{...(7.44)}$$

If we assume that initially the capacitor is discharged, $Q_0 = 0$

$\therefore$ Equation (7.44) becomes

$$E = RI(s) + \frac{1}{C}\left[\frac{I(s)}{s}+0\right]$$

$$= \left(R+\frac{1}{Cs}\right)I(s) = \frac{R}{s}\left(s+\frac{1}{RC}\right)I(s)$$

$$\therefore \quad I(s) = \frac{E}{R}\frac{s}{\left(s+\frac{1}{RC}\right)} = \frac{E}{R}\left[1-\frac{1/RC}{s+\frac{1}{RC}}\right]$$

$$= \frac{E}{R}\left[1-\frac{1/T}{s+\frac{1}{T}}\right] \qquad \text{...[7.44(a)]}$$

$(\because RC = T$, the time constant)

Hence, the inverse of equation (7.45) gives

$$i(t) = \frac{E}{R}\delta(t) - \frac{E}{RT}e^{-\frac{1}{T}\cdot t}\text{ A.}$$

7.13 IMPULSE RESPONSE OF SERIES *RL* NETWORK

Figure 7.16 represents a series *R-L* circuit being excited by an *impulse function* $E\,\delta(t)$. Let us assume that the circuit is initially de-energized. Using KVL,

$$E\,\delta(t) = Ri(t) + L\frac{di(t)}{dt} \qquad \text{...(7.45)}$$

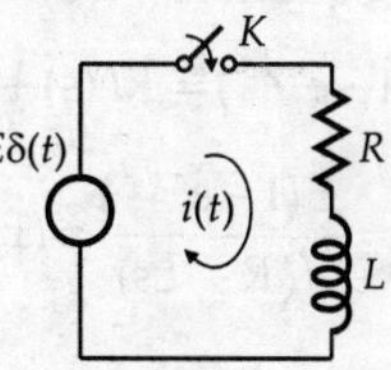

Fig. 7.16 *R-L* circuit excited by impulse function.

Taking the Laplace transform of equation (7.45),

$$E = RI(s) + L[sI(s) - i(0+)] \qquad \text{...(7.46)}$$

However, following the initial condition, $i(0+) = 0$. Thus from equation (7.46),

$$E = RI(s) + Ls\,I(s)$$

or, $$I(s) = \frac{E}{R+Ls} = \frac{E}{L\left(s+\frac{R}{L}\right)} = \frac{E}{L}\cdot\frac{1}{\left(s+\frac{R}{L}\right)}$$

Taking the inverse of Laplace transformation,

$$i(t) = \frac{E}{L}e^{-\frac{R}{L}\cdot t}.$$

7.14 RESPONSE OF *RL* CIRCUIT WITH PULSE INPUT

A pulse $E(t)$ as shown in Fig. 7.17(*a*) is applied to a *RL* circuit [Fig. 7.17(*b*)] at $t=0$ by switching a switch *K*. Application of KVL in the loop of Fig. 7.17(*b*) yields

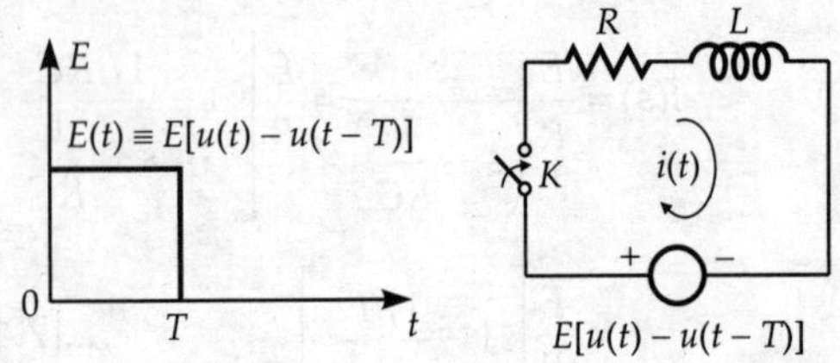

(a) Pulse input (b) Pulse input applied to RL series circuit

Fig. 7.17

$$E(t) = Ri(t) + L\frac{di(t)}{dt}$$

or, $$E[u(t) - u(t-T)] = R.i(t) + L\frac{di(t)}{dt} \quad ...(7.47)$$

The Laplace transform of equation (7.47) gives

$$£\,E\,u(t) - £\,u(t-T) = £\left[Ri(t) + L\frac{di(t)}{dt}\right]$$

or, $$\frac{E}{s} - \frac{E}{s}e^{-Ts} = RI(s) + L[sI(s) - i(0+)] \quad ...(7.48)$$

Assuming the circuit to the initially de-energized, $i(0+) = 0$. Thus equation (7.48) becomes

$$\frac{E}{s}(1-e^{-Ts}) = RI(s) + LsI(s)$$

or, $$I(s) = \frac{E(1-e^{-Ts})}{s(R+Ls)} = (1-e^{-Ts})\frac{E}{L}\frac{1}{s\left(s+\frac{R}{L}\right)} \quad ...(7.49)$$

However, by partial fraction,

$$\frac{E/L}{s\left(s+\frac{R}{L}\right)} = \frac{A}{s} + \frac{B}{s+\frac{R}{L}},$$

when $$A = \left[\frac{E/L}{s+\frac{R}{L}}\right]_{s=0} = \frac{E}{R};$$

$$B = \left[\frac{E/L}{s}\right]_{s=-\frac{R}{L}} = -\frac{E}{R}$$

Thus, equation (7.49) becomes

$$I(s) = (1-e^{-Ts})\left[\frac{E/R}{s} + \frac{(-E/R)}{s+\frac{R}{L}}\right]$$

$$= \frac{E/R}{s} - \frac{E/R}{s}e^{-Ts} - \frac{E/R}{s+\frac{R}{L}} + \frac{E/R}{s+\frac{R}{L}}e^{-Ts}$$

Thus the inverse Laplace transform is given by

$$i(t) = \frac{E}{R}u(t) - \frac{E}{R}u(t-T) - \frac{E}{R}e^{-\frac{R}{L}t} + \frac{E}{R}e^{-\frac{R}{L}t}u(t-T)$$

7.15 PULSE RESPONSE OF SERIES *RC* CIRCUIT

A pulse $E(t)$ [Fig. 7.18(*a*)] is applied to *RC* circuit through a switch *K*, the circulating current being $i(t)$ [Fig. 7.18(*b*)]. We assume the initial charge to be zero in the capacitor. Application of KVL in the loop of Fig. 7.18(*b*) yields

$$E(t) = Ri(t) + \frac{1}{C}\int i(t)\,dt$$

or, $$E[u(t) - u(t-T)] = Ri(t) + \frac{1}{C}\int i(t)\,dt \quad ...(7.50)$$

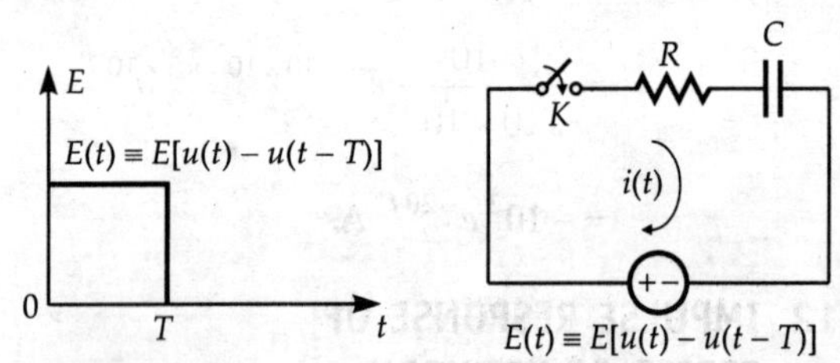

(a) Pulse input (b) Pulse input in *RC* circuit

Fig. 7.18

Taking the Laplace Transform,

$$RI(s) + \frac{1}{C}\left[\frac{Q_0}{s} + \frac{I(s)}{s}\right] = \frac{E}{s}[1-e^{-Ts}] \quad ...(7.51)$$

But $Q_0 = 0$ [following the initial condition]

Thus equation (7.51) becomes,

$$RI(s) + \frac{1}{C}\left[\frac{I(s)}{s}\right] = \frac{E}{s}(1-e^{-Ts})$$

$$\therefore \quad I(s) = \frac{E}{s}\frac{1-e^{-Ts}}{R+\frac{1}{Cs}} = \frac{E}{R}\frac{1-e^{-Ts}}{s+\frac{1}{RC}}$$

$$= \frac{E}{R}\left[\frac{1}{s+\frac{1}{RC}} - \frac{e^{-Ts}}{s+\frac{1}{RC}}\right] \quad ...(7.52)$$

Taking the inverse of equation (7.52),

$$i(t) = \frac{E}{R}\left[e^{-\frac{t}{RC}} - e^{-\frac{t}{RC}}u(t-T)\right].$$

EXAMPLE 7.24 *In the circuit of Fig. E7.10 obtain the expression for the current i(t) when the switch is moved from position (1) to position (2) at t = 0.*

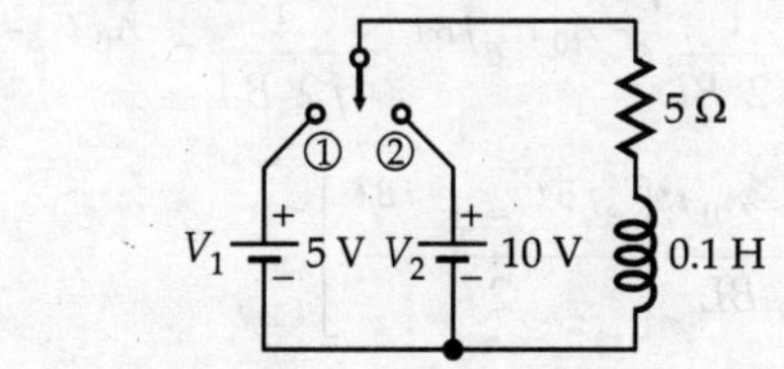

Fig. E7.10

Solution. Assuming the switch to be at position (2), application of KVL in Fig. E7.11 yields

$$5i(t) + 0.1\frac{di(t)}{dt} = 10.$$

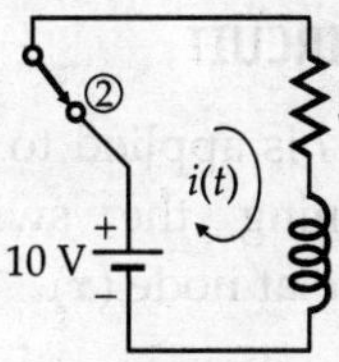

Fig. E7.11

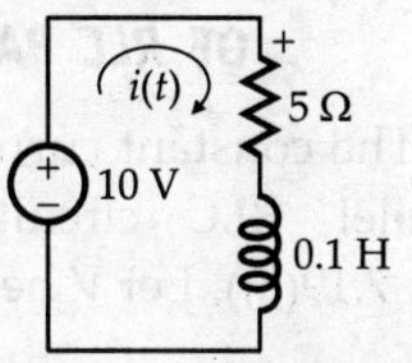

(at $t = 0+$)

Fig. E7.12

Taking Laplace transform of the above equation

$$5I(s) + 0.1[sI(s) - i(0+)] = \frac{10}{s} \qquad ...(a)$$

$i(0+)$ being the current in the *R-L* circuit just after switching.

Obviously $i(0)$ at $t = 0^+$ (*i.e.*, at the instant just after switching) will be equal to the value of $i(0)$ at $t = 0^-$ (*i.e.* at the instant just before switching) as the inductance will not allow the current to flow through it immediately with change of switching status.

However, $i(0)$ at $t = 0^-$ is given by

$$\frac{\text{voltage source } V_1}{\text{resistance } 5\,\Omega} = 1\text{ A}$$

as the current at $t = 0^-$ means the switch at position (1) and the circuit in steady state, inductance being of no effect.

Thus, $i(0+) = 1$ A.

Thus, equation (*a*) becomes,

$$5\,I(s) + 0.1[s\,I(s) - 1] = \frac{10}{s}$$

or,
$$I(s)[5 + 0.1\,s] - 0.1 = \frac{10}{s}$$

$$\therefore \quad I(s) = \frac{(10/s) + 0.1}{5 + 0.1\,s}$$

$$= \frac{10 + 0.1s}{s(0.1\,s + 5)} = \frac{s + 100}{s(s + 50)}$$

However,

$$\frac{s + 100}{s(s + 50)} = \frac{A}{s} + \frac{B}{s + 50}.$$

$$A = \left.\frac{s + 100}{s + 50}\right|_{s=0} = 2$$

$$B = \left.\frac{s + 100}{s}\right|_{s=-50} = -1$$

$$\therefore \quad I(s) = \frac{2}{s} + \frac{(-1)}{s + 50} = \frac{2}{s} - \frac{1}{s + 50}$$

$$\therefore \quad i(t) = 2 - e^{-50\,t}\text{ A.}$$

7.16(A) STEP RESPONSE OF *RLC* SERIES CIRCUIT

In the circuit shown in Fig. 7.19(*a*), a unit step voltage $u(t)$ is applied across an *RLC* series circuit having zero initial conditions $[V_c(0^-) = 0;\, I_L(0^-) = 0]$.

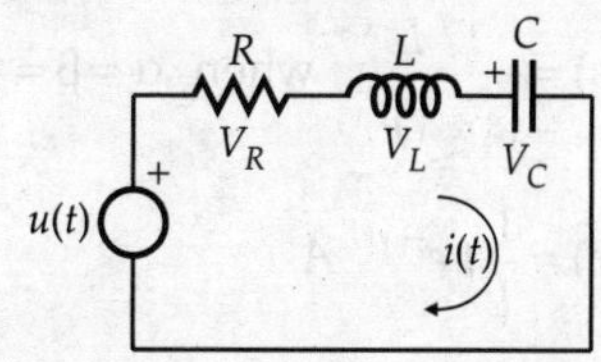

Fig. 7.19 (*a*) *Series RLC circuit excited by step voltage.*

In Laplace domain, the current through the circuit is given by

$$I(s) = \frac{1/s}{R + Ls + \dfrac{1}{Cs}}$$

$$\left[\because \pounds\,u(t) = \frac{1}{s};\; Z(s) = R + Ls + \frac{1}{Cs}\right]$$

$$= \frac{1}{Rs + Ls^2 + \dfrac{1}{C}} = \frac{1/L}{s^2 + \dfrac{R}{L}s + \dfrac{1}{LC}}$$

$$= \frac{1/L}{(s + \alpha)(s + \beta)} \qquad ...(7.53)$$

$$\text{where, } \alpha, \beta = -\frac{R}{2L} \pm \sqrt{\left(\frac{R}{2L}\right)^2 - \frac{1}{LC}} \qquad ...(7.54)$$

It may be noted here that there are *three* possible solutions for $I(s)$:

Case A. Both α and β are real and not equal $\left[\dfrac{R}{2L} > \dfrac{1}{\sqrt{LC}}\right]$

Here $I(s) = \dfrac{1/L}{(s+\alpha)(s+\beta)} = \dfrac{K_1}{s+\alpha} + \dfrac{K_2}{s+\beta}$.

where $K_1 = \left.\dfrac{1/L}{(s+\beta)}\right|_{s=-\alpha} = \dfrac{1}{L(\beta-\alpha)}$

$K_2 = \left.\dfrac{1/L}{(s+\alpha)}\right|_{s=-\beta} = \dfrac{1}{L(\alpha-\beta)}$,

Thus, $I(s) = \dfrac{1/L}{(s+\alpha)(s+\beta)}$

$$= \frac{1/L(\beta-\alpha)}{(s+\alpha)} + \frac{1/L(\alpha-\beta)}{(s+\beta)} \quad ...(7.55)$$

$$\therefore \quad i(t) = \left[\frac{1}{L(\beta-\alpha)} e^{-\alpha t} + \frac{1}{L(\alpha-\beta)} e^{-\beta t}\right] \text{A} \quad ...(7.56)$$

Case B. α and β are equal to each other $[\alpha = \beta = \gamma]$

i.e., $\dfrac{R}{2L} = \dfrac{1}{\sqrt{LC}}$

$$I(s) = \frac{1/L}{(s+\gamma)^2} \quad \text{when } \alpha = \beta = \gamma$$

$$\therefore \quad i(t) = \frac{1}{L} t e^{-\gamma t} \text{ A} \quad ...(7.57)$$

Case C. $\left[\dfrac{R}{2L}\right] < \dfrac{1}{\sqrt{LC}}$ and $\alpha = \beta^*$

Let $\alpha = -A_0 + jB$ and $\beta = -A_0 - jB$.

$$\left[\text{Here } |A_0| = \frac{R}{2L} \text{ and } |B| = \sqrt{\frac{1}{LC} - \left[\frac{R}{2L}\right]^2}\,\right]$$

Using partial fraction expansion,

$$I(s) = \frac{1/L}{(s+A_0-jB)(s+A_0+jB)}$$

$$= \frac{K_3}{(s+A_0-jB)} + \frac{K_3^*}{(s+A_0+jB)}$$

Here $K_3 = (s+A_0-jB)\,I(s)\big|_{s=-A_0+jB}$.

$$K_3 = \left.\frac{1/L}{(s+A_0+jB)}\right|_{s=-A_0+jB} = \frac{1}{(j2B)L}$$

i.e., $K_3^* = -\dfrac{1}{(j2B)L}$

$$\therefore \quad I(s) = \frac{1/(j2B)L}{(s+A_0-jB)} - \frac{1/(j2BL)}{(s+A_0+jB)}$$

$$\therefore i(t) = \frac{1}{j2BL} e^{-A_0 t} e^{jBt} - \frac{1}{j2BL} e^{-A_0 t} e^{-jBt}$$

$$= \frac{e^{-A_0 t}}{BL}\left[\frac{e^{jBt} - e^{-jBt}}{2j}\right]$$

or, $$i(t) = \left[\frac{e^{-A_0 t}}{BL} \sin Bt\right] \quad ...(7.58)$$

Equations (7.56), (7.57) and (7.58) represent $i(t)$ at $t = 0^+$ for the given circuit.

7.16(B) STEP CURRENT RESPONSE OF *RLC* PARALLEL CIRCUIT

The constant current source I is applied to the parallel *RLC* circuit by opening the switch (Fig. 7.19(*b*)). Let V be the voltage at node (x).

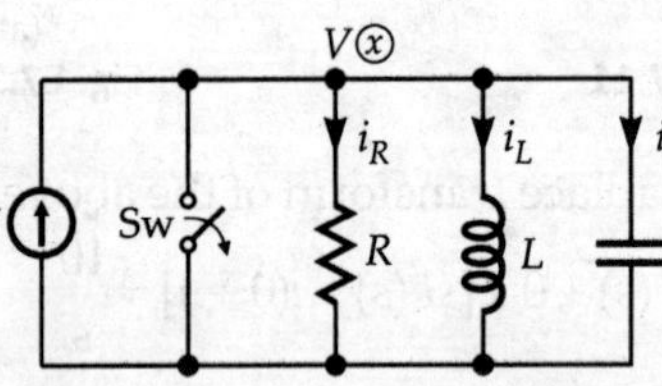

Fig. 7.19 (*b*) Step current applied to parallel *RLC* circuit.

Using nodal analysis for node (x), we can write

$$I = \frac{V}{R} + \frac{1}{L}\int v\,dt + C\frac{dv}{dt}$$

Taking Laplace transformation,

$$\frac{I(s)}{s} = \frac{V(s)}{R} + \frac{1}{L}\frac{V(s)}{s} + sCV(s)$$

[We assume switching at $t = 0$ and zero initial condition for L, R and C at $t = 0$ – when the switch was closed]

i.e., $$\frac{I(s)}{s} = V(s)\left[\frac{1}{R} + \frac{1}{Ls} + Cs\right]$$

$$= V(s)\left[\frac{1}{RC}s + \frac{1}{LC} + s^2\right]\frac{C}{s} \quad ...(7.59)$$

Assuming the current source to be a unit step function, we can write for equation (7.59),

$$V(s) = \frac{1/C}{s^2 + \dfrac{1}{RC}.s + \dfrac{1}{LC}} \quad ...(7.60)$$

For convenience we assume

$$\frac{1}{RC} = 2\,\xi\,\omega_0 \quad \text{and} \quad \frac{1}{LC} = \omega_0^2$$

$\therefore$ The expression of $V(s)$ can now be written as

$$V(s)=\frac{1/C}{s^2+2\,\xi\,\omega_0\,.\,s+\omega_0^2}$$

$$=\frac{1/C}{s^2+2\,\xi\,\omega_0\,s+(\xi\,\omega_0)^2+\omega_0^2-(\xi\omega_0)^2}$$

$$=\frac{1}{C\omega_d}\cdot\frac{\omega_d}{(s+\xi\omega_0)^2+\omega_d^2}$$

where $\omega_d=\sqrt{\omega_0^2-(\xi\omega_0)^2}=\omega_0\sqrt{1-\xi^2}$

Also, $\omega_d=\sqrt{\omega_0^2-(\xi\omega_0)^2}=\sqrt{\frac{1}{LC}-\left(\frac{1}{2\,RC}\right)^2}$

Hence, in time domain,

$$v(t)=\frac{1}{\omega_d\,C}e^{-\xi\,\omega_0\,.\,t}\sin\omega_d t \qquad ...(7.61)$$

$$\therefore \quad i_R=\frac{v(t)}{R}=\frac{1}{\omega_d\;CR}e^{-\xi\,\omega_0 t}\sin\omega_d t \qquad ...(7.62)$$

and $\quad i_L=\frac{1}{L}\int_0^t v(t)\,dt$

$$=\frac{1}{L}\int_0^t\frac{1}{\omega_d\,.\,C}e^{-\xi\,\omega_0\,.\,t}\sin\omega_d t\,.\,dt$$

$$=\frac{1}{\omega_d\,LC}\int_0^t e^{-\xi\omega_0\,.\,t}\sin\omega_d\,.\,t\,dt$$

$$=\frac{1}{\omega_d\,.\,LC}\left[\frac{e^{-\xi\omega_0\,.\,t}}{\sqrt{(\xi\omega_0)^2+\omega_d^2}}\times\sin(\omega_d t-\phi)\right] \qquad ...(7.63)$$

where $\phi=-\tan^{-1}\frac{\omega_d}{\xi\,\omega_0}$.

i.e., $\quad i_L(t)=\frac{1}{\omega_d LC}\left[\frac{e^{-\xi\,\omega_0\,.\,t}}{\sqrt{(\xi\omega_0)^2+\omega_d^2}}\times\sin\left(\omega_d t+\tan^{-1}\frac{\omega_d}{\xi\omega_0}\right)\right] \qquad ...(7.64)$

Again, $\quad i_C(t)=C\frac{dv(t)}{dt}$

Let $\xi\omega_0=a$ and $\omega_d=b$

$$\therefore \quad i_C=C\left(\frac{1}{bC}\right)[-ae^{-at}\sin b\,.\,t+be^{-at}\cos bt]$$

$$=\frac{1}{b}e^{-at}[b\cos bt-a\sin bt]$$

$$=\frac{1}{b}e^{-at}[\sqrt{a^2+b^2}]\sin(bt-\phi)$$

where $\phi=\tan^{-1}\frac{b}{a}=\tan^{-1}\frac{\omega_d}{\xi\omega_0}$

$$\therefore \quad i_C(t)=\frac{e^{-\xi\omega_0 t}}{\omega_d}[\sqrt{(\xi\omega_0)^2+\omega_d^2}]\sin\left(\omega_d t-\tan^{-1}\frac{\omega_d}{\xi\,\omega_0}\right) \qquad ...(7.65)$$

EXAMPLE 7.25 *Fig. E7.13 represents a parallel RLC circuit. The switch is suddenly opened at t = 0. Assuming no charge on the capacitor and no current in the inductor before switching find the voltage across the switch.*

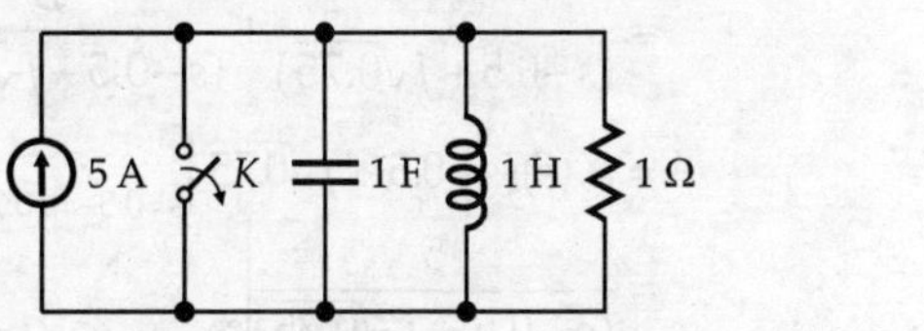

Fig. E7.13

SOLUTION. Let the strength of the current source be $I(=5\text{ A})$, the current through the capacitor be $i_C(t)$, current through the inductor be $i_L(t)$ and current through the resistor be $i_R(t)$ just after switching K [it may be noted that before switching off K, as K was closed, no current passed through R, L or C and hence there was no energy stored in L or C during steady state condition. The circuit components R, L and C will be energized only after K is off.]

As per KCL

$$i(t)=i_R(t)+i_L(t)+i_C(t)$$

or, $$5=\frac{v}{R}+\frac{1}{L}\int_{-\infty}^{t}v\,dt+C\frac{dv}{dt}$$

[assuming the voltage across the switch after its opening to be v]

or, $$5=v+\int_{-\infty}^{t}v\,dt+\frac{dv}{dt}.$$

or, $$5=v+\int_{-\infty}^{0}v\,dt+\int_0^t v\,dt+\frac{dv}{dt} \qquad ...(i)$$

CHAPTER 7

Taking Laplace transform of (*i*),

$$V(s) + £\left[\int_{-\infty}^{0} v\,dt\right] + \frac{V(s)}{s} + [sV(s) - v(0+)] = \frac{5}{s}$$

However, following zero initial condition,

$$V(s) + \frac{V(s)}{s} + sV(s) = \frac{5}{s}$$

$$V(s)\left[1 + \frac{1}{s} + s\right] = \frac{5}{s}$$

or, $$V(s) = \frac{5}{s\left(1 + \frac{1}{s} + s\right)} = \frac{5}{(s + 1 + s^2)}$$

$$= \frac{5}{(s - 0.5 + j\sqrt{0.75})(s - 0.5 - j\sqrt{0.75})}$$

$$= \frac{A}{(s - 0.5 + j\sqrt{0.75})} + \frac{B}{(s - 0.5 - j\sqrt{0.75})}$$

$$A = V(s)(s - 0.5 + j\sqrt{0.75}\,\Big|_{s=0.5-j\sqrt{0.75}}$$

$$= \frac{5}{(s - 0.5 - j\sqrt{0.75})}\Bigg|_{s=0.5-j\sqrt{0.75}}$$

$$= \frac{5}{-2j\sqrt{0.75}} = \frac{j\,10\sqrt{0.75}}{4 \times 0.75} = j\,2.887$$

$$B = V(s)(s - 0.5 - j\sqrt{0.75}\,\Big|_{s=0.5+j\sqrt{0.75}}$$

$$= \frac{5}{(s - 0.5 + j\sqrt{0.75})}\Bigg|_{s=0.5+j\sqrt{0.75}}$$

$$= \frac{5}{2j\sqrt{0.75}} = -\frac{10j\sqrt{0.75}}{4 \times 0.75} = -j\,2.887$$

$$\therefore\ V(s) = \frac{j\,2.887}{s - 0.5 + j\sqrt{0.75}} + \frac{-j\,2.887}{s - 0.5 - j\sqrt{0.75}}$$

Inverse of $v(s)$ then gives

$$v(t) = j\,2.887\,(e^{(0.5 - j\sqrt{0.75})t}) - j\,2.887\,(e^{(0.5 + j\sqrt{0.75})t})\ \text{V}$$

EXAMPLE 7.26 *Function in s-domain is given by*

$$F(s) = \frac{s^2 + 3s + 1}{s(s^2 + 3s + 2)}$$

Find (i) f (t) and (ii) the steady state solution using final value theorem.

SOLUTION. $$F(s) = \frac{s^2 + 3s + 1}{s(s^2 + 3s + 2)}$$

$$= \frac{P}{s} + \frac{Q}{(s+2)} + \frac{R}{s+1}$$

However,

$$P = \frac{s^2 + 3s + 1}{(s+2)(s+1)}\Bigg|_{s=0} = \frac{1}{2}$$

$$Q = \frac{s^2 + 3s + 1}{s(s+1)}\Bigg|_{s=-2} = -\frac{1}{2}$$

$$R = \frac{s^2 + 3s + 1}{s(s+2)}\Bigg|_{s=-1} = 1$$

$$\therefore\ F(s) = \frac{1/2}{s} + \frac{(-1/2)}{s+2} + \frac{1}{s+1}\ \text{giving}$$

$$f(t) = \frac{1}{2} - \frac{1}{2}e^{-2t} + e^{-t}$$

Here the expression $f(t)$ has steady state solution value 1/2 and the transient part $\left(-\frac{1}{2}e^{-2t} + e^{-t}\right)$.

However, to obtain the steady state value by final value theorem,

$$F(s)\ \text{at}\ \infty = \lim_{s \to 0} sF(s) = \lim_{s \to 0} \frac{s^2 + 3s + 1}{s(s^2 + 3s + 2)}.s$$

$$= \lim_{s \to 0} \frac{s^2 + 3s + 1}{(s+1)(s+2)} = \frac{1}{2}.$$

$\therefore$ Final value of the function $= \frac{1}{2}$.

EXAMPLE 7.27 *A time domain network is shown in Fig. E7.14. Find the loop currents (following switching) in Laplace domain as well as in time domain when $r_1 = r_2 = r_3 = 1\,\Omega$, L = 1 H and C = 1 F. Initial potential in the capacitor is e_0 though the initial currents through the inductor and capacitor are zero.*

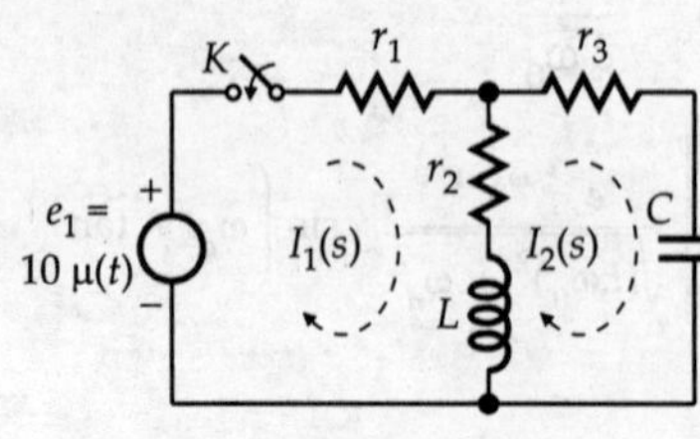

Fig. E7.14

SOLUTION. Let the loop currents be $I_1(s)$ and $I_2(s)$ as shown in Fig. E7.14. In time domain the application of KVL in the loops after switching of the switch *K* yields

$$r_1 i_1(t) + r_2 [i_1(t) - i_2(t)] + L\frac{d}{dt}[i_1(t) - i_2(t)] = e_1 \quad ...(1)$$

and $$r_2 [i_2(t) - i_1(t)] + L\frac{d}{dt}[i_2(t) - i_1(t)] + r_3 i_2(t) + \frac{1}{C}\int i_2\, dt = -e_0 \quad ...(2)$$

On rearrangement, these equations become,

$$(r_1 + r_2) i_1(t) - r_2 i_2(t) + L\frac{di_1(t)}{dt} - L\frac{di_2(t)}{dt} = e_1 \quad ...(1A)$$

and $$-r_2 i_1(t) - L\frac{di_1(t)}{dt} + L\frac{di_2(t)}{dt} + (r_2 + r_3) i_2(t) + \frac{1}{C}\int i_2\, dt = -e_0 \quad ...(2A)$$

Taking the Laplace transform of three equations, we get,

$$(r_1 + r_2) I_1(s) - r_2 I_2(s) + sLI_1(s) - Li_1(0^+) - sLI_2(s) + Li_2(0^+) = E_1(s) \quad ...(1B)$$

and $$-r_2 I_2(s) - sLI_1(s) + Li_1(0^+) + sLI_2(s) - Li_2(0^+) + (r_2 + r_3) I_2(s) + \frac{1}{sC} I_2(s) = -E_0(s) \quad ...(2B)$$

On rearrangement, equations (1B) and (2B) become

$$(r_1 + r_2 + sL) I_1(s) - (r_2 + sL) I_2(s) = E_1(s) + L[i_1(0^+) - i_2(0^+)] \quad ...(1C)$$

and $$-(r_2 + sL) I_1(s) + \left(r_2 + r_3 + sL + \frac{1}{Cs}\right) I_2(s) = -E_0(s) + L[i_2(0^+) - i_1(0^-)] \quad ...(2C)$$

However,

$$r_1 = r_2 = r_3 = 1\,\Omega,\ L = 1\,\text{H},\ C = 1\,\text{F},\ e_0 = 4\,\text{V}$$

and $i_1(0^+) = i_2(0^+) = 0.$

∴ Equations (1C) and (2C) become

$$(s+2) I_1(s) - (s+1) I_2(s) = \frac{10}{s} \quad ...(1D)$$

and $$-(s+1) I_1(s) + \frac{s^2 + 2s + 1}{s} I_2(s) = -\frac{4}{s} \quad ...(2D)$$

$$\therefore I_1(s) = \frac{\begin{vmatrix} (10/s) & -(s+1) \\ -4/s & \dfrac{s^2+2s+1}{s} \end{vmatrix}}{\begin{vmatrix} (s+2) & -(s+1) \\ -(s+1) & \dfrac{s^2+2s+1}{s} \end{vmatrix}} = \frac{\dfrac{2}{s^2}(3s+5)(s+1)}{\dfrac{2}{s}(s+1)^2}$$

$$= \frac{3s+5}{s(s+1)}$$

$$I_2(s) = \frac{\begin{vmatrix} s+2 & 10/s \\ -(s+1) & -4/s \end{vmatrix}}{\dfrac{2}{s}(s+1)^2} = \frac{3s+1}{(s+1)^2}$$

Now

$$I_1(s) = \frac{3s+5}{s(s+1)} = \frac{A}{s} + \frac{B}{s+1}$$

$$A = \left.\frac{3s+5}{s+1}\right|_{s=0} = 5$$

$$B = \left.\frac{3s+5}{s}\right|_{s=-1} = -2$$

$$\therefore I_1(s) = \frac{\mathbf{5}}{\mathbf{s}} - \frac{\mathbf{2}}{\mathbf{s+1}} \text{ giving } i_1(t) = \mathbf{5 - 2e^{-t}\ A.}$$

Similarly,

$$I_2(s) = \frac{3s+1}{(s+1)^2} = \frac{\mathbf{3}}{\mathbf{s+1}} - \frac{\mathbf{2}}{\mathbf{(s+1)^2}}$$

or, $$i_2(t) = \mathbf{3\,e^{-t} - 2t\,e^{-t}\ A.}$$

EXAMPLE 7.28 *In the circuit of Fig. E7.15 steady state exists when switch K is in position 1. At t = 0, it is moved to position 2. Obtain the expression for current using Laplace transformation.*

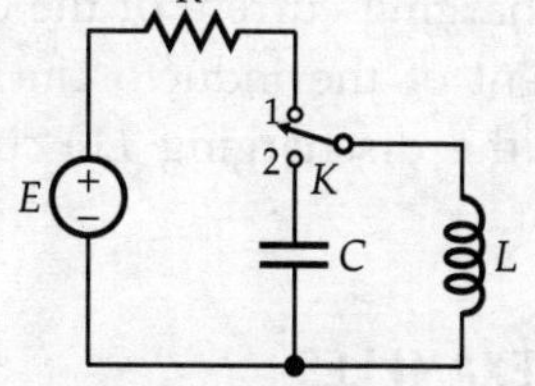

Fig. E7.15

SOLUTION. When the switch is at 1, steady state is reached and the current through the circuit is

$$I_{in} = \frac{E}{R} \quad ...(1)$$

[it may be noted here that at the time of switching, *i.e.*, at $t = 0$, the circuit current is thus (E/R)]

when the switch is moved to position 2, the tapped energy in L starts discharging through C. The mesh equation is then given by

$$L\frac{di(t)}{dt}+\frac{1}{C}\int i\,dt=0 \qquad ...(1)$$

or, $$sLI(s)+Li(0+)+\frac{1}{Cs}I(s)+\frac{Q_0}{Cs}=0 \qquad ...(2)$$

[Taking the Laplace transform of (1) and assuming the initial current through the inductor as $i(0+)$ at $t=0+$ which would obviously same as $i(0^-)$; the initial change of the capacitor being Q_0 which is zero as per this problem]

Thus, we get from (2)

$$\frac{1}{Cs}I(s)+sLI(s)+\left(-\frac{E}{R}L\right)=0 \qquad ...(3)$$

Here, the initial current I_{in} (*i.e.*, the steady state current before switching) was flowing in the clockwise direction in the loop through L while following switching, the current flow though L being reversed (discharging current), $i(0+)$ is –ve and thus equal to $(-E/R)$. Thus from (3),

$$I(s)=\frac{\frac{E}{R}s}{s^2+\frac{1}{LC}}=\frac{E}{R}\frac{s}{s^2+a^2}$$

where, $a=\sqrt{\frac{1}{LC}}$

The inverse of $I(s)$ gives,

$$i(t)=\frac{E}{R}\cos\sqrt{\frac{1}{LC}}\,t=\frac{E}{R}\cos\left(\frac{t}{\sqrt{LC}}\right)\text{A.}$$

It may be noted that $i(t)$ is the discharging current of the inductor and charging current of the capacitor in the first half cycle of the cosine wave while the discharging current of the capacitor and charging current of the inductor in the next half cycle making the discharging LC circuit to be a *oscillator* circuit.

ADDITIONAL EXAMPLES

Example 7.29 *Find the Laplace inverse of transform*

$$F(s)=\frac{1}{s^2(s+\theta)^3}$$

Solution. The function $F(s)$ can be expanded in partial fractions as follows :

$$F(s)=\frac{A_1}{s}+\frac{A_2}{s^2}+\frac{B_1}{(s+\theta)}+\frac{B_2}{(s+\theta)^2}+\frac{B_3}{(s+\theta)^3}$$

Here,

$$A_1=\frac{1}{\underline{|1}}\frac{d}{ds}\left[\frac{1}{(s+\theta)^3}\right]\Bigg|_{s=0}=-\frac{3}{\theta^4}$$

$$A_2=\frac{1}{(s+\theta)^3}\Bigg|_{s=0}=\frac{1}{\theta^3}$$

$$B_1=\frac{1}{\underline{|2}}\frac{d^2}{ds^2}\left[\frac{1}{s^2}\right]\Bigg|_{s=-\theta}=\frac{3}{\theta^4}$$

$$B_2=\frac{1}{\underline{|1}}\frac{d}{ds}\left[\frac{1}{s^2}\right]\Bigg|_{s=-\theta}=\frac{2}{\theta^3}$$

$$B_3=\frac{1}{s^2}\Bigg|_{s=-\theta}=\frac{1}{\theta^2}$$

$$\therefore F(s)=\frac{1}{\theta^4}\left[-\frac{3}{s}+\frac{\theta}{s^2}+\frac{3}{s+\theta}+\frac{2\theta}{(s+\theta)^2}+\frac{\theta^2}{(s+\theta)^3}\right]$$

Taking the inverse of Laplace transform,

$$f(t)=\frac{1}{\theta^4}[-3+\theta t+3e^{-\theta t}+2\theta te^{-\theta t}+\theta^2t^2e^{-\theta t}]$$

$$=\frac{1}{\theta^4}[-3+\theta t+e^{-\theta t}(3+2\theta t-\theta^2t^2)].$$

Example 7.30 *Find the inverse of Laplace transform*

$$F(s)=\frac{s-1}{s(s+1)^3}.$$

Solution. The function can be expanded in the partial fraction as

$$F(s)=\frac{A_0}{s}+\frac{B_1}{s+1}+\frac{B_2}{(s+1)^2}+\frac{B_3}{(s+1)^3}$$

Here

$$A_0=sF(s)\Big|_{s=0}=\frac{s-1}{(s+1)^3}\Bigg|_{s=0}=-1$$

$$B_1=\frac{1}{\underline{|2}}\frac{d^2}{ds^2}[(s+1)^3F(s)]\Big|_{s=-1}$$

$$=\frac{1}{2}\frac{d}{ds}\left[\frac{1}{s^2}\right]\Bigg|_{s=-1}=-\frac{1}{s^3}\Bigg|_{s=-1}=+1$$

$$B_2=\frac{d}{ds}[(s+1)^3F(s)]\Big|_{s=-1}$$

$$=\frac{d}{ds}\left[\frac{s-1}{s}\right]\Bigg|_{s=-1}=\frac{1}{s^2}\Bigg|_{s=-1}=1$$

$$B_3 = (s+1)^3 \; F(s) \Big|_{s=-1} = \frac{s-1}{s}\Big|_{s=-1} = 2$$

$$\therefore \; F(s) = -\frac{1}{s} + \frac{1}{s+1} + \frac{1}{(s+1)^2} + \frac{2}{(s+1)^3}$$

Taking the inverse of Laplace transform,

$$f(t) = (-1 + e^{-t} + te^{-t} + 2t^2 e^{-t}).$$

EXAMPLE 7.31 *Find the inverse of the Laplace transform*

$$F(s) = \frac{s^3 + 6s^2 + 11s + 7}{s^2 + 5s + 6}$$

SOLUTION. In Laplace transformation, a rational function $F(s)$ can be represented by

$$F(s) = \frac{M(s)}{N(s)} = \frac{b_p s^p + b_{p-1} s^{p-1} + ... + b_1 s + b_0}{a_q s^q + a_{q-1} s^{q-1} + ... + a_1 s + a_0}$$

when a' s and b' s are real constants.

If "p", the degree of $M(s)$ is equal or greater than "q", the degree of $N(s)$, the constants of the partial fraction of the polynomial of $F(s)$ can be obtained by long division.

$\therefore$ In this problem we first perform the long division.

$$s^2 + 5s + 6 \,)\, s^3 + 6s^2 + 11s + 7 \,(\, s + 1$$
$$\underline{s^3 + 5s^2 + 6s}$$
$$s^2 + 5s + 7$$
$$\underline{s^2 + 5s + 6}$$
$$1$$

$$\therefore \quad F(s) = s + 1 + \frac{1}{s^2 + 5s + 6}$$

Now

$$\frac{1}{s^2 + 5s + 6} = \frac{1}{(s+2)(s+3)} = \frac{A}{s+2} + \frac{B}{s+3}$$

$$\therefore \quad A = (s+2)\frac{1}{(s+2)(s+3)}\Big|_{s=-2} = 1$$

$$B = (s+3)\frac{1}{(s+2)(s+3)}\Big|_{s=-3} = -1$$

Thus $F(s) = s + 1 + \dfrac{1}{s+2} - \dfrac{1}{s+3}$

Taking the inverse of Laplace,

$$f(t) = u_1(t) + \delta(t) + e^{-2t} - e^{-3t}.$$

$[\because \; £^{-1}(1) = \delta(t)$ *i.e.*, the impulse function,

$\therefore \quad £^{-1}(s) = u_1(t)$ *i.e.*, the unit doublet function]*

EXAMPLE 7.32 *A function in s-domain is given by*

$$G(s) = \frac{s+1}{s(s+2)}.$$

Find the initial value of g(t).

SOLUTION. $G(s)$ in s-domain being a proper function, the initial theorem is valid.

$$\therefore \quad g(0^+) = \lim_{s\to\infty} sG(s) = \lim_{s\to\infty}\frac{s+1}{s+2} = 1$$

i.e., $\quad g(0^+) = \mathbf{1}.$

EXAMPLE 7.33 *Find the Laplace transform of*

$$f(t) = 1 - e^{-2t}.$$

SOLUTION. $\quad f(t) = 1 - e^{-2t} = f_x(t) + f_y(t)$

where $f_x(t) = 1$ and $f_y(t) = -e^{-2t}$

$$\therefore \; £[f(t)] = £[f_x(t)] + £[f_y(t)]$$
$$= £[1] + £[-e^{-2t}]$$
$$= \frac{1}{s} - \frac{1}{s+2} = \frac{\mathbf{2}}{\mathbf{s(s+2)}}.$$

EXAMPLE 7.34 *Find the Laplace transform of the function* $x(t) = u(t) - u(t-\theta)$.

SOLUTION. $£[x(t)] = £[u(t) - u(t-\theta)]$

$$= £[u(t)] - £[u(t-\theta)] = \frac{1}{s} - e^{-s\theta}.\frac{1}{s}$$
$$= \frac{\mathbf{1}}{\mathbf{s}}[\mathbf{1} - e^{-s\theta}] \text{ (also refer to Ex. 7.3)}$$

EXAMPLE 7.35 *A function is given as*

$$z(s) = \frac{3(s+1)}{s(s+2)(s+3)}.$$

Find final value of z(t) by final value theorem.

SOLUTION. $z(t)_\infty = \lim_{s\to 0} sF(s)$

$$= \lim_{s\to 0}\frac{3(s+1)}{(s+2)(s+3)}$$
$$= \frac{3}{6} = \frac{1}{2}.$$

$\therefore$ Final value of the function $= \mathbf{1/2}$.

* Please see Ch. 8, Art. 8.2.

C H A P T E R 7

EXAMPLE 7.36 *A function in Laplace domain is given by*

$$M(s)=\frac{s^2+10s+15}{(s+1)(s+2)(s+3)}. \text{ Find } M(t).$$

SOLUTION. $$M(s)=\frac{s^2+10s+15}{(s+1)(s+2)(s+3)}$$

$$=\frac{A_1}{s+1}+\frac{A_2}{s+2}+\frac{A_3}{s+3}$$

where

$$A_1=(s+1)M(s)\Big|_{s=-1}=\frac{s^2+10s+15}{(s+2)(s+3)}\Big|_{s=-1}=\frac{6}{2}=3$$

$$A_2=(s+2)M(s)\Big|_{s=-2}=\frac{s^2+10s+15}{(s+1)(s+3)}\Big|_{s=-2}=1$$

$$A_3=(s+3)M(s)\Big|_{s=-3}=\frac{s^2+10s+15}{(s+1)(s+2)}\Big|_{s=-3}=-3$$

$$\therefore \quad M(s)=\frac{s^2+10s+15}{(s+1)(s+2)(s+3)}$$

$$=\frac{3}{s+1}+\frac{1}{s+2}+\frac{-3}{s+3}$$

Taking the inverse of the Laplace transform,

$$M(t)=3e^{-t}+e^{-2t}-3e^{-3t}.$$

EXAMPLE 7.37 *In s-domain, a function is given by*

$$F(s)=\frac{5s^2+2s-1}{s(s^2+2s+5)}. \text{ Find } f(t).$$

SOLUTION. $$F(s)=\frac{5s^2+2s-1}{s(s^2+2s+5)}$$

$$=\frac{5s^2+2s-1}{s(s+1+j2)(s+1-j2)}$$

or, $$\frac{5s^2+2s-1}{s(s+1+j2)(s+1-j2)}=\frac{K_1}{s}+\frac{K_2}{s+1+j2}+\frac{K_3}{s+1-j2}$$

[K_3 is complex conjugate of K_2]

where, $$K_1=sF(s)\Big|_{s=0}=\frac{5s^2+2s-1}{s^2+2s+5}\Big|_{s=0}=-\frac{1}{5}.$$

$$K_2=(s+1+j2)F(s)\Big|_{s=-1-j2}$$

$$=\frac{5s^2+2s-1}{s(s+1-j2)}\Big|_{s=-1-j2}=2.6-j0.7$$

$$\therefore \quad K_2=(2.6-j0.7) \text{ and } K_3=2.6+j0.7$$

or, $$K_2=a+j(-b) \text{ and } K_3=a-j(-b)$$

However,

$$\frac{K_2}{s+\alpha+j\beta}+\frac{K_3}{s+\alpha-j\beta}$$

$$=\frac{[a+j(-b)][s+\alpha-j\beta]+[a-j(-b)][s+\alpha+j\beta]}{(s+\alpha+j\beta)(s+\alpha-j\beta)}$$

$$=\frac{2a(s+\alpha)}{(s+\alpha)^2+\beta^2}+\frac{2(-b)\beta}{(s+\alpha)+\beta^2}$$

Thus here,

$$F(s)=-\frac{1/5}{s}+\frac{2.6-j0.7}{s+1+j2}+\frac{2.6+j0.7}{s+1-j2}$$

$$=-\frac{1}{5}\cdot\frac{1}{s}+\frac{5.2(s+1)}{(s+1)^2+2^2}+\frac{2(-0.7)2}{(s+1)^2+2^2}$$

$$=-\frac{1}{5}\cdot\frac{1}{s}+\frac{5.2(s+1)}{(s+1)^2+2^2}-\frac{2.8}{(s+1)^2+2^2}$$

$$f(t)=\left[-\frac{1}{5}u(t)+5.2(e^{-t}\cos 2t)-(e^{-t}\sin 2t)\times 1.4\right]$$

EXAMPLE 7.38 *A function is given by*

$$P(s)=\frac{2s^2+3s+2}{s^2+2s-3}. \text{ Find } p(t).$$

SOLUTION. As the powers of the polynomial in the numerator and denominator are same, the coefficients of the partial fraction can be obtained by long division method.

$$s^2+2s-3\,\big)\,2s^2+3s+2\,\big(\,2$$
$$\underline{2s^2+4s-6}$$
$$-s+8$$

$$\therefore \quad P(s)=\frac{2s^2+3s+2}{s^2+2s-3}=2-\frac{s-8}{s^2+2s-3}$$

$$=2-\frac{s-8}{(s-1)(s+3)}$$

However,

$$\frac{s-8}{s^2+2s-3}=\frac{K_1}{s-1}+\frac{K_2}{s+3}$$

$$\therefore \quad K_1=(s-1)\left(\frac{s-8}{(s-1)(s+3)}\right)\Big|_{s=1}=-\frac{7}{4}$$

$$K_2=(s+3)\frac{s-8}{(s-1)(s+3)}\Big|_{s=-3}=\frac{11}{4}.$$

$$\therefore \quad P(s) = 2 - \frac{s-8}{(s-1)(s+3)}$$

$$= 2 - \frac{-\frac{7}{4}}{(s-1)} + \frac{11/4}{(s+3)}$$

The inverse Laplace transform is then given by

$$p(t) = \mathbf{2\,\delta\,(t) + -7/4\, e^{t} + \frac{11}{4}\, e^{-3t}}.$$

EXAMPLE 7.39 *In a RC series circuit, for a step input voltage, determine the initial current at $t=0^+$ following switching on at $t=0$ using the initial value theorem. Assume the initial charge to be $+Q_0$ in the capacitor.*

SOLUTION. In the text, with step input voltage E, the current in the RC circuit has been shown to be

$$I(s) = \frac{E - \frac{Q_0}{C}}{R}\left[\frac{1}{s+\frac{1}{RC}}\right]$$

Using initial value theorem,

$$i(0+) = \lim_{s\to\infty} \frac{E - \frac{Q_0}{C}}{R}\left[\frac{s}{s+\frac{1}{RC}}\right]$$

$$\left[\because f(0+) = \lim_{s\to\infty} \{sF(s)\}\right]$$

$$= \frac{E - \frac{Q_0}{C}}{R}.\ \text{i.e., } i(0+) = \frac{\mathbf{E - \frac{Q_0}{C}}}{\mathbf{R}}.$$

EXAMPLE 7.40 *Find the final value of the current in a RL circuit following step response using final value theorem.*

SOLUTION. In a RL circuit, following switching at $t=0$ against a step response, the current is given by

$$I(s) = \frac{E/R}{s} + \frac{-E/R}{s+\frac{R}{L}} = \frac{E}{R}\left\{\frac{1}{s} - \frac{1}{s+\frac{R}{L}}\right\}$$

Following the final value theorem,

$$i(\infty) = \lim_{s\to 0} \frac{E}{R}\left[\frac{s}{s} - \frac{s}{s+\frac{R}{L}}\right] = \frac{E}{R}$$

i.e., $\quad i(\infty) = \mathbf{\frac{E}{R}}.$

EXAMPLE 7.41 *Find $i(t)$ in Fig. E7.16 following switching at $t=0$. Assume initial charge on capacitor 250 μ coulombs as shown in the figure.*

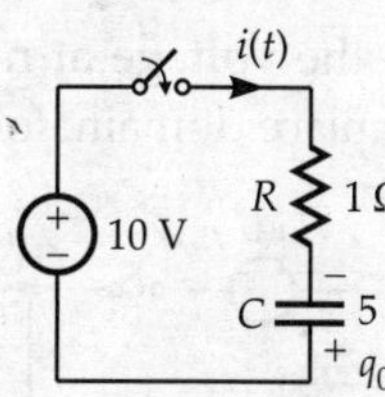

Fig. E7.16

SOLUTION. Following switching, the differential equation representing the circuit is

$$i(t)\,R + \frac{1}{C}\int i(t)\,dt = V = 10$$

or, $$i(t) + \frac{1}{5\times 10^{-6}}\int i(t)\,dt = 10$$

Taking Laplace transformation,

$$I(s) + \frac{I(s)}{5\times 10^{-6}\,s} + \frac{Q_0}{5\times 10^{-6}\,s} = \frac{10}{s}$$

However, $\quad Q_0 = -250\times 10^{6}\ \mu\text{C}$

This gives

$$I(s) + \frac{I(s)}{5\times 10^{-6}\,s} - \frac{250\times 10^{-6}}{5\times 10^{-6}\,s} = \frac{10}{s}$$

or, $$I(s) + \frac{I(s)}{5\times 10^{-6}\,s} = \frac{10}{s} + \frac{50}{s}$$

$$= \frac{10+50}{s} = \frac{60}{s}$$

or, $$I(s) + \frac{10^5\times 2}{s}\,I(s) = \frac{60}{s}$$

or, $$I(s)\left[1 + \frac{2\times 10^5}{s}\right] = \frac{60}{s}$$

or, $$I(s)\left[\frac{s+2\times 10^5}{s}\right] = \frac{60}{s}$$

$$\therefore \quad I(s) = \frac{60}{s+2\times 10^5}.$$

Taking inverse of Laplace transform,

$$i(t) = \mathbf{60\, e^{-2\times 10^5\, t}\ A}.$$

EXAMPLE 7.42 *Apply nodal analysis to find the voltage at node (A) in the circuit of Fig. E7.17 in s-domain. [Assume initial current through the inductor to be zero].*

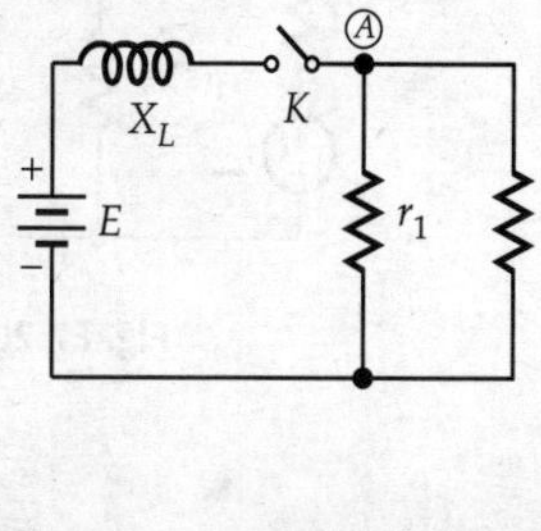

Fig. E7.17

Solution. Let the voltage at node (A) be V_A in time domain. In Laplace domain, following Fig. E7.18

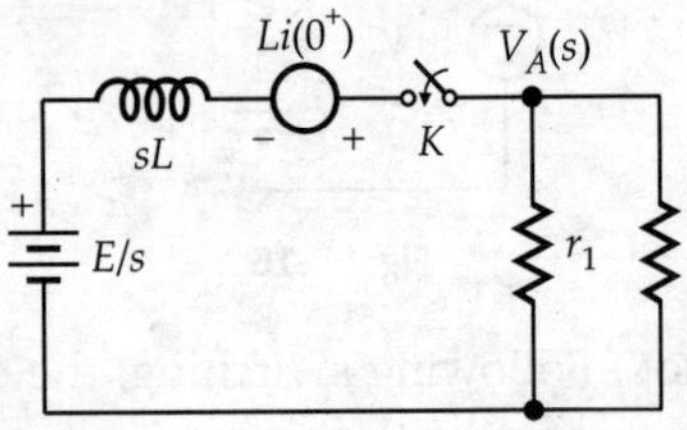

Fig. E7.18

which is the Laplace domain circuit of the given time domain circuit, we write the nodal equation at (A) as

$$\frac{V_A(s)}{r_1}+\frac{V_A(s)}{r_2}+\frac{V_A(s)-Li(0+)-\dfrac{E}{s}}{sL}=0$$

or, $$V_A(s)\left[\frac{1}{r_1}+\frac{1}{r_2}+\frac{1}{sL}\right]=\frac{E/s+Li(0+)}{sL}.$$

However, the initial current through the inductance being zero, $i(0+)=0$

$\therefore$ We obtain, $V_A(s)=\dfrac{E}{s}\left(\dfrac{r_1r_2}{r_1r_2+sLr_2+sLr_1}\right).$

Example 7.43 *A voltage source E with internal resistance r_i feeds a parallel R-C circuit while C is only switchable (Fig. E7.19). Assuming a zero initial charge, using mesh analysis, obtain the s-domain equations for the network.*

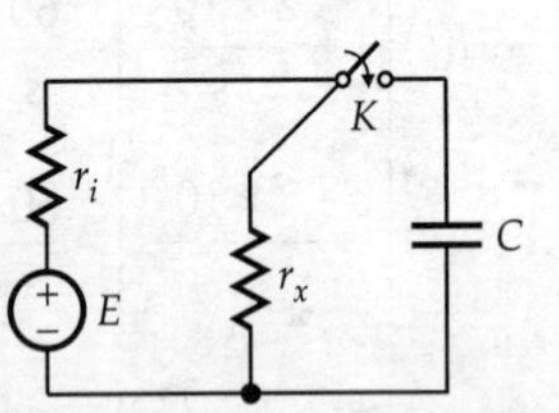

Fig. E7.19 (*K* is the switch)

Solution. Let us transfer the time domain circuit of Fig. E7.19 into laplace domain circuit (Fig. E7.20) with corresponding mesh currents.

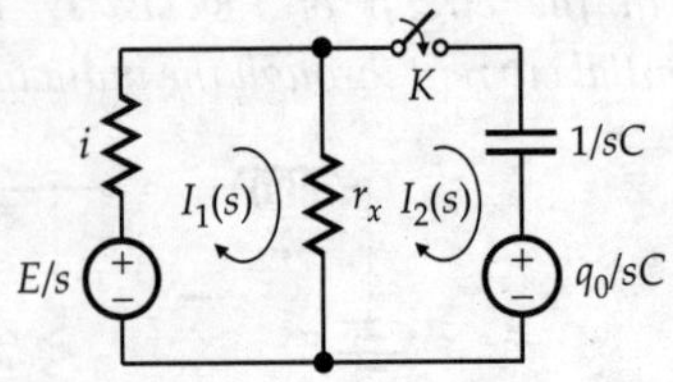

Fig. E7.20

The mesh equations are as follows :

in left handed loop

$$I_1(s)r_i+[I_1(s)-I_2(s)].r_x=\frac{E}{s}$$

or, $$\mathbf{I_1(s)[r_i+r_x]-I_2(s)r_x=\frac{E}{s}} \quad ...(1)$$

and in right handed loop

$$r_x[I_2(s)-I_1(s)]+\frac{1}{sC}I_2(s)+\frac{q_0}{sC}=0$$

Actually, in this problem, $q_0=0$ but to show the generalisation, the term q_0/sC is added. It may also be noticed that with the designated polarity, q_0/sC is +ve while in case of reversed polarity, $\dfrac{q_0}{sC}$ would be –ve.

Here, $$r_x[I_2(s)-I_1(s)]+I_2(s)\frac{1}{sC}=0$$

or, $$\left(r_x+\frac{1}{sC}\right)I_2(s)-r_xI_1(s)=0$$

i.e., $$\mathbf{-r_xI_1(s)+\left(r_x+\frac{1}{sC}\right)I_2(s)=0} \quad ...(ii)$$

Equations (i) and (ii) represent the **mesh equation in s-domain.**

Example 7.44 *Assuming the initial current to be 2 A through the inductor, find $V_0(t)$ in Fig. E7.21. What will be $V_0(t)$ if the supply is $10e^{-t}u(t)$?*

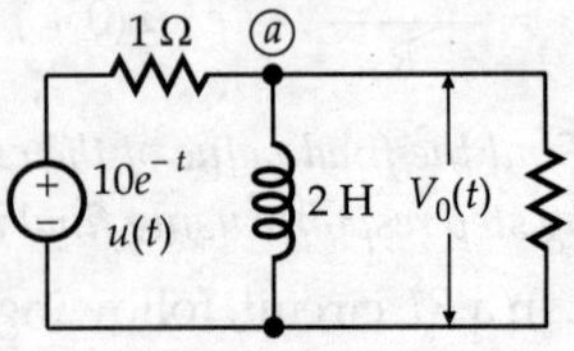

Fig. E7.21

Solution. Application of nodal analysis at (a) reveals,

$$\frac{V_0(t)}{4}+\frac{1}{L}\int V_0(t)\,dt+2\text{ A}+\frac{V_0(t)-10\,u(t)}{1}=0$$

or, $$\frac{V_0(s)}{4}+\frac{2}{s}+\frac{V_0(s)}{Ls}+V_0(s)-\frac{10}{s}=0$$

[Taking the Laplace transform of the nodal equation]

or, $$V_0(s)\left[1+\frac{1}{2s}+\frac{1}{4}\right]=\frac{10}{s}-\frac{2}{s}=\frac{8}{s}$$

$$\therefore \quad V_0(s) = \frac{8/s}{\frac{5}{4}+\frac{1}{2s}} = \frac{8/s}{\frac{5s+2}{2s}} = \frac{16}{5s+2}$$

$$= \frac{3.2}{s+0.4}$$

[Here the supply is assumed to be $10\,u(t)$]

$$\therefore \quad V_0(t) = \mathbf{3.2}\, e^{-0.4\,t}\ \mathbf{V}.$$

On the other hand, if the supply is assumed to be $10\,e^{-t}\,u(t)$, its Laplace transform is $V_0(s) = \dfrac{10}{s+1}$.

$\therefore$ From the same nodal analysis, we get

$$\frac{V_0(s)}{4} + \frac{2}{s} + \frac{V_0(s)}{Ls} + V_0(s) - \frac{10}{s+1} = 0$$

or,
$$V_0(s)\left[1+\frac{1}{2s}+\frac{1}{4}\right] = \frac{10}{s+1} - \frac{2}{s}$$

$$= \frac{10\,s - 2\,(s+1)}{s(s+1)} = \frac{8s-2}{s(s+1)}$$

or,
$$V_0(s) = \frac{8s-2}{s(s+1)} \times \frac{1}{\frac{5}{4}+\frac{1}{2s}} = \frac{(8s-2)(4s)}{s(s+1)(5s+2)}$$

$$= \frac{32\,s-8}{(s+1)(5s+2)}$$

$$\therefore \quad V_0(s) = \frac{32\,s-8}{5\,(s+1)(s+0.4)}$$

$$= \frac{6.4\,s-1.6}{(s+1)(s+0.4)} = \frac{A}{s+1} + \frac{B}{s+0.4}$$

Here
$$A = \left.\frac{6.4\,s-1.6}{(s+1)(s+0.4)}(s+1)\right|_{s=-1}$$

$$= \frac{-6.4-1.6}{-1+0.4} = \frac{-8}{-0.6} = 13.33$$

$$B = \left.\frac{6.4\,s-1.6}{(s+1)(s+0.4)}.(s+0.4)\right|_{s=-0.4}$$

$$= \frac{-2.56-1.6}{(-0.4+1)} = \frac{-4.16}{0.6} = -6.933$$

$$\therefore \quad V_0(s) = \frac{13.33}{s+1} - \frac{6.933}{s+0.4}$$

Then, taking Laplace inverse,

$$V_0(t) = (\mathbf{13.33}\, e^{-t} - \mathbf{6.933}\, e^{-0.4\,t})\ \mathbf{V}.$$

EXAMPLE 7.45 *For the circuit shown in Fig. E7.22, obtain the current through the capacitor (C) at t = 0 + following switching at t = 0. Assume the capacitor to be initially discharged.*

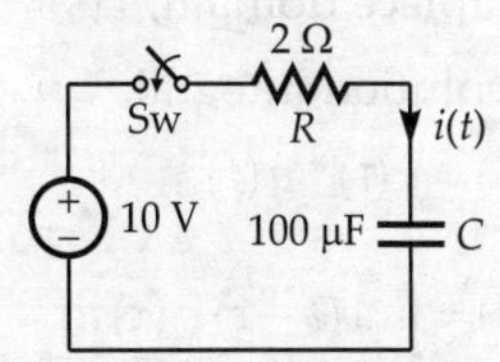

Fig. E7.22

SOLUTION. Applying KVL, the network equation becomes, following switching,

$$\frac{1}{C}\int_0^t i(t)\,dt + Ri(t) = V$$

Taking the Laplace transformation,

$$\frac{1}{Cs}I(s) + \frac{q(0+)}{s} + RI(s) = \frac{V}{s}.$$

However, $q(0+) = 0$ as the capacitor is initially discharged giving $q(0-) = q(0+) = 0$

$$\therefore \; I(s)\left[R+\frac{1}{Cs}\right] = \frac{V}{s} \quad \text{or} \quad I(s) = \frac{V/R}{s+\frac{1}{RC}}$$

Taking the inverse of this,

$$i(t) = \frac{V}{R}e^{-t/RC}, \text{ for } t \ge 0. \text{ and } = 0 \text{ or } t < 0.$$

However, $V = 10$ V, $R = 2\,\Omega$,

$$C = 100\,\mu\text{F} = 100 \times 10^{-6}\ \text{F}$$

$$\therefore \; \boldsymbol{i(t) = 5\, e^{-t/200 \times 10^{-6}}\ \text{A};\ i(0+)\ 5\ \text{A}.}$$

EXAMPLE 7.46 *A series RL circuit is energized by a d.c. voltage of 1.0 V by switching it at t = 0. If R = 1Ω and L = 1 H, find the expression of the current using the convolution integral.*

SOLUTION. The circuit is drawn in Fig. E7.23

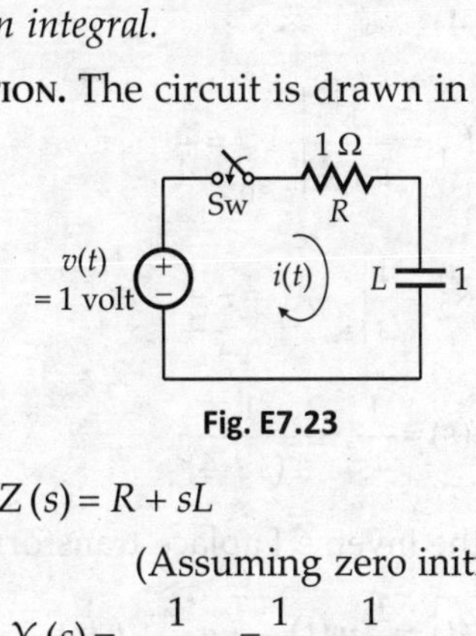

Fig. E7.23

Here $Z(s) = R + sL$

(Assuming zero initial condition)

$$\therefore \quad Y(s) = \frac{1}{R+sL} = \frac{1}{L}\frac{1}{s+R/L}$$

CHAPTER 7

Taking the inverse transform,

$$y(t) = \frac{1}{L} e^{(-R/L)t}$$

Also, in Laplace domain, $I(s) = Y(s) V(s)$

or, using convolution integral,

$$i(t) = y(t) * v(t)$$

or, $$i(t) = \int_0^t y(t-\tau) v(\tau) d\tau$$

$$= \frac{1}{L} \int_0^t e^{(-R/L)(t-\tau)} .1 \, d\tau$$

$$= \frac{1}{R}(1 - e^{(-R/L)t})$$

However, $R = 1\,\Omega$ and $L = 1\,\text{H}$

$\therefore$ $\quad i(t) = \mathbf{1 - e^{-t}}$ **A.**

Example 7.47 *Assuming $v_0(t) = tu(t)$, find $i(t)$ in the RC circuit of Fig. E7.24.*

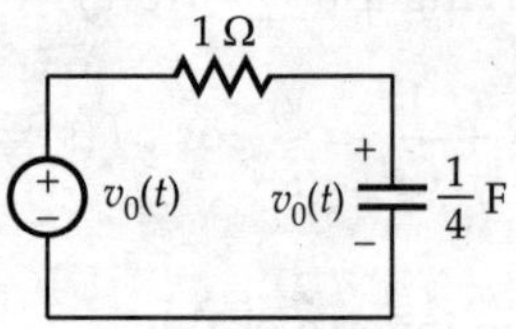

Fig. E7.24

Solution. $$I(s) = \frac{V_0(s)}{Z(s)} = \frac{(1/s^2)}{R + \dfrac{1}{Cs}}$$

$$= \frac{1}{s^2\left(1 + \dfrac{4}{s}\right)} = \frac{s}{s^2(s+4)} = \frac{1}{s(s+4)}$$

but $$\frac{1}{s(s+4)} = \frac{K_1}{s} + \frac{K_2}{s+4}$$

Here $$K_1 = \left.\frac{1}{s+4}\right|_{s=0} = \frac{1}{4}$$

$$K_2 = \left.\frac{1}{s}\right|_{s=-4} = -\frac{1}{4}$$

$\therefore$ $$I(s) = \frac{1}{4s} - \frac{1}{4(s+4)}$$

Taking the inverse Laplace transform,

$$\mathbf{i(t) = \frac{1}{4} u(t) - \frac{1}{4} e^{-4t} u(t).}$$

Example 7.48 *The Laplace transform of a voltage across a capacitor is*

$$V_c(s) = \frac{s+1}{s^3 + s^2 + s + 1}$$

If the capacitor has the value of 2F, find the current through the capacitor at $t = 0+$.

Solution. At $t = 0+$, s tends to infinity. In the numerator, $s >> 1$ as $s \to \infty$ at $t = 0+$. On the other hand, in the denominator, at $s \to \infty$,

$$s^3 >> s^2 >> s >> 1$$

i.e., $$\underset{s\to\infty}{\text{Lt}}\ V_c(s) = \frac{s}{s^3} = \frac{1}{s^2}$$

$\therefore$ $$\underset{s\to\infty}{\text{Lt}}\ sI(s) = s\frac{V_c(s)}{\dfrac{1}{Cs}} = \underset{s\to\infty}{s\,V_c(s)\,Cs} = c = 2\ \text{A}.$$

$\therefore$ Current at $t = 0+$ through the capacitor is **2 A.**

Example 7.49 *Determine the solution of the following second order differential equation having initial conditions at $f(0+) = 4$ and $\dfrac{df(0+)}{dt} = 1$*

$$\frac{d^2 f(t)}{dt^2} + 3\frac{df}{dt} - 4f(t) = e^{-3t}.$$

Solution. Taking the Laplace transform of the differential equation,

$$s^2 F(s) - sf(0+) - \frac{df(0+)}{dt}$$

$$+ 3[sF(s) - f(0+)] - 4F(s) = \frac{1}{s+3}$$

or $$s^2 F(s) - 4s - 1 + 3[sF(s) - 4] - 4F(s) = \frac{1}{s+3}$$

or $$F(s)[s^2 + 3s - 4] - 4s - 13 = \frac{1}{s+3}$$

or $$F(s)[s^2 + 4s - s - 4] = \frac{1}{s+3} + 4s + 13$$

$$= \frac{1 + 4s^2 + 13s + 12s + 39}{s+3}$$

or $$F(s)[(s+4)(s-1)] = \frac{4s^2 + 25s + 40}{s+3}$$

$\therefore$ $$F(s) = \frac{4s^2 + 25s + 40}{(s-1)(s+3)(s+4)}$$

$$= \frac{K_1}{s-1} + \frac{K_2}{s+3} + \frac{K_3}{s+4}$$

where $K_1 = (s-1)\left.\dfrac{4s^2+25s+40}{(s-1)(s+3)(s+4)}\right|_{s=1} = 3.45$

$$K_2 = (s+3)\left.\frac{4s^2+25s+40}{(s-1)(s+3)(s+4)}\right|_{s=-3} = -0.25$$

$$K_3 = (s+4)\left.\frac{4s^2+25s+40}{(s-1)(s+3)(s+4)}\right|_{s=-4} = 0.8$$

$$\therefore\ F(s) = \frac{3.45}{s-1} + \frac{-0.25}{s+3} + \frac{0.8}{s+4}$$

i.e., $\quad f(t) = \mathbf{3.45\, e^{+t} - 0.25\, e^{-3t} + 0.8\, e^{-4t}}$.

EXAMPLE 7.50 *In the circuit of Fig. E7.25, find $i_1(t)$ and $I_2(s)$. Assume zero initial condition.*

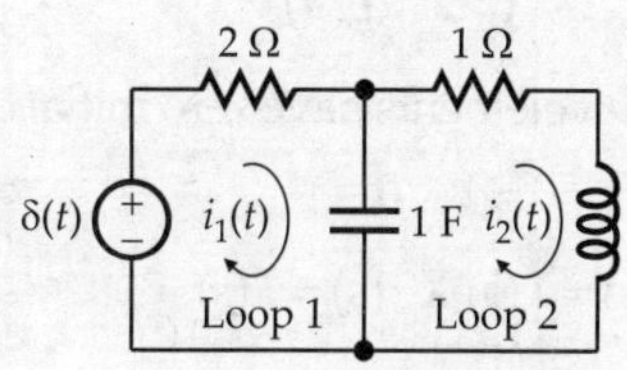

Fig. E7.25

SOLUTION. *In loop 1,* KVL provides

$$\delta(t) = i_1(t)\times 4 + \frac{1}{1}\int [i_1(t) - i_2(t)]\, dt$$

Taking Laplace transform,

$$1 = 4I_1(s) + \frac{1}{s}[I_1(s) - I_2(s)] + \frac{q(0+)}{s}$$

or, $\quad I_1(s)\left[\dfrac{1}{s} + 4\right] - I_2(s)\dfrac{1}{s} = 1 \qquad ...(a)$

$\left(\text{Applying zero initial condition, } \dfrac{q(0+)}{s} = 0\right)$

Similarly, *in loop 2,* KVL provides

$$0 = i_2(t)\times 1 + \frac{di_2(t)}{dt} + \frac{1}{1}\int (i_2(t) - i_1(t))\, dt$$

Taking the Laplace transform,

$$I_2(s) + sI_2(s) - i_2(0+) + [I_2(s) - I_1(s)]\frac{1}{s} + \frac{q(0+)}{s} = 0$$

or, $\quad I_1(s).\dfrac{1}{s} = I_2(s)\left[s + 1 + \dfrac{1}{s}\right]$

or, $\quad I_1(s) = I_2(s)[s^2 + s + 1] \qquad ...(b)$

Substituting the value of $I_1(s)$ from (*b*) in (*a*),

$$I_2(s)[s^2+s+1]\left[\frac{1}{s} + 4\right] - I_2(s)\frac{1}{s} = 1$$

or, $\quad I_2(s)\left[s + 1 + \dfrac{1}{s} + 4s^2 + 4s + 4\right] - I_2(s)\dfrac{1}{s} = 1$

or, $\quad I_2(s)\left[4s^2 + 5s + \dfrac{1}{s} + 5 - \dfrac{1}{s}\right] = 1$

or, $\quad I_2(s) = \dfrac{1}{\mathbf{4s^2+5s+5}}$

$$\therefore\quad I_1(s) = \frac{1}{4s^2+5s+5}\times(s^2+s+1)$$

$$= \frac{\mathbf{s^2+s+1}}{\mathbf{4s^2+5s+5}}. \qquad \text{[Using } (b)\text{]}$$

EXAMPLE 7.50(a) *Find i(t) in Fig. E7.25(a). Assume zero initial response.*

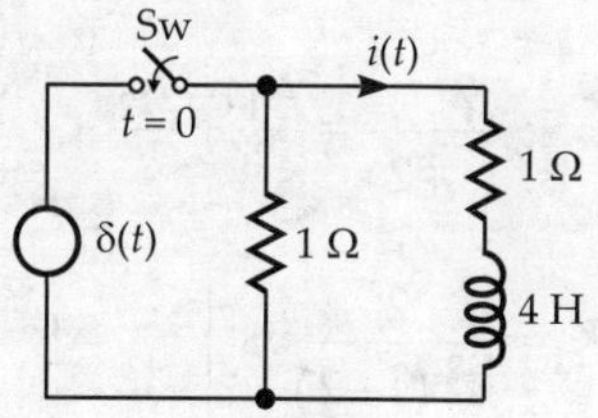

Fig. E7.25 (a)

SOLUTION. With reference to the transformed circuit [Fig. E7.25(*b*)],

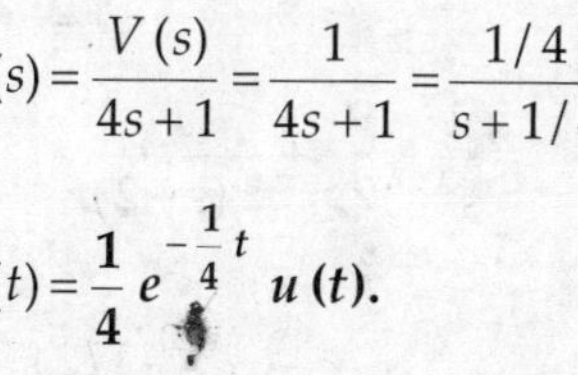

Fig. E7.25 (b)

$$I(s) = \frac{V(s)}{4s+1} = \frac{1}{4s+1} = \frac{1/4}{s+1/4}$$

$$\therefore\quad i(t) = \frac{\mathbf{1}}{\mathbf{4}}\, e^{-\frac{1}{4}t}\, \mathbf{u(t)}.$$

EXAMPLE 7.51 *In a series RC circuit, the resistance is of 2 Ω while the capacitor is of 1/4 F. Find the transfer function of voltage and the drop across the capacitor assuming the supply voltage to be $V_0(t) = t\,u(t)$.*

SOLUTION. Let *H*(*s*) be the transfer function in the *RC* circuit while

$$H(s) = \frac{V_c(s)}{V_0(s)}$$

[assuming the supply to be $V_0(t)$ and the voltage across the capacitor to be $V_c(t)$].

$$= \frac{I(s)\,X_c(s)}{I(s)\,Z(s)} = \frac{X_c(s)}{Z(s)} = \frac{\dfrac{1}{\frac{1}{4}.s}}{2+\dfrac{1}{\frac{1}{4}s}}$$

$$= \frac{\frac{4}{s}}{2+\frac{4}{s}} = \frac{4}{2s+4} = \frac{2}{s+2} \qquad ...(1)$$

Also, $V_0(s) = £\,V_0(t) = \dfrac{1}{s^2}$

and $\quad V_c(s) = V_0(s)\,H(s) = \dfrac{1}{s^2}\cdot\dfrac{2}{s+2} = \dfrac{2}{s^2(s+2)} \qquad ...(2)$

Let $\quad \dfrac{2}{s^2(s+2)} = \dfrac{K_1}{s^2} + \dfrac{K_2}{s} + \dfrac{K_3}{s+2}.$

Here $\quad K_1 = \left.\dfrac{2}{s^2(s+2)}.s^2\right|_{s=0} = 1$

$$K_2 = \left.\frac{d}{ds}\left[\frac{2}{s^2(s+2)}.s^2\right]\right|_{s=0}$$

$$= \left.\frac{-2}{(s+2)^2}\right|_{s=0} = -\frac{1}{2}$$

$$K_3 = \left.\frac{2}{s^2(s+2)}.(s+2)\right|_{s=-2} = \frac{1}{2}$$

$\therefore \quad V_c(s) = \dfrac{1}{s^2} + \dfrac{(-1/2)}{s} + \dfrac{1/2}{s+2}$

$$= \frac{1}{s^2} - \frac{1}{2s} + \frac{1}{2(s+2)}$$

Thus,

$$H(s) = \frac{V_c(s)}{V_0(s)} = \frac{\dfrac{1}{s^2} + \dfrac{(-1/2)}{s} + \dfrac{1/2}{s+2}}{\dfrac{1}{s^2}}$$

$$= \mathbf{\frac{1}{s^2}\left[\frac{1}{s^2} - \frac{1}{2s} + \frac{1}{2(s+2)}\right]}.$$

Taking the inverse of Laplace transform of $V_c(s)$,

$$V_c(t) = \mathbf{tu(t) - \frac{1}{2}u(t) + \frac{1}{2}e^{-2t}\,u(t)}.$$

Example 7.52 *In a series LC circuit, a 50 dc is applied at $t=0$. Find the voltage across the capacitor at $t=\infty$. Assume zero initial condition in the circuit elements.*

Solution. $Z(s)$ [impedance of the LC circuit at s-domain]

$$= sL + \frac{1}{Cs}.$$

$$\therefore \quad I(s) = \frac{V(s)}{Z(s)} \left[\begin{array}{l} V(s) = \text{Supply voltage} = \dfrac{50}{s} \\ I(s) = \text{current in LC circuit} \end{array}\right]$$

$$= \frac{50/s}{sL+\dfrac{1}{sC}} = \frac{50\,C}{s^2\,LC+1} = \frac{50}{s^2\,L+\dfrac{1}{C}}$$

$$= \frac{50}{L\left(s^2+\dfrac{1}{LC}\right)}$$

$\because$ The circuit elements have zero initial conditions,

$$V_c(0+) = 0 = V_c(0-)$$

Thus $V_c(s) = I(s)\,X_c(s) = I(s)\dfrac{1}{Cs}$

$$= \frac{50}{LCs\left(s^2+\dfrac{1}{LC}\right)}$$

To find $V_c(s)$ at $t\to\infty$, let us apply final value theorem.

Then, $\displaystyle\lim_{s\to 0} sV_c(s) = \lim_{s\to 0}\frac{50s}{LCs\left(s^2+\dfrac{1}{LC}\right)} = 50\text{ V}$

$\therefore$ At $\quad t\to\infty,\ V_c(t) = \mathbf{50\ V}.$

Example 7.53 *Two simultaneous differential equations are given by*

$$\frac{df_1(t)}{dt} + 4\,f_1(t) + 2\,\frac{df_2(t)}{dt} + 5\,f_2(t) = 4\,u(t)$$

$$2\,\frac{df_1(t)}{dt} + f_1(t) + \frac{df_2(t)}{dt} + 4\,f_2(t) = 5\,\delta(t).$$

With zero initial condition, form the matrix for $F_1(s)$ and $F_2(s)$.

Solution. Taking the Laplace transformation of the given equations,

$$[sF_1(s) - f_1(0+)] + 4F_1(s) + 2\,[sF_2(s) - f_2(0+)] + 5\,F_2(s) = \frac{4}{s}$$

and $\quad 2\,[sF_1(s) - f_1(0+)] + F_1(s) + [sF_2(s) - f_2(0+)] + 4\,F_2(s) = 5$

The pair of equations reduces to,

$$F_1(s)[s+4]+F_2(s)[2s+5]=\frac{4}{s}$$

and $$F_1(s)[2s+1]+F_2(s)[s+4]=5$$

Thus in matrix form

$$\begin{bmatrix}F_1(s)\\F_2(s)\end{bmatrix}\begin{bmatrix}s+4 & 2s+5\\2s+1 & s+4\end{bmatrix}=\begin{bmatrix}4/s\\5\end{bmatrix}.$$

$F_1(s)$ and $F_2(s)$ can be determined employing usual matrix methods.

EXAMPLE 7.54 *If $f_1(t)=2\,u(t)$ and $f_2(t)=e^{-3t}\,u(t)$, determine the convolution between $f_1(t)$ and $f_2(t)$.*

SOLUTION. As $f_1(t)=2u(t)$ $\quad\therefore\ F_1(s)=\frac{2}{s}$

and as $$f_2(t)=e^{-3t}\,u(t)\ \therefore\ F_2(s)=\frac{1}{s+3}$$

As $F(s)=F_1(s)*F_2(s)$, we find

$$F(s)=\int_0^t f_1(t)\,f_2(t-\tau)\,d\tau=\int_0^t 2e^{-3(t-\tau)}\,d\tau$$

$$=2e^{-3t}\int_0^t e^{3\tau}\,d\tau=2e^{-3t}\left[\frac{e^{3\tau}}{3}\right]_0^t$$

$$=\frac{2}{3}e^{-3t}\,[e^{3t}-1]=\frac{2}{3}\,(1-e^{-3t}).$$

EXAMPLE 7.55 *A function in laplace domain is given by*

$$F(s)=\frac{2(s+4)}{(s+3)(s+8)}.$$

Find the initial and final value by initial and final value theorem.

SOLUTION. $$F(s)=\frac{2(s+4)}{(s+3)(s+8)}=\frac{K_1}{s+3}+\frac{K_2}{s+8}$$

where, $$K_1=(s+3)\left.\frac{2(s+4)}{(s+3)(s+8)}\right|_{s=-3}=\frac{2}{5}$$

$$K_2=(s+8)\left.\frac{2(s+4)}{(s+3)(s+8)}\right|_{s=-8}=\frac{8}{5}$$

$$\therefore\quad F(s)=\frac{2/5}{s+3}+\frac{8/5}{s+8}$$

i.e., $$f(t)=\frac{2}{5}e^{-3t}+\frac{8}{5}e^{-8t}$$

$$\therefore\quad f(0+)=\lim_{s\to\infty}[sF(s)]$$

$$=\lim_{s\to\infty}\left[\frac{2}{5}\cdot\frac{s}{s+3}+\frac{8}{5}\cdot\frac{s}{s+8}\right]=\mathbf{2}$$

and $$f(\infty)=\lim_{s\to 0}[sF(s)]$$

$$=\lim_{s\to 0}\left[\frac{2}{5}\cdot\frac{s}{s+3}+\frac{8}{5}\cdot\frac{s}{s+8}\right]=\mathbf{0}.$$

EXAMPLE 7.56 *In Fig. E7.26, the initial voltage in the capacitor is 1 V in the polarity shown. Find the voltage appearing across the capacitor with application of the step voltage.*

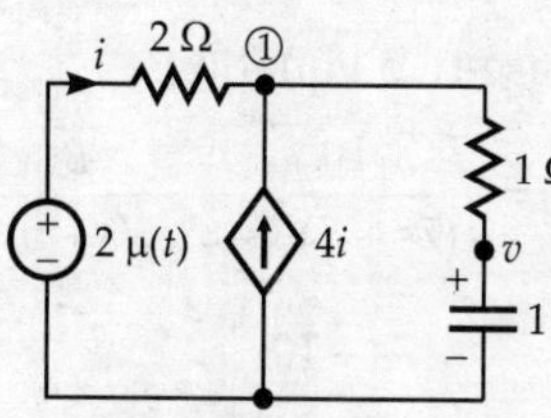

Fig. E7.26

SOLUTION. Let us first transform the circuit to laplace domain (Fig. E7.27). Let the voltage at node (1) be $V_1(s)$.

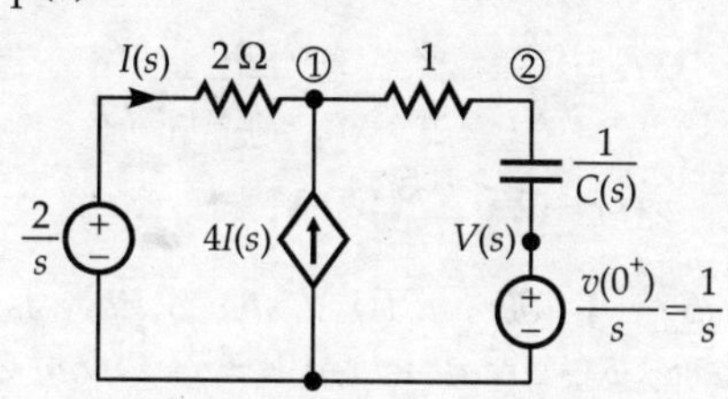

Fig. E7.27

$\therefore$ At node (1),

$$\frac{V_1(s)-V(s)}{1}=4\,I(s)+I(s)=5I(s)$$

or, $$V_1(s)-V(s)=5I(s) \qquad \text{...(A)}$$

Also, using KCL in the right handed loop of Fig. E7.27, at node (2),

$$\frac{V_1(s)-V(s)}{1}=\frac{V(s)-\frac{v(0+)}{s}}{1/Cs}\left(=\frac{V(s)-1/s}{1/s}\right)$$

or, $$V_1(s)-V(s)=\frac{sV(s)-1}{1}=sV(s)-1$$

or, $$V_1(s)-V(s)[s+1]=-1 \qquad \text{...(B)}$$

However,

$$I(s)=\frac{\frac{2}{s}-V_1(s)}{2} \qquad \text{...(C)}$$

Thus from (*A*) and (C),

$$V_1(s) - V(s) = 5\,\frac{\frac{2}{s} - V_1(s)}{2} = 5 \times \frac{1}{s} - \frac{5}{2} V_1(s)$$

$$V_1(s) + \frac{5}{2} V_1(s) - V(s) = \frac{5}{s}$$

or,
$$\frac{7 V_1(s)}{2} - V(s) = \frac{5}{s} \qquad \text{...(D)}$$

Thus we finally got two equations [(D) and (B)] as

$$\frac{7}{2} V_1(s) - V(s) = \frac{5}{s} \text{ and } V_1(s) - V(s)[s+1] = -1$$

Solving these two equations,

$$V(s) = \frac{7s+10}{s(7s+5)} = \frac{A}{s} + \frac{B}{7s+5}$$

Here,
$$A = s.\frac{7s+10}{s(7s+5)}\bigg|_{s=0} = 2$$

$$B = (7s+5)\frac{7s+10}{s(7s+5)}\bigg|_{s=-\frac{5}{7}} = -7$$

$$\therefore \quad V(s) = \frac{2}{s} - \frac{7}{7s+5} = \frac{2}{s} - \frac{1}{s+5/7}$$

$$\therefore \quad v(t) = \mathbf{(2 - e^{-5/7\,t})\ V.}$$

EXAMPLE 7.57 *A 100 t u (t) V step voltage is applied across a series RC circuit where R = 5 kΩ and C = 4 μF. Find the drop across the 5 kΩ resistor using Laplace transformation.*

SOLUTION. In the *RC* circuit, in Laplace domain,

$$V_{in}(s) = \frac{100}{s^2}$$

and
$$Z(s) = R + \frac{1}{Cs}$$

[$V_{in}(s)$ = input voltage = £ $V_{in}(t)$]

$Z(s)$ = impedance of the series circuit

$I(s)$ = through current]

$$\therefore \quad I(s) = \frac{V_{in}(s)}{Z(s)} = \frac{100/s^2}{R + \frac{1}{Cs}}$$

$$= \frac{100/s^2}{5\times 10^3 + \frac{1}{4\times 10^{-6} s}}$$

$$= \frac{100 \times 4 \times 10^{-6} s}{(20\times 10^3 \times 10^{-6} s + 1) s^2}$$

$$= \frac{4\times 10^{-4}}{(2\times 10^{-2} s + 1) s}$$

∴ $V_R(s)$, *i.e.* the drop across the 5 Ω resistor is

$$V_R(s) = I(s) \times 5 \times 10^3 = \frac{5\times 10^3 \times 4 \times 10^{-4}}{(2\times 10^{-2} s + 1) s}$$

$$= \frac{2}{s}$$

[∵ 2×10^{-2} s is very small and can be neglected]

$$\therefore \quad \mathbf{V_R\ (t) = 2\ V.}$$

EXAMPLE 7.58 *A 10 volts step voltage is applied across a RC series circuit at t = 0. Find i (t) at t = 0+ and obtain the value of di / dt $|_{t=0+}$. Assume R = 100 Ω, C = 100 μF.*

SOLUTION. The supply voltage is given by

$$V(s) = £\, V(t) = £\, 10\, u(t) = \frac{10}{s}.$$

Also,
$$Z(s) = R + \frac{1}{Cs} = 100 + \frac{1}{100\times 10^{-6} s}$$

$$= 100 + \frac{10^4}{s}$$

$$\therefore \quad I(s) = \frac{V(s)}{Z(s)} = \frac{10/s}{100 + 10^4/s}$$

$$= \frac{1}{s(10 + 1000/s)} = \frac{1}{1000 + 10 s}$$

or,
$$I(s) = \frac{1}{(s+100)10}$$

∴ $i(t)$, the inverse of Laplace transform in

$$i(t) = \mathbf{0.1\, e^{-100\, t}\ A}$$

$$\therefore \quad \frac{di(t)}{dt}\bigg|_{t=0+} = 0.1\, e^{-100\,t}(-100)\bigg|_{t=0}$$

$$= \mathbf{-10\ A/sec.}$$

EXAMPLE 7.59 *A network has been shown in Fig. E7.28. The switch K is closed at t = 0. Find the current in R_L using*

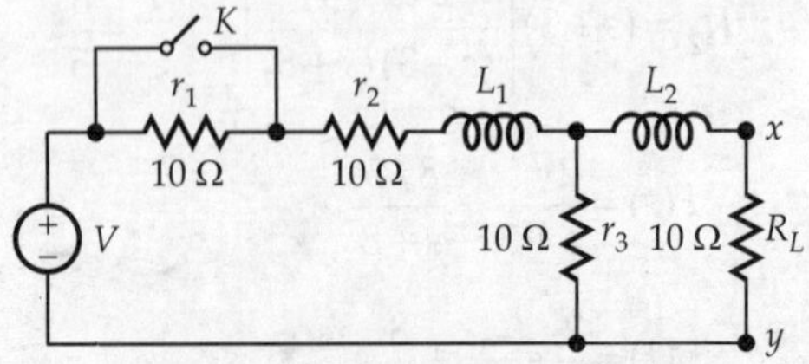

Fig. E7.28

Thevenin's theorem. Assume steady state condition before switching.

$[r_1 = r_2 = 10\,\Omega,\ L_1 = L_2 = 1\ H,\ r_3 = 10\,\Omega,\ V = 100\ V]$

Solution. When the switch K was open, steady state condition was existing and L_1 and L_2, both the inductances were acting as short circuit.

$\therefore$ I, the steady state current from the battery at this condition would be

$$I = \frac{V}{(r_3 \,||\, R_L) + r_2 + r_1}$$

$$= \frac{100}{\dfrac{10 \times 10}{10 + 10} + 10 + 10} = 4\text{ A}$$

By the formula of current division, then, the current through R_L would be given by

$$I_{R_L} = I\frac{r_3}{r_3 + R_L} = 4\frac{10}{10 + 10} = 2\text{ A}$$

When the switch K is now closed at $t = 0$, r_1 will immediately get shorted. Laplace transform of the given network is shown in Fig. E7.29.

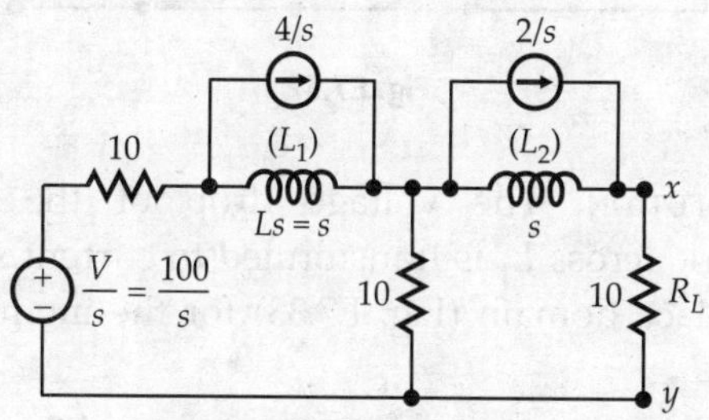

Fig. E7.29

[For transformation of inductive drop to current source in Laplace domain, please refer to Fig. 7.10]

In order to apply the Thevenin's theorem, the load resistor (R_L) is to be removed from x-y terminals of Fig. E7.29 and the circuit is redrawn in Fig. E7.30.

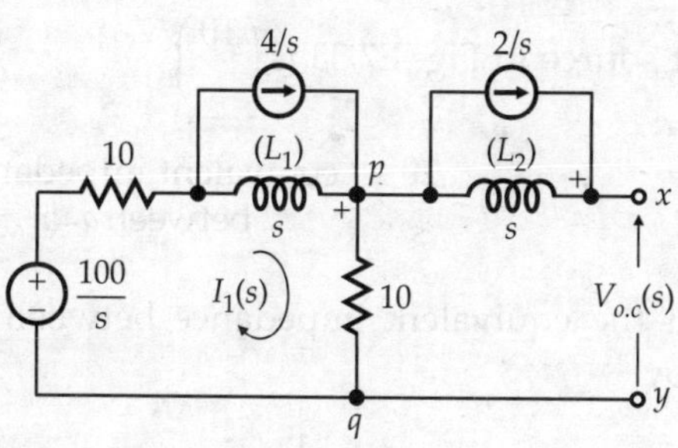

Fig. E7.30

The loop equations in s-domain are then given by

$$\frac{100}{s} = 10\,I_1(s) + \left[I_1(s) - \frac{4}{s}\right]s + 10\,I_1(s)$$

or, $$I_1(s)[20 + s] = \left[\frac{100}{s} + 4\right]$$

or $$I_1(s) = \frac{100 + 4s}{(20 + s)s} = \frac{4(25 + s)}{s(20 + s)}$$

Thus, the open circuit voltage $V_{o.c}(s)$ across x-y is given by

$$V_{o.c}(s) = \begin{matrix}\text{drop across } 10\,\Omega \\ \text{resistor in } s\text{-domain}\end{matrix} + \begin{matrix}\text{drop across the inductor} \\ L_2 \text{ in } s\text{-domain}\end{matrix}$$

$$= V_{p-q}(s) + V_{p-x}(s)$$

However,

$$V_{p-q}(s) = 10\,I_1(s) = 10\frac{4(25 + s)}{s(20 + s)} = \frac{40(25 + s)}{s(20 + s)}.$$

and $$V_{p-x}(s) = \frac{2}{s} \times s = 2$$

[with +ve polarity being at x terminal]

$$\therefore \quad V_{o.c}(s) = \frac{40(25 + s)}{s(20 + s)} + 2$$

$$= \frac{40(25 + s) + 2s(20 + s)}{s(20 + s)}$$

$$= \frac{2s^2 + 80s + 1000}{s(20 + s)}$$

Next, to find the internal impedance (R_{Th}) of the given circuit, the constant sources are deactivated *i.e.*, the voltage sources are shorted while the current sources are opened.

Then,

$$R_{Th}(s) = \frac{10(10 + s)}{10 + 10 + s} + s$$

$$= \frac{100 + 10s + 20s + s^2}{(20 + s)}$$

$$= \frac{s^2 + 30s + 100}{(s + 20)}$$

Following Fig. E7.31, Thevenin's equivalent circuit, current through R_L is given by

$$I_{R_L}(s)\ \text{(after switching)} = \frac{V_{o.c}}{R_{\text{int}} + R_L}$$

$$= \frac{\dfrac{2s^2 + 80s + 1000}{s(s+20)}}{\dfrac{s^2 + 30s + 100}{s+20} + 10}$$

$$= \frac{2s^2 + 80s + 1000}{s(s^2 + 40s + 300)}$$

or, $$I_{R_L}(s) = \frac{2s^2 + 80s + 1000}{s(s+10)(s+30)}$$

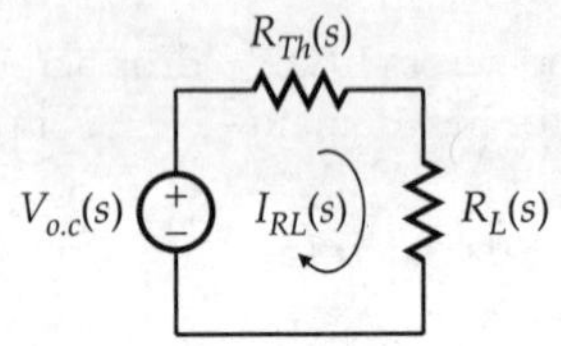

Fig. E7.31

Using the method of partial fractions we have

$$\frac{2s^2 + 80s + 1000}{s(s+10)(s+30)} = \frac{A}{s} + \frac{B}{s+10} + \frac{C}{s+30}$$

where $$A = s.\frac{2s^2 + 80s + 1000}{s(s+10)(s+30)}\Bigg|_{s=0} = \frac{10}{3}$$

$$B = \frac{2s^2 + 80s + 1000}{s(s+10)(s+30)}(s+10)\Bigg|_{s=-10} = -2$$

$$C = \frac{2s^2 + 80s + 1000}{s(s+10)(s+30)}(s+30)\Bigg|_{s=-30} = \frac{2}{3}.$$

Thus $$I_{R_L}(s) = \frac{A}{s} + \frac{B}{s+10} + \frac{C}{s+30}$$

$$= \frac{10/3}{s} + \frac{(-2)}{s+10} + \frac{2/3}{s+30}$$

Taking the inverse of Laplace transform,

$$i(t) = \mathbf{\frac{10}{3} + (-2)\,e^{-10t} + \frac{2}{3}\,e^{-30t}}.$$

where $i(t)$ is the current through R_L.

EXAMPLE 7.60 *Find the Laplace inverse of* $\dfrac{s+4}{(2s^2+5s+3)}$

SOLUTION. $$\frac{s+4}{2s^2+5s+3} = \frac{s+4}{(s+1)(2s+3)}$$

$$= \frac{A}{s+1} + \frac{B}{2s+3}.$$

However,

$$A = \frac{s+4}{(s+1)(2s+3)}.(s+1)\Bigg|_{s=-1} = 3$$

$$B = \frac{s+4}{(s+1)(2s+3)}(2s+3)\Bigg|_{s=-3/2} = -5$$

$$\therefore \quad \frac{s+4}{(s+1)(2s+3)} = \frac{3}{s+1} - \frac{5}{2s+3}$$

Thus, the Laplace inverse is given by

$$\pounds^{-1}\left[\frac{s+4}{(s+1)(2s+3)}\right] = \mathbf{3e^{-t} - 2.5\,e^{-3/2\,t}}.$$

EXAMPLE 7.61 *Initially, K is at x. At t = 0, the switch is shifted to y. Find the voltage at t > 0 across a-b. Assume zero initial condition for L_2 (Fig. E7.32).*

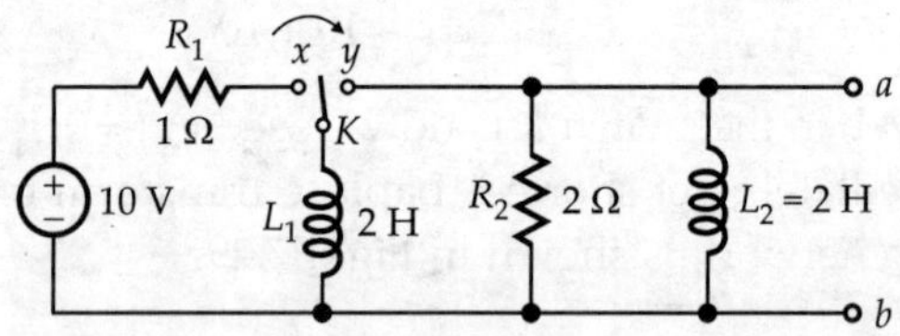

Fig. E7.32

SOLUTION. The voltage drop of the given network across L_1 is transformed to current source in Laplace domain (Fig. E7.33) for the moment of $t = 0+$.

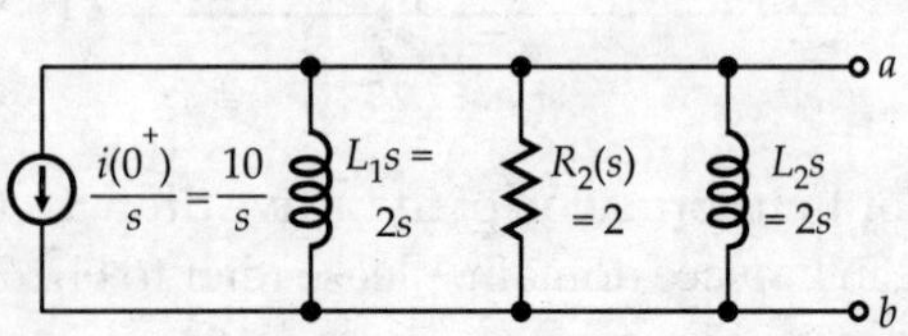

Fig. E7.33

As $i(0+) = \dfrac{10}{R_1} = 10$ A, hence the strength of the current source in Fig. E7.33 is $\left(\dfrac{10}{s}\right)$

$$\therefore \quad V_{a-b}(s) = \frac{10}{s} \times \left(\begin{array}{c}\text{equivalent impedance}\\ \text{between } a\text{-}b\end{array}\right)$$

But the equivalent impedance between *a-b* is given by

$$Z(s) = \frac{1}{\text{equivalent admittance between } a\text{-}b}$$

$$= \frac{1}{\text{summation of admittances of individual branches}}$$

$$= \frac{1}{\frac{1}{2s}+\frac{1}{2}+\frac{1}{2s}} = \frac{1}{\frac{2+s}{2s}} = \frac{2s}{2+s}$$

Thus $\quad V_{a-b}(s) = \frac{10}{s} \times \frac{2s}{2+s} = \frac{20}{2+s}$

i.e., $\quad V_{a-b}(t) = \mathbf{20\, e^{-2t}\ V.}$

Notice that as the direction of the current source is anticlockwise, the +ve polarity for $V_{a-b}(t)$ is at b terminal.

EXAMPLE 7.62 *Initial voltage retained by the capacitor C_1 is 100 V while there is no initial voltage stored in C_2. Switch K is closed at $t=0$. Find the voltage drops across the capacitors C_1 and C_2 at $t=\infty$ (Fig. E7.34).*

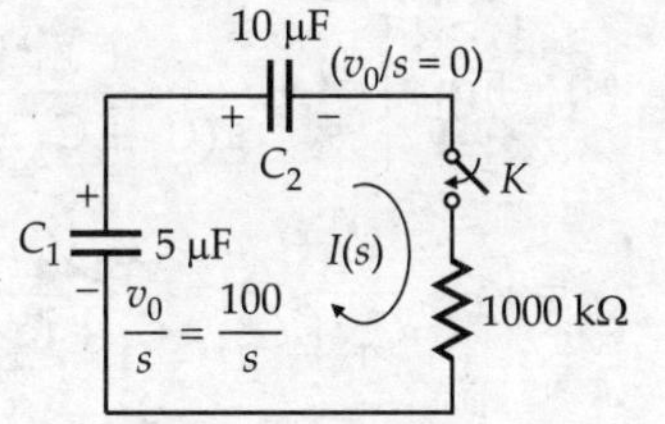

Fig. E7.34

SOLUTION. Following operation of the switch, let the loop current be $I(s)$ in Laplace domain.

Also, $\quad X_{C_1}(s) = \frac{1}{C_1 s} = \frac{10^6}{5s};$

$$X_{C_2}(s) = \frac{1}{C_2 s} = \frac{10^6}{10s}$$

Since the voltage stored in C_1 is 100 V at $t=0$, application of KVL in the loop at $t=0+$ gives

$$\frac{100}{s} = I(s)\left[\frac{10^6}{5s} + \frac{10^6}{10s} + 10^6\right]$$

$$= I(s) \times 10^6 \left[\frac{2+1+10s}{10s}\right]$$

$$= 10^6\, I(s)\left[\frac{10s+3}{10s}\right]$$

$$\therefore \quad I(s) = \frac{100\times 10^{-6} \times 10s}{s(10s+3)} = \frac{10^{-4}}{(s+0.33)}$$

Thus $V_{C_1}(s)$ [drop across C_1]

$$= \frac{100}{s} - I(s)\, X_{C_1}(s)$$

[$\because$ drop across C_1 would be the difference of the initial voltage across C_1 and the final voltage across C_1 during discharge]

$$= \frac{100}{s} - \frac{10^{-4}}{(s+0.33)} \times \frac{10^6}{5s}$$

$$= \frac{100}{s} - \frac{20}{s(s+0.33)}$$

$\therefore \lim_{s\to 0} sV_{C_1}(s) = \lim_{t\to\infty} V_{C_1}(t)$ [steady state V_{C_1}]

$$= s\left[\frac{100}{s} - \frac{20}{s(s+0.33)}\right]\Bigg|_{s=0}$$

$$= 100 - \frac{20}{0.33} = 39.39 \text{ V}$$

Similarly,

$$V_{C_2}(s) = I(s)\, X_{C_2}(s)$$

[$\because$ it had no initial voltage]

$$= \frac{10^{-4}}{s+0.33} \times \frac{10^6}{10s} = \frac{10}{s(s+0.33)}$$

$\therefore \quad \lim_{s\to 0} s\,V_{C_2}(s)$

[*i.e.*, the voltage across C_2 at steady state]

$$= \frac{10}{s(s+0.33)}.s\Bigg|_{s\to 0} = \frac{10}{s+0.33}\Bigg|_{s\to 0}$$

$$= 30.3 \text{ V}$$

Thus at $t=\infty$, $V_{C_1} = \mathbf{39.39\ V}$ and $V_{C_2} = \mathbf{30.3\ V.}$

EXAMPLE 7.63 *The current through a circuit element is $\frac{4s^2}{s+7}$. Find the current in t domain at $s\to 0$ and $s\to\infty$.*

SOLUTION. Using initial and final value theorem,

$$\underset{s\to 0}{\text{Lt}}\ s\,I(s) = \underset{s\to 0}{\text{Lt}}\ s.\frac{4s^2}{s+7} = 0$$

i.e., current at $s\to 0$ [or at $t\to\infty$] is **zero.**

Also, $\quad \underset{s\to\infty}{\text{Lt}}\ s\,I(s) = \underset{s\to\infty}{\text{Lt}}\ s\frac{4s^2}{s+7} = \infty$

$\therefore$ Current at $s\to\infty$ [or at $t\to 0$] is **infinity.**

The circuit element is possibly a capacitor as at $t=0$, the current is infinity *i.e.*, acting as short circuit. On the other hand, at $t=\infty$, the current ceases.

CHAPTER 7

Example 7.64 *A RL series circuit is energized by a voltage $V_0(t) = 3t\, u(t)$. Find $i(t)$. Assume $R = 2\,\Omega$, $L = 1$ H.*

Solution. In the *R-L* circuit, $I(s) = \dfrac{V_0(s)}{z(s)}$

But $V_0(s) = \pounds\, V_0(t) = \pounds\,[3t\, u(t)] = \dfrac{3}{s^2}$

and $Z(s) = 2 + s.1 = s + 2$

$$\therefore \quad I(s) = \frac{3/s^2}{s+2} = \frac{3}{s^2(s+2)}$$

Let
$$\frac{3}{s^2(s+2)} = \frac{A}{s+2} + \frac{B}{s} + \frac{C}{s^2}$$

$$\therefore \quad A = \left.\frac{3}{s^2}\right|_{s=-2} = \frac{3}{4}$$

$$B = \frac{d}{ds}\left[\frac{3}{s+2}\right]\Bigg|_{s=0} = -\left.\frac{3}{(s+2)^2}\right|_{s=0} = -\frac{3}{4}$$

$$C = \left.\frac{3}{s+2}\right|_{s=0} = \frac{3}{2}$$

$$\therefore \quad I(s) = \frac{3}{4(s+2)} - \frac{3}{4s} + \frac{3}{2s^2}$$

The inverse of Laplace transform is then

$$\boldsymbol{i(t) = \left[\frac{3}{4}e^{-2t} - \frac{3}{4} + \frac{3}{2}t\right] u(t).}$$

Example 7.65 *In the network of Fig. E7.35, C_1 is initially charged at V_1 potential, polarities being marked in the figure. With switching of K at $t = 0$, find the distribution of voltage in C_1 and C_2 at $t = \infty$ assuming zero initial charge across C_2.*

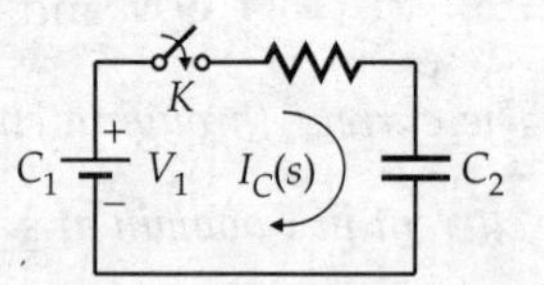

Fig. E7.35

Solution. Let $I_C(s)$ be the circulating current in s-domain in the circuit following switching at $t = 0$. The circuit has been transformed to Laplace domain as shown in Fig. E7.35(*a*).

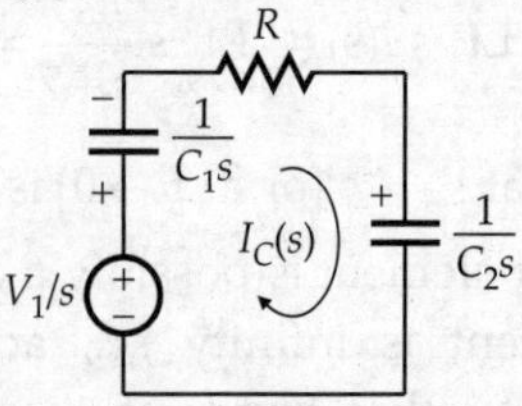

Fig. E7.35 (*a*)

Here, in s-domain, the voltage $V(s)$ across C_1 is

$$V(s) = \frac{V_1}{s} + \frac{I(s)}{C_1 s} \quad \left[i.e.,\ V(s) = \frac{V_1}{s} + V_{C_1}(s)\right]$$

But for the entire loop,

$$\frac{V_1}{s} + \frac{1}{C_1 s} I(s) + \frac{1}{C_2 s} I(s) = 0$$

or,
$$I(s) = \frac{-V_1 C_1 C_2}{C_1 + C_2 + Rs(C_1 C_2)}$$

$$\therefore \quad V_{C_1}(s) = \frac{V_1}{s} - \frac{V_1 C_1 C_2}{C_1 + C_2 + Rs(C_1 C_2)} \times \frac{1}{C_1 s}$$

and
$$V_{C_2}(s) = I(s)\, X_{C_2}(s)$$
$$= \frac{-V_1 C_1 C_2}{C_1 + C_2 + Rs(C_1 C_2)} \times \frac{1}{C_2 s}$$

At $t = \infty$ [or at $s \to 0$], $V_{C_1}(s)$ is obtained as

$$\lim_{s\to 0} sV_{C_1}(s) = \lim_{s\to 0} s\left[\frac{V_1}{s} - \frac{V_1 C_2}{s(C_1 + C_2 + RsC_1C_2)}\right]$$
$$= V_1 - \frac{V_1 C_2}{C_1 + C_2} = \frac{\boldsymbol{C_1 V_1}}{\boldsymbol{C_1 + C_2}}.$$

At $t = \infty$ (or at $s \to 0$), $V_{C_2}(s)$ is obtained as

$$\lim_{s\to 0} sV_{C_2}(s) = \lim_{s\to 0}\left[\frac{-V_1 C_1}{C_1 + C_2 + RsC_1C_2}\right]$$
$$= \frac{\boldsymbol{-V_1 C_1}}{\boldsymbol{C_1 + C_2}}.$$

Example 7.66 *In the initial condition, K is closed and a steady state is reached in the network of Fig. E7.36. At $t = 0$, the switch is opened. What is the current through the inductor ?*

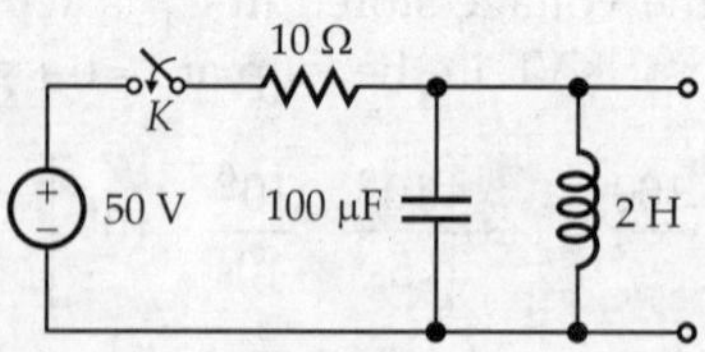

Fig. E7.36

Solution. Assuming *K* closed initially, the current will be limited by the resistance only as the inductor behaves as open circuit and the capacitor as short circuit at steady state.

$$i_{in}\ [i.e.\ \text{at}\ t = 0(-)] = \frac{50}{10} = 5\ \text{A}$$

Also, the capacitor acts as open circuit and $v_C(0-) = 0$.

At $t = 0$, the switch is opened.

$$Z(s) = Ls + \frac{1}{Cs}$$

$$= 2s + \frac{1}{100 \times 10^{-6}\, s} = 2s + \frac{10^4}{s} = \frac{2s^2 + 10^4}{s}$$

Thus, the current through inductor becomes $\frac{V(s)}{Z(s)}$.

Obviously $V(s)$ being the voltage drop across the inductor, it is actually the current source across the inductor at $t = 0+$.

Here it is $\frac{i(0+)}{s} = \frac{i(0-)}{s} = \frac{5}{s}$

This would cause a drop of $\left(\frac{5}{s} \times Ls\right)$ *i.e.*, $\frac{5}{s} \times 2s = 10$ across the inductor.

$$\therefore \quad V(s) = 10.$$

Finally, $I_L(s)$, the current through the inductor

$$= \frac{V(s)}{Z(s)} = \frac{10}{\dfrac{2s^2 + 10^4}{s}} = \frac{10\, s}{2s^2 + 10^4}$$

or $$I_L(s) = \frac{5\, s}{s^2 + 5 \times 10^3}.$$

Taking the Laplace inverse,

$$I_L(t) = \mathbf{5 \cos (5 \times 10^3)\, t.}$$

EXAMPLE 7.67 *Find Laplace transform of* $[M \sin(\omega t + \phi)]$.

SOLUTION.

Since $\sin(\omega t + \phi) = \sin \omega t \cos \phi + \cos \omega t \sin \phi$,

$$F(s) = £[M \sin(\omega t + \phi)] = M\left[\frac{\omega \cos \phi}{s^2 + \omega^2} + \frac{s \sin \phi}{s^2 + \omega^2}\right]$$

Similarly,

$$£[M \cos(\omega t + \phi)] = M\left[\frac{s \cos \phi}{s^2 + \omega^2} - \frac{\omega \sin \phi}{s^2 + \omega^2}\right].$$

EXAMPLE 7.68 *It is given that* $f(t) = \sin \omega\left(t - \frac{T}{2}\right) u\left(t - \frac{T}{2}\right)$. *Find its Laplace transform.*

SOLUTION. $f(t) = \sin \omega\left(t - \frac{T}{2}\right) u\left(t - \frac{T}{2}\right)$

$$\therefore \quad £ f(t) = F(s) = \frac{\omega e^{-\frac{T}{2}.s}}{s^2 + \omega^2}$$

Here it may be noted that since a first half cycle of a sine wave is obtained by adding a $(\sin \omega t)$ function with $\sin \omega\left(t - \frac{T}{2}\right)$ function, hence, the Laplace transform of a single half wave of a sine function is given by

$$£ f(t) = £\left[\sin \omega t\, u(t) + \sin \omega\left(t - \frac{T}{2}\right) u\left(t - \frac{T}{2}\right)\right]$$

$$= \frac{\omega}{s^2 + \omega^2} + \frac{\omega e^{-\frac{T}{2}s}}{s^2 + \omega^2} = \frac{\omega}{s^2 + \omega^2}\left(1 + e^{-\frac{T}{2}.s}\right).$$

EXAMPLE 7.69 *In a series RLC network, $R = 0.5\,\Omega$, $L = 1$ H and $C = 1$ F. If the initial voltage on the capacitor is 4 V, find $i(t)$ following switching of a voltage $10\,u(t)$ into the circuit. Assume zero initial condition for the inductor and the polarity of charge on the capacitor as shown in Fig. E7.37.*

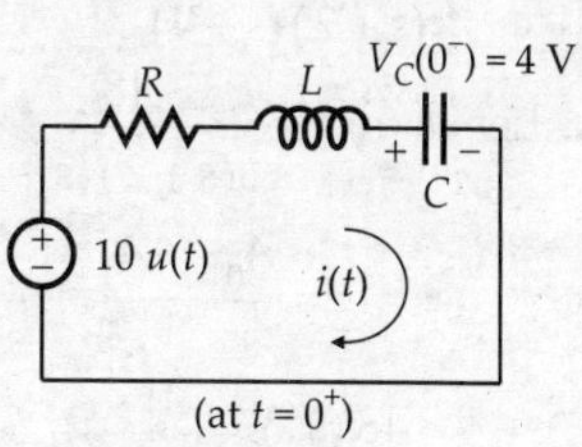

Fig. E7.37

SOLUTION. Since $R = \frac{1}{2}\,\Omega$, $L = 1$ H, $C = 1$ F, hence in Laplace domain,

$$Z(s) = R + Ls + \frac{1}{Cs} = \frac{1}{2} + s + \frac{1}{s} = \frac{s^2 + s + 2}{2s}$$

$$\therefore \quad Y(s) = \frac{2s}{s^2 + s + 2}$$

[$Z(s)$ = impedance; $Y(s)$ = admittance in s-domain]

$$= \frac{2s}{(s + 0.25 - j0.968)(s + 0.25 + j0.968)}$$

However,

$I(s) = Y(s)\, V(s)$ or, $i(t) = Y(t)\, V(t)$

$$= \{K_1 e^{[-0.25 + j\,0.968]\,t} + K_2 e^{[-0.25 - j\,0.968]\,t}\}\, 10\, u(t)$$

$$= 10\, K e^{-0.25\,t} \cos\{0.968\, t + \phi\}\, u(t)$$

Due to zero initial condition of the inductor,

$$i(0-)=i(0+)=0$$

$$\therefore \quad 0=10\,K\cos\phi$$

or, $\phi=\pm\pi/2$ (giving also $K=0$).

Also, $\left.\dfrac{di}{dt}\right|_{t=0+}$ (*i.e.*, drop across the inductor)

$$=10-4=6\text{ V}$$

[$\because$ at $t=0+$, drop across the inductor is the difference of supply voltage and initial voltage on the capacitor]

or, $6=10\,K[-0.25\cos\phi-0.968\sin\phi]$

$$=10\,K\left[-0.25\cos\left(\frac{\pi}{2}\right)-0.968\sin(-\pi/2)\right]$$

$$=10\,K\times(+0.968)$$

$$\therefore\ K=\frac{6}{9.68}=0.62$$

Thus

$$i(t)=0.62\times 10\,e^{-0.25t}\cos\{0.968\,t+(-\pi/2)\}\,u(t)$$

or, $\boldsymbol{i(t)=6.2\,e^{-0.25t}\sin\{0.968\,t\}\,u(t)}$ **A.**

EXAMPLE 7.70 *Find inverse Laplace transform of*

$$F(s)=\frac{48}{s^2(s+2)(s+4)}.$$

SOLUTION. Let $F(s)=\dfrac{48}{s^2(s+2)(s+4)}$

$$=\frac{A_0}{s}+\frac{A_1}{s^2}+\frac{A_2}{s+2}+\frac{A_3}{s+4}$$

Here $A_1=\left.\dfrac{48(s^2)}{s^2(s+2)(s+4)}\right|_{s=0}=6$

A_0 is obtained taking $\dfrac{d}{ds}$ of the equation $\dfrac{48}{(s+2)(s+4)}$ at $s=0$.

Now, $\dfrac{d}{ds}\left[\dfrac{48}{(s+2)(s+4)}\right]_{s=0}$

$$=\left.\frac{(s^2+6s+8)(0)-48(2s+6)}{(s^2+6s+8)^2}\right|_{s=0}=A_0$$

$$\therefore\quad A_0=-\frac{9}{2}.$$

$$A_2=\left.\frac{48}{s^2(s+2)(s+4)}.(s+2)\right|_{s=-2}=6$$

$$A_3=\left.\frac{48}{s^2(s+2)(s+4)}.(s+4)\right|_{s=-4}=-\frac{3}{2}$$

$$\therefore\quad F(s)=-\frac{9/2}{s}+\frac{6}{s^2}+\frac{6}{s+2}+\frac{-\frac{3}{2}}{s+4}$$

$$\therefore\ \pounds^{-1}(F(s))=-\frac{9}{2}+6\,e^{-2t}+6t-\frac{3}{2}\,e^{-4t}$$

or, $\boldsymbol{f(t)=6t-\dfrac{9}{2}+6e^{-2t}-\dfrac{3}{2}\,e^{4t}}$.

EXAMPLE 7.71 *Using Laplace transformation technique, find $i_2(t)$ at $t=0+$ following switching at $t=0$ of switch K in Fig. E7.38. Assume the network previously deenergized.*

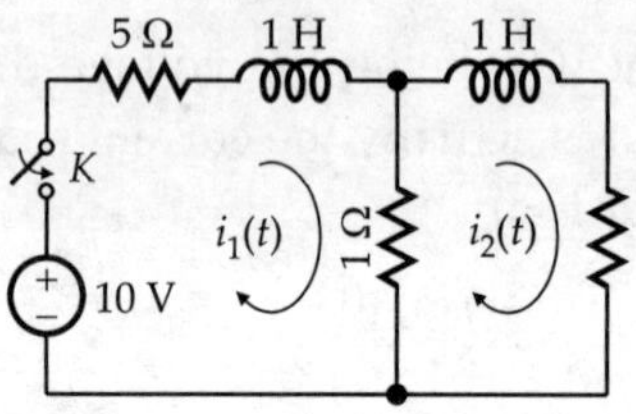

Fig. E7.38

SOLUTION. Loop equation for the left loop is given by

$$5i_1(t)+\frac{di_1(t)}{dt}+1[i_1(t)-i_2(t)]=10\,u(t) \quad ...(1)$$

and the same for the right loop is

$$\frac{di_2(t)}{dt}+5i_2(t)+1[i_2(t)-i_1(t)]=0 \quad ...(2)$$

Taking Laplace transform of both the equations, we get

$$5I_1(s)+sI_1(s)+I_1(s)-I_2(s)=\frac{10}{s} \quad ...[1(a)]$$

and $sI_2(s)+5I_2(s)+I_2(s)-I_1(s)=0 \quad ...[2(a)]$

Simplification of (1*a*) gives

$$I_1(s)[6+s]-I_2(s)=\frac{10}{s} \quad ...(3)$$

and simplification of 2(*a*) yields

$$-I_1(s)+I_2(s)[6+s]=0$$

or, $I_1(s)=I_2(s)(6+s) \quad ...(4)$

Substitution of (4) in (3),

$$I_2(s)(6+s)^2-I_2(s)=\frac{10}{s}$$

or, $I_2(s)[(6+s)^2-1]=\dfrac{10}{s}$

or, $I_2(s)=[36+s^2+12\,s-1]=\dfrac{10}{s}$

or, $I_2(s)=\dfrac{10}{s(s^2+12\,s+35)}=\dfrac{10}{s(s^2+7s+5s+35)}$

$$=\frac{10}{s(s+7)(s+5)}=\frac{K_1}{s}+\frac{K_2}{s+7}+\frac{K_3}{s+5}$$

where $K_1=\left.\dfrac{10}{(s+7)(s+5)}\right|_{s=0}=\dfrac{10}{35}=\dfrac{2}{7}$; $K_2=\left.\dfrac{10}{s(s+5)}\right|_{s=7}$

and $=\dfrac{10}{84}$; $K_3=\left.\dfrac{10}{s(s+7)}\right|_{s=5}=\dfrac{1}{6}$

$\therefore\quad I_2(s)=(2/7).\dfrac{1}{s}+\left(\dfrac{10}{84}\right)\dfrac{1}{s+7}+\dfrac{1}{6}.\dfrac{1}{s+5}$

$$=\frac{2/7}{s}+\frac{10/84}{s+7}+\frac{1/6}{s+5}.$$

i.e., $i_2(t)=\pounds^{-1}[I_2(s)]$

$$=\left(\frac{\mathbf{2}}{\mathbf{7}}+\frac{\mathbf{10}}{\mathbf{84}}\,e^{-7t}-\frac{\mathbf{1}}{\mathbf{6}}\,e^{-5t}\right)\textbf{A.}$$

EXAMPLE 7.72 *Find $V_c(t)$ and $I_L(t)$ in the circuit of Fig. E7.39 assuming zero initial conditions.*

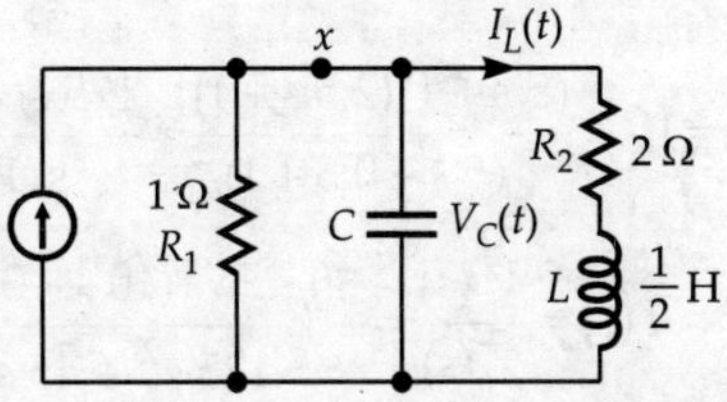

Fig. E7.39

SOLUTION. Applying nodal analysis in the circuit of Fig. E7.39,

$$\delta(t)=\frac{V_C(t)}{R_1}+\frac{V_C(t)}{X_C}+\frac{V_C(t)}{Z_L}\qquad ...(1)$$

However,

$$R_1=1\,\Omega;\ X_C=\frac{1}{(j\,\omega)\,C}=\frac{1}{j\,\omega}\quad [C=1\,\text{F}]$$

and $\quad Z_L=R_2+(j\,\omega)\,L=2+(j\,\omega)\dfrac{1}{2}$

Taking Laplace transform of equation (1),

$$1=\frac{V_C(s)}{1}+\frac{V_C(s)}{\frac{1}{s}}+\frac{V_C(s)}{2+\frac{s}{2}}$$

$$\left[\begin{array}{l}\because\ X_C(s)=\dfrac{1}{Cs}=\dfrac{1}{s}\\ Z_L(s)=R+Ls=2+\dfrac{s}{2}\end{array}\right]$$

or, $\quad V_C(s)\left[1+s+\dfrac{1}{2+\frac{s}{2}}\right]=1$

$\therefore\quad V_C(s)=\dfrac{1}{1+s+\dfrac{1}{2+\frac{s}{2}}}$

$$=\frac{1}{1+s+\dfrac{1}{\left(\frac{4+s}{2}\right)}}=\frac{1}{1+s+\dfrac{2}{4+s}}$$

$$=\frac{s+4}{4+s+s(4+s)+2}=\frac{s+4}{s^2+5s+6}$$

$$=\frac{s+4}{(s+3)(s+2)}=\frac{A}{s+3}+\frac{B}{s+2}$$

Here $\quad A=\left.\dfrac{s+4}{(s+3)(s+2)}(s+3)\right|_{s=-3}=\dfrac{1}{-1}=-1$

$\quad B=\left.\dfrac{s+4}{(s+3)(s+2)}(s+2)\right|_{s=-2}=2$

$\therefore\quad V_C(s)=-\dfrac{1}{s+3}+\dfrac{2}{s+2}.$

Taking laplace inverse,

$$V_C(t)=-\boldsymbol{e^{-3t}}+\mathbf{2}\boldsymbol{e^{-2t}}\ \textbf{V.}$$

Again,

$$I_L(s)=\frac{V_C(s)}{Z_L(s)}=\frac{\dfrac{s+4}{(s+3)(s+2)}}{2+\dfrac{s}{2}}$$

$$=\frac{\dfrac{s+4}{(s+3)(s+2)}}{\dfrac{4+s}{2}}=\frac{2}{(s+3)(s+2)}$$

$$=\frac{K_1}{s+3}+\frac{K_2}{s+2}$$

Here, $\quad K_1=\left.\dfrac{2}{s+2}\right|_{s=-3}=-2$

and $\quad K_2=\left.\dfrac{2}{s+3}\right|_{s=-2}=2$

$\therefore\quad I_L(s)=-\dfrac{2}{s+3}+\dfrac{2}{s+2}$

Taking Laplace inverse,

$$I_L(t)=-\mathbf{2}\boldsymbol{e^{-3t}}+\mathbf{2}\boldsymbol{e^{-2t}}\ \textbf{A.}$$

EXAMPLE 7.73 *The system response of a function in frequency domain is described by the following equation :*

$$s^2\,F(s)+sF(s)=\frac{2}{s^2}.\ \text{Find } f(t).$$

SOLUTION. Given that $s^2\,F(s)+sF(s)=\dfrac{2}{s^2}$

or, $$F(s)\,[s^2+s]=\frac{2}{s^2}$$

or, $$F(s)=\frac{2}{s^3\,(s+1)}$$

$$=\frac{A_0}{s^3}+\frac{A_1}{s^2}+\frac{A_2}{s}+\frac{A_4}{s+1}\ \text{(say)}$$

Here, $$A_0=\left.\frac{2}{s^3\,(s+1)}\,.\,s^3\right|_{s=0}=2$$

To find A_1, the derivative of $\dfrac{2}{s+1}$ is taken at $t=0$

This leads to $$\left.\frac{(s+1)0-2\,(1)}{(s+1)^2}\right|_{s=0}=A_1$$

$\therefore$ $A_1=-2.$

Next A_2 is found in the same manner taking the derivative of

$$\frac{(s+1).0-2\,(1)}{(s+1)^2}\ \text{at } s=0$$

We find $$\left.\frac{(s+1)^2.0-(-2)(s+1)1}{(s+1)^4}\right|_{s=0}=A_2$$

or, $A_2=2.$

However, $$A_4=\left.\frac{2}{s^3\,(s+1)}.(s+1)\right|_{s=-1}=-2$$

$$\therefore\quad F(s)=\frac{2}{s^3}+\frac{-2}{s^2}+\frac{2}{s}-\frac{2}{s+1}$$

$$=\frac{2}{s^3}-\frac{2}{s^2}+\frac{2}{s}-\frac{2}{s+1}$$

$$\therefore\quad \boldsymbol{f(t)=\pounds^{-1}\,F(s)=t^2-2t+2-2e^{-t}}.$$

EXAMPLE 7.74 *Assume no initial charge on either of the capacitors in Fig. E7.40. The switch is closed at $t=0$. Find i at $t=0+$. Apply initial and final value theorem.*

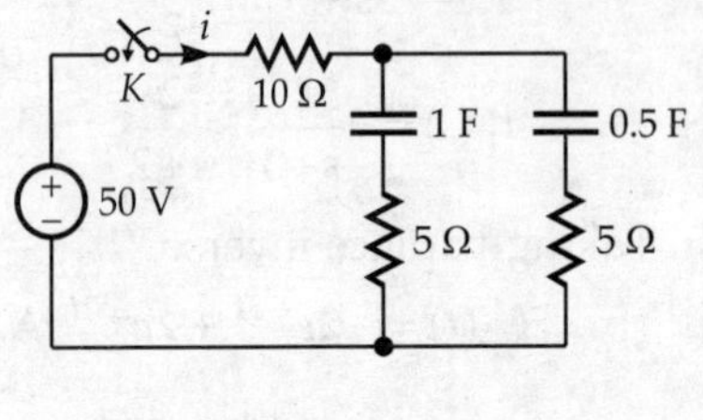

Fig. E7.40

SOLUTION. The given circuit is first converted to s-domain (at $t=0+$) and is exhibited in Fig. E7.41.

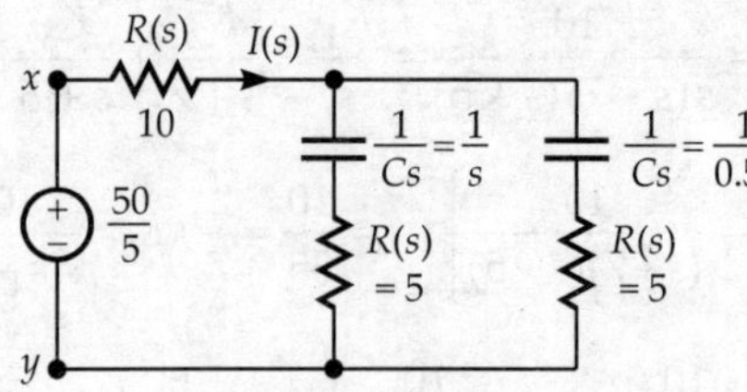

Fig. E7.41

the impedance of the given circuit across x-y in s-domain is given by

$$Z(s)=10+\frac{\left(5+\dfrac{1}{s}\right)\left(5+\dfrac{1}{0.5\,s}\right)}{\left(10+\dfrac{1}{s}+\dfrac{1}{0.5\,s}\right)}$$

$$=10+\frac{\dfrac{5\,s+1}{s}\cdot\dfrac{2.5\,s+1}{0.5\,s}}{\dfrac{5\,s+0.5+1}{0.5\,s}}$$

$$=10+\frac{(5\,s+1)(2.5\,s+1)}{s\,(5\,s+0.5+1)}=\frac{125\,s^2+45\,s+2}{s\,(10\,s+3)}$$

$$\therefore\quad I(s)=\frac{V(s)}{Z(s)}=\frac{50}{s}\cdot\frac{s\,(10\,s+3)}{125\,s^2+45\,s+2}$$

$$=\frac{4\,(s+0.3)}{(s+0.308)\,(s+0.052)}$$

$$=\frac{K_1}{(s+0.308)}+\frac{K_2}{(s+0.052)}$$

Here

$$K_1=\left.\frac{4\,(s+0.3)}{(s+0.308)\,(s+0.052)}.(s+0.308)\right|_{s=-0.308}$$

$$=\frac{4\,(-0.308+0.3)}{(-0.308+0.052)}=0.125$$

$$K_2=\left.\frac{4\,(s+0.3)}{(s+0.308)\,(s+0.052)}.(5+0.052)\right|_{s=-0.052}$$

$$=\frac{4\,(-0.052+0.3)}{(-0.052+0.308)}=3.875.$$

$$\therefore\quad I(s)=0.125/(s+0.308)+3.875/(s+0.052)$$

$$=0.125\,e^{-0.308\,t}+3.875\,e^{-0.052\,t}$$

Applying the initial and final value theorem, we get

$$i(0+) = \lim_{s\to\infty} [sI(s)]$$

$$= \lim_{s\to\infty} \left[\left(\frac{s\times 0.125}{s+0.308}\right)+\left(\frac{3.875\, s}{s+0.052}\right)\right] = \mathbf{4\ A}$$

and $$i(\infty) = \lim_{s\to 0} [sI(s)]$$

$$= \lim_{s\to 0}\left[0.125\frac{s}{s+0.308}+3.875\frac{s}{s+0.052}\right] = \mathbf{0.}$$

This is reasonable as at $t=0+$, capacitors would behave as short circuit and $i = \frac{50}{12.5} = 4$ A and at $t=\infty$, capacitors would behave as open circuit and $i=0$.

EXAMPLE 7.75 *In the series RC circuit of Fig. E7.42, find an expression for $V_C(t)$ using nodal analysis if $V_0(t) = u(t) - u(t-1)$ and $v_C(0^-) = 2$ V.*

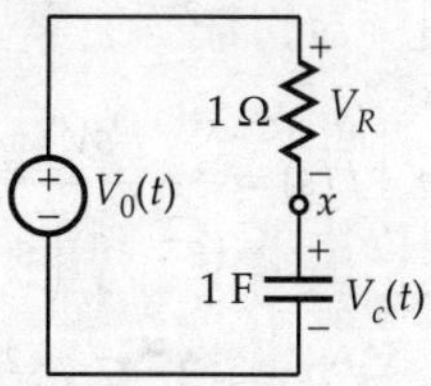

Fig. E7.42

SOLUTION. Let the selected node be (x) in the circuit of Fig. E7.42.

Using nodal analysis,

$$\frac{V_C(t)-V_0(t)}{R}+C\frac{dV_C(t)}{dt}=0$$

or, $$\frac{V_C(t)-[u(t)-u(t-1)]}{R}+\frac{d\,V_C(t)}{dt}=0$$

Here $R=C=1$.

$$\therefore \quad V_C(t)+\frac{d\,V_C(t)}{dt}=u(t)-u(t-1)$$

Taking Laplace transform for both the sides of the above equation,

$$V_C(s)+[s\,V_C(s)-V_C(0)]=\frac{1}{s}-\frac{1}{s}e^{-s}$$

However, $V_C(0-)=V_C(0+)$

[following application of switching]

$=2$ volts

$$\therefore \quad V_C(s)+[sV_C(s)-2]=\frac{1}{s}(1-e^{-s})$$

or, $$V_C(s)[1+s]=2+\frac{1}{s}(1-e^{-s})$$

or, $$V_C(s)=\frac{2}{s+1}+\frac{1}{s(s+1)}-\frac{e^{-s}}{s(s+1)}$$

Using the concept of partial fraction,

$$\frac{1}{s(s+1)}=\frac{1}{s}-\frac{1}{s+1}.$$

$$\therefore \quad V_C(s)=\left[\frac{1}{s}-\frac{1}{s+1}\right]-e^{-s}\left[\frac{1}{s}-\frac{1}{s+1}\right]+\frac{2}{s+1}$$

Taking the inverse Laplace transform,

$$V_C(t)=[1-e^{-t}]\,u(t)-(1-e^{-(t-1)})\,u(t-1)+2e^{-t}u(t)$$

$$=(1+e^{-t})\,u(t)-(1-e^{-(t-1)})\,u(t-1)$$

However, $u(t)=0$ if $t<0$ and $=1$ if $t>0$

Also, $u(t-1)=0$ if $t<1=1=$ if $t>1$;

$\therefore$ **for $1>t>0$,** $\quad$ **$V_C(t)=(1+e^{-t})$ V**

and **for $t>1$,** $\quad$ **$V_C(t)=(e^{-(t-1)}+e^{-t})$ V**

It may be noted here that Fig. E7.42 represents the circuit at $t=0+$.

EXAMPLE 7.76 *A differential equation is represented by*

$$\frac{d^2x}{dt^2}-x=e^{-t}$$

Assuming zero initial condition, find $x(t)$ at $t>0$.

SOLUTION. $$\frac{d^2x}{dt^2}-x=e^{-t} \qquad ...(1)$$

In Laplace domain (1) becomes

$$s^2X(s)-X(s)=\frac{1}{s+1}$$

or, $$X(s)=\frac{1}{(s+1)(s^2-1)}=\frac{1}{(s+1)^2(s-1)}$$

$$=\frac{A_0}{(s+1)^2}+\frac{A_1}{(s+1)}+\frac{A_2}{s-1}$$

$$\therefore \quad A_0=\left.\frac{1}{(s+1)^2(s-1)}(s+1)^2\right|_{s=-1}=-\frac{1}{2}$$

A_1 can be evaluated by taking the derivative $\frac{d}{ds}$ of $\left(\frac{1}{s-1}\right)$ at $s=-1$.

CHAPTER 7

Here $A_1 = \left.\dfrac{(s-1)0-(1)(1)}{(s-1)^2}\right|_{s=-1} = -\dfrac{1}{4}.$

However, $A_2 = \left.\dfrac{1\,(s-1)}{(s+1)^2\,(s-1)}\right|_{s=+1} = \dfrac{1}{4}$

Thus $X(s) = \dfrac{-1/2}{(s+1)^2} + \dfrac{-1/4}{s+1} + \dfrac{1/4}{s-1}$

$$= -\frac{1/2}{(s+1)^2} - \frac{1/4}{s+1} + \frac{1/4}{s-1}$$

$$\therefore \quad x(t) = £^{-1}\left[-\frac{1/2}{(s+1)^2} - \frac{1/4}{s+1} + \frac{1/4}{s-1}\right]$$

$$= -\frac{1}{2}\,t\,e^{-t} - \frac{1}{4}\,e^{-t} + \frac{1}{4}\,e^{t}.$$

Example 7.77 *A voltage is given by*

$$v(t) = 4\delta(t) + 2e^{-2t}\,u(t) + \cos(2t)\,u(t) + e^{3t}\,u(t).$$

Find its Laplace transform.

Solution.

$$v(t) = 4\delta(t) + 2e^{-2t}\,u(t) + \cos(2t)\,u(t) + e^{3t}\,u(t)$$

$$\therefore \quad V(s) = £[4\delta(t)] + £[2e^{-2t}\,u(t)] + £[\cos(2t)\,u(t)] + £[e^{3t}\,u(t)]$$

$$= 4 + \frac{2}{s+2} + \frac{s}{s^2+4} + \frac{1}{s-3}$$

$$= \frac{4(s+2)(s^2+4)(s-3) + 2(s^2+4)(s-3) + (s+2)(s^2+4)}{(s+2)(s^2+4)(s-3)}$$

$$= \frac{4(s^3+4s+2s^2+8)(s-3) + 2(s^3-3s^2+4s-12) + (s^3+4s+2s^2+8)}{(s+2)(s-3)(s^2+4)}$$

$$= \frac{4(s^4+4s^2+2s^3+8s-3s^3-12s-6s^2-24) + 2s^3-6s^2+8s-24+s^3+4s+2s^2+8}{(s+2)(s-3)(s^2+4)}$$

$$= \frac{4s^4+16s^2+8s^3+32s-12s^3-48s-24s^2-96 + 2s^3-6s^2+8s-24+s^3+4s+2s^2+8}{(s+2)(s-3)(s^2+4)}$$

$$= \frac{\mathbf{4s^4 - s^3 - 12s^2 - 4s - 112}}{\mathbf{(s+2)\,(s-3)\,(s^2+4)}}.$$

Example 7.78 *In a series LC circuit, the supply voltage being $v = V_{max}\cos(t)$, find $i(t)$ at $t = 0+$ following switching at $t = 0$ with zero initial conditions. Assume $L = 1$ H; $C = 1$ F in Fig. E7.43.*

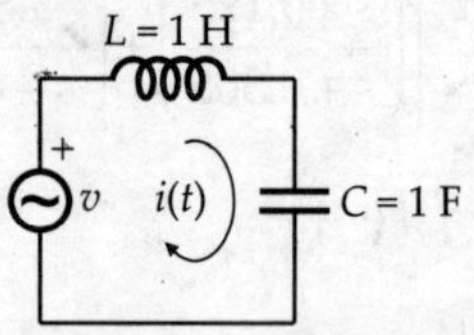

(Circuit at $t = 0^+$ following switching)

Fig. E7.43

Solution. (Fig. E7.43). Application of KVL at $t = 0+$ in Laplace domain,

$$I(s)\left[Ls + \frac{1}{Cs}\right] = £\,v = \frac{sV_m}{s^2+1}$$

or $$I(s)\left[s + \frac{1}{s}\right] = \frac{sV_m}{s^2+1}$$

or $$I(s) = \frac{sV_m}{(s^2+1)\left(s+\dfrac{1}{s}\right)}$$

$$= \frac{V_m\,s^2}{(s^2+1)(s^2+1)}$$

$\left[\begin{array}{c}\text{multiplying the numerator}\\ \text{and denominator by } s/s\end{array}\right]$

$$= \frac{s^2\,V_m}{(s^2+1)^2}$$

Before we find the partial fraction expansion, the roots are $+j, -j, +j$ and $-j$.

$$\therefore \quad I(s) = \frac{s^2\,V_m}{(s+j)(s-j)(s+j)(s-j)}$$

$$= \frac{s^2\,V_m}{(s+j)^2\,(s-j)^2}$$

$$= \frac{K_1}{(s-j)^2} + \frac{K_1^*}{(s+j)^2} + \frac{K_2}{(s-j)} + \frac{K_2^*}{s+j}$$

$$\therefore \quad K_1 = I(s)(s-j)^2\Big|_{s=j} = \left.\frac{s^2V_m}{(s+j)^2}\right|_{s=j}$$

$$= \frac{j^2V_m}{(2j)^2} = \frac{V_m}{4}$$

$$K_2 = \left| \frac{1}{\lfloor 2-1} \frac{d}{ds}(s-j)^2\, I(s) \right|_{s=j}$$

$$= \left| \frac{(s+j)^2\, V_m\, 2s - V_m\, s^2 \times 2\,(s+j)}{(s+j)^4} \right|_{s=j}$$

$$= -j\, \frac{V_m}{4}$$

$$\therefore \quad K_1^* = \frac{V_m}{4} \text{ and } K_2^* = j\, \frac{V_m}{4}$$

Thus,

$$I(s) = \frac{V_m/4}{(s-j)^2} + \frac{V_m/4}{(s+j)^2} + \frac{-j\,V_m/4}{s-j} + \frac{j\,V_m/4}{s+j}$$

$$= \frac{V_m}{4}\left[\frac{1}{(s-j)^2} + \frac{1}{(s+j)^2} - \frac{j}{s-j} + \frac{j}{s+j}\right]$$

Inverse of Laplace transform gives

$$I(t) = \frac{V_m}{4}\,[t\,e^{jt} + t\,e^{-jt} - j\,e^{jt} + je^{-jt}]$$

$$= \frac{V_m}{4}\left[2t.\frac{e^{jt}+e^{-jt}}{2} - j\,(2\,j)\frac{e^{jt}-e^{-jt}}{(2\,j)}\right]$$

$$= \frac{V_m}{2}\,[\mathbf{t\,cos\,t + sin\,t}].$$

Example 7.79 *If the initial voltage in the capacitor is 1 V with the polarity as shown, find the voltage appearing across the capacitor with application of step voltage 3.*

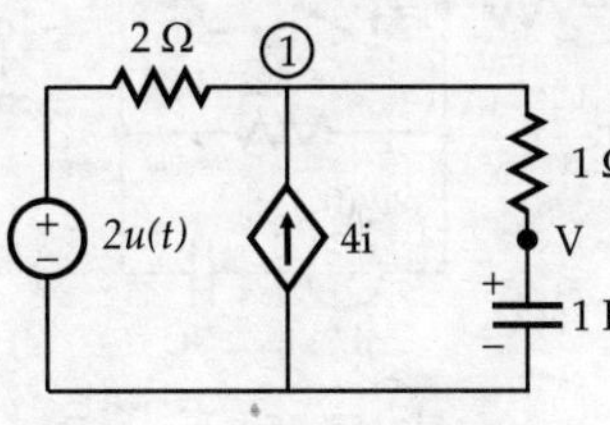

Fig. E7.44

Solution. Transform the circuit to Laplace domain [Fig. 7.44(*a*)]. Let the voltage at node (1) be $V_1(s)$.

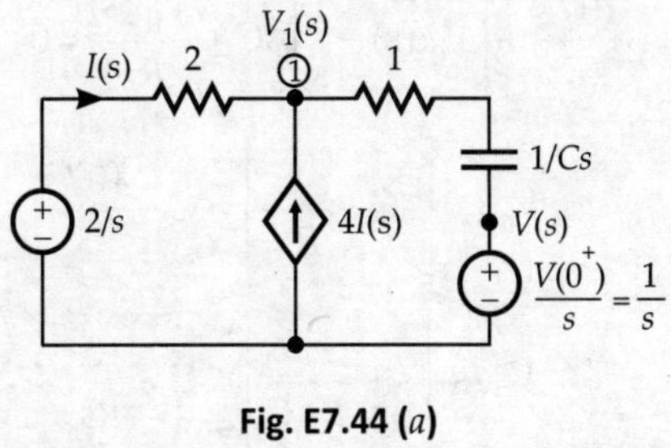

Fig. E7.44 (*a*)

At node (1), we have

$$\frac{V_1(s) - V(s)}{1} = 4I(s) + I(s) = 5I(s)$$

$$\therefore \quad V_1(s) - V(s) = 5I(s) \qquad ...(1)$$

Using KCL in the right hand loop of Fig. 7.44(*a*) at node (2),

$$\frac{V_1(s) - V(s)}{1} = \frac{V(s) - \dfrac{V(0^+)}{s}}{\dfrac{1}{Cs}\,.\,s}$$

$$= \frac{V(s) - \dfrac{1}{s}}{s}$$

or
$$V_1(s) - V(s) = \frac{s\,V(s) - 1}{1} = sV(s) - 1$$

$$V_1(s) - V(s)[s+1] = -1 \qquad ...(2)$$

$$I(s) = \frac{2/s - V_1(s)}{2} \qquad ...(3)$$

However, from equations (1) and (3), we get

$$V_1(s) - V(s) = 5\frac{2/s - V_1(s)}{2}$$

$$= 5 \times \frac{1}{s} - \frac{5}{2}\, V_1(s)$$

$$V_1(s) + 5/2\, V_1(s) - V(s) = \frac{5}{s}$$

$$\frac{7\,V_1(s)}{2} - V(s) = \frac{5}{s} \qquad ...(4)$$

From equations (4) and (2), we have

$$\frac{7}{2}\, V_1(s) - V(s) = \frac{5}{s}$$

$$V_1(s) - V(s)\,[s+1] = -1$$

Solving these two equations

$$V(s) = \frac{7s+10}{s\,(7s+5)} = \frac{A}{s} + \frac{B}{7s+5}$$

i.e.,
$$A = s \times \left.\frac{(7s+10)}{s\,(7s+5)}\right|_{s=0} = 2$$

$$B = \left.\frac{(7s+5)\,(7s+10)}{(s)\,(7s+5)}\right|_{s=-\frac{5}{7}} = -7$$

$$V(s) = \frac{2}{s} - \frac{7}{7s+5} = \frac{2}{s} - \frac{1}{s+\dfrac{5}{7}}$$

Taking the Laplace Inverse

$$V(t) = \mathbf{(2 - e^{-5/7t})} \text{ volts.}$$

EXAMPLE 7.80 *In an LC series circuit (Fig. E7.45), the initial current through the inductor being 2 A, the initial voltage is 10 V. Assume L = 1 H and C = $\frac{1}{2}$ F. Find the voltage across the capacitor at t = 0 +.*

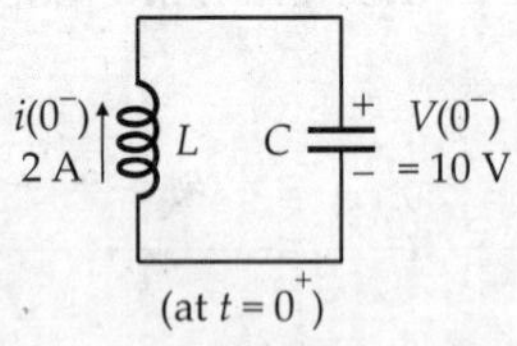

Fig. E7.45

SOLUTION. Let us first transform the given circuit using initial conditions [Fig. E7.45(*a*)] and

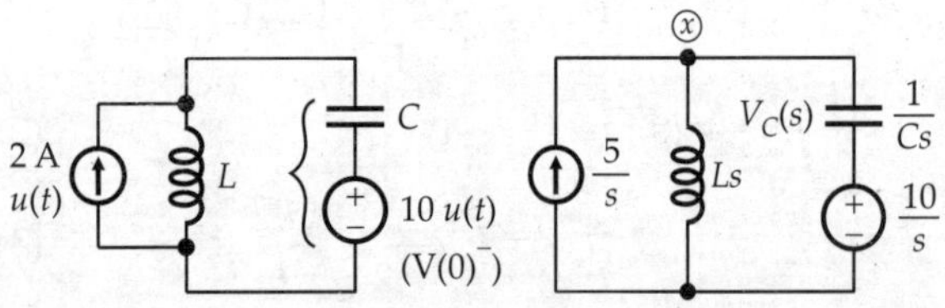

Fig. E7.45 (*a*) (*b*)

then transform the same to Laplace domain [Fig. E7.45(*b*)]. Application of nodal analysis at node (*x*) yields

$$\frac{5}{s} = \frac{V_C(s)}{Ls} + \frac{V_C(s) - \frac{10}{s}}{\frac{1}{Cs}}$$

$$= \frac{V_C(s)}{s} + \frac{V_C(s) - \frac{10}{s}}{\frac{1}{\frac{1}{2}s}}$$

$$= \frac{V_C(s)}{s} + \frac{s\,V_C(s)}{2} - 5$$

or, $$\frac{5}{s} = V_C(s)\left[\frac{1}{s} + \frac{s}{2}\right] - 5 \text{ or } \frac{5}{s} + 5 = V_C(s)\left[\frac{1}{s} + \frac{s}{2}\right]$$

$$\therefore \quad V_C(s) = \frac{\frac{5}{s} + 5}{\frac{1}{s} + \frac{s}{2}} = \frac{\left(\frac{5}{s} + 5\right)s}{\left(\frac{1}{s} + \frac{s}{2}\right)s}$$

$$= \frac{5s + 5}{\frac{s^2}{2} + 1} = \frac{5s}{\frac{s^2}{2} + 1} + \frac{5}{\frac{s^2}{2} + 1}$$

or, $$V_C(s) = \frac{10\,s}{s^2 + 2} + \frac{10}{s^2 + 2}$$

$$= 10\left[\frac{s}{s^2 + 2} + \frac{1}{s^2 + 2}\right]$$

$$= 10\left[\frac{s}{s^2 + (\sqrt{2})^2} + \frac{1}{s^2 + (\sqrt{2})^2}\right]$$

$$= 10\left[\frac{s}{s^2 + (\sqrt{2})^2} + \frac{1}{\sqrt{2}}\frac{\sqrt{2}}{s^2 + (\sqrt{2})^2}\right]$$

$$\therefore \quad \mathbf{V_C(t) = 10\left[\cos\sqrt{2}\,t + \frac{1}{\sqrt{2}}\sin\sqrt{2}\,t\right] V.}$$

EXAMPLE 7.81 *Find $V_0(t)$ at t = 0 +. Assume initial charge in the capacitor to be V [Fig. E7.46].*

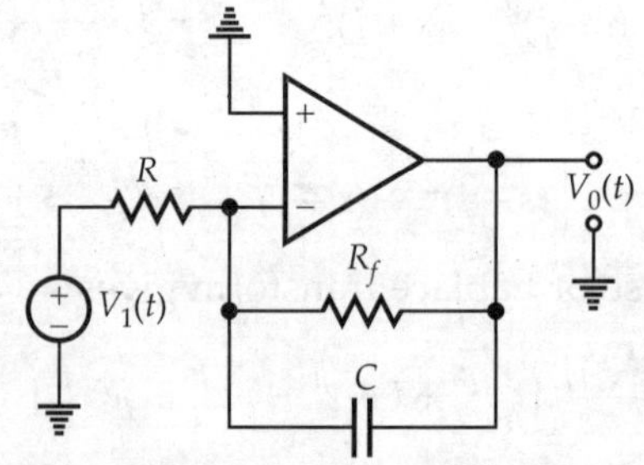

[$R = 10\ \Omega$; $R_f = 10\ \Omega$; $C = 1$ F ; $V_1(t) = 10$ V]

Fig. E7.46

SOLUTION. Let us first convert the given *op*-amp circuit to Laplace domain [Fig. E7.46(*a*)].

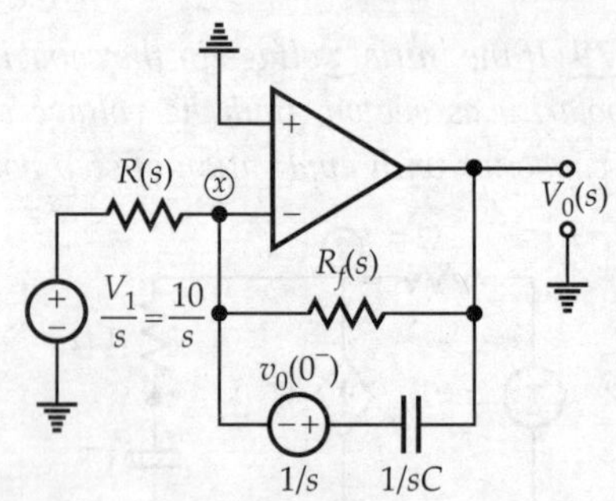

Fig. E7.46(*a*)

Applying KCL at node (*x*),

$$\frac{V_1(s)}{R} + \frac{V_0(s) - v_0(0-)}{1/sC} + \frac{V_0(s)}{R_f} = 0$$

or, $$\frac{10/s}{R} + \left[V_0(s) - \frac{1}{s}\right]sC + \frac{V_0(s)}{R_f} = 0$$

or, $$V_0(s)\left[sC + \frac{1}{R_f}\right] = C - \frac{10/s}{R}$$

or, $$V_0(s)\left[s + \frac{1}{R_f C}\right] = C - \frac{10}{Rs}$$

$$\therefore \quad V_0(s) = \frac{C - 10/Rs}{s + \dfrac{1}{R_f C}}$$

$$= \frac{C}{s + \dfrac{1}{R_f C}} - \frac{10}{Rs\left(s + \dfrac{1}{R_f C}\right)}.$$

Substituting the numerical values,

$$V_0(s) = \frac{1}{s + \dfrac{1}{10}} - \frac{10}{10\,s\left(s + \dfrac{1}{10}\right)}$$

$$= \frac{1}{(s+0.1)} - \frac{1}{s(s+0.1)}$$

However, $$\frac{1}{s(s+0.1)} = \frac{K_1}{s} + \frac{K_2}{s+0.1}$$

when $$K_1 = \frac{1}{s(s+0.1)}\cdot s\Bigg|_{s=0} = 10$$

$$K_2 = \frac{1}{s(s+0.1)}(s+0.1)\Bigg|_{s=-0.1} = -10$$

$$\therefore \quad V_0(s) = \frac{1}{s+0.1} - \frac{10}{s} + \frac{10}{s+0.1}$$

This gives

$$V_0(t) = -10 + e^{-0.1t} + 10\,e^{-0.1t}$$

$$= \mathbf{-10 + 11\,e^{-0.1t}\ V.}$$

EXAMPLE 7.82 *Steady state conditions exist at $t = 0\,(-)$ and switch S is closed at $t = 0$ (Fig. E7.47). Find i_a and i_b in Laplace domain.*

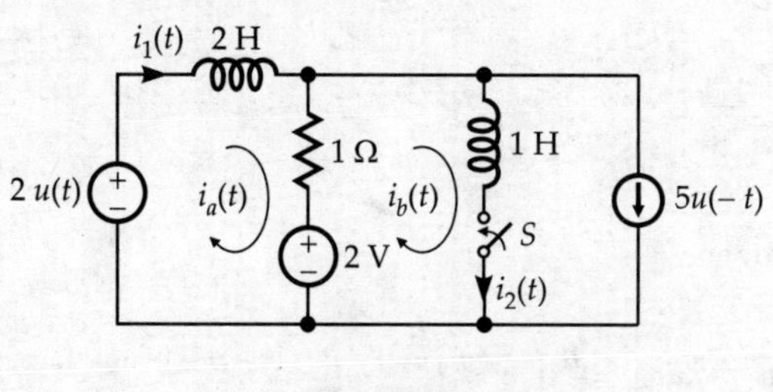

Fig. E7.47

SOLUTION. It may be noted that at $t = 0-$, *i.e.* before switching, the current source was supplying 5 A but the voltage source at the first loop *i.e.*, $2u(t)$ was zero. However 2 V source being constant, it remained active in the circuit. The condition of the circuit at $t = 0\,(-)$ is shown in Fig. E7.48. It may also

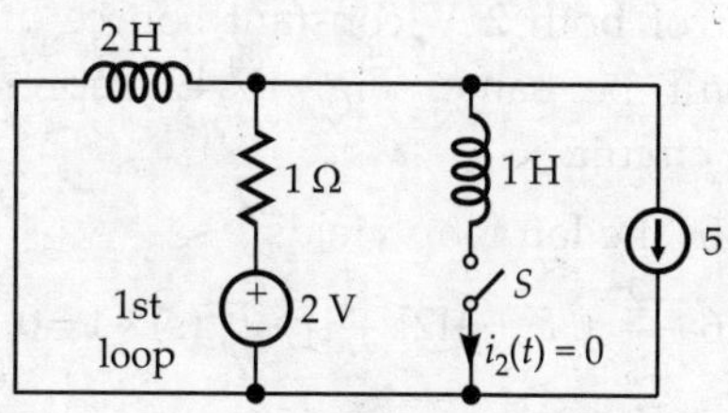

Fig. E7.48

be noted that as the switch remained open at $t = 0\,(-)$ hence, $i_2(t) = 0$. The 2 Henry inductor at in the 1st loop was acting as short circuited and the final equivalent circuit at $t = 0\,(-)$ is shown in Fig. 7.48(*a*).

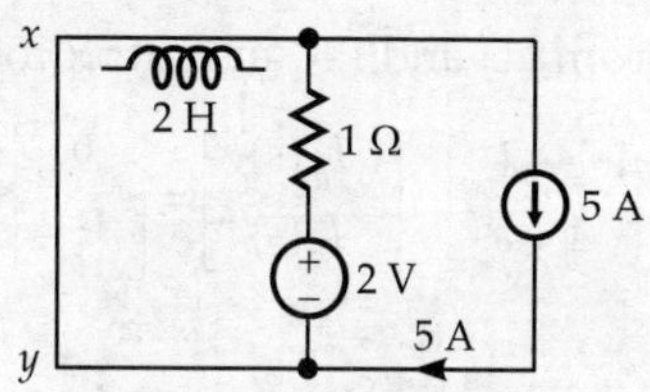

Fig. E7.48 (*a*)

It may be noted here that 2 V source would drive a current $\left(\frac{2}{1}\right)$ A *i.e.*, 2 A through *x-y* branch *i.e.*, through the shorted inductor while 5 A source would drive 5 A current through the shorted inductor at $t = 0\,(-)$. As the two currents are reverse directed, hence, $i_1(t)$, the net current through the inductor at $t = 0\,(-)$ is $(+5\text{ A} - 2\text{ A})$ *i.e.*, 3 A (clockwise through the inductor). Thus we finally obtain $i_2(t) = 0$ and $i_1(t) = 2$ A at $t = 0\,(-)$.

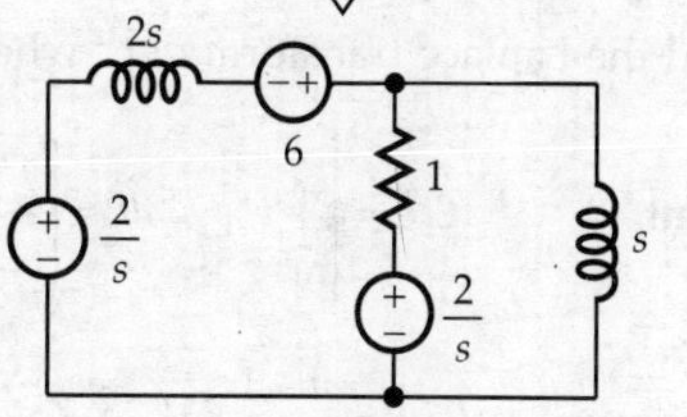

Fig. E7.49

Next, the circuit is converted to *s*-domain at $t = 0^+$. The current source $5\,u(-t)$ will cease to operate as it existed for $t = 0\,(-)$ only. The Laplace transform of both 2 V constant source and 2 $u(t)$ source will be same. Fig. E7.49 represent the s-domain circuit.

KVL in the left loop yields

$$-\frac{2}{s}-6+\frac{2}{s}+I_a(s)[2s+1]-I_b(s)\times 1=0$$

or,
$$I_a(s)[2s+1]-I_b(s)=6 \qquad ...(1)$$

KVL in the right loop yields

$$sI_b(s)-\frac{2}{s}+I_b(s)\times 1-I_a(s)\times 1=0$$

or
$$-I_a(s)+I_b(s)[1+s]=\frac{2}{s} \qquad ...(2)$$

Thus, from (1) and (2), in matrix form,

$$\begin{bmatrix} 2s+1 & -1 \\ -1 & 1+s \end{bmatrix}\begin{bmatrix} I_a(s) \\ I_b(s) \end{bmatrix}=\begin{bmatrix} 6 \\ \frac{2}{s} \end{bmatrix}$$

$$\therefore \quad I_a(s)=\frac{\begin{vmatrix} 6 & -1 \\ \frac{2}{s} & 1+s \end{vmatrix}}{\begin{vmatrix} 2s+1 & -1 \\ -1 & 1+s \end{vmatrix}}=\frac{6+6s-\frac{2}{s}}{2s+2s^2+1+s+1}$$

$$=\frac{\mathbf{6s^2+6s-2}}{\mathbf{s\,(2s^2+3s+2)}}$$

and
$$I_b(s)=\frac{\begin{vmatrix} 2s+1 & 6 \\ -1 & \frac{2}{s} \end{vmatrix}}{\begin{vmatrix} 2s+1 & -1 \\ -1 & 1+s \end{vmatrix}}=\frac{4+\frac{2}{s}-6}{(2s^2+3s+2)}$$

$$=\frac{\mathbf{-2s+2}}{\mathbf{s\,(2s^2+3s+2)}}$$

Thus we have obtained $I_a(s)$ and $I_b(s)$

EXAMPLE 7.83 *A voltage is expressed as*

$$V(s)=\frac{s+1}{s(s^2+4s+4)}.$$

If this voltage is applied across a resistance of 0.25 Ω only, find the current through the resistor in time domain.

SOLUTION. We can write $V(s)$ as

$$V(s)=\frac{s+1}{s(s+2)^2}$$

$$=\frac{K_1}{s}+\frac{K_2}{s+2}+\frac{K_3}{(s+2)^2}$$

Here $$K_1=\left.\frac{s+1}{(s+2)^2}\right|_{s=0}=\frac{1}{4}$$

$$K_3=\left.\frac{s+1}{s}\right|_{s=-2}=\frac{1}{2}$$

Also, $$K_2=-\frac{1}{4}.$$

$$\therefore \quad V(s)=\frac{1/4}{s}-\frac{1/4}{s+2}+\frac{1/2}{(s+2)^2}$$

Taking inverse of $V(s)$, we get

$$v(t)=\frac{1}{4}-\frac{1}{4}e^{-2t}+\frac{1}{2}te^{-2t} \text{ volts}$$

Since $i(t)=\frac{v(t)}{R}$, we get

$$\mathbf{i(t)=(1-e^{-2t}-2te^{-2t})\ A.}$$

EXERCISES

1. Find the Laplace transform of t^n where n is a positive integer.

[**Hint.** $$£t^n=\left[\int_0^\infty t^n e^{-st}dt=\left[\frac{t^n e^{-st}}{s}\right]_0^\infty-\int_0^\infty \frac{e^{-st}}{-s}nt^{n-1}dt\right]=\frac{n}{s}\int_0^\infty e^{-st}t^{n-1}dt=\frac{n}{s}£t^{n-1}$$

Similarly $$£t^{n-1}=\frac{n-1}{s}£t^{n-2}$$

$$\therefore \quad £t^n=\frac{n}{s}\cdot\frac{n-1}{s}\cdot\frac{n-2}{s}\cdots\cdots\frac{2}{s}\cdot\frac{1}{s}£(t^{n-n})=\frac{n!}{s^n}\times\frac{1}{s}=\frac{n!}{s^{n+1}}\Big]$$

2. Obtain the Laplace transform of "cosh rt".

[**Hint.** $\pounds(\cosh rt) = \int_0^\infty \cos h(rt)\, e^{-st}\, dt = \int_0^\infty \left[\frac{e^{rt} + e^{-rt}}{2}\right] e^{-st}\, dt$

$= \frac{1}{2}\int_0^\infty e^{-(s-r)t}\, dt + \frac{1}{2}\int_0^\infty e^{-(s+r)t}\, dt = \frac{1}{2}\frac{1}{(s-r)} + \frac{1}{2}\frac{1}{(s+r)} = \frac{s}{s^2 - r^2}$.]

3. Obtain the Laplace transform of sin h (rt)

[**Hint.** $\pounds(\sin h\, rt) = \int_0^\infty \sin h(rt)\, dt$

$= \int_0^\infty \left[\frac{e^{rt} - e^{-rt}}{2}\right] e^{-st}\, dt = \frac{a}{s^2 - a^2}$.]

4. Find the Laplace transform of the function $f(t) = \cos^2 \theta$.

[**Hint.** $\pounds(\cos^2\theta) = \pounds\left(\frac{1+\cos 2\theta}{2}\right) = \pounds\left(\frac{1}{2}\right) + \pounds\left(\frac{\cos 2\theta}{2}\right)$

$= \frac{1}{2s} + \frac{1}{2}\cdot\frac{s}{s^2+4} = \frac{2s^2+4}{2s\,(s^2+4)}$.]

5. Find the value of $\frac{d}{ds}F(s)$ in usual Laplace transform form.

[**Hint.** $\frac{d}{ds}F(s) = \frac{d}{ds}\int_0^\infty f(t)\, e^{-st}\, dt = \int_0^\infty \frac{\partial}{\partial s}[f(t)\, e^{-st}]\, dt = \int_0^\infty f(t)[-te^{-st}]\, dt$

$= -\int_0^\infty [tf(t)]\, e^{-st}\, dt = -\pounds[t\, f(t)]$

Also, $\pounds[t\, f(t)] = -\frac{d}{ds}F(s)$]

6. Find the Laplace transform of $f(t) = t \sin 2t$

[**Hint.** $f_1(t) = \sin 2t \quad \therefore \quad \pounds f_1(t) = \pounds[\sin 2t] = F_1(s)$

$\therefore \quad F_1(s) = \frac{2}{s^2+4}$, Hence $\pounds[t\, f_1(t)] = \pounds(t \sin 2t)$

$= -\frac{d}{ds}\left[\frac{2}{s^2+4}\right] = \frac{4s}{(s^2+4)^2}$.]

7. Find the initial value of the following functions (*i*) $2e^{-3t}$ (*ii*) $2 - e^{3t}$ (*iii*) $e^{-\theta}(\sin 3\theta + \cos 5\theta)$

[**Hint.** (*i*) $f(t) = 2e^{-3t} \quad \therefore F(s) = \frac{2}{s+3}$ or, $sF(s) = \frac{2s}{(s+3)} \quad \therefore \quad \underset{s\to\infty}{\text{Lt}}\ sF(s) = \underset{s\to\infty}{\text{Lt}}\ \frac{2}{s+3/s} = 2$

(*ii*) $f(t) = 2 - e^{5t} \quad \therefore F(s) = \pounds(2 - e^{5t}) = (2/s) - (1/(s-5))$

(*iii*) $\pounds[e^{-\theta}(\sin 3\theta + \cos 5\theta)] = F(s) = \pounds\, e^{-\theta}\sin 3\theta + \pounds\, e^{-\theta}\cos 5\theta$

$= \frac{3}{(s+1)^2+3^2} + \frac{s+1}{(s+1)^2+5^2}$

$\therefore \ sF(s) = \frac{3s}{s^2\left(1+\frac{2}{s}+\frac{10}{s}\right)} + \frac{s^2+s}{s^2\left(1+\frac{2}{s}+\frac{26}{s^2}\right)} = \frac{3}{s\left(1+\frac{2}{s}+\frac{10}{s^2}\right)} + \frac{1}{\left(1+\frac{2}{s}+\frac{26}{s^2}\right)} + \frac{1}{s\left(1+\frac{2}{s}+\frac{26}{s^2}\right)}$

$\therefore \quad \underset{s\to\infty}{\text{Lt}}\ sF(s) = 1$]

8. Find the final value of the following functions :

(*i*) $1 + e^{-2t}\cos 5t$ (*ii*) $2 - 2e^{-t}$. (*iii*) $e^{-t}(\sin 3t + \cos 5t)$

CHAPTER 7

[**Hint.** *(i)* $f(t) = 1 + e^{-2t}\cos 5t \quad \therefore \; F(s) = \frac{1}{s} + \frac{s+2}{(s+2)^2 + 25} \quad \therefore \; sF(s) = 1 + \frac{s(s+2)}{(s+2)^2 \; 25}$ or, $\underset{s \to 0}{\text{Lt}}\; sF(s) = 1$

(ii) $f(t) = 2 - 2e^{-t} \quad \therefore \; F(s) = \frac{2}{s} - \frac{2}{s+1} \quad \therefore \; sF(s) = 2 - \frac{2s}{(s+1)}$ or, $\underset{s \to 0}{\text{Lt}}\; sF(s) = 2$

(iii) As done in the previous problem, if $f(t) = e^{-t}(\sin 3t + \cos 5t)$,

$$sF(s) = \frac{3}{s\left(1 + \frac{2}{s} + \frac{10}{s^2}\right)} + \frac{1}{1 + \frac{2}{s} + \frac{26}{s^2}} + \frac{1}{s\left(1 + \frac{2}{s} + \frac{26}{s^2}\right)} \quad \therefore \; \underset{s \to 0}{\text{Lt}}\; sF(s) = 0. \;]$$

9. Find the inverse transfer of by $\left(\frac{s+3}{s+5}\right)$.

[**Hint.** Let $F(s) = \log\left(\frac{s+3}{s+5}\right) \quad \therefore \; \frac{d}{ds}F(s) = \frac{d}{ds}\left[\log\frac{(s+3)}{(s+5)}\right] = \frac{1}{s+3} - \frac{1}{s+5}$

However, $£^{-1}\left[\frac{d}{ds}F(s)\right] = -t\, f(t) \quad \therefore \; £^{-1}\left[\frac{d}{ds}F(s)\right] = £\left[\frac{1}{s+3} - \frac{1}{s+5}\right] = e^{-3t} - e^{-5t}$

$\therefore \quad f(t) = -\frac{1}{t}(e^{-3t} - e^{-5t}) = \frac{e^{-5t} - e^{-3t}}{t}$.]

10. A ramp voltage of $v = 5\,r(t-2)$ is applied in a series RC circuit. Find the response if $R = 1\,ohm$ and $C = (1/4)$ Farad.

[**Hint.** $Ri(t) + \frac{1}{C}\int_{-\infty}^{t} i(t)\,dt = v(t) = 5r(t-2)$

$$\therefore \quad I(s) = \frac{5(e^{-2s}/s^2)}{\left(R + \frac{1}{Cs}\right)} = 5\frac{e^{-2s}}{s^2}\cdot\frac{1}{1 + \frac{4}{s}} = \frac{5e^{-2s}}{s(s+4)} = \frac{5}{4}\left[\frac{e^{-2s}}{s} - \frac{e^{-2s}}{s+4}\right]$$

$$\therefore \quad \frac{1}{s(s+4)} = \frac{1}{4}\left(\frac{1}{s} - \frac{1}{s+4}\right).$$

Here $i(t) = \frac{5}{4}[u(t-2) - e^{-4(t-2)}\,u(t-2)]$.]

11. A step voltage of 10 V is applied at $t = 0$ in a series RC circuit where $R = 1\Omega$ and $C = 2$F. The initial charge of the capacitor is nil. Using Laplace transformation, find $i(t)$.

[**Hint.** for the text, $i(t) = \left(\frac{E}{R} - \frac{Q_0}{RC}\right)e - \frac{t}{RC}$ However, here $Q_0 = 0. \quad \therefore \; i(t) = \frac{E}{R}e^{-t/RC} = 10\,e^{-0.5t}$.]

12. A series RL circuit experiences an exponential voltage $v = 10\,e^{-100t}$ after closing a switch at $t = 0$. Assume $R = 1\Omega$, $L = 0.1$ H.

[**Hint.** $Ri(t) + L\frac{di(t)}{dt} = v = 10e^{-100t}$

Laplace transform of this equation gives $RI(s) + sLI(s) - Li(0+) = \frac{10}{s+100}$.

Assuming, $i(0) = 0$, $\quad I(s) = \frac{10/(s+100)}{(R+sL)} = \frac{10/(s+100)}{(1+0.1s)}$

$$\frac{10}{(s+100)}\cdot\frac{10}{(10+s)} = \frac{100}{(s+10)(s+10)} = \frac{K_1}{s+10} + \frac{K_2}{s+100}.$$

$$K_1 = \frac{100}{90}, \; K_2 = -\frac{100}{90}.$$

$$\therefore \quad I(s) = \frac{100}{90(s+10)} - \frac{100}{10(s+100)} = \frac{10}{9(s+10)} - \frac{10}{9(s+100)} \quad \therefore \; i(t) = \frac{10}{9}[e^{-10t} - e^{-100t}]\,\text{A}. \;]$$

13. A function in s-domain is given by $F(s) = \dfrac{2s^2 + 6s + 1}{(2s^2 + 5s + 3)\, s}$. Find (*i*) $f(t)$ and (*ii*) the final value.

[**Hint.** Solve in same way as done in Example 7.26]

14. In the circuit of Fig. P7.1, steady state is reached with the switch at position "*a*". At $t = 0$, switching is done to "*b*" such that the circuit goes to discharging mode. Obtain the expression for the circuit current at $t = 0+$.

[**Hint.** Refer to Example 7.28]

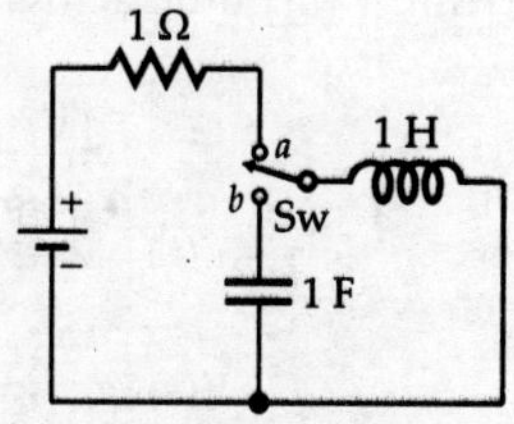

Fig. P7.1

15. Find $f(t)$ when $F(s) = \dfrac{1}{s^2 (s + \alpha)^3}$.

[**Hint.** Solve as done in Example 7.29]

16. Find $f(t)$ when $F(s) = \dfrac{2s^3 + 4s^2 + 10s + 5}{s^2 + 5s + 6}$

[**Hint.** Solve as done in Example 7.31]

17. A function in Laplace domain is given by

$$X(s) = \frac{2s^2 + 10\,s + 5}{(s + 1)(s + 2)(s + 3)}$$

[**Hint.** Refer to Example 7.36]

18. Find $i(t)$ following switching at $t = 0$. Assume initial charge on capacitor as 100 μC (Fig. P7.2).

[**Hint.** Refer to Example 7.41]

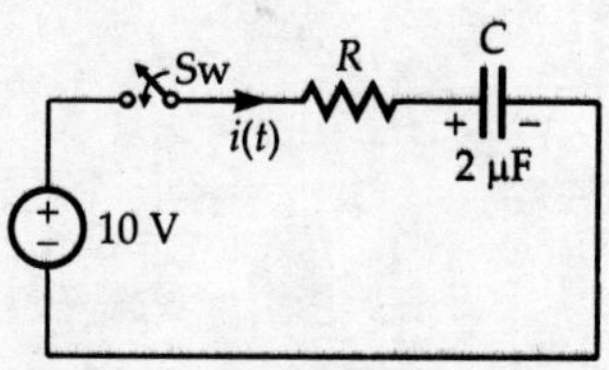

Fig. P7.2

19. A second order differential equation is given by

$$\frac{d^2 f(t)}{dt^2} + 3\frac{df(t)}{dt} + 2f(t) = 2e^{-t}.$$

Solve the equation using Laplace transform subject to the initial conditions of $f(0+) = 2$ and $\dfrac{df(0+)}{dt} = 0$

[**Hint.** Do in the same way as done in Example 7.49]

20. A function is given by $X(s) = \dfrac{2(s + 2)}{(s + 1)(s + 3)}$. Find its value using the initial and final value theorem.

[**Hint.** Refer to Example 7.55]

21. It is given that $F(s) = \dfrac{s^4 + 2s^3 + s^2 + 1}{s(s + 3)}$. Find the partial fraction expression.

[**Hint.** Dividing $(s^4 + 2s^3 + s^2 + 1)$ by $(s^2 + 3s)$, the quotient is $(s^2 - s + 4)$ and remainder is $(-12s + 1)$.

$$\therefore \quad \frac{s^4 + 2s^3 + s^2 + 1}{s^2 + 3s} = (s^2 - s + 4) + \frac{-12s + 1}{s(s + 3)}$$

Let $\dfrac{-12s + 1}{s(s + 3)} = \dfrac{A}{s} + \dfrac{B}{s + 3}$ where $A = \dfrac{(-12s + 1)}{s(s + 3)} \cdot s \Big|_{s=0} = \dfrac{1}{3}$

and $B = \dfrac{-12s + 1}{s(s + 3)} \cdot (s + 3)\Big|_{s=-3} = -\dfrac{37}{3}$.

$$\therefore \quad \frac{-12s + 1}{s(s + 3)} = \frac{1/3}{s} + \frac{-37/3}{s + 3} = \frac{1/3}{s} - \frac{37/3}{s + 3}$$

$$\therefore \quad \frac{s^4 + 2s^3 + s^2 + 1}{s(s + 3)} = s^2 - s + 4 + \frac{1/3}{s} - \frac{37/3}{s + 3} \quad \text{(Partial fraction obtained).}\ ]$$

22. Given $V(t) = 5u(t)$. Find the output $V_0(t)$ for $t > 0$ in Fig. P7.3. Assume steady state deenergized condition of the circuit at $t < 0$.

[**Hint.** $V(t)$ = drop across $2\,\Omega + V_0(t)$

$$= i(t) \times 2 + V_0(t) = C\frac{dV_0(t)}{dt} \times 2 + V_0(t)$$

or, $$V(t) = 2\frac{dV_0(t)}{dt} + V_0(t)$$

$\therefore$ $$V(s) = 2[s\,V_0(s) - v_0(0-)] + V_0(s)$$

$\therefore$ $$V_0(s) = \frac{1}{2s+1}V(s) + \frac{2V_0(0-)}{2s+1} = \frac{0.5}{s+0.5}\,.\,V(s)$$

$$(\because\ v_0(0-) = 0)$$

or, $$\frac{0.5}{s+0.5}\ \pounds\ 5u(t) = V_0(s) = \frac{0.5 \times 5}{(s+0.5)\,s}$$

or, $$V_0(s) = \frac{2.5}{s(s+0.5)} = \frac{K_1}{s} + \frac{K_2}{s+0.5}$$

when $K_1 = 5,\ K_2 = -5$

$\therefore$ $$V_0(s) = \frac{5}{s} - \frac{5}{s+0.5} \quad \text{or,} \quad V_0(t) = 5 - 5e^{-0.5t}\,.\,]$$

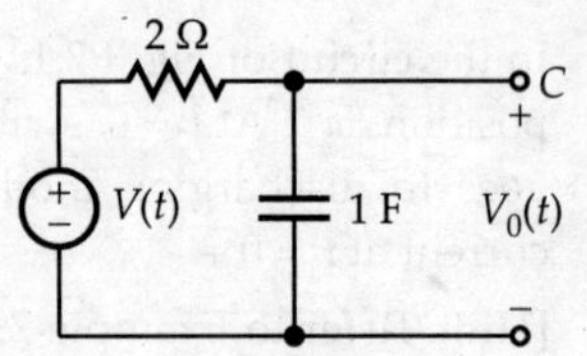

Fig. P7.3

CHAPTER 8

Analysis of Special Signal Waveforms

8.1 INTRODUCTION

Circuits frequently experience response of the sources having complicated waveforms such as rectangular, pulse, square wave, ramp type etc. in addition to step d.c., exponential or sinusoidal (the circuit responses to these signals have been discussed amply in the other parts of this book). The signals may be recurrent type or non-recurrent type and mostly involve the passive circuits. This chapter deals with analysis of these basic types of signals, termed as *special signals*, which are reasonably common.

8.2 BASIC TYPES OF SPECIAL SIGNALS

Shifted Unit Step Function

This function remains at zero value till $t = a$ and at $t = a$, it abruptly changes from 0 to unity.

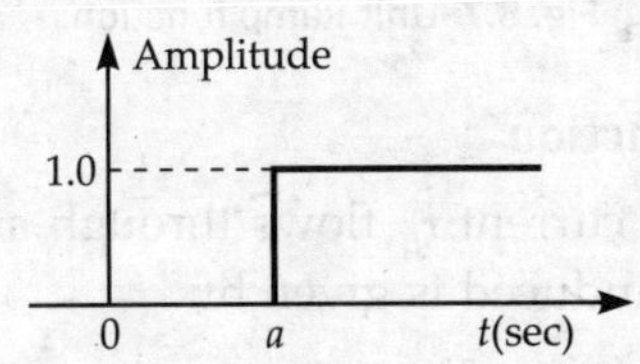

Fig. 8.1 Shifted Unit Step function $u(t - a)$.

It is expressed as

$$u(t-a) = \begin{cases} 0, & t < a \\ 1, & t \geq a \end{cases}$$

and is shown in Fig. 8.1 [the quantity $(t - a)$ is called the *argument* of the function].

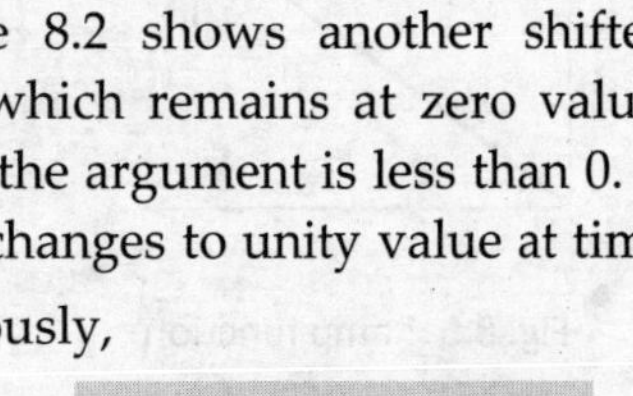

Fig. 8.2 Shifted Unit step function $u(t + a)$.

Figure 8.2 shows another shifted unit step function which remains at zero value as long as $(t + a)$ *i.e.,* the argument is less than 0. The function abruptly changes to unity value at time $t = -a$.

Obviously,

$$u(t+a) = \begin{cases} 0, & t < -a \\ 1, & t \geq -a \end{cases}$$

Similarly, two other forms of shifted unit step functions are shown in Figs. 8.3 and 8.4. The function in Fig. 8.3 is $u(a - t)$ and remains zero so long as $(a - t)$, the argument, is negative *i.e.,* $(a - t) < 0$ or $t > a$.

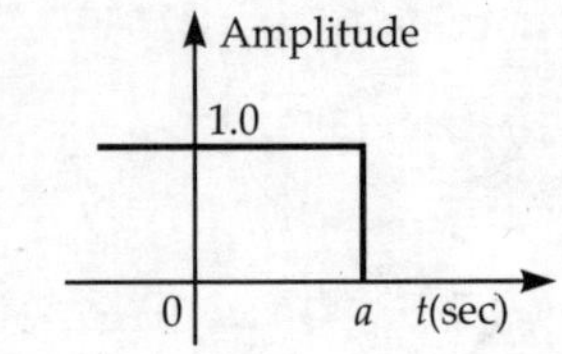

Fig. 8.3 Shifted Unit Step function $u(a-t)$.

It abruptly rises to unity value for positive value of argument $(a-t)$ *i.e.*, when $t<a$.

Obviously, $$u(a-t)=\begin{cases}0, & t>a\\ 1, & t\le a\end{cases}$$

Figure 8.4 represents another form of shifted unit step function which remains of zero value as long as the argument $(-a-t)$ is negative *i.e.*, till $(-t-a)<0$ or,

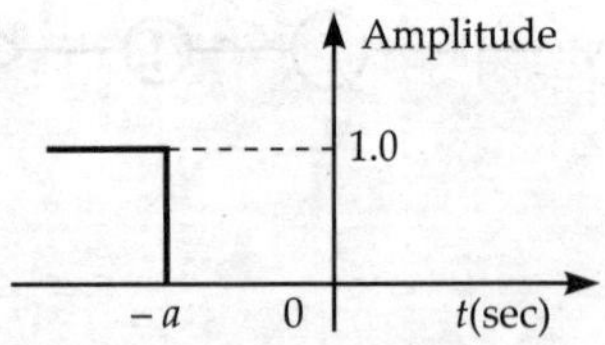

Fig. 8.4 Shifted Unit Step function $u(-t-a)$.

$t>-a$. The value of the function abruptly becomes unity at $t=-a$ and remains so for $t<-a$.

It is represented as

$$u(-t-a)=\begin{cases}0, & t>-a\\ 1, & t\le -a\end{cases}$$

Ramp Function

When a time variant current or voltage increases linearly with time, it is known as *ramp function* or simply an ordinary *ramp* (Fig. 8.5).

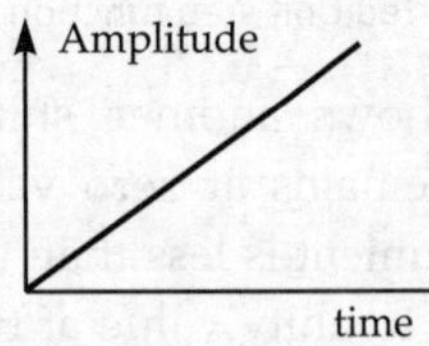

Fig. 8.5 Ramp function

To give a practical example of a ramp function, let us consider a unit step voltage applied to an inductor of L Henry (Fig. 8.6).

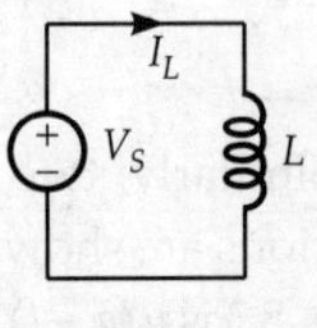

Fig. 8.6 Example to show ramp function.

Obviously, $$I_L=\frac{1}{L}\int_{-\infty}^{t} V_S\,dt$$

where $V_S=u(t)=1.0$

Assuming zero initial condition, $i_L(0+)=0$.

$$\therefore \qquad I_L=\frac{t}{L}.$$

This response current constitutes the ramp function where the inductor current is seen to vary linearly with time (Fig. 8.6(a)).

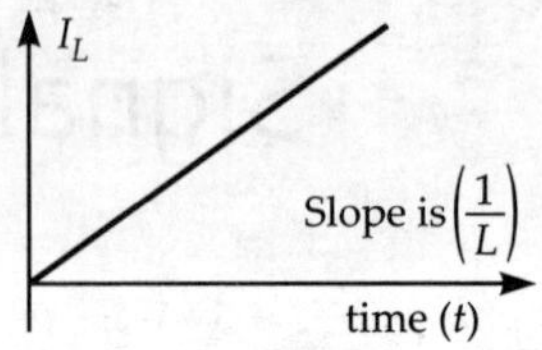

Fig. 8.6 (a) Inductor current *vs* time.

Similarly, if a unit step current is applied to a capacitor C, the capacitor voltage would be

$$V_C=\frac{1}{C}\int_{-\infty}^{t} i_C\,dt=\frac{1}{C}\int_{-\infty}^{t} u(t)\,dt.$$

This, with zero initial condition gives [*i.e.*, V_C at $0^+=0$]

$$V_C=\frac{t}{C}.$$

This voltage response constitutes the ramp function where the capacitor voltage is seen to vary linearly with time. Thus, the response of unit step function of voltage to inductor and of current to capacitor gives us the ramp function of response *i.e.*, the inductor current and capacitor voltage. To clarify further, it can be said that the *integration of unit step function results in unit ramp function* (Fig. 8.7).

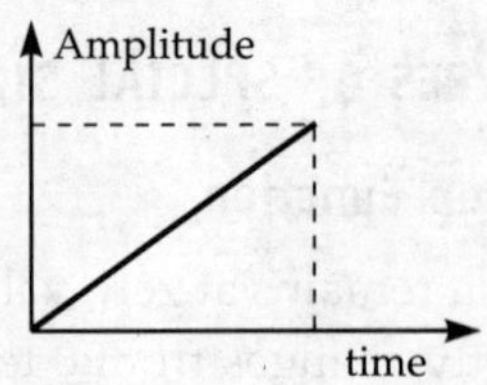

Fig. 8.7 Unit Ramp function.

Impulse Function

When a current i_L flows through an inductor, the voltage induced is given by

$$v_L=L\frac{di_L}{dt}\quad (v_L \text{ is directed to oppose } i_L)$$

Assuming $i_L = u(t)$, the step function, $\frac{di_L}{dt} = 0$.

Thus the derivative $\frac{di_L}{dt}$ is zero for all time except $t = 0$ *i.e.,* at the moment when stepping occurs. At $t = 0$, the slope would become infinite as $\frac{di_L}{dt}$ is infinite at $t = 0$. Thus the response of step current at the inductor makes an impulse [*i.e.,* the function is infinite at $t = 0$ and zero at $t > 0$] (Fig. 8.8). Similarly, application of unit step voltage to a capacitor C results in impulse current given by

$$i_C = C\frac{dv_C}{dt}$$

$$\left[\text{obviously, } \frac{dv_C}{dt} = 0 \text{ at } t > 0 \text{ and infinity at } t = 0\right]$$

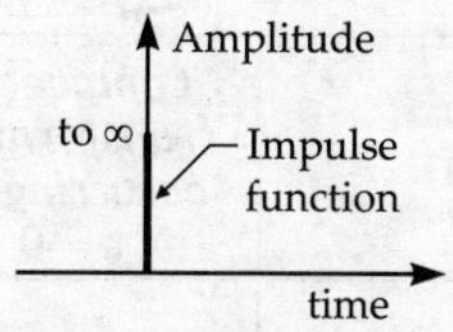

Fig. 8.8 Impulse function.

The above examples clearly show that :

Differentiation of step function results in impulse function.

$$\frac{d}{dt}u(t - t_1) = \delta(t - t_1) = \begin{cases} 0 & \text{for } t \neq t_1 \\ = \infty & \text{for } t = t_1. \end{cases}$$

An unit impulse function is denoted by $\delta(t - t_1)$, where t_1 is the instant of time at which the pulse occurs. Obviously, if the pulse occurs at origin of the axis, $t_1 = 0$ leading to the unit impulse function to be $\delta(t)$. Further, as the differentiation of step function results to impulse function, hence we can say that :

The integration of unit impulse function would result in a unit step function.

i.e., $$\int_{-\infty}^{t} \delta(t - t_1)\,dt \begin{cases} = 0 & \text{for } t < t_1 \\ = 1 & \text{for } t \geq t_1 \end{cases}$$

Figure 8.9 indicates the transformation of impulse and step function.

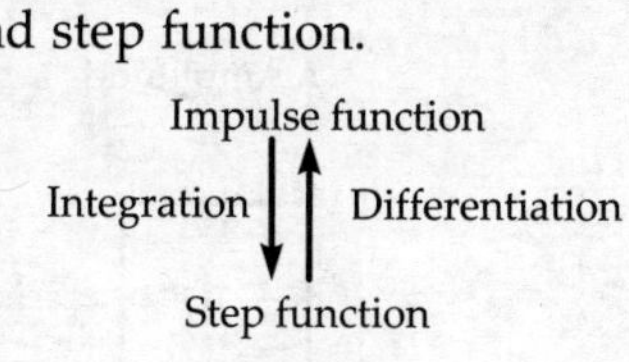

Fig. 8.9

Unit Doublet Function

Differentiating a unit impulse function with respect to t, we find

$$\frac{d}{dt}\delta(t - t_1)\begin{cases} = 0, & t \neq t_1 \\ = +\infty \text{ and } -\infty, & t = t_1. \end{cases}$$

The function $\frac{d}{dt}\delta(t - t_1)$ is called *unit doublet function*. Fig. 8.10 represents such a function. For academic interest, it may be noted that starting from unit step function, successive integrations result in new functions (as discussed above and summarised below in Fig. 8.11).

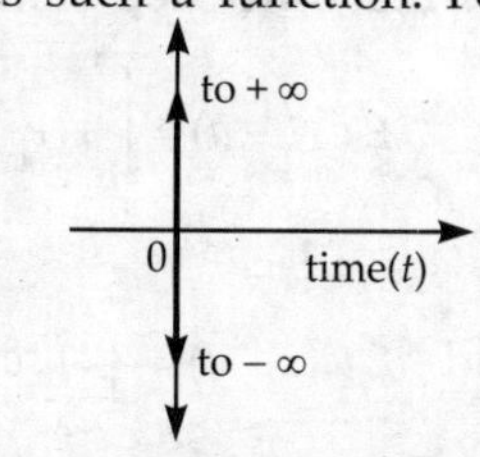

Fig. 8.10 Unit doublet function.

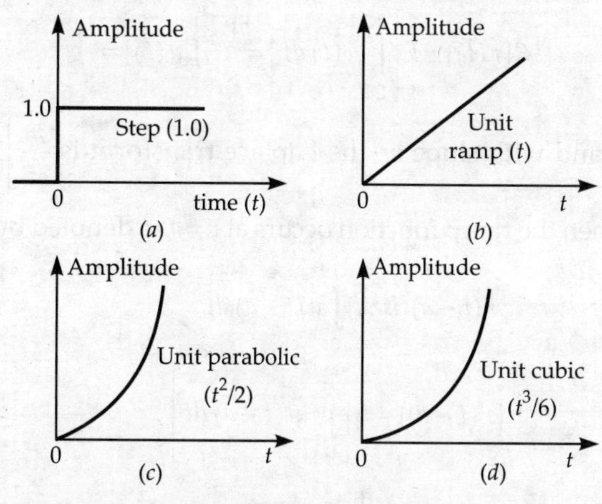

Fig. 8.11 Successive integration of unit step function ; (on integration of unit step function of Fig. *(a)* results to unit ramp of Fig. *(b)* which on further integration leads to unit parabolic of Fig. *(c)* and then to unit cubic function of Fig. *(d)*)

It may be recalled here that :

Differentiation of unit step function gives unit impulse function which on further differentiation gives unit doublet function (Fig. 8.12).

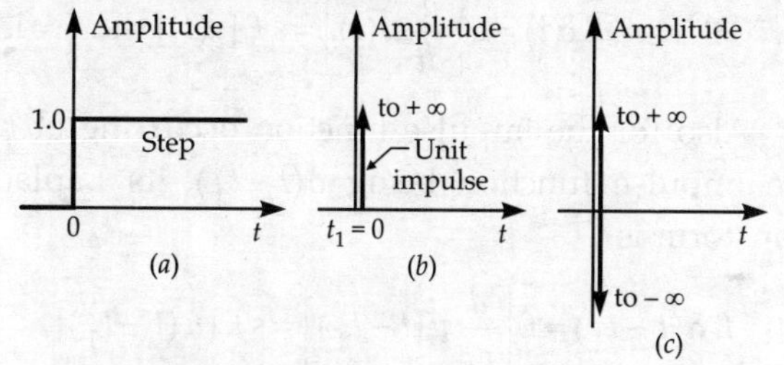

Fig. 8.12 Differentiation of Fig. *(a)* gives Fig. *(b) i.e.,* unit impulse function which on further differentiation gives unit doublet function (Fig. *(c)*)

8.3 LAPLACE TRANSFORMATION OF SPECIAL SIGNAL WAVEFORMS

Unit Step Function

$$\pounds\, u(t) = \int_0^{\infty} 1.e^{-st}\, dt = \left[\frac{-e^{-st}}{s}\right]_0^{\infty} = \frac{1}{s}.$$

Shifted Unit Step Function

$$\pounds\, u(t-a) = \int_a^{\infty} 1.e^{-st}\, dt = \left[\frac{-e^{-st}}{s}\right]_a^{\infty} = \left(\frac{1}{s}\right) e^{-as}$$

and $\pounds\, u(t+a) = \int_{-a}^{\infty} 1.e^{-st}\, dt = \left[\frac{-e^{-st}}{s}\right]_{-a}^{\infty} = \left(\frac{1}{s}\right) e^{as}.$

Ramp Function

$$\pounds[r(t)] = \pounds\left[\int_0^t u(t)\, dt\right] = \frac{1}{s}\pounds[u(t)] = \frac{1}{s^2},$$

$\left[\text{and with slope } m\text{, the Laplace transform is } \frac{m}{s^2}\right]$

when the ramp function occurs at $t = a$, is denoted by

$$r(t-a) \text{ i.e., } \int_0^t u(t-a)\, dt\,;$$

$$\therefore \quad \pounds[r(t-a)] = \pounds\left[\int_0^t u(t-a)\, dt\right];$$

$$= \frac{1}{s}\pounds\, u(t-a)$$

$$= \frac{1}{s}.\frac{1}{s}.e^{-as} = \frac{e^{-as}}{s^2}.$$

[with slope m, the ramp function becomes $m\frac{e^{-as}}{s^2}$ in s-domain].

Impulse Function

$$\pounds\, \delta(t) = \pounds\left[\frac{d}{dt}u(t)\right] = s\,\pounds[u(t)] = s.\frac{1}{s} = 1.$$

Also for the impulse function occurring at t_1, the impulse function being $\delta(t-t_1)$, its Laplace transform is

$$\pounds\, \delta(t-t_1) = \pounds\left[\frac{d}{dt}u(t-t_1)\right] = s\,\pounds[u(t-t_1)]$$

$$= s.\frac{e^{-t_1 s}}{s} = e^{-t_1 s}.$$

Unit Doublet Function

Let the function occurs at t_1. The function is then represented by $\delta'(t-t_1)$.

Obviously,

$$\delta'(t-t_1) = \frac{d}{dt}\delta(t-t_1)$$

$$\pounds[\delta'(t-t_1)] = \pounds\left[\frac{d}{dt}\delta(t-t_1)\right]$$

$$= s\pounds\, \delta(t-t_1) = se^{-t_1 s}.$$

Obviously, $\delta'(t) = s$ and the Laplace transform of a doublet function with slope m is

$$\pounds[m\delta'(t-t_1)] = m\pounds[\delta'(t-t_1)] = mse^{-t_1 s}.$$

The following table shows the Laplace transform of unit functions.

Table 8.1 *Laplace Transform of Unit Functions*

Function	Laplace transform occurring at t = 0	Laplace transform occurring at t = a
$u(t)$ [unit step function]	$\frac{1}{s}$	$\frac{1}{s}e^{-as}$
$r(t)$ [ramp function]	$\frac{1}{s^2}$	$\frac{e^{-as}}{s^2}$
$\delta(t)$ [impulse function]	1	$e^{-t_1 s}$ [$a = t_1$ here]
$\delta'(t)$ [doublet function]	s	se^{-as}
$p(t)$ [unit parabolic function]	$\frac{1}{s^3}$	$\frac{1}{s^3}e^{-as}$

EXAMPLE 8.1 *A series R-L circuit has $R = 2\,\Omega$ and $L = 1$ H. A pulse voltage of magnitude 4 V and width θ is applied at $t = 0$. Assuming initial current through the inductor to be zero, find $i(t)$.*

SOLUTION. A pulse voltage of magnitude 4 V, width θ is shown in Fig. E8.1 and can be represented by $[u(t) - u(t-\theta)]\,4$. At $t = 0$, this impulse being applied in the R-L circuit, the KVL yields

$$Ri(t) + L\frac{di(t)}{dt} = 4\,[u(t) - u(t-\theta)].$$

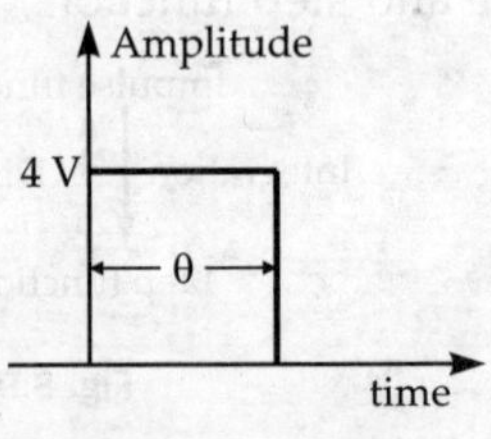

Fig. E8.1

Laplace transformation of this equation yields

$$RI(s) + L[sI(s) - i(0+)] = \frac{4}{s}[1 - e^{-\theta s}].$$

However, $i(0+) = 0$. Thus finally,

$$RI(s) + Ls\,I(s) = \frac{4}{s}(1 - e^{-\theta s})$$

or,
$$I(s) = \frac{4}{s}\,\frac{1 - e^{-\theta s}}{R + Ls} = \frac{4}{s}\,\frac{1 - e^{-\theta s}}{2 + s}$$

$$= \frac{4}{s(s+2)}.(1 - e^{-\theta s}).$$

However, $\dfrac{4}{s(s+2)} = \dfrac{K_1}{s} + \dfrac{K_2}{s+2}$

where $K_1 = \left.\dfrac{4}{s+2}\right|_{s=0} = 2$;

$$K_2 = \left.\frac{4}{s}\right|_{s=-2} = -2$$

i.e., $\dfrac{4}{s(s+2)} = \dfrac{2}{s} - \dfrac{2}{s+2}$.

Thus $I(s) = \left[\dfrac{2}{s} - \dfrac{2}{s+2}\right][1 - e^{-\theta s}]$

$$= \frac{2}{s} - \frac{2e^{-\theta s}}{s} - \frac{2}{s+2} + \frac{2e^{-\theta s}}{s+2};$$

$$\therefore \quad \boldsymbol{i(t) = 2\,[u(t) - u(t)\,e^{-2t} - u(t-\theta) + u(t-\theta)\,e^{-2(t-\theta)}].}$$

Example 8.2 *In a R-L series circuit assume $R = 10\,\Omega$ while L = 2 H. Assuming the initial current through the inductor to be zero, find i (t) following the application of an unit impulse voltage at t = 0.*

Solution. The unit impulse voltage being represented by $\delta(t)$ in time domain, application of KVL in the *R-L* circuit yields

$$L\frac{di(t)}{dt} + R\,i(t) = \delta(t).$$

By Laplace transformation of the above equation,

$$L[sI(s) - i(0+)] + RI(s) = 1.$$

However, $\quad i(0+) = 0$

$$\therefore \quad sL\,I(s) + RI(s) = 1$$

or, $I(s) = \dfrac{1}{R + sL} = \dfrac{1}{L\left(s + \dfrac{R}{L}\right)} = \dfrac{1}{2\,(s+5)}$.

$\therefore$ Inverse Laplace transformation yields

$$\boldsymbol{i(t) = \frac{1}{2}\,e^{-5t}.}$$

Example 8.3 *Develop the equation of the function shown in Fig. E8.2 in terms of ramp function.*

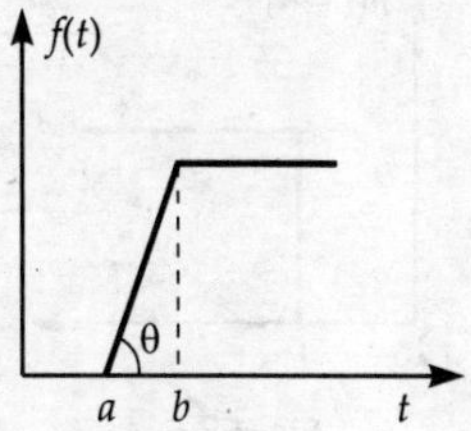

Fig. E8.2

Solution. The function of Fig. E8.2 is graphically segregated into following functions (Ref. Fig. E8.3).

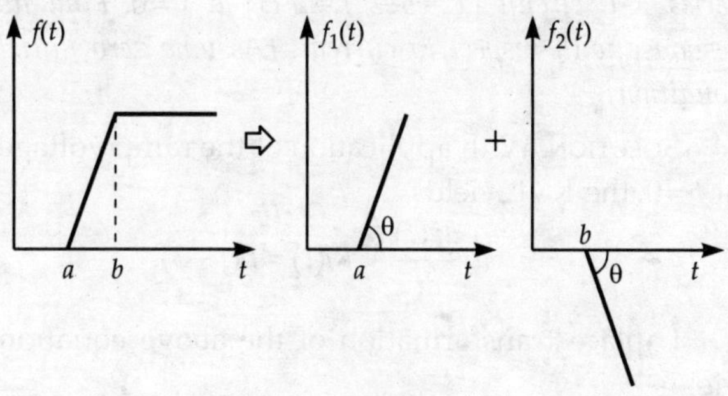

Fig. E8.3

Here, $f(t) = f_1(t) + f_2(t)$

$$= K[r(t-a)] + \{-K[r(t-b)]\}$$

$$= Kr(t-a) - Kr(t-b)$$

$$= K[r(t-a) - r(t-b)].$$

Thus, finally $f(t) = K[r(t-a) - r(t-b)]$

when $\quad \boldsymbol{K = \tan\theta}$.

Example 8.4 *Express the function shown in Fig. E8.4 as a product of two step functions.*

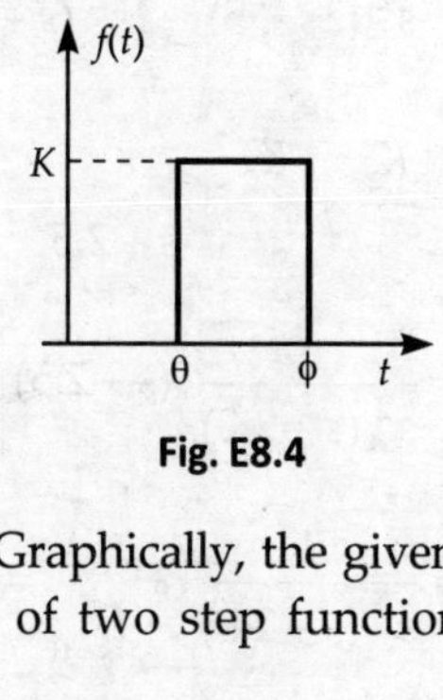

Fig. E8.4

Solution. Graphically, the given pulse function is the product of two step functions as shown in Fig. E8.5.

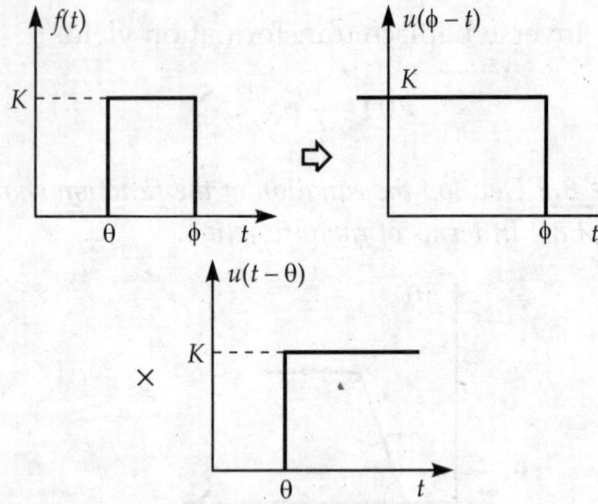

Fig. E8.5

Obviously, with reference to Fig. E8.5,

$$f(t) = \boldsymbol{Ku\,(t-\theta)\,.\,u\,(\phi - t)}.$$

Example 8.5 *A unit ramp voltage $r(t-3)$ is applied to a series R-L circuit [$R=5\Omega$; $L=2$ H] at $t=0$. Find its response with respect to current. [Assume zero initial condition]*

Solution. With application of the ramp voltage at $t=0$, the KVL yields

$$L\frac{di\,(t)}{dt} + Ri(t) = r(t-3).$$

Laplace transformation of the above equation yields

$$L[sI\,(s) - i\,(0+)] + RI\,(s) = \frac{1}{s^2}e^{-3s}.$$

However, due to zero initial condition, $i\,(0+) = 0$.

Thus we obtain,

$$sLI\,(s) + RI\,(s) = \frac{1}{s^2}e^{-3s};$$

however, $L = 2$ H, $R = 5\,\Omega$;

This gives, $(2s+5)\,I\,(s) = \frac{1}{s^2}e^{-3s}$.

$$\therefore \quad I\,(s) = \frac{e^{-3s}}{s^2\,(2s+5)} = \frac{e^{-3s}}{2s^2\,(s+2.5)}.$$

However,

$$\frac{1}{s^2\,(s+2.5)} = \frac{K_1}{s} + \frac{K_2}{s^2} + \frac{K_3}{s+2.5} \qquad ...(a)$$

$$\text{Hence } K_3 = \frac{1}{s^2\,(s+2.5)}\,.(s+2.5)\bigg|_{s=-2.5} = 0.16$$

$$K_2 = \frac{1}{s^2\,(s+2.5)}\,.\,s^2\bigg|_{s=0} = 0.4$$

Let us now multiply equation (*a*) by s^2. This gives

$$\frac{1}{s+2.5} = K_1 s + K_2 + \frac{K_3 s^2}{s+2.5}. \qquad ...(b)$$

Differentiating (*b*) with respect to (*a*), we get

$$-\frac{1}{(s+2.5)^2} = K_1 + K_3\frac{(s+2.5)\,(2s) - s^2}{(s+2.5)^2}. \qquad ...(c)$$

Putting $s=0$ in (*c*),

$$K_1 = -\frac{1}{(2.5)^2} = -0.16$$

$$\text{Hence,} \quad I(s) = \left[\frac{1}{s}(-0.16) + \frac{0.4}{s^2} + \frac{0.16}{s+2.5}\right]\frac{e^{-3s}}{2}.$$

i.e.,

$$\boldsymbol{i\,(t) = \frac{1}{2}[-0.16\,u\,(t-3) + 0.4\,r\,(t-3) + 0.16\,e^{-2.5\,(t-3)}\,u\,(t-3)]\text{ A.}}$$

Example 8.6 *A unit step voltage $u(t-2)$ is applied to a series L-R circuit at $t=0$ when, $L=1$ H, $R=2\,\Omega$. Find i (t) assuming zero initial condition.*

Solution. With application of KVL in the series *LR* circuit with unit step voltage of $u(t-2)$ being applied at $t=0$, we get

$$L\frac{di\,(t)}{dt} + Ri(t) = u\,(t-2).$$

Laplace transformation gives,

$$L[sI\,(s) - i\,(0+)] + RI\,(s) = \frac{e^{-2s}}{s}.$$

With zero initial condition, $i\,(0+) = 0$. Thus,

$$I\,(s)\,[sL + R] = \frac{e^{-2s}}{s}$$

or,

$$I\,(s)\,[s+2] = \frac{e^{-2s}}{s} \qquad [\because R = 2\Omega, L = 1\text{ H}]$$

or,

$$I\,(s) = \frac{1}{s\,(s+2)}e^{-2s}$$

$$\text{Obviously,} \quad \frac{1}{s\,(s+2)} = \frac{K_1}{s} + \frac{K_2}{s+2}$$

$$\text{where, } K_1 = \frac{1}{s\,(s+2)}\,.\,s\bigg|_{s=0} = 0.5$$

$$K_2 = \frac{1}{s\,(s+2)}\,.\,(s+2)\bigg|_{s=-2} = -0.5$$

$$\text{Then,} \quad I(s) = \left[\frac{0.5}{s} - \frac{0.5}{s+2}\right]e^{-2s}.$$

Inverse Laplace transformation gives,

$$i(t) = 0.5\,u(t-2) - 0.5\,e^{-2(t-2)}\,u(t-2)$$

i.e., $$\mathbf{i(t) = 0.5\,u(t-2)\,[1 - e^{-2(t-2)}]}.$$

EXAMPLE 8.7 *A unit impulse function of voltage is applied at $t=0$ to a series RC circuit. Find $i(t)$ assuming the initial charge stored in the capacitor to be zero. Assume $R = 5\,\Omega$, $C = 2$ F.*

SOLUTION. Applying KVL at the series RC circuit, we can write

$$Ri(t) + \frac{1}{C}\int_{-\infty}^{t} i(t)\,dt = \delta(t)$$

[$\because$ applied voltage is a unit impulse function],

or, $$Ri(t) + \frac{1}{C}\int_{-\infty}^{0} i(t)\,dt + \frac{1}{C}\int_{0}^{t} i(t)\,dt = \delta(t).$$

Laplace transformation yields

$$RI(s) + \frac{1}{C}\cdot\frac{q(0+)}{s} + \frac{1}{C}\,\frac{I(s)}{s} = 1.$$

However, as the initial charge stored in C is zero, hence $q(0+) = 0$. Thus, we get

$$RI(s) + \frac{1}{Cs}I(s) = 1$$

or, $$I(s) = \frac{1}{R + \dfrac{1}{Cs}}$$

$$= \frac{1}{R}\,\frac{s}{s + \dfrac{1}{RC}} = \frac{1}{5}\,\frac{s}{s + \dfrac{1}{10}}$$

$$= 0.2\,\frac{s}{s+0.1}$$

$$= 0.2\left[1 - \frac{0.1}{s+0.1}\right].$$

Inverse Laplace transformation yields

$$\mathbf{i(t) = 0.2\,[\delta(t) - 0.1\,e^{-0.1t}]\ A.}$$

EXAMPLE 8.8 *In the above problem assume the excitation voltage to be a shifted impulse function $\delta(t-a)$. Assuming zero initial condition, find $i(t)$.*

SOLUTION. Here, application of KVL yields

$$Ri(t) + \frac{1}{C}\int_{-\infty}^{0} i(t)\,dt + \frac{1}{C}\int_{0}^{t} i(t)\,dt = \delta(t-a).$$

Laplace transformation yields

$$RI(s) + \frac{1}{C}\frac{q(0+)}{s} + \frac{1}{C}\frac{I(s)}{s} = e^{-as}.$$

With zero initial condition, we get

$$RI(s) + \frac{1}{Cs}I(s) = e^{-as}$$

$$\therefore \quad I(s) = \frac{e^{-as}}{\left(R + \dfrac{1}{Cs}\right)}$$

$$= \frac{e^{-as}}{5 + \dfrac{1}{2s}} = \frac{2s\,e^{-as}}{10s+1} = 2e^{-as}\left[\frac{s}{10s+1}\right]$$

$$= e^{-as}\,\frac{(2\times 0.1)\,s}{s+0.1} = 0.2\,e^{-as}\,\frac{s}{s+0.1}$$

$$= 0.2\,e^{-as}\left[1 - \frac{0.1}{s+0.1}\right].$$

$\therefore$ Inverse of Laplace transformation yields

$$i(t) = 0.2\,[\delta(t-a) - \delta(t-a)\,e^{-0.1(t-a)} \times 0.1],$$

i.e., $$\mathbf{i(t) = 0.2\delta(t-a) - 0.02\delta(t-a)\,e^{-0.1(t-a)}\ A.}$$

EXAMPLE 8.9 *A unit step voltage $2u(t-\theta)$ is applied in a series RC circuit with $R = 2\,\Omega$, $C = 1$ F. Assuming zero initial condition, find $i(t)$.*

SOLUTION. Here, KVL in RC series circuit yields

$$Ri(t) + \frac{1}{C}\int_{-\infty}^{t} i(t)\,dt = 2u(t-\theta)$$

which, after Laplace transformation with zero initial condition gives

$$I(s)\left[R + \frac{1}{Cs}\right] = 2\,\frac{1}{s}\,e^{-\theta s}$$

i.e., $$I(s) = \frac{2e^{-\theta s}}{s\left(R + \dfrac{1}{Cs}\right)} = \frac{2e^{-\theta s}}{s\left(2 + \dfrac{1}{s}\right)} = \frac{2e^{-\theta s}}{2s+1}$$

$$= \frac{e^{-\theta s}}{s+0.5}.$$

Inverse Laplace transformation yields

$$\mathbf{i(t) = u(t-\theta)\,e^{-0.5(t-\theta)}\ A.}$$

EXAMPLE 8.10 *A ramp voltage $2r(t-2)$ is applied in a series RC circuit at $t=0$ where $R = 3\,\Omega$, $C = 1$ F. Assuming zero initial conditions, find $i(t)$.*

SOLUTION. With ramp voltage $2r(t-2)$ being applied in series RC circuit,

$$Ri(t) + \frac{1}{C}\int_{-\infty}^{t} i(t)\,dt = 2r(t-2).$$

Laplace transformation provides

$$RI(s)+\frac{1}{C}\frac{q(0+)}{3}+\frac{1}{C}\frac{I(s)}{s}=2\frac{1}{s^2}e^{-2s}$$

However, the initial condition being zero, $q(0+)=0$.

$\therefore$ We get,

$$RI(s)+\frac{1}{C}\frac{I(s)}{s}=2\frac{1}{s^2}e^{-2s}$$

or, $$I(s)\left[R+\frac{1}{Cs}\right]=\frac{2\,e^{-2s}}{s^2}$$

or, $$I(s)=\frac{2e^{-2s}}{s^2\left(R+\frac{1}{Cs}\right)}=\frac{2e^{-2s}}{s^2\left(3+\frac{1}{s}\right)}=2\frac{e^{-2s}}{s(3s+1)}$$

$$=\frac{2}{3}\frac{e^{-2s}}{s(s+0.33)}.$$

However, $$\frac{1}{s(s+0.33)}=\frac{K_1}{s}+\frac{K_2}{s+0.33}$$

where, $$K_1=\frac{1}{s(s+0.33)}.s\bigg|_{s=0}=3$$

$$K_2=\frac{1}{s(s+0.33)}(s+0.33)\bigg|_{s=-0.33}=-3$$

$\therefore$ $$I(s)=\frac{2}{3}\left[\frac{3}{s}-\frac{3}{s+0.33}\right]e^{-2s}.$$

Using inverse of Laplace transformation,

$i(t)=0.67\,[3u(t-2)-3u(t-2)\,e^{-0.33(t-2)}]$ A.

Thus the expression of the current becomes

$$\mathbf{i(t)=2.01\,u(t-2)-2.01\,u(t-2)\,e^{-0.33(t-2)}\ A.}$$

EXAMPLE 8.11 *A function f(t) is shown in Fig. E8.6. Write its equation in terms of step functions.*

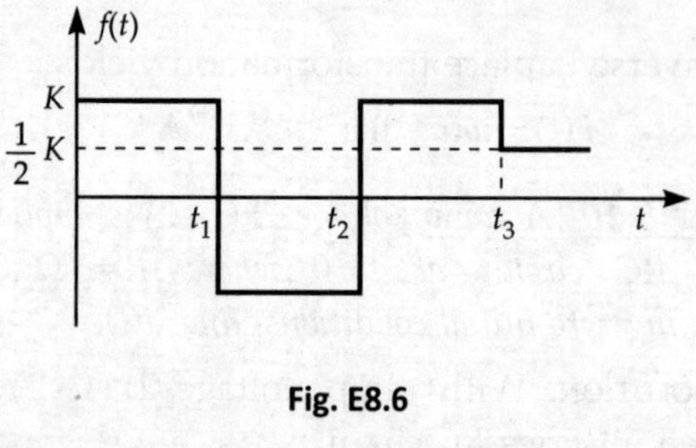

Fig. E8.6

SOLUTION. The waveform analysis shows that the given waveform is a combination of a number of step functions as shown below (Fig. E8.7).

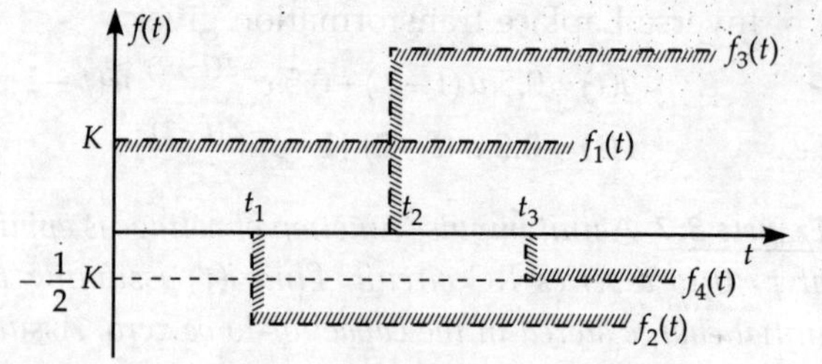

Fig. E8.7

Obviously,

$$f(t)=f_1(t)+f_2(t)+f_3(t)+f_4(t)$$

where $$f_1(t)=Ku(t)$$
$$f_2(t)=-2\,Ku(t-t_1)$$
$$f_3(t)=2\,Ku(t-t_2)$$
$$f_4(t)=-\frac{1}{2}\,K\,u(t-t_3);$$

i.e., the equation of the given waveform is

$$f(t)=f_1(t)+f_2(t)+f_3(t)+f_4(t)$$

or, $$\mathbf{f(t)=K\left[u(t)-2u(t-t_1)+2u(t-t_2)-\frac{1}{2}u(t-t_3)\right]}.$$

EXAMPLE 8.12 *Obtain the waveform of the figure shown in Fig. E8.8.*

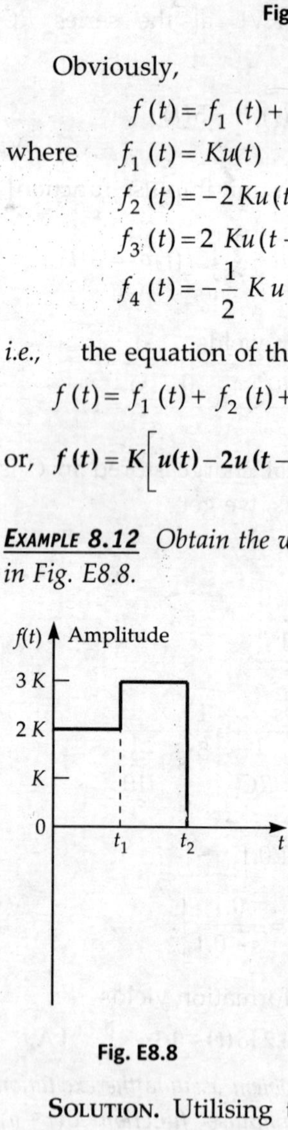

Fig. E8.8

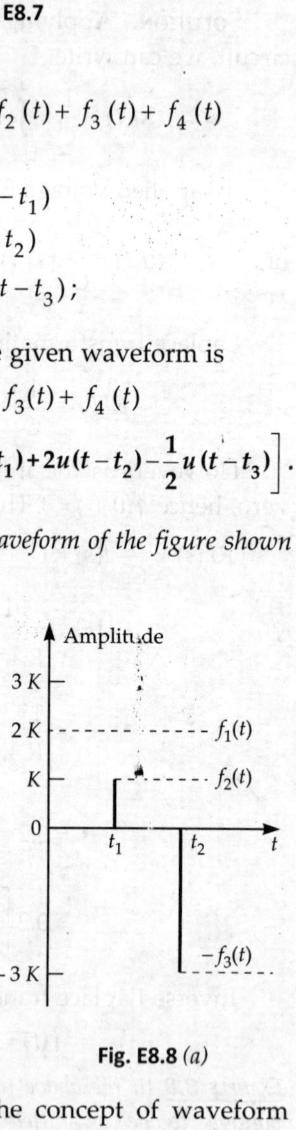

Fig. E8.8 *(a)*

SOLUTION. Utilising the concept of waveform analysis, the given waveform is shown in Fig. E8.8*(a)*.

Obviously, $$f(t)=f_1(t)+f_2(t)+f_3(t)$$

where $$f_1(t)=2K\,u(t);\ f_2(t)=K\,u(t-t_1)$$
$$f_3(t)=-3\,Ku(t-t_2).$$

$\therefore$ The wave equation is given by

$$f(t)=\mathbf{2Ku(t)+Ku(t-t_1)-3\,Ku(t-t_2)}.$$

EXAMPLE 8.13 *A wave equation is given by*

$$f(t)=6u(t-t_1)+2u(t-t_2)-10u(t-t_3)$$

Draw the waveform.

SOLUTION. Let

$$f_1(t)=6u(t-t_1)$$

$$f_2(t)=2u(t-t_2)$$

$$f_3(t)=10\,u(t-t_3)$$

As $f(t)=f_1(t)+f_2(t)+f_3(t)$, the waveforms are drawn in Fig. E8.9.

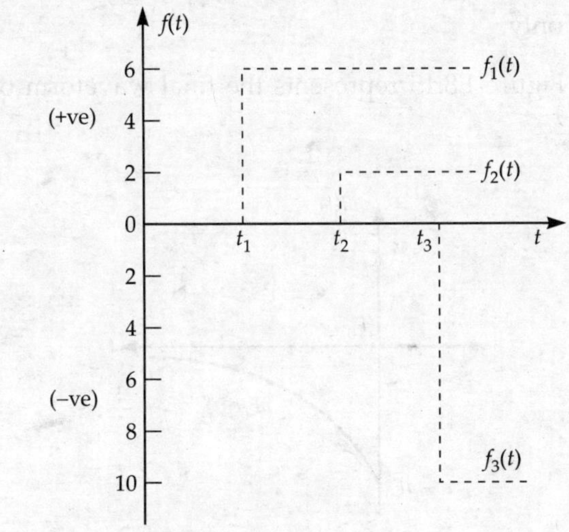

Fig. E8.9

The **resultant waveform is shown by hatched line in Fig. E8.10.**

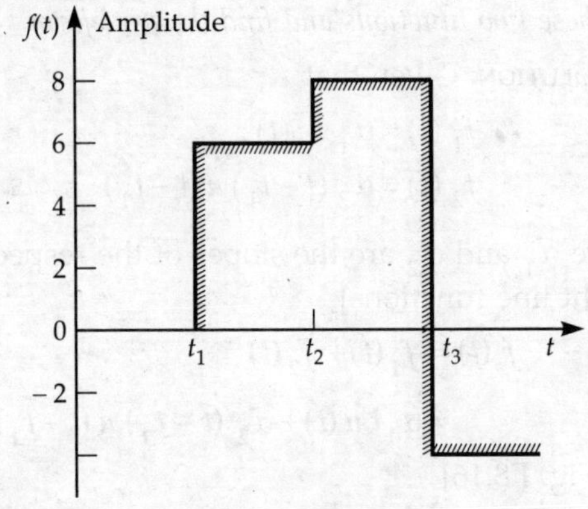

Fig. E8.10

EXAMPLE 8.14 *A ramp function, having slope "m" starts at $t=t_x$ sec. Obtain its equation.*

SOLUTION. As the unit ramp function is given by $r(t)[=tu(t)]$, hence here, m being the slope, the function being starting at $t=t_x$, we can write, the ramp function $=\boldsymbol{m(t-t_x)\,u(t-t_x)}$.

EXAMPLE 8.15 *A function is given by $f(t)=(t_1-t)$. Between the interval $-t_2\le t\le t_2$, sketch the waveforms of*

(i) $f(t)\,u(t)$ *(ii)* $f(t)\,u(t-t_1)$

(iii) $f(t)\,u(-t)$.

SOLUTION. The product of $f(t)\,u(t)$ is shown below (Fig. E8.12). The hatched graph in Fig. 8.11 shows $f(t)\,u(t)$ within $-t_2\le t\le t_2$ **(Ans. of (*i*))**.

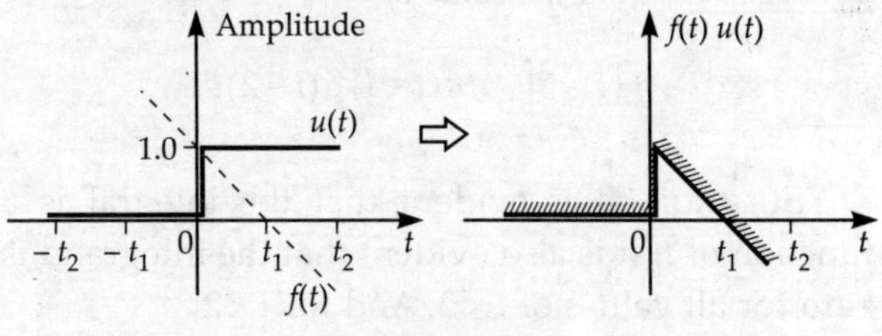

Fig. E8.11

The product of $f(t)\,u(t-t_1)$ is shown in Fig. E8.12, the hatched graph is the final waveform of $f(t)\,u(t-t_1)$ within $-t_2\le t\le t_2$. **(Ans. of (*ii*))**

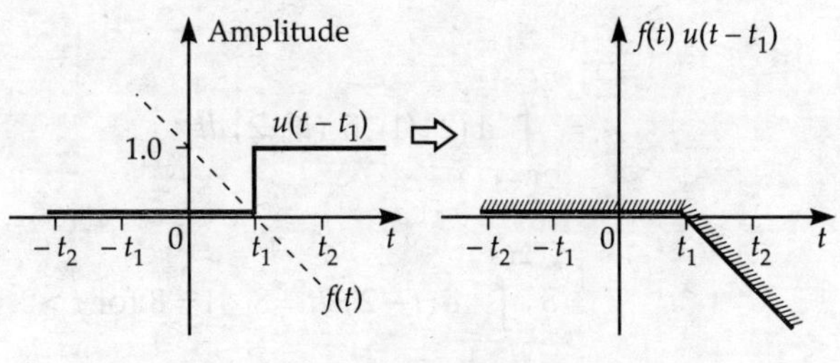

Fig. E8.12

The product of $f(t)\,u(-t)$ is shown in Fig. E8.13, the hatched graph being the final waveform of $f(t)\,u(-t)$. **(Ans. of (*iii*))**

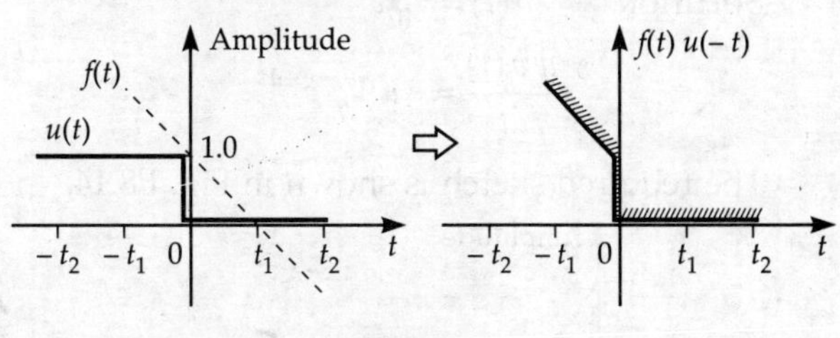

Fig. E8.13

EXAMPLE 8.16 *Find the value of* $M=\int_{-\infty}^{+\infty} 10\delta(t)\,dt$.

SOLUTION. It is obvious that $\delta(t)$ is zero everywhere except at $t=0$. Thus the limits of integrations can be put as $0(-)$ to $0(+)$ *i.e.*, just before and after zero instead of $-\infty$ to $+\infty$.

CHAPTER 8

$$\therefore \quad M = \int_{0(-)}^{0(+)} 10\,\delta(t)\,dt = 10 \int_{0(-)}^{0(+)} \delta(t)\,dt.$$

However, $\int_{0(-)}^{0(+)} \delta(t)\,dt$ is simply the area of the unit impulse $\delta(t)$.

$$\therefore \quad M = 10\,(1) = \mathbf{10}.$$

Example 8.17 *Find the value of*

$$f(t) = \int_{-\infty}^{t} 4tu(t-1)\,\delta(t-2)\,dt.$$

Solution. It is evident that the integral is a function of t. It is also evident that the integrand is **zero** for all values of $t < 2$. And for $t < 2$,

$$f(t) = \int_{-\infty}^{t} 0\,.\,dt = 0.$$

However, for $t > 2$,

$$f(t) = \int_{-\infty}^{t} 4t\,u(t-1)\,\delta(t-2)\,dt$$

$$= \int_{2(-)}^{2(+)} 4\,(2)\,(1)\;\delta\,(t-2)\,dt$$

$$= 8 \int_{2(-)}^{2(+)} \delta(t-2)\,dt = 8 \times 1 = \mathbf{8} \text{ for } t > 2.$$

Example 8.18 *An exponential waveform is given by* $v(t) = V_0\,e^{-at}$. *Sketch the derivative waveform of this function.*

Solution. $v(t) = V_0\,e^{-at}$

$$\therefore \quad \frac{d\,v(t)}{dt} = \boldsymbol{-a\,V_0\,e^{-at}}.$$

The required sketch is shown in Fig. E8.14.

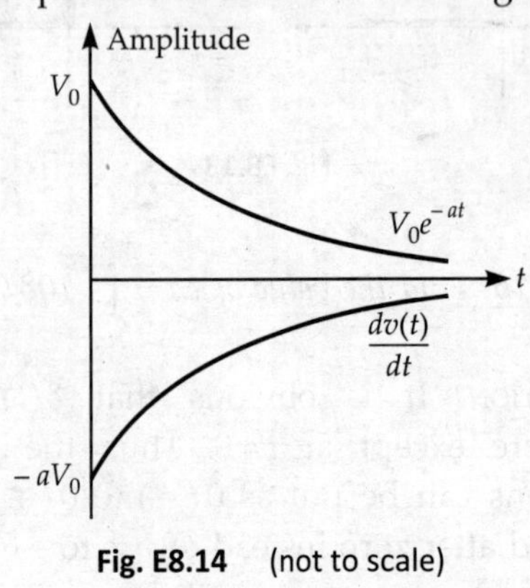

Fig. E8.14 (not to scale)

Example 8.19 *A function is given by*

$$f(t) = F_0\,e^{-at}\,u(t)$$

Find its derivative and sketch the waveform.

Solution. $f(t) = F_0\,e^{-at}\,u(t)$

$$\therefore \quad \frac{df(t)}{dt} = F_0\,[e^{-at}\,\delta(t) - ae^{-at}\,u(t)]$$

$$= \mathbf{F_0\,[\delta(t) - ae^{-at}\,u(t)]}.$$

It may be noted that the impulse function is only valid at $t = 0$. Thus at $t = 0$, $e^{-at}\,\delta(t)$ becomes $\delta(t)$ only.

Figure E8.15 represents the final waveform of $\frac{df(t)}{dt}$.

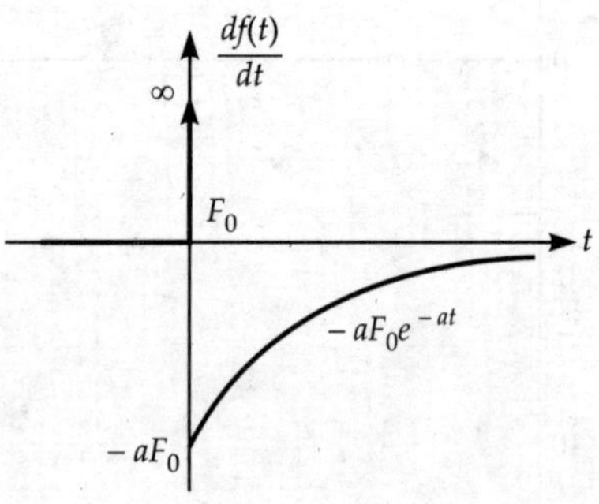

Fig. E8.15

Example 8.20 *Two positive straight line functions are given by* $f_1(t) = \alpha_1\,t\,u(t)$ *and* $f_2(t) = \alpha_2(t - t_1)\,u(t - t_1)$. *Add these two functions and find the waveform.*

Solution. Given that

$$f_1(t) = \alpha_1\,t\,u(t);$$
$$f_2(t) = \alpha_2\,(t - t_1)\,u(t - t_1)$$

[where α_1 and α_2 are the slopes of the respective straight line functions].

$$\mathbf{f(t) = f_1(t) + f_2(t)}$$

$$\mathbf{= \alpha_1 t\,u(t) + \alpha_2\,(t - t_1)\,u(t - t_1)}$$

[Ref. Fig. E8.16]

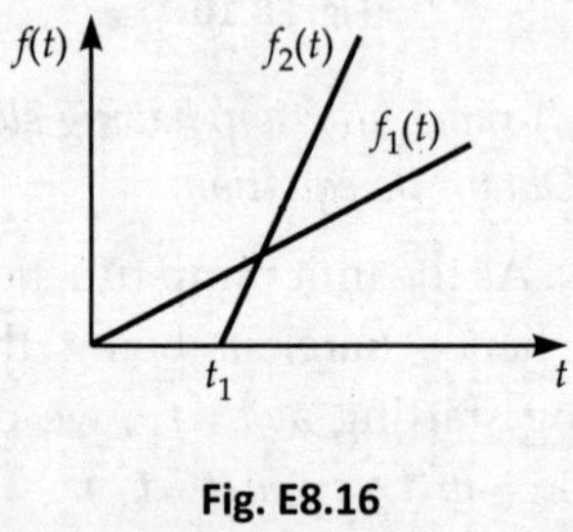

Fig. E8.16

The waveform of $f(t)$ is shown in Fig. E8.17.

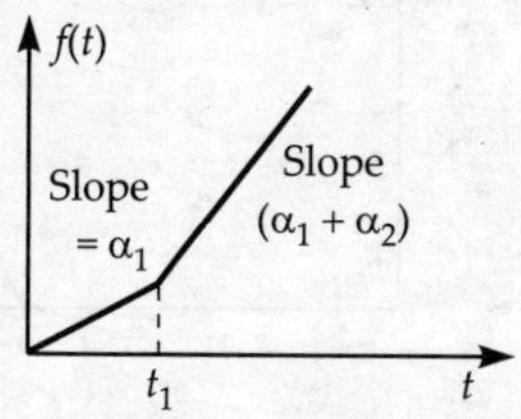

Fig. E8.17

EXAMPLE 8.21 *A triangular pulse waveform is shown in Fig. E8.18. By waveform analysis, draw the component functions.*

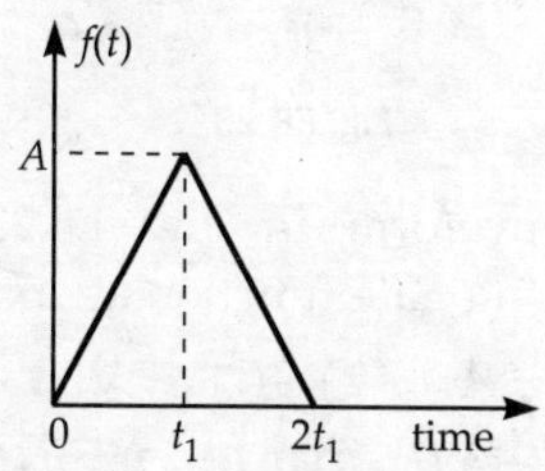

Fig. E8.18

SOLUTION. To obtain the components of the triangular pulse, from time 0 to t_1, we draw a ramp function with slope (A/t_1) and is denoted by $f_1(t)$ (Ref. Fig. E8.19). We then add another ramp with a slope $(-2A/t_1)$, delayed by t time and denoted by $f_2(t)$ (Fig. E8.20). Since the function is zero at all time intervals greater than $2t$, we add another ramp with a +ve slope of (A/t_1) at $t = 2t$. It is denoted by $f_3(t)$ [Ref. Fig. E8.21].

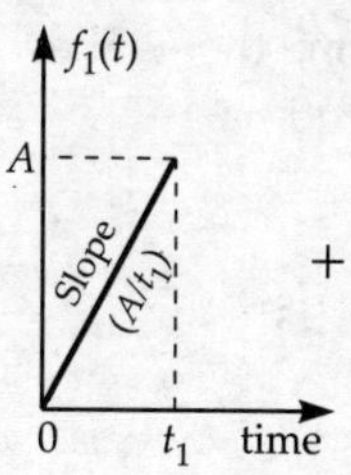

Fig. E8.19

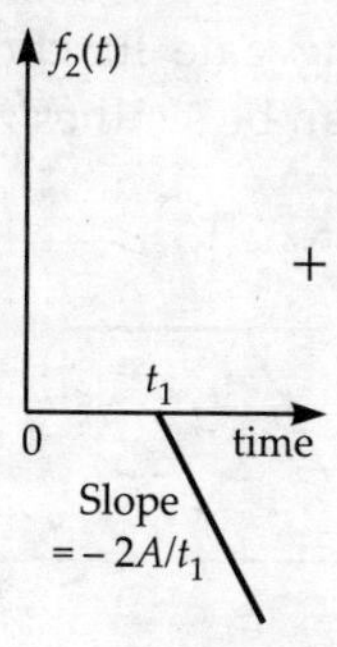

Fig. E8.20

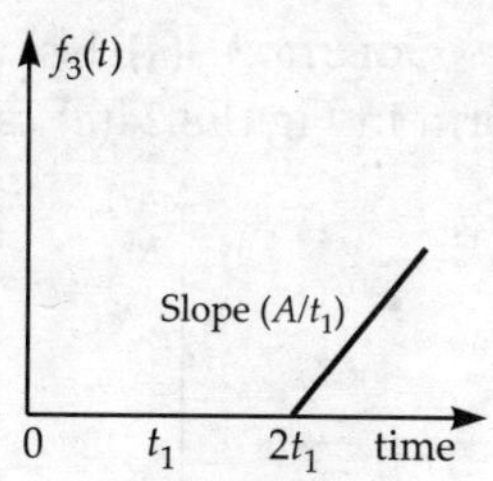

Fig. E8.21

Obviously,

$$f(t) = f_1(t) + f_2(t) + f_3(t).$$

$$= \frac{A}{t_1} tu(t) - \frac{2A}{t_1}(t - t_1)\, u(t - t_1) + \frac{A}{t_1}(t - 2t_1)\, u(t - 2t_1).$$

8.4 GATE FUNCTION

A rectangular pulse of unit height (*i.e.*, having amplitude of one unit), initiating at $t = a$ and ending at $t = b$ with duration T is defined as a gate function. It is expressed in terms of unit step function and can be represented by (also see Fig. 8.13)

$$G(t) = u(t - a) - u(t - b)$$
$$= u(t - a) - u(t - a - T)$$

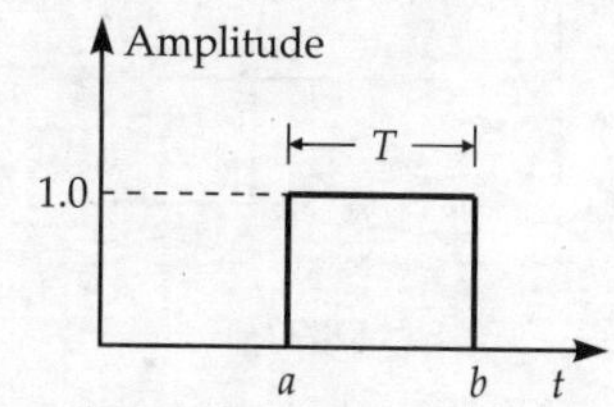

Fig. 8.13 Graphical representation of a gate function.

In Laplace transform,

$$G(s) = e^{-as} \times \frac{1}{s} - e^{-(a+T)s} \times \frac{1}{s}$$

$$= \frac{e^{-as}}{s}[1 - e^{-T.s}]$$

When the gate function starts from zero, *i.e.*, from origin (Fig. 8.14)

$$G(t) = u(t) - u(t - a)$$

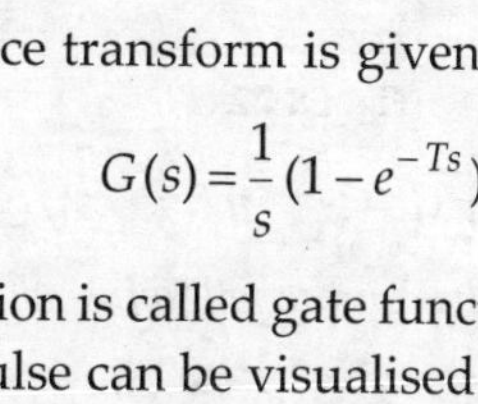

Fig. 8.14 Gate function starting from origin.

The Laplace transform is given by

$$G(s) = \frac{1}{s}(1 - e^{-Ts})$$

This function is called gate function because the rectangular pulse can be visualised as a "gate" just opening at $t = a$ and closing at $t = b$. As the gate opens at $t = a$, its value becomes 1.0 (amplitude) and as it closes at $t = b$, its value becomes 0.

If any function is multiplied by a gate function then that function will have zero value outside the interval of the gate function while the value of the function remains unchanged within the duration of the gate function.

CHAPTER 8

EXAMPLE 8.22 *Synthesize the given gate function (Fig. E8.22) using addition and multiplication of two unit step functions.*

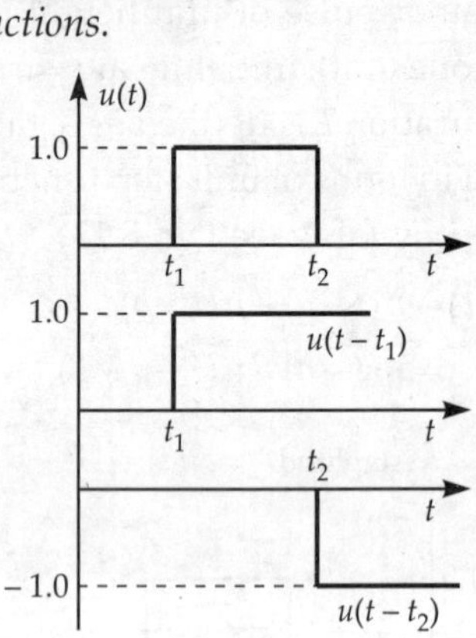

Fig. E8.22

SOLUTION. Figure E8.22 represents a gate function $g(t)$. The waveform analysis reveals that this function can be represented by the sum of two unit step functions as shown in Fig. E8.22.

i.e.,
$$g(t) = u(t-t_1) + [-u(t-t_2)]$$
$$= u(t-t_1) - u(t-t_2).$$

Also, using the concept of waveform analysis, the gate function can also be represented by the product of two unit step functions as shown in Fig. E8.22(*a*).

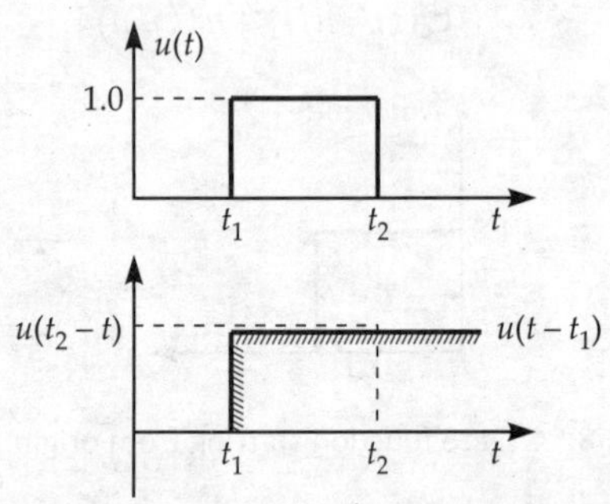

Fig. E8.22 (*a*)

Here, $g(t) = \mathbf{u(t - t_1) \,.\, u(t_2 - t)}$.

EXAMPLE 8.23. *Synthesize the following waveforms using gate function.*

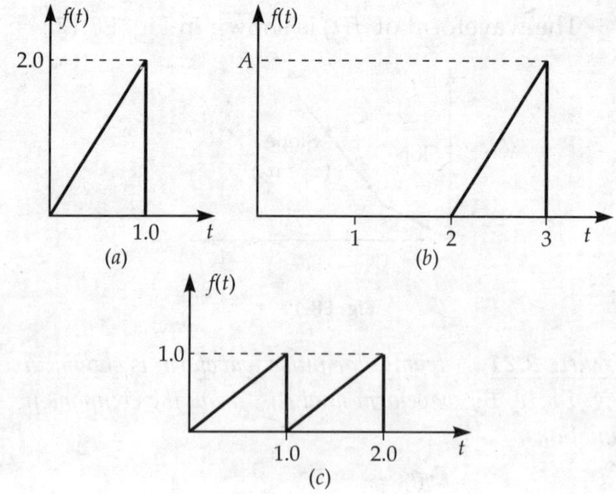

Fig. E8.23

SOLUTION. (*a*) Using gate function, we can synthesize the waveform in Fig. E8.23(*a*) as

$$f(t) = 2t \,.\, G(t)$$

[∵ the equation of the given function is $\left(\frac{2}{1} \times t + 0\right)$ in terms of $(mx + c)$]

or, $$f(t) = \mathbf{2t\,[u(t) - u(t-1)]}.$$

(*b*) The waveform in Fig. E8.23(*b*) can be synthesized, using gate function as

$$f(t) = A(t-2)\,G(t)$$
$$= \mathbf{A\,(t-2)\,[u\,(t-2) - u\,(t-3)]}.$$

(*c*) For the waveform in Fig. E8.23(*c*), we can use gate function as

$$f(t) = 1.t\,G(t)_{0-1} + 1.(t-1)\,G(t)_{1-2}$$
$$= t\,[u(t) - u(t-1)] + (t-1)[u(t-1) - u(t-2)]$$
$$= t\,u(t) - t\,u(t-1) + tu(t-1) - u(t-1) - tu(t-2) + u(t-2)$$

$$\therefore \quad \mathbf{f\,(t) = t\,u\,(t) - u\,(t-1) - (t-1)\,u\,(t-2)}.$$

EXAMPLE 8.24 *Synthesize the following waveforms using gate function :*

SOLUTION. (*a*) Using gate function, the waveform in Fig. E8.24(*a*) can be synthesized as

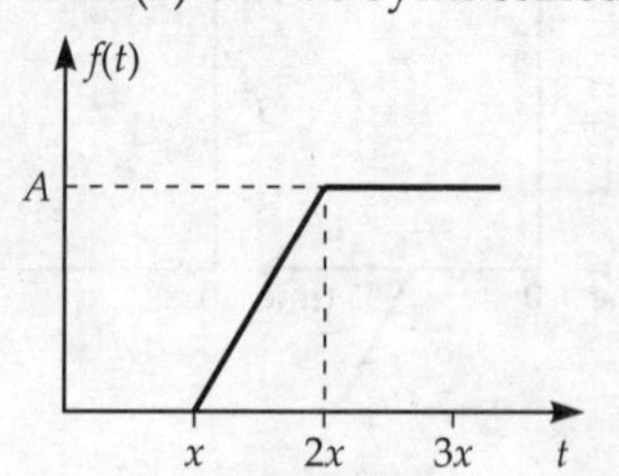

Fig. E8.24 (*a*)

$$f(t) = \frac{A}{x}(t-x)\,G(t)_{x-2x} + AG(t)_{2x-\infty}$$

[∵ the given waveform can be assumed to be sum of two functions—one is from x to $2x$ and the other is from $2x$ to infinity. The equation of the function from x to $2x$ is $\frac{A}{x}(t-x)$ while that from $2x$ to infinity is A.]

$$\therefore \quad f(t) = \frac{A}{x}(t-x)[u(t-x) - u(t-2x)] + Au(t-2x)$$

$$= \frac{A}{x}(t-x)\,u(t-x) - \frac{A}{x}(t-x)\,u(t-2x) + Au(t-2x)$$

$$= \frac{A}{x}(t-x)\,u(t-x) - Au(t-2x)\left[\frac{1}{x}(t-x)+1\right]$$

$$= \frac{A}{x}(t-x)\,u(t-x) - \frac{Au}{x}(t-2x)\,.\,t$$

$$= \frac{A}{x}(t-x)u(t-x) - \frac{A}{x}\,.\,tu(t-2x).$$

(*b*) We synthesize the given triangular wave in Fig. E8.24(*b*) as sum of two functions, one from 0 to *x* and another from *x* to 2*x*.

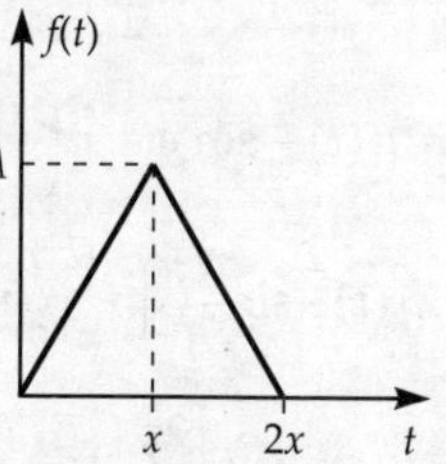

Fig. E8.24 (*b*)

$$f(t) = \frac{A}{x}\,.\,t\,.\,G(t)_{0-x} + \frac{-A}{x}(t-2x)\,G(t)_{x-2x}$$

$$= \frac{A}{x}\,.\,t\,[u(t) - u(t-x)] - \frac{A}{x}(t-2x)\,[u(t-x) - u(t-2x)]$$

$$= \frac{A}{x}\,.\,tu(t) - \frac{A}{x}\,.\,tu(t-x) - \frac{A}{x}(t-2x)\,u(t-x) + \frac{A}{x}(t-2x)\,u(t-2x)$$

$$= \frac{A}{x}\,t\,u(t) - \frac{A}{x}\,u(t-x)[t+t-2x] + \frac{A}{x}(t-2x)\,u(t-2x)$$

$$= \frac{A}{x}\,t\,u(t) - \frac{A}{x}\,u(t-x)\,2\,(t-x) + \frac{A}{x}(t-2x)\,u(t-2x)$$

$$= \boldsymbol{\frac{A}{x}\,tu(t) - \frac{2A}{x}(t-x)\,u(t-x) + \frac{A}{x}(t-2x)\,u(t-2x)}$$

Example 8.25 *Synthesize the following waveforms using gate function :*

Solution. (*a*) The given waveform [Fig. E8.25(*a*)] can be synthesized as

$$f(t) = 1 \times G(t)_{0-x} + 1 \times G(t)_{2x-3x}$$

$$= 1\,[u(t) - u(t-x)] + 1\,[u(t-2x) - u(t-3x)]$$

$$= \boldsymbol{u(t) - u(t-x) + u(t-2x) - u(t-3x).}$$

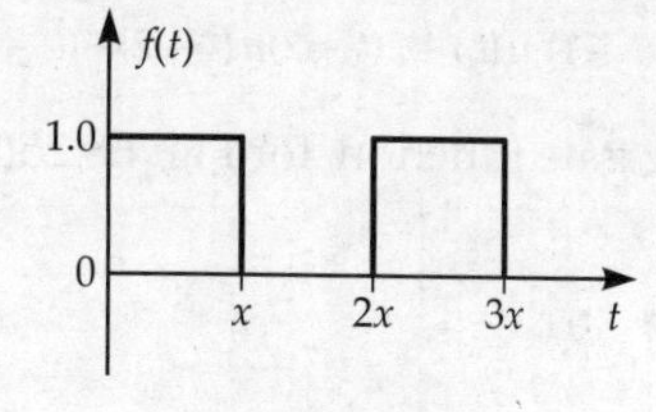

Fig. E8.25 (*a*)

(*b*) The given waveform [Fig. E8.25(*b*)] can be synthesized in terms of gate function as :

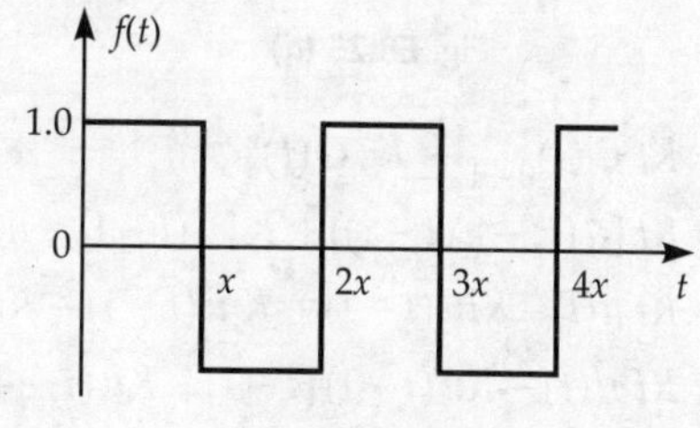

Fig. E8.25 (*b*)

$$f(t) = 1 \times G(t)_{0-x} + (-1)\,G(t)_{x-2x} + 1 \times G(t)_{2x-3x} + (-1)\,G(t)_{3x-4x} + \ldots\ldots$$

$$= 1\,[u(t) - u(t-x)] - 1\,[u(t-x) - u(t-2x)] + 1\,[u(t-2x) - u(t-3x)] - 1\,[u(t-3x) - u(t-4x)] + \ldots\ldots$$

$$= \boldsymbol{u(t) - 2u(t-x) + 2u(t-2x) - 2u(t-3x) + \ldots}$$

(*c*) Using gate function, the waveform in Fig. E8.25(*c*) can be synthesized as

$$f(t) = (At - A)[G(t)_{0-2}] + (-At + 3A)[G(t)_{2-4}]$$

$$= (At - A)\,[u(t) - u(t-2)] + (-At + 3A)\,[u(t-2) - u(t-4)]$$

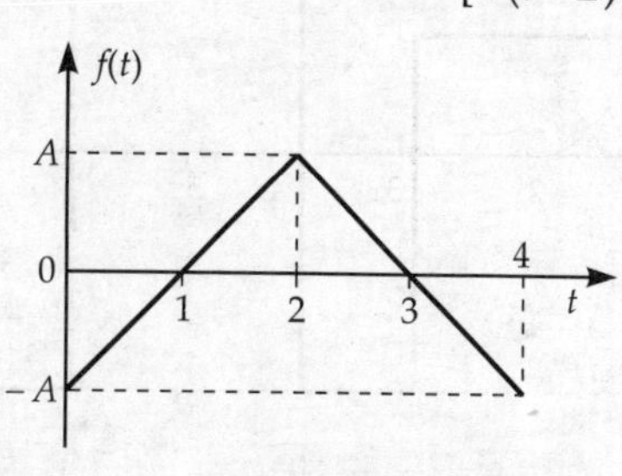

Fig. E8.25 (*c*)

CHAPTER 8

$$= At\,u(t) - Au(t) - Atu(t-2) + Au(t-2) - At\,u(t-2) + 3Au(t-2) + At\,u(t-4) - 3Au(t-4)$$

$$= (At - A)\,u(t) - (2At - 4A)\,u(t-2) + (At - 3A)\,u(t-4)$$

$$= A(t-1)\,u(t) - 2A(t-2)\,u(t-2) + A(t-3)\,u(t-4)$$

or, $\mathbf{f(t) = A[(t-1)\,u(t) - 2(t-2)u(t-2) + (t-3)\,u(t-4)]}$

(*d*) Using gate function, for Fig. E8.25(*d*), we can write

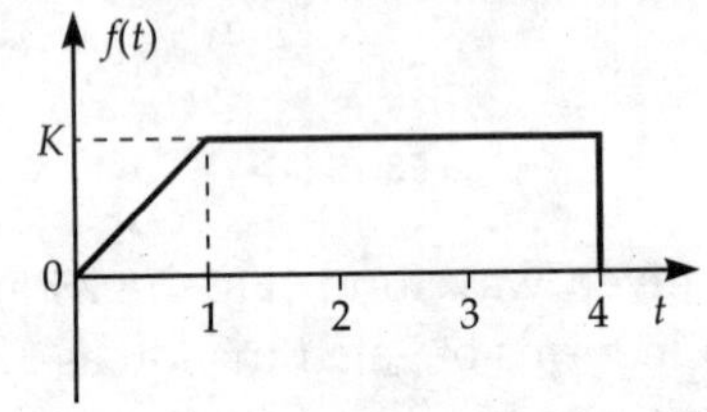

Fig. E8.25 (*d*)

$$f(t) = Kt\,G(t)_{0-1} + K.G(t)_{1-4}$$

$$= Kt[u(t) - u(t-1)] + K[u(t-1) - u(t-4)]$$

$$= Kt\,u(t) - Ktu(t-1) + K\,u(t-1) - Ku(t-4)$$

$$= Kt\,u(t) - Ku(t-1)[t-1] - Ku(t-4)$$

$$\mathbf{= Kt\,u(t) - K(t-1)\,u(t-1) - Ku(t-4).}$$

EXAMPLE 8.26 *Synthesize the following waveforms in terms of gate functions.*

SOLUTION. (*a*) Using gate function, the waveform in Fig. E8.26(*a*) can be synthesized as

$$f(t) = 1 \times G(t)_{0-3x} + (-2) \times G(t)_{3x-4x} + 2 \times G(t)_{4x-6x} + (-2)\,G(t)_{6x-7x}$$

$$= 1[u(t) - u(t-3x)] - 2[u(t-3x) - u(t-4x)] + 2[u(t-4x) - u(t-6x)] - 2[u(t-6x) - u(t-7x)]$$

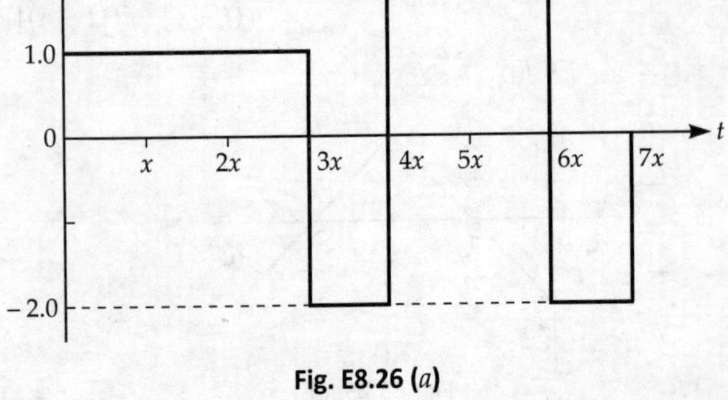

Fig. E8.26 (*a*)

$$= u(t) - u(t-3x) - 2u(t-3x) + 2u(t-4x) + 2u(t-4x) - 2u(t-6x) - 2u(t-6x) + 2u(t-7x)$$

$$\mathbf{= u(t) - 3u(t-3x) + 4u(t-4x) - 4u(t-6x) + 2u(t-7x).}$$

(*b*) For the waveform in Fig. E8.26(*b*), we can use gate function to get the following result :

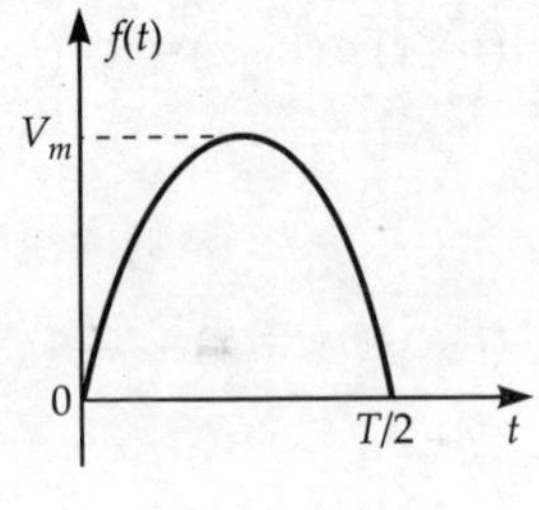

Fig. E8.26 (*b*)

$$v(t) = V_m \sin\omega t\,.\,G(t)$$

$$= V_m \sin\omega t\left[u(t) - u\left(t - \frac{T}{2}\right)\right]$$

$$= V_m\left[\sin\omega t\,.\,u(t) - \sin\omega t\,.\,u\left(t - \frac{T}{2}\right)\right]$$

$$= V_m\left[\sin\omega t.u(t) - \sin\frac{2\pi}{T}\left(t - \frac{T}{2} + \frac{T}{2}\right).u\left(t - \frac{T}{2}\right)\right]$$

$$= V_m\left[\sin\omega t\,.\,u(t) - \sin\left\{\frac{2\pi}{T}\left(t - \frac{T}{2}\right) + \pi\right\}u\left(t - \frac{T}{2}\right)\right]$$

$$\mathbf{= V_m\left[\sin\omega t\,.\,u(t) + \sin\left\{\frac{2\pi}{T}\left(t - \frac{T}{2}\right)\right\}u\left(t - \frac{T}{2}\right)\right]}$$

(*c*) For the waveform shown in Fig. E8.26(*c*), we write :

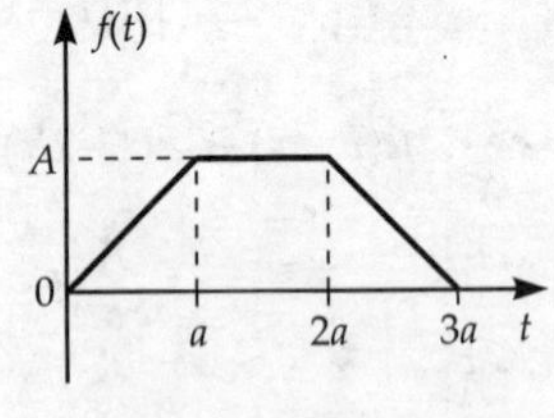

Fig. E8.26 (*c*)

$$f(t) = \frac{A}{a}.t.G(t)_{0-a} + A.G(t)_{a-2a} + \left[\left(-\frac{A}{a}\right)t + 3a\right]G(t)_{2a-3a}$$

$$= \frac{A}{a}t[u(t) - u(t-a)] + A[u(t-a) - u(t-2a)] - \left(\frac{A}{a}.t - 3a\right)[u(t-2a) - u(t-3a)]$$

$$= \frac{A}{a}.t\,u(t) - \frac{A}{a}.t\,u(t-a) + Au(t-a) - Au(t-2a)$$

$$- \frac{A}{a}.tu(t-2a) + 3au(t-2a)$$

$$+ \frac{A}{a}.t\,u(t-3a) - 3au(t-3a)$$

$$= \frac{A}{a}.t.u(t) - Au(t-a)\left[\frac{1}{a}.t - 1\right]$$

$$- u(t-2a)\left[A + \frac{A}{a}.t - 3a\right]$$

$$+ u(t-3a)\left[\frac{A}{a}.t - 3a\right]$$

or, $$\boldsymbol{f(t) = \frac{A}{a}.t.u(t) - \frac{A}{a}(t-a)\,u(t-a)}$$

$$\boldsymbol{- \frac{A}{a}\left(a + t - \frac{3a^2}{A}\right)u(t-2a)}$$

$$\boldsymbol{+ \frac{1}{a}(At - 3a^2)\,u(t-3a).}$$

(*d*) For the diagram shown in Fig. E8.26(*d*) use of gate function is helpful in solving the synthesization problem of the given waveform.

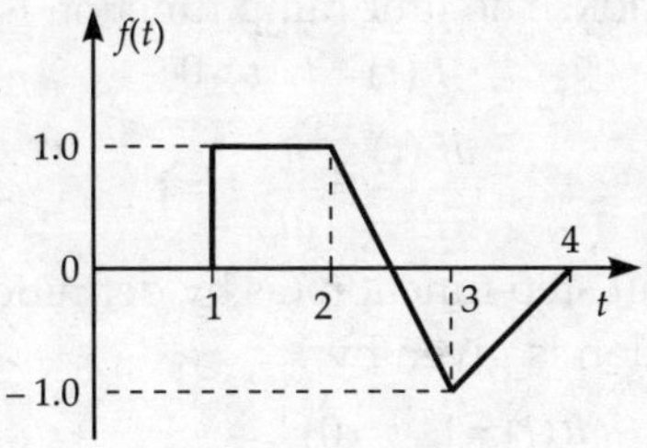

Fig. E8.26 (*d*)

Here,

$$f(t) = 1 \times G(t)_{1-2} + \{(-1)t + 5\}\,G(t)_{2-3} + (t-4)\,G(t)_{3-4}$$

$$= [u(t-1) - u(t-2)] + (-2t+5)[u(t-2) - u(t-3)] + (t-4)[u(t-3) - u(t-4)]$$

$$= u(t-1) - u(t-2) - 2tu(t-2) + 2tu(t-3) + 5u(t-2) - 5u(t-3) + tu(t-3) - tu(t-4) - 4u(t-3) + 4u(t-4)$$

$$= u(t-1) - t(t-2)(2t-4) + u(t-3)(3t-9) - u(t-4).(t-4)$$

or, $$\boldsymbol{f(t) = u(t-1) - 2(t-2)\,u(t-2) + 3(t-3)\,u(t-3) - (t-4)\,u(t-4).}$$

EXAMPLE 8.27 *Synthesize the following waveforms in terms of gate function :*

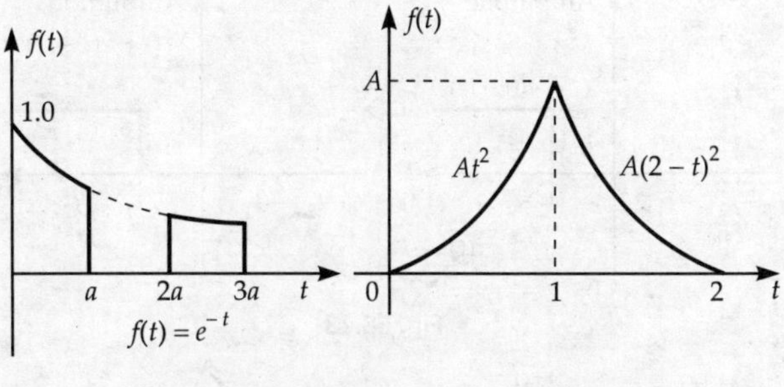

Fig. E8.27 (*a*) (*b*)

SOLUTION. (*a*) The gate function can be utilised as follows for the waveform as shown in Fig. E8.27(*a*)

$$f(t) = e^{-t}.G(t)_{0-a} + e^{-t}.G(t)_{2a-3a}$$

$$= e^{-t}[u(t) - u(t-a)] + e^{-t}[u(t-2a) - u(t-3a)]$$

$$\boldsymbol{= e^{-t}[u(t) - u(t-a) + u(t-2a) - u(t-3a)].}$$

(*b*) For the waveform shown in Fig. E8.27(*b*), we find that

$$f(t) = At^2.G(t)_{0-1} + A(2-t)^2\,G(t)_{1-2}$$

$$= At^2[u(t) - u(t-1)] + A(2-t)^2[u(t-1) - u(t-2)]$$

$$= At^2[u(t) - u(t-1)] + A(4 - 4t + t^2)[u(t-1) - u(t-2)]$$

$$= At^2[u(t) - u(t-1)] + 4Au(t-1) - 4Au(t-2) - 4At\,u(t-1) + 4At\,u(t-2) + At^2\,u(t-1) - At^2\,u(t-2)$$

$$= At^2\,u(t) - Au(t-1)\,t^2 + Au(t-1).4 - Au(t-1).4t + Au(t-2).4t - Au(t-2).t^2 - Au(t-2).4 + At^2\,u(t-1)$$

$$= At^2\,u(t) - Au(t-1)[t^2 - 4 + 4t - t^2] + Au(t-2)[4t - t^2 - 4]$$

$$= A[t^2\,u(t) - 4u(t-1).(t-1) - u(t-2)(2-t)^2]$$

$$\boldsymbol{= A\,[t^2\,u(t) - 4(t-1)\,u(t-1) - (2-t)^2\,u(t-2)].}$$

ADDITIONAL EXAMPLES

EXAMPLE 8.28 *A function is given by* $X(t) = (t_1 - t)$. *Sketch the waveform between* $-t_2 \le t \le t_2$ *of the following :*

(*i*) $X(t) + u(t - t_1)$ (*ii*) $X(t - t_2).u(t)$

(*iii*) $X(t - t_2)\,u(t + t_1)$.

SOLUTION. The addition of function $X(t)$ and $u(t-t_1)$ is shown in Fig. E8.28. **(Ans. of (*i*)).**

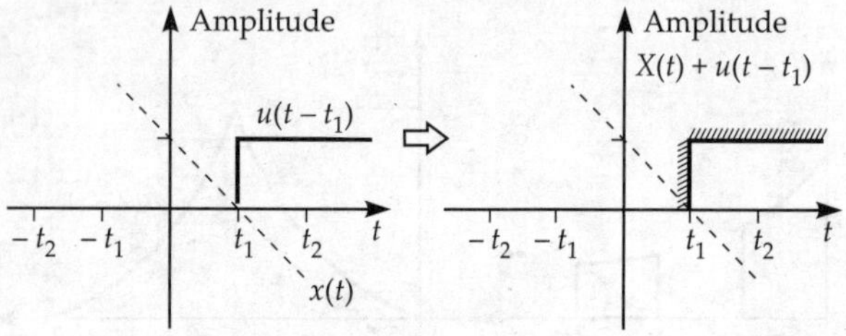

Fig. E8.28

The multiplication of functions $X(t-t_2)$ and $u(t)$ is shown in Fig. E8.29. **(Ans. of (*ii*))**

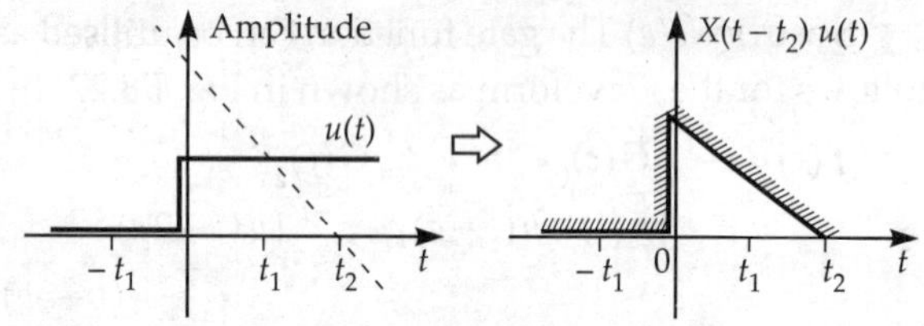

Fig. E8.29

The multiplication of functions $X(t-t_2)$ and $u(t+t_1)$ is shown below (Fig. E8.30) **(Ans. of (*iii*))**

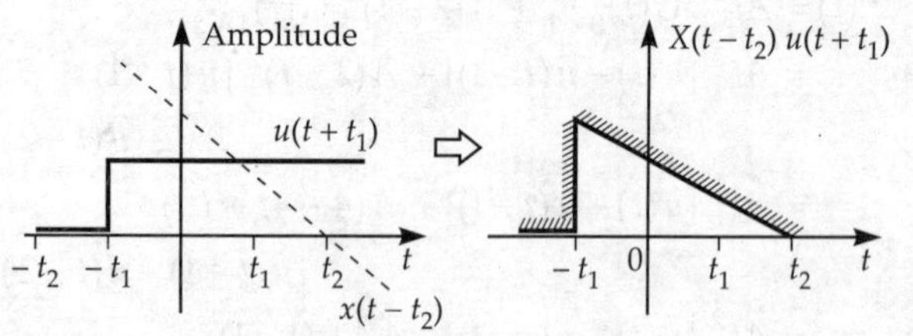

Fig. E8.30

EXAMPLE 8.29 *A function is given by*

$$G(t)=\int_{-\infty}^{t} f(t)\,dt \text{ where } f(t)=K_0\,e^{-\theta t}\,u(t).$$

Evaluate the function G(t) for t <0, and t >0.

SOLUTION. Given that,

$$G(t)=\int_{-\infty}^{t} f(t)\,dt=\int_{-\infty}^{t} K_0 e^{-\theta t}u(t)\,dt,$$

or, $$G(t)=K_0\int_{0}^{t} e^{-\theta t}dt \; [t \text{ being greater than } 0]$$

$$=K_0\left.\frac{e^{-\theta t}}{-\theta}\right|_{t=0}^{t}=-\frac{K_0}{\theta}(e^{-\theta t}-e^{0})$$

$$=\frac{\mathbf{K_0}}{\theta}\,(\mathbf{1-e^{-at}})\,[t>0].$$

Again, for $t<0$, as $u(t)=0$,

$$G(t)=\int_{-\infty}^{t} 0\,.\,dt=\mathbf{0}.$$

It may be noted that for all t,

$$\mathbf{G(t)=\frac{K_0}{\theta}\,(1-e^{-\theta t})\,u(t)}$$

EXAMPLE 8.30 *A parabolic function is given by*

$$f(t)=\begin{cases}0 & \text{for } t<0\\ t^2/2 & \text{for } t>0.\end{cases}$$

Obtain its derivative.

SOLUTION. $\frac{d}{dt}f(t)=\frac{d}{dt}(t^2/2)$ for $t>0$ *i.e.*, the derivative of the parabolic function becomes "t" at $t>0$ as $\frac{d}{dt}\frac{t^2}{2}=\mathbf{t}.$

However $f'(t)=t$ represents a ramp function.

Thus, it is observed that the derivative of a parabolic function becomes a ramp function.

EXAMPLE 8.31 *Show that the derivative of an unit ramp function is a step function.*

SOLUTION. The unit ramp function is given by

$$f(t)=t,\; t>0$$

$$\therefore \qquad \frac{df(t)}{dt}=\frac{d}{dt}\,.\,t=\mathbf{1}.$$

i.e., the unit step function (as by definition, the unit step function is given by

$$u(t)=1,\; t>0).$$

In a similar way we can find the derivative of unit step function as $\frac{du(t)}{dt}=0$ at $t>0$. This means that for all values of t except zero, the slope (*i.e.*, the derivative) is zero. Only the function exists at $t=0$ when the slope is not zero. This means that **the derivative of the unit step function represents the unit impulse function as by definition, unit impulse function exists only at t = 0].**

EXAMPLE 8.32 *Obtain the waveform equation of the square train wave shown in Fig. E8.31. What is its Laplace transformation ?*

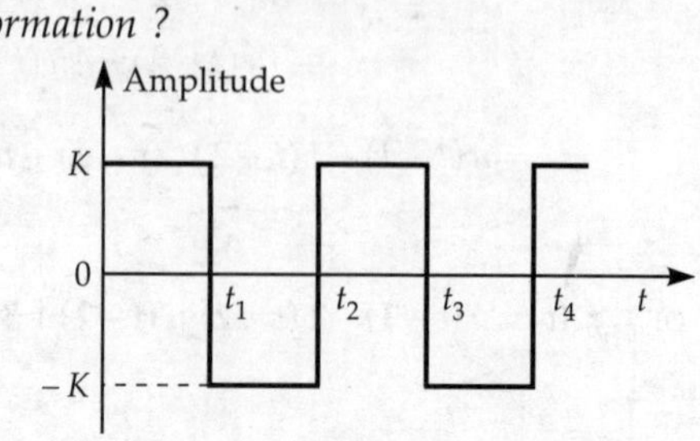

Fig. E8.31

Solution. By waveform analysis, it is evident that the given square wave waveform can be analysed as shown in Fig. E8.32.

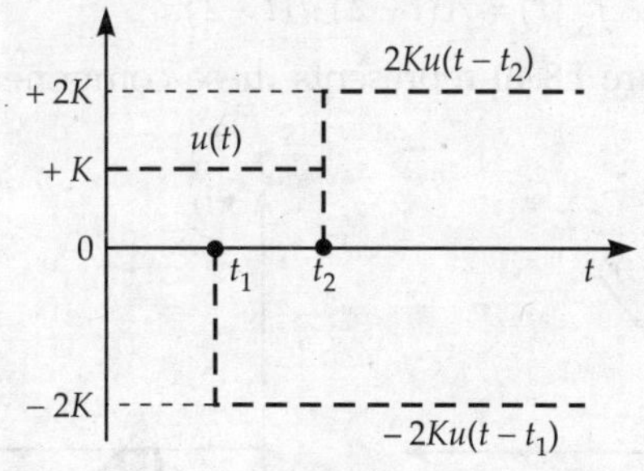

Fig. E8.32

Thus, $f(t) = Ku(t) - 2\,Ku(t-t_1) + 2\,Ku(t-t_2)$
$- 2\,Ku(t-t_3) + \ldots\ldots,$

i.e., the waveform equation becomes

$$f(t) = K[u(t) - 2u(t-t_1) + 2u(t-t_2) - 2u(t-t_3) + \ldots].$$

Its Laplace transformation is

$$\mathbf{F(s)} = \frac{\mathbf{K}}{\mathbf{s}}[\mathbf{1} - \mathbf{2}e^{-t_1 s} + \mathbf{2}e^{-t_2 s} - \mathbf{2}e^{-t_3 s} + \ldots].$$

Example 8.33 *Obtain the equation of f (t) for the figure shown in Fig. E8.33.*

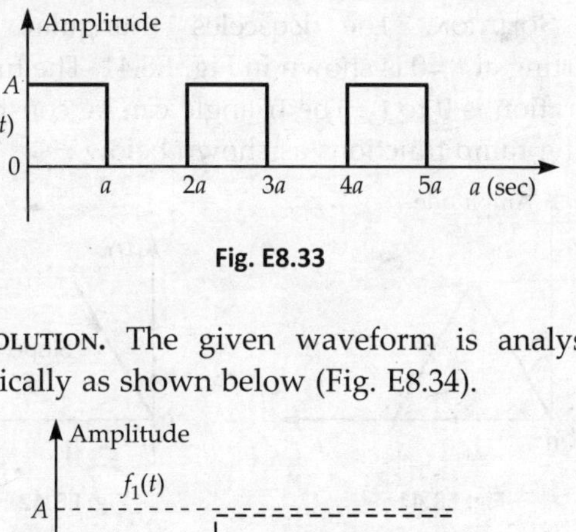

Fig. E8.33

Solution. The given waveform is analysed graphically as shown below (Fig. E8.34).

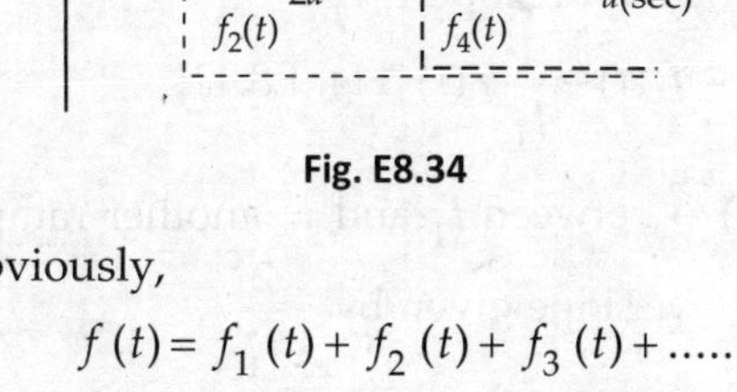

Fig. E8.34

Obviously,

$$f(t) = f_1(t) + f_2(t) + f_3(t) + \ldots..$$
$$= Au(t) - Au(t-a) + Au(t-2a) - Au(t-3a) + Au(t-4a)\ldots..,$$

i.e, wave equation is given by

$$\mathbf{f(t) = A[u(t) - u(t-a) + u(t-2a) - u(t-3a) + u(t-4a) \ldots]}.$$

Example 8.34 *A function is given by*

$$v(t) = V_m \cos(\omega t + \theta).$$

Sketch the time derivative function of v (t).

Solution. As $v(t) = V_m \cos(\omega t + \theta)$

$$\therefore \quad \frac{d}{dt}v(t) = -\omega V_m \sin(\omega t + \theta).$$

Figures E8.35 and **E8.36** represent the original and the time derivative functions.

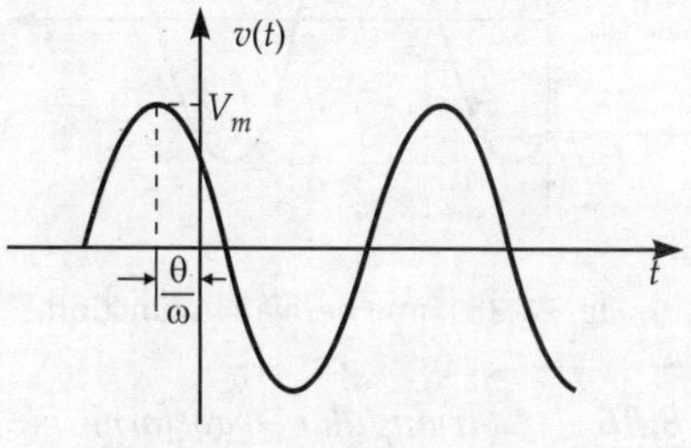

Fig. E8.35 Original function.

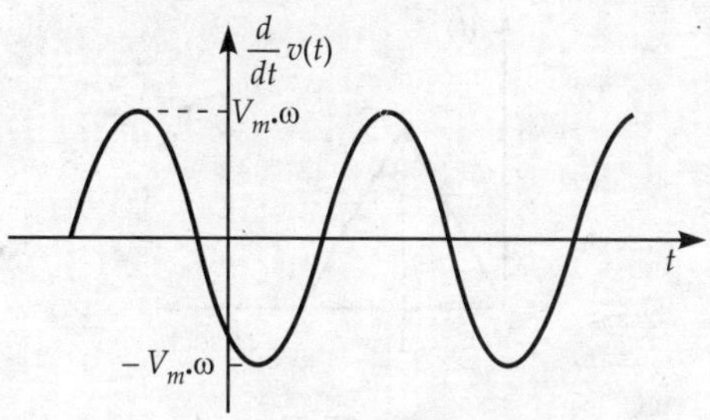

Fig. E8.36 Time derivative function.

Example 8.35 *If* $i(t) = I_m \cos(\omega t + \phi)\,u(t)$, *find* $\frac{d}{dt}i(t)$.

Solution. Let

$$f(t) = \frac{d}{dt}i(t)$$

where, $i(t) = I_m \cos(\omega t + \phi)\,u(t)$;

$$\therefore \quad f(t) = \frac{d}{dt}[I_m \cos(\omega t + \phi)\,u(t)]$$

$$= I_m \cos(\omega t + \phi)\,\delta(t) - I_m\,.\,\omega \sin(\omega t + \phi)\,u(t)$$

$$= \mathbf{I_m \cos\phi\,\delta(t) - \omega I_m \sin(\omega t + f)\,u(t)}.$$

The sketches are shown in Figs. E8.37 and E8.38.

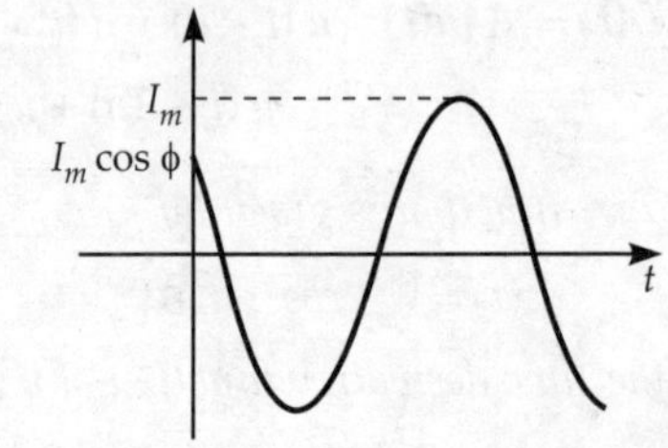

Fig. E8.37 Original function.

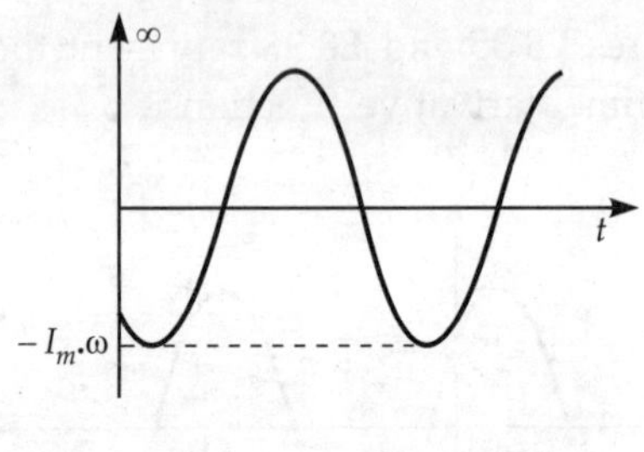

Fig. E8.38 Time derivative function.

EXAMPLE 8.36 *A triangular waveform is shown in Fig. E8.39. Find the component waveforms.*
[Ref. Example 8.22 also]

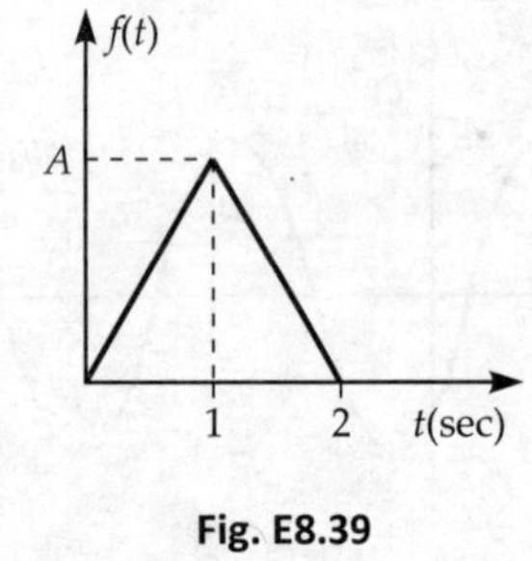

Fig. E8.39

SOLUTION. The waveform components are as under :

$f_1(t)$: *between 0 and 1 sec.* a ramp function of slope $(A/1)$ *i.e*, A.

i.e., $f_1(t) = A \,.\, tu(t) = Atu(t)$;

$f_2(t)$: *between 1 and 2 sec.* another ramp function of double the slope of the former one with negative magnitude is to be added.

$$f_2(t) = -\frac{2A}{1}(t-2)\,u(t-2)$$

$$= -2A(t-2)\,u(t-2).$$

$f_3(t)$ *at* $t = 2$ *sec.* As the triangular function is zero for $t > 2$ and as the summation of slopes of $f_1(t)$ and $f_2(t)$ gives the slope $A - 2A = -A$, hence to make the net function zero at $t = 2$, the slope of $f_3(t)$ must be $A/1$ *i.e.,* A.

i.e., $f_3(t) = A(t-2)\,u(t-2)$.

Figure **E8.40** represents these component waveforms.

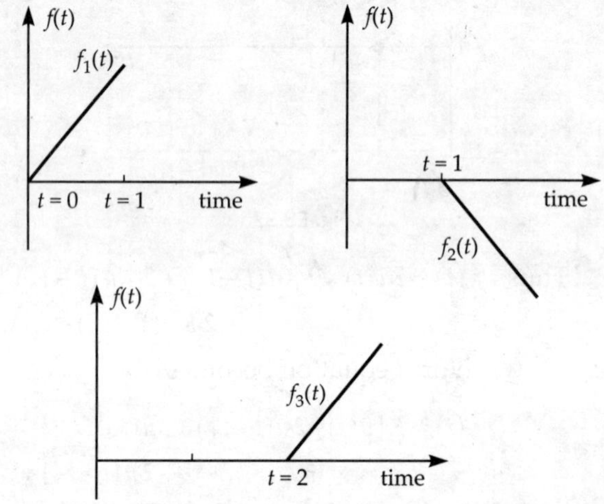

Fig. E8.40

EXAMPLE 8.37 *Using the concept of waveform analysis, obtain the waveform components of an isosceles triangular pulse in terms of ramp functions and find its Laplace transform.*

SOLUTION. The isosceles triangular pulse, starting at $t = 0$ is shown in Fig. E8.41. The function duration is 0 to t_2. The triangle can be constructed using ramp functions as shown below :

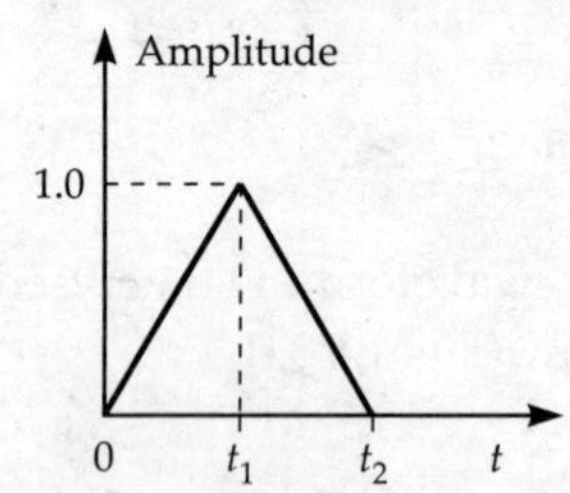

Fig. E8.41

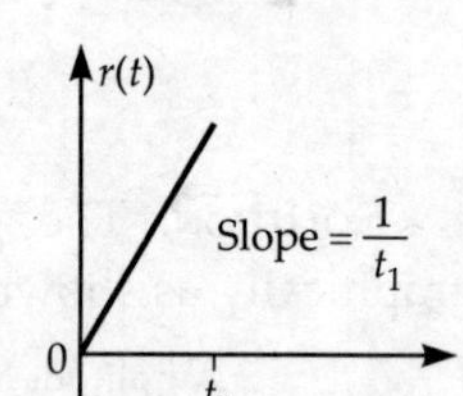

Fig. E8.42

$f_1(t) \to$ between 0 and t_1, $f_1(t)$ represents a ramp function of slope $1/t_1$.

i.e., $f_1(t) \simeq \frac{1}{t_1} r(t)$ [Fig. E8.42]

$f_2(t) \to$ between t_1 and t_2 another ramp starts with the –ve slope given by $-\frac{2}{t_1}$.

$\therefore$ $f_2(t) = -\frac{2}{t_1} r(t - t_1)$.

This is shown in Fig. E8.43

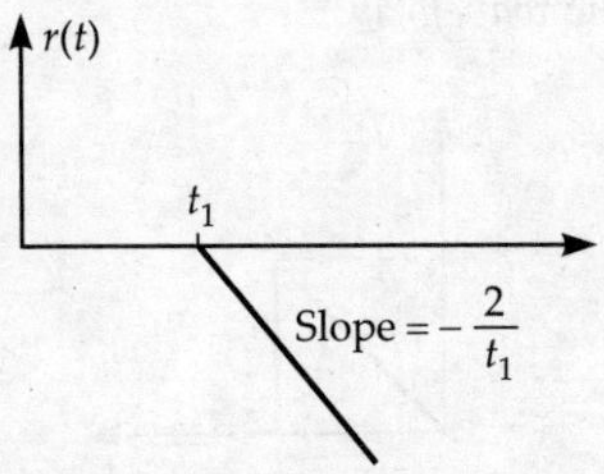

Fig. E8.43

$f_3(t) \rightarrow$ the third ramp is at $t = t_2$ (*i.e.*, at $2t_1$) and has slope $\frac{1}{t_1}$

$$\left[\because \text{ sum of slopes of } f_1(t) \text{ and } f_2(t) \text{ is } \frac{1}{t_1} - \frac{2}{t_1} = -\frac{1}{t_1}\right]$$

so that the slope of $f_1(t) + f_2(t)$ cancels slope of $f_3(t)$ making the net slope zero at $t = t_2$.

$$\therefore \quad f_3(t) = \frac{1}{t_1} r(t - t_2) \equiv \frac{1}{t_1} r(t - 2t_1),$$

[Ref. Fig. E8.44].

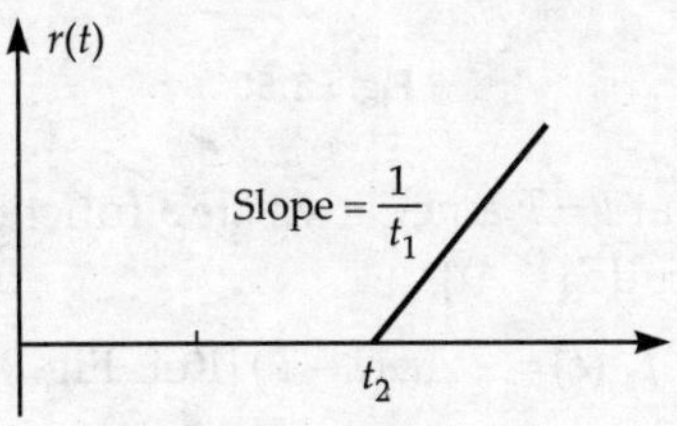

Fig. E8.44

This gives

$$f(t) = f_1(t) + f_2(t) + f_3(t)$$

$$= \frac{1}{t_1} r(t) - \frac{2}{t_1} r(t - t_1) + \frac{1}{t_1} r(t - 2t_1).$$

The Laplace transform of $f(t)$ is then given by

$$F(s) = \frac{1}{t_1} \cdot \frac{1}{s^2} - \frac{2}{t_1} \cdot \frac{e^{-t_1 s}}{s^2} + \frac{1}{t_1} \frac{e^{-2t_1 s}}{s^2}$$

$$= \frac{1}{t_1 s^2}\left[1 - 2e^{-t_1 s} + e^{e^{-2t_1 s}}\right] = \frac{(1 - e^{-t_1 s})^2}{t_1 s^2}.$$

i.e., Laplace transform of the triangular isosceles waveform is given by

$$\left[\frac{\mathbf{1}}{\boldsymbol{t_1 s^2}} (\mathbf{1} - \boldsymbol{e^{-t_1 s}})^{\mathbf{2}}\right].$$

EXAMPLE 8.38 *A pulse waveform is shown in Fig. E8.45. Obtain its Laplace transformation.*

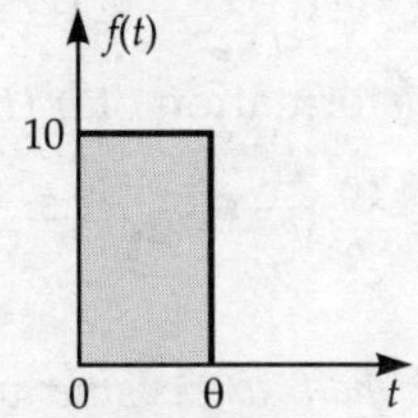

Fig. E8.45

SOLUTION. The pulse can be represented as

$$f(t) = 10\,[u(t) - u(t - \theta)].$$

The Laplace transformation of the above equation is then given by

$$F(s) = \frac{10}{s}[1 - e^{-\theta s}].$$

$\therefore$ The Laplace transform of the required waveform is given by

$$\left[\frac{\mathbf{10}}{\boldsymbol{s}} (\mathbf{1} - \boldsymbol{e^{-\theta s}})\right].$$

EXAMPLE 8.39 *A pulse waveform is shown in Fig. E8.46. Obtain its Laplace transform.*

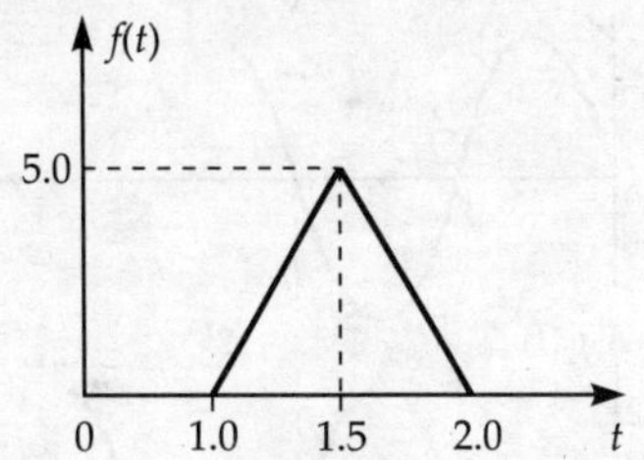

Fig. E8.46

SOLUTION. The waveform analysis technique reveals that the given waveform is combination of three waveforms $f_1(t)$, $f_2(t)$ and $f_3(t)$ where

$f_1(t) \rightarrow$ ramp function between $t = 1.0$ and 1.5 sec.

$f_2(t) \rightarrow$ ramp function between $t = 1.5$ and 2.0 sec.

$f_3(t) \rightarrow$ ramp function $t = 2.0$ sec.

Thus

$$f_1(t) = \frac{5}{(1.5 - 1)} r(t - 1);$$

$$f_2(t) = \frac{2 \times 5}{(1.5 - 1)} r(t - 1.5)$$

and $$f_3(t) = +\frac{5}{(1.5 - 1)} r(t - 2);$$

C H A P T E R 8

$$\therefore \quad f(t) = f_1(t) + f_2(t) + f_3(t)$$
$$= 10r(t-1) - 20r(t-1.5) + 10r(t-2).$$

Laplace transformation of $f(t)$ is thus

$$F(s) = \frac{10}{s^2}[e^{-s} - 2e^{-1.5s} + e^{-2s}].$$

EXAMPLE 8.40 *A half wave sine wave is shown in Fig. E8.47. Synthesize the waveform.*

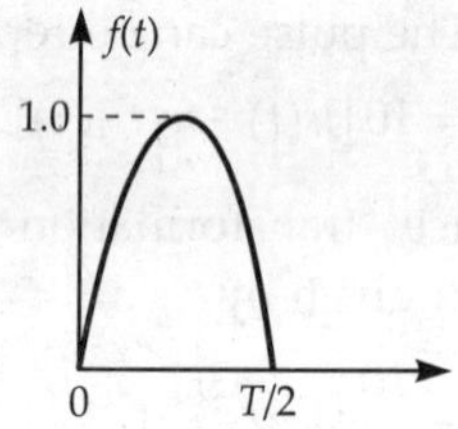

Fig. E8.47

SOLUTION. Using waveform analysis, it is evident that the given wave is the summation of two sine waves as shown in Fig. E8.48.

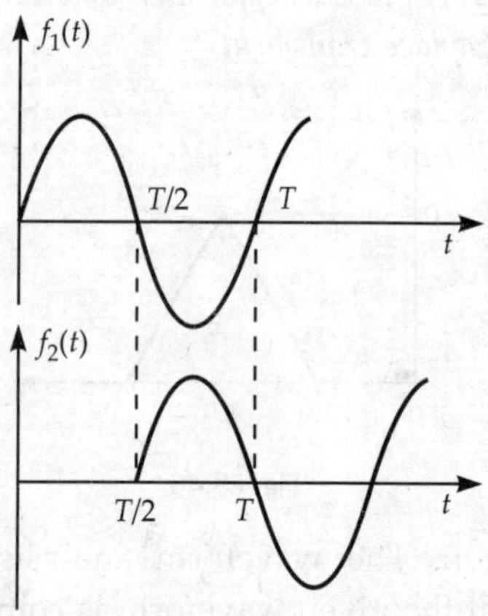

Fig. E8.48

Here, $f_1(t) = \sin 2\pi\,\omega\, u(t) = \sin 2\pi \frac{t}{T} u(t)$,

$$f_2(t) = \sin 2\pi\left(t - \frac{T}{2}\right) . u\left(t - \frac{T}{2}\right)$$

[the waveform of $f_1(t)$ and $f_2(t)$ are shown in Fig. E8.48].

Here

$$f(t) = \sin\frac{2\pi t}{T} u(t) + \sin\frac{2\pi}{T}\left(t - \frac{T}{2}\right) . u\left(t - \frac{T}{2}\right).$$

EXAMPLE 8.41 *A sawtooth pulse is shown in Fig. E8.49. Synthesize the waveform.*

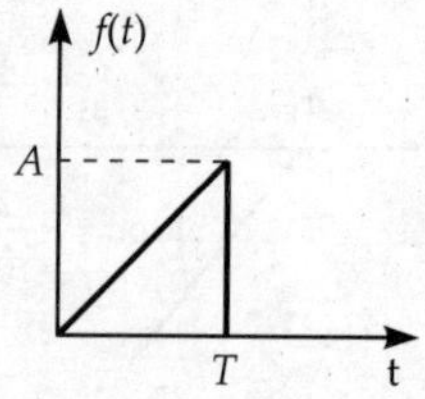

Fig. E8.49

SOLUTION. To synthesize the pulse, a ramp function $f_1(t)$ is generated between 0 and T with slope $\frac{A}{T}$ (Ref. Fig. E8.50).

$$\therefore \quad f_1(t) = \frac{A}{T} t\, u(t).$$

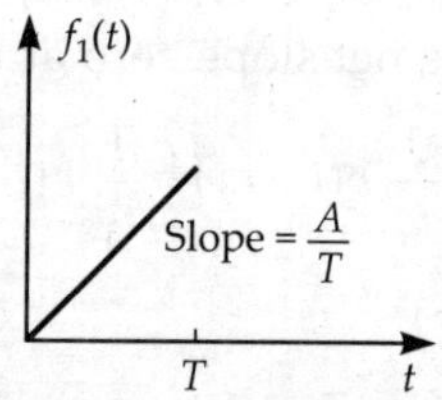

Fig. E8.50

Then, at $t = T$ a negative step function is added [of magnitude $(-A)$].

$$\therefore \quad f_2(t) = -Au(t-T) \text{ [Ref. Fig. E8.51]}.$$

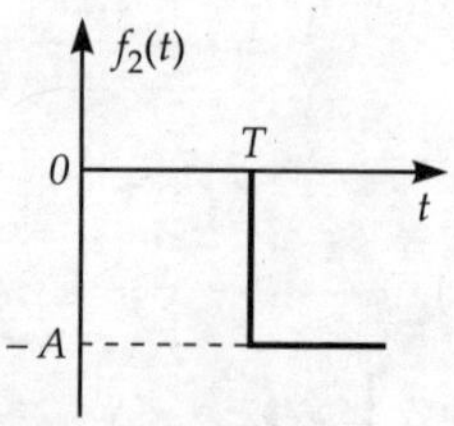

Fig. E8.51

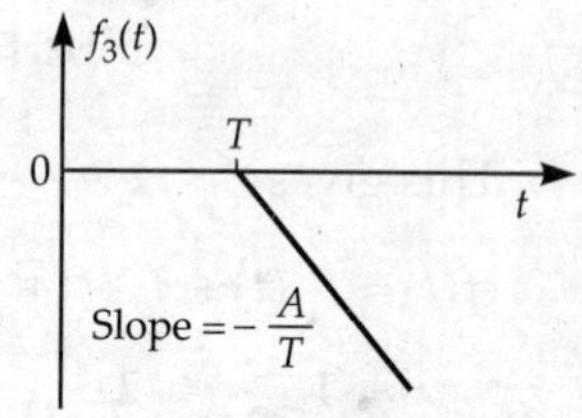

Fig. E8.51(*a*)

At $t = T$, another negative ramp function is to be added since the sawtooth pulse is to be made zero at $t = T$ finally.

This ramp has a negative slope of $-\frac{A}{T}$ at $t = T$.

$$\therefore \quad f_3(t) = -\frac{A}{T}(t-T)\,u(t-T).$$

Thus,

$$f(t) = f_1(t) + f_2(t) + f_3(t)$$
$$= \frac{A}{T} tu(t) - Au(t-T) - \frac{A}{T}(t-T)\,u(t-T).$$

EXAMPLE 8.42 *Two sawtooth waveform pulses are shown in Fig. E8.52. Synthesize the waveform.*

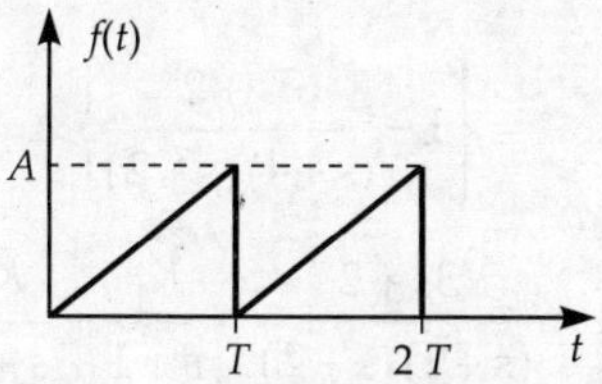

Fig. E8.52

SOLUTION. The first pulse in Fig. E8.52 is synthesized in the same manner as shown in the previous example.

The first pulse is synthesized as

$$f(t) = \frac{A}{T} t\, u(t) - Au(t-T) - \frac{A}{T}(t-T)\, u(t-T).$$

In a similar way, the second pulse is given as

$$f'(t) = \frac{A}{T}(t-T)\, u(t-T) - Au(t-2T) - \frac{A}{T}(t-2T)\, u(t-2T);$$

$f(t)$ and $f'(t)$ represent the synthesized components.

EXAMPLE 8.43 *Synthesize the halfwave shown in Fig. E8.53, where each time interval is T sec.*

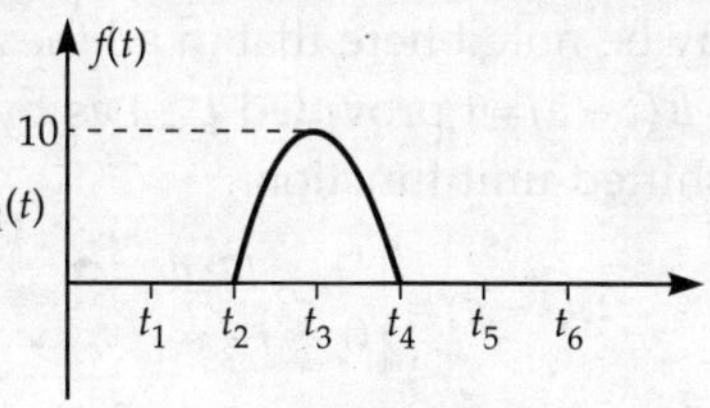

Fig. E8.53

SOLUTION. The given waveform is the addition of two sine waves as shown below [Fig. E8.54].

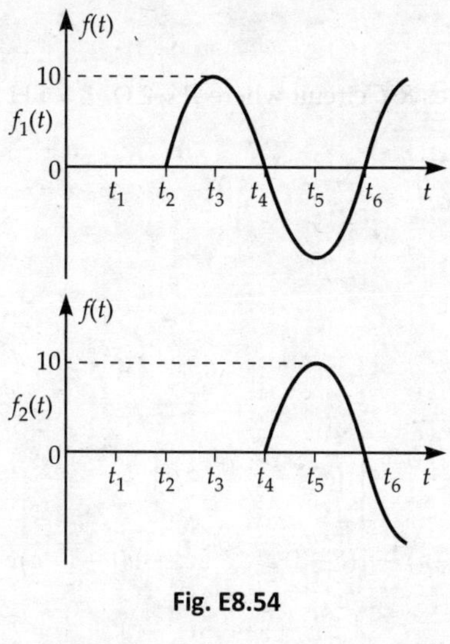

Fig. E8.54

Here $f(t) = f_1(t) + f_2(t)$;

where $f_1(t) = 10 \sin \frac{2\pi}{4T}(t-t_2)\, u(t-t_2)$,

$$f_2(t) = 10 \sin \frac{2\pi}{4T}(t-t_4)\, u(t-t_4)$$

$$\therefore \quad f(t) = f_1(t) + f_2(t)$$

$$= \mathbf{10}\left[\sin \frac{2\pi}{4T}(t-t_2)\, u(t-t_2) + \sin \frac{2\pi}{4T}(t-t_4)\, u(t-t_4)\right].$$

EXAMPLE 8.44 *Find the expression of i (t) in the following circuits when a shifted unit doublet function is applied in :*

(i) a series R-L circuit where $R = 2\,\Omega$, $L = 1$ H,

(ii) a series R-C circuit where $R = 5\,\Omega$, $C = 1$ F,

(iii) a series R-L-C circuit where $R = 3\,\Omega$, $L = 1$ H, $C = \frac{1}{2}$ F.

In all the cases, assume zero initial condition.

SOLUTION. Let the shifted doublet function be represented by $\delta'(t-a)$.

∴ In *R-L* series circuit the application of KVL yields

$$L\frac{di(t)}{dt} + Ri(t) = \delta'(t-a).$$

Applying Laplace transformation, with zero initial conditions, we get

$$I(s)[sL + R] = se^{-as}$$

$$\therefore \quad I(s) = \frac{se^{-as}}{sL+R} = \frac{s}{(2+s)}e^{-as}$$

$$= e^{-as}\left[1 - \frac{2}{s+2}\right].$$

Inverse Laplace transformation yields

$$i(t) = \delta(t-a)\, u(t-a) - 2e^{-2(t-a)}\, u(t-a)$$

i.e., $\quad \mathbf{i(t) = u(t-a)\,[\delta(t-a) - 2e^{-2(t-a)}]\; A.}$

(ii) Doublet function be $\delta'(t-a)$, its application in the *R-C* series circuit leads the formation of the voltage equation as

$$Ri(t) + \frac{1}{C}\int_{-\infty}^{t} i(t)\, dt = \delta'(t-a).$$

CHAPTER 8

Laplace transformation and application of initial conditions yield

$$I(s)\left[R+\frac{1}{Cs}\right]=se^{-as}$$

or,
$$I(s)=\frac{se^{-as}}{R+\frac{1}{Cs}}=\frac{Cs^2 e^{-as}}{RCs+1}=\frac{s^2 e^{-as}}{5s+1}$$

$$=0.2\,e^{-as}\left[\frac{s^2}{s+0.2}\right]$$

$$=0.2\,e^{-as}\left[s-0.2+\frac{0.04}{s+0.2}\right]$$

$$=0.2\,s\,e^{-as}-0.04\,e^{-as}+\frac{0.008\,e^{-as}}{s+0.2}.$$

Inverse Laplace transform yields

$$\boldsymbol{i(t)=0.2\,\delta\,(t-a)-0.04\delta\,(t-a)}$$
$$\boldsymbol{+\,0.008\delta\,(t-a)\,e^{(-0.2(t-a))}\ A.}$$

(*iii*) In a *RLC* circuit Laplace transformation of the voltage equation with zero initial conditions leads to

$$I(s)\left[R+Ls+\frac{1}{Cs}\right]=\pounds\,\delta\,(t-a)=se^{-as};$$

$$\therefore\quad I(s)=\frac{se^{-as}}{R+sL+\frac{1}{sC}}=\frac{s^2 e^{-as}}{\frac{1}{C}+Rs+s^2 L}$$

$$=\frac{s^2 e^{-as}}{\frac{1}{1/2}+3s+s^2}$$

$$=\frac{s^2 e^{-as}}{s^2+3s+2}=\frac{s^2}{(s+1)(s+2)}e^{-as}$$

$$=\left\{1-\frac{3s+2}{(s+1)(s+2)}\right\}e^{-as}.$$

However,
$$\frac{3s+2}{(s+1)(s+2)}=\frac{K_1}{s+1}+\frac{K_2}{s+2}$$

where
$$K_1=\frac{3s+2}{(s+1)(s+2)}.(s+1)\Big|_{s=-1}=-1$$

$$K_2=\frac{3s+2}{(s+1)(s+2)}.(s+2)\Big|_{s=-2}=4$$

$$=-\frac{1}{s+2}+\frac{4}{s+2}.$$

$$\therefore\quad I(s)=\left\{1+\frac{1}{s+1}-\frac{4}{s+2}\right\}e^{-as}$$

$$=e^{-as}+\frac{e^{-as}}{s+1}-\frac{4e^{-as}}{s+2}.$$

Inverse Laplace transformation yields

$$\boldsymbol{i(t)=\delta(t-a)+e^{-(t-a)\,u(t-a)-4\,e^{-2(t-a)}}\,u(t-a).}$$

It may be noted here that in all the above cases the term $u(t-a)=1$ provided $t\ge a$ as by definition, for any shifted unit function,

$$u(t-a)=\begin{cases}1, & t\ge a\\ 0, & t<a.\end{cases}$$

EXERCISES

1. A pulse of width "*a*" begins at $t = 1$. This pulse is applied in a series *R-L* circuit where $R = 2\,\Omega$, $L = 1$ H. Assuming zero initial condition, find $i(t)$.

   [**Hint.** The equation of the pulse would be $u(t-1)-u[(t-1)-a]$

   whose Laplace transformation is $\left[\frac{1}{s}e^{-s}-\frac{1}{s}e^{-(1+a)s}\right]$

   With zero initial condition, the circuit equation becomes

   $$I(s)\,[Ls+R]=\frac{1}{s}\left[e^{-s}-e^{-(1+a)s}\right]$$

   $$\therefore\quad I(s)=\frac{1}{s(s+2)}\left[e^{-s}-e^{-(1+a)s}\right]=\left[\frac{0.5}{s}-\frac{0.5}{s+2}\right]\,[e^{-s}-e^{-(1+a)s}]$$

   $$=0.5\,u(t-1)-0.5\,u(t-1-a)-u(t-1)\,e^{-2(t-1)}+u(t-1-a)e^{-2(t-1-a)}$$

2. A unit impulse voltage $\delta(t-2)$ is applied in a series R-L circuit where $L = 1$ H and $R = 3\,\Omega$. If the impulse voltage is applied at $t = 0$ while the initial condition of the circuit is $i(0) = 0$, find $i(t)$.

[**Hint.** Here, $L\dfrac{di(t)}{dt} + Ri(t) = \delta(t-2)$

with $i(0+) = 0$, Laplace transformation yields

$$I(s) = \frac{e^{-2s}}{sL+R} = \frac{e^{-2s}}{s+3} \qquad \therefore\; i(t) = e^{-3(t-2)}\,u(t-2) \text{ A.}]$$

3. Find $i(t)$ in an RLC circuit provided $R = 3\,\Omega$, $L = 1$ H, $C = \frac{1}{2}$ F and an impulse voltage $3\delta(t-2)$ is applied at $t = 0$. Assume zero initial condition.

[**Hint.** $I(s)\left[R + Ls + \dfrac{1}{Cs}\right] = £\,3\,\delta(t-2) = 3e^{-2s}$

$$\therefore \quad I(s) = \frac{3e^{-2s}}{3+s+\dfrac{2}{s}} = \frac{3s\,e^{-2s}}{3s+s^2+2} = \frac{3s}{(s+1)(s+2)}\,e^{-2s}$$

Now $$\frac{3s}{(s+1)(s+2)} = \frac{K_1}{s+1} + \frac{K_2}{s+2} \qquad \text{where } K_1 = \left.\frac{3s}{s+2}\right|_{s=-1} = -3$$

i.e., $$\frac{3s}{(s+1)(s+2)} = -\frac{3}{s+1} + \frac{6}{s+2} \qquad K_2 = \left.\frac{3s}{s+1}\right|_{s=-2} = 6$$

$$\therefore \quad I(s) = e^{-2s}\left[-\frac{3}{s+1} + \frac{6}{s+2}\right].$$

Take inverse laplace transform to get the result $i(t)$].

4. In the above exercise if the applied voltage be a step voltage $u(t-a)$, find $i(t)$, other things being same as the previous problem.

[**Hint.** $I(s)\left[R + Ls + \dfrac{1}{Cs}\right] = £(t-a) = \dfrac{1}{s}e^{-as}$

$$\therefore \quad I(s) = \frac{e^{-as}}{s\left(R+Ls+\dfrac{1}{Cs}\right)} = \frac{e^{-as}}{s\left(3+s+\dfrac{2}{s}\right)}$$

$$= \frac{s\,e^{-as}}{s(3s+s^2+2)} = \frac{e^{-as}}{s^2+3s+2} = \frac{1}{(s+1)(s+2)}\,e^{-as}.$$

Next apply partial fraction method and find $I(s)$. Taking the inverse of $I(s)$, $i(t)$ will be obtained.]

5. A unit step voltage $5u(t-t_1)$ is applied in a series R-C circuit with $R = 5\,\Omega$, $C = 2$ F. Assuming zero initial condition, find $i(t)$.

[**Hint.** Solve as shown in Example 8.9]

6. A ramp voltage $r(t-1)$ is applied in series RC circuit at $t = 0$. Assuming zero initial conditions and $R = 2\,\Omega$, $C = \frac{1}{2}$ F, find $i(t)$.

[**Hint.** Solve as shown in Example 8.10.]

7. The waveform of a function $f(t)$ is shown in Fig. P8.1. Write down its equations in terms of step functions.

[**Hint.** Refer Example 8.12]

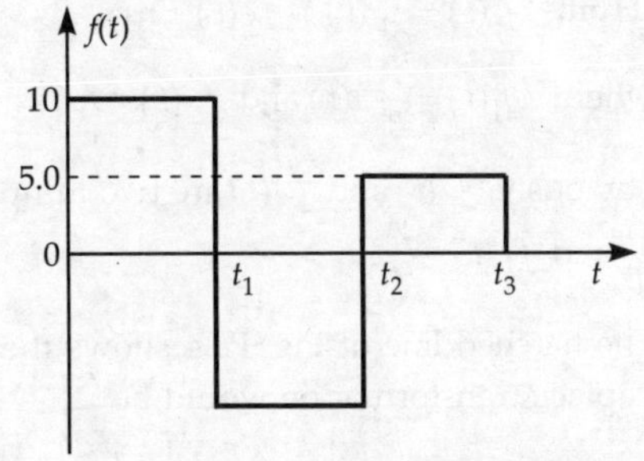

Fig. P8.1

8. A wave equation is given by $f(t) = 2u(t - t_1)t + 4u(t - t_2) - u(t - t_3)$. Sketch the waveform.
[**Hint.** Refer Example 8.14.]

9. If $f(t) = K_0 \cos(\omega t + \phi)\, u(t)$, find $G(t)$ when $G(t) = \int_{-\infty}^{t} f(t)\, dt$

[**Hint.** $G(t) = K_0 \int_0^t \cos(\omega t + \phi)\, dt = \frac{K_0}{\omega} \sin(\omega t + \phi)\Big|_0^t = \frac{K_0}{\omega}[\sin(\omega t + \phi) - \sin\phi.]$

10. Two ramp functions are given by

$$f_1(t) = mt\, u(t) \quad \text{and} \quad f_2(t) = -m'(t - a)\, u(t - a)$$

where m and m' are two slopes (+ve) and $m > m'$. Sketch the waveform by adding these two functions.
[**Hint.** $f(t) = mt\, u(t) - m'(t - a)\, u(t - a)$, the sketch being shown in Fig. P8.2.]

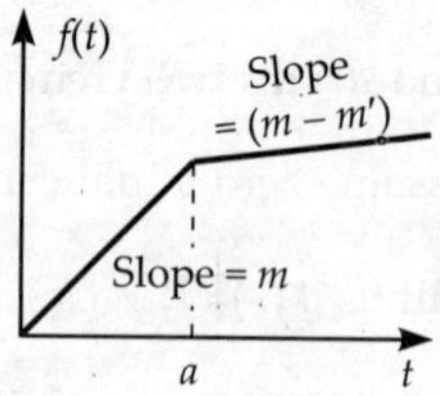

Fig. P8.2

11. A stepped waveform is shown in Fig. P8.3. Find its equation.
[**Hint.** $f(t) = u(t - 1) + u(t - 2)\, u(t - 3) - 3u(t - 4)$.]

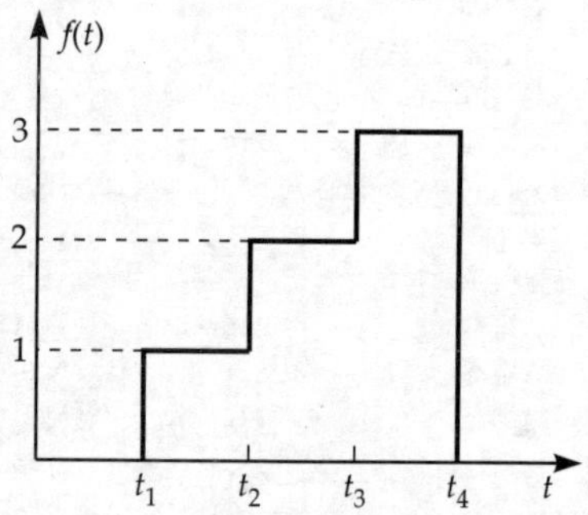

Fig. P8.3

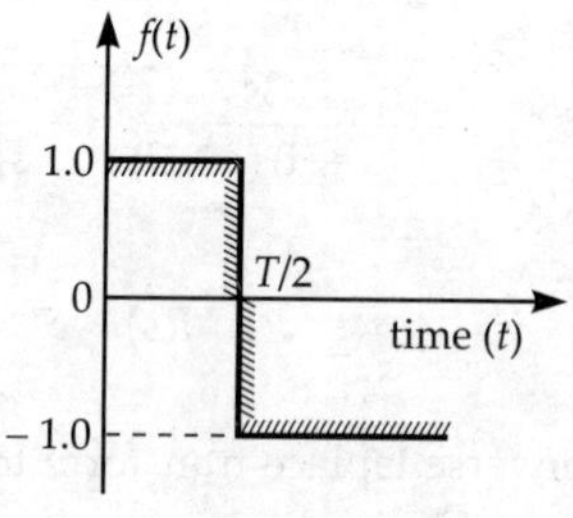

Fig. P8.4

12. A waveform is shown in Fig. P8.4. Find the wave equation.
[**Hint.** $f(t) = f_1(t) + f_2(t) = u(t) + [-2u(t - T/2)] = u(t) - 2u(t - T/2)$].

13. Find the Laplace transform of the waveform shown in Fig. P8.5.
[**Hint.** $f(t) = f_1(t) + f_2(t)$

where $\quad f_1(t) = 5[u(t - 1) - u(t - 2)]$

and $\quad f_2(t) = 5[u(t - 3) - u(t - 4)]$

$$\pounds\, f(t) = \frac{5}{s}[e^{-s} - e^{-2s} + e^{-3s} - e^{-4s}].\,]$$

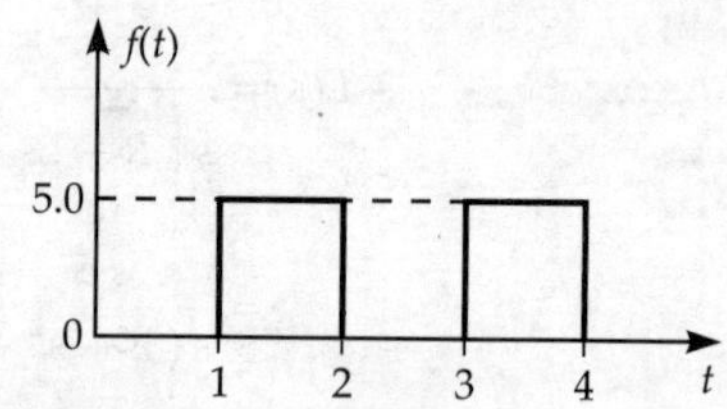

Fig. P8.5

14. A waveform equation is given by

$f(t) = \frac{A}{T} r(t) - \frac{A}{T} r(t - T)$. Draw the waveform.

[**Hint.** $f(t) = f_1(t) + f_2(t)$

where $f_1(t) = \frac{A}{T} r(t)$ and $f_2(t) = -\frac{A}{T} r(t - T)$;

obviously, $f_1(t)$ and $f_2(t)$ are two ramp functions, $f_1(t)$ having slope $\frac{A}{T}$ and $f_2(t) - \frac{A}{T}$.

The hatched line of Fig. P8.4 shows the truncated ramp function. Its Laplace transformation would be

$$\frac{A}{T}\left[\frac{1}{s^2} - \frac{1}{s^2} e^{-Ts}\right]$$

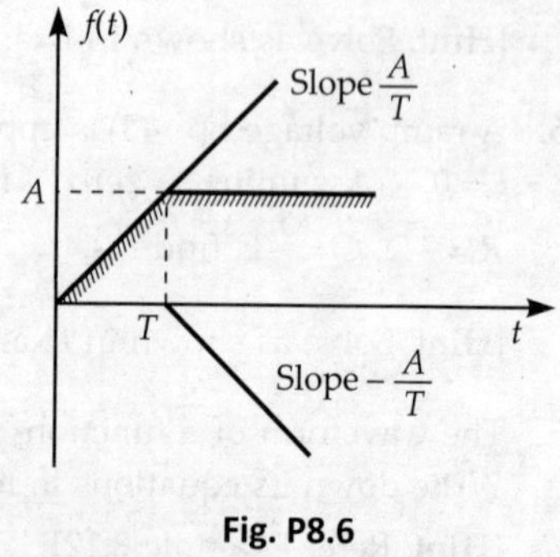

Fig. P8.6

CHAPTER 9

Analysis of Coupled Circuits

9.1 INTRODUCTION

In this chapter, the aim is to analyse magnetically *coupled circuits i.e.,* the interconnected loops of an electric network through magnetic fields.

9.2 SELF INDUCTANCE

When a current changes in a circuit, the magnetic flux linking the same circuit changes (and vice versa) and an e.m.f is induced in the circuit. This induced emf is proportional to the rate of change current.

i.e., $$v = L\frac{di}{dt} \qquad \text{...(9.1)}$$

where v = induced voltage

$\frac{di}{dt}$ = rate of change of current

L = constant of proportionality called *self-inductance.*

[The unit of self-inductance is *Henry*]

However, from the concepts of basic Electrical Engineering, this inductance is also expressed as

$$L = \frac{N\phi}{i} \qquad \text{...(...(9.2)}$$

$$\begin{bmatrix} \text{N = no. of turns in the circuit} \\ \phi = \text{flux linkage} \end{bmatrix}$$

Substitution of (9.2) in (9.1) yields

$$v = L\frac{d\left(\frac{N\phi}{L}\right)}{dt}$$

or $$v = L \times \frac{1}{L} \times N\frac{d\phi}{dt} = N\frac{d\phi}{dt} \qquad \text{...(9.3)}$$

Comparing (9.1) and (9.3),

$$L\frac{di}{dt} = N\frac{d\phi}{dt}$$

or $$L = N\frac{d\phi}{di} \qquad \text{...(9.4)}$$

Expression (9.4) represents the magnitude of self-inductance.

9.3 MUTUAL INDUCTANCE

In Fig. 9.1 let two coils carry currents i_1 and i_2 [both alternating currents]. Each coil will have

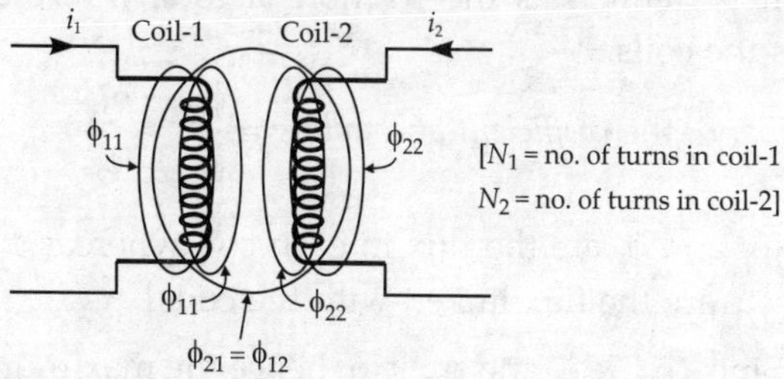

Fig. 9.1 Linking of Flux.

leakage flux (ϕ_{11} and ϕ_{22} for coil 1 and coil 2 respectively) as well as mutual flux (ϕ_{21} or ϕ_{12} where, the flux of coil-2 links coil-1 or flux of coil-1 links coil-2).

The induced voltage of coil-2 is given by

$$v_{L_2} = N_2 \frac{d\phi_{12}}{dt} \quad ...(9.5)$$

Again, since ϕ_{12} is related to the current of coil-1 and the induced voltage is proportional to the rate of change of i_1

$$\therefore \quad v_{L_2} = M \frac{di_1}{dt} \quad ...(9.6)$$

[M = constant of proportionality termed as *mutual inductance* between the two coils]

Comparing equations (9.5) and (9.6),

$$M \frac{di_1}{dt} = N_2 \frac{d\phi_{12}}{dt}$$

$$\therefore \quad M = N_2 \frac{d\phi_{12}}{di_1} \quad ...(9.7)$$

Similarly,

$$M = N_1 \frac{d\phi_{21}}{di_2} \quad ...(9.8)$$

When the coils are linked with air as medium, the flux and current are linearly related and the expressions of mutual inductance are modified as

$$M = N_2 \frac{\phi_{12}}{i_1} \quad ...9.7(A)$$

and
$$M = N_1 \frac{\phi_{21}}{i_2} \quad ...9.8(A)$$

It may be observed at this stage that the mutual inductance is the bilateral property of the linked coils.

9.4 COEFFICIENT OF COUPLING

It is defined as the fraction of total flux that links the coils.

i.e., K, the *coefficient of coupling* $= \dfrac{\phi_{12}}{\phi_1} = \dfrac{\phi_{21}}{\phi_2}$

[ϕ_1 and ϕ_2 are the flux in each coil whereas ϕ_{12} and ϕ_{21} are the flux linked with the coils]

Since, $\phi_{12} < \phi_1$ and $\phi_{21} < \phi_2$ hence the maximum value of K is unity.

Multiplying equations (9.7(A)) and (9.8(A)), we get

$$M^2 = N_1 N_2 \frac{\phi_{21}\,\phi_{12}}{i_1\, i_2} = N_1 N_2 \frac{K\phi_1 \cdot K\phi_2}{i_1 . i_2}$$

$$= K^2 N_1 \frac{\phi_1}{i_1} . N_2 \frac{\phi_2}{i_2}$$

$$= K^2 L_1 L_2 \qquad \left[\because \; L = \frac{N\phi}{i}\right]$$

$$\therefore \quad M = K\sqrt{L_1 L_2} \quad ...(9.9)$$

9.5 SERIES CONNECTION OF COUPLED COILS

Let two coils, of self-inductances L_1 and L_2 be connected in series such that the voltage induced in coil-1 is v_{L_1} and that in coil-2 is v_{L_2} while a current i flows through them. Let M_{12} be the mutual inductance.

$$\therefore \quad v_{L_1} = L_1 \frac{di}{dt} + M_{12} \frac{di}{dt} = (L_1 + M_{12}) \frac{di}{dt} \quad ...(9.10)$$

and
$$v_{L_2} = L_2 \frac{di}{dt} + M_{12} \frac{di}{dt} = (L_2 + M_{12}) \frac{di}{dt} \quad ...(9.11)$$

$\therefore$ Net voltage

$$= v_L = v_{L_1} + v_{L_2}$$

$$= (L_1 + M_{12}) \frac{di}{dt} + (L_2 + M_{12}) \frac{di}{dt}$$

$$= \frac{di}{dt} [L_1 + M_{12} + L_2 + M_{12}]$$

or
$$v_L = (L_1 + L_2 + 2M) \frac{di}{dt}$$

[putting $M_{12} = M$]

$\therefore$ In case of series connection, as shown in Fig. 9.2, the total inductance

$$L = L_1 + L_2 + 2M \quad ...(9.12)$$

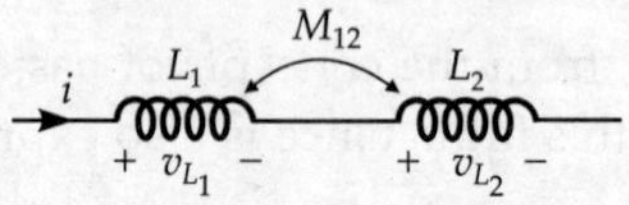

Fig. 9.2 Mutually Coupled coils in Series [Here the fluxes of both the coils mutually assist each other]

However, in Fig. 9.3, where the coils are still series connected but the fluxes of both the coils oppose each other,

$$v_{L_1} = (L_1 - M_{12})\frac{di}{dt}$$

and $$v_{L_2} = (L_2 - M_{12})\frac{di}{dt},$$

giving $$v_L = (L_1 + L_2 - 2M_{12})\frac{di}{dt}.$$

The net inductance, here, is thus

$$\mathbf{L = (L_1 + L_2 - 2M)} \qquad ...(9.13)$$

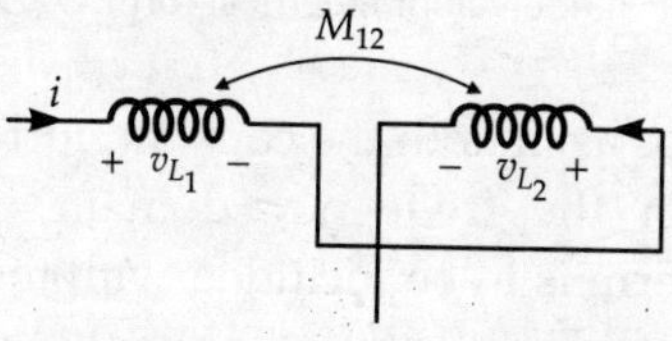

Fig. 9.3 Mutually Coupled coils in Series [Here the fluxes of both the coils mutually oppose each other]

9.6 MODELING OF COUPLED CIRCUITS

In Fig. 9.4, each circuit contains a voltage source and the respective mesh currents being i_1 and i_2, application of KVL yields

$$v_1 = R_1 i_1 + L_1\frac{di_1}{dt} \pm M\frac{di_2}{dt} \qquad ...(9.14)$$

and $$v_2 = R_2 i_2 + L_2\frac{di_2}{dt} \pm M\frac{di_1}{dt} \qquad ...(9.15)$$

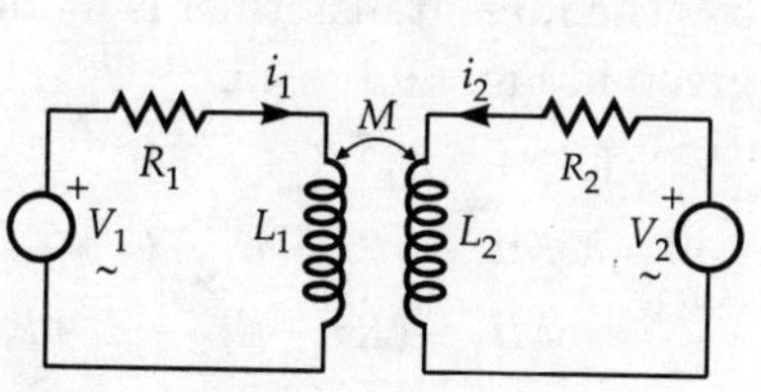

Fig. 9.4 Coupled coils fed by voltage sources

If the fluxes of both the coils oppose each other, equations (9.14) and (9.15) modify as

$$v_1 = R_1 i_1 + L_1\frac{di_1}{dt} - M\frac{di_2}{dt} \qquad ...(9.14(A))$$

$$v_2 = R_2 i_2 + L_2\frac{di_2}{dt} - M\frac{di_1}{dt} \qquad ...(9.15(A))$$

Assuming sinusoidal voltage sources, at steady state, equations (9.14(A)) and (9.15(A)) are further modified as

$$v_1 = I_1 R_1 + j\omega L_1 I_1 - j\omega M I_2$$

$$v_2 = I_2 R_2 + j\omega L_2 I_2 - j\,\omega M I_1$$

i.e., $$v_1 = (R_1 + j\omega L_1) I_1 - j\omega M I_2 \qquad ...(9.14(B))$$

$$v_2 = -j\,\omega M I_1 + (R_2 + j\omega L_2) I_2 \qquad ...(9.15(B))$$

In matrix form,

$$\begin{bmatrix} v_1 \\ v_2 \end{bmatrix} = \begin{bmatrix} Z_{11} & Z_{12} \\ Z_{21} & Z_{22} \end{bmatrix}\begin{bmatrix} I_1 \\ I_2 \end{bmatrix} \qquad ...(9.16)$$

where $Z_{11} = R_1 + j\omega L_1$ $\quad Z_{12} = -j\omega M$

$Z_{21} = -j\,\omega M$ $\quad Z_{22} = R_2 + j\omega L_2$

On the other hand, if the fluxes of both coils assists, each other, we can write

$$v_1 = R_1 i_1 + L_1\frac{di_1}{dt} + M\frac{di_2}{dt}$$

and $$v_2 = R_2 i_2 + L_2\frac{di_2}{dt} + M\frac{di_1}{dt}$$

This time $Z_{12} = Z_{21} = +j\omega M$

9.7 DOT CONVENTION IN COUPLED COILS

To determine the relative polarity of the induced voltage in the coupled coil, the coils are marked with *dots*. On each coil, a dot is placed at the terminals which are instantaneously of the same polarity on the basis of mutual inductance alone. When the currents through *each* of the mutually coupled coils are going away from the dot or towards the dot, the mutual inductance is +ve while for the case when the current through the coil is leaving the dot for one coil and entering the other, the mutual inductance is –ve [Figs. 9.5(*a*) and (*b*)].

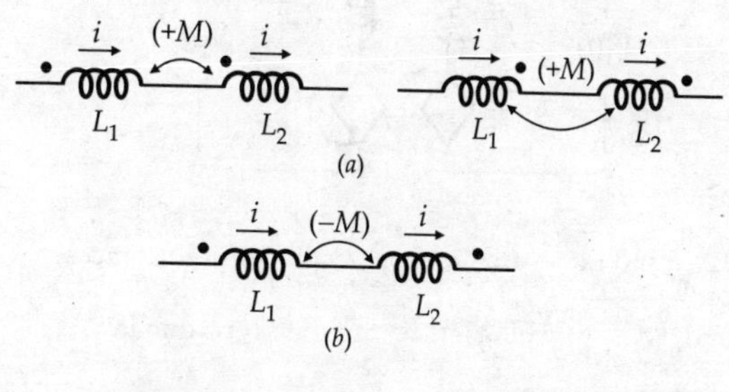

Fig. 9.5 +ve and –ve dot convention for series connected mutually coupled coils.

The dot convention of few possibilities of mutually coupled transformer coils is indicated below (Fig. 9.6).

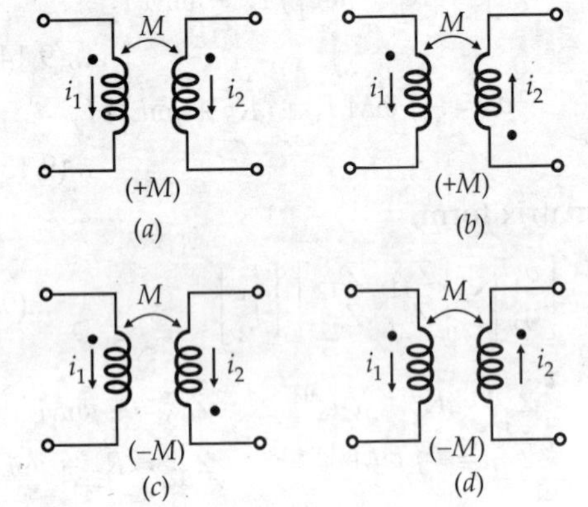

[Physically (– M) means that the windings of the coil are wound in reverse way from one another]

Fig. 9.6 Dot convention of transformer coils.

9.8 ELECTRICAL EQUIVALENTS OF MAGNETICALLY COUPLED CIRCUITS

Figure 9.7 represents circuit in time domain. In electrical equivalent representation of this circuit

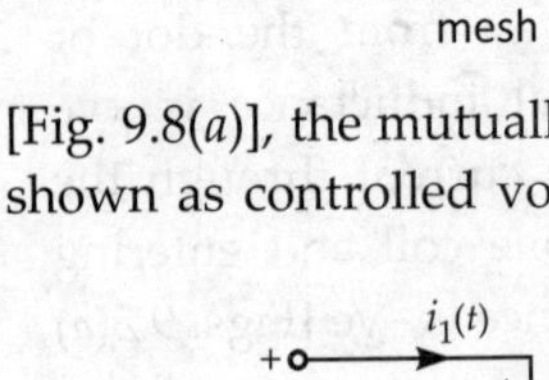

$$\begin{cases} v_1(t) = L_1 \dfrac{di_1(t)}{dt} + M\dfrac{di_2(t)}{dt} \\ v_2(t) = L_2 \dfrac{di_2(t)}{dt} + M\dfrac{di_1(t)}{dt} \end{cases}$$

Fig. 9.7 Coupled circuit and the instantaneous mesh equations.

[Fig. 9.8(a)], the mutually induced voltages may be shown as controlled voltage sources (M is +ve for

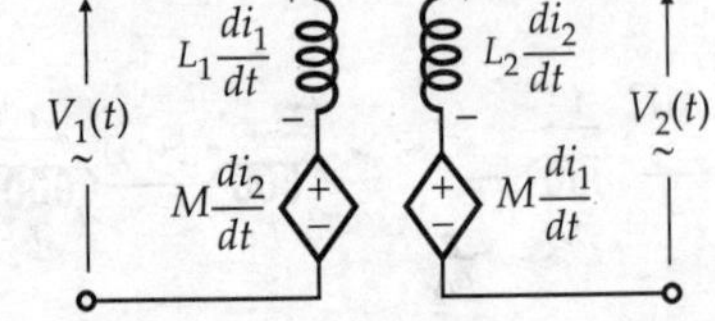

$L_1\dfrac{di_1}{dt}$ and $L_2\dfrac{di_2}{dt}$ are the drops in the self-inductances and $M\dfrac{di_1}{dt}$ as well as $M\dfrac{di_2}{dt}$ are the drops due to mutual inductance.

(a) Time domain representation of coupled circuits

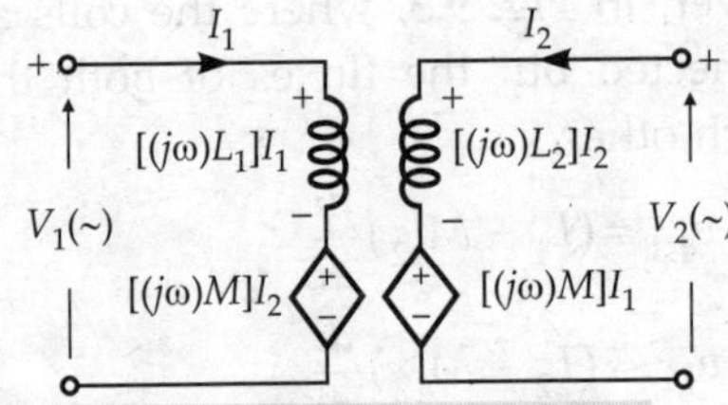

Here $V_1 = [(j\omega)L_1]I_1 + [(j\omega)M]I_2]$
$V_2 = [(j\omega)M]I_1 + [(j\omega)L_2]I_2]$

(b) Frequency-domain representation of coupled circuit

Fig. 9.8 Representation of coupled circuits in equivalent electrical form.

both the loops as in both the coils the currents enter the dots). In the frequency domain equivalent circuit, '$j\omega$' term is to be included with the induced voltages [Ref. Fig. 9.8(b)]. Table 9.1 represents different combinations of couplings and their equivalent circuits.

EXAMPLE 9.1 *For an ideal transformer (Fig. E9.1) find the input impedance. Assume load impedance to be Z_L.*

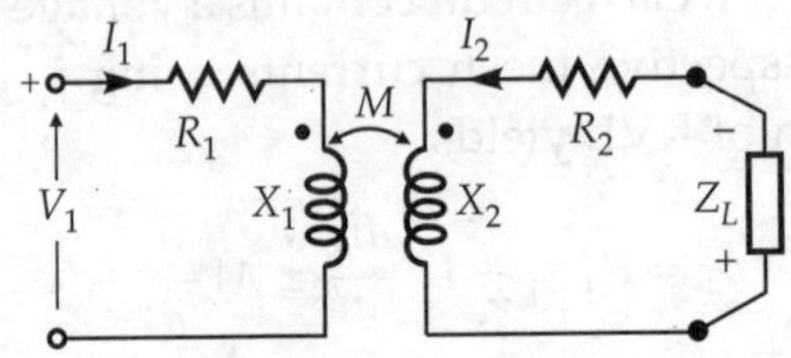

Fig. E9.1

SOLUTION. The ideal transformer is modelled in the circuit given in Fig. E9.1.

Here, $V_1 = (R_1 + jX_1)I_1 + j\omega M I_2$

and $0 = j\omega M I_1 + (R_2 + jX_2)I_2 + Z_L I_2$

$= j\omega M I_1 + (R_2 + jX_2 + Z_L)I_2$

In matrix form,

$$\begin{bmatrix} V_1 \\ 0 \end{bmatrix} = \begin{bmatrix} (R + jX_1) & j\omega M \\ j\omega M & (R_2 + X_2 + Z_L) \end{bmatrix} \begin{bmatrix} I_1 \\ I_2 \end{bmatrix}$$

Elimination of I_2 from the first equation results

$$V_1 = (R_1 + jX_1)I_1 + j\omega M\left[-\frac{j\omega M I_1}{R_2 + jX_2 + Z_L}\right]$$

$$\therefore \quad Z_{\text{input}} = \frac{V_1}{I_1} = (R_1 + jX_1) + \frac{\omega^2 M^2}{R_2 + jX_2 + Z_L}$$

$$\mathbf{Z_{in} = (R_1 + jX_1) + \frac{\omega^2 M^2}{R_2 + jX_2 + Z_L}}.$$

Table 9.1

Different Combination of Coupling	*Time Domain Equivalent Circuit*	*Frequency Domain Equivalent Circuit*
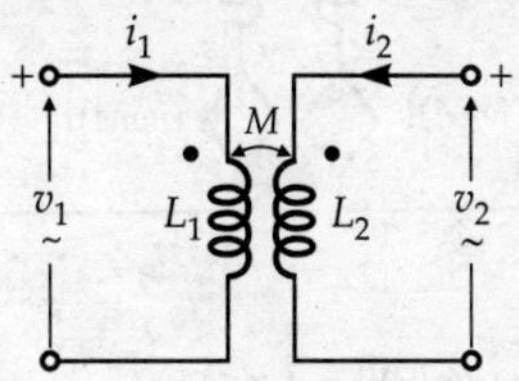 [In both the coils, the currents enter the dot end and hence M term would be +ve in both the loops]	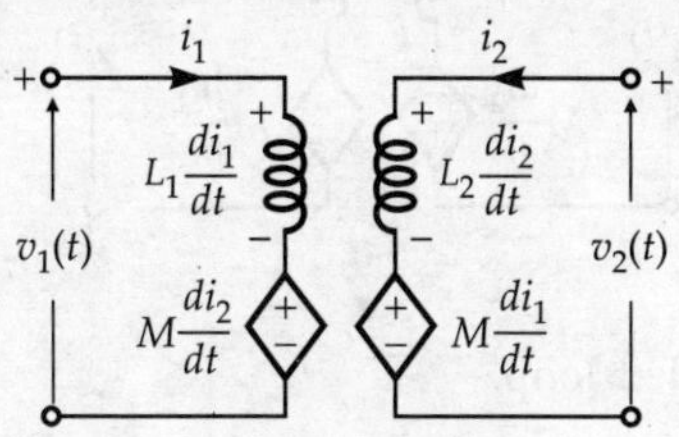 $v_1 = L_1 \frac{di_1}{dt} + M\frac{di_2}{dt}$ $v_2 = L_2 \frac{di_2}{dt} + M\frac{di_1}{dt}$	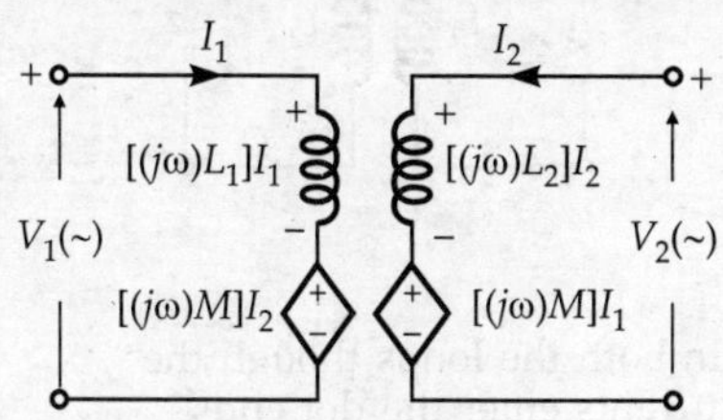 $V_1 = j\omega L_1 . I_1 + j\omega M . I_2$ $V_2 = j\omega M . I_1 + j\omega L_2 . I_2$
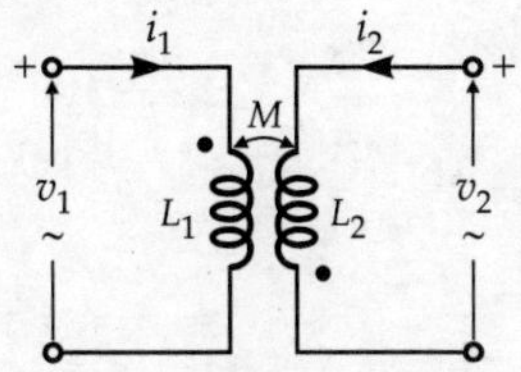 [In left loop, the current enters the dot end while in right loop, the current comes out of the dot end. Hence M terms will be –ve]	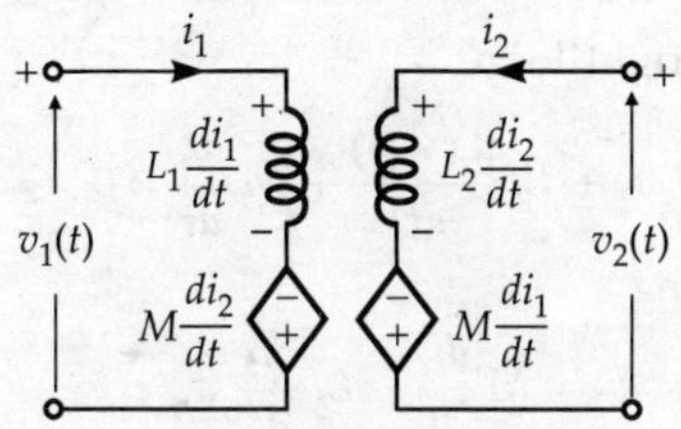 $v_1 = L_1 \frac{di_1}{dt} - M\frac{di_2}{dt}$ $v_2 = L_2 \frac{di_2}{dt} - M\frac{di_1}{dt}$	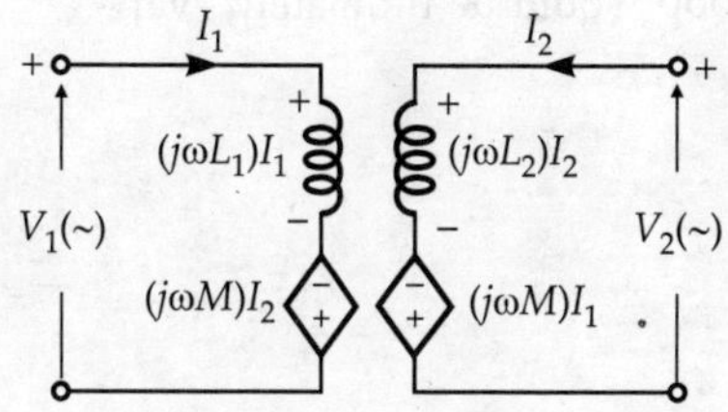 $V_1 = (j\omega L_1) I_1 - (j\omega M) I_2$ $V_2 = -(j\omega M) I_1 + (j\omega L_2) I_2$
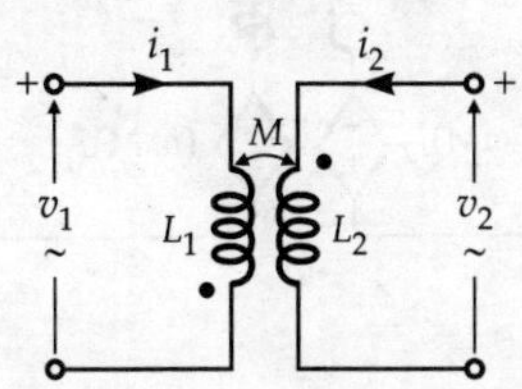 [In left hand coil current comes out of the dot while in the right hand coil, the current enters the coil through dot end. Hence M terms would be –ve in both the loops]	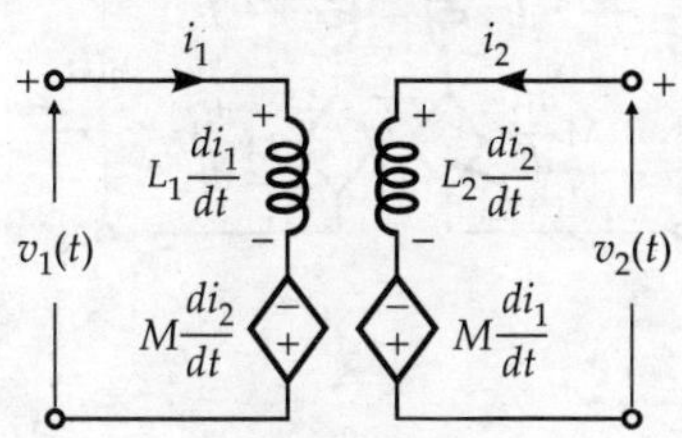 $v_1 = L_1 \frac{di_1}{dt} - M\frac{di_2}{dt}$ $v_2 = L_2 \frac{di_2}{dt} - M\frac{di_1}{dt}$	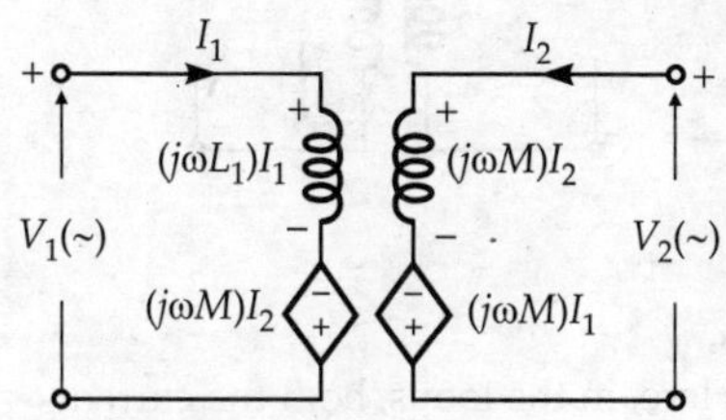 $V_1 = (j\omega L_1) I_1 - (j\omega M) I_2$ $V_2 = -(j\omega M) I_1 + (j\omega L_2) I_2$
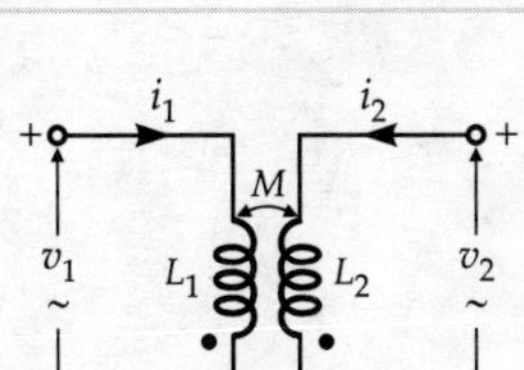 [In both the coils, the currents are coming out of dot ends. Hence in both the loops, the M terms would be +ve]	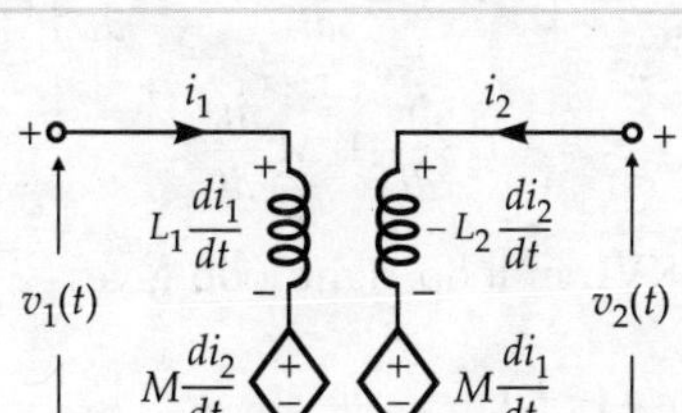 $v_1 = L_1 \frac{di_1}{dt} + M\frac{di_2}{dt}$ $v_2 = L_2 \frac{di_2}{dt} + M\frac{di_1}{dt}$	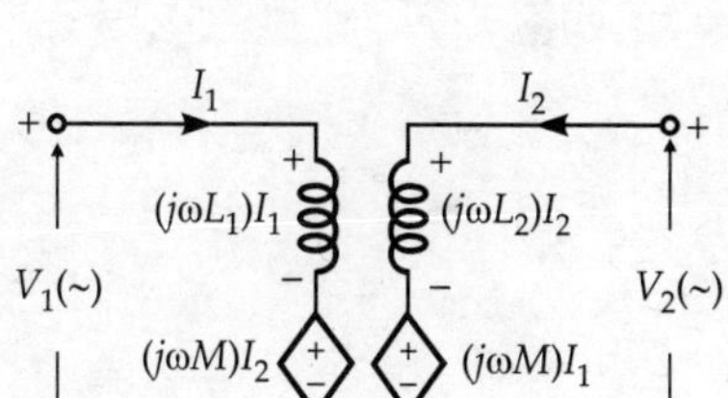 $V_1 = (j\omega L_1) I_1 + (j\omega M) I_2$ $V_2 = (j\omega M) I_1 + (j\omega L_2) I_2$

(*Contd...*)

Different Combination of Coupling	Time Domain Equivalent Circuit	Frequency Domain Equivalent Circuit
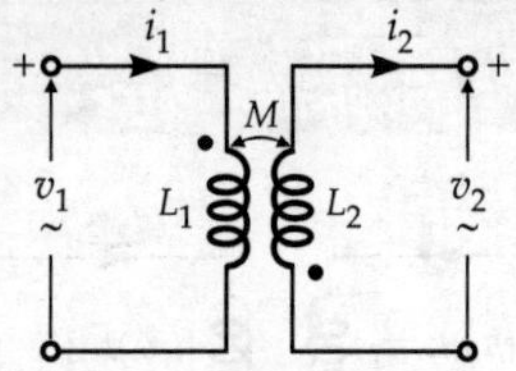	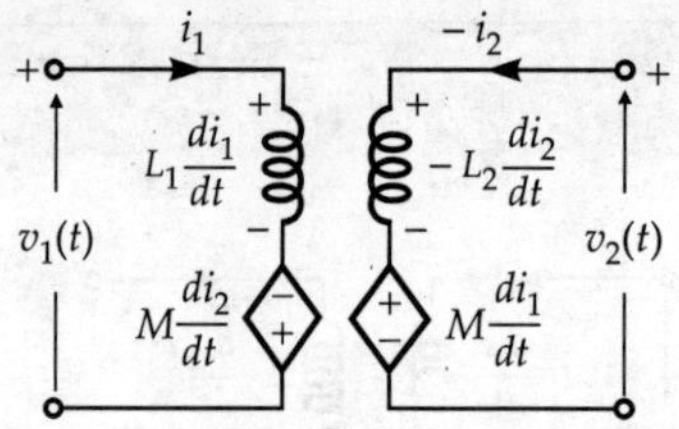	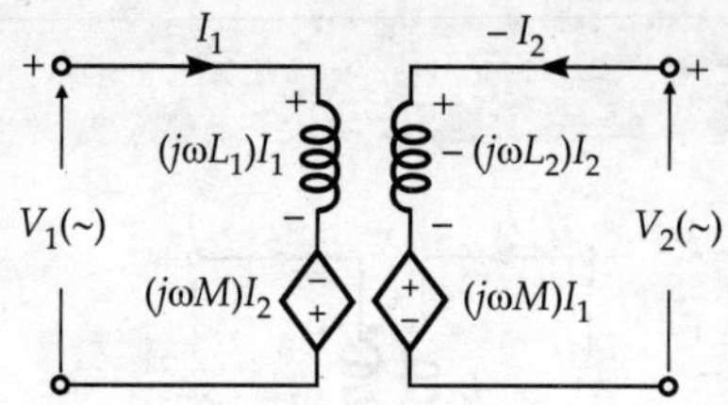
[In both the loops though the currents enter the dot ends indicating M terms in both the loops to be +ve, but it may be observed that the direction of i_2 here is reverse than that of the conventional one. Hence the M term in the equation of left hand loop would be ultimately –ve]	for left loop, $v_1 = L_1 \frac{di_1}{dt} + M \frac{d(-i_2)}{dt}$ giving $v_1 = L_1 \frac{di_1}{dt} - M \frac{di_2}{dt}$ for right loop, $-v_2 + L_2 \frac{d(-i_2)}{dt} + M \frac{di_1}{dt} = 0$ giving $v_2 = M \frac{di_1}{dt} - L_2 \frac{di_2}{dt}$	$V_1 = (j\omega L_1) I_1 - (j\omega M) I_2$ $V_2 = (j\omega M) I_1 - (j\omega L_2) I_2$
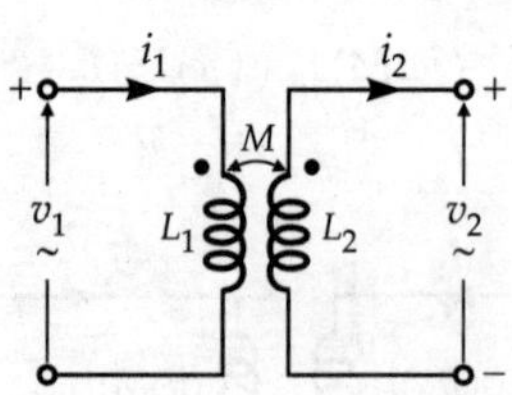	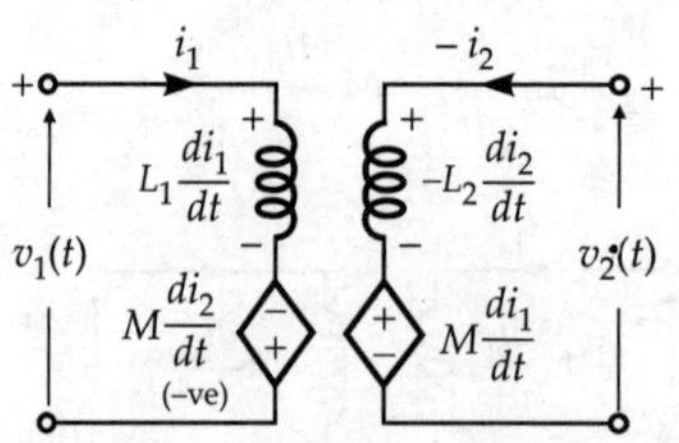	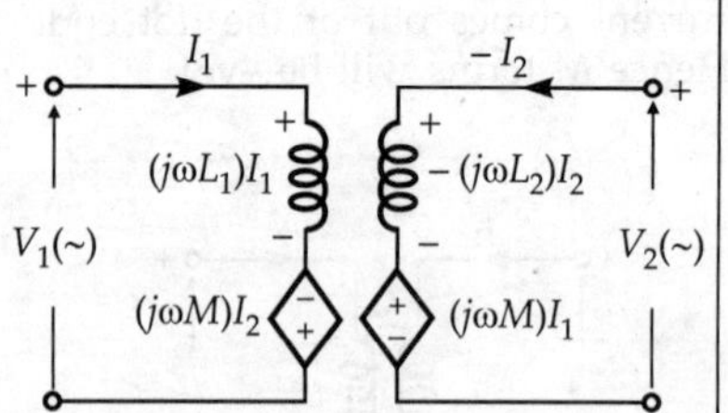
[Here, in the loops, both the currents i_1 and $(-i_2)$ enter the dot ends. This will make M to be +ve in both the loop equations. However, the direction of i_2 is reversed here than that of the conventional figures]	for left loop, $v_1 = L_1 \frac{di_1}{dt} - M \frac{di_2}{dt}$ $\left[\because v_1 = L_1 \frac{di_1}{dt} + M\left(-\frac{di_2}{dt}\right)\right]$ $v_2 = -L_2 \frac{di_2}{dt} + M \frac{di_1}{dt}$ [∵ KVL in loop right loop gives $L_2 \frac{d(-i_2)}{dt} + M \frac{di_1}{dt} - v_2 = 0$]	$V_1 = (j\omega L_1) I_1 - (j\omega M) I_2$ $V_2 = (j\omega L_2) I_2 - (j\omega M) I_1$

(Contd...)

Different Combination of Coupling	Time Domain Equivalent Circuit	Frequency Domain Equivalent Circuit
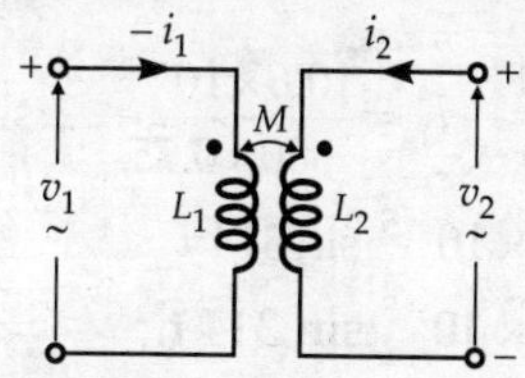	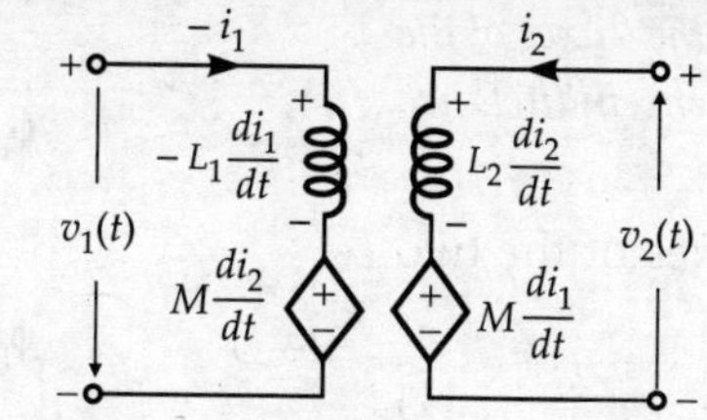	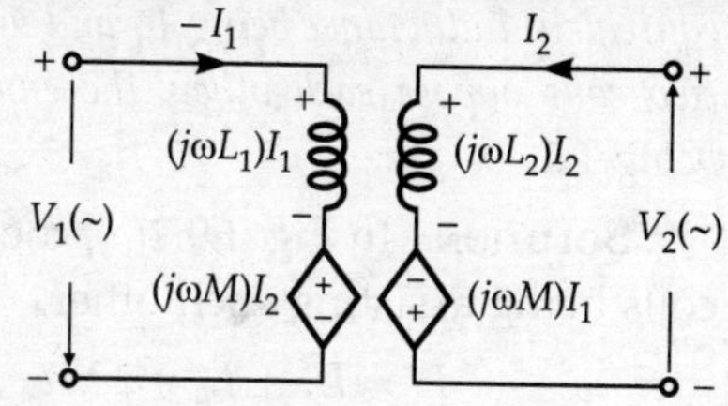
[In the left hand loop, $(-i_1)$ enters the dot end while for the right handed loop, i_2 enters the dot end. This will make both the M terms at first of +ve signs but as i_1 is –ve hence ultimately the M term of r.h. loops involving i_1 would be –ve]	for left loop $-v_1 - L_1\dfrac{di_1}{dt} + M\dfrac{di_2}{dt} = 0$ giving $v_1 = -L_1\dfrac{di_1}{dt} + M\dfrac{di_2}{dt}$ for the right loop, $v_2 = L_2\dfrac{di_2}{dt} + M\dfrac{d(-i_1)}{dt}$ giving $v_2 = L_2\dfrac{di_2}{dt} - M\dfrac{di_1}{dt}$	$V_1 = -(j\omega L_1)I_1 + (j\omega M)I_2$ $V_2 = -(j\omega M)I_2 + (j\omega L_2)I_1$
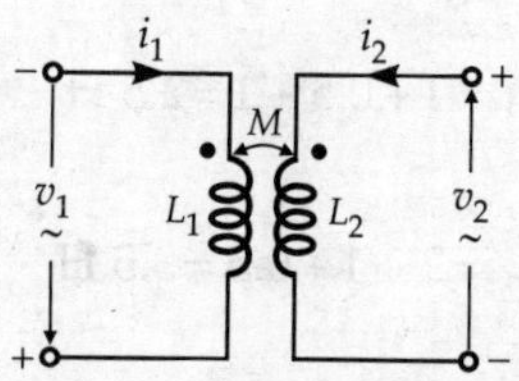	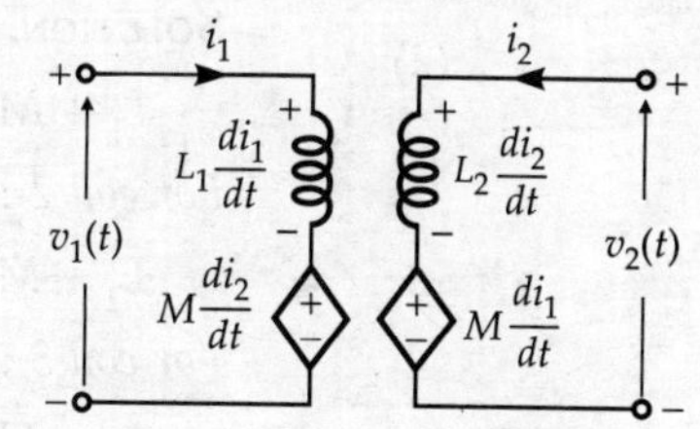	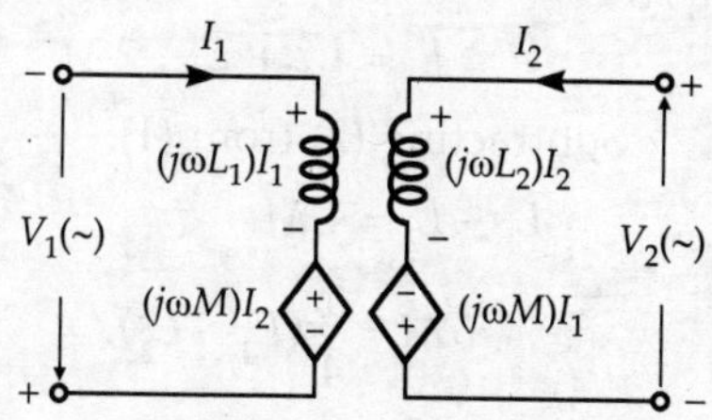
[In both the loops currents enter the dotted ends. Thus M terms in equations of both the loops will be +ve]. Note that polarity of V_1 is reversed.	$-v_1 = L_1\dfrac{di_1}{dt} + M\dfrac{di_2}{dt}$ $v_2 = L_2\dfrac{di_2}{dt} + M\dfrac{di_1}{dt}$	$-V_1 = (j\omega L_1)I_1 + (j\omega M)I_2$ $V_2 = (j\omega L_2)I_2 + (j\omega M)I_1$
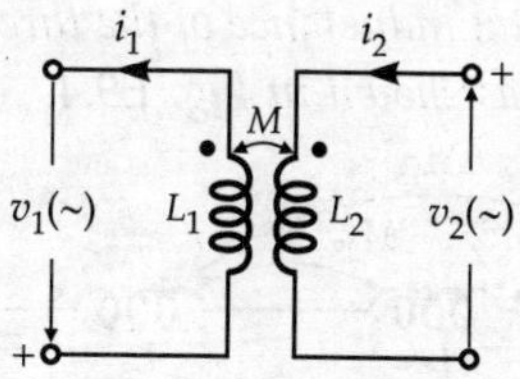	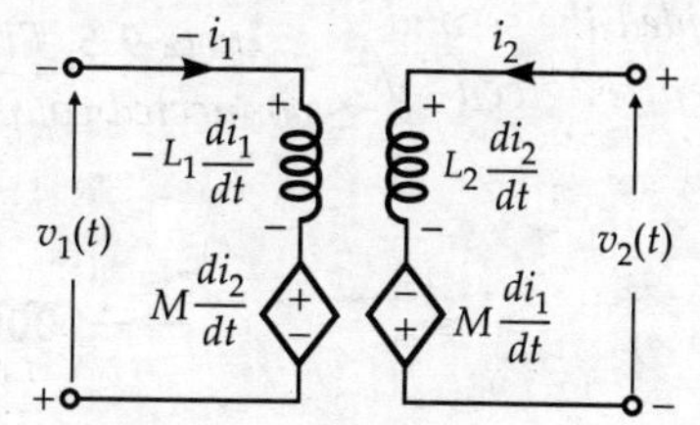	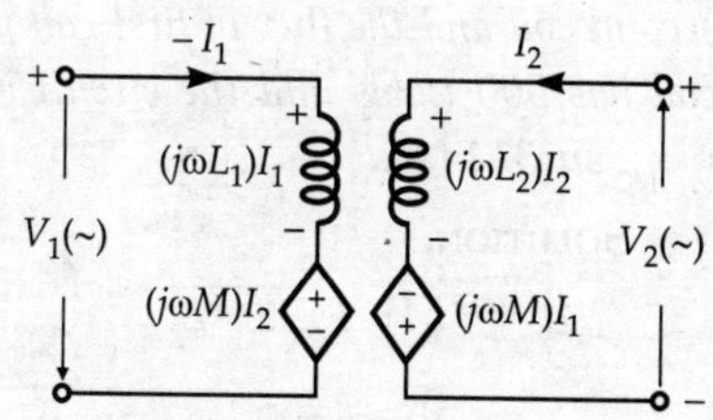
[In left loop i_1 leaves the dot end while in right loop, $(-i_2)$ also leaves the dot end. Thus M will be +ve. However, as basically i_1 is reverse direction in the actual circuit hence the terms involving i_1 will be –ve]	$\left(-v_1 = L_1\dfrac{d(-i_1)}{dt} + M\dfrac{di_2}{dt}\right)$ $v_1 = L_1\dfrac{di_1}{dt} - M\dfrac{di_2}{dt}$ $\left(v_2 = L_2\dfrac{di_2}{dt} + M\dfrac{d(-i_1)}{dt}\right)$ $v_2 = L_2\dfrac{di_2}{dt} - M\dfrac{di_1}{dt}$	$V_1 = (j\omega L_1)I_1 - (j\omega M)I_2$ $V_2 = (j\omega L_2)I_2 - (j\omega M)I_1$

EXAMPLE 9.2 *Find the expression for the mutual inductance in the series connection of two coupled coils, when the flux of the two coils assist each other, the net equivalent inductance being L_1 and when the fluxes of the two coils oppose each other, the equivalent inductance being L_2.*

SOLUTION. In Fig. E9.2(*a*), the fluxes of the two coils being assisting each other,

$$L_1 = L_A + L_B + 2M \qquad \text{...(1)}$$

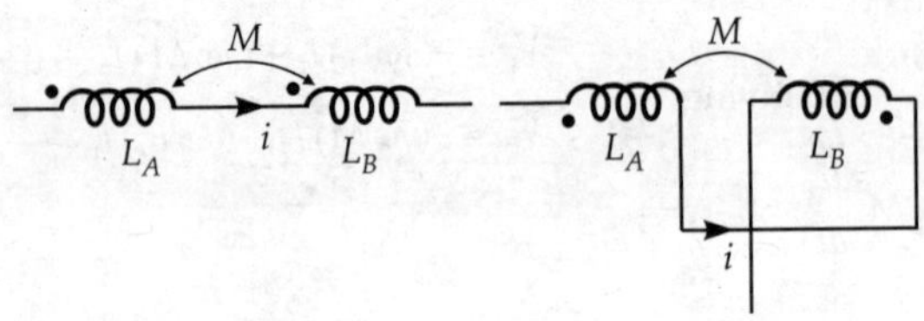

(*a*) (*b*)

Fig. E9.2

In Fig. E9.2(*b*), the fluxes of the coils being opposing each other,

$$L_2 = L_A + L_B - 2M \qquad \text{...(2)}$$

Subtracting (2) from (1),

$$L_1 - L_2 = 4\,M$$

$$\therefore \qquad \boldsymbol{M = \frac{1}{4}(L_1 - L_2).}$$

This gives the expression for the mutual inductance for the given series connected coils.

EXAMPLE 9.3 *Two coupled coils have self-inductances $L_1 = 10 \times 10^{-3}$ H and $L_2 = 20 \times 10^{-3}$ H. The coefficient of coupling (K) being 0.75 in the air, find voltage in the second coil and the flux of first coil provided the second coil has 500 turns and the circuit current is given by $i_1 = 2 \sin 314\, t$ A.*

SOLUTION.

$$M = K\sqrt{L_1 L_2}$$

$$= 0.75\sqrt{10 \times 10^{-3} \times 20 \times 10^{-3}}$$

$$= 10.6 \times 10^{-3} \text{ H}$$

The voltage induced in the second coil is

$$v_{L_2} = M\frac{di_1}{dt} = M\frac{di}{dt}$$

$$= 10.6 \times 10^{-3} \frac{d}{dt}(2 \sin 314\, t)$$

$$= 10.6 \times 10^{-3} \times 2 \times 314 \cos 314\, t$$

$$= \mathbf{(6.66 \cos 314\, t)\ V.}$$

The magnetic circuit being linear,

$$M = \frac{N_2\, \phi_{12}}{i_1} = \frac{500 \times (K\phi_1)}{i_1}$$

$$\therefore \qquad \phi_1 = \frac{M}{500 \times K} i_1 = \frac{10.6 \times 10^{-3}}{500 \times 0.75} .2 \sin 314\, t$$

$$= 5.66 \times 10^{-5} \sin 314\, t$$

i.e., $\qquad \boldsymbol{\phi_1 = 5.66 \times 10^{-5} \sin 314\, t.}$

EXAMPLE 9.4 *Find the total inductance of the three series connected coupled coils in Fig. E9.3.*

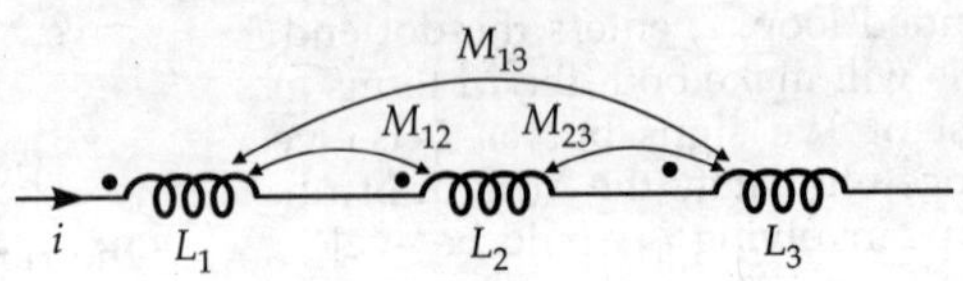

Fig. E9.3

[*Given*: $L_1 = 1\,H$; $L_2 = 2\,H$: $L_3 = 5\,H$
$M_{12} = 0.5\,H$; $M_{23} = 1\,H$; $M_{13} = 1\,H$]

SOLUTION. *For coil 1 :*

$$L_1 + M_{12} + M_{13} = 1 + 0.5 + 1 = 2.5 \text{ H}$$

For coil 2 :

$$L_2 + M_{23} + M_{12} = 2 + 1 + 0.5 = 3.5 \text{ H}$$

For coil 3 :

$$L_3 + M_{13} + M_{23} = 5 + 1 + 1 = 7 \text{ H}$$

∴ The net inductance

$$= (L_1 + M_{12} + M_{13}) + (L_2 + M_{23} + M_{12}) + (L_3 + M_{13} + M_{23})$$

$$= 2.5 + 3.5 + 7 = \mathbf{13\ H.}$$

EXAMPLE 9.5 *Find the total inductance of the three series connected coupled coils as shown in Fig. E9.4.*

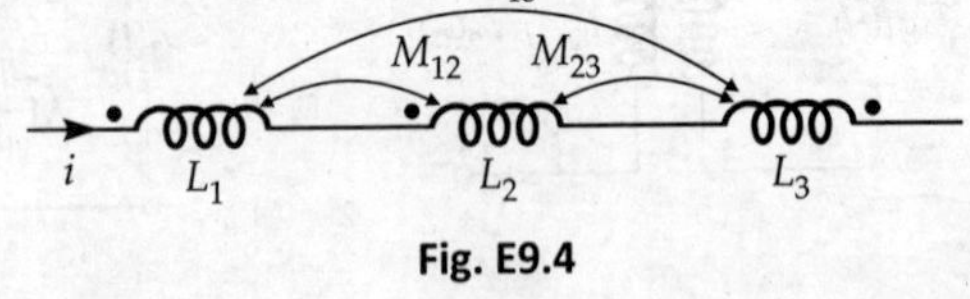

Fig. E9.4

[*Self and mutual inductances of the coils are as given in Example 9.4*]

SOLUTION. *For coil 1 :*

$$L_1 + M_{12} - M_{13} = 1 + 0.5 - 1 = 0.5 \text{ H}$$

For coil 2 :

$$L_2 + M_{12} - M_{23} = 2 + 0.5 - 1 = 1.5 \text{ H}$$

For coil 3 :

$$L_3 - M_{23} - M_{13} = 5 - 1 - 1 = 3 \text{ H}$$

$\therefore$ Net inductance

$$= (L_1 + M_{12} - M_{13}) + (L_2 + M_{12} - M_{23}) + (L_3 - M_{23} - M_{13})$$

$$= 0.5 + 1.5 + 3 = \mathbf{5\ H.}$$

EXAMPLE 9.6 *In the coupled circuit of Fig. E9.5, find the input impedance as well as the net inductance.*

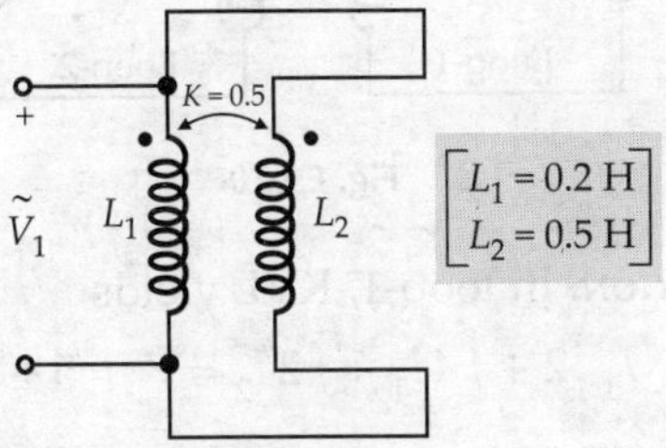

Fig. E9.5

SOLUTION. The circuit is redrawn in Fig. E9.6 and the KVL is applied in both the circuits with assumed currents I_1 and I_2.

$$\boldsymbol{V_1 = (I_1 - I_2)\, j\omega L_1 + j\omega M I_2}$$

or, $$V_1 = j\,\omega L_1 I_1 + I_2\,[j\omega M - j\omega L_1]$$

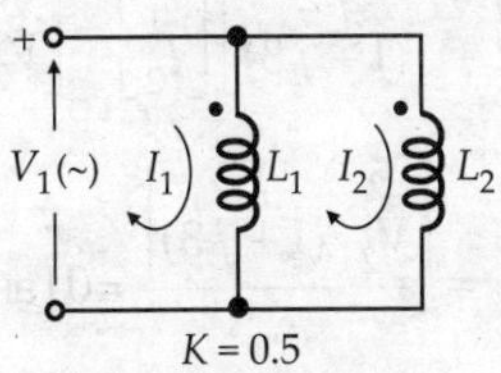

Fig. E9.6

Here, $L_1 = 0.2$ H, $M = K\sqrt{L_1 L_2}$

$$= 0.5\sqrt{0.2 \times 0.5} = 0.158\text{ H.}$$

$$\therefore \quad V_1 = j\,\omega(0.2)\,I_1 - j\,\omega(0.042)\,I_2 \qquad ...(1)$$

Again, in second loop,

$$0 = (I_2 - I_1)j\,\omega L_1 + I_2\,.\,j\omega L_2 + j\omega M I_1$$

$$= j\omega I_1\,(M - L_1) + j\omega I_2\,(L_1 + L_2)$$

$$= -(0.042)\,j\omega I_1 + j\omega I_2\,(0.7)$$

or $$j\omega I_2 = \frac{j\omega \times 0.042}{0.7} I_1 \qquad ...(2)$$

Using (2) in (1),

$$V_1 = j\omega(0.2)\,I_1 - 0.042 \times \frac{j\omega \times 0.042}{0.7} I_1$$

$$= j\omega I_1\,(0.2 - 0.00252) = j\omega(0.1975)\,I_1$$

or $$Z_{in} = \frac{V_1}{I_1} = j\omega\,(0.1975)\,\Omega$$

This gives $L_{\text{equivalent}} = \mathbf{0.1975\ Henry.}$

EXAMPLE 9.7 *Following data refers to two coupled coils 1 and 2 (Fig. E9.7). $\phi_{11} = 0.5$ mWb; $\phi_{12} = 0.3$ mWb; $N_1 = 100$ turns; $N_2 = 500$ turns; $i_1 = 1$ A.*

Find, K, the coefficient of coupling, the inductances L_1 and L_2 and M, the mutual inductance.

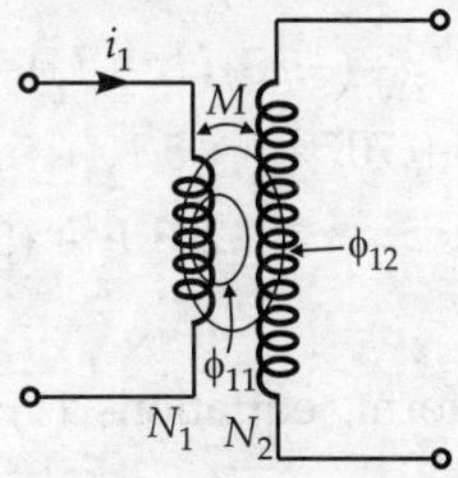

Fig. E9.7

SOLUTION. Total flux of coil-1

$$\phi_1 = \phi_{11} + \phi_{12} = 0.8\text{ mWb.}$$

Assuming the magnetic circuits to be linear,

$$L_1 = \frac{N_1\,\phi_1}{I_1} = 100 \times \frac{0.8 \times 10^{-3}}{1} = 0.08\text{ H}$$

Again, the coupling coefficient

$$K = \frac{\phi_{12}}{\phi_1} = \frac{0.3}{0.8} = 0.375$$

Mutual inductance

$$M = \frac{N_2\,\phi_{12}}{i_1} = \frac{500 \times 0.3 \times 10^{-3}}{1} = 0.15\text{ H}$$

But $$M = K\sqrt{L_1 L_2}$$

$$\therefore \quad L_2 = \frac{M^2}{K^2 L_1} = \frac{0.15^2}{0.375^2 \times 0.08} = \mathbf{2\ H.}$$

EXAMPLE 9.8 *Find the drop across R_L (Fig. E9.8).*

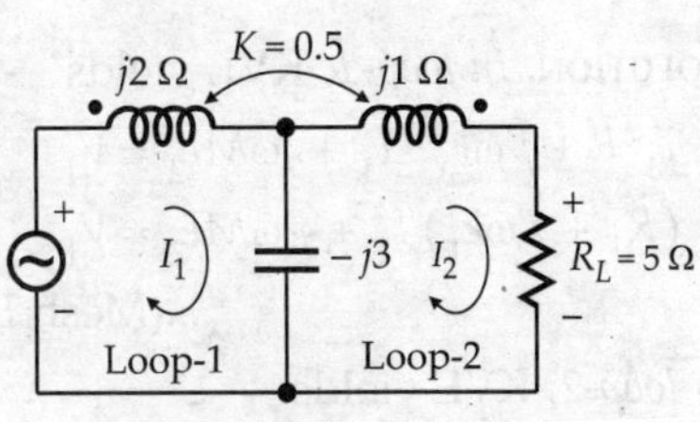

Fig. E9.8

SOLUTION. It is evident from the given figure that reactance of coil-1 is $j\,\omega L_1 = j\,2\Omega$ while that of coil-2 is $j\omega L_2 = j\,1\Omega$ and the coefficient of coupling is $K = 0.5$.

$$\therefore \quad \omega M = X_M = 0.5\sqrt{2 \times 1} = 0.707\,\Omega.$$

Applying KVL in *loop-1*,

$$10 + j\,0 = I_1 \times j\,2 + (I_1 - I_2)(-j3) - j\,0.707\, I_2$$

or $$j\,2\, I_1 - j\,3\, I_1 + j3I_2 - j\,0.707\, I_2 = 10$$

or $$-j\,1.\,I_1 + I_2 \times j\,2.293 = 10 \quad ...(1)$$

Applying KVL *in loop-2*,

$$j\,1.0\, I_2 + 5\, I_2 + (-j\,3)(I_2 - I_1) - j\,0.70\, I_1 = 0$$

or $$(+j\,3\, I_1 - 0.707\, I_1) + 5\, I_2 + j\, I_2 - j\,3I_2 = 0$$

or, $$2.293\, I_1 + (5 - j\,2)\, I_2 = 0 \quad ...(2)$$

In matrix form, equations (1) and (2) can be oriented as

$$\begin{bmatrix} 10 \\ 0 \end{bmatrix} = \begin{bmatrix} -j & 2.293 \\ 2.293 & 5 - j\,2 \end{bmatrix} \begin{bmatrix} I_1 \\ I_2 \end{bmatrix}$$

$$\therefore \quad I_2 = \frac{\begin{vmatrix} -j & 10 \\ 2.293 & 0 \end{vmatrix}}{\begin{vmatrix} -j & 2.293 \\ 2.293 & 5 - j2 \end{vmatrix}} = \frac{22.93}{5.25 + 5j + 2}$$

$$= \frac{22.93}{7.25 + j\,5} = 2.6 \angle -34.6° \text{ A.}$$

Then drop across R_L

$$= I_2 \times R_L = 2.6 \angle -34.6° \times 5$$

$$= \mathbf{13 \angle -34.6° \ V.}$$

EXAMPLE 9.9 *Write the mesh equations for the transformer circuit shown in Fig. E9.9.*

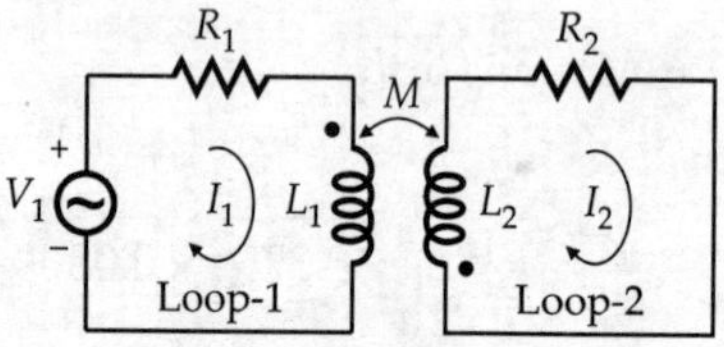

Fig. E9.9

SOLUTION. *In loop-1*, KVL yields

$$I_1\, R + j\,\omega L_1 \,.\, I_1 + j\omega M I_2 = V_1$$

or $$(R_1 + j\,\omega L_1)\, I_1 + j\,\omega M I_2 = V_1$$

...(Mesh Equation # 1)

In loop-2, KVL yields

$$I_2\, R_2 + j\,\omega L_2\, I_2 + j\omega M I_1 = 0$$

or $$j\omega M\, I_1 + (R_2 + j\omega L_2)\, I_2 = 0$$

...(Mesh Equation # 2)

Thus, the required mesh equations are

$$(R_1 + j\omega L_1)\, I_1 + j\omega M\, I_2 = V_1$$

and

$$j\omega M\, I_1 + (R_2 + j\omega L_2)\, I_2 = 0$$

EXAMPLE 9.10 *Find V_2 in the circuit of Fig. E9.10 such that current in the left hand loop (loop-1) is zero. Assume $V_1 = 5\angle 0°$ V.*

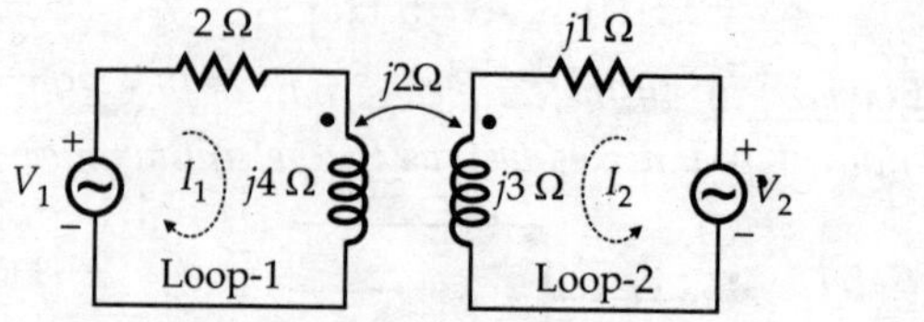

Fig. E9.10

SOLUTION. In loop-1, KVL yields

$$I_1\,.2 + j\,4I_1 + j\,2I_2 = V_1 = 5 + j\,0 \quad ...(1)$$

In loop-2, KVL gives,

$$I_2\,.1 + j\, I_2\,.3 + j\,2\,.\, I_1 = V_2 \quad ...(2)$$

[In both loops, currents enter the dot ends. Hence M is +ve in both the loop equations]

In matrix form, the loop equations can be written as

$$\begin{bmatrix} (2 + j\,4) & j\,2 \\ j\,2 & (1 + j\,3) \end{bmatrix} \begin{bmatrix} I_1 \\ I_2 \end{bmatrix} = \begin{bmatrix} 5 \\ V_2 \end{bmatrix}$$

$$\therefore \quad I_1 = \frac{\begin{vmatrix} 5 & j\,2 \\ V_2 & (1 + j\,3) \end{vmatrix}}{\Delta} = 0 \text{ [as given]}$$

where $$\Delta = \begin{vmatrix} 2 + j\,4 & j\,2 \\ j\,2 & 1 + j\,3 \end{vmatrix}$$

or $$5\,(1 + j\,3) - j\,2\,.\,V_2 = 0$$

i.e., $$V_2 = \frac{5\,(1 + j\,3)}{j\,2} = -j\,2.5\,(1 + j\,3)$$

$$= (7.5 - j\,2.5)\text{ V}$$

Thus the value of $\mathbf{V_2 = (7.5 - j\,2.5)\ V}$ such that $I_1 = 0$.

9.9 TUNED COUPLED CIRCUITS

In radio frequency range, the amplification of signals is done by *tuned coupled circuits*. There are *two* types of tuned circuits—the *single tuned* and *double tuned* circuits. In the single tuned circuit, the secondary is only tuned while in double tuned circuit, both the primary and secondary of the coupled coils are tuned. The tuned circuits find application in broadcasting receivers, TV receivers to couple the antenna to the RF stage. Isolation of input circuit from output circuit can be achieved using coupled circuits. Single tuned circuits are also applied in band stop filters. Double tuned circuits are used in tuned amplifiers.

9.9.1 Single Tuned Coupled Coils

Referring to Fig. 9.9, for the case of single tuned coupled coils,

$$Z_{11} = R_0 + (R_p + j\omega L_p)$$

$$= R_1 + j\,\omega L_p = R_1 + j\,X_1 \simeq R_1$$

[for tuned coil, $X_1 \to 0$]

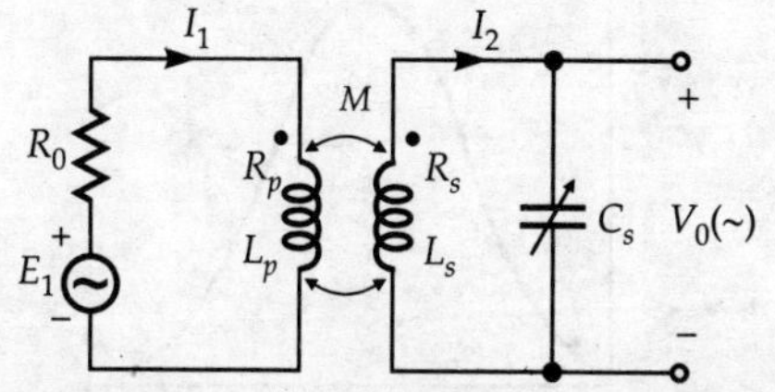

Z_{11} = driving point impedance at input
R_0 = source resistance
E_1 = source voltage
R_p, L_p = resistance and inductance of primary *wdg*
Z_{22} = driving point impedance at output
Z_{12}, Z_{21} = transfer impedance
R_s, L_s = resistance and inductance of secondary *wdg*
C_s = variable capacitor at secondary for tuning
V_0 = output voltage.

Fig. 9.9

Also, $$Z_{22} = R_2 + j\left(\omega L_s - \frac{1}{\omega C_s}\right) = R_2 + j\,X_2.$$

and $$Z_{12} = Z_{21} = j\omega M$$

The loop equations are given by

$$Z_{11}\,I_1 - Z_{12}\,I_2 = E_1$$
$$-Z_{21}\,I_1 + Z_{22}\,I_2 = 0 \qquad \text{...(9.17)}$$

Here using Cramar's rule,

$$I_2 = \frac{\begin{vmatrix} Z_{11} & E_1 \\ -Z_{12} & 0 \end{vmatrix}}{\begin{vmatrix} Z_{11} & -Z_{12} \\ -Z_{12} & Z_{22} \end{vmatrix}} \qquad \text{...(9.18)}$$

$$= \frac{E_1\,Z_{12}}{Z_{11}\,Z_{22} - Z_{12}^2}$$

$$= \frac{E_1\,(j\omega M)}{R_1\,(R_2 + j\,X_2) + \omega^2\,M^2} \qquad \text{...(9.19)}$$

$$\therefore \quad I_2 = \frac{E_1\,(j\omega M)}{R_1\left[R_2 + j\left(\omega L_s - \frac{1}{\omega C_s}\right)\right] + \omega^2\,M^2} \qquad \text{...(9.20)}$$

Again,

$$V_0 = \frac{I_2}{j\omega C_s}.$$

$$= \frac{E_1\,M}{C_s\left[R_1\left\{R_2 + j\left(\omega L_s - \frac{1}{\omega C_s}\right)\right\} + \omega^2\,M^2\right]} \qquad \text{...(9.21)}$$

Thus amplification,

$$A \simeq \frac{V_0}{E_1}$$

$$= \frac{M}{R_1\left\{R_2 + j\left(\omega L_s - \frac{1}{\omega C_s}\right)\right\} + \omega^2\,M^2} \cdot \frac{1}{C_s} \qquad \text{...(9.22)}$$

By varying C_s, for any specified value of M, tuning can be obtained when $\omega L_s = \frac{1}{\omega C_s}$. The resonant frequency is given by ω_r. Variation of V_0 with ω is shown in Fig. 9.10. It may be seen that peak value of V_0 occurs at an angular frequency slightly less than ω_r (the resonant frequency). This is because the Q factors remain constant for primary and secondary near the angular frequency and for such cases the voltage at resonant frequency is equal to the peak voltage V_0.

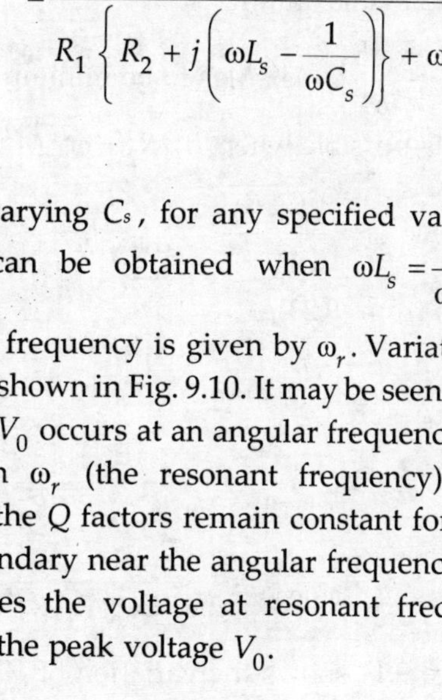

Fig. 9.10 Profile of V_0 vs. ω

At the frequency of resonance,

$$I_{2_{\text{res.}}} = \frac{E_1\ \omega_r\ M}{R_1\ R_2 + \omega_r^2 M^2}$$
$$V_{0_{\text{res.}}} = \frac{E_1\ M/C_s}{R_1\ R_2 + \omega_r^2\ M^2} \quad \text{...(9.23)}$$
$$A_{0_{\text{res.}}} = \frac{M/C_s}{R_1\ R_2 + \omega_r^2\ M^2}$$

The above equations are valid for a specified value of M. However, $M = K\sqrt{L_s\ L_p}$. If K is varied, this will result in variation in M. There will be one value of K that will result in a value of M so that $(V_{0_{res}})$ is maximum. This particular value of K is called *critical coefficient of coupling* (K_{crit}).

As $$V_{0_{\text{res.}}} = \left\{ \frac{E_1/C_s}{\dfrac{R_1\ R_2}{M} + \omega_r^2\ M} \right\}$$

for $V_{0_{res}}$ to be maximum,

$$\frac{R_1\ R_2}{M} + \omega_r^2\ M \text{ is to be minimum.}$$

This is possible when $R_1\ R_2 = \omega_r^2\ M^2$.

$$\therefore \quad M_{\text{opt}} = \frac{\sqrt{R_1\ R_2}}{\omega_r} = K_{\text{crit}}\sqrt{L_p\ L_s}.$$

Thus, from (9.23),

$$I_{2_{\text{res (opt)}}} = \frac{E_1}{2\sqrt{R_1\ R_2}}$$
$$V_{0_{\text{res (opt)}}} = \frac{E_1}{2\,\omega_r\ C_s\sqrt{R_1\ R_2}}$$
$$A_{\text{res (opt)}} = \frac{1}{2\,\omega_r\ C_s\sqrt{R_1\ R_2}}$$

Figure 9.11 shows the variation of V_0 *vs* ω for different values of K. This shows the *selectivity* of coils for different values of K.

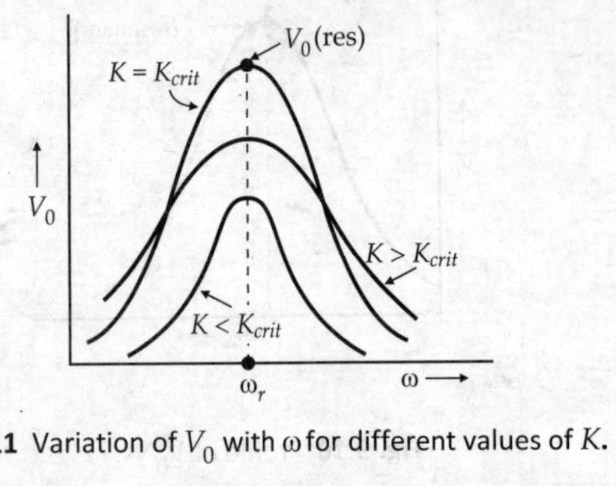

Fig. 9.11 Variation of V_0 with ω for different values of K.

With reference to Example 9.1, it is evident that the secondary impedance reflected to primary side in the form of coupled impedance is given by

$$\frac{(\omega M)^2}{R_s + j\omega L_s - \dfrac{j}{\omega C_s}}.$$

This impedance has the maximum value of $[(\omega M)^2/R_s]$ at the resonance frequency of the secondary. Fig. 9.12 represents the profile of this impedance *vs* frequency.

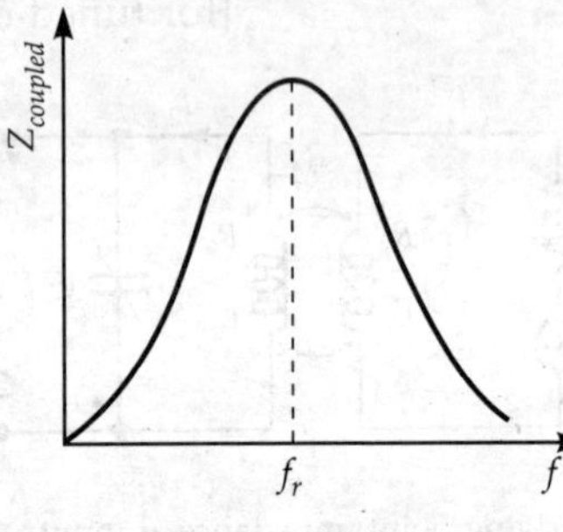

Fig. 9.12 Z-coupled vs. f profile

9.9.2 Double-Tuned Coupled Coils

Figure 9.13 represents a double tuned coupled coil where tuning capacitors are placed both in primary and secondary as shown.

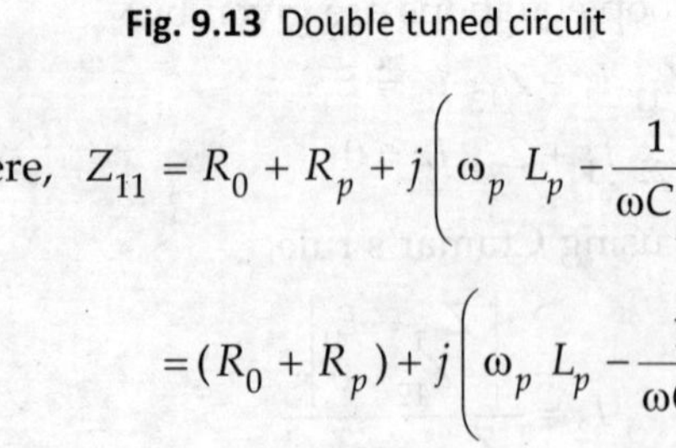

Fig. 9.13 Double tuned circuit

Here, $$Z_{11} = R_0 + R_p + j\left(\omega_p\ L_p - \frac{1}{\omega C_p}\right)$$
$$= (R_0 + R_p) + j\left(\omega_p\ L_p - \frac{1}{\omega C_p}\right)$$
$$= R_1 + j\,X_1 \quad \text{...(9.24)}$$
$$Z_{22} = R_s + j\left(\omega L_s - \frac{1}{\omega C_s}\right) = R_2 + j\,X_2 \quad \text{...(9.25)}$$
$$Z_{12} = Z_{21} = j\,\omega M \quad \text{...(9.26)}$$

Forming the loop equations and solving for I_2, we get

$$I_2 = \frac{E_1 \, Z_{12}}{Z_{11} \, Z_{12} - Z_{12}^2}$$

$$= \frac{E_1 \, (j \, \omega M)}{(R_1 + j \, X_1)(R_2 + j \, X_2) + \omega^2 \, M^2}$$

$$V_0 = \frac{I_2}{j\omega C_s}$$

$$= \frac{E_1 \, M}{C_s \, [(R_1 + j \, X_1)(R_2 + j \, X_2) + \omega^2 \, M^2]}$$

$$A = \frac{V_0}{E_1} = \frac{M}{C_s[(R_1 + jX_1)(R_2 + jX_2) + \omega^2 M^2 \,]} \quad ...(9.27)$$

At resonant frequency, $\omega_r \left(\frac{1}{\sqrt{L_p \, C_p}} = \frac{1}{\sqrt{L_s \, C_s}} \right)$,

$$I_{2_{res}} = \frac{E_1 \, \omega_r \, M}{R_1 \, R_2 + \omega_r^2 \, M^2}$$

$$V_{0_{res}} = \frac{E_1 \, M / C_s}{R_1 \, R_2 + \omega_r^2 \, M^2} \quad ...(9.28)$$

$$A_{res} = \frac{M / C_s}{R_1 \, R_2 + \omega_2^2 \, M^2}$$

Similar to single tuned circuits, at the value of M_{opt},

$$V_{0_{res}} = \frac{E_1 \, / \, C_s}{(R_1 \, R_2 \, / \, M) + \omega_r^2 \, M} \quad ...(9.29)$$

$V_{0_{res}}$ to be maximum,

$$\frac{R_1 \, R_2}{M} = \omega_r^2 \, M$$

This gives

$$M_{opt} = \frac{\sqrt{R_1 \, R_2}}{\omega_r} = K_{crit} \sqrt{L_p \, L_s} \quad ...(9.30)$$

Thus finally,

$$I_{2 \text{ res opt}} = \frac{E_0}{2 \sqrt{R_1 \, R_2}}$$

$$V_{0_{\text{res opt}}} = \frac{E_0}{2\omega_r \, . \, C_s \sqrt{R_1 \, R_2}} \quad ...(9.31)$$

$$A_{\text{res opt}} = \frac{1}{2\omega_r \, C_s \sqrt{R_1 \, R_2}}$$

The expression of V_0 can be rewritten as

$$V_0 = \frac{E_1 \, M / C_s}{\left[R_1 + j\left(\omega L_p - \frac{1}{\omega C_s} \right) \right] \left[R_2 + j\left(\omega L_s - \frac{1}{\omega C_s} \right) \right] + \omega^2 M^2} \quad ...(9.31(a))$$

while the total impedance* seen by the primary

$$= R_p + j\left(\omega L_p - \frac{j}{\omega C_p} \right) + \frac{\omega^2 \, M^2}{R_s + j\left(\omega L_s - \frac{1}{\omega C_s} \right)}$$

Figure 9.14 represents the variation of V_0 with respect to ω

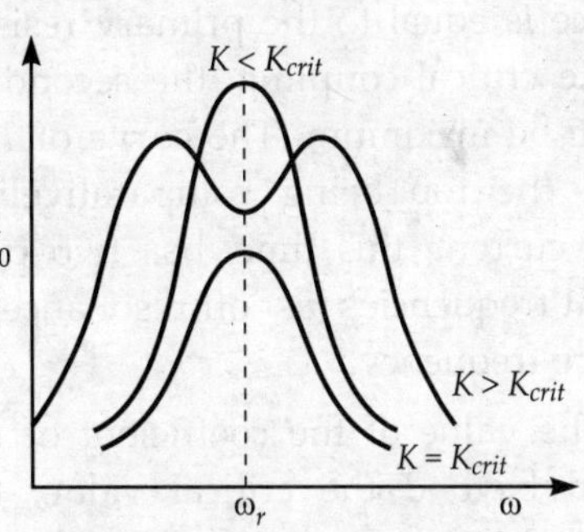

Fig. 9.14 Variation of V_0 with ω

However, for values of $K > K_{crit}$, the voltage profile is double peaked.

$V_{0_{peak}}$ occurs near ω_r for $K = K_{crit}$ and $K < K_{crit}$. For $K > K_{crit}$, the peak occurs twice.

The coupled impedance is *maximum* at resonance, it becomes *inductive* below resonance and is *capacitive* above resonance. When such coupled impedance is added to the primary circuit

* The total input impedance consists of inpedance of primary without the secondary and the coupled impedance due to the presence of secondary given by

$$\left(\frac{\omega^2 M^2}{R_s + j\left(\omega L_s - \frac{1}{\omega C_s} \right)} \right)$$

impedance due to coupling, significant effects are produced. The magnitude of primary current, the secondary current and the voltage output across the capacitor in the secondary is affected.

When the coefficient of coupling is small, the effect of coupled impedance is negligible; the profile of I_p vs f would follow the series resonance curve of the primary circuit. The secondary current is small and varies with frequency in such a way that it has much more peaky response then the resonance curve of the secondary circuit, had it been considered individually.

As the coefficient of coupling is enhanced, the effect of coupled impedance increases the total impedance of the primary circuit. This results in reduction in the primary current magnitude and the curve of primary current becomes broader. At the same time, the secondary current peak becomes higher and the curve of secondary current broadens.

This effect is continued until the increased coupling is such that the resistance which the secondary circuit couples into the primary at resonance is equal to the primary resistance. This being the critical coupling, the secondary current will then be maximum. The curve of I_s would be broader, the top being comparatively flat. The primary current, this time, has two peaks, being greater at frequencies just off resonance than at the resonance frequency.

As the value of the coefficient of coupling is increased beyond the critical value, the double humps in the primary current become more prominent, peaks being departing from each other further. The secondary current would now display double humps too. During this time, the magnitude of the primary current at peaks becomes smaller as the coupling coefficient is increased.

9.10 CONDUCTIVELY COUPLED EQUIVALENT CIRCUITS

In Fig. 9.15(a), the loop equations are

$$v_1 = L_1 \frac{di_1}{dt} + M\frac{di_2}{dt}$$
$$v_2 = L_2 \frac{di_2}{dt} + M\frac{di_1}{dt} \quad ...(9.32)$$

[M is +ve as i_1 and i_2 both enter the coils through dot ends]

Again in Fig. 9.15(b),

$$v_1 = (L_1 - M)\frac{di_1}{dt} + M\frac{d}{dt}(i_1 + i_2)$$
$$v_2 = (L_2 - M)\frac{di_2}{dt} + M\frac{d}{dt}(i_1 + i_2) \quad ...(9.33)$$

which, on simplification become

$$v_1 = L_1 \frac{di_1}{dt} + M\frac{di_2}{dt}$$
$$v_2 = L_2 \frac{di_2}{dt} + M\frac{di_1}{dt}$$

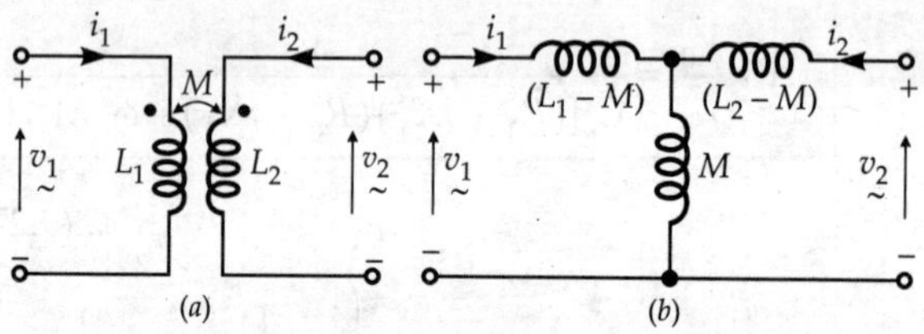

Fig. 9.15 Conductively coupled equivalent circuits.

Thus we see that both the Figures 9.15(a) and 9.15(b) are equivalent. Fig. 9.15(b) is thus called the *conductively equivalent of the magnetic circuit.* Here we may represent $Z_A = L_1 - M$,

$$Z_B = (L_2 - M) \text{ and } Z_C = M.$$

note In case M is +ve and both the currents through the common branch are additive, then $Z_A = L_1 - M$; $Z_B = L_2 - M$ and $Z_C = M$.

Also, if M is –ve and currents in the common branch opposite to each other,

$$Z_A = L_1 - M, Z_B = L_2 - M, Z_C = M.$$

But, on the other hand, if M is +ve but the two currents in the common branch are opposite to each other,

$$Z_A = L_1 + M, Z_B = L_2 + M \text{ and } Z_C = -M.$$

Similarly, if M is –ve but the two currents in the common branch are additive, then also

$$Z_A = L_1 + M, \ Z_B = L_2 + M \text{ and } Z_C = -M.$$

Further, Z_A, Z_B and Z_C may also be assumed to be the T equivalent of the circuit shown in Fig. 9.15(b).

EXAMPLE 9.11 *Draw T equivalent circuit of the coupled network (Fig. E9.11).*

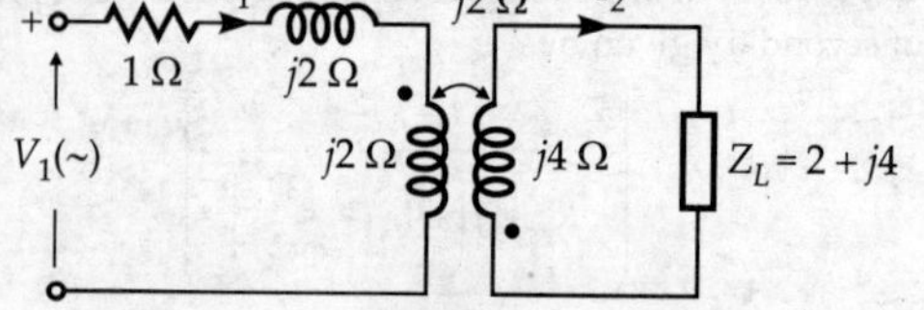

Fig. E9.11

SOLUTION. I_1 enters $j\,2\,\Omega$ branch through dot end while I_2 also enters $j\,4\,\Omega$ branch through dot end. Thus M is +ve. However, the currents in the coupled circuit (the common branch) are in opposite direction. Hence Z_A, Z_B and Z_C in the conductively equivalent circuit given as

$$Z_A = L_1 + M;\; Z_B = L_2 + M;\; Z_C = -M$$

i.e., here, $Z_A = j\,2 + j\,2 = j\,4\,\Omega$

$$Z_B = L_2 + M = j\,4 + j\,2 = j\,6\,\Omega$$

$$Z_C = -j\,2\,\Omega$$

The conductively coupled equivalent circuit is shown in **Fig. E9.12.**

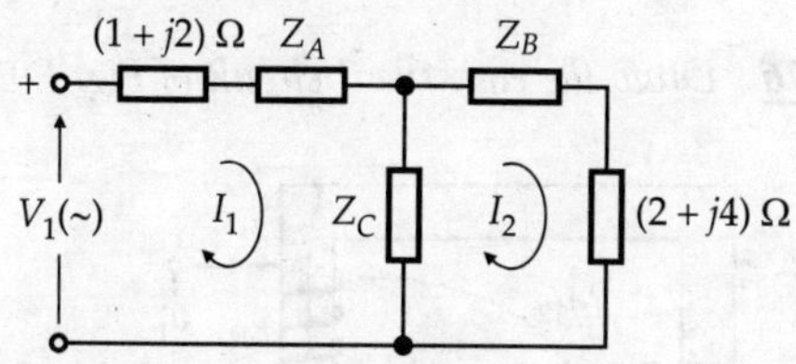

Fig. E9.12

EXAMPLE 9.12 *Find the conductively coupled equivalent circuit for the network shown in Fig. E9.13.*

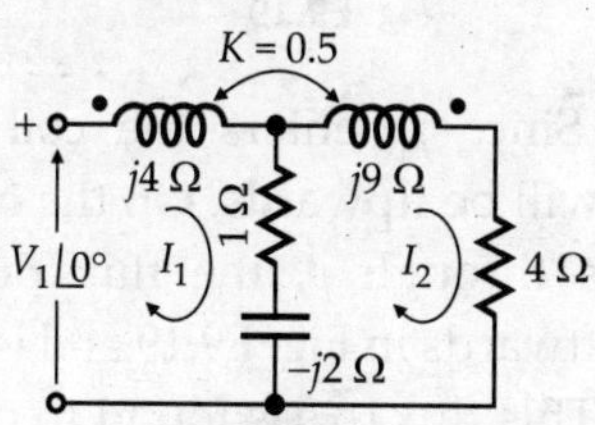

Fig. E9.13

SOLUTION. $K = 0.5$

As $X_M = K\sqrt{X_1 X_2}$

$\therefore$ here $X_M = 0.5\sqrt{4 \times 9} = 3\,\Omega$

Again, M is –ve as I_1 enters $j\,4\,\Omega$ coil through dot end, I_2 enters $j\,9\,\Omega$ coil through undot end. In the common branch, I_1 and I_2 are directed opposite. Thus, from the theory of conductivity coupled circuits,

$$Z_A = L_1 - M,\; Z_B = L_2 - M,\; Z_C = M$$

Here $Z_A = j\,4 - j\,3 = j\,1\,\Omega$

$$Z_B = j\,9 - j\,3 = j\,6\,\Omega$$

$$Z = j\,3\,\Omega$$

The conductively coupled equivalent circuit is shown in **Fig. E9.14.**

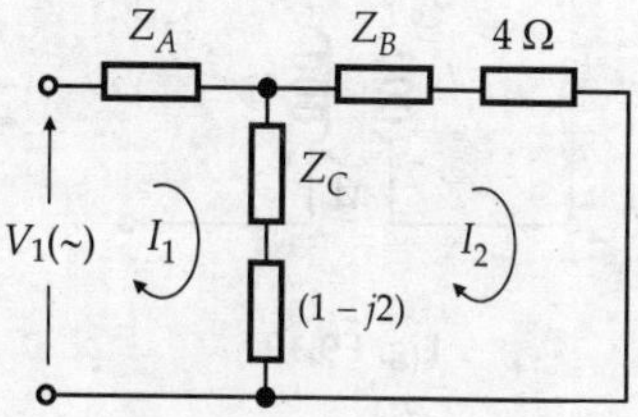

Fig. E9.14

ADDITIONAL EXAMPLES

EXAMPLE 9.13 *Draw the equivalent circuit with the dot notation of the coupled circuit in Fig. E9.15. Also write the loop equations.*

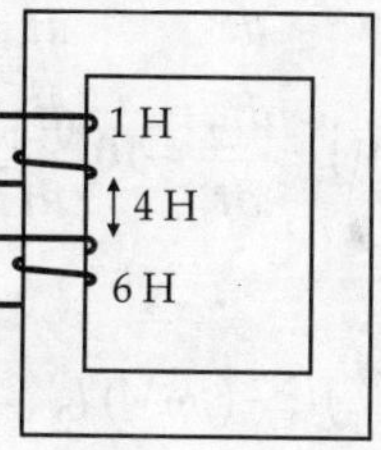

Fig. E9.15

SOLUTION. Assuming currents entering terminals 1 and 3, the fluxes of both the coils would assist each other. Thus the equivalent circuit with dot convention is drawn in **Fig. E9.16.**

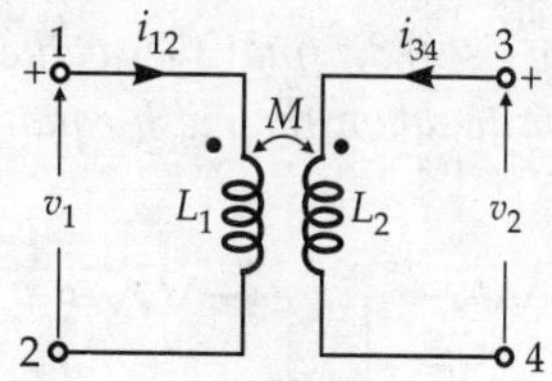

Fig. E9.16

The loop equations are,

$$v_1 = L_1 \frac{di_{12}}{dt} + M\frac{di_{34}}{dt}$$

$$v_2 = L_2 \frac{di_{34}}{dt} + M\frac{di_{12}}{dt}.$$

EXAMPLE 9.14 *In the circuit of Fig. E9.17, write the loop equation in time domain as well as in s-domain if $L_1 = L_2 = 1\,H$, $v_1 = 10 \sin \omega t$, $v_2 = 5 \sin(\omega t + 30°)$. Assume $M = 10$ H.*

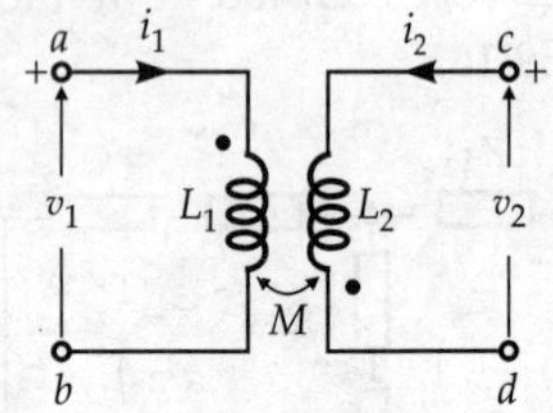

Fig. E9.17

SOLUTION. The loop equations are

$$v_1 = L_1\frac{di_1}{dt} - M\frac{di_2}{dt}$$
in time domain
$$v_2 = L_2\frac{di_2}{dt} - M\frac{di_1}{dt}$$

i.e.,
$$\mathbf{10\,sin\,\omega t} = \frac{di_1}{dt} - 10\frac{di_2}{dt}$$
in time domain
$$\mathbf{5\,sin\,(\omega t + 30°)} = \frac{di_2}{dt} - 10\frac{di_2}{dt}$$

In s-domain :

$$V_1 = (j\omega L_1)I_1 - (j\omega M)I_2$$
in s-domain
$$V_2 = -(j\omega M)I_1 + (j\omega L_2)I_2$$

i.e.,
$$\mathbf{V_1 = (j\omega)\,I_1 - (10\,j\omega)\,I_2}$$
in s-domain
$$\mathbf{V_2 = (-\,j\omega 10)\,I_1 + (j\omega)\,I_2}$$

EXAMPLE 9.15 *Fig. E9.18 represents a coupled coil circuit where $L_1 = 20$ mH, $L_2 = 50$ mH. If the coefficient of mutual induction is 0.8, find the value of mutual inductance and write down the mesh equations in time domain.*

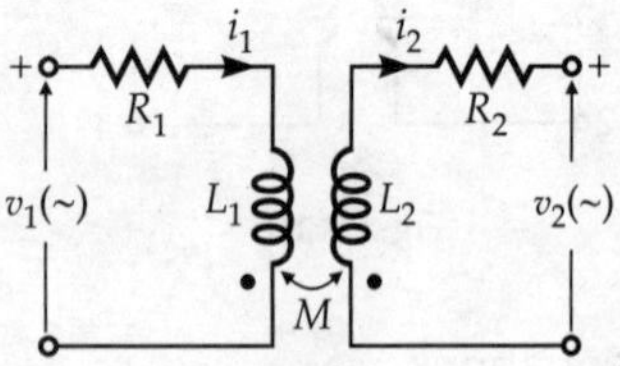

Fig. E9.18

SOLUTION. $M = K\sqrt{L_1 L_2}$

$$= 0.8\sqrt{20\times10^{-3}\times50\times10^{-3}}$$

$$= 0.025 \text{ H.}$$

The voltage equation in the left loop is

$$v_1 = L_1\frac{di_1}{dt} - M\frac{di_2}{dt}$$

i.e.,
$$v_1 = 0.02\frac{di_1}{dt} - 0.025\frac{di_2}{dt}$$

while, the voltage equation for the right hand loop is

$$v_2 = M\frac{di_1}{dt} - L_2\frac{di_2}{dt} = 0.025\frac{di_1}{dt} - 0.05\frac{di_2}{dt}.$$

Hence, the given circuit has mutual inductance given by

$$\mathbf{M = 0.025\ H}$$

and the voltage equations in the loops are

$$v_1 = \mathbf{0.02}\frac{di_1}{dt} - \mathbf{0.025}\frac{di_2}{dt}$$

$$v_2 = \mathbf{0.025}\frac{di_1}{dt} - \mathbf{0.05}\frac{di_2}{dt}.$$

EXAMPLE 9.16 *Draw the equivalent circuit of Fig. E9.19.*

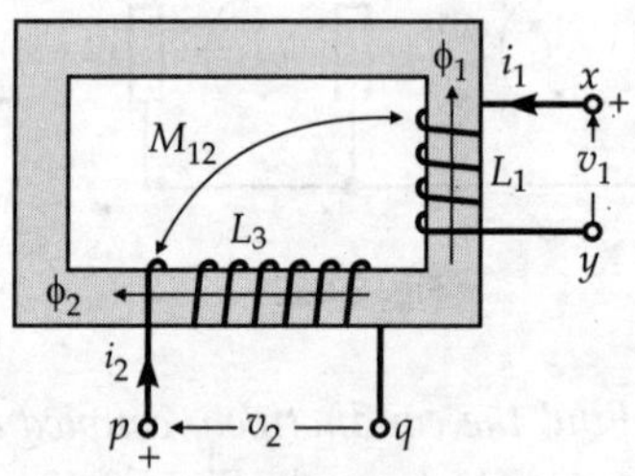

Fig. E9.19

SOLUTION. Since i_1 enters the coil at x flux produced (ϕ_1) will be upwards. On the other hand, since i_2 enters through p, the flux produced is horizontally leftwards in Fig. E9.19 and is shown by dotted arrow. This flux (ϕ_2) is found to oppose ϕ_1.

Thus the M term would be negative and the dot convention indicates that terminal p and x are of opposite polarities (Ref. **Fig. E9.20**)

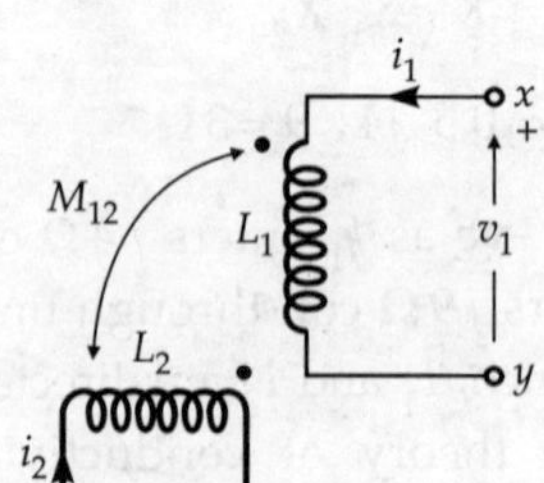

Fig. E9.20

EXAMPLE 9.17 *Write the voltage equation for the following Figs. (E9.21-9.23) showing coupled coil equivalent circuits.*

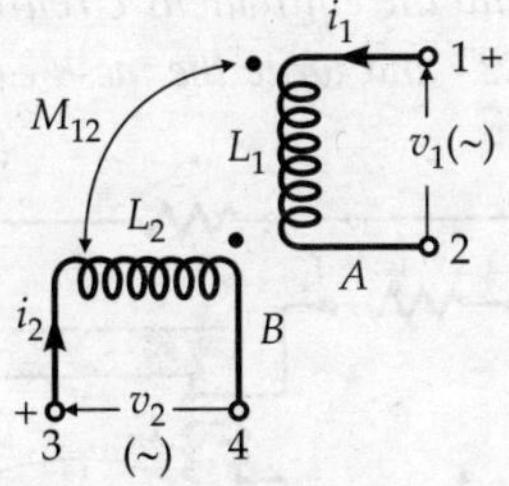

Fig. E9.21

Solution. *(Fig. E9.21)* Since in coil *A*, current enters towards the dot, while in coil *B* the current comes out of the dot hence *M* term would be –ve. The voltage equations for the coils are then,

$$v_1 = L_1 \frac{di_1}{dt} - M_{12} \frac{di_2}{dt}$$

$$v_2 = L_2 \frac{di_2}{dt} - M_{12} \frac{di_1}{dt} \qquad \text{in time domain}$$

while in the **frequency domain,**

$$V_1 = (j\,\omega L_1)\, I_1 - (j\omega M)\, I_2$$

and $$V_2 = (j\,\omega L_2)\, I_2 - (j\,\omega M)\, I_1$$

(Fig. E9.22) For coils *A* and *B*, currents enter through dot terminals and hence M_{12} would be +ve. For coils *B* and *C*, current enters through dot terminal in coil *B* and comes out of the dot terminal in coil *C*. Hence M_{23} would be –ve. Same reasoning holds good for coils *A* and *C*. Thus M_{13} would be –ve.

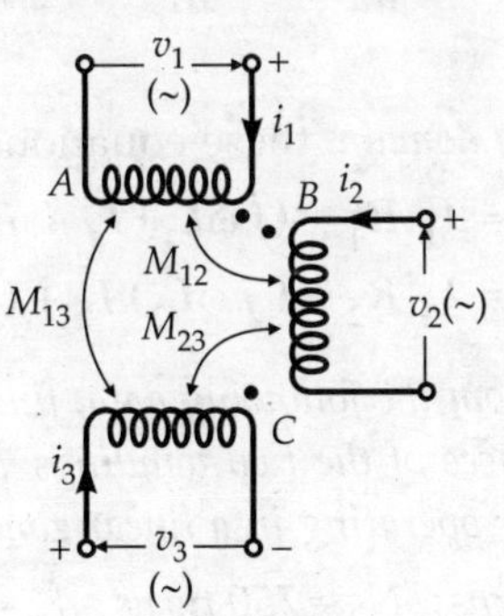

Fig. E9.22

The voltage equations are

$$v_1 = L_1 \frac{di_1}{dt} + M_{12} \frac{di_2}{dt} - M_{13} \frac{di_3}{dt}$$

$$v_2 = L_2 \frac{di_2}{dt} + M_{12} \frac{di_1}{dt} - M_{23} \frac{di_3}{dt}$$

$$v_3 = L_3 \frac{di_3}{dt} - M_{23} \frac{di_2}{dt} - M_{13} \frac{di_1}{dt}$$

in *time domain*

and $$V_1 = (j\,\omega L_1)\, I_1 + (j\,\omega M_{12})\, I_2 - (j\,\omega M_{13})\, I_3$$

$$V_2 = (j\,\omega L_2)\, I_2 + (j\,\omega M_{12})\, I_1 - (j\,\omega M_{23})\, I_3$$

$$V_3 = (j\,\omega L_3)\, I_3 - (j\,\omega M_{23})\, I_2 - (j\,\omega M_{13})\, I_1$$

in *frequency domain*

(Fig. E9.23) Current i_1 enters the dot end of coil-1 while i_2 also enters the dot end of coil 2. Hence M_{12} (or M_{21}) is +ve. Between coils 1 and 3, i_1

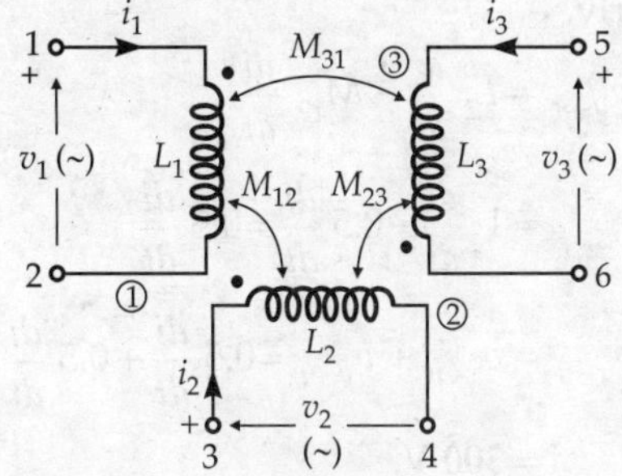

Fig. E9.23

enters the dot end of coil 1 while i_3 comes out of the dot and for coil 3. Thus M_{13} (or M_{31}) is –ve. Same reasoning holds good for coils 3 and 2 and hence M_{23} (or M_{32}) is –ve. The voltage equations are then,

$$v_1 = L_1 \frac{di_1}{dt} + M_{12} \frac{di_2}{dt} - M_{13} \frac{di_3}{dt}$$

$$v_2 = M_{12} \frac{di_1}{dt} + L_2 \frac{di_2}{dt} - M_{23} \frac{di_3}{dt}$$

$$v_3 = - M_{31} \frac{di_1}{dt} - M_{23} \frac{di_2}{dt} + L_3 \frac{di_{13}}{dt}$$

in *time domain*

and $$V_1 = (j\,\omega L_1)\, I_1 + (j\,\omega M_{12})\, I_2 - (j\,\omega M_{13})\, I_3$$

$$V_2 = (j\,\omega M_{12})\, I_1 + (j\,\omega L_2)\, I_2 - (j\,\omega M_{23})\, I_3$$

$$V_3 = -(j\,\omega M_{31})\, I_1 - (j\,\omega M_{23})\, I_2 + (j\,\omega L_3)\, I_3$$

in *frequency domain*

Example 9.18 *With reference to Fig. E9.24 find* $v_{x\text{-}y}$*, if* $\frac{di}{dt} = 300\ A/\sec$*. Assume* $L_1 = L_2 = 1\ H$ *and* $M_{12} = \frac{1}{2}\ H$.

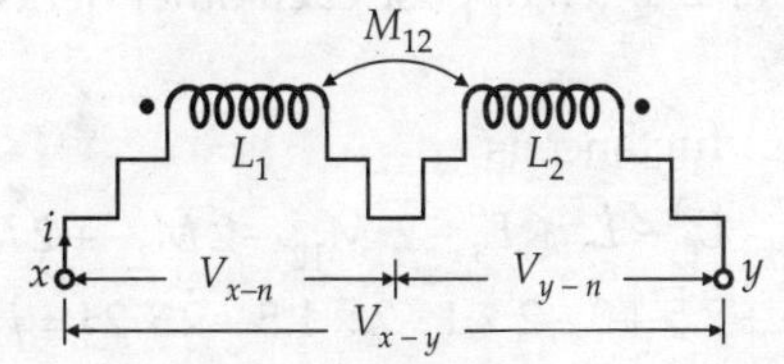

Fig. E9.24

SOLUTION. Applying KVL in the respective loops,

$$v_{x-n} = L_1 \frac{di}{dt} - M_{12} \frac{di}{dt}$$

[As the coils are electrically in series, hence, the same current i passes through the coils ; M is negative]

or, $$v_{x-n} = \frac{di}{dt} - 0.5 \frac{di}{dt} = 0.5 \frac{di}{dt} \quad ...(1)$$

Similarly,

$$v_{y-n} = L_2 \frac{di}{dt} - M_{12} \frac{di}{dt}$$

$$= 1.\frac{di}{dt} - 0.5 \frac{di}{dt} = 0.5 \frac{di}{dt} \quad ...(2)$$

$$\therefore \quad v_{x-y} = v_{x-n} + v_{y-n} = 0.5 \frac{di}{dt} + 0.5 \frac{di}{dt} = \frac{di}{dt}.$$

i.e., $|v_{x-y}|$ = **300 V.**

EXAMPLE 9.19 *Find the equivalent circuit and the net inductance of the iron cored coupled coils in series connection (Fig. E9.25).*

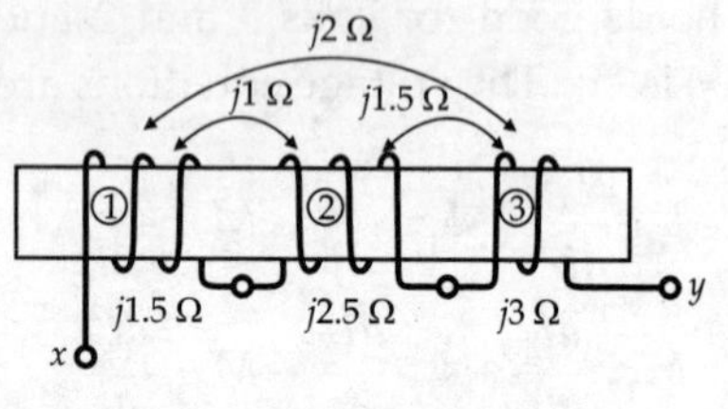

Fig. E9.25

SOLUTION. The equivalent circuits of the coils are drawn in Fig. E9.26.

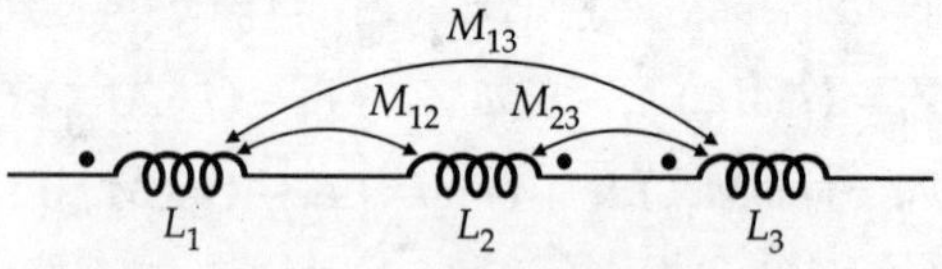

Fig. E9.26

Assuming a current in the coils from terminal x to y, it may be observed that fluxes of coils 1 and 2 oppose each other while flux of 1 in same direction to that of coil 3. Thus M_{12} is –ve, M_{13} is positive. As fluxes of coils 2 and 3 oppose each other hence, M_{23} is also –ve.

$\therefore$ Net inductance is

$$L_1 + L_2 + L_3 - 2\,M_{12} - 2\,M_{23} + 2\,M_{13}$$

i.e., $j\,[1.5 + 2.5 + 3 - 2 \times 1 - 2 \times 1.5 + 2 \times 2] = j\,6\,\Omega.$

$\therefore$ Net inductance of the coils = $\boldsymbol{j\,6\,\Omega}$.

EXAMPLE 9.20 *Draw the equivalent circuit of the coupled circuits in Fig. E9.27 and write the mesh equations.*

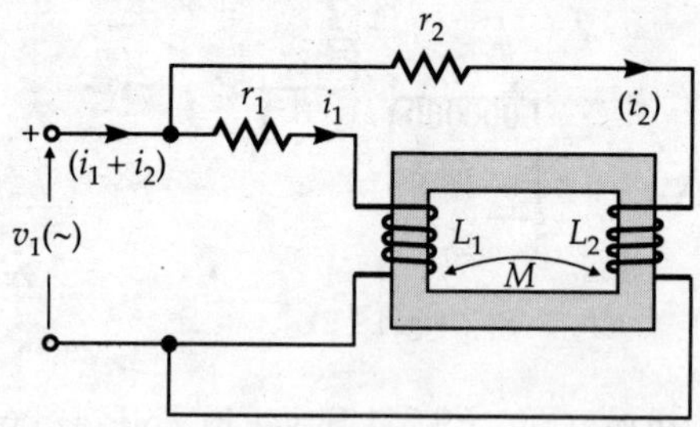

Fig. E9.27

SOLUTION. The equivalent circuit is drawn in Fig. E9.28.

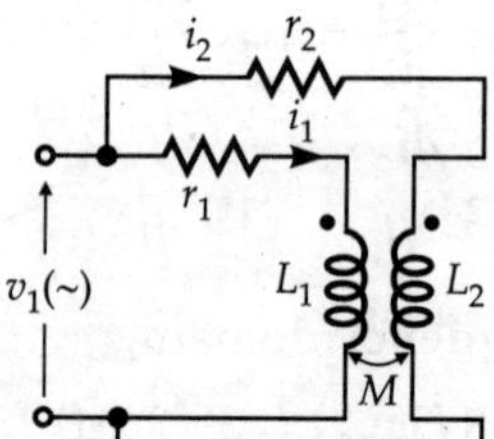

Fig. E9.28

The loop equations are as under

$$v_1 = i_1 r_1 + L_1 \frac{di_1}{dt} + M \frac{di_2}{dt} \quad ...(1)$$

and $$v_1 = i_2 r_2 + L_2 \frac{di_2}{dt} + M \frac{di_1}{dt} \quad \textbf{(in time domain)} \quad ...(2)$$

In frequency domain, these equations would be

$$V_1 = I_1 R_1 + (j\,\omega L_1)\,I_1 + j\,\omega M\,I_2$$
$$V_2 = I_2 R_2 + (j\,\omega L_2)\,I_2 + (j\,\omega M)\,I_1$$

EXAMPLE 9.21 *From the following data, find the self and mutual inductances of the two windings 1 and 2 of an ideal transformer operating in a linear zone.*

$$N_1 = 500 \text{ turns};\; N_2 = 750 \text{ turns};\; I_1 = 2 \text{ A}$$
$$\phi_1 = 10 \text{ mwb};\; \phi_{12} = 6 \text{ mwb}.$$

SOLUTION. $K = \dfrac{\phi_{12}}{\phi_1} = \dfrac{6}{10} = 0.6$

As the transformer is operating in the linear zone, hence,

$$L_1 = N_1 \frac{\phi_1}{I_1} = 500 \times \frac{0.01}{2} = 2.5 \text{ H}$$

$$M = N_2 \frac{\phi_{12}}{I_1} = 750 \times \frac{0.006}{2.0} = 2.25 \text{ H}$$

However,

$$M = K\sqrt{L_1 L_2}$$

i.e.,
$$L_2 = \frac{M^2}{K^2 L_1} = \frac{2.25^2}{0.6^2 \times 2.5} = 5.625 \text{ H}$$

$$\therefore \quad \mathbf{L_1 = 2.5\ H}, \quad \mathbf{L_2 = 5.625\ H}, \quad \mathbf{M = 2.25\ H.}$$

EXAMPLE 9.22 *In an ideal transformer, the mutual inductance = 10 H; No. of primary and secondary terms are 50 and 200. Obtain the value of primary current to produce 0.5 wb flux to link with the secondary coil.*

SOLUTION. $N_1 = 50$, $N_2 = 200$, $M = 10$ H;

But
$$M = N_2 \frac{\phi_{12}}{I_1} = 200 \times \frac{0.5}{I_1}$$

or,
$$10 = \frac{100}{I_1} \quad \therefore \quad I_1 = 10 \text{ A}$$

∴ The value of the primary current = **10 A.**

EXAMPLE 9.23 *For an ideal transformer, show that* $\frac{V_1}{V_2} = \sqrt{\frac{L_1}{L_2}}$ *where,* L_1 *and* L_2 *are the self-inductances of the primary and secondary windings.*

SOLUTION. For an ideal transformer, Fig. E9.29 $K = 1$, $R_1 = R_2 = 0$.

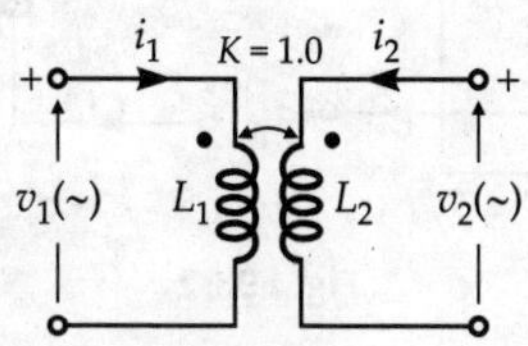

Fig. E9.29

Applying KVL in the primary and secondary loops, we get,

$$V_1 = (j\,\omega L_1)\,I_1 + (j\,\omega M)\,I_2$$

$$V_2 = (j\,\omega L_2)\,I_2 + (j\,\omega M)\,I_1$$

[In this case I_1 and I_2 both enter through the dot ends; thus, ∴ M is +ve]

Hence,

$$\frac{V_1}{V_2} = \frac{L_1 I_1 + M I_2}{M I_1 + L_2 I_2} \qquad ...(1)$$

For an ideal transformer, since $K = 1$,

$$M = \sqrt{L_1 L_2}$$

i.e.,
$$\frac{V_1}{V_2} = \frac{L_1 I_1 + \sqrt{L_1 L_2}\, I_2}{\sqrt{L_1 L_2}\, I_1 + L_2 I_2}$$

$$= \sqrt{\frac{L_1}{L_2}} \left[\frac{\sqrt{L_1} \cdot I_1 + \sqrt{L_2} \cdot I_2}{\sqrt{L_1}\, I_1 + \sqrt{L_2}\, I_2} \right]$$

or
$$\frac{V_1}{V_2} = \sqrt{\frac{L_1}{L_2}}.$$

In a linear circuit $\frac{L_1}{L_2} = \frac{N_1^2}{N_2^2}$, where N_1 and N_2 are the number of turns

$$\therefore \quad \frac{V_1}{V_2} = \frac{N_1}{N_2} = \text{turns ratio} = n \text{ (say)}$$

i.e., $V_1 = nV_2$ (this is a very important relationship in transformer theory)

As the ideal transformer is lossless,

the primary coil power = secondary coil power

i.e.,
$$V_1 I_1 = -V_2 I_2,$$

the –ve sign indicates entry of power in secondary coil.

i.e.,
$$-\frac{I_1}{I_2} = \frac{V_2}{V_1}.$$

Thus in ideal transformer,

$$\frac{V_1}{V_2} = \frac{N_1}{N_2} = -\frac{I_2}{I_1} = n.$$

EXAMPLE 9.24 *Show that in an ideal transformer, the input impedance looking through the primary terminals is the square of turns ratio times the secondary impedance.*

SOLUTION. We have just proved in the previous example that for an ideal transformer (Fig. E9.30),

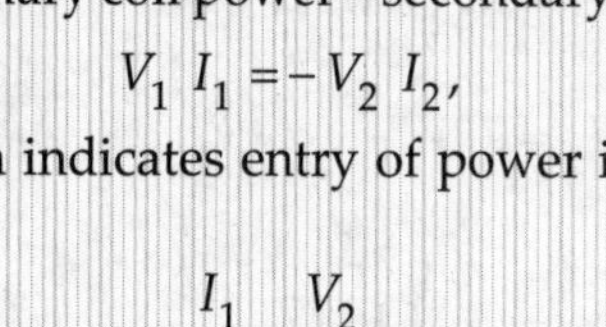

Fig. E9.30

$$\frac{V_1}{V_2} = \frac{N_1}{N_2} \text{ and } -\frac{I_1}{I_2} = \frac{N_2}{N_1}.$$

i.e.,
$$\frac{V_1/I_1}{V_2/I_2} = \left(\frac{N_1}{N_2}\right)^2$$

CHAPTER 9

or, $\frac{Z_{in}}{Z_{sec}} = n^2$

$$\left[\because \frac{V_1}{I_1} = Z_{\text{input}} \text{ and } \frac{V_2}{I_2} = Z_{\text{secondary}}\right]$$

i.e., $\mathbf{Z_{in} = n^2 \cdot Z_{sec}}$.

EXAMPLE 9.25 *Show that for an ideal transformer, $AD - BC = 1$ where A, B, C, D are transmission parameters in the two port network.*

SOLUTION. In Example 9.23, we have proved that

$$\frac{V_1}{V_2} = \frac{N_1}{N_2} = n \quad i.e., \; V_1 = nV_2 \quad ...(1)$$

and $$\frac{I_1}{I_2} = -\frac{N_2}{N_1} = -\frac{1}{n} \quad i.e., \; I_2 = -n\,I_1 \quad ...(2)$$

We can rewrite equations (1) and (2) as

$$V_1 = nV_2 + 0 \,.\, I_2$$

$$I_1 = 0 \,.\, V_2 + \frac{1}{n}(-I_2)$$

i.e., $$\begin{bmatrix} V_1 \\ I_1 \end{bmatrix} = \begin{bmatrix} n & 0 \\ 0 & \frac{1}{n} \end{bmatrix} \begin{bmatrix} V_2 \\ -I_2 \end{bmatrix}.$$

Comparing this equation with the standard forms of *ABCD* parameters,

$$A = n,\; B = 0,\; C = 0,\; D = \frac{1}{n}.$$

Hence $AD - BC = n \times \frac{1}{n} - 0 \times 1 = 1$

Thus in ideal transformers, $\mathbf{AD - BC = 1}$.

The circuit is reciprocal.

EXAMPLE 9.26 *Two impedances Z_1 and Z_2 are connected in series with the primary and secondary winding of an ideal transformer where the primary coil has $j\,2\,\Omega$ and the secondary coil has $j\,3\,\Omega$ reactance (Fig. E9.31). Find the mutual reactance and inductance if ω= 100 rad / sec.*

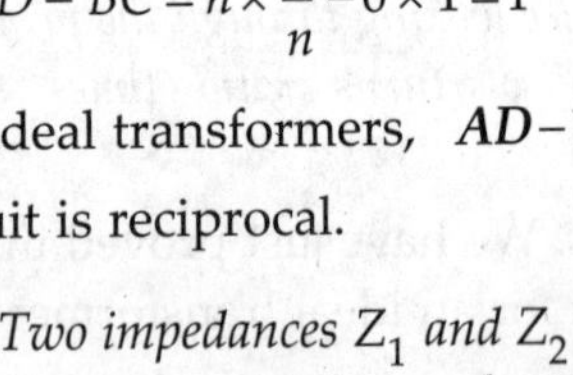

Fig. E9.31

SOLUTION. In ideal transformer, $K = 1$.

$\therefore \quad M = \sqrt{L_1 L_2}$

i.e., $X_M = \sqrt{X_1 X_2}$

[X_1 = reactance of primary coil ;
X_2 = reactance of secondary coil ;
X_M = mutual reactance]

i.e., $X_M = \sqrt{j\,2 \times j\,3} = j\,2.45\,\Omega$

But $X = 2\pi fL$

$\therefore \quad L_M = \frac{X_M}{2\pi f} = \frac{X_M}{\omega} = \frac{2.45}{100} = 2.45 \times 10^{-2}$ H

i.e., Mutual reactance $= \mathbf{2.45\,\Omega}$

and Mutual inductance $= \mathbf{2.45 \times 10^{-2}\ H}$.

EXAMPLE 9.27 *Find net inductance in the series connected coupled coils [Figs. E9.32(a) to 9.32(d)].*

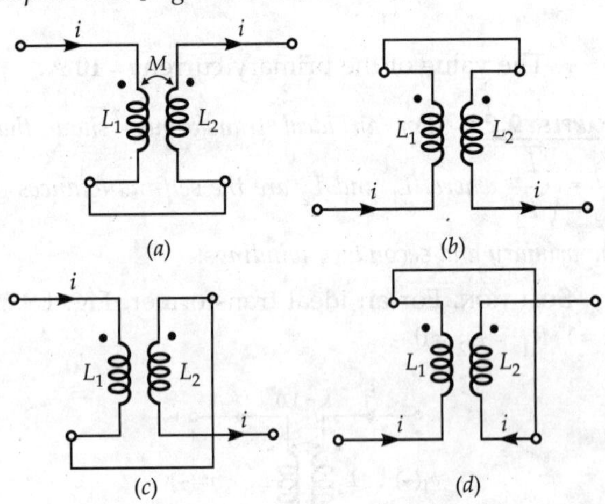

Fig. E9.32

SOLUTION. *Fig. E9.32(a)* : *i* enters L_1 through dot end and leaves L_2 through dot end.

$\therefore$ M is –ve.

Then, $\quad L_{eq} = L_1 + L_2 - 2M$

Figure E9.32(b) : *i* enters L_1 through undotted end and enters L_2 through dot end. Thus M is –ve here also.

$$L_{eq} = L_1 + L_2 - 2M.$$

Figure E9.32(c) : *i* enters L_1 as well as L_2 through dot end. Thus M is +ve.

$\therefore \quad L_{eq} = L_1 + L_2 + 2M$

Figure E9.32(d) : In both the coupled coils, *i* leaves though the dot end. Thus M is +ve.

$\therefore \quad L_{eq} = L_1 + L_2 + 2M.$

EXAMPLE 9.28 *Two coupled coils have $K = 0.8$, $N_1 = 500$ turns, $N_2 = 1000$ turns and the mutual flux being 0.9 wb, find the primary coil flux. If the primary current be 10 A, find the primary coil inductance. Also obtain the secondary inductance.*

SOLUTION. Let $\phi_1 =$ primary flux,

$\phi_{12} =$ mutual flux,

$K =$ coefficient of coupling,

$I_1 = 10$ A

Again, $\phi_{12} = K\phi_1$ or $0.9 = 0.8\,\phi_1$

$\therefore \quad \phi_1 = 1.125$ wb.

Primary coil flux = **1.125 wb.**

$$\text{Again } L_1 = N_1 \frac{\phi_1}{I_1} = 500 \times \frac{1.125}{10} = 56.25 \text{ H}$$

$\therefore$ Primary coil inductance = **56.25 H**

Also, $M = K\sqrt{L_1 L_2}$

But $M = N_2 \dfrac{\phi_{12}}{I_1}$

gives $M = 1000 \times \dfrac{0.9}{10} = 90$ H;

K being 0.8, we can write

$$10 = 0.8\sqrt{56.25 \times L_2}$$

or, $$L_2 = \frac{10^2}{0.8^2 \times 56.25} = 2.78 \text{ H}$$

$\therefore$ Secondary coil inductance = **2.78 H.**

EXAMPLE 9.29 *In the network of Fig. E9.33, $L_1 = 1$ H; $L_2 = 2$ H, $M = 1.2$ H. Assuming the inductance coils to be ideal, find the amount of energy stored after 0.1 sec of the circuit connected to a d.c. source of 10 V.*

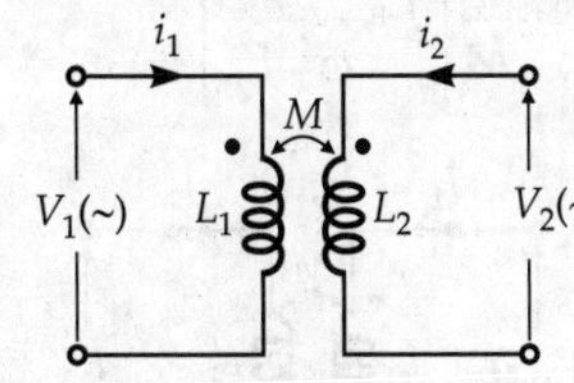

Fig. E9.33

SOLUTION. Applying KVL in the left loop, just after switching the 10 V source as V_1,

$$10 = L_1 \frac{di_1}{dt} + M \frac{di_2}{dt} \text{ and at the right loop,}$$

$$0 = L_2 \frac{di_2}{dt} + M \frac{di_1}{dt}$$

[$\therefore$ i_1 and i_2 both enter the respective coils through dotted ends hence M is +ve]

or, $$\frac{di_2}{dt} = -\frac{M}{L_2}\frac{di_1}{dt}$$

Utilising the value of $\dfrac{di_2}{dt}$ in the first equation,

$$10 = L_1 \frac{di_1}{dt} + M\left(-\frac{M}{L_2}\frac{di_1}{dt}\right) = \frac{di_1}{dt}\left[L_1 - \frac{M^2}{L_2}\right]$$

$$= \frac{L_1 L_2 - M^2}{L_2} \cdot \frac{di_1}{dt}.$$

This indicates that the equivalent inductance is given by

$$\frac{L_1 L_2 - M^2}{L_2} \quad i.e., \quad \frac{1 \times 2 - 1.44}{2} = 0.28 \text{ H}$$

i.e., $\quad L_{\text{equiv.}} = 0.28$ H

or, $$\frac{di_1}{dt} = \frac{10}{0.28} = 35.7$$

$$\therefore \quad i_1 = \int_0^t 35.7\, dt = 35.7\, t$$

The stored energy after 0.1 sec is thus

$$E_{\text{stored}} = \frac{1}{2} LI^2$$

$$= \frac{1}{2} \times 0.28 \times (35.7)^2\, t^2$$

$$= \frac{1}{2} \times 0.28 \times 35.7^2 \times 0.1^2 = 1.785 \text{ J}$$

i.e., energy stored after 0.1 sec = **1.785 J.**

EXAMPLE 9.30 *Find the net impedance for the central mesh and then find the input impedance of the circuit shown in Fig. E9.34.*

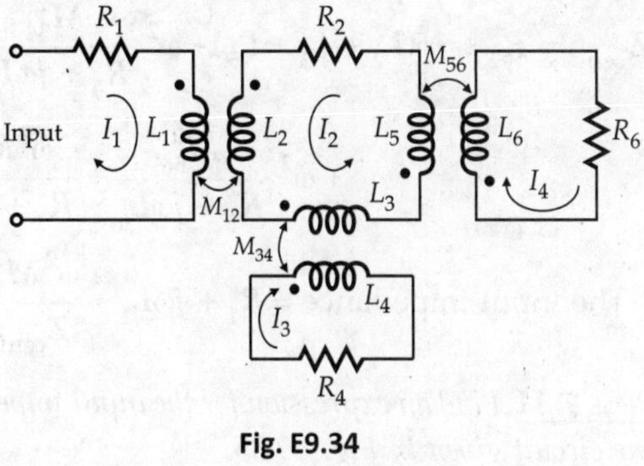

Fig. E9.34

CHAPTER 9

Solution. Applying KVL in the central loop (Fig. 9.34),

$$0 = I_2 R_2 + j\, I_2\, (\omega L_2 + \omega L_3 + \omega L_5) + j\, I_3\, (\omega M_{34}) + j\, I_4\, (\omega M_{56}) + jI_1\, (\omega M_{12}) \quad ...(1)$$

However, in the bottommost loop,

$$(R_4 + j\omega L_4)\, I_3 + j\, \omega M_{34}\, I_2 = 0$$

$$\therefore \quad I_3 = I_2 \cdot \left(-\frac{j\, \omega M_{34}}{R_4 + j\, \omega L_4} \right) \quad ...(2)$$

Similarly, for the rightmost loop,

$$(R_6 + j\, \omega L_6)\, I_4 + j\omega M_{56} \cdot I_2 = 0$$

or,
$$I_4 = I_2 \left(-\frac{j\, \omega M_{56}}{R_6 + j\omega L_6} \right) \quad ...(3)$$

Utilising (2) and (3) in (1),

$$0 = I_2\, [R_2 + j\, (\omega L_2 + \omega L_3 + \omega L_5)] + j\, I_2\, (\omega M_{34}) \left(-\frac{j\omega M_{34}}{R_4 + j\omega L_4} \right) + j\, I_2\, (\omega M_{56}) \left(-\frac{j\, \omega M_{56}}{R_6 + j\omega L_6} \right) + jI_1\, (\omega M_{12})$$

Next, applying KVL in the leftmost loop,

Simplification yields,

$$I_1 = \frac{V_1 - j\omega M_{12}\, I_2}{R_1 + j\omega L_1} = \frac{V_1}{R_1 + j\omega L_1} - \frac{j\omega M_{12}\, I_2}{R_1 + j\omega L_1}$$

$\therefore$ Finally,

$$0 = I_2 \left[R_2 + j\, \omega(L_2 + L_3 + L_5) + \frac{\omega^2\, M^2{}_{34}}{R_4 + j\, \omega L_4} + \frac{\omega^2\, M_{56}^2}{R_6 + j\omega L_6} + \frac{\omega^2\, M_{12}^2}{R_1 + j\omega L_1} \right] + j\, \frac{\omega M_{12}\, V_1}{R_1 + j\omega L_1}$$

$\therefore$ Net impedance of the central loop

$$\mathbf{Z_{cent.} = R_2 + j\omega(L_2 + L_3 + L_5) + \omega^2 \frac{M_{34}^2}{R_4 + j\omega L_4} + \omega^2 \frac{M_{56}^2}{R_6 + j\omega L_6} + \frac{\omega^2 M_{12}^2}{R_1 + j\omega L_1}}$$

The input impedance $= \mathbf{R_1 + j\omega L_1 + \dfrac{\omega^2 M_{12}^2}{Z_{cent.}}}$.

Example 9.31 *Find an expression for the input impedance of the circuit given in Fig. E9.35.*

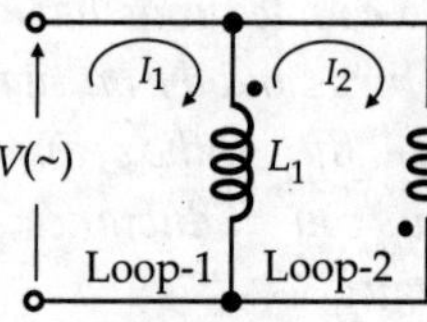

Fig. E9.35

Solution. In coil-1, current $(I_1 - I_2)$ enters through the dot end while for the coil-2, the current I_2 comes out of the dot end.

$\therefore$ *In loop-1,*

$$V = (j\, \omega L_1)(I_1 - I_2) - (j\, \omega M)\, I_2 = (j\, \omega L_1)\, I_1 - j\, \omega(L_1 + M)\, I_2 \quad ...(1)$$

Using KVL *in loop-2,*

$$0 = j\, \omega L_1\, (I_2 - I_1) + j\, \omega L_2\, I_2 + j\, \omega M\, I_2 + j\, \omega M (I_2 - I_1)$$
$$= -\, j\, \omega(L_1 + M)\, I_1 + j\, \omega(L_1 + L_2 + 2M)\, I_2$$

or,
$$I_2 = \frac{L_1 + M}{L_1 + L_2 + 2M} \cdot I_1 \quad ...(2)$$

Substituting the value of I_2 from (2) in (1),

$$V = (j\, \omega L_1)\, I_1 - j\, \omega(L_1 + M) \frac{L_1 + M}{L_1 + L_2 + 2M} \cdot I_1$$

$$\therefore \quad \frac{V}{I_1} = j\, \omega L_1 - j\, \omega(L_1 + M) \frac{L_1 + M}{L_1 + L_2 + 2M} = j\, \omega \frac{(L_1 L_2 - M^2)}{L_1 + L_2 + 2M}$$

i.e., $\mathbf{Z_{in} = j\omega \dfrac{(L_1 L_2 - M^2)}{L_1 + L_2 + 2M}}$.

Example 9.32 *In the coupled coil circuit of Fig. E9.36, prove that*

$$\frac{|\, I_1\, |}{|\, I_2\, |} = \frac{L_2}{M} \left[1 + \frac{R_2^2}{\omega^2\, L_2^2} \right]^{1/2}.$$

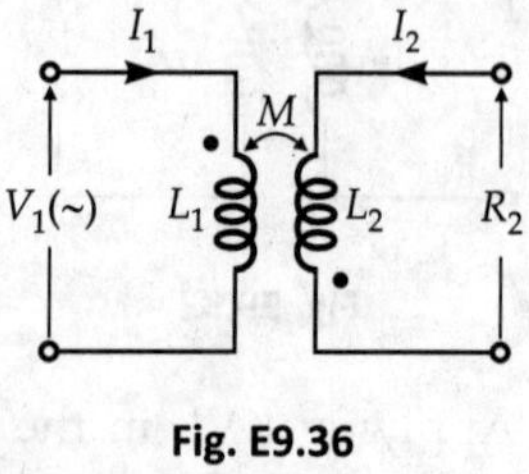

Fig. E9.36

Solution. As I_1 enters L_1 through dot end and I_2 comes out from L_2 through dot end hence M is negative.

The loop equation in the output loop is

$$(R_2 + j\,\omega L_2)\,I_2 - (j\,\omega M)\,I_1 = 0$$

$$\therefore \quad \frac{I_1}{I_2} = \frac{R_2 + j\,\omega L_2}{j\,\omega M}$$

$$\text{i.e.,} \quad \frac{|\,I_1\,|}{|\,I_2\,|} = \frac{\sqrt{R_2^2 + \omega^2 L_2^2}}{\omega M} = \frac{L_2}{M}\left(1 + \frac{R_2^2}{\omega^2 L_2^2}\right)^{1/2}$$

It is proved that $\dfrac{|\,I_1\,|}{|\,I_2\,|} = \dfrac{L_2}{M}\left(1 + \dfrac{R_2^2}{\omega^2 L_2^2}\right)^{1/2}$.

EXAMPLE 9.33 *Show that for an ideal transformer, $L_1 L_2 - M^2 = 0$.*

SOLUTION. For an ideal transformer (Fig. E9.37).

$$R_1 = R_2 = 0 \text{ and } K = 1$$

[∵ the coils do not have any resistance].

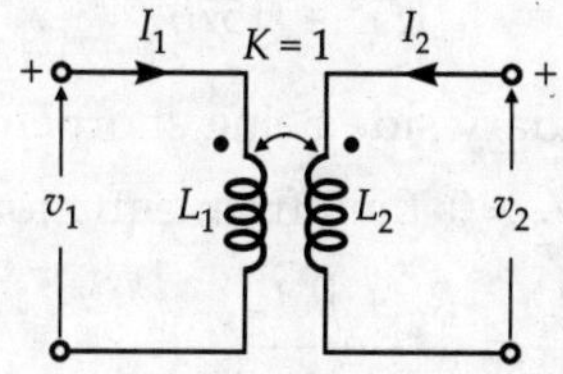

Fig. E9.37

$$\text{Since} \quad K = \frac{M}{\sqrt{L_1 L_2}}.$$

$$\therefore \quad M = \sqrt{L_1 L_2}$$

i.e., $\mathbf{L_1 L_2 - M^2 = 0}$.

EXAMPLE 9.34 *Show that the network shown in Fig. E9.38 is reciprocal.*

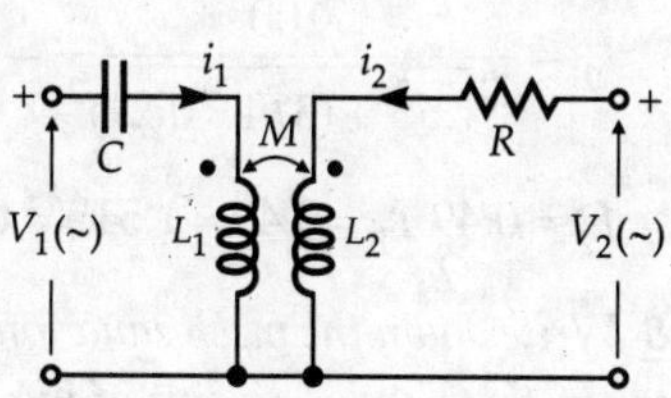

Fig. E9.38

SOLUTION. For the given network the loop equations are (transforming the components in *s*-domain)

$$V_1(s) = \left(\frac{1}{sC} + sL_1\right) I_1(s) + sMI_2(s)$$

$$V_2(s) = (R + sL_2)\,I_2(s) + sMI_1(s)$$

[M is +ve here as i_1 and i_2 enter the coupled circuit coils through dot ends]

Thus,

$$\begin{bmatrix} V_1(s) \\ V_2(s) \end{bmatrix} = \begin{bmatrix} \dfrac{1}{sC} + sL_1 & sM \\ sM & R + sL_2 \end{bmatrix} \begin{bmatrix} I_1(s) \\ I_2(s) \end{bmatrix}$$

$$= \begin{bmatrix} Z_{11}(s) & Z_{21}(s) \\ Z_{12}(s) & Z_{22}(s) \end{bmatrix} \begin{bmatrix} I_1(s) \\ I_2(s) \end{bmatrix}$$

$$\therefore \quad \mathbf{Z_{12}(s) = sM = Z_{21}(s).}$$

Thus the given circuit is reciprocal.

EXAMPLE 9.35 *Find the open circuit output voltage (v_{x-y}) in terms of M in Fig. E9.39.*

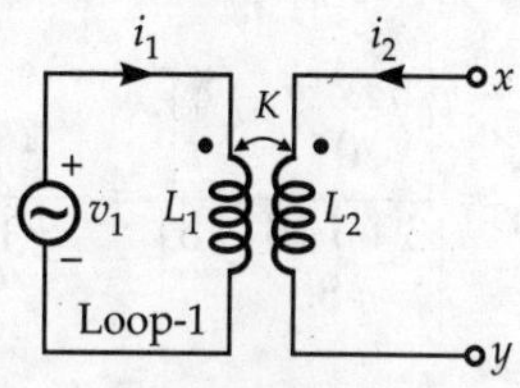

Fig. E9.39

SOLUTION. Applying KVL in loop-1,

$$v_1 = L_1 \frac{di_1}{dt} + M \frac{di_2}{dt} \quad \text{...(1)}$$

But, $\quad i_2 = 0 \quad$ [∵ output is open-circuited]

$$\therefore \quad v_1 = L_1 \frac{di_1}{dt}.$$

$$\therefore \quad \frac{di_1}{dt} = \frac{v_1}{L_1} \quad \text{...(2)}$$

Again, in the output loop,

$$v_2 = M\frac{di_1}{dt} + L_2\frac{di_2}{dt} = M\frac{di_1}{dt} \quad [\because i_2 = 0]$$

$$\text{or,} \quad v_2 = M.\frac{v_1}{L_1} \quad [v_2 \equiv v_{x-y}] \quad \text{...(3)}$$

Thus, output

$$\mathbf{v_2 = M\frac{v_1}{L_1}.}$$

EXAMPLE 9.36 *In Fig. E9.40, find the drop across the capacitor and the resistor.*

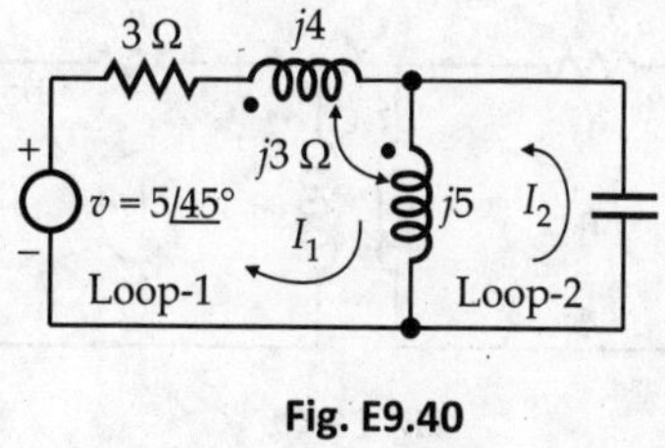

Fig. E9.40

SOLUTION. Applying KVL in loop-1,

$$3I_1 + j\,4I_1 + j\,5(I_1+I_2) + j\,3(I_2+I_1) + j\,3\,I_1 = 5\,\angle 45°$$

or, $$I_1\,(3+j\,15) + j\,8\,I_2 = 5\angle 45°$$

Applying KVL in loop-2,

$$j\,5(I_1+I_2) - j\,6.I_2 + j\,3\,I_1 = 0.$$

or, $$j\,8I_1 - j\,I_2 = 0.$$

In matrix form

$$\begin{bmatrix} 3+j\,15 & j\,8 \\ +j\,8 & -j \end{bmatrix}\begin{bmatrix} I_1 \\ I_2 \end{bmatrix} = \begin{bmatrix} 5\,\angle 45° \\ 0 \end{bmatrix}$$

$$\therefore \quad I_1 = \frac{\begin{vmatrix} 5\angle 45° & j\,8 \\ 0 & -j \end{vmatrix}}{\begin{vmatrix} 3+j\,15 & j\,8 \\ j\,8 & -j \end{vmatrix}} = \frac{5\,\angle -45°}{-j\,3+15+64}$$

$$= \frac{5\,\angle -45°}{79 - j\,3} = \frac{5\,\angle -45°}{79\,\angle -2.175°}$$

$$= 0.063\,\angle -47.175°\text{ A}$$

$$I_2 = \frac{\begin{vmatrix} 3+j\,15 & 5\,\angle 45° \\ j\,8 & 0 \end{vmatrix}}{\begin{vmatrix} 3+j\,15 & j\,8 \\ j\,8 & -j \end{vmatrix}} = \frac{-40\,\angle 135°}{79\,\angle -2.175°}$$

$$= -0.506\angle 132.83°\text{ A}$$

$\therefore$ Drop across 3 Ω resistor

$$= 3\times I_1 = \mathbf{0.189\,\angle -47.175°\ V}$$

and drop across $-j\,6\,\Omega$ capacitor

$$= (-j\,6)(-0.506\,\angle 132.83°)$$

$$= 6\,\angle -90° \times -0.506\,\angle 132.83°$$

$$= \mathbf{-3.036\,\angle 42.83°\ V}$$

It may be noted that the polarity of drop across the capacitance will be such that +ve terminal is at the top and the current in loop-2 is clockwise.

EXAMPLE 9.37 *Two coils A and B having resistances of 1.5 Ω and 5 Ω and self inductances of 5 H and 20 H respectively have mutual inductance of 9.8 H. Coil A is connected to 100 V, 50 Hz supply [See Fig. E9.41].*

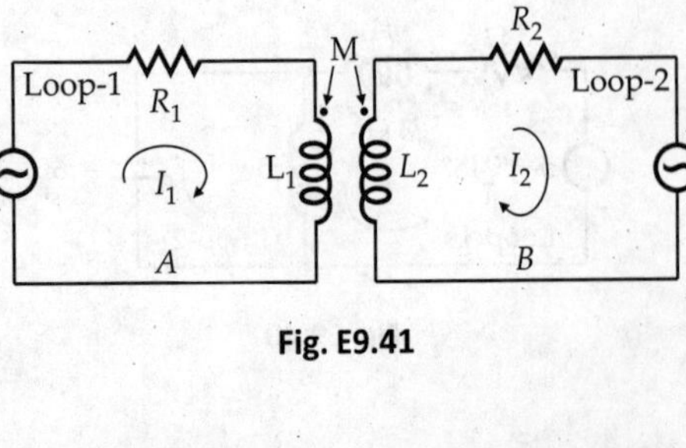

Fig. E9.41

Obtain

(a) *primary current with the secondary terminals being open circuited*

(b) *primary current and secondary current with the secondary terminal short circuited.*

SOLUTION. Applying KVL to loop-1 [Fig. 9.41)]

$$V_1 = (R_1 + j\omega L_1)\,I_1 - j\omega M I_2 \qquad \text{...(A)}$$

for loop-2, we have

$$V_2 = -\,j\omega M I_1 + (R_2 + j\omega L_2) I_2 \qquad \text{...(B)}$$

(*a*) With secondary side open circuited, $I_2 = 0$

From equations (*A*) and (*B*) we then have

$$I_1 = \frac{V_1}{R_1 + j\omega L_1} = \frac{100}{1.5 + j2\,\pi \times 50 \times 5}$$

i.e., $$|\,I_1\,| = \frac{100}{\sqrt{1.5^2 + (1570)^2}} = 0.0637\text{ A}$$

(*b*) Secondary side being short circuited,

$V_2 = 0$, then from equation (*B*)

$$\frac{I_1}{I_2} = \frac{R_2 + j\omega L_2}{j\omega M}$$

or $$\left|\frac{I_1}{I_2}\right| = \sqrt{\frac{25 + (2\pi\times 50\times 20)^2}{(2\pi\times 50\times 9.8)^2}} = 2.04$$

With $I_2 = 0.49\,I_1$,

From equation (*A*) we get,

$$100 = (1.5 + j314\times 5 - j314\times 9.8\times 0.49)$$

$$= (1.5 + j0.21\times 314)\,I_1$$

i.e., $$I_1 = \frac{100}{\sqrt{1.5^2 + (314\times 0.21)^2}} = \mathbf{1.515\ A}$$

Also, $I_2 = 0.49\,I_1 = 0.49\times 1.515 = \mathbf{0.743\ A.}$

EXAMPLE 9.38 *Write down the mesh equation for the loops abcd and pqrs in the coupled circuit of Fig. E9.42.*

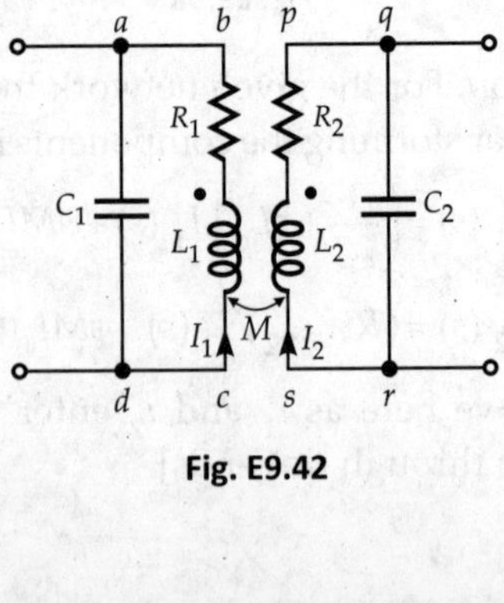

Fig. E9.42

Solution. Applying KVL in the loop *abcd*,

$$I_1 R_1 + I_1 (j\,\omega L_1) - j\frac{1}{\omega C_1} \cdot I_1 + (j\,\omega M)\, I_2 = 0$$

It may be noted that $\frac{1}{j\,\omega C_1} = -j\frac{1}{\omega C_1}$ and as I_1 and I_2 enter L_1 and L_2 through undotted ends hence M is positive.

i.e., $$\mathbf{I_1\left[R_1 + j\left(\omega L_1 - \frac{1}{\omega C_1}\right)\right] + (j\,\omega M)\, I_2 = 0} \quad ...(1)$$

Applying KVL in the loop *pqrs*,

$$I_2 R_2 + I_2 (j\omega L_2) - j\frac{1}{\omega C_2} \cdot I_2 + j\omega M\, I_1 = 0$$

or, $$\mathbf{j\,\omega M \cdot I_1 + I_2\left[R_2 + j\left(\omega L_2 - \frac{1}{\omega C_2}\right)\right] = 0.} \quad ...(2)$$

Example 9.39 *Find the conductively coupled equivalent circuit of Fig. E9.43.*

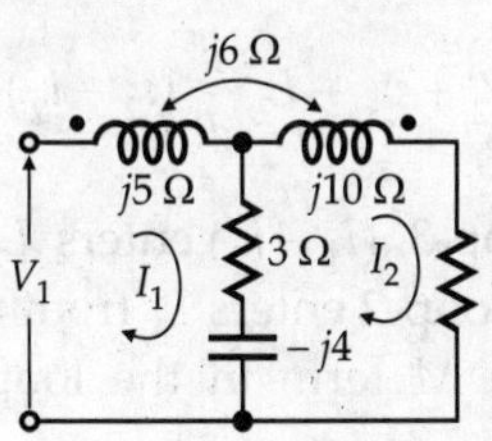

Fig. E9.43

Solution. From the theory of conductively coupled equivalent circuit,

$$Z_A = (L_1 - M) = j\,5 - j\,6 = -j\,\Omega$$
$$Z_B = (L_2 - M) = j\,10 - j\,6 = j\,4\,\Omega$$
$$Z_C = M = j\,6\,\Omega$$

M is –ve for Z_A and Z_B because in Fig. E9.43, I_1 enters $j\,5\,\Omega$ through dot end while I_2 enters $j\,10\,\Omega$ through undot end.

The circuit configuration of the equivalent circuit is drawn in **Fig. E9.44.**

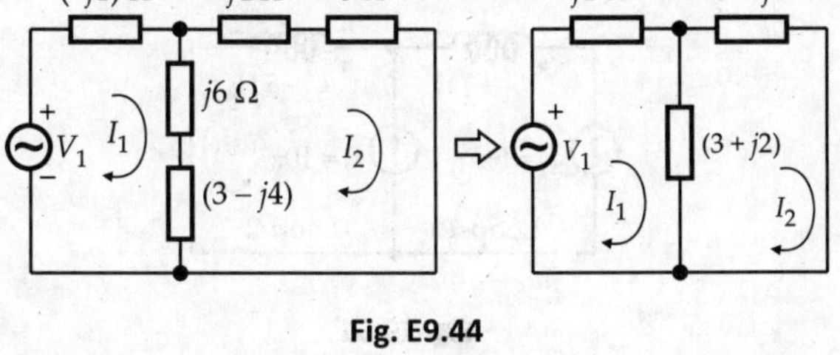

Fig. E9.44

Example 9.40 *Find the conductively coupled equivalent circuit of the network shown in Fig. E9.45. [Assume M = 2 Ω]*

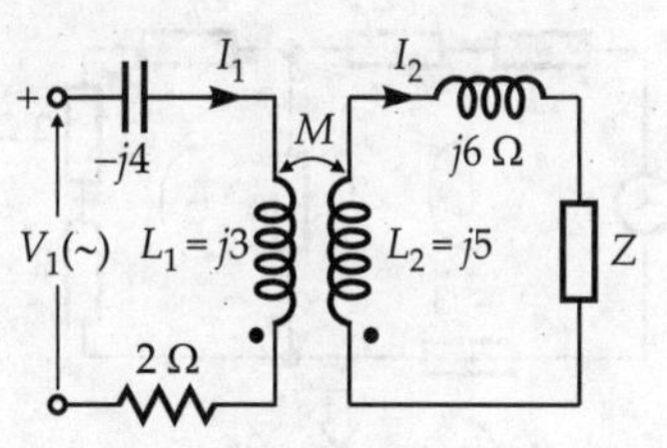

Fig. E9.45

Solution. Here M is –ve as in L_1, I_1 enters through undotted end but in L_2, I_2 enters through dot end. **(Fig. E9.45).**

∴ In the conductively coupled equivalent circuit [Fig. E9.46],

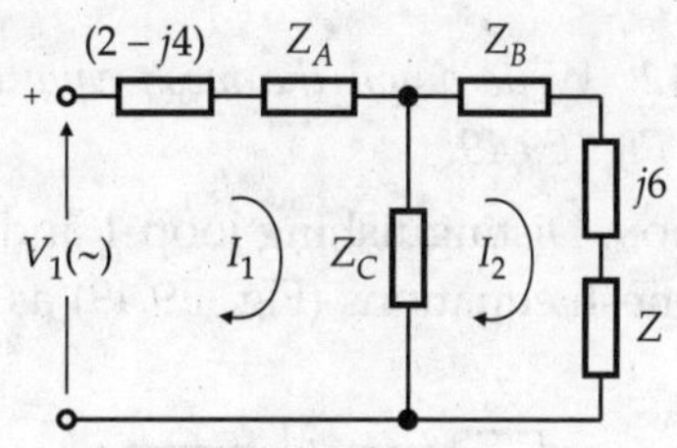

Fig. E9.46

$$\mathbf{Z_A = L_1 - M = j\,3 - j\,2 = j\,1\,\Omega}$$
$$\mathbf{Z_B = L_2 - M = j\,5 - j\,2 = j\,3\,\Omega}$$
$$\mathbf{Z_C = M = j\,2\,\Omega}$$

Example 9.41 *Find the conductively coupled equivalent circuit of the network in Fig. E9.47.*

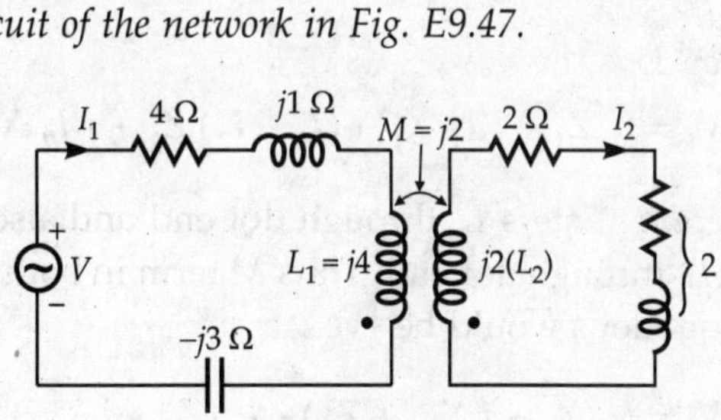

Fig. E9.47

Solution. In this network, M is +ve as I_1 enters L_1 through undotted end as well as I_2 enters L_2 through undotted end.

∴ In the conductively coupled equivalent circuit,

$$Z_A = L_1 + M = j\,4 + j\,2 = j\,6$$
$$Z_B = L_2 + M = j\,2 + j\,2 = j\,4$$
$$Z_C = -M = -j\,2\,\Omega$$

The conductively equivalent circuit figures are drawn in **Fig. E9.48.**

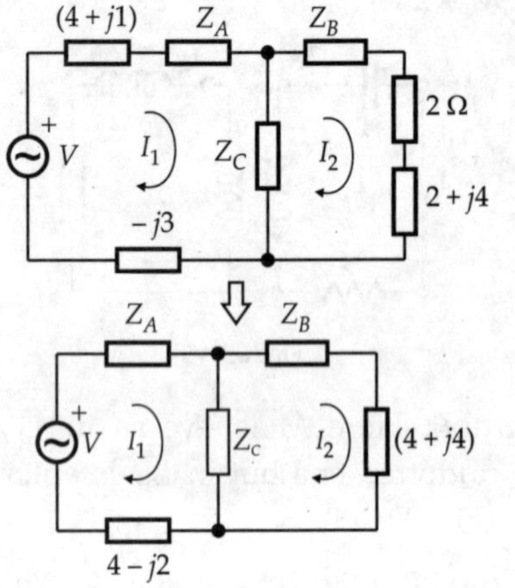

Fig. E9.48

EXAMPLE 9.42 *Write down the mesh equations for the network in Fig. E9.49.*

SOLUTION. Distinguishing loop-1 and loop-2 we write the mesh equations (Fig. E9.49) as follows :

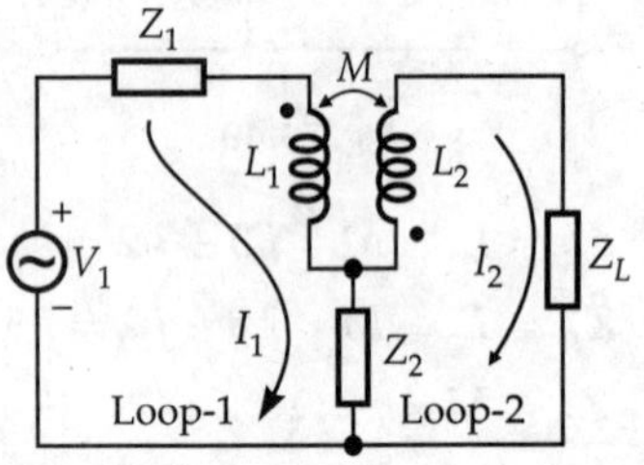

Fig. E9.49

Loop-1,

$$V_1 = I_1\, Z_1 + j\, I_1\, X_{L_1} + (I_1 - I_2)\, Z_2 + j\, I_2\, X_m$$

Here, I_1 enters L_1 through dot end and also I_2 enters L_2 through dot end. Thus M term in both the loop equations would be +ve.

or, $$V_1 = I_1\,(Z_1 + j\,X_{L_1} + Z_2) - I_2\,(Z_2 - j\,X_M) \qquad ...(1)$$

Loop-2,

$$0 = (I_2 - I_1)\, Z_2 + j\, I_2\, X_{L_2} + I_2\, Z_L + j\, I_1\, X_M$$

or, $$0 = -\,I_1\,(Z_2 - j\,X_M) + I_2\,(Z_2 + j\,X_{L_2} + Z_L) \qquad ...(2)$$

In matrix form

$$\begin{bmatrix} V_1 \\ 0 \end{bmatrix} = \begin{bmatrix} Z_1 + jX_{L_1} + Z_2 & -(Z_2 - jX_M) \\ -(Z_2 - jX_M) & (Z_2 + jX_{L_2} + Z_L) \end{bmatrix} \begin{bmatrix} I_1 \\ I_2 \end{bmatrix}$$

EXAMPLE 9.43 *Write down the mesh equations in the coupled circuits of Fig. E9.50.*

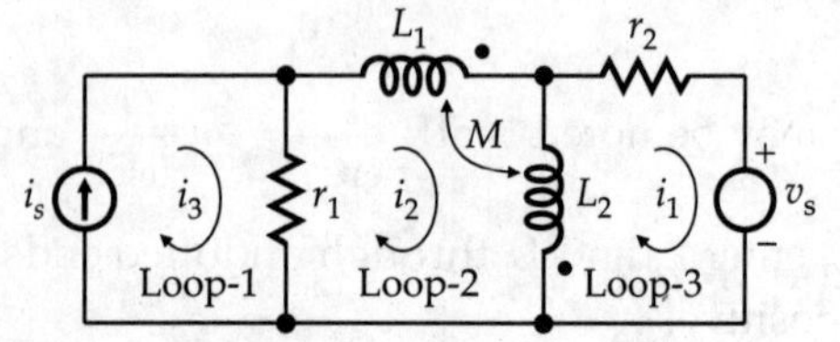

Fig. E9.50

SOLUTION. Let us first draw the circuit currents in the loops as shown in Fig. E9.50.

In loop-1, $$i_3 = i_s \qquad ...(1)$$

In loop-2, $$L_1 \frac{di_2}{dt} + r_1\,(i_2 - i_s) + M\frac{di_2}{dt} + M\frac{d}{dt}(i_2 - i_1) + L_2\,\frac{d}{dt}(i_2 - i_1) = 0$$

As i_2 enters L_1 through undotted end while $(i_2 - i_1)$ enters L_2 through undotted end, hence M terms in the loop equation of loop-2 would be +ve.

In loop-3,

$$i_1\, r_2 + v_s + L_2\,\frac{d}{dt}(i_1 - i_2) - M\frac{di_2}{dt} = 0$$

Here, in loop-3, $(i_1 - i_2)$ enters L_2 through dot end while i_2 of loop-2 enters L_1 from undotted end. This makes the M term in the loop equation of loop-2 –ve.

Reorienting the loop equation we ultimately get

$$\mathbf{i_3 = i_s} \qquad ...(1)$$

$$\frac{di_1}{dt}[-M - L_2] + \frac{di_2}{dt}[L_1 + 2M + L_2] + r_1(i_2 - i_s) = \mathbf{0} \qquad ...(2)$$

$$\frac{di_1}{dt}\,[L_1] + \frac{di_2}{dt}[-L_2 - M] + i_1 r_2 + v_s = \mathbf{0} \qquad ...(3)$$

EXAMPLE 9.44 *Find the instantaneous voltages v_1 and v_2 in the coupled inductances in the circuit to Fig. E9.51.*

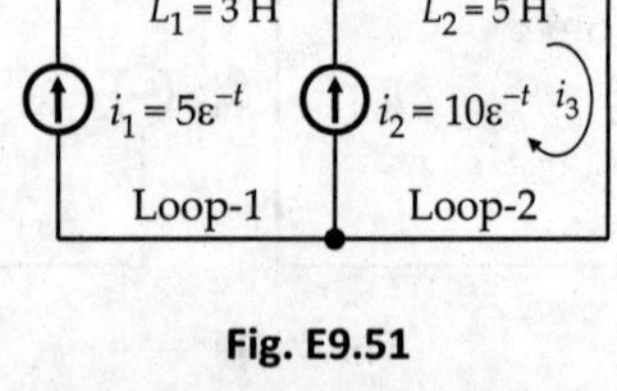

Fig. E9.51

SOLUTION. $i_1 = 5e^{-t}$ A,

$$i_3 = i_1 + i_2 = (5e^{-t} + 10\,e^{-t})\,\text{A} = 15\,e^{-t}\ \text{A},$$

The loop equations are written below (Fig. E9.51) :

Loop-1,

$$v_1 = L_1\frac{di_1}{dt} + M\frac{di_3}{dt}$$

$$= 3\frac{d}{dt}(5e^{-t}) + 2\frac{d\,(15\,e^{-t})}{dt}$$

$$= -15\,e^{-t} + (-30\,e^{-t}) = -45\,e^{-t}.$$

[Note that the actual polarity of v_1 is opposite to that of assumed across L_1].

$\therefore$ $\quad v_1 = \mathbf{-45\,e^{-t}\ V}.$

Loop-2,

$$v_2 = L_2\frac{di_3}{dt} + M\frac{di}{dt}$$

$$= 5\frac{d}{dt}(15e^{-t}) + 2\frac{d}{dt}(5\,e^{-t})$$

$$= -75\,e^{-t} - 10\,e^{-t} = -85\,e^{-t}\ \text{V}.$$

[Here also the polarity of actual v_2 would be opposite to that of assumed across L_2].

i.e., $\quad v_2 = \mathbf{-85\,e^{-t}\ V.}$

EXAMPLE 9.45 *Find v_1 and v_2 in the circuit of Fig. E9.52.*

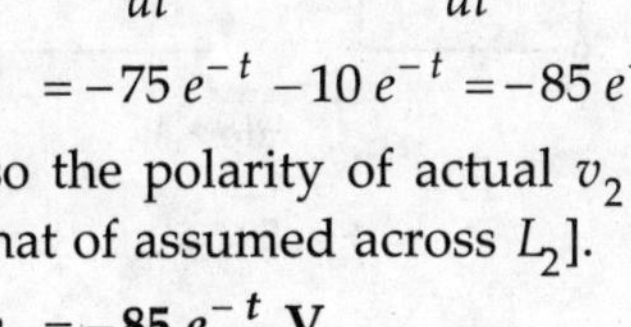

Fig. E9.52

SOLUTION. In Fig. E9.52,

$$i_1 = 10\,e^{-t}\ \text{A}$$

Also, $\quad i_2 = 10\,e^{-t}$ A.

$\therefore$ $\quad i_3 = i_1 + i_2 = 20\,e^{-t}$ A.

M is +ve in both the loop equations as i_1 enters L_1 through dot end while i_3 also enters L_2 through dot end.

In loop-1,

$$v_1 = L_1\frac{di_1}{dt} + M\frac{di_3}{dt}$$

$$= 2\frac{d\,(10\,e^{-t})}{dt} + 2\frac{d}{dt}(20\,e^{-t})$$

$$= -20\,e^{-t} - 40\,e^{-t} = -60\,e^{-t}\ \text{V}$$

In loop-2,

$$v_2 = L_2\frac{di_3}{dt} + M\frac{di_1}{dt}$$

$$= 4\frac{d}{dt}(20e^{-t}) + 2\frac{d}{dt}(10\,e^{-t})$$

$$= -80\,e^{-t} - 20\,e^{-t} = -100\,e^{-t}\ \text{V}$$

$$v_1 = -60\,e^{-t}\text{V}$$

$\therefore$ $\quad v_2 = \mathbf{-100\,e^{-t}V}$

It may be noted that for Fig. E9.53, the loop equation would be as follows :

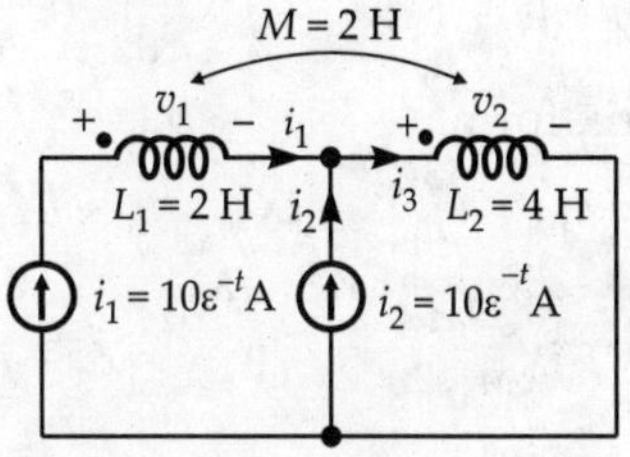

Fig. E9.53

$$v_1 = L_1\frac{di}{dt} - M\frac{di_3}{dt}$$

$$v_2 = L_2\frac{di_3}{dt} - M\frac{di_1}{dt}$$

as M is –ve here, current i_1 being entering L_1 through dot end while current i_3 enters L_2 through undotted end.

EXAMPLE 9.46 *Develop the mesh equation of the Auto-transformer circuit in Fig. E9.54.*

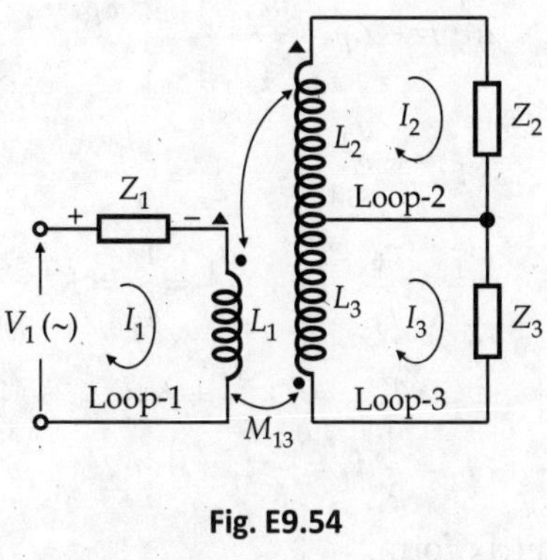

Fig. E9.54

SOLUTION. The dot convention here is applied between L_1 and L_2 and it is observed that M_{12} – ve. Applying dot convention between L_1 and L_3 we find that M_{13} +ve.

CHAPTER 9

The loop equations are as follows :

(i) For loop-1,

$$V_1 = I_1 Z_1 + j I_1 X_{L_1} + j X_{M_{13}} I_3 - j X_{M_{12}} I_2$$

or, $$V_1 = I_1 (Z_1 + j X_{L_1}) - jX_{M_{12}} I_2 + j X_{M_{13}} I_3$$

(ii) For loop-2,

$$0 = I_2 Z_2 + j I_2 X_{L_2} - j X_{M_{12}} I_1$$

or, $$0 = - j X_{M_{12}} I_1 + I_2 (Z_2 + j X_{L_2})$$

(iii) For loop-3,

$$0 = I_3 Z_3 + j I_3 X_{L_3} + j X_{M_{13}} I_1$$

or, $$j X_{M_{13}} I_1 + I_3 (Z_3 + j X_{L_3}) = 0$$

In matrix form,

$$\begin{bmatrix} V_1 \\ 0 \\ 0 \end{bmatrix} = \begin{bmatrix} (Z_1 + jX_{L_1}) & -jX_{M_{12}} & +jX_{M_{13}} \\ -jX_{M_{12}} & Z_2 + jX_{L_2} & 0 \\ jX_{M_{13}} & 0 & Z_3 + jX_{L_3} \end{bmatrix} \begin{bmatrix} I_1 \\ I_2 \\ I_3 \end{bmatrix}.$$

EXAMPLE 9.47 *Show that NIC (negative impedance converter) is a non-reciprocal device.*

SOLUTION. An ideal NIC has the property that the impedance seen at the input port (NIC is a two port device) is equal to the negative of the load impedance. Fig. E9.55 represents NIC with load impedance Z_L.

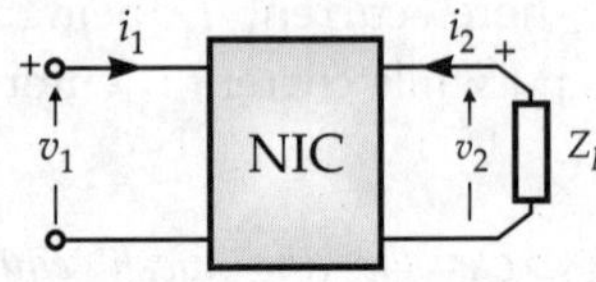

Fig. E9.55

Here $$Z_{in} = - Z_L = \frac{v_1}{i_1}$$

But $$Z_L = -\frac{v_2}{i_2}$$

$$\therefore \quad \frac{v_1}{i_1} = \frac{v_2}{i_2} \;\; i.e., \;\; \frac{v_1}{v_2} = \frac{i_1}{i_2} = K$$

or, $$v_1 = Kv_2 = 0 \times i_1 + K \times v_2$$

and $$i_2 = \frac{1}{K} i_1 = \frac{1}{K} i_1 + 0 . v_2$$

In matrix form,

$$\begin{bmatrix} v_1 \\ i_2 \end{bmatrix} = \begin{bmatrix} 0 & K \\ \frac{1}{K} & 0 \end{bmatrix} \begin{bmatrix} i_1 \\ v_2 \end{bmatrix}$$

Comparing with the standard form of h-parameter network form,

$$h_{11} = 0 ; \; h_{12} = K$$

$$h_{21} = \frac{1}{K} ; \; h_{22} = 0$$

As $(-h_{12}) \neq h_{21}$, hence **NIC is a non-reciprocal device.**

[As for NIC $v_1 = Kv_2$ and $i_2 = Ki_2$ hence it is evident that NIC inverts the direction of current and keep the polarity of the voltage unchanged.]

EXAMPLE 9.48 *Show that a gyrator is a non-reciprocal device.*

SOLUTION. A gyrator is a two port network when it gyrates the current of one port into the voltage of the other port and vice versa and is having the gyration constant or gyration ratio α. (Fig. E9.56).

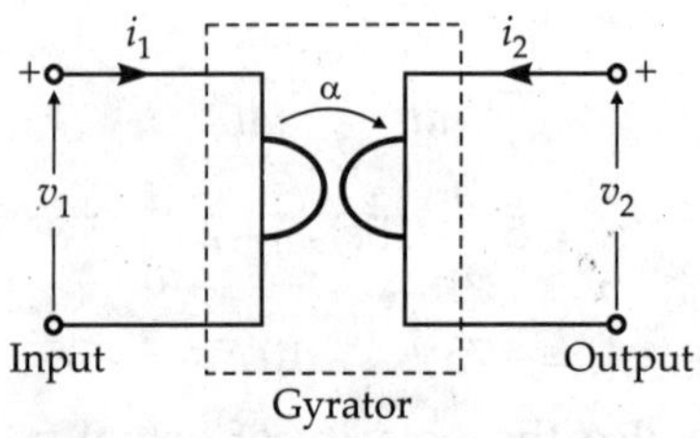

Fig. E9.56

$$\therefore \quad v_1 = - \alpha \, i_2 \quad \text{[–ve sign appears as } i_2 \text{ flows inwards at output]}$$

$$v_2 = \alpha \, i_1 \quad \text{[+ve sign appears with } \alpha \text{ as } i_1 \text{ flows inwards at input]}$$

i.e., $$v_1 = 0 . i_1 + (-\alpha) i_2$$

$$v_2 = \alpha \, i_1 + 0 . i_2$$

In matrix form $$\begin{bmatrix} v_1 \\ v_2 \end{bmatrix} = \begin{bmatrix} 0 & -\alpha \\ \alpha & 0 \end{bmatrix} \begin{bmatrix} i_1 \\ i_2 \end{bmatrix}$$

Also we can reorient the equations as

$$v_1 = 0 . I_1 - (\alpha) i_2 , \; i_1 = \frac{1}{\alpha} v_2 - 0 . i_2$$

In matrix form $$\begin{bmatrix} v_1 \\ i_1 \end{bmatrix} = \begin{bmatrix} 0 & \alpha \\ \frac{1}{\alpha} & 0 \end{bmatrix} \begin{bmatrix} v_2 \\ -i_2 \end{bmatrix}$$

Comparing with the standard form of transmission parameters,

$$A = 0, \; B = \alpha, \; C = \frac{1}{\alpha}, \; D = 0.$$

$$\therefore \quad AD - BC = 0 - 1 = -1.$$

As the transmission parameter network can only be reciprocal if $AD - BC = 1$, hence it is concluded that a **gyrator is a non-reciprocal device.**

EXERCISES

1. Two coupled coils have self-inductances $L_1 = 50$ mH and $L_2 = 70$ mH. The coefficient of coupling (K) being 0.65 in the air, find voltage in the second coil and the flux of the first coil provided the second coil has 500 turns and the circuit current is given by $i_1 = 5 \sin 314t$ Amps.
   [Hint. Ref. Ex. 9.3]
2. In the coupled circuit of Fig. P9.1, find the input impedance and net inductance.
   [Hint. Ref. Ex. 9.6]

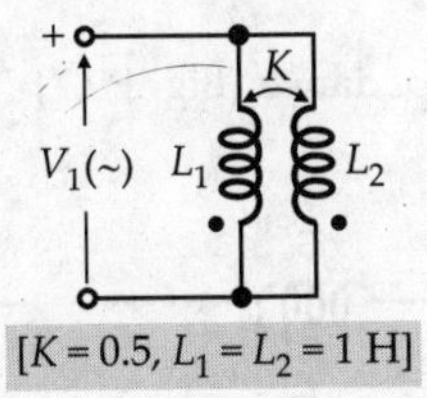

Fig. P9.1

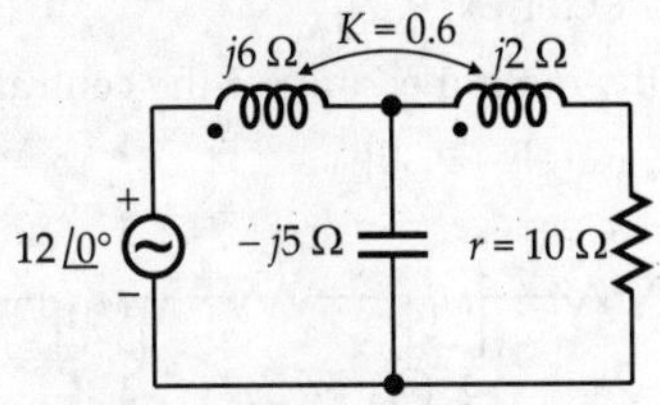

Fig. P9.2

3. Find the voltage drop across the resistance "r" in the network of Fig. P9.2.
   [Hint. Ref. Ex.9.8]
4. Find the conductively coupled equivalent circuit for the network shown in Fig. P9.3.
   [Hint. Do in the same way as shown in Ex.9.12]

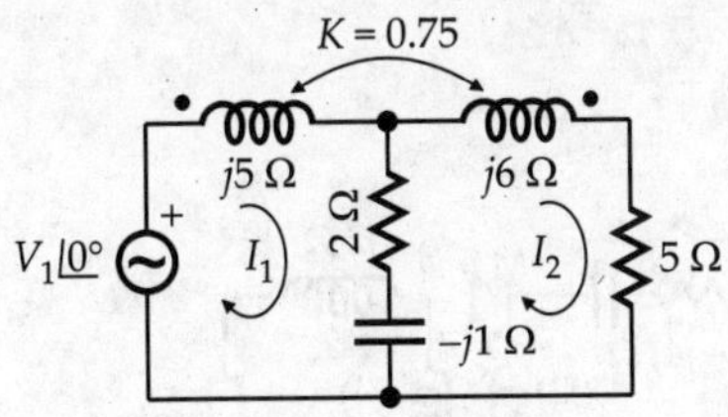

Fig. P9.3

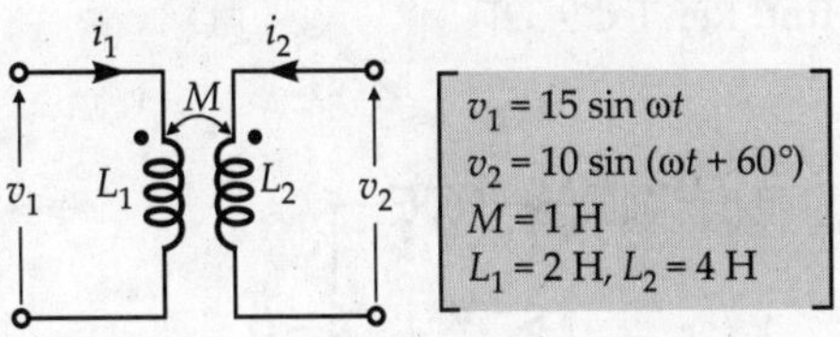

Fig. P9.4

5. In the circuit of Fig. P9.4, write down the loop equations in time domain as well as in frequency domain.
   [Hint. Ref. Ex. 9.14]
6. Write down the loop equations in each of the coupled coils in time as well as in frequency domain (Fig. P9.5).
   [Hint. Ref. Ex 9.17]

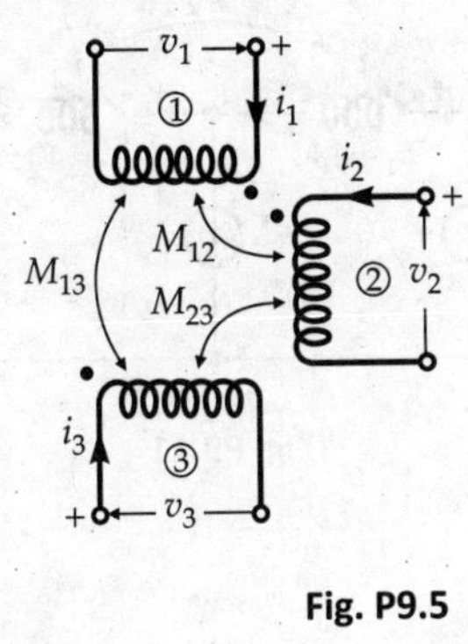

Fig. P9.5

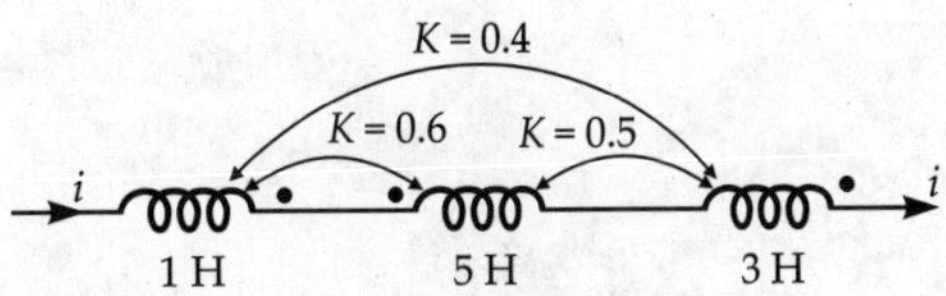

Fig. P9.6

7. Find the equivalent circuit and the net inductance of the series connected coupled coils in Fig. P9.6.
   [Hint. Ref. Ex 9.19]

8. What are the values of the self and mutual inductances for the two coupled coils 1 and 2 if $K = 1$ and $N_1 = 500$ turns, $N_2 = 750$ turns, $I_1 = 5$ A, $\phi_1 = 50$ m wb, $\phi_2 = 60$ m wb.
[**Hint.** Do in the same way as done in Ex. 9.21]

9. Two coupled coils have $K = 0.6$, $N_1 = 250$ turns, $N_2 = 500$ turns and the mutual flux being 0.7 wb, find the primary coil flux. If the primary current be 10 A, find the primary coil inductance. Also obtain the secondary inductance.
[**Hint.** Do in the same way as done in Ex. 9.28]

10. Two coils, of self-inductances $L_1 = 2$ H; $L_2 = 4$ H are coupled in such a way that $M = 1.5$ H. Assuming the mutual inductance to be +ve as per the dot convention, find the amount of energy stored after 0.2 sec for the circuit connected to a d.c. source of 12 V.
[**Hint.** Refer Ex. 9.29]

11. Find the net impedance of the central mesh and then find the net input impedance [Fig. P9.7]
[**Hint.** Ref. Ex. 9.30]

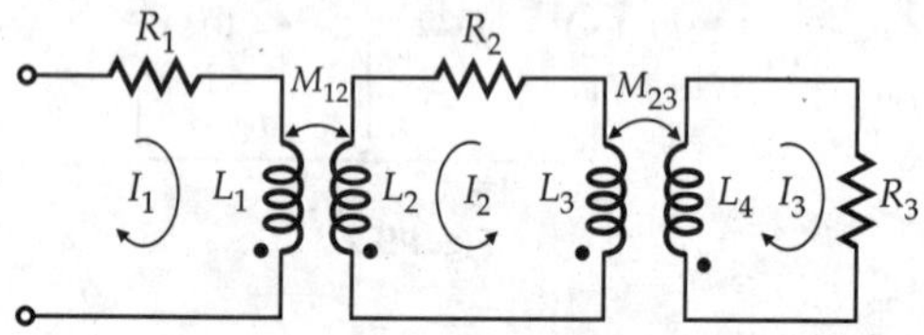

Fig. P9.7

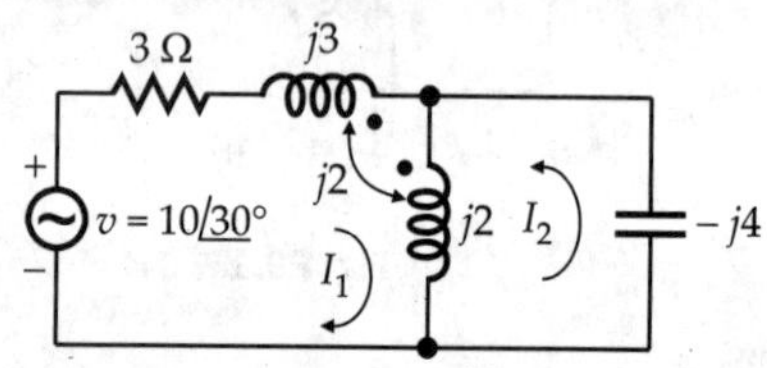

Fig. P9.8

12. Find the drop across the capacitor and the resistor (Fig. P9.8).
[**Hint.** Ref. Ex. 9.36]

13. Find the conductively coupled equivalent circuit of (Fig. P9.9).
[**Hint.** Ref. Ex. 9.39]

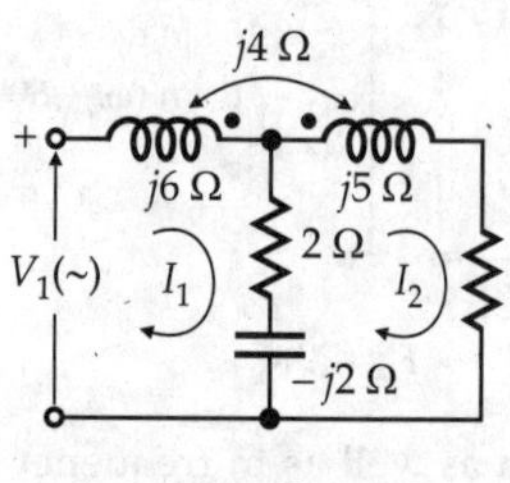

Fig. P9.9

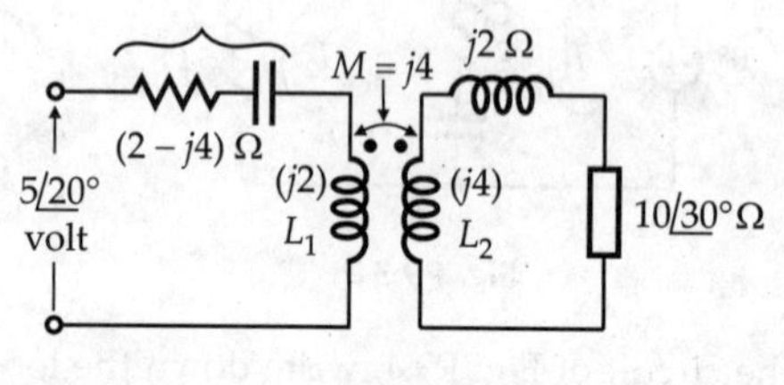

Fig. P9.10

14. Find the conductively coupled equivalent circuit of the network shown in Fig. P9.10.
[**Hint.** Ref. Ex. 9.40]

15. In Fig. P9.11, $i_j = 5e^{-2t}$ A ; $i_2 = 15\,e^{-2t}$ A. Find v_1 and v_2.
[**Hint.** Ref. Ex. 9.45]

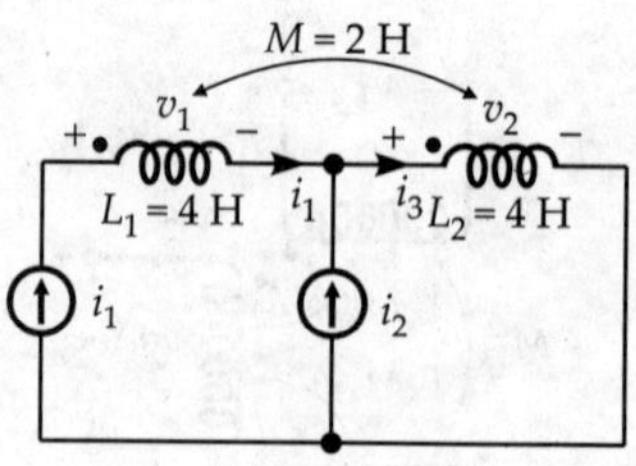

Fig. P9.11

CHAPTER

10

Application of Network Theorems in AC Circuits

10.1 INTRODUCTION

When two or more sources are present in a network and they are connected in such a way that they are not mutually in series or in parallel, special network solution methods like *mesh analysis* or *nodal analysis* must be employed. The application of these two techniques being described earlier for d.c. networks, they are well applied in a.c. network analysis too. The difference is that in a.c. application the *complex numbers* (*i.e.*, impedances) are used as the *coefficients of the equations* (instead of real numbers *i.e.*, resistances as done in d.c. applications) and the *variables* (like currents and voltages) have phasors instead of scalar voltage or currents.

In addition to application of mesh or nodal analysis in a.c. networks, application of network theorems like *Thevenin's theorem, Norton theorem, superposition theorem, Millman's theorem, Reciprocity theorem* and *Maximum Power Transfer theorems* are also shown in this chapter in steady state conditions. Since the discussion of theoretical aspects have been well covered in the chapter showing their d.c. applications, hence in theoretical discussions regarding these theorems here, only the variations required in a.c. application are considered.

10.2 MESH ANALYSIS

Mesh current analysis for a.c. networks can be done exactly in the same manner like d.c. network, the only difference is that the coefficients in the mesh current equations of the a.c. network have complex numbers (*i.e.*, impedances) instead of real numbers (resistances) and having phasors instead of real currents or voltages as the unknowns.

The mesh current analysis technique is applied for all networks with independent sources or networks with dependent sources where the controlling variables are not a part of the network under investigation. If the controlling variable is part of the network being examined, additional care must be taken when applying the above technique.

EXAMPLE 10.1 *Find the transfer function* (V_2 / V_1) *for the network shown in Fig. E10.1 using mesh analysis.*

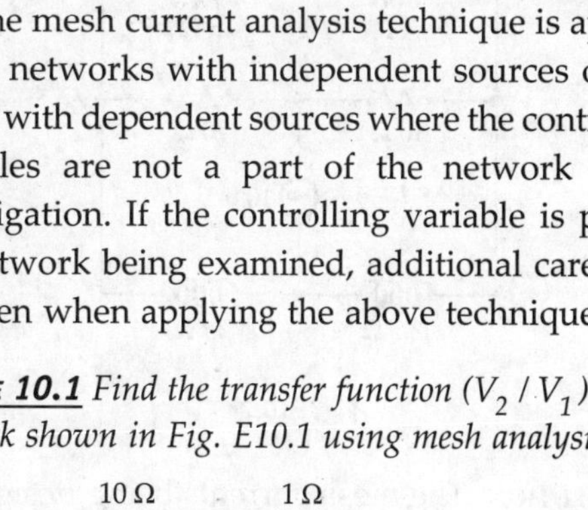

Fig. E10.1

SOLUTION. The mesh currents being designated by dotted arrows, *mesh analysis* yields :

$$(10 + j\,2)\,I_1 - j2\,(I_2) = V_1 \qquad ...(1)$$

and
$$(-j\,2)\,I_1 + (1 + j\,7)\,I_2 = 0 \qquad ...(2)$$

In matrix form, we can rearrange as

$$\begin{bmatrix} (10+j\,2) & -(j\,2) \\ (-j\,2) & (1+j\,7) \end{bmatrix}\begin{bmatrix} I_1 \\ I_2 \end{bmatrix} = \begin{bmatrix} V_1 \\ 0 \end{bmatrix}$$

However, at the output,

$$V_2 = (j\,5)\,I_2 \qquad ...(3)$$

Solving for I_2,

$$I_2 = \frac{\begin{vmatrix} 10+j\,2 & V_1 \\ -j\,2 & 0 \end{vmatrix}}{\begin{bmatrix} 10+j\,2 & -j\,2 \\ -j\,2 & 1+j\,7 \end{bmatrix}}$$

$$= \frac{(j\,2)\,V_1}{10 + j\,70 + j\,2 - 14 + 4} = \frac{(j\,2)\,V_1}{+j\,72}$$

$$\therefore \quad V_2 = (j.5)\frac{(j\,2)\,V_1}{j\,72} = -\frac{10\,V_1}{j\,72}$$

$$= -0.138\,\angle 90°\,V_1$$

$\therefore$ **$(V_2 / V_1) = 0.138\angle 90°$** (Taking magnitude only) (*i.e.*, the required transfer function.)

EXAMPLE 10.2 *Find the current through Z_L using mesh analysis for the network shown in Fig. E10.2.*

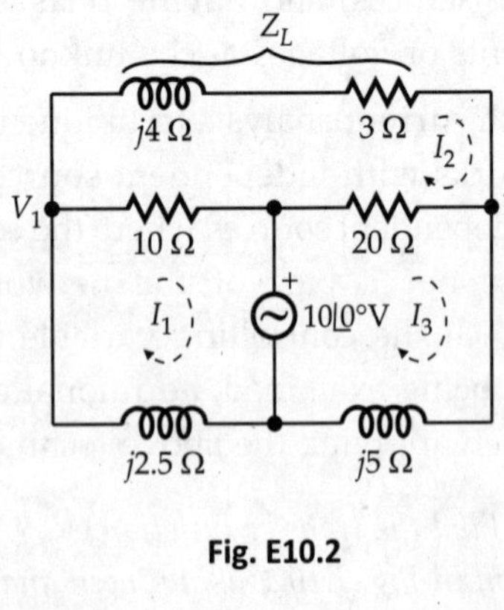

Fig. E10.2

SOLUTION. The mesh currents being designated by dotted arrowhead lines, *mesh analysis* gives

$$(10 + j\,2.5)\,I_1 - 10\,I_2 = -10\,\angle 0° \qquad ...(1)$$

$$(20 + j\,5)\,I_3 - 20\,I_2 = 10\,\angle 0° \qquad ...(2)$$

$$-10\,I_1 - 20\,I_3 + I_2\,(33 + j\,4) = 0 \qquad ...(3)$$

Rearranging in matrix form,

$$\begin{bmatrix} (10+j2.5) & -10 & 0 \\ 0 & -20 & (20+j\,5) \\ -10 & (33+j4) & -20 \end{bmatrix}\begin{bmatrix} I_1 \\ I_2 \\ I_3 \end{bmatrix} = \begin{bmatrix} -10\angle 0° \\ 10\angle 0° \\ 0 \end{bmatrix}$$

$$\therefore I_2 = \frac{\begin{vmatrix} 10+j\,2.5 & -10\,\angle 0° & 0 \\ 0 & 10\angle 0° & 20+j\,5 \\ -10 & 0 & -20 \end{vmatrix}}{\begin{vmatrix} (10+j\,2.5) & -10 & 0 \\ 0 & -20 & (20+j\,5) \\ -10 & (33+j\,4) & -20 \end{vmatrix}}$$

$$= \frac{(10+j2.5)\,10\angle 0° \times (-20) - (-10\angle 0°)\,\{10\,(20+j\,5)\}}{\Delta Z},$$

where ΔZ = determinant of the matrix in the denominator;

$$= \frac{-2000 - j\,500 + 2000 + j\,500}{\Delta Z} = \frac{0}{\Delta Z} = \mathbf{0}.$$

Thus, it is seen that no current would flow through Z_L, since I_2 is found to be zero and at the starting of the solution, I_2 had been the current flowing through Z_L.

EXAMPLE 10.3 *Using mesh current analysis, find the drop in the capacitor for the network shown in Fig. E10.3.*

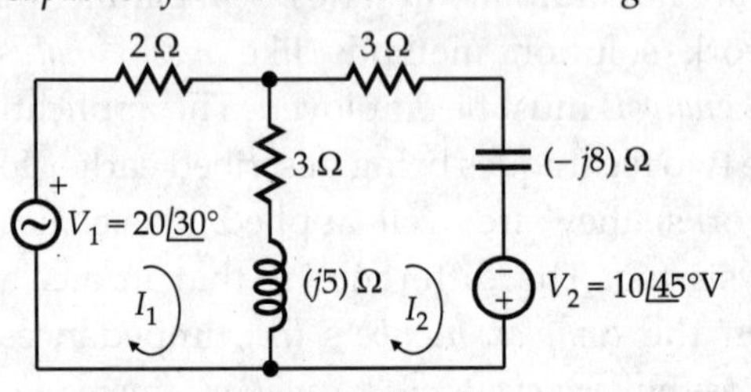

Fig. E10.3

SOLUTION. Let us first designate the mesh currents as I_1 and I_2. Application of *loop analysis* yields

$$(2 + 3 + j5)\,I_1 - (3 + j\,5)\,I_2 = V_1$$

or
$$(5 + j\,5)\,I_1 - (3 + j\,5)\,I_2 = V_1 = 20\,\angle 30°\text{ V} \qquad ...(1)$$

and
$$(3 - j\,8 + 3 + j\,5)\,I_2 - (3 + j\,5)\,I_1 = 10\,\angle 45°$$

or
$$(6 - j\,3)\,I_2 - (3 + j\,5)\,I_1 = 10\,\angle 45° \qquad ...(2)$$

In matrix form equations (1) and (2) are rearranged as

$$\begin{bmatrix} (5+j\,5) & -(3+j\,5) \\ -(3+j\,5) & (6-j\,3) \end{bmatrix}\begin{bmatrix} I_1 \\ I_2 \end{bmatrix} = \begin{bmatrix} 20\,\angle 30° \\ 10\,\angle 45° \end{bmatrix}$$

$$\therefore I_2 = \frac{\begin{vmatrix} 5+j5 & 20\angle 30° \\ -(3+j5) & 10\angle 45° \end{vmatrix}}{\begin{vmatrix} 5+j5 & -(3+j5) \\ -(3+j5) & (6-j3) \end{vmatrix}}$$

$$= \frac{\begin{vmatrix} 7.07\angle 45° & 20\angle 30° \\ -5.83\angle 59° & 10\angle 45° \end{vmatrix}}{\begin{vmatrix} 7.07\angle 45° & -5.83\angle 59° \\ -5.83\angle 59° & 6.71\angle -26.56° \end{vmatrix}}.$$

$$= \frac{70.7\angle 90° + 116.6\angle 89°}{47.44\angle 18.44 - 33.99\angle 118°}$$

$$= \frac{j70.7 + 2.03 + j116.58}{45 + j15 + 15.96 - j30} = \frac{2.03 + j187.28}{60.96 - j15}$$

$$= \frac{187.29\angle 89.38°}{62.78\angle -13.81} = 2.98\angle 103.29° \text{ A.}$$

$\therefore$ Drop in the capacitor

$= I_2(-j8) = \mathbf{23.84\angle 13.19° \text{ V.}}$

EXAMPLE 10.4 *Find the drop across 4 Ω and 10 Ω resistors using mesh current analysis. (Fig. E10.4).*

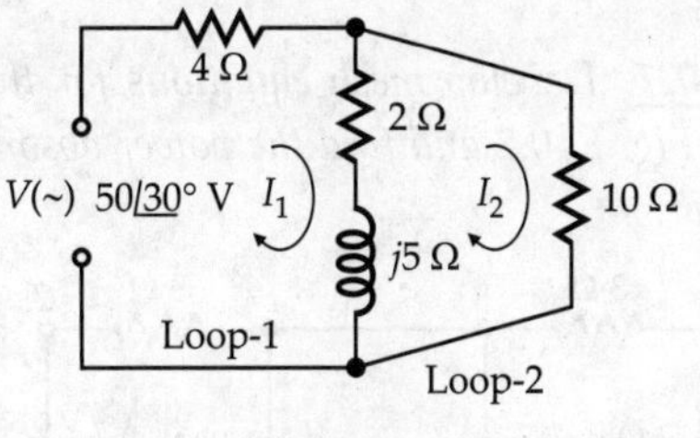

Fig. E10.4

SOLUTION. Let us first designate the mesh currents by arrowhead lines indicating the loops.

In *loop-1*, mesh current analysis provides

$$(4 + 2 + j5)I_1 - (2 + j5)I_2 = 50\angle 30°$$

or $\quad (6 + j5)I_1 - (2 + j5)I_2 = 50\angle 30° \quad$ ...(1)

In *loop-2*, mesh analysis provides

$$-(2 + j5)I_1 + (2 + 10 + j5)I_2 = 0$$

or $\quad -(2 + j5)I_1 + (12 + j5)I_2 = 0 \quad$ ...(2)

Rearranging (1) and (2) in matrix form,

$$\begin{bmatrix} (6+j5) & -(2+j5) \\ -(2+j5) & (12+j5) \end{bmatrix}\begin{bmatrix} I_1 \\ I_2 \end{bmatrix} = \begin{bmatrix} 50\angle 30° \\ 0 \end{bmatrix}$$

$$\therefore I_1 = \frac{\begin{vmatrix} 50\angle 30° & -(2+j5) \\ 0 & (12+j5) \end{vmatrix}}{\begin{vmatrix} (6+j5) & -(2+j5) \\ -(2+j5) & (12+j5) \end{vmatrix}}$$

$$= \frac{50\angle 30(12 + j5)}{(6 + j5)(12 + j5) - (2 + j5)(2 + j5)}$$

$$= \frac{650\angle 52.62°}{72 + j30 + j60 - 25 - 4 - j10 - j10 + 25}$$

$$= \frac{650\angle 52.62°}{68 + j70}$$

$$= \frac{650\angle 52.62°}{97.60\angle 45.83°} = 6.66\angle 6.79° \text{ A.}$$

$\therefore$ Drop across 4 Ω resistor is

$$4 \times I_1 = 4 \times 6.66\angle 6.79° \text{ i.e., } 26.64\angle 6.79° \text{ V.}$$

Similarly,

$$I_2 = \frac{\begin{vmatrix} 6+j5 & 50\angle 30° \\ -(2+j5) & 0 \end{vmatrix}}{\begin{vmatrix} (6+j5) & -(2+j5) \\ -(2+j5) & (12+j5) \end{vmatrix}}$$

$$= \frac{50\angle 30°(2 + j5)}{68 + j70}$$

$$= \frac{5.385\angle 68.19° \times 50\angle 30°}{97.60\angle 45.83°} = 2.76\angle 52.36° \text{ A.}$$

Thus, drop across 10 Ω resistor is

$$10\,I_2 = 10 \times 2.76\angle 52.36°$$

$$= \mathbf{27.6\angle 52.36° \text{ V.}}$$

EXAMPLE 10.5 *What is the value of V_2 such that the current in $(2 + j3)\Omega$ impedance is zero (Fig. E10.5) ?*

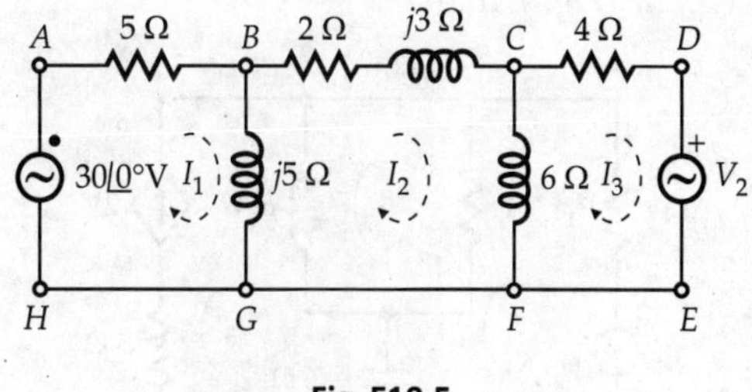

Fig. E10.5

SOLUTION. Let us first designate the loops alongwith the loop currents in Fig. E10.5.

C
H
A
P
T
E
R
10

In loop ABGH, mesh analysis gives

$$5I_1 + j\,5I_1 - j\,5I_2 = 30\angle 0°$$

or $$I_1\,(5 + j\,5) - j\,5I_2 = 30\,\angle 0° \qquad ...(1)$$

In loop BCFG, mesh analysis gives

$$(2 + j3 + 6 + j\,5)\,I_2 - j\,5I_1 - 6I_3 = 0$$

or $$(8 + j\,8)\,I_2 - j\,5\,I_1 - 6\,I_3 = 0 \qquad ...(2)$$

In loop CDEF, mesh analysis gives

$$(4 + 6)\,I_3 - 6I_2 = -V_2$$

or $$10\,I_3 - 6\,I_2 = -V_2 \qquad ...(3)$$

Rearranging the three equations in matrix form,

$$\begin{bmatrix} (5 + j\,5) & -j\,5 & 0 \\ -j\,5 & 8 + j\,8 & -6 \\ 0 & -6 & 10 \end{bmatrix}\begin{bmatrix} I_1 \\ I_2 \\ I_3 \end{bmatrix} = \begin{bmatrix} 30\,\angle 0° \\ 0 \\ -V_2 \end{bmatrix} \qquad ...(4)$$

$$\therefore \quad I_2 = \frac{\begin{vmatrix} (5 + j\,5) & 30\,\angle 0° & 0 \\ (-j\,5) & 0 & -6 \\ 0 & -V_2 & 10 \end{vmatrix}}{\Delta Z}$$

[where ΔZ is the determinant of the matrix equation (4)]

$$= \frac{(5 + j5)(-6V_2) - 30\,\angle 0°(-j5 \times 10)}{\Delta Z}$$

But I_2 being the current through $(2 + j\,3)\,\Omega$, as per the question, $I_2 = 0$.

i.e., $$(5 + j5)(-6\,V_2) - 30\,\angle 0° \times (-j\,50) = 0$$

$$-V_2\,(5 + j5) = 5\,\angle 0° \times (-j\,50) = -j\,250.$$

$$\therefore \quad V_2 = \frac{j250}{5 + j5} = 35.36\angle 45°\text{ V.}$$

Thus, $V_2 = \mathbf{35.36\,\angle\,45°\ V.}$

EXAMPLE 10.6 *Find the mesh transformation matrix of the given circuit (Fig. E10.6).*

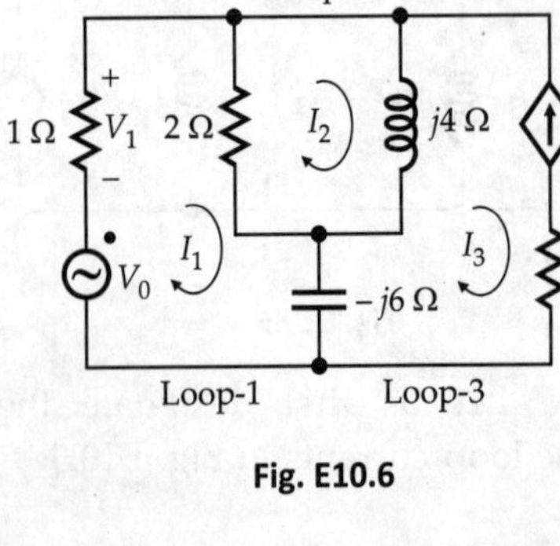

Fig. E10.6

SOLUTION. Let us first designate the loops as shown in the given figure.

Application of KVL around *loop-1* yields

$$-V_0 + 1.\,I_1 + 2\,(I_1 - I_2) + (-j\,6)(I_1 - I_3) = 0$$

or $$I_1\,(3 - j\,6) - 2I_2 + j\,6\,.\,I_3 = V_0 \qquad ...(1)$$

Application of KVL at the *loop-2* yields

$$2\,(I_2 - I_1) + j\,4(I_2 - I_3) = 0$$

or $$-2I_1 + I_2\,(2 + j\,4) - (j\,4)\,I_3 = 0 \qquad ...(2)$$

Presence of current source in the *third loop* makes the use of KVL redundant and using KCL,

$$I_3 = -2\,V_1 = -2I_1$$

or $$I_3 + 2I_1 = 0 \qquad ...(3)$$

Thus, arranging (1), (2) and (3) in matrix form, we get

$$\begin{bmatrix} (3 - j6) & -2 & +j6 \\ -2 & (2 + j4) & (-j4) \\ 2 & 0 & 1 \end{bmatrix}\begin{bmatrix} I_1 \\ I_2 \\ I_3 \end{bmatrix} = \begin{bmatrix} V_0 \\ 0 \\ 0 \end{bmatrix}$$

Left hand matrix in the above eqn. gives *mesh transformation matrix*.

EXAMPLE 10.7 *Develop mesh equations for the network shown in Fig. E10.7 and find the power absorbed by the 3 Ω resistor.*

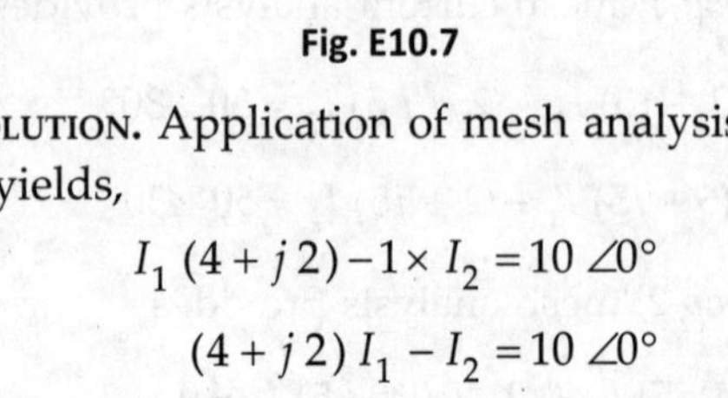

Fig. E10.7

SOLUTION. Application of mesh analysis in loop *ABEF* yields,

$$I_1\,(4 + j\,2) - 1 \times I_2 = 10\,\angle 0°$$

or $$(4 + j\,2)\,I_1 - I_2 = 10\,\angle 0° \qquad ...(1)$$

Similarly, in *loop BCDE*, mesh analysis yields

$$(5 + j\,1)\,I_3 + I_2 - I_1 = 0$$

or $$-I_1 + I_2 + (5 + j\,1)\,I_3 = 0 \qquad ...(2)$$

But it is evident from the given figure that

$$I_3 - I_2 = 1\angle 0° \qquad ...(3)$$

Next, subtracting equation (3) from (1),

$$(4+j2)\,I_1 - I_3 = 10\,\angle 0^\circ - 1\,\angle 0^\circ = 9$$

or $$I_3 = [(4+j2)\,I_1 - 9] \qquad ...(4)$$

Also, adding equation (1) to (2), we get

$$(4+j2)\,I_1 - I_1 + (5+j1)\,I_3 = 10\,\angle 0^\circ$$

or $$(3+j2)\,I_1 + (5+j1)[(4+j2)\,I_1 - 9] = 10$$

or $$3I_1 + j2I_1 + (5+j1)(4+j2)\,I_1 - 9(5+j1) = 10$$

or $$3\,I_1 + j\,2I_1 + 20\,I_1 + j\,10\,I_1 + j\,4\,I_1 - 2\,I_1 - 45 - j\,9 = 10$$

or $$21\,I_1 + j\,16\,I_1 = 10 + 45 + j\,9 = 55 + j\,9$$

or $$I_1 = \frac{55+j\,9}{21+j\,16} = \frac{55.73\,\angle 9.29^\circ}{26.4\,\angle 37.3^\circ}$$

$$= 2.11\,\angle -28.01^\circ \text{ A.}$$

∴ Power absorbed by the 3 Ω resistor is

$$(2.11)^2 \times 3 = \mathbf{13.36\ W.}$$

EXAMPLE 10.8 *Find the drop across 2Ω resistor in the network of Fig. E10.8 using mesh analysis.*

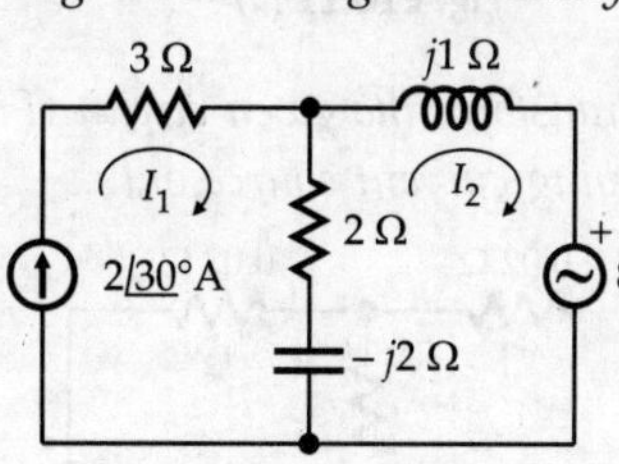

Fig. E10.8

SOLUTION. Due to presence of the current source, the loop current of the left loop is $I_1 = 2\angle 30^\circ$ A while that of the right loop is assumed to be I_2 A.

Obviously, the current through 2 Ω resistor is $(I_1 - I_2)$, the vector difference.

Application of KVL at the *right hand loop* yields

$$(j1)\,I_2 + (2-j\,2)\,I_2 - 2\,\angle 30\,(2-j2) = -8\,\angle 45^\circ$$

or $$I_2 = \frac{2\,\angle 30\,(2-j\,2) - 8\,\angle 45^\circ}{(2-j\,1)}$$

$$= 3.18\,\angle -65^\circ \text{ A.}$$

However, since the drop across the 2 Ω resistor is $2\,(I_1 - I_2)$ hence we find $V_{\text{drop}(2\Omega)} = 2\,(I_1 - I_2)$

$$= 2\,(2\,\angle 30^\circ - 3.18\,\angle -65^\circ)$$

$$= 2\,(0.38 + j\,3.88) = (0.76 + j\,7.76)\text{ V}$$

$$= \mathbf{7.80\,\angle 84.41^\circ\ V.}$$

10.3 SOURCE CONVERSIONS

When applying the network theorems in the a.c. networks, it may be necessary to convert a current source to voltage source and vice versa. This can be accomplished in the same manner as we do for d.c. networks, except now we shall be using phasors and impedances instead of real numbers and resistors.

10.4 NODAL ANALYSIS

Node voltage analysis of a.c. networks is identical to that of d.c. networks. In the frequency domain network having *n*-principal nodes, one of them is designated as the reference node and we require $(n-1)$ node voltage equations to solve for the desired result. Regarding *sign convention* of nodal currents, we take the currents entering the nodes as –ve while the currents leaving the nodes are +ve.

10.5 INDEPENDENT AND DEPENDENT SOURCES

The term *independent* indicates that the magnitude of the source is independent of the network to which it is applied and that it exhibits its terminal characteristics even if completely isolated.

A *dependent* or *controlled* source is that whose magnitude is governed by a current or voltage of the system in which it is situated.

The diagrammatic representation of the dependent sources is similar to that we have shown in analysing the d.c. network.

EXAMPLE 10.9 *Convert the given current source (Fig. E10.9) to voltage source.*

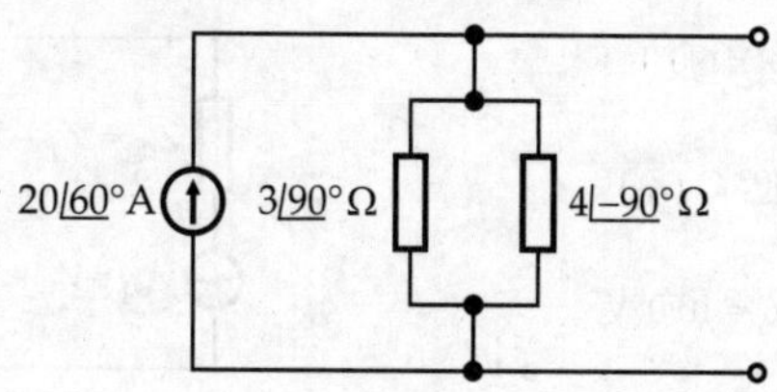

Fig. E10.9

SOLUTION. $Z_{\text{equivalent}}$ (Fig. E10.9)

$$= \frac{3\,\angle 90^\circ \times 4\,\angle -90^\circ}{3\,\angle 90^\circ + 4\,\angle -90^\circ}$$

$$= \frac{j\,3 \times (-j\,4)}{j\,3 - j\,4} = \frac{12}{-j} = 12\,\angle 90^\circ\,\Omega$$

$\therefore$ V (equivalent voltage source)

$$= I \times Z_{equivalent}$$

$$= 20 \angle 60° \times 12 \angle 90° = 240 \angle 150° \text{ V}$$

Thus, the equivalent voltage source of the given current source becomes **240 ∠150° V** [Fig. E10.9(*a*)].

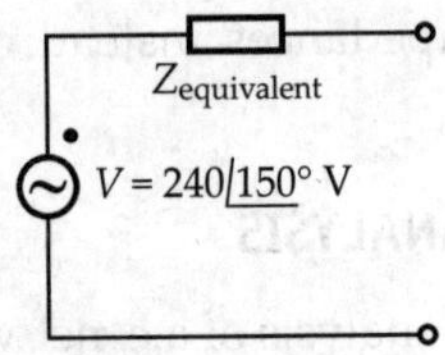

Fig. E10.9 (*a*)

Example 10.10 *Convert the current source circuit (Fig. E10.10) to a single voltage source circuit.*

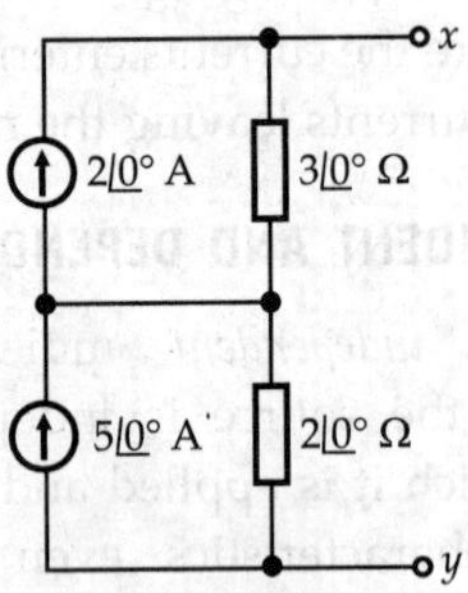

Fig. E10.10

Solution. The current sources are converted into equivalent voltage source as shown in Fig. E10.10(*a*) and then to single equivalent voltage source as shown in Fig. E10.10(*b*).

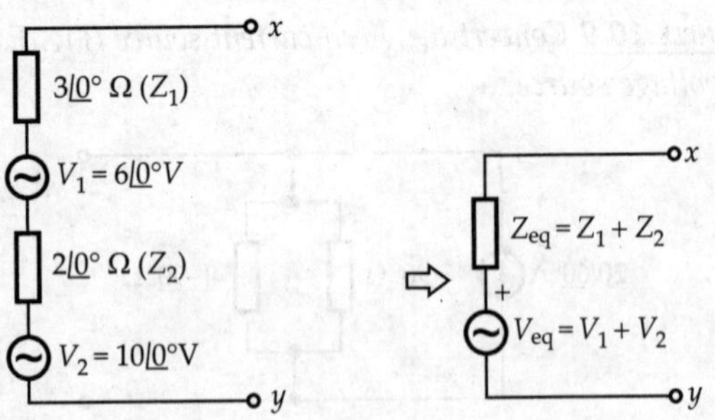

Fig. E10.10 (*a*) (*b*)

In Fig. E10.10(*b*),

$$V_{eq.} = V_1 + V_2 = 2 \angle 0° \times 3 \angle 0° + 5 \angle 0° \times 2 \angle 0°$$

$$= 6 \angle 0° + 10 \angle 0° = \mathbf{16 \angle 0° \text{ V}}$$

$$Z_{eq.} = 3 \angle 0° + 2 \angle 0° = \mathbf{5 \angle 0° \Omega.}$$

Example 10.11 *Convert the given voltage source (Fig. E10.11) to a current source.*

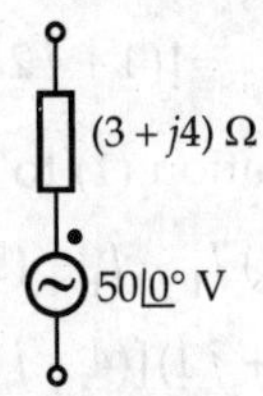

Fig. E10.11

Solution. Figure E10.11(*a*) represents the conversion of voltage source to equivalent current source when,

$$I_{eq} = \frac{V}{Z} = \frac{50 \angle 0°}{(3 + j\,4)} = \frac{50 \angle 0°}{5 \angle 53.13°} = \mathbf{10 \angle -53.13° \text{ A.}}$$

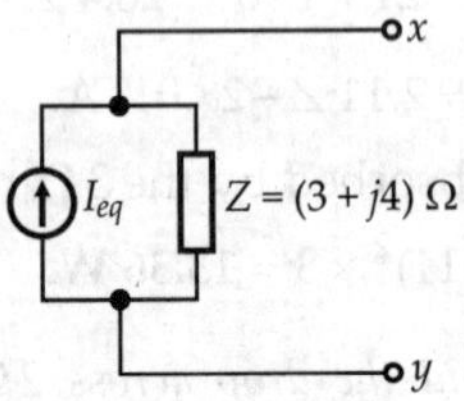

Fig. E10.11 (*a*)

Example 10.12 *Transform the given circuit (Fig. E10.12) to the circuit having current source only.*

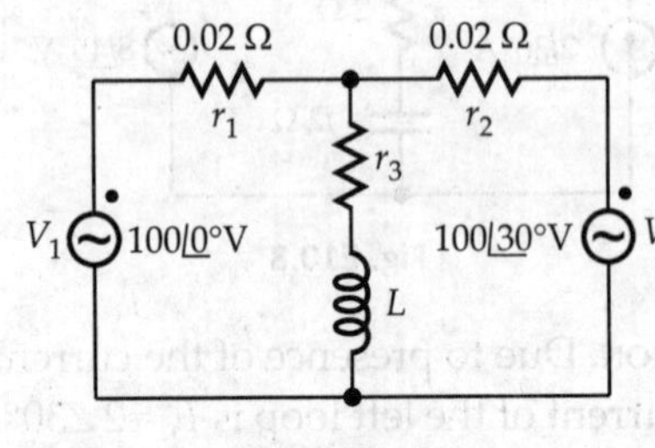

Fig. E10.12

Solution. Figure E10.12(*a*) represents the conversion of the given circuit from voltage source fed circuit to current source fed circuit.

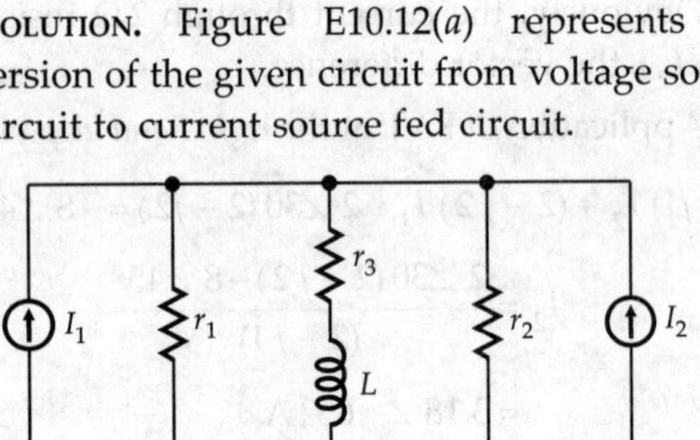

Fig. E10.12 (*a*)

Here, $\quad I_1 = V_1 / r_1 = \dfrac{100 \angle 0°}{0.02} = \mathbf{5000 \angle 0° \text{ A}}$

and $\quad I_2 = V_2 / r_2 = \dfrac{100 \angle 30°}{0.02} = \mathbf{5000 \angle 30° \text{ A.}}$

EXAMPLE 10.13 *Write the node transformation matrix of the network shown in Fig. E10.13.*

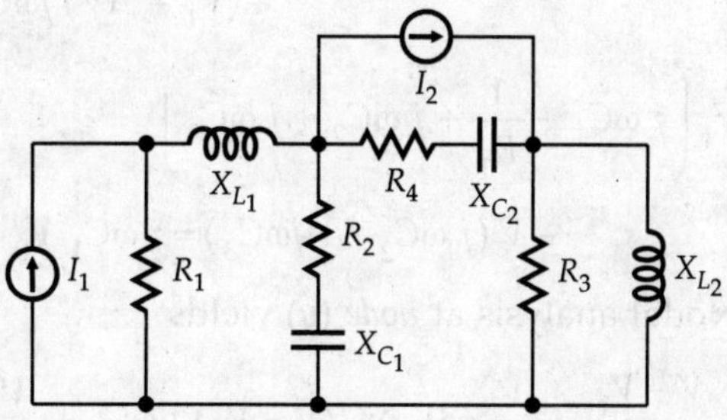

Fig. E10.13

SOLUTION. Let the given network be formatised as shown in Fig. E10.13(*a*) indicating the respective node voltages.

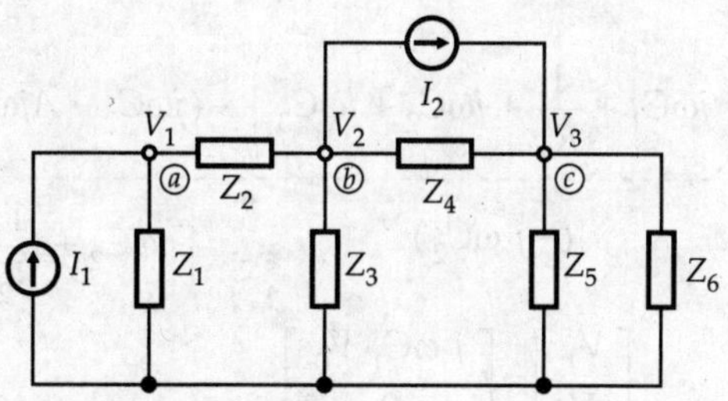

Fig. E10.13 (*a*)

The nodal equations are as follows :

At node (a),

$$\frac{V_1}{Z_1}+\frac{V_1-V_2}{Z_2}=I_1$$

or $$V_1\left(\frac{1}{Z_1}+\frac{1}{Z_2}\right)-\frac{V_2}{Z_2}=I_1$$

or $$V_1\,(Y_1+Y_2)-V_2\,Y_2=I_1 \qquad \text{...(1)}$$

where $Y_1=\dfrac{1}{Z_1}$; $Y_2=\dfrac{1}{Z_2}$

At node (b),

$$\frac{V_2-V_1}{Z_2}+\frac{V_2}{Z_3}+\frac{V_2-V_3}{Z_4}+I_2=0$$

or $$-V_1\cdot\frac{1}{Z_2}+V_2\left(\frac{1}{Z_2}+\frac{1}{Z_3}+\frac{1}{Z_4}\right)-V_3\cdot\frac{1}{Z_4}=-I_2$$

or $$-V_1\,Y_2+V_2\,(Y_2+Y_3+Y_4)-V_3\,Y_4=-I_2 \qquad \text{...(2)}$$

where $Y_3=\dfrac{1}{Z_3}$; $Y_4=\dfrac{1}{Z_4}$

At node (c),

$$\frac{V_3}{Z_5}+\frac{V_3}{Z_6}+\frac{V_3-V_2}{Z_4}=I_2$$

or $$-V_2\cdot\frac{1}{Z_4}+V_3\left(\frac{1}{Z_4}+\frac{1}{Z_5}+\frac{1}{Z_6}\right)=I_2$$

or $$-V_2\,Y_4+V_3\,(Y_3+Y_5+Y_6)=I_2 \qquad \text{...(3)}$$

where $Y_5=\dfrac{1}{Z_5}$; $Y_6=\dfrac{1}{Z_6}$.

In matrix form, the three equations can be shown as

$$\begin{bmatrix}(Y_1+Y_2) & (-Y_2) & 0\\ (-Y_2) & (Y_2+Y_3+Y_4) & (-Y_4)\\ 0 & (-Y_4) & (Y_3+Y_5+Y_6)\end{bmatrix}\begin{bmatrix}V_1\\ V_2\\ V_3\end{bmatrix}=\begin{bmatrix}I_1\\ -I_2\\ I_2\end{bmatrix}$$

The matrix in the left hand side is called *node transformation matrix.*

EXAMPLE 10.14 *Form node-transformation matrix for the given network using a.c nodal analysis (Fig. E10.14).*

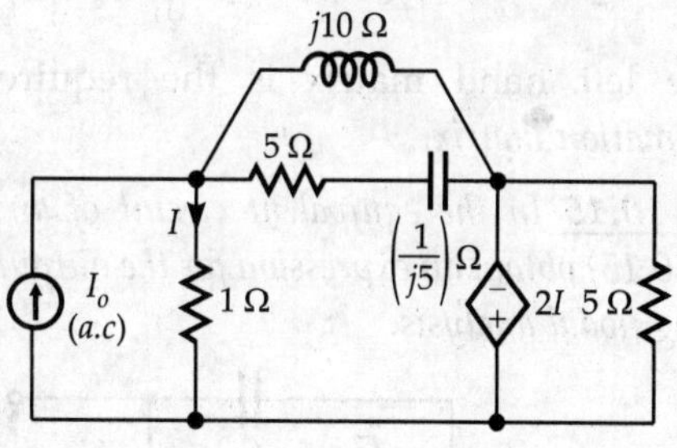

Fig. E10.14

SOLUTION. Let us first designate nodes as shown in Fig. E10.14(*a*) with assumed nodal voltages.

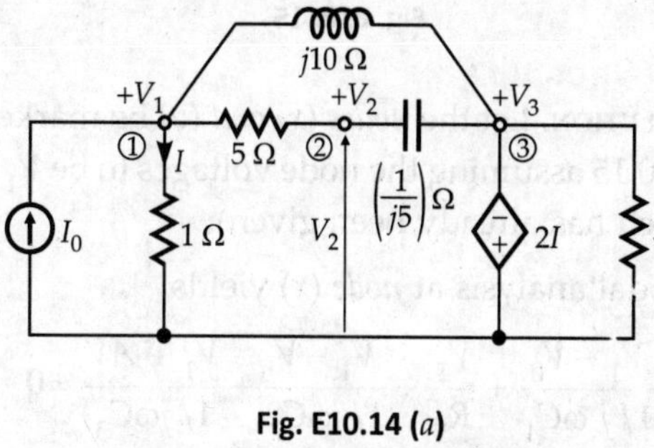

Fig. E10.14 (*a*)

At *node-1*, nodal equation can be written as

$$-I_0+\frac{V_1}{1}+\frac{V_1-V_2}{5}+\frac{V_1-V_3}{j10}=0$$

or $V_1(1+0.2-0.1j)+V_2(-0.2)+V_3(+0.1j)=I_0$

or $V_1(1.2-j0.1)-0.2V_2+0.1jV_3=I_0$ ...(1)

At *node-2*, nodal equation can be written as

$$\frac{V_2-V_1}{5}+\frac{V_2-V_3}{\frac{1}{j5}}=0$$

or $-0.2V_1+0.2V_2+j5V_2-j5V_3=0$

or $-0.2V_1+V_2(0.2+j5)-j5V_3=0$ ...(2)

At *node-3*, the nodal equation is

$$V_3=-2I=-2\left(\frac{V_1}{1}\right)=-2V_1$$

or $2V_1+0.V_2+V_3=0$ ...(3)

Thus, in matrix form, equations (1), (2) and (3) are

$$\begin{bmatrix}(1.2-j0.1) & -0.2 & j0.1\\ -0.2 & (0.2+j5) & -j5\\ 2 & 0 & 1\end{bmatrix}\begin{bmatrix}V_1\\V_2\\V_3\end{bmatrix}=\begin{bmatrix}I_0\\0\\0\end{bmatrix}$$

The left hand matrix is the required *node transformation matrix*.

EXAMPLE 10.15 *In the equivalent circuit of an op-amp (Fig. E10.15) obtain an expression for the output voltage V_L using nodal analysis.*

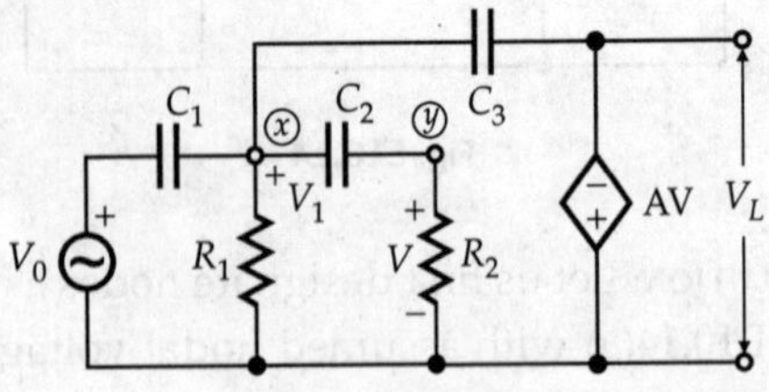

Fig. E10. 15

SOLUTION. Let the *nodes (x) and (y)* be marked in Fig. E10.15 assuming the node voltages to be V_1 and V (which has already been given).

Nodal analysis at *node (x)* yields

$$\frac{V_1-V_0}{1/j\omega C_1}+\frac{V_1}{R_1}+\frac{V_1-V}{1/j\omega C_2}+\frac{V_1+AV}{1/j\omega C_3}=0$$

or $(V_1-V_0)j\omega C_1+V_1\cdot\frac{1}{R_1}+(V_1-V)j\omega C_2+(V_1+AV)j\omega C_3=0$

or $$V_1\left(j\omega C_1+\frac{1}{R_1}+j\omega C_2+j\omega C_3\right)-V(j\omega C_2-Aj\omega C_3)=j\omega C_1V_0 \quad ...(1)$$

Nodal analysis at *node (y)* yields

$$\frac{V-V_1}{1/j\omega C_2}+\frac{V}{R_2}=0 \text{ or } (V-V_1)j\omega C_2+\frac{V}{R_2}=0$$

or $$-V_1(j\omega C_2)+V\left(j\omega C_2+\frac{1}{R_2}\right)=0 \quad ...(2)$$

In matrix form, (1) and (2) can be arranged as

$$\begin{bmatrix}\left(j\omega C_1+\frac{1}{R_1}+j\omega C_2+j\omega C_3\right) & -(j\omega C_2-Aj\omega C_3)\\ (-j\omega C_2) & \left(j\omega C_2+\frac{1}{R_2}\right)\end{bmatrix}\begin{bmatrix}V_1\\V\end{bmatrix}=\begin{bmatrix}j\omega C_1V_0\\0\end{bmatrix}$$

$$\therefore\quad V=\frac{\begin{vmatrix}\frac{1}{R_1}+j\omega(C_1+C_2+C_3) & j\omega C_1V_0\\ -j\omega C_2 & 0\end{vmatrix}}{\begin{vmatrix}\frac{1}{R_1}+j\omega(C_1+C_2+C_3) & -(j\omega C_2-j\omega C_3A)\\ -j\omega C_2 & j\omega C_2+\frac{1}{R_2}\end{vmatrix}}$$

$$=\frac{-\omega^2C_1C_2V_0}{\left[\frac{1}{R_1}+j\omega(C_1+C_2+C_3)\right]\left(j\omega C_2+\frac{1}{R_2}\right)-j\omega C_2(j\omega C_2-j\omega C_3A)}$$

$$=\frac{-\omega^2C_1C_2R_1R_2V_0}{1+j\omega[R_2C_2+R_1(C_1+C_2+C_3)]-\omega^2R_1R_2C_2(C_1+C_3+C_3A)}\text{ V.}$$

By observation, it is revealed that

$$V_L\text{ (output voltage)}=-AV$$

$$\therefore V_L=\frac{(-A)(-\omega^2C_1C_2R_1R_2V_0)}{\{1+j\omega[R_2C_2+R_1(C_1+C_2+C_3)]-\omega^2R_1R_2C_2(C_1+C_3+C_3A)\}}\text{ V.}$$

EXAMPLE 10.16 *Assuming the circuit variables to be a.c. phasor quantities, find V as well as V_0 using nodal analysis in the circuit of Fig. E10.16.*

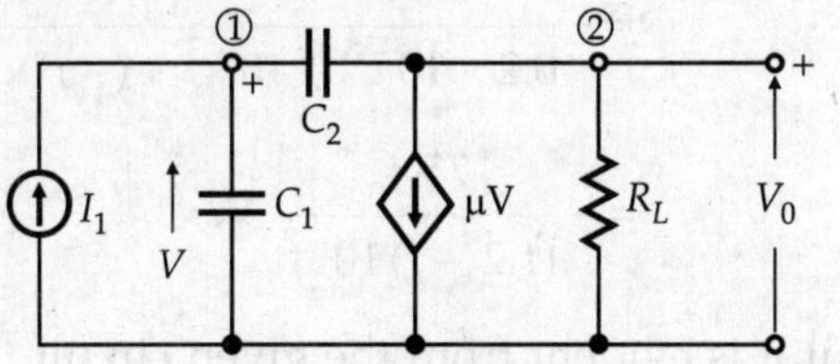

Fig. E10.16

SOLUTION. Application of nodal analysis at the input *node (1)*, nodal analysis yields

$$\frac{V}{1/j\omega C_1}+\frac{V-V_0}{1/j\omega C_2}-I_1=0$$

[Output node being (2) having nodal voltage V_0]

$$V_1(j\omega C_1)+(V-V_0)\,j\omega C_2=I_1$$

or $$(j\omega C_1+j\omega C_2)V-j\omega C_2\,V_0=I_1 \qquad ...(1)$$

Similarly, at *node (2)*, nodal analysis reveals

$$\frac{(V_0-V)}{1/j\omega C_2}+\mu V+\frac{V_0}{R_L}=0$$

$$(V_0-V)\,j\omega C_2+\mu V+\frac{V_0}{R_L}=0$$

or $$(\mu-j\omega C_2)V+\left(j\omega C_2+\frac{1}{R_L}\right)V_0=0 \qquad ...(2)$$

In matrix form, (1) and (2) can be arranged as follows :

$$\begin{bmatrix}(j\omega C_1+j\omega C_2) & (-j\omega C_2)\\ (\mu-j\omega C_2) & \left(j\omega C_2+\frac{1}{R_L}\right)\end{bmatrix}\begin{bmatrix}V\\ V_0\end{bmatrix}=\begin{bmatrix}I_1\\ 0\end{bmatrix}$$

Solving for V,

$$V=\frac{\begin{vmatrix}I_1 & -j\omega C_2\\ 0 & j\omega C_2+\frac{1}{R_L}\end{vmatrix}}{\begin{vmatrix}j\omega(C_1+C_2) & (-j\omega C_2)\\ (\mu-j\omega C_2) & \left(j\omega C_2+\frac{1}{R_L}\right)\end{vmatrix}}$$

$$=\frac{I_1\left(j\omega C_2+\frac{1}{R_L}\right)}{j\omega(C_1+C_2)\left(j\omega C_2+\frac{1}{R_L}\right)+j\omega C_2(\mu-j\omega C_2)}$$

and $$V_0=\frac{\begin{vmatrix}j\omega(C_1+C_2) & I_1\\ (\mu-j\omega C_2) & 0\end{vmatrix}}{\begin{vmatrix}j\omega(C_1+C_2) & (-j\omega C_2)\\ (\mu-j\omega C_2) & \left(j\omega C_2+\frac{1}{R_L}\right)\end{vmatrix}}$$

$$=\frac{-I_1(\mu-j\omega C_2)}{j\omega(C_1+C_2)\left(j\omega C_2+\frac{1}{R_L}\right)+j\omega C_2(\mu-j\omega C_2)}.$$

EXAMPLE 10.17 *If $Z_L=-j\,2\,\Omega$, find V_L in the circuit of Fig. E10.17 using nodal analysis.*

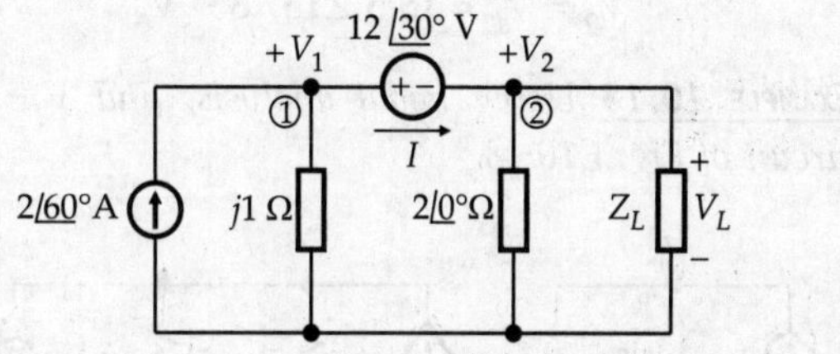

Fig. E10.17

SOLUTION. Let us mark nodes alongwith the node voltages in the given figure.

Applying nodal equations at respective nodes,

At node (1) :

$$\frac{V_1}{j1}-2\angle 60°=-I_1 \qquad ...(1)$$

At node (2) :

$$\frac{V_2}{2}+\frac{V_2}{Z_L}+I_2=0$$

or $$\frac{V_1-12\angle 30°}{2}+\frac{V_1-12\angle 30°}{-j2}=-I_2 \qquad ...(2)$$

[∵ using KVL, $-V_1+12\angle 30°+V_2=0$ or, $V_2=(V_1-12\angle 30°)$ V]

But actually $I_2=-I_1$,

∴ (2) becomes $$\frac{V_1-12\angle 30°}{2}+\frac{V_1-12\angle 30°}{-j2}=I_1 \qquad ...(3)$$

Comparing (1) and (3),

$$\frac{V_1}{j1}-2\angle 60°=-\left[\frac{V_1-12\angle 30°}{2}+\frac{V_1-12\angle 30°}{-j2}\right]$$

or $$\frac{V_1}{j1}+\frac{V_1-12\angle 30°}{2}+\frac{V_1-12\angle 30°}{-j2}=2\angle 60°$$

or $V_1\left(\frac{1}{j1}+\frac{1}{2}+\frac{1}{-j2}\right)=2\angle 60°+\frac{12\angle 30°}{2}-\frac{12\angle 30°}{j2}$

or $(0.71\angle -45°)\,V_1 = 3.2 + j\,9.93$

$\therefore \quad V_1 = 14.7\angle 117°\text{ V}.$

But we have seen earlier,

$$V_2 = (V_1 - 12\angle 30°)\text{ V}$$

$$\therefore \quad V_2 = 14.7\angle 117° - 12\angle 30°$$
$$= -6.7 + j\,13.07 - 10.4 - j\,6$$
$$= -17.1 + j\,7.07 = 18.5\angle 157.55°\text{ V}.$$

By inspection,

$$V_2 = V_L = \mathbf{18.5\angle 157.55°\ V.}$$

EXAMPLE 10.18 *Using nodal analysis, find V_L in the circuit of Fig. E10.18.*

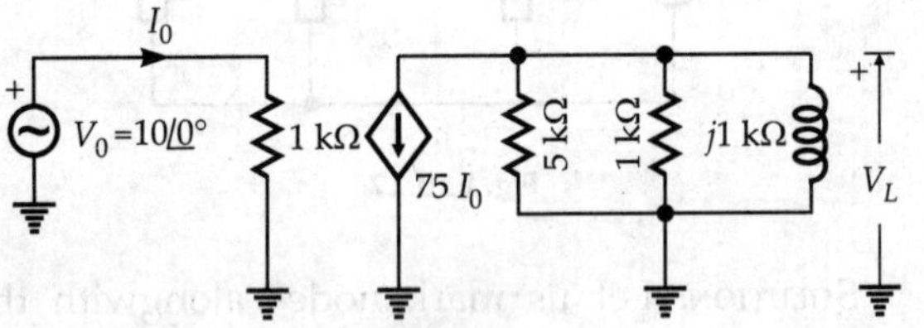

Fig. E10.18

SOLUTION. Let us simplify the figure as shown in Fig. E10.18 (*a*) where

$$Y_1 = \frac{1}{5\times 10^3} = 0.2\times 10^{-3}\ \angle 0°\text{ mho.}$$

$$Y_2 = \frac{1}{1\times 10^3} = 1\times 10^{-3}\ \angle 0°\text{ mho.}$$

$$Y_3 = \frac{1}{j1\times 10^3} = 1\times 10^{-3}\ \angle -90°\text{ mho,}$$
$$= -j\,(1\times 10^{-3})\text{ mho.}$$

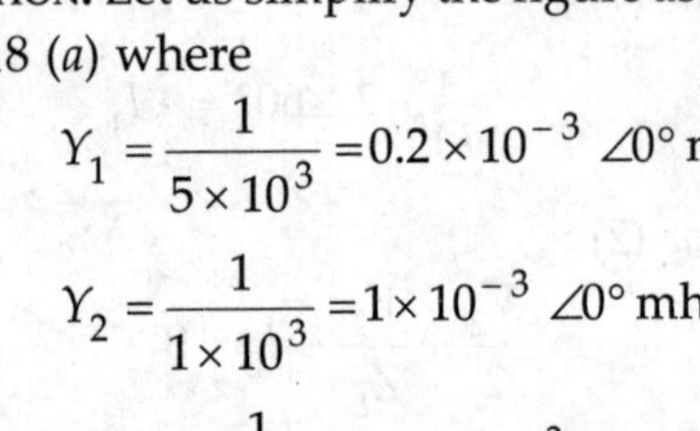

Fig. E10.18(*a*)

Application of nodal analysis at the load node (voltage being V_L),

$$-75\,I_0 = V_L\,(Y_1 + Y_2 + Y_3)$$

[$\because$ current in $Y_1 = V_1\,Y_1$, in $Y_2 = V_2\,Y_2$ and in $Y_3 = V_3\,Y_3$]

or $$V_L = -\frac{75\,I_0}{Y_1+Y_2+Y_3}$$
$$= -\frac{75\,I_0}{0.2\times 10^{-3}+10^{-3}+(-j)\times 10^{-3}}$$
$$= -\frac{75\,I_0}{(1.2-j)10^{-3}}\text{ V.}$$

But it is evident from the given circuit that

$$I_0 = \frac{V_0}{1\text{k}\Omega} = \frac{10\angle 0°}{1000} = 0.01\angle 0°\text{ A};$$

$$\therefore \quad V_L = -\frac{75\times 0.01\times 10^3}{1.2-j} = -\frac{750\,(1.2+j)}{2.44}$$
$$= -307.38\,(1.2+j)$$
$$= (-368.86 - j\,307.38)\text{ V}$$
$$= \mathbf{480\angle -140.2°\ V.}$$

10.6 THEVENIN'S AND NORTON'S THEOREM

The *Thevenin's theorem* is changed only in the a.c. application to include the impedance instead of resistance. Since the reactances of a circuit are frequency dependent, the Thevenin's circuit found for a particular network is applicable only at the specified frequency.

For independent and dependent sources (with a control variable *not* in the network under study) the application of the Thevenin's theorem in the a.c. circuits needs modification only for inclusion of impedances instead of resistances, as stated above, and using current and or voltage phasors. However, for dependent sources of the special type where the control variable is governed by the network variable, any of the following methods is to be applied to find the Thevenin's impedance.

Method-1

Removing the load impedance, $V_{o.c.}$ is obtained. Next, these terminals being shorted, the short circuit current ($I_{s.c.}$) is determined though the shorted link. Established network solution techniques like node voltage or loop current methods can be used for these purposes.

Then, $$Z_{int} = \frac{V_{o.c}}{I_{s.c}}$$

Method-2

Open circuiting the load impedance, a source voltage (V) is applied. The source current (I), entering through the load terminals is determined, the original source voltage of the network being set to zero.

The Thevenin impedance is then given by

$$Z_{\text{int}} = \frac{V}{I}$$

where $V \equiv V_{o.c}$

In the application of *Norton's theorem* in a.c. circuits, the resistances are replaced by impedances, the circuit variables being current and or voltage phasors. For independent sources and dependent sources (where the control variable does not contain any network variable) the internal impedance of the network (being same to that for Thevenin's theorem application) can be determined by the usual procedure as described for d.c. networks. On the other hand, where the network does have the dependent sources, whose control variables depend on network parameters, the way of finding the internal impedance of the network is same as the two methods described for Thevenin's network.

Also, the Norton's equivalent circuit, like the Thevenin's equivalent circuit, is applicable only on one frequency since the reactances are frequency dependent.

The Norton's and Thevenin's equivalent circuits can also be found from each other by using the source transformation as illustrated in Fig. 10.1.

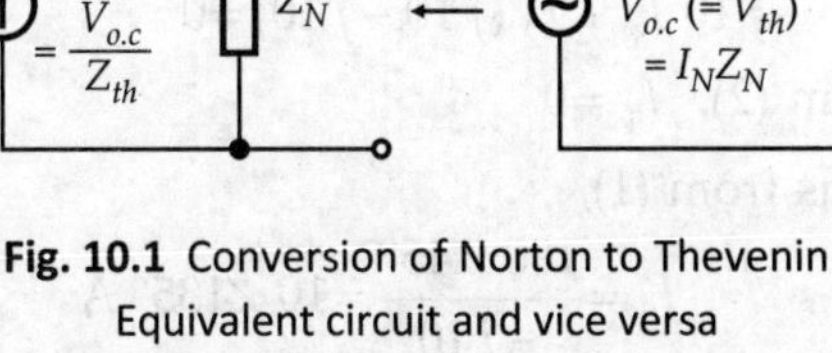

Fig. 10.1 Conversion of Norton to Thevenin Equivalent circuit and vice versa

$$[Z_N \equiv Z_{th} \equiv Z_{\text{int}}\,;\, V_{Th} \equiv V_{o.c.}\,;\, I_N \equiv I_{s.c}]$$

EXAMPLE 10.19 *If $I = 33\angle -13°$ A, find the Thevenin's equivalent circuit to the left of terminals x-y in the network of Fig. E10.19.*

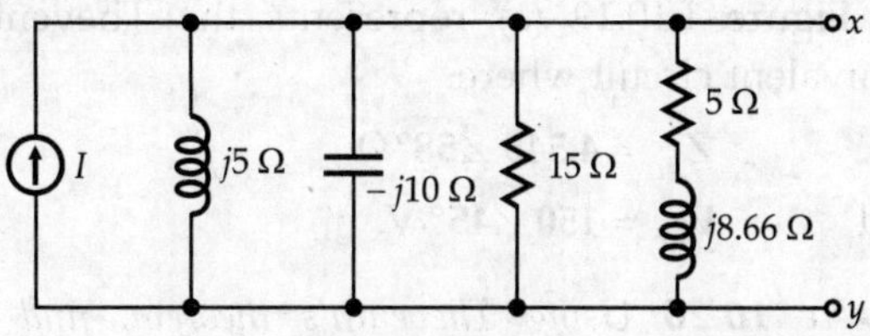

Fig. E10.19

SOLUTION. Let us first find the equivalent impedance across the current source. However, assuming the equivalent admittance to be Y_{eq}, we find that

$$Y_{eq} = Y_1 + Y_2 + Y_3 + Y_4$$

where Y_1 .... Y_4 is the branch admittance of each branch.

Obviously,

$$Y_1 = \frac{1}{j5} = -j0.2 \text{ mho};$$

$$Y_2 = \frac{1}{-j10} = j0.1 \text{ mho}$$

$$Y_3 = \frac{1}{15} = 0.067 \text{ mho}$$

$$Y_4 = \frac{1}{5 + j8.66} = \frac{1}{10\angle 60°}$$

$$= (0.05 - j0.0866) \text{ mho},$$

$$\therefore \quad Y_{eq.} = (0.117 - j0.1866) \text{ mho}$$

Then,

$$V_{x-y} (= V_{o.c}) = I / Y_{eq}$$

$$= 33\angle -13 / (0.117 - j0.1866)$$

$$= 33\angle -13 / 0.22\angle -58°$$

$$= 150\angle 45° \text{ V}.$$

To find Z_{in} ($= Z_{Th}$), the current source is deactivated and by inspection it is observed that

$$Z_{in} = \frac{1}{Y_{eq}} = \frac{1}{0.117 - j0.1866}$$

$$= \frac{1}{0.22\angle -58°} = 4.545\angle 58° \text{ ohm}.$$

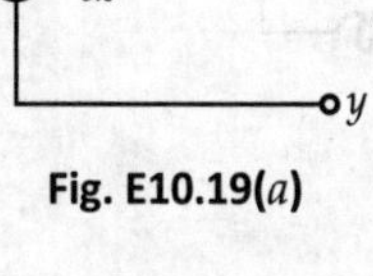

Fig. E10.19(a)

Figure E10.19 (*a*) represents the Thevenin's equivalent circuit where

$$Z_{in} = \mathbf{4.545\ \angle 58°\ \Omega}$$

and $V_{o.c} = \mathbf{150\ \angle 45°\ V.}$

EXAMPLE 10.20 *Using Thevenin's theorem, find the Thevenin's equivalent circuit of the network across x-y in Fig. E10.20.*

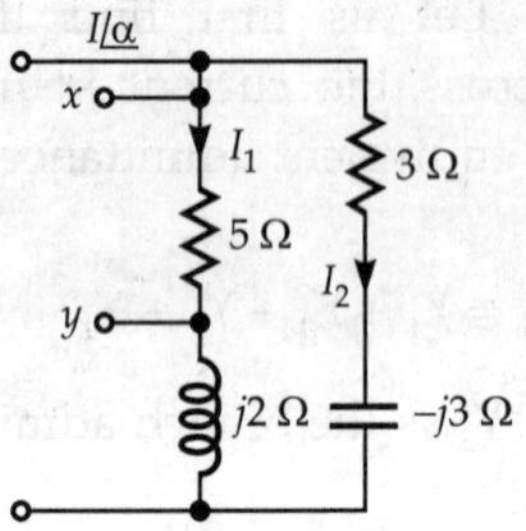

Fig. E10.20

SOLUTION. Given : $I_2 = 15\ \angle 0°$ A.

∴ Drop across $(3 - j\,3)\,\Omega$ branch is

$$V_{drop} = (3 - j\,3)\,15\ \angle 0° = 63.6\ \angle -45°\ \text{V}$$

This gives

$$I_1 = \frac{V_{drop}}{5 + j\,2} = \frac{63.6\ \angle -45°}{5 + j\,2}$$

or $$I_1 = 11.8\ \angle -66.8°\ \text{A} = (4.64 - j\,10.85)\ \text{A}.$$

∴ $V_{o.c}$(*i.e.*, V_{x-y}, the drop across *xy* terminal) is given by

$$V_{o.c} = 5\,(4.64 - j\,10.85)$$

$$[\because V_{o.c} = (I_1 \times 5\,\Omega)\ \text{V}]$$

$$= 59\ \angle -66.8\ \text{V}$$

In order to find Z_{int} $(= Z_{Th})$ we deactivate the current source and find the internal impedance (Z_{int}) across *x-y* looking into the circuit through *x-y* [Fig. E10.20(*a*)].

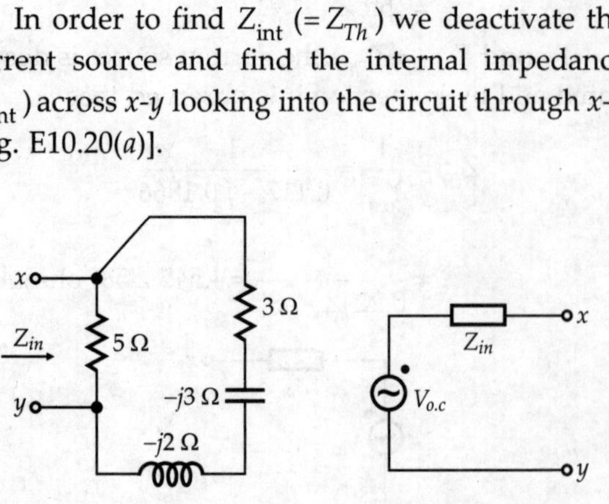

Fig. E10.20 (*a*) (*b*)

Here $Z_{in} = (3 - j\,3 + j\,2)\,||\,5$

$$= \frac{(3 - j\,1)\,5}{3 - j\,1 + 5} = \frac{15 - j\,5}{8 - j\,1}$$

$$= \frac{15.81\ \angle -18.42°}{8.06\ \angle -7.125}\ \Omega$$

$$= 1.96\ \angle -11.295°\,\Omega$$

Thus, Thevenin's equivalent circuit is obtained as shown in E10.20(*b*) where

$$Z_{in} = \mathbf{1.96\,\Omega\ \angle -11.295°}$$

$$V_{o.c.} = \mathbf{59\ \angle -66.8°\ V.}$$

EXAMPLE 10.21 *Find the current through 10 Ω resistor using Thevenin's Theorem. (Fig. E10.21).*

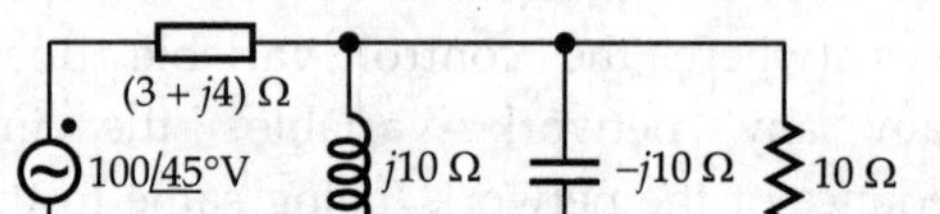

Fig. E10.21

SOLUTION. Let us first remove the 10 Ω resistor and designate the open circuit voltage across it by $V_{o.c}$ [Fig. E10.21 (*a*)]. Let the mesh currents be I_1 and I_2.

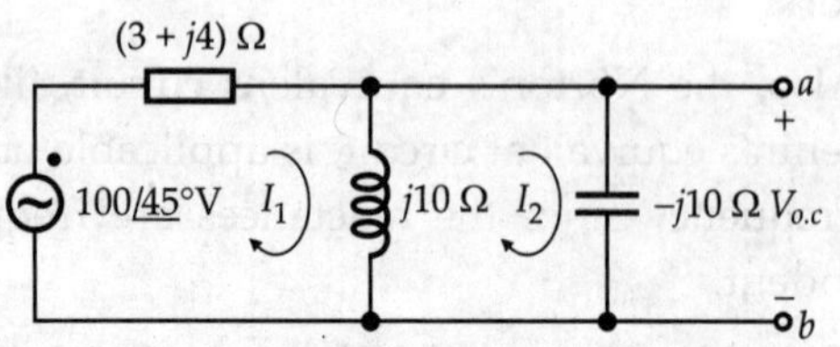

Fig. E10.21 (*a*)

The mesh equations are as follows :

$$(3 + j\,4)\,I_1 + j\,10\,.\,I_1 - j\,10\,I_2 = 100\ \angle 45°$$

or $$(3 + j\,14)\,I_1 - j\,10\,I_2 = 100\ \angle 45° \quad ...(1)$$

also, $$-j\,10\,I_1 + I_2\,(j\,10 - j\,10) = 0 \quad ...(2)$$

From (2), $I_1 = 0$

Thus from (1),

$$I_2 = \frac{100\ \angle 45°}{-j\,10} = 10\ \angle 135°\ \text{A}$$

and $V_{a-b}\,(= V_{o.c}) = -j\,10 \times 10\ \angle 135° = 100\ \angle 45°$ V.

It may be noted here since in the parallel branches, $X_L = X_C$, resonance would appear making $I_1 = 0$. Since $I_1 = 0$, $V_{o.c} \equiv V_{supply}$.

To find the internal impedance of the circuit through a-b, let us deactivate the voltage source [Fig. E10.21(*b*)].

$$Z_{\text{int}} = \frac{1}{Y_{\text{int}}} = \frac{1}{\frac{1}{-j\,10} + \frac{1}{j\,10} + \frac{1}{3 + j\,4}} = (3 + j\,4) \text{ ohm.}$$

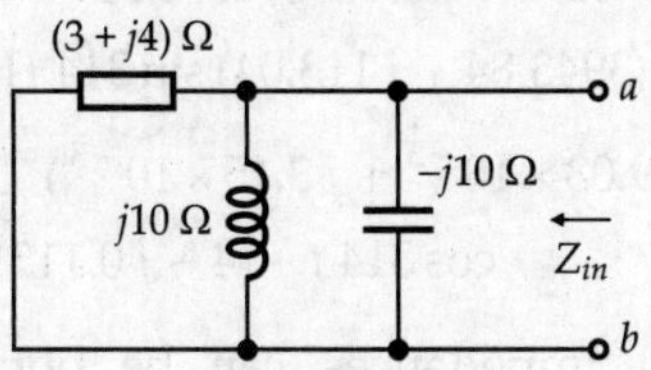

Fig. E10.21 (*b*)

In Fig. E10.21(*c*), the Thevenin's equivalent circuit is drawn where $Z_{in} = (3 + j\,4)\,\Omega$ and $V_{o.c.} = 100 \angle 45°$ V.

$$I_L = \frac{V_{o.c}}{Z_{in} + Z_L} = \frac{100 \angle 45°}{(3 + j\,4) + 10} = 7.35 \angle 28.3° \text{ A}$$

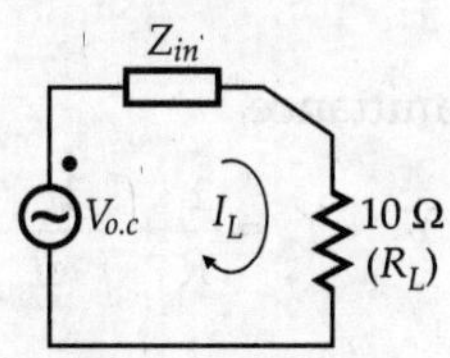

Fig. E10.21 (*c*)

Hence, **the current through the 10 Ω resistor is 7.35 ∠28.3° A.**

Example 10.22 *Find Thevenin's equivalent circuit of the network shown in Fig. E10.22.*

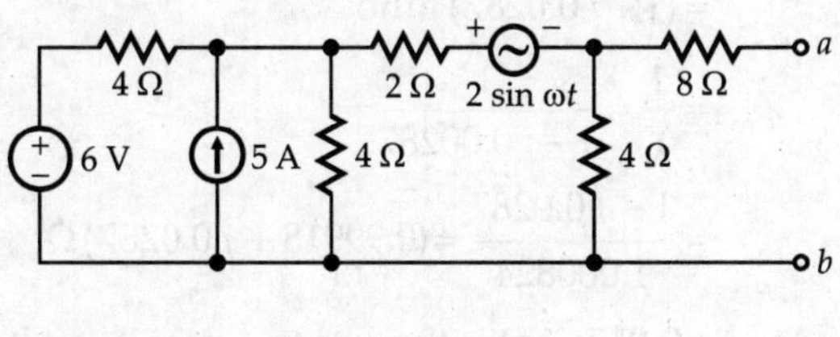

Fig. E10.22

Solution. Let us redraw the given network with mesh currents indicated [Fig. E10.22(*a*)]. Let the open circuit voltage across *a-b* be $V_{o.c.}$ It may be noted here that the 5 A current source has been converted to necessary voltage source as shown in the figure.

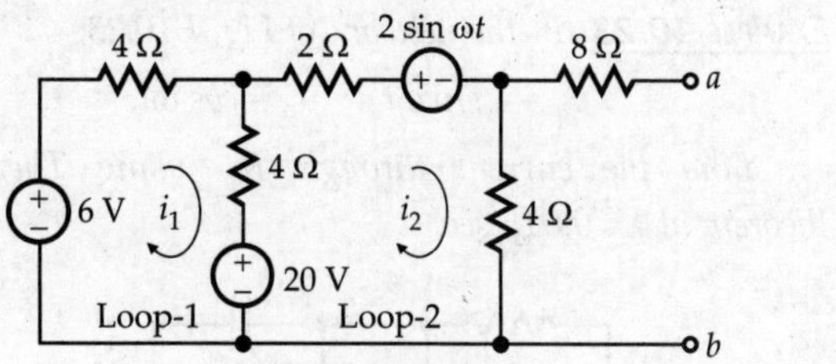

Fig. E10.22 (*a*)

In *loop 1*, mesh analysis gives

$$(4 + 4)\, i_1 - 4 i_2 = 6 - 20 = -14$$

or $$8 i_1 - 4 i_2 = -14 \quad \text{...(1)}$$

In *loop-2*, mesh analysis gives

$$i_2\,(2 + 4 + 4) - 4 i_1 = 20 - 2 \sin \omega t$$

or $$-4 i_1 + 10\, i_2 = 20 - 2 \sin \omega t$$

or $$-2 i_1 + 5 i_2 = 10 - \sin \omega t \quad \text{...(2)}$$

From (1),

$$8\, i_1 = 4\, i_2 - 14$$

or $$i_1 = 0.5\, i_2 - 1.75 \quad \text{...(3)}$$

Using the value of i_1 from (3) in (2),

$$-2\,(0.5\, i_2 - 1.75) + 5 i_2 = 10 - \sin \omega t$$

or $$-i_2 + 3.5 + 5\, i_2 = 10 - \sin \omega t$$

or $$4\, i_2 = 6.5 - \sin \omega t$$

$$\therefore \quad i_2 = 1.625 - 0.25 \sin \omega t \quad \text{...(4)}$$

$$\therefore \quad V_{o.c} = i_2 \times 4 = V_{a-b} = (1.625 - 0.25 \sin \omega t)\, 4$$

or $$V_{o.c} = 6.5 - \sin \omega t$$

To find the Thevenin's internal resistance, the sources are replaced by their internal resistances and the network is then shown in Fig. E10.22(*b*).

$$R_{in} = [\{(4 \,||\, 4) + 2\} \,||\, 4] + 8 = 10\,\Omega$$

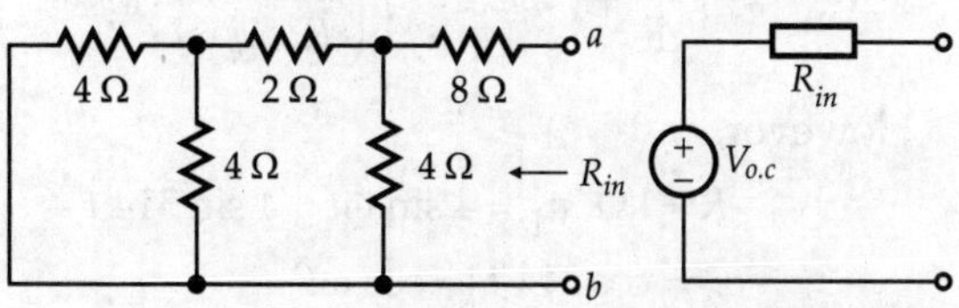

Fig. E10.22 (*b*) (*c*)

The Thevenin's equivalent circuit is formed where

$$\mathbf{V_{o.c.} = (6.5 - \sin \omega t)\ V}$$

and $$\mathbf{R_{in}\ (= R_{th}) = 10\,\Omega.}$$

[Refer to Fig. E10.22(*c*)].

CHAPTER 10

EXAMPLE 10.23 *In the network of Fig. E10.23,*

$$v_1 = 4 \sin \omega t \; ; \quad v_2 = \cos \omega t.$$

Find the current through R_L using Thevenin's theorem at $t = 0.015$ sec.

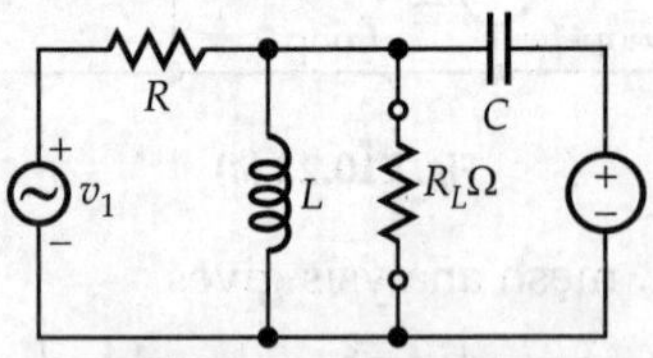

[$f = 50$ Hz, $R = 1\ \Omega$, $L = 0.1$ H, $C = 10\ \mu$F, $R_L = 10\ \Omega$]

Fig. E10.23

SOLUTION. Let R_L be removed and the circuit is drawn as shown in Fig. E10.23(*a*). Let the open circuit voltage be $v_{o.c}$

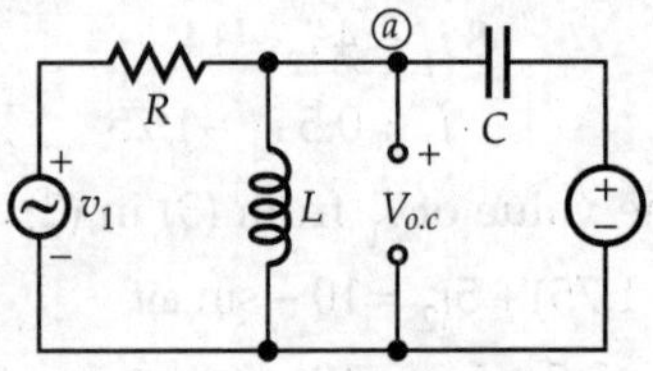

Fig. E10.23 (*a*)

Application of nodal analysis at node "*a*" gives:

$$\frac{v_{o.c} - v_2}{X_C} + \frac{v_{o.c.}}{X_L} + \frac{V_{o.c} - v_1}{R} = 0$$

$$\text{or} \quad v_{o.c}\left[\frac{1}{R} + \frac{1}{j\,\omega L} + j\,\omega C\right] - \frac{v_1}{R} - j\,\omega C\, v_2 = 0$$

$$\left[\because X_C = \frac{1}{j\omega C}; X_L = j\,\omega L\right]$$

$$\text{or} \quad v_{o.c.} = -\left(\frac{v_1}{R} + j\,\omega C\, v_2\right) \Bigg/ \left(\frac{1}{R} + \frac{1}{j\,\omega L} + j\,\omega C\right).$$

However,

$$R = 1\Omega, v_1 = 4 \sin \omega t = 4 \sin 314\, t$$

$$v_2 = \cos 314\, t\, (= \cos \omega t)$$

$$\omega = 2\pi f = 2 \times \pi \times 50 = 314 \text{ rad/sec}$$

$$L = 0.1\text{ H}; C = 10\,\mu\text{ F}$$

$$\therefore \quad v_{o.c} = \frac{\left(\frac{4}{1}\sin 314t + j \times 314 \times 10^{-6} \times 10 \cos 314t\right)}{\left(\frac{1}{1} + \frac{1}{j\,314 \times 0.1} + j\,314 \times 10 \times 10^{-6}\right)}$$

$$= \frac{(4 \sin 314\, t + j\,3.14 \times 10^{-3} \cos 314\, t)}{1 + \frac{1}{j\,31.4} + j\,3.14 \times 10^{-3}} \text{ V}$$

$$= \frac{-0.099 \cos 314\, t + j\,125.6 \sin 314\, t}{0.9 + j\,31.4}$$

$$= [(-0.0891 + j\,3.1086) \cos 314\, t + (3943.84 + j\,113.04) \sin 314\, t] \times (1/986.77)$$

$$= [(-9.03 \times 10^{-5} + j\,3.15 \times 10^{-3}) \cos 314\, t + (4 + j\,0.115) \sin 314\, t] \text{ V}$$

Internal impedances can be obtained from Fig. E10.23(*b*).

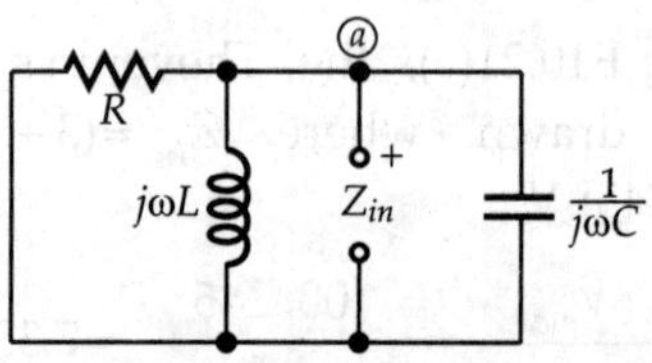

Fig. E10.23 (*b*)

Here the admittance

$$Y = Y_1 + Y_2 + Y_3 = \frac{1}{R} + \frac{1}{j\,\omega L} + \frac{1}{(1/j\,\omega C)}$$

$$\text{or} \quad Y = \frac{1}{R} + \frac{1}{j\omega L} + j\,\omega C = \frac{1}{R} - \frac{j}{\omega L} + j\,\omega C$$

$$= \frac{1}{R} + j\left(\omega C - \frac{1}{\omega L}\right)$$

$$= 1 + j\left(314 \times 10 \times 10^{-6} - \frac{1}{314 \times 0.1}\right)$$

$$= (1 - j\,0.0287) \text{ mho}$$

$$\therefore Z_{in} = \frac{1}{Y} = \frac{1}{1 - j\,0.00287}$$

$$= \frac{1 + j\,0.0287}{1.000824} = (0.99918 + j\,0.0287)\,\Omega$$

At $t = 0.015$ sec, the open circuit voltage (Thevenin's voltage) becomes

$$v_{o.c} = -9.03 \times 10^{-5} \cos 314 \times 0.015 + j\,0.115 \sin 314 \times 0.015 + j\,3.15 \times 10^{-3} \cos 314 \times 0.015 + 4.0 \sin 314 \times 0.015$$

$$= 2.16 \times 10^{-7} - 0.115j - j\,7.53 \times 10^{-6} - 4$$

$$= (-4 - j\,0.115) \text{ V}.$$

Thevenin's equivalent circuit being drawn in Fig. E10.23(c), at t = 0.015 sec,

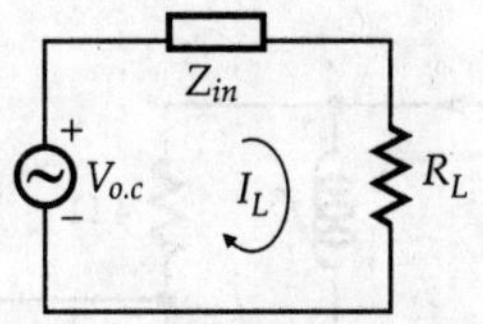

Fig. E10.23 (c)

$$I_L \text{ (current through } R_L) = \frac{v_{o.c.}}{Z_{in} + R_L}$$

$$= \frac{(-4 - j\,0.115)}{0.99918 + j\,0.0287 + 10}$$

$$= \frac{4\,\angle -178.35^\circ}{10.992\,\angle 0.15^\circ}$$

$$= \mathbf{0.364\,\angle -178.49^\circ\ A.}$$

Example 10.24 *Using Thevenin's theorem, find the current through the coil* $(5 + j\,4)\,\Omega$ *in the bridge circuit shown in Fig. E10.24.*

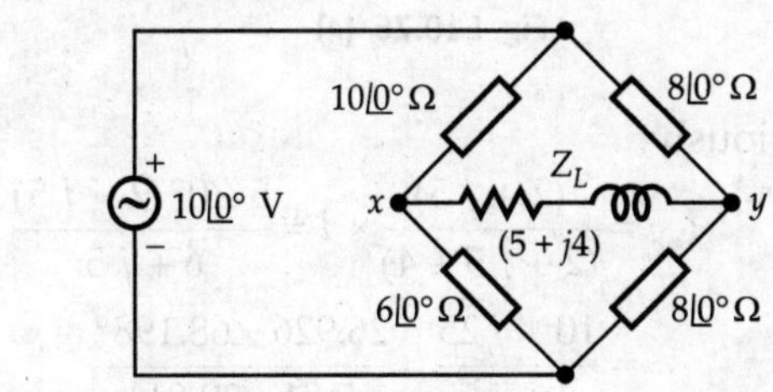

Fig. E10.24

Solution. Let us first remove Z_L [Fig. E10.24(a)].

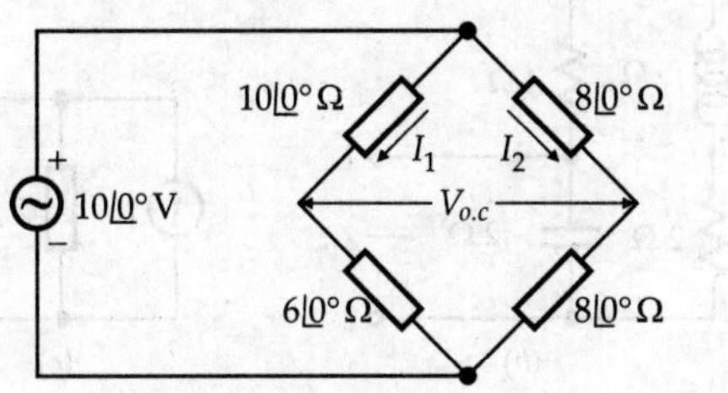

Fig. E10.24 (a)

$$I_1 = \frac{10\angle 0^\circ}{10+6} = 0.625\,\angle 0^\circ \text{ A};$$

$$I_2 = \frac{10\,\angle 0^\circ}{8+8} = 0.625\,\angle 0^\circ \text{ A.}$$

$$\therefore \quad V_{o.c} = V_{xy} \text{ (the Thevenin's voltage)}$$

$$= -6I_1 + 8I_2$$

$$= -6 \times 0.625\,\angle 0^\circ + 8 \times 0.625\,\angle 0^\circ$$

$$= -3.75\,\angle 0^\circ + 5.0\,\angle 0^\circ = 1.25\,\angle 0^\circ \text{ V}$$

To calculate Z_{int} (Thevenin's impedance), the voltage source is deactivated [Fig. E10.24(b)].

$$Z_{\text{int}} = \frac{10 \times 6}{10+6} + \frac{8 \times 8}{8+8} = 7.75\,\Omega$$

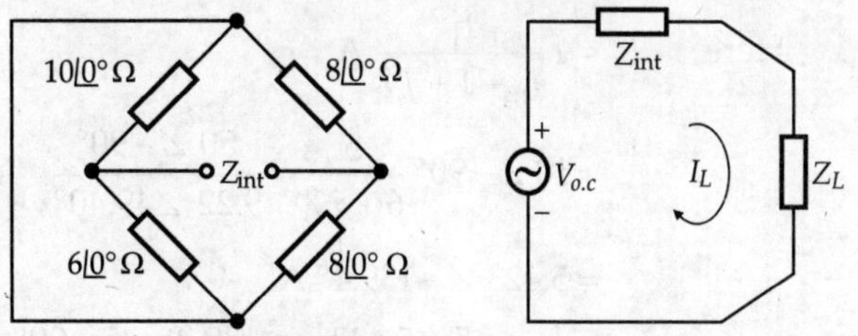

Fig. E10.24 (b) (c)

Thevenin's equivalent circuit can now be formed where,

$$V_{o.c} = 1.25\,\angle 0^\circ \text{ V} \quad \text{and} \quad Z_{\text{int}} = 7.75\,\angle 0^\circ\,\Omega$$

[Fig. E10.24(c)]

Here,

$$I_L = \frac{V_{o.c}}{Z_{\text{int}} + Z_L} = \frac{1.25\,\angle 0^\circ}{7.75 + 5 + j\,4} = \frac{1.25\,\angle 0^\circ}{13.36\,\angle 17.4^\circ}$$

$$= 0.094\,\angle -17.4^\circ \text{ A.}$$

The load current though Z_L would be **0.094 ∠– 17.4° A.**

Example 10.25 *Find Thevenin's equivalent network at the left of terminals x-y in the network of Fig. E10.25.*

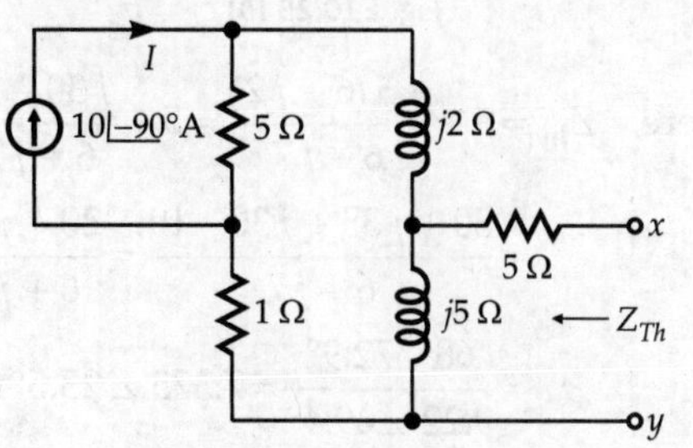

Fig. E10.25

Solution. Let us redraw the circuit as shown in Fig. E10.25(a). Voltage across x-y being $V_{\text{o.c.}}$, no current would flow through r_2. The current division has been shown in Fig. E10.25(a).

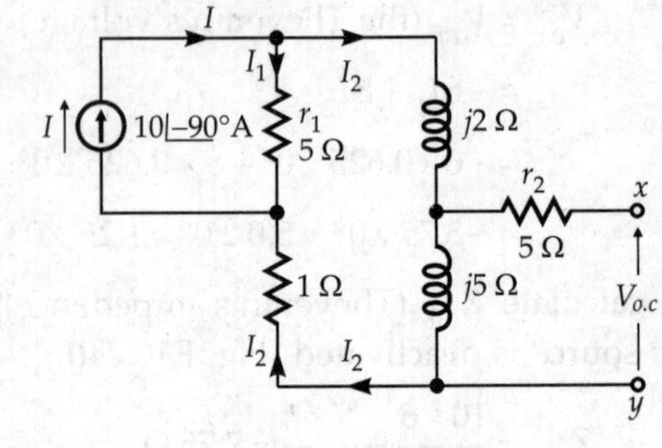

Fig. E10.25 (*a*)

Here $I_2 = I \dfrac{r_1}{r_1 + 1 + j7}$ A

$$= 10 \angle -90^\circ \frac{5}{6 + j7} = \frac{50 \angle -90^\circ}{9.22 \angle 49.40^\circ}$$

$$= 5.423 \angle -139.4^\circ \text{ A.}$$

$$\therefore \quad V_{o.c.} = I_2 \times j\,5 = 5.423 \angle -139.4^\circ \times 5 \angle 90^\circ$$

$$= 27.115 \angle -49.4^\circ \text{ V.}$$

The internal impedance across *x-y* can be obtained as shown in Fig. E10.25(*b*).

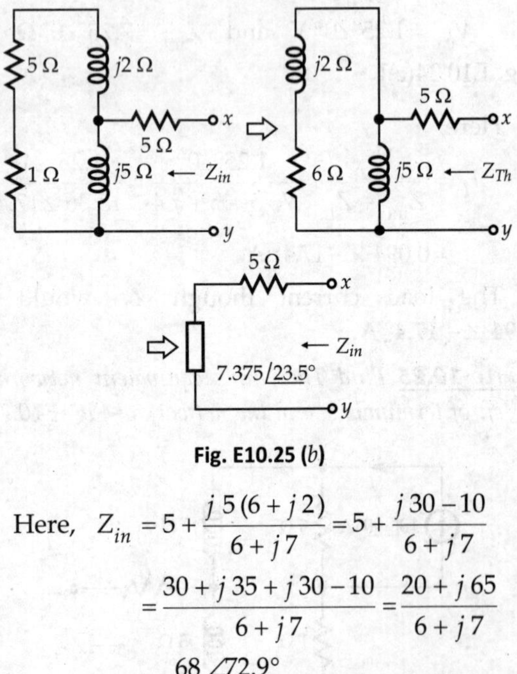

Fig. E10.25 (*b*)

Here, $Z_{in} = 5 + \dfrac{j\,5\,(6 + j\,2)}{6 + j\,7} = 5 + \dfrac{j\,30 - 10}{6 + j\,7}$

$$= \frac{30 + j\,35 + j\,30 - 10}{6 + j\,7} = \frac{20 + j\,65}{6 + j\,7}$$

$$= \frac{68 \angle 72.9^\circ}{9.22 \angle 49.4^\circ} = 7.375 \angle 23.5^\circ \,\Omega.$$

The Thevenin's equivalent circuit is shown in Fig. E10.25(*c*) where

$\mathbf{V_{o.c.}} = \mathbf{27.115 \angle -49.4^\circ}$ **V**

$\mathbf{Z_{int}} = \mathbf{7.375 \angle 23.5^\circ \,\Omega}$**.**

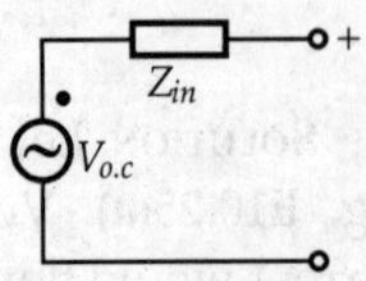

Fig. E10.25 (*c*)

EXAMPLE 10.26 *Find Norton's equivalent circuit for the network shown in Fig. E10.26 at the left of terminals 1-2. Assume I = 5 ∠0° A.*

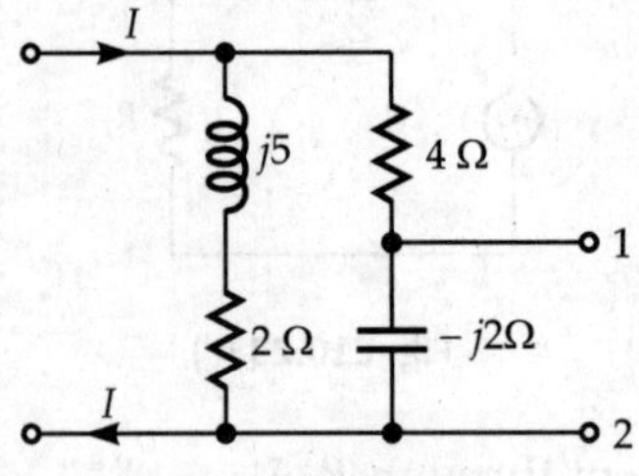

Fig. E10.26

SOLUTION. Terminals 1-2 are shorted [Fig. E10.26(*a*)]. No current would flow through (– *j* 2 Ω) capacitive reactance due to shorting of terminal 1-2.

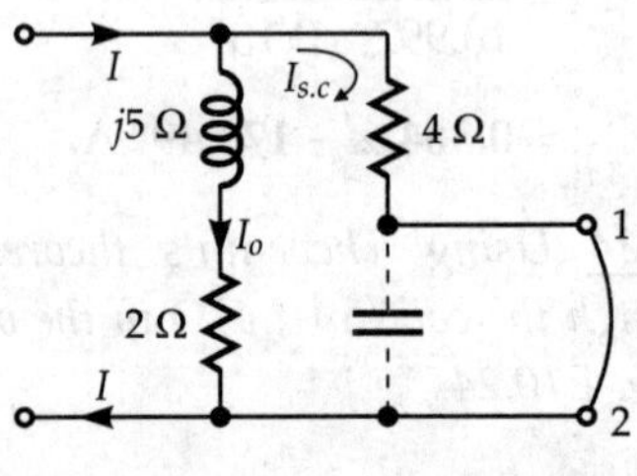

Fig. E10.26 (*a*)

Obviously,

$$I_{s.c} = \frac{(2 + j\,5)}{(2 + j\,5 + 4)} \times I = \frac{5 \angle 0^\circ (2 + j\,5)}{6 + j\,5}$$

$$= \frac{10 + j\,25}{6 + j\,5} = \frac{26.926 \angle 68.198^\circ}{7.81 \angle 39.81^\circ}$$

$$= 3.45 \angle 28.39^\circ \text{ A.}$$

Internal impedance can be obtained from Fig. E10.26(*b*) deactivating the current source.

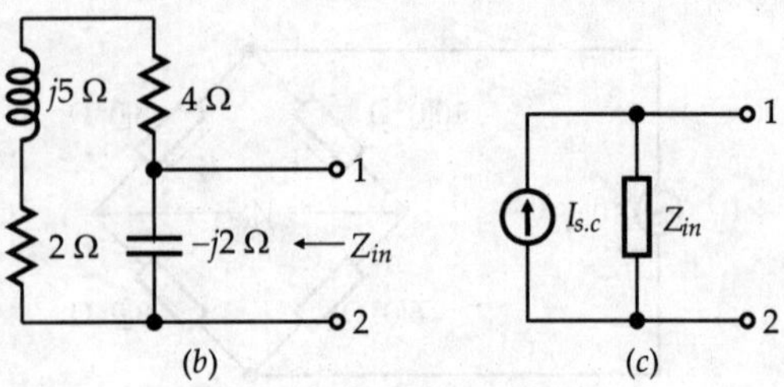

Fig. E10.26

$$Z_{in} = \frac{-j\,2\,(4 + 2 + j\,5)}{-j\,2 + 4 + j\,5 + 2} = \frac{-j\,8 - j\,4 + 10}{6 + j\,3}$$

$$= \frac{10 - j\,12}{6 + j\,3} = \frac{15.62 \angle -50.19^\circ}{6.71 \angle 26.56^\circ}$$

$$= 2.33 \angle -76.75^\circ \,\Omega.$$

Norton's equivalent circuit is shown in Fig. E10.26(*c*) where

$$\boldsymbol{I_{s.c} = 3.45 \angle 28.39° \text{ A};}$$

$$\boldsymbol{Z_{in} = 2.33 \angle -76.75° \,\Omega.}$$

EXAMPLE 10.27 *Find Thevenin's equivalent network across x-y (Fig. E10.27).*

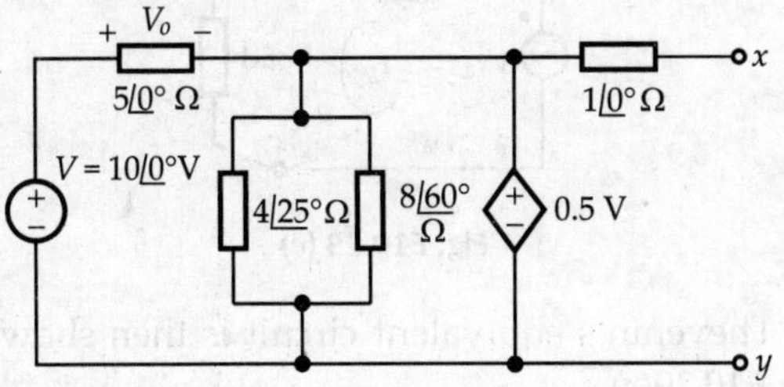

Fig. E10.27

SOLUTION. The circuit is simplified as shown in Fig. E10.27(*a*)

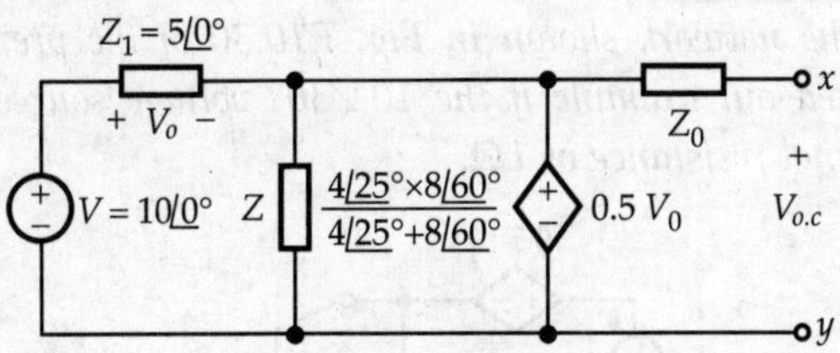

Fig. E10.27 (*a*)

Here $\quad Z = \dfrac{4 \angle 25° \times 8 \angle 60°}{4 \angle 25° + 8 \angle 60°}$

$$= \frac{32 \angle 85°}{7.625 + j\,8.62} = \frac{32 \angle 85°}{11.51 \angle 48.5°}$$

$$= 2.78 \angle 36.5° \,\Omega$$

Let the current through Z be I.

By inspection, $IZ = 0.5\, V_0 = V_{o.c}$

[$\because$ no current flows through Z_0]

Also, in the leftmost loop,

$$-V + V_0 + 0.5\, V_0 = 0 \qquad [\because IZ = 0.5\, V_0]$$

or $\quad V_0 = \dfrac{V}{1.5} = \dfrac{10 \angle 0°}{1.5} = 6.67 \angle 0° \text{ V}.$

$\therefore \quad V_{o.c} = 0.5\, V_0 = 0.5 \times 6.67 \angle 0°$

$$= \mathbf{3.335 \angle 0° \text{ V}.}$$

To find Z_{int}, a current source of $1 \angle 0°$ A is applied at *x-y* deactivating the voltage source [Fig. E10.27(*b*)].

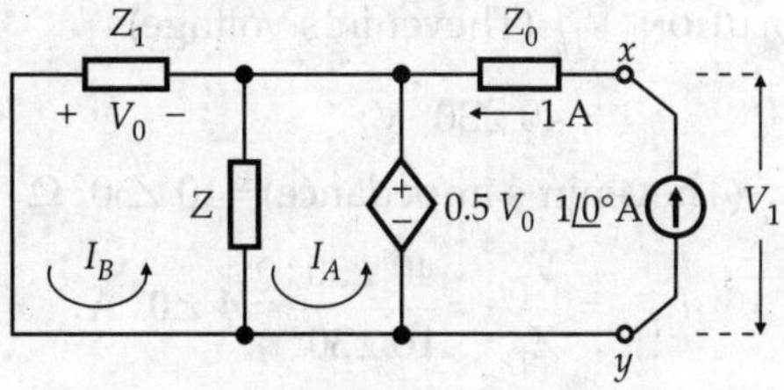

Fig. E10.27 (*b*)

Here, $-V_1 + 1 \angle 0 \times 1 \angle 0° + 0.5\, V_0 = 0$

or $\quad V_1 = 0.5\, V_0 + 1 \qquad$ ...(1)

Also, $\quad -0.5\, V_0 + (I_A - I_B)\, Z = 0$

or $\quad 0.5\,(I_B\, Z_1) + (I_A - I_B)\, Z = 0$

$$[\because -I_B\, Z_1 = V_0\,]$$

or $\quad I_B\,(0.5\, Z_1 - Z) + I_A\, Z = 0 \qquad$ ...(2)

Again in the leftmost loop,

$$I_B\, Z - I_A\, Z + I_B\, Z_1 = 0$$

or $\quad -I_A\, Z + I_B\,(Z + Z_1) = 0 \qquad$ ...(3)

Using (2) in (3),

$$I_B\,(0.5\, Z_1 - Z) + I_B\,(Z + Z_1) = 0$$

or $\quad 1.5\, I_B\, Z_1 = 0 \qquad \therefore \quad I_B = 0$

Thus from (1),

$$V_1 = 1 \text{ or } \frac{V_1}{1} = 1\,\Omega \quad i.e.,\ \mathbf{Z_{int} = 1\,\Omega.}$$

Figure E10.27(*c*) represents the Thevenin's equivalent source across *x-y* where $V_{o.c} = 3.335 \angle 0°$ and $Z_{int} = 1\,\Omega$.

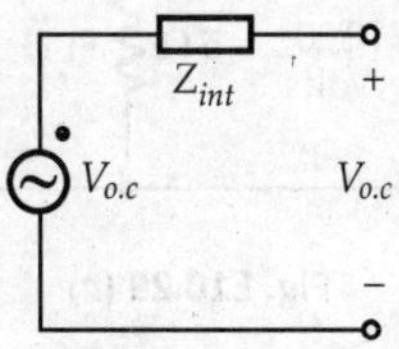

Fig. E10.27 (*c*)

EXAMPLE 10.28 *The Thevenin's equivalent voltage and Thevenin's equivalent impedance of a circuit are 40 $\angle 30°$ volts and 10 $\angle 30°\,\Omega$ respectively (Fig. E10.28). Determine the Norton equivalent circuit.*

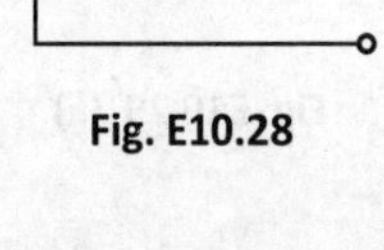

Fig. E10.28

CHAPTER 10

Solution. V_{Th} (Thevenin's voltage)

$$= 40 \angle 30° \text{ V};$$

Z_{Th} (Thevenin's impedance) $= 10 \angle 30° \, \Omega$

$$\therefore \quad I_{Nor} = \frac{V_{Th}}{Z_{Th}} = \frac{40 \angle 30°}{10 \angle 30°} = \mathbf{4 \angle 0° \text{ A.}}$$

Obviously, Thevenin's impedance being equal to Norton's impedance,

$$Z_{Nor} = Z_{Th} = \mathbf{10 \angle 30° \, \Omega.}$$

Example 10.29 *Find Thevenin's equivalent circuit of the network shown in Fig. E10.29 across the load.*

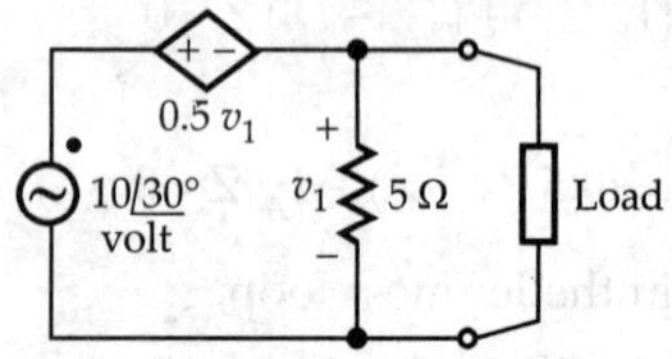

Fig. E10.29

Solution. Removing the load, assuming the open circuit voltage to be $V_{o.c}$, it is seen that $V_{o.c} = v_1$. Applying KVL in the left loop of Fig. E10.29(*a*),

$$-10 \angle 30° + 0.5 \, v_1 + v_1 = 0$$

or $\quad 1.5 \, v_1 = 10 \angle 30°$

$$\therefore \quad v_1 = 6.67 \angle 30° \text{ V} \qquad (= V_{o.c}).$$

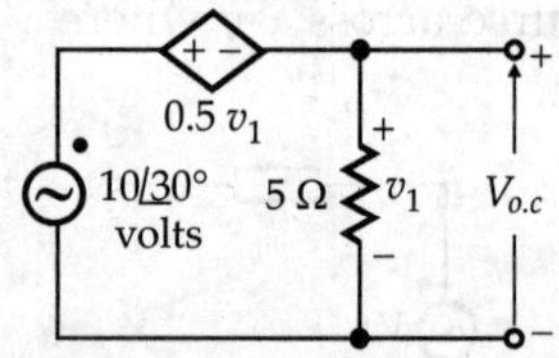

Fig. E10.29 (*a*)

Applying short circuit across the output, following Fig. E10.29(*b*), it is evident that $v_1 = 0$ (since the output is short-circuited). This makes the dependent source also to be zero.

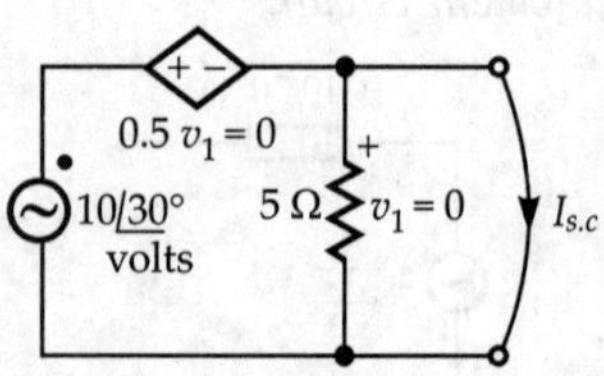

Fig. E10.29 (*b*)

$$\therefore \quad I_{s.c} = \frac{10 \angle 30° \text{ V}}{0} \quad \text{[Since there is no other impedance in the loop]}$$

i.e., $\quad I_{s.c} = \infty.$

$$\therefore \quad Z_{int} = \frac{V_{o.c}}{I_{s.c}} = \frac{V_{o.c}}{\infty} = 0 \, \Omega.$$

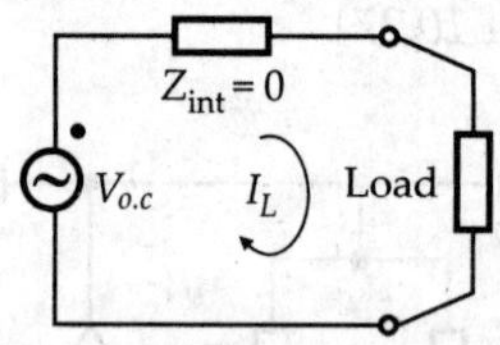

Fig. E10.29 (*c*)

Thevenin's equivalent circuit is then shown in Fig. E10.29(*c*).

$$\left[I_L = \frac{V_{o.c.}}{Z_{int} + Z_{Load}} \right]$$

Example 10.30 *Find the Thevenin's equivalent network for the network shown in Fig. E10.30 of the previous worked out example if the $10 \angle 30°$ voltage source has internal resistance of 1Ω.*

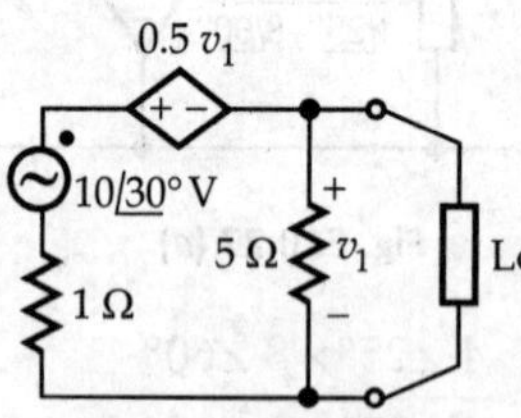

Fig. E10.30

Solution. Let us redraw the network with 1Ω internal resistance of the $10 \angle 30°$ V source [Fig. E10.30(*a*)].

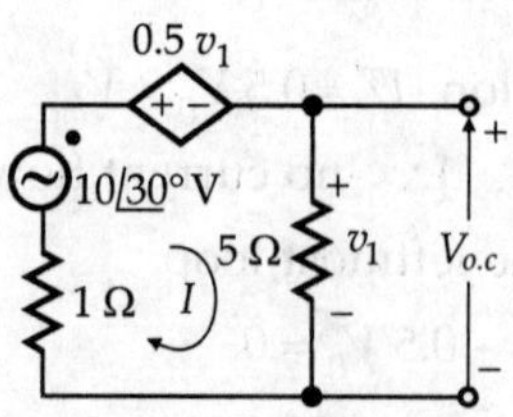

Fig. E10.30 (*a*)

Next, the load being removed, the loop equation in the left loop gives [Fig. E10.30(*a*)]

$$-10 \angle 30° + 0.5 \, v_1 = 5 \, I + 1 \, I$$

However, $\quad I = \dfrac{V_{o.c}}{5};$

$$\therefore \; -10(\cos 30° + j\sin 30°) + 0.5\,v_1 = 5.\frac{V_{o.c.}}{5} + 1\frac{V_{o.c.}}{5}$$

or $\quad -8.66 - j\,5 = V_{o.c} - 0.5\,V_{o.c} + 0.2\,V_{o.c.}$

$$[\because V_{o.c} \equiv v_1]$$

or $\quad V_{o.c} = (-8.66 - j\,5)/0.7$

$$= -12.37 - j\,7.14 \text{ V}$$

To find Z_{Th}, let the output be shorted [Fig. E10.30(*b*)]. No current passes through 5 Ω resistor and $v_1 = 0$. This leads to $0.5\,v_1$ to be zero also.

$$\therefore \quad I_{s.c.} = \frac{10\angle 30°}{1\Omega} = 10\angle 30° \text{ A.}$$

$$\text{Thus, } Z_{\text{int}} = \frac{V_{o.c.}}{I_{s.c.}} = \frac{-12.37 - j\,7.14}{8.66 + j\,5}$$

$$\therefore \quad Z_{\text{int}} = \frac{14.28\angle -150°}{9.999\angle 30°} = 1.43\angle -180°.$$

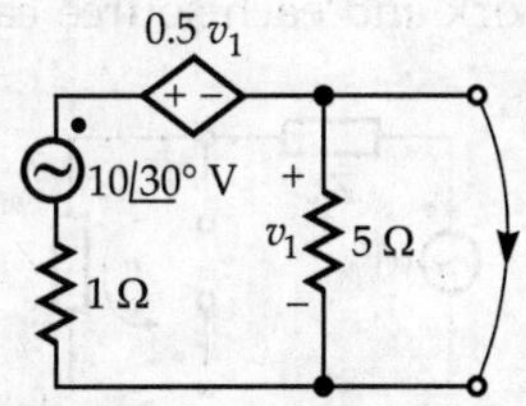

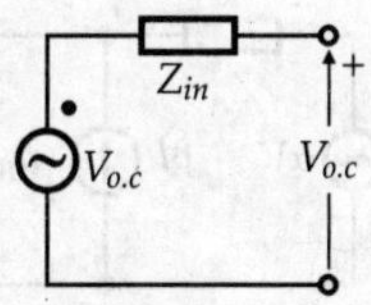

Fig. E10.30 (*b*) (*c*)

Thevenin's circuit is drawn in Fig. E10.30(*c*) so that

$$\mathbf{V_{o.c} = (-12.37 - j7.14)\ V}$$

$$\mathbf{Z_{int} = 1.43\angle -180°\,\Omega.}$$

EXAMPLE 10.31 *Find Thevenin's equivalent network of the circuit shown across x-y and find the current through the 1 Ω resistor. Verify the result using Norton's theorem (Fig. E10.31).*

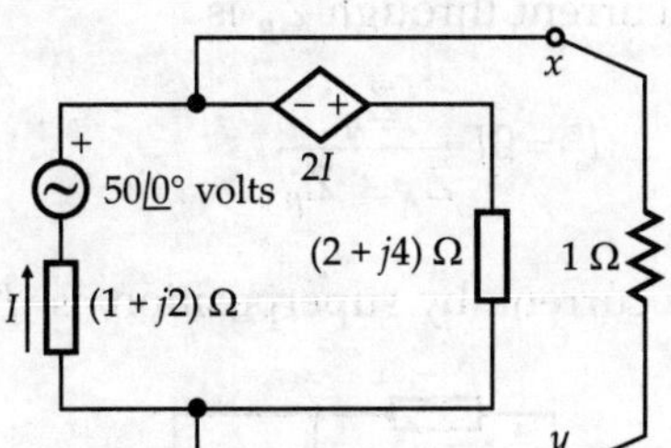

Fig. E10.31

SOLUTION. Let us remove 1 Ω resistor from *x-y* and keep it open circuited [Fig. E10.31(*a*)].

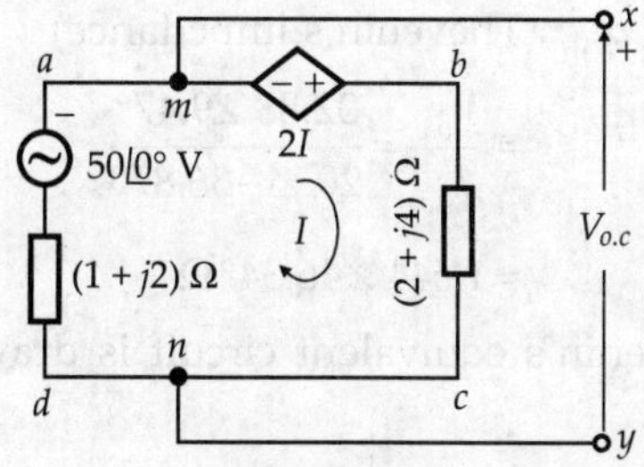

Fig. E10.31 (*a*)

Application of loop equation in loop *abcd* yields

$$-50\angle 0° - 2I + I(2 + j\,4 + 1 + j\,2) = 0$$

or $\quad -50 = 2I - I(3 + j\,6)$

or $\quad I(-1 - j\,6) = -50$

$$\therefore \quad I = \frac{50}{1 + j\,6} = (1.35 - j\,8.11) \text{ A}$$

Application of loop equation in *loop amnd* yields

$$(1 + j\,2)\,I - 50 + V_{o.c} = 0$$

or $\quad V_{o.c} = 50 - I(1 + j\,2)$

$$\therefore \quad V_{o.c} = 50 - (1.35 - j\,8.11)(1 + j\,2)$$

$$= 50 - [(17.57 - j\,5.41)]$$

$$= (32.43 + j\,5.41) \text{ V} = 32.88\angle 9.47° \text{ V.}$$

Next, short circuit is applied across *x-y* [Fig. E10.31(*b*)]

$$I_1 = \frac{50\angle 0°\,V}{(1 + j\,2)\Omega} = 22.36\angle -63.43° \text{ A,}$$

$$I_2 = \frac{2I_1}{(2 + j\,4)} = \frac{2 \times 22.36\angle -63.434°}{4.472\angle 63.434°}$$

$$= 10\angle -126.87° \text{ A}$$

$$\therefore \quad I_{s.c} = I_1 - I_2$$

$$= 22.36\angle -63.43° - 10\angle -126.87°$$

$$= 10 - j\,20 + 6 + j\,8 = (16 - j\,12) \text{ A}$$

$$= 20\angle -36.87° \text{ A}$$

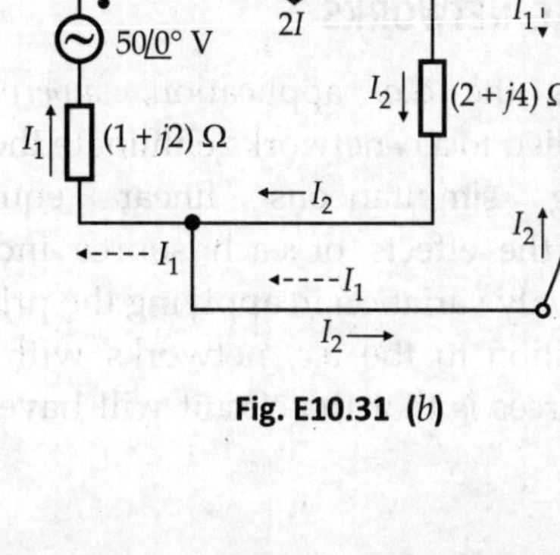

Fig. E10.31 (*b*)

Thus, Z_{in} (Thevenin's impedance)

$$= \frac{V_{o.c}}{I_{s.c}} = \frac{32.88 \angle 9.47°}{20 \angle -36.87°}$$

$$= 1.644 \angle 46.34° \Omega$$

Thevenin's equivalent circuit is drawn in Fig. E10.31(*c*).

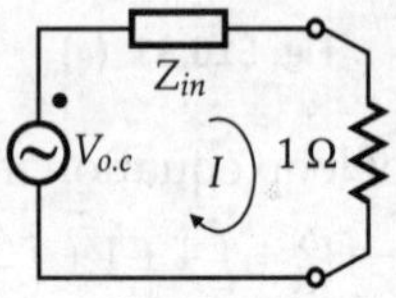

Fig. E10.31 (*c*)

I_L (= current through 1 Ω resistor) is then given by

$$I_L = \frac{V_{o.c}}{Z_{in}+1} = \frac{32.88 \angle 9.47°}{1.644 \angle 46.34° + 1}$$

$$= \frac{32.88 \angle 9.47°}{1.135 + j\,1.19 + 1} = \frac{32.88 \angle 9.47°}{2.44 \angle 29.13°}$$

$$= \mathbf{13.475 \angle -19.66° \text{ A}}.$$

Also, to establish the validity of the result obtained, Norton's theorem can be applied when,

$I_{s.c}$ (already obtained) $= 20 \angle -36.87°$ A

Z_{in} (also obtained above) $= 1.644 \angle 46.34° \Omega$.

$\therefore I_L$ (current though 1 Ω resistor)

$$= I_{s.c} \times \frac{Z_{in}}{Z_{in}+1}$$

$$= \frac{20 \angle -36.87 \times 1.644 \angle 46.34°}{1.644 \angle 46.34 + 1}$$

$$= \mathbf{13.475 \angle -19.66° \text{ A}}.$$

Thus the validity of the result obtained through Thevenin's theorem is established by Norton's Theorem.

10.7 SUPERPOSITION THEOREM FOR AC NETWORKS

Just like the d.c. application, *superposition theorem,* applied to a.c. networks eliminate the need for solving simultaneous linear equations considering the effects of each source independently. The only variation in applying the principle of superposition to the a.c. networks with independent sources is that the circuit will have to be worked out with impedances and phasors (*i.e.,* operation with complex numbers) instead of just resistors and real numbers.

For dependent sources in which the control variable is determined by the network to which the theorem is to be applied, the dependent source cannot be set to zero unless controlling variable is also zero. For networks where both the independent and dependent sources exist, the superposition principle is to be applied for each independent source and each dependent source *not* having a controlling variable in the portions of the network under investigation.

In order to explain the above let us illustrate as follows :

In Fig. 10.2, both the sources have control variable V and I but it is to be noted that V and I does not make the source dependent on the variable of any portion of the network and each source can be treated as independent source. To apply superposition to find the current through Z_B, let us first remove the current source (Fig. 10.3).

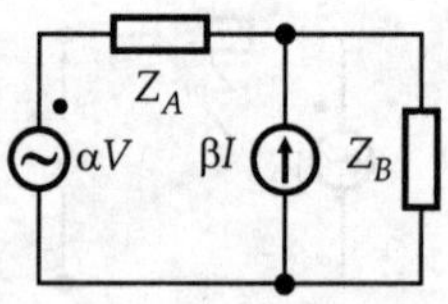

Fig. 10.2 Application of superposition theorem.

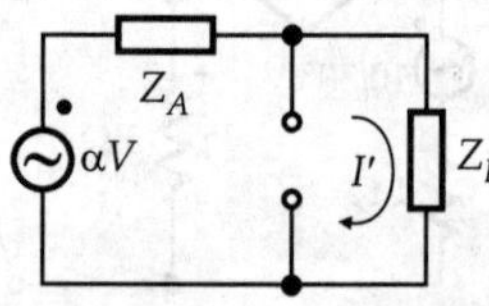

Fig. 10.3 Current due to voltage source only.

$$I' = \frac{\alpha V}{Z_A + Z_B}.$$

Next, the voltage source being removed, (Fig. 10.4), the current through Z_B is

$$I'' = \beta I \frac{Z_A}{Z_A + Z_B}.$$

$\therefore$ Net current, by superposition, is $I' + I''$.

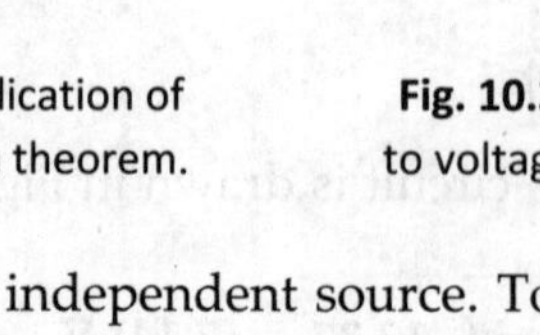

Fig. 10.4 Current due to current source only.

On the other hand, for another circuit (Fig. 10.5), it may be noted that the controlling variable V is determined by the network to be analysed. If the current source is set to zero, the drop across R would vanish and this will make $\alpha V = 0$. Thus the network would then lack of any source.

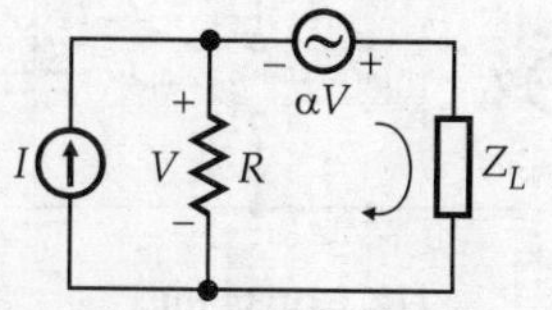

Fig. 10.5 Circuit where source variable depends on network to be analysed.

Hence, it becomes evident that the *superposition principle cannot be applied at a circuit where the dependent source existing within the circuit contains the variable determined by the network to be analysed.* However, for the circuit with dependent variable source, where the source does not depend on the network variable, the principle of superposition can be well applied.

EXAMPLE 10.32 *Find the current through $j\,3\,\Omega$ inductive reactance using the principle of superposition.*

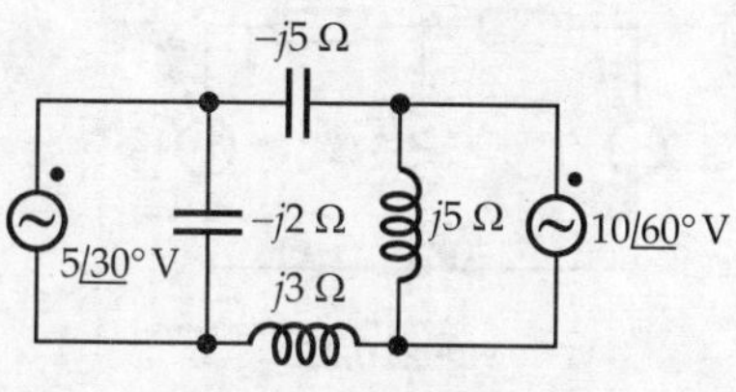

Fig. E10.32

SOLUTION. Using the principle of superposition, the given circuit is fed by each of the two sources at a time [Fig. E10.32(*a*) and (*b*)]

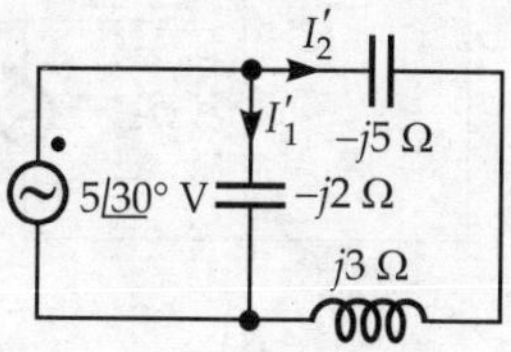

[($j5$) Ω inductive reactance gets shorted here]

Fig. E10.32 (*a*)

Here, $I_2' = \dfrac{5\angle 30°}{-j5 + j3} = \dfrac{5\angle 30°}{-j2} = 2.5\angle 30° + 90°$

$= 2.5\angle 120°$ A. [Fig. E10.31(*a*)]

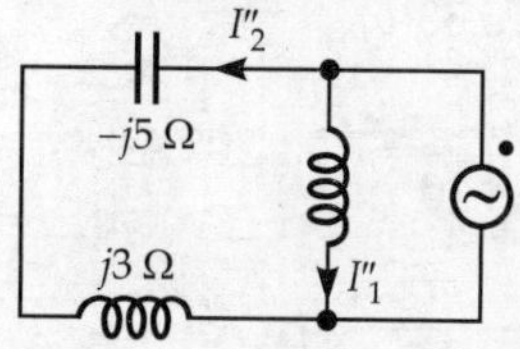

[($-j2$) Ω capacitive reactance gets shorted here]

Fig. E10.32 (*b*)

and for Fig. E10.32(*b*),

$$I_2'' = \frac{10\angle 60°}{-j\,5 + j\,3} = \frac{10\angle 60°}{-j\,2} = 5\angle 150° \text{ A}.$$

$\therefore I_2$ (following the principle of superposition),

$I_2' - I_2'' = 2.5\angle 120° - 5\angle 150°$

[$\because I_2'$ and I_2'' are directed opposite].

$= -1.25 + j\,2.165 + 4.33 - j\,2.5$

$= (3.08 - j\,0.335) = \mathbf{3.1\angle 6.2°\ A.}$

EXAMPLE 10.33 *Find, by the principle of superposition, the current through 5Ω resistor (Fig. E10.33).*

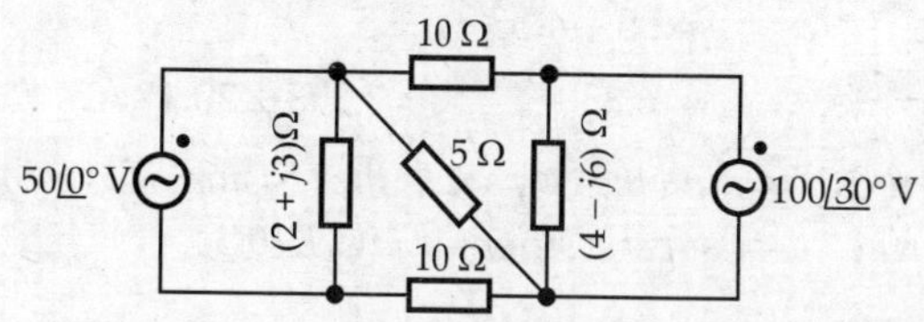

Fig. E10.33

SOLUTION. Superposition theorem is applied to the given network as shown in Fig. E10.33(*a*) and (*b*) deactivating one source at a time.

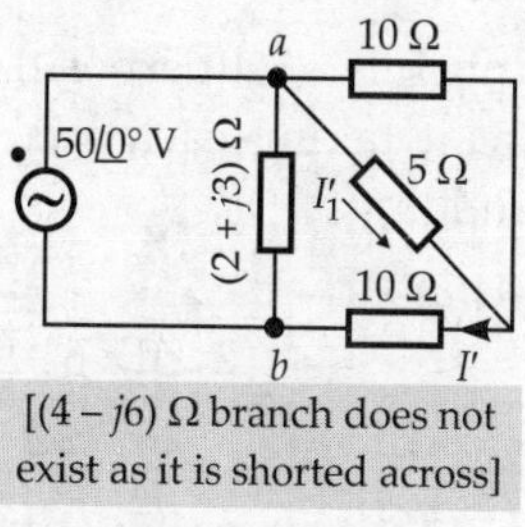

[($4 - j6$) Ω branch does not exist as it is shorted across]

Fig. E10.33 (*a*)

In Fig. E10.33(*a*)

$$I' = \frac{50\angle 0°}{(10\,||\,5) + 10} = \frac{50\angle 0°}{13.33} = 3.75\angle 0° \text{ A}.$$

$$\therefore \quad I_1' = I'\,\frac{10}{10+5} = \frac{3.75 \times 10}{15} = 2.5\ A\angle 0°.$$

CHAPTER 10

Again from Fig. E10.33(*b*),

$$I'' = \frac{100\ \angle 30^\circ}{10\,||\,5+10} = 7.5\ \angle 30^\circ \text{ A.}$$

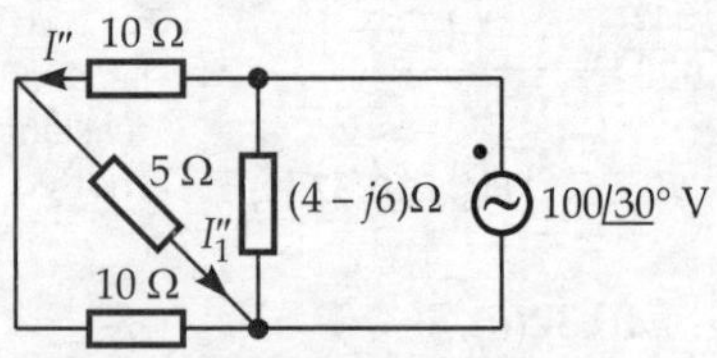

[(2 + *j*3) Ω branch does not exist as it is shorted across]

Fig. E10.33 (*b*)

This gives

$$I_1'' = I''\frac{10}{10+5} = \frac{7.5\ \angle 30^\circ \times 10}{10+5}$$

$$= 5\ \angle 30^\circ \text{ A.}$$

Thus, the current through 5 Ω resistor, using the principle of superposition is

$$I_{5\Omega} = I_1' + I_1'' = 2.5\ \angle 0^\circ + 5\ \angle 30^\circ$$

$$= 2.5 + 4.33 + j\,2.5$$

$$= (6.83 + j\,2.5) = \mathbf{7.273\ \angle 20.1^\circ\ A.}$$

EXAMPLE 10.34 *Find the current in the resistor* (R_L) *using the principle of superposition in Fig. E10.34.*

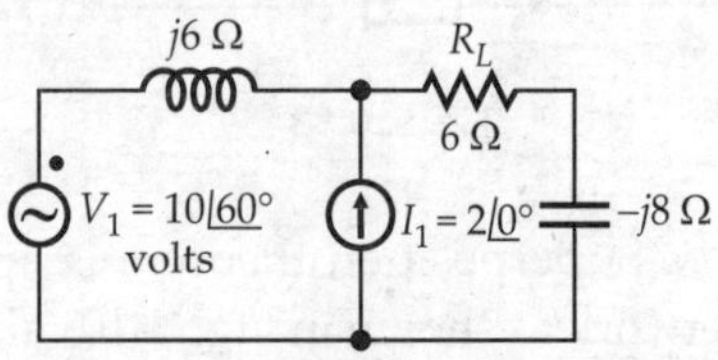

Fig. E10.34

SOLUTION. Principle of superposition is applied in the given circuit taking each source at a time [Fig. E10.34(*a*) and (*b*)].

In Fig. E10.34(*a*),

$$I_1' = I\frac{j\,6}{j6+6+(-j\,8)} = \frac{2\ \angle 0 \times 6\ \angle 90^\circ}{6-j\,2}$$

$$= \frac{12\ \angle 90^\circ}{6.32\ \angle -18.43^\circ} = 1.9\ \angle 108.43^\circ \text{ A.}$$

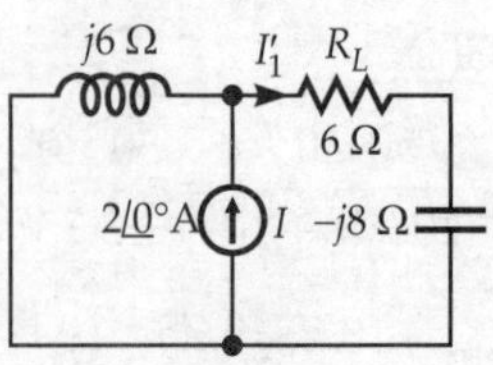

Fig. E10.34 (*a*)

On the other hand, in Fig. E10.33(*b*),

$$I_1'' = \frac{V_1}{j\,6+6-j\,8} = \frac{10\ \angle 60^\circ}{6-j\,2} = \frac{10\ \angle 60^\circ}{6.32\ \angle -18.43^\circ}$$

$$= 1.58\ \angle 78.43^\circ \text{ A.}$$

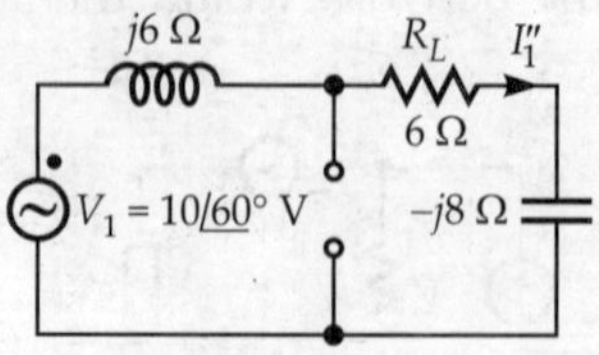

Fig. E10.34 (*b*)

∴ *I*, the total current through R_L is $I = I_1' + I_1''$ (since both are directed in the same direction)

$$= 1.9\ \angle 108.43^\circ + 1.58\ \angle 78.43^\circ$$

$$= -0.6 + j\,1.8 + 0.32 + j\,1.55$$

$$= (-0.28 + j\,3.35)$$

$$= \mathbf{3.362\ \angle 94.78^\circ\ A.}$$

EXAMPLE 10.35 *In the network of Fig. E10.35 the current flowing through the 5 Ω resistor is equal when each of the voltage sources acts separately on the circuit. What is the value of the ratio of the two sources ?*

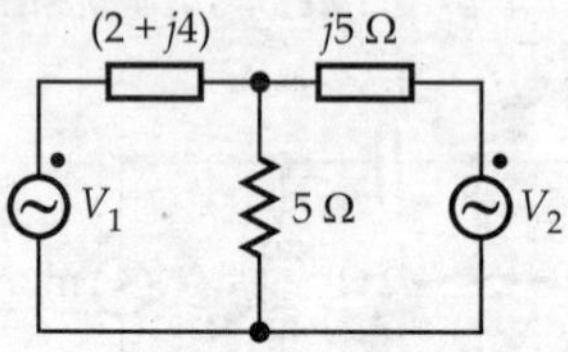

Fig. E10.35

SOLUTION. Principle of superposition is applied in the network taking each voltage source at a time [Fig. E10.35(*a*) and (*b*)].

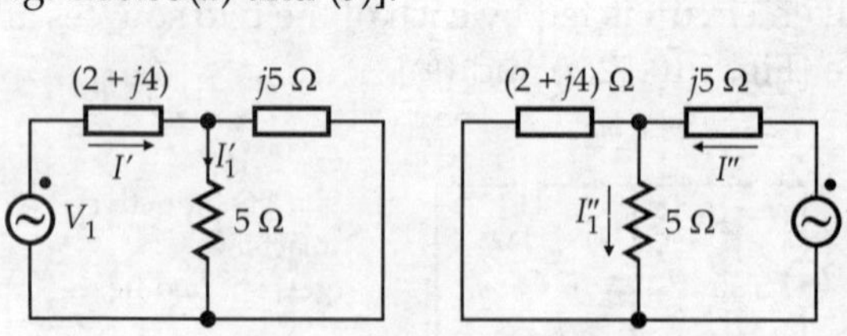

Fig. E10.35 (*a*) (*b*)

Here, in Fig. E10.35(*a*),

$$Z' = \left[\frac{j\,5 \times 5}{j\,5+5} + (2+j\,4)\right]\ \Omega,$$

where *Z′* is the impedance of the network across V_1]

$$= \frac{j\,25 + j\,30 - 10}{(5 + j\,5)} = \frac{(-10 + j\,55)}{(5 + j\,5)}$$

$$= \frac{55.9\ \angle 100.3°}{7.07\ \angle 45°} = 7.91\ \angle 55.3°\ \Omega$$

$$\therefore \quad I' = \frac{V_1}{7.91\ \angle 55.3°}\ \text{A.}$$

and $$I_1' = I' \frac{j\,5}{5 + j\,5} = \frac{V_1}{7.91\ \angle 55.3°} \times \frac{5\ \angle 90°}{7.07\ \angle 45°}$$

$$= \frac{V_1\,(5\ \angle 90°)}{55.9\ \angle 100.3°}$$

$$= V_1\,(0.0894\ \angle -10.3°)\ \text{A}$$

In Fig. E10.35(b), Z'' (impedance across V_2)

$$= \left[\frac{5\,(2 + j\,4)}{(5 + 2 + j\,4)} + j\,5\right]\ \Omega = \frac{10 + j\,20}{7 + j\,4} + j\,5$$

$$= \frac{10 + j\,20 + j\,35 - 20}{7 + j\,4} = \frac{-10 + j\,55}{7 + j\,4}$$

$$= \frac{55.9\ \angle 100.3°}{8.062\ \angle 29.75°} = 6.933\ \angle 70.55°\ \Omega$$

$$\therefore\ I'' = \frac{V_2}{Z''} = \frac{V_2}{6.933\ \angle 70.55°}\ \text{A}$$

Then

$$I_1'' = I'' \frac{(2 + j\,4)}{2 + j\,4}$$

$$= \frac{V_2}{6.933\ \angle 70.55°} \times \frac{4.47\ \angle 63.43°}{8.062\ \angle 29.75°}$$

$$= V_2\ 0.08\ \angle -36.87°\ \text{A}$$

As per the question,

$$I_1' = I_1''$$

or $$V_1\,(0.0894\ \angle -10.3°) = V_2\,(0.08\ \angle -36.87°)$$

$$\therefore \quad \frac{V_1}{V_2} = \frac{0.08\ \angle -36.57°}{0.0894\ \angle -10.3°} = 0.89 \angle -26.57°$$

Thus the ratio of the voltages is **0.89 $\angle$ – 26.57° only.**

EXAMPLE 10.36 *Obtain the steady state current through the 10 V battery in time domain in the circuit of Fig. E10.36 using superposition theorem.*

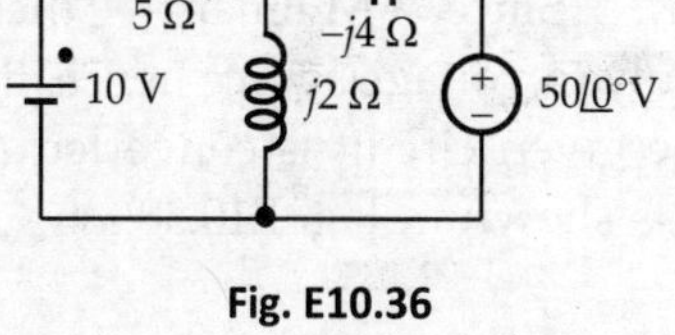

Fig. E10.36

SOLUTION. Superposition principle is applied in the circuit of Fig. E10.36 taking one source at a time as shown in Figs. E10.36 (a) and (b).

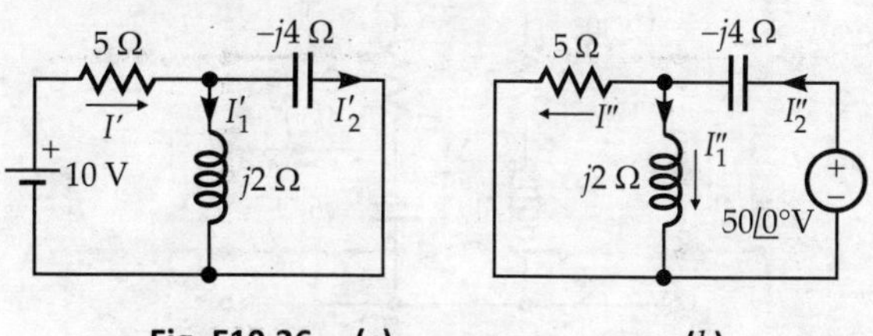

Fig. E10.36 (a) (b)

Since $j2\ \Omega$ inductive reactance would act as short circuit while $-j4\ \Omega$ capacitive reactance would act as open circuit while encountering 10 V d.c. source, the currents I_1' is equal to I' and $I_2' = 0$.

$$\therefore \quad I'\ (= I_1') = \frac{10}{5} = 2\ \text{A}$$

In Fig. E10.36(b),

$$Z'' = \frac{(j\,2\ \Omega)(5\ \Omega)}{j\,2 + 5} + (-j\,4)\ \Omega$$

where Z'' is the impedance of the circuit shown in Fig. E10.36(b) across the a.c. source.

$$\therefore \quad Z'' = \frac{j\,10}{5 + j\,2} - j\,4 = \frac{j\,10 - j\,20 + 8}{5 + j\,2}$$

$$= \left(\frac{8 - j\,10}{5 + j\,2}\right)\Omega$$

or $$Z'' = \frac{12.8\ \angle -51.34°}{5.385\ \angle 21.8°} = 2.377\ \angle -73.14°\ \Omega.$$

$$\therefore \quad I_2'' = \frac{50\ \angle 0°}{2.377\ \angle -73.14°} = 21.04\ \angle 73.14°\ \text{A.}$$

$$\therefore \quad I'' = I_2'' \frac{j\,2}{5 + j\,2}$$

or $$I'' = 21.04\ \angle 73.14° \ \frac{2\ \angle 90°}{5.385\ \angle 21.8°}$$

$$= \frac{42.08\ \angle 163.14°}{5.385\ \angle 21.8°} = 7.81\ \angle 141.34°\ \text{A.}$$

In time domain, the instantaneous value is

$$i'' = \sqrt{2} \times 7.81 \sin(\omega t + 141.34°)$$

$\therefore$ Net current through the resistor, using the principle of superposition, is

$$I = I' - i'' = 2 - 11 \sin(\omega t + 141.34°)\ \text{A.}$$

Thus, the battery current, in time domain, is

(2 – 11 sin (ωt + 141.34°) A.

CHAPTER 10

EXAMPLE 10.37 *Find the current in the* $(-j\,6\,\Omega)$ *capacitive reactance using superposition theorem in the circuit of Fig. E10.37.*

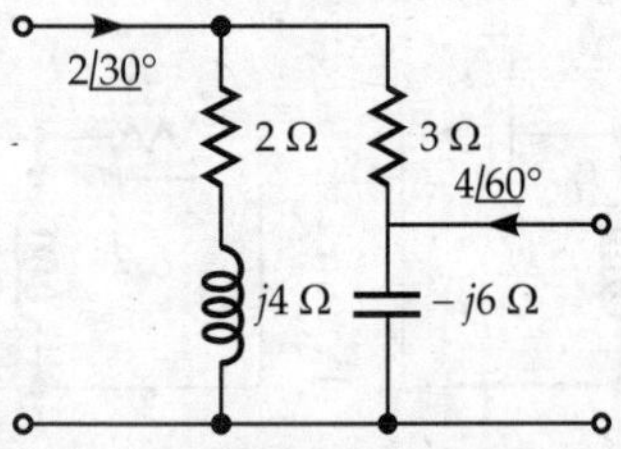

Fig. E10.37

SOLUTION. Let us apply superposition theorem [Figs. E10.37(*a*) and (*b*)] deactivating one source at a time.

$$I_2' = 2\ \angle 30° \frac{(2 + j\,4)}{(2 + j\,4) + (3 - j\,6)} \quad \text{[Fig. E10.37(a)]}$$

$$= \frac{8.944\ \angle 93.44°}{5 - j\,2} = \frac{8.944\ \angle 93.44°}{5.385\ \angle -21.80°}$$

$$= 1.661\ \angle 115.24\ \text{A.}$$

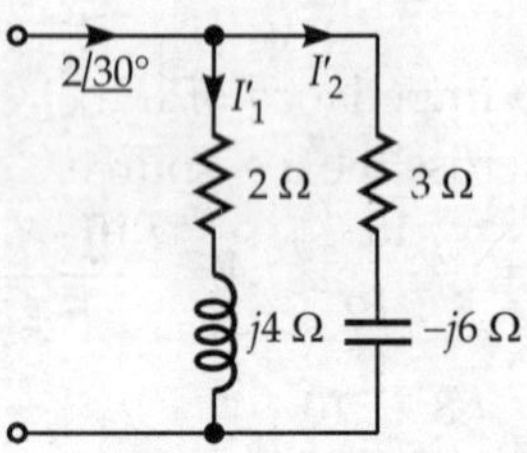

Fig. E10.37 (*a*)

In Fig. E10.37(*b*),

$$I_2'' = 4\ \angle 60° \frac{(3 + 2 + j\,4)}{(3 + 2 + j\,4) - j\,6}$$

$$= \frac{4\ \angle 60° (5 + j\,4)}{(5 - j\,2)}$$

$$= \frac{4\ \angle 60° \times 6.4\ \angle 38.66°}{5.385\ \angle -21.80°}$$

$$= 4.754\ \angle 120.46°\ \text{A.}$$

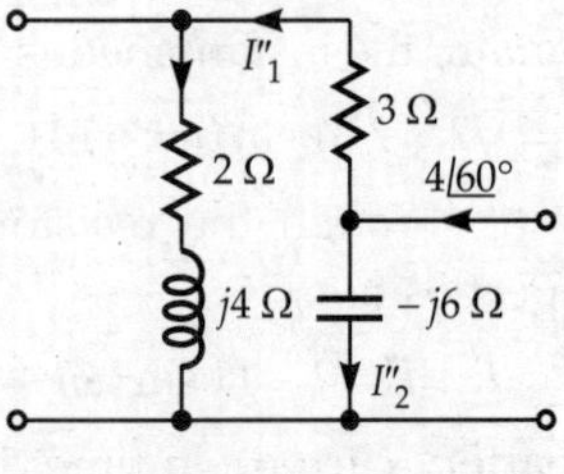

Fig. E10.37 (*b*)

Using the principle of superposition,

$$I_2 = I_2' + I_2''$$

$$= 1.661\ \angle 115.24 + 4.754\ \angle 120.46°$$

$$= -0.7083 + j\,1.5 - 2.41 + j\,4.098$$

$$= -3.118 + j\,5.598 = 6.41\ \angle 119.117°\ \text{A}$$

Thus, the current through the capacitor is **6.41 ∠119.117° A.**

10.8 MILLMAN'S THEOREM FOR AC NETWORKS

Millman's theorem states that if there are "*n*" number of voltage sources having magnitude $V_1, V_2, V_3, \ldots V_n$ having internal impedances $Z_1, Z_2, \ldots, Z_n$ respectively, then these sources may be replaced by a single voltage source V_m having equivalent series internal impedance Z_m given by the equations

$$V_m = \frac{V_1Y_1 + V_2Y_2 + V_3Y_3 + \ldots + V_nY_n}{Y_1 + Y_2 + \ldots + Y_n} \quad \ldots(10.1)$$

$$\text{and } Z_m = \frac{1}{Y_1 + Y_2 + Y_3 + \ldots + Y_n} \quad \ldots(10.2)$$

where $Y_1, Y_2, \ldots Y_n$ are the admittances corresponding to $Z_1, Z_2, Z_3, \ldots, Z_n$ (Fig. 10.6).

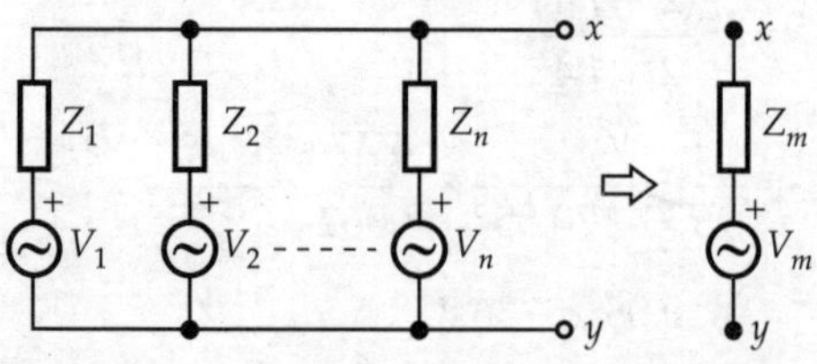

Fig. 10.6 Millman's Equivalent circuit

EXAMPLE 10.38 *Using Millman's theorem find the current in the load* Z_L *in Fig. E10.38.*

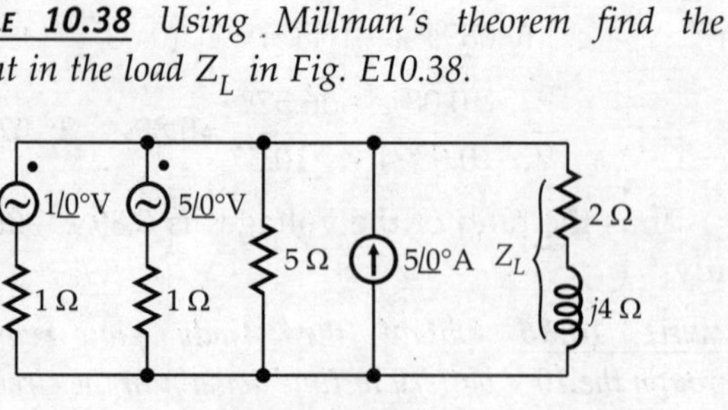

Fig. E10.38

SOLUTION. Since Millman's theorem is applicable only to voltage source hence, the current source in the given circuit is converted to voltage source first as shown in Fig. E10.38(*a*).

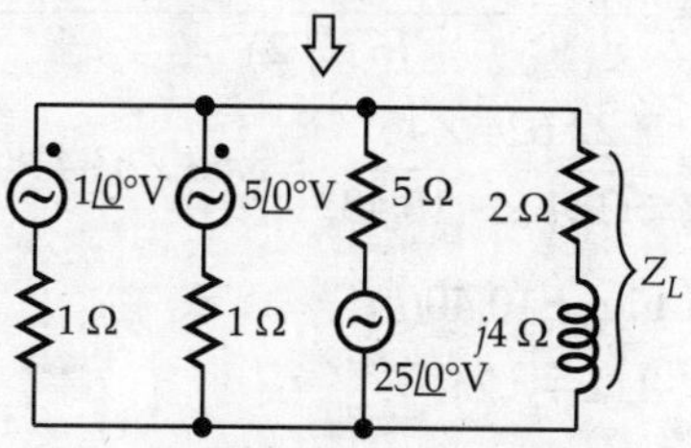

Fig. E10.38 (*a*)

As per Millman's theorem, the equivalent voltage source is given by

$$E = \frac{E_1 Y_1 + E_2 Y_2 + E_3 Y_3}{Y_1 + Y_2 + Y_3}$$

$$= \frac{1\angle 0° \times \frac{1}{1} + 5\angle 0° \times \frac{1}{1} + 25\angle 0° \times \frac{1}{5}}{\frac{1}{1} + \frac{1}{1} + \frac{1}{5}}$$

$$= \frac{1\angle 0° + 5\angle 0° + 0.2 \times 25\angle 0°}{1 + 1 + 0.2}$$

$$= \frac{11}{2.2} = 5\angle 0° \text{ V.}$$

$$\therefore \quad I_L = \frac{E}{Z_L} = \frac{5\angle 0°}{2 + j\,4} = \mathbf{1.12\angle -63.43° \text{ A.}}$$

10.9 RECIPROCITY THEOREM FOR AC NETWORK

This theorem can be stated as follows :

> *For a linear network containing generators and impedances, the ratio of a voltage V introduced in one loop to the current I produced in any other loop is the same as the ratio of voltage and current obtained if the position of voltage source V and the current measured are interchanged.*

To illustrate the reciprocity theorem, let voltage V in Fig. 10.7(*a*) produce a current I_3 in the branch having impedance Z_3. In Fig. 10.7(*b*), we just interchange the voltage source and ammeter. As per reciprocity theorem,

$$\frac{V}{I_3} = \frac{V}{I_1} \quad \text{i.e.,} \quad I_3 = I_1.$$

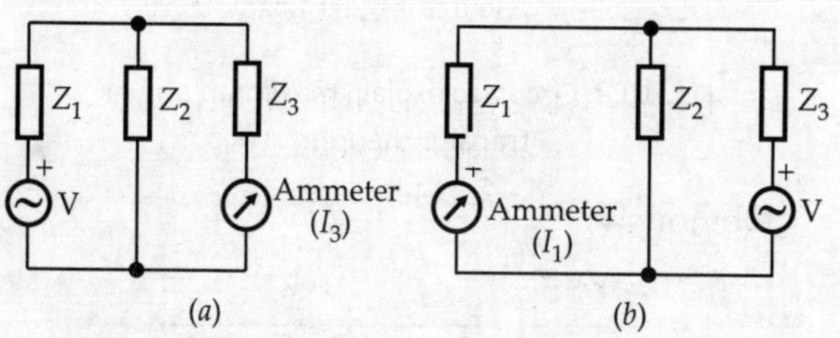

Fig. 10.7 Application of Reciprocating Theorem.

EXAMPLE 10.39 *Verify the reciprocity theorem in the circuits E10.39(a) and (b).*

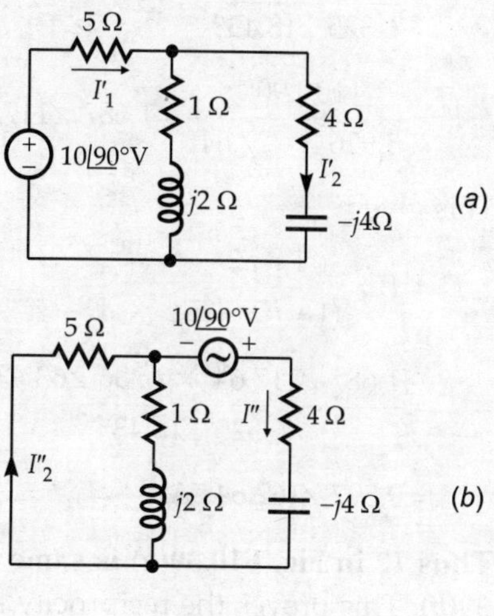

Fig. E10.39

SOLUTION. In Fig. E10.39(*a*), the impedance of the circuit across the voltage source $10\angle 90°$ V is given by

$$Z_{in} = 5 + \frac{(1 + j\,2)(4 - j\,4)}{1 + j\,2 + 4 - j\,4}$$

$$= \frac{5\,(5 - j\,2) + (1 + j\,2)(4 - j\,4)}{(5 - j\,2)}$$

$$= \frac{(25 - j\,10) + (4 - j\,4 + j\,8 + 8)}{(5 - j\,2)} = \frac{37 - j\,6}{5 - j\,2}$$

$$= \frac{37.48\angle -9.21°}{5.385\angle -21.8°} = 6.96\angle 12.59°\,\Omega$$

$$\therefore \quad I' = \frac{10\angle 90°}{6.96\angle 12.59°} = 1.437\angle 77.41° \text{ A.}$$

and $$I'_2 = I' \frac{(1 + j\,2)}{(1 + j\,2) + (4 - j\,4)}$$

$$= \frac{1.437\angle 77.41° \times 2.236\angle 63.43°}{5.385\angle -21.8°}$$

$$= 0.597\angle 162.64° \text{ A.}$$

In Fig. E10.39(*b*),

Z_{in}, the impedance across the voltage source is

$$Z_{in} = \frac{5(1+j2)}{5+1+j2} + (4-j4) = \frac{5+j10}{6+j2} + (4-j4)$$

$$= \frac{5+j10+24+j8-j24+8}{6+j2} = \frac{37-j6}{6+j2}$$

$$= \frac{37.48\angle -9.21^\circ}{6.325\angle 18.43^\circ} = 5.926\angle -27.64^\circ\,\Omega$$

$$\therefore\ I'' = \frac{10\angle 90^\circ}{5.926\angle -27.64^\circ} = 1.687\angle 117.64^\circ\text{ A}$$

This gives

$$I_2'' = I'' \times \frac{1+j2}{(1+j2)+5}$$

$$= \frac{1.687\angle 117.64^\circ \times 2.236\angle 63.43^\circ}{6.325\angle 18.43^\circ}$$

$$= 0.597\angle 162.64^\circ\text{ A.}$$

Thus I_2' in Fig. E10.39(*a*) is same as I_2'' in Fig. E10.39(*b*). This proves the reciprocity theorem.

EXAMPLE 10.40 *In Figs. E10.40(a) and (b) obtain V_0 and establish the reciprocity theorem.*

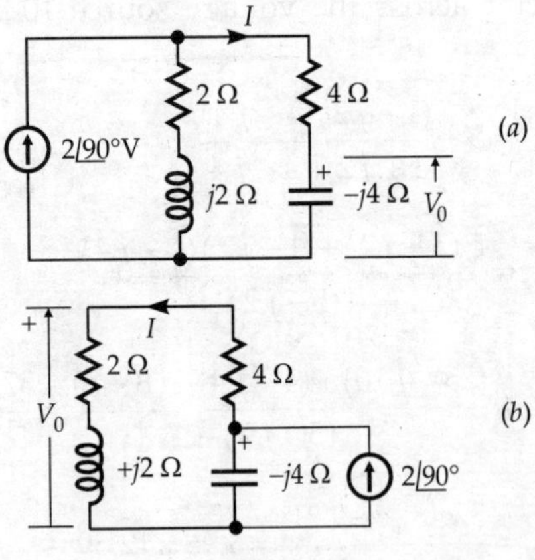

Fig. E10.40

SOLUTION. From Fig. E10.40(*a*),

$$I = 2\angle 90^\circ \cdot \frac{(2+j2)}{(4-j4)+(2+j2)}$$

$$\therefore\quad V_0 = (-j4)\,I$$

$$= (-j4)2\angle 90^\circ \cdot \frac{(2+j2)}{(4-j4)+(2+j2)}$$

$$= \frac{2\angle 90^\circ \times 4\angle -90^\circ \times 2.828\angle 45^\circ}{(6-j2)}$$

$$= \frac{22.624\angle 45^\circ}{6.324\angle -18.43^\circ} = 3.58\angle 63.43^\circ\text{ V.}$$

From Fig. E10.40(*b*),

$$V_0 = I(2+j2)$$

$$= 2\angle 90^\circ \frac{-j4}{-j4+4+2+j2}(2+j2)$$

$$= \frac{2.828\angle 45^\circ \times 2\angle 90^\circ \times 4\angle -90^\circ}{6-j2}$$

$$= 3.58\angle 63.43^\circ\text{ V.}$$

Thus we see that in both the figures, **V_0 is same with interchange of sources.** This proves the reciprocity theorem.

10.10 MAXIMUM POWER TRANSFER THEOREM IN AC CIRCUITS

In a.c. network, the maximum power transfer theorem is stated as follows :

> In a linear network having energy sources and impedances, maximum amount of power is transferred from source to load impedance if the load impedance is the complex conjugate of the total impedance of the network, *i.e.*, if the source impedance is $(R_g \pm j\,X_g)\,\Omega$, to have maximum power transfer, the load impedance must be $(R_g \mp j\,X_g)\Omega$.

To prove it, we assume a circuit (Fig. 10.8) where load impedance is Z_L and source impedance is Z_g, connected in series with the source V_g. Let I be the current through the load.

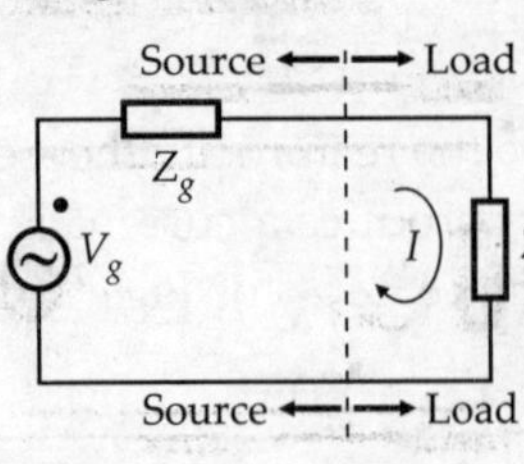

Fig. 10.8 Circuit to explain maximum power transfer theorem.

Obviously,

$$I = \frac{V_g}{Z_g + Z_L} = \frac{V_g}{(R_g + R_L) + j(X_g + X_L)}$$

$\therefore$ Power (real power) $P_L = I^2 R_L$

$$= \frac{V_g^2}{(R_g + R_L)^2 + (X_g + X_L)^2} \times R_L \qquad ...(10.3)$$

Let us first find the condition of maximum power flow from source to load when X_L is varied keeping X_g constant. This is possible when mathematically

$$\frac{dP_L}{dX_L} = 0$$

However, from (10.3),

$$\frac{dP_L}{dX_L} = \frac{d}{dX_L}\left[\frac{V^2 R_L}{(R_g + R_L)^2 + (X_g + X_L)^2}\right]$$

$$= \frac{-V^2 R_L \times 2\,(X_g + X_L)}{[(R_g + R_L)^2 + (X_g + X_L)^2]^2} \qquad ...(10.4)$$

Setting $\frac{dP_L}{dX_L} = 0$, we get from (10.4),

$$X_g = -X_L.$$

Next, substituting $X_g = -X_L$ in (10.3),

$$P_L = \frac{V_g^2 R_L}{(R_g + R_L)^2} = \frac{V_g^2}{4R_g}\left[1 - \left(\frac{R_g - R_L}{R_g + R_L}\right)^2\right] \qquad ...(10.5)$$

It may be seen that P_L would attain maximum value provided $R_g = R_L$. Thus, maximum power transfer takes place in a.c. network provided $R_g = R_L$ and $X_g = -X_L$ or in other words $(R_g + j X_g) = (R_L - jX_L)$ *i.e.,* $Z_g = Z_L^*$. This means that the load impedance is the complex conjugate of the source impedance. Consequently, the *amount of maximum power transfer becomes* $\frac{V_g^2}{4R_L}$, *the efficiency being 50 %.*

In solving the problems, the internal impedance of the network across the load is to be determined as done for problems dealing with application of Thevenin's theorem. The load impedance, for which power transfer becomes maximum is then the complex conjugate of the source impedance. Next, the open circuit voltage ($V_{o.c}$, the Thevenin's voltage) is determined across the open circuited terminals and amount of maximum power transfer is $(V_{o.c}^2 / 4\,R_L)$ watts.

EXAMPLE 10.41 *Find the load impedance in Fig. E10.41 for maximum power to the load. Find the amount of maximum power.*

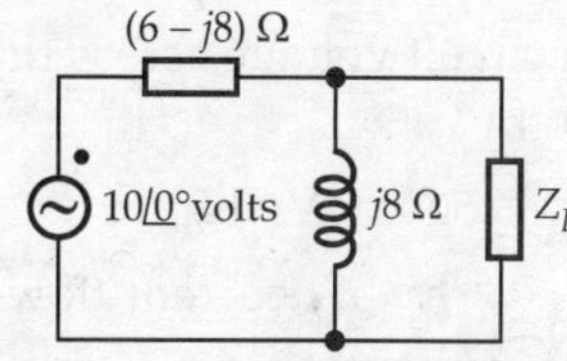

Fig. E10.41

SOLUTION. Let us remove the load impedance Z_L first. Looking back into the network through the open circuited load terminals,

$$Z_{\text{int}} = \frac{j\,8\,(6 - j\,8)}{6 - j\,8 + j\,8} = \frac{64 + j\,48}{6} = (10.67 + j\,8)\,\Omega.$$

Also, $V_{o.c}$ [Thevenin's voltage] $= I\,(j\,8)$ V

[Refer to Fig. E10.41(*a*)]

$$= \frac{10\,\angle 0°}{(6 - j\,8 + j\,8)} \times (j\,8) = 13.33\angle 90°\text{ V}.$$

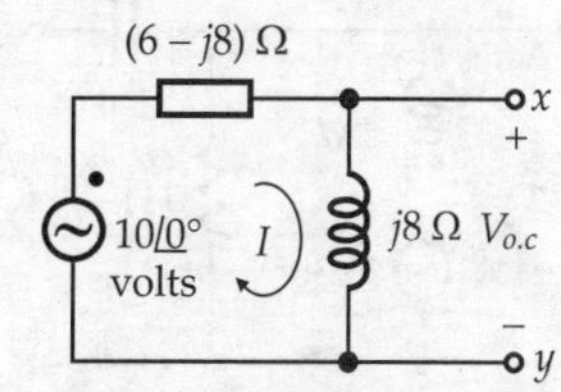

Fig. E10.41 (*a*)

As per maximum power transfer theorem, the load impedance (Z_L) must be the complex conjugate of the source impedance (*i.e.,* internal impedance Z_{int}).

i.e., $Z_L = Z_{\text{int}}^* = \mathbf{(10.67 - j8)\,\Omega}$

Maximum power is given by

$$P_{\max} = \frac{V_{o.c}}{4R_L} = \frac{13.33^2}{4 \times 10.67} = \mathbf{4.163\ W.}$$

[R_L being the resistive part of Z_L]

EXAMPLE 10.42 *Find the value of R_L in Fig. E10.42 that results in maximum power transfer and find the maximum power delivered to load.*

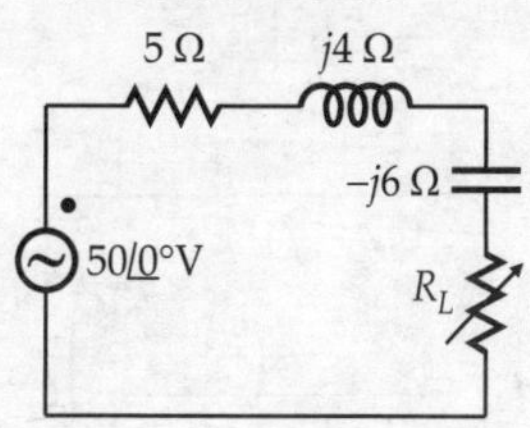

Fig. E10.42

SOLUTION. Let us remove R_L. The internal impedance of the circuit, deactivating the source, is

$$Z_{int} = 5 + j\,4 - j\,6 = (5 - j\,2)\,\Omega.$$

The open circuit voltage across the open circuit of R_L is given by

$$V_{o.c} = 50\,\angle 0°\,\text{Volts}.$$

[∵ no current flows in the loop]

As per maximum power transfer theorem, the load resistance must be equal to the source resistance

i.e., R_{Load} = real part of Z_{int} = **5 Ω.**

P_{max} (maximum power transfer)

$$= \frac{V_{o.c}^2}{4 \times R_L} = \frac{50^2}{4 \times 5} = \mathbf{125\ W.}$$

EXAMPLE 10.43 *What should be the value of R_L so the maximum power can be transferred from the source to R_L in Fig. E10.43 ?*

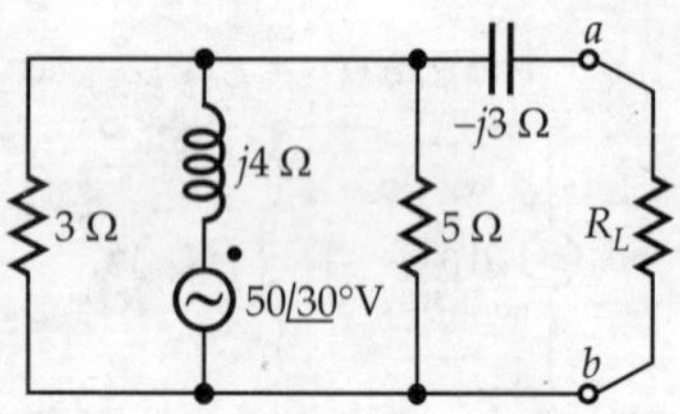

Fig. E10.43

SOLUTION. Removing R_L, deactivating the source, the internal impedance can be found out as follows [Fig. E10.43(*a*)];

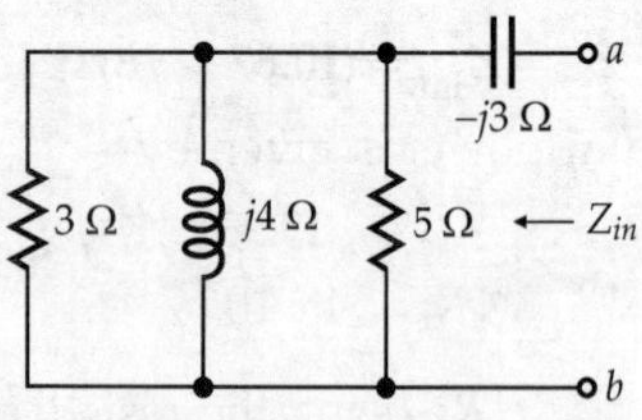

Fig. E10.43 (*a*)

$$Z_{int} = (-j\,3) + \frac{1}{\frac{1}{5} + \frac{1}{j\,4} + \frac{1}{3}}$$

$$= (-j\,3) + \frac{1}{0.2 - j\,0.25 + 0.333}$$

$$= \left[-j\,3 + \frac{1}{(0.533 - j\,0.25)}\right]\Omega$$

$$= -j\,3 + \frac{1}{0.589\,\angle -25.1°}$$

$$= -j\,3 + 1.698\,\angle 25.1°$$

$$= -j\,3 + 1.54 + j\,0.718$$

$$= 1.54 - j\,2.282 = 2.75\angle -56°\,\Omega.$$

Following Fig. E10.43(*b*),

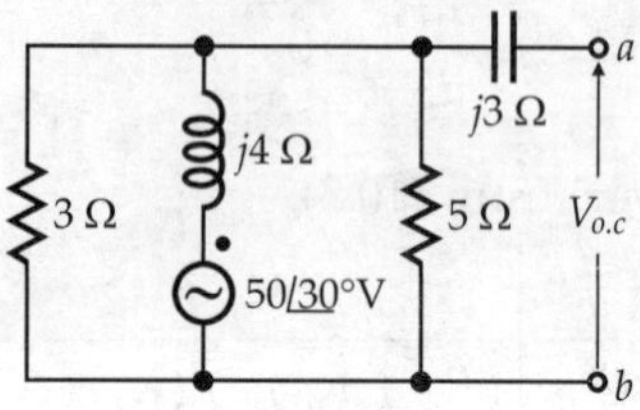

Fig. E10.43 (*b*)

Current from 50∠30° V source is

$$I = \frac{50\angle 30°}{j\,4 + \frac{5 \times 3}{5 + 3}}\,\text{A} = \frac{50\,\angle 30°}{j\,4 + 1.875}$$

$$= 11.32\,\angle -34.89°\,\text{A}.$$

$$\therefore \quad V_{o.c} = I \times \frac{5 \times 3}{5 + 3} = 11.32\,\angle -34.89° \times 1.875$$

$$= 21.225\angle -34.9°\,\text{V}.$$

Thus, maximum power transfer will take place from source to load provided R_L = real part of Z_{int} = **1.54 Ω**

$$P_{max}\ (\text{maximum power}) = \frac{V_{o.c}^2}{4R_L}$$

$$= \frac{21.225^2}{4 \times 1.54} = \mathbf{73.13\ W.}$$

EXAMPLE 10.44 *In the network of Fig. E10.44, find the value of Z_L so that the power transfer from the source is maximum. Also find P_{max}.*

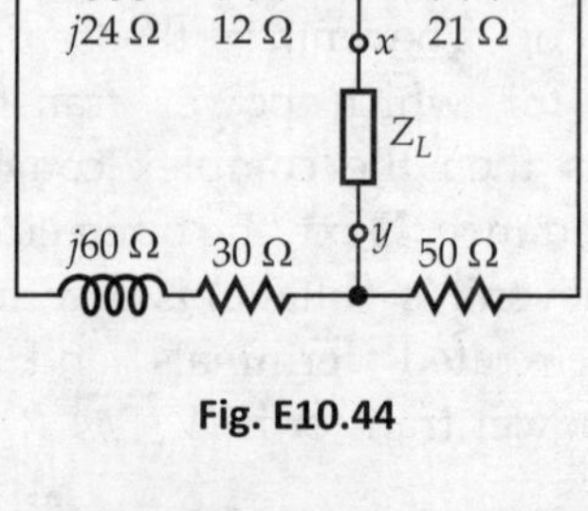

Fig. E10.44

Solution. Let us remove Z_L and the circuit is redrawn. The internal impedance of the circuit looking through *x*-*y* is given by

$$Z_{in} = \frac{21(12+j\,24)}{21+12+j\,24} + \frac{50\,(30+j\,60)}{50+30+j\,60}$$

[Refer to Fig. E10.44(*a*) where 10 $\angle 0°$ source is deactivated]

$$= \frac{252+j\,504}{33+j\,24} + \frac{1500+j\,3000}{80+j\,60}$$

$$= \frac{563.44\angle 63.43°}{40.8\angle 36°} + \frac{3354.10\angle 63.43°}{100\angle 36.87°}$$

$$= 13.81\angle 27.43° + 33.54\angle 26.56°$$

$$= (42.26 + j\,21.35)\,\Omega$$

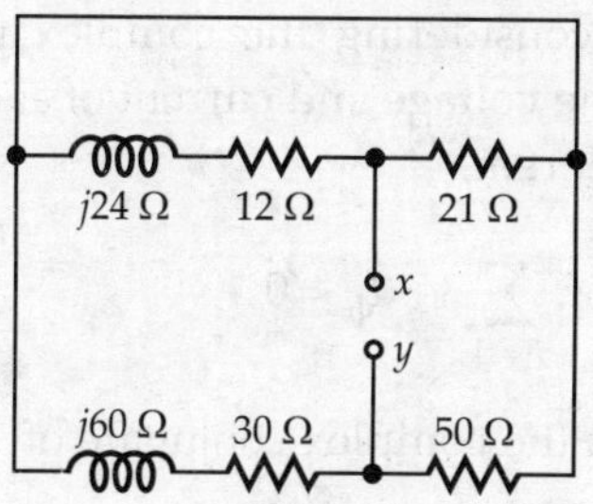

Fig. E10.44 (*a*)

As per maximum power transfer theorem, Z_L should be complex conjugate of Z_{in}.

$$\therefore \quad Z_L = Z_{in}^* = \mathbf{(42.26 - j\,21.35)\,\Omega.}$$

Next, with *x*-*y* terminal open but source present, let the voltage across *x*-*y* be $V_{o.c.}$ while potential at point *x* is V_x and potential at point *y* is V_y.

However potential

$$V_x = \frac{12+j\,24}{12+j\,24+21} \times 10\angle 0°$$

[as per voltage division formulae]

$$= \frac{268.33\angle 63.43°}{40.8\angle 36°} = 6.577\angle 27.43°\text{ V.}$$

Similarly,

$$V_y = \frac{30+j\,60}{30+j\,60+50} \times 10\angle 0°$$

$$= \frac{670.82\angle 63.43°}{80+j\,60}$$

$$= \frac{670.82\angle 63.43°}{100\angle 36.87°} = 6.71\angle 26.56°\text{ V.}$$

$$\therefore \quad V_{o.c} = V_x - V_y \text{ (vectorial)}$$

$$= 6.577\angle 27.43° - 6.71\angle 26.56°$$

$$= 5.837 + j\,3.029 - 6 - j\,3$$

$$= -0.163 + j\,0.029$$

$$= 0.1657\angle 170°\text{ V.}$$

$\therefore P_{max}$ (max. power transfer)

$$= \frac{V_{o.c}^2}{4\,R_L} = \frac{0.1657^2}{4 \times 42.16} = \mathbf{0.1624\ mW.}$$

Example 10.45 *Find the value of Z_L to have maximum power transfer from the 10 $\angle 0°$ voltage source. Also determine the amount of maximum power (Fig. E10.45).*

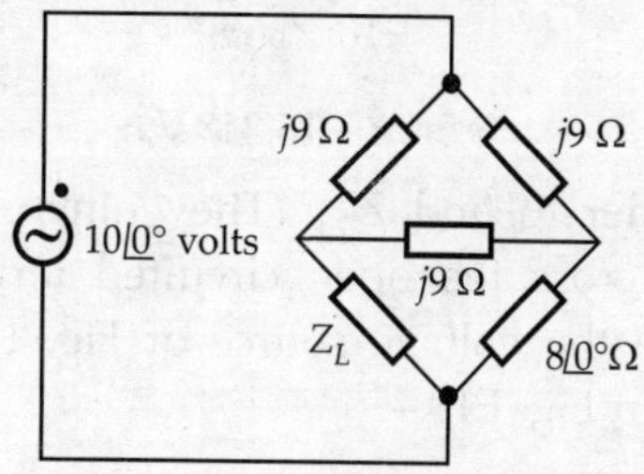

Fig. E10.45

Solution. Let us first remove Z_L and obtain the open circuit voltage ($V_{o.c}$) across the open circuited terminals [Fig. E10.45(*a*)]

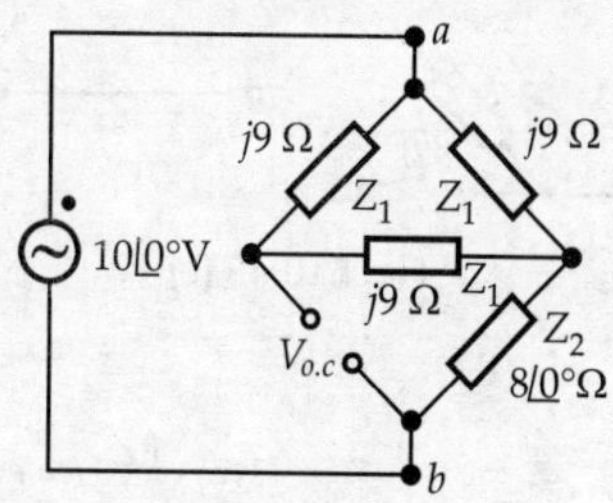

Fig. E10.45 (*a*)

Converting the three Z_1 impedance (connected in Δ) to star [Fig. E10.45(*b*)], we find

$$Z_{1(eq.)} = \frac{Z_1}{3} = \frac{j\,9}{3} = j\,3\,\Omega$$

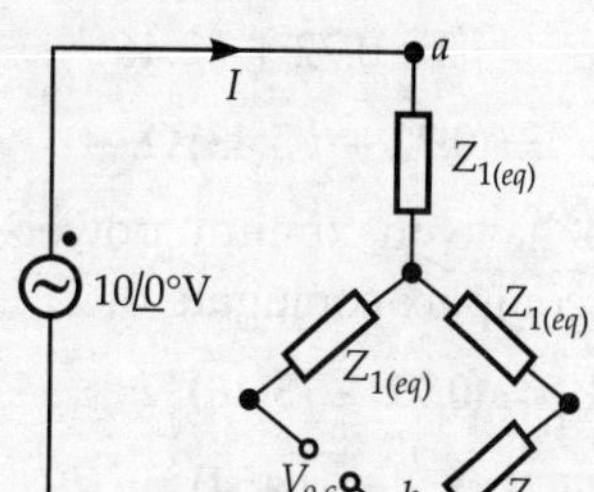

Fig. E10.45 (*b*)

Thus, in Fig. E10.45(b),

$$I = \frac{10\angle 0°}{Z_2 + Z_{1(eq)} + Z_{1(eq)}}$$

$$= \frac{10\angle 0°}{8 + j3 + j3} = \frac{10\angle 0°}{(8 + j6)} \text{ A}$$

Observation reveals that

$$V_{o.c} = \text{drop across}\,(Z_{1(eq)} + Z_2)$$
$$= I(Z_{1(eq.)} + Z_2)$$
$$= \frac{10\angle 0°}{(8 + j6)} \times (8 + j3)$$
$$= \frac{8.54\angle 20.56° \times 10\angle 0°}{10\angle 36.87°}$$
$$= 8.54\angle -16.31° \text{ V}.$$

In order to find Z_{int} (Thevenin's impedance) looking across the open circuited terminals, we deactivate the voltage source of Fig. E10.45(b) as redrawn in Fig. E10.45(c).

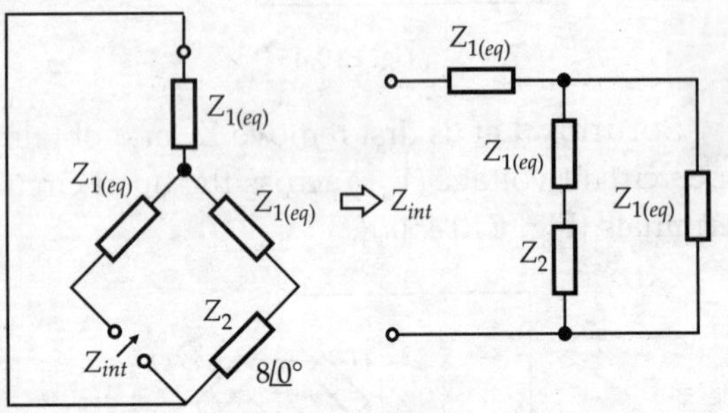

Fig. E10.45 (c)

Here

$$Z_{int} = Z_{1(eq)} + \frac{Z_{1(eq)}\,(Z_{1(eq)} + Z_2)}{Z_{1(eq)} + Z_{1(eq)} + Z_2}$$

$$= j3 + \frac{j3\,(j3 + 8)}{j3 + j3 + 8} = j3 + \frac{-9 + j24}{8 + j6}$$

$$= j3 + \frac{(-9 + j24)(8 - j6)}{64 + 36}$$

$$= j3 + 0.72 + j2.46$$

$$= (0.72 + j5.46)\,\Omega.$$

Thus, to have maximum power transfer, Z_L must be the complex conjugate of Z_{int}

i.e., $Z_L =$ **(0.72 – j5.46) Ω.**

Also, $P_{max} = \frac{V_{o.c}^2}{4R_L} = \frac{(8.54)^2}{4 \times 0.72} =$ **25.32 W.**

10.11 TELLEGEN'S THEOREM

The basic concept of the theorem being identical in d.c. or a.c. systems, for the application in a.c. systems, it can be stated as follows :

> *In any linear, non-linear, passive, active time variant network, excited by alternating sources, the summation of instantaneous or complex power of the sources is zero.*

For a network excited by sinusoidal sources, if the number of branches be "b",

$$\sum_{b=1}^{b} v_b\, i_b = 0$$

where v_b and i_b represent the instantaneous voltage and current of source at each branch.

When considering the complex power, if V_b and I_b be the voltage and current of each branch, as per this theorem,

$$\sum_{b=1}^{b} V_b\, I_b^* = 0$$

where I_b^* is the complex conjugate of I_b.

10.11.1 Proof of Tellegen's Theorem

With reference to the network shown in Fig. 10.9, let the node voltages be V_1, V_2 and V_3 at nodes 1, 2 and 3 respectively. The current directions are shown arbitrarily.

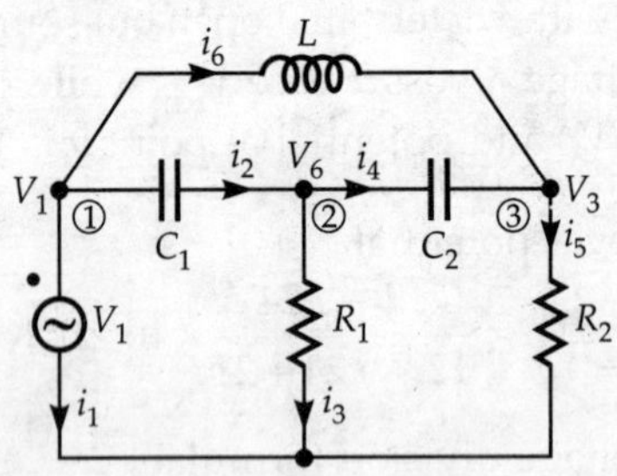

Fig. 10.9 Application of Tellegen's theorem.

The summation of instantaneous power in the network is given by

$$\sum_{b=1}^{b} v_b\, i_b = V_1 i_1 + V_{C_1} i_2 + V_{R_1} i_3 + V_{C_2} i_4 + V_{R_2} i_5 + V_L i_6$$

[where, V_{C_1}, V_{C_2}, V_L, V_{R_1} etc. indicate the respective voltages across the elements C_1, C_2, L, R_1 etc.]

or $$\sum_{b=1}^{b} v_b i_b = V_1 i_1 + (V_1 - V_2)\, i_2 + V_2 i_3 + (V_2 - V_3)\, i_4 + V_3\, i_5 + (V_1 - V_3)\, i_6$$

$$= V_1\,(i_1 + i_2 + i_6) + V_2\,(i_3 - i_2 + i_4) + V_3\,(i_5 - i_4 - i_6)$$

Application of KCL at *node (1)* reveals that $i_1 + i_2 + i_6 = 0$, at *node (2)*, $i_3 + i_4 - i_2 = 0$ and at *node (3)*, $i_5 - i_4 - i_6 = 0$.

Thus finally,

$$\sum_{b=1}^{b} v_b\, i_b = V_1 \times 0 + V_2 \times 0 + V_3 \times 0 = 0$$

Hence the theorem is proved.

EXAMPLE 10.46 *In the network shown in Fig. E10.46, $V_1 = 10$ V, $V_2 = 4$ V, $V_4 = 6$ V. Also it is given that $I_1 = 2$ A $= I_2$ while $I_3 = 4$ A. Check the validity of Tellegen's theorem.*

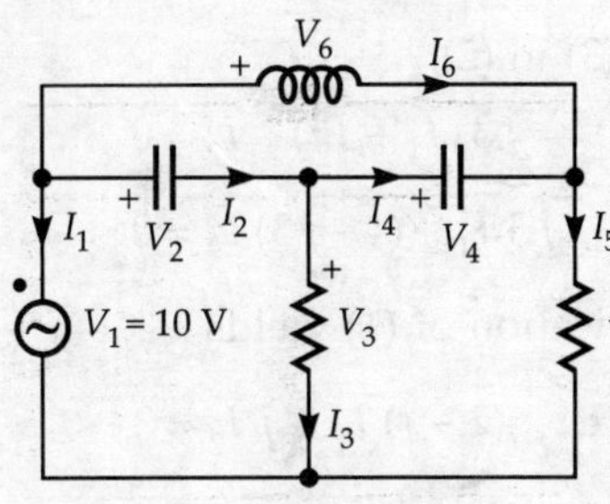

Fig. E10.46

SOLUTION. Let us redraw the given circuit with node representation [Fig. E10.46(*a*)] and loop formations.

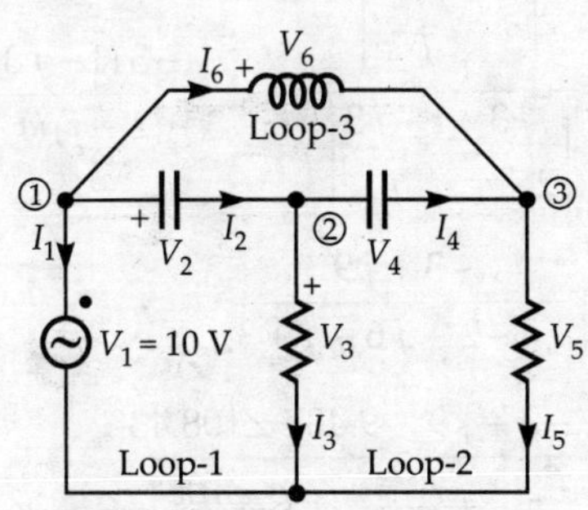

Fig. E10.46 (*a*)

In *loop-1*, KVL yields

$$-V_1 + V_2 + V_3 = 0$$

or $$V_3 = V_1 - V_2 = 10 - 4 = 6 \text{ V}.$$

In *loop-2*, KVL yields

$$-V_3 + V_4 + V_5 = 0$$

or $$V_5 = V_3 - V_4 = 6 - 6 = 0 \text{ V}.$$

Similarly, for *loop-3*, KVL yields

$$V_6 - V_4 - V_2 = 0$$

or $$V_6 = V_4 + V_2 = 6 + 4 = 10 \text{ V}.$$

Next, application of KCL at *node (1)* yields :

$$I_2 + I_1 + I_6 = 0$$

$$\therefore \quad I_6 = -I_2 - I_1 = -4 \text{ A}.$$

Also, application of KCL at *node (2)* yields

$$I_2 = I_3 + I_4$$

or $$I_4 = I_2 - I_3 = 2 - 4 = -2 \text{ A}.$$

Similarly, for node (3),

$$I_5 = I_4 + I_6 \text{ or } I_5 = -2 + (-4) = -6 \text{ A}.$$

$\therefore$ Summation of branch voltages and currents are

$$\sum_{b=1}^{b} v_b\, i_b = V_1\, I_1 + V_2\, I_2 + V_3\, I_3 + V_4\, I_4 + V_5\, I_5 + V_6\, I_6$$

$$= 10 \times 2 + 4 \times 2 + 6 \times 4 + 6 \times (-2) + (0)(-6) + 10 \times (-4)$$

$$= 20 + 8 + 24 - 12 + 0 - 40 = 0.$$

Hence the **Tellegen's theorem is Verified.**

It may be noted that for the application of Tellegen's theorem, it is also true that when voltages and currents in the network branches are measured at different instants t_1 and t_2, the set of voltage corresponding to time t_1 can be paired to the set of currents corresponding to time t_2 and vice versa.

i.e., $$\sum_{b=1}^{b} v_b\,(t_1)\, i_b\,(t_2) = \sum_{b=1}^{b} v_b\,(t_2)\, i_b\,(t_1) = 0.$$

ADDITIONAL EXAMPLES

EXAMPLE 10.47 *Find the current coming out from $150\angle 120°$ volts source in Fig. E10.47 by mesh current analysis.*

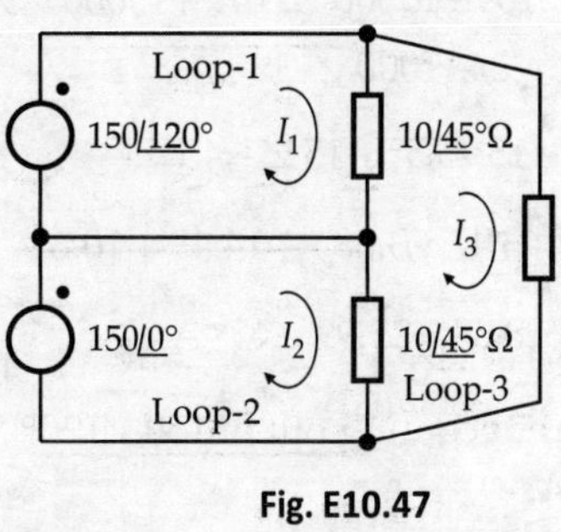

Fig. E10.47

SOLUTION. Applying mesh analysis in *loop-1,*

$$10\angle 45°(I_1)-10\angle 45°(I_3)=150\angle 120° \quad ...(1)$$

then for *loop-2,* mesh analysis gives

$$(I_2)10\angle 45°-(I_3)10\angle 45°=150\angle 0° \quad ...(2)$$

Loop analysis for *loop-3* gives

$$(-I_1)10\angle 45°+(-I_2)10\angle 45°+(I_3)30\angle 45°=0 \quad ...(3)$$

Rearranging the three equations in matrix form,

$$\begin{bmatrix} 10\angle 45° & 0 & -10\angle 45° \\ 0 & 10\angle 45° & -10\angle 45° \\ -10\angle 45° & -10\angle 45° & 30\angle 45° \end{bmatrix}\begin{bmatrix} I_1 \\ I_2 \\ I_3 \end{bmatrix} = \begin{bmatrix} 150\angle 120° \\ 150\angle 0° \\ 0 \end{bmatrix}$$

The determinant of Z of the above equation is given by

$$\Delta Z=10\angle 45°[10\angle 45°\times 30\angle 45°-10\angle 45°\times 10\angle 45°] -10\angle 45°[10\angle 45°\times 10\angle 45°]$$

$$=10\angle 45°[300\angle 90°-100\angle 90°] -10\angle 45°\times 100\angle 90°$$

$$=3000\angle 135°-1000\angle 135°-1000\angle 135°$$

$$=1000\angle 135°$$

$$\therefore I_1=I_A=\frac{\begin{vmatrix} 150\angle 120° & 0 & -10\angle 45° \\ 150\angle 0° & 10\angle 45° & -10\angle 45° \\ 0 & -10\angle 45° & 30\angle 45° \end{vmatrix}}{\Delta Z}$$

[I_A is the current coming out of 150 ∠120° V source]

$$=\frac{150\angle 120°[10\angle 45°\times 30\angle 45°-10\angle 45°\times 10\angle 45°]+(-10\angle 45°)[-10\angle 45°\times 150\angle 0°]}{\Delta Z}$$

$$=\frac{45000\angle 210°-15000\angle 210°+15000\angle 90°}{1000\angle 135°}$$

$$=45\angle 75°-15\angle 75°+15\angle -45°$$

$$=11.65+j\,43.47-3.88-j\,14.49+10.6-j\,10.6$$

$$=18.37+j\,18.38=25.99\angle 45°\text{ A.}$$

∴ The current coming out of 150 ∠120° V source is **25.99 ∠45° A.**

EXAMPLE 10.48 *Determine the values of I_1 and I_2 in Fig. E10.48 using mesh analysis.*

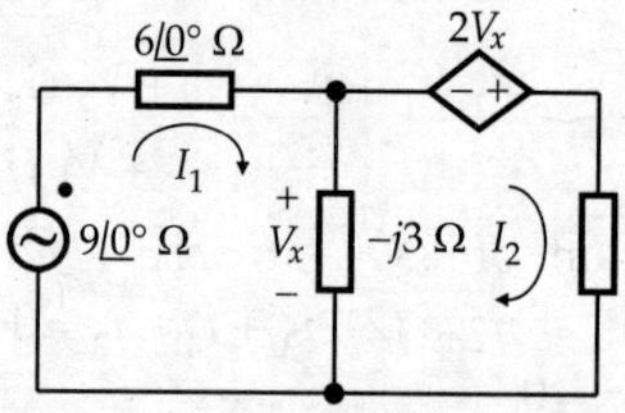

Fig. E10.48

SOLUTION. Using mesh analysis at the *left loop,*

$$6\angle 0°\times I_1-(j3)[I_1-I_2]=9\angle 0° \quad ...(1)$$

Mesh analysis at the *right side loop* yields

$$-V_x-2V_x+3\angle 0°.I_2=0$$

or $$-3V_x+3I_2=0$$

or $$-V_x+I_2=0 \quad ...(2)$$

But $$V_x=(-j3)(I_1-I_2) \quad ...(3)$$

Using (3) in (2),

$$j3(I_1-I_2)+I_2=0$$

or $$j3I_1+(1-j3)I_2=0 \quad ...(4)$$

Simplification of (1) yields

$$(2-j)I_1+jI_2=3. \quad ...(5)$$

Equations (4) and (5) can be arranged in matrix form as

$$\begin{bmatrix} j3 & 1-j3 \\ 2-j & j \end{bmatrix}\begin{bmatrix} I_1 \\ I_2 \end{bmatrix}=\begin{bmatrix} 0 \\ 3 \end{bmatrix}$$

$$\therefore I_1=\frac{\begin{vmatrix} 0 & 1-j3 \\ 3 & j \end{vmatrix}}{\begin{vmatrix} j3 & 1-j3 \\ 2-j & j \end{vmatrix}}=\frac{-3(1-j3)}{-3-(2-j)(1-j3)}$$

$$=\frac{-3+j9}{-3-2+j6+j+3}$$

$$=\frac{-3+j9}{-2+j7}=\frac{9.487\angle 108.43°}{7.28\angle 106°}$$

$$=\mathbf{1.30\angle 2.43°\ A.}$$

and $$I_2=\frac{\begin{vmatrix} j3 & 0 \\ 2-j & 3 \end{vmatrix}}{-2+j7}=\frac{j9}{7.28\angle 106°}$$

$$=\mathbf{1.24\angle -16°\ A.}$$

EXAMPLE 10.49 *Obtain the output voltage V_0 across x-y using mesh analysis in the network of Fig. E10.49.*

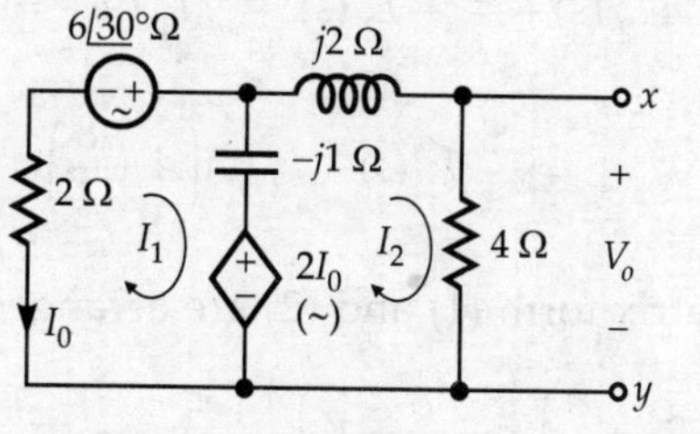

Fig. E10.49

SOLUTION. Let us first designate the mesh currents I_1 and I_2. It may be noted here that $I_0 \equiv I_1$.

Loop equation at the *left loop* is :

$$2\,I_1 + (I_1 - I_2)(-j\,1) = 6\,\angle 30° - 2\,I_0$$

or $$4I_1 - j\,1.I_1 + j.1.I_2 = 6\,\angle 30° \quad ...(1)$$

Similarly, in the *right sided loop,*

$$-I_1(-j\,1) + I_2(4 + j\,2) - 2\,I_0 + I_2(-j\,1) = 0$$

or $$I_1(-2 + j\,1) + I_2(4 + j\,1) = 0$$

$$[\because I_1 = I_0] \quad ...(2)$$

These two equations can be configured in matrix form as

$$\begin{bmatrix} 4 - j1 & j1 \\ -2 + j1 & 4 + j1 \end{bmatrix}\begin{bmatrix} I_1 \\ I_2 \end{bmatrix} = \begin{bmatrix} 6\,\angle 30° \\ 0 \end{bmatrix}$$

Here $$I_2 = \frac{\begin{vmatrix} 4 - j1 & 6\,\angle 30° \\ -2 + j1 & 0 \end{vmatrix}}{\begin{vmatrix} 4 - j1 & j1 \\ -2 + j1 & 4 + j1 \end{vmatrix}}$$

$$= \frac{6\,\angle 30\,(2 - j\,1)}{(4 - j\,1)(4 + j\,1) - (j\,1)(-2 + j\,1)}$$

$$= \frac{6\,\angle 30° \times 2.24\,\angle -26.565°}{16 + 1 + j\,2 + 1}$$

$$= \frac{13.44\,\angle 3.435°}{18 + j\,2}$$

$$= \frac{13.44\,\angle 3.435°}{18.11\,\angle 6.34°} = 0.742\,\angle -2.91$$

$\therefore V_0$ (output voltage) $= 4I_2 = \mathbf{2.96\,\angle -2.91°\ V.}$

EXAMPLE 10.50 *Using mesh current analysis, find V_2 such that the source current of V_2 is zero.*

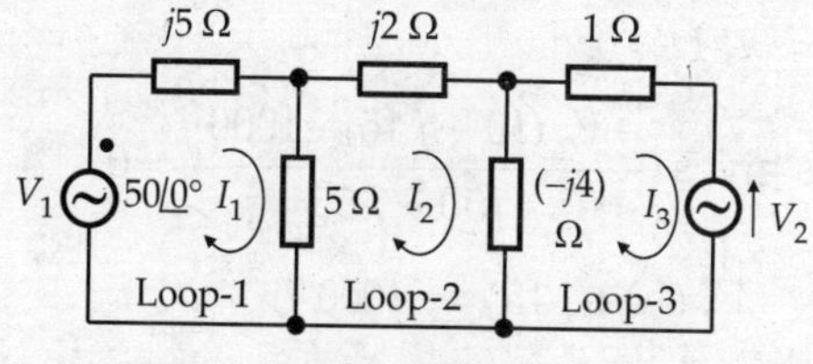

Fig. E10.50

SOLUTION. In *loop-1,* mesh analysis yields

$$(5 + j\,5)\,I_1 - 5I_2 = 50\,\angle 0° \quad ...(1)$$

Mesh analysis in *loop-2* yields

$$-5\,I_1 + [(j\,2 + \{-j\,4\}) + 5]\,I_2 - (-j\,4)\,I_3 = 0$$

or $$-5\,I_1 + (5 - j\,2).\,I_2 + j\,4\,I_3 = 0 \quad ...(2)$$

On the other hand, mesh analysis in loop-3 yields

$$-(-j\,4)\,I_2 + [(-j\,4) + 1]\,I_3 = -V_2$$

or $$j\,4I_2 + (1 - j\,4)\,I_3 = -V_2 \quad ...(3)$$

In matrix form, the three equations can be rearranged as

$$\begin{bmatrix} (5 + j\,5) & -5 & 0 \\ -5 & (5 - j\,2) & j\,4 \\ 0 & j\,4 & (1 - j\,4) \end{bmatrix}\begin{bmatrix} I_1 \\ I_2 \\ I_3 \end{bmatrix} = \begin{bmatrix} 50\,\angle 0° \\ 0 \\ -V_2 \end{bmatrix}$$

$$\therefore I_3 = \frac{\begin{vmatrix} 5 + j\,5 & -5 & 50\,\angle 0 \\ -5 & (5 - j\,2) & 0 \\ 0 & j\,4 & -V_2 \end{vmatrix}}{\begin{vmatrix} 5 + j\,5 & -5 & 0 \\ -5 & (5 - j\,2) & j\,4 \\ 0 & j\,4 & 1 - j\,4 \end{vmatrix}}$$

$$= \frac{(5 + j5)\,[\{(5 - j2) \times (-V_2)\}] + 5\,[(-5)\,(-V_2)] + 50\,\angle 0°(-j\,20)}{(5 + j\,5)\,[(5 - j2)\,(1 - j4) - j^2 16] + 5\,[(-5)\,(1 - j4)]}$$

$$= \frac{-(5 + j\,5)(5 - j2)\,V_2 + 25\,V_2 - j\,1000}{[(5 + j\,5)(-3 - j\,22 + 16) + 5\,(-5 + j\,20)]}$$

$$= \frac{V_2\,(-10 - j\,15) - j\,1000}{175 - j\,45 + j\,100 - 25}$$

$$= \frac{-V_2\,(10 + j\,15) - j\,1000}{150 + j\,55}$$

But as per the question, the current through V_2 or coming out from V_2 must be zero.

$$\therefore \quad I_3 = 0.$$

This gives $\dfrac{-V_2(10+j15)-1000j}{150+j55}=0$

or $\quad V_2(10+j15) = -1000j$

$$\therefore \quad V_2 = \frac{-j1000}{(10+j15)} = \frac{-1000\angle 90°}{18.03\angle 56.31}$$

$$= -55.46\angle 33.69° \text{ V}.$$

Thus, the value of V_2 is $\mathbf{-55.46\angle 33.69°\ V}$.

EXAMPLE 10.51 *Transform the circuit given in Fig. E10.51 to s-domain and apply mesh analysis to find the current through the dependent voltage source (in s-domain).*

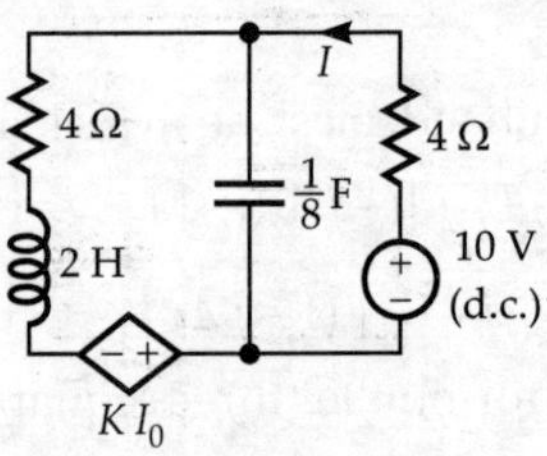

Fig. E10.51

SOLUTION. Figure 10.51(*a*) represents the s-domain form of the given circuit.

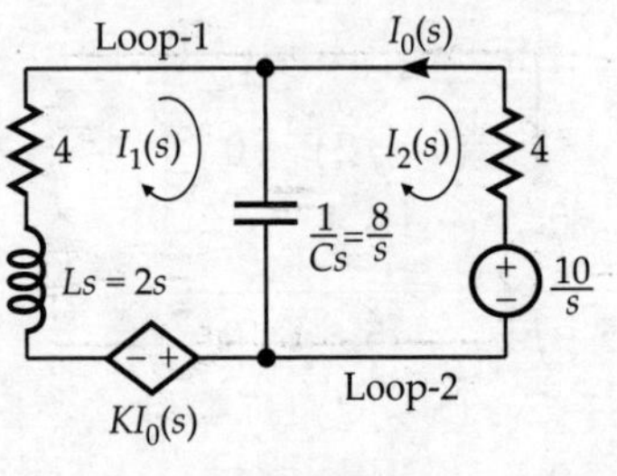

Fig. E10.51 (*a*)

In *loop-1* :

$$\left(4+2s+\frac{8}{s}\right)\ I_1(s) - \frac{8}{s}I_2(s) + K\,I_0(s) = 0$$

or $$\left(4+2s+\frac{8}{s}\right) I_1(s) - \frac{8}{s}I_2(s) - KI_2(s) = 0$$

$$[\because\ I_0(s) = -I_2(s)]$$

or $$\left(4+2s+\frac{8}{s}\right)\ I_1(s) - I_2(s)\left(\frac{8}{s}+K\right) = 0 \quad ...(1)$$

In *loop-2* :

$$4I_2(s) + \frac{10}{s} + I_2(s).\frac{8}{s} - I_1(s)\frac{8}{s} = 0$$

or $$-\frac{8}{s}I_1(s) + I_2(s)\left(4+\frac{8}{s}\right) = -\frac{10}{s} \quad ...(2)$$

In matrix form (1) and (2) are arranged as

$$\begin{bmatrix} \left(4+2s+\frac{8}{s}\right) & -\left(\frac{8}{s}+K\right) \\ -\frac{8}{s} & \left(4+\frac{8}{s}\right) \end{bmatrix} \begin{bmatrix} I_1(s) \\ I_2(s) \end{bmatrix} = \begin{bmatrix} 0 \\ -\frac{10}{s} \end{bmatrix}$$

$\therefore$ $I_1(s)$, the current through the dependent source is given by

$$I_1(s) = \frac{\begin{vmatrix} 0 & -\frac{8}{s}-K \\ -\frac{10}{s} & 4+\frac{8}{s} \end{vmatrix}}{\begin{vmatrix} 2s+4+\frac{8}{s} & -\frac{8}{s}-K \\ -\frac{8}{s} & 4+\frac{8}{s} \end{vmatrix}} = \frac{\mathbf{-10-s\left(\frac{10}{8}K\right)}}{\mathbf{s(s^2+4s+8-K)}}.$$

EXAMPLE 10.52 *Using nodal analysis, find the node voltage V_1 and V_2 (Fig. E10.52).*

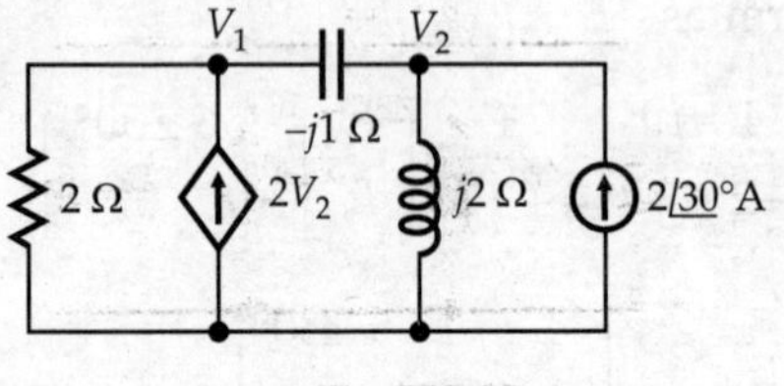

Fig. E10.52

SOLUTION. The respective nodal equations are :

$$\frac{V_1}{2} + \frac{V_1 - V_2}{-j1} - 2V_2 = 0$$

or $$\frac{V_1}{2} + \frac{V_1 - V_2}{-j1} = 2V_2 \quad ...(1)$$

and $$\frac{V_2 - V_1}{-j1} + \frac{V_2}{j2} - 2\angle 30° = 0$$

or $$\frac{V_2 - V_1}{-j1} + \frac{V_2}{j2} = 2\angle 30° \quad ...(2)$$

Simplification of equations (1) and (2) leads

$$\left(\frac{1}{2}+j.1\right)V_1 - (2+j1)V_2 = 0 \quad ...(3)$$

$$-(j.1)\,V_1 + \left(j\frac{1}{2}\right)V_2 = 2\angle 30° \qquad ...(4)$$

or
$$\begin{bmatrix} \left(\frac{1}{2}+j1\right) & -(2+j1) \\ (-j.1) & \left(j\frac{1}{2}\right) \end{bmatrix} \begin{bmatrix} V_1 \\ V_2 \end{bmatrix} = \begin{bmatrix} 0 \\ 2\angle 30° \end{bmatrix}$$

$$\therefore \quad V_1 = \frac{\begin{vmatrix} 0 & -(2+j1) \\ 2\angle 30° & j.\frac{1}{2} \end{vmatrix}}{\begin{vmatrix} \left(\frac{1}{2}+j1\right) & -(2+j1) \\ (-j1) & \left(j.\frac{1}{2}\right) \end{vmatrix}}$$

$$= \frac{(2\angle 30°)(2+j1)}{\frac{1}{2}-j1.75} = \frac{4.48\angle 56.57°}{1.82\angle -74.05°}$$

$$= 2.46\angle 130.62°\text{ V}$$

and
$$V_2 = \frac{\begin{vmatrix} \left(\frac{1}{2}+j1\right) & 0 \\ (-j1) & 2\angle 30° \end{vmatrix}}{\begin{vmatrix} \left(\frac{1}{2}+j1\right) & -(2+j1) \\ (-j1) & \left(j.\frac{1}{2}\right) \end{vmatrix}}$$

$$= \frac{2\angle 30° \times 1.12\angle 63.43°}{1.82\angle -74.05°}$$

$$= 1.23\angle 167.48°\text{ V}$$

Thus, $V_1 = \mathbf{2.46\angle 130.62°\ V}$

and $V_2 = \mathbf{1.23\angle 167.48°\ V.}$

Example 10.53 *Assuming $\alpha = \beta = 90$, $V_0 = 1\angle 0°$ V, find the voltage V_L at load node in the circuit of Fig. E10.53 using nodal analysis.*

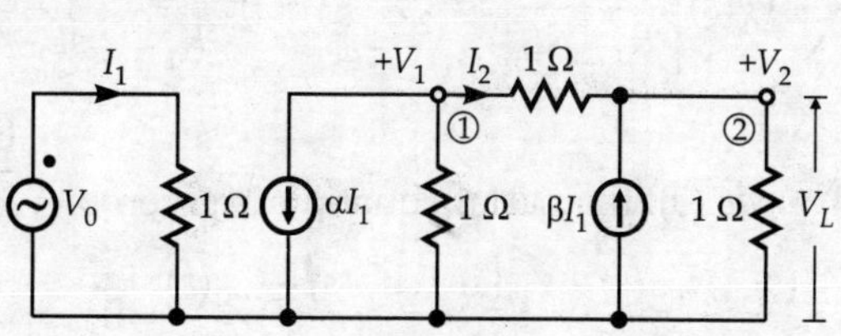

Fig. E10.53

Solution. In the left hand loop of the given circuit,

$$I_1 = \frac{V_0}{1} = 1\angle 0°\text{ A} \qquad ...(1)$$

Let us designate the nodal voltages at the right hand part of the given network designating the nodes as shown in Fig. E10.53.

By inspection, at *node (1)*,

$$\frac{V_1}{1} + \frac{V_1 - V_2}{1} + \alpha\, I_1 = 0$$

or
$$V_1(1+1) - V_2 = -\alpha\, I_1 \qquad ...(2)$$

Similarly, at *node (2)*,

$$\frac{V_2}{1} + \frac{V_2 - V_1}{1} = \beta\, I_2$$

or
$$V_2(1+1) - V_1 = \beta I_2$$

or
$$2V_2 - V_1 = \beta(V_1 - V_2) \qquad ...(3)$$

$$\left[\because\ I_2 = \frac{V_1 - V_2}{1} = (V_1 - V_2)\right]$$

Reorienting (2) and (3),

$$2V_1 - V_2 = -\alpha\, I_1 \qquad ...(4)$$

and
$$-(1+\beta)\,V_1 + (2+\beta)\,V_2 = 0 \qquad ...(5)$$

From (4) and (5),

$$V_2 = V_L$$

$$= \frac{\begin{vmatrix} 2 & -\alpha\, I_1 \\ -(1+\beta) & 0 \end{vmatrix}}{\begin{vmatrix} 2 & -1 \\ -(1+\beta) & (2+\beta) \end{vmatrix}} = \frac{\begin{vmatrix} 2 & -\alpha \\ -(1+\beta) & 0 \end{vmatrix}}{\begin{vmatrix} 2 & -1 \\ -(1+\beta) & (2+\beta) \end{vmatrix}}$$

[Since $I_1 = 1\angle 0°$ from (1)]

$$\therefore \quad V_L = \frac{-\alpha(1+\beta)}{2(2+\beta) - 1(1+\beta)} = \left[\frac{-\alpha(1+\beta)}{3+\beta}\right]$$

$$= \frac{-90 \times 91}{3+90} = -88.065\text{ V}$$

Thus $V_L = \mathbf{-88.065\ V.}$

Example 10.54 *Taking $I(s) = \dfrac{2\omega}{s^2+\omega^2}$, find $V_L(s)$ in Fig. E10.54 using Nodal analysis.*

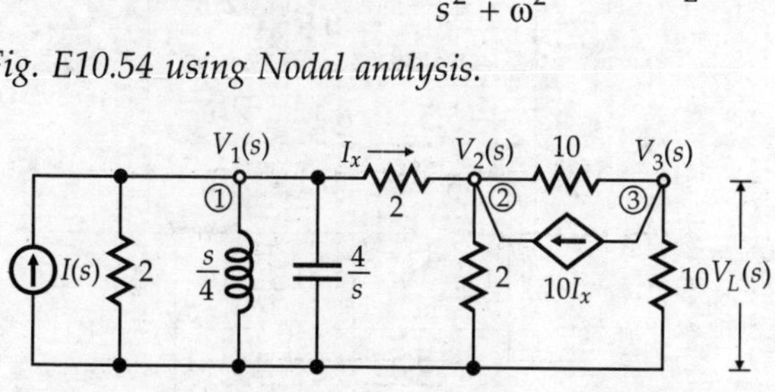

Fig. E10.54

Solution. Let us designate the voltages at the nodes marked (1), (2) and (3) as $V_1(s)$, $V_2(s)$ and $V_3(s)$.

Application of nodal analysis at node (1) yields

$$\frac{V_1(s)}{2}+\frac{V_1(s)}{\frac{s}{4}}+\frac{V_1(s)}{\frac{4}{s}}+\frac{V_1(s)-V_2(s)}{2}=I(s)$$

$$=\frac{2\omega}{s^2+\omega^2}$$

or $$V_1(s)\left[1+\frac{4}{s}+\frac{s}{4}\right]-0.5\,V_2(s)=\frac{2\omega}{s^2+\omega^2} \quad ...(1)$$

At *node (2)*, nodal analysis yields,

$$\frac{V_2(s)-V_1(s)}{2}+\frac{V_2(s)}{2}+\frac{V_2(s)-V_3(s)}{10}=10\,I_x$$

or $$-0.5V_1(s)+V_2(s)[0.5+0.5+0.1]-0.1V_3(s)=10I_x$$

or $$-0.5\,V_1(s)+1.1\,V_2(s)-0.1\,V_3(s)=10\,I_x \quad ...(2)$$

At *node (3)*, nodal analysis yields,

$$\frac{V_3(s)-V_2(s)}{10}+\frac{V_3(s)}{10}+10I_x=0$$

or $$-0.1\,V_2(s)+V_3(s)(0.1+0.1)=-10\,I_x$$

or $$-0.1\,V_2(s)+0.2\,V_3(s)=-10\,I_x \quad ...(3)$$

But $$I_x=\frac{V_1(s)-V_2(s)}{2}=0.5\,V_1(s)-0.5\,V_2(s) \quad ...(4)$$

Using (4) in (2) and (3), we get

$$-5.5\,V_1(s)+6.1\,V_2(s)-0.1\,V_3(s)=0 \quad ...(5)$$

and $$5V_1(s)-5.1\,V_2(s)-0.2\,V_3(s)=0 \quad ...(6)$$

Rearranging equations (1), (5) and (6) in matrix form,

$$\begin{bmatrix}\left(1+\frac{s}{4}+\frac{s}{4}\right) & -0.5 & 0\\ -5.5 & 6.1 & -0.1\\ 5 & -5.1 & 0.2\end{bmatrix}\begin{bmatrix}V_1(s)\\ V_2(s)\\ V_3(s)\end{bmatrix}=\begin{bmatrix}\frac{2\omega}{s^2+\omega^2}\\ 0\\ 0\end{bmatrix}$$

$$\therefore \quad V_3(s)=\frac{\begin{vmatrix}1+\frac{4}{s}+\frac{s}{4} & -0.5 & \frac{2\omega}{s^2+\omega^2}\\ -5.5 & 6.1 & 0\\ 5 & -5.1 & 0\end{vmatrix}}{\begin{vmatrix}1+\frac{4}{s}+\frac{s}{4} & -0.5 & 0\\ -5.5 & 6.1 & -0.1\\ 5 & -5.1 & 0.2\end{vmatrix}}$$

On simplification,

$$V_3(s)=\frac{-27.61\,s\,\omega}{(s^2+\omega^2)(s^2+2.31\,s+16)}=V_L(s)$$

$\therefore$ Load voltage (in *s*-domain)

$$=\frac{-27.61\,s\omega}{(s^2+\omega^2)(s^2+2.31\,s+16)}.$$

Example 10.55 *Obtain node voltage equations for the network shown in Fig. E10.55 in s-domain.*

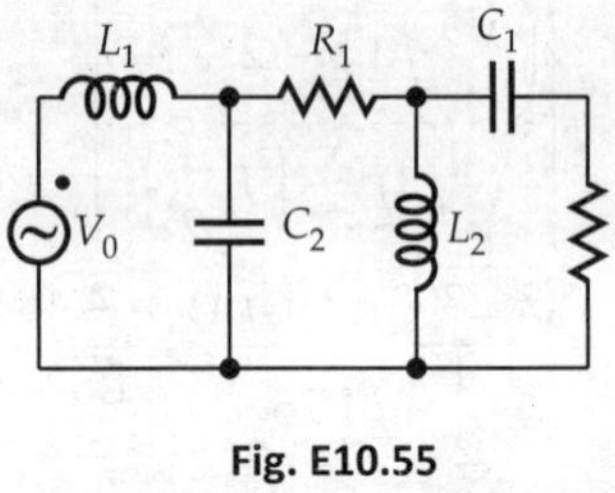

Fig. E10.55

Solution. Let us first transfer the given circuit to *s*-domain and mark the nodes and the node voltages as shown in Fig. E10.55(*a*).

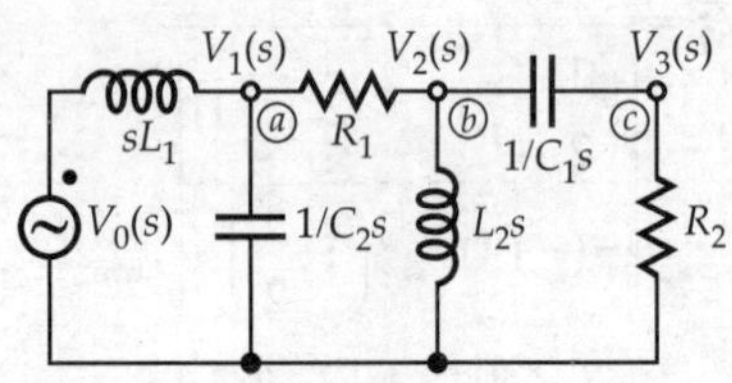

Fig. E10.55 (*a*)

At node (a), the nodal equation is given by :

$$\frac{V_1(s)-V_0(s)}{sL_1}+\frac{V_1(s)}{\frac{1}{C_2s}}+\frac{V_1(s)-V_2(s)}{R_1}=0$$

or $$V_1(s)\left[\frac{1}{R_1}+\frac{1}{sL_1}+C_2s\right]-V_2(s).\frac{1}{R_1}=\frac{V_0(s)}{sL_1} \quad ...(1)$$

At node (b), the nodal equation is given by :

$$\frac{V_2(s)}{sL_2}+\frac{V_2(s)-V_1(s)}{R_1}+\frac{V_2(s)-V_3(s)}{\frac{1}{C_1\,s}}=0$$

or $$-\frac{1}{R_1}V_1(s)+V_2(s)\left[\frac{1}{R_1}+\frac{1}{sL_2}+C_1s\right]-V_3(s).sC_1=0 \quad ...(2)$$

At node (*c*), the nodal equation is given by

$$\frac{V_3(s)}{R_2} + \frac{V_3(s) - V_2(s)}{1/C_1 s} = 0$$

or $$-C_1 s . V_2(s) + V_3(s)\left[\frac{1}{R_2} + sC_1\right] = 0 \qquad ...(3)$$

Equations (1), (2) and (3) represent the **required nodal equations.**

EXAMPLE 10.56 *In the op. amp. circuit of Fig. E10.56, find V_0 using nodal analysis.*

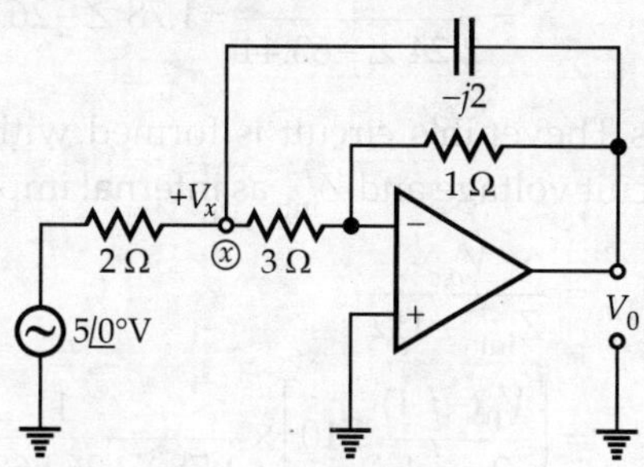

Fig. E10.56

SOLUTION. Let us assume that the node voltage at *node (x)* be V_x.

Application of nodal analysis at *node (x)* leads to

$$\frac{V_x - 5\angle 0°}{2} + \frac{V_x}{3} + \frac{V_x - V_0}{-j2} = 0$$

or $$V_x\left(\frac{1}{2} + \frac{1}{3} - \frac{1}{j2}\right) + \frac{V_0}{j2} = (5\angle 0)/2$$

or $$V_x(0.83 + j0.5) - j0.5\,V_0 = 2.5 \qquad ...(1)$$

Application of KCL at the inverting input of the op. amp.,

$$\frac{V_x}{3} + \frac{V_0}{1} = 0 \quad \text{or} \quad V_x = -3\,V_0 \qquad ...(2)$$

Substitution of V_x from (2) in (1), we get

$$-3V_0(0.83 + j0.5) - j0.5\,V_0 = 2.5$$

or $$V_0[-2.49 - j1.5 - j0.5] = 2.5$$

$$\therefore \quad V_0 = \frac{2.5}{-2.49 - j2} = \frac{2.5\angle 0°}{3.19\angle -141.23°}$$

$$= \mathbf{0.784\angle 141.23° \ V.}$$

EXAMPLE 10.57 *If $E_2 = 10\angle 0°$ V, find E_1 in Fig. E10.57 such that there is no current through the capacitor in Fig. E10.57.*

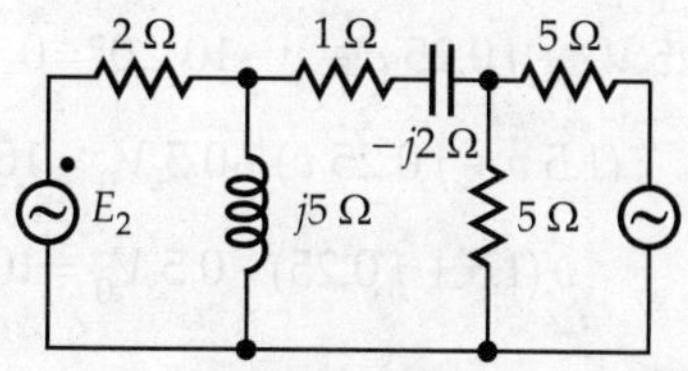

Fig. E10.57

SOLUTION. Let us redraw the circuit with capacitor branch $[(1 - j2)\Omega]$ removed. The open

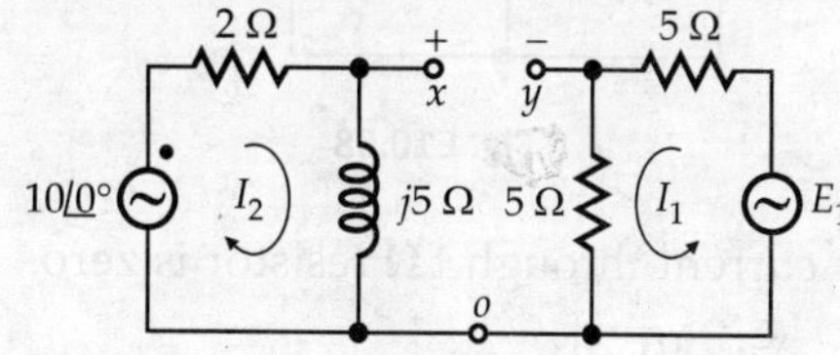

Fig. E10.57 (*a*)

circuit voltage across *x-y* is then $V_{o.c.}$ (say). In Fig. E10.57(*a*),

$$I_1 = \frac{E_1}{10\angle 0°} \text{ A.}$$

$$I_2 = \frac{10\angle 0°}{(2 + j5)\Omega} = \frac{10\angle 0°}{5.38\angle 68.198°}$$

$$= 1.86\angle -68.198° \text{ A.}$$

$$\therefore \quad V_{x-0} = I_2(j5) = 1.86$$
$$\angle -68.198° \times 5\angle 90° = 9.3\angle 21.8° \text{ V.}$$

while $$V_{yo} = I_1(5\Omega) = \frac{E_1}{10}.5 = \frac{1}{2}E_1.$$

Thus $$V_{x-y} = V_{x-0} - V_{y-0} = 9.3\angle 21.8° - 0.5E_1$$

But, since there is no current flowing through the capacitor,

$$V_{x-y} = 0.$$

Thus, $$9.3\angle 21.8° - 0.5E_1 = 0$$

or $$0.5\,E_1 = 9.3\angle 21.8°$$

i.e., $$E_1 = \frac{9.3}{0.5}\angle 21.8° = \mathbf{18.6\angle 21.8° \ V.}$$

EXAMPLE 10.58 *Find V_0 such that the current through 1Ω resistor is zero. Use Nodal analysis.*

SOLUTION. Let the potential at *node x* be *v*. Using nodal analysis,

$$\frac{v - V_0}{2} + \frac{v}{-j4} + \frac{v - 10\angle 0°}{1} = 0$$

[Fig. E10.58]

or $0.5\,v - 0.5\,V_0 + j\,0.25\,v + v - 10\,\angle 0° = 0$

or $(1.5\,v + j\,0.25\,v) - 0.5\,V_0 = 10\,\angle 0°$

or $v\,(1.5 + j\,0.25) - 0.5\,V_0 = 10\,\angle 0°$ ...(1)

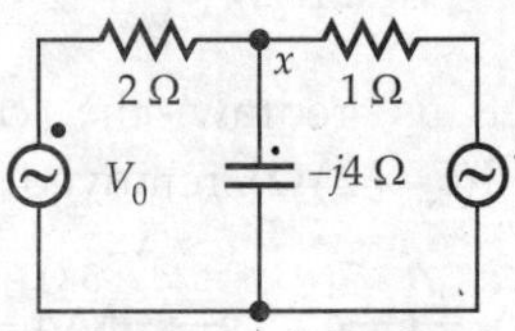

Fig. E10.58

But current through 1 Ω resistor is zero.

i.e., $\dfrac{v - 10\,\angle 0°}{1} = 0$ *i.e.,* $v = 10\,\angle 0°$

Thus from (1),

$10\,(1.5 + j\,0.25) - 0.5\,V_0 = 10$

or $15 + j\,2.5 - 10 = 0.5\,V_0$

or $V_0 = \mathbf{(10 + j\,5)\ V.}$

This problem can also be solved by Thevenin's theorem as follows :

Let us first remove the 1 Ω resistor [Fig. E10.58(*a*)],

$$I = \frac{V_0}{2 - j\,4}\ \text{A}$$

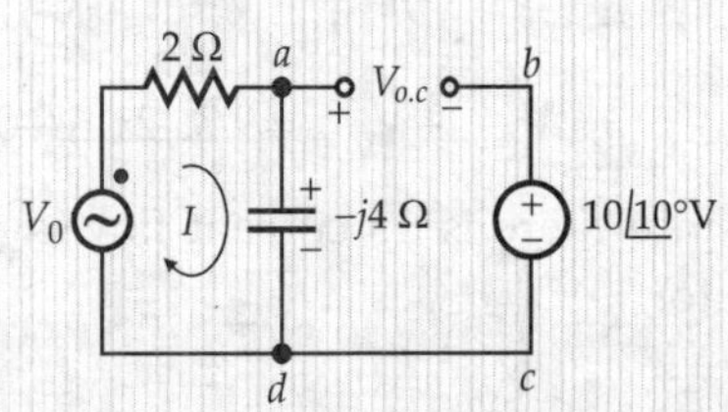

Fig. E10.58 (*a*)

$\therefore$ Drop across $-j\,4\,\Omega$ reactance

$$= I(-j\,4) = \frac{V_0\,(-j\,4)}{(2 - j\,4)}\ \text{V.}$$

In loop *abcd*,

$$-\left[\frac{V_0\,(-j\,4)}{2 - j\,4}\right] + V_{o.c} + 10\,\angle 0° = 0$$

$$V_{o.c} = \left[\frac{V_0\,(-j\,4)}{2 - j\,4} - 10\right]\ \text{V.}$$

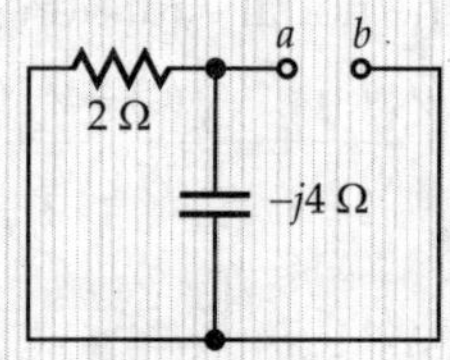

Fig. E10.58 (*b*)

In Fig. E10.58(*b*),

$$Z_{int} = Z_{ab} = \frac{-j\,4 \times 2}{-j\,4 + 2} = \frac{-j\,8}{2 - j\,4} = \frac{-j\,4}{1 - j\,2}$$

$$= \frac{4\,\angle -90°}{2.24\,\angle -63.44} = 1.78\,\angle -26.56°\,\Omega.$$

Thus Thevenin's circuit is formed with $V_{o.c}$ as open circuit voltage and Z_{int} as internal impedance.

$$\therefore \quad I_{Th} = \frac{V_{o.c}}{Z_{int} + 1\,\Omega}$$

$$= \left[\frac{V_0(-j\,4)}{2 - j\,4} - 10\right] \times \frac{1}{1.78\angle -26.56° + 1\angle 0°}$$

However, as per question, $I_{Th} = 0$,

$$\therefore \quad \left[\frac{V_0\,(-j\,4)}{2 - j\,4} - 10\right] \times \frac{1}{1.78\,\angle -26.56° + 1\,\angle 0°} = 0$$

or $$\left[\frac{V_0\,(-j\,4)}{2 - j\,4} - 10\right] = 0$$

or $$\frac{V_0\,(-j\,4)}{2 - j\,4} = 10$$

or $$V_0 = (10 + j\,5)\ \text{V}$$

as obtained above using mesh analysis.

Example 10.59 *Find Thevenin's equivalent across x-y in Fig. E10.59.*

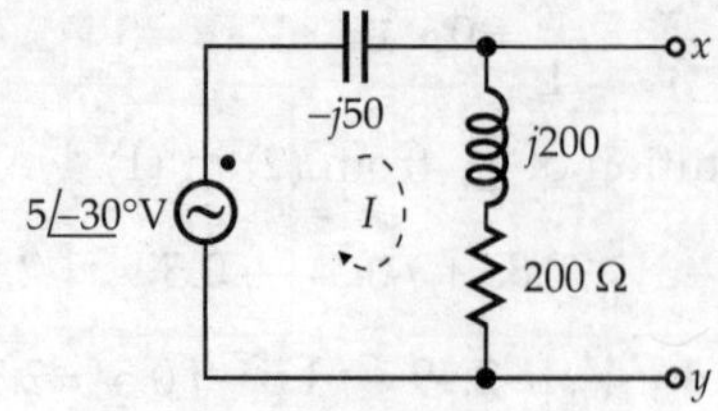

Fig. E10.59

Solution. Let us find $V_{o.c}$ *i.e.,* voltage drop across $x - y$.

Obviously, $V_{o.c} = V_{x-y} = I\,(200 + j\,200)$

where I is the circulating current in the loop as shown by dotted line.

Again $I = \dfrac{5\angle -30^\circ}{200 + j\,200 - j\,50} = \dfrac{5\angle -30^\circ}{200 + j\,150}$

$$= \frac{5\angle -30^\circ}{250\angle 36.87^\circ} = 0.02\angle -66.87^\circ \text{ A.}$$

$$\therefore \quad V_{o.c.} = [0.02\angle -66.87^\circ][200 + j\,200]$$

$$= 0.02\angle -66.87^\circ \times 282.85\angle 45^\circ$$

$$= \mathbf{5.66\angle -21.87^\circ \text{ V.}}$$

Again, the internal impedance of the circuit deactivating the source and looking from *x-y* terminal is

$$Z_{int} = \frac{(j\,200 + 200)(-j\,50)}{j\,200 + 200 - j\,50}$$

$$= (8 - j\,56)\,\Omega = \mathbf{56.57\angle -81.87^\circ\,\Omega.}$$

Figure E10.59(*a*) represents the Thevenin's equivalent circuit across *x-y*.

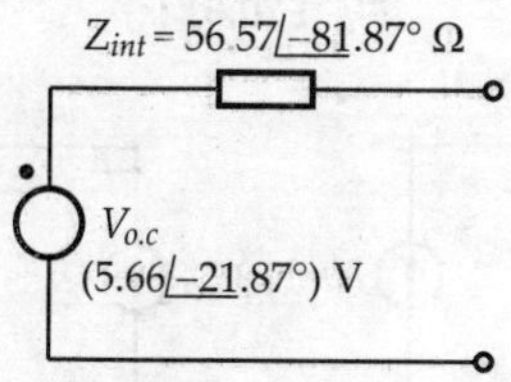

Fig. E10.59 (*a*)

Example 10.60 *Find the Norton's equivalent circuit at the left of x-y in Fig. E10.60 (the previous problem) and check the validity of the results obtained above.*

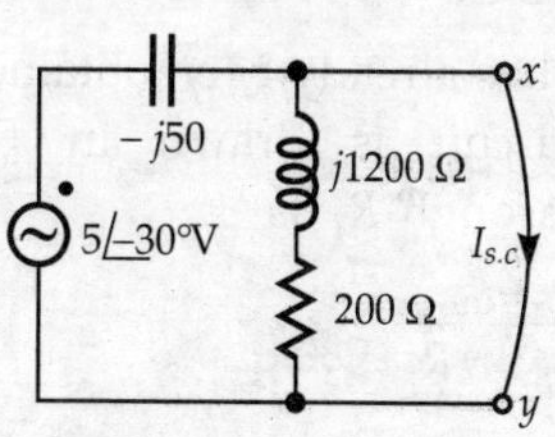

Fig. E10.60

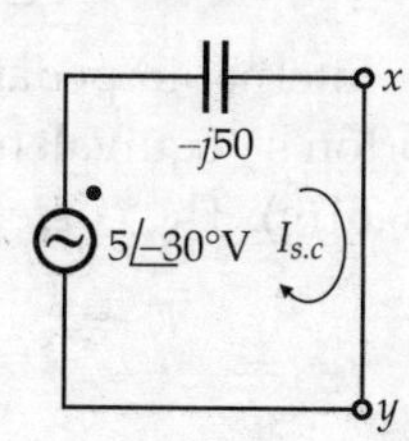

Fig. E10.60 (*a*)

Solution. Applying short circuit across *x-y*,

$$I_{s.c} = \frac{5\angle -30^\circ}{-j\,50}$$

[$\because$ no current would pass through $(200 + j\,200)\,\Omega$ branch due to shorting of *x-y*]

$$= 0.1\angle(-30^\circ + 90^\circ) = 0.1\angle 60^\circ \text{ A.}$$

[Fig. E10.60(*a*)]

As obtained in the previous problem,

$$Z_{int} = \mathbf{56.57\angle -81.87^\circ\,\Omega,}$$

Norton's equivalent circuit is drawn as shown in **Fig. E10.60(*b*).**

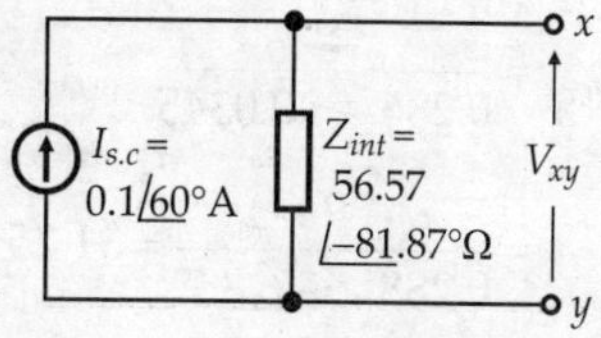

Fig. E10.60 (*b*)

To check the validity of the results of $V_{o.c.}$ obtained in the previous problem using Thevenin's theorem, observation reveals that

$$V_{o.c} = V_{x-y} = I_{s.c} \times Z_{int}$$

i.e.,

$$V_{o.c} = 0.1\angle 60^\circ \times 56.57\angle -81.87^\circ\,\Omega$$

$$= \mathbf{5.66\angle -21.87^\circ \text{ V.}}$$

(*i.e.,* $V_{o.c.}$ obtained in the previous problem.)

Example 10.61 *In the circuit of Fig. E10.61, find the current through R_L connected across x-y terminals by utilising Thevenin's theorem. Verify the result by Norton Theorem also. $I_0 = 5\angle 0^\circ$ A.*

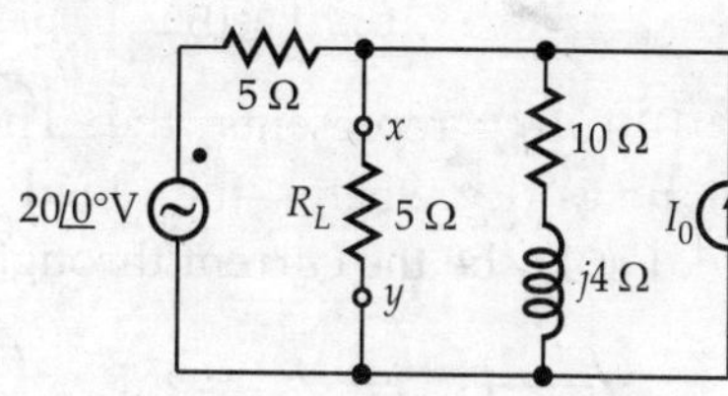

Fig. E10.61

Solution. Let us first remove the 5 Ω resistor from *x-y* [Fig. E10.61(*a*)], the voltage at node *x* being $V_{o.c.}$

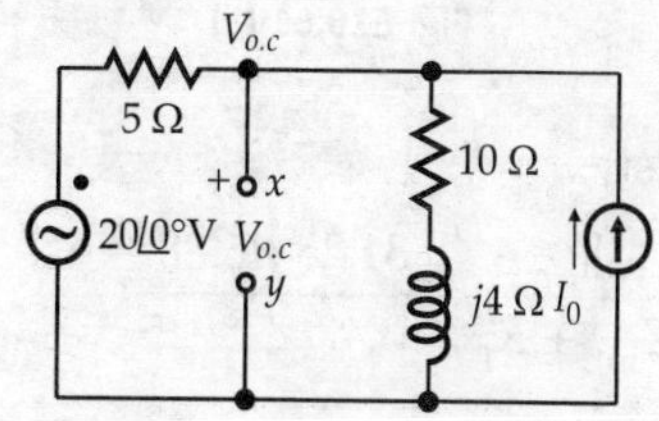

Fig. E10.61 (*a*)

Application of node analysis at node "*x*" yields

$$\frac{V_{o.c.} - 20\angle 0^\circ}{5} + \frac{V_{o.c.}}{10 + j\,4} = I_0 = 5\angle 0^\circ \text{ A}$$

or

$$\frac{V_{o.c.}}{5} - 4\angle 0^\circ + \frac{V_{o.c.}(10 - j\,4)}{116} = 5\angle 0^\circ$$

or $0.2\,V_{o.c} + 0.086\,V_{o.c} - j\,0.0345\,V_{o.c} = 5 + 4 = 9$

or $V_{o.c}\,(0.286 - j\,0.0345) = 9$

$$\therefore \quad V_{o.c} = \frac{9}{0.286 - j\,0.0345}$$

$$= \frac{9}{0.288\,\angle -6.88^\circ} = 31.25\,\angle +6.88^\circ \text{ V}.$$

The internal impedance is obtained by deactivating the voltage and current sources as shown in Fig. E10.61(*b*).

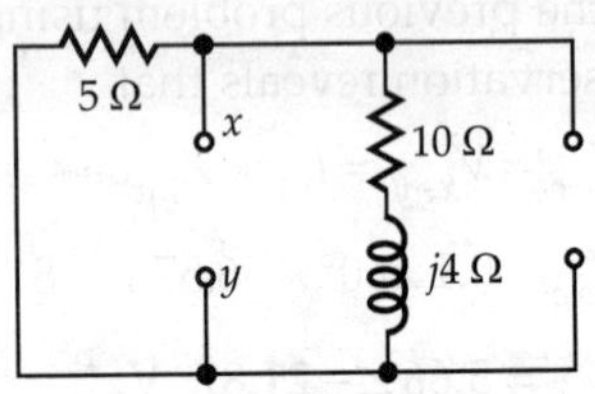

Fig. E10.61 (*b*)

$$Z_{\text{int}} \text{ (between } x - y) = \frac{5\,(10 + j\,4)}{10 + j\,4 + 5} = \frac{50 + j\,20}{15 + j\,4}$$

$$= \frac{53.85\,\angle 22^\circ}{15.52\,\angle 15^\circ} = 3.47\,\angle 7^\circ\,\Omega.$$

Figure E10.61(*c*) represents the Thevenin's equivalent network where the load R_L is reconnected. Let I_{Th} be the current through R_L.

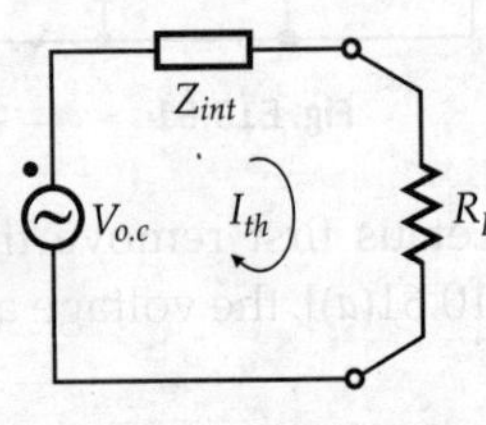

Fig. E10.61 (*c*)

Obviously,

$$I_{Th} = \frac{V_{o.c}}{Z_{\text{int}} + R_L} = \frac{31.25\,\angle 6.88^\circ}{3.47\,\angle 7^\circ + 5}$$

$$= \frac{31.25\,\angle 6.88^\circ}{8.45 + j\,0.423} = \frac{31.25\,\angle 6.88^\circ}{8.46\,\angle 2.865^\circ}$$

$$\simeq \mathbf{3.7\angle 4^\circ \text{ A.}}$$

Next, Norton's Theorem is applied to solve the network of Fig. E10.61. Let the load resistance R_L be removed from *x*-*y* terminal and *x*-*y* be shorted [Fig. E10.61(*d*)].

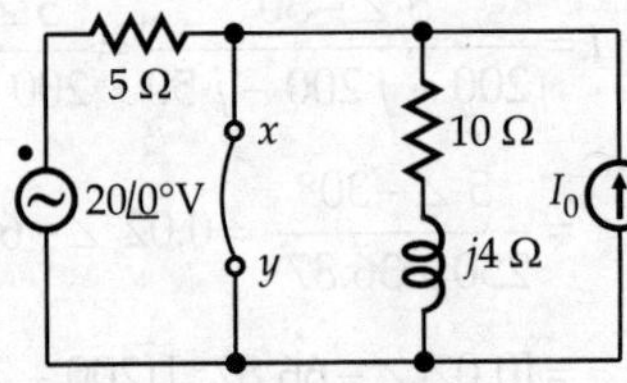

Fig. E10.61 (*d*)

To simplify the given network, let the voltage source be converted to current source [Fig. E10.61(*e*)]. The equivalent network is drawn in Fig. E10.61(*f*).

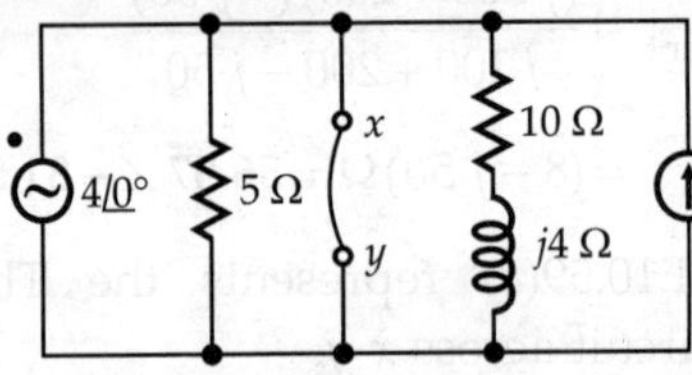

Fig. E10.61 (*e*)

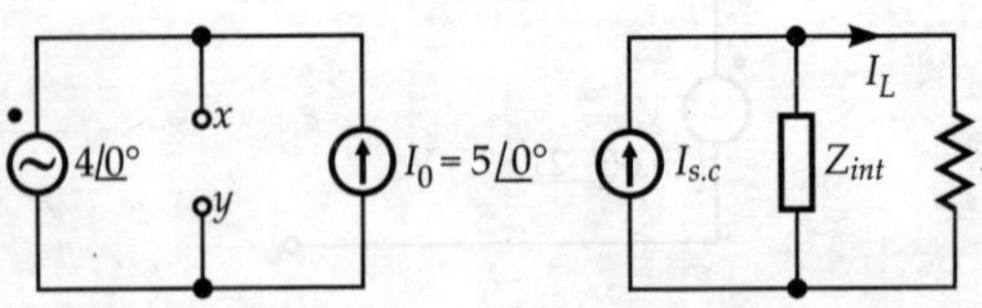

Fig. E10.61 (*f*) (*g*)

Obviously, $I_{s.c}$ (Current through shorted link)

$$= 4\,\angle 0^\circ + 5\,\angle 0^\circ = 9 \text{ A}$$

Internal impedance has already been obtained, Norton's equivalent circuit is drawn in Fig. E10.61(*g*). The current through R_L is

$$I_L = I_{s.c} \times \frac{Z_{\text{in}}}{Z_{in} + R_L}$$

$$= 9\,\angle 0^\circ\,\frac{3.475\,\angle 7^\circ}{3.475\,\angle 7^\circ + 5} \simeq \mathbf{3.7\,\angle 4^\circ \text{ A.}}$$

Thus the result obtained above has been verified.

Example 10.62 *Find I_L in the circuit of Fig. E10.62 using Thevenin's theorem.*

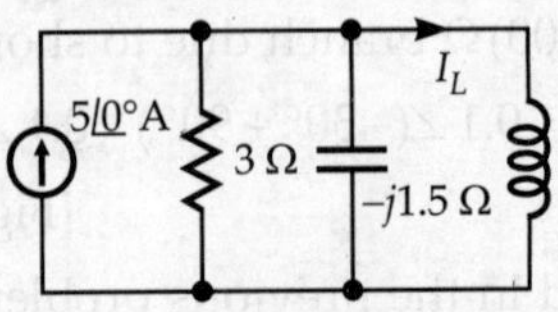

Fig. E10.62

Solution. Let us first remove the $j\,1\,\Omega$ inductive reactance, the open circuit voltage becoming $V_{o.c}$ [Fig. E10.62(*a*)].

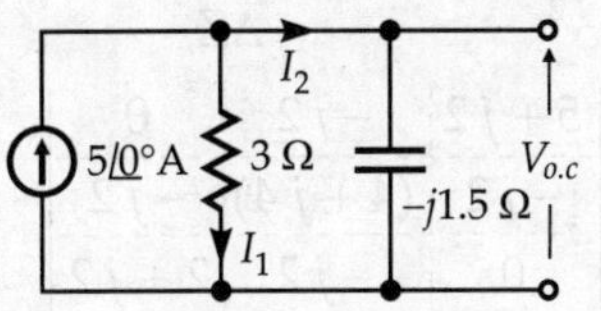

Fig. E10.62 (*a*)

Here

$$I_2 = 5\angle 0^\circ \frac{3\angle 0^\circ}{3 - j\,1.5} = \frac{15\angle 0^\circ}{3.354\angle -26.56^\circ}$$

$$= 4.47\angle 26.56^\circ \text{ A.}$$

$$\therefore \quad V_{o.c} = I_2 \times (-j\,1.5)$$

$$= 4.47\angle -26.56^\circ \times 1.5\angle -90^\circ$$

$$= 6.705\angle -116.56^\circ \text{ V.}$$

Again, to find internal impedance, the current source is removed and then following Fig. E10.62(*b*),

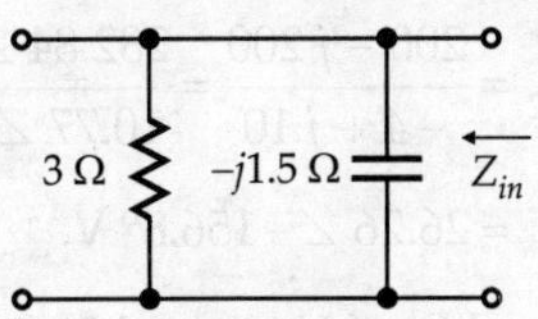

Fig. E10.62 (*b*)

$$Z_{in} = \frac{3(-j\,1.5)}{3 - j\,1.5} = \frac{-j\,3}{(2 - j)}\,\Omega$$

$$= \frac{-j\,3\,(2 + j)}{5} = \frac{3 - j\,6}{5} = \frac{6.71\angle -63.43^\circ}{5}$$

$$= 1.342\angle -63.43^\circ\,\Omega.$$

Figure E10.62(*c*) represents Thevenin's equivalent circuit.

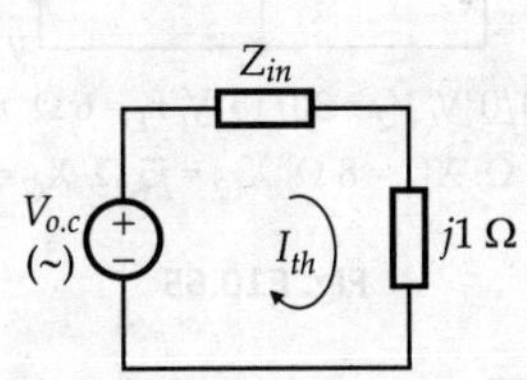

Fig. E10.62 (*c*)

Here, I_{Th} (Thevenin's equivalent current *i.e.*, the current through $j\,1\,\Omega$ inductive reactance)

$$= \frac{V_{o.c}}{Z_{in} + j\,1} = \frac{6.705\angle -116.56^\circ}{1.342\angle -63.43^\circ + j\,1}$$

$$= \frac{6.705\angle -116.56^\circ}{0.6 - j\,1.2 + j\,1} = \frac{6.705\angle -116.56^\circ}{0.6 - j\,0.2}$$

$$= \frac{6.705\angle -116.56^\circ}{0.632\angle -18.42^\circ} = 10.6\angle 98.14^\circ \text{ A.}$$

i.e., $I_L\ (\equiv I_{Th}) = \mathbf{10.6\angle -98.14^\circ\ A.}$

Example 10.63 *Obtain Thevenin's equivalent circuit across A-B terminals in Fig. E10.63, $V_S = 10\angle 0^\circ$ V.*

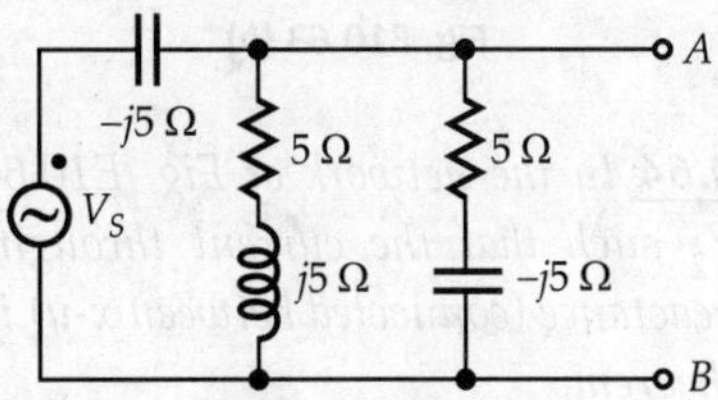

Fig. E10.63

Solution. Let the open circuit voltage at *A-B* is $V_{o.c}$ appearing with + ve polarity at *A* terminal when V_S is +ve.

Nodal analysis at *A* gives

$$\frac{V_{o.c.} - V_S}{-j\,5} + \frac{V_{o.c.}}{5 + j\,5} + \frac{V_{o.c.}}{5 - j\,5} = 0$$

or $$V_{o.c.}\left[\frac{1}{-j\,5} + \frac{1}{5 + j\,5} + \frac{1}{5 - j\,5}\right] = \frac{V_S}{-j\,5}$$

or $$V_{o.c.}\left(0.2\,j + \frac{5 - j\,5 + 5 + j\,5}{50}\right) = j\,0.2\,V_S$$

or $$V_{o.c.}\,(j\,0.2 + 0.2) = j\,0.2\,V_S = j\,0.2 \times 10\angle 0^\circ$$

$$\therefore \quad V_{o.c.} = \frac{2\angle 90^\circ}{0.2 + j\,0.2} = \frac{2\angle 90^\circ}{0.283\angle 45^\circ} = 7.07\angle 45^\circ \text{ V.}$$

The internal impedance of the given circuit can be obtained as shown in Fig. E10.63(*a*) by deactivating the source and looking back to the circuit through *A-B* terminal.

$$Z_{in} = \frac{(5 + j\,5)(5 - j\,5)}{5 + j\,5 + 5 - j\,5} - j\,5 = (5 - j\,5)$$

$$= 7.071\angle -45^\circ\,\Omega.$$

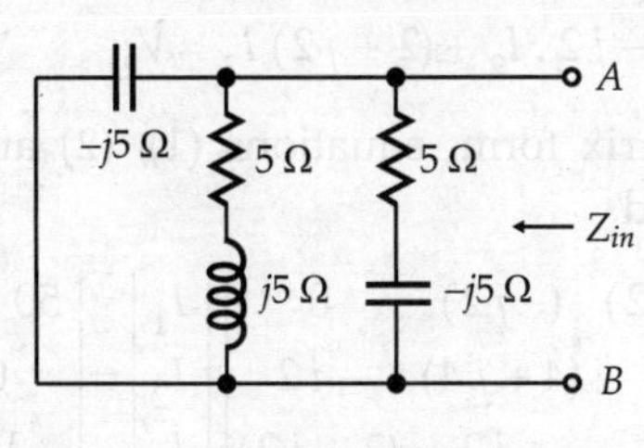

Fig. E10.63 (*a*)

CHAPTER 10

Thevenin's equivalent circuit is shown in Fig. E10.63(b)

where $V_{o.c} = 7.07 \angle 45° \text{ V}$

and $Z_{\text{int}} = 7.07 \angle -45° \Omega.$

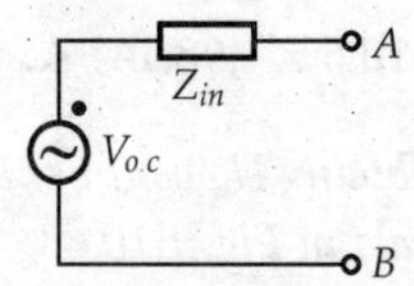

Fig. E10.63 (b)

Example 10.64 *In the network of Fig. E10.64, find the value of V_2 such that the current through the $j\,4\,\Omega$ inductive reactance (connected between x-y) is zero. Use Norton's theorem.*

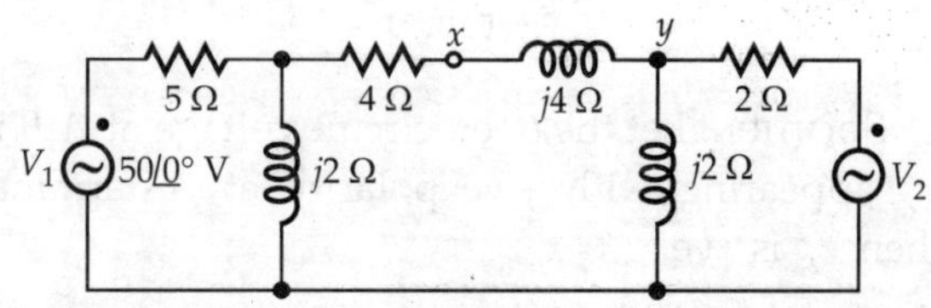

Fig. E10.64

Solution. Let us first remove the $j\,4\,\Omega$ inductive reactance and short the terminals x-y [Fig. E10.64(a)]. Let the loop currents be marked.

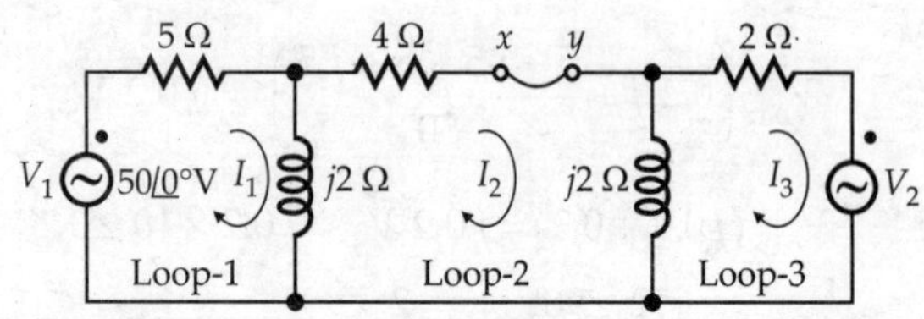

Fig. E10.64 (a)

Loop equations are as follows :

for loop-1,

$$I_1 (5 + j\,2) - j\,2 \,.\, I_2 = V_1 = 50 \angle 0° \quad ...(1)$$

for loop-2,

$$-I_1 \,.\, j\,2 + (4 + j\,4)\, I_2 - j\,2\, I_3 = 0 \quad ...(2)$$

for loop-3,

$$-j\,2 \,.\, I_2 + (2 + j\,2)\, I_3 = V_2 \quad ...(3)$$

In matrix form, equations (1), (2) and (3) are re-arranged

$$\begin{vmatrix} (5 + j\,2) & (-j\,2) & 0 \\ -j\,2 & (4 + j\,4) & -j\,2 \\ 0 & -j\,2 & (2 + j\,2) \end{vmatrix} \begin{vmatrix} I_1 \\ I_2 \\ I_3 \end{vmatrix} = \begin{vmatrix} 50 \angle 0° \\ 0 \\ V_2 \end{vmatrix}$$

$$\therefore \quad I_2 = \frac{\begin{vmatrix} 5 + j\,2 & 50 & 0 \\ -j\,2 & 0 & -j\,2 \\ 0 & V_2 & (2 + j\,2) \end{vmatrix}}{\Delta Z}$$

$$\text{where } \Delta Z = \begin{vmatrix} 5 + j\,2 & -j\,2 & 0 \\ -j\,2 & (4 + j\,4) & -j\,2 \\ 0 & -j\,2 & 2 + j\,2 \end{vmatrix}$$

$$= \frac{(5 + j2)(j2V_2) - 50\,(-j2)(2 + j2)}{\Delta Z}$$

$$= \frac{-4V_2 + j\,10\,V_2 - (4 \times 50 - j\,4 \times 50)}{\Delta Z}$$

$$= \frac{-4\,V_2 + j\,10\,V_2 - 200 + j\,200}{\Delta Z}$$

But as per the question, $I_2\ (= I_{s.c}) = 0$

This gives,

$$(-4V_2 + j\,10\,V_2 - 200 + j\,200)/(\Delta Z) = 0$$

or

$$V_2\,(-4 + j\,10) + 200\,(-1 + j\,1) = 0$$

$$\therefore \quad V_2 = \frac{200 - j\,200}{-4 + j\,10} = \frac{282.84 \angle -45°}{10.77 \angle 111.8°}$$

$$= 26.26 \angle -156.8° \text{ V}.$$

Thus, the value of V_2 would be **26.26 ∠ – 156.8°** volts so that there is no current though $j\,4\,\Omega$ inductor.

Example 10.65 *Obtain Thevenin's equivalent network for the circuit at the left of terminal x-y in the network shown in Fig. E10.65.*

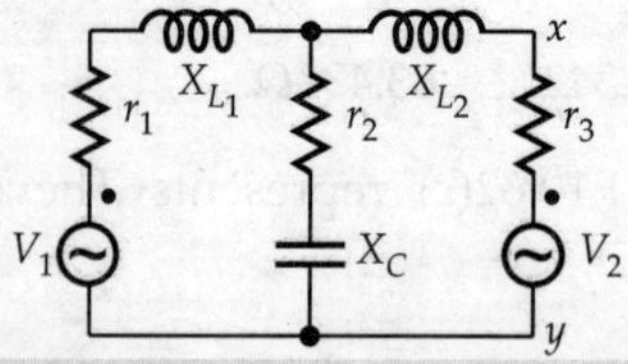

[$V_1 = 10\underline{/0°}$V, $V_2 = 30\underline{/15°}$V, $r_1 = 6\,\Omega$, $r_2 = 3\,\Omega$, $r_3 = 7\,\Omega$, $X_{L1} = 8\,\Omega$, $X_{L2} = j5\,\Omega$, $X_C = 4\,\Omega$]

Fig. E10.65

Solution. The given circuit has been reduced as shown in Fig. E10.65(a) with the branch between x-y being removed.

Here $Z_A = r_1 + j\,X_{L_1} = (6 + j\,8)\,\Omega,$

$Z_B = j\,X_{L_2} = j\,5\,\Omega,$

$Z_C = R_2 - j\,X_C = (3 - j\,4)\,\Omega.$

Inspection of the circuit in Fig. E10.65(a) reveals that

$$V_{o.c} = IZ_C = \frac{V_1}{Z_A + Z_C} \cdot Z_C$$

$$= \frac{(10\angle 0^\circ)(3 - j\,4)}{6 + j\,8 + 3 - j\,4} = \frac{10\angle 0^\circ \times 5\angle -53^\circ}{9.85\angle 24^\circ}$$

$$= \frac{50\angle -53^\circ}{9.85\angle 24^\circ} = 5.08\angle -77^\circ \text{ V.}$$

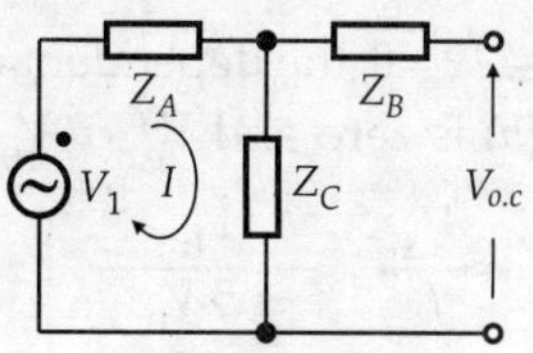

Fig. E10.65 (a)

Deactivating the constant source, the internal impedance Z_{in} is obtained as

$$Z_{in} = \frac{Z_A\,Z_C}{Z_A + Z_C} + Z_B = \frac{(6 + j\,8)(3 - j\,4)}{(6 + j\,8) + (3 - j\,4)} + j\,5$$

$$= \frac{10\angle 53^\circ \times 5\angle -53^\circ}{9.85\angle 24^\circ} + 5\angle 90^\circ$$

$$= 5.08\angle -24^\circ + 5\angle 90^\circ$$

$$= 4.64 + j\,2.95 = 5.5\angle 32.45^\circ\,\Omega.$$

Thevenin's equivalent circuit has been shown in **Fig. E10.65(b).**

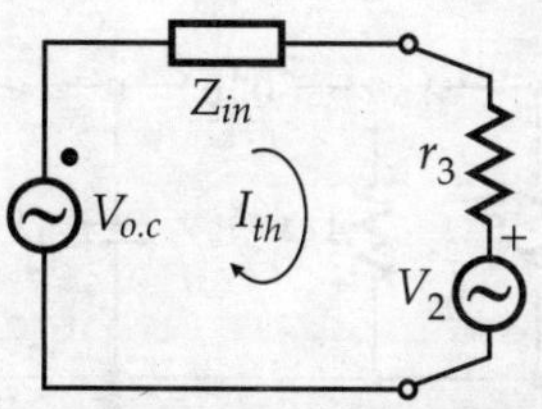

[$r_{o.c} = 5.08\,\underline{/-77^\circ}$, $Z_{in} = 5.5\,\underline{/32.37^\circ}\,\Omega$,
$r_3 = 7\,\Omega$; $r_2 = 30\,\underline{/15^\circ}$ V]

Fig. E10.65 (b)

EXAMPLE 10.66 *Find Norton's equivalent of the circuit shown in Fig. E10.66 across point x-y.*

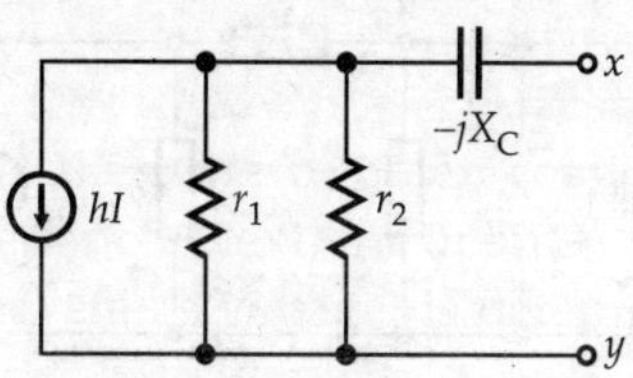

Fig. E10.66

SOLUTION. Let us short terminals x-y [Fig. E10.66(a)].

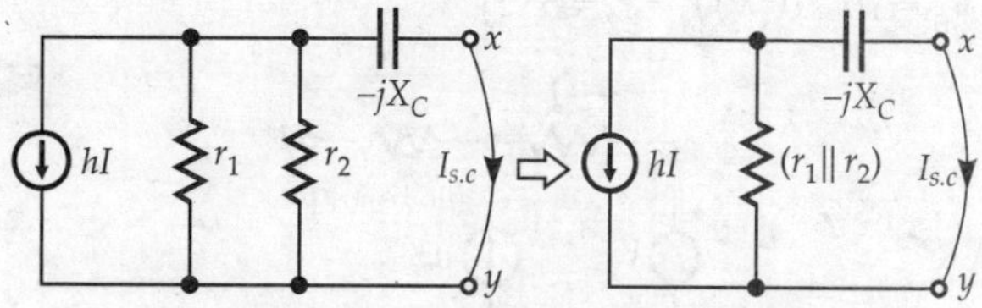

Fig. E10.66 (a)

$$I_{s.c} = (-hI)\frac{r_1 \| r_2}{(r_1 \| r_2) - j\,X_C}$$

[–ve sign with (hI) is due to opposite polarity w.r.t. $I_{s.c}$]

$$= (-h\,I)\frac{\dfrac{r_1\,r_2}{r_1 + r_2}}{\dfrac{r_1\,r_2}{r_1 + r_2} - j\,X_C}$$

$$= \frac{-hI\,(r_1\,r_2)}{r_1\,r_2 - j\,(r_1 + r_2)\,X_C}$$

The internal impedance of the given circuit can be obtained by removing the shorting link and looking into the circuit through x-y and deactivating the current source [Fig. E10.66(b)].

$$Z_{in} = (r_1 \| r_2) + (-j\,X_C) = \frac{r_1\,r_2}{r_1 + r_2} - j\,X_C$$

$$= \frac{r_1\,r_2 - j\,X_C\,(r_1 + r_2)}{(r_1 + r_2)}$$

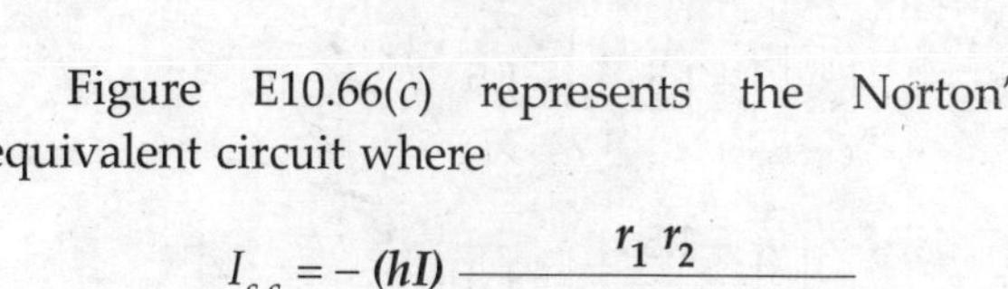

(b) (c)

Fig. E10.66

Figure E10.66(c) represents the Norton's equivalent circuit where

$$I_{s.c} = -\,(\boldsymbol{hI})\,\frac{r_1\,r_2}{r_1 r_2 - j\,(r_1 + r_2)\,X_C}$$

and $$Z_{in} = \frac{r_1\,r_2 - j\,X_C\,(r_1 + r_2)}{(r_1 + r_2)}$$

EXAMPLE 10.67 *Find Norton's equivalent circuit of the network shown in Fig. E10.67 across terminals 1-2.* [$V_0 = 10\ \angle 0°\ V; r_1 = r_2 = 5\,\Omega$]

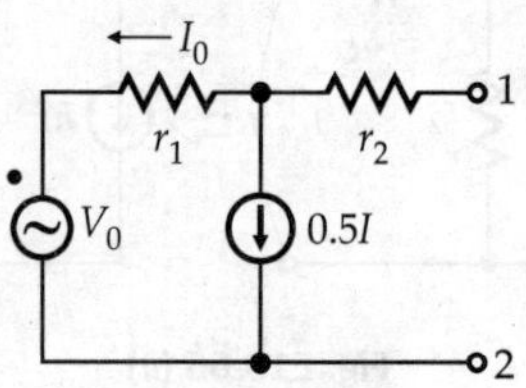

Fig. E10.67

SOLUTION. Let us first apply short circuit across 1-2 terminals [Fig. E10.67(*a*)]

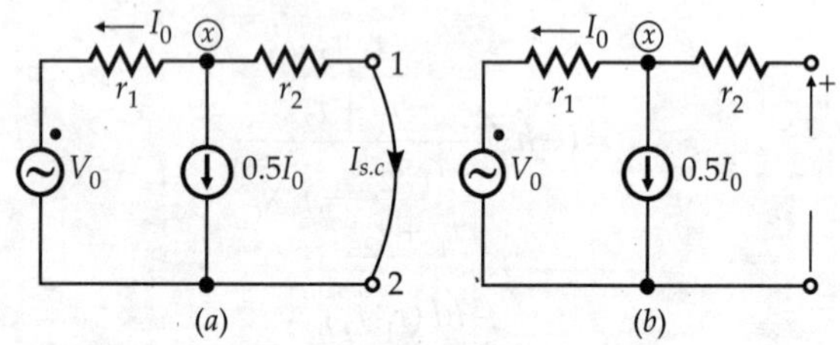

Fig. E10.67

Applying KCL at *node (x)*,

$$I_0 + 0.5\, I_0 + I_{s.c} = 0$$

or
$$I_{s.c} = -1.5\, I_0 \quad ...(1)$$

Applying KVL in the outer loop,

$$I_0\, r_1 + V_0 - I_{s.c}\, r_2 = 0$$

or
$$I_0 = \frac{I_{s.c}\, r_2 - V_0}{r_1} \quad ...(2)$$

Using (2) in (1),

$$I_{s.c} = -1.5\, \frac{I_{s.c}\, r_2 - V_0}{r_1}$$

or
$$I_{s.c} = -1.5\, \frac{I_{s.c} \cdot r_2}{r_1} + 1.5\, \frac{V_0}{r_1}$$

or
$$I_{s.c}\left(1 + 1.5\, \frac{r_2}{r_1}\right) = 1.5\, \frac{V_0}{r_1}$$

or
$$I_{s.c}\left(\frac{r_1 + 1.5\, r_2}{r_1}\right) = 1.5\, \frac{V_0}{r_1}$$

or
$$I_{s.c} = \frac{1.5\, V_0}{r_1 + 1.5\, r_2} = I_{\text{Norton}}.$$

Next, due to presence of dependent source, Z_{in} (internal impedance) of the given circuit is to be determined as follows :

> let the output terminals (1-2) be opened such that output voltage = $V_{o.c.}$

At *node (x)*,

$$0 = I_0 + 0.5\, I_0 = 1.5\, I_0$$

$$\therefore \quad I_0 = 0.$$

As soon as, $I_0 = 0$, the dependent current source in Fig. E10.67(*b*) is zero and $V_{o.c.} \equiv V_0$.

Thus,
$$Z_{in} = \frac{V_{o.c}}{I_{s.c}} = \frac{V_0}{\dfrac{1.5\, V_0}{r_1 + 1.5\, r_2}}$$

$$= \frac{1}{1.5} \times \frac{r_1 + 1.5\, r_2}{1} = \frac{r_1 + 1.5\, r_2}{1.5}.$$

Thus Norton's equivalent circuit now can be formulated where

$$I_{s.c.} = I_N = \frac{1.5\, V_0}{r_1 + 1.5\, r_2} = \frac{1.5 \times 10}{5 + 1.5 \times 5}$$

$$= \mathbf{1.2A\ \angle 0°\ A.}$$

and
$$Z_{in} = \frac{r_1 + 1.5\, r_2}{1.5} = \mathbf{8.33\ \Omega\ (resistive).}$$

EXAMPLE 10.68 *Find the current through the* 5 Ω *resistor in the network of Fig. E10.68 using Thevenin's theorem.*

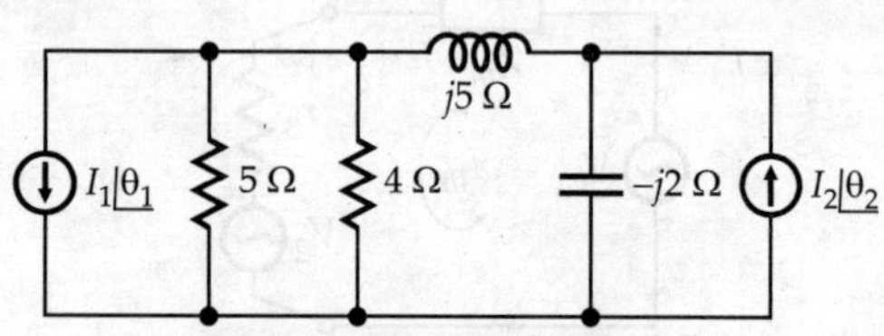

[$I_1|\theta_1 = 6\underline{|0°}$; $I_2|\theta_2 = 4\underline{|0°}$A]

Fig. E10.68

SOLUTION. Let us remove the 5 Ω resistor and the circuit is simplified as shown in Fig. E10.68(*a*).

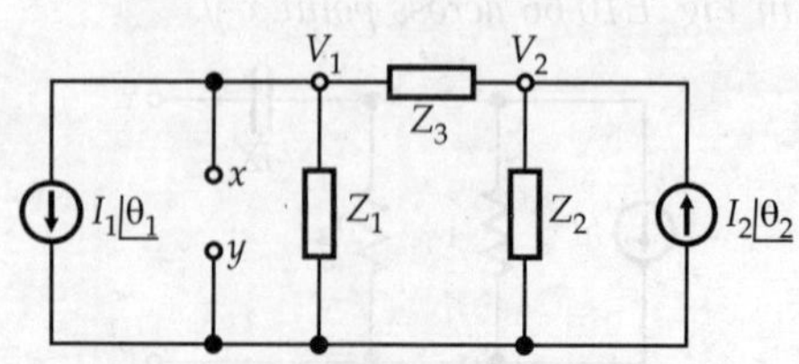

Fig. E10.68 (*a*)

Here $Z_1 = 4\,\Omega$ (resistive)

$Z_2 = -j\,2\,\Omega$

$Z_3 = j\,5\,\Omega$

Let nodal voltage at node (x) be V_1 and that at node (Z) be V_2. Little observation reveals that $V_1 \equiv V_{o.c}$ *i.e.*, Thevenin's equivalent voltage across x-y.

Here nodal analysis at *node (x)* yields

$$V_1\,(Y_1 + Y_3) - V_2\,(Y_3) = -\,I_1\,\angle\theta_1 \qquad ...(1)$$

and at *node (y)* yields

$$V_2\,(Y_2 + Y_3) - V_1\,(Y_3) = I_2\,\angle\theta_2 \qquad ...(2)$$

$$\left[Y_1 = \frac{1}{Z_1}\,;\,Y_2 = \frac{1}{Z_2}\,;\,Y_3 = \frac{1}{Z_3}\right]$$

In matrix form, these two equations can be arranged as shown below :

$$\begin{bmatrix} Y_1 + Y_3 & -Y_3 \\ -Y_3 & Y_2 + Y_3 \end{bmatrix}\begin{bmatrix} V_1 \\ V_2 \end{bmatrix} = \begin{bmatrix} I_1\,\angle\theta_1 \\ I_2\,\angle\theta_2 \end{bmatrix}$$

$$\therefore \quad V_1 = \frac{\begin{vmatrix} -I_1\,\angle\theta_1 & -Y_3 \\ I_2\,\angle\theta_2 & Y_2 + Y_3 \end{vmatrix}}{\begin{vmatrix} Y_1 + Y_3 & -Y_3 \\ -Y_3 & Y_3 + Y_2 \end{vmatrix}}$$

$$= \frac{-(Y_2 + Y_3)\,I_1\,\angle\theta_1 + I_2\,\angle\theta_2\,.\,Y_3}{(Y_1 + Y_3)(Y_3 + Y_2) - Y_3^2}$$

$$= \frac{-(Y_2 + Y_3)\,I_1\,\angle\theta_1 + I_2\,\angle\theta_2\,.\,Y_3}{Y_1\,Y_3 + Y_2\,Y_3 + Y_1\,Y_2}$$

$$= \frac{-\left[\left(\frac{1}{-j\,2}\right) + \frac{1}{j\,5}\right]\,6\,\angle 0° + 4\,\angle 0°\left(\frac{1}{j\,5}\right)}{\frac{1}{4}\times\frac{1}{j\,5} + \frac{1}{-j\,2}\times\frac{1}{j\,5} + \frac{1}{4}\times\frac{1}{-j\,2}}$$

$$= \frac{-(j\,0.5 - j\,0.2)6 + 4(-j\,0.2)}{\frac{1}{-j\,8} + \frac{1}{10} + \frac{1}{j\,20}}$$

$$= \frac{-0.3\,\angle 90° \times 6\,\angle 0° + 4\,\angle 0° \times 0.2\,\angle -90°}{j\,0.125 + 0.1 - j\,0.05}$$

$$= \frac{-1.8\,\angle 90° + 0.8\,\angle -90°}{0.1 + j\,0.075} = \frac{2.6\,\angle -90°}{0.125\,\angle 36.87°}$$

$$= 20.8\,\angle -126.87°\text{ V.}$$

Thus, $\quad V_1\,(\equiv V_{o.c.}) = 20.8\,\angle -126.87°\text{ V}.$

The internal impedance can be found out by deactivating the current sources as shown in Fig. E10.68(b).

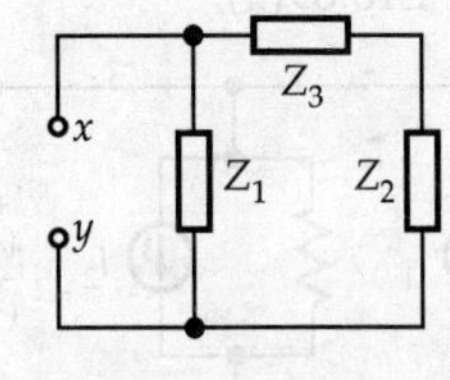

Fig. E10.68 (b)

$$\text{Here } Z_{int} = \frac{Z_1\,(Z_2 + Z_3)}{Z_1 + Z_2 + Z_3} = \frac{4(-j\,2 + j\,5)}{4 + j\,5 - j\,2}$$

$$= \frac{j\,12}{4 + j\,3} = \frac{12\,\angle 90°}{5\,\angle 36.87°} \simeq 2.4\,\angle 53.13°\,\Omega.$$

Thevenin's equivalent circuit is then drawn in Fig. E10.68(c)

where $V_{o.c} = 20.8\,\angle -126.87°$ V ;

$Z_{\text{int}} = 2.4\,\angle 53.13°\,\Omega.$

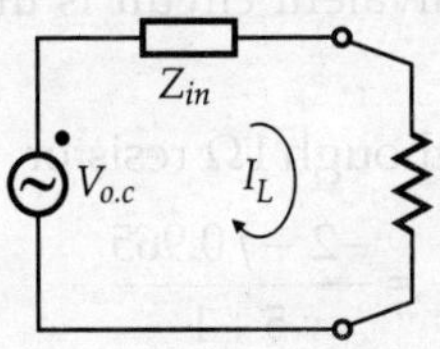

Fig. E10.68 (c)

The current through the load resistor (5Ω) would now be

$$I_L = \frac{V_{o.c.}}{Z_{in} + 5} = \frac{20.8\,\angle -126.87°}{2.4\,\angle 53.13° + 5}$$

$$= \frac{20.8\,\angle -126.87°}{1.44 + j\,1.92 + 5}$$

$$= \frac{20.8\,\angle -126.87°}{6.44 + j\,1.92} = \frac{20.8\,\angle -126.87°}{6.72\,\angle 16.6°}$$

$$= \mathbf{3.095\,\angle -143.47°\text{ A.}}$$

EXAMPLE 10.69 *Find the current through the 1Ω resistor in Fig 10.69 using both Thevenin's theorem and Norton's theorem.*

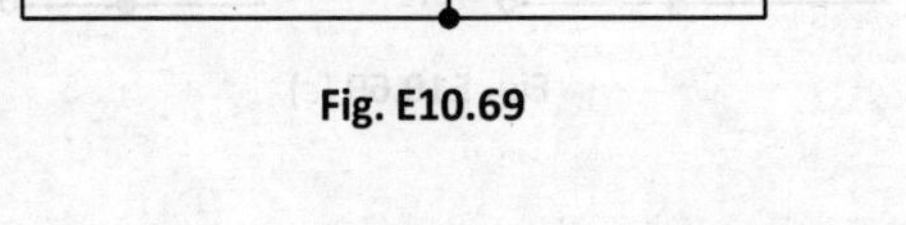

Fig. E10.69

SOLUTION. Let us first apply Thevenin's theorem and remove the 1Ω resistor. Assuming the open circuit voltage across the open circuited terminals to be $V_{o.c.}$ in Fig. E10.69(*a*),

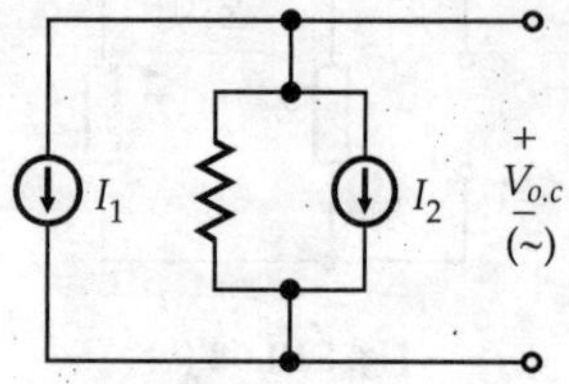

Fig. E10.69 (*a*)

$$V_{o.c.} = \text{drop across } 5\,\Omega \text{ resistor}$$
$$= (I_1 - I_2)\,5 = [0.5\,\angle 90° - 0.8\,\angle 60°]\,5$$
$$= (j\,0.5 - 0.4 - j\,0.693)\,5 = (-0.4 - j\,0.193)\,5$$
$$= (-2 - j\,0.965)\text{ V}.$$

To find internal inspection of the given circuit, the sources are deactivated and it can be found easily that $Z_{in} = 5\,\Omega$.

Thevenin's equivalent circuit is then drawn in Fig. E10.69(*b*)

when I_L = current though 1Ω resistor

$$= \frac{V_{o.c.}}{Z_{in} + R_L} = \frac{-2 - j\,0.965}{5+1}$$

$$= \mathbf{(-0.333 - j\,0.161)\ A.}$$

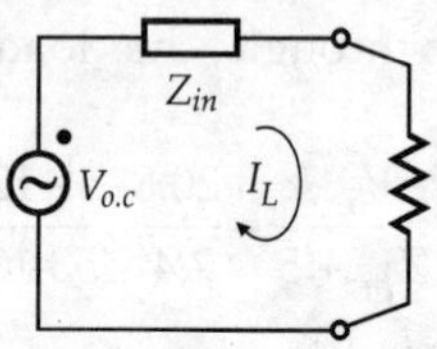

Fig. E10.69 (*b*)

To apply Norton's Theorem, let the 1Ω resistor be removed and the respective terminals be shorted. No current would flow though 5Ω resistor [Fig. E10.69(*c*)].

Here $\quad I_{s.c} (= I_N) = I_1 - I_2$
$$= 0.5\,\angle 90° - 0.8\,\angle 60°$$
$$= (0.4 - j\,0.193)\text{ A}.$$

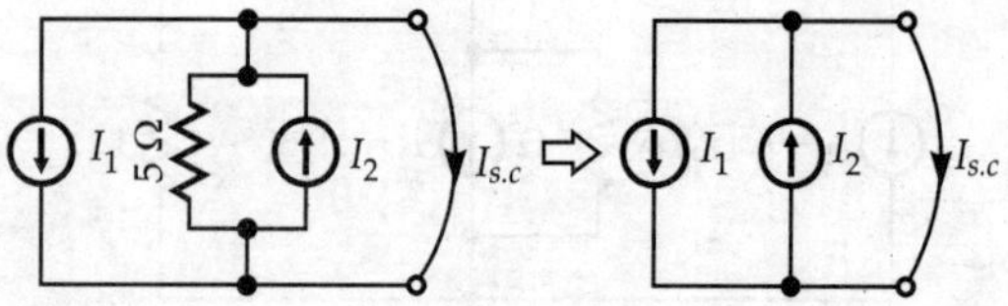

Fig. E10.69 (*c*)

Norton's equivalent circuit is then drawn in Fig. E10.69(*d*) [Z_{in} remains the same] and the load resistance (1Ω) is reconnected. The current though 1Ω resistor (I_L) is then

$$I_L = I_{s.c}\,\frac{Z_{in}}{Z_{in}+1} = (-0.4 - j\,0.193)\,\frac{5}{5+1}$$
$$= (-0.333 - j\,0.161)\text{ A}$$

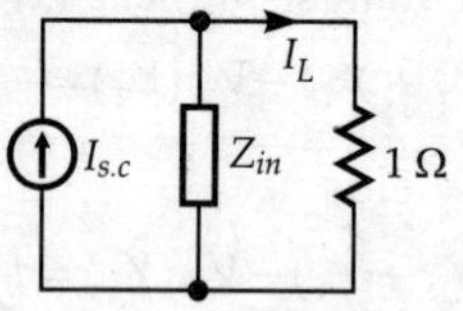

Fig. E10.69 (*d*)

Thus we see that $I_L = (-0.333 - j\,0.161)$ A as obtained by **Thevenin's and Norton's theorem both.**

EXAMPLE 10.70 *In the circuit of Fig. E10.70, obtain the Thevenin's equivalent circuit across x-y.*

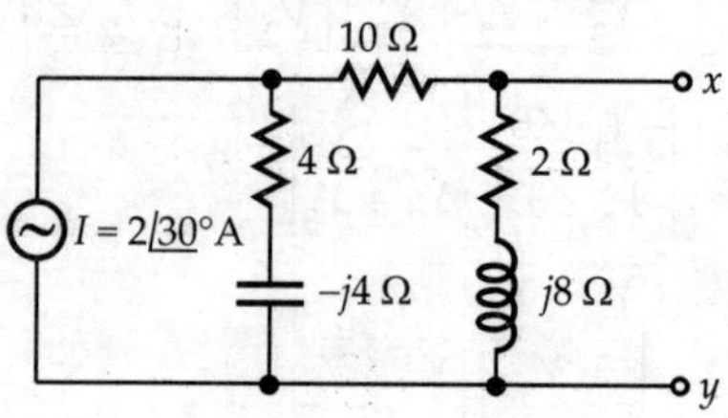

Fig. E10.70

SOLUTION. The given network is redrawn after deactivating the current source as shown in Fig. E10.70(*a*).

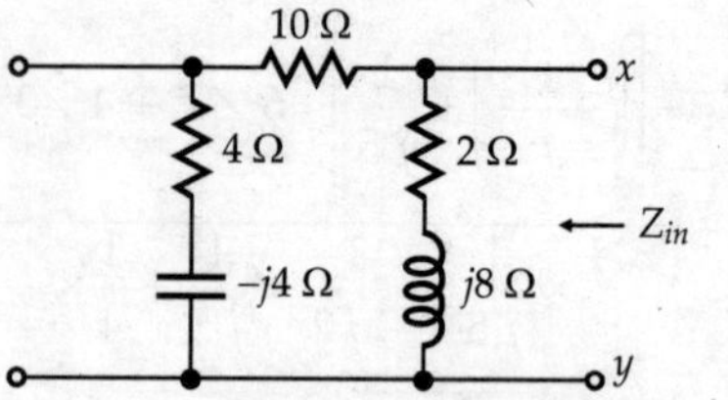

Fig. E10.70 (*a*)

Here, $$Z_{in} = \frac{(2 + j\,8)(10 + 4 - j\,4)}{2 + j\,8 + 10 + 4 - j\,4}$$
$$= \frac{(2 + j\,8)(14 - j\,4)}{(16 + j\,4)}$$
$$= \frac{28 - j\,8 + j\,112 + 32}{16 + j\,4} = \frac{60 + j\,104}{16 + j\,4}$$
$$= \frac{120\,\angle 60°}{16.49\,\angle 14.04°} = 7.28\,\angle 45.96°\,\Omega$$

On open circuit of *x-y*, let current *I* in Fig. 10.70 be divided into I_1 and I_2 as shown in Fig. E10.70(*b*).

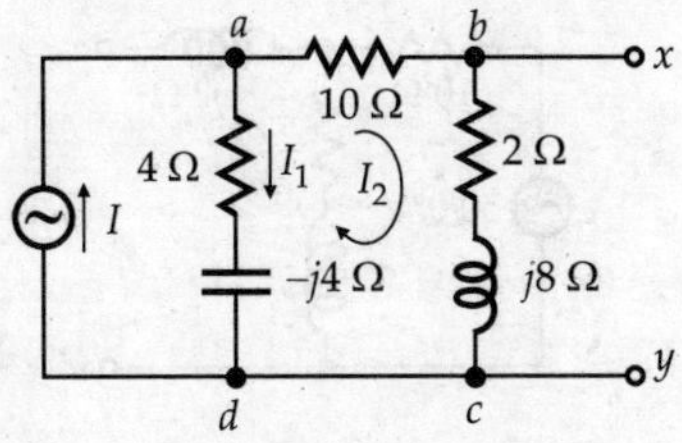

Fig. E10.70 (*b*)

Here, $$I_2 = I\frac{4 - j\,4}{4 - j\,4 + 10 + 2 + j\,8}$$

$$= I\frac{5.66\,\angle -45^\circ}{16 + j\,4}$$

$$= \frac{2\,\angle 30^\circ \times 5.66\,\angle -45^\circ}{16.49\,\angle 14.04^\circ}$$

$$= 0.686\,\angle -29.04^\circ \text{ A}$$

$$\therefore \quad V_{o.c.} = I_2 \times \text{imp. of branch } bc$$

$$= 0.686\,\angle -29.04^\circ \times (2 + j\,8)$$

$$= 0.686 \times 8.25\,\angle(-29.04^\circ + 76^\circ)$$

$$= 5.66\,\angle 46.96^\circ \text{ V}$$

Then, Thevenin's equivalent circuit can now be formed with

$$\mathbf{V_{o.c.} = 5.66\,\angle 46.96^\circ \text{ V}}$$

and $$\mathbf{Z_{in} = 7.28\,\angle 45.96^\circ\,\Omega.}$$

Example 10.71 *Find Norton's equivalent of the circuit shown in Fig. E10.71 in the previous Example.*

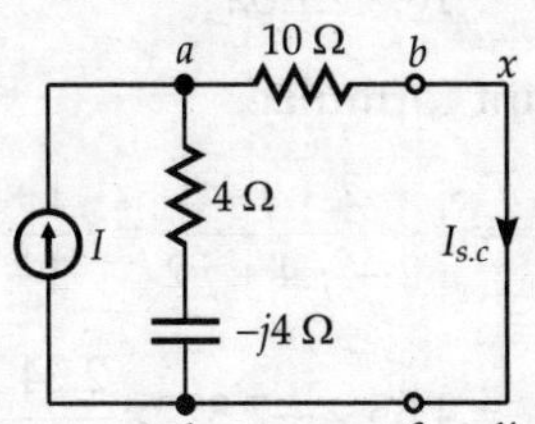

Fig. E10.71

Solution. It may be noted that the equivalent Norton's impedance *i.e.*, the internal impedance of the given network across *x-y* with the source deactivated has already been obtained in Ex. 10.70 and is rewritten here

$$Z_{in} = 7.28\,\angle 45.96^\circ\,\Omega.$$

In order to find Norton's equivalent current source, *x-y* is shorted. It is evident that no current would flow through $(2 + j\,8)\Omega$ branch as *x-y* is shorted (Fig. E10.70)

$$I_{s.c.} = I\frac{4 - j\,4}{4 - j\,4 + 10} = 2\,\angle 30^\circ\frac{4 - j\,4}{14 - j\,4}$$

$$= \frac{2\,\angle 30^\circ \times 5.657\,\angle -45^\circ}{13.56\,\angle -16^\circ} = 0.78\,\angle 1^\circ$$

Norton's equivalent circuit is shown in **Fig. E10.71(*a*).**

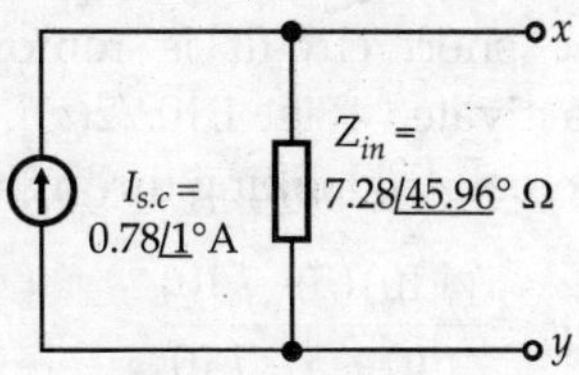

Fig. E10.71 (*a*)

Check

It may be observed that V_{drop} across Z_{in} is $I_{s.c} \times Z_{in}$ from Norton's equiv. circuit

$$= 0.78\,\angle 1^\circ \times 7.28\,\angle 45.96^\circ$$

$$= 5.68\,\angle 46.96^\circ \text{ V } (= V_{x-y})$$

In the previous example, the Thevenin's equivalent voltage has been found to be $5.66\,\angle 46.96^\circ$ V, which is actually V_{x-y} of Norton's circuit.

Example 10.72 *In the circuit of Fig. E10.72, find Norton's equivalent across AB. Verify the result using Thevenin's Theorem.*

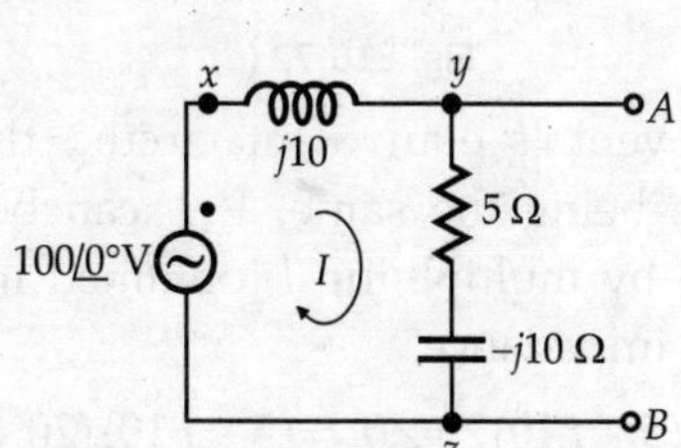

Fig. E10.72

Solution. The current in the loop *x-y-z-p* is shown by an arrow in Fig. E10.72 and is denoted by *I*.

$$I = \frac{100\,\angle 0^\circ}{(5 - j\,10) + j\,10} = 20\,\angle 0^\circ \text{ A} \quad ...(1)$$

Next, A-B terminal is shorted [Fig. E10.72(a)]

$$\therefore \quad I_{s.c.} = \frac{100\ \angle 0^\circ}{j\,10} = 10\ \angle -90^\circ \text{ A.}$$

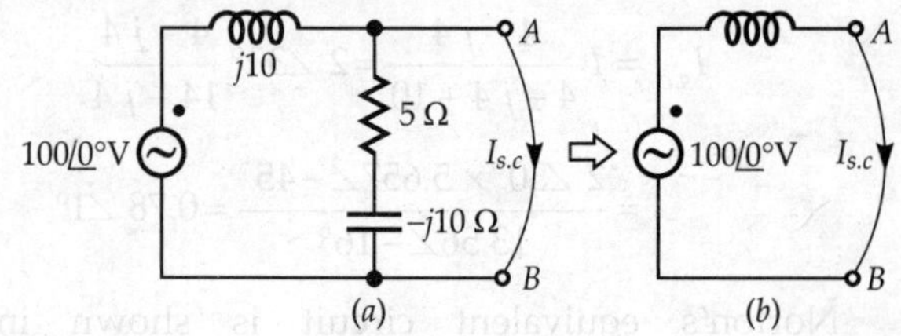

Fig. E10.72

Next, the short circuit is removed and the source is deactivated [Fig. E10.72(c)]. The internal impedance across A-B looking through A-B is then

$$Z_{in} = \frac{(j\,10)\,(5 - j\,10)}{j\,10 + 5 - j\,10}$$

$$= j\,2\,(5 - j\,10) = (20 + j\,10)\,\Omega.$$

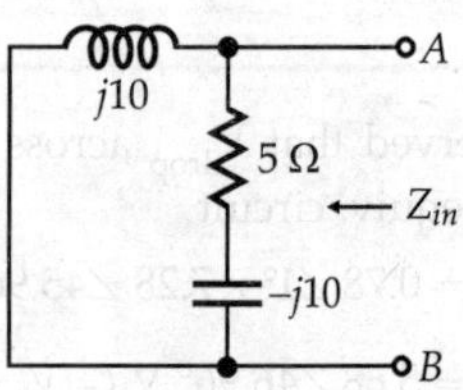

Fig. E10.72 (c)

Norton's equivalent circuit is shown in **Fig. E10.72(d).**

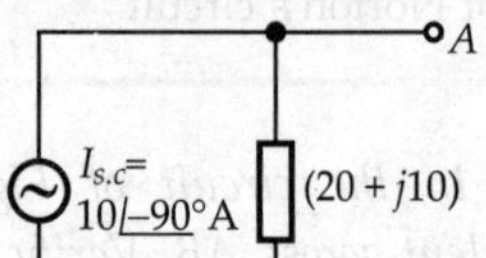

Fig. E10.72 (d)

In Thevenin's equivalent circuit, the internal impedance being the same, $V_{o.c.}$ can be obtained across A-B by multiplying I [obtained in (1)] with $(5 - j\,10)\,\Omega$ impedance.

i.e., $V_{o.c.} = (5 - j\,10)\,20\ \angle 0^\circ = (5 - j\,10)\,(20 + j\,0)$

$= (100 - j\,200)$ V

Figure 10.72(e) represents the Thevenin's equivalent circuit.

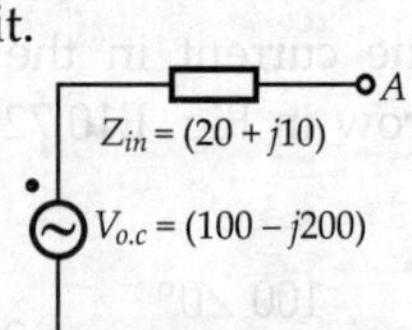

Fig. E10.72 (e)

EXAMPLE 10.73 *Find Norton's equivalent circuit across x-y [Fig. E10.73].*

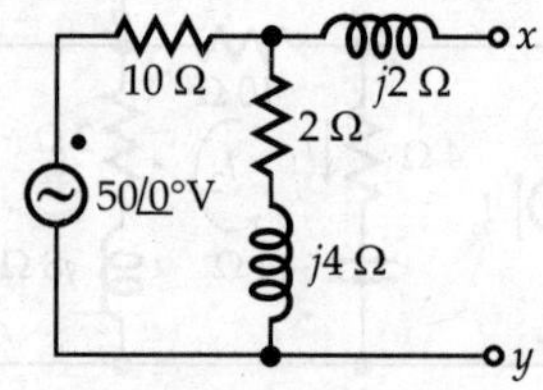

Fig. E10.73

SOLUTION. x-y is shorted [Fig. E10.73(a)]

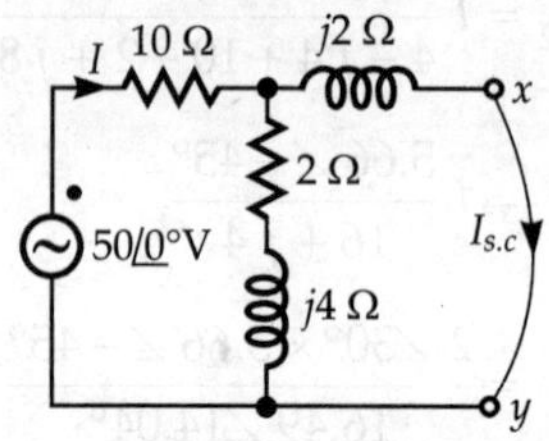

Fig. E10.73 (a)

The impedance (Z) across the voltage source is given by

$$Z = \frac{(j\,2)\,(2 + j\,4)}{j\,2 + 2 + j\,4} + 10$$

$$= \frac{-8 + j\,4}{2 + j\,6} + 10 = \frac{-8 + j\,4 + 20 + j\,60}{2 + j\,6}$$

$$= \frac{(12 + j\,64)}{(2 + j\,6)} = \frac{65.11\ \angle 79.38^\circ}{6.32\ \angle 71.56^\circ}$$

$$= 10.3\ \angle 7.82^\circ\,\Omega.$$

$$\therefore \quad I = \frac{50\ \angle 0^\circ}{10.3\ \angle 7.82^\circ} = 4.85\ \angle -7.82^\circ \text{ A.}$$

Using shunt formulae,

$$I_{s.c.} = I\,\frac{2 + j\,4}{2 + j\,4 + j\,2} = I\,\frac{1 + j\,2}{1 + j\,3}$$

$$= 4.85\ \angle -7.82^\circ \times \frac{2.24\ \angle 63.43^\circ}{3.16\ \angle 71.56^\circ}$$

$$= 4.85\ \angle -7.82^\circ \times 0.71\ \angle -8.13^\circ$$

$$= 3.4435\ \angle -15.95^\circ \text{ A.}$$

Internal impedance (Z_{in}) of the network looking from x-y can be obtained by deactivating $50\ \angle 0^\circ$ V source and removing the short.

$$\text{Here} \quad Z_{in} = \frac{10\,(2 + j\,4)}{10 + 2 + j\,4} + j\,2 = \frac{20 + j\,40}{12 + j\,4} + j\,2$$

$$= \frac{5+j\,10}{3+j\,1} + j\,2 = \frac{5+j\,10+j\,6-2}{3+j\,1}$$

$$= \frac{16.279\ \angle +79.4°}{3.16\ \angle 18.43°} = 5.44\ \angle 60.97°\,\Omega.$$

Norton's equivalent circuit is shown in **Fig. E10.73(*b*).**

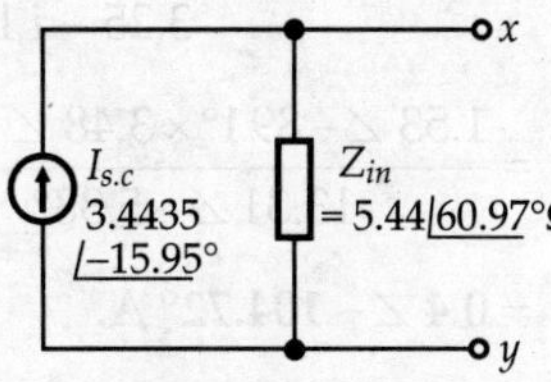

Fig. E10.73 (*b*)

***Example* 10.74** *In the network of Fig. E10.74, find the power loss in the 10 Ω resistor.*

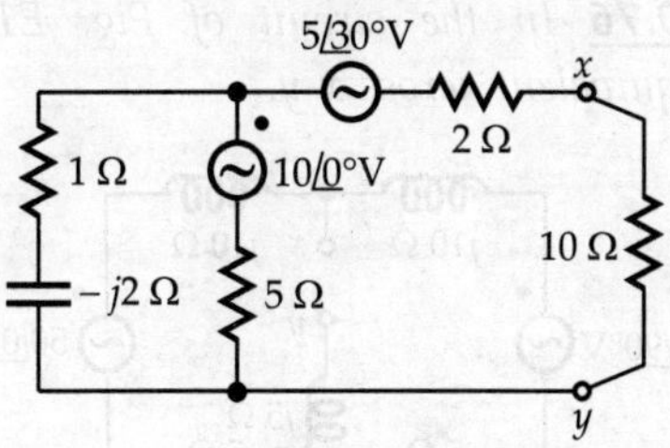

Fig. E10.74

Solution. Let us open terminal *x-y* [Fig. E10.74(*a*)]

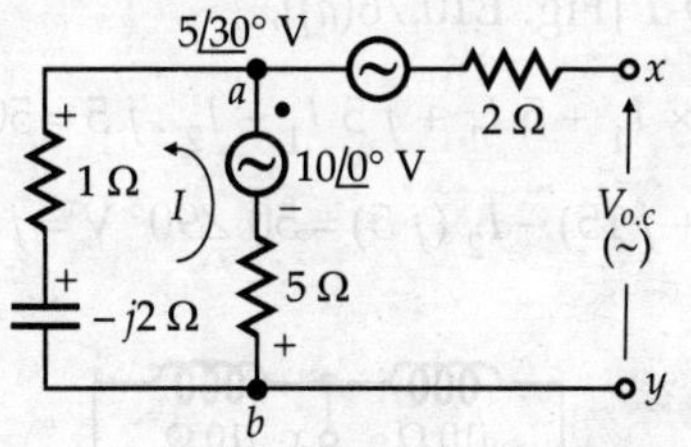

Fig. E10.74 (*a*)

Here, $I = \dfrac{10\ \angle 0°}{5+1-j\,2} = \dfrac{10\ \angle 0°}{6.32\ \angle -18.43°}$

$$= 1.58\ \angle 18.43°\ \text{A}.$$

Then, voltage drop across 5 Ω resistor is

$$V_{5\Omega} = (5\,\Omega)\,I = 5 \times 1.58\ \angle 18.43°\ \text{V}$$

$$= 7.91\ \angle 18.43°\ \text{V}$$

[The polarities are shown in Fig. E10.74(*a*)].

Next, in *loop baxy*, application of KVL yields

$$V_{5\Omega} - 10\ \angle 0° + 5\ \angle 30° + V_{o.c} = 0$$

[∵ no current is flowing through 2 Ω resistor]

or $\quad 7.91\ \angle 18.43 - 10\ \angle 0° + 5\ \angle 30° + V_{o.c} = 0$

or $\quad 7.91\,(\cos 18.43 + j\,\sin 18.43) - 10\,(\cos 0° + j\,\sin 0°) + 5\,(\cos 30° + j\,\sin 30°) + V_{o.c} = 0$

or $\quad 7.504 + j\,2.5 - 10 + 4.33 + j\,2.5 + V_{o.c} = 0.$

or $\quad 1.834 + j\,5 = -V_{o.c}$

or $\quad V_{o.c} = -1.834 - j\,5 = 5.325\ \angle -110°\ \text{V}.$

Deactivating the voltage sources, the internal circuit looking through *x-y* terminal is

$$Z_{in} = \frac{(1-j\,2)\,5}{1-j\,2+5} + 2 = \left(\frac{5-j\,10}{6-j\,2} + 2\right)$$

$$= \frac{5-j10+12-j4}{6-j\,2} = \frac{17-j14}{6-j\,2}$$

$$= \frac{22\angle -39.47°}{6.32\angle -18.42°} = 3.48\ \angle -21°\,\Omega.$$

Thus the Thevenin's equivalent circuit consists of

$$V_{o.c} = 5.325\ \angle -110°\ \text{V}$$

and $\quad Z_{in} = 3.48\ \angle -21°\,\Omega \quad$ [Fig. E10.74(*b*)].

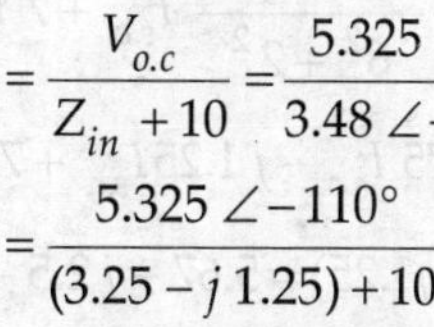

Fig. E10.74 (*b*)

Here $\quad I_{Th} = \dfrac{V_{o.c}}{Z_{in}+10} = \dfrac{5.325\ \angle -110°}{3.48\ \angle -21° + 10}$

$$= \frac{5.325\ \angle -110°}{(3.25 - j\,1.25) + 10} = \frac{5.325\ \angle -110°}{13.31\ \angle -5.39°}$$

$$= 0.4\ \angle -104.61\ \text{A}.$$

∴ Power loss $= (0.4)^2 \times 10 =$ **1.6 W.**

***Example* 10.75** *Find the current through the 10 Ω resistor in the previous problem (Ex. 10.74) using Norton's Theorem.*

Solution. We have obtained in the previous problem

$$Z_{in} = 3.48\ \angle -21°\,\Omega.$$

To find Norton's equivalent current source, terminals x-y is shorted (Fig. E10.75).

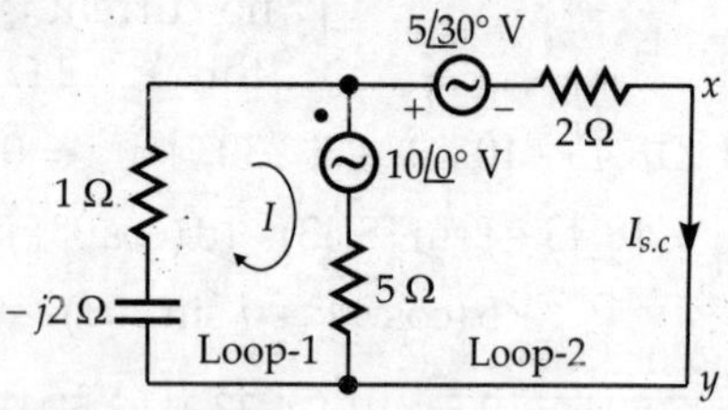

Fig. E10.75

In *loop-1*, mesh equation yields

$$I \times 1 + 10 \angle 0° + I \times 5 - I_{s.c} \times 5 + I(-j2) = 0$$

or $$6I - 5I_{s.c} - j2I = -10$$

or $$I(6 - j2) - 5I_{s.c} = -10 \quad ...(1)$$

In *loop-2*, mesh equation yields

$$5\angle 30° + 2 \times I_{s.c} + 5I_{s.c} - 5I - 10\angle 0° = 0$$

or $$7I_{s.c} - 5I = 10 - 5\angle 30°$$

$$= 10 - 4.33 - j2.5 = 5.67 - j2.5$$

or $$-5I + 7I_{s.c} = 5.67 - j2.5 \quad ...(2)$$

From (1),

$$I = \frac{-10 + 5I_{s.c}}{6 - j2} \quad ...(3)$$

Using (3) in (2),

$$-5\frac{(-10 + 5I_{s.c})}{(6 - j2)} + 7I_{s.c} = 5.67 - j2.5$$

or $$\frac{(50 - 25I_{s.c})}{(6 - j2)} + 7I_{s.c} = 5.67 - j2.5$$

or $$\frac{50(6 + j2)}{6^2 + 2^2} - \frac{25(6 + j2)}{6^2 + 2^2}I_{s.c} + 7I_{s.c} = 5.67 - j2.5$$

or $$7.5 + j2.5 - 3.75I_{s.c} - j1.25I_{s.c} + 7I_{s.c} = 5.67 - j2.5$$

or $$I_{s.c}(7 - 3.75 - j1.25) = 5.67 - j2.5 - 7.5 - j2.5$$

or $$I_{s.c} = \frac{-1.83 - j5}{3.25 - j1.25} = \frac{5.324\angle -110.1°}{3.482\angle -21°}$$

$$= 1.53\angle -89.1° \text{ A.}$$

Norton's equivalent circuit is shown in Fig. E10.75(*a*).

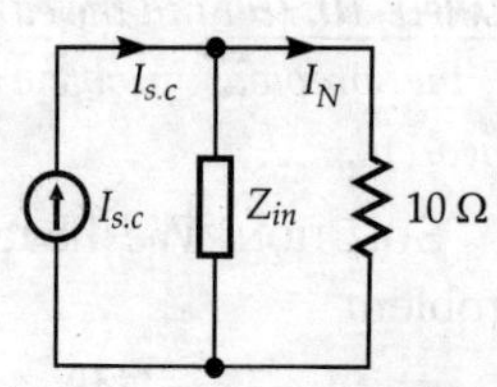

Fig. E10.75 (*a*)

Here current though 10 Ω resistor is

$$I_N = I_{s.c}\frac{Z_{in}}{Z_{in} + 10}$$

$$= 1.53\angle -89.1° \frac{3.48\angle -21°}{3.48\angle -21° + 10\angle 0°}$$

$$= 1.53\angle -89.1° \frac{3.48\angle -21°}{3.25 - j1.248 + 10}$$

$$= \frac{1.53\angle -89.1° \times 3.48\angle -21°}{13.31\angle -5.38°}$$

$$= \mathbf{0.4\angle -104.72° \text{ A.}}$$

Thus, using Norton's theorem, we got the current through the 10 Ω resistor to be $0.4\angle -104.72°$ A which we had obtained in the previous problem using Thevenin's theorem.

Example 10.76 *In the circuit of Fig. E10.76, find Norton's equivalent across x-y.*

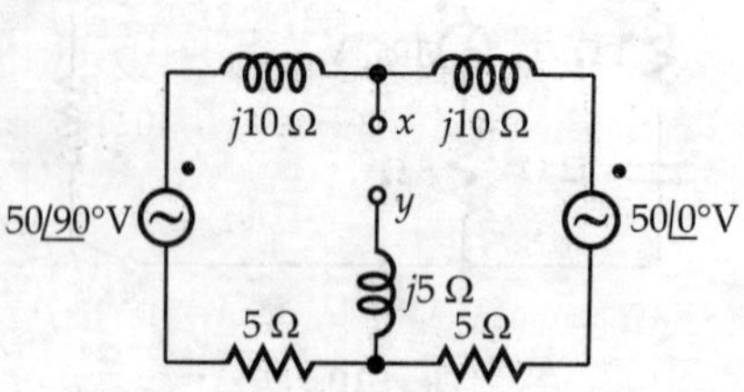

Fig. E10.76

Solution. Let us first short x-y.

In *loop-1* [Fig. E10.76(*a*)],

$$j10 \times I_1 + 5I_1 + j5I_1 - I_2 \cdot j5 = 50\angle 90° \text{ V}$$

or $$I_1(5 + j15) - I_2(j5) = 50\angle 90° \text{ V} = j50 \quad ...(1)$$

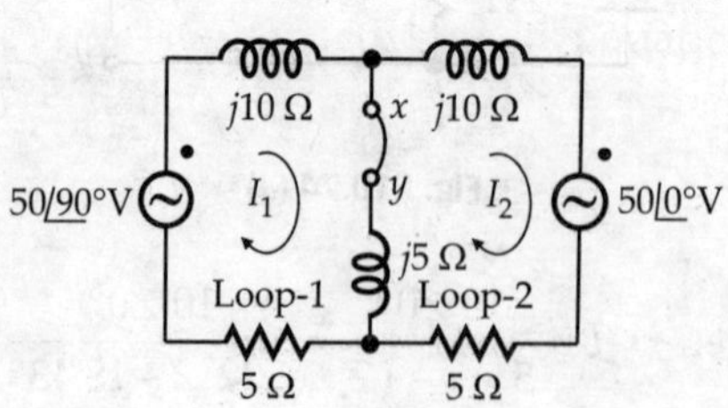

Fig. E10.76 (*a*)

Similarly, in *loop-2*,

$$-I_1 \cdot j5 + j5I_2 + j10 \cdot I_2 + 5I_2 = -50\angle 0°$$

or $$-j5 \cdot I_1 + j15I_2 + 5I_2 = -50$$

or $$-j5 \cdot I_1 + I_2(5 + j15) = -50 \quad ...(2)$$

In matrix form,

$$\begin{vmatrix} (5+j\,15) & -j\,5 \\ -j\,5 & (5+j\,15) \end{vmatrix} \begin{vmatrix} I_1 \\ I_2 \end{vmatrix} = \begin{vmatrix} j\,50 \\ -50 \end{vmatrix}$$

$$\therefore\ I_1 = \frac{\begin{vmatrix} j\,50 & -j\,5 \\ -50 & (5+j\,15) \end{vmatrix}}{\begin{vmatrix} (5+j\,15) & -j\,5 \\ -j\,5 & 5+j\,15 \end{vmatrix}}$$

$$= \frac{j\,250 - 750 - j\,250}{25 + j\,75 + j\,75 - 225 + 25} = \frac{-750}{-175 + j\,150}$$

$$= \frac{-15}{-3.5 + j\,3} = 3.25\ \angle 40.6°$$

$$I_2 = \frac{\begin{vmatrix} 5+j\,15 & j\,50 \\ -j\,5 & -50 \end{vmatrix}}{\begin{vmatrix} 5+j\,15 & -j\,5 \\ -j\,5 & 5+j\,15 \end{vmatrix}}$$

$$= \frac{-250 - j\,750 - 250}{-175 + j\,150} = \frac{-500 - j\,750}{-175 + j\,150}$$

$$= \frac{-10 - j\,15}{-3.5 + j\,3} = \frac{18.03\ \angle -123.69°}{4.61\ \angle 139.40°}$$

$$= 3.91\ \angle 96.91\ \text{A}$$

$\therefore$ Current $I_{s.c.}$ through x-y link is

$$I_1 - I_2 = 3.25\ \angle 40.6 - 3.91\ \angle 96.91°$$
$$= 2.47 + j\,2.12 + 0.47 - j\,3.88$$
$$= 2.94 - j\,1.76 = 3.43 \angle -30.91°\ \text{A}$$

The internal impedance of the circuit across x-y can be obtained by network reduction as shown in Fig. E10.76(b) (Opening the shorting link across x-y and deactivating the sources)

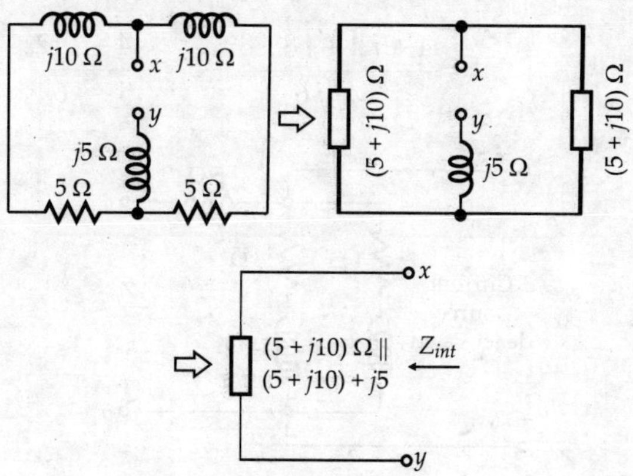

Fig. E10.76 (b)

Here,

$$Z_{\text{int}} = \frac{(5+j\,10)(5+j\,10)}{(5+j\,10)+(5+j\,10)} + j\,5$$
$$= 2.5 + j\,5 + j\,5 = 2.5 + j\,10$$
$$= 10.31\ \angle 75.96°\ \Omega$$

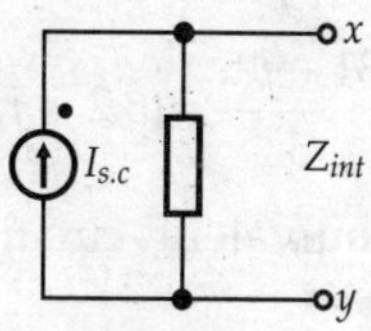

Fig. E10.76 (c)

Norton's Equivalent circuit is then drawn in Fig. E10.76(c) where

$$\mathbf{I_{s.c.} = 3.43\ \angle -30.91°\ A}$$
$$\mathbf{Z_{int} = 10.31\ \angle 75.96°\ \Omega}.$$

EXAMPLE 10.77 *Using Thevenin's theorem find the power in* $(4+j\,6)\,\Omega$ *impedance connected across terminals x-y in Fig. E10.77.*

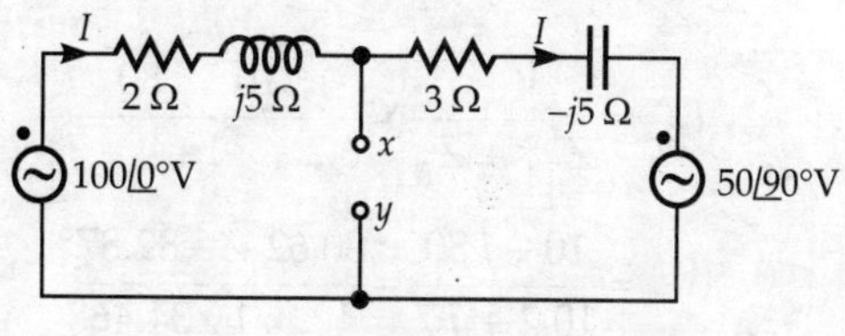

Fig. E10.77

Solution. Let the circulating current be I in the loop as shown in the given circuit of Fig. E10.77(a).

$$I = \frac{100\ \angle 0° - 50\ \angle 90°}{2 + j\,5 + 3 - j\,5} = \frac{100 - j\,50}{5}$$
$$= (20 - j\,10)\ \text{A}.$$

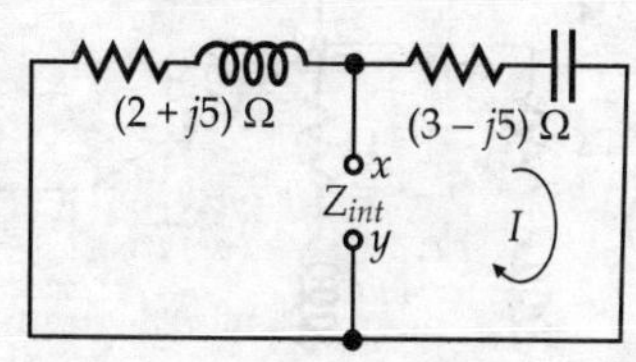

Fig. E10.77 (a)

$$\therefore\quad V_{x-y} = 100\ \angle 0°\ \text{V - dorp in}(2 + j\,5)\,\Omega.$$
$$= 100\ \angle 0° - (20 - j\,10)(2 + j\,5)$$
$$= 100 - [40 + j\,100 - 20\,j + 50]$$
$$= (10 - j\,80)\ \text{V}\ [= V_{o.c.}].$$

The internal impedance can be found out from Fig. E10.77(a) deactivating all sources.

$$Z_{int} = \frac{(2+j\,5)(3-j\,5)}{2+j\,5+3-j\,5}$$

$$= \frac{6-j\,10+j\,15+25}{5}$$

$$= \frac{31+j\,5}{5} = (6.2+j\,1)\,\Omega.$$

Thevenin's equivalent circuit is then drawn with

$$V_{o.c} = (10-j\,80)\text{ V}$$

and $Z_{int} = (6.2+j\,1)\,\Omega.$ [Fig. E10.77(b)]

where $Z_L = (4+j\,6)\,\Omega$;

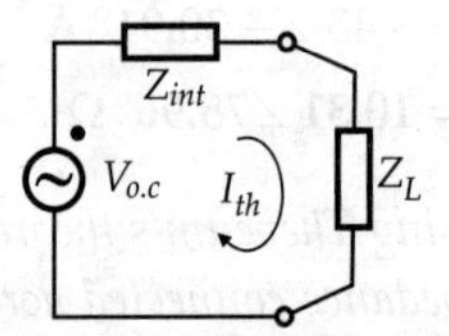

Fig. E10.77 (b)

$$\therefore \quad I_{Th} = \frac{V_{o.c.}}{Z_{int}+Z_L} = \frac{10-j\,80}{6.2+j\,1+4+j\,6}$$

$$= \frac{10-j\,80}{10.2+j\,7} = \frac{80.62\angle-82.87°}{12.371\angle 34.46°}$$

$$= 6.52\angle-117.33°\text{ A.}$$

$\therefore P_{loss}$ in $(4+j\,6)\,\Omega$ impedance

$$= (6.52)^2 \times 4 \simeq \mathbf{170\ W}.$$

EXAMPLE 10.78 *Obtain Norton's equivalent circuit at terminals a-b [Fig. E10.78]. Assume* $I_0 = 10\angle 30°$ *A.*

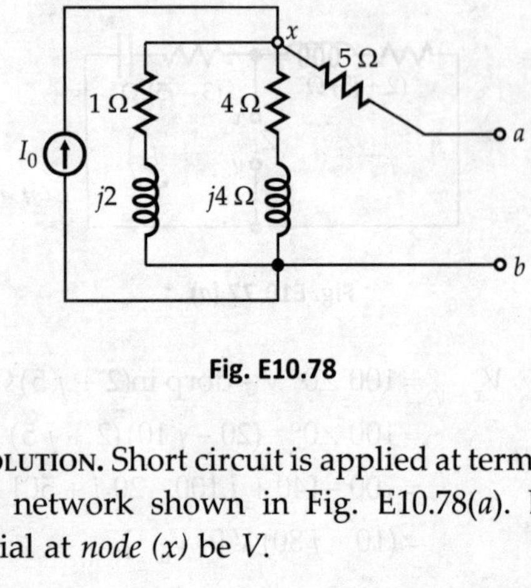

Fig. E10.78

SOLUTION. Short circuit is applied at terminal a-b of the network shown in Fig. E10.78(a). Let the potential at *node* (x) be V.

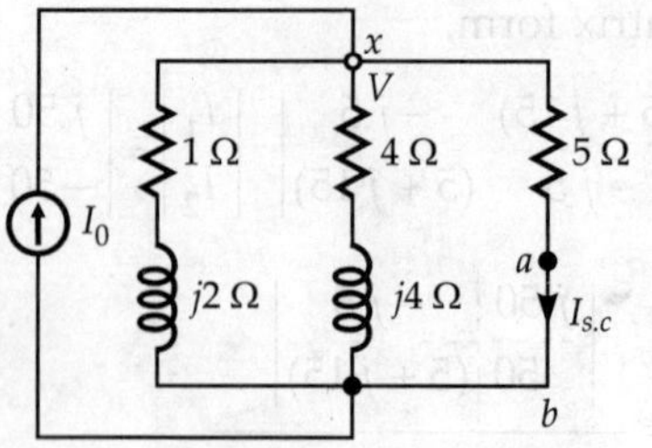

Fig. E10.78 (a)

Using Node analysis,

$$\frac{V}{1+j\,2} + \frac{V}{4+j\,4} + \frac{V}{5} = I_0$$

[Refer to Fig. E 10.78(a)]

or $$V\left[\frac{1-j\,2}{5} + \frac{4-j\,4}{32} + 0.2\right] = 10\,(\cos 30 + j\sin 30°)$$

or $$V\,[0.2-j\,0.4+0.125-j\,0.125+0.2] = 8.66+j\,5$$

or $$V = \frac{8.66+j5}{0.525-j\,0.525} = \frac{10\angle 30°}{0.743\angle-45°} = 13.46\angle 75°\text{ V.}$$

Thus, potential at node (x) in Fig. E10.78(a) is $13.46\angle 75°$ V. However, observation leads that the current through shorted a-b terminal being $I_{s.c.}$, it is the current through $5\,\Omega$ resistor in Fig. E10.78(a).

Obviously,

$$I_{s.c} = \frac{V}{5\angle 0} = \frac{13.46\angle 75°}{5\angle 0°} = 2.69\angle 75°\text{ A.}$$

Next, the internal impedance of the circuit is obtained as

$$Z_{int} = \left[\frac{(1+j\,2)(4+j\,4)}{1+j\,2+4+j\,4} + 5\right]\Omega$$

[refer Fig. E10.78(b)]

$$= \frac{4+j\,4+j\,8-8}{5+j\,6} + 5 = \frac{-4+j\,12}{5+j\,6} + 5$$

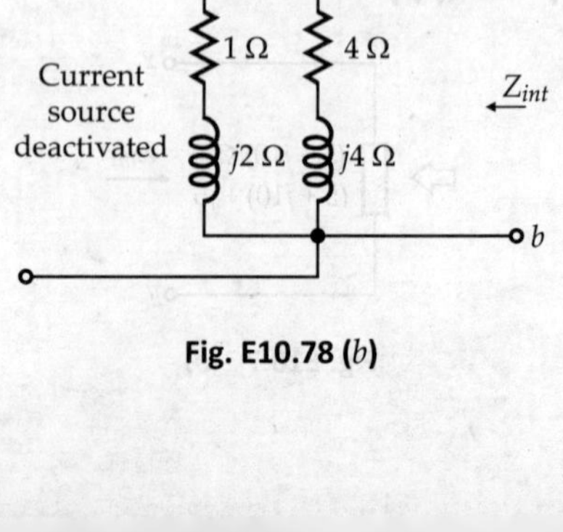

Fig. E10.78 (b)

$$= \frac{12.65\ \angle 108.43^\circ}{7.81\ \angle 50.2^\circ} + 5$$

$$= 1.62\ \angle 58.23^\circ\,\Omega + 5$$

$$= \mathbf{6.01\ \angle 13.24^\circ\,\Omega}.$$

Norton's equivalent circuit is then drawn in **Fig. E10.78(*c*).**

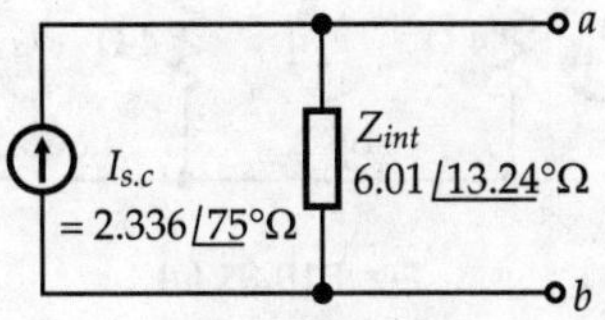

Fig. E10.78 (*c*)

Example 10.79 *Find Norton's equivalent circuit across x-y for the network shown in Fig. E10.79.*

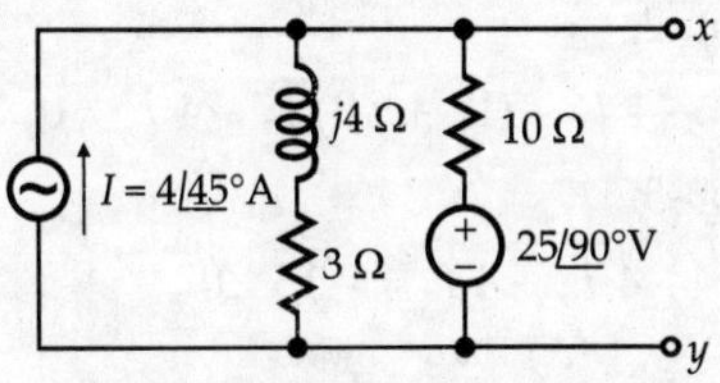

Fig. E10.79

Solution. Let us apply short circuit across *x-y*. Obviously, no current would pass through $(3 + j\,4)\,\Omega$ impedance branch and the total current through the short circuit becomes additive [Fig. E10.79(*a*)].

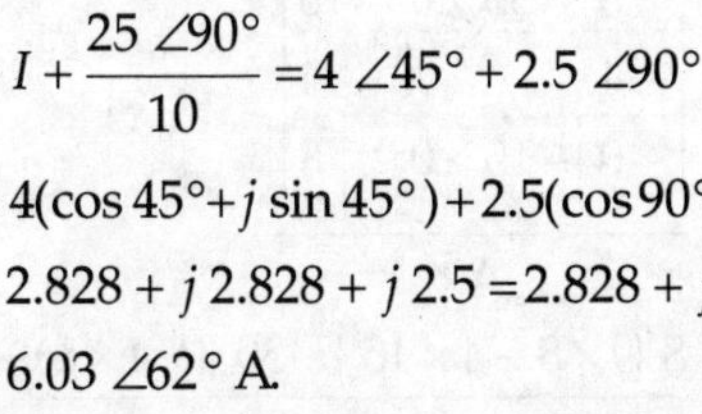

Fig. E10.79 (*a*)

i.e., $I_{s.c.} = I + \frac{25\ \angle 90^\circ}{10} = 4\ \angle 45^\circ + 2.5\ \angle 90^\circ$

$$= 4(\cos 45^\circ + j \sin 45^\circ) + 2.5(\cos 90^\circ + j \sin 90^\circ)$$

$$= 2.828 + j\,2.828 + j\,2.5 = 2.828 + j\,5.328$$

$$= 6.03\ \angle 62^\circ\ \text{A}.$$

Thus, Norton's equivalent current is **6.03 ∠62° A.**

Internal impedance can be obtained by activating the source and looking back to the circuit through $x-y$ terminals, short circuit being removed [Fig. E10.79(*b*)].

$$Z_{int} = \frac{10\,(3 + j\,4)}{10 + 3 + j\,4} = \frac{30 + j\,40}{13 + j\,4} = 3.68\ \angle 36^\circ\,\Omega.$$

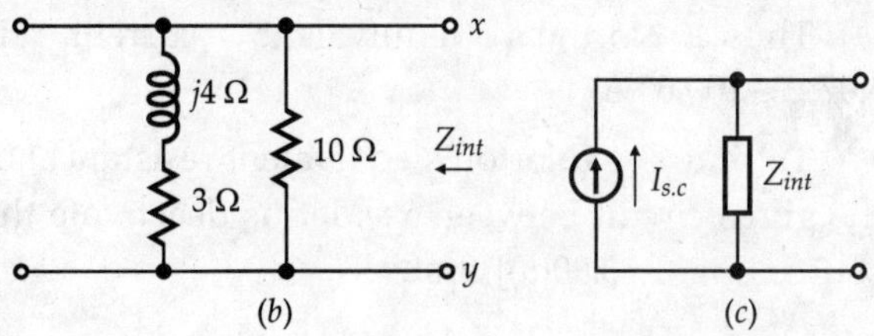

Fig. E10.79

Norton's equivalent circuit can now be drawn, where

$$\mathbf{Z_{int} = 3.68\ \angle 36^\circ\,\Omega \ \text{ and } \ I_{s.c} = 6.03\ \angle 62^\circ\ A.}$$

[Fig. E10.79(*c*)]

Example 10.80 *Find current through R_L using Norton's theorem (Fig. E10.80).*

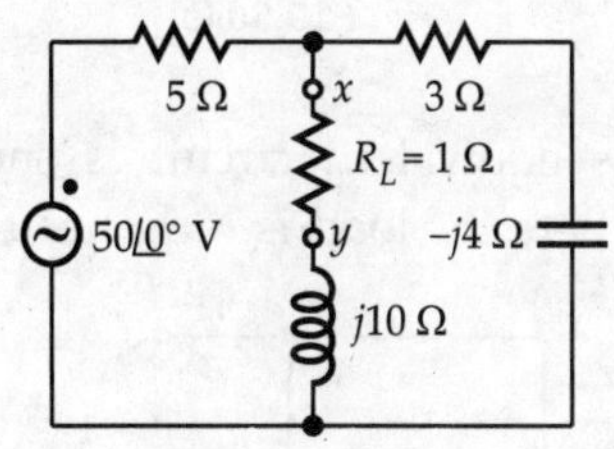

Fig. E10.80

Solution. Let us remove R_L across *x-y* terminal and apply short circuit across *x-y* [Fig. E10.80(*a*)].

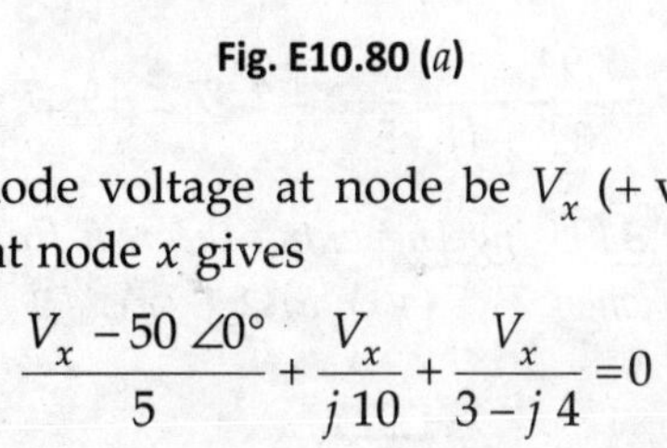

Fig. E10.80 (*a*)

Let the node voltage at node be V_x (+ ve). Nodal analysis at node *x* gives

$$\frac{V_x - 50\ \angle 0^\circ}{5} + \frac{V_x}{j\,10} + \frac{V_x}{3 - j\,4} = 0$$

or $$V_x = \frac{10\ \angle 0^\circ}{0.326\ \angle 10.6^\circ} = 30.7\ \angle -10.6^\circ\ \text{V}.$$

Also, $$I_{s.c} = \frac{V_x}{j\,10} = \frac{30.7\ \angle -10.6^\circ}{j\,10}$$

$$= \frac{30.7\ \angle -10.6^\circ}{10\ \angle 90^\circ} = 3.07\ \angle -100.6^\circ\ \text{A}.$$

Thus Norton's equivalent current is $3.07 \angle -100.6°$ A.

To find Z_{int} (Norton's equivalent resistance) of the given circuit between x-y, let us deactivate the source [Fig. E10.80(*b*)] first.

$$Z_{in} = j\,10 + \frac{5\,(3 - j\,4)}{5 + 3 - j\,4} = j\,10 + 2.5 - j\,1.25$$

$$= 9.1 \angle 74.05° \text{ ohm.}$$

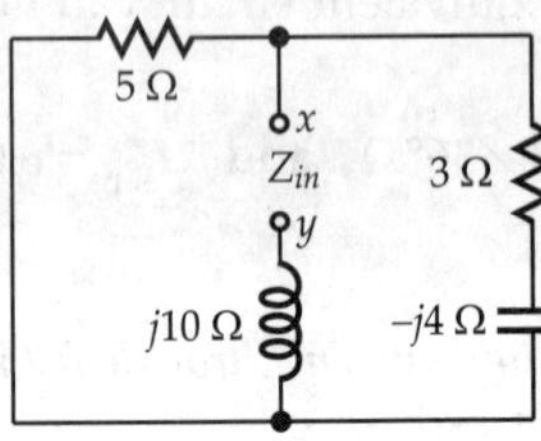

Fig. E10.80 (*b*)

Norton's equivalent circuit is shown in Fig. E10.80(*c*), where the load is reconnected.

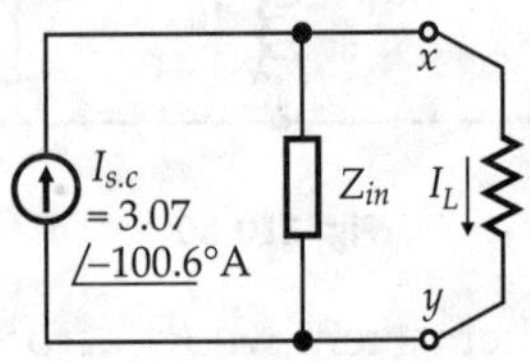

Fig. E10.80 (*c*)

The current through R_L (1Ω) resistor is

$$I_L = I_{s.c.}\,\frac{Z_{in}}{Z_{in} + R_L}$$

$$= \frac{3.07 \angle -100.6° \times 9.1 \angle 74.05°}{9.1 \angle 74.05° + 1 \angle 0°}$$

$$= \frac{27.94 \angle -26.55°}{3.5 + j\,8.75} = \mathbf{2.97 \angle -94.75°\ A.}$$

EXAMPLE 10.81 *Using Thevenin's theorem, find the power loss in* Z_L *when* $Z_L = (4 + j\,8)\,\Omega$.

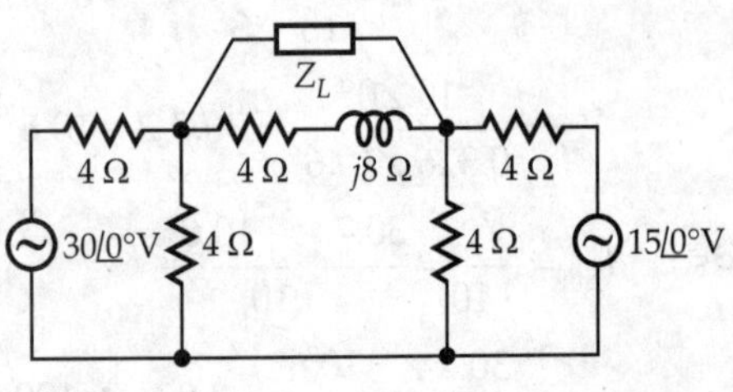

Fig. E10.81

Solution. Let us remove first the load impedance Z_L [Refer to Fig. E10.81(*a*)], the loop currents being marked.

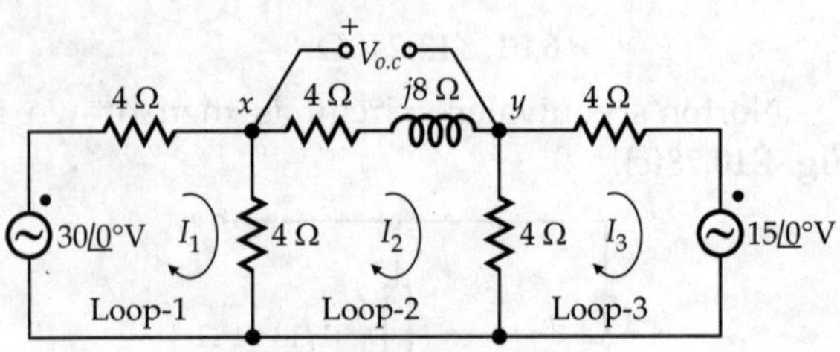

Fig. E10.81 (*a*)

The loop equations are :

for loop-1,

$$8\,I_1 - 4\,I_2 = 30 \angle 0°$$

for loop-2,

$$-4\,I_1 + (12 + j\,8)\,I_2 - 4\,I_3 = 0$$

for loop-3,

$$-4\,I_2 + 8\,I_3 = -15 \angle 0°$$

In matrix form, these equations can be reoriented as

$$\begin{vmatrix} 8 & -4 & 0 \\ -4 & 12 + j\,8 & -4 \\ 0 & -4 & 8 \end{vmatrix} \begin{vmatrix} I_1 \\ I_2 \\ I_3 \end{vmatrix} = \begin{vmatrix} 30 \angle 0° \\ 0 \\ -15 \angle 0° \end{vmatrix}$$

The determinant ΔZ is then given by

$$\Delta Z = 8\,\{(12 + j\,8)8 - 16\} + 4\,\{(-4)8 - 0(-4)\}$$

$$= 8\,\{96 - 16 + j\,64\} + 4(-32)$$

$$= 8\,(80 + j\,64) - 128 = 640 - 128 + j\,512$$

$$= (512 + j\,512)$$

$$= 724.08 \angle 45°.$$

$$\therefore\ I_2 = \frac{\begin{vmatrix} 8 & 30 \angle 0° & 0 \\ -4 & 0 & -4 \\ 0 & -15 \angle 0° & 8 \end{vmatrix}}{\Delta Z}$$

$$= \frac{8\,\{0 \times 8 - 4 \times 15\} - 30\,\{(-4 \times 8) - 0(-4)\}}{\Delta Z}$$

$$= \frac{8 \times (-60) - 30(-32)}{\Delta Z} = \frac{-480 + 960}{724.08 \angle 45°}$$

$$= 0.66 \angle -45°\text{ A.}$$

$$\therefore\quad V_{o.c} = I_2 \times (4 + j\,8)$$

$$= 0.66 \angle -45° \times 8.94 \angle 63.43°$$

$$= 5.9 \angle 18.43°\text{ V}$$

The internal impedance (Z_{in}) can be obtained across x-y by network elimination after deactivating the sources as shown in Fig. E10.81(b).

$$\text{Here} \quad Z_{in} = \frac{4(4+j8)}{8+j8} = \frac{4+j8}{2+j2} = \frac{2+j4}{1+j1}$$

$$= \frac{4.472\angle 63.44°}{1.414\angle 45°} = 3.16\angle 18.44°\,\Omega.$$

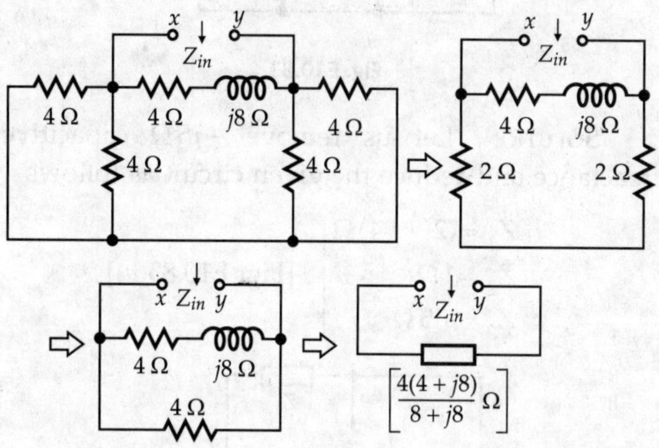

Fig. E10.81 (b)

Thevenin's equivalent circuit is then drawn in Fig. 10.81(c).

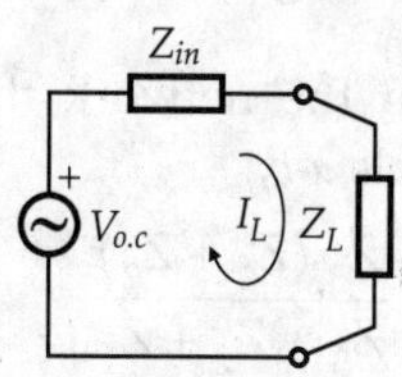

Fig. E10.81 (c)

$$\text{Here,} \quad I_L = \frac{V_{o.c}}{Z_{in}+Z_L} = \frac{5.9\angle 18.43°}{3.16\angle 18.44° + (4+j8)}$$

$$= \frac{5.9\angle 18.43°}{3+j1+4+j8}$$

$$= \frac{5.9\angle 18.43°}{7+j9} = \frac{5.9\angle 18.43°}{11.4\angle 52.13°}$$

$$= 0.52\angle -33.7°\text{ A}$$

$\therefore$ Power loss (P_L) in Z is given by

$$(0.52)^2 \times 4 = \mathbf{1.0816\ W.}$$

EXAMPLE 10.82 *In the network of Fig. E10.82, $V_2 = 10\angle 90°$. Find Thevenin's equivalent network across x-y. Also check your result using Norton's Theorem.*

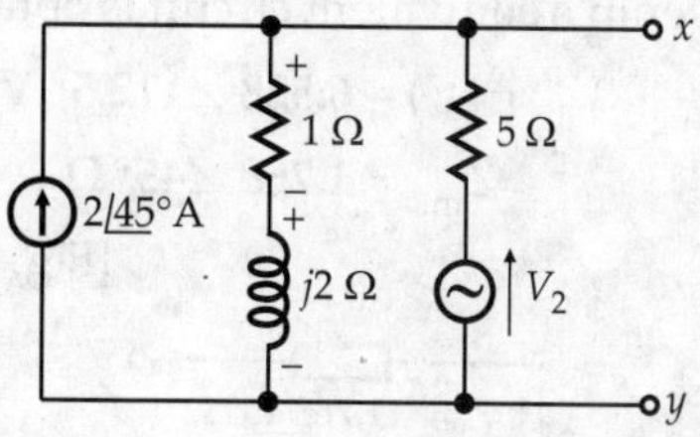

Fig. E10.82

SOLUTION. The internal impedance of the network can be obtained by deactivating the sources as shown in Fig. E10.82(a).

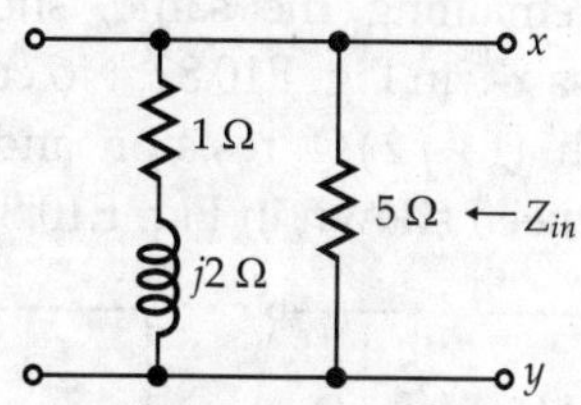

Fig. E10.82(a)

$$\text{Here,} \quad Z_{int} = \frac{(1+j2)5}{1+j2+5} = \frac{5+j10}{6+j2}$$

$$= \frac{11.18\angle 63.43°}{6.324\angle 18.43°}$$

$$= 1.768\angle 45°\,\Omega.$$

Next, in Fig. E10.82, let the potential at x be V. Nodal analysis yields

$$\frac{V}{1+j2} + \frac{V-V_2}{5} = 2\angle 45°$$

$$\text{or} \quad \frac{V(1-j2)}{5} + \frac{V}{5} - \frac{V_2}{5} = 2(\cos 45° + j\sin 45°)$$

$$= 1.414 + j1.414$$

$$\text{or} \quad 0.2V - j0.4V + 0.2V - \frac{10\angle 90°}{5} = 1.414 + j1.414$$

$$\text{or} \quad 0.4V - j0.4V - j2 = 1.414 + j1.414$$

$$\text{or} \quad 0.4(1-j)V = 1.414 + j3.414$$

$$\therefore \quad V = \frac{1.414 + j3.414}{0.4(1-j)}$$

$$= \frac{3.695\angle 67.5°}{0.566\angle -45°}$$

$$= 6.528\angle 112.5°\text{ V.}$$

Thus Thevenin's equivalent circuit is obtained with

$$V_{o.c}\ (=V) = \mathbf{6.528\ \angle 112.5^\circ\ V}$$

and $$Z_{int} = \mathbf{1.768\ \angle 45^\circ\ \Omega}$$

[Fig. E10.82(*b*)].

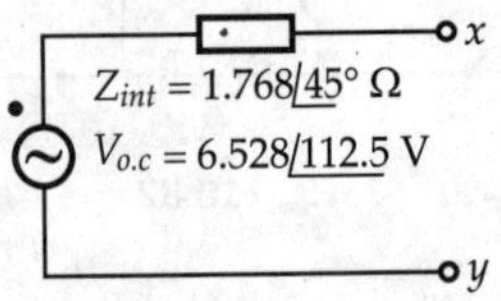

Fig. E10.82 (*b*)

While Norton's theorem is utilised, the internal impedance remaining the same, short circuit is applied across *x-y* in Fig. E10.82. No current would flow through $(1+j\,2)\Omega$ resistor and the circuit diagram has been shown in Fig. E10.82(*c*).

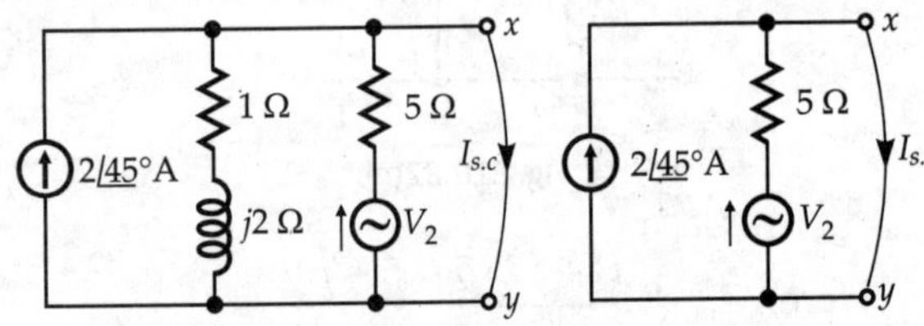

Fig. E10.82 (*c*)

Obviously,

$$I_{s.c} = 2\ \angle 45^\circ + \frac{V_2}{5} = 2\ \angle 45^\circ + \frac{10\ \angle 90^\circ}{5}$$

$$= 2(\cos 45^\circ + j \sin 45^\circ) + 2\,(\cos 90^\circ + j \sin 90^\circ)$$

$$= 1.414 + j\,1.414 + j\,2$$

$$= (1.414 + j\,3.414)\ \text{A}.$$

We have obtained the internal impedance as

$$\mathbf{Z_{int} = 1.768\ \angle 45^\circ\ \Omega.}$$

The equivalent Norton's circuit is drawn in Fig. 10.82(*d*); where

$$V_{x-y} = V_{o.c}\ (\text{of Thevenin's circuit}) = I_{s.c} \times Z_{int}$$

$$= (1.414 + j\,3.414)(1.768\ \angle 45^\circ)$$

$$= 3.695\ \angle 67.5^\circ \times 1.768\ \angle 45^\circ$$

$$= \mathbf{6.533\ \angle 112.5^\circ\ V}$$

Nearly same result we have obtained while solving the problem using Thevenin's theorem.

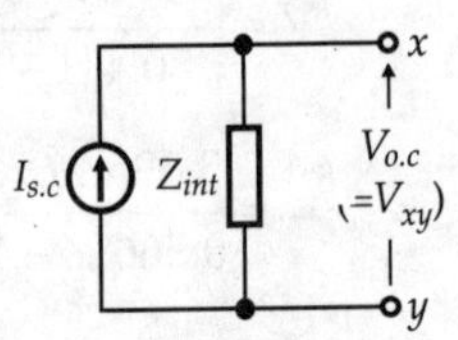

Fig. E10.82 (*d*)

EXAMPLE 10.83 *Find Norton's equivalent circuit across the* $-j5\,\Omega$ *capacitor in the network of Fig. E10.83.*

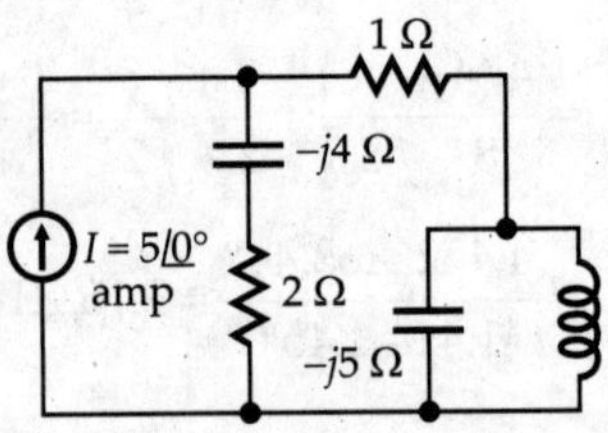

Fig. E10.83

SOLUTION. Let us remove $-j5\,\Omega$ capacitive reactance and reduce the given circuit as follows :

$$\left.\begin{aligned} Z_1 &= (2 - j\,4)\,\Omega \\ Z_2 &= 1\,\Omega \\ Z_3 &= j\,5\,\Omega \end{aligned}\right\} \quad \text{[Fig. E10.83(}a\text{)]}$$

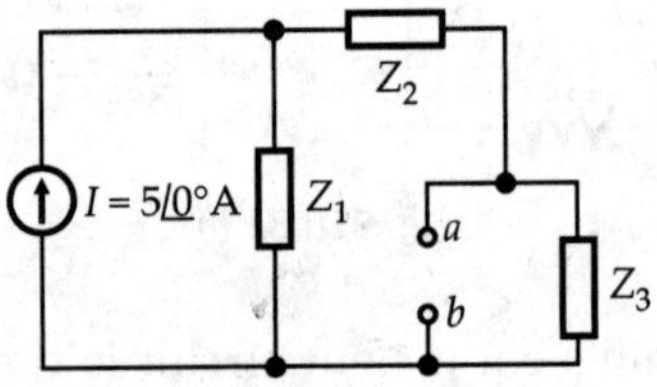

Fig. E10.83 (*a*)

Looking into the network through the open circuited terminals *a-b*,

$$Z_{in} = \frac{Z_3\,(Z_1 + Z_2)}{Z_3 + Z_2 + Z_1}$$

[Ref. Fig. E10.83(*b*) source deactivated]

$$= \frac{j\,5\,(2 - j\,4 + 1)}{j\,5 + 1 + 2 - j\,4} = \frac{5\ \angle 90^\circ\,(3 - j\,4)}{3 + j\,1}$$

$$= \frac{5\ \angle 90^\circ \times 5\ \angle -53.1^\circ}{3.16\ \angle 18.43^\circ}$$

$$= 7.91\ \angle 18.47^\circ\ \Omega.$$

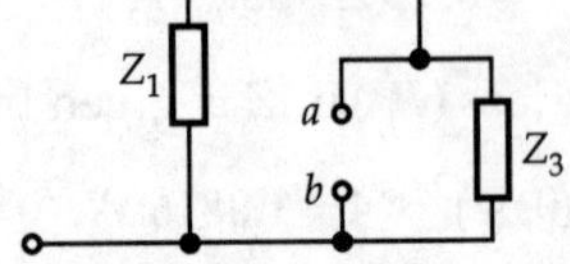

Fig. E10.83 (*b*)

Next, short circuit is applied at terminals *a-b* of Fig. E10.83(*a*) assuming the current through *a-b* terminals being $I_{s.c.}$ Let the circuit configuration be redrawn as shown in Fig. E10.83(*c*).

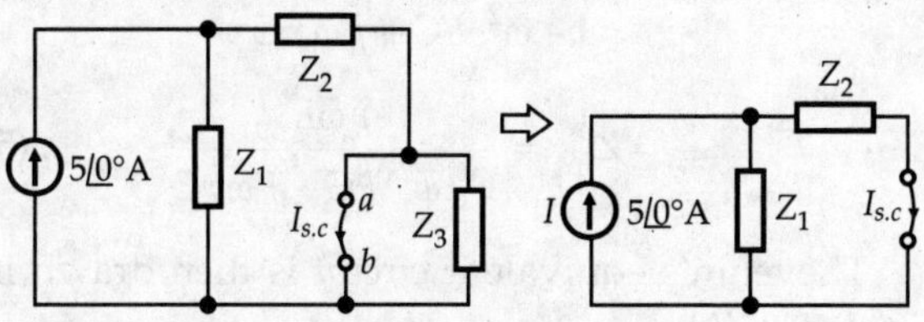

Fig. E10.83(*c*)

$$I_{s.c.} = I\frac{Z_1}{Z_1+Z_2} = 5\angle 0^\circ \frac{2-j4}{(2-j4)+1}$$

$$= \frac{22.36\angle -63.43^\circ}{(3-j4)} = \frac{22.36\angle -63.43^\circ}{5\angle -53.13^\circ}$$

$$= 4.472\angle -10.30^\circ \text{ A}$$

Norton's equivalent circuit is drawn in **Fig. E10.83(*d*)**.

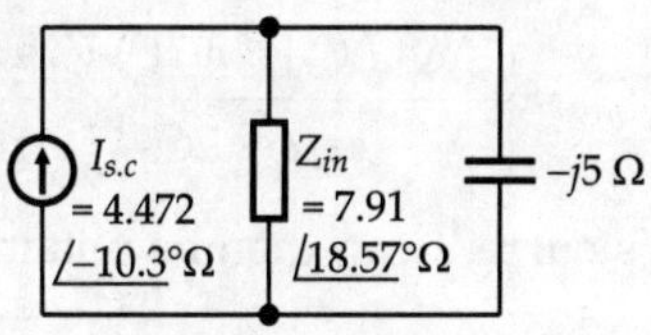

Fig. E10.83(*d*)

EXAMPLE 10.84 *In Fig. 10.84, find Thevenin's equivalent circuit across terminals a-b. Take* $I = 1\angle 0^\circ$ *A,* $R = 1\Omega$.

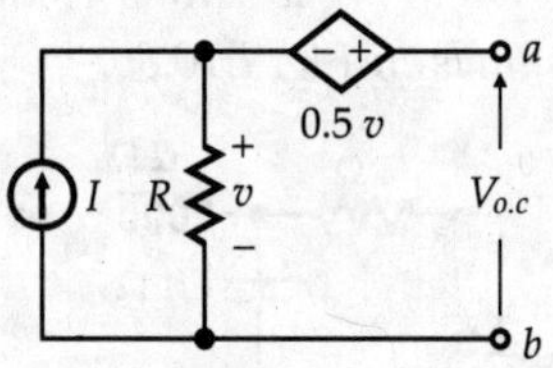

Fig. E10.84

SOLUTION. Let the open circuit voltage across *a-b* terminals be $V_{o.c.}$ in Fig. E10.84.

Obviously, in the right handed open circuited loop,

$$-v - 0.5\,v + V_{o.c} = 0 \quad \text{or} \quad V_{o.c.} = 1.5\,v.$$

However, in the left loop,

$$v = IR = 1\angle 0^\circ \times 1 = 1\angle 0^\circ \text{ V}.$$

$$\therefore \quad V_{o.c} = 1.5 \times 1\angle 0^\circ = 1.5\angle 0^\circ \text{ V}.$$

Since the circuit contains dependent source hence to find Z_{in} (internal impedance) of the given circuit, following method is adopted :

Let *a-b* terminal be shorted as shown in Fig. E10.84(*a*)

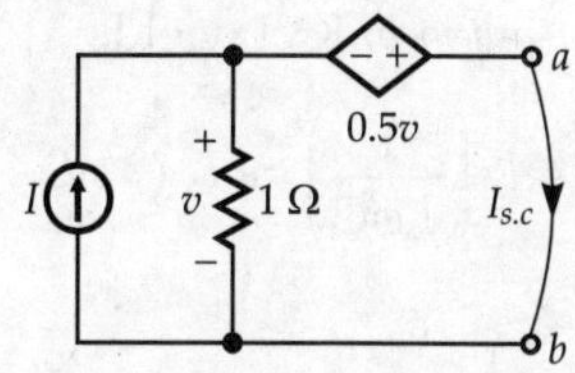

Fig. E10.84(*a*)

In the right hand loop,

$$-v - 0.5\,v = 0$$

or
$$v = 0 \qquad \text{...(1)}$$

Substitution of $v = 0$ leads to the result that the dependent source $0.5\,v$ does not exist when *a-b* terminals are shorted [Fig. E10.84(*b*)]. Also, no current would flow through *R* and finally

$$I_{s.c.} = I$$

$$\therefore \quad Z_{in} = \frac{V_{o.c}}{I_{s.c.}} = \frac{1.5\angle 0^\circ}{1\angle 0^\circ} = 1.5\,\Omega$$

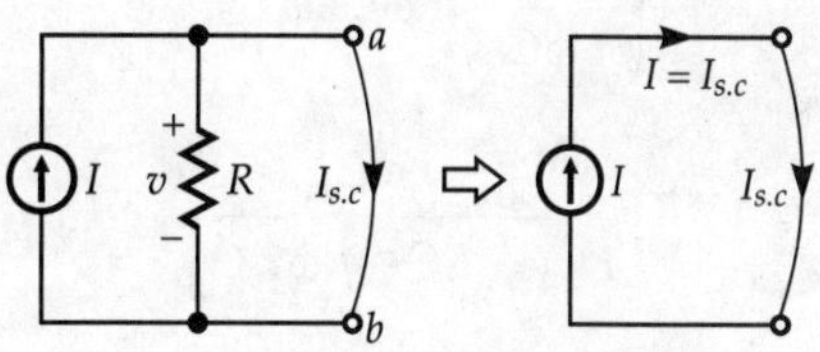

Fig. E10.84(*b*)

Thus, the Thevenin's equivalent circuit can be formed with

$$\mathbf{V_{o.c} = 1.5\angle 0^\circ \text{ V} \text{ and } Z_{in} = 1.5\angle 0^\circ\,\Omega.}$$

EXAMPLE 10.85 *Obtain Thevenin's and Norton's equivalent circuit of the network shown in Fig. E10.85 across x-y.*

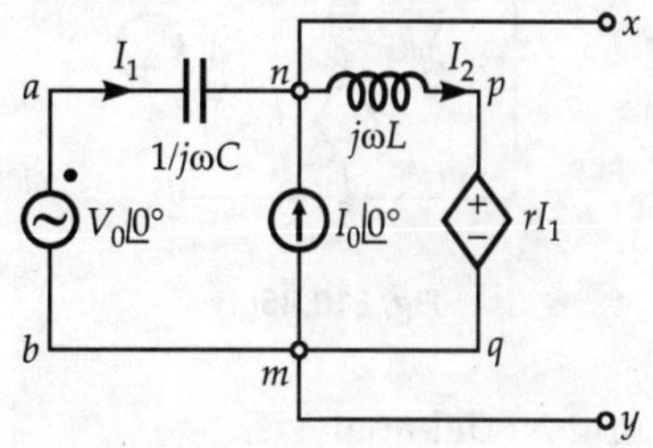

Fig. E10.85

SOLUTION. Let $V_{o.c.}$ be the open circuit voltage across *x-y*.

Obviously, at the central *node n*,

$$I_2 = I_1 + I_0 \qquad \text{[vector sum]}$$

In *loop a-n-p-q-m-b*, KVL yields

$$-V_0 + I_1\left(\frac{1}{j\,\omega C}\right) + I_2\,(j\,\omega L) + rI_1 = 0$$

or $$-V_0 + I_1\left(\frac{1}{j\,\omega C}\right) + (I_1 + I_0)\,j\,\omega L + r\,I_1 = 0$$

$$[\because I_2 = I_1 + I_0]$$

$$\therefore \quad I_1 = \frac{V_0 - j\,\omega L\,I_0}{\dfrac{1}{j\,\omega C} + j\,\omega L + r} \qquad ...(1)$$

The open circuit voltage across *x-y* terminal being the voltage across nodes *n-m*, we find that

$$V_{o.c} = V_0 - I_1\left(\frac{1}{j\,\omega C}\right)$$

$$= V_0 - \left(\frac{V_0 - j\,\omega L\,I_0}{\dfrac{1}{j\,\omega C} + j\,\omega L + r}\,\frac{1}{j\,\omega C}\right)$$

$$= V_0 - \left[\frac{V_0 - j\,\omega L\,I_0}{1 - \omega^2\,LC + j\,\omega\,r\,C}\right]$$

$$= \frac{(-\omega^2\,LC + j\,\omega\,r\,C)\,V_0 + j\,\omega L\,I_0}{1 - \omega^2\,LC + j\,\omega\,r\,C} \qquad ...(2)$$

To find the Thevenin's equivalent impedance Z_{int}, the independent sources of the network are set to zero and a source (*V*) is applied at *x-y* terminals [Fig. E10.85(*a*)].

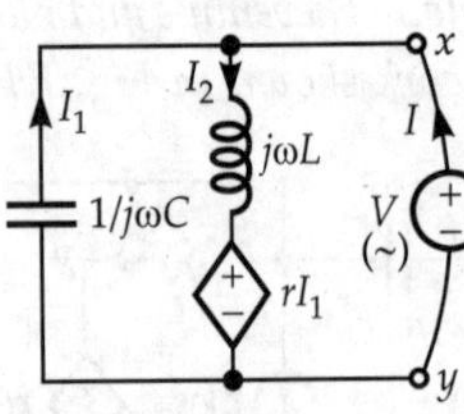

Fig. E10.85(*a*)

Applying Nodal analysis,

$$\frac{V}{1/j\,\omega C} + \frac{V - r\,I_1}{j\,\omega L} = I \qquad ...(3)$$

But $$I_1 = -j\,\omega C\,V \qquad ...(4)$$

Using (4) in (3),

$$V = I\,\frac{j\,\omega L}{1 - \omega^2\,LC + j\,\omega\,r\,C}$$

$$\therefore \quad \frac{V}{I} = Z_{int} = \frac{j\,\omega L}{1 - \omega^2\,LC + j\,\omega\,rC} \qquad ...(5)$$

Thevenin's equivalent circuit is then drawn in **Fig. E10.85(*b*)**.

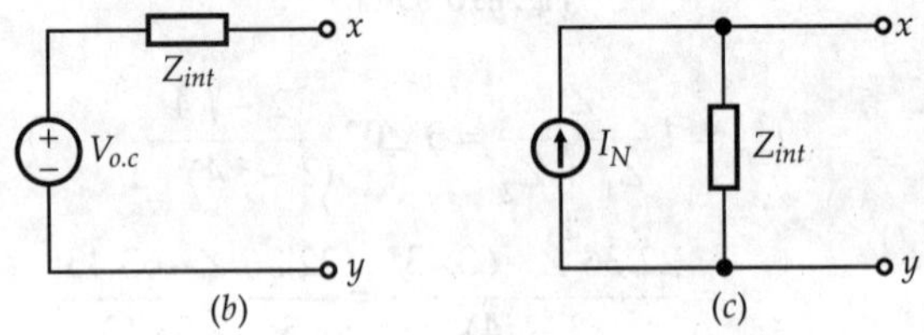

Fig. E10.85

Here $$Z_{int} = \frac{j\,\omega L}{1 - \omega^2\,LC + j\,\omega\,rC}$$

and $$V_{o.c} = \frac{(-\omega^2\,LC + j\,\omega\,rC)\,V_0 + j\,\omega L\,I_0}{1 - \omega^2\,LC + j\,\omega\,rC}$$

Norton's current can then be obtained as

$$I_N = \frac{V_{o.c}}{Z_{int}} = I_0 + \left(j\,\omega + \frac{r}{L}\right)CV_0 \qquad ...(6)$$

Fig. E10.85(*c*) represents Norton's equivalent circuit.

EXAMPLE 10.86 *Obtain Thevenin's equivalent network across x-y terminals in Fig. E10.86.*

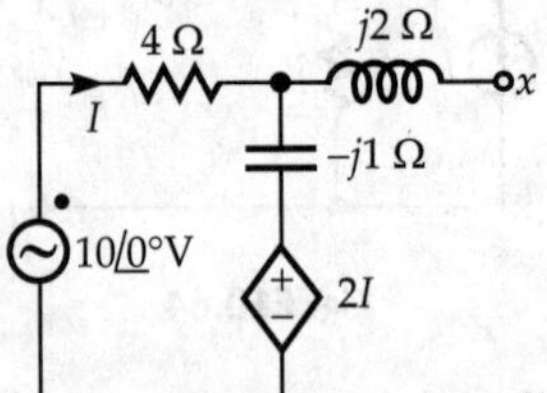

Fig. E10.86

SOLUTION. Let us redraw the network with node markings [Fig. E10.86(*a*)]. Applying KVL in *loop abcd*,

$$-10 + 4\,I - j\,1(I) + 2\,I = 0$$

or $$I\,(6 - j) = 10$$

$$\therefore \quad I = \frac{10}{6 - j} = \frac{10\,\angle 0^\circ}{6.083\,\angle -9.46^\circ}$$

$$= 1.64\,\angle 9.46^\circ \text{ A.}$$

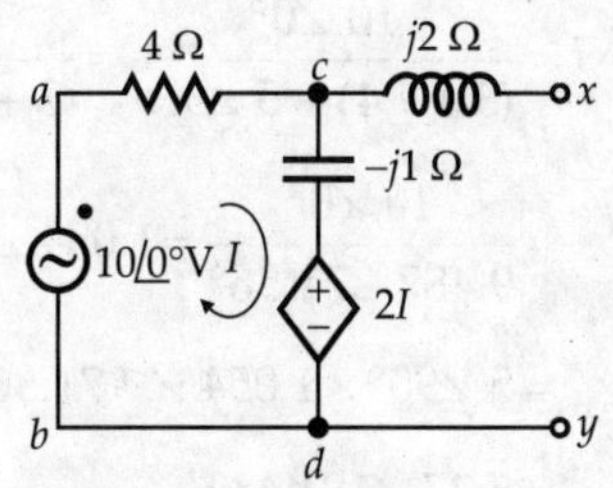

Fig. E10.86(*a*)

$$\therefore V_{x-y} (= V_{Th}) = (-j\,1)\,I + 2I$$

$$= I(2 - j\,1) = 1.64\,\angle 9.46° \times 2.24\,\angle -26.56°$$

$$= 3.674\,\angle -17.1°\text{ V}.$$

Let us now apply short circuit across *x-y* [Fig. E10.86(*b*)].

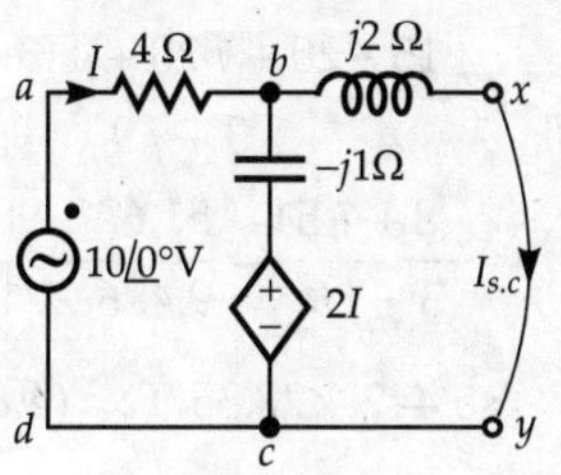

Fig. E10.86(*b*)

In *loop a-b-c-d*,

$$-10 + 4I + I(-j\,1) + 2I - I_{s.c.}(-j\,1) = 0$$

or $$I(6 - j\,1) + j\,I_{s.c.} = 10 \quad ...(1)$$

In *loop b-x-y-c*,

$$j\,2(I_{s.c.}) - 2I + I_{s.c.}(-j\,1) - I(-j\,1) = 0$$

or $$I(2 - j) = I_{s.c.}(j\,1)$$

$$\therefore \quad I = j\frac{I_{s.c.}}{2 - j} = \frac{j\,(2 + j)}{4 + 1} I_{s.c.}$$

$$= 0.2\,I_{s.c}(-1 + j\,2) \quad ...(2)$$

Substituting (2) in (1),

$$0.2\,I_{s.c}(-1 + j\,2)(6 - j\,1) + j\,I_{s.c.} = 10.$$

or $$0.2\,I_{s.c}[-6 + j\,1 + j\,12 + 2] + j\,I_{s.c.} = 10$$

or $$I_{s.c}[-0.8 + j\,2.6] + j\,I_{s.c.} = 10$$

$$\therefore \quad I_{s.c}[-0.8 + j\,3.6] = 10$$

$$\therefore \quad I_{s.c} = \frac{10}{-0.8 + j\,3.6} = \frac{10}{3.69\,\angle 102.53°}$$

or $$I_{s.c} = 2.71\,\angle -102.53°\text{ A}.$$

Thus

$$Z_{\text{int}}\,(Z_{th}) = \frac{V_{o.c.}}{I_{s.c.}} = \frac{V_{th}}{I_{s.c.}} = \frac{3.674\,\angle -17.1°}{2.71\,\angle -102.53°}$$

$$= 1.356\,\angle 85.43°\,\Omega.$$

Thevenin's equivalent circuit can now be drawn as shown in **Fig. E10.86(*c*)**.

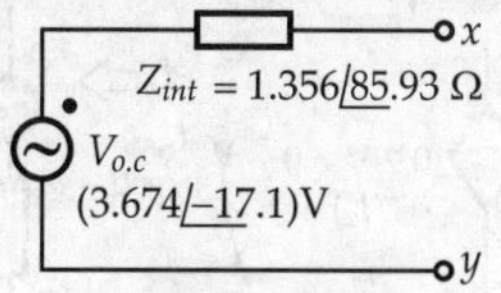

Fig. E10.86(*c*)

EXAMPLE 10.87 *Find Thevenin's equivalent circuit across terminal a-b for the left part of the network of the circuit shown in Fig. E10.87.*

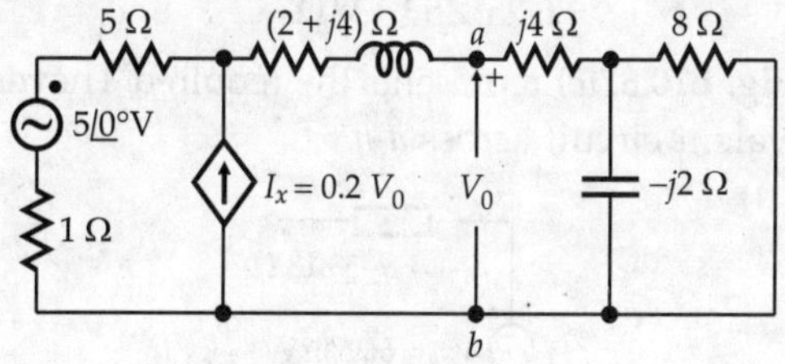

Fig. E10.87

SOLUTION. Let us remove the portion of the network to the right of terminals *a-b*, the open circuit voltage being $V_{o.c.}$ Applying KVL at the left loop of Fig. E10.87(*a*),

$$I_x\,(1) + 5\,\angle 0° = V_{o.c} \quad ...(1)$$

[∵ no current flows through (2 + *j* 4) Ω impedance]

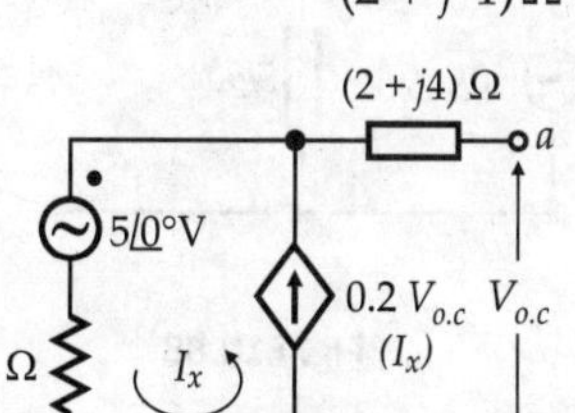

Fig. E10.87(*a*)

But $$I_x = 0.2\,V_{o.c.},$$

∴ From (1),

$$V_{o.c.} = \frac{5}{0.8} = 6.25\text{ V}.$$

To find Z_{int}, let short circuit be applied across *a-b* terminal. This makes $V_0 = 0$ leading to zero value of the dependent source too.

[Fig. E10.87(*b*)]

$$I_{s.c.} = \frac{5\angle 0^\circ}{1 + j0 + 2 + j4} = \frac{5\angle 0^\circ}{3 + j4}$$

$$= 1\angle -53.13^\circ \text{ A;}$$

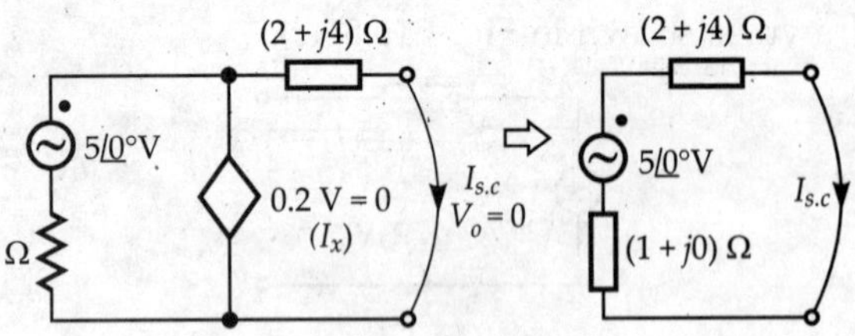

Fig. E10.87(*b*)

$$\therefore \quad Z_{\text{int}} = \frac{V_{o.c.}}{I_{s.c.}} = \frac{6.25\angle 0^\circ}{1\angle -53.13^\circ}$$

$$= 6.25\angle 53.13^\circ \, \Omega.$$

Fig. E10.87(*c*) represents the required Thevenin's equivalent circuit across *a-b*.

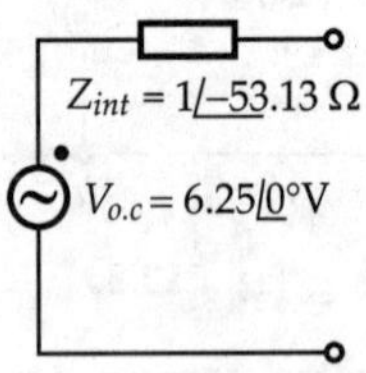

Fig. E10.87 (*c*)

Example 10.88 *Find current through $(-j4\,\Omega)$ capacitor using Thevenin's theorem in Fig. E10.88.*

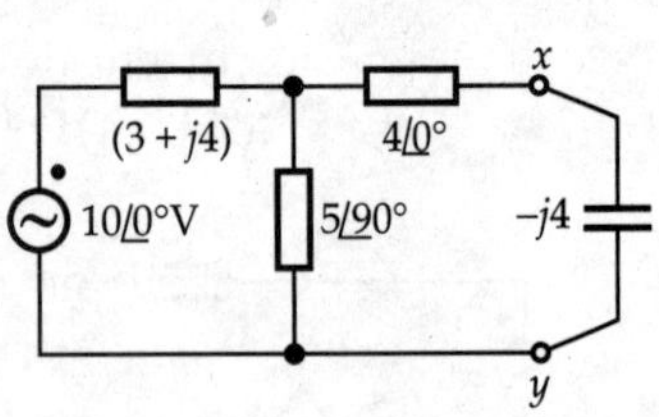

Fig. E10.88

Solution. Let us open the *x-y* terminal removing the capacitor. Let the open circuit voltage be $V_{o.c.}$ [Fig. E10.88(*a*)].

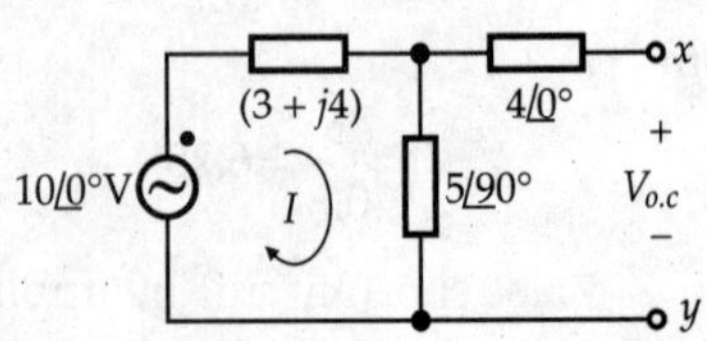

Fig. E10.88(*a*)

$$I = \frac{10\angle 0^\circ}{(3 + j4) + 5\angle 90^\circ} = \frac{10\angle 0^\circ}{(3 + j4) + j5}$$

$$= \frac{10\angle 0^\circ}{9.487\angle 71.56^\circ} = 1.054\angle -71.56^\circ \text{ A;}$$

$$\therefore \quad V_{o.c} = 5\angle 90^\circ \times 1.054\angle -71.56^\circ$$

$$= 5.27\angle 18.44^\circ \text{ V.}$$

Internal impedance can be obtained as

$$Z_{\text{int}} = \frac{(3 + j4)\,5\angle 90^\circ}{(3 + j4) + 5\angle 90^\circ} + 4\angle 0^\circ$$

[deactivating the 10 ∠0° V source as shown in Fig. E10.88(*b*)]

$$= \frac{(3 + j4)\,j5}{(3 + j4) + j5} + 4$$

or $$Z_{in} = \frac{j15 - 20 + j20 + 4(3 + j4)}{3 + j9}$$

$$= \frac{-8 + j51}{3 + j9} = \frac{51.62\angle 98.91^\circ}{9.486\angle 71.56^\circ}$$

$$= 5.442\angle 27.35^\circ \, \Omega = (4.834 + j2.5)\,\Omega.$$

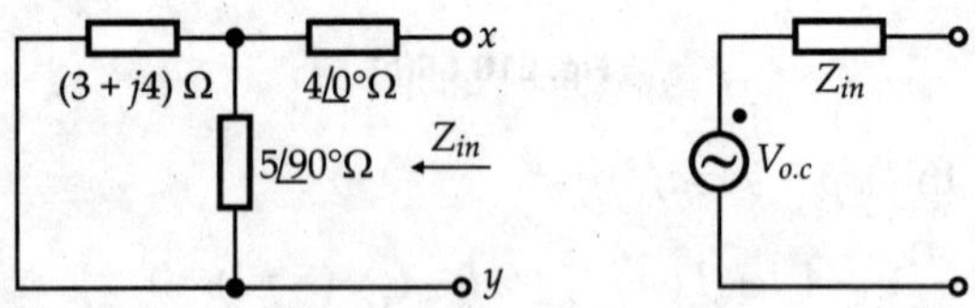

Fig. E10.88 (*b*) (*c*)

Thevenin's equivalent circuit is shown in Fig. E10.88(*c*). The load (the capacitor) being reconnected, the current through it is,

$$I_L = \frac{V_{o.c.}}{Z_{in} + (-j4)} = \frac{5.27\angle 18.44^\circ}{4.834 + j2.5 - j4}$$

$$= \frac{5.27\angle 18.44^\circ}{5.06\angle -17.24} = \mathbf{1.041\angle 35.68^\circ \text{ A.}}$$

Example 10.89 *Find Thevenin's equivalent circuit across the output terminals for the given transistor equivalent circuit shown in Fig. E10.89.*

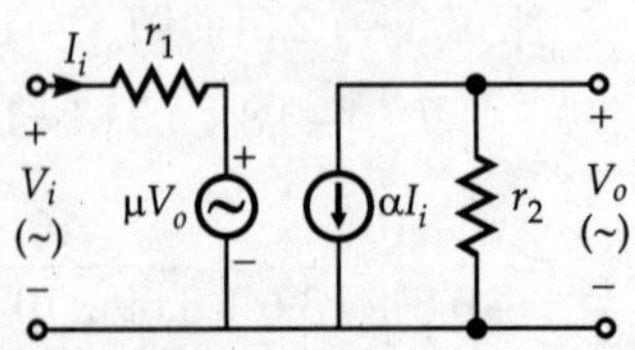

Fig. E10.89

SOLUTION. Inspection reveals that $V_0 \equiv V_{o.c}$ while we are thevenising the given circuit. Also I_i being the input current shown by an arrow in the left loop of Fig. E10.89.

Obviously,

$$I = \frac{V_i - \mu V_0}{r_1} = \frac{V_i - \mu V_{o.c.}}{r_1} \quad ...(1)$$

Also, in the right loop, $\alpha I \times r_2 = -V_{o.c.}$ [-ve sign is due to the reverse direction flow of (αI) current];

or $$V_{o.c} = -I \alpha r_2 = -\alpha r_2 \left(\frac{V_i - \mu V_{o.c.}}{r_1} \right)$$

$$= \frac{-\alpha r_2 V_i}{r_1} + \frac{\alpha \mu r_2 V_{o.c.}}{r_1}$$

or $$V_{o.c} \left(1 - \frac{\alpha \mu r_2}{r_1} \right) = \frac{-\alpha r_2 V_i}{r_1}$$

or $$V_{o.c} (r_1 - \alpha \mu r_2) = -\alpha r_2 V_i$$

$\therefore$ $$V_{o.c} = -\frac{\alpha r_2 V_i}{r_1 - \alpha \mu r_2}. \quad ...(2)$$

Next, the output terminals are shorted [Fig. E10.89(*a*)]. Since $V_0 = 0$ due to shorting of output terminals hence the dependent source μV_0 in the left loop will have no existance. Also, no current would flow through r_2 in the right loop and hence

$$I_{s.c.} = -\alpha I_i = -\alpha \frac{V_i}{r_1} \quad ...(3)$$

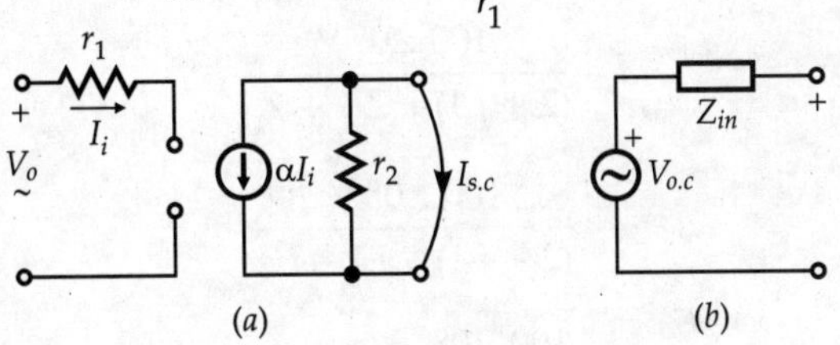

Fig. E10.89(*a*)

$\therefore$ From (2) and (3),

$$Z_{in} = \frac{V_{o.c.}}{I_{s.c.}} = \frac{-\alpha \dfrac{r_2 V_i}{r_1 - \alpha \mu r_2}}{-\alpha \dfrac{V_i}{r_1}} = \frac{(r_1 r_2)}{(r_1 - \alpha \mu r_2)}$$

Thevenin's equivalent circuit is then shown in **Fig. E10.89(*b*).**

when $$V_{o.c.} = -\frac{\alpha r_2 V_i}{r_1 - \alpha \mu r_2} \text{ V}$$

$$Z_{in} = \frac{r_1 r_2}{r_1 - \alpha \mu r_2} \Omega.$$

EXAMPLE 10.90 *Find the Norton's equivalent for the circuit shown in the preceding example (Ex. 10.89).*

SOLUTION. We have seen that

$$V_{o.c.} = -\frac{\alpha r_2 V_i}{r_1 - \alpha \mu r_2} \text{ volts,}$$

while $V_{o.c.}$ represents the Thevenin's voltage at the output while the internal impedance Z_{in} is given by

$$Z_{in} = \frac{r_1 r_2}{r_1 - \alpha \mu r_2} \text{ ohm.}$$

Converting the equivalent Thevenin's circuit to current source circuit (*i.e.*, Norton's circuit),

$$I_N = \frac{V_{o.c.}}{Z_{in}} = \frac{-\alpha \dfrac{r_2 V_i}{r_1 - \alpha \mu r_2}}{\dfrac{r_1 r_2}{r_1 - \alpha \mu r_2}} = -\alpha \frac{V_i}{r_1}$$

[which has been determined as $I_{s.c}$ in the previous example]

Norton's equivalent circuit is then drawn in Fig. E10.90.

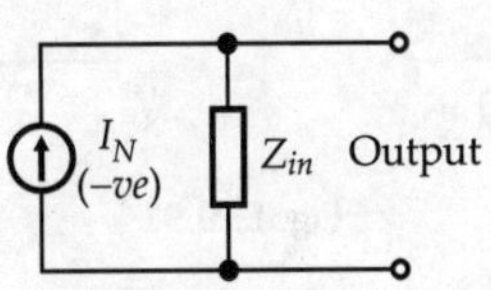

Fig. E10.90

Here, $\mathbf{I_N} = -\alpha \dfrac{V_i}{r_1}$ **V** and $\mathbf{Z_{in}} = \dfrac{r_1 r_2}{r_1 - \alpha \mu r_2} \Omega.$

EXAMPLE 10.91 *Fig. E10.91 represents a steady state circuit in s-domain. Find its Thevenin's equivalent at the right of terminal x-y.*

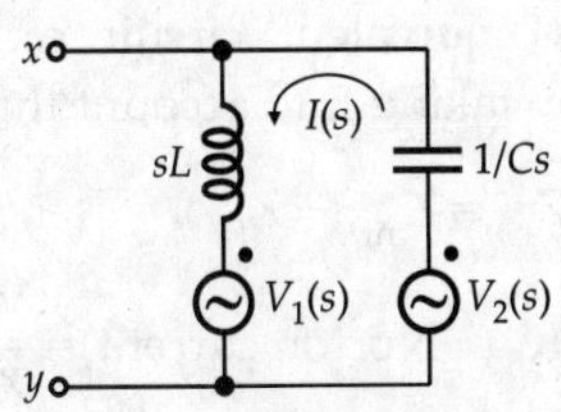

Fig. E10.91

SOLUTION. Let $I(s)$ be the circulating loop current as shown in Fig. E10.91. Obviously,

$$I(s) = \frac{V_2(s) - V_1(s)}{sL + \dfrac{1}{Cs}}$$

Assuming the open circuit voltage across x-y terminal to be $V_{o.c.}$, application of KVL gives

$$V_{o.c} = sL.\, I(s) + V_1(s)$$

$$= V_1(s) + sL \frac{V_2(s) - V_1(s)}{sL + \frac{1}{Cs}}$$

$$= \frac{V_1(s) + s^2 LC\, V_2(s)}{s^2 LC + 1}$$

With independent sources deactivated, [Fig. E10.91(a)] the Thevenin's impedance (internal impedance of the network looking through x-y terminal) is given by

$$Z_{int} = sL || \frac{1}{Cs} = \frac{sL(1/Cs)}{sL + \frac{1}{Cs}} = \frac{sL}{s^2 LC + 1}$$

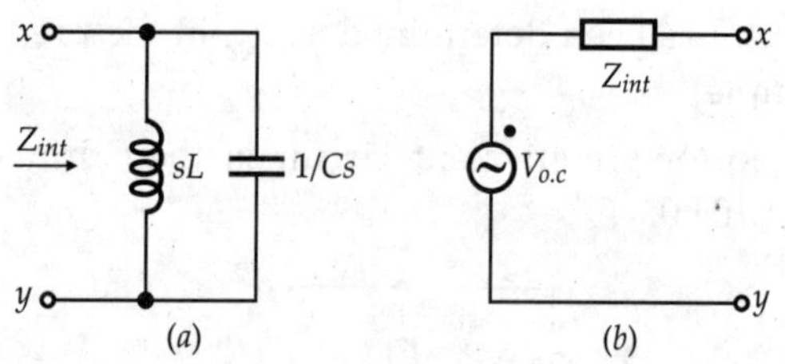

Fig. E10.91

Figure E10.91(b) represents the Thevenin's equivalent circuit,

$$\mathbf{V_{o.c.}} = \frac{\boldsymbol{V_1(s) + s^2 LC\, V_2(s)}}{\boldsymbol{s^2 LC + 1}}$$

and $$\boldsymbol{Z_{int}} = \frac{\boldsymbol{sL}}{\boldsymbol{s^2 LC + 1}}$$

[Norton's equivalent circuit can be formed from above by taking into account that

$$Z_N \equiv Z_{int} \; (= Z_{Th})$$

and $$I_N \; (= \text{Norton current}) = \frac{V_{o.c.}}{Z_{int}}$$

$$= \frac{\dfrac{V_1(s) + s^2 LC\, V_2(s)}{s^2 LC + 1}}{\dfrac{sL}{s^2 LC + 1}}$$

or $$I_N = \frac{\boldsymbol{V_1(s) + s^2 LC\, V_2(s)}}{\boldsymbol{sL}}.$$

EXAMPLE 10.92 *Obtain equivalent circuit across x-y terminals in Fig. E10.92 and find the value of Z_L to have maximum power transfer.*

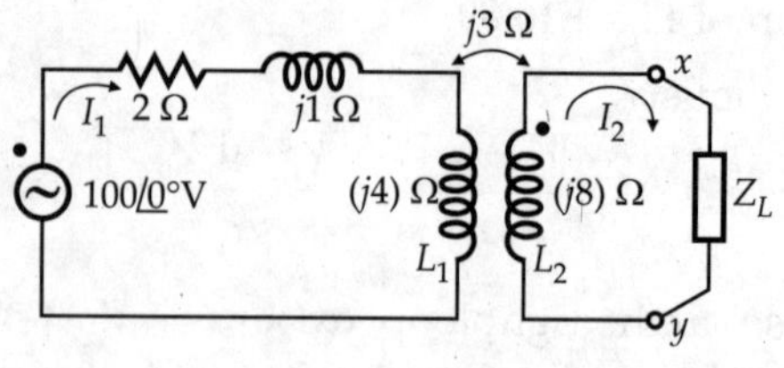

Fig. E10.92

SOLUTION. From the theory of conductively coupled circuit, M here is –ve as in L_1, I_1 enters through dotted terminals while I_2 leaves dotted terminal in L_2.

$\therefore$ In the equivalent circuit, referring Fig. E10.92(a),

$$Z_A = L_1 - M = j\,4 - j\,3 = +\,j\,1\,\Omega$$
$$Z_B = L_2 - M = j\,8 - j\,3 = j\,5\,\Omega$$
$$Z_C = M = j\,3\,\Omega.$$

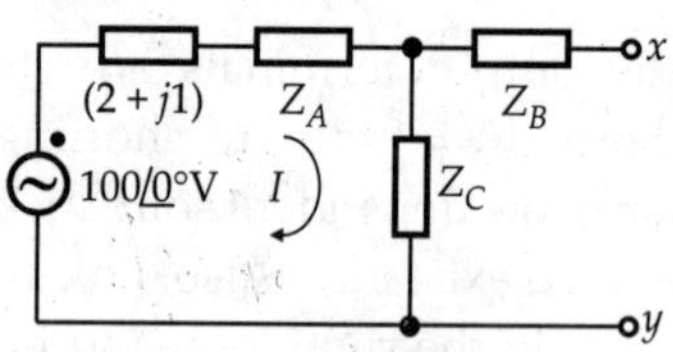

Fig. E10.92(*a*)

$$\therefore \quad I = \frac{100\,\angle 0°\text{ V}}{(2 + j\,1) + Z_A + Z_C}$$

$$= \frac{100\,\angle 0°\text{ V}}{(2 + j\,1) + j\,1 + j\,3}$$

$$= \frac{100\,\angle 0°}{(2 + j\,5)} = 18.57\,\angle -68.19°\text{ A.}$$

Thus, $V_{o.c.} \; (= V_{x-y}) = I(Z_C)$

$$= 18.57\,\angle -68.19 \times j\,3$$
$$= 55.71\,\angle 21.81°\text{ V}$$

The internal impedance (Z_{int}) may be obtained by deactivating the source in Fig. E10.92(a), where

$$Z_{int} = \frac{[Z_A + (2 + j\,1)]\, Z_C}{Z_A + 2 + j\,1 + Z_C} + Z_B$$

$$= \frac{\{(j\,1) + (2 + j\,1)\}(j\,3)}{j\,1 + 2 + j\,1 + j\,3} + j\,5$$

$$= \frac{(2+j2)\,j3}{2+j5} + j5$$

$$= \frac{-6+j6}{2+j5} + j5 = \frac{-6+j6+j10-25}{(2+j5)}$$

$$= \frac{-31+j16}{2+j5} = \frac{34.89\angle 152.7^\circ}{5.385\angle 68.19^\circ}$$

$$\therefore \quad Z_{int} = 6.48\angle 84.51^\circ\,\Omega = (0.62 + j6.45)\,\Omega.$$

Figure E10.92(*b*) represents the Thevenin's equivalent circuit across *x*-*y* where

$\mathbf{V_{o.c.} = 55.71\angle 21.81^\circ}$ **V and** $\mathbf{Z_{int} = 6.48\angle 84.51^\circ\,\Omega}$**.**

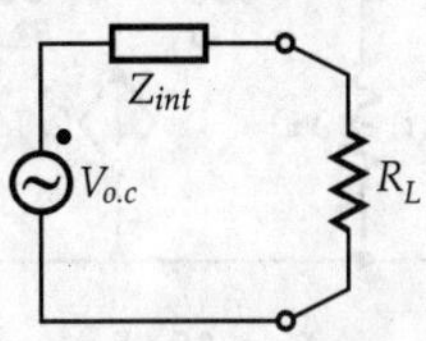

Fig. E10.92(*b*)

Again, as per maximum power transfer theorem,

$$Z_L = Z_{in}^{*} \text{ (complex conjugate)}$$

$$\therefore \quad \mathbf{Z_L = (0.62 - j\,6.45)\,\Omega}$$

$$P_{max} = \frac{V_{o.c}^2}{4R_L} = \frac{55.71^2}{4\times 0.62} \simeq \mathbf{1251.5\ W.}$$

Example 10.93 *Find Norton's equivalent circuit across x-y in s-domain (Fig. E10.93). Hence find Thevenin's equivalent circuit too.*

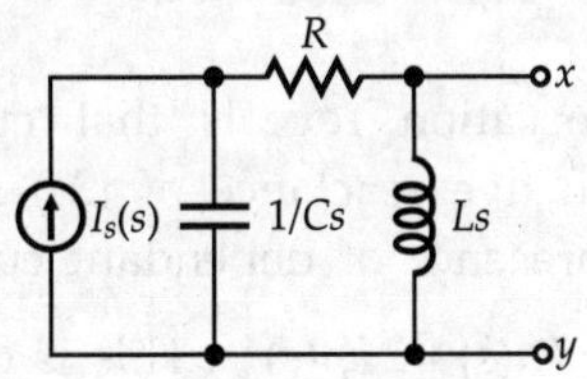

Fig. E10.93

Solution. Let us apply short circuit across *x*-*y* as shown in Fig. E10.93(*a*).

$$I_{s.c}(s) = I_s(s)\frac{\frac{1}{Cs}}{\frac{1}{Cs}+R}$$

[by current division formulae]

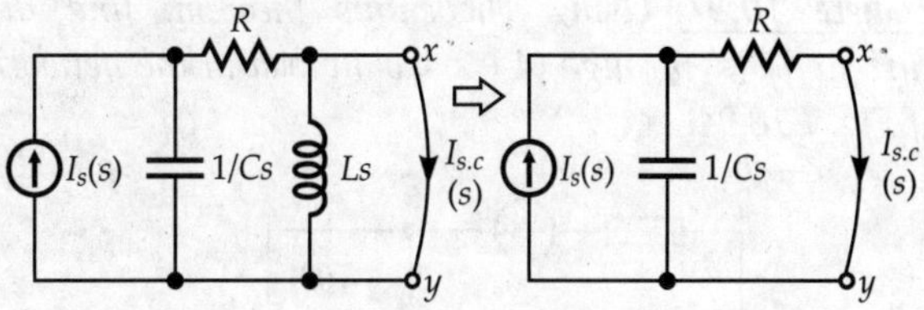

Fig. E10.93(*a*)

To find Z_{int}, the current source is deactivated and the shorting is removed. Looking back into the circuit through *x*-*y*, following Fig. E10.93(*b*),

$$Z_{int} = \frac{\left(R+\frac{1}{Cs}\right)Ls}{\frac{1}{Cs}+R+Ls} = \frac{s^2\left(R+\frac{1}{Cs}\right)}{s^2+\left(\frac{R}{L}\right)s+\frac{1}{LC}}$$

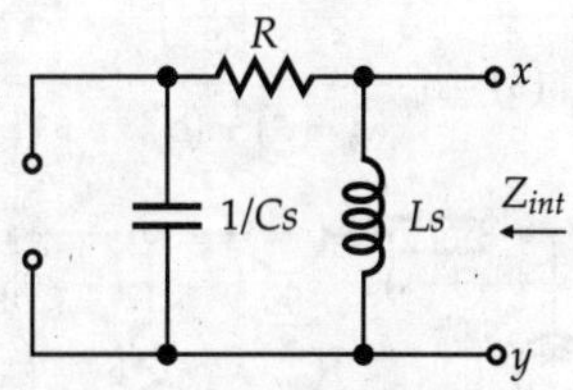

Fig. E10.93(*b*)

Figure E10.93(*c*) denotes the Norton's equivalent source while Thevenin's equivalent voltage can be obtained as

$$V_{o.c.} = I_{s.c.}(s)\times Z_{int}$$

$$= I_s(s)\left(\frac{\frac{1}{Cs}}{\frac{1}{Cs}+R}\right)\left(\frac{R+\frac{1}{Cs}}{\frac{1}{Cs}+R+Ls}\right).Ls$$

$$= \frac{(1/C)\,sI_s(s)}{s^2+(R/L)s+1/LC}$$

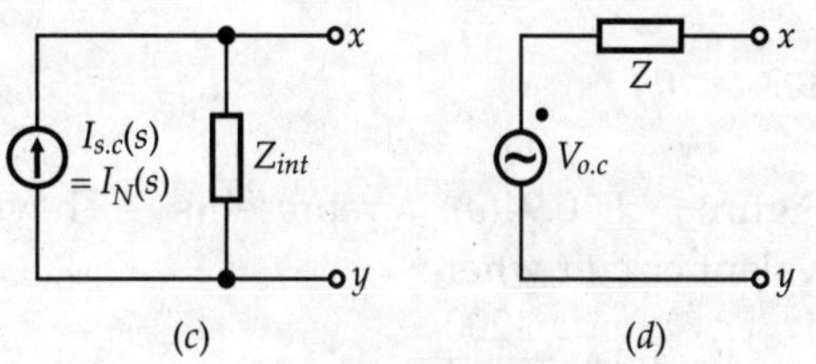

Fig. E10.93

Figure **E10.93(*d*)** represents Thevenin's equivalent circuit derived from Norton's circuit [it may be noted that the internal impedance remains the same].

EXAMPLE 10.94 *Using Thevenin's theorem, find the current $I_L(s)$ through $(4+2s)$ ohm load in the network of Fig. E10.94.*

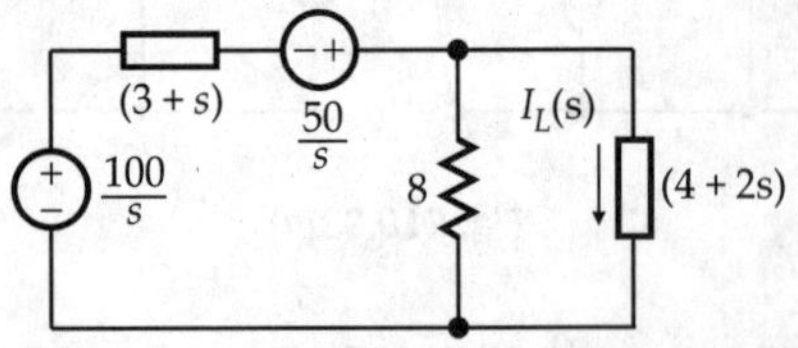

Fig. E10.94

SOLUTION. Let us remove $(4+2s)$ from the circuit [Fig. E10.94(*a*)]. Let the open circuit voltage be $V_{o.c.}(s)$. Let $I(s)$ be the circulating current in the loop and $V_{o.c.}(s) = 8 \times I(s)$.

$$\text{or} \qquad V_{o.c}(s) = 8\,\frac{\left(\dfrac{100}{s}+\dfrac{50}{s}\right)}{(3+s)+(8)} = \frac{1200}{s(11+s)}.$$

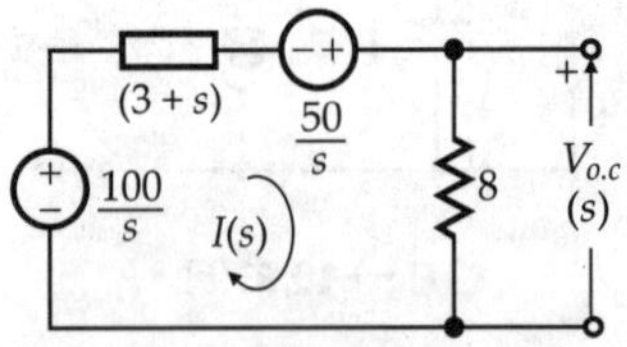

Fig. E10.94(*a*)

$Z_{in}(s)$, the internal impedance in the s-domain is obtained by deactivating the constant sources as shown in Fig. E10.94(*b*).

$$Z_{in}(s) = \frac{8(s+3)}{8+s+3} = \frac{8s+24}{(s+11)}\,\Omega.$$

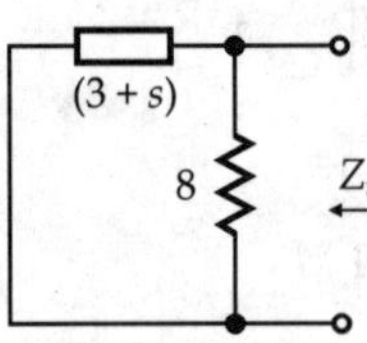

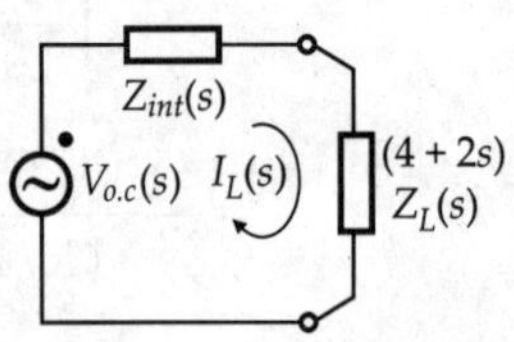

Fig. E10.94 (*b*) (*c*)

Figure E10.94(*c*) represents Thevenin's equivalent circuit where

$$V_{o.c}(s) = \frac{1200}{s(s+11)}$$

$$\text{and} \qquad Z_{in}(s) = \frac{8s+24}{(s+11)}.$$

$$\therefore \qquad I_L(s) = \frac{V_{o.c}(s)}{Z_{in}(s)+Z_L(s)}$$

$$\text{or} \qquad I_L(s) = \frac{\dfrac{1200}{s(s+11)}}{\dfrac{8s+24}{s+11}+4+2s}$$

$$= \frac{1200}{s(8s+24+4s+2s^2+44+22\,s}$$

$$= \frac{\mathbf{1200}}{\mathbf{s\,(2s^2+34\,s+68)}}.$$

EXAMPLE 10.95 *Transform the circuit shown in Fig. E10.95 into s-domain and find Thevenin's equivalent circuit in s-domain.*

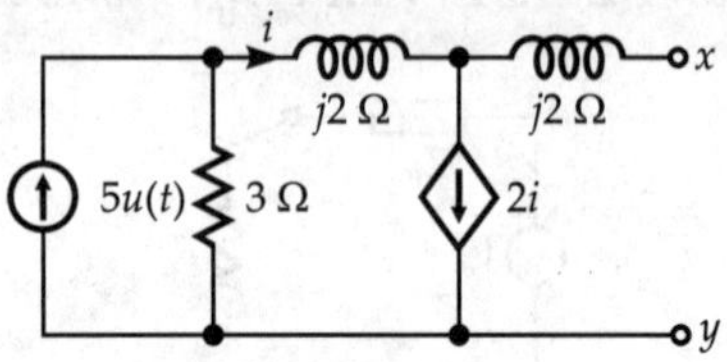

Fig. E10.95

SOLUTION. Figure E10.95(*a*) exhibits the given circuit transformed into s-domain. Let the output voltage be $V_0(s)$. Applying nodal analysis we get

$$\frac{5}{s} = I_2(s) + I_1(s)$$

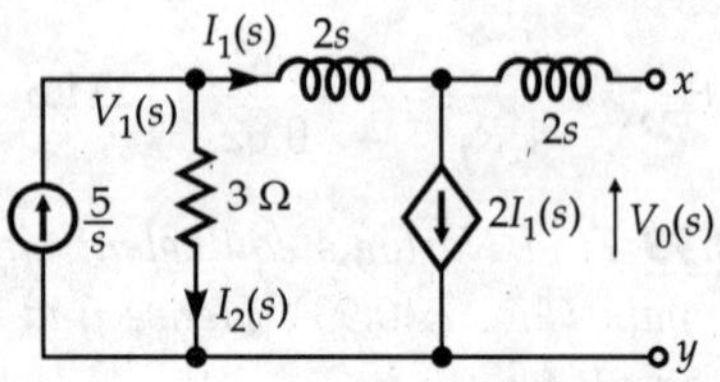

Fig. E10.95(*a*)

But observation reveals that current flows through inductive reactance of $(2s)$ is $2I_1(s)$ too because of presence of dependant current source $\left[i.e., \text{ also, } \dfrac{5}{s} = I_2(s) + 2I_1(s)\right]$. This is only possible if $I_1(s) = 0$.

$$\therefore \qquad V_0(s) = 3\,I_2(s) = 3\left(\frac{5}{s}\right) = \frac{15}{s}$$

To find $Z_{int}(s)$ let us apply a voltage $V_0(s)$ at x-y deactivating the current source so that input current is $I_0(s)$ [Fig. E10.95(*b*)].

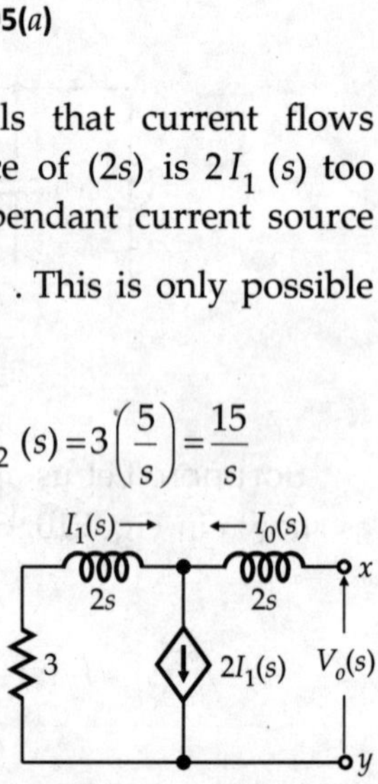

Fig. E10.95(*b*)

At *node (1)*,

$$I_1(s) + I_0(s) = 2I_1(s)$$

$$\therefore \quad I_0(s) = I_1(s)$$

and

$$V_0(s) = 2s\,I_0(s) - I_1(s)(3+2s)$$

$$= I_0(s).2s - I_0(s)(3+2s)$$

$$[\because I_0(s) = I_1(s)]$$

$$\therefore \quad V_0(s) = -3I_0(s)$$

$$\therefore \quad \frac{V_0(s)}{I_0(s)} = -3$$

Neglecting the –ve sign, it is obtained that $Z_{int}(s)$, *i.e.*, the Thevenin's impedance is 3 Ω.

Thevenin's equivalent circuit is shown in Fig. E10.95(*c*) when

$$\mathbf{V_0(s) = \frac{15}{s}\ ;\ Z_{int}(s) = 3\,\Omega.}$$

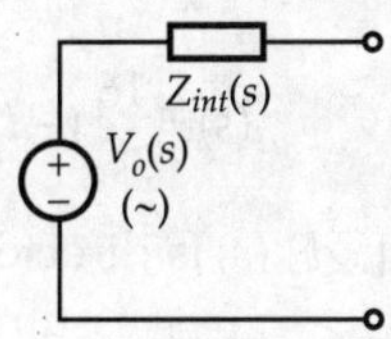

Fig. E10.95(*c*)

Example 10.96 *Obtain Norton's equivalent network at terminals a-b (Fig. E10.96).*

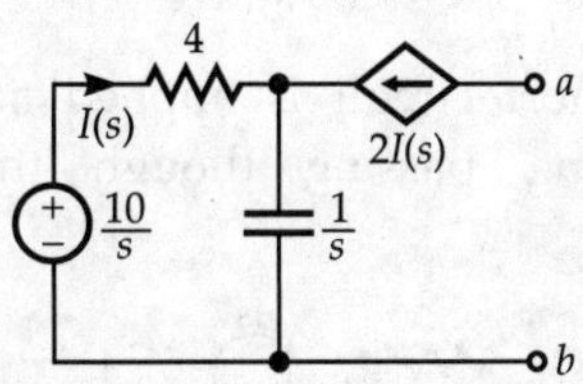

Fig. E10.96

Solution. Let us apply short circuit across *a-b* [Fig. E10.96(*a*)]. Let $V_x(s)$ be the voltage at *node (x)* in the circuit.

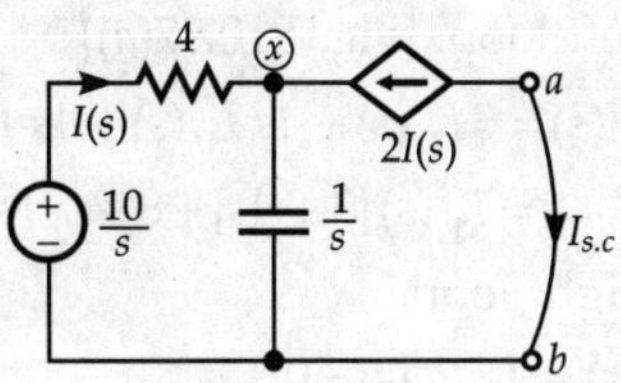

Fig. E10.96 (*a*)

Then, by nodal analysis,

$$\frac{V_x(s)}{\frac{1}{s}} = 2I(s) + I(s) = 3I(s)$$

$$\therefore \quad sV_x(s) = 3I(s)$$

or

$$V_x(s) = \frac{3I(s)}{s} \qquad ...(1)$$

Also,

$$4 \times I(s) = \frac{10}{s} - V_x(s)$$

$$= \frac{10}{s} - \frac{3I(s)}{s} \qquad \text{[Using (1)]}$$

or

$$I(s)\left[4 + \frac{3}{s}\right] = \frac{10}{s}$$

or

$$I(s) = \frac{10/s}{4+\frac{3}{s}} = \frac{10}{4s+3} \qquad ...(2)$$

Again, inspection reveals that

$$-2I(s) = I_{s.c}(s)$$

or

$$I_{s.c}(s) = -2\frac{10}{4s+3} = -\frac{20}{4s+3} \qquad ...(3)$$

This $I_{s.c.}(s)$ is the Norton's equivalent current.

Let us now remove the short circuit across *a-b* as shown in Fig. E10.96(*b*) and apply a voltage source $V_0(s)$ so that input current is $I_0(s).\left(\frac{10}{s}\right)$ source is deactivated.

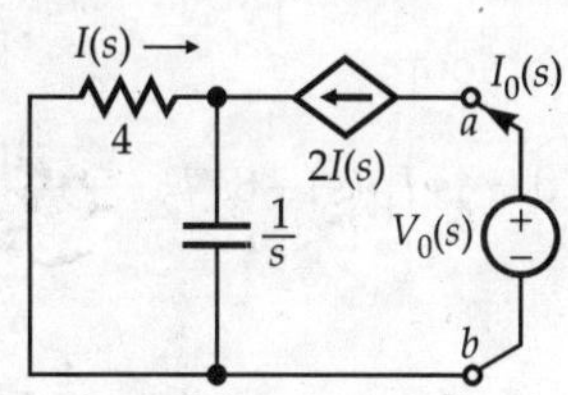

Fig. E10.96 (*b*)

At *node x*, nodal analysis yields

$$\frac{V_x(s)}{1/s} = I(s) + 2I(s) = 3\,I(s)$$

or

$$sV_x(s) = 3I(s) \qquad ...(4)$$

Also, from the leftmost loop,

$$I(s) = -V_x(s)/4 \qquad ...(5)$$

Using (5) in (4) we find that

$$V_x(s) = 0;\ I(s) = 0$$

Thus, $I_0(s)[=2I(s)]$ becomes zero.

CHAPTER 10

Thus $Z_{int}(s) = \dfrac{V_0(s)}{I_0(s)} = \infty.$

Figure E10.96(*c*) represents the Norton's equivalent circuit where $\mathbf{Z}_{int} = \infty$

and $I_{s.c.}(s) = -\dfrac{20}{4s+3}$.

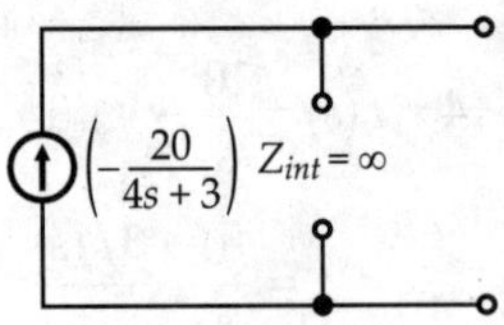

Fig. E10.96 (*c*)

Example 10.97 *Fig. E10.97 represents a coupled circuit in s-domain. Obtain Thevenin's equivalent at the terminal x-y.*

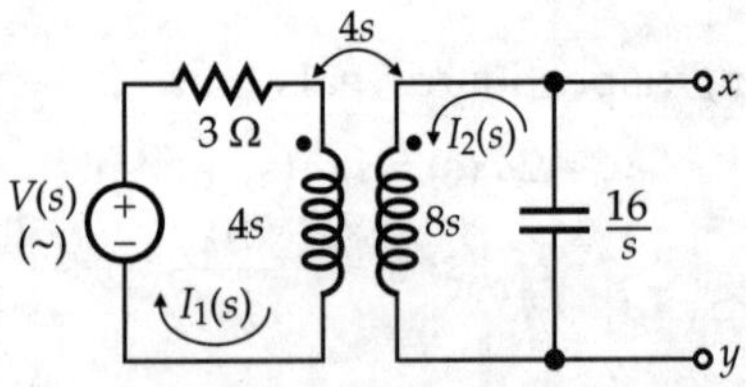

Fig. E10.97

Solution. Let I_1 and I_2 be the loop currents as shown in Fig. E10.97 by dotted arrows.

In the left loop,

$$V(s) = (3+4s)\, I_1(s) + 4s\, I_2(s) \qquad ...(1)$$

and in the right loop,

$$0 = 4s\, I_1(s) + 8s\, I_2(s) + \frac{16}{s} I_2(s) \qquad ...(2)$$

From (2),

$$0 = sI_1(s) + 2sI_2(s) + \frac{4}{s} I_2(s)$$

$$= sI_1(s) + I_2(s)\left[2s + \frac{4}{s}\right]$$

or

$$I_1(s) = -I_2(s)\frac{2s+\frac{4}{s}}{s} = -I_2(s)\frac{2s^2+4}{s^2}$$

$$= -2I_2(s)\left[\frac{s^2+2}{s^2}\right] \qquad ...(3)$$

Substituting the value of $I_1(s)$ from (3) in (1),

$$V(s) = (3+4s)\left[-2I_2(s)\left\{\frac{s^2+2}{s^2}\right\}\right] + 4s\, I_2(s)$$

$$= -6I_2(s)\frac{s^2+2}{s^2} - 8sI_2(s).\frac{s^2+2}{s^2} + 4sI_2(s)$$

$$= I_2(s)\left[-8s\frac{s^2+2}{s^2} - 6\frac{s^2+2}{s^2} + 4s\right]$$

$$= I_2(s)\left[-\frac{8(s^2+2)}{s} - 6\frac{s^2+2}{s^2} + 4s\right]$$

$$= I_2(s)\left[\frac{-8s(s^2+2) - 6(s^2+2) + 4s^3}{s^2}\right]$$

$$\therefore \quad I_2(s) = \frac{s^2}{4s^3 - 8s^3 - 16s - 6s^2 - 12} V(s)$$

$$= \frac{s^2 V(s)}{-4s^3 - 6s^2 - 16s - 12}$$

$$= -\frac{s^2 V(s)}{4s^3 + 6s^2 + 16s + 12} \qquad ...(4)$$

However,

$$V_{o.c.}(s) = V_{x-y}(s) = \frac{16}{s}(-I_2(s))$$

[$\because I_2(s)$ is directed opposite to the assumed +ve direction]

$$\therefore \quad V_{o.c.}(s) = \frac{16}{s} \times \frac{s^2 V(s)}{4s^3 + 6s^2 + 16s + 12} \qquad ...(5)$$

or

$$V_{o.c.}(s) = \frac{4s\, V(s)}{s^3 + 1.5s^2 + 4s + 3}$$

Next, short circuit is applied across *x*-*y*, no current being passing though the capacitive reactance.

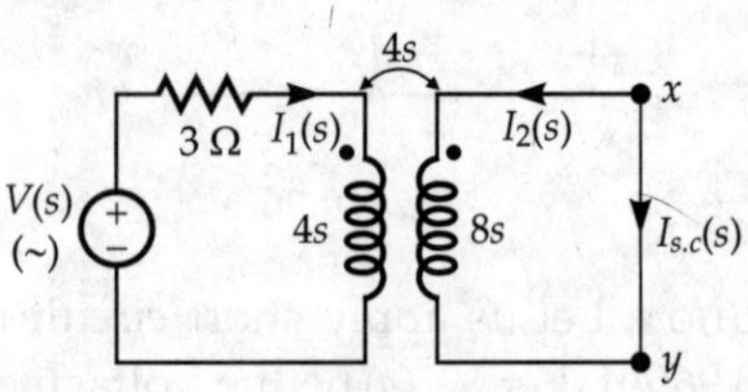

Fig. E10.97(*a*)

In the left loop, [Fig. E10.97(*a*)]

$$V(s) = 3I_1(s) + 4s\, I_1(s) + 4s\, I_2(s)$$

$$= I_1(s)[3+4s] + 8s\, I_2(s) \qquad ...(6)$$

In the right loop,

$$8s\, I_2(s) + 4s\, I_1(s) = 0$$

or

$$I_1(s) = -\frac{8s}{4s} I_2(s) = -2\, I_2(s) \qquad ...(7)$$

Applying (7) in (6),

$$V(s) = -2I_2(s)[3+4s] + 8s\, I_2(s)$$

or $$V(s) = -6I_2(s)$$

or $$I_2(s) = -\frac{1}{6}V(s) \quad \text{...(8)}$$

But $$I_{s.c.}(s) = -I_2(s)$$

$\therefore$ $$I_{s.c.}(s) = \frac{1}{6}V(s) \quad \text{...(9)}$$

Thus from (5) and (9),

$$Z_{int}(s) = \frac{V_{o.c}(s)}{I_{s.c.}(s)} = \frac{\dfrac{16}{s} \times \dfrac{s^2\, V(s)}{4s^3 + 6s^2 + 16s + 12}}{\dfrac{1}{6}V(s)}$$

$$= \frac{16s \times 6}{4s^3 + 6s^2 + 16s + 12}$$

$$= \frac{24s}{s^3 + 1.5s^2 + 4s + 3}$$

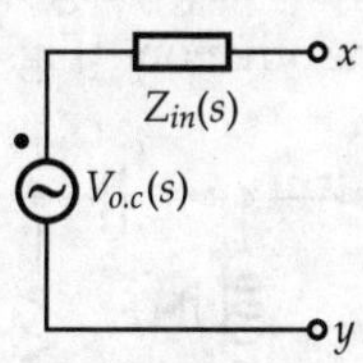

Fig. E10.97(*b*)

Thevenin's equivalent circuit can now be formed [Fig. E10.97(*b*)] where

$$V_{o.c.} = \frac{4s\, V(s)}{s^3 + 1.5s^2 + 4s + 3}$$

and $$Z_{in}(s) = \frac{24s}{s^3 + 1.5s^2 + 4s + 3}.$$

Example 10.98 *Find the current through the capacitor of $(-j5)\,\Omega$ reactance in Fig. E10.98 using Superposition Theorem.*

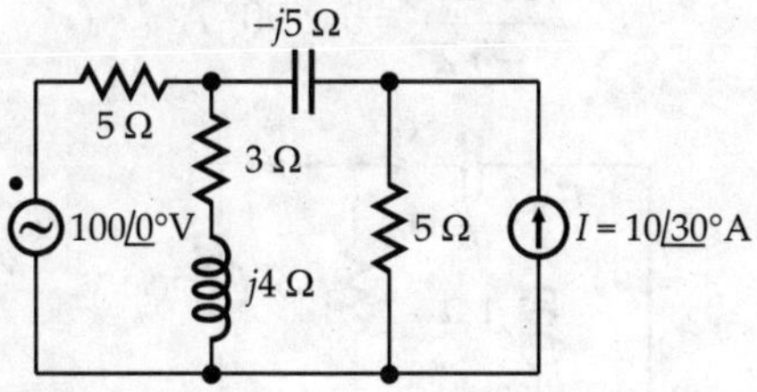

Fig. E10.98

Solution. Superposition is applied in the given circuit as shown in Fig. E10.98(*a*) and 10.98(*b*) deactivating each source at time.

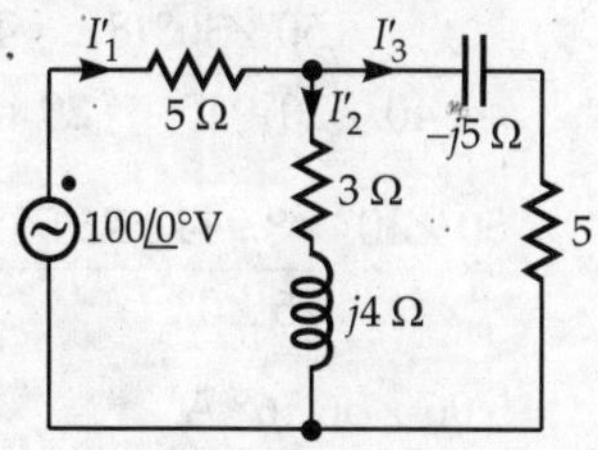

Fig. E10.98 (*a*)

In Fig. E10.98(*a*) the impedance Z' across $100\angle 0°$ V is

$$Z' = 5 + \frac{(5-j5)(3+j4)}{5-j5+3+j4}$$

$$= 5 + \frac{15+j20-j15+20}{8-j1}$$

$$= \frac{40-j5+15+j20-j15+20}{8-j1}$$

$$= \frac{75\angle 0°}{8.062\angle -7.125°}$$

$$= 9.3\angle 7.125°\,\Omega.$$

$\therefore$ $$I_1' = \frac{100\angle 0°}{9.3\angle 7.125°} = 10.75\angle -7.125°\text{ A}.$$

Thus

$$I_3' = I_1' \frac{3+j4}{3+j4-j5+5}$$

$$= \frac{10.75\angle -7.125° \times 5\angle 53.13°}{8-j1}$$

$$= \frac{53.75\angle 46°}{8.062\angle -7.125°} = 6.67\angle 53.125°\text{ A}.$$

On the other hand, in Fig. E10.98(*b*),

$$I_3'' = I\frac{5\angle 0°}{-j5 + \dfrac{(3+j4)5}{3+j4+5} + 5}$$

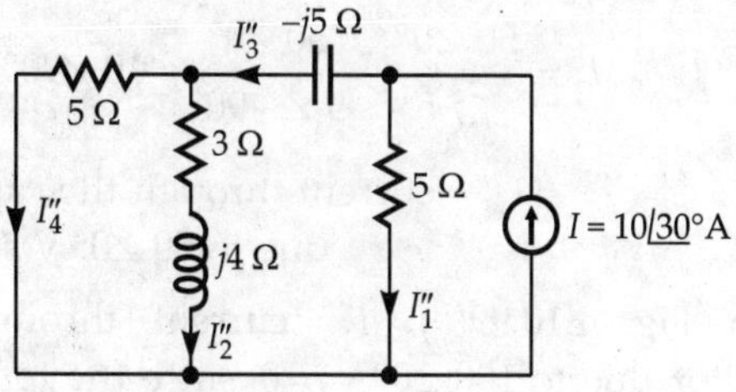

Fig. E10.98 (*b*)

$$= \frac{10\angle 30^\circ \times 5\angle 0^\circ}{-j\,5 + \dfrac{15 + j\,20}{8 + j\,4} + 5}$$

$$= \frac{50\angle 30^\circ (8 + j\,4)}{-j\,40 + 20 + 15 + j\,20 + 40 + j\,20}$$

$$= \frac{50\angle 30^\circ \times 8.944\angle 26.56^\circ}{75\angle 0^\circ}$$

$$= 5.96\angle 56.56^\circ \text{ A.}$$

Using the principle of superposition,

$$\begin{aligned} I_3 &= I_3' - I_3'' \text{ (vectorial)} \\ &= 6.67\angle 53.125^\circ - 5.96\angle 56.56^\circ \\ &= 4 + j\,5.33 - 3.28 - j\,4.979 \\ &= 0.72 + j\,0.351 \\ &= \mathbf{0.801\angle 26^\circ \text{ A.}} \end{aligned}$$

EXAMPLE 10.99 *Find the current through the capacitor by superposition theorem. (Fig. E10.99).*

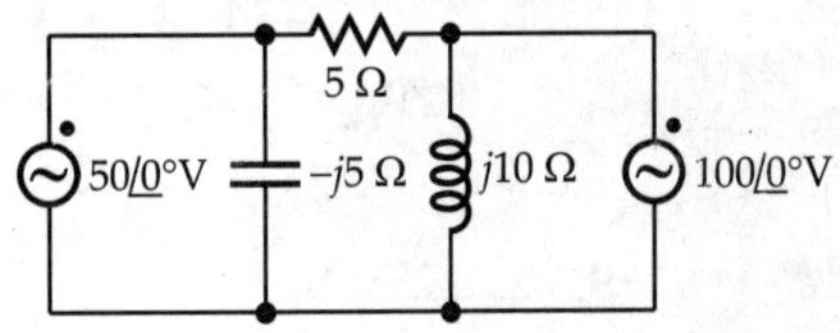

Fig. E10.99

SOLUTION. Superposition principle is applied in the circuit as shown in Fig. E10.99(*a*) and (*b*) deactivating one source at a time.

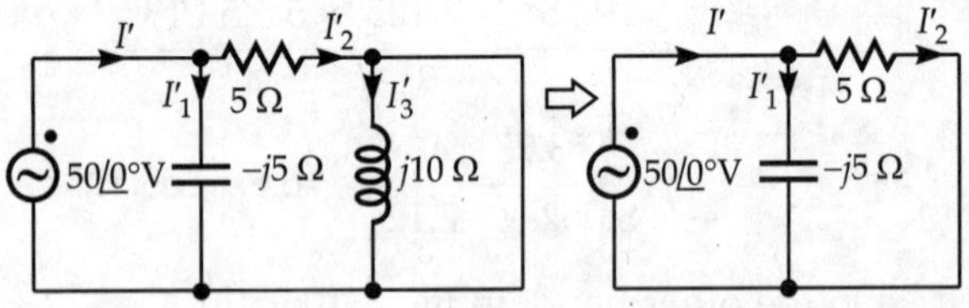

Fig. E10.99(*a*)

In Fig. E10.99(*a*),

$$I_1' = \frac{50\angle 0^\circ}{-j\,5} = \frac{50\angle 0^\circ}{5\angle -90^\circ} = 10\angle 90^\circ \text{ A.}$$

[I_1' = current through the capacitor due to 50 $\angle 0^\circ$ V source].

In Fig. E10.99(*b*), I_1'' (current through the capacitor due to 100 $\angle 0^\circ$ V) = 0, since the terminals are seen to be shorted.

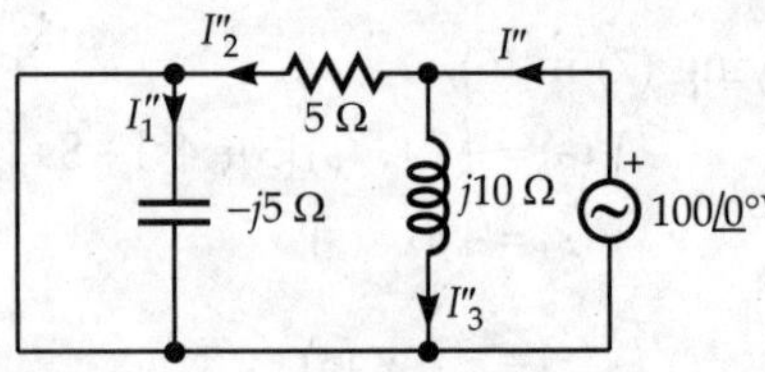

Fig. E10.99(*b*)

∴ Net current through the capacitor

$$= I_1' + I_1'' = \mathbf{10\angle 90^\circ \text{ A.}}$$

EXAMPLE 10.100 *In the circuit of Fig. E10.100, find the current through the inductor as well as through the capacitor using the principle of superposition.*

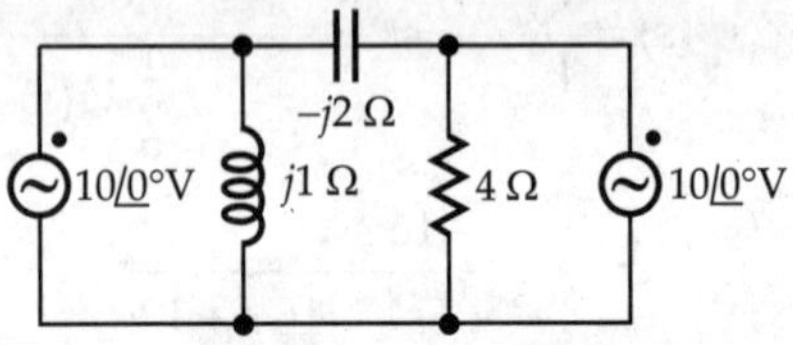

Fig. E10.100

SOLUTION. Principle of superposition is applied in the given circuit by applying one source at a time and deactivating the other one [Fig. E10.100(*a*) and (*b*)].

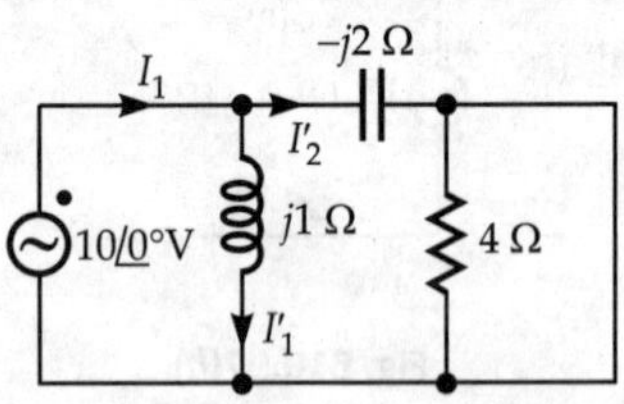

Fig. E10.100(*a*)

In Fig. E10.100(*a*),

$$I_1' = \frac{10\angle 0^\circ}{j\,1} = 10\angle -90^\circ \text{ A.}$$

$$I_2' = \frac{10\angle 0^\circ}{-j\,2} \quad [\because 4\,\Omega \text{ resistor is shorted}]$$

$$= 5\angle 90^\circ \text{ A.}$$

In Fig. E10.100(*b*), $I_1'' = 0$

[∵ the terminals of $j\,1\Omega$ are shorted]

$$I_2'' = \frac{10\angle 0^\circ}{-j\,2} = 5\angle 90^\circ \text{ A}$$

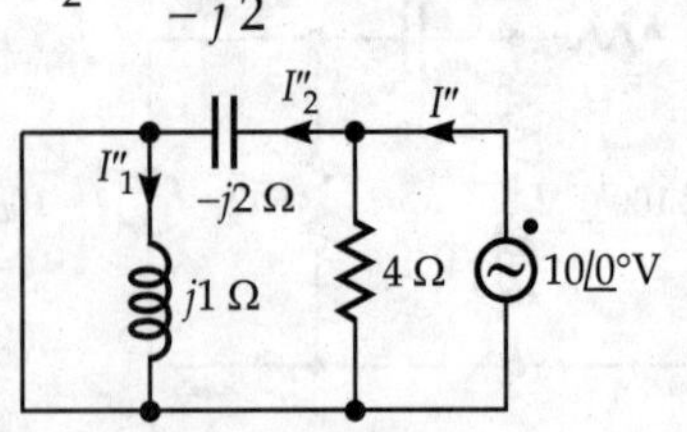

Fig. E10.100(*b*)

Using the principle of superposition,

$$I_1 = I_1' + I_1'' = 10\angle -90^\circ + 0$$
$$= 10\angle -90^\circ \text{ A}$$

and $I_2 = I_2' + (-I_2'')$ [$\because$ the direction of I_2 and I_2'' are opposite]

$$= 5\angle 90^\circ - 5\angle 90^\circ = 0$$

Thus, using the principle of superposition, the current though $j1\Omega$ inductive reactance is **10 ∠ – 90° A** and that through the capacitor is **zero.**

Example 10.101 *In Fig. E10.101, $E_1 = 10\sin(314t + 45^\circ)$ V and $I_1 = 5\cos(314t + 30^\circ)$ A. Using the principle of superposition, find the power delivered to the 1Ω resistor in the central branch.*

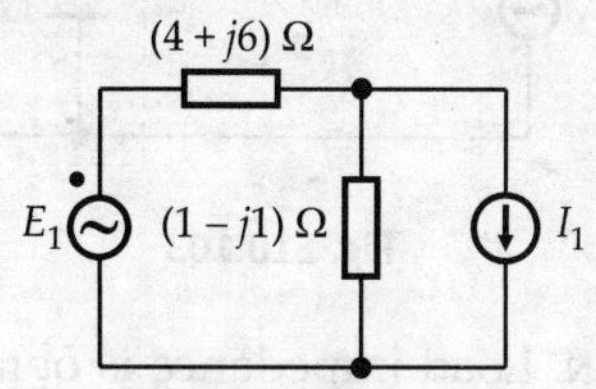

Fig. E10.101

Solution. The principle of superposition is applied as shown in Fig. 10.101(*a*) and (*b*). Here $E_1 = 10\angle 45^\circ$ V from the given data [Fig. E10.101(*a*)].

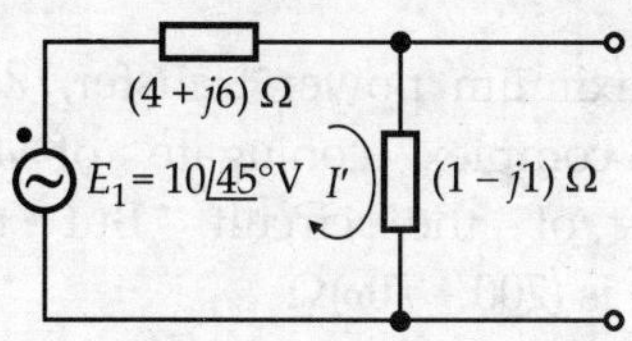

(*a*)

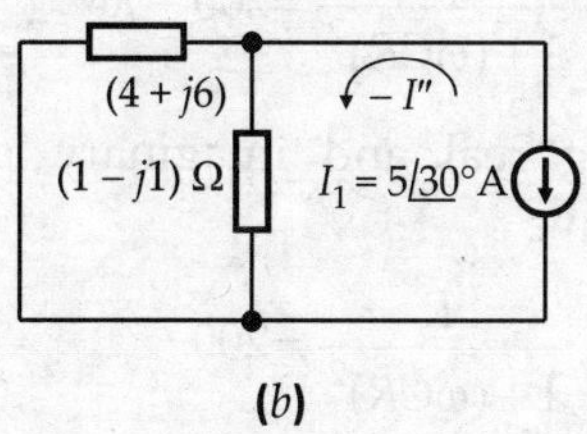

Fig. E10.101 (*b*)

$$\therefore \quad I' = \frac{10\angle 45^\circ}{4 + j6 + 1 - j1}$$
$$= \frac{10\angle 45^\circ}{5 + j5} = \frac{10\angle 45^\circ}{7.07\angle 45^\circ}$$
$$= 1.414\angle 0^\circ \text{ A (max. value)}$$

$\therefore$ Power delivered to the load of 1Ω by the voltage source E_1 is

$$\frac{1}{2}(1.414)^2 \times 1 = 1\text{ W.} \quad \left[\because \; I'_{rms} = \left(\frac{1.414}{\sqrt{2}}\right)^2\right]$$

In Fig. E10.101(*b*),

$$-I'' = \frac{4 + j6}{4 + j6 + 1 - j1} \times 5\angle 30^\circ$$
$$= \frac{7.211\angle 56.31^\circ}{(5 + j5)} \times 5\angle 30^\circ$$
$$= \frac{36.055\angle 86.31^\circ}{7.07\angle 45^\circ} = 5.1\angle 41.31^\circ \text{ A}$$

$\therefore$ Power delivered to the load of 1Ω by the current source is

$$\frac{1}{2}(5.1)^2 \times 1 = 13\text{ W.}$$

By the principle of superposition, the power delivered to the load due to both the sources is (1 W + 13 W) = **14 W.**

Example 10.102 *Find the value of Z_L such that maximum power transfer takes place from source to Z_L in Fig. E10.102.*

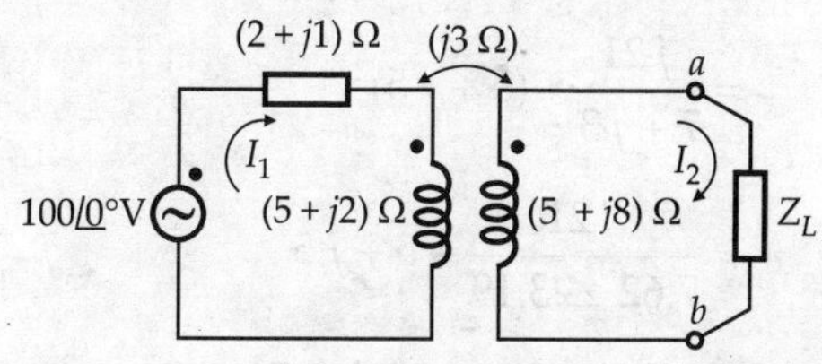

Fig. E10.102

Solution. Let us first draw the conductively coupled equivalent circuit of the given coupled network [Fig. E10.102(*a*)].

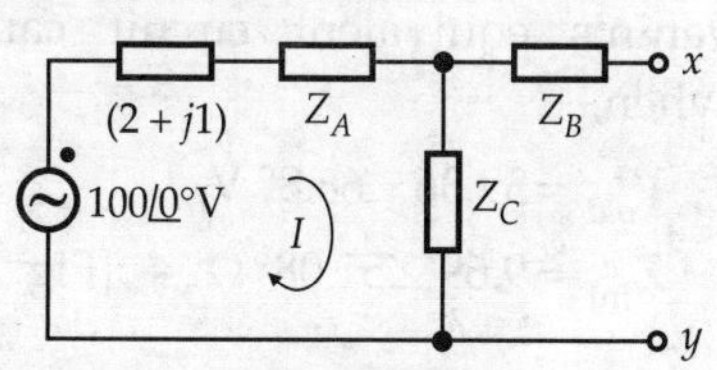

Fig. E10.102 (*a*)

From the theory of coupled circuit,

$$Z_A = (5 + j2) - j3 = (5 - j1)\Omega$$
$$Z_B = (5 + j8) - j3 = (5 + j5)\Omega$$
$$Z_C = jM = j3\Omega.$$

Here, $V_{o.c.}$ (Thevenin's voltage across *x*-*y*)

$$= \frac{100\angle 0^\circ}{(2 + j1) + Z_A + Z_C} \times Z_C$$

$$= \frac{100 \angle 0°}{(2+j1)+(5-j1)+j3} = \frac{100 \angle 0° \times j3}{(7+j3)}$$

$$= \frac{100 \angle 0° \times 3 \angle 90°}{7.62 \angle 23.19°} = 39.36 \angle 66.8° \text{ V.}$$

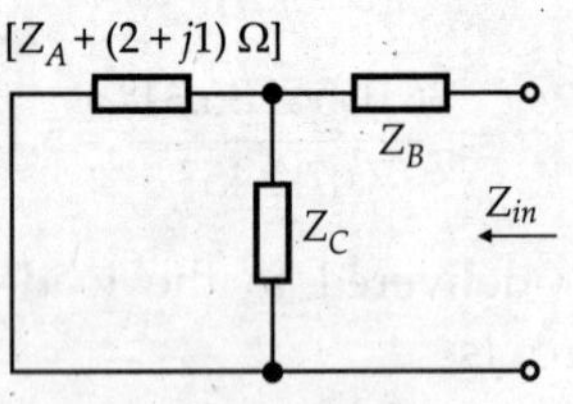

Fig. E10.102 (*b*)

Following Fig. E10.102(*b*),

$$Z_{int} = \frac{Z_C \{Z_A + (2+j1)\}}{Z_C + Z_A + 2 + j1} + Z_B$$

$$= \frac{j3\{5 - j1 + 2 + j1\}}{j3 + 5 - j1 + 2 + j1} + 5 + j5$$

$$= \frac{j21}{7+j3} + (5+j5)$$

$$= \frac{j21}{7.62 \angle 23.19} + 5 + j5$$

$$= 2.76 \angle (90° - 23.2°) + 5 + j5$$

$$= 2.76 \angle 66.8° + 5 + j5$$

$$= (1.087 + j2.537) + 5 + j5$$

$$= 6.087 + j7.537 = 9.69 \angle 51.08° \, \Omega$$

Thevenin's equivalent circuit can now be formed when,

$$V_{o.c.} = 39.36 \angle 66.8° \text{ V},$$

and $$Z_{int} = 9.69 \angle 51.08° \, \Omega \quad \text{[Fig. E10.102(c)]}$$

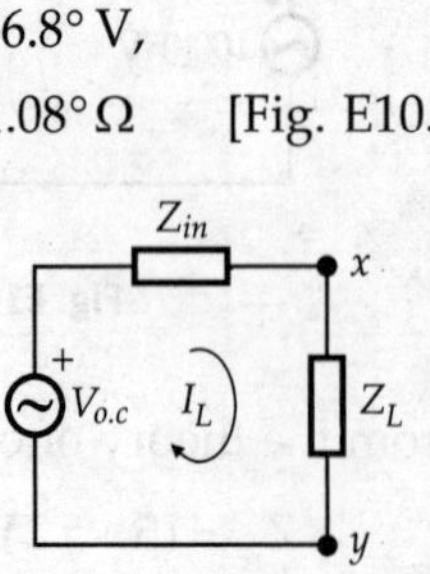

Fig. E10.102 (*c*)

As per maximum power transfer theorem, maximum power would flow from source to load provided the load impedance is the complex conjugate of the source impedance (*i.e.*, the internal impedance) ;

$$\therefore \quad Z_L = Z_{int}^* = \mathbf{(6.087 - j\,7.537)\,\Omega.}$$

Maximum power is obtained as

$$P_{max} = \frac{V_{o.c.}^2}{4R_L} = \frac{39.36^2}{4 \times 6.087} = \mathbf{63.63 \text{ W.}}$$

$$[R_L = \text{resistive part of } Z_L]$$

EXAMPLE 10.103 *In the circuit shown in Fig. E10.103 determine the values of R and C so that maximum power is absorbed by R. Determine the power for these values. Assume frequency supply as* $\omega = 200$ *rad / sec for* $V_S = 200 \angle 0°$ V.

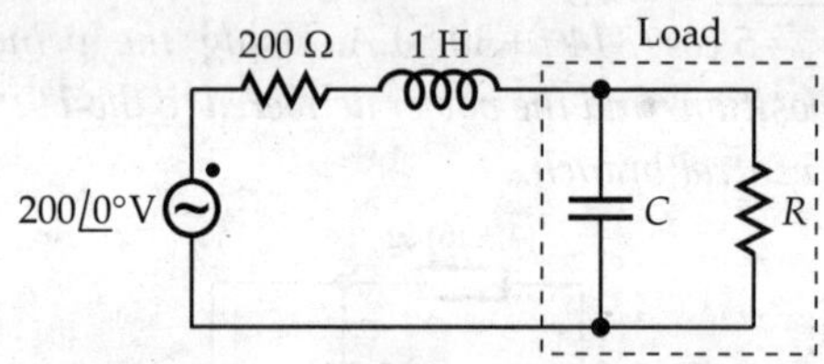

Fig. E10.103

SOLUTION. Load impedance is obtained as

$$Z_L = R \,||\, \frac{1}{j\omega C} = \frac{R}{1 + j\omega CR}$$

$$= \frac{R - j\omega CR^2}{1 + (\omega CR)^2}$$

For maximum power transfer, Z_L should be equal to complex conjugate of the internal impedance of the circuit. But the internal impedance is $(200 - j1\omega)\Omega$

$$\therefore \quad \frac{R - j\omega CR^2}{1 + (\omega CR)^2} = 200 - j\omega$$

Equating real and imaginary parts of both sides, we have

$$\frac{R}{1 + (\omega CR)^2} = 200 \quad \text{...(1)}$$

and $$\frac{\omega CR^2}{1 + (\omega CR)^2} = \omega \quad \text{...(2)}$$

Using equation (2) in equation (1), we get

$$200\,CR = 1$$

i.e., $$C = \frac{1}{200\,R}$$

With this value of C from equation (1), we get

$$R = 400 \, \Omega$$

and $$C = 12.5 \, \mu F$$

$$\text{Maximum power} = \frac{V^2}{4R_L}$$

where $R_L = R_i\ (= R_{th}) = 200\ \Omega]$

$$= \frac{(200)^2}{4 \times 400} = \mathbf{25\ watts.}$$

EXAMPLE 10.104 *Verify Tellegen's theorem for a network having four branches where voltages and currents as functions of time are given as*

$$v_1(t) = 10 \cos \omega t + 4 \sin \omega t$$
$$i_1(t) = 2 \cos \omega t + 0.8 \sin \omega t$$
$$v_2(t) = 8 \cos \omega t - 4 \sin \omega t$$
$$i_2(t) = 4 \cos \omega t + 1 \sin \omega t$$
$$v_3(t) = 8 \cos \omega t - 5 \sin \omega t$$
$$i_3(t) = -3 \cos \omega t - 1.5 \sin \omega t$$
$$v_4(t) = -10 \cos \omega t - 3.5 \sin \omega t$$
$$i_4(t) = 2 \cos \omega t + 1.2 \sin \omega t$$

SOLUTION. Tellegen's theorem can be verified if we associate voltages at time $t_1 = \frac{\pi}{2\omega}$ with currents at time $t_2 = 0$ since Tellegen's theorem states that for the set of measurements at t_1 and t_2,

$$\sum_{b=1}^{b} v_b(t_1)\, i_b(t_2) = 0.$$

Here, $v_1(t_1) = 4;\quad v_2(t_1) = -4$

$v_3(t_1) = -5;\quad v_4(t_1) = -3.5$

and $i_1(t_2) = 2;\quad i_2(t_2) = 4$

$i_3(t_2) = -3;\quad i_4(t_2) = 2$

$$\therefore \sum_{b=1}^{b} v_b(t_1)\, i_b(t_2) = v_1(t_1)\, i_1(t_2) + v_2(t_1)\, i_2(t_2) + v_3(t_1)\, i_3(t_2) + v_4(t_1)\, i_4(t_2)$$

$$= (4) \times (2) + (-4) \times (4) + (-5) \times (-3) + (-3.5) \times (2)$$

$$= 8 - 16 + 15 - 7 = 0.$$

Hence, Tellegen's theorem is verified.

EXAMPLE 10.105. *Verify Tellegen's Theorem in the network shown in Fig. E10.104.*

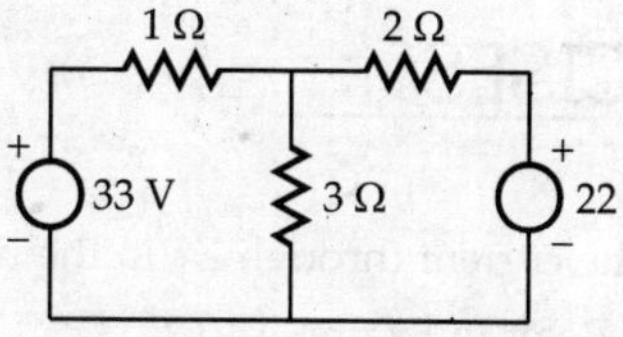

Fig. E10.104

SOLUTION. Let us first redraw the circuit as shown in Fig. E10.104(*a*)

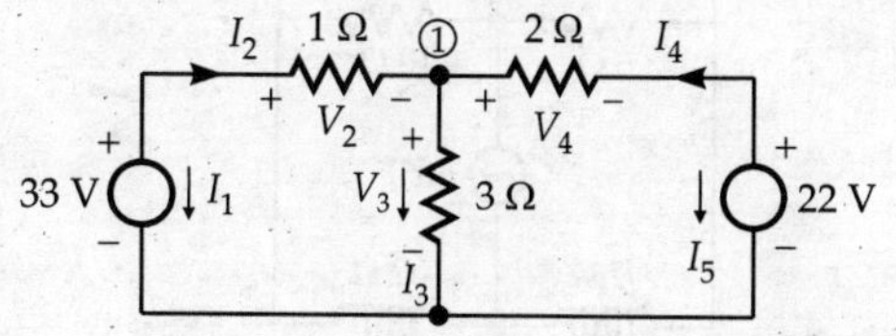

Fig. E10.104 (*a*)

Let $V_1 = 33$ V and $V_5 = 22$ V

Applying KVL, we get

$$33 = 1I_2 + 3I_3$$

or $$33 = I_2 + 3I_3 \quad \text{...(1)}$$

and $$22 = 2I_4 + 3I_3 \quad \text{...(2)}$$

or $$22 = 2I_4 + 3I_3$$

Applying KCL at node (1), we get

$$I_2 + I_4 = I_3 \quad \text{...(3)}$$

From equations (1), (2) and (3), we have

$$I_2 = 9\ \text{A},$$
$$I_3 = 8\ \text{A},$$
$$I_4 = -1\ \text{A}$$

Therefore,

$$I_2 + (-I_2) = -9\ \text{A}$$

and $$I_5 = -I_4 = 1\ \text{A}$$
$$V_2 = 1I_2 = 9\ \text{V}$$
$$V_3 = 3I_3 = 24\ \text{V}$$
$$V_4 = 2I_4 = -2\ \text{V}$$

We then can write,

$$\sum_{i=1}^{5} V_i I_i = 33 \times (-9) + 9 \times 9 + 24 \times 8 + (-2) \times (-1) + 22 \times 1$$

$$= -297 + 81 + 192 + 2 + 22$$

$$= -297 + 297 = 0$$

Hence, Tellegen's Theorem is verified.

EXERCISES

1. Find the current through Z_L in the network of Fig. P10.1 using mesh analysis.
[**Hint.** Refer to Example 10.2]

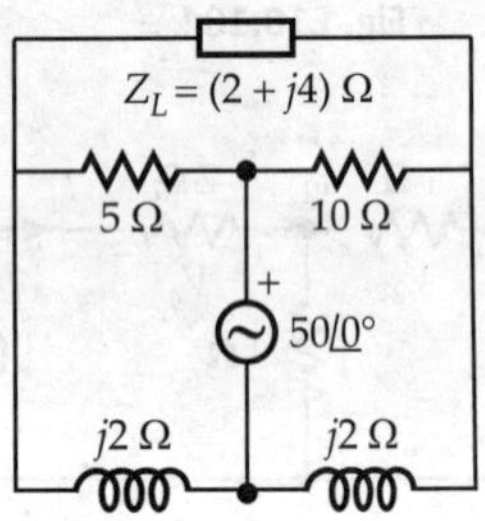

Fig. P10.1

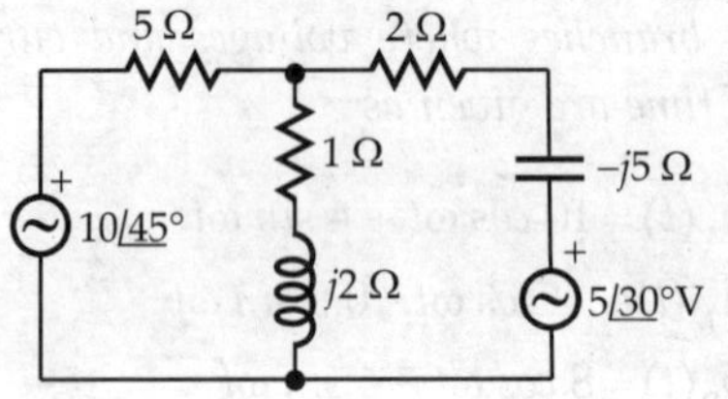

Fig. P10.2

2. Find the drop in the capacitor for the network shown in Fig. P10.2.
[**Hint.** Refer to Example 10.3]

3. What is the value of V_2 such that the current through $(4 + j\,6)\ \Omega$ impedance is zero ? (Refer to Fig. P10.3)
[**Hint.** Refer to Example 10.5]

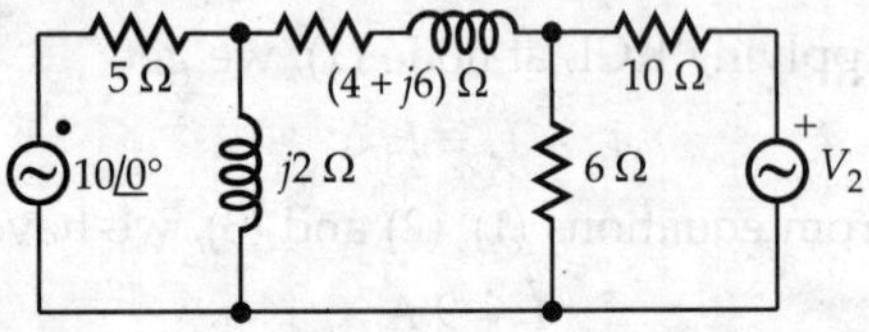

Fig. P10.3

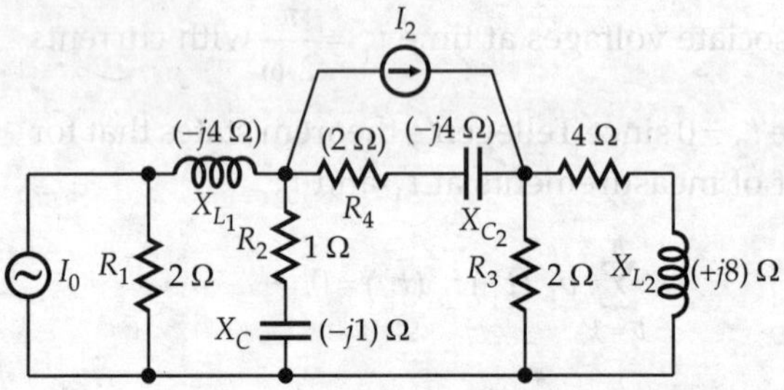

Fig. P10.4

4. In the network of Fig. P10.4, write down the node transformation matrix taking $I_1 = I_2 = 5\angle 0°$ A.
[**Hint.** Refer to Example 10.13]

5. Using nodal analysis, taking $A = 0.5$, find V_L for the circuit shown in Fig. P10.5.
[**Hint.** Refer to Example 10.15]

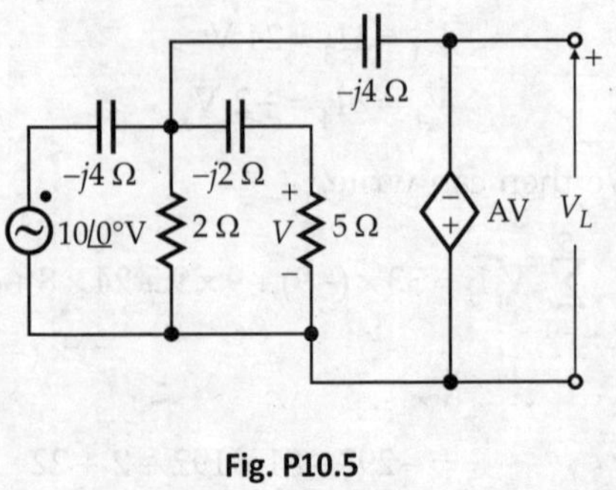

Fig. P10.5

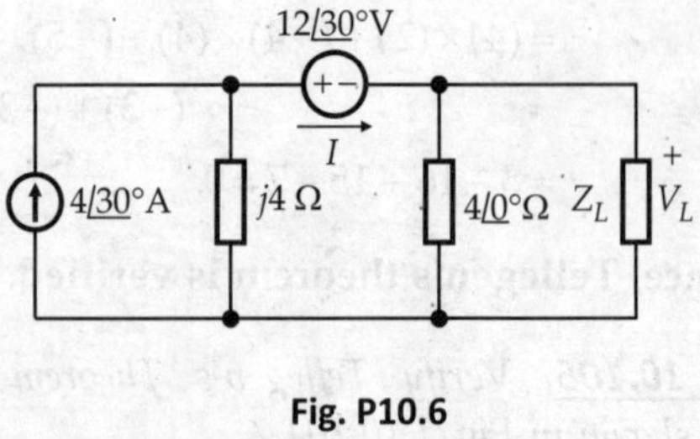

Fig. P10.6

6. Using nodal analysis, find the load voltage (V_L) across Z_L in the circuit of Fig. P10.6 if $Z_L\ (4 - j\,4)\ \Omega$.
[**Hint.** Refer to Example 10.17].

7. If $R_L = 5\,\Omega$, find the power loss in R_L using Thevenin's theorem (Fig. P10.7).
[**Hint.** Refer to Example 10.21].

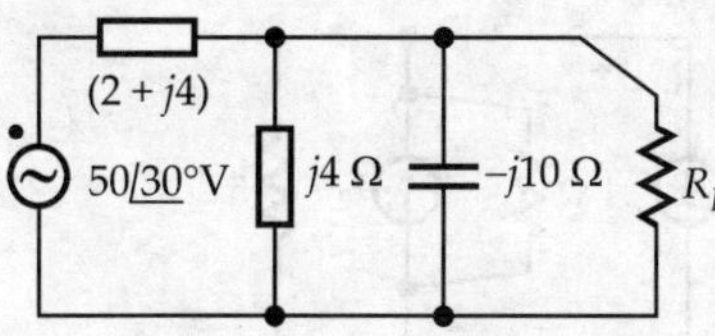

Fig. P10.7

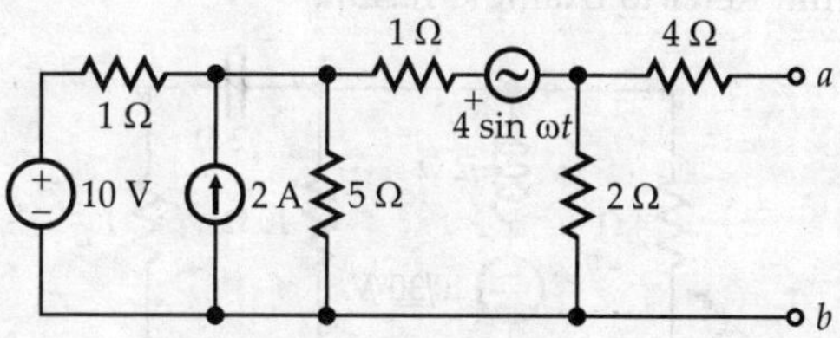

Fig. P10.8

8. Find Thevenin's equivalent circuit for the network shown in Fig. P10.8.
[**Hint.** Refer to Example 10.22].

9. Using Thevenin's theorem, find the current through $(2 + j\,2)\,\Omega$ impedance in Fig. P10.9.
[**Hint.** Refer to Example 10.24].

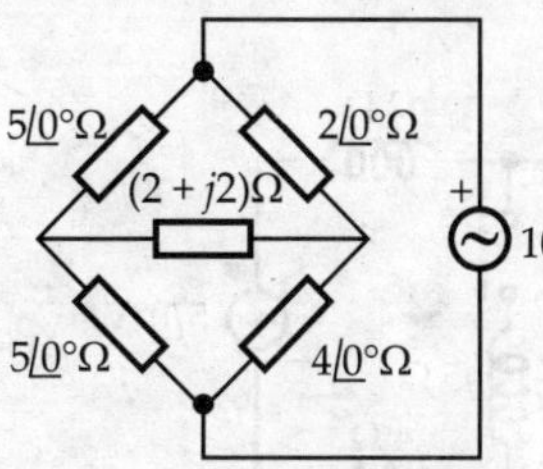

Fig. P10.9

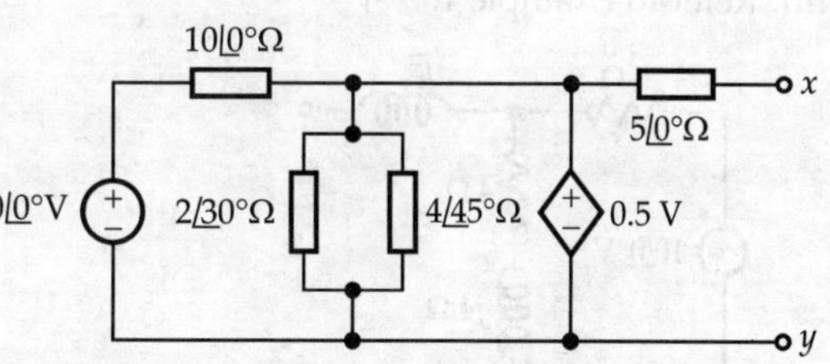

Fig. P10.10

10. In Fig. P10.10, find Thevenin's equivalent circuit across x-y.
[**Hint.** Refer to Example 10.27].

11. Find Thevenin's equivalent circuit across a-b [Fig. P10.11] and find the current through $10\,\Omega$ resistor.
[**Hint.** Refer to Example 10.31].

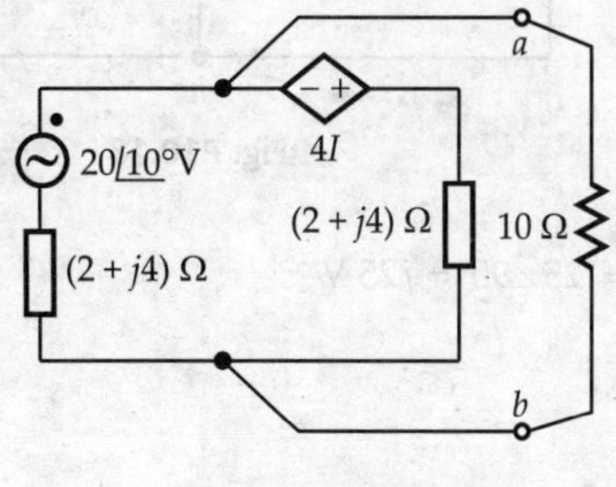

Fig. P10.11

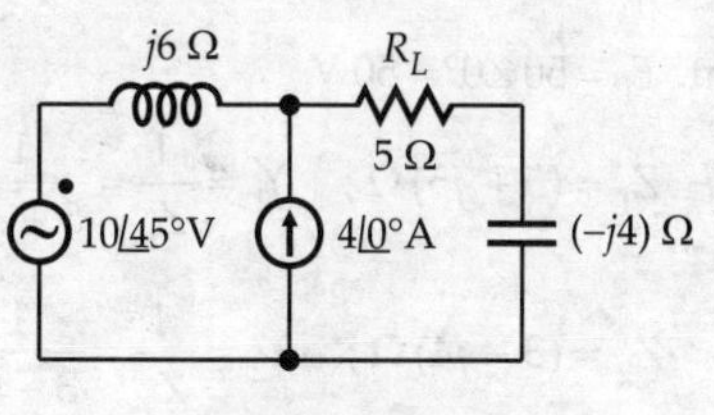

Fig. P10.12

12. Verify the results obtained in problem 11 (Fig. P10.11) using Norton's theorem.

[**Hint.** Refer to Example 10.31]

13. Find the power loss in the resistor R_L using the principle of superposition in the circuit of Fig. P10.12.

[**Hint.** Refer to Example 10.33].

14. Find, using the principle of superposition, the current in $(-j\,4)\,\Omega$ impedance in the circuit of Fig. P10.13.

[**Hint.** Refer to Example 10.37].

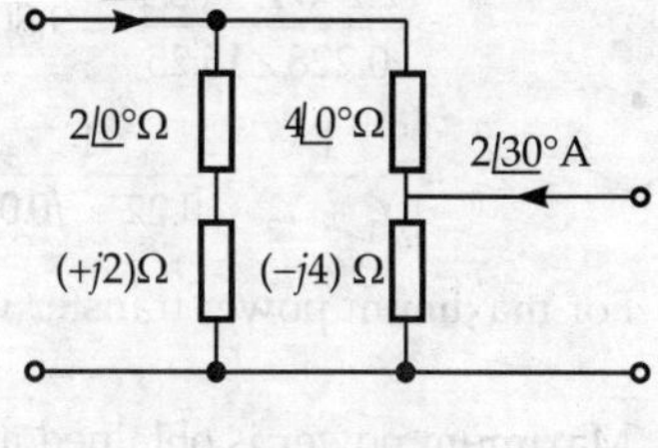

Fig. P10.13

15. What should be the value of R_L in Fig. P10.14 such that maximum power transfer occurs from the source to load ?

[**Hint.** Refer to Example 10.43]

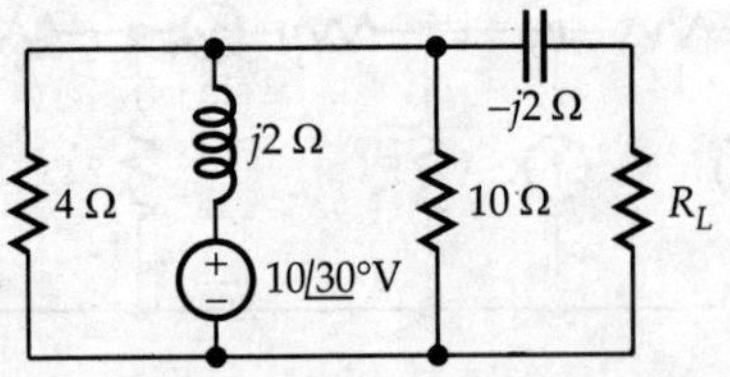

Fig. P10.14

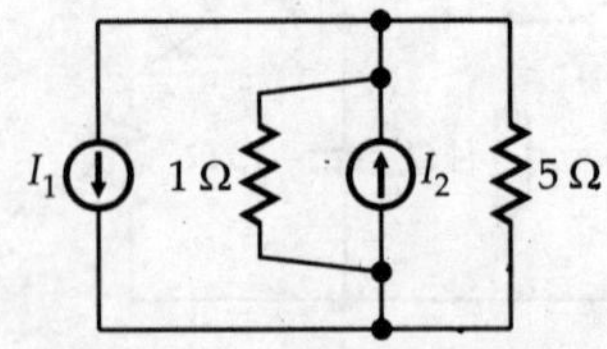

Fig. P10.15

16. In the circuit of Fig. P10.15, find the current through the 5 Ω resistor using Norton's Theorem. [$I_1 = 1\angle 60°$ A ; $I_2 = 0.5\angle 90°$ A]

[**Hint.** Refer to Example 10.69].

17. Find Norton's equivalent circuit across *a-b* in the network of Fig. P10.16.

[**Hint.** Refer to Example 10.73]

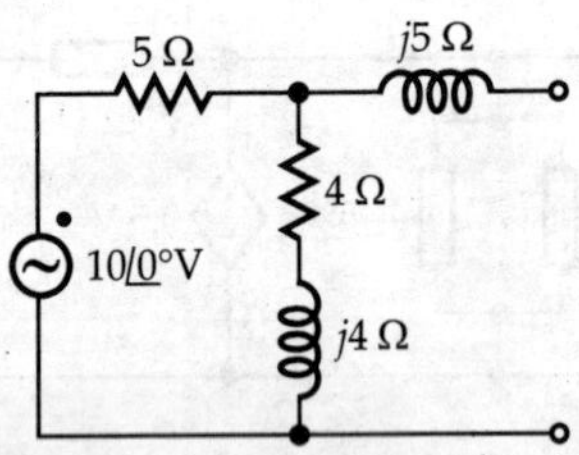

Fig. P10.16

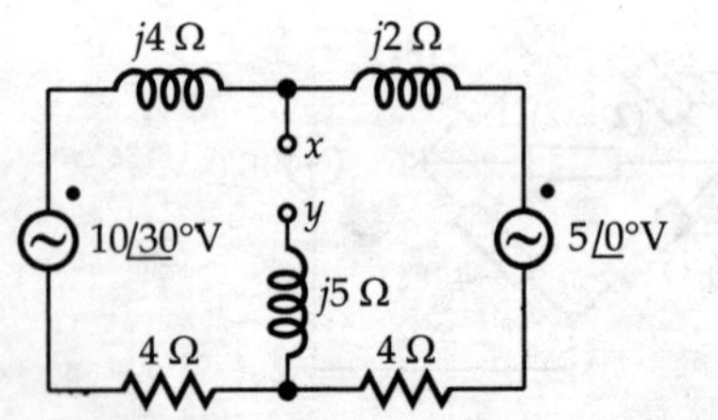

Fig. P10.17

18. In the network of Fig. P10.17, find Norton's equivalent circuit across *x-y*.

[**Hint.** Refer to Example 10.76]

19. In the circuit shown in Fig. P10.18 two voltage sources act on the load impedance connected to terminal *ab*. If the load impedance is variable, what load Z_L will draw maximum power ? Applying Milliman Theorem, also calculate maximum power.

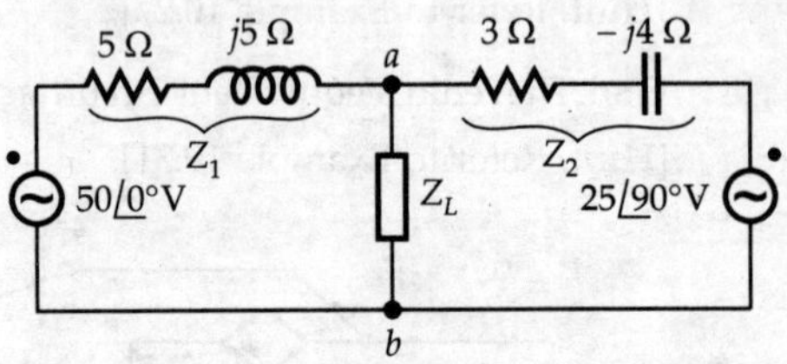

Fig. P10.18

[**Hint.** $E_1 = 50\angle 0° = 50$ V

$$Z_1 = (5 + j5)\,\Omega\,;\quad Y_1 = \frac{1}{Z_1} = \frac{1}{5 + j5} = (0.1 - j0.1)\text{ mho}\,;\quad E_2 = 25\angle 90° = j25\text{ V}$$

$$Z_2 = (3 - j4)\,\Omega\,;\quad Y_2 = \frac{1}{Z_2} = \frac{1}{3 - j4} = (0.12 + j0.16)\text{ mho}$$

$$V_m = \frac{E_1Y_1 + E_2Y_2}{Y_1 + Y_2} = \frac{50\,(0.1 - j0.1) + j25\,(0.12 + j0.16)}{(0.1 - j0.1) + (0.12 + j0.16)} = \frac{5 - j5 + j3 - 4}{0.22 + j0.06}$$

$$= \frac{2.236\angle -63.4}{0.228\angle 15.25} = 9.807\angle -78.65°\text{ volts}$$

$$Z_m = \frac{1}{Y_1 + Y_2} = \frac{1}{0.22 + j0.06} = 4.385\angle -15.25° = (4.23 - j1.15)\,\Omega$$

For maximum power transfer we have $Z_L = Z_m^* = 4.385\angle -15.25° = (4.23 - j1.15)\,\Omega$

Maximum power is obtained as $P_{max} = \dfrac{E_m^2}{4R_L} = \dfrac{(9.807)^2}{4 \times 4.23} = 5.68$ watts.]

CHAPTER

11

Analysis of Two Port Network

11.1 INTRODUCTION

When a number of impedances are connected together to form a system that consists of set(s) interconnected circuits performing specific or assigned functions, it is called a "network" or "circuit". An "electrical network" with which the present text is concerned, is a combination of numerous electric elements (*e.g.*, resistance (*R*), inductance (*L*), capacitance (*C*) etc.)

11.2 REVIEW OF CONCEPTS

11.2.1 Linear and Non-linear Elements

A network element is a component of a circuit having different characteristics.

A linear element shows linear characteristics of voltage *vs* current. Simple resistors, inductors and capacitors are linear elements and their resistances, inductances and capacitances do not change with a change in applied voltage or the circuit current.

For a *non-linear element* the current passing through it does not change linearly with the linear change in applied voltage at a particular frequency. Semiconductor devices are usually examples of non-linear elements.

11.2.2 Active and Passive Elements

If a circuit element has the capability of enhancing the energy level of a signal passing through it, it is called an *active element*.

Vacuum tubes and semiconductor devices (such as transistors op. amps. etc.) are active elements. On the other hand, resistors, inductors, capacitors, thermistors etc. are *passive elements* as they do not have any intrinsic means of signal boosting.

11.2.3 Unilateral and Bilateral Elements

If the magnitude of the current passing through an element is affected due to change in the polarity of the applied voltage, the element is called *unilateral element*. On the other hand, if the current magnitude remains the same even if the applied *e.m.f.'s* polarity is changed, it is called a *bilateral element*. Unilateral elements offer varying impedances with variations in flow of current while bilateral elements offer same impedance irrespective of flow of current. A resistor, inductor, capacitor are bilateral network elements while diodes, transistors are unilateral elements.

11.2.4 Classification of Network

The network being a conducting path through which electric current flows or intends to flow, contains resistance, inductance and capacitance. These elements are also called network parameters and may be in form of *lumped* or *distributed*.

Similar to those described in the previous article, there are different types of classifications of networks too :

(*a*) ***Linear circuits.*** It is the circuit whose parameters remain constant with change in applied voltage or current. Examples are a resistance, inductance or capacitance.

(*b*) ***Non-linear circuits.*** It is a circuit whose parameters change with voltage or current. A semi-conductor resistor is an example of this circuit.

A linear circuit obeys Ohm's law *i.e.*, current remains directly proportional with applied voltage, while in non-linear circuit, Ohm's law is not satisfied.

(*c*) ***Unilateral circuit.*** When the direction of current is changed, the characteristics or properties of the circuit may change. In this case, the circuit is an unilateral circuit (*e.g.*, diode, transistor etc.)

(*d*) ***Bilateral circuit.*** When with change in direction of current, the characteristic or properties of the circuit may not change, it is then called a bilateral circuit. Mostly, elements made of high conductivity material are bilaterial circuits.

(*e*) ***Active network.*** It is a network which contains one or more than one sources of *e.m.f.* An active network consists of an active element like a battery or transistor [Fig. 11.1(*a*)].

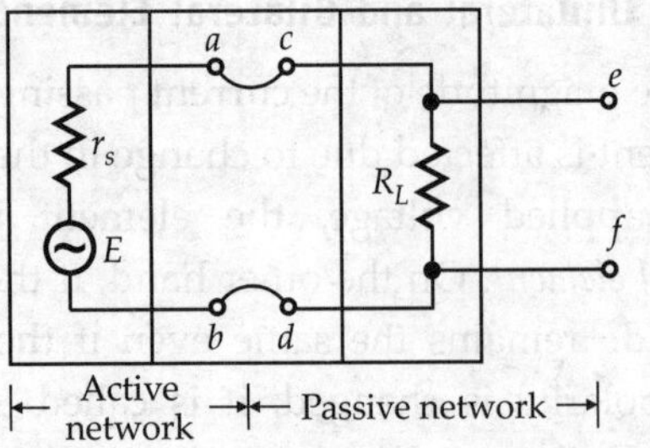

Fig. 11.1 (*a*) Schematic representation of active and assive network

[In Fig. 11.1(*a*),
$a, b \rightarrow$ driving port of active network (output port)
$c, d \rightarrow$ input port of passive network
$e, f \rightarrow$ output port of passive network]

(*f*) ***Passive network.*** When the network does not contain any source of *e.m.f.*, it is called passive network. A passive network consists of resistance, inductance or capacitance as passive elements. A passive network does not contain any source of energy and the input port serves as load terminal. It may have output terminals [Fig. 11.1(*a*)].

(*g*) ***Lumped and distributed network.*** Physically separate network elements like *R*, *L* or *C* are known as lumped elements. A transmission line or a cable on the other hand, is an example of distributed parameter network as throughout the line they are not physically separate. If the network is fabricated with its elements in lumped form, it is called a *lumped network* and if in distributed form it is called *distributed network.*

(*h*) ***Recurrent and non-recurrent network.*** When a large circuit consists of similar networks connected one after another, the network is called as *recurrent network* or *cascaded network*. It may also be called as *ladder network*. On the other hand, a single network is called *non-recurrent network*.

11.2.5 Different Parameters of the Network

Resistance, inductance and capacitance being the most fundamental parameters of a network, the *resistance* is defined as the ratio of voltage drop and current across a conducting path. Its unit being ohm, it also represents the capability of a circuit by virtue of which it opposes flow of steady state current through it.

Symbolically, $R = \dfrac{V}{I}$.

Self-inductance is an element which accounts for the storage of energy in a magnetic field associated with the current. The energy stored being $\frac{1}{2}LI^2$, inductance in steady state is applicable in *a.c.* circuits only.

Mathematically, $e = -L\dfrac{di}{dt}$ volts where *e* is the induced *e.m.f.* due to rate of change of current $\left(\dfrac{di}{dt}\right)$ in a circuit in a magnetic field, the direction of *e* being reverse to the change.

Self-inductance is the property of a conductor (say a coil) by virtue of which it opposes change of direction and or any increase or decrease of current or flux through it. The property is analogous to inertia in a material body. Quantitatively, the self-inductance is measured in terms of coefficient of self-inductance L, the unit being Henry.

$$L=\frac{N\phi}{I}\text{ Henry}$$

where, N represents the number of turns, ϕ, the flux set up by the coil current I.

However, the flux produced in a magnetic circuit is given by

$$\text{Flux}=\frac{\text{m.m.f.}}{\text{reluctance}}=\frac{NI}{\dfrac{l}{\mu_0\mu_r A}}$$

where, l is the length of the magnetic path, A, the area, μ_0 and μ_r are the absolute and relative permeabilities.

$$\therefore\quad \frac{\phi}{I}=\frac{N}{\dfrac{l}{\mu_0\mu_r A}}$$

But $$L=N\frac{\phi}{I}=N\frac{N}{\dfrac{l}{\mu_0\mu_r A}}$$

$$=\frac{N^2}{\dfrac{l}{\mu_0\mu_r A}}=\frac{N^2}{S}\text{ Henry.}$$

Expression $(L=N\phi/I)$ gives the value of self-inductance in terms of current flowing through it, flux and number of turns while the expression $(L=N^2/S)$ gives the same in terms of the dimensions of solenoid.

Mutual inductance is another property which is defined as the ability of one coil (or circuit) to produce an induced voltage in a nearby coil by electromagnetic induction when the current in the first coil changes, the action being vice versa. Mutual inductance is measured in terms of the coefficient of mutual induction M.

Node. A node is the junction in a network where two or more circuit elements are connected together.

Branch. It is a portion of a network which lies between two junctions of the network.

Let I_1 be the current in first coil producing a flux ϕ_1 in it. The flux linkings by the second coil of N_2 turns, *i.e.*, the coefficient of mutual induction, is then given by,

$$M=\frac{N_2\,\phi_1}{I_1}\text{ Henry}$$

Again flux in the first coil

$$\phi_1=\frac{N_1 I_1}{\dfrac{l}{\mu_0\mu_r A}}\qquad\left[\because \text{Flux}=\frac{\text{m.m.f.}}{\text{reluctance}}\right]$$

or $$\frac{\phi_1}{I_1}=\frac{N_1}{\dfrac{l}{\mu_0\mu_r A}}$$

But $$M=\frac{N_2\,\phi_1}{I_1}=N_2\frac{N_1}{\dfrac{l}{\mu_0\mu_r A}}$$

$$=\frac{\mu_0\mu_r A N_1 N_2}{l}\text{ Henry}$$

$$=\frac{N_1 N_2}{\dfrac{l}{\mu_0\mu_r A}}=\frac{N_1 N_2}{S}\text{ Henry}$$

Expression $\left(M=\dfrac{N_2\,\phi_1}{I_1}\right)$ being the general form of representing the coefficient of mutual induction, the above expression $\left(M=\dfrac{N_1 N_2}{S}\right)$ represents the same in terms of dimension of the coils.

The concept of *coefficient of coupling* is associated with inductance.

Considering two magnetically coupled coils A and B having number of turns N_1 and N_2 respectively with self-inductances L_1 and L_2, we can write

$$L_1=\frac{N_1^2}{\dfrac{l}{\mu_0\mu_r A}}\text{ and }L_2=\frac{N_2^2}{\dfrac{l}{\mu_0\mu_r A}}$$

Flux produced in coil A due to flow of current I_1 is given by

$$\phi_1=\frac{N_1 I_1}{\dfrac{l}{\mu_0\mu_r A}}$$

Also, flux linked in coil B is given by

$$M=\frac{K_1\,\phi_1\,N_2}{I_1}$$

CHAPTER 11

K_1 being the fraction of the flux linking with coil B

$$= K_1 \frac{N_1 N_2}{\frac{l}{\mu_0 \mu_r A}}$$

[substituting the value of ϕ_1]

Then, when I_1 current flows through coil A producing flux ϕ_1 and assuming flux $K_1 \phi_1$ to be linked with coil B, the coefficient of mutual induction is given by expression $\left(M = \frac{K_1 \phi_1 N_2}{I_1} \right)$.

Similarly, if I_2 be the current flowing through coil B, producing flux ϕ_2, assuming a flux $K_2 \phi_2$ linking coil A, the coefficient of mutual induction, in this case, is given by

$$M = \frac{K_2 \phi_2 N_2}{I_2} = K_2 \frac{N_1 N_2}{\frac{l}{\mu_0 \mu_r A}}$$

Multiplying the above two equations relating M, we get

$$M^2 = K_1 K_2 \frac{N_1^2}{\frac{l}{\mu_0 \mu_r A}} \times \frac{N_2^2}{\frac{l}{\mu_0 \mu_r A}}$$

or $$M^2 = K_1 K_2 L_1 L_2$$

$\therefore$ $$M = K\sqrt{L_1 L_2} \text{ where } K = \sqrt{K_1 K_2}.$$

Constant K is called *coefficient of coupling*. If the flux due to one coil completely links with the other, $K = 1$. On the other hand, if the flux of one coil does not at all link with the other, $K = 0$.

Next to resistance and inductance, *capacitance* C is the characteristic of the element in a circuit which describes the capability of the circuit to store electric charge. Capacitance accounts for the storage of energy in the associated electric field.

$C = Q/V$ where Q is the charge taken and V is the voltage across the capacitance. The unit of C is Farad.

11.2.6 Combination of Resistances, Inductances and Capacitances

If the resistances are in series, the equivalent resistance is the algebraic sum of individual resistances.

i.e., $$R_{\text{equiv.}} = R_1 + R_2 + R_3 + \ldots$$

On the other hand, if the resistances are in parallel, the equivalent resistance can be obtained as follows :

$$\frac{1}{R_{\text{equiv.}}} = \frac{1}{R_1} + \frac{1}{R_2} + \frac{1}{R_3} + \ldots\ldots$$

In the series combination of inductances, if the fluxes are additive [Fig. 11.1(*b*)].

$$L_{\text{equiv.}} = L_1 + L_2 + 2M$$

and if the fluxes are opposite to each other, [Fig. 11.1(*c*)]

$$L_{\text{equiv.}} = L_1 + L_2 - 2M.$$

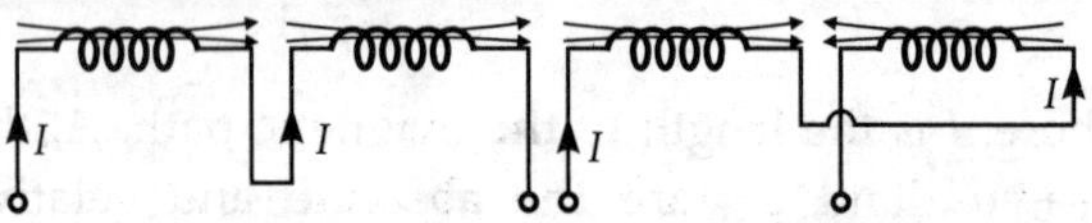

(*b*) Fluxes are additive (*c*) Fluxes are opposite

Fig. 11.1

M being the coefficient of mutual inductance. On the other hand, if L_1 and L_2 are parallel,

$$L_{\text{equiv.}} = \frac{L_1 L_2 - M^2}{L_1 + L_2 - 2M};$$

if the mutual flux helps the individual flux and

$$L_{\text{equiv.}} = \frac{L_1 L_2 - M^2}{L_1 + L_2 + 2M}$$

when the mutual flux opposes the individual flux.

In case of series combination of capacitance, the equivalent capacitance is given by

$$\frac{1}{C_{\text{equiv.}}} = \frac{1}{C_1} + \frac{1}{C_2} + \frac{1}{C_3} + \ldots..$$

and in case of parallel combination, the equivalent capacitance is given by

$$C_{\text{equiv.}} = C_1 + C_2 + C_3 + \ldots\ldots$$

11.3 PORT IN NETWORK

(*a*) One port network

Any network may diagrammatically be represented by a rectangular box. In order to connect it with other network, it must have two terminals. This rectangular box then represents one port or a two terminal network (Fig. 11.2). Any active or passive network having only two terminals can be represented by an *one port network*.

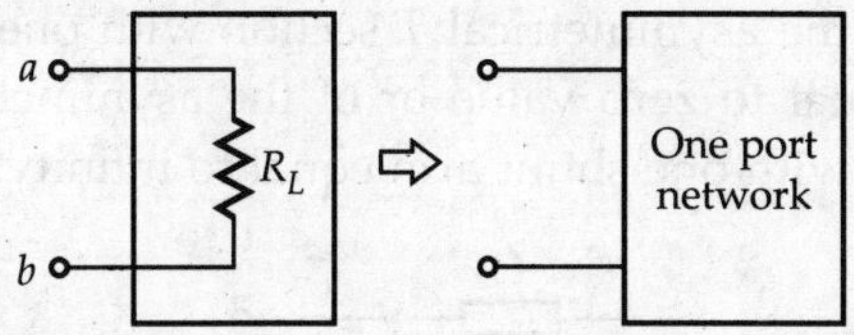

Fig. 11.2 Schematic representation of one port network.

(*b*) Two port network

If the rectangular box that represents a network, consists of two pairs of terminals (*i.e.*, four terminals) where one pair of terminals can be designated as input, the other pair being output, it is called a *two port network* (or *a four terminal network*). Fig. 11.3 represents the diagrammatic representation of a two port network. In such a network, the driving source may be connected at the pair of input terminals while the other pair of terminals serves as output.

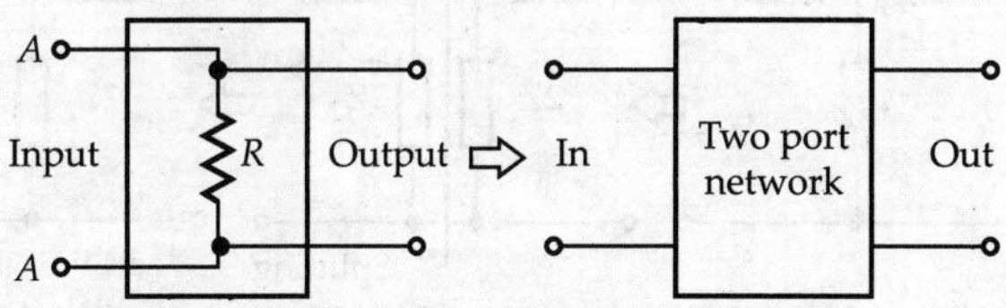

Fig. 11.3 Diagrammatic representation of two port network.

(*c*) *n*-port network

If the network representation contains of '*n*'-number of pairs of terminals, it is called a *n* port network. In *n* port network, the driving source may be connected in more than one number of pairs of terminals. The block diagram of an *n*-port network has been shown in Fig. 11.4.

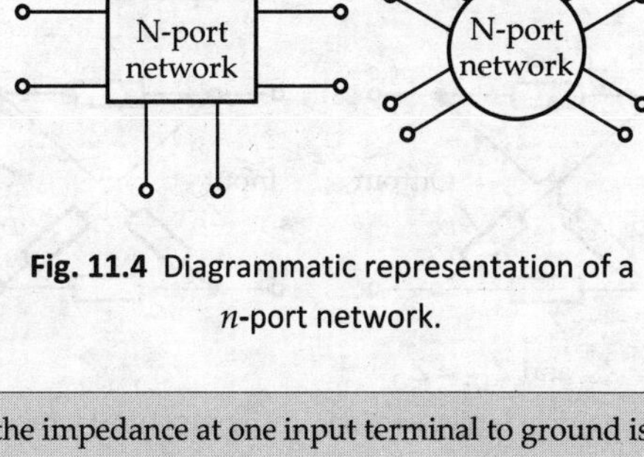

Fig. 11.4 Diagrammatic representation of a *n*-port network.

11.4 NETWORK CONFIGURATION

Depending on the configuration of impedance a network can be specified as follows :

(*i*) *T*-section

When a network section looks like a "*T*", it is known as *T-section*. Figs. 11.5(*a*) and (*b*) represent *unsymmetrical* and *symmetrical T*-sections.

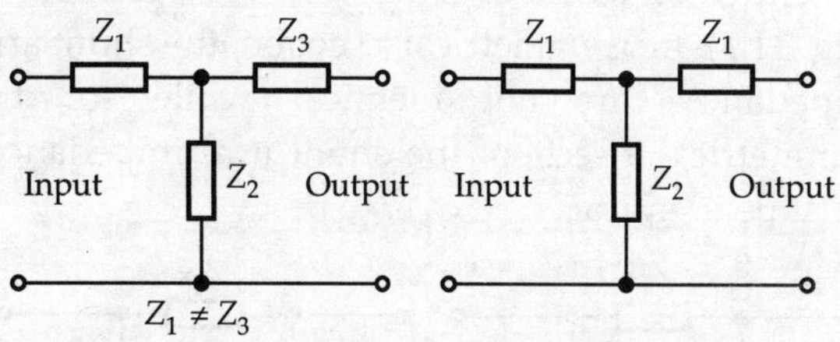

(*a*) Unsymmetrical *T*-section (*b*) Symmetrical *T*-section

Fig. 11.5 Symmetrical and unsymmetrical *T*-sections.

The figure indicates that in a symmetrical section, the series arm impedance is equal in both the sides of the shunt arm impedance. It may be observed that in unsymmetrical section, the impedances Z_1 and Z_3 are not equal to each other. The net series arm impedance of the unsymmetrical section is $(Z_1 + Z_3)$ ohm while that for the symmetrical section is $(2\ Z_1)$ ohm. The shunt arm impedance in both the cases is given by Z_2 ohm.

Balanced and ***unbalanced**** configuration of a *T*-section has been shown in Fig. 11.6. The balanced *T*-section has also been termed as *H-section*.

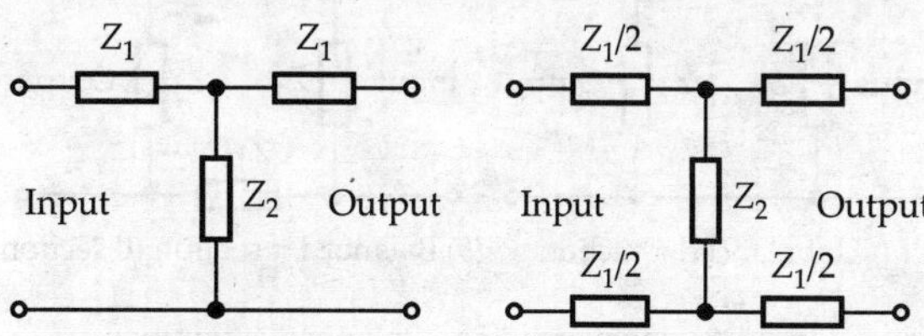

(*a*) Unbalanced symmetrical *T*-section (*b*) Balanced symmetrical *T*-section (*H*-section)

Fig. 11.6 Representation of Balanced and Unbalanced *T*-sections.

Though Fig. 11.6 represents the balanced and unbalanced configuration of a symmetrical *T*-section, asymmetrical *T*-section can also be similarly configured. It may also be noted that both the

* If the impedance at one input terminal to ground is same as the impedance at corresponding output terminal and ground, it is a *balanced* network. If the condition is not satisfied, it is called *unbalanced* network.

balanced and unbalanced *T*-sections have identical transmission characteristics under identical mode of connection and hence there is exact equivalence between balanced and unbalanced section.

(*ii*) π-section

In an identical manner, symmetrical and asymmetrical π section (*i.e.* the section whose structure looks like a π) can be configured (Fig. 11.7). In asymmetrical π section, the shunt arm impedances are not identical while for the symmetrical π section, the shunt arm impedances must be identical.

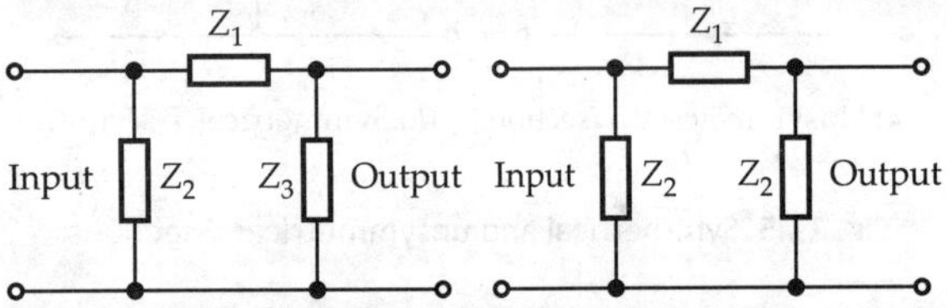

(*a*) Asymmetrical π section (*b*) Symmetrical π section

Fig. 11.7 Asymmetrical and symmetrical representation of π section.

Here, the net series arm impedance being Z_1 in each case, the shunt arm impedance is the parallel combination of the individual shunt arms.

Figure 11.8 represents the unbalanced and balanced π sections in exactly similar way to that in *T*-section.

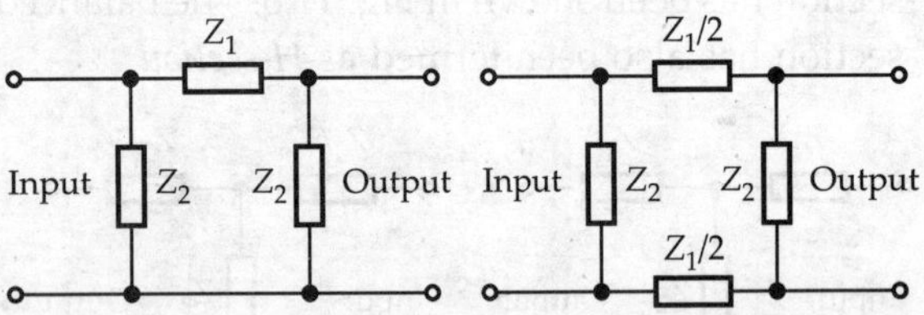

(*a*) Unbalanced π section (*b*) Balanced π section (0 section)

Fig. 11.8 Unbalanced and Balanced π-sections.

An asymmetrical π section can also be represented in the form of balanced and unbalanced modes and the equivalence between modes exists till the mode of connection is same. A balanced form of π network is known as a "O" section also.

(*iii*) L-section

When the network section looks like 'L', the configuration is termed as *L section* [Fig. 11.8(*c*)]. It may be observed that *L* section is merely a specific case of the asymmetrical *T* section with one series arm equal to zero value or of the asymmetrical π section with one shunt arm equal to infinity.

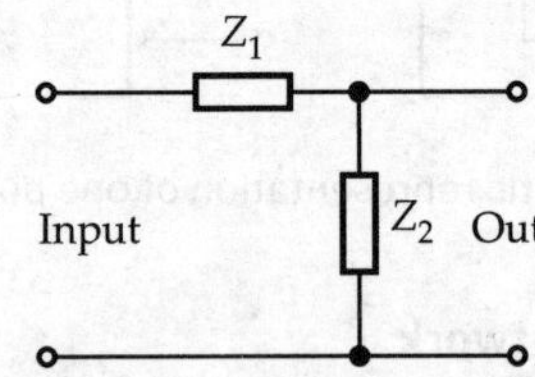

Fig. 11.8 (*c*) Representation of an *L*-section.

(*iv*) Half-section

It is obvious that both the symmetrical *T* or π section can be split into *two halves*. Each half is then known as half section [Fig. 11.9].

Configurationwise, an half section looks like an *L*-section.

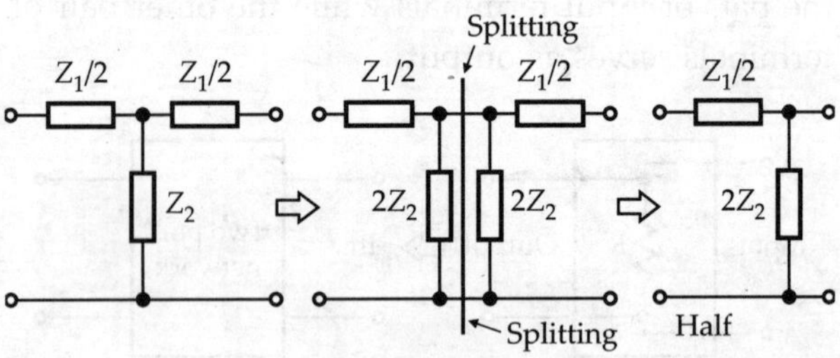

(*a*) Splitting of a *T*-section

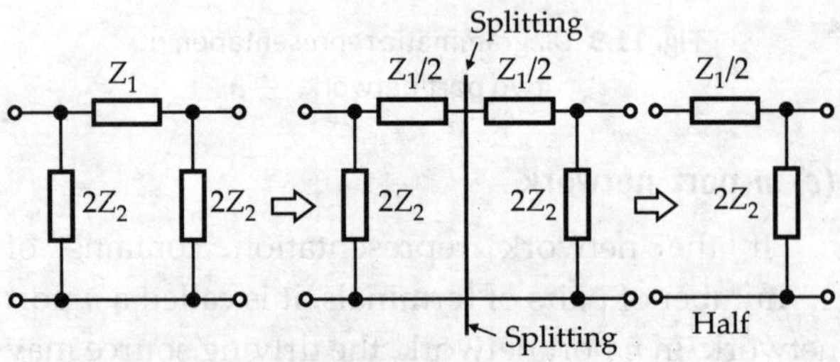

(*b*) Splitting of a π section

Fig. 11.9 Formation of a half-section.

(*v*) Lattice section

Figure 11.10 represents a *lattice section* where the *series arms* are given by the impedances between

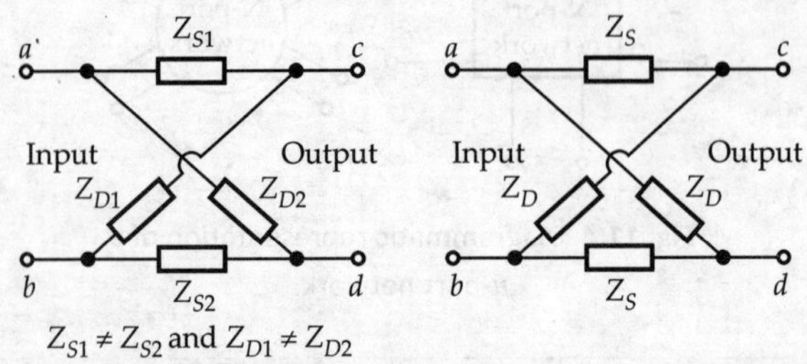

$Z_{S1} \neq Z_{S2}$ and $Z_{D1} \neq Z_{D2}$

(*a*) Asymmetrical lattice section (*b*) Symmetrical lattice section

Fig. 11.10 Lattice Section.

(*a* and *c*) and (*b* and *d*). The diagonal arms are frequently termed as *cross arms*. Fig. 11.10(*a*) represents the asymmetrical lattice section while Fig. 11.10(*b*) represents symmetrical lattice section. The lattice section is usually a *balanced* structure. Fig. 11.11 represents 'bridge' form of a lattice section.

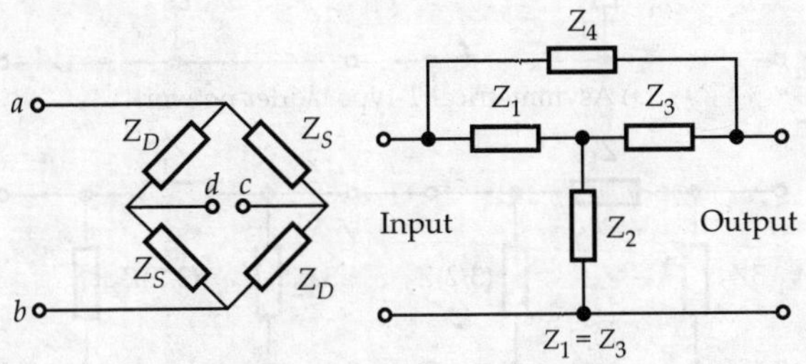

Fig. 11.11 Bridge representation.

(*vi*) Bridged *T*-section

When the series arms of a *T*-section are bridged by an impedance, the section is termed as bridged *T*-section. Fig. 11.12 represents *asymmetrical* and *symmetrical* bridged *T*-sections.

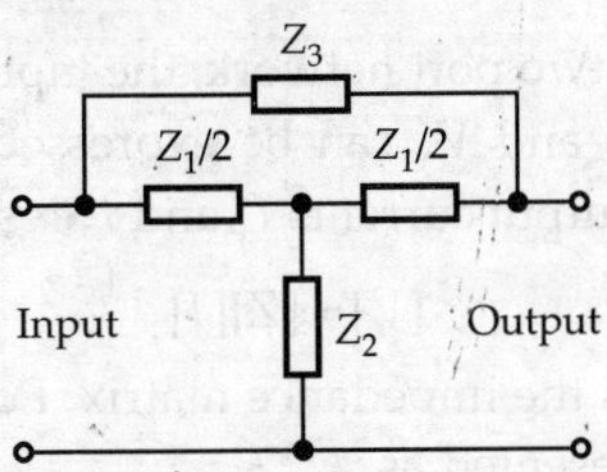

Fig. 11.12 Bridge *T*-representation.

Figure 11.13 represents a balanced and unbalanced form of a bridged *T*-section.

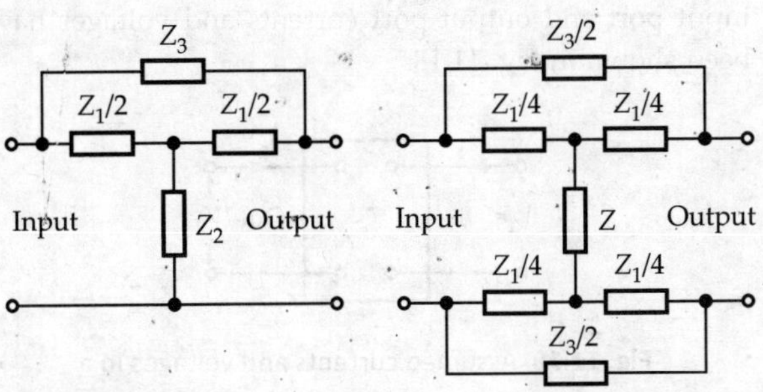

(*a*) Unbalanced bridged *T*-section

(*b*) Balanced bridged *T*-section

Fig. 11.13 Unbalanced and Balanced bridged *T*-sections.

11.5 RECURRENT NETWORK

A cascade of repeated sections of network is known as *recurrent network*. Recurrent network as shown in Fig. 11.14 is most commonly used in line transmission and is also known as ladder network.

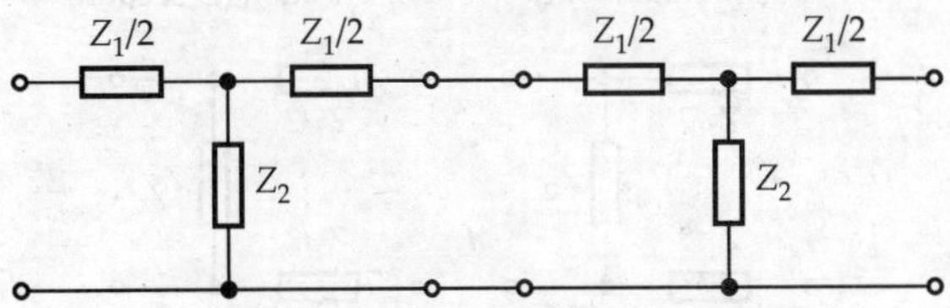

(*a*) Unbalanced ladder (*T*-sections)

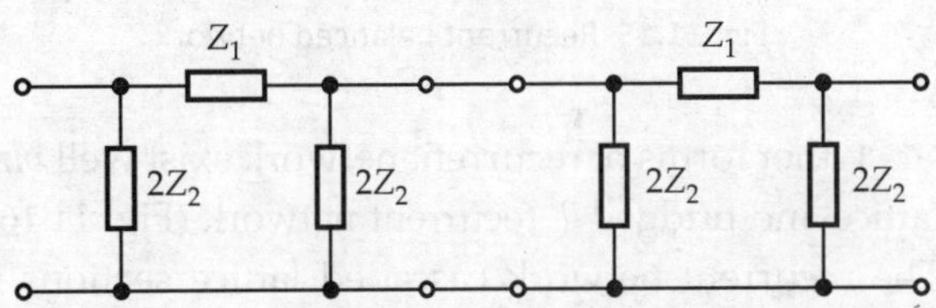

(*b*) Unbalanced ladder (π sections)

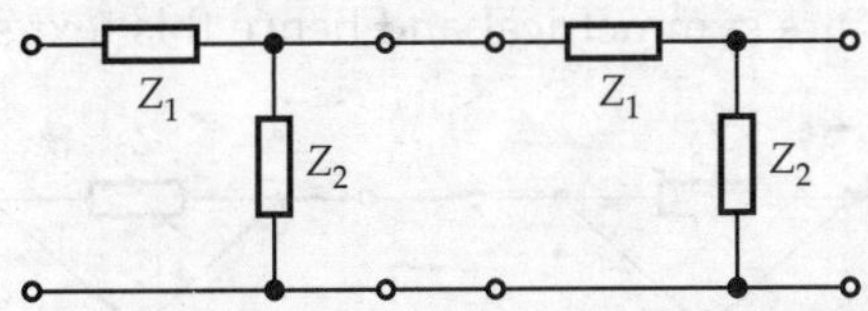

(*c*) Unbalanced ladder network composed of *L* sections

Fig. 11.14 Recurrent unbalanced networks.

The ladder network may be a balanced or unbalanced form of recurrent network. Common forms of recurrent (or ladder) networks are *T*, π, *L* in unbalanced form and *H*, *O* and *C* in balanced form. The sections are arranged in such a way so that the total series impedance is Z_1 ohm and the total shunt impedance is Z_2 ohm. Figs 11.14(*a*), (*b*) & (*c*) represent unbalanced form of ladder network while Figs. 11.15(*a*), (*b*) & (*c*) show the balanced forms.

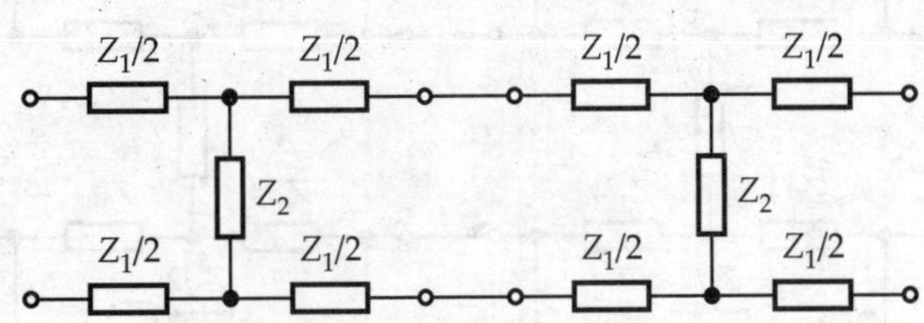

(*a*) Balanced ladder network of *T* section (*H* section)

Fig. 11.15

CHAPTER 11

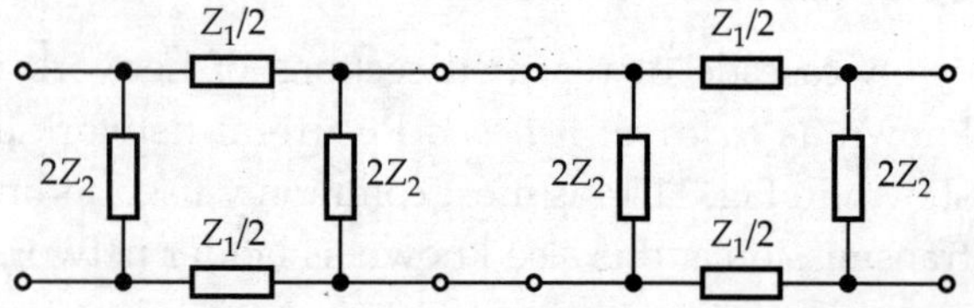

(*b*) Balanced ladder network of π section (*O* section)

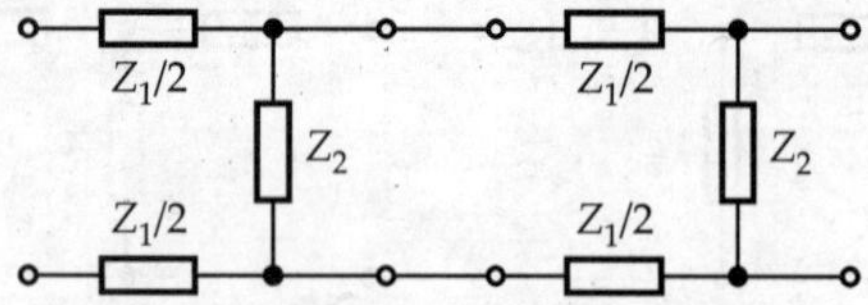

(*c*) Balanced ladder network of *I* section

Fig. 11.15 Recurrent balanced network.

Other forms of recurrent network exist well *viz.*, lattice and bridged *T* recurrent network (Fig. 11.16). The recurrent network cascaded lattice sections is usually a balanced one while that for bridged *T* may be unbalanced also. Usually the recurrent networks are symmetrical and hence this text stresses only on the symmetrical recurrent networks. *T* and π type asymmetrical recurrent network have been shown in Fig. 11.17.

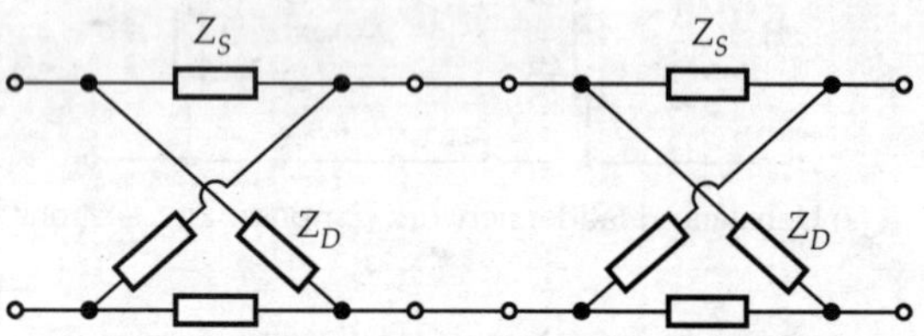

(*a*) Recurrent lattice network

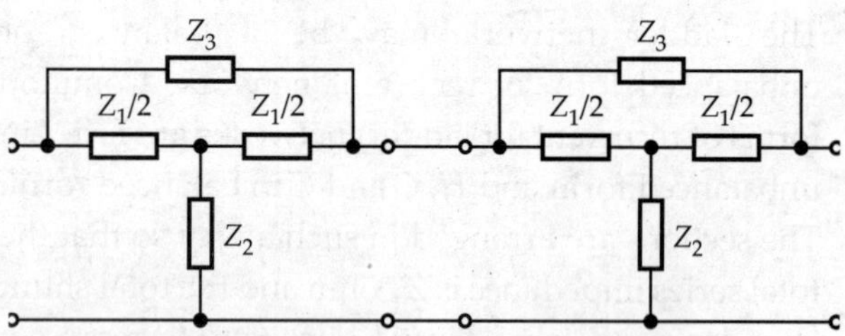

(*b*) Recurrent unbalanced bridge *T* network

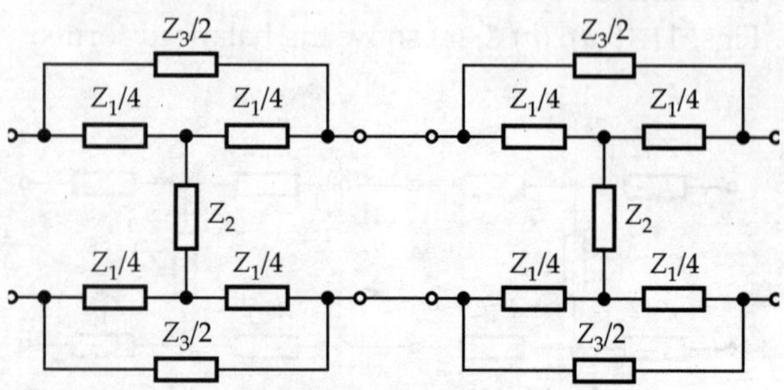

(*c*) Recurrent bridge *T* balanced network

Fig. 11.16 Recurrent bridge *T* balanced network.

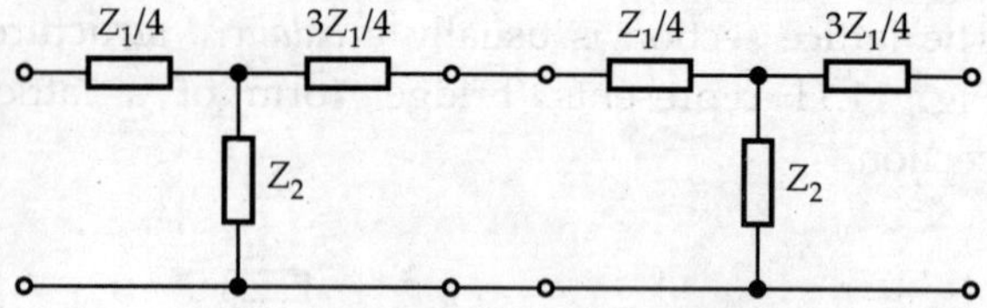

(*a*) Asymmetrical *T*-type ladder network

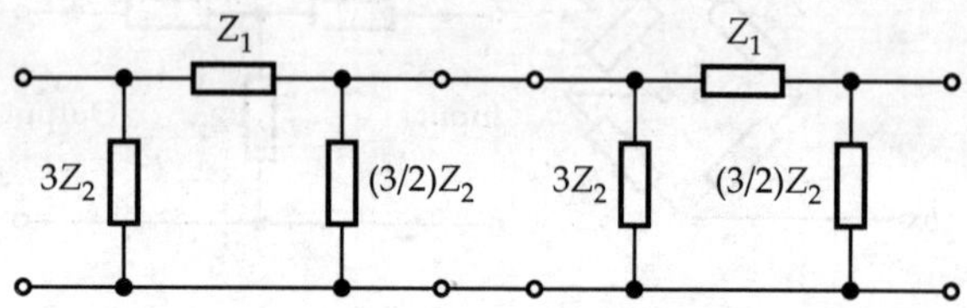

(*a*) Asymmetrical π-type ladder network

Fig. 11.17 Recurrent asymmetrical ladder network.

PARAMETER REPRESENTATION

11.6 Z-PARAMETERS (OPEN CIRCUIT IMPEDANCE PARAMETERS)

For the two port network, the input and output voltages V_1 and V_2 can be expressed in terms of input and output currents I_1 and I_2 respectively as

$$[V] = [Z][I] \qquad ...(11.1)$$

where $[Z]$ is the impedance matrix. Equation (11.1) can be represented as

$$\begin{bmatrix} V_1 \\ V_2 \end{bmatrix} = \begin{bmatrix} Z_{11} & Z_{12} \\ Z_{21} & Z_{22} \end{bmatrix} \begin{bmatrix} I_1 \\ I_2 \end{bmatrix} \qquad ...(11.2)$$

In a two port network representation, the network is assumed to be a rectangular box and the directions of input port and output port currents and voltages have been shown in Fig. 11.18.

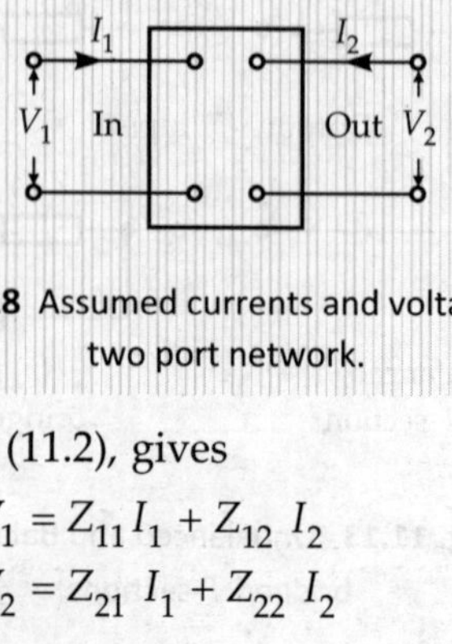

Fig. 11.18 Assumed currents and voltages in a two port network.

Equation (11.2), gives

$$V_1 = Z_{11} I_1 + Z_{12} I_2 \qquad ...(11.3)$$

and

$$V_2 = Z_{21} I_1 + Z_{22} I_2 \qquad ...(11.4)$$

Assuming the output of the two port network to be open-circuited,

$$I_2 = 0$$

Thus, from equation (11.3), with

$$I_2 = 0,$$

$$Z_{11} = \frac{V_1}{I_1} \qquad \text{...(11.5)}$$

With $I_2 = 0$, from equation (11.4),

$$Z_{21} = \frac{V_2}{I_1} \qquad \text{...(11.6)}$$

Again, assuming the input port of the same two port network to be open circuited,

$$I_1 = 0$$

This gives, from equation (11.3)

$$Z_{12} = \frac{V_1}{I_2} \qquad \text{...(11.7)}$$

and, from equation (11.4),

$$Z_{22} = \frac{V_2}{I_2} \qquad \text{...(11.8)}$$

Then, $Z_{11} = \left(\left.\frac{V_1}{I_1}\right|_{I_2=0}\right)$ and $Z_{22} = \left(\left.\frac{V_2}{I_2}\right|_{I_1=0}\right)$

are called *input and output driving point impedances* respectively while

$$Z_{12} = \left(\left.\frac{V_1}{I_2}\right|_{I_1=0}\right) \text{ and } Z_{21} = \left(\left.\frac{V_2}{I_1}\right|_{I_2=0}\right)$$

are called *reverse and forward transfer impedances.*

$Z_{11}, Z_{12}, Z_{21}, Z_{22}$ are also called *impedance parameters* or *open circuit parameters* of the two port network.

Equations (11.3) and (11.4) can further be represented as

$$V_1 = (Z_{11} - Z_{12})\, I_1 + Z_{12}\,(I_1 + I_2) \qquad \text{...(11.9)}$$

and $V_2 = (Z_{21} - Z_{12})\, I_1 + (Z_{22} - Z_{12})\, I_2 + Z_{12}(I_1 + I_2)$ ...(11.10)

Figure 11.19 represents the *equivalent circuit* utilising equations (11.3) and (11.4) and Fig. 11.20 represent the same utilising equations (11.9) and (11.10).

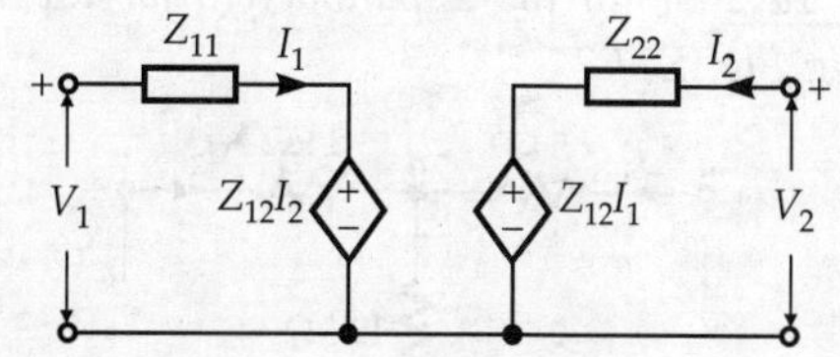

Fig. 11.19 Basic Z parameter equivalent circuit.

It may be noted that Z_{11}.......Z_{22} are expressed in ohm.

$Z_{12}\, I_2$ and $Z_{21}\, I_1$ in Fig. 11.19 while $(Z_{21} - Z_{12})\, I_1$ in Fig. 11.20 represent "current controlled voltage sources".

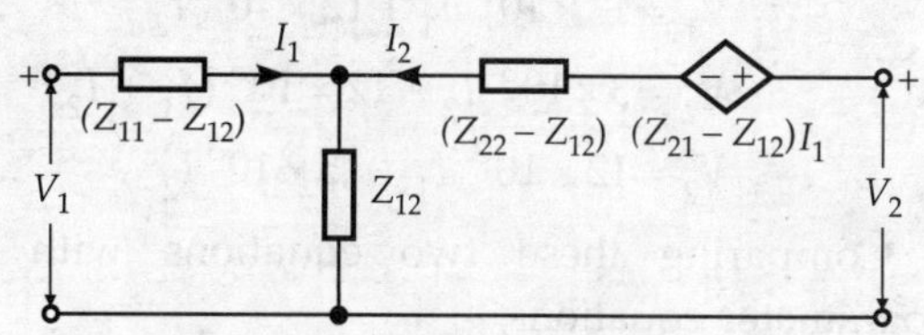

Fig. 11.20 Another form of equivalent circuit with open circuit (Z) parameters

WORKED EXAMPLES

EXAMPLE 11.1 *Find the Z-parameters for the following network.*

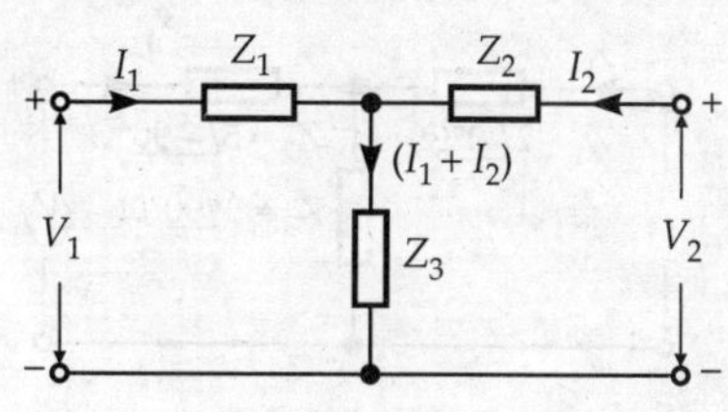

Fig. E11.1

SOLUTION. Using KVL in Fig. E11.1, the loop equations can be written as

$$V_1 = I_1 Z_1 + (I_1 + I_2)\, Z_3$$

or $$V_1 = (Z_1 + Z_3)\, I_1 + Z_3 I_2 \qquad \text{...}(i)$$

and $$V_2 = I_2\, Z_2 + (I_2 + I_2)\, Z_3$$

or $$V_2 = Z_3 I_1 + (Z_2 + Z_3)\, I_2 \qquad \text{...}(ii)$$

Comparing equations (*i*) and (*ii*) with the standard Z-parameter equations,

$$Z_{11} = Z_1 + Z_3;\; Z_{12} = Z_3;$$

$$Z_{21} = Z_3\,;\; Z_{22} = Z_2 + Z_3$$

EXAMPLE 11.2 *Find the Z-parameters for the network shown in Fig. E11.2.*

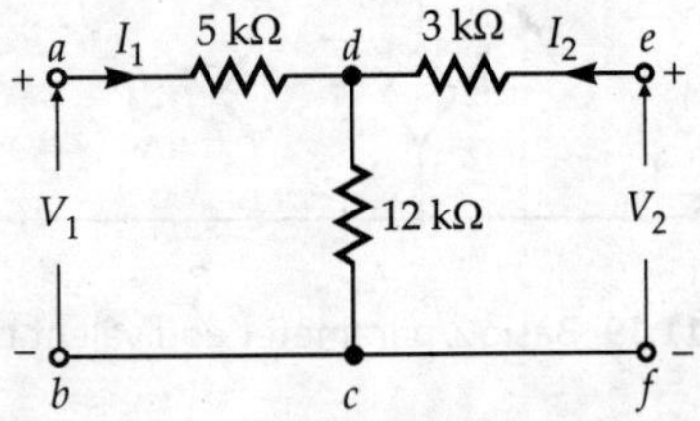

Fig. E11.2

SOLUTION. Using KVL for loops *abcd* and *cdef*, the loop equations for Fig. E11.2 are given by

$$V_1 = 5\times 10^3\ I_1 + 12\times 10^3\ (I_1 + I_2)$$

or $$V_1 = 17\times 10^3\ I_1 + 12\times 10^3\ I_2 \quad ...(i)$$

and $$V_2 = 3\times 10^3\ I_2 + 12\times 10^3\ (I_1 + I_2)$$

or $$V_2 = 12\times 10^3\ I_1 + 15\times 10^3\ I_2 \quad ...(ii)$$

Comparing these two equations with the Z-parameter equations,

$$\mathbf{Z_{11} = 17\times 10^3\ \Omega}$$
$$\mathbf{Z_{12} = 12\times 10^3\ \Omega}$$
$$\mathbf{Z_{21} = 12\times 10^3\ \Omega}$$
$$\mathbf{Z_{22} = 15\times 10^3\ \Omega.}$$

EXAMPLE 11.3 *In a T network of Fig. E11.3, $Z_1 = 2\angle 0°$, $Z_2 = 5\angle -90°$, $Z_3 = 3\angle 90°$, find the Z-parameters.*

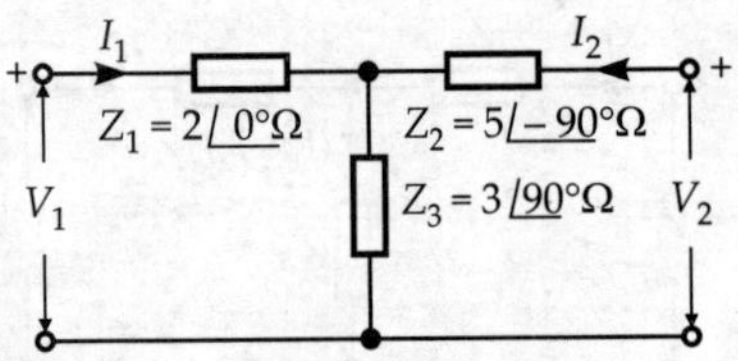

Fig. E11.3

SOLUTION. Using KVL, the loop equations are

$$V_1 = 2\angle 0°\ I_1 + 3\angle 90°\ (I_1 + I_2)$$

or $$V_1 = [2\angle 0° + 3\angle 90°]\ I_1 + 3\angle 90°\ I_2$$

$$V_2 = 5\angle -90°\ I_2 + 3\angle 90° (I_1 + I_2)$$

or $$V_2 = 3\angle 90°\ I_1 + [5\angle -90° + 3\angle 90°]\ I_2$$

These equations give

$$Z_{11} = 2\angle 0° + 3\angle 90° = 2 + 3j$$
$$= \mathbf{3.605\angle +56°\ \Omega}$$
$$Z_{12} = \mathbf{3\angle 90°\ \Omega}$$
$$Z_{21} = \mathbf{3\angle 90°\ \Omega}$$
$$Z_{22} = 5\angle -90° + 3\angle 90°$$
$$= -5j + 3j = -2j = \mathbf{2\angle -90°\ \Omega.}$$

EXAMPLE 11.4 *The following readings are obtained experimentally for an unknown two-port network :*

	V_1	V_2	I_1	I_2
Output open	100 V	60 V	10 A	0
Input open	30 V	40 V	0	3 A

Compute the Z-parameters.

SOLUTION. From the theory of Z-parameters, we know,

$$Z_{11} = \left.\frac{V_1}{I_1}\right|_{I_2=0} = \frac{100}{10} = \mathbf{10\ \Omega}$$

$$Z_{12} = \left.\frac{V_1}{I_2}\right|_{I_1=0} = \frac{30}{3} = \mathbf{10\ \Omega}$$

$$Z_{21} = \left.\frac{V_2}{I_1}\right|_{I_2=0} = \frac{60}{10} = \mathbf{6\ \Omega};$$

$$Z_{22} = \left.\frac{V_2}{I_2}\right|_{I_1=0} = \frac{40}{3} = \mathbf{13.33\ \Omega.}$$

EXAMPLE 11.5 *Determine the Z-parameters for a π-type attenuator section (Fig. E11.4).*

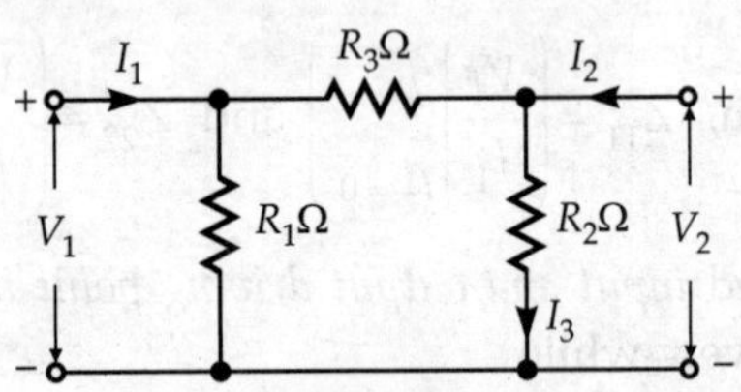

Fig. E11.4

SOLUTION. The π attenuator section has been drawn in Fig. E11.4.

Let us first assume that the output port is open-circuited.

$$\therefore \quad I_2 = 0$$

and $$Z_{11} = \left.\frac{V_1}{I_1}\right|_{I_2=0} \equiv (R_2 + R_3) \| R_1$$

$$= \frac{R_1 (R_2 + R_3)}{R_1 + R_2 + R_3} \quad ...(i)$$

However,

$$I_3 = I_1 \frac{R_1}{R_1 + R_2 + R_3}$$

[Output being open circuited] ...(*ii*)

But $V_2 = I_3 R_2$

$$= I_1 \frac{R_1 R_2}{R_1 + R_2 + R_3} \quad \text{[using (ii)]} \qquad ...(iii)$$

$$\text{Again, } Z_{21} = \left.\frac{V_2}{I_1}\right|_{I_2=0} = \frac{R_1 R_2}{R_1 + R_2 + R_3} \quad \text{[using (iii)]}$$

Hence with output open circuited,

$$Z_{11} = \frac{R_1 (R_2 + R_3)}{R_1 + R_2 R_3}$$

and
$$Z_{21} = \frac{R_1 R_2}{R_1 + R_2 + R_3}$$

Let us now assume, input is open circuited such that

$$I_1 = 0$$

$$\therefore \quad Z_{22} = \left.\frac{V_2}{I_2}\right|_{I_1=0} = (R_1 + R_3) || R_2$$

$$= \frac{R_2 (R_1 + R_3)}{R_1 + R_2 + R_3} \qquad ...(iv)$$

Again current I_3' [*i.e.*, the current through R_1 when input port is open and current entering from the output side is I_2] is given by

$$I_3' = I_2 \frac{R_2}{R_1 + R_2 + R_3} \qquad ...(v)$$

But
$$V_1 = I_3' R_1 = I_2 \frac{R_1 R_2}{R_1 + R_2 + R_3} \quad \text{[using (v)]}$$

$$\text{Again } Z_{12} = \left.\frac{V_1}{I_2}\right|_{I_1=0} = \frac{R_1 R_2}{R_1 + R_2 + R_3}$$

With input open-circuited we obtained the values of Z_{12} and Z_{22} as

$$Z_{12} = \frac{R_1 R_2}{R_1 + R_2 + R_3}$$

and
$$Z_{22} = \frac{R_2 (R_1 + R_3)}{R_1 + R_2 + R_3}.$$

EXAMPLE 11.6 *Draw an equivalent circuit of the Z-parameter model of the two port network.*

SOLUTION. Let us draw a T circuit representation of the two port network as shown in Fig. E11.5.

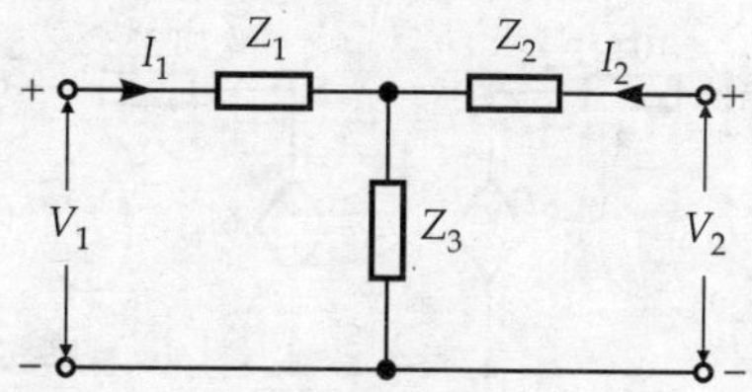

Fig. E11.5

The Z parameter equations are then given by

$$V_1 = (Z_1 + Z_3) I_1 + Z_3 I_2$$

and
$$V_2 = Z_3 I_1 + (Z_2 + Z_3) I_2$$

Thus we write these two equations in the form of standard Z-parameter form as

$$V_1 = Z_{11} I_1 + Z_{12} I_2$$

and
$$V_2 = Z_{21} I_1 + Z_{22} I_2$$

where, $Z_{11} = (Z_1 + Z_3)$; $Z_{12} = Z_3$;
$Z_{21} = Z_3$; $\quad Z_{22} = (Z_2 + Z_3)$

In the equivalent circuit, for loop 1, $Z_{12} I_2$ is the controlled voltage source while $Z_{11} I_1$ is the drop. I_1 being the loop current. In loop 2, $Z_{21} I_1$ becomes the controlled source while $Z_{22} I_2$ is the drop due to loop current I_2. The equivalent circuit has been shown in Fig. E11.6.

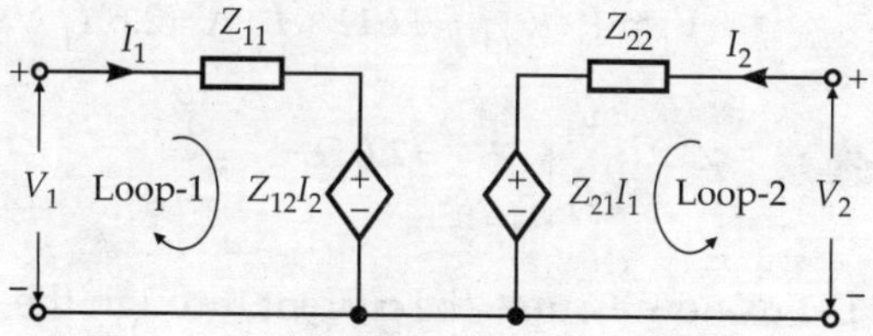

Fig. E11.6

EXAMPLE 11.7 *Draw the Z-parameter equivalent circuit of Example 11.4.*

SOLUTION. From the said Example,

$$Z_{11} = 10\,\Omega;\ Z_{12} = 10\,\Omega;$$
$$Z_{21} = 6\,\Omega \text{ and } Z_{22} = 13.33\,\Omega.$$

Thus the Z-parameter equation can be written as

$$V_1 = 10\, I_1 + 10\, I_2$$
$$V_2 = 6 I_1 + 13.33\, I_2$$

[Here, $10\, I_1$ and $11.33\, I_2$ are the voltage drops at loop 1 and 2 while $10\, I_2$ and $6\, I_1$ are the controlled sources].

CHAPTER 11

Figure E11.7 represents the equivalent circuit of the Z-parameter form.

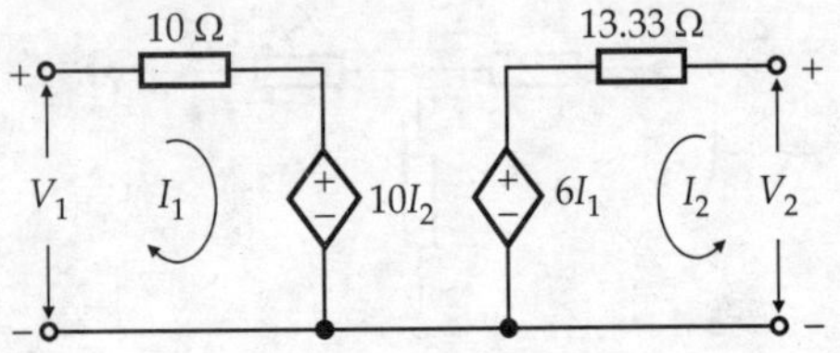

Fig. E11.7

EXAMPLE 11.8 *Find the Z parameters for the circuit shown in Fig. E11.8.*

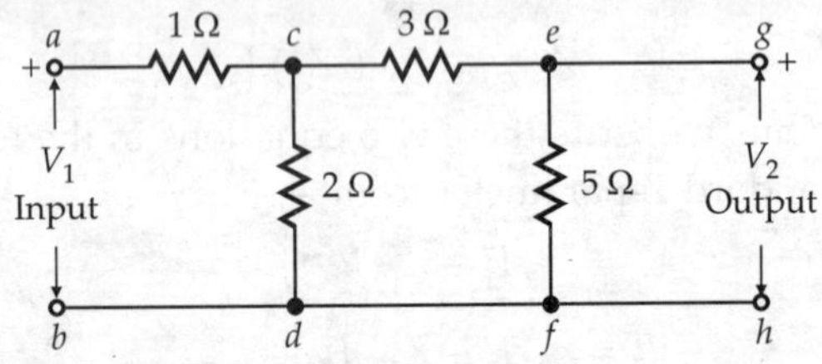

Fig. E11.8

SOLUTION. Assuming first that the output is open-circuited, $I_2 = 0$.

Looking back to the network from terminals *ab*.

$$R_{eq1} = [(3+5)||2]+1 = \frac{16}{10}+1 = 2.6\,\Omega$$

Let us assume I_1 to be the input current such that

$$V_1 = I_1\, R_{eq1} = 2.6\,\Omega \times I_1 \text{ A} = 2.6\, I_1 \text{ V}$$

$$\therefore \quad Z_{11} = \left.\frac{V_1}{I_1}\right|_{I_2=0} = \mathbf{2.6\,\Omega.}$$

Let us now assume the current through the 5 Ω resistor be I_x.

$$\text{Then} \quad I_x = I_1 \times \frac{2}{2+3+5} = \frac{I_1}{5} \text{ A}$$

[Output being open]

$$\therefore \quad V_2 = \frac{I_1}{5} \times 5 = I_1 \text{ volt.}$$

$$\text{This gives } Z_{21} = \left.\frac{V_2}{I_1}\right|_{I_2=0} = \mathbf{1\,ohm.}$$

Next, assuming the input to be open, $I_1 = 0$. The equivalent resistance of the network looking back from terminal *gh* is given by

$$R_{eq2} = (3+2)||5 = 2.5\,\Omega$$

Assuming I_2 to be the current entering through the output port,

$$V_2 = I_2\, R_{eq2} = 2.5\, I_2 \text{ volt.}$$

$$\therefore \quad Z_{22} = \left.\frac{V_2}{I_2}\right|_{I_1=0} = \mathbf{2.5\,\Omega.}$$

Let I_Y be the current through the 2 Ω resistor,

$$\therefore \quad I_Y = I_2 \frac{5}{5+3+2} = \frac{I_2}{2} \text{ A}$$

With terminal *a-b* open, $V_{a-b} \equiv V_{c-d}$, *i.e.,* the voltage across *c-d* terminal is V_1 too.

$$\text{Hence} \quad V_1 = I_Y \times 2 = \frac{I_2}{2} \times 2 = I_2 \text{ volts.}$$

This gives

$$Z_{12} = \left.\frac{V_1}{I_2}\right|_{I_1=0} = \mathbf{1\,ohm}$$

note In this problem, $Z_{12} = Z_{21}$ indicating bilateral property of the network.

EXAMPLE 11.9 *Two identical T sections, as one shown in Fig. E11.9 are connected in series. Determine the Z-parameters of the combination.*

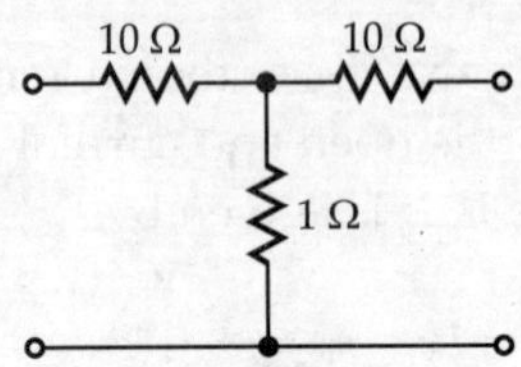

Fig. E11.9

SOLUTION. The series connection of the two identical *T* sections has been shown in Fig. E11.10.

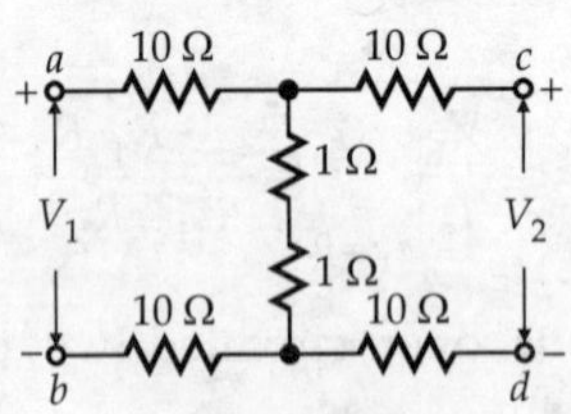

Fig. E11.10

First, the output is open-circuited and V_1 is applied at *a-b* terminals (input). Let I_1 be the current entering into the network.

R_{eq1} the equivalent resistance of the network looking back at the network through *a-b* terminals is given by

$$R_{eq1} = (10+1+1+10)\,\Omega = 22\,\Omega$$

$\therefore \quad V_1 = I_1 \times R_{eq1} = 22\, I_1.$

$$\therefore \quad Z_{11} = \left.\frac{V_1}{I_1}\right|_{I_2=0} = 22\,\Omega$$

As output is open, $V_2 = I_1 \times (1+1) = 2\, I_1$.

$$\therefore \quad Z_{21} = \left.\frac{V_2}{I_1}\right|_{I_2=0} = 2 \text{ ohms.}$$

Next, it is assumed that terminal *a-b* is open and V_2 is applied voltage at *c-d* terminals (output) when I_2 current enters into the network from the output.

Here also R_{eq2} is 22 ohms and

$$V_2 = I_2\, R_{eq2} = 22\, I_2.$$

$$\therefore \quad Z_{22} = \left.\frac{V_2}{I_2}\right|_{I_1=0} = 22\,\Omega$$

As *a-b* terminals are open,

$$V_1 = (1+1)\, I_2$$

or $$\left.\frac{V_1}{I_2}\right|_{I_1=0} = Z_{12} = 2\,\Omega$$

Hence $Z_{11} = Z_{22} = 22\,\Omega$ and $Z_{12} = Z_{21} = 2\,\Omega$.

[The same result can also be obtained from direct calculation (refer article 11.13)]

EXAMPLE 11.10 *Determine the Z-parameters of the network shown in Fig. E11.11.*

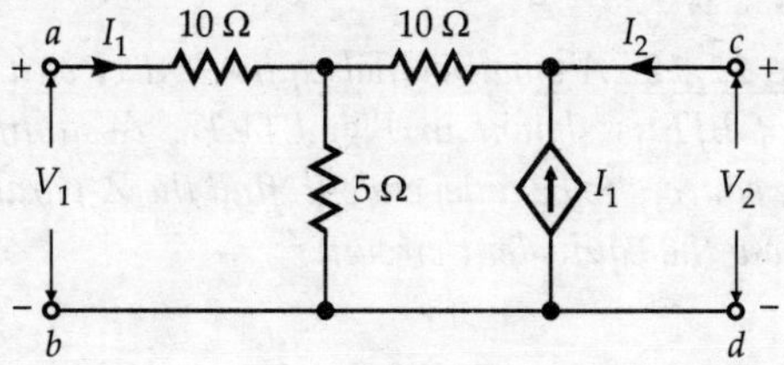

Fig. E11.11

SOLUTION. With open circuiting the output port *c-d*, and applying a voltage source V_1 at the input port (terminal *a-b*), the loop equations are given by (refer to Fig. E11.12).

$$V_1 = I_1\,(10+5) - I_2' \times 5$$

or $$V_1 = 15\, I_1 - 5I_2' \qquad ...(i)$$

However, $I_2 = 0$, output being open circuited,

$$-I_2' = I_1$$

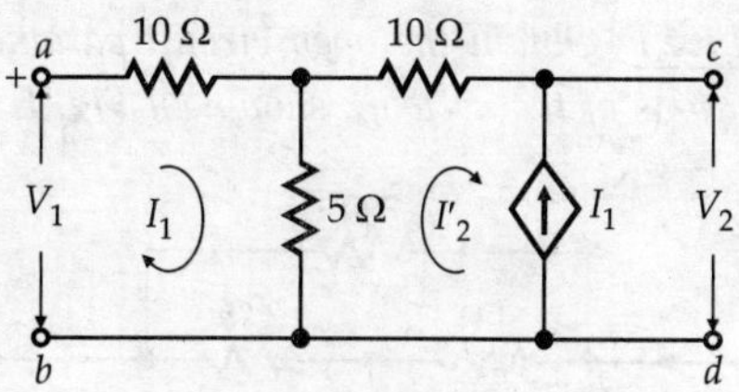

Fig. E11.12

$\therefore$ Equation (*i*) becomes

$$V_1 = 15\, I_1 + 5I_1 = 20\, I_1$$

$$\therefore \quad \left.\frac{V_1}{I_1}\right|_{I_2=0} = Z_{11} = 20\,\Omega$$

and $$I_2' = -I_1 = -\frac{V_1}{20}\text{ A.} \qquad ...(ii)$$

Again

$$V_2 = (I_1 - I_2')\,5 - 10\, I_2'$$
$$= (I_1 + I_1)\,5 + 10\, I_1 \qquad [\because I_1 = -I_2']$$
$$= 10\, I_1 + 10\, I_1 = 20\, I_1$$

$$\therefore \quad \left.\frac{V_2}{I_1}\right|_{I_2=0} = Z_{21} = 20\,\Omega.$$

In the next step, the input is opened and V_2 is applied at the output (terminal *c-d*). The current source becomes useless as with input open, $I_1 = 0$. The network configuration has been shown in Fig. E11.13.

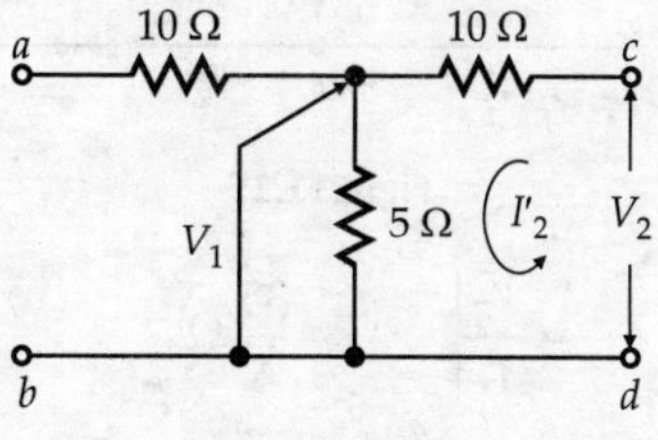

Fig. E11.13

Here $\quad I_2 \equiv I_2'$

and $\quad V_2 = I_2'\,(10+5) = 15\, I_2' = 15\, I_2$

or $$Z_{22} = \left.\frac{V_2}{I_2}\right|_{I_1=0} = 15\,\Omega.$$

Also, $\quad V_1 = I_2' \times 5 = 5\, I_2$

$$\therefore \quad Z_{12} = \left.\frac{V_1}{I_2}\right|_{I_1=0} = 5\,\Omega$$

$\therefore \quad$ **$Z_{11} = 20\,\Omega$; $\quad Z_{12} = 5\,\Omega$**

$Z_{21} = 20\,\Omega$; $\quad Z_{22} = 15\,\Omega$.

EXAMPLE 11.11 *Obtain the open circuit parameters and loop equations of the network shown in Fig. E11.14.*

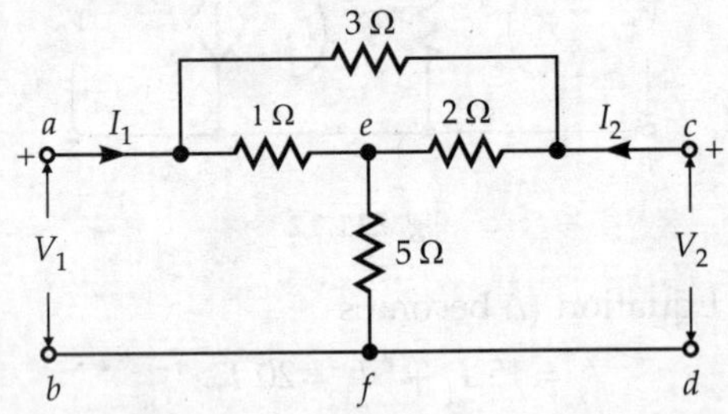

Fig. E11.14

SOLUTION. Let us first assume the output terminals (c-d) are open circuited and V_1 is applied at a-b terminals (input port). The circuit configuration has been shown in Fig. E11.15. The equivalent resistance looking from the terminals a-b is given as

$$R_{eq1} = [(3+2)||1] + 5 = \frac{35}{6}\,\Omega$$

$$\therefore \quad V_1 = I_1 \times R_{eq1} = \frac{35}{6} I_1.$$

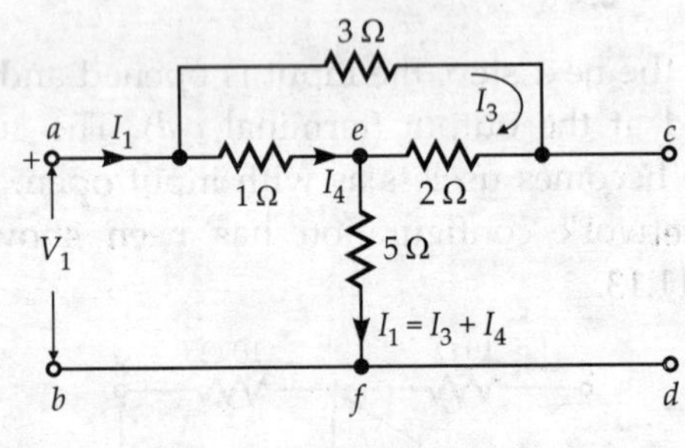

Fig. E11.15

$$\text{Hence } Z_{11} = \left.\frac{V_1}{I_1}\right|_{I_2=0} = \frac{35}{6}\,\Omega.$$

$$\text{Again, } I_3 = I_1 \frac{1}{1+3+2} = \frac{1}{6} I_1$$

Thus drop V_2 across terminal c-d is given by

$$I_3 \times 2 + I_1 \times 5 = V_2$$

$$\text{i.e.,} \quad \frac{I_1}{3} + I_1 \times 5 = V_2 \qquad \left[\because \frac{I_1}{6} = I_3\right]$$

$$\text{or} \quad \left.\frac{V_2}{I_1}\right|_{I_2=0} = Z_{21} = \frac{16}{3}\,\Omega$$

Let us now open terminals a-b (input port) applying the voltage V_2 at terminals c-d (output port). The circuit has been shown in Fig. E11.16.

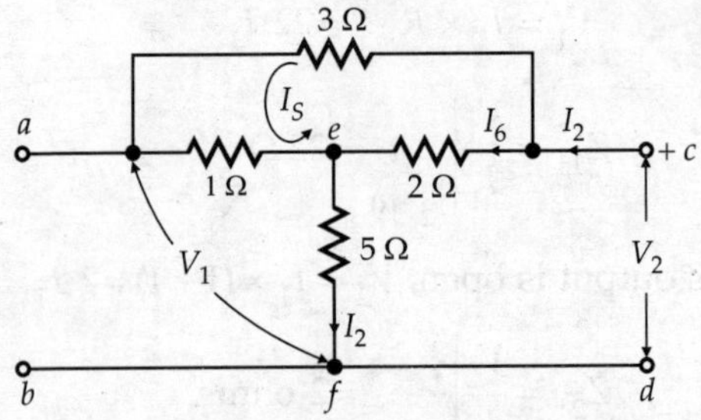

Fig. E11.16

The equivalent resistance of the network looking from output port (terminal c-d) is given by

$$R_{eq2} = [(3+1)||2] + 5 = \frac{19}{3}\,\Omega$$

$$\therefore \quad V_2 = I_2 \times R_{eq2} = \frac{10}{3} I_2$$

$$\text{i.e.} \quad \left.\frac{V_2}{I_2}\right|_{I_1=0} = Z_{22} = \frac{10}{3}\,\Omega.$$

$$\text{Again, } I_5 = I_2 \frac{2}{2+3+1} = \frac{I_2}{3}\text{ A.}$$

$$\text{Hence, } V_1 = \left(\frac{I_2}{3}\right) \times 1 + 5I_2 = \frac{16}{3} I_2$$

$$\text{or} \quad \left.\frac{V_1}{I_2}\right|_{I_1=0} = Z_{12} = \frac{16}{3}\,\Omega.$$

$$\therefore \quad \mathbf{Z_{11} = \frac{35}{6}\,\Omega;\ Z_{12} = \frac{16}{3}\,\Omega}$$

$$\mathbf{Z_{21} = \frac{16}{3}\,\Omega;\ Z_{22} = \frac{19}{3}\,\Omega.}$$

EXAMPLE 11.12 *A small signal equivalent circuit of CB mode of BJT is shown in Fig. E11.17. Assuming the voltage sources to be independent, find the Z-parameters and draw the equivalent circuit.*

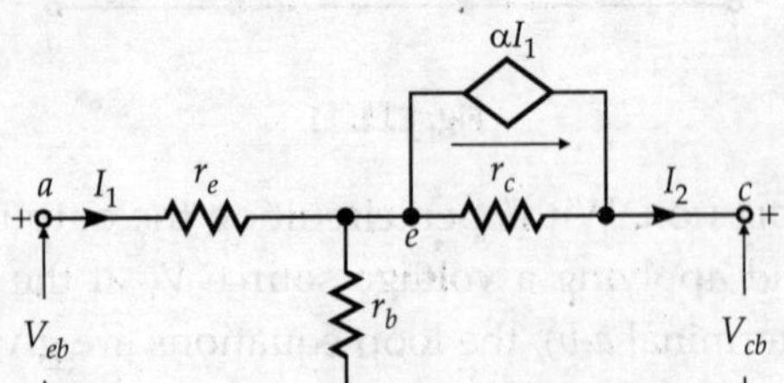

Fig. E11.17

SOLUTION. Applying KVL to the loops,

$$v_{eb} = I_1 r_e + r_b (I_1 - I_2)$$

or $\quad v_{eb} = I_1 r_e + I_1 r_b - I_2 r_b$

$\quad\quad = I_1 (r_e + r_b) - I_2 r_b$

and $\quad -v_{cb} = (I_2 - I_1) r_b + (I_2 - \alpha I_1) r_c$

or $\quad -v_{cb} = -I_1 r_b - \alpha r_c I_1 + I_2 r_b + I_2 r_c$

or $\quad v_{cb} = +(r_b + \alpha r_c) I_1 - (r_b + r_c) I_2$

$\therefore$ We ultimately obtained

$$v_{eb} = (r_e + r_b) I_1 - r_b I_2$$

$$v_{cb} = +(r_b + \alpha r_c) I_1 - (r_b + r_c) I_2$$

i.e.,
$$\begin{bmatrix} v_{eb} \\ v_{cb} \end{bmatrix} = \begin{bmatrix} (r_e + r_b) & r_b \\ (r_b + \alpha r_c) & (r_b + r_c) \end{bmatrix} \begin{bmatrix} I_1 \\ -I_2 \end{bmatrix}$$

($-I_2$ indicates the current at the output opposite to the assumed direction of I_2 of the original two port Z parameter representation).

Comparing with the original Z-parameter representation,

$$\mathbf{Z_{11} = (r_e + r_b); Z_{12} = (r_b)}$$

$$\mathbf{Z_{21} = (r_b + r_c); Z_{22} = (r_b + r_e).}$$

Figure E11.18 represents Z parameter equivalent circuit.

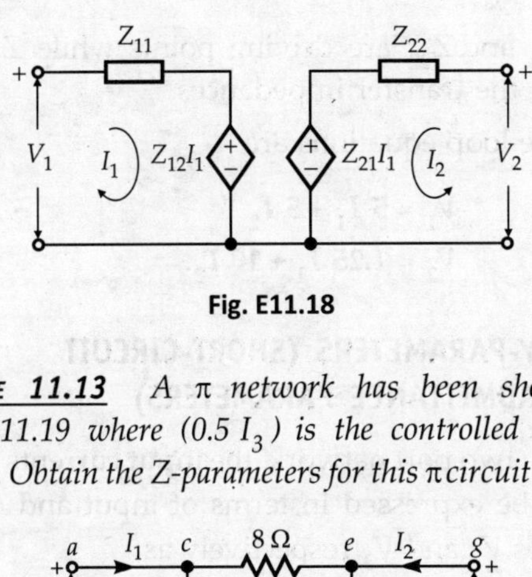

Fig. E11.18

EXAMPLE 11.13 *A π network has been shown in Fig. E11.19 where ($0.5 I_3$) is the controlled current source. Obtain the Z-parameters for this π circuit model.*

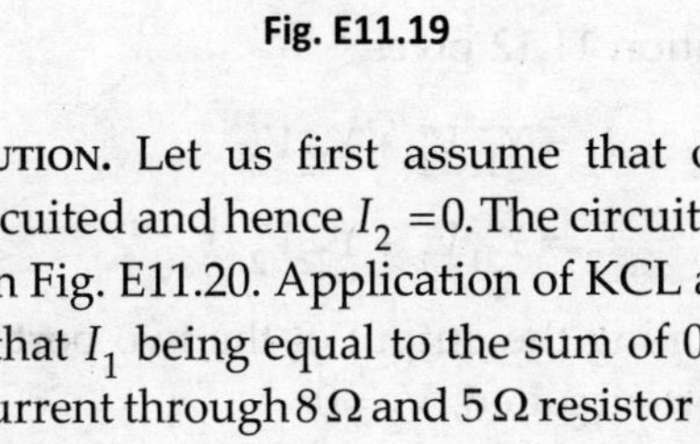

Fig. E11.19

SOLUTION. Let us first assume that output is open-circuited and hence $I_2 = 0$. The circuit has been shown in Fig. E11.20. Application of KCL at node C reveals that I_1 being equal to the sum of $0.5 I_3$ and I_3, the current through 8 Ω and 5 Ω resistor being I_3.

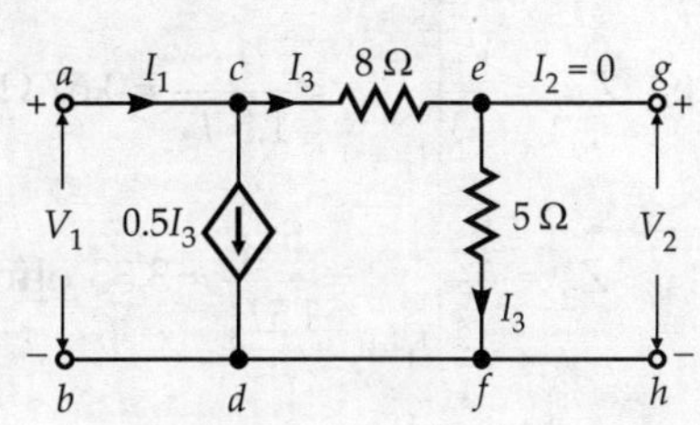

Fig. E11.20

However, $\quad I_3 = \dfrac{V_{c-d}}{8+5} = \dfrac{V_1}{13}$ A $\quad [\because V_{c-d} \equiv V_{c-f}]$

$\therefore$ From $I_1 = (I_3 + 0.5 I_3)$ at *c node*, we get,

$$I_1 = 1.5 I_3 = 1.5 \frac{V_1}{13} \text{ A}$$

Hence,

$$Z_{11} = \left.\frac{V_1}{I_1}\right|_{I_2=0} = \frac{V_1}{1.5 \frac{V_1}{13}} = 8.67 \text{ ohms}$$

Also, $\quad I_3 = \dfrac{V_2}{5}$

$$\left[\because I_3 = \frac{V_{e-f}}{5}, V_{e-f} \text{ being identical to } V_2\right]$$

Hence, finally, $\quad I_1 = 1.5 I_3 = 1.5 \dfrac{V_2}{5}$.

Thus, $\quad Z_{21} = \left.\dfrac{V_2}{I_1}\right|_{I_2=0} = \dfrac{V_2}{1.5 \frac{V_2}{5}} = 3.33$ ohms

Now, with input open-circuited, $I_1 = 0$.

With $I_1 = 0$, application of KCL at *node e* results,

$$I_2 = I_3 + 0.5 I_3 = 1.5 I_3 \text{ (Fig. E11.21).}$$

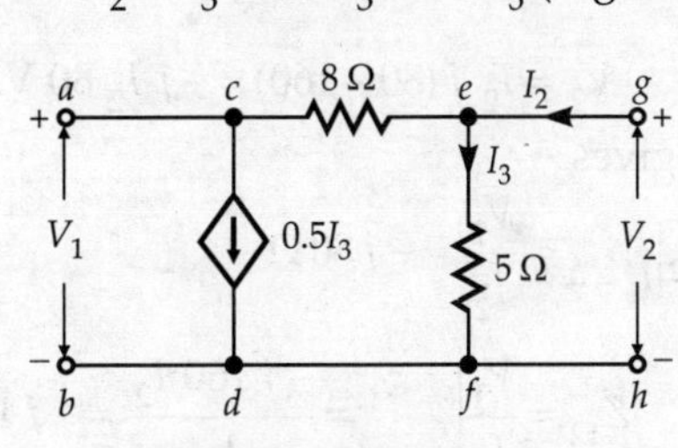

Fig. E11.21

Application of KVL in loop *cedf* (ref. Fig. E11.21) results

$$V_{e-f} = 8 \times 0.5 I_3 + V_{c-d}$$

or $\quad V_1 = V_2 - 8 \times 0.5 I_3$

$$[V_{e-f} \equiv V_2 \text{ and } V_{c-d} \equiv V_1]$$

or $\quad V_1 = 5 I_3 - 4 I_3 = I_3$

Hence, $Z_{12} = \left.\dfrac{V_1}{I_2}\right|_{I_1=0} = \dfrac{I_3}{1.5\,I_3} = 0.67\,\Omega$

and $Z_{22} = \left.\dfrac{V_2}{I_2}\right|_{I_1=0} = \dfrac{5I_3}{1.5I_3} = 3.33$ ohms.

Hence we obtained

$$\mathbf{Z_{11} = 8.67 \text{ ohms } Z_{21} = 3.33 \text{ ohms}}$$

$$\mathbf{Z_{12} = 0.67 \text{ ohms } Z_{22} = 3.33 \text{ ohms.}}$$

Example 11.14 *Find the open circuit parameter of the two port network shown in Fig. E11.22.*

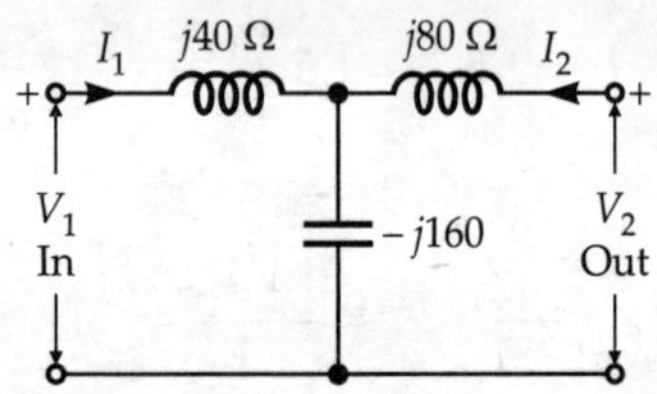

Fig. E11.22

Solution. Assuming open circuit at the output terminals (Fig. E11.22).

$$V_1 = I_1\, j\,(40 - 160)\text{ V}$$

Then $Z_{11} = \left.\dfrac{V_1}{I_1}\right|_{I_2=0} = -j\,120$ ohms.

and since $V_2 = I_1\,(-j\,160)$ V,

$\therefore \quad Z_{21} = \left.\dfrac{V_2}{I_1}\right|_{I_2=0} = -j\,160$ ohms.

Similarly, assuming input terminals to be open circuited.

$$V_2 = I_2\, j\,(80 - 160) = -j\, I_2\, 80\text{ V.}$$

This gives

$$Z_{22}\big|_{I_1=0} = \frac{V_2}{I_2} = -j\,80\,\Omega$$

and $Z_{12} = \left.\dfrac{V_1}{I_2}\right|_{I_1=0} = \dfrac{-j\,160\,I_2}{I_2} = -j\,160$ ohm

$$[\because V_1 = I_2\,(-j\,160)\text{ V}]$$

Thus in this network

$$\mathbf{Z_{11} = -j\,120\,\Omega}$$

$$\mathbf{Z_{12} = -j\,160\,\Omega}$$

$$\mathbf{Z_{21} = -j\,160\,\Omega}$$

$$\mathbf{Z_{22} = -j\,80\,\Omega.}$$

Example 11.15 *Following measurements are obtained on a two terminal network :*

(a) When a voltage of 100 ∠0° volts applied at input port with output port open, $I_1 = 20\angle 0°$ A and $V_2 = 25\angle 0°$ V.

(b) When a voltage of 100∠0° V applied at output port with input open, $I_2 = 10\angle 0°$ A and $V_1 = 50\angle 0°$ V.

Write the loop equations for the network and determine the driving point and transfer impedance.

Solution.

$$Z_{11}\big|_{I_2=0} = \left.\frac{V_1}{I_1}\right|_{I_2=0} = \frac{100\angle 0°}{20\angle 0°} = 5\,\Omega$$

$$Z_{21} = \left.\frac{V_2}{I_1}\right|_{I_2=0} = \frac{25\angle 0°}{20\angle 0°} = 1.25\,\Omega$$

$$Z_{22} = \left.\frac{V_2}{I_2}\right|_{I_1=0} = \frac{100\angle 0°}{10\angle 0°} = 10\,\Omega$$

$$Z_{12} = \left.\frac{V_1}{I_2}\right|_{I_1=0} = \frac{50\angle 0°}{10\angle 0°} = 5\,\Omega.$$

Z_{11} and Z_{22} are driving points while Z_{21} and Z_{12} are the transfer impedances.

The loop equations are

$$\boldsymbol{V_1 = 5\,I_1 + 5\,I_2}$$

$$\boldsymbol{V_2 = 1.25\,I_1 + 10\,I_2.}$$

11.7 *Y*-PARAMETERS (SHORT-CIRCUIT ADMITTANCE PARAMETERS)

In a two port network, the input currents I_1 and I_2 can be expressed in terms of input and output voltages V_1 and V_2 respectively as

$$[I] = [Y][V] \qquad \text{...(11.11)}$$

where $[Y]$ is the admittance matrix.

$$\begin{bmatrix} I_1 \\ I_2 \end{bmatrix} = \begin{bmatrix} Y_{11} & Y_{12} \\ Y_{21} & Y_{22} \end{bmatrix} \begin{bmatrix} V_1 \\ V_2 \end{bmatrix} \qquad \text{...(11.12)}$$

Equation 11.12 gives

$$I_1 = Y_{11}V_1 + Y_{12}V_2 \qquad \text{...(11.13)}$$

and $$I_2 = Y_{21}V_1 + Y_{22}V_2 \qquad \text{...(11.14)}$$

Assuming the output of the two port network to be short-circuited, $V_2 = 0$.

Thus, from equation (11.13), with $V_2 = 0$,

$$Y_{11} = \frac{I_1}{V_1} \qquad ...(11.15)$$

With $V_2 = 0$, from equation (11.14)

$$Y_{21} = \frac{I_2}{V_1} \qquad ...(11.16)$$

Similarly, assuming the input port to be short-circuited, $V_1 = 0$; with $V_1 = 0$, from equations (11.13) and (11.14), we get,

$$Y_{12} = \frac{I_1}{V_2} \qquad ...(11.17)$$

and

$$Y_{22} = \frac{I_2}{V_2} \qquad ...(11.18)$$

Here, $Y_{11} = \left(\left. \frac{I_1}{V_1} \right|_{V_2 = 0} \right)$ and $Y_{22} = \left(\left. \frac{I_2}{V_2} \right|_{V_1 = 0} \right)$

are called *input and output driving point admittances* while

$$Y_{12} = \left(\left. \frac{I_1}{V_2} \right|_{V_1 = 0} \right) \text{ and } Y_{21} = \left(\left. \frac{I_2}{V_1} \right|_{V_2 = 0} \right)$$

are called *reverse and forward transfer admittances*, all expressed in mho.

Equations (11.13) and (11.14) can be further represented as

$$I_1 = (Y_{11} + Y_{12})\, V_1 - Y_{12}\,(V_1 - V_2) \qquad ...(11.19)$$

and $I_2 = (Y_{21} - Y_{12})\, V_1 + (Y_{22} + Y_{12})\, V_2 - Y_{12}\,(V_2 - V_1)$ ...(11.20)

Figure 11.21 represents the *equivalent circuit* utilising equations (11.13) and (11.14) while Fig. 11.22 represents the same for equations (11.19) and (11.20) respectively for the admittance parameter representation of the two port network.

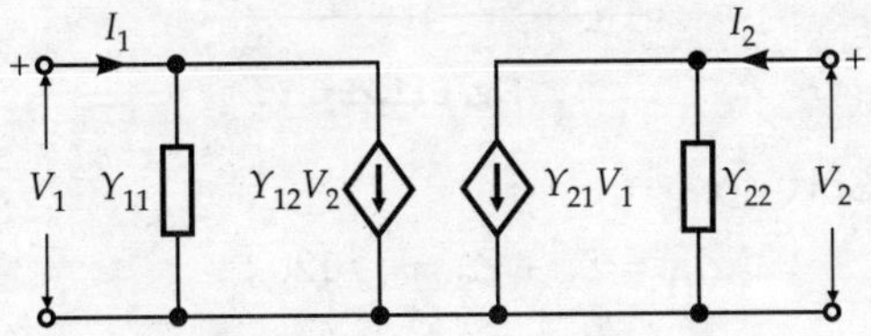

Fig. 11.21 Equivalent circuit representation of short circuit (*Y*) parameters.

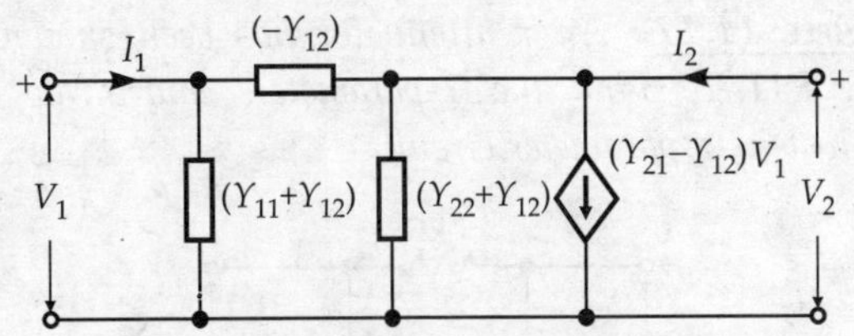

Fig. 11.22 Another form of equivalent circuit with short circuit (*Y*) parameters.

In Figs. 11.21 and 11.22, $Y_{12}V_2$, $Y_{21}V_1$ and $(Y_{21} - Y_{12})\, V_1$ are called "voltage controlled current sources".

EXAMPLE 11.16 *Find the Y-parameters of the following π-circuit (Fig. E11.23) and draw the Y-parameter model.*

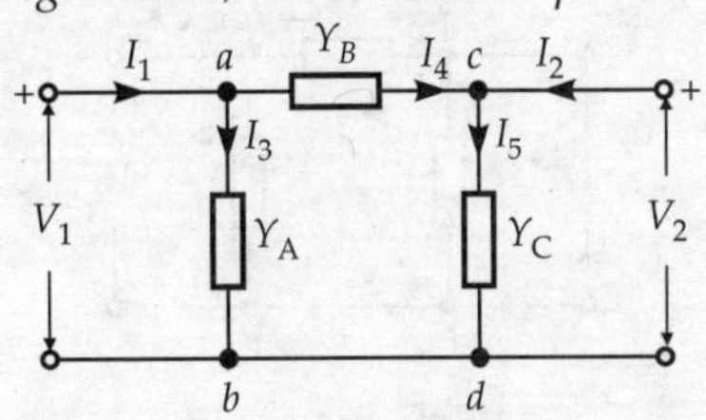

Fig. E11.23

SOLUTION. Using KCL at *node a*,

$$I_1 = I_3 + I_4$$
$$I_1 = V_1 Y_A + (V_1 - V_2)\, Y_B$$

or
$$I_1 = V_1\,(Y_A + Y_B) + (-Y_B)\, V_2 \qquad ...(i)$$

Application of KCL at *node c* results

$$I_2 = I_5 - I_4$$

or
$$I_2 = V_2 Y_C - (V_1 - V_2)\, Y_B$$

or
$$I_2 = (-Y_B)\, V_1 + (Y_C + Y_B)\, V_2 \qquad ...(ii)$$

Comparing these two equations (*i*) and (*ii*) with the developed equations of Y-parameter representation as shown in the text.

$$\mathbf{Y_{11} = (Y_A + Y_B)\,;\; Y_{12} = -Y_B}$$
$$\mathbf{Y_{21} = -Y_B\,;\; Y_{22} = Y_C + Y_B.}$$

Observation of equations (*i*) and (*ii*) reveals that $(Y_A + Y_B)\, V_1$ and $(Y_C + Y_B)\, V_2$ being the current through admittances Y_{11} and Y_{22}, $Y_B V_2$ and $Y_B V_1$ are the controlled current sources. The equivalent circuit has been shown in **Fig. 11.24.**

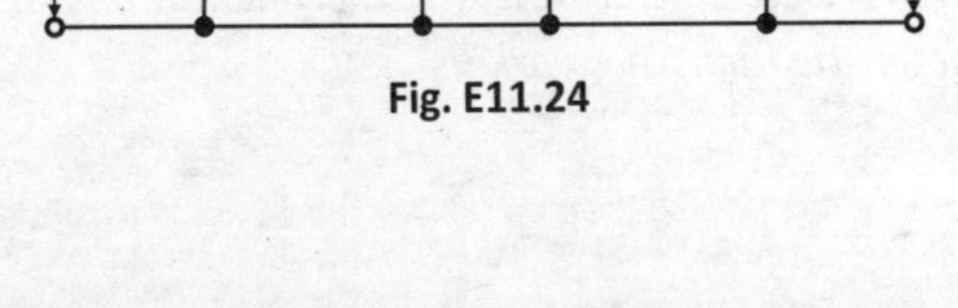

Fig. E11.24

EXAMPLE 11.17 *An π attenuator has been shown in Fig. E11.25. Find the Y-parameters and draw the equivalent Y-parameter circuit.*

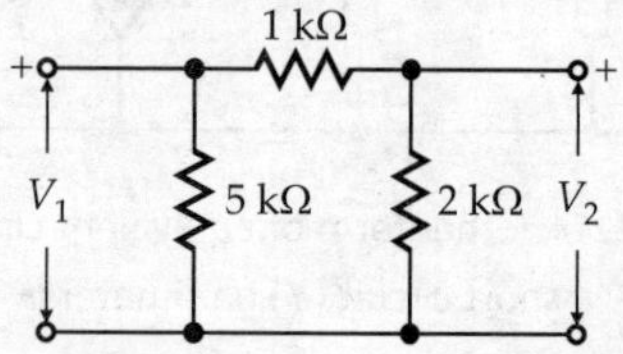

Fig. E11.25

SOLUTION. The values of the arm impedences of the π network are given in ohms. In form of admittances, Fig. E11.25 is redrawn as in Fig. E11.26.

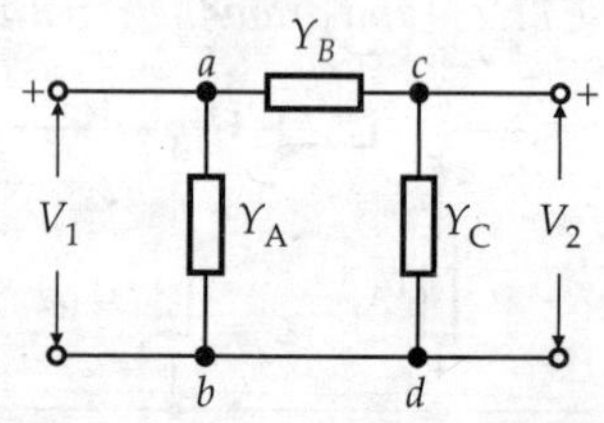

Fig. E11.26

$$\therefore \quad Y_A = \frac{1}{5\text{ k}\Omega} = 0.2 \times 10^{-3} \text{ mho}$$

$$Y_B = \frac{1}{1\text{ k}\Omega} = 10^{-3} \text{ mho}$$

$$Y_C = \frac{1}{2\text{ k}\Omega} = 0.5 \times 10^{-3} \text{ mho.}$$

The Y-parameters are

$$\mathbf{Y_{11} = Y_A + Y_B = 1.2 \times 10^{-3} \text{ mho}}$$
$$\mathbf{Y_{12} = -10^{-3} \text{ mho}}$$
$$\mathbf{Y_{21} = -10^{-3} \text{ mho}}$$
$$\mathbf{Y_{22} = Y_B + Y_C = 1.5 \times 10^{-3} \text{ mho.}}$$

The Y-parameter equivalent circuit has been shown in **Fig. E11.27.**

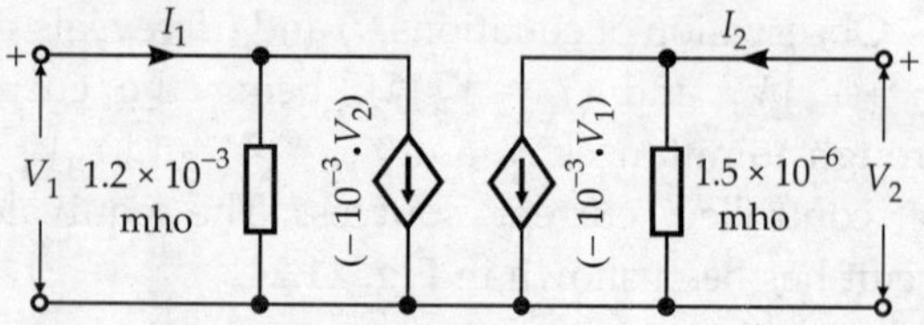

Fig. E11.27

EXAMPLE 11.18 *On short circuit test, the currents and voltages were determined experimentally for an unknown two port network as*

$$\left.\begin{aligned} I_1 &= 1\,mA \\ I_2 &= -0.5\,mA \\ V_1 &= 25\,V \end{aligned}\right|_{\text{at } V_2=0} \quad \left.\begin{aligned} I_1 &= -1\,mA \\ \text{and } I_2 &= -10\,mA \\ V_2 &= 50\,V \end{aligned}\right|_{\text{at } V_1=0}$$

Determine the Y-parameters and draw the Y-parameter model.

SOLUTION. From the text,

$$Y_{11} = \left.\frac{I_1}{V_1}\right|_{V_2=0} = \frac{1 \times 10^{-3}}{25} = 40\ \mu \text{ mho}$$

$$Y_{21} = \left.\frac{I_2}{V_1}\right|_{V_2=0} = -\frac{0.5 \times 10^{-3}}{25} = -20\ \mu \text{ mho}$$

$$Y_{12} = \left.\frac{I_1}{V_2}\right|_{V_1=0} = -\frac{1 \times 10^{-3}}{50} = -20\ \mu \text{ mho}$$

$$Y_{22} = \left.\frac{I_2}{V_2}\right|_{V_1=0} = -\frac{10 \times 10^{-3}}{50} = -200\ \mu \text{ mho.}$$

The governing equations are then

$$I_1 = 40 \times 10^{-6}\, V_1 + (-20 \times 10^{-6})\, V_2$$

and $\quad I_2 = (-20 \times 10^{-6})\, V_1 + (-200 \times 10^{-6})\, V_2$

The equivalent circuit of the Y-parameter model is drawn in **Fig. E11.28.**

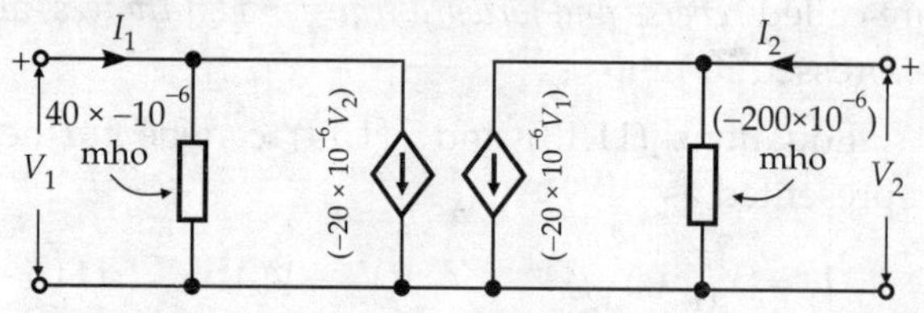

Fig. E11.28

EXAMPLE 11.19 *Find Y-parameters of network shown in Fig. E11.29 from Z-parameters.*

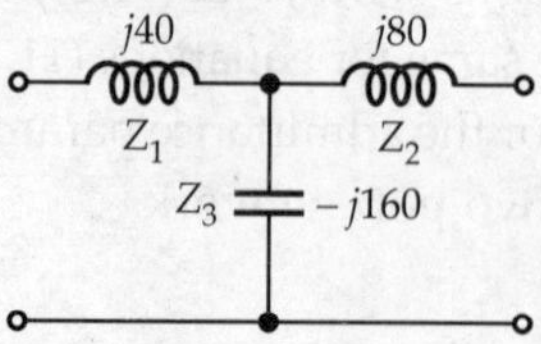

Fig. E11.29

SOLUTION.

$$Z_{11} = Z_1 + Z_3 = -j\,120\,;$$
$$Z_{12} = Z_3 = -j\,160$$
$$Z_{21} = Z_3 = -j\,160\,;$$
$$Z_{22} = Z_2 + Z_3 = -j\,80$$

Here,

$$Y_{11} = \frac{Z_{22}}{Z_{11}Z_{22} - Z_{12}Z_{21}}$$

$$= \frac{-j\,80}{(-j\,120)(-j\,80) - (-j\,160)^2}$$

$$= \frac{-j\,80}{16{,}000} = \frac{-j}{\mathbf{200}}\ \textbf{mho.}$$

$$Y_{12} = Y_{21} = \frac{-Z_{12}}{Z_{11}Z_{22} - Z_{12}Z_{21}}$$

$$= \frac{j\,160}{16{,}000} = \frac{j}{\mathbf{100}}\ \textbf{mho.}$$

$$Y_{22} = \frac{Z_{11}}{Z_{11}Z_{22} - Z_{12}Z_{21}}$$

$$= \frac{-j\,120}{16{,}000} = \frac{-j}{\mathbf{133.33}}\ \textbf{mho.}$$

EXAMPLE 11.20 *Find the parameters Y_a, Y_b and Y_c of the equivalent π network shown in Fig. E11.30 to represent a*

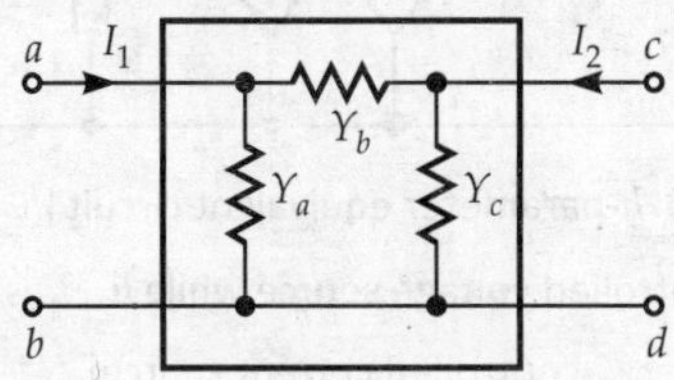

Fig. E11.30

2-port network for which following measurements were taken :

(a) *With terminal pairs c-d short circuited, a voltage of 10 ∠0° V applied at terminal-pairs a-b resulting in $I_1 = 2.50\ \angle 0°$ A and $I_2 = -0.50\ \angle 0°$ A.*

(b) *With the terminal-pair a-b short-circuited, the same applied voltage at terminal-pair c-d the current at output port resulted is $I_2 = (1.50\ \angle 0°\ A)$.*

SOLUTION. With terminal-pair *c-d* short-circuited

$$V_1 = I_1 / (Y_a + Y_b)$$

or $$Y_a + Y_b = \frac{I_1}{V_1} = \frac{2.50\ \angle 0°}{10} = 0.25\ \text{mho.}$$

Also $$-I_2 / Y_b = V_1$$

or $$Y_b = \frac{-I_2}{V_1} = \frac{0.50\ \angle 0°}{10}$$

$$= 0.05\ \text{mho};$$

$$\therefore\quad \mathbf{Y_a = 0.20\ mho\ ;\ Y_b = 0.05\ mho}$$

With terminal-pair *a-b* short circuited

$$V_2 = I_2 / (Y_b + Y_c)$$

or $$Y_b + Y_c = \frac{I_2}{V_2} = \frac{1.50}{10} = 0.15\ \text{mho}$$

$$\therefore\quad \mathbf{Y_c = 0.10\ mho.}$$

EXAMPLE 11.21 *In a π network, the series arm impedance is $0.05 \times 10^{-3} \angle -90°$ mho and shunt arm impedences are $0.1 \times 10^{-3} \angle 0°$ and 0.2×10^{-3} 90° mho. Find the Y-parameters.*

SOLUTION. For the π network, representing in Y-parameter form,

$$Y_{11} = Y_A + Y_B\ ;\ Y_{12} = Y_{21} = -Y_B\ ;\ Y_{22} = Y_B + Y_C$$

In this problem,

$$Y_A = 0.1 \times 10^{-3}\ \angle 0° = 0.1 \times 10^{-3}\ \text{mho}$$

$$Y_B = 0.05 \times 10^{-3}\ \angle -90° = -j\,0.05 \times 10^{-3}\ \text{mho}$$

$$Y_C = 0.2 \times 10^{-3}\ \angle 90° = +j\,0.2 \times 10^{-3}\ \text{mho};$$

$$\therefore\quad \mathbf{Y_{11} = (0.1 - j\,0.05) \times 10^{-3}\ mho}$$

$$\mathbf{Y_{12} = Y_{21} = j\,0.05 \times 10^{-3}\ mho}$$

$$\mathbf{Y_{22} = j\,0.15 \times 10^{-3}\ mho.}$$

EXAMPLE 11.22 *Following short circuit currents and voltages are obtained experimentally for a two port network :*

(a) *With output short-circuited,*

$$I_1 = 5\ mA;\ I_2 = -0.3\ mA;\ V_1 = 25\ V.$$

(b) *With input short-circuited,*

$$I_1 = -5\ mA;\ I_2 = 10\ mA;\ V_2 = 30\ V.$$

Determine Y-parameters.

SOLUTION. From the text, we know, for Y-parameter representation,

$$Y_{11} = \left.\frac{I_1}{V_1}\right|_{V_2 = 0};\quad Y_{12} = \left.\frac{I_1}{V_2}\right|_{V_1 = 0}$$

$$Y_{21} = \left.\frac{I_2}{V_1}\right|_{V_2 = 0};\quad Y_{22} = \left.\frac{I_2}{V_2}\right|_{V_1 = 0}$$

From the condition (*a*) given in the problem,

$$Y_{11} = \frac{0.005}{25} = \mathbf{0.0002\ mho}$$

$$Y_{21} = -\frac{0.3 \times 10^{-3}}{25} = \mathbf{-0.000012\ mho.}$$

and from the condition (*b*) given in the problem,

$$Y_{12} = \left.\frac{I_1}{V_2}\right|_{V_1=0} = -\frac{5 \times 10^{-3}}{30} = \mathbf{-0.00017\ mho,}$$

and $Y_{22} = \dfrac{10 \times 10^{-3}}{30} = \mathbf{0.00033\ mho.}$

11.8 HYBRID PARAMETERS (*h*-PARAMETER REPRESENTATION)

h-parameter representation is widely used in modelling of electronic components and circuits, particularly transistors. As both short circuit and open circuit terminal conditions are utilized hence, this parameter representation is known as *hybrid parameter* representation. In this form of representation, the voltage of the input port and the current of the output port are expressed in terms of the current of the input port and the voltage of the output port.

Here, $\begin{bmatrix} V_1 \\ I_2 \end{bmatrix} = \begin{bmatrix} h_{11} & h_{12} \\ h_{21} & h_{22} \end{bmatrix} \begin{bmatrix} I_1 \\ V_2 \end{bmatrix}$ ...(11.21)

or $V_1 = h_{11} I_1 + h_{12} V_2$ ...(11.22)

and $I_2 = h_{21} I_1 + h_{22} V_2$ ...(11.23)

Assuming short circuit conditions at the output, $V_2 = 0$. This gives, from equation (11.22)

$$h_{11} = \frac{V_1}{I_1} \quad ...(11.24)$$

and from equation 11.23

$$h_{21} = \frac{I_2}{I_1} \quad ...(11.25)$$

Here, $h_{11} = \left(\left.\dfrac{V_1}{I_1}\right|_{V_2=0}\right)$

and $h_{21} = \left(\left.\dfrac{I_2}{I_1}\right|_{V_2=0}\right)$

are called *input impedance and forward current gain.* h_{11} is expressed in ohms while h_{21} is a unitless quantity.

In a similar way, from equations (11.22) and (11.23), for the input open-circuited condition, with $I_1 = 0$,

$$h_{12} = \frac{V_1}{V_2} \quad ...(11.26)$$

and $h_{22} = \dfrac{I_2}{V_2}$ ...(11.27)

Then, $h_{12} = \left(\left.\dfrac{V_1}{V_2}\right|_{I_1=0}\right)$

and $h_{22} = \left(\left.\dfrac{I_2}{V_2}\right|_{I_1=0}\right)$

are called *reverse voltage gain* and *output admittance.* h_{12} has got no unit while h_{22} has unit of mho.

The equivalent circuit of the hybrid parameter representation is shown in Fig. 11.23.

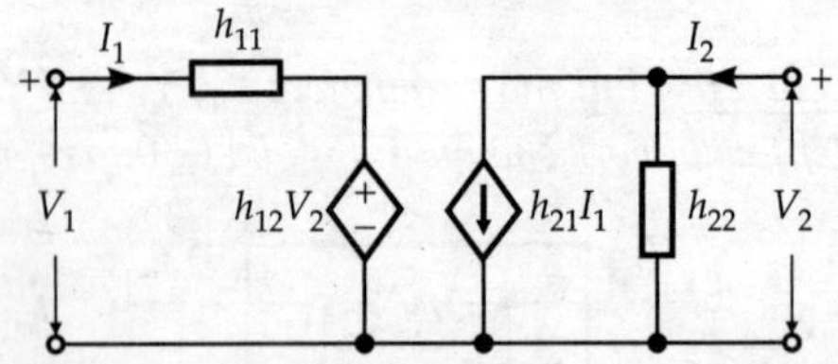

Fig. 11.23 *h*-parameter equivalent circuit [$h_{12}V_2$ is the controlled voltage source while $h_{21}I_1$ is the controlled current source]

EXAMPLE 11.23 *A common emitter transistor amplifier hardware circuit can be represented by a four terminal network. The signal source strength being 1 mV, a resistive load of 10 kΩ is applied at the output of the network. The following data are given :*

(*i*) *Short circuit input impedance* $(h_i) = 2\ k\Omega$.

(*ii*) *Short circuit forward current ratio* $(h_f) = 50$

(*iii*) *Open circuit output admittance* $(h_o) = 25 \times 10^{-6}$ *mho.*

(*iv*) *Open circuit reverse voltage ratio* $(h_r) = 3 \times 10^{-4}$

Expressing these values in terms of h-parameter representation, determine

(*i*) *h-parameter equivalent circuit*

(*ii*) *voltage drop across the load*

(*iii*) *load current*

(*iv*) *voltage gain*

(*v*) *current gain.*

Solution. From the given data,

$$h_{11} = h_i = 2000\,\Omega\,;\; h_{12} = h_r = 3\times 10^{-4}$$

$$h_{21} = h_f = 50\,;\, h_{22} = h_o = 25\times 10^{-6}\ \text{mho.}$$

(*i*) The *h*-parameter equation being

$$V_1 = h_{11}\, I_1 + h_{12}\, V_2 \ \text{ and } \ I_2 = h_{21} I_1 + h_{22} V_2,$$

the equivalent circuit has been drawn below **(Fig. E11.31)**

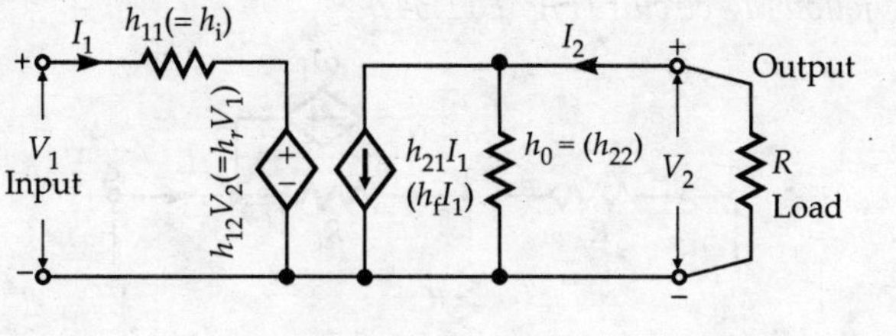

Fig. E11.31

(*ii*) Again, the loop equation at the input port is given by

$$V_1 = h_i I_1 + h_r V_2$$

[refer to equivalent circuit]

or $\quad 1\times 10^{-3} - 3\times 10^{-4}\, V_2 = 2000\, I_1 \qquad \text{...}(i)$

The loop equation at the output port is given by

$$I_2 = h_f\, I_1 + h_o V_2$$

or $\quad -\dfrac{V_2}{R_{\text{load}}} = h_f\, I_1 + h_o V_2$

or $\quad -h_f\, I_1 = \left[h_o + \dfrac{1}{R_{\text{load}}}\right] V_2$

or $\quad -50\, I_1 = \left[25\times 10^{-6} + \dfrac{1}{10\times 10^3}\right] V_2$

$$= 10^{-6}\,[25 + 100]\, V_2$$

$\therefore \quad I_1 = -\dfrac{125\times 10^{-6}}{50} V_2 \qquad \text{...}(ii)$

Substituting the value of I_1 from (*ii*) in (*i*),

$$10^{-3} - 3\times 10^{-4}\, V_2 = 2000\left(-\frac{125\times 10^{-6}}{50}\right) V_2$$

or $\quad V_2 = -0.213\ \text{V.}$

Thus the drop across the load resistor is **– 0.021 V** and against the assumed direction of I_2.

(*iii*) The load current is given by

$$I_L = \frac{V_2}{R_L} = \frac{-0.213}{10\times 10^3} = -\mathbf{21.3\ \mu\ A.}$$

(–ve I_L indicates the actual flow of current opposite to the assumed direction)

(*iv*) The voltage gain of the circuit is given by

$$\frac{V_2}{V_1} = \frac{-0.213}{0.001} = -\mathbf{213}$$

[–ve sign in voltage gain indicates 180° phase shift].

The current gain is given by $\dfrac{I_2}{I_1}$.

In the equivalent circuit,

$$I_2 = h_f\, I_1 \frac{\dfrac{1}{h_o}}{\dfrac{1}{h_o} + R_{\text{load}}}$$

[h_0 having unit mho, the representation in ohm will be $\dfrac{1}{h_0}$]

$$= \frac{h_f I_1}{1 + h_o\, R_{\text{load}}}$$

$$\therefore \quad \frac{I_2}{I_1} = \frac{h_f}{1 + h_o\, R_{\text{load}}}$$

$$= \frac{50}{1 + 25\times 10^{-6}\times 10\times 10^3}$$

$$= \frac{50}{1 + 0.25} = \mathbf{40.}$$

Example 11.24 *For the h-parameter equivalent network (Fig. E11.32) find the voltage gain. Assume the load resistance to be R_L.*

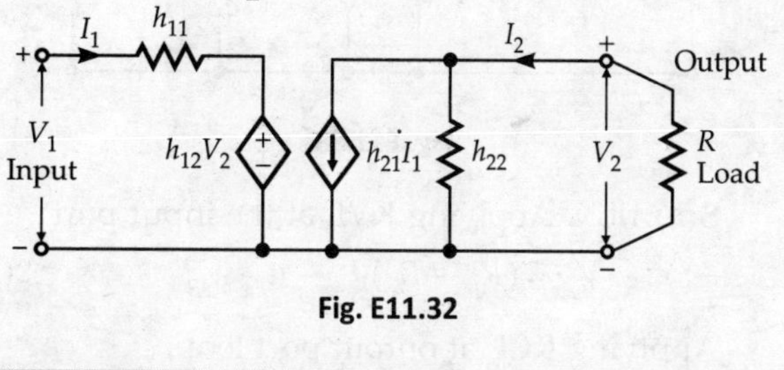

Fig. E11.32

The expression for $\dfrac{I_2}{I_1}$, the current gain, can then be generalised as $\dfrac{h_f}{1 + h_o R_L}$.

Solution. The *h*-parameter equivalent circuit has been shown in Fig. E11.32

At the input port,

$$I_1 = \frac{V_1 - h_{12} V_2}{h_{11}} \quad ...(1)$$

At the output port,

$$I_2 = -\frac{V_2}{R_L}$$

Also, $I_2 = h_{21} I_1 + h_{22} V_2$

or $$-\frac{V_2}{R_L} = h_{21} I_1 + h_{22} V_2 \quad ...(2)$$

Utilising equation (1) for substitution of I_1 in (2),

$$-\frac{V_2}{R_L} = h_{21}\left[\frac{V_1 - h_{12} V_2}{h_{11}}\right] + h_{22} V_2$$

$$-\frac{V_2}{R_L} + \frac{h_{12} h_{21}}{h_{11}} V_2 - h_{22} V_2 = \frac{h_{21}}{h_{11}} V_1$$

or $$V_2\left[\frac{h_{12} h_{21}}{h_{11}} - h_{22} - \frac{1}{R_L}\right] = \frac{h_{21}}{h_{11}} V_1$$

or $$V_2\left[\frac{h_{12} h_{21} R_L - h_{11} h_{22} R_L - h_{11}}{R_L}\right] = V_1 \cdot h_{21}$$

$\therefore$ $$\frac{V_2}{V_1} = \text{voltage gain}$$

$$= \frac{h_{21} R_L}{-h_{11}(1 + h_{22} R_L) + h_{12} h_{21} R_L}.$$

Example 11.25 *CE transistor equivalent circuit has been shown in Fig. E11.33. Find the h-parameters.*

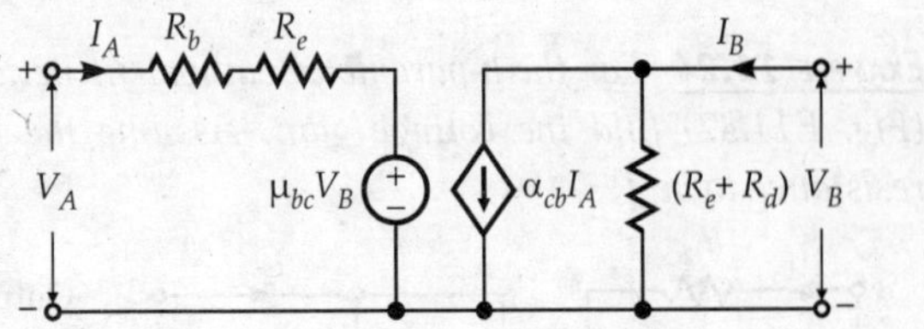

Fig. E11.33

Solution. Applying KVL at the input port,

$$V_A = (R_b + R_e) I_A + \mu_{bc} V_B \quad ...(i)$$

Applying KCL at output port loop,

$$I_B = \alpha_{cb} I_A + \frac{V_B}{R_e + R_d}$$

i.e., in matrix form,

$$\begin{bmatrix} V_A \\ I_B \end{bmatrix} = \begin{bmatrix} (R_b + R_e) & \mu_{bc} \\ \alpha_{cb} & \left(\dfrac{1}{R_e + R_d}\right) \end{bmatrix} \begin{bmatrix} I_A \\ V_B \end{bmatrix}$$

i.e., $$\boldsymbol{h_{11} = (R_b + R_e)\,;\ h_{12} = \mu_{bc}}$$

$$\boldsymbol{h_{21} = \alpha_{cb}\,;\ h_{22} = \frac{1}{(R_e + R_d)}}.$$

Example 11.26 *Find the hybrid parameter of the following circuit (Fig. E11.34).*

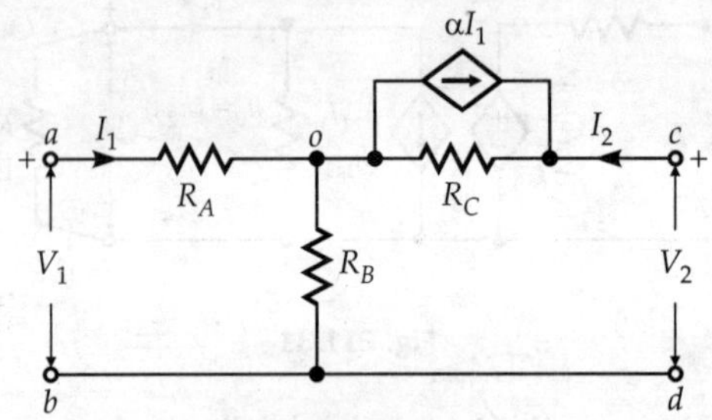

Fig. E11.34

Solution. Let us assume that the output port is short-circuited ; *i.e.*, $V_2 = 0$. The voltage at point *O* is *V* with respect to –ve terminal *b*.

As soon as the output port is shorted, R_B and R_C become parallel such that current through R_B and R_C becomes

$$\frac{V}{\dfrac{R_B R_C}{R_B + R_C}} = \frac{V(R_B + R_C)}{R_B R_C}$$

Applying KCL at point *O*,

$$I_1 = \frac{V(R_B + R_C)}{R_B R_C} + \alpha I_1$$

or $$I_1(1 - \alpha) = \frac{V(R_B + R_C)}{R_B R_C}$$

$\therefore$ $$V = \frac{(1 - \alpha) I_1 R_B R_C}{(R_B + R_C)}$$

Next, applying KVL at input port,

$$V_1 = I_1 R_A + V.$$

However, $$h_{11} = \left.\frac{V_1}{I_1}\right|_{V_2 = 0}$$

Here, $$h_{11} = \frac{V_1}{I_1} = R_A + \frac{(1 - \alpha) R_B R_C}{R_B + R_C}$$

$$= \boldsymbol{\frac{R_A(R_B + R_C) + (1 - \alpha) R_B R_C}{R_B + R_C}}\ \textbf{ohm.}$$

Again by inspection of Fig. E11.34 it is evident that

$$I_2 = -\left(\alpha\, I_1 + \frac{V}{R_C}\right)$$

or $$I_2 = -\alpha I_1 - \frac{(1-\alpha)\, I_1\, R_B}{(R_B + R_C)}$$

$$\therefore \quad h_{21} = \left.\frac{I_2}{I_1}\right|_{V_2=0} = -\alpha - \frac{(1-\alpha)\, R_B}{(R_B + R_C)}$$

$$= -\frac{(\alpha\, R_C + R_B)}{(R_B + R_C)}.$$

Next, the voltage V_2 is applied at the output port and input port is opened such that $I_1 = 0$. This makes $\alpha\, I_1 = 0$. Thus the circuit configuration becomes simpler and has been shown in Fig. E11.35.

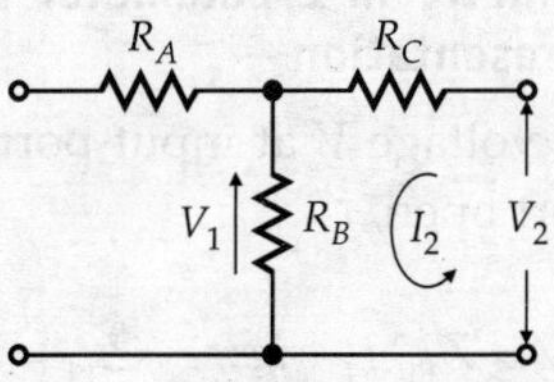

Fig. E11.35

Applying KVL at output port,

$$V_2 = I_2\,(R_B + R_C)$$

or $$\left.\frac{I_2}{V_2}\right|_{I_1=0} = h_{22} = \left(\frac{1}{R_B + R_C}\right) \text{mho.}$$

Again, under this condition,

$$V_1 = I_2\, R_B$$

$$\therefore \quad h_{12} = \left.\frac{V_1}{V_2}\right|_{I_1=0} = \frac{I_2\, R_B}{I_2\,(R_B + R_C)}$$

$$= \frac{R_B}{R_B + R_C}.$$

11.9 *ABCD* (TRANSMISSION) PARAMETERS

ABCD parameters are widely used in analysis of power transmission engineering where they are termed as "Circuit Parameters". *ABCD* parameters are also called as "Transmission Parameters".

It is conventional to designate the input port as sending end and the output port as receiving end while representing *ABCD* parameters. Moreover, the output current direction, assumed in Fig. 11.24, is taken reverse.

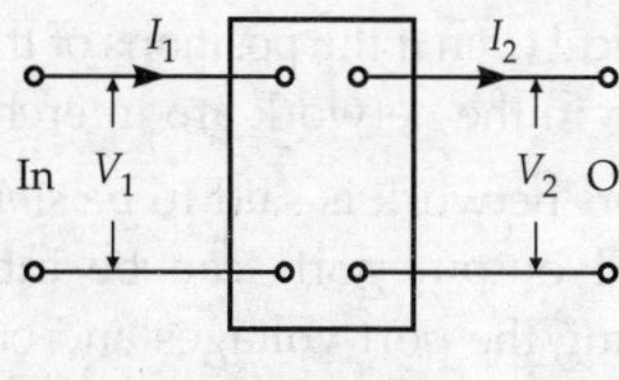

Fig. 11.24 Representation of input and output voltages and currents in two-port network for *ABCD* parameter representation.

Here, the *ABCD* parameter equations are given as

$$\begin{bmatrix} V_1 \\ I_1 \end{bmatrix} = \begin{bmatrix} A & B \\ C & D \end{bmatrix} \begin{bmatrix} V_2 \\ -I_2 \end{bmatrix} \quad \text{...(11.28)}$$

such that $$V_1 = AV_2 + B(-I_2) \quad \text{...(11.29)}$$

and $$I_1 = CV_2 + D(-I_2) \quad \text{...(11.30)}$$

Assuming the receiving end to be open-circuited, $I_2 = 0$.

This gives, from equation (11.29),

$$A = \frac{V_1}{V_2} \quad \text{...(11.31)}$$

and from equation (11.30)

$$C = \frac{I_1}{V_2} \quad \text{...(11.32)}$$

Being a ratio of voltages, '*A*' is called *reverse voltage ratio* and does not have any unit. '*C*' is known as *transfer admittance* and has the unit mho.

Next, let us assume that the receiving end be short-circuited. Then from equations (11.28) and (11.30), with $V_2 = 0$,

$$B = \frac{V_1}{-I_2} \quad \text{...(11.33)}$$

while $$D = \frac{I_1}{-I_2} \quad \text{...(11.34)}$$

"*D*" being a ratio of two currents, it is called *reverse current ratio*; it is an unitless quantity while '*B* is expressed in ohm and is termed as *transfer impedance*.

CHAPTER 11

11.10 CONDITION OF RECIPROCITY AND SYMMETRY IN TWO PORT PARAMETER REPRESENTATION

A network is termed to be reciprocal if the ratio of the *response variable* to the *excitation variable* remains identical even if the positions of the response and excitation in the network are interchanged.

A two port network is said to be *symmetrical* if the input and output ports can be interchanged without altering the port voltages and currents.

11.10.1 Reciprocity in Z-parameter Representation

Let the Z parameter based two port network be represented as shown in Fig. 11.25.

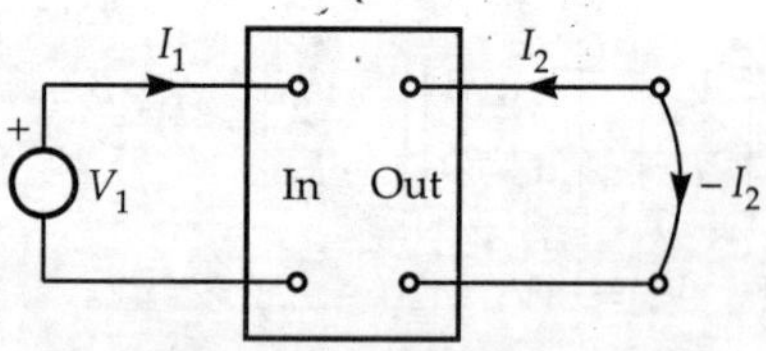

Fig. 11.25 Two port network representation (here I_2 is assumed to be in reversed direction of I_2 assumed in Fig. 11.24)

Here, from the governing Z-parameter network equations (11.3) and (11.4), we write

$$V_1 = Z_{11}\, I_1 - Z_{12}\, I_2 \quad ...(11.35)$$

and

$$0 = Z_{21}\, I_1 - Z_{22}\, I_2 \quad ...(11.36)$$

[here I_2 is –ve as its direction is reversed to the originally assumed direction, V_2 is zero as output is shorted].

From equations (11.35) and (11.36),

$$I_2 = \frac{V_1\, Z_{21}}{Z_{11}\, Z_{22} - Z_{21}\, Z_{12}} \quad ...(11.37)$$

Let us now interchange the input and output voltage and currents (Fig. 11.26).

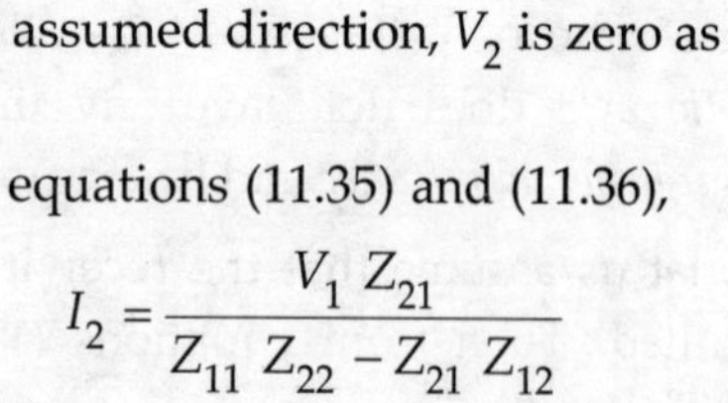

Fig. 11.26 Voltage and currents are interchanged for the two port network.

Here, from the same set of governing equations of Z parameter network,

$$0 = -Z_{11}\, I_1 + Z_{12}\, I_2 \quad ...(11.38)$$

and

$$V_2 = -Z_{21}\, I_1 + Z_{22}\, I_2 \quad ...(11.39)$$

Here, I_1 is negative as its direction is opposite to that originally assumed, V_1 is zero as input terminals are shorted.

Solving equations (11.38) and (11.39)

$$I_1 = \frac{V_2\, Z_{12}}{Z_{11}\, Z_{22} - Z_{12}\, Z_{21}} \quad ...(11.40)$$

Assuming $V_1 = V_2$, comparison of (11.37) and (11.40) yields

$$Z_{12} = Z_{21} \quad ...(11.41)$$

Equation (11.41) represents the condition of *reciprocity*.

11.10.2 Symmetry in *Z*-parameter Representation

Applying voltage V at input port and keeping the output port open,

$$V = Z_{11}\, I_1 \quad i.e., \quad Z_{11} = \left.\frac{V}{I_1}\right|_{I_2=0}$$

Again, applying voltage V at output port and keeping open circuit at input port,

$$V = I_2\, Z_{22} \quad i.e., \quad Z_{22} = \left.\frac{V}{I_2}\right|_{I_1=0}$$

Condition of symmetry is observed when $(V/I_1) = (V/I_2)$ leading to the condition

$$Z_{11} = Z_{22} \quad ...(11.42)$$

11.10.3 Condition of Reciprocity and Symmetry in *Y*-Parameter Representation

From the governing equation (11.12) of the *Y*-parameter network,

$$-I_2 = Y_{21}\, V_1$$

[due to shorting of output terminals, $V_2 = 0$; –ve sign of I_2 indicates the direction of flow of I_2 is outward of the network (Fig. 11.25)].

i.e.,

$$Y_{21} = -\frac{I_2}{V_1} \quad ...(11.43)$$

With interchanging of response and excitation of the two port network the new network is as per Fig. 11.26 and here $V_1 = 0$, I_1 is flowing outward of the network.

$$\therefore \quad -I_1 = Y_{12} V_2$$

$$\therefore \quad Y_{12} = -\frac{I_1}{V_2} \qquad \text{...(11.44)}$$

If the voltage V_1 is same to V_2, the left hand side of equations (11.43) and (11.44) will be identical provided the circuit is *reciprocal*. Thus for the Y-parameter representation, the circuit will be reciprocal provided

$$Y_{21} = Y_{12} \qquad \text{...(11.45)}$$

The Y-parameter form of the two port network will be symmetric if the input and output ports can be interchanged without changing the voltage or current at each port. This is only possible if $Y_{11} = Y_{22}$. Thus for the *symmetrical* network,

$$Y_{11} = Y_{22} \qquad \text{...(11.46)}$$

11.10.4 Condition of Reciprocity and Symmetry in *ABCD* Parameters

The governing equations of the $ABCD$ network are given by

$$V_1 = AV_2 - BI_2 \qquad \text{...(11.47)}$$

and

$$I_1 = CV_2 - DI_2 \qquad \text{...(11.48)}$$

With excitation V_1 at input port and shorting link at output port, equation (11.47) gives

$$V_1 = -BI_2$$

or

$$\frac{I_2}{V_1} = -\frac{1}{B} \qquad \text{...(11.49)}$$

With interchange of excitation and response, the voltage source V_2 is at the output port while the short circuit current I_1 is obtained at input port. This time, the parameter equations (11.47) and (11.48) become

$$0 = AV_2 - BI_2 \text{ and } I_1 = CV_2 - DI_2$$

These equations give

$$I_2 = \frac{AV_2}{B} \text{ and } I_1 = CV_2 - \frac{ADV_2}{B}$$

$$= V_2\left(\frac{BC - AD}{B}\right)$$

or

$$\frac{I_1}{V_2} = \frac{BC - AD}{B} = -\frac{AD - BC}{B} \qquad \text{...(11.50)}$$

when $V_1 = V_2$, the left hand sides of equations (11.49) and (11.50) will be identical provided $[AD - BC] = 1$.

Thus the *condition of reciprocity* is given by

$$AD - BC = 1 \text{ or } \begin{vmatrix} A & B \\ C & D \end{vmatrix} = 1 \qquad \text{...(11.51)}$$

Again, from the concept of *symmetry* for Z-parameter network,

$$Z_{11} = \left.\frac{V_1}{I_1}\right|_{I_2=0} = \left.\frac{AV_2 - BI_2}{CV_2 - DI_2}\right|_{I_2=0} = \frac{A}{C}$$

$$[\because I_2 = 0]$$

$$\text{Also,} \quad Z_{22} = \left.\frac{V_2}{I_2}\right|_{I_1=0} = \frac{D}{C} \qquad \text{...(11.52)}$$

[$\because$ when $I_1 = 0$, from $I_1 = CV_2 - DI_2$ we get, $0 = CV_2 - DI_2$ or, $(V_2 / I_2) = (D / C)$]

For a symmetrical Z-parameter network $Z_{11} = Z_{22}$. This gives, for the $ABCD$ parameters, $\frac{A}{C} = \frac{D}{C}$ or, $A = D$ as *condition of symmetry*.

11.10.5 Condition of Reciprocity and Symmetry in *h*-parameter Network

In h-parameter representation,

$$V_1 = h_{11} I_1 + h_{12} V_2$$

With output terminals shorted, $V_2 = 0$. This gives,

$$V_1 = h_{11} I_1 \qquad \text{...(11.53)}$$

Similarly, for the h-parameter equation

$$I_2 = h_{21} I_1 + h_{22} V_2$$

for

$$V_2 = 0, -I_2 = h_{21} I_1 \qquad \text{...(11.54)}$$

[with shorted output, the direction of I_2 gets reversed]

Dividing equation (11.54) by (11.53)

$$\frac{I_2}{V_1} = -\frac{h_{21}}{h_{11}} \qquad \text{...(11.55)}$$

The excitation and responses are then interchanged such that voltage V_2 is applied at output terminals while input terminals are shorted. The direction of I_1 is now reversed.

Thus, from the h-parameter representation,

$$0 = -h_{11} I_1 + h_{12} V_2$$

or, $$\frac{I_1}{V_2} = \frac{h_{12}}{h_{11}} \quad \text{...(11.56)}$$

Assuming $V_1 = V_2$, following the principle of reciprocity, the left hand sides of equations (11.55) and (11.56) will be same. This is possible provided,

$$h_{21} = -h_{12} \quad \text{...(11.57)}$$

Thus, $h_{21} = -h_{12}$ exhibits the *condition of reciprocity*.

For establishing the condition of symmetry, let us incorporate the concept of Z-parameter network again.

By definition, when the output is shorted, $I_2 = 0$ and then

$$Z_{11} = \frac{V_1}{I_1} = \frac{h_{11} I_1 + h_{12} V_2}{I_1} = h_{11} + h_{12} \frac{V_2}{I_1}$$

$$= h_{11} - h_{12} \frac{h_{21}}{h_{22}}$$

$$\left[\because \text{ from } I_2 = h_{21} I_1 + h_{22} V_2, \text{ for } I_2 = 0, \frac{V_2}{I_1} = -\frac{h_{21}}{h_{22}} \right]$$

$$= \frac{h_{11} h_{22} - h_{12} h_{21}}{h_{22}} = \frac{\Delta h}{h_{22}} \quad \text{...(11.58)}$$

where $\Delta h = h_{11} h_{22} - h_{12} h_{21}$.

Again, with input ports shorted, $I_1 = 0$. This gives, for the Z parameter representation,

$$Z_{22} = \left. \frac{V_2}{I_2} \right|_{I_1 = 0} = \frac{V_2}{h_{22} V_2}$$

[in the expression, $I_2 = h_{21} I_1 + h_{22} V_2$, for $I_1 = 0, I_2 = h_{22} V_2$]

$$\therefore \quad Z_{22} = \frac{1}{h_{22}} \quad \text{....(11.59)}$$

The condition of symmetry ($Z_{11} = Z_{22}$) leads to $\Delta h = 1$ such that equations (11.58) and (11.59) are identical. Thus the *condition of symmetry* is given by

$$\begin{vmatrix} h_{11} & h_{12} \\ h_{21} & h_{22} \end{vmatrix} = 1$$

Table 11.1 Conditions for Reciprocity and Symmetry in Terms of Various Parameters

Parameter	*Condition for reciprocity*	*Condition for symmetry*
Z	$Z_{12} = Z_{21}$	$Z_{11} = Z_{22}$
Y	$Y_{12} = Y_{21}$	$Y_{11} = Y_{21}$
h	$h_{12} = -h_{21}$	$\Delta h = 1$
$ABCD$	$AD - BC = 1$	$A = D$

EXAMPLE 11.27 *Find Z-parameters for the lattice network shown in Fig. E11.36.*

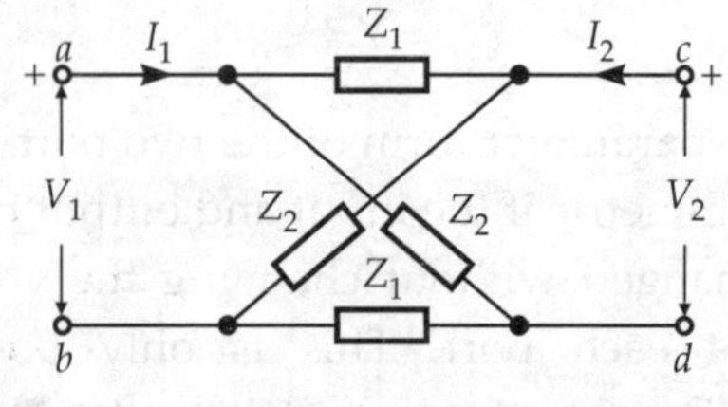

Fig. E11.36

SOLUTION. In the first step, the output terminals are open-circuited with V_1 at the input. The network is redrawn with I_1 as the input current (Fig. E11.37). The equivalent impedance of the network looking back from the input terminals is

$$(Z_1 + Z_2) \| (Z_2 + Z_1) \text{ i.e.,} \left(\frac{Z_1 + Z_2}{2} \right).$$

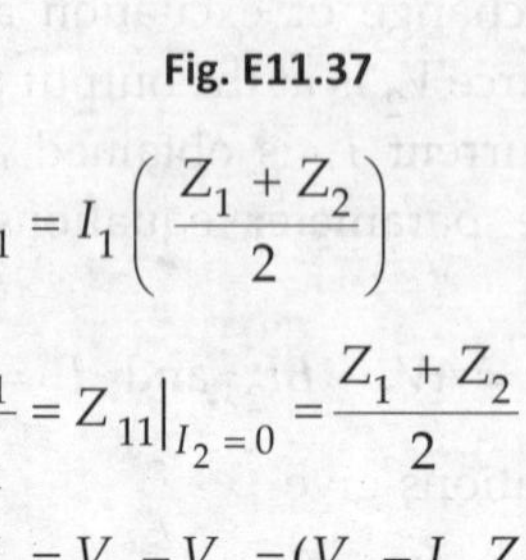

Fig. E11.37

Hence, $V_1 = I_1 \left(\frac{Z_1 + Z_2}{2} \right)$

or $$\frac{V_1}{I_1} = Z_{11}\big|_{I_2 = 0} = \frac{Z_1 + Z_2}{2}$$

Now, $V_2 = V_c - V_d = (V_1 - I_3 Z_1) - (V_1 - I_4 Z_2)$

$$= I_4 Z_2 - I_3 Z_1$$

[V_c and V_d being the potentials at point c and d]

However,

$$I_3 = I_1 \frac{(Z_2 + Z_1)}{(Z_1 + Z_2) + (Z_2 + Z_1)} = \frac{I_1}{2}$$

$$\left[\text{impedances in branch } ab \text{ and } xy \text{ are same hence } I_3 = I_4 = \frac{I_1}{2} \right]$$

Also, $I_4 = \frac{I_1}{2}$

Hence $V_2 = \frac{I_1}{2} \times Z_2 - \frac{I_1}{2} \times Z_1 = \frac{Z_2 - Z_1}{2} \cdot I_1$

$$\therefore \quad \frac{V_2}{I_1} = Z_{21} \bigg|_{I_2=0} = \frac{Z_2 - Z_1}{2}$$

As the given network is symmetrical Z_{12} must be equal to Z_{21} and Z_{22} should be equal to Z_{11}.

Hence $\mathbf{Z_{11} = Z_{22} = \frac{Z_1 + Z_2}{2}}$

and $\mathbf{Z_{12} = Z_{21} = \frac{Z_2 - Z_1}{2}}$.

Example 11.28 *Obtain Z parameter of the following network [Fig. E11.38(a) and Fig. 11.38(b)].*

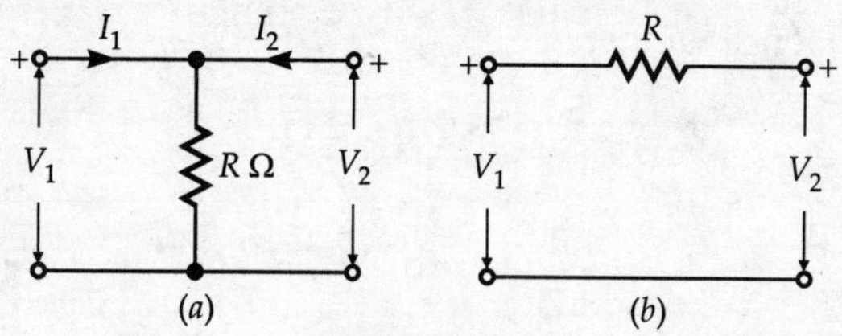

Fig. E11.38

Solution. In Fig. 11.38(a), with output open-circuited, $I_2 = 0$.

$$\therefore \quad V_1 = I_1 R \text{ giving } \frac{V_1}{I_1} = Z_{11}\,(I_2 = 0) = R$$

Also, $I_1 R = V_2 \;\therefore\; \frac{V_2}{I_1}\bigg|_{I_2=0} = Z_{21} = R$

Again with input open-circuited, $I_1 = 0$

$$\therefore \quad V_2 = I_2 R \text{ giving } \frac{V_2}{I_2} = Z_{22} = R\,(\text{at } t_1 = 0)$$

and $\quad I_2 R = V_1$ giving $\frac{V_1}{I_2}\bigg|_{I_1=0} = Z_{12} = R$

$$\therefore \quad \mathbf{Z_{11} = R;\; Z_{12} = R}$$
$$\mathbf{Z_{21} = R;\; Z_{22} = R.}$$

In **Fig. E11.38(b)** since I_1 and I_2 are not independent, **Z parameters cannot be determined.**

[As soon as V_1 will be applied I_1 will flow causing I_2 to flow as $(-I_1)$. Then I_1 and I_2 are not independent].

Example 11.29 *Obtain Z parameter for Fig. E11.39.*

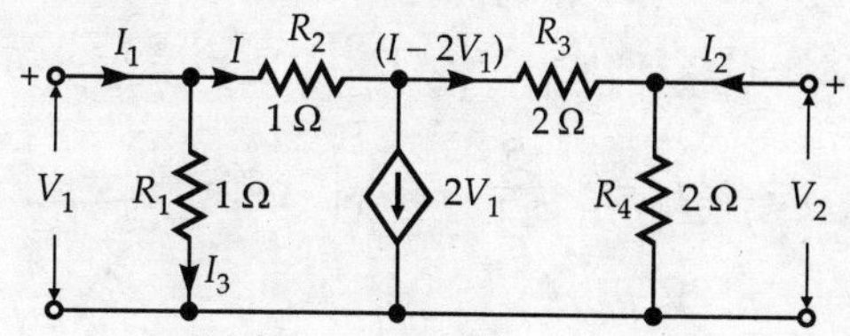

Fig. E11.39

Solution. Let us first assume

$I_2 = 0$ [output is open-circulated. Refer to Fig. E11.40]

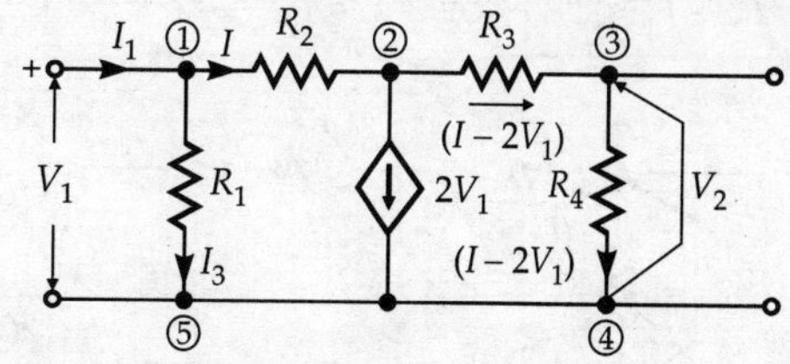

Fig. E11.40

At *node (1)*,

$$I_1 = I_3 + I$$

or $$I = I_1 - I_3 = I_1 - \frac{V_1}{R_1} = \left(I_1 - \frac{V_1}{1}\right)$$

$$= (I_1 - V_1) \quad \ldots(i)$$

However,

$$I = \frac{\text{Voltage at node (1)} - \text{Voltage at node (2)}}{R_2}$$

$$= \frac{V_1 - (I - 2V_1)4}{1} \quad \ldots(ii)$$

Comparing (i) and (ii),

$$(I_1 - V_1) = \frac{V_1 - (I - 2V_1)4}{1}$$

$$= \frac{V_1 - [(I_1 - V_1) - 2V_1]4}{1}$$

or $$I_1 - V_1 = \frac{V_1 - [4I_1 - 4V_1 - 8V_1]}{1}$$

or $\quad I_1 - V_1 = V_1 - 4I_1 + 4V_1 + 8V_1$

or $\quad 5I_1 = 14V_1$

$$Z_{11} = \frac{V_1}{I_1}\bigg|_{I_2=0} = \frac{5}{14}\,\Omega.$$

$\therefore$ Again, denoting V_2 as the drop against R_4 when $I_2 = 0$,

$$V_2 = (I - 2V_1)2 = (I_1 - V_1 - 2V_1)2 = 2I_1 - 6V_1$$

$$= +2I_1 - 6 \times \frac{5}{14}I_1 = I_1\left(+2 - \frac{15}{7}\right) = -\frac{1}{7}I_1$$

$$\therefore \quad Z_{21} = \frac{V_2}{I_1}\bigg|_{I_2=0} = -\frac{1}{7}\,\Omega$$

In the next step, let $I_1 = 0$ *i.e.*, input is open-circuited (Refer to Fig. E11.41). Then, at *node 3*,

$$I_2 = I_4 + I'.$$

or $\quad I_2 - I_4 = I'$; or, $I' = I_2 - \dfrac{V_2}{2}$ ...(*iii*)

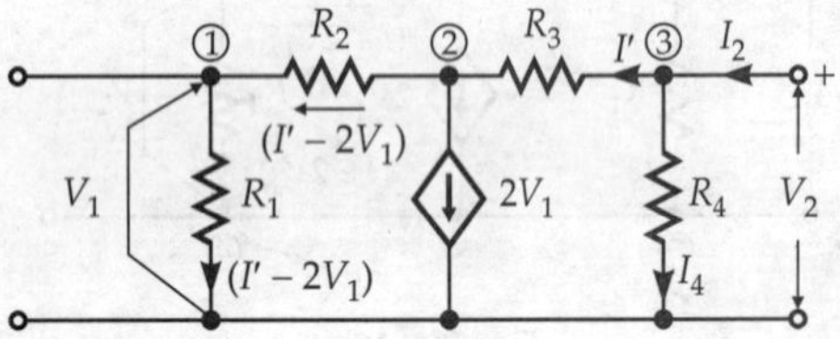

Fig. E11.41

But

$$I' = \frac{\text{Voltage at node (3)} - \text{Voltage at node (2)}}{R_3}$$

$$I' = \frac{V_2 - (R_2 + R_1)(I' - 2V_1)}{2} = \frac{V_2 - 2(I' - 2V_1)}{2} \quad \text{...(iv)}$$

Comparing equations (*iii*) and (*iv*),

$$I_2 - \frac{V_2}{2} = \frac{V_2 - 2(I' - 2V_1)}{2}$$

or
$$I_2 - \frac{V_2}{2} = \frac{V_2 - 2\left(I_2 - \dfrac{V_2}{2} - 2V_1\right)}{2}$$

or
$$I_2 - \frac{V_2}{2} = \frac{V_2}{2} - I_2 + \frac{V_2}{2} + 2V_1$$

or
$$2I_2 = \frac{3}{2}V_2 + 2V_1 \quad \text{...(v)}$$

But $\quad V_1 = (I' - 2V_1)R_1 = \left(I_2 - \dfrac{V_2}{2} - 2V_1\right)$

[since $R_1 = 1\Omega$]

or $\quad 3V_1 = I_2 - \dfrac{V_2}{2}$

or
$$V_1 = \left(\frac{I_2}{3} - \frac{V_2}{6}\right) \quad \text{...(vi)}$$

Substitution of (*vi*) in (*v*) results

$$2I_2 = \frac{3}{2}V_2 + 2\left(\frac{I_2}{3} - \frac{V_2}{6}\right)$$

or
$$2I_2 = \frac{3}{2}V_2 + \frac{2}{3}I_2 - \frac{V_2}{3}$$

or
$$\frac{4}{3}I_2 = \frac{7}{6}V_2\text{ ; or } 4I_2 = \frac{7}{2}V_2$$

$$\therefore \quad \frac{V_2}{I_2}\bigg|_{I_1=0} = Z_{22} = \frac{8}{7}\,\Omega.$$

Equation $4I_2 = V_2 \times \dfrac{7}{2}$ gives from equation (*v*)

$$2I_2 = \frac{3}{2} \times \frac{8}{7}I_2 + 2V_1 \text{ or } \frac{V_1}{I_2} = Z_{12} = \frac{1}{7}\,\Omega.$$

Hence we get,

$$\mathbf{Z_{11} = \frac{5}{14}\,\Omega\text{; } Z_{12} = \frac{1}{7}\,\Omega}$$

$$\mathbf{Z_{21} = -\frac{1}{7}\,\Omega \text{ and } Z_{22} = \frac{8}{7}\,\Omega.}$$

EXAMPLE 11.30 *For Fig. E11.42 obtain Z-parameters and show that the network is not reciprocal.*

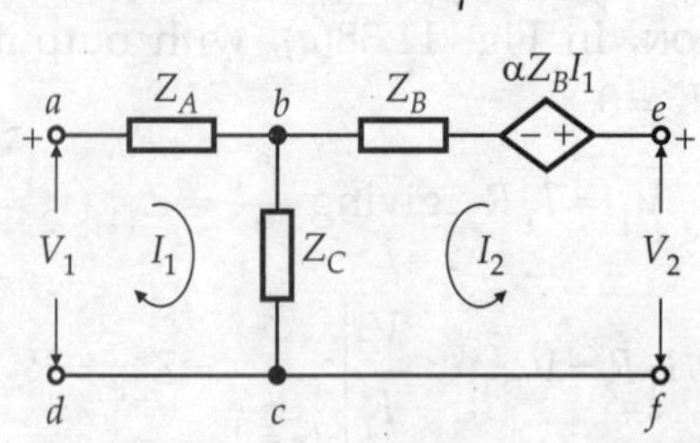

Fig. E11.42

SOLUTION. Applying KVL at loop *abcd* (Fig. E11.42)

$$V_1 = (Z_A + Z_C)I_1 + Z_C I_2 \quad \text{...(i)}$$

and applying KVL at loop *bcfe*,

$$V_2 = \alpha Z_B I_1 + (Z_B + Z_C)I_2 + Z_C I_1$$

$$= (\alpha Z_B + Z_C)I_1 + (Z_B + Z_C)I_2 \quad \text{...(ii)}$$

Comparing equations (*i*) and (*ii*) with the governing equation of Z parameter representation,

$$\mathbf{Z_{11} = Z_A + Z_C; Z_{21} = (\alpha Z_B + Z_C)}$$
$$\mathbf{Z_{12} = Z_C ; Z_{22} = (Z_B + Z_C)}$$

It may be observed that $Z_{12} \neq Z_{21}$

∴ The network is not reciprocal.

EXAMPLE 11.31 *Find the Z-parameter of the network drawn in Fig. E11.43.*

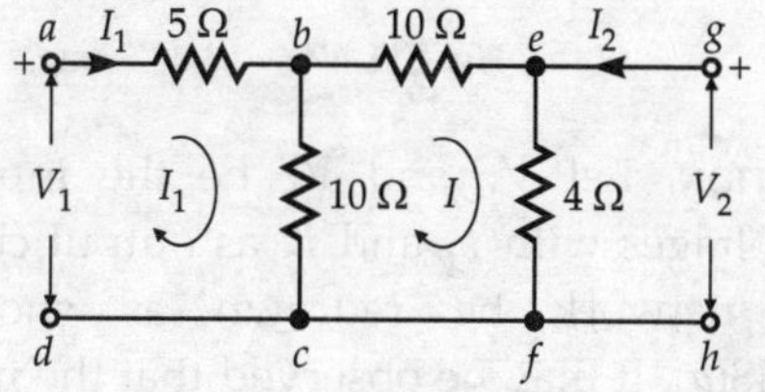

Fig. E11.43

SOLUTION. The loop currents are drawn in Fig. E11.43. Let us first assume the output (*g-h* terminal) be open-circuited.

$$\therefore \quad V_{e-f} = V_2 \text{ (say)} = I \times 4 \ \textit{i.e.,}\ V_2 = 4I$$

and in *loop bcfe*, with KVL,

$$10(I_1 - I) + 10I + 4I = 0$$

or $$10 I_1 = (10 + 10 + 4) I = 24I = 6V_2$$

$$[\because V_2 = 4I]$$

$$\therefore \quad \frac{V_2}{I_1} = Z_{21} \text{ (at } I_2 = 0) = \frac{10}{6} = 1.67\,\Omega.$$

Again, in *loop abcd*,

$$V_1 = 5I_1 + 10(I_1 - I)$$
$$= 5I_1 + 10\left(I_1 - \frac{10}{24} I_1\right)$$

$$[\because 24 I = 10 I_1 \text{ just shown above}]$$

$$= I_1\left[5 + 10 \times \frac{14}{24}\right] = I_1 \times 10.83$$

or $$Z_{11} = \left.\frac{V_1}{I_1}\right|_{I_2=0} = 10.83 \text{ ohm.}$$

Next, let us assume that the input port is shorted and voltage V_2 is applied at output port.

This gives, for $I_1 = 0$,

$$V_2 = I_2 \times [(10 + 10) \,||\, 4] = \frac{80}{24} I_2$$

$$\therefore \quad Z_{22} = \left.\frac{V_2}{I_2}\right|_{I_1=0} = \frac{80}{24} = 3.33 \text{ ohms.}$$

Again, $V_1 = 10 I$

and in *loop bcfe*,

$$4(I - I_2) + 10I + 10I = 0$$

or, $$4 I_2 = I(10 + 10 + 4) = 24 I = 2.4 V_1$$

$$\therefore \quad \frac{V_1}{I_2} = Z_{12} \text{ (at } I_1 = 0) = \frac{4}{2.4} = 1.67 \text{ ohm.}$$

[It may be noted that in this network $Z_{12} = Z_{21}$]

Thus $\mathbf{Z_{11} = 10.83\,\Omega ; Z_{12} = 1.67\,\Omega}$

$\mathbf{Z_{21} = 1.67\,\Omega ; Z_{22} = 3.33\,\Omega.}$

EXAMPLE 11.32 *Find the Y-parameters for the network of Fig. E11.44.*

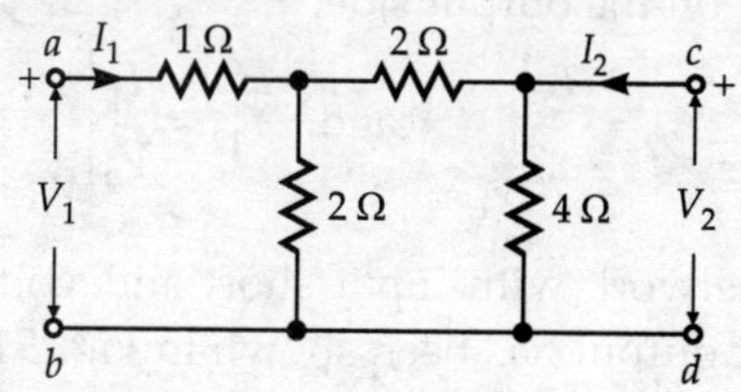

Fig. E11.44

SOLUTION. As $Y_{11} = \left.\frac{I_1}{V_1}\right|_{V_2=0.}$

hence to find Y_{11}, the output is short-circuited (*i.e.* $V_2 = 0$) and a source V_1 is applied at input as shown in Fig. E11.45.

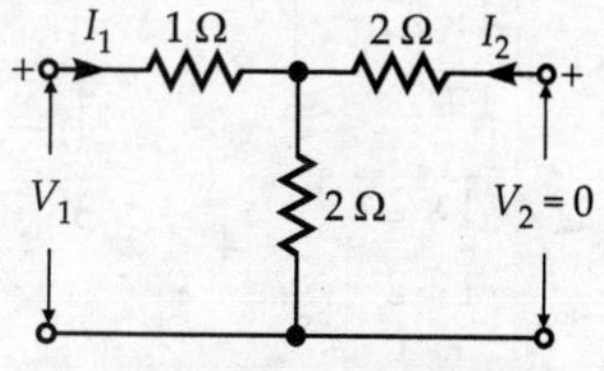

Fig. E11.45

From the figure,

$$Y_{11} = \frac{I_1}{V_1} = \frac{1}{1 + \frac{2 \times 2}{2 + 2}} = \frac{1}{2} \textbf{ mho,}$$

where $$I_1 = \frac{V_1}{1 + \frac{2 \times 2}{2 + 2}}$$

[$\because$ With output shorted, no current will flow though 4 Ω resistance]

CHAPTER 11

Also $Y_{21} = \left.\dfrac{I_2}{V_1}\right|_{V_2=0}$

So for finding Y_{21} we again keep output short-circuited.

Hence, $I_2 = \dfrac{-I_1 \times 2}{2+2}$

[–ve sign indicates reverse direction of I_2]

$$= \frac{-\left(\dfrac{V_1}{2}\right) \times 2}{2+2} = -\frac{V_1}{4}$$

or $$Y_{21} = \left.\frac{I_2}{V_1}\right|_{V_2=0} = -\frac{1}{4}\ \textbf{mho.}$$

For finding Y_{22} and Y_{12}, the short circuit will have to be placed on the input side and source V_2 is connected on the output side.

Thus, $Y_{22} = \left.\dfrac{I_2}{v_2}\right|_{V_1=0}$ and $Y_{12} = \left.\dfrac{I_1}{V_2}\right|_{V_1=0}$

The network with input short and voltage V_2 applied at output has been shown in Fig. E11.46.

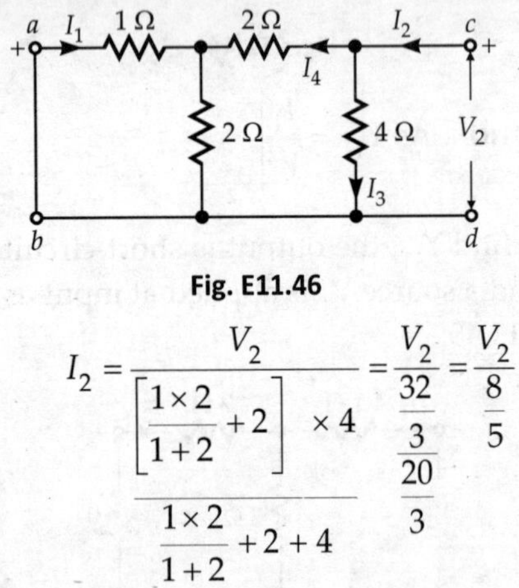

Fig. E11.46

$$I_2 = \frac{V_2}{\dfrac{\left[\dfrac{1\times 2}{1+2}+2\right]\times 4}{\dfrac{1\times 2}{1+2}+2+4}} = \frac{V_2}{\dfrac{\frac{32}{3}}{\frac{20}{3}}} = \frac{V_2}{\frac{8}{5}} = \frac{5\,V_2}{8}$$

$\therefore$ $$Y_{22} = \left.\frac{I_2}{V_2}\right|_{V_1=0} = \frac{5}{8}\ \textbf{mho.}$$

Again, $I_4 + I_3 = I_2$

or $$I_4 = I_2 - I_3 = \frac{5V_2}{8} - \frac{V_2}{4} = \frac{3}{8}V_2$$

$\therefore$ $$I_1 = -\frac{3}{8}V_2 \times \frac{2}{2+1} = -\frac{1}{4}V_2$$

$\therefore$ $$Y_{12} = \left.\frac{I_1}{V_2}\right|_{V_1=0} = -\frac{1}{4}\,\Omega$$

Example 11.33 *Obtain the Y-parameter of the network shown in Fig. E11.47.*

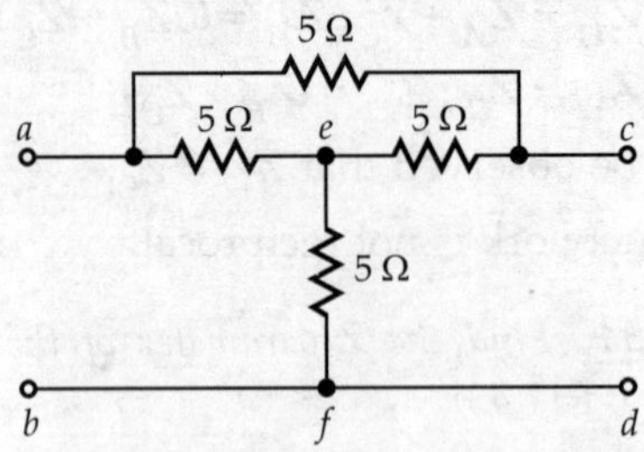

Fig. E11.47

Solution. Let V_1 and V_2 be the input and output voltages with I_1 and I_2 as output currents. Let the network be redrawn as shown in Fig. E11.48(*a*). It may be observed that the network is a combination of two networks when R_4 is parallel to the *T* network comprising R_1, R_2 and R_3. Thus a bridged *T* network is the combination of the *T* network with the bridge network [Figs. E11.48(*b*) and (*c*)].

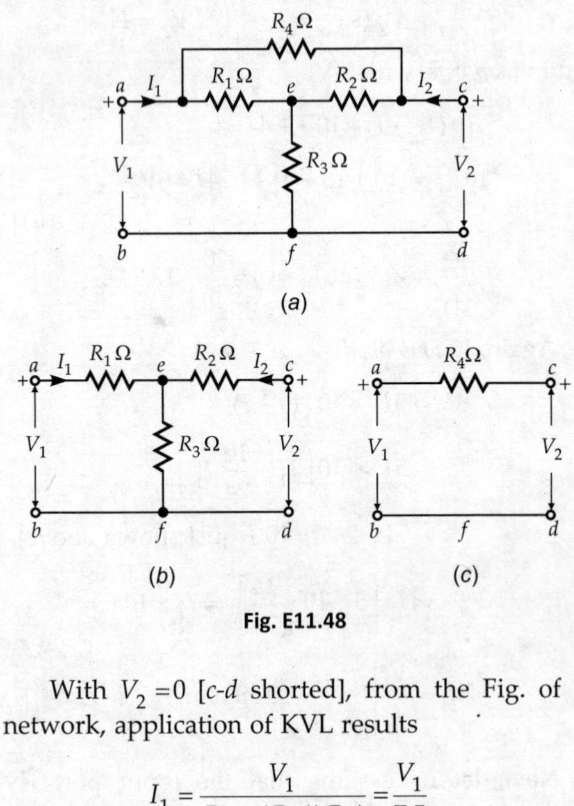

Fig. E11.48

With $V_2 = 0$ [*c-d* shorted], from the Fig. of *T* network, application of KVL results

$$I_1 = \frac{V_1}{R_1 + (R_2 \parallel R_3)} = \frac{V_1}{7.5}$$

$$Y_{11} = \left.\frac{I_1}{V_1}\right|_{V_2=0} = \frac{1}{7.5}\ \text{mho}$$

Again, $I_2 = -I_1 \times \dfrac{R_3}{R_2 + R_3} = -\dfrac{I_1}{2} = -\dfrac{V_1}{15}$

$$\therefore \quad Y_{21} = \left.\frac{I_2}{V_1}\right|_{V_2=0} = -\frac{1}{15} \text{ mho.}$$

Also, with

$$V_1 = 0.\ I_2 = \frac{V_2}{R_2 + (R_1 \| R_3)} = \frac{V_2}{7.5}$$

$$\therefore \quad Y_{22} = \left.\frac{I_2}{V_2}\right|_{V_1=0} = \frac{1}{7.5} \text{ mho}$$

and $\quad I_1 = -I_2 \dfrac{R_3}{R_1 + R_3} = -\dfrac{V_2}{15}$

$$\therefore \quad Y_{12} = \left.\frac{I_1}{V_2}\right|_{V_1=0} = -\frac{1}{15} \text{ mho}$$

Thus $\;Y_{11} = Y_{22} = \dfrac{1}{7.5}$ mho while

$$Y_{21} = Y_{12} = -\frac{1}{15} \text{ mho.}$$

In a similar way, the Y-parameter of the bridge network only is

$$Y_{11} = \left.\frac{I_1}{V_1}\right|_{V_2=0} = \frac{1}{5} \text{ mho}$$

$$\left[\because \text{ with } V_2 = 0,\ I_1 = V_1 / R_4 = \frac{V_1}{5}\right]$$

and $\quad Y_{21} = \left.\dfrac{I_2}{V_1}\right|_{V_2=0} = -\dfrac{1}{5}$ mho

$$\left[\because \text{ with } V_2 = 0,\ V_1 = -I_2 R_4 \ \therefore I_2 = -\frac{V_1}{R_4} = -\frac{V_1}{5}\right]$$

It is evident that Y_{22} and Y_{12} can be determined for the bridge network [Fig. E11.48(*a*)] in exactly the similar way where,

$$Y_{22} = \frac{1}{5} \text{ mho}\,;\ Y_{12} = -\frac{1}{5} \text{ mho}$$

As the T network and the bridge network are parallel forming the bridged T network hence the combined Y parameter of the two network will be

$$Y_{\text{net}} = \begin{bmatrix} \dfrac{1}{7.5} & -\dfrac{1}{15} \\ -\dfrac{1}{15} & \dfrac{1}{7.5} \end{bmatrix} + \begin{bmatrix} \dfrac{1}{5} & -\dfrac{1}{5} \\ -\dfrac{1}{5} & \dfrac{1}{5} \end{bmatrix} = \begin{bmatrix} \dfrac{1}{3} & -\dfrac{4}{15} \\ -\dfrac{4}{15} & \dfrac{1}{3} \end{bmatrix}$$

EXAMPLE 11.34 *In the circuit shown in Fig. E11.49, find the h-parameter.*

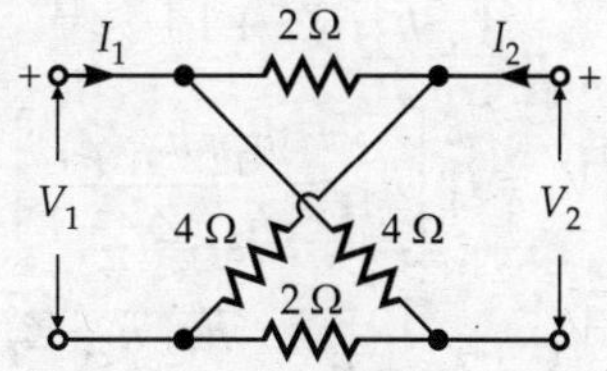

Fig. E11.49

SOLUTION. The h-parameter can be determined from the Z-parameters directly as we have already seen the Z-parameters of this lattice network.

$$Z_{11} = 3\,\Omega;\ Z_{21} = 1\,\Omega$$

$$Z_{12} = 1\,\Omega;\ Z_{22} = 3\,\Omega \quad \text{[Ref. to Ex. 11.27]}$$

Here $\quad h_{11} = \dfrac{\Delta Z}{Z_{22}} = \dfrac{8}{3}$ **ohm**

$$h_{22} = \frac{1}{Z_{22}} = \frac{1}{3} \textbf{ mho}$$

$$h_{12} = \frac{Z_{12}}{Z_{22}} = \frac{1}{3}$$

$$h_{21} = -\frac{Z_{21}}{Z_{22}} = -\frac{1}{3}.$$

EXAMPLE 11.35 *In the circuit of Fig. E11.50 determine the input and output impedances.*

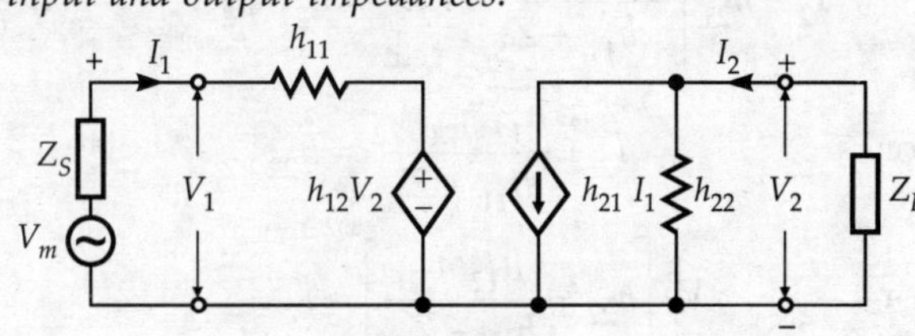

Fig. E11.50

SOLUTION. Applying KVL at input port loop,

$$V_1 = h_{11}\, I_1 + h_{12}\, V_2$$

or $\quad V_1 - h_{12}\, V_2 = h_{11}\, I_1 \qquad$ ...(*i*)

Application of KCL at output port gives,

$$I_2 = h_{22}\, V_2 + h_{21}\, I_1$$

or $\quad -\dfrac{V_2}{Z_L} = h_{22}\, V_2 + h_{21}\, I_1$

or $\quad -h_{21}\, I_1 = V_2 \left[h_{22} + \dfrac{1}{Z_L}\right]$

or $\quad V_2 = -\dfrac{h_{21}\, I_1}{h_{22} + \dfrac{1}{Z_L}} = -\dfrac{h_{21}\, I_1\, Z_L}{h_{22}\, Z_L + 1} \qquad$ ...(*ii*)

CHAPTER 11

Substitution of V_2 from (*ii*) in (*i*),

$$V_1 - h_{12}\left(-\frac{h_{21}\, I_1\, Z_L}{h_{22}\, Z_L + 1}\right) = h_{11} I_1$$

or
$$V_1 = I_1\left[h_{11} - \frac{h_{12}\, h_{21}\, Z_L}{h_{22}\, Z_L + 1}\right]$$

or
$$\frac{V_1}{I_1} = Z_{in} = \boldsymbol{h_{11}} - \frac{\boldsymbol{h_{12}\, h_{21}\, Z_L}}{\boldsymbol{h_{22}\, Z_L + 1}} \qquad ...(iii)$$

Then the input impedance Z_{in} is obtained by equation (*iii*).

To determine Z_{out}, the source voltage V_m is made zero with Z_S being maintained, Z_S being the source impedance.

Applying KVL at input port loop,

$$h_{12}\, V_2 = -I_1\, h_{11} - Z_S\, I_1$$

or
$$-h_{12}\, V_2 = I_1\,(h_{11} + Z_S) \qquad ...(iv)$$

At the output port, the KCL application yields

$$I_2 - h_{21}\, I_1 = h_{22}\, V_2 \qquad ...(v)$$

From (*iv*), $I_1 = -\dfrac{h_{12}}{h_{11} + Z_S} . V_2$

Substituting the value of I_1 thus obtained in (*v*),

$$I_2 - h_{21}\left[-\frac{h_{12}}{h_{11} + Z_S} . V_2\right] = h_{22}\, V_2$$

or
$$I_2 + \frac{h_{12}\, h_{21}\, V_2}{h_{11} + Z_S} = h_{22} V_2$$

or
$$V_2\left[h_{22} - \frac{h_{12}\, h_{21}}{h_{11} + Z_S}\right] = I_2$$

$$\therefore \quad \frac{V_2}{I_2} = Z_{out} = \frac{\boldsymbol{1}}{\left[\boldsymbol{h_{22}} - \dfrac{\boldsymbol{h_{12}\, h_{21}}}{\boldsymbol{h_{11} + Z_S}}\right]} \qquad ...(vi)$$

Z_{out}, the output impedance, is obtained in equation (*vi*).

Example 11.36 *Obtain transmission parameter of the network shown in Fig. E11.51.*

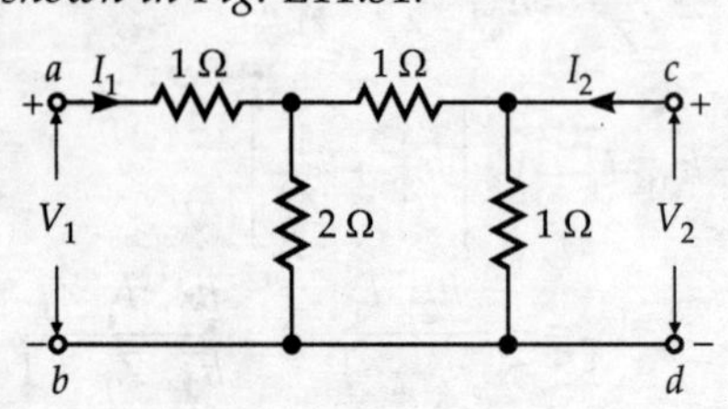

Fig. E11.51

Solution. Let us first keep terminals *c*-*d* open circuit and apply voltage V_1 at input port (*a*-*b*). The circuit has been shown in Fig. E11.52.

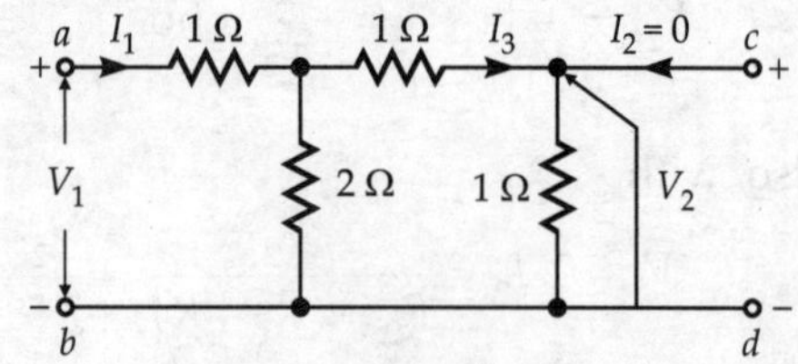

Fig. E11.52

Applying KVL the mesh equations are

$$V_1 = I_1 \times 1 + (I_1 - I_3)2$$

or
$$V_1 = 3I_1 - 2I_3 \qquad ...(i)$$

and
$$0 = (I_3 - I_1)2 + I_3\,(1 + 1) = 4I_3 - 2I_1$$

$$\therefore \quad I_3 = \frac{1}{2} I_1 \qquad ...(ii)$$

Utilising (*ii*) in (*i*),

$$V_1 = 3I_1 - 2 \times \frac{1}{2} I_1 = 2I_1 \qquad ...(iii)$$

∴ Again,

$$V_2 = I_3 \times 1 = \frac{1}{2} I_1 \qquad ...(iv)$$

$$\therefore \quad \left.\frac{I_1}{V_2}\right|_{I_2 = 0} = 2 \text{ mho} = C.$$

Dividing equation (*iii*) by (*iv*),

$$\left.\frac{V_1}{V_2}\right|_{I_2 = 0} = 4 = A.$$

Now at output port (*c*-*d*), short circuit is applied and at input port (*a*-*b*) same voltage V_1 is applied (refer to Fig. E11.53).

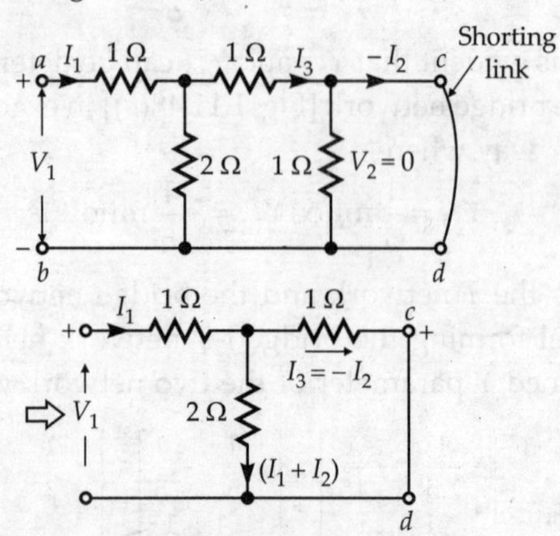

Fig. E11.53

Applying KVL in the loops, the loop equation is given by

$$V_1 = I_1 + (I_1 + I_2)2$$
$$= 3I_1 + 2I_2 \qquad ...(v)$$

and $\quad (I_3 - I_1)2 + I_3 = 0$

or $\quad -(I_1 + I_2)2 - I_2 = 0 \qquad (\because I_3 = -I_2)$

or $\quad 2I_1 + 3I_2 = 0$

$$\therefore \quad I_1 = -\frac{3}{2} I_2 . \qquad ...(vi)$$

Utilising equation, in (v),

$$V_1 = -\frac{9}{2} I_2 + 2I_2 = -\frac{5}{2} I_2$$

$$\therefore \quad \left.\frac{V_1}{-I_2}\right|_{V_2=0} = \frac{5}{2} \text{ ohm} = B.$$

From (vi) $\quad \dfrac{I_1}{-I_2} = \dfrac{3}{2} = D.$

Hence the transmission parameters are

$$\begin{bmatrix} A & B \\ C & D \end{bmatrix} = \begin{bmatrix} 4 & \frac{5}{2} \\ 2 & \frac{3}{2} \end{bmatrix}$$

Here $AD - BC = 1$ and $A \neq D$

Thus the circuit is reciprocal but not symmetrical.

EXAMPLE 11.37 *Find ABCD parameters of the following lattice network (Fig. E11.54).*

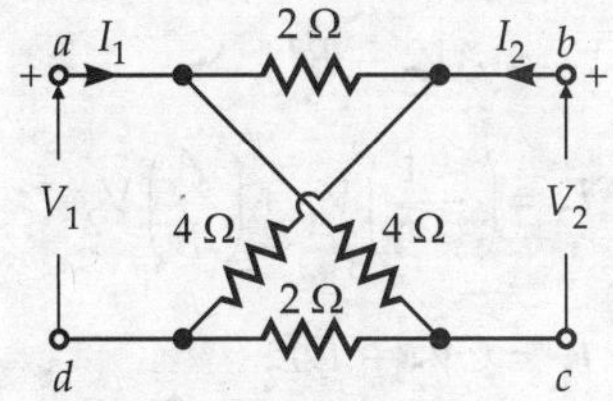

Fig. E11.54

SOLUTION. Here with output port open-circuited, (refer to Fig. E11.55)

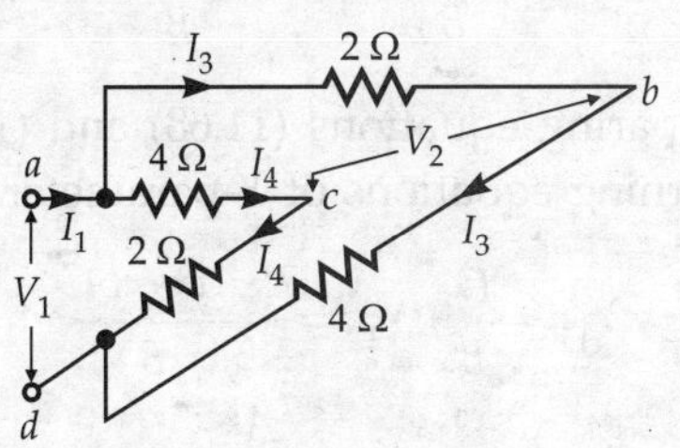

Fig. E11.55

$$V_1 = I_1 \{(2+4) \| (4+2)\} = I_1 \times 3$$

$$\therefore \quad \left.\frac{V_1}{I_1}\right|_{I_2=0} = Z_{11} = 3\,\Omega.$$

Again, the voltage between nodes b and c being V_2,

$$V_2 = (V_1 - 2I_3) - (V_1 - 4I_4) = 4I_4 - 2I_3 \qquad ...(i)$$

However,

$$V_1 = 4I_4 + 2I_4 = 2I_3 + 4I_3 \quad \text{or} \quad I_3 = I_4 \qquad ...(ii)$$

Thus we get,

$$V_2 = 4I_4 - 2I_3 = 2I_4 \text{ [using } (ii) \text{ in } (i)]$$

But $\quad I_3 = I_4$

$$\therefore \quad I_1 = 2I_3 = 2I_4 \qquad [\because I_1 = I_3 + I_4]$$

Hence $\quad V_2 = 2I_4 = I_1$

$$\therefore \quad \left.\frac{V_2}{I_1}\right|_{I_2=0} = 1\,\Omega = Z_{21}$$

Again open-circuiting the input port and applying voltage V_2 at output port, in a similar way

$$Z_{12} = 1\,\Omega \text{ and } Z_{22} = 3\,\Omega$$

thus $\quad \begin{bmatrix} Z_{11} & Z_{12} \\ Z_{21} & Z_{22} \end{bmatrix} = \begin{bmatrix} 3 & 1 \\ 1 & 3 \end{bmatrix}.$

$ABCD$ parameters may then be determined as follows (See Art. 11.11.7) :

$$A = \frac{Z_{11}}{Z_{21}} = \frac{3}{1} = 3, \quad B = \frac{\Delta Z}{Z_{21}} = 8\,\Omega$$

$$C = \frac{1}{Z_{21}} = \frac{1}{1} = 1 \text{ mho}, \quad D = \frac{Z_{22}}{Z_{21}} = 3$$

and $\quad AD - BC = 1.$

Also, $\quad A = D.$

Thus the circuit is reciprocal and also symmetrical.

11.11 INTER-RELATIONSHIPS BETWEEN PARAMETERS OF TWO PORT NETWORK

11.11.1 *Z*-parameters in Terms of *Y*-parameters

Z being the impedance and Y being the admittance,

$$[Z] = [Y]^{-1}$$

or $\quad \begin{bmatrix} Z_{11} & Z_{12} \\ Z_{21} & Z_{22} \end{bmatrix} = \begin{bmatrix} Y_{11} & Y_{12} \\ Y_{21} & Y_{22} \end{bmatrix}^{-1}$

CHAPTER 11

Thus $Z_{11} = \frac{Y_{22}}{\Delta Y}, Z_{12} = -\frac{Y_{12}}{\Delta Y}$

$$Z_{21} = -\frac{Y_{21}}{\Delta Y} \text{ and } Z_{22} = \frac{Y_{11}}{\Delta Y} \quad ...(11.60)$$

$$\left[\text{Here } \Delta Y = \begin{bmatrix} Y_{11} & Y_{12} \\ Y_{21} & Y_{22} \end{bmatrix} = Y_{11}\,Y_{22} - Y_{12}\,Y_{21}\right]$$

11.11.2 *Z*-parameters in Terms of *ABCD* Parameters

From the governing equation

$I_1 = CV_2 - DI_2$, we can write

$$V_2 = \frac{1}{C} \cdot I_1 + \frac{D}{C} \cdot I_2 \quad ...(11.61)$$

Similarly, from another governing equation

$$V_1 = AV_2 - BI_2,$$

$$V_1 = \left[\frac{1}{C} \cdot I_1 + \frac{D}{C} \cdot I_2\right] \; A - BI_2$$

$$= \frac{A}{C} \cdot I_1 + \frac{AD - BC}{C} \cdot I_2 \quad ...(11.62)$$

Comparing these two equations with the governing equations of *Z*-parameter network, we can write

$$Z_{11} = \frac{A}{C}, Z_{12} = \frac{AD - BC}{C}$$

$$Z_{21} = \frac{1}{C}, Z_{22} = \frac{D}{C}.$$

11.11.3 *Z*-parameters in Terms of Hybrid Parameters

The governing equations of the *h*-parameter network are given by

$$V_1 = h_{11}\, I_1 + h_{12}\, V_2 \quad ...(11.63)$$

$$I_2 = h_{21}\, I_1 + h_{22}\, V_2 \quad ...(11.64)$$

From equation (11.64),

$$V_2 = -\frac{h_{21}}{h_{22}} \cdot I_1 + \frac{1}{h_{22}} \cdot I_2 \quad ...[11.64(a)]$$

From equation (11.63),

$$V_1 = h_{11} I_1 + h_{12}\, V_2$$

$$= h_{11}\, I_1 + h_{12}\left[-\frac{h_{21}}{h_{22}}\, I_1 + \frac{1}{h_{22}} \cdot I_2\right]$$

$$= \frac{\Delta h}{h_{22}}\, I_1 + \frac{h_{12}}{h_{22}} \cdot I_2 \quad ...(11.65)$$

Comparing equations (11.64) and (11.65) with the governing equations of *Z*-parameter network, here,

$$Z_{11} = \frac{\Delta h}{h_{22}}, \quad Z_{12} = \frac{h_{12}}{h_{22}}$$

$$Z_{21} = -\frac{h_{21}}{h_{22}}, Z_{22} = \frac{1}{h_{22}} \quad ...(11.66)$$

$$[\text{Here } \Delta h = h_{11}\, h_{22} - h_{21}\, h_{12}]$$

11.11.4 *Y*-parameters in Terms of *Z*-parameter

We know, $[I] = [Y][V] = [Y][Z][I]$

$$(\because [V] = [Z][I])$$

or $[Y] = [Z]^{-1}$

or $\begin{bmatrix} Y_{11} & Y_{12} \\ Y_{21} & Y_{22} \end{bmatrix} = \begin{bmatrix} Z_{11} & Z_{12} \\ Z_{21} & Z_{22} \end{bmatrix}^{-1}$

Thus, $Y_{11} = \frac{Z_{22}}{\Delta Z}, \quad Y_{12} = -\frac{Z_{12}}{\Delta Z}$

$$Y_{21} = -\frac{Z_{21}}{\Delta Z}, Y_{22} = \frac{Z_{11}}{\Delta Z} \quad ...(11.67)$$

$$[\text{ Here, } \Delta Z = Z_{11}\, Z_{22} - Z_{12}\, Z_{21}]$$

11.11.5 *Y*-parameters in Terms of Transmission parameters (*ABCD* parameters)

Utilising the *ABCD* parameter representation, the governing equations are

$$V_1 = AV_2 - BI_2$$

giving $I_2 = \left(-\frac{1}{B}\right) V_1 + \left(\frac{A}{B}\right) V_2 \quad ...(11.68)$

and $I_1 = CV_2 - DI_2$

$$= CV_2 - D\left[\left(-\frac{1}{B}\right) V_1 + \frac{A}{B}\, V_2\right]$$

$$= \left(\frac{D}{B}\right) V_1 - \frac{AD - BC}{B} \cdot V_2 \quad ...(11.69)$$

Comparing equations (11.68) and (11.69) with the governing equations of *Y*-parameter network,

$$Y_{11} = \frac{D}{B}, Y_{12} = -\frac{AD - BC}{B}$$

$$Y_{21} = -\frac{1}{B}, Y_{22} = \frac{A}{B} \quad ...(11.70)$$

11.11.6 *Y*-parameter in Terms of *h*-parameter

The governing equations of *h*-parameter network are given by

$$V_1 = h_{11}\, I_1 + h_{12}\, V_2$$

giving
$$I_1 = \left(\frac{1}{h_{11}}\right) V_1 + \left(-\frac{h_{12}}{h_{11}}\right) V_2 \quad ...(11.71)$$

and
$$I_2 = h_{21}\, I_1 + h_{22}\, V_2$$

or,
$$I_2 = h_{21}\left[\left(\frac{1}{h_{11}}\right) V_1 - \left(\frac{h_{12}}{h_{11}}\right) V_2\right] I_1 + h_{22}\, V_2$$

$$= \left(\frac{h_{21}}{h_{11}}\right) V_1 + \left(\frac{h_{11}h_{22} - h_{12}h_{21}}{h_{11}}\right) V_2 \quad ...(11.72)$$

Comparing these two equations with the governing equations of *Y*-parameter network,

$$Y_{11} = \frac{1}{h_{11}};\ Y_{12} = -\frac{h_{12}}{h_{11}};$$
$$Y_{21} = \frac{h_{21}}{h_{11}};\ Y_{22} = \frac{h_{11}\,h_{22} - h_{12}\,h_{21}}{h_{11}}.$$

11.11.7 *ABCD* parameter in Terms of *Z*-parameter

The Z-parameter equations are given by

$$V_2 = Z_{21}\, I_1 + Z_{22} I_2$$

which gives
$$I_1 = \left(\frac{1}{Z_{21}}\right) V_2 + \left(\frac{Z_{22}}{Z_{21}}\right)(-I_2) \quad ...(11.73)$$

and
$$V_1 = Z_{11}\, I_1 + Z_{12}\, I_2$$

giving
$$V_1 = Z_{11}\left\{\left(\frac{1}{Z_{21}}\right) V_2 + \left(-\frac{Z_{22}}{Z_{21}}\right) I_2\right\} + Z_{12} I_2$$

$$= \left(\frac{Z_{11}}{Z_{21}}\right) V_2 + (-I_2)\left[\frac{Z_{22}Z_{11} - Z_{12}Z_{21}}{Z_{21}}\right] \quad ...(11.74)$$

Comparing these two equations (11.73) and (11.74) with the governing equations of *ABCD* parameters, we find that

$$A = \frac{Z_{11}}{Z_{21}};\quad B = \frac{Z_{22}Z_{11} - Z_{12}\,Z_{21}}{Z_{21}}$$
$$C = \frac{1}{Z_{21}};\quad D = \frac{Z_{22}}{Z_{21}} \quad ...(11.75)$$

11.11.8 *ABCD* parameters in Terms of *Y*-parameters

Y-parameter equations are given by

$$I_2 = Y_{21}\, V_1 + Y_{22}\, V_2$$

giving
$$V_1 = \left(-\frac{Y_{22}}{Y_{21}}\right) V_2 + \left(-\frac{1}{Y_{21}}\right)(-I_2)$$

or,
$$V_1 = \left(-\frac{Y_{22}}{Y_{21}}\right) V_2 - \left(-\frac{1}{Y_{21}}\right) I_2 \quad ...(11.76)$$

and
$$I_1 = Y_{11}\, V_1 + Y_{12}\, V_2$$

$$= Y_{11}\left[\left(-\frac{Y_{22}}{Y_{21}}\right) V_2 + \left(\frac{1}{Y_{21}}\right) I_2\right] + Y_{12}\, V_2$$

$$= \left[-\frac{Y_{11}\,Y_{22} - Y_{12}\,Y_{21}}{Y_{21}}\right] V_2 + \left(-\frac{Y_{11}}{Y_{21}}\right)(-I_2)$$

$$= \left[-\frac{Y_{11}\,Y_{22} - Y_{12}\,Y_{21}}{Y_{21}}\right] V_2 - \left(-\frac{Y_{11}}{Y_{21}}\right) I_2 \quad ...(11.77)$$

Comparing equations (11.74) and (11.77) with the governing equations of *ABCD* parameters,

$$A = \left(-\frac{Y_{22}}{Y_{21}}\right);\quad B = \left(-\frac{1}{Y_{21}}\right)$$
$$C = \left[-\frac{Y_{11}\,Y_{22} - Y_{12}\,Y_{21}}{Y_{21}}\right];\ D = \left(-\frac{Y_{11}}{Y_{21}}\right) \quad ...(11.78)$$

11.11.9 *ABCD* parameters in Terms of *h*-parameters

From the governing equations of *h*-parameter network, we get

$$I_2 = h_{21}\, I_1 + h_{22}\, V_2$$

giving
$$I_1 = \left(-\frac{h_{22}}{h_{21}}\right) V_2 + \left(-\frac{1}{h_{21}}\right)(-I_2) \quad ...(11.79)$$

and
$$V_1 = h_{11} I_1 + h_{12}\, V_2$$

giving
$$V_1 = h_{11}\left[\left(-\frac{h_{22}}{h_{21}}\right) V_2 + \left(-\frac{1}{h_{21}}\right)(-I_2)\right] h_{12} V_2$$

CHAPTER 11

or $$V_1 = \left(-\frac{h_{11}\,h_{22} - h_{12}h_{21}}{h_{21}}\right)V_2 + \left(-\frac{h_{11}}{h_{21}}\right)(-I_2)$$

or $$V_1 = \left(-\frac{h_{11}\,h_{22} - h_{12}\,h_{21}}{h_{21}}\right)V_2 - \left(-\frac{h_{11}}{h_{21}}\right)(I_2) \qquad ...(11.80)$$

Comparing equations (11.79) and (11.80) with the original *ABCD* parameter equations, we observe

$$A = \left(-\frac{h_{11}\,h_{22} - h_{12}\,h_{21}}{h_{21}}\right),\ B = -\left(\frac{h_{11}}{h_{21}}\right)$$
$$C = \left(-\frac{h_{22}}{h_{21}}\right),\ D = \left(-\frac{1}{h_{21}}\right) \qquad ...(11.81)$$

11.11.10 *h*-parameter in Terms of *Z*-parameters

Utilising the governing equation

$$V_2 = Z_{21}\,I_1 + Z_{22}\,I_2$$

or the *Z*-parameter representation, we can write

$$I_2 = \left(-\frac{Z_{21}}{Z_{22}}\right)I_1 + \left(\frac{1}{Z_{22}}\right)V_2 \qquad ...(11.82)$$

Also from the other governing equation

$V_1 = Z_{11}\,I_1 + Z_{12}\,I_2$, which can be written as

$$V_1 = Z_{11}\,I_1 + Z_{12}\left[\left(-\frac{Z_{21}}{Z_{22}}\right)I_1 + \left(\frac{1}{Z_{22}}\right)V_2\right]$$

$$= \left(\frac{Z_{11}\,Z_{22} - Z_{12}\,Z_{21}}{Z_{22}}\right)I_1 + \left(\frac{Z_{12}}{Z_{22}}\right)V_2 \qquad ...(11.83)$$

Comparing these two equations (11.82) and (11.83) with the governing equations of the *h*-parameter network,

$$h_{11} = \frac{Z_{11}\,Z_{22} - Z_{21}\,Z_{12}}{Z_{22}}$$

$$h_{12} = \frac{Z_{12}}{Z_{22}} \qquad ...(11.84)$$

$$h_{21} = -\frac{Z_{21}}{Z_{22}}$$

and $$h_{22} = \frac{1}{Z_{22}}.$$

11.11.11 *h*-parameters in Terms of the *Y*-parameters

The governing equations of the *Y*-parameter equations are

$$I_1 = Y_{11}\,V_1 + Y_{12}\,V_2$$

and $$I_2 = Y_{21}\,V_1 + Y_{22}\,V_2$$

The first equation gives

$$V_1 = \left(\frac{1}{Y_{11}}\right)I_1 + \left(-\frac{Y_{12}}{Y_{11}}\right)V_2 \qquad ...(11.85)$$

Thus the second equation becomes

$$I_2 = Y_{21}\,V_1 + Y_{22}\,V_2$$

$$= Y_{21}\left[\left(\frac{1}{Y_{11}}\right)I_1 - \left(\frac{Y_{12}}{Y_{11}}\right)V_2\right] + Y_{22}V_2$$

$$= \left(\frac{Y_{21}}{Y_{11}}\right)I_1 + \left(\frac{Y_{11}\,Y_{22} - Y_{12}\,Y_{21}}{Y_{11}}\right)V_2 \qquad ...(11.86)$$

Comparing equations (11.85) and (11.86) with the original *h*-parameter equations,

$$h_{11} = \frac{1}{Y_{11}}$$

$$h_{12} = -\frac{Y_{12}}{Y_{11}}$$

$$h_{21} = \frac{Y_{21}}{Y_{11}} \qquad ...(11.87)$$

$$h_{22} = \frac{Y_{11}\,Y_{22} - Y_{12}\,Y_{21}}{Y_{11}}$$

11.11.12 *h*-parameter in Terms of *ABCD* parameters

The *ABCD* parameter equations are given by

$$I_1 = CV_2 - DI_2$$

giving $$I_2 = \left(-\frac{1}{D}\right)I_1 + \left(\frac{C}{D}\right)V_2 \qquad ...(11.88)$$

and $$V_1 = AV_2 - BI_2$$

giving $$V_1 = AV_2 - B\left[\left(-\frac{1}{D}\right)I_1 + \left(\frac{C}{D}\right)V_2\right]$$

$$= \left(\frac{B}{D}\right)I_1 + \left(\frac{AD - BC}{D}\right)V_2 \qquad ...(11.89)$$

Comparing these two equations (11.88 and 11.89) with the h-parameter equations,

$$h_{11} = \left(\frac{B}{D}\right)$$

$$h_{12} = \left(\frac{AD - BC}{D}\right)$$

$$h_{21} = \left(-\frac{1}{D}\right)$$

$$h_{22} = \left(\frac{C}{D}\right)$$

11.12 EXPRESSION OF INPUT AND OUTPUT IMPEDANCES IN TERMS OF TWO PORT PARAMETERS

11.12.1 Input and Output Impedances in Terms of Z-parameters

Rewriting the Z-parameter equations,

$$V_1 = Z_{11} I_1 + Z_{12} I_2 \quad ...(11.90)$$

$$V_2 = Z_{21} I_1 + Z_{22} I_2 \quad ...[11.90(a)]$$

However, in actual circuit, the load current flows outwards from the network, the load impedance being connected at output port, and hence

$$V_2 = (-I_2) Z_R \quad ...[11.90(b)]$$

Z_R being the load impedance. Utilising equation [11.90(*b*)] in [11.90(*a*)],

$$-I_2 Z_R = Z_{21} I_1 + Z_{22} I_2$$

or $$I_2 = -\frac{Z_{21}}{Z_{22} + Z_R} I_1 \quad ...[11.90(c)]$$

Substituting the value of I_2 from equation [11.90(*c*)] in 11.90

$$V_1 = Z_{11} I_1 + Z_{12}\left[-\frac{Z_{21}}{Z_{22} + Z_R}\right] I_1$$

or $$\frac{V_1}{I_1} = Z_{in} = \frac{Z_{11} Z_{22} - Z_{12} Z_{21} + Z_{11} Z_R}{Z_{22} + Z_R} \quad ...(11.91)$$

Equation (11.91) represents the general expression for *input impedance* of a two port network in terms of Z-parameters.

Now, assuming open circuit condition at output, $Z_R = \infty$.

Thus,

$$Z_{in} = \operatorname*{Lt}_{Z_R \to \infty} \frac{Z_{11} Z_{22} - Z_{12} Z_{21} + Z_{11} Z_R}{Z_{22} + Z_R}$$

$$= \operatorname*{Lt}_{Z_R \to \infty} \frac{\dfrac{Z_{11} Z_{22}}{Z_R} - \dfrac{Z_{12} Z_{21}}{Z_R} + Z_{11}}{\dfrac{Z_{22}}{Z_R} + 1} = Z_{11}$$

Hence, for an *open-circuited* condition, the input impedance looking through the input terminals towards the network (Z_{in}) is only Z_{11}.

On the other hand, when the output port is short-circuited *i.e.*, $Z_R = 0$, the input impedance (Z_{in}) looking through the input sides to the network is given by

$$Z_{in} = \frac{Z_{11} Z_{22} - Z_{12} Z_{21} + Z_{11} \times 0}{Z_{22} + 0}$$

i.e., $$Z_{in} = \frac{Z_{11} Z_{22} - Z_{12} Z_{21}}{Z_{22}}$$

Under *short-circuited* output condition,

$$Z_{in} = \frac{Z_{11} Z_{22} - Z_{12} Z_{21}}{Z_{22}}$$

To determine the *output impedance*, the load (Z_R) is connected to the input side and the input current I_1 flows outwards from the network in the actual circuit.

Thus, $V_1 = (-I_1) Z_R$

This gives from equation (11.90),

$$-I_1 Z_R = Z_{11} I_1 + Z_{12} I_2$$

or $$I_1 = -\frac{Z_{12}}{Z_{11} + Z_R} . I_2 \quad ...(11.92)$$

Substituting the expression of I_1 in equation [11.90(*a*)]

$$V_2 = Z_{21}\left(-\frac{Z_{12}}{Z_{11} + Z_R}\right) I_2 + Z_{22} I_2$$

or $$\frac{V_2}{I_2} = Z_{out} = \left(\frac{Z_{11} Z_{22} - Z_{12} Z_{21} + Z_{22} Z_R}{(Z_{11} + Z_R)}\right)$$

However, if the input is open-circuited, $Z_R = \infty$.

CHAPTER 11

Thus, $Z_{out} = \underset{Z_R \to \infty}{\text{Lt}} \dfrac{Z_{11} Z_{22} - Z_{12} Z_{21} + Z_{22} Z_R}{Z_{11} + Z_R}$

$$= \frac{\dfrac{Z_{11} Z_{22}}{Z_R} - \dfrac{Z_{12} Z_{21}}{Z_R} + Z_{22}}{(Z_{11}/Z_R)+1} = Z_{22} \quad \text{...[11.92}(a)\text{]}$$

and if the input is short-circuited,

$$Z_R = 0$$

$$\text{Then, } Z_{out} = \frac{Z_{11} Z_{22} - Z_{12} Z_{21}}{Z_{11}} \quad \text{...(11.93)}$$

11.12.2 Input and Output Impedance in Terms of Transmission Parameters

The transmission parameter equations are given by

$$V_1 = AV_2 - BI_2$$

and $\quad I_1 = CV_2 - DI_2$

Assuming the load impedance Z_R at the output side the direction of I_2 is towards the load.

This gives,

$$V_2 = (-I_2) Z_R \quad \text{...(11.94)}$$

Thus from the second equation of *ABCD* parameter equations, we can write

$$I_1 = C(-I_2 Z_R) - DI_2$$

or $\quad I_1 = -I_2 (CZ_R + D)$

or $\quad I_2 = -\dfrac{I_1}{(CZ_R + D)} \quad$ ...(11.95)

Substituting the value of I_2 from equation (11.95) in the first expression of *ABCD* parameter representation,

$$V_1 = AV_2 - B\left(-\frac{I_1}{CZ_R + D}\right)$$

or $\quad = A(-I_2 Z_R) + \dfrac{BI_1}{CZ_R + D}$

$$= +\frac{AI_1}{CZ_R + D} . Z_R + \frac{BI_1}{CZ_R + D}$$

or $\quad V_1 = I_1 \left(\dfrac{AZ_R + B}{CZ_R + D}\right)$

$$\therefore \quad \frac{V_1}{I_1} = Z_{in} = \frac{AZ_R + B}{CZ_R + D}$$

For open-circuited output,

$$Z_R = \infty.$$

$$\therefore \quad Z_{in} = \underset{Z_R \to \infty}{\text{Lt}} \frac{(AZ_R + B)}{(CZ_R + D)} = \frac{A}{C} \quad \text{...(11.96)}$$

and for short-circuited output,

$$Z_R = 0.$$

This gives

$$Z_{in} = \frac{B}{D} \quad \text{...(11.97)}$$

Thus the *input impedance* (Z_{in}) looking from the input side is A/C when the output is *open-circuited* and is B/D when the output is *short-circuited.*

To determine the *output impedance,* the load is assumed to be connected at the input side such that the current I_1 flows outwards from the network.

Thus $\quad V_1 = -I_1 Z_R$

Substitution of V_1 in the transmission parameter network equation,

$$-I_1 Z_R = AV_2 - BI_2 \quad \text{...(11.98)}$$

Also, $\quad I_1 = CV_2 - DI_2 \quad$ ...(11.99)

Division of eqn. (11.98) by (11.99)

$$-Z_R = \frac{AV_2 - BI_2}{CV_2 - DI_2}$$

or $\quad -Z_R (CV_2) + Z_R (DI_2) = AV_2 - BI_2$

or $\quad -V_2 (CZ_R + A) = -I_2 (DZ_R + B)$

$$\therefore \quad \frac{V_2}{I_2} = Z_{out} = \frac{DZ_R + B}{CZ_R + A} \quad \text{...(11.100)}$$

When the input port is *open-circuited,*

$$Z_R = \infty$$

$$\therefore \quad Z_{out} = \underset{Z_R \to \infty}{\text{Lt}} \frac{DZ_R + B}{CZ_R + A} = \underset{Z_R \to \infty}{\text{Lt}} \frac{D + \dfrac{B}{Z_R}}{C + \dfrac{A}{Z_R}}$$

or $\quad Z_{out} = \dfrac{D}{C} \quad$ ...(11.101)

On the other hand, if the input port is *short-circuited,*

$$Z_R = 0$$

$$\therefore \quad Z_{out} = \frac{D \times 0 + B}{C \times 0 + A} = \frac{B}{A} \quad \text{...(11.102)}$$

11.12.3 Input and Output Impedance in Terms of Hybrid Parameters

The hybrid parameter equations are given by

$$V_1 = h_{11} I_1 + h_{12} V_2 \quad ...(11.103)$$

and

$$I_2 = h_{21} I_1 + h_{22} V_2 \quad ...(11.104)$$

Assuming the output impedance Z_R to be connected at the output,

$$V_2 = -I_2 Z_R$$

Substituting the value of V_2 in equation (11.104)

$$I_2 = h_{21} I_1 + h_{22}(-I_2 Z_R)$$

or

$$I_2 = \frac{h_{21}}{1+h_{22} Z_R} . I_1 \quad ...(11.105)$$

Again, substitution of value of I_2 from (11.105) in (11.104)

$$\frac{h_{21}}{1+h_{22} Z_R} . I_1 = h_{21} I_1 + h_{22} V_2$$

or

$$h_{22} V_2 = I_1\left(-h_{21} + \frac{h_{21}}{1+h_{22} Z_R}\right)$$

$$= -I_1 . \frac{h_{21} h_{22} Z_R}{1+h_{22} Z_R}$$

or

$$V_2 = -\frac{h_{21} Z_R I_1}{1+h_{22} Z_R} \quad ...(11.106)$$

Substituting the value of V_2 from (11.106) in (11.103)

$$V_1 = h_{11} I_1 - h_{12} \frac{h_{21} Z_R I_1}{1+h_{22} Z_R}$$

or,

$$Z_{in} = \frac{V_1}{I_1} = h_{11} - h_{12} \frac{h_{21} Z_R}{1+h_{22} Z_R}$$

If the output is *open-circuited*, $Z_R = \infty$. This gives

$$Z_{in} = \frac{h_{11} h_{22} - h_{12} h_{21}}{h_{22}}$$

On the other hand, if the output is short-circuited, $Z_R = 0$.

This gives

$$Z_{in} = h_{11} \quad ...(11.107)$$

The output impedance can be obtained by connecting the load impedance Z_R at the input.

Thus $V_1 = -I_1 Z_R$

From the hybrid parameter equation

$$V_1 = h_{11} I_1 + h_{12} V_2,$$

we then get

$$-I_1 Z_R = h_{11} I_1 + h_{12} V_2$$

or

$$-I_1(Z_R + h_{11}) = h_{12} V_2$$

or

$$I_1 = -\frac{h_{12}}{(h_{11}+Z_R)} . V_2$$

Then, from equation $I_2 = h_{21} I_1 + h_{22} V_2$,

$$I_2 = h_{21}\left(-\frac{h_{12}}{(h_{11}+Z_R)}\right) V_2 + h_{22} V_2$$

$$= V_2\left[h_{22} - \frac{h_{12} h_{21}}{(h_{11}+Z_R)}\right]$$

$$\therefore (V_2/I_2) = Z_{out} = \frac{1}{h_{22} - \dfrac{h_{12} h_{21}}{(h_{11}+Z_R)}}$$

$$\therefore \quad Z_{out} = \frac{h_{11}+Z_R}{(h_{11} h_{22} - h_{12} h_{21}) + h_{22} Z_R} \quad ...(11.108)$$

EXAMPLE 11.38 *Find the open circuit impedance parameter of the circuit shown in Fig. E11.56. Also find the Y parameters.*

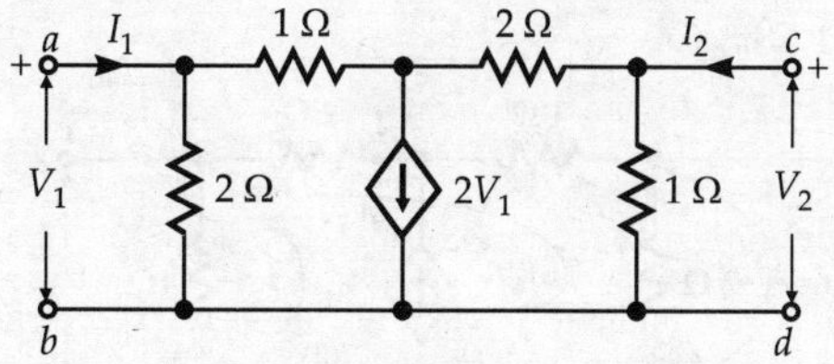

Fig. E11.56

SOLUTION. Assuming the output port (port *cd*) to the open-circuited, $I_2 = 0$. The circuit configuration alongwith loop currents has been shown in Fig. E11.57.

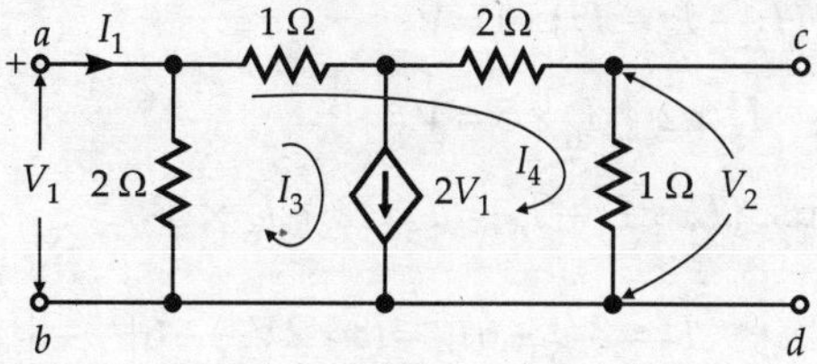

Fig. E11.57

Here,

$$I_4 \times 1 = V_2\ ;\ (I_1 - I_3 - I_4)2 = V_1\ ;$$

$$I_3 \times 1 + I_4 \times 4 = V_1.$$

Thus,

$$2I_1 - 2I_3 - 2I_4 = I_3 + 4I_4$$

or, $I_1 = 1.5\, I_3 + 3\, I_4 = 1.5 \times 2V_1 + 3 \times V_2$

$$= 3V_1 + 3\left(-\frac{1}{4} V_1\right) = \frac{9}{4} V_1.$$

$$\left[\because V_1 = 4I_4 + I_3 = 4V_2 + 2V_1 \text{ or } V_2 = -\frac{1}{4} V_1\right]$$

$$\therefore \quad \frac{V_1}{I_1} = Z_{11} = \frac{4}{9}\,\Omega.$$

Also, $(2 + 1)\, I_4 + I_3 + V_2 = V_1$

or $3I_4 + I_3 + V_2 = V_1$

or $\left(\frac{V_2}{1}\right)3 + I_3 + V_2 = V_1 \qquad \left[\because I_4 = \frac{V_2}{1\Omega}\right]$

or $4V_2 + 2V_1 = V_1 \qquad [\because I_3 = 2\, V_1]$

or $4V_2 = -V_1 = -\frac{4}{9} I_1 \qquad [\because 4I_1 = 9V_1]$

or $Z_{21} = \left.\frac{V_2}{I_1}\right|_{I_2 = 0} = -\frac{1}{9}\,\Omega.$

Let us now open the circuit of Fig. E11.58 and apply voltage at input port (port *a-b*). With $I_1 = 0$, the circuit under this condition is redrawn in Fig. E11.58.

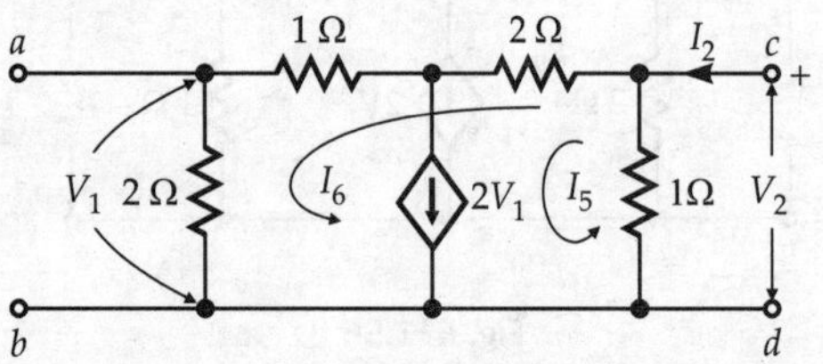

Fig. E11.58

Here, $I_5 = 2V_1; 2 \times I_6 = V_1$

Also utilising KVL,

$$(I_2 - I_5 - I_6) \times 1 = V_2$$

and $I_5 \times 2 + I_6 \times 5 = V_2$

Thus, $(I_2 - I_5 - I_6) = I_5 \times 2 + I_6 \times 5$

or $I_2 = 3I_5 + 6I_6 = (3 \times 2V_1) + 6\left(\frac{V_1}{2}\right)$

$$[\because I_5 = 2V_1 \text{ and } 2I_6 = V_1]$$

$$= 6V_1 + 3V_1 = 9V_1$$

$$\therefore \quad Z_{12} = \left.\frac{V_1}{I_2}\right|_{I_1 = 0} = \frac{1}{9} \text{ ohm}$$

Again, $5I_6 + 2I_5 = V_2$

or $\frac{5}{2} V_1 + 4V_1 = V_2$

$$[\because I_5 = 2V_1 \text{ and } 2I_6 = V_1]$$

or $\frac{5}{2} \times \frac{I_2}{9} + 4\frac{I_2}{9} = V_2 \qquad \left[\because \frac{V_1}{I_2} = \frac{1}{9}\right]$

or $\frac{13}{18} I_2 = V_2$

or $\left.\frac{V_2}{I_2}\right|_{I_1 = 0} = Z_{22} = \frac{13}{18}$ ohm

$\therefore$ Z parameters are given by,

$$Z = \begin{bmatrix} (4/9) & (1/9) \\ (-1/9) & (13/18) \end{bmatrix}$$

i.e., $\text{Det}\,[Z] = \left(\frac{4}{9}\right)\left(\frac{13}{18}\right) + \left(\frac{1}{9}\right)\left(\frac{1}{9}\right) = \frac{1}{3}$

Thus Y parameters are given as

$$Y_{11} = \frac{Z_{22}}{\text{Det}\,[Z]} = \frac{\mathbf{13/18}}{\mathbf{1/3}} = \frac{\mathbf{13}}{\mathbf{6}} \textbf{ mho.}$$

$$Y_{21} = -\frac{Z_{21}}{\text{Det}\,[Z]} = \frac{1/9}{1/3} = \frac{\mathbf{1}}{\mathbf{3}} \textbf{ mho}$$

$$Y_{12} = -\frac{Z_{12}}{\text{Det}\,[Z]} = -\frac{\mathbf{(1/9)}}{\mathbf{1/3}} = -\frac{\mathbf{1}}{\mathbf{3}} \textbf{ mho}$$

$$Y_{22} = \frac{Z_{11}}{\text{Det}\,[Z]} = \frac{\mathbf{4/9}}{\mathbf{1/3}} = \frac{\mathbf{4}}{\mathbf{3}} \textbf{ mho.}$$

EXAMPLE 11.39 *The Z-parameters of a circuit are given by*

$$\begin{bmatrix} 4 & 1 \\ 3 & 3 \end{bmatrix}$$

Obtain the transmission parameters.

SOLUTION. The Z parameters equations are given by

$$V_1 = 4I_1 + I_2 \qquad ...(i)$$

$$V_2 = 3I_1 + 3I_2 \qquad ...(ii)$$

From equation (*ii*),

$$I_1 = \frac{V_2}{3} + (-I_2) \qquad ...(iii)$$

and from equation (*i*)

$$V_1 = 4\left[\frac{V_2}{3} + (-I_2)\right] + I_2$$

or $V_1 = \frac{4}{3} V_2 + 3(-I_2) \qquad ...(iv)$

Rewriting the equations (*iii*) and (*iv*),

$$\begin{bmatrix} V_1 \\ I_1 \end{bmatrix} = \begin{bmatrix} \frac{4}{3} & 3 \\ \frac{1}{3} & 1 \end{bmatrix} \begin{bmatrix} V_2 \\ -I_2 \end{bmatrix}$$

This gives,

$$\begin{bmatrix} A & B \\ C & D \end{bmatrix} = \begin{bmatrix} \frac{4}{3} & 3 \\ \frac{1}{3} & 1 \end{bmatrix}.$$

EXAMPLE 11.40 *In the network shown in Fig. E11.59 find the transmission parameters.*

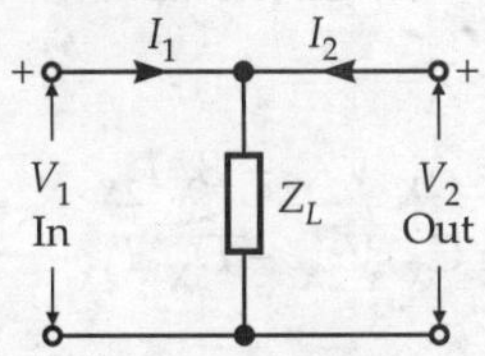

Fig. E11.59

SOLUTION. The loop becomes

$$V_1 = Z_L\,(I_1 + I_2) = Z_L\, I_1 + Z_L\, I_2$$

$$V_2 = Z_L\,(I_1 + I_2) = Z_L\, I_1 + Z_L\, I_2$$

or

$$\begin{bmatrix} V_1 \\ V_2 \end{bmatrix} = \begin{bmatrix} Z_L & Z_L \\ Z_L & Z_L \end{bmatrix} \begin{bmatrix} I_1 \\ I_2 \end{bmatrix}$$

Hence, the Z parameters become

$$Z_L \begin{bmatrix} 1 & 1 \\ 1 & 1 \end{bmatrix}$$

Hence the transmission parameters can be written as

$$\frac{1}{Z_{21}} \begin{bmatrix} Z_{11} & \Delta Z \\ 1 & Z_{22} \end{bmatrix} = \begin{bmatrix} 1 & 0 \\ 1/Z_L & 1 \end{bmatrix}$$

where $\Delta Z = Z_{11}\, Z_{22} - Z_{12}\, Z_{21} = 0$.

EXAMPLE 11.41 *Fig. E11.60 represents a two port network feeding an impedance load Z_L. Determine the transmission parameters, voltage gain, output and input impedances.*

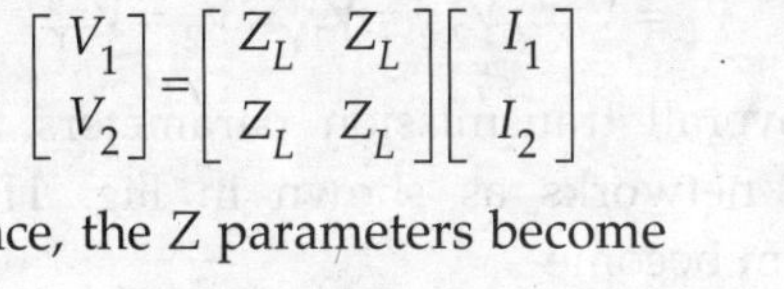

Fig. E11.60

SOLUTION. The $ABCD$ parameters of the two port network are given by $\begin{bmatrix} A_1 & B_1 \\ C_1 & D_1 \end{bmatrix}$ while those for the load Z_L are given by $\begin{bmatrix} 1 & 0 \\ 1/Z_L & 1 \end{bmatrix}$.

As both the networks are in cascade, thus the transmission parameters are obtained as

$$\begin{bmatrix} A & B \\ C & D \end{bmatrix} = \begin{bmatrix} A_1 & B_1 \\ C_1 & D_1 \end{bmatrix} \begin{bmatrix} 1 & 0 \\ 1/Z_L & 1 \end{bmatrix}$$

$$= \begin{bmatrix} A_1 + B_1 Z_L & B_1 \\ C_1 + D_1/Z_L & D_1 \end{bmatrix}$$

$$\therefore \quad A = A_1 + B_1/Z_L$$

$$B = B_1$$

$$C = C_1 + D_1/Z_1$$

$$D = D_1.$$

Voltage gain is given by

$$\frac{V_2}{V_1} = \frac{1}{A} = \frac{1}{A_1 + B_1/Z_L}$$

The input impedance is given by

$$Z_1 = \left.\frac{V_1}{I_1}\right|_{I_2=0} = \frac{A}{C}$$

$$= (A_1 + B_1/Z_L)/(C_1 + D_1/Z_L).$$

The output impedance,

$$Z_2 = \left.\frac{V_2}{I_2}\right|_{V_1=0} = \frac{B}{A} = \frac{B_1}{A_1 + B_1/Z_L} = \frac{B_1}{A_1}$$

$$[\because Z_L = \infty]$$

11.13 DIFFERENT TYPES OF INTERCONNECTIONS OF TWO PORT NETWORKS

11.13.1 Series Connection

The open circuit impedance parameter is highly useful in characterising the *series connected* two port networks. Though here only two numbers of two port networks are shown to be connected in series, this result can be generalised for any number of two port network in series.

Let network A and B be the two port networks connected in series (Ref. Fig. 11.27).

CHAPTER 11

All input and output currents and voltages have been shown in Fig. 11.27.

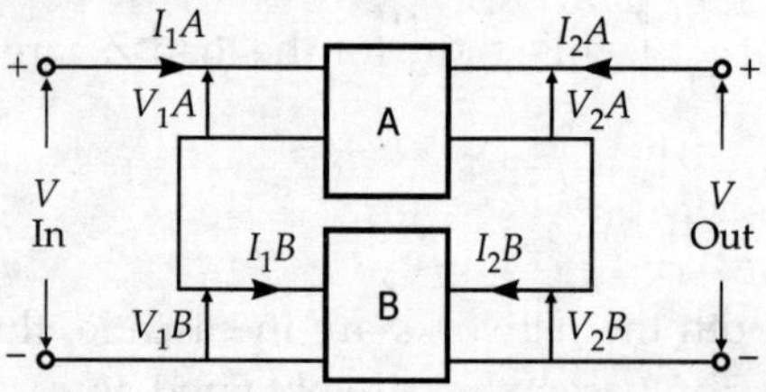

Fig. 11.27 Series connection of two 2-port networks.

For network A,

$$V_{1A} = Z_{11A}\, I_{1A} + Z_{12A}\, I_{2A}$$

$$V_{2A} = Z_{21A}\, I_{1A} + Z_{22A}\, I_{2A}$$

and for network B,

$$V_{1B} = Z_{11B}\, I_{1B} + Z_{12B}\, I_{2B}$$

$$V_{2B} = Z_{21B}\, I_{1B} + Z_{22B}\, I_{2B}$$

Referring to Fig. 11.27, the interconnection results

$$I_1 \equiv I_{1A} \equiv I_{1B}$$

$$I_2 \equiv I_{2A} \equiv I_{2B}$$

$$V_2 = V_{2A} + V_{2B}$$

However,

$$\begin{aligned} V_1 &= V_{1A} + V_{1B} \\ &= (Z_{11A} I_{1A} + Z_{12A} I_{2A}) + Z_{11B} I_{1B} + Z_{12B} I_{2B} \\ &= I_1 (Z_{11A} + Z_{11B}) + I_2 (Z_{12A} + Z_{12B}) \end{aligned}$$

and $V_2 = V_{2A} + V_{2B}$

$$= (Z_{21A} I_{1A} + Z_{22A} I_{2A}) + (Z_{21B} I_{1B} + Z_{22B} I_{2B})$$

or $V_2 = I_1 (Z_{21A} + Z_{21B}) + I_2 (Z_{22A} + Z_{22B})$

Thus we get, for the series connected two numbers two port networks,

$$V_1 = (Z_{11A} + Z_{11B})\, I_1 + (Z_{12A} + Z_{12B})\, I_2$$

$$V_2 = (Z_{21A} + Z_{21B})\, I_1 + (Z_{22A} + Z_{22B})\, I_2$$

or, in matrix form,

$$\begin{bmatrix} V_1 \\ V_2 \end{bmatrix} = \begin{bmatrix} Z_{11A} + Z_{11B} & Z_{12A} + Z_{12B} \\ Z_{21A} + Z_{21B} & Z_{22A} + Z_{22B} \end{bmatrix} \begin{bmatrix} I_1 \\ I_2 \end{bmatrix} . \qquad ..(11.109)$$

Thus it has been observed that the overall Z parameter matrix for series connected two port networks is simply the sum of Z matrices of each individual network.

11.13.2 Cascade Connection

ABCD parameters are highly useful in characterising *cascaded* two port networks.

In Fig. 11.28 let X and Y be two networks connected in cascade. The results may be generalised for any number of networks.

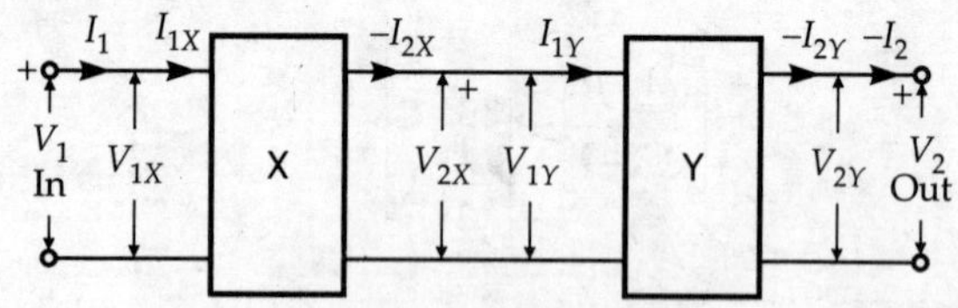

Fig. 11.28 Cascade connected two numbers two port network.

For network X,

$$V_{1X} = A_X\, V_{2X} - B_X I_{2X}$$

$$I_{IX} = C_X\, V_{2X} - D_X\, I_{2X}$$

and for network Y,

$$V_{1Y} = A_Y\, V_{2Y} - B_Y I_{2Y}$$

$$I_{1Y} = C_Y V_{2Y} - D_Y I_{2Y}$$

For the cascade connection,

$$I_1 = I_{1X}\, ; -I_{2X} = I_{1Y}\, ; I_2 = I_{2Y}$$

$$V_1 = V_{IX}\, ; V_{2X} = V_{1Y}\, ; V_2 = V_{2Y}$$

The overall transmission parameters for the combined networks as shown in Fig. 11.28, in matrix form become

$$\begin{aligned} \begin{bmatrix} V_1 \\ I_1 \end{bmatrix} = \begin{bmatrix} V_{1X} \\ I_{1X} \end{bmatrix} &= \begin{bmatrix} A_X & B_X \\ C_X & D_X \end{bmatrix} \begin{bmatrix} V_{2X} \\ -I_{2X} \end{bmatrix} \\ &= \begin{bmatrix} A_X & B_X \\ C_X & D_X \end{bmatrix} \begin{bmatrix} V_{1Y} \\ I_{1Y} \end{bmatrix} \\ &= \begin{bmatrix} A_X & B_X \\ C_X & D_X \end{bmatrix} \begin{bmatrix} A_Y & B_Y \\ C_Y & D_Y \end{bmatrix} \begin{bmatrix} V_{2Y} \\ -I_{2Y} \end{bmatrix} \\ &= \begin{bmatrix} A_X & B_X \\ C_X & D_X \end{bmatrix} \begin{bmatrix} A_Y & B_Y \\ C_Y & D_Y \end{bmatrix} \begin{bmatrix} V_Y \\ -I_Y \end{bmatrix} \\ &= \begin{bmatrix} A & B \\ C & D \end{bmatrix} \begin{bmatrix} V_Y \\ -I_Y \end{bmatrix} \qquad ...(11.110) \end{aligned}$$

where, $\begin{bmatrix} A & B \\ C & D \end{bmatrix} = \begin{bmatrix} A_X & B_X \\ C_X & D_X \end{bmatrix} \begin{bmatrix} A_Y & B_Y \\ D_Y & D_Y \end{bmatrix}$

The overall ABCD parameter network matrix for cascaded network is then the matrix product of ABCD matrices of individual network.

11.13.3 Parallel Connection

Let network A and B be connected in *parallel* as shown in Fig. 11.29. Y-parameter representation is very much useful.

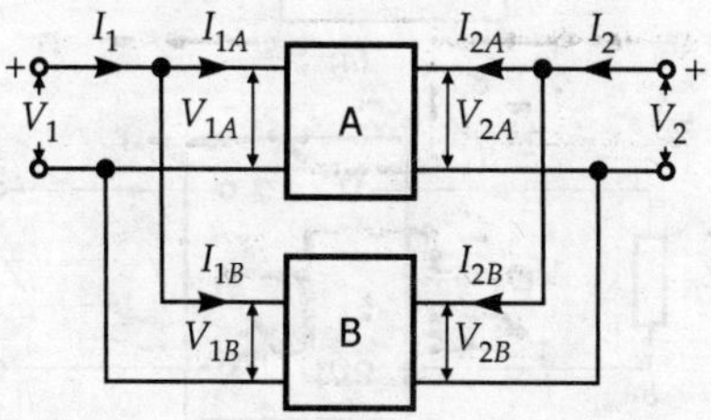

Fig. 11.29 Parallel connection of two 2-port networks.

For network A,

$$I_{1A} = Y_{11A}\, V_{1A} + Y_{12A}\, V_{2A}$$
$$I_{2A} = Y_{21A}\, V_{1A} + Y_{22A}\, V_{2A}$$

and for network B,

$$I_{1B} = Y_{11B}\, V_{1B} + Y_{12B}\, V_{2B}$$
$$I_{2B} = Y_{21B}\, V_{1B} + Y_{22B}\, V_{2B}$$

For the parallel connection as shown in the figure,

$$V_1 = V_{1A} = V_{1B};\ V_2 = V_{2A} = V_{2B}$$
$$I_1 = I_{1A} + I_{1B}\ ;\ I_2 = I_{2A} + I_{2B}$$

Thus,

$$\begin{aligned} I_1 &= I_{1A} + I_{1B} \\ &= (Y_{11A}V_{1A} + Y_{12A}V_{2A}) + (Y_{11B}V_{1B} + Y_{12B}V_{2B}) \\ &= (Y_{11A} + Y_{11B})\, V_1 + (Y_{12A} + Y_{12B})\, V_2 \end{aligned}$$

$$\begin{aligned} I_2 &= I_{2A} + I_{2B} \\ &= (Y_{21A}V_{1A} + Y_{22A}V_{1B}) + (Y_{21B}V_{1B} + Y_{22B}V_{2B}) \\ &= (Y_{21A} + Y_{21B})\, V_1 + (Y_{22A} + Y_{22B})\, V_2 \end{aligned}$$

Thus we finally obtain

$$I_1 = (Y_{11A} + Y_{11B})\, V_1 + (Y_{12A} + Y_{12B})\, V_2$$
$$I_2 = (Y_{21A} + Y_{21B})\, V_1 + (Y_{22A} + Y_{22B})\, V_2$$

Thus, in matrix form, the combined network parameter equations become,

$$\begin{bmatrix} I_1 \\ I_1 \end{bmatrix} = \begin{bmatrix} Y_{11A} + Y_{11B} & Y_{12A} + Y_{12B} \\ Y_{21A} + Y_{21B} & Y_{22A} + Y_{22B} \end{bmatrix} \begin{bmatrix} V_1 \\ V_2 \end{bmatrix} \qquad ...(11.111)$$

This result may be generalised for any number of Y parameter network paralleling. *The overall Y parameter matrix is then simply the summation of Y matrices of each individual two port network.*

11.14 OPEN CIRCUIT AND SHORT CIRCUIT IMPEDANCES AND THE *ABCD* CONSTANTS

Let us consider the following relationships for the two port network of Fig. 11.30.

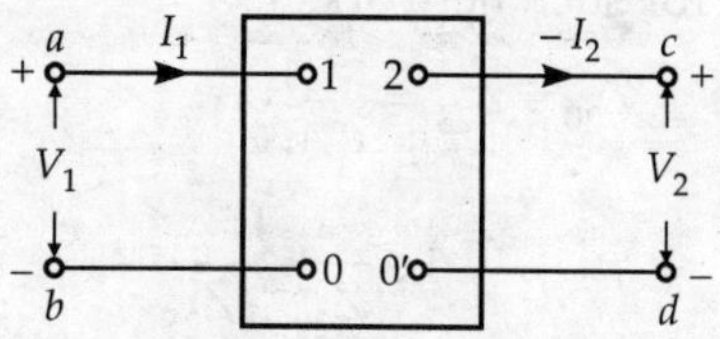

Fig. 11.30 *ABCD* constants in terms of o.c and s.c impedances.

$$V_1 = AV_2 - BI_2 \qquad ...(11.112)$$
$$I_1 = CV_2 - DI_2 \qquad ...(11.113)$$

With receiving end (c-d) open-circuited, $I_2 = 0$. So that equations (11.112) and (11.113) become $V_1 = AV_2$ and $I_1 = CV_2$

i.e.,
$$\frac{V_1}{I_1} = \frac{A}{C} = Z_{10} \qquad ...(11.114)$$

where Z_{10} is the impedance measured at end a-b (sending end) with end c-d (receiving end) open.

Similarly, if receiving end is short-circuited

$$V_2 = 0$$

and
$$\frac{V_1}{I_1} = \frac{B}{D} = Z_{1S} \qquad ...(11.115)$$

where Z_{1S} refers to the impedance measured at end a-b with end c-d short-circuited. (The suffix S refers to the short circuit).

Now if the network is viewed from the opposite end, Eqn. (11.112) and (11.113) become respectively

$$Z_{20} = \frac{D}{C} \qquad ...(11.116)$$

and
$$Z_{2S} = \frac{B}{A} \qquad ...(11.117)$$

where Z_{20} is the impedance measured at end c-d with the other end, (*i.e.,* end a-b) open and Z_{2S} is the impedance measured at end c-d with end a-b shorted.

From Eqns. (11.114) to (11.117) the ratio of short-circuit to open-circuit impedance at the two ends is

$$\frac{Z_{1S}}{Z_{10}} = \frac{Z_{2S}}{Z_{20}} = \frac{B}{D} \cdot \frac{C}{A} \qquad ...(11.118)$$

In order to find $ABCD$ constants from $o.c$ and $s.c$ impedances, from Eqns. (11.116) and (11.117)

$$Z_{20} - Z_{2S} = \frac{D}{C} - \frac{B}{A} = \frac{AD - BC}{CA}$$

Since for reciprocal networks $AD - BC = 1$, therefore, for such networks

$$Z_{20} - Z_{2S} = \frac{1}{CA}$$

or
$$CA = \frac{1}{Z_{20} - Z_{2S}} \qquad ...(11.119)$$

Also from Eqn. (11.114), $\frac{A}{C} = Z_{10}$

Multiplying these two equations (11.119 and 11.114) and taking square root

$$A = \pm \sqrt{\frac{Z_{10}}{Z_{20} - Z_{2S}}} \qquad ...(11.120)$$

$$C = \frac{A}{Z_{10}} = \pm \sqrt{\frac{1}{Z_{10}(Z_{20} - Z_{2S})}}$$

Thus
$$B = Z_{2S}\, A = \pm Z_{2S} \sqrt{\frac{Z_{10}}{Z_{20} - Z_{2S}}}$$

and
$$D = \frac{B}{Z_{1S}} = \frac{Z_{2S}}{Z_{1S}} A = \frac{Z_{20}}{Z_{10}} A \qquad ...(11.121)$$

$$= \pm Z_{20} \sqrt{\frac{1}{Z_{10}(Z_{20} - Z_{2S})}}$$

[The ambiguity of sign in eqns. (11.120 and 11.121) is inherent since the impedances will not distinguish between two circuits which differ only in polarity.]

11.15 IMAGE IMPEDANCES IN TERMS OF *ABCD* PARAMETERS

In a two-port network, if the impedance at input port with Z_{i2} at output port be Z_{i1} and simultaneously the impedance looking back from output port with Z_{i1} at input port (Fig. 11.31) is Z_{i2} then Z_{i1} and Z_{i2}, are termed as the "image" impedances of the network.

We can conveniently express the image impedances in terms of $ABCD$ constants. In Fig. 11.31,

$$Z_{i1} = \frac{V_1}{I_1} = \frac{AV_2 - BI_2}{CV_2 - DI_2}$$

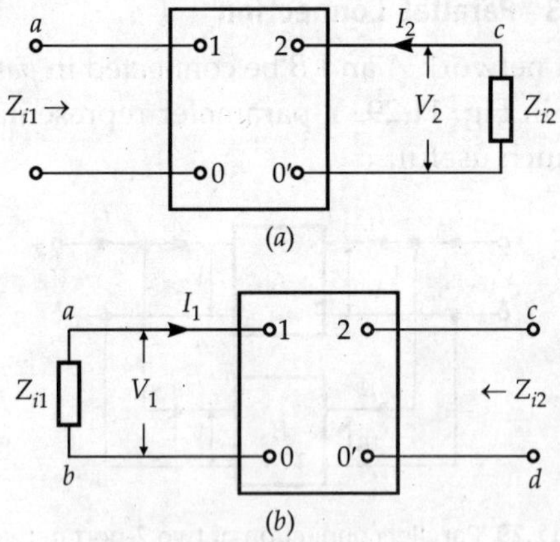

Fig. 11.31 Image impedances.

But as $\frac{V_2}{-I_2} = Z_{i2}$

therefore, $V_2 = -Z_{i2}\, I_2$

so that
$$Z_{i1} = \frac{-AZ_{i2} - B}{-CZ_{i2} - D} = \frac{AZ_{i2} + B}{CZ_{i2} + D} \qquad ...(11.122)$$

(a) $Z_{i1} = V_1/I_1 \quad Z_{i2} = V_2/(-)I_2$

(b) $Z_{i1} = V_1/(-)I_1 \quad Z_{i2} = V_2/I_2$

(Note carefully the direction of currents in the figures).

Now consider Fig. 11.31(b).

From Eqs.

$$V_1 = AV_2 - BI_2 \quad I_1 = CV_2 - DI_2$$

we get
$$V_2 = \frac{DV_1}{AD - BC} - \frac{BI_1}{AD - BC}$$

and
$$I_2 = \frac{CV_1}{AD - BC} - \frac{AI_1}{AD - BC}$$

or
$$Z_{i2} = \frac{V_2}{I_2} = \frac{DV_1 - BI_1}{CV_1 - AI_1}$$

As
$$\frac{V_1}{-I_1} = Z_{i1}$$

$$\therefore \quad Z_{i2} = \frac{DZ_{i1} + B}{CZ_{i1} + A} \qquad ...(11.123)$$

Solving Eqs. (11.122) and (11.123)

and
$$Z_{i1} = \sqrt{\frac{AB}{CD}}\,; \quad Z_{i2} = \sqrt{\frac{BD}{AC}} \qquad ...(11.124)$$

Expressions in equation (11.124) represent the image impedances of an *ABCD* network. The roots with +ve real parts are chosen (since resistances are positive with +ve real roots).

However, image impedances do not completely define a network. We need another parameter which we shall get from the voltage and current ratios. Assuming the receiving impedance to be the image impedance Z_{i2}, then

$$V_1 = AV_2 - BI_2 = \left(A + \frac{B}{Z_{i2}}\right) V_2$$

$$I_1 = CV_2 - DI_2 = -(CZ_{i2} + D)\, I_2$$

Remembering that $Z_{i2} = \sqrt{\frac{BD}{AC}}$,

$$\frac{V_1}{V_2} = A + B\sqrt{\frac{AC}{BD}} = A + \frac{\sqrt{ABCD}}{D}$$

and $$\frac{I_1}{I_2} = -\left(C\sqrt{\frac{BD}{AC}} + D\right) = -\left(D + \frac{\sqrt{ABCD}}{A}\right)$$

Now

$$\frac{-V_1}{V_2} \cdot \frac{I_1}{I_2} = \left(A + \frac{\sqrt{ABCD}}{D}\right)\left(D + \frac{\sqrt{ABCD}}{A}\right)$$

$$= AD + 2\sqrt{ABCD} + BC$$

$$= (\sqrt{AD} + \sqrt{BC})^2$$

Therefore,

$$\sqrt{\frac{-V_1 I_1}{V_2 I_2}} = \sqrt{AD} + \sqrt{BC}$$

$$= \sqrt{AD} + \sqrt{AD - 1} \quad \left[\begin{array}{l} \because AD - BC = 1 \\ \therefore AD - 1 = BC \end{array}\right]$$

Let $\sqrt{AD} = \cosh\theta$

then $\sqrt{AD-1} = \sinh\theta$

and $$\sqrt{\frac{-V_1 I_1}{V_2 I_2}} = \cosh\theta + \sinh\theta = e^{\theta}$$

whence $$\theta = \ln\sqrt{\frac{-V_1 I_1}{V_2 I_2}} = \frac{1}{2}\ln\left(\frac{-V_1 I_1}{V_2 I_2}\right)$$

θ is called the *image transfer constant* and is the third complex parameter.

In general, $$\theta = \frac{1}{2}\ln\left(\frac{-V_1 I_1}{V_2 I_2}\right) \quad ...(11.125)$$

In the above derivation the sign of θ is ambiguous, Either sign of θ will satisfy equations $\sqrt{AD} = \cosh\theta$ or $\sqrt{BC} = \sinh\theta$. For the normal direction of propagation, the magnitude of $V_1 I_1$ will usually exceed that of $V_2 I_2$ and, therefore, the real part of θ will be positive.

We will normally assume θ to have *a +ve real part.*

Since $V_1 = Z_{i1} I_1$ and $V_2 = -Z_{i2} I_2$, the image transfer constant may be written as

$$\theta = \frac{1}{2}\ln\frac{Z_{i1}}{Z_{i2}} + \ln\frac{I_1}{I_2} \quad ...(11.126)$$

Other forms are

$$\theta = \cosh^{-1}\sqrt{AD} = \sinh^{-1}\sqrt{BC}$$

$$= \tanh^{-1}\sqrt{\frac{BC}{AD}} \quad ...(11.127)$$

11.16 RELATIONSHIP BETWEEN THE IMAGE PARAMETERS AND THE SHORT-CIRCUIT AND OPEN CIRCUIT IMPEDANCES

From equation (11.124),

$$Z_{i1} = \sqrt{\frac{AB}{CD}}$$

$$Z_{i2} = \sqrt{\frac{BD}{AC}}$$

and from equation (11.127)

$$\theta = \tanh^{-1}\sqrt{\frac{BC}{AD}}$$

Also we have seen that $Z_{10} = \frac{A}{C}$

$$Z_{1S} = \frac{B}{D}$$

$$\therefore \quad Z_{i1} = \sqrt{Z_{10} \cdot Z_{1S}} \quad ...(11.128)$$

Again,

$$Z_{20} = \frac{D}{C}$$

$$Z_{2S} = \frac{B}{A}$$

$$\therefore \quad Z_{i2} = \sqrt{Z_{20}\, Z_{2S}} \quad ...(11.129)$$

$$\theta = \tanh^{-1}\sqrt{\frac{Z_{1S}}{Z_{10}}} = \tanh^{-1}\sqrt{\frac{Z_{2S}}{Z_{20}}} \quad ...(11.130)$$

CHAPTER 11

These relationships are the easiest way of determining the image parameters from physical measurements, the short circuit and open-circuit impedances being measured.

In general image transfer constant (θ) will be a complex number. The real part of θ is called the *image-attenuation constant* and the imaginary part is called the *image phase constant.*

In the case of symmetrical networks there is a considerable simplification. The image impedance characteristic impedance, designated by Z_o, and the image transfer constant is called the *propagation constant* γ.

For symmetrical *ABCD* networks $A = D$.

However, $$Z_{i1} = \sqrt{\frac{AB}{CD}}$$

and $$Z_{i2} = \sqrt{\frac{BD}{AC}}.$$

With $$A = D, Z_{i1} = Z_{i2} = \sqrt{\frac{B}{C}} = Z_0 \quad ...(11.131)$$

$$\theta = \gamma = \ln\sqrt{\frac{V_1\, I_1}{V_2\, I_2}} = \ln\sqrt{\frac{Z_0\, I_1^2}{Z_0\, I_2^2}}$$

or $$\gamma = \ln\frac{I_1}{I_2} \quad ...(11.132)$$

As in the case of θ, γ is in general a complex number

i.e. $\gamma = \alpha + j\beta$,

where α is called the attenuation constant and is measured in radians.

Also $$\gamma = \cosh^{-1}\sqrt{AD} = \cosh^{-1} A \quad [\because A = D]$$

$$= \sinh^{-1}\sqrt{BC} \quad ...(11.133)$$

Again $$Z_0 = \sqrt{Z_{1S}\, Z_{20}} = (Z_{2S}\, Z_{20})^{1/2} \quad ...(11.134)$$

The *ABCD* constants of a symmetrical network in terms of Z_0 and γ are then as follows :

$$A = D = \cosh\gamma$$

$$B = \sqrt{\frac{B}{C}} \times \sqrt{BC} = Z_0 \sinh\gamma \quad ...(11.135)$$

$$C = \sqrt{\frac{C}{B}} \times \sqrt{BC} = \frac{1}{Z_0} \sinh\gamma$$

11.17 EQUIVALENT *T*-AND π-SECTION REPRESENTATION IN PARAMETER FORMS

T and π networks are the two networks which are used frequently to represent the equivalence of transmission lines, filters etc.

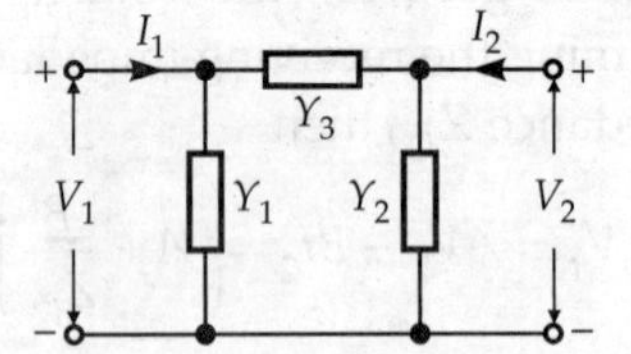

Fig. 11.32 A π-network.

The π network is represented by the model shown in Fig. 11.32. We will find Y_1, Y_2 and Y_3 in terms of *Y*-parameters. With a short circuit at output port, the network takes the form shown in Fig. 11.33.

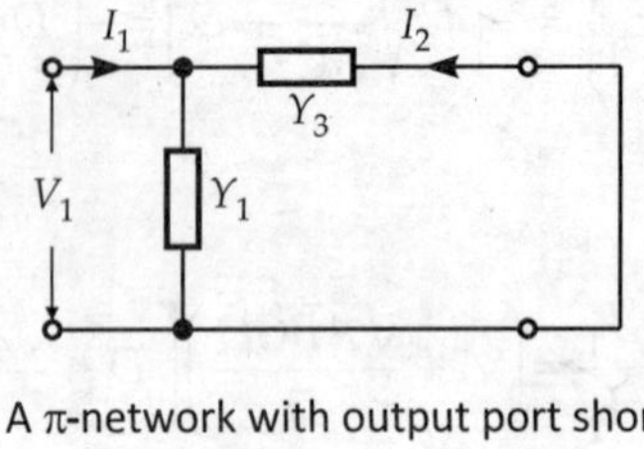

Fig. 11.33 A π-network with output port short-circuites.

For this network,

$$I_1 = V_1\, Y_1 + V_1\, Y_3 = V_1\,(Y_1 + Y_3)$$

$$\therefore \quad Y_{11} = \left.\frac{I_1}{V_1}\right|_{V_2=0} = Y_1 + Y_3 \quad ...(11.136)$$

Again, $$Y_{21} = \left.\frac{I_2}{V_1}\right|_{V_2=0}$$

Here $-I_2 = V_1\, Y_3$

$$\therefore \quad Y_{21} = \frac{-V_1\, Y_3}{V_1} = -Y_3 \quad ...(11.137)$$

Similarly, we can find Y_{12} and Y_{22} by short-circuiting input port

Here, $Y_{22} = Y_2 + Y_3\,;\, Y_{12} = -Y_3$ ...(11.138)

Using equations (11.136) to (11.138) we can express Y_1, Y_2 and Y_3 in terms of *Y*-parameters.

Thus $$\begin{aligned} Y_1 &= Y_{11} + Y_{12} \\ Y_2 &= Y_{22} + Y_{12} \\ Y_3 &= -Y_{12} \end{aligned} \quad ...(11.139)$$

Therefore, if Y-parameters of a network are known, the equivalent π-network can be constructed by using above equations.

If Z-parameters of a network are known then it is convenient to construct an equivalent T-model rather than an equivalent π-model. The T-network

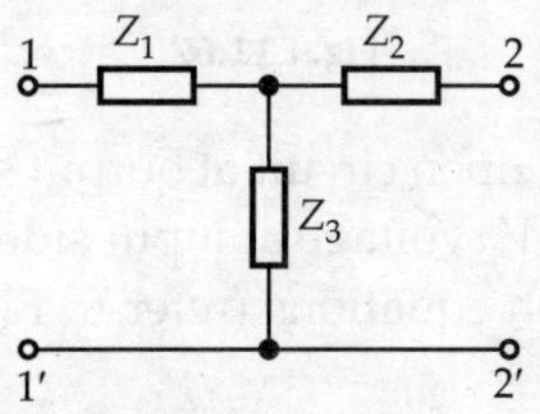

Fig. 11.34 A T-network

is shown in Fig. 11.34. With an open circuit at output port we have,

$$V_1 = I_1 (Z_1 + Z_3)$$

or $$Z_{11} = \left.\frac{V_1}{I_1}\right|_{I_2=0} = Z_1 + Z_3 \quad ...(11.140)$$

Also, $V_2 = I_1 Z_3$ when output is open,

$$\therefore \quad Z_{21} = \left.\frac{V_2}{I_1}\right|_{I_2=0}$$

i.e., $$Z_{21} = \frac{I_1 Z_3}{I_1} = Z_3 \quad ...(11.141)$$

Again, keeping the input port open, for voltage V_2 at output port, it can be shown that

$$Z_{22} = Z_2 + Z_3 \quad ...(11.142)$$

an $$Z_{12} = Z_3 \quad ...(11.143)$$

From equations (11.140) to (11.142) the elements of T-network, Z_1, Z_2 and Z_3 can be expressed in terms of Z-parameters.

i.e., $$Z_1 = Z_{11} - Z_{12}$$
$$Z_2 = Z_{22} - Z_{12} \quad ...(11.144)$$
$$Z_3 = Z_{12}$$

Therefore, if Z-parameters of a network are known, then the equivalent T-network model can be constructed by using equation (11.144).

11.18 LADDAR NETWORK

A general laddar network is shown in Fig. 11.35. Each Z or Y may contain a number of resistances, inductances and capacitances in series

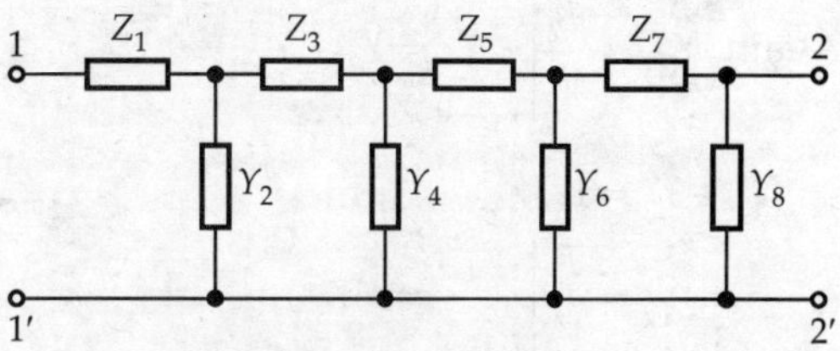

Fig. 11.35 A π-network.

or parallel or both. The driving point impedance at port 1, with port 2 open, can be easily verified to be

$$Z_{11} = Z_1 + \cfrac{1}{Y_2 + \cfrac{1}{Z_3 + \cfrac{1}{Y_4 + \cfrac{1}{Z_5 + \cfrac{1}{Y_6 + \ldots\ldots}}}}} \quad ...(11.145)$$

This type of equation is referred to as a *continuous fraction.*

EXAMPLE 11.42 *The currents I_1 and I_2 at input and output port respectively of a two-port network can be expressed as :*

$$I_1 = 5V_1 - V_2 \quad ...(1)$$
$$I_2 = -V_1 + V_2 \quad ...(2)$$

(a) *Find the equivalent π-network.*

(b) *Find the input impedance when a load of (3 + j5) ohms is connected across the output port.*

SOLUTION. (a) Let the equivalent π network be represented by Fig. E11.61.

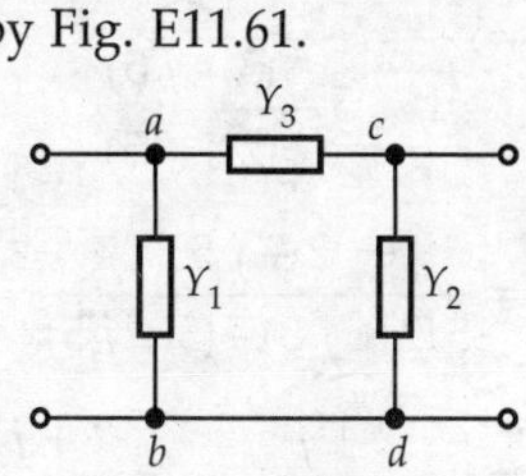

Fig. E11.61

Comparing Eqns. (1) and (2) with conventional Y-parameter equations, we get

$$Y_{11} = 5 \text{ mhos}, Y_{12} = Y_{21} = -1 \text{ mho}, Y_{22} = 1 \text{ mho}.$$

From Fig. E11.61,

$$Y_{11} = \left.\frac{I_1}{V_1}\right|_{V_2=0} = Y_1 + Y_3$$

or $$Y_1 + Y_3 = 5 \quad ...(3)$$

CHAPTER 11

$$\text{Again } Y_{22} = \left.\frac{I_2}{V_2}\right|_{V_1=0} = Y_2 + Y_3$$

$$\text{or} \quad Y_2 + Y_3 = 1 \quad \text{...(4)}$$

$$Y_{12} = \left.\frac{I_1}{V_2}\right|_{V_1=0} = -Y_3$$

$$Y_{21} = \left.\frac{I_2}{V_1}\right|_{V_2=0} = -Y_3$$

$$\text{or} \quad Y_3 = 1 \quad \text{...(5)}$$

Solving Eqns. (3), (4), (5)

$$\mathbf{Y_3 = 1\ mho,\ Y_1 = 4\ mhos,\ Y_2 = 0.}$$

Thus all the elements of equivalent π-network are obtained.

(*b*) When a load of $(3 + j5)$ ohms is connected across the output, we have

$$V_2 = -I_2 Z_L = -(3 + j\,5)\,I_2$$

Substituting this relationship in Eqns. (1) and (2)

$$I_1 = 5\,V_1 + (3 + j5)\,I_2 \quad \text{...(6)}$$

$$I_2 = (3 + j\,5)\,I_2 + V_1 \quad \text{...(7)}$$

From Eqn. (7)

$$I_2 = \frac{V_1}{-(2 + j5)}$$

Substituting this in Eqn. (6)

$$I_1 = 5V_1 - \frac{(3 + j\,5)}{(2 + j\,5)}\,V_1$$

$$\text{or} \quad Z_{in} = \frac{V_1}{I_1} = \frac{1}{5 - \dfrac{(3 + j\,5)}{(2 + j\,5)}}$$

$$= \frac{2 + j\,5}{5\,(2 + j\,5) - (3 + j\,5)}$$

$$= \frac{2 + j\,5}{10 + j\,25 - j\,5} = \frac{2 + j\,5}{7 + j\,20}$$

$$= \frac{5.39\,\angle 68.2^\circ}{21.2\,\angle 70.7^\circ} = \mathbf{0.254\,\angle -2.5^\circ\ ohms.}$$

EXAMPLE 11.43 *Two networks have been shown in Fig. E11.62. Obtain the transmission parameters of the resulting circuit when both the circuits are in cascade.*

SOLUTION. As both the circuits are identical hence let us find the transmission parameters of any one circuit.

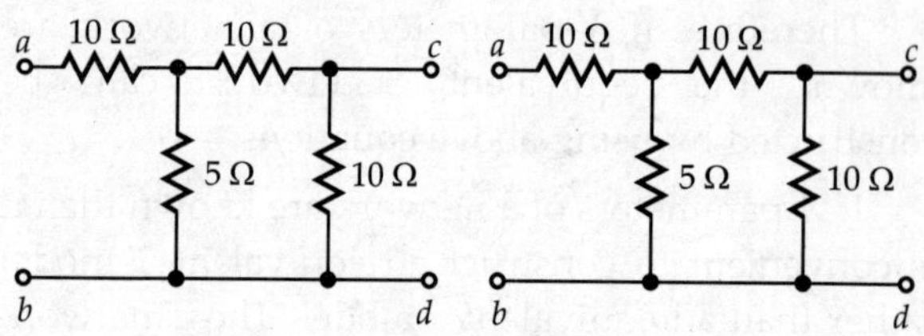

Fig. E11.62

Assuming open circuit at output side, for $I_2 = 0$, application of V_1 voltage at input side results in the following mesh equations (refer to Fig. E11.63)

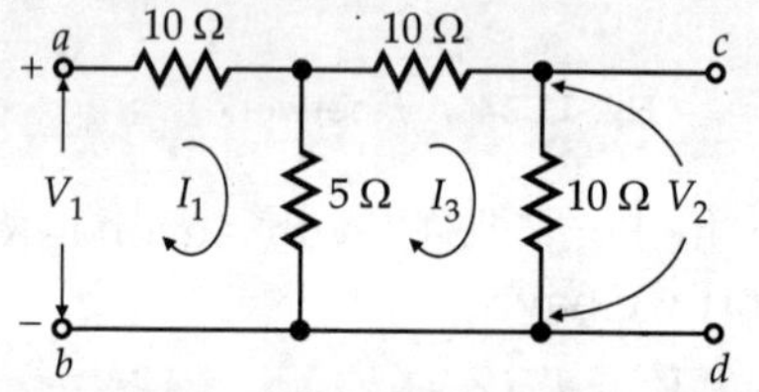

Fig. E11.63

$$V_1 = 10\,I_1 + (I_1 - I_3)\,5 = 15\,I_1 - 5\,I_3 \quad \text{...}(i)$$

$$\text{and} \quad 0 = (I_3 - I_1)\,5 + 20\,I_3$$

$$\text{or} \quad 25 I_3 = 5\,I_1$$

$$\therefore \quad I_3 = \frac{1}{5}\,I_1 \quad \text{...}(ii)$$

Utilising (*ii*) in (*i*),

$$V_1 = 14\,I_1 \quad \text{...}(iii)$$

Again, with $I_2 = 0$,

$$V_2 = 10\,I_3 = 2\,I_1 \quad \text{...}(iv)$$

$$\therefore \quad \left.\frac{I_1}{V_2}\right|_{I_2=0} = \frac{1}{2}\ \text{mho} = C_1$$

Dividing (*iii*) by (*iv*),

$$\left.\frac{V_1}{V_2}\right|_{V_2=0} = 7 = A_1$$

Again applying same voltage V_1 at input and keeping the output port short circuit, for $V_2 = 0$, the configuration has been shown in Fig. E11.64.

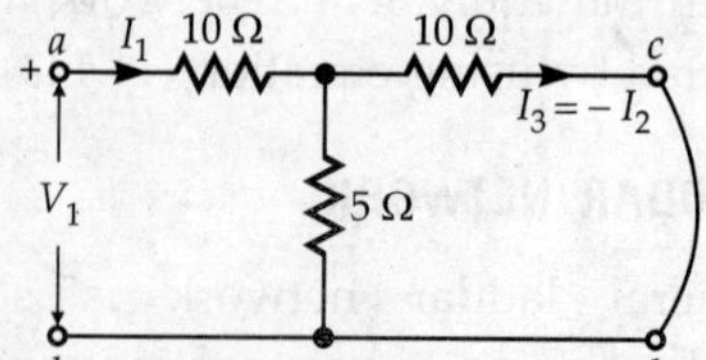

Fig. E11.64

Here $V_1 = 10\,I_1 + (I_1 - I_3)5$

$$= 10\,I_1 + (I_1 + I_2)5 = 15\,I_1 + 5I_2 \qquad ...(v)$$

and $0 = (I_3 - I_1)5 + 10\,I_3$

$$= -(I_1 + I_2)5 - 10\,I_2$$

or $5I_1 + 15I_2 = 0$

or $I_1 = -3I_2 \qquad ...(vi)$

Eq. (*vi*) gives

$$\left.\frac{I_1}{-I_2}\right|_{V_2=0} = 3 = D_1$$

and substituting equation (*vi*) in (*v*),

$$V_1 = -45\,I_2 + 5I_2 = -40\,I_2$$

$$\therefore \quad \left.\frac{V_1}{-I_2}\right|_{V_2=0} = 40\,\Omega = B_1$$

∴ *ABCD* parameters become,

$$\begin{bmatrix} A_1 & B_1 \\ C_1 & D_1 \end{bmatrix} = \begin{bmatrix} 7 & 40 \\ \frac{1}{2} & 3 \end{bmatrix}$$

It may be noted that the circuit of Fig. E11.62(*a*) is reciprocal $(AD - BC = 1)$ and not symmetrical $A \neq D$.

Both the circuits are identical

$$\therefore \quad \begin{bmatrix} A_1 & B_1 \\ C_1 & D_1 \end{bmatrix} \equiv \begin{bmatrix} A_2 & B_2 \\ C_2 & D_2 \end{bmatrix}$$

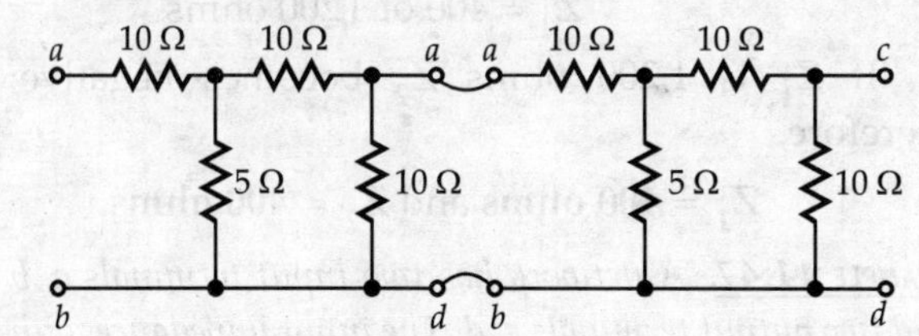

Fig. E11.65

Figure E11.65 represents the cascaded circuit of Fig. E11.62 and from the text it is evident that the net transmission parameters are given

$$\begin{bmatrix} A & B \\ C & D \end{bmatrix} = \begin{bmatrix} A_1 & B_1 \\ C_1 & D_1 \end{bmatrix}\begin{bmatrix} A_2 & B_2 \\ C_2 & D_2 \end{bmatrix}$$

$$= \begin{bmatrix} 7 & 40 \\ \frac{1}{2} & 3 \end{bmatrix}\begin{bmatrix} 7 & 40 \\ \frac{1}{2} & 3 \end{bmatrix} = \begin{bmatrix} \mathbf{69} & \mathbf{400} \\ \mathbf{5} & \mathbf{29} \end{bmatrix}.$$

Example 11.44 *Find out the ABCD parameters of the network shown in Fig. E11.66. Also find the image parameters for the network.*

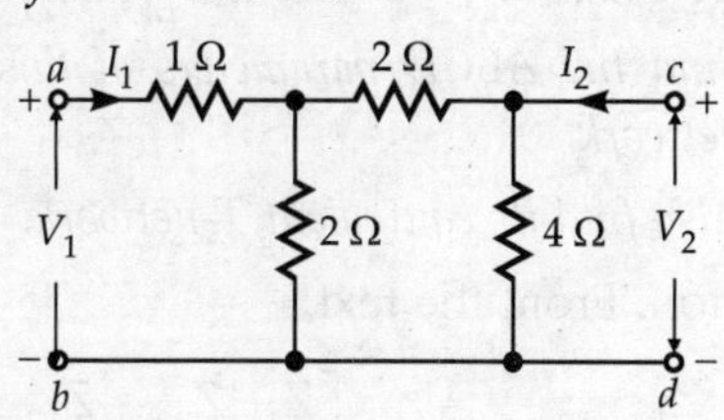

Fig. E11.66

Solution. *Z*-parameters for this two port network can be obtained as $Z_{11} = 2.5$ ohms, $Z_{22} = 2$ ohms, $Z_{12} = Z_{21}$ and $Z_{22} = 1$ ohm. *ABCD* parameters are then given by

$$A = \frac{Z_{11}}{Z_{21}} = \frac{2.5}{1} = \mathbf{2.5}$$

$$B = \frac{Z_{11}\,Z_{22} - Z_{12}\,Z_{21}}{Z_{21}} = \frac{2.5 \times 2 - 1 \times 1}{1} = \mathbf{4\ ohms}$$

$$C = \frac{1}{Z_{21}} = \frac{1}{1} = \mathbf{1\ mho}$$

$$D = \frac{Z_{22}}{Z_{21}} = \frac{2}{1} = \mathbf{2}$$

Image impedance at port *a-b*

$$Z_{i1} = \sqrt{\frac{AB}{CD}} = \sqrt{\frac{2.5 \times 4}{1 \times 2}} = \mathbf{2.24\ ohms.}$$

Image impedance at port *c-d*,

$$Z_{i2} = \sqrt{\frac{BD}{AC}} = \sqrt{\frac{4 \times 2}{2.5 \times 1}} = \mathbf{1.79\ ohms.}$$

Image transfer constant

$$\theta = \tanh^{-1}\sqrt{\frac{BC}{AD}}.$$

Let $u = \sqrt{\frac{BC}{AD}} = \sqrt{\frac{4 \times 1}{2.5 \times 2}} = \mathbf{0.895}\,;$

then $u = \tanh\theta = \frac{e^{\theta} - e^{-\theta}}{e^{\theta} + e^{-\theta}} = \frac{e^{2\theta} - 1}{e^{2\theta} + 1}$

Hence $e^{2\theta} = \frac{1+u}{1-u} = \frac{1 + 0.895}{1 - 0.895} = \frac{1.895}{0.105} = 18.05$

or $2\theta = \log_e 18.05$

or $2\theta = 2.303\,\log_{10} 18.05 = 2.90$

or $\theta = \mathbf{1.45.}$

EXAMPLE 11.45 *The Z-parameters of a two-port network are*

$Z_{11} = 10$ *ohms,* $Z_{22} = 20$ *ohms,* $Z_{12} = Z_{21} = 5$ *ohms.*

(*a*) *Find the ABCD parameters of this two-port network.*

(*b*) *Also find its equivalent T-network.*

SOLUTION. From the text,

$$A = \frac{Z_{11}}{Z_{12}}, \quad B = \frac{\Delta Z}{Z_{21}} = \left[\frac{Z_{11}\,Z_{22} - Z_{12}\,Z_{21}}{Z_{21}}\right]$$

$$C = \frac{1}{Z_{21}}, \quad D = \frac{Z_{22}}{Z_{21}}$$

Hence $A = \frac{10}{5} = \mathbf{2}$

$$B = \frac{10 \times 20 - 5 \times 5}{5} = \frac{175}{5} = \mathbf{35\ ohms}$$

$$C = \frac{1}{5} = \mathbf{0.2\ mho}$$

$$D = \frac{20}{5} = \mathbf{4}$$

(*b*) The equivalent *T*-network is shown in Fig. E11.67.

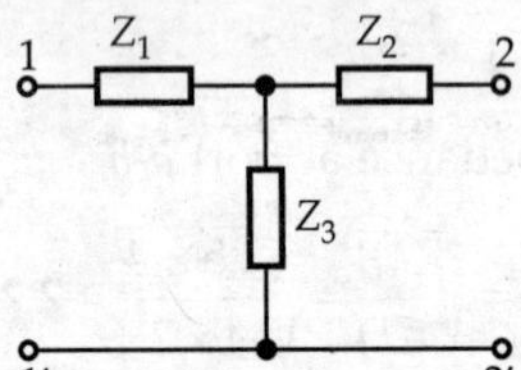

Fig. E11.67

Again, $$Z_{11} = \left.\frac{V_1}{I_1}\right|_{I_2=0} = Z_1 + Z_3$$

or $$Z_1 + Z_3 = 10 \qquad ...(1)$$

$$Z_{22} = \left.\frac{V_2}{I_2}\right|_{I_1=0} = Z_2 + Z_3$$

or $$Z_2 + Z_3 = 20 \qquad ...(2)$$

$$Z_{12} = \left.\frac{V_1}{I_2}\right|_{I_1=0} = Z_3$$

$$Z_{21} = \left.\frac{V_2}{I_1}\right|_{I_2=0} = Z_3$$

or $$Z_3 = 5 \qquad ...(3)$$

From Eqns. (1), (2), (3)

$$\mathbf{Z_1 = 5, Z_2 = 15 \text{ and } Z_3 = 5 \text{ ohms.}}$$

[Alternatively we may directly use relationships developed in Art. 11.17. Thus all the elements of equivalent *T* are known].

EXAMPLE 11.46 *A symmetrical T-section has the following o.c and s.c impedances :*

$$Z_{o.c} = 800 \text{ ohms } Z_{s.c} = 600 \text{ ohms}$$

Determine T section parameters to represent the two port network.

SOLUTION. Referring to Fig. E11.68 under o.c condition,

$$Z_1 + Z_2 = 800 \qquad ...(1)$$

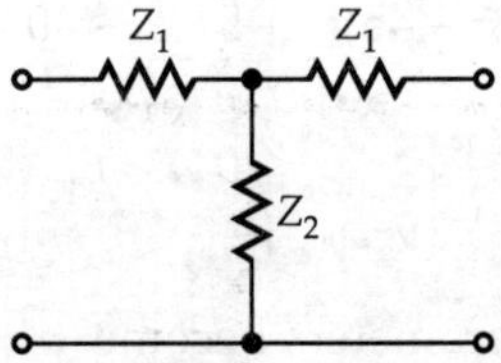

Fig. E11.68

and under *s.c* condition,

$$Z_1 + \frac{Z_1\,Z_2}{Z_1 + Z_2} = 600 \qquad ...(2)$$

or $$Z_1 + \frac{Z_1\,(800 - Z_1)}{800} = 600 \quad \text{[utilising (1)]}$$

or $$Z_1^2 - 1{,}600\,Z_1 + 48 \times 10^4 = 0$$

or $$(Z_1 - 800)^2 = (\pm\,400)^2$$

or $$Z_1 = 400 \text{ or } 1{,}200 \text{ ohms}$$

If Z_1 is 1,200 ohms Z_2 becomes negative; therefore,

$$\mathbf{Z_1 = 400 \text{ ohms and } Z_2 = 400 \text{ ohms.}}$$

EXAMPLE 11.47 *A network has two input terminals a, b and two output terminals c, d. The input impedance with c-d open circuited is (250 + j 100) ohms and with c-d short-circuited is (400 + j 300) Ω. The impedance across c-d with a-b open-circuited is 200 ohms. Determine the equivalent T network parameters.*

SOLUTION. Referring to Fig. 11.69 we observe for *c-d* terminal open,

$$Z_A + Z_B = 250 + j\,100 \qquad ...(1)$$

But for *c-d* terminals shorted,

$$Z_A + \frac{Z_B\,Z_C}{Z_B + Z_C} = 400 + j\,300 \qquad ...(2)$$

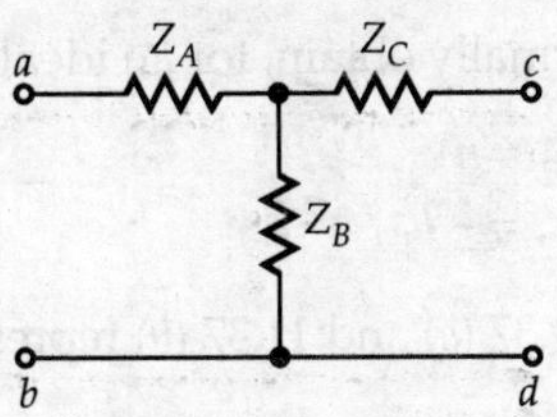

Fig. E11.69

Again, with a-b terminals open,

and $\quad Z_B + Z_C = 200 \qquad ...(3)$

Subtracting (1) from (2),

$$\frac{Z_B Z_C}{Z_B + Z_C} - Z_B = 150 + j\,200$$

or $Z_B Z_C - Z_B Z_C - Z_B^2 = 200\,(150 + j\,200)$

or
$$Z_B^2 = 200\,(-150 - j\,200)$$
$$= 10^4\,(-3 - j\,4)$$
$$= 10^4\,(1 - j\,2)^2$$

Therefore, $\quad \mathbf{Z_B = 100 - j200 \text{ ohms}}$

and $\quad \mathbf{Z_A = 150 + j300 \text{ ohm};}$

$$\mathbf{Z_C = 100 + j200 \text{ ohms.}}$$

EXAMPLE 11.48 *For the lattice two port network of Fig. E11.70, find the image impedance and the image transfer constant.*

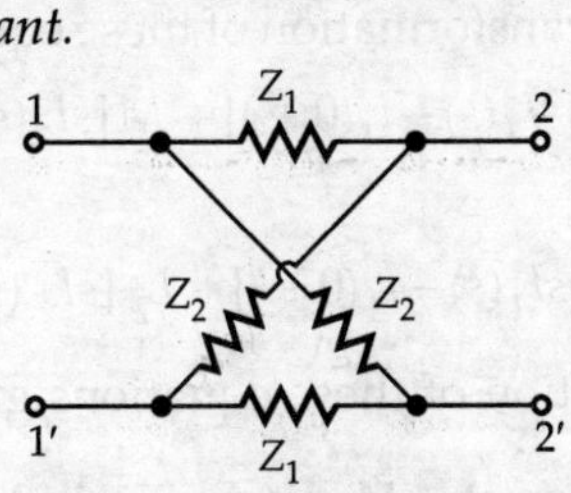

Fig. E11.70

SOLUTION. Open circuit and short circuit impedances can be obtained for this network by inspection :

$$Z_{o.c} = \frac{Z_1 + Z_2}{2} \text{ and } Z_{s.c} = \frac{2 Z_1 Z_2}{Z_1 + Z_2}$$

Image impedance,

$$Z_i = \sqrt{Z_{o.c}\, Z_{s.c}} = \sqrt{\mathbf{Z_1 Z_2}} \qquad ...(1)$$

Image transfer constant θ is given by

$$\tanh\theta = \sqrt{\frac{Z_{s.c}}{Z_{o.c}}} = \frac{2\sqrt{Z_1 Z_2}}{Z_1 + Z_2} = \frac{2Z_i}{Z_1 + Z_2}$$

or
$$\frac{e^{\theta} - e^{-\theta}}{e^{\theta} + e^{-\theta}} = \frac{2Z_i}{Z_1 + Z_2} \qquad ...(2)$$

From Eqn. (1) we substitute for Z_2 in Eqn. (2)

$$\frac{e^{\theta} - e^{-\theta}}{e^{\theta} + e^{-\theta}} = \frac{2Z_i}{Z_1 + \dfrac{Z_i^2}{Z_1}}$$

or
$$\frac{e^{2\theta} - 1}{e^{2\theta} + 1} = \frac{2Z_i Z_1}{Z_1^2 + Z_i^2}$$

or
$$e^{2\theta} = \frac{(Z_1 + Z_i)^2}{(Z_i - Z_1)^2}$$

or
$$e^{\theta} = \pm \frac{1 + \dfrac{Z_1}{Z_i}}{1 - \dfrac{Z_1}{Z_i}} \qquad ...(3)$$

$$= \pm \frac{1 + \sqrt{\dfrac{Z_1}{Z_2}}}{1 - \sqrt{\dfrac{Z_1}{Z_2}}} \qquad ...(4)$$

Thus θ may be obtained from equations (3) and (4).

11.19 CIRCUIT MODELLING OF AN IDEAL TRANSFORMER

The coefficient of coupling of a transformer being defined by K (refer to the chapter : Coupled Circuits),

$$K = \frac{M}{\sqrt{L_1 L_2}}$$

[With reference to Fig. 11.36,

L_1 = Self induction of the primary coil

L_2 = Self induction of the secondary coil

M = mutual inductance between the primary and secondary coils]

[Refer to Fig. 11.36].

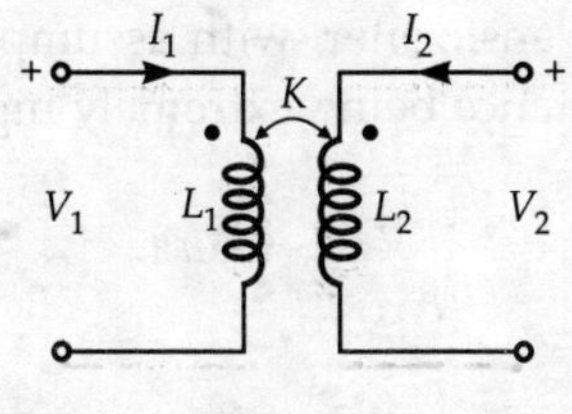

Fig. 11.36 Circuit model of a transformer.

An ideal transformer has perfect coupling with $K = 1$.

Here, $V_1 = j\omega L_1 I_1 + j\omega M I_2$

i.e., $$I_1 = \frac{V_1 - j\omega M I_2}{j\omega L_1} \quad ...(11.146)$$

and also, $V_2 = j\omega M I_1 + j\omega L_2 I_2$

giving $$V_2 = j\omega M\left(\frac{V_1 - j\omega M I_2}{j\omega L_1}\right) + j\omega L_2 I_2$$

$$= \frac{MV_1}{L_1} - \frac{j\omega M^2 I_2}{L_1} + j\omega L_2 I_2$$

However, with perfect coupling ($K = 1$),

$$M = \sqrt{L_1 L_2}$$

$$\therefore \quad V_2 = \frac{\sqrt{L_1 L_2}\, V_1}{L_1} - \frac{j\omega L_1 L_2 I_2}{L_1} + j\omega L_2 I_2$$

$$= \sqrt{\frac{L_2}{L_1}}\, V_1$$

$$= nV_1 \quad \left[\text{Say } \sqrt{\frac{L_2}{L_1}} = n \text{ the turn ratio}\right]$$

However, n_1 and n_2 being the number of turns of primary and secondary from the theory of basic electrical engineering,

$$L_1 = Kn_1^2 \text{ and } L_2 = Kn_2^2$$

This gives,

$$n = \sqrt{\frac{L_2}{L_1}} = \sqrt{\frac{Kn_2^2}{Kn_1^2}} = \frac{n_2}{n_1}$$

Thus, from equation (11.146),

$$I_1 = \frac{V_1}{j\omega L_1} - \frac{MI_2}{L_1} = \frac{V_1}{j\omega L_1} - \frac{\sqrt{L_1 L_2}\, I_2}{L_1}$$

$$= \frac{V_1}{j\omega L_1} - \sqrt{\frac{L_2}{L_1}}\, I_2$$

In ideal transformer, with assumption that L_1, the self inductance being extremely high,

$$I_1 = -\sqrt{\frac{L_2}{L_1}}\, I_2 = -n I_2$$

or, $$I_2 = -\frac{I_1}{n}$$

Thus we finally obtain, for an ideal transformer,

$$\left.\begin{aligned} V_2 &= nV_1 \\ I_2 &= -I_1/n \end{aligned}\right\} \quad ...(11.147)$$

Figures 11.37 (*a*) and 11.37 (*b*) represent the circuit models.

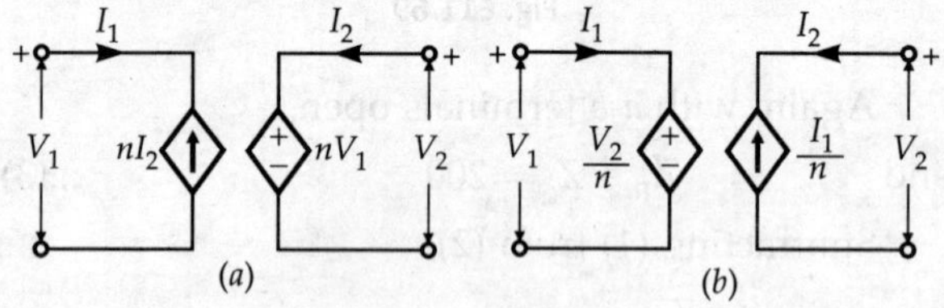

Fig. 11.37 Current and voltage source equivalents of transformer.

Total instantaneous power absorbed by the transformer

$$= p_1 + p_2 = v_1 i_1 + v_2 i_2$$
$$= v_1 i_1 + (nv_1)(-i_1/n) = 0.$$

Thus ideal transformer is a lossless device.

Let us now rewrite the voltage equations of the ideal transformer again—

$$V_1 = j\omega L_1 I_1 + j\omega M I_2$$

and $$V_2 = j\omega M I_1 + j\omega L_2 I_2$$

Laplace transformation of these equations give

$$V_1(s) = L_1[sI_1(s) - i_1(0+)] + M[sI_2(s) - i_2(0+)] \quad ...(11.148)$$

$$V_1(s) = M[sI_1(s) - i_1(0+)] + L_2[sI_2(s) - i_2(0+)]$$

Reorientation of these equations gives

$$V_1(s) = L_1 sI_1(s) + Ms\, I_2(s) - [L_1 i_1(0+) + M i_2(0+)]$$
$$...(11.149)$$
$$V_2(s) = Ms\, I_1(s) + L_2 sI_2(s) - [M i_1(0+) + L_2 i_2(0+)]$$

These two circuit equations can then be diagrammatically represented as shown below (Fig. 11.38).

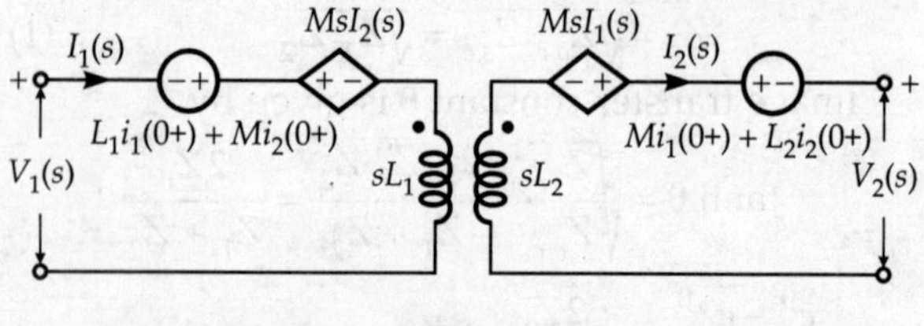

Fig. 11.38 Representation of circuit model of an ideal transformer.

However, assuming zero initial condition, the equations of V_1 (s) and V_2 (s) reduce to

$$V_1(s) = L_1\, sI_1(s) + Ms\, I_2(s)$$
$$V_2(s) = Ms\, I_1(s) + L_2\, sI_2(s) \quad ...(11.150)$$

The diagrammatic representation is then shown in Fig. 11.39.

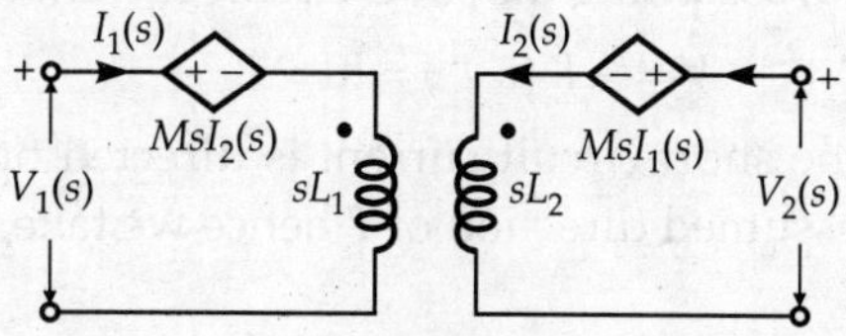

Fig. 11.39 Diagrammatic representation of the circuit model of a transformer.

11.20 MODELING OF NETWORK COMPONENTS

1. Transformer

The governing equations for an ideal transformer are given by (as shown in equation 11.147)

$$V_2 = nV_1$$
$$I_2 = -I_1/n.$$

For our convenience we can rewrite these two equations as

$$V_1 = \frac{1}{n}.V_2$$
$$I_2 = \left(-\frac{1}{n}\right).I_1$$

In matrix form, these equations are shown as

$$\begin{bmatrix} V_1 \\ I_2 \end{bmatrix} = \begin{bmatrix} 0 & 1/n \\ -1/n & 0 \end{bmatrix} \begin{bmatrix} I_1 \\ V_2 \end{bmatrix} \quad ...(11.151)$$

Equation (11.151) exhibits the modeling form in terms of *h*-parameter concept.

We can also write the governing equations of an ideal transformer in the following forms (as shown in Art 11.19)

$$V_1(s) = sL_1 . I_1(s) + sM . I_2(s)$$
$$V_2(s) = sM . I_1(s) + sL_2 . I_2(s)$$

Thus, in Z-parameter form, these equations can be shown as

$$\begin{bmatrix} V_1(s) \\ V_2(s) \end{bmatrix} = \begin{bmatrix} sL_1 & sM \\ sM & sL_2 \end{bmatrix} \begin{bmatrix} I_1(s) \\ I_2(s) \end{bmatrix} \quad ...(11.152)$$

The governing equations can further be reoriented in following fashion :

$$V_1 = \frac{1}{n}.V_2 + 0.(-I_2)$$

and $$I_1 = 0.V_2 + n(-I_2)$$

Thus, in *ABCD* parameter form we can write

$$\begin{bmatrix} V_1 \\ I_1 \end{bmatrix} = \begin{bmatrix} \frac{1}{n} & 0 \\ 0 & n \end{bmatrix} \begin{bmatrix} V_2 \\ -I_2 \end{bmatrix} \quad ...(11.153)$$

It may be noted here that the ideal transformer being a lossless device (explained in Art 11.19) it is neither storing nor dissipating energy and hence it is a passive device (however, practical transformers being composed of resistances in winding, they cannot be treated as passive device since the practical transformer dissipates energy). Also, it may be observed from above that with $L_1 = L_2$, in Z parameter form $Z_{11} = Z_{22}$ for the ideal transformer. Also from *ABCD* parameter representation, it is evident that $AD - BC = 1$, for ideal transformer, making it a reciprocal device.

Thus, the ideal transformer model exhibits that it is a passive element and has both symmetry and reciprocity.

2. Gyrator

The *gyrator* is an inverting circuit element commonly used in electronic circuits. We will show the model of gyrator as a two port network and its properties rather describing the hardware of a gyrator. A gyrator is shown as a two port device as exhibited in Fig. 11.40.

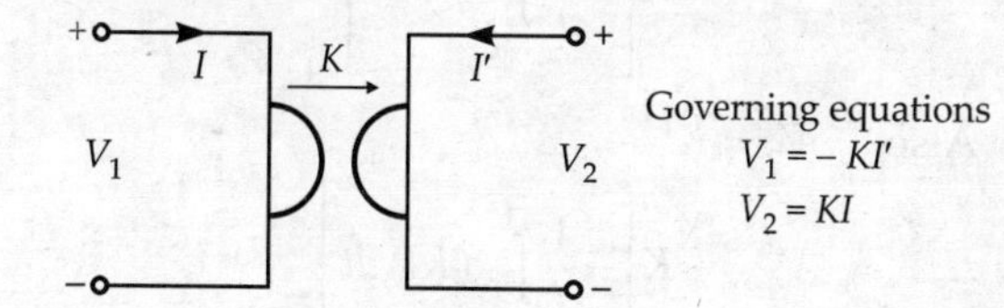

Fig. 11.40 Representation of a gyrator.

Let us assume first that the gyrator is terminated by a resistor R (Fig. 11.41).

Here, $V_2 = -I'R$, ...(11.154*a*)

$$V_1 = -KI' \quad ...(11.154b)$$

(since the gyrator is characterised by $V_1 = -KI'$ and $V_2 = KI$)

Substituting the value of I' from (11.154*a*) in (11.154*b*), we get

$$V_1 = -K\left(-\frac{V_2}{R}\right) = K\left(\frac{V_2}{R}\right) = K\left(\frac{KI}{R}\right) = K^2\left(\frac{I}{R}\right)$$

$$= K^2 (G)\, I, \quad \text{where } G = \text{conductance} = \frac{1}{R}.$$

$$\therefore \quad \frac{V_1}{I} = K^2\, G. \qquad \text{...(11.155)}$$

Thus the equivalent resistance at the input terminals is equal to the conductance at output terminals multiplied by K^2. This is a very clear example of inverting property of a gyrator.

Let us now explore another important inverting property of a gyrator. We assume the gyrator is terminated by an inductor in Fig. 11.41 instead of a resistor.

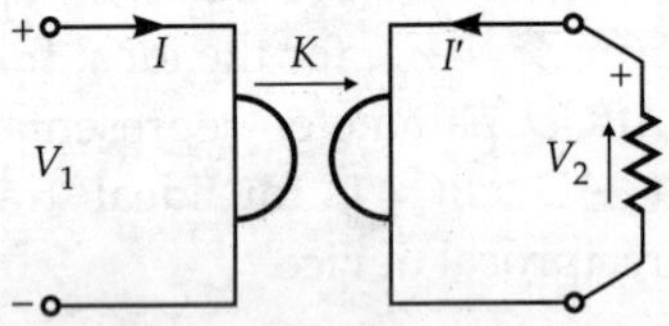

Fig. 11.41 Gyrator termination by resistance.

Obviously,

$$I' = -\frac{1}{L}\int_{-\infty}^{t} V_2 \, . \, dt$$

But $V_1 = -KI'$

$\therefore$ We can write,

$$V_1 = -K\left[-\frac{1}{L}\int_{-\infty}^{t} V_2 \, dt\right]$$

Also, $V_2 = KI$

$$\therefore \quad V_1 = -K\left[-\frac{1}{L}\int_{-\infty}^{t} (KI)\, dt\right]$$

$$= \frac{K^2}{L}\int_{-\infty}^{t} I \, . \, dt = \frac{1}{(L/K^2)}\int_{-\infty}^{t} I \, . \, dt$$

$$= \frac{1}{C}\int_{-\infty}^{t} I \, . \, dt,$$

where C is equivalent to (L/K^2).

Thus we see the termination of the gyrator by the inductance L is equivalent to input capacitance of (L/K^2). In electronic circuits it may be difficult to have inductors of high values ; these inductors can then be simulated by capacitors using gyrator circuits.

Next we check whether the gyrator is a reciprocal device or not. Let us apply a voltage V at the input terminals keeping the output short circuited, assuming the short circuit current to be I'.

$$\therefore \quad V = -K(-I') = KI'$$

[since the short circuit current is directed opposite to our assumed direction of I' hence we take I' to be – ve].

$$\therefore \quad I' = \frac{V}{K} \qquad \text{...(11.156)}$$

Repeating the same exercise *i.e.*, applying voltage V at the output and keeping input terminals short circuited, we can write

$$V = K(-I);$$

I being the short circuit current directed opposite to our assumed direction of I.

$$\therefore \quad V = -KI \text{ giving } I = -\frac{V}{K} \qquad \text{...(11.157)}$$

Comparing equations (11.156) and (11.157) we find that $I = -I'$. This violates the reciprocity principle. Thus the gyrator is antireciprocal device.

Next we check the total energy input to the gyrator ;

$$E = \int_{-\infty}^{t} [v_1 i_1 + v_2 i_2]\, dt$$

$$= \int_{-\infty}^{t} [-Ki_2 i_1 + Ki_1 i_2]\, dt = 0$$

Thus the gyrator neither stores nor dissipates any energy. It is thus a passive device.

The input impedance of a gyrator is

$$Z_{in} = \frac{V_1}{I} = \frac{-KI'}{V_2/K} = K^2\left(-\frac{I'}{V_2}\right) = K^2 \times \frac{1}{Z_L} \qquad \text{...(11.158)}$$

[Since, the termination of the zyrator by Z_L gives $V_2 = (-I')\, Z_L$; I' being negative as the direction of I' is reversed as we connect Z_L at the output].

Thus, the gyrator is a passive device and can be used as an inverting device. It is also an antireciprocal element.

3. Negative convertor

The governing equations for the negative convertors are as under :

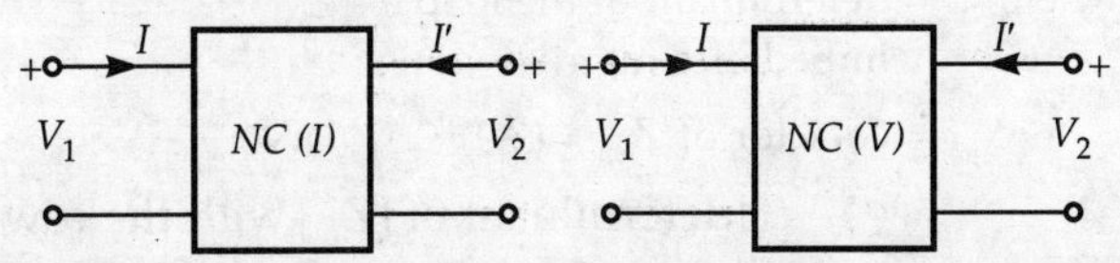

Governing equations	Governing equations
$V_1 = KV_2$	$V_1 = -KV_2$
$I' = KI$	$I' = -KI$
$\therefore \begin{bmatrix} V_1 \\ I' \end{bmatrix} = \begin{bmatrix} 0 & K \\ K & 0 \end{bmatrix} \begin{bmatrix} I \\ V_2 \end{bmatrix}$	$\therefore \begin{bmatrix} V_1 \\ I' \end{bmatrix} = \begin{bmatrix} 0 & -K \\ -K & 0 \end{bmatrix} \begin{bmatrix} I \\ V_2 \end{bmatrix}$

[K is the conversion ratio]

Fig. 11.42 Representation of negative convertors.

In $NC(I)$, I' and I being directed opposite, K converts the sign making $I' = KI$ while in $NC(V)$, V_1 and V_2 having same polarity, K converts them in such a way so that $V_1 = -KV_2$. Thus $NC(I)$ is a *negative current convertor* while $N_C\ (V)$ is a *negative voltage convertor.*

If we assume an inductance L is connected across a negative convertor, we can write, for $N_C\ (I)$,

$$V_2 = -L\frac{dI'}{dt}$$

But $\quad V_1 = KV_2$

$$\therefore \quad V_1 = K\left(-L\frac{dI'}{dt}\right)$$

or

$$V_1 = -KL\frac{d}{dt}(KI)$$

$$= -K^2 L.\frac{dI}{dt}.$$

From $NC(V)$, we can write,

$$V_1 = -KV_2 = KL\frac{dI'}{dt}$$

$$= KL\frac{d}{dt}(-KI) = -K^2 L.\frac{dI}{dt}$$

Thus for inductive termination at the output, the equivalent inductance is proportional to the negative of the terminating inductance. The same result holds good for both R and C termination. Hence this device is known as *negative convertor.*

ADDITIONAL PROBLEMS

EXAMPLE 11.49 *Find Y parameters of the bridge T network shown in Fig. E11.71 and check whether the network is symmetrical and reciprocal.*

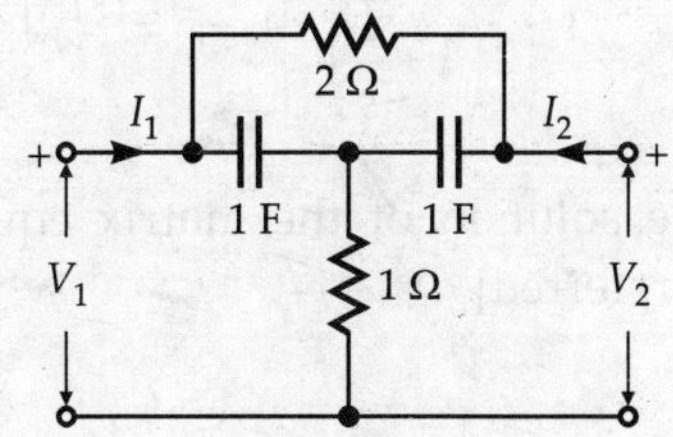

Fig. E11.71

SOLUTION. Let us first transform the given network of Fig. E11.71 to Laplace domain (Fig. E11.72)

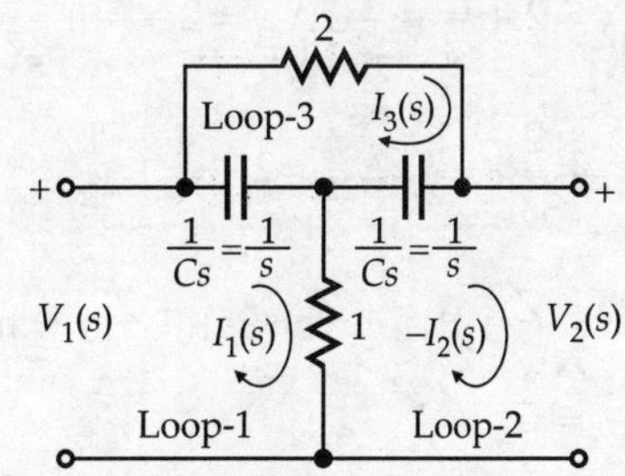

Fig. E11.72

The loop equations are then—

For loop-1

$$I_1(s)\left[1+\frac{1}{s}\right] - [-I_2(s)\times 1] - I_3(s)\frac{1}{s} = V_1(s)$$

$$\left[1+\frac{1}{s}\right] I_1(s) - (1)[-I_2(s)] - \frac{1}{s} I_3(s) = V_1(s) \quad ...(i)$$

For loop-2

$$-I_2(s)\left[1+\frac{1}{s}\right] - I_1(s)\times 1 - I_3(s)\frac{1}{s} = V_2(s)$$

or $\quad -(1)[I_1(s)] + \left[1+\frac{1}{s}\right](-I_2(s)) - \frac{1}{s} I_3(s) = V_2(s)$

$$...(ii)$$

and *for loop-3*

$$\left(2+\frac{1}{s}+\frac{1}{s}\right) I_3(s) - \frac{1}{s} I_1(s) - [-I_2(s)]\frac{1}{s} = 0$$

or $\quad -\frac{1}{s}[I_1(s)] - \frac{1}{s}[-I_2(s)] + \left(2+\frac{2}{s}\right) I_3(s) = 0$

or $\quad -\frac{1}{s}[I_1(s)] - \frac{1}{s}[-I_2(s)] + 2\left(1+\frac{1}{s}\right) I_3(s) = 0 \quad ...(iii)$

The three equations in matrix form give

$$\begin{bmatrix} 1+\frac{1}{s} & -1 & -\frac{1}{s} \\ -1 & 1+\frac{1}{s} & -\frac{1}{s} \\ -\frac{1}{s} & -\frac{1}{s} & 2\left(1+\frac{1}{s}\right) \end{bmatrix} \begin{bmatrix} I_1(s) \\ -I_2(s) \\ I_3(s) \end{bmatrix} = \begin{bmatrix} V_1(s) \\ V_2(s) \\ 0 \end{bmatrix}$$

[For the solution of the matrix equation, the footnote is referred]

Here,

$$\Delta_{11} = (-1)^2 \begin{vmatrix} 1+\frac{1}{s} & -\frac{1}{s} \\ -\frac{1}{s} & 2\left(1+\frac{1}{s}\right) \end{vmatrix} = 2 + \frac{4}{s} + \frac{1}{s^2}$$

$$\Delta_{12} = 2 + \frac{2}{s} + \frac{1}{s^2}, \Delta_{21} = 2 + \frac{2}{s} + \frac{1}{s^2}$$

$$\Delta_{31} = \frac{2}{s} + \frac{1}{s^2}, \Delta_{22} = 2 + \frac{4}{s} + \frac{1}{s^2}$$

$$\therefore \quad \Delta = Z_{11}\,\Delta_{11} + Z_{21}\,\Delta_{21} + Z_{31}\,\Delta_{31}$$

$$= \frac{4}{s} + \frac{2}{s^2}.$$

For a *n*-loop network, (Fig. 11.73)

$$\begin{bmatrix} Z_{11} & Z_{12}\; Z_{13} \ldots\ldots Z_{1n} \\ Z_{21} & Z_{22}\; Z_{23} \ldots\ldots Z_{2n} \\ \vdots & \\ Z_{n1} & Z_{n2}\; Z_{n3} \ldots\ldots Z_{nn} \end{bmatrix} \begin{bmatrix} I_1 \\ -I_2 \\ \vdots \\ I_n \end{bmatrix} = \begin{bmatrix} V_1 \\ -V_2 \\ \vdots \\ 0 \end{bmatrix}$$

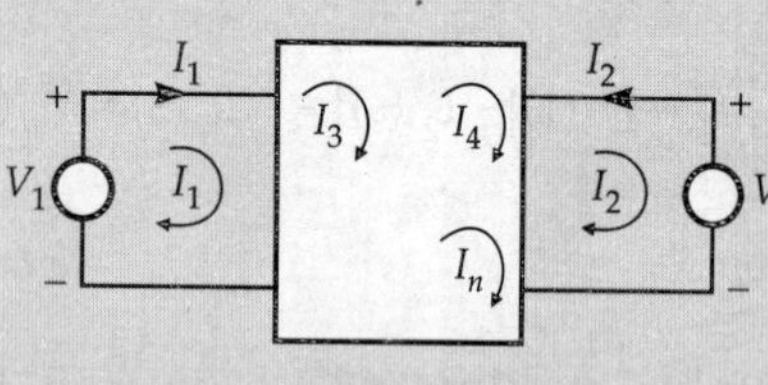

Fig. E11.73

Here,

$$I_1 = \frac{\Delta_{11}}{\Delta} V_1 + \frac{\Delta_{21}}{\Delta}(-V_2) = \frac{\Delta_{11}}{\Delta} V_1 + \left(-\frac{\Delta_{21}}{\Delta}\right) V_2$$

$$I_2 = \frac{\Delta_{12}}{\Delta}(-V_1) + \frac{\Delta_{22}}{\Delta} V_2 = \left(-\frac{\Delta_{12}}{\Delta}\right) V_1 + \frac{\Delta_{22}}{\Delta} V_2$$

...(*A*)

However, the *Y*-parameter network equations are given by

$$I_1 = Y_{11} V_1 + Y_{12} V_2$$
$$I_2 = Y_{21} V_1 + Y_{22} V_2 \qquad \ldots(B)$$

Comparing the two sets of equations (*A*) and (*B*),

$$Y_{11} = \frac{\Delta_{11}}{\Delta}, Y_{12} = -\frac{\Delta_{21}}{\Delta}, Y_{21} = -\frac{\Delta_{12}}{\Delta}, Y_{22} = \frac{\Delta_{22}}{\Delta}$$

when, Δ = determinant of the loop impedance metrix

Δ_{pq} = cofactor of $Z_{pq} = (-1)^{p+q}$

[determinant of $[Z_L]$ with the row and *q*th column deleted]

$$Y_{11} = \frac{\Delta_{11}}{\Delta} = \frac{2 + \frac{4}{s} + \frac{1}{s^2}}{\frac{4}{s} + \frac{2}{s^2}} = \frac{2s^2 + 4s + 1}{2s(1+2s)}$$

and

$$Y_{12} = -\frac{\Delta_{21}}{\Delta} = -\frac{1 + 2s + 2s^2}{2s(1+2s)}$$

In this problem,

$$\Delta_{11} = \Delta_{22}, \; \Delta_{12} = \Delta_{21},$$
$$Y_{11} = Y_{22}, \; Y_{21} = Y_{12}$$

$\therefore$ **The network is symmetrical and reciprocal.**

EXAMPLE 11.50 *Obtain the Z-parameters of the network shown in Fig. E11.74.*

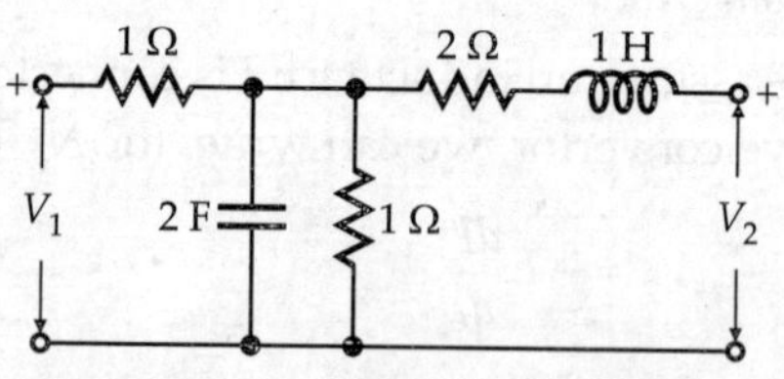

Fig. E11.74

SOLUTION. The network is first transformed to the *s*-domain (Fig. E11.75)

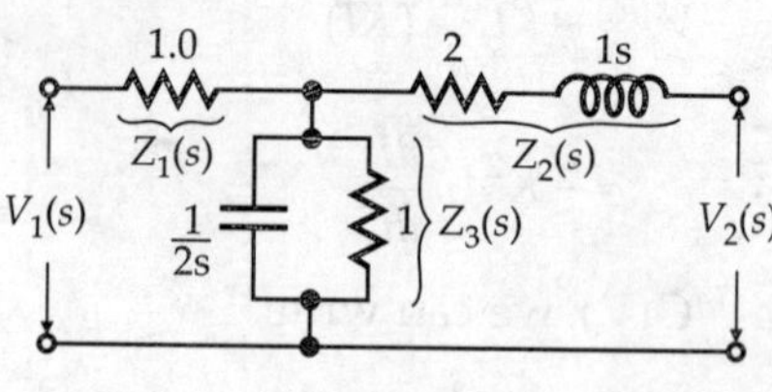

Fig. E11.75

The net impedance of the shunt circuit is then

$$Z_3(s) = 1 \,||\, \frac{1}{2s} = \frac{1 \times \frac{1}{2s}}{1 + \frac{1}{2s}} = \frac{1}{2s+1}$$

However,

$$Z_1(s) = 1, Z_2(s) = 2 + s$$

$$\therefore \quad Z_{11}(s) = \frac{V_1}{I_1}\bigg|_{I_2=0}^{s\text{-domain}} = Z_1(s) + Z_3(s)$$

$$= 1 + \frac{1}{2s+1} = \frac{2(s+1)}{2s+1} = \frac{s+1}{s+0.5}$$

$$Z_{12}(s) = \frac{V_1}{I_1}\bigg|_{I_1=0}^{s\text{-domain}} = Z_3(s) = \frac{1}{2s+1}$$

$$Z_{21}(s) = \frac{V_2}{I_1}\bigg|_{I_2=0}^{s\text{-domain}} = Z_3(s) = \frac{1}{2s+1}$$

$$Z_{22}(s) = \frac{V_2}{I_2}\bigg|_{I_1=0}^{s\text{-domain}}$$

$$= Z_2(s) + Z_3(s) = (2+s) + \frac{1}{2s+1}$$

$$= \frac{(2+s)(2s+1)+1}{(2s+1)}$$

$$= \frac{4s+2+2s^2+s+1}{2s+1}$$

$$= \frac{2s^2+5s+3}{2s+1}.$$

$\therefore$ The Z-parameters in s-domain are

$$\mathbf{Z_{11}(s) = \frac{s+1}{s+0.5}}$$

$$\mathbf{Z_{12}(s) = \frac{1}{2s+1}}$$

$$\mathbf{Z_{21}(s) = \frac{1}{2s+1}}$$

$$\mathbf{Z_{22}(s) = \frac{2s^2+5s+3}{2s+1}}.$$

EXAMPLE 11.51 *A network is shown in Fig. E11.76. Determine the Z-parameters.*

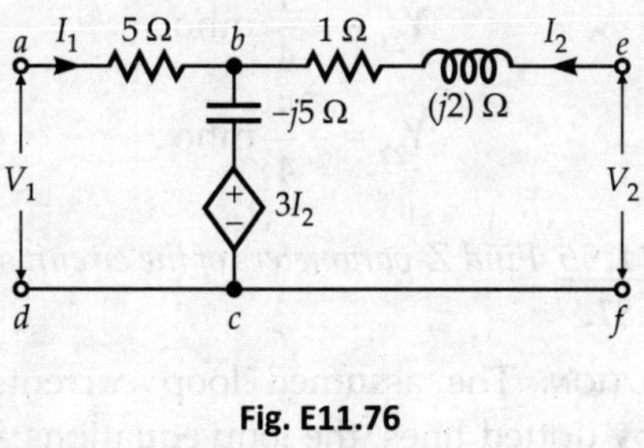

Fig. E11.76

SOLUTION. Writing KVL for loop *abcd*, from Fig. E11.76,

$$V_1 = 5I_1 - j5I_1 + (3I_2) + (-j5I_2)$$

or $$V_1 = (5-j5)I_1 + (3-j5)I_2 \qquad ...(i)$$

Next, applying KVL for loop *bcfe*,

$$I_2(1+j2-j5) + I_1(-j5) + 3I_2 - V_2 = 0$$

or $$V_2 = (-j5)I_1 + (4-j3)I_2 \qquad ...(ii)$$

Thus we obtained two equations,

$$V_1 = (5-j5)I_1 + (3-j5)I_2$$

and $$V_2 = (-j5)I_1 + (4-j3)I_2$$

or in matrix form, $$\begin{bmatrix} V_1 \\ V_2 \end{bmatrix} = \begin{bmatrix} 5-j5 & 3-j5 \\ -j5 & 4-j3 \end{bmatrix} \begin{bmatrix} I_1 \\ I_2 \end{bmatrix}$$

Thus,

$$\mathbf{Z_{11} = (5-j5)\,W;\ Z_{12} = (3-j5)\,\Omega}$$

$$\mathbf{Z_{21} = (-j5)\,W;\ Z_{22} = (4-j3)\,\Omega.}$$

EXAMPLE 11.52 *In a T network, the arm impedances are shown in Fig. E11.77. Find Z parameters.*

[Assume $Z_A = \mathbf{(4+j3)}\Omega$ *;* $Z_B = \mathbf{1\angle -90^\circ}$

$Z_C = \mathbf{(2+j3)\Omega}$*].*

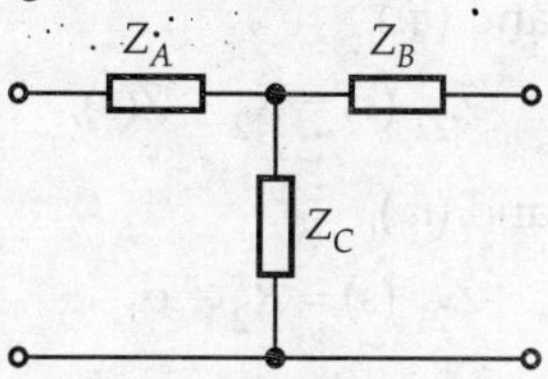

Fig. E11.77

SOLUTION. From the theory of Z parameters,

$$\mathbf{Z_{11}} = Z_A + Z_C \ ;\ \mathbf{Z_{12}} = Z_C$$

$$\mathbf{Z_{21}} = Z_C \ ;\ \mathbf{Z_{22}} = Z_B + Z_C$$

$$\mathbf{Z_{11} = (6+j6)\Omega}$$

$$\mathbf{Z_{12} = (2+j3)\Omega}$$

$$\mathbf{Z_{21} = (2+j3)\Omega}$$

$$\mathbf{Z_{22}} = 1\angle -90^\circ + (2+j3) = \mathbf{(2+j2)\Omega}.$$

EXAMPLE 11.53 *In Fig. E11.78, find the Z-parameters in s-domain.*

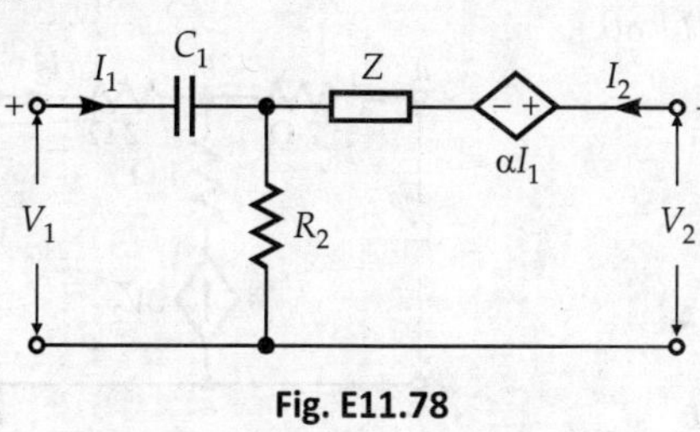

Fig. E11.78

Solution. Comparing the Laplace form of the given circuit (Fig. E11.79) with the equivalent circuit

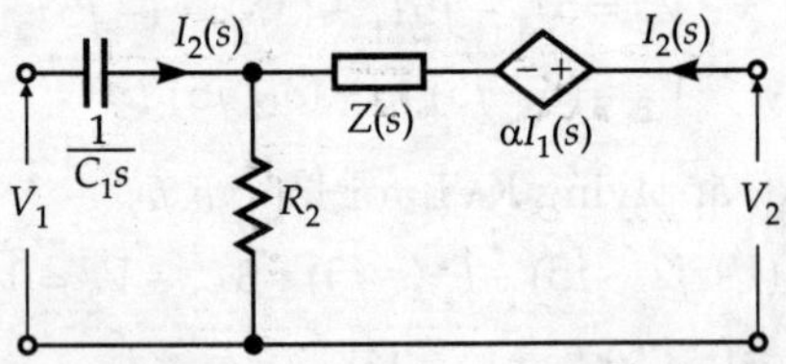

Fig. E11.79

of Z-parameter network in the text (Fig. 11.20), we can write

$$Z_{11}(s) - Z_{12}(s) = \frac{1}{C_1 s} \quad ...(i)$$

$$Z_{12}(s) = R_2 \quad ...(ii)$$

$$Z_{22}(s) - Z_{12}(s) = Z(s) \quad ...(iii)$$

$$[Z_{21}(s) - Z_{12}(s)]\, I_1(s) = \alpha\, I_1(s) \quad ...(iv)$$

From (*i*) and (*ii*),

$$Z_{11}(s) = R_2 + \frac{1}{C_1 s},$$

From (*ii*) and (*iii*),

$$Z_{22}(s) = R_2 + Z(s),$$

From (*ii*) and (*iv*),

$$Z_{21}(s) = R_2 + \alpha,$$

and from (*ii*),

$$Z_{12}(s) = R_2$$

The Z-parameters of the given network in s-domain are

$$\mathbf{Z_{11}(s) = R_2 + \frac{1}{C_1 s}}$$

$$\mathbf{Z_{12}(s) = R_2}$$

$$\mathbf{Z_{21}(s) = R_2 + \alpha}$$

$$\mathbf{Z_{22}(s) = R_2 + Z(s)}.$$

Example 11.54 *Find Y-parameters of the network shown in Fig. E11.80.*

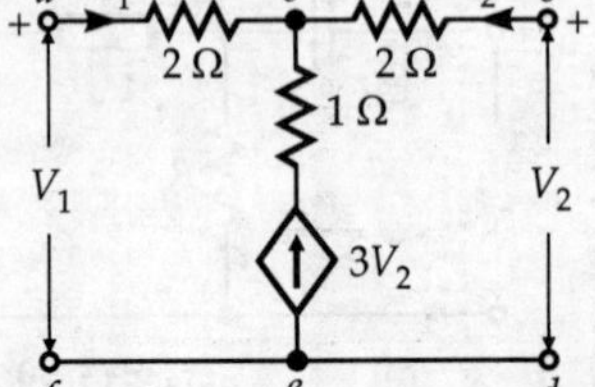

Fig. E11.80

Solution. Let us first apply KVL at the outer loop of the given circuit (*abcdef*), assuming the currents I_1 and I_2 entering the circuit from the input and output sides with application of voltages V_1 and V_2 at the input and output respectively.

We thus obtain,

$$-V_1 + 2I_1 - 2I_2 + V_2 = 0 \quad ...(a)$$

Applying KCL at node (*b*),

$$I_1 + I_2 + 3V_2 = 0$$

or
$$I_1 = -I_2 - 3V_2 \quad ...(b)$$

i.e.,
$$I_2 = -I_1 - 3V_2 \quad ...(c)$$

Substituting the value of I_2 from (*c*) in (*a*),

$$-V_1 + 2I_1 - 2(-I_1 - 3V_2) + V_2 = 0$$

or
$$-V_1 + 4I_1 + 7V_2 = 0$$

or
$$I_1 = -\frac{7}{4}V_2 + \frac{1}{4}V_1 \quad ...(d)$$

Again substituting the value of I_1 from (*b*) in (*a*),

$$-V_1 + 2(-I_2 - 3V_2) - 2I_2 + V_2 = 0$$

or
$$-V_1 - 2I_2 - 6V_2 - 2I_2 + V_2 = 0$$

or
$$-V_1 - 4I_2 - 5V_2 = 0$$

$$\therefore \quad I_2 = -\frac{1}{4}V_1 - \frac{5}{4}V_2 \quad ...(e)$$

Rearranging equations (*d*) and (*e*),

$$I_1 = \frac{1}{4}V_1 - \frac{7}{4}V_2$$

$$I_2 = -\frac{1}{4}V_1 - \frac{5}{4}V_2$$

Comparing these equations with the standard form of the Y-parameter equation,

$$\mathbf{Y_{11} = \frac{1}{4}\ \text{mho}}$$

$$\mathbf{Y_{12} = -\frac{7}{4}\ \text{mho}}$$

$$\mathbf{Y_{21} = -\frac{1}{4}\ \text{mho}}$$

$$\mathbf{Y_{22} = -\frac{5}{4}\ \text{mho}}.$$

Example 11.55 *Find Z-parameters of the circuit shown in Fig. E11.81.*

Solution. The assumed loop currents being shown by dotted lines, the loop equations are :

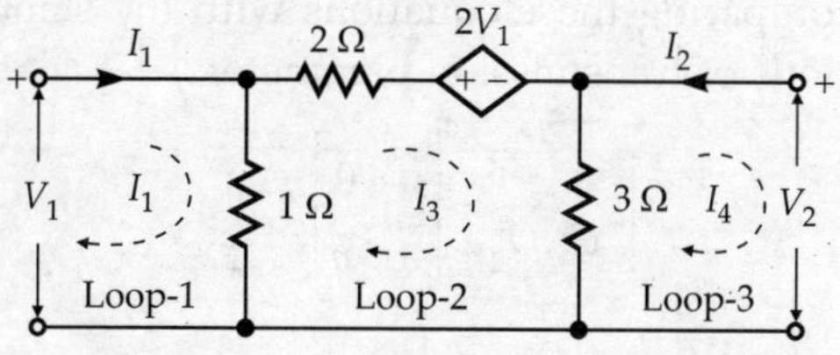

Fig. E11.81

For *loop-1*

$$I_1 - I_3 = V_1 \quad ...(a)$$

For *loop-2*

$$2I_3 + 2V_1 + 3(I_3 - I_4) + 1(I_3 - I_1) = 0$$

or $$-I_1 + 2V_1 + 6I_3 - 3I_4 = 0$$

or $$-I_1 + 3I_2 + 6I_3 = -2V_1, \quad ...(b)$$

$$[\because I_4 \equiv -I_2]$$

For *loop-3*

$$3(I_4 - I_3) + V_2 = 0$$

or $$V_2 = 3(I_3 - I_4)$$

or $$V_2 = 3I_3 + 3I_2 \quad ...(c)$$

Thus the equations are rearranged as

$$I_1 + 0.I_2 - I_3 = V_1 \quad ...(a)$$

$$-I_1 + 3I_2 + 6I_3 = -2V_1 \quad ...(b)$$

$$0.I_1 + 3I_2 + 3I_3 = V_2 \quad ...(c)$$

From (*a*), $I_3 = I_1 - V_1$

Then from (*b*),

$$-I_1 + 3I_2 + 6(I_1 - V_1) = -2V_1$$

or $$5I_1 + 3I_2 = 4V_1$$

or $$V_1 = \frac{5}{4}I_1 + \frac{3}{4}I_2 \quad ...(d)$$

Again, using (*a*) in (*c*),

$$+3I_2 + 3(I_1 - V_1) = V_2$$

or $$+3I_2 + 3I_1 - 3V_1 = V_2$$

or $$V_2 = 3I_2 + 3I_1 - 3\left[\frac{5}{4}I_1 + \frac{3}{4}I_2\right]$$

$\therefore$ $$V_2 = 3I_1 - \frac{15}{4}I_1 + 3I_2 - \frac{9}{4}I_2$$

or $$V_2 = -\frac{3}{4}I_1 + \frac{3}{4}I_2 \quad ...(e)$$

Comparing (*d*) and (*e*) with the standard equations of *Z*-parameter,

$$\mathbf{Z_{11} = \frac{5}{4}\Omega;\ Z_{12} = \frac{3}{4}\Omega;\ Z_{21} = -\frac{3}{4}\Omega;\ Z_{22} = \frac{3}{4}\Omega}$$

EXAMPLE 11.56 *A transistorised two port network is represented by the following values of h-parameters :*

Generator impedance $(Z_S) = 1\,k\Omega$
Short circuit input impedance $(h_i) = 1\,k\Omega$
Short circuit forward current ratio $(h_f) = 40$
Open circuit reverse voltage ratio $(h_r) = 350 \times 10^{-6}$
Open circuit output admittance $(h_0) = 30 \times 10^{-6}$ *mho*
Load impedance $(Z_L) = 10\,k\Omega$

Draw the equivalent h-parameter model, determine the input impedance, output impedance, voltage gain, current gain.

SOLUTION. From the given data

$$h_i = h_{11} = 1000 \text{ ohms};\ h_f = h_{21} = 40$$

$$h_r = h_{12} = 350 \times 10^{-6};\quad h_o = h_{22} = 30 \times 10^{-6} \text{ mho.}$$

The governing equation of the *h*-parameter representations then become

$$V_1 = h_{11}I_1 + h_{12}V_2;\quad I_2 = h_{21}I_1 + h_{22}V_2$$

The equivalent circuit has been drawn in Fig. E11.82.

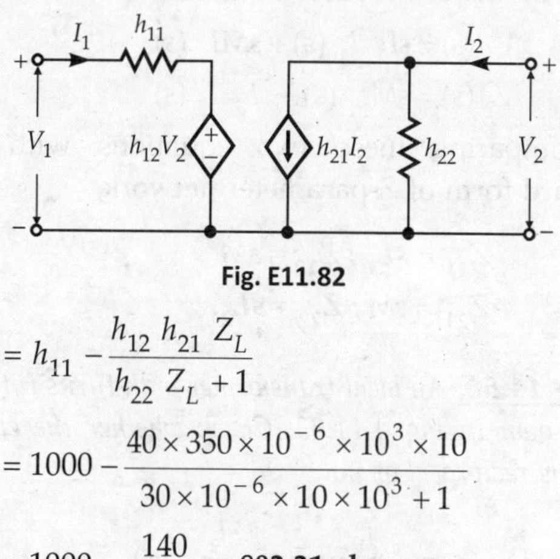

Fig. E11.82

$$Z_{in} = h_{11} - \frac{h_{12}h_{21}Z_L}{h_{22}Z_L + 1}$$

$$= 1000 - \frac{40 \times 350 \times 10^{-6} \times 10^3 \times 10}{30 \times 10^{-6} \times 10 \times 10^3 + 1}$$

$$= 1000 - \frac{140}{1 + 0.3} = \mathbf{892.31\ ohms}$$

$$Z_{out} = \frac{1}{\left[h_{22} - \frac{h_{12}h_{21}}{h_{11} + Z_s}\right]}$$

$$= \frac{1}{30 \times 10^{-6} - \frac{40 \times 350 \times 10^{-6}}{1000 + 1000}}$$

$$= \frac{1}{10^{-6}\left(30 - \frac{14000}{2000}\right)}$$

$$= \frac{1}{10^{-6}(30 - 7)} = 0.0435 \times 10^6 = \mathbf{43.5\ k\,\Omega.}$$

$$\text{Voltage gain} = \frac{h_{21}\,R_L}{h_{12}\,h_{21}\,R_L - h_{11}\,(1 + h_{22}\,R_L)}$$

$$= \frac{40 \times 10 \times 10^3}{40 \times 350 \times 10^{-6} \times 10 \times 10^3 - 1000\,(1 + 30 \times 10^{-6} \times 10^4)}$$

$$= \frac{4 \times 10^5}{140 - 1000\,(1 + 0.3)} = \mathbf{-3.4 \times 10^2.}$$

[–ve voltage gain means 180° phase shift between V_2 and V_1].

Current gain

$$= \frac{h_{21}}{1 + h_{22}\,R_L} = \frac{40}{1 + 30 \times 10^{-6} \times 10^4}$$

$$= \frac{40}{1 + 0.3} = \mathbf{30.76.}$$

EXAMPLE 11.57 *Obtain Z-parameters of an ideal transformer.*

SOLUTION. From the text, the equations for the circuit model of the ideal transformer are given by

$$V_1\,(s) = sL_1\,I_1\,(s) + sMI_2\,(s)$$
$$V_2\,(s) = sMI_1\,(s) + sL_2\,I_2\,(s)$$

Comparing these two equations with the standard form of Z-parameter network,

$$\mathbf{Z_{11} = sL_1\,;\ Z_{12} = sM}$$
$$\mathbf{Z_{21} = sM\,;\ Z_{22} = sL_2.}$$

EXAMPLE 11.58 *An ideal transformer with turns ratio n : 1 is shown in Fig. E11.83. Check whether the circuit model is reciprocal or not.*

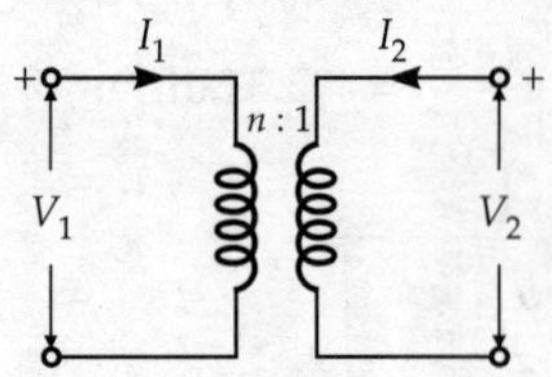

Fig. E11.83

SOLUTION. Here, $V_1 = \frac{1}{n} . V_2$

$I_1 = -n\,I_2$ [refer to the text]

These equations can be configured as

$$V_1 = \frac{1}{n} V_2 + 0\,(-I_2)$$

$$I_1 = 0.V_2 + n\,(-I_2)$$

Comparing these equations with the standard equations of transmission parameters,

$$\begin{bmatrix} A & B \\ C & D \end{bmatrix} = \begin{bmatrix} \frac{1}{n} & 0 \\ 0 & n \end{bmatrix}$$

Here, $\quad AD - BC = \frac{1}{n} \times n - 0 = 1$

$\therefore$ **The ideal transformer is reciprocal.**

EXAMPLE 11.59 *Find the transmision parameter matrix of Fig. E11.84.*

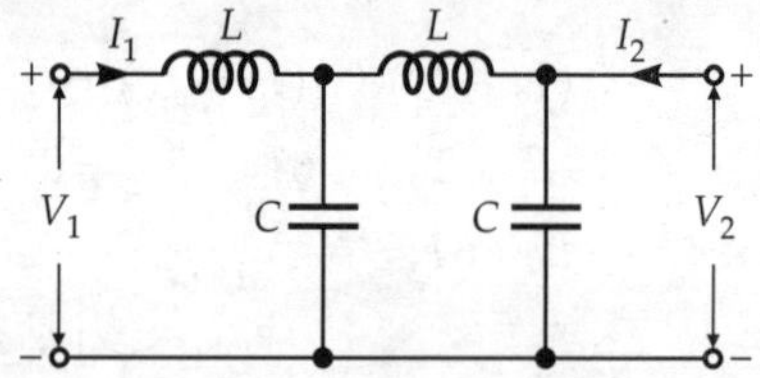

Fig. E11.84

SOLUTION. Let us first transform the given network of Fig. E11.84 into *s*-domain. The Laplace configuration of the network is shown in Fig. E11.85.

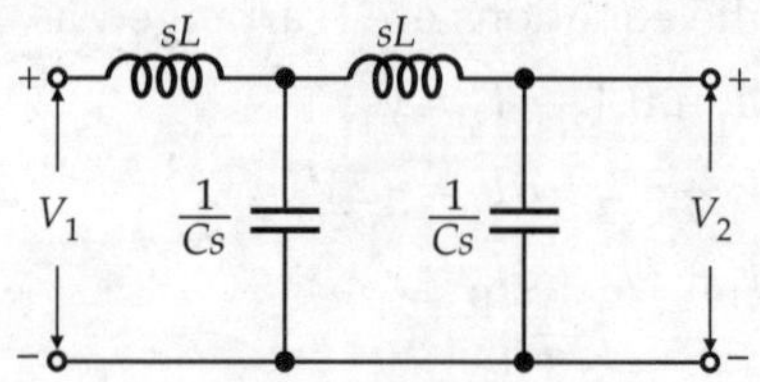

Fig. E11.85

It may be observed that this circuit is a cascaded combination of the two networks as shown in Fig. E11.86.

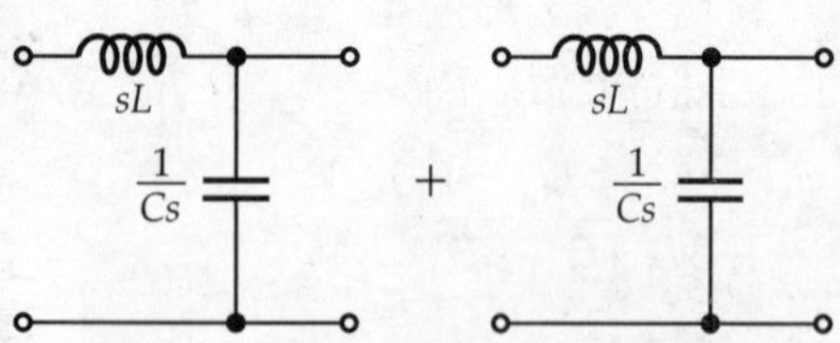

Fig. E11.86

Again each of the two cascaded networks can be assumed to be cascade connection of one series element with one shunt element.

Here, $V_1 = ZI_1 + V_2$ and $I_1 = -I_2$ for the series network [Fig. E11.87(*b*)]

i.e.,
$$\begin{bmatrix} A_1 & B_1 \\ C_1 & D_1 \end{bmatrix} = \begin{bmatrix} 1 & Z \\ 0 & 1 \end{bmatrix}$$

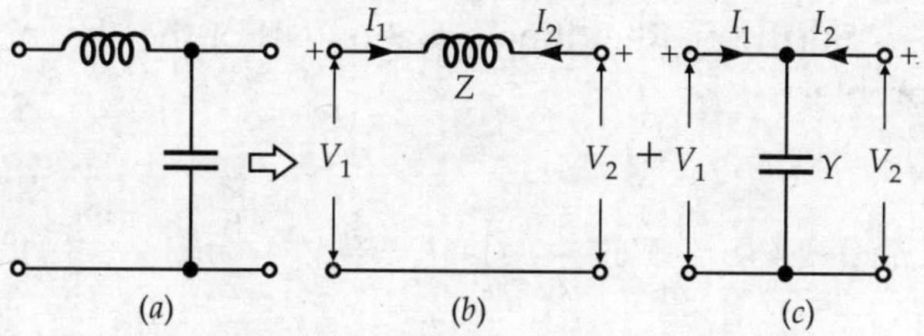

Fig. E11.87

and $\quad V_1 = V_2 \; ; \; I_1 = YV_2 - I_2$

for the shunt network [Fig. E11.87(c)]

i.e.,
$$\begin{bmatrix} A_2 & B_2 \\ C_2 & D_2 \end{bmatrix} = \begin{bmatrix} 1 & 0 \\ Y & 1 \end{bmatrix}$$

$\therefore$ For Fig. E11.87(a),

$$\begin{bmatrix} A' & B' \\ C' & D' \end{bmatrix} = \begin{bmatrix} A_1 & B_1 \\ C_1 & D_1 \end{bmatrix}\begin{bmatrix} A_2 & B_2 \\ C_2 & D_2 \end{bmatrix}$$

$$= \begin{bmatrix} 1 & Z \\ 0 & 1 \end{bmatrix}\begin{bmatrix} 1 & 0 \\ Y & 1 \end{bmatrix}$$

$$= \begin{bmatrix} 1 & Ls \\ 0 & 1 \end{bmatrix}\begin{bmatrix} 1 & 0 \\ Cs & 1 \end{bmatrix} = \begin{bmatrix} 1+s^2 LC & sL \\ sC & 1 \end{bmatrix}$$

Referring back to Fig. E11.85,

$$\begin{bmatrix} A & B \\ C & D \end{bmatrix} = \begin{bmatrix} A' & B' \\ C' & D' \end{bmatrix}\begin{bmatrix} A' & B' \\ C' & D' \end{bmatrix}$$

$$= \begin{bmatrix} 1+s^2 LC & sL \\ sC & 1 \end{bmatrix}^2$$

$$= \begin{bmatrix} \mathbf{1+3s^2 LC+s^4 L^2C^2} & \mathbf{sL\,(2+s^2 LC)} \\ \mathbf{sC\,(2+s^2 LC)} & \mathbf{1+s^2 LC} \end{bmatrix}.$$

EXAMPLE 11.60 *What is the voltage and power gain of the circuit shown in Fig. E11.88 ? Assume* $n = \frac{1}{10}$.

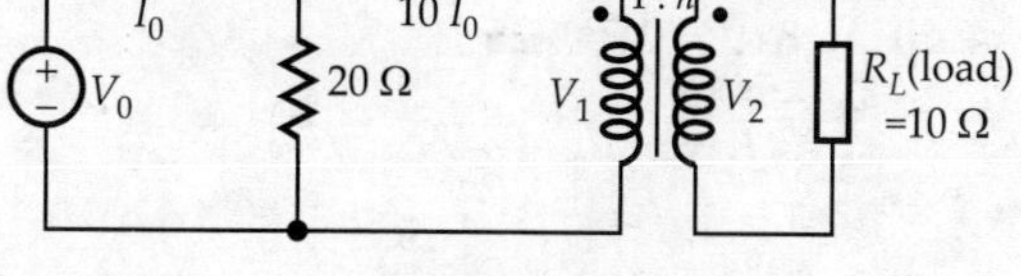

Fig. E11.88

SOLUTION. Let us designate the currents in the loops and drops across the windings of the transformer.

Applying KVL in the leftmost loop,

$$V_0 = 100\, I_0 + 20\,(I_0 - I_1)$$

$$= 100\, I_0 + 20\,(I_0 + 10\, I_0) \qquad [\because I_1 = -10\, I_0\,]$$

$$= 100\, I_0 + 220\, I_0$$

or
$$I_0 = \frac{V_0}{320}\, \text{A}$$

Also, $\quad I_1 = -10\, I_0 = -10\,\dfrac{V_0}{320} = -\dfrac{V_0}{32}.$

From the theory of ideal transformer,

$$I_2 = -\frac{I_1}{n} = -\frac{I_1}{\frac{1}{10}} = +\frac{V_0}{32} \times 10 = \frac{10\, V_0}{32}$$

Thus $\quad V_2 = -R_L\, I_2 = -10 \times \dfrac{10\, V_0}{32} = -\dfrac{100}{32}\, V_0\,,$

or Voltage gain $= \dfrac{V_2}{V_0} = -\dfrac{100}{32} = \mathbf{-3.125}$

To find power gain, first let us calculate the power supplied (instantaneous) by the independent voltage source (V_0).

$$\therefore \qquad p_0 = v_0\, i_0 = v_0 \times \frac{v_o}{320} = \frac{v_0^2}{320}.$$

Power absorbed by the load resistor (r_L) is

$$p_2 = \frac{V_2^2}{10} = \frac{\left(-\dfrac{100}{32}\, v_0\right)^2}{10} = \frac{10^3}{1024}\, v_0^2$$

$$\therefore \text{ Power gain} = \frac{p_2}{p_0} = \frac{10^3}{1024} \times 320 = \mathbf{312.5.}$$

EXAMPLE 11.61 *Obtain short circuit parameters of the network shown in Fig. E11.89.*

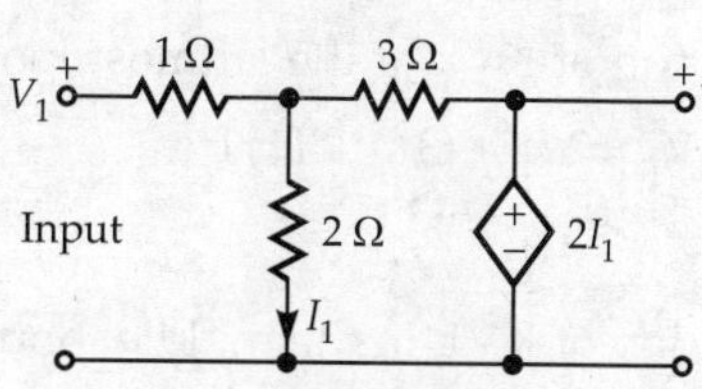

Fig. E11.89

SOLUTION. To obtain the short circuit parameters (*i.e.*, *Y*-parameters), short circuit is applied at the output port. (Fig. E11.90). Under this condition,

$$2 I_1 = 0$$

i.e.,
$$I_1 = 0$$

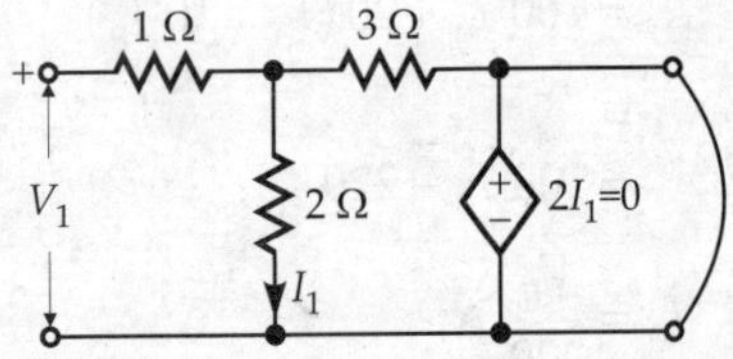

Fig. E11.90

However, I_1 should be a finite quantity as V_1, the voltage applied at the input port is a nonzero quantity. This apparent paradox indicates that the solution of the network though Y-parameter concept is not possible and *it can be concluded that the Y-parameters of the network do not exist.*

EXAMPLE 11.62 *Find Z-parameters of the network shown in Fig. E11.91.*

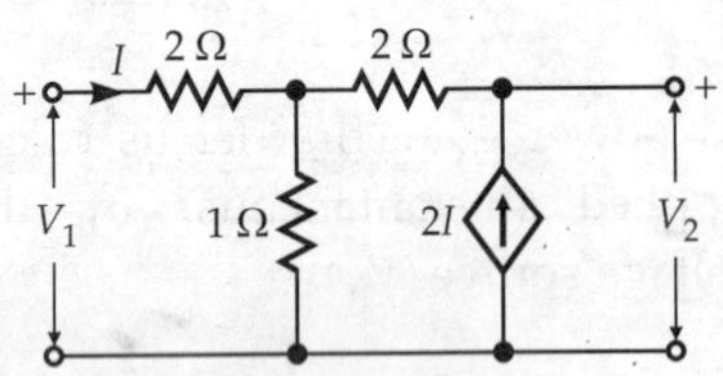

Fig. E11.91

SOLUTION. Let us redraw the given circuit with respective branch currents (Fig. E11.92).

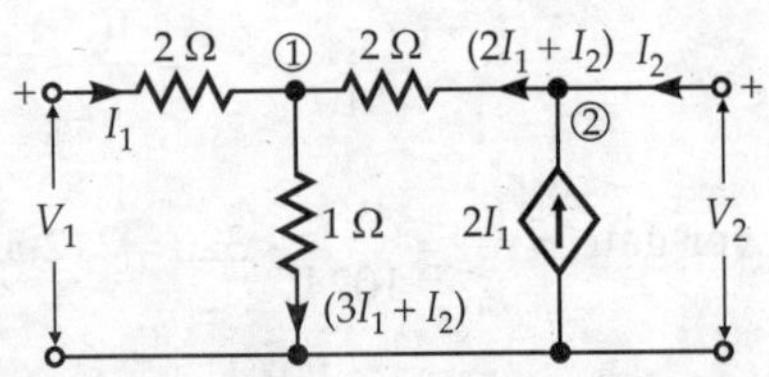

Fig. E11.92

Application of KVL at the leftmost loop yields

$$V_1 = 2I_1 + (3I_1 + I_2)1$$

or $$V_1 = 5I_1 + I_2 \qquad ...(A)$$

Application of KVL in the middle loop [*i.e.*, the loop involving the nodes (1) and (2)] gives

$$+2(2I_1 + I_2) + (3I_1 + I_2)1 - V_2 = 0$$

or $$V_2 = +7I_1 + 3I_2 \qquad ...(B)$$

From equations (A) and (B),

$$Z_{11} = 5\,\Omega,\ Z_{12} = 1\,\Omega,\ Z_{21} = 7\,\Omega,\ Z_{22} = 3\,\Omega.$$

EXAMPLE 11.63 *Find the transmission parameters of the network shown in Fig. E11.91.*

SOLUTION. Rewriting equation (A) of the above problem,

$$V_1 = 5I_1 + I_2$$

$$= 5\left(\frac{1}{7}V_2 - \frac{3}{7}I_2\right) + I_2 = \frac{5}{7}V_2 - \frac{8}{7}I_2 \qquad ...(A)$$

and from equation (B) of the same problem,

$$I_1 = \frac{1}{7}V_2 - \frac{3}{7}I_2 \qquad ...(C)$$

Comparing equations (A) and (C) with the standard form of the equations of $ABCD$ parameters, $\mathbf{A = \frac{5}{7}, B = \frac{8}{7}\,\Omega, C = \frac{1}{7}}$ **mho**, $\mathbf{D = \frac{3}{7}}$.

EXAMPLE 11.64 *In a two port network,*

$$Z_{11} = 2\,\Omega,\ Z_{12} = Z_{21} = 5\,\Omega,\ Z_{22} = 1\,\Omega$$

Find : (i) Y-parameters (ii) h-parameters (iii) ABCD parameters.

SOLUTION. Z-parameter equations are given by

$$V_1 = Z_{11}\,I_1 + Z_{12}\,I_2$$

and $$V_2 = Z_{21}\,I_1 + Z_{22}\,I_2$$

With the given values,

$$V_1 = 2I_1 + 5I_2 \qquad ...(1)$$

$$V_2 = 5I_1 + I_2 \qquad ...(2)$$

To find Y-parameters the equations in (1) are modified as follows :

$$2.5\,V_1 = 5I_1 + 12.5I_2 \qquad ...(3)$$

Subtracting (3) from (2),

$$V_2 - 2.5\,V_1 = I_2 - 12.5\,I_2 = -11.5\,I_2$$

$$\therefore \quad I_2 = +\frac{2.5}{11.5}V_1 - \frac{1}{11.5}V_2$$

or $$I_2 = 0.217\,V_1 - 0.087\,V_2 \qquad ...(4)$$

Again multiplying equation (2) by 5 and subtracting from equation (1), we get

$$V_1 - 5V_2 = 2I_1 - 25\,I_1$$

or $$23\,I_1 = -V_1 + 5\,V_2$$

or $$I_1 = -\frac{1}{23}V_1 + \frac{5}{23}V_2$$

$$= -0.0434\,V_1 + 0.217\,V_2 \qquad ...(5)$$

Thus from equations (4) and (5),

$\mathbf{Y_{11} = -0.0434}$ **mho** ; $\mathbf{Y_{12} = 0.217}$ **mho**

$\mathbf{Y_{21} = 0.217}$ **mho** ; $\mathbf{Y_{22} = -0.087}$ **mho.**

To obtain *h*-parameters, equation (5) is rewritten as

$$0.0434\ V_1 = -I_1 + 0.217\ V_2$$

or $$V_1 = -23\ I_1 + 5\ V_2 \quad ...(6)$$

and equation (2) is rewritten as

$$I_2 = -5I_1 + V_2 \quad ...(7)$$

Comparing equations (6) and (7) with those of standard *h*-parameter equations,

$$\boldsymbol{h_{11} = -23,\ h_{12} = 5}$$

$$\boldsymbol{h_{21} = -5,\ h_{22} = 1.0.}$$

To obtain *ABCD* parameters, equation (4) is rearranged as

$$0.217\ V_1 = 0.087\ V_2 + I_2$$

or $$V_1 = 0.4\ V_2 + 4.61\ I_2 \quad ...(8)$$

Rearranging equation (2), we get

$$5I_1 = V_2 - I_2$$

or $$I_1 = 0.2\ V_2 - 0.2\ I_2 \quad ...(9)$$

Comparing equations (8) and (9) with standard equation of transmission parameters,

$$\boldsymbol{A = 0.4,\ B = -4.61\ \Omega}$$

$$\boldsymbol{C = 0.2\ \text{mho},\ D = 0.2.}$$

EXAMPLE 11.65 *Find Z parameters of the following network (Fig. E11.93).*

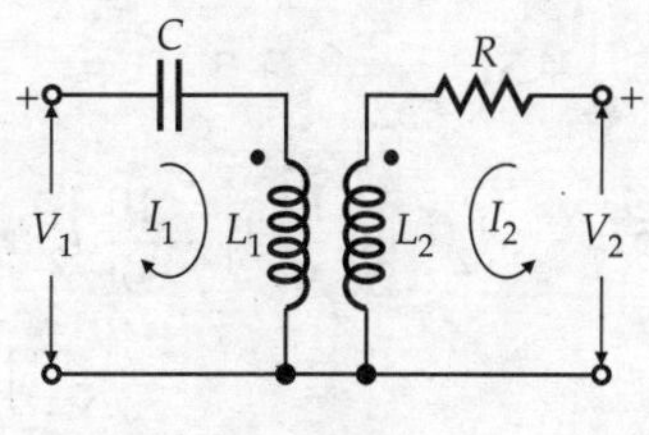

Fig. E11.93

SOLUTION. Let us first transform the network of Fig. E11.94 in Laplace domain.

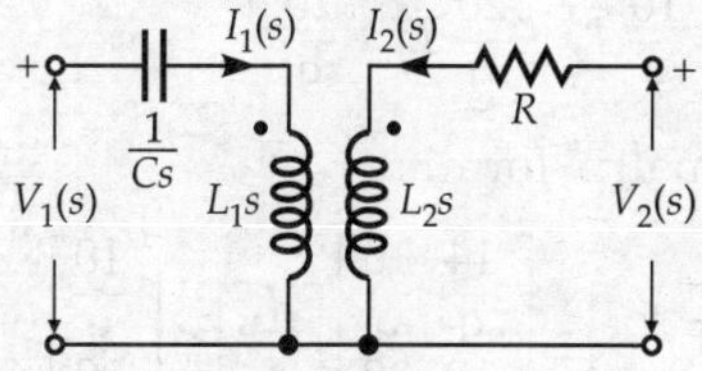

Fig. E11.94

Using KVL,

$$V_1(s) = \left(L_1 s + \frac{1}{Cs}\right) I_1(s) + sMI_2(s) \quad ...(1)$$

and $$V_2(s) = (R + L_2 s)\ I_2(s) + sMI_1(s)$$

or $$V_2(s) = sMI_1(s) + (R + L_2 s)\ I_2(s) \quad ...(2)$$

Thus from equations (1) and (2),

$$\boldsymbol{Z_{11} = L_1 s + \frac{1}{Cs},\ Z_{12}(s) = sM}$$

$$\boldsymbol{Z_{21} = sM\ Z_{22} = R + L_2 s}$$

It may also be noted that as

$$Z_{12}(s) = Z_{21}(s) = sM.$$

∴ The given circuit is also reciprocal.

EXAMPLE 11.66 *Find Z parameters of the following circuit (Fig. E11.95).*

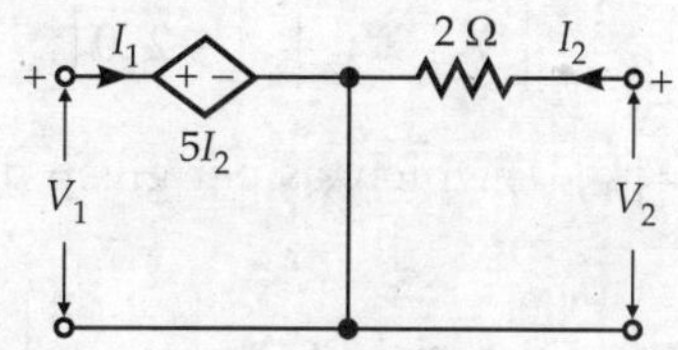

Fig. E11.95

SOLUTION. Applying KVL in the left handed loop,

$$V_1 = 0.I_1 + 5I_2 \quad ...(1)$$

Applying KVL in the right handed loop,

$$V_2 = 2I_2 + 0.(I_1 + I_2)$$

$$= 0.I_1 + 2I_2 \quad ...(2)$$

From (1) and (2), we get

$$\boldsymbol{Z_{11} = 0\ \Omega,\ Z_{12} = 5\ \Omega}$$

$$\boldsymbol{Z_{21} = 0,\ Z_{22} = 2\ \Omega}$$

It may be noted that for this circuit,

$$Z = \begin{bmatrix} 0 & 5 \\ 0 & 2 \end{bmatrix} \text{ and } Y = [Z]^{-1}$$

However, it is evident that with the given values of Z, $Y\ (=[Z]^{-1})$ does not exist.

∴ For the given circuit, Y parameter does not exist. Also, it can be observed that in this circuit, V_1 and V_2 can not be chosen independently justifying the absence of Y parameter.

EXAMPLE 11.67 *If the current through 1Ω resistor is I_0 A, find Y and Z parameters of the network shown in Fig. E11.96.*

CHAPTER 11

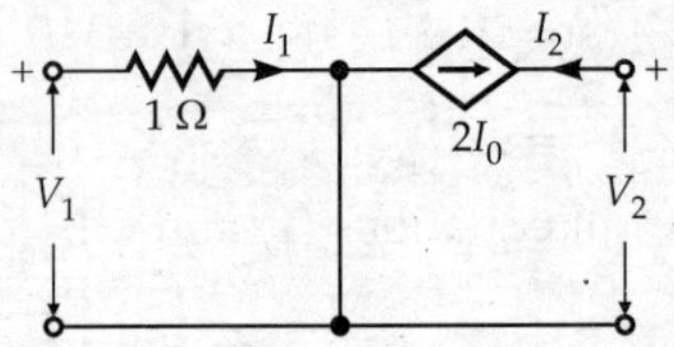

Fig. E11.96

SOLUTION.

$$V_1 = I_1 \times 1 + 0.(I_1 + I_2) = I_1 = I_0$$

$\therefore \quad I_1 = V_1 + 0.V_2$ ...(1)

Also, $\quad I_2 = -2I_0 = -2V_1 + 0.V_2$ ...(2)

Then from (1) and (2)

$$Y = \begin{bmatrix} Y_{11} & Y_{12} \\ Y_{21} & Y_{22} \end{bmatrix} = \begin{bmatrix} 1 & 0 \\ -2 & 0 \end{bmatrix}$$

But $Z = [Y]^{-1}$, which, as per given data can not exist.

$\therefore$ For the given circuit, $\mathbf{Y} = \begin{bmatrix} \mathbf{1} & \mathbf{0} \\ -\mathbf{2} & \mathbf{0} \end{bmatrix}$ and **Z does not exist.**

It may also be observed that as I_1 and I_2 can not be chosen independently hence Z parameters in this circuit can not exist.

EXAMPLE 11.68 *In the network of Fig. E11.97, Find (i) Z-parameters (ii) Y-parameters.*

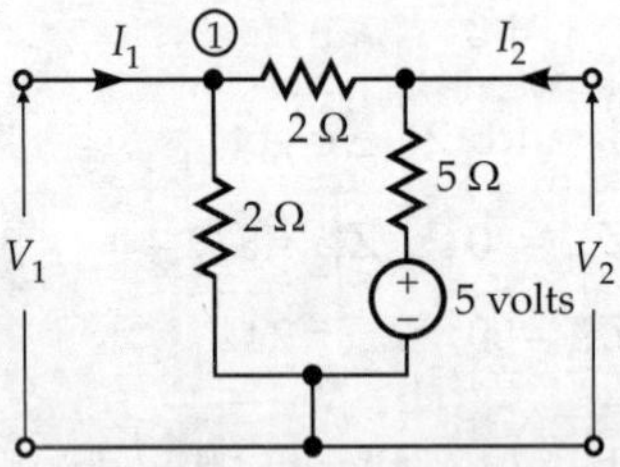

Fig. E11.97

SOLUTION. Let the circuit be redrawn with the branch currents as shown in Fig. E11.98.

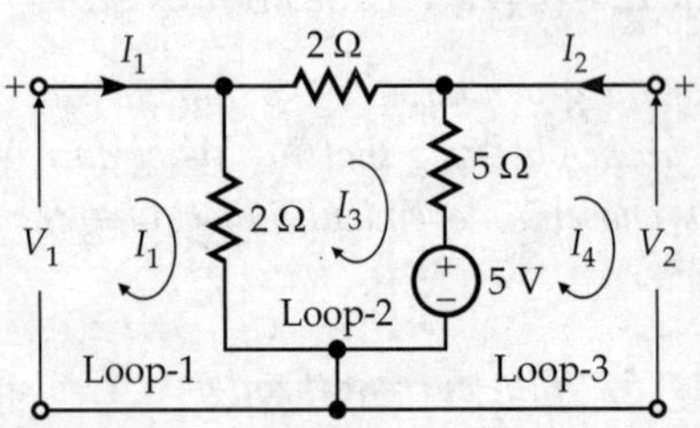

Fig. E11.98

In *loop-1*, KVL yields,

$$2(I_1 - I_3) = V_1$$

or $\quad 2I_3 = 2I_1 - V_1$

or $\quad I_3 = I_1 - \frac{1}{2}V_1$ ...(1)

In *loop-2*, KVL yields

$$2I_3 + 5(I_3 - I_4) + 5 + 2(I_3 - I_1) = 0$$

or $\quad 9I_3 - 5I_4 - 2I_1 = -5$

but, $\quad I_4 = -I_2$

$\therefore$ We get,

$$9I_3 + 5I_2 - 2I_1 = -5$$

or $\quad 9\left[I_1 - \frac{V_1}{2}\right] + 5I_2 - 2I_1 = -5$ [utilising (1)]

or $\quad 7I_1 + 5I_2 = \frac{9}{2}V_1 - 5$

i.e., $\quad V_1 = \frac{14}{9}I_1 + \frac{10}{9}I_2 + \frac{10}{9}$ ...(2)

For *loop-3*, application of KVL yields

$$5(I_4 - I_3) + V_2 - 5 = 0$$

or $\quad -5I_3 - 5I_2 + V_2 - 5 = 0$ $\quad [\because I_4 = -I_2]$

or $\quad -5\left(I_1 - \frac{1}{2}V_1\right) - 5I_2 + V_2 - 5 = 0$

or $\quad -5I_1 - 5I_2 + \frac{5}{2}V_1 + V_2 - 5 = 0$

or $\quad V_2 = 5I_1 + 5I_2 - \frac{5}{2}V_1 + 5$

$$= 5I_1 + 5I_2 - \frac{5}{2}\left[\frac{14}{9}I_1 + \frac{10}{9}I_2 + \frac{10}{9}\right] + 5$$

[utilising (2)]

$$= 5I_1 + 5I_2 - \frac{35}{9}I_1 - \frac{25}{9}I_2 - \frac{25}{9} + 5$$

$$= \frac{10}{9}I_1 + \frac{20}{9}I_2 + \frac{20}{9}$$

or $\quad V_2 = \frac{10}{9}I_1 + \frac{20}{9}I_2 + \frac{20}{9}$ ...(3)

$\therefore$ In matrix form

$$\begin{bmatrix} V_1 \\ V_2 \end{bmatrix} = \begin{bmatrix} \frac{14}{9} & \frac{10}{9} \\ \frac{10}{9} & \frac{20}{9} \end{bmatrix} \begin{bmatrix} I_1 \\ I_2 \end{bmatrix} + \begin{bmatrix} \frac{10}{9} \\ \frac{20}{9} \end{bmatrix}$$

i.e., $\quad \mathbf{Z_{11} = \frac{14}{9}}\,\Omega$; $\mathbf{Z_{12} = Z_{21} = \frac{10}{9}}\,\Omega$

$$\mathbf{Z_{22} = \frac{20}{9}}\,\Omega.$$

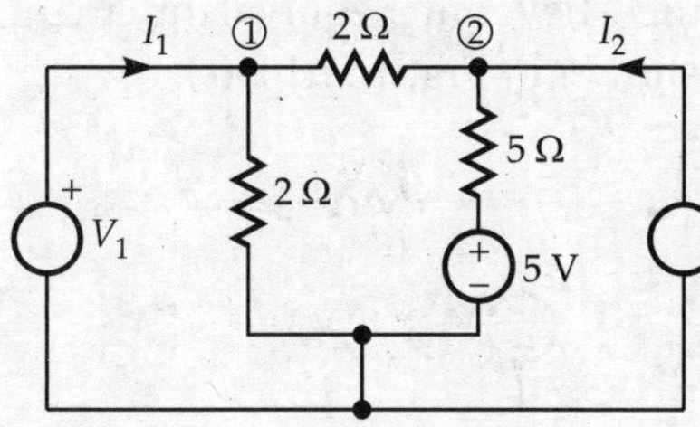

Fig. E11.99

In order to find the Y parameters, the given circuit is redrawn with respective nodes (Fig. E11.99).

At *node (1)*,

$$I_1 = \frac{V_1}{2} + \frac{V_1 - V_2}{2}$$

or $$I_1 = V_1 - \frac{V_2}{2} \qquad ...(1)$$

At *node (2)*,

$$I_2 = \frac{V_2 - 5}{5} + \frac{V_2 - V_1}{2}$$

or $$I_2 = -\frac{V_1}{2} + \frac{7}{10} V_2 - 1 \qquad ...(2)$$

∴ In matrix form

$$\begin{bmatrix} I_1 \\ I_2 \end{bmatrix} = \begin{bmatrix} 1 & -\frac{1}{2} \\ -\frac{1}{2} & \frac{7}{10} \end{bmatrix} \begin{bmatrix} V_1 \\ V_2 \end{bmatrix} - \begin{bmatrix} 0 \\ +1 \end{bmatrix}$$

i.e., $$\mathbf{Y_{11} = 1 \text{ mho}, Y_{12} = Y_{21} = -\frac{1}{2} \text{ mho},}$$

$$\mathbf{Y_{22} = \frac{7}{10} \text{ mho.}}$$

EXAMPLE 11.69 *In the network of Fig. E11.100, $r_1 = 10\ k\,\Omega$, $r_2 = 40\ k\Omega$, $\beta = 3 \times 10^{-4}$, $\alpha = 25$, $R_L = 50\ k\Omega$.*

Find : (i) h-parameters, (ii) voltage gain, (iii) input impedance.

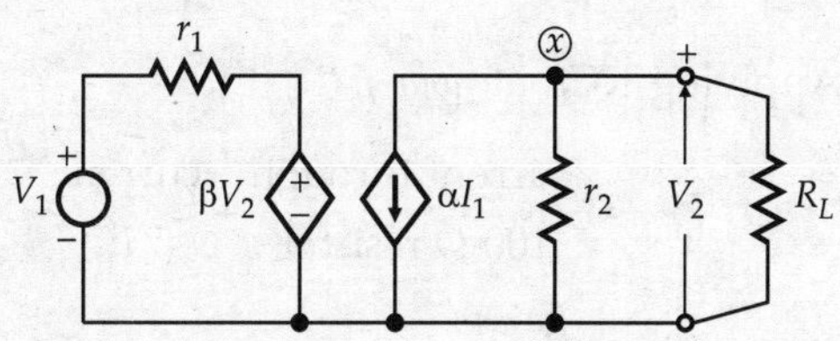

Fig. E11.100

SOLUTION. Let us first redraw the h-parameter circuit (Fig. E11.101).

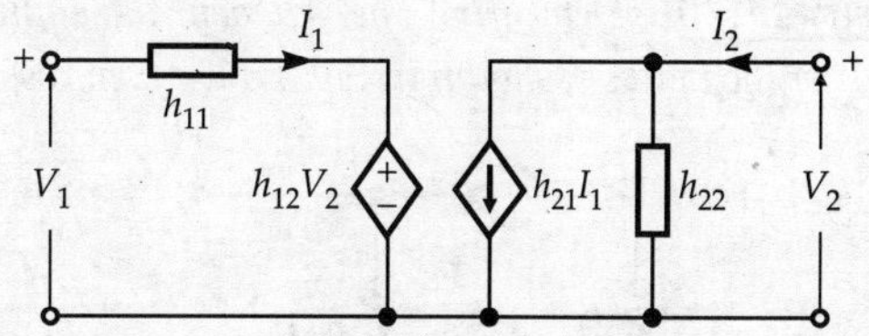

Fig. E11.101

Comparison of Fig. E11.100 and Fig. E11.101 reveals,

$$\mathbf{h_{11} = r_1 = 10\ k\Omega}$$
$$\mathbf{h_{12} = \beta = 3 \times 10^{-4}}$$
$$\mathbf{h_{21} = \alpha = 25}$$
$$\mathbf{h_{22} = (1/r_2) = \frac{1}{40 \times 10^3} \text{ mho} = 25 \times 10^{-6} \text{ mho}}$$

To find voltage gain, let us apply KCL at node (x) in Fig. E11.100. We thus find

$$25\ I_1 + \frac{V_2}{50{,}000} + \frac{V_2}{40{,}000} = 0$$

or $$5 \times 10^6\ I_1 + 9V_2 = 0 \qquad ...(i)$$

But $$I_1 = \frac{V_1 - 3 \times 10^{-4}\ V_2}{10{,}000} \qquad ...(ii)$$

Substitution of (*ii*) in (*i*), we get

$$5 \times 10^6 \times \frac{V_1 - 3 \times 10^{-4}\ V_2}{10{,}000} + 9\ V_2 = 0$$

or $$500\ V_1 - \frac{15\ V_2}{100} + 9V_2 = 0$$

or $$500\ V_1 + 8.85\ V_2 = 0$$

$$\therefore \quad V_2 / V_1 = -\frac{500}{8.85} = -56.5 \text{ (Voltage gain).}$$

Thus **voltage gain of the given network = 56.5**

Also, from (*ii*),

$$I_1 = \frac{V_1 - 3 \times 10^{-4} \times (-56.5)\ V_1}{10{,}000}$$
$$= \frac{V_1 + 0.017\ V_1}{10{,}000} = \frac{1.017}{10{,}000} V_1$$
$$= 1.017 \times 10^{-4}\ V_1$$

$$\therefore \ V_1 / I_1 = \text{input impedance}$$
$$= \frac{1}{1.017 \times 10^{-4}} = 9.83 \times 10^3\ \Omega.$$

∴ Input impedance of the given circuit

$$\mathbf{= 9.83 \times 10^3\ \Omega.}$$

CHAPTER 11

EXAMPLE 11.70 *Determine the Thevenin's equivalent circuit of the network shown in Fig. E11.102 across a-b.*

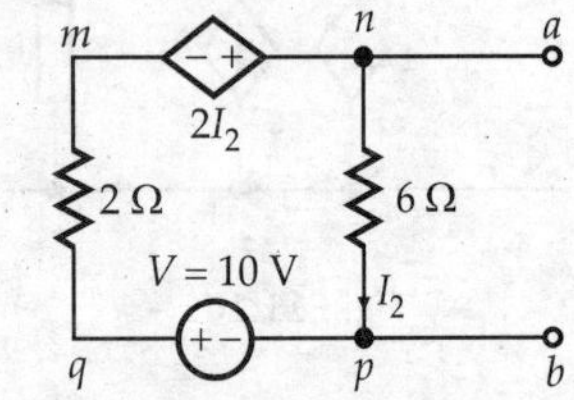

Fig. E11.102

SOLUTION. Let us first short circuit terminal *ab*. This will make the current through the 6 Ω resistor zero as the current will flow through the terminals *a-b*, being shorted "by passing" 6 Ω resistor.

$$\therefore \quad I_2 = 0$$

Thus in loop *mnpq*, the dependent voltage source $2I_2$ is zero. Fig. E11.102 is then redrawn as Fig. E11.103(*a*).

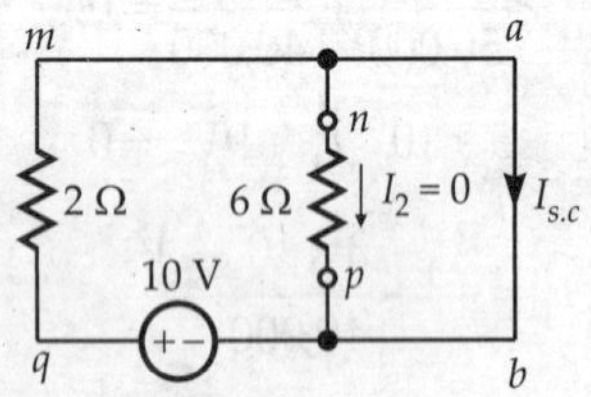

Fig. E11.103 (*a*)

Here KVL in loop *mabq* leads

$$10 = I_{s.c} \times 2\,; \qquad \therefore\ I_{s.c} = \mathbf{5\ A}$$

Let us now keep terminal *a-b* open in Fig. 11.103(*b*). KVL application in loop *mnpq* leads

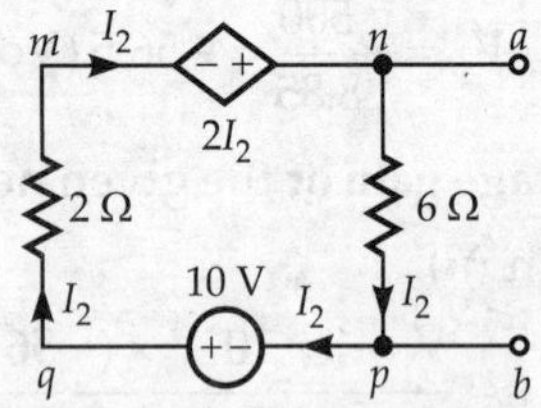

Fig. E11.103 (*b*)

$$-10 + I_2 \times 2 - 2I_2 + 6I_2 = 0$$

or
$$-10 + 6I_2 = 0$$
$$I_2 = 1.67\ \text{A}$$

This gives $V_{o.c}$ (*i.e.* voltage across *a-b*)

$$= 1.67 \times 6 = \mathbf{10\ V}$$

$$R_{\text{int}} = \frac{V_{o.c}}{I_{s.c}} = \frac{10}{5} = \mathbf{2\ \Omega}$$

Thus the Thevenin's equivalent circuit, can be drawn as shown in **Fig. E11.103(*c*).**

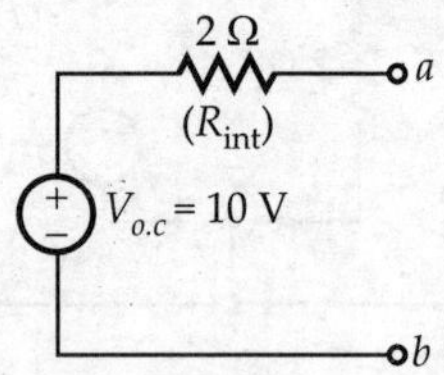

Fig. E11.103 (*c*)

[The Norton's equivalent circuit can also be drawn as shown in **Fig. E11.103(*d*)**].

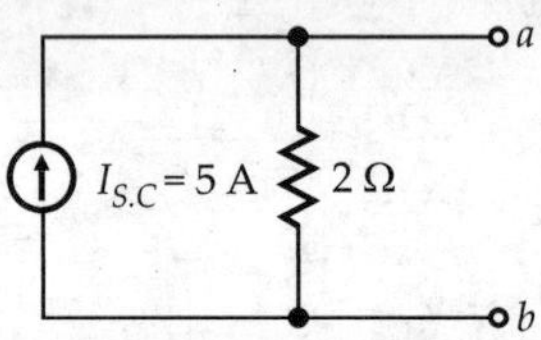

Fig. E11.103 (*d*)

EXAMPLE 11.71 *Find Thevenin's equivalent circuit at terminal a-b (Fig. E11.104).*

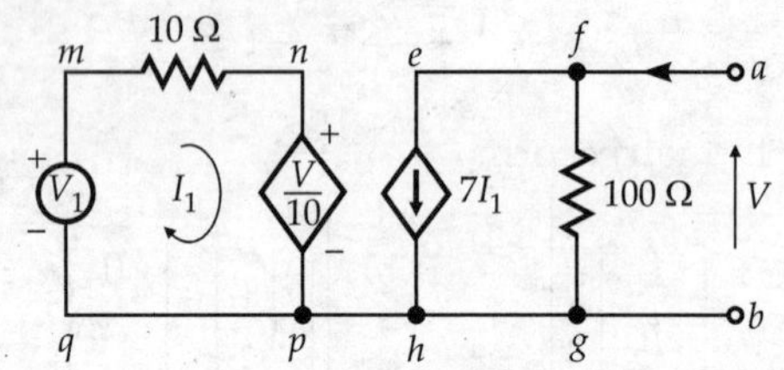

Fig. E11.104

SOLUTION. Let us keep *a-b* open-circuited first. In loop *mnpq*, KVL yields

$$-V_1 + I_1 \times 10 + \frac{V_{o.c}}{10} = 0$$

[Let voltage across *a-b* this time be $V_{o.c}$]

$$I_1 = \left[\left(V_1 - \frac{V_{o.c.}}{10}\right) \times \frac{1}{10}\right] \text{A}$$

Applying KCL at *node f*,

$$I_{\text{output}} = \begin{matrix}\text{current through} \\ 100\ \Omega\ \text{resistor}\end{matrix} + \begin{matrix}\text{current} \\ (7I_1)\end{matrix}$$

or
$$0 = \frac{V_{o.c}}{100} + 7I_1$$

$$\left[\begin{matrix}\because a-b\ \text{is open circuit} \\ \therefore I_{\text{output}} = 0\end{matrix}\right]$$

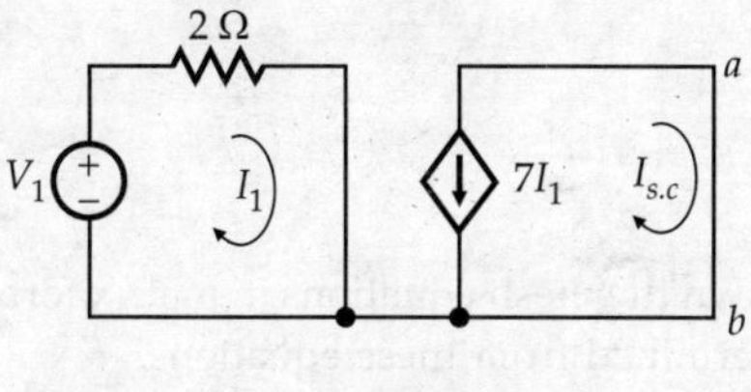

Fig. E11.105

or $$\frac{V_{o.c}}{100}+7\left[\left(V_1-\frac{V_{o.c}}{10}\right)\frac{1}{10}\right]=0$$

[substituting the value of I_1]

or $$\frac{V_{o.c}}{100}+0.7\,V_1-0.07\,V_{o.c}=0$$

or $$-0.06\,V_{o.c}=-0.7\,V_1$$

$$\therefore \quad V_{o.c}=\mathbf{(11.67\,V_1)}.$$

Let us now apply short circuit at *a-b*. This gives $V=0$ and current through *a-b* as $I_{s.c}$ The figure is redrawn below (Fig. E11.105).

Now $$I_1=\frac{V_1}{10}.$$

Applying KCL at *node a,*

$$I_{s.c}+7I_1=0$$

$$\therefore \quad I_{s.c}=-7I_1=-7\left(\frac{V_1}{10}\right)=-0.7\,V_1$$

Now we can find R_{int} of the circuit from terminal (*a-b*) for Fig. E11.105.

Hence $$R_{int}=\frac{V_{o.c}}{I_{s.c}}=\frac{11.67\,V_1}{0.7\,V_1}=\mathbf{16.67\,\Omega.}$$

(negative sign of $I_{s.c}$ being neglected)

The Thevenin's equivalent circuit is drawn below **Fig. E11.106.**

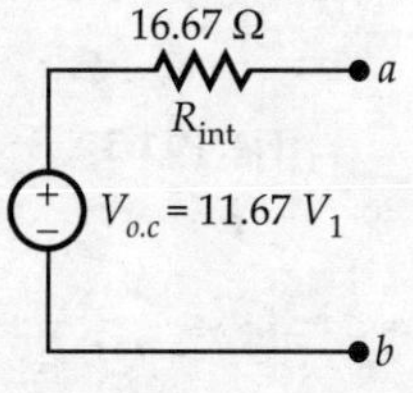

Fig. E11.106

EXAMPLE 11.72 *A gyrator is terminated by a series R-L circuit at its output. Find its equivalent network.*

SOLUTION. Fig. E11.107 represents a gyrator being connected to a series *R-L* network at its output.

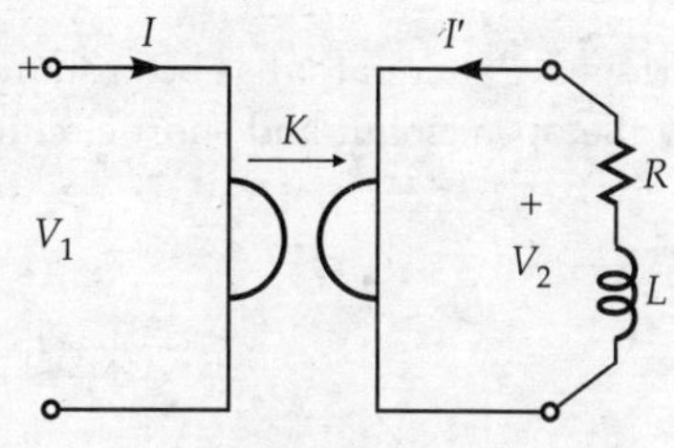

Fig. E11.107

Here, $V_1=-KI'$

$V_2=KI$

Also, $$V_2=R(-I')+L\frac{d}{dt}(-I')$$

$$=-RI'-L\frac{dI'}{dt}$$

$$=-R\left[-\frac{V_1}{K}\right]-L\frac{d}{dt}\left(-\frac{V_1}{K}\right)$$

$$=\frac{R}{K}V_1+\frac{L}{K}\frac{dV_1}{dt}$$

or $$KI=\frac{R}{K}.V_1+\frac{L}{K}\frac{dV_1}{dt}$$

$$\therefore \quad I=\frac{R}{K^2}.V_1+\frac{L}{K^2}.\frac{dV_1}{dt} \qquad ...(a)$$

From equation (*a*) we then can draw the equivalent circuit as shown in **Fig. E11.107(*a*)**

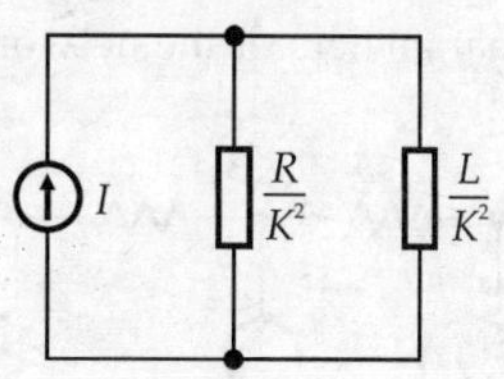

Fig. E11.107(*a*)

Equation (*a*) can be rewritten as

$$I=R'\,V+C\frac{dV_1}{dt}$$

where $R'=\frac{1}{K^2}.R$ and $C=\frac{L}{K^2}$

Thus, the gyrator terminated by a series *R-L* circuit is equivalent to parallel *R-C* circuit at its input.

EXERCISES

1. A bridged T attenuator has been shown in Fig. P11.1. Write down the mesh equations in matrix form and state how the open circuit and short circuit impedances can be determined from these equations.

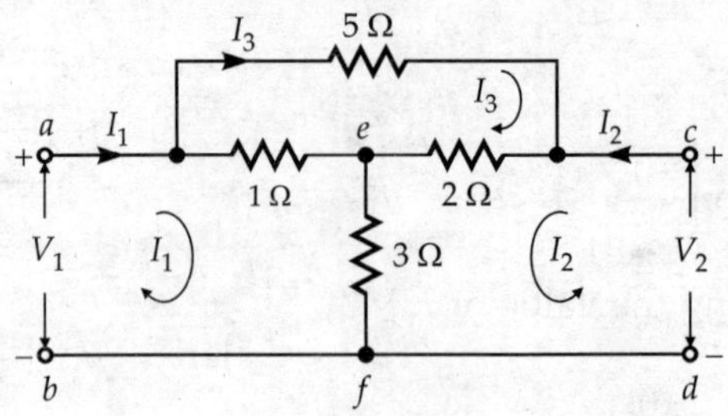

Fig. P11.1

[**Hints.** The mesh equations are written below

$$V_1 = I_1 (1+3) + I_2 \times 3 - I_3 \times 1 = 4\, I_1 + 3\, I_2 - I_3 \qquad ...(1)$$

$$V_2 = (2+3)\, I_2 + I_1 \times 3 + 2\, I_3 = 5\, I_2 + 3\, I_1 + 2\, I_3 \qquad ...(2)$$

$$0 = 5\, I_3 + 2(I_3 + I_2) + 1(I_3 - I_1) = 8I_3 + 2I_2 - I_1 \qquad ...(3)$$

Equations (1), (2) and (3) can be arranged in matrix form

$$\begin{bmatrix} V_1 \\ V_2 \\ 0 \end{bmatrix} = \begin{bmatrix} 4 & 3 & -1 \\ 3 & 5 & 2 \\ -1 & 2 & 8 \end{bmatrix} \begin{bmatrix} I_1 \\ I_2 \\ I_3 \end{bmatrix}$$

$$I_1 = \frac{D_1}{\Delta} \text{ where } D_1 = \begin{bmatrix} V_1 & 3 & -1 \\ 3 & 5 & 2 \\ -1 & 2 & 8 \end{bmatrix} \quad \text{and} \quad \Delta = \begin{bmatrix} 4 & 3 & -1 \\ 3 & 5 & 2 \\ -1 & 2 & 8 \end{bmatrix}$$

Thus ratio V_1 and I_1 can be obtained].

2. Find Y parameters of the network shown in Fig. P11.2.

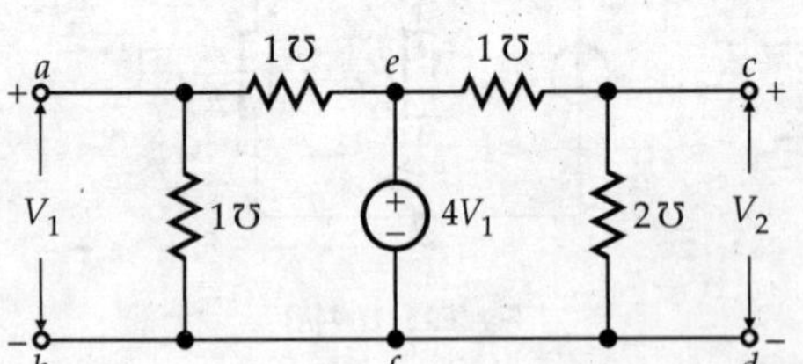

Fig. P11.2

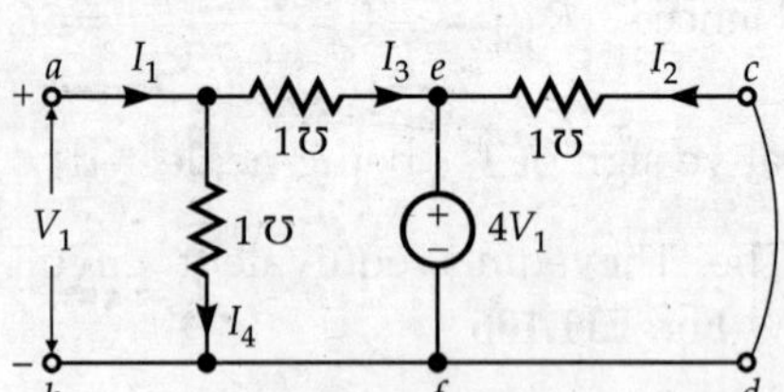

Fig. P11.3

[**Hint.** In the first step c-d is short-circuited (Refer to Fig. P11.3)

$$4V_1 = -(I_2)/1\,\text{mho} \qquad \text{or, } I_2 = -4\, V_1$$

$$V_1 = 4\, V_1 + \frac{I_3}{1\Omega} \qquad \text{or, } I_3 = -3\, V_1$$

$$I_1 = I_3 + I_4 = -3\, V_1 + V_1/1 = -2\, V_1$$

$\therefore \qquad Y_{11} = -2$ mho

$\qquad\quad Y_{21} = -4$ mho

Next, short terminal *a-b* (refer to Fig. P11.4)

Note that $4\,V_1 = 0$ as $V_1 = 0$ due to s.c. at terminal (*a-b*)

$$V_2 = I_2\,(2+1) = 3\,I_2 \qquad \therefore\; Y_{22} = 3 \text{ mho}$$

also $\quad V_2 = -I_1 \times 1 \qquad \therefore\; Y_{12} = -1$ mho]

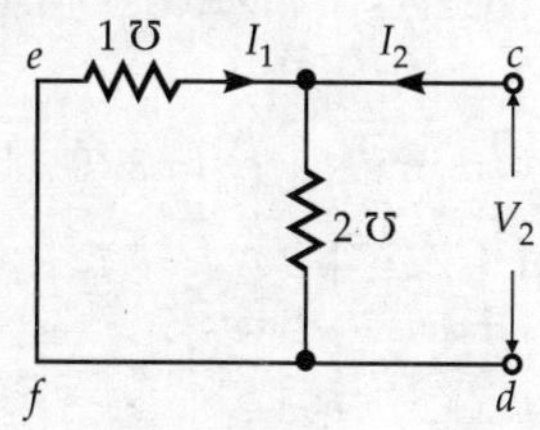

Fig. P11.4

3. Find *Z*-parameters for the attenuator network shown in Fig. P11.5.

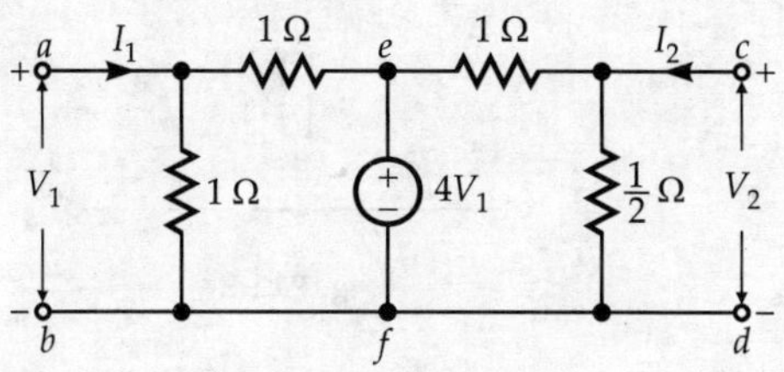

Fig. P11.5

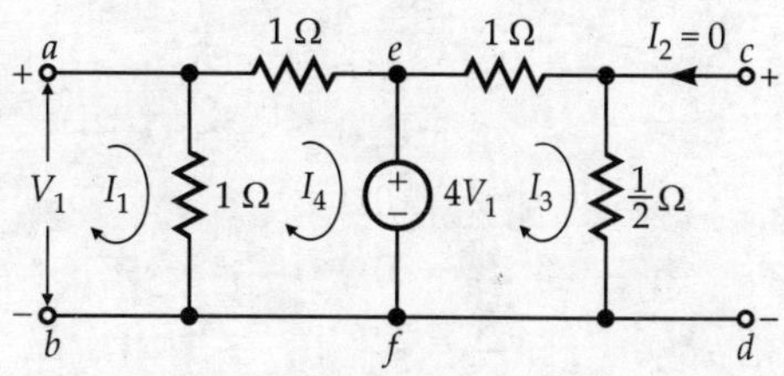

Fig. P11.6

[**Hint.** Open circuit output port (Fig. P11.6)

$$V_2 = \frac{1}{2} \times I_3 \quad \text{or} \quad V_2 = \frac{I_3}{2} - 4\,V_1 + I_3\left(1 + \frac{1}{2}\right) = 0$$

or $$I_3 = \frac{4}{1.5}\,V_1$$

$$4V_1 + I_4\,(1+1) - I_1 \times 1 = 0 \qquad \text{or} \qquad 4V_1 + 2I_4 - I_1 = 0$$

$$V_1 = I_1 \times 1 - I_4 \times 1 \quad \text{or} \qquad V_1 = I_1 - I_4$$

From the above four equations find Z_{11} and Z_{21}.

Next make terminal *a-b* open (Fig. P11.7),

$$V_1 = I_5 \times 1$$

$$2\,I_5 = 4\,V_1$$

$$\frac{1}{2}(I_6 - I_2) + I_6 \times 1 + 4\,V_1 = 0$$

$$\frac{1}{2}(I_2 - I_6) = V_2$$

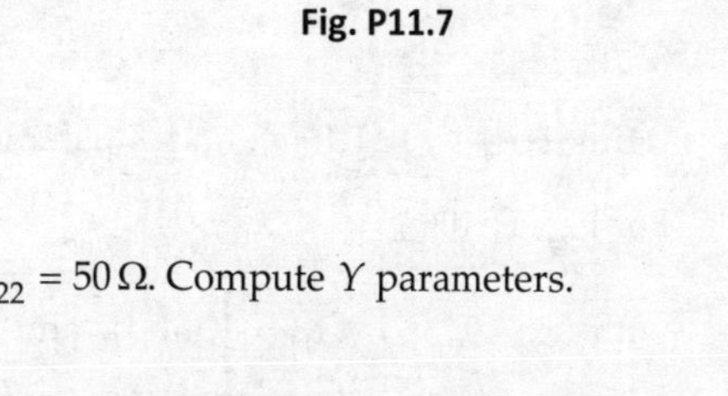

Fig. P11.7

From these equations, Z_{22} and Z_{12} can be found out.]

4. In a two port network, $Z_{11} = 100\,\Omega$, $Z_{21} = 120\,\Omega$, $Z_{12} = 120\,\Omega$, $Z_{22} = 50\,\Omega$. Compute *Y* parameters.
[**Hint.** Ref. Article 11.11].

5. Compute the transmission parameters of the network whose data of Z parameters have been shown in problem 4.
[**Hint.** Ref. Article 11.11].

6. In a two port network, *Y*-parameters are given as $Y_{11} = 0.3$ mho, $Y_{12} = Y_{21} = -0.1$ mho and $Y_{22} = 0.2$ mho. Determine transmission parameters and write down governing equations.
[**Hint.** Ref. Art. 11.11].

7. The voltages at the two ports of a two port network are represented as

$$V_1 = 5I_1 + 5I_2\,; \qquad V_2 = I_1 + 2I_2$$

If a load impedance of 3∠0° ohm is connected at the output port, determine the input impedance.

[**Hint.** $V_2 = I_1 + 2I_2 = -I_2 R_1 = -3\,I_2 \quad \therefore \quad I_2 = -\frac{1}{5}I_1$

Thus $V_1 = 5I_1 + 5\left(-\frac{1}{5}I_1\right) = 4\,I_1 \quad \therefore \quad Z_{11} = 4\,\Omega$]

8. Z-parameters for a two port network are given as $Z_{11} = 25\,\Omega$, $Z_{12} = Z_{21} = 20\,\Omega$, $Z_{22} = 50\,\Omega$ Find the equivalent T network.

[**Hint.** Fig. P11.8 $Z_A = Z_C(= Z_{11}) = 25\,\Omega$

$Z_{21} = Z_C = 20\,\Omega$

$Z_{22} = Z_B + Z_C = 50\,\Omega$

$\therefore \quad Z_A = 10\,\Omega$

$Z_B = 30\,\Omega$

$Z_C = 20\,\Omega$].

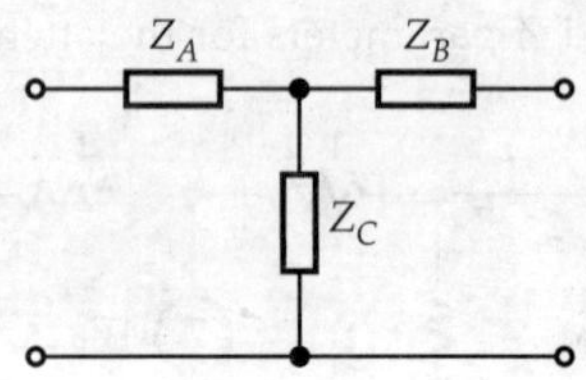

Fig. P11.8

9. Determine Y-parameters for the bridge-T network shown in Fig. P11.9.

[**Hint.** In Ex. 11.27, Z parameters of this circuit have been obtained,

As $Y_{11} = \frac{Z_{22}}{\Delta Z}\,;\; Y_{12} = -\frac{Z_{12}}{\Delta Z}$

$Y_{21} = -\frac{Z_{21}}{\Delta Z}\,;\; Y_{22} = \frac{Z_{11}}{\Delta Z}$

Hence Y parameters can be determined].

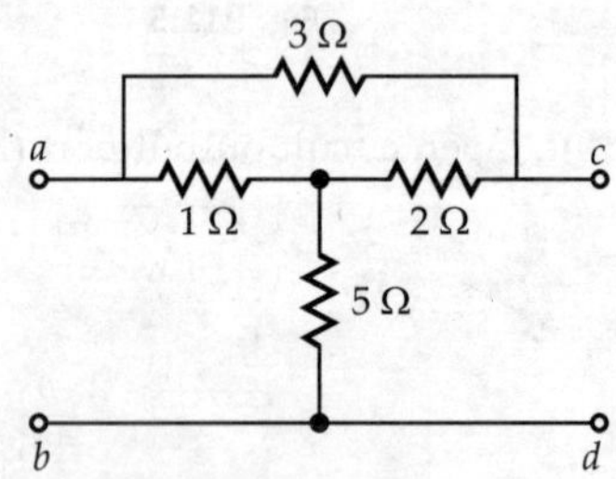

Fig. P11.9

10. Determine Y parameters of the circuits shown in Figs. P11.10 (*a*) and 11.10 (*b*),

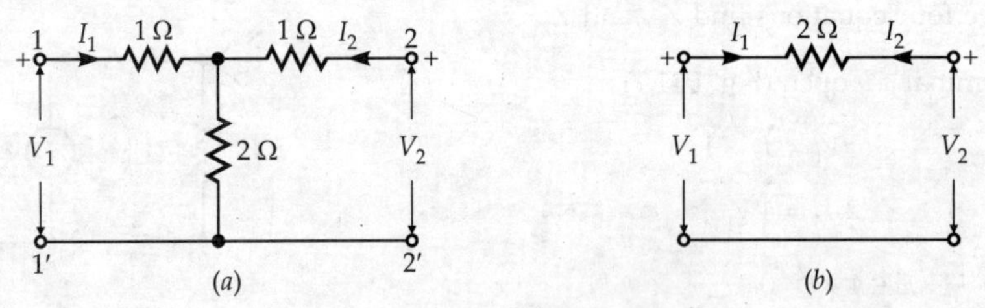

Fig. P11.10

[**Hint.** For Fig. P11.10(*a*), find Z parameters and then find Y parameters from there.

For Fig. 11.10(*b*),

with $V_2 = 0$, $\quad Y_{11} = \frac{1}{2}$ mho and $Y_{21} = \frac{1}{2}$ mho

with $V_1 = 0$, $\quad Y_{22} = \frac{1}{2}$ mho and $Y_{12} = -\frac{1}{2}$ mho].

11. Obtain T and π equivalent circuits for the network of Fig. P11.11 by using impedance and admittance parameters respectively.

[**Hint.** First obtain Z parameters of the bridged T network as well as Y parameters then ref. Art. 11.17.

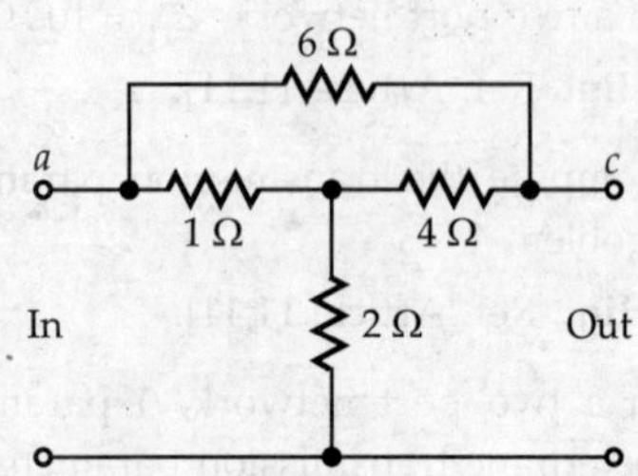

Fig. P11.11

Thus $Z_1 = Z_{11} - Z_{12}$; $Z_2 = Z_{22} - Z_{12}$; $Z_3 = Z_{12}$

and $Y_1 = Y_{11} + Y_{12}$; $Y_2 = Y_{22} + Y_{12}$; $Y_3 = - Y_{12}$].

12. Determine Y parameters of the network shown in Fig. P11.12.

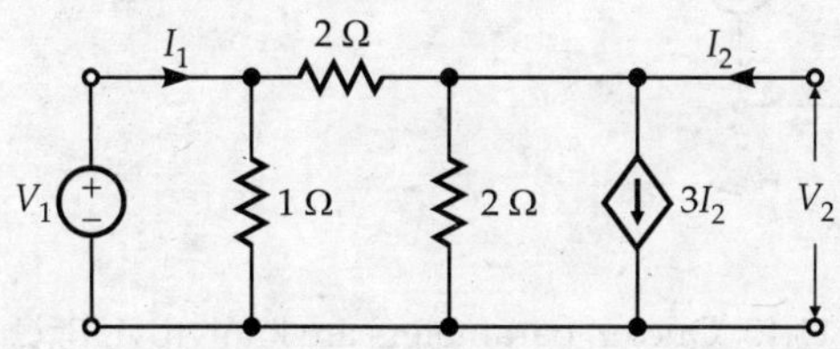

Fig. P11.12

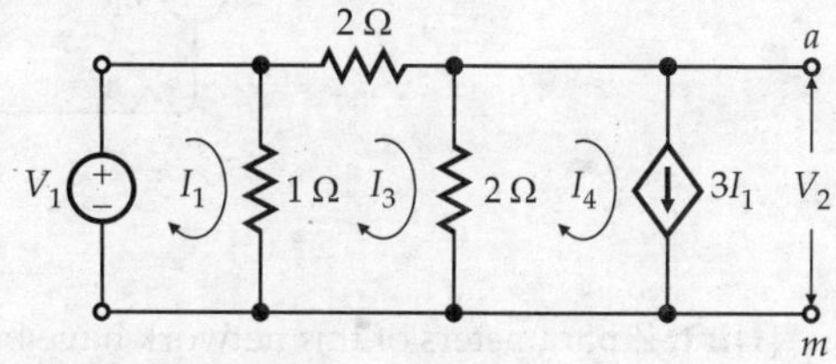

Fig. P11.13

[**Hint.** Let us first find Z parameters, With $I_2 = 0$,

Loop equations become (Refer to Fig. P11.13)

$$V_1 = (I_1 - I_3)\,1 \quad \text{...(1)}$$

$$0 = (I_3 - I_1)\,1 + 2\,I_3 + (I_3 - I_4)\,2 \quad \text{...(2)}$$

$$V_2 = 2\,(I_3 - I_4) \quad \text{...(3)}$$

$$I_4 = 3\,I_1 \quad \text{...(4)}$$

From (2), utilising (4),

$$0 = I_3 - I_1 + 2\,I_3 + 2\,I_3 - 6\,I_1 \quad \text{or} \quad 5\,I_3 = 7\,I_1$$

$$\therefore \quad I_3 = \frac{7}{5}\,I_1$$

$$\therefore \text{ From (1)} \quad V_1 = I_1 - \frac{7}{5}\,I_1 = -\frac{2}{5}\,I_1$$

$$\therefore \quad Z_{11} = \left.\frac{V_1}{I_1}\right|_{I_2=0} = -0.4\,\Omega$$

Also, from (3) and (4),

$$V_2 = 2\,(I_3 - 3\,I_1) = 2\left(\frac{7}{5}\,I_1 - 3\,I_1\right) = -\frac{16}{5}\,I_1 \quad \therefore \quad Z_{21} = -3.2\,\Omega$$

Next input port is opened (Fig. P11.14), $I_1 = 0$,

$$V_2 = (I_2 - I_5)\,2 \quad \text{...(5)}$$

and $$0 = 2\,(I_5 - I_2) + 3\,I_5 \quad \text{...(6)}$$

or $$I_5 = \frac{2}{5}\,I_2$$

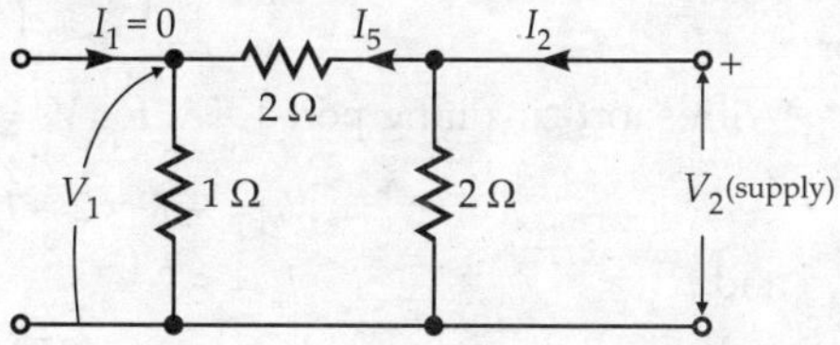

Fig. P11.14

Thus from (5), $V_2 = \left(I_2 - \frac{2}{5}\,I_2\right)2 = 2\,I_2 - \frac{4}{5}\,I_2 = \frac{6}{5}\,I_2$

$$\therefore \quad Z_{22} = \frac{6}{5} = 1.2\,\Omega$$

Also, $V_1 = I_5 \times 1 = \frac{2}{5}\,I_2 \quad \therefore \quad \frac{V_1}{I_2} = Z_{12} = \frac{2}{5} = 0.4\,\Omega$

Thus $$\begin{bmatrix} Z_{11} & Z_{12} \\ Z_{21} & Z_{22} \end{bmatrix} = \begin{bmatrix} -0.4 & 0.4 \\ -3.2 & 1.2 \end{bmatrix}$$

From these values of Z, referring to Art 11.11, the value of Y parameters can be determined].

13. Determine transmission parameters of the circuit shown in Fig. P11.15.

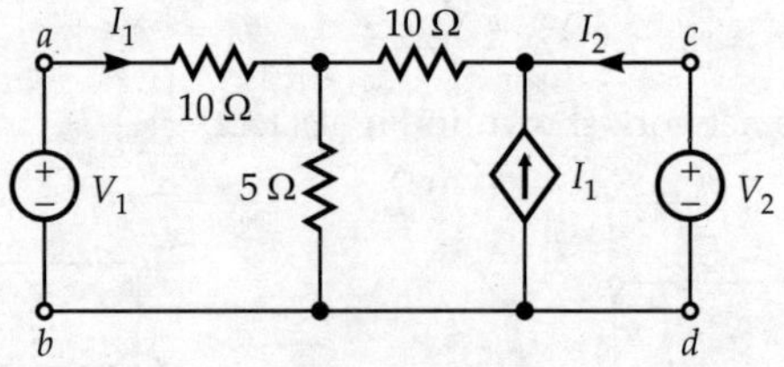

Fig. P11.15

[**Hint.** *Z* parameters of this network have been obtained in Ex. 11.13. Once *Z* parameters are known, *A, B, C, D* parameters can be determined utilising their inter-relationship].

14. Determine *Y* parameters of the network shown in Fig. P11.16.

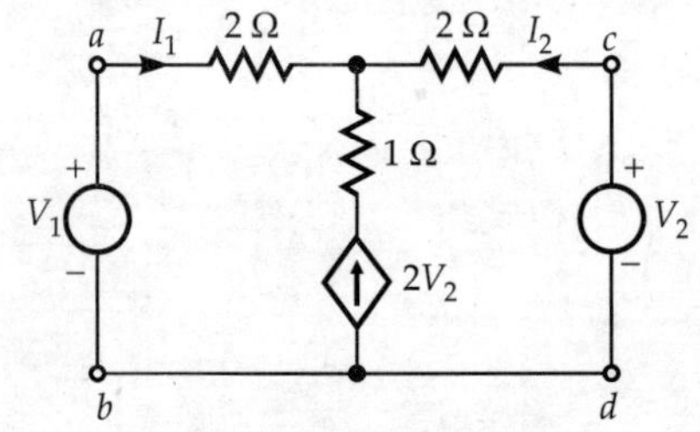

Fig. P11.16

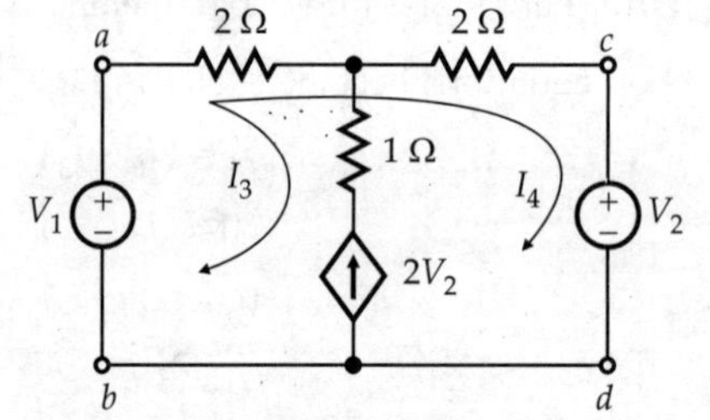

Fig. P11.17

[**Hint.** Here, in Fig. P11.17

$$V_1 - V_2 = I_3 \times 2 + I_4 \times 4 \qquad \text{...(1)}$$

$$I_3 = -2\,V_2 \qquad \text{...(2)}$$

With $V_2 = 0$, *i.e.,* with output short-circuited, I_3 becomes zero.

$\therefore$ With $I_3 = 0$, $V_1 = 4\,I_4$

or $$I_4 = \frac{V_1}{4}$$

$\therefore$ $$I_1 = I_3 + I_4 = 0 + \frac{V_1}{4} = \left(\frac{V_1}{4}\right) \quad \text{or} \quad Y_{11} = \frac{V_1}{I_1} = \frac{1}{4} \text{ mho}$$

Also, $$I_2 = -I_4 = -\frac{V_1}{4} \quad \text{or} \quad Y_{21} = \frac{I_2}{V_1} = -\frac{1}{4} \text{ mho}$$

With short-circuiting port-1, *i.e.,* for $V_1 = 0$,

$$V_2 = -I_3 \times 2 - I_4 \times 4 = -2\,I_3 - 4\,I_4$$

and $$I_3 = -2\,V_2$$

$\therefore$ $$V_2 = -2(-2V_2) - 4\,I_4 = +4\,V_2 - 4\,I_4$$

$\therefore$ $$I_4 = \frac{3}{4}V_2$$

Again $$I_2 = -I_4 = -\frac{3}{4}V_2$$

$\therefore$ $$\frac{I_2}{V_2} = -\frac{3}{4} \text{ mho} \quad \text{and} \quad I_1 = I_3 + I_4 = -2\,V_2 + \frac{3}{4}V_2 = -\frac{5}{4}V_2$$

$\therefore$ $$\frac{I_1}{V_2} = Y_{12} = -\frac{5}{4} \text{ mho} \text{]}.$$

15. Obtain Y and Z parameters of the network shown in Fig. P11.18.

[**Hint.** Mesh equations are formed first applying short circuit at output

$$I_1 = \text{loop 1 current}$$
$$I_3 = \text{loop 2 current}$$
$$I_2 = \text{output current}$$

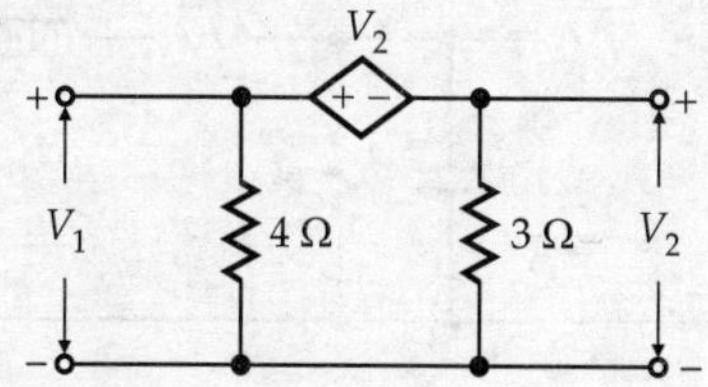

Fig. P11.18

$$\begin{bmatrix} 6 & -4 & 0 \\ -4 & 7 & 3 \\ 0 & 3 & 3 \end{bmatrix} \begin{bmatrix} I_1 \\ I_3 \\ I_3 \end{bmatrix} = \begin{bmatrix} V_1 \\ 0 \\ 0 \end{bmatrix}$$

By Cramer's Rule,

$$I_1 = \frac{\begin{vmatrix} V_1 & -4 & 0 \\ 0 & 7 & 3 \\ 0 & 3 & 3 \end{vmatrix}}{\Delta}$$

$$I_2 = \frac{\begin{vmatrix} 6 & 4 & V_1 \\ -4 & 7 & 0 \\ 0 & 3 & 0 \end{vmatrix}}{\Delta}$$

$$\Delta = \begin{vmatrix} 6 & 4 & 0 \\ -4 & 7 & 3 \\ 0 & 3 & 3 \end{vmatrix}$$

Solving the above expressions,

$$\frac{I_1}{V_1} (= Y_{11}) \text{ and } \frac{I_2}{V_1} (= Y_{21}) \text{ can be found out.}$$

In a similar way, applying short circuit at input port, the mesh equations become

$$\begin{bmatrix} 3 & 3 & 0 \\ 3 & 7 & -4 \\ 0 & -4 & 6 \end{bmatrix} \begin{bmatrix} I_2 \\ I_3 \\ I_1 \end{bmatrix} = \begin{bmatrix} V_2 \\ -V_2 \\ 0 \end{bmatrix}$$

$$I_2 = \frac{\begin{vmatrix} V_2 & 3 & 0 \\ -V_2 & 7 & -4 \\ 0 & -4 & 6 \end{vmatrix}}{\Delta}$$

$$I_1 = \frac{\begin{vmatrix} 3 & 3 & V_2 \\ 3 & 7 & -V_2 \\ 0 & -4 & 0 \end{vmatrix}}{\Delta}$$

$$\Delta = \begin{vmatrix} 3 & 3 & 0 \\ 3 & 7 & -4 \\ 0 & -4 & 6 \end{vmatrix}$$

Solving the above expressions,

$$\frac{I_2}{V_2} \text{ or } Y_{22} \text{ and } \frac{I_1}{V_2} \text{ or } Y_{12} \text{ can be obtained.}$$

Once Y parameters are obtained, Z parameters can be obtained.]

16. Obtain Z-parameters for the network shown in Fig. P11.19.
[**Hint.** Refer to Example 11.50]

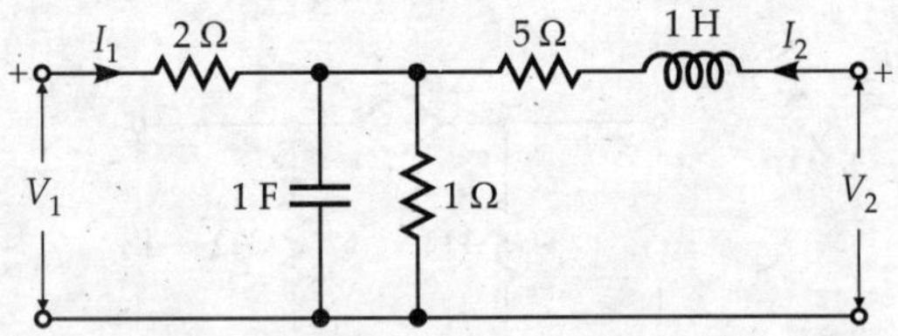

Fig. P11.19

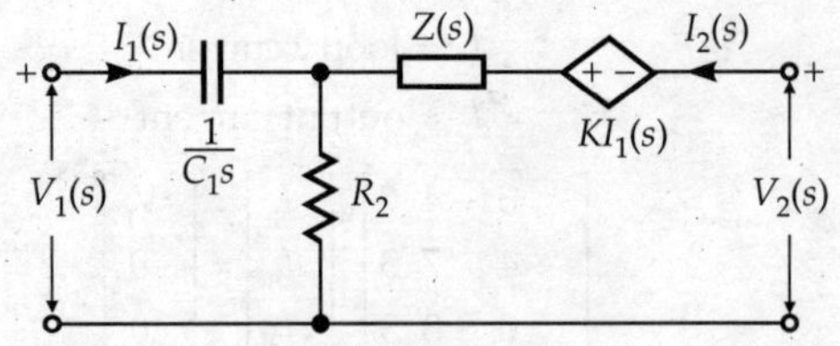

Fig. P11.20

17. Find Z-parameters of the network represented in s-domain in Fig. P11.20.
[**Hint.** Refer to Example 11.53]

18. Obtain Y-parameters of the network shown in Fig. P11.21.
[**Hint.** Refer to Example 11.54]

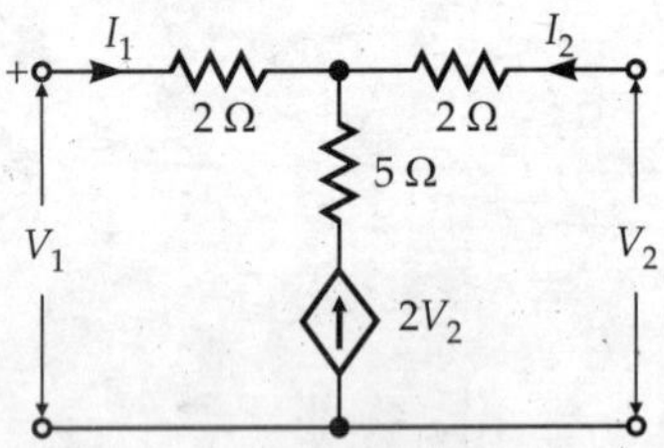

Fig. P11.21

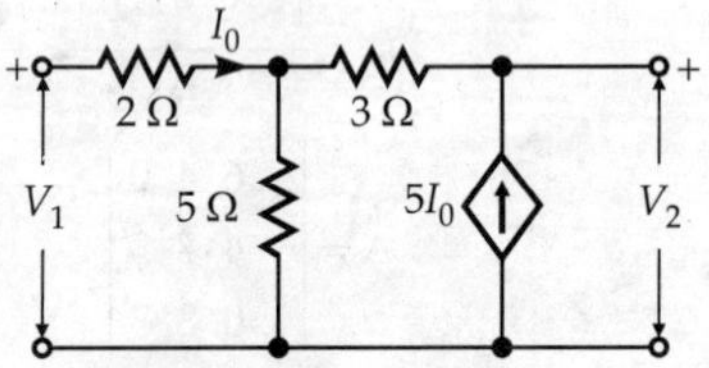

Fig. P11.22

19. Obtain Z-parameters and transmission of parameters of the network shown in Fig. P11.22.
[**Hint.** Refer to Example 11.61]

CHAPTER

12

Properties of Network Functions

12.1 INTRODUCTION

The basic definition of one port and two port network being discussed earlier, here we will discuss about the *transform of excitation and response* alongwith their relations. A *network function* exhibits the relationship between the transform of the source or excitation to the transform of the response for a electrical network. Further to this, we will discuss the stability of the network function mathematically formulating the network function through "pole-zero" concept.

12.2 DRIVING POINT IMPEDANCE AND ADMITTANCE

The *driving point impedance* of a one port network is defined as

$$Z(s) = \frac{V(s)}{I(s)} \qquad ...(12.1)$$

while the driving point admittance is given as

$$Y(s) = \frac{I(s)}{V(s)} \qquad ...(12.2)$$

for the one port network.

Similarly, for the two port network, the *driving point impedance* and *admittance at port* 1 is defined as

$$Z_{11}(s) = \frac{V_1(s)}{I_1(s)} \qquad ...(12.3)$$

and

$$Y_{11}(s) = \frac{I_1(s)}{V_1(s)} \qquad ...(12.4)$$

While the *driving point impedance and admittance at the port 2* are designated as

$$Z_{22}(s) = \frac{V_2(s)}{I_2(s)} \qquad ...[12.4(a)]$$

and

$$Y_{22}(s) = \frac{I_2(s)}{V_2(s)} \qquad ...(12.5)$$

12.3 TRANSFER IMPEDANCE AND ADMITTANCE

Transfer impedance is defined as the ratio of transformed voltage at output port to the transformed current at the input port of a two port network.

This gives,
$$Z_{12}(s) = \frac{V_2(s)}{I_1(s)} \qquad ...(12.6)$$

In a similar way, the *transfer admittance* is defined as the ratio of current transform at output port to the voltage tranform at the input port. It is given as

$$Y_{12}(s) = \frac{I_2(s)}{V_1(s)} \qquad ...(12.7)$$

12.4 VOLTAGE AND CURRENT TRANSFER RATIO

Voltage and current transfer ratios are basically transfer functions. *Voltage transfer ratio* is the ratio of voltage transform at output port to the voltage transform at the input port. It is usually denoted by $G(s)$. Thus,

$$G_{12}(s) = \frac{V_2(s)}{V_1(s)} \qquad ...(12.8)$$

In a similar way, the ratio of transform of current at output port to that at the input port of a two port network gives the *current transfer ratio.* It is reprosented by $\alpha(s)$. Thus,

$$\alpha_{12}(s) = \frac{I_2(s)}{I_1(s)} \qquad ...(12.9)$$

EXAMPLE 12.1 *A series R-L circuit is in parallel with a capacitance. Find the input impedance in Laplace domain.*

SOLUTION. Figure E12.1 represents the parallel combination of one series *R-L* circuit with a capacitance in Laplace domain. The input impedance is $Z(s)$ which is obviously

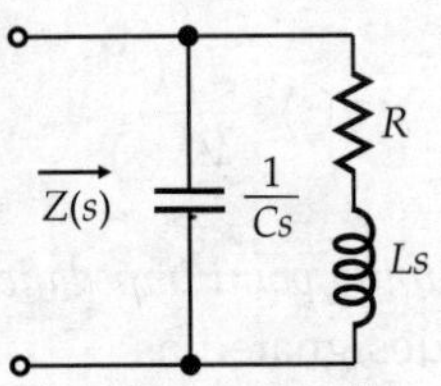

Fig. E12.1

$$Z(s) = \frac{(1/Cs)(R+Ls)}{\frac{1}{Cs} + (R+Ls)}$$

$$= \frac{R+Ls}{1+RCs+LCs^2}$$

$$= \frac{s+\frac{R}{L}}{C\left(s^2+\frac{R}{L}s+\frac{1}{LC}\right)}$$

$\therefore$ Input impedance

$$Z(s) = \frac{s+(R/L)}{C\left(s^2+\frac{R}{L}s+\frac{1}{LC}\right)}.$$

EXAMPLE 12.2 *Find $Z_{11}(s), Z_{21}(s)$ in the following circuit. (Fig. E12.2)*

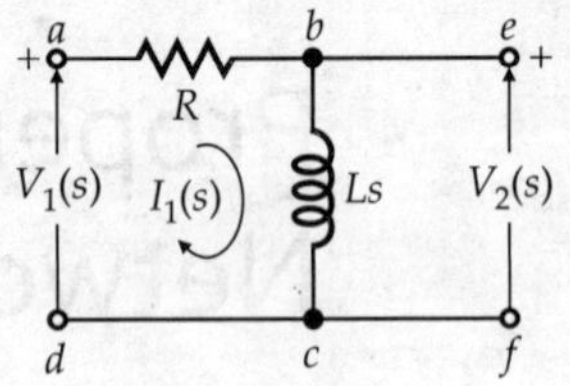

Fig. E12.2

SOLUTION. KVL gives for *loop abcd*,

$$RI_1(s) + I_1(s)\,Ls = V_1(s) \qquad ...(i)$$

or, $$I_1(s)(R+Ls) = V_1(s)$$

$$\therefore \quad Z_{11}(s) = \frac{V_1(s)}{I_1(s)} = (R+Ls) \qquad ...(ii)$$

Again in *loop bcfe*, KVL yields

$$V_2(s) = I_1(s)\,Ls$$

which gives, $$Z_{12}(s) = \frac{V_2(s)}{I_1(s)} = Ls. \qquad ...(iii)$$

Equations (*ii*) and (*iii*) give the required result.

EXAMPLE 12.3 *Obtain the transfer function $V_2(s)/V_1(s)$ in Fig. E12.3.*

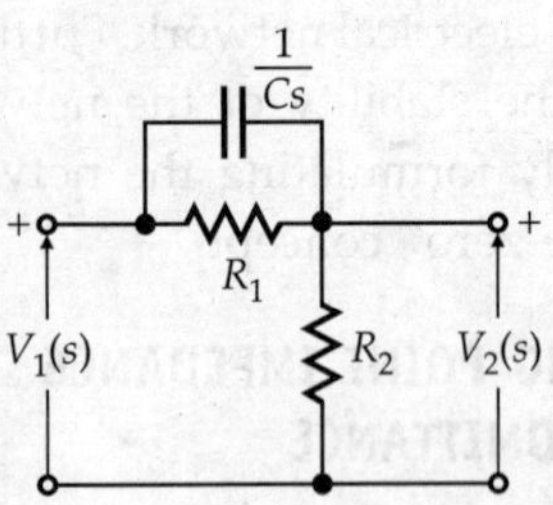

Fig. E12.3

SOLUTION. The equivalent impedance of $\frac{1}{Cs}$ and R_1 is given by $Z(s)$.

Obviously,

$$Z(s) = \frac{R_1 \times \frac{1}{Cs}}{R_1 + \frac{1}{Cs}} = \frac{R_1}{R_1 Cs + 1}.$$

Applying KVL in *left loop* of Fig. E12.3, we get

$$V_1(s) = I_1(s)[Z(s) + R_2]$$

$$V_2(s) = R_2\, I_1(s).$$

$$\therefore \quad V_2(s)/V_1(s) = \frac{R_2}{R_2 + Z(s)}$$

$$= \frac{R_2}{R_2 + \dfrac{R_1}{R_1 Cs + 1}}$$

$$= \frac{R_2(1 + R_1 Cs)}{R_2 + R_1 R_2 Cs + R_1}$$

$$= \frac{R_2 + R_1 R_2 Cs}{R_1 + R_2 + R_1 R_2 Cs}$$

$$= \frac{R_2 R_1 C\left(s + \dfrac{1}{R_1 C}\right)}{R_2 R_1 C\left(s + \dfrac{R_1 + R_2}{R_2 R_1 C}\right)}$$

i.e., Voltage transfer ratio

$$= \frac{\mathbf{R_2 R_1 C\left(s + \dfrac{1}{R_1 C}\right)}}{\mathbf{R_2 R_1 C\left(s + \dfrac{R_1 + R_2}{R_1 R_2 C}\right)}}.$$

EXAMPLE 12.4 *Obtain $Z_{12}(s)$ for a parallel R-C network where $R = 1\Omega$; $C = 1$ F.*

SOLUTION. In Fig. E12.4,

$$V_2(s) = I_1(s)\left[\frac{R \times \dfrac{1}{Cs}}{R + \dfrac{1}{Cs}}\right]$$

$$\text{or,} \quad \frac{V_2(s)}{I_1(s)} = \frac{R}{RCs + 1} = \frac{1}{\left(s + \dfrac{1}{RC}\right)C}$$

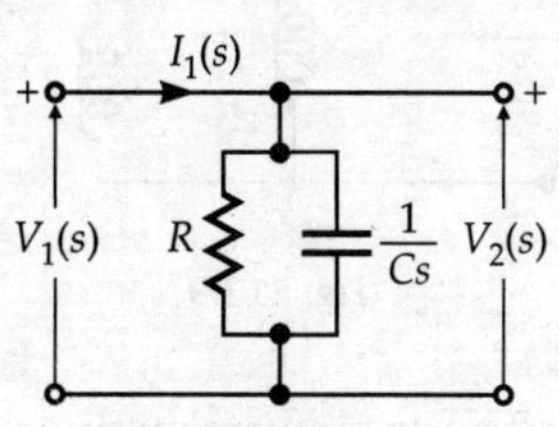

Fig. E12.4

$$\therefore \quad Z_{12}(s) = \frac{V_2(s)}{I_1(s)}$$

$$= \frac{1}{C\left(s + \dfrac{1}{RC}\right)} = \frac{1}{1(s+1)}$$

$$\therefore \quad Z_{12}(s) = \frac{\mathbf{1}}{\mathbf{s+1}}.$$

EXAMPLE 12.5 *Find (V_2/V_1) and (V_2/I_1) in Fig. E12.5.*

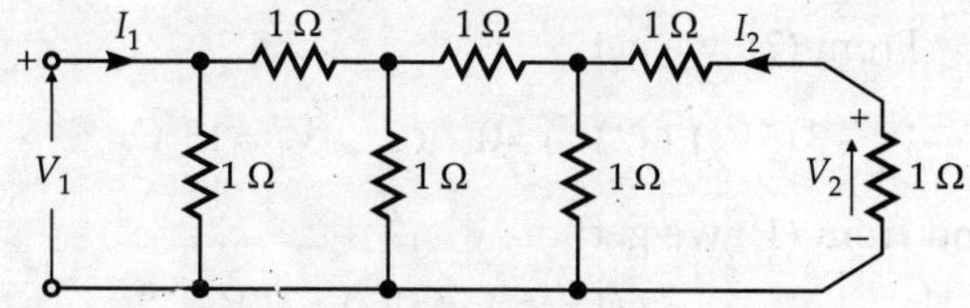

Fig. E12.5

SOLUTION. The figure is redrawn (Fig. E12.6) with marking of nodes and voltages at the node.

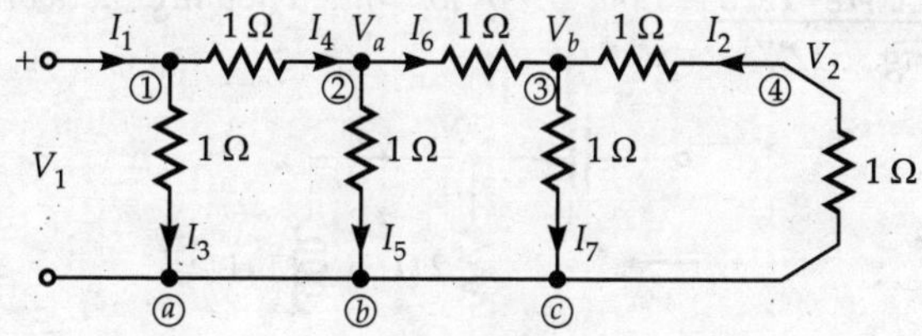

Fig. E12.6

At *node (1)*, application of KCL yields

$$I_1 = I_3 + I_4 = \frac{V_1}{1} + \frac{V_1 - V_a}{1} = 2V_1 - V_a \quad \text{...(1)}$$

At *node (2)*,

$$I_4 = I_5 + I_6$$

$$\text{or,} \quad \frac{V_1 - V_a}{1} = \frac{V_a}{1} + \frac{V_a - V_b}{1}$$

$$\text{or,} \quad V_1 - V_a = V_a + V_a - V_b$$

$$\text{or,} \quad V_1 - 3V_a + V_b = 0 \quad \text{...(2)}$$

At *node (3)*,

$$I_6 = I_7 - I_2$$

$$\text{or} \quad \frac{V_a - V_b}{1} = \frac{V_b}{1} - \frac{V_2 - V_b}{1}$$

$$\text{or,} \quad V_a - V_b = V_b - V_2 + V_b$$

$$\text{or} \quad V_2 + V_a - 3V_b = 0 \quad \text{...(3)}$$

CHAPTER 12

At *node (4)*, KCL yields,

Current through load of 1Ω = Current flows between nodes (3) and (4)

i.e., $$\frac{V_2}{1} = \frac{V_b - V_2}{1}$$

or $$2V_2 - V_b = 0 \qquad ...(4)$$

From (4), $V_b = 2V_2$ and from (3) we then get $V_a = 5V_2$

From (2), we get

$$V_1 - 3(5V_2) + (2V_2) = 0 \quad \text{or,} \quad V_1 = 13\,V_2$$

and from (1), we get

$$I_1 = 2\,(13\,V_2) - (5V_2) = 21\,V_2$$

Then finally, we get

$$V_2 / V_1 = \frac{\mathbf{1}}{\mathbf{13}} \text{ and } V_2 / I_1 = \frac{\mathbf{1}}{\mathbf{21}}.$$

EXAMPLE 12.6 *Find Z(s) for the following network (Fig. E12.7).*

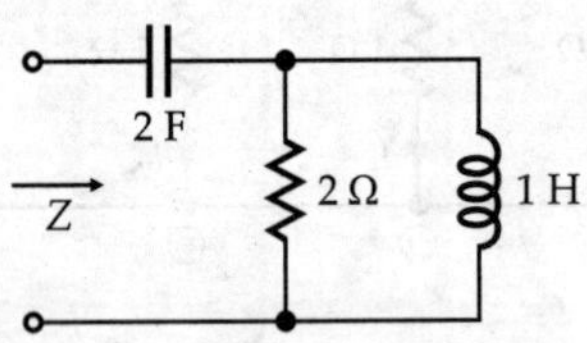

Fig. E12.7

SOLUTION. The transform network is shown in Fig. E12.7(*a*).

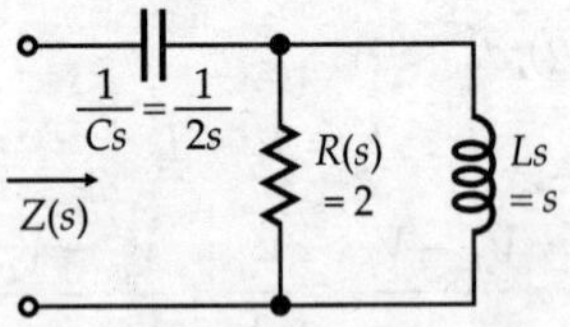

Fig. E12.7 (*a*)

$$Z(s) = [R(s) \,||\, Ls] + \frac{1}{Cs} = \frac{2 \times s}{2 + s} + \frac{1}{2s},$$

$$= \frac{4s^2 + s + 2}{2s(s+2)} = \frac{4s^2 + s + 2}{2s^2 + 4s}$$

$$\therefore \quad Z(s) = \frac{\mathbf{4s^2 + s + 2}}{\mathbf{2s^2 + 4s}}.$$

EXAMPLE 12.7 *Find the driving point impedance for the network shown in Fig. E12.8.*

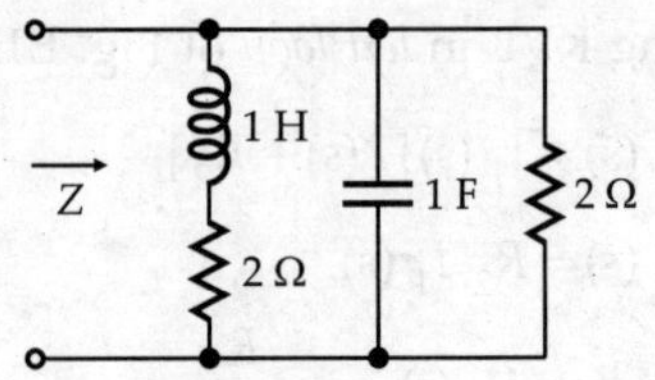

Fig. E12.8

SOLUTION. The transfer network is shown in Fig. E12.8(*a*).

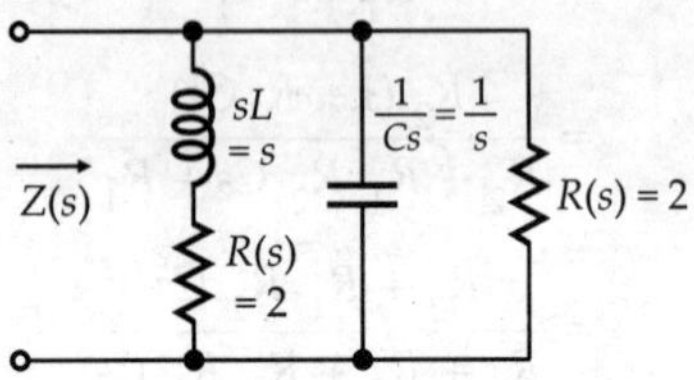

Fig. E12.8 (*a*)

Here $$Z(s) = \left[R_2(s) \,||\, \frac{1}{Cs}\right] \,||\, [SL + R_1(s)]$$

$$= \frac{2 \times \frac{1}{s}}{2 + \frac{1}{s}} \,||\, (2+s) = \frac{\frac{2}{s}}{\frac{2s+1}{s}} \,||\, (2+s)$$

$$= \frac{2}{(2s+1)} \,||\, (2+s) = \frac{\frac{2}{(2s+1)} \times (2+s)}{\frac{2}{2s+1} + 2 + s}$$

$$= \frac{2\,(s+2)}{2 + 4s + 2 + 2s^2 + s}$$

$$= \frac{2\,(s+2)}{2s^2 + 5s + 4}.$$

i.e., Z (s), the driving point impedance $= \dfrac{\mathbf{2\,(s+2)}}{\mathbf{2s^2 + 5s + 4}}.$

EXAMPLE 12.8 *Find the driving point admittance of the network shown in Fig. E12.9.*

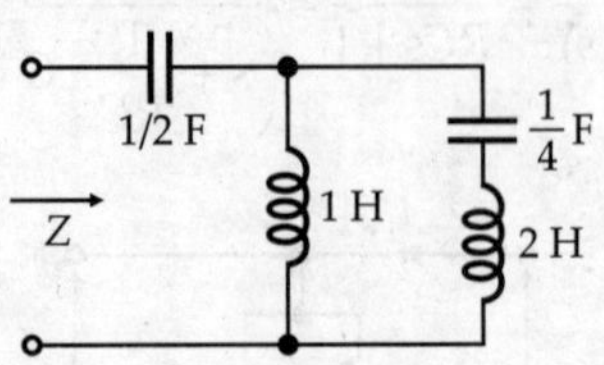

Fig. E12.9

SOLUTION. The transform network is shown in Fig. E12.9(*a*)

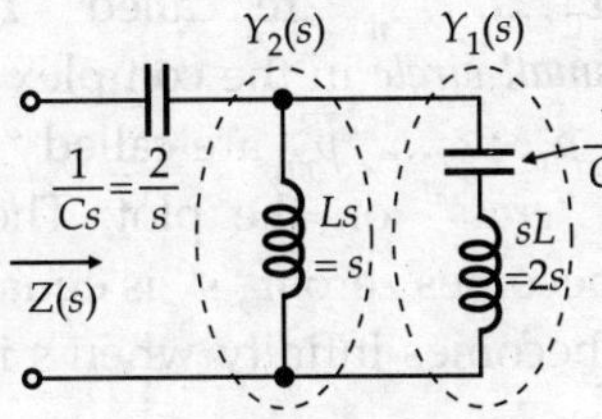

Fig. E12.9 (*a*)

$$\text{Here } Y_1(s) = \frac{1}{2s + \frac{4}{s}} = \frac{1}{\frac{2s^2+4}{s}} = \frac{s}{2s^2+4}$$

$$Y_2(s) = \frac{1}{s}$$

$$\therefore \quad Y_E(s) = Y_1(s) + Y_2(s) = \frac{s}{2s^2+4} + \frac{1}{s}$$

$$= \frac{3s^2+4}{2s^3+4s}$$

$$\therefore \quad Z_E(s) = \frac{1}{Y(s)} = \frac{2s^3+4s}{3s^2+4}$$

$$\text{Thus } Z(s) = Z_E(s) + \frac{1}{Cs}$$

$$= \frac{2s^3+4s}{3s^2+4} + \frac{2}{s}$$

$$= \frac{2s^4+10s^2+8}{3s^3+4s}$$

$$\because \quad Y(s) = \frac{1}{Z(s)},$$

here $$Y(s) = \frac{\mathbf{3s^3+4s}}{\mathbf{2s^4+10s^2+8}}.$$

EXAMPLE 12.9 *Find the transfer function of the network shown in Fig. E12.10.*

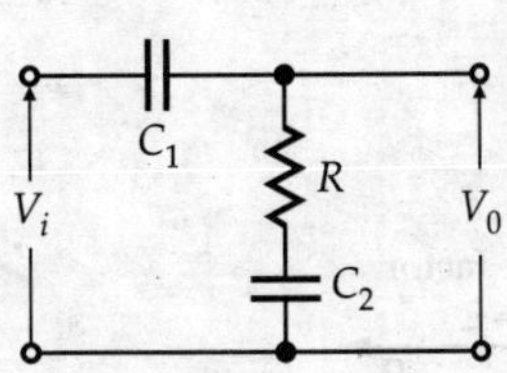

Fig. E12.10

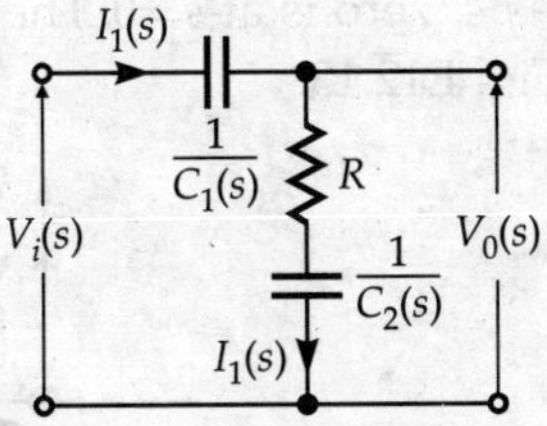

Fig. E12.10 (*a*)

SOLUTION. Transforming the given network in the Laplace domain [Fig. E12.10(*a*)].

$$V_i(s) = I_1(s)\left[R + \frac{1}{C_1 s} + \frac{1}{C_2 s}\right] \quad \text{...(1)}$$

and $$V_0(s) = I_1(s)\left[R + \frac{1}{C_2 s}\right]$$

$$\therefore \quad \frac{V_0(s)}{V_i(s)} = \frac{R + \frac{1}{C_2 s}}{R + \frac{1}{C_1 s} + \frac{1}{C_2 s}}$$

$$= \frac{(RC_2 s + 1)C_1 s}{(RC_1 C_2 s^2 + C_1 s + C_2 s)}$$

$$= \frac{C_1(1 + RC_2 s)}{C_1 + C_2 + RC_1 C_2 s}$$

i.e., the transfer function (voltage transfer ratio) is given by

$$\left[\frac{\mathbf{C_1(1+RC_2 s)}}{\mathbf{C_1+C_2+RC_1 C_2 s}}\right].$$

EXAMPLE 12.10 *Find the expression of voltage transfer ratio for the network shown in Fig. E12.11.*

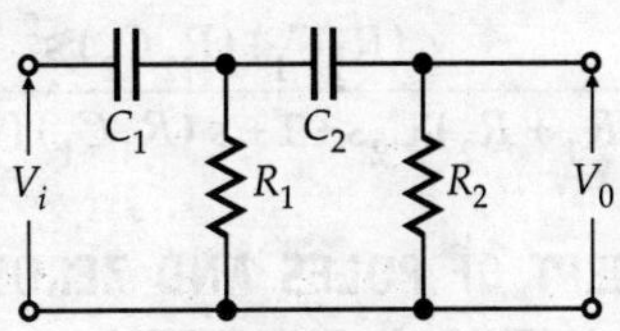

Fig. E12.11

SOLUTION. The equivalent circuit of Fig. E12.11 in Laplace domain is shown in Fig. E12.11(*a*).

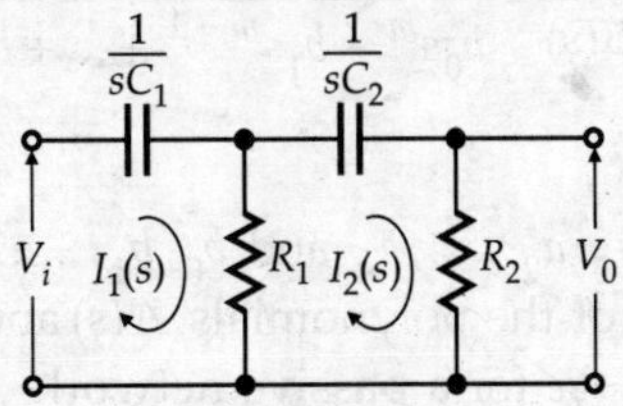

Fig. E12.11 (*a*)

Here, in the *leftmost loop*,

$$V_i(s) = I_1(s)\left[R_1 + \frac{1}{C_1 s}\right] - R_1 I_2(s) \quad \text{...(a)}$$

in the *second loop*,

$$-R_1 I_1(s) + \left(R_1 + R_2 + \frac{1}{C_2 s}\right) I_2(s) = 0 \quad \text{...(b)}$$

and in the *rightmost loop*,

$$R_2 I_2(s) = V_0(s) \quad \text{...(c)}$$

CHAPTER 12

Solving for $I_2(s)$,

$$I_2(s) = \frac{\begin{vmatrix} R_1 + \frac{1}{C_1 s} & V_i(s) \\ -R_1 & 0 \end{vmatrix}}{\begin{vmatrix} R_1 + \frac{1}{C_1 s} & -R_1 \\ -R_1 & R_1 + R_2 + \frac{1}{C_2 s} \end{vmatrix}}$$

or, $$I_2(s) = \frac{R_1 V_i(s) C_1 s C_2 s}{(R_1 + R_2) C_2 s + 1 + R_1 C_1 s (R_2 C_2 s + 1)}$$

∴ From (c),

$$V_0(s) = I_2(s) R_2$$

$$= \frac{R_1 R_2 V_i(s) C_1 s C_2 s}{(R_1 + R_2) C_2 s + 1 + R_1 C_1 S (R_2 C_2 s + 1)}$$

i.e.,

$$\frac{V_0(s)}{V_i(s)} = \frac{R_1 R_2 C_1 s C_2 s}{(R_1 + R_2) C_2 s + 1 + R_1 C_1 s (R_2 C_2 s + 1)}$$

i.e., Voltage transfer ratio

$$= \frac{(R_1 C_1)(R_2 C_2) s^2}{(R_1 + R_2) C_2 s + 1 + s (R_1 C_1)(R_2 C_2 s + 1)}.$$

12.5 CONCEPT OF POLES AND ZEROS IN A NETWORK FUNCTION

A network function $H(s)$ may be written as

$$H(s) = \frac{A(s)}{B(s)} = \frac{a_0 s^n + a_1 s^{n-1} + \ldots + a_{n-1} s + a_n}{b_0 s^m + b_1 s^{m-1} + \ldots + b_{m-1} s + b_m} \qquad \ldots(12.10)$$

where, $a_0, a_1, a_2, \ldots, a_n$ and $b_0, b_1, \ldots, b_m$ are the coefficients of the polynomials $A(s)$ and $B(s)$. They are *real and +ve* for a passive network.

Factorising the numerator and denominator, the network function can be rewritten as

$$H(s) = \frac{A(s)}{B(s)} = \frac{a_0 (s - z_1)(s - z_2) \ldots (s - z_n)}{b_0 (s - p_1)(s - p_2) \ldots (s - p_m)} \qquad \ldots(12.11)$$

where, $z_1, z_2, \ldots, z_n$ are the n roots for $A(s) = 0$;

$p_1, p_2, \ldots, p_m$ are the m roots for $B(s) = 0$;

(a_0 / b_0) is a constant (say K) and is called *scale factor.*

Here, $z_1, z_2, \ldots, z_n$ are called *"zeros"* and denoted by a *small circle* in the complex frequency diagram while $p_1, p_2, \ldots, p_m$ are called *"poles"* and denoted by a *"cross"* on the plot. The network function $H(s)$ becomes zero if "s" is equal to any of the zeros and becomes infinity when s is equal to any of the poles.

The network function is said to be having *simple poles or simple zeros* if the poles and zeros are not repeated. On the other hand, if the poles and zeros are repetitive, the function is said to have *multiple poles or zeros.*

EXAMPLE 12.11 *A function is given by* $Z(s) = \frac{s+4}{s}$. *Find the pole-zero plot.*

SOLUTION. In the function $Z(s) = \frac{s+4}{s}$, the zero is at $s = -4$ and pole is at $s = 0$. This gives the pole-zero plot as shown in Fig. E12.12.

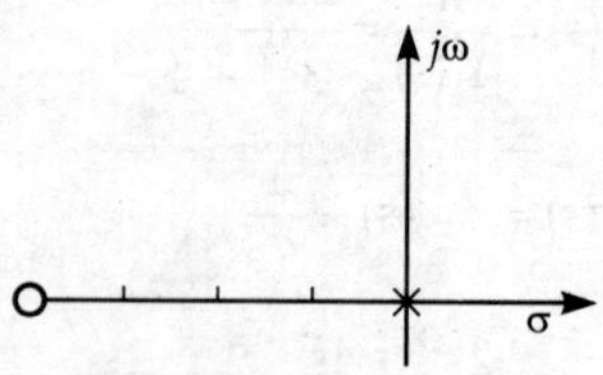

Fig. E12.12

EXAMPLE 12.12 *A function is given by* $Z(s) = \frac{2s}{s^2 + 16}$. *Draw its pole zero plot.*

SOLUTION. For the given function factorisation of denominator gives

$$(s^2 + 16) = (s + j4)(s - j4)$$

$$\therefore \quad Z(s) = \frac{2s}{(s + j4)(s - j4)}$$

The scale factor is 2, poles are at $s = +j4$ and $-j4$, zero is at $s = 0$. The pole-zero plot is shown in Fig. E12.13.

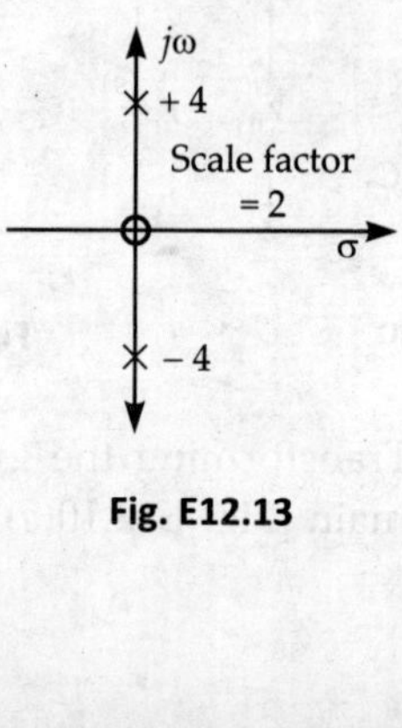

Fig. E12.13

EXAMPLE 12.13 *An admittance function is given by*

$$Y(s)=\frac{1}{s+2}.$$

Find the pole-zero plot.

SOLUTION. For the given function, the pole is at $s=-2$ and the zero is at infinity. The plot is shown in Fig. E12.14.

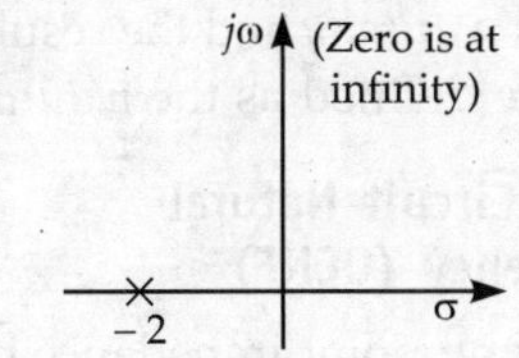

Fig. E12.14

EXAMPLE 12.14 *A network function is given by*

$$P(s)=\frac{2s}{(s+2)(s^2+2s+2)}$$

Obtain the pole-zero diagram.

SOLUTION. In the given function, on factorisation, the denominator is obtained as

$$(s+2)(s+1-j\,1)(s+1+j\,1).$$

Hence, the function becomes

$$P(s)=\frac{2s}{(s+2)(s+1-j\,1)(s+1+j\,1)}.$$

Then the poles are located at $s=-2,(-1+j\,1)$, $(-1-j\,1)$ and the zero is at $S=0$.

The scale factor is 2. [Fig. E12.15]

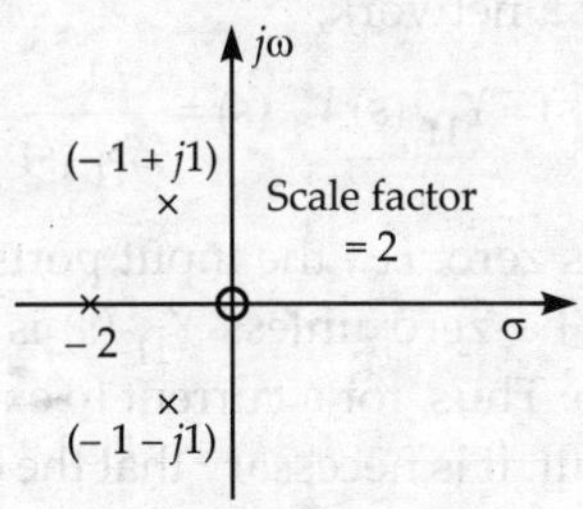

Fig. E12.15

12.6 RESTRICTION ON LOCATION OF POLES AND ZEROS IN DRIVING POINT FUNCTIONS

The following list provides the listing of restrictions of locations of poles and zeros in driving point function :

(*a*) The co-efficients of the polynomials $A(s)$ and $B(s)$ of the network function $H(s)$ must be real and positive.

(*b*) Poles and zeros, if complex or imaginary, must occur in conjugate pairs.

(*c*) The real parts of all poles and zeros must be zero or negative.

[If the real part is zero, then the pole and zero must be simple]

(*d*) The polynomial $A(s)$ or $B(s)$ cannot have any missing term between those of highest and lowest order values unless all even order or all odd order terms are missing.

(*e*) The degree of $A(s)$ and $B(s)$ may differ by zero or one only.

(*f*) The lowest degree in $A(s)$ and $B(s)$ may differ in degree by at the most one.

EXAMPLE 12.15 *Check, if the driving point impedance* $Z(s)$, *given by* $Z(s)=\dfrac{s^4+s^2+1}{s^3+2s^2-2s+10}$ *can represent a passive one port network.*

SOLUTION. The given function is not suitable to represent the impedance of a one port network due to following reasons :

(*i*) In the numerator, one coefficient is missing.

(*ii*) In the denominator, one coefficient is negative.

EXAMPLE 12.16 *Explain, with reasons, why the following expression for the driving point impedance Z(s) is not suitable for representing a passive network.*

$$Z(s)=\frac{s^4-s^3+2s^2}{s+5}$$

SOLUTION. The given function is not suitable for representating the driving point impedance due to following reasons :

(*i*) In the numerator, one coefficient is –ve

(*ii*) The degree of numerator is 4 while that of denominator is 1. Thus a difference of 3 exists between the degree of numerator and denominator and is not permitted.

(*iii*) The numerator gives $s^2(s^2-s+2)$ *i.e.*, double zero, at $s=0$, $s=-0.5+j\sqrt{\frac{7}{4}}$ and $s=-0.5-j\sqrt{\frac{7}{4}}$. This is not permitted.

(*iv*) The term of the lowest degree in numerator is of 2 while that in the denominator is zero.

CHAPTER 12

12.7 NECESSARY CONDITIONS FOR TRANSFER FUNCTIONS

The limitations on pole and zero location in transfer function are as follows :

(*i*) The coefficients of polynomials $A(s)$ and $B(s)$ are to be real; coefficients of $B(s)$ must be +ve though few coefficients of $A(s)$ may be –ve.

(*ii*) The poles and zeros; if complex or imaginary, must be in conjugate.

(*iii*) The real part of poles must be negative or zero. If the real part is zero, the pole must be simple.

(*iv*) The polynomial $A(s)$ may have missing terms between the lowest and highest degree. However, polynomial $B(s)$ should not have any missing term between the highest and lowest degree unless all even or all odd terms are missing.

(*v*) Degree of $A(s)$ may be zero, independent of the degree of $B(s)$.

(*vi*) For the voltage or current transfer ratio, the maximum degree of $A(s)$ must equal the degree of $B(s)$.

(*vii*) For the transfer impedance and admittance, the maximum degree of $A(s)$ must equal the degree of $B(s)$ plus one.

12.8 NATURAL RESPONSE OF A NETWORK

The *natural response* of a network is the response that occurs when the source *excitation is reduced to zero value* and the system responds to its *initial conditions* (*i.e.*, initial stored energy). It is then also called *source free response* or *zero state behaviour*.

Basically, the source free response is the *complementary* solution of the homogeneous differential equation. It is called the *transient response* too. It depends only on the values of the elements and their interconnection but independent of the excitation. The natural response of the system may also be described as the response to *unit impulse excitation* and is characterised by the natural frequencies of oscillation of the system (*natural frequencies* being defined as those to which a network responds when excited by unit impulse function).

On the other hand, if a source excitation is applied with frequency ω_0, the network is forced to react at that frequency. However, the source "being unit impulse function, it does not force any specific frequency in the network and simple introduces some energy instantaneously and then leaves the network to react naturally".

Thus, a network, being exited by an impulse function, reacts *naturally* and the resulting response singularities are defined as the *natural frequencies*.

12.8.1 Open Circuit Natural Frequency (OCNF)

Let the drivng point impedance be given as

$$Z_{11}(s) = K\frac{(s-z_1)(s-z_2)...(s-z_n)}{(s-p_1)(s-p_2)...(s-p_m)} \quad ...(12.12)$$

Also, $V_1(s) = Z_{11}(s)\, I_1(s)$.

With $I_1(s) = 0$, $V_1(s)$ becomes zero unless $Z_{11}(s)$ be infinite *i.e.*, a voltage to exist at the open circuit input with no excitation, it is necessary that $Z_{11}(s)$, the driving point impedance is infinite. The poles of $Z_{11}(s)$ *i.e.*, $p_1, p_2, \ldots, p_n$ are then the *natural frequencies* of the network with input open. These frequencies are called *open circuit natural frequencies* of that network.

12.8.2 Short Circuit Natural Frequencies (SCNF)

Also, for a network,

$$I_1(s) = Y_{11}(s)\, V_1(s) = \frac{1}{Z_{11}(s)} V_1(s).$$

If $V_1(s)$ is zero, *i.e.*, the input ports are shorted, $I_1(s)$ would be zero unless $Y_{11}(s)$ is infinite *i.e.*, $Z_{11}(s)$ is zero. Thus, for a current to exist with short circuited input, it is necessary that the driving point impedance is zero. Then the zeros of $Z_{11}(s)$ *i.e.*, $z_1, z_2, \ldots$ represent the short circuit natural frequencies of the network.

EXAMPLE 12.17 *Find the pole-zero plots of the driving point and transfer impedances of the network shown in Fig. E12.16.*

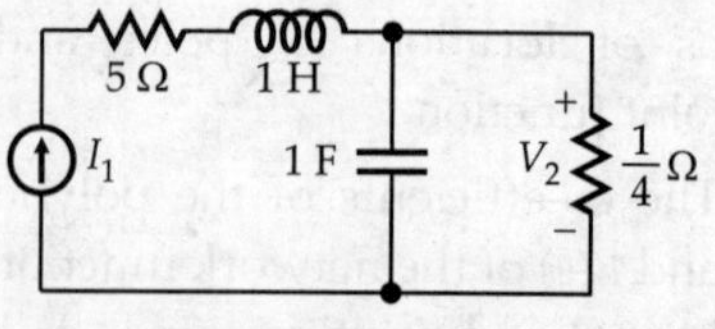

Fig. E12.16

SOLUTION. Let us first transform the given circuit to s-domain as shown in Fig. E12.17 ; where $Z_L(s)$ is the impedance of circuit across terminals x-y.

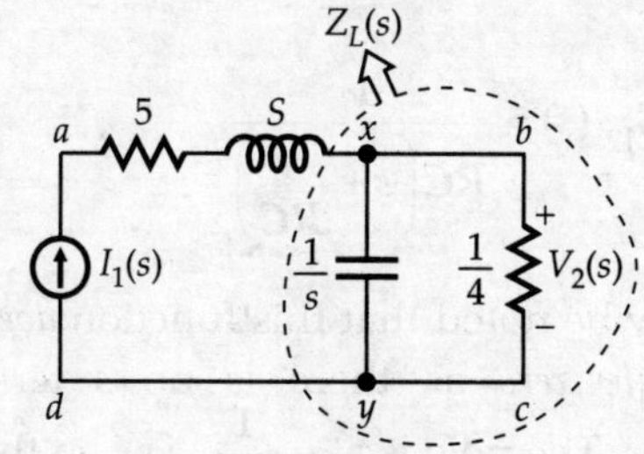

Fig. E12.17

Obviously, $Z_L(s) = \dfrac{1}{Y_L(s)} = \dfrac{1}{s+4}$

$\because$ $V_2(s) = I_1(s)\, Z_L(s)$

$$\frac{V_2(s)}{I_1(s)} = Z_L(s) = \frac{1}{s+4}$$

Also, if $V_1(s)$ be the voltage across the current source, application of KVL in the *loop abcd* (Fig. E12.17) yields,

$$(5+s)\, I_1(s) + V_2(s) = V_1(s)$$

or,
$$V_1(s) = I_1(s)\left[s + 5 + \frac{1}{s+4}\right]$$

$$= I_1(s)\left[\frac{s^2 + 9s + 20 + 1}{s+4}\right]$$

$$\therefore \quad \frac{V_1(s)}{I_1(s)} = \frac{s^2 + 9s + 21}{s+4}$$

i.e., we ultimately obtained

$$Z_{11}(s) = \frac{s^2 + 9s + 21}{s+4}$$

$$Z_{12}(s) = \frac{1}{s+4}$$

Pole-zero plot of $Z_{11}(s)$

The numerator of $Z_{11}(s)$ has roots

$$s_{1,2} = \frac{-9 \pm \sqrt{81-84}}{2} = -4.5 \pm j\frac{\sqrt{3}}{2}$$

$\therefore$ $Z_{11}(s)$ has zeros at $\left(\mathbf{-4.5 \pm j\frac{\sqrt{3}}{2}}\right)$ while pole at **– 4** on s plane.

Pole zero plot of $Z_{21}(s)$

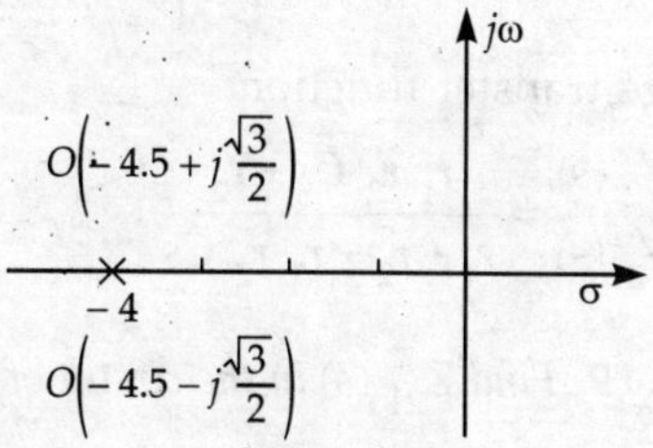

Fig. E12.18

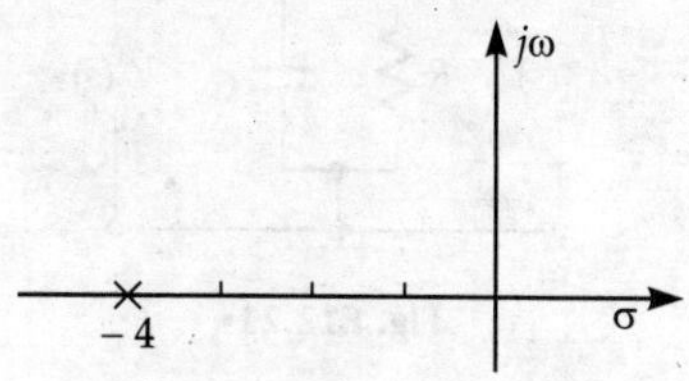

Fig. E12.19

As there is no "s" term in the numerator of $Z_{21}(s)$, it has **no define** *zero* while the pole is at – 4 on s plane.

EXAMPLE 12.18 *In the circuit of Fig. E12.20, find* $Z_{in}(s)$. *Also find the voltage transfer function.*

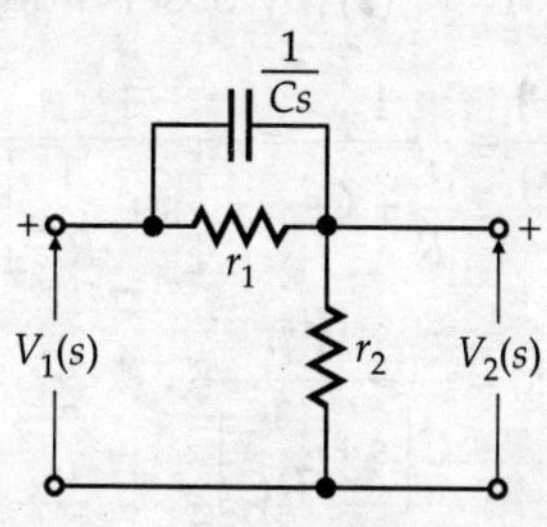

Fig. E12.20

SOLUTION. $Z_{in}(s) = \left(r_1 \,||\, \dfrac{1}{Cs}\right) + r_2$

$$= \frac{\dfrac{r_1}{Cs}}{r_1 + \dfrac{1}{Cs}} + r_2 = \frac{r_1}{r_1\, Cs + 1} + r_2$$

i.e.,
$$Z_{in}(s) = \frac{\mathbf{r_1 + r_1\, r_2\, Cs + r_2}}{\mathbf{(r_1\, Cs + 1)}}.$$

$$\therefore \quad I(s) = \frac{V_1(s)}{Z_{in}(s)} = \frac{V_1(s)}{\dfrac{r_1 + r_1\, r_2\, Cs + r_2}{r_1\, Cs + 1}}$$

$$= V_1(s)\frac{r_1\, Cs + 1}{r_1 + r_2\, r_1\, Cs + r_2}$$

CHAPTER 12

$$\therefore \quad V_2(s) = r_2\, I(s) = V_1(s)\frac{r_1 r_2 Cs + r_2}{r_1 + r_2 + r_1 r_2 Cs}$$

i.e., Voltage transfer function

$$\frac{V_2(s)}{V_1(s)} = \frac{r_1 r_2 Cs + r_2}{r_1 + r_2 + r_1 r_2 Cs}.$$

EXAMPLE 12.19 *Find Z_{21} (s) in the circuit of Fig. E12.21.*

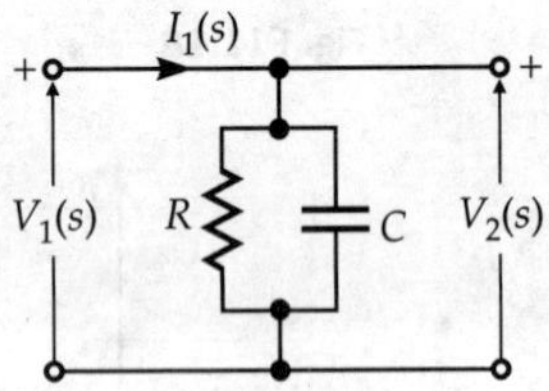

Fig. E12.21

SOLUTION. $Y_{(\text{input})}(s) = \frac{1}{R} + Cs$

However,

$$I_1(s) = V_1(s)\, Y_{in}(s)$$

or,
$$I_1(s) = V_1(s)\left[\frac{1}{R} + Cs\right]$$

But $V_2(s) = V_1(s)$ [by observation] ;

$$\therefore \quad \frac{V_2(s)}{I_1(s)} = \frac{1}{\frac{1}{R} + Cs} = \frac{1}{C\left[s + \frac{1}{RC}\right]}$$

i.e.,
$$Z_{12}(s) = \frac{\mathbf{1}}{\mathbf{C}\left[\mathbf{s} + \frac{\mathbf{1}}{\mathbf{RC}}\right]}.$$

EXAMPLE 12.20 *Find G_{21} (s), Voltage transfer for ratio, for the network shown in Fig. E12.22.*

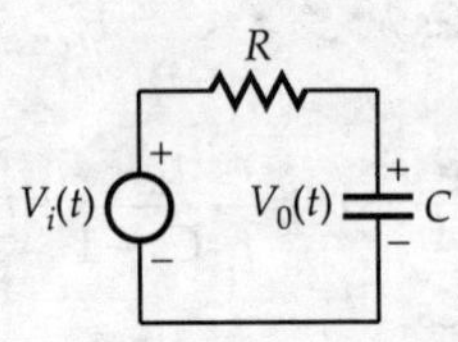

Fig. E12.22

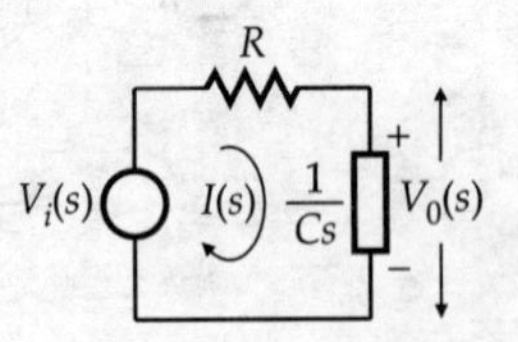

Fig. E12.22 (*a*)

SOLUTION. Transforming the given circuit of Fig. E12.22(*a*), into the s-domain circuit, we get,

$$V_i(s) = I(s)\left[R + \frac{1}{Cs}\right] \quad ...(1)$$

and
$$V_0(s) = I(s)\cdot\frac{1}{Cs} \quad ...(2)$$

$$\therefore \quad \frac{V_0(s)}{V_i(s)} = \frac{1/Cs}{R + \frac{1}{Cs}} = \frac{1}{1 + sCR} = \frac{1}{CR}\left[\frac{1}{s + \frac{1}{RC}}\right]$$

Then,

$$G_{12}(s) = \frac{\mathbf{1}}{\mathbf{RC}\left(\mathbf{s} + \frac{\mathbf{1}}{\mathbf{RC}}\right)}.$$

It may be noted that this function *does not have any definite zero* as there is no *s* term in the numerator. The pole is at $-\frac{\mathbf{1}}{\mathbf{RC}}$, *i.e.,* on the –ve real axis.

EXAMPLE 12.21 *In the network of Fig. E12.23, find $\frac{V_C}{V}$. Also find the pole zero locations.*

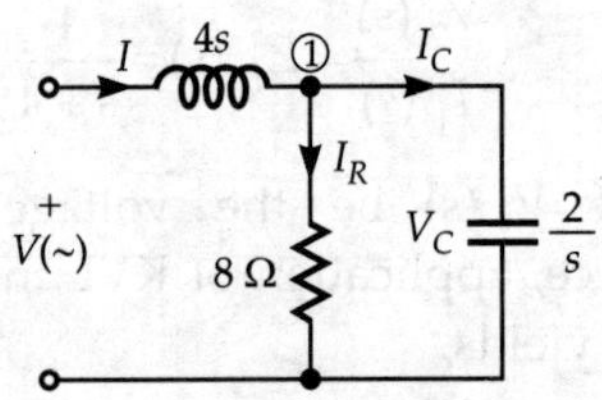

Fig. E12.23

SOLUTION. Using KCL at *node (1),*

$$\frac{V_C - V}{4s} + \frac{V_C}{8} + \frac{V_C}{2/s} = 0$$

or,
$$\frac{V_C}{4s} - \frac{V}{4s} + \frac{V_C}{8} + \frac{V_C \cdot s}{2} = 0$$

or,
$$V_C\left[\frac{1}{4s} + \frac{1}{8} + \frac{s}{2}\right] = \frac{V}{4s}$$

or,
$$V_C\left[\frac{2 + s + 4s^2}{8s}\right] = \frac{V}{4s}$$

$$\therefore \quad V_C = V\frac{2}{2 + s + 4s^2}$$

giving
$$\frac{V_C}{V} = \frac{2}{4s^2 + s + 2}$$

Again, $\frac{V_C}{V} = \frac{\mathbf{2}}{\mathbf{4s^2 + s + 2}} = H(s)$, Say.

i.e.,
$$G_{12}(s) = \frac{2}{\left(s + \frac{1}{8} - j\frac{\sqrt{31}}{8}\right)\left(s + \frac{1}{8} + j\frac{\sqrt{31}}{8}\right)}$$

This function $H(s)$ **does not have any zero** as the s term is absent in the numerator. The poles are at $\left(-\frac{1}{8}+j\frac{\sqrt{31}}{8}\right)$ and at $\left(-\frac{1}{8}-j\frac{\sqrt{31}}{8}\right)$ in the s-plane (Fig. E12.24).

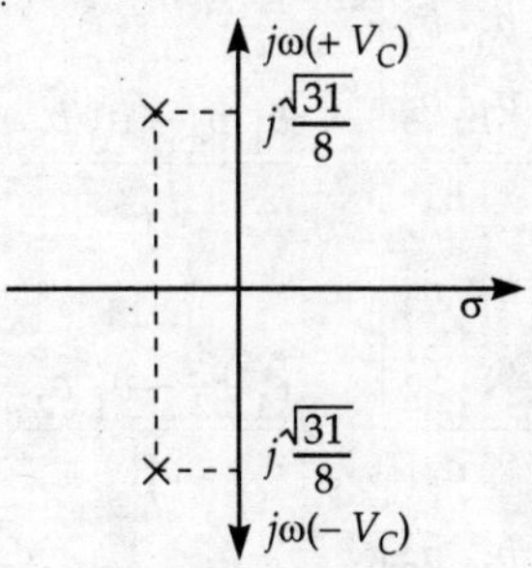

Fig. E12.24

Example 12.22 *Find the pole zero locations of the current transfer ratio* I_2 / I_1 *in s-domain for circuit shown in Fig. E12.25.*

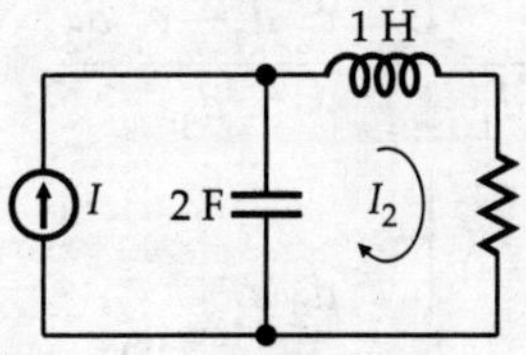

Fig. E12.25

Solution. By the current division formula, the current $I_2(s)$ in Fig. E12.25(*a*) (the *s*-domain circuit of the given network) is given by

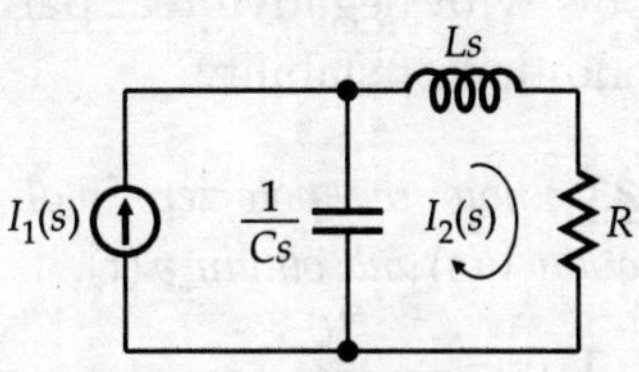

Fig. E12.25 (*a*)

$$I_2(s) = I_1(s)\frac{\frac{1}{Cs}}{R+Ls+\frac{1}{Cs}}$$

or,

$$\frac{I_2(s)}{I_1(s)} = \frac{\frac{1}{Cs}}{R+Ls+\frac{1}{Cs}}$$

$$= \frac{1}{1+sCR+s^2 LC}$$

$$= \frac{1}{1+200\,s+2s^2} = \frac{1}{D}$$

where $D = 1+200\,s+2s^2$

$$\therefore \quad s_1, s_2 = \frac{-200 \pm \sqrt{200^2-8}}{2}$$

$$= -100 \pm \sqrt{10{,}000-2}$$

$$= -100 \pm 99.99 \simeq \text{either } 0 \text{ or } -200.$$

i.e., **"zero" being not existing** (as numerator of $I_2(s)/I_1(s)$ does not contain *s* term), the **poles are either at zero or at – 200.**

12.9 MAGNITUDE AND PHASE ANGLE OF THE COEFFICIENTS IN THE NETWORK FUNCTION

Let the network function be rewritten as shown in eqn. (12.11).

$$H(s) = \frac{A(s)}{B(s)} = K\frac{(s-z_1)(s-z_2)\ldots\ldots(s-z_n)}{(s-p_1)(s-p_2)\ldots\ldots(s-p_m)}$$

$$= \frac{K_a}{s-p_1} + \frac{K_b}{s-p_2} + \ldots + \frac{K_r}{(s-p_r)} + \ldots + \frac{K_m}{(s-p_m)} \qquad \ldots(12.13)$$

Here,

$$K_r = K\frac{(s-z_1)(s-z_2)\ldots(s-z_n)}{(s-p_1)(s-p_2)\ldots(s-p_r)\ldots(s-p_m)}\cdot(s-p_r)\Bigg|_{s=p_r}$$

$$\text{or, } K_r = K\frac{(p_r-z_1)(p_r-z_2)\ldots(p_r-z_n)}{(p_r-p_1)(p_r-p_2)\ldots(p_r-p_m)} \qquad \ldots(12.14)$$

Expression (12.14) consists of factors of the general form $(p_r - p_n)$, where p_r and p_n are known *complex numbers.* The difference of two complex numbers is also another complex number which may be written in polar form as

$$(p_r - p_n) = M_{nr}\, e^{j\phi_{nr}} \qquad \ldots(12.15)$$

M_{nr} being the magnitude of the phasor $(p_r - p_n)$ and ϕ_{nr} the phase angle of the same phasor.

Thus,

$$K_r = K\frac{M_{1r}\cdot M_{2r}\cdot M_{3r}\ldots\ldots M_{nr}}{M_{ar}\cdot M_{br}\cdot M_{cr}\ldots\ldots M_{mr}}\; e^{j(\phi_{1r}+\phi_{2r}+\ldots\ldots-\phi_{ar}-\phi_{br}-\ldots\ldots)} \qquad \ldots(12.16)$$

The above equation (12.16) gives the magnitude and phase angle of the coefficient *Kr*. Thus all the coefficients from K_a to K_m can be evaluated.

The magnitude of $M_{1r}, M_{2r}, \ldots\ldots$ and $M_{ar}, M_{br}\ldots\ldots$ can be evaluated from pole and zero plot on the *s*-plane. In a similar way, the phase angles $\phi_{1r}, \phi_{2r}\ldots\ldots$ and $\phi_{ar}, \phi_{br}\ldots\ldots$ can also be measured from the same pole-zero plot.

The graphical procedure/steps for determining the quantities in equation (12.16) can be done as shown below :

Step 1 On the complex *s*-plane, plot the poles and zeros of the given network function to scale.

Step 2 Calculate (or measure) the distances M_{1r}, M_{2r}..... of a given pole from each of the zeros. Also calculate (or measure) the distances M_{ar}, M_{br},.... of the same pole from each of the other finite poles.

Step 3 Calculate or measure the angle from each of the other finite poles (*i.e.*, ϕ_{ar}, ϕ_{br}......) as well as from each of the other zeros (ϕ_{1r}, ϕ_{2r}.....).

Step 4 Substitute these values in equation (12.16) to get the value of K_r.

Step 5 Repeat the above procedure for all the coefficients K_a, K_b,.....

12.10 ROUTH-HURWITZ CRITERION OF STABILITY OF NETWORK FUNCTION

The *stability* of a network function can be observed utilising following steps –

(*i*) The array is to be constructed first.

(*ii*) Two rows of coefficients are formed, first row containing even numbered coefficients and the second row odd number coefficients.

(*iii*) The array is to be completed.

Illustration

Let the polynomial be

$$B(s) = b_0 s^m + b_1 s^{m-1} + b_2 s^{m-2} + \ldots + b_m.$$

First row and second row coefficients give

$$\begin{matrix} b_0 & b_2 & b_4 \ldots\ldots \\ b_1 & b_3 & b_5 \ldots\ldots \end{matrix}$$

Let $m = 5$, the array will contain $(m+1)$ *i.e.* 6 rows.

Array

s^5	b_0	b_2	b_4
s^4	b_1	b_3	b_5
s^3	c_1	c_2	
s^2	d_1	d_2	
s^1	e_1		
s^0	f_1		

where,

$$c_1 = \frac{\begin{vmatrix} b_0 & b_2 \\ b_1 & b_3 \end{vmatrix}}{b_1} = \frac{b_1 b_2 - b_0 b_3}{b_1}$$

$$c_2 = \frac{\begin{vmatrix} b_0 & b_4 \\ b_1 & b_5 \end{vmatrix}}{b_1} = \frac{b_1 b_4 - b_0 b_5}{b_1}$$

$$d_1 = \frac{\begin{vmatrix} b_1 & b_3 \\ c_1 & c_2 \end{vmatrix}}{c_1} = \frac{c_1 b_3 - b_1 c_2}{c_1}$$

$$d_2 = \frac{\begin{vmatrix} b_1 & b_5 \\ c_1 & 0 \end{vmatrix}}{c_1} = \frac{b_5 c_1}{c_1} = b_5$$

$$e_1 = \frac{\begin{vmatrix} c_1 & c_2 \\ d_1 & d_2 \end{vmatrix}}{d_1} = \frac{c_2 d_1 - c_1 d_2}{d_1}$$

$$f_1 = \frac{\begin{vmatrix} d_1 & d_2 \\ e_1 & 0 \end{vmatrix}}{e_1} = \frac{d_2 e_1}{e_1} = d_2$$

According to *Routh Hurwitz criterion,* the system is said to be stable, *if and only if, there are no changes in signs of the first column of the array*. This gives the roots with negative real parts and hence gives the condition of stability.

EXAMPLE 12.23 *Show the pole-zero plot of the given network function V(s) and obtain v (t).*

$$V(s) = \frac{10\,s}{(s+3)\,(s+2)}$$

SOLUTION. Using the techniques of partial fraction,

$$V(s) = \frac{10\,s}{(s+3)(s+2)} = \frac{K_1}{(s+3)} + \frac{K_2}{(s+2)}$$

$$v(t) = K_1\, e^{-3t} + K_2\, e^{-2t} \qquad \ldots(i)$$

The pole zero plot is shown in Fig. E12.26.

First we consider the pole at –2.

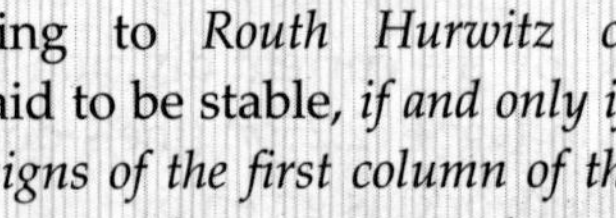

Fig. E12.26

$\therefore M_{02}$ (distance between "zero" to "pole" at $-2) = 2$

and $\phi_{02} = 180°$

Also, $M_{32} = 1$ and $\phi_{32} = 0°$

[$\because$ the distance between pole at -3 and pole at -2 is 1 unit and ϕ_{32} is directed in opposite sense to ϕ_{02}]

$$\therefore \quad K_2 = H\frac{M_{02}\, e^{j\phi_{02}}}{M_{32}\, e^{j\phi_{32}}} = 10\frac{2e^{j180°}}{e^{j0°}}$$

$$= 20\, e^{j180°} = -20.$$

Next we consider the pole at -3.

$$\therefore \quad M_{03} = 3\,;\ \phi_{03} = 180°$$

Also, $M_{23} = 1\,;\ \phi_{23} = 180°$

$$\therefore \quad K_1 = H\frac{M_{03}\, e^{j\phi_{03}}}{M_{23}\, e^{j\phi_{23}}}$$

$$= 10\frac{3\, e^{j180°}}{e^{j180°}} = 30$$

This gives $\boldsymbol{v(t) = 30\, e^{-3t} - 20\, e^{-2t}}$.

Example 12.24 *Obtain the pole zero diagram of the given function and obtain the time domain response.*

$$I(s) = \frac{2s}{(s+1)(s^2+2s+4)}$$

Solution. Using partial fraction,

$$I(s) = \frac{2s}{(s+1)(s^2+2s+4)}$$

$$= \frac{K_1}{(s+1)} + \frac{K_2}{(s+1-j\sqrt{3})} + \frac{K_3}{(s+1+j\sqrt{3})}$$

$$\therefore i(t) = K_1\, e^{-t} + K_2\, e^{-(1-j\sqrt{3})t} + K_3\, e^{-(1+j\sqrt{3})t}$$

The pole zero plot has been exhibited in the figure (Fig. E12.27).

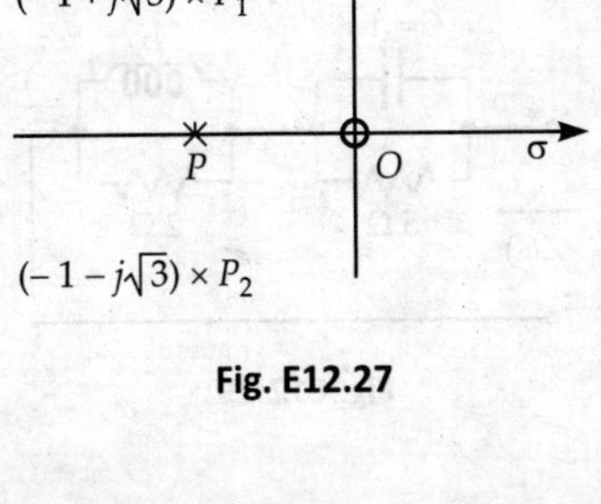

Fig. E12.27

$$K_1 = H\frac{M_{OP}\, e^{j\phi_{OP}}}{M_{P_1-P}\, M_{P_2-P}\, e^{j(\phi_{P_1-P}+\phi_{P_2-P})}}$$

$$= 2\frac{1.\, e^{j180}}{(\sqrt{3}\times\sqrt{3})\, e^{j(-90°+90°)}}$$

$$[\because M_{OP} = 1\,;\ M_{P_1-P} = M_{P_2-P} = \sqrt{3}$$
$$\phi_{OP} = 180°\,;\ \phi_{P_1-P} = -90°\,;\ \phi_{P_2-P} = 90°]$$

$$\therefore \quad K_1 = 0.67\, e^{j180°} = -0.67$$

and
$$K_2 = H\frac{M_{OP_1}\, e^{j\phi_{OP_1}}}{M_{P-P_1}\, M_{P_2-P_1}\, e^{j(\phi_{P-P_1}+\phi_{P_2-P_1})}}$$

(Please check with Fig. E12.28)

$$= 2\frac{2e^{j\left[\tan^{-1}\frac{OP}{PP_1}+90°\right]}}{(\sqrt{3}\times 2\sqrt{3})\, e^{j(90°+90°)}}$$

$$= 0.67\, e^{j\left[\tan^{-1}\frac{OP}{PP_1}+90°-180°\right]}$$

$$= 0.67\, e^{-j(60°)}$$

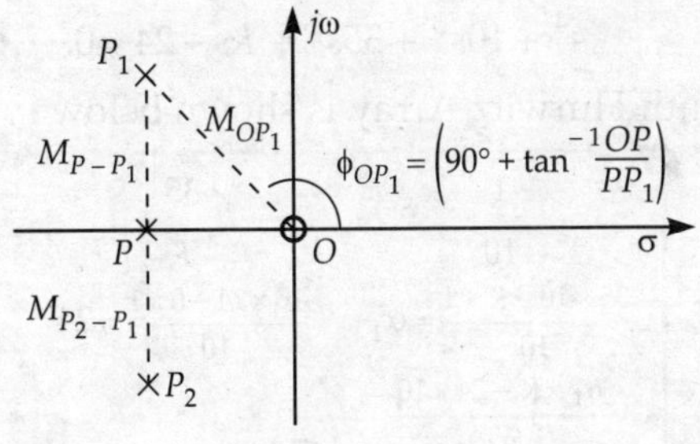

Fig. E12.28

$\therefore K_3$, being the conjugate of K_2 will be given by

$$K_3 = 0.67\, e^{j(60°)}\ [K_3 = K_2^*]$$

$$\therefore \quad \boldsymbol{i(t) = -0.67\, e^{-t} + 0.67\, e^{+j(60°)}\, e^{-(1+j\sqrt{3})t}}$$
$$\boldsymbol{+ 0.67\, e^{-j(60°)}\, e^{-(1-j\sqrt{3})t}}$$

Example <u>12.25(a)</u> *Check the stability of the following polynomial by applying Routh-Hurwitz criterion :*

$$P(s) = s^4 + 2s^3 + 4s^2 + 12\,s + 10$$

Solution. Routh array of the polynomial can be obtained from the following coefficients.

$$b_0 = 1\,;\ b_2 = 4\,;\ b_4 = 10\,;\ b_1 = 2\,;\ b_3 = 12$$

$$c_1 = \frac{b_1\, b_2 - b_0\, b_3}{b_1} = \frac{8-12}{2} = -2$$

CHAPTER 12

$$\therefore \quad c_2 = \frac{b_1 b_4 - b_0 b_5}{b_1} = \frac{20 - 1 \times 0}{2} = 10$$

$$d_1 = \frac{c_1 b_3 - b_1 c_2}{c_1} = \frac{-2 \times 12 - 2 \times 10}{-2} = 22$$

$$d_2 = b_5 = 0$$

$$e_1 = \frac{c_2 d_1 - c_1 d_2}{d_1} = \frac{10 \times 16 - (-2) \times 0}{16} = 10$$

$$f_1 = d_2 = 0$$

This gives

s^4	1	4	10
s^3	2	12	
s^2	−2	10	
s^1	22	0	
s^0	10		

There is a sign change in the 1st column of the array. Hence the system **is not stable.**

EXAMPLE 12.25(b) *For what value of 'K' the polynomial $s^4 + 10s^3 + 35s^2 + Ks + 24 = 0$ is said to be stable ? Solve by using Routh Hurwitz Array.*

SOLUTION. Given Polynomial is

$$s^4 + 10s^3 + 35s^2 + Ks + 24 = 0.$$

Routh Hurwitz Array is shown below

s^4	1	35	24
s^3	10	K	
s^2	$\frac{35 \times 10 - K \times 1}{10} = \alpha_1$	$\frac{10 \times 24 - 0 \times 1}{10} = 24$	
s^1	$\frac{\alpha_1 \times K - 24 \times 10}{\alpha_1}$		
s^0	24		

For stability of the network, $\alpha_1 > 0$

i.e., $\quad \frac{350 - K}{10} > 0 \quad$ or $\quad K < 350.$

Hence the range K is **$(0 < K < 350)$.**

EXAMPLE 12.26(a) *A polynomial is given by*

$$P(s) = s^3 + 2s^2 + 4s + M.$$

"M" is adjustable. Apply Routh Hurwitz criterion.

SOLUTION. Routh array gives

s^3	1	4
s^2	2	M
s^1	$\frac{8 - M}{2}$	
s^0	M	

We see that if M is less than 8, the system is stable. There will be no change in the sign of 1st column. If $M = 8$, then also there is no change in sign in the first column and hence the **system will also be stable.**

EXAMPLE 12.26(b) *Check whether the following polynomial $P(s) = s^4 + s^3 + 2s^2 + 2s + 3$ is stable or not. Comment on your findings.*

SOLUTION. Given polynomial is

$$P(s) = s^4 + s^3 + 2s^2 + 25 + 3$$

where total number of rows are $(4 + 1) = 5$

Routh Hurwitz Array is shown below :

s^4	1	2	3
s^3	1	2	
s^2	$\frac{2 - 2 = 0}{1} = 0$	3	
s^1	∞		
s^0			

In above array, we found third row of first column has a zero value. Hence the subsequent value is infinite. Let us now assume a small value ε in place of the zero value. The modified array is given below :

s^4	1	2	3
s^3	1	2	
s^2	ε	3	
s^1	$\frac{2\varepsilon - 3}{\varepsilon} > 0$		
s^0	3		

For stability point of view, $\varepsilon > 0$ *i.e.,* $\frac{2\varepsilon - 3}{\varepsilon} > 0.$

This gives $\varepsilon > \mathbf{3/2}$

Hence to have the stability of the function, we should have any value of ε more than $(3/2)$.

EXAMPLE 12.27 *What should be the value of L such that $Z(s) = 1$ in the network of Fig. E12.29 ?*

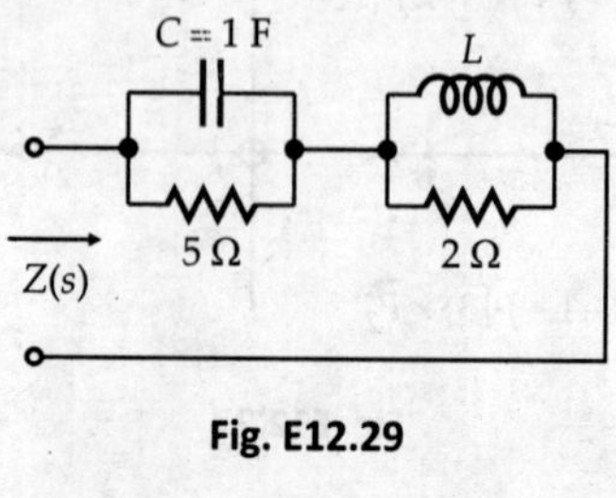

Fig. E12.29

SOLUTION. Let us first convert the network of Fig. E12.29 to s-domain [Fig. E12.29(a)]

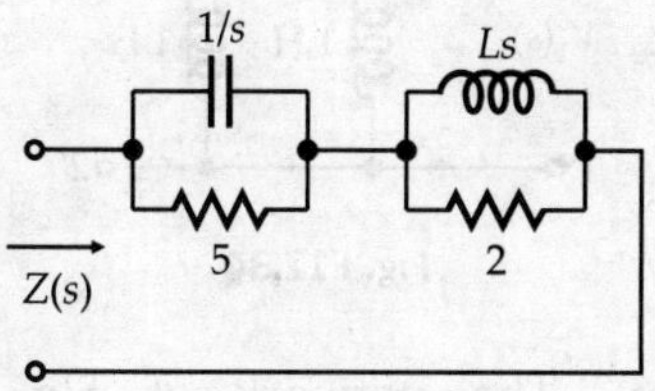

Fig. E12.29 (a)

$$Z(s)=\frac{5\times\dfrac{1}{Cs}}{5+\dfrac{1}{Cs}}+\frac{2\times Ls}{2+Ls}=\frac{5}{5s+1}+\frac{2\ Ls}{2+Ls}$$

$$=\frac{10+5\ Ls+10\ Ls^2+2\ Ls}{(5s+1)(2+Ls)}$$

$$=\frac{10+7Ls+10\ Ls^2}{(5s+1)(2+lS)}$$

However, $Z(s)=1$

$$\therefore\quad \frac{10+7\ Ls+10Ls^2}{10\ s+5Ls^2+2+Ls}=1$$

or, $$5Ls^2+6Ls-10\ s+8=0$$

$$\therefore\ L=\frac{\mathbf{10\ s+8}}{\mathbf{s\ (5s+6)}}.$$

ADDITIONAL EXAMPLES

EXAMPLE 12.28 *Find Z_{in} in Laplace domain in the circuit of Fig. E12.30 and find the voltage transfer function of the same network if a voltage $V_1(s)$ is applied at 1 - 1′ terminal that produces a drop $V_2(s)$ across r_2.*

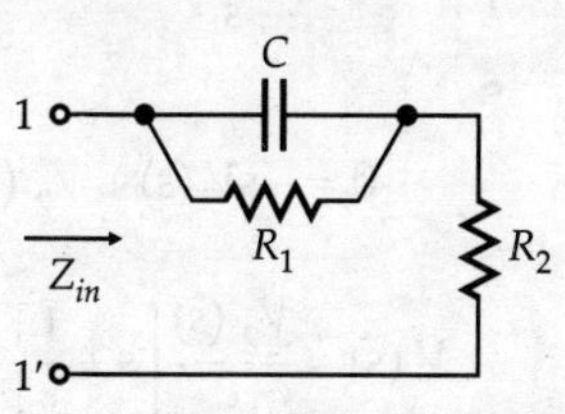

Fig. E12.30

SOLUTION. Let us transform the given network to s-domain first (Fig. E12.31)

$$Z_{in}(s)=\left[\frac{1}{Cs}\,||\,R_1\right]+R_2=\frac{R_1}{1+R_1\,Cs}+R_2$$

$$=\frac{R_1+R_2+R_1\,R_2\,Cs}{1+R_1\,Cs}$$

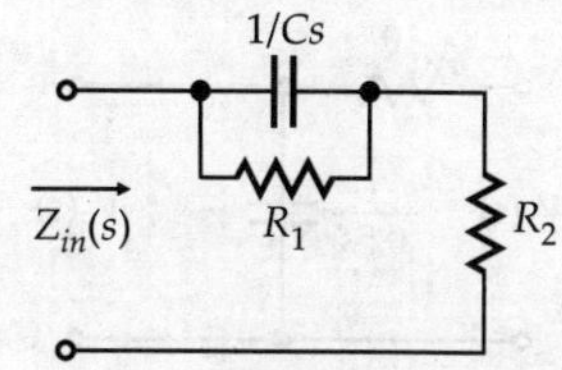

Fig. E12.31

or, $$Z_{in}(s)=\frac{s+\dfrac{1}{R_2\,C}+\dfrac{1}{R_1\,C}}{s+\dfrac{1}{R_1\,C}}\cdot\frac{R_1\,R_2\,C}{R_1\,C}$$

i.e., $$Z_{in}(s)=R_2\cdot\frac{s+\dfrac{1}{R_2\,C}+\dfrac{1}{R_1C}}{s+\dfrac{1}{R_1\,C}}$$

$$\text{Voltage transfer ratio}=\frac{V_2(s)}{V_1(s)}=\frac{I(s).R_2}{I(s).Z_{in}(s)}$$

$$=\frac{R_2}{Z_{in}(s)}=\frac{R_2}{R_2\dfrac{s+\dfrac{1}{R_2\,C}+\dfrac{1}{R_1\,C}}{s+\dfrac{1}{R_1\,C}}}$$

$$=\frac{s+\dfrac{1}{R_1\,C}}{s+\dfrac{1}{R_2\,C}+\dfrac{1}{R_1\,C}}$$

$$\therefore\ \text{Voltage transfer ratio}=\frac{\mathbf{s+\dfrac{1}{R_1\,C}}}{\mathbf{s+\dfrac{1}{R_2\,C}+\dfrac{1}{R_1\,C}}}.$$

EXAMPLE 12.29 *Obtain the transfer function $\dfrac{V_2(s)}{V_1(s)}$ of the network shown in Fig. E12.32. Find $V_2(t)$ when $V_1(t)=10\,e^{-2t}$ V.*

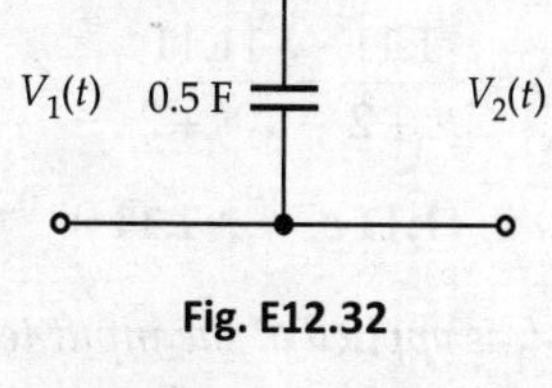

Fig. E12.32

SOLUTION. Let the network be transformed to s-domain (Fig. E12.33).

C
H
A
P
T
E
R
12

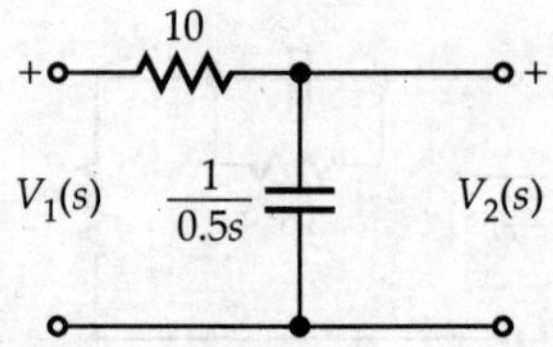

Fig. E12.33

Here, $V_1(s) = \left(10 + \frac{1}{0.5\,s}\right) I_1(s) = \left(10 + \frac{2}{s}\right) I_1(s)$

Also, $V_2(s) = I_1(s) \times \frac{1}{0.5\,s} = \frac{2}{s} I_1(s)$

$\therefore$ Thus, the required transfer function

$$= \frac{V_2(s)}{V_1(s)} = \frac{\frac{2}{s}}{10 + \frac{2}{s}}$$

$\therefore$ Voltage transfer function $= \dfrac{2}{s\left(10 + \frac{2}{s}\right)}$

However,

$$V_1 = 10\,e^{-2t} \text{ i.e., } V_1(s) = \frac{10}{(s+2)}$$

$$\because \quad V_2(s) = V_1(s) \cdot \frac{2}{s\left(10 + \frac{2}{s}\right)},$$

hence $\quad V_2(s) = \dfrac{10}{(s+2)} \dfrac{2}{s(10 + 2/s)}$

$$= \frac{20s}{s(s+2)(10s+2)}$$

$$= \frac{K_1}{s+2} + \frac{K_2}{10s+2}$$

$$K_1 = \left.\frac{20}{(10s+2)}\right|_{s=-2} = -1.11$$

$$K_2 = \left.\frac{20}{(s+2)}\right|_{s=-\frac{2}{10}} = 11.11.$$

$$\therefore \quad V_2(s) = -\frac{1.11}{s+2} + \frac{11.11}{10s+2}$$

$$\therefore \quad \mathbf{V_2(t) = -1.11\,e^{-2t} + 1.11\,e^{-0.2t}}.$$

EXAMPLE 12.30 *V_1 is applied at the input terminals 1 – 1′. Find the voltage transfer ratio G_{21} in the network of Fig. E12.34.*

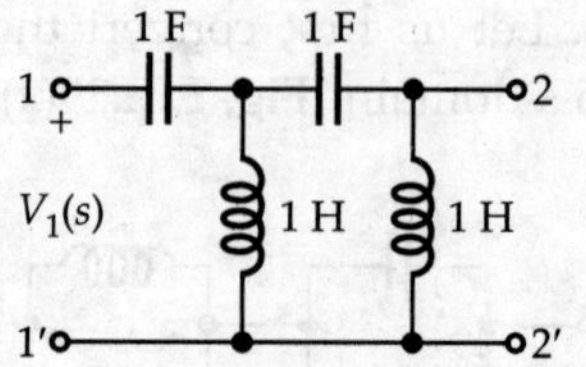

Fig. E12.34

SOLUTION. The network of Fig. E12.34 is redrawn in s-domain in Fig. E12.35 alongwith assumed voltages and currents.

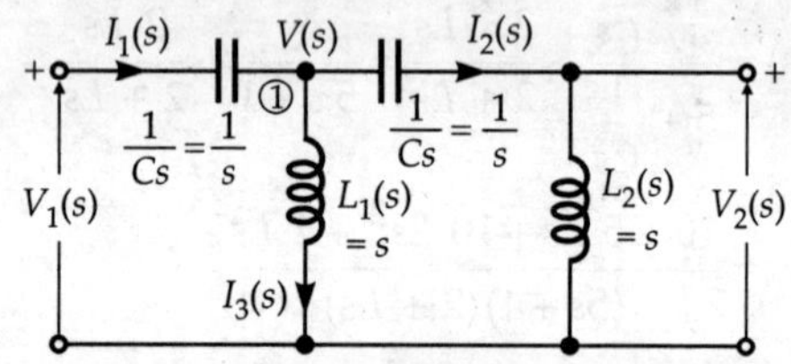

Fig. E12.35

In the leftmost loop, applying KCL at node (1),

$$I_1(s) = I_2(s) + I_3(s)$$

or,
$$\frac{V_1(s) - V(s)}{\frac{1}{s}} = \frac{V(s)}{s} + \frac{V(s) - V_2(s)}{\frac{1}{s}}$$

or,
$$sV_1(s) = V(s)\left[2s + \frac{1}{s}\right] - sV_2(s) \qquad ...(1)$$

By observation, it is evident that $I_2(s)$ flows through $L_2(s)$ too producing output voltage $V_2(s)$ across 2-2′ terminal.

$$\therefore \quad \frac{V(s) - V_2(s)}{\frac{1}{s}} = \frac{V_2(s)}{s}$$

or,
$$0 = -sV(s) + V_2(s)\left[s + \frac{1}{s}\right]$$

or,
$$V(s) = \frac{V_2(s)}{s}\left[s + \frac{1}{s}\right] \qquad ...(2)$$

Substituting the value of $V(s)$ from (2) in (1),

$$sV_1(s) = \left[\frac{V_2(s)}{s}\left(s + \frac{1}{s}\right)\right]\left[2s + \frac{1}{s}\right] - sV_2(s)$$

$$= V_2(s)\left[\left\{\frac{1}{s}\left(s + \frac{1}{s}\right)\right\}\left\{2s + \frac{1}{s}\right\} - s\right]$$

$$= V_2(s)\left[\left(1 + \frac{1}{s^2}\right)\left(2s + \frac{1}{s}\right) - s\right]$$

$$= V_2(s)\left[2s + \frac{1}{s} + \frac{2}{s} + \frac{1}{s^3} - s\right]$$

$$= V_2(s)\left[\frac{2s^4 + s^2 + 2s^2 - s^4 + 1}{s^3}\right]$$

$$= V_2(s)\left[\frac{s^4 + 3s^2 + 1}{s^3}\right]$$

$$\therefore \quad \frac{V_2(s)}{V_1(s)} = \frac{s^4}{s^4 + 3s^2 + 1} = G_{21}(s)$$

i.e., $$G_{12}(s) = \frac{s^4}{s^4 + 3s^2 + 1}.$$

***Example* 12.31** *Find $G_{21}(s)$ for the network shown in Fig. E12.36 when $V_1(s)$ is the applied voltage at the input terminals.*

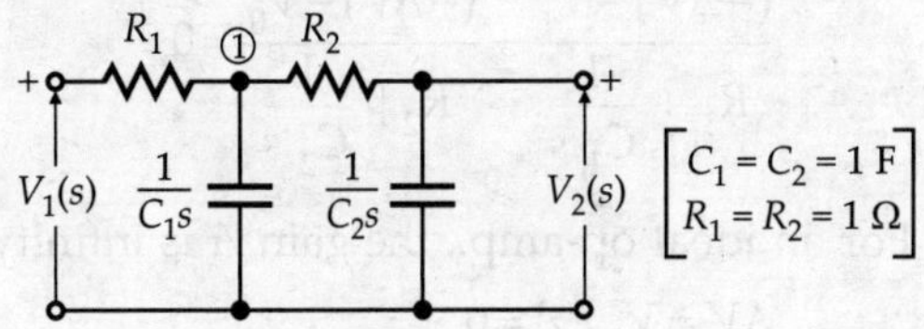

Fig. E12.36

Solution. In the *s*-domain network of Fig. E12.36, let $V_3(s)$ be the potential at the junction of R_1, R_2, C_1 *i.e.,* at *node (1).*

Applying KCL at node (1),

$$\frac{V_1(s) - V_3(s)}{R_1} + \frac{V_2(s) - V_3(s)}{R_2} = \frac{V_3(s)}{\dfrac{1}{C_1 s}}$$

$$= V_3(s)\, C_1 s$$

or, $$\frac{V_1(s)}{R_1} = V_3(s)\left[sC_1 + \frac{1}{R_1} + \frac{1}{R_2}\right] - \frac{V_2(s)}{R_2} \quad \text{...(1)}$$

It may also be evident that the current passing through R_2 also passes through C_2

i.e., $$\frac{V_3(s) - V_2(s)}{R_2} = \frac{V_2(s)}{\dfrac{1}{sC_2}}$$

or, $$0 = \left[\frac{-V_3(s)}{R_2}\right] + V_2(s)\left[sC_2 + \frac{1}{R_2}\right]$$

i.e., $$V_3(s) = V_2(s)\left[sC_2 R_2 + 1\right] \quad \text{...(2)}$$

Utilising (2) in (1),

$$\frac{V_1(s)}{R_1} = V_2(s)\left[1 + sC_2 R_2\right]\left[sC_1 + \frac{1}{R_1} + \frac{1}{R_2}\right] - \frac{V_2(s)}{R_2}$$

or, $$V_1(s) = V_2(s)\left[\{R_1 + sC_2 R_2 R_1\}\left\{sC_1 + \frac{1}{R_1} + \frac{1}{R_2}\right\} - \frac{R_1}{R_2}\right]$$

or, $$\frac{V_2(s)}{V_1(s)} = G_{12}(s)$$

$$= \frac{1}{\left[\{R_1 + sC_2 R_1 R_2\}\left\{sC_1 + \dfrac{1}{R_1} + \dfrac{1}{R_2}\right\} - \dfrac{R_1}{R_2}\right]}$$

$$= \frac{1}{[\{1 + s\}\{s + 1 + 1\} - 1]} = \frac{1}{(s + 1)[(s + 2) - 1]}$$

i.e., $$G_{12(s)} = \frac{1}{(s+1)^2}.$$

***Example* 12.32** *Obtain the voltage transfer function of the network shown in Fig. E12.37.*

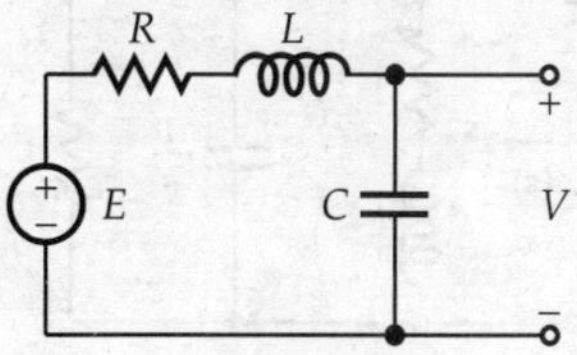

Fig. E12.37

Solution. Let us first transform the network to frequency domain (Fig. E12.38).

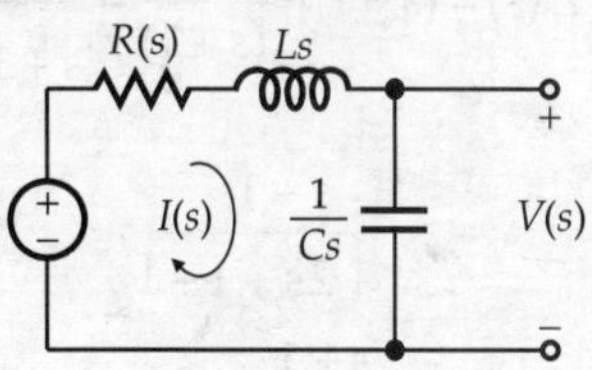

Fig. E12.38

Here, $$I(s) = \frac{E(s)}{R + Ls + \dfrac{1}{Cs}}$$

$$\therefore \quad V(s) = I(s) \times \frac{1}{Cs} = \frac{E(s)}{R + Ls + \dfrac{1}{Cs}} \cdot \frac{1}{Cs}$$

$$\therefore \quad \frac{V(s)}{E(s)} = \frac{\dfrac{1}{Cs}}{R + Ls + \dfrac{1}{Cs}} = \frac{1}{LCs^2 + RCs + 1}$$

Obviously, $\dfrac{V(s)}{E(s)}$ gives the voltage transfer ratio and

$$\frac{V(s)}{E(s)} = \frac{1}{LCs^2 + RCs + 1}.$$

EXAMPLE 12.33 *Find the driving point impedance of the network shown in Fig. E12.39. Find the poles and zeros of the network and locate them in the S-plane.*

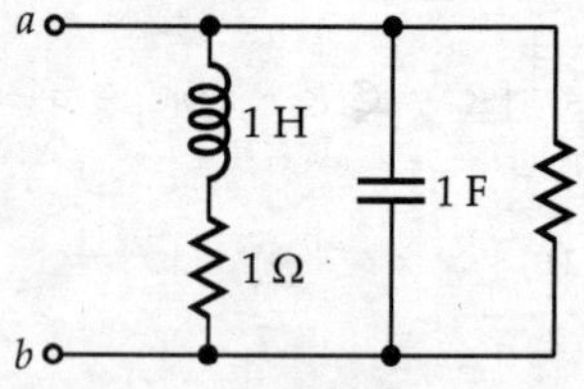

Fig. E12.39

SOLUTION. Let us first transform the impedance to s-domain (Fig. E12.40).

$$Z_1(s) = \frac{1 \times \frac{1}{s}}{1 + \frac{1}{s}} = \frac{1}{s+1}$$

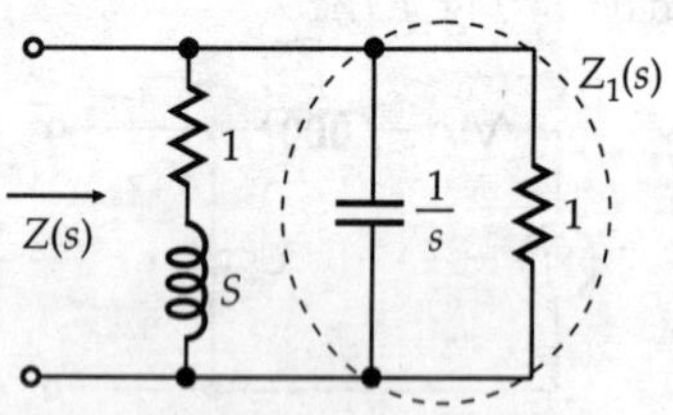

Fig. E12.40

$$\therefore \quad Z(s) = (s+1) \,||\, \frac{1}{(s+1)} = \frac{(s+1)\frac{1}{s+1}}{s+1+\frac{1}{s+1}}$$

$$= \frac{s+1}{s^2 + 2s + 1 + 1}.$$

$$\therefore \quad Z(s) = \frac{s+1}{s^2 + 2s + 2}.$$

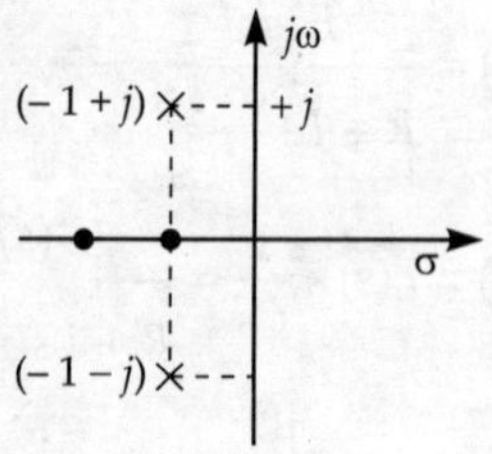

Fig. E12.41

$Z(s)$ being the driving point impedance.

$$\text{or,} \quad Z(s) = \frac{s+1}{(s+1+j)(s+1-j)}.$$

Thus the **poles are at $-1-j$ and $-1+j$ and there is one zero at -1.**

EXAMPLE 12.34 *Find the voltage transfer ratio of the ideal Op-Amp model shown in Fig. E12.42.*

[Assume $\Delta V = V_0 / A$, A being the gain].

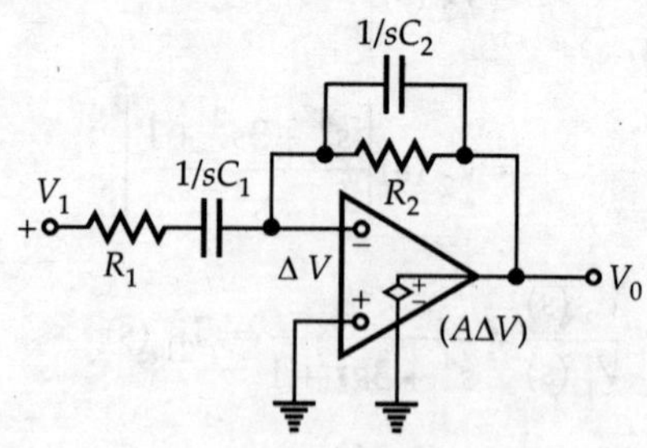

Fig. E12.42

SOLUTION. Application of KCL at the negative terminal of the input of the Op-amp in Fig. E12.42, gives

$$\frac{(-\Delta V) - V_1}{R_1 + \frac{1}{C_1 s}} + \frac{(-\Delta V) - V_0}{R_2 \,||\, \frac{1}{C_2 s}} = 0 \qquad \text{...(1)}$$

For an ideal op-amp., the gain A is infinity.

$$\therefore \quad \Delta V = V_0 / A = 0$$

Using $\Delta V = 0$ in (1),

$$-\frac{V_1}{R_1 + \frac{1}{C_1 s}} - \frac{V_0}{\dfrac{R_2 \times \frac{1}{C_2 s}}{R_2 + \frac{1}{C_2 s}}} = 0$$

$$\text{or,} \quad \frac{V_1 (C_1 s)}{(R_1 C_1 s + 1)} + \frac{V_0 \left(R_2 + \frac{1}{C_2 s}\right)}{\frac{R_2}{C_2 s}} = 0$$

$$\text{or,} \quad \frac{V_1 (C_1 s)}{1 + R_1 C_1 s} + \frac{V_0 (R_2 C_2 s + 1)}{R_2} = 0$$

$$\therefore \quad \frac{V_0}{V_1} = -\left(\frac{C_1 s}{1 + R_1 C_1 s}\right)\left(\frac{R_2}{1 + R_2 C_2 s}\right)$$

The above expression gives the voltage transfer ratio.

EXAMPLE 12.35 *What is the value of Z_{21} in the circuit of Fig. E12.43 ?*

SOLUTION. Let the voltage at node (1) be V_1. Application of KCL at *node* (1) gives

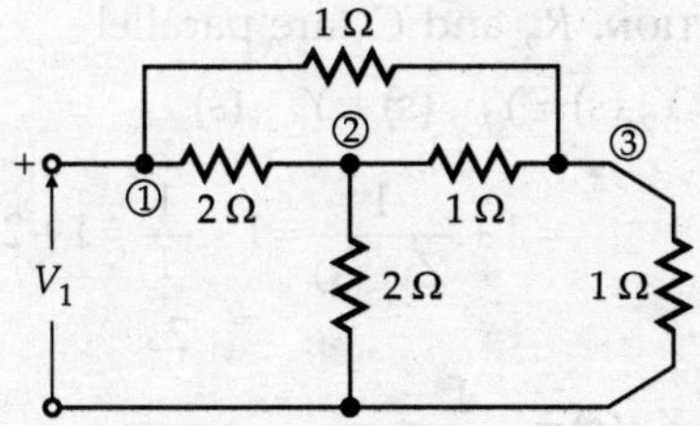

Fig. E12.43

$$I_1 = \frac{V_1 - V_0}{2} + \frac{V_1 - V_2}{1}$$

$$= 0.5\, V_1 - 0.5\, V_0 + V_1 - V_2$$

[node voltage at (2) being V_0]

$$I_1 = 1.5\, V_1 - 0.5\, V_0 - V_2 \quad ...(1)$$

At *node* (2), application of KCL at node (2) gives

$$\frac{V_1 - V_0}{2} - \frac{V_0 - V_2}{1} = \frac{V_0}{2}$$

or, $\quad 0.5\, V_1 - 0.5\, V_0 - V_0 + V_2 = 0.5\, V_0$

or, $\quad 0.5\, V_1 - 2V_0 + V_2 = 0 \quad ...(2)$

At *node* (3), application of KCL yields

$$\frac{V_1 - V_2}{1} = \frac{V_2 - V_0}{1} + \frac{V_2}{1}$$

or, $\quad V_1 - V_2 = V_2 - V_0 + V_2$

or, $\quad 0 = -V_1 - V_0 + 3V_2$

or, $\quad V_1 + V_0 - 3V_2 = 0 \quad ...(3)$

Multiplying equation (2) by 3, we get

$1.5\, V_1 - 6V_0 + 3V_2 = 0 \quad ...(4)$

Adding (3) and (4),

$$-5V_0 + 2.5\, V_1 = 0 \text{ or } V_0 = 0.5\, V_1$$

Also, from (2),

$\therefore \quad V_0 = V_2$

$\therefore$ Utilising the values of V_0 and V_2 in (1), we get

$$I_1 = 1.5\, V_1 - 0.5 \times 0.5\, V_1 - 0.5\, V_1$$

$$= 0.75\, V_1$$

$\therefore \quad \frac{V_1}{I_1} = \frac{1}{0.75}$ *i.e.*, $\mathbf{Z_{11} = 1.33\,\Omega}$.

Also, from (1), putting $V_1 = 2V_2$ [from (2)] and $V_0 = 0.5\, V_1$, we get

$$I_1 = 1.5\, V_1 - 0.5\, V_0 - V_2$$

$$= 1.5 \times 2V_2 - 0.5 \times V_2 - V_2 = 1.5\, V_2$$

$\therefore \quad \frac{V_2}{I_1} = Z_{21} = \frac{1}{1.5} = 0.667\,\Omega$

i.e., $\quad \mathbf{Z_{21} = 0.667\,\Omega}$.

EXAMPLE 12.36 *Obtain the current transfer ratio of the network shown in Fig. E12.44.*

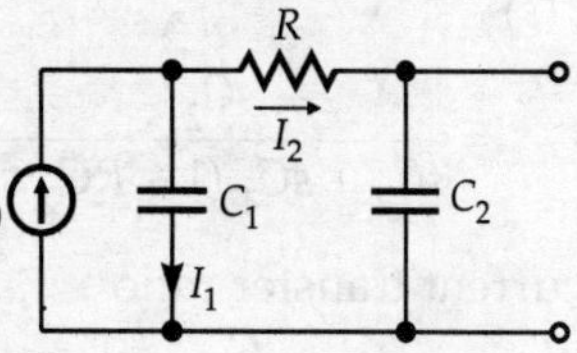

Fig. E12.44

SOLUTION. In Fig. E12.45, the s-domain network of Fig. E12.44.

$$I_0(s) = I_1(s) + I_2(s) = V_1(s)[Y_1(s) + Y_2(s)]$$

where $Y_1(s)$ is the admittance of branch *a-b* and $Y_2(s)$ is that of branch *acd*.

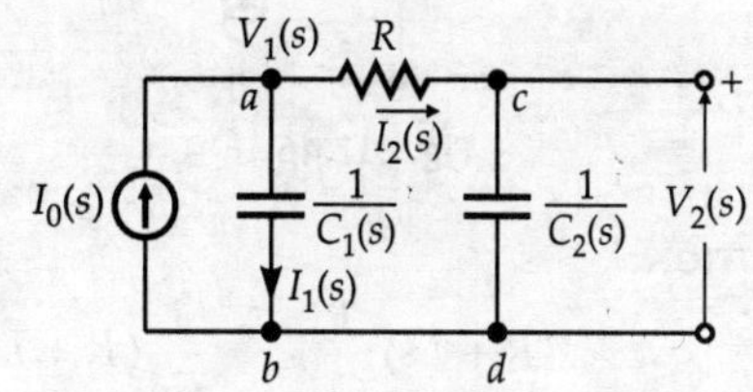

Fig. E12.45

However,

$$I_2(s) = Y_2(s)\, V_1(s)$$

$$\therefore \quad I_2(s) = Y_2(s)\frac{I_0(s)}{Y_1(s) + Y_2(s)}$$

$$= I_0(s)\frac{Y_2(s)}{Y_1(s) + Y_2(s)}$$

$$\therefore \quad \frac{I_2(s)}{I_0(s)} = \text{current transfer ratio}$$

$$= \frac{Y_2(s)}{Y_1(s) + Y_2(s)}$$

However,

$$Y_1(s) = C_1 s; \quad Y_2(s) = \frac{1}{R + \frac{1}{C_2 s}} = \frac{sC_2}{RC_2 s + 1}$$

This gives,

$$I_2(s) = I_0(s)\frac{\dfrac{C_2 s}{1+RC_2 s}}{C_1 s + \dfrac{C_2 s}{1+RC_2 s}}$$

$$= I_0(s)\frac{C_2 s}{C_1 s(1+RC_2 s)+C_2 s};$$

$$\frac{I_2(s)}{I_0(s)} = \text{Current transfer ratio}$$

$$= \frac{sC_2}{sC_2 + sC_1(1+RC_2 s)}$$

Thus, current transfer ratio

$$= \frac{C_2}{C_2 + C_1(1+RC_2 s)}.$$

EXAMPLE 12.37 *Obtain the driving point admittance of the network shown in Fig. E12.46.*

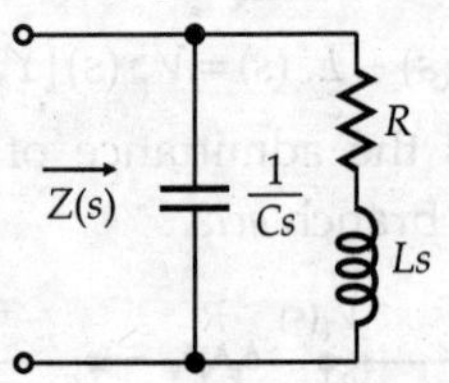

Fig. E12.46

SOLUTION.

$$Z(s) = \frac{(R+Ls)\dfrac{1}{Cs}}{R+Ls+\dfrac{1}{Cs}} = \frac{\dfrac{1}{Cs}(R+Ls)}{\dfrac{1+RCs+LCs^2}{Cs}}$$

$$= \frac{R+Ls}{1+RCs+LCs^2}$$

$\therefore$ $Y(s)$, the driving point admittance

$$= \frac{1}{Z(s)} = \frac{LCs^2+RCs+1}{R+Ls},$$

i.e.,

$$\mathbf{Y(s) = \frac{1+RCs+LCs^2}{R+Ls}}.$$

EXAMPLE 12.38 *Find the driving point impedance of the network shown in Fig. E12.47.*

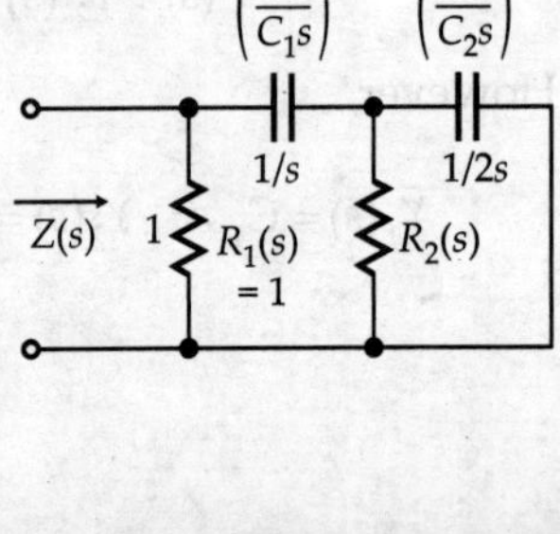

Fig. E12.47

SOLUTION. R_2 and C_2 are parallel

$$\therefore \quad Y_2(s) = Y_{R_2}(s) + Y_{C_2}(s)$$

$$= 1 + \frac{1}{Z_{C_2}(s)} = 1 + \frac{1}{\dfrac{1}{2s}} = 1+2s$$

i.e.,

$$Z_2(s) = \frac{1}{1+2s}$$

However, $Z_2(s)$ is in series with C_1

$$\therefore \quad Z_1(s) = Z_2(s) + \frac{1}{C_1 s} = \frac{1}{1+2s} + \frac{1}{s} = \frac{3s+1}{s(2s+1)}$$

$$\therefore Y_1(s) = \frac{s(2s+1)}{3s+1}$$

Again $Z_1(s)$ and $R_1(s)$ are in parallel.

$$\therefore \quad Y(s) = \frac{1}{Z_1(s)} + \frac{1}{R_1(s)}$$

$$= \frac{s(2s+1)}{3s+1} + 1 = \frac{2s^2+4s+1}{3s+1}$$

$$\therefore \quad Z(s) = \frac{1}{Y(s)} = \frac{3s+1}{2s^2+4s+1}$$

i.e., Driving point impedance $= \mathbf{\dfrac{3s+1}{2s^2+4s+1}}$.

EXAMPLE 12.39 *In the network of Fig. E12.48, find pole-zero plot.*

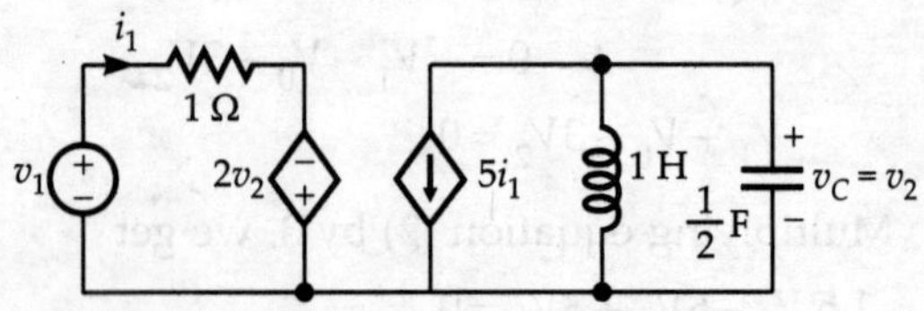

Fig. E12.48

SOLUTION. Let us first convert Fig. E12.48 to s-domain circuit (Fig. E12.49).

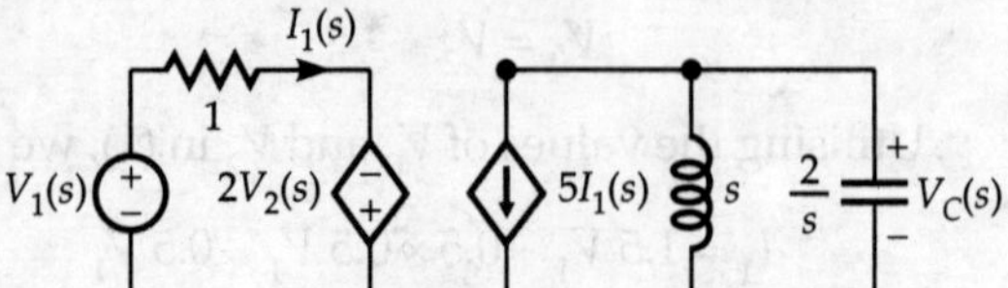

Fig. E12.49

Using KCL at *right hand loop,*

$$5I_1(s) + \frac{V_C(s)}{s} + \frac{V_C(s)}{2/s} = 0 \quad \text{...(1)}$$

While at *left loop,*

$$I_1(s) = \frac{V_1(s) + 2V_C(s)}{1} \qquad \text{...(2)}$$

Using (2) in (1),

$$5 \cdot \frac{V_1(s) + 2V_c(s)}{1} + \frac{V_C(s)}{s} + \frac{s\,V_C(s)}{2} = 0$$

or, $$10\,V_C(s) + \frac{V_C(s)}{s} + \frac{s\,V_C(s)}{2} + 5V_1(s) = 0$$

or, $$V_C(s)\frac{20\,s + 2 + s^2}{2s} = -5\,V_1(s)$$

or, $$\frac{V_C(s)}{V_1(s)} = G_{12}(s) = -\frac{10\,s}{20\,s + 2 + s^2}$$

$\therefore$ Zero is at $s = 0$.

Poles are at $\left(-\frac{1}{20} + j\frac{\sqrt{76}}{40}\right)$ and $\left(-\frac{1}{20} - j\frac{\sqrt{76}}{40}\right)$

The **pole-zero plot is shown in Fig. E12.50.**

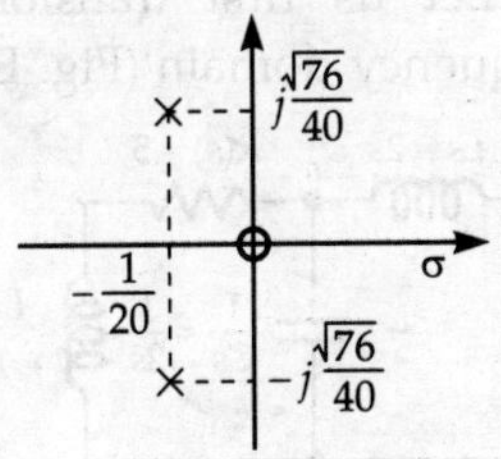

Fig. E12.50

EXAMPLE 12.40 *Find the driving point admittance function and the respective pole-zero plot for Fig. E12.51.*

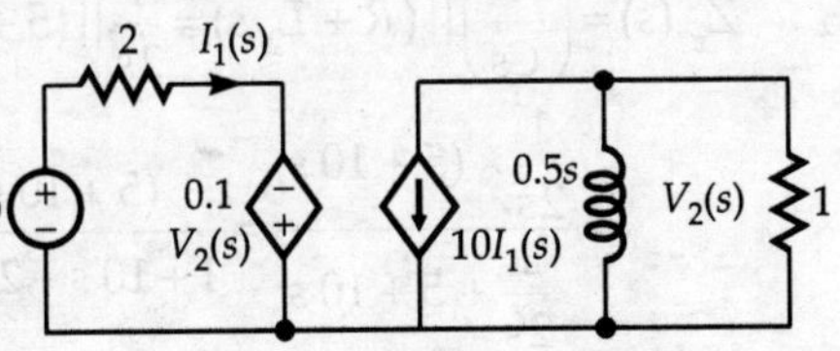

Fig. E12.51

SOLUTION. In the left loop,

$$I_1(s) = \frac{V_1(s) + 0.1\,V_2(s)}{2}, \qquad \text{...(1)}$$

and in the right hand loop, applying KCL,

$$\frac{V_2(s)}{0.5s} + \frac{V_2(s)}{1} + 10\,I_1(s) = 0$$

or, $$\frac{2}{s}V_2(s) + V_2(s) + 10\,I_1(s) = 0.$$

or, $$V_2(s)\left[\frac{2}{s} + 1\right] = -10\,I_1(s)$$

or, $$V_2(s)\left[\frac{2+s}{s}\right] = -10\,I_1(s)$$

or, $$V_2(s) = -\frac{10}{\frac{2+s}{s}}I_1(s) = -\frac{10\,s}{s+2}I_1(s) \qquad \text{...(2)}$$

Using (2) in (1),

$$I_1(s) = \frac{V_1(s) + 0.1\left[-\frac{10\,s}{s+2}\right]I_1(s)}{2}$$

$$= \frac{1}{2}V_1(s) + 0.05\,I_1(s)\left[-\frac{10\,s}{s+2}\right]$$

or, $$I_1(s)\left[1 + \frac{0.5\,s}{s+2}\right] = 0.5\,V_1(s)$$

$\therefore$ Driving point admittance

$$= \frac{I_1(s)}{V_1(s)} = \frac{0.5}{1 + \frac{0.5\,s}{s+2}} = \frac{\mathbf{0.5\,(s+2)}}{\mathbf{s+2+0.5\,s}}.$$

or, $$Y_{11}(s) = \frac{0.5\,(s+2)}{2 + 1.5\,s} = \frac{0.5\,s + 1}{1.5\,s + 2}$$

i.e., **pole at $-\frac{4}{3}$; Zero at -2.**

Pole zero Plot is shown in Fig. **E12.52.**

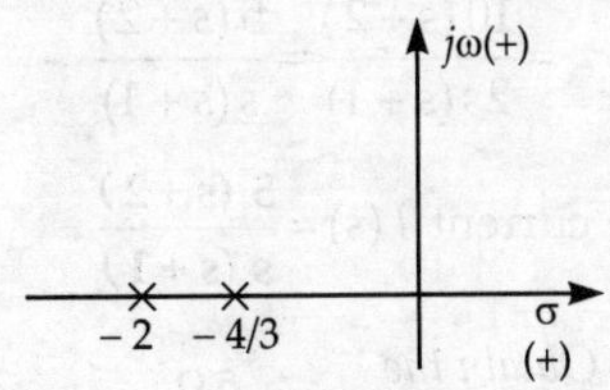

Fig. E12.52

EXAMPLE 12.41 *In the network of Fig. E12.53, "S" is switched on at $t = 0$. Find the driving point impedance and the source current in s-domain.*

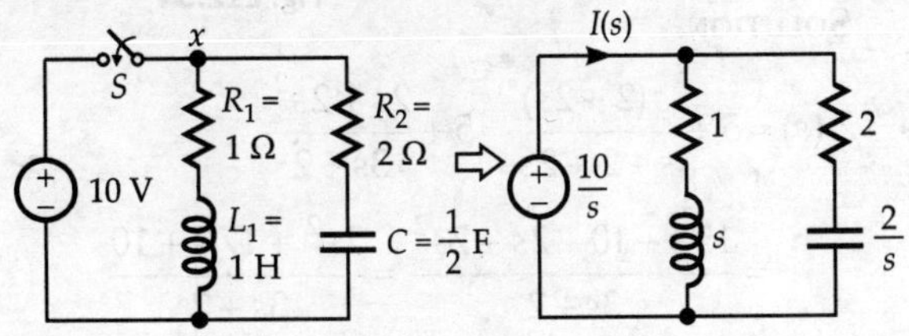

Fig. E12.53

Solution. Let $Z_1(s)$ be the impedance of *R-L* branch and $Z_2(s)$ be that of *RC* branch.

$$\therefore \quad Z_1(s) = R_1 + sL_1 = (1+s) \text{ i.e., } Y_1(s) = \frac{1}{1+s}$$

$$Z_2(s) = \left(R_2 + \frac{1}{Cs}\right) = \left(2 + \frac{1}{\frac{1}{2}s}\right)$$

$$= \left(2 + \frac{2}{s}\right) = \frac{2s+2}{s}$$

i.e.,
$$Y_2(s) = \frac{s}{2s+2}$$

$\therefore \quad Y(s)$ = admittance of the network across terminals *x-y*

$$= Y_1(s) + Y_2(s) = \frac{1}{1+s} + \frac{s}{2s+2}$$

$$= \frac{1}{s+1} + \frac{s}{2(s+1)} = \frac{2+s}{2(s+1)} = \frac{(s+2)}{2(s+1)}$$

$$\therefore \quad Z(s) = \mathbf{\frac{2(s+1)}{(s+2)}}$$

[$Z(s)$ is the driving point impedance]

However,

$$Z(s) = \frac{V(s)}{I(s)}$$

$$\therefore \quad I(s) = \frac{V(s)}{Z(s)} = \frac{(10/s)}{\frac{2(s+1)}{(s+2)}} = \frac{10}{s} \times \frac{s+2}{2(s+1)}$$

$$= \frac{10(s+2)}{2s(s+1)} = \frac{5(s+2)}{s(s+1)}$$

$\therefore$ Source current $I(s) = \mathbf{\frac{5(s+2)}{s(s+1)}}$.

Example 12.42 *Obtain the pole zero plot in the s-plane of the driving point impedance function for the network shown in Fig. E12.54.*

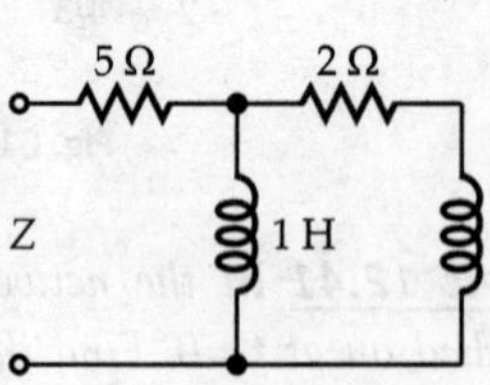

Fig. E12.54

Solution.

$$Z(s) = 5 + \frac{s(2+2s)}{s+2+2s} = 5 + \frac{2s+2s^2}{3s+2}$$

$$= \frac{15s+10+2s+2s^2}{3s+2} = \frac{2s^2+17s+10}{3s+2}$$

$$= \frac{(s+4.25+3.61)(s+4.25-3.61)}{(3s+2)}$$

This gives, zeros

at $-4.25+3.61$ and $-4.25-3.61$

i.e., **at -0.64 and -7.86 and pole at $-\frac{2}{3}$.**

The pole zero plot is shown in Fig. E12.55.

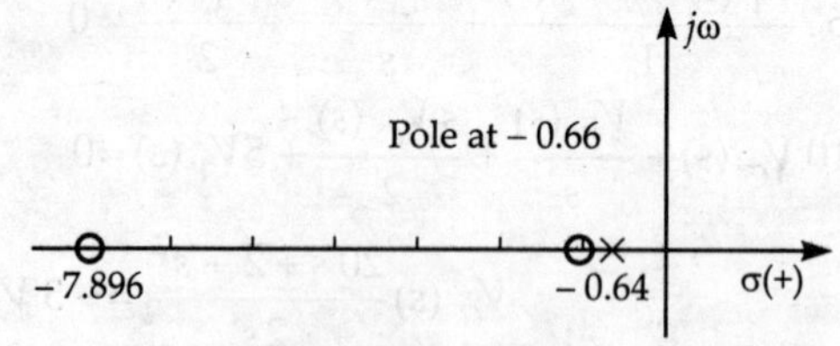

Fig. E12.55

Example 12.43 *What is the impedance and admittance functions in the circuit of Fig. E12.56 in complex frequency domain ?*

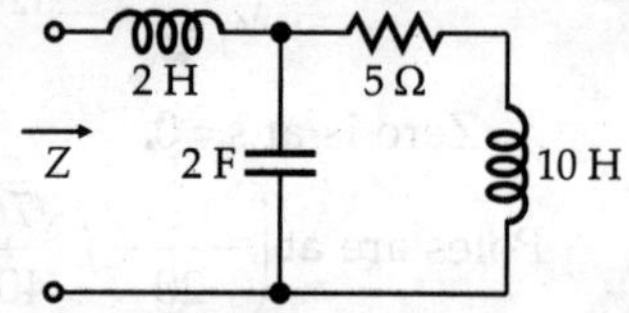

Fig. E12.56

Solution. Let us first transform the given network to frequency domain (Fig. E12.57).

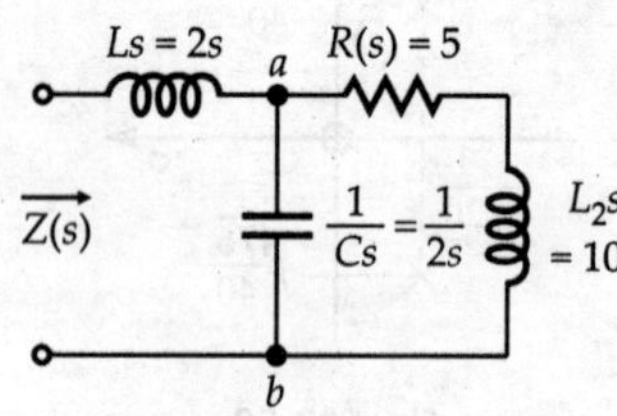

Fig. E12.57

Here, $Z_e(s)$, the equivalent impedance across *a-b* points is given by

$$Z_e(s) = \left(\frac{1}{Cs}\right) || (R + L_2 s) = \frac{1}{2s} || (5+10s)$$

$$= \frac{\frac{1}{2s} \times (5+10s)}{\frac{1}{2s} + 5 + 10s} = \frac{(5+10s)}{1+10s+20s^2}$$

$$\therefore \quad Z(s) = Z_e(s) + L_1 s = \frac{5+10s}{1+10s+20s^2} + 2s$$

$$= \frac{5+10s+2s+20s^2+40s^3}{1+10s+20s^2}$$

$\therefore \quad Z(s)$ = impedance function

$$= \frac{40s^3+20s^2+12s+5}{s^2+10s+1}$$

and $\mathbf{Y(s)}$ = admittance function

$$= \mathbf{\frac{1}{Z(s)} = \frac{20s^2+10s+1}{40s^3+20s^2+12s+5}}.$$

***EXAMPLE 12.44** In the coupled circuit of Fig. 12.58, find input impedance forward voltage and current transfer functions.*

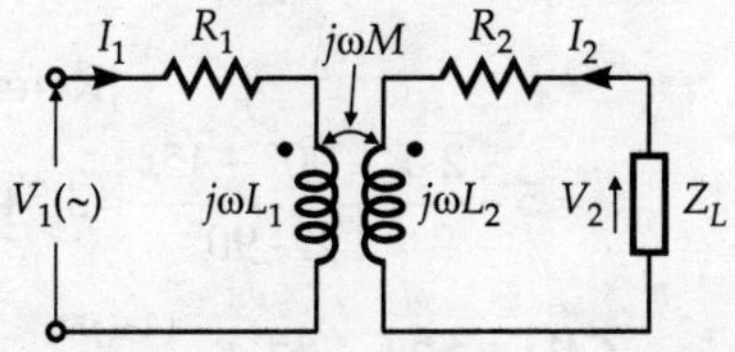

Fig. E12.58

SOLUTION. The matrix equation of this coupled circuit (Fig. E12.58) is given by [Refer to Chapter *Coupled Circuits*]

$$\begin{bmatrix} V_1 \\ 0 \end{bmatrix} = \begin{bmatrix} Z_{11} & Z_{12} \\ Z_{21} & Z_{22}+Z_L \end{bmatrix} \begin{bmatrix} I_1 \\ I_2 \end{bmatrix}$$

where, $Z_{11} = R_1 + j\omega L_1$, $Z_{12} = Z_{21} = j\,\omega\, M$,

$Z_{22} = R_2 + j\omega L_2$

The determinant of the impedance matrix is given by $\Delta_z = Z_{11}\,(Z_{22}+Z_L) - Z_{12}\,Z_{21}$

Using Cramer's Rule,

$$I_1 = \frac{\begin{vmatrix} V_1 & Z_{12} \\ 0 & Z_{22}+Z_L \end{vmatrix}}{\Delta_Z} = \frac{(Z_{22}+Z_L)}{\Delta_Z} V_1$$

and
$$I_2 = \frac{\begin{vmatrix} Z_{11} & V_1 \\ Z_{21} & 0 \end{vmatrix}}{\Delta_Z} = \frac{-Z_{21}}{\Delta_Z} . V_1$$

The input impedance is thus given by

$$Z_1 = \frac{V_1}{I_1} = \frac{V_1}{\frac{(Z_{22}+Z_L)}{\Delta_Z} V_1} = \frac{\Delta_Z}{Z_{22}+Z_L}$$

$$= \frac{Z_{11}\,(Z_{22}+Z_L) - Z_{12}\,Z_{21}}{Z_{22}+Z_L}$$

i.e., Z_1 (input impedance)

$$= \frac{\mathbf{Z_{11}\,(Z_{22}+Z_L) - Z_{12}\,Z_{21}}}{\mathbf{Z_{22}+Z_L}}$$

Again, $V_2 = -I_2\,Z_L = +\frac{Z_{21}}{\Delta_Z} . V_1\,Z_L$

$$\therefore \quad \frac{\mathbf{V_2}}{\mathbf{V_1}} = \text{forward voltage transfer function} = \frac{\mathbf{Z_{21}\,Z_L}}{\mathbf{\Delta_Z}}$$

and
$$\frac{\mathbf{I_2}}{\mathbf{I_1}} = \frac{-\frac{\mathbf{Z_{21}}}{\mathbf{\Delta_Z}} . \mathbf{V_1}}{\frac{\mathbf{(Z_{22}+Z_L)}}{\mathbf{\Delta_Z}} . \mathbf{V_1}} = -\frac{\mathbf{Z_{21}}}{\mathbf{Z_{22}+Z_L}}$$

where $\frac{I_2}{I_1}$ is the forward current transfer function.

***EXAMPLE 12.45** What is the driving point and transfer impedance of the network shown in Fig. E12.59 ?*

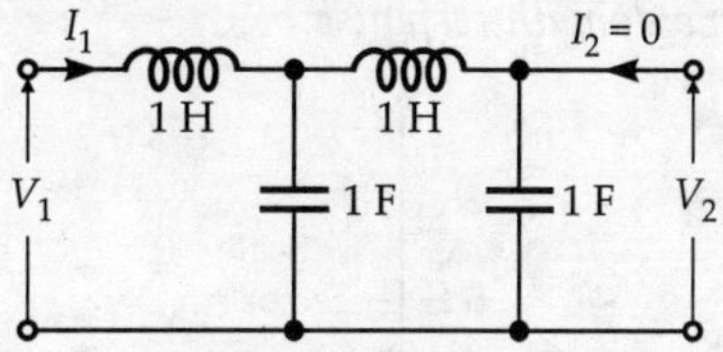

Fig. E12.59

SOLUTION. Let us first transform the given circuit to *s*-domain (Refer to Fig. E12.60).

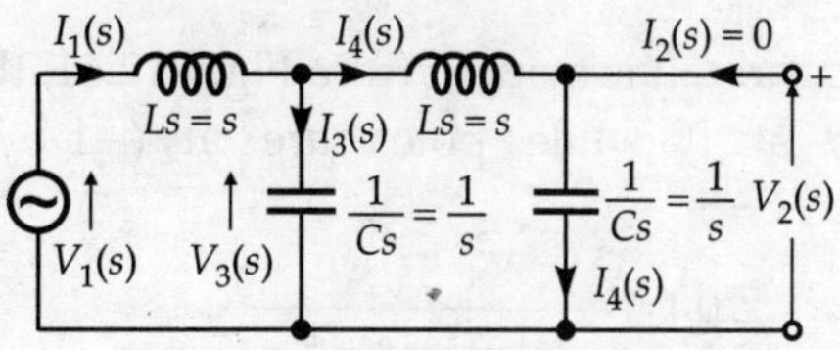

Fig. E12.60

Here, $I_4\,(s) = \frac{V_2\,(s)}{\frac{1}{Cs}} = sV_2\,(s)$

Also $V_3\,(s) = V_2\,(s) + I_4\,(s).\,Ls$

$= V_2\,(s) + sV_2\,(s).\,Ls$

$= V_2\,(s)\,[s^2\,L+1] = V_2\,(s)\,[1+s^2]$

$I_1\,(s) = I_3\,(s) + I_4\,(s) = \frac{V_3\,(s)}{1/Cs} + sV_2\,(s)$

$= CsV_2\,(s)\,(1+s^2) + sV_2\,(s)$

$= V_2\,(s)\,[s\,(1+s^2)+s]$

$= V_2\,(s)\,[s^3+2s]$

Now, $V_1(s) = V_3\,(s) + I_1\,(s)\,Ls$

$= V_2\,(s)\,[1+s^2] + V_2\,(s)\,[s^3+2s]\,s$

$= V_2\,(s)\,[1+s^2+s^4+2s^2]$

$= V_2\,(s)\,[s^4+3s^2+1]$

$\therefore$ Driving point impedance

$$= \frac{V_1\,(s)}{I_1\,(s)} = \frac{V_2\,(s)\,[s^4+3s^2+1]}{V_2\,(s)\,[s^3+2s]},$$

or, driving point impedance $= \frac{\mathbf{1+3s^2+s^4}}{\mathbf{2s+s^3}}$.

Transfer impedance

$$= \frac{V_2\,(s)}{I_1\,(s)} = \frac{V_2\,(s)}{V_2\,(s)\,[s^3+2s]} = \frac{1}{s^3+2s}$$

i.e., transfer impedance $= \frac{\mathbf{1}}{\mathbf{s^3+2s}}$.

EXAMPLE 12.46 *The pole zero plot of the driving point impedance of a circuit is shown in Fig. E12.61 in s-plane. Find the time domain response.*

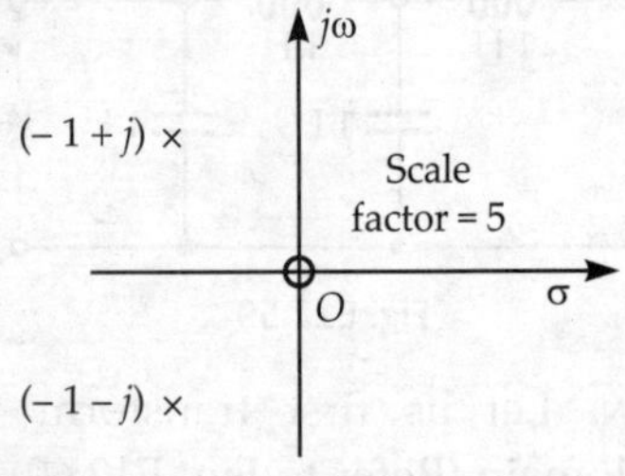

Fig. E12.61

SOLUTION. It is evident from Fig. E12.61, that the zero is at 0 while poles are at $(-1+j)$ and $(-1-j)$, $H=5$

$$\therefore \quad Z(s)=\frac{5s}{(s+1+j)(s+1-j)}$$

$$\text{i.e.,} \quad Z(t)=K_1\, e^{-(1+j)t}+K_2\, e^{-(1-j)t}.$$

To find K_1 and K_2, Fig. E12.62 and E12.63 may be referred.

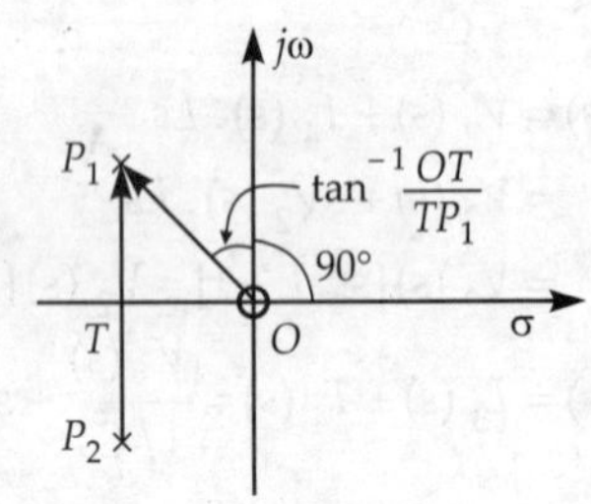

Fig. E12.62

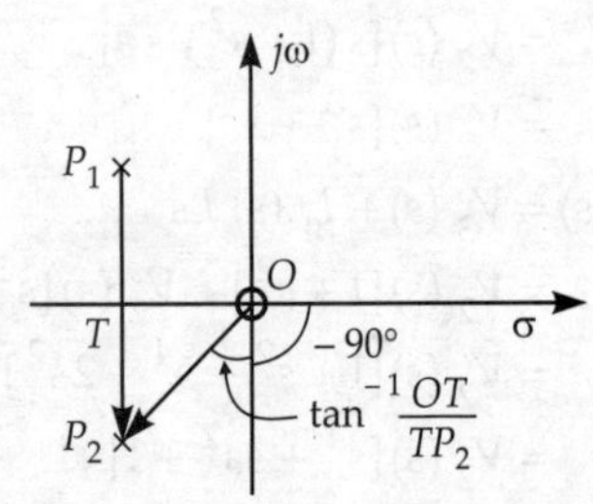

Fig. E12.63

With reference to the text,

$$K_1=H\frac{M_{O-P_1}\ \angle 90^\circ+\tan^{-1}\dfrac{OT}{TP_1}}{M_{P_2-P_1}\ \angle +90^\circ}$$

[Refer to Fig. E12.62]

$$=5\frac{\sqrt{OT^2+TP_1^2}\ \angle 90^\circ+(+45^\circ)}{2\times 1\angle +90^\circ}$$

$$=5\frac{\sqrt{2}\ \angle 135^\circ}{2\ \angle +90^\circ}=3.54\ \angle 45^\circ$$

$$K_2=H\frac{M_{O-P_2}\ \angle -90^\circ-\tan^{-1}\dfrac{OT}{TP_2}}{M_{P_1-P_2}\ \angle -90^\circ}$$

[Refer to Fig. E12.63]

$$=5\frac{\sqrt{2}\ \angle -90^\circ-45^\circ}{2\times 1\angle -90^\circ}=3.54\ \angle -45^\circ$$

$$\therefore \quad \mathbf{Z(t)=3.54\ \angle 45^\circ\, e^{-(1+j)t}+3.54\ \angle -45^\circ\, e^{-(1-j)t}\Omega.}$$

EXAMPLE 12.47 *A current transfer function is given by*

$$I(s)=\frac{5s}{(s+2)(s^2+2s+2)}.$$

Obtain its time domain response.

SOLUTION. The given transfer function is

$$I(s)=\frac{5s}{(s+2)(s^2+2s+2)}$$

$$=\frac{5s}{(s+2)(s+1-j)(s+1+j1)}$$

$\therefore$ The zero is at origin and the poles are at $(-2), -(1\pm j1)$

$$\therefore \quad I(s)=\frac{5s}{\{s-(-2)\}\{(s-(-1+j)\}\{s-(-1-j)\}}$$

$$=\frac{K_1}{[s-(-2)]}+\frac{K_2}{\{s-(-1+j)\}}+\frac{K_3}{\{s-(-1-j)\}}$$

Thus, the function response in time domain is given by

$$I(t)=K_1\, e^{-2t}+K_2\, e^{(-1+j)t}+K_3\, e^{(-1-j)t}$$

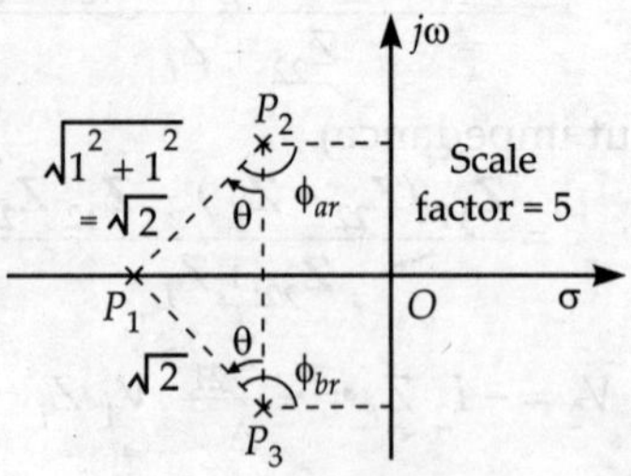

Fig. E12.64

Here

$$K_1=5\frac{M_{OP_1}\ \angle \text{ of } P_1 \text{ with respect to zero } (\phi_{1r})}{M_{P_2P_1}\ \angle\phi_{ar}\times M_{P_3P_1}\ \angle\phi_{br}}$$

[Refer to Fig. E12.64]

where ϕ_{ar} = angle of $P_2\,P_1$ and ϕ_{br} = angle of $P_3\,P_1$

$$= 5\,\frac{2\,\angle 180^\circ}{\sqrt{2}\,\angle -(90^\circ + \theta) \times \sqrt{2}\,\angle (90^\circ + \theta)}$$

$$\left[\text{where } \theta = \tan^{-1}\frac{1}{1} = 45^\circ\right]$$

$$= 5\,\frac{2\,\angle 180^\circ}{\sqrt{2}\,\angle -135^\circ \times \sqrt{2}\,\angle 135^\circ} = 5\,\angle 180^\circ$$

To find K_2, let us refer to Fig. E12.65.

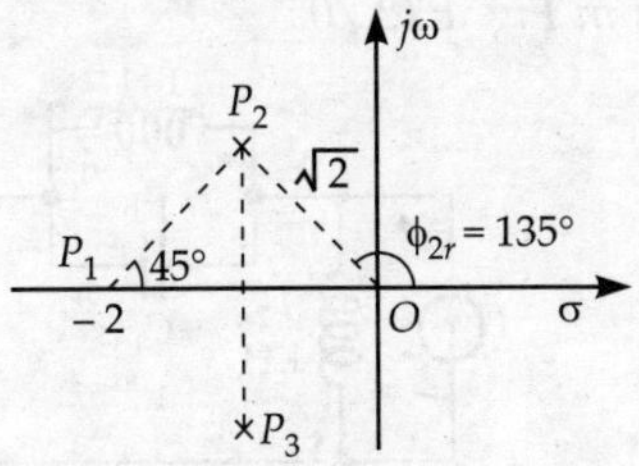

Fig. E12.65

$$K_2 = 5\,\frac{M_{OP_2}\ \angle \text{ of } OP_2\,(\phi_{2r})}{M_{P_1P_2}\ \angle \text{of } P_1P_2(\phi_{P_2r}) \times M_{P_3P_2}\ \angle \text{of } P_3P_2(\phi_{P_3r})}$$

$$= 5\,\frac{\sqrt{2}\,\angle 135^\circ}{\sqrt{2}\,\angle 45^\circ \times 2\,\angle 90^\circ} = 2.5\,\angle 0^\circ = 2.5 + j\,0 = 2.5$$

and $K_3 = K_2^* = 2.5 - j\,0 = 2.5$

$$\therefore \quad I(t) = 5\,\angle 180^\circ\, e^{-2t} + 2.5\, e^{(-1+j)\,t} + 2.5\, e^{(-1-j)\,t}$$

$$= \mathbf{[-5e^{-2t} + 2.5\, e^{(-1+j)\,t} + 2.5\, e^{(-1-j)\,t}]\ A.}$$

Example 12.48 *A transfer admittance is given by*

$$Y(s) = \frac{s\,(s^2+2)}{s^2+1}.$$

Find the pole-zero plot.

Solution.

$$Y(s) = \frac{s\,(s + j\sqrt{2})(s - j\sqrt{2})}{(s + j\,1)(s - j\,1)}$$

$\therefore$ The zeros would occur at $s = \pm j\sqrt{2}$ and at origin $(s = 0)$ while the poles would occur at $S = \pm j\,1$. **The pole zero plot is shown in Fig. E12.66.**

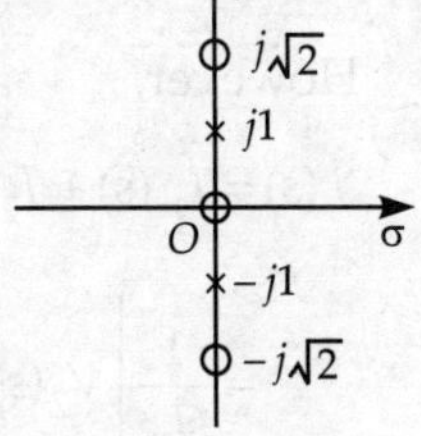

Fig. E12.66

Example 12.49 *A driving point impedance is given by*

$$Z(s) = \frac{s^2 - 7s + 10}{s^2 + s + 50}.\ \textit{Find pole zero plot.}$$

Solution. The numerator of the given function can be factorised as follows :

$$s^2 - 7s + 10 = s^2 - 5s - 2s + 10$$

$$= s\,(s-5) - 2\,(s-5) = (s-2)(s-5).$$

$\therefore$ Zeros would appear at $s = 2,\ s = 5$.

However, the denominator being $s^2 + s + 50$, the roots are

$$\frac{-1 \pm \sqrt{1-200}}{2} = -0.5 \pm j\,\frac{\sqrt{199}}{2}$$

$\therefore$ The poles would appear at

$$s = -0.5 + j\,\frac{\sqrt{199}}{2} \text{ and } s = -0.5 - j\,\frac{\sqrt{199}}{2}.$$

The pole zero plot is shown in Fig. E12.67.

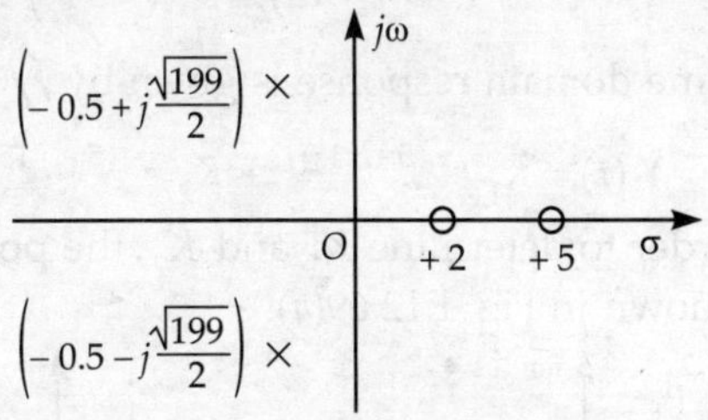

Fig. E12.67

Example 12.50 *A transfer function is given by* $Y(s) = \dfrac{50}{s^2 + 2s + 2}$. *Find the pole zero plot.*

Solution. As there is no s term in the numerator of the function, hence there will be no finite zero in the function. The denominator can be factored as

$$(s^2 + 2s + 2) = (s + 1 + j)(s + 1 - j)$$

$\therefore$ Poles will appear at $s = -1 - j, -1 + j$

The pole zero plot is shown in Fig. E12.68.

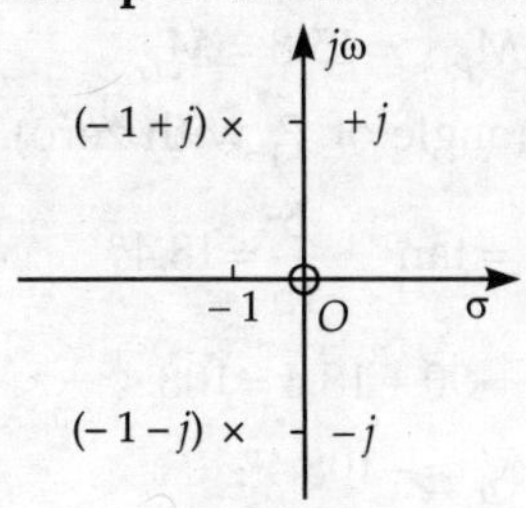

Fig. E12.68

Example 12.51 *The transfer function of a network is given by* $T(s) = \dfrac{1}{1 + sCR}$. *Find its impulse response.*

Solution. Impulse response is given by

$$I(t) = £^{-1}\,T(s) = £^{-1}\left[\frac{1}{1 + sCR}\right]$$

$$= £^{-1}\left[\frac{1/RC}{s + 1/RC}\right] = \frac{1}{RC}\,e^{-t/RC},$$

i.e., impulse response $= \mathbf{\dfrac{1}{RC}\,e^{-t/RC}}$.

EXAMPLE 12.52 *A transfer function is given by*

$$Y(s) = \frac{10\,s}{[(s+5+j\,15)(s+5-j\,15)]}.$$

Find the time domain response.

SOLUTION. The given function can be written as

$$Y(s) = \frac{10(s-0)}{[s-(-5+j\,15)][s-(-s-j\,15)]}$$

$$= \frac{K_1}{s-(-5+j\,15)} + \frac{K_2}{s-(-5-j\,15)}$$

∴ Time domain response is given by

$$Y(t) = K_1\,e^{-(5+j\,15)\,t} + K_2\,e^{-(5-j\,15)\,t}.$$

In order to determine K_1 and K_2, the pole-zero plot is shown in Fig. E12.69(*a*).

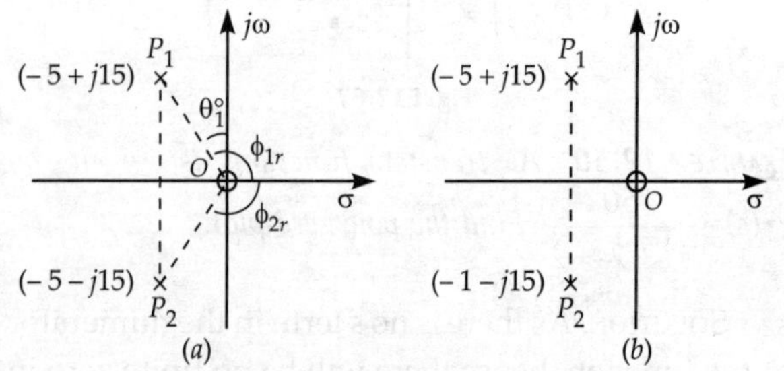

Fig. E12.69

Here, M_{P_2r} [distance of the pole P_2 from the zero] is given by,

$$M_{P_2r} = OP_2 = \sqrt{5^2+15^2} = 15.8 = M_{2r}$$

Similarly, $M_{P_1r} = 15.8 = M_{1r}$

Again ϕ_{1r} (angle of P_1 with zero) $= 90° + \theta_1$

where $\theta_1 = \tan^{-1}\dfrac{5}{15} = 18.4°$

∴ $\phi_{1r} = 90 + 18.4 = 108.4°$

Similarly, $\phi_{2r} = -108.4°$.

Next, redrawing the pole zero plot, following Fig. E12.69(*b*).

M_{ar} [the distance between two poles P_1 and P_2] is given by,

$$M_{ar} = 15 + 15 = 30$$

while $\phi_{ar(P_1)} = 90°$ and $\phi_{ar(P_2)} = -90°$

[where $\phi_{ar(P_1)}$ is the angle of P_1 with left *x*-axis

and $\phi_{ar(P_2)}$ is the angle of P_2 with left *x*-axis]

$$\therefore\quad K_1 = 10\,\frac{M_{1r}\angle\phi_{1r}}{M_{ar}\angle\phi_{ar(P_1)}} = 10\,\frac{15.8\angle 108.4°}{30\angle 90°}$$

$$= 5.26\angle 18.4°$$

and

$$K_2 = 10\,\frac{M_{2r}\angle\phi_{2r}}{M_{ar(P_2)}\angle\phi_{br}} = 10\,\frac{15.8\angle -108.4°}{30\angle -90°}$$

$$= 5.26\angle -18.4°$$

Thus,

$$Y(t) = \mathbf{5.26\angle 18.4°\,e^{-(5+j\,15)t} + 5.26\angle -18.4°\,e^{-(5-j\,15)\,t}}.$$

EXAMPLE 12.53 *Obtain the transfer impedance for the circuit shown in Fig. E12.70.*

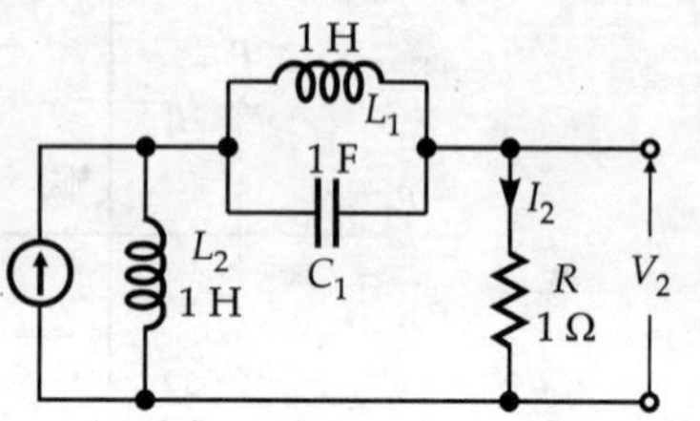

Fig. E12.70

SOLUTION. Let us first transform the given network to *s*-domain [Fig. E12.70(*a*)].

Here, $V_2(s) = I_2(s)\,.\,R$ ...(1)

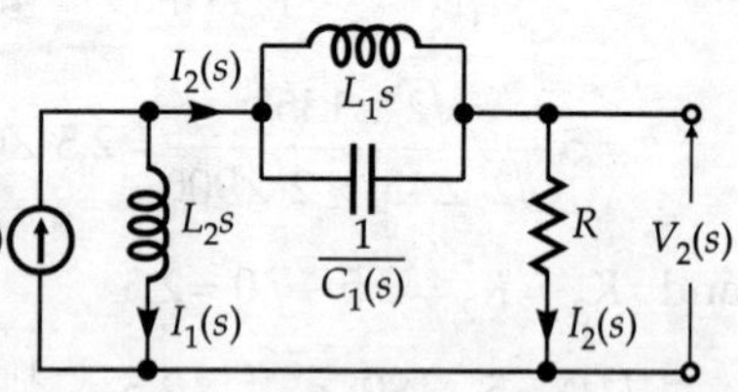

Fig. E12.70 (*a*)

Voltage across the inductor is given by using KVL

$$V_L(s) = V_2(s) + I_2(s)\left[\frac{1}{\left(sC_1 + \dfrac{1}{sL_1}\right)}\right]$$

$$= V_2(s) + \frac{V_2(s)}{R}\cdot\frac{sL_1}{1+s^2L_1C_1} \qquad ...(2)$$

However,

$$I(s) = I_1(s) + I_2(s) = \frac{V_L(s)}{sL_2} + \frac{V_2(s)}{R}$$

$$= \frac{1}{sL_2}\left[V_2(s)\left\{1+\frac{1}{R}\cdot\frac{sL_1}{1+s^2L_1C_1}\right\}\right] + \frac{V_2(s)}{R}$$

$$= V_2(s)\left[\frac{1}{sL_2}\left\{1+\left(\frac{1}{R}\right)\left(\frac{sL_1}{1+s^2L_1C_1}\right)\right\} + \frac{1}{R}\right]$$

$$= V_2(s)\left[\frac{R(1+s^2L_1C_1)+sL_1+sL_2(1+s^2L_1C_1)}{sL_2\,R\,(1+s^2\,L_1\,C_1)}\right]$$

$$= V_2(s)\left[\frac{s^3L_1L_2C_1 + s(L_1+L_2) + R + RL_1C_1s^2}{sL_2\,R\,(1+s^2\,L_1\,C_1)}\right]$$

$$\therefore \ Z_{12}(s) = \frac{V_2(s)}{I(s)}$$

$$= \frac{sL_2 R(1+s^2 L_1 C_1)}{s^3 L_1 L_2 C_1 + s(L_1+L_2) + R + RL_1 C_1 s^2}$$

Substituting the numerical values

$$Z_{12}(s) = \frac{s(1+s^2)}{s^3+s^2+2s+1}.$$

EXAMPLE 12.54 *In a linear two port network, $v_1(t)$ and $v_2(t)$ be the input voltage and its response at the output, $v_2(t) = te^{-2t}\,u(t)$. If the response to an impulse voltage be given by $v(t) = (e^{-1} + e^{-2t})\,u(t)$, find $v_1(t)$ as well as the transfer function of the network.*

SOLUTION. The transfer function $T(s)$ of the network is given by

$$T(s) = \pounds\{(e^{-t} + e^{-2t})\,u(t)\}$$

$$= \frac{1}{s+1} + \frac{1}{s+2} = \frac{(s+2)+(s+1)}{(s+1)(s+2)}$$

or, $\quad T(s) = (2s+3)/(s+1)(s+2)$

Again,

$$v_2(t) = te^{-2t}\,u(t) \text{ [given]}$$

$$\therefore \quad V_2(s) = \frac{1}{(s+2)^2}$$

$$\{\because \pounds\, v_2(t) = V_2(s) = \pounds[te^{-2t}\,u(t)]\}$$

But $\quad V_2(s) = T(s)\,V_1(s)$

$$\therefore \quad V_1(s) = \frac{V_2(s)}{T(s)} = \frac{1}{(s+2)^2} \times \frac{(s+1)(s+2)}{(2s+3)}$$

$$= \frac{(s+1)}{(s+2)(2s+3)} = \frac{K_1}{s+2} + \frac{K_2}{2s+3}$$

Using partial fraction method,

$$K_1 = 1;\ K_2 = -1$$

$$\therefore \quad V_1(s) = \frac{1}{s+2} + \frac{(-1)}{2s+3} = \frac{1}{s+2} - \frac{1/2}{s+1.5}$$

i.e., $\quad v_1(t) = [e^{-2t} - 0.5\,e^{-1.5t}]\,u(t)$

i.e., $\quad T(s) = \text{transfer function} = \dfrac{\mathbf{2s+3}}{\mathbf{(s+1)(s+2)}}$

and $\quad \boldsymbol{v_1(t) = [e^{-2t} - 0.5\,e^{-1.5t}]\,u(t).}$

EXAMPLE 12.55 *In the coupled circuit of Fig. E12.71, $L_1 = 4H$, $L_2 = 6H$, $C = \frac{1}{18}$ F, $R_1 = 9\,\Omega$, $M = 2H$. Find : (i) the voltage transfer function (ii) input impedance of the network seen from the source size.*

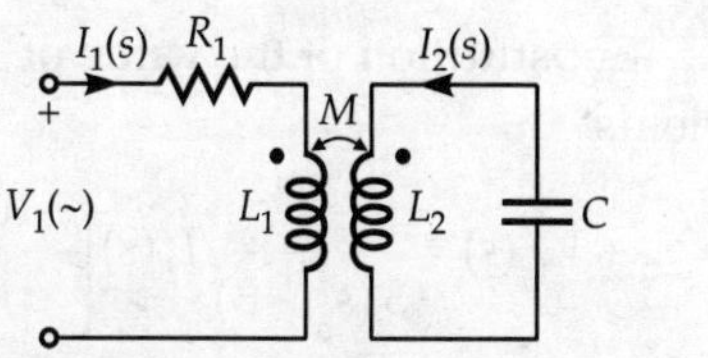

Fig. E12.71

SOLUTION. From the concept of coupled theory,

$$V_1(s) = (R_1 + L_1 s)\,I_1(s) + Ms\,I_2$$

or, $$V_1(s) = (9+4s)\,I_1(s) + 2s\,I_2(s) \quad \text{...(1)}$$

Utilising KVL in the output loop,

$$0 = Ms\,I_1(s) + sL_2\,I_2(s) + I_2(s) \times \frac{1}{Cs}$$

$$= 2s\,I_1(s) + 6sI_2(s) + \frac{18}{s}\,I_2(s)$$

or, $$I_1(s) = -\left(3 + \frac{9}{s^2}\right) I_2(s) = -3\left(\frac{s^2+3}{s^2}\right) I_2(s) \quad \text{...(2)}$$

Substitution of the value of $I_1(s)$ from (2) to (1),

$$V_1(s) = (9+4s)\left[-3\left(\frac{s^2+3}{s^2}\right)\right] I_2(s) + 2s\,I_2(s)$$

$$= I_2(s)\left[-(9+4s)3\left(\frac{s^2+3}{s^2}\right) + 2s\right]$$

$$= I_2(s)\left[-27 - \frac{81}{s^2} - 12\,s - \frac{36}{s} + 2s\right]$$

$$= I_2(s)\left[\frac{-27\,s^2 - 81 - 12\,s^3 - 36\,s + 2s^3}{s^2}\right]$$

$$= I_2(s)\left[\frac{-10\,s^3 - 27\,s^2 - 36\,s - 81}{s^2}\right] \quad \text{...(3)}$$

$$\therefore \quad I_2(s) = \frac{-s^2\,V_1(s)}{10\,s^3 + 27\,s^2 + 36\,s + 81}$$

However, the output voltage $V_2(s)$ is given by

$$V_2(s) = -I_2(s) \times \frac{1}{Cs} = \frac{18}{s}[-I_2(s)]$$

$$= \frac{18}{s}\left[\frac{s^2\,V_1(s)}{10\,s^3 + 27\,s^2 + 36\,s + 81}\right]$$

$$\therefore \quad \frac{V_2(s)}{V_1(s)} = \frac{18\,s}{10\,s^3 + 27\,s^2 + 36\,s + 81}$$

= voltage transfer function.

We can rewrite equation (2) as

$$I_2(s) = \frac{-s^2}{3(s^2+3)}\,I_1(s) \quad \text{...(4)}$$

Substitution of the value of I_2 (s) from (4) in (3) yields

$$V_1(s) = \frac{-s^2}{3(s^2+3)} I_1(s) \left[\frac{-10s^3 - 27s^2 - 36s - 81}{s^2}\right]$$

$$\therefore \frac{V_1(s)}{I_1(s)} = \frac{10s^3 + 27s^2 + 36s + 81}{3(s^2+3)}$$

= **input impedance.**

EXAMPLE 12.56 *For the network of Fig. E12.72 find the current ratio transfer function given by* $\alpha = (I_2 / I_1)$.

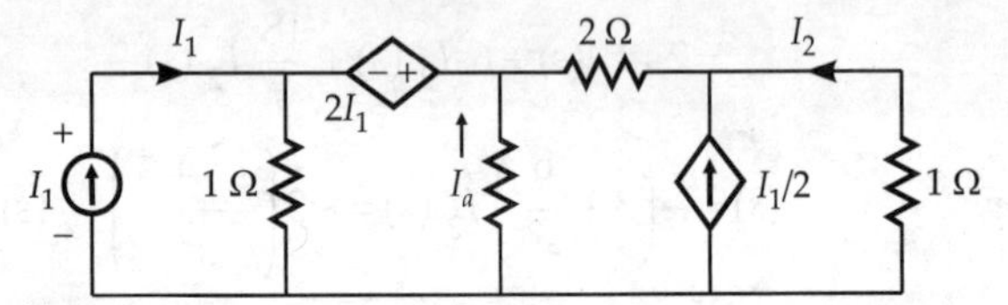

Fig. E12.72

SOLUTION. First, we cc. vert current source into equivalent voltage source as shown in Fig. E12.72(*a*).

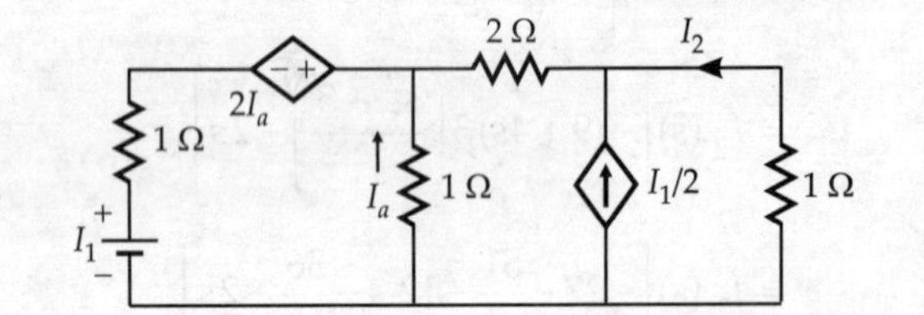

Fig. E12.72 (*a*)

Let I be the current in First (leftmost) loop. Applying KVL we get

$$I_1 = I - 2I_a - I_a \quad ...(i)$$

$$I = -\left(I_a + \frac{I_1}{2} + I_2\right) \quad ...(ii)$$

From equations (*i*) and (*ii*), eliminating I, we get

$$I_1 = -\left(I_a + \frac{I_1}{2} + I_2\right) - 2I_a - I_a$$

$$I_a = -\frac{1}{4}\left(\frac{3I_1}{2} + I_2\right) \quad ...(iii)$$

Next applying KVL in the external loop consisting resistances 1 Ω, 2 Ω and 1 Ω we have from Fig. E12.72(*a*)

$$I_2 + 2\left(I_2 + \frac{I_1}{2}\right) - I_a = 0$$

or
$$3I_2 + I_1 - I_a = 0 \quad ...(iv)$$

From equations (*iii*) and (*iv*), eliminating I_a, we obtain

$$3I_2 + I_1 + \frac{1}{4}\left(\frac{3I_1}{2} + I_2\right) = 0$$

$$3I_2 + \frac{1}{4}I_2 + I_1 \frac{3}{8} I_1 = 0$$

$$\frac{13}{4}I_2 + \frac{11}{8}I_1 = 0$$

$$\alpha = \frac{I_2}{I_1} = -\frac{\mathbf{11}}{\mathbf{26}}.$$

EXAMPLE 12.57. *Find the driving point admittance function and respective pole-zero location plot of the network shown in Fig. E12.73.*

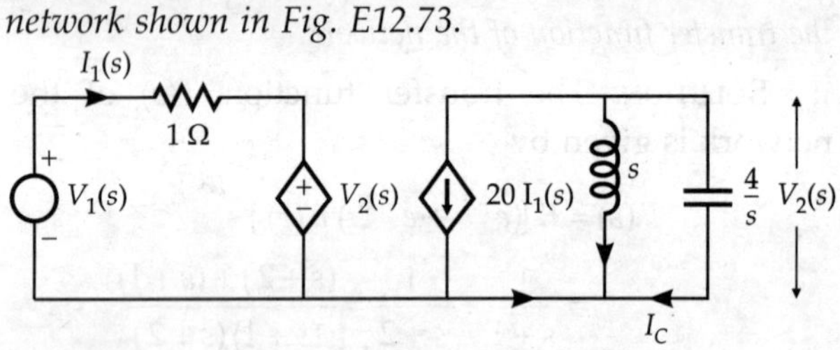

Fig. E12.73

SOLUTION. Considering left hand side loop (Fig. E12.73), for KVL we can write,

$$V_1(s) - I_1(s) + V_2(s) = 0$$

i.e.,
$$I_1(s) = V_1(s) + V_2(s) \quad ...(i)$$

Similarly, for right hand loop, applying KCL we get

$$20I_1(s) - I_L + I_C = 0 \quad ...(ii)$$

or
$$20I_1(s) + \frac{V_2(s)}{s} + \frac{V_2(s)}{\frac{4}{s}} = 0$$

or
$$20\,I_1(s) = -V_2(s)\left[\frac{1}{s} + \frac{s}{4}\right] = -V_2(s)\left[\frac{4+s^2}{4s}\right]$$

$$\therefore \quad V_2(s) = \frac{-20 \times 4s}{(4+4s^2)} I_1(s) = \frac{-80\,s}{s^2+4} \times I_1(s).$$

Substituting the value of V_2 (s) from equation (*i*) in equation (*ii*) we get

$$I_1(s) = V_1(s) + \left(\frac{-80\,s}{s^2+4} I_1(s)\right)$$

or
$$I_1(s)^0 \left[1 + \frac{80s}{s^2+4}\right] = V_1(s)$$

∴ Driving point admittance

$$= \frac{I_1(s)}{V_1(s)} = 1 + \frac{80s}{s^2+4} = \frac{\mathbf{s^2 + 4 + 80s}}{\mathbf{s^2+4}}.$$

EXERCISES

1. Find $Y_{11}(s)$ of the circuit shown in Fig. P12.1.

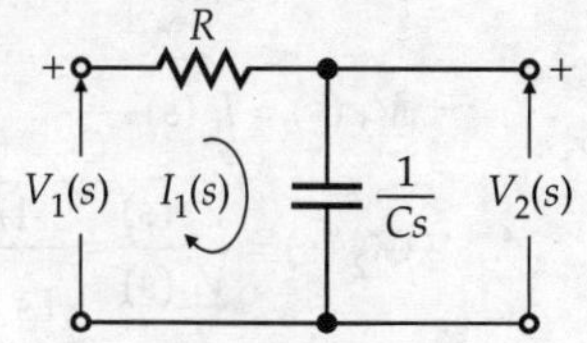

Fig. P12.1

[Hint. $V_1(s) = I_1(s)\left[R + \dfrac{1}{Cs}\right]$

$$\therefore \quad Y_{11}(s) = \frac{I_1(s)}{V_1(s)} = \frac{1}{\left(R + \dfrac{1}{Cs}\right)} = \frac{1}{R}\left[\frac{s}{s + \dfrac{1}{R}}\right] \;]$$

2. Find $V_2(s)/V_1(s)$ in Fig. P12.2.

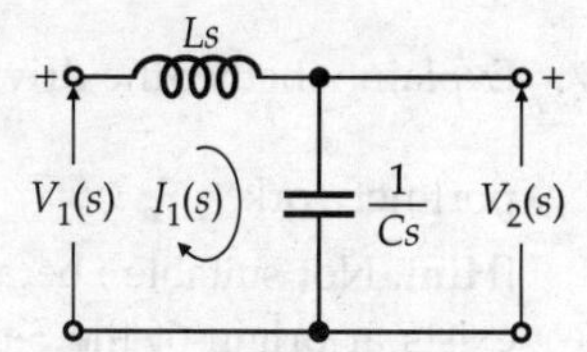

Fig. P12.2

[Hint. KVL gives, $V_1(s) = I_1(s)\left[Ls + \dfrac{1}{Cs}\right]$; $V_2(s) = \dfrac{1}{Cs}\,.\,I_1(s)$

$$\therefore \quad \frac{V_2(s)}{V_1(s)} = \frac{1/Cs}{Ls + 1/Cs} = \frac{1/LC}{s^2 + (1/LC)} \;]$$

3. Obtain $Z_{21}(s)$ for the network shown in Fig. P12.3.

[Hint. $I_1(s) = I'(s) + I_2(s) = V_1(s)\,Y'(s) + V_2(s)\,Y''(s)$

where $Y'(s)$ and $Y''(s)$ are the admittances of *dc* and *db*.

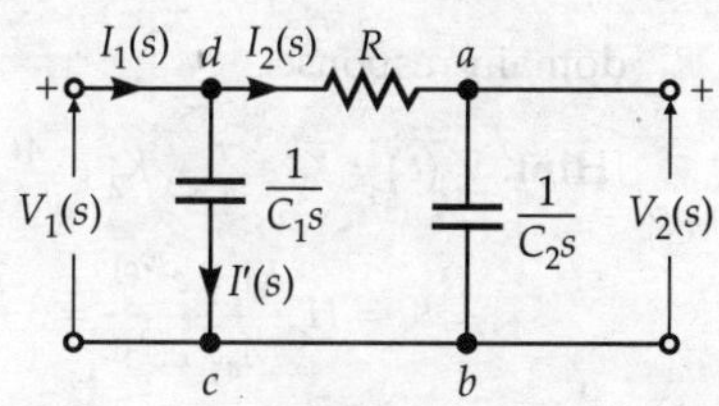

Fig. P12.3

Again $\quad I_2(s) = Y''(s)\,V_1(s) = \dfrac{Y''(s)}{Y'(s) + Y''(s)}\,.\,I_1(s)$

$$\because \quad V_1(s) = \frac{I_1(s)}{Y''(s) + Y''(s)}.$$

$$\therefore \quad \frac{I_2(s)}{I_1(s)} = \frac{Y''(s)}{Y'(s) + Y''(s)}$$

Again $\quad Z_{12}(s) = \dfrac{V_2(s)}{I_1(s)} = \dfrac{I_2(s)\dfrac{1}{C_2\,s}}{I_1(s)} = \dfrac{1}{C_2(s)}\,.\,\dfrac{I_2(s)}{I_1(s)} = \dfrac{1}{C_2(s)}\,.\,\dfrac{Y''(s)}{Y'(s) + Y''(s)}$

But $\quad Y''(s) = \dfrac{1}{R_1 + \dfrac{1}{C_2\,s}} = \dfrac{C_2(s)}{R_1\,C_2\,s + 1} = \dfrac{s/R_1}{s + \dfrac{1}{R_1\,C_2}}$ and $Y'(s) = \dfrac{1}{1/C_1(s)} = C_1\,s.$

Then $Z_{12}(s)$ can be obtained.]

4. In the network of Fig. P12.4, find the driving point impedance $Z_{11}(s)$ and the driving point admittance $Y_{11}(s)$

[Hint. Apply $V_1(s)$ at port-1. Current flow is $I_1(s)$, drop across inductor is $V_2(s)$.

$\therefore$ KVL gives, $\quad V_1(s) = I_1(s)\,[5 + s] \quad$ and $\quad V_2(s) = S\,.\,I_1(s)$

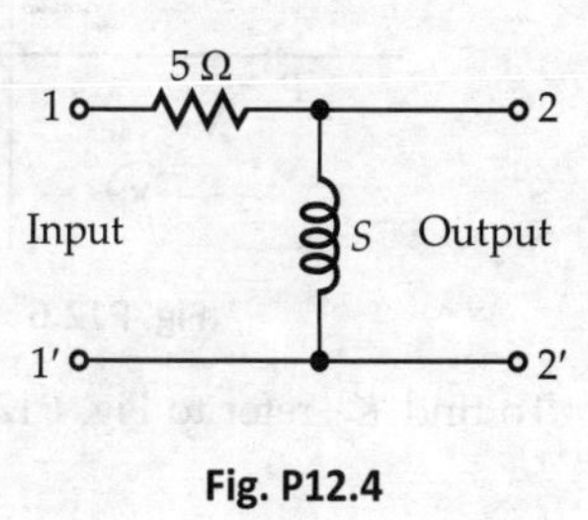

Fig. P12.4

$$\therefore \quad Z_{11}(s) = \frac{V_1(s)}{I_1(s)} = (s + 5)$$

and $\quad Y_{11}(s) = \dfrac{I_1(s)}{Y_1(s)} = \dfrac{1}{S + 5}$]

5. In the above problem, find $Z_{21}(s)$.

[Hint. $Z_{12}(s) = \dfrac{V_2(s)}{I_1(s)} = s$]

6. A network is shown in Fig. P12.5, find the voltage transfer ratio and transfer impedances.

[**Hint.** Apply $V_1(s)$ at 1-1′ and the current flow through the inductor and capacitor is $I_1(s)$; assume 2-2′ open.

$\therefore \quad V_1(s) = I_1(s)\left[Ls + \frac{1}{Cs}\right]$

$V_2(s) = I_1(s) \cdot \frac{1}{Cs}$.

$\therefore \quad G_{12}(s) = \frac{V_2(s)}{V_1(s)} = \frac{1/Cs}{Ls + \frac{1}{Cs}}$; now simplify.

$Z_{12}(s) = \frac{V_2(s)}{I_1(s)} = \frac{1}{Cs}$]

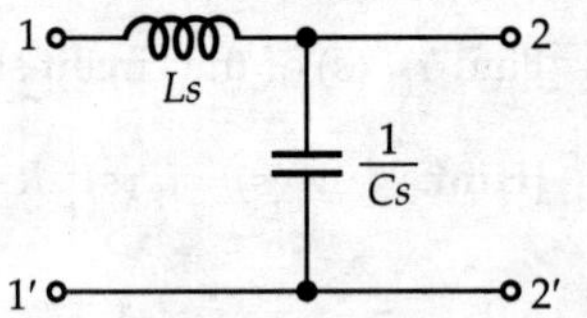

Fig. P12.5

7. Explain whether the driving point impedance $Z(s) = \frac{s^2 + S + 3}{s^4 + 5s^3 + 6s^2}$ is suitable for representing a passive one port network.

[**Hint.** Not suitable ; because the degree of numerator is 2 while that of denominator is 4. Also a double pole exists at origin of the S-plane. The term of lowest degree in the numerator is of degree O while that in the denominator is 2. This is also not permitted].

8. A transform voltage is given by $V(s) = \frac{3s}{(s+1).(s+4)}$. Plot the pole-zero in the S-plane and obtain the time domain response.

[**Hint.** $V(t) = K_1 e^{-t} + K_2 e^{-4t}$

$$K_1 = H\frac{M_{01}\, e^{j\phi_{01}}}{M_{41}\, e^{j\phi_{41}}} = 3\frac{1.\, e^{j180°}}{3\, e^{j0}} = -1 \;; \qquad K_2 = H\frac{M_{04}\, e^{j\phi_{04}}}{M_{14}\, e^{j\phi_{14}}} = 3\frac{4.\, e^{j180°}}{3.\, e^{j180°}} = 4 \;]$$

9. The transform current $I(s)$ in a given network is given by $I(s) = \frac{s}{(s+2)(s^2 + 2S + 2)}$. Obtain the pole zero plot and hence the time domain response.

[**Hint.** $i(t) = K_1 e^{-2t} + K_2 e^{-(1-j)t} + K_3 e^{-(1+j)t}$.

$$K_1 = H\frac{M_{OP}\, e^{j\phi_{OP}}}{M_{P_1-P}\, M_{P_2-P}\, e^{j(\phi_{P_1-P} + \phi_{P_2-P})}} \quad \text{[refer to Fig. P12.6]}$$

$H = 1$; $M_{OP} = 2$; $\phi_{OP} = 180°$

$M_{P_1-P} = \sqrt{2} = M_{P_2-P}$

$\phi_{P_1-P} = -135°$; $\phi_{P_2-P} = +135°$ (geometrically)

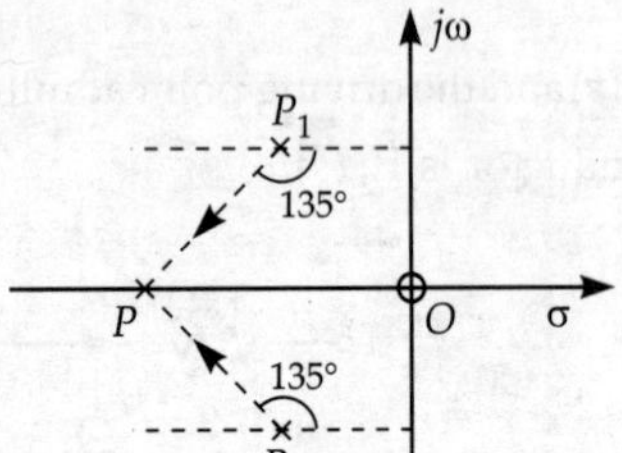

Fig. P12.6

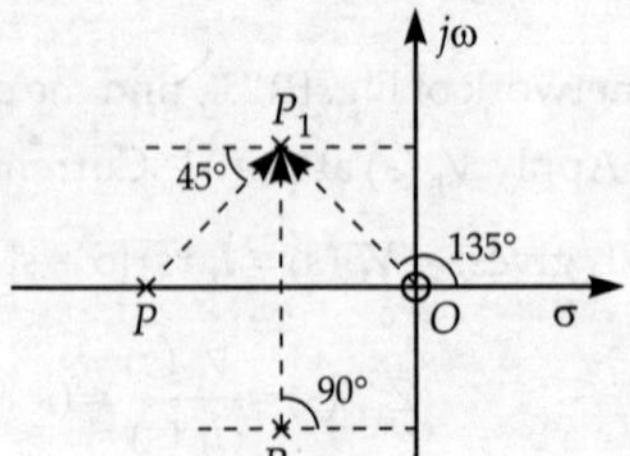

Fig. P12.7

To find K_2, refer to Fig. P12.7.

$$K_2 = H\frac{M_{OP_1}\, e^{j\phi_{OP_1}}}{M_{P-P_1}\, M_{P_2 P_1}\, e^{j(\phi_{P-P_1} + \phi_{P_2-P_1})}}$$

$$H = 1 ; M_{OP_1} = \sqrt{2} ; \phi_{OP_1} = 135°$$

$$M_{P-P_1} = \sqrt{2} ; M_{P_2 - P_1} = 2$$

$$\phi_{P-P_1} = 45° ; \phi_{P_2 - P_1} = 90°$$

K_3 will be the conjugate of K_2. Substituting the values of K_1, K_2 and K_3, we will get the time domain response.]

10. Check the stability of the following system expressed of the polynomial $P(s) = s^3 + 2s^2 + 2s + 40$. Apply Routh Hurwitz criterion.

[**Hint.** Tabulate the Routh Array and check the sign of the first column elements. The system will not be stable as there will be change in sign in the first column.]

11. Find the voltage transfer ratio in the network in Fig. P12.8.

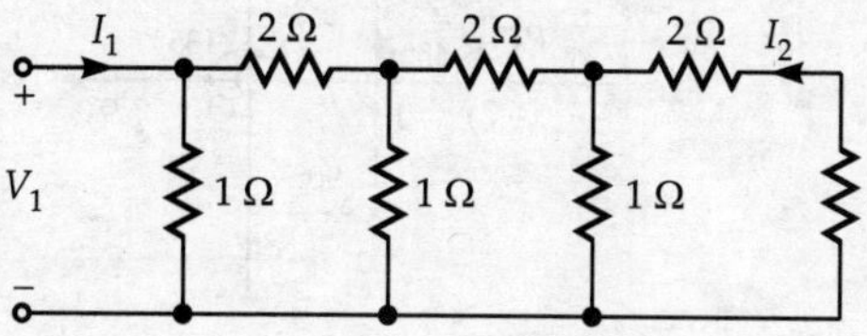

Fig. P12.8

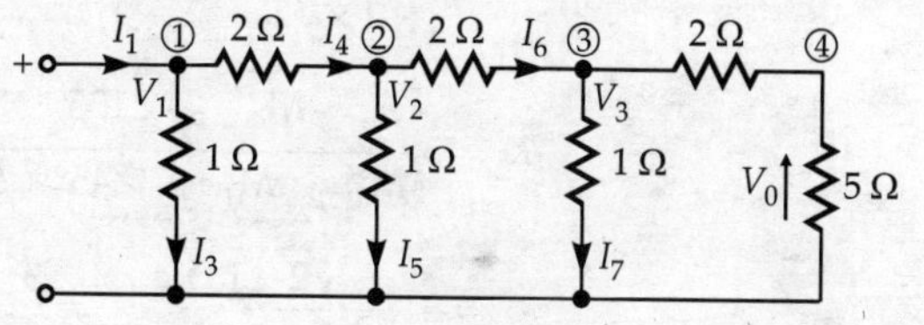

Fig. P12.9

[**Hint.** Fig. P12.8 is redrawn as Fig. P12.9 at *node (1)*

$$I_1 = I_3 + I_4 = \frac{V_1}{1} + \frac{V_1 - V_2}{2}$$

or, $\quad I_1 = 1.5\,V_1 - 0.5\,V_2 \quad$ ...(*a*)

At *node (2)* : $\quad I_4 = I_5 + I_6$

$$\frac{V_1 - V_2}{2} = \frac{V_2}{1} + \frac{V_2 - V_3}{2}$$

or, $\quad 0.5\,V_1 - 2V_2 + 0.5\,V_3 = 0 \quad$ ...(*b*)

At *node (3)* : $\quad I_6 = I_7 + (-I_2)$

or, $$\frac{V_2 - V_3}{2} = \frac{V_3}{1} - \frac{V_0 - V_3}{2}$$

or, $\quad 0.5\,V_2 - 2V_3 + 0.5\,V_0 = 0 \quad$ ...(*c*)

At *node (4)* : $$\frac{V_0}{5} = -\frac{V_0 - V_3}{2}$$

or, $\quad 0.7\,V_0 - 0.5\,V_3 = 0 \quad$ ...(*d*)

Solving these four equations, the voltage transfer ratio, V_0 / V_1 can be obtained]

12. The transfer function of a network is given by

$$T(s) = \frac{3s}{(s+2)(s^2 + 2s + 2)}$$

Plot the pole-zero diagram and obtain $T(t)$.

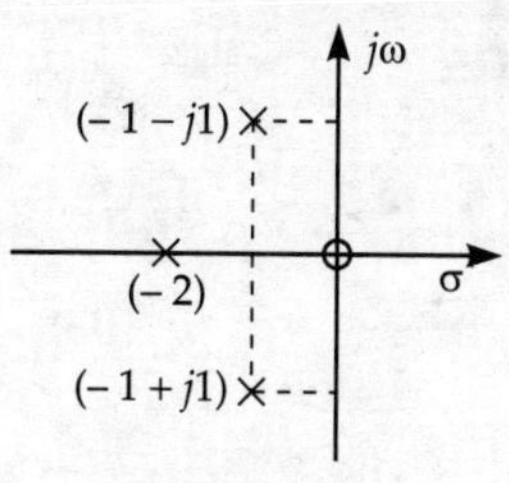

Fig. P12.10

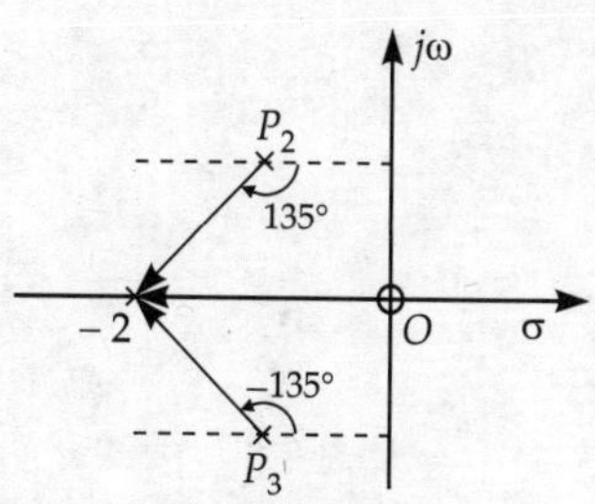

Fig. P12.11

[**Hint.** $T(s) = \dfrac{3s}{(s+2)(s+1-j\,1)(s+1+j\,1)}$

$\therefore$ Poles are at $-2, -1+j\,1, -1-j\,1$ zero is at 0, origin.

i.e., $$T(s) = \frac{3\,s}{(s+2)(s+1-j\,1)(s+1+j\,1)}$$

$\therefore$ $$T(t) = K_1\,e^{-2t} + K_2\,e^{(-1+j1)t} + K_3\,e^{(-1-j1)t}$$

$$K_1 = 3\,\frac{M_{OP_1}\ \angle 180°}{M_{P_2-P_1}\ M_{P_3-P_1}\ \angle 135° + (-135°)}$$

$$= 3\,\frac{2\ \angle 180°}{\sqrt{2}\times\sqrt{2}} = 3\ \angle 180°$$

$$K_2 = 3\,\frac{M_{O-P_2}\ \angle 135°}{M_{P_1P_2}\ M_{P_3P_2}\ \angle 45° + 90°}$$

$$= 3\,\frac{\sqrt{2}\ \angle 135°}{\sqrt{2}\times 2\ \angle 45° + 90°} = \frac{3}{2}.$$

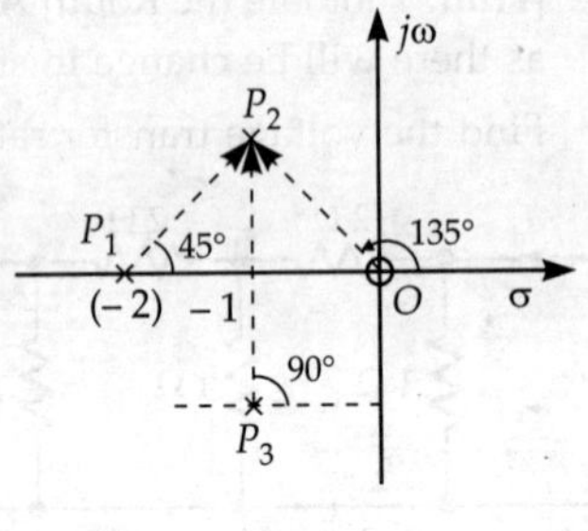

Fig. P12.12

$$K_3 = K_2^*\ \text{(Complex conjugate)} = \frac{3}{2}.$$

$\therefore$ $$T(t) = 3e^{j180°}\,e^{-2t} + \frac{3}{2}\,e^{(-1+j)t} + \frac{3}{2}\,e^{(-1-j)t}$$

$$= -3e^{-2t} + \frac{3}{2}\,e^{(-1+j)t} + \frac{3}{2}\,e^{(-1-j)t}\ ]$$

13. *Find the poles and zero location of the current transfer ratio I_2 / I_1 in s-domain in the circuit shown in Fig. P12.13.*

[**Hint.** In the given circuit, $I_2 = I_1 \times \dfrac{3s}{2+4s}$

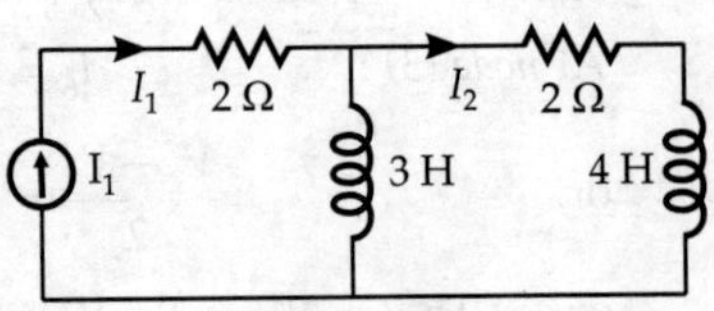

Fig. P12.13

$\Rightarrow$ $$\frac{I_2}{I_1} = \frac{3s}{2+4s} = \frac{\frac{3}{4}s}{5+0.5}$$

$$= \frac{3}{4}\left(\frac{s}{s+0.5}\right) = K\,.\,\frac{P}{Q}$$

Here, scale factor $(K) = \dfrac{3}{4}$

For zero, $P(s) = 0$ *i.e.*, $s = 0$ for pole, value $Q(s) = 0$ *i.e.*, $s + 0.5 = 0$

or $s = -0.5$

Pole zero plot is shown in Fig. P12.13(*a*)].

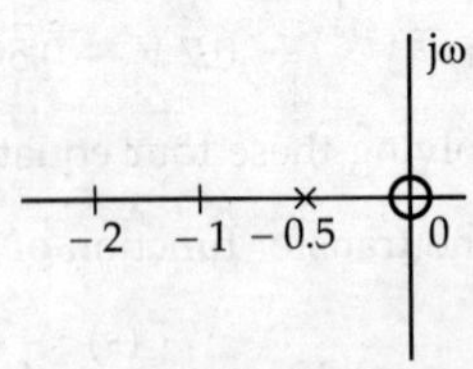

Fig. P12.13 (*a*)

CHAPTER

13

Network Topology (*Graph Theory*)

13.1 CONCEPT OF A NETWORK GRAPH

When all the elements (*e.g.* resistors, inductors, capacitors etc.) in a network are replaced by lines with circles or dots at both ends, the configuration is then called the *graph* of the network. The graph of any network is drawn by keeping all the points of intersection of two or more branches and representing the network elements of lines, voltages and current sources by their internal impedances. The point of intersection of two or more branches is called a *node*. Small letters (*a*, *b*, *c*,....) may be used to denote the nodes while numbers (1, 2,...) may be given to identify elements.

13.2 TERMINOLOGY USED IN NETWORK GRAPH

Branch. A *branch* is a line segment representing one network element or a combination of elements connected between two points. Though the line segment with its two distinct end points represents a branch, it does not indicate anything about the type of elements.

Node. A *node point* is defined as an end point of a line segment and exists at the junction between two branches or at the ends of an isolated branch.

Degree of a Node. It is the number of branches incident to it.

Tree. It is an interconnected open set of branches which include all the nodes of the given graph. In a tree of the graph there cannot be any closed loop.

Tree branch. It is any branch of a tree. It is also named as *twig*.

Tree link (or chord). It is that branch of the graph that does not belong to the particular tree. It is simply called a *link*.

Loop. This is the closed contour selected in a graph.

Cut-set. It is that set of elements or branches of a graph that separates two main parts of a network. If any branch of the cut-set is not removed, the network remains connected. The term *cut-set* is derived from the property designated by the way by which the network can be divided into two parts.

A cut-set is shown on a graph by a dashed line, where the dashed line passes through the branches defining the *cut-set*. A graph should have at least one cut-set though there may be more than one cut-set in any graph.

Tie-set. It is a unique set with respect to a given tree of a connected graph containing one chord and all of the free branches contained in the free path formed between two vertices of the chord.

Network Variables. A network, in the present discussion, consists of a passive elements as well as sources of energy. In order to find out the response of the network the through current and voltages across each branch of the network are to be obtained.

In order to analyse the network on *voltage basis,* we are to force the tree branch voltage to zero making all branch voltages zero. Then, the tree branch voltage alone forms the independent variables and it is possible to express the tree link voltages in terms of tree branch voltages. Then, if B represents the number of branches and N the number of nodes, the *minimum number of variables* involved in analysing a network is equal to $(N-1)$.

When a network is analysed on *current basis,* removal of all the links destroys all the closed paths making all the branch currents zero. All branch currents can be expressed in terms of link currents. Hence, out of B branch currents only *link currents are independent* while remaining branch currents are dependent variables.

Directed (or oriented) Graph

A graph is said to be *directed* (*or oriented*) when all nodes and branches are numbered and directions are assigned to the branches by arrows (it is customary to assign +ve reference direction to all branch currents and voltages).

Subgraph. A graph G_S is said to be the *subgraph* of a graph G if every node of G_S is a node of G and every branch of G_S is also a branch of G.

Path. An ordered sequence of branches traversing from one node to another is called a *path* in a graph.

Connected Graph. When at least one path along branches between every pair of nodes of a graph exists, it is called a *connected graph.*

Incidence matrix. Any oriented graph can be described completely in a compact matrix form. Here, we specify the orientation of each branch in the graph and the nodes at which this branch is incident. This matrix is called *incident matrix*.

When one row is deleted from the complete incidence matrix, the remaining matrix is then termed as reduced incidence matrix.

Isomorphism. It is the property between two graphs so that both have got same incidence matrix.

13.3 RELATION BETWEEN TWIGS AND LINKS

The number of twigs on a tree is always one less than the number of nodes.

Let N = no. of nodes; then number of twigs will be $(N-1)$.

Also, if L represents the total number of links while B the total number of branches, then

$$L = B-(N-1) = B-N+1 \qquad ...(13.1)$$

13.4 PROPERTIES OF A TREE IN A GRAPH

(*i*) It consists of all the nodes of the graph.

(*ii*) If the graph has N no. of nodes, the tree will have $(N-1)$ branches.

(*iii*) There will be no closed path in the tree.

(*iv*) There can be many possible different trees for a given graph depending on the number of nodes and branches.

EXAMPLE 13.1 *Draw the nodes and branches of the network elements and sources shown in Figs. E13.1(a) to (f).*

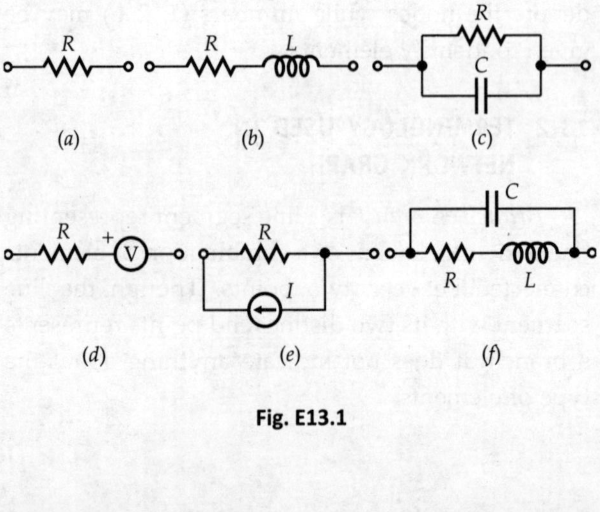

Fig. E13.1

Solution. The node and branch of the network elements [Figs. E13.1(*a*) and 13.1(*b*)] are shown below :

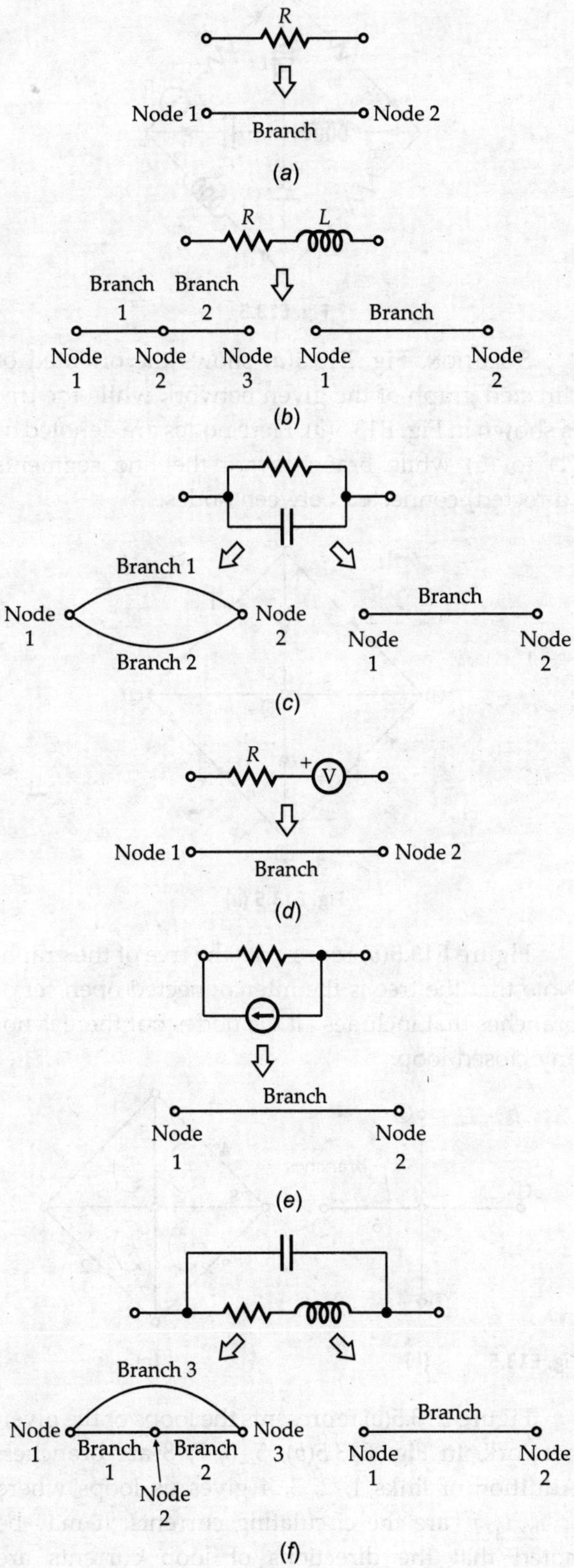

Fig. E13.1

It may be observed that a branch also represents a combination of elements and hence in Fig. E13.1(*b*), two types of branch-node equivalent diagrams are shown. The choice of branches and nodes with respect to network elements is flexible. This concept is thus also applicable in drawing the branch of Figs. E13.1(*c*) and (*f*). Since the energy sources are replaced by their internal impedances hence, in Figs. E13.1(*d*) and (*e*), the voltage and current sources are replaced by short circuit and open circuit respectively. The following list of figures show the respective branches with corresponding nodes with their given network equivalents.

Example 13.2 *A network is shown in Fig. E13.2. Draw its graph.*

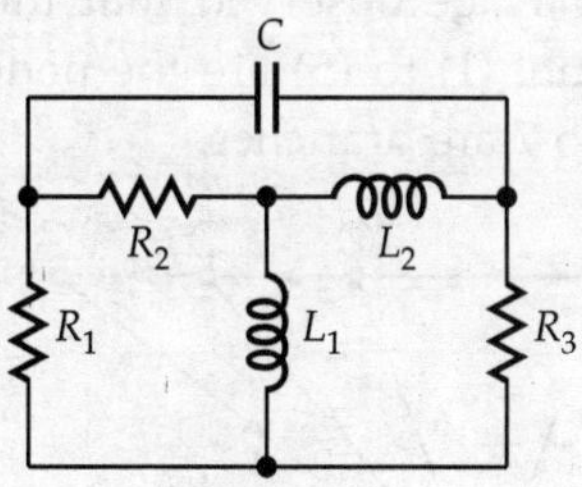

Fig. E13.2

Solution. Let us draw the line segments between the nodes of the given network. It then represents a graph as shown in Fig. E13.2(*a*). The nodes are represented by encircled numbers while the branches are drawn by line segments connecting the nodes.

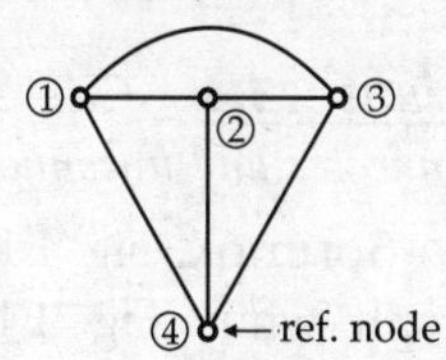

Fig. E13.2 (*a*)

Example 13.3 *Draw the graph of the networks shown in Figs. E13.3(a) to (c).*

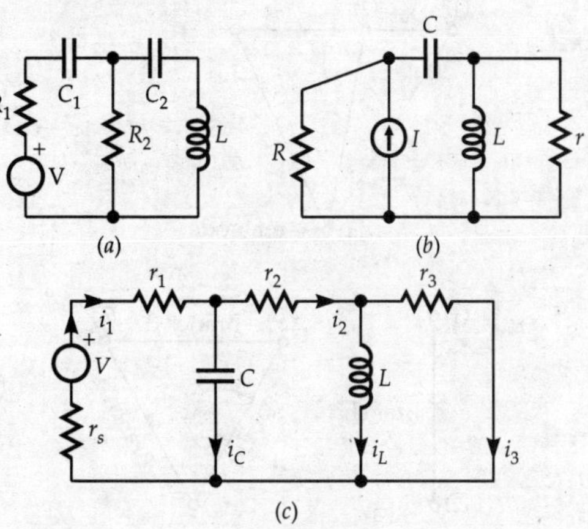

Fig. E13.3

CHAPTER 13

SOLUTION. Voltage sources being replaced by short circuits in the graph, the current sources are to be replaced by open circuit. Figs. E13.3(*d*) and (*e*) represent the required graph of Figs. E13.3(*a*) and (*b*) respectively. The respective nodes are encircled.

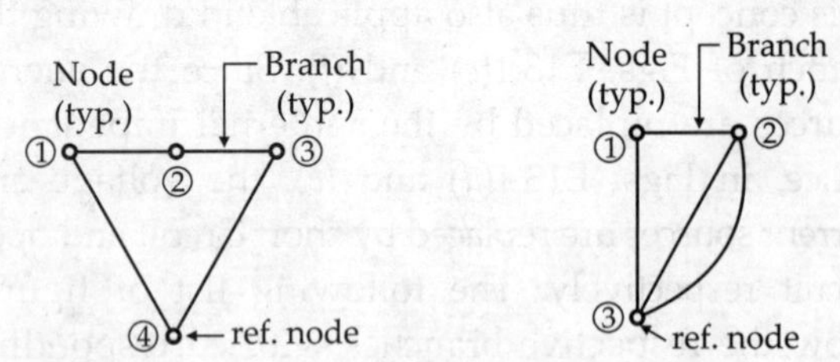

Fig. E13.3 (*d*) (*e*)

Figure E13.3(*f*) represents the graph of Fig. E13.3(*c*). It may be observed that this graph is a directed graph. (1) to (5) are the nodes while line segments 1 to 7 are branches.

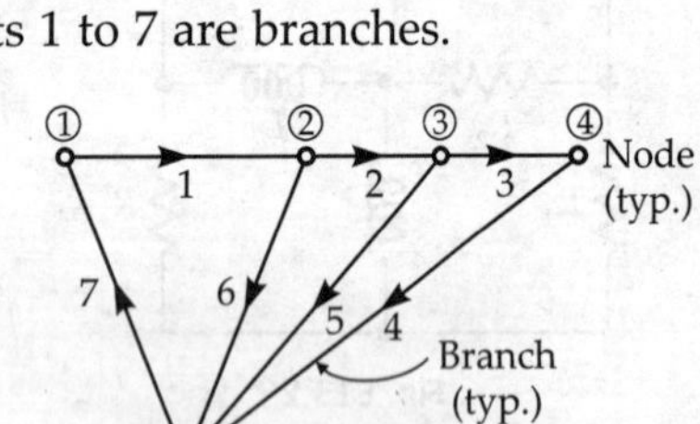

Fig. E13.3 (*f*)

EXAMPLE 13.4 *Give suitable diagrams to illustrate connected and unconnected graphs.*

SOLUTION. Fig. E13.4(*a*) represents a connected graph while Fig. E13.4(*b*) represents an unconnected graph. The connected graph may be defined as such a graph where at least one path along branches between every pair of nodes of a graph exists.

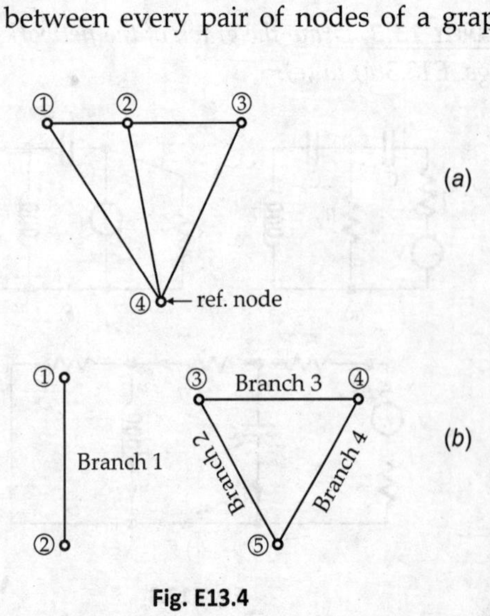

Fig. E13.4

EXAMPLE 13.5 *A network is shown in Fig. E13.5. Draw the directed graph, tree and show the loops.*

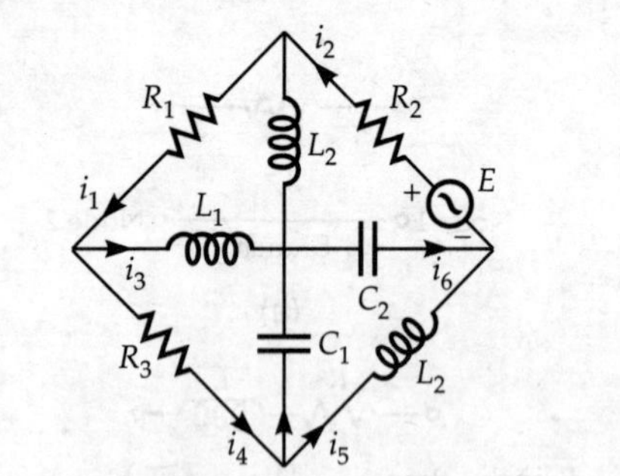

Fig. E13.5

SOLUTION. Fig. E13.5(*a*) shows the oriented or directed graph of the given network while the tree is shown in Fig. E13.5(*b*). Here nodes are denoted as (1) to (5) while branches are the line segments (directed) connected between nodes.

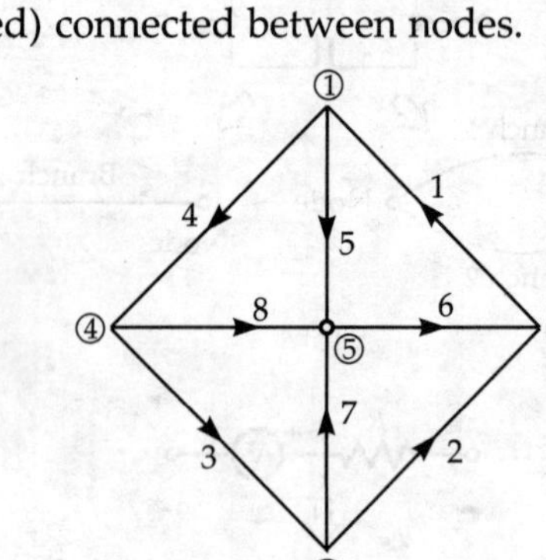

Fig. E13.5 (*a*)

Figure **E13.5(*b*)** represents the tree of the graph. Note that the tree is the interconnected open set of branches that includes all the nodes but there is not any closed loop.

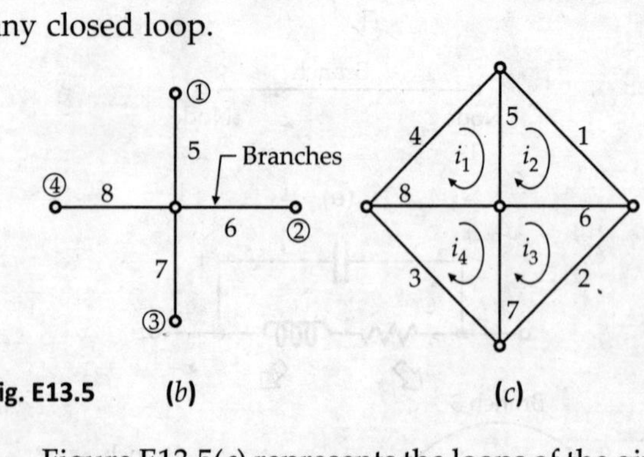

Fig. E13.5 (*b*) (*c*)

Figure E13.5(*c*) represents the loops of the given network. In Fig. E13.5(*b*), 5, 6, 7, 8 are branches. Addition of links 1, 2, 3, 4 gives us loops where i_1, i_2, i_3, i_4 are the circulating currents. It may be noted that the directions of loop currents are arbitrary [Fig. E13.5(*c*)].

EXAMPLE 13.6 *Fig. E13.6 represents a graph of a network. Show the tree, twigs and links.*

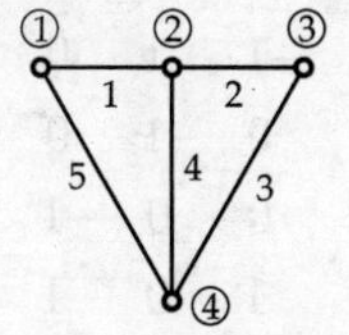

Fig. E13.6

SOLUTION. A simple graph may have many different trees (*i.e.*, consisting of a number of interconnected set of branches that include all the nodes but do not form any closed loop). The trees of the given graph are shown below [Fig. E13.6(*a*)].

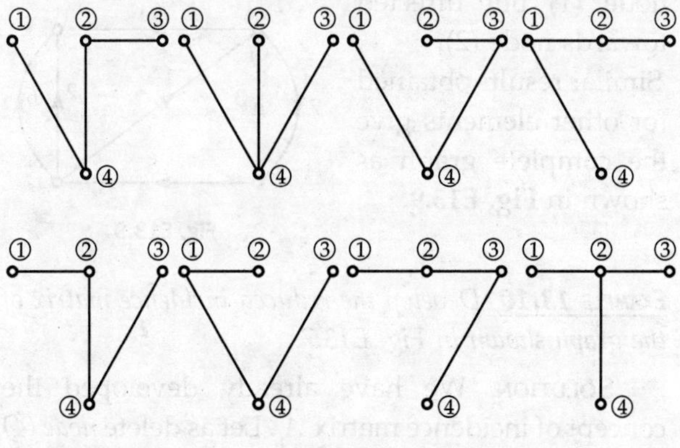

Fig. E13.6 (*a*)

The twigs and links are shown by bold and dotted lines respectively in Fig. E13.6(*b*) for each of the trees shown in Fig. E13.6(*a*). It may be noted that twigs being the branches of any particular / corresponding tree, the links do not belong to any particular tree.

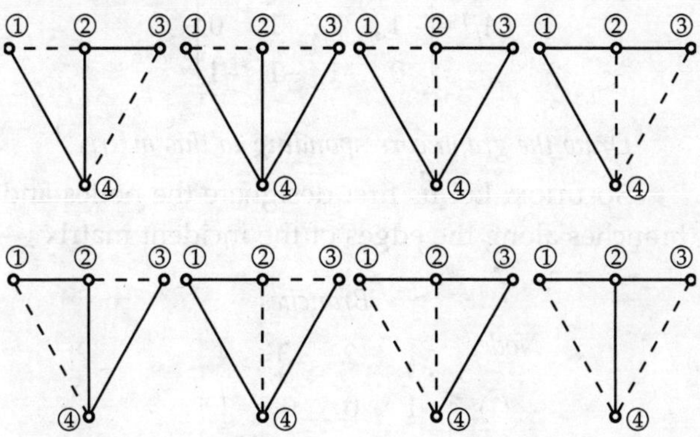

Fig. E13.6 (*b*)

13.5 FORMATION OF INCIDENCE MATRIX $[A_i]$

This matrix shows which branch is incident to which node. Each row of the matrix being representing the corresponding node of the graph, each column corresponds to a branch. When a graph does have N nodes and B branches, the complete incidence matrix $[A_i]$ is $[a_{ij}]$ and is $N \times B$ rectangular matrix whose elements (a_{ij}) are defined by

(*i*) If branch j is incident at node i and is *oriented away* from the node, $a_{ij} = 1$. In other words, when $a_{ij} = 1$, branch j leaves away node i.

(*ii*) If branch j is incident at node i and is *oriented towards* node i, $a_{ij} = -1$. In other words, branch j enters node i.

(*iii*) If branch j is *not incident* at node i, $a_{ij} = 0$.

The complete set of incidence matrix is called *augmented incidence matrix.*

EXAMPLE 13.7 *Obtain the incidence matrix of the graph shown in Fig. E13.7.*

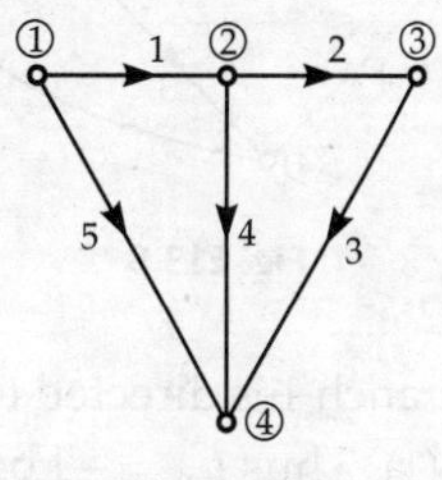

Fig. E13.7

SOLUTION. We observe that branch 1 is incident to node (1) as well as node (2) but oriented away from node (1) and oriented towards node (2). Thus $a_{11} = 1$, but $a_{21} = -1$. Since branch 1 is not incident to nodes (3) or (4) hence, $a_{31} = 0; a_{41} = 0$. However, branch 5 is incident on node (1) but away from it. Hence $a_{15} = 1$. Similarly, other a_{ij} elements can be calculated. The complete **incidence matrix** is shown below :

Branches

Nodes	1	2	3	4	5
(1)	1	0	0	0	1
(2)	−1	1	0	1	0
(3)	0	−1	1	0	0
(4)	0	0	−1	−1	−1

$= [A_i]$

13.5.1 Properties of Incidence Matrix

(*i*) *Algebraic sum of the column entries of an incidence matrix is zero.*

(*ii*) *Determinant of the incidence matrix of a closed loop is zero.*

13.5.2 Reduced Incidence Matrix [*A*]

It is possible to remove any one row from $[A_i]$ without sacrificing any information in $[A_i]$. When one row is deleted from the complete incidence matrix A_i, the remaining matrix is called a *reduced incidence matrix [A]*.

Thus, for a graph when there are N nodes and B branches, the order of the incidence matrix is $[(N-1)\times B]$. This means $[A]$ has $(N-1)$ rows and B columns.

EXAMPLE 13.8 *Draw the incidence matrix of the following graph (Fig. E13.8).*

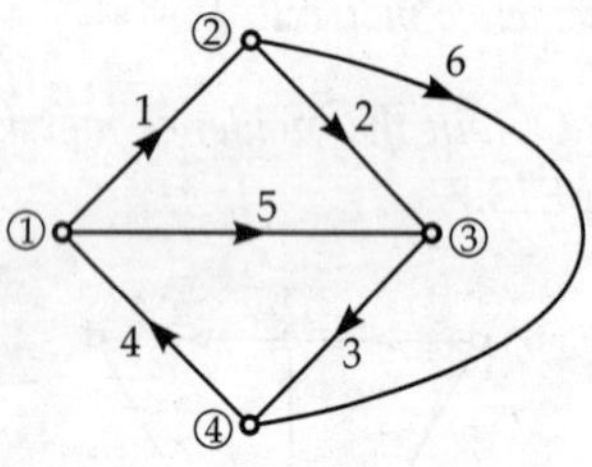

Fig. E13.8

SOLUTION. Branch 1 is directed towards node (2) but away from (1). Thus $a_{21}=-1$ but $a_{11}=1$.

Branch 2 is directed towards node (3) but away from node (2). Thus $a_{32}=-1$ while $a_{22}=1$.

Similar reasonings are applied for other elements and the **incidence matrix** is formed as shown below.

Nodes \ Branches	1	2	3	4	5	6
(1)	1	0	0	−1	1	0
(2)	−1	+1	0	0	0	+1
(3)	0	−1	+1	0	−1	0
(4)	0	0	−1	+1	0	−1

It may be observed that the sum of entries of each column is zero.

EXAMPLE 13.9 *Incidence matrix of a graph is given below. Draw the directed graph.*

Nodes \ Branches	1	2	3	4	5	6	7
(1)	−1	0	−1	1	0	0	1
(2)	0	−1	0	−1	0	−1	0
(3)	1	1	0	0	−1	1	0
(4)	0	0	1	0	1	0	−1

SOLUTION. It is evident from the given incidence matrix that branch 1 is directed towards node (1) but away from node (3) as is evident from a_{11} and a_{31}. Thus branch 1 is a line segment directed from node (3) to node (1). Similarly, branch 3 is directed towards node (1) $[a_{13}]$ but directed away from node (4) $[a_{43}]$. Branch 4 is directed away from node (1) but directed towards node (2). Similar results obtained for other elements give the complete graph as shown in **Fig. E13.9.**

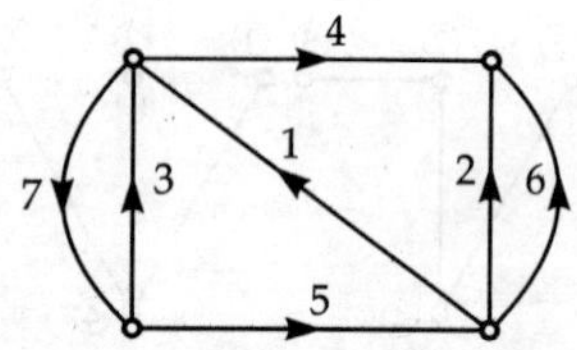

Fig. E13.9

EXAMPLE 13.10 *Develop the reduced incidence matrix of the graph shown in Fig. E13.7.*

SOLUTION. We have already developed the concept of incidence matrix A_i. Let as delete *node (4)* such that the 4th row is removed. The **reduced incidence matrix** is then given by

$$[A]=\begin{bmatrix} 1 & 0 & 0 & 0 & -1 \\ -1 & 1 & 0 & 1 & 0 \\ 0 & -1 & 1 & 0 & 0 \end{bmatrix}$$

EXAMPLE 13.11(a) *An incidence matrix is given by*

$$[A_i]=\begin{bmatrix} 1 & 0 & 0 & 1 \\ -1 & 1 & 1 & 0 \\ 0 & -1 & -1 & -1 \end{bmatrix}$$

Draw the graph corresponding to this matrix.

SOLUTION. Let us first designate the nodes and branches along the edges of the incident matrix ;

Nodes \ Branches	1	2	3	4
(1)	1	0	0	1
(2)	−1	1	1	0
(3)	0	−1	−1	−1

$\therefore\ a_{11} = 1;\ a_{12} = 0;\ a_{13} = 0;\ a_{14} = 1;$

i.e., the branches 1 and 4 are incident on nodes (1) and (4) but both are away from the nodes. Branch 1 is oriented away from node (1) but directed towards node (2). Similarly, for other nodes and branches, applying similar reasoning, we can draw the respective branches that give the graph (**Fig. E13.10**).

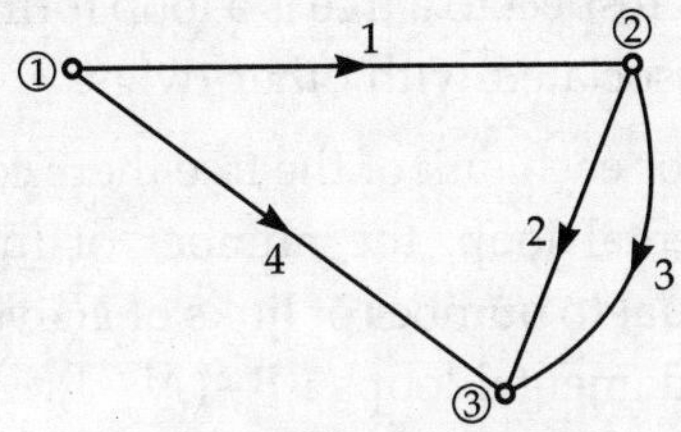

Fig. E13.10

13.5.3 Twig Matrix and Link Matrix

Let us assume as oriented graph of a network as shown in Fig. 13.1(*a*). Let us write first the incidence matrix $[A_i]$ as

$$[A_i] = \begin{array}{c} \\ 1 \\ 2 \\ 3 \\ 4 \end{array} \begin{array}{c} \begin{matrix} 1 & 2 & 3 & 4 & 5 & 6 \end{matrix} \\ \begin{bmatrix} 1 & 1 & 0 & 0 & 0 & 1 \\ 0 & -1 & 1 & -1 & 0 & 0 \\ 0 & 0 & 0 & 1 & 1 & -1 \\ -1 & 0 & -1 & 0 & -1 & 0 \end{bmatrix} \end{array}$$

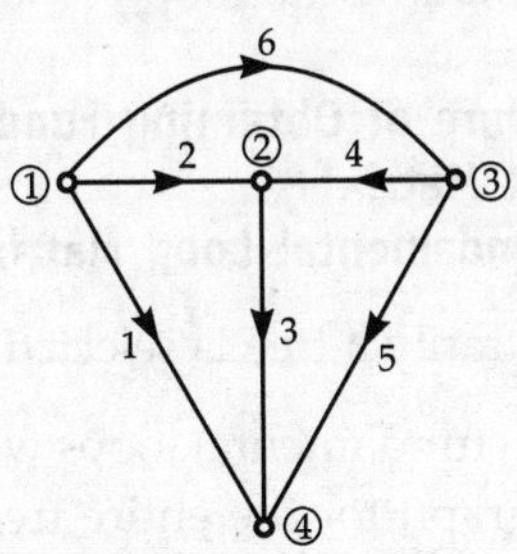

Fig. 13.1 (*a*) Oriented graph of a network

Eliminating node (3) we write then the reduced incidence matrix $[A]$ as

$$[A] = \begin{bmatrix} 1 & 1 & 0 & 0 & 0 & 1 \\ 0 & -1 & 1 & -1 & 0 & 0 \\ -1 & 0 & -1 & 0 & -1 & 0 \end{bmatrix}$$

(here we have eliminated the third row.)

If a tree is now selected as shown in Fig. 13.1(*b*), and if we form $[A]$ by arranging columns such that

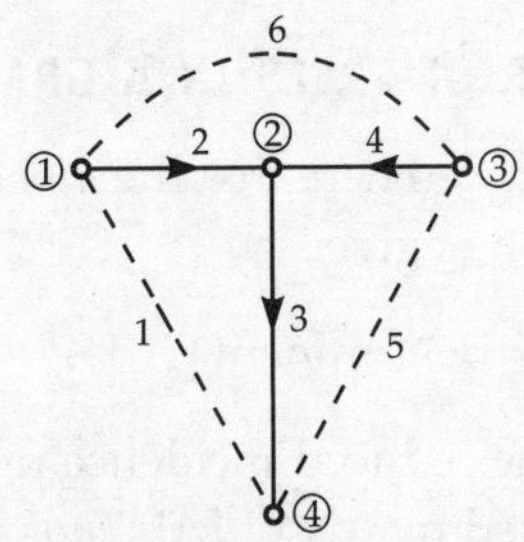

Fig. 13.1 (*b*) Tree of the given graph

[Twigs : (2, 3, 4)
Links : (1, 5, 6)]

first $(N-1)$ columns correspond to twigs of the selected tree and last $[B-(N-1)]$ branches correspond to links of the selected tree, we can write the matrix $[A]$ as

$$[A] = \begin{array}{c} \begin{matrix} 2 & 3 & 4 & & 1 & 5 & 6 \end{matrix} \\ \left[\begin{array}{ccc|ccc} 1 & 0 & 0 & 1 & 0 & 1 \\ -1 & 1 & -1 & 0 & 0 & 0 \\ 0 & -1 & 0 & -1 & -1 & 0 \end{array}\right] \end{array}$$

Matrix of Twigs — Matrix of Links

Now we see that matrix $[A]$ is subdivided into two submatrices $[A_T]$ and $[A_L]$.

$[A_T]$ is called Twig Matrix and $[A_L]$ is the Link Matrix.

Also, $[A] = [A_T : A_L]$ ...(13.2)

However,

$$[A_T] = \begin{bmatrix} 1 & 0 & 0 \\ -1 & 1 & -1 \\ 0 & -1 & 0 \end{bmatrix}$$

$\therefore$ Determinant of $[A_T]$ is given by

$$1\begin{vmatrix} 1 & -1 \\ -1 & 0 \end{vmatrix} - 0\begin{vmatrix} -1 & -1 \\ 0 & 0 \end{vmatrix} + 0\begin{vmatrix} -1 & 1 \\ 0 & -1 \end{vmatrix}$$

or $\qquad \text{Det}\,[A_T] = -1$

i.e., matrix A_T is non-singular. This is a very general result and we may conclude that for matrix A_T, it is always *non-singular* and the determinant will be either (−1) or (+1). It may also be observed from above that rank of matrix $[A]$ is same as that of submatrix A_T [here both are 3]. For an nth order submatrix A_T, the matrix will also be non-singular and if the connected graph has N number of nodes, the rank of its incidence matrix will also be having same rank as the submatrix A_T which will be equal to $(N-1)$.

13.6 NUMBER OF TREES IN A GRAPH

It may be noted here that the *number* of possible trees of a graph is given by

$$T = \text{determinant}\,[A][A^t]$$

where $[A]$ is the reduced incidence matrix and $[A^t]$ is the transposed matrix of $[A]$. *Thus in order to find the possible number of trees in a graph it is required only to find determinant* $[A][A^t]$.

Example 13.11(b) *A reduced incidence matrix of a graph is given by*

$$[A] = \begin{bmatrix} 1 & 1 & 0 & 0 & 0 & 1 \\ 0 & -1 & 1 & -1 & 0 & 0 \\ -1 & 0 & -1 & 0 & -1 & 0 \end{bmatrix}$$

Obtain the number of possible trees.

Solution. The transpose of the given matrix is given by

$$[A^T] = \begin{bmatrix} 1 & 0 & -1 \\ 1 & -1 & 0 \\ 0 & 1 & -1 \\ 0 & -1 & 0 \\ 0 & 0 & -1 \\ 1 & 0 & 0 \end{bmatrix}$$

Since number of possible trees is

$$T = \text{Det}\,[A][A^T]$$

[refer to Article 13.6]

hence we can write here

$$T = \text{Det}\left\{\begin{bmatrix} 1 & 1 & 0 & 0 & 0 & 1 \\ 0 & -1 & 1 & -1 & 0 & 0 \\ -1 & 0 & -1 & 0 & -1 & 0 \end{bmatrix}\begin{bmatrix} 1 & 0 & -1 \\ 1 & -1 & 0 \\ 0 & 1 & -1 \\ 0 & 0 & -1 \\ 1 & 0 & 0 \end{bmatrix}\right\}$$

$$= \text{Det}\begin{bmatrix} 3 & -1 & -1 \\ -1 & 3 & -1 \\ -1 & -1 & 3 \end{bmatrix}$$

$$= 3\,[9-1] + [-4][1] - 1[1+3] = 16$$

∴ **Number of possible trees = 16.**

13.7 TIE-SET MATRIX [OR LOOP MATRIX] $[B_a]$

It is the matrix that is used to find the branch currents. For a given tree of a graph, addition of each link forms a closed path. In a closed path, there flows a circulating current which is also the link current. The current in any branch of a graph can be found by using link currents and its directions.

13.8 FUNDAMENTAL TIE-SET MATRIX (OR FUNDAMENTAL LOOP MATRIX) [*B*]

A *fundamental loop* or a *fundamental tie-set* of a graph with respect to a tree is a loop formed by only one link associated with other twigs.

Since for each link of the tree there corresponds a fundamental loop, the number of fundamental loops is equal to number of links of a given tree; *i.e.*, No. of fundamental loops : $B-(N-1)$.

KVL is applicable in each loop and in order to apply KVL to each fundamental loop, a reference direction of the loop is to be taken that coincides with the reference direction of the link concerning that loop. If the direction of any branch is oriented in the same way as the reference direction of the loop current, the corresponding element in the matrix (b_{ij}) is positive while the corresponding element (b_{ij}) would be negative if the reference direction of any branch (link or twig) is opposite to that of the reference direction of the loop current; b_{ij} would be zero when the corresponding branch does not link the fundamental loop.

13.8.1 Procedure of Obtaining Fundamental Tie-set Matrix (or Fundamental Loop Matrix)

Step 1 Arbitrarily a tree is selected in the graph.

Step 2 Form fundamental loops with each link in the graph for the entire tree.

Step 3 Assume directions of loop currents oriented in the same direction as that of the link.

Step 4 Form fundamental tie-set matrix $[b_{ij}]$ where

$b_{ij} = 1$ when branch b_j is in the fundamental loop i and their reference directions are oriented same,

$b_{ij} = -1$ when branch b_j is in the fundamental loop i but their reference direction are oriented opposite,

$b_{ij} = 0$ when branch b_j is not in the fundamental loop i.

An illustration

Given graph being shown in Fig. 13.2, the tree is selected in Fig. 13.2(*a*) arbitrarily and the loops are formed as shown in Fig. 13.2(*b*).

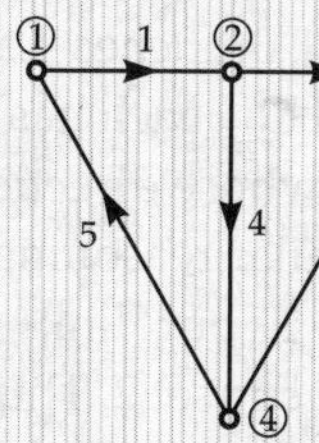

Fig. 13.2 A network graph

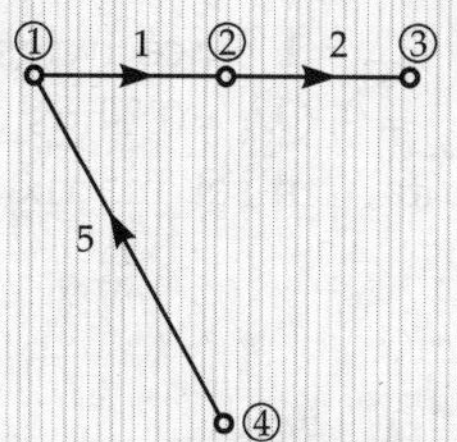

Fig. 13.2 (*a*)
An arbitrary tree

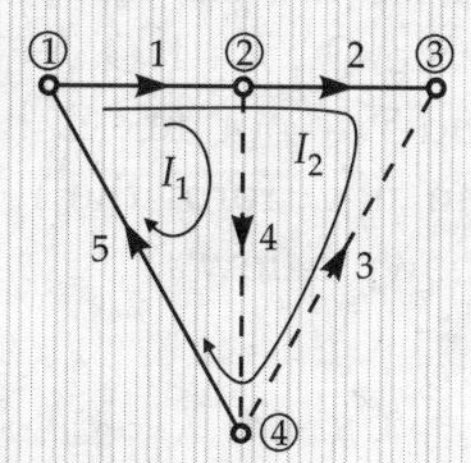

Fig. 13.2 (*b*)
Loops selected for the given graph

Note that there are two fundamental loops as there are two links only. Loop-1 has current I_1 and is formed with branches 1, 4 and 5 while Loop-2 has current I_2 and is formed with branches 1, 2, 3 and 5.

It may be noted that branches 1 and 4 are linked with loop-1 and having the orientation same as I_1 hence, in the loop matrix, b_{11} and b_{14} are $+1$ each while b_{15} is also $+1$ with the same reasoning. Other branches like 2 and 3 are not linked with loop-1 and hence b_{12} and b_{13} both has zero values. Similarly, for loop-2, orientation of branch 1, 2, 5 are same as I_2 orientation while branch 3 has orientation opposite to that of orientation of I_2. Then in loop matrix, for I_2 row, $b_{21} = +1;\ b_{22} = +1;\ b_{23} = -1;\ b_{25} = 1$ while $b_{24} = 0$. Since branch 4 does not link this loop.

The fundamental tie-set matrix is shown below :

Tie-sets (or loop currents)	*Branches* 1	2	3	4	5
I_1	1	0	0	1	1
I_2	1	1	−1	0	1

If $v_1, v_2, \ldots$ are the branch voltages, the voltage loop equation for each loop is then obtained as summation of each row voltages—

$$v_1 + v_4 + v_5 = 0\,;\ v_1 + v_2 - v_3 + v_5 = 0.$$

Similarly, each branch current is given by the algebraic sum of the link currents below the corresponding column of the branch number in the tie-set matrix.

Thus, $I_1 + I_2 = j_1;\quad I_2 = j_2;\quad -I_3 = j_3\,;$

$$I_1 = j_4;\quad I_1 + I_2 = j_5$$

(where $j_1, j_2, \ldots$ represent the branch currents). Thus the tie-set matrix gives the branch currents in terms of link currents too.

Matrix $[B]$ can also be partitioned into two submatrices $[B_T]$ and $[B_L]$ where $[B_T]$ is the matrix with twigs and $[B_L]$ is matrix with links only. Also, $[B] = [B_T : B_L]$.

13.9 FUNDAMENTAL CUT-SET

A fundamental cut-set of a graph with respect to a tree is a cut-set formed *by one and only one twig and a set of links*. Thus, in a graph, for each twig of a chosen tree, there would be a fundamental cut-set. *For a graph having N nodes there will be* $(N-1)$ *fundamental cut-sets* (*i.e.*, equal to the number of twigs).

As a convention, the orientation of cut-set is so chosen that it coincides with the orientation of its twig.

13.10 CUT-SET MATRIX $[Q_a]$

This matrix provides a compact and effective means of writing algebraic equations giving branch voltages in terms of tree branches.

The number of independent node-pair terminals is equal to the number of tree branches. Since all the tree branches are connected to all the nodes in the graph, it is possible to express the potential difference in terms of tree branch voltages. A cut-set consists of one and only one branch of the network tree, together with any links which must be cut to divide the network into two parts.

13.10.1 Procedure of Forming Fundamental Cut-Set Matrix [Q]

Step 1 Arbitrarily a tree is selected in the graph.

Step 2 Form fundamental cut-sets with each twig in the graph for the entire tree.

Step 3 Assume directions of the cut-sets oriented in the same direction of the concerned twig.

Step 4 Form fundamental cut-set matrix $[Q_{Kj}]$

where,

$Q_{Kj} = 1$ when branch b_j has same orientation of the cut-set K.

$Q_{Kj} = -1$ when branch b_j has opposite orientation of the cut-set K.

$Q_{Kj} = 0$ when b_j is not in the cut-set K.

An illustration

An oriented graph is shown in Fig. 13.3. Let us first select a tree arbitrarily [Fig. 13.3(*a*)]. Next, cut-sets are formed in Fig. 13.3(*b*). Note that there are three fundamental cut-sets as the graph has three twigs represented by bold lines. Each cut-set has only one twig.

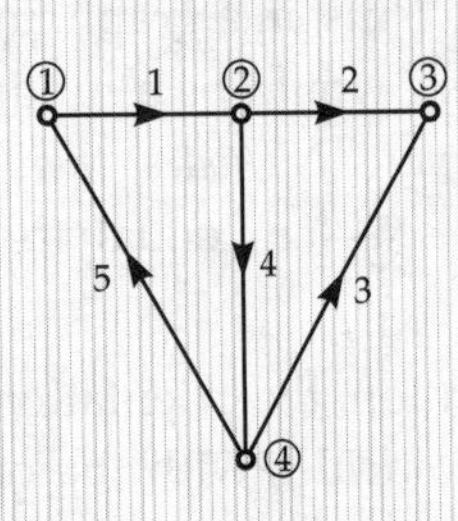

Fig. 13.3 An oriented graph

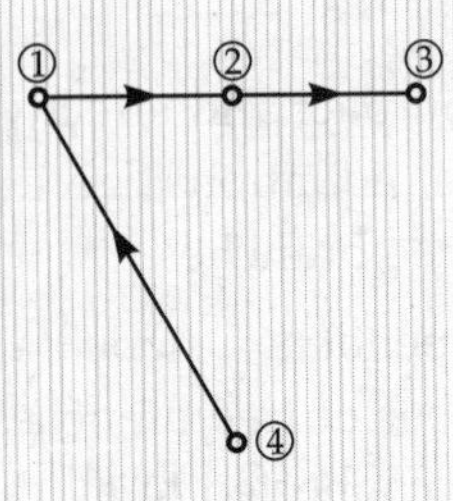

Fig. 13.3 (*a*) Selected tree

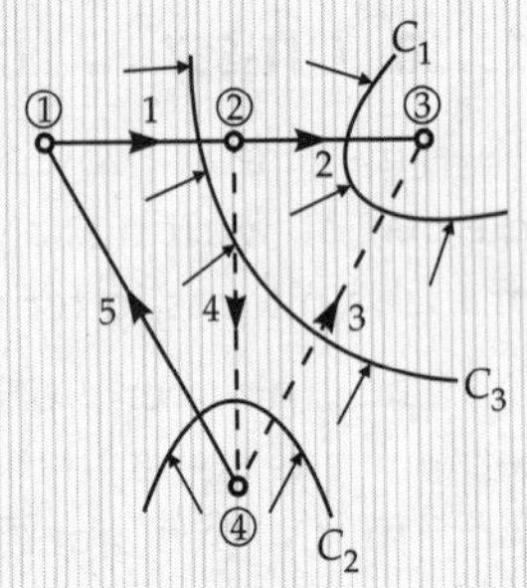

Fig. 13.3 (*b*) Cut-sets in selected tree

Cut-set C_1. Twig 2, link 3.

Cut-set C_2. Twig 5, link 3 and 4

Cut-set C_3. Twig 1, link 4 and 3.

It may be noted that for cut-set C_1, Q_{11} (*i.e.*, the branch-1 linking cut-set C_1) has coefficient *O* since branch 1 does not link C_1. On the other hand, branch 2 has same orientation of cut-set C_2 and hence $Q_{12} = +1$. Link 3 has also same direction like C_1 and hence $Q_{13} = +1$. Branches 4 and 5 do not link C_1 and hence Q_{14} and Q_{15} each has zero coefficient. Cut-set 2 links twig 5 whose direction is the same as C_2. Thus $Q_{25} = +1$. Similar reasonings hold for link 3 and hence Q_{23} is $+1$, but link 4 has direction opposite to that of the cut-set 2. Thus $Q_{24} = -1$. Since branches 1 and 2 do not link C_2 hence Q_{21} and Q_{22} are 0 each. Cut-set 3 links twig 1 and links 4 and 3. Observing the directions of these branches we can write $Q_{31} = +1, Q_{34} = -1$ and $Q_{33} = 1$. Since twigs 2 and 5 do not link C_3 hence $Q_{32} = 0, Q_{35} = 0$. Thus we can now form the fundamental cut-set matrix as shown below :

Cut-sets	*Branches* 1	2	3	4	5
C_1	0	+1	+1	0	0
C_2	0	0	+1	−1	+1
C_3	+1	0	+1	−1	0

The current balance equations can be obtained from the cut-set matrix as follows :

$$i_2 + i_3 = 0 ; i_3 - i_4 + i_5 = 0 ; i_3 - i_4 = 0$$

Arrows on cut-set indicate the direction of cut-set.

EXAMPLE 13.12 *With reference to Fig. E13.11, draw the graph and write down the tie-set matrix.*

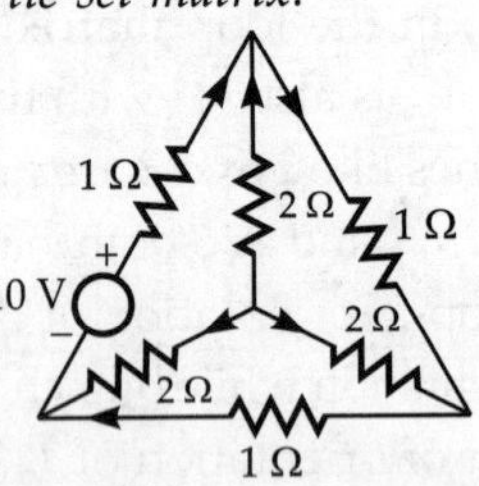

Fig. E13.11

SOLUTION. The graph of the given network is shown in Fig. E13.11(*a*). The loops are shown in Fig. E13.11(*b*) selecting the tie-set.

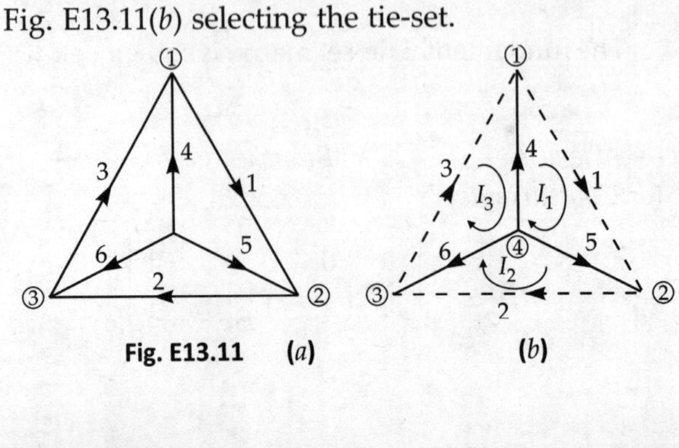

Fig. E13.11 (*a*) (*b*)

The **tie-set matrix** is shown below :

Tie-set (loop)	Branches 1	2	3	4	5	6
I_1	1	0	0	1	−1	0
I_2	0	1	0	0	1	−1
I_3	0	0	1	−1	0	1

EXAMPLE 13.13 *In the tree-link graph of Fig. E13.12 develop the fundamental cut-set matrix and equilibrium equations on nodal basis.*

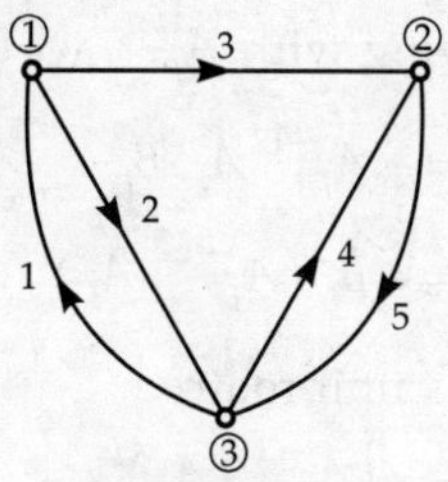

Fig. E13.12

SOLUTION. Cut-sets C_1 and C_2 are shown in Fig. E13.12(*a*). We take the matrix element as +1 when the corresponding branch is oriented in the same direction as cut-set. Otherwise the element is −1 when the orientation of the cut-set and branch is opposite. The **cut-set matrix** is shown below.

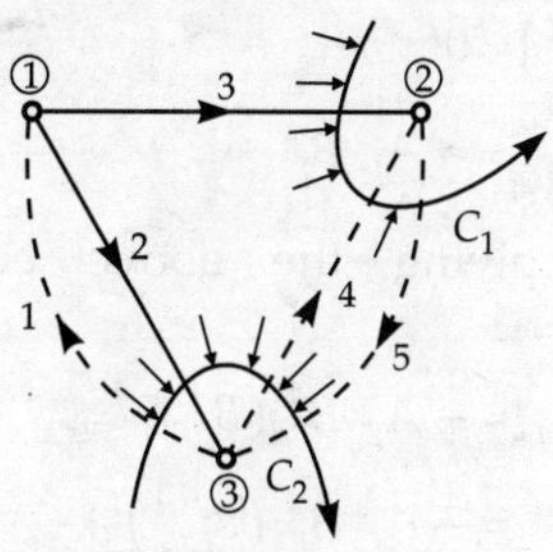

Fig. E13.12 (*a*)

Cut-Sets	Branches 1	2	3	4	5
C_1	0	0	1	1	−1
C_2	−1	1	0	−1	1

The equilibrium equations formed on nodal basis in orientation of the cut-set matrix are

$$i_3 + i_4 - i_5 = 0 \quad \text{and} \quad -i_1 + i_2 - i_4 + i_5 = 0$$

It may be noted that the cut-sets are not applied at node (1) since that would have involved two twigs (branches 2 and 3).

EXAMPLE 13.14 *For the resistive network shown in Fig. E13.13, draw the graph and tree of the network. Also develop the fundamental cut-set matrix.*

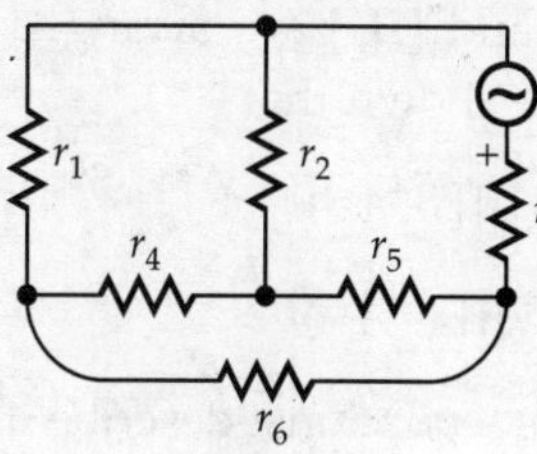

Fig. E13.13

SOLUTION. The graph and tree of the given network are shown in Figs. E13.13(*a*) and E13.13(*b*).

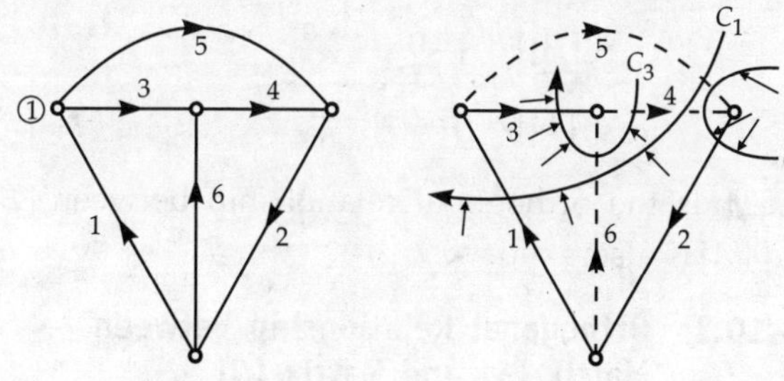

Fig. E13.13 (*a*) (*b*)

In Fig. E13.13(*b*) arbitrarily the tree is chosen with branches 1, 2 and 3. The links are 4, 5 and 6. The three cut-sets are shown in Fig. E13.13(*b*) as C_1, C_2 and C_3. The directions of cut-sets are also chosen in the direction of the corresponding twigs.

In the cut-set matrix, if the direction of the branch or link is in the same direction cut-set, we will take the matrix element as +1. On the other hand, if the direction of the branch or link is opposite to that of the cut-set, the matrix element would be −1. In case the branch does not link the cut-set, the matrix element would be zero.

Following this rule we have prepared the cut-set matrix below :

Fundamental Cut-set Matrix

Cut-sets	Branches 1	2	3	4	5	6
C_1 [1, 6, 4]	1	0	0	−1	0	1
C_2 [2, 4, 5]	0	1	0	−1	−1	0
C_3 [3, 6, 4]	0	0	+1	−1	0	+1

CHAPTER 13

13.10.2 Orthogonal Relationship between Matrix [*A*] and Matrix [*B*]

For a linear graph, if the columns of the two matrices $[A_i]$ and $[B_a]$ are arranged in the same order, it can be shown that

$$[A_i][B_a^t] = 0$$

i.e., $$[B_a][A_i^t] = 0$$

The above equations describe the *orthogonal relationship* between $[A_i]$ and $[B_a]$.

If reduced incidence matrix [*A*] and fundamental tie set matrix [*B*] are written for the same tree, it is also valid that

$$[A][B^t] = 0$$

or $$[B][A^t] = 0$$

Thus the orthogonal relationship between [*B*] and [*A*] is also valid.

13.10.3 Orthogonal Relationship between Matrix [*B*] and Matrix [*Q*]

If the columns of two Matrices $[B_a]$ and $[Q_a]$ are arranged in the same order,

$$[Q_a][B_a^t] = 0 \qquad \text{...(13.3)}$$

or $$[B_a][Q_a^t] = 0$$

Similarly, if the fundamental tie set matrix [*B*] and fundamental cutset matrix [*Q*] are written for the same tree,

$$[B][Q^t] = 0 \qquad \text{...(13.4)}$$

or $$[Q][B^t] = 0.$$

Thus, orthogonal relationship between [*B*] and [*Q*] is also valid.

13.11 RELATIONSHIP AMONG SUBMATRICES OF *A*, *B* AND *Q*

Let us arrange the columns of matrices *A*, *B* and *Q* with twigs for a given tree first and then the links. In partioned form we get

$$[A] = [A_T : A_L] \qquad \text{...(13.5a)}$$

$$[B] = [B_T : B_L] = [B_T : U] \qquad \text{...(13.5b)}$$

$$[Q] = [Q_T : Q_L] = [U : Q_L] \qquad \text{...(13.5c)}$$

From the orthogonal relation, $(AB^t = 0)$, we can write

$$[AB^t] = [A_T : A_L]\begin{bmatrix} B_T^t \\ \cdots\cdots \\ B_L^t \end{bmatrix}$$

$$\therefore \quad A_T\, B_L^t + A_L\, B_L^t = 0$$

or, $$A_T\, B_L^t = -A_L\, B_L^t \qquad \text{...(13.6)}$$

Since $[A_T]$ is non-singular. (*i.e.,* $|A| \neq 0$), Inverse of $[A_T]$ exists.

Premultiplying with A_T^{-1}, we get from (13.6),

$$[B_T^t] = -A_T^{-1}\, A_L\, B_L^t$$

$$\therefore \quad [B_T] = -B_L\,(A_T^{-1} . A_L)^t \qquad \text{...(13.7)}$$

Since B_L is a unit matrix

$$\therefore \quad [B_T] = -(A_T^{-1} . A_L)^t$$

Hence matrix *B* is written as

$$[B] = [-(A_T^{-1} . A_L)^t : U] \qquad \text{...(13.8)}$$

We know that,

$$[AB^t] = 0$$

$$\therefore \quad A_L\, B_L^t = -A_T\, B_T^t \qquad \text{...(13.8a)}$$

Postmultiplying the above equation with $[B_L^t]^{-1}$,

$$A_L = -A_T\, B_T^t\,(B_L^t)^{-1}$$

$$= -A_T\, B_T^t\,(B_L^{-1})^t$$

$$= -A_T\,(B_L^{-1} . B_T)^t \qquad \text{...(13.9)}$$

Thus matrix *A* can be written as,

$$[A] = [A_T : -A_T\,(B_L^{-1} . B_T)^t]$$

$$= A_T\,[U : -(B_L^{-1} . B_T)^t] \qquad \text{...(13.10)}$$

Similarly,

$$[Q] = [U : -(B_L^{-1} . B_T)^t] \qquad \text{...(13.11)}$$

From equations 13.10 and 13.11, we can write

$$[A] = [A_T][Q] \qquad \text{...(13.12)}$$

$$\therefore \quad [Q] = [A_T^{-1}][A] \qquad \text{...(13.13)}$$

$$= [A_T]^{-1}[A_T : A_L]$$

$$= [U : A_T^{-1}\, A_L] \qquad \text{...(13.14)}$$

We have shown that

$$B_T = -(A_T^{-1} . A_L)^t \quad ...(13.15)$$

$$\therefore \quad B_T^t = -(A_T^{-1} . A_L)$$

From (13.14), then we can write

$$[Q] = [U : - B_T^t]$$

$$\text{or} \quad [Q_L] = [- B_T^t]. \quad ...(13.16)$$

13.12 KIRCHOFF'S VOLTAGE LAW IN TOPOLOGICAL FORM

KVL states that if v_k be the voltage drop across k^{th} branch then $\Sigma v_k = 0$, the sum being taken over all the branches in a given loop.

If '*l*' is the number of loops then there will be '*l*' number of KVL equations, one for each loop. The KVL equation for loop '*h*' can then be written as

$$\sum_{k=1}^{b} b_{hk} \, v_k = 0 \quad (h = 1, 2, ..., l) \quad ...(13.17)$$

where b_{hk} is the elements of the tieset matrix *B*, *b* being the number of branches. In matrix form, the set of '*l*' KVL equations are given by

$$[B][V_b] = 0 \quad ...(13.18)$$

$$\text{where} \quad [V_b] = \begin{bmatrix} v_1 \\ v_2 \\ \vdots \\ v_b \end{bmatrix}$$

V_b is a column vector of branch voltages and $[B]$ is *fundamental circuit matrix* (*f*-loop matrix).

Illustration of KVL in Topological Form

We assume a graph shown in Fig. 13.4(*a*). The graph consists of four nodes and six branches. Let us form a tree of the graph as shown in Fig. 13.4(*b*) [the twigs being given by branches 1, 2 and 3]. The links being branches 4, 5 and 6, we form fundamental loops by adding one link (dotted line) at a time as represented in Figs. 13.4(*c*), (*d*) and (*e*). The orientation of the loops is same as that of the link.

Let us now write the voltage equation for the *f*-loops taking one at a time. We assume voltages $v_1, v_2, ..., v_6$ represent the voltages of the respective branches.

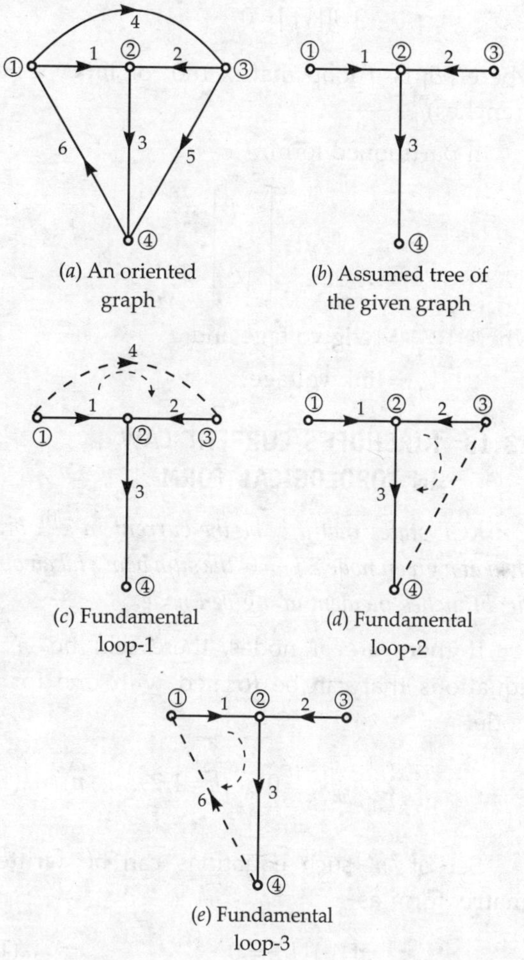
(*a*) An oriented graph (*b*) Assumed tree of the given graph (*c*) Fundamental loop-1 (*d*) Fundamental loop-2 (*e*) Fundamental loop-3

Fig. 13.4 Illustration graph.

$\therefore$ for *f*-loop-1,

$$-v_1 + v_2 + v_4 = 0$$

for *f*-loop-2,

$$-v_2 - v_3 + v_5 = 0$$

for *f*-loop-3,

$$v_1 + v_3 + v_6 = 0$$

[the branch voltage polarity, it coincides with the orientation of the *f*-loop, is taken as positive]

$\therefore$ In matrix form we can write

$$\begin{bmatrix} -1 & +1 & 0 & +1 & 0 & 0 \\ 0 & -1 & -1 & 0 & +1 & 0 \\ +1 & 0 & +1 & 0 & 0 & +1 \end{bmatrix} \begin{bmatrix} v_1 \\ v_2 \\ v_3 \\ v_4 \\ v_5 \\ v_6 \end{bmatrix} = \begin{bmatrix} 0 \\ 0 \\ 0 \end{bmatrix}$$

i.e., $[B][V_b]=0$

where $[B]$ is f-loop matrix (no. of links × no. of branches).

In partitioned form,

$$[V_b]=\begin{bmatrix} V_T \\ \vdots \\ V_L \end{bmatrix},$$

where V_T = twig voltage and

V_L = link voltage.

13.13 KIRCHOFF'S CURRENT LAW IN TOPOLOGICAL FORM

KCL states that if i_k be the current in k^{th} branch, then at a given node $\Sigma\, i_k = 0$, the sum being taken over all the branches incident at a given node.

If there are 'n' nodes, there will be 'n' such equations that can be formed with one for each node.

$$\therefore \quad \sum_{k=1}^{b} a_{hk}\, i_k = 0 \quad (h = 1, 2, \ldots\ldots, n) \quad \ldots(13.19)$$

Set of 'n' such equations can be written in matrix form as

$$[A_i][I_b]=0 \quad \ldots(13.20)$$

where $$[I_b]=\begin{bmatrix} i_1 \\ i_2 \\ \vdots \\ i_b \end{bmatrix}$$

I_b is a column vector of branch currents and $[A_i]$ is the complete incidence matrix.

If one node is taken as reference node (or datum node), we can rewrite the above equation as,

$$[A][I_b]=0 \quad \ldots(13.21)$$

where $[A]$ is the incidence matrix of order $[(n-1)\times b]$.

Illustration of KCL in Topological Form

Let us take an example of the graph shown in Fig. 13.4(*a*). We redraw the graph highlighting the branch currents assuming directed as that of the graph [see Fig. 13.5]. We assume node-4 to be the datum node as we assume in nodal analysis.

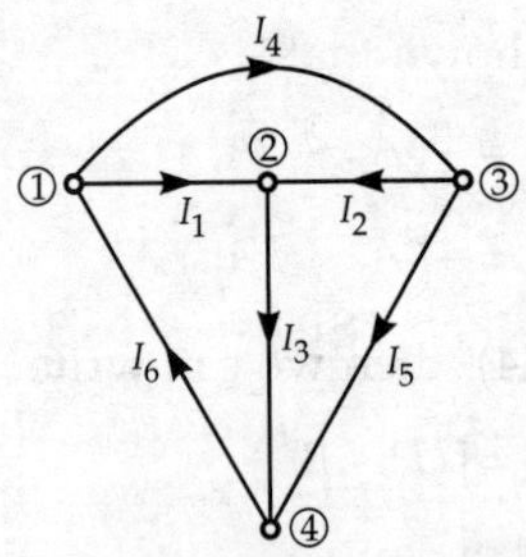

Fig. 13.5 Branch currents in the given graph.

∴ At node-1,

$$I_1 + I_4 - I_6 = 0$$

At node-2

$$-I_1 - I_2 + I_3 = 0$$

At node-3,

$$I_2 - I_4 + I_5 = 0$$

In matrix form we now can write

$$\begin{bmatrix} +1 & 0 & 0 & +1 & 0 & -1 \\ -1 & -1 & +1 & 0 & 0 & 0 \\ 0 & +1 & 0 & -1 & +1 & 0 \end{bmatrix}\begin{bmatrix} I_1 \\ I_2 \\ I_3 \\ I_4 \\ I_5 \\ I_6 \end{bmatrix}=\begin{bmatrix} 0 \\ 0 \\ 0 \end{bmatrix}$$

i.e., $[A][I_b]=0$

where $[A]$ is the incidence matrix of order [(no. of nodes − 1) × no. of branches].

Also from equation (13.12),

$$[A]=[A_T][Q]$$

Thus from above

$$[A_T][Q][I_b]=0 \quad \ldots(13.22)$$

Premultiplying with A_T^{-1}, we get

$$[A_T^{-1}][A_T][Q][I_b]=[A_T^{-1}].0$$

or $[I][Q][I_b]=0$

i.e., $[Q][I_b]=0 \quad \ldots(13.22a)$

where Q is fundamental cutset matrix.

We thus see that KCL is also applicable to a cut set of a network. KCL may be stated as follows for a cut set :

The algebraic sum of all the cut set branch currents in a lumped passive linear network is equal to zero.

Let us again take the graph of Fig. 13.4(*a*) for illustration. We assume that if the branch currents are directed in the same direction as that of the orientation of the cut set, they are positive currents and if these branch currents are directed in the opposite direction of the orientation of the cut set, they are negative. Since we would like to explain the physical form of equation (13.22*a*) we draw the fundamental cut set of the graph shown in Fig. 13.4(*a*) and with tree as shown in Fig. 13.4(*b*). The *f*-cutset is shown in Fig. 13.6.

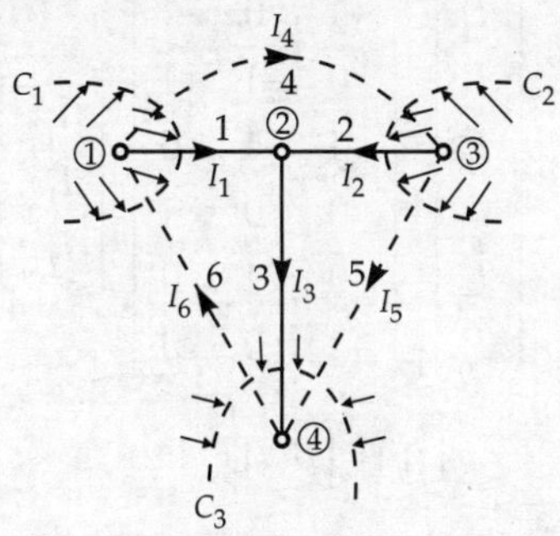

Fig. 13.6 Cut-sets.

Cut-sets are numbered as follows :

$C_1 = \{1, 4, 6\}$ where 1 is the twig.

$C_2 = \{2, 4, 5\}$ where 2 is the twig.

$C_3 = \{3, 5, 6\}$ where 3 is the twig.

We can also write,

for node-1, $\quad I_1 + I_4 - I_6 = 0$

for node-3, $\quad I_2 + I_5 - I_4 = 0$

and for node-4, $\quad -I_3 - I_5 + I_6 = 0$

In matrix form, we can write

$$\begin{bmatrix} +1 & 0 & 0 & +1 & 0 & -1 \\ 0 & +1 & 0 & -1 & +1 & 0 \\ 0 & 0 & -1 & 0 & -1 & +1 \end{bmatrix} \begin{bmatrix} I_1 \\ I_2 \\ I_3 \\ I_4 \\ I_5 \\ I_6 \end{bmatrix} = \begin{bmatrix} 0 \\ 0 \\ 0 \end{bmatrix}$$

i.e., $\quad [Q][I_b] = 0$

where $[Q]$ is *f*-cutset matrix and is given by

	1	2	3	4	5	6
C_1	+1	0	0	+1	0	−1
C_2	0	+1	0	−1	+1	0
C_3	0	0	−1	0	−1	+1

13.14 RELATION BETWEEN BRANCH VOLTAGE MATRIX $[V_b]$, TWIG VOLTAGE MATRIX $[V_T]$ & NODE VOLTAGE MATRIX $[V_n]$

We know that (eqn. 13.18)

$$[B][V_b] = 0$$

$$\therefore \quad [B_T : B_L] \begin{bmatrix} V_T \\ \cdots\cdots \\ V_L \end{bmatrix} = 0 \qquad \text{(Using eqn. 13.5}b\text{)}$$

$$\therefore \quad B_T V_T + B_L V_L = 0$$

or, $$B_L V_L = -B_T V_T$$

Pre-multiplying with B_L^{-1}, we can write

$$V_L = -B_L^{-1} B_T V_T$$

$$= -(B_L^{-1} B_T) V_T \qquad \text{...(13.23)}$$

$$\text{Now } [V_b] = \begin{bmatrix} V_T \\ \cdots\cdots \\ V_L \end{bmatrix}$$

$$= \begin{bmatrix} V_T \\ \cdots\cdots\cdots\cdots \\ -(B_L^{-1} B_T) V_T \end{bmatrix}$$

$$= \begin{bmatrix} U \\ \cdots\cdots\cdots\cdots \\ -(B_L^{-1} B_T) \end{bmatrix} . V_T$$

or, $$[V_b] = [Q^t][V_T] \qquad \text{...(13.24)}$$

Also $$[Q] = [A_t^{-1}][A]$$

$$\therefore \quad [Q^t] = [A^t][(A_T^{-1})^t]$$

$$= [A^t][(A_T^t)^{-1}] \qquad \text{...(13.25)}$$

Hence equation (13.24) can be written as,

$$[V_b] = [A^t][(A_T^t)^{-1}][V_T]$$

$$= [A^t][(A_T^t)^{-1}][V_T]$$

$$= [A^t][V_n] \qquad \text{...(13.26)}$$

where $[V_n]$ is node voltage matrix.

Also, $$[V_b] = [Q^t][V_T] \qquad \text{...(13.26}a\text{)}$$

or, $$[V_b] = [A^t][V_n]$$

$$= [A^t][(A_T^t)^{-1}][V_T] = [Q^t][V_T]$$

CHAPTER 13

13.15 RELATION BETWEEN BRANCH CURRENT MATRIX $[I_b]$ AND LOOP CURRENT MATRIX $[I_L]$

Since $[A]\,[I_b]=0$ (equation 13.21)

$$\therefore\quad [A_T : A_L]\begin{bmatrix} I_T \\ \cdots\cdots \\ I_L \end{bmatrix}=0$$

$$\therefore\quad A_T\, I_T + A_L\, I_L = 0$$

i.e., $$A_T I_T = -A_L\, I_L \qquad \text{...(13.27)}$$

Pre-multiplying with A_t^{-1}.

$$I_T = -A_T^{-1}\, A_L\, I_L$$

$$= -(A_T^{-1}\, A_L)\, I_L \qquad \text{...(13.28)}$$

$$\text{Now}\quad [I_b]=\begin{bmatrix} I_T \\ \cdots\cdots\cdots \\ I_L \end{bmatrix}$$

$$=\begin{bmatrix} -(A_T^{-1}\, A_L)\, I_L \\ \cdots\cdots\cdots\cdots\cdots\cdots\cdots \\ I_L \end{bmatrix}$$

$$=\begin{bmatrix} -(A_T^{-1}\, A_L) \\ \cdots\cdots\cdots\cdots\cdots \\ U \end{bmatrix} . I_L$$

$$[I_b]=[B^t][I_L] \qquad \text{...(13.29)}$$

An Illustration

Let us redraw the oriented graph of Fig. 13.4(*a*) comprising of twigs and links (see Fig. 13.7). We assume the branch current to be positive if directed along the orientation of the corresponding loop current (the loop current orientation being identical to the orientation of the link).

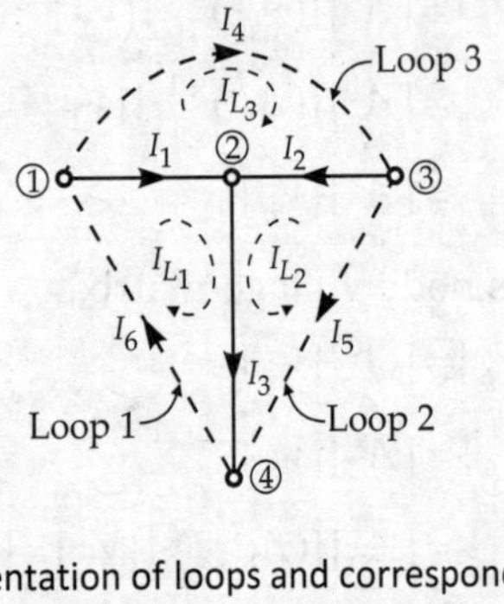

Fig. 13.7 Orientation of loops and corresponding currents.

We observe,

$$I_1 = I_{L_1} - I_{L_3}$$
$$I_2 = -I_{L_2} + I_{L_3}$$
$$I_3 = I_{L_1} - I_{L_2}$$
$$I_4 = I_{L_3}$$
$$I_5 = I_{L_2}$$
$$I_6 = I_{L_1}$$

In matrix form we can write

$$\begin{bmatrix} I_1 \\ I_2 \\ I_3 \\ I_4 \\ I_5 \\ I_6 \end{bmatrix} = \begin{bmatrix} +1 & 0 & -1 \\ 0 & -1 & +1 \\ +1 & -1 & 0 \\ 0 & 0 & +1 \\ 0 & +1 & 0 \\ +1 & 0 & 0 \end{bmatrix} \begin{bmatrix} I_{L_1} \\ I_{L_2} \\ I_{L_3} \end{bmatrix} \qquad \text{...}(a)$$

i.e., $$[I_b]=[B^t][I_L]$$

where $[B^t]$ is the transpose of the *f*-tie set matrix.

The fundamental tie set matrix (*B*) being given by

f-tie sets	*Branches* 1	2	3	4	5	6
I_{L_1}	+1	0	+1	0	0	+1
I_{L_2}	0	−1	−1	0	+1	0
I_{L_3}	−1	+1	0	+1	0	0

It is thus observed that taking transpose of $[B]$ we obtain $[B^t]$ given in equation (*a*) above.

13.16 NETWORK EQUILIBRIUM EQUATIONS

KVL Equation

Assuming a voltage source v_{sk} in branch k having impedance z_k and carrying current i_k, we can write from Fig. 13.8,

$$v_k = z_k\, i_k + v_{sk} \qquad (k = 1, 2, \ldots\ldots, b)$$

In matrix form, we then write

$$[V_b]=[Z_b][I_b]+[V_s] \qquad \text{...(13.30)}$$

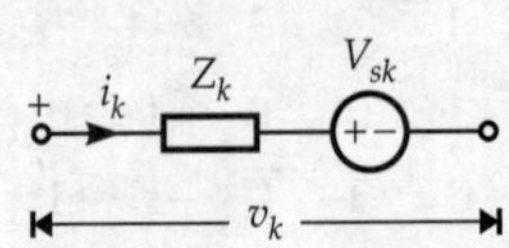

Fig. 13.8 A voltage source in series with an impedance.

where $[Z_b]$ is the branch impedance matrix, $[I_b]$ is column vector of branch currents and $[V_s]$ is column vector of source voltages. Since KVL equation can be written as

$$[B][V_b]=0,$$

we can write $[B]([Z_b][I_b]+[V_s])=0$

or,
$$[B][Z_b][I_b]=-[B][V_s] \quad ...(13.31)$$

Also $[I_b]=[B^t][I_L]$ (equation 13.29)

$$\therefore\ [B][Z_b][B^t][I_L]=-[B][V_s] \quad ...(13.32)$$

or
$$[Z][I_L]=-[E]$$

where
$$[E]=[B][V_s]$$

and
$$[Z]=[B][Z_b][B^t] \quad ...(13.32a)$$

The matrix $[Z]$ is called *loop impedance matrix* and $[Z]=[B][Z_b][B^t]$

If there be a voltage source in series with an impedance and a current source in parallel with the combination (as shown in Fig. 13.9), we can write,

$$i_k=\frac{(v_k-v_{sk})}{z_k}+i_{sk}$$

$$\therefore\quad v_k=z_k i_k-z_k i_{sk}+v_{sk}$$

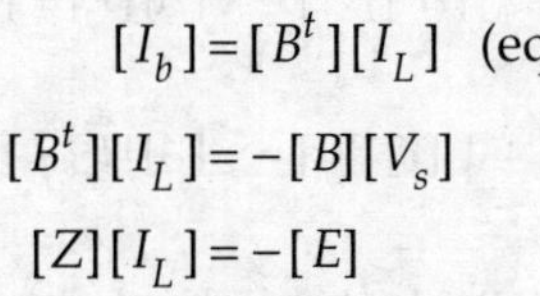

Fig. 13.9 Voltage source in series with impedance and in parallel to current source.

In matrix form, we can write,

$$[V_b]=[Z_b][I_b]-[Z_b][I_s]+[V_s] \quad ...(13.33)$$

or
$$[B][V_b]=[B][([Z_b][I_b]-[Z_b][I_s]+[V_s])] \quad ...(13.33(a))$$

$$\therefore\quad [B][Z_b][I_b]=-[B][V_s]+[B][Z_b][I_s]$$

[Since $[B][V_b]=0$]

But $[I_b]=[B^t][I_L]$

$$\therefore\quad [B][Z_b][B^t][I_L]=-[B][V_s]+[B][Z_b][I_s]$$

$$\therefore\quad [Z][I_L]=-[B][V_s]+[B][Z_b][I_s] \quad ...(13.34)$$

where $[Z]=[B][Z_b][B^t]$
and is called *loop impedance matrix*.

Branch Impedance Matrix (Z_b)

It is a matrix of the order (no. of branches × no. of branches), having branch impedances as diagonal elements and the mutual impedances between the branches as off-diagonal elements. It may be noted here that for a network where there is no transformer or any mutual coupling between branches, the off diagonal elements of (Z_b) would be zero ; only diagonal elements would be present. We can express the general form of (Z_b) as follows :

$$[Z_b]=\begin{bmatrix} Z_{11} & Z_{12} & Z_{13} & \cdots\cdots & Z_{1n} \\ Z_{21} & Z_{22} & Z_{23} & \cdots\cdots & Z_{2n} \\ \vdots & \vdots & \vdots & \cdots\cdots & \vdots \\ Z_{n1} & Z_{n2} & Z_{n3} & \cdots\cdots & Z_{nn} \end{bmatrix}$$

where, n represents the number of branches. $Z_{11}, Z_{22}, \ldots\ldots, Z_{nn}$ are all self impedances of branches $1, 2, \ldots\ldots, n$ respectively and are called *diagonal elements*. $Z_{12}, Z_{13}, Z_{23}, \ldots\ldots Z_{nn}$ etc. are all *off diagonal elements* and basically all mutual impedances.

Loop Impedance Matrix (Z_l)

The loop impedance matrix is of the order $(l \times l)$ where l denotes the number of loops. In general form

$$[Z_l]=\begin{bmatrix} Z_{l11} & Z_{l12} & \cdots\cdots & Z_{l1m} \\ Z_{l21} & Z_{l22} & \cdots\cdots & Z_{l2m} \\ \vdots & \vdots & \cdots\cdots & \vdots \\ Z_{lm1} & Z_{lm2} & \cdots\cdots & Z_{lmm} \end{bmatrix}$$

where $Z_{l11}, Z_{l22}, \ldots\ldots, Z_{lmm}$ are the self impedances of loops $1, 2, \ldots\ldots, m$ respectively and are *diagonal elements*. They are the sum of all the impedances of the branches in the respective loops. $Z_{l12}, Z_{l13}, \ldots\ldots, Z_{lm3}$ are the mutual impedances between loop 1 and 2, loop 1 and 3 and so on.

$$[Z_l]=[B][Z_b][B^t]$$

KCL Equation

If the branch k contains an input current source i_{sk} and an admittance y_k (Fig. 13.10), then

$$i_k=y_k\, v_k-i_{sk} \qquad (k=1,2,\ldots\ldots,b)$$

In the matrix form,

$$[I_b]=[Y_b][V_b]-[I_s] \quad ...(13.35)$$

where Y_b is branch admittance matrix.

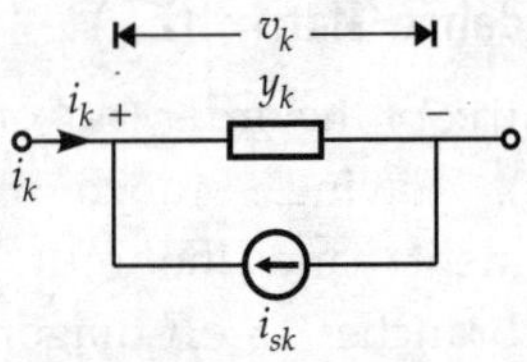

Fig. 13.10 Current source in parallel to an admittance.

KCL equation is given by,

$$[A][I_b]=0$$

or $$[A]([Y_b][V_b]-[I_s])=0$$

$$[A][Y_b][V_b]=[A][I_s] \quad ...(13.35a)$$

Also $$[V_b]=[A^t][V_n]$$

$$\therefore [A][Y_b][A^t][V_n]=[A][I_s] \quad ...(13.36)$$

$$\therefore \quad [Y][V_n]=[I] \quad ...(13.37)$$

where $$[Y]=[A][Y_b][A^t]$$

and $$[I]=[A][I_s]$$

The matrix $[Y]$ is called node admittance matrix. This is the KCL equation in matrix form.

KCL equation can also be written as,

$$[Q][I_b]=0$$

$$[Q]([Y_b][V_b]-[V_s])=0$$

$$[Q][Y_b][V_b]=[Q][I_s]$$

Also $$[V_b]=[Q^t][V_T]$$

$$\therefore [Q][Y_b][Q^t][V_T]=[Q][I_s] \quad ...(13.38)$$

$$\therefore \quad [Y][V_t]=[I] \quad ...(13.39)$$

where $$[Y]=[Q][Y_b][Q^t]$$

and $$[I]=[Q][I_s]$$

This is the KCL equation in matrix form in terms of fundamental cutset matrix.

If there is voltage source in series with an impedance and a current source in parallel with the combination as shown in Fig. 13.11, we can write

$$y_k = \frac{1}{z_k}$$

$$\therefore \quad i_k = y_k\, v_k - y_k\, v_{sk} + i_{sk}$$

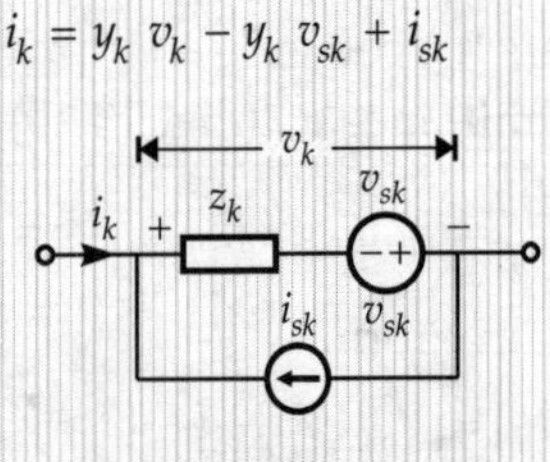

Fig. 13.11 Current source in parallel to admittance and voltage source.

In matrix form,

$$[I_b]=[Y_b][V_b]-[Y_b][V_s]+[I_s] \quad ...(13.40)$$

KCL equation is then given by

$$[A][I_b]=0$$

$$[A]([Y_b][V_b]-[Y_b][V_s]+[I_s])=0$$

$$[A][Y_b][V_b]=-[A][I_s]+[A][Y_b][V_s] \quad ...(13.41)$$

Also $$[V_b]=[A^t][V_n]$$

$$\therefore \quad [A][Y_b][A^t][V_n]=-[A][I_s]+[A][Y_b][V_s] \quad ...(13.42)$$

$$\therefore \quad [Y][V_n]=-[A][I_s]+[A][Y_b][V_s] \quad ...(13.43)$$

where $[Y]=[A][Y_b][A^t]$ is node admittance matrix.

KCL equation can also be written as,

$$[Q][I_b]=0$$

$$[Q]([Y_b][V_b]-[Y_b][V_s]+[I_s])=0$$

$$[Q][Y_b][V_b]=-[Q][I_s]+[Q][Y_b][V_s] \quad ...(13.44)$$

Also $$[V_b]=[Q^t][V_T]$$

$$\therefore \quad [Q][Y_b][Q^t][V_T]=(-[Q][I_s]+[Q][Y_b][V_s]) \quad ...(13.45)$$

$$\therefore \quad [Y][V_T]=-[Q][I_s]+[Q][Y_b][V_s] \quad ...(13.46)$$

This is generalised KCL equation in terms of fundamental cutset matrix.

Branch Admittance Matrix (Y_b)

It is a matrix of the order (no. of branches × no. of branches), containing the branch admittances as *diagonal elements* and mutual admittances (between the branches) as *off diagonal elements*. It may be noted that in the network if there be no transformer or any mutual coupling between the branches, all off diagonal terms are zero in $[Y_b]$. In general form we may write

$$[Y_b]=\begin{bmatrix} y_{11} & y_{12} & \cdots\cdots & y_{1n} \\ y_{21} & y_{22} & \cdots\cdots & y_{2n} \\ \vdots & \vdots & \cdots\cdots & \vdots \\ y_{n1} & y_{n2} & \cdots\cdots & y_{nn} \end{bmatrix}$$

where, $y_{11}, y_{12}, \ldots\ldots, y_{nn}$ represent the self admittances of branches $1, 2, \ldots\ldots, n$ respectively ; n being the number of branches. The off diagonal elements y_{12}, y_{13} ...... etc. represent the mutual admittances between branches 1 and 2, 1 and 3 and so on.

Node Admittance Matrix [Y]

The node admittance matrix [Y] is of the order $[(K-1)\times(K-1)]$ where K is the number of nodes.

In general form we may write

$$[Y]=\begin{bmatrix} y_{aa} & y_{ab} & y_{ac} & y_{ad} & \cdots\cdots & y_{aN} \\ y_{ba} & y_{bb} & y_{bc} & y_{bd} & \cdots\cdots & y_{bN} \\ \vdots & \vdots & \vdots & \vdots & \cdots\cdots & \vdots \\ y_{Na} & y_{Nb} & y_{Nc} & y_{Nd} & \cdots\cdots & y_{NN} \end{bmatrix}$$

Here N is the $(K-1)^{\text{th}}$ node. $y_{aa}, y_{bb}, \ldots, y_{NN}$ are the self admittances of nodes $a, b, \ldots, N$ (*i.e.*, the total admittances of the branches connected to nodes $a, b, \ldots\ldots, N$). Also, $y_{ab}, y_{ac}, \ldots\ldots, y_{Nb}$ are the admittances between nodes a and b, a and c and so on.

Another Illustration showing topological application of KVL

For the network shown in Fig. 13.12 the tieset matrix and network equilibrium equation in matrix form (using KVL) can be written. The loop currents and branch currents can also be calculated.

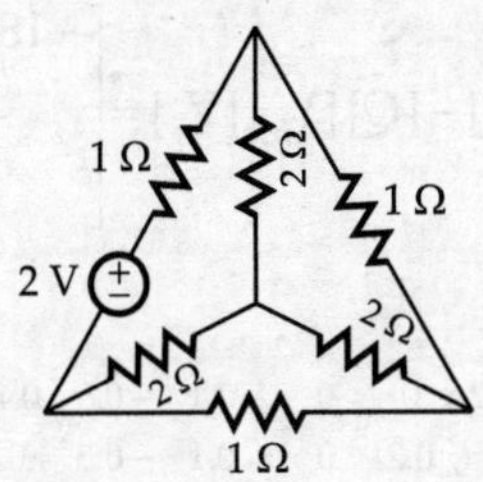

Fig. 13.12 Illustration network.

Figure 13.12(*a*) and (*b*) depict the oriental graph and one selected tree.

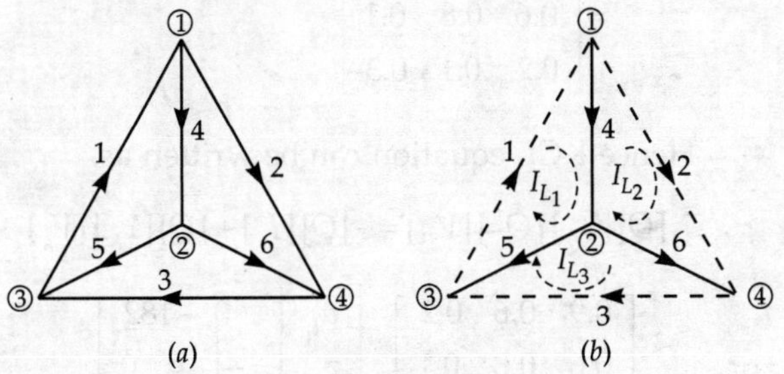

Fig. 13.12

Tieset Matrix **[B]** is obtained as

	1	2	3	4	5	6
1	1	0	0	1	1	0
2	0	1	0	−1	0	−1
3	0	0	1	0	−1	1

$$[B]=\begin{bmatrix} 1 & 0 & 0 & 1 & 1 & 0 \\ 0 & 1 & 0 & -1 & 0 & -1 \\ 0 & 0 & 1 & 0 & -1 & 1 \end{bmatrix}$$

∵ The KVL equation in matrix form is given by,

$$-[B][V_s]=[B][Z_b][B^t][I_L] \quad \text{(equation 13.32)}$$

$$[B][V_s]=\begin{bmatrix} 1 & 0 & 0 & 1 & 1 & 0 \\ 0 & 1 & 0 & -1 & 0 & -1 \\ 0 & 0 & 1 & 0 & -1 & 1 \end{bmatrix}\begin{bmatrix} 2 \\ 0 \\ 0 \\ 0 \\ 0 \\ 0 \end{bmatrix}$$

$$=\begin{bmatrix} 2 \\ 0 \\ 0 \end{bmatrix}$$

$$[B][Z_b]=\begin{bmatrix} 1 & 0 & 0 & 1 & 1 & 0 \\ 0 & 1 & 0 & -1 & 0 & -1 \\ 0 & 0 & 1 & 0 & -1 & 1 \end{bmatrix}\begin{bmatrix} 1 & 0 & 0 & 0 & 0 & 0 \\ 0 & 1 & 0 & 0 & 0 & 0 \\ 0 & 0 & 1 & 0 & 0 & 0 \\ 0 & 0 & 0 & 2 & 0 & 0 \\ 0 & 0 & 0 & 0 & 2 & 0 \\ 0 & 0 & 0 & 0 & 0 & 2 \end{bmatrix}$$

$$=\begin{bmatrix} 1 & 0 & 0 & 2 & 2 & 0 \\ 0 & 1 & 0 & -2 & 0 & -2 \\ 0 & 0 & 1 & 0 & -2 & 2 \end{bmatrix}$$

$$[B][Z_b][B^t]=\begin{bmatrix} 1 & 0 & 0 & 2 & 2 & 0 \\ 0 & 1 & 0 & -2 & 0 & -2 \\ 0 & 0 & 1 & 0 & -2 & 2 \end{bmatrix}\begin{bmatrix} 1 & 0 & 0 \\ 0 & 1 & 0 \\ 0 & 0 & 1 \\ 1 & -1 & 0 \\ 1 & 0 & -1 \\ 0 & -1 & 1 \end{bmatrix}$$

$$=\begin{bmatrix} 5 & -2 & -2 \\ -2 & 5 & -2 \\ -2 & -2 & 5 \end{bmatrix}$$

The KVL equation in matrix form is given by,

$$-\begin{bmatrix} 2 \\ 0 \\ 0 \end{bmatrix}=\begin{bmatrix} -5 & -2 & -2 \\ -2 & 5 & -2 \\ -2 & -2 & 5 \end{bmatrix}\begin{bmatrix} I_{L_1} \\ I_{L_2} \\ I_{L_3} \end{bmatrix}$$

Solution of this matrix equation yields

$$I_{L_1}=-0.568\text{ A};\quad I_{L_2}=-0.67\text{ A};\quad I_{L_3}=-0.67\text{ A}$$

The branch currents are given by,

$$[I_b]=[B^t][I_L] \quad \text{(equation 13.29)}$$

$$\begin{bmatrix} i_1 \\ i_2 \\ i_3 \\ i_4 \\ i_5 \\ i_6 \end{bmatrix}=\begin{bmatrix} 1 & 0 & 0 \\ 0 & 1 & 0 \\ 0 & 0 & 1 \\ 1 & -1 & 0 \\ 1 & 0 & -1 \\ 0 & -1 & 1 \end{bmatrix}\begin{bmatrix} -0.568 \\ -0.67 \\ -0.67 \end{bmatrix}=\begin{bmatrix} -0.568 \\ -0.67 \\ -0.67 \\ +0.102 \\ +0.102 \\ 0 \end{bmatrix}.$$

Another Illustration for topological application of KCL

We are required to find this voltages for the given network (Fig. 13.13).

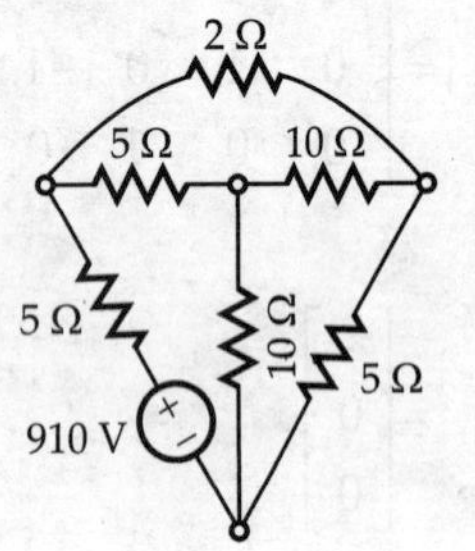

Fig. 13.13 Topological application of KCL.

The oriented graph and one of the tree are shown in Figs. 13.13(*a*) and (*b*).

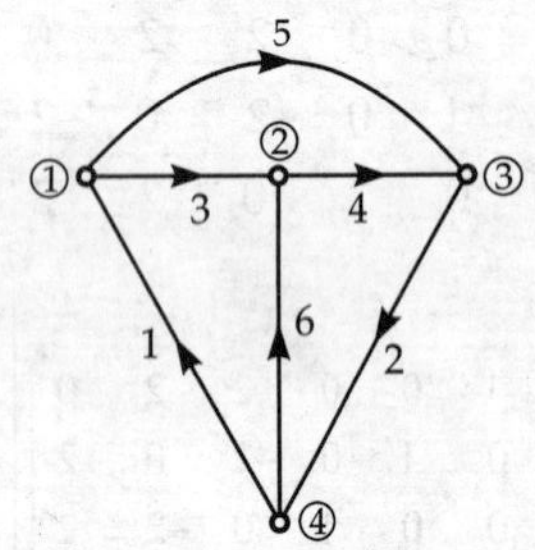

(*a*)

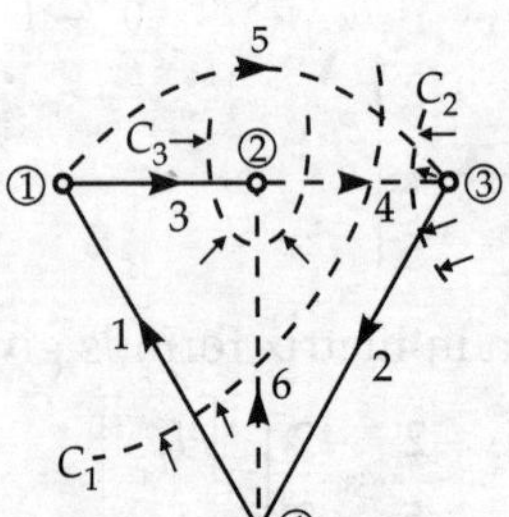

Tieset 1 : [1, 6, 4, 5]
Tieset 2 : [2, 4, 6]
Tieset 3 : [3, 4, 6]

Fig. 13.13 (*b*)

	1	2	3	4	5	6
1	1	0	0	−1	−1	1
2	0	1	0	−1	−1	0
3	0	0	1	−1	0	1

$$[Q] = \begin{bmatrix} 1 & 0 & 0 & -1 & -1 & 1 \\ 0 & 1 & 0 & -1 & -1 & 0 \\ 0 & 0 & 1 & -1 & 0 & 1 \end{bmatrix}$$

The network equilibrium equation can be written as

$$[Q][Y_b][Q^t][V_T] = -[Q][I_s] + [Q][Y_b][V_s] \quad \text{(equation 13.45)}$$

$$[Q][I_s] = \begin{bmatrix} 1 & 0 & 0 & -1 & -1 & 1 \\ 0 & 1 & 0 & -1 & -1 & 0 \\ 0 & 0 & 1 & -1 & 0 & 1 \end{bmatrix} \begin{bmatrix} 0 \\ 0 \\ 0 \\ 0 \\ 0 \\ 0 \end{bmatrix} = \begin{bmatrix} 0 \\ 0 \\ 0 \end{bmatrix}$$

$$[Q][Y_b] = \begin{bmatrix} 1 & 0 & 0 & -1 & -1 & 1 \\ 0 & 1 & 0 & -1 & -1 & 0 \\ 0 & 0 & 1 & -1 & 0 & 1 \end{bmatrix} \begin{bmatrix} 0.2 & 0 & 0 & 0 & 0 & 0 \\ 0 & 0.2 & 0 & 0 & 0 & 0 \\ 0 & 0 & 0.2 & 0 & 0 & 0 \\ 0 & 0 & 0 & 0.1 & 0 & 0 \\ 0 & 0 & 0 & 0 & 0.5 & 0 \\ 0 & 0 & 0 & 0 & 0 & 0.1 \end{bmatrix}$$

$$[Q][Y_b][V_s] = \begin{bmatrix} 0.2 & 0 & 0 & -0.1 & -0.5 & 0.1 \\ 0 & 0.2 & 0 & -0.1 & -0.5 & 0 \\ 0 & 0 & 0.2 & -0.1 & 0 & 0.1 \end{bmatrix} \begin{bmatrix} 910 \\ 0 \\ 0 \\ 0 \\ 0 \\ 0 \end{bmatrix}$$

$$= \begin{bmatrix} 182 \\ 0 \\ 0 \end{bmatrix}$$

$$\therefore \quad [Q][I_s] - [Q][Y_b][V_s] = \begin{bmatrix} -182 \\ 0 \\ 0 \end{bmatrix}$$

$$[Q][Y_b][Q^t] = \begin{bmatrix} 0.2 & 0 & 0 & -0.1 & -0.5 & 0.1 \\ 0 & 0.2 & 0 & -0.1 & -0.5 & 0 \\ 0 & 0 & 0.2 & -0.1 & 0 & 0.1 \end{bmatrix} \begin{bmatrix} 1 & 0 & 0 \\ 0 & 1 & 0 \\ 0 & 0 & 1 \\ -1 & -1 & -1 \\ -1 & -1 & 0 \\ 1 & 0 & 1 \end{bmatrix}$$

$$= \begin{bmatrix} 0.9 & 0.6 & 0.2 \\ 0.6 & 0.8 & 0.1 \\ 0.2 & 0.1 & 0.3 \end{bmatrix}$$

Hence KCL equation can be written as,

$$[Q][Y_b][Q^t][V_T] = -[Q][I_s] + [Q][Y_b][V_s]$$

or,
$$\begin{bmatrix} 0.9 & 0.6 & 0.2 \\ 0.6 & 0.8 & 0.1 \\ 0.2 & 0.1 & 0.3 \end{bmatrix} \begin{bmatrix} v_{t_1} \\ v_{t_2} \\ v_{t_3} \end{bmatrix} = - \begin{bmatrix} -182 \\ 0 \\ 0 \end{bmatrix}$$

Solving this matrix equation, we get

$$V_{T_1} = +460 \text{ V}$$
$$V_{T_2} = -320 \text{ V}$$
$$V_{T_3} = -200 \text{ V.}$$

Twig voltages

13.17 PRINCIPLE OF DUALITY

Circuits where the cutset matrix of one corresponds to Tieset matrix of the other are Duals of each other.

Let us consider the following two circuits shown in Fig. 13.14.

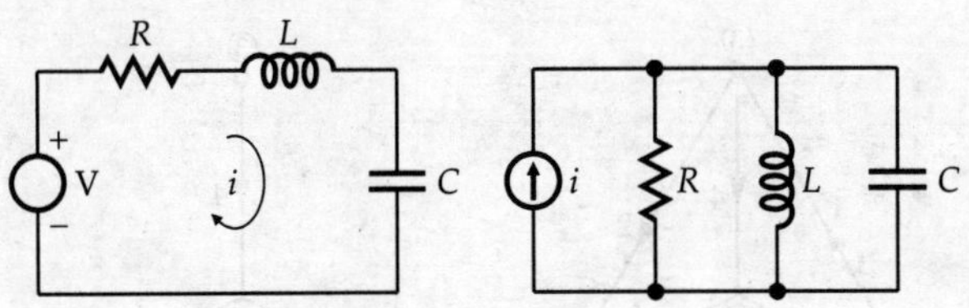

Fig. 13.14 (*a*) (*b*)

By KVL in Fig. 13.14(*a*) we get :

$$V = iR + L.\frac{di}{dt} + \frac{1}{C}.\int_0^t idt. \qquad ...(13.47)$$

By KCL in Fig. 13.14(*b*) we get :

$$i = vG + C.\frac{dv}{dt} + \frac{1}{L}.\int_0^t v\,dt. \qquad ...(13.48)$$

The KVL and KCL of either figures are identical and this illustrates the principle of Duality.

Conversion of Dual Electrical Circuit

Loop Basis	*Node Basis*
1. Current	Voltage
2. Resistance	Conductance
3. Inductance	Capacitance
4. Branch current	Branch Voltage
5. Mesh	Node
6. Short Circuit	Open circuit
7. Parallel Path	Series Path

13.17.1 Construction of a Dual Network

1. Put a dot per mesh loop current *i.e.*, in each mesh of the given network. These interval dots correspond to independent nodes in the dual network.
2. Put one reference dot for reference node outside the circuit.
3. Connect one element from an internal dot to adjoining dot or to the reference taking only one element at a time.
4. Draw the dual between the same two nodes in steps.
5. Magnitude of dual in step 4 will be same. Only the unit will be dual unit (for example 15 Ω will be dual at 15 MHos)
6. Clockwise current cutting at a node will reject as current into the node of the dual.

ADDITIONAL EXAMPLES

EXAMPLE 13.15 *Draw the oriented graph of the network shown in Fig. E13.14 and write the incidence matrix by inspection.*

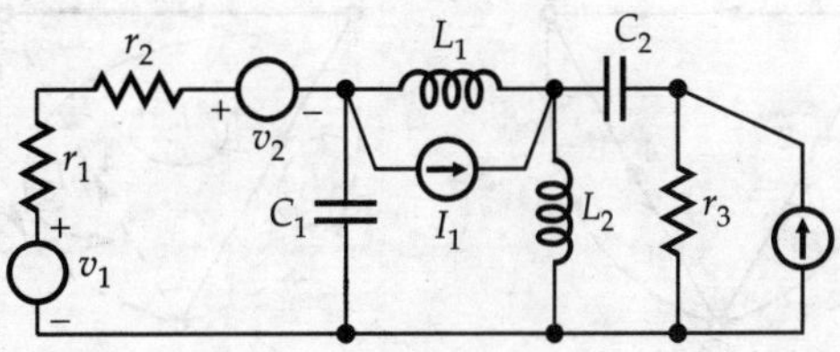

Fig. E13.14

SOLUTION. The oriented graph of the network shown in Fig. E13.14 is drawn in **Fig. E13.14(*a*).** Here nodes are numbered and encircled. Branches are line segments.

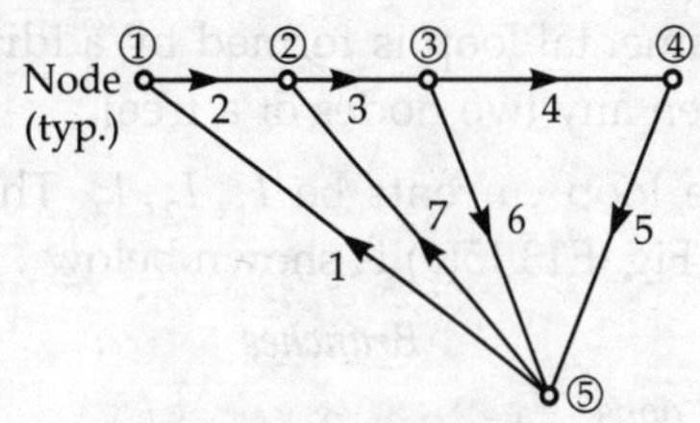

Fig. E13.14 (*a*)

The **incidence matrix** is shown below :

Branches

Nodes	1	2	3	4	5	6	7
(1)	−1	1	0	0	0	0	0
(2)	0	−1	1	0	0	0	−1
(3)	0	0	−1	1	0	1	0
(4)	0	0	0	−1	1	0	0
(5)	1	0	0	0	−1	−1	1

it may be noted that the sum of column entries is zero for each column.

EXAMPLE 13.16 *Develop the graph of the network shown in Fig. E13.15. Obtain the tie-set matrix selecting a tree.*

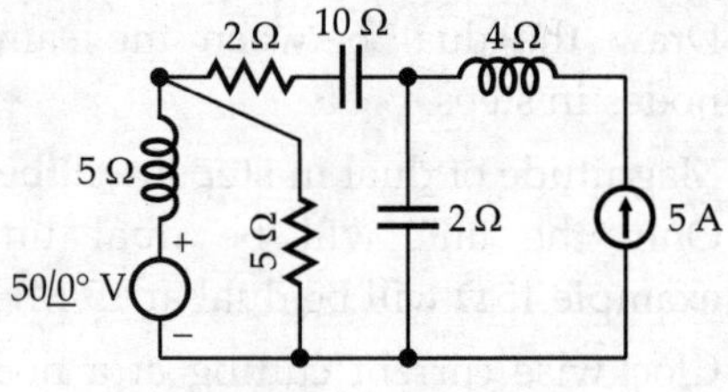

Fig. E13.15

SOLUTION. The graph of the given network is shown in Fig. E13.15(*a*), where nodes are numbered with encircles and branches are denoted by line segments.

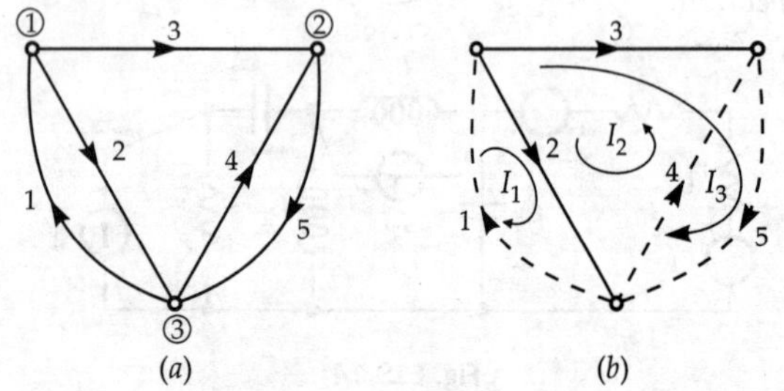

Fig. E13.15

A tree is selected from the graph and is shown by bold lines in Fig. E13.15(*b*). The links are shown dotted. The fundamental loops are 1-2, 2-3-4, 2-3-5.

[Fundamental loop is formed by addition of a link between any two nodes of a tree].

Let the loop currents be I_1, I_2, I_3. The **tie-set matrix** for Fig. E13.15(*b*) is shown below :

Branches

Loops	1	2	3	4	5
I_1	1	1	0	0	0
I_2	0	1	–1	1	0
I_3	0	–1	1	0	1

EXAMPLE 13.17 *Write down the fundamental loop matrix of the network shown in Fig. E13.16.*

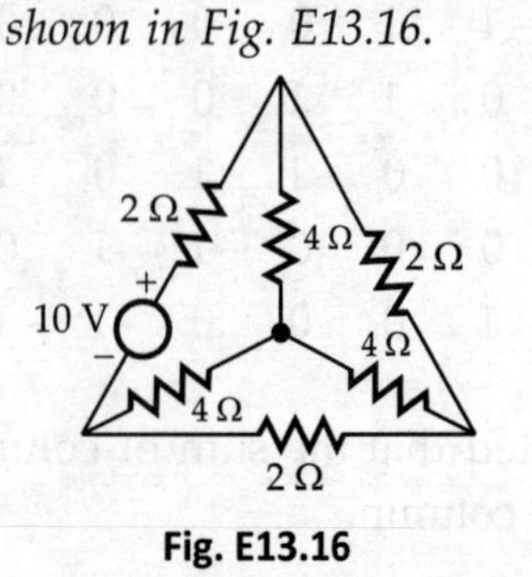

Fig. E13.16

SOLUTION. The oriented graph of the given figure is first drawn [Fig. E13.16(*a*)]. Arbitrarily a fundamental tree is then chosen [Fig. E13.16(*b*)]. The twigs are shown as solid lines and links as dotted lines. Fundamental loops are also marked as arrows associated with markings I_1, I_2, I_3 [Fig. E13.16(*c*)].

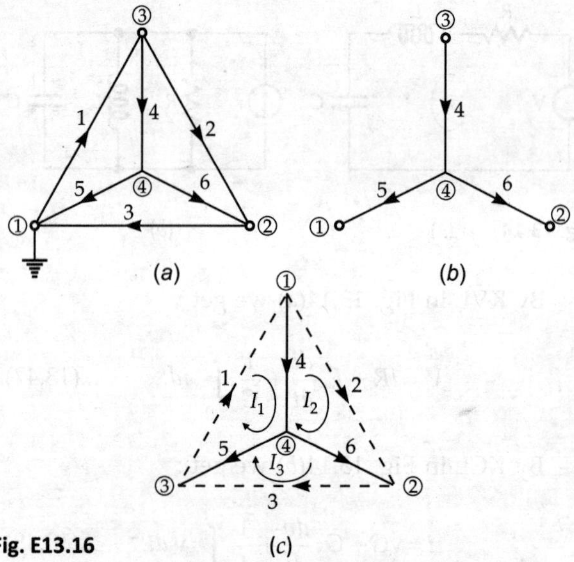

Fig. E13.16

The **fundamental loop matrix** is shown below :

Branches

Fund. loops	1	2	3	4	5	6
(1)	1	0	0	1	1	0
(2)	0	1	0	–1	0	–1
(3)	0	0	1	0	–1	1

If the branch orientation is in the same direction as the loop orientation *i.e.*, if the branch arrow is directed towards the loop arrow, the corresponding matrix element is + 1, if they are oppositely directed, the element is – 1

EXAMPLE 13.18 *Figure E13.17 represents a resistive circuit. Determine the number of branches, number of nodes and number of links. Write down the incidence matrix for the given network. Also develop the network equilibrium equation.*

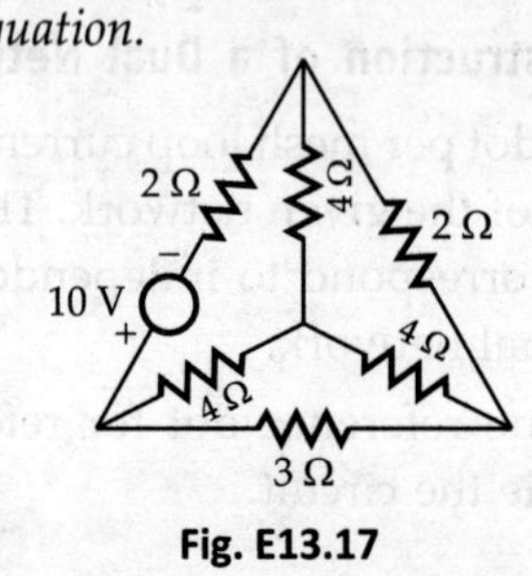

Fig. E13.17

Solution. We have seen earlier that if N represents number of nodes, the number of twigs is $(N-1)$ and if B represents number of branches, number of links (L) is $[B-(N-1)]$.

Thus, from Fig. E13.17,

$$B=6\,;\;\; N=4,$$

$$L=B-(N-1)=6-(4-1)=3.$$

Next, in order to find the incidence matrix, let us draw the oriented graph (Fig. E13.18).

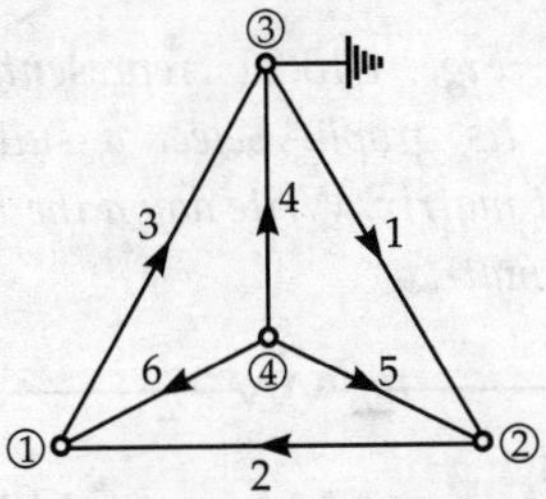

[o→ nodes ; - → branches]

Fig. E13.18

Following the conventions of signs, the **incidence matrix** is drawn below :

Branches

Nodes	1	2	3	4	5	6
(1)	0	−1	1	0	0	−1
(2)	−1	1	0	0	−1	0
(3)	1	0	−1	−1	0	0
(4)	0	0	0	+1	+1	+1

In order to obtain the network equilibrium equation, let v_1 indicates the drop in branch-1, v_2 in branch-2 and like this.

Applying KVL in loop of I_1, $v_1 - v_5 + v_4 = 0$

Applying KVL in loop of I_2, $v_5 + v_2 - v_6 = 0$

Applying KVL in loop of I_3, $v_3 - v_4 + v_6 = 0$.

loop of I_1 is formed by nodes (3), (2) and (4);
loop of I_2 is formed by nodes (2), (1) and (4);
loop of I_3 is formed by nodes (3), (4) and (1).

Assuming the branch currents as $j_1, j_2, j_3 \ldots$ and expressing then in terms of $I_1, I_2, \ldots$

$$j_1 = I_1\,;\; j_2 = I_2\,;\; j_3 = I_3\,;\; j_4 = I_1 - I_3,$$

$$j_5 = I_2 - I_1\,;\; j_6 = I_3 - I_2.$$

However, Ohm's law gives,

$$v_1 = j_1 r_1 = r_1 I_1 = 2I_1$$

$$v_2 = j_2 r_2 = r_2 I_2 = 2I_2$$

$$v_3 = j_3 r_3 - 10 = r_3 I_3 - 10 = 2I_3 - 10$$

$$v_4 = j_4 r_4 = (I_1 - I_3) r_4 = (I_1 - I_3)4$$

$$v_5 = j_5 r_5 = (I_2 - I_1) r_5 = (I_2 - I_1)4$$

$$v_6 = j_6 r_6 = (I_3 - I_2) r_6 = (I_3 - I_2)4.$$

Substituting the values of $v_1, v_2 \ldots$ in KVL equation,

$$2I_1 - (I_2 - I_1)4 + (I_1 - I_3)4 = 0$$

or, $$2I_1 - 4I_2 - 4I_3 = 0 \quad \ldots(1)$$

$$(I_2 - I_1)4 + 2I_2 - (I_3 - I_2)4 = 0$$

or, $$4I_1 - I_2 + 4I_3 = 0 \quad \ldots(2)$$

$$2I_3 - 10 - (I_1 - I_3)4 + (I_3 - I_2)4 = 0$$

or, $$4I_1 - 4I_2 + 2I_3 = 10 \quad \ldots(3)$$

Network equilibrium equations in matrix form,

$$\begin{bmatrix} 2 & -4 & -4 \\ 4 & -1 & 4 \\ 4 & -4 & 2 \end{bmatrix} \begin{bmatrix} I_1 \\ I_2 \\ I_3 \end{bmatrix} = \begin{bmatrix} 0 \\ 0 \\ 10 \end{bmatrix}.$$

Example 13.19 *Draw the oriented graph of the given coupled circuit network (Fig. E13.19) and develop the tie-set matrix.*

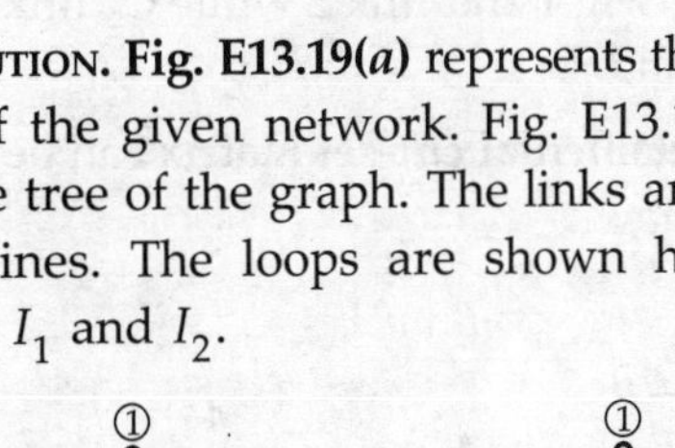

Fig. E13.19

Solution. Fig. E13.19(*a*) represents the necessary graph of the given network. Fig. E13.19(*b*) represents the tree of the graph. The links are drawn as dotted lines. The loops are shown having loop currents I_1 and I_2.

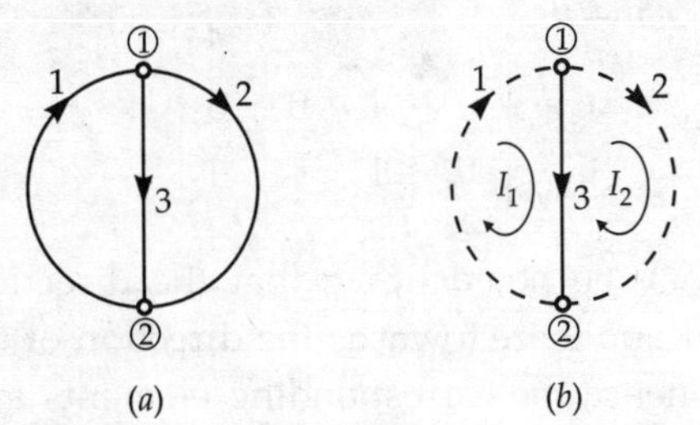

(*a*) (*b*)

Fig. E13.19

C H A P T E R 13

The **tie-set matrix** is shown below :

$$\begin{array}{c} \\ \text{Loops} \\ I_1 \\ I_2 \end{array} \begin{array}{c} \textit{Branches} \\ \begin{matrix} 1 & 2 & 3 \end{matrix} \\ \begin{bmatrix} 1 & 0 & 1 \\ 0 & 1 & -1 \end{bmatrix} \end{array}$$

EXAMPLE 13.20 *Develop the fundamental cut-set matrix of the network shown in Fig. E13.20.*

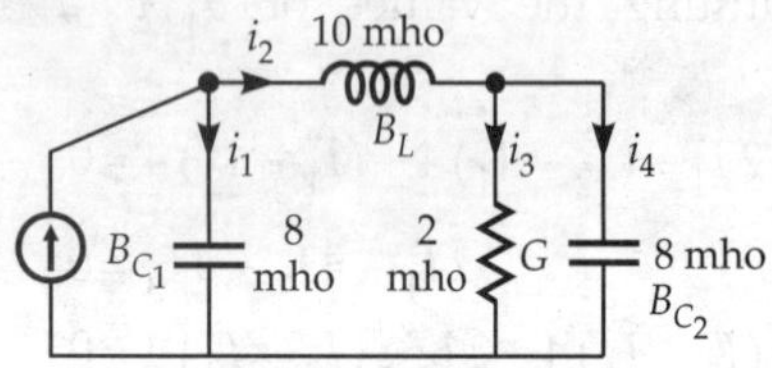

Fig. E13.20

SOLUTION. Fig. E13.20(*a*) represents the graph of the network where nodes are encircled and branches are numbered.

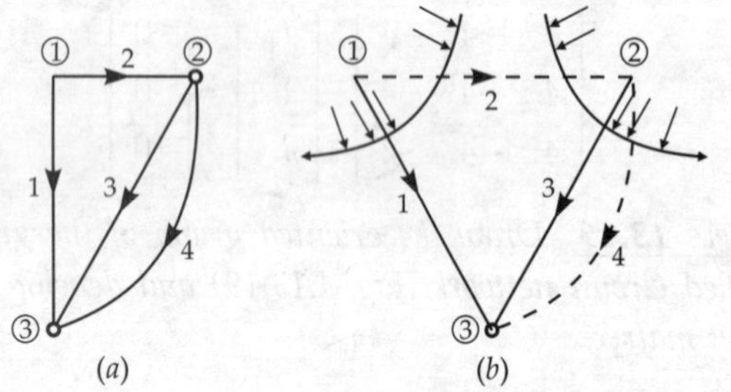

Fig. E13.20

Figure E13.20(*b*) shows the tree and link, where the twigs are bold lines but links are dotted lines. The cut-sets C_1 and C_2 are shown also in the same figure.

C_1 links twig 1 and link 2 while C_2 links twig 3 and links 2 and 4.

The **fundamental cut-set matrix** can be formed as shown below :

$$\begin{array}{c} \\ \text{Cut-sets} \\ C_1 \\ C_2 \end{array} \begin{array}{c} \textit{Branches} \\ \begin{matrix} 1 & 2 & 3 & 4 \end{matrix} \\ \begin{bmatrix} 1 & 1 & 0 & 0 \\ 0 & -1 & 1 & 1 \end{bmatrix} \end{array}$$

It may be noted down that the directions of branch 1 and 2 are towards the direction of cut-set C_1 and hence the corresponding elements are +ve while for branch 2 the direction is opposite to the direction of C_2 making the element – ve. However directions of branch 3 and 4 with respect to cut-set C_2 are same to that of C_2 and hence the corresponding elements are +ve.

It may also be noted that for fundamental cut-set matrix formation, cut-sets are done in such a way so that only and only one twig with link(s) are concerned. *Thus cut-sets at node (1) and (2) are fundamental cut-sets while cut-set at node (3) cannot be defined as fundamental as that would involve two twigs.*

EXAMPLE 13.21 *Fig. E13.21 represents a resistive network. Draw its graph. Select a suitable tree and obtain the tie-set matrix. Write down the KVL equations from the tie-set matrix.*

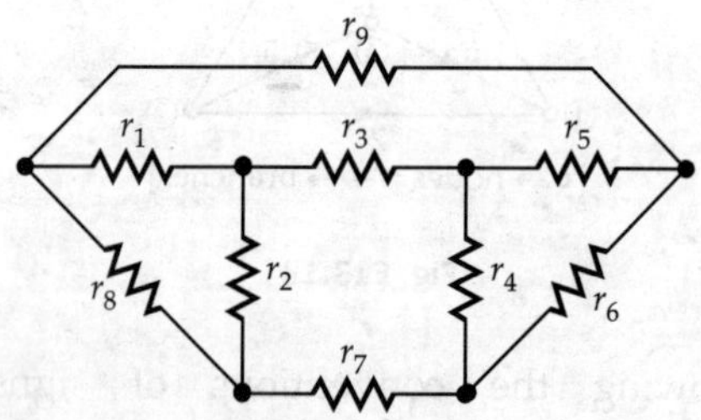

Fig. E13.21

SOLUTION. The graph of the given resistive network is shown in **Fig. E13.21(*a*).** The graph is oriented arbitrarily and nodes are encircled while line segments are marked as branches.

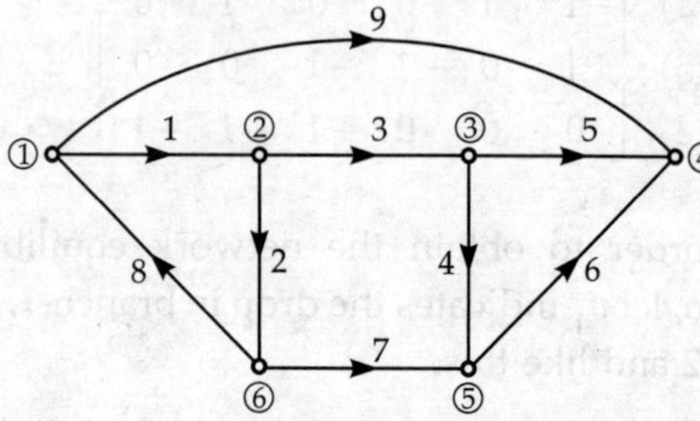

Fig. E13.21 (*a*)

The tree is arbitrarily selected using bold lines for the twigs. The links are marked by dotted lines while the loops are marked by I_1, I_2,...... [Fig. E13.21(*b*)].

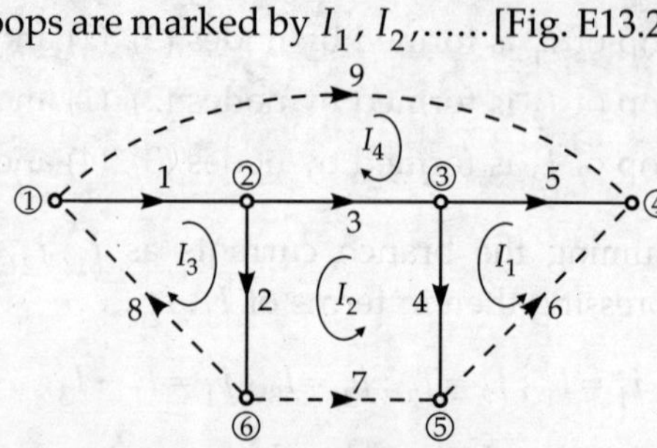

Fig. E13.21 (*b*)

The *tie-set matrix* is shown below :

Loop Current	*Branches* 1	2	3	4	5	6	7	8	9
I_1	0	0	0	+1	−1	+1	0	0	0
I_2	0	+1	−1	−1	0	0	+1	0	0
I_3	+1	+1	0	0	0	0	0	+1	0
I_4	−1	0	−1	0	−1	0	0	0	+1

The **KVL equations** are as follows :

$$\left.\begin{aligned} v_4 - v_5 + v_6 &= 0 \\ v_2 - v_3 - v_4 + v_7 &= 0 \\ -v_1 - v_3 - v_5 + v_9 &= 0 \end{aligned}\right\}$$

where $v_1, v_2, \ldots, v_9$ are corresponding branch voltages.

Example 13.22 *For the network shown in Fig. E13.22, draw (i) the graph (oriented), (ii) Select a tree, (iii) Obtain the cut-set matrix.*

Also find the number of twigs and links.

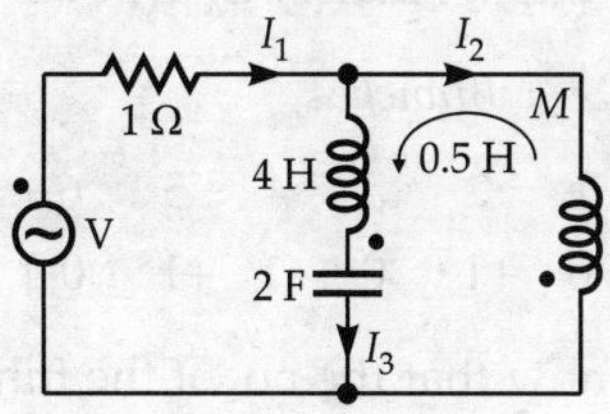

Fig. E13.22

Solution. (*i*) The graph of the network is shown in **Fig. E13.22(*a*)**. The nodes and branches are also shown.

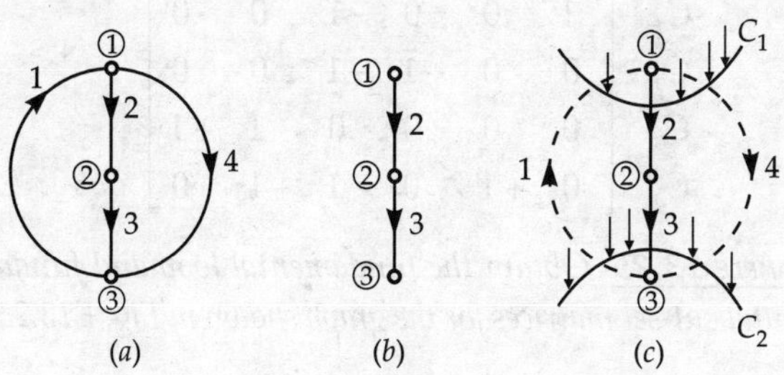

Fig. E13.22

(*ii*) The tree (arbitrarily selected) is shown in **Fig. E13.22(*b*)**.

(*iii*) To obtain the cut-set matrix, the links are used to form complete graph [Fig. E13.22(*c*)].

The **fundamental cut-set matrix** is shown below :

Cut-set	*Branches* 1	2	3	4
C_1	−1	+1	0	+1
C_2	−1	0	+1	+1

[Two cut-sets are formed by taking one twig for each of the cut-sets]

(*iv*) No. of branches $(B) = 4$

No. of Nodes $(N) = 3$

$\therefore$ No. of Twigs $= N - 1 = \mathbf{2}$

and No. of links $(l) = B - (N-1) = 4 - 2 = 2.$

Example 13.23 *Draw the oriented graph of a network with fundamental cutset matrix as shown below :*

Twigs 1	2	3	4	Links 5	6	7
1	0	0	0	−1	0	0
0	1	0	0	1	0	1
0	0	1	0	0	1	1
0	0	0	1	0	1	0

Solution.

No. of links $\quad L = B - N + 1$

$\therefore$ No. of nodes $\quad N = B - L + 1$

$= 7 - 3 + 1 = 5$

fundamental cutsets are written as,

$C_1 : \{1, 5\}$

$C_2 : \{2, 5, 7\}$

$C_3 : \{3, 6, 7\}$

$C_4 : \{4, 6\}$

Then oriented graph is then drawn as shown below **(Fig. E12.23)** :

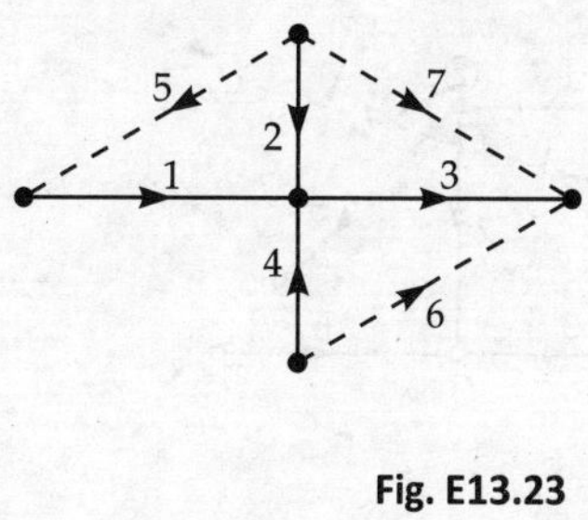

Twigs : {1, 2, 3, 4} ;
Links : {5, 6, 7}

Fig. E13.23

EXAMPLE 13.24 *Show the cut-sets for the graph of the network shown in Fig. E13.24 and develop the fundamental cut-set matrix.*

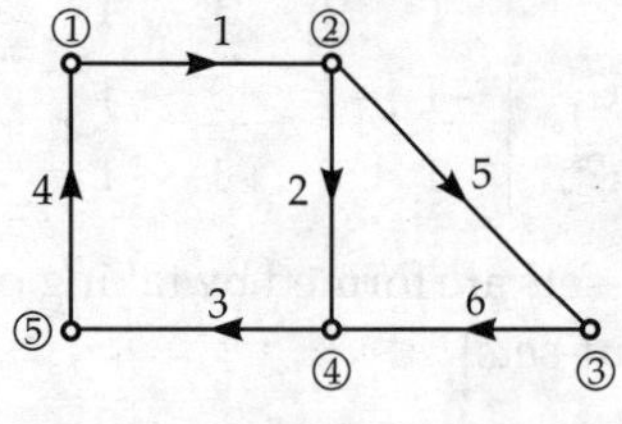

Fig. E13.24

SOLUTION. The cut-sets are shown in Figs. E13.24(*a*) to (*d*) with individual cut-set row. Tree is assumed to be formed by branch 1-2-3-6.

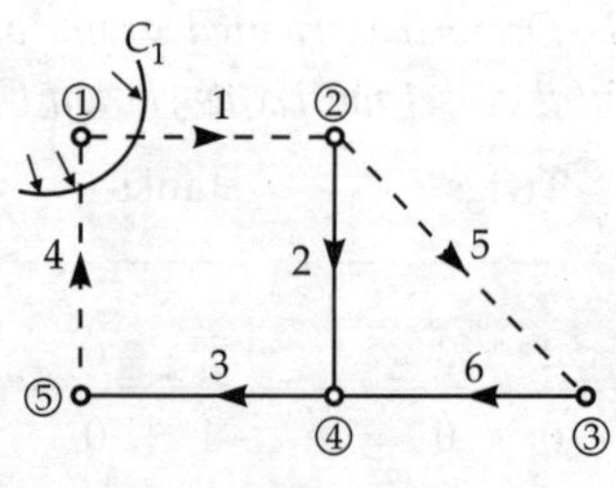

(*a*)

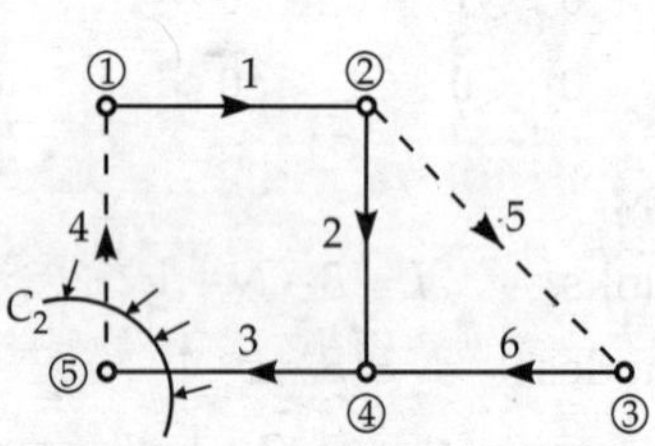

(*b*)

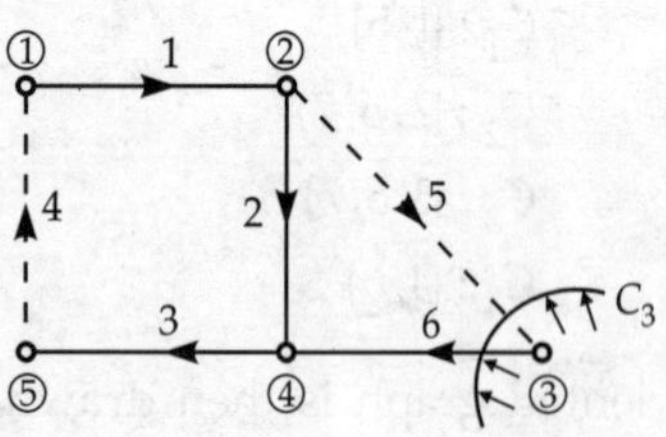

(*c*)

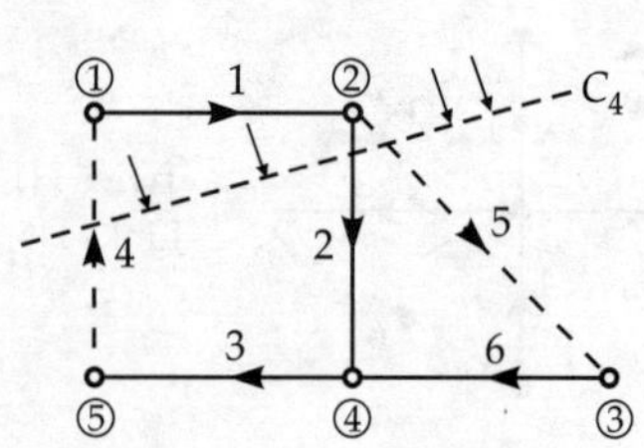

Fig. E13.24 (*d*)

C_1 is formed linking twig 1 and link 4 [Fig. E13.24(*a*)]. The cut set matrix for C_1 will be

Cut-set	*Branches* 1	2	3	4	5	6
C_1	1	0	0	–1	0	0

C_2 formed linking twig 3 and link 4 [Fig. E13.24(*b*)]. The cut set matrix for C_2 would be

Cut-set	*Branches* 1	2	3	4	5	6
C_2	0	0	1	–1	0	0

C_3 is formed linking twig 6 and link 5 [Fig. E13.24(*c*)]. The cut-set matrix C_3 would be then

Cut-set	*Branches* 1	2	3	4	5	6
C_3	0	0	0	0	–1	1

C_4 is formed with twig 2 and links 4 and 5 [Fig. E13.24(*d*)]. The cut-set matrix C_4 will be

Cut-set	*Branches* 1	2	3	4	5	6
C_4	0	+1	0	–1	+1	0

Since we know that the no. of the fundamental cut-sets must be equal to no. of nodes minus one hence here, we could obtain the four cut-sets and the **cut-set matrix** is shown below :

Cut-sets	*Branches* 1	2	3	4	5	6
C_1	1	0	0	–1	0	0
C_2	0	0	+1	–1	0	0
C_3	0	0	0	0	–1	+1
C_4	0	+1	0	–1	+1	0

EXAMPLE 13.25 *Obtain the fundamental loop and fundamental cut-set matrices for the graph shown in Fig. E13.25.*

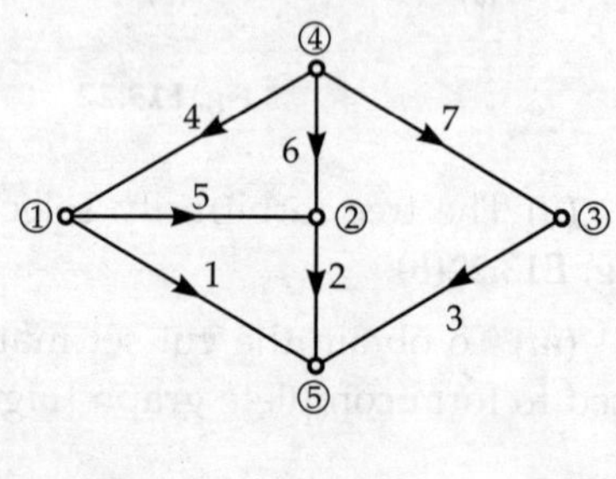

Fig. E13.25

Solution. The tree is arbitrarily selected [Fig. E13.25(*a*)] with branches 4-1-2-3. Thus the twigs are these branches (bold lines) while the links are dotted lines.

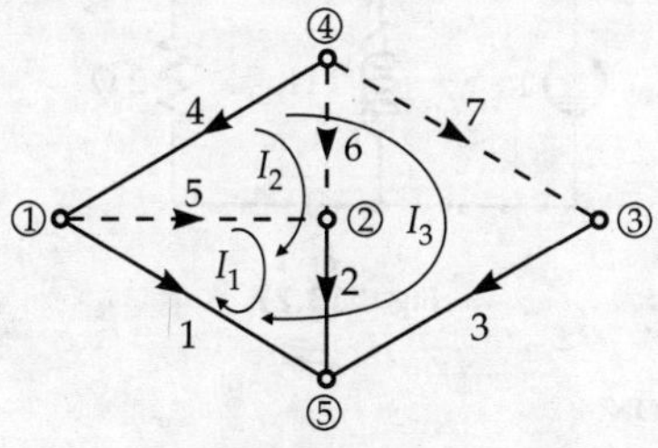

Fig. E13.25 (*a*)

Tie-set-1 (loop current I_1)—

formed by twigs 1 and 2 with link 5.

Tie-set-2 (loop current I_2)—

formed by twigs 1, 2 and 4 with link 6.

Tie-set-3 (loop current I_3)—

formed by twigs 3, 1, 4 and link 7.

[*each loop contains one link only in fundamental tie-set matrix*]

The **tie-set matrix** is shown below :

Loop currents	*Branches* 1	2	3	4	5	6	7
I_1	−1	+1	0	0	+1	0	0
I_2	−1	+1	0	−1	0	1	0
I_3	−1	0	1	−1	0	0	1

To obtain the cut-set matrix, the graph is redrawn with twigs in bold and links in dotted line [Fig. E13.25(*b*)].

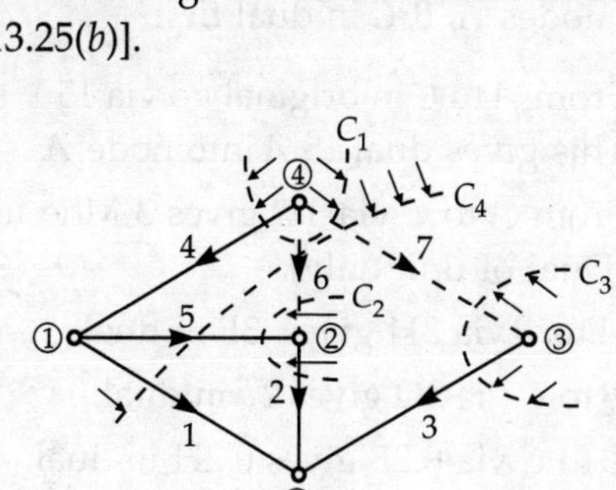

Fig. E13.25 (*b*)

Cut-sets are formed taking one twig at a time.

C_1, *Cut-set-1*. Twig 4, links 6 and 7

C_2, *Cut-set-2*. Twig 2, links 5 and 6

C_3, *Cut-set-3*. Twig 3, links 7

C_4, *Cut-set-16*. Twig 1, links 5, 6, 7.

[Note that total number of fundamental cut-sets = No. of nodes − 1 = 5 − 1 = 4].

The necessary **cut-set matrix** is shown below :

Cut-set	*Branches* 1	2	3	4	5	6	7
C_1	0	0	0	+1	0	+1	+1
C_2	0	+1	0	0	−1	+1	0
C_3	0	0	+1	0	0	0	−1
C_4	+1	0	0	0	+1	+1	+1

Example 13.26 *A graph is shown in Fig. E13.26. Find the tie-set and cut-set matrices and obtain the KCL and KVL equations [the bold lines indicate twigs while the dotted lines the links].*

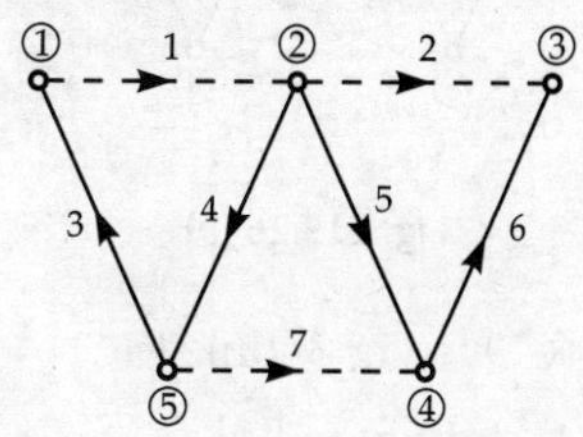

Fig. E13.26

Solution. The fundamental loops are located by loop currents I_1, I_2 and I_3. All these loops contain only one link each [Fig. E13.26(*a*)].

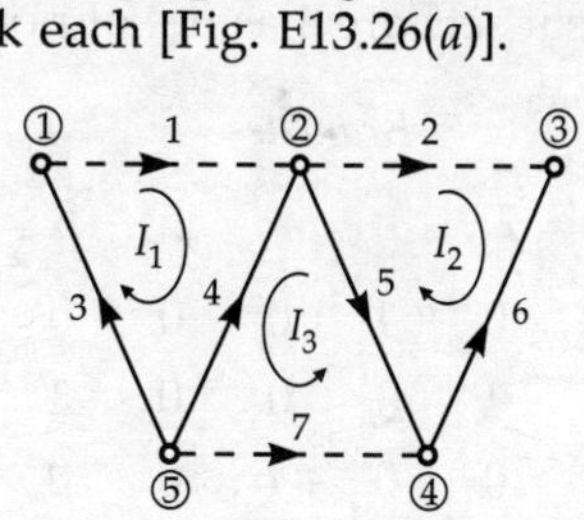

Fig. E13.26 (*a*)

The **tie-set matrix** is shown below :

Loop current	*Branches* 1	2	3	4	5	6	7
I_1	+1	0	+1	−1	0	0	0
I_2	0	+1	0	0	−1	−1	0
I_3	0	0	0	−1	−1	0	+1

Thus from the loop current matrix [Columns giving branch currents in terms of loop currents],

$$j_3 = I_1, j_4 = -I_1 - I_3, j_5 = -I_2 - I_3,$$
$$j_6 = -I_2, j_1 = I_1$$
$$j_2 = I_2, j_7 = I_3$$

[$j_1, j_2, \ldots$ are the branch currents]

At the respective loops the **KVL equations** are

$$v_1 + v_3 - v_4 = 0;$$
$$v_2 - v_5 - v_6 = 0;$$
$$-v_4 - v_5 + v_7 = 0.$$

To form the **cut-set matrix** we redraw the figure with twigs and links [Fig. E13.26(*b*)].

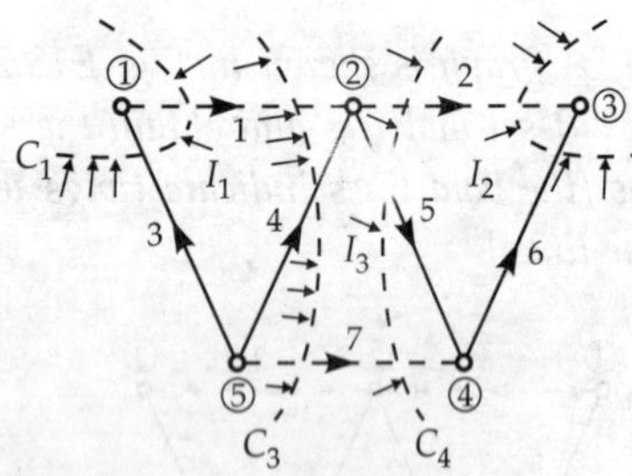

Fig. E13.26 (*b*)

Cut-set-1. (C_1): twig 3, link 1

Cut-set-2 (C_2): twig 6, link 2

Cut-set-3 (C_3): twig 4, link 1, link 7

Cut-set-4 (C_4): twig 5, link 2, link 7

[It may be noted that the number of fundamental cut-sets are 4 as no. of nodes is 5

Cut-sets	*Branches* 1	2	3	4	5	6	7
C_1	−1	0	+1	0	0	0	0
C_2	0	+1	0	0	0	+1	0
C_3	+1	0	0	+1	0	0	+1
C_4	0	+1	0	0	+1	0	+1

KCL equations can now be written for these 4 no-pairs by using the coefficients in the rows of the cut-set matrix.

$$-j_1 + j_3 = 0;$$
$$j_2 + j_6 = 0;$$
$$j_1 + j_4 + j_7 = 0;$$
$$+j_2 + j_5 + j_7 = 0.$$

EXAMPLE 13.27 *Draw the dual network as shown in Fig. E13.27.*

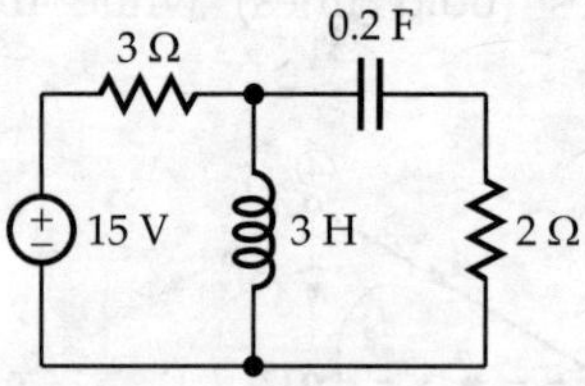

Fig. E13.27

SOLUTION.

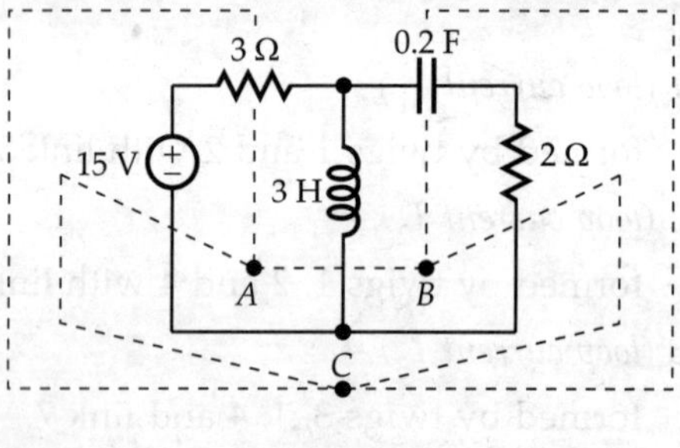

Fig. E13.27 (*a*)

Mark node *C* as reference and one dot per mesh *A* and *B*.

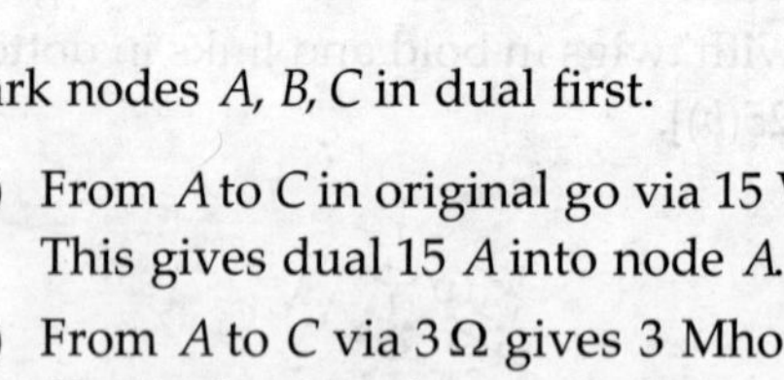

Fig. E13.27 (*b*)

Mark nodes *A, B, C* in dual first.

(*i*) From *A* to *C* in original go via 15 V source. This gives dual 15 *A* into node *A*.

(*ii*) From *A* to *C* via 3 Ω gives 3 Mho in Dual. (Dual of unit only).

(*iii*) *A* to *B* via 3H gives. 3F in dual.

(*iv*) *B* to *C* via 2Ω gives 2*v* in dual.

(*v*) *B* to *C* via 0.2F gives 0.2H in dual.

The dual is drawn **(Fig. E13.27(*b*))**.

note Clockwise current via (+ve) terminal of voltage source connected to node and vice-versa is dual.

Example 13.28 *Draw the dual of the network shown in Fig. E13.28.*

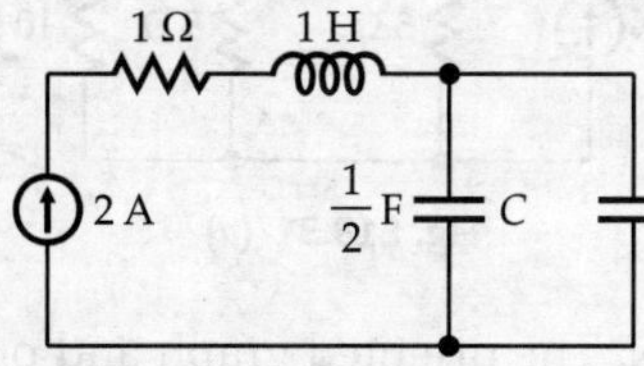

Fig. E13.28

Solution. Figure E13.28 shows the dual.

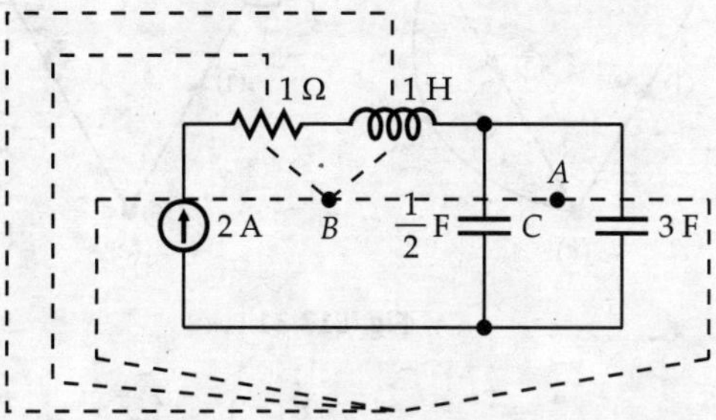

(*a*)

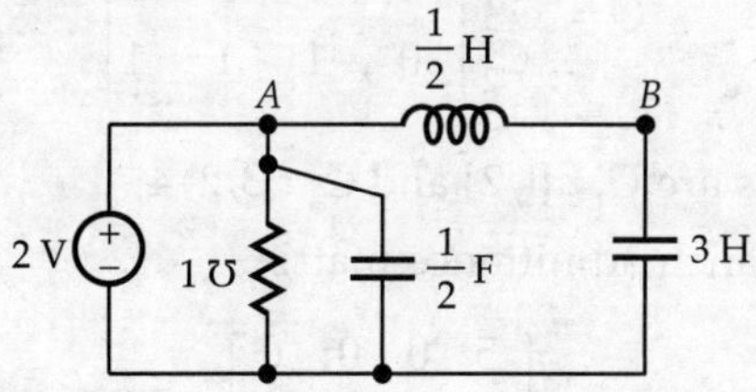

Fig. E13.28 (*b*)

Example 13.29 *Draw the dual of the network shown in Fig. E13.29.*

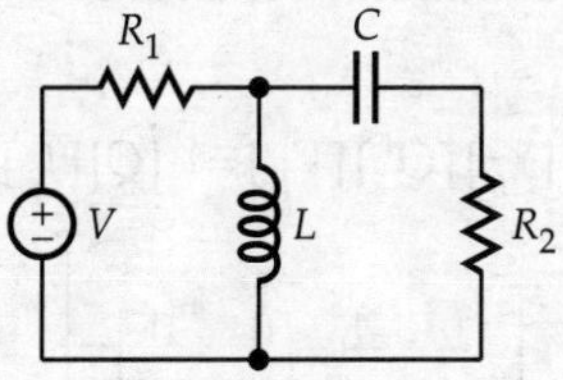

Fig. E13.29

Solution.

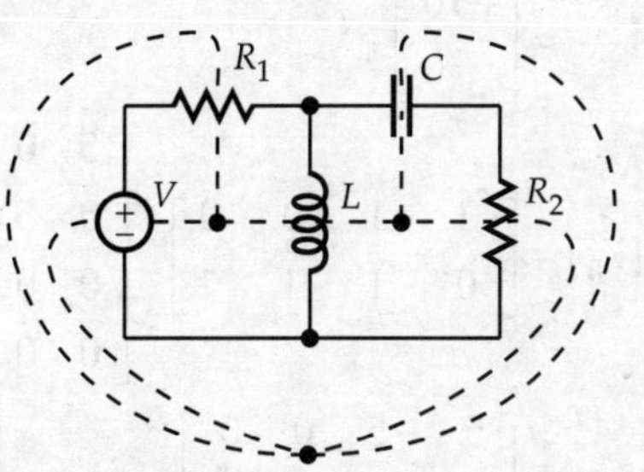

Fig. E13.29 (*a*)

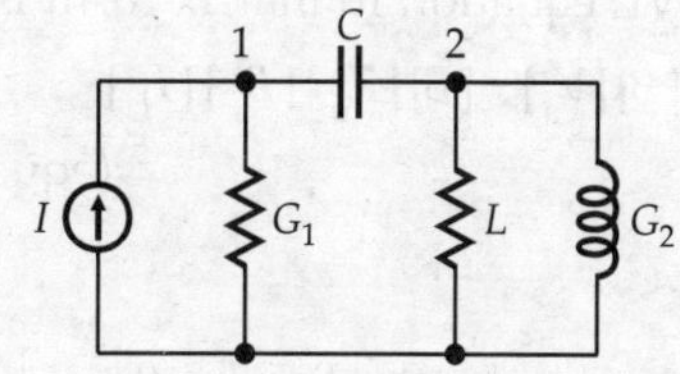

Fig. E13.29 (*b*)

Proceed as done in previous example and draw the dual (**Fig. E13.29(*b*)**).

Example 13.30 *A network has been shown in Fig. E13.30(a). Write down the tieset matrix and obtain network equilibrium equation in matrix form using KVL. Calculate loop currents.*

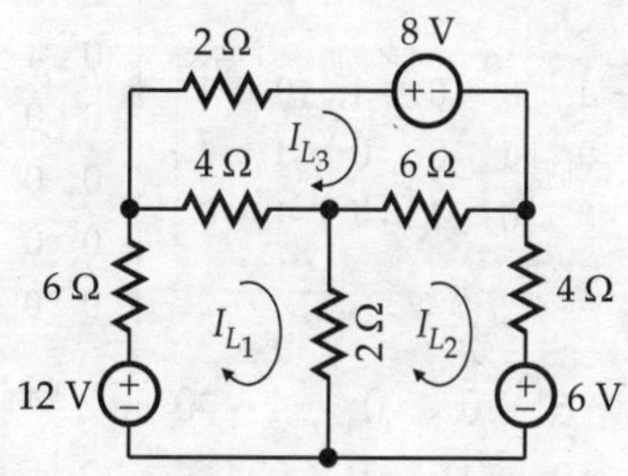

Fig. E13.30 (*a*)

Solution. The oriented graph and its selected tree are shown in Figs. E13.30(*b*) and (*c*).

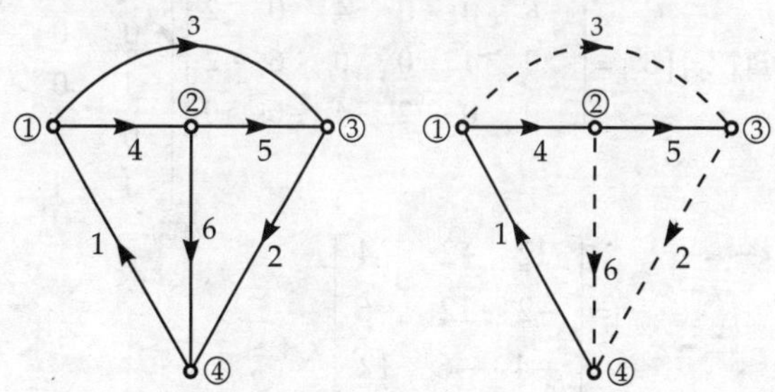

(*b*) (*c*)

Fig. E13.30

Tieset Matrix [*B*] is written form Fig. E13.30(*c*) as

$$[B] = \begin{array}{c} \\ 1 \\ 2 \\ 3 \end{array} \begin{array}{c} \begin{matrix} 1 & 2 & 3 & 4 & 5 & 6 \end{matrix} \\ \begin{bmatrix} 1 & 0 & 0 & 1 & 0 & 1 \\ 0 & 1 & 0 & 0 & 1 & -1 \\ 0 & 0 & 1 & -1 & -1 & 0 \end{bmatrix} \end{array}$$

Tieset 1 : [1, 4, 6]

Tieset 2 : [2, 5, 6]

Tieset 3 : [3, 5, 6]

The KVL equation in matrix form is given by,

$$[B][V_s]=[B][Z_b][B^t][I_L]$$

(equation 13.32)

$$\text{or}\quad [B][V_s]=\begin{bmatrix}1&0&0&1&0&1\\0&1&0&0&1&-1\\0&0&1&-1&-1&0\end{bmatrix}\begin{bmatrix}12\\-6\\-8\\0\\0\\0\end{bmatrix}$$

$$=\begin{bmatrix}12\\-6\\-8\end{bmatrix}$$

$$[B][Z_b]=\begin{bmatrix}1&0&0&1&0&1\\0&1&0&0&1&-1\\0&0&1&-1&-1&0\end{bmatrix}\begin{bmatrix}6&0&0&0&0&0\\0&4&0&0&0&0\\0&0&2&0&0&0\\0&0&0&4&0&0\\0&0&0&0&6&0\\0&0&0&0&0&2\end{bmatrix}$$

$$=\begin{bmatrix}6&0&0&4&0&2\\0&4&0&0&6&-2\\0&0&2&-4&-6&0\end{bmatrix}$$

$$[B][Z_b][B^t]=\begin{bmatrix}6&0&0&4&0&2\\0&4&0&0&6&-2\\0&0&2&-4&-6&0\end{bmatrix}\begin{bmatrix}1&0&0\\0&1&0\\0&0&1\\1&0&-1\\0&1&-1\\1&-1&0\end{bmatrix}$$

$$=\begin{bmatrix}12&-2&-4\\-2&12&-6\\-4&-6&12\end{bmatrix}$$

Hence the **KVL equation** in matrix form is given by,

$$\begin{bmatrix}12\\-6\\-8\end{bmatrix}=\begin{bmatrix}12&-2&-4\\-2&12&-6\\-4&-6&12\end{bmatrix}\begin{bmatrix}I_{L_1}\\I_{L_2}\\I_{L_3}\end{bmatrix}$$

Solving this matrix equation, we get

$\boldsymbol{I_{L_1}}=0.55\text{ A}$; $\boldsymbol{I_{L_2}}=-0.866\text{ A}$; $\boldsymbol{I_{L_3}}=-0.916\text{ A}$.

EXAMPLE 13.31 *Obtain equilibrium equation using nodal equations for the network shown in Fig. E13.31(a). Also find node voltages at X and Y.*

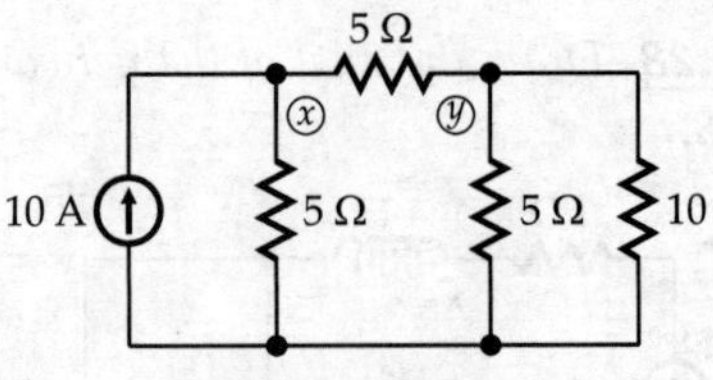

Fig. E13.31 (*a*)

SOLUTION. The oriented graph and one selected tree has been shown in Figs. E13.31(*b*) and (*c*).

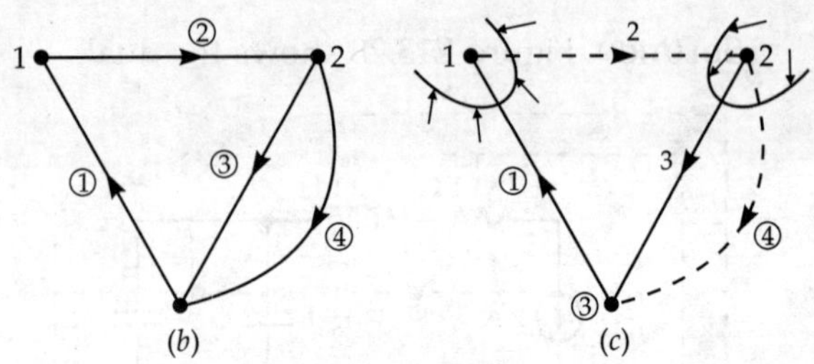

Fig. E13.31

$$Q=\begin{array}{c}\\ C_1\\ C_2\end{array}\begin{array}{c}\begin{matrix}1&2&3&4\end{matrix}\\ \begin{bmatrix}1&-1&0&0\\0&-1&1&1\end{bmatrix}\end{array};$$

Cutsets are $C_1:\{1,2\}$ and $C_3:\{3,2,4\}$

Branch admittance matrix

$$[Y_b]=\begin{bmatrix}5&0&0&0\\0&5&0&0\\0&0&5&0\\0&0&0&10\end{bmatrix}$$

$\because$ KCL equation in matrix form (eqn. 13.28) is given by,

$$[Q][Y_b][Q^t][V_T]=-[Q][I_s],\ \text{here,}$$

$$[Q][I_s]=\begin{bmatrix}1&-1&0&0\\0&-1&1&1\end{bmatrix}\begin{bmatrix}+10\\0\\0\\0\end{bmatrix}$$

$$=\begin{bmatrix}+10\\0\end{bmatrix}$$

$$[Q][Y_b]=\begin{bmatrix}1&-1&0&0\\0&-1&1&1\end{bmatrix}\begin{bmatrix}5&0&0&0\\0&5&0&0\\0&0&5&0\\0&0&0&10\end{bmatrix}$$

$$=\begin{bmatrix}5&-5&0&0\\0&-5&5&10\end{bmatrix}$$

and $$[Q][Y_b][Q^t] = \begin{bmatrix} 5 & -5 & 0 & 0 \\ 0 & -5 & 5 & 10 \end{bmatrix} \begin{bmatrix} 1 & 0 \\ -1 & -1 \\ 0 & 1 \\ 0 & 1 \end{bmatrix}$$

$$= \begin{bmatrix} 10 & 5 \\ 5 & 20 \end{bmatrix}$$

Hence KCL equation can be written as,

$$\begin{bmatrix} 10 & 5 \\ 5 & 20 \end{bmatrix} \begin{bmatrix} V_{T_1} \\ V_{T_3} \end{bmatrix} = -\begin{bmatrix} +10 \\ 0 \end{bmatrix}$$

Solving this matrix equation, we get

$$V_{T_1} = -\frac{8}{7}\text{ V}$$

$$V_{T_3} = \frac{2}{7}\text{ V}$$

V_{T_1} and V_{T_3} are the twig voltages indicating nodes X and Y voltages respectively.

Example 13.32 *Draw the dual of the network shown in Fig. E13.32.*

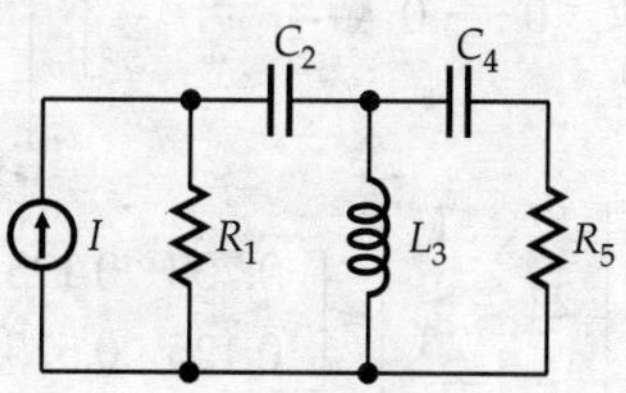

Fig. E13.32

Solution. Fig. E13.32(*b*) is the dual

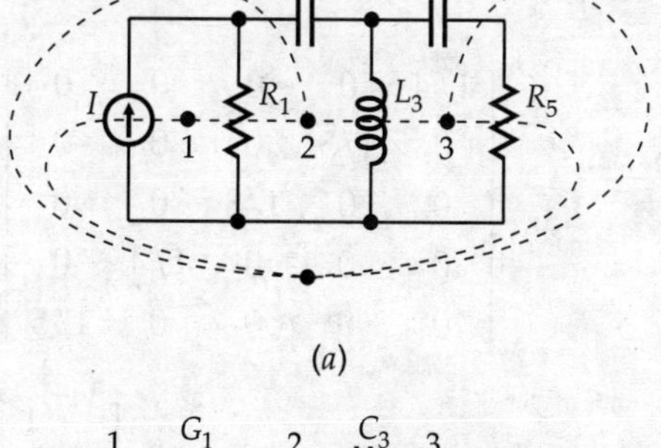

(*a*)

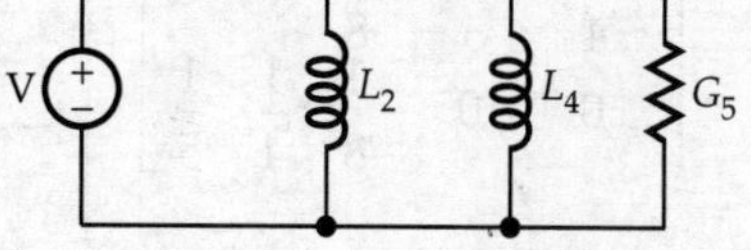

Fig. E13.32 (*b*)

Dual Network.

Example 13.33 *Draw the dual of the network in Fig. E13.33.*

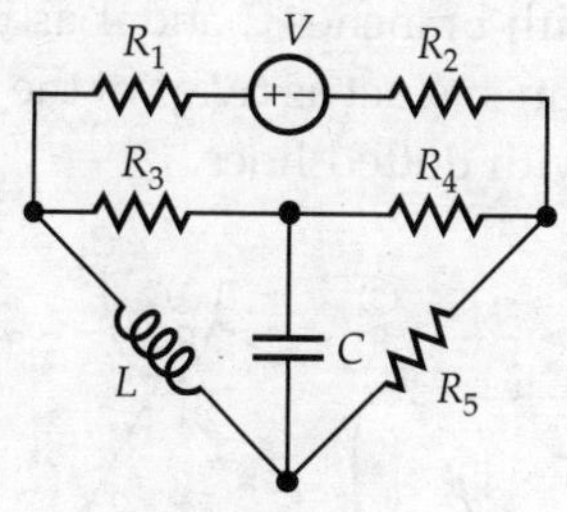

Fig. E13.33

Solution. Proceeding exactly in the similar way, we get **Fig. E13.33** as dual.

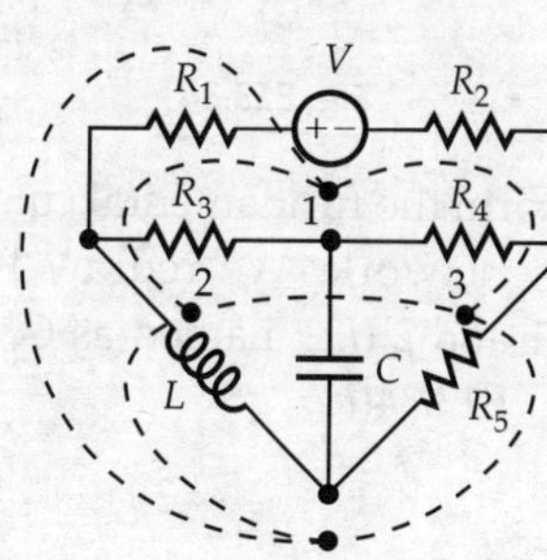

(*a*)

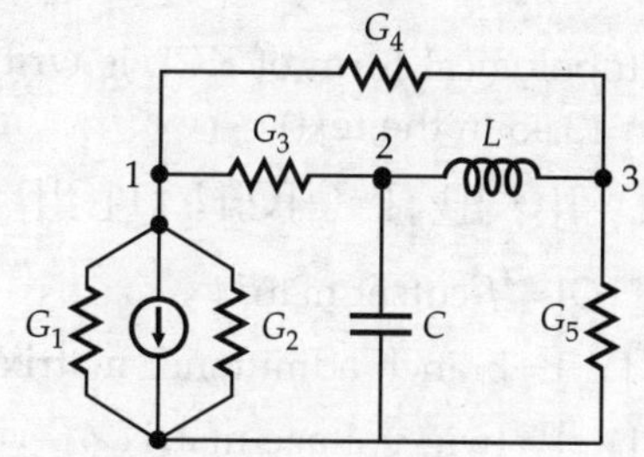

Fig. E13.33 (*b*)

Example 13.34 *A network has been displayed in Fig. E13.34. Draw a graph of the network and select a tree with branches having resistances 3 Ω and 4 Ω (branches 2 and 4). Draw the cut-set matrix. Using topological form of KCL equation, find various branch voltages and currents. The branch numbers are marked with integers in the figure while node numbers are encircled.*

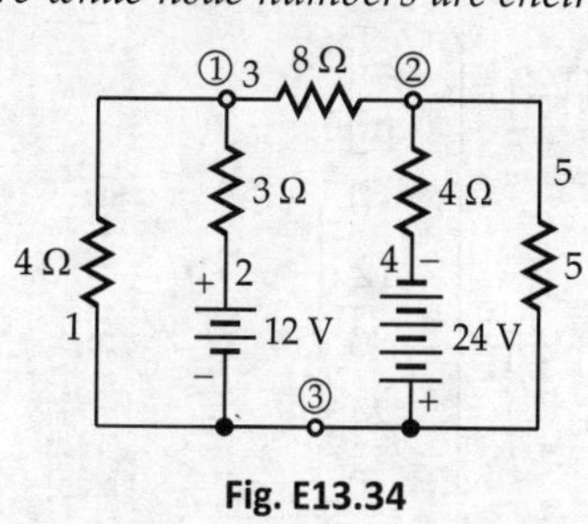

Fig. E13.34

CHAPTER 13

Solution. The graph (oriented arbitrarily) of the given network is shown in Fig. 13.34(a). The tree is formed with branches 2 and 4 as bold lines and these two branches act as twigs of the tree. The links are shown with dotted lines.

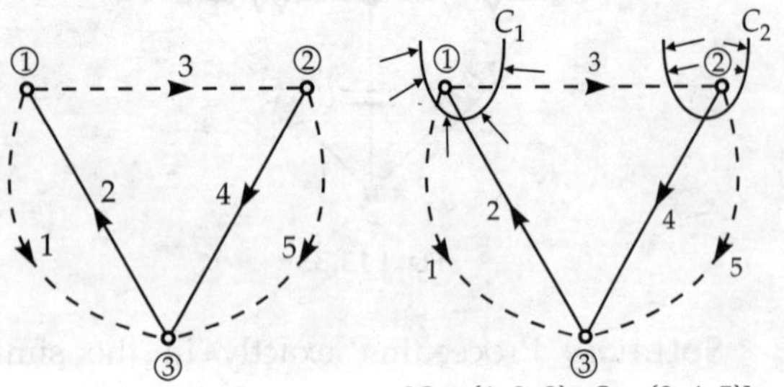

[C_1 = {1, 2, 3} ; C_2 = {3, 4, 5}]

(a) (b)

Fig. E13.34

We first form the fundamental cutset matrix [Q] for the given network. We redraw Fig. E13.34(a) with cutsets 1 and 2 ($i.e.$, named as C_1 and C_2) and shown in Fig. E13.34(b).

$$Q = \begin{array}{c} \\ C_1 \\ C_2 \end{array}\begin{array}{c} \begin{matrix} 1 & 2 & 3 & 4 & 5 \end{matrix} \\ \begin{bmatrix} -1 & +1 & -1 & 0 & 0 \\ 0 & 0 & -1 & +1 & +1 \end{bmatrix} \end{array}$$

The topological form of KCL is written below (equation 13.45 in the text) :

$$[Q][Y_b][Q^t][V_T] = (-[Q][I_s] + [Q][Y_b][V_s])$$

where, $[Q]$ = f-cutset matrix

$[Y_b]$ = branch admittance matrix

$[V_T]$ = twig voltage matrix

$[I_s]$ = current source matrix

$[V_s]$ = voltage source matrix.

$$\text{Here, } [Y_b] = \begin{bmatrix} 1/4 & 0 & 0 & 0 & 0 \\ 0 & 1/3 & 0 & 0 & 0 \\ 0 & 0 & 1/8 & 0 & 0 \\ 0 & 0 & 0 & 1/4 & 0 \\ 0 & 0 & 0 & 0 & 1/5 \end{bmatrix}$$

$$[V_T] = \begin{bmatrix} V_2 \\ V_4 \end{bmatrix}$$

$$[V_s] = \begin{bmatrix} 0 \\ -12 \\ 0 \\ -24 \\ 0 \end{bmatrix}$$

In the network the polarity of connection of 12 V and 24 V source is reverse but here, in the $[V_s]$ matrix, both the sources are substituted with their values prefixed by –ve signs. This is because the orientation of the graphs for these two branches are directed from –ve to +ve ; [Fig. E13.34(a)]

$$[I_s] = \begin{bmatrix} 0 \\ 0 \end{bmatrix}, \text{ a null matrix.}$$

$$\therefore\ [Q][Y_b][Q^t] = \begin{bmatrix} -1 & +1 & -1 & 0 & 0 \\ 0 & 0 & -1 & +1 & +1 \end{bmatrix}$$

$$\begin{bmatrix} 1/4 & 0 & 0 & 0 & 0 \\ 0 & 1/3 & 0 & 0 & 0 \\ 0 & 0 & 1/8 & 0 & 0 \\ 0 & 0 & 0 & 1/4 & 0 \\ 0 & 0 & 0 & 0 & 1/5 \end{bmatrix} \begin{bmatrix} -1 & 0 \\ +1 & 0 \\ -1 & -1 \\ 0 & +1 \\ 0 & +1 \end{bmatrix}$$

$$= \begin{bmatrix} -\frac{1}{4} & +\frac{1}{3} & -\frac{1}{8} & 0 & 0 \\ 0 & 0 & -\frac{1}{8} & \frac{1}{4} & \frac{1}{5} \end{bmatrix} \begin{bmatrix} -1 & 0 \\ +1 & 0 \\ -1 & -1 \\ 0 & +1 \\ 0 & +1 \end{bmatrix}$$

$$= \begin{bmatrix} \frac{17}{24} & \frac{1}{8} \\ \frac{1}{8} & \frac{23}{40} \end{bmatrix} = \begin{bmatrix} 0.708 & 0.125 \\ 0.125 & 0.575 \end{bmatrix}$$

Also, $[Q][I_s] = 0$ (since $[I_s]$ is a null matrix)

$$\text{Again, } [Q][Y_b][V_s] = \begin{bmatrix} -1 & +1 & -1 & 0 & 0 \\ 0 & 0 & -1 & +1 & +1 \end{bmatrix}$$

$$\begin{bmatrix} 1/4 & 0 & 0 & 0 & 0 \\ 0 & 1/3 & 0 & 0 & 0 \\ 0 & 0 & 1/8 & 0 & 0 \\ 0 & 0 & 0 & 1/4 & 0 \\ 0 & 0 & 0 & 0 & 1/5 \end{bmatrix} \begin{bmatrix} 0 \\ -12 \\ 0 \\ -24 \\ 0 \end{bmatrix}$$

$$= \begin{bmatrix} -\frac{1}{4} & +\frac{1}{3} & -\frac{1}{8} & 0 & 0 \\ 0 & 0 & -\frac{1}{8} & \frac{1}{4} & \frac{1}{5} \end{bmatrix} \begin{bmatrix} 1 \\ -12 \\ 0 \\ -24 \\ 0 \end{bmatrix}$$

$$= \begin{bmatrix} -4 \\ -6 \end{bmatrix}$$

From the KCL equilibrium equation we can write

$$\begin{bmatrix} 0.708 & 0.125 \\ 0.125 & 0.575 \end{bmatrix} \begin{bmatrix} V_2 \\ V_4 \end{bmatrix} = \begin{bmatrix} -4 \\ -6 \end{bmatrix}$$

i.e., $0.708V_2 + 0.125V_4 = -4$ ...(1)

and $0.125V_2 + 0.575V_4 = -6$ ...(2)

Solving equations (1) and (2) we get the twig voltages V_2 and V_4 as

$$V_2 = -3.96 \text{ volts} \quad \text{and} \quad V_4 = -9.57 \text{ volts}.$$

The branch voltages can be determined as

$$[V_b] = [Q^t][V_T]$$

(equation 13.26(*a*), in text)

$$\text{Here } [V_b] = \begin{bmatrix} -1 & 0 \\ +1 & 0 \\ -1 & -1 \\ 0 & +1 \\ 0 & +1 \end{bmatrix} \begin{bmatrix} -3.96 \\ -9.57 \end{bmatrix} = \begin{bmatrix} 3.96 \\ -3.96 \\ 13.53 \\ -9.57 \\ -9.57 \end{bmatrix}$$

$\therefore$ V_{b_1} **= 3.96 volts ;** V_{b_2} **= – 3.96 volts ;**
V_{b_3} **= 13.53 volts ;** V_{b_4} **= – 9.57 volts ;**
V_{b_5} **= – 9.57 volts.**

The branch currents can be obtained from the following equation (equation 13.40 in the text)

$$[I_b] = [Y_b][V_b] - [Y_b][V_s] + [I_s]$$
$$= [Y_b]\left([V_b] - [V_s] \right) + [I_s]$$

Here we can write

$$\begin{bmatrix} I_1 \\ I_2 \\ I_3 \\ I_4 \\ I_5 \end{bmatrix} = \begin{bmatrix} 1/4 & 0 & 0 & 0 & 0 \\ 0 & 1/3 & 0 & 0 & 0 \\ 0 & 0 & 1/8 & 0 & 0 \\ 0 & 0 & 0 & 1/4 & 0 \\ 0 & 0 & 0 & 0 & 1/5 \end{bmatrix} \begin{bmatrix} 3.96 + 0 \\ -3.96 + 12 \\ 13.53 + 0 \\ -9.57 + 24 \\ -9.57 + 0 \end{bmatrix} + \begin{bmatrix} 0 \\ 0 \end{bmatrix}$$

$$= \begin{bmatrix} 0.99 \\ 2.68 \\ 1.69 \\ 3.61 \\ -1.92 \end{bmatrix}$$

$\therefore I_1$ **= 0.99 A ;** I_2 **= 2.68 A ;** I_3 **= 1.69 A ;**
I_4 **= 3.61 A;** I_5 **= – 1.92 A**

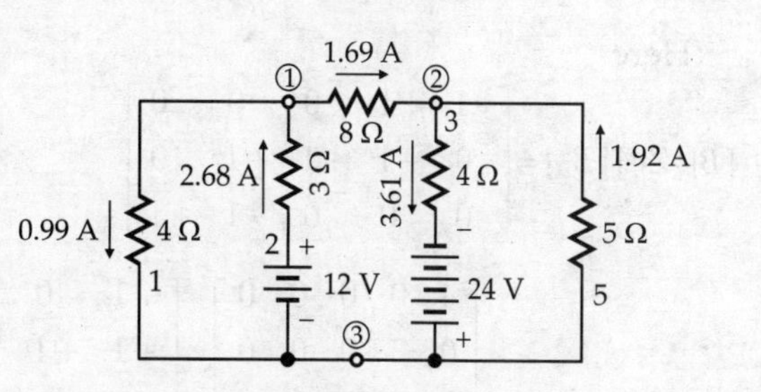

Fig. E13.34 (*c*)

EXAMPLE 13.35 *For the network shown in Fig. E13.34 [Ex. 13.34] write down the equilibrium equation with loop currents as variables. Find various branch voltages and currents using topological form of KVL equation.*

SOLUTION. Let us redraw the graph of the network shown in Fig. E13.34 with loop currents I_{L_1}, I_{L_2} and I_{L_3} in fundamental loops 1, 2 and 3. (Refer to Fig. E13.35).

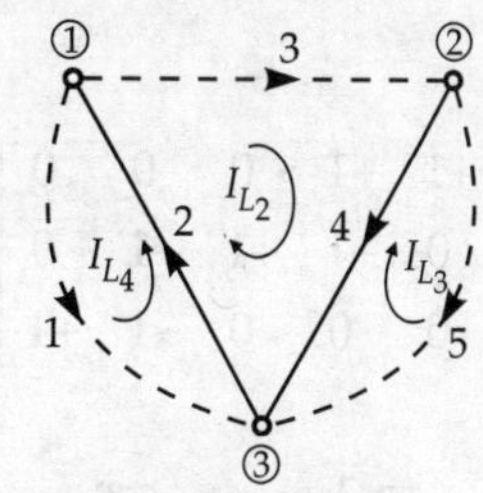

Fig. E13.35

The positive directions of the branch currents coincide with the orientation of the loop. The fundamental tie set matrix is given by

loop \ branches	1	2	3	4	5
1	+1	+1	0	0	0
2	0	+1	+1	+1	0
3	0	0	0	−1	+1

$[B] =$ the matrix above.

The branch impedance matrix $[Z_b]$ is given by

$$[Z_b] = \begin{bmatrix} 4 & 0 & 0 & 0 & 0 \\ 0 & 3 & 0 & 0 & 0 \\ 0 & 0 & 8 & 0 & 0 \\ 0 & 0 & 0 & 4 & 0 \\ 0 & 0 & 0 & 0 & 5 \end{bmatrix}$$

However, the network equilibrium equation following KVL is given by (equation 13.34 in text)

$$[B][Z_b][B^t][I_L] = -[B][V_s] + [B][Z_b][I_s] \quad ...(1)$$

Here

$$[B][Z_b][B^t] = \begin{bmatrix} +1 & +1 & 0 & 0 & 0 \\ 0 & +1 & +1 & +1 & 0 \\ 0 & 0 & 0 & -1 & +1 \end{bmatrix} \begin{bmatrix} 4 & 0 & 0 & 0 & 0 \\ 0 & 3 & 0 & 0 & 0 \\ 0 & 0 & 8 & 0 & 0 \\ 0 & 0 & 0 & 4 & 0 \\ 0 & 0 & 0 & 0 & 5 \end{bmatrix} \begin{bmatrix} +1 & 0 & 0 \\ +1 & +1 & 0 \\ 0 & +1 & 0 \\ 0 & +1 & -1 \\ 0 & 0 & +1 \end{bmatrix}$$

$$= \begin{bmatrix} 7 & 3 & 0 \\ 3 & 15 & -4 \\ 0 & -4 & 9 \end{bmatrix}$$

Also, $[B][Z_b][I_s]=0,$; since $[I_s]$ is a null matrix, the circuit being having no current source.

Again

$$[B][V_s] = \begin{bmatrix} +1 & +1 & 0 & 0 & 0 \\ 0 & +1 & +1 & +1 & 0 \\ 0 & 0 & 0 & -1 & +1 \end{bmatrix} \begin{bmatrix} 0 \\ -12 \\ 0 \\ -24 \\ 0 \end{bmatrix}$$

$$= \begin{bmatrix} -12 \\ -36 \\ +24 \end{bmatrix}$$

$\therefore$ We can write, following equation (1)

$$\begin{bmatrix} 7 & 3 & 0 \\ 3 & 15 & -4 \\ 0 & -4 & 9 \end{bmatrix} \begin{bmatrix} I_{L_1} \\ I_{L_2} \\ I_{L_3} \end{bmatrix} = - \begin{bmatrix} -12 \\ -36 \\ +24 \end{bmatrix}$$

$$\therefore \quad \mathbf{7I_{L_1} + 3I_{L_2} = 12}$$

$$\mathbf{3I_{L_1} + 15I_{L_2} - 4I_{L_3} = 36}$$

$$\mathbf{-4I_{L_2} + 9I_{L_3} = -24}$$

Solving these three equations we obtain the values of I_{L_1}, I_{L_2} and I_{L_3} as

$$I_{L_1} = 0.99 \text{ A};$$

$$I_{L_2} = 1.69;$$

$$I_{L_3} = -1.92 \text{ A}$$

$\therefore$ Branch currents are given by

$$[I_b] = [B^t][I_L]$$

$$= \begin{bmatrix} +1 & 0 & 0 \\ +1 & +1 & 0 \\ 0 & +1 & 0 \\ 0 & +1 & -1 \\ 0 & 0 & +1 \end{bmatrix} \begin{bmatrix} 0.99 \\ 1.69 \\ -1.92 \end{bmatrix}$$

$$= \begin{bmatrix} 0.99 \\ 2.68 \\ 1.69 \\ 3.61 \\ -1.92 \end{bmatrix}$$

$\therefore$ $\mathbf{I_{b_1} = 0.99\ A;\ I_{b_2} = 2.68\ A;\ I_{b_3} = 1.69\ A;}$
$\mathbf{I_{b_4} = 3.61\ A;\ I_{b_5} = -1.92\ A.}$

It may be observed that these results are identical so that we obtain in Ex. 13.34.

The various branch voltages are given by the following matrix equation (equation 13.33 in text)

$$[V_b] = [Z_b][I_b] - [Z_b][I_s] + [V_s]$$

Since $[I_s]=0$, here we can write,

$$[V_b] = \begin{bmatrix} 4 & 0 & 0 & 0 & 0 \\ 0 & 3 & 0 & 0 & 0 \\ 0 & 0 & 8 & 0 & 0 \\ 0 & 0 & 0 & 4 & 0 \\ 0 & 0 & 0 & 0 & 5 \end{bmatrix} \begin{bmatrix} I_{b_1} \\ I_{b_2} \\ I_{b_3} \\ I_4 \\ I_5 \end{bmatrix} + \begin{bmatrix} 0 \\ -12 \\ 0 \\ -24 \\ 0 \end{bmatrix}$$

$$= \begin{bmatrix} 4 & 0 & 0 & 0 & 0 \\ 0 & 3 & 0 & 0 & 0 \\ 0 & 0 & 8 & 0 & 0 \\ 0 & 0 & 0 & 4 & 0 \\ 0 & 0 & 0 & 0 & 5 \end{bmatrix} \begin{bmatrix} 0.99 \\ 2.68 \\ 1.69 \\ 3.61 \\ -1.92 \end{bmatrix} + \begin{bmatrix} 0 \\ -12 \\ 0 \\ -24 \\ 0 \end{bmatrix}$$

$$= \begin{bmatrix} 3.96 \\ -3.96 \\ 13.52 \\ -9.56 \\ -9.56 \end{bmatrix}$$

$\therefore$ $\mathbf{V_{b_1} = 3.96\ volts;\quad V_{b_2} = -3.96\ volts;}$

$\mathbf{V_{b_3} = 13.52\ volts;\quad V_{b_4} = -9.56\ volts.;}$

$\mathbf{V_{b_5} = -9.56\ volts.}$

These results are also mostly identical to that we obtained earlier.

EXAMPLE 13.36 *Solve Example 13.34 for the network shown in Fig. E13.34 using KCL equation in topological form involving branch admittance matrix and node voltage matrix. Obtain the branch voltages and currents.*

SOLUTION. The KCL equation in topological form involving branch admittance matrix and node voltage matrix is given by (equation 13.42).

$$[A][Y_b][A^t][V_n] = -[A][I_s] + [A][Y_b][V_s]$$

Here, for the graph shown in Fig. E13.34*a*, the reduced incidence matrix [*A*] is obtained as

$$[A] = \begin{bmatrix} +1 & -1 & +1 & 0 & 0 \\ 0 & 0 & -1 & +1 & +1 \end{bmatrix}$$

Also, the branch admittance matrix $[Y_b]$ can be obtained as

$$[Y_b] = \begin{bmatrix} 1/4 & 0 & 0 & 0 & 0 \\ 0 & 1/3 & 0 & 0 & 0 \\ 0 & 0 & 1/8 & 0 & 0 \\ 0 & 0 & 0 & 1/4 & 0 \\ 0 & 0 & 0 & 0 & 1/5 \end{bmatrix}$$

$$\therefore\ [A][Y_b][A^t] = \begin{bmatrix} +1 & -1 & +1 & 0 & 0 \\ 0 & 0 & -1 & +1 & +1 \end{bmatrix}$$

$$\begin{bmatrix} 1/4 & 0 & 0 & 0 & 0 \\ 0 & 1/3 & 0 & 0 & 0 \\ 0 & 0 & 1/8 & 0 & 0 \\ 0 & 0 & 0 & 1/4 & 0 \\ 0 & 0 & 0 & 0 & 1/5 \end{bmatrix} \begin{bmatrix} +1 & 0 \\ -1 & 0 \\ +1 & -1 \\ 0 & +1 \\ 0 & +1 \end{bmatrix}$$

$$= \begin{bmatrix} \frac{17}{24} & -\frac{1}{8} \\ -\frac{1}{8} & \frac{23}{40} \end{bmatrix}$$

$$\text{Also } [A][Y_b][V_s] = \begin{bmatrix} +1 & -1 & +1 & 0 & 0 \\ 0 & 0 & -1 & +1 & +1 \end{bmatrix}$$

$$\begin{bmatrix} 1/4 & 0 & 0 & 0 & 0 \\ 0 & 1/3 & 0 & 0 & 0 \\ 0 & 0 & 1/8 & 0 & 0 \\ 0 & 0 & 0 & 1/4 & 0 \\ 0 & 0 & 0 & 0 & 1/5 \end{bmatrix} \begin{bmatrix} 0 \\ -12 \\ 0 \\ -24 \\ 0 \end{bmatrix}$$

$$= \begin{bmatrix} \frac{1}{4} & -\frac{1}{3} & \frac{1}{8} & 0 & 0 \\ 0 & 0 & -\frac{1}{8} & \frac{1}{4} & \frac{1}{5} \end{bmatrix} \begin{bmatrix} 0 \\ -12 \\ 0 \\ -24 \\ 0 \end{bmatrix} = \begin{bmatrix} 4 \\ -6 \end{bmatrix}$$

Since there is no current source,

$$[A][I_s] = \begin{bmatrix} 0 \\ 0 \\ 0 \end{bmatrix}$$

$\therefore$ The equilibrium equation in final form is given by (in terms of node voltages V_1 and V_2)

$$\begin{bmatrix} \frac{17}{24} & -\frac{1}{8} \\ -\frac{1}{8} & \frac{23}{40} \end{bmatrix} \begin{bmatrix} V_1 \\ V_2 \end{bmatrix} = +\begin{bmatrix} 4 \\ -6 \end{bmatrix}$$

(it may be noted that V_3 is the datum node voltage *i.e.*, $V_3 = 0$)

The node voltages are obtained from the two equations

$$\frac{17}{24} V_1 - \frac{1}{8} V_2 = +4$$

$$-\frac{1}{8} V_1 + \frac{23}{40} V_2 = -6$$

Solving these two equations we obtain

$$V_1 = 3.96 \text{ volts}$$

$$V_2 = -9.57 \text{ volts}$$

$\therefore$ Branch voltages can be obtained as follows (refer to Fig. 13.34*a*) :

$$V_{b_1} \equiv V_1 = 3.96 \text{ volts}$$

$$V_{b_2} \equiv -V_1 = -3.96 \text{ volts}$$

$$V_{b_3} \equiv V_1 - V_2 = 13.53 \text{ volts}$$

$$V_{b_4} \equiv V_2 = -9.57 \text{ volts}$$

$$V_{b_5} \equiv V_2 = -9.57 \text{ volts.}$$

Various branch currents are then obtained as

$$I_{b_1} = \frac{V_1}{4} = 0.99 \text{ A}$$

$$I_{b_2} = \frac{12 - V_1}{3} = 2.68 \text{ A}$$

$$I_{b_3} = \frac{V_1 - V_2}{8} = 1.69 \text{ A}$$

$$I_{b_4} = \frac{V_2 + 24}{4} = 3.607 \text{ A}$$

$$I_{b_5} = \frac{V_2}{5} = -1.914 \text{ A}$$

CHAPTER 13

EXERCISES

1. A network is shown in Fig. P13.1. Draw the graph.

   [**Hint.** In graph current source is open circuited while voltage source is represented by short circuit provided they are ideal. Also refer to Ex. 13.2].

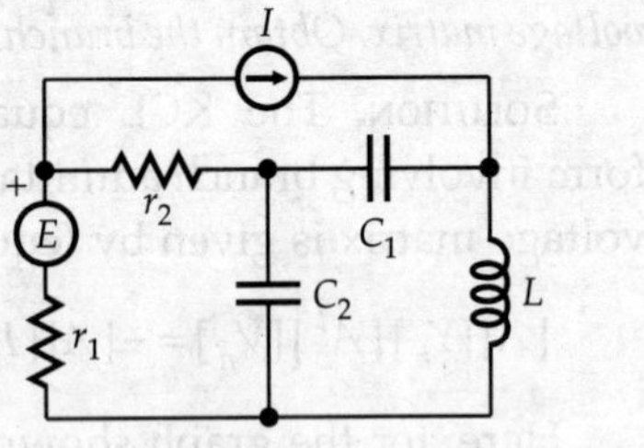

Fig. P13.1

2. Draw the oriented graph of the networks shown in Figs. P13.2 (*a*) and P13.2 (*b*).

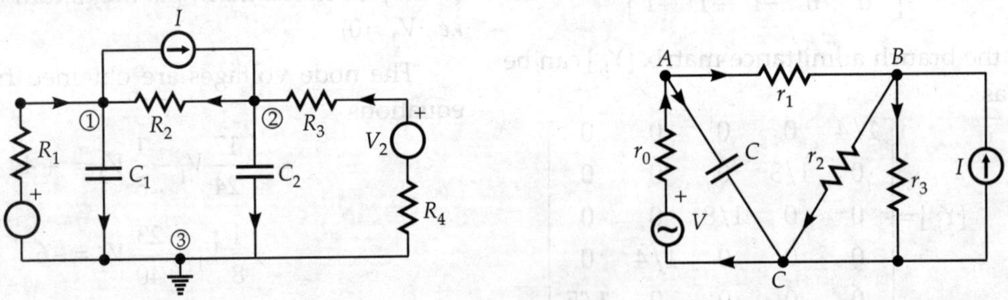

Fig. P13.2 (*a*) (*b*)

   [**Hint.** Refer to Figs. P13.3(*a*) and P13.3(*b*)]

(*a*) (*b*)

Fig. P13.3

3. Fig. P13.4 represents a network. Draw the directed graph, tree and show the loops.

   [**Hint.** Refer to Ex. 13.5]

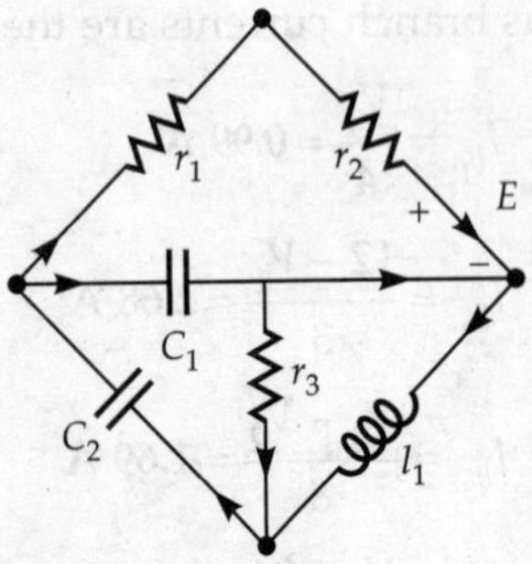

Fig. P13.4

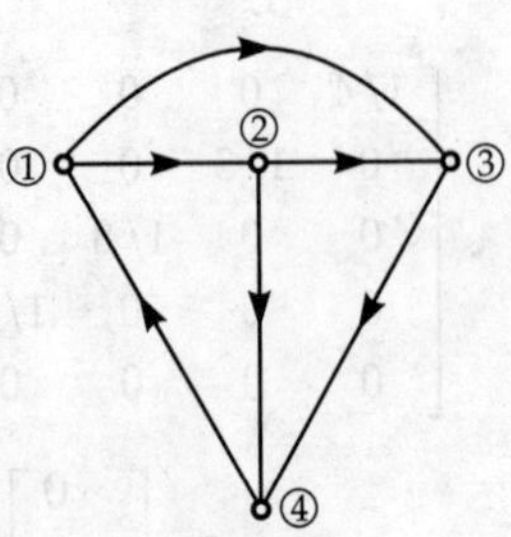

Fig. P13.5

4. Fig. P13.5 represents the oriented graph of a network. Show the tree, twigs and links.

   [**Hint.** Refer to Ex. 13.6]

5. An oriented graph is shown in Fig. P13.6. Obtain the incidence matrix.
[**Hint.** Refer to Ex. 13.8]

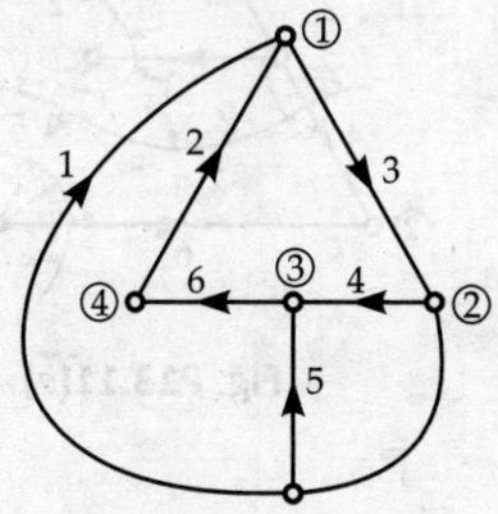

Fig. P13.6

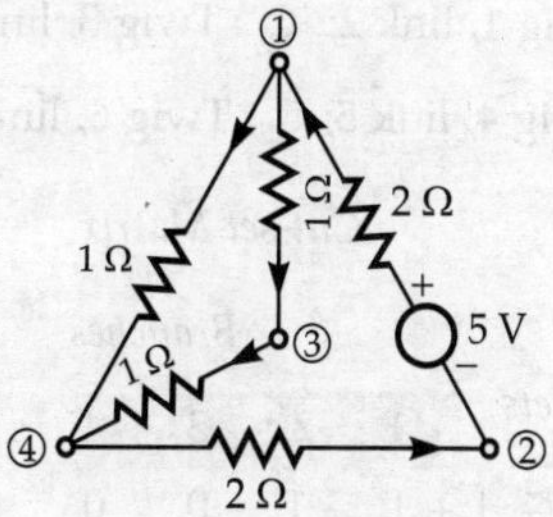

Fig. P13.7

6. For the network of Fig P13.7, find the no. of twigs and links. Obtain the tie set matrix.
[**Hint.** Refer to Ex. 13.12]

7. A network is shown in Fig. P13.8. Draw the graph and possible trees. Find the number of twigs and links.

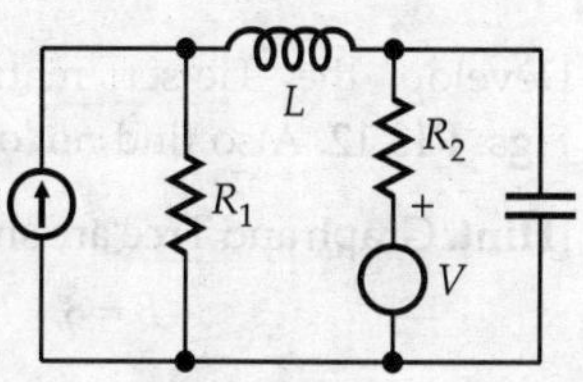

Fig. P13.8

[**Hint.** $B = 4$; $N = 3$ (Graph shown) in Fig. P13.9(*a*)

$\therefore$ Twigs $= 3 - 1 = 2$ and Links $= B - (N - 1) = 2$

Possible trees are shown in Fig. P13.9(*b*)]

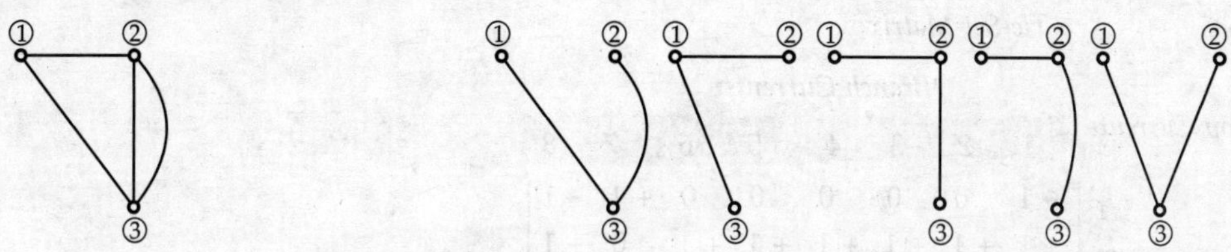

Fig. P13.9 (*a*) (*b*)

8. Obtain the fundamental tie-set matrix for Fig. P13.8 for any arbitrary tree.

[**Hint.** Branches are arbitrarily named and directed.

Loop-1 is formed with link 2 and twigs 3, 1.

Loop-2 is formed with link 4 and twigs 3, 1 (Fig. P13.10)]

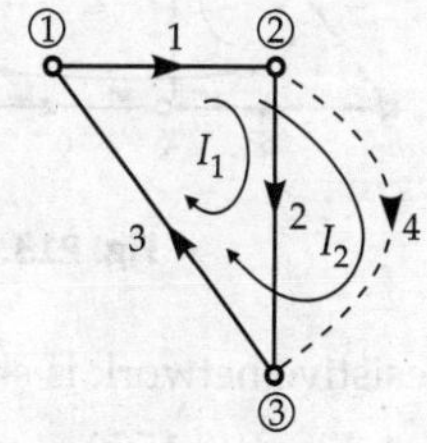

Fig. P13.10

Tie-set matrix

Loop Nos.	*Branches* 1	2	3	4
I_1	1	1	1	0
I_2	1	0	1	1

9. A resistive network is shown in Fig. P13.11. Obtain the cut-set matrix.

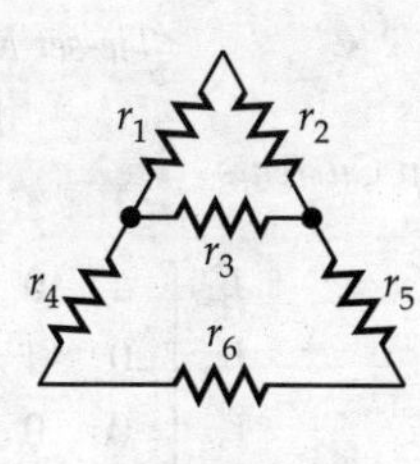

Fig. P13.11

[**Hint.** The tree is shown in Fig. P13.11(*a*) where bold lines represent twigs and dotted lines represent links.

C_1 : Twig 1, link 2; C_2 : Twig 3, links 2, 5

C_3 : Twig 4, link 5; C_4 : Twig 6, link 5]

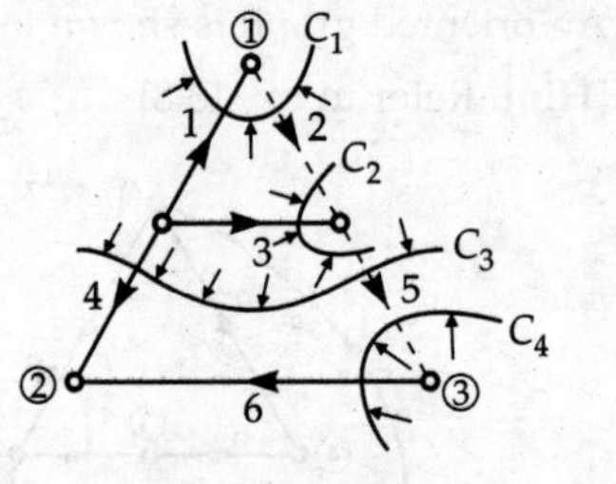

Fig. P13.11(*a*)

Cut-set Matrix

Branches

Cut-Sets	1	2	3	4	5	6
C_1	+1	−1	0	0	0	0
C_2	0	+1	+1	0	−1	0
C_3	0	0	0	+1	+1	0
C_4	0	0	0	0	−1	+ 1

10. Develop the Tie-set matrix of the circuit shown in Figs. P13.12. Also find no. of links.

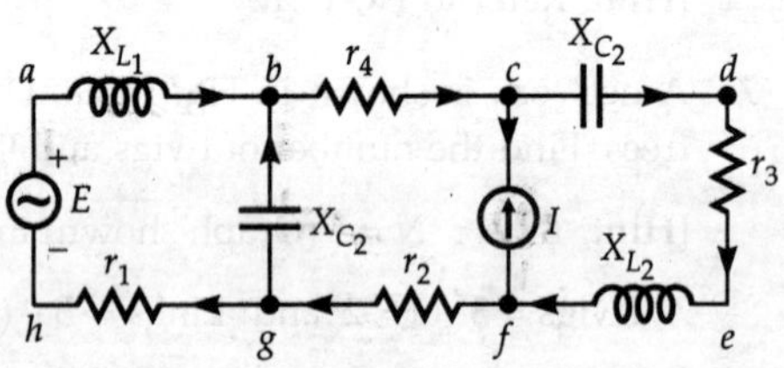

Fig. P13.12

[**Hint.** Graph and Tree are shown in Figs. P13.13 and P13.14.

$$B = 8, \quad N = 7$$

$\therefore$ No. of twigs = $N - 1 = 6$

No. of Links = $B - (N - 1) = 2$

Tie-Set Matrix

Branch Currents

Loop Currents	1	2	3	4	5	6	7	8
I_1	−1	0	0	0	0	0	+1	−1
I_2	+1	+1	+1	+1	+1	+1	0	+1

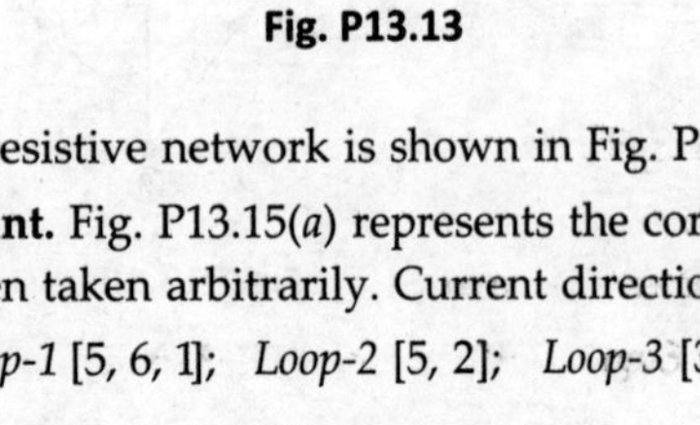

Fig. P13.13

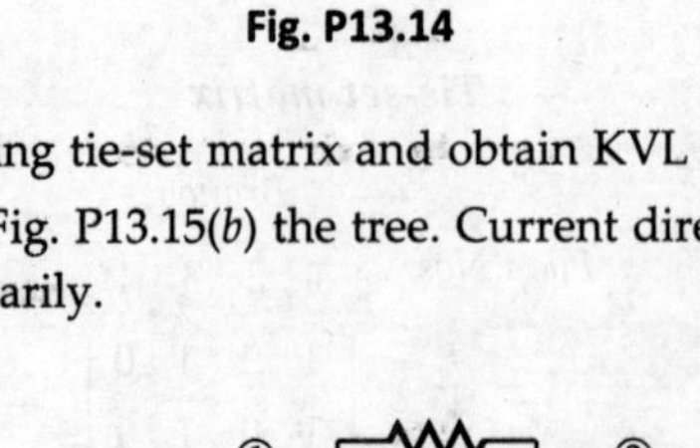

Fig. P13.14

11. A resistive network is shown in Fig. P13.15. Set up corresponding tie-set matrix and obtain KVL equation.

[**Hint.** Fig. P13.15(*a*) represents the corresponding graphs and Fig. P13.15(*b*) the tree. Current directions have been taken arbitrarily. Current direction have been taken arbitrarily.

Loop-1 [5, 6, 1]; *Loop-2* [5, 2]; *Loop-3* [3, 6]; *Loop-4* [4, 5, 6]

Tie-set Matrix

Branches

Loop Currents	1	2	3	4	5	6
I_1	1	0	0	0	1	1
I_2	0	1	0	0	−1	0
I_3	0	0	1	0	0	−1
I_4	0	0	0	1	1	1

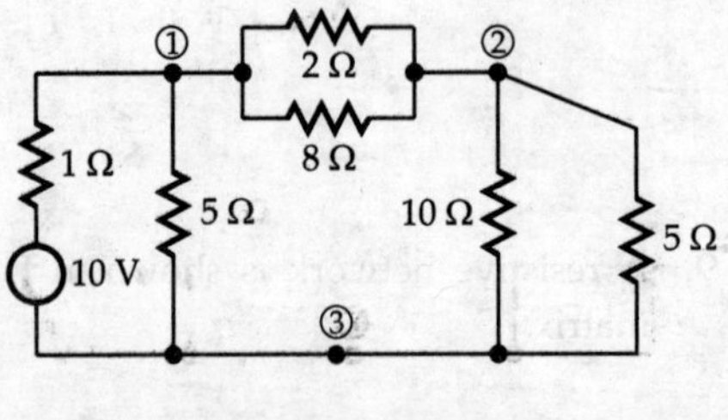

Fig. P13.15

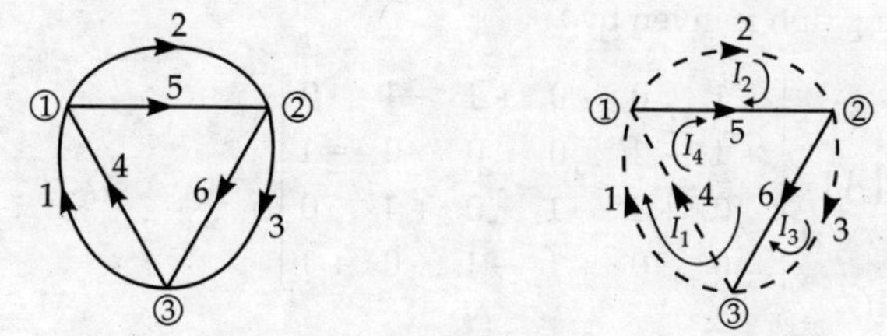

Fig. P13.15 (*a*) (*b*)

The rows give,

$$v_1 + v_5 + v_6 = 0; \quad v_2 - v_5 = 0; \quad v_3 - v_6 = 0; v_4 + v_5 + v_6 = 0$$

The columns give

$$j_1 = I_1\ ;\ j_2 = I_2;\ j_3 = I_3\ ;\ j_4 = I_4\ ;\ j_5 = I_1 - I_2 + I_4;\ j_6 = I_1 - I_3 + I_4.$$

But $\quad v_1 = r_1\, j_1 - 10 = j_1 - 10\ ;\ v_2 = r_2\, j_2 = 2j_2\ ;\ v_3 = r_3\, j_3 = 5j_3\ ;$

$$v_4 = r_4\, j_4 = 5j_4\ ;\ v_5 = r_5\, j_5 = 8\, j_5\ ;\ v_6 = r_6\, j_6 = 10\, j_6.$$

Substitution of values of v_1, v_2,..... with corresponding j_1, j_2,... yields the desired result of forming the necessary KVL equations.]

12. Draw the oriented graph of the figure shown in Fig. P13.16. Also obtain the fundamental cut-set matrix.

[**Hint.** The graph (oriented) and the tree are shown in Fig. P13.16(*a*)

C_1 is formed by twig 2 and links 5, 3

C_2 is formed by twig 4 and links 3, 6

C_3 is formed by twig 1 and links 5, 3, 6.

[Fig. P13.16(*b*)].

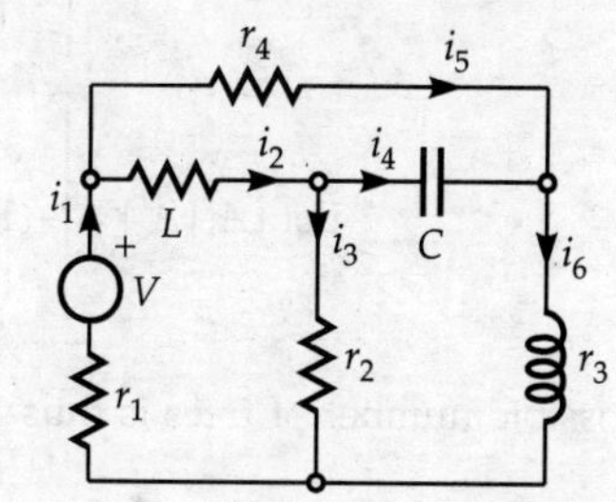

Fig. P13.16

Fig. P13.16 (*a*) (*b*)

Cut-set Matrix

Branches

Cut-Sets

	1	2	3	4	5	6
C_1	0	+1	−1	0	−1	0
C_2	0	0	−1	+1	0	−1
C_3	+1	0	−1	0	−1	−1

13. The incidence matrix of a graph is given by

$$[A_i] = \begin{bmatrix} -1 & 0 & 0 & +1 & -1 & 0 \\ +1 & -1 & 0 & 0 & 0 & -1 \\ 0 & +1 & -1 & 0 & +1 & 0 \\ 0 & 0 & +1 & -1 & 0 & +1 \end{bmatrix}$$

Determine possible number of trees.

[**Hint.** The reduced incidence matrix is obtained by deleting one of the rows, say the bottom most row.

$$[A] = \begin{bmatrix} -1 & 0 & 0 & +1 & -1 & 0 \\ +1 & -1 & 0 & 0 & 0 & -1 \\ 0 & +1 & -1 & 0 & +1 & 0 \end{bmatrix}$$

when $$[A^t] = \begin{bmatrix} -1 & +1 & 0 \\ 0 & -1 & +1 \\ 0 & 0 & -1 \\ +1 & 0 & 0 \\ -1 & 0 & +1 \\ 0 & 1 & 0 \end{bmatrix}$$

$$\therefore \qquad \det [A][A^t] = \begin{vmatrix} 3 & -1 & -1 \\ -1 & 3 & -1 \\ -1 & -1 & 3 \end{vmatrix} = 16$$

Possible number of trees is thus 16].

CHAPTER 14

Fourier Analysis

14.1 INTRODUCTION

Jean Baptiste Joseph Fourier (1768—1830) developed a technique of analysing non-sinusoidal waveforms applicable to a wide range of engineering problems. Later it was applied to analyse electric circuits excited by non-sinusoidal waveforms.

14.2 EXPONENTIAL FORM OF FOURIER SERIES

In his work, Fourier demonstrated that a periodic function $f(t)$ can be expressed as a sum of sinusoidal functions.

As per Fourier representation,

$$f(t) = a_0 + \sum_{n=1}^{\infty} M_n \cos(n\,\omega_0 t + \theta_n) \quad ...(14.1)$$

where $\omega_0 = \dfrac{2\pi}{T_0}$,

T_o being the time period (when $n=1$, one cycle covers T_o seconds while $M_1 \cos(\omega_0 t + \theta_1)$ is termed as *fundamental*). Taking $n=2$, T_o represents the two cycles within T_o seconds while the term $M_2 \cos(2\omega_0 t + \theta_2)$ is called the *2nd harmonic.* In the continued fashion thus for $n = K$, K cycles fall within T_o seconds and $M_K \sin(K\omega_0 t + \theta_K)$ is the *Kth harmonic term.*

Using Euler identity,

$$f(t) = a_0 + \sum_{\substack{n=-\infty \\ n \neq 0}}^{\infty} C_n\, e^{jn\omega_0 t}$$

[C_n = Complex Fourier coefficients]

$$= a_0 + \sum_{n=1}^{\infty} a_n \cos n\omega_0 t + b_n \sin n\omega_0 t \quad ...(14.2)$$

Fourier coefficients C_n can be evaluated as follows :

$$\because \quad f(t) = \sum_{n=-\infty}^{\infty} C_n\, e^{jn\omega_0 t},$$

multiplying both sides of the above expression by $e^{-jK\omega_0 t}$ and integrating over the interval t_1 to $(t_1 + T_0)$, we get

$$\int_{t_1}^{t_1+T_0} f(t)\, e^{-jK\omega_0 t} dt = \int_{t_1}^{t_1+T_0} \left(\sum_{n=-\infty}^{\infty} C_n e^{jn\omega_0 t} \right) e^{-jK\omega_0 t}\, dt$$

$$= C_K\, T_0$$

$$\text{Since,} \quad \int_{t_1}^{t_1+T_0} e^{\,j(n-K)\omega_0 t}\, dt = \begin{cases} 0 & \text{for } n \neq K \\ T_0 & \text{for } n = K \end{cases}$$

$\therefore$ The *Fourier coefficients* are defined by the expression [given in (14.3)]

$$\mathbf{C_n = \frac{1}{T_0} \int_{t_1}^{t_1+T_0} f(t)\, e^{-jn\omega_0 t}\, dt} \quad ...(14.3)$$

Expression (14.3) represents the *exponential form* of Fourier Series.

14.3 TRIGONOMETRIC FORM OF FOURIER SERIES

From equation (14.3), we can write

$$2C_n = \frac{2}{T_0}\int_{t_1}^{t_1+T_0} f(t)\, e^{-jn\omega_0 t}\, dt$$

$$= \frac{2}{T_0}\int_{t_1}^{t_1+T_0} f(t)\,[\cos n\omega_0 t - j\sin n\,\omega_0 t]\, dt$$

[Using Euler's identity]

$$\text{or,}\quad 2C_n = \frac{2}{T_0}\int_{t_1}^{t_1+T_0} f(t)\cos n\omega_0 t\, dt - j\frac{2}{T_0}\int_{t_1}^{t_1+T_0} f(t)\sin n\,\omega_0 t\, dt \qquad ...(14.4)$$

However, C_n being a complex coefficient,

$$2C_n = a_n - jb_n \qquad ...(14.5)$$

Comparing (14.4) and (14.5),

$$\boldsymbol{a_n = \frac{2}{T_0}\int_{t_1}^{t_1+T_0} f(t)\cos n\omega_0 t\, dt} \qquad ...[14.6(a)]$$

$$\boldsymbol{b_n = \frac{2}{T_0}\int_{t_1}^{t_1+T_0} f(t)\sin n\omega_0 t\, dt} \qquad ...[14.6(b)]$$

Assuming $t_1 = 0$, T_o corresponding to 2π radians,

$$a_n = \frac{2}{2\pi}\int_0^{2\pi} F(\psi)\cos n\psi\, d\psi$$

$$= \frac{1}{\pi}\int_0^{2\pi} F(\psi)\cos n\psi\, d\psi$$

$$\equiv \frac{1}{\pi}\int_{-\pi}^{\pi} F(\psi)\cos n\psi\, d\psi$$

$$= \frac{1}{\pi}\int_{-T_0/2}^{T_0/2} F(\psi)\cos n\psi\, d\psi \qquad ...[14.6(a)(i)]$$

$$\text{and}\quad b_n = \frac{2}{2\pi}\int_0^{2\pi} F(\psi)\sin n\psi\, d\psi = \frac{1}{\pi}\int_0^{2\pi} F(\psi)\sin n\psi\, d\psi$$

$$= \frac{1}{\pi}\int_{-\pi}^{\pi} F(\psi)\sin n\psi\, d\psi$$

$$= \frac{1}{\pi}\int_{-T_0/2}^{T_0/2} F(\psi)\sin n\,\psi\, d\psi \qquad ...[14.6(b)(i)]$$

where $\psi = \omega t$ and $F(\psi) \equiv f(\psi/\omega)$.

Also, from equation (14.3), C_0, being written here as a_0 and is given by

$$\boldsymbol{a_0 = \frac{1}{T_0}\int_{t_1}^{t_1+T_0} f(t)\, dt} \qquad ...(14.7)$$

The *average value* (a_0) *of the waveform* then can be directly evaluated from the waveform.

Since the periodic function can be represented as a sum of sinusoidal functions we can rewrite equation (14.1) as

$$f(t) = a_0 + \sum_{n=1}^{\infty} a_n \cos n\alpha + \sum_{n=1}^{\infty} b_n \sin n\alpha$$

where a_0 = a constant.

$a_1, a_2, a_3, ..., a_n$ and $b_1, b_2, ,..., b_n$ are the amplitudes of different harmonies,

α = a variable and n = an integer 1, 2, ...

Fourier series can also be expressed in terms of either sine or cosine terms.

Let us assume

$$M = a_n \cos n\alpha + b_n \sin n\alpha$$

$$= \sqrt{a_n^2 + b_n^2}\left[\frac{a_n}{\sqrt{a_n^2+b_n^2}}.\cos n\alpha + \frac{b_n}{\sqrt{a_n^2+b_n^2}}\sin n\alpha\right]$$

Let us now assume

$$\frac{a_n}{\sqrt{a_n^2 + b_n^2}} = \sin\phi_n$$

$$\text{and}\quad \frac{b_n}{\sqrt{a_n^2 + b^2}} = \cos\phi_n$$

$$\therefore M = \sqrt{a_n^2 + b_n^2}\,[\sin\phi_n \cos n\alpha + \cos\phi_n \sin n\alpha]$$

$$= K_n \sin(n\alpha + \phi_n)$$

where $K_n = \sqrt{a_n^2 + b_n^2}$

Thus, finally we can write

$$f(t) = a_0 + K_1 \sin(\alpha + \phi_1) + K_2 \sin(2\alpha + \phi_2) + ... + K_n \sin(n\alpha + \phi_n) \qquad ...(14.8)$$

$$\text{Here}\quad \tan\phi_n = \frac{\sin\phi_n}{\cos\phi_n} = \frac{a_n}{b_n}. \qquad ...(14.8a)$$

On the other hand if we represent

$$\frac{a_n}{\sqrt{a_n^2 + b_n^2}} = \cos\phi_n\ ;\quad \frac{b_n}{\sqrt{a_n^2 + b_n^2}} = \sin\phi_n,$$

$$M = \sqrt{a_n^2 + b_n^2}\,[\cos\phi_n \sin n\alpha + \sin\phi_n \sin n\alpha]$$
$$= K_n \cos(n\alpha - \phi_n)$$

i.e., $f(t) = a_0 + K_1 \cos(\alpha - \phi_1) + K_2 \cos(2\alpha - \phi_2) + \ldots + K_n \sin(n\alpha - \phi_n)$ ...(14.9)

Here $\tan\phi_n = \dfrac{\sin\phi_n}{\cos\phi_n} = \dfrac{b_n}{a_n}$. ...(14.9*a*)

14.4 SYMMETRY IN FOURIER SERIES

When a signal exhibits symmetrical properties, simplification procedure can be adopted in Fourier analysis. There are *three* types of symmetry :

(*a*) Even function symmetry

(*b*) Odd function symmetry

(*c*) Half wave symmetry.

(a) Even Function Symmetry

A function is said to be even if

$$f(t) = f(-t) \quad \text{...(14.10)}$$

An even function is symmetrical about the vertical axis. In order to determine the Fourier coefficients, the condition of symmetry being applied, let $t_1 = -T_0/2$.

$$\therefore a_0 = \frac{1}{T_0}\int_{t_1}^{t_1+T_0} f(t)\,dt = \frac{1}{T_0}\int_{-T_0/2}^{-T_0/2+T_0} f(t)\,dt$$

$$= \frac{1}{T_0}\int_{-T_0/2}^{T_0/2} f(t)\,dt$$

$$= \frac{1}{T_0}\int_{-T_0/2}^{0} f(t)\,dt + \frac{1}{T_0}\int_{0}^{T_0/2} f(t)\,dt$$

Let us now change the variable of the first integral so that $t \equiv (-x)$ in the first integral.

Then, $f(-x) = f(x)$, $dt = d(-x) = -dx$, while the range of integration is from $x = T_0/2$ to 0.

$$\therefore a_0 = \frac{1}{T_0}\int_{T_0/2}^{0} f(x)(-dx) + \frac{1}{T_0}\int_{0}^{T_0/2} f(t)\,dt$$

$$= \frac{1}{T_0}\int_{0}^{T_0/2} f(x)\,dx + \frac{1}{T_0}\int_{0}^{T_0/2} f(t)\,dt$$

$$\therefore \quad a_0 = \frac{2}{T_0}\int_{0}^{T_0/2} f(t)\,dt \quad \text{...(14.11)}$$

Similarly,

$$a_n = \frac{2}{T_0}\int_{-T_0/2}^{0} f(t)\cos n\omega_0 t\,dt + \frac{2}{T_0}\int_{0}^{T_0/2} f(t)\cos n\omega_0 t\,dt$$

$$= \frac{2}{T_0}\int_{T_0/2}^{0} f(x)\cos(-n\,\omega_0 x)(-dx) + \frac{2}{T_0}\int_{0}^{T_0/2} f(t)\cos n\,\omega_0 t\,dt$$

$$= \frac{2}{T_0}\int_{0}^{T_0/2} f(x)\cos(n\,\omega_0 x)\,dx + \frac{2}{T_0}\int_{0}^{T_0/2} f(t)\cos(n\omega_0 t)\,dt$$

$$\text{or,} \quad a_n = \frac{4}{T_0}\int_{0}^{T_0/2} f(t)\cos(n\omega_0 t)\,dt. \quad \text{...(14.12)}$$

Also, for the other coefficient,

$$b_n = \frac{2}{T_0}\int_{-T_0/2}^{0} f(t)\sin(n\omega_0 t)\,dt + \int_{0}^{T_0/2} f(t)\sin(n\,\omega_0 t)\,dt$$

$$= \frac{2}{T_0}\int_{T_0/2}^{0} f(x)\sin(-n\,\omega_0 x)(-dx) + \frac{2}{T_0}\int_{0}^{T_0/2} f(t)\sin(n\omega_0 t)\,dt$$

$$= -\frac{2}{T_0}\int_{0}^{T_0/2} f(x)\sin(n\,\omega_0 x)(dx) + \frac{2}{T_0}\int_{0}^{T_0/2} f(t)\sin(n\omega_0 t)\,dt = 0.$$

...[14.13(*a*)]

i.e., $b_n = 0$

Thus we see that, for even function symmetry,

$$a_0 = \frac{2}{T_0}\int_{0}^{T_0/2} f(t)\,dt,$$

$$a_n = \frac{4}{T_0}\int_{0}^{T_0/2} f(t)\cos(n\,\omega_0 t)\,dt,$$

$$b_n = 0.$$

CHAPTER 14

The cosine wave is an even function and the sum or product of two or more even functions is an even function. With addition of a constant, the even nature is still preserved.

(*b*) Odd Function Symmetry

A function is said to be odd if

$$f(t) = -f(-t) \qquad ...(14.14)$$

However, we have seen that

$$a_0 = \frac{1}{T_0}\int_{-T_0/2}^{0} f(t)\,dt + \frac{1}{T_0}\int_{0}^{T_0/2} f(t)\,dt.$$

Here, for $t = -x$, the first integral becomes

$$\frac{1}{T_0}\int_{+T_0/2}^{0} -f(x)(-dx)$$

since $-f(-t) = -f(x)$ and $dt = -dx$ when the integral is $T_0/2$ to 0.

$$\therefore a_0 = \frac{1}{T_0}\int_{T_0/2}^{0} -f(x)(-dx) + \frac{1}{T_0}\int_{0}^{T_0/2} f(t)\,dt$$

$$= \frac{1}{T_0}\int_{T_0/2}^{0} f(x)\,dx + \frac{1}{T_0}\int_{0}^{T_0/2} f(t)\,dt$$

$$= -\frac{1}{T_0}\int_{0}^{T_0/2} f(x)\,dx + \frac{1}{T_0}\int_{0}^{T_0/2} f(t)\,dt = 0.$$

note Two examples of even and odd symmetry are shown in Fig. 14.1 to illustrate the difference. In Fig. 14.1(*a*), the function is of even symmetry as $f(-x) = f(x)$ when $t = -x$ *i.e.*, about the vertical axis, the waveform is symmetrical. (it means, about the vertical axis, the area of wave *oxpq* is same to area of wave *ox′ p′ q* while time axis for the left part of the wave about the vertical axis is -ve or $ox' \equiv -ox$ in time scale).

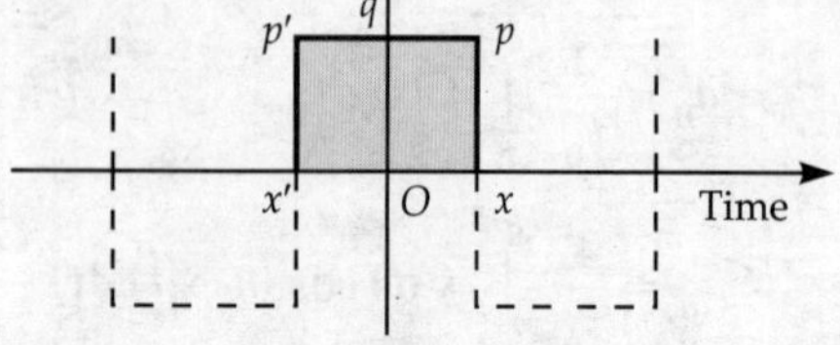

Fig. 14.1 (*a*) Even symmetry.

On the other hand, for the odd symmetry, $-f(-x) = f(t)$ when $t = -x$ *i.e.*, at equivalent -ve time, the left part of the waveform is symmetrical to the right part [in Fig. 14.1(*b*), *oxpq* is same as *ox′ p′ q′* but for time $x' (= -x)$, the wave form is symmetrically inverted].

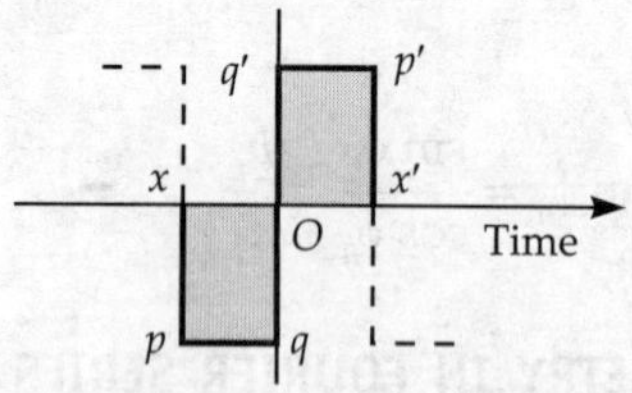

Fig. 14.1 (*b*) Odd symmetry.

In a similar way,

$$a_n = \frac{2}{T_0}\int_{-T_0/2}^{0} f(t)\cos(n\omega_0 t)\,dt + \frac{2}{T_0}\int_{0}^{T_0/2} f(t)\cos(n\omega_0 t)\,dt$$

$$= \frac{2}{T_0}\int_{+T_0/2}^{0} -f(x)\cos(-n\omega_0 x)(-dx) + \frac{2}{T_0}\int_{0}^{T_0/2} f(t)\cos(n\omega_0 t)\,dt$$

$$= \frac{2}{T_0}\int_{T_0/2}^{0} f(x)\cos(n\omega_0 x)\,dx + \frac{2}{T_0}\int_{0}^{T_0/2} f(t)\cos(n\omega_0 t)\,dt$$

$$= -\frac{2}{T_0}\int_{0}^{T_0/2} f(x)\cos(n\omega_0 x)\,dx + \frac{2}{T_0}\int_{0}^{T_0/2} f(t)\cos(n\omega_0 t)\,dt = 0.$$

and $$b_n = \frac{2}{T_0}\int_{-T_0/2}^{0} f(t)\sin(n\omega_0 t)dt + \int_{0}^{T_0/2} f(t)\sin(n\omega_0 t)dt$$

$$= \frac{2}{T_0}\int_{T_0/2}^{0} -f(x)\sin(-n\omega_0 x)(-dx) + \frac{2}{T_0}\int_{0}^{T_0/2} f(t)\sin(n\omega_0 t)\,dt$$

$$= -\frac{2}{T_0}\int_{T_0/2}^{0} f(x)\sin(n\,\omega_0 x)\,dx$$

$$+\frac{2}{T_0}\int_{0}^{T_0/2} f(t)\sin(n\omega_0 t)\,dt$$

$$= \frac{2}{T_0}\int_{0}^{T_0/2} f(x)\sin(n\omega_0 x)\,dx$$

$$+\frac{2}{T_0}\int_{0}^{T_0/2} f(t)\sin(n\omega_0 t)\,dt$$

$$= \frac{4}{T_0}\int_{0}^{T_0/2} f(t)\sin(n\omega_0 t)\,dt. \qquad ...(14.15)$$

Thus, we see, for a odd symmetry,

$$a_n = 0\,;$$

$$b_n = \frac{4}{T_0}\int_{0}^{T_0/2} f(t)\sin(n\omega_0 t)\,dt \text{ while } a_0 = 0.$$

(c) Half-wave Symmetry

A function is said to have half wave symmetry if

$$f(t) = -f\left(t - \frac{T_0}{2}\right). \qquad ...(14.16)$$

i.e., the half cycle is an inverted version of the adjacent half cycle (*i.e.*, if the waveform from $-T_0/2$ to 0 is inverted and if it becomes identical to the waveform from 0 to $T_0/2$, it is said to have half symmetry).

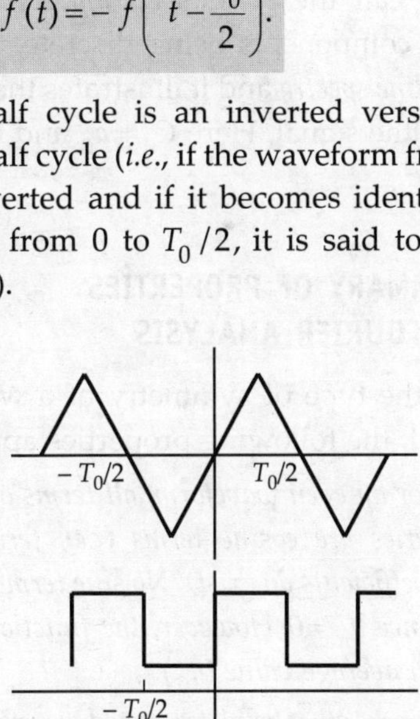

Fig. 14.2 Represents wave of half symmetry

Mathematically it can be shown that by changing the first variable of the Fourier coefficient expression for $t = x + T_0/2$ and $f(t) = -f(t - T_0/2)$,

$$a_0 = 0$$

$$a_n = b_n = 0 \quad \text{when } n \text{ is even}$$

and $$a_n = \frac{4}{T_0}\int_{0}^{T_0/2} f(t)\cos(n\omega_0 t)\,dt \text{ when } n \text{ is odd}, \qquad ...(14.17)$$

$$b_n = \frac{4}{T_0}\int_{0}^{T_0/2} f(t)\sin(n\omega_0 t)\,dt \text{ when } n \text{ is odd}. \qquad ...(14.18)$$

It may be noted that the sum of two or more odd functions is an odd function, but unlike to the property of even function, the addition of a constant removes the odd nature of the function. The product of two odd functions is an even function.

Figure 14.3 represents some examples of even, odd and half wave functions.

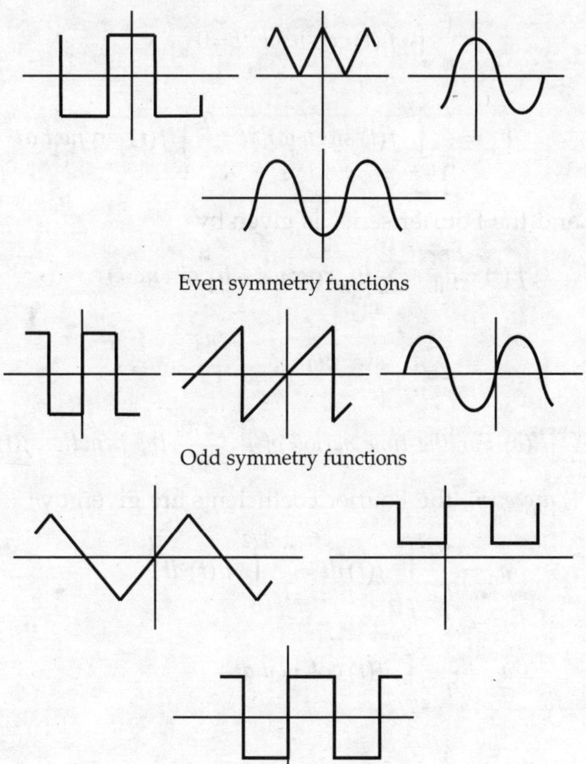

Fig. 14.3 Waveform Symmetry.

CHAPTER 14

Summary of Fourier Coefficients and Fourier Series

(a) When the period of the waveform is 2π *and* $f(t)$ *is even,* the Fourier coefficients are given by

$$a_0 = \frac{1}{2\pi}\int_{-\pi}^{\pi} f(t)dt = \frac{1}{\pi}\int_{0}^{\pi} f(t)\,dt.$$

$$a_n = \frac{1}{\pi}\int_{-\pi}^{\pi} f(t)\cos n\,\omega t\,dt = \frac{2}{\pi}\int_{0}^{\pi} f(t)\cos n\omega t\,dt$$

$$b_n = \frac{1}{\pi}\int_{-\pi}^{\pi} f(x)\sin n\omega t\,dt = 0$$

and the Fourier series is given by

$$f(t) = a_0 + \sum_{n=1}^{\infty}(a_n \cos n\omega t + b_n \sin n\omega t)$$
$$= a_0 + \sum_{n=1} a_n \cos n\omega t$$

On the other hand, the period being remaining 2π but $f(t)$ becoming odd, the Fourier coefficients are given by

$$a_0 = \frac{1}{2\pi}\int_{-\pi}^{\pi} f(t)\,dt = 0$$

$$a_n = \frac{1}{\pi}\int_{-\pi}^{\pi} f(t)\cos n\,\omega t\,dt = 0$$

$$b_n = \frac{1}{\pi}\int_{-\pi}^{\pi} f(t)\sin n\,\omega\,t\,dt = \frac{2}{\pi}\int_{0}^{\pi} f(t)\sin n\omega t\,dt$$

and the Fourier series is given by

$$f(t) = a_0 + \sum_{n=1}^{\infty}(a_n \cos n\omega t + b_n \sin n\omega t)$$
$$= \sum_{n=1}^{\infty} b_n \sin n\omega t$$

(b) For the time period of $T = \frac{2\pi}{\omega}$, the function f(t) being even, the Fourier coefficients are given by

$$a_0 = \frac{1}{T}\int_{-T/2}^{T/2} f(t)\,dt = \frac{2}{T}\int_{0}^{T/2} f(t)\,dt$$

$$a_n = \frac{2}{T}\int_{-T/2}^{T/2} f(t)\cos n\omega t\,dt$$
$$= \frac{4}{T}\int_{0}^{T/2} f(t)\cos n\omega t\,dt$$

$$b_n = \frac{2}{T}\int_{-T/2}^{T/2} f(t)\cos n\omega t\,dt = 0$$

and the Fourier series is given by

$$f(t) = a_0 + a_0 + \sum_{n=1}^{\infty} a_n \cos n\omega t + b_n \sin n\omega t$$
$$= a_0 + \sum_{n=1}^{\infty} a_n \cos n\omega t.$$

On the other hand, if for the same time period, f(t) be odd, the Fourier coefficients are given by

$$a_0 = \frac{1}{T}\int_{-T/2}^{T/2} f(t)\,dt = 0$$

$$a_n = \frac{2}{T}\int_{0}^{T/2} f(t)\cos n\omega t\,dt = 0$$

$$b_n = \frac{2}{T}\int_{-T/2}^{T/2} f(t)\cos n\omega t\,dt = \frac{4}{T}\int_{0}^{T/2} f(t)\sin n\omega t\,dt$$

and the Fourier series is given by

$$f(t) = \sum_{n=1}^{\infty} b_n \sin n\omega t.$$

14.5 FREQUENCY SPECTRUM

The *frequency spectrum* of the function $f(t)$ expressed as a Fourier series consists of a plot of the amplitude of the harmonics versus frequency (commonly known as *amplitude spectrum*) and the plot of phase of the harmonics versus frequency, which we call the *phase spectrum*. However, the frequency components being discrete, the spectra are called *line spectra* and it illustrates the frequency content of the signal. Here $C_0 = a_0$ and C_n is given by $\sqrt{a_n^2 + b_n^2}$.

14.6 SUMMARY OF PROPERTIES OF FOURIER ANALYSIS

Once the type of symmetry of a waveform is established, the following properties appear :

(a) *For an even waveform, all terms of its Fourier series are cosine terms (i.e., terms with a_n coefficients do exist). No sine terms are present since $b_n = 0$. However, the function does have an average value (a_0).*

(b) *On the other hand, for an odd waveform, the series contains only sine terms. There is no average value ($a_0 = 0$) and no cosine terms since $a_n = 0$. In special cases the given waveform may be odd only after its average value is subtracted.*

(c) *If the given waveform is of halfwave symmetry, only odd harmonics are present in the series. The series would contain both sine and cosine terms when n is odd. The average value is zero.*

EXAMPLE 14.1 *Obtain the coefficients of the exponential Fourier series for the waveform shown in Fig. E14.1.*

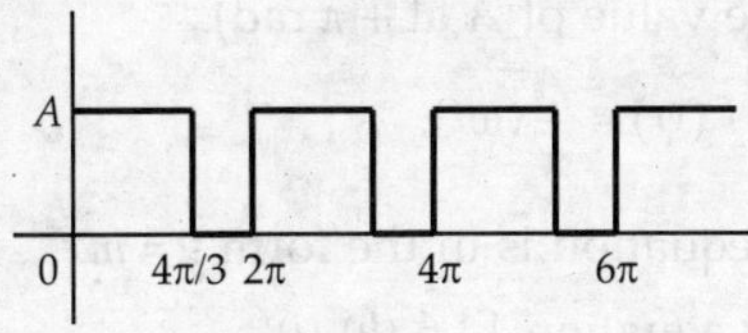

Fig. E14.1

SOLUTION.

$$C_n = \frac{1}{T_0}\int_0^{T_0} f(t)\, e^{-jn\omega_0 t}\, dt$$

$$= \frac{1}{2\pi}\int_0^{2\pi} f(t)\, e^{-jn\omega_0 t}\, dt$$

$$= \frac{1}{2\pi}\int_0^{4\pi/3} A e^{-jn\left(2\pi \times \frac{1}{T_0}\right)t}\, dt$$

$$= \frac{1}{2\pi}\int_0^{4\pi/3} A e^{-jnt}\, dt$$

$$= \frac{jA}{2\pi n}\left[e^{-j\left(\frac{4\pi n}{3}\right)} - 1\right].$$

EXAMPLE 14.2 *Find the waveform symmetry of the following waveforms (Fig. E14.2).*

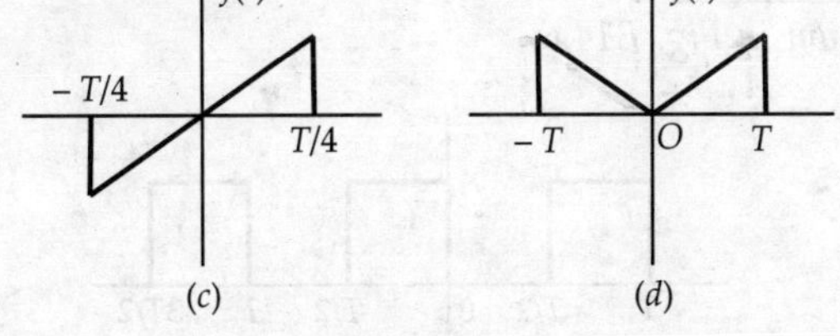

Fig. E14.2

SOLUTION. By inspection, for Fig. E14.2(*a*) the given waveform is an **odd function**, while for Fig. E14.2(*b*), the given waveform is also another **odd function**.

For Fig. E14.2(*c*), the given waveform is an **odd function** but for Fig. E14.2(*d*), the given waveform is an **even function**.

EXAMPLE 14.3 *Find the amplitude of the 5th harmonic of the given waveform (Fig. E14.3).*

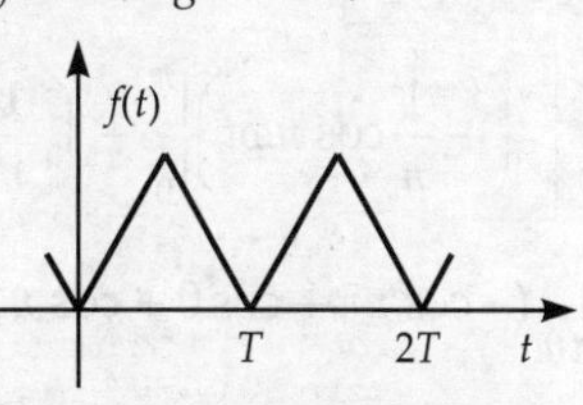

Fig. E14.3

SOLUTION. Since the given waveform is an even function, only cosine terms would be present.

$$\therefore \qquad a_5 = \frac{4}{T}\int_0^{T/2} \frac{2t}{T}\cos\left(\frac{2\pi}{T}\right)(5\,t)\,dt$$

$$= \frac{2}{25\,\pi^2}(\cos 5\pi - 1) = -\frac{\mathbf{4}}{\mathbf{25\,\pi^2}}.$$

EXAMPLE 14.4 *A square waveform is shown in Fig. E14.4. Obtain the Fourier series.*

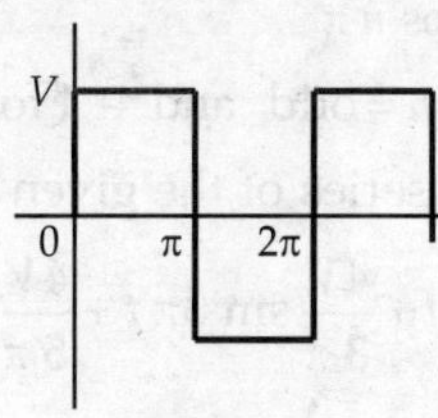

Fig. E14.4

SOLUTION. It may be observed that in the interval $0 < \omega t < \pi$, $f(t) = V$ while in the interval $\pi < \omega t < 2\pi$, $f(t) = -V$. Hence the given waveform possesses symmetry.

$\therefore$ The series does not contain any cosine term and the average value would be zero.

i.e., $\qquad a_n = 0;\ a_0 = 0.$

However sine terms would be present, *i.e.*, b_n would be present.

Here

$$a_n = \frac{1}{\pi}\left[\int_0^{\pi} V\cos n\omega t\, d(\omega t) + \int_{\pi}^{2\pi} (-V)\cos n\omega t\, d(\omega t)\right]$$

$$= \frac{V}{\pi}\left[\left(\frac{1}{n}\sin n\omega t\right)\Bigg|_0^{\pi} - \left(\frac{1}{n}\sin n\,\omega\, t\right)\Bigg|_{\pi}^{2\pi}\right]$$

$$= \frac{V}{\pi}\left[\frac{1}{n}\sin n\pi - \frac{1}{n}\sin n(2\pi) + \frac{1}{n}\sin n\pi\right]$$

$$= 0 \text{ for any value of } n.$$

and $b_n = \frac{1}{\pi}\left[\int_0^{\pi} V\sin(n\omega t)d(\omega t) + \int_{\pi}^{2\pi}(-V)\cos(n\omega t)d(\omega t)\right]$

$$= \frac{V}{\pi}\left[\left(-\frac{1}{n}\cos n\omega t\right)\Big|_0^{\pi} + \left(\frac{1}{n}\cos n\,\omega\, t\right)\Big|_{\pi}^{2\pi}\right]$$

$$= \frac{V}{\pi n}(-\cos n\pi + \cos 0 + \cos n2\pi - \cos n\,\pi)$$

$$= \frac{2V}{n\pi}(1 - \cos n\,\pi);$$

for $n = 1$, $b_n = \frac{4V}{\pi}$

for $n = 2$, $b_n = 0$

for $n = 3$, $b_n = \frac{4V}{3\pi}$

for $n = 4$, $b_n = 0$

for $n = 5$, $b_n = \frac{4\,V}{5\,\pi}$

and so on, since $\cos n\,\pi$

$= -1$ for $n =$ odd and $+1$ for $n =$ even.

$\therefore$ The Fourier series of the given waveform is

$$f(t) = \frac{4V}{\pi}\sin\omega\,t + \frac{4V}{3\,\pi}\sin 3\pi\,t + \frac{4V}{5\,\pi}\sin 5\,\omega + \ldots.$$

EXAMPLE 14.5 *Find the Fourier expansion of the given waveform (Fig. E14.5).*

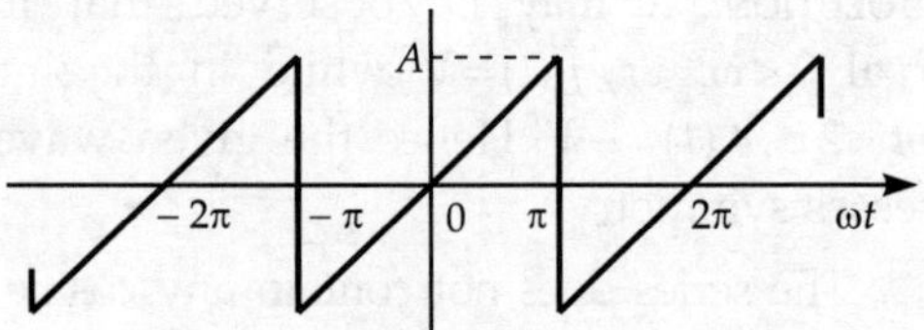

Fig. E14.5

SOLUTION. By inspection, the given function is having odd symmetry.

$\therefore$ $a_0 = 0\,;\, a_n = 0.$

Also, $T_0 = (2\,\pi)$ rad.

It may be revealed that if the period $0 - 2\,\pi$ is considered, the function and integration are to be carried out in two parts, *i.e.*, from 0 to π and again from π to $2\,\pi$ since the function is different for the two spans. On the other hand, from $-\pi$ to $+\pi$, in one way, the full period is covered and also, the function has one form and hence there will be one integral (*i.e.*, from $-\pi$ to π, the waveform is a single straight line equation with a zero intercept and having the value of A at $+\pi$ rad).

$$\therefore \quad f(\psi) = \frac{A}{\pi}(\omega t),$$

since the equation is in the form $y = mx$.

Using equation 14.6 (*b*) (*i*),

$$b_n = \frac{1}{\pi}\int_{-\pi}^{\pi} F(\psi)\sin\psi\,d\psi$$

$$= \frac{1}{\pi}\int_{-\pi}^{\pi}\frac{A}{\pi}(\omega\,t)\sin(n\,\omega\,t)\,d(\omega t)$$

$$= \frac{A}{\pi^2}\left[\frac{1}{n^2}\sin(n\,\omega\,t) - \frac{\omega t}{n}\cos n\omega t\right]_{-\pi}^{\pi}$$

$$= -\frac{2\,A}{n\pi}(\cos n\pi).$$

$\therefore$ For $n = 1$, $b_1 = \frac{2\,A}{\pi}$, for $n = 2$, $b_2 = -\frac{2\,A}{2\pi}$;

for $n = 3$, $b_3 = \frac{2\,A}{3\pi}$,

and so on; (with the knowledge that for $n =$ even number, $\cos n\pi$ is $+1$ and for $n =$ odd numbers, $\cos n\,\pi = -1$).

$\therefore$ The Fourier series becomes

$$f(t) = \frac{2\,A}{\pi}\sin\omega t - \frac{2\,A}{2\pi}\sin 2\,\omega\,t + \frac{2\,A}{3\pi}\sin 3\,\omega t - \frac{2\,A}{4\pi}\sin 4\,\omega\,t + \ldots..$$

$$= \frac{2A}{\pi}\left[\sin\omega t - \frac{1}{2}\sin 2\omega t + \frac{1}{3}\sin 3\omega t - \frac{1}{4}\sin 4\omega t + \ldots\right]$$

EXAMPLE 14.6 *Determine the Fourier series of the wave shown in Fig. E14.6.*

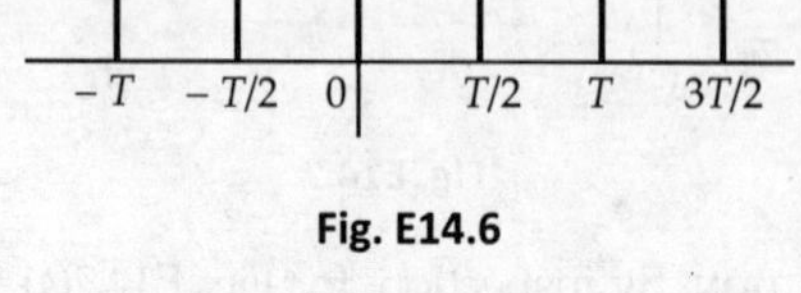

Fig. E14.6

SOLUTION. By inspection, it may be seen that

$$f(t) = A \text{ when } 0 < t < \frac{T}{2}$$

$$= 0 \text{ when } \frac{T}{2} < t < T.$$

$$\therefore\ a_0 = \frac{1}{T}\int_0^T f(t)\,dt$$

$$= \frac{1}{T}\left(\int_0^{T/2} A\,dt + \int_{T/2}^{T} 0\,.\,dt\right) = \frac{A}{T}\,.\,t\Big|_0^{T/2} = \frac{A}{2}.$$

$$a_n = \frac{2}{T}\int_0^T f(t)\cos(n\omega_0 t)\,dt$$

$$= \frac{2}{T}\left[\int_0^{T/2} A\cos\frac{2\pi n}{T}\,.\,tdt + \int_{T/2}^{T} 0.\cos\frac{2\pi n}{T}\,.\,tdt\right]$$

$$= \frac{2A}{T}\left(\frac{T}{2\pi n}\right)\sin\left(\frac{2\pi n}{T}\right)t\Big|_0^{T/2}$$

$$= \frac{A}{n\pi}\sin n\pi = 0 \text{ for any value of } n\,(1, 2, ...)$$

$$b_n = \frac{2}{T}\int_0^T f(t)\sin(n\,\omega_0 t)\,dt$$

$$= \frac{2}{T}\left[\int_0^{T/2} A\sin(n\omega_0 t)\,dt + \int_{T/2}^{T} 0.\sin(n\omega_0 t)dt\right]$$

$$= \frac{2}{T}\left[\int_0^{T/2} A\sin(n\,\omega_0 t)\,dt\right]$$

$$= \frac{2}{T}\int_0^{T/2} A\sin\left(\frac{2\pi n}{T}\right)t\,dt$$

$$= \frac{2A}{T}\left(-\frac{T}{2\pi n}\right)\cos\left(\frac{2\pi n}{T}\right)t\Big|_0^{T/2}$$

$$= -\frac{A}{n\pi}[\cos(n\pi) - 1].$$

However, when n is even, $\cos n\pi$ is $+1$ and hence $b_n = 0$ for any even value of n. On the other hand, for any odd value of n, since $\cos n\pi = -1$, hence, $b_n = \dfrac{2A}{n\pi}$ when n is odd.

$\therefore f(t)$, the Fourier series becomes

$$f(t) = \frac{A}{2} + \frac{2A}{\pi}\sin(\omega_0 t) + \frac{2A}{3\pi}\sin(3\,\omega_0 t) + \frac{2A}{5\pi}\sin(5\,\omega_0\,.\,t) + \ldots$$

$$= \frac{A}{2} + \frac{2A}{\pi}\left[\sin(\omega_0 t) + \frac{1}{3}\sin(3\omega_0 t) + \frac{1}{5}\sin(5\,\omega_0 t) + \ldots\right]$$

EXAMPLE 14.7 *Obtain the Fourier analysis of the waveform shown in Fig. E14.7.*

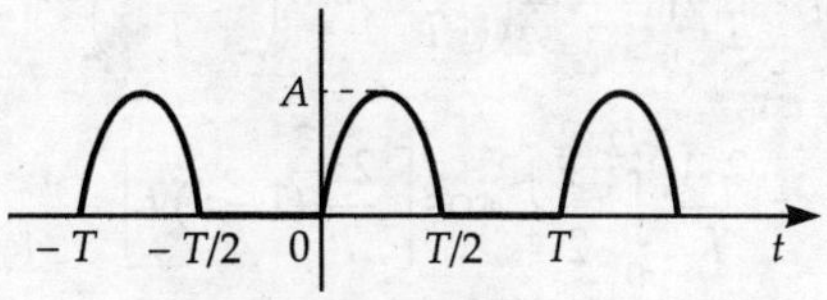

Fig. E14.7

SOLUTION. By inspection it is seen that the function is described by

$$f(t) = A\sin\left(\frac{2\pi t}{T}\right), \text{ when } 0 \le t \le \frac{T}{2}$$

$$= 0, \text{ when } \frac{T}{2} \le t \le T.$$

$$\therefore\quad a_0 = \frac{1}{T}\int_0^{T/2} A\sin\left(\frac{2\pi t}{T}\right)dt$$

$$= \frac{1}{T}\left(-\frac{T}{2\pi}\right)A\cos\left(\frac{2\pi t}{T}\right)\Big|_0^{T/2}$$

$$= -\frac{A}{2\pi}(\cos\pi - 1) = \frac{A}{\pi}$$

Similarly,

$$a_n = \frac{2}{T}\int_0^{T/2} A\sin\left(\frac{2\pi t}{T}\right)\cos\left(\frac{2\pi nt}{T}\right)dt$$

$$= \frac{2A}{T}\int_0^{T/2}\frac{1}{2}\left\{\sin\left[\frac{2\pi}{T}(1+n)t\right] + \sin\left[\frac{2\pi}{T}(1-n)t\right]\right\}dt$$

$$= -\frac{A}{T}\left\{\frac{T}{2\pi(1+n)}\cos\left[\frac{2\pi}{T}(1+n)t\right] + \frac{T}{2\pi(1-n)}\cos\left[\frac{2\pi}{T}(1-n)t\right]\right\}_0^{T/2}$$

$$= -\frac{A}{2\pi}\left\{\frac{1}{1+n}\{\cos[\pi(1+n)] - 1\} + \frac{1}{1-n}\{\cos[\pi(1-n)] - 1\}\right\}$$

For n odd, $\cos[\pi(1+n)] = \cos[\pi(1-n)] = 1$ and for n even, $\cos[\pi(1+n)] = \cos[\pi(1-n)] = -1.$

$\therefore a_n = 0$ for all cases when n is odd.

$$a_n = \frac{2A}{\pi(1-n^2)} \text{ for all cases when } n \text{ is even.}$$

In a similar way

$$b_n = \frac{2}{T}\int_0^{T/2} A\sin\left(\frac{2\pi t}{T}\right)\sin\left(\frac{2\pi nt}{T}\right)dt$$

$$= \frac{2A}{T}\int_0^{T/2}\frac{1}{2}\left\{\cos\left[\frac{2\pi}{T}(1-n)\,t\right] - \cos\left[\frac{2\pi}{T}(1+n)\,t\right]\right\}dt$$

$$= \frac{A}{2\pi}\left\{\frac{1}{1-n}\sin\left[\frac{2\pi}{T}(1-n)\,t\right] - \frac{1}{1+n}\sin\left[\frac{2\pi}{T}(1+n)\,t\right]\right\}_0^{T/2}$$

$$= \frac{A}{2\pi}\left\{\frac{1}{1-n}\{\sin[\pi(1-n)]\} - \frac{1}{1+n}\{\sin[\pi(1+n)]\}\right\}$$

For all n, except $n=1$,

$$\sin[\pi(1-n)] = \sin[\pi(1+n)] = 0$$

as well as $b_n = 0$.

for $n=1$, $\quad b_1 = \frac{2A}{T}\int_0^{T/2}\sin^2\left(\frac{2\pi t}{T}\right)dt$

$$= \frac{A}{T}\int_0^{T/2}\left[1-\cos\left(\frac{4\pi t}{T}\right)\right]dt$$

$$= \frac{A}{2} - \frac{A}{4\pi}\sin\left(\frac{4\pi t}{T}\right)\Bigg|_0^{T/2} = \frac{A}{2}.$$

$\therefore$ The Fourier series becomes

$$f(t) = \frac{A}{\pi} + \frac{A}{2}\sin\left(\frac{2\pi t}{T}\right) - \frac{2A}{3\pi}\cos\left(\frac{4\pi t}{T}\right) - \frac{2A}{15\pi}\cos\left(\frac{8\pi t}{T}\right) + \ldots$$

$$= \frac{A}{\pi} + \frac{A}{2}\sin(\omega_0 t) - \frac{2A}{3\pi}\cos(2\omega_0 t) - \frac{2A}{15\pi}\cos(4\omega_0 t) + \ldots$$

EXAMPLE 14.8 *Find the line spectrum of the following waves using Fourier analysis (Figs. E14.8(a) to (c)).*

SOLUTION. In Fig. E14.8(a), the desired Fourier series has already been obtained as

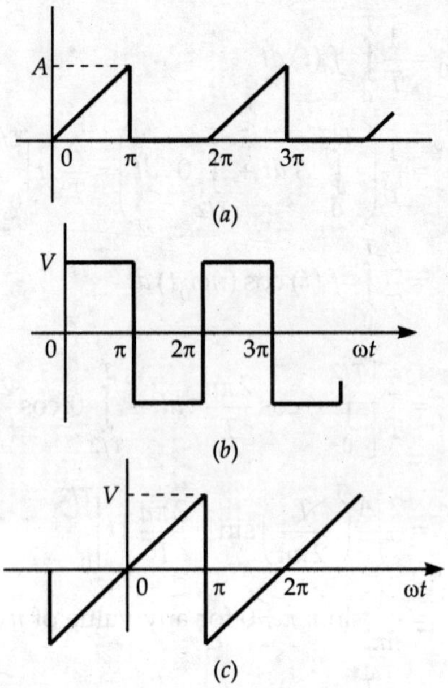

Fig. E14.8

$$f(t) = \frac{A}{4} - \frac{2A}{\pi^2}\cos\omega_0 t - \frac{2A}{9\pi^2}\cos 3\omega_0 t - \frac{2A}{25\pi^2}\cos 5\omega_0 t - \ldots + \frac{V}{\pi}\sin\omega_0 t - \frac{V}{2\pi}\sin 2\omega_0 t + \frac{V}{3\pi}\sin 3\omega_0 t - \ldots\ldots$$

Here $C_0 = |a_0| = \frac{A}{4}$.

For n = odd numbers the series contains both sine and cosine terms. Thus for n = odd,

$$C_n = \sqrt{a_n^2 + b_n^2}.$$

$$\therefore \quad C_1 = \sqrt{\left(\frac{2A}{\pi^2}\right)^2 + \left(\frac{V}{\pi}\right)^2}$$

$$C_3 = \sqrt{\left(\frac{2A}{(3\pi)^2}\right)^2 + \left(\frac{V}{3\pi}\right)^2}$$

However, for n = even number, the line spectrum amplitudes are directly given by b_n since there is no a_n terms for n = even.

Fig. E14.8(d) shows the line spectrum.

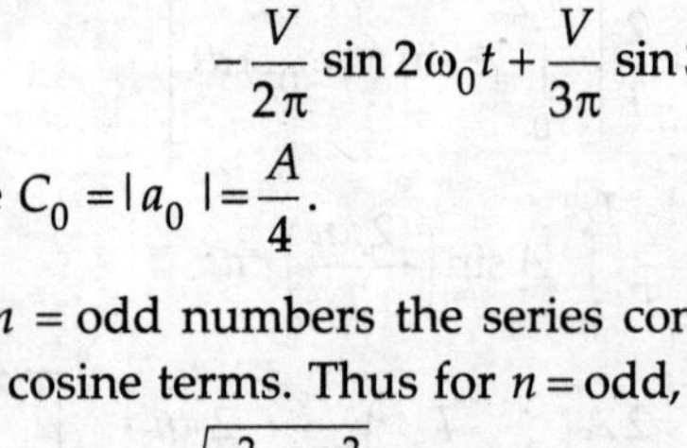

Fig. E14.8 (d)

For Fig. E14.8(*b*), the Fourier series is given by

$$f(t) = \frac{4V}{\pi}\sin\omega t + \frac{4V}{3\pi}\sin 3\pi t + \frac{4V}{5\pi}\sin 5\,\omega t + \ldots$$

Since the series contains only odd harmonics (b_n terms for $n = 1, 3, \ldots.$) hence line spectrum would appear only at the odd harmonics and is given by $\frac{4V}{n\pi}$.

Fig. E14.8(*e*) represents the line spectrum.

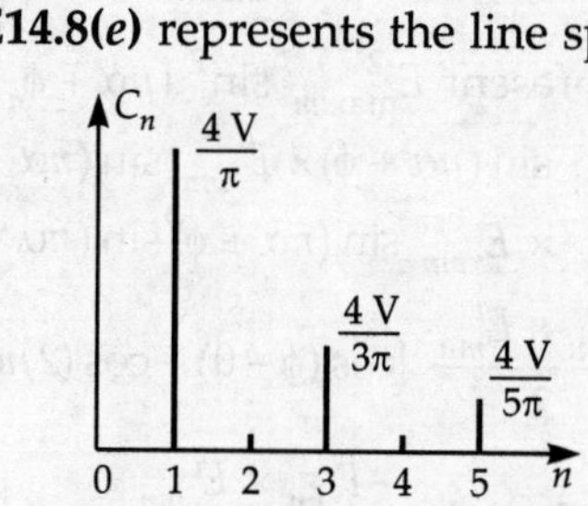

Fig. E14.8 (*e*)

For Fig. E14.8(*c*), the required Fourier series waveform is given by

$$f(t) = \frac{2A}{\pi}\left[\sin\omega t - \frac{1}{2}\sin 2\,\omega t + \frac{1}{3}\sin 3\omega t - \frac{1}{4}\sin 4\,\omega t + \ldots.\right]$$

Thus it is evident that the coefficients decrease by $\frac{1}{n}$ and the series does not contain any cosine term. The required line spectrum is shown in **Fig. E14.8(*f*)**.

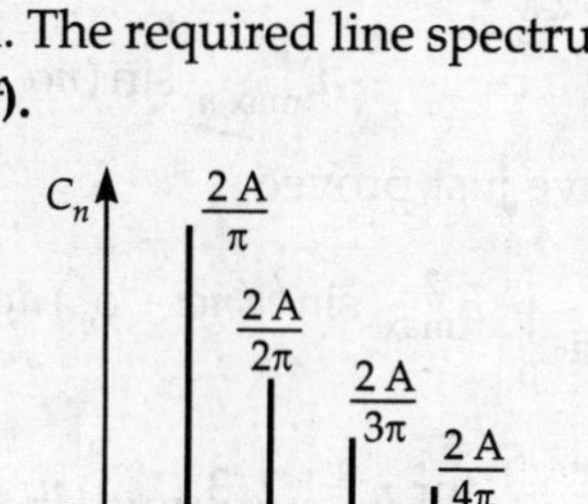

Fig. E14.8 (*f*)

EXAMPLE 14.9 *Find a and b coefficients of Fourier series of the given waveform (Fig. E14.9).*

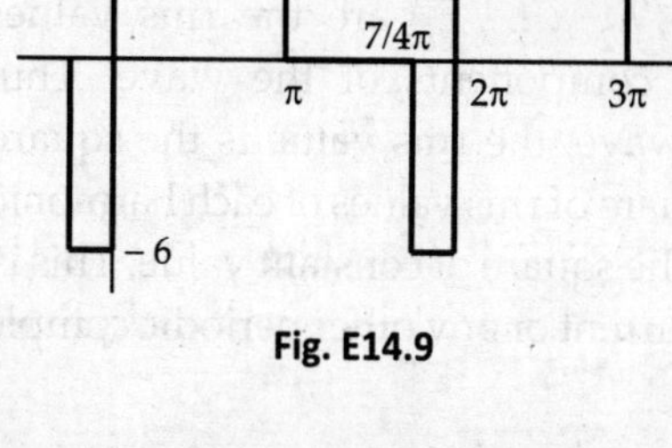

Fig. E14.9

SOLUTION.

$$a_0 = \frac{1}{T}\int_0^T f(t)\,dt$$

$$= \frac{1}{2\pi}\left[\int_0^{\pi} 4\,(\omega t)\,d\,(\omega t) - \int_{7/4\,\pi}^{2\pi} 6\,(\omega t)\,d\,(\omega\,t)\right]$$

$$= \frac{4}{2\pi}\left[\frac{(\omega t)^2}{2}\right]_0^{\pi} - \frac{6}{2\pi}\left[\frac{(\omega t)^2}{2}\right]_{7/4\,\pi}^{2\pi}$$

$$= \frac{2}{\pi}\times\frac{\pi^2}{2} - \frac{6}{2\pi}\cdot\frac{4\pi^2}{2} + \frac{6}{2\pi}\cdot\frac{49\,\pi^2}{32}$$

$$= \pi - 6\pi + \frac{147\,\pi}{32} = \mathbf{-1.2756.}$$

$$a_n = \frac{2}{T_0}\int_0^{T_0} f(t)\cos(n\omega t)\,d(t)$$

$$= \frac{2}{2\pi}\int_0^{2\pi} f(t)\cos(n\,\omega t)\,dt$$

$$= \frac{1}{\pi}\int_0^{2\pi} f(t)\cos(n\,\omega t)\,dt$$

$$= \frac{1}{\pi}\int_0^{\pi} 4\cos(n\,\omega\,t)\,d\,\omega t + \frac{1}{\pi}\int_{\pi}^{7/4\,\pi} 0\,.\cos(n\,\omega t)\,d\,(\omega t) + \frac{1}{\pi}\int_{7/4\,\pi}^{2\pi}(-6)\cos(n\,\omega t)\,d\,(\omega t)$$

$$= \frac{1}{\pi}\left[\left|\frac{4\sin n\omega t}{n}\right|_0^{\pi} + 0 + \left|\frac{(-6)\sin n\omega t}{n}\right|_{7/4\,\pi}^{2\pi}\right]$$

$$= \frac{4}{\pi n}[\sin n\pi] + \frac{-6}{n\,\pi}[\sin n(2\,\pi)] + \frac{6}{n\pi}\left[\sin n\frac{7\pi}{4}\right]$$

$$= \frac{\mathbf{6}}{\boldsymbol{n\,\pi}}\,\mathbf{sin}\,\boldsymbol{n}\,.\,\frac{\mathbf{7\pi}}{\mathbf{4}}.\quad [\because \sin n\pi = 0 \text{ for } n = 1, 2, \ldots \text{ however } \sin n\,\pi \neq 0 \text{ for } n = \text{any fraction}]$$

Similarly,

$$b_n = \frac{2}{T_0}\int_0^{T_0} f(t)\sin(n\omega t)\,d\,(\omega t)$$

$$= \frac{1}{\pi}\int_0^{\pi} 4\sin(n\omega t)d(\omega t) + \frac{1}{\pi}\int_{\pi}^{7\pi/4} 0.\sin(n\omega t)d(\omega t) + \frac{1}{\pi}\int_{7\pi/4}^{2\pi} -6\sin(n\,\omega t)\,d\,(\omega t).$$

$$= \frac{1}{\pi}\left[\frac{4(-\cos n\omega t)}{n}\Bigg|_0^{\pi} + 0 - 6\left(\frac{-\cos n\omega t}{n}\right)\Bigg|_{7\pi/4}^{2\pi}\right]$$

$$= \frac{1}{n\pi}\left[-4(\cos n\pi - 1) + 6\left(1 - \cos\frac{7\pi}{4}\right)\right].$$

Thus we obtained, $a_0 = 1.276$; $a_n = \frac{6}{n\pi}\sin n\frac{7\pi}{4}$

$$b_n = \frac{1}{n\pi}\left[-4(\cos n\pi - 1) + 6\left(1 - \cos\frac{7n\pi}{4}\right)\right].$$

14.7 AVERAGE VALUE OF A PERIODIC COMPLEX WAVE

Let us assume a periodic complex wave (non-sinusoidal)

$$e = E_0 + E_{\max 1}\sin(\alpha+\phi_1) + E_{\max 2}\sin(\alpha+\phi_2) + \ldots + E_{\max n}\sin(n\alpha+\phi_n)$$

represented in Fourier series where $\alpha = \omega t$ and e is the instantaneous voltage, E_0 is the constant value.

Since the average value of a periodic function is represented as

$$f(t)_{av} = \frac{1}{T}\int_0^T f(t)\,dt, \text{ we can write}$$

$$E_{av} = \frac{1}{T}\int_0^T e\,d\alpha,$$

where T represents the period of the wave. Since the integration of any sine function between 0 and T (when $T = 2\pi$) is zero, here we can write

$$E_{av} = E_0 + 0 + 0 + \ldots\ldots$$
$$= E_0$$

$\therefore$ *For any periodic complex wave, the average value is given by the constant term of the Fourier series representing the periodic wave.* This is true for voltage, current and any other periodic complex wave.

14.8 RMS VALUE OF PERIODIC COMPLEX WAVE

Since the rms value x_{rms} for any periodic function is given by

$$x_{rms} = \sqrt{\frac{1}{T}\int_0^T x(t)^2\,dt},$$

for our case when the periodic non-sinusoidal complex voltage wave is represented by

$$e = E_0 + E_{\max 1}\sin(\alpha+\phi_1) + E_{\max 2}\sin(\alpha+\phi_2) + \ldots + E_{\max n}\sin(\alpha+\phi_n),$$

we can write

$$E_{rms} = \sqrt{\frac{1}{2\pi}\int_0^{2\pi}[E_0 + E_{\max 1}\sin(\alpha+\phi_1) + \ldots + E_{\max n}\sin(n\alpha+\phi_n)]^2\,.\,d\alpha}$$

Let us represent $E_{\max m}^2\sin^2(n\alpha+\phi_n)$ as

$$P(\alpha) = E_{mn}\sin(n\alpha+\phi)\times E'_{mn}\sin(n\alpha+\theta)$$
$$= E_{mn}\times E'_{mn}\sin(n\alpha+\phi)\sin(n\alpha+\theta)$$
$$= \frac{E_{mn}\times E'_{mn}}{2}\{\cos(\phi-\theta) - \cos(2n\alpha+\phi+\theta)\}$$

$$\therefore \frac{1}{2\pi}\int_0^{2\pi}P(\alpha)\,d\alpha = \frac{E_{mn}\times E'_{mn}}{2}\cos(\phi-\theta)$$

$[\because \alpha$ is the only variable and $\int_0^{2\pi}\cos(2n\alpha+\phi+\theta) = 0]$

With $E_{mm} = E'_{mn}$ and $\phi = \theta$,

$$\frac{1}{2\pi}\int_0^{2\pi}P(\alpha)\,d\alpha = \frac{E_{mn}^2}{2}.$$

$$\therefore E_{rms} = \sqrt{\frac{1}{2\pi}\int_0^{2\pi}[E_0 + E_{\max 1}\sin(\alpha+\phi_1) + \ldots + E_{\max n}\sin(n\alpha+\phi_n)]^2\,.\,d\alpha}$$

But we have just proved

$$\frac{1}{2\pi}\int_0^{2\pi}E_{\max}^2\sin^2(n\alpha+\phi_n)\,d\alpha$$
$$= \frac{E_{\max n}^2}{2} \text{ for } n = 1, 2, 3, \ldots\ldots, n.$$

$$E_{rms} = \sqrt{E_0^2 + \frac{E_{\max 1}^2}{2} + \frac{E_{\max 2}^2}{2} + \ldots + \frac{E_{\max n}^2}{2}}$$
$$= \sqrt{E_0^2 + \left(\frac{E_{\max 1}}{\sqrt{2}}\right)^2 + \left(\frac{E_{\max 2}}{\sqrt{2}}\right)^2 + \ldots + \left(\frac{E_{\max n}}{\sqrt{2}}\right)^2}$$
$$= \sqrt{E_0^2 + E_1^2 + \ldots\ldots + E_n^2}$$

where $E_1, E_2, \ldots\ldots, E_n$ are the rms values of the harmonic components of the wave. Thus, for a complex wave, the rms value is the square root of sum of square of rms values of each harmonic component and the square of constant value. This is true for voltage, current or any other periodic complex wave.

14.9 EXPRESSION OF POWER WITH NON-SINUSOIDAL VOLTAGE AND CURRENT

We have shown earlier (*see* eqn. 14.8) that the non-sinusoidal complex wave (say a voltage wave) can be expressed as

$$e = E_0 + E_{\max 1} \sin(\alpha + \phi_1) + E_{\max 2} \sin(2\alpha + \phi_2) + ... + E_{\max n} \sin(n\alpha + \phi_n) \quad ...(14.19)$$

where e represents the instantaneous voltage, E_0 the constant value, n the integer and $\alpha = \omega t$. $E_{\max 1}, E_{\max 2}, ...$ are the peak amplitudes of various harmonics and $\phi_1, \phi_2, ..., \phi_n$ are the angles measured from the origin to the point of crossing from negative to positive values of component waves. Similarly, the non-sinusoidal current wave is expressed as :

$$i = I_0 + I_{\max 1} \sin(\alpha + \phi_1 + \psi_1) + I_{\max 2} \sin(2\alpha + \phi_2 + \psi_2) + ... + I_{\max n} \sin(n\alpha + \phi_n + \psi_n)$$

where ψ_n represents the phase angle between the nth harmonic voltage and corresponding current wave.

The average power P, is then given by

$$P = \frac{1}{2\pi} \int_0^{2\pi} e \,.\, i \,.\, d\alpha \quad ...(14.20)$$

However, expressions of e and i (from equations (14.19) and (14.20) may further be represented as

$$e = E_0 + \sum_{n=1}^{n} E_{\max n} \sin(n\alpha + \phi_n) ... \quad ...(14.21)$$

and $$i = I_0 + \sum_{n=1}^{n} I_{\max n} \sin(n\alpha + \phi_n + \psi_n) \quad ...(14.22)$$

Thus from (14.20) we can write

$$P = \frac{1}{2\pi} \int_0^{2\pi} \left[\left\{ E_0 + \sum_{n=1}^{n} E_{\max n} \sin(n\alpha + \phi_n) \right\} \times \left\{ I_0 + \sum_{n=1}^{n} I_{\max n} \sin(n\alpha + \phi_n + \psi_n) \right\} \right] d\alpha$$

or $$P = \frac{1}{2\pi} \int_0^{2\pi} [E_0 I_0 + E_0 \sum_{n=1}^{n} I_{\max n} \sin(n\alpha + \phi_n + \psi_n) + I_0 \sum_{n=1}^{n} E_{\max n} \sin(n\alpha + \phi_n)] + \left[\left\{ \sum_{n=1}^{n} E_{\max n} \sin(n\alpha + \phi_n) \right\} \times \left\{ \sum_{n=1}^{n} I_{\max n} \sin(n\alpha + \phi_n + \psi_n) \right\} \right] d\alpha$$

or $$P = E_0 I_0 + \frac{E_{\max 1} I_{\max 1}}{2} \cos\psi_1 + \frac{E_{\max 2} I_{\max 2}}{2} \cos\psi_2 + ... + \frac{E_{\max n} I_{\max n}}{2} \cos\psi_n$$

$$= E_0 I_0 + E_1 I_1 \cos\psi_1 + E_2 I_2 \cos\psi_3 + ... + E_n I_n \cos\psi_n$$

14.10 SHIFTING OF FUNCTION

In order to compute the Fourier series coefficients for a given waveform, it is important to consider whether the waveform possesses any or all of the symmetries (*i.e.*, whether the given waveform is an even function, or an odd function or whether does it have an even symmetry). It is also worthwhile to investigate whether an amplitude or time shift of the function will make these properties.

It may be observed that for any time function, a shift in level of the function only affects the *dc* term a_0. In case a function is shifted up or down by an amount Z, then $f(t) = F(t) - Z$; $F(t)$ is expanded in Fourier series and this amplitude shift can be accounted for by subtracting M from a_0 in the $F(t)$ expansion. On the other hand, a time shift will not affect whether a function has half-wave symmetry but will effect whether it is an odd or even function.

When $f(t)$ is shifted by K in time axis,

$$F(t) = f(t + K)$$

When shifting is performed for both amplitude and time,

$$F(t) = f(t + K) - Z$$

or, $$f(t) = F(t - K) + Z.$$

14.11 APPLICATION IN CIRCUIT ANALYSIS

When a non-sinusoidal waveform of voltage is applied to a linear network, its Fourier analysis gives the harmonic voltages. Utilising the principle of Superposition, the corresponding harmonic terms of the currents can be obtained. Each term of the Fourier series of voltage is then assumed to represent the voltage as a single source. The equivalent impedance of the network at each harmonic frequency *nw* is used to compute the current at that harmonic. The sum of these individual responses provides the total response of the current.

14.12 COMPARISON BETWEEN LAPLACE AND FOURIER TRANSFORM

The Laplace transform is represented by the following expression :

$$F(s) = \int_{0}^{\infty} f(t) = e^{-st}\, dt$$

While the Fourier transform is given by

$$F(j\omega) = \int_{-\infty}^{\infty} f(t)\, e^{-j\omega t}\, dt$$

We observe that $(j\omega)$ term in the Fourier transform has the same position as the term(s) in the Laplace transform. However, the limits of integration in the Fourier transform is $(-\infty)$ to $(+\infty)$ *i.e.*, two-sided of the zero axis while the Laplace transform integral limits are only one sided [0 to $+\infty$; though instead of 0, the lower limit may be (0 –) to include the network condition just before switching].

In Laplace transform if $f(t) = 0$ for the interval $t < 0$, we can write

$$£\, f(t) = £[f(t)\, e^{-\sigma t}]$$

i.e., the Laplace transform becomes identical to Fourier transform of $f(t)$ multipled by $(e^{-\sigma t})$.

The Fourier transform is a function only of the real variable (ω) while the Laplace transform is a function of the complex variable (s). Also the inverse Laplace is given by

$$£^{-1}[F(s)] = f(t) = \frac{1}{2\pi j} \int_{\sigma_0 - j\omega}^{\sigma_0 + j\omega} F(s)\, e^{st}\, ds$$

while inverse of Fourier transform is given by

$$F^{-1}[F(j\omega)] = \frac{1}{2\pi} \int_{-\infty}^{\infty} F(j\omega)\, e^{j\omega t}\, dt$$

Thus, the contour of integration of Fourier transform is along imaginary axis while those for Laplace transform is displaced by σ.

The Fourier analysis is advantageous for arbitrary periodic function and transient non-periodic functions. However using Fourier analysis it is difficult to arrive at a solution in a closed form obtained by summing the response of all component responses, though it is relatively simple to obtain the solution of a system for each of the frequency components when the input is non-sinusoidal. However, a big difficulty arises to analyse a system with Fourier analysis if the input is either a unit step function or an undamped sinusoidal as these functions do not have necessary Fourier Transform. Laplace transform is usually proved to be more convenient to use to electrical engineers particularly with sinusoidal input circuits as well as when the circuit is subjected to conventional signal waveforms.

EXAMPLE 14.10 *Obtain the Fourier series of the waveform shown in Fig. E14.10.*

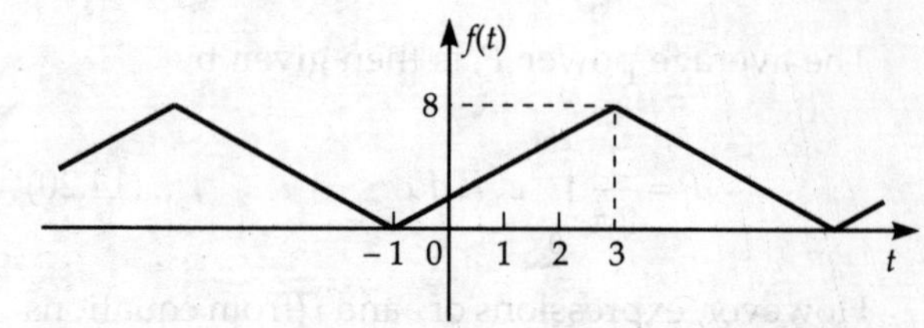

Fig. E14.10

SOLUTION. Since the average value is 4, we may shift the function down in amplitude axis as shown in Fig. E14.10(*a*). In addition, by shifting the function to leftwards (the time axis), the final shifted waveform is obtained as shown in Fig. E14.10(*a*).

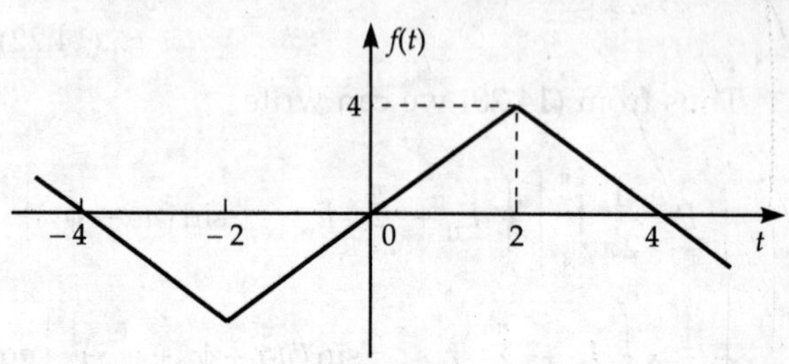

Fig. E14.10 (*a*)

For amplitude shift,

$$F(t) = f(t+1) - 4$$

while for time shift,

$$f(t) = F(t-1) + 4.$$

Fig. E14.10(*a*) represents a odd function symmetry.

Here, $a_0 = 0$

$a_n = 0$ for all *n*.

b_n can be calculated in a way as shown in Example 14.22.

It has been shown in Example 14.22 that

$$b_n = \frac{8V}{(n\pi)^2} \sin\left(\frac{n\pi}{2}\right)$$

$$= \frac{32}{(n\,\pi)^2} \sin\left(\frac{n\pi}{2}\right).$$

[Here, *V* corresponds to 4, the average value]

However,

for $n = 1, 5, 9, \ldots, \sin\left(\frac{n\pi}{2}\right) = +1$

for $n = 3, 7, 11, \ldots, \sin\left(\frac{n\pi}{2}\right) = -1$

for $n = 2, 4, 6, \ldots, \sin\left(\frac{n\pi}{2}\right) = 0$

Thus, $b_1 = \frac{32}{\pi^2}, \quad b_2 = 0, \quad b_3 = -\frac{32}{9\pi^2},$

$b_4 = 0, \quad b_5 = \frac{32}{25\,\pi^2}$ and so on.

$\therefore F(t)$, the shifted waveform series is given by

$$F(t) = \frac{32}{\pi^2} \sin(\omega_0 t) - \frac{32}{9\,\pi^2} \sin(3\,\omega_0 t) + \frac{32}{25\,\pi^2} \sin(5\,\omega_0 t) + \ldots\ldots$$

However,

$$F(t) = f(t+1) + 5$$

$$= 5 + \frac{32}{\pi^2} \sin\left[\frac{\pi}{4}(t-1)\right] - \frac{32}{9\pi^2} \sin\left[\frac{3\pi}{4}(t-1)\right] + \ldots$$

$$\therefore\ \boldsymbol{f(t) = 5 + \frac{32}{\pi^2}\left[\sin\left(\frac{\pi t}{4}\right)\cos\left(\frac{\pi}{4}\right) - \cos\left(\frac{\pi t}{4}\right)\sin\left(\frac{\pi}{4}\right)\right]}$$

$$\boldsymbol{-\frac{32}{9\pi^2}\left[\sin\left(\frac{3\pi t}{4}\right)\cos\left(\frac{3\pi}{4}\right) - \cos\left(\frac{3\pi t}{4}\right)\sin\left(\frac{3\pi}{4}\right)\right] + \ldots}$$

ADDITIONAL EXAMPLES

EXAMPLE 14.11 *Obtain the exponential Fourier series of the waveform shown in Fig. E14.11.*

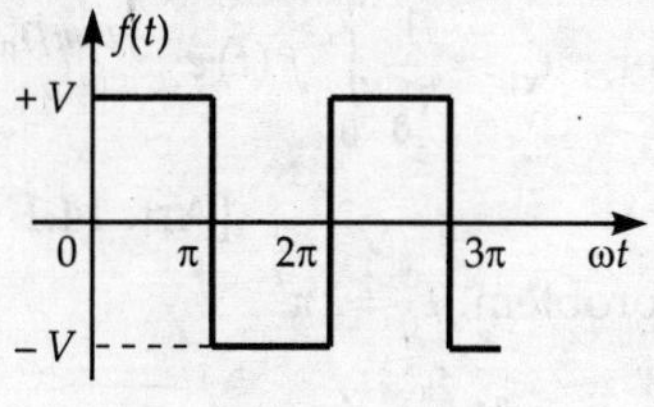

Fig. E14.11

SOLUTION. By inspection,

$$f(t) = V \quad \text{for } 0 < \omega t < \pi$$

$$= -V \text{ for } -\pi < \omega t < 0.$$

Hence the wave possesses odd symmetry.

$\therefore \quad a_0 = 0$

[*i.e.*, the average value of the wave is zero];

$$C_n = \frac{1}{T_0}\left[\int_{-\pi}^{0} (-V)e^{-jn\omega t}\,d(\omega t) + \int_{0}^{\pi} (V)e^{-jn\omega t}\,d(\omega t)\right]$$

$$= \frac{V}{2\pi}\left[-\left(\frac{1}{-j\,n}\right)e^{-jn\omega t}\Big|_{-\pi}^{0} + \left(\frac{1}{-j\,n}\right)e^{-jn\omega t}\Big|_{0}^{\pi}\right]$$

$$= \frac{V}{(-j\,2\pi\,n)}(-e^0 + e^{jn\pi} + e^{-jn\pi} - e^0)$$

$$= j\,\frac{V}{n\pi}(e^{jn\pi} - 1).$$

For $n =$ even, $e^{jn\pi} = 1$ and $C_n = 0$

For $n =$ odd, $e^{jn\pi} = -1$ and $C_n = -j\left(\frac{2V}{n\pi}\right)$.

$\therefore$ The Fourier series is

$$\boldsymbol{f(t) = \ldots + j\frac{2V}{3\pi}e^{-j3\omega t} + j\frac{2V}{\pi}e^{-j\omega t} - j\frac{2V}{\pi}e^{j\omega t} - j\frac{2V}{3\pi}e^{j3\omega t} \ldots}$$

EXAMPLE 14.12 *Find the exponential Fourier series of the given waveform (Fig. E14.12).*

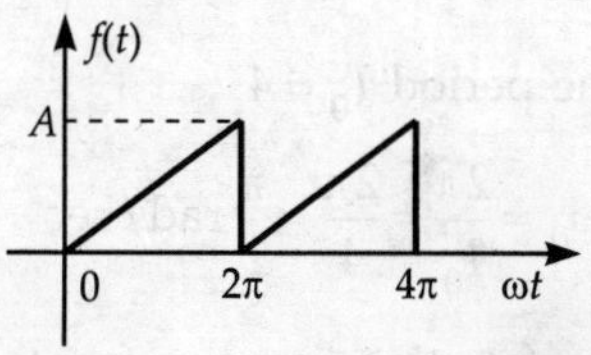

Fig. E14.12

SOLUTION. By inspection,

$$f(t) = \frac{A}{2\pi}(\omega t) \text{ for } 0 < \omega t < 2\pi.$$

However, $$C_n = \frac{1}{T_0}\int_0^{T_0} f(t)\, e^{-j2\pi nt/T_0}\, dt$$

[Art. 14.1 in the text]

In this problem, $T_0 = 2\pi$

$$\therefore \quad C_n = \frac{1}{2\pi}\int_0^{2\pi} \frac{A}{2\pi}\, \omega t\, e^{-jn\omega t}\, d(\omega t)$$

$$= \frac{A}{(2\pi)^2}\left[\frac{e^{-jn\omega t}}{(-j\, n)^2}(-j\, \omega n\, t - 1)\right]_0^{2\pi}$$

$$= -j\frac{A}{2\pi n}$$

$$\therefore \quad f(t) = \sum_{n=-\infty}^{\infty} C_n\, e^{jn\omega t}$$

$$= \sum_{n=-\infty}^{\infty} -j\frac{A}{2\pi n}\, e^{jn\omega t}$$

$$= -\ldots - j\frac{A}{4\pi}e^{-j2\omega t} - j\frac{A}{2\pi}e^{-j\omega t} + \frac{A}{2} + j\frac{A}{2\pi}e^{j\omega t} + j\frac{A}{4\pi}e^{j2\omega t} + \ldots.$$

[Here the average value is $\frac{A}{2}$ which can easily be derived].

EXAMPLE 14.13 *Obtain the Fourier Series for the waveform shown in Fig. E14.13.*

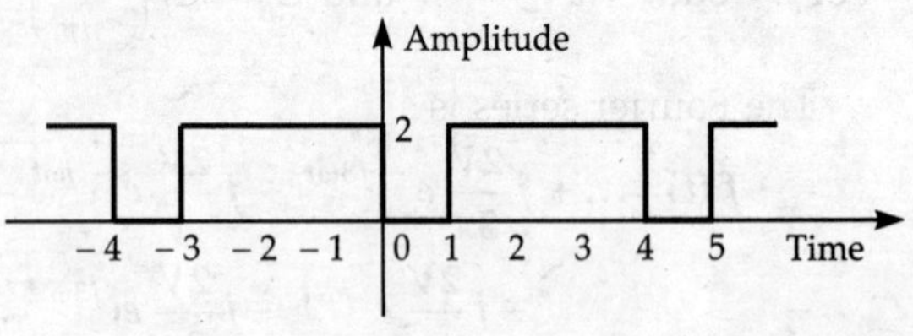

Fig. E14.13

SOLUTION. By inspection, $f(t) = \begin{cases} 0 \text{ for } 0 < t < 1 \\ 2 \text{ for } 1 < t < 4 \end{cases}$

Also, time period $T_0 = 4$

and $$\omega_0 = \frac{2\pi}{T_0} = \frac{2\pi}{4} = \frac{\pi}{2} \text{ rad/sec}$$

Since the function is zero for $t = 0$ to 1, the integrals need only extend from 1 to 4 sec.

To start with, the average value is first found out.

$$a_0 = \frac{1}{T_0}\int_0^{T_0} f(t)\, dt = \frac{1}{4}\int_1^4 2\, dt = \frac{2}{4}(4-1) = \frac{3}{2}.$$

Next task is to obtain the cosine coefficient ;

$$a_n = \frac{2}{T_0}\int_0^{T_0} f(t)\cos(n\,\omega_0 t)\,(dn\,\omega_0 t)$$

$$= \frac{2}{4}\int_1^4 f(t)\cos\left(\frac{n\pi t}{2}\right) d\left(\frac{n\pi t}{2}\right)$$

$$= \frac{1}{2}\int_1^4 2\cos\left(\frac{n\pi t}{2}\right) d\left(\frac{n\pi t}{2}\right)$$

$$= \frac{1}{n\pi}\left[\sin\left(\frac{n\pi t}{2}\right)\right]_1^4$$

$$= \frac{1}{n\pi}\left[\sin(2\,n\,\pi) - \sin\left(\frac{n\pi}{2}\right)\right]$$

$$= -\frac{1}{n\pi}\sin\left(\frac{n\pi}{2}\right).$$

To find b_n, we proceed as follows :

$$b_n = \frac{2}{T_0}\int_0^{T_0} f(t)\sin(n\,\omega_0 t)\, d(n\,\omega_0 t)$$

$$= \frac{2}{4}\int_1^4 2\sin\left(\frac{n\pi t}{2}\right) d\left(\frac{n\pi t}{2}\right)$$

$$= -\frac{1}{n\pi}\left[\sin\left(\frac{n\pi t}{2}\right)\right]_1^4$$

$$= -\frac{1}{n\pi}\left[\cos(2\,n\,\pi) - \cos\left(\frac{n\pi}{2}\right)\right]$$

$$= -\frac{1}{n\pi}\left[1 - \cos\left(\frac{n\pi}{2}\right)\right]$$

Thus the Fourier series coefficients can be found out as follows :

for $n = 1$, $a_1 = -\frac{1}{\pi}$; $b_1 = -\frac{1}{\pi}$

$n = 2$, $a_2 = 0$; $b_2 = -\frac{1}{\pi}$

$n = 3$, $a_3 = \frac{1}{3\pi}$; $b_3 = -\frac{1}{3\pi}$

$n = 4$, $a_4 = 0$; $b_4 = 0$

$n = 5$, $a_5 = -\frac{1}{5\pi}$; $b_5 = -\frac{1}{5\pi}$ and so on;

$$\therefore \quad f(t)=\frac{3}{2}-\frac{1}{\pi}\cos\left(\frac{\pi t}{2}\right)-\frac{1}{\pi}\sin\left(\frac{\pi t}{2}\right)-\frac{1}{\pi}\sin\frac{2\pi t}{2}$$

$$-\frac{1}{3\pi}\cos\frac{3\pi t}{2}-\frac{1}{3\pi}\sin\frac{3\pi t}{2}$$

$$-\frac{1}{5\pi}\cos\frac{5\pi t}{2}-\frac{1}{5\pi}\sin\frac{5\pi t}{2}\ldots$$

$$=\frac{3}{2}-\frac{1}{\pi}\left[\cos\left(\frac{\pi t}{2}\right)+\sin\left(\frac{\pi t}{2}\right)+\sin(\pi t)+\frac{1}{3}\cos\frac{3\pi t}{2}+\frac{1}{3}\sin\frac{3\pi t}{2}+\frac{1}{5}\cos\frac{5\pi t}{2}+\frac{1}{5}\sin\frac{5\pi t}{2}+\ldots\ldots\right]$$

EXAMPLE 14.14 *Find the complex Fourier coefficient of the waveform shown in Fig. E14.14.*

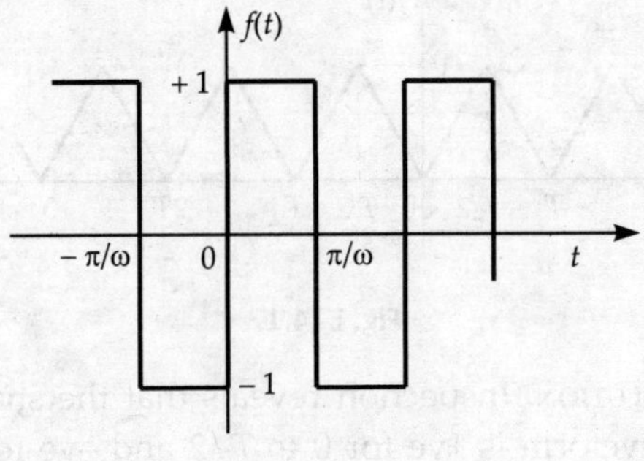

Fig. E14.14

SOLUTION. The function in Fig. E14.14 is given by

$$f(t)=-1 \text{ for } -\frac{\pi}{\omega}<t<0$$

$$=+1 \text{ for } 0<t<\frac{\pi}{\omega}.$$

The general form being given in Eq. (14.3) here

$$C_n=\frac{\omega}{2\pi}\left[\int_{-\pi/\omega}^{\pi/\omega} f(t)\,e^{-j\omega nt}\,dt\right]$$

$$=\frac{\omega}{2\pi}\left[\int_{-\pi/\omega}^{0} f(t)e^{-j\omega nt}dt+\int_{0}^{\pi/\omega} f(t)e^{-j\omega nt}dt\right]$$

$$=\frac{\omega}{2\pi}\left[\int_{-\pi/\omega}^{0}(-1)e^{-j\omega nt}dt+\int_{0}^{\pi/\omega}(1)e^{-j\omega nt}dt\right]$$

$$=\frac{\omega}{n\pi}(1-e^{jn\pi})\int_{0}^{\pi/\omega}e^{-jn\omega t}\,dt$$

$$=\frac{(1-e^{-jn\pi})(1-e^{j\omega n})}{2jn\pi}=\frac{1-\cos n\pi}{jn\pi}$$

$\therefore C_n = 0$ for n being 0 or even and $C_n = \frac{2}{jn\pi}$ if n be odd.

EXAMPLE 14.15 *Find the Fourier series of the function shown in Fig. E14.15 and is represented by*

$$f(t)=\begin{cases}0 \text{ for } 0<t<T/2\\ A \text{ for } \frac{T}{2}<t<T\end{cases}$$

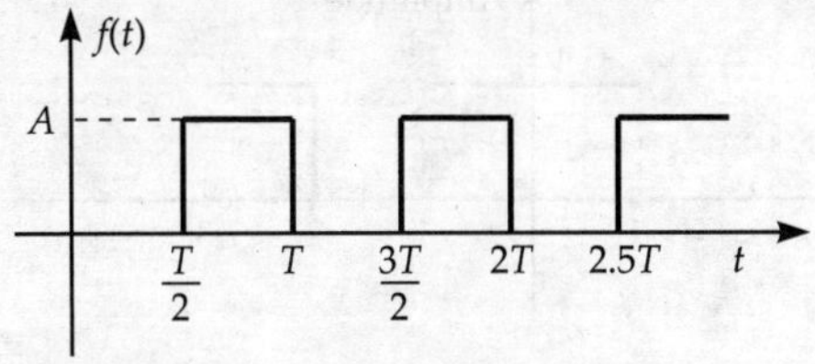

Fig. E14.15

SOLUTION. With reference to Fig. E14.15,

$$a_0=\frac{1}{T_0}\int_t^{t+T_0} f(t)\,dt=\frac{1}{T}\int_{T/2}^{T}A\,dt=\frac{A}{2}.$$

$$a_n=\frac{2}{T_0}\int_t^{t+T_0} f(t)\cos(n\omega_0 t)\,dt$$

$$=\frac{2}{T}\int_0^T f(t)\cos\frac{2n\pi}{T}.t\,dt$$

$$=\frac{2A}{T}\int_{T/2}^{T}\cos\frac{2n\pi}{T}.t\,dt=\frac{2A}{T}.\frac{T}{2n\pi}\left[\sin\frac{2n\pi}{T}.t\right]_{T/2}^{T}$$

$$=\frac{A}{n\pi}[\sin 2n\pi-\sin n\pi]=0$$

Again

$$b_n=\frac{2}{T_0}\int_t^{t+T_0} f(t)\sin(n\omega_0 t)\,dt$$

$$=\frac{2A}{T}\int_{T/2}^{T}\sin\frac{2n\pi}{T}.t\,dt$$

$$=-\frac{2A}{T}.\frac{T}{2n\pi}\left[\cos\frac{2n\pi}{T}.t\right]_{T/2}^{T}$$

$$=-\frac{A}{n\pi}[\cos 2n\pi-\cos n\pi]=-\frac{A}{n\pi}[1-(-1)^n]$$

$\therefore b_n$ is zero when n is even and is $\left(-\frac{2A}{n\pi}\right)$ when n is odd.

CHAPTER 14

This gives $b_1 = \frac{2A}{\pi};\ b_2 = 0;\ b_3 = -\frac{2A}{3\pi};$

$$b_4 = 0;\quad b_5 = -\frac{2A}{5\pi}\ \ldots\ldots$$

∴ The Fourier series is then obtained as

$$f(t) = \frac{A}{2} - \frac{2A}{\pi}\left[\sin\omega_0 t + \frac{1}{3}\sin 3\omega_0 t + \frac{1}{5}\sin 5\omega_0 t + \ldots\right]$$

EXAMPLE 14.16 *Find the Fourier series of the single rectangular pulse shown in Fig. E14.16.*

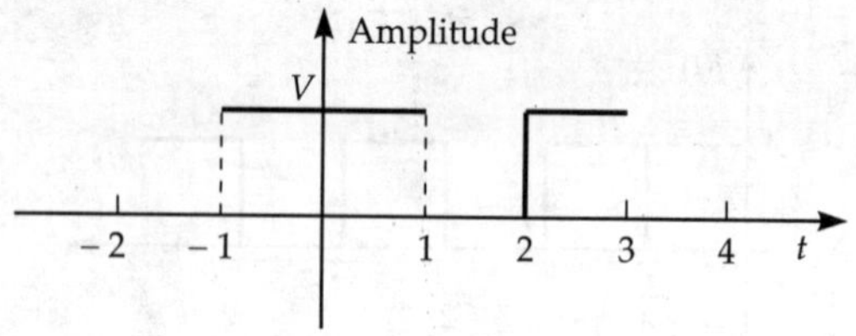

Fig. E14.16

SOLUTION. The waveform is given by

$$f(t) = \begin{cases} 0 \text{ when } -2 < t < -1 \\ V \text{ when } -1 < t < 1 \\ 0 \text{ when } \quad 1 < t < 2 \end{cases}$$

Here, $a_0 = \frac{1}{T_0}\int_{t_1}^{t_1+T_0} f(t)\,dt$ gives

$$a_0 = \frac{1}{4}\int_{-1}^{+1} V\,dt = \frac{V}{2}$$

Again, $a_n = \frac{2}{T_0}\int_{t_1}^{t_1+t_0} f(t)\cos(n\omega_0 t)\,dt$

$$= \frac{2}{T_0}\int_{-T_0/2}^{T_0/2} f(t)\cos n\frac{2\pi}{T_0}t\,dt$$

$$= \frac{2V}{4}\int_{-1}^{+1}\cos\frac{n\pi t}{2}\,dt$$

$$= \frac{V}{2}\left[\frac{\sin\frac{n\pi t}{2}}{\frac{n\pi}{2}}\right]_{-1}^{+1}$$

$$= \frac{2V}{n\pi}\cdot\sin\frac{n\pi}{2}.$$

[it may be observed here that a_n will be zero for even values of n].

$$b_n = \frac{2}{T_0}\int_{t_1}^{t_1+T_0} f(t)\sin(n\omega_0 t)\,dt$$

$$= \frac{2}{T}\int_{-T_0/2}^{T_0/2} f(t)\sin\frac{n2\pi}{T_0}t\,dt$$

$$= \frac{2V}{4}\int_{-1}^{1}\sin\frac{n\pi t}{2}\,dt = 0.$$

∴ The Fourier series is

$$f(t) = \frac{V}{2} + \frac{2V}{\pi}\left[\cos\frac{\pi}{2}.t - \frac{1}{3}\cos\frac{3\pi}{2}.t + \ldots\right]$$

EXAMPLE 14.17 *Find the Fourier coefficients of the waveform shown in Fig. E14.17.*

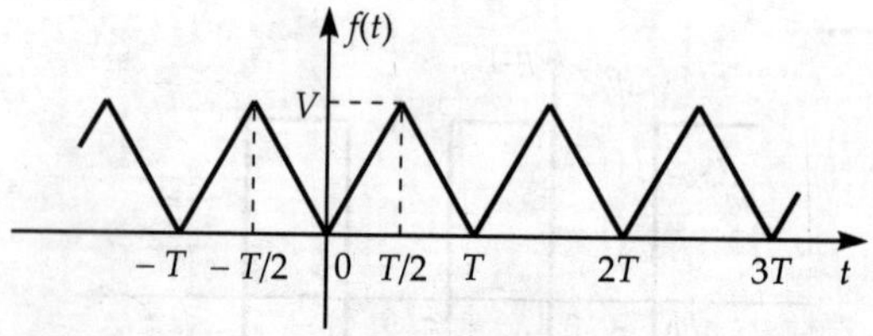

Fig. E14.17

SOLUTION. Inspection reveals that the shape of the waveform is +ve for 0 to $T/2$ and –ve for 0 to $-T/2$. The gradient of the straight line of the waveform (*i.e.*, the shape) being $V/(T/2)$ *i.e.*, $\frac{2V}{T}$, we can write

$$f(t) = \begin{cases} \frac{2V}{T}(t) \text{ when } 0 \le t \le T/2 \\ -\frac{2V}{T}(t) \text{ when } -\frac{T}{2} \le t \le 0 \end{cases}$$

Inspection also reveals that the given waveform has even symmetry.

Thus $b_n = 0$.

$$a_0 = \frac{2}{T_0}\int_0^{T_0/2} f(t)\,dt$$

$$= \frac{2}{2T}\left[\int_{-T/2}^{0}\left(-\frac{2V}{T}\right)(t)\,dt + \int_0^{T/2}\left(\frac{2V}{T}\right)(t)\,dt\right]$$

[∵ T_o, the time period is equivalent to $2T$ in this problem]

[Since, T_o (the time period) is $2T$ in this problem and integral is $-\frac{T}{2}$ to $\frac{T}{2}$ in Fig. E14.17.]

$$= \frac{1}{T}\left[\left(-\frac{2V}{T}\right)\frac{t^2}{2}\Big|_{-T/2}^{0} + \left(\frac{2V}{T}\right)\frac{t^2}{2}\Big|_{0}^{T/2}\right]$$

$$= \frac{2V}{T^2} \times \frac{T^2}{8} + \frac{2V}{T^2} \times \frac{T^2}{8} = \frac{V}{2}$$

Again,

$$a_n = \frac{4}{T_0}\int_0^{T_0/2} f(t)\cos(n\,\omega_0 t)\,dt$$

Here T_0, the time period $= 2\pi$

$$\therefore \quad a_n = \frac{4}{2\pi}\left[\int_0^{T/2} \frac{2V}{T}(t)\cos(n\omega_0 t)\,dt\right]$$

$$= \frac{2}{\pi}\left[\int_0^{T/2} \frac{2V}{T}(t)\cos(n\,\omega_0 t)\,dt\right]$$

$$= \frac{4V}{\pi T}\int_0^{T/2} t\cos n\,\omega_0 t\,dt$$

$$= \frac{4V}{\pi T}\left[\frac{1}{n^2\,\omega_0^2}\cos n\,\omega_0 t + \frac{1}{n\,\omega_0} t\sin(n\,\omega_0 t)\right]_0^{T/2}$$

$$= \frac{4V}{\pi T}\left[\frac{1}{n^2\,\omega_0^2}\cos n\,\omega_0 t\right]_0^{T/2},$$

since $\frac{1}{n\,\omega_0} t\sin(n\,\omega_0 t) = 0$ for $n = 1, 2, 3, \ldots..;$

$$\therefore a_n = \frac{4V}{\pi T}\left[\frac{1}{n^2\,\omega_0^2}\cos n\,\omega_0 T/2 - \frac{1}{n^2\,\omega_0^2}\cos 0°\right]$$

Replacing T by π,

$$a_n = \frac{4V}{\pi^2}\left[\frac{1}{n^2\,\omega_0^2}\cos\left(\frac{n\,\pi}{2}\right)\omega_0 - 1/(n^2\,\omega_0^2)\right]$$

But for $n = 1, 2, 3, \ldots\ldots$, $\cos n\,\pi/2 = 0$

$$\therefore a_n = -\frac{4V}{n^2\,\pi^2}$$

$$\left[\because\ \omega_0^2 = (2\,\pi\,f)^2 = \left(2\pi \times \frac{1}{\text{Time period}}\right)2\right.$$

$$= 1, \quad \text{since time period is } 2\,\pi\,]$$

Thus, for the given waveform,

$$\mathbf{a_0 = \frac{V}{2},\ a_n = -\frac{4V}{n^2\,\pi^2},\ b_n = 0.}$$

EXAMPLE 14.18 *Obtain Fourier series of the given waveform (Fig. E14.18).*

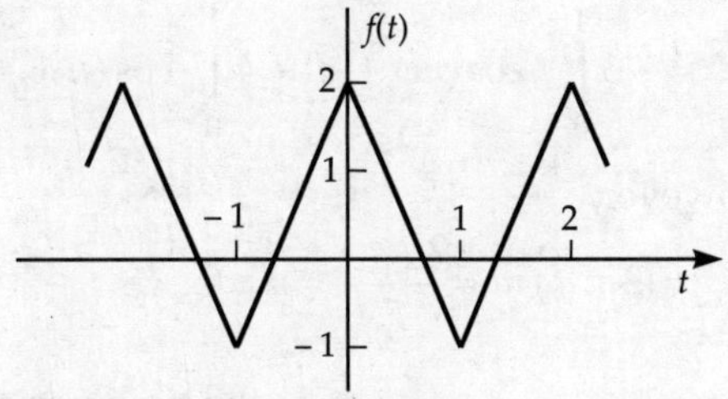

Fig. E14.18

SOLUTION. Since the given waveform possesses even symmetry, as is evident from the figure, hence $b_n = 0$.

It may be observed from the given figure that the equation of the waveform from $t = 0$ to $t = 1$ is

$$f(t) = mt + \text{intercept}$$

$$= -\frac{3}{1}t + 2 = -3\,t + 2$$

and that from $t = -1$ to $t = 0$ is $f(t) = 3t + 2$.

i.e.,

$$f = (3\,t + 2) \quad \text{when } -1 \le t \le 0$$

$$= (-3t + 2) \quad \text{when } \ 0 \le t \le 1$$

Also,

$$a_0 = \frac{2}{T_0}\int_0^{T_0/2} f(t)\,dt = \frac{2}{2}\int_0^1 (-3t + 2)\,dt$$

$$= -3\int_0^1 t\,dt + 2\int_0^1 dt = -3\frac{t^2}{2}\Big|_0^1 + 2\,t\,\Big|_0^1$$

$$= -\frac{3}{2} + 2 = \frac{1}{2} = 0.5$$

and

$$a_n = \frac{2}{T_0}\int_0^{T_0} f(t)\cos(n\omega_0 t)\,dt$$

$$= \frac{2}{2}\int_{-1}^{0} (3t + 2)\cos(n\,\omega_0 t)\,dt$$

$$+ \frac{2}{2}\int_0^1 (-3\,t + 2)\cos(n\,\omega_0 t)\,dt$$

$$= \int_0^1 (-3t + 2)\cos(n\,\omega_0 t)\,dt$$

$$+ \int_0^1 (-3t + 2)\cos(n\omega_0 t)\,dt$$

CHAPTER 14

$$= 2\int_0^1 (-3t+2)\cos(n\,\omega_0 t)\,dt$$

$$= -6\int_0^1 t\cos(n\omega_0 t)\,dt + 4\int_0^1 \cos(n\,\omega_0 t)\,dt$$

However,

$$n\,\omega_0 t = (2\,\pi\,f)\,nt = \frac{2\,n\,\pi\,t}{T_0} = n\,\pi\,t$$

$$(\because T_0, \text{ the time period} = 2)$$

$\therefore$ We can write,

$$a_n = -6\int_0^1 t\cos(n\,\pi\,t)\,dt + 4\int_0^1 \cos(n\,\pi\,t)\,dt$$

$$= -\frac{6}{(n\pi)^2}[\cos(n\,\pi) - 1]$$

However, for $n =$ even, $\cos(n\pi) = +1$ and all a_n for even n become zero.

$$\therefore \text{ for } \quad n = 1, a_1 = -\frac{6}{\pi^2}(-1-1) = \frac{12}{\pi^2}$$

$$\text{for} \quad n = 3, a_3 = \left(-\frac{6}{9\pi^2}\right)(-1-1) = \frac{12}{9\,\pi^2}$$

$$\text{for} \quad n = 5, a_5 = \left(-\frac{6}{25\,\pi^2}\right)(-1-1) = \frac{12}{25\,\pi^2}$$

and so on, since for $n =$ odd, $\cos(n\,\pi) = -1$.

$\therefore$ The Fourier series becomes

$$f\,(t) = 0.5 + \frac{12}{\pi^2}\left[\cos(\pi t) + \frac{1}{9}\cos(3\pi t) + \frac{1}{25}\cos(5\pi t) + \ldots\right]$$

EXAMPLE 14.19 *Find the Fourier series of the waveform shown in Fig. E14.19.*

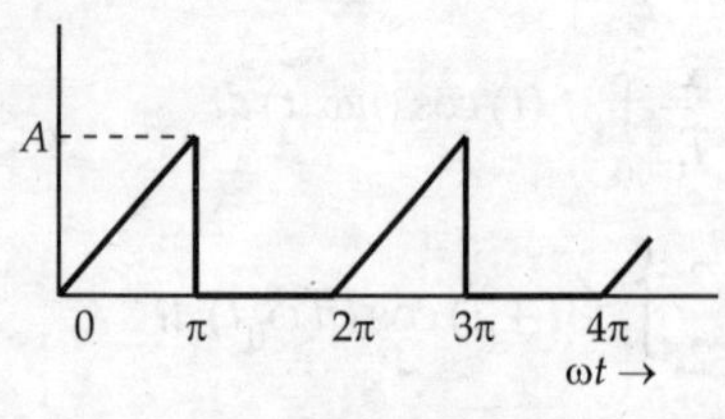

Fig. E14.19

SOLUTION. By inspection, it is observed that the given waveform is neither odd nor even. Thus the series will contain both sine and cosine terms.

Also, $f\,(t) = \left(\frac{A}{\pi}\right)\omega_0 t$, for $0 < \omega_0 t < \pi$

and $\quad = 0, \quad$ for $\pi < \omega_0 t < 2\pi$

Here

$$a_0 = \frac{1}{T_0}\int_0^{T_0} f\,(t)\,dt$$

$$= \frac{1}{T}\left[\int_0^{T_0/2} \frac{A}{\pi}\,\omega_0 t\,d\,(\omega_0 t) + \int_{T_0/2}^{T_0} 0\,.\,d\,(\omega_0 t)\right]$$

$$= \frac{1}{T_0}\int_0^{T_0/2} \frac{A}{\pi}(\omega_0 t)d(\omega_0 t)$$

$$= \frac{1}{2\pi}\int_0^{\pi} \frac{A}{\pi}(\omega_0 t)d(\omega_0 t)$$

$$= \frac{A}{2\pi^2}\cdot\left.\frac{(\omega_0 t)^2}{2}\right|_0^{\pi} = \frac{A}{4}.$$

Next,

$$a_n = \frac{2}{T_0}\int_0^{T_0} f\,(t)\cos n\,\omega_0 t\,d\,(\omega_0 t)$$

$$= \frac{2}{T_0}\int_0^{T_0/2} f\,(t)\cos(n\omega_0 t)\,d\,(\omega_0 t)$$

[$\because f\,(t) = 0$ for $\pi < \omega\,t < 2\pi, \therefore$ The integral is given for 0 to π *i.e.*, for 0 to $T_0/2$ only].

$$= \frac{2}{2\pi}\int_0^{\pi} \frac{A}{\pi}\,\omega_0 t\cos(n\,\omega_0 t)\,d\,(\omega_0 t)$$

$$= \frac{1}{\pi}\int_0^{\pi} \frac{A}{\pi}(\omega_0 t)\cos(n\,\omega_0 t)\,d\,(\omega_0 t)$$

$$= \frac{A}{\pi^2}\left[\frac{1}{n^2}\cos(n\,\omega_0 t) + \frac{\omega_0 t}{n}\sin(n\,\omega_0 t)\right]_0^{\pi}$$

$$= \frac{A}{\pi^2\,n^2}(\cos n\,\pi - 1)$$

We know that when n is even, $\cos(n\,\pi) - 1 = 0$; thus, $a_2, a_4, a_6 \ldots$ terms are zero. On the other hand, when n is odd, $a_n = -\frac{2A}{\pi^2\,n^2}$; since, $\cos n\,\pi = -1$.

$$\therefore a_1 = -\frac{2A}{\pi^2}\,;\, a_3 = -\frac{2A}{9\pi^2}\,;\, a_5 = -\frac{2\,A}{25\,\pi^2} \text{ and so on.}$$

We next obtain the b_n coefficients as shown below :

$$b_n = \frac{2}{T_0}\int_0^{T_0} f\,(t)\sin(n\,\omega_0 t)\,d\,(\omega_0 t)$$

$$= \frac{2}{2\pi}\int_0^{\pi} f(t)\sin(n\,\omega_0 t)\, d(\omega_0 t)$$

$$[\because \text{from } \pi \text{ to } 2\pi,\ f(t) = 0]$$

$$= \frac{1}{\pi}\int_0^{\pi} \frac{A}{\pi}(\omega_0 t)\sin n\,\omega_0 t\, d(\omega_0 t)$$

$$= \frac{A}{\pi^2}\left[\frac{1}{n^2}\sin(n\omega_0 t) - \frac{\omega_0 t}{n}\cos n\,\omega_0 t\right]_0^{\pi}$$

$$= -\frac{A}{n\pi}(\cos n\,\pi)$$

for n = odd numbers, $\cos n\,\pi$ is -1 and hence,

$$b_n\ (n \text{ being odd}) = +\frac{A}{n\,\pi}.$$

Whereas for n = even numbers, $\cos n\,\pi = 1$ giving

$$b_n = -\frac{A}{n\,\pi}$$

$\therefore$ The desired Fourier series becomes

$$f(t) = \frac{A}{4} - \frac{2A}{\pi^2}\cos\omega_0 t - \frac{2A}{9\pi^2}\cos 3\,\omega_0 t - \frac{2A}{25\,\pi^2}\cos 5\,\omega_0 t$$

$$- \ldots + \frac{V}{\pi}\sin\omega_0 t - \frac{V}{2\pi}\sin 2\,\omega_0 t + \frac{V}{3\pi}\sin 3\,\omega_0 t - \ldots$$

EXAMPLE 14.20 *Obtain Fourier coefficients for the function given by*

$$f(t) = (t+\pi)\ \textit{when}\ -\pi < t < \pi;\ f(x+2\pi) = f(x).$$

SOLUTION. The given function has been represented in Fig. E14.20.

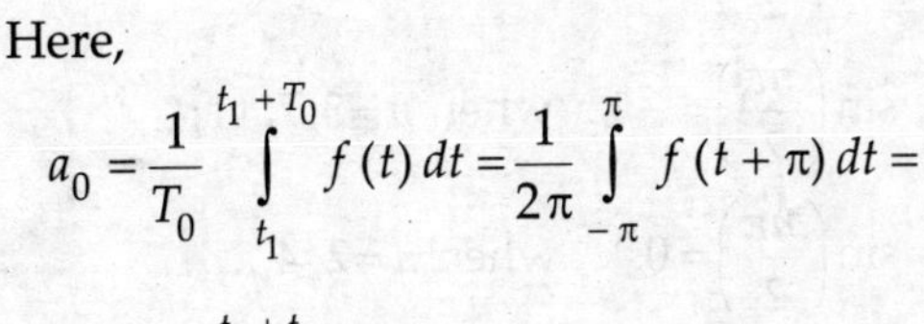

Fig. E14.20

Here,

$$a_0 = \frac{1}{T_0}\int_{t_1}^{t_1+T_0} f(t)\, dt = \frac{1}{2\pi}\int_{-\pi}^{\pi} f(t+\pi)\, dt = \pi.$$

$$a_n = \frac{2}{T_0}\int_{t_1}^{t_1+t_0} f(t)\cos(n\omega_0 t)\, dt$$

$$= \frac{1}{\pi}\int_{-\pi}^{\pi} (t+\pi)\cos n\omega_0 t\, dt = 0$$

$$b_n = \frac{2}{T_0}\int_{t_1}^{t_1+T_0} f(t)\sin(n\omega_0 t)\, dt$$

$$= \frac{1}{\pi}\int_{-\pi}^{\pi} (t+\pi)\sin(n\omega_0 t)\, dt$$

$$= -\frac{2}{n}\cos n\pi = -\frac{2}{n}(-1)^n = (-1)^{n+1}\,\frac{2}{n}.$$

Thus $\boldsymbol{a_0 = \pi;\ a_n = 0}$ **and** $\boldsymbol{b_n = (-1)^{n+1}\frac{2}{n}}$.

EXAMPLE 14.21 *Obtain the Fourier coefficients of the waveform shown in Fig. E14.21.*

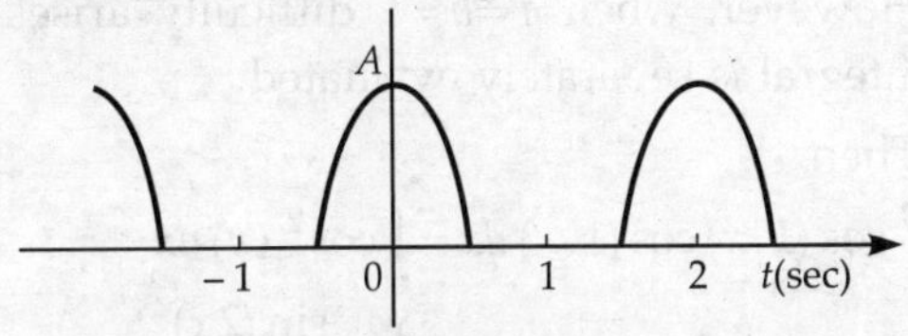

Fig. E14.21

SOLUTION. By inspection,

(*i*) T_o (time period) = 2 sec

(*ii*) The waveform possesses even symmetry;

$$b_n = 0$$

(*iii*) $f(t) = A\cos\dfrac{2\,\pi\, t}{T_0} = A\cos\pi\, t$

for $-0.5 < t < 0.5$ and $f(t) = 0$ for $0.5 < t < 1.5$.

[It may be observed that the given waveform is 90° shifted sine waveform and thus it represents cosine waveform]

Here

$$a_0 = \frac{1}{T_0}\int_0^{T_0/2} f(t)\, dt = \frac{1}{2}\int_{-0.5}^{0.5} 5\cos(\pi\, t)\, dt$$

$$= \frac{5}{2\,\pi}\sin(\pi\, t)\Big|_{-0.5}^{0.5} = \frac{5}{\pi}$$

and $$a_n = \frac{5}{\pi}\int_{-0.5}^{0.5} \cos(\pi\, t)\cos(n\,\pi\, t)\, d(\pi\, t)$$

$\Big[\because a_n = \dfrac{2}{T_0}\displaystyle\int_0^{T_0} f(t)\cos(n\,\omega_0 t)\, dt$, here, $0 \to T_0$ is equivalent to -0.5 to $+0.5$ in time axis while $\omega_0 t \equiv \pi\, t$. Since $T_0 = 2$ sec, replacing t by $\omega_0 t$, *i.e.*, converting time t from second to radians, we have replaced dt by $d(\omega_0 t)$ *i.e.*, by $d(\pi\, t)$. Again "T_o" being 2 sec or 2 π rad/sec, $\dfrac{2}{T_0} \equiv \dfrac{2}{2\,\pi} = \dfrac{1}{\pi}\Big]$

However, from texts of Calculus,

$$\int \cos(ax)\cos(bx)\,dx = \frac{\sin[(a-b)x]}{2(a-b)} + \frac{\sin[(a+b)x}{2(a+b)}$$

Here, $a=1, b\equiv n, x\equiv \pi t$.

$$\therefore a_n = \frac{5}{\pi}\left[\frac{\sin[\pi t(1-n)]}{2(1-n)} + \frac{\sin[\pi t(1+n)]}{2(1+n)}\right]_{-0.5}^{0.5}$$

$$= \frac{5}{\pi}\left[\frac{\sin[\pi(n-1)/2]}{(n-1)} + \frac{\sin[\pi(n+1)/2]}{n+1}\right]$$

However, when $a=b=1$, difficulty arises and the integral is separately evaluated.

Then,

$$\int \cos(1.x)\cos(1.x)\,dx = \int \cos^2(x)\,dx$$

$$= \frac{x}{2} + \frac{\sin(2x)}{4}$$

$$\therefore a_1 = \frac{5}{\pi}\left[\frac{\pi t}{2} + \frac{\sin(2\pi t)}{4}\right]_{-0.5}^{0.5} = 2.5$$

Thus, we finally obtain

$$\mathbf{a_0 = \frac{5}{\pi};\ a_1 = 2.5}$$

$$\mathbf{a_n = \frac{5}{\pi}\left[\frac{\sin[\pi(n-1)/2}{(n-1)} + \frac{\sin[\pi(n+1)/2]}{n+1}\right]}$$

for values of $n=2,3,\ldots\ldots$ and $\mathbf{b_n = 0}$.

EXAMPLE 14.22 *Obtain the Fourier series of the waveform shown in Fig. E14.22.*

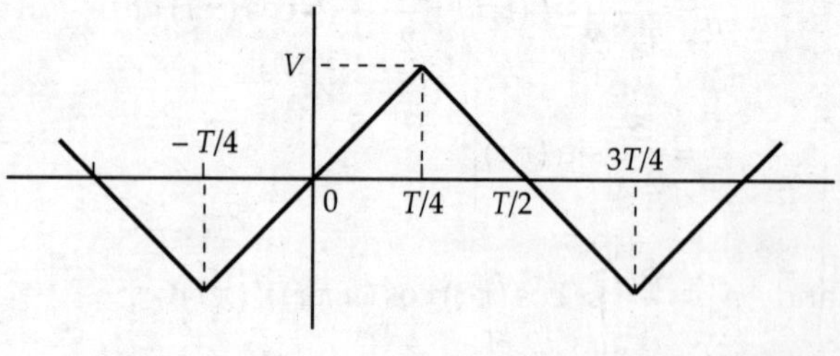

Fig. E14.22

SOLUTION. Inspection reveals that the function is described by

$$f(t) = \frac{4V}{T}t \qquad \text{when } 0 \le t \le \frac{T}{4}$$

$$= -\frac{4V}{T}t + 2V \qquad \text{when } \frac{T}{4} \le t \le 3\frac{T}{4}$$

$$= \frac{4V}{T}t - 4V \qquad \text{when } \frac{3T}{4} \le t \le T$$

Also, it is revealed that the function being odd, $a_0 = 0$ and $a_n = 0$. The sine coefficient is then given by

$$b_n = \frac{4}{T}\int_0^{T/2} f(t)\sin(n\omega_0 t)\,dt$$

$$= \frac{4}{T}\left[\int_0^{T/4}\left(\frac{4V}{T}t\right)\sin\left(\frac{2\pi n}{T}\right)t\,dt + \int_{T/4}^{T/2}\left(-\frac{4V}{T}t + 2V\right)\sin\left(\frac{2\pi n}{T}\right)t\,dt\right]$$

$$= \frac{16V}{T^2}\cdot\frac{T^2}{(2\pi n)^2}\left[\sin\left(\frac{2\pi n}{T}\right)t - \frac{2\pi n}{T}\cos\left(\frac{2\pi n}{T}\right)t\right]_0^{T/4}$$

$$-\frac{16V}{T^2}\cdot\frac{T^2}{(2\pi n)^2}\left[\sin\left(\frac{2\pi n}{T}\right)t - \frac{2\pi n}{T}t\cos\left(\frac{2\pi n}{T}\right)t\right]_{T/4}^{T/2}$$

$$-\frac{8V}{T}\cdot\frac{T}{2\pi n}\cos\left(\frac{2\pi n}{T}t\right)\Bigg|_{T/4}^{T/2}$$

$$= \frac{4V}{(n\pi)^2}\left[\sin\left(\frac{n\pi}{2}\right) - \frac{n\pi}{2}\cos\left(\frac{n\pi}{2}\right) - \sin(n\pi) + n\pi\cos(n\pi) + \sin\left(\frac{n\pi}{2}\right) - \frac{n\pi}{2}\cos\left(\frac{n\pi}{2}\right)\right]$$

$$-\frac{4V}{4\pi}\left[\cos(n\pi) - \cos\left(\frac{n\pi}{2}\right)\right]$$

$$= \frac{8V}{(n\pi)^2}\sin\left(\frac{n\pi}{2}\right)$$

$$\therefore\ n=1,\ b_n = \frac{8V}{\pi^2}$$

$$n=2,\ b_n = 0$$

$$n=3,\ b_n = -\frac{8V}{(3\pi)^2} = -\frac{8V}{9\pi^2}$$

$$n=4,\ b_n = 0$$

$$n=5,\ b_n = \frac{8V}{(5\pi)^2} = \frac{8V}{25\pi^2}$$

$$\sin\left(\frac{n\pi}{2}\right) = +1, \quad \text{when } n = 1,5,9;$$

$$\sin\left(\frac{n\pi}{2}\right) = -1, \quad \text{when } n = 3,7,11;$$

$$\sin\left(\frac{n\pi}{2}\right) = 0, \quad \text{when } n = 2,4,\ldots\ldots$$

$\therefore$ Fourier series is given by

$$\mathbf{f(t) = \frac{8A}{\pi^2}\sin(\omega_0 t) - \frac{8A}{9\pi^2}\sin(3\omega_0 t) + \frac{8A}{25\pi^2}\sin(5\omega_0 t)\ldots}$$

EXERCISES

1. Determine the effective value of $f(t)$ of the waveform shown in Fig. P14.1.

[**Hint.** $f(t) = \frac{A}{T} t$ for one complete cycle.

$$\therefore \text{(Effective value)}^2 = \frac{1}{T}\int_0^T [f(t)]^2\, dt = \frac{1}{T}\int_0^T \left(\frac{A}{T}.t\right)^2 dt$$

$$= \frac{1}{T}.\frac{A^2}{T^2}\int_0^T t^2\, dt = \frac{A^2}{T^3}.\left(\frac{t^3}{3}\right)\Bigg|_0^T = \frac{A^2}{3}$$

$\therefore$ Effective value $= (A/\sqrt{3})$]

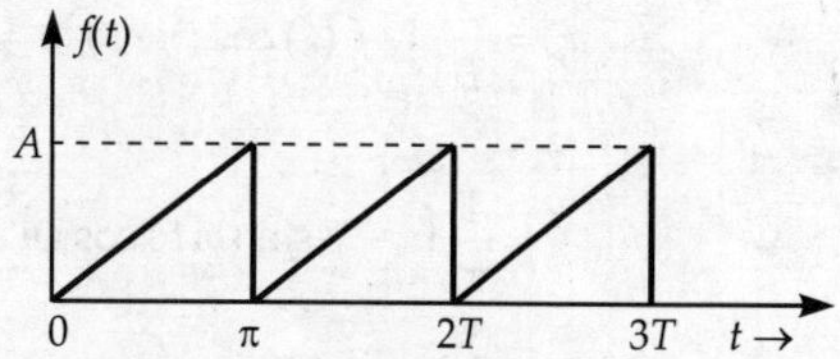

Fig. P14.1

2. Obtain the Fourier series of the function shown in Fig. P14.1 with $T = 2\pi$

[**Hint.** $a_0 = \frac{A}{2}$; $a_n = \frac{2}{T_0}\int_0^{T_0} \frac{A}{2\pi}.\, \omega t \cos(n\omega t)\, d(\omega t) = \frac{A}{2\pi^2}\left[\frac{\omega t}{n}\sin(n\omega t) + \frac{1}{n^2}\cos(n\omega t)\right]_0^{2\pi}$ (using $T_0 = 2\pi$).

$$\therefore \quad a_n = 0$$

$$b_n = \frac{1}{\pi}\int_0^{2\pi}\left(\frac{A}{2\pi}\right)\omega t \sin(\omega t)\, d(\omega t) = \frac{A}{2\pi^2}\left[-\frac{\omega t}{n}\cos(n\omega t) + \frac{1}{n^2}\sin(n\omega t)\right]_0^{2\pi} = -\frac{A}{n\pi}$$

$$\therefore \quad f(t) = \frac{A}{2} - \frac{A}{\pi}\sin(\omega t) - \frac{A}{2\pi}\sin 2\omega t - \frac{A}{3\pi}\sin 3\omega t \;]$$

3. Obtain the Fourier Coefficients of the waveform shown in Fig. P14.2.

[**Hint.** $a_0 = \frac{2}{T_0}\int_0^{T_0} f(t)\, dt = \frac{2}{2\pi}\int_0^{2\pi} f(t)\, dt$

$$= \frac{1}{\pi}\int_0^{\pi}(10)\sin\omega t\, d(\omega t) = \frac{10}{\pi}[-\cos\omega t]_0^{\pi} = \frac{10}{\pi}$$

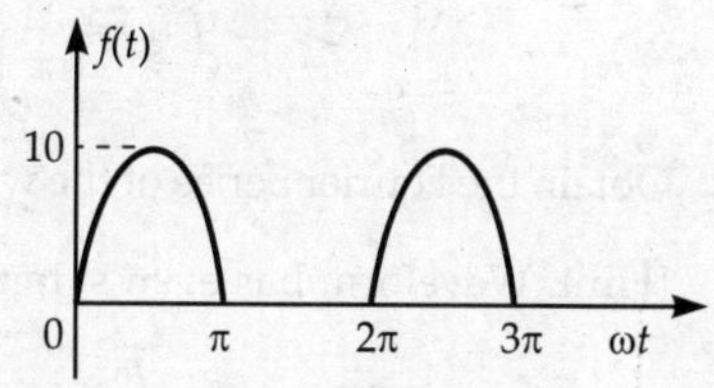

Fig. P14.2

$$a_n = \frac{2}{T_0}\int_0^{T_0} f(t)\cos(n\omega t)\, d(\omega t) = \frac{1}{\pi}\int_0^{\pi}(10)\sin\omega t\cos(n\omega t)\, d(\omega t)$$

$$= \frac{10}{\pi}\left[\frac{-n(\sin(\omega t)\sin(n\omega t) - \cos(n\omega t)\cos(\omega t))}{-n^2+1}\right]_0^{\pi} = \frac{10}{\pi(1-n^2)}(\cos n\pi + 1)$$

For odd values of n, $a_n = 0$; for even values of n,

$$a_n = \frac{2V}{\pi(1-n^2)};$$

for $n = 1$, $$a_1 = \frac{1}{\pi}\int_0^{\pi} 10\sin\omega t\cos\omega t\, d\,\omega t = \frac{10}{\pi}\int_0^{\pi}\frac{1}{2}\sin 2\omega t\, d\,\omega t = 0$$

$$b_n = \frac{1}{\pi}\int_0^{\pi} f(t)\sin(n\omega t)\, d(\omega t) = \frac{1}{\pi}\int_0^{\pi} 10\sin(\omega t)\sin(n\omega t)\, d(\omega t)$$

$$= \frac{10}{\pi}\left[\frac{n\sin(\omega t)\cos(n\omega t) - \sin(n\omega t)\cos(\omega t)}{-n^2+1}\right]_0^{\pi} = 0$$

$$b_1 = \frac{1}{\pi}\int_0^{\pi} 10\sin(\omega t)\sin(\omega t)\, d(\omega t) = \frac{10}{\pi}\int_0^{\pi}\sin^2\omega t\, d(\omega t) = \frac{10}{\pi}\left[\frac{\omega t}{2} - \frac{\sin 2\omega t}{4}\right]_0^{\pi} = \frac{10}{2} = 5. \;]$$

4. Obtain Fourier Series of the waveform shown in Fig. P14.3.

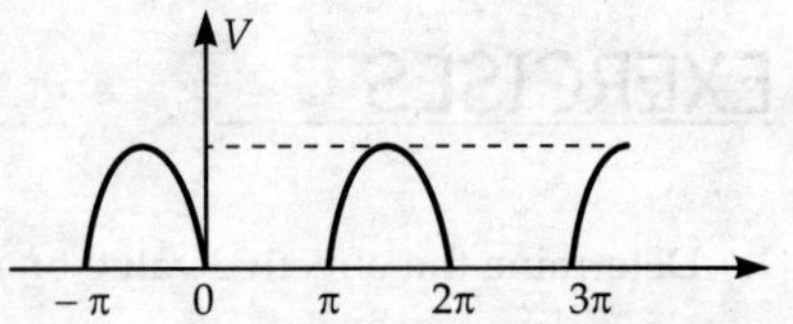

Fig. P14.3

[**Hint.** $f(t) = -V \sin \omega t$ for $-\pi < \omega t < 0$

a_0 = Same as done in the previous exercise $\left(i.e., \dfrac{V}{\pi} \right)$

$$a_n = \frac{2}{T_0}\int_0^{T_0} f(t)\cos(n\omega t)\,dt = \frac{2}{2\pi}\int_0^{2\pi} f(t)\cos(n\omega t)\,dt$$

$$= \frac{1}{\pi}\int_{-\pi}^{0} -V\sin(\omega t)\cos(n\omega t)\,d(\omega t) \qquad \{\because f(t) = 0, \text{ for } 0 \text{ to } \pi\} = \frac{V}{\pi(1-n^2)}(1+\cos n\pi)$$

when n is even, $\quad a_n = \dfrac{2V}{\pi(1-n^2)}$;

when n is odd, $\quad a_n = 0$;

when $n = 1$, $\quad a_1 = \dfrac{1}{\pi}\displaystyle\int_{-\pi}^{0} (-V\sin\omega t)\cos(\omega t)\,d(\omega t) = 0$

Again, $\quad b_n = \dfrac{1}{\pi}\displaystyle\int_{-\pi}^{0} (-V\sin\omega t)\sin(n\omega t)\,d(\omega t) = 0$

but for $n = 1$, $\quad b_1 = \dfrac{1}{\pi}\displaystyle\int_{-\pi}^{0} (-V)\sin^2\omega t\,d(\omega t) = -\dfrac{V}{2}$

$$\therefore \quad f(t) = \frac{V}{\pi}\left\{1 - \frac{\pi}{2}\sin(\omega t) - \frac{2}{3}\cos 2(\omega t) - \frac{2}{15}\cos 4\,\omega t \ldots\right\}$$

5. Obtain the Fourier Series of the waveform shown in Fig. P14.4.

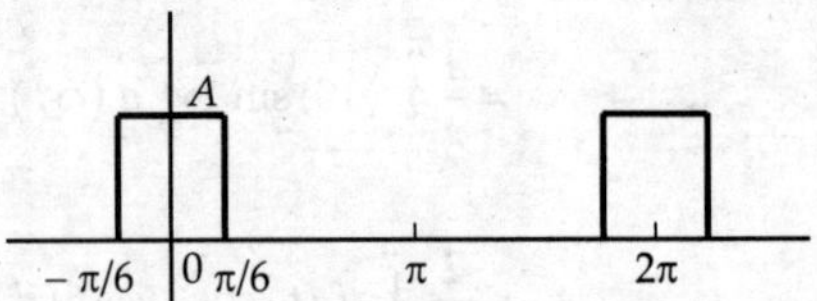

Fig. P14.4

[**Hint.** Waveform has even symmetry.

$$\therefore \quad a_0 = \frac{1}{2\pi}\int_{-\pi/6}^{\pi/6} A\,d(\omega t) = \frac{A}{6}$$

$$a_n = \frac{1}{\pi}\int_{-\pi/6}^{\pi/6} A\cos(n\omega t)\,d(\omega t) = \frac{2A}{n\pi}\sin\frac{n\pi}{6}$$

for $n = 1, 2, 3, \ldots$, $\sin\dfrac{n\pi}{6} = \dfrac{1}{2}, \dfrac{\sqrt{3}}{2}, 1, \ldots$

$$\therefore \quad f(t) = \frac{A}{6} + \frac{2A}{\pi}\sum_{n=1}^{\infty}\frac{1}{n}\sin\left(\frac{n\pi}{6}\right)\cos(n\omega t)\Bigg]$$

6. Obtain the Fourier Series for the waveform shown in Fig. P14.5.

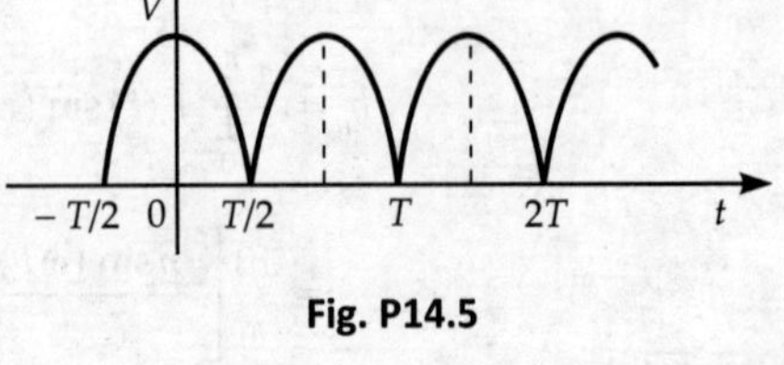

Fig. P14.5

[**Hint.** $f(t) = V\cos\dfrac{\pi t}{T}$ for $-\dfrac{T}{2} \le t \le \dfrac{T}{2}$

$$a_0 = \frac{2}{T_0}\int_0^{T_0/2} f(t)\,dt = \frac{2}{T}\int_0^{T/2} V\cos\frac{\pi t}{T}\,dt = \frac{2V}{\pi}$$

$$a_1 = \frac{4}{T_0}\int_0^{T_0/2} V\cos\frac{\pi t}{T}\cos(n\omega t)\,dt = \frac{4}{T}\int_0^{T/2} V\cos\frac{\pi t}{T}\cos\frac{2\pi nt}{T}\,dt$$

$b_n = 0$ $\qquad$ ($\because$ wave has even symmetry)]

CHAPTER

15

Analysis of Passive Filters

15.1 INTRODUCTION

A filter is an electrical network that can transmit signals within a specified frequency range. This frequency range is called *pass band* and other frequency band where the signals are suppressed is called *attenuation band* or *stop band*. The frequency that separates the pass and attenuation bands is known as *cut-off frequency*. There may also be two *cut off frequencies* in the entire zone of operation of the filter. The cut off frequency is usually symbolised as f_c in case its value is unique or by f_1 and f_2 in case the cut off frequencies are more than one (f_1 indicates lower cut off while the f_2 indicates higher cut off frequency).

15.2 IDEAL FILTER

An ideal filter would transmit signals under the pass band frequencies without attenuation and completely suppress the signal with attenuation band of frequencies with a sharp cut off profile.

15.3 PRACTICAL FILTERS

Practical filters do not ideally transmit the pass band signal unattenuated due to absorption, reflection or due to other loss. This results in loss of signal power. Also, the filters do not completely suppress the signal in attenuation bands. In passive filters, the circuit components – capacitor and inductor – are arranged in different circuit configurations to make the passive filter.

15.4 PROPERTIES OF FILTER

The chief properties of a passive filter section are generally characterised by the following properties :

(*a*) ***Characteristic impedance.*** The characteristic impedance (Z_0) of a filter matches with the circuit to which it is connected throughout the pass band. This prevents reflection loss in the combination. Special attention must be taken for choosing a filter, so that it can be inserted into a given line or between two pieces of equipment.

(*b*) ***Pass band characteristic.*** The filter should have minimum attenuation in its pass band range and high attenuation in the stop band range. The degree of attenuation is generally expressed by the attenuation constant α, its unit being *Neper* or *decibel*.

(*c*) ***Cut-off frequency characteristic.*** The filter should possess frequency distinguishing property in the pass band or stop band. It should be capable of identifying lower as well as higher cut-off frequency for transmitting signals through it. The transition frequency region between the pass and stop band must be very small.

In real life, ideal filters are difficult to be implemented. However, attempts are being made to fabricate filters having characteristics in close proximity of ideal filter.

15.5 USE OF FILTERS

Filters are frequently used in numerous fields of electrical and electronic engineering. The filter being a frequency selecting device, it can be utilised for selecting a particular band or frequency from a wide range of frequency spectrum. In voice frequency telegraphy, multichannel communication is possible by utilising a number of band pass filters with different pass bands. In telephony or radio and TV broadcasting, several numbers of information are transmitted by modulating different carrier frequencies which can be received by utilising filter circuits. In radio receivers, intermediate carrier frequency selection is also possible by using filters in the communication network. In AM detection, high pass filters (HPF) are generally used in order to separate carrier frequency signal from the audio frequency.

Many filters are used in various stages in TV receivers, where they can be used for producing intermediate combined sound and picture carrier frequency and then can separate sound carrier from the composite video signal. It also selects horizontal and vertical synchronising pulses from the composite video signal in addition to separating colour signals.

In audio amplifiers, filters are used to reduce harmonic distortion and voice rejection. In regulated power supply units, filters are used to provide smooth d.c. output from a.c. input.

In many electronic measuring equipments, filters are also used to study particular band of frequencies. Different instruments/equipments may be protected using filter circuits.

In electrical engineering, LPF and HPF (low pass filter and high pass filter) are also utilised in order to eliminate the undesired frequency components resulting from thyristor controlled circuits.

15.6 CLASSIFICATION OF FILTERS

Filters may be classified according to the following *two* philosophies :

(*a*) depending upon the relation between the arm impedances (*i.e.*, series arm impedance Z_1 and shunt arm impedance Z_2), the filters are categorised as

(*i*) constant *K*-filter or prototype filter

(*ii*) *m*-derived filter.

(*b*) identifying their frequency characteristic, the filters are differentiated as

(*i*) low pass filters (LPF)

(*ii*) high pass filters (HPF)

(*iii*) band pass filters (BPF)

(*iv*) band stop filter (BSF) or band elimination filter (BEF).

Table 15.1 shows the main classifications with their corresponding frequency limits.

Table 15.1

Types of filter	*Pass band*	*Attenuation band*
Low pass	$0 \to f_c$	$f_c \to \infty$
High pass	$f_c \to \infty$	$0 \to f_c$
Band pass	$f_2 \to f_1$	$0 \to f_2,\ f_1 \to \infty$
Band stop	$0 \to f_1,\ f_2 \to \infty$	$f_1 \to f_2$

Constant *K* filter (Prototype Filter)

In this filter, the series and shunt impedances (Z_1 and Z_2) are such that, $Z_1 Z_2 = R_0^2 = K$ (constant) where, R_0 is a real number and independent of frequency. It is conventionally known as *design impedance* of the section. Any filter, where this relationship is maintained is known as constant *K* or prototype filter. It can also be classified utilising low pass, high pass, band pass and band stop configurations.

Constant *K* Low Pass Filter (LPF)

It is the simplest type of filter which allows all frequencies, upto the specified cut off frequency, to pass through it and attenuates all the other frequencies above the cut off frequency. *Cut off frequency* demarcates the pass band and the stop band.

Figure 15.1 represents the *T* and π configuration of a typical low pass filter section alongwith its zone of frequency operation.

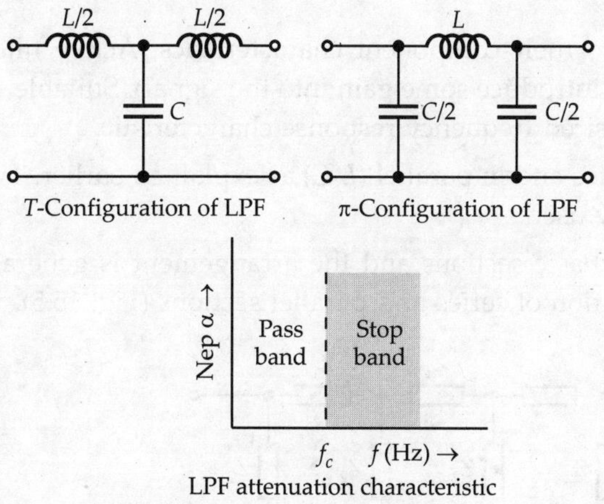

Fig. 15.1 Low pass prototype filter representation.

Constant *K* High Pass Filter

Simply speaking, a high pass filter is the reverse of a low pass filter. This filter attenuates all frequency below the cut off frequency and allows to pass all other frequencies above the cut off frequency. Configurations of typical high pass filters are shown in Fig. 15.2 alongwith its zone of frequency of operation.

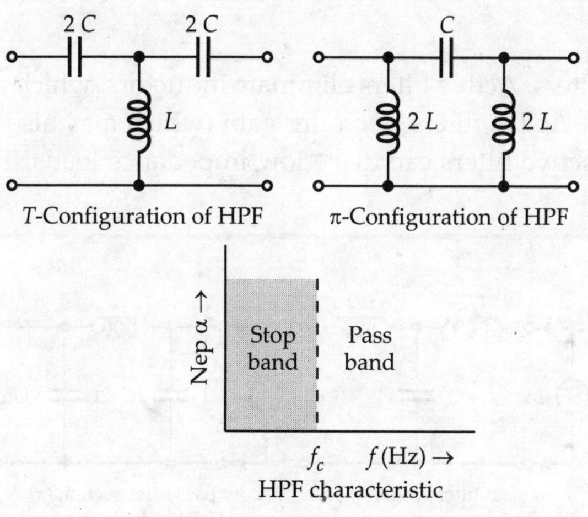

Fig. 15.2 High pass prototype filter representation.

Constant *K* Band Pass Filter

A band pass filter allows transmission of a limited band of frequencies ($f_2 \to f_1$) and rejects all other frequencies below or above frequency band. A band pass filter has series tuned circuit in series arm and parallel tuned circuit in the shunt arm. Fig. 15.3 represents different configurations of the filter and its frequency zone of operation.

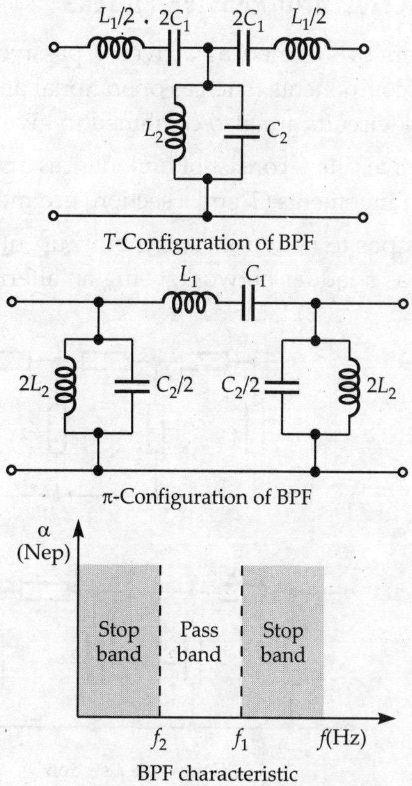

Fig. 15.3 Band pass prototype filter representation.

Constant *K* Band Stop Filter

A band elimination or band stop filter rejects transmission of a limited band of frequencies but it allows transmission of all other frequencies. Fig. 15.4 shows different configurations of band stop filter and its zone of frequency of operation.

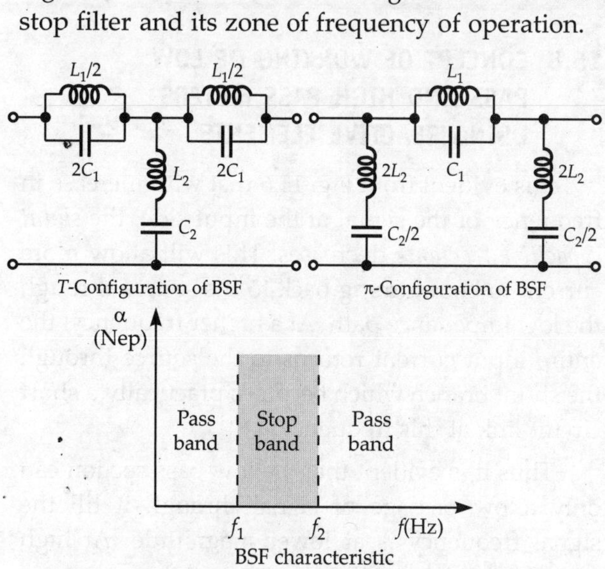

Fig. 15.4 Band stop prototype filter representation.

CHAPTER 15

15.7 ACTIVE AND PASSIVE FILTERS

Filters are termed as active or passive according to their component characteristics. Active filters contain components (such as operational amplifiers that introduce some gain into the signal). Suitable *RC* feedback circuits are also combined to give them the desired frequency response characteristic.

Passive filters consist of impedances arranged in series and in parallel (*L-C*) as explained earlier. Two basic arrangements (*T* and π section) are most commonly used.

Composite network can be built up utilising these basic sections and the arrangement is generally termed as a ladder network, being an alternate combination of series and parallel sections (Fig. 15.5).

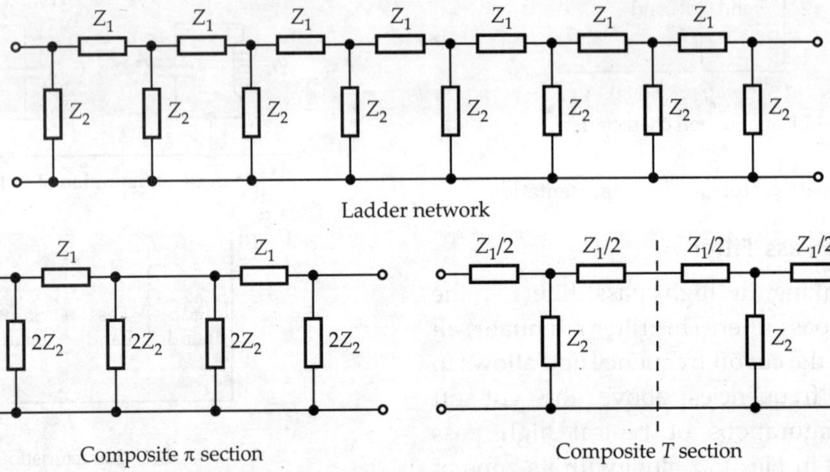

Fig. 15.5 Composite filter sections.

Advantages of active filters over passive filters

Active filters have several advantages over passive filters. Active filters eliminate inductors, which are bulky and are very much expensive at lower frequencies. Active filters also offer gain (which may also be variable). Moreover, it is easy to tune active filters and active filters can drive low impedance loads. The present text mainly deals with passive filters.

15.8 CONCEPT OF WORKING OF LOW PASS AND HIGH PASS FILTERS USING REACTIVE ELEMENTS

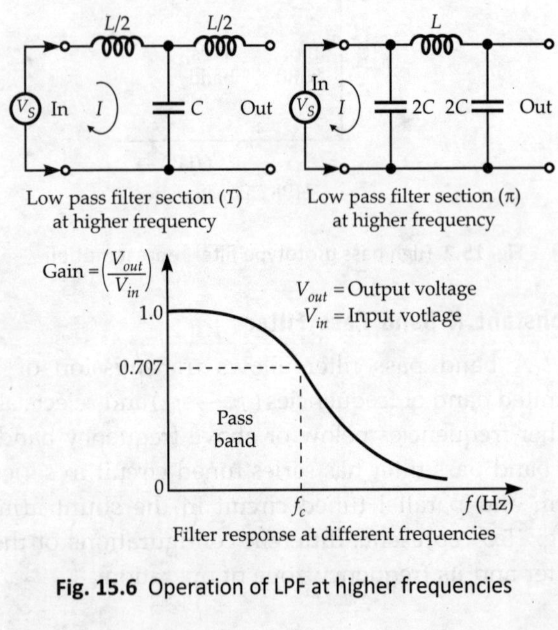

Fig. 15.6 Operation of LPF at higher frequencies

It is evident from Fig. 15.6 that with increase in frequency of the signal at the input side, the *shunt capacitive reactance* decreases. This will allow more current to be returning back to the source through the low impedance path. At a higher frequency, the entire input current returns to the source through the shunt branch which becomes practically a short circuit link at this frequency.

Thus it is evident that the low pass section can only allow passage of signal through it till the signal frequency is at lower magnitude. At high frequency, the inductive reactance in the series arm also increases to a very high value rendering the blockage of the input signal. In practice, LPF operation is said to be satisfactory for increasing frequencies till the voltage gain is 0.707 p.u.

In case of high pass filter, the action is just the reverse and with enhancement of frequency, capacitive reactance in the series arm decreases while the inductive reactance in the shunt arm increases. Thus the section allows the passage of higher order frequencies blocking the lower order frequencies. At lower frequencies, the series capacitor behaves as if a very high reactance while the shunt path offers low reactance. Fig. 15.7 shows the filter sections operating at *low frequency* and the corresponding gain frequency plot f_c indicates the cut off frequency at the point where the voltage gain equals to 0.707 p.u.

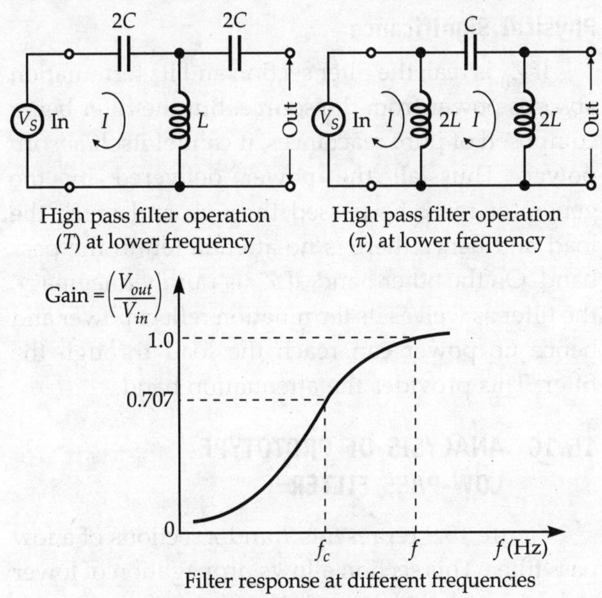

Fig. 15.7 Operation of HPF at lower frequency.

15.9 ANALYSIS OF A PROTOTYPE FILTER SECTION

Considering a simple T section having series and shunt reactances X_1 and X_2 respectively (Fig. 15.8), the characteristic impedance (Z_{0T}) is given by

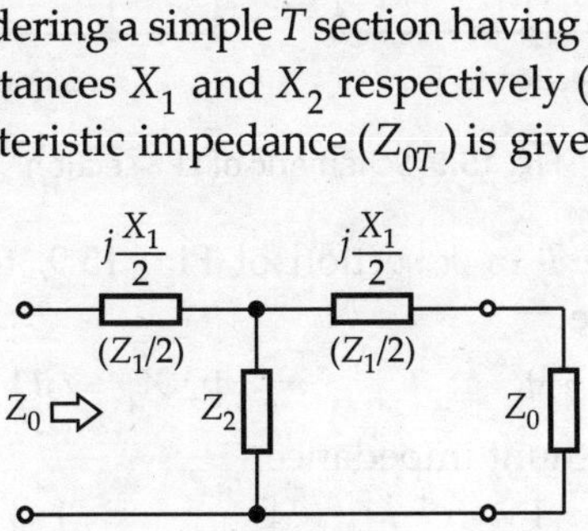

Fig. 15.8 T section with load Z_0.

$$Z_{0T} = \sqrt{\frac{Z_1^2}{4} + Z_1 Z_2} \qquad ...(15.1)$$

while the propagation and attenuation are given by

$$e^{\gamma} = \frac{I_S}{I_R} = 1 + \frac{Z_1}{2Z_2} + \frac{Z_0}{Z_2} \qquad ...(15.2)$$

and

$$\alpha = 20 \log_{10} \left|\frac{I_S}{I_R}\right| \text{ dB} \qquad ...(15.3)$$

In this case, say, $Z_1 = jx_1$ and $Z_2 = jx_2$

Equation (15.1) then becomes

$$Z_0 = \sqrt{\frac{(jx_1)^2}{4} + jx_1\, jx_2}$$

$$= j\sqrt{\frac{x_1^2}{4} + x_1 x_2} = j\sqrt{M} \text{ (say)} \qquad ...(15.4)$$

while equation (15.2) becomes

$$\frac{I_S}{I_R} = 1 + \frac{x_1}{2x_2} - j\,\frac{Z_0}{x_2} \qquad ...(15.5)$$

It may be observed from equation 15.4 that if the sign of "M" is –ve.

$$Z_0 = j\sqrt{-M} = -\sqrt{M}$$

$$[\because \sqrt{-1} = j \text{ and } j^2 = -1] \qquad ...(15.6)$$

Thus if M is – ve, Z_0 becomes real (Eqn. 15.6 does not contain "j").

On the other hand, if sign of "M" is +ve,

$$Z_0 = j\sqrt{+M} = \text{imaginary}$$

$$[\because \text{"}j\text{" remains in this expression}]$$

Again, from equation (15.5), we get,

$$\frac{I_S}{I_R} = \left[1 + \frac{x_1}{2x_2}\right] - j\left[\frac{Z_0}{x_2}\right]$$

$$= \left[1 + \frac{x_1}{2x_2}\right] - j\left[\frac{\sqrt{M}}{x_2}\right] \qquad ...(15.7)$$

Thus, from equation (15.7)

$$\left|\frac{I_S}{I_R}\right| = \sqrt{\left(1 + \frac{x_1}{2x_2}\right)^2 + \left(\frac{\sqrt{M}}{x_2}\right)^2}$$

$$= \sqrt{1 + \frac{x_1^2}{4x_2^2} + \frac{x_1}{x_2} + \frac{M}{x_2^2}}$$

$$= \sqrt{1 + \frac{x_1^2}{4x_2^2} + \frac{x_1}{x_2} - \frac{\{x_1^2/4 + x_1 x_2\}}{x_2^2}}$$

[utilising equation (15.4) and assuming M to be –"ve"]

$$= \sqrt{1 + \frac{x_1^2}{4x_2^2} + \frac{x_1}{x_2} - \frac{x_1^2}{4x_2^2} - \frac{x_1}{x_1}} = 1 \quad ...(15.8)$$

Thus, the attenuation

$$\alpha = 20 \log_{10} \left| \frac{I_S}{I_R} \right| \text{ becomes}$$

$$\alpha = 0. \qquad \left[\because \left| \frac{I_S}{I_R} \right| = 1 \right]$$

Hence, if "M' is –ve, Z_0 is real and the attenuation α is zero ... (proposition – 1)

Again, if Z_0 is imaginary, *i.e.*, when M is +ve, from equation (15.5),

$$\frac{I_S}{I_R} = \left[1 + \frac{x_1}{2x_2} \right] - j \left[\frac{Z_0}{x_2} \right]$$

$$= \left[1 + \frac{x_1}{2x_2} \right] - j \left[\frac{j\sqrt{M}}{x_2} \right]$$

$$= 1 + \frac{x_1}{2x_2} + \frac{\sqrt{M}}{x_2}$$

$$\text{Thus,} \quad \left| \frac{I_S}{I_R} \right| = 1 + \frac{x_1}{2x_2} + \frac{\sqrt{\frac{x_1^2}{4} + x_1 x_2}}{x_2} \quad ...(15.9)$$

Observing equation (15.9), it is evident that though α is real but not equal to unity.

This proves that if "M' is +ve, Z_0 is imaginary, the attenuation being constant and not equal to zero ... (proposition – 2)

From propositions (1) and (2), it can be concluded that during pass band [*i.e.*, when α, the attenuation, is zero], the characteristic impedance is *real* and for attenuation band, when $\alpha \neq 0$, the characteristic impedance is *imaginary*.

Again, as

$$Z_0 = \sqrt{\frac{Z_1^2}{4} + Z_1 Z_2}$$

and as $Z_1 = jX_1$ and $Z_2 = jX_2$, where X_1 and X_2 are pure reactances, hence,

$$Z_0 = \sqrt{\frac{-X_1^2}{4} - X_1 X_2} = \sqrt{-X_1 \left(\frac{X_1}{4} + X_2 \right)} \quad ...(15.10)$$

It is thus evident that if X_1 and $\left(\frac{X_1}{4} + X_2 \right)$ have only opposite signs, Z_0 will be *real i.e.*, the attenuation will be zero indicating operation in pass band. On the other hand, if X_1 and $\left(\frac{X_1}{4} + X_2 \right)$ have the same sign, Z_0 will become a purely *imaginary* quantity when the filter will attenuate the signal (attenuation band) (Fig. 15.10).

Physical Significance

If Z_0 is real, the filter section and its termination absorbs power from the source. But the filter being composed of pure reactances, it cannot itself absorb power. Thus all the power delivered by the generator must be passed through and reach the load and hence there is no attenuation in the pass band. On the other hand, if Z_0 is purely imaginary, the filter as well as its termination reflect power and hence no power can reach the load through the filter. This provides the attenuation band.

15.10 ANALYSIS OF PROTOTYPE LOW-PASS FILTER

Figure 15.9 represents T and π sections of a low pass filter. This section allows propagation of lower order frequencies through it.

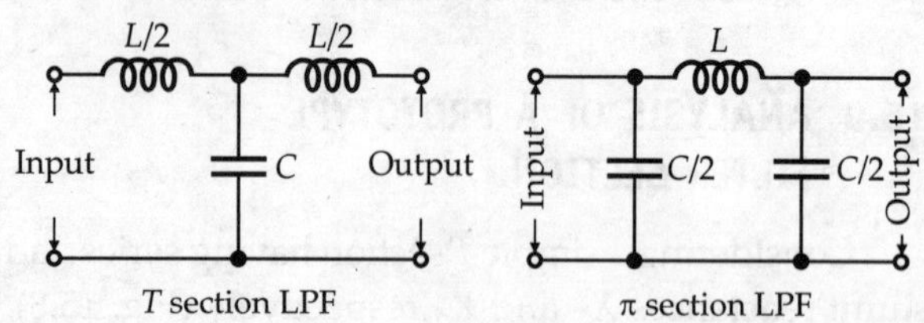

Fig. 15.9 Schematic of LPF section.

In the T or π section of Fig. 15.9, total series impedance

$$Z_1 = j\omega L \qquad [\because X_1 = \omega L] \quad ...(15.11)$$

and total shunt impedance

$$Z_2 = \frac{1}{j\omega C} = -\frac{j}{\omega C} \qquad \left[\because X_2 = -\frac{1}{\omega C} \right] \quad ...(15.12)$$

Multiplying both the equations (15.11) and (15.12)

$$Z_1 Z_2 = j\omega L\left(-\frac{j}{\omega C}\right) = \frac{L}{C} = R_0^2 \text{ (say)} \quad ...(15.13)$$

$\left[\frac{L}{C} \text{ being a real quantity}\right]$

Again $$\frac{Z_1}{4Z_2} = -\frac{\omega^2 LC}{4} \quad ...(15.14)$$

But from two port network,

$$Z_{0T} = \sqrt{Z_1 Z_2\left(1+\frac{Z_1}{4Z_2}\right)} \quad ...(15.15)$$

where Z_{0T} indicates the characteristic impedance of the T section of the reactance characteristic has been shown in Fig. 15.10.

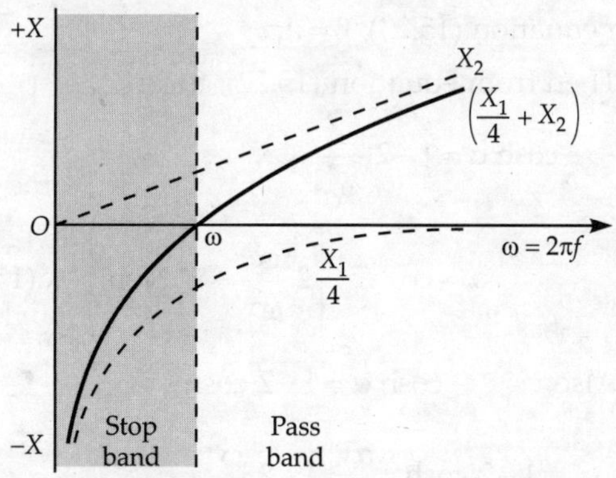

Fig. 15.10 Reactance frequency characteristic of LPF.

Substituting the value of Z_1Z_2 and $\frac{Z_1}{4Z_2}$ from equations (15.13) and (15.14) respectively, equation (15.15) gives

$$Z_{0T} = \sqrt{\frac{L}{C}}\sqrt{1-\frac{\omega^2 LC}{4}}$$

$$= R_0\sqrt{1-\frac{\omega^2 LC}{4}} = R_0\sqrt{1-\frac{\omega^2}{4/LC}}$$

or $$Z_{0T} = R_0\sqrt{1-\frac{\omega^2}{\omega_C^2}} \quad \left[\text{where } \omega_C^2 = \frac{4}{LC}\right]$$

$$= R_0\sqrt{1-\left(\frac{f}{f_C}\right)^2} \quad ...(15.16)$$

Thus, it is evident from above that $Z_{0T} = \left(= R_0\sqrt{1-\frac{\omega^2 LC}{4}}\right)$ is *real* if $\frac{\omega^2 LC}{4} < 1$ and *imaginary* if $\frac{\omega^2 LC}{4} > 1$ *i.e.,* Z_{0T} indicates the characteristic impedance of the pass band when $\frac{\omega^2 LC}{4} < 1$ [as Z_{0T} remains real] and Z_{0T} becomes the characteristic impedance for the stop band if $\frac{\omega^2 LC}{4} > 1$ [as Z_{0T} becomes imaginary]. Obviously, the *cut off frequency* will be at a particular condition when, $\frac{\omega^2 LC}{4} = 1\left[i.e., \omega_C = \frac{2}{\sqrt{LC}}\right]$. Hence the low pass filter possesses a cut off frequency given by

$$\omega_C = \frac{2}{\sqrt{LC}} \text{ or } f_C = \frac{1}{\pi\sqrt{LC}} \quad ...(15.17)$$

It is also evident from the reasonings cited above in relevance to equation (15.16), that in the pass band (*i.e.,* when Z_{0T} is real) $f < f_C$ and in the stop band (*i.e.,* when Z_{0T} is imaginary), $f > f_C$.

For the π section, the characteristic impedance is given by (ref. to two port network theories),

$$Z_{0\pi} = \frac{Z_1 Z_2}{Z_{0T}} = \frac{R_0^2}{R_0\sqrt{1-\left(\frac{f}{f_C}\right)^2}} = \frac{R_0}{\sqrt{1-\left(\frac{f}{f_C}\right)^2}} \quad ...(15.18)$$

Here, in the pass band, $f < f_C$, so that $Z_{0\pi}$ is real and positive quantity. When $f > f_C$, $Z_{0\pi}$ becomes an imaginary quantity. Fig. 15.11 represents the Z_{0T} and $Z_{0\pi}$ characteristics of the LPF in the pass band.

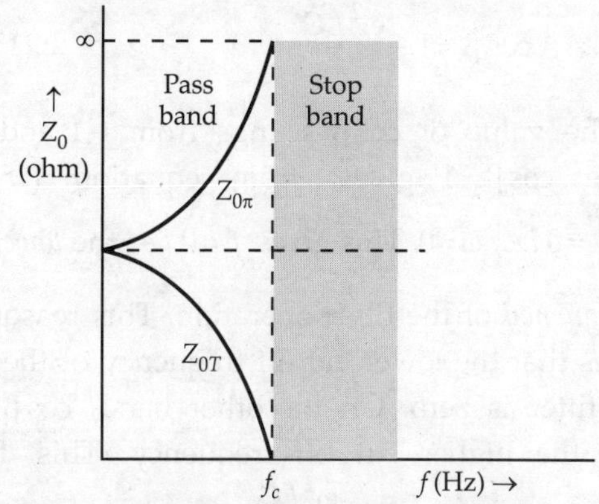

Fig. 15.11 Characteristic impedance profile of π and T sections of an LPF.

Attenuation (α) and Phase Shift (β) Characteristics of LPF Section

From the treatise in *two* port network,

$$\cosh\gamma = 1 + \frac{Z_1}{2Z_2} \quad ...(15.19)$$

where, $\gamma = \alpha + j\beta$

In a filter section, $Z_1 = jx_1$ and $Z_2 = jx_2$, where x_1 and x_2 are the reactances of the series and shunt branch. For an LPF section $x_1 = j\omega L$ and $x_2 = -\frac{j}{\omega C}$ (Refer to Fig. 15.9).

Also, for the same LPF T section,

$$\left(1 + \frac{Z_1}{2Z_2}\right) = 1 - \frac{\omega^2 LC}{2} \qquad \left[\because \frac{Z_1}{4Z_2} = -\frac{\omega^2 LC}{4}\right]$$

i.e., $$\cosh\gamma = 1 - \frac{\omega^2 LC}{2}$$

or $$\cosh(\alpha + j\beta) = 1 - \frac{\omega^2 LC}{2} \quad ...(15.20)$$

or $$\cosh\alpha\cos\beta + j\sinh\alpha\sin\beta = 1 - \frac{\omega^2 LC}{2} \quad ...(15.21)$$

Equating the real and imaginary parts of equation (15.21),

$$\cosh\alpha\cos\beta = 1 - \frac{\omega^2 LC}{2} \quad ...(15.22)$$

and $$\sinh\alpha\sin\beta = 0 \quad ...(15.23)$$

From equation (15.23), either $\alpha = 0$ or $\beta = n\pi$, n being an integer.

For pass band. In the pass band, there is no *attenuation*. Hence $\alpha = 0$.

This gives, from equation (15.22)

$$\cos\beta = 1 - \frac{\omega^2 LC}{2} \quad ...(15.24)$$

The value of $\cos\beta$ swings from +1 and −1. Hence $\cos\beta = 1$ gives, from equation (15.24), $\frac{\omega^2 LC}{2} = 0$ *i.e.,* $\omega = 0$. This gives $f = 0$ *i.e.,* the *lower cut off frequency* of the filter operation. This reasoning proves that the lower cut off frequency of the low pass filter is zero. On the other hand, $\cos\beta = -1$ gives the higher cut off frequency. This, from equation (15.24) gives, $\frac{\omega^2 LC}{2} = 2$

i.e., $\omega_C = \frac{2}{\sqrt{LC}}$ giving $f_C = \frac{1}{\pi\sqrt{LC}}$

(*i.e.,* the higher cut-off frequency)

Again, from equation (15.24),

$$\cos\beta = 1 - \frac{\omega^2 LC}{2} = 1 - \frac{\omega^2}{2/LC} = 1 - 2\frac{\omega^2}{\omega_C^2}$$

$$\therefore \quad \beta = \cos^{-1}\left[1 - 2\frac{\omega^2}{\omega_C^2}\right] \text{ radian} \quad ...(15.25)$$

Also, $\cos\beta = 1 - 2\sin^2\frac{\beta}{2} = 1 - \frac{\omega^2 LC}{2}$

or $$2\sin^2\frac{\beta}{2} = 2\frac{\omega^2}{\omega_C^2}$$

i.e., $$\beta = 2\sin^{-1}\frac{\omega}{\omega_C} \text{ rad}$$

For attenuation band. In attenuation band it is obvious that $\alpha \neq 0$. Hence, it is justified to answer, from equation (15.23), $\beta = n\pi$.

Then from equation (15.22), for $n = 1$,

$$-\cosh\alpha = 1 - 2\frac{\omega^2}{\omega_C^2}$$

or $$\alpha = \cosh^{-1}\left[2\frac{\omega^2}{\omega_C^2} - 1\right] \text{ Nep.} \quad ...(15.26)$$

Also, $$-\cosh\alpha = 1 - 2\cosh^2\frac{\alpha}{2}$$

or $$1 - 2\cosh^2\frac{\alpha}{2} = 1 - 2\frac{\omega^2}{\omega_C^2}$$

which gives

$$\alpha = 2\cosh^{-1}\left(\frac{\omega}{\omega_C}\right) \text{ Nep.} = 2\cosh^{-1}\left(\frac{f}{f_C}\right) \text{ Nep.} \quad ...(15.27)$$

The attenuation (α) and phase shift (β) characteristics of LPF section have been shown in Fig. 15.12.

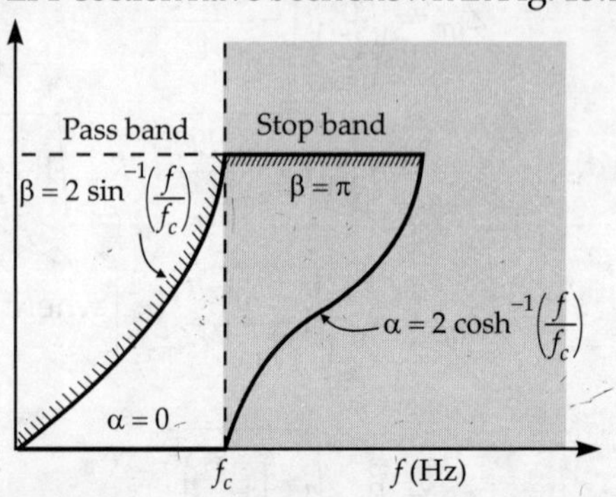

Fig. 15.12 α and β characteristic of LPF section.

15.11 DESIGN OF A PROTOTYPE LPF SECTION

One of the most important parts of filter analysis is selection of its components R_0 being known as design impedance, cut off frequency being f_C, both being given in equations

$$R_0 = \sqrt{\frac{L}{C}} \quad \text{(equation 15.13)}$$

and

$$f_C = \frac{1}{\pi\sqrt{LC}} \quad \text{(equation 15.17)}$$

The expressions for the inductance and capacitance are then given by

$$L = \frac{R_0}{\pi f_c} \qquad ...(15.28)$$

and

$$C = \frac{1}{\pi R_0 f_C} \qquad ...(15.29)$$

15.12 ANALYSIS OF A PROTOTYPE HIGH PASS FILTER

Figure 15.13 represents T and π sections of a prototype HPF section. In both the sections, total series impedance is given by

$$Z_1 = \frac{1}{j\omega C} \qquad ...(15.30)$$

and shunt impedance

$$Z_2 = j\omega L \qquad ...(15.31)$$

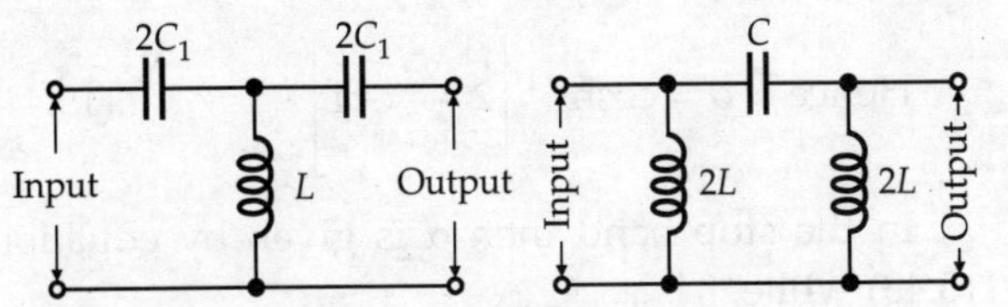

Fig. 15.13 T and π section of a prototype HPF section.

Hence,

$$Z_1 Z_2 = \frac{1}{j\omega C} \times j\omega L = \frac{L}{C} = R_0^2 \text{ (say)} \qquad ...(15.32)$$

[R_0 being a real quantity]

The characteristic impedance of a T section being given by

$$Z_{0T} = \sqrt{\frac{Z_1^2}{4} + Z_1 Z_2} \qquad ...(15.33)$$

The reactance frequency characteristic has been shown in Fig. 15.14.

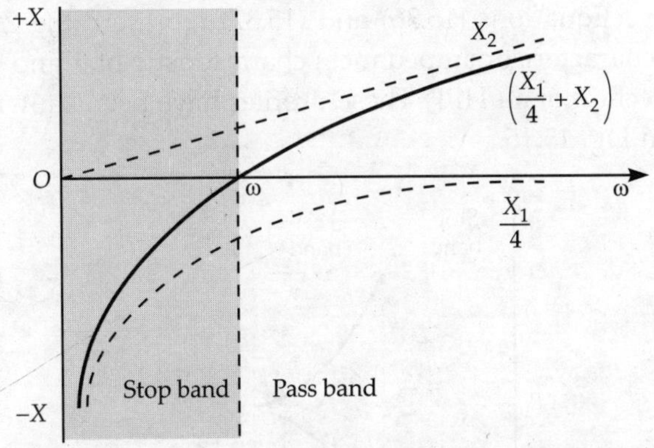

Fig. 15.14 Reactance frequency characteristic of HPF.

In case of the prototype HPF section.

$$Z_{0T} = \sqrt{-\frac{1}{4\omega^2 C^2} + \frac{L}{C}}$$

[utilising equations (15.31) and (15.32) in (15.33)]

$$= \sqrt{\frac{L}{C}}\sqrt{1 - \frac{1}{4\omega^2 CL}}$$

$$= R_0 \sqrt{1 - \frac{1}{4\omega^2 LC}} \qquad ...(15.34)$$

If $4\omega^2 LC > 1$, Z_{0T} is real and the filter works in the pass band. However, if $4\omega^2 LC < 1$, Z_{0T} is imaginary, and the filter's operation lies in the attenuation band. Obviously, the cut off frequency is given by

$$4\omega_C^2 LC = 1 \qquad \textit{i.e.,} \qquad \omega_C = \frac{1}{2\sqrt{LC}}$$

or

$$f_c = \frac{1}{4\pi\sqrt{LC}} \qquad ...(15.35)$$

Also, $$Z_{0T} = R_0 \sqrt{1 - \frac{1}{4\omega^2 LC}}$$

$$= R_0 \sqrt{1 - \frac{\omega_C^2}{\omega^2}} = R_0 \sqrt{1 - \frac{f_C^2}{f^2}} \qquad ...(15.36)$$

where $\omega_C^2 = (1/4\,LC)$

Hence,

$$Z_{0\pi} = \frac{R_0^2}{Z_{0T}} = \frac{R_0^2}{R_0\sqrt{1 - \frac{\omega_C^2}{\omega^2}}} = \frac{R_0}{\sqrt{1 - \frac{\omega_C^2}{\omega^2}}}$$

$$= \frac{R_0}{\sqrt{1 - \frac{f_C^2}{f^2}}} \qquad ...(15.37)$$

Equations (15.36) and (15.37) represent the Z_0 (characteristic impedance) characteristic of T and π section of an HPF. These profiles have been shown in Fig. 15.15.

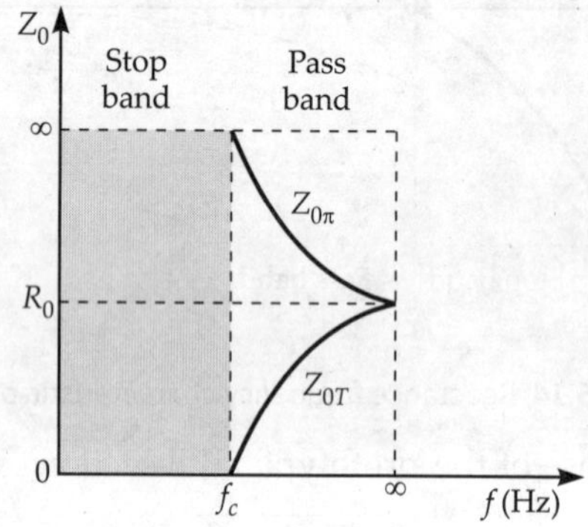

Fig. 15.15 Z_0 profile of HPF.

Attenuation (α) and phase shift (β) characteristic of HPF

For a T network, the propagation constant (γ) is given by the relation

$$\cosh \gamma = 1 + \frac{Z_1}{2Z_2} \qquad ...(15.38)$$

But

$$1 + \frac{Z_1}{2Z_2} = 1 + \frac{1/j\omega C}{2j\omega L} = 1 + \frac{1}{j\omega C} \times \frac{1}{2j\omega L}$$

$$= 1 - \frac{1}{2\omega^2 LC} \qquad ...(15.39)$$

But $\qquad \gamma = \alpha + j\beta \qquad ...(15.40)$

Comparing the equations (15.39) and (15.40) for real and imaginary parts, either,

$$\sinh \alpha \sin \beta = 0 \qquad ...(15.40a)$$

or $\cosh \alpha \cos \beta = 1 - \dfrac{1}{2\omega^2 LC} \qquad ...(15.40b)$

From equation (15.40*a*), it is evident that

either $\alpha = 0$ or $\beta = n\pi$, n being an integer.

For Pass Band. In pass band, $\alpha = 0$ (as there is no attenuation). However, phase shift exists giving the value of $\cos \beta = 1 - \dfrac{1}{2\omega^2 LC}$ when $\alpha = 0$ in equation (15.40*b*). It is evident that the value of $\cos \beta$ swings from +1 and −1. However, $\cos \beta = 1$ gives cut off frequency (as with $\cos \beta = 1$, from equation $\cos \beta = 1 - \dfrac{1}{2\omega^2 LC}$, $\omega = \infty$ *i.e.*, $f = \infty$). This has been referred to as *higher cut off frequency*.

Assuming $\cos \beta$ to be −1, from the expression (15.40*b*),

$$-1 = 1 - \frac{1}{2\omega^2 LC}$$

giving $\qquad \omega_C^2 = \dfrac{1}{4LC} \qquad$ [ω_C represents a particular value of ω when $\cos \beta = -1$]

Hence, the *lower cut off frequency*

$$\omega_C = \frac{1}{2\sqrt{LC}} \qquad ...(15.41)$$

or $\qquad f_c = \dfrac{1}{4\pi\sqrt{LC}} \qquad ...(15.42)$

Also, from $\qquad \cos \beta = 1 - \dfrac{1}{2\,\omega^2 LC}$

$$\cos \beta = 1 - 2\,\frac{\omega_C^2}{\omega^2}$$

$$\therefore \qquad \beta = \cos^{-1}\left(1 - \frac{2\omega_C^2}{\omega^2}\right) = \cos^{-1}\left(1 - \frac{2f_C^2}{f^2}\right)$$

Again,

$$\cos \beta = 1 - 2\sin^2\frac{\beta}{2} = 1 - 2\,\frac{\omega_C^2}{\omega^2}$$

or $\qquad \beta = 2\sin^{-1}\dfrac{\omega_C}{\omega}$ rad $\qquad ...(15.43)$

For Attenuation Band. Utilising $\beta = \pi$ in equation (15.40*b*), α being not equal to zero,

$$\cosh \alpha = -1 + \frac{1}{2\omega^2 LC} = -1 + 2\,\frac{\omega_C^2}{\omega^2}$$

Hence $\qquad \alpha = \cosh^{-1}\left[2\,\dfrac{\omega_C^2}{\omega^2} - 1\right] \qquad ...(15.44)$

In the stop band then α is given by equation (15.43) while, β is π.

Figure 15.16 represents the profiles of α and β, the attenuation and phase shift of a HPF section.

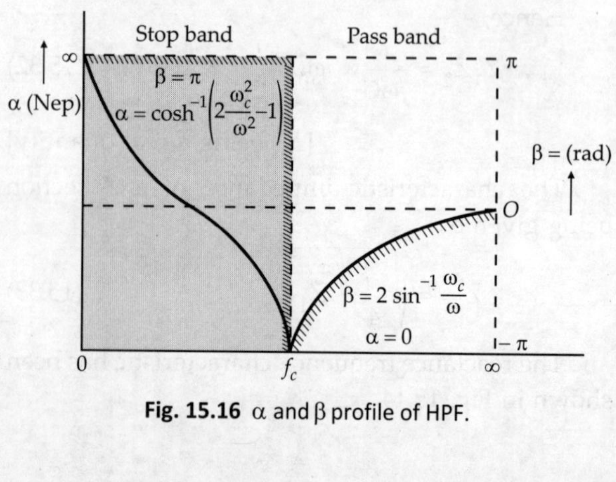

Fig. 15.16 α and β profile of HPF.

15.13 DESIGN OF A PROTOTYPE HPF SECTION

The design impedance being R_0 and the cut off frequency being f_C, both being known, the design components L and C of the filter can be found out from the following two equations derived earlier.

$$R_0 = \sqrt{\frac{L}{C}} \text{ (equation 15.32)}$$

and $$f_C = \frac{1}{4\pi\sqrt{LC}} \text{ (equation 15.42)}$$

Solving these two questions,

$$L = \frac{R_0}{4\pi f_C} \qquad \text{...(15.45)}$$

and $$C = \frac{1}{4\pi R_0 f_C} \qquad \text{...(15.46)}$$

Example 15.1 *In a simple T section, a low pass filter has a design impedance R_0. Find $Z_{0\pi}$ at 0.9 f_C.*

Solution. $\dfrac{f}{f_C} = 0.9$ (given)

However, for LPF,

$$Z_{0\pi} = \frac{R_0}{\sqrt{1-\left(\frac{f}{f_C}\right)^2}}$$

$$= \frac{R_0}{\sqrt{[1-(0.9)^2]}} = \mathbf{2.3\ R_0}.$$

Example 15.2 *Design a constant K-low pass filter having cut-off frequency 2.5 kHz and design resistance $R_0 = 700\,\Omega$. Also find the frequency at which this filter produces attenuation of 19.1 dB. Find its characteristic impedances and phase constant at pass band and stop or attenuation band.*

Solution. Here from the given data,

$$f_c = 2.5 \text{ kHz} = 2500 \text{ Hz}; \quad R_o = 700\,\Omega$$

$$\text{Attenuation } \alpha = 19.1 \text{ dB} = \frac{19.1}{8.686} = 2.199 \text{ nepers}$$

The design elements of LPF are L and C given by the relations

$$L = \frac{R_o}{\pi f_c} = \frac{700}{\pi \times 2500} \text{ H} = 89.127 \text{ mH}$$

and $$C = \frac{1}{\pi R_o f_c} = \frac{1}{\pi \times 700 \times 2500} \text{ F} = 0.182\ \mu\text{F}$$

Attenuation in attenuation band of a low pass filter is given by the relation

$$\alpha = 2\cosh^{-1}\left(\frac{f}{f_c}\right)$$

where, f be the frequency at which this filter produces attenuation 19.1 dB or 2.199 nepers.

Hence, $$\frac{f}{f_c} = \cosh\left(\frac{\alpha}{2}\right)$$

or $$\frac{f}{2500} = \cosh\left(\frac{2.199}{2}\right) = 1.6678509$$

or $$f = 2500 \times 1.6678509 \text{ Hz} = 4.170 \text{ kHz}.$$

The characteristic impedances of a T-type and π-type LPF are given by the relations,

$$Z_{oT} = R_o\sqrt{1-\left(\frac{f}{f_c}\right)^2}$$

and $$Z_{o\pi} = \frac{R_o}{\sqrt{1-\left(\frac{f}{f_c}\right)^2}}$$

But, in this case $f > f_c$, therefore the characteristic impedance **Z_{oT} and $Z_{o\pi}$ are imaginary.**

The phase constant (β) in pass band is given by,

$$\beta = 2\sin^{-1}\left(\frac{f}{f_c}\right) = 2\sin^{-1}\left(\frac{4.170}{2.500}\right) \text{ radians}$$

But as $f > f_c$, **β in pass band is imaginary** or impracticable, but in attenuation band the phase constant (β) is given by

$$\beta = \pi \text{ radians}$$

The required T and π-section low pass filters are as shown below (Fig. E15.1).

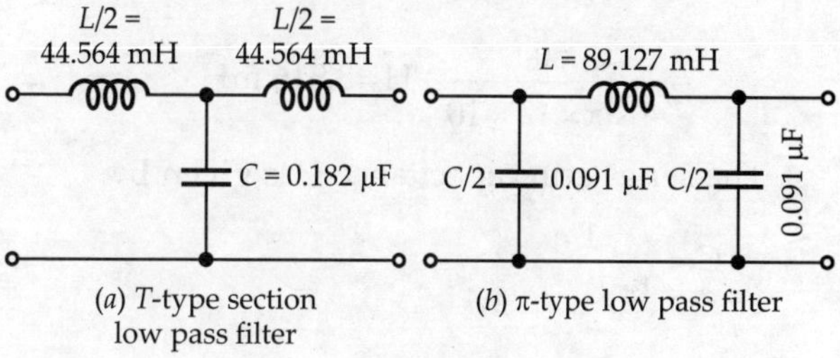

Fig. E15.1

EXAMPLE 15.3 *A T-section low pass filter has series inductance 80 mH and shunt capacitance 0.022 μF. Determine the cut-off frequency and nominal design impedance (R_o). Also design an equivalent π-section.*

SOLUTION. Here from the given data,

$$L = 80 \text{ mH and } C = 0.022 \text{ μF}$$

Therefore, the cut-off frequency (f_c) is given by,

$$f_c = \frac{1}{\pi\sqrt{LC}}$$

$$= \frac{1}{\pi\sqrt{(80\times10^{-3})(0.022\times10^{-6})}} \text{ Hz}$$

$$\therefore \quad f_c = \mathbf{7.587 \text{ kHz.}}$$

The nominal design impedance (R_o) is given by,

$$R_o = \sqrt{\frac{L}{C}}$$

$$= \sqrt{\frac{80\times10^{-3}}{0.022\times10^{-6}}}\ \Omega = \mathbf{1.907\ K\Omega}.$$

The required T and π-section low pass filters are as shown below (Fig. E15.2).

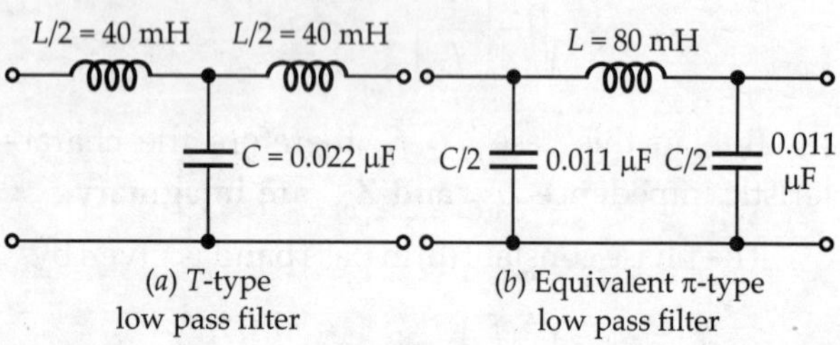

Fig. E15.2

EXAMPLE 15.4 *Design a T and π section constant-K high pass filter having cut-off frequency of 12 kHz and nominal impedance $R_o = 500\,\Omega$. Also find : (i) Its characteristic impedance and phase constant at 24 kHz and (ii) attenuation at 4 kHz.*

SOLUTION. The shunt arm inductance L is given by,

$$L = \frac{R_o}{4\pi f_c}$$

$$= \frac{500}{4\times\pi\times12\times10^3} \text{ H} = 3.316 \text{ mH}$$

The series arm capacitance C is given by,

$$C = \frac{1}{4\pi R_o f_c}$$

$$= \frac{1}{4\times\pi\times500\times12\times10^3} \text{ F} = 0.0132 \text{ μF}$$

Hence, the required T and π-section high pass filters are as shown below (Fig. E15.3).

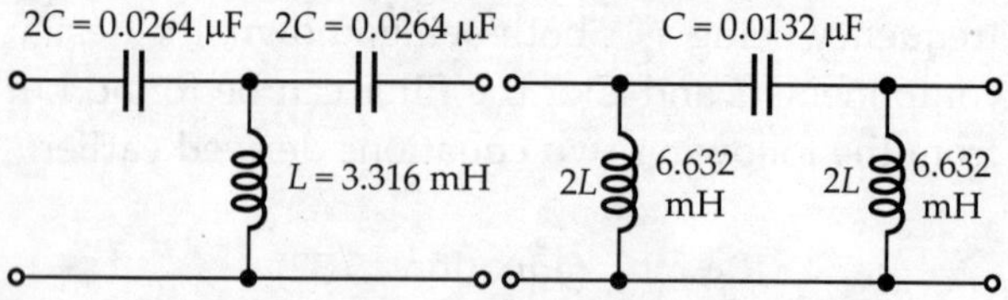

Fig. E15.3 T and π section filters.

(*i*) If $f = 24$ kHz, the characteristic impedances of T and π-section are given by,

$$Z_{oT} = R_o\sqrt{1-\left(\frac{f_c}{f}\right)^2}$$

$$= 500\sqrt{1-\left(\frac{12\times10^3}{24\times10^3}\right)^2} = \mathbf{433.013\ \Omega}$$

and

$$Z_{o\pi} = \frac{R_o}{\sqrt{1-\left(\frac{f_c}{f}\right)^2}}$$

$$= \frac{500}{\sqrt{1-\left(\frac{12\times10^3}{24\times10^3}\right)^2}} = \mathbf{577.350\ \Omega}$$

The phase constant (β) in pass band is given by,

$$\beta = 2\sin^{-1}\left(\frac{f_c}{f}\right)$$

$$= 2\sin^{-1}\left(\frac{12\times10^3}{24\times10^3}\right) = \mathbf{60°}.$$

(*ii*) In the attenuation band, α is given by, at frequency 4 kHz.

$$\alpha = 2\cosh^{-1}\left(\frac{f_c}{f}\right) \text{ neper}$$

$$= 2\cosh^{-1}\left(\frac{12\times10^3}{4\times10^3}\right) \text{ neper} = \mathbf{3.525 \text{ neper.}}$$

EXAMPLE 15.5 *Design a constant K-low pass filter having $f_c = 2$ kHz and design impedance $R_o = 600\,\Omega$. Obtain the value of attenuation at 4 kHz.*

SOLUTION. The values of the elements of constant K-low pass filter are :

The series arm inductance,

$$L = \frac{R_o}{\pi f_c} = \frac{600}{\pi\times2\times10^3} \text{ H} = 95.493 \text{ mH}$$

The shunt capacitance,

$$C = \frac{1}{\pi f_c R_o} = \frac{1}{\pi \times 2 \times 10^3 \times 600} \text{ F} = 0.265 \ \mu\text{F}$$

Let attenuation at 4 kHz be α, where α is given by the relation,

$$\alpha = 2 \cosh^{-1}\left(\frac{f_\alpha}{f_c}\right)$$

$$= 2 \cosh^{-1}\left(\frac{4000}{2000}\right) \text{ nepers} = \mathbf{2.634 \ nepers.}$$

The required *T* and π-section low pass filters are as shown below (Fig. E15.4).

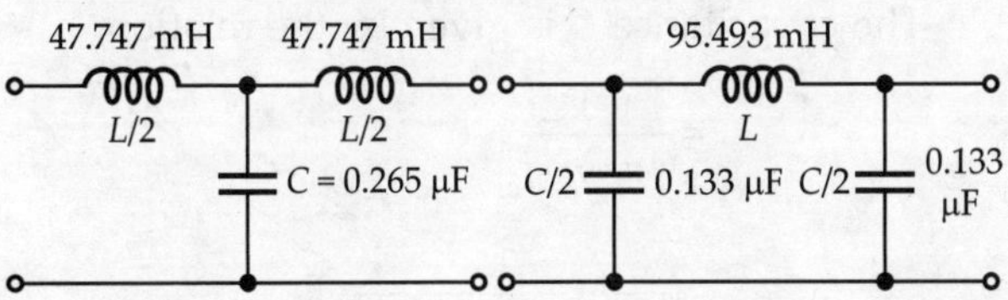

Fig. E15.4 *T* and π section LPF.

Example 15.6 *Design a constant K-high pass filter, having $f_c = 4$ kHz and design impedance $R_o = 600\,\Omega$ (π-section).*

Solution. From the theory of high pass filter, the series arm capacitance (*C*) and shunt arm inductance (*L*) are given by

$$C = \frac{1}{4\pi R_o f_c} = \frac{1}{4 \times \pi \times 600 \times 4000} \text{ F}$$

$$= 0.033 \ \mu\text{F}$$

and $$L = \frac{R_o}{4\pi f_c}$$

$$= \frac{600}{4 \times \pi \times 4000} \text{ H}$$

$$= 11.937 \text{ mH.}$$

The required constant *K* π-section high pass filter is shown as below (Fig. E15.5).

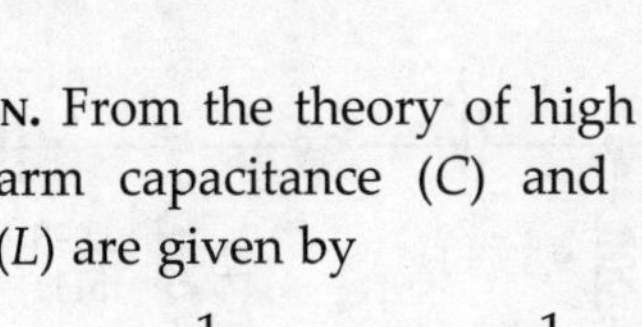

Fig. E15.5 Constant *K* π section HPF.

Example 15.7 *Design a T-section constant K-high pass filter having cut-off frequency of 10 kHz and design impedance $R_o = 600\,\Omega$. Find its characteristic impedance and phase constant at 25 kHz.*

Solution. Let the characteristic impedance of a *T*-section high pass filter is Z_{oT} and the phase constant is β. Here from the given data, $f_c = 10$ kHz, $R_o = 600\,\Omega$ and attenuation frequency $f = 25$ kHz.

The design elements [series capacitance (*C*) and shunt inductance (*L*)] are given by,

$$C = \frac{1}{4\pi R_o f_c} = \frac{1}{4 \times \pi \times 600 \times 10 \times 10^3} \text{ F}$$

$$= 0.013 \ \mu\text{F}$$

and $$L = \frac{R_o}{4\pi f_c} = \frac{600}{4 \times \pi \times 10 \times 10^3} \text{ H} = 4.777 \text{ mH}$$

The characteristic impedance of *T*-section high pass filter is given by,

$$Z_{oT} = R_o \sqrt{1 - \left(\frac{f_c}{f}\right)^2}$$

$$= 600 \sqrt{1 - \left(\frac{10 \times 10^3}{25 \times 10^3}\right)^2} = \mathbf{549.909 \ \Omega}$$

The phase constant (β) in the pass band is given by,

$$\beta = \pm 2 \sin^{-1}\left(\frac{f_c}{f}\right)$$

$$= \pm 2 \sin^{-1}\left(\frac{10 \times 10^3}{25 \times 10^3}\right)$$

$$= \pm 47.156° = \pm \mathbf{47°9'22.8''}$$

And at attenuation band the phase constant (β) is given by,

$$\beta = \pi \text{ radians}$$

The required *T*-section high pass filter is shown as below (Fig. E15.6).

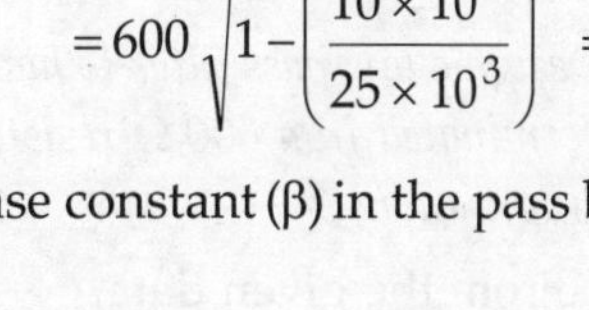

Fig. E15.6 *T* section HPF.

EXAMPLE 15.8 *Design a constant-K-low pass filter to match with a line having characteristic impedance of 500 Ω and to pass frequency upto 5 kHz.*

SOLUTION. Here, the given data provides

$$f_c = 5 \text{ kHz} = 5000 \text{ Hz}$$

and $$R_o = 500\,\Omega$$

The values of series inductance (*L*) and shunt capacitance (*C*) are given by,

$$L = \frac{R_o}{\pi f_c} = \frac{500}{\pi \times 5000} \text{ H} = 31.837 \text{ mH}$$

and $$C = \frac{1}{\pi R_o f_c} = \frac{1}{\pi \times 500 \times 5000} \text{ F} = 0.127\,\mu\text{F}$$

The required *T* and π-section low pass filter is as shown below (Fig. E15.7).

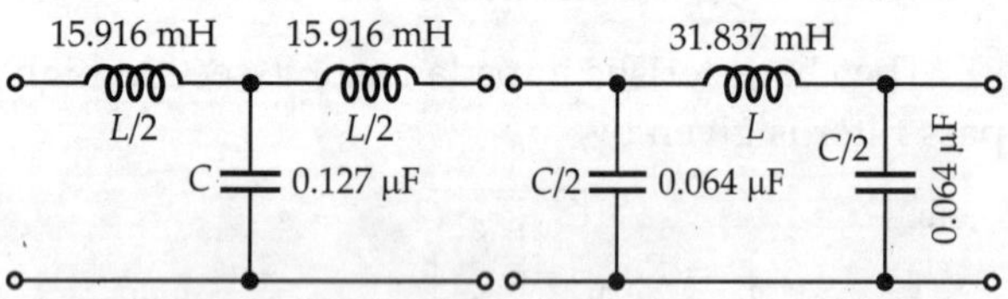

Fig. E15.7 *T* and π section LPF.

EXAMPLE 15.9 *Design a low pass filter to have a cut-off at 796 Hz when terminated in a 600 Ω resistance, in both the T and π configurations.*

SOLUTION. From the given data,

$$f_c = 796 \text{ Hz}$$

and $$R_o = 600\,\Omega$$

∴ The series inductance

$$L = \frac{R_o}{\pi f_c} = \frac{600}{\pi \times 796} = 240 \text{ mH}$$

And the shunt capacitance

$$C = \frac{1}{\pi R_o f_c} = \frac{1}{\pi \times 600 \times 796} \text{ F} = 0.666\,\mu\text{F}$$

The required *T* and π-section filters are as shown in Fig. E15.8.

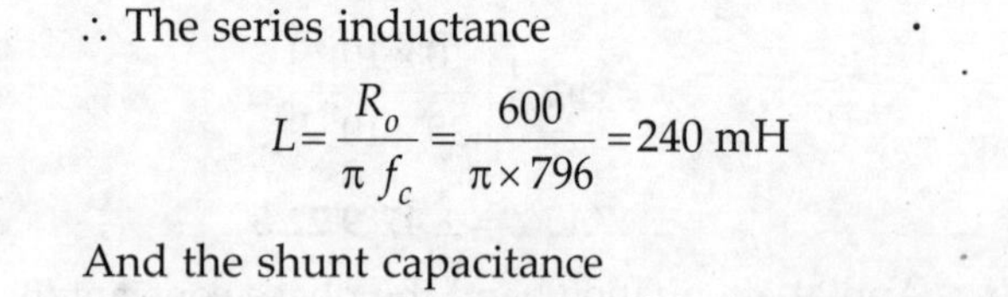

Fig. E15.8 *T* and π section of Ex. 15.9.

EXAMPLE 15.10 *Design constant K-high pass filter T and π-section having f_c = 5 kHz and nominal characteristic impedance R_o = 600 Ω.*

SOLUTION. Let total series capacitance and shunt inductances of *T* and π-section HPF are *C* and *L* respectively.

The inductance *L* is given by the relation,

$$L = \frac{R_o}{4\pi f_c}$$

$$= \frac{600}{4 \times \pi \times 5000}$$

$$= 9.55 \text{ mH}$$

The capacitance *C* is given by the relation,

$$C = \frac{1}{4\pi R_o f_c}$$

$$= \frac{1}{4 \times \pi \times 600 \times 5000} \text{ F}$$

$$= 0.027\,\mu\text{F}$$

The required *T* and π-sections of high pass filters are shown in Fig. E15.9.

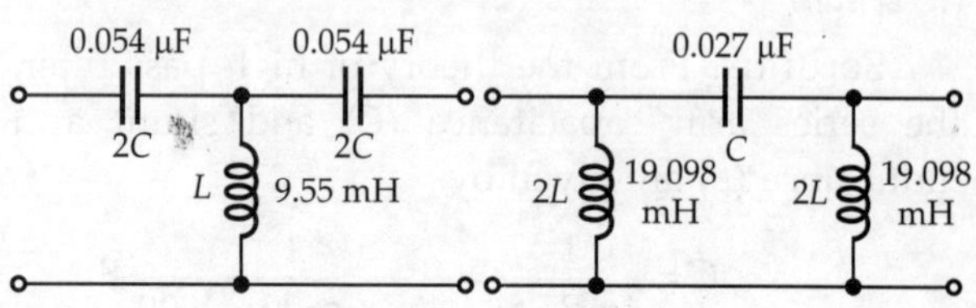

Fig. E15.9 *T* and π sections of HPF.

15.14 ANALYSIS OF A BAND PASS FILTER (BPF)

This filter is a combination of two parallel tuned circuits (Fig. 15.17). This is a special type of *LC* filter alongwith a particular bandwidth frequency to be allowed through it. Let Z_1 be the impedance of the series arm and Z_2 be that of the shunt arm. The operation is initiated when the shunt arm as well as the series arms are in resonance. At resonance, the shunt arm behaves as a rejector circuit offering a very high impedance in the shunt arm while the series arm at resonance offers least impedance (acceptor circuit) ; thus, any electric signal, incident at the input of the filter allows its transmission through it within the pass band.

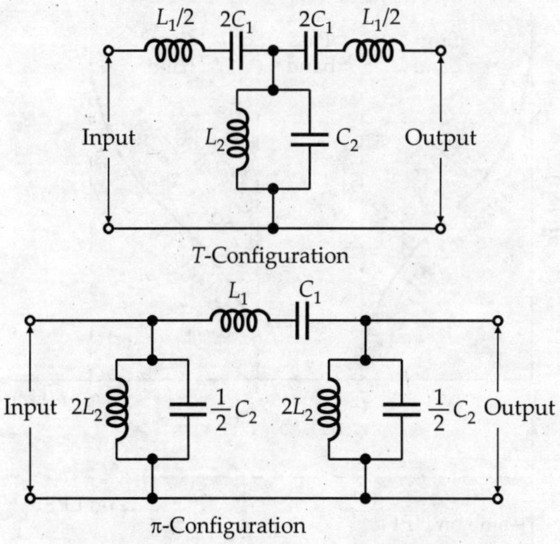

Fig. 15.17 *T* and π configuration of BPF.

Hence, at resonance, for each of the series and shunt arm,

$$\omega_0^2 L_1 C_1 = 1 \quad ...(15.47)$$

and $$\omega_0^2 L_2 C_2 = 1 \quad ...(15.48)$$

$\left[\because \text{ at resonance } f_0 = \dfrac{1}{2\pi\sqrt{LC}} \text{ and } \omega_0 = \dfrac{1}{LC},\right.$ f_0 and ω_0 being the resonance frequency in Hz or rad/sec$\left.\right]$

Comparing equations (15.47) and (15.48),

$$\frac{L_1}{C_2} = \frac{L_2}{C_1} \quad ...(15.49)$$

Now, $$Z_1 = j\,\omega L_1 + \frac{1}{j\,\omega C_1}$$

$$= j\left[\frac{\omega^2 L_1 C_1 - 1}{\omega C_1}\right] \quad ...(15.50)$$

and $$Z_2 = \frac{j\,\omega L_2\left[\dfrac{1}{j\,\omega C_2}\right]}{j\,\omega L_2 + \dfrac{1}{j\,\omega C_2}} = j\,\frac{\omega L_2}{1-\omega^2 L_2 C_2} \quad ...(15.51)$$

Multiplying equation (15.50) by (15.51)

$$Z_1 Z_2 = j\left[\frac{\omega^2 L_1 C_1 - 1}{\omega C_1}\right] \times j\,\frac{\omega L_2}{1-\omega^2 L_2 C_2}$$

$$= \frac{L_2\,(\omega^2 L_1 C_1 - 1)}{C_1\,(\omega^2 L_2 C_2 - 1)} \quad ...(15.52)$$

Finally,

$$Z_1 Z_2 = \frac{L_2}{C_1}\left(i.e., = \frac{L_1}{C_2} \text{ using Eqn. (15.49)}\right)$$

$$= R_0^2 \text{ (say)}$$

$$\therefore \quad Z_1 Z_2 = R_0^2,\ R_0 \text{ being a real quantity.} \quad ...(15.53)$$

The characteristic impedance Z_0 of any *T* section being given by

$$Z_{0T}^2 = \frac{Z_1^2}{4} + Z_1 Z_2,$$

normalisation for Z_1 yields,

$$\frac{Z_{0T}^2}{Z_1} = \frac{Z_1}{4} + Z_2$$

or $$\frac{Z_{0T}^2}{Z_1 Z_2} = \frac{Z_1}{4Z_2} + 1 \quad ...(15.54)$$

[Dividing both sides by Z_2]

From equation (15.54), it can be observed that the *limiting condition* $(Z_{0T} = 0)$ is achieved if

$$\frac{Z_1}{4Z_2} = -1.$$

Thus, for $$\frac{Z_1}{4Z_2} = -1,$$

$$Z_1 = -4Z_2$$

or $$Z_1 Z_1 = -4 Z_1 Z_2$$

or $$Z_1^2 = -4 Z_1 Z_2 = -4 Z_0^2 = -4 R_0^2$$

or $$Z_1 = \pm\, j\, 2 R_0 \quad ...(15.55)$$

Equation (15.55) indicates that Z_1 is either positive or negative at the limiting condition. It follows that Z_1 is positive for a particular frequency f_1 and Z_1 is negative for another particular frequency, f_2. Substituting the values of Z_1 from equation (15.50) in equation (15.55).

$$j\left(\frac{\omega_1^2 L_1 C_1 - 1}{\omega_1 C_1}\right) = j 2 R_0$$

[taking +ve value of Z_1 and corresponding frequency as f_1]

or $$\omega_1^2 L_1 C_1 - 1 = 2 R_0 \omega_1 C_1$$

or $$\omega_1^2 L_1 C_1 - 2 R_0\, \omega_1 C_1 - 1 = 0$$

CHAPTER 15

or $$\omega_1 = \frac{2R_0C_1 \pm \sqrt{4R_0^2C_1^2 + 4L_1C_1}}{2L_1C_1} \quad ...(15.56)$$

i.e., $$f_1 = \frac{2R_0\,C_1 \pm \sqrt{4R_0^2\,C_1^2 + 4L_1C_1}}{2\pi \times 2L_1C_1}$$

$$= \frac{R_0 + \sqrt{R_0^2 + \dfrac{L_1}{C_1}}}{2\pi L_1} \quad ...[15.56(a)]$$

Then, equation 15.56(*a*) provides *the particular one of the cut off frequencies* of the BPF when Z_1 behaves as a positive impedance. Assuming f_2 to be the other particular frequency, when Z_1 behaves as negative impedance, in a similar way,

$$j\left(\frac{\omega_2^2L_1C_1 - 1}{\omega_2C_1}\right) = -j\,2R_0$$

or $$\omega_2^2L_1C_1 - 1 = -2R_0\,\omega C_1$$

or $$\omega_2^2L_1C_1 + 2R_0\,\omega_2C_1 - 1 = 0$$

This gives

$$\omega_2 = \frac{-2R_0C_1 \pm \sqrt{4R_0^2C_1 + 4L_1C_1}}{2L_1C_1} \quad ...(15.57)$$

i.e., $$f_2 = \frac{-2R_0C_1 \pm \sqrt{4R_0^2C_1^2 + 4L_1C_1}}{2\pi \times 2L_1C_1}$$

$$= \frac{-R_0 \pm \sqrt{R_0^2 + \dfrac{L_1}{C_1}}}{2\pi L_1}$$

$$\therefore \quad f_2 = -\left[\frac{R_0 + \sqrt{R_0^2 + \dfrac{L_1}{C_1}}}{2\pi L_1}\right] \quad ...[15.57(a)]$$

Expression [15.57(*a*)] gives the *second cut off frequency* of the BPF.

As negative frequency does not carry any physical meaning hence the sign of the root of f_1 and f_2 both are taken to be positive. Fig. 15.18 represents the profiles of attenuation (α), phase shift (β) and Z_0 (characteristic impedance) of the prototype band pass filter. Fig. 15.19 represents the reactance frequency characteristic of BPF.

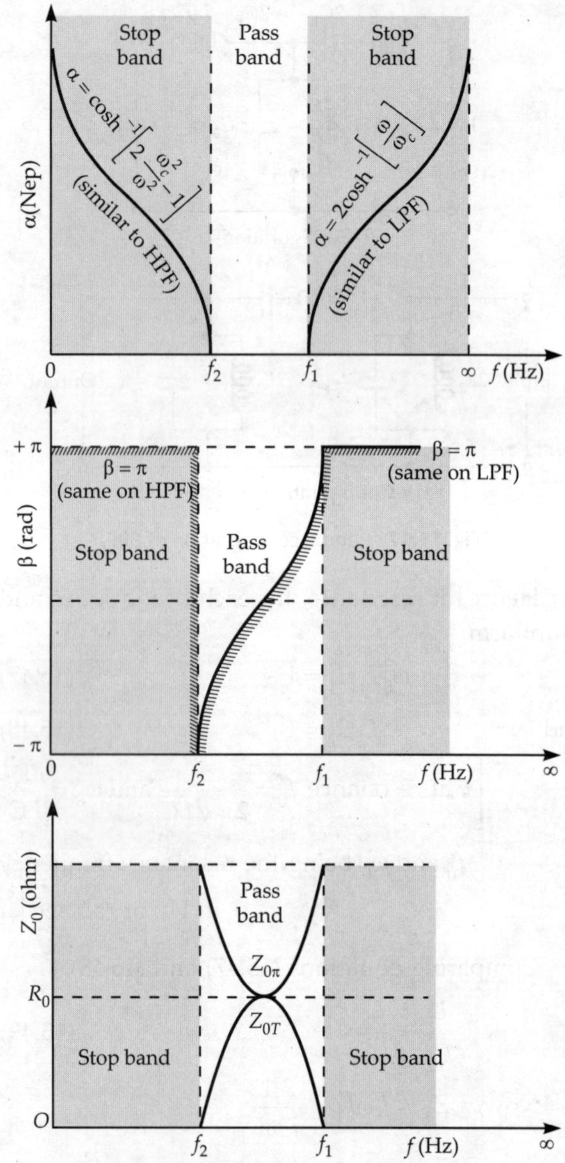

Fig. 15.18 Characteristic of BPF section.

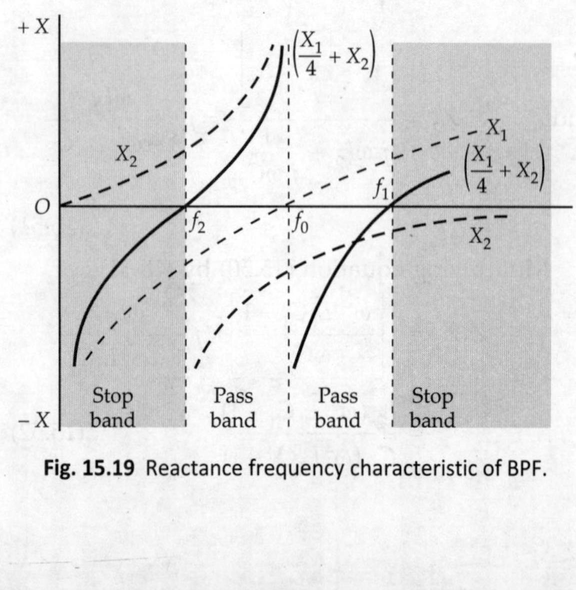

Fig. 15.19 Reactance frequency characteristic of BPF.

15.15 DESIGN OF PROTOTYPE BAND PASS FILTER

Taking $Z_1 = -j\,2R_0$, substituting the values of Z_1, as done in the preceding part,

$$\frac{\omega_2^2 L_1 C_1 - 1}{\omega_2 C_1} = -2R_0$$

[ω_2 being the frequency in rad/sec when $Z_1 = -j\,2R_0$]

or $$\frac{1-\omega_2^2 L_1 C_1}{\omega_2 C_1} = 2R_0$$

or $$1-\omega_2^2 L_1 C_1 = 2R_0\omega_2 C_1$$

or $$1-\frac{\omega_2^2}{\omega_0^2} = 2R_0\omega_2 C_1 \qquad \left[\because\ L_1C_1 = L_2C_2 = \frac{1}{\omega_0^2}\right]$$

or $$1-\frac{f_2^2}{f_0^2} = 2R_0 \times 2\pi f_2 \times C_1$$

[f_2 in Hz corresponds to ω_2 in rad/sec]

or $$1-\frac{f_2^2}{f_1 f_2} = 4\pi f_2 R_0 C_1$$

[$\because f_0^2 = f_1 f_2$, (as shown in the footnote)]

As the magnitude of Z_1 remains same at f_1 and f_2, the only difference being the change of sign between f_1 and f_2, hence it is justified to write,

$$Z_1 \text{ at } f_1 = Z_2 \text{ at } f_2$$

or $$\left(j\omega_1 L_1 + \frac{1}{j\omega_1 C_1}\right) = -\left(j\omega_2 L_1 + \frac{1}{j\omega_2 C_1}\right)$$

or $$\left(\omega_1 L_1 - \frac{1}{\omega_1 C_1}\right) = -\left(\omega_2 L_1 - \frac{1}{\omega_2 C_1}\right)$$

or $$\frac{\omega_1^2 L_1 C_1 - 1}{\omega_1 C_1} = -\frac{\omega_2^2 L_1 C_1 - 1}{\omega_2 C_1}$$

or $$\left(\frac{\omega 1^2}{\omega_0^2} - 1\right)/\,\omega_1 = -\left(\frac{\omega_2^2}{\omega_0^2} - 1\right)/\,\omega_2$$

or $$\left(\frac{f_1^2}{f_0^2} - 1\right)/\,f_1 = -\left(\frac{f_2^2}{f_0^2} - 1\right)/\,f_2$$

or $$1-\frac{f_1^2}{f_0^2} = \frac{f_1}{f_2}\left[\frac{f_2^2}{f_0^2} - 1\right]$$

or $$1-\frac{f_1^2}{f_0^2} = \frac{f_1 f_2}{f_0^2} - \frac{f_1}{f_2}$$

or $$1+\frac{f_1}{f_2} = \frac{f_1 f_2}{f_0^2} + \frac{f_1^2}{f_0^2} = \frac{f_1 f_2 + f_1^2}{f_0^2}$$

$$\frac{f_1 + f_2}{f_2} = \frac{f_1 f_2 + f_1^2}{f_0^2}$$

$$f_0^2 = \frac{(f_1 f_2 + f_1^2)\, f_2}{f_1 + f_2} = f_1 f_2$$

$$f_0 = \sqrt{f_1 f_2} \qquad ...(15.58)$$

$\therefore$ $$1-\frac{f_2}{f_1} = 4\pi f_2 R_0 C_1$$

or $$f_1 - f_2 = 4\pi f_1 f_2 R_0 C_1$$

$\therefore$ $$C_1 = (f_1 - f_2) \times \frac{1}{4\pi f_1 f_2 R_0} \text{ Farad} \qquad ...(15.59)$$

Again, from $L_1 C_1 = \dfrac{1}{\omega_0^2}$,

$\therefore$ $$L_1 = \frac{1}{\omega_0^2 C_1} = \frac{1}{(2\pi f_0)^2 \times C_1}$$

$$= \frac{1}{4\pi^2 f_1 f_2 (f_1 - f_2)\dfrac{1}{4\pi f_1 f_2 R_0}}$$

(utilising eqn. (15.59)

$$= \frac{R_0}{\pi(f_1 - f_2)} \text{ Henry} \qquad ...(15.60)$$

Also, from

$$R_0 = \sqrt{\frac{L}{C}},\quad L = R_0^2\, C \ \text{ i.e. } L_2 = R_0^2 C_1$$

$$\left[\because\ \frac{L_2}{C_1} = \frac{L_1}{C_2} = R_0^2\right]$$

or $$L_2 = R_0^2 C_1 = (f_1 - f_2)\frac{1}{4\pi f_1 f_2 R_0} R_0^2$$

$$= \frac{R_0 (f_1 - f_2)}{4\pi f_1 f_2} \text{ Henry} \qquad ...(15.61)$$

Similarly, $C_2 = \dfrac{L_1}{R_0^2}$ gives

$$C_2 = \frac{R_0/\pi(f_1 - f_2)}{R_0^2}$$

$$= \frac{1}{\pi R_0 (f_1 - f_2)} \text{ Farad} \qquad ...(15.62)$$

Equations (15.59), (15.60), (15.61) and (15.62) give the design equations of the BPF filter for determining the values of its components.

CHAPTER 15

15.16 ANALYSIS OF A PROTOTYPE BAND STOP FILTER (BSF)

A band stop filter, in its simplest form, is a tandem of a low pass filter with a high pass filter (Fig. 15.20). Here, the cut off frequency of high pass filter is higher than the cut off frequency of the low pass filter. The overlapping attenuation band of the two filters then constitutes the stop band of the band stop filter. In practice, the actions of LPF and HPF are combined into a single band stop filter. Z_1 becomes the series impedance of a parallel tuned circuit and Z_2 is the shunt impedance of a series tuned circuit.

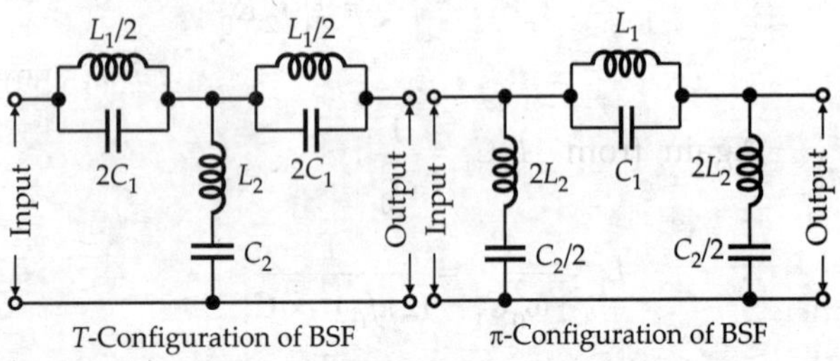

Fig. 15.20 T and π configuration of Band stop filter section.

Operation is initiated when resonance occurs so that shunt impedance (Z_2) becomes minimum and series impedance (Z_1) becomes maximum. Thus incident signal is blocked at this particular condition.

Thus at resonance,

$$\omega_0^2 L_1 C_1 = 1 \quad \text{...(15.63)}$$

and

$$\omega_0^2 L_2 C_2 = 1 \quad \text{...(15.64)}$$

But

$$L_1 C_1 = L_2 C_2 = \frac{1}{\omega_0^2} \quad \text{...(15.65)}$$

[from eqns. (15.63) and (15.64)]

However,

$$Z_1 = 2\left[\frac{j\dfrac{\omega L_1}{2}\left(\dfrac{1}{2j\,\omega C_1}\right)}{j\dfrac{\omega L_1}{2} + \dfrac{1}{2j\,\omega C_1}}\right] = j\frac{\omega L_1}{1-\omega^2 L_1 C_1} \quad \text{...(15.66)}$$

$$Z_2 = j\omega L_2 + \frac{1}{j\,\omega C_2} = j\left[\frac{\omega^2 L_2 C_2 - 1}{\omega C_2}\right] \quad \text{...(15.67)}$$

Therefore,

$$Z_1 Z_2 = j\frac{\omega L_1}{1-\omega^2 L_1 C_1} \times j\left[\frac{\omega^2 L_2 C_2 - 1}{\omega C_2}\right]$$

$$= \frac{L_1}{C_2} = \frac{L_2}{C_1} = R_0^2 \quad \text{...(15.67(a))}$$

$$\left[\because \frac{L_1}{C_2} = \frac{L_2}{C_1} = R_0^2\right]$$

However, the characteristic impedance being given by

$$Z_{0T}^2 = \frac{Z_1^2}{4} + Z_1 Z_2$$

normalisation by Z_1 and division by Z_2 gives

$$\frac{Z_{0T}^2}{Z_1 Z_2} = \frac{Z_1}{4Z_2} + 1$$

Here,

$$\frac{Z_1}{4Z_2} = -1$$

gives the critical condition as with

$$\frac{Z_1}{4Z_2} = -1,$$

$$Z_{0T} = 0$$

Thus with

$$\frac{Z_1}{4Z_2} = -1,$$

$$Z_1 = -4Z_2$$

or

$$Z_1^2 = -4Z_1 Z_2$$

[multiplying both sides by Z_1]

$$= -4R_0^2$$

Hence

$$Z_1 = \pm j\,2R_0$$

Citing similar reasoning as done for the BPF, it can be commented that Z_1 will be positive with f_1 and Z_2 will be negative with system frequency f_2.

Considering Z_1 to be positive,

$$Z_1 = +j\,2R_0$$

or

$$j\frac{\omega_1 L_1}{1-\omega_1^2 L_1 C_1} = j\,2R_0$$

or

$$\omega_1 L_1 = 2R_0(1-\omega_1^2 L_1 C_1)$$

or

$$\omega_1^2 L_1 C_1 \cdot 2R_0 + \omega_1 L_1 - 2R_0 = 0$$

$$\therefore \quad \omega_1 = \frac{-L_1 \pm \sqrt{L_1^2 + 4L_1C_1 \cdot 4R_0^2}}{2L_1C_1 \cdot 2R_0}$$

$$= \frac{-L_1 \pm \sqrt{L_1^2 + 16L_1C_1R_0^2}}{2L_1C_1 \cdot 2R_0}$$

$$f_1 = \frac{-L_1 \pm \sqrt{L_1^2 + 16L_1C_1R_0^2}}{8\pi L_1C_1R_0}$$

$$= \frac{-1 \pm \sqrt{1 + 16\frac{C_1}{L_1}R_0^2}}{8\pi C_1R_0} \text{ Hz} \quad ...(15.68)$$

Equation (15.68) provides the *lower root of frequency* of the Band stop filter.

Considering the negative impedance of Z_1 for f_2,

$$Z_1 = -j\,2R_0$$

or $$j\frac{\omega_2L_1}{1-\omega_2^2L_1C_1} = -j\,2R_0$$

[ω_2 being the frequency at which $Z_1 = -j\,2R_0$]

or $$\frac{\omega_2L_1}{\omega_2^2L_1C_1 - 1} = 2R_0$$

or $$\omega_2L_1 = 2R_0(\omega_2^2L_1C_1 - 1)$$

or $$2R_0 \cdot \omega_2^2L_1C_1 - \omega_2L_1 - 2R_0 = 0$$

or $$\omega_2 = \frac{L_1 \pm \sqrt{L_1^2 + 16R_0^2 \cdot L_1C_1}}{4R_0L_1C_1}$$

$$= \frac{1 \pm \sqrt{1 + 16R_0^2 \cdot \frac{C_1}{L_1}}}{4R_0C_1}$$

or $$f_2 = \frac{1 \pm \sqrt{1 + 16R_0^2\frac{C_1}{L_1}}}{8\pi R_0C_1} \text{ Hz} \quad ...(15.69)$$

f_2 gives the higher cut-off frequency and hence equations (15.68) and (15.69) give the two *cut off frequencies* of the Band Stop Filter.

15.17 DESIGN OF A BAND STOP FILTER

From $Z_1 = j\,2R_0$

$$j\left[\frac{\omega_1L_1}{1-\omega_1^2L_1C_1}\right] = j\,2R_0$$

or $$1 - \omega_1^2L_1C_1 = \frac{\omega_1L_1}{2R_0}$$

or $$1 - \frac{\omega_1^2}{\omega_0^2} = \frac{\omega_1L_1}{2R_0}$$

or $$1 - \frac{f_1^2}{f_0^2} = \frac{\pi f_1L_1}{R_0}$$

or $$1 - \frac{f_1^2}{f_1f_2} = \frac{\pi f_1L_1}{R_0} \qquad [\because\ f_0^2 = f_1f_2]$$

or $$1 - \frac{f_1}{f_2} = \frac{\pi f_1L_1}{R_0}$$

or $$f_2 - f_1 = \frac{\pi f_1f_2L_1}{R_0}$$

or $$L = \frac{R_0(f_2 - f_1)}{\pi f_1f_2} \text{ Henry} \quad ...(15.70)$$

But $\omega_0^2L_1C_1 = 1$

$$\therefore \quad C_1 = \frac{1}{\omega_0^2L_1} = \frac{1}{4\pi^2f_0^2L_1}$$

$$= \frac{1}{4\pi R_0(f_2 - f_1)} \text{ Farad} \quad ...(15.71)$$

From $C_2 = \frac{L_1}{R_0^2}$

$$C_2 = \frac{R_0(f_2 - f_1)/\pi f_1f_2}{R_0^2}$$

$$= \frac{f_2 - f_1}{\pi f_1f_2R_0} \text{ Farad} \quad ...(15.72)$$

Also, $L_2 = C_1R_0^2$

$$\therefore \quad L_2 = \frac{R_0}{4\pi^2(f_2 - f_1)} \text{ Henry} \quad ...(15.73)$$

Equations (15.70) to (15.73) give the analytical expression for the design of the components of the Band Stop Filter.

Figure 15.21 represents the profile of attenuation (α), phase shift (β) and Z_0 (characteristic impedance of BSF). Fig. 15.22 represents the reactance frequency characteristic of BSF.

CHAPTER 15

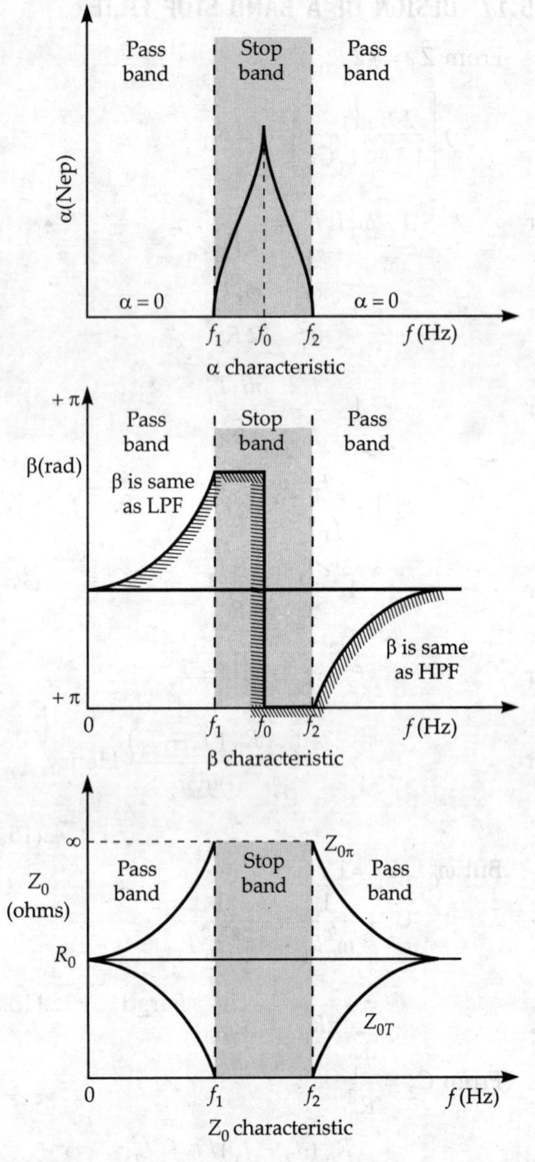

Fig. 15.21 α, β **and** Z_0 **profile of the BSF**

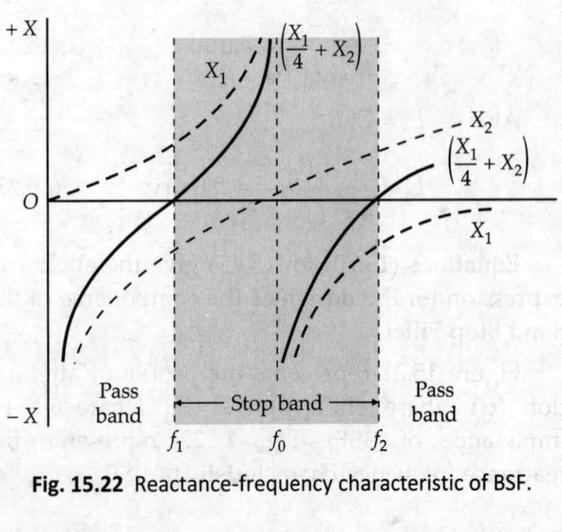

Fig. 15.22 Reactance-frequency characteristic of BSF.

EXAMPLE 15.11 *Design a prototype bandpass filter section (T and π) having cut-off frequencies of 3000 Hz and 6000 Hz and nominal characteristic impedance of 600 Ω. Also find the resonant frequency of shunt arm or series arm.*

SOLUTION. Here from the given data,

$$f_2 = 3000 \text{ Hz and } f_1 = 6000 \text{ Hz and } R_o = 600\,\Omega$$

The series arm inductance of a band pass filter is given by

$$L_1 = \frac{R_o}{\pi(f_2 - f_1)} = \frac{600}{\pi(6000 - 3000)} \text{ H}$$

$$= 63.662 \text{ mH}$$

Hence, $\dfrac{L_1}{2} = \dfrac{63.662}{2} = 31.831$ mH

The series arm capacitance (C_1) is given by,

$$C_1 = \frac{(f_1 - f_2)}{4\pi R_o f_1 f_2}$$

$$= \frac{(6000 - 3000)}{4 \times \pi \times 600 \times 3000 \times 6000} \text{ F}$$

$$= 0.022\ \mu\text{F}$$

Hence,

$$2C_1 = 0.044\ \mu\text{F}$$

Again, the shunt arm inductance (L_2) and capacitance (C_2) are given by,

$$L_2 = \frac{R_o(f_1 - f_2)}{4\pi f_1 f_2}$$

$$= \frac{600\,(6000 - 3000)}{4 \times \pi \times 3000 \times 6000} \text{ F} = 7.96 \text{ mH}$$

Hence,

$$2L_2 = 15.92 \text{ mH}$$

and

$$C_2 = \frac{1}{\pi R_o (f_1 - f_2)}$$

$$= \frac{1}{\pi \times 600\,(6000 - 3000)} \text{ F} = 0.177\ \mu\text{F}$$

Hence, $\dfrac{C_2}{2} = 0.0885\ \mu$F.

Now the resonant frequency (f_o) of the band pass filter is given by

$$f_o = \sqrt{f_1 f_2} = \sqrt{3000 \times 6000}$$

$$= \mathbf{4242.640 \text{ Hz}}$$

The band pass filter (T and π-section) is as shown in Fig. E15.10.

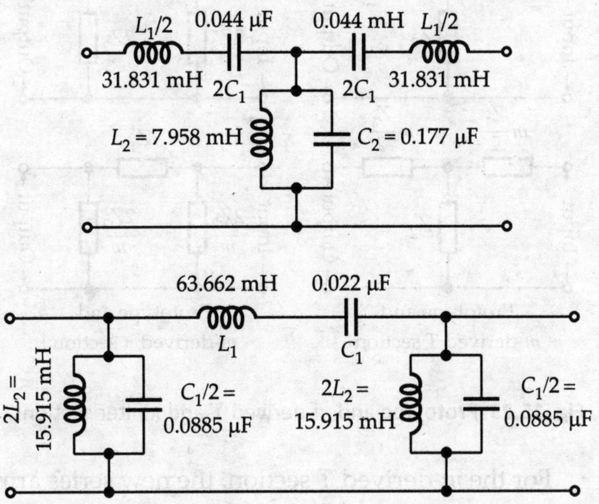

Fig. E15.10 T and π section BPF.

Example 15.12 *Design a prototype band stop filter section having cut-off frequencies of 2000 Hz and 5000 Hz and design resistance of 600 Ω.*

Solution. The series arm inductance (L_1) and capacitance (C_1) are given by,

$$L_1 = \frac{R_o(f_2 - f_1)}{\pi f_1 f_2}$$

$$= \frac{600\,(5000 - 2000)}{\pi \times 2000 \times 5000} \text{ H} = 57.32 \text{ mH}$$

Hence, $\frac{L_1}{2} = \frac{57.32}{2} = 28.66$ mH

and $$C_1 = \frac{1}{4\pi R_o (f_2 - f_1)}$$

$$= \frac{1}{4 \times \pi \times 600 \times (5000 - 2000)} \text{ F}$$

$$= 0.044 \ \mu\text{F}$$

Hence, $2C_1 = 2 \times 0.044 \ \mu\text{F} = 0.088 \ \mu\text{F}$

Again, the shunt inductance (L_2) and capacitance (C_2) are given by,

$$L_2 = \frac{R_o}{4\pi(f_2 - f_1)}$$

$$= \frac{600}{4 \times \pi \times (5000 - 2000)} \text{ H}$$

$$= 15.92 \text{ mH}$$

and $$C_2 = \frac{(f_2 - f_1)}{\pi R_o f_1 f_2}$$

$$= \frac{(5000 - 2000)}{\pi \times 600 \times 2000 \times 5000} \text{ F} = 0.159 \ \mu\text{F}$$

The required band stop T-section filter is as shown below (Fig. E15.11)

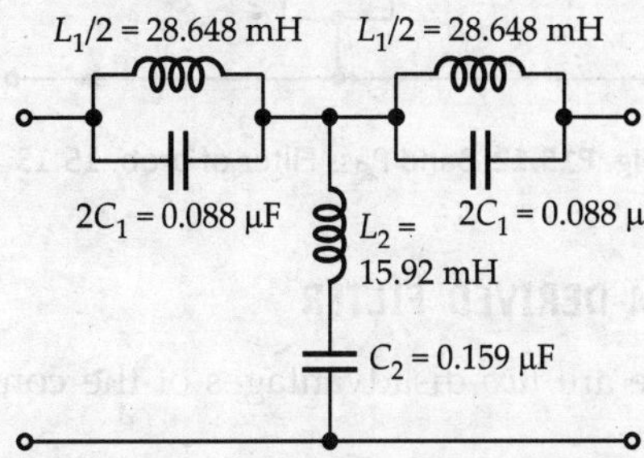

Fig. E15.11 Band stop T section filter.

Example 15.13 *Design a prototype band pass filter to match with a load of 600 Ω and to allow frequencies between 3 kHz and 6 kHz.*

Solution. Let series arm capacitance and inductance are C_1 and L_1 respectively and the shunt arm inductance and capacitance are L_2 and C_2 respectively.

Hence, from the given data

$$R_o = 600 \ \Omega$$

Lower cut-off frequency (f_2) = 3 kHz = 3000 Hz

and upper cut-off frequency (f_1) = 6 kHz = 6000 Hz

Hence C_1 and L_1 are given by,

$$C_1 = \frac{(f_1 - f_2)}{4\pi R_o f_1 f_2}$$

$$= \frac{(6000 - 3000)}{4 \times \pi \times 600 \times 3000 \times 6000} \text{ F} = 0.022 \ \mu\text{F}$$

and $$L_1 = \frac{R_o}{\pi(f_1 - f_2)}$$

$$= \frac{600}{\pi\,(6000 - 3000)} \text{ H} = 63.662 \text{ mH}$$

$$= \frac{1}{\pi \times 600\,(6000 - 3000)} \text{ F} = 0.177 \ \mu\text{F}$$

and $$L_2 = \frac{R_o\,(f_1 - f_2)}{4\pi f_1 f_2}$$

$$= \frac{600\,(6000 - 3000)}{4 \times \pi \times 3000 \times 6000} \text{ H} = 7.958 \text{ mH}$$

CHAPTER 15

The required band pass filter is as shown below (Fig. E15.12).

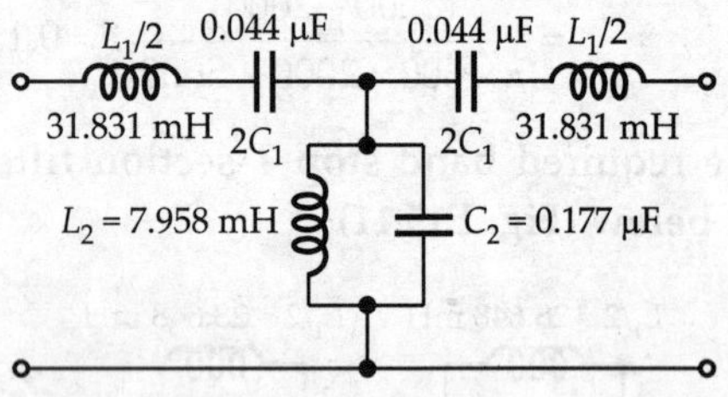

Fig. E15.12 Band Pass Filter of prob. 15.13

15.18 M-DERIVED FILTER

There are *two* disadvantages of the constant *K* filters *viz.*,

(*i*) the attenuation does not increase rapidly beyond cut-off frequencies.

(*ii*) characteristic impedance varies widely in the pass band from the desired value.

In order to overcome these disadvantages of constant *K* (prototype) filters, a special type of filter called *m-derived filter*, has been implemented. A *m*-derived filter is a filter that mostly removes these two disadvantages. Here, it is possible to design a filter to have the same impedance throughout the pass band and stop band like prototype (or constant *K*) filter, but with a different degree of attenuation outside the pass band. In the *m*-derived filter, it becomes possible to get very rapid attenuation rise in the stop band and just beyond the cut-off frequency. However, it fails to provide constant characteristic impedance over the entire pass band.

15.19 THEORY OF M-DERIVED FILTER SECTION

A prototype and *m*-derived *T* and π sections of the passive filter have been shown in Fig. 15.23.

The prototype sections are identical to that of the *m*-derived sections except the series arm of *T* section is multiplied by *m* and shunt arms of π section are divided by *m*. In case of *m* derived filters '*m*' is a constant whose value is to be determined. Inclusion of "*m*" with the prototype filter modifies it in such a way so that the characteristic impedances of both the filters remain identical. The constant '*m*' has been assumed to be less than 1 but greater than 0.

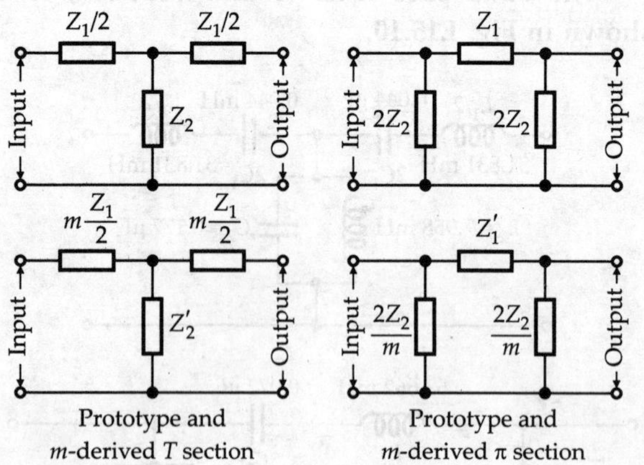

Fig. 15.23 Prototype and *m*-derived *T* and π filter sections.

For the *m*-derived *T* section, the new series arm impedance of the *m*-derived filter is then given by $[(mZ_1)/2]$ in each half of the series arm instead of $(Z_1/2)$ only.

However, for the prototype *T* section,

$$Z_{OT} \text{ (characteristic impedance)} = \sqrt{\frac{Z_1^2}{4} + Z_1 Z_2} \quad ...(15.74)$$

For the new, *m*-derived *T* filter section,

$$Z'_{OT} = \sqrt{\frac{m^2 Z_1^2}{4} + mZ_1 Z'_2} \quad ...(15.75)$$

(Z'_2 being the new shunt impedance of the *m*-derived filter and Z'_{OT} the characteristic impedance of the *m*-derived filter section).

From the basic assumption $Z_{OT} = Z'_{OT}$

$$\sqrt{\frac{Z_1^2}{4} + Z_1 Z_2} = \sqrt{\frac{m^2 Z_1^2}{4} + mZ_1 Z'_2}$$

This gives

$$Z'_2 = \frac{Z_2}{m} + \frac{(1-m^2)}{4m} Z_1 \quad ...(15.76)$$

From equation (15.76), it is indicated that Z'_2 must be an impedance composed of two impedances $\left(\frac{Z_2}{m}\right)$ and $\left[\frac{(1-m^2)}{4m} Z_1\right]$ and both of these impedances can be realised if $0 < m < 1$.

Thus in the *m*-derived *T* section,

$$Z'_1 = m\frac{Z_1}{2} \text{ and } Z'_2 = \frac{Z_2}{m} + \frac{1-m^2}{4m} Z_1 \quad ...(15.77)$$

Figure 15.24 represents the complete T section of the m-derived filter.

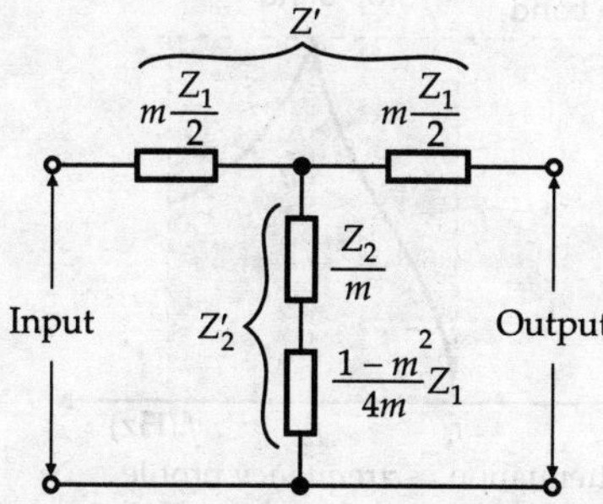

Fig. 15.24 Complete configuration of m-derived T section filter.

Similarly, for a π section of the m-derived filter, Z_1' being the series impedance, $2Z_2'$ being the shunt impedance, with the similar reasoning,

$$2Z_2' = \frac{2Z_2}{m} \quad \text{...(15.78)}$$

$Z_{0\pi}$ being the characteristic impedance of the prototype section and $Z_{0\pi}'$ being the same of the m-derived section,

$$Z_{0\pi} = \sqrt{\frac{Z_1 Z_2}{1+\dfrac{Z_1}{4Z_2}}} \quad \text{...(15.79)}$$

and

$$Z_{0\pi}' = \sqrt{\frac{Z_1'\dfrac{Z_2}{m}}{1+\dfrac{Z_1'}{4\dfrac{Z_2}{m}}}} \quad \text{...(15.80)}$$

Considering the basic assumption that $Z_{0\pi} = Z_{0\pi}'$, from equations (15.79) and (15.80),

$$\frac{Z_1'\dfrac{Z_2}{m}}{1+\dfrac{Z_1'}{4\dfrac{Z_2}{m}}} = \frac{Z_1 Z_2}{1+\dfrac{Z_1}{4Z_2}}$$

or

$$Z_1' = Z_1 m\left[1+\frac{Z_1'}{4\dfrac{Z_2}{m}}\right]\times\frac{1}{1+\dfrac{Z_1}{4Z_2}}$$

$$= \left[Z_1 m+\frac{Z_1 Z_1' m}{4\dfrac{Z_2}{m}}\right]\times\frac{1}{1+\dfrac{Z_1}{4Z_2}}$$

or

$$Z_1'\left[1-\frac{\dfrac{mZ_1}{4Z_2+Z_1}}{m}\right] = \frac{mZ_1}{1+\dfrac{Z_1}{4Z_2}}$$

or

$$Z_1'\left[1-\frac{m^2 Z_1}{4Z_2+Z_1}\right] = \frac{4mZ_1Z_2}{Z_1+4Z_2}$$

or

$$Z_1'\left[\frac{4Z_2+Z_1(1-m^2)}{4Z_2+Z_1}\right] = \frac{4mZ_1Z_2}{Z_1+4Z_2}$$

or

$$Z_1' = \frac{4mZ_1Z_2}{4Z_2+Z_1(1-m^2)}$$

or

$$Z_1' = \frac{mZ_1\left(\dfrac{4m}{1-m^2}\right)Z_2}{\left(\dfrac{4m}{1-m^2}\right)Z_2+mZ_1} \quad \text{...(15.81)}$$

Thus, it is evident that for the π section Z_1' is a combination of two parallel impedances namely mZ_1 and $\frac{4m}{1-m^2}Z_2$. Fig. 15.25 represents the configuration of the m-derived π section filter.

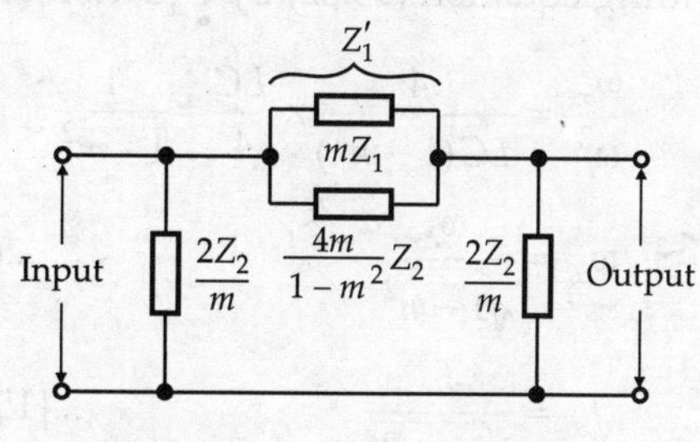

Fig. 15.25 Complete configuration of m-derived π section filter

15.20 ANALYSIS OF m-DERIVED LOW PASS FILTER (FIG. 15.26)

For the m-derived sections, at a particular frequency the shunt arm of T section or series arm of π-section will be in resonance giving a *short circuit* to the input for T section and *open circuit* for π section causing infinite attenuation. This particular frequency is denoted by f_∞.

The resonance frequency is given by

$$\omega_\infty^2 = \frac{1}{\left(\dfrac{1-m^2}{4m}\cdot L\right)(mC)} = \frac{4}{LC(1-m^2)} \quad \text{...(15.82)}$$

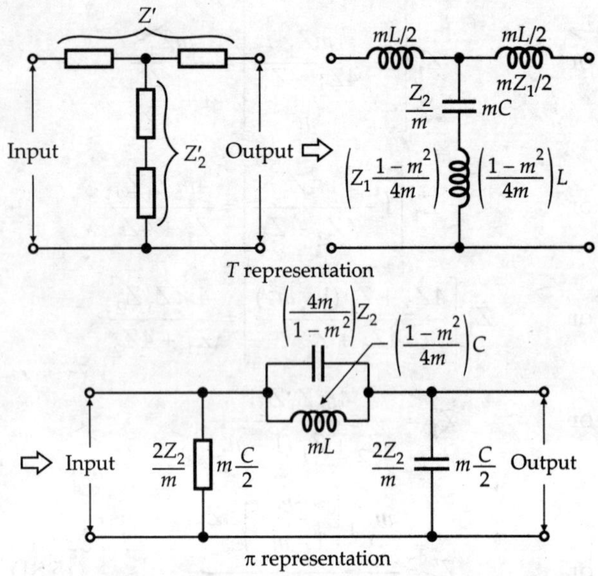

Fig. 15.26 Circuit representation of the *m*-derived LPF.

However, $$\omega_C^2 = \frac{4}{LC} \quad ...(15.83)$$

$$\left[f_c = \frac{1}{\pi\sqrt{LC}} \text{ in case of prototype LPF}\right]$$

Dividing equation (15.82) by equation (15.83),

$$\frac{\omega_\infty^2}{\omega_C^2} = \frac{4}{LC(1-m^2)} \times \frac{LC}{4} = \frac{1}{1-m^2}$$

$$\therefore \quad \omega_\infty = \frac{\omega_c}{\sqrt{1-m^2}} \quad ...(15.84)$$

and $$f_\infty = \frac{f_c}{\sqrt{1-m^2}} \quad ...[15.84(a)]$$

Also, $$\frac{f_\infty}{f_c} = \frac{1}{\sqrt{1-m^2}}, \text{ which gives} \quad ...(15.85)$$

$$m = \sqrt{1 - \frac{f_c^2}{f_\infty^2}} \quad ...(15.86)$$

The frequency of resonance of π section will be of same value $\left(f_\infty = \frac{f_c}{\sqrt{1-m^2}}\right)$ as the resonance frequencies for series and parallel *LC* circuits are identical.

The attenuation (α), phase shift (β) and characteristic impedance (Z_0) profile of the *m*-derived LPF has been shown in Fig. 15.27.

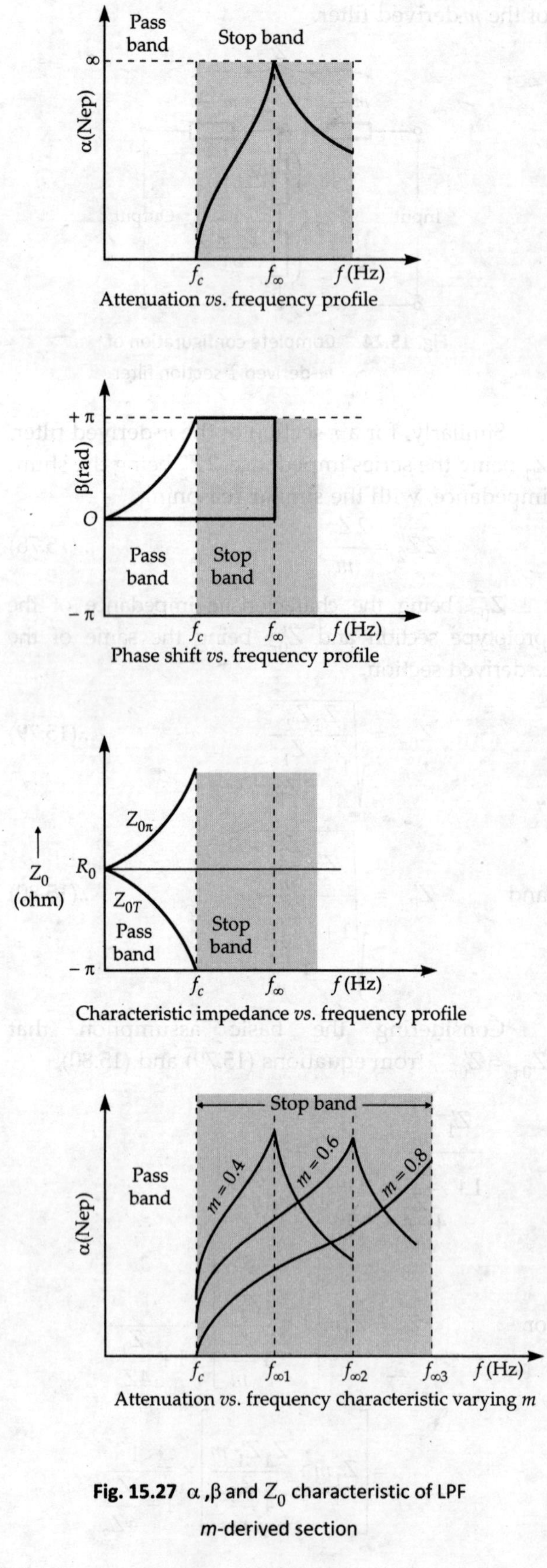

Fig. 15.27 α, β and Z_0 characteristic of LPF *m*-derived section

15.21 ANALYSIS OF *m*-DERIVED HIGH PASS FILTER (FIG. 15.28)

The shunt arm is constituted by a series combination of a capacitance $\frac{4m}{1-m^2}C\left(i.e., \frac{1-m^2}{4m}Z_1\right)$ and inductance $\frac{L}{m}\left(i.e., \frac{Z_2}{m}\right)$.

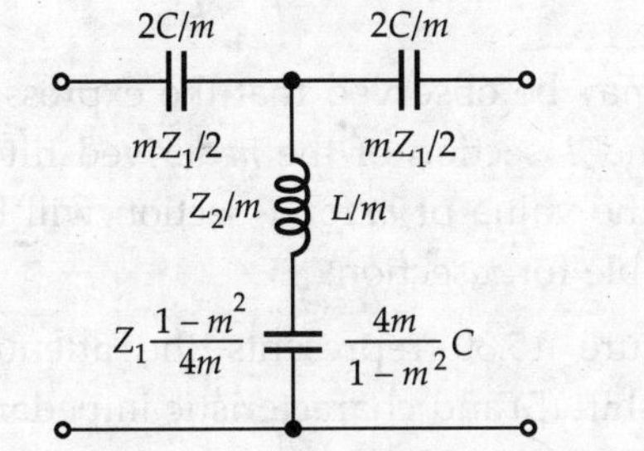

Fig. 15.28 Circuit representation of *m*-derived HPF section (*T*-type)

The shunt impedance Z_2' is given by

$$Z_2' = j\omega\frac{L}{m} + \frac{1}{j\omega C\dfrac{4m}{1-m^2}}$$

$$= \frac{Z_2}{m} + \frac{1-m^2}{4m}Z_1 \qquad ...(15.87)$$

The total series impedance Z_1' is given by

$$Z_1' = \frac{1}{j\omega C\left(\dfrac{4m}{1-m^2}\right)}$$

$$= \frac{1-m^2}{4m}\cdot\frac{1}{j\omega C} = \frac{1-m^2}{4m}Z_1 \qquad ...(15.88)$$

where, Z_1 and Z_2 are the impedances of the series and shunt arm of the corresponding prototype filter.

The shunt arm is a series *LC* circuit that offers almost zero impedance at the frequency of its series resonance. At this resonant frequency, f_∞, the transmission through the filter is zero *i.e.*, the attenuation becomes infinite. Also, at resonance, the inductive reactance (X_L) is *equal* to the capacitive reactance (X_C).

Hence, $$\frac{1}{\dfrac{4m}{1-m^2}\cdot\omega_\infty\cdot C} = \frac{\omega_\infty L}{m}$$

or $$\omega_\infty^2 = \frac{1-m^2}{4LC}$$

or $$\omega_\infty = \frac{\sqrt{1-m^2}}{2\sqrt{LC}} \qquad ...(15.89)$$

or $$f_\infty = \frac{\sqrt{1-m^2}}{4\pi\sqrt{LC}} \qquad ...(15.90)$$

However cut-off frequency (f_c) is given by, for a prototype HPF,

$$f_c = \frac{1}{4\pi\sqrt{LC}}\text{ Hz} \qquad ...(15.91)$$

$$\left[\text{or, } \omega_C = \frac{1}{2\sqrt{LC}}\text{ rad/sec}\right]$$

Now, from the equation (15.89), utilising (15.91)

$$\omega_\infty = (\sqrt{1-m^2})\,\omega_c \qquad ...(15.92)$$

Similarly,

$$f_c = (\sqrt{1-m^2})\,f_c \qquad ...(15.93)$$

Thus '*m*' is obtained from equations (15.92) or (15.93) as

$$m = \sqrt{1-\left(\frac{f_\infty}{f_c}\right)^2} = \sqrt{1-\left(\frac{\omega_\infty}{\omega_C}\right)^2} \qquad ...(15.94)$$

For the π section (Fig. 15.29), it may be observed that the series arm is a *parallel tuned circuit* which offers infinitely large impedance at the frequency of its parallel resonance. At this frequency, the transmission through the filter is zero, *i.e.*, the attenuation is infinite.

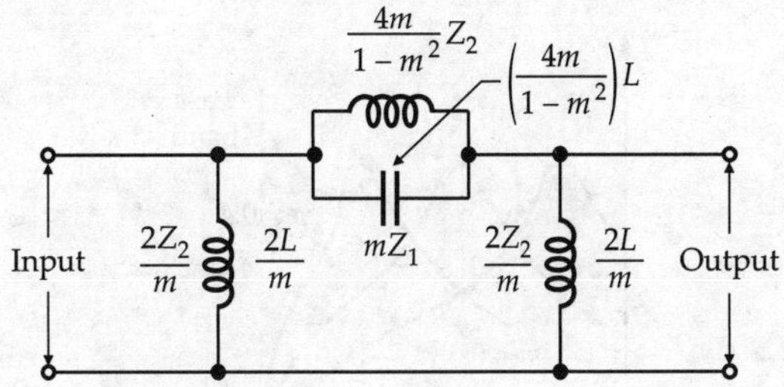

Fig. 15.29 *m*-derived π HPF filter section.

However, at resonance, X_L, the inductive reactance must be equal to the capacitive reactance X_C in the series arm.

Thus, $$\omega_\infty \frac{4m}{1-m^2} L = \frac{1}{\dfrac{\omega_\infty C}{m}}$$

or $$\omega_\infty = \frac{\sqrt{1-m^2}}{2\sqrt{LC}} \qquad ...(15.95)$$

and $$f_\infty = \frac{\sqrt{1-m^2}}{4\pi\sqrt{LC}} \qquad ...(15.96)$$

It may be observed that the expression for f_∞ for π and T section of the m-derived filter is same hence the value of m for T section will be equally applicable for π section.

Figure 15.30 represents the attenuation (α), phase shift (β) and characteristic impedance (Z_0) of the HPF m-derived section.

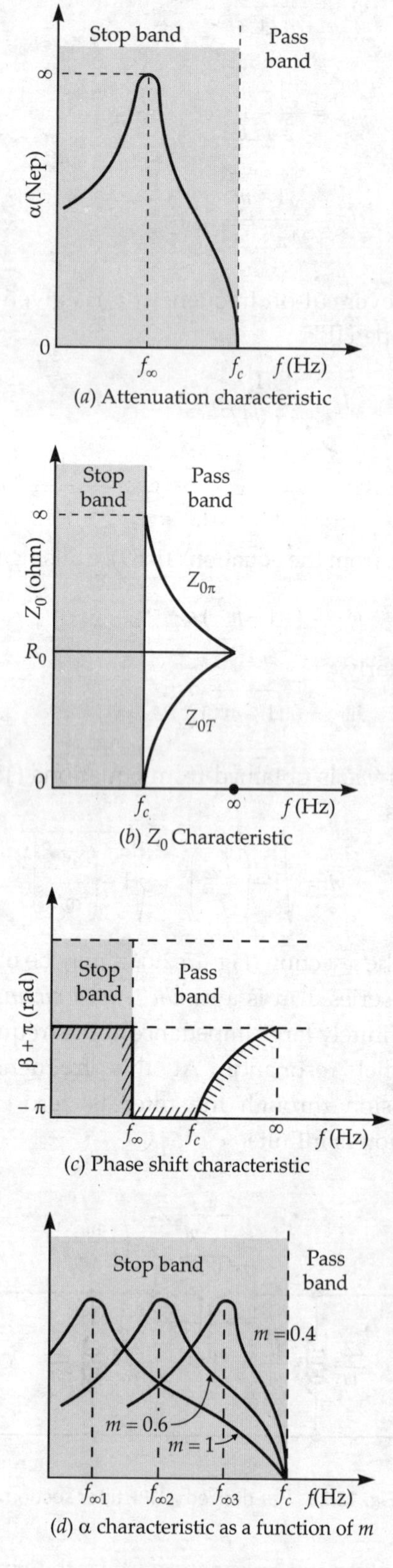

(a) Attenuation characteristic

(b) Z_0 Characteristic

(c) Phase shift characteristic

(d) α characteristic as a function of m

Fig. 15.30 Operating characteristics of m-derived HPF filter.

15.22 COMPARISON BETWEEN *m*-DERIVED AND PROTOTYPE FILTERS

The m-derived filter has a sharper frequency cut off characteristic with steep rise at the cut off frequency. The slope of the rise curve is adjustable by fixing the bandwidth between f_c and f_∞.

The characteristic impedance of the filter will be more uniform within the pass band for m-derived filter. The m-derived filter can be utilised so that it is possible to construct composite filters to have any desired attenuation/frequency characteristic.

In m-derived filter $Z_1 Z_2 \neq K^2$ while in prototype filter $Z_1 Z_2 = K^2$, Z_1 and Z_2 being the impedances of the series and shunt arms and K the constant. K is a real quantity and is independent of the frequency. The attenuation level of m-derived filters rises more sharply in the stop band in comparison to that of prototype filters. The reflection of energy from the load is more for the prototype filters at different frequencies.

15.23 IMPEDANCE MATCHING OF FILTERS

A filter being composed of a number of sections, it is essential that the impedance at each junction is to be correctly matched. As the characteristic impedance of an equivalent π or T section does not match with each other hence a T section should not be simply joined to a p section. In case it is desirable to construct a filter consisting of π and T sections, a half section should be used for impedance matching between the π and T sections. As the input impedance of the half section is the characteristic impedance of a T section while the output impedance of the half section is same as the characteristic impedance of the π section, hence matching can be obtained if a half section is connected in between a T and π section. When an *m*-derived section is segregated into half sections, the impedance at the point of bisection is dependent upon the value of *m*. It has been fortunately found that with $m=0.6$, the impedance at the bisection remains nearly equal to R_0 and is constant in the entire pass band.

Figure 15.31 shows the use of prototype half section for matching T and π sections. If a filter is matched throughout, the overall attenuation of the filter will be simply the sum of the attenuation of individual sections or half section, there being no internal reflection or mis-match loss.

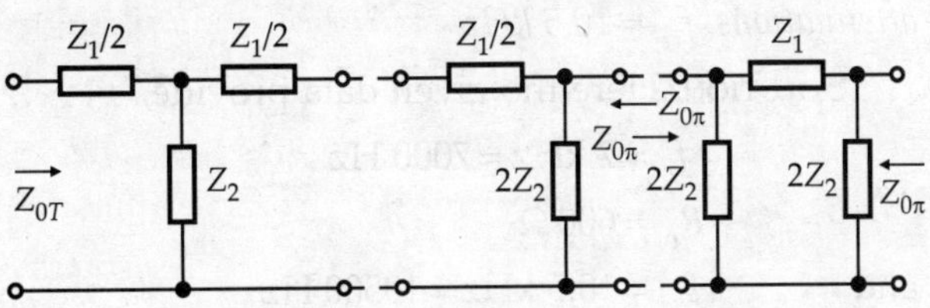

Fig. 15.31 Impedance matching of filters.

EXAMPLE 15.14 *Design an m-derived low pass filter (T and π section having design resistance $R_o = 500\,\Omega$, cut-off frequency $f_c = 1500$ Hz and infinite attenuation frequency $f_\alpha = 2000$ Hz.*

SOLUTION. From the theory of *m*-derived filter,

$$m=\sqrt{1-\left(\frac{f_c}{f_\alpha}\right)^2}=\sqrt{1-\left(\frac{1500}{2000}\right)^2}=0.661$$

For the prototype low pass filter, for $f_c = 1500$ Hz and $R_\alpha = 500\,\Omega$, series arm inductance (L) is given by :

$$\frac{R_o}{\pi f_c}=\frac{500}{\pi\times 1500}\text{ H}=106.86\text{ mH}$$

and shunt arm capacitance is given by,

$$C=\frac{1}{\pi R_o f_c}=\frac{1}{\pi\times 500\times 1500}\text{ F}$$

$$=0.424\,\mu\text{F}$$

In the T-section of *m*-derived low pass filter, the values of the elements are :

$$\frac{mL}{2}=\frac{0.661\times 106.86}{2}\text{ mH}=35.09\text{ mH}$$

$$mC=0.661\times 0.424\,\mu\text{F}=0.280\,\mu\text{F}$$

$$\frac{1-m^2}{4m}L=\frac{1-(0.661)^2}{4\times 0.661}\times 106.86=22.596\text{ mH}$$

In the π-section of *m*-derived low pass filter, the values of the elements are :

$$\frac{mC}{2}=\frac{0.661\times 0.424}{2}\,\mu\text{f}=\mathbf{0.140\,\mu F}$$

$$mL=0.661\times 106.86\text{ mH}=\mathbf{70.134\text{ mH}}$$

$$\frac{1-m^2}{4m}C=\frac{1-(0.661)^2}{4\times 0.661}\times 0.424\,\mu\text{F}=\mathbf{0.090\,\mu F.}$$

EXAMPLE 15.15 *Design T and π-section of m-derived high pass filter having design impedance of 600 Ω cut-off frequency 4 kHz and infinite attenuation at 3.6 kHz.*

SOLUTION. From the theory of *m*-derived high pass filter,

$$m=\sqrt{1-\left(\frac{f_\infty}{f_c}\right)^2}=\sqrt{1-\left(\frac{3.6\times 10^3}{4\times 10^3}\right)^2}=0.436$$

For the constant K-high pass filter having

$$f_c = 4\text{ kHz}\quad\text{and}\quad R_o = 600\,\Omega$$

The series arm capacitance,

$$C=\frac{1}{4\pi f_c R_o}=\frac{1}{4\times\pi\times 4\times 10^3\times 600}\text{ F}$$

$$=0.033\,\mu\text{F}$$

and the shunt arm inductance,

$$L=\frac{R_o}{4\pi f_c}=\frac{600}{4\pi\times 4\times 10^3}\text{ H}=11.94\text{ mH}$$

In T-section of *m*-derived high pass filter, the values of the circuit elements are :

$$\frac{2C}{m}=\frac{2\times 0.033}{0.436}\,\mu\text{F}=0.151\,\mu\text{F}$$

$$\frac{L}{m}=\frac{11.94}{0.436}\text{ mH}=27.39\text{ mH}$$

$$\frac{4m}{1-m^2}\cdot C=\frac{4\times 0.436}{1-(0.436)^2}\times 0.033\,\mu\text{F}=0.071\,\mu\text{F}$$

CHAPTER 15

In *m*-derived π-section high pass filter, the values of the circuit elements are :

$$\frac{2L}{m} = \frac{2 \times 11.94}{0.436} \text{ mH} = \mathbf{54.78 \text{ mH}}$$

$$\frac{C}{m} = \frac{0.033}{0.436} \mu\text{F} = \mathbf{0.076\ \mu F}$$

$$\frac{4m}{1-m^2} \cdot L = \frac{4 \times 0.436}{1-(0.436)^2} \times 11.937 \text{ mH}$$

$$= \mathbf{25.704 \text{ mH.}}$$

EXAMPLE 15.16 *Design an m-derived low pass filter to match a line having characteristic impedance of 500 Ω and to pass signals upto 1 kHz with infinite attenuation occurring at 1.2 kHz.*

SOLUTION. From the theory of *m*-derived filter,

$$m = \sqrt{1-\left(\frac{f_c}{f_\infty}\right)^2} = \sqrt{1-\left(\frac{1000}{1200}\right)^2} = 0.553$$

For the prototype low pass filter, for $f_c = 1000$ Hz and $R_o = 500\,\Omega$.

The series arm inductance, $L = \frac{R_o}{\pi f_c}$

$$= \frac{500}{\pi \times 1000} \text{ H} = 159.24 \text{ mH}$$

and shunt arm capacitance,

$$C = \frac{1}{\pi R_o f_c} = \frac{1}{\pi \times 500 \times 1000} \text{ F} = 0.637\ \mu\text{F}$$

The values of the elements of *T*-section of *m*-derived low pass filter are :

$$\frac{mL}{2} = \frac{0.553 \times 159.24}{2} \text{ mH} = 44.03 \text{ mH}$$

$$mC = 0.553 \times 0.637\ \mu\text{F} = 0.352\ \mu\text{F}$$

$$\frac{1-m^2}{4m} L = \frac{1-(0.553)^2}{4 \times 0.553} \times 159.155 \text{ mH}$$

$$= 49.948 \text{ mH}$$

And the values of elements of π-section *m*-derived low pass filter are :

$$\frac{mC}{2} = \frac{0.553 \times 0.637}{2} \mu\text{F} = 0.176\ \mu\text{F}$$

$$mL = 0.553 \times 159.24 \text{ mH} = 88.06 \text{ mH}$$

$$\frac{1-m^2}{4m} C = \frac{1-(0.553)^2}{4 \times (0.553)} \times 0.637\ \mu\text{F} = 0.074\ \mu\text{F}$$

The required *T* and π-section *m*-derived low pass filter is shown in Fig. E15.13.

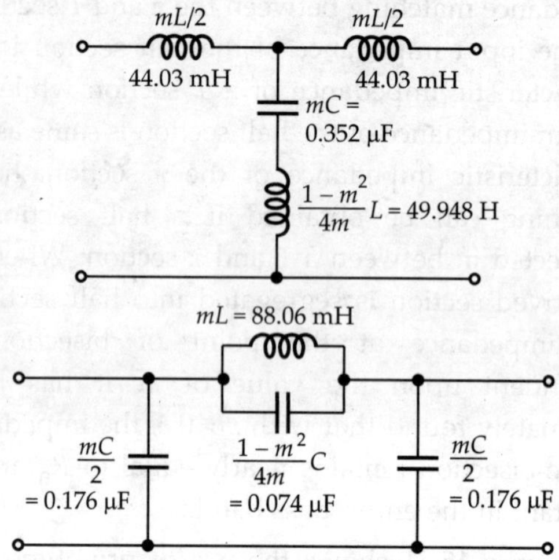

Fig. E15.13 *m*-derived LPF.

EXAMPLE 15.17 *Design an m-derived T-section low pass filter having cut-off frequency* $(f_c) = 7$ *kHz, design impedance* $R_o = 600\,\Omega$ *and frequency of infinite attenuations* $f_\alpha = 10.5$ *kHz.*

SOLUTION. Here the given data provide,

$$f_c = 7 \text{ kHz} = 7000 \text{ Hz}$$

$$R_o = 600\,\Omega$$

and $$f_\infty = 10.5 \text{ kHz} = 10500 \text{ Hz}$$

The constant term *m* is given by

$$m = \sqrt{1-\left(\frac{f_c}{f_\infty}\right)^2} = \sqrt{1-\left(\frac{7000}{10500}\right)^2}$$

$$= 0.745$$

For the prototype low pass filter, for $f_c = 7000$ Hz and $R_o = 600\,\Omega$

The series arm inductance (*L*) is given by,

$$L = \frac{R_o}{\pi f_c}$$

$$= \frac{600}{\pi \times 7000} \text{ H} = 27.284 \text{ mH}$$

and the shunt arm capacitance (C) is given by,

$$C = \frac{1}{\pi R_o f_c}$$

$$= \frac{1}{\pi \times 600 \times 7000} \text{ F} = 0.076\ \mu\text{F}$$

The values of the elements of *m*-derived *LPF* are :

$$\frac{mL}{2} = \frac{0.745 \times 27.284}{2} \text{ mH} = 10.163 \text{ mH}$$

$$mC = 0.745 \times 0.076 \ \mu\text{F} = 0.057 \ \mu\text{F}$$

and $$\left(\frac{1-m}{4m}\right)^2 L = \frac{1-(0.745)^2}{4 \times 0.745} \times 27.284 \text{ mH}$$

$$= 4.074 \text{ mH}$$

Desired *T*-section *m*-derived low pass filter is shown in Fig. E15.14.

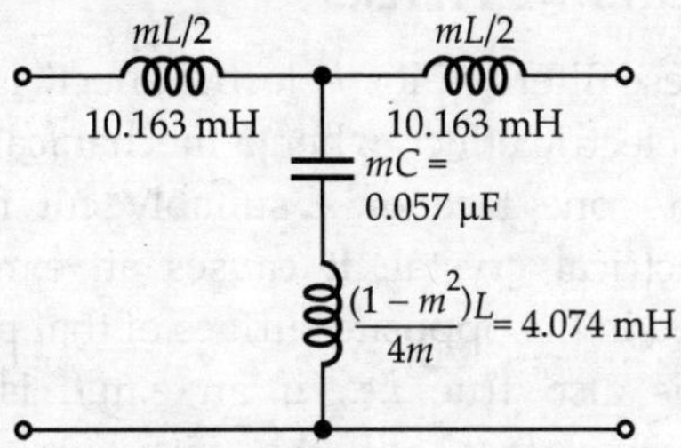

Fig. E15.14 *m*-derived *T* section LPF.

Example 15.18 *Design an m-derived high pass filter having a design impedance of 600 Ω, cut-off frequency of 5 kHz and m = 0.35. Also determine the frequency of infinite attenuation.*

Solution. Here from the given data

$$R_o = 600 \ \Omega$$

$$f_c = 5 \text{ kHz} = 5000 \text{ Hz}$$

and $$m = 0.35$$

Let the frequency of infinite attenuation = f_∞.

f_∞ is given by the relation,

$$m = \sqrt{1 - \left(\frac{f_\infty}{f_c}\right)^2}$$

$$\text{Here, } 0.35 = \sqrt{1 - \left(\frac{f_\infty}{5000}\right)^2}$$

or $$\left(\frac{f_\infty}{5000}\right)^2 = 1 - (0.35)^2$$

or $$(f_\infty)^2 = 0.8775 \times 25 \times 10^6$$

or $$f_\infty = \mathbf{4.684 \text{ kHz}}$$

Therefore the frequency of infinite attenuation is $f_\infty = 4.684$ kHz. For the prototype high pass filter, the series capacitance (*C*) is given by the relation,

$$C = \frac{1}{4\pi f_c R_o}$$

$$= \frac{1}{4 \times \pi \times 5000 \times 600} \text{ F} = 0.026 \ \mu\text{F}$$

and the shunt arm inductance (*L*) is given by the relation,

$$L = \frac{R_o}{4\pi f_c} = \frac{600}{4 \times \pi \times 5000} \text{ H} = 9.55 \text{ mH}$$

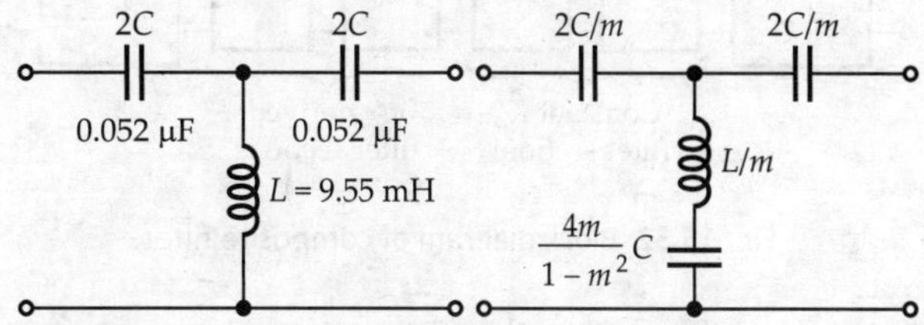

Fig. E15.15 *T* section of constant *K* and *m*-derived filter

T-sections of constant *K*-filter and *m*-derived filter have been shown in the adjacent figure (Fig. E15.15). The values of the circuit elements are :

$$\frac{2C}{m} = \frac{2 \times 0.026}{0.35} \ \mu\text{F} = \mathbf{0.148 \ \mu F}$$

$$\frac{L}{m} = \frac{9.549}{0.35} \text{ mH} = \mathbf{27.298 \text{ mH}}$$

and $$\frac{4m}{1-m^2} C = \frac{4 \times 0.35}{1-(0.35)^2} \times 0.026 \ \mu\text{F} = \mathbf{0.041 \ \mu F}$$

The π-section of constant *K* and *m*-derived high pass filters are shown below (Fig. E15.16).

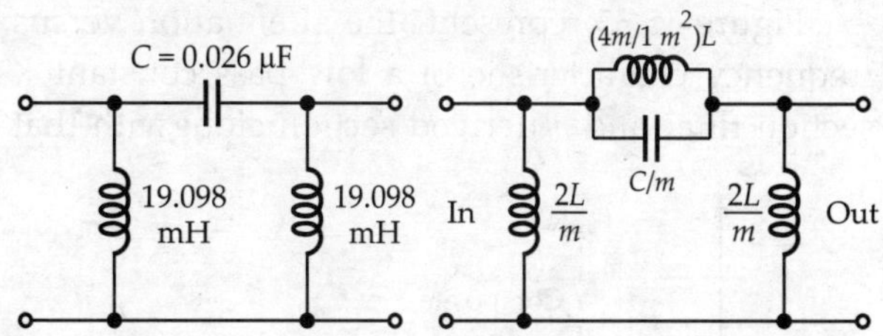

Fig. E15.16 π section of constant *K* and *m*-derived filter.

The values of the π-circuit elements are :

$$\frac{2L}{m} = \frac{2 \times 9.55}{0.35} \text{ mH} = \mathbf{54.595 \text{ mH}}$$

$$\frac{C}{m} = \frac{0.026}{0.35} \ \mu\text{F} = \mathbf{0.074 \ \mu F}$$

and $$\frac{4m}{1-m^2} L = \frac{4 \times 0.35}{1-(0.35)^2} \times \mathbf{9.55 \text{ mH}}$$

$$= \mathbf{15.24 \text{ mH}}$$

CHAPTER 15

15.24 COMPOSITE FILTER

The attenuation of a prototype filter in the stop band increases slowly from zero while in the *m*-derived filter, attenuation reaches a very high value at a frequency (f_∞) very close to the cut off

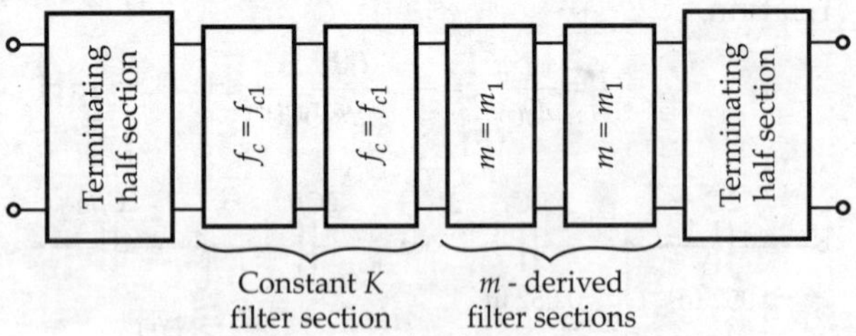

Fig. 15.32 Block diagram of composite filter.

frequency. However, the attenuation decreases for frequency beyond f_∞. In order to avoid these undesired results, a special type of filter may be used being termed as composite filter. A composite filter (Fig. 15.32) consists of

(*i*) One or more constant *K* sections to produce a specific cut off frequency *i.e.*, transition from pass band to the stop band is feasible at a specified frequency (f_c).

(*ii*) One or more *m*-derived sections in order to provide infinite attenuation at a frequency close to f_c.

(*iii*) Two number of terminating half sections to provide almost constant input and output impedances.

Figure 15.33 represents the attenuation versus frequency characteristic of a low pass constant *K* section filter and *m*-derived section alongwith that

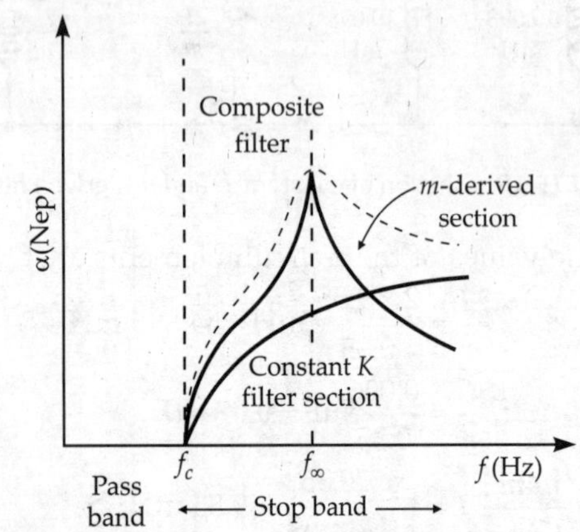

Fig. 15.33 Attenuation characteristic of composition.

of a composite filter forming a combination of the two sections (*K* section and *m*-derived section). Each of the constant *K* and *m*-derived filters fail to achieve desirable attenuation versus frequency characteristic but the combination of these two filters forms a composite section when the attenuation versus frequency curve is desirable. In such a combination, the attenuation rises very rapidly with frequency in the range of f_c to f_∞, the attenuation falls only marginally with frequency.

15.25 CRYSTAL FILTERS

In these filters, "piezo-electric effect" is utilised. In piezo-electric effect, when a mechanical strain is applied to one face of a suitably cut face of a piezo-electrical crystal, it causes an e.m.f. to be developed in the opposite surface of that piece. The reverse is also true *i.e.*, if an e.m.f. is applied between two faces of the piece, it causes a mechanical deformation.

Slice cut from a quartz crystal has also important property. It behaves electrically as a series resonant circuit of extremely high *Q* factor. It is resonant at the natural frequency of mechanical vibration of the slice. If a quartz crystal slice is placed between two metal plates (Fig. 15.34), it

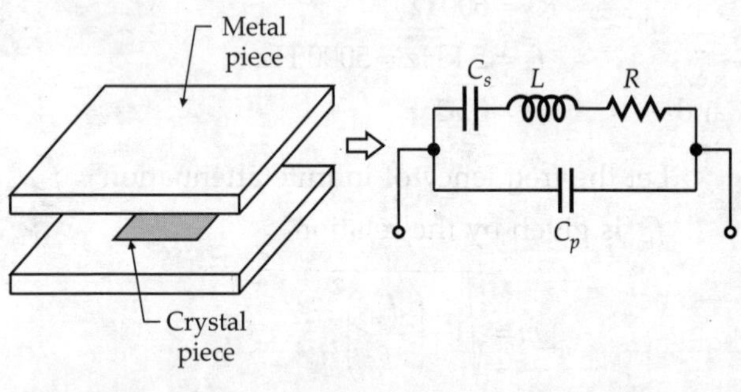

Fig. 15.34 Crystal piece within two metal plates and its equivalent circuit.

behaves like an equivalent electrical circuit shown in the same figure. C_S, *L* and *R* are the electrical equivalent of the crystal and C_P is the capacitance between the faces of the crystal. C_S, *L* and *R* provide a resonance frequency, say f_R which is also the mechanical resonant frequency of the crystal. This circuit also has an antiresonant frequency, say f_A. The ratio of C_P / C_S is such that,

$$f_A / f_R = 1.004.$$

The approximate values of typical C_S, L and C_P are given by

$$L = 115\frac{XY}{Z}\ \text{Henry},\ C = 0.0032\frac{YZ}{x}\ \mu\mu\text{F}$$

$$C_P = 0.4\frac{YZ}{x}\ \mu\mu\text{F},$$

X, Y and Z being the length, breadth and height of the crystal. R is very low for the crystal. Q factor is very high, of the order of 5000 to 20,000. Crystal filters are categorised as following types, like,

(1) Single crystal band pass filter.
(2) Double crystal band pass filter.
(3) T-type crystal band pass filter.
(4) Lattice-type crystal band pass filter.
(5) Broad-band lattice filter.

15.25.1 Single Crystal Band Pass Filter

Figure 15.35 shows a crystal filter where it presents a low impedance at its resonant frequency and almost infinite impedance at its anti-resonance

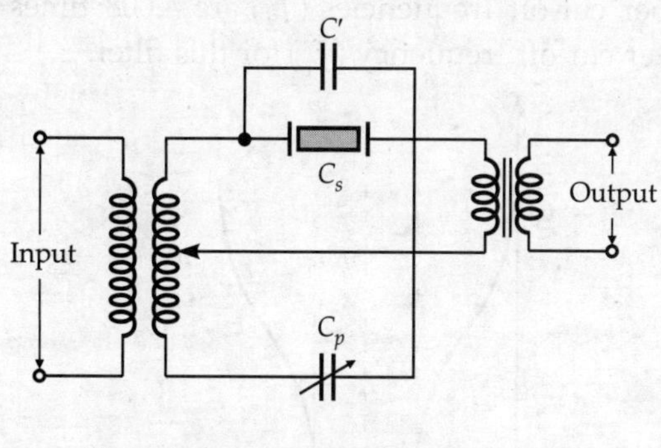

Fig. 15.35 Single crystal band pass filter.

frequency. It offers a high impedance at all other frequencies. The attenuation frequency curve of this filter has been shown in Fig. 15.36.

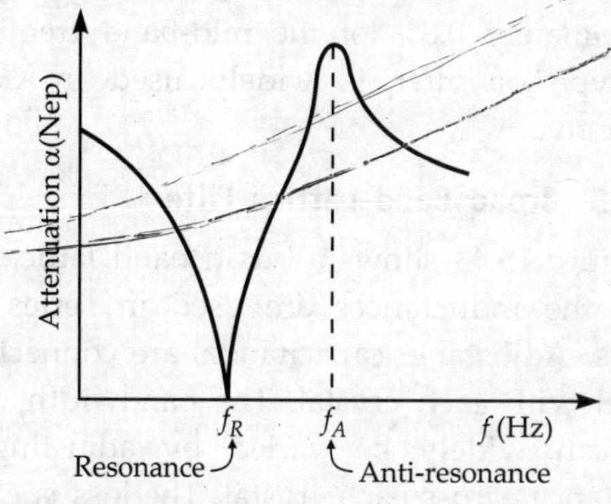

Fig. 15.36 α vs f characteristic of crystal filter.

The capacitance "C_S" can be varied by adjusting as balance capacitor "C_P" thus the anti-resonance frequencies can be altered. These types of filters are generally used to transmit signal with one particular frequency and to attenuate other frequencies completely. C' is used to create anti-resonance.

15.25.2 Double Crystal Band Pass Filter

Two crystals are used instead of one in this filter (Fig. 15.37). The balance capacitance "C_P" is

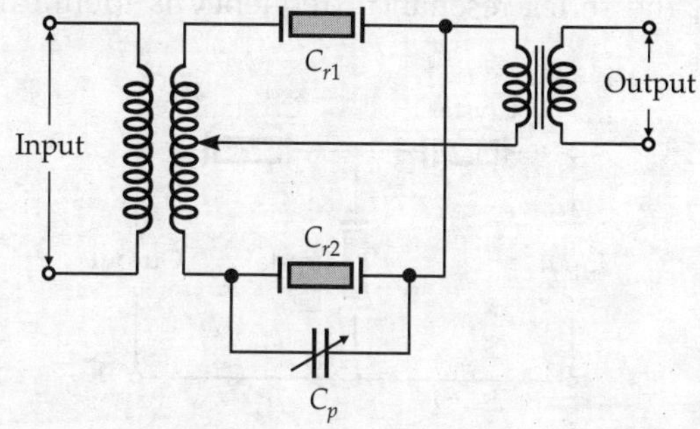

Fig. 15.37 Schematic of double crystal band pass filter.

usually of higher value. The balance capacitance "C_P" being increased, the total capacitance of the second filter increases and this changes the bandwidth of the filter. This type of filter circuit provides a pass band upto about 1% of the mid band frequency as shown in Fig. 15.38.

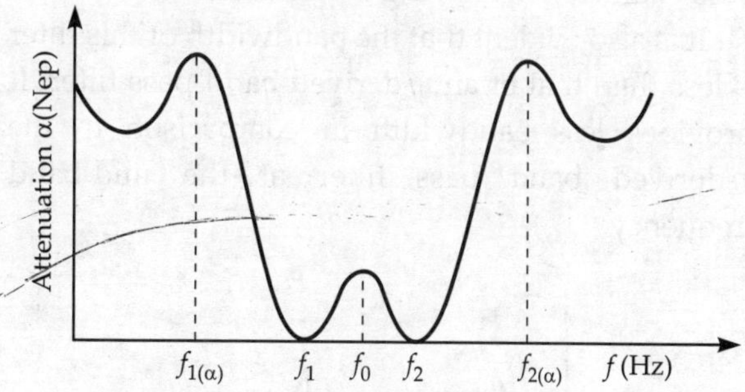

Fig. 15.38 α vs f characteristic of double crystal band pass filter.

The resonant frequencies of the two crystals are designed to be at the lower and upper edges of the pass band respectively. The input and output circuits being tuned to the mid band frequencies, the outputs from the two crystals are in antiphase. From Fig. 15.38 it is evident that the attenuation increases at the centre of the pass band, wider the pass band more is the increase. A low attenuation is obtained between two resonant frequencies (f_1 and f_2) of the two crystals. This type of filter is used where the bandwidth is less than 1% of the mid band frequency.

15.25.3 *T*-type Crystal Filter

It consists of two crystals in the series arm while one crystal is in the shunt arm (Fig. 15.39). The crystals in the series arm are so selected such that the series resonance frequency is identical to

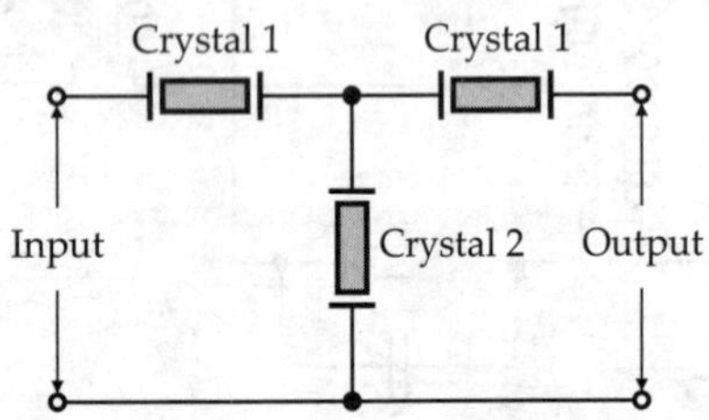

Fig. 15.39 *T*-type crystal filter.

the resonance frequency of the crystal of the shunt arm. The bandwidth being very less, the attenuation frequency characteristic is almost same to that of *m*-derived band pass section. Fig. 15.40 represents the attenuation *vs.* Frequency characteristic for a *T*-type band pass filter with a band pass characteristic having a pass band from f_1 and f_2. It is also evident that the bandwidth of this filter is less than that of an *m*-derived band pass filter. It provides less bandwidth in comparison to the *m*-derived band pass filter at the mid-band frequency.

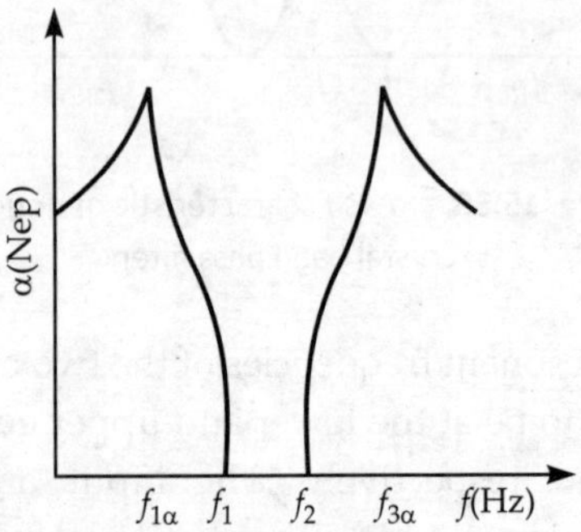

Fig. 15.40 α vs *f* characteristic of crystal *T*-type BPF (crystal).

15.25.4 Lattice Crystal Band Pass Filter

In lattice type crystal filters, series elements (C_{r1}) and other diagonal elements (C_{r2}) are formed as shown in Fig. 15.41. The section will have band pass filter characteristics as soon as the series

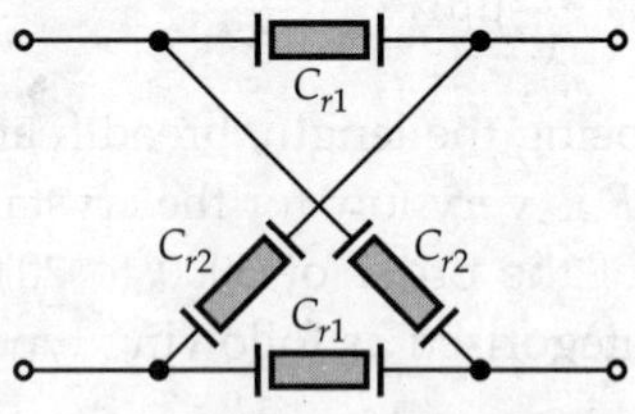

Fig. 15.41 Lattice crystal filter (BPF)

resonant frequency of one pair coincides with the anti-resonant frequency of the other. The characteristic impedance of such section has been given by,

$$Z_0 = \sqrt{Z_{r1} \times Z_{r2}}$$

where Z_{r1} is the series arms impedance and Z_{r2} is the diagonal impedance. The frequency vs attenuation characteristic has been shown in Fig. 15.42. The upper cut-off frequencies (f_2) are 4.008 times the lower cut-off frequency (f_1) for this filter.

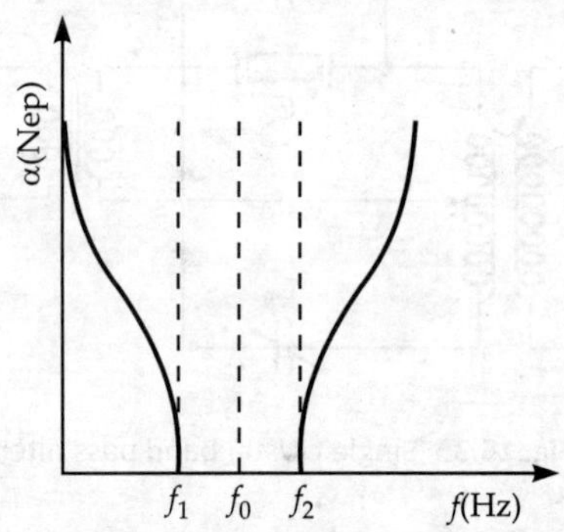

Fig. 15.42 α vs *f* characteristic of lattice crystal filter.

The bandwidth of such a filter ($f_2 - f_1$) is approximately 0.8% of the mid-band frequency. This type of filter is widely used in Carrier Telephony.

15.25.5 Broad Band Lattice Filter

Figure 15.43 shows a broad band lattice filter where the inductances are used in series with crystals. Adjustable capacitances are connected in parallel with each crystal. The bandwidth of the filter can widely be varied by adjusting the capacitance across each crystal. The loss is caused by the resistance of the inductance in the filter.

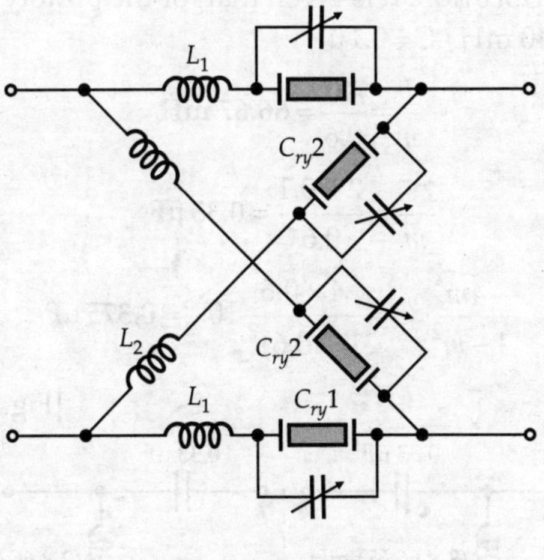

Fig. 15.43 Schematic of Broad Band Lattice Filter.

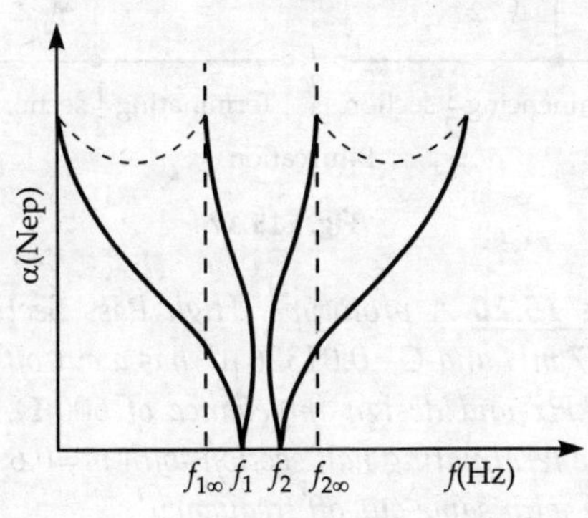

Fig. 15.44 α vs *f* characteristic of Broad Band Lattice Filter.

Ordinary inductance and capacitor filters are generally for bandwidth greater than 13%. A broadband crystal filter has a low characteristic impedance in the order of 100 Ω.

15.26 MISMATCH LOSS IN FILTER

By using suitable *m*-derived half-section, it is possible to match the filter to purely resistive circuits. This matching is practically feasible over about 9/10th of the pass band. However, in the attenuation band, the characteristic impedance of the filter is a pure reactance and the filter is terminated in a pure resistance, the design impedance being R_o. But the filter should always be correctly terminated in its characteristic impedance in the pass band and in a pure reactance in the stop or attenuation band.

The effect of this mis-termination may produce a loss by the filter given by the equation.

Insertion (Neper) loss

$$= A + \log_e \left| \frac{Z_o + Z_{i1}}{2\sqrt{Z_o Z_{i1}}} \right| + \log_e \left| \frac{Z_L + Z_{i2}}{2\sqrt{Z_L Z_{i2}}} \right| - \log_e \left| \frac{Z_o + Z_L}{2\sqrt{Z_o Z_L}} \right| + \log_e \left| 1 - \frac{Z_{i1} - Z_o}{Z_{i1} + Z_o} \cdot \frac{Z_{i2} - Z_L}{Z_{i2} + Z_L} e^{-2\theta} \right| \quad ...(15.97)$$

[Z_{i1} and Z_{i2} being the iterative impedances at input and output respectively]

However, since a filter has a high value of attenuation in the attenuation band, the fact that the termination is not equal to the characteristic impedance has little effect on the input impedance of the filter.

The mismatch in the attenuation band affects the overall attenuation of the section. It gives rise to an additional "mismatch loss" over the calculated attenuation of the filter. When an *m*-derived half section, used as a termination section, is terminated in its design impedance, the mismatch loss is a function of the difference between the attenuation of the prototype half section and that of the *m*-derived half section.

15.27 EFFECT OF RESISTANCE ON FILTER OPERATION

As reactances used in practical filters are not ideal and contain resistance hence in LPF this resistance appears as series resistance and is often comparable in magnitude with the reactance. Its effect is to introduce attenuation in the pass band. The effect of resistance in the capacitor in a LPF appears as a high shunt resistance and is usually negligible. Fig. 15.45 and Fig. 15.46 show the characteristics of a practical low pass constant *K* section and a *m*-derived section.

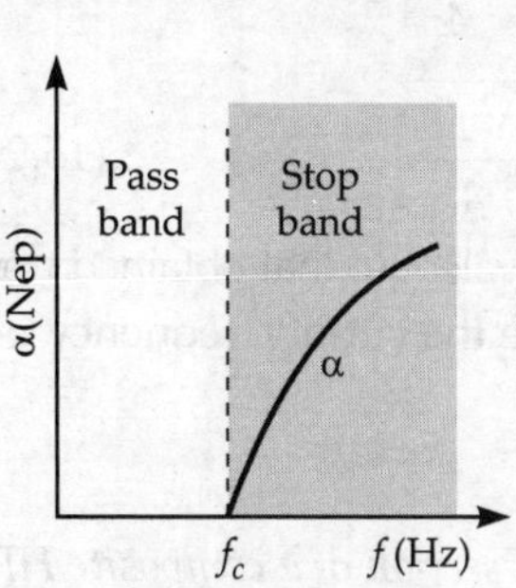

Fig. 15.45 α characteristic of prototype LPF with resistance.

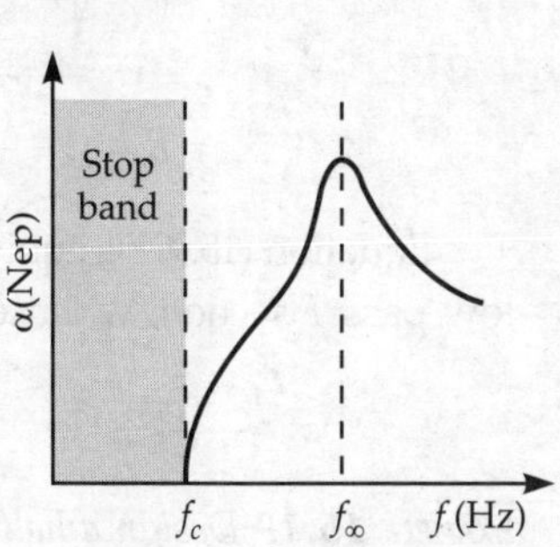

Fig. 15.46 α characteristic of *m*-derived LPF with resistance.

CHAPTER 15

The operating characteristics of all the filters are affected due to resistance effect in series with the inductance and capacitance. In case the resistance appears in the series arm, the attenuation increases while the effect of resistance in the shunt arm causes higher shunt impedance in the filter.

15.28 LATTICE FILTER

A ladder network may be converted into lattice filter section with the use of suitable components. The equivalences of *T* section and lattice section are shown in Fig. 15.47.

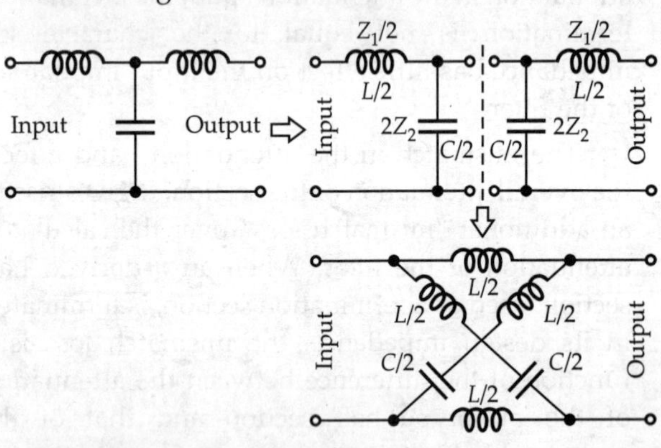

Fig. 15.47 Equivalence of *T* and lattice section.

The characteristic impedance of this equivalent lattice section is

$$Z_o = \sqrt{Z_S\, Z_D} \qquad \text{...(15.98)}$$

when, Z_S and Z_D are series and diagonal arm impedances.

$$\text{Here,} \quad Z_S = j\frac{\omega L}{2} \text{ and } Z_D = \frac{1}{j}\left(\frac{2}{\omega C} - \frac{\omega L}{2}\right)$$

$$\text{Thus} \quad Z_o = \sqrt{\frac{j\omega L}{2} \cdot \frac{1}{j}\left(\frac{2}{\omega C} - \frac{\omega L}{2}\right)}$$

$$= \sqrt{\frac{L}{C}}\sqrt{1 - \frac{\omega^2 LC}{4}}$$

$$= R_o\sqrt{1 - \frac{\omega^2 LC}{4}} \qquad \text{...(15.99)}$$

Equation (15.99) is equivalent to that obtained from low pass *T* section, whence the cut-off frequency is

$$f_C = \frac{1}{\pi\sqrt{LC}}.$$

Example 15.19 *Design a half section of a composite HPF section consisting of a prototype HPF with L = 40 mH, C = 0.1 μF. The load is 600 ohms and cut-off frequency is 1 kHz. Take m = 0.6.*

Solution. It is given that for the prototype HPF, $L = 40$ mH; $C = 0.1\,\mu$F

$$\therefore \quad \frac{L}{m} = \frac{40}{0.6} = \mathbf{66.67\ mH}$$

$$\frac{2C}{m} = \frac{2 \times 0.1}{0.6} = \mathbf{0.33\ \mu F}$$

$$\frac{4m}{1-m^2}C = \frac{4 \times 0.6}{1-(0.6)^2}.0.1 = \mathbf{0.375\ \mu F}$$

[Fig. E15.17]

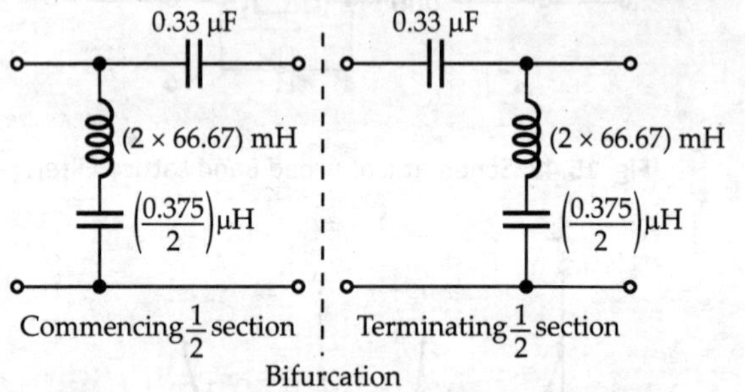

Fig. E15.17

Example 15.20 *A prototype 'High Pass Section' with L = 4.77 mH and C = 0.01326 μF has a cut-off frequency of 10 kHz and design impedance of 600 Ω. Design a suitable terminating half section with m = 0.6 such as to operate with same cut-off frequency.*

Solution. It is given that

$L = 4.77$ mH, $C = 0.01326\,\mu$F — For prototype HPF

Thus its equivalent *m*-derived section will have

$$\frac{L}{m} = \frac{4.77}{0.6} = 7.957 \text{ mH}$$

$$\frac{2C}{m} = 0.0442\ \mu\text{F}$$

With these component values the required *m*-derived *T* sections have been shown below : (Fig. E15.18)

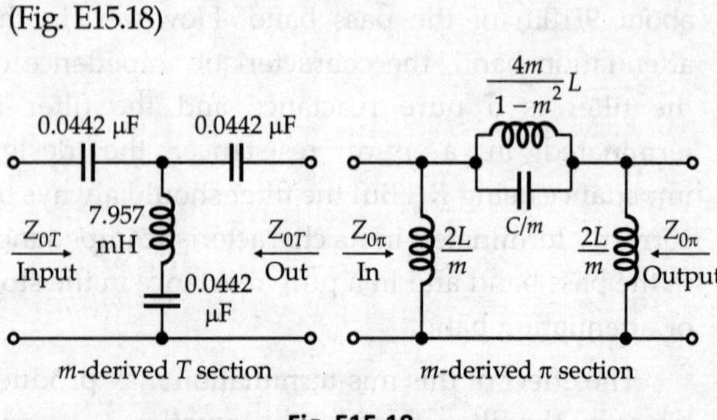

Fig. E15.18

In the *m*-derived equivalent π section,

$$\frac{4m}{1-m^2}L = \mathbf{17.89\ mH}$$

$$\frac{2L}{m} = \mathbf{15.9\ mH}$$

$$\frac{C}{m} = \mathbf{0.0221\ \mu F}$$

Thus the half sections can be formed by symmetrically dividing the *m*-derived *T* and π sections as shown below (Fig. E15.19) :

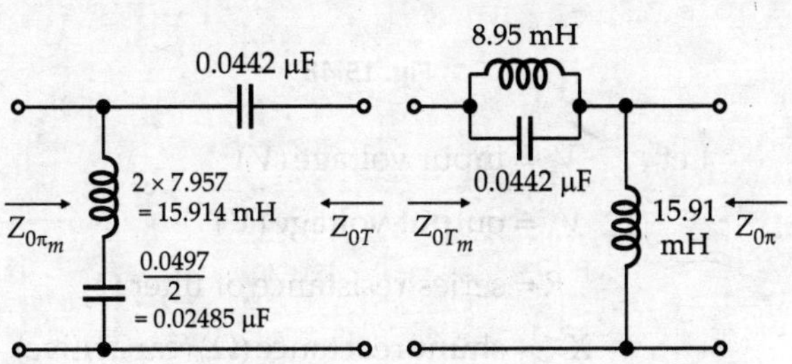

Fig. E15.19

Example 15.21 *Design a low pass composite filter to operate with a design impedance 500 ohms, m = 0.2 and cut-off frequency = 2000 Hz.*

Solution. For prototype *T* section LPF,

$$L = \frac{R_0}{\pi f_C} = 0.08\ \text{H}$$

$$C = \frac{1}{\pi f_C R_0} = \frac{1}{\pi \times 2000 \times 500} = 31.8\ \mu\text{F}$$

Hence, *m*-derived equivalent section will be (*T* section) (Fig. E15.20).

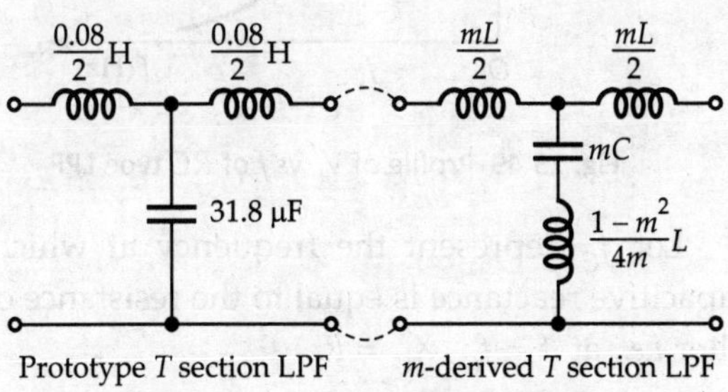

Fig. E15.20

$$\text{Here,}\quad \frac{mL}{2} = \frac{0.2 \times 0.08}{2} \times 0.008\ \text{H}$$

$$mC = 0.2 \times 31.8 = 6.36\ \mu\text{F}$$

$$\frac{1-m^2}{4m} \cdot L = 0.096\ \text{H}$$

The composite filter consists of the prototype LPF and *m*-derived LPF in cascade.

In order to design the composite filter we are to split the *m*-derived section taking *m* = 0.6 and make terminating half sections. Thus, taking the prototype *T* section as the primary, in the new *m*-derived section

$$\frac{mL}{2} = \frac{0.6 \times 0.08}{2} = 0.024\ \text{H}$$

$$mC = 0.6 \times 31.8 = 19.08\ \mu\text{F}$$

$$\frac{1-m^2}{4m}L = \frac{1-0.36}{4 \times 0.6} \cdot 0.08 = 0.021\ \text{H}$$

Thus, this section is bifurcated as shown to give *m*-derived terminating half section (Fig. E15.21).

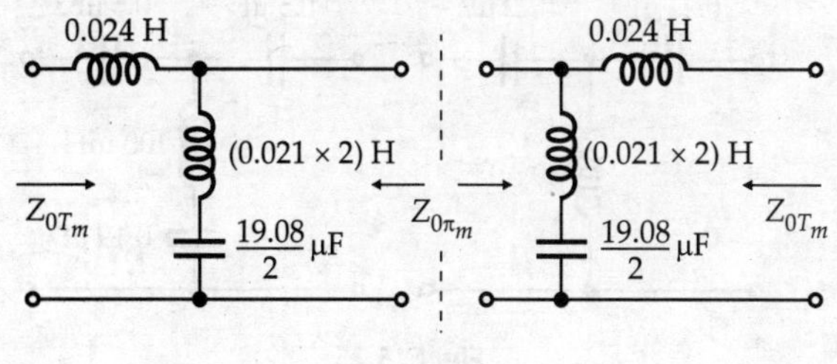

Fig. E15.21

The complete section is shown in Fig. E15.22.

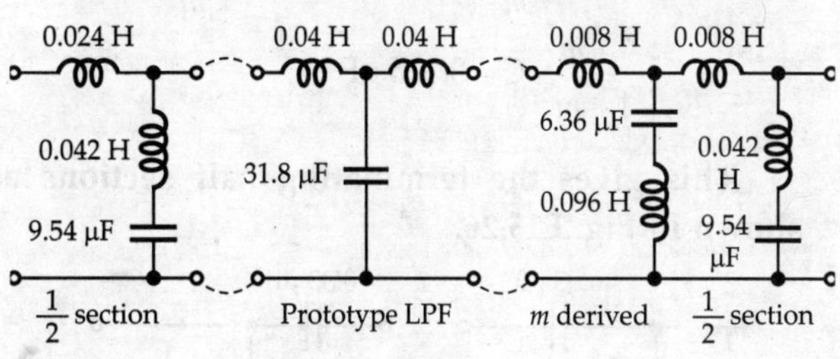

Fig. E15.22

Example 15.22 *Design a complete composite HP filter having a m-derived section m = 0.4, and prototype HPF with L = 40 mH and C = 0.1 μF.*

Solution. For the prototype HPF,

$$L = 40\ \text{mH}$$

$$C = 0.1\ \mu\text{F}$$

The *T* section of HPF is shown in Fig. E15.23.

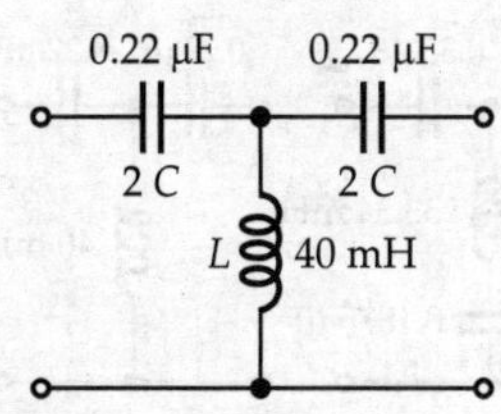

Fig. E15.23

The equivalent m-derived T section will be as shown in Fig. E15.24.

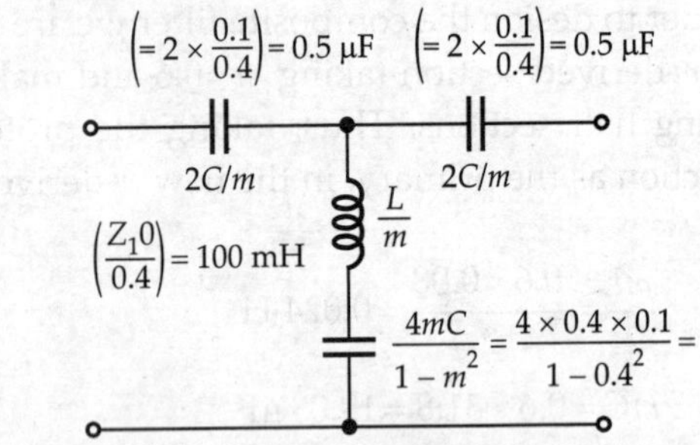

Fig. E15.24

Thus the filter section (without the terminating section) looks like that in Fig. E15.25. To design a suitable terminating half section, let m=0.6.

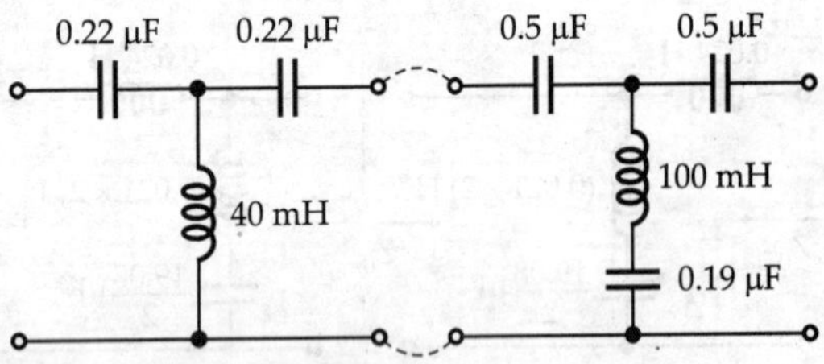

Fig. E15.25

With this value of m=0.6

$$\frac{L}{m} = 66.67 \text{ mH} \; ; \qquad \frac{2C}{m} = 0.33\ \mu\text{F}$$

$$\frac{4m}{1-m^2} C = 0.375\ \mu\text{F}$$

This gives the terminating half sections as shown in Fig. E15.26.

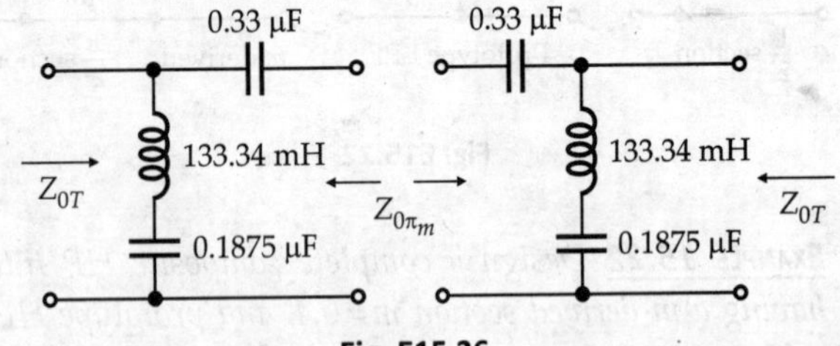

Fig. E15.26

The complete composite section has been shown in Fig. E15.27.

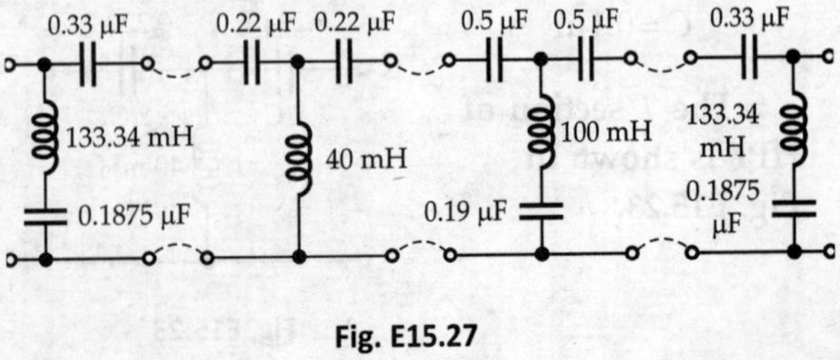

Fig. E15.27

15.29 LPF FILTER WITH *RC* AND *RL* CIRCUITS

15.29.1 *R-C* Filter

Figure 15.48 represents the circuit of an RC filter used extensively in rectifier circuits.

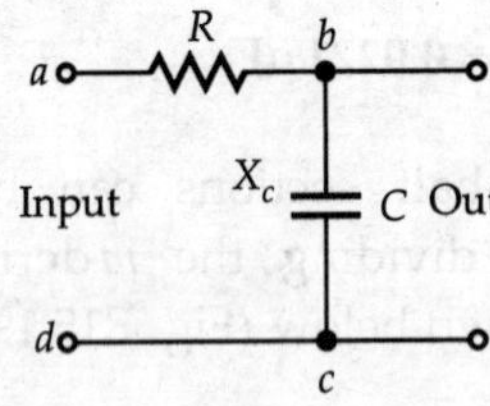

Fig. 15.48

Let V_i = input voltage (V)

V_0 = output voltage (V)

R = series resistance of filter Ω

X_C = shunt reactance (Ω) (capacitive)

Applying KVL in loop $abcd$,

$$V_0 = V_i \cdot \frac{X_C}{\sqrt{R^2 + X_C^2}} \qquad ...(15.100)$$

The profile of V_0 is qualitatively plotted in Fig. 15.49.

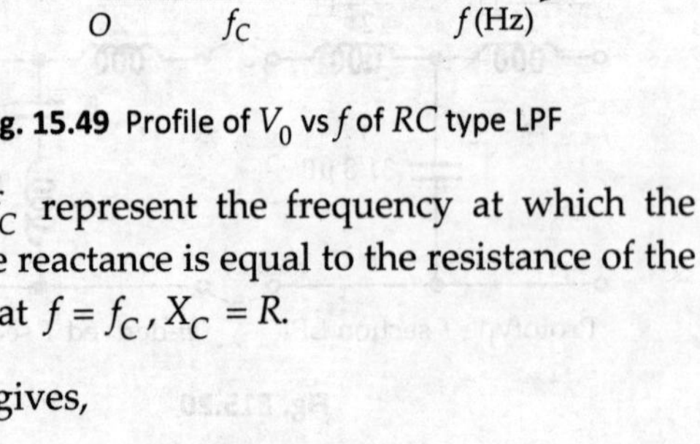

Fig. 15.49 Profile of V_0 vs f of RC type LPF

Let f_C represent the frequency at which the capacitive reactance is equal to the resistance of the filter *i.e.*, at $f = f_C$, $X_C = R$.

This gives,

$$V_0 = V_i \frac{X_C}{\sqrt{2X_C^2}} = 0.707\ V_i \qquad ...(15.101)$$

Thus the pass band (of frequency 0 to f_C) gives the bandwidth also.

Substituting $V_0 = 0.707\,V_i$ from (15.101) in (15.100)

$$(0.707)^2 = \frac{X_C^2}{R^2 + X_C^2}$$

or $$R = X_C \left(= \frac{1}{2\pi f_C C} \right) \text{Farad}$$

$$\therefore \quad C = \frac{1}{2\pi f_C\, R} \qquad \text{...(15.102)}$$

This filter acts as a low pass filter (LPF) where cut-off frequency is given by

$$f_C = \frac{1}{2\pi\, CR}\ \text{Hz} \qquad \text{...(15.103)}$$

15.29.2 *RL* Filter

Figure 15.50 represents the schematic of another LPF.

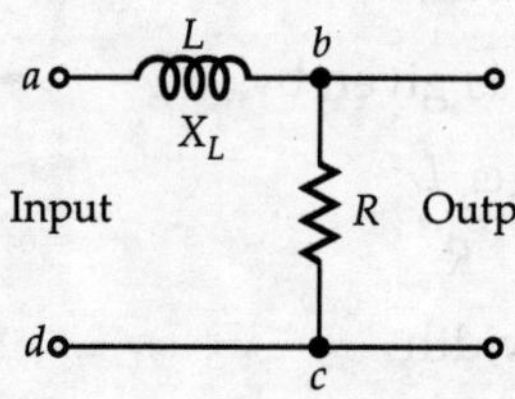

Fig. 15.50 Schematic of *RL* LPF.

Here, from KVL in loop *abcd*,

$$V_0 = V_i \frac{R}{\sqrt{R^2 + X_L^2}} \qquad \text{...(15.104)}$$

similar to R-C filter, at $f = f_C, X_L = R$.

$$\therefore \quad V_0 = 0.707\, V_i \qquad \text{...(15.105)}$$

Thus, utilising (15.105) in (15.104)

$$(0.707)^2 = \frac{R^2}{R^2 + X_L^2}$$

or, $$R = X_L = 2\pi f_C L$$

$$\therefore \quad L = \frac{R}{2\pi f_C}\ \text{Henry} \qquad \text{...(15.106)}$$

and $$f_C = \frac{R}{2\pi f L}\ \text{Hz} \qquad \text{...(15.107)}$$

The output voltage profile (V_0) vs frequency (f) is similar to that shown in Fig. 15.49.

15.30 HPF FILTER WITH *RC* AND *RL* CIRCUITS

15.30.1 *RC* Filter

By interchanging the circuit elements of the *RC* circuit, the high pass filter can be constituted. The plot of V_0 vs frequency has been shown in Fig. 15.51.

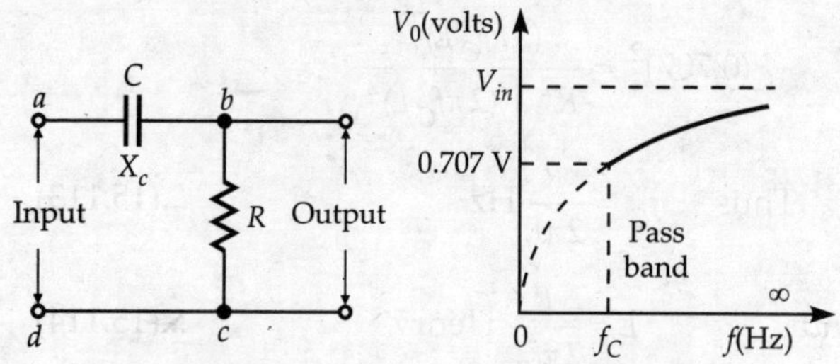

(*a*) Schematic (*b*) Characteristic

Fig. 15.51 *RC* HPF circuit.

Here, application of KVL in loop *abcd*

$$V_0 = V_i \frac{R}{\sqrt{R^2 + X_C^2}} \qquad \text{...(15.108)}$$

at $f = f_C, X_C = R$.

This gives

$$V_0 = V_i \frac{R}{\sqrt{2R^2}} = 0.707\, V_i \qquad \text{...(15.109)}$$

Thus, from (15.105),

$$(0.707)^2 = \frac{R^2}{R^2 + X_C^2}$$

or $$R = X_C \left(= \frac{1}{2\pi f_C C} \right) \Omega \qquad \text{...(15.110)}$$

Here, $$f_C = \frac{1}{2\pi RC}\ \text{Hz} \qquad \text{...(15.111)}$$

15.30.2 *RL* Filter

In a similar way, an *R-L* circuit can be used as HPF filter (Fig. 15.52).

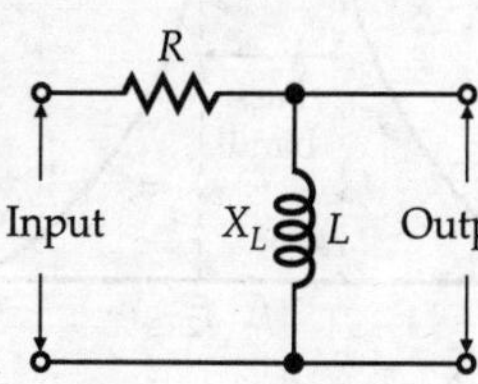

Fig. 15.52 Schematic of *R-L* HPF.

CHAPTER 15

Here, $V_0 = V_i \dfrac{X_L}{\sqrt{R^2 + X_L^2}}$ ...(15.112)

At cut-off, $f = f_C$ giving $R = X_L$

This gives $V_0 = 0.707\, V_i$

With this, from (15.112),

$$(0.707)^2 = \frac{(2\pi f_C L)^2}{R^2 + (2\pi f_C L)^2}$$

Thus $f_C = \dfrac{R}{2\pi L}$ Hz ...(15.113)

and $L = \dfrac{R}{2\pi f_C}$ Henry ...(15.114)

The output voltage frequency (f) profile of HPF *R-L* circuit is similar to that of HPF *R-C* filter.

15.31 BANDPASS FILTER WITH *RLC* CIRCUITS

Figure 15.53 represents a *R-L-C* type band pass filter. Fig. 15.54 is its equivalent circuit.

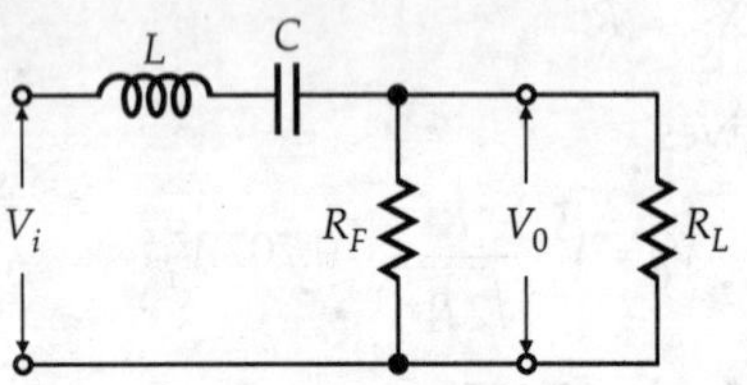

Fig. 15.53 *RLC* BP filter.

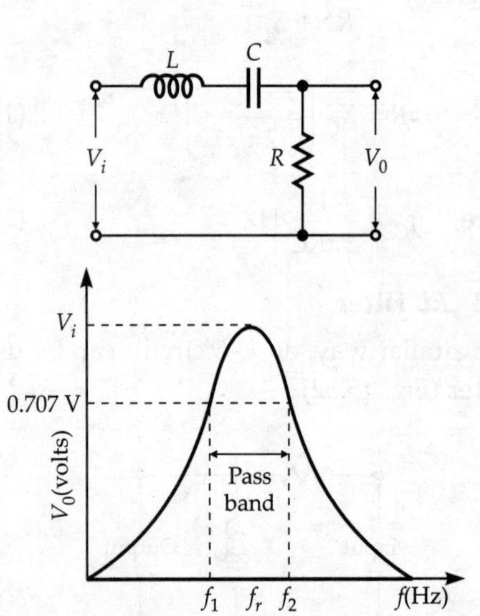

Fig. 15.54 *RLC* type BPF and its characteristic of *LCR* BPF.

Here, $V_0 = V_i \dfrac{R}{\sqrt{R^2 + (X_L - X_C)^2}}$

$$= V_i \frac{R}{\sqrt{R^2 + \left[2\pi f L - \dfrac{1}{2\pi f C}\right]^2}} \text{ volts}$$

...(15.115)

Here $R = \dfrac{R_F \times R_L}{R_F + R_L}$ ohms ...(15.116)

R_F = Filter resistance
R_L = Load resistance
V_i = Input voltage
V_0 = Output voltage

From the theory of series resonance, the resonance frequency is given by

$$f_r = \frac{1}{2\pi\sqrt{LC}} \text{ Hz} \quad ...(15.117)$$

The *Q* factor is given by

$$Q\,\text{factor} = \frac{\omega_r L}{R}, \quad ...(15.118)$$

The *B* bandwidth

$$(\text{BW}) = \frac{f_r}{Q} \text{ Hz} \quad ...(15.119)$$

while $f_1 = f_r - \dfrac{\text{Bandwidth}}{2}$ Hz ...(15.120)

and $f_2 = f_r + \dfrac{\text{Bandwidth}}{2}$ Hz ...(15.121)

[f_1 and f_2 being the lower and higher cut-off frequencies]

LCR type band pass filter can also be made utilising the circuit shown in Fig. 15.55, with its equivalent in Fig. 15.56.

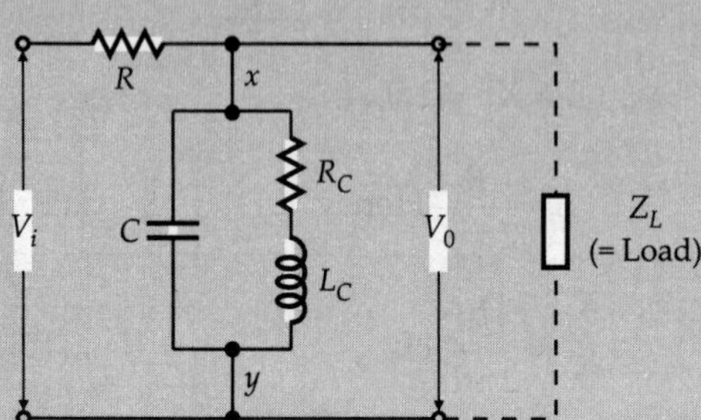

Fig. 15.55 A BPF circuit

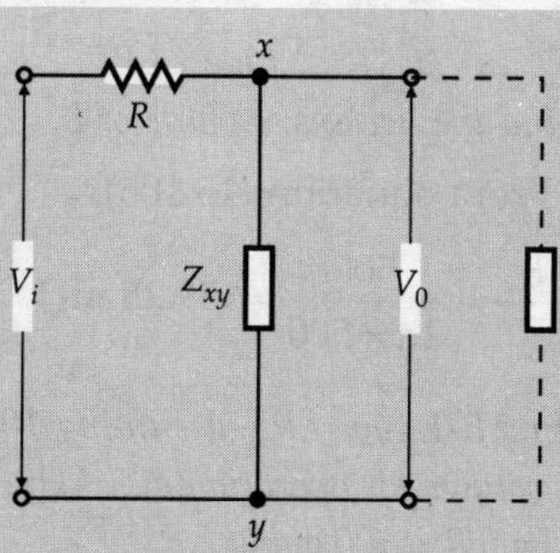

Fig. 15.56 Equivalent circuit of Fig. 15.55

Here,

$$Z_{XY} = \frac{(R_C + jX_L)(-jX_C)}{(R_C + jX_L) + (-jX_C)} \text{ ohms} \quad ...(15.122)$$

and $$V_0 = V_i \frac{Z_{XY}}{R + Z_{XY}} \text{ volts} \quad ...(15.123)$$

15.32 BAND STOP FILTER WITH *RLC* CIRCUITS

Figure 15.57 represents the schematic of a band stop filter (BSF) or a band elimination filter (BEF).

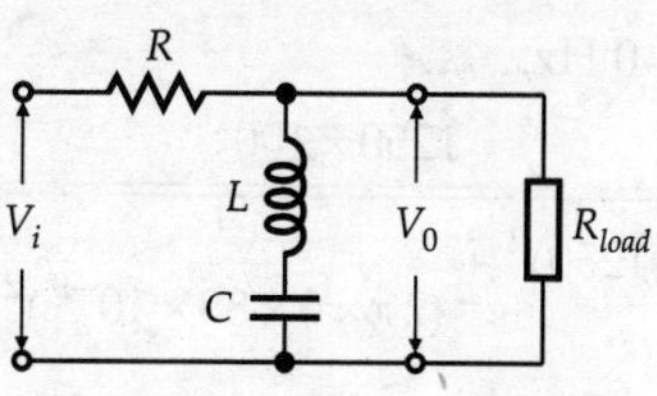

Fig. 15.57 Series *R-L-C* type band stop filter.

The equivalent circuit is shown in Fig. 15.58(*a*). The characteristic of such a filter has been represented by the profile shown in Fig. 15.58(*b*).

Here $$Z = j(X_L - X_C) \text{ ohms} \quad ...(15.124)$$

and the net impedance of the circuit [Fig. 15.58(*a*)] is given by

$$Z_{total} = R + j(X_L - X_C) \text{ ohms} \quad ...(15.125)$$

Applying KVL in loop *abcd* of Fig. 15.58(*a*),

$$V_0 = V_i \frac{|Z|}{|Z_{total}|}$$

or $$V_0 = V_i \frac{\sqrt{(X_L - X_X)^2}}{\sqrt{R^2 + (X_L - X_C)^2}} \quad ...(15.126)$$

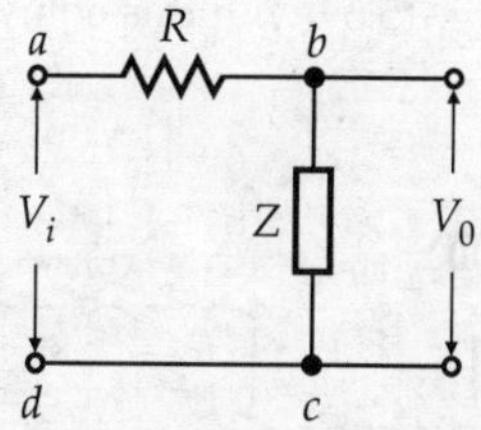

(*a*) Equivalent circuit

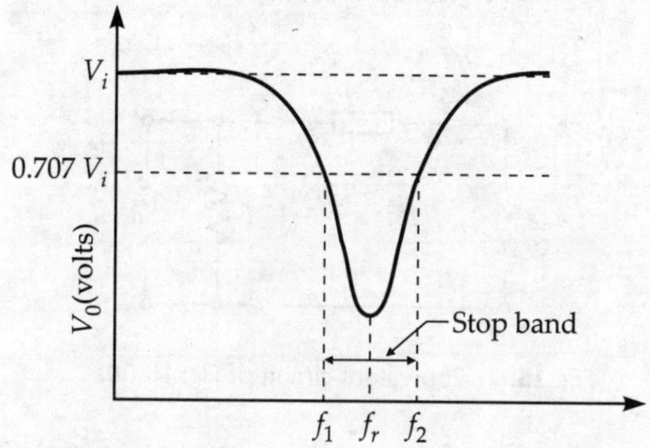

Fig. 15.58 Equivalent circuit and characteristic of BSF (*R-L-C* type)

From the theory of series resonance, the resonant frequency (f_r) is given by

$$f_r = \frac{1}{2\pi\sqrt{LC}} \text{ Hz} \quad ...(15.127)$$

and the Q factor is given by

$$Q = \frac{\omega_r L}{R} \quad ...(15.128)$$

while band width (BW)

$$= \frac{f_r}{Q} \text{ Hz} \quad ...(15.129)$$

Here,

$$f_1 = \left(f_r - \frac{\text{BW}}{2}\right) \text{Hz}$$

and $$f_2 = \left(f_r + \frac{\text{BW}}{2}\right) \text{Hz}$$

[f_1 and f_2 being the lower and higher cut-off frequencies]

CHAPTER 15

LCR type BS filters can also be made utilising the circuit shown in Fig. 15.59 with this equivalent circuit in Fig. 15.60.

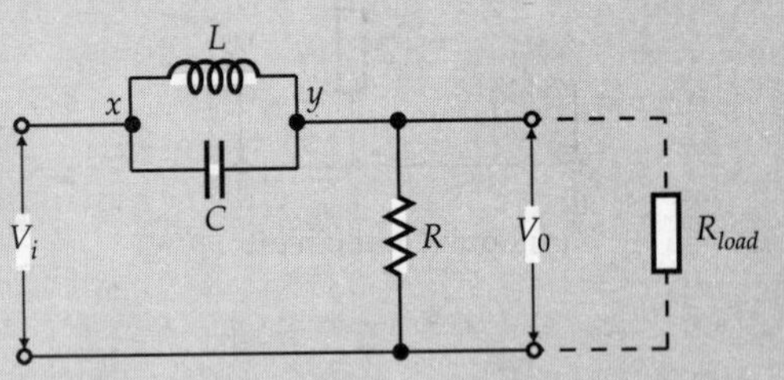

Fig. 15.59 A BSF circuit

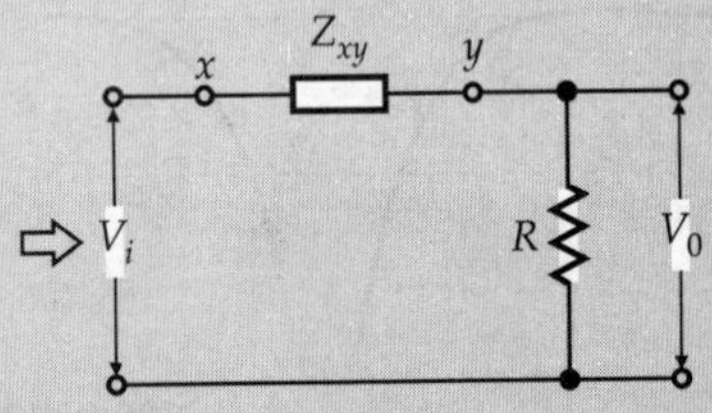

Fig. 15.60 Equivalent circuit of Fig. 15.59.

Here,

$$Z_{XY} = \frac{(jX_L)\times(-jX_C)}{jX_L - jX_C}$$

$$= -j\frac{X_L X_C}{(X_L - X_C)} \text{ ohm} \quad ...(15.130)$$

$$V_0 = V_i \frac{R}{R + Z_{XY}} \text{ volts} \quad ...(15.131)$$

Example 15.23 *The cut-off frequency of an LPF with R-C configuration is 500 Hz. Assuming $R = 500\,\Omega$, find the value of C.*

Solution. From equation (15.103), for a RC LPF,

$$f_C = \frac{1}{2\pi CR} = \frac{1}{2\pi \times 500 \times 500} = \mathbf{636.6\ nF.}$$

Example 15.24 *In a RC type LPF, the cut-off frequency is 2000 Hz. Assuming the capacitance to be 80 nF, determine the value of the resistance.*

Solution. From equation (15.102), we can write

$$R = \frac{1}{2\pi f_C C}$$

or
$$R = \frac{1}{2\pi \times 2000 \times 800 \times 10^{-8}}$$

$\therefore$ $R = \mathbf{9.95\ ohms.}$

Example 15.25 *In a RL type LPF, $R = 500\,\Omega$, $f_C = 500$ Hz. Find the necessary value of L.*

Solution. From equation (15.106),

$$L = \frac{R}{2\pi f_C} = \frac{500}{2\pi \times 500} = \mathbf{159.25\ mH.}$$

Example 15.26 *In a R-L type LPF, assuming 10 V input, find the output voltage for operation at 1 kHz. Assume L = 159.15 mH and R = 500 ohms.*

Solution. Utilising equation (15.104),

$$V_0 = 10\frac{500}{\sqrt{(500)^2 + (2\pi f \times 159.15 \times 10^{-3})}} \text{ volts}$$

for $f = 1000$ Hz

$$V_{out} = \mathbf{9.99\ V.}$$

Example 15.27 *In a HP R-C filter, find V_0 at 0 Hz (b) 100 kHz for a 100 V input. Assume the capacitance to be 80 nF and the resistance to be 1250 ohms.*

Solution. From equation (15.108)

$$V_0 = 100\frac{1250}{\sqrt{(1250)^2 + (2\pi f \times 80 \times 10^{-9})^2}}$$

(*a*) at $f = 0$ Hz,

$$V_0 = \frac{1250 \times 100}{\sqrt{(1250)^2 + \frac{1}{(2\pi \times 0 \times 80 \times 10^{-9})^2}}} = 0 \text{ volt}$$

i.e., the filter does not allow to pass the signal at $f = 0$ Hz

(*b*) at $f = 100 \times 10^3$ Hz

$$V_0 = \frac{1250 \times 100}{\sqrt{(1250)^2 + \frac{1}{(2\pi \times 100 \times 10^3 \times 80 \times 10^{-9})^2}}}$$

$$\simeq \mathbf{100\ volts}$$

$\therefore$ at $f = 100$ kHz, the filter allows complete flow of the input signal.

Example 15.27(a) *Design an R-L HP filter with $f_C = 2$ kHz and having $R = 2$ kΩ.*

Solution. Utilising equation (15.114),

$$L = \frac{R}{2\pi f_C}$$

$$= \frac{2 \times 10^3}{2\pi \times 2 \times 10^3} = \mathbf{159.25\ mH.}$$

ADDITIONAL EXAMPLES

EXAMPLE 15.28 *Determine the output voltage of an R-L HPF having working frequency 0 Hz, 500 Hz and R = 2 kΩ, = L = 159.15 mH. Assume input voltage to be 10 volts.*

SOLUTION. Utilising equation (15.112),

$$V_0 = 10\frac{2\pi f \times 159.25 \times 10^{-3}}{\sqrt{(2000)^2 + (2\pi f + 159.25 \times 10^{-3})^2}}$$

at $f = 0$ Hz,

$$V_0 = 10 \times 0 = 0 \text{ volts}$$

i.e., the filter operates at stop band.

$f = 500$ Hz,

$$V_0 = 10\frac{2\pi \times 500 \times 159.25 \times 10^{-3}}{\sqrt{(2000)^2 + (2\pi \times 500 \times 159.25 \times 10^{-3})^2}}$$

$$= \mathbf{2.42\ volts}$$

∴ at 500 Hz, the filter partially allows the input to pass through it.

EXAMPLE 15.29 *In a series LCR type BPF, L = 50 mH, C = 127 nF and R_F = 63 ohms. Determine*

(i) the resonance frequency

(ii) the band width

(iii) the cut-off frequencies.

Assume the load resistance to be 600 ohms.

SOLUTION. Utilising equation (15.117), the resonant frequency f_r is given by

$$f_r = \frac{1}{2\pi\sqrt{LC}} \text{ Hz}$$

$$= \frac{1}{2\pi\sqrt{50 \times 10^{-3} \times 127 \times 10^{-9}}} = \mathbf{2\ kHz}$$

Again, using equation (15.116),

$$R = \frac{R_F \times R_L}{R_F + R_L} = \frac{63 \times 600}{63 + 600} = 57 \text{ ohms}$$

∴ BW (band width)

$$= \frac{f_r}{Q} = \frac{2 \times 10^3}{11}$$

$$\left[\because Q = \frac{\omega_r L}{R} = \frac{2\pi \times 0.05}{57} = 11\right]$$

$$= 181.8 \text{ Hz} \simeq \mathbf{182\ Hz}$$

f_1 = lower cut-off frequency

$$= f_r - \frac{BW}{2}$$

[Equations (15.120) and (15.121)]

$$= 2 \times 10^3 - \frac{182}{2} = 1909 \text{ Hz}$$

f_2 = Higher cut-off frequency

$$= f_r + \frac{BW}{2}$$

$$= 2 \times 10^3 + \frac{182}{2} = \mathbf{2091\ Hz.}$$

EXAMPLE 15.30 *In Example 15.29, find the output voltage for an input ac voltage of 10 volts (rms) at f_r, f_1 and f_2.*

SOLUTION. At f_r, $X_L = X_C$

$$\therefore \quad V_0 = V_i \frac{R}{\sqrt{R^2 + 0}}$$

[Refer to equation (15.115)]

$$= V_i = 10 \text{ volts}$$

∴ at resonance frequency, the signal passes unattenuated.

At $f_1 = 1909$ Hz,

$$X_L = 2\pi f_1 L = 2\pi \times 1909 \times 0.05 = 600\,\Omega$$

$$X_C = \frac{1}{2\pi f_1 C} = \frac{1}{2\pi \times 1909 \times (127 \times 10^{-9})}$$

$$= 658\,\Omega$$

$$\therefore \quad V_0 = 10 \times \frac{57}{\sqrt{(57)^2 + (600 - 658)^2}}$$

[utilising equation 15.115]

$$= 7 \text{ volt}$$

At $f_2 = 2091$ Hz

$$X_L = 2\pi f_2 L = 2\pi \times 2091 \times 0.05$$

$$= 656 \text{ ohms}$$

$$X_C = \frac{1}{2\pi f_2 C} = \frac{1}{2\pi \times 2091 \times (127 \times 10^{-9})}$$

$$= 600 \text{ ohms}$$

$$\therefore \quad V_0 = 10 \times \frac{57}{\sqrt{(57)^2 + (656 - 600)^2}} = \mathbf{7\ volts}$$

Thus at f_1 and f_2, 70% of the signal passes out.

Example 15.31 *A series LCR type BPF is to work with cut-off frequencies 23 kHz and 25 kHz. Assume L= 45 mH, while load resistance is 50 kΩ. Design the BPF.*

Solution. As $BW = f_2 - f_1$,

Here, $BW = (25-23)\text{ kHz} = 2\text{ kHz}$

As f_r lies in between f_1 and f_2 hence

$$f_r = 24\text{ kHz}$$

$$\left[\text{Also, } f_r = f_2 - \frac{BW}{2} = 25000 - \frac{2000}{2}\right]$$

$$= 24\text{ kHz}$$

But $f_r = \dfrac{1}{2\pi\sqrt{LC}} = \dfrac{1}{2\pi\sqrt{0.045\times C}}$

$$\therefore\ 24\times10^3 = \frac{1}{2\pi\sqrt{0.045\times C}}$$

or $C \simeq 977\text{ pF}$

$$Q = \frac{f_r}{BW} = \frac{24{,}000}{2000} = 12 = \frac{\omega_r L}{R}$$

$$\therefore\quad R = \frac{\omega_r L}{12} = \frac{2\pi\times24000\times0.045}{12}$$

$$\simeq 565.2\text{ ohms}$$

However,

$$R = \frac{R_F\times R_L}{R_F + R_L}$$

or $565.2 = \dfrac{R_F\times50\times10^3}{R_F+50\times10^3}$

$$\simeq 588.88\text{ ohms}$$

∴ The BPF filter configurations are

L = **45 mH**

C = **977 pF**

R = **558.88 ohms.**

Example 15.32 *In a series resonance type BPF, C = 1.8 pF, L= 25 mH, R_F = 52 Ω and R_L = 9 kΩ. Find f_r and BW.*

Solution. Utilising equation (15.117),

$$f_r = \frac{1}{2\pi\sqrt{LC}} = \frac{1}{2\pi\sqrt{0.025\times1.8\times10^{-12}}}$$

$$\simeq 751\text{ kHz}$$

Again, utilising equation (15.116)

$$R = \frac{52\times9000}{52+9000} \simeq 52\text{ ohms}$$

∴ From equation (15.119),

$$Q_{factor} = \frac{\omega_r L}{R} = \frac{2\pi\times751\times25\times10^{-3}}{52}$$

$$\simeq 2270$$

Thus $BW = \dfrac{f_r}{Q}$ [Refer to equation (15.119)]

$$= \frac{751\times10^3}{2270} = 331\text{ Hz}$$

f_1 and f_2 can also be found out as

$$f_1 = f_r - \frac{BW}{2} = 751\times10^3 - \frac{331}{2}$$

$$= 750.849\text{ kHz}$$

and $f_2 = f_r + \dfrac{BW}{2} = \mathbf{751.162\ kHz.}$

Example 15.33 *In a LCR type band stop filter, R = 1 kΩ, L= 115 mH, C= 400 pF. Determine (i) the bandwidth (ii) cut-off frequencies (iii) output voltage at f_r, f_1 and f_2.*

Solution. Utilising equation (15.127),

$$f_r = \frac{1}{2\pi\sqrt{LC}} = \frac{1}{2\pi\sqrt{0.155\times400\times10^{-12}}}$$

$$= 20.50\text{ kHz}$$

However,

$$Q = \frac{\omega_r L}{R}\ \text{[from equation(15.128)]}$$

$$= \frac{2\pi(20.55\times10^2)\times0.155}{1\times10^3} = 19.46$$

$$\simeq 20\text{ Hz}$$

But it is evident that $Q = \dfrac{f_r}{BW}$

[Refer to equation (15.129)]

$$\therefore\quad BW = \frac{f_r}{Q} = \frac{20.50\times10^3}{20} = \mathbf{1025\ Hz}$$

Also, $f_1 = f_r - \dfrac{BW}{2} = 20\times10^3 - \dfrac{1025}{2}$

$$= \mathbf{19.49\ kHz}$$

and $f_2 = f_r + \frac{BW}{2} = 20 \times 10^3 + \frac{1025}{2}$

$= \mathbf{20.51\ kHz}$

Referring to Art. 15.32, we observe that for the *BSF* given in the question,

$$|Z| = (X_L - X_C)$$

and $$|Z_T| = \sqrt{R^2 + (X_L - X_C)^2}$$

at $f_r, X_L = X_C$

$\therefore$ $|Z| = 0$ and $|Z_T| = R$

This gives $V_0 = V_i \cdot \frac{0}{R} = 0$ at f_r

i.e., at $f = f_r$, the signal is completely attenuated.

at $f = f_1$,

$$X_L = 2\pi \times 19.49 \times 10^3 \times 0.155 = 18.97\ \text{k}\Omega$$

$$X_C = \frac{1}{2\pi \times 19.49 \times 10^3 \times 400 \times 10^{-12}}$$

$$= 20.4\ \text{k}\Omega$$

$$\therefore \quad |X_L - X_C| = -1410\ \Omega$$

$$\therefore \quad V_0 = V_i \frac{\sqrt{(-1410)^2}}{\sqrt{(1000)^2 + (-1410)^2}}$$

$$= 0.81\ V_i \text{ volts}$$

at $f = f_2$,

$$X_L = 2\pi \times 20.51 \times 10^3 \times 0.155 = 19.97\ \text{k}\Omega$$

$$X_C = \frac{1}{2\pi \times 20.51 \times 10^3 \times 400 \times 10^{-12}}$$

$$= 19.45\ \text{k}\Omega$$

$$\therefore |X_L - X_C| = 1150\ \Omega$$

$$\therefore V_0 \text{ at } f = f_2 \text{ is } V_i \frac{\sqrt{1150^2}}{\sqrt{(1000)^2 + (1150)^2}}$$

$$= \mathbf{0.75\ V_i\ volts}$$

i.e., 75% of the signal will pass at $f = f_2$

Ideally 70.7% signal should have passed through for $f = f_1$ or f_2. The error has come due to negligence of resistance in the inductance coil which should be taken into account for all accurate calculations.

EXAMPLE 15.34 *Find out the capacitance required for a series LCR type BSF that will block a signal at 85 kHz. Assume the filter reactor has inductance and resistance of 60 mH and 15 ohms respectively. The load resistance is 1.4 MΩ while the filter series resistance is 2 kΩ. Find also the band width.*

SOLUTION. As per the given data,

$$R = 2000\ \Omega$$

$$C = \text{unknown}$$

$$L = 60 \times 10^{-3}\ \text{H};\ r = 15\Omega$$

resistance (r) in inductance $= 15\ \Omega$

$$R_L = 1.4\ \text{M}\Omega$$

Figure E15.28 shows the filter.

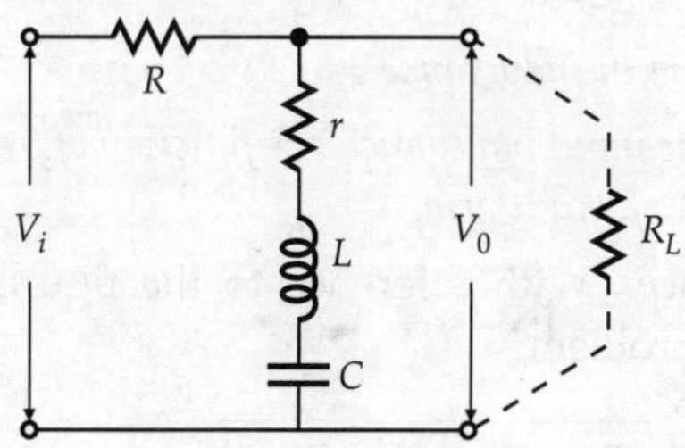

Fig. E15.28

Here, $f_r = \frac{1}{2\pi\sqrt{LC}}$ [equation (15.127)]

or $85 \times 10^3 = \frac{1}{2\pi\sqrt{0.06 \times C}}$

[$\because$ f_r = given = 85 kHz]

$\therefore$ $C = \mathbf{58\ pF}$

Utilising equation (15.129),

$$BW = \frac{f_r}{Q}$$

However,

$$Q = \frac{2\pi \times 85 \times 10^3 \times 0.06}{(15 + 2000)}$$

[utilising equation 15.128]

It may be noted that net resistance of filter $= r = R = (15 + 2000)\ \Omega$

This gives

$$Q = 15.9$$

$$\therefore \quad BW = \frac{85 \times 10^3}{16} = \mathbf{5313\ Hz}$$

[Assuming $Q = 15.9 \simeq 16$]

C H A P T E R 15

f_1 and f_2 can be determined as follows :

$$f_1 = f_r - \frac{BW}{2}$$

$$= 85 \times 10^3 - \frac{5313}{2} = 82.34 \text{ kHz}$$

$$f_2 = f_r + \frac{BW}{2}$$

$$= 85 \times 10^3 + \frac{5313}{2} = \mathbf{87.66 \text{ kHz.}}$$

EXAMPLE 15.35 *In a BSF (series resonant type),*

$$R = 2\ k\Omega$$
$$C = 58 \times 10^{-12}\ F$$
$$L = 60 \times 10^{-3}\ H$$

resistance (r) in inductance $= 15\,\Omega$

Find the input impedance as a function of frequency. Also find Z of shunt arm.

SOLUTION. With reference to the figure in the previous problem,

$$Z_{in} = \sqrt{(R+r)^2 + (X_L - X_C)^2}$$

$$= \sqrt{(2015)^2 + \left(2\pi f \times 0.06 - \frac{1}{2\pi f \times 58 \times 10^{-12}}\right)^2}$$

Again,

$$Z_{shunt\ arm} = \sqrt{r^2 + (X_L - X_C)^2}$$

$$= \sqrt{(15)^2 + \left(2\pi f \times 0.06 - \frac{1}{2\pi f \times 58 \times 10^{-12}}\right)^2}$$

EXAMPLE 15.36 *For the example 15.34, determine* V_0 *in terms of frequency and input voltage* V_i.

SOLUTION. Referring to the figure of Example 15.34 and expressions of Z_{in} and $Z_{shunt\ arm}$, the expression for the output voltage can be written as

$$V_0 = V_i \frac{Z_{shunt\ arm}}{Z_{in}}$$

$$= V_i \frac{\sqrt{(15)^2 + \left(2\pi f \times 0.06 - \frac{1}{2\pi f \times 58 \times 10^{-12}}\right)^2}}{\sqrt{(2015)^2 + \left(2\pi f \times 0.06 - \frac{1}{2\pi f \times 58 \times 10^{-12}}\right)^2}}$$

Numerical values of V_0 can be obtained for different values of f utilising the above expression.

EXAMPLE 15.37 *A typical filter is shown in Fig. E15.29. Obtain a relationship between input and output voltage. Find the frequency of resonance and Q factor.*

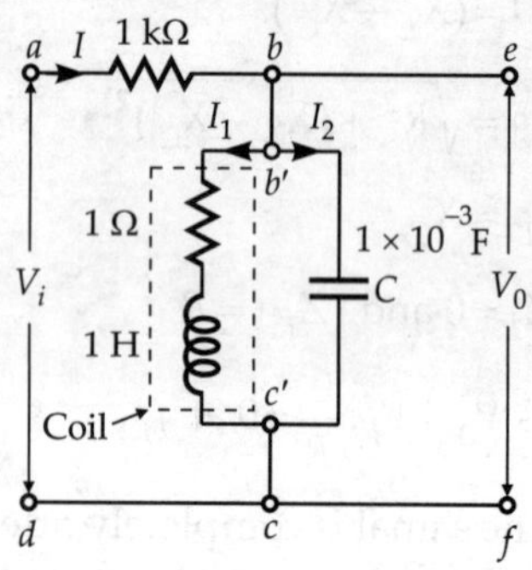

Fig. E15.29

SOLUTION. Let us assume that the input terminals be *a-b* and the output terminals be *e-f*. The directions of current flows (I, I_1 and I_2) are shown in the figure for applied voltage V_i at (*a-b*) terminals and obtained voltage V_0 at (*e-f*) terminals.

As per KCL,

$$I = I_1 + I_2$$

or
$$\frac{V_{ad} - V_{bc}}{1\,k\Omega} = \frac{V_{bc}}{1 + j\omega} + \frac{V_{bc}}{1/j\omega \times 1 \times 10^{-3}}$$

or
$$\frac{V_i - V_0}{1000} = \frac{V_0}{1 + j\omega} + \frac{V_0}{1000/j\omega}$$

$$= V_0\left(\frac{j\omega}{1000} + \frac{1}{1 + j\omega}\right)$$

$$\therefore \quad \frac{V_0}{V_i} = \frac{1 + j\omega}{(1 + j\omega)^2 + 1000}$$

Frequency of resonance is given by

$$\omega_r = \frac{1}{\sqrt{LC}}$$

$$= \frac{1}{\sqrt{1 \times 10^3}} = \mathbf{31.6\ rad/sec.}$$

$$Q_{factor} = \frac{\omega_\gamma L}{R}$$

$$= \frac{31.6 \times 1}{1} = \mathbf{31.6}$$

EXERCISES

1. A *T*-section of a low pass filter has series inductance of 100 mH and shunt capacitance of 0.025 μF. Find the cut-off frequency and nominal design impedance. Also design an equivalent π-section.

[Hint. Find 'f_c' from the given data utilising the relation $f_c = \dfrac{1}{\pi\sqrt{LC}}$, then determine R_o from $R_o = \sqrt{\dfrac{L}{C}}$]

2. Design the *T* and π section of a prototype *HPF* having cut-off frequency of 20 kHz and design impedance of 450 ohms. Also find its characteristic impedance and phase constant at 25 kHz as well as determine the attenuation at 4 kHz.

[Hint. $L = \dfrac{R_o}{4\pi f_c}$ and $C = \dfrac{1}{4\pi f_o f_c}$

Thus find *L* and *C* of the HPF section.

From the expression, $Z_{0T} = R_0\sqrt{1-\left(\dfrac{f_c}{f}\right)^2}$, find Z_{0T} at f = 24 kHz.

Similarly, find $Z_{0\pi}$. Find β and α utilising the relationship $\beta = 2\sin^{-1}\left(\dfrac{f_c}{f}\right)$, $\alpha = 2\cosh^{-1}\left(\dfrac{f_c}{f}\right)$].

3. Design a prototype BPF (*T* and π) having cut-off frequencies of 5 kHz and 10 kHz. The nominal characteristic impedance being 600 ohms ; find the resonant frequency of the shunt or series arm.

[Hint. Find L_1 and C_1 utilising $L_1 = \dfrac{R_0}{\pi(f_2 - f_1)}$ and $C_1 = \dfrac{(f_2 - f_1)}{4\pi R_0 f_1 f_2}$

Similarly, find L_2 and C_2. But $f_c = \sqrt{f_1 f_2}$; thus find the resonant frequency]

4. Design a constant *K*-type band stop filter having cut-off frequencies of 2 kHz and 4 kHz and design impedance of 500 ohms.

[Hint. Find 4, C_1, L_2 and C_2 utilising established relationships].

5. Design an *m*-derived LPF (*T* and π section) having design resistance of 500 ohms, cut-off frequency of 1 kHz and infinite attenuation frequency f_∞ = 2 kHz.

[Hint. Find '*m*' utilising $m = \sqrt{1-\left(\dfrac{f_C}{f_\infty}\right)^2}$. Then find *L* and *C* utilising the relationships of LPF prototype filter.

The filter elements will then be $\dfrac{mL}{2}$, mC, $\dfrac{1-m^2}{4m}$, $\dfrac{mC}{2}$, mL, $\dfrac{1-m^2}{4m}$ C.]

6. Design an *m*-derived LPF to match a line having characteristic impedance of 450 ohms and to pass signals upto 1.5 kHz with infinite attenuation frequency of 1.8 kHz.

[Hint. Do in the same way as you have done in the previous problem]

7. Design *T* and π section of *m*-derived HPF having design impedance of 500 ohms, cut-off frequency 5 kHz and infinite attenuation frequency at 4.5 kHz.

[Hint. Find '*m*' utilising the relationship $m = \sqrt{1-\left(\dfrac{f_\infty}{f_C}\right)^2}$

Then find *L* and *C* prototype filter. The elements of the *m*-derived filter will then be $\dfrac{2C}{m}$, $\dfrac{L}{m}$, $\dfrac{4m}{1-m^2}$ C for the *T*-section and $\dfrac{2C}{m}$, $\dfrac{L}{m}$ and $\dfrac{4m}{1-m^2}$ C for the π section.]

CHAPTER 15

8. Design an *m*-derived *T*-section LPF having cut-off frequency $f_c = 8$ kHz, design impedance $R_0 = 600$ ohms and frequency of infinite attenuation $f_\infty = 10$ kHz.

[**Hint.** Proceed in the same way as you have done in the previous problems.]

9. Design a prototype LPF to have a cut-off frequency at 760 Hz when terminated in a 500 ohms resistance, in both π and *T* configurations.

[**Hint.** Find *L* from $L = \dfrac{R_0}{\pi f_c}$ and C from $C = \dfrac{1}{\pi R_0 f_c}$]

10. Design an *m*-derived HPF having a design impedance of 500 ohms, cut-off frequency of 5 kHz and $m = 0.32$. Also determine the frequency of infinite attenuation.

[**Hint.** Find f_∞ utilising the relationship $m = \sqrt{1 - \left(\dfrac{f_\infty}{f_c}\right)^2}$.

Then find the value of the circuit elements in the usual way.]

11. In a series resonance type band pass filter, $L = 60$ mH, $C = 150$ nF and $R = 70$ ohms. Determine (*i*) the resonance frequency in Hz, (*ii*) the bandwidth (*iii*) the cut-off frequencies. Assume the load resistance to be 600 ohms.

[**Hint.** Refer to solved example 15.31]

12. A series LCR type band stop filter has $R = 1.5$ kΩ, $L = 140$ mH and $C = 300$ pF. Find the (*i*) frequency of resonance and (*ii*) the bandwidth. Also find the cut-off frequencies.

[**Hint.** Refer to solved example 15.35]

13. Figure P15.1 represents a special filter (double resonant type). The two resonance frequencies are for the tank circuit and for the series ckt. Assuming $C_1 = 3500$ μF, determine the other parameters in the series arm such that the filter rejects a 100 kHz signal but accepts 50 kHz.

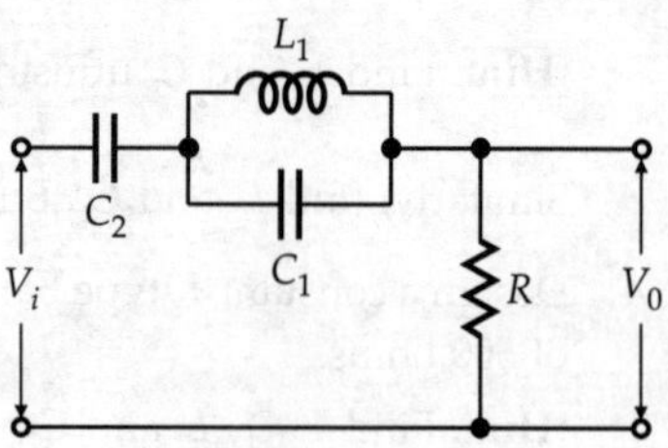

Fig. P15.1

[**Hint.** Determine L_1 using $f_r = \dfrac{1}{2\pi\sqrt{L_1 C_1}}$ for $f_r = 100$ kHz

Find X_{L1} at f_r as well as X_C at f_r. Then find $Z_{tank}\left(= \dfrac{jX_{L1} \cdot jC_1}{j(X_{L1} - X_{C1})}\right)$

To have a series resonance, $|Z_{tank}| = |X_{C2}|$

From this find C_2 assuming $f_r' = 50$ kHz

It may be noted that the concepts of rejecting the signal at resonance by a tank circuit and accepting the signal by a series circuit at resonance have been utilised.]

14. Figure P15.2 represents another double resonating filter. Assume $L_1 = 2.0$ mH. Design the other parameters (L_2 and C_1) so that the filter accepts 200 kHz but rejects 150 kHz.

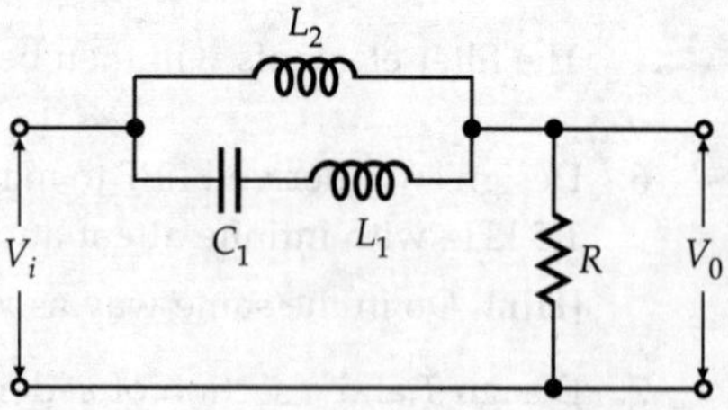

Fig. P15.2

[**Hint.** Series resonance will occur for L_1 and C_1.

This will cause pass band for the filter accepting 200 kHz ($= f_r$) signal.

Thus from the expression

$$f_r = \frac{1}{2\pi\sqrt{L_1 C_1}}, \text{ find } C_1$$

At resonance frequency of 150 kHz, the tank circuit will behave as a rejector circuit.

The impedance of the series is given by $Z = j(X_{L1} - X_{C1})$ at $f_r' = 150$ kHz.

To have a resonance in the tank circuit, this series Z must be equal to the inductive reactance of the parallel branch.

$\therefore \quad |Z| = |X_{L2}|$ at 150 kHz.

This gives L_2].

CHAPTER

16

Fundamentals of Active Filters

16.1 INTRODUCTION

From the earlier texts it may be observed that the design of passive filters (prototype and *m*–derived) largely depends on response of characteristic impedance variation and also on the matching between filter sections. The load on any particular section of the filter becomes the image impedance of the following circuit/section. On the other hand, the modern design of filters takes into consideration the transfer function in order to achieve the desired characteristics. *Active filters* are thus designed using operational amplifiers (op-amps). Active filters have some more advantages as listed below :

(*a*) Bulky inductors are dispensed with in active filter design and only resistors, capacitors and op-amps are used. This saves cost, makes the design more compact and reduces the loss.

(*b*) Active filters have much higher gain and have inherently high input impedance with low output impedance.

(*c*) Active filters are easily made compatible with IC circuits due to absence of inductors in the circuits.

(*d*) *Q* factor is comparatively higher in case of active filter circuits.

However, the active filters require high grade technology for selected components and to achieve the desired characteristic and control. One more drawback of such a filter is that the selectivity and the cut-off frequency becomes a function of gain of the op-amp and the value of feedback components. Moreover, at very low frequencies, the stability of the active filter is inferior then that of passive filters.

16.2 THEORY OF ACTIVE FILTERS

A filter being a two-port network transmitting signals in a specified range of frequencies (without attenuation), the transfer function can be represented by the ratio of following polynomials

$$H(s) = \frac{a_2 s^2 + a_1 s + a_0}{b_2 s^2 + b_1 s + b_0}$$

$$= A\frac{(s+s_1)(s+s_2)}{(s+s_a)(s+s_b)} \qquad ...(16.1)$$

Here, *a* being the pass band gain, $-s_1$ and $-s_2$ are the zeros while $-s_a$ and $-s_b$ are the poles of the biquadratic polynomials. Since there are only two poles existing in the denominator polynomial hence this particular representation is referred to a *second order filter* representation. The *order* of the filter is referred to as the number of poles in the denominator of the transfer function.

In case of a first order low pass filter, single pole will appear in the denominator of the transfer function and the magnitude of the transfer function will fall with $\frac{1}{\omega}\left(\text{or } \frac{1}{f}\right)$ at all frequencies above the cut-off frequency. The transfer function of the second order low pass filter will decrease with $\frac{1}{\omega^2}\left(\text{or } \frac{1}{f^2}\right)$ with presence of the two poles in the denominator of the polynomial. In this case the transition zone from pass-band to stop band will be steeper than the transition characteristic of the first order LP filter. It has been observed that filter with higher order have sharper transition characteristics.

The fact that a second order filter introduces $\frac{1}{\omega^2}$ form at high frequencies can be evident by adjusting the polynomial coefficients b_0, b_1, b_2 of the denominator for the given transfer function of the second order filter under consideration. The overall behaviour of the filter *i.e.*, whether this will behave as LP, HP, BP or BS would be established by adjusting the coefficient a_0, a_1, a_2 of the numerator polynomial.

Since $H(s) = \frac{a_2 s^2 + a_1 s + a_0}{b_2 s^2 + b_1 s + b_0}$,

by adjusting $a_1 = a_2 = 0$ we find

$$H(s) = \frac{a_0}{b_2 s^2 + b_1 s + b_0}$$

$$= \frac{\frac{a_0}{b_2}}{s^2 + \left(\frac{b_1}{b_2}\right)s + \frac{b_0}{b_2}}$$

Normalising by ω_0, the cut-off frequency, the transfer function becomes $\frac{a_0}{b_2\left(\frac{s}{\omega_0}\right)^2 + b_1\left(\frac{s}{\omega_0}\right) + b_0}$

i.e., $$H(s) = \frac{K\omega_0^2}{s^2 + \left(\frac{\omega_0}{Q}\right) + \omega_0^2} \quad ...(16.2)$$

where, K, ω_0 and Q can be expressed in terms of a_1, b_1, a_0 and b_0.

Since by adjusting the coefficients of the polynomials it is possible to realise the different type of filter characteristics, if evident from the transfer function that

(*i*) **With $a_2 = a_1 = 0$,**

$$H(s) = \frac{a_0}{b_2 s^2 + b_1 s + b_0}$$

At frequencies near $s = j\omega = 0$,

$$H(s) = \frac{a_0}{b_0} = \text{constant}$$

and at high frequencies,

$$H(s) = \frac{a_0}{b_2 s^2}.$$

Since $s = j\omega$, $|H(j\omega)|$ decreases with increase of ω^2 and as $|H(j\omega)|$ signifies gain, it is evident that the increase of frequency makes the gain extremely low thus achieving the LP filter characteristics (Fig. 16.1)

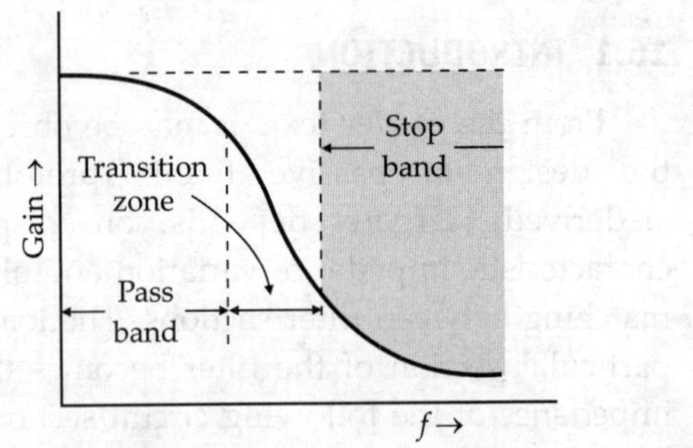

Fig. 16.1 LP filter characteristic.

(*ii*) Again, **with $a_1 = a_0 = 0$,**

$$H(s) = \frac{a_2 s^2}{b_2 s^2 + b_1 s + b_0};$$

at frequency near $s = j\omega = 0$,

$$H(s) = 0;$$

i.e., at very low frequency/frequencies, the gain is almost nil indicating stop band at lower range of frequencies.

On the other hand, at high frequencies,

$$H(s) \simeq \frac{a_2 s^2}{b_2 s^2} \simeq \frac{a_2}{b_2} = \text{constant}.$$

Thus, at higher range of frequencies, the signal passes through thus representing the HP filter characteristics (Fig. 16.2).

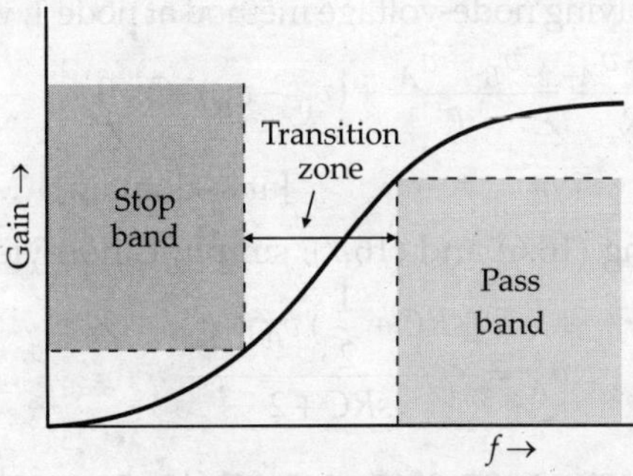

Fig. 16.2 HP filter characteristic.

In a similar way, by adjusting the coefficients of the numerator and denominator polynomials, the band pass and band stop filters can also be realised.

For band pass (BP) filter,

$$H(s) = \frac{a_1 s}{b_2 s^2 + b_1 s + b_0} \qquad \text{...(16.3)}$$

With $s = j\omega$, at very low ω, $H(s) \to 0$ while for very high ω, $H(s)$ becomes extremely small due to presence of s^2 term in the denominator. $H(s)$ remains constant at a middle frequency range.

Also, for $a_1 = 0$

$$H(s) = \frac{a_2 s^2 + a_0}{b_2 s^2 + b_1 s + b_0}$$

gives the band stop filter characteristics.

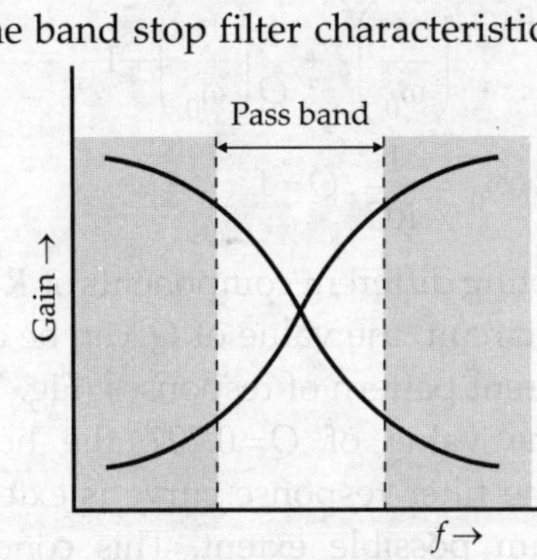

Fig. 16.3 BP characteristic.

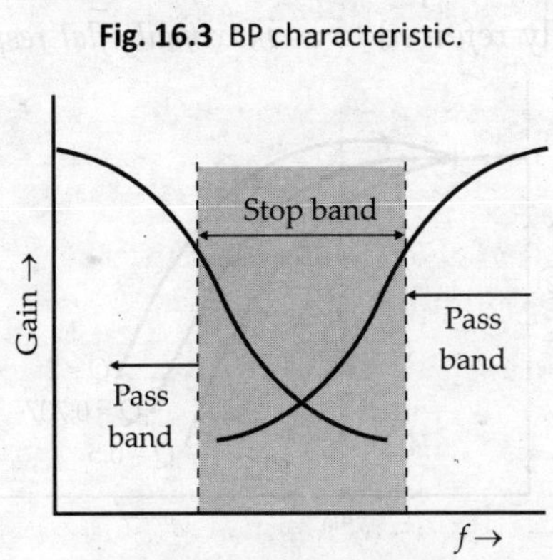

Fig. 16.4 BS characteristic.

16.3 REALISATION OF ACTIVE LPF

(i) First order LPF

Figure 16.5 represents an op-amp. based active filter circuit. This circuit is basically a non-inverting amplifier relating v_A and v_0. Let us first analyse the non-inverting amplifier circuit only (Fig. 16.5).

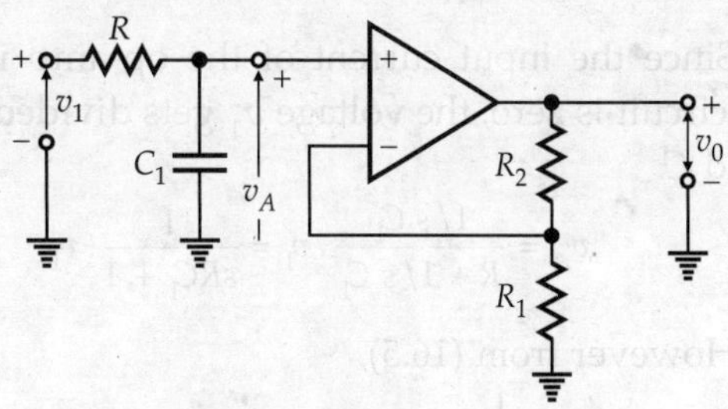

Fig. 16.5 OP-amp based Action LPF.

The input signal is applied at the non-inverting terminal. v_2 being +ve, v_0 would be positive, i is also +ve. Voltage $v_1\ (= iR_1)$ is applied to the inverting terminal as –ve voltage feedback signal. Assuming the op-amp to be ideal, $i_{in} = 0$, $v_d \simeq 0$; $v_1 \simeq v_2$.

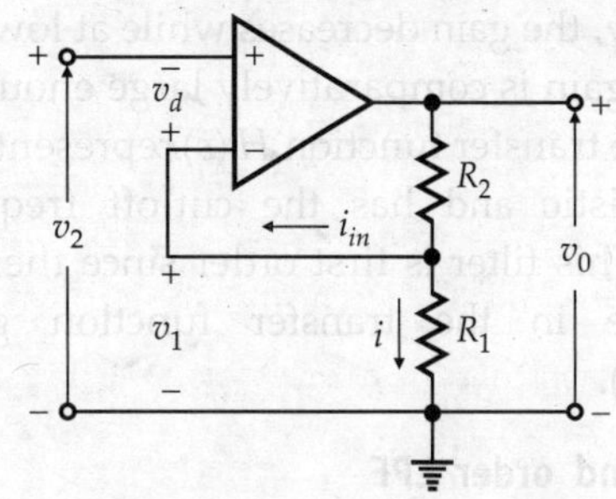

Fig. 16.6 Schematic or non-inverting of amp.

Since $i_{in} = 0$, the current through R_2 and R_1 must be same,

i.e., $$\frac{v_0 - v_1}{R_2} = \frac{v_1}{R_1}$$

or, $$\frac{v_0}{R_2} - \frac{v_1}{R_2} = \frac{v_1}{R_1}$$

or, $$\frac{v_0}{R_2} = v_1\left(\frac{1}{R_1} + \frac{1}{R_2}\right)$$

or, $$v_0 / v_1 = \frac{R_1 + R_2}{R_1}$$

or $$\frac{v_0}{v_1} = \left(1 + \frac{R_2}{R_1}\right). \qquad \text{...(16.4)}$$

Applying this concept in Fig. 16.5, with $v_A \equiv v_2$ for the particular case when $R_1 = R_2$, the gain in the non-inverting amplifier of the LPF circuit is given as

$$\frac{v_0}{v_A} = \left(1 + \frac{R_1}{R_1}\right) = 2$$

or $$v_0 = 2v_A \qquad ...(16.5)$$

Since the input current of the op-amp in the LPF circuit is zero, the voltage v_1 gets divided over R and C.

i.e., $$v_A = \frac{1/sC_1}{R + 1/sC_1} \cdot v_1 = \frac{1}{sRC_1 + 1} \cdot v_1$$

However from (16.5),

$$v_A = \frac{1}{2} v_0.$$

$$\therefore \quad v_A = \frac{1}{2} v_0 = \frac{1}{sRC_1 + 1} \cdot v_1$$

or $$\frac{v_0}{v_1} = \frac{2}{sRC_1 + 1} \quad (= H(s))$$

Since v_0 / v_1 is the net gain of the LPF circuit and $s = j\omega$ hence, with higher value of ω, the frequency, the gain decreases while at lower values of ω, the gain is comparatively large enough. Thus, the above transfer function $H(s)$ represents the LPF characteristic and has the cut-off frequency of $1/RC_1$. This filter is first order since there is only one pole in the transfer function given by $(-1/RC_1)$.

(ii) Second order LPF

It has been obtained earlier that for the non-inverting amplifier, the output voltage v_0 is related to v_B (Fig. 16.7) by the relation

$$v_0 = \left(1 + \frac{R_1}{R_1}\right) v_B = 2\,v_B \qquad ...(16.6)$$

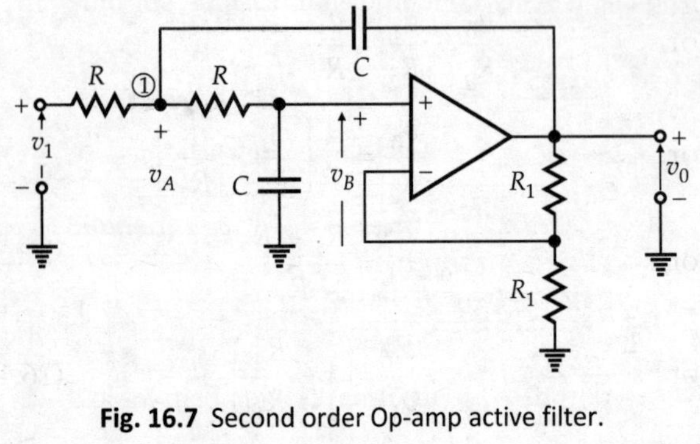

Fig. 16.7 Second order Op-amp active filter.

Applying node-voltage method at node 1, we get

$$\frac{v_1 - v_A}{R} + \frac{v_B - v_A}{R} + (v_0 - v_B)\,sC = 0$$

[at s–domain] ...(16.7)

Using (16.6) and (16.7), simplification yields

$$v_A = \frac{(sRC + \frac{1}{2})\,v_0 + v_1}{sRC + 2} \qquad ...(16.8)$$

Assuming op-amp current to be negligibly small, the input voltage division is as follows :

$$v_B\left(-\frac{1}{2} v_0\right) = \frac{1/sC}{R + 1/sC} v_A \qquad ...(16.9)$$

Substituting for v_A from (16.8) in (16.10) simplification yields

$$\frac{v_0}{v_1} = \frac{\frac{2}{(RC)^2}}{s^2 + \left(\frac{1}{RC}\right)s + \left(\frac{1}{RC}\right)^2} \quad (= H(s))$$

$$= \frac{K\omega_0^2}{s^2 + \left(\frac{\omega_0}{Q}\right)s + \omega_0^2}$$

i.e., $$\frac{v_0}{v_1} = \frac{K}{\left(\frac{s}{\omega_0}\right)^2 + \frac{1}{Q}\left(\frac{s}{\omega_0}\right) + 1}$$

where, $K = 2$, $\omega_0 = \frac{1}{RC}$, $Q = 1$.

By adjusting different components of R and C in the op-amp circuit, the value of Q can be adjusted to give different pattern of responses (Fig. 16.8). By adjusting the value of $Q = 0.707$, the horizontal portion of the filter response curve is extended to the maximum possible extent. This condition is frequently referred to as *maximally flat response.*

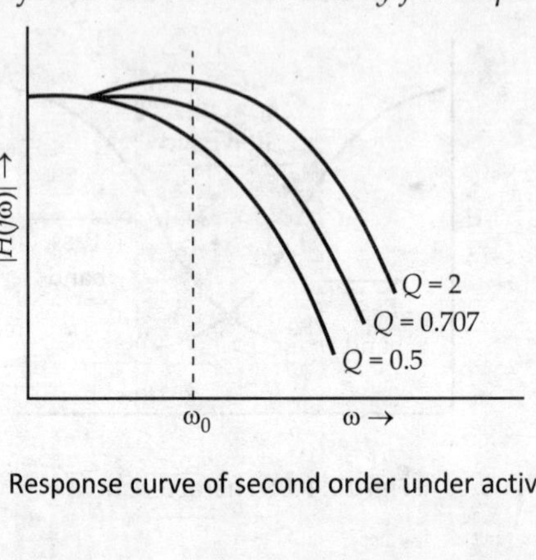

Fig. 16.8 Response curve of second order under active filter.

(iii) First Order HPF

Figure 16.9 represents a first order HPF using op-amp circuitry. Following the relation for non-inverting amplifier relating v_A and v_0, for this particular circuit,

$$v_0 = \left(1 + \frac{R_1}{R_1}\right) V_A = 2V_A \quad \text{...(16.11)}$$

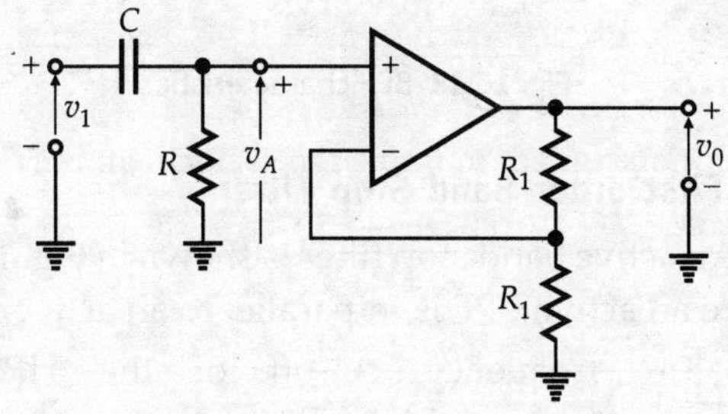

Fig. 16.9 Schematic of a first order HPF.

Since the op-amp is assumed to be ideal, there is practically no input current of the op-amp and the voltage division for V_1 would be across the capacitor and R only (in Fig. 16.9). Thus, in laplace domain,

$$V_A = \frac{R}{R + 1/sC} v_1 = \frac{sRC}{sRC + 1} v_1 \quad \text{...(16.12)}$$

From (16.11), $V_A = \frac{v_0}{2}$; using the expression for v_A in (16.12), we get,

$$\frac{v_0}{2} = \frac{sRC}{sRC + 1} v_1$$

or, $$\frac{v_0}{v_1} = \frac{2 . sRC}{sRC + 1} \quad \text{...(16.13)}$$

Expression (16.13) reveals that using $s = j\omega$, the gain becomes high and constant at higher values of ω while it is very low at lower order frequencies. Thus the circuit shown in Fig. 16.9 represents that of a HP filter circuit, the cut-off frequency is $1/RC$.

(iv) Second Order HPF

The active component of the circuit shown in Fig. 16.10 is a non-inverting amplifier ; v_A and v_0 are related by

$$v_0 = \left(1 + \frac{R}{R}\right) v_A = 2\, v_A \quad \text{...(16.14)}$$

Applying node-voltage analysis at node (1), we get

$$\frac{(v_1 - v_B)}{1/sC} + \frac{v_A - v_B}{1/sC} + \frac{v_0 - v_B}{R} = 0$$

or $(v_1 - v_B)sC + (v_A - v_B)sC + (v_0 - v_B)/R = 0.$ ...(16.15)

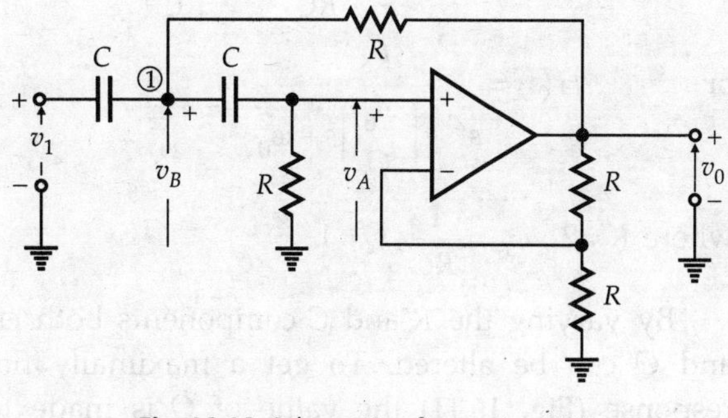

Fig. 16.10 Schematic of an active HPF.

Using $v_A = \frac{v_0}{2}$ from (16.14), and substituting in (16.15) rearrangement results

$$v_B = \frac{\left(\frac{1}{2} sRC + 1\right) v_0 + sRC\, v_1}{S.2\, RC} \quad \text{...(16.16)}$$

Assuming the op-amp to be ideal, voltage division results for the circuit shown in Fig. 16.10

$$v_A\left(= \frac{1}{2} v_0\right) = \frac{R}{R + 1/sC} . v_B$$

$$= \frac{sRC}{sRC + 1} . v_B \quad \text{...(16.17)}$$

Using (16.16) and (16.17) rearrangement results

$$\frac{v_0}{v_1} = \frac{2s^2}{s^2 + \frac{1}{RC} . s + \left(\frac{1}{RC}\right)^2} \quad \text{...(16.18)}$$

Thus the transfer takes the form of

$$H(s) = \left(= \frac{v_0}{v_1}\right) = \frac{a_2 s^2}{b_2 s^2 + b_1 s + b_0}$$

i.e., that of HPF.

The presence of s^2 term in the numerator and denominator makes the gain very high and constant when the input frequency is very high. On the other hand, for lower ranges of frequencies, $H(s)$ becomes appreciably low. Thus, the given circuit (Fig. 16.10) represents a HP filter. Due to presence of two poles in the denominator in the expression of the gain of the HPF, this representation is commonly called **second order filter.**

The transfer function $H(s)$ for this filter can be represented in the following form :

$$H(s) = \frac{v_0}{v_1} = \frac{2s^2}{s^2 + \frac{1}{RC}.s + \left(\frac{1}{RC}\right)^2}$$

or $$H(s) = \frac{Ks^2}{s^2 + \left(\frac{\omega_0}{Q}\right)s + \omega_0^2}$$

where $K = 2$; $\omega_0 = \frac{1}{RC}$, $Q = 1$.

By varying the R and C components both ω_0 and Q can be altered. To get a maximally flat response (Fig. 16.11) the value of Q is made to be 0.707.

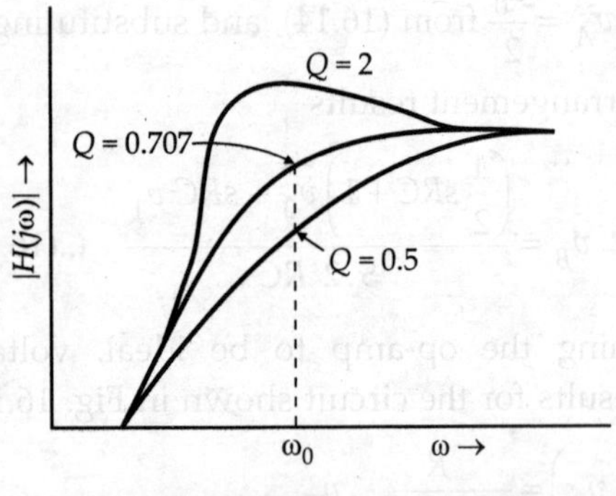

Fig. 16.11 Active HPF characteristic.

(v) First order BP filter

Figure 16.12 represents active band-pass filter obtained by cascading one active LPF with one HPF where $f_1 = \frac{1}{2\pi R_1 C_1}$ and $f_2 = \frac{1}{2\pi R_0 C_0}$

$f_1 \rightarrow$ high frequency cut-off of LPF ;

$f_2 \rightarrow$ low frequency cut-off HPF.

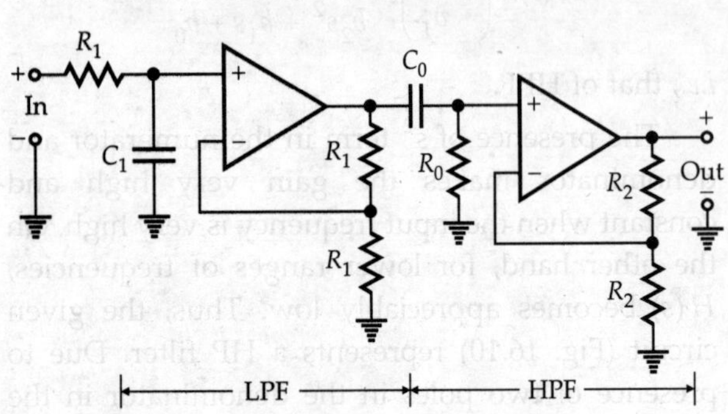

Fig. 16.12 Active band-pass filter.

The characteristic of active BPF is shown below (Fig. 16.13) :

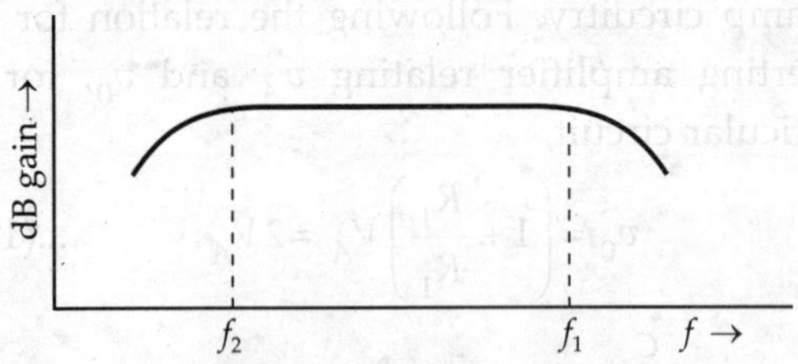

Fig. 16.13 BPF characteristic.

(vi) First order Band Stop Filter

An active band stop filter is shown in Fig. 16.14, where an active LPF is in parallel to an active HPF. The low frequency cut-off of the HPF is $f_2 = \frac{1}{2\pi R_1 C_1}$ while high freq-cut-off of LPF is $f_1 = \frac{1}{2\pi R_0 C_0}$ The final op. amp. stage acts as a summer.

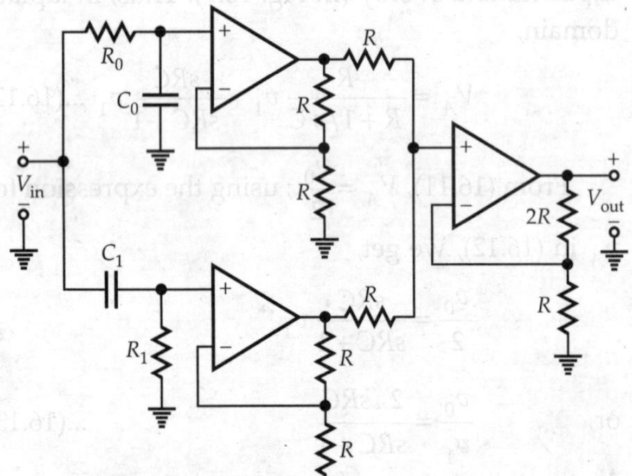

Fig. 16.14 An active band stop filter.

The characteristic of an active BSF is shown in Fig. 16.15.

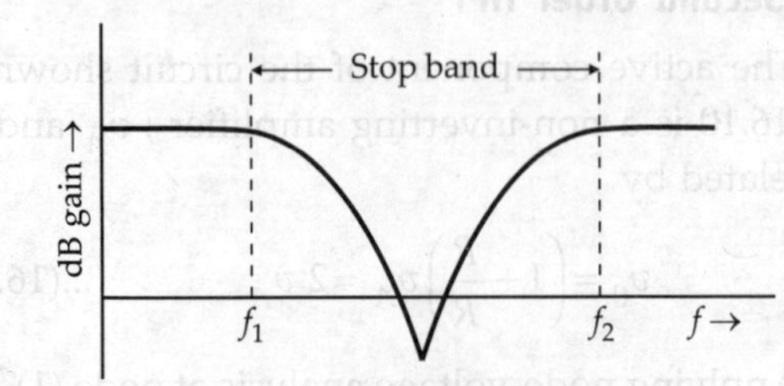

Fig. 16.15 Active BSF characteristic.

16.4 CASCADING OF SIMILAR FILTERS

Cascading similar types of active filters produce filter transfer function of increased order. The overall transfer function of the cascaded similar type of filters becomes equal to the product of transfer functions of each of the individual stages. In general, the higher the order of a filter cascade, the more closely its transfer function approaches the ideal response of the filters.

Since the various poles in a cascade act jointly to produce the overall response, it is convenient to describe the response of the filter in terms of the magnitude squared of its transfer function $H(s)$. $|H(s)|^2$ becomes $|H(j\omega)|^2$ in sinusoidal steady state analysis with $s = j\omega$ The transfer function then becomes a function of ω^2.

The ideal low pass filter having a response of magnitude of $\frac{a_0}{b_0}(=A_0)$ in the pass band, the cascaded filter response can be generalised as

$$|H(j\omega)^2| = A_0^2 \quad \text{for } 0 < \omega < \omega_0$$
$$= 0 \quad \text{for } \omega > \omega_0$$

Also,

$$|H(\omega)|^2 = A_0^2 \cdot \frac{1 + a_1\omega^2 + a_2\omega^4 + \ldots + a_m\omega^{2m}}{1 + b_1\omega^2 + b_2\omega^4 + b_m\omega^{2m} + b_{m+1}\omega^{2m+1} + \ldots + b_n\omega^{2n}}$$

Here the transfer function $|H(\omega)|^2$ is made as flat as possible at $\omega=0$. Then $|H(\omega)|^2$ is termed as **maximally flat magnitude squared** (MFMS) function. The function is assumed to be a ratio of polynomials, maximally flat response is activated as follows ;

Expanding $|H(\omega)|^2$ $(=T(\omega))$ function in a McLaurian series about $\omega=0$, we get

$$T = 1 + \frac{T^2}{2!}\omega^2 + \frac{T^4}{4!}\omega^4 + \ldots \quad \ldots(16.119)$$

where T^2 represents $\frac{d^2T}{d\omega^2}$, T^4 represents $\frac{d^4T}{d\omega^4}$ and so on.

For $m < n$, the numerator is divided by the denominator in a long division and then

$$T = 1 + (a_1 - b_1)\,\omega^2 + [(a_2 - b_2) - b_1(a_1 - b_1)]\,\omega^4 + \ldots \quad \ldots(16.20)$$

Since the requirement of the maximal flatness of T is that all the derivatives $T^2, T^4 \ldots$ equal to zero, we find by comparing (16.19) and (16.20),

$$a_1 = b_1$$
$$a_2 = b_2$$
$$\ldots\ldots\ldots$$
$$a_m = b_m$$
$$b_{m+1} = b_{m+2} = \ldots = b_{2n-1} = 0\,;\, b_n \neq 0.$$

$$\therefore\ |H(\omega)|^2 = T(\omega) = A_0^2 = \frac{(1 + a_1\omega^2 + a_2\omega^4 + \ldots + a_m\omega^{2m})}{(1 + a_1\omega^2 + a_2\omega^4 + \ldots + a_m\omega^{2m} + b_n\omega^{2n})}$$

Adjusting all a's to be zero,

$$a_1 = a_2 = \ldots = a_m = 0.$$

$$\text{Thus, } T(\omega) = \frac{A_0^2 \times 1}{1 + b_n\omega^{2n}} = \frac{A_0^2}{1 + f(\omega)^2}$$

For LPF, $f(\omega)^2$ must be chosen in such a way so that

$$f(\omega)^2 << 1 \quad \text{for} \quad \omega < \omega_0$$
$$f(\omega)^2 >> 1 \quad \text{for} \quad \omega > \omega_0.$$

For HPF, $f(\omega)^2$ must be chosen in the reverse way such that

$$f(\omega)^2 >> 1 \quad \text{for} \quad \omega < \omega_0$$
$$f(\omega)^2 << 1 \quad \text{for} \quad \omega > \omega_0.$$

Choice of $f(\omega)^2$ makes the realisation of *Butterworth* or *Chebyshev* type filters.

16.5 BUTTERWORTH FILTER

In the general form of cascaded LPF transfer function $|H(\omega)|^2 = \frac{A_0^2}{1 + f(\omega)^2}$ if we select $f(\omega)^2$ as $(\omega^2/\omega_0^2)^n$, the cascaded transfer function takes the form of

$$|H(\omega)|^2 = \frac{A_0^2}{1 + \left(\frac{\omega}{\omega_0}\right)^{2n}} = \frac{A_0^2}{B_n^2(\omega)}$$

where $B_n^2(\omega) = 1 + \left(\frac{\omega}{\omega_0}\right)^{2n}$ and is called *Butterworth polynomial*, n being a positive integer indicating the

CHAPTER 16

order of filter cascade. Fig. 16.16 represents the normalised frequency response for various values of n. It may observed that for higher values of n, the response of the Butterworth filter approaches the ideal response of low pass filter.

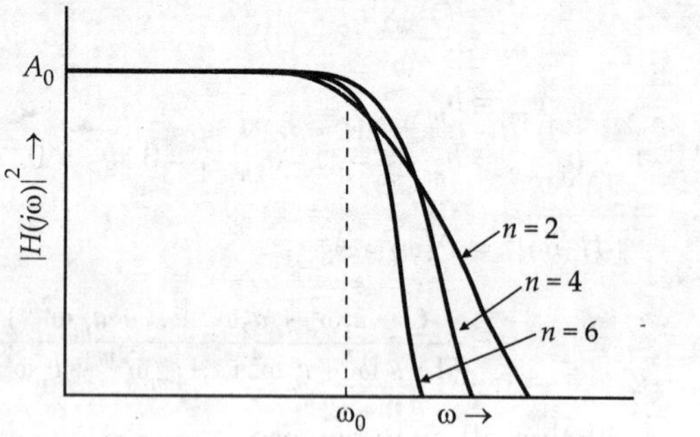

Fig. 16.16 Response of Butterworth LPF.

16.6 REALISATION OF ACTIVE BUTTERWORTH FILTER

(i) First order LPF

Figure 16.17 represents an active LPF (Butterworth type). Here v_0 and v are related by

$$v_0 = \left(1 + \frac{R_2}{R_1}\right) v$$

or
$$\frac{v_0}{v} = \left(1 + \frac{R_2}{R_1}\right) = A_0.$$

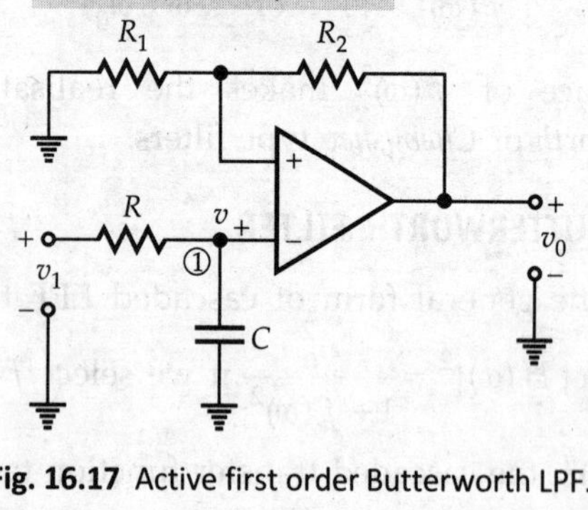

Fig. 16.17 Active first order Butterworth LPF.

Assuming the input current of op.amp to be zero, nodal analysis at node (1) gives

$$\frac{v - v_1}{R} + \frac{v}{1/sC} = 0$$

or
$$v\left(\frac{1}{R} + sC\right) = \frac{v_1}{R}$$

or
$$v / v_1 = \frac{1}{sRC + 1}$$

or
$$\frac{v}{v_0} \cdot \frac{v_0}{v_1} = \frac{1}{1 + sRC}$$

or
$$\frac{v_0}{v_1} = \frac{A_0}{1 + sRC} \qquad \left[\because \frac{v_0}{v} = A_0\right]$$

i.e.,
$$H(s) = \frac{A_0}{1 + sRC} = \frac{A_0}{1 + \left(\dfrac{s}{\omega_0}\right)} \qquad \text{...(16.21)}$$

Here expression (16.21) represents the standard form of Butterworth expression for $n = 1$. It may be observed that $\omega_0 = \frac{1}{RC}$ representing the cut-off frequency.

(ii) Second order LPF

Figure 16.18 represents a second order active Butterworth LPF. As before, the voltages v and v_0 are related by the following relation

$$v_0 = v\left(1 + \frac{R_2}{R_1}\right)$$

or
$$\frac{v_0}{v} = A_0 = \left(1 + \frac{R_2}{R_1}\right) \qquad \text{...(16.22)}$$

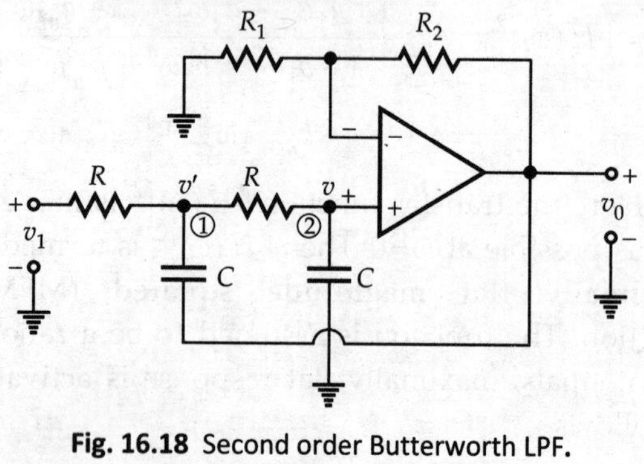

Fig. 16.18 Second order Butterworth LPF.

Applying nodal analysis at node (1),

$$\frac{-v_1 + v'}{R} + \frac{v'}{1/sC} + \frac{v' - v}{R} = 0 \qquad \text{...(16.23)}$$

and for node (2),

$$\frac{v' - v}{R} + \frac{v}{1/sC} = 0 \qquad \text{...(16.24)}$$

[assuming op-amp input current to be zero]

Eliminating v' and substituting $A_0 = \frac{v_0}{v}$,

$$H(s) = \frac{v_0}{v_1} = \frac{A_0}{\left(\dfrac{s}{\omega_0}\right)^2 + (3 - A_0)\left(\dfrac{s}{\omega_0}\right) + 1}.$$

The above form of representation is a second order form of LPF and may also be written in the form of

$$H(s) = \frac{A_0}{\left(\frac{s}{\omega_0}\right)^2 + 2K\left(\frac{s}{\omega_0}\right) + 1}$$

where $2K = (3 - A_0)$ or, $A_0 = (3 - 2K)$ and $\omega_0 = (1/RC)$; $A_0 = 1 + \frac{R_2}{R_1}$.

16.7 BUTTERWORTH HIGH PASS FILTER

Transformation of the concept of LPF to HPF is possible by applying the following transformation in the expression of $H(s)$.

$$\left.\frac{s}{\omega_0}\right|_{LPF} \Rightarrow \left.\frac{s}{s/\omega_0}\right|_{HPF}$$

Since for LPF, $H(s) = \frac{1}{H\left(\frac{s}{\omega_0}\right)}$,

for HPF, following the transformation,

$$H(s) = \frac{1}{1 + \frac{1}{s/\omega_0}} = \frac{s/\omega_0}{1 + s/\omega_0}. \quad ...(16.24)$$

The physical significance of this transformation is interchange of R and C in the active LPF circuit whether it is of first order or of higher order (Fig. 16.19) (see also article 16.13).

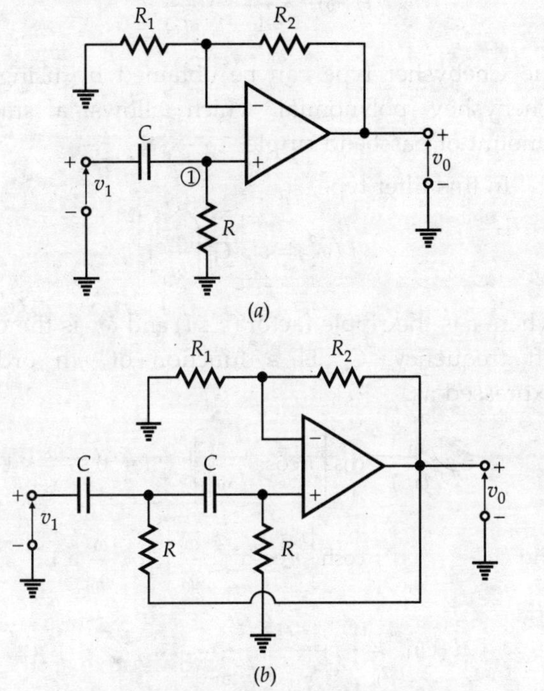

Fig. 16.19 (*a*) First order active Butterworth HPF. (*b*) Second order active Butterworth HPF.

16.8 FOURTH ORDER ACTIVE BUTTERWORTH LPF AND HPF

Here we cascade two LP and HP filters of second order so as to arrange for fourth order LPF or HPF (Fig. 16.20 and Fig. 16.21).

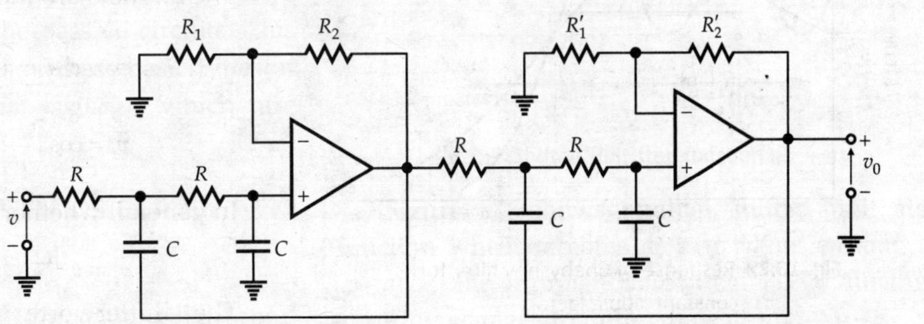

Fig. 16.20 Fourth order active Butterworth LPF

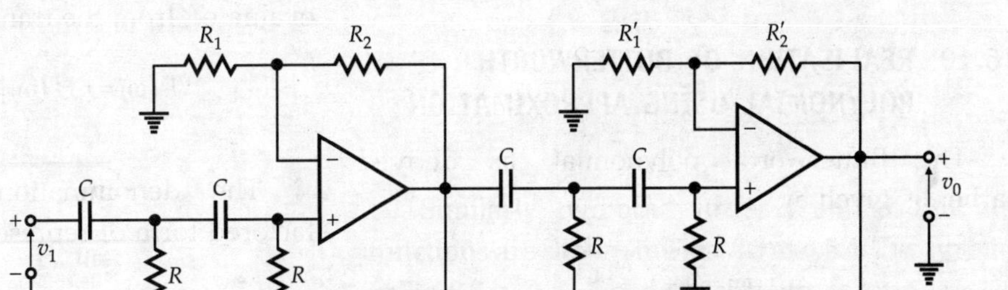

Fig. 16.21 Fourth order active Butterworth HPF

16.9 CHEBYSHEV FILTER

Since the filter response can be approximated by the following function

$$|H(\omega)|^2 = \frac{A_0^2}{1+f(\omega^2)},$$

the Chebysher type can be obtained by using a Chebyshev polynomial which allows a small amount of passband ripple.

In this filter type,

$$f(\omega^2) = \varepsilon^2\left[C_n\left(\frac{\omega}{\omega_0}\right)\right]^2$$

where ε is the ripple factor ($\varepsilon \le 1$) and ω_0 is the cut off frequency. C_n is a function of nth order expressed as

$$C_n\left(\frac{\omega}{\omega_0}\right) = \cos\left[n\cos^{-1}\frac{\omega}{\omega_0}\right] \quad \text{for } 0 \le \frac{\omega}{\omega_0} \le 1$$

and

$$= \cosh\left[n\cosh^{-1}\frac{\omega}{\omega_0}\right] \quad \text{for } \frac{\omega}{\omega_0} \ge 1$$

$$\therefore |H(\omega)|^2 = \frac{A_0^2}{1+\varepsilon^2 C_n^2\left(\frac{\omega}{\omega_0}\right)}$$

Figure 16.22 represents the response of Chebyshev's filter.

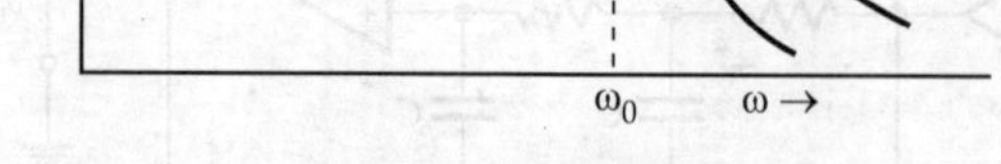

Fig. 16.22 Response of Chebyshev filter for constant ripple factor.

16.10 REALISATION OF BUTTERWORTH POLYNOMIAL USING APPROXIMATION

The Butterworth polynomial, as derived earlier, is given by

$$B_n^2(\omega) = 1+\left(\frac{\omega}{\omega_0}\right)^{2n}.$$

Normalising for $\omega_0 = 1$ rad/sec.,

$$\therefore \quad B_n^2(\omega) = 1+\omega^{2n}$$

However,

$$B_n^2(\omega) \equiv |B_n(j\omega)|^2$$

$$= B_n(s)\,B_n(-s)|_{s=j\omega}$$

$$= 1+(-s^2)^n|_{s^2=-\omega^2}$$

The zeros ($2n$ numbers) of $[B_n(s)\,B_n(-s)]$ are obtained by solving $1+(-1)^n s^{2n} = 0$.

Case 1. [n is even]

The equation $1+(-1)^n s^{2n} = 0$ reduces to $s^{2n} = -1$ which can also be written in form of $s^{2n} = -1 = e^{j(2i-1)\pi}$.

Obviously, the $2n$ roots are given by

$$p_i = e^{j\frac{2i-1}{2n}.\pi}, i = 1, 2, \ldots, 2n$$

or

$$p_i = \cos\left(\frac{2i-1}{2n}.\pi\right) + j\sin\left(\frac{2i-1}{2n}.\pi\right).$$

Case 2. [n is odd]

The equation $1+(-1)^n s^{2n} = 0$ reduces to $s^{2n} = 1$; which can be further written as

$$s^{2n} = 1 = e^{j2i\pi}$$

The $2n$ roots are then given by

$$p_i = e^{j\frac{i}{n}.\pi}, i = 0, .1, \ldots (2n-1)$$

i.e.,

$$p_i = \cos\left(\frac{i}{n}\pi\right) + j\sin\left(\frac{i}{n}\pi\right).$$

In general, whether n is odd or even,

$$p_i = e^{j[(2i+n-1)/2n]\pi}.$$

The Butterworth polynomial can then be evaluated from the transfer formation

$$T(\omega) = |H(\omega)|^2 = \frac{A_0^2}{B_n^2(\omega)}$$

The denomination polynomial can have factored form of representation as follows :

$$B_n^2(s) = (s+e^{j\theta_1})(s+e^{-j\theta_1}), \text{ for } n = 2$$

(where $\theta_1 = \frac{2i-1}{2n} . \pi$ for $i = 1, 2, ..., 2n$)

$$= s^2 + s(e^{j\theta_1} + e^{-j\theta_1}) + 1$$

$$= s^2 + 2\left[\frac{e^{j\theta_1} + e^{-j\theta_1}}{2}\right] s + 1$$

$$= s^2 + 2\cos\theta_1 . s + 1$$

$$= s^2 + 2\cos\frac{\pi}{4} . s + 1$$

$$= s^2 + \sqrt{2}\, s + 1$$

In general form, the Butterworth polynomial (for $n =$ even) is given by

$$B_n^2(s) = \prod_{i=1}^{n/2} (s^2 + 2\cos\theta_i\, s + 1)$$

for $\theta_i = \frac{2i-1}{2n} . \pi$

Again, for $n = 3$,

$$B_n^2(s) = (s+1)(s + e^{j\theta_1})(s + e^{-j\theta_1})$$

$$= (s+1)(s^2 + 2\cos\theta_1 s + 1)$$

where $\theta_1 = \frac{\pi}{n}$ for $n = 3$ giving $\theta_1 = \frac{\pi}{3}$.

$$\therefore \quad B_n^2(s) = (s+1)\left(s^2 + 2\cos\frac{\pi}{3} + 1\right)$$

$$= (s+1)(s^2 + s + 1)$$

$$= s^3 + 2s^2 + 2s + 1.$$

In general form, the Butterworth polynomial (for $n =$ odd) is given by

$$B_n^2(s) = \left[\prod_{i=1}^{(n-1)/2} (s^2 + 2\cos\theta_i\, s + 1)\right](s+1)$$

for $\theta_i = \frac{\pi}{n}$

Similarly, for $n = 4$, the Butterworth polynomial is given by

$$(s + e^{j\frac{5}{8}\pi})(s + e^{j\frac{7}{8}\pi})(s + e^{j\frac{9}{8}\pi})(s + e^{j\frac{11}{8}\pi})$$

$$= (s^2 + 0.76536\, s + 1)(s^2 + 1.84775\, s + 1).$$

CHAPTER 16

Table 16.1 represents the Butterworth polynomials in tabular form upto 7th order.

Table 16.1 Butterworth Polynomial

n	*Roots*	*Factors*	*Polynomials*
1.	-1	$(s + 1)$	$(s + 1)$
2.	$-\cos\frac{\pi}{4} \pm j\sin\frac{\pi}{4}$	$(s^2 + \sqrt{2}\, s + 1)$	$(s^2 + 1.414\, s + 1)$
3.	$-1, -\cos\frac{\pi}{3} \pm j\sin\frac{\pi}{3}$	$(s + 1)(s^2 + s + 1)$	$(s^3 + 2s^2 + 2s + 1)$
4.	$-\cos i\frac{\pi}{8} \pm j\sin i\frac{\pi}{8} (i = 1, 3)$	$(s^2 + 0.765\, s + 1)\ (s^2 + 1.848 + 1)$	$(s^4 + 2.613\, s^3 + 3.414\, s^2 + 2.613\, s + 1)$
5.	$-1, -\cos\frac{i\pi}{5} \pm j\sin\frac{i\pi}{5} (i = 1, 2)$	$(s+ 1)(s^2 + 0.618s + 1)(s^2 + 1.618s + 1)$	$(s^5 + 3.236\, s^4 + 5.236\, s^3 + 5.236\, s^2 + 3.236\, s + 1)$
6.	$-\cos i\frac{\pi}{12} \pm j\sin i\frac{\pi}{12} (i = 1, 3, 5)$	$(s^2 + 0.518\, s + 1)(s^2 + 1.414\, s + 1)(s^2 + 1.932\, s + 1)$	$(s^6 + 3.864 s^5 + 7.464\, s^4 + 9.142\, s^3 + 7.464\, s^2 + 3.864\, s + 1)$
7.	$-1, -\cos i . \frac{\pi}{7} \pm j\sin i\frac{\pi}{7} (i = 1, 2, 3)$	$(s + 1)(s^2 + 0.44\, s + 1)(s^2 + 1.247\, s + 1), (s^2 + 1.802\, s + 1)$	$(s^7 + 4.494\, s^6 + 10.098\, s^5 + 14.92\, s^4 + 14.592\, s^3 + 10.098\, s^2 + 4.494\, s + 1)$

16.11 REALISATION OF CHEBYSHEV'S POLYNOMIAL USING APPROXIMATION

We have earlier seen that the C_n function in the Chebyshev polynomial is represented as

$$\cos\left(n\cos^{-1}\frac{\omega}{\omega_0}\right) \quad \text{for } 0 \le \frac{\omega}{\omega_0} \le 1$$

and as $$\cosh\left(n\cosh^{-1}\frac{\omega}{\omega_0}\right) \quad \text{for } \frac{\omega}{\omega_0} \ge 1.$$

Normalising with $\omega_0 = 1$,

$$C_n(\omega) = \cos(n\cos^{-1}\omega) \quad \text{for } |\omega| \le 1$$

and $$= \cosh(n\cosh^{-1}\omega) \quad \text{for } |\omega| \ge 1$$

i.e., $$C_n(\omega) = \text{Re}|e^{jn\phi}|$$

$$= \text{Re}|\cos\phi + j\sin\phi|^n;\ \phi = \cos^{-1}\omega$$

i.e., $$\cos\phi = \omega,\ \sin\phi = \sqrt{1-\omega^2}$$

Binomial expansion of the above expression results

$$C_n(\omega) = \text{Re}\,[\omega + j(1-\omega^2)]^n$$

$$= \omega^n - \frac{n(n-1)}{2!}\omega^{n-2}(1-\omega^2)$$

$$+ \frac{n(n-1)(n-2)(n-3)}{4!}\omega^{n-4}(1-\omega^2)^2 \ldots$$

$$\therefore\ C_0(\omega) = 1;\ C_1(\omega) = \omega$$

$$C_2(\omega) = \omega^2 - \frac{2(2-1)}{2!}\omega^{2-2}(1-\omega^2) = 2\omega^2 - 1$$

$$C_3(\omega) = \omega^3 - \frac{3(3-1)}{2!}\omega^{3-2}(1-\omega^2) = 4\omega^3 - 3\omega.$$

Table 16.2 represents the Chebyshev's polynomials.

Table 16.2

n	
0.	1
1.	ω
2.	$2\omega^2 - 1$
3.	$4\omega^3 - 3\omega$
4.	$8\omega^4 - 8\omega^2 + 1$
5.	$16\omega^5 - 20\omega^3 + 5\omega$
6.	$32\omega^6 - 48\omega^4 + 18\omega^2 - 1$
7.	$64\omega^7 - 112\omega^5 + 56\omega^3 - 7\omega$

In order to apply the Chebyshev's polynomial to low pass filter approximation, let us consider the function $\varepsilon^2 C_n^2(\omega)$ where ε is real and small in comparison to 1. $\varepsilon^2 C_n^2(\omega)$ would then vary between 0 and ε^2 in the interval $|\omega| \le 1$. When 1 is added to it, the function $1 + \varepsilon^2 C_n^2(\omega)$ varies between 1 and $1 + \varepsilon^2$ *i.e.*, between 1 and a quantity slightly greater than unity for $|\omega| \le 1$.

Thus with $|\omega| \le 1$, $|H(j\omega)|^2 = \left[\dfrac{1}{1+\varepsilon^2 C_n^2(\omega)}\right]$

will oscillate about unity such that the maximum value is 1 and the minimum is $\dfrac{1}{1+\varepsilon^2}$. Outside this interval, $C_n^2(\omega)$ becomes very large so that ω when increases, a point is reached where $\varepsilon^2 C_n^2(\omega) \ge 1$ and $|H(j\omega)|^2$ approaches zero. Thus Chebysher's filter can be used as LP filter. We reproduce the Chebyshev's filter characteristic again (Fig. 16.23) for better understanding. In pass band, $|H(j\omega)|$ is between 1 and $\dfrac{1}{(1+\varepsilon^2)^{1/2}}$

and ripple $= 1 - \dfrac{1}{(1+\varepsilon^2)^{1/2}}$

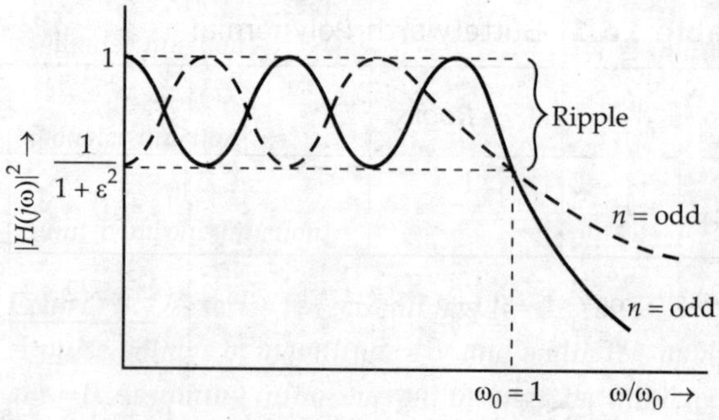

Fig. 16.23 Chebyshev's filter characteristics for n = odd/even.

At $$\omega_{cutoff} = 1,\ C_n^2(1) = 1$$

and $$|H(j\omega)| = \frac{1}{(1+\varepsilon^2)^{1/2}}$$

In stop band $|\omega| > 1$ and then at a certain stage $\varepsilon^2 C_n^2(\omega) \ge 1$ and so for $\omega > \omega_c$

$$|H(j\omega)| = \frac{1}{\varepsilon\, C_n\,.\,\omega}.$$

16.12 ELLIPTIC FILTER APPROXIMATION (CAUER FILTER)

In order to improve the performance of the Chebyshev's filter it is required to allow equiripple response in both pass and stop band. this leads to narrower transition band (Fig. 16.24).

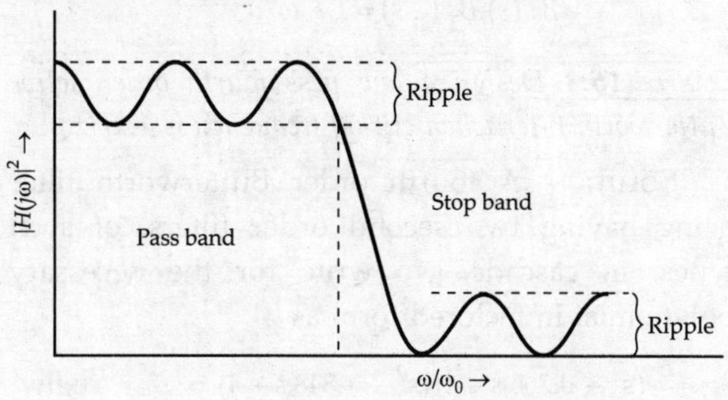

Fig. 16.24 Characteristic of elliptic filter.

Following Cauer polynomial, the polynomial is arranged in such a fashion that $C_n^2(\omega)$ is replaced by $R_n^2(\omega)$ so that

$$R_n\left(\frac{1}{\omega}\right)=\frac{1}{R_n(\omega)}$$

i.e., the polynomial poles and zeros are reciprocal to each other. This ensures that the value of $R_n(\omega)$ at a frequency ω_K in $0 \le \omega \le 1$ is reciprocal of its value at $\frac{1}{\omega_K}, 1 \le \omega \le \infty$.

16.13 FREQUENCY TRANSFORMATION

We have earlier obtained expressions for transfer function of low pass filter. We can obtain the transfer function of other variables (say of HP filter) by transformation of the frequency variable in the expression of transfer function of LPF. This is called frequency transformation and it is understandable once the reader has a knowledge of "frequency normalisation".

Let p be the complex variable for the normalised transfer function $H(p)$. Let ω_0 be given and then the complex variable be s. Thus the relation between p and s is given by

$$p=\frac{s}{\omega_0}.$$

[*i.e.*, s being normalised to ω_0 given p]

Now, considering the second order LP Butterworth filter expressed in normalised variable p, we can write (for cut-off frequency $\omega_C = 1$),

$$B_2(p)=\frac{1}{p^2+\sqrt{2}\,p+1}$$

When the cut-off frequency is ω_C instead of unity,

$$B_2\left(\frac{s}{\omega_C}\right)=\frac{1}{\left(\frac{s}{\omega_C}\right)^2+\sqrt{2}\left(\frac{s}{\omega_C}\right)+1}$$

$$=\frac{\omega_C^2}{s^2+\sqrt{2}\,\omega_C\,s+\omega_C^2}$$

Next we will see frequency transformation of LP to HP.

Let p be the variable for LP and s for HP. For normalised LPF, the pass band is from $\omega=0$ to $\omega=1$ and for HP, ω ranges from 1 to ∞.

$$\therefore\ p=\frac{1}{s}\quad \text{or,}\quad j\omega_p=\frac{1}{j\omega_s}\quad \text{or,}\quad \omega_p=-\frac{1}{\omega_s}$$

We have seen above that for LPF (Butterworth)

$$B_e(p)=\frac{1}{p^2+\sqrt{2}\,p+1}$$

which for HP can easily be written

$$B_2(s)=\frac{1}{\left(\frac{1}{s}\right)^2+\sqrt{2}\left(\frac{1}{s}\right)+1},$$

replacing p by $\frac{1}{s}$.

or, $$B_2(s)=\frac{s^2}{s^2+\sqrt{2}\,s+1}$$

Here $\omega_C=1$; for $\omega_C \ne 1$, we can replace s by $\frac{s}{\omega_C}$ and then,

$$B_2(s)=\frac{\left(\frac{s}{\omega_C}\right)^2}{\left(\frac{s}{\omega_C}\right)^2+\sqrt{2}\left(\frac{s}{\omega_C}\right)+1}$$

$$=\frac{s^2}{s^2+\sqrt{2}\,(\omega_C-s)+\omega_C^2}, \text{ for HPF.}$$

EXAMPLE 16.1 *Design a second order Butterworth low pass filter with cut-off frequency of 1 kHz.*

SOLUTION. For the second order filter, the Butterworth polynomial ($n=2$) is given by $(s^2+\sqrt{2}\,s+1)$. Comparing with the denominator of the transfer function of the second order Butterworth filter,

$$2\,k_1 = \sqrt{2}\ (= 1.414)\,;$$

$$A_0 = 3 - 2\,k_1 = 3 - 1.414$$

$$= 1.586 = 1 + \frac{R_2}{R_1}$$

Assuming $R_1 = 10\ \text{k}\Omega$, $R_2 = 5.86\ \text{k}\Omega$

Again, cut-off frequency $\omega_0 = \dfrac{1}{RC}$

$$\therefore \quad C = \frac{1}{\omega_0\,R} = \frac{1}{2\pi\,f_0\,R}$$

Assuming $R = 1\ \text{k}\Omega$

$$C = \frac{1}{2\pi \times 1000 \times 1000} = 0.16\ \mu\text{F}.$$

Figure E16.1 represents the desired filter.

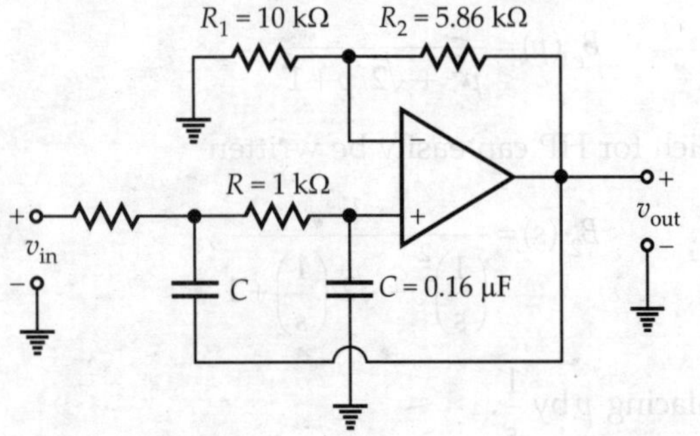

Fig. E16.1

EXAMPLE 16.2 *For a Butterworth polynomial for $n=3$, show that $B_3(s), B_3(-s) = 1+\omega^6$ for $s = j\omega$.*

SOLUTION. For $n=3$, the Butterworth polynomial is given by

$$B_3(s) = (s+1)(s^2+s+1)$$

With $s = j\,\Omega$,

$$B_3(j\,\omega) = (j\,\omega+1)(-\omega^2 + j\,\omega + 1)$$

And for $s = -j\,\omega$,

$$B_3(-j\,\omega) = (-j\,\omega+1)(-\omega^2 - j\,\omega+1)$$

$$\therefore\ B_3(s)\,B_3(-s)\Big|_{s=-j\omega}$$

$$= (j\,\omega+1)(-\omega^2+j\,\omega+1)(-j\,\omega+1)(-\omega^2-j\,\omega+1)$$

$$= (1+\omega^2)(1-\omega^2+\omega^4) = 1+\omega^6$$

$\therefore$ for $s = j\,\omega$,

$$B_3(s)\,B_3(-s) = \mathbf{1+\omega^6}.$$

EXAMPLE 16.3 *Design a low pass fourth order active Butterworth filter when cut-off frequency is 1 kHz.*

SOLUTION. A fourth order Butterworth filter being having two second order filters, of such types, in cascade, we write for the necessary polynomial in factored form as

$$(s^2 + 0.765\,s + 1)(s^2 + 1.848\,s + 1)$$

$$\therefore \quad 2\,k_1 = 0.765 \text{ and } 2\,k_2 = 1.848\,;$$

for the first stage,

$$A_{0_1} = 1 + \frac{R_2}{R_1} = 3 - 2\,k_1$$

or,
$$\frac{R_2}{R_1} = (3 - 2\,K_1) - 1$$

$$= (3 - 0.765) - 1 = 1.235$$

Assuming $R_1 = 10\ \text{k}\Omega$,

$R_2 = 12.35\ \text{k}\Omega$

Next, for the second state,

$$A_{0_2} = 1 + \frac{R_2}{R_1} = 3 - 2\,K_2$$

$$= 3 - 1.848 = 1.152$$

$$\therefore \quad \frac{R_2}{R_1} = 0.152$$

With $R_1 = 10\ \text{k}\Omega$,

R_2 (2nd stage) $= 1.52\ \text{k}\Omega$

The cut-off frequency being 1.0 kHz, from

$f_0 = \dfrac{1}{2\pi\,RC}$, we can write,

$$C = \frac{1}{f_0 \times 2\pi\,R} = \frac{1}{1000 \times 2 \times \pi \times 1000}$$

[assuming $R = 1\ \text{k}\Omega$]

$$= 0.16\ \mu\text{F}.$$

Figure E16.2 represents the fourth order Butterworth filter.

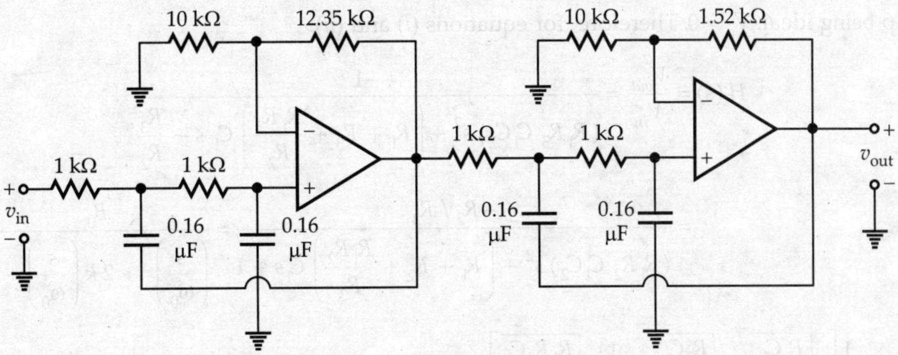

Fig. E16.2

EXERCISES

1. Design an active sixth order Butterworth low pass filter with a cut off frequency of 1 kHz.
[**Hint :** See Example 16.3. Take Butterworth polynomial as $(s^2 + 0.518\,s + 1)(s^2 + 1.414\,s + 1)(s^2 + 1.932\,s + 1)$

and for first stage $2k_1 = 0.518$, $A_{01} = 3 - 2k_1$

for second stage $2k_2 = 0.414$, $A_{02} = 3 - 2k_2$

for third stage $2k_3 = 1.932$, $A_{03} = 3 - 2k_3$

and for each stage $A_0 = 1 + \dfrac{R_2}{R_1}$.

Take $R_1 = 10\ \text{k}\Omega$ for each stage and calculate R_2 for each stage.

Also, $f_0 = \dfrac{1}{2\pi RC}$. With $f_0 = 1\ \text{kHz}$, $C = 0.16\ \mu\text{F}$ for $R = 1\ \text{k}\Omega$.]

2. For a second order Butterworth polynomial, show that $B_2(s)\,B_2(-s) = 1 + \omega^4$ for $s = j\omega$.
[**Hint :** See Example 16.2. Take the polynomial as $(s^2 + \sqrt{2}\,s + 1)$.]

3. For the circuit shown in Fig. P16.1 find $H(s) = \dfrac{V_0}{V_{in}}$.

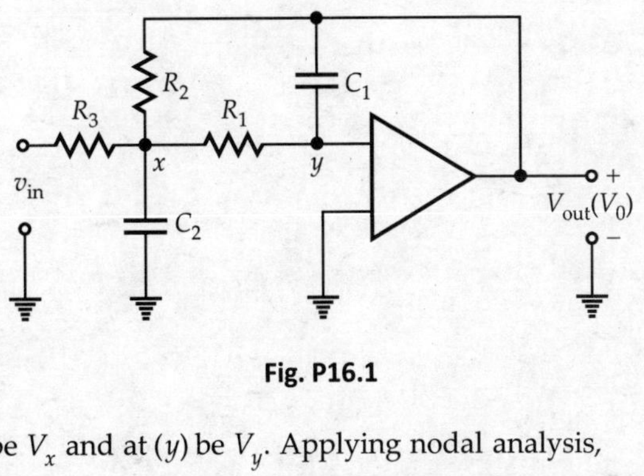

Fig. P16.1

[**Hint :** Let voltage at (x) be V_x and at (y) be V_y. Applying nodal analysis,

$$\frac{V_x - V_{in}}{R_3} + \frac{V_x}{1/s\,C_2} + \frac{V_x - V_{out}}{R_2} + \frac{V_x - V_y}{R_1} = 0 \qquad \text{...(16.}i\text{)}$$

and $$\frac{V_y - V_x}{R_1} + \frac{V_y - V_0}{1/sC_1} = 0 \qquad ...(16.ii)$$

Op-amp being ideal, $V_y = 0$. Therefore, for equations (*i*) and (*ii*),

$$H(s) = \frac{V_{out}}{V_{in}} = \frac{-1}{(R_1 R_3\, C_1 C_2)\, s^2 + \left(R_1 + R_3 + \frac{R_1 R_3}{R_2}\right) C_1\, s + \frac{R_3}{R_2}}$$

$$= \frac{-R_2 / R_3}{(R_1 R_2\, C_1 C_2)\, s^2 + \left(R_1 + R_2 + \frac{R_1 R_2}{R_3}\right) C_1 s + 1} = \frac{B_0}{\left(\frac{s}{\omega_0}\right)^2 + 2k\left(\frac{s}{\omega_0}\right) + 1}$$

where $k = \frac{1}{2}\left[\sqrt{\frac{R_1 C_1}{R_2 C_2}} + \sqrt{\frac{R_2 C_1}{R_1 C_2}} + \frac{1}{R_3}\sqrt{\frac{R_1 R_2 C_1}{C_2}}\right]$

and $$\omega_0^2 = \frac{1}{R_1 R_2\, C_1 C_2},\ A_0 = -R_2 / R_3 .]$$

CHAPTER 17

High Frequency Transmission Lines

17.1 INTRODUCTION

The transmission line is a medium for transmitting electrical energy from one place to another. Transmission lines are used between transmitter and receiver with the help of "antenna" as linking element. It may consist of a pair of uniform wires throughout their entire length. Thus the transmission line utilises its conducting medium transporting electrical energy from one place to another place by utilising electrical conductors. It may be open wire (*e.g.*, telegraph or telephone lines) or insulated (*e.g.*, underground cable or submarine cable).

17.2 APPLICATION

Transmission line is utilised for the purpose :

(*i*) to transmit electrical energy from one place to another place,

(*ii*) to transmit communication signal from a transmitter to receiver,

(*iii*) to work as circuit elements like inductor, capacitor, transformer, filter etc. particularly at high frequency,

(*iv*) to act as a measuring device in order to obtain impedance matching between source and load.

17.3 TYPES OF TRANSMISSION LINES

Basically, a transmission line may be any of the following types :

(*i*) ***Parallel wire transmission line.*** This is the commonest form of line on insulator and on poles. This is open wire line *i.e.*, there is no insulation on the conductor. Telephone lines, telegraphy lines and power lines are of this variety.

(*ii*) ***Coaxial type line.*** Here, the main conductor being a hollow tube, another conductor is laid inside this tube. Both the tubes are coaxial. Each tube is insulated from another by a dielectric medium.

(*iii*) ***Wave guide type cable.*** This is required for VHF/UHF transmission. There is also a hollow conducting tube of uniform cross-section when energy is transmitted by reflection from the inner walls of the guide (optical fibre).

Advantages of open wire lines are that they are cheaper and can be easily constructed. Since there is no insulation around the line conductors hence there is little dielectric loss. Fields of open wire lines are balanced. However, open wire lines are not suitable for operation beyond 100 MHz because of significant energy loss due to radiation effect. In co-axial cables, there is no radiation loss. However, these cables are costlier and have higher dielectric loss. At frequencies above 1 GHz this loss is significantly high. Wave guides are suitable for transmission of energy at very high frequency.

17.4 INFINITE LINE

Before proceeding into the details of theory of transmission lines, the concept of the infinite line should be clear.

Let the propagation of electricity along any uniform and symmetrical transmission line be assumed in a hypothetical line of infinite length having electrical constants per unit length identical to those of the line under construction.

The infinite line will have the following important characteristics :

(*a*) Since the line is of infinite length, no electric wave will ever reach the distant end. Then there will be no possibility of reflection of electric energy at the distant end and consequently no reflected wave also.

(*b*) The voltage being applied at the sending end, the current will depend only on the characteristic impedance Z_0, and will not be affected by the terminating impedance Z_R at the remote end. Considering an infinite line, the impedance will be Z_0 looking from input terminals. Even if a short section of the line at the end of the line is removed, so that the line now starts at the cut section, the impedance looking through the cut section will again be Z_0. The removal of the short section does not affect in any way the infinite nature of the line. The currents and voltages at all the points along the length of the line would be exactly the same as if it were terminated in an infinite length of the line.

Therefore, from the logical point of view, it follows that a short line terminated in Z_0 behaves electrically, at all points along its length, as if it were an infinite line.

When an alternating voltage is applied at the sending end of an infinite line, a finite current flows (due to the capacitance effect and the leakage conductance) between the two wires constituting the transmission. The ratio of the voltage applied to the currents flowing, gives the input impedance of the line (commonly termed as the characteristic impedance Z_0, a vector quantity having a modulus $|Z_0|$). The magnitude of Z_0 usually lies between 200 ohms and 1600 ohms with an angle between (−45°) and (0°). The modulus and angle of the characteristic impedance will be dependent on frequency and the frequency at which the impedance has been measured should be stated.

17.5 CHARACTERISATION OF A TRANSMISSION LINE

The transmission line is generally characterised by a few parameters like primary constants, (R, L, C and G) secondary constants (Z_0 and γ).

17.5.1 Primary Constants

A transmission line may electrically be represented as a circuit consisting of a series resistance (R) and series inductance (L) alongwith a shunt capacitance (C) and leakage conductance (G) (Fig. 17.1). When the circuit elements (equivalent) are assumed to be lumped as single parameters like a single resistance, inductance, capacitance etc., this equivalent representation is called *lumped parameter concept* and is generally represented in terms of T or π network for simplicity of analysis. The parameters may also be assumed to be distributed throughout the entire line and is then known as distributed parameter concept.

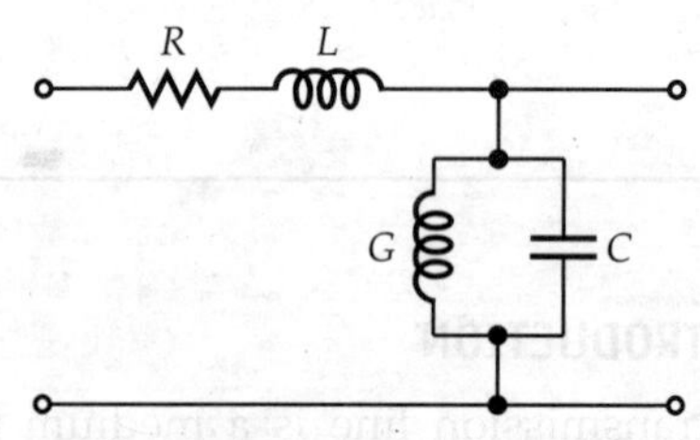

Fig. 17.1 Circuit representation of a transmission line section.

The four line parameters, R, L, C and G are termed as primary constants of the transmission line. The magnitudes of L and C vary with frequency while R does not vary with frequency. When assumed to be only the inverse of insulation resistance, G also does not vary with frequency.

Primary constants may be represented by *lower case letters* like l, c, r and g when

l = loop inductance/unit length (H/km)

c = shunt capacitance/unit length (F/km)

r = loop resistance/unit length (Ohm/km)

g = shunt conductance/unit length (mho/km)

The total series impedance can thus be represented as

$$z = (r + j\omega l) \text{ Ohm/km} \quad ...(17.1)$$

and shunt admittance

$$y = (g + j\omega c) \text{ mho / km} \quad ...(17.2)$$

[Capital letters generally indicate the net value of the corresponding parameter over the entire line.]

17.5.2 Secondary Constants

Characteristic impedance Z_0 and propagation constant γ are called the secondary constants of the transmission line. These two secondary constants indicate about the electrical properties of the transmission line.

In order to find a relationship between the primary and secondary constants, let an infinite line be assumed where Fig. 17.2 represents a very small length (Δx) for which the analysis is to be done.

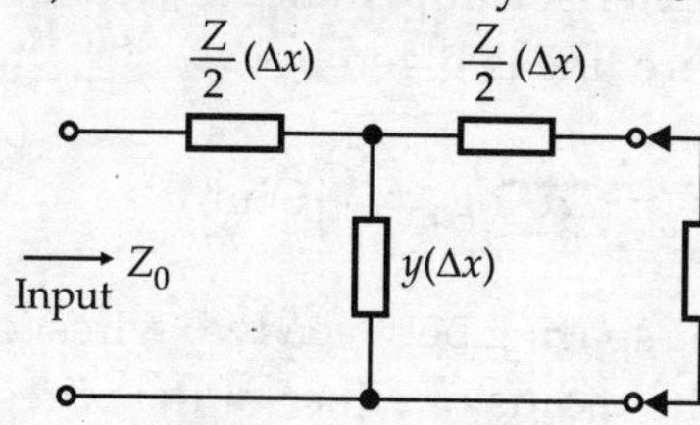

Fig. 17.2 Small length of T section for analysis.

Assuming it to be terminated by z_0,

$$z_0 = \frac{z}{2}(\Delta x) + \frac{\left[\frac{z}{2}(\Delta x) + z_0\right]\frac{1}{y(\Delta x)}}{\left[\frac{z}{2}(\Delta x) + z_0 + \frac{1}{y(\Delta x)}\right]} \text{ Ohm} \quad ...(17.3)$$

where, y = admittance/unit length

z = series impedance/unit length.

Representing the transmission line of length (Δx) by a T circuit, solving equation (17.3) for z_0,

$$z_0 = \sqrt{\frac{z}{y} + \frac{z^2}{4}(\Delta x)^2} = \sqrt{\frac{z}{y}\left\{1 + \frac{zy}{4}(\Delta x)^2\right\}} \quad ...(17.4)$$

Assuming (Δx) to be extremely small, $\Delta x \to 0$

i.e., from equation (17.4),

$$z_0 = \sqrt{\frac{z}{y}} = \sqrt{\frac{r + j\omega l}{g + j\omega c}} \text{ Ohm/km} \quad ...(17.5)$$

i.e., $$z_0 = \sqrt{\frac{z \times \text{length}}{y \times \text{length}}} = \sqrt{\frac{R + j\omega L}{G + j\omega C}} \text{Ohm} \quad ...[17.5(a)]$$

for the entire line length.

For any lossless line, $R = 0$, $G = 0$. [In a lossless line, $I^2 R = 0$, *i.e.*, R must be zero as I cannot be zero. Moreover, there is no shunt leakage as the insulation resistance is assumed to be infinite (*i.e.*, $G = 0$)].

Z_0 is independent of line length.

Hence $z_{0(\text{lossless line})} = \sqrt{\frac{L}{C}}$.

On the other hand, the propagation constant, 'γ', representing the square root of the product of the series impedance (z) and shunt admittance (y), is then given by

$$\gamma = \sqrt{zy} = \sqrt{(\gamma + j\omega l)(g + j\omega c)} \quad ...(17.6)$$

The equivalent circuit of an infinite line has been shown in Fig. (a).

Here, $I_R = \dfrac{Z_2}{Z_2 + \dfrac{Z_1}{2} + Z_0} . I_S$

However, by definition, $e^{\gamma} = \dfrac{I_S}{I_R} = 1 + \dfrac{Z_1}{2Z_2} + \dfrac{Z_0}{Z_2}$

Thus, $\gamma = \log_e\left[1 + \dfrac{Z_1}{2Z_2} + \dfrac{Z_0}{Z_2}\right]$

and for the length of line l, $e^{\gamma L} = 1 + \dfrac{Z_1}{2Z_2} + \dfrac{Z_0}{Z_2}$

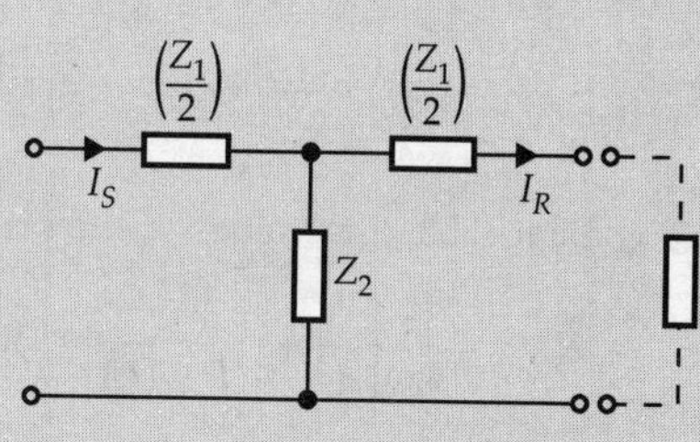

Fig. (a) Equivalent circuit of an infinite line.

However, for line length l, $Z_1 = (r + j\omega l)L$; $Z_2 = \dfrac{1}{(g + j\omega c)L}$

$$\therefore \quad e^{\gamma L} = 1 + \frac{(r + j\omega l)(g + j\omega c)L^2}{2} + \sqrt{\frac{r + j\omega l}{g + j\omega c}}(g + j\omega c)L \qquad \left[\text{Substituting } Z_0 = \sqrt{\frac{r + j\omega l}{g + j\omega c}}\right]$$

$$= 1 + \sqrt{(r + j\omega l)(g + j\omega c)}.L + \frac{(\gamma + j\omega l)(g + j\omega c)L^2}{2} \quad ...(i)$$

However, from the theory of exponential series,

$$e^{\gamma L} = 1 + \gamma L + \frac{\gamma^2 L^2}{2!} + ...$$

As $L \to 0$, terms containing L^3 and higher may be neglected.

$$e^{\gamma L} = 1 + \gamma L + \frac{\gamma^2 L^2}{2} \quad ...(ii)$$

Comparison of equations (i) and (ii) yields $\gamma = \sqrt{(r + j\omega l)(g + j\omega c)}$; for lossless line, $\gamma = j\omega\sqrt{lc}$.

It may be noted that Z_0, the characteristic impedance, may be representing input or output impedance of the line where

$$\left.\begin{aligned} Z_{0(\text{input})} &= \frac{V_S}{I_S} \\ \text{and} \quad Z_{0(\text{output})} &= \frac{V_R}{I_R} \end{aligned}\right\} \quad ...(17.7)$$

V_S, I_S represent the source side voltage and current while V_R, I_R represent the receiving end side voltage and current.

If $Z_{0(\text{input})} = Z_{0(\text{output})}$, the characteristic impedance is called the *surge impedance*. It may be noted that Z_0 is not the simple impedance of the line but is determined by the characteristic of the line per unit length. Z_0 does not depend on line length or type of load connected. If r and g be neglected, Z_0 becomes $\sqrt{l/c}$ (a real quantity) and is thus *independent of frequency*.

17.6 CHARACTERISTIC IMPEDANCE OF A LINE

Characteristic impedance of a uniform transmission line may be defined as the steady state vector ratio of the voltage to the current at the input of an infinite line. It is the impedance looking into an infinite length of transmission line from the input side. For a lossless line, the characteristic impedance (Z_0) is called "surge impedance", the unit being ohms (Ω). Z_0 does not depend on the length of the line or on the character of the terminating load.

The characteristic impedance (Z_0) for open wire or parallel wire line is given by

$$Z_0 = 276 \log_{10}\left(\frac{S}{r}\right) \text{Ohm} \quad ...(17.8)$$

where, S is the spacing between two wires (centre to centre), r is the radius of either of the wires.

The characteristic impedance (Z_0) for coaxial cable is given by

$$Z_0 = 138 \log_{10}\left(\frac{D}{d}\right) \Omega \quad ...(17.9)$$

(D being the outer diameter and d the inner diameter)

17.6.1 Analytical Expression of Z_0 for a Short Line in Terms of o/c and s/c Parameters

Figure 17.3(a) shows an infinite line with input terminals $a-b$. By definition, the impedance looking into the terminals will be Z_0. If a short section of line

* For open wire line, the values of primary constants can be evaluated from the following expressions :

$$R_{(d.c.)} = \frac{2\rho}{\pi R^2} \text{ohm/mt} \; ; \quad L = \frac{\mu_0}{\pi} \ln\left(\frac{S}{R}\right) \text{Henry/mt} \; ; \quad C = \pi\varepsilon_0 \cdot \frac{1}{\ln\left(\frac{S}{R}\right)} \text{Farad/mt}$$

For coaxial cable, the values of the primary constants are given by

$$R_{(d.c.)} = \frac{1}{4\pi g}\left[\frac{1}{d^2} + \left\{\frac{1}{(D-D_1)}\right\}^2\right] \text{ohms/mt} \; ; \quad R_{(a.c.)} = \sqrt{\frac{\mu f}{\pi}}\left(\frac{1}{D} + \frac{1}{d}\right) \text{ohms/mt}$$

$$L = \frac{\mu}{2\pi} \ln\left(\frac{D}{d}\right) \text{Henry/mt} \; ; \quad C = \frac{2\pi\varepsilon}{\ln\left(\frac{D}{d}\right)} \text{Farad/mt}$$

where, ρ = resistivity
R = radius of cross-sectional area of the open conductor
S = spacing between the conductors
μ_0 = absolute permeability
g = conductivity of coaxial cable conductor
d = diameter of the inner conductor
D = diameter of the outer conductor
D_1 = inner diameter of the outer conductor
f = frequency
ε_0 = absolute permittivity
ε and μ = permittivity and permeability of the insulating medium

be removed from the infinite line, as shown in Fig. 17.3(*b*), the impedance looking through terminals *c* and *d* will still be Z_0. Hence, the removed short section (say *AB*) may be assumed to be terminated in an impedance Z_0 at *B* having the current and voltage at all points along its length to be exactly the same as if it were terminated in an infinite line. This type of line and termination is popularly known as "short line terminated in Z_0" [Fig. 17.3(*c*)].

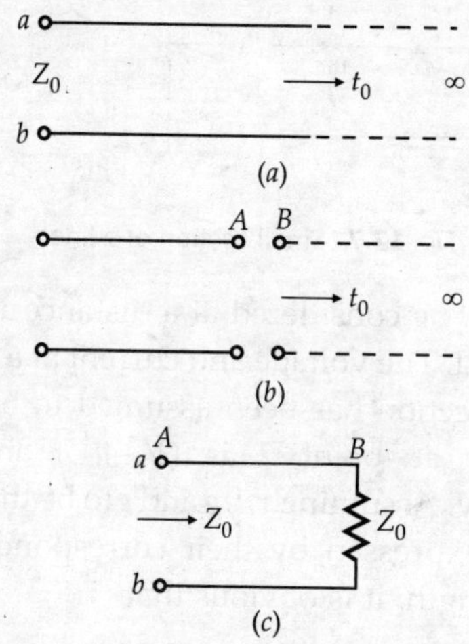

Fig. 17.3 Short line terminated in Z_0.

The short line, being a complex electrical network, may be represented by a *T* section having an input impedance Z_0 as shown in Fig. 17.4.

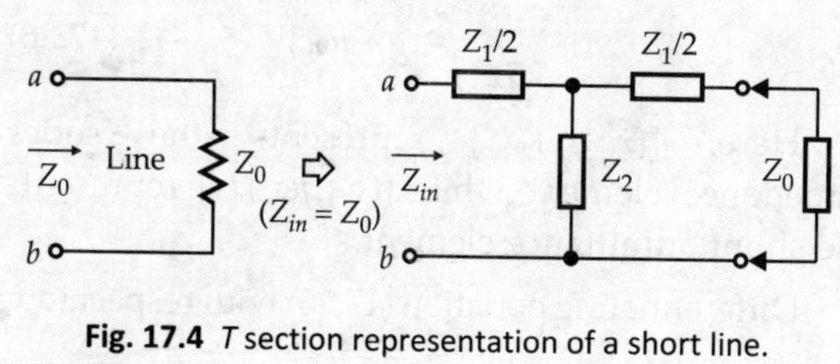

Fig. 17.4 *T* section representation of a short line.

Here, $$Z_{in} = \frac{Z_1}{2} + \frac{Z_2\left(\frac{Z_1}{2} + Z_0\right)}{\frac{Z_1}{2} + Z_2 + Z_0} \quad ...(17.10)$$

But $Z_{in} \equiv Z_0$.

Simplification of equation (17.10) results,

$$Z_0^2 = \frac{Z_1^2}{4} + Z_1 Z_2$$

or, $$Z_0 = \sqrt{\frac{Z_1^2}{4} + Z_1 Z_2} \quad ...(17.11)$$

However, the open circuit impedance of the short line looking from terminal *a-b* and removing Z_0 is given by

$$Z_{o/c} = \frac{Z_1}{2} + Z_2 \quad ...(17.12)$$

Shorting the output terminals of the short line, the short-circuit impedance of this short line looking from terminals *a-b* is given by

$$Z_{s/c} = \frac{Z_1}{2} + \frac{\frac{Z_1 Z_2}{2}}{\frac{Z_1}{2} + Z_2} = \frac{\frac{Z_1^2}{4} + Z_1 Z_2}{\frac{Z_1}{2} + Z_2} \quad ...(17.13)$$

Substitution of equations (17.11) and (17.12) in equation (17.13) yields

$$Z_{s/c} = \frac{Z_0^2}{Z_{o/c}}$$

or, $$Z_0 = \sqrt{Z_{o/c} \cdot Z_{s/c}} \quad ...(17.14)$$

Expression (17.14) represents the *characteristic impedance* of a short line in terms of open circuit and short-circuit impedances.

17.6.2 Propagation Constant

The propagation constant is defined as the natural logarithm of the ratio of the input to the output current and is usually denoted by γ.

Hence, $$\gamma = \log_e \frac{I_S}{I_R} \quad ...(17.15)$$

i.e., $$\frac{I_S}{I_R} = e^{\gamma} \quad ...(17.16)$$

γ, the propagation constant, is thus a vector quantity and can be represented by $\gamma = \alpha + j\beta$, where α is the attenuation constant and β the phase constant. When β is multiplied by the total length of the line, it gives the *electrical length* of the line. However, if α is multiplied by the length of the line, the product gives *total attenuation*. α is expressed in Neper or decibel and β is expressed in radian.

17.6.3 Attenuation Constant and Phase Shift Constants of a Transmission Line

The propagation constant γ being given by $\gamma = (\alpha + j\beta)$, α represents the real part determining the reduction or *attenuation in voltage and current* along the line while β represents the imaginary part determining the *variation of the phase position* of voltage and current along the line.

Also, $\gamma = \sqrt{Z_\gamma} = \sqrt{(R+j\omega L)(G+j\omega C)}$

i.e., $\alpha + j\beta = \sqrt{(R+j\omega L)(G+j\omega C)}$ ...(17.17)

Squaring both sides,

$$\gamma^2 = (\alpha+j\beta)^2 = [\sqrt{(R+j\omega L)(G+j\omega c)}]^2 = (R+j\omega L)(G+j\omega C) \quad ...(17.18)$$

Equating the real part of this equation (17.18),

$$\alpha^2 - \beta^2 = RG - \omega^2 LC \quad ...(17.19)$$

On the other hand, equating the imaginary part of equation (17.18),

$$2\alpha\beta = \omega RC + \omega LG \quad ...(17.20)$$

Again, the magnitude of γ is given by

$$|\gamma| = \sqrt{\alpha^2 + \beta^2} \quad ...(17.21)$$

i.e., $$\alpha^2 + \beta^2 = \sqrt{R^2 + (\omega L)^2}\sqrt{G^2 + (\omega C)^2} \quad ...(17.22)$$

Adding equations (17.19) and (17.22),

$$2\alpha^2 = (RG - \omega^2 LC) + \sqrt{(R^2 + \omega^2 L^2)(G^2 + \omega^2 C^2)}$$

$$\therefore\ \alpha = \sqrt{\frac{1}{2}\{(RG - \omega^2 LC) + \sqrt{(R^2+\omega^2L^2)(G^2+\omega^2C^2)}\}} \quad ...(17.23)$$

Similarly, subtracting equation (17.22) from equation (17.19), simplification yields

$$\beta = \sqrt{\frac{1}{2}\{(\omega^2 LC - RG) + \sqrt{(R^2+\omega^2L^2)(G^2+\omega^2C^2)}\}} \quad ...(17.24)$$

Expressions (17.23) and (17.24) represent the relation between the primary constant R, L, C and G in terms of α and β, the secondary constants. The profiles of α and β with respect to ω are shown in Figs. 17.5 and 17.6.

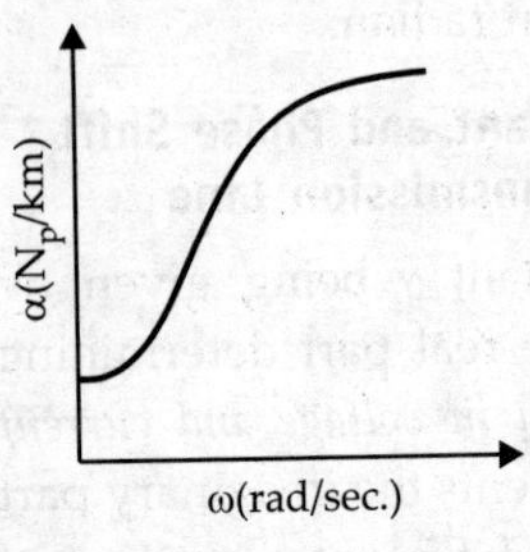

Fig. 17.5 Profile of α *vs.* ω.

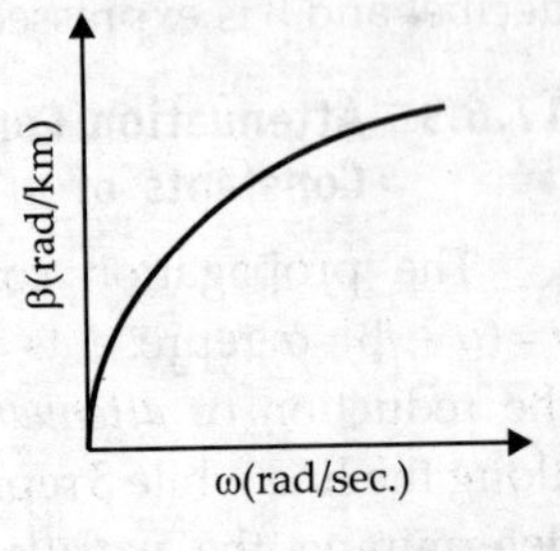

Fig. 17.6 Profile of β *vs.* ω.

17.7 LINE EQUATION

17.7.1 Analytical Expression

Figure 17.7 shows current and voltage distribution in a transmission line having a length l km. Let Z_0 be the characteristic impedance, γ the propagation constant. Let a small section of the line

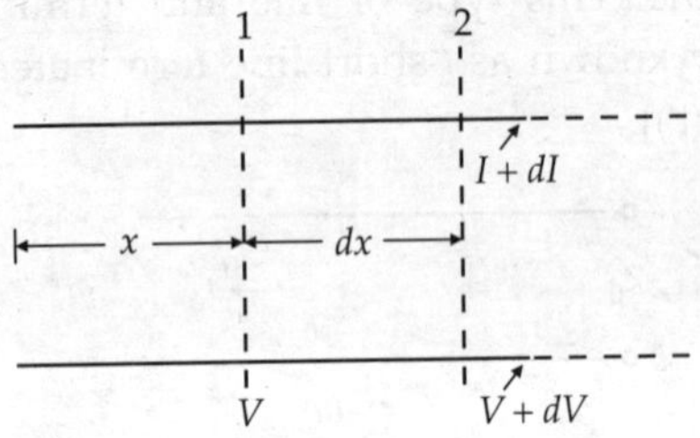

Fig. 17.7 Small section of a line.

of length dx be considered at a distance x from the sending end. The voltage and current at a point 1 of the small section has been assumed to be V and I while that at point 2 is $(V+dV)$ and $(I+dI)$ respectively. Assuming r, l, g and c to be the primary constants expressed by their corresponding units per unit length, it is obvious that

$$V - (V + dV) = I(r + j\omega l)\,dx$$

$$\therefore\ \frac{dV}{dx} = -(r + j\omega l)I \quad ...(17.25)$$

and $$I - (I + dI) = V(g + j\omega c)\,dx$$

or, $$\frac{dI}{dx} = -(g + j\omega c)V \quad ...(17.26)$$

Here, $[(r + j\omega l)dx]$ represents the series impedance element while $[(g + j\omega c)dx]$ represents the shunt admittance element.

Differentiating equation (17.26) with respect to x,

$$\frac{d^2 I}{dx^2} = -(g + j\omega c)\frac{dV}{dx} \quad ...(17.27)$$

Substitution of equation (17.25) in equation (17.27), yields

$$\frac{d^2 I}{dx^2} = (g + j\omega c)(r + j\omega l)I = \rho I \quad ...(17.28)$$

where, $\rho = (g + j\omega c)(r + j\omega l)$

[or, $\sqrt{\rho} = \sqrt{(r + j\omega l)(g + j\omega c)} = \gamma$]

Solution of the differential equation (17.28) yields

$$I = ae^{\sqrt{\rho}x} + be^{-\sqrt{\rho}x} \quad ...(17.29)$$

where a and b are constants.

However, $e^{\sqrt{\rho}x} = \cos h\sqrt{\rho}x + \sin h\sqrt{\rho}x$ ...(17.30)

and $e^{-\sqrt{\rho}x} = \cos h\sqrt{\rho}x - \sin h\sqrt{\rho}x$ ...(17.31)

Utilising equations (17.30) and (17.31) in equation (17.29),

$$I = (a+b)\cos h\sqrt{\rho}x + (a-b)\sin h\sqrt{\rho}\,x$$

or, $$I = A\cos h\sqrt{\rho}x + B\sin h\sqrt{\rho}x \quad ...(17.32)$$

where, $A = (a+b)$ and $B = (a-b)$

Again, differentiating equation (17.32) with respect to x,

$$\frac{dI}{dx} = \sqrt{\rho}(A\sin h\sqrt{\rho}x + B\cos h\sqrt{\rho}x) \quad ...(17.33)$$

Rewriting equation (17.26) as follows,

$$V = -\frac{1}{(g+j\omega c)}\frac{dI}{dx} \quad ...(17.34)$$

Substitution for $\frac{dI}{dx}$ from equation (17.33), equation (17.34) becomes

$$V = -\frac{\sqrt{\rho}}{(g+j\omega c)}(A\sin h\sqrt{\rho}x + B\cos h\sqrt{\rho}x)$$

or, $$V = -q(A\sin h\sqrt{\rho}x + B\cos h\sqrt{\rho}x) \quad ...(17.35)$$

where, $$q = \frac{\sqrt{\rho}}{(g+j\omega c)} = \frac{\sqrt{(r+j\omega l)(g+j\omega c)}}{(g+j\omega c)}$$

$$= \sqrt{\frac{r+j\omega l}{g+j\omega c}}\ (= Z_0) \quad ...(17.36)$$

Equations (17.32) and (17.35) represent *general line equation* of a transmission line.

17.7.2 Determination of Values of Constants *A* and *B*

(i) When conditions at the sending end of the line are known :

It is obvious that at the sending end $x = 0$.

$$\therefore \quad I \equiv I_S = A\cos h\sqrt{\rho}.0 + B\sin h\sqrt{\rho}.0$$
$$= A\times 1\times B\times 0.$$

$$\therefore \quad A = I_S \quad ...(17.37)$$

Also, $V \equiv V_S = -q(A\sin h\sqrt{\rho}.0 + B\cos h\sqrt{\rho}.0)$
$= -Z_0 B$

[$\because q = Z_0$ provided r and g are neglected]

$$\therefore \quad B = -\frac{V_S}{Z_0} \quad ...(17.38)$$

Thus, $$I = I_S\cos h\sqrt{\rho}x - \frac{V_S}{Z_0}\sin h\sqrt{\rho}x$$

or, $$I = I_S\cos h\gamma x - \frac{V_S}{Z_0}\sin h\gamma x \quad ...(17.39)$$

and $$V = V_S\cos h\sqrt{\rho}x - I_S Z_0\sin h\sqrt{\rho}x$$

or, $$V = V_S\cos h\gamma x - I_S Z_0\sin h\gamma x \quad ...(17.40)$$

(ii) When conditions at the receiving end are known :

It is obvious that in this case $x = L$.

$$\therefore \quad I \equiv I_R = A\cos h\sqrt{\rho}L + B\sin h\sqrt{\rho}L \quad ...(17.41)$$

Similarly,

$$V \equiv V_R = -BZ_0\cos h\sqrt{\rho}L - AZ_0\sin h\sqrt{\rho}L \quad ...(17.42)$$

Dividing equation (17.41) by equation (17.42), after rearrangement,

$$\frac{I_R - A\cos h\sqrt{\rho}L}{V_R + AZ_0\sin h\sqrt{\rho}L} = -\frac{B\sin h\sqrt{\rho}L}{BZ_0\cos h\sqrt{\rho}L}$$

or, $$-I_R Z_0\cos h\sqrt{\rho}L + AZ_0\cos h^2\sqrt{\rho}L = V_R\sin h\sqrt{\rho}L + AZ_0\sin h^2\sqrt{\rho}L$$

i.e., $$A = \frac{V_R}{Z_0}\sin h\sqrt{\rho}L + I_R\cos h\sqrt{\rho}L \quad ...(17.43)$$

Similarly, $$\frac{I_R - B\sin h\sqrt{\rho}L}{V_R + BZ_0\cos h\sqrt{\rho}L} = \frac{A\cos h\sqrt{\rho}L}{-AZ_0\sin h\sqrt{\rho}L}$$

or, $$-I_R Z_0\sin h\sqrt{\rho}L + BZ_0\sin h^2\sqrt{\rho}L = V_R\cos h\sqrt{\rho}L + BZ_0\cos h^2\sqrt{\rho}L$$

i.e., $$B = -I_R\sin h\sqrt{\rho}L - \frac{V_R}{Z_0}\cos h\sqrt{\rho}\,L \quad ...(17.44)$$

Thus from equations (17.32) and (17.35), utilising equations (17.43) and (17.44)

$$I = \left[I_R\cos h\sqrt{\rho}L + \frac{V_R}{Z_0}\sin h\sqrt{\rho}\,L\right]\cos h\sqrt{\rho}x$$
$$-\left[I_R\sin h\sqrt{\rho}L + \frac{V_R}{Z_0}\cos h\sqrt{\rho}L\right]\sin h\sqrt{\rho}x$$

Equations (17.39) and (17.40) can also be expressed as

$$I = I_S\left[\left(\frac{e^{\gamma x}+e^{-\gamma x}}{2}\right) - \frac{Z_S}{Z_0}\left(\frac{e^{\gamma x}-e^{-\gamma x}}{2}\right)\right] \quad \text{and} \quad V = V_S\left[\left(\frac{e^{\gamma x}+e^{-\gamma x}}{2}\right) - \frac{Z_0}{Z_S}\left(\frac{e^{\gamma x}-e^{-\gamma x}}{2}\right)\right]$$

i.e., $I = I_R \cos h\,\gamma[L-x] + \frac{V_R}{Z_0}\sin h\gamma(L-x)$ ...(17.45)

and $V = [I_R Z_0 \sin h\sqrt{\rho}\,L + V_R \cos h\sqrt{\rho}\,L]\cos h\sqrt{\rho}\,x$
$\quad -[I_R Z_0 \cos h\sqrt{\rho}\,L + V_R \sin h\sqrt{\rho}\,L]\sin h\sqrt{\rho}\,.x$

or, $V = V_R \cos h\gamma(L-x) + I_R Z_0 \sin h\gamma(L-x)$ ...(17.46)

Plots of $\sin h\gamma L$, its angle, $\cos h\gamma L$ and its angle are shown in Fig. 17.8.

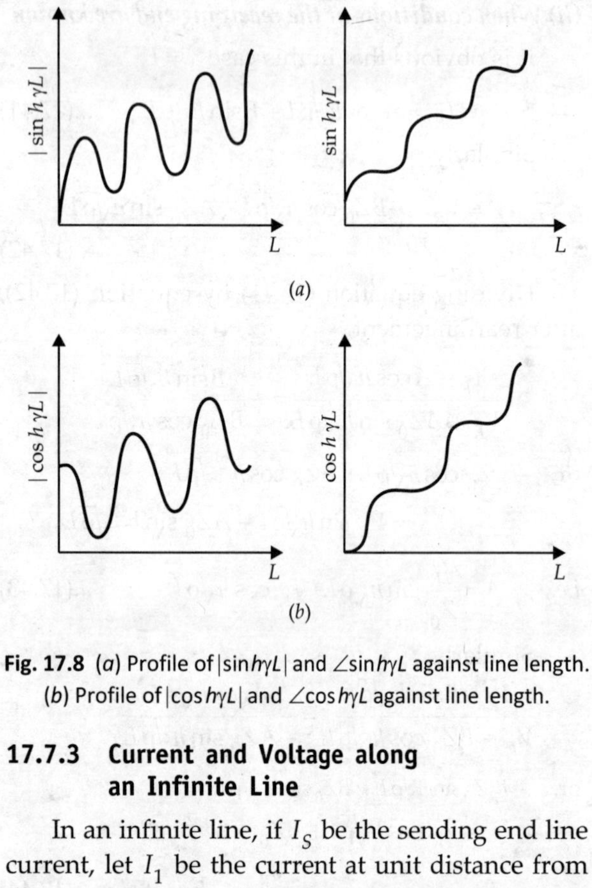

Fig. 17.8 (*a*) Profile of $|\sin h\gamma L|$ and $\angle \sin h\gamma L$ against line length. (*b*) Profile of $|\cos h\gamma L|$ and $\angle \cos h\gamma L$ against line length.

17.7.3 Current and Voltage along an Infinite Line

In an infinite line, if I_S be the sending end line current, let I_1 be the current at unit distance from the sending side down the line. Due to loss introduced by the line, the current I_1 will be less than the current I_S. Additionally, a phase shift will also be introduced.

From the definition of the propagation constant, for an unit length,

$$e^{\gamma} = \frac{I_S}{I_1} \qquad \text{...(17.47)}$$

Then, at a distance x unit down the line,

$$e^{x\gamma} = \frac{I_S}{I_R}, \qquad \text{...(17.48)}$$

assuming I_R be the current at the distance x.

But $\quad \gamma = \alpha + j\beta$

Equation (17.48) becomes

$$\frac{I_S}{I_R} = e^{x\gamma} = e^{\alpha x}\angle\beta x$$

or, $$I_R = I_S e^{-\alpha x}\angle -\beta x \qquad \text{...(17.49)}$$

Equation (17.49) represents the equation of the current at a distance x down the line. Similarly, the voltage V_R, at any point x down the line is given by

$$V_R = V_S e^{-\alpha x}\angle -\beta x \qquad \text{...(17.50)}$$

Figure 17.9 represents these exponential relations of current and voltages down the line.

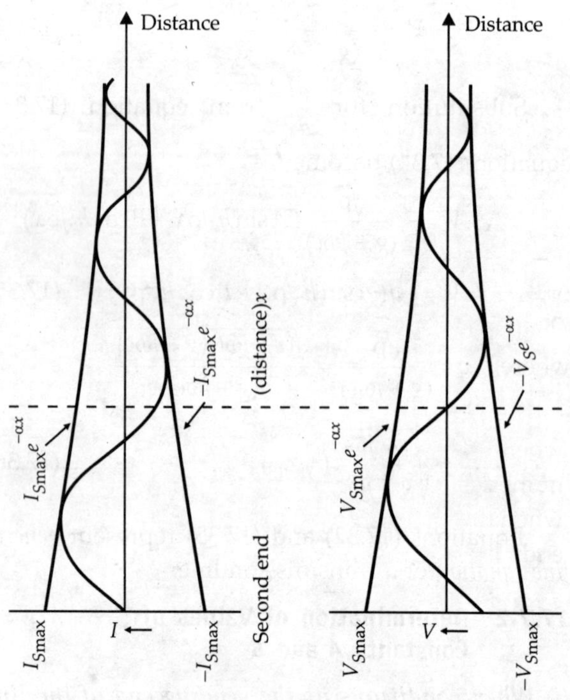

Fig. 17.9 Current and voltage at any point x along the infinite line.

17.8 INPUT IMPEDANCE OF FINITE LINE

17.8.1 Considering Open Circuit at Distant End

Figure 17.10 shows a open-circuited finite line of length 'l' km. Let $Z_{o/c}$ be the input impedance $\left(\frac{V_S}{I_S}\right)$ of the line.

For the open-circuited line

$$\left.\begin{array}{l} x = l \\ I_R = 0 \end{array}\right\} \qquad \text{...(17.51)}$$

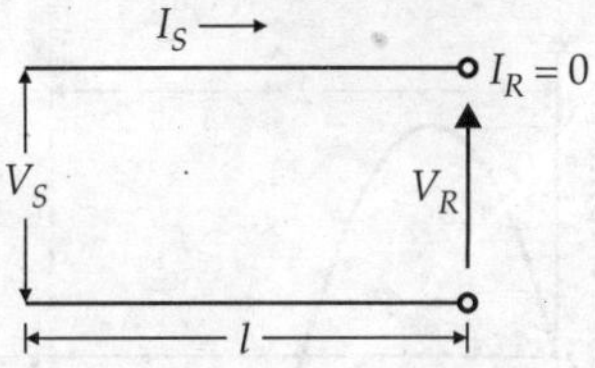

Fig. 17.10 Open-circuited finite line.

However, the general line equation for current is given by

$$I = A\cos h\sqrt{\rho}x + B\sin h\sqrt{\rho}x,$$

which for this case, with $x = l,\ A = I_S,\ B = -\dfrac{V_S}{Z_0}$;

$\therefore$ With $I \equiv I_R$,

$$I_R = I_S \cos h(\gamma l) - \frac{V_S}{Z_0}\sin h(\gamma l)$$

[Assuming $\gamma = \sqrt{\rho}$, being evident from equation (17.28)]

or, $$0 = I_S \cos h(\gamma l) - \frac{V_S}{Z_0}\sin h(\gamma l)$$

[$\because$ with open circuit, $I_R = 0$]

or, $$\frac{V_S}{I_S} = Z_0 \frac{\cos h(\gamma l)}{\sin h(\gamma l)}$$

i.e., $$Z_{o/c} = Z_0 \cot h(\gamma l) \qquad \text{...(17.52)}$$

when γl is very large, $\cot h(\gamma l)$ turns to be numerically equal to one. This gives $Z_{o/c} = Z_0$, when the line length is long and open at the distant end.

17.8.2 Considering Short-Circuit at Distant End

For the same line, let $Z_{s/c}$ be the input impedance of the line given by $\left(\dfrac{V_S}{I_S}\right)$ and short-circuited at the distant end (Fig. 17.11).

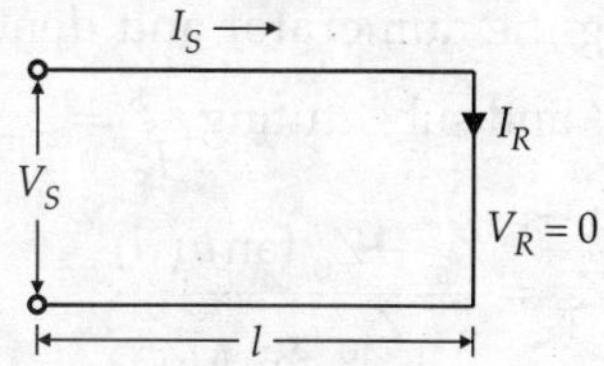

Fig. 17.11 Short-circuited finite line.

For the short-circuited line,

$$\left.\begin{aligned} x &= l \\ V_R &= 0 \end{aligned}\right\} \qquad \text{...(17.53)}$$

The general line equation being given by,

$$V = -q[A\sin h\sqrt{\rho}x + B\cos h\sqrt{\rho}x],$$

which, for this case with $x = l,\ A = I_S,\ B = -\dfrac{V_S}{Z_0}$, $q = Z_0$ the line equation becomes

$$0 = V_S \cos h(\gamma l) - I_S Z_0 \sin h(\gamma l)$$

or, $$\frac{V_S}{I_S} = Z_0 \frac{\sin h(\gamma l)}{\cos h(\gamma l)} = Z_0 \tan h(\gamma l)$$

or, $$Z_{s/c} = Z_0 \tan h(\gamma l) \qquad \text{...(17.54)}$$

From above equation (17.54), it is evident that when (γl) is very large, $\tan h(\gamma l)$ is unity. Hence $Z_{s/c}$ approaches the characteristic impedance (Z_0) if line length is very long.

17.8.3 Considering Termination by any Impedance Z_R

Considering the line of length 'l' being terminated by an impedance Z_R, the general line equation of voltage and currents becomes,

$$V_R = V_S \cos h(\gamma l) - I_S Z_0 \sin h(\gamma l)$$

$$I_R = I_S \cos h(\gamma l) - \frac{V_S}{Z_0}\sin h(\gamma l)$$

The terminating impedance Z_R is then given by

$$Z_R = \frac{V_R}{I_R} = \frac{V_S \cos h(\gamma l) - I_S Z_0 \sin h(\gamma l)}{I_S \cos h(\gamma l) - \dfrac{V_S}{Z_0}\sin h(\gamma l)}$$

Relation between $Z_{o/c}$ and $Z_{s/c}$. Multiplication of equation (17.52) with equation (17.53) yields

$$Z_{o/c}.Z_{s/c} = Z_0 \coth(\gamma l).Z_0 \tanh(\gamma l)$$

Hence $$Z_0 = \sqrt{Z_{s/c} Z_{o/c}} \qquad \text{...(i)}$$

On the other hand, division of equation (17.52) with equation (17.54) yields

$$\frac{Z_{o/c}}{Z_{s/c}} = \frac{Z_0 \coth(\gamma l)}{Z_0 \tanh(\gamma l)}$$

or, $$\frac{Z_{s/c}}{Z_{o/c}} = \tanh^2(\gamma l) \quad i.e., \quad \tanh(\gamma l) = \sqrt{\frac{Z_{s/c}}{Z_{o/c}}} \qquad \text{...(ii)}$$

Dividing the numerator and denominator by "$I_S \cos h(\gamma l)$" and substituting $\frac{V_S}{I_S} = Z_{in}$,

$$Z_R = \frac{Z_{in} - Z_0 \tan h(\gamma l)}{1 - \frac{Z_{in}}{Z_0} \tan h(\gamma l)}$$

or, $$Z_R = \frac{Z_0 Z_{in} - Z_0^2 \tan h(\gamma l)}{Z_0 - Z_{in} \tan h(\gamma l)}$$

or, $Z_{in}\{Z_0 + Z_R \tan h(\gamma l)\} = Z_0\{Z_R + Z_0 \tan h(\gamma l)\}$

Hence $$Z_{in} = Z_0 \frac{Z_R + Z_0 \tan h(\gamma l)}{Z_0 + Z_R \tan h(\gamma l)} \quad ...(17.55)$$

17.8.4 Considering Termination by Characteristic Impedance Z_0

Substituting Z_0 for Z_R in equation (17.55),

$$Z_{in} = Z_0 \frac{Z_0 + Z_0 \tan h(\gamma l)}{Z_0 + Z_0 \tan h(\gamma l)} = Z_0 \quad ...[17.55(a)]$$

Thus, the *input impedance* of a finite line of length 'l', terminated in its characteristic impedance Z_0, is the characteristic impedance Z_0.

In such a line, the voltage and current, at any point x from the sending end are given by

$$V_x = V_S \cos h\gamma x - I_S Z_0 \sin h\gamma x$$

$$I_x = I_S \cos h\gamma x - \frac{V_S}{Z_0} \sin h\gamma x$$

Substituting the value of Z_0 as $\frac{V_S}{I_R}$, simplification yields

$$V_x = V_S(\cos h\gamma x - \sin h\gamma x) = V_{se}^{-\gamma x}$$

$$I_x = I_S(\cos h\gamma x - \sin h\gamma x) = I_{se}^{-\gamma x}$$

These equations confirm the results we obtained earlier.

17.9 WAVELENGTH AND VELOCITY OF PROPAGATION

It is defined as the *distance* that an electric wave traverses along a line in order that the total phase shift of input energy is 2π radians. The wavelength is generally denoted by "λ", the unit being meter (Fig. 17.12).

$\therefore$ $\beta\lambda = 2\pi$, where, β is the phase shift

i.e., $$\lambda = \frac{2\pi}{\beta} \text{ mt.}$$

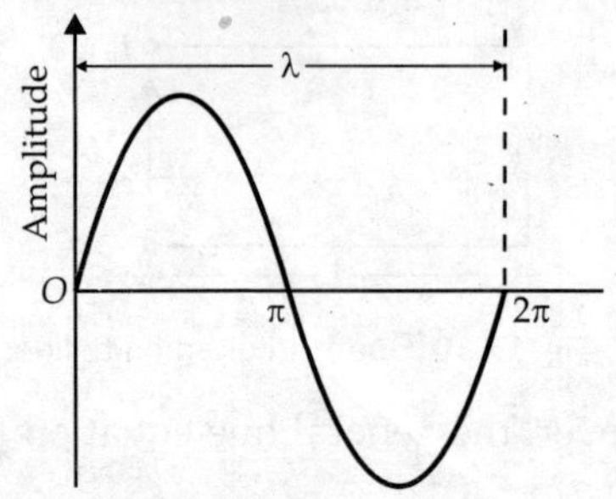

Fig. 17.12 Representation of wavelength.

In case of radio frequency transmission with air as dielectric, λ is approximately equal to the wavelength of wave of radio transmission. In case of cable transmission, the wavelength is approximately equal to the wavelength of the wave in radio frequency transmission divided by a factor $\sqrt{k}$, k being the dielectric constant of the medium.

The velocity of propagation or phase velocity is defined by the *magnitude* of velocity with which a signal of single frequency propagates and is denoted by v_p, its unit being km/sec.

It is evident that change of 2π represents one cycle operation and hence

$$\lambda = v_p \times t \quad ...(17.56)$$

But t, the time period $= \frac{1}{f}$ ...[17.56(a)]

Substituting the value of t from equation [17.56(a)] in equation (17.56)

$$\lambda = v_p \times \frac{1}{f}$$

or, $$v_p = \lambda . f \quad ...(17.57)$$

Substituting the value of $\lambda \left(= \frac{2\pi}{\beta}\right)$ in equation (17.57)

$$v_p = \frac{2\pi}{\beta} \times f = \frac{\omega}{\beta} \quad ...(17.58)$$

In practical transmission line, with air as dielectric, v_p is approximately equal to the velocity of light. In lines with chemical or solid dielectric medium, v_p is the velocity of light divided by $\sqrt{k}$. Velocity of propagation cannot exceed velocity of light.

17.10 ANALYTICAL EXPRESSION FOR VOLTAGE AND CURRENT OF A LINE AT ANY POINT OF LENGTH "x" FROM THE SENDING END

Figure 17.13 shows the transmission line of length l terminated by Z_R. Let the voltage across the load be V_R.

Hence, $V_R = I_R Z_R$

or, $$I_R = \frac{V_R}{Z_R} \quad ...(17.59)$$

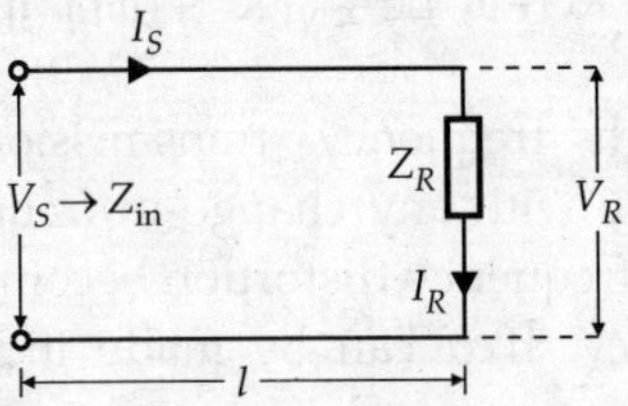

Fig. 17.13 Transmission line terminated by Z_R.

However, from the general line equations

$$V_R = V_S \cos h(\gamma l) - I_S Z_0 \sin h(\gamma l) \quad ...(17.60)$$

$$I_R = I_S \cos h(\gamma l) - \left(\frac{V_S}{Z_0}\right) \sin h(\gamma l) \quad ...(17.61)$$

Substituting the values of V_R and I_R from equations (17.60) and (17.61) in equation (17.59),

$$\left[I_S \cos h(\gamma l) - \left(\frac{V_S}{Z_0}\right) \sin h(\gamma l)\right] = \left[\frac{V_S}{Z_0} \cos h(\gamma l) - \frac{I_S Z_0}{Z_R} \sin h(\gamma l)\right]$$

or, $$I_S \cos h(\gamma l) + \frac{I_S Z_0}{Z_R} \sin h(\gamma l) = \frac{V_S}{Z_R} \cos h(\gamma l) + \frac{V_S}{Z_0} \sin h(\gamma l)$$

or, $$I_S = \frac{\frac{V_S}{Z_R} \cos h(\gamma l) + \frac{V_S}{Z_0} \sin h(\gamma l)}{\cos h(\gamma l) + \frac{Z_0}{Z_R} \sin h(\gamma l)}$$

$$= \frac{V_S [Z_0 \cos h(\gamma l) + Z_R \sin h(\gamma l)]}{Z_0 [Z_R \cos h(\gamma l) + Z_0 \sin h(\gamma l)]} \quad ...(17.62)$$

However, the sending end impedance or input impedance as viewed from the sending end is given by

$$Z_{in} = \frac{V_S}{I_S} = \frac{V_S}{\frac{V_S}{Z_0}\left[\frac{[Z_0 \cos h(\gamma l) + Z_R \sin h(\gamma l)]}{[Z_R \cos h(\gamma l) + Z_0 \sin h(\gamma l)]}\right]}$$

or, $$Z_{in} = Z_0 \left[\frac{[Z_R \cos h(\gamma l) + Z_0 \sin h(\gamma l)]}{[Z_0 \cos h(\gamma l) + Z_R \sin h(\gamma l)]}\right] \quad ...(17.63)$$

$$= Z_0 \left[\frac{Z_R + Z_0 \tan h(\gamma l)}{Z_0 + Z_R \tan h(\gamma l)}\right] \quad ...[17.63(a)]$$

Let V_x and I_x represent the voltage and current at any point "P" at a distance x from the sending end (Fig. 17.14).

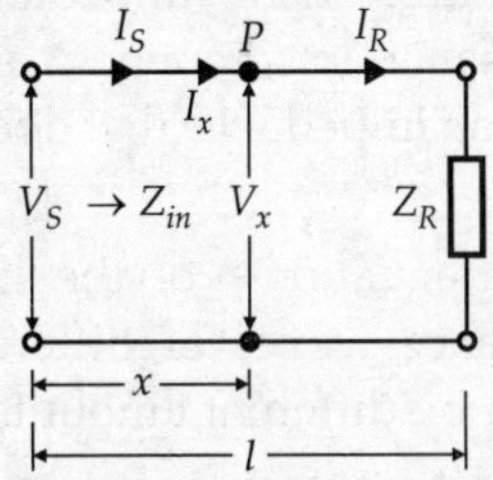

Fig. 17.14 Voltage and current at any point P of the line.

Substituting the value of I_S from equation (17.62) in equation (17.60),

$$V_x = V_S \cos h(\gamma x) - Z_0 \left[\frac{V_S}{Z_0}\left\{\frac{Z_0 \cos h(\gamma l) + Z_R \sin h(\gamma l)}{Z_R \cos h(\gamma l) + Z_0 \sin h(\gamma l)}\right\}\right] \times \sin h(\gamma x)$$

$$= V_S \left[\frac{\{Z_R \cos h(\gamma x) \cos h(\gamma l) + Z_0 \sin h(\gamma l) \cos h(\gamma x)\} - \{Z_0 \sin h(\gamma x) \cos h(\gamma l) + Z_R \sin h(\gamma x) \sin h(\gamma l)\}}{Z_R \cos h(\gamma l) + Z_0 \sin h(\gamma l)}\right]$$

or, $$V_x = V_S \left[\frac{Z_R \cos h \gamma (l-x) + Z_0 \sin h \gamma (l-x)}{Z_R \cos h(\gamma l) + Z_0 \sin h(\gamma l)}\right] \quad ...(17.64)$$

Similarly, the current equation at a distance x from the sending end becomes,

$$I_x = \frac{V_S}{Z_0}\left[\frac{Z_0 \cos h \gamma (l-x) + Z_R \sin h \gamma (l-x)}{Z_R \cos h(\gamma l) + Z_0 \sin h(\gamma l)}\right] \quad ...(17.65)$$

17.11 DISTORTION IN A TRANSMISSION LINE

Signals transmitted over transmission lines are mostly complex and consist of maximum frequency components. While passing through distortion occurs in the signal. This is commonly known as *line distortion*.

CHAPTER 17

In ideal transmission line, it is intended that the waveform at receiving end of the line must be identical to the waveform of the signal in the sending end. The line is then said to be *distortionless line* or *distortion-free line*.

It has been seen that distortion in the waveform exists if all frequencies in the complex waveform do not have same attenuation and same delay during propagation.

17.11.1 Causes of Distortion

Distortion is caused due to the following *three* reasons :

(*i*) The characteristic impedance of the line varies with change in frequency* and line may be terminated in an impedance that does not vary with frequency.

(*ii*) The attenuation** of the line varies with frequency. Hence waves of different frequencies are attenuated by different amounts.

(*iii*) The velocity of propagation varies with frequency. Hence waves of different frequencies arrive at different times at the end of the line.

The wavelength is given by $\lambda = \dfrac{2\pi}{\beta}$,

β being the phase shift constant, velocity of propagation is then,

$$v_p = f \times \lambda = \frac{2\pi f}{\beta} = \frac{\omega}{\beta}$$

This indicates how the velocity (v_p) depends on ω and hence on the frequency of the signal. Thus, for a line to be distortionless, the characteristic impedance (Z_0), α and β should be independent of frequency.

17.11.2 Types of Distortion

There are two types of distortion *viz.*, (*a*) *Frequency distortion* and (*b*) *Delay distortion*.

Frequency Distortion

It is a particular type of distortion in which the various frequency components of a transmitting signal undergo different attenuations. Frequency distortion is governed by attenuation constant α where,

$$\alpha = \frac{1}{\sqrt{2}}\sqrt{RG - \omega^2 LC + \sqrt{[R^2 + (\omega L)^2][G^2 + (\omega C)^2]}}$$

In high frequency transmission, α varies significantly with any change in frequency (*i.e.*, ω) and hence frequency distortion becomes a function of frequency. If α can be made independent of frequency, frequency distortion does not occur.

Delay Distortion

It is another type of distortion where the time required to transmit the various frequency components of the complex waveform vary over the line. This causes consequent delay in transmission of signal components and hence the delays are not constant. It is directly related with β, the phase constant which is given by

$$\beta = \frac{1}{\sqrt{2}}\sqrt{\omega^2 LC - RG + \sqrt{[R^2 + (\omega L)^2][G^2 + (\omega C)^2]}}$$

This particular type of distortion is known as delay distortion or phase distortion. It can be evident from the above equation that β is governed by ω and normally the delay distortion is a function of frequency.

---

* We know that $Z_0 = \sqrt{\dfrac{R + j\omega L}{G + j\omega C}} = \left[\dfrac{\sqrt{R^2 + (\omega L)^2},\ \angle\tan^{-1}\dfrac{\omega L}{R}}{\sqrt{G^2 + \omega^2 C^2},\ \angle\tan^{-1}\dfrac{\omega L}{G}}\right]^{\frac{1}{2}} = \sqrt{\left[\dfrac{R^2 + \omega^2 L^2}{G^2 + \omega^2 C^2}\right]^{\frac{1}{2}}}\ \angle\dfrac{1}{2}\left[\tan^{-1}\dfrac{G}{\omega C} - \tan^{-1}\dfrac{R}{\omega L}\right]$

when ω is small, $Z_0 = \sqrt{R/G}$ and for large values of ω, $Z_0 = \sqrt{L/C}$.

Since (R/G) is in all cases greater than (L/C), the variation of Z_0 with frequency for a practical line has been shown in Fig. (*b*).

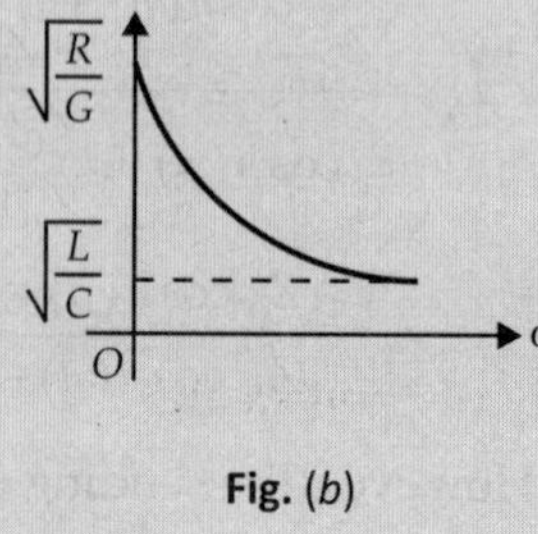

Fig. (*b*)

** The phase constant has been shown to be

$$\beta = \sqrt{\frac{1}{2}\{\sqrt{(R^2 + \omega^2 L^2)(G^2 + \omega^2 C^2)} - (RG - \omega^2 LC)\}}$$

and, the attenuation constant

$$\alpha = \sqrt{\frac{1}{2}\{\sqrt{(R^2 + \omega^2 L^2)(G^2 - \omega^2 C^2)} + (RG - \omega^2 LC)\}}$$

This shows the variation of α and β with ω.

17.11.3 Reduction of Distortion

In a high quality transmission, the frequency distortion is reduced or eliminated utilising a network known as equalizer. The equalizer has the attenuation versus frequency characteristic just opposite to that of the line. The total attenuation thus becomes constant in a particular frequency band and is minimum. In telecommunication lines, the attenuation problem is also eliminated by using large gain amplifiers. This enables practically frequency distortionless transmission of the signal.

Equaliser has also been used to reduce delay distortion. Here, the equalizer is made in such a way so that $\beta = \omega\sqrt{LC}$ *i.e.*, ω is always multiplied by a constant (*i.e.*, $\sqrt{LC}$). So, $v_p = \dfrac{\omega}{\beta}$ becomes $v_p = \dfrac{\omega}{\omega\sqrt{LC}}$ utilising equalizer. Here, $v_p = \dfrac{1}{\sqrt{LC}}$ which is constant and becomes independent of frequency.

In audio transmission, frequency distortion causes serious problem in output while delay distortion is not taken as a serious problem. However, in picture signal transmission both may create problem in the output.

17.11.4 Distortionless Line

In distortionless line, the input signal is propagated to the output terminals without any distortion (*i.e.*, there is no frequency or delay distortion).

Again, $\gamma = \sqrt{ZY} = \sqrt{(R + j\omega L)(G + j\omega C)}$

$$= \sqrt{L\left(\frac{R}{L} + j\omega\right)C\left(\frac{G}{C} + j\omega\right)}$$

or, $$\gamma = \sqrt{LC\left(\frac{R}{L} + j\omega\right)\left(\frac{G}{C} + j\omega\right)} \quad ...(17.66)$$

When, $\dfrac{R}{L} = \dfrac{G}{C}$, from equation (17.66)

$$\left.\begin{aligned} &\text{either } \gamma = \sqrt{LC}\left[\frac{R}{L} + j\omega\right] \text{ i.e., } \gamma = \frac{R}{L}\sqrt{LC} + j\omega\sqrt{LC} \\ &\text{or, } \gamma = \sqrt{LC}\left[\frac{G}{C} + j\omega\right] \text{ i.e., } \gamma = \frac{G}{C}\sqrt{LC} + j\omega\sqrt{LC} \end{aligned}\right\} \quad ...[17.66(a)]$$

Also $$\gamma = \alpha + j\beta \quad ...[17.66(b)]$$

Hence, comparison of Eqs. 17.66(*a*) and 17.66(*b*) reveals

$$\alpha = \frac{R}{L}\sqrt{LC} \quad \text{or,} \quad \frac{G}{C}\sqrt{LC} \quad \text{and,} \quad \beta = \omega\sqrt{LC}$$

Then, it is evident that α is *independent* of ω and β is *dependent* on ω. However, ω is a real component and β is associated with imaginary component.

Again, as $\beta = \omega\sqrt{LC}$, hence it is evident $\sqrt{LC}$ being a constant quantity, β is then a constant quantity multiplied by ω.

Also $v_p = \dfrac{\omega}{\beta} = \dfrac{\omega}{\omega\sqrt{LC}} = \dfrac{1}{\sqrt{LC}}$; hence the velocities of the components propagating along the line are same indicating no effect of delay distortion.

Again, $$Z_0 = \sqrt{\frac{R + j\omega L}{G + j\omega C}} = \sqrt{\frac{L}{C}\left[\frac{\frac{R}{L} + j\omega}{\frac{G}{C} + j\omega}\right]}$$

If $$\frac{R}{L} = \frac{G}{C}, \quad Z_0 = \sqrt{\frac{L}{C}}$$

Z_0 being a real quantity, all frequency components will have some attenuation and phase velocity. This makes the line free from delay distortion. Hence, the line becomes totally distortionless provided $\dfrac{R}{L} = \dfrac{G}{C}$.

17.11.5 Practical Ways to make the Line Distortionless

In an actual transmission line,

$$\frac{R}{L} >> \frac{G}{C}.$$

Hence, to make a line distortionless, either $\dfrac{R}{L}$ is to be decreased or $\dfrac{G}{C}$ is to be increased. There are *three* methods by which this can be achieved.

Method 1 *Reduction of the resistance R results in reduction of* $\dfrac{R}{L}$.

Disadvantages

Reduction of R, the resistance, requires large conduction or combination of parallel conductors. This is an expensive affair and is not normally feasible. Another disadvantage of reduction of R is that it reduces Z_0. This causes undamped oscillation and reflection of energy from the load ends.

Advantage

I^2R loss in the line is reduced with decrease in R.

CHAPTER 17

Method 2 *Increasing L, i.e., the inductance, the value of the quantity $\frac{R}{L}$ decreases.*

Disadvantage

This requires additional amount of reactive power in the line.

Advantages

This is the best method because it can be easily achieved by changing the configuration of conductors and using low cost (high inductance) conductors. It also decreases α and hence reduces distortion. It also improves the value of Z_0 and hence does not cause energy reflection from the load. Method of increasing L is known as "loading of lines".

Method 3 *Decreasing C, $\frac{G}{C}$ can be increased.*

Disadvantage

It results in abnormal increase in Z_0 which may not be acceptable. It also increases installation cost and if cables are used, total cost increases.

Advantage

Decrease of C is generally done by increasing the spacing between conductors. This also results in lowering of α.

Adjustment in G, though theoretically can be done, is not generally acceptable because increase of G means increase in leakage current. This is not a proper solution because of increased dielectric loss and degradation in conductor quality.

17.12 CONDITION FOR MINIMUM ATTENUATION

In continuous line, attenuation plays a vital role in decreasing the amplitude of the input wave signal. In long lines, this may create problem in reception. The signal received may be too low to serve any useful purpose. Hence, it is needed that the communication lines should have minimum attenuation *i.e.*, minimum α.

However,

$$\alpha = \sqrt{\frac{1}{2}[\{\sqrt{(R^2+\omega^2L^2)(G^2+\omega^2C^2)}\}+(RG-\omega^2LC)]}$$

Squaring both sides,

$$2\alpha^2 = \left[\sqrt{(R^2+\omega^2L^2)(G^2+\omega^2C^2)}+(RG-\omega^2LC)\right]$$

If L is regarded as a variable and R, G and C are assumed to be constant, the optimum value of L to provide minimum attenuation may be found by differentiating the above expression with respect to L and equating the result to be zero.

This gives

$$4\alpha\frac{d\alpha}{dL} = \left[\frac{\omega^2L(G^2+\omega^2G^2)}{\sqrt{(R^2+\omega^2L^2)(G^2+\omega^2C^2)}}-\omega^2C\right] \quad ...(17.67)$$

The condition for minimum attenuation being $\frac{d\alpha}{dL}=0$, from equation (17.67),

$$\frac{\omega^2L(G^2+\omega^2C^2)}{\sqrt{(R^2+\omega^2L^2)(G^2+\omega^2C^2)}} = \omega^2C$$

or, $$L^2(G^2+\omega^2C^2) = C^2(R^2+\omega^2L^2)(G^2+\omega^2C^2)$$

or, $$L^2G^2+\omega^2L^2C^2 = C^2R^2+\omega^2L^2C^2$$

or, $$\frac{L}{C} = \frac{R}{G}$$

i.e., the condition of minimum attenuation becomes

$$\frac{R}{L} = \frac{G}{C} \quad ...(17.68)$$

Assuming L to be variable,

$$L = \frac{RC}{G}\text{ Henry} \quad ...(17.69)$$

To have minimum attenuation the value of L is to be adjusted in such a way so that it satisfies equation (17.69).

Value of C, the shunt capacitance of the line, can also be obtained from equation (17.69) for minimum attenuation and is given by

$$C = \frac{LG}{R}\text{ Farad} \quad ...(17.70)$$

In practice, C is normally greater than the desired value of $\frac{LG}{R}$, and to reduce the attenuation it would be necessary to decrease the capacitance of the line.

The value of R and G for minimum attenuation can be obtained for minimum attenuation as

$$R = \frac{GL}{C}\text{ Ohm}$$

and $$G = \frac{RC}{L}\text{ mho}$$

It may be observed that in a line, if $R=0$ and $G=0$ *i.e.*, the line is lossless, the attenuation α is zero. Hence for practical purposes, R and G should be kept minimum.

Thus, from the above analysis, it is evident that the condition $\frac{R}{L}=\frac{G}{C}$ indicates the condition of minimum distortion as well as minimum attenuation.

When this relationship holds, the received signal is an exact replica of the sending end signal. It is also evident that the transmission properties of a line can be greatly improved if either L can be increased or C can be decreased such that $\frac{R}{L}=\frac{G}{C}$.

C depends on the construction of the line and cannot readily be reduced. Due to this cause, attempts are being made to increase L. This process has been termed as "loading" whereas the inductance of a line is artificially increased to reduce attenuation and distortion. No attempt has been made to increase the value of G, the conductance as it reduces the quality of transmission and increases dielectric loss.

17.13 LOADING OF LINES

As increase of L decreases $\frac{R}{L}$ value, hence by increasing L, the value $\frac{R}{L}$ is approximately equal to $\frac{G}{C}$. In normal transmission line $\frac{R}{L}>>\frac{G}{C}$ causing the line not free from distortion. To make it distortionless, one should make $\frac{R}{L}=\frac{G}{C}$. This is possible by making L higher. This is obtained by changing the line configuration and spacing and using high inductance wires. This method is popularly known as "Loading of lines".

Loading of line means artificial enhancement of the inductance and the line is then termed as "loaded line". There are various ways by which line loading can be increased *viz.*, (*a*) by adding induction in lumped form at specific locations (this is also known as stub matching) in a particular form ; (*b*) by installation of coaxial cable in series with the line such that line inductance increases.

17.13.1 Types of Loading

There are *two* types of loading in general :

(*a*) Continuous loading

(*b*) Lumped loading

(*a*) Continuous Loading

Figure 17.15 shows a continuously loaded cable. A steel tape or some other magnetic material such as a mumetal is wound round the conductor to be loaded. This increases the permeability of the surrounding medium and thereby increasing the inductance. The increase in inductance is

$$L \simeq \frac{\mu}{\frac{D}{n.t}+1} \text{ mH}$$

where, μ = permeability of iron tape

D = dia. of copper conductor

n = number of layers

t = thickness per layer of iron wire

This method may be useful in order to give an increase in inductance upto approximately 100 mH/mile, though the cost is excessive due to difficulties in construction. Also, the large apparent increase in the primary constant R, due to eddy current losses and hysteresis losses in the magnetic material, cause problem. Moreover, small differences in mechanical pressure between the tape and conductor may cause large variation in the primary constant.

Nowadays the continuous loading is widely used only on submarine cables due to problem of making watertight joints at loading points. The continuous loaded cable (Fig. 17.15) has definite advantage over the lumped loaded cable. The attenuation (α) increases smoothly with increase in frequency and the attenuation versus frequency curves of continuous loaded cable and lumped loaded cable and unloaded cable are shown in Fig. 17.15.

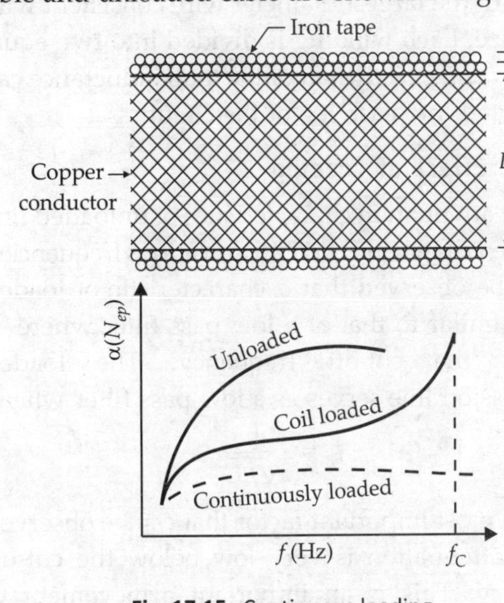

Fig. 17.15 Continuous loading.

CHAPTER 17

(b) Lumped Loading

The inductance of a transmission line may also be increased by the introduction of inductance coils at uniform and definite interval along the length of the line. The line then behaves, at all frequencies and upto a certain frequency called the "cut-off" frequency, as a distortionless line provided the spacings are uniform. Attenuation (α) increases rapidly above the cut-off frequency and therefore the lumped-loaded line behaves as a low pass filter. This method of loading is more convenient than continuous loading in practice.

There is, however, a practical limitation by which the inductance of the line may be increased to reduce attenuation. The inductance coils possess a certain resistance and thus increase of L also increases R. If R increases the hysteresis and eddy current losses are increased in loading coils and hence the distortion increases in the line. If the coils are not carefully designed, the distortion may again be introduced in the line.

Loading Coils

Low resistance, low core loss, maintenance of circuit balance, avoidance of interference between circuits and small size are the most important aspects of design and application of loading coils.

The core is usually a toroidal type and made of permalloy or molybdenum-permalloy dust, bound by shellac. This type of construction permits the loading coil of high inductance with small dimension and low eddy current loss. The coil is wound of wire with the largest diameter wire consistent with small size. Each winding is divided into two equal parts, so that exactly half of the total inductance can be inserted into each leg of the circuit.

17.13.2 Effect of Loading

The attenuation characteristics of unloaded line have been shown in Fig. 17.16 for various frequencies. It may be observed that α characteristic of loaded line is similar to that of a low pass filter where f_c denotes the cut-off frequency. The loaded transmission line serves as a low pass filter when,

$$f_c = \frac{1}{\pi\sqrt{LC}}$$

The most important factor that can be observed is that attenuation is very low below the cut-off frequency. This is an important achievement to make minimum attenuation in the line. Proper loading of line makes $\frac{R}{L}$ approximately equal to G/C thus making the line almost distortionless.

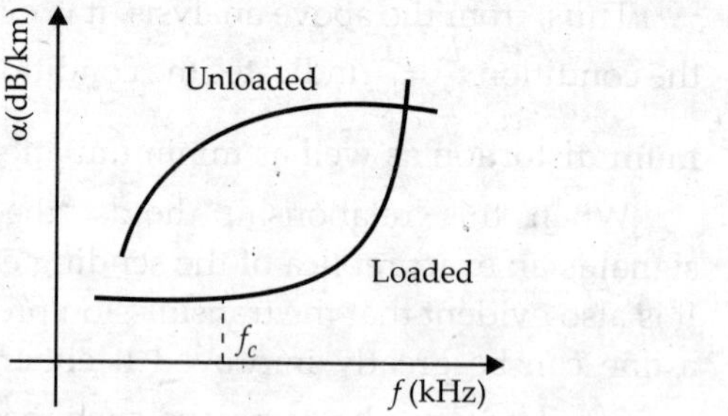

Fig. 17.16 α characteristic.

17.13.3 Effect of Loading on the Secondary Constant

(a) Z_0 is increased and becomes practically a pure resistance.

(b) α is reduced and becomes practically constant over the working range.

(c) β is increased and the velocity of propagation is reduced to a value which is practically constant over the working range.

17.14 LOSSES IN TRANSMISSION LINE

In practical transmission line, energy input at one place suffers some loss while being transmitted to another place at output.

There are *three* types of losses, *i.e.*,

(a) Radiation loss,

(b) Dielectric loss and

(c) Copper loss or conductor heating loss or thermal loss

(a) *Radiation loss.* This loss arises when the line may act as an antenna and is particularly evident when the separation of conductor is high. This loss is more in open wire lines than that in co-axial cables.

In case of high frequency transmission through open wire transmission lines, radiation loss occurs due to rise in electromagnetic field surrounding the conductors : this loss of energy due to radiation effect is proportional to the square of the frequency and increases with the spacing between the line conductors.

(*b*) *Dielectric loss.* In transmission line, air generally acts as dielectric medium between conductors and earth while in coaxial cable the dielectric medium may be chemical compounds. The dielectric medium possesses finite conductivity and there is leakage of current as well as loss of energy between conductor being separated by the dielectric medium. This energy loss appears as heat in dielectric medium.

Dielectric loss *i.e.,* the energy loss, is proportional to the voltage across the dielectric and inversely proportional to the characteristic impedance Z_0 of the dielectric medium for any power transmitted. This loss increases with frequency for solid and chemical dielectric medium. However, for air, dielectric heat loss is negligible. In practical capacitors dielectric loss appears due to the imperfectness of a power capacitance. In transmission lines dielectric loss appears for imperfectness of the dielectric medium.

(*c*) *Copper loss* (*Conductor heating loss or thermal loss*). It is the energy loss in the form of heat being dissipated in the surrounding medium by the line conductors. This loss appears due to existence of resistance in the line conductors. In analysis it is expressed as I^2R loss, where I is the current through the conductor and R is resistance.

Conventionally, this is known as copper loss or conductors heat loss or thermal loss. This loss is proportional to the square of current flowing through and inversely proportional to the characteristic impedance.

[Because of "skin effect" *ac* and *dc* copper losses are different. *AC* copper loss is more and increases with frequency of operation.]

17.15 REFLECTION IN TRANSMISSION LINES

If a line, at any point along its length, is connected to an impedance that has a value different from Z_0, part of the wave travelling down the line will be reflected back from point of interconnection. This phenomenon is known as *reflection in transmission line*. If a line is uniform along its entire length and is terminated by an impedance Z_R, reflection will occur at the distant end. This reflection will be maximum when the line is open-circuited ($Z_R = \infty$) or short-circuited ($Z_R = 0$) and will be zero when $Z_R = Z_0$.

17.15.1 Reflection Coefficient

In a transmission line, reflection occurs whenever there is an impedance *mismatch* between two networks. The ratio of amplitudes of reflected voltage (E_R) to the incident voltage (E_i) at the receiving end of a line has been termed as the reflection coefficient (K).

$$\therefore \quad K = \frac{E_R}{E_i}\left(= -\frac{I_R}{I_i}\right)$$

Let network A represents the transmission line of characteristic impedance Z_0 and network B represents the load of impedance Z_R (Fig. 17.17).

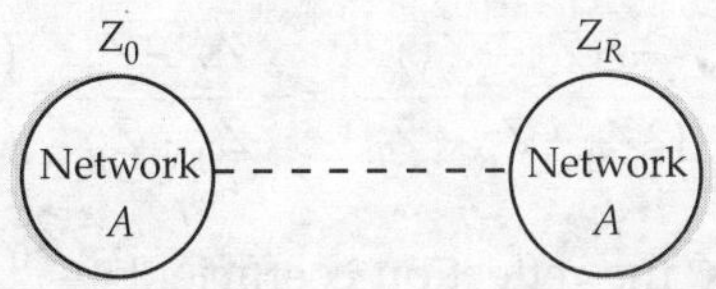

Fig. 17.17 Two networks connected.

Replacing network A by a generator *emf* E and impedance Z_0 and network B by the combination of two impedances Z_0 and Z'_R (such that $Z_0 + Z'_R = Z_R$), the entire network looks like Fig. 17.18.

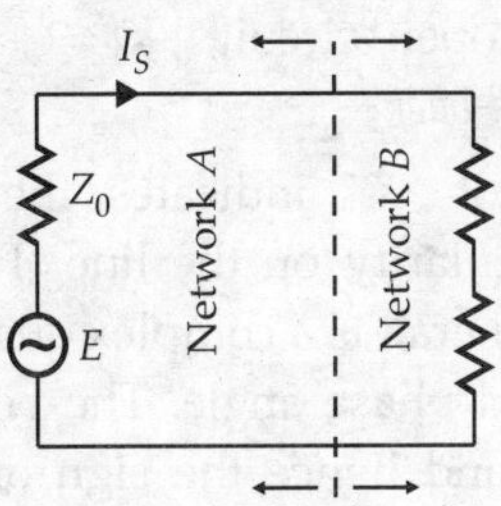

Fig. 17.18 Representation of two networks.

Figure 17.19 shows the final equivalent representation of the network shown in Fig. 17.17 with equivalent *emf* source ($-IZ'_R$) responsible for the reflected current I_R, the incident current being I_i.

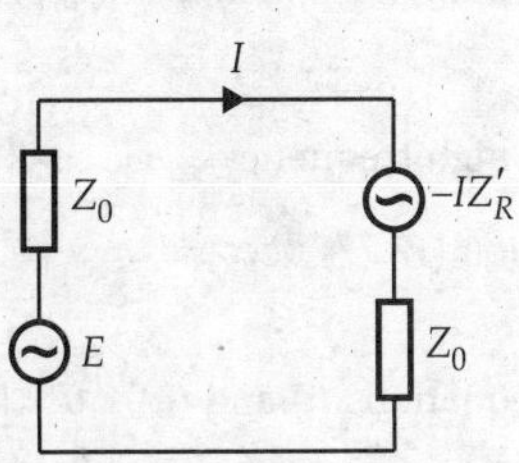

Fig. 17.19 Equivalent circuit.

The resultant current in steady is I.

$$\therefore \quad I = I_i + I_R \qquad \text{...(17.71)}$$

Also, $I = \dfrac{E - IZ'_R}{2Z_0}$

i.e., $E = I(2Z_0 + Z'_R)$ ...(17.72)

However, utilising the concept of superposition theorem,

$$I_i = \frac{E}{2Z_0}, \quad I_R = -\frac{IZ'_R}{2Z_0}$$

$$\therefore \quad \frac{I_R}{I_i} = \frac{-IZ'_R}{E} = \frac{-IZ'_R}{I(2Z_0 + Z'_R)}$$

[Utilising 17.72]

But $Z'_R = Z_R - Z_0$

Hence,

$$\frac{I_R}{I_i} = \frac{-I(Z_R - Z_0)}{I(2Z_0 + Z_R - Z_0)} = -\frac{Z_R - Z_0}{Z_0 + Z_R} = \frac{(Z_0 - Z_R)}{(Z_0 + Z_R)}$$

Thus K, the reflection coefficient $= \dfrac{Z_0 - Z_R}{Z_0 + Z_R}$ ...(17.73)

If a line is terminated in its characteristic impedance (Z_0), then $K=0$ and there is no reflection. The line is said to be *non-resonant* or *flat line*. On the other hand, if the line is terminated in a short-circuit or open circuit, $|K|=1$ and the total power is *reflected back.*

The value of 'K' indicates the amount of impedance irregularity on the line. The reflection coefficient, in general, is a complex quantity having a magnitude and phase angle. The polarity of the reflected wave and hence the sign of K depends upon the magnitudes and angles of Z_R, the load impedance and Z_0, the characteristic impedance of the line.

17.15.2 Standing Wave

Whenever reflection takes place in line transmission, at some points, the incident and reflected signals are in phase and both the components add together ; on the other hand, at some other points, two components may oppose each other. The net or resultant graphical profile of both of these incident and reflected waves is called *standing wave* ; the points where the resultant signal (voltage or current) is maximum are known as *voltage* or *current maxima.* On the other hand, the points where the resultant signal (voltage or current) is minimum are called *voltage* or *current minima.* There will be standing waves corresponding to the resultant voltage or current signal. Thus, it is evident that :

$$|V_{max}| = |V_i| + |V_r| \ ; \qquad |I_{max}| = |I_i| + |I_r|$$

$$|V_{min}| = |V_i| - |V_r| \ ; \qquad |I_{min}| = |I_i| - |I_r|$$

Voltage Standing Wave Ratio (VSWR)

This is defined as the ratio of magnitudes maximum and minimum voltage of the standing wave,

i.e., $VSWR = S = \dfrac{|V_{max}|}{|V_{min}|}$ ...(17.74)

Here, the standing wave has been specified in terms of voltage. In high frequency transmission*, standing wave problem is very common.

[In a similar way, *current standing wave ratio* may be defined by the ratio of maximum to the minimum current on the standing wave. Voltage standing wave ratio (VSWR) is more popular since it is easy to measure VSWR at different points of the line by just a voltmeter while for measurement of current standing wave ratio, we require an ammeter to be connected in series at different maxima and minima points which is cumbersome].

---

* A major disadvantage of high frequency lines is that it has got appreciable ohmic and dielectric loss (because of the fact that X_L is high but X_C is low). However, in analysis, the effect of this loss is usually disregarded since the physical length of the line is small. In high frequency lines, propagation constant γ is given by

$$\gamma = \sqrt{ZY} = \sqrt{(R + j\omega L)(G + j\omega C)} \quad ...(i)$$

However, at high frequency, $\omega L >> R$ and $\omega C >> G$.

Hence equation (17.77) becomes $\gamma = \sqrt{j\omega L . j\omega C} = j\omega\sqrt{LC}$ ...(ii)

But $\gamma = \alpha + j\beta$ ...(iii)

Comparing equations (*i*) and (*ii*), $\alpha = 0$, $\gamma = j\beta$, where $\beta = \omega\sqrt{LC}$

The velocity of signal is then given by $v_p = \dfrac{\omega}{\beta} = \dfrac{1}{\sqrt{LC}}$ km/sec.

Also, when $\omega L >> R$ and $\omega C >> G$, $Z_0 = \sqrt{\dfrac{R + j\omega L}{G + j\omega C}} = \sqrt{\dfrac{L}{C}}$

Figure 17.20 represents the profiles of voltage and current standing waves. It may be noted that as the power of the wave must remain same at any point on the line hence current and voltages are opposite in phase *i.e.*, at voltage maximum point the current is minimum and vice-versa. In this figure, λ represents wavelength and it may be noted that the maximum impedance and minimum impedance points can be determined by the ratios of (V_{max} and I_{min}) and (V_{min} and I_{max}) respectively. It may also be noted that current minimum and voltage minimum or the current maximum and voltage maximum points are $(\lambda/4)$ distance apart from each other.

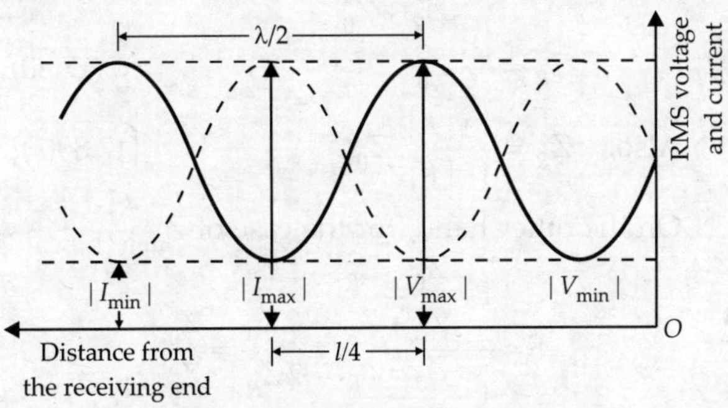

Fig. 17.20 Standing wave patterns on a HF line.

In case of *open-circuited line*, the load current is zero. This clearly indicates that the incident and reflected currents at load are equal in magnitude but opposite in sign so that I_i and I_r cancel each other. Thus at load the current minima point is found. Obviously the voltage maximum point will be located here also and at a distance $(\lambda/4)$ from the load end along the line, the conditions are opposite and at $(\lambda/4)$, the current will be maximum while the voltage will be minimum.

On the other hand, when the load end of the line is *short-circuited*, load current is maximum at this point and load voltage is zero. Thus, incident and reflected voltages cancel each other at load point and the voltage minima, current maxima point is located at the load. At a distance $(\lambda/4)$ along the line from the load points the condition is reversed and voltage maxima current minima point is reached.

If the load at the termination of the line is very high *i.e.*, more than Z_0 (but not infinity like the open-circuited case) the voltage maxima-current minima point is also reached at the load but the magnitude of this voltage maxima is smaller than its value in the open-circuited line. Though current minima occurs at this point still it is not zero.

On the other hand, if the load is very low *i.e.*, less than Z_0 (but not zero), the voltage minima-current maxima point is reached at the load point like the case of short-circuited line. However, this time, the magnitude of current maxima is not so high like the short-circuited one and the voltage is not zero at load.

17.16 REFLECTION COEFFICIENT

It has been defined in the usual way *i.e.*, $K=\frac{|V_R|}{|V_i|}$, the ratio of reflected and incident voltage. K is a vector quantity.

17.16.1 Relation between VSWR and K

It is obvious that

$$|V_{max}| = |V_i| + |V_R|$$

$$|V_{min}| = |V_i| - |V_R|$$

But $\text{VSWR} = \frac{|V_{max}|}{|V_{min}|} = \frac{|V_i|+|V_R|}{|V_i|-|V_R|}$

$$= \frac{1+\left|\frac{V_R}{V_i}\right|}{1-\left|\frac{V_R}{V_i}\right|} = \frac{1+|K|}{1-|K|}$$

or, $$S = \frac{1+|K|}{1-|K|} \qquad \text{...(17.75)}$$

or, $S(1-|K|) = (1+|K|)$

or, $S - S|K| = 1 + |K|$

or, $S - 1 = |K| + S|K| = |K|(1+S)$

$\therefore$ $$|K| = \frac{S-1}{S+1} \qquad \text{...(17.76)}$$

17.16.2 Determination of VSWR

(a) For an open wire line. An open wire line is energized by a generator (Fig. 17.21). A sliding contact *ac* voltmeter is used to measure the voltage at different points along the line by sliding the contacts. The voltmeter will read the maximum and

CHAPTER 17

minimum voltages at different points. Let $V_{max_{av}}$ and $V_{min_{av}}$ indicate the respective two averages of the values.

Here $S = \text{VSWR} = \dfrac{|V_{max_{av}}|}{|V_{min_{av}}|}$.

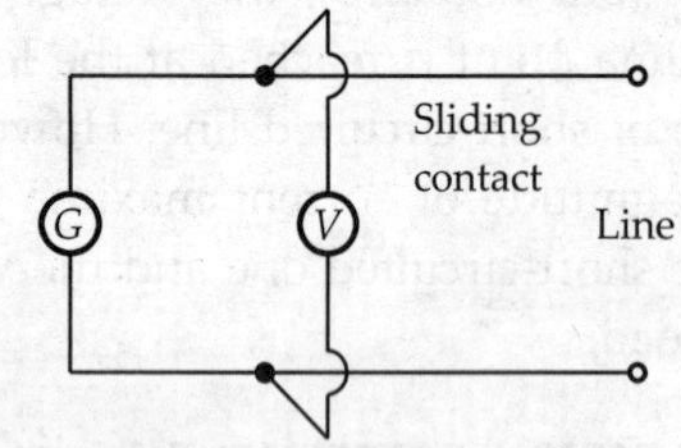

Fig. 17.21 An open wire line.

(*b*) *SWR for a cable.* In high frequency transmission, coaxial cables are frequently used. Here, a wire probe is inserted into the air dielectric of the coaxial cable as a sensor device for voltage measurement. A high frequency oscillator (with sine wave output) is operated with a single frequency and is connected at one end of the coaxial cable. A fixed attenuator (*PAD*) between the oscillator and the cable is utilised to avoid reflection entering the oscillator and thereby causing secondary reflection and disturbing the measurement.

The probe is displaced along the length and several values of voltages at different points are recorded. V_{max} and V_{min} values are averaged and '*S*' is then calculated from the ratio of these two values.

17.16.3 Relation between VSWR and Load Impedance

It is known that when the load impedance is high (greater than Z_0), at load, voltage maximum and current minima points occur and the ratio of voltage maxima and current minima becomes maximum (Z_{max}).

As $Z_R >> Z_0$,

$$K = \frac{Z_0 - Z_R}{Z_0 + Z_R} = -\text{ve} \qquad ...(17.77)$$

i.e., to have +ve *K*, we should write

$$K = \frac{Z_R - Z_0}{Z_0 + Z_R} \qquad ...(17.78)$$

On the other hand, if the load impedance is very low (less than Z_0), at load, the current maximum-voltage minimum points occur and the ratio of voltage minima to current maxima becomes minimum (Z_{min}).

This time $Z_R << Z_0$,

Thus $K = \dfrac{Z_0 - Z_R}{Z_0 + Z_R}$ remains +ve ...(17.79)

Now, $S = \dfrac{1+|K|}{1-|K|}$

Hence, for the case of Z_{max},

$$S = \frac{1 + \dfrac{Z_R - Z_0}{Z_R + Z_0}}{1 - \dfrac{Z_R - Z_0}{Z_R + Z_0}} = \frac{2Z_R}{2Z_0} = \frac{Z_R}{Z_0}$$

i.e., $$Z_R = S \times Z_0 \qquad ...(17.80)$$

Also, $$Z_R = \frac{1+|K|}{1-|K|} . Z_0 \qquad [17.80(a)]$$

On the other hand, for the case of Z_{min},

$$S = \frac{1 + \dfrac{Z_0 - Z_R}{Z_0 + Z_R}}{1 - \dfrac{Z_0 - Z_R}{Z_0 + Z_R}} = \frac{2Z_0}{2Z_R} = \frac{Z_0}{Z_R}$$

or, $$Z_R = \frac{Z_0}{S} \qquad ...(17.81)$$

i.e., $$Z_R = \frac{1-|K|}{1+|K|} . Z_0 \qquad [17.81(a)]$$

Expressions (17.80) and [17.80(*a*)] indicate the relationship between the load impedances and VSWR while expressions (17.81) and [17.81(*a*)] indicate the relationship between the load impedances and reflection coefficient. It may be observed that,

(*i*) When $K = 0$ *i.e.*, when there is no reflection,

$$S = \frac{1+0}{1-0} = 1 \quad i.e., \; V_{max} = V_{min}$$

Also, $K = 0$ means $Z_0 = Z_R$. Thus the line terminated by characteristic impedance will have no reflection and is evident from the above reasonings.

(*ii*) When $K = +1$, there is complete reflection,

$$S = \frac{1+1}{1-1} = \infty.$$

Also, $K = +1$ means that $Z_R = 0$ *i.e.*, the load terminals are short-circuited. Then $S = \infty$ indicates complete reflection from distant end, the distant end being short-circuited.

(*iii*) When $K=-1$, there is also complete reflection.

Here, $S=\dfrac{1-1}{1+1}=0.$

Also $S=\dfrac{Z_0}{Z_R}$ (equation 17.80)

Here $Z_R=\infty$ with $S=0$. This means that the distant end is open-circuited.

It may be observed that in open and short-circuits, the reflection is complete (*i.e.*, $K=1$), only the sign of K is reversed. This indicates that the reflection in case of distant end being short-circuited is with same polarity while that for open-ended line, the polarity is just opposite.

17.16.4 Power Expression

In a *HF* line, the maxima of current and voltages are always a quarter wavelength apart.

Also, $|V_{max}|=|V_i|+|V_r|$

But, $|V_i|=|I_i|Z_0$ and $|V_r|=|I_r|Z_0$

$\therefore$ We get $|V_{max}|=[\,|I_i|+|I_r|\,]Z_0$

or, $$|V_{max}|=|I_{max}|Z_0 \qquad ...(17.82)$$

In a similar way, it can be shown that

$$|V_{min}|=|I_{min}|Z_0 \qquad ...(17.83)$$

At the point of maximum voltage and minimum current, Z_{max} occurs. Also, at this point

$$V_{max}=I_{min}\cdot Z_{max}$$

$$=I_{min}\times SZ_0 \quad [\because \text{ at } Z_{max}, Z_R=SZ_0]$$

$$\therefore \quad \text{Power } (P)=|V_{max}||I_{min}|=\frac{|V_{max}|^2}{SZ_0} \qquad ...(17.84)$$

$$\text{Also,} \quad P=|V_{min}||I_{max}|=\frac{S|V_{max}|^2}{Z_0} \qquad ...(17.85)$$

Power can also be expressed as

$$P=\frac{|V_{max}||V_{min}|}{Z_0}$$

$$\text{or,} \quad P=\frac{(|V_i|+|V_r|)(|V_i|-|V_r|)}{Z_0}=\frac{|V_i|^2}{Z_0}-\frac{|V_r|^2}{Z_0} \qquad ...(17.86)$$

Equations (17.84), (17.85) and (17.86) represent different expressions of power.

17.17 COAXIAL CABLE

This is a special type of signal transmission medium consisting of two (or more) coaxial cylindrical tubes (or conductors). The outermost tube (or conductor) is generally earthed. The dielectric between the two tubular surfaces may be solid or gaseous medium. The outer conductor works as an electrostatic shield to avoid external interference. Hence a coaxial cable forms an excellent transmission line, particularly for high frequency signals.

In coaxial cable conductor heating loss as well as 'skin effect' is reduced. Moreover, dielectric heating being negligible, coaxial cable is not affected or does not affect by external interference.

Coaxial cables are frequently used as distributed parameter configuration of 'L' and 'C' and are used to transmit high frequency signal in television, ratio and VHF or microwave sets. For impedance matching also co-axial cable is utilised. In transmission line, the coaxial cable is utilised as a distributed loading element. When waveguides are used, coaxial cables are utilised as a connector between the equipment and the waveguide.

The characteristics impedance of any coaxial cable is given by :

$$Z_0=\sqrt{\frac{L}{C}}=\sqrt{\frac{\mu}{4\pi^2 K}}\log_e\left(\frac{D}{d}\right) \qquad ...(17.87)$$

$$\text{or,} \quad Z_0=\sqrt{\frac{\mu_0\mu_r}{4\pi^2 K_0 K_n}}\log_e\left(\frac{D}{d}\right)$$

$$=138\sqrt{\frac{\mu_r}{K_n}}\times\log_{10}\left(\frac{D}{d}\right)=138\log_{10}\left(\frac{D}{d}\right)$$

(Assuming μ_r and K_n as unity) ...(17.88)

where, D = Inner diameter of the outer conductor of the coaxial cable

d = Diameter of the inner conductor

μ_o, K_0 = Absolute permeability

μ_r, K_n = Relative permittivity

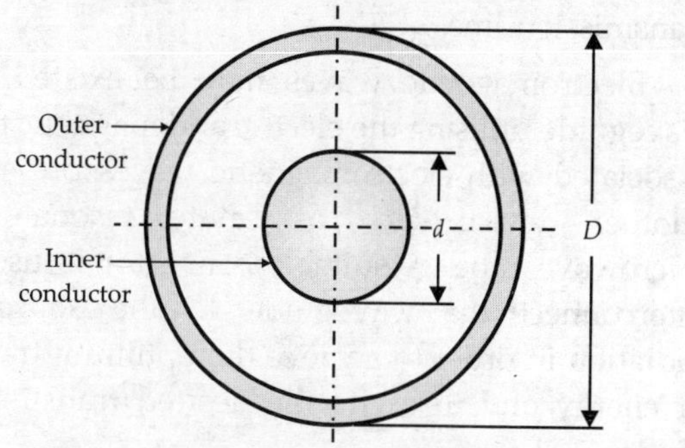

Fig. 17.22 Cross-section of a coaxial cable.

17.18 WAVEGUIDE

A transmission line consisting of a suitably shaped hollow conductor, which may be fitted with a dielectric material and is used to guide electromagnetic waves of ultra high frequency propagated along its length, is called a waveguide. The transmitted wave is reflected back by the internal walls of the waveguide and the resulting distribution associated with the wave causes the transmission mode (transmission mode is any one of different states of oscillation of an electromagnetic wave of given frequency). The mode of an electromagnetic wave is governed by the configuration of the vectors describing the wave. The main types of wave configurations are :

(*i*) *TE* wave (*Transverse Electric Wave*)

(*ii*) *TM* wave (*Transverse Magnetic Wave*)

(*iii*) *TEM* wave (*Transverse Electromagnetic Wave*)

TEM mode is one of the most commonly excited modes in coaxial cables. It cannot be propagated in a waveguide. In a waveguide, each component of the wave contains a factor given by $e^{(j\omega t - \gamma_{m,n} Z)}$ where, $\omega = 2\pi f$ and $\gamma_{m,n}$ is the propagation coefficient determining the phase and amplitude of the wave components.

For each mode of transmission, a lower limit exists where the complex quantity $\gamma_{m,n}$ becomes purely real and is equal to the attenuation constant $\alpha_{m,n}$.

The amplitude of the component then decreases exponentially and the frequency goes below cut-off and the wave does not propagate when $\gamma_{m,n}$ is imaginary, the phase of the wave then varies with distance and the wave then propagates without any attenuation. In practice, $\gamma_{m,n}$ can never be purely imaginary and hence some attenuation always occurs due to energy loss in the transmission line.

Electromagnetic waves may be excited in a waveguide utilising the electric and magnetic fields associated with electromagnetic waves present in another device such as cavity resonator or microwave tube. A suitable connector is used to interconnect the waveguide to the source of radiation in order to achieve the optimum transfer of energy and to excite the desired transmission mode.

A waveguide in which no reflected wave occurs at any of the transverse sections in known as a "Matched Waveguide".

In construction of a waveguide, bends are usually made smooth in order to prevent unwanted reflections. If the direction of polarisation has to be changed, a special joint, known as 'Rotator' is used.

It is possible to create localised concentration of electric or magnetic energy within a waveguide by inserting suitably shaped metallic or dielectric pieces as lumped parameters. Capacitance elements can be formed from screws while inductive element can be formed from diaphragms. Installation of *L* and *C* is necessary when the impedances of different sections of a waveguide transformer (known as Quarter Wavelength line and is generally used for impedance matching). Unwanted frequencies or modes of transmission are eliminated using a waveguide filter.

Waveguides are widely used in communicating 'network' for the transmission of electromagnetic waves. Electromagnetic energy may also be stored by using a section of waveguide, short-circuited at each end to form a "cavity resonator". Like transmission lines, waveguides allow to pass different signals simultaneously.

However, different signals being propagated through a line must have different frequency, but in a waveguide they can have same frequency provided that each is propagated in different mode. This is a kind of multiplex transmission.

Waveguides are comparatively simpler with respect to coaxial cable from the point of view of manufacturing. Power handling capacity of waveguides is higher than the coaxial cables. Moreover, in waveguide, the power loss is low due to the fact that propagation of energy is by means of reflection from the walls.

17.19 LINE IMPEDANCE OF HF LINES

It is defined as the ratio of the line voltage and current at any point on the line when a line is not properly terminated ; standing waves are set up due to reflection affecting line impedance.

It has been deduced earlier, for an open-circuited line,

$$Z_{in} = Z_0 \coth(\gamma l)$$

$$= Z_0 \coth j\beta l$$

$$[\because \gamma = \alpha + j\beta = 0 + j\beta \text{ ; in h.f. lines, } \alpha = 0]$$

$$= -jZ_0 \cot \beta l \quad \text{...(17.89)}$$

when $l = 0$, $\beta l = 0$ and $\cot \beta l = \infty$

Hence the input impedance becomes infinity.

Again, when $l = \lambda/4$, $\beta l = \pi/2$ and $\cot \beta l = 0$.

This gives $Z_{in} = 0$.

Figure 17.23 is a plot of open circuit line impedance for different line lengths.

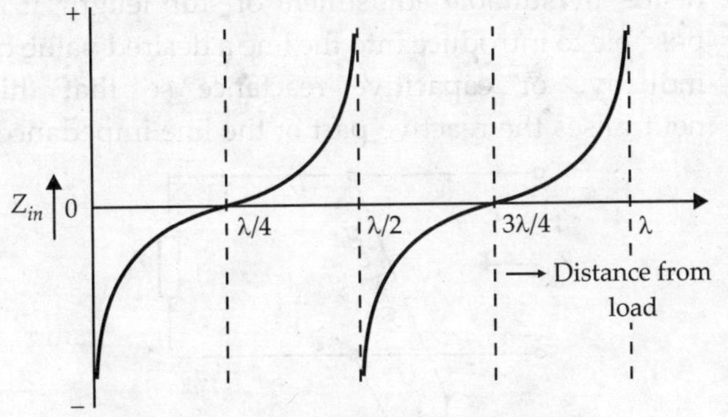

Fig. 17.23 Line impedance of a line with $Z_R = \infty$.

It may be observed from the graph that for line lengths less than $(\lambda/4)$, the line impedance behaves a capacitive reactance while for line lengths more than $(\lambda/4)$, this impedance is inductive. The line acts as a *series resonant circuit* when the length is $(\lambda/4)$ and line impedance is zero. At $(\lambda/2)$, the input impedance is infinite and the line behaves as *parallel resonant circuit*.

Similarly, it can be shown, for short-circuited line,

$$Z_{in} = jZ_0 \tan \beta l \quad \text{...(17.90)}$$

when $l = 0$, $\tan \beta l = 0$ and hence

$Z_{in} = 0$. When $l = \lambda/4$, $\beta l = \pi/2$

and hence $Z_{in} = \infty$. Figure 17.24 represents the profile of Z_{in} (line impedance) against line length under short-circuit condition.

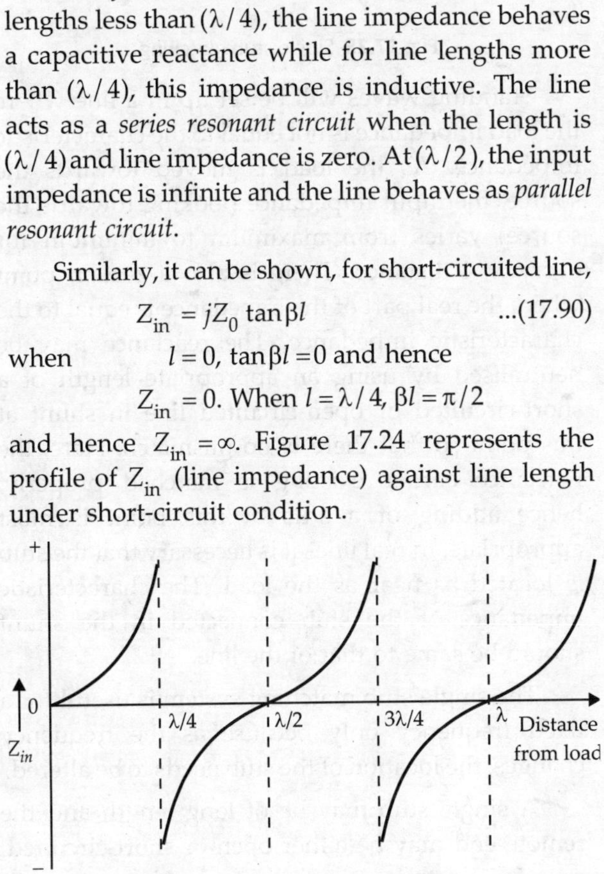

Fig. 17.24 Profile of Z_{in} for short-circuited line.

It may be observed that the line impedance behaves as inductive reactance for line length below $(\lambda/4)$ while for line lengths above $(\lambda/4)$ the line impedance is capacitive till the line length is $(\lambda/2)$. At line length $(\lambda/4)$, the line impedance is infinity while at $(\lambda/2)$ it is zero. Thus at $(\lambda/4)$, this line acts at a *parallel resonant circuit* while at $(\lambda/2)$ it acts as a *series resonant circuit*.

Thus it has been seen that lines with open and short termination act as a resonant circuit, provided their lengths are properly selected.

17.20 MATCHING

In most of the transmission line applications, it is an essential requirement that the load be *matched* with the line itself such that the power transfer is maximum from the line to the load (as per the maximum power transfer theorem). This also happens when the impedance of either source or load is the *complex conjugate* of the impedance of the load or source. This condition being achieved, it is called *impedance matching* and the devices employed to achieve this matching are called *impedance matching elements* and are briefly described below :

17.20.1 Quarter Wave Transformer

A transmission line of length equal to one-fourth of the wavelength of the fundamental frequency of the wave propagating through it is called a quarter wave transformer. It is used for impedance matching, particularly at high frequency as well as for suppression of even order of harmonics in filter network and for coupling of feeders with aerials.

The input impedance of uniform line being given by

$$Z_{in} = Z_0 \left[\frac{Z_R \cosh(\gamma l) + Z_0 \sinh(\gamma l)}{Z_0 \cosh(\gamma l) + Z_R \sinh(\gamma l)} \right]$$

(Equation 17.63 given earlier)

At high frequencies, line has been considered as lossless.

Here, $\alpha = 0$ and $\gamma = j\beta$

This gives

$$Z_{in} = Z_0 \left[\frac{Z_R \cosh j\beta l + Z_0 \sinh j\beta l}{Z_R \cosh j\beta l + Z_R \sinh j\beta l} \right] \quad \text{...(17.91)}$$

CHAPTER 17

For a line which is of quarter wavelength, $l = \frac{\lambda}{4}$, $\beta = \frac{2\pi}{\lambda}$. This gives $\beta l = \frac{2\pi}{\lambda} \cdot \frac{\lambda}{4} = \frac{\pi}{2}$.

Hence, from equation (17.91),

$$Z_{in} = Z_0 \frac{Z_R \cos\frac{\pi}{2} + jZ_0 \sin\frac{\pi}{2}}{Z_0 \cos\frac{\pi}{2} + jZ_R \sin\frac{\pi}{2}}$$

$$= Z_0 \cdot \frac{j Z_0}{j Z_R} = \frac{Z_0^2}{Z_R} \quad ...(17.92)$$

or, $$Z_0 = \sqrt{Z_{in} \times Z_R} \quad ...[17.92(a)]$$

Equation (17.92) shows that the impedance at the input of a quarter wave line depends upon the load impedance and characteristic impedance of the transmission line. Thus if Z_0 is varied, the impedance seen at the input of quarterwave transformer will also change accordingly. The load then is matching to the characteristic impedance of the main line. This is identical to varying the turns ratio of a transformer to obtain a required value of the input impedance for any given value of load impedance. [Equation (17.92) shows that where Z_R is high, the input impedance is low and vice versa, Z_0 being constant. If the load is inductive, the input impedance is capacitive and vice versa. A quarter wave line thus serves as an impedance inverter]. The quarter wave transformer has the length of $\lambda/4$ at only one frequency and then is highly frequency dependent.

17.20.2 Stubs

A section of transmission line can be used as impedance matching element by inserting it between the load and source. It is also possible to connect sections of open or short-circuited line* called "stub" in shunt with the main line at some points in order to achieve impedance matching. The process is known as *stub matching* and has the following advantages :

(*a*) Length of the main line remains unaltered.

(*b*) Characteristic impedance of the line remains constant.

(*c*) At the higher frequency, the stub may be made adjustable to suit a variety of loads and to operate over a wide range of frequencies.

Basically, the stub matching is of two types :

(*i*) Single stub matching

(*ii*) Double stub matching.

17.20.3A Single Stub Matching (Fig. 17.25)

In single stub matching, a short-circuited transmission line of a specific length is connected in shunt with the main line at a certain distance from the receiving end. As the stub impedance is inductive or capacitive, depending on its length, hence, by suitable adjustment of stub length, it is possible to introduce into the line a desired value of inductive or capacitive reactance so that this neutralises the reactive part of the line impedance.

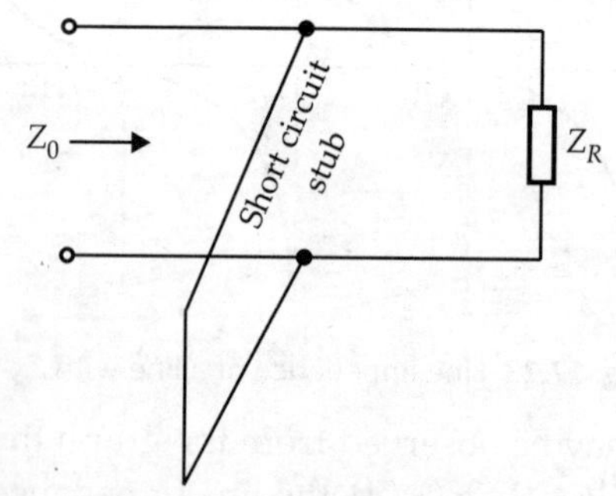

Fig. 17.25 Single stub matching.

Standing waves will be set up in a line where the load impedance is not equal to the characteristic impedance. As the load is moved towards the source, the input impedance (looking towards the source) varies from maximum to minimum for every $\lambda/4$ distance. There is also a certain point where the real part of the impedance is equal to the characteristic impedance. The reactance may be neutralised by using an appropriate length of a short-circuited or open-circuited line in shunt at this point so that there is no mismatch. Here, the reactance earlier existing is matched properly, hence adding of a stub at this point is most appropriate. In real lines it is necessary that the stub is located as near as the load. The characteristic impedance of the stub connected in the shunt should be same to that of the line.

The single stub matching system is useful for a fixed frequency only because as the frequency changes, the location of the stub needs to be altered.

A single stub may be of long length and the remote end may be either open or short-circuited.

* A small section of a line is termed as a stub.

For the short-circuited stub, the impedance of the stub can be adjusted by varying the line length. Additionally, the short-circuited stub is simpler and is of robust mechanical construction. Moreover, in this case, the spacing between line conducting remains fixed. Hence it is preferred.

17.20.3B Double Stub Matching (Fig. 17.26)

The major disadvantage of single stub matching is that it is only effective for a fixed frequency system.

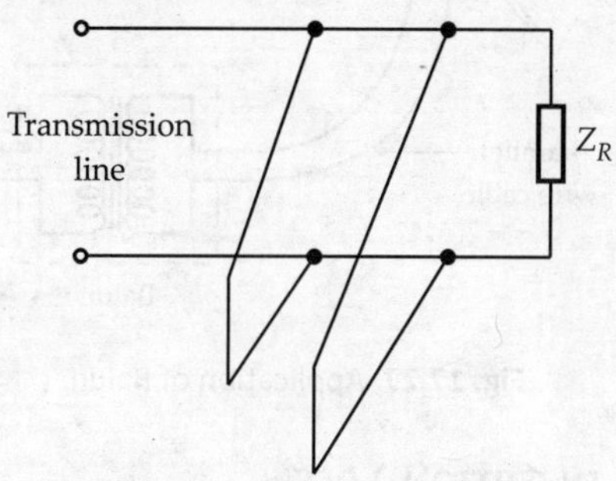

Fig. 17.26 Double stub matching.

In case the frequency of the signal changes, the location of the stub needs to be readjusted. To overcome this problem two short-circuited stubs, whose lengths are adjustable, are installed and is known as double stub matching. Here the stub positions are fixed and are generally employed at HF transmission. Conventionally, two stubs are placed at $\lambda/8$ distance apart. It provides good impedance matching though in some of the cases, double stub matching system may be inferior than single stub matching because of the fact that stub matching is most effective when locations are variables.

17.21 ANALYTICAL EXPRESSIONS FOR DETERMINATION OF LENGTH OF STUB

We know, the input impedance of a transmission line is given by

$$Z_{\text{in}} = Z_0 \frac{Z_R \cos h(\gamma l) + Z_0 \sin h(\gamma l)}{Z_0 \cos h(\gamma l) + Z_R \sin h(\gamma l)}$$

[Equation (17.63)]

For a high frequency line,

$$\alpha = 0, \ \gamma = j\beta$$

$$\therefore \quad Z_{\text{in}} = Z_0 \frac{Z_R \cos \beta l + j Z_0 \sin \beta l}{Z_0 \cos \beta l + j Z_R \sin \beta l}$$

$\therefore$ The input admittance Y_{in} is given by

$$Y_{\text{in}} = \frac{1}{Z_{\text{in}}} = \frac{1}{Z_0}\left[\frac{Z_0 \cos\beta l + j Z_R \sin\beta l}{Z_R \cos\beta l + j Z_0 \sin\beta l}\right]$$

$$= \frac{1}{Z_0}\left[\frac{Z_0 + j Z_R \tan\beta l}{Z_R + j Z_0 \tan\beta l}\right]$$

$$= \frac{1}{Z_0}\left[\frac{(Z_0 + j Z_R \tan\beta l)(Z_R - j Z_0 \tan\beta l)}{(Z_R + j Z_0 \tan\beta l)(Z_R - j Z_0 \tan\beta l)}\right]$$

$$= \left[\frac{Z_R Z_0 + Z_R Z_0 \tan^2\beta l + jZ_R^2 \tan\beta l - jZ_0^2 \tan\beta l}{Z_R^2 - jZ_0 Z_R \tan\beta l + jZ_0 Z_R \tan\beta l + Z_0^2 \tan^2\beta l}\right] \cdot \frac{1}{Z_0}$$

$$= \frac{Z_R(1+\tan^2\beta l)}{Z_R^2 + Z_0^2 \tan^2\beta l} + j\frac{(Z_R^2 - Z_0^2)\tan\beta l}{Z_R^2 + Z_0^2 \tan\beta l} \cdot \frac{1}{Z_0}$$

$$= \left[\frac{Z_R(1+\tan^2\beta l)}{Z_R^2 + Z_0^2 \tan^2\beta l}\right] + j\frac{1}{Z_0} \cdot \left[\frac{(Z_R^2 - Z_0^2)\tan\beta l}{Z_R^2 + Z_0^2 \tan\beta l}\right]$$

$$= G_{\text{in}} + jB_{\text{in}} \qquad \text{...(17.93)}$$

where G_{in} is the input conductance and B_{in} is the input susceptance.

The above expression shows that the input conductance (G_{in}) as well as the input susceptance (B_{in}) are line length dependent terms. If l is properly selected, the conductance, as well as the susceptance, can be matched with $Y_0(G_0 + jB_0)$ such that the characteristic conductance is equal to the line conductance first.

Then, $$G_{\text{in}} = \frac{1}{Z_0} = \frac{Z_R(1+\tan^2\beta l)}{Z_R^2 + Z_0^2 \tan^2\beta l}$$

or, $$Z_0 Z_R(1+\tan^2\beta l) = Z_R^2 + Z_0^2 \tan^2\beta l$$

or, $$Z_0 Z_R + Z_0 Z_R \tan^2\beta l = Z_R^2 + Z_0^2 \tan^2\beta l$$

or, $$(Z_0^2 - Z_0 Z_R)\tan^2\beta l = Z_0 Z_R - Z_R^2$$

or, $$\tan\beta l = \left[\frac{Z_R(Z_0 + Z_R)}{Z_0(Z_0 - Z_R)}\right]^{\frac{1}{2}} = \sqrt{\frac{Z_R}{Z_0}}$$

$$\therefore \quad (\beta l) = \tan^{-1}\left(\sqrt{\frac{Z_R}{Z_0}}\right) \qquad \text{...(17.94)}$$

i.e., l, the required line length

$$= \frac{1}{\beta}\tan^{-1}\sqrt{\frac{Z_R}{Z_0}} \qquad \text{...(17.95)}$$

$$= \frac{\lambda}{2\pi}\tan^{-1}\sqrt{\frac{Z_R}{Z_0}} \qquad \text{...[17.95(a)]}$$

CHAPTER 17

In a similar way, for the required line length of the stub, the input susceptance of the line $\left(jB_{\text{in}} = j\dfrac{1}{Z_0}\left[\dfrac{(Z_R^2 - Z_0^2)\tan\beta l}{Z_R^2 + Z_0^2 \tan^2 \beta l}\right]\right)$ will be same to input susceptance of the stub $\left(= \dfrac{1}{jZ_0 \tan\beta l_X}\right)$

[l_X is the required length]

Thus we get

$$\frac{1}{j\,Z_0 \tan\beta l_X} = -j\frac{1}{Z_0}\frac{(Z_R^2 - Z_0^2)\tan\beta l}{Z_R^2 + Z_0^2 \tan^2 \beta l}$$

or, $$\left(-\frac{j}{Z_0}\right)\cot\beta l_X = \left(-\frac{j}{Z_0}\right)\frac{(Z_R^2 - Z_0^2)\tan\beta l}{Z_R^2 - Z_0^2 \tan^2 \beta l}$$

or, $$\cot\beta l_X = \frac{(Z_R^2 - Z_0^2)\sqrt{Z_R/Z_0}}{Z_R^2 + Z_0^2(Z_R/Z_0)}$$

$$= \frac{(Z_R - Z_0)\sqrt{Z_R/Z_0}}{Z_R}$$

$$= \frac{Z_R - Z_0}{\sqrt{Z_R \cdot Z_0}} \quad ...(17.96)$$

$$\therefore\ \tan(\beta l_L) = \frac{\sqrt{Z_R Z_0}}{Z_R - Z_0}$$

$$\therefore\quad l_X = \frac{1}{\beta}\tan^{-1}\frac{\sqrt{Z_R Z_0}}{Z_R - Z_0}$$

or, $$l_X = \frac{\lambda}{2\pi}\tan^{-1}\frac{\sqrt{Z_R Z_0}}{Z_R - Z_0} \quad ...(17.97)$$

To achieve perfect matching, both the equations (17.95) and (17.97) are to be satisfied.

17.22 BALUN

It is a special type of transformer utilised for interconnection of a balanced line (parallel wire line) with an unbalance line (antenna) which is shown in Fig. 17.27. It effectively serves as an impedance matching element between a balanced and an unbalanced line. It may also be termed as a transmission line or choke or sleeve. The cable from the dipole antenna offers reasonably high output impedance which does not match with the input impedance of the TV receiver. A transformer is thus required that matches the output impedance of the parallel wire cable with input impedance of the TV set. This transformer is known as balun and has got few turns of winding on a ferrite core.

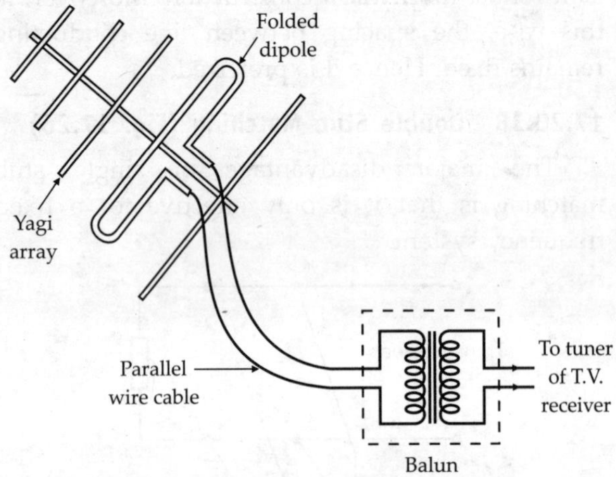

Fig. 17.27 Application of Balun.

17.23 INSERTION LOSS

When a network is introduced between a source and load for impedance matching, attenuation etc., there is a reduction in power level. This is known as *Insertion Loss.*

> Insertion loss = Input power − Output power
> [the difference is a vectorial difference]

If the receiving end current without the inserted network be I_1 and the receiving end current with the inserted network be I_2, then

$$\text{Insertion loss} = \log_e \frac{|I_1|}{|I_2|}$$

$$= 20\log_{10}\frac{I_1}{I_2}\ \text{Nep}$$

In most of the network insertions, I_1 is greater than I_2 and insertion loss is a positive quantity. However, if I_2 is greater than I_1, insertion loss is a negative quantity and has been termed as "Insertion Gain".

The insertion loss is governed by the value of source and load impedance and is not a fixed quantity. In some cases, insertion of a network causes phase shift between I_1 and I_2 in addition to insertion loss. This phase shift is known as "Insertion shift".

17.24 CHARACTERISTIC OF TELEPHONE CABLES

Telephone cables are primarily used for transmission of low voltage signals. This leads to negligible inductance as well as negligible shunt conductance. This is achieved by special construction and the cable works at audio frequencies.

Here, $Z = r + j\omega l \simeq r$ ohm/km

$Y = j\omega C$ mho/km

$$\therefore \quad Z_0 = \sqrt{\frac{Z}{Y}} = \sqrt{\frac{Z}{j\omega C}} = \sqrt{\frac{r}{\omega C}} \angle -45°$$

$$\text{also,} \quad \gamma = \sqrt{ZY} = \sqrt{r \times j\omega C} = \sqrt{\omega r C} \angle 45°$$

$$\text{Thus,} \quad \gamma = \alpha + j\beta = \sqrt{\omega r C} \angle 45° \quad \text{...(17.98)}$$

$$\text{i.e.,} \quad \alpha + j\beta = \sqrt{\omega r C} \angle 45°$$

$$= \sqrt{\omega r C}\,[\cos 45° + j \sin 45°]$$

$$= \sqrt{\omega r C}\left[\frac{1}{\sqrt{2}} + j\frac{1}{\sqrt{2}}\right]$$

$$= \frac{\sqrt{\omega r C}}{\sqrt{2}}[1 + j] \quad \text{...(17.99)}$$

$$\text{Hence,} \quad \alpha = \sqrt{\frac{\omega r C}{2}}, \beta = \sqrt{\frac{\omega r C}{2}} \quad \text{...(17.100)}$$

17.25 SMITH CHART

The Smith Chart, first developed by P.H. Smith in 1938-39 is plotted within a circle of unit radius of *reflection coefficient i.e.,* it is a circular chart drawn with an outside radius that represents unit magnitude of reflection coefficient $(K = 1)$. The magnitude of K is represented by the radius from the centre. Superimposed on this chart are lines representing constant values of r and x (*i.e.,* resistance and reactance). The lines of constants r and x form two *orthogonal families of circles*. The Smith Chart plots K in polar co-ordinates and has lines corresponding to (Z_R / Z_0) *i.e.,* normalised (Z). The chart shows the relation between normalised line impedance (Z) and the complex ratio of reflected to incident voltage, K. The phase angle of the reflection coefficient has been arbitrarily plotted in terms of *distant scale*. The scale is used in relative manner and the location of the zero is of no essential importance. The value of θ, the phase angle of K, corresponding to any given reading the distance scale can be determined by use of the outer circle.

Distance scale

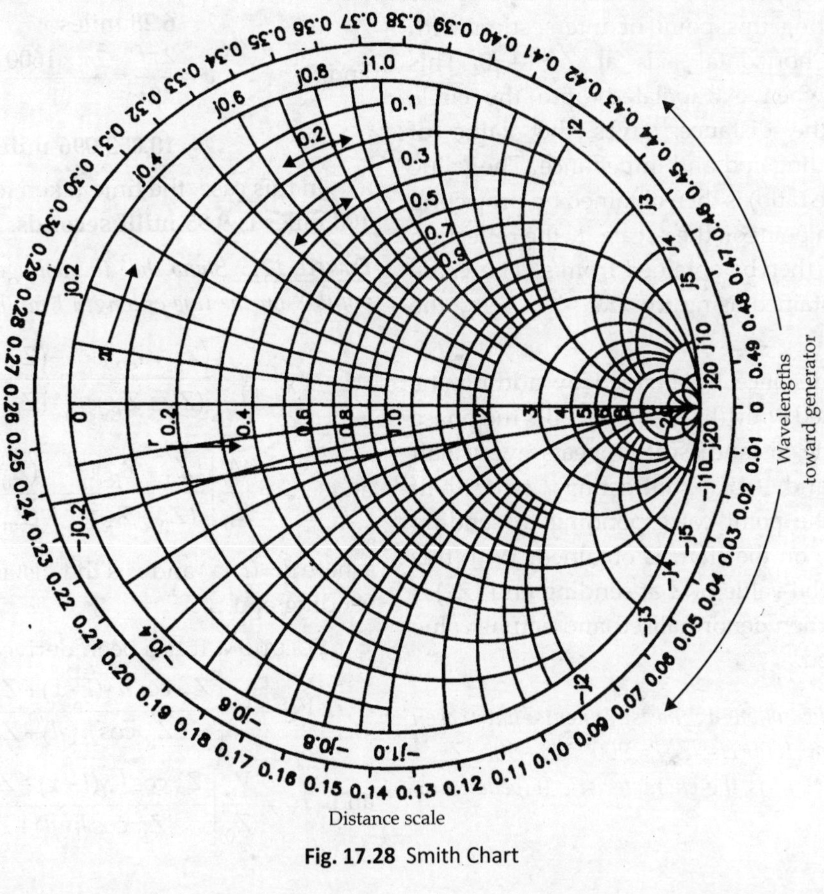

Distance scale

Fig. 17.28 Smith Chart

The sending and reflection coefficient is given by

K	s	K	s
0	1	0.75	7
0.2	1.5	0.875	15
0.5	3	0.9375	31

$$K_s = K\varepsilon^{-2\alpha d}$$

where, α is attenuation in neper per K_m and d the length of the line.

The advantages of Smith Chart are that the lines are less crowded in the low impedance region and also that all the usual values of K and Z are contained within a finite area. The values of Z are much easier to read when plotted. A typical Smith Chart (Fig. 17.28) is shown.

17.25.1 Use of Smith Chart

To find the input impedance, first the ratio of $Z_R / Z_0 (= Z)$ is to be obtained. With the value of Z, in form of $r + jx$, the point corresponding to real part r is obtained alongwith the imaginary part x at their intersection (say point m). A straight line is the drawn connecting this point of intersection with the point on horizontal axis at $Z = 1 + j0$. This straight line, when extrapolated upto the circle representing the distance, gives the value of location of sending end and impedance. The value of s (stand wave ratio) is then obtained by projecting an arc line from point on the r-scale. K, the reflection coefficient, can then be obtained from s. The value of K_s can be obtained using $K_s = K\varepsilon^{-2\alpha l}$, l being the distance.

The final distance is obtained by adding the distance obtained with $[(\beta/2\pi)l]$ where β is the phase constant. As the distance scale repeats every half wavelength and so, subtracting two half wavelengths, the point corresponding to sending end impedance on the chart is obtained. With this value and K_s, the value of Z at sending end (Z_s) is obtained. It is then denormalised and actual value of Z_s is obtained.

EXAMPLE 17.1 *The following measurements have been made on a line at 1600 c/s, $Z_{oc} = 900\ \Omega\angle{-30°}$, $Z_{sc} = 100\ \Omega\angle{-10°}$. What is the characteristic impedance of the line at 1600 c/s ?*

SOLUTION. We know

$$Z_0 = \sqrt{Z_{oc} \cdot Z_{sc}}$$

$$= \sqrt{[900\angle{-30°}][100\angle{-10°}]}$$

$$= \sqrt{90{,}000\angle{-40°}} = \mathbf{300\angle{-20°}\ Ohm.}$$

EXAMPLE 17.2 *Find the wavelength of the wave travelling for the above line when β = 0.055 rad/sec. Compare the velocity of propagation for β = 0.055 rad/sec and β = 1 rad/sec. How much time will be taken by wave to travel 100 miles ? Assume f = 1600 Hz.*

SOLUTION. We know

$$\lambda = \frac{2\pi}{\beta} = \frac{2\pi}{0.055} = 114.2 \text{ miles}$$

and, velocity of propagation $(v) = \dfrac{\omega}{\beta}$

$$= \frac{10053}{0.055} \quad [\omega = 2\pi f = 10053 \text{ rad/sec}]$$

$$= \mathbf{182782\ mile/sec.}$$

Therefore, the time taken for a wave of this frequency to travel 100 miles is **0.547** milliseconds.

In the second case, for the cable,

$$\beta = 1.0 \text{ radian/mile}$$

$$\therefore \quad \lambda = 6.28 \text{ miles}$$

$$\text{and,} \quad v = \frac{2\pi f}{\beta} = \frac{2\pi \times 1600}{1}$$

$$= \mathbf{10{,}053.096\ miles/sec}$$

In this case, the time taken for a signal to travel 100 miles is **9.95 milli seconds.**

EXAMPLE 17.3 *Show that the voltage and current at any point X on the line of length l can be represented as*

$$V_X = V_S \left[\frac{(Z_0 + Z_R)e^{\gamma d} - (Z_0 - Z_R)e^{-\gamma d}}{(Z_0 + Z_R)e^{\gamma l} - (Z_0 - Z_R)e^{-\gamma l}} \right]$$

$$\text{and } I_X = \frac{V_S}{Z_0} \left[\frac{(Z_0 + Z_R)e^{\gamma d} + (Z_0 - Z_R)e^{-\gamma d}}{(Z_0 + Z_R)e^{\gamma l} - (Z_0 - Z_R)e^{-\gamma l}} \right]$$

where $d = (l - x)$ and x is the distance of point x from sending end.

SOLUTION. It has been derived in the text that

$$V_X = V_S \left[\frac{Z_R \cos h\,\gamma(l-x) + Z_0 \sin h\,\gamma(l-x)}{Z_R \cos h(\gamma l) + Z_0 \sin h(\gamma l)} \right]$$

$$\text{and } I_X = \frac{V_S}{Z_0} \left[\frac{Z_0 \cos h\,\gamma(l-x) + Z_R \sin h\,\gamma(l-x)}{Z_R \cos h(\gamma l) + Z_0 \sin h(\gamma l)} \right]$$

Taking $(l-x)=d$, these equations become

$$V_X = V_S\left[\frac{Z_R \cosh(\gamma d)+Z_0 \sinh(\gamma d)}{Z_R \cosh(\gamma l)+Z_0 \sinh(\gamma l)}\right]$$

and $$I_X = \frac{V_S}{Z_0}\left[\frac{Z_0 \cosh(\gamma d)+Z_R \sinh(\gamma d)}{Z_R \cosh(\gamma l)+Z_0 \sinh(\gamma l)}\right]$$

However, $$\cosh(\gamma d)=\left(\frac{e^{\gamma d}+e^{-\gamma d}}{2}\right)$$

$$\cosh(\gamma l)=\left(\frac{e^{\gamma l}+e^{-\gamma l}}{2}\right)$$

$$\sinh(\gamma d)=\left(\frac{e^{\gamma d}-e^{-\gamma d}}{2}\right)$$

$$\sinh(\gamma l)=\left(\frac{e^{\gamma l}-e^{-\gamma l}}{2}\right)$$

$$V_X = V_S\left[\frac{Z_R\left(\frac{e^{\gamma d}+e^{-\gamma d}}{2}\right)+Z_0\left(\frac{e^{\gamma d}-e^{-\gamma d}}{2}\right)}{Z_R\left(\frac{e^{\gamma l}+e^{-\gamma l}}{2}\right)+Z_0\left(\frac{e^{\gamma l}-e^{-\gamma l}}{2}\right)}\right]$$

$$= V_S\left[\frac{(Z_0+Z_R)e^{\gamma d}-(Z_0-Z_R)e^{-\gamma d}}{(Z_0+Z_R)e^{\gamma l}-(Z_0-Z_R)e^{-\gamma l}}\right]$$

In the similar way,

$$I_X = \frac{V_S}{Z_0}\left[\frac{(Z_0+Z_R)e^{\gamma d}+(Z_0-Z_R)e^{-\gamma d}}{(Z_0+Z_R)e^{\gamma l}-(Z_0-Z_R)e^{-\gamma l}}\right].$$

EXAMPLE 17.4 *Show that, in a transmission line, the input impedance is given by*

$$Z = Z_0\,\frac{(Z_R+Z_0)e^{\gamma l}+(Z_R-Z_0)e^{-\gamma l}}{(Z_R+Z_0)e^{\gamma l}-(Z_R-Z_0)e^{-\gamma l}}$$

SOLUTION. We know,

$$Z_{in} = Z_0\left[\frac{Z_R \cosh(\gamma l)+Z_0 \sinh(\gamma l)}{Z_0 \cosh(\gamma l)+Z_R \sinh(\gamma l)}\right]$$

But $$\cosh(\gamma l)=\left(\frac{e^{\gamma l}+e^{-\gamma l}}{2}\right)$$

and $$\sinh(\gamma l)=\left(\frac{e^{\gamma l}-e^{-\gamma l}}{2}\right)$$

$$\therefore\ Z_{in} = Z_0\left[\frac{Z_R\frac{e^{\gamma l}}{2}+Z_R\frac{e^{-\gamma l}}{2}+Z_0\frac{e^{\gamma l}}{2}-Z_0\frac{e^{-\gamma l}}{2}}{Z_0\frac{e^{\gamma l}}{2}+Z_0\frac{e^{-\gamma l}}{2}+Z_R\frac{e^{\gamma l}}{2}-Z_R\frac{e^{-\gamma l}}{2}}\right]$$

$$= \left[\frac{\frac{e^{\gamma l}}{2}(Z_R+Z_0)+\frac{e^{-\gamma l}}{2}(Z_R-Z_0)}{\frac{e^{\gamma l}}{2}(Z_0+Z_R)-\frac{e^{-\gamma l}}{2}(Z_R-Z_0)}\right]\times Z_0$$

$$Z_{in} = \left[\frac{(Z_R+Z_0)e^{\gamma l}+(Z_R-Z_0)e^{-\gamma l}}{(Z_0+Z_R)e^{\gamma l}-(Z_R-Z_0)e^{-\gamma l}}\right]Z_0.$$

EXAMPLE 17.5 *Represent voltage at any point "X" on a transmission line in terms of quantities at the receiving end and in both exponential as well as in hyperbolic forms.*

SOLUTION. We know (Ex. 17.3)

$$V_X = V_S\left[\frac{(Z_0+Z_R)e^{+\gamma d}-(Z_0-Z_R)e^{-\gamma d}}{(Z_0+Z_R)e^{\gamma l}-(Z_0-Z_R)e^{-\gamma l}}\right] \quad ...(a)$$

where V_X is the voltage at any point "X" on the line. When V_X is to be expressed in terms of receiving end, $d=0$ and $V_X \equiv V_R$.

This gives

$$V_R = V_S\,\frac{2Z_R}{(Z_0+Z_R)e^{\gamma l}-(Z_0-Z_R)e^{-\gamma l}} \quad ...(b)$$

i.e., $$V_S = \frac{V_R}{2Z_R}[(Z_0+Z_R)e^{\gamma l}-(Z_0-Z_R)e^{-\gamma l}] \quad ...(c)$$

Substituting the value of V_S from (*c*) in (*a*), we get

$$V_X = \frac{V_R}{2Z_R}[(Z_0+Z_R)e^{\gamma d}-(Z_0-Z_R)e^{-\gamma d}]$$

$$= \frac{I_R}{2}[(Z_0+Z_R)e^{\gamma d}-(Z_0-Z_R)e^{-\gamma d}] \quad ...(d)$$

In the similar way,

$$I_X = \frac{I_R}{2Z_0}[(Z_0+Z_R)e^{\gamma d}+(Z_0-Z_R)e^{-\gamma d}] \quad ...(e)$$

The above expressions (*d*) and (*e*) representing V_X and I_X are in exponential form. Rewriting the expressions of V_X and I_X in terms of receiving end quantities,

$$V_X = \frac{V_R}{2Z_R}[Z_0(e^{\gamma l}-e^{-\gamma d})+Z_R(e^{\gamma d}+e^{-\gamma d})]$$

$$= V_R\left[\left(\frac{e^{\gamma d}+e^{-\gamma d}}{2}\right)+\frac{Z_0}{Z_R}\left(\frac{e^{\gamma d}-e^{-\gamma d}}{2}\right)\right]$$

$$= V_R\left[\cosh(\gamma d)+\frac{Z_0}{Z_R}\sinh(\gamma d)\right]$$

i.e., $$\mathbf{V_X = [V_R \cosh(\gamma d)+I_R Z_0 \sinh(\gamma d)]} \quad ...(f)$$

CHAPTER 17

Similarly,

$$I_X = \frac{I_R}{2Z_0}[Z_0(e^{\gamma d} + e^{-\gamma d}) + Z_R(e^{\gamma d} - e^{-\gamma d})]$$

$$\therefore\ \mathbf{I_X} = \left[\mathbf{I_R \cosh(\gamma d) + \frac{V_R}{Z_0}\sinh(\gamma d)}\right] \quad ...(g)$$

Expressions (*f*) and (*g*) represent the expressions of voltage and current at any point '*X*' in terms of hyperbolic forms.

EXAMPLE 17.6 *Find the expressions for the input impedance of the line (Z_{in}) in terms of exponential form.*

SOLUTION. We have seen that

$$V_X = \frac{I_R}{2}[(Z_0 + Z_R)e^{\gamma d} - (Z_0 - Z_R)e^{-\gamma d}]$$

and $$I_X = \frac{I_R}{2Z_0}[(Z_0 + Z_R)e^{\gamma d} + (Z_0 - Z_R)e^{-\gamma d}]$$

Letting $d = l$ and $V_X = V_S$

and $I_X = I_S$, we get, from the above expressions,

$$V_S = \frac{I_S}{2}[(Z_0 + Z_R)e^{\gamma l} - (Z_0 - Z_R)e^{-\gamma l}]$$

and $$I_S = \frac{I_R}{2Z_0}[(Z_0 + Z_R)e^{\gamma l} + (Z_0 - Z_R)e^{-\gamma l}]$$

$$\therefore\ Z_{in} = \frac{V_S}{I_S} = Z_0\left[\frac{(Z_0 + Z_R)e^{\gamma l} - (Z_0 - Z_R)e^{-\gamma l}}{(Z_0 + Z_R)e^{\gamma l} + (Z_0 - Z_R)e^{-\gamma l}}\right]$$

$$= \mathbf{Z_0}\frac{\mathbf{1 - \left(\frac{Z_0 - Z_R}{Z_0 + Z_R}\right)e^{-2\gamma l}}}{\mathbf{1 + \frac{Z_0 - Z_R}{Z_0 + Z_R}e^{-2\gamma l}}}.$$

EXAMPLE 17.7 *The values of primary constants of an open wire line per loop km are : $R = 15\ \Omega$, $L = 4\ mH$, $C = 0.008\ \mu F$ and $G = 0.5\ \mu$ mho. For a signal frequency of 1000 Hz, determine the characteristic impedance, propagation constant, attenuation and phase constant. Also find the wavelength and phase velocity.*

SOLUTION.

$$z = r + j\omega l = 15 + j \times 2\pi \times 1000 \times 4 \times 10^{-3}$$
$$= 15 + j25.13 = 29.26\ \angle 59°\Omega/\text{km}$$
$$y = g + j\omega c$$
$$= 0.6 \times 10^{-6} + j \times 2 \times \pi \times 1000 \times 0.008 \times 10^{-6}$$
$$= 10^{-6}(0.5 + j6.28 \times 0.008 \times 1000)$$
$$= 50.25 \times 10^{-6}\ \angle 89.43°\ \text{mho/km}$$

$\therefore\ Z_0$ (characteristic impedance)

$$= \sqrt{\frac{z}{y}} = \sqrt{\frac{29.26}{50.25 \times 10^{-6}}} = \mathbf{763\ Ohms}$$

Propagation constant $(\gamma) = \sqrt{(\gamma + j\omega l)(g + j\omega c)}$

$$= \sqrt{29.26\angle 59° \times 10^{-6} \times 50.25\ \angle 89.43°}$$
$$= \sqrt{29.26 \times 50.25 \times 10^{-6}}\ \angle \frac{59° + 89.43°}{2}$$
$$= 0.038\ \angle 74.22°$$

$$\therefore\ \gamma = 0.038\ \angle 74.22°$$
$$= 0.038(\cos 74.22° + j\sin 74.22°)$$
$$= \mathbf{0.0103 + j\,0.04} = \alpha + j\beta$$

$\therefore\ \alpha$ (attenuation constant) $= \mathbf{0.0103\ Np/km}$

β (phase constant) $= \mathbf{0.04\ rad/km}$

$$\text{Wavelength } (\lambda) = \frac{2\pi}{\beta} = \frac{6.28}{0.04} = \mathbf{157\ km}$$

$$\text{Phase velocity, } v_p = \frac{\omega}{\beta} = \frac{2\pi \times 1000}{0.04}$$
$$= 157079.63 \simeq \mathbf{157080\ km/sec.}$$

EXAMPLE 17.8 *A line has $Z_0 = 500\angle -12°$ ohms, $\alpha = 0.0075$ Nep. per km, $\beta = 0.035$ radian per km. The line being 100 km long and is terminated by a pure resistance of 200 ohms. If the sending end voltage is 5 volts, calculate the line impedance from the input side. Also find the sending end current.*

SOLUTION. Given that

$$Z_0 = 500\ \angle -12° = (489 - j104)\Omega$$
$$Z_R = 200\ \angle 0° = 200 + j0$$
$$\beta l = 0.035 \times 100 = 3.5\ \text{rad} = 200.5°$$

[l being the line length]

$$e^{\gamma l} = e^{0.75 + j3.5} = e^{0.75}\ \angle 200.5°$$

[$\because\ \alpha l = 0.0075 \times 100 = 0.75$ Nep.]

$$= -1.99 - j0.74$$

Similarly,

$$e^{-\gamma l} = e^{-0.75}\ \angle -200.5° = -0.442 + j\,0.156$$

However, the input impedance (Z_{in}) is given by

$$Z_{in} = \left[\frac{(Z_0 + Z_R)e^{\gamma l} + (Z_R - Z_0)e^{-\gamma l}}{(Z_0 + Z_R)e^{\gamma l} - (Z_R - Z_0)e^{-\gamma l}}\right] Z_0$$

$$= (489 - j104)\left[\frac{(200 + 489 - j104)e^{\gamma l} + (200 - 489 + j104)e^{-\gamma l}}{(200 + 489 - j104)e^{\gamma l} - (200 - 489 + j104)e^{-\gamma l}}\right]$$

$$=(489-j104)\left[\frac{(689-j104)(-1.99-j0.74)+(-289+j104)(-0.442+j0.156)}{(689-j104)(-1.99-j0.74)-(-289+j104)(-0.442+j0.156)}\right]$$

$$= \mathbf{442\angle-3.3° \text{ ohms}}$$

$$I_S=\frac{V_S}{Z_{in}}=\frac{5}{442\angle-3.3°}$$

$$= \mathbf{0.0113\angle-3.3° \text{ A} = 11.3 \text{ mA at } \angle 3.3°.}$$

EXAMPLE 17.9 *A transmission line is 100 km long. It has a characteristic impedance given by (685 – j 92) ohms, attenuation and phase constants as 0.00497 Nep./km and 0.0352 rad/km at 1000 Hz. The line is terminated in a pure resistive load of 2000 ohms. If the signal generator at the sending end is of 10 volts capacity and having an internal impedance of 700 ohms (resistive), find the sending end impedance, current voltage and power.*

SOLUTION. In this problem,

$$\beta l = 0.0352 \times 100 = 3.52 \text{ rad} \qquad (= 202 \text{ degree})$$

$$e^{\gamma l} = e^{0.00497\times100 + j0.03.52\times100}$$

$$= e^{0.497+j3.52} = e^{0.497}\angle 202° = (-1.52 - j0.615)$$

Similarly, $e^{-\gamma l} = e^{-0.497}\angle -202° = (-0.567 + j0.23)$

However, the input impedance (Z_{in}) is given by

$$Z_{in}=\left[\frac{(Z_0+Z_R)e^{\gamma l}+(Z_R-Z_0)e^{-\gamma l}}{(Z_0+Z_R)e^{\gamma l}-(Z_R-Z_0)e^{-\gamma l}}\right]Z_0$$

$$=\left[\frac{(2000+685-j92)e^{\gamma l}+(2000-685+j92)e^{-\gamma l}}{(2000+685-j92)e^{\gamma l}-(2000-685+j92)e^{-\gamma l}}\right](685-j92)$$

$$=(685-j92)\left[\frac{(2685-j92)e^{\gamma l}+(1315+j92)e^{-\gamma l}}{(2685-j92)e^{\gamma l}-(1315+j92)e^{-\gamma l}}\right]$$

$$=691\angle-7.7° . \frac{5060\angle 14.5°}{3810\angle 27.5°} = 919\angle-20.5°$$

$$= \mathbf{(861 - j\,325) \text{ ohms}}$$

$$|I_S|=\left|\frac{E_g}{Z_g+Z_S}\right|=\left|\frac{10}{700+861-j325}\right|$$

[Here E_g = generator voltage = 10 V

Z_g = internal impedance of generator

$= 700\,\Omega$

$Z_S = Z_{in}$ = input impedance]

$$=\frac{10}{1596} = \mathbf{6.3 \times 10^{-3} \text{ Amp(rms)}}$$

Again $|V_S| = |I_S||Z_S| = 6.3 \times 10^{-3} \times 919$

$$= \mathbf{5.75 \text{ Volts (rms)}}$$

$$P_S = |V_S||I_S| = 5.75 \times 6.3 \times 10^{-3}$$

$$= \mathbf{34 \times 10^{-3} \text{ W.}}$$

EXAMPLE 17.10 *Find the sending end line impedance for a HF line having characteristic impedance of 50 ohms. The line is of length (1.185 λ) and is terminated in a load of (110 + j 80) ohms.*

SOLUTION. We know, $Z_{in} = Z_0 \dfrac{Z_R + j Z_0 \tan\beta l}{Z_0 + Z_R \tan\beta l}$

However, as given,

$$Z_0 = 50\,\Omega, \quad Z_R = (110 + j\,80)\Omega$$

$$\beta l = \frac{2\pi}{\lambda}.l = \frac{2\pi}{\lambda}.(1.185\lambda)$$

$$= 7.44 \text{ rad} \simeq 426° \text{ or, } 66°$$

$$\therefore \quad Z_{in} = 50\frac{(110+j80)+j\,50\tan 66°}{50+(110+j80)\tan 66°}$$

$$= 50\frac{110+j\,192.3}{160+j\,180}$$

$$= 50\left[\frac{(110+j192.3)(160-j180)}{(160+j180)(160-j180)}\right]$$

$$= 50\left[\frac{17600-j\,19800+j\,30768+34614}{25600-j\,28800+j\,28800+32400}\right]$$

$$= 8.62\times10^{-4}[52214-j\,10968]$$

$$= \mathbf{(45 - j\,9.45) \text{ ohm}}.$$

EXAMPLE 17.11 *A cable pair has the following primary co-efficients at an angular frequency of 5000 radians/sec.*

$$R = 30\ \Omega/\text{km}\ ; \qquad G = 1\ \mu \text{ mho/km}$$

$$L = 1.1 \text{ mH/km}\ ; \qquad C = 0.2\ \mu\text{F/km}$$

Calculate :

(i) The characteristic impedance

(ii) The attenuation co-efficient

(iii) The phase change co-efficient

(iv) The attenuation in decible over a length of 15 km.

SOLUTION. The angular frequency being given by (ω)

$$= 5000 \text{ rad/sec.}$$

The series impedance (Z)

$$= R + j\omega L$$

$$= 30 + j \times 5000 \times 1.1 \times 10^{-3}$$

$$= 30 + j\,5.5 = 30.5\angle 10.39° \text{ Ohm.}$$

CHAPTER 17

Shunt admittance Y

$$= G + j\omega C$$
$$= 10^{-6} + j \times 5000 \times 0.2 \times 10^{-6}$$
$$= 10^{-6} + j10^{-3} \simeq 10^{-3} \angle 90° \text{ mho}$$

The characteristics impedance (Z_0) is given by the relation

$$Z_0 = \sqrt{\frac{Z}{Y}} = \sqrt{\frac{30.5 \angle 10.39°}{10^{-3} \angle 90°}}$$
$$= 30500 \times \frac{1}{2} \angle 10.4° - 90°$$
$$= \mathbf{30500 \angle -39.81° \Omega}$$

And propagation constant (γ) is given by the relation

$$\gamma = \sqrt{Z \times Y}$$
$$= \sqrt{30.5 \times 10^{-3} \times \tfrac{1}{2} \angle 10.39 + 90°}$$
$$= 0.1746 \angle 50.195°$$
$$= 0.1746\,[\cos(50.195°) + j\sin(50.195°)]$$
$$= \mathbf{0.1118 + j\,0.1356}$$

But $\gamma = \alpha + j\beta$

where, α and β is the attenuation co-efficient and phase change co-efficient respectively.

Hence,

$$\alpha = 0.1118 \text{ nepers/km} = \mathbf{1.677 \text{ Nep for 15 km}}$$
$$\beta = 0.1356 \text{ radians/km} = \mathbf{2.034 \text{ rad for 15 km}}$$

The attenuation in dB over length of 15 km is

$$1.677 \times \frac{1}{0.115} = \mathbf{14.58 \text{ dB.}} \quad \left[\because dB = \frac{1}{0.115} \times \text{Neper}\right]$$

EXAMPLE 17.12 *(a) A loss free transmission line has an inductance of 1.2 mH/km and a capacitance of 0.05 μF / km. Calculate the characteristic impedance and propagation constant of the line. (b) For 0.4 km of wavelength, find*

(i) the frequency at which the line length is equivalent to one wavelength and

(ii) the velocity of propagation.

Assume $\omega = 5000$ rad/sec.

SOLUTION. (*a*) Here $R = 0, G = 0$, since the line is lossless

$$L = 1.2 \times 10^{-3} \text{ H/km and } C = 0.05 \times 10^{-6} \text{ F/km}$$

The characteristic impedance

$$Z_0 = \sqrt{\frac{R + j\omega L}{G + j\omega C}} = \sqrt{\frac{L}{C}} = \sqrt{\frac{1.2 \times 10^{-3}}{0.05 \times 10^{-6}}} = \mathbf{154.92\ \Omega}$$

The propagation constant

$$\gamma = \sqrt{(R + j\omega L)(G + j\omega C)} = j\omega\sqrt{LC}$$
$$\therefore \quad |\gamma| = \omega\sqrt{LC}$$
$$= 5000\sqrt{1.2 \times 10^{-3} \times 0.05 \times 10^{-6}}$$
$$= \mathbf{0.0387.}$$

(*b*) Since the line is lossless, $\alpha = 0$ and

$$\gamma = \alpha + jB = j\beta$$
$$|\gamma| = |\beta| = 0.0387 \text{ rad/km}$$

The velocity of propagation at the assumed frequency of 5000 radians/sec is

$$v = \frac{\omega}{\beta} = \frac{5000}{0.0387} = \mathbf{1.292 \times 10^5 \text{ km/sec.}}$$

And, also $v = f \times \lambda$

where λ = wavelength = 0.4 km

$$\therefore \quad f = \frac{v}{0.4} = \frac{1.292 \times 10^5}{0.4} = \mathbf{323 \text{ kHz.}}$$

EXAMPLE 17.13 *The permissible approximations for unloaded underground cables at audio frequencies are $\omega C >> G$ and that $\omega L << R$. Calculate Z_0, α, β under these approximations. Also find the velocity of propagation.*

SOLUTION. The characteristic impedance Z_0 is given by

$$Z_0 = \sqrt{\frac{R + j\omega L}{G + j\omega C}}$$

When $R >> \omega L$ and $\omega C >> G$,

$$Z_0 \cong \sqrt{\frac{R}{j\omega C}} = \sqrt{\frac{R}{\omega C}} \angle \frac{1}{2}(0 - 90°)$$
$$\cong \mathbf{\sqrt{\frac{R}{\omega C}} \angle -45°}$$

Propagation constant

$$\gamma = \sqrt{(R + j\omega L)(G + j\omega C)} \cong \sqrt{j\omega CR}$$
$$= \sqrt{\omega CR} \angle 45°$$
$$= \sqrt{\omega CR}\cos 45° + j\sqrt{\omega CR}\sin 45°$$
$$= \sqrt{\frac{\omega CR}{2}} + j\sqrt{\frac{\omega CR}{2}}$$

But $\gamma = \alpha + j\beta$

$$\therefore \quad \alpha = \sqrt{\frac{\omega CR}{2}} \text{ nepers/km}$$

and

$$\beta = \mathbf{\sqrt{\frac{\omega CR}{2}} \text{ nepers/km}}$$

The wavelength λ is the distance between any two consecutive points along the line at which the current (or voltage) is in the same phase. If β is the phase shift on the line, then wavelength λ is given by

$$\lambda = \frac{2\pi}{\beta}$$

And the velocity of propagation

$$v = \text{frequency} \times \text{wavelength}$$

$$= f \times \lambda = 2\pi f/\beta = \frac{\omega}{\beta}$$

But $\quad \beta = \sqrt{\dfrac{\omega CR}{2}}$

and $\quad v = \sqrt{\dfrac{2\omega}{CR}}$ **km/sec.**

Example 17.14 *A cable has been uniformly loaded by an inductance such that $\omega L >> R$. Assuming leakage conductance to be nil, deduce an expression for attenuation and phase constant without neglecting R.*

Solution. Given that $G = 0$ and $\omega L >> R$

However, R is not to be neglected.

$\therefore \quad Z = R + j\omega L$

and $\quad |Z| = \sqrt{R^2 + (\omega L)^2} \angle \dfrac{\pi}{2} - \dfrac{R}{\omega L}$

[The angle being nearly $\frac{\pi}{2}$ as $(\omega L) >> (R)$]

Also $\quad Y = j\omega C \qquad [\because G = 0]$

$\therefore \quad \gamma = \sqrt{ZY}$

$$= \sqrt{\left\{[R^2 + (\omega L)^2]^{1/2} \angle \frac{\pi}{2} - \frac{R}{\omega L}\right\} . \omega C \angle \frac{\pi}{2}}$$

$$= \omega\sqrt{LC}\left(1 + \frac{R^2}{\omega^2 L^2}\right)^{1/4} \angle \frac{\pi}{2} - \frac{R}{2\omega L}$$

$$\left[\because \sqrt{\angle \frac{\pi}{2} - \frac{R}{\omega L} + \frac{\pi}{2}} = \frac{1}{2}\angle\left(\pi - \frac{R}{\omega L}\right) \frac{\pi}{2} - \frac{R}{2\omega L}\right]$$

Since $\omega L >> R$, $\dfrac{R^2}{\omega^2 L^2}$ may be neglected

$\therefore \quad \gamma = \omega\sqrt{LC} . \dfrac{R}{2\omega L} + j\omega\sqrt{LC} = \alpha + j\beta$

$\therefore \quad \boldsymbol{\alpha = \dfrac{R}{2}\sqrt{\dfrac{C}{L}}}$

$$\boldsymbol{\beta = \omega\sqrt{LC}}$$

[the phase velocity can also be found out as $v_p = \dfrac{\omega}{\beta} = \dfrac{1}{\sqrt{LC}}$]

ADDITIONAL EXAMPLES

Example 17.15 *A coaxial cable has following parameters : $Z_0 = 50\angle 0°$ ohms, $L = 20$ km.*

If the power input is 1 watt and the attenuation constant (α) is 1.5 db/km, find the output power of the cable provided it is terminated by Z_0. Also determine the output current.

Solution. Attenuation for the entire length

$$= \alpha . L = 1.5 \times 20 = 30 \text{ dB}$$

$$= 30 \times (0.115 \text{ Nep}) = 3.45 \text{ Nep}$$

Hence $\quad \ln\left|\dfrac{I_S}{I_R}\right| = 3.45$

or, $\quad \left|\dfrac{I_S}{I_R}\right| = e^{3.45} = 31.5$

Power ratio $\left(\dfrac{P_S}{P_r}\right) = \left(\dfrac{I_S}{I_R}\right)^2 = (31.5)^2 = 992.25$

But $\quad P_S = 1$ watt

Hence received power

$$(P_R) = \frac{1}{992.25} = \mathbf{1 \times 10^{-3}\ watt}$$

It is given that $Z_0 = 50\angle 0$ ohms

Hence $\quad P_S = |I_S|^2 |Z_0|$

$\therefore \quad |I_S|^2 = \dfrac{P_S}{Z_0} = \dfrac{1}{50} = 0.02$

$\therefore \quad I_S = 0.1414$ A

and receiving end (output) current is then given from the relation,

$$\left|\frac{I_S}{I_R}\right| = 31.5$$

$\therefore \quad I_R = \dfrac{I_S}{31.5} = \mathbf{4.49 \times 10^{-3}\ A.}$

Example 17.16 *A lossless transmission line has a shunt capacitance of 100 pF/m and a series inductance of 4 μH / m. What is its characteristic impedance ?*

Solution. In a lossless line having $\dfrac{R}{L} = \dfrac{G}{C}$

the characteristic impedance, Z_0 is given by

$$Z_0 = \sqrt{\frac{L}{C}}$$

$$= \sqrt{\frac{4 \times 10^{-6}}{100 \times 10^{-12}}} = \sqrt{\frac{4 \times 10^{-6}}{100}} = \mathbf{200\ \Omega.}$$

CHAPTER 17

EXAMPLE 17.17 *The characteristic impedance of uniform transmission line is 2039.6 Ω at 800 Hz. At this frequency the propagation constant was found to be 0.054∠87.9°. Determine the values of primary constants R, L, G and C of the line.*

SOLUTION. Here the given data are :

$$Z_0 = 2039.6\ \Omega$$

and $\gamma = 0.054\ \angle 87.9°$

Since $f = 800$ Hz

$$\omega = 2\pi \times 800 = 5026.548 \text{ rad/sec}$$

However, $Z_0 = \sqrt{\dfrac{R+j\omega L}{G+j\omega C}}$

and $\gamma = \sqrt{(R+j\omega L)(G+j\omega C)}$

Multiplying Z_0 and γ, we have

$\therefore \quad Z_0 \times \gamma = (R+j\omega L)$

or, $2039.6 \times 0.054 \underline{/87.6°} = R + j\omega L$

or, $R + j\omega L = 110.138\ \underline{/87.6°}$

Now, $R^2 + \omega^2 L^2 = (110.138)^2$

or, $R^2 + \omega^2 L^2 = 12130.379$

or, $R^2(1+743.7) = 12130.379$

$[\because \tan(87.9)° = \dfrac{\omega L}{R}$ or $\omega L = R \times 27.271$

or $\omega^2 L^2 = R^2 \times 743.71]$

or, $R = \sqrt{\dfrac{12130.379}{743.71}} = \mathbf{4.038\ \Omega}$

Now, $L = \sqrt{\dfrac{R \times 27.271}{\omega}} = \dfrac{4.038 \times 27.271}{5026.548} = \mathbf{0.0219\ H}$

But dividing γ by Z_0 we have,

$$\frac{\gamma}{Z_0} = (G + j\omega C)$$

or, $\dfrac{0.054}{2039.6}\underline{/87.9°} = G + j\omega C$

or, $G + j\omega C = 2.648 \times 10^{-5}$

Now, $G^2 + \omega^2 C^2 = (2.648 \times 10^{-5})^2$

or, $G^2 + \omega^2 C^2 = 7.012 \times 10^{-10}$

But $\tan(87.9°) = \dfrac{\omega C}{G}$

or, $\omega C = G 27.271$

$\therefore \quad G^2[1 + (27.271)^2] = 7.012 \times 10^{-10}$

or, $G = \sqrt{\dfrac{7.012 \times 10^{-10}}{743.707}}$

or, $G = 3.07 \times 10^{-6}$ mho $= \mathbf{3.07\ \mu\ mho}$

and $C = \dfrac{G \times 27.271}{\omega}$

$$= \frac{9.703 \times 10^{-7} \times 27.271}{5026.548}$$

$$= \mathbf{5.264 \times 10^{-9}\ F = 5.264\ nF}$$

Hence $R = 4.038\ \Omega$, $L = 0.0219$ H, $G = 3.07\ \mu$ mho, $C = 5.264\ nF$.

EXAMPLE 17.18 *Open and short circuit impedances of a transmission line at 1.6 kHz are 900∠–30°Ω and 400 ∠–10°Ω. Calculate the characteristic impedance of the line.*

SOLUTION. Here the given data are,

$$Z_{oc} = 900\ \angle{-30°}$$

and $Z_{sc} = 400\ \angle{-10°}$

Now the characteristic impedance of the line is

$$Z_0 = \sqrt{Z_{oc} \times Z_{sc}}$$

$$= \sqrt{900 \times 400} \times \tfrac{1}{2}(\angle{-30°} - 10°)$$

$$= \mathbf{600\ \angle{-20°}\Omega.}$$

EXAMPLE 17.19 *A telephone line has the following primary constant per km loop. R = 20Ω, L = 10 mH, C = 0.1μF and G = 10 μ mho. Find its characteristic impedance at angular frequency of 5×10^3 radians/second.*

SOLUTION. The characteristic impedance of the telephone line per km loop, is given by the relation,

$$Z_0 = \sqrt{\frac{R + j\omega L}{G + j\omega C}} \quad ...(i)$$

But $R + j\omega L = 20 + j \times 5 \times 10^3 \times 10 \times 10^{-3}$

$$= 20 + j\,50 = 53.852 \angle 68.19° \text{ ohm}$$

and $G + j\omega L = 10 \times 10^{-6} + j \times 5 \times 10^3 \times 0.1 \times 10^{-6}$

$$= 10^{-6}(10 + j5 \times 10^3 \times 0.1)$$

$$= 10^{-6}(10 + j\,5000)$$

$$= 5000 \times 10^{-6}\ \angle 89.88°$$

Putting the value of $(R + j\omega L)$ and $(G + j\omega C)$ in equation (i), we have

$$Z_0 = \sqrt{\frac{53.852}{5000 \times 10^{-6}}} \times \frac{1}{2}\underline{/68.19° - 89.88°}$$

$$= \mathbf{103.78\underline{/-10.85°}\ \Omega.}$$

EXAMPLE 17.20 *Calculate the primary constant of a transmission line having Z_0 = 710∠–14.24°Ω and γ = 0.0185∠74.81° at f = 1 kHz.*

Solution. We know that,

$$Z_0 = \sqrt{\frac{R+j\omega L}{G+j\omega C}} \quad ...(i)$$

and $$\gamma = \sqrt{(R+j\omega L)(G+j\omega C)} \quad ...(ii)$$

Multiplying (*i*) and (*ii*),

$$Z_0 \cdot \gamma = R+j\omega L$$

or, $$710 \times 0.0185 \underline{/-14.24° + 74.81°} = R+j\omega L$$

or, $$13.135(\cos 60.6° + j\sin 60.6°) = R+j\omega L$$

or, $$6.45 + j11.44 = R+j\omega L \quad ...(iii)$$

Separating real and imaginary parts, equation (*iii*) becomes

$$R = 6.45 \text{ Ohms}$$

$$\omega L = 11.44$$

i.e., $$L = \frac{11.44}{2\pi f} = \frac{11.44}{2\pi \times 1000}$$

$$= 1.82 \times 10^{-3} \text{ Henry} = 1.82 \text{ mH}$$

Dividing (*ii*) by (*i*),

$$\frac{\gamma}{Z_0} = G+j\omega C$$

or, $$\frac{0.0185 \angle 74.81°}{710 \angle -14.24°} = G+j\omega C$$

or, $$2.6 \times 10^{-5} \angle 89° = G+j\omega C$$

or, $$2.6 \times 10^{-5}(\cos 89° + j\sin 89°) = G+j\omega C$$

or, $$0.045 \times 10^{-5} + j2.6 \times 10^{-5} = G+j\omega C \quad ...(iv)$$

Separating real and imaginary parts of (*iv*)

$$G = 0.045 \times 10^{-5} \text{ mho} = 0.45 \times 10^{-6} \text{ mho}$$
$$= 0.45 \ \mu \text{ mho}$$

and $$C = \frac{2.6 \times 10^{-5}}{2\pi f} = 0.414 \times 10^{-8} \text{ F} = 4.14 \times 10^{-9} \text{ F}$$

Here **$R = 6.45$ ohms, $L = 1.82$ mH,**

$G = 0.45\ \mu$ mho, $C = 4.14$ nF.

Example 17.21 *The primary constants of a line working at 1 MHz are : $r = 83.4\,\Omega/km$, $l = 2.29 \times 10^{-3}\ H/km$, $c = 4.85 \times 10^{-2}\ \mu F/km$, and $g = 0$. Calculate the values of Z_0, β, λ and v_p.*

Solution. The characteristic impedance is given by the relation

$$Z_0 = \sqrt{\frac{r+j\omega l}{g+j\omega c}}$$

Here, $$\omega = 2\pi f = 2\pi \times 1 \times 10^6 \text{ radians/sec}$$
$$= 6.283 \times 10^6 \text{ rad/sec}$$

$$r + j\omega l = 83.4 + j \times 6.283 \times 10^6 \times 2.29 \times 10^{-3}$$
$$= 83.4 + j\,14.388 \times 10^3$$
$$= 14388 \angle 89.67° \text{ Ohm per km}$$

and $$G + j\omega C = 0 + j \times 6.283 \times 10^6 \times 4.85 \times 10^{-2} \times 10^{-6}$$
$$= 0 + j\,30.473 \times 10^{-2}$$
$$= 0.305 \underline{/90°} \text{ mho per km}$$

$$\therefore \quad Z_0 = \sqrt{\frac{r+j\omega l}{g+j\omega c}}$$

$$= \sqrt{\frac{14388}{0.305}} \times \frac{1}{2}\underline{/89.67° - 90°}$$

$$= \mathbf{217.197 \underline{/-0.165°} \text{ ohm}}$$

Again, the propagation constant is given by

$$\gamma = \alpha + j\beta = \sqrt{(r+j\omega l)(g+j\omega c)}$$
$$= \sqrt{14388 \times 0.305}\,\frac{1}{2}\underline{/89.67° + 90°}$$
$$= 66.245 \underline{/89.83°}$$
$$= \mathbf{0.1965 + j\,66.24}$$

$$\therefore \quad \alpha = 0.1965 \text{ nepers/km} = \mathbf{1.71 \text{ dB/km}}$$

and $$\beta = 66.24 \text{ rad/km}$$
$$= 66.24 \times \frac{180}{\pi} \text{ degree/km}$$
$$= \mathbf{3795.27 \text{ degree/km}}$$

Again,

$$\beta = \omega\sqrt{LC}$$
$$= 6.283 \times 10^6 \sqrt{2.29 \times 10^{-3} \times 4.85 \times 10^{-2} \times 10^{-6}}$$
$$= 6.619 \text{ rad/km}$$

The wavelength λ is given by the relation

$$\lambda = \frac{2\pi}{\beta} = \frac{2 \times \pi}{6.619} = \mathbf{9.949 \text{ km}}$$

The velocity of propagation will be,

$$v_p = \frac{2\pi f}{\beta} = \frac{\omega}{\beta}$$

$$= \frac{6.283 \times 10^6}{6.619} = 949236.8 \text{ km/sec}$$

Also $$v_p = \frac{\mathbf{1}}{\sqrt{LC}} \textbf{ km/sec.}$$

Example 17.22 *A low loss coaxial cable of characteristic impedance of 50 Ω is terminated in a resistive load of 75Ω. The peak voltage across the load is found to be 30 volts. Calculate :*

(*i*) *The reflection co-efficient of the load.*

(*ii*) *The amplitude of the forward and reflected voltage waves.*

(*iii*) *The amplitude of the forward and reflected current waves.*

(*iv*) *The V.S.W.R.*

Solution. From the given data

$$Z_R = 75\,\Omega \text{ and } Z_0 = 50\,\Omega$$

(*i*) The reflection co-efficient

$$K = \frac{Z_0 - Z_R}{Z_R + Z_0} = \frac{50-75}{75+50} = -\frac{25}{125} = -\mathbf{0.2}$$

(*ii*) Let, amplitude of the forward voltage wave and reflected voltage wave V_i and V_R respectively.

$$K = \frac{V_R}{V_i},$$

or, $$-0.2 = \frac{V_R}{V_i},$$

or, $$V_R = -0.2\,V_i$$

But from the given data, $V_R + V_i = 30$

Hence $V_i - 0.2\,V_i = 30$

or, $$V_i = \frac{30}{0.8} = 37.5 \text{ Volts.}$$

and $$V_R = -0.2\,V_i$$

$$= -0.2 \times 37.5 = -7.5 \text{ Volts}$$

$\therefore$ $|V_i| = \mathbf{37.5\ Volt}$; $|V_R| = \mathbf{7.5\ Volts}$

(*iii*) Peak value of the current at the terminated end

$$= \frac{\text{Total voltage}}{\text{Load resistance}} = \frac{30}{75} = 0.4 \text{ Amp.}$$

But $I_R + I_i = 0.4$

where I_R and I_i is the reflected and forward current respectively.

Here $-K = \frac{I_R}{I_i}$ or, $I_R = +0.2\,I_i$ $[\because K = -0.2]$

[The direction of the reflected current is the reverse of the incident current]

Hence from, $I_R + I_i = 0.4$

or, $$I_i + 0.2\,I_i = 0.4$$

or, $$I_i = \frac{0.4}{1.2} = \mathbf{0.33\ Amp}$$

and $$I_R = 0.2 \times 0.33 = \mathbf{0.066\ Amp}$$

(*iv*) $$VSWR = \frac{1-K}{1+K} = \frac{1-0.2}{1+0.2} = \frac{0.8}{1.2} = \mathbf{0.66.}$$

Example 17.23 *A transmission line with a characteristic impedance of 300Ω is terminated in a purely resistive load. It is found by measurement that the minimum value of voltage upon it is 5 μV and maximum voltage is 7.5 μV. What is the value of the load resistance ?*

Solution. Here the given data are :

$$Z_0 = 300\,\Omega,\ E_{max} = 7.5\,\mu V,\ E_{min} = 5\,\mu V$$

$\therefore$ The voltage standing wave ratio is given by the relation,

$$S = \frac{|E_{max}|}{|E_{min}|} = \frac{7.5}{5} = 1.5$$

Let, the reflection co-efficient = K

and, load resistance = Z_R

Again, $$S = \frac{1+|K|}{1-|K|}$$

or, $$1.5 = \frac{1+|K|}{1-|K|}$$

or, $$2.5\,|K| = 0.5$$

$$|K| = \frac{0.5}{2.5} = 0.2$$

But, $$K = -\frac{Z_R - Z_0}{Z_R + Z_0}$$

or, $$0.2 = -\frac{Z_R - 300}{Z_R + 300}$$

or, $(0.2+1)Z_R = 240$

or, $Z_R = \mathbf{200\ \Omega.}$

Example 17.24 *A lossless line of characteristic impedance 300Ω is terminated in a pure resistance of 200Ω. Find the value of standing wave ratio.*

Solution. In a lossless line, the reflection coefficient is given by

$$|K| = \frac{|Z_0| - |Z_R|}{|Z_0| + |Z_R|} = \frac{300-200}{200+300} = 0.2$$

Therefore, the standing wave ratio of a lossless line is given by the relation,

$$S = \frac{1+|K|}{1-|K|} = \frac{1+0.2}{1-0.2} = \frac{1.2}{0.8} = \mathbf{1.5.}$$

Example 17.25 *In a transmission line the VSWR is given by 2.5. The characteristic impedance is 50 ohms and the line is to transmit a power of 25 watts. Determine the magnitudes of the maximum and minimum voltage and current. Also find the magnitude of the receiving end voltage [Assume $Z_R = (110 - j80)\Omega$].*

SOLUTION.

$$P = \frac{|V_{max}|^2}{Z_{max}} = \frac{|V_{max}|^2}{SZ_0}$$

or, $$25 = \frac{|V_{max}|^2}{2.5 \times 50}$$

$\therefore$ $|V_{max}| = \mathbf{56\ Volts}$

Again, as $|V_{max}| = S|V_{min}|$

$$\therefore \quad |V_{min}| = \frac{|V_{max}|}{S} = \frac{56}{2.5} = \mathbf{22.5\ Volts}$$

$$|I_{max}| = \frac{|E_{max}|}{Z_0} \qquad [\because |E_{max}| = |I_{max}||Z_0|]$$

$$= \frac{56}{50} = \mathbf{1.12\ Amps}$$

$$|I_{min}| = \frac{|E_{min}|}{Z_0} = \frac{22.5}{50} = \mathbf{0.45\ Amp}$$

As powers at sending end and receiving end are same, hence,

$$P = |I_R|^2 R_R$$

or, $$25 = |I_R|^2 \times 110$$

$$I_R = 0.476 \text{ Amp}$$

Thus $|V_R| = |I_R||Z_R|$

$$= 0.476 \times \sqrt{(110)^2 + (80)^2}$$

$$= \mathbf{64.9\ Volts.}$$

EXAMPLE 17.26 *The input impedance (Z) that terminates a HF line can be determined from the standing wave ratio, S, the characteristic impedance, Z_0, and the distance from the load to the first voltage minimum, d.*

Show that $$Z_R = Z_0 \left[\frac{1 - jS\tan\left(\frac{2\pi d}{\lambda}\right)}{S - j\tan\left(\frac{2\pi d}{\lambda}\right)}\right].$$

SOLUTION. We know (from equation 17.63(*a*)) that

$$Z_{in} = Z = Z_0 \left[\frac{Z_R + Z_0 \tan h(\gamma l)}{Z_0 + Z_R \tan h(\gamma l)}\right]$$

However, in a high frequency line,

$$\alpha = 0; \quad \gamma = j\beta = j\frac{2\pi}{\lambda}$$

$$\therefore Z = Z_0 \left[\frac{\frac{Z_R}{Z_R} + \frac{Z_0}{Z_R}\tan h\left(j\frac{2\pi}{\lambda}\right)l}{\frac{Z_0}{Z_R} + \frac{Z_R}{Z_R}\tan h\left(j\frac{2\pi}{\lambda}\right)l}\right]$$

$$= Z_0 \left[\frac{1 - j\frac{Z_0}{Z_R}\tan\frac{2\pi l}{\lambda}}{\frac{Z_0}{Z_R} - j\tan\left(\frac{2\pi l}{\lambda}\right)}\right]$$

However, at voltage minimum, Z is Z_{min}.

Hence from the text, at the point of Z_{min}.

$$\frac{Z_0}{Z_R} = S$$

Thus, $$Z = Z_0 \left[\frac{1 - jS\tan\left(\frac{2\pi l}{\lambda}\right)}{S - j\tan\left(\frac{2\pi l}{\lambda}\right)}\right].$$

EXAMPLE 17.27 *A low loss transmission line has characteristic impedance of 70 ohms and is terminated by another impedance of $(115 - j80)$ ohms. The wavelength on the line is 2.5 mt. Find the standing wave ratio, maximum and minimum line impedances. Also, determine the distance between the load and the first voltage minimum.*

SOLUTION. It is given that

$$Z_0 = 70 \text{ Ohms}$$

$$Z_R = (115 - j80) \text{ Ohms} = 140\angle -34.8° \Omega$$

$$\lambda = 2.5 \text{ mt}$$

Reflection co-efficient

$$K = \frac{Z_0 - Z_R}{Z_0 + Z_R} = \frac{70 - (115 - j80)}{70 + (115 - j80)}$$

$$= \frac{-45 + j80}{185 - j80} = \frac{91.79}{201.5}\angle -60.6° + 23.38°$$

$$= 0.46\angle -37.22°$$

$$\therefore \quad |K| = 0.46$$

However, $$S = \frac{1 + K}{1 - K} = \frac{1.46}{0.54} = \mathbf{2.7}$$

Again from the text, it has been established that

at Z_{max}, $Z = SZ_0 = 2.7 \times 70 = \mathbf{189\ \Omega}$

at Z_{min}, $Z = \frac{Z_0}{S} = \frac{70}{2.7} = \mathbf{25.9\ \Omega}$

CHAPTER 17

Thus, the maximum line impedance is 189Ω and minimum line impedance is 25.9 Ω.

The distance between the load and first voltage minimum will be given by

$$d = \frac{\lambda}{4} + \frac{Z_0}{Z_R} = \frac{2.5}{4} + \frac{70}{140} = \mathbf{1.125\ mt.}$$

EXAMPLE 17.28 *A HF transmission line is operated at a frequency of 1000 kHz. It has a characteristic impedance of 685 ohms (resistive) and the phase constant is 20 radians/km. The line is terminated by a pure resistive load of 350 ohms. If the voltage drop across the load is 5 volts, determine the magnitude and phases of voltages and current at a distance of $\frac{1}{2}$ km from the load. Also calculate the reflection coefficient.*

SOLUTION. We have seen

$$V_X = V_R \cos\beta d + jR_0 I_R \sin\beta d$$

Here $\beta = 20$ rad/km

$$d = \frac{1}{2} \times \frac{180}{\pi}$$

[∵ β is given in radians/km, d is expressed in radians]

$$R_0 = 685\ \Omega$$

$$I_R = \frac{5}{350}\ \text{A}$$ [voltage across the load is 5 V and line is terminated by a pure resistance of 350 Ω]

$$\therefore \quad V_X = 5\cos\left(\frac{20\times 1/2\times 180}{\pi}\right) + j\frac{685\times 5}{350}\sin\left(\frac{20\times 1/2\times 180}{\pi}\right)$$

$$= -4.2 - j5.32 = \mathbf{6.78\ \angle 52^\circ\ Volts}$$

$$I_X = I_R \cos\beta d + j\frac{V_R}{R_0}\sin\beta d$$

$$= \frac{5}{350}\cos\left(\frac{20\times 1/2\times 180}{\pi}\right) + j\frac{5}{685}\sin\left(\frac{20\times 1/2\times 180}{\pi}\right)$$

$$= -0.012 - j\,0.00397$$

$$= \mathbf{0.013\angle 18^\circ\ Amps.}$$

$|K|$(reflection coefficient)

$$= \left|\frac{R_R - R_0}{R_R + R_0}\right| = \frac{350-685}{350+683} = \left|\frac{335}{1035}\right| = |\mathbf{0.32}|.$$

EXAMPLE 17.29 *Derive expressions of voltage and current for different line terminations (open circuit, short circuit and termination by Z_0) in terms of receiving end parameters.*

SOLUTION. We have derived the expression for voltage at any point on the line in terms of receiving end quantities as

$$V_X = \frac{V_R}{2Z_R}[(Z_0 + Z_R)e^{\gamma d} - (Z_0 - Z_R)e^{-\gamma d}] \quad ...(a)$$

Assuming K to be the reflection co-efficient in a lossless line,

$\alpha = 0, \gamma = j\beta$ and $Z_0 = R_0$, so that

$$V_X = \frac{V_R}{2Z_R}(Z_R + R_0)(e^{j\beta d} - Ke^{-j\beta d})$$

$$\left[\because K = \frac{Z_0 - Z_R}{Z_0 + Z_R}\right]$$

Also, from (*a*),

$$V_X = \frac{V_R}{Z_R}\left[Z_R\frac{e^{j\beta d} + e^{-j\beta d}}{2} + jR_0\frac{e^{j\beta d} - e^{-j\beta d}}{2j}\right]$$

$$= V_R \cos\beta d + jR_0 I_R \sin\beta d \quad ...(b)$$

$$I_X = \frac{I_R}{2Z_0}[(Z_0 + Z_R)e^{\gamma d} + (Z_0 - Z_R)e^{-\gamma d}] \quad ...(c)$$

$$= \frac{I_R}{R_0}\left[jZ_R\frac{e^{j\beta d} - e^{-j\beta d}}{2j} + R_0\frac{e^{j\beta d} + e^{-j\beta d}}{2}\right]$$

$$= I_R \cos\beta d + j\frac{V_R}{R_0}\sin\beta d \quad ...(d)$$

Also, from (c)

$$I_X = \frac{I_R(Z_0 + Z_R)}{2Z_0}\left[e^{\gamma d} - \left(\frac{Z_R - Z_0}{Z_R + Z_0}\right)e^{-\gamma d}\right]$$

$$= \frac{I_R(Z_R + R_0)}{2R_0}[e^{j\beta d} + Ke^{-j\beta d}] \quad ...(e)$$

Since $\beta = \frac{2\pi}{\lambda}$, the above expressions can further be simplified as

$$V_X = V_R\cos\left(\frac{2\pi}{\lambda}.d\right) + j\,I_R R_0 \sin\left(\frac{2\pi}{\lambda}.d\right)$$

$$I_X = I_R\cos\left(\frac{2\pi}{\lambda}.d\right) + j\frac{V_R}{R_0}\sin\left(\frac{2\pi}{\lambda}.d\right)$$

If the line is open-circuited at the receiving end,

$$I_R = 0$$

$$\therefore \quad V_X \equiv V_{o/c} = V_R \cos\left(\frac{2\pi}{\lambda}.d\right)$$

and
$$I_X \equiv I_{o/c} = j\frac{V_R}{R_0}\sin\left(\frac{2\pi}{\lambda}.d\right)$$

On the other hand, if the line is short-circuited at the receiving end,

$$V_R = 0$$

$$\therefore \quad V_X \equiv V_{s/c} = jI_R R_0 \sin\left(\frac{2\pi}{\lambda}.d\right)$$

and
$$I_X \equiv I_{s/c} = I_R \cos\left(\frac{2\pi}{\lambda}.d\right)$$

If the line is terminated by R_0, the reflection co-efficient K becomes zero and $Z_R \equiv R_0$. Thus from equations (*a*) and (*c*),

$$V_X = V_R e^{j\beta d} \text{ and } I_X = I_R e^{j\beta d}$$

[These equations indicate that the voltage and current magnitudes remain constant and there is no attenuation with continuously increasing phase angle along the line].

EXAMPLE 17.30 *It is required to match a 200 Ω load to a 300Ω transmission line, to reduce the VSW along the line to 1. What must be the characteristic impedance of the quarter wave transformer used for this purpose, if it is connected directly to the load.*

SOLUTION. When the line is made $\lambda/4$ long, the input impedance becomes,

$$Z_s(\lambda/4) = \frac{Z_0^2}{Z_R} \text{ at any value of } S.$$

But when standing wave ratio S is equal to 1 then $Z_R = Z_0$

$$\therefore \quad Z_s(\lambda/4) = \frac{Z_0^2}{Z_0} = Z_0$$

$\therefore$ Here $Z_s(\lambda/4) = 300\Omega = Z_{in}$

Hence, the characteristic impedance of the quarter wave transformer should be **300 Ω.**

EXAMPLE 17.31 *The distributed circuit coefficients of a transmission line at frequency of 1100 Hz are R = 0.053 Ω/m, L= 0.62 × 10^{-6} H/m, G= 950 μ mho/m and C = 39.5 μF. Find the current gradient along the line at point Z where the phasor voltage is 16.5 volts.*

SOLUTION. Using equation (17.26),

$$\frac{dI}{dx} = -(g + j\omega C)V$$

$$\frac{dI}{dx} = -[950\times10^{-12} + j(2\pi\times1100)(39.5\times10^{-12})]16.5$$
$$= -(0.015 + j\,4.52)10^{-6}\text{ A/m}$$

Thus, the current gradient along the line at point Z given by

$$-\mathbf{(0.015 + j\,4.52)10^{-6}\,A/m}$$

[The value obtained is the rms value and the maximum value of the gradient can be obtained as

$$\sqrt{2}\times\frac{dI}{dx} = \sqrt{2}\,|0.016 + j4.51|\times10^{-6}$$
$$= \mathbf{6.39\times10^{-6}\,A/m}\text{].}$$

EXAMPLE 17.32 *At a particular frequency power is transmitted from a source to a load by a $\frac{1}{2}$ km length of uniform transmission line. The voltage at the source is 250 V (rms) while that at the load is 220 V (rms). What is the total attenuation of the line ? Obtain the value of attenuation factor ? Assume no reflection of voltage or current waves at load.*

SOLUTION. Since $e^{-\alpha} = \dfrac{V_{out}}{V_{in}}$

$\therefore$ Here $e^{-\alpha} = \dfrac{220}{250} = 0.88$

or, $-\alpha = \log_e 0.88 = -0.129$

$\therefore$ $\alpha = \mathbf{0.129\ Neper}$

Attenuation factor is α per unit length.

$$\therefore \text{ Attenuation factor} = \frac{0.129\text{ Neper}}{500\text{ mt}}$$
$$= \mathbf{2.56\times10^{-4}\ Nep/m.}$$

EXAMPLE 17.33 *A transmission line (50 km long) has attenuation constant of 1.5× 10^{-4} Nep/m at frequency of 1 kHz. If the input current to the line is 650 mA, what is the line current at its load end if the reflection of current is not considered ?*

SOLUTION. αl (Attenuation for the entire line)

$$= (50\times10^3)(1.5\times10^{-4}) = 7.5\text{ Nep}$$

As $e^{-\alpha} = \dfrac{I_2}{I_1}$; I_1 = input current

I_2 = load current

$$\therefore \quad e^{-7.5} = \frac{I_2}{650} \text{ or } I_2 = \mathbf{0.36\ mA}$$

Then the load current is 0.36 mA.

EXAMPLE 17.34 *The phase constant factor for a transmission line is 0.123 rad/m at a frequency 4.5 MHz. Assuming the line length to be 500 m, find the wavelength and phase velocity of waves on the line. What is the phase difference between the voltages at the two ends of the line ?*

Solution.

Wavelength $\lambda = \frac{2\pi}{\beta} = 51$ mt

Phase velocity $v_p = \frac{\omega}{\beta} = \frac{2\pi f}{\beta} = 2.3 \times 10^8$ mt/sec

Phase difference for the entire line $= \beta l = 61.51$ rad.

Example 17.35 *A section of a lossless transmission line is 0.4 λ long and is terminated in a short circuit. The characteristic impedance of the line being $(73 + j0)\Omega$, determine the input impedance of the line section. Assume the operating frequency to be 200 MHz.*

Solution.

$Z_{in} = jZ_0 \tan\beta l$, for the shorted end of the line.

$$\therefore \quad Z_{in} = jZ_0 \tan\frac{2\pi l}{\lambda}$$

$$= j(73 + j0)\tan(2.51 \text{ rad}) = -j\,53.5\Omega$$

It is a capacitive reactance.

The equivalent capacitance is then given by

$$C_{in} = \frac{1}{53.5\omega} = \frac{1}{53.4 \times 2\pi \times 200 \times 10^6} = \mathbf{14.9\ \mu F.}$$

Example 17.36 *A transmission line operates at 400 MHz and characteristic impedance of 50Ω. If the terminating impedance is $(20 - j80)\Omega$, obtain the value of VSWR.*

Solution.

$$K = \frac{\frac{Z_R}{Z_0} - 1}{\frac{Z_R}{Z_0} + 1} = \frac{(0.4 - j1.6) - 1}{(0.4 - j1.6) + 1} = 0.8 \angle 5.2 \text{ rad.}$$

$$\therefore \quad S = \frac{1+K}{1-K} = \frac{1.8}{0.2} = \mathbf{9.0}$$

[Here K = reflection coefficient

and S = voltage standing wave ratio]

Example 17.37 *A transmission line with characteristic impedance Z_0 $(= 50 + j0)$ ohms is terminated in an impedance of $(25 - j100)$ ohms. Determine the reflection coefficient at the load end using Smith Chart.*

Solution. The given impedance of $(25 - j100)$ is first normalised

$$Z_{in} = \frac{25 - j100}{50 + j0} = (0.5 - j2)$$

This value of $(0.5 - j2)$ is located in the Smith Chart (using the r circle of 0.5 value and $-jx$ circle with $-j2$ value) to obtain the point of intersection (point m in Fig. E17.37). Thus, the coordinate of "m" is $(0.5, -2)$.

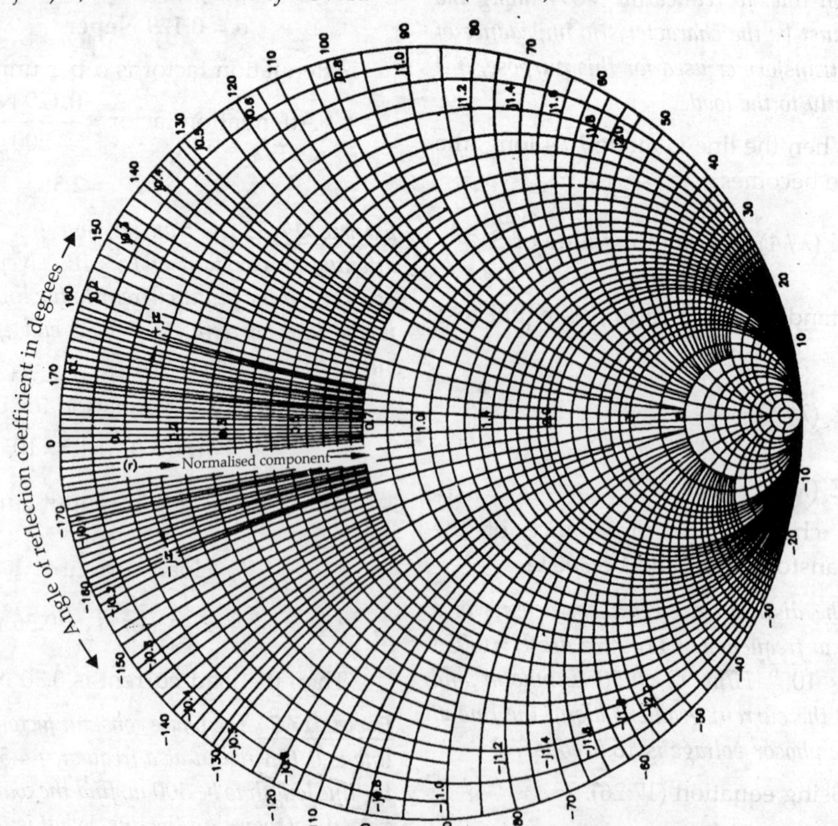

Fig. E17.37

In order to find S, the VSWR, a straight line is joined between the point m and point 1.0 on r-axis as shown in the figure. With this line as the radius, an arc is drawn with point 1.0 as centre. This arc touches the r-axis at 8.5.

$$\therefore \qquad S = 8.5$$

We can now find K, the reflection coefficient as

$$K = \frac{S-1}{S+1}$$

$$\text{Here} \qquad K = \frac{8.5-1}{8.51} = \frac{7.5}{9.5} = 0.8.$$

Thus, the value of the reflection coefficient at the load end is **0.8.**

In order to find the angle of K, the line joining 1.0 and m is extended upto the outer circle where we find that the angle becomes $-51°$.

$$\therefore \qquad K = 0.8\angle -51° \quad \text{or,} \quad \mathbf{0.8\angle -309°}.$$

EXAMPLE 17.38 *The normalised load impedance of a line is (2.5 + j1.0). The line being 28° long find the value of the VSWR and reflection coefficient. What is the value of the input impedance of the line ?*

SOLUTION. The normalised load impedance being $(2.5 + j1.0)$, the point of intersection of r circle with $+jx$ circle (with respective values of $r_n = 2.5$, $jx_n = j\,1.0$) is obtained in Fig. E17.38 (point n). The point n and the point of value 1.0 on r-axis are joined by a line. With this line as the radius and point (1.0) as centre on r-axis, an arc is drawn that intersects the r-axis at 3.0. This value gives S.

$$\therefore \qquad \text{VSWR} = S = 3.0$$

$$\therefore \qquad K = \frac{3-1}{3+1} = 0.5$$

The reflection coefficient is thus 0.5. The angle of reflection coefficient is obtained by projecting the line joining 1.0 to n upto the outer circle when the reading of the angle in degree is 17°.

$$\therefore \qquad K = 0.5\angle 17°$$

It may further be observed that the line joining 1.0 on r-axis to n can be extended to meet the outer-most circle (distance scale) at 0.227 λ. However the line length being 28°, in the distance scale, it is

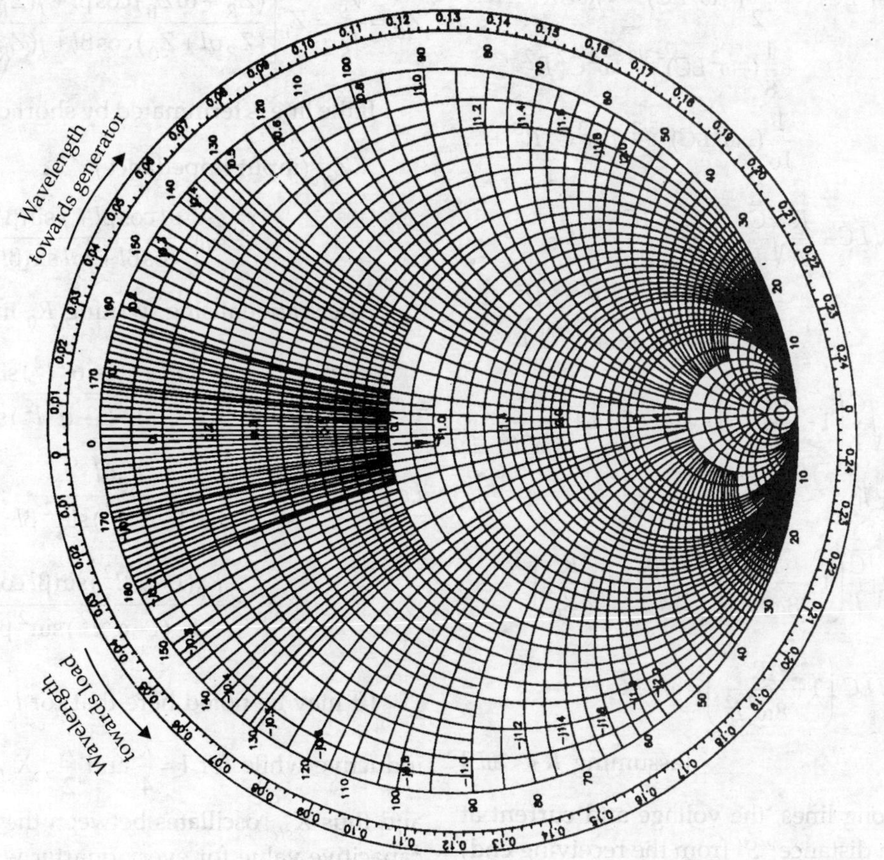

Fig. E17.38

equivalent to $\frac{28°}{360°} = 0.078\ \lambda$. Total value is thus $(0.078\ \lambda + 0.227\ \lambda)$ *i.e.*, $0.305\ \lambda$. This means that in the lower half of the circle the value is $0.5\ \lambda - 0.305\ \lambda = 0.195\ \lambda$. Locating this value on the lower half of the Smith Chart, another line from 1.0 at *r*-axis is drawn to meet the outer circle at $0.195\ \lambda$ at lower half. Next, the arc from $S = 3$ is extended to meet this new line at X. The co-ordinate of X is $(\mathbf{1.6 - j1.35})$. This gives the input impedance of the line.

EXAMPLE 17.39 *Obtain the expression for the "Bandwidth" for a transmission line while it acts as a resonant circuit.*

SOLUTION. At high frequencies, the transmission line has got low value of dissipation such that

$R << \omega L$ and $G \simeq 0$

$$\therefore \qquad \gamma = \sqrt{\gamma Z} = \sqrt{j\omega C(R + j\omega L)}$$

$$\text{or,} \qquad \gamma = (-\omega^2 LC + j\omega CR)^{1/2}$$

Using Binomial Theorem,

$$r = (-\omega^2 LC)^{1/2} + \frac{1}{2}(-\omega^2 LC)^{-1/2} j\omega CR + \frac{1}{8}(-\omega^2 LC)^{-3/2}.\omega^2 C^2 R^2 - \frac{1}{16}(-\omega^2 LC)^{-5/2}.j\,\omega^3 C^3 R^3 + \ldots$$

$$= j\omega\sqrt{LC} + \frac{R}{2}\sqrt{\frac{C}{L}} + j\frac{R^2}{8\omega L}\sqrt{\frac{C}{L}} - \frac{1}{16}\frac{R^3}{\omega^2 L^2}\sqrt{\frac{C}{L}} + \ldots$$

$$= \frac{R}{2}\sqrt{\frac{C}{L}}\left(1 - \frac{R^2}{8\omega^2 L^2}\right) + j\omega\sqrt{LC}\left(1 + \frac{R^2}{8\omega^2 L^2}\right)$$

$$= \alpha + j\beta$$

$$\text{where, } \alpha = \frac{R}{2}\sqrt{\frac{C}{L}}\left(1 - \frac{R^2}{8\omega^2 L^2}\right) \simeq \frac{R}{2}\sqrt{\frac{C}{L}} = \left(\frac{R}{2R_0}\right)$$

$$\beta = \omega\sqrt{LC}\left(1 + \frac{R^2}{8\omega^2 L^2}\right) = \omega\sqrt{LC}$$

[assuming $R << \omega L$]

Also for long lines, the voltage and current at any point (at a distance "S" from the receiving end) is given by

$$V_S = \frac{V_R}{2Z_R}(Z_R + Z_0)(e^{rS} + Ke^{-rS})$$

[For derivation, refer to Example 17.5]

$$I_S = \frac{V_R}{2Z_0}(Z_R + Z_0)(e^{rS} - Ke^{-rS})$$

[Here since $Z_R > Z_0$, K is assumed to be $\left(\frac{Z_R - Z_0}{Z_0 + Z_R}\right)$]

Again $e^{rS} = e^{\alpha S} e^{j\beta S} = (1 + \alpha S)(\cos\beta S + j\sin\beta S)$

and $\qquad e^{-rS} = e^{-\alpha S} e^{-j\beta S} = (1 - \alpha S)(\cos\beta S - j\sin\beta S)$

Thus, the voltage and current relations become

$$V_S = V_R\left[\left(1 + \alpha S\frac{Z_0}{Z_R}\right)\cos\beta S + j\left(\alpha S + \frac{Z_0}{Z_R}\right)\sin\beta S\right]$$

$$\text{and } I = \left\{\frac{V_R}{Z_0}\right\}\left[\left(\alpha S + \frac{Z_0}{Z_R}\right)\cos\beta S + j\left(1 + \alpha S\frac{Z_0}{Z_R}\right)\sin\beta S\right]$$

For $S = l$, the finite length of the line,

$$Z_S = \frac{V_S}{I_S} = Z_0\left[\frac{(Z_R + \alpha l Z_0)\cos\beta l + j(Z_R\alpha l + Z_0)\sin\beta l}{(Z_R\alpha l + Z_0)\cos\beta l + j(Z_R + \alpha l Z_0)\sin\beta l}\right]$$

If the line is terminated by short circuit, $Z_R = 0$.

$\therefore Z_{s/c}$ (input impedance)

$$= Z_0\left(\frac{\alpha l\cos\beta l + j\sin\beta l}{\cos\beta l + j\alpha l\sin\beta l}\right)$$

After rationalising, writing R_0 instead of Z_0,

$$Z_{s/c} = R_0\left[\frac{\alpha l + j(1 - \alpha^2 l^2)\sin\beta l\cos\beta l}{1 - (1 - \alpha^2 l^2)\sin^2\beta l}\right]$$

i.e.,
$$R_{s/c} = \frac{R_0\alpha l}{1 - (1 - \alpha^2 l^2)\sin^2\beta l};$$

$$X_{s/c} = \frac{R_0(1 - \alpha^2 l^2)\sin\beta l\cos\beta l}{1 - (1 - \alpha^2 l^2)\sin^2\beta l}$$

[It may be noted here that for $l = 0$ to $\frac{\lambda}{4}$, $X_{s/c}$ is inductive while for $l = \frac{\lambda}{4}$ and $\frac{\lambda}{2}$, $X_{s/c}$ is capacitive and thus $X_{s/c}$ oscillates between the inductive and capacitive value for every quarter wavelength].

A transmission line being able to act as a resonant circuit [Art 17.9], we must have two frequencies, f_2 and f_1 about f_0, at which the power is $\frac{1}{2}$ of the value at resonant frequency f_0. It is evident that for operating frequency f_1, the line being short circuited, the resistance of the line equals to the reactance and hence, for $R_{s/c} = X_{s/c}$, we can write,

$$\frac{R_0 \alpha l}{1-(1-\alpha^2 l^2)\sin^2 \beta_1 l} = \frac{R_0(1-\alpha^2 l^2)\sin\beta_1 l\cos\beta_1 l}{1-(1-\alpha^2 l^2)\sin\beta_1 l}$$

or, $$R_0 \alpha l = R_0(1-\alpha^2 l^2)\sin\beta_1 l\cos\beta_1 l$$

or, $$\frac{1}{2}(\sin 2\beta_1 l) = \frac{\alpha l}{1-\alpha^2 l^2}$$

If αl is small, $\alpha^2 l^2$ can be neglected.

$\therefore$ $$2\beta_1 l = \sin^{-1}[(\alpha l)\times 2]$$

or, $$\beta_1 l = \frac{\pi}{2} - \alpha l$$

[Since αl is small, $\sin \alpha l$ can be replaced by αl]

or, $$\frac{\omega_1}{v_p}.l = \frac{\pi}{2} - \alpha l$$

$$\left[\because \beta = \frac{\omega}{v_p};\ v_p \text{ being the phase velocity}\right]$$

or, $$\omega_1 = \frac{v_p}{l}\left[\frac{\pi}{2} - \alpha l\right]$$

or, $$f_1 = \frac{v_p}{2\pi l}\left(\frac{\pi}{2} - \alpha l\right).$$

Again, dividing the numerator and denominator by Z_R and setting $Z_R = \infty$, for the open circuited line, the expression for Z_S derived earlier becomes

$$Z_{o/c} = Z_0\left[\frac{\cos\beta l + j\alpha l\sin\beta l}{\alpha l\cos\beta l + j\sin\beta l}\right]$$

Rationalising and substituting R_0 and Z_0,

$$Z_{o/c} = R_0\left[\frac{\alpha l - j(1-\alpha^2 l^2)\sin\beta l\cos\beta l}{1-(1-\alpha^2 l^2)\cos^2\beta l}\right]$$

i.e., $$R_{o/c} = \frac{R_0 \alpha l}{1-(1-\alpha^2 l^2)\cos^2\beta l}$$

$$X_{o/c} = \frac{-R_0(1-\alpha^2 l^2)\sin\beta l\cos\beta l}{1-(1-\alpha^2 l^2)\cos^2\beta l}$$

[For values of l between 0 and $\frac{\lambda}{4}$, $X_{o/c}$ is capacitive while for values of l between $\frac{\lambda}{4}$ and $\frac{\lambda}{2}$, $X_{o/c}$ is inductive]. Since, at $\frac{\lambda}{4}$, the line is resonant, for the open circuited line also, there will be a frequency f_2, around f_0 where the resistance would be equal to the reactance [as in the case for the short circuited line].

With this $R_{o/c} = X_{o/c}$

or, $$\frac{R_0 \alpha l}{1-(1-\alpha^2 l^2)\cos^2\beta_2 l} = \frac{-R_0(1-\alpha^2 l^2)\sin\beta_2 l\cos\beta_2 l}{1-(1-\alpha^2 l^2)\cos^2\beta_2 l}$$

or, $$R_0 \alpha l = -R_0(1-\alpha^2 l^2)\sin\beta_2 l\cos\beta_2 l$$

or, $$\frac{\sin 2\beta_2 l}{2} = \frac{\alpha l}{1-\alpha^2 l^2}$$

Neglecting $\alpha^2 l^2$, assuming $\sin \alpha l \simeq \alpha l$, we finally obtain,

$$\beta_2 l = \frac{\pi}{2} + \alpha l$$

$\therefore$ $$f_2 = \frac{v_p}{2\pi l}\left(\frac{\pi}{2} + \alpha l\right)$$

The bandwidth of the line is then given by

$$\frac{\Delta f}{f_0} = \frac{f_2 - f_1}{f_0} \quad \text{[normalising across } f_0]$$

or, $$\frac{\Delta f}{f_0} = \frac{\frac{v_p}{2\pi l}\left(\frac{\pi}{2} + \alpha l - \frac{\pi}{2} + \alpha l\right)}{f_0}$$

or, $$\frac{\Delta f}{f_0} = \frac{2\alpha}{\beta} \quad \left[\because \beta = \frac{2\pi f}{v_p}\right]$$

$$\left[\text{Since } Q \text{ is reciprocal of Bandwidth, } Q = \frac{\beta}{2\alpha}\right]$$

C H A P T E R 17

Exercises

1. The following measurements have been obtained on a transmission line at 1 kHz : $Z_{o/c} = 1000\,\Omega\angle -30°$; $Z_{s/c} = 100\,\Omega\angle -10°$. What is the characteristic impedance of the line ?

   [**Hint.** Find Z_0 from $Z_0 = \sqrt{Z_{o/c} . Z_{s/c}}$]

2. A communication cable has the following primary coefficients at an angular frequency of 10×10^3 rad/sec : $R = 25$ Ohms/km, $G = 1\mu$ mho/km, $L = 1$ mH/km, $C = 0.01\ \mu$G /km. Find Z_0 and r.

   [**Hint.** Refer to Solved Examples]

3. A coaxial cable of characteristic impedance 40 ohms has been terminated in a resistive load of 100 ohm. The peak voltage across the load has been obtained as 30 volts. Calculate (*a*) the reflection coefficient, (*b*) the amplitude of the forward and reflected voltage wave, (*c*) VSWR.

   [**Hint.** Find K from $K = \dfrac{Z_0 - Z_R}{Z_R + Z_0}$;

   Also $K = \dfrac{V_R}{V_i}$ and from the data given, $V_R + V_i = 30$.

   Find V_R and V_i from these two equations.

   Also $S = \dfrac{1+K}{1-K}$. K is known, hence S can be calculated.]

4. A lossless transmission line has an inductance of 1.5 mH/km and a capacitance of 0.02 μF / km. Calculate Z_0 and γ of the line. Assume $\omega = 5000$ rad/sec. Find the velocity of wave propagation and frequency of the wave for wavelength of 0.5 km.

   [**Hint.** Do in the same way as has been done in Ex. 17.5].

5. A lossless line has a shunt capacitance of 130 pF/mt and a series inductance of 4 μH/ mt. What is its characteristic impedance ?

   [**Hint.** Find Z_0 from $Z_0 = \sqrt{\dfrac{L}{C}}$.]

6. Z_0 for an uniform transmission line is 2100 ohm at 1000 Hz. The propagation constant being $0.05\angle 88°$, find the magnitudes of the primary constants of the line.

   [**Hint.** Proceed in the same way as has been shown in Ex. 17.9].

7. A line has following primary constants per km loop. $R = 26\,\Omega$, $L = 16$ mH, $C = 0.2$ μF, $G = 5$ μmho. Find the characteristic impedance at $\omega = 7500$ rad/sec

   $\left[\textbf{Hint. } Z_0 = \sqrt{\dfrac{R + j\omega L}{G + j\omega C}}\right.$. Find Z_0 from the given data.]

8. Calculate the primary constants of a line having $Z_0 = 500\angle -10.5°$ Ohm, $\gamma = 0.02\angle 75°$ at $f = 1.5$ kHz.

   $\left[\textbf{Hint. } Z_0 = \sqrt{\dfrac{R + j\omega L}{G + j\omega C}}, \gamma = \sqrt{(R + j\omega L)(G + j\omega C)}\right.$

   Multiplying, we get $(R + j\omega L)$ from where, separating real and imaginary parts, the value of R and L can be obtained. Similarly, dividing the equations, we get $(G + j\omega C)$ from where, again we can get the value of G and C by separating the real and imaginary parts].

9. A lossless line is terminated in a pure resistance of 500 ohms. If the characteristic impedance of the line is 400 ohms, find the value of the standing wave ratio.

   $\left[\textbf{Hint. } K = \dfrac{Z_0 - R_R}{Z_0 + Z_R} . S = \dfrac{1+K}{1-K}\right]$

10. An open wire line has $R = 85$ ohm/loop km, $G = 0$, $L = 2.3$ mH/loop km and $C = 5$ nF/loop km. Determine Z_0, β, λ and v_p. (Assume operating frequency of 1 kHz)

$$\left[\textbf{Hint. } Z_0 = \sqrt{\frac{R + j\omega L}{j\omega C}}\,\Omega, \beta = \omega\sqrt{LC} \text{ rad/km}; \lambda = \frac{2\pi}{\beta} \text{mt and } v_p = \frac{\omega}{\beta} = \frac{2\pi f}{\beta}.\text{mt/sec.}\right]$$

11. A lossless line of 200 ohm characteristic impedance is required to have input impedance of 8 δH at a frequency of 70 MHz under short circuit condition at the receiving end. What should be the length of line ?

$$\left[\textbf{Hint. } Z_{s/c} = jZ_0 \tan\left(\frac{2\pi l}{\lambda}\right)\right.$$

Here $Z_0 = 200\,\Omega$; $Z_{s/c} = j2\pi \times f \times 8 \times 10^{-3}\Omega$

$$\therefore \quad \frac{2\pi l}{\lambda} = \tan^{-1}\left[\frac{Z_{s/c}}{Z_0}\right]$$

∴ l, in terms of λ can be found out. In the similar way, using the formula for open circuit condition, the required length can be used also. Obviously, the results of l obtained during both the condition will differ.]

12. A transmission cable has following primary parameters : $R = 52\,\Omega$/loop km, $L = 0.5$ H/loop km, $C = 0.04\,\mu$F / km. The cable is loaded by loading coils of inductance 250 mH and resistance 7 ohms each at standard interval of 12.6 km. Calculate the values of characteristic impedance, attenuation and phase constants. Assuming the operating frequency of 1 kHz, also find the phase velocity of the wave. (Assume $G = 0$)

[**Hint.** $Z = R + j\omega L$; $Y = G + j\omega C$; first find $Z_0\left(= \sqrt{\frac{Z}{Y}}\right)$ and $\gamma(= \sqrt{ZY})$

As $\gamma = \alpha + j\beta$, get α and β from the real and imaginary components of γ.

Also, phase velocity $= \frac{\omega}{\beta}$.

Total inductance of the cable after loading is given by $L' = \left(L + \frac{250 \times 10^{-3}}{12.6}\right)$ H/ km.

Similarly, R' (total inductance) $= \left(+\frac{7}{12.6}\right)\Omega$ / km

$$\therefore \quad Z_{0(\text{new})} = \sqrt{\frac{L'}{C}}\,\Omega \quad \Rightarrow \quad \alpha = \frac{R}{2}\sqrt{\frac{C}{L}} \text{ (Np/km) [see text for the derivation]}$$

$$\beta = \omega\sqrt{LC} \text{ rad/km}; \; v_p = \frac{1}{\sqrt{LC}} \text{km / sec.]}$$

13. The characteristic impedance of an open wire transmission line is $690\angle -12°$ and propagation constant is $0.04\angle +77°$. The transmission line is 200 km long. A generator supplies power at 5 volts at the sending end. The internal impedance (resistive) of the generator is 600 ohms. If this line is terminated by its characteristic impedance, find the receiving end current and power.

[**Hint.** Work out Z_0 in complex form.

$$I_S = \frac{V_g}{Z_0 + Z_i} \quad (Z_i \text{ being the internal resistance of sending end generator})$$

$$I_R = I_S e^{-re} = I_S e^{-(\alpha l + j\beta l)}$$

Again $|V_R| = |I_R| Z_0$

$P_R = |V_R||I_R| \cos\phi$, ϕ being the angle of V_R and I_R which can be obtained from the complex calculation of V_R.]

14. A parallel wire transmission line has $Z_0 = (700 - j150)\,\Omega$ at a frequency 8 kHz. If a signal voltage of 10 volts runs at 8 kHz is connected to the input terminals of the line, what is the input current and what is the average power supplied by the signal source to the line ?

$$\textbf{[Hint. } I_{\text{input}} = \frac{V}{Z} = \frac{10 + j.0}{700 - j150} = 13.7 + j\,2.95 \text{ mA}; P = I^2_{\text{input}} \times R_{\text{input}} = (14 \times 10^{-3})^2 \times 700 \text{W]}$$

CHAPTER 17

15. A signal at a frequency of 2.5×10^6 Hz is applied to the input of a transmission line 125 mt long. If the line is terminated by its characteristic impedance, and the wavelength of the signal is 92 m, find the time delay between the instant of connecting the source to the line and the arrival of signal at the terminal load.

[**Hint.** $v_p = f\lambda = 92 \times 2.5 \times 10^6 = 2.3 \times 10^8$ m/sec.

$$\therefore \quad \text{time} = \frac{\text{length}}{v_p} = 0.54 \times 10^{-6} \text{ sec}]$$

16. What is the phase difference between the voltage at the two ends of the line in the previous problem ?

[**Hint.** $\beta = \dfrac{2\pi}{\lambda} = 0.068$ rad/m ; βl is the phase difference *i.e.*, $\beta l = 8.5$ rad]

17. A coaxial cable of 900 m long has following distributed parameters : $R = G = 0$; $L = 0.425$ mH/m ; $C = 0.0715\,\mu$F/m. Assuming no reflection, how long a signal be delayed in transmission ? When the rms voltage at a particular point is 5 V, what is the rms signal current ?

[**Hint.** For loss-line $\beta = \omega\sqrt{LC}$ and $Z_0 = \sqrt{\dfrac{L}{C}}$; $v_p = \dfrac{\omega}{\beta} = \dfrac{1}{\sqrt{LC}}$;

$$\text{time} = \frac{\text{length}}{\text{velocity}} ; \; I = \frac{V}{Z_0} ; \text{ signal power} = \frac{V^2}{Z_0} \;]$$

CHAPTER

18

Synthesis of Passive Network

18.1 CONCEPT OF STABILITY OF A SYSTEM (POLYNOMIAL RATIO) FROM POLE ZERO CONCEPT

Let a *system* (denoted by ratio of polynomials) be represented as

$$F(s) = \frac{s(s-1+j2)(s-1-j2)}{(s+2)(s+j1)(s-j1)}$$

[$F(s)$ is a rational function with real coefficients]

It may be observed that $F(s)$ becomes *zero* for $s=0, (1-j2)$ and $(1+j2)$ while becomes *infinity* for $s=-2, -j1$ and $j1$. Thus any of the roots of the denominator of $F(s)$ (here $s=-2, -j1$ and $j1$) define a *pole* while any of the roots of the numerator [here $s=0, (1-j2), (1+j2)$] of the same system defines a *zero*. In the complex *s*-plane (σ real part, $j\omega$ imaginary part) the pole is denoted by a *small cross* and zero by a *small circle*. Fig. 18.1 represents the pole-zero diagram of the given function.

Next a unit step-function being considered, its *s*-domain representation is $\left(\frac{1}{s}\right)$.

i.e., $\quad F(s) = \frac{1}{s}$

Hence, there will be a no zero but only one pole at $s=0$ (origin) exist.

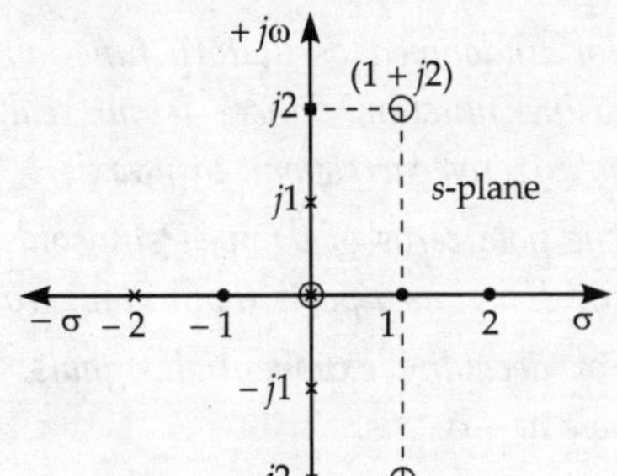

Fig. 18.1 Pole-zero plot of $F(s)$.

Suppose a cosine function being taken, then

$$F(s) = \frac{s}{s^2+\omega^2}.$$

Here poles exist at $s=\pm j\omega$ [conjugate poles] (Fig. 18.2) while zero is at the origin ($s=0$).

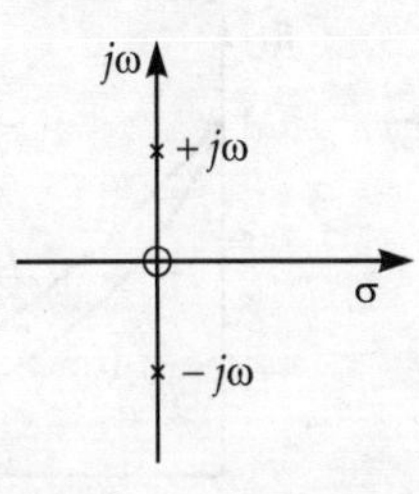

Fig. 18.2 Pole-zero plot of cosine function in *s*-domain.

Let us now examine the pole zero plot of a damped cosine wave whose s-domain representation is

$$F(s) = \frac{s+\sigma_0}{(s+\sigma_0)^2+\omega_0^2}.$$

The pole zero plot is shown in Fig. 18.3.

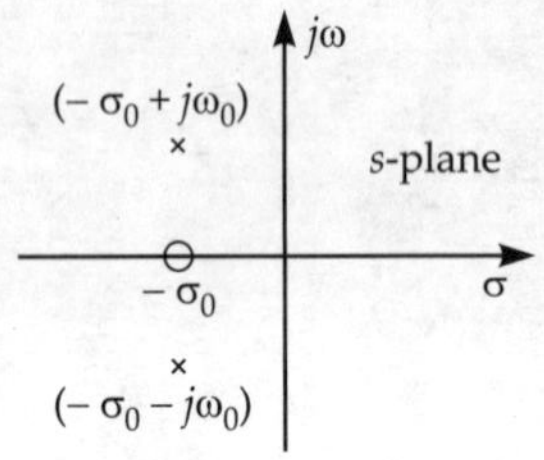

Fig. 18.3 Pole-zero plot of damped sinusoid.

Also, the normal exponential signal $e^{-\sigma_0 t}$ $(\sigma_0 > 0)$ having transform $F(s) = \frac{1}{s+\sigma_0}$, has the pole at $(-\sigma_0)$ while no zero exists.

Thus, following things are observed from above illustrations

(i) *For undamped oscillatory functions (say the cosine function), there is no real part and poles/zeros correspond to $j\omega$-axis.*

(ii) *The pole zeros of damped sinusoids have real and imaginary parts (both non zero).*

(iii) *For decaying exponential signals, there is a pole at $-\sigma$ axis.*

In the next section we consider two exponential functions $f_1(t)$ and $f_2(t)$ where

$$f_1(t) = Me^{-\sigma_1 t}$$

and $\quad f_2(t) = Me^{-\sigma_2 t}$ (Fig. 18.4) $\quad (\sigma_2 > \sigma_1 > 0)$

Obviously, $f_2(t)$ decays faster than $f_1(t)$.

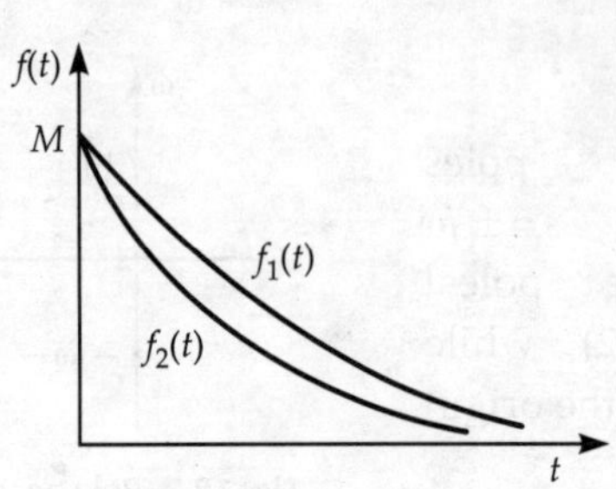

Fig. 18.4 Exponential functions in time domain.

Transforms are given by

$$F_1(s) = \frac{1}{s+\sigma_1}$$

$$F_2(s) = \frac{1}{s+\sigma_2},$$

The pole-zero diagram (Fig. 18.5) clearly illustrates that in the $(-\sigma)$ axis, the pole of $F_2(s)$ (*i.e.*, $-\sigma_2$) is further away from that (pole of $F_1(s)$ is $-\sigma_1$) of $F_1(s)$. Since the decay of $f_2(t)$ is more rapid than that of $f_1(t)$ hence we can make a thumb rule to say that *the distance of the pole in the negative real axis being more, the exponential function decays faster.*

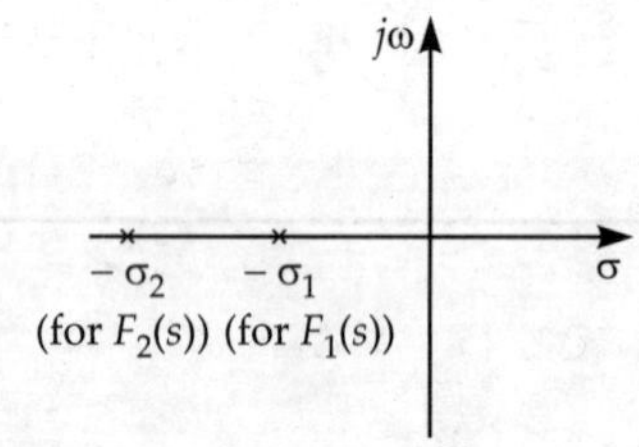

Fig. 18.5 Pole-zero plot of exponential functions.

Next we analyse the pole zero plot of two sine waves given by

$$f(t) = \sin \omega_1 t, \quad f'(t) = \sin \omega_2 t.$$

The poles are shown in Fig. 18.6.

$$F(s) = \frac{\omega_1}{s^2+\omega_1^2}; \quad F'(s) = \frac{\omega_2}{s^2+\omega_2^2}$$

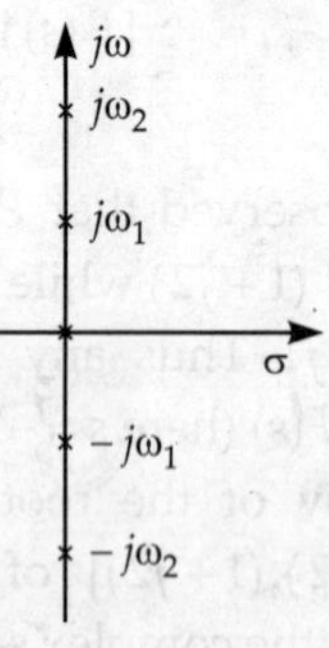

Fig. 18.6 Pole plot of sine functions.

For the first one, the poles are at $\pm j\omega_1$ and for the second one poles are at $\pm j\omega_2$. Obviously, zeros do not exist. It is evident that assuming $\omega_2 > \omega_1 > 0$, $j\omega_2 > j\omega_1$ and hence the frequency of oscillation of $f'(t)$ is more; *i.e., greater the distance of the pole in the $j\omega$ axis, greater is the frequency of oscillation.*

Next, another set of two functions is considered. The first function $f_X(t)$ has pole pairs (*i.e.*, conjugate poles) (say) s_1, s_1^* while the second function $f_Y(t)$ has pole pairs (say) s_2, s_2^*, the plot being shown in Fig. 18.7.

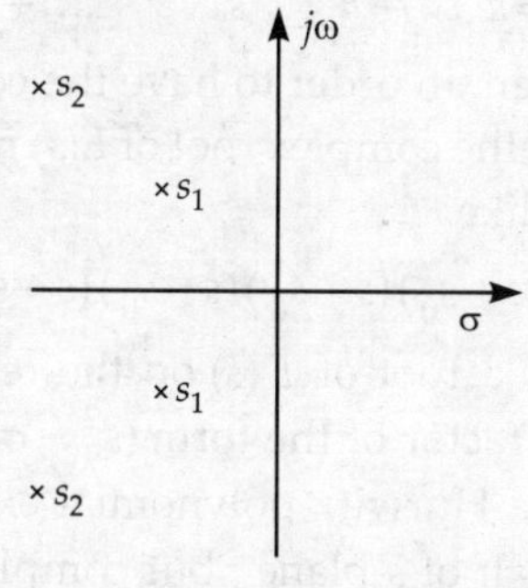

Fig. 18.7 Pole plot of a pair of functions.

From the previous analysis it is evident that the function $f_Y(t)$ will decay faster than $f_X(t)$ [since the real part of poles of $f_Y(t)$ is further away from that $f_X(t)$ in $(-\sigma)$ axis], but the frequency of $f_Y(t)$ would be higher [since the imaginary part of poles of $f_Y(t)$ is further away in the $j\omega$ axis than those of $f_X(t)$].

Let us now consider an entirely different scenario. A function $f(t) = Ke^{p_0 t}$ is considered while (p_0) being the root $(\sigma_0 + j\omega)$ of the exponential function. The transform of $f(t)$ is given by

$$F(s) = \frac{K}{s - p_0} = \frac{K}{s - (\sigma_0 + j\omega)}$$

[*K* is a constant]

It is evident that the real part of the pole is +ve $(\sigma_0 > 0)$ and hence the function $f(t)$ is an exponentially increasing sinusoid [it may be noted here the pole in this case has positive real part and is then placed at right half of *s*-plane].

It is then evident that pressure of *a pole in the right half of s-plane gives rise to exponentially increasing transient response. Then, a system function that has poles in the right half of s-plane is basically unstable.*

Again, suppose a function has double poles given by

$$F(s) = \frac{s}{(s^2 + \omega_1^2)^2}$$

The pole zero diagram is shown in Fig. 18.8.

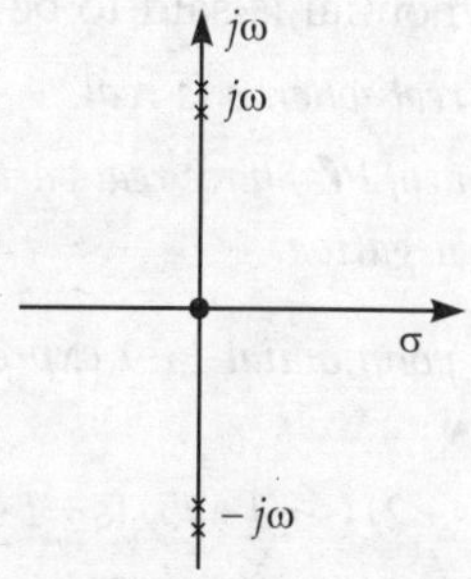

Fig. 18.8 Presence of multiple poles.

Since the inverse function of this transform is given by

$$f(t) = \frac{1}{2\omega_1} \sin \omega_1 t,$$

it is evident that *the system becomes unstable with presence of multiple poles in the jω axis.*

18.1.1 Necessary Conditions of Stability of a Network Function [*F*(*s*)]

Thus, from the preceding discussion we find that for a network function to be stable the following three conditions must be satisfied :

1. *F*(*s*) cannot have poles in the right half of *s*-plane.
2. *F*(*s*) should not have any multiple poles in the $j\omega$ axis.
3. The degree of the numerator of *F*(*s*) can not exceed the degree of the denominator by more than unity, *i.e.*, if

$$F(s) = \frac{a_n s^n + a_{n-1} s^{n-1} + \ldots + a_1 s + a_0}{b_m s^m + b_{m-1} s^{m-1} + \ldots + b_m s + b_0},$$

then the order of *n* cannot exceed the order of *m* by more than unity *i.e.*, $n - m \le 1$. However, if $n - m > 1$, it would simple mean multiple poles at $s = \infty$ which impairs the stability

18.2 HURWITZ POLYNOMIALS

We have just observed that for a system function (represented by ratio of two polynomials) to be stable, *the poles must exist at the left half of s-plane* (*i.e.*, on or left side of $j\omega$ axis). Also the poles should be *simple* (*i.e.*, there will be no multiple poles). The denominator polynomial $P(s)$ of the system function is then termed as *Hurtwitz polynomial.*

Then a polynomial is said to be *Hurwitz* iff

(*i*) *P(s) is real when s is real.*

(*ii*) *The roots of P(s) have real parts which are to be zero or negative.*

Example 18.1 *A polynomial P(s) expressed in factored form is given by*

(*i*) $P_1(s) = (s+2)(s+1+j5)(s+1-j5)$

(*ii*) $P_2(s) = (s-2)(s+1)(s+3)$

Check whether both the polynomials are Hurwitz or not.

Solution. In $P_1(s)$, all the roots have non zero negative real parts $[-2, -1-j5, -1+j5]$ and hence obviously $P_1(s)$ is Hurwitz. On the other hand, $P_2(s)$ is not Hurwitz because of presence +ve real part of one of the roots $[s=2]$.

18.3 PROPERTIES OF HURWITZ POLYNOMIALS

A *Hurwitz polynomial P(s) can have following three types of roots :*

(*a*) $s = -r$, *r* being real and positive ;

(*b*) $s = \pm j\omega$, ω being real;

(*c*) $s = -\sigma \pm j\omega$, σ being real and positive ;

∴ The polynomial can be written as

$$P(s) = (s+r)(s+\omega^2)[(s+\sigma)^2 + \omega^2].$$

Thus it follows that $P(s)$ is the product of terms with only *positive coefficients.* This marks $P(s)$ positive.

Hence, for a Hurwitz polynomial, *all the coefficients of P(s) i.e.,* $a_n, a_{n-1}, a_{n-2}, \ldots, a_1$ etc. *are positive* when the polynomial is expressed as $P(s) = a_n s^n + a_{n-1} s^{n-1} + \ldots + a_1 s + a_0$.

A corollary can then easily be extracted as follows :

Between the highest order term in s and the lowest order term, none of the coefficients may be zero (unless the polynomial is even or odd). It clearly indicates that provided the polynomial is neither only even nor only odd, '*a*' coefficients of *P*(*s*) must not be zero. Also it means that *for a Hurwitz polynomial being neither even nor odd, there should not be any missing s terms.*

Both the odd and even parts of a Hurwitz polynomial *P*(*s*) have roots on *j*ω axis only [this is evident from the following explanation :

Let us consider a real even polynomial written as

$$E(s) = a_n s^n + a_{n-2} s^{n-2} + \ldots + a_0$$

where *n* is even. In order to have the coefficients of *E*(*s*) to be real, the complex root of *E*(*s*) must occur in quadriplates like

$$(s+s_0)(s+s_0^*)(s-s_0)(s-s_0^*).$$

Similarly, a root of $E(s)$ on the real axis must give rise to a factor of the form $(s^2 - \sigma_0^2)$. Now, the definition of a Hurwitz polynomial excludes roots in the right half of *s*-plane ; but complex roots of a real even polynomial occur in quadruplets, the real axis being occurring at $s = \pm\sigma_0$. Thus exclusion of right half plane roots of a real even polynomial immediately excludes their "images" in the open left half plane. On the other hand, purely imaginary root of *E*(*s*) occur in conjugate pair in the form $(s^2 + \omega_0^2)$, ω_0 being real and provided they are simple. *Therefore, for a real even polynomial to be Hurwitz, it must have only simple roots on the imaginary axis.* This logic is equally valid for odd polynomial too.

Denoting the odd part of $P(s)$ as $N(s)$ and the even part as $M(s)$, we can write

$$P(s) = N(s) + M(s)$$

$M(s)$ and $N(s)$ have roots on the jω-axis only. Thus, if $P(s)$ is either even or odd only, all its roots are on the imaginary axis of s-plane.

Again, separating the even and odd parts of *P* (*s*) we can write

$$M(s) = a_n s^n + a_{n-2} s^{n-2} + \ldots$$

$$N(s) = a_{n-1} s^{n-1} + a_{n-3} s^{n-3} + \ldots$$

where, for *n* even, *M*(*s*) is even and *N*(*s*) is odd and for *n* odd, *M*(*s*) is odd and *N*(*s*) is even.

Next, we obtain the continued fraction of $P(s) = \dfrac{M(s)}{N(s)}$ by successive division and inversion as follows :

$$\frac{M(s)}{N(s)} = \frac{a_n s^n + a_{n-2} s^{n-2} + \ldots}{a_{n-1} s^{n-1} + a_{n-3} s^{n-3} + \ldots}$$

$$= \frac{a_n}{a_{n-1}} s + \frac{d'_{n-2} s^{n-2} + d'_{n-4} s^{n-4} + \ldots}{a_{n-1} s^{n-1} + a_{n-3} s^{n-3} + \ldots}$$

$$= \alpha_1 s + \frac{M_1 (s)}{N(s)} \quad \ldots(18.1)$$

$\alpha_1 s$ is the quotient resulting from the first division and $M_1 (s)/N(s)$ is the remainder.

Inverting the remainder and dividing again,

$$\frac{M(s)}{N(s)} = \alpha_1 s + \frac{1}{N(s)/M_1 (s)}$$

$$= \alpha_1 s + \frac{1}{\alpha_2 s + N_2 (s)/M_1 (s)} \quad \ldots(18.2)$$

The process of division and inversion is repeated until the function $M(s)/N(s)$ is exhausted. The result is the *continued fraction expansion* of $M(s)/N(s)$ of the form

$$\frac{M(s)}{N(s)} = \alpha_1 s + \cfrac{1}{\alpha_2 s + \cfrac{1}{\alpha_3 s + \cfrac{}{\ddots + \cfrac{1}{\alpha_n s}}}} \quad \ldots(18.3)$$

Now, the necessary and sufficient condition for $P(s) = M(s) + N(s)$ to be strictly Hurwitz is that all the n quotients in the continued fraction expansion be strictly positive.

i.e., $\alpha_i > 0, i = 1, 2, \ldots n.$

A corollary of this states that if the continued expansion of the odd to even or even to odd parts of a polynomial yields *positive terms* the polynomial is Hurwitz to within a multiplicative factor $W(s)$ *i.e.*, if we write

$$F(s) = W(s) F_1 (s) \quad \ldots(18.4)$$

then $F(s)$ is Hurwitz if $W(s)$ and $F_1 (s)$ are Hurwitz.

Next, let us assume that all the α_i s after α_K in the continued fraction method are zero. The process of continued fraction then terminates prematurely or abruptly giving a zero remainder and indicating that $M(s)$ and $N(s)$ have a common factor, which is an even polynomial (because M is odd and N is even or vice versa) that is identified as the numerator of the remainder in the division immediately preceding the zero remainder step.

A simple procedure for determining whether an even polynomial E (s) has only simple pure imaginary roots, is to differentiate E (s) to obtain E′ (s) $\left[E'(s) = \frac{d}{ds} E(s) \right]$.

Then the required condition is that $E(s) + E'(s)$ be strictly Hurwitz (i.e., the continued fraction expansion of $E(s)/E'(s)$ yields all positive quotients).

To summarise, the properties of the Hurwitz polynomials are listed below :

A polynomial *P*(*s*) is Hurwitz when the following conditions are satisfied :

(*i*) *P*(*s*) is *real* when *s* is real.

(*ii*) The *roots of P*(*s*) *have real parts* which are zero or negative.

The Hurwitz polynomial has the following properties (usually being expressed as

$$P(s) = a_n s^n + a_{n-1} s^{n-1} + \ldots + a_1 s + a_0.$$

(*a*) The coefficients of the *s* terms must be *positive* (*i.e.*, a_i coefficients in the above representation are all +ve).

(*b*) Both the odd and even parts of the Hurwitz polynomial have *roots on the imaginary axis* ($j\omega$ axis) only.

i.e., if $P(s) = M(s) + N(s)$, $M(s)$ being representing the even parts while $N(s)$ the odd parts of the polynomial respectively, $M(s)$ and $N(s)$ both have roots on $j\omega$ axis only.

(*c*) The continued fraction expansion of the ratio of even to odd parts (or the odd to even parts) of the Hurwitz polynomial gives *all positive quotient terms* ; *i.e.*, supposing $Z(s) = \frac{M(s)}{N(s)} \left(\text{or } \frac{N(s)}{M(s)} \right)$ the continued fraction can be written as

$$Z(s) = \alpha_1 s + \cfrac{1}{\alpha_2 s + \cfrac{1}{\alpha_3 s + \cfrac{1}{\alpha_4 s + \cfrac{}{\ddots + \cfrac{1}{\alpha_n s}}}}}$$

CHAPTER 18

where $\alpha_1, \alpha_2, \ldots, \alpha_n$ are the quotients in each step of the division

$$\frac{M(s)}{N(s)} \text{ or } \frac{N(s)}{M(s)}.$$

These coefficients must be *positive* when the polynomial $P(s)$ is Hurwitz.

(*d*) If the polynomial satisfies the condition of *Hurwitz*, the polynomial then is Hurwitz to an even multiplicative factor $W(s)$; *i.e.*, if $P_1(s) = W(s)\,P(s)$ and $P(s)$ is Hurwitz, $P_1(s)$ must be Hurwitz.

(*e*) If the ratio of the polynomial $P(s)$ and its derivative $(P'(s))$ gives a continued fraction expansion with all positive coefficients, then $P(s)$ is Hurwitz. In case the polynomial is either *only even* or *only odd*, the method of continued fraction is *not possible* and this method is then beneficial.

The definition of the Hurwitz polynomial presented in this text was developed by Brune and later illustrated by Van Valkenburg and Kuo. This definition refers the criteria of the polynomial to be Hurwitz bounded by characterisation of poles of the system. Guillemin as well as Van Valkenburg had also bounded the criteria of polynomial to be Hurwitz by characterisation of zeros of the polynomial as mentioned below :

The characterisation of Hurwitz poynomial by zeros states that a real polynomial $P(s)$ [*i.e.*, polynomial with real coefficients] is termed as a Hurwitz if all its zeros lie in the left half plane (*i.e.*, $\text{Re}(s) \le 0$) with those on the imaginary axis being simple ($P(s)$ is said to be strictly Hurwitz provided $j\omega$ axis zeros are excluded *i.e.*, all the zeros occur in the left half side of S plane only ($\text{Re}(s) < 0$)). It may be noted that both these approaches result in identical concept as it is evident that if system function being represented by a ratio of polynomials and the denominator being analysed for its poles in order to determine the stability of the system, it is same thing if the zeros of the numerator are analysed for stability, *i.e.*, the analysis of pole of a system is identical to analysing the zeros of the polynomial in of the system function.

18.4 PROCEDURE OF TESTING OF A GIVEN POLYNOMIAL FOR HURWITZ CHARACTER

Physical Testing

The necessary but *not* sufficient conditions for $P(s)$ to be Hurwitz are as follows :

1. All the coefficients of the polynomial must be positive and real.
2. There must not be any power of s missing between the highest degree and lowest degree of the polynomial (unless the polynomial is completely even or completely odd).

Analytic Testing

The necessary and sufficient condition for $P(s)$ to be Hurwitz is as follows :

The quotients $(\alpha_1, \alpha_2 \ldots)$ in the continued fraction expansion of $Z(s)\left[= \dfrac{M(s)}{N(s)}\right.$ where $M(s)$ represents the even part of $P(s)$ and $N(s)$ the odd part] *must be real and positive.* However if due to a common factor between $M(s)$ and $N(s)$, if the continued fraction method is prematurely terminated, then the quotients in the continued fraction expansion of $\psi(s)\left[\psi(s) = \dfrac{P(s)}{P'(s)}\right.$, $P'(s)$ being the first derivative of $P(s)\Big]$ must be all real and positive.

Use of $\psi(s)$ is also suitable if the given polynomial is either only even or only odd.

EXAMPLE 18.2 *Check whether the polynomial*

$$s^5 + 9s^4 + 7s^3 + s^2 + 4s$$

is Hurwitz or not.

SOLUTION.

$$P(s) = s^5 + 9\,s^4 + 7\,s^3 + s^2 + 4\,s$$
$$= M(s) + N(s)$$

where $M(s) = 9\,s^4 + s^2 = s^2(1 + 9\,s^2)$

$$N(s) = s^5 + 7\,s^3 + 4\,s = s(4 + 7\,s^2 + s^4)$$

Let $Z(s)=\dfrac{N(s)}{M(s)}=\dfrac{s^5+7s^3+4s}{9s^4+s^2}$

$$=\frac{s^4+7s^2+4}{s(9s^2+1)}\;[s\neq 0].$$

It is obvious that the above function $Z(s)$ has a zero at the origin. The quotient of the continued function of $N(s)/M(s)$ also gives negative value. This proves that the given **polynomial is not Hurwitz**.

Example 18.3 *Check whether the polynomial* $s^8+s^7+s^6-2s^5+4s^3-s^2+s+1$ *is Hurwitz or not.*

Solution. By inspection it is evident that the given **polynomial is not Hurwitz** because the coefficients of the s^5 and s^2 term are negative.

Example 18.4 *Indicate, with proper reasoning which of the following polynomials are Hurwitz :*

(*a*) $s^2+4s+10$

(*b*) $s^4+s^3+2s^2+3s+2$

(*c*) $s^4+11s^3+39s^2+51s+20$

Solution. (*a*) $P(s)=s^2+4s+10$

The given **polynomial is Hurwitz** because it is a quadratic, with no missing term and all its coefficients are of positive sign.

(*b*) $P(s)=s^4+s^3+2s^2+3s+2$

$M(s)=s^4+2s^2+2$

$N(s)=s^3+3s$

$\therefore\quad Z(s)=\dfrac{M(s)}{N(s)}=\dfrac{s^4+2s^2+2}{s^3+3s}$

Using continued fraction method, the function $Z(s)=\dfrac{M(s)}{N(s)}$ is tested as follows :

$s^3+3s\,)\;s^4+2s^2+2\;(\;s$

$\quad s^4+3s^2$

$\quad -s^2+2\,)\;s^3+3s\;(\;-s$

$\qquad s^3-2s$

$\qquad 5s\,)\;-s^2+2\;(\;-\dfrac{s}{5}$

$\qquad\quad -s^2$

$\qquad\quad 2\,)\;5s\;(\;\dfrac{5s}{2}$

$\qquad\qquad 5s$

$\qquad\qquad \times$

Since the continued fraction contains negative quotients hence the **given polynomial is not Hurwitz.**

(*c*) $P(s)=s^4+11s^3+39s^2+51s+20$

$=M(s)+N(s)$

$=\underbrace{(s^4+39s^2+20)}_{M(s)}+\underbrace{(11s^3+51s)}_{N(s)}$

Let us now use the continued fraction method as shown below :

$11s^3+51s\,)\;s^4+39s^2+20\;(\;\dfrac{s}{11}$

$\quad s^4+\dfrac{51}{11}s^2$

$\quad \dfrac{378}{11}s^2+20\,)\;11s^3+51s\;(\;\dfrac{121}{378}s$

$\qquad 11s^3+\dfrac{1210}{189}s$

$\qquad \dfrac{8429}{189}s\,)\;\dfrac{378}{11}s^2+20\;(\;\dfrac{378\times 189}{8429\times 11}s$

$\qquad\quad \dfrac{378}{11}s^2$

$\qquad\quad 20\,)\;\dfrac{8429}{189}s\;(\;s\times\dfrac{8429}{189\times 20}$

$\qquad\qquad \dfrac{8429}{189}s$

$\qquad\qquad \times$

Since the continued fraction has all +ve quotients hence the **given polynomial is Hurwitz.**

Example 18.5 *Determine whether the given polynomial* $(s+2)(s^2+4s+6)(s^2+3s+2)$ *is Hurwitz or not.*

Solution. The polynomial is given in form of factors. No further factorisation is needed. Also all the factors are Hurwitz. Thus the **given polynomial is Hurwitz.**

Example 18.6 *Check whether the following polynomials are Hurwitz or not :*

(*a*) $s^4+7s^3+4s^2+18s+6$

(*b*) $s^4+s^3+6s^2+3s+6$

(*c*) $s^4+s^3+2s^2+4s+1.$

Solution. (*a*)

$$P(s)=s^4+7s^3+4s^2+18s+6$$

$$=M(s)+N(s)$$

where $\quad M(s)=s^4+4s^2+6$

and $\quad N(s)=7s^3+18s.$

Using continued fraction method, from

$$Z(s)=\frac{M(s)}{N(s)},$$

$$7s^3+18s\;)\;s^4+4s^2+6\;(\;\frac{s}{7}$$
$$s^4+\frac{18s^2}{7}$$
$$\frac{10s^2}{7}+6\;)\;7s^3+18s\;(\;s.\frac{49}{10}$$
$$7s^3+\frac{147}{5}s$$
$$-\frac{57}{5}s\;)\;\frac{10s^2}{7}+6\;(\;-\frac{50}{7\times 57}s$$
$$\frac{10s^2}{7}$$
$$6\;)\;-\frac{57}{5}s\;(\;-\frac{57}{30}s$$
$$-\frac{57}{5}s$$
$$\times$$

Since the continued fraction contains the negative quotient, hence the **given polynomial is not Hurwitz.**

(*b*) $P(s)=s^4+s^3+6s^2+3s+6=M(s)+N(s)$

where $M(s)=s^4+6s^2+6\,;\quad N(s)=s^3+3s.$

Let us now perform the continued fraction expansion of $P(s)$ by dividing $M(s)$ by $N(s)$ and then inverting and dividing again as given below :

$$s^3+3s\;)\;s^4+6s^2+6\;(\;s$$
$$s^4+3s^2$$
$$3s^2+6\;)\;s^3+3s\;(\;\frac{1}{3}s$$
$$s^3+2s$$
$$s\;)\;3s^2+6\;(\;3s$$
$$3s^2$$
$$6\;)\;s\;(\;\frac{s}{6}$$
$$s$$
$$\times$$

The continued fraction is then

$$P(s)=s+\cfrac{1}{\cfrac{s}{3}+\cfrac{1}{3s+\cfrac{1}{\cfrac{s}{6}}}}.$$

Since all the quotient terms of the continued fraction expansion are positive, ***P*(*s*) is Hurwitz.**

(*c*) $P(s)=s^4+s^3+2s^2+4s+1=M(s)+N(s)$

where $M(s)=s^4+2s^2+1;\quad N(s)=s^3+4s$

Using the method of continued fraction,

The continued fraction yields

$$s^3+4s\;)\;s^4+2s^2+1\;(\;s$$
$$s^4+4s^2$$
$$-2s^2+1\;)\;s^3+4s\;(\;-\frac{s}{2}$$
$$s^3-\frac{s}{2}$$
$$\frac{9s}{2}\;)\;-2s^2+1\;(\;-\frac{4}{9}s$$
$$-2s^2$$
$$1\;)\;\frac{9s}{2}\;(\;\frac{9s}{2}$$
$$\frac{9s}{2}$$
$$\times$$

The given **polynomial is not Hurwitz** because of presence of the negative quotient in the continued fraction.

Example 18.7 *Check whether a polynomial expressed as* $P(s)=s^3+6s^2+11s+6$ *is Hurwitz or not.*

Solution. Separating $P(s)$ into odd and even parts,

$$M(s)=s^3+11s\,;\;N(s)=6s^2+6$$

The continued fraction expansion of $M(s)/N(s)$ is obtained as follows :

$$6s^2+6\;)\;s^3+11s\;(\;\frac{1}{6}s$$
$$s^3+\;s$$
$$10s\;)\;6s^2+6\;(\;\frac{3}{5}s$$
$$6s^2$$
$$6\;)\;10s\;(\;\frac{5}{3}s$$
$$10s$$
$$\times$$

Since the quotients in the continued fraction method become all positive, **the polynomial is Hurwitz.**

EXAMPLE 18.8 *Test whether the polynomial $s^5 + s^3 + s$ is Hurwitz or not.*

SOLUTION. $P(s) (= s^5 + s^3 + s)$ consists of only odd functions, as a result of which it is not possible to perform the continued fraction expansion. Let us then take the derivative of $P(s)$. Assume derivative of $P(s)$ as $P'(s)$],

i.e., $$P(s) = 5s^4 + 3s^2 + 1.$$

Let $$\psi(s) = \frac{P(s)}{P'(s)} = \frac{s^5 + s^3 + s}{5s^4 + 3s^2 + 1}$$

and let us now proceed with continued fraction method as shown below :

$$5s^4 + 3s^2 + 1)\; s^5 + s^3 + s\; (\frac{s}{5}$$
$$s^5 + \frac{3}{5}s^3 + \frac{s}{5}$$
$$\frac{2}{5}s^3 + \frac{4}{5}s)\; 5s^4 + 3s^2 + 1\; (\frac{25}{2}s$$
$$5s^4 + 10s^2$$
$$-7s^2 + 1)\; \frac{2}{5}s^3 + \frac{4}{5}s\; (-\frac{2}{35}s$$
$$\frac{2}{5}s^3 - \frac{2}{35}s$$
$$\frac{6}{7}s)\; -7s^2 + 1\; (-\frac{49}{6}s$$
$$-7s^2$$
$$1)\; \frac{6s}{7}\; (\frac{6s}{7}$$
$$\frac{6s}{7}$$
$$\times$$

In the continued fraction of the above function, the third and fourth quotients are negative. Hence, the **given polynomial is not Hurwitz.**

EXAMPLE 18.9 *Test whether the following functions are Hurwitz or not :*

(*i*) $s^5 + 3s^4 + 3s^3 + 4s^2 + s + 1$

(*ii*) $s^4 + 3s^2 + 2$

SOLUTION. (*i*)

$$P(s) = s^5 + 3s^4 + 3s^3 + 4s^2 + s + 1 = M(s) + N(s)$$

where $$M(s) = 3s^4 + 4s^2 + 1;$$

$$N(s) = s^5 + 3s^3 + s$$

Let $$Z(s) = \frac{N(s)}{M(s)}$$ [∵ degree of $N(s)$ is higher than that of $M(s)$]

Testing of continued fraction is performed in the following steps :

$$3s^4 + 4s^2 + 1)\ s^5 + 3s^3 + s\ (\ \frac{s}{3}$$
$$s^5 + \frac{4}{3}s^3 + \frac{s}{3}$$
$$\frac{5}{3}s^3 + \frac{2}{3}s\ )\ 3s^4 + 4s^2 + 1\ (\ \frac{9}{5}s$$
$$3s^4 + \frac{18}{15}s^2$$
$$\frac{42}{15}s^2 + 1\ )\ \frac{5}{3}s^3 + \frac{2}{3}s\ (\ \frac{75}{126}s$$
$$\frac{5}{3}s^3 + \frac{75}{126}s$$
$$\frac{9}{126}s\ )\ \frac{42}{15}s^2 + 1\ (\ \frac{126 \times 42}{9 \times 15}s$$
$$\frac{42}{15}s^2$$
$$1\ )\ \frac{9}{126}s\ (\ \frac{9}{126}s$$
$$\frac{9}{126}s$$
$$\times$$

Since the continued fraction contains all +ve quotients hence the **given polynomial is Hurwitz.**

(*ii*) $P(s) = s^4 + 3s^2 + 2$;

since $P(s)$ only contains even polynomials, continued fraction is not ordinarily possible. Let us take the derivative of $P(s)$ as $P'(s) = 4s^3 + 6s$

Next, coming back to continued fraction method, we have

$$4s^3 + 6s\ )\ s^4 + 3s^2 + 2\ (\ \frac{s}{4}$$
$$s^4 + \frac{6}{4}s^2$$
$$\frac{3}{2}s^2 + 2\ )\ 4s^3 + 6s\ (\ \frac{8}{3}s$$
$$4s^3 + \frac{16}{3}s$$
$$\frac{2}{3}s)\ \frac{3}{2}s^2 + 2\ (\ \frac{9}{4}s$$
$$\frac{3}{2}s^2$$
$$2\ )\ \frac{2}{3}s\ (\ \frac{1}{3}s$$
$$\frac{2}{3}s$$
$$\times$$

Since all the quotients in the continued fraction method are +ve, the **given polynomial is Hurwitz.**

EXAMPLE 18.10 *Test the following polynomial for its Hurwitz character :*

$$P(s) = s^8 + 3s^7 + 10s^6 + 24s^5 + 35s^4 + 57s^3 + 50s^2 + 36s + 24$$

SOLUTION. $M(s) = s^8 + 10\,s^6 + 35\,s^4 + 50\,s^2 + 24$

$N(s) = 3\,s^7 + 24\,s^5 + 57\,s^3 + 36\,s$

Performing the continued fraction expansion of $M(s)/N(s)$, we find

$$\begin{array}{l} 3s^7 + 24s^5 + 57s^3 + 36s \,)\, s^8 + 10s^6 + 35s^4 + 50s^2 + 24 \,(\, \frac{s}{3} \\ \qquad\qquad\qquad\qquad\quad \underline{s^8 + 8s^6 + 19s^4 + 12s^2} \\ \qquad\qquad\qquad\qquad\quad 2s^6 + 16s^4 + 38s^2 + 24 \,)\, 3s^7 + 24s^5 + 57s^3 + 36s \,(\, \frac{3}{2}s \\ \qquad\qquad\qquad\qquad\qquad\qquad\qquad\qquad\qquad\qquad \underline{3s^7 + 24s^5 + 57s^3 + 36s} \\ \qquad\qquad\qquad\qquad\qquad\qquad\qquad\qquad\qquad\qquad\qquad\quad \times \end{array}$$

Though the first two quotients are positive, the process has terminated after two steps, giving a zero remainder. Thus it is evident that $M(s)$ and $N(s)$ have the even polynomial $(2s^6 + 16\,s^4 + 38\,s^2 + 24)$ as a common factor.

Therefore $P(s)$ has an even factor

$$E(s) = s^6 + 8s^4 + 19\,s^2 + 12$$

Differentiating $E(s)$, $\quad E'(s) = 6s^5 + 32\,s^3 + 38\,s$

Performing then the continued fraction of $E(s)/E'(s)$, six positive partial quotients are obtained as

$$\frac{s}{6}, \frac{9s}{4}, \frac{16\,s}{21}, \frac{49\,s}{60}, \frac{25\,s}{7} \text{ and } \frac{s}{10}.$$

Hence the polynomial $E'(s) + E(s)$ is Hurwitz. Since first two quotients in the expansion of $M(s)/N(s)$ are also positive, we ultimately conclude that **the given polynomial is Hurwitz.**

EXAMPLE 18.11 *Check whether* $P(s) = 4s^6 + 2s^5 + 17s^4 + 8s^3 + 16\,s^2 + 6s + 3$ *is Hurwitz.*

SOLUTION. By physical observation it is revealed that all the a_i coefficients are real and positive and there is no missing power of s between the highest and lowest degree of $P(s)$.

Next we break $P(s)$ in even odd powers of s as follows :

$$P(s) = M_1(s) + N_1(s)$$

where $M_1(s) = 4s^6 + 17\,s^4 + 16\,s^2 + 3$

$N_1(s) = 2s^5 + 8s^3 + 6s$

$$\therefore \qquad Z(s) = \frac{M_1(s)}{N_1(s)} = \frac{4s^6 + 17\,s^4 + 16\,s^2 + 3}{2s^5 + 8s^3 + 6s}$$

Dividing $M_1(s)$ by $N_1(s)$,

$$\begin{array}{l} 2s^5 + 8s^3 + 6s \,)\, 4s^6 + 17s^4 + 16s^2 + 3 \,(\, 2s \\ \qquad\qquad\qquad\quad \underline{4s^6 + 16s^4 + 12s^2} \\ \qquad\qquad\qquad\qquad\quad s^4 + 4s^2 + 3 \,)\, 2s^5 + 8s^3 + 6s \,(\, 2s \\ \qquad\qquad\qquad\qquad\qquad\qquad\qquad\quad \underline{2s^4 + 4s^3 + 6s} \\ \qquad\qquad\qquad\qquad\qquad\qquad\qquad\qquad\quad \times \end{array}$$

The continued fraction expansion abruptly terminates. The last divisor $(s^4 + 4s^2 + 3)$ is therefore one of the factors of $P(s)$.

Dividing $P(s)$ by $s^4 + 4s^2 + 3$, the other factor is obtained as shown below :

$$s^4 + 4s^2 + 3 \;)\; 4s^6 + 2s^5 + 17s^4 + 8s^3 + 16s^2 + 6s + 3 \;(\; 4s^2 + 2s + 1$$

$$4s^6 \quad + 16s^4 \quad + 12s^2$$

$$2s^5 + s^4 + 8s^3 + 4s^2 + 6s + 3$$

$$2s^5 \quad + 8s^3 \quad + 6s$$

$$s^4 + 4s^2 + 3$$

$$s^4 + 4s^2 + 3$$

$$\times$$

i.e., $$4s^6 + 2s^5 + 17s^4 + 8s^3 + 16s^2 + 6s + 3 = (s^4 + 4s^2 + 3)(4s^2 + 2s + 1)$$

$P(s)$ will be Hurwitz provided its factors are Hurwitz.

Let us take the quadratic factor $4s^2 + 2s + 1$, and apply continued fraction method.

$$P'(s) = 4s^2 + 2s + 1 = M_2(s) + N_2(s)$$

where $M_2(s) = 4s^2 + 1 \,;\, N_2(s) = 2s$

$$2s \;)\; 4s^2 + 1 \;(\; 2s$$

$$4s^2$$

$$1 \;)\; 2s \;(\; 2s$$

$$2s$$

$$\times$$

Since the quotients in continued fraction are positive hence $4s^2 + 2s + 1$ is a Hurwitz.

In fact, any quadratic equation in form of $ax^2 + bx + c$ with positive real coefficients is a Hurwitz.

Next we take another factor $(s^4 + 4s^2 + 3)$ of $P(s)$. We use the continued fraction method by dividing $(s^4 + 4s^2 + 3)$ by its first derivative.

i.e., $$\psi(s) = \frac{s^4 + 4s^2 + 3}{\frac{d}{ds}[s^4 + 4s^2 + 3]} = \frac{s^4 + 4s^2 + 3}{4s^3 + 8s}$$

$$4s^3 + 8s \;)\; s^4 + 4s^2 + 3 \;(\; \frac{1}{4}s$$

$$s^4 + 2s^2$$

$$2s^2 + 3 \;)\; 4s^3 + 8s \;(\; 2s$$

$$4s^3 + 6s$$

$$2s \;)\; 2s^2 + 3 \;(\; s$$

$$2s^2$$

$$3 \;)\; 2s \;(\; \frac{2s}{3}$$

$$2s$$

$$\times$$

Thus, all the quotients of the continued fraction expansion of $(s^2 + 4s^2 + 3)$ are +ve and real. Then $(s^2 + 4s^2 + 3)$ is Hurwitz. Hence it is concluded that the **entire polynomial $P(s)$ is Hurwitz.**

EXAMPLE 18.12 *Check whether the following function is Hurwitz or not*

(i) $P(s) = s^7 + 3s^5 + s^3 + 2s$ (ii) $P(s) = s^4 + s^3 + 3s^2 + 2s + 2$

SOLUTION. (i) Since $P(s) = s^7 + 3s^5 + s^3 + 2s$ contains only odd powers of s hence checking of Hurwitz character by continued fraction method is not possible. Thus we take $P'(s)$ as the denominator while $P(s)$ is in the numerator. To apply the method of continued fraction, we proceed as follows :

$$\psi(s) = \frac{P(s)}{P'(s)} = \frac{s^7 + 3s^5 + s^3 + 2s}{\frac{d}{ds}(s^7 + 3s^5 + s^3 + 2s)} = \frac{s^7 + 3s^5 + s^3 + 2s}{7s^6 + 15s^4 + 3s^2 + 2}$$

Applying the method of continued fraction, we get

$$7s^6 + 15s^4 + 3s^2 + 2 \;)\; s^7 + 3s^5 + s^3 + 2s \;(\; \frac{s}{7}$$

$$s^7 + \frac{15}{7}s^5 + \frac{3}{7}s^3 + \frac{2}{7}s$$

$$\frac{6}{7}s^5 + \frac{4}{7}s^3 + \frac{12}{7}s \;)\; 7s^6 + 15s^4 + 3s^2 + 2 \;(\; \frac{49}{6}s$$

$$7s^6 + \frac{14}{3}s^4 + 14s^2$$

$$\frac{31}{3}s^4 - 11s^2 + 2 \;)\; \frac{6}{7}s^5 + \frac{4}{7}s^3 + \frac{12}{7}s \;(\; \frac{6 \times 3}{31 \times 7}s$$

$$\frac{6}{7}s^5 - \frac{18 \times 11}{31 \times 7}s^3 + \frac{36}{217}s$$

$$\frac{322}{217}s^3 + \frac{336}{217}s \;)\; \frac{31}{3}s^4 - 11s^2 + 2 \;(\; \frac{217 \times 31}{322 \times 3}s$$

$$\frac{31}{3}s^4 + \frac{56 \times 31}{161}s^2$$

$$-\frac{3497}{161}s^2 + 2$$

$$-\frac{3497}{161}s^2 + 2 \;)\; \frac{322}{217}s^3 + \frac{336}{217}s \;(\; -\frac{161 \times 322}{3497 \times 217}s$$

$$\frac{322}{217}s^3 - \frac{2 \times 161 \times 322}{3497 \times 217}s$$

Without proceeding further we observe that the last quotient in the continued fraction of $\frac{P(s)}{P'(s)}$ has become –ve. Then **the given polynomial P (s) is not Hurwitz.**

EXAMPLE 18.13 $P(s) = s^4 + s^3 + 3s^2 + 2s + 2 = M(s) + N(s)$

where $M(s) = s^4 + 3s^2 + 2$

$N(s) = s^3 + 2s$ *Check the Hurwitzness of* $P(s)$.

SOLUTION. Using continued fraction method,

$$s^3 + 2s \;)\; s^4 + 3s^2 + 2 \;(\; s$$

$$s^4 + 2s^2$$

$$s^2 + 2 \;)\; s^3 + 2s \;(\; s$$

$$s^3 + 2s$$

$$\times$$

The continued fraction ends here abruptly.

Obviously this is due to the presence of the common fraction (s^2+2) between $M(s)$ and $N(s)$.

In order to find another factor of $P(s)$, let us divide $P(s)$ by (s^2+2)

$$
\begin{array}{r|l}
s^2+2 \,)\; s^4+s^3+3s^2+2s+2 & (\; s^2+s+1 \\
s^4 \quad\;\; + 2s^2 & \\
\hline
s^3+s^2+2s+2 & \\
s^3 \quad\;\; + 2s & \\
\hline
s^2+2 & \\
s^2+2 & \\
\hline
\times &
\end{array}
$$

Thus, $\quad s^4+s^3+3s^2+2s+2=(s^2+s+1)(s^2+2)$

Since s^2+s+1 is a quadratic expression with all +ve real coefficients hence it is a Hurwitz. On the other hand, if we factor s^2+2, we get

$$
\begin{aligned}
s^2+2 &= (s+\sqrt{2}+\sqrt{2.82s})(s+\sqrt{2}-\sqrt{2.82\,s}) \\
&= ((\sqrt{s})^2+\sqrt{2.82}\,\sqrt{s}+\sqrt{2})((\sqrt{s})^2-\sqrt{2.82}\,\sqrt{s}+\sqrt{2})
\end{aligned}
$$

The first expression is again Hurwitz but the second expression has –ve real coefficient; hence it is not Hurwitz. **Thus the original expression is not Hurwitz.**

EXAMPLE 18.14 *Check whether the polynomial*

$$F(s)=s^3+4s^2+2s+8 \text{ is Hurwitz or not.}$$

SOLUTION. $\quad F(s)=s^3+4s^2+2s+8=M(s)+N(s)$

where, $\quad M(s)=4s^2+8;$

$\quad N(s)=s^3+2s.$

Let us now apply the method of continued fraction as shown below when $Y(s)=\dfrac{N(s)}{M(s)}=\dfrac{s^3+2s}{4s^2+8}$

[It may be noted here that the degree of $N(s)$ is more than the degree of $M(s)$ hence, instead of $\dfrac{M(s)}{N(s)}$, here the polynomial will be tested for $\dfrac{N(s)}{M(s)}$]

Next,

$$
\begin{array}{r|l}
4s^2+8 \,)\; s^3+2s & (\; \dfrac{s}{4} \\
s^3+2s & \\
\hline
\times &
\end{array}
$$

We find that the division has been terminated abruptly by a common factor (s^3+2s). Next, we apply analytic testing when

$$\psi(s)=\frac{s^3+4s^2+2s+8}{3s^2+8s+2}$$

Continued fraction reveals that –ve quotients are appearing. Hence the **original polynomial is not Hurwitz.**

EXAMPLE 18.15 *Find the range of values of m in P(s), so that P(s) is Hurwitz.*

Assume $P(s) = 2s^4 + s^3 + ms^2 + s + 2.$

SOLUTION.

$$P(s) = 2s^4 + s^3 + ms^2 + s + 2$$
$$= (2s^4 + ms^2 + 2) + (s^3 + s) = M(s) + N(s)$$

Applying the continued fraction expansion,

$$s^3 + s\ )\ 2s^4 + ms^2 + 2\ (\ 2s$$
$$2s^4 + 2s^2$$
$$(m-2)s^2 + 2\ )\ s^3 + s\ \left(\frac{s}{m-2}\right.$$
$$s^3 + \frac{2s}{m-2}$$
$$\left(1 - \frac{2}{m-2}\right)s$$

The quotients of the continued fraction expansion would be +ve only when $m > 2$ and $1 > \frac{2}{m-2}$ *i.e.,* $m > 4$.

Thus the range is **$m > 4$ for $P(s)$ to be Hurwitz.**

18.5 POSITIVE REAL (PR) FUNCTIONS

It has already been known to us that the driving point impedance function $[Z(s)]$ as well as the driving point admittance function $[Y(s)]$ of one port network can be represented in the form of

$$F(s) = \frac{A(s)}{B(s)}$$
$$= \frac{a_0 s^n + a_1 s^{n-1} + \ldots\ldots + a_{n-1} s + a_n}{b_0 s^m + b_1 s^{m-1} + \ldots\ldots + b_{m-1} s + b_m}$$

The function $F(s)$ is called a *positive real (or PR) function** iff

(*a*) $F(s)$ is *real* for s real

(*b*) $B(s)$ is *Hurwitz* polynomial

(*c*) If $F(s)$ has *poles* on $(j\omega)$ axis, the poles are *simple* and the residues thereof are *real* and *positive.*

(*d*) Real $F(j\omega) \geq 0$ for all values of ω

[*i.e.,* when real part of is greater then zero, $\text{Re}(F(s) = \sigma > 0]$

To illustrate the concept of PR function in practical circuit theory, let us analyse the following examples of PR functions :

(*a*) Let $F(s)$ [= Ls, L being real and positive] be a PR function. If $F(s)$ denotes an *impedance function, L becomes an inductance.*

(*b*) Let $F(s)$ [= R, R being real and positive] be another PR function. $F(s)$ being denoting an *impedance*, R is a resistance.

(*c*) $F(s) = \left[\frac{K}{s}, K \text{ being real and positive}\right]$ be a PR function, when s is real, $F(s)$ is real. Also when $\text{Re}(s) > 0$, $\text{Re}\, F(s) > 0\ [= \sigma]$

$$i.e., \ \text{Re}\left(\frac{K}{s}\right) = \frac{K.\sigma}{\sigma^2 + \omega^2} > 0$$

If $F(s)$ represents an impedance, the corresponding element becomes a *capacitor of 1/K Farads.*

We thus find that the passive impedances are all *PR functions. Similarly, the admittance functions are also PR functions. Also, all driving point immittances of passive networks are PR functions.*

18.5.1 Properties of PR Functions

Let $F(s) = \frac{A(s)}{B(s)}$

The properties of PR functions are as below :

(*i*) Both $A(s)$ and $B(s)$ polynomials are *Hurwitz.* They may have factors of the form $(s^2 + \omega^2)$ *i.e.,* the poles and zeros of a PR function cannot have +ve real parts *i.e.,* they cannot be in the right half of the *s*-plane. Only simple poles with +ve real residues can exist on the $j\omega$ axis.

(*ii*) The highest and lowest powers of $A(s)$ and $B(s)$ differ by *unity.* This condition prohibits multiple pole and zeros at $s = \infty$ and at $s = 0$ respectively.

(*iii*) If $F(s)$ is a PR function, the reciprocal of $F(s)$ is also a *PR function* (this implies that if the driving point impedance is a *PR function,* the driving point admittance is also a *PR function*).

(*iv*) The *sum* of PR functions is also a PR function (though the *difference* of two PR functions is not necessarily a PR function)

* A real function whose real part is positive for values of s with positive real part is called a ***positive real function.***

The above properties characterise the stability of the function representing the passive (*RLC*) network. Another property of the *RLC* network is its energy absorbing character which evidently manifests that for the passive network, the average energy is always positive. This results to the introduction of the following theorem :

18.5.2 Theorem

Statement. *All real parts of the driving point immitances (impedance or admittance) of RLC networks (passive networks) must be PR functions.*

For a passive network, the average power dissipated has always a positive real value.

$$i.e., \; P_{av} = \frac{1}{2} Re[Z_{in}(j\omega)] |i|^2 \geq 0$$

$$\text{or,} \qquad Re[Z_{in}(j\omega)] \geq 0$$

$\therefore$ for any passive network, $Re[Z_{in}(j\omega)] \geq 0$.

i.e., the *real parts of the driving point impedance are a PR function.*

18.5.3 Procedure of Testing of PR Function

Let the function be represented by

$$F(s) = \frac{s+\alpha}{s^2+\beta s+\gamma},$$

where α, β and γ are the coefficients.

We know, if $Re\, F(j\omega) > 0$, $F(s)$ will be PR function. In order to find whether $Re\, F(j\omega) \geq 0$ for all ω, the following procedure is adopted :

$$\text{Let} \quad F(s) = \frac{M_1(s)+N_1(s)}{M_2(s)+N_2(s)}$$

where $M_1(s)$ and $M_2(s)$ are the even parts of the numerator and denominator polynomial and $N_1(s)$ and $N_2(s)$ are the odd parts of the numerator and denominator polynomials. Next, rationalising,

$$F(s) = \frac{M_1+N_1}{M_2+N_2} \times \frac{M_2-N_2}{M_2-N_2}$$

$$= \frac{M_1 M_2 - N_1 N_2}{M_2^2 - N_2^2} + \frac{M_2 N_1 - M_1 N_2}{M_2^2 - N_2^2} \qquad ...(18.5)$$

Here, even part of $Z(s)$ is given by

$$Ev.F(s) = \frac{M_1 M_2 - N_1 N_2}{M_2^2 - N_2^2}$$

$$\therefore \quad \text{Real } F(s) = \left.\frac{M_1 M_2 - N_1 N_2}{M_2^2 - N_2^2}\right|_{S=j\omega}$$

$$= \frac{D(s)}{M_2^2 - N_2^2} \qquad ...(18.6)$$

Since, $(M_2^2 - N_2^2)$ is always positive for $s = j\omega$, $F(j\omega) \geq 0$ provided $D(j\omega) \geq 0$ for any ω.

For the given function,

$$M_1(s) = \alpha; \quad M_2(s) = s^2 + \gamma$$

$$N_1(s) = s; \quad N_2(s) = \beta s$$

$$\therefore \quad M_1 M_2 - N_1 N_2$$

$$= \alpha(s^2+\gamma) - s.\beta s$$

$$= \alpha[(j\omega)^2 + \gamma] - \beta(j\omega)^2$$

$$= \alpha[-\omega^2 + \gamma] + \beta\omega^2$$

$$= (\beta - \alpha)\omega^2 + \alpha\gamma \qquad ...(18.7)$$

Thus $(M_1 M_2 - N_1 N_2) \geq 0$,

$$(\beta-\alpha)\omega^2 + \alpha\gamma \geq 0 \qquad ...(18.8)$$

i.e., β **must be greater than** or **at least to be equal to** α **(**$\beta \geq \alpha$**)**.

This also means when $\beta = 0, \alpha = 0$.

Thus, $F(s)$ to be PR function,

(*i*) α, β and $\gamma \geq 0$

(*ii*) $\beta \geq \alpha$.

Thus it is very much evident that for any function represented by

$$F(s) = \frac{s+\alpha}{s^2+\beta s+\gamma},$$

$F(s)$ would be PR if, α, β and γ are greater than or equal to zero and $\beta \geq \alpha$.

Let us now take another type of function given by

$$F'(s) = \frac{s+\alpha}{s^2+\gamma}, (\beta \text{ being zero})$$

It is evident that here poles will appear in the $j\omega$ axis.

$$\text{Also,} \quad F'(s) = \frac{s}{s^2+\gamma} + \frac{\alpha}{s^2+\gamma}$$

Comparing with the previous function $F(s) = \dfrac{s+\alpha}{s^2+\beta s+r}$, here we see $F'(s)$ in identical to $F(s)$ except here $\beta = 0$. However we just have established that to become PR function $(\beta-\alpha)\omega^2+\alpha\gamma \geq 0$. Thus if $\beta=0, \alpha$ must be zero. However in the given function $F'(s), \beta=0$ but $\alpha \neq 0$. Thus $F'(s)$ *is not a PR function.*

On the other hand, with $\alpha=\beta=0, F''(s)=\dfrac{s}{s^2+c}$ is a PR function

Again, if a function is represented in the form of

$$F(s)=\frac{s^2+\alpha_1 s+\alpha_0}{s^2+\beta_1 s+\beta_0},$$

it will be a PR function provided

$$\alpha_1 \beta_1 \geq (\sqrt{\alpha_0}-\sqrt{\beta_0})^2 \qquad ...(18.9)$$

For proof of this condition, please refer to Kuo's book on Network Analysis and Synthesis.

Testing of positiveness of real function by use of 'residue' is also helpful.

Say a function is given by

$$F(s)=\frac{as^2+b}{s(s^2+c)}=\frac{K_1}{s}+\frac{K_2}{s^2+c}$$

$$\therefore \quad K_1=\left.\frac{as^2+b}{s^2+c}\right|_{s=0}=b$$

$$K_2=\left.\frac{as^2+b}{s}\right|_{s^2=-c}=\frac{-ac+b}{j(c)^{1/2}}$$

$$=\frac{-j(-ac+b)}{c^{1/2}}=\frac{jac-bj}{\sqrt{c}}$$

$\therefore K_2$ is imaginary and hence the condition of PR function is violated (since for a PR function, the residues must be real and positive).

Thus $F(s)=\dfrac{as+b}{s(s^2+c)}$ can not be a PR function.

On the other hand, functions in form of

$$F(s)=\frac{Ks}{s+a} \quad \text{or} \quad \frac{K}{s+b}$$

are PR function when a, b and K are real positive quantities.

Again, let us suppose a function be represented by

$$F(s)=\frac{s+b}{s+a}, b, a \geq 0$$

Since $F(s)=\dfrac{s+b}{s+a}=\dfrac{s}{s+a}+\dfrac{b}{s+a}$,

hence $F(s)$ is a PR *function as* $\dfrac{b}{s+a}$ *is PR function as well as* $\dfrac{s}{s+a}$ *is also a PR function and sum of two PR functions is also a PR function.*

Thus we can summarise the requirements of a PR function as listed below :

1. Function being of type $F(s)=\dfrac{s+\alpha}{s^2+\beta s+\gamma}$,

   α, β and γ being real, $F(s)$ *will be a PR function iff* $\alpha, \beta, \gamma \geq 0$ *and* $\beta \geq \alpha$.

2. Function being of type $F(s)=\dfrac{Ks}{s^2+a}$,

   a and K being real, $F(s)$ *will be a PR function iff* $\alpha, K \geq 0$.

3. Function being of type

   $$F(s)=\frac{s+b}{s+a},$$

   a, b being real, $F(s)$ *will be a PR function iff* $a, b \geq 0$.

4. Function being of type

   $$F(s)=\frac{s^2+a_1 s+a_0}{s^2+b_1 s+b_0},$$

   a_0, a_1, b_0 and b_1 being real, *F(s) will be a PR function iff*

   $$a_0, a_1, b_0, b_1 > 0; \quad a_1 b_1 \geq [\sqrt{a_0}-\sqrt{b_0}]^2$$

For testing of a rational function, following tests can be performed to check its positive realness. The *necessary but not sufficient* conditions are —

1. *All the coefficients of the polynomial must be real and positive.*
2. *Imaginary axis poles and zeros must be simple.*
3. *Degree of numerator and denominator polynomial may differ by at most unity.*
4. *Terms in the lowest degree of numerator and denominator polynomials also may differ by at most unity.*
5. *Unless the polynomial is either even or odd completely, there would be no missing term between the highest and lowest degree in numerator and denominator polynomials.*

CHAPTER 18

The *necessary and sufficient conditions* of positive realness of a given rational function are as follows :

1. $F(s)$ must have simple poles on $j\omega$ axis with real and positive residues.
2. If $F(s)=\dfrac{P(s)}{Q(s)}$, then $P(s)+Q(s)$ must be Hurwitz. (ref. the analytic testing of Hurwitz character).
3. If $F(s)=\dfrac{P(s)}{Q(s)}=\dfrac{M_1(s)+N_1(s)}{M_2(s)+N_2(s)}$, M being the even parts and N being the odd parts, then for positive realness of $F(s)$, $M_1 M_2 - N_1 N_2\big|_{s=j\omega} \geq 0$ for all ω such that $Re[F(j\omega)] \geq 0$ for all ω

EXAMPLE 18.16 *Check whether* $F(s)=\dfrac{s+2}{s+1}$ *is a PR function.*

SOLUTION. Let us apply the tests of PR function one by one :

(*i*) Since all the quotient terms of $F(s)$ are real hence $F(s)$ is real if s is real.

(*ii*) It is also evident that the pole and zero of the given function lie on the left half of the s-plane.

pole at -1 on σ axis and zero at -2 on σ axis; no pole or zero on $j\omega$ axis]. Obviously the denominator is Hurwitz.

(*iii*) $\operatorname{Re} F(j\omega) = \operatorname{Re}\left[\dfrac{j\omega+2}{j\omega+1}\right]$

$$= \operatorname{Re}\left[\frac{j\omega+2}{j\omega+1}\right]\left[\frac{-j\omega+1}{-j\omega+1}\right]$$

$$= \operatorname{Re}\left[\frac{\omega^2+j\omega-2j\omega+2}{\omega^2+1}\right]$$

$$= \frac{\omega^2+2}{\omega^2+1}$$

$\therefore$ For all values of ω, $\operatorname{Re}[F(j\omega)] \geq 0$.

The above tests certify that the **given function is a PR function.**

EXAMPLE 18.17 *Check whether*

$$Z(s)=\frac{4s+1}{s+2} \text{ is a PR function.}$$

SOLUTION. Let us apply the tests of PR function one by one :

(*i*) Observation reveals that all the quotient terms of $Z(s)$ are real and hence $Z(s)$ is real if s is real.

(*ii*) It is also evident that the pole of the given function is -2, lying on the left half of the s-plane and the zero is at $(-1/4)$, also lying on the left half of the s-plane. Thus, it is needless to state the denominator is also Hurwitz.

$$\operatorname{Re} Z(j\omega) = \operatorname{Re}\left[\frac{j\omega.4+1}{j\omega+2}\right]$$

$$= \operatorname{Re}\left[\frac{j\omega.4+1}{j\omega+2}\right]\left[\frac{-j\omega+2}{-j\omega+2}\right]$$

$$= \operatorname{Re}\left[\frac{4\omega^2+8j\omega-j\omega+2}{\omega^2+4}\right]$$

$$= \frac{4\omega^2+2}{\omega^2+4}$$

$\therefore$ For all values of ω, $Re\,F(j\omega) \geq 0$.

The above tests certify that the **given function is a PR function.**

EXAMPLE 18.18 *Check whether the function*

$$Z(s)=\frac{8-s}{s+1} \text{ is a PR function or not.}$$

SOLUTION. PR function tests reveal that all the quotients of the polynomial in the numerator are not +ve and also, there is a zero on the right half of the s-plane. This clearly proves that the **given function is not a PR** function. No more confirmatory testing is needed.

EXAMPLE 18.19 *Check whether the function of*

$$F(s)=\frac{s^2-1}{-s+8} \text{ is a PR function or not.}$$

SOLUTION. PR function tests reveal that all the quotients of the polynomial in the numerator are not +ve and there is a zero on the $j\omega$ axis. This clearly proves that the **given function is not a PR function**. Further testing is not needed.

EXAMPLE 18.20 *Check the positive realness of the function*

$$F(s)=\frac{s^2+10s+4}{s+2}$$

Solution. Let us apply the tests of PR function :

(*i*) Since all the coefficients of the polynomials in the numerator and denominator are +ve hence $F(s)$ is real if s is real.

(*ii*) It is also evident that the pole of the function lies on the left half of the *s*-plane [the zeros, $(-5 \pm \sqrt{21})$ also lie on the left half of the s plane].

(*iii*) $\text{Re}[F(j\,\omega)]$

$$= \text{Re}\left[\frac{-\omega^2 + 10\,j\,\omega + 4}{j\,\omega + 2}\right]\left[\frac{-j\,\omega + 2}{-j\,\omega + 2}\right]$$

$$= \text{Re}\left[\frac{-2\,\omega^2 + 20\,j\,\omega + 8 + j\,\omega^3 + 10\,\omega^2 - 4\,j\,\omega}{\omega^2 + 4}\right]$$

$$= \text{Re}\left[\frac{8\,\omega^2 + 16\,j\,\omega + j\,\omega^3 + 8}{\omega^2 + 4}\right]$$

$$= \text{Re}\left[\frac{(8\,\omega^2 + 8) + j\,(\omega^3 + 16\,\omega)}{\omega^2 + 4}\right] = \frac{8\,\omega^2 + 8}{\omega^2 + 4}$$

Since for all values of ω, $Re[Z(j\,\omega)] \geq 0$.

The function $Z(s)$ is **thus a PR function.**

Example 18.21 *Check the positive realness of the function*

$$Y(s) = \frac{s^2 + 2s + 20}{s + 10}.$$

Solution. Let us apply the tests of PR function to the given function.

In the function $Y(s)$, all the quotient terms are real and for *s* to a real quantity $Y(s)$ is real. Also the poles and zeros are on the left half of the *s*-plane for the given function.

Next, let us see the positive realness of the given function in the $(j\,\omega)$ domain.

$$\text{Re}[Y(j\,\omega) = \text{Re}\left[\frac{(j\,\omega)^2 + 2\,(j\,\omega) + 20}{j\,\omega + 10}\right]$$

$$= \text{Re}\left[\frac{-\omega^2 + 2\,j\,\omega + 20}{j\omega + 10}\right]\left[\frac{-j\,\omega + 10}{-j\,\omega + 10}\right]$$

$$= \text{Re}\left[\frac{+j\omega^3 + 2\omega^2 - 20\,j\omega - 10\,\omega^2 + 20\,j\omega + 200}{\omega^2 + 100}\right]$$

$$= \left[\frac{-8\,\omega^2 + 200 + j\,\omega^3}{\omega^2 + 100}\right] = \frac{-8\,\omega^2 + 200}{\omega^2 + 100}$$

Since for all values of ω, $\text{Re}[Y(j\,\omega)] \ngeq 0$ *i.e.*, this test certifies that the **function is not a positive real function.**

Example 18.22 *A function is given by*

$$Z(s) = \frac{s^3 + 5s^2 + 9s + 3}{s^3 + 4s^2 + 7s + 9}.$$

Find the positive realness of the function.

Solution. Let us proceed with the testing of the function for positive realness—

(*i*) Since all the coefficients in the numerator and denominator are having +ve values hence, for real value of *s*, $Z(s)$ is real.

(*ii*) To find whether the poles are on the left half of the *s*-plane, let us apply the Hurwitz criterion to the denominator using continued fraction method.

Let $P(s) = s^3 + 4\,s^2 + 7s + 9 = M_2(s) + N_2(s)$

where $M_2(s) = 4s^2 + 9$ and $N_2(s) = s^3 + 7\,s.$

Application of continued fraction method is shown below.

$$\psi(s) = \frac{N_2(s)}{M_2(s)} = \frac{s^3 + 7\,s}{4\,s^2 + 9}$$

$4s^2 + 9\ )\ s^3 + 7\,s\ (\ \frac{s}{4}$

$s^3 + \frac{9s}{4}$

$\frac{19\,s}{4}\ )\ 4s^2 + 9\ (\ \frac{16}{19}\,s$

$4s^2$

$9\ )\ \frac{19\,s}{4}\ (\ \frac{19\,s}{4 \times 9}$

$\frac{19\,s}{4}$

×

Since all the quotients are +ve in the continued fraction expansion, hence, the polynomial of $Z(s)$ in the denominator is Hurwitz.

(*iii*) In order to find whether $\text{Re}\,Z(j\,\omega) \geq 0$ for all ω, let us adopt slightly more mathematical manipulation.

Let $$Z(s) = \frac{M_1(s) + N_1(s)}{M_2(s) + N_2(s)}$$

where

$$M_1(s) = 5s^2 + 3$$
$$N_1(s) = s^3 + 9s$$
$$M_2(s) = 4s^2 + 9$$
$$N_2(s) = s^3 + 7s$$

Rationalising,

$$Z(s) = \frac{M_1 + N_1}{M_2 + N_2} \cdot \frac{M_2 - N_2}{M_2 - N_2}$$
$$= \frac{M_1 M_2 - N_1 N_2}{M_2^2 - N_2^2} + \frac{N_1 M_2 - M_1 N_2}{M_2^2 - N_2^2}$$

Here, even part of $Z(s)$ is $\dfrac{M_1 M_2 - N_1 N_2}{M_2^2 - N_2^2}$

$$\therefore \text{ Real } Z(j\omega) = \left.\frac{M_1 M_2 - N_1 N_2}{M_2^2 - N_2^2}\right|_{s=j\omega}$$
$$= \frac{D(s)}{M_2^2 - N_2^2}$$

Since, $(M_2^2 - N_2^2)$ is always +ve for $s = j\omega$, $Z(j\omega) \geq 0$ provided $D(j\omega) \geq 0$ for any ω.

In this present example,

$$D(s) = M_1 M_2 - N_1 N_2$$
$$= (5s^2 + 3)(4s^2 + 9) - (s^3 + 9s)(s^3 + 7s)$$
$$= 20s^4 + 45s^2 + 12s^2 + 27$$
$$-s^6 - 7s^4 - 9s^4 - 63s^2$$
$$= -s^6 + 4s^4 - 6s^2 + 27$$
$$\therefore \quad D(j\omega) = -(j\omega)^6 + 4(j\omega)^4 - 6(j\omega)^2 + 27$$
$$= \omega^6 + 4\omega^4 + 6\omega^2 + 27$$

i.e., $D(j\omega) > 0$ for any value of ω.

Thus, $Z(j\omega) \geq 0$ for any value of ω.

The above tests certify that the **given function is a PR function.**

EXAMPLE 18.23 *Check whether the function*

$$Z(s) = \frac{2s^2 + 2s + 1}{s^3 + 2s^2 + s + 2} \text{ is a PR function.}$$

SOLUTION. Application of PR function tests yields following results :

(*i*) All the coefficients of the polynomial in numerator and denominator are +ve coefficients. Hence $Z(s)$ will be +ve if s is +ve.

(*ii*) The denominator of $Z(s)$ can be factorised as

$$s^3 + 2s^2 + s + 2 = s^2(s+2) + 1(s+2)$$
$$= (s^2 + 1)(s + 2).$$

This shows that the poles of the given function are at $\pm j1$ and -2. Since the poles are on $j\omega$ axis, we have to determine the residue.

Let $Z(s) = \dfrac{A.s}{s^2+1} + \dfrac{B}{s+2}$.

$$A = \left.\frac{2s^2 + 2s + 1}{s(s+2)}\right|_{s^2 = -1} = 1$$

and

$$B = \left.\frac{(2s^2 + 2s + 1)}{s^2 + 1}\right|_{s=-2} = 1$$

$\therefore$ The residues are +ve and real.

(*iii*) Also, let

$$Z(s) = \frac{(2s^2 + 1) + (2s + 0)}{(2s^2 + 2) + (s^3 + s)} = \frac{M_1(s) + N_1(s)}{M_2(s) + N_2(s)}$$

Following the same procedure that we have followed in the previous problem, we find here

$$D(s) = M_1(s)\, M_2(s) - N_1(s)\, N_2(s)$$
$$= (2s^2 + 1)(2s^2 + 2) - (2s)(s^3 + s)$$
$$= 4s^4 + 4s^2 + 2s^2 + 2 - 2s^4 - 2s^2$$
$$= 2s^4 + 4s^2 + 2$$
$$= 2(s^4 + 2s^2 + 1) = 2(s^2 + 1)^2$$
$$\therefore \quad D(j\omega) = 2[(j\omega)^2 + 1]^2$$
$$= 2[-\omega^2 + 1]^2 \equiv (1 - \omega^2)^2$$

i.e., $D(j\omega)$ is +ve for all values of ω.

Thus $\text{Re}[D(s)] \geq 0$

The above tests certify that the **given function is a PR function.**

18.6 CONCEPT OF NETWORK SYNTHESIS

Let us start the discussion considering two one port network forms (Fig. 18.9). Basically, these two networks are equivalent provided.

$$Z(s) = Z_1(s) + Z_2(s) \qquad \text{[Fig. 18.9(a)]}$$

and

$$Y(s) = Y_1(s) + Y_2(s) \qquad \text{[Fig. 18.9(b)]}$$

Network synthesis then refers to the operational procedures in which a positive real function is given for $Z(s)$ *or* $Y(s)$ [it may be recalled here that we have

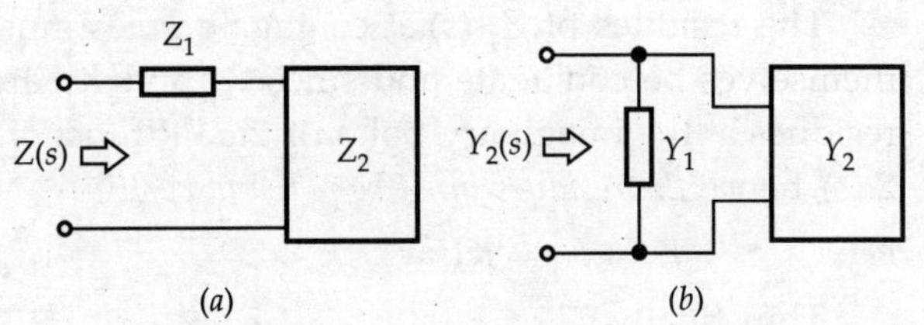

Fig. 18.9 Sum of Networks in impedance and admittance form.

shown that all immitance functions of passive networks are PR functions] *and it is required to select appropriate forms of* Z_1 *and* Z_2 *or* Y_1 *and* Y_2. For this we require the positive realness of each function Z_1 and Z_2 or Y_1 and Y_2 so that their sum would be obviously a PR function. When one of the functions in the sum is recognizable from the simplicity of its form of expression, the other can be determined through the steps of synthesis. *The synthesis is complete when all the elements (obviously network elements) of the sum are known or identified.* Usually *expansion technique* (long division procedure) is adopted in order to perform the steps of synthesis.

Let us start demonstrating the process of synthesis taking into account the network shown in Fig. 18.9(*a*).

Solving for Z_2 (*s*), we then can write

$$Z_2(s) = Z(s) - Z_1(s)$$

[Seggreation of Z_2 (*s*) from $Z(s)$ is identical of 'removing' Z_1 (*s*) from $Z(s)$ and this technique is very common in synthesis.]

Obviously, if Z_1 (*s*) is removed from $Z(s)$, the poles and zeros of Z_1 (*s*) would obviously be removed from $Z(s)$. The different removal operations are shown below :

(*i*) Removal of a Pole at Infinity

If the impedance function $Z(s)$ *has a pole at infinity, it is required that the numerator polynomial of* $Z(s)$ *is of degree one larger than the degree of the denominator polynomial.*

i.e.,
$$Z(s) = \frac{a_{n+1}\, s^{n+1} + a_n s^n + \ldots + a_1\, s + a_0}{b_n\, s^n + b_{n-1}\, s^{n-1} + \ldots + b_1 s + b_0} \qquad \ldots(18.10)$$

By ordinary long division, we get

$$Z(s) = Hs + \frac{C_n\, s^n + C_{n-1}\, s^{n-1} + \ldots + C_1\, s + C_0}{b_n\, s^n + b_{n-1}\, s^{n-1} + \ldots + b_1 s + b_0}$$

where $H = \dfrac{a_{n+1}}{b_n}$.

Let $Z_1\,(s) = Hs$

and
$$Z_2\,(s) = \frac{c_n\, c^n + c_{n-1}\, s^{n-1} + \ldots + c_1 s + c_0}{b_n\, s^n + b_{n-1}\, s^{n-1} + \ldots + b_1\, s + b_0} \qquad \ldots(18.11)$$

$$\therefore\; Z_2\,(s) = \frac{C_n\, s^n + C_{n-1}\, s^{n-1} + \ldots + C_1\, s + C_0}{b_n s^n + b_{n-1}\, s^{n-1} + \ldots + b_1 s + b_0}$$

$$= Z(s) - Hs$$

Simple reasoning in circuit theory reveals that Z_1 (*s*) being equivalent to *Hs*, it represents an inductor having $L = H\left(= \dfrac{a_{n+1}}{b_n}\right)$ since for inductor, $Z_L\,(s) = Ls$.

On the other hand, comparison of equations (18.10) and (18.11) reveals that $Z(s)$ and $Z_2(s)$ have the same poles. Since $Z(s)$ is a PR function (basic postulate), all poles of Z_2 (*s*) would also lie in left half of *s*-plane (or on the imaginary axis). Also, all poles of Z_2 (*s*) on the imaginary axis are simple. The real part of Z_1 (*s*) (= *Hs*) for ($s = j\omega$) is zero.

$$\therefore \qquad \text{Re}\, Z_2\,(j\omega) = Re\, Z(j\omega) \ge 0$$

for all values of ω

Thus, Z_2 (*s*) *is also a PR function.*

Since we have seen that Z_1 (*s*) is equivalent to an inductor hence it can be concluded that *removal of a pole at infinity corresponds to the removal of an inductor from the network Z (s)* leaving only $Z_2(s)$ [if the function is originally considered to be $Y(s)$ instead of $Z(s)$, *i.e.*, an admittance function, then $Y_1(s) \equiv Hs$. Obviously, in this case (*Hs*) corresponds to the *admittance* of a capacitor since $Y_C\,(s) = Cs$ and the configuration for Y_1 (*s*) is a capacitor having the value $C = H$ Farad $\left(= \dfrac{a_{n+1}}{b_n}\right)$. *In this case the removal of* Y_1 (*s*) *corresponds to the removal of a capacitor from* $Y(s)$.]

(*ii*) Removal of a pole at zero

If the impedance function Z (s) has a pole at zero, it is required that the denominator polynomial of Z (s) is of degree one larger than the degree of numerator polynomial.

i.e., $$Z(s) = \frac{a_0 + a_1 s + \ldots + a_{n-1} s^{n-1} + a_n s^n}{b_1 s + b_2 s^2 + \ldots + b_n s^n}$$

By long division we obtain,

$$Z(s) = \frac{K_0}{s} + \frac{c_1 + c_2 s + \ldots + c_n s^{n-1}}{b_1 + b_2 s + \ldots + b_n s^{n-1}}$$

$$= Z_1(s) + Z_2(s) \, [K_0 \text{ being } a_0 / b_1] \quad \ldots(18.12)$$

Here also $Z_2(s)$ is positive real like $Z(s)$ following the same concept of reasoning used in the previous case (removal of a pole at infinity). Also, we find that since $Z_c(s) = \frac{1}{sC}$, in the present context $Z_1(s) = Z_c(s)$, C being of value $1/K.\left(=\frac{b_1}{a_0}\right)$. *Thus removal of a pole at zero indicates actually the removal of a capacitor from the original network* (the given function being $Z(s)$).

If the function is originally considered to be admittance $Y(s)$ instead of impedance $Z(s)$, then $Y_1(s) = K_0/s$. Since $Y_L(s) = \frac{1}{Ls}$, hence from simple reasoning it is ascertained that $L = 1/K_0 \left(=\frac{b_1}{a_0}\right)$ and *removal of a pole at zero would mean the removal of an inductor from Y(s).*

(*iii*) Removal of conjugate imaginary poles

$Z(s)$ being containing poles on the imaginary axis $(z = \pm j\omega_1)$, $Z(s)$ will then have factors in complex conjugate form [since the denominator will be in the form $(s^2 + \omega_1^2)$ this time, the denominator factors would be $(s + j\omega_1)(s - j\omega_1)$]. The impedance function can then be written as

$$Z(s) = \frac{P(s)}{(s^2 + \omega_1^2)\, Q_1(s)}$$

In partial form, $Z(s)$ can be written as

$$Z(s) = \frac{K_1}{s - j\omega_1} + \frac{K_1^*}{s + j\omega_1} + Z_2(s) \quad \ldots(18.13)$$

The residues of $Z_1(s)$ at conjugate poles must themselves be conjugate and since K_1 and K_1^* are residues at the imaginary poles of the PR function, $Z(s)$, hence *the residues must be real and positive*

i.e., $$K_1 = K_1^* = K \text{ (say)}.$$

Thus finally,

$$Z(s) = \frac{2Ks}{s^2 + \omega_1^2} + Z_2(s) = Z_1(s) + Z_2(s) \quad \ldots(18.14)$$

Next we find that

$$\text{Re}[Z_1(j\omega)] = \text{Re}\left[\frac{2K_1(j\omega)}{-\omega^2 + \omega_1^2}\right]$$

Thus, $\text{Re}\, Z_2(j\omega)$ becomes zero or positive for any value of ω since $Z(s)$ is a *PR* function.

Synthesization of $Z_1(s)$ gives

$$Z_1(s) = \frac{2Ks}{s^2 + \omega_1^2} = \frac{1}{\frac{s}{2K} + \frac{\omega_1^2}{2K_1 s}}$$

$$= \frac{1}{Y_a(s) + Y_b(s)} = \frac{1}{Y(s)} \quad \ldots(18.15)$$

Here $Y_a(s) = \frac{s}{2K}$ represents the admittance of a capacitor with $C = \frac{1}{2K}$ while $Y_b(s) = \frac{\omega_1^2}{2Ks}$ is the admittance of an inductor of value $L = \frac{2K}{\omega_1^2}$. Obviously these two elements are connected in *parallel* to form $Z_1(s)$.

If the original PR function is an *admittance* function, instead of $Z_1(s)$, we write $Y_1(s)$ as

$$Y_1(s) = \frac{1}{Z_a(s) + Z_b(s)} \quad \ldots(18.16)$$

Here, $Z_a(s)\left(=\frac{s}{2K}\right)$ representing the *impedance of an inductor having the value* $L = \frac{1}{2K}$ *and* $Z_b(s)\left(=\frac{\omega_1^2}{2Ks}\right)$ *as the impedance of a capacitor with* $C = \frac{2K}{\omega_1^2}$.

It is also observed that $Z_a(s)$ and $Z_b(s)$ are connected in *series*.

We thus finally see that for an impedance function, location of a pole at $(s \to \infty)$ indicates a series inductor while location of a pole at $(s \to 0)$ indicates the presence of a series capacitor. Location of a pole at imaginary axis indicates the presence of parallel LC elements.

On the other hand, if the given function is an admittance function, location of a pole at $(s \to \infty)$ means a parallel capacitance while location of a pole at zero $(s \to 0)$ indicates presence of parallel inductance. Location of a pole in $(j\omega)$ axis in such a case indicates presence of series LC element.

It may be noticed here that it is also possible to remove a constant (a real number R) from $Z(s)$ such that $Z_2(s) = Z(s) - R$. $Z_2(s)$ is a PR function if $R \le$ min. value of $Re[Z(j\omega)]$. Thus it becomes evident that in this case R represents the magnitude of a resistor. If the original *PR* function be given in form of $Y(s)$ instead of $Z(s)$, R indicates a conductance.

Thus to generalise we can say that if a PR function $Z(s)$ has simple poles at $j\omega$ axis $(s = \pm j\omega_i, i = 1, 2, \ldots, m)$ as well as simple poles at $s = 0$ and $s = \infty$, then $Z(s)$ can be expressed as

$$Z(s) = \frac{K_0}{s} + \sum_{i=1}^{m} \frac{2K_i s}{s^2 + \omega_i^2} + K_\infty s + Z_2(s) \quad \ldots(18.17)$$

$$[= Z_1(s) + Z_2(s)]$$

The constituent terms in $Z(s)$ can be interpreted as

(*a*) $\dfrac{K_0}{s}$ results from a possible pole at $s = 0$.

(*b*) $K_\infty s$ results from a possible pole at $s = \infty$

(*c*) $\dfrac{2K_i s}{s^2 + \omega_i^2}$ results from a pair of conjugate poles on the $j\omega$ axis.

$$\left[\frac{2K_i s}{s^2 + \omega_i^2} \equiv \frac{K_i}{s + j\omega_i} + \frac{K_i'}{s - j\omega_i} = \frac{(K_i + K_i')s - j(K_i - K_i')\omega_i}{s^2 + \omega_i^2}\right]$$

In order that they give a real term after combination, it is essential that the residues K_i and K_i' must be equal.

The residues K_0, K_∞ and $2K_i$ can be calculated as follows

$$K_0 = \{sZ(s)\}_{s=0}$$

$$K_\infty = \lim_{s \to \infty} \left\{\frac{Z(s)}{s}\right\} \quad \ldots(18.18)$$

$$2K_i = \left\{\frac{s^2 + \omega_i^2}{s} Z(s)\right\}_{s = j\omega_i}$$

Also, from the explanations cited in the previous portions it is evident that $Z_2(s)$ being a *PR* function,

$$Z_2(s) = Z(s) - \frac{K_0}{s} - \sum_{i=1}^{m} \frac{2K_i s}{s^2 + \omega_i^2} - K_\infty s \quad \ldots(18.19)$$

We have stated earlier about the removal of poles from a given $Z(s)$ and observed that $Z_2(s)$ *remain PR provided Z(s) is a PR function. In other words, it means that a PR function maintains its positive realness after removal (or extraction) of all or some of its poles on the imaginary axis (those at 0 and ∞ included). The degree of function gets diminished by the number of extracted poles.*

We have also observed in the preceding parts that the term (K_0/s) is the impedance of a capacitor while $K_\infty s$ (*i.e., Hs*) is the impedance of an inductor. The term $\dfrac{2K_i s}{s^2 + \omega_i^2}$ is the impedance of a parallel *LC* circuit when, $Z_i(s) = \dfrac{(1/C_i)s}{s^2 + \dfrac{1}{L_i C_i}}$.

Since these terms are extracted from an impedance, the corresponding circuits are placed in series (Fig. 18.10).

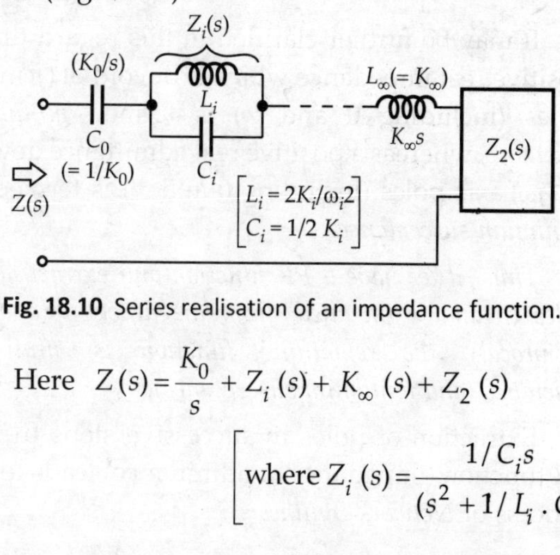

Fig. 18.10 Series realisation of an impedance function.

Here $Z(s) = \dfrac{K_0}{s} + Z_i(s) + K_\infty(s) + Z_2(s)$

$$\left[\text{where } Z_i(s) = \frac{1/C_i s}{(s^2 + 1/L_i \cdot C_i}\right]$$

CHAPTER 18

We thus see the removal of poles from an impedance function (PR function) can be interpreted as a (jω) axis pole extraction.

Similarly, for an admittance function,

$$Y_2(s) = Y(s) - \frac{K'_0}{s} - \sum_{i=1}^{r} \frac{2K'_i}{s^2 + \omega_i^2} - K'_\infty s \quad ...(18.20)$$

Obviously, $Y_2(s)$ being again a PR function (since $Y(s)$ is a *PR* function), K'_0/s is the admittance of an inductor while $K_\infty{}'s$ is that of a capacitor. Term $\frac{2K'_i s}{s^2+\omega_i^2}$ is the admittance of a series $L_i\,C_i$ network $\left[Y_i(s) = \frac{\frac{1}{L_i}.s}{s^2 + \frac{1}{L_i C_i}}\right]$.

Figure 18.11 represents an admittance function realisation.

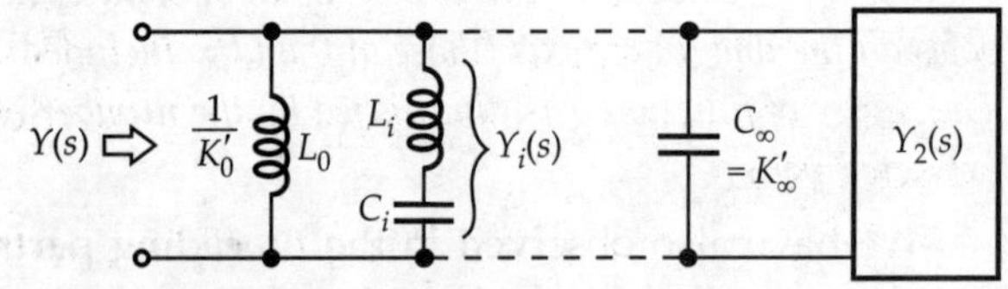

Fig. 18.11 Realisation of an admittance function.

$$\left[L_0 = \frac{1}{K'_0};\ C_\infty = K'_\infty h\right.$$

$$L_i = \frac{1}{2K'_i};\ C_i = \frac{2K'_i}{\omega_i^2}$$

$$\left.Y(s) = \frac{K'_0}{s} + \frac{2K'_i s}{s^2+\omega_i^2} + K'_\infty s + Y_2(s)\right]$$

It may be further clarified in this regard that a positive real impedance which is devoid of (jω) axis poles (including 0 and ∞) is termed *minimum reactance,* whereas a positive real admittance devoid of (jω) axis poles (including 0 and ∞) is termed as *minimum susceptance.*

Thus, if we have a PR function and extract all jω poles (0 and ∞ included) from the function (and its reciprocal), the remaining function is minimum reactance (and minimum susceptance).

Extraction of poles in successive steps from a PR function (impedance or admittance) leads to the process of *Network Synthesis.*

18.7 SUMMARY OF PROCEDURE OF SYNTHESIS

Step 1

The given function being a *PR* function, it must be either in form of $Z(s)$ or $Y(s)$. In this first step substitute $j\omega$ for s in the expression of $Z(s)$ or $Y(s)$, rationalise and find the real part of the function. Find the minimum value of the real part $[ReF(j\omega)]_{min.}$ [This is done by differentiating the real part of the rationalised function with respect to ω and equating it to zero and obtaining the value of ω for which the real part of the function would be minimum. Substituting the value of ω in the real part of the rationalised function find $Re[F(j\omega)]_{min}$.].

Step 2

If the functions given in form of $Z(s)$, the $[Re\,Z(j\omega)]_{min}$ is then a constant term signifying the presence of a series resistance whose magnitude is equal to the minimum real value just obtained. However if given in form of $Y(s)$, the obtained min. value is that of a shunt resistor.

Step 3

In case the given function does not have any real part, then it becomes evident that the given function $[Z(s)$ or $Y(s)]$ does not have any resistive part and contains either inductance or capacitance.

Step 4

In this step check whether the numerator of the given function has one '*s*' term higher. If the numerator has one '*s*' term higher, pole appears at $s=\infty$; on the other hand if the denominator has one *s* term higher, pole appears at $s=0$ This can be explained as follows :

$$\text{Say } Z(s) = \frac{a_{n+1}s^{n+1} + a_n s^n + ... + a_1 s + a_0}{b_n s^n + b_{n-1}s^{n-1} + ... + b_1 s + b_0}$$

By long division,

$$Z(s) = K_0\, s + \frac{\text{Remainder}}{b_n s^n + b_{n-1}s^{n-1} + ... + b_1 s + b_0} \quad ...(18.21)$$

It can now be observed that $Z(s)$ will have a pole at $s=\infty$.

On the other hand, if

$$Z(s) = \frac{a_0 + a_1 s + \ldots + a_{n-1} s^{n-1} + a_n s^n}{b_1 s + b_2 s^2 + \ldots + b_n s^n},$$

by long division,

$$Z(s) = \frac{K_0}{s} + \frac{\text{remainder}}{b_1 + b_2 s + \ldots + b_{n-1} s^{n-1}} \quad \ldots(18.22)$$

It can be observed that $Z(s)$ will have a pole at $s = 0$.

In the former case, if the original function is expressed in impedance form, the first term then becomes a series inductor; if the original expression of the function is in admittance form, the former can reveal the presence of a shunt capacitor.

Also, for the case when there is one higher s term in the denominator, the first term is a series capacitor provided the function is expressed in impedance form. If the function is expressed in admittance form, this case reveals the presence of a shunt inductor.

Step 5

Perform the first long division to obtain the first quotient. In the first case of step 4, the quotient will be (K_0 s) indicating the value of the series inductor (if the function is originally expressed in Z form) to be K_0 Henry. If the function is originally expressed in Y form, ($K_0 s$) indicates the presence of a shunt capacitor of value K_0 Farad. On the other hand if the first quotient is $\frac{K_0}{s}$ in step 4, the magnitude of the series capacitor is ($1/K_0$) Farad when the original function is expressed in Z form. If the original function be expressed in Y form, this $\frac{K_0}{s}$ quotient indicates that the first element being shunt inductor, its value is ($1/K_0$) Henry.

Step 6

Once the first part of the given function is realised, the remainder is inverted and the realisation is again commenced starting from step-1.

This process continuous till the last element is realised.

EXAMPLE 18.24 *The driving point impedance of a network is given by*

$$Z(s) = \frac{s^3 + 4s}{s^2 + 2}. \textit{ Realise the network.}$$

SOLUTION. ***Step 1.*** Since the degree of numerator polynomial is one higher than that of denominator polynomial hence it is evident that $Z(s)$ will have a pole at $s = \infty$ indicating the presence of a series inductor whose value can be determined by long division of the numerator of $Z(s)$ by its denominator.

Step 2.

$$\begin{array}{l} s^2 + 2\,)\; s^3 + 4s\;(\,s \\ \qquad\quad \underline{s^3 + 2s} \\ \qquad\qquad 2s \end{array}$$

i.e., $Z(s) = s + \frac{2s}{s^2 + 2} = Z_1(s) + Z_2(s)$

Thus $Z_1(s)[= 1.s]$ indicates that the series inductance would have value of 1 H.

Step 3. Since $Z_2(s) = \frac{2s}{s^2 + 2}$, $Y_2(s) = \frac{s^2 + 2}{2s}$.

Presence of pole at $s = \infty$ is evident as the degree of numerator is still one higher. For the admittance function $Y_2(s)$, presence of pole at $s = \infty$ indicates a parallel capacitance whose value can be determined by breaking $Y_2(s)$ in partial fraction.

Step 4. $Y_2(s) = \frac{s}{2} + \frac{1}{s} = Y_3(s) + Y_4(s)$

$Y_3(s) = \left(\frac{1}{2} s\right)$ indicates the value of the capacitance to be $\frac{1}{2}$ Farad in parallel to $Y_4(s)\left(= \frac{1}{s}\right)$ which is evidently an inductor of $L = 1$ Henry. **The complete realisation is shown in Fig. E18.1.**

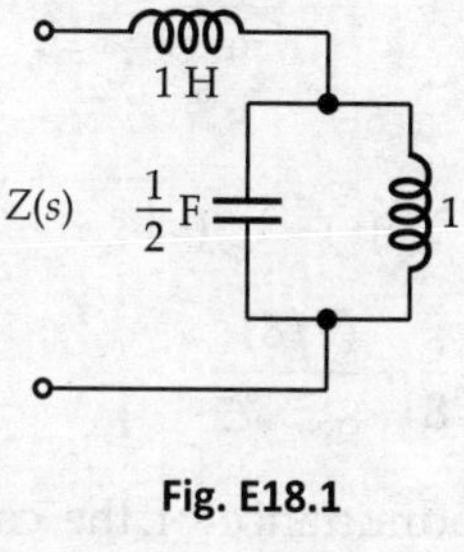

Fig. E18.1

EXAMPLE 18.25 *Realise the network whose impedance is given as* $Z_1(s) = \frac{s^4 + 10 s^2 + 7}{s^3 + 2s}$

CHAPTER 18

SOLUTION. *Step 1.* Substitution of $s = j\omega$ reveals that $Z_1(s)$ does not have any real part and hence it can be inferred that $Z_1(s)$ would not have any resistance element.

Since the degree of s term in numerator is one higher than the degree of s in denominator hence it is evident that $Z_1(s)$ has a pole at infinity indicating presence of an series inductor. The magnitude of the series inductance can be obtained by using long division method.

Step 2. $s^3 + 2s\ )\ s^4 + 10s^2 + 7\ (\ s$

$$\frac{s^4 + 2s^2}{8s^2 + 7}$$

$$\therefore\ Z_1(s) = \frac{s^4 + 10s^2 + 7}{s^3 + 2s} = s + \frac{8s^2 + 7}{s^3 + 2s}$$

$$= Z_2(s) + Z_3(s)$$

Thus the inductor has an impedance of $Z_2(s)$ being denoted by s *i.e.*, the inductance is 1 Henry.

Step 3. Since $Z_3(s) = \frac{8s^2 + 7}{s^3 + 2s}$, inverting it we get,

$$Y_3(s) = \frac{s^3 + 2s}{8s^2 + 7}.$$

Also for $Y_3(s)$, the degree of s in numerator is one more ;

$\therefore\ Y_3(s)$ would have a pole at infinity resulting a parallel capacitor.

Step 4. Again by long division, we find,

$8s^2 + 7\ )\ s^3 + 2s\ (\ \frac{s}{8}$

$$\frac{s^3 + \frac{7}{8}s}{\frac{9}{8}s}$$

$$\therefore\quad Y_3(s) = Y_4(s) + Y_5(s)$$

$$= \frac{s}{8} + \frac{(9/8)s}{8s^2 + 7}.$$

i.e., $Y_4(s)$ is the admittance of the capacitor being given by $\frac{s}{8}$. This indicates than the capacitor has a capacitance of $\frac{1}{8}$ Farad.

Step 5. Next, converting $Y_5(s)$ to impedance form,

$$Z_5(s) = \frac{8s^2 + 7}{(9/8)s} = \frac{64}{9}s + \frac{56}{9s} = Z_6(s) + Z_7(s)$$

Since expression of $Z_5(s)$ has s in numerator one degree higher than that in denominator, hence it is evident that $Z_6(s)$ is a series inductor having inductance of $\frac{64}{9}$ H.

Step 6. Again inversion of $Z_7(s)$ in admittance form $\left[Y_7(s) = \frac{9s}{56}\right]$ reveals the presence of a pole at infinity indicating the presence of a shunt capacitor of $\frac{9}{56}$ Farad.

The complete synthesis is shown in Fig. E18.2.

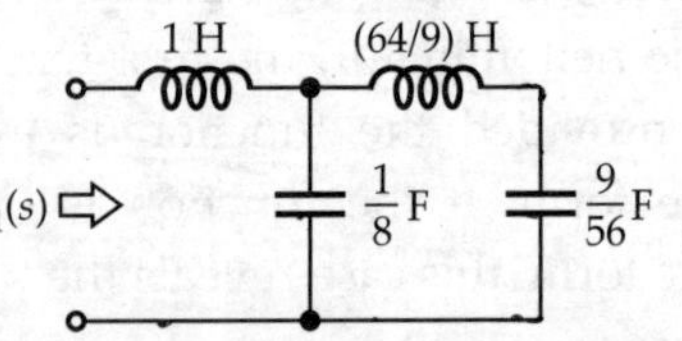

Fig. E18.2

EXAMPLE 18.26 *Realise the network having impedance function*

$$Z(s) = \frac{s^2 + 4s + 40}{s(s+10)}.$$

SOLUTION. *Step 1.* Inspection of $Z(s)$ reveals that the pole is at origin $(s = 0)$ for the given impedance function.

$\therefore$ Location of a pole at $s = 0$ indicates the presence of a series capacitor whose value can be determined using long division of numerator of $Z(s)$ by its denominator (Step 2).

Step 2. $s^2 + 10s\ )\ s^2 + 4s + 40\ (\ \frac{4}{s}$

$$\frac{4s + 40}{s^2}$$

i.e.,
$$Z(s) = \frac{s^2 + 4s + 40}{s(s+10)} = \frac{4}{s} + \frac{s^2}{s^2 + 10s}$$

$$= \frac{4}{s} + \frac{s}{s+10} = Z_1(s) + Z_2(s)$$

Then $Z_1(s) = \frac{4}{s}$ indicates the capacitor having $C_1 = \frac{1}{4}$ Farad in series with $Z_2(s)$ [Fig. E18.3(*a*)]

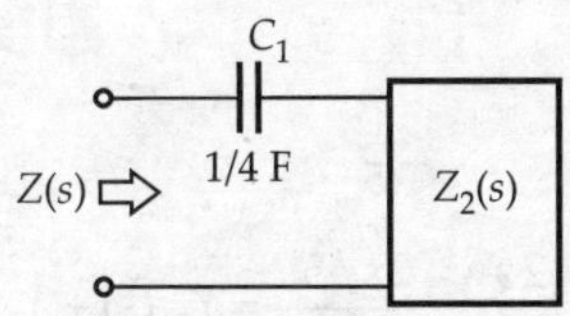

Fig. E18.3 (*a*)

Step **3.** We will now realise $Z_2(s)$ by first inverting it as $Y_2(s)$.

$$\therefore \quad Y_2(s) = \frac{1}{Z_2(s)} = \frac{s+10}{s}.$$

Since $Y_2(s)$ has a pole at $s=0$, it is evident that this indicates a parallel inductance determined by dividing the numerator $(s+10)$ by s (step 4)

Step 4. $s\;)\;s + 10\;(\;1$

$\quad\quad\; s$

$\quad\quad\; \overline{10}$

$$\text{i.e.,} \quad Y_2(s) = \frac{s+10}{s} = 1 + \frac{10}{s}$$

$$= \frac{10}{s} + 1 = Y_3(s) + Y_4(s)$$

$\therefore Y_3(s) = \frac{10}{s}$ indicates an inductor in parallel to $Y_4(s)$. Obviously if $Y_3(s) = \frac{10}{s}$, for an inductor, $Z_3(s) = \frac{s}{10} = L_3 s$ indicating $L_3 = \frac{1}{10}$ Henry.

The circuit is realised in Fig. E18.3(*b*) :

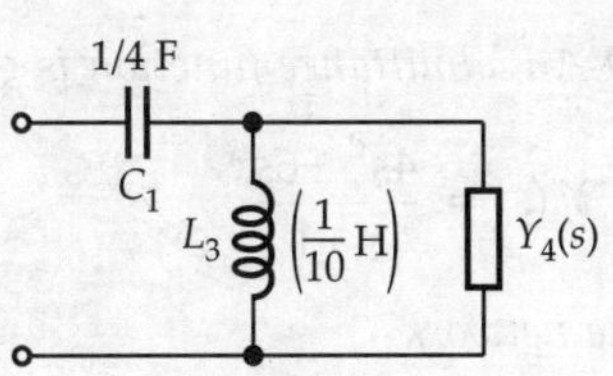

Fig. E18.3 (*b*)

Step **5.** Removing $Y_3(s)$ from $Y_2(s)$ it is evident that the left out portion is $Y_4(s)[=1]$. Since it is independent of s term hence it is evident that it is a constant term representing a resistance of $1\,\Omega$.

Step **6. The complete realisation is then shown below (Fig. E18.3(*c*))**

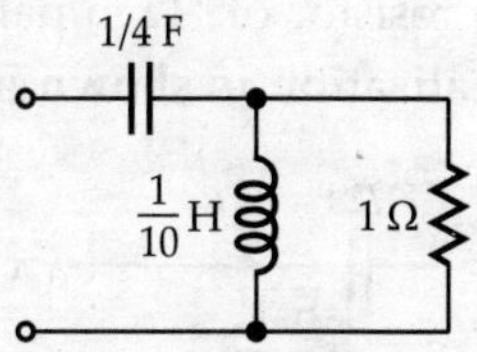

Fig. E18.3 (*c*)

EXAMPLE 18.27 *Realise the network having impedance function :*

$$Z(s) = \frac{s^2 + 2s + 10}{s(s+5)}.$$

SOLUTION. ***Step 1.*** We observe that $Z(s)$ has a pole at $s=0$. Location of a pole at $s=0$ indicates the presence of a series capacitor whose value can be determined using long division of numerator of $Z(s)$ by its denominator (Step 2).

Step 2. $s^2 + 5s\;)\;s^2 + 2s + 10\;(\;\frac{2}{s}$

$\quad\quad\quad\quad\quad\quad 2s + 10$

$\quad\quad\quad\quad\quad\quad \overline{s^2}$

$$\therefore \quad Z(s) = \frac{2}{s} + \frac{s^2}{s^2 + 5s} = \frac{2}{s} + \frac{s}{s+5}$$

$$= Z_1(s) + Z_2(s)$$

Thus $Z_1(s) = \frac{2}{s}$ indicates the value of the series capacitance to be $\frac{1}{2}$ Farad.

Step **3.** To realise $Z_2(s)$, it is inverted to gives $Y_2(s)$.

$$Y_2(s) = \frac{s+5}{s} = 1 + \frac{5}{s}$$

$$= \frac{5}{s} + 1 = Y_3(s) + Y_4(s)$$

Since $Y_2(s)$ has a pole at $s=0$, it is then evident that there exists a parallel inductance in $Y_3(s)$. Its value is indicated in step-4.

Step 4. $Z_3(s) = \frac{1}{Y_3(s)} = \frac{s}{5} = \frac{1}{5}.s(= L_3 s)$

Thus the parallel inductance has a value of $\frac{1}{5}$ Henry.

CHAPTER 18

Step 5. The only left portion being $Y_4(s)$, in this problem it is 1Ω. Thus $Y_4(s)=1$ indicates $Z_4(s)=1$ *i.e.*, presenting a resistor of 1Ω in parallel to $Y_3(s)$. **The complete realisation is shown in Fig. E18.4.**

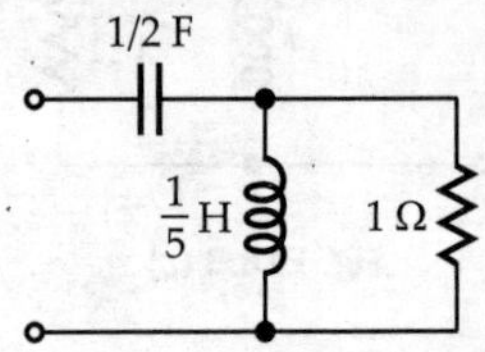

Fig. E18.4

EXAMPLE 18.28 *The impedance function of a network is given by*

$$Z(s) = \frac{6s^3+5s^2+6s+4}{2s^3+2s}$$

Realise the network.

SOLUTION.

$$Z(s) = \frac{6s^3+5s^2+6s+4}{2s^3+2s}$$

$$= \frac{6s^3+5s^2+6s+4}{s(2s^2+2)}.$$

It may be observed that $Re[Z(s)]$ at $s=j\omega$ has terms devoid of s terms and its minimum real value is a constant term with $\omega=0$. Thus the first element is a resistance term whose value can be found out by long division method.

$$2s^3+2s\;)\;6s^3+5s^2+6s+4\;(\;3$$
$$\underline{6s^3 \qquad\quad +6s}$$
$$5s^2+4$$

$$\therefore \quad Z(s) = 3 + \frac{5s^2+4}{2s^3+2s} = Z_1(s) + Z_2(s)$$

Thus, $Z_1(s)$ being realised as a s-free quantity, if is obviously a series resistor (of 3Ω).

Next we observe $Z_2(s)$. It is inverted and then

$$Y_2(s) = \frac{2s^3+2s}{5s^2+4}$$

$Y_2(s)$ has no real part and hence it would not have any resistor. Again, since the numerator has one degree higher than denominator, $Y_2(s)$ has a pole at $s=\infty$ indicating the presence of a parallel capacitor.

By long division,

$$5s^2+4\;)\;2s^3+2s\;(\;\frac{2s}{5}$$
$$\underline{2s^3+\frac{8s}{5}}$$
$$\frac{2s}{5}$$

$$\therefore \quad Y_2(s) = \frac{2s}{5} + \frac{2s/5}{5s^2+4} = Y_3(s) + Y_4(s)$$

$Y_3(s) = \left(\frac{2}{5}\cdot s\right)$ indicates that the parallel capacitance is of $\frac{2}{5}$ Farad.

Next, we invert $Y_4(s)$ to obtain $Z_4(s)$

$$Z_4(s) = \frac{5s^2+4}{2s/5} = \frac{25s^2+20}{2s}$$

Since the degree of s is higher in numerator than denominator, $Z_4(s)$ would have a pole at $s=\infty$. This indicates a series inductor.

Also, $\quad Z_4(s) = 12.5\,s + \frac{10}{s} = Z_5(s) + Z_6(s)$

Thus the inductor $Z_5(s)$ would be of 12.5 Henry while $Z_6(s)$ would be a series capacitor of $\frac{1}{10}$ Farad.

The complete realisation is shown in Fig. E18.5.

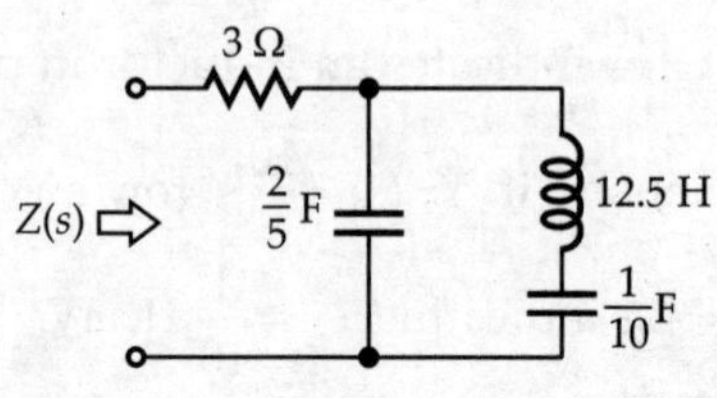

Fig. E18.5

EXAMPLE 18.29 *An admittance function is given as*

$$Y(s) = \frac{4s^2+6s}{s+1}.$$

Realise the network.

SOLUTION. ***Step 1.*** We observe that the numerator polynomial is of one degree higher than the denominator polynomial. Thus a pole exists at $s=\infty$. This clearly indicates that for the given impedance function, for pole at $s=\infty$, a parallel capacitor exists whose value can be determined by long division method (Step-2)

Step 2. $s + 1 \,)\; 4s^2 + 6s \;(\; 4s$

$\quad\quad\quad\quad 4s^2 + 4s$

$\quad\quad\quad\quad\quad 2s$

i.e., $$Y(s) = 4s + \frac{2s}{s+1} = Y_1(s) + Y_2(s)$$

$Y_1(s) = 4s$ indicates that the value of the capacitor would be 4 F.

Step 3. Next $Y_2(s)$ is inverted such that

$$Z_2(s) = \frac{s+1}{2s} = \frac{1}{2} + \frac{1}{2s}$$

$$= \frac{1}{2s} + \frac{1}{2} = Z_3(s) + Z_4(s)$$

However, $Z_2(s)$ being having a pole at $s = 0$, it is evident that there will be a series capacitor represented by $Z_3(s)$ in series with $Z_4(s)$. Obviously $Z_3(s)$ being $\frac{1}{2s}$, the capacitor would be of 2 Farad.

Step 4. $Z_4(s)$ being devoid of s, it is a resistance of $\frac{1}{2}\,\Omega$ in series with $Z_3(s)$.

The complete realisation is shown in Fig. E18.6.

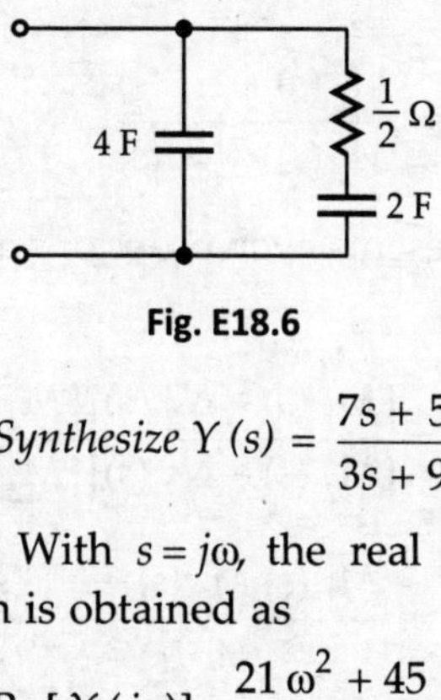

Fig. E18.6

EXAMPLE 18.30 *Synthesize* $Y(s) = \dfrac{7s+5}{3s+9}$.

SOLUTION. With $s = j\omega$, the real part of $Y(j\omega)$ appears which is obtained as

$$\text{Re}[Y(j\omega)] = \frac{21\,\omega^2 + 45}{9\omega^2 + 81}$$

The minimum real part occurs at $\omega = 0$.

$$\therefore \quad \text{Min}[\text{Re}\,Y(j\omega)] = \frac{5}{9}.$$

Thus the resistive part in $Y(s)$ is obtained but since the expression is given in admittance form hence the value obtained is actually conductance instead of resistance. This, clearly indicates the resistance of $\frac{5}{9}$ ohm is connected in parallel as first element.

The left out portion of $Y(s)$ is thus

$$Y'(s) = Y(s) - \frac{5}{9} = \frac{7s+5}{3s+9} - \frac{5}{9}$$

$$= \frac{16\,s}{9s+27}$$

$$\therefore \quad Z'(s) = \frac{9s+27}{16s} = \frac{9}{16} + \frac{27}{16s}$$

i.e., the presence of a series resistor of $\frac{9}{16}$ ohm is obtained in this step.

The remaining portion is $\frac{27}{16s}$ which indicates a pole at zero. This reveals the identity of a series capacitor of $\frac{16}{27}$ Farad. **The complete realisation is shown in Fig. E18.7.**

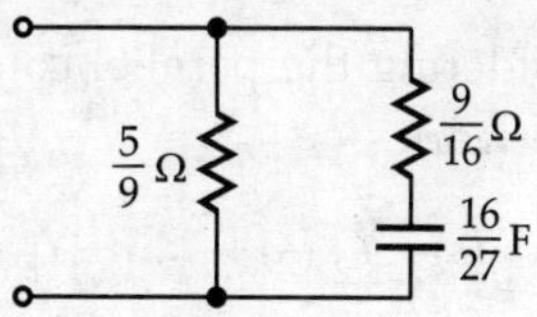

Fig. E18.7

18.8 REACTIVE NETWORKS

Any *L-C* one port network contains no resistive element and is thus dissipationless. The driving point immittance (either impedance or admittance) can be obtained by combining impedance or admittance expression for the elements of the network. LC networks are usually called the *reactive networks.*

Any given reactive network may be split up into either series or parallel combination of *L-C* elements. In series combination, the total impedance $Z(s)$ of the combination (in frequency domain) is given by

$$Z(s) = Z_1(s) + Z_2(s) + \ldots.. + Z_n(s) \qquad \ldots(18.23)$$

or, $$Z(s) = (L_1 + L_2 + \ldots\ldots + L_n)\,s + \left(\frac{1}{C_1} + \frac{1}{C_2} + \ldots.. + \frac{1}{C_n}\right)\frac{1}{s} \qquad \ldots(18.23(a))$$

[$\because$ the inductor L has impedance Ls while a capacitor C has impedance $\frac{1}{Cs}$]

or, $$Z(s) = L_{eq}\ s + \frac{1}{C_{eq}\ s} \quad \text{...(18.24)}$$

where L_{eq} is the equivalent inductance of the series system and C_{eq} is the equivalent capacitance of the series system.

Thus, the series combination of L and C may be represented by L_{eq} in series with C_{eq} (Refer to Fig. 18.12)

or, $$Z(s) = L_{eq}\ \frac{s^2 + \dfrac{1}{L_{eq}\ C_{eq}}}{s} \quad \text{...(18.25)}$$

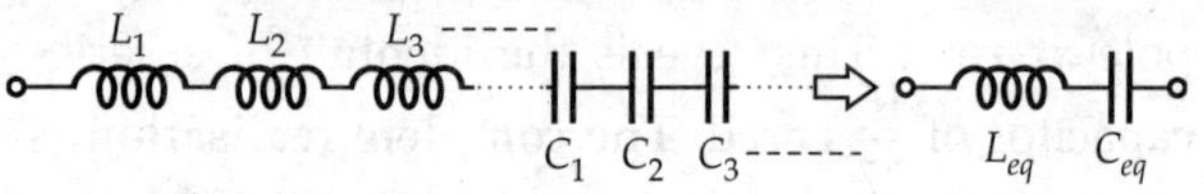

Fig. 18.12 Series combination of Reactive network.

Next, considering the parallel configuration of the reactive network,

$$Y(s) = Y_1\ (s) + Y_2\ (s) + \ldots\ldots + Y_n\ (s) \quad \text{...(18.26)}$$

[where $Y(s)$ represents the net shunt admittance of the network and $Y_1\ (s), Y_2\ (s),\ldots.$ the shunt admittance of each branch]

or, $$Y(s) = (C_1 + C_2 + \ldots.. + C_n)\ s + \left(\frac{1}{L_1} + \frac{1}{L_2} + \ldots\ldots + \frac{1}{L_n}\right)\frac{1}{s} \quad \text{...(18.27)}$$

[$\because$ The inductor has an admittance of $\frac{1}{Ls}$ while the capacitor has admittance of Cs]

or, $$Y(s) = C_{eq}\ s + \frac{1}{L_{eq}\ s} \quad \text{...(18.28)}$$

[here, C_{eq} represents the equivalent capacitance of the parallel combination of elements while L_{eq} is the equivalent inductance of the parallel combination of elements]

Thus, $$Y(s) = C_{eq}\ \frac{s^2 + \dfrac{1}{L_{eq}\ C_{eq}}}{s} \quad \text{...(18.29)}$$

Thus, the parallel combination of L and C can be exhibited by L_{eq} in parallel with C_{eq} as shown in Fig. 18.13.

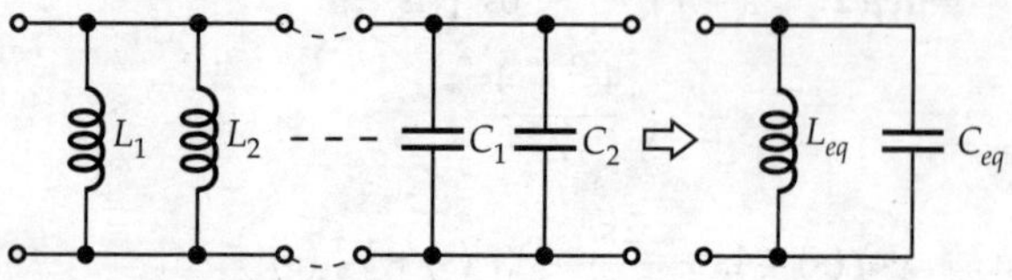

Fig. 18.13 Parallel combination of Reactive network.

Thus we find that

(*i*) *the driving point impedance for a complex network consisting of series reactive elements is obtained by adding the impedances and reciprocals of admittances and*

(*ii*) *the driving point admittances of a complex network consisting of parallel reactive network elements is obtained by adding the admittance and the reciprocal of impedances.*

18.9 PROPERTIES OF DRIVING POINT IMMITTANCES OF *LC* NETWORKS

Let us consider an impedance function $Z(s)$ which is intrinsically a PR function. If it has to represent an LC network, $Re\,[Z(j\omega)] = 0$ for all ω

However,

$$Z(s) = \frac{M_1\ (s) + N_1\ (s)}{M_2\ (s) + N_2\ (s)}$$

[where M represents even order of s and N and the odd order of s]

i.e., $$Z(s) = \frac{[M_1\ (s) + N_2\ (s)][M_2\ (s) - N_2\ (s)]}{[M_2\ (s) + N_2\ (s)][M_2\ (s) - N_2\ (s)]}$$

$$= \frac{M_1\ (s)\ M_2\ (s) - N_1\ (s)\ N_2\ (s)}{M_2^2\ (s) - N_2^2\ (s)} + \frac{M_2\ (s)\ N_1\ (s) - M_1\ (s)\ N_2\ (s)}{M_2^2\ (s) - N_2^2\ (s)}$$

Since the product of two even functions or two odd functions is itself an even function while the product of an even and odd function is odd, we find that the first term of RHS of the above equation is even while the second term is odd.

i.e., $$Ev\,[Z(s)] = \frac{M_1\ (s)\ M_2\ (s) - N_1\ (s)\ N_2\ (s)}{M_2^2\ (s) - N_2^2\ (s)}$$

However, the real part of $Z(j\omega)$ is given as

$$\text{Re}[Z(j\omega)] = Ev\left[Z(s)\Big|_{s=j\omega}\right]$$

Since for LC networks, $Re\,Z(j\omega)=0$ hence it follows that $Ev\ Z(s)=0$

i.e., $$\frac{M_1(s)M_2(s) - N_1(s)N_2(s)}{M_2^2(s) - N_2^2(s)} = 0$$

i.e., $$M_1(s)M_2(s) - N_1(s)N_2(s) = 0.$$

This is possible if

$$M_1(s)=0 \quad \text{and} \quad N_2(s)=0$$

or $$M_2(s)=0 \quad \text{and} \quad N_1(s)=0$$

or $$M_1(s)M_2(s) - N_1(s)N_2(s) = 0.$$

The first condition reveals that

$$Z(s) = \frac{N_1(s)}{M_2(s)},$$

while the second condition reveals that

$$Z(s) = \frac{M_1(s)}{N_2(s)}.$$

The third condition is redundant since it already takes care of first two conditions.

Thus we observe that for a LC network, $Z(s)$ [and obviously $Y(s)$] is a ratio of two polynomials in s and either it is a ratio of odd to even or an even to odd polynomials. It can also be inferred from here that since the driving point immittance is the ratio of odd to even or even to odd polynomials, their degrees must differ by exactly unity (since for a PR function, the highest powers of the numerator and denominator polynomials may differ by at most unity otherwise multiple pole or zero at $\omega = \infty$ would result). The same statement is also valid about the lowest powers of the numerator and denominator polynomials. Moreover, the numerator and denominator of $Z(s)$ or $Y(s)$ must be Hurwitz such that $Z(s)$ or $Y(s)$ could be a PR function. We have also seen that all the zeros of a Hurwitz polynomial (even or odd) must be simple and on the $(j\omega)$ axis. Then all the poles and zeros of the reactance functions are simple and lie on $(j\omega)$ axis.

Furthermore, the residues of the function (and obviously its reciprocal) at the poles are real and positive. In this context we also observe that since the immittance function is the ratio of either odd to even or even to odd polynomials hence at infinity, $Z(s)$ would here either a pole or a zero depending on whether the even or odd function is of higher degree.

Thus we can summarise the properties of an LC immittance function as listed below :

1. *All the expressions of driving point immittances are quotients of polynomials in s (with a constant multiplier).*
2. *Z(s) or Y(s) of the LC network is the ratio of either even to odd or odd to even polynomials (if the numerator polynomial contains term in only odd powers of s, the denominator polynomial must contain term in only even powers of s and vice versa).*
3. *The highest powers of numerator and denominator polynomials must differ by one, the lowest powers also differ by one.*
4. *The poles and zeros of the driving point immittances are simple and lie on the $j\omega$ axis.*
5. *There must be a pole or zero at the origin and infinity.*
6. *The residues of the immittance function at the poles are real and positive.*

CHAPTER 18

EXAMPLE 18.31 *Find an expression for the driving point impedance in s-domain for the reactive network shown in Fig. E18.8.*

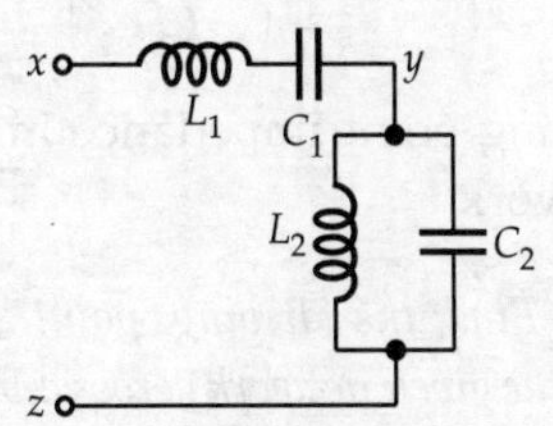

Fig. E18.8

SOLUTION. Let us first transfer the given network in s-domain [Fig. E18.8(*a*)].

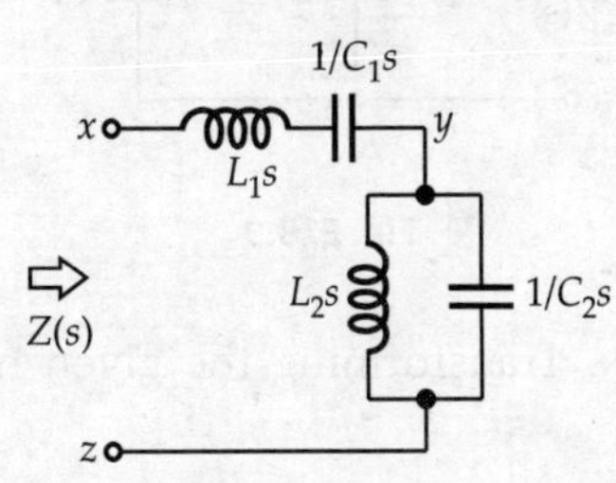

Fig. E18.8 (*a*)

$Z(s)$ = impedance between terminals x-z.

$$= Z(s)\,(\text{between } x\text{-}y) + Z(s)\,(\text{between } y\text{-}z)$$

$$= Z_{xy}(s) + \frac{1}{Y_{yz}(s)} = L_1 s + \frac{1}{C_1 s} + \frac{1}{C_2 s + \dfrac{1}{L_2 s}}$$

$$= L_1 \frac{s^2 + \dfrac{1}{L_1 C_1}}{s} + \frac{s}{C_2\left(s^2 + \dfrac{1}{L_2 C_2}\right)}$$

$$= L_1 \frac{s^2 + \dfrac{1}{L_1 C_1}}{s} + \frac{s/C_2}{\left(s^2 + \dfrac{1}{L_2 C_2}\right)}$$

$$= L_1 \frac{s^4 + \dfrac{s^2}{L_2 C_2} + \dfrac{s^2}{L_1 C_1} + \dfrac{1}{L_1 C_1 L_2 C_2} + \dfrac{s^2}{L_1 C_2}}{s^3 + \dfrac{s}{L_2 C_2}}$$

$$= L_1 \frac{s^4 + s^2\left(\dfrac{1}{L_1 C_1} + \dfrac{1}{L_2 C_2} + \dfrac{1}{L_1 C_2}\right) + \dfrac{1}{L_1 C_1 L_2 C_2}}{s^3 + \dfrac{s}{L_2 C_2}}$$

Thus

$$Z(s) = L_1 \frac{s^4 + s^2\left(\dfrac{1}{L_1 C_1} + \dfrac{1}{L_2 C_2} + \dfrac{1}{L_1 C_2}\right) + \dfrac{1}{L_1 C_1 L_2 C_2}}{\left(s^3 + \dfrac{s}{L_2 C_2}\right)}$$

gives the driving point impedance in s-domain of the given network.

***Example* 18.32** *Find the driving point impedance in Laplace form of the given network across a-b (Fig. E18.9).*

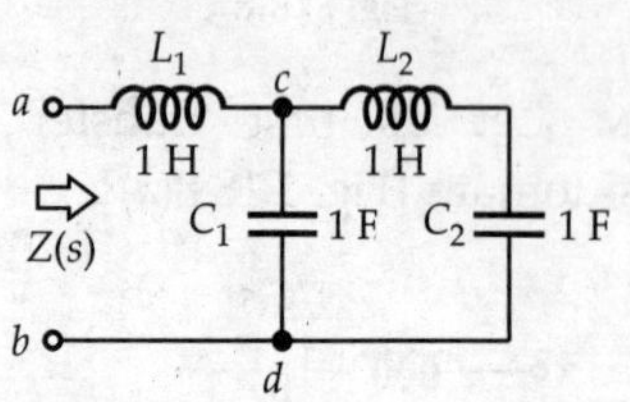

Fig. E18.9

Solution. Transforming the given network in s-domain,

$$Z_{ab}(s) = Z_{L_1}(s) + Z_{c-d}(s) \qquad \text{[Fig. E18.9(a)]}$$

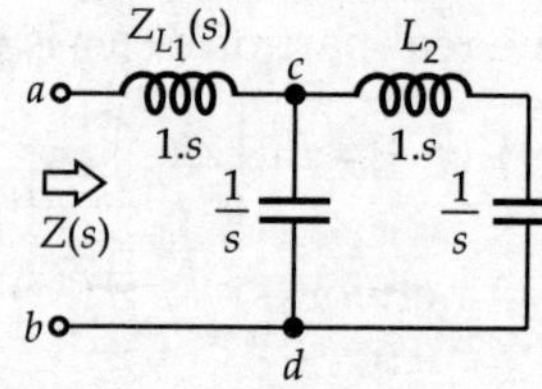

Fig. E18.9 *(a)*

$$\text{where } Z_{c-d}(s) = \left[\left(s + \frac{1}{s}\right) \| \frac{1}{s}\right] = \frac{s\left(s + \dfrac{1}{s}\right)}{s + s + \dfrac{1}{s}}$$

$$= \frac{s\left(s + \dfrac{1}{s}\right)}{2s + \dfrac{1}{s}} = \frac{s(s^2+1)}{2s^2+1}.$$

Also, $Z_{L_1}(s) = s.$

$$\therefore \quad Z_{ab}(s) = s + \frac{s(s^2+1)}{2s^2+1}$$

$$= \frac{2s^3 + s + s^3 + s}{2s^2+1} = \frac{3s^3 + 2s}{2s^2+1}$$

$$= \mathbf{\frac{s\,(3s^2+2)}{2s^2+1}}.$$

***Example* 18.33** *Obtain the value of Z(s) in Fig. E18.10 in s-domain.*

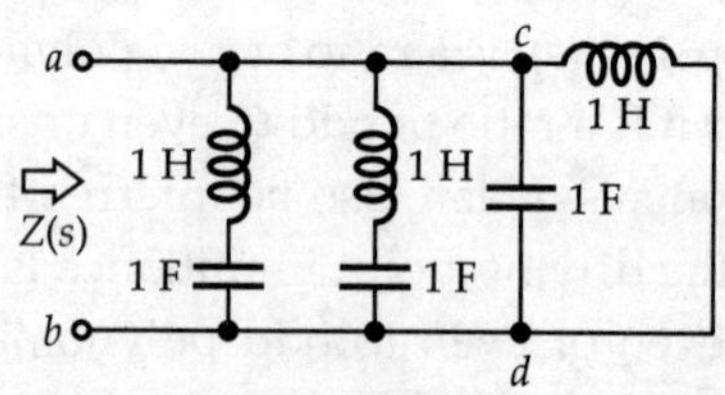

Fig. E18.10

Solution. Let us first transform the given circuit to s-domain [Fig. E18.10(a)]

$$Z(s) = \frac{1}{Y(s)};\; Y(s) = Y_1(s) + Y_2(s) + Y_{c-d}(s)$$

where, $Y_1(s)$ and $Y_2(s)$ are the admittances of individual branches.

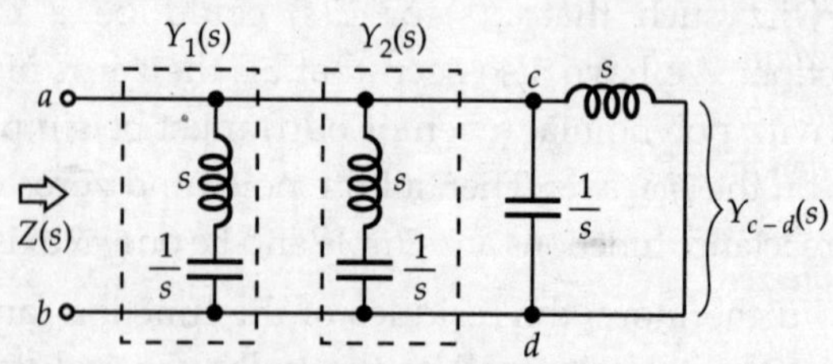

Fig. E18.10 *(a)*

Here,

$$Y_1(s) = Y_2(s) = \frac{1}{Z_1(s)} = \frac{1}{s + \frac{1}{s}} = \frac{s}{s^2 + 1}$$

$$Y_{c-d}(s) = \frac{1}{1/s} + \frac{1}{s} = s + \frac{1}{s} = \frac{s^2 + 1}{s}$$

$$\therefore \quad Y(s) = \frac{s}{s^2+1} + \frac{s}{s^2+1} + \frac{s^2+1}{s}$$

$$= \frac{2s^2 + (s^2+1)^2}{s(s^2+1)}$$

$$= \frac{2s^2 + s^4 + 1 + 2s^2}{s(s^2+1)}$$

$$= \frac{s^4 + 4s^2 + 1}{s^3 + 1}$$

$$\therefore \quad Z(s) = \frac{1}{Y(s)} = \frac{s^3 + 1}{s^4 + 4s^2 + 1}.$$

18.10 POLE ZERO INTERPRETATIONS IN *LC* NETWORKS

The driving point impedance of the *LC* network has been shown to be

$$Z(s) = \frac{a_n s^n + a_{n-2} s^{n-2} + \ldots.. + a_0}{b_m s^m + b_{m-2} s^{m-2} + \ldots. + b_1 s}$$

where n is an even and m is an odd integer.

Let us now consider that $(j\omega)$ (*i.e.*, s), tends to infinity. The above equation then can be written as

$$\lim_{s\to\infty} Z(s) = \lim_{s\to\infty} \frac{a_n s^n}{b_m s^m} \qquad \text{...(18.30)}$$

However, integers m and n can never be equal and differ only by unity at the most.

Hence, at $s \to \infty$, $Z(s)$ approaches zero when $m > n$. $Z(s)$ approaches infinity when $n > m$ *In other words, for a reactive network, in the driving point impedance function if the order of the polynomial in the numerator is greater than the order of the polynomial in the denominator, then there is a simple pole at infinity. On the other hand, if the converse is true, then there is a simple zero at infinity.*

Again, when $(j\omega)$ (*i.e., s*) is very small, only the lowest ordered terms in $Z(s)$ expression are retained and

$$Z(s) = \frac{\ldots.. + a_0 s^2 + a_0}{\ldots.. + b_2 s^2 + b_1 s};$$

when $a_0 \neq 0$,

$$\lim_{s\to 0} Z(s) = \lim_{s\to 0} \frac{H}{s} = +\infty \qquad \text{...[18.30(a)]}$$

i.e., there is a pole at zero frequency.

But with $a_0 = 0$,

$$\lim_{s\to 0} Z(s) = \lim_{s\to 0} Hs = 0 \qquad \text{...[18.30(b)]}$$

Thus, *a zero exists at zero frequency.*

To summarise, for a driving point function, at $\omega \to \infty$, when the order of polynomial in the denominator is higher, a simple zero exists at infinity and if the polynomial of the numerator is higher, a simple pole exists at infinity. On the other hand, when $\omega \to 0$, for the case when the lowest ordered term in the numerator is higher than that in the denominator, there is a simple pole at zero frequency. However for the same condition, when $\omega \to 0$, but the lowest ordered term in the numerator is lesser than that in the denominator, then a zero exists at zero frequency.

EXAMPLE 18.34 *State whether the following functions are driving point immittances of LC network or not :*

$$(a)\ Z(s) = \frac{10(s^2+4)(s^2+6)}{(s^2+1)(s^2+9)},$$

$$(b)\ Z(s) = \frac{5s(s^2+4)}{(s^2+1)(s^2+3)}.$$

SOLUTION. Since *LC* immittance functions are a ratio of either odd to even or even to odd polynomials hence, both the numerator and denominator polynomial should contain the polynomial order differing by unity in the highest and lowest case. However for the function given in (*a*)

$$\left[Z(s) = \frac{10(s^2+4)(s^2+16)}{(s^2+1)(s^2+9)} \right]$$

has same highest power of the polynomial in the numerator and denominator. Thus the **given function cannot be an *LC* function.**

In (*b*) the given function is $\left[Z(s) = \frac{5s(s^2+4)}{(s^2+1)(s^2+3)} \right]$; the poles and zeros do not alternate (even though they are on the $j\omega$). Hence the given **function cannot be an immittance function.**

CHAPTER 18

18.11 *LC* NETWORK SYNTHESIS

Any *LC* network can be synthesized in two forms designated by the names of the proposers *Foster and Cauer*.

18.11.1 Foster's Canonic Form

A positive real impedance Z (*s*) of LC network being a ratio of either even to odd or odd to even polynomials, it can be synthesized by *Foster form. Since the synthesis is performed with the least number of elements hence the synthesis gives birth to a network with* ***least*** *number of LC elements and termed as canomic form of network.*

In Foster synthesis there are two types of networks for realisation of one port reactive networks. The first type is a series combination of parallel *LC* networks while the other is the parallel combination of series LC networks. (Figs. 18.14 and 18.15)

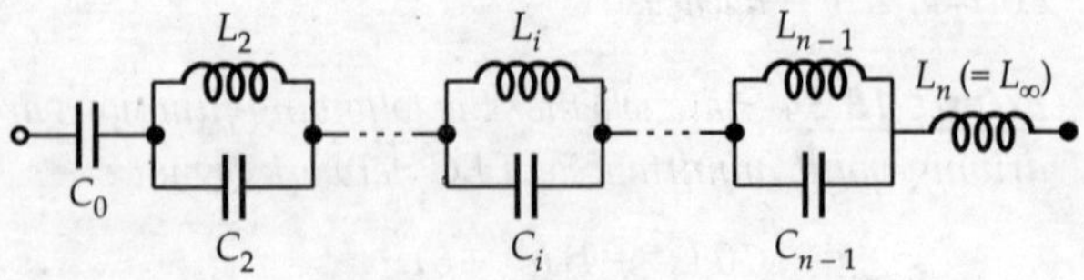

Fig. 18.14 First form of Foster *LC* network (Impedance Form).

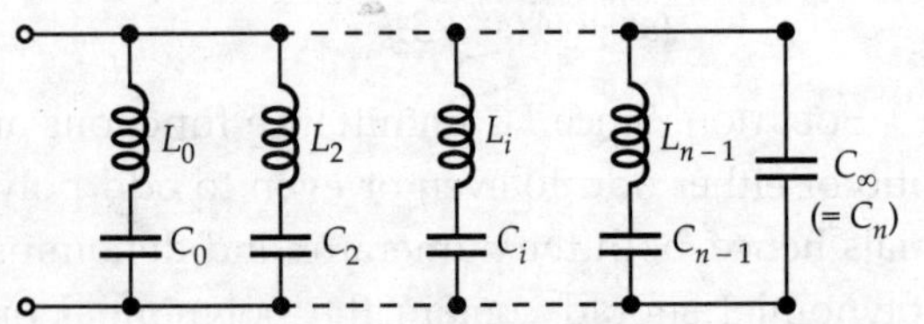

Fig. 18.15 Second form of Foster *LC* network (Admittance Form).

$Z(s)$ is a *PR* function, having simple poles at $j\omega$ axis $[s = \pm j\omega_i, i = 1, 2, \ldots, m]$ as well as simple poles at $s = 0$ and $s = \infty$, using partial fraction, $Z(s)$ can be expressed as

$$Z(s) = \frac{A_0}{s} + \sum_{i=2}^{n-1} \frac{2A_i s}{s^2 + \omega_i^2} + H.s \qquad \text{...(18.31)}$$

when the constituent terms in $Z(s)$ can be interpreted as

(*a*) $\frac{A_0}{s}$ results from a possible pole at $s = 0$ [$\frac{A_0}{s}$ is the first term]

(*b*) $H.s$ results from a possible pole at $s = \infty$ [$H.s$ is the last (*n*th) term]

(*c*) $\frac{2A_i s}{s^2 + \omega_i^2}$ results from a pair of conjugate poles on the $j\omega$ axis and obviously,

$$\frac{2A_i s}{s^2 + \omega_i^2} = \frac{A_i'}{s + j\omega_i} + \frac{A_i'}{s - j\omega_i}$$

$$= \frac{(A_i + A_i')s - j(A_i - A_i')\omega_i}{s^2 + \omega_i^2} \qquad \text{...(18.32)}$$

In order that they give a real term after combination, it is essential that the residues A_i and A_i' must be equal.

Following Fig. 18.14, for the parallel combination of *L, C*,

$$Z(s) = \frac{1}{Cs + \frac{1}{Ls}}$$

i.e.,

$$Z(s) = \frac{\left(\frac{1}{C}\right)s}{s^2 + \frac{1}{LC}} \qquad \text{...(18.33)}$$

However, from equation (18.31),

$$Z(s) = \frac{A_0}{s} + \frac{2A_2 s}{s^2 + \omega_2^2} + \ldots + \frac{2A_{n-1} s}{s^2 + \omega_{n-1}^2} + H.s \qquad \text{...(18.34)}$$

Also, $Z(s) = Z_1(s) + Z_2(s) + \ldots + Z_n(s)$ ...(18.35)

Comparing equations (18.34) and (18.35),

$$Z_1(s) = \frac{A_0}{s} \qquad \text{...(18.36)}$$

$$Z_n(s) = H.s \qquad \text{...(18.37)}$$

It is evident that equation (18.36) represents that $Z_1(s)$ *is an impedance representing a capacitor* C_0 *of value* $(1/A_0)$ and from equation (18.37), it is evident that $Z_n(s)$ *represents an inductor of inductance H henry* (L_∞). *The remaining intermediate terms represent parallel combination of an inductor and a capacitor*. Comparing Eq. (18.33) with the mid-terms of equation (18.31), we get,

$$C_i = \frac{1}{2A_i} \text{ and } L_i = \frac{2A_i}{\omega_i^2} \qquad \text{...(18.38)}$$

[*i*th term refers to $(2A_i s / s^2 + \omega_i^2)$ in equation (18.31)].

The above realisation is known as First *Form of Foster Realisation of LC network.*

The *second form of Foster network is a parallel combination of series LC networks* (Fig. 18.15). As all the series branches are connected in parallel, it is convenient to consider the driving point admittance ($Y(s)$).

If we write the expression for *LC* series combination,

$$Y_{\text{series}}(s)=\frac{1}{Ls+\frac{1}{Cs}}=\frac{(s/L)}{s^2+\frac{1}{LC}} \quad ...(18.39)$$

However equation (18.31) can be written as

$$Y(s)=\frac{B_0}{s}+\frac{2B_2\,s}{s^2+\omega_2^2}+...+\frac{2B_i\,s}{s^2+\omega_i^2}+...$$
$$+\frac{2B_{n-1}\,s}{s^2+\omega_{n-1}^2}+H.s \quad ....(18.40)$$

[n refers to the term $(2B_n s/s^2+\omega_n^2)$ in eqn. (18.40)].

Also, if we take the total admittance into a parallel combination of branch admittances,

$$Y(s)=Y_1(s)+Y_2(s)+....+Y_n(s) \quad ...(18.41)$$

Comparing equations (18.40) and (18.41), $Y_1(s)=(B_0/s)$ *represent an inductor* L_0 of value $(1/B_0)$ while $Y_n(s)=Hs$, *represents a capacitor* C_∞ *of value H Farad. The intermediate terms represent series combination of an inductor and capacitor*. By comparing eqns. (18.39) and (18.40), we have

$$L_i=\frac{1}{2B_i};\;C_i=\frac{2B_i}{\omega_i^2}$$

18.12 SIGNIFICANCE OF ELEMENTS IN THE FOSTER FORM

First Foster Form

(*a*) The capacitor C_0 represents the term $\left(\frac{A_0}{s}\right)$ that corresponds to a pole at the origin.

(*b*) The inductor L_∞ represents the term *Hs* that corresponds to a pole at the infinity.

(*c*) The parallel $L_i\,C_i$ networks represent the term $(s^2+\omega_i^2)$ in the denominator of $Z(s)$. ω_i, the frequency represents a pole frequency. Parallel resonance of L_i and C_i would result in a pole of $Z(s)$. Reactance of each parallel circuit changes sign as frequency increases and at some frequency the reactance of a certain group of these parallel circuits is equal and opposite to the reactance of all remaining parallel circuits. This results in a zero of $Z(s)$.

(*d*) When there is no *s* term in the denominator of $Z(s)$, there will be no $\left(\frac{A_0}{s}\right)$ term in the partial fraction expansion of $Z(s)$. C_0 is absent and replaced by short circuit.

Again, when the order of the numerator polynomial is less than that of the denominator polynomial, there will be no (*Hs*) factor in the partial expansion fraction of $Z(s)$ and hence there would be no inductor L_0 in the circuit. L_0 will then be replaced by a short circuit.

Second Foster Form

(*a*) The inductor L_0 represents the term $\left(\frac{B_0}{s}\right)$ in the partial fraction form of $Y(s)$ corresponding a pole at the origin.

(*b*) The capacitor C_∞ represents the term (*Hs*) corresponding a pole at infinity.

(*c*) The series $L_i\,C_i$ network represents the term $(s^2+\omega_i^2)$ in the denominator of $Y(s)$. Frequency ω_n represents a pole frequency that is associated with series resonance of the *LC* network. Series resonance within these *LC* combinations causes the network to have a pole of admittance. Susceptance of series circuit changes sign as frequency increases. At some frequency the susceptance of a certain group of these series circuits is equal and opposite to that of the remaining series circuits. This yields a zero of $Y(s)$.

(*d*) In case there is no pole either at $\omega=0$ or at $\omega=\infty$, or at both, the presence of zero is signified with absence of end elements. The second form of Foster network can then be realised by the absence of C_0 and L_∞, the first and end elements.

To conclude with the discussion about the two forms of Foster networks, it may be said that the first form of realisation is actually the series impedance realisation of the driving point impedance $Z(s)$. The second form is a parallel admittance realisation of driving point admittance $Y(s)$. $Y(s)$ can be obtained by inversion of $Z(s)$. However, this process of inversion interchanges poles and zeros.

To summarise, we thus can say that if there is a pole at $\omega = 0$, the first element C_0 is present in the network of first Foster form. Similarly, if there is a pole at $\omega = \infty$, the last element L_∞ is present in it. In the second form of network, if there is a pole at $\omega = 0$, the first element L_0 is present while for $\omega = \infty$, the last element C_∞ is present.

EXAMPLE 18.35 *The driving point impedance of an LC network is given by*

$$Z(s) = 10\,\frac{(s^2+4)(s^2+16)}{s(s^2+9)}$$

Obtain the first form of Foster network.

SOLUTION. Observation reveals that there is s^4 term in the numerator while s^3 term in denominator. Since the numerator contains an excess term, while the denominator has one s term, hence two poles exist at $\omega = 0$ and at $\omega = \infty$. Thus, the network consists of first and last element in the Foster first form.

By taking the partial fraction expansion of $Z(s)$, we find

$$Z(s) = \frac{A_0}{s} + \frac{A_2}{s+j3} + \frac{A_2^*}{s-j3} + Hs$$

where

$$A_0 = \left.\frac{10(s^2+4)(s^2+16)}{(s^2+9)}\right|_{s=0}$$

$$= \frac{10\times 4\times 16}{9} = 71.11$$

$$A_2 = \left.\frac{10(s^2+4)(s^2+16)}{s(s-j3)}\right|_{s=-j3}$$

$$= \frac{10[\{(-j3)^2+4\}\{(-j3)^2+16\}]}{(-j3)(-j3-j3)}$$

$$= 10\left[\frac{(-9+4)(-9+16)}{-18}\right]$$

$$= \frac{350}{18} = 19.45$$

$$\therefore \quad C_0 = \frac{1}{A_0} = \frac{1}{71.11}\,F = 0.0141\ \text{F}$$

$$L_\infty = H = 10\ \text{H}$$

By inspection, the constant multiplier term is 10 *i.e.*, $H = 10$

$$C_2 = \frac{1}{2A_2} = \frac{1}{2\times 19.45} = 0.0257\ \text{F}$$

$$L_2 = \frac{2A_2}{\omega_n^2} = \frac{2\times 19.45}{3^2}$$

[$\omega_n = 3$ since the denominator contains s^2+3^2 in the form of $s^2+\omega_n^2$]

$$= 4.322\ \text{H.}$$

The first form of Foster network is shown in Fig. E18.11.

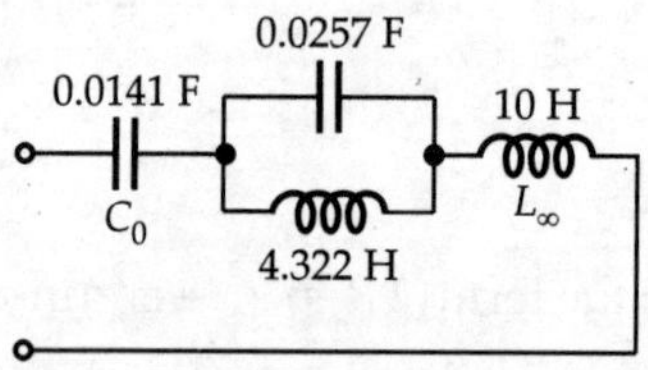

Fig. E18.11

EXAMPLE 18.36 *Find the second Foster Form of the admittance function :*

$$Y(s) = \frac{s(s^2+9)}{10(s^2+4)(s^2+25)}.$$

SOLUTION. Since there is an s term in the numerator and an excess term in the denominator than in the numerator, two zeros exist at $\omega = 0$ and $\omega = \infty$. Thus, there is no question of first and last element and the given network consists of LC combinations of parallel elements.

$$Y(s) = \frac{2B_1 s}{s^2+4} + \frac{2B_2 s}{s^2+25}$$

$$B_1 = \left.\frac{1}{10}\frac{s(s^2+9)}{(s-j2)(s^2+25)}\right|_{s=-j2}$$

$$= \frac{1}{10}\frac{-j2(-4+9)}{(-j4)(-4+25)} = \frac{1}{10}\cdot\frac{-10}{-84} = \frac{1}{84}$$

$$B_2 = \left.\frac{1}{10}\frac{s(s^2+9)}{(s^2+4)(s-j5)}\right|_{s=-j5}$$

$$= \frac{1}{10}\frac{(-j5)(-25+9)}{(-25+4)(-j10)} = \frac{1}{10}\frac{80}{210} = \frac{1}{26.25}.$$

∴ The values of elements in the 2nd form of Foster network,

$$L_1 = \frac{1}{2B_1} = 42 \text{ H}$$

$$C_1 = \frac{2B_1}{\omega_1^2} = \frac{2 \times 1/84}{2^2} = \frac{1}{168} \text{ F}$$

$$L_2 = \frac{1}{2B_2} = 26.25/2 = 13.125 \text{ H}$$

$$C_2 = \frac{2B_2}{\omega_2^2} = \frac{2 \times 1/26.25}{5^2} = \frac{2}{656.25} \text{ F.}$$

Figure E18.12 represents the second form of Foster network.

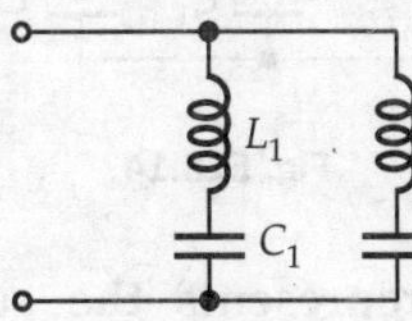

Fig. E18.12

EXAMPLE 18.37 *The driving point impedance of a one port LC network is given by*

$$Z(s) = \frac{2\,(s^2+9)\,(s^2+16)}{s\,(s^2+4)}$$

Obtain the Foster form of LC network realisation.

SOLUTION. Observation of the expression of $Z(s)$ reveals that there is a s^4 term in the numerator while there is only s^3 term in the denominator. Since the numerator has one excess term while the denominator has one s term, hence two poles exist at $\omega = 0$ and at $\omega = \infty$. The given network thus consists of first and last elements in the first form of Foster network.

The partial fraction expansion gives

$$Z(s) = \frac{A_0}{s} + \frac{A_2}{s+j2} + \frac{A_2^*}{s-j2} + Hs$$

where, $$A_0 = \left.\frac{2\,(s^2+9)(s^2+16)}{s^2+4}\right|_{s=0}$$

$$= \frac{2 \times 9 \times 16}{4} = 72$$

$$A_2 = \left.\frac{2\,(s^2+9)(s^2+16)}{s(s-j2)}\right|_{s=-j2}$$

$$= \frac{2\,(-4+9)(-4+16)}{(-j2)(-j4)}$$

$$= \frac{2 \times 5 \times (12)}{-8} = -15$$

Since A_2 has come out to be –ve hence Foster realisation is not possible.

As per Foster realisation, the coefficients of the partial fraction expansion must be real and +ve. Also the poles and zeros of $Z(s)$ do not interlace and hence $Z(s)$ is not basically an LC function.

EXAMPLE 18.38 *The driving point impedance of a one port LC network is given by*

$$Z(s) = \frac{8\,(s^2+4)\,(s^2+25)}{s\,(s^2+16)}$$

Obtain the first and second Foster form of equivalent networks.

SOLUTION. Since the order of the numerator polynomial exceeds that of the denominator polynomial hence there is a simple pole at $\omega = \infty$. On the other hand, the lowest order term of the numerator is of order lower than that of the denominator. Hence there is a simple pole at $\omega = 0$. This indicates that both first and last elements would be present.

Thus, the partial fraction expansion gives

$$Z(s) = \frac{A_0}{s} + \frac{A_2}{s+j4} + \frac{A_2^*}{s-j4} + Hs$$

Here, $$A_0 = \left.\frac{8\,(s^2+4)(s^2+25)}{s^2+16}\right|_{s=0}$$

$$= \frac{8 \times 4 \times 25}{16} = 50$$

$$A_2 = \left.\frac{8\,(s^2+4)(s^2+25)}{s(s-j4)}\right|_{s=-j4}$$

$$= \frac{8\,(-16+4)(-16+25)}{-j4 \times -j8}$$

$$= \frac{8 \times (-12) \times 9}{-32} = 27$$

By inspection, $H = 8$.

CHAPTER 18

$\therefore$ In the first form of Foster network,

$$C_0 = \frac{1}{A_0} = \frac{1}{50} \text{ Farad}$$

$$L_\infty = H = 8 \text{ Henry}$$

$$C_2 = \frac{1}{2A_2} = \frac{1}{54} \text{ Fared}$$

$$L_2 = \frac{2A_2}{\omega_n^2} = \frac{54}{4^2} = 3.375 \text{ Henry.}$$

Figure E18.13 represents the first form of Foster network.

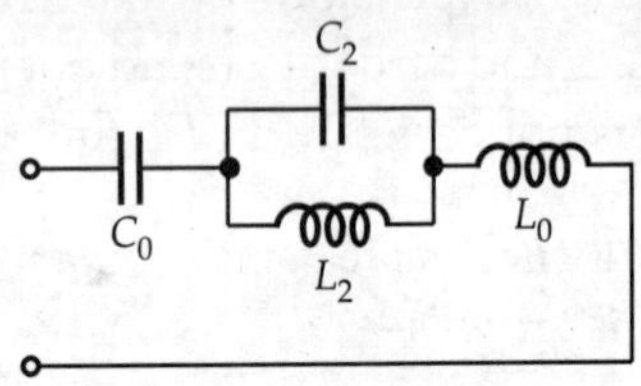

Fig. E18.13

In order to find the second Foster form, we shall have to represent the given function into admittance form.

$$Y(s) = \frac{s(s^2+16)}{8(s^2+4)(s^2+25)}$$

Since there is one s term in the numerator and an excess term in the denominator than in the numerator, two zeros exist at $\omega = 0$ and at $\omega = \infty$. Thus, the given network is only a LC parallel combination. The presence of zero indicates that there would be no end elements in the 2nd form of Foster Network. The partial fraction expansion is then

$$Y(s) = \frac{2B_1 s}{s^2+4} + \frac{2B_2 s}{s^2+25}$$

$$B_1 = \frac{1}{8} \cdot \frac{s(s^2+16)}{(s-j2)(s^2+25)}\bigg|_{s=-j2}$$

$$= \frac{-j2 \times 12}{8(-j4 \times 21)} = \frac{24}{84 \times 8} = 0.0357$$

$$B_2 = \frac{1}{8} \frac{s(s^2+16)}{(s^2+4)(s-j5)}\bigg|_{s=-j5}$$

$$= \frac{1}{8} \frac{-j5 \times (-9)}{-21 \times -j10} = 0.027$$

$\therefore$ The values of elements in the 2nd form are then

$$L_1 = \frac{1}{2B_1} = \frac{1}{0.0714} \text{ Henry}$$

$$C_1 = \frac{2B_1}{\omega_1^2} = \frac{2 \times 0.0357}{2^2} = 0.0178 \text{ F}$$

$$L_2 = \frac{1}{2B_2} = \frac{1}{2 \times 0.027} = 18.52 \text{ Henry}$$

$$C_2 = \frac{2B_2}{\omega_2^2} = \frac{2 \times 0.027}{5^2} = 0.00216 \text{ Farad.}$$

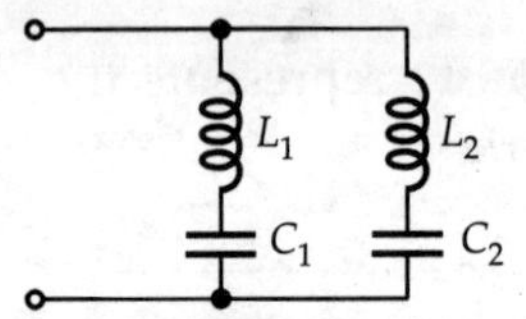

Fig. E18.14

Fig. E18.14 represents the second form of Foster network.

EXAMPLE 18.39 *The driving point impedance of a one port reactive network is given by*

$$Z(s) = 4\frac{s(s^2+4)}{(s^2+1)(s^2+16)}$$

Obtain the Foster forms of LC network realisation.

SOLUTION. Observation reveals that the order of the numerator is less than that of the denominator [in numerator the order is s^3 while in denominator it is s^4]. Hence there is a simple zero at $\omega = \infty$. Further, the lowest ordered term in the numerator is of higher order than the lowest order term of the denominator. Thus there is a simple zero at $\omega = 0$. This indicates that in the first form of the Foster network, there will be no end elements. *i.e.,* there will be no (A_0/s) term and (Hs) terms in the partial fraction expansion.

The partial fraction of $Z(s)$ becomes,

$$Z(s) = \frac{2A_1 s}{s^2+1} + \frac{2A_2 s}{s^2+4^2}.$$

Here $$A_1 = \frac{4s(s^2+4)}{(s-j1)(s^2+16)}\bigg|_{s=-j1}$$

$$= \frac{4(-j1)(-1+4)}{-j2(-1+16)} = \frac{12}{30} = \frac{2}{5} = 0.4.$$

$$A_2 = \left.\frac{4s(s^2+4)}{(s^2+1)(s-j4)}\right|_{s=-j4}$$

$$= \frac{4(-j4)(-16+4)}{(-16+1)(-j8)}$$

$$= \frac{4\times(-j4)(-12)}{(-15)(-j8)} = 1.6.$$

$\therefore$ In Foster first form,

$$C_1 = \frac{1}{2A_1} = \frac{1}{0.8}\text{ F}$$

$$L_1 = \frac{2A_1}{\omega_1^2} = \frac{2\times 0.4}{1^2} = 0.8\text{ H}$$

$$C_2 = \frac{1}{2A_2} = \frac{1}{2\times 1.6} = \frac{1}{3.2}\text{ F}$$

$$L_2 = \frac{2A_2}{\omega_2^2} = \frac{2\times 1.6}{4^2} = 0.2\text{ H.}$$

Figure E18.15 represents Foster first form of network.

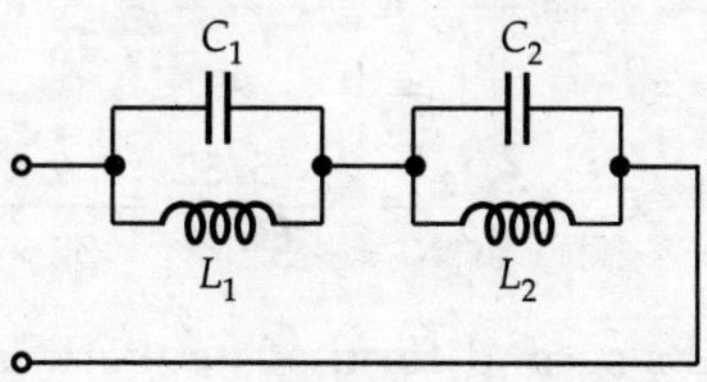

Fig. E18.15

In order to determine the second Foster form, first we consider the admittance function $Y(s)$.

$$Y(s) = \frac{1}{Z(s)} = \frac{(s^2+1)(s^2+16)}{4s(s^2+4)}$$

The numerator polynomial is of order s^4 and the denominator polynomial is of order s^3. The numerator has one excess term and the denominator has s term. Thus the given function has two poles at $\omega=0$ and $\omega=\infty$. The given network would then contain the end elements in the Foster second form.

The partial fraction expansion gives

$$Y(s) = \frac{B_0}{s} + \frac{B_2}{s+j2} + \frac{B_2^*}{s-j2} + Hs$$

$$B_0 = \left.\frac{(s^2+1)(s^2+16)}{4(s^2+4)}\right|_{s=0} = 1$$

$$B_2 = \left.\frac{(s^2+1)(s^2+16)}{4s(s-j2)}\right|_{s=-j2}$$

$$= \frac{(-4+1)(-4+16)}{4\times(-j2)(-j4)}$$

$$= \frac{-3\times 12}{-32} = 1.125.$$

By observation of $Y(s)$, $H = \frac{1}{4} = 0.25$

$$\therefore \quad L_0 = \frac{1}{B_0} = 1\text{ H}$$

$$C_\infty = H = 0.25\text{ F}$$

$$L_2 = \frac{1}{2B_2} = \frac{1}{2\times 1.125} = \frac{1}{2.25}\text{ H}$$

$$C_2 = \frac{2B_2}{\omega_2^2} = \frac{2\times 1.125}{2^2} = 0.5625\text{ F.}$$

Figure E18.16 represents the second form of Foster network.

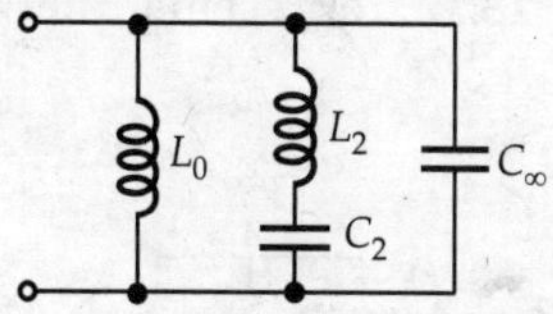

Fig. E18.16

Example 18.40 *Find the first and second Foster form of the driving point impedance function*

$$Z(s) = \frac{2(s^2+1)(s^2+9)}{s(s^2+4)}$$

Solution. Since the order of the numerator polynomial exceeds that of the denominator polynomial hence there is a simple pole at $\omega=\infty$. On the other hand, the lowest order term of the numerator is of the order lower than that of the denominator. Hence there is a simple pole at $\omega=0$. Thus there would be first and last elements present in the first form of Foster Network.

Thus, the partial expansion gives

$$Z(s) = \frac{A_0}{s} + \frac{A_2}{s+j2} + \frac{A_2^*}{s-j2} + Hs$$

where, $$A_0 = \left.\frac{2(s^2+1)(s^2+9)}{s^2+4}\right|_{s=0} = \frac{2\times 9}{4} = 4.5$$

$$A_2 = \left.\frac{2(s^2+1)(s^2+9)}{s(s-j2)}\right|_{s=-j2}$$

$$= \frac{2(-4+1)(-4+9)}{(-j2)\times(-j4)}$$

$$= \frac{-3\times 2\times 5}{-8} = 3.75$$

By inspection, $H = 2$

$\therefore$ In the first form of Foster network,

$$C_0 = \frac{1}{A_0} = \frac{1}{4.5}\ \text{F}$$

$$L_\infty = \text{H} = 2\ \text{Henry}$$

$$C_2 = \frac{1}{2A_2} = \frac{1}{2\times 3.75} = \frac{1}{7.5}\ \text{F}$$

$$L_2 = \frac{2A_2}{\omega_2^2} = \frac{2\times 3.75}{2^2} = 1.875\ \text{H}.$$

Figure E18.17 represents the first form of Foster network.

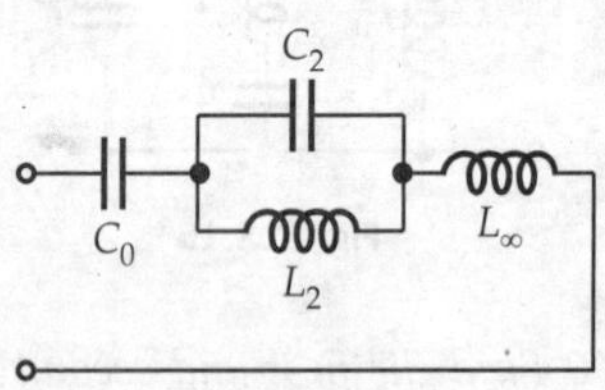

Fig. E18.17

In order to find the second Foster form, we will represent the given function into admittance form.

$$Y(s) = \frac{s(s^2+4)}{2(s^2+1)(s^2+9)}.$$

Since there is one s term in the numerator and an excess term in the denominator than in the numerator, two zeros exist at $\omega = 0$ and at $\omega = \infty$. Thus, the given network is simply a LC parallel combination. The presence of zero indicates that there would be no end elements in the second form of network.

The partial fraction expansion is then

$$Y(s) = \frac{2B_1 s}{s^2+1} + \frac{2B_2 s}{s^2+25}$$

where $$B_1 = \left.\frac{1}{2}\cdot\frac{s(s^2+4)}{(s-j1)(s^2+9)}\right|_{s=-j1}$$

$$= \frac{1}{2}\frac{(-j1)(-1+4)}{(-j2)(-1+9)} = \frac{3}{32}$$

$$B_2 = \left.\frac{1}{2}\frac{s(s^2+4)}{(s^2+1)(s-j3)}\right|_{s=-j3}$$

$$= \frac{1}{2}\frac{(-j3)(-9+4)}{(-9+1)(-j6)}$$

$$= \frac{15}{48\times 2} = \frac{15}{96} = \frac{5}{32}.$$

The values of elements in the second form are thus

$$L_1 = \frac{1}{2B_1} = \frac{16}{3}\ \text{H}$$

$$L_2 = \frac{1}{2B_2} = 3.2\ \text{H}$$

$$C_1 = \frac{2B_1}{\omega_1^2} = \frac{2\times 3/32}{1} = \frac{3}{16}\ \text{F}$$

$$C_2 = \frac{2B_2}{\omega_2^2} = \frac{2\times 5/32}{5^2} = \frac{2\times 5}{32\times 5^2} = \frac{1}{80}\ \text{F}.$$

Foster's second form of network is shown in Fig. E18.18.

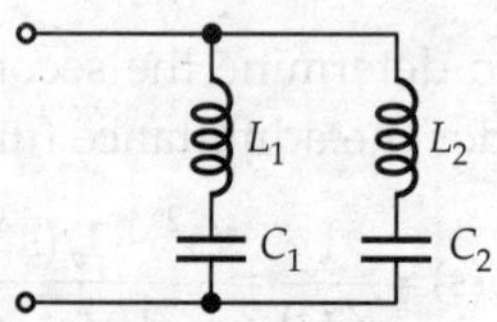

Fig. E18.18

18.13 CAUER CANONIC FORM OF REACTIVE NETWORKS

W. Cauer, in 1927 introduced realisation of one port LC networks in two configurations (commonly known as *Cauer-I and Cauer-II* forms) *using the*

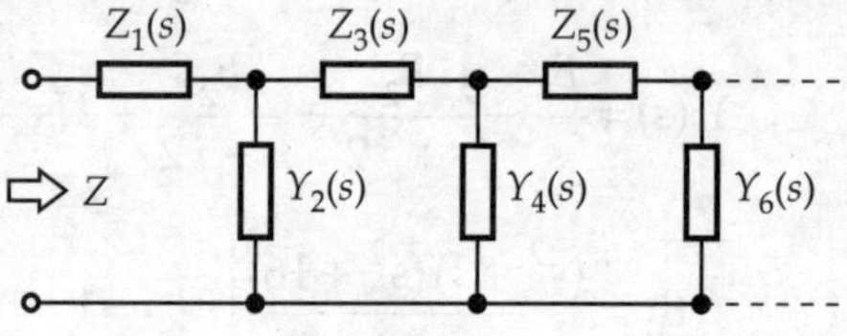

Fig. 18.16 Ladder Network.

continued fraction expansion of the driving point impedance. The basic form of the Cauer realisation being a ladder type network, the driving point impedance of this network (Fig. 18.16) may be represented in the form of continued fraction as

$$Z(s) = Z_1(s) + \cfrac{1}{Y_2(s) + \cfrac{1}{Z_3(s) + \cfrac{1}{Y_4(s) + \cfrac{1}{Z_5(s) + \ldots}}}} \qquad \text{..(18.42)}$$

The driving point impedance is expressed as

$$Z(s) = \frac{a_n s^n + a_{n-2} s^{n-2} + \ldots}{b_m s^m + b_{m-2} s^{m-2} + \ldots} \qquad \text{...(18.43)}$$

where n is even and m is odd. First form of realisation is possible with either pole at infinity $(\omega = \infty)$ or with zero at infinity $(\omega = \infty)$. If $n > m$, a pole is evident at $\omega = \infty$ and it is possible to represent $Z(s)$ in the continued function form *by dividing the numerator by denominator, inverting and dividing until the expansion terminates.* Cauer considered, in its first form, the ladder network to be having series arm with inductors and shunt arm with capacitors. This form of realisation is represented in equation (18.44) and Fig. 18.17.

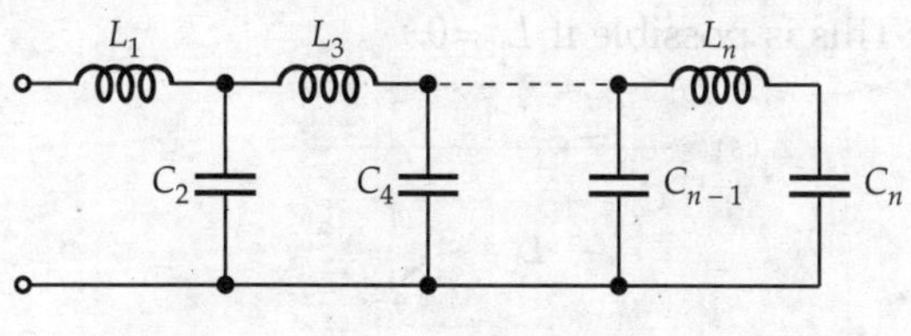

Fig. 18.17 First form of Cauer realisation with pole at $\omega = \infty$ (*i.e.*, $n > m$).

$$\text{Here,} \quad Z(s) = L_1 s + \cfrac{1}{C_2 s + \cfrac{1}{L_3 s + \cfrac{1}{C_4 s + \ldots}}} \qquad \text{...(18.44)}$$

[*i.e., the inductors are connected in series while the capacitors are connected in shunt*]

On the other hand, in equation (18.42) if $n < m$, *i.e.*, the order of the polynomial of the denominator is more than that of the numerator, a zero appears at infinity $(\omega = \infty)$. The continued fraction expansion can now be performed *by inverting the driving point function.* In this case, *the continued fraction will give a capacitive admittance as first element and then a series inductance.* The form of expansion is then,

$$Z(s) = \cfrac{1}{Y_2(s) + \cfrac{1}{Z_3(s) + \cfrac{1}{Y_4(s) + \cfrac{1}{Z_5(s) + \ldots}}}} \qquad \text{...(18.45)}$$

Comparing equation (18.42) with (18.45), it is evident that only difference between the two is that in (18.45), $Z_1(s) = 0$. *Since $Z_1(s) = 0$, the first series inductance is absent.* It is also evident from eqn. (18.44) that with $s \to \infty$, if $Z(s)$ is to be zero, it is only possible iff $L_1 = 0$. *Thus, the first element in this form of Cauer network is a shunt capacitor.* Thus we see that *if $Z(s)$ expression is in form of equation (18.43), $n > m$, a pole exists at $\omega = \infty$ denoting the first element in the Cauer network of form one to be a series inductor.*

On the other hand, in the expression of (18.43), if $m > n$, a zero exists at $\omega = \infty$ denoting the first element in the Cauer network (form-1) to be a shunt capacitor.

In a similar way, if a zero appears in $Z(s)$ [expression (18.43)] with $\omega = 0$, it implies an inductor as the last element. A pole, appearing in $Z(s)$, with $\omega = 0$, implies the capacitor as last element [as capacitor offers infinite impedance *i.e.*, open circuit at $\omega = 0$ indicating termination].

To summarise, Cauer-I first form, network can be realised by pole zero configuration of driving point function where, for $n > m$, pole appears at $\omega = \infty$ which represents the first element to be a series inductor. In the same expression zero appears with $\omega = 0$ indicating the last element to be an inductor. On the other hand, for $m > n$, zero appears for $\omega = \infty$ indicating the first element to be a shunt capacitor and pole appears with $\omega = 0$ indicating the last element to be capacitor.

The second form of ladder network developed by Cauer consists of capacitors in the series arms and inductors in the shunt arms. Thus in the expression of (18.42), for Cauer-II network, the impedance of the first element is $Z_1(s) = 1/C_1 s$, while the admittance of the second element in shunt path is $Y_2(s) = \frac{1}{L_2 s}$. The continued fraction expansion is then obtained as

$$Z(s)=\frac{1}{C_1 s}+\cfrac{1}{\cfrac{1}{L_2 s}+\cfrac{1}{\cfrac{1}{C_3 s}+\cfrac{1}{(1/L_4 s)+.....}}}$$
...(18.46)

It may be noted down here that since we considered the value of $\omega=\infty$ that makes $s\to\infty$ in the expression of $Z(s)$ in the First Cauer form (Cauer-I) in order to determine pole zero configuration, the continued fraction is performed with the numerator and the denominator polynomial both in descending order. On the other hand, here the function is considered for $\omega=0$ making $s\to 0$. *Thus in the Second Cauer form (Cauer-II), the continued fraction expansion is to be performed with the numerator and denominator, both polynomials in ascending order.*

We have earlier seen that if the lowest ordered term of the numerator is higher order than that of the denominator, the driving point impedance becomes zero with $s\to 0$ (*i.e.*, $\omega=0$). A simple zero appears at zero frequency. Thus, with $s\to 0$, $Z(s)$ to be zero, from equation (18.46), it is evident that C_1 must be zero. On the other hand, for the case when the lowest ordered term in the denominator is greater than that in the numerator, the driving point impedance function becomes infinity for $s\to 0$ (*i.e.*, $\omega=0$). Thus a pole appears at zero. Here, if $Z(s)$ is to be infinity at $s\to 0$, a capacitor C_1 must appear as the first series element of the network as is evident from eqn. (18.46).

Next, with $\omega=\infty$ since a capacitor offers zero impedance, thus, with $\omega=\infty$ (*i.e.*, with $s\to\infty$) if $Z(s)$ gives a pole ($Z(s)$ becoming infinity), the end termination of the second form of Cauer network is an inductor. On the other hand, with $\omega=\infty$, s being turning to ∞, if $Z(s)$ becomes zero *i.e.*, a zero appears in $Z(s)$, it indicates the last element to be a capacitor.

Article 18.13.1 represents the first element and end element determination concepts with respect to pole zero configuration of the first form as well as the same for the second form.

18.13.1 Summary of Cauer form of Realisation of *LC* Network

First form of Cauer Network

[Cauer proposed the first form to have L in series and C in shunt in the ladder pattern].

$$Z(s)=\frac{a_n s^n + a_{n-2} s^{n-2} + ... + a_0}{b_m s^m + b_{m-2} s^{m-2} + ... + b_1 s}$$

$$\therefore \quad \lim_{s\to\infty}\frac{a_n s^n}{b_m s^m}\begin{cases}=\infty \text{ if } n>m\\ =0 \text{ if } m>n\end{cases}$$

(*i*) $\underset{s\to\infty}{Z(s)}\to\infty$ if $n>m$ [Fig. 18.18(*a*)]

$\therefore$ Pole is formed at $s\to\infty$. This gives L_1 having finite value and

$$Z(s)=L_1 s+\cfrac{1}{C_2 s+\cfrac{1}{L_3 s+\cfrac{1}{C_4 s+....}}}$$

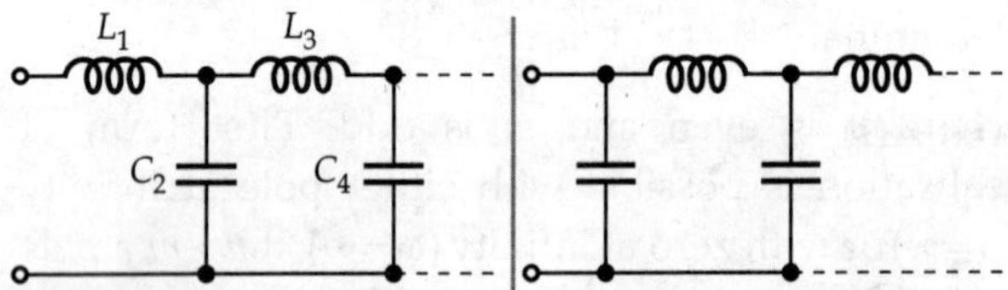

(*a*) 1st series element = L_1 (*b*) 1st shunt element = C_2 (No first series element L_1)

Fig. 18.18 First element representation in Cauer first form [at $\omega=\infty$ *i.e.*, at $s\to\infty$].

(*ii*) $\underset{s\to\infty}{Z(s)}\to 0$ if $n<m$, [Fig. 18.18(*b*)]

$\therefore$ Zero is formed at $s\to\infty$

This is possible if $L_1=0$.

i.e.,
$$Z(s)=\cfrac{1}{C_2 s+\cfrac{1}{L_3 s+\cfrac{1}{C_4 s}....}}$$

Last term determination of Cauer *L-C* type network in its first form, has been explained in Fig. 18.19.

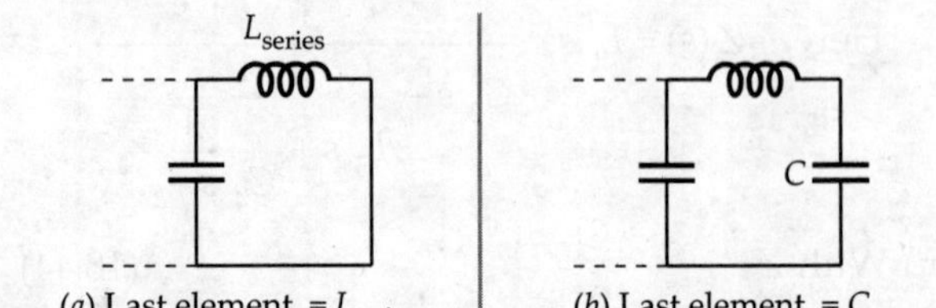

(*a*) Last element = L_{series} (If $Z(s)$ is zero with $\omega=0$, *i.e.*, for $s\to 0$, the inductive path is conductive. Thus the last element is inductor when $Z(s)$ gives a zero at $\omega=0$)

(*b*) Last element = C (If $Z(s)$ is infinity with $\omega=0$, *i.e.*, when $s\to 0$, a pole appears with $Z(s)$. This indicates that a capacitor is present as ending element of the network.)

Fig. 18.19 Last element determination in Cauer first form [at $s\to 0$].

Second Form of Cauer Network

[Cauer proposed the second form to have C in series and L in shunt in the ladder pattern].

$$\left[Z(s) = \frac{a_n s^n + a_{n-2} s^{n-2} + \ldots + a_0}{b_m s^m + b_{m-2} s^{m-2} + \ldots\ldots + b_1 s} \right]$$

$$\therefore \quad \lim_{s \to 0} Z(s) = \lim_{s \to 0} \frac{H}{s} = \infty \text{ when } a_0 \neq 0$$

(lowest ordered term in the polynomial of the denominator is higher than that of the numerator).

$$\text{Also,} \quad \lim_{s \to 0} Z(s) = \lim_{s \to 0} Hs = 0 \quad \text{when } a_0 = 0$$

(*i.e.*, the lowest ordered term in the polynomial of the numerator is higher than that of the denominator).

(*i*) If $Z(s) \to \infty$, with $s \to 0$ a pole appears in $Z(s)$ and since

$$Z(s) = \frac{1}{C_1 s} + \cfrac{1}{\cfrac{1}{L_2 s} + \cfrac{1}{\cfrac{1}{C_3 s} + \cfrac{1}{L_4 s + \ldots}}}$$

hence C_1 must have some definite value [Fig. 18.20(*a*)].

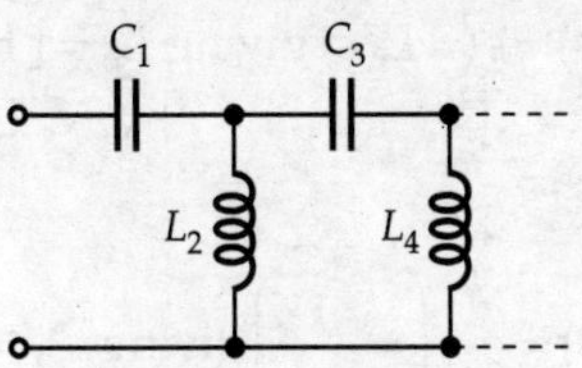

(*a*) 1st series element = C_1
1st shunt element = L_2

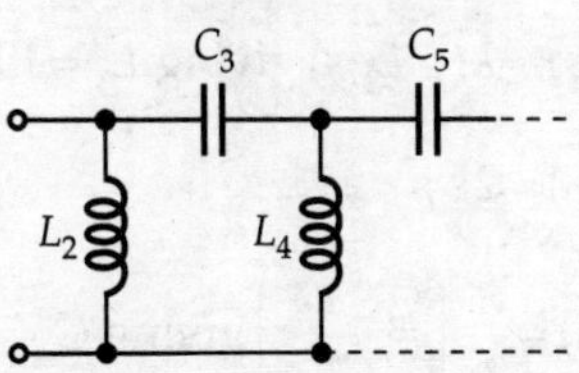

(*b*) 1st shunt element = L_2
(No first series element)

Fig. 18.20 First element representation in Cauer second form [at $s \to 0$].

(*ii*) With $\lim_{s \to 0} Z(s) \to 0$,

$$\text{since} \quad Z(s) = \frac{1}{C_1 s} + \cfrac{1}{\cfrac{1}{L_2 s} + \cfrac{1}{\cfrac{1}{C_3 s} + \cfrac{1}{L_4 s + \ldots}}}$$

hence C_1 must be zero [Fig. 18.20(*b*)].

Figure 18.21 represents the method of determination of last term in Cauer second form of LC network.

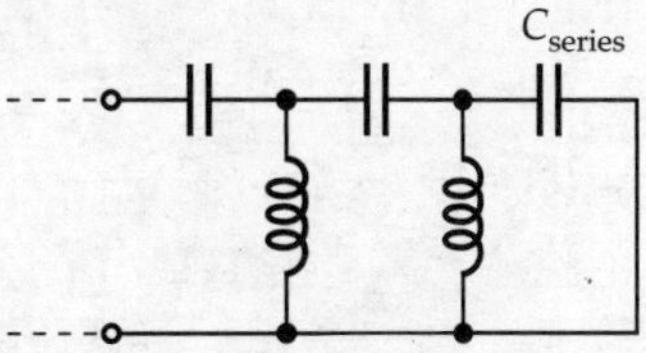

(*a*) Last element = C_{series}
[If $Z(s) \to 0$ with $s \to \infty$ *i.e.*, for $\omega = \infty$, the last element must appear as capacitor]

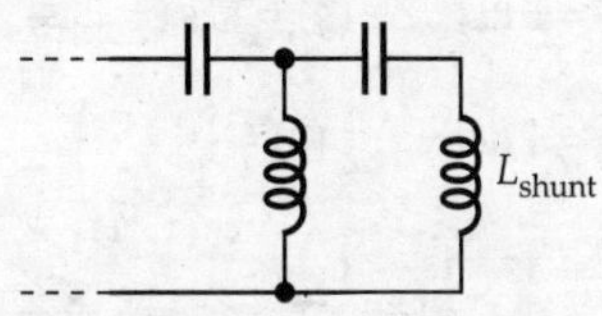

(*b*) Last element = L_{shunt}
[If $Z(s) \to \infty$ with $s \to \infty$ *i.e.*, for $\omega = \infty$, the last element must be an inductor]

Fig. 18.21 Last element determination in Cauer second form [at $s \to \infty$].

EXAMPLE 18.41 *A driving point impedance is given by*

$$Z_{LC}(s) = \frac{s(s^2+4)(s^2+6)}{(s^2+1)(s^2+5)}$$

Obtain the first form of Cauer network.

SOLUTION.

$$Z_{LC}(s) = \frac{s(s^4 + 6s^2 + 4s^2 + 24)}{(s^4 + 5s^2 + s^2 + 5)} = \frac{s^5 + 10s^3 + 24s}{s^4 + 6s^2 + 5}$$

Continued fraction expansion is shown below :

$s^4 + 6s^2 + 5)\ s^5 + 10s^3 + 24s\ (s$
$\quad s^5 + 6s^3 + 5s$
$\quad\quad 4s^3 + 19s)\ s^4 + 6s^2 + 5\ (\frac{s}{4}$
$\quad\quad\quad s^4 + \frac{19}{4}s^2$
$\quad\quad\quad\quad \frac{5}{4}s^2 + 5)\ 4s^3 + 19s\ (\frac{16}{5}s$
$\quad\quad\quad\quad\quad 4s^3 + 16s$
$\quad\quad\quad\quad\quad\quad 3s$
$\quad\quad\quad\quad\quad 3s)\ \frac{5}{4}s^2 + 5\ (\frac{5}{12}s$
$\quad\quad\quad\quad\quad\quad \frac{5}{4}s^2$
$\quad\quad\quad\quad\quad\quad\quad 5)\ 3s\ (\frac{3s}{5}$
$\quad\quad\quad\quad\quad\quad\quad\quad 3s$
$\quad\quad\quad\quad\quad\quad\quad\quad \times$

Here, $Z_{LC}(s) \to \infty$ with $s \to \infty$; also $Z_{LC}(s) \to 0$ with $s \to 0$. Thus for the function $Z_{LC}(s)$ having $n > m$, the first element is L_1 and the last element is also an inductor.

$$\therefore \quad Z_{LC}(s) = s + \cfrac{1}{\cfrac{s}{4} + \cfrac{1}{\cfrac{16\,s}{5} + \cfrac{1}{\cfrac{5s}{12} + \cfrac{1}{\cfrac{3s}{5}}}}}$$

Thus, $L_1 = 1\,\text{H};\; Z_1(s) = 1.s\,(= L_1 s)$

$C_2 = 1/4\,\text{F};\; Y_2(s) = \frac{s}{4}$

giving $Z_2(s) = \frac{4}{s} = \frac{1}{\frac{s}{4}} = \frac{1}{Cs}$

$L_3 = \frac{16}{5}\,\text{H};\; Z_3(s) = \frac{16}{5}s\,(= L_3 s)$

$C_4 = \frac{5}{12}\,\text{F};\; Y_4(s) = \frac{5}{12}s$

giving $Z_4(s) = \frac{1}{\frac{5}{12}s}$

$L_5 = \frac{3}{5}\,\text{H}:\; Z_5(s) = \frac{3}{5}s\,(= L_5 s)$

Figure E18.19 represents the first Cauer form at network.

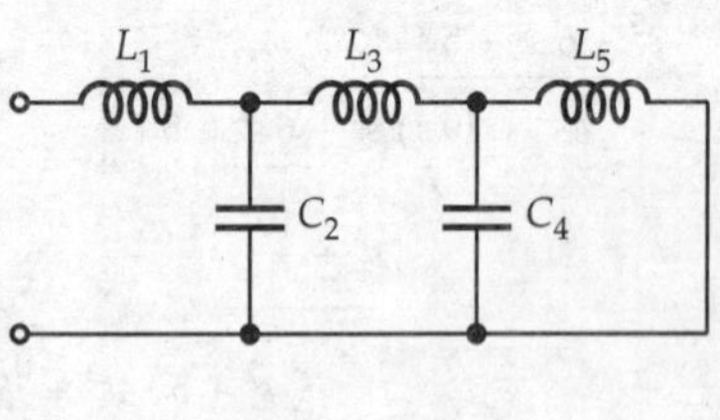

Fig. E18.19

EXAMPLE 18.42 *Develop the Cauer-1 network for the given function*

$$Z(s) = \frac{s^5 + 5s^3 + 3s}{s^4 + 3s^2 + 1}.$$

SOLUTION. The continued fraction is shown below :

$s^4 + 3s^2 + 1)\; s^5 + 5s^3 + 3s\; (\,s$
$\quad s^5 + 3s^3 + s$
$\quad 2s^3 + 2s)\; s^4 + 3s^2 + 1\; (\,\frac{s}{2}$
$\quad\quad s^4 + s^2$
$\quad\quad 2s^2 + 1)\; 2s^3 + 2s\; (\,s$
$\quad\quad\quad 2s^3 + s$
$\quad\quad\quad s)\; 2s^2 + 1\; (\,2s$
$\quad\quad\quad\quad 2s^2$
$\quad\quad\quad\quad 1)\; s\; (\,s$
$\quad\quad\quad\quad\quad s$
$\quad\quad\quad\quad\quad \times$

Here $Z(s) \to \infty$ with $s \to \infty$ and $Z(s) \to 0$ with $s \to 0$. Since in $Z(s)$, $n > m$, thus it can be concluded that in Cauer-1 form of $Z(s)$, first element is an inductor as well as the last element.

$$\therefore \quad Z(s) = s + \cfrac{1}{\cfrac{s}{2} + \cfrac{1}{s + \cfrac{1}{2s + \cfrac{1}{s}}}}$$

$\therefore \quad Z_1(s) = s\,(= L_1 s)$ giving $L_1 = 1\,\text{H}$

$Y_2(s) = \frac{s}{2};$

$Z_2(s) = \frac{1}{\frac{1}{2}s}\left(= \frac{1}{C_2 s}\right)$ giving $C_2 = \frac{1}{2}\,\text{F}$

$Z_3(s) = s\,(= L_3 s)$ giving $L_3 = 1\,\text{H}$

$Y_4(s) = 2s;$

$Z_4(s) = \frac{1}{2s}\left(= \frac{1}{C_4 s}\right)$ giving $C_4 = 2\,\text{F}$

$Z_5(s) = s\,(= L_5 s)$ giving $L_5 = 1\,\text{H}$

Figure E18.20 represents the first form of Cauer Network.

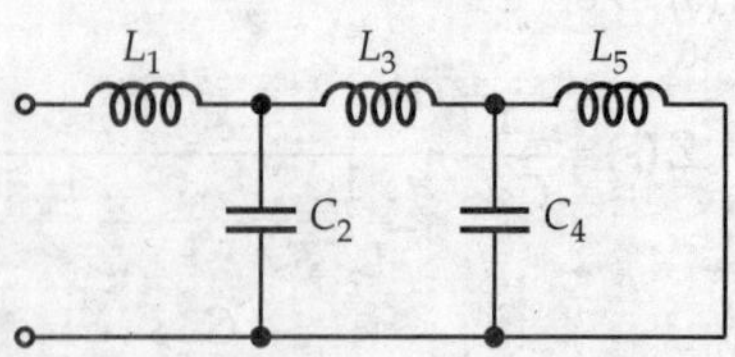

Fig. E18.20

EXAMPLE 18.43 *Justify the termination of Cauer-1 network of Examples 18.41 and 18.42 by inductors.*

SOLUTION. In Example 18.41, the impedance function in the continued fraction form has been found to be

$$Z(s)=s+\cfrac{1}{\cfrac{s}{4}+\cfrac{1}{\cfrac{16s}{5}+\cfrac{1}{\cfrac{5s}{12}+\cfrac{1}{\cfrac{3s}{5}}}}}$$

We know, for inductor as end element, $Z(s)\to 0$ for $\omega=0$ *i.e.*, for $s\to 0$. It is evident from the above expression that for $s\to 0$, $Z(s)$ turns to be zero.

For Example 18.42 also, if we put $s\to\infty$ in the expression of

$$Z(s)\left[=s+\cfrac{1}{\cfrac{s}{2}+\cfrac{1}{s+\cfrac{1}{2s+\cfrac{1}{s}}}}\right]$$, it turns to be a pole.

Thus the end elements must be inductors (which is also evident from the above Examples).

EXAMPLE 18.44 *Synthesize the network having driving point impedance*

$$Z(s)=\frac{2s^5+10s^3+10s}{s^4+4s^2+3} \text{ in the first Cauer form.}$$

SOLUTION. Proceeding with the continued fraction expansion,

$s^4+4s^2+3\ )\ 2s^5+10s^3+10s\ (\ 2s$

$\quad 2s^5+8s^3+6s$

$\quad\quad 2s^3+4s\ )\ s^4+4s^2+3\ (\ \frac{s}{2}$

$\quad\quad\quad s^4+2s^2$

$\quad\quad\quad\quad 2s^2+3\ )\ 2s^3+4s\ (\ s$

$\quad\quad\quad\quad\quad 2s^3+3s$

$\quad\quad\quad\quad\quad\quad s\ )\ 2s^2+3\ (\ 2s$

$\quad\quad\quad\quad\quad\quad\quad 2s^2$

$\quad\quad\quad\quad\quad\quad\quad\quad 3\ )\ s\ (\ \frac{s}{3}$

$\quad\quad\quad\quad\quad\quad\quad\quad\quad s$

$\quad\quad\quad\quad\quad\quad\quad\quad\quad \times$

In $Z(s)$, $n>m$; also $Z(s)\to\infty$ with $s\to\infty$ and $Z(s)\to 0$ with $s\to 0$. Thus in Cauer first form of synthesis, both the first and last elements are inductors.

$$\therefore\quad Z(s)=2s+\cfrac{1}{\cfrac{s}{2}+\cfrac{1}{s+\cfrac{1}{2s+\cfrac{1}{\cfrac{s}{3}}}}}$$

$$\therefore\quad Z_1(s)=2s(=L_1 s) \text{ giving } L_1=2\,\text{H}$$

$$Y_2(s)=\frac{s}{2};$$

i.e., $$Z_2(s)=\frac{2}{s}=\frac{1}{\frac{s}{2}}\left(=\frac{1}{C_2 s}\right) \text{ giving } C_2=\frac{1}{2}\,\text{F}$$

$$Z_3(s)=s(=L_3 s) \text{ giving } L_3=1\,\text{H.}$$

$$Y_4(s)=2s(=C_4 s) \text{ giving } C_4=2\,\text{F}$$

$$Z_5(s)=s/3=(L_5 s) \text{ giving } L_5=\frac{1}{3}\,\text{H}$$

[At $s=0$, $Z(s)\to 0$. From the continued fraction expression this confirms the presence of inductor as the last element].

The Cauer first form of network is shown in Fig. E18.21.

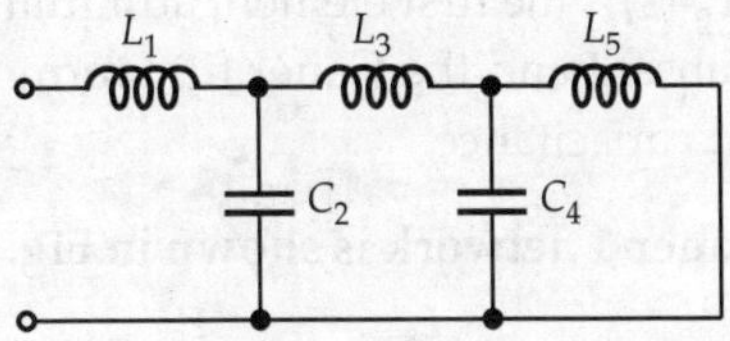

Fig. E18.21

EXAMPLE 18.45 *The driving point impedance of a network is given by*

$$Z(s)=\frac{6s^3+2s}{9s^4+4s^2+(1/6)}.$$

Find the first form of Cauer network.

SOLUTION. Since the order of polynomial of denominator is higher than that of the numerator, hence we first invert the function and then proceed with continued fraction. It may also be observed that zero is formed at $s\to\infty$ (since denominator polynomial is of one term higher) and it indicates absence of first element. However, with $s\to 0$, $Z(s)\to 0$. Since here $m>n$, the last element is inductor.

The continued fraction is obtained as

$$6s^3 + 2s\ )\ 9s^4 + 4s^2 + (1/6)\ (\ \frac{3}{2}s$$
$$\underline{9s^4 + 3s^2}$$
$$s^2 + (1/6)\ )\ 6s^3 + 2s\ (\ 6s$$
$$\underline{6s^3 + s}$$
$$s\ )\ s^2 + \frac{1}{6}\ (\ s$$
$$\underline{s^2}$$
$$\frac{1}{6}\ )\ s\ (\ 6s$$
$$\underline{s}$$
$$\times$$

$$\therefore \quad Z(s) = \cfrac{1}{\cfrac{3s}{2} + \cfrac{1}{6s + \cfrac{1}{s + \cfrac{1}{6s}}}}$$

$\therefore \quad Y_2(s) = \frac{3}{2}s$ giving $C_2 = \frac{3}{2}$ **F.**

$Z_3(s) = 6s$ giving $L_3 = 6$ **H.**

$Y_4(s) = s$ giving $C_4 = 1$ **F.**

$Z_5(s) = 6s$ giving $L_5 = 6$ **H.**

Since $Y_2(s)$ is the first element admittance hence L_1 will be absent and the Cauer first form will start from shunt capacitance.

The Cauer-1 network is shown in Fig. E18.22.

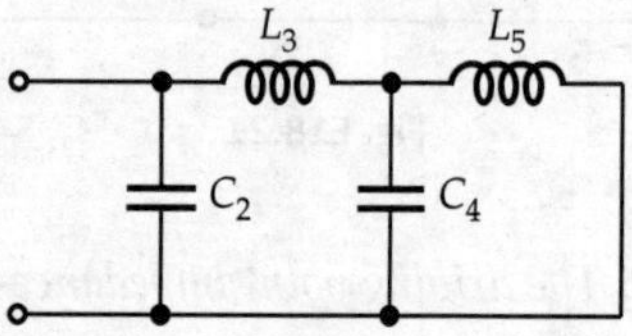

Fig. E18.22

EXAMPLE 18.46 *The driving point impedance of a reactive network is given by*

$$Z(s) = \frac{s^4 + 4s^2 + 3}{2s^3 + 3s}.$$

Find the second form of Cauer network.

SOLUTION. In order to find the second form of Cauer network, the impedance function is rearranged as below :

$$Z(s) = \frac{3 + 4s^2 + s^4}{3s + 2s^3}$$

The continued fraction expansion shows :

$$3s + 2s^3\ )\ 3 + 4s^2 + s^4\ (\ \frac{1}{s}$$
$$\underline{3 + 2s^2}$$
$$2s^2 + s^4\ )\ 3s + 2s^3\ (\ \frac{3}{2s}$$
$$\underline{3s + \frac{3}{2}s^3}$$
$$\frac{1}{2}s^3\ )\ 2s^2 + s^4\ (\ 4/s$$
$$\underline{2s^2}$$
$$s^4\ )\ \frac{1}{2}s^3\ (\ \frac{1}{2s}$$
$$\underline{\frac{1}{2}s^3}$$
$$\times$$

With $s \to 0$, $Z(s) \to \infty$. Thus the first element is capacitor in Cauer-2 form. Also with $s \to 0$, $Z(s) \to \infty$. This indicates the last term to be inductor.

$$\therefore \quad Z(s) = \frac{1}{s} + \cfrac{1}{\cfrac{3}{2s} + \cfrac{1}{\cfrac{4}{s} + \cfrac{1}{\cfrac{1}{2s}}}}$$

[1st element will be present as $Z(s) \to \infty$ with $s \to 0$]

$$\therefore Z_1(s) = \frac{1}{s}\left(= \frac{1}{C_1 s}\right) \text{ representing } C_1 = 1\ \text{F}$$

$$Y_2(s) = \frac{3}{2s} = \frac{1}{\frac{2}{3}s}\left(= \frac{1}{L_2 s}\right) \text{ representing } L_2 = \frac{2}{3}\ \text{H}$$

$$Z_3(s) = \frac{4}{s} = \frac{1}{\frac{1}{4}s}\left(= \frac{1}{C_4 s}\right) \text{ representing } C_4 = \frac{1}{4}\ \text{F}$$

$$Y_4(s) = \frac{1}{2s}\left(= \frac{1}{L_4 s}\right) \text{ representing } L_4 = 2\ \text{H.}$$

The required second form of Cauer network is shown in Fig. E18.23.

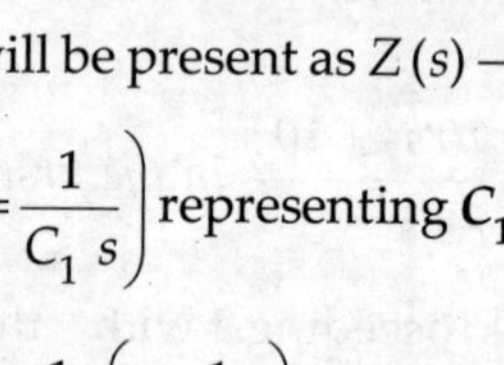

Fig. E18.23

Example 18.47 *An impedance function of LC network is given by*

$$Z(s) = \frac{12\,s^3 + 4s}{3s^4 + 10\,s^2 + 2}.$$

Synthesize the function to draw the Cauer-2 network.

Solution. Let us first reorient the function as shown below to get the Cauer-2 network.

$$Z(s) = \frac{4s + 12\,s^3}{2 + 10\,s^2 + 3s^4}$$

Figure E18.24 represents the 2nd form of Cauer network the elements of which can be found out as shown below.

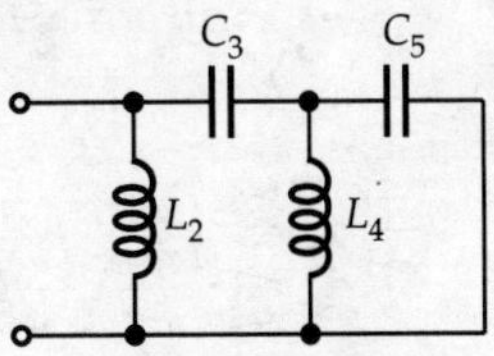

Fig. E18.24

Since $Z(s) \to 0$ with $s \to 0$, the first element C_1 is absent and with $s \to \infty, Z(s) \to 0$; then the last element is a capacitor.

In this case,

$$Z(s) = \cfrac{1}{Y_2(s) + \cfrac{1}{Z_3(s) + \cfrac{1}{Y_4(s) + \cfrac{1}{Z_5(s)}}}}$$

or,

$$Z(s) = \cfrac{1}{\cfrac{1}{L_2 s} + \cfrac{1}{\cfrac{1}{C_3 s} + \cfrac{1}{\cfrac{1}{L_4 s} + \cfrac{1}{1/C_5 s}}}}$$

The continued fraction is then obtained on inverting and dividing as shown below :

$$4s + 12\,s^3\;)\;2 + 10\,s^2 + 3s^4\;\left(\frac{1}{2s}\right.$$
$$\underline{2 + 6s^2}$$
$$4s^2 + 3s^4\;)\;4s + 12\,s^3\;\left(\frac{1}{s}\right.$$
$$\underline{4s + 3s^3}$$
$$9s^3\;)\;4s^2 + 3s^4\;\left(\frac{4}{9s}\right.$$
$$\underline{4s^2}$$
$$3s^4\;)\;9s^3\;\left(\frac{3}{s}\right.$$
$$\underline{9s^3}$$
$$\times$$

$$\therefore \quad Y(s) = \cfrac{1}{\cfrac{1}{Y_2(s) + \cfrac{1}{Z_3(s) + \cfrac{1}{Y_4(s) + \ldots}}}}$$

[reciprocal of $Z(s)$]

Since first element is absent, hence, $C_1 = 0$ and the first element would now be shunt inductor. [Here $Z(s) \to 0$ with $s \to 0$]

Here, $Y_2(s) = \frac{1}{2s}$ giving $L_2 = 2$ **H**

$Z_3(s) = \frac{1}{s}$ giving $C_3 = 1$ **F**

$Y_4(s) = \frac{4}{9s}$ giving $L_4 = \frac{9}{4}$ **H**

$Z_5(s) = \frac{3}{s} = \frac{1}{s/3}$ giving $C_5 = \frac{1}{3}$ **F.**

Example 18.48 *Synthesize the following network function in Cauer-2 form :*

$$Z(s) = \frac{8s^3 + 10\,s}{5 + 6s^2 + s^4}.$$

Solution. For using $Z(s)$ in continued fraction form, it is arranged in descending order polynomial form for both the numerator and denominator.

$$Z(s) = \frac{10\,s + 8s^3}{5 + 6s^2 + s^4} = \cfrac{1}{\cfrac{5 + 6s^2 + s^4}{10\,s + 8\,s^3}}$$

Let us now use the function in continued fraction expansion form :

$$10\,s + 8s^3\;)\;5 + 6s^2 + s^4\;\left(\frac{1}{2s}\right.$$
$$\underline{5 + 4s^2}$$
$$2s^2 + s^4\;)\;10\,s + 8s^3\;\left(\frac{5}{s}\right.$$
$$\underline{10\,s + 5\,s^3}$$
$$3s^3\;)\;2s^2 + s^4\;\left(\frac{2}{3s}\right.$$
$$\underline{2s^2}$$
$$s^4\;)\;3s^3\;\left(\frac{3}{s}\right.$$
$$\underline{3s^3}$$
$$\times$$

CHAPTER 18

With $s \to 0$, $Y(s) \to \infty$. *i.e.,* $Z(s) \to 0$. The first element is absent. Also with $s \to \infty$, $Z(s) \to 0$. The last term is thus a capacitor.

In continued fraction,

$$Y(s) = \cfrac{1}{Z_1(s) + \cfrac{1}{Y_2(s) + \cfrac{1}{Z_3(s) + \cfrac{1}{Y_4(s) + \cfrac{1}{Z_5(s) + \cfrac{1}{Y_6(s)}}}}}}$$

Thus

$$Y_2(s) = \frac{1}{2s}\left(= \frac{1}{L_2 s}\right) \quad \text{giving } \mathbf{L_2 = 2\,H}$$

$$Z_3(s) = \frac{5}{s} = \frac{1}{\frac{1}{5}s}\left(= \frac{1}{C_3 s}\right) \quad \text{giving } \mathbf{C_3 = \frac{1}{5}\,F}$$

$$Y_4(s) = \frac{2}{3s}\left(= \frac{1}{L_4 s}\right) \quad \text{giving } \mathbf{L_4 = \frac{3}{2}\,H}$$

$$Z_5(s) = \frac{3}{s} = \frac{1}{\frac{1}{3}s}\left(= \frac{1}{C_5 s}\right) \quad \text{giving } \mathbf{C_5 = \frac{1}{3}\,F.}$$

Figure E18.25 represents the second form of Cauer Network.

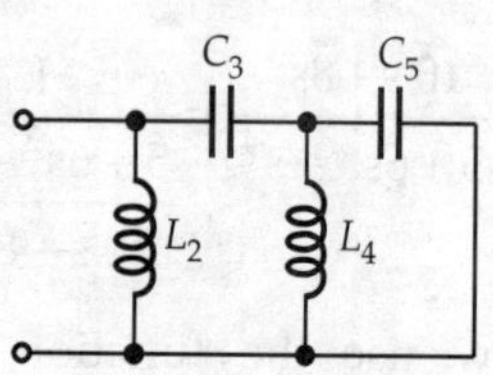

Fig. E18.25

EXAMPLE 18.49 *Realise the network function in Cauer-2 form*

$$Z(s) = \frac{(s^2+2)(s^2+4)}{s(s^2+3)}.$$

SOLUTION. $Z(s) = \dfrac{s^4 + 6s^2 + 8}{s^3 + 3s}$

Using the continued fraction method for the driving point impedance for the Cauer-2 form, using $Z(s)$ in descending order,

$$Z(s) = \frac{8 + 6s^2 + s^4}{s^3 + 3s}$$

$$3s + s^3 \;)\; 8 + 6s^2 + s^4 \;\left(\frac{8}{3s}\right.$$
$$\underline{8 + \frac{8}{3}s^2}$$
$$\frac{10}{3}s^2 + s^4 \;)\; 3s + s^3 \;\left(\frac{9}{10\,s}\right.$$
$$\underline{3s + \frac{9}{10}s^3}$$
$$\frac{1}{10}s^3 \;)\; \frac{10}{3}s^2 + s^4 \;\left(\frac{100}{3s}\right.$$
$$\underline{\frac{10}{3}s^2}$$
$$s^4 \;)\; \frac{1}{10}s^3 \;\left(\frac{1}{10\,s}\right.$$
$$\underline{\frac{1}{10}s^3}$$
$$\times$$

$$\therefore \quad Z(s) = \frac{8}{3s} + \cfrac{1}{\cfrac{9}{10\,s} + \cfrac{1}{\cfrac{100}{3s} + \cfrac{1}{\cfrac{1}{10\,s}}}}$$

$Z(s)$ turns to ∞ in the given expression and hence first element is present. Also with $S \to \infty$, $Z(s) \to \infty$ indicating presence inductor as last element

Thus,

$$Z_1(s) = \frac{8}{3s}\left(= \frac{1}{C_1 s}\right) \text{giving } \mathbf{C_1 = \frac{3}{8}\,F}$$

$$Y_2(s) = \frac{9}{10\,s}$$

$$= \frac{1}{\frac{10}{9}s}\left(= \frac{1}{L_2 s}\right) \text{representing } \mathbf{L_2 = \frac{10}{9}\,H}$$

$$Z_3(s) = \frac{100}{3s}$$

$$= \frac{1}{\frac{3}{100}s}\left(= \frac{1}{C_3 s}\right) \text{representing } \mathbf{C_3 = \frac{3}{100}\,F}$$

$$Y_4(s) = \frac{1}{10\,s}\left(= \frac{1}{L_4 s}\right) \text{representing } \mathbf{L_4 = 10\,H.}$$

Figure E18.26 represents the Cauer-2 form of network.

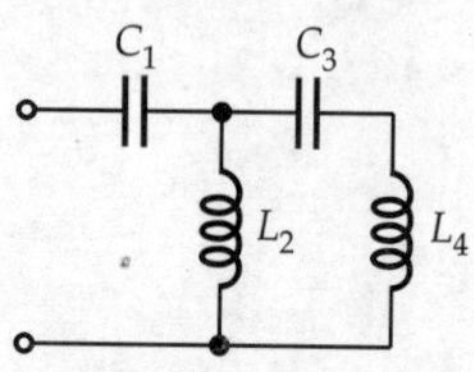

Fig. E18.26

18.14 APPLICABILITY OF FOSTER AND CAUER FORMS

It may be noted in this context that in both forms of Foster as well as Cauer network realisations, the number of elements is one greater than the number of internal critical frequencies [critical frequency being the frequency at which the system function becomes a zero or a pole] excluding those at $s = 0$ and $s = \infty$. Both the Foster and Cauer forms give the minimum number of elements for a specified driving point function and hence both the forms represent "Canonical" forms.

In conclusion, it is desirable to point out that the Cauer form of realisation serve another very useful purpose. If it is necessary to decide whether a given function is realisable as a reactance, the cauer development provides a simple and direct way of doing this. For a higher order polynomial since the process of locating poles and zeros is a difficult task, synthetic division is to be performed for the continued fraction expansion. If it is reactance, the remainders of any step in the synthetic division can not be a negative number. The following example illustrates this.

EXAMPLE 18.50 $Z(s)=\dfrac{s^9+4s^7+3s^5+2s^3+2s}{s^8+s^6+s^4+s^2+1}$. *Check whether Z (s) represents a reactance.*

SOLUTION. The synthetic division is performed below :

$$s^8+s^6+s^4+s^2+1)\ s^9+4s^7+3s^5+2s^3+2s\ (s$$
$$\underline{s^9+s^7+s^5+s^3+s}$$
$$3s^7+2s^5+s^3+s)\ s^8+s^6+s^4+s^2+1\ (\frac{s}{3}$$
$$\underline{s^8+\frac{2}{3}s^6+\frac{s^4}{3}+\frac{s^2}{3}}$$
$$\frac{s^6}{3}+\frac{2s^4}{3}+\frac{2s^2}{3}+1)\ 3s^7+2s^5+s^3+s\ (9s$$
$$\underline{3s^7+6s^5+6s^3+9s}$$
$$-4s^5-5s^3-8s$$

Since negative numbers occur in the last step, it is not worthwhile to continue further and it is concluded that the **function cannot be a reactance.**

EXAMPLE 18.51 *An impedance is given by*

$$Z(s)=\frac{8\,(s^2+1)\,(s^2+3)}{s\,(s^2+2)\,(s^2+4)}.$$

Realise the network in Foster-I, II and Cauer-I, II form.

SOLUTION.

Foster-I Form

$$Z\,(s)=\frac{8\,(s^2+1)(s^2+3)}{s\,(s^2+2)(s^2+4)}$$

Since the denominator has one *s*-term hence *Z*(*s*) becomes a pole at $s = 0$ indicating the presence of first element (C_0) in the Foster first form. When $s \to \infty$, $Z(s) \to 0$. It indicates the absence of the last element L_∞.

By taking the partial fraction of the given impedance function,

$$Z\,(s)=\frac{A_0}{s}+\frac{2A_1\,s}{s^2+2}+\frac{2A_2\,s}{s^2+4}$$

$$\text{Here}\quad A_0=\left.\frac{8(s^2+1)(s^2+3)}{(s^2+2)(s^2+4)}\right|_{s=0}=\frac{8\times 3}{2\times 4}=3$$

$$A_1=\left.\frac{8\,(s^2+1)(s^2+3)}{s\,(s-j\sqrt{2})(s^2+4)}\right|_{s=-j\sqrt{2}}$$

$$=\frac{8\,(-2+1)(-2+3)}{-j\sqrt{2}\,(-2\,j\sqrt{2})(-2+4)}$$

$$=\frac{-8}{-j\sqrt{2}\times -4\,j\sqrt{2}}=1$$

CHAPTER 18

$$A_2 = \left.\frac{8(s^2+1)(s^2+3)}{s(s^2+2)(s-j2)}\right|_{s=-j2}$$

$$= \frac{8(-4+1)(-4+3)}{-j2(-4+2)(-j4)}$$

$$= \frac{8\times 3}{-8\times(-2)} = 1.5.$$

$$\therefore \quad C_0 = \frac{1}{A_0} = \frac{1}{3}\text{ F}$$

$$C_1 = \frac{1}{2A_1} = \frac{1}{2\times 1} = \mathbf{\frac{1}{2}\ F}$$

$$L_1 = \frac{2A_1}{\omega_1^2} = \frac{2\times 1}{(\sqrt{2})^2} = \mathbf{1\ H}$$

$$C_2 = \frac{1}{2A_2} = \frac{1}{2\times 1.5} = \mathbf{\frac{1}{3}\ F}$$

$$L_2 = \frac{2A_2}{\omega_2^2} = \frac{2\times 1.5}{4} = \mathbf{\frac{3}{4}\ H.}$$

The Foster first form of realisation is shown in Fig. E18.27.

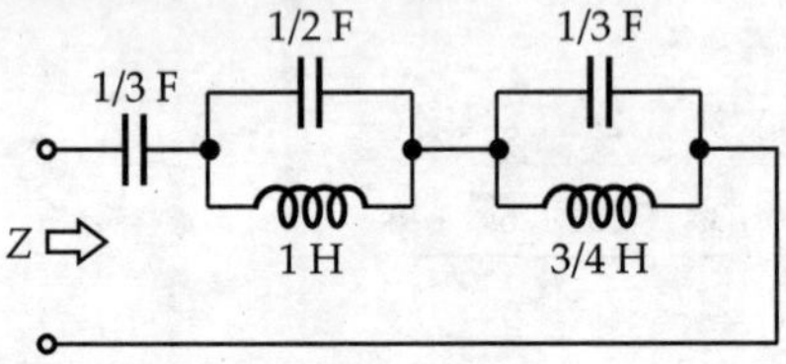

Fig. E18.27

Foster-II Form

$$Y(s) = \frac{1}{Z(s)} = \frac{s(s^2+2)(s^2+4)}{8(s^2+1)(s^2+3)}$$

At $s=0$, $Y(s)=0$. It indicates that for $Y(s)$ where numerator polynomial is one term higher than denominator is having a zero at $s=0$. Then, there will be no first element in Foster-II form. On the other hand, for $s\to\infty$, $Y(s)$ shows a pole. It indicates the presence of last element in Foster-II form.

Expansion of $Y(s)$ in Foster-II form suggests

$$Y(s) = \frac{2B_1 s}{s^2+1} + \frac{2B_2 s}{s^2+3} + Hs$$

while $$B_1 = \left.\frac{1}{8}\,\frac{s(s^2+2)(s^2+4)}{(s-j1)(s^2+3)}\right|_{s=-j1}$$

$$= \frac{1}{8}\,\frac{(-1+2)(-1+4)(-j1)}{-2j\times(-1+3)}$$

$$= \frac{1\times 3(-j1)}{8\times(-j1)\times 2\times 2} = \frac{3}{32}$$

$$B_2 = \left.\frac{1}{8}\,\frac{(s^2+2)(s^2+4)}{(s^2+1)(s-j\sqrt{3})}\right|_{s=-j\sqrt{3}}$$

$$= \frac{(-j\sqrt{3})(-3+2)(-3+4)}{(-3+1)(-2j\sqrt{3})\times 8}$$

$$= \frac{(-j\sqrt{3})(-1)(1)}{(-2)(-2)(j\sqrt{3})}\times\frac{1}{8} = \frac{1}{32} \qquad \left[H = \frac{1}{8}\right]$$

$$\therefore \quad L_1 = \frac{1}{2B_1} = \frac{1}{2}\times\frac{32}{3} = \mathbf{\frac{16}{3}\ H}$$

$$L_2 = \frac{1}{2B_2} = \frac{1}{2}\times 32 = \mathbf{16\ H}$$

$$C_1 = \frac{2B_1}{\omega_1^2} = \frac{2\times\frac{3}{32}}{1} = \mathbf{\frac{3}{16}\ F}$$

$$C_2 = \frac{2B_2}{\omega_2^2} = \frac{2\times\frac{1}{32}}{3} = \mathbf{\frac{1}{48}\ F}$$

$$C_\infty = H = \mathbf{\frac{1}{8}\ F.}$$

Foster II network is realised below : (Fig. E18.28).

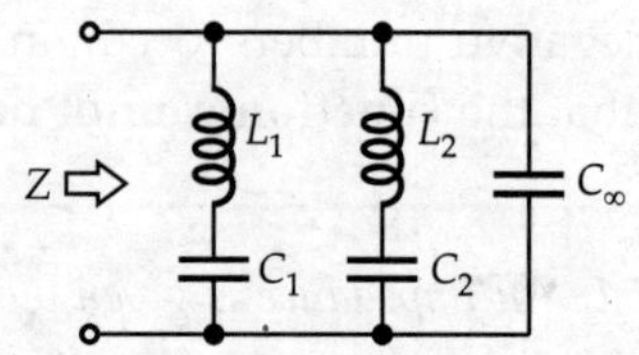

Fig. E18.28

Cauer-I Realisation

$$Z(s) = \frac{8(s^2+1)(s^2+3)}{s(s^2+2)(s^2+4)} = \frac{8s^4+32s^2+24}{s^5+6s^3+8s}$$

With $s\to\infty$, $Z(s)\to 0$. This indicates absence of the first element L_1 [Here the denominator polynomial is one higher degree than numerator polynomial].

However, $$Y(s) = \frac{1}{Z(s)} = \frac{s^5+6s^3+8s}{8s^4+32s^2+24}$$

Let us now perform the continued fraction :

$$8s^4 + 32s^2 + 24\,)\; s^5 + 6s^3 + 8s\; (\; \frac{s}{8}$$
$$s^5 + 4s^3 + 3s$$
$$2s^3 + 5s\,)\; 8s^4 + 32s^2 + 24\; (\; 4s$$
$$8s^4 + 20s^2$$
$$12s^2 + 24\,)\; 2s^3 + 5s\; (\; \frac{s}{6}$$
$$2s^3 + 4s$$
$$s\,)\; 12s^2 + 24\; (\; 12s$$
$$12s^2$$
$$24\,)\; s\; (\; \frac{s}{24}$$
$$s$$
$$\times$$

Since $Y(s) = \cfrac{1}{\cfrac{1}{Y_2(s) + \cfrac{1}{Z_3(s) + \cfrac{1}{Y_4(s) + \ldots}}}} = \cfrac{1}{\cfrac{1}{C_2 s + \cfrac{1}{L_3 s + \cfrac{1}{C_4\, s + \ldots}}}}$

$\therefore$ Here, $C_2 s = \frac{1}{8}s;\; L_3 s = 4s;\; C_4 s = s \times \frac{1}{6};\; L_5 s = 12s;\; C_6 s = \frac{1}{24}s$

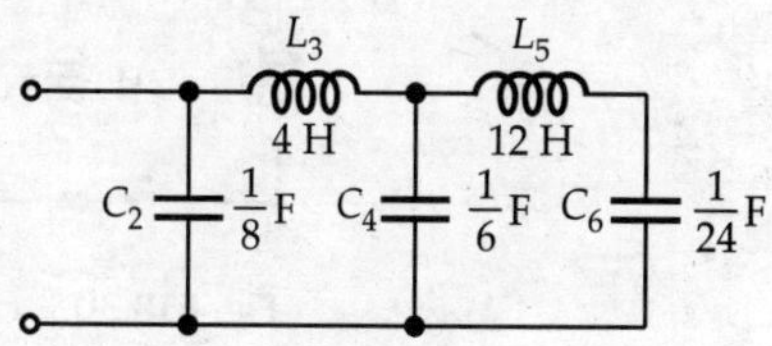

Fig. E18.29

The Cauer-I realisation is shown in Fig. E18.29 where

$$C_2 = \frac{1}{8}\text{ F},\; L_3 = 4\text{ H},\; C_4 = \frac{1}{6}\text{ F},\; L_5 = 12\text{ H},\; C_6 \text{ (last element)} = \frac{1}{24}\text{ F}$$

Cauer-II realisation

Given : $Z(s) = \dfrac{8s^4 + 32s^4 + 24}{s^5 + 6s^3 + 8s}$. In Cauer II form we write $Z(s) = \dfrac{24 + 32s^2 + 8s^4}{8s + 6s^3 + s^5}$

With $s \to 0, Z(s) \to \infty$. Then a pole exists with $s \to 0$. The first element C_1 is then present. With $s \to \infty, Z(s) \to 0$. The last element is then a capacitor. Let us now perform continued fraction expansion :

$$8s + 6s^3 + s^5\,)\; 24 + 32s^2 + 8s^4\; (\; \frac{3}{s}$$
$$24 + 18s^2 + 3s^4$$
$$14s^2 + 5s^4\,)\; 8s + 6s^3 + s^5\; (\; \frac{4}{7}s$$
$$8s + \frac{20}{7}s^3$$
$$\frac{22}{7}s^3 + s^5\,)\; 14s^2 + 5s^4\; (\; \frac{49}{11}/s$$
$$14s^2 + \frac{49}{11}s^4$$
$$\frac{6s^4}{11}\,)\; \frac{22}{7}s^3 + s^5\; (\; \frac{121}{21s}$$
$$\frac{22}{7}s^3$$
$$s^5\,)\; \frac{6s^4}{11}\; (\; \frac{6}{11s}$$
$$\frac{6s^4}{11}$$
$$\times$$

CHAPTER 18

$$\therefore \quad Z(s)=\frac{3}{s}+\cfrac{1}{\cfrac{4}{7s}+\cfrac{1}{\cfrac{49}{11s}+\cfrac{1}{\cfrac{121}{21s}+\cfrac{1}{\cfrac{6}{11s}}}}}$$

This gives

$$C_1=\frac{1}{3}\text{ F},\ L_2=\frac{7}{4}\text{ H},$$

$$C_3=\frac{11}{49}\text{ F},\ L_4\ \frac{21}{121}\text{ H},\ C_5=\frac{11}{6}\text{ F}.$$

The Cauer-II form of realisation is shown below : (Fig. E18.30)

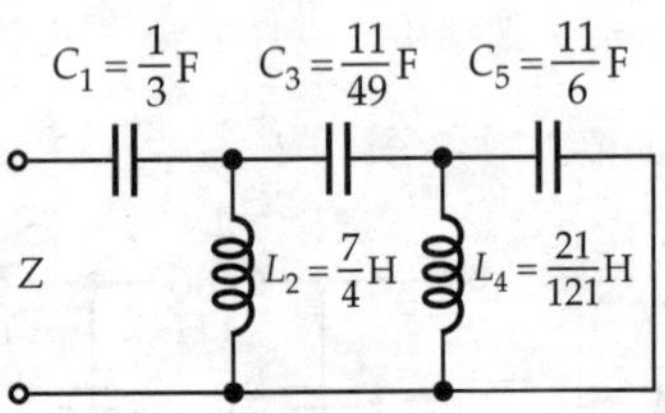

Fig. E18.30

18.15 FOSTER FORM OF SYNTHESIS OF LOSSY NETWORKS

RL or *RC* networks are called lossy networks due to presence of resistance element. The following article shows Foster realisation of *RC* and *RL* networks.

18.15.1 *RC* Network Synthesis by Foster Form

Comparing with the Foster form of *LC* network, the *RC* network in Foster form can be represented, as shown in Fig. 18.22.

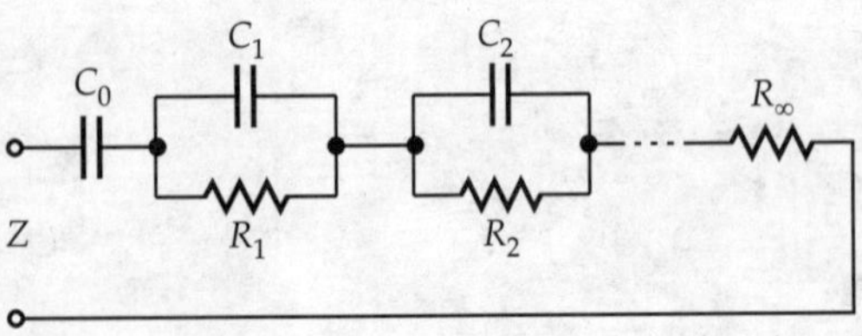

Fig. 18.22 Foster form of *RC* Network.

A parallel *RC* network can be represented as

$$Z_{RC}(s)=\frac{1}{C}\left[\frac{1}{s+\frac{1}{RC}}\right] \quad \text{...(18.47)}$$

while the admittance of a series *RC* network is given as

$$Y_{RC}(s)=\frac{1}{R}\left[\frac{s}{s+\frac{1}{RC}}\right] \quad \text{...(18.48)}$$

$\therefore$ From Fig. 18.22,

$$Z(s)=\frac{A_0}{s}+\frac{A_1}{s+\sigma_1}+\frac{A_2}{s+\sigma_2}+\ldots+A_\infty \quad \text{...(18.49)}$$

where, $C_0=\frac{1}{A_0};C_1=\frac{1}{A_1};R_1=\frac{A_1}{\sigma_1};R_\infty=A_\infty$

$$R_2=\frac{A_2}{\sigma_2},$$

$$C_2=\frac{1}{A_2}\left[\sigma_1=\frac{1}{R_1C_1};\sigma_2=\frac{1}{R_2\ C_2}\right]$$

Thus we observe

(*i*) The poles of an *RC* driving point impedance are on negative real axis $(-\sigma)$.

(*ii*) The residues of the poles (A_i) are real and positive for the *RC* driving point impedance.

Let us now examine the behaviour of the *RC* network (Fig. 18.22) at frequencies $\sigma=0$ and $\sigma=\infty$. At $\sigma=0$, *i.e.*, for *dc* application, if the first element C_0 is present, it offers infinite reactance *i.e.*, it behaves as an open circuit.

Thus *Z*(*s*) offers a pole at $\sigma=0$ if C_0 is present. On the other hand, if C_0 is absent, at $\sigma=0$ (*dc*), all the parallel branched capacitors $(C_1, C_2, \ldots)$ behave as open circuit and hence the net impedance is then given by

$$Z(s)=R_1+R_2+\ldots+R_\infty. \quad \text{...(18.50)}$$

Thus to summarise, if $Z(s)=\infty$ *for* $\sigma=0$, C_0 *is present ; but if* $Z(s)=\Sigma R$ *for* $\sigma=0$ *i.e., if* $Z(s)$ *is constant for* $\sigma=0$, *it is evident that* C_0 *is absent.*

Again for $\sigma=\infty$, all the capacitors in the Foster circuit show short circuited. Thus all the resistances across the parallel capacitances are bypassed and only R_∞ is of use.

$\therefore$ *if* $Z(s)=R_\infty$ *i.e., a constant term in the Foster circuit appears for* $\sigma=\infty$, *then we can say that last term is present. On the other hand, if* $Z(s)=0$, *for* $0=\infty$, *it becomes evident that* R_∞ *is missing.*

We have just established that the critical frequency nearest the origin must be a pole and the critical frequency nearest $\sigma = \infty$ must be zero. Thus, if a *RC* impedance function be given as

$$Z(s) = \frac{(s+\sigma_2)(s+\sigma_4)}{(s+\sigma_1)(s+\sigma_3)},$$

it is evident that the singularity nearest the origin must be a pole i.e., pole appears at $s = -\sigma_1$. The singularity furthest from the origin must be a zero *i.e.*, it appears at $s = -\sigma_4$.

Next, let us examine the slope of $Z(\sigma)$ along the $-\sigma$ axis [since poles and zeros of *RC* impedances are on $-\sigma$ axis].

Replacing s by σ,

$$Z(\sigma) = \frac{A_0}{\sigma} + A_\infty + \frac{A_1}{\sigma+\sigma_1} + \frac{A_2}{\sigma+\sigma_2} + \ldots$$

and $$\frac{dZ(\sigma)}{d\sigma} = -\frac{A_0}{\sigma^2} + \frac{-A_1}{(\sigma+\sigma_1)^2} + \frac{-A_2}{(\sigma+\sigma_2)^2} + \ldots \quad \ldots(18.51)$$

It is clear from eqn. (18.51) that $\frac{dZ(\sigma)}{d\sigma} \leq 0$.

i.e., the slope of $Z(\sigma)$ is always positive as $-\sigma$ increases. $Z(\sigma)$ must increase until the pole $s = -\sigma_1$ is reached. At $\sigma = -\sigma_1$, $Z(\sigma)$ changes sign and becomes negative until the next critical frequency is reached. The next critical frequency is zero for $s = -\sigma_2$. The third critical frequency must be a pole at $s = -\sigma_3$. Thus we see that the *poles and zeros alternate* on $-\sigma$ axis for the *RC* impedance function.

Summarising, the properties of *RC* driving point impedance are listed below :

1. *Poles and zeros lie on negative real axis.*
2. *Poles and zeros alternate on negative real axis.*
3. *The singularity nearest to (or at) the origin must be a pole whereas the singularity nearest to (or at) $\sigma = \infty$ must be a zero.*
4. *The residues of the poles must be real and positive.*

Similarly, if

$$Y(s) = B_0 + \frac{B_1 s}{s+\sigma_1} + \ldots + \frac{B_i s}{s+\sigma_i} + \ldots + Hs, \quad \ldots(18.52)$$

then the realisation can be achieved by representing $Y(s) = Y_1(s) + Y_2(s) + \ldots + Y_i(s) + \ldots + Y_n(s)$ where $Y_1(s)$ is actually a resistance $R_0 \left[= \frac{1}{B_0} \right]$ and the last term is a capacitance C_∞ $(= H)$. The intermediate terms $Y_i(s)$ can be represented as

$$Y_i(s) = \frac{1}{Z_i(s)} = \frac{1}{R_i + \frac{1}{C_i s}};$$

where $$R_i = \frac{1}{B_i}$$

and $$C_i = \frac{1}{\sigma_i R_i}$$

The network is shown in Fig. 18.23 and is termed as *Foster RC Network Realisation of Second Form.*

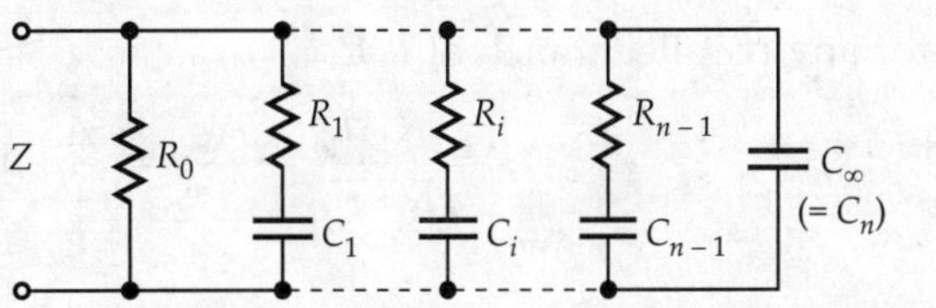

Fig. 18.23 Foster Second *RC* type network.

Obviously, for $\sigma = 0$ if $Z(s) = R_0$ (a constant), it becomes evident that $C_1, \ldots, C_\infty$ all represent open circuit and $Z(s)$ becomes only equal to R_0 in Fig. 18.23.

On the other hand, for $\sigma_i = \infty$, $C_1, \ldots, C_\infty$ will act as short circuits and all resistance branches will be parallel being shorted by the last branch C_∞. Thus $Z(s) = 0$.

i.e., if $Z(s) = R_0$ for $\sigma = 0$, first element remains.

But if $Z(s) = \infty$ for $\sigma = 0$, first element is absent ;

and if $Z(s) = 0$ for $\sigma = \infty$, last element is present.

On the other hand, if $Z(s) = \Sigma \frac{1}{R}$ for $\sigma = \infty$, it indicates the absence of the last element. It may also be noted that *in the first form, partial fraction of $Z(s)$ gives real and positive residues while in the second form, the partial exapansion of $Y(s)$ will give real and negative residue though $\frac{Y(s)}{s}$ expansion would give real and positive residue.*

18.15.2 *RL* Network Synthesis by Foster Form

The impedance of a *RL* network in Foster first form (Fig. 18.24) can be represented as

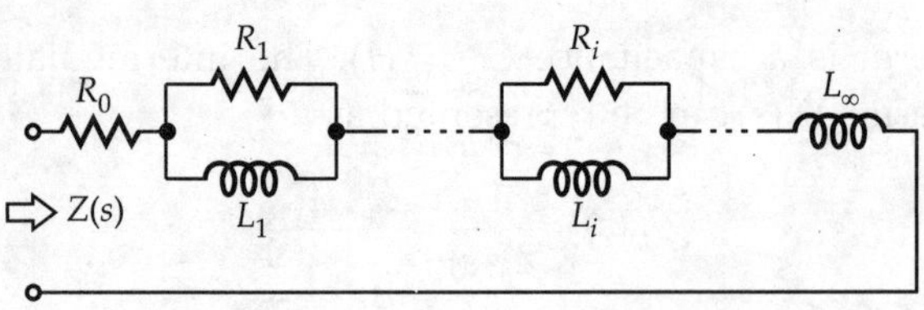

Fig. 18.24 First form of *R-L* Foster Network

$$Z(s) = A_0 + \frac{A_1 s}{s+\sigma_1} + \ldots + \frac{A_i s}{s+\sigma_i} + \ldots + A_\infty s$$

where, $A_0 = R_0, A_i = R_1$

$$\sigma_1 = \frac{R_1}{L_1};\ L_1 = \frac{A_1}{\sigma_1};\ A_\infty = L$$

[for any parallel branch of *R-L*,

$$Z_{R-L}(s) = \frac{R.sL}{R+sL} = \frac{R.s}{s+\dfrac{R}{L}} = \frac{As}{s+\sigma}\ ]$$

Similar to the properties of *R-C* impedance functions, without going into derivations, the properties can be tabulated below :

1. *Poles and zeros of the RL impedance functions are located on the negative real axis and they interface (alternate).*
2. *The singularity nearest to (or at) the origin is a zero. The singularity nearest to (or at) $s = \infty$ must be a pole.*
3. *The residues of the poles must be real and negative for Z(s).*

For $\frac{Z(s)}{s}$ expansion, the residues are positive and real.

At $\sigma = 0$, each inductance offer short circuit and hence $Z(s) = \Sigma R_0$ *i.e.*, a constant term and is evident from Fig. 18.24. In case R_0 is absent, all $R_1, \ldots, R_i$ are shorted by respective inductances at $\sigma = 0$; it indicates that $Z(s) = 0$.

On the other hand, for $\sigma = \infty$, if L_∞ is present the first form of Foster network represents an open circuit and $Z(s) = \infty$. But if L_∞ is absent, for $\sigma = \infty$, $L_1, \ldots, L_i$ represent open circuits and hence from Fig. 18.24 it is evident that this time $Z(s) = \Sigma R$.

To summarise, for Foster first form

	if $Z(s) = R_0$	for $\sigma = 0$, R_0 is present ;
but	if $Z(s) = 0$	for $\sigma = 0$, R_0 is absent.
Also,	if $Z(s) = \infty$	for $\sigma = \infty$, L_∞ is present
but	if $Z(s) = \Sigma R$	for $\sigma = \infty$, L_∞ is absent.

Similarly, the driving point admittance function of *RL* network (*Foster second form*) can be represented by

$$Y(s) = \frac{B_0}{s} + \frac{B_i}{s+\sigma_i} + \ldots + H \qquad \ldots[18.53(a)]$$

$$= Y_1(s) + Y_2(s) + \ldots + Y_n(s) \qquad \ldots[18.53(b)]$$

Comparing [18.53 (*a*)] and [18.53 (*b*)], the first term of equation [18.53 (*a*)] represents $\frac{B_0}{s}$ *i.e.*, the inductance of value $L_0 = 1/B_0$ while the last term represents a resistance R_∞ (= *H*). The intermediate terms represent admittance function of the parallel connected series network

$$\left[Y_i(s) = \frac{1}{R_i + sL_i} \right]$$

The second form of Foster network can thus be realised with parallel connected *R-L* series network with starting element as L_0 and ending element as R_∞. (Fig. 18.25).

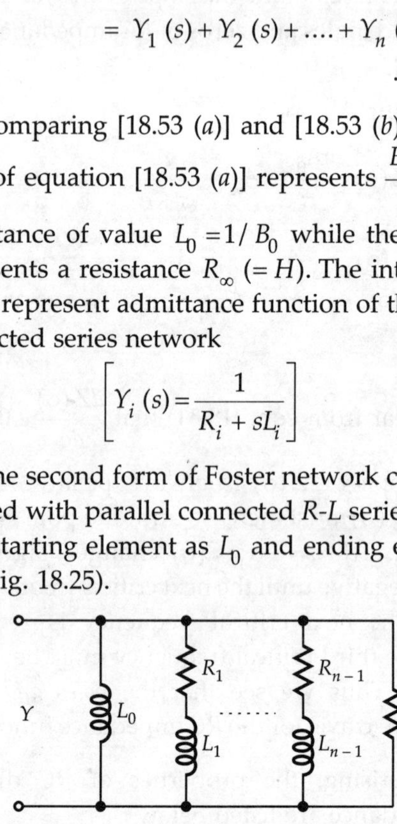

Fig. 18.25 Second form of Foster representation of *RL* network.

It has following properties :

(*i*) *The poles and zeros are located on the negative real axis of the complex plane.*

(*ii*) *Poles and zeros alternate along the negative real axis.*

(*iii*) *The residues at the poles of Y(s) are real and +ve.*

(*iv*) *The singularity nearest to (or at) the origin gives a pole while the singularity nearest to (or at) $s = \infty$ must give a zero.*

It is thus evident that for $\sigma = 0$, $L_0, L_1, \ldots$ would offer short circuit and hence $Z(s) = 0$. If L_0 is absent, $Z(s) = \Sigma R$, a constant term for $\sigma = 0$. On the other hand, for $\sigma = \infty$, $L_0, L_1, \ldots$ would offer open circuit and with R_∞ present, $Z(s) = R_\infty$ (= constant). But if R_∞ is absent, $Z(s) = \infty$ when $\sigma = \infty$.

Thus, to summarise, for Foster second form of *RL* network,

if $Z(s) = 0$ for $\sigma = 0$, L_0 is present,

but if $Z(s) = \Sigma R$ for $\sigma = 0$, L_0 is absent.

Also, if $Z(s) = R_\infty$ for $\sigma = \infty$, R_∞ is present,

but if $Z(s) = \infty$ for $\sigma = \infty$, R_∞ is absent.

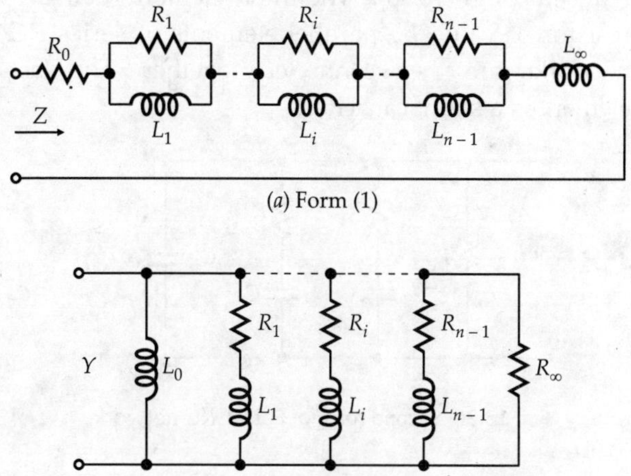

(*a*) Form (1)

(*b*) Form (2)

Fig. 18.26 Foster realisation of *RL* network.

18.16 IDENTIFICATION OF FOSTER FORM OF *R-L*/*R-C* NETWORK (FROM ANY GIVEN FUNCTION)

The following tips help the reader to identify the type of foster *RL* or *RC* network at a glance :

If the given function represents driving point impedance, $Z(s)$, it is the first form of Foster *RL* network provided the driving point impedance function can be represented in the following form :

$$\left.\begin{aligned} Z(s) &= A_0 + \ldots + \frac{A_i\, s}{s+\sigma_i} + \ldots + Hs \\ &= Z_1(s) + \ldots + Z_i(s) + \ldots + Z_n(s) \end{aligned}\right\}$$

The residues at the poles of $Z(s)$ must be real and negative though the residues of $\dfrac{Z(s)}{s}$ are real but positive.

On the other hand, if the given function represents the admittance function $Y(s)$ and can be represented by

$$\left.\begin{aligned} Y(s) &= \frac{B_0}{s} + \ldots + \frac{B_i}{s+\sigma_i} + \ldots + H \\ &= Y_1(s) + \ldots + Y_i(s) + \ldots Y_n(s) \end{aligned}\right\}$$

and also, the residues at the poles of the function are real and +ve, the network can be realised in Foster second form of *RL* network.

Figures 18.26(*a*) and 18.26(*b*) represent both these forms of the network.

Again if $Z(s)$ be given in such a form so that the residues at the poles are real and positive and

$$\left.\begin{aligned} Z(s) &= Z_1(s) + \ldots + Z_i(s) + \ldots + Z_n(s) \\ &= \frac{A_0}{s} + \ldots + \frac{A_i}{s+\sigma_i} + \ldots + H \end{aligned}\right\}$$

the network realisation is done in Foster's first form of *RC* network where the starting element is $C_0\left(=\dfrac{1}{A_0}\right)$ and the end element is R_∞ $(= H)$ [Fig. 18.27].

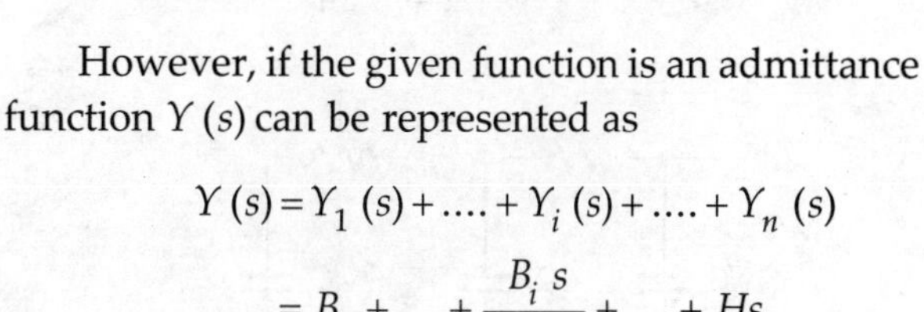

Fig. 18.27 Foster realisation of *RC* network (first form).

However, if the given function is an admittance function $Y(s)$ can be represented as

$$\begin{aligned} Y(s) &= Y_1(s) + \ldots + Y_i(s) + \ldots + Y_n(s) \\ &= B_0 + \ldots + \frac{B_i\, s}{s+\sigma_i} + \ldots + Hs, \end{aligned}$$

with partial fraction expansion giving the residue as real but negative. While the partial fraction expansion of $[Y(s)/s]$ becoming +ve and real, the second form of Foster *RC* network can then be realised (Fig. 18.28). The first element being a resistor of value B_0, parallel elements of series RC networks are then connected together. The last element is a shunt capacitor.

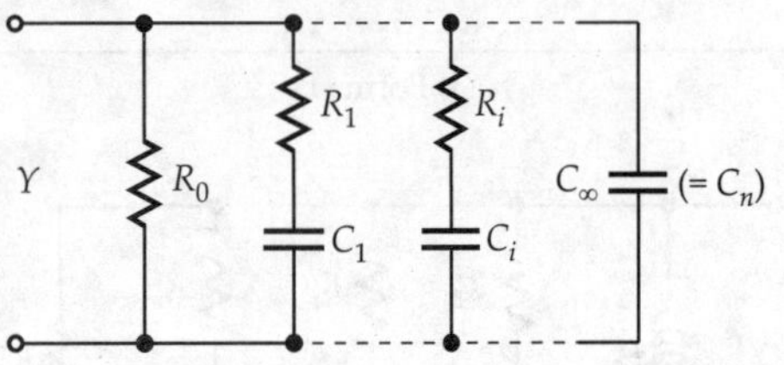

Fig. 18.28 Second form of Foster RC network.

18.17 CAUER FORM OF SYNTHESIS OF LOSSY NETWORKS

18.17.1 Synthesis of *RC* Network in Cauer Form

If the driving point impedance function is represented as

$$Z(s) = R_1 + \cfrac{1}{Y_2(s) + \cfrac{1}{R_3 + \cfrac{1}{Y_4(s) + \ldots}}},$$

the first form of Cauer network can be realised. However, in the network if $Z(s)$ is zero at $s \to \infty$, the first element is shunt capacitor while for $Z(s)$ a constant at $s \to \infty$, the first element is series R_1 [Figs. 18.29(a) and (b)].

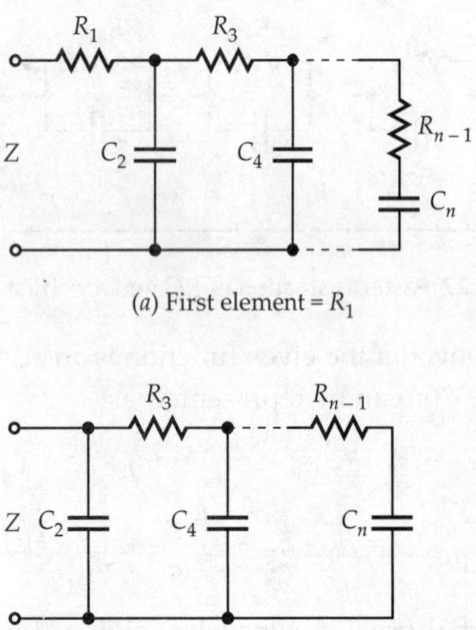

(a) First element = R_1

(b) First element = C_2

Fig. 18.29 First Form of Cauer RC networks.

On the other hand, if the continued fraction expansion is performed such that the result is

$$Z(s) = \frac{1}{C_1 s} + \cfrac{1}{\cfrac{1}{R_2} + \cfrac{1}{\cfrac{1}{C_3 s} + \cfrac{1}{\cfrac{1}{R_4 + \ldots}}}}$$

and the value of $Z(s)$ is infinity at $s \to 0$ [*i.e.*, a pole exists at $s \to 0$], the second form of Cauer network can be formed and is shown in Fig. 18.30(a) while for $Z(s)$ having a constant value at $s \to 0$ the second form of the RC network can also be formed and is shown in Fig. 18.30(b).

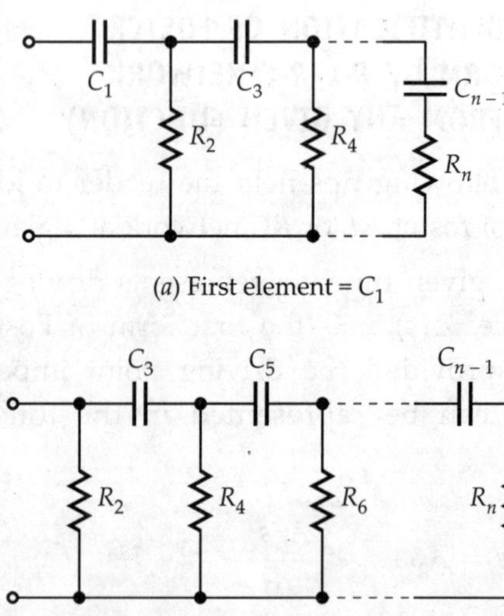

(a) First element = C_1

(b) First element = R_2

Fig. 18.30 Second Form of Cauer RC networks.

18.17.2 Synthesis of *RL* Network in Cauer Form

In Cauer first form (Fig. 18.31),

$$Z(s) = sL_1 + \cfrac{1}{\cfrac{1}{R_2} + \cfrac{1}{sL_3 + \cfrac{1}{R_4 + \ldots}}}$$

(in continued fraction form)

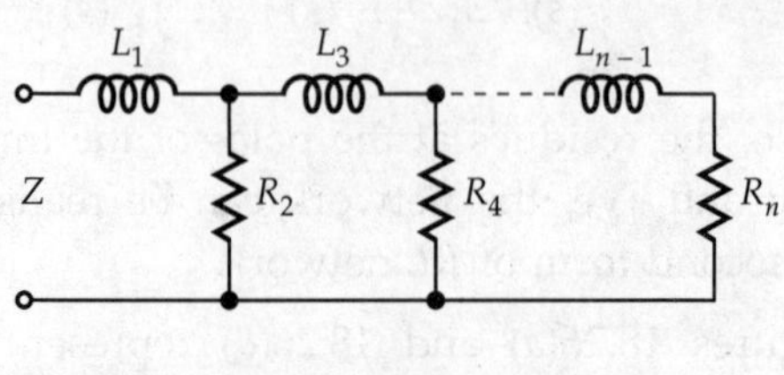

Fig. 18.31 Cauer First Form of RL network.

If $Z(s) \to \infty$ for $s \to \infty$, the first element L_1 exists but if $Z(s)$ is constant for $s \to \infty$, L_1 does not exist.

On the other hand, if $Z(s)$ has a constant value at $s \to \infty$, the first element is R_1 (Fig. 18.32) [Cauer Second form] when $Z(s)$ is expressed as

$$Z(s) = R_1 + \cfrac{1}{\cfrac{1}{sL_2} + \cfrac{1}{R_3 + \cfrac{1}{\cfrac{1}{sL_4} + \cfrac{1}{R_5 + \ldots}}}} \qquad \ldots(18.54)$$

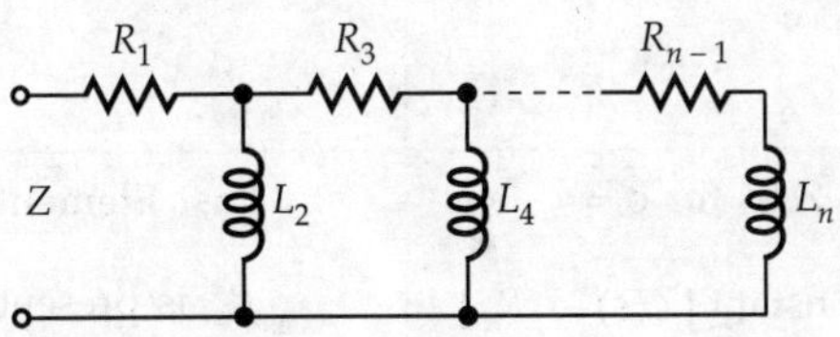

Fig. 18.32 Cauer Second Form of *RL* network.

It may also be noted that if $Z(s)$ has a zero at $s = 0$, the last element is L_n. If $Z(s)$ is constant at $s = 0$, the last element is R_n.

18.18 IDENTIFICATION OF AN IMMITTANCE FUNCTION IN CAUER FORM OF *RC* NETWORK

Step 1

If the function represents a constant value at $s \to \infty$ [$Z_s(\infty)$] as well as another constant value at $s \to 0$ [$Z_s(0)$], and if $Z_s(\infty) < Z_s(0)$, it is an impedance function that can be of Cauer first form of *RC* network [Fig. 18.33(*a*)].

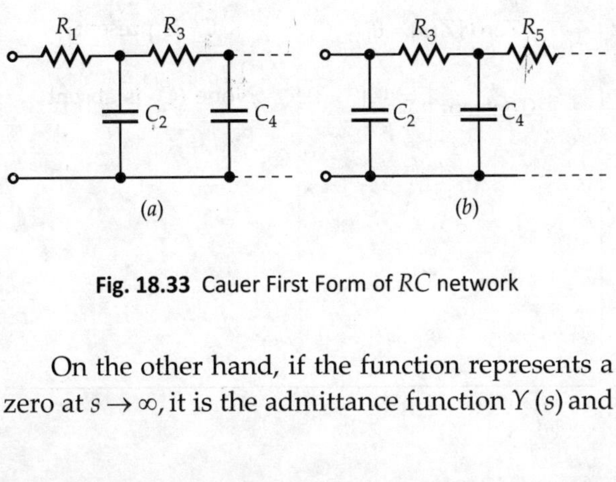

Fig. 18.33 Cauer First Form of *RC* network

On the other hand, if the function represents a zero at $s \to \infty$, it is the admittance function $Y(s)$ and it can also be represented also by Cauer first form of *RC* network [Fig. 18.33(*b*)] *but without the first element* R_1.

In both these forms of representation, the necessary form of Cauer network can be represented by arranging both the numerator polynomial and denominator polynomial in descending order of *s* and dividing the numerator by denominator.

Step 2

Comparing $Z_s(\infty)$ at $s \to \infty$ and for $Z_s(0)$ at $s \to 0$ [if, $Z_s(0) < Z_s(\infty)$], realisation is possible by Cauer second form of *RC* network. This time the network function is the impedance function $Z(s)$.

On the other hand, if the function represents a constant value with $s \to 0$ (and not infinity), the given function is then an admittance function $Y(s)$.

In both the above cases, the functions $Z(s)$ or $Y(s)$ can be realised by the second form of Cauer *RC* network. To realise the network elements, the polynomials of both the numerator and denominator are to be arranged in the ascending order and then the numerator is to be divided by the denominator. Realisation of $Z(s)$ in second Cauer form is shown in Fig. 18.34(*a*) while the realisation also in Cauer second form is shown in Fig. 18.34(*b*) without the first element.

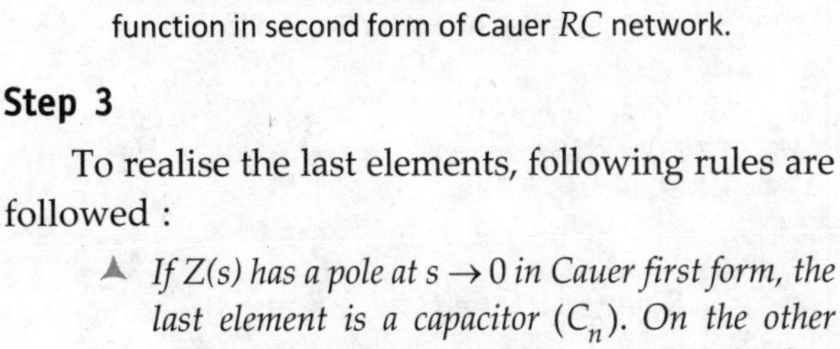

Fig. 18.34 Realisation of Impedance and admittance function in second form of Cauer *RC* network.

Step 3

To realise the last elements, following rules are followed :

- *If $Z(s)$ has a pole at $s \to 0$ in Cauer first form, the last element is a capacitor (C_n). On the other hand, if $Z(s)$ is constant at $s \to 0$ in the first form of Cauer network, the last element is a resistance (R_n).*
- *In the second form of Cauer network, if $Z(s)$ has a zero at $s \to \infty$, the last element is a capacitor (C_n) while for $Z(s)$ a constant at $s \to \infty$, the last element is a resistance (R_n).*

CHAPTER 18

18.19 SUMMARY OF DETERMINATION OF END ELEMENTS IN FOSTER AND CAUER *RC* NETWORK

Table 18.1 represents the summarised procedure determination of end elements in Foster Network (*RC*) while Table 18.2 represents the same for Cauer Network.

Table 18.1 (Foster RC Network) Determination of First and Last Elements

Types of Network	**$Z(s)$ for $\sigma = 0$**	**First Element**
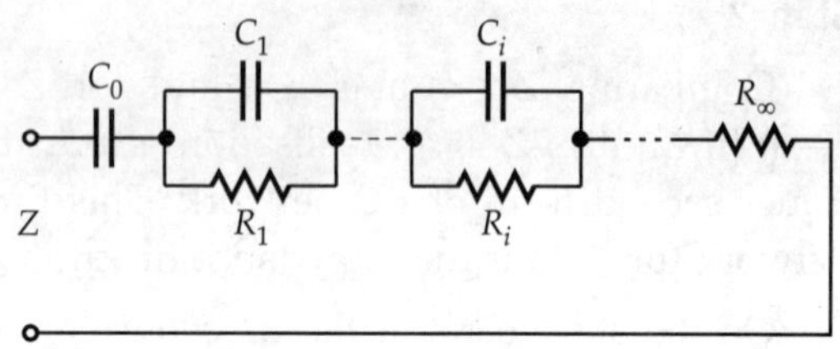	Pole $[Z(s) \to \infty]$	C_0 is present
	Constant $[Z(s) = \Sigma R]$	None (C_0 is absent)
Fig. 18.35 Foster first form.	**$Z(s)$ for $\sigma = \infty$**	**Last Element**
$Z(s) = \frac{A_0}{s} + \frac{A_1}{s+\sigma_1} + \ldots + \frac{A_i}{s+\sigma_i} + \ldots + A_\infty$	Constant $[Z(s) \to R_\infty]$	R_∞ is present
$C_0 = (1/A_0)$; $C_1 = (1/A_1)$; $R_1 = (A_1/\sigma_1)$; $C_i = (1/A_i)$; $R_i = (A_i/\sigma_i)$; $R_\infty = A_\infty$ $\sigma_i = \frac{1}{R_i C_i}$	Zero $[Z(s) = 0]$	None (R_∞ is absent)
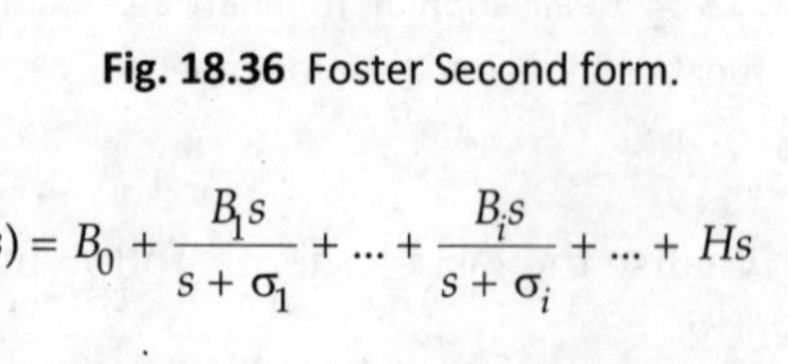	**$Z(s)$ for $\sigma = 0$**	**First Element**
	Constant $[Y(s) = R_0]$	R_0 is present
	Pole $[Y(s) = \infty]$	None (R_0 is absent)
Fig. 18.36 Foster Second form.	**$Z(s)$ for $\sigma = \infty$**	**Last Element**
$Y(s) = B_0 + \frac{B_1 s}{s+\sigma_1} + \ldots + \frac{B_i s}{s+\sigma_i} + \ldots + Hs$	Zero $[Z(s) = 0]$	C_∞ is present
$R_0 = \frac{1}{B_0}$; $C_\infty = H$; $R_1 = \frac{1}{B_1}$; $R_i = \frac{1}{B_i}$ $C_1 = \frac{1}{\sigma_1 R_1}$; $C_i = \frac{1}{\sigma_i R_i}$	Constant $\left[\Sigma \frac{1}{R}\right]$	None (C_∞ is absent)

Table 18.2 (Cauer RC Network) Determination of First and Last Elements

Types of Network	**Z (s) at s = ∞**	**First Element**
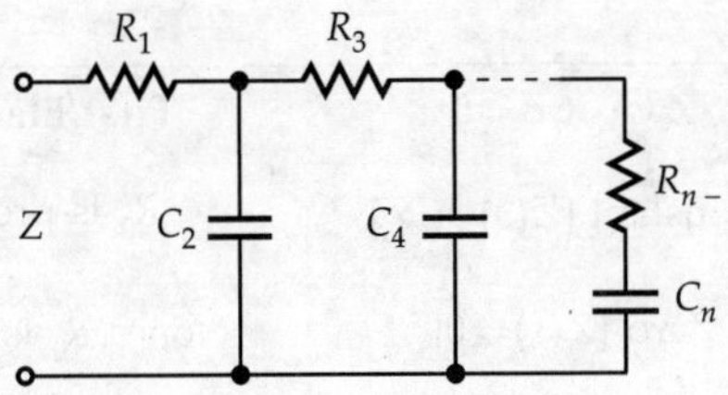 Fig. 18.37 Cauer first form.	$Z(s)$ = Constant	R_1
	$Z(s)$ = Zero	C_2 (R_1 is absent)
	Z (s) at s = 0	**Last Element**
$Z(s) = R_1 + \cfrac{1}{C_2 s + \cfrac{1}{R_3 + \cfrac{1}{C_4 s + \ldots}}}$	Pole $[Z(s) \to \infty]$	C_n
	$Z(s)$ = Constant	R_n (C_n is absent)
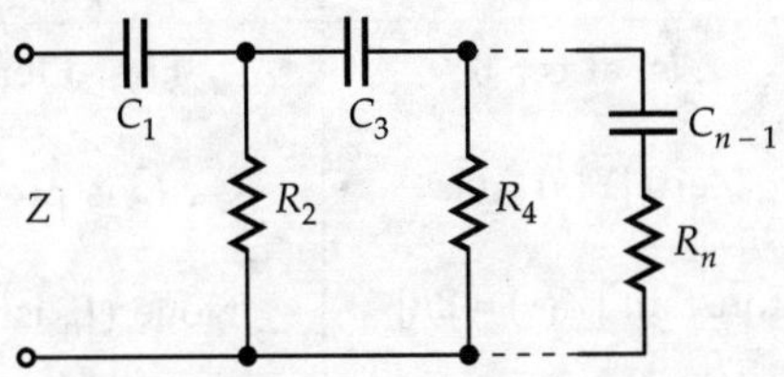 Fig. 18.38 Cauer Second form.	**Z (s) at s = 0**	**First Element**
	Pole $[Z(s) \to \infty]$	C_1
	$Z(s)$ = Constant	R_2 (C_1 is absent)
	Z (s) at s → ∞	**Last Element**
$Z(s) = \dfrac{1}{C_1 s} + \cfrac{1}{\cfrac{1}{R_2} + \cfrac{1}{\cfrac{1}{C_3 s} + \cfrac{1}{\cfrac{1}{R_4 + \ldots}}}}$	$Z(s)$ = Constant	R_n
	Zero $[Z(s) = 0]$	C_{n-1} (R_n is absent)

CHAPTER 18

18.20 SUMMARY OF DETERMINATION OF END ELEMENTS IN FOSTER AND CAUER *RL* NETWORK

Table 18.3 exhibits the procedure of determining the end elements of Foster *RL* network while Table 18.4 represents the same for *Cauer representation*.

Table 18.3 (Foster *RL* Network) Determination of First and Last Elements

Types of Network	$Z(s)$ at $\sigma = 0$	First Element
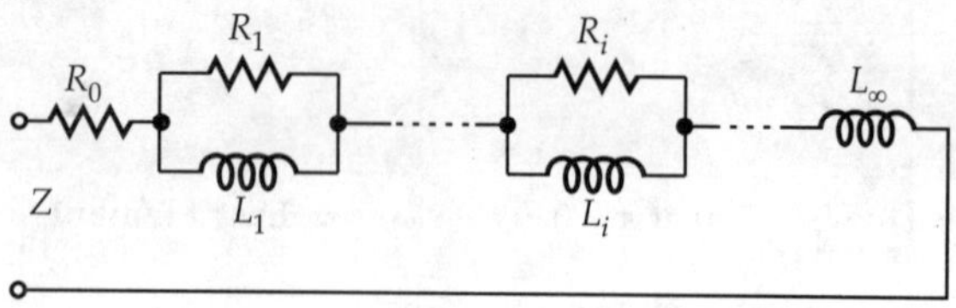 **Fig. 18.39** First form of Foster Network.	Constant $[Z(s) \to \infty]$ Zero $[Z(s) = 0]$	R_0 is present None (R_0 is absent)
	$Z(s)$ at $\sigma = \infty$	**Last Element**
$Z(s) = A_0 + \dfrac{A_1 s}{s+\sigma_1} + \ldots + \dfrac{A_i s}{s+\sigma_i} + \ldots + A_\infty$ $A_0 = R_0$; $A_i = R_i$; $L_i = A_i / \sigma_i$; $A_\infty = L$	Pole $[Z(s) \to \infty]$ Constant $[Z(s) = \Sigma R]$	L_∞ is present None (L_∞ is absent)
	$Z(s)$ at $\sigma = 0$	**First Element**
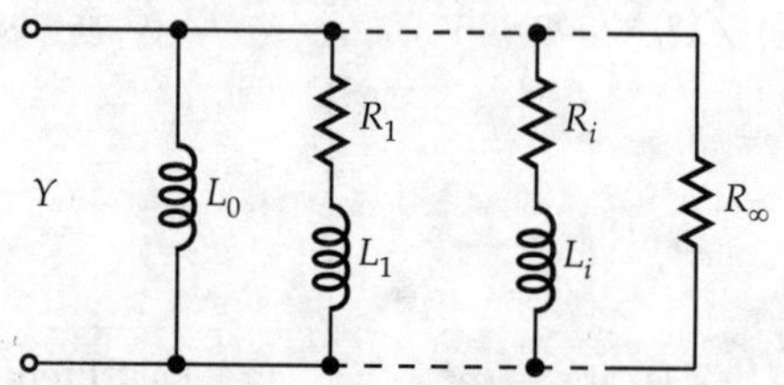 **Fig. 18.40** Second form of Foster Network.	Zero $[Y(s) = 0]$ Constant $[Z(s) = \Sigma R]$	L_0 is present None (L_0 is absent)
	$Z(s)$ at $\sigma = \infty$	**Last Element**
$Y(s) = \dfrac{B_0}{s} + \dfrac{B_1}{s+\sigma_1} + \ldots + \dfrac{B_{is}}{s+\sigma_i} + \ldots + H$ $L_0 = \dfrac{1}{B_0}$; $R_\infty = H$; $\sigma_i = \dfrac{R_i}{L_i}$; $L_i = \dfrac{1}{B_i}$; $R_i = L_i \sigma_i$	Constant $[Z(s) = R_\infty]$ Pole $[Z(s) \to \infty$	R_∞ is present None (R_∞ is absent)

Table 18.4 (Cauer RL Network) Determination of First and Last Elements

Types of Network	**Z (s) at s = ∞**	**First Element**
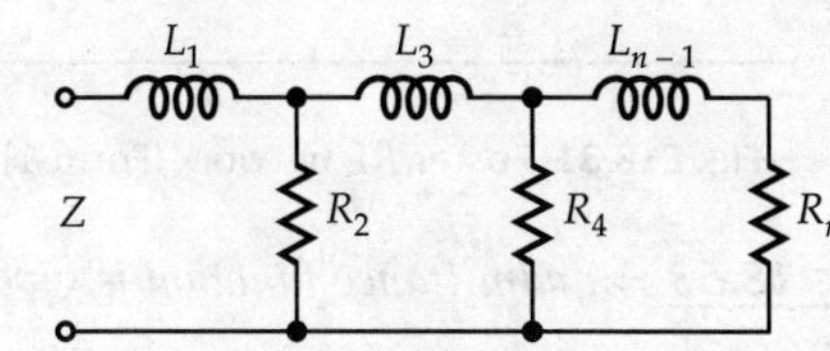	Pole $[Z(s) \to \infty]$	L_1
	$Z(s)$ = Constant	R_2 [L_1 does not exist]
Fig. 18.41 Cauer first form.	**Z (s) at s = 0**	**Last Element**
	$Z(s)$ = Constant	R_n
$Z(s) = sL_1 + \cfrac{1}{\cfrac{1}{R_2} + \cfrac{1}{sL_3 + \cfrac{1}{\cfrac{1}{R_4} + \dots}}}$	Zero $[Z(s) \to 0]$	L_{n-1} (R_n does not exist)
	Z (s) at s = 0	**First Element**
	$Z(s)$ = Constant	R_1
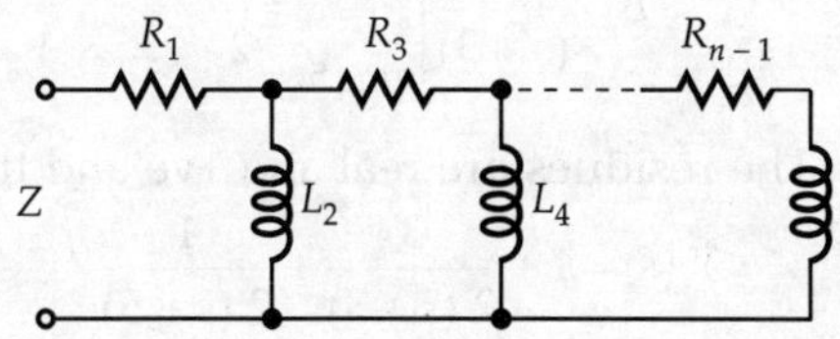	Zero $[Z(s) \to 0]$	L_2 (R_1 is absent)
Fig. 18.42 Cauer Second form.	**Z (s) at s → ∞**	**Last Element**
	$Z(s)$ = Constant	L_n
$Z(s) = R_1 + \cfrac{1}{\cfrac{1}{sL_2} + \cfrac{1}{R_3 + \cfrac{1}{\cfrac{1}{sL_4} + \cfrac{1}{R_5 + \dots}}}}$	Zero $Z(s) = 0$	L_n (R_{n-1} is absent)

C H A P T E R 18

ADDITIONAL EXAMPLES

EXAMPLE 18.52 *An impedance function is given by*

$$Z(s) = \frac{2(s+1)(s+3)}{(s+2)(s+4)}.$$

Find the R-L representation of Foster first form of network.

SOLUTION. $Z(s) = \dfrac{2(s+1)(s+3)}{(s+2)(s+4)}$

$$= 2 - \frac{1}{s+2} - \frac{3}{s+4}.$$

Thus the residues are real but negative and poles and zeros alternate on negative real axis.

$$\therefore \quad \frac{Z(s)}{s} = \frac{2(s+1)(s+3)}{s(s+2)(s+4)}$$

$$= \frac{K_1}{s} + \frac{K_2}{s+2} + \frac{K_3}{s+4}$$

$$K_1 = \left.\frac{2(s+1)(s+3)}{(s+2)(s+4)}\right|_{s=0} = \frac{6}{8} = \frac{3}{4}$$

$$K_2 = \left.\frac{2(s+1)(s+3)}{s(s+4)}\right|_{s=-2}$$

$$= \frac{2\times(-1)\times(1)}{(-2)(-2+4)} = \frac{1}{2}$$

$$K_3 = \left.\frac{2(s+1)(s+3)}{s(s+2)}\right|_{s=-4}$$

$$= \frac{2\times(-3)(-1)}{(-4)(-2)} = \frac{3}{4}$$

$$\therefore \quad Z(s) = \frac{3}{4s} + \frac{1}{2(s+2)} + \frac{3}{4(s+4)}$$

Multiplying both sides by s,

$$Z(s) = \frac{3}{4} + \frac{s}{2(s+2)} + \frac{3s}{4(s+4)}$$

$$[\because \quad A_0 = R_0 \text{ ; here } A_0 = 3/4\text{ ;}$$

$$L_1 = A_1/\sigma_1 = \left(\frac{1}{2}\right)/2 = \frac{1}{4}\text{ H}$$

$$L_2 = A_2/\sigma_2 = \left(\frac{3}{4}\right)/4 = \frac{3}{16}\text{ H}$$

$$R_1 = A_1 = \frac{1}{2}\,\Omega\text{ ; } R_2 = A_2 = \frac{3}{4}\,\Omega\text{]}$$

Hence the impedance can be realised (Foster first form) as shown in Fig. E18.31.

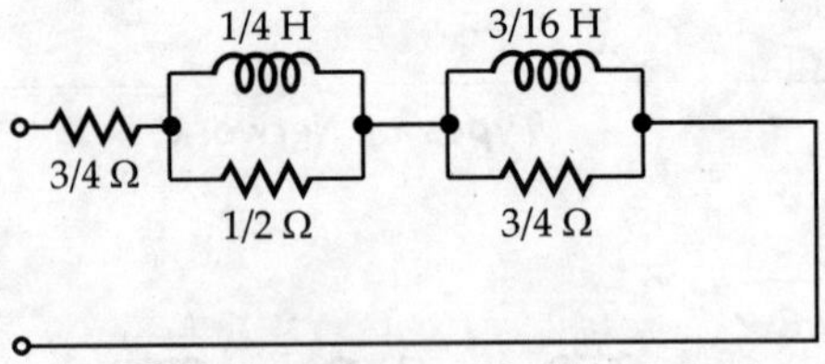

Fig. E18.31 Foster *RL* network (Form-1).

EXAMPLE 18.53 *An admittance function is given by*

$$Y(s) = \frac{(s+4)(s+6)}{(s+3)(s+5)}.$$

Find the R-L network following Foster form of realisation.

SOLUTION.

$$Y(s) = \frac{(s+4)(s+6)}{(s+3)(s+5)} = \frac{s^2+10s+24}{s^2+8s+15}$$

$$= 1 + \frac{2s+9}{s^2+8s+15} = 1 + \frac{A}{s+3} + \frac{B}{s+5}$$

$$A = \left.\frac{2s+9}{(s+5)}\right|_{s=-3} = \frac{3}{2};$$

$$B = \left.\frac{2s+9}{(s+3)}\right|_{s=-5} = \frac{1}{2}$$

$\therefore$ The residues are real and +ve and then

$$Y(s) = 1 + \frac{3}{2(s+3)} + \frac{1}{2(s+5)}$$

$$= 1 + \frac{1}{\frac{2s}{3}+2} + \frac{1}{2s+10}$$

$\therefore$ In Foster *R-L* network (second form),

$$\mathbf{R_\infty = 1\,\Omega,}$$

$$\mathbf{R_1 = 2\,\Omega\text{ ; } L_1 = \frac{2}{3}\text{ H}}$$

$$\mathbf{R_2 = 10\,\Omega\text{ ; } L_2 = 2\text{ H}}$$

Figure E18.32 represents this network.

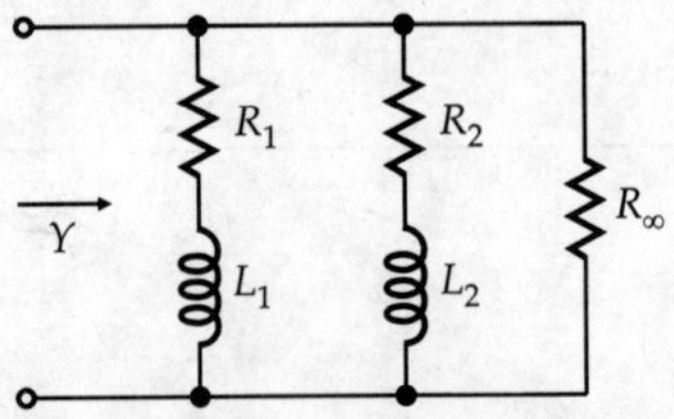

Fig. E18.32

In the above two problems it may be noted that if the residues at the poles are real and negative, first form of Foster network is to be adopted (Ex. 18.52). On the other hand, if the residues are real but positive, second form of the Foster network is to be implemented (Ex 18.53).

EXAMPLE 18.54 *Diagnose whether the following impedance function represents a RL or RC network and find its first Cauer form.*

$$Z(s)=\frac{(s+4)(s+6)}{(s+3)(s+5)}.$$

SOLUTION. It is evident by inspection that the singularity of the function nearest to the origin is a pole $[Z(s)=\infty$ for $s=-3]$ whereas for $s=-6$, the singularity of it becomes a pole. Also poles and zeros lie on the negative real axis and they interface (*i.e.* they alternate). Next we check the residues;

$$Z(s)=\frac{s^2+10s+24}{s^2+8s+15}=1+\frac{K_1}{s+3}+\frac{K_2}{s+5}$$

$$K_1=\left|\frac{(s+4)(s+6)}{(s+5)}\right|_{s=-3}=\frac{1\times 3}{2}=\frac{3}{2}$$

(real and +ve)

$$K_2=\frac{(s+4)(s+6)}{s+3}\bigg|_{s=-5}=\frac{-1\times 1}{-2}=\frac{1}{2}$$

(real and +ve)

i.e., $$Z(s)=\frac{3}{2(s+3)}+\frac{1}{2(s+5)}+1$$

$\therefore Z(s)$, when expanded over partial fraction, possesses +ve real residues.

From above, it is thus evident that the given impedance function $Z(s)$ is a RC impedance function.

In order to realise the given network in Cauer-I form, we observe that $Z(s)=$ a constant $\left(\frac{24}{15}\right)$ with $s\to 0$. Thus the last element would be a resistance. Also, with $s\to\infty, Z(s)=1$, another constant term. Thus, the first term is also a resistor.

Thus, the Cauer form I realisation would be

$$Z(s)=R_1+\cfrac{1}{Y_2(s)+\cfrac{1}{R_3+\cfrac{1}{Y_4(s)+\ldots}}}$$

The elements can be determined using continued fraction method.

$$s^2+8s+15\,)\,s^2+10s+24\,(\,1\to Z_1$$
$$\underline{s^2+8s+15}$$
$$2s+9\,)\,s^2+8s+15\,(\,\tfrac{s}{2}\to Y_2$$
$$\underline{s^2+\tfrac{9}{2}s}$$
$$7/2\,s+15\,)\,2s+9\,(\,\tfrac{4}{7}\to Z_3$$
$$\underline{2s+\tfrac{60}{7}}$$
$$\tfrac{3}{7}\,)\,\tfrac{7}{2}s+15\,(\,\tfrac{49}{6}s\to Y_4$$
$$\underline{\tfrac{7}{2}s}$$
$$15\,)\,\tfrac{3}{7}\,(\,\tfrac{1}{35}\to Z_5$$
$$\underline{\tfrac{3}{7}}$$
$$\times$$

Thus in Cauer-I form the expansion can be written as

$$Z(s)=1+\cfrac{1}{\frac{1}{2}s+\cfrac{1}{\frac{4}{7}+\cfrac{1}{\frac{49}{6}s+\cfrac{1}{\frac{1}{35}}}}}$$

Here, $R_1=1\,\Omega,\ C_2=\frac{1}{2}\text{F},\ R_3=\frac{4}{7}\,\Omega,$

$C_4=\frac{49}{6}\text{F},\ R_5=\frac{1}{35}\,\Omega.$

The Cauer-I network realisation is shown below (Fig. E18.33)

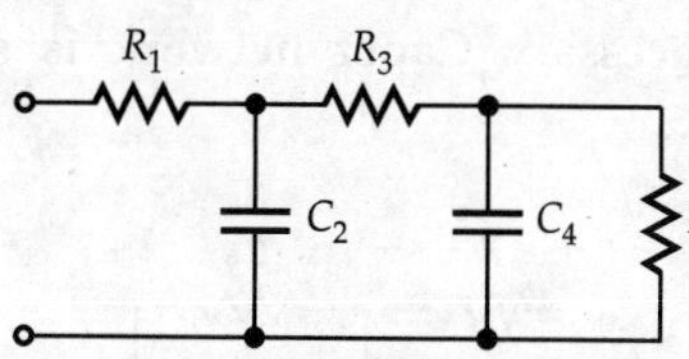

Fig. E18.33

EXAMPLE 18.55 *Consider the driving point impedance Z(s) to be*

$$Z(s)=\frac{(s+3)(s+5)}{s(s+4)}.$$

Find the Cauer form of RC network.

CHAPTER 18

Solution. $Z(s) = \dfrac{(s+3)(s+5)}{s(s+4)} = \dfrac{s^2+8s+15}{s^2+4s}$

$Z(s) = 0$ for $s \to \infty$; $Z(s) = \infty$ for $s \to 0$. Since $Z(s)$ at $s \to 0$ is higher than $Z(s)$ at $S \to \infty$ hence first form of RC network is to be realised.

In continued fraction expansion form,

$$s^2+4s\,)\; s^2+8s+15\; (\,1$$
$$s^2+4s$$
$$4s+15\,)\; s^2+4s\; (\,\frac{s}{4}$$
$$s^2+\frac{15}{4}s$$
$$\frac{s}{4}\,)\; 4s+15\; (\,16$$
$$4s$$
$$15\,)\; \frac{s}{4}\; (\,\frac{s}{60}$$
$$\frac{s}{4}$$
$$\times$$

$$\therefore \quad Z(s) = 1 + \cfrac{1}{\cfrac{s}{4} + \cfrac{1}{16 + \cfrac{1}{\cfrac{s}{60}}}}$$

$$= R_1 + \cfrac{1}{C_2\, s + \cfrac{1}{R_3 + \cfrac{1}{C_4\, s}}}$$

[*i.e.*, form-1 of Cauer RC network].

Here, $R_1 = 1\,\Omega$; $C_2 = \frac{1}{4}$ **F**; $R_3 = 16\,\Omega$, $C_4 = \frac{1}{60}$ **F**

The necessary Cauer network is shown in Fig. E18.34.

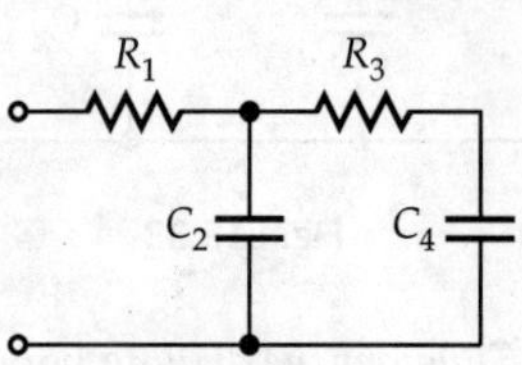

Fig. E18.34

It may be observed that for $s \to 0, Z(s) \to \infty$. Thus the last element must be a capacitor.

Example 18.56 *An impedance function at the input of a network is represented by*

$$Z(s) = \frac{s^2+5s+4}{s^2+2s}.$$

Express it in both the Foster forms.

Solution.

$$Z(s) = \frac{s^2+5s+4}{s^2+2s} = \frac{(s+1)(s+4)}{s(s+2)}$$

$$= 1 + \frac{3s+4}{s(s+2)} = 1 + \frac{K_1}{s} + \frac{K_2}{s+2}$$

$$\text{where } K_1 = \left.\frac{3s+4}{s+2}\right|_{s=0} = 2 \; ; \; K_2 = \left.\frac{3s+4}{s}\right|_{s=-2} = 1$$

$$\text{Thus, } Z(s) = 1 + \frac{2}{s} + \frac{1}{s+2} = 1 + \frac{1}{s/2} + \frac{1}{s+2}$$

Here, the residues are +ve and real and in the expression of $Z(s)$, zeros are at $-1, -4$ while poles are at $0, -2$; thus the poles and zeros alternate in the –ve real axis. Thus the given function can be realised as a RC network **(Fig. E18.35)** in first form of Foster network.

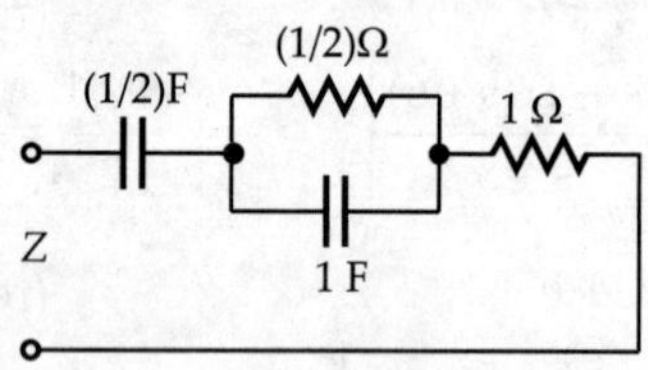

Fig. E18.35

To obtain Foster second form, let us invert the given function and obtain,

$$Y(s) = \frac{s^2+2s}{s^2+5s+4} = 1 - \frac{3s+4}{(s+1)(s+4)}$$

$$= 1 - \frac{K_1}{s+1} - \frac{K_2}{s+4}$$

Since negative coefficients appear hence, we take $\dfrac{Y(s)}{s}$.

However,

$$\frac{Y(s)}{s} = \frac{s(s+2)}{s(s+1)(s+4)} = \frac{s+2}{(s+1)(s+4)}$$

$$= \frac{K_1}{s+1} + \frac{K_2}{s+4}.$$

$$\therefore \quad K_1 = \left.\frac{s+2}{s+4}\right|_{s=-1} = \frac{1}{3};$$

$$K_2 = \left.\frac{s+2}{s+1}\right|_{s=-4} = \frac{2}{3}$$

$$\therefore \quad \frac{Y(s)}{s} = \frac{1/3}{s+1} + \frac{2/3}{s+4}$$

or
$$Y(s) = \frac{s}{3(s+1)} + \frac{2s}{3(s+4)}$$

or
$$Y(s) = \frac{s}{3s+3} + \frac{s}{\frac{3}{2}s+6} = \frac{1}{3+\frac{3}{s}} + \frac{1}{\frac{3}{2}+\frac{6}{s}}$$

$$= \frac{1}{3+\frac{1}{\frac{1}{3}s}} + \frac{1}{\frac{3}{2}+\frac{1}{\frac{1}{6}s}}.$$

Foster second form of *RC* network is shown in Fig. E18.36.

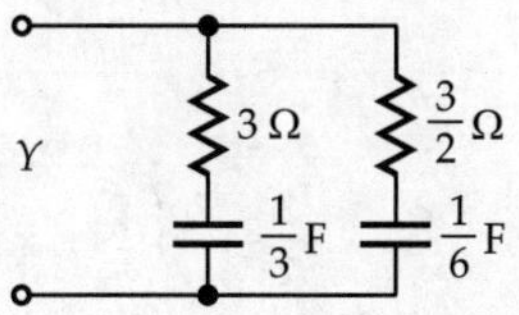

Fig. E18.36

EXAMPLE 18.57 *Find the first and second forms of Cauer network for the function :*

$$Z(s) = \frac{s^2+5s+4}{s^2+2s}.$$

SOLUTION. Applying the steps outlined in the text, it becomes evident that the given function is an *RC* network which is to be realised in Cauer forms.

First form of Cauer Network

$s^2 + 2s$) $s^2 + 5s + 4$ (1
$s^2 + 2s$
$3s + 4$) $s^2 + 2s$ ($\frac{s}{3}$
$s^2 + \frac{4s}{3}$
$\frac{2s}{3}$) $3s + 4$ ($\frac{9}{2}$
$3s$
4) $\frac{2s}{3}$ ($\frac{s}{6}$
$\frac{2s}{3}$
$\times$

$$\therefore \quad Z(s) = 1 + \frac{1}{\frac{s}{3} + \frac{1}{\frac{9}{2}+\frac{1}{\frac{s}{6}}}}$$

The necessary first form of Cauer network is shown in Fig. E18.37.

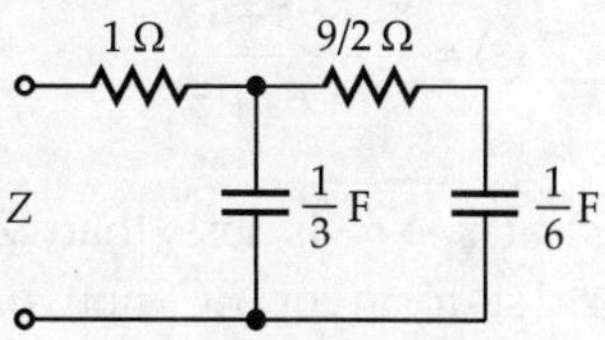

Fig. E18.37

Second form of Cauer Network

The second form can be realised by arranging the numerator and denominator polynomials of *Z(s)* in ascending order of *s* and taking the continued expansion form.

$2s + s^2$) $4 + 5s + s^2$ ($\frac{2}{s}$
$4 + 2s$
$3s + s^2$) $2s + s^2$ ($\frac{2}{3}$
$2s + \frac{2}{3}s^2$
$\frac{1}{3}s^2$) $3s + s^2$ ($\frac{9}{s}$
$3s$
s^2) $\frac{1}{3}s^2$ ($\frac{1}{3}$
$\frac{1}{3}s^2$
$\times$

$$\therefore \quad Z(s) = \frac{2}{s} + \frac{1}{\frac{2}{3} + \frac{1}{\frac{9}{s}+\frac{1}{\frac{1}{3}}}}$$

Figure E18.38 represents the second form of Cauer Network.

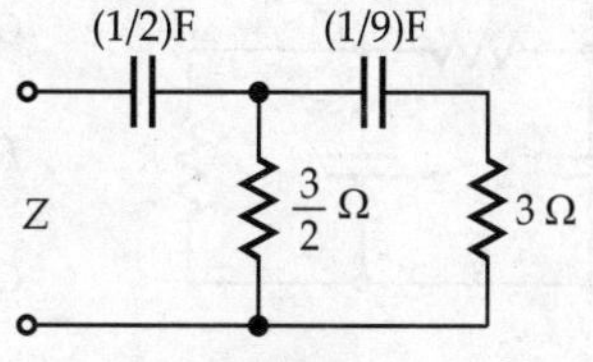

Fig. E18.38

EXAMPLE 18.58 *Find the first Cauer form of RC network*

$$Z(s)=\frac{(s+3)(s+6)}{(s+1)(s+5)}.$$

SOLUTION. The continued fraction expansion is done as shown below after rewriting $Z(s)$ expression.

$$Z(s)=\frac{s^2+9s+18}{s^2+6s+5}$$

Here $Z(s)$ at $s\to\infty$ is less than $Z(s)$ at $s=0$. Hence Cauer 1st form of RC network is to be realised.] Also, since $Z(s)$ is contact at $s\to\infty$, first element is present ; $Z(s)$ at $s\to 0$ is also constant. Thus last element is R_n.

$$s^2+6s+5\;)\; s^2+9s+18\;(\,1$$
$$\underline{s^2+6s+5}$$
$$3s+13\;)\; s^2+6s+5\;(\,\frac{s}{3}$$
$$\underline{s^2+\frac{13s}{3}}$$
$$\frac{5}{3}s+5\;)\;3s+13\;(\,\frac{9}{5}$$
$$\underline{3s+9}$$
$$4\;)\;\frac{5}{3}s+5\;(\,\frac{5}{12}s$$
$$\underline{\frac{5}{3}s}$$
$$5\;)\;4\;(\,\frac{4}{5}$$
$$\underline{4}$$
$$\times$$

$$\therefore\quad Z(s)=1+\cfrac{1}{\frac{1}{3}s+\cfrac{1}{\frac{9}{5}+\cfrac{1}{\frac{5}{12}s+\cfrac{1}{4/5}}}}$$

The necessary form of RC Cauer network is shown in Fig. E18.39.

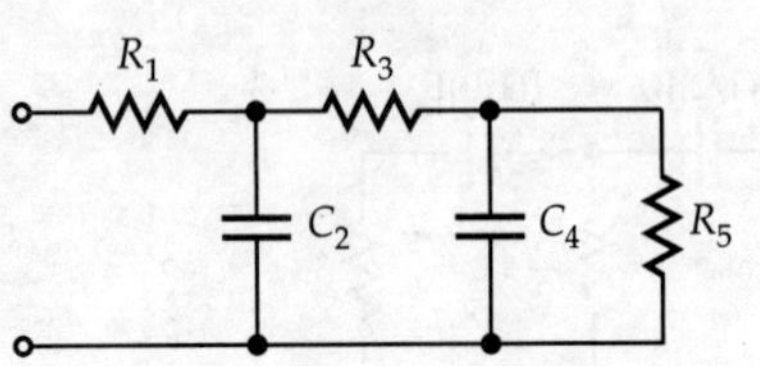

Fig. E18.39

$R_1=1\Omega$; $C_2=\frac{1}{3}F$; $R_3=\frac{9}{5}\Omega$; $C_4=\frac{5}{12}F$; $R_5=\frac{4}{5}\Omega$.

EXAMPLE 18.59 *A driving point function is given by*

$$F(s)=\frac{s^2+6s+8}{s^2+4s+3}.$$

Show that the function can be realised in both the Cauer RC and RL forms.

SOLUTION. $F(s)=\dfrac{s^2+6s+8}{s^2+4s+3}=\dfrac{(s+2)(s+4)}{(s+1)(s+3)}$

Since the poles and zeros alternate on the negative real axis and in both the cases $F(s)$ at $s\to 0$ is greater than $Z(s)$ at $s\to\infty$, hence both the RC and RL first Cauer forms are realisable. Let us first realise the RC network by continued fraction expansion taking $F(s)=Z(s)$ of RC network.

$$s^2+4s+3\;)\;s^2+6s+8\;(\,1$$
$$\underline{s^2+4s+3}$$
$$2s+5\;)\;s^2+4s+3\;(\,\frac{s}{2}$$
$$\underline{s^2+\frac{5s}{2}}$$
$$\frac{3}{2}s+3\;)\;2s+5\;(\,\frac{4}{3}$$
$$\underline{2s+4}$$
$$1\;)\;\frac{3}{2}s+3\;(\,\frac{3}{2}s$$
$$\underline{\frac{3}{2}s}$$
$$3\;)\;1\;(\,\frac{1}{3}$$
$$\underline{1}$$
$$\times$$

$$\therefore\quad Z(s)=1+\cfrac{1}{\frac{s}{2}+\cfrac{1}{\frac{4}{3}+\cfrac{1}{\frac{3}{2}s+\cfrac{1}{\frac{1}{3}}}}}$$

In RC network form [Cauer-1, RC type]

$$Z(s)=R_1+\cfrac{1}{Y_2(s)+\cfrac{1}{R_3+\cfrac{1}{Y_3(s)\ldots\ldots}}}$$

$\therefore$ Here in Cauer-1, RC network,

$$R_1=1\Omega;\quad Y_2(s)=\frac{1}{2}s$$

giving $\quad C_2 = \frac{1}{2}\,\text{F};\ R_3 = \frac{4}{3}\,\Omega;\ Y_4(s) = \frac{3}{2}\,s$

giving $\quad C_4 = \frac{3}{2}\,\text{F}$ and $R_5 = \frac{1}{3}\,\Omega.$

The required network is shown in Fig. E18.40.

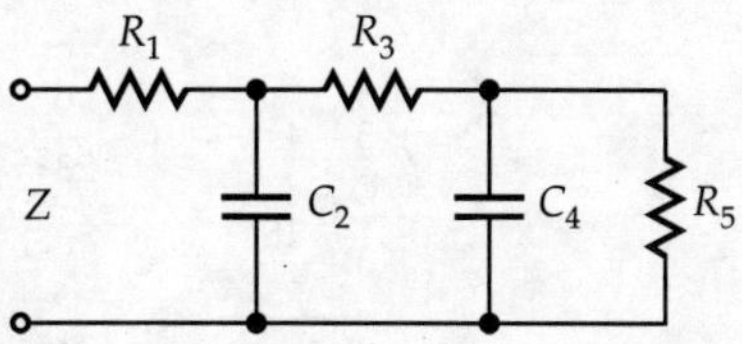

Fig. E18.40

Had the given function been in impedance form, the first form of Cauer-1 *RL* representation, would then become

$$Z(s) = sL_1 + \cfrac{1}{\cfrac{1}{R_2} + \cfrac{1}{sL_3 + \cfrac{1}{\cfrac{1}{R_4} + \ldots}}},$$

Since *RC* impedance is equivalent to *RL* admittance hence this time *F*(*s*) should be an admittance function and $F(s) = 1/Z(s)$

In our case we find that

$L_1 = 0$ and $R_2 = 1\Omega$, $L_3 = \frac{1}{2}\,\text{H}$, $R_4 = \frac{3}{4}\,\Omega$,

$L_5 = \frac{3}{2}\,\text{H}$, $R_6 = 3\Omega$

$$\because \quad Z(s) = \cfrac{1}{1 + \cfrac{1}{\cfrac{s}{2} + \cfrac{1}{\cfrac{4}{3} + \cfrac{1}{\cfrac{3s}{2} + \cfrac{1}{\frac{1}{3}}}}}}$$

The required *RL* network is drawn in Fig. E18.41.

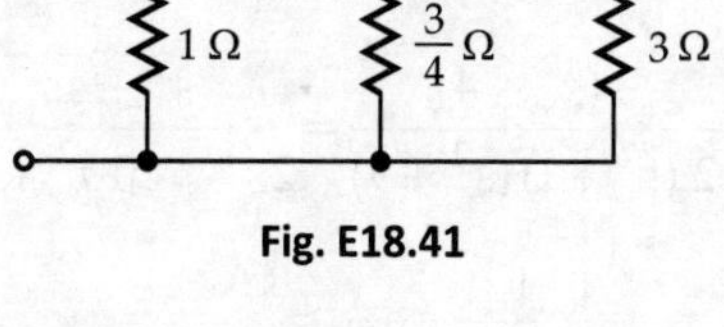

Fig. E18.41

The above forms of representation are called *dual forms of representation.*

EXAMPLE 18.60 *Realise the following impedance functions in both the Cauer forms of LC network :*

$$Z(s) = \frac{12\,s^4 + 10\,s^2 + 1}{3s^3 + 2s}.$$

SOLUTION. Let us first keep the polynomials in the numerator and denominator in the descending power and perform the continued fraction.

$$3s^3 + 2s\,)\ 12\,s^4 + 10\,s^2 + 1\ (\ 4s$$
$$12\,s^4 + 8s^2$$
$$2s^2 + 1\,)\ 3s^3 + 2s\ (\ \tfrac{3}{2}s$$
$$3s^3 + \tfrac{3}{2}s$$
$$\tfrac{1}{2}s\,)\ 2s^2 + 1\ (\ 4s$$
$$2s^2$$
$$1\,)\ \tfrac{s}{2}\ (\ \tfrac{s}{2}$$
$$\tfrac{s}{2}$$
$$\times$$

With $n > m$ in $Z(s)$, for $s \to \infty$, $Z(s) \to \infty$. The first element is inductor. Also, with $s \to 0$, $Z(s) \to \infty$ the last term is thus a capacitor.

$$\therefore \quad Z(s) = 4\,s + \cfrac{1}{\cfrac{3s}{2} + \cfrac{1}{4s + \cfrac{1}{s/2}}}$$

The resulting Cauer first form of network is shown below [Fig. E18.42].

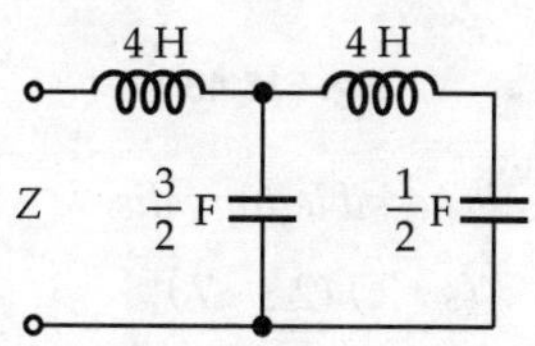

Fig. E18.42

To realise the second form of Cauer Network, we take the polynomials in the *Z*(*s*) function in the ascending form both in numerator and denominator.

$$\therefore \quad Z(s) = \frac{1 + 10\,s^2 + 12\,s^4}{2s + 3s^3}$$

CHAPTER 18

Let us perform now the continued fraction expansion.

$$2s+3s^3\ )\ 1+10s^2+12s^4\ \left(\frac{1}{2s}\right.$$
$$1+\frac{3}{2}s^2$$
$$\overline{\frac{17}{2}s^2+12s^4}\ )\ 2s+3s^3\ \left(\frac{4}{17s}\right.$$
$$2s+\frac{48}{17}s^3$$
$$\overline{\frac{3}{17}s^3}\ )\ \frac{17}{2}s^2+12s^4\ \left(\frac{289}{6s}\right.$$
$$\frac{17}{2}s^2$$
$$\overline{12s^4}\ )\ \frac{3}{17}s^3\ \left(\frac{3}{17\times 12s}\right.$$
$$\frac{3}{17}s^3$$
$$\times$$

With $s\to 0$, $Z(s)\to\infty$ the first term is a capacitor. With $s\to\infty$, $Z(s)\to\infty$ the last term is thus an inductor.

$$\therefore\quad Z(s)=\frac{1}{2s}+\cfrac{1}{\cfrac{4}{17s}+\cfrac{1}{\cfrac{289}{6s}+\cfrac{1}{\cfrac{3}{204s}}}}$$

The second form of Cauer *LC* network is shown in Fig. E18.43.

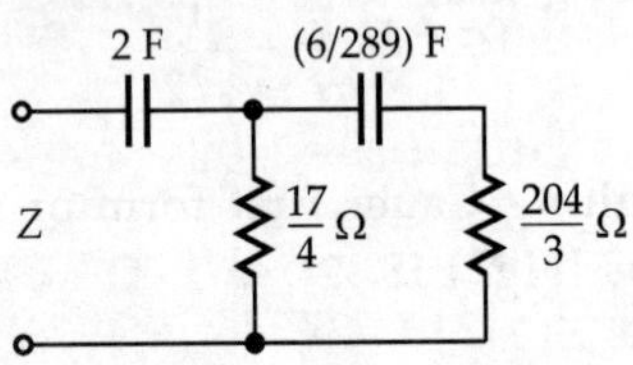

Fig. E18.43

EXAMPLE 18.61 *Is it possible to realise*

$$Y(s)=\frac{(s+2)(2s+7)}{(s+1)(s+3)}$$

in the second form of RC Cauer network ?

SOLUTION.

$$Y(s)=\frac{2s^2+7s+4s+14}{s^2+4s+3}=\frac{2s^2+11s+14}{s^2+4s+3}$$

In the second form of representation we require to arrange the numerator and denominator in the ascending order of s.

$$i.e.,\qquad Y(s)=\frac{14+11s+2s^2}{3+4s+s^2}$$

Let us now perform the continued fraction

$$3+4s+s^2\ )\ 14+11s+2s^2\ \left(\frac{14}{3}\right.$$
$$14+\frac{56}{3}s$$
$$\overline{-\frac{23}{3}s+2s^2}\ )\ 3+4s+s^2\ \left(-\frac{9}{23s}\right.$$
$$3+\frac{18}{23}s$$

Since a negative quotient has appeared in the expression of continued fraction, hence it is evident that Cauer 2nd form of representation is not possible.

Also, to be represented in Cauer second form of *RC* network, $Z(s)$ should be infinity at $s\to 0$.

$$\text{Here}\quad Z(s)=\frac{s^2+4s+3}{2s^2+11s+14}.$$

Obviously, this is not infinity at $s\to 0$.

Thus for the given function, it is not possible to represent it in Cauer second forms of *RC* network.

EXAMPLE 18.62 *Realise the function*

$$Z(s)=\frac{s(s^2+4)}{2(s^2+1)(s^2+9)}$$

in both the Cauer and Foster forms of LC networks.

SOLUTION. (*i*) Cauer-I form :

Observation reveals that the polynomial order of numerator (n) is less than that of the denominator (m) *i.e.*, $n<m$.

Also, with $s\to\infty$, $Z(s)\to 0$. This gives the continued fraction of the Cauer-1 form (*LC* network) as

$$Z(s)=\cfrac{1}{C_2 s+\cfrac{1}{L_3 s+\cfrac{1}{C_4 s+\ldots}}}$$

The continued fraction expansion is performed from

$$Z(s)=\frac{s(s^2+4)}{2(s^2+1)(s^2+9)}=\frac{s^3+4s}{2s^4+20s^2+18}$$

$$=\cfrac{1}{\cfrac{2s^4+20s^2+18}{s^3+4s}}$$

when the continued expression is obtained as

$$s^3 + 4s\,)\ 2s^4 + 20s^2 + 18\ (\ 2s$$
$$\underline{2s^4 + 8s^2}$$
$$12s^2 + 18\,)\ s^3 + 4s\ (\ \frac{s}{12}$$
$$\underline{s^3 + \frac{18s}{12}}$$
$$\frac{30}{12}s\,)\ 12s^2 + 18\ (\ \frac{144\,s}{30} = \frac{24}{5}s$$
$$\underline{12s^2}$$
$$18\,)\ \frac{30}{12}s\ (\ \frac{30}{18\times 12}s = \frac{5}{36}s$$
$$\underline{\frac{30\,s}{12}}$$
$$\times$$

$$\therefore \quad Z(s) = \cfrac{1}{2s + \cfrac{1}{\cfrac{s}{12} + \cfrac{1}{\cfrac{24}{5}s + \cfrac{1}{\cfrac{5}{36}s}}}}$$

Here, $C_2 = 2$ **H**, $L_3 = \frac{1}{12}$ **H**

$C_4 = \frac{24}{5}$ **F** $L_5 = \frac{5}{36}$ **H.**

Figure E18.44 represents the first form of Cauer *LC* network.

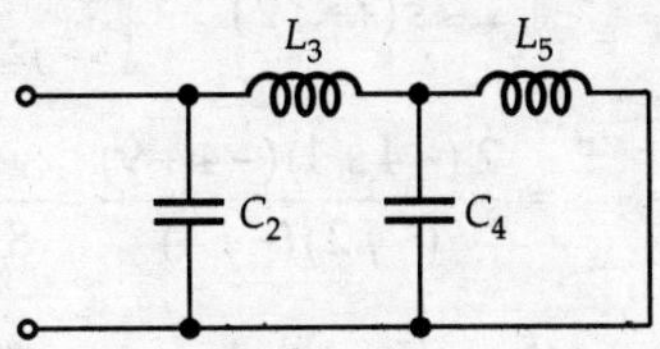

Fig. E18.44

(*ii*) **Cauer-II form**

Here we observe, *n* being less than *m*, with $s \to 0, Z(s) \to 0$. This gives the second form of Cauer network in the form of

$$Z(s) = \cfrac{1}{L_2 s + \cfrac{1}{\cfrac{1}{C_3 s} + \cfrac{1}{1/L_4 s + \ldots}}}$$

To realise the network elements we are to invert the order of polynomials both in the numerator and denominator for continued fraction.

$$Z(s) = \cfrac{1}{\cfrac{18 + 20s^2 + 2s^4}{4s + s^3}}$$

$$4s + s^3\,)\ 18 + 20s^2 + 2s^4\ (\ \frac{9}{2s}$$
$$\underline{18 + \frac{9}{2}s^2}$$
$$\frac{31s^2}{2} + 2s^4\,)\ 4s + s^3\ (\ \frac{8}{31\,s}$$
$$\underline{4s + \frac{16\,s^3}{31}}$$
$$\frac{15\,s^3}{31}\,)\ \frac{31}{2}s^2 + 2s^4\ (\ \frac{961}{30\,s}$$
$$\underline{\frac{31}{2}s^2}$$
$$2s^4\,)\ \frac{15}{31}s^3\ (\ \frac{15}{62\,s}$$
$$\underline{\frac{15}{31}s^3}$$
$$\times$$

$$\therefore \quad Z(s) = \cfrac{1}{\cfrac{9}{2s} + \cfrac{1}{\cfrac{8}{31s} + \cfrac{1}{\cfrac{961}{30\,s} + \cfrac{1}{\cfrac{15}{62\,s}}}}}$$

$$= \cfrac{1}{Y_2(s) + \cfrac{1}{Z_3(s) + \cfrac{1}{Y_4(s) + \ldots}}}$$

Thus,

$$Y_2(s) = \frac{9}{2s}\left(= \frac{1}{L_2\,s}\right) \text{ giving } L_2 = \frac{2}{9}\text{ H}$$

$$Z_3(s) = \frac{8}{31\,s}\left(= \frac{1}{C_3\,s}\right) \text{ giving } C_3 = \frac{31}{8}\text{ F}$$

$$Y_4(s) = \frac{961}{30\,s}\left(= \frac{1}{L_4\,s}\right) \text{ giving}$$

$$L_4 = \frac{30}{961}\text{ H;}$$

$$Z_5(s) = \frac{15}{62\,s}\left(= \frac{1}{C_5\,s}\right) \text{ giving } C_5 = \frac{62}{15}\text{ F}$$

Figure E18.45 gives the second form of Cauer Network (*LC*).

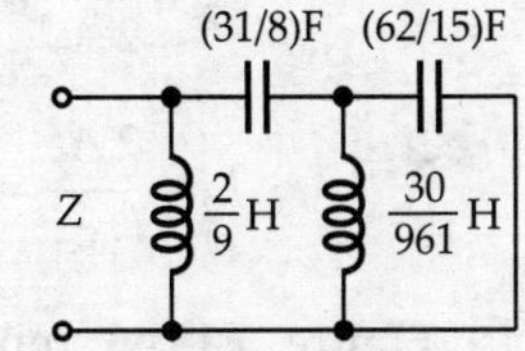

Fig. E18.45

(iii) **Foster first form**

$$Z(s) = \frac{s^3 + 4s}{2s^4 + 20s^2 + 18} = \frac{1}{2}\frac{s(s^2+4)}{(s^2+1)(s^2+9)}$$

Observation reveals that the order of the numerator is less than the order of the denominator. Hence there is a simple zero at $s \to \infty$. Also, lowest ordered term in the numerator is greater than the lowest ordered term in the denominator. Hence there is a simple pole at $s \to 0$. This indicates that in the Foster first form, there will be no first element as well as no end element. There will also be no (A_o / s) term and Hs term in the partial fraction expansion.

$$\therefore \quad Z(s) = \frac{2A_1 s}{s^2+1} + \frac{2A_2 s}{s^2+9}$$

$$A_1 = \left.\frac{\frac{1}{2}s(s^2+4)}{(s^2+9)(s-j1)}\right|_{s=-j1}$$

$$= \frac{\frac{1}{2}(-j1)(-1+4)}{(-1+9)(-j2)} = \frac{\frac{3}{2}(-j1)}{(-j1)(16)} = \frac{3}{32}$$

$$A_2 = \left.\frac{\frac{1}{2}s(s^2+4)}{(s^2+1)(s-j3)}\right|_{s=-j3}$$

$$= \frac{\frac{1}{2}(-j3)(-9+4)}{(-9+1)(-j6)} = \frac{-\frac{15}{2}(-j1)}{(-8)(-j6)} = \frac{15}{96} = \frac{5}{32}.$$

In Foster form,

$$C_1 = \frac{1}{2A_1} = \frac{32}{6} = \mathbf{\frac{16}{3}\ F};$$

$$L_1 = \frac{2A_1}{\omega_1^2} = \frac{2\times 3/32}{1} = \mathbf{\frac{3}{16}\ H}$$

$$C_2 = \frac{1}{2A_2} = \mathbf{\frac{16}{5}\ F};$$

$$L_2 = \frac{2A_2}{\omega_2^2} = \frac{2\times 5/32}{9} = \left(\mathbf{\frac{5}{144}}\right)\mathbf{H}.$$

Figure E18.46 represents the first form of Foster *LC* network.

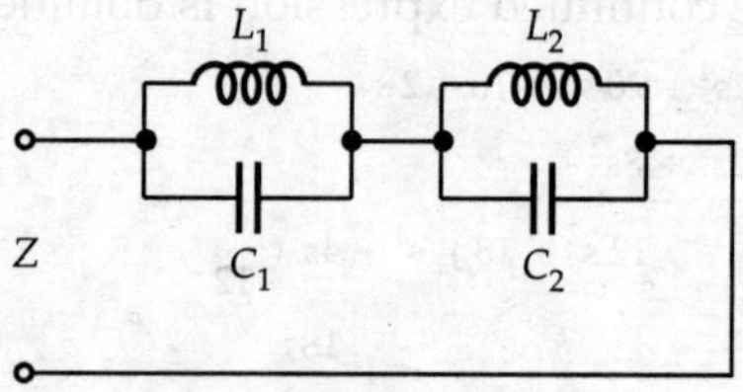

Fig. E18.46

(iv) **Second form of Foster Network**

In order to determine the second form, we consider the admittance function $Y(s)$.

$$Y(s) = \frac{1}{Z(s)} = 2\frac{(s^2+1)(s^2+9)}{s(s^2+4)}$$

The numerator polynomial is of higher order and the numerator has one excess term while the denominator has one s term. Thus the given function has two poles at $s \to 0$ and $s \to \infty$.

Further,

$$Y(s) = \frac{B_0}{s} + \frac{B_2}{s+j2} + \frac{B_2^*}{s-j2} + Hs$$

$$B_0 = \left.\frac{2(s^2+1)(s^2+9)}{(s^2+4)}\right|_{s=0} = \frac{18}{4} = \frac{9}{2}$$

$$B_2 = \left.\frac{2(s^2+1)(s^2+9)}{s(s-j2)}\right|_{s=-j2}$$

$$= \frac{2(-4+1)(-4+9)}{(-j2)(-j4)} = \frac{30}{8} = \frac{15}{4}$$

By observation, $H = 2$.

$$\therefore \quad L_0 = \frac{1}{B_0} = \frac{2}{9}\ \text{H};\ C_\infty = H = 2\ \text{F}.$$

$$L_2 = \frac{1}{2B_2} = \frac{1}{2\times\frac{15}{4}} = \frac{2}{15}\ \text{H};$$

$$C_2 = \frac{2B_2}{\omega_2^2} = \frac{2\times 15/4}{2} = \frac{30}{16} = \frac{15}{8}\ \text{F}.$$

Figure E18.47 represents the second form of Foster network.

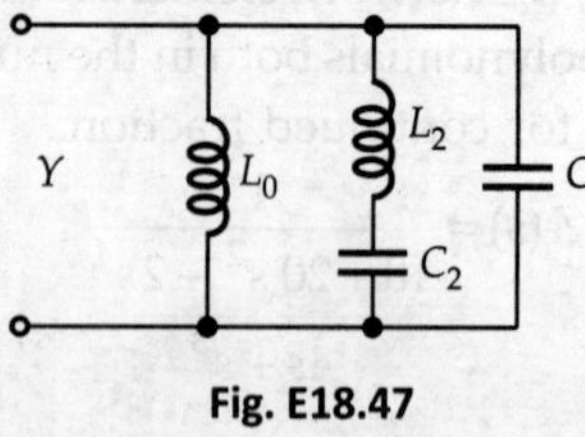

Fig. E18.47

EXERCISES

1. Check whether the following polynomials are Hurwitz :

(a) $s^4 + 3s^2 + 6s + 20$ [**Hint.** s^2 term is missing hence not Hurwitz]

(b) $2s^6 + 4s^5 + 4s^4 - 2s^3 + s^2 + s + 3$ [**Hint.** Not Hurwitz because one coefficient is –ve]

(c) $s^2 + 4s + 7$

[**Hint.** The given polynomial is a second order polynomial with no missing term and all the coefficients are of same sign (+ve). Also the test function $F(s) = \dfrac{s^2+7}{4s}$ gives all +ve quotients in the continued fraction. Hence the given function is Hurwitz]

(d) $-2s^2 - 4s - 12$

[**Hint.** No missing term of s in polynomial; all the coefficients are of same sign (–ve) and $\dfrac{-(2s^2+16)}{-6s}$ in continued fraction gives all +ve quotients. Thus the given polynomial is Hurwitz]

(e) $s^5 + s^3 + s$

[**Hint.** Since the polynomial has only odd s powers hence the first derivative gives $5s^4 + 3s^2 + 1$. However, $\dfrac{s^5+s^3+s}{5s^4+3s^2+1}$ in continued fraction gives negative quotients. Thus the given polynomial is not Hurwitz.]

2. Check whether the following functions are *PR* :

(a) $F(s) = \dfrac{s^2 - s - 8}{s^2 + 2s - 2}$

[**Hint.** Numerator polynomial is not Hurwitz as well as the denominator polynomial. Hence $F(s)$ is not *PR*.]

(b) $P(s) = \dfrac{s^2 + s + 4}{s^2 + s + 1}$

[**Hint.** It may be observed that the numerator and denominator polynomials have their zeros in the left half plane. However, $Re\, P(s)|_{s=j\omega}$ is not positive for any value of ω. Thus all the conditions of PR functions are not satisfied and hence the given function is not *PR*.]

(c) $F(s) = \dfrac{s^2 + s + 1}{s^2 + s + 4}$

[**Hint.** Re $F(s)|_{s=j\omega} > 0$; actually Re $F(s)\Big|_{s=j\omega} = \dfrac{(s^2+2)^2}{s^4+7s^2+16} = \dfrac{(-\omega^2+2)^2}{\omega^4 - 7\omega^2 + 16}$

Thus Re $F(s)$ is +ve for any value of ω. Moreover, both numerator and denominator are both Hurwitz. Hence $F(s)$ is a *PR* function.]

3. A function is given by $Z(s) = \dfrac{(s^2+1)(s^2+16)}{s(s^2+4)}$. Realise it in the first and second form of Foster *LC* forms.

Hint. $Z(s) = s + \dfrac{13s^2 + 16}{s(s^2+4)} = s + \dfrac{A}{s} + \dfrac{B}{s+j2} + \dfrac{C}{s-j2}$, where $A = 4,\ B = 9/2,\ C = 9/2$

$$\therefore \quad Z(s) = s + \frac{4}{s} + \frac{9}{2}\left(\frac{1}{s+j2} + \frac{1}{s-j2}\right) = s + \frac{4}{s} + \frac{\frac{9s}{4}\cdot\frac{9}{s}}{\frac{9}{4}s + \frac{9}{s}}$$

C H A P T E R 18

Figure P18.1 gives the first Foster form.

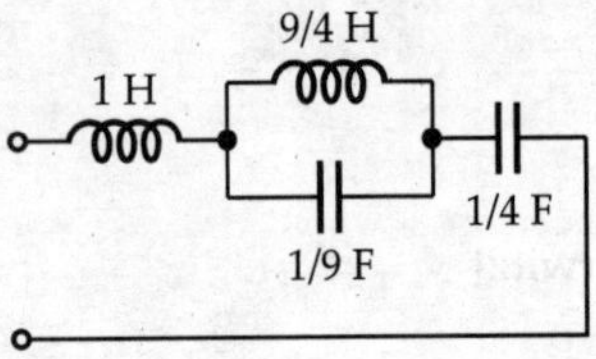

Fig. P18.1

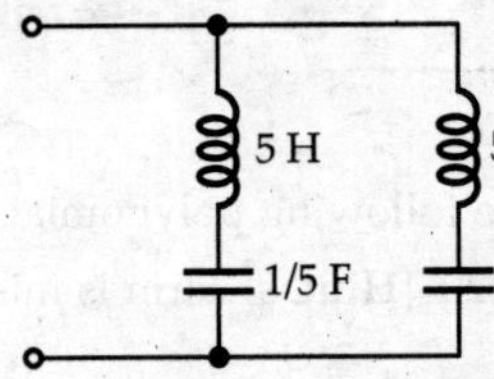

Fig. P18.2

To find second form,

$$Y(s) = \frac{s(s+4)}{(s^2+1)(s^2+16)}$$

$$= \frac{1}{s+j} + \frac{B}{s-j} + \frac{C}{s+j4} + \frac{D}{s-j4} = \frac{1/10}{s+j} + \frac{1/10}{s-j} + \frac{2/5}{s+j4} + \frac{2/5}{s-j4}$$

$$\therefore \quad Y(s) = \frac{1}{10}\left(\frac{1}{s+j} + \frac{1}{s-j}\right) + \frac{2}{5}\left(\frac{1}{s+j4} + \frac{1}{s-j4}\right) = \frac{s/5}{s^2+1} + \frac{\frac{4s}{5}}{s^2+4^2} = \frac{1}{5s+\frac{5}{s}} + \frac{1}{\frac{5}{4}s+\frac{20}{5}}.$$

Figure P18.2 gives the 2nd form of Foster *LC* network.]

4. Represent $Z(s) = \dfrac{s^4+7s^2+9}{s(s^2+4)}$ in the form of Cauer *LC* network.

[**Hint.** $\dfrac{s^4+7s^2+9}{s^3+4s} = s + \cfrac{1}{\cfrac{s}{3} + \cfrac{1}{3s + \cfrac{1}{\frac{1}{9}s}}}$ (in continued fraction)

Figure P18.3 gives the first form of Cauer Network.

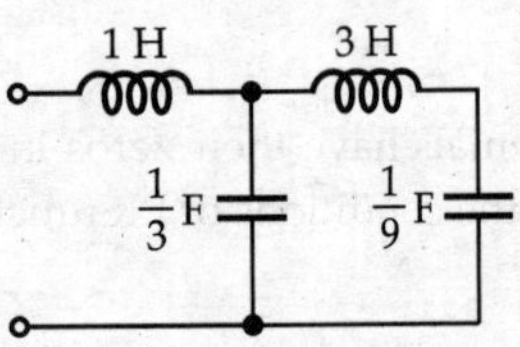

Fig. P18.3

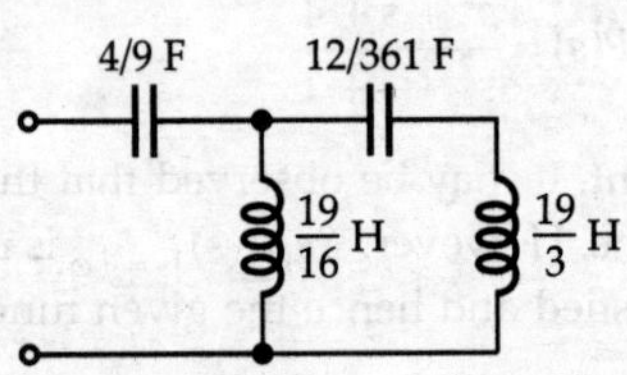

Fig. P18.4

Using continued fraction for $\dfrac{9+7s^2+s^4}{4s+s^3}$, the second form of Cauer network is obtained (Fig. P18.4)].

5. The driving point impedance of an *LC* network is given by

$$Z(s) = \frac{10s^4+12s^2+1}{2s(s^2+1)}.$$

Obtain the first form of Cauer *LC* network.

[**Hint.** Figure P18.5 gives the required network]

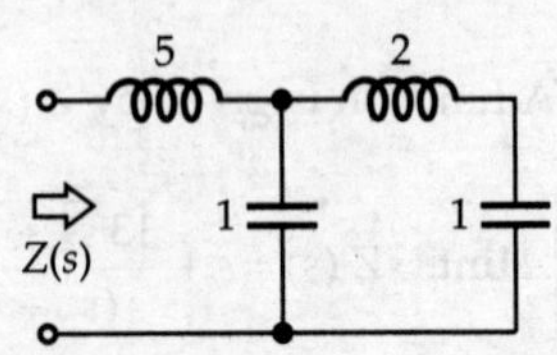

Fig. P18.5

CHAPTER

19

Review Problems

Harder Worked out Problems Covering Concepts Furnished in Different Chapters

Example 19.1 *In Fig. E19.1 find R_{net} (resistance between X-Y).*

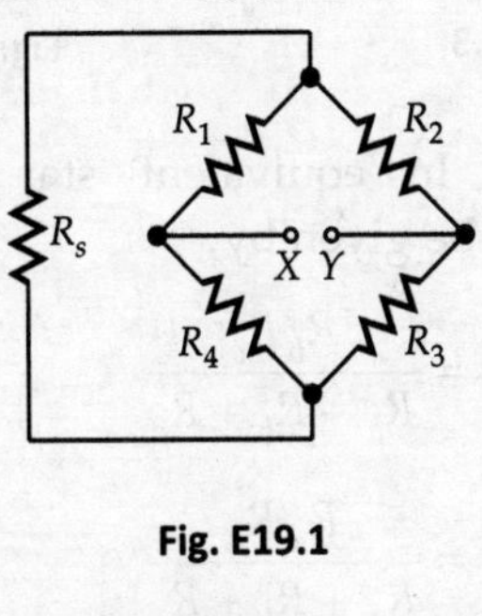

Fig. E19.1

Solution. The network reduction is shown below [Fig. E19.1(*a*)]. Finally the network can be simplified as shown in Fig. E19.1(*b*).

$$R_B = R_s + R_2 + \frac{R_s R_2}{R_1}$$

$$= \frac{R_1 R_s + R_1 R_2 + R_s R_2}{R_1}$$

$$R_A = R_s + R_1 + \frac{R_1 R_s}{R_2} = \frac{R_s R_2 + R_1 R_2 + R_1 R_s}{R_2}$$

$$R_C = R_1 + R_2 + \frac{R_1 R_2}{R_s} = \frac{R_1 R_s + R_2 R_s + R_1 R_2}{R_s}$$

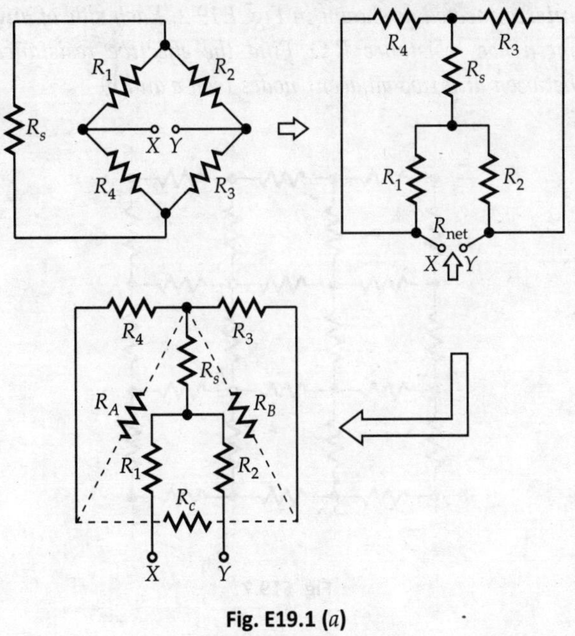

Fig. E19.1 (*a*)

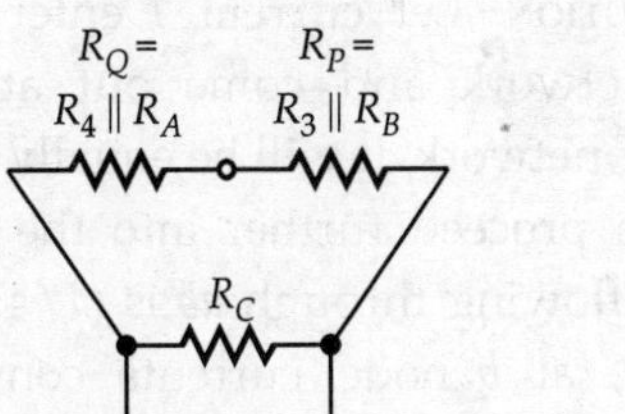

Fig. E19.1 (*b*)

$$R_Q = \frac{R_4 R_A}{R_4 + R_A}$$

$$= \frac{R_4 R_s R_2 + R_4 R_1 R_2 + R_4 R_1 R_s}{R_2 (R_4 + R_A)}$$

$$= \frac{R_2 R_4 R_s + R_1 R_2 R_4 + R_1 R_4 R_s}{R_2 R_4 + R_s R_2 + R_1 R_2 + R_1 R_s}$$

$$R_P = \frac{R_3 R_B}{R_3 + R_B}$$

$$= \frac{R_3 R_1 R_3 + R_1 R_2 R_3 + R_3 R_2 R_s}{R_1 R_3 + R_1 R_s + R_1 R_2 + R_s R_2}$$

$$\therefore \quad R_{net} = R_c \,||\, (R_P + R_Q)$$

or

$$R_{net} = \frac{\mathbf{R_C (R_P + R_Q)}}{\mathbf{R_C + R_P + R_Q}}.$$

Substituting the values of R_P, R_Q and R_C we can find R_{net}.

EXAMPLE 19.2 *An infinite number of square meshes are interconnected as shown in Fig. E19.2. Each side of any mesh has resistance R Ω. Find the effective resistance between any two adjacent nodes (say a and b).*

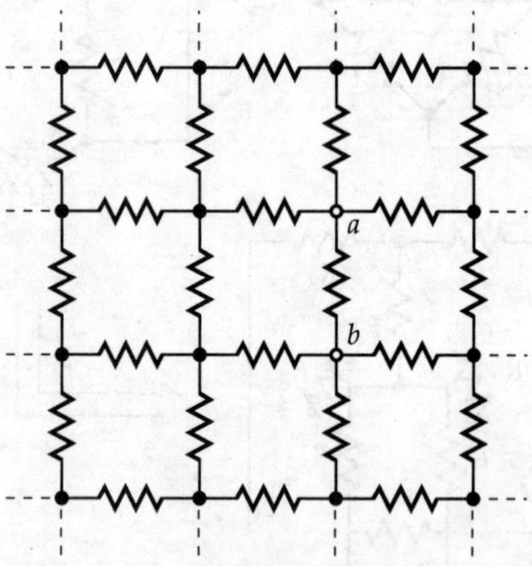

Fig. E19.2

SOLUTION. Let current I enter from a in the mesh network and come out at b. At a, after entering network, it will be equally divided in four paths to proceed further into the network. Thus current flowing through ab is $(I/4)$. Similarly, we can say, at b node currents converge from its adjacent four branches to come out finally as I. Thus, current coming out through ab branch is $(I/4)$.

Hence the total current flowing through branch ab is $\left(I_4 + \frac{I}{4}\right)$ *i.e.*, $\left(\frac{I}{2}\right)$. The voltage drop across ab is thus $\left(R \times \frac{I}{2}\right)$ as R is ab branch resistance.

The effective resistance between ab is thus given by

$$R_{eff} = \frac{R \times \frac{I}{2}}{I} = \frac{\mathbf{R}}{\mathbf{2}} \textbf{ Ohm.}$$

EXAMPLE 19.3 *Fig. E19.3 represents a delta connected resistor assembly. Fig. E19.3(a) represents an equivalent star. Show that if all elements of the delta connection are scaled by a factor 'K' where K>0, the elements of the corresponding star equivalent will also be scaled by a factor of K.*

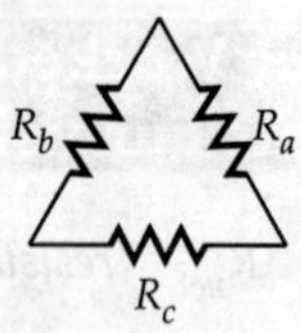

Fig. E19.3

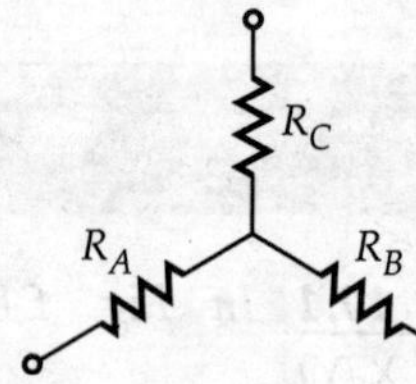

Fig. E19.3 (*a*)

SOLUTION. In equivalent star network the resistance can be given by

$$R_A = \frac{R_b R_c}{R_a + R_b + R_c}$$

$$R_B = \frac{R_a R_c}{R_a + R_b + R_c}$$

$$R_C = \frac{R_b R_a}{R_a + R_b + R_c}$$

If the components of delta network are scaled by K, then,

$$R'_A = \frac{(KR_b)(KR_c)}{K(R_a + R_b + R_c)}$$

$$= K\frac{R_b R_c}{R_a + R_b + R_c} = KR_A$$

Similarly $R'_B = KR_B$; $R'_C = KR_C$

Thus, the elements of equivalent star are also scaled by a factor K.

Example 19.4 *Figure E19.4 represents a waveform of a voltage across a 10 Ω resistor. Find the energy delivered to the resistor for 0 to 5 sec.*

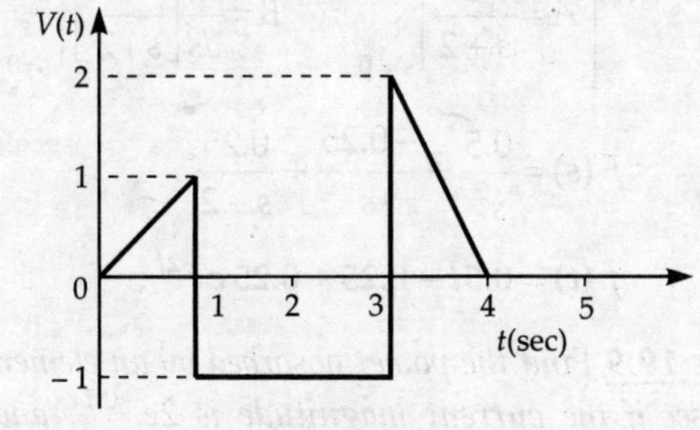

Fig. E19.4

Solution. The voltage-time equations for the applied voltage as per the given profile at different time intervals are as follows :

$$V(t) = t \qquad \text{for } 0 \le t < 1$$
$$V(t) = -1 \qquad \text{for } 1 \le t < 3$$
$$V(t) = -2(t-4) \qquad \text{for } 3 \le t \le 4$$
$$V(t) = 0 \qquad \text{for } 4 \le t \le 5$$

Now, $\text{Energy} = \int_{t_0}^{t} p(t)\,dt$

where power $p(t) = [V(t)]^2 \times \dfrac{1}{R}$.

∴ for 0 – 5 sec, the energy delivered is the sum of energy delivered for 0 – 1, 1 – 3, 3 – 4 and 4 – 5 sec.

i.e., Energy (0 – 5) = Energy (0 – 1) + Energy (1 – 3) + Energy (3 – 4) + Energy (4 – 5).

$$= \frac{1}{10}\int_0^1 t^2\,dt + \frac{1}{10}\int_1^3 (-1)^2\,dt + \frac{1}{10}\int_3^4 [-2(t-4)]^2\,dt + \frac{1}{10}\int_4^5 0\,.\,dt$$

$$= \frac{1}{10}\left[\frac{t^3}{3}\right]_0^1 + \frac{1}{10}[t]_1^3 + \frac{1}{10}\int_3^4 (4t^2 + 32t + 64)\,dt + 0$$

$$= \frac{1}{30} + \frac{3}{10} - \frac{1}{10} + \frac{1}{10}\left[\frac{1}{3}.4t^3 - \frac{1}{2}.32t^2 + 64t\right]_3^4$$

$$= \frac{1}{30} + \frac{3}{10} - \frac{1}{10} + \frac{1}{10}\left[\frac{256}{3} - \frac{512}{2} + 256\right] - \frac{1}{10}\left[\frac{108}{3} - \frac{288}{2} + 192\right]$$

$$= \frac{1}{30} + \frac{2}{10} + \frac{1}{10}\left[\frac{148}{3} - \frac{224}{2} + 64\right]$$

$$= \frac{7}{30} + \frac{148}{30} - \frac{144}{30} = \frac{11}{30} \text{ Joules.}$$

$$\therefore \text{ Energy } (0-5 \text{ sec}) = \mathbf{\frac{11}{30} \text{ Joules.}}$$

Example 19.5 *An alternating voltage wave, represented by $e = E_{max} \sin(\omega t - \theta)$, has been shown in Fig. E19.5. Assuming $\theta = 30°$, $\omega = 314$ rad / sec, $E_{max} = 100$ volts, find the instantaneous value after 0.05 sec. What is the rms value ?*

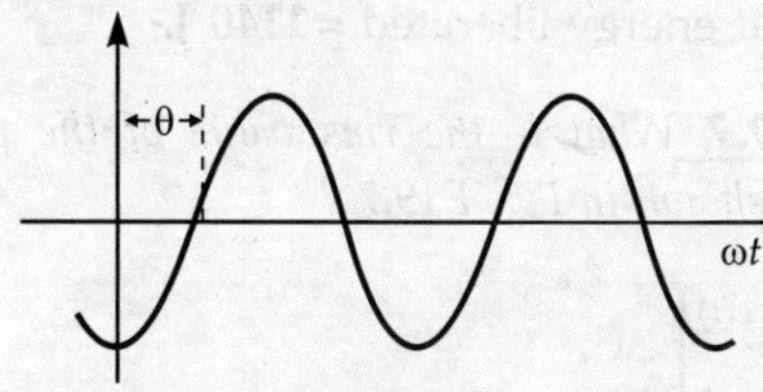

Fig. E19.5

Solution. $e = E_{\max} \sin(\omega t - \theta)$

$$= 100 \sin(314\,t - 30°)$$
$$= 100 \sin(314 \times 0.05 - 0.52)$$
$$[\because 30° = 0.52 \text{ rad.}]$$
$$= 49.71 \text{ volts.}$$

$$\text{rms value} = \frac{E_{\max}}{\sqrt{2}} = \frac{100}{\sqrt{2}} = 70.7 \text{ Volts.}$$

Thus, for the given a.c. wave, instantaneous value after 0.05 sec is **49.71 volts** and rms value is **70.7 volts.**

Example 19.6 *Fig. E19.6 shows a plot of stepped d.c. voltage applied to a resistor of 5 Ω for 15 seconds. Determine the total heat energy liberated.*

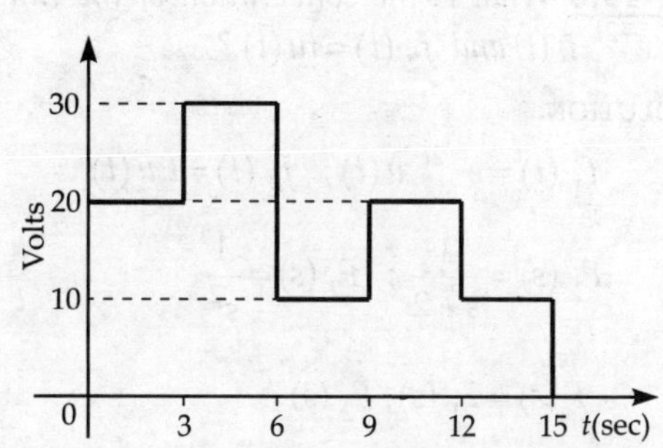

Fig. E19.6

SOLUTION.

$$W = \Sigma\ Pt = \Sigma\ \frac{V^2}{R}.t$$

$$= \frac{20^2}{5} \times 3 + \frac{30^2}{5} \times (6-3) + \frac{10^2}{5}(9-6)$$

$$+ \frac{20^2}{5}(12-9) + \frac{10^2}{5}(15-12)$$

$$= \frac{3}{5}[400 + 900 + 100 + 400 + 100]$$

$$= \frac{5700}{5} = 1140 \text{ J.}$$

$\therefore$ Heat energy liberated = **1140 J.**

EXAMPLE 19.7 *What is the rms value of the periodic waveform shown in Fig. E19.7 ?*

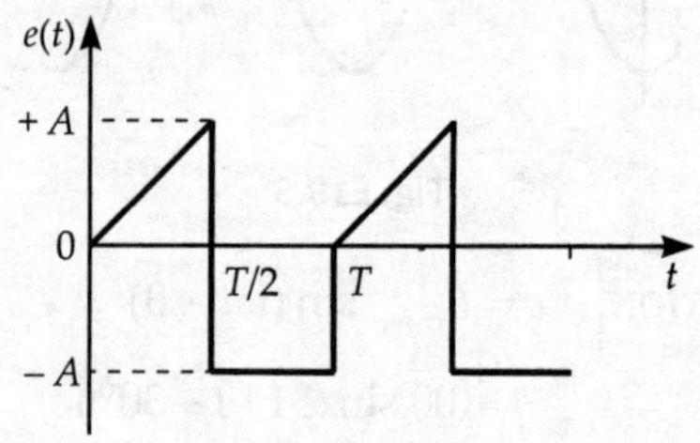

Fig. E19.7

SOLUTION. RMS value

$$= \sqrt{\frac{1}{T}\int_0^T e(t)\,dt}$$

$$= \frac{1}{T}\left[\int_0^{T/2}\left[\frac{2At}{T}\right]^2 + \int_{T/2}^{T} A^2\,dt\right]$$

$$= \sqrt{\frac{1}{T}\left[\frac{4A^2}{T^2}\cdot\frac{1}{3}\frac{T^3}{8} + A^2\frac{T}{2}\right]} = \sqrt{\frac{2A^2}{3}} = \sqrt{\frac{\mathbf{2}}{\mathbf{3}}}.\mathbf{A.}$$

EXAMPLE 19.8 *What is the convolution of the functions $f_1(t) = e^{-2t}\ u(t)$ and $f_2(t) = tu(t)$?*

SOLUTION.

$$f_1(t) = e^{-2t}\ u(t);\ f_2(t) = t\,u(t)$$

$$\therefore \quad F_1(s) = \frac{1}{s+2};\ F_2(s) = \frac{1}{s^2}$$

$$\therefore \quad F(s) = F_1(s).F_2(s)$$

$$= \frac{1}{s^2(s+2)} = \frac{A}{s^2} + \frac{B}{s} + \frac{C}{s+2}$$

Using partial fraction technique,

$$A = 0.5, \quad B = -0.25, \quad C = 0.25$$

$$\left[A = \frac{1}{s+2}\bigg|_{s=0}\ ; \quad B = \frac{d}{ds}\left[\frac{1}{s+2}\right]\bigg|_{s=0}\right]$$

$$\therefore \quad F(s) = \frac{0.5}{s^2} + \frac{-0.25}{s} + \frac{0.25}{s+2}$$

$$\therefore \quad \mathbf{f(t) = 0.5t - 0.25 + 0.25\,e^{-2t}.}$$

EXAMPLE 19.9 *Find the power absorbed by an element for $t = 10$ sec if the current magnitude is $2e^{-0.1t}$ and the voltage across the element is $v = 6\frac{di}{dt}$.*

SOLUTION.

$$p(t) = i(t)\,v(t)$$

$$= 2e^{-0.1t} \times 6\frac{di}{dt}$$

$$= 2e^{-0.1t} \times 6 \times (-0.1)(2)\,e^{-0.1t}$$

$$= -2.4\,e^{-0.1t}\ e^{-0.1t}$$

$$= -2.4\,e^{-0.2t} \text{ Watt}$$

$\therefore$ for $t = 10$ sec,

$$p(10) = -2.4\,e^{-0.2(10)}$$

$$= \mathbf{-0.325\ Watt.}$$

i.e., actually the element is supplying power.

EXAMPLE 19.10 *A voltage $v(t) = t^2e^{-2t}$ is applied to a 4F capacitor for the time interval 0 to 10 sec. Find the magnitude of stored energy.*

SOLUTION. Energy

$$= \int_{t_0}^{t} vi\,dt = \int_{t_0}^{t} v.C\frac{dv}{dt}.dt$$

$$= \int_{v(t_0)}^{v(t)} Cv\,dv = C\int_{v(t_0)}^{v(t)} v\,dv$$

$$= C \times \frac{1}{2}[(v(t))^2 - (v(t_0))^2]$$

But $\quad v(t) \equiv v(10) = 10^2\,e^{-20}$

$[\because v(t) = t^2\,e^{-2t}$ and $t = 10]$

and $v(0) = 0$.

$$\therefore \text{ Energy} = 4 \times \frac{1}{2}[(10^2\,e^{-20})^2 - 0^2]$$

$$= 2\,[(20.6 \times 10^{-7})^2] \text{ Joule}$$

i.e. $\quad$ Energy = $\mathbf{8.6 \times 10^{-14}}$ **Joule.**

EXAMPLE 19.11 *Find the resonant frequency of the circuit shown in Fig. E19.8.*

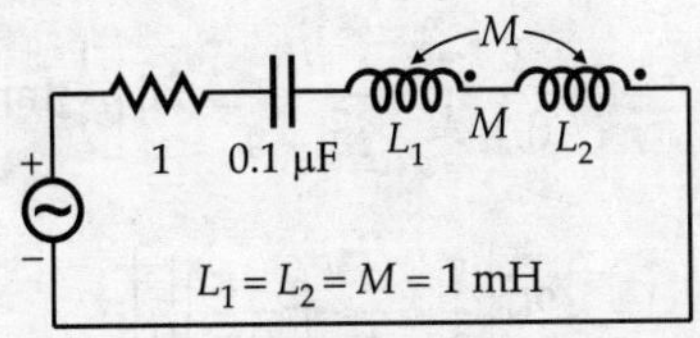

Fig. E19.8

SOLUTION. $L_{eq} = L_1 + L_2 + 2M = 4$ mH

$$f_n = \frac{1}{2\pi\sqrt{L_{eq}C}} = \frac{1}{2\pi\sqrt{4\times10^{-3}\times0.1\times10^{-6}}}$$

$$= \frac{50}{2\pi}\text{ kHz} = \mathbf{7.962\ Hz}$$

EXAMPLE 19.12 *Find the Thevenin's resistance of the given circuit in Fig. E19.9.*

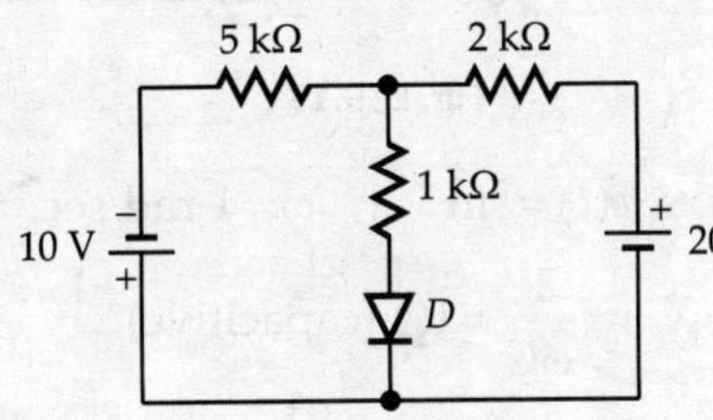

Fig. E19.9

Solution. Since diode is a non-linear element hence we deactivate the voltage sources and the diode. Fig. 19.9(*a*) represents the circuit.

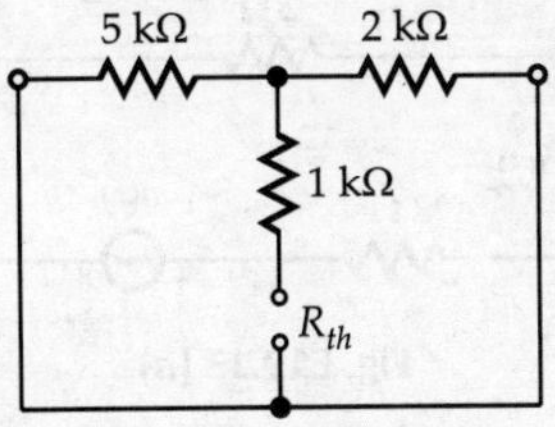

Fig. E19.9(*a*)

$$\therefore \quad R_{th} = 1 + \frac{2\times5}{7} = \frac{17}{7} = \mathbf{2.43\ k\Omega}$$

EXAMPLE 19.13 *What is the value of L_{eq} (Fig. E19.10) ?*

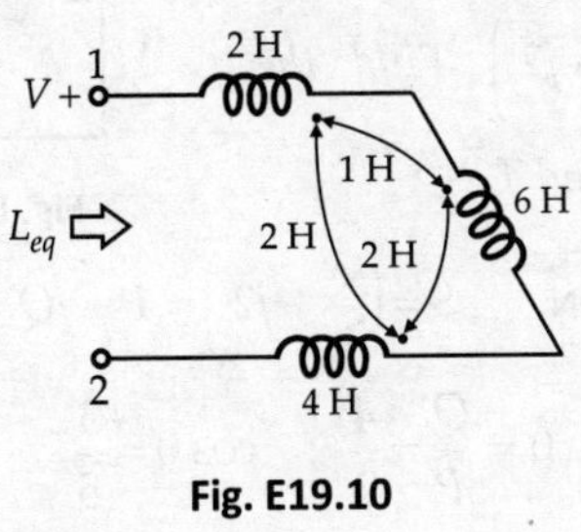

Fig. E19.10

Solution. Using loop equation,

$$-V + 2\frac{di}{dt} - 1.\frac{di}{dt} - 2\frac{di}{dt} + 6\frac{di}{dt} - 1.\frac{di}{dt}$$

$$+ 2\frac{di}{dt} + 4\frac{di}{dt} - 2\frac{di}{dt} + 2\frac{di}{dt} = 0$$

[Assuming circulating current to be *i*]

$$\therefore \quad V = 16\frac{di}{dt} - 6\frac{di}{dt} = 10\frac{di}{dt} = L_{eq}\frac{di}{dt}$$

$$\therefore \quad \mathbf{L_{eq} = 10\ H.}$$

EXAMPLE 19.14 *Find the frequency of resonance of the network shown in Fig. E19.11.*

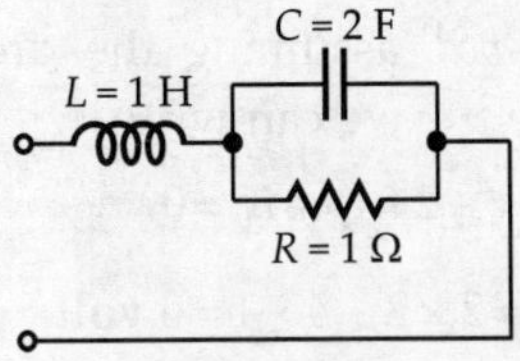

Fig. E19.11

SOLUTION. $Z_{\text{input}} = jX_L + \dfrac{R\times\dfrac{1}{j\omega C}}{R + \dfrac{1}{j\omega C}}$

$$= j\omega + \frac{1\times\dfrac{1}{2j\omega}}{1 + \dfrac{1}{j2\omega}} = j\omega - \frac{j}{2\omega - j}\times\frac{2\omega + j}{2\omega + j}$$

$$= j\omega - \frac{j2\omega - 1}{4\omega^2 + 1}$$

For resonance, the imaginary part must be zero. Thus,

$$j\omega_n - \frac{j2\omega_n - 1}{4\omega_n^2 + 1} = 0$$

This gives, on simplification, ω_n **= 0.5 rad / sec.**

EXAMPLE 19.15 *At steady state find the drop across the capacitor C_C (100 μF) and the accumulated charge (Fig. E19.12).*

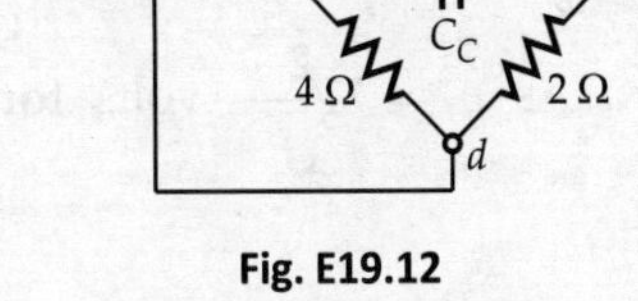

Fig. E19.12

CHAPTER 19

Solution. At steady state, across the dc supply, the capacitor acts as open circuit [see Fig. E19.12(*a*)].

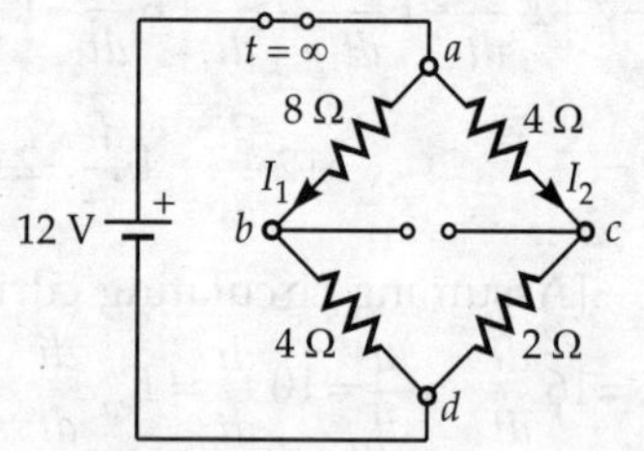

Fig. E19.12 (*a*)

$$\therefore \quad I_1 = \frac{12}{8+4} = 1\,\text{A}; \quad I_2 = \frac{12}{4+2} = 2\text{ A}$$

$\therefore$ In loop *bcd*, assuming the drop across the capacitor to be v_C, we can write

$$-v_C + 2I_2 - 4I_1 = 0$$

or $$v = 2\times 2 - 4\times 1 = \mathbf{0\ volt.}$$

$\therefore$ Charge accumulated in the capacitor

$$q = Cv_C = 100\times 10^{-6}\times 0 = \mathbf{0\ coulomb.}$$

Example 19.16 *The charge in a capacitor is given by*

$$q = v + \frac{1}{3}v^3.$$

If the voltage across this capacitor be $v(t) = \sin t$, *find* $i(t)$, *the current through the capacitor.*

Solution. $i(t) = \dfrac{dq}{dt}$.

However, $q = v + \dfrac{1}{3}v^3$ and hence $\dfrac{dq}{dv} = 1 + v^2$.

Also, $v = \sin t$.

$$\therefore \quad \frac{dv}{dt} = \cos t$$

$$\therefore \quad i(t) = \frac{dq}{dv}\cdot\frac{dv}{dt} = \frac{dq}{dt}.$$

or $$i(t) = (1+v^2)\cos t = (1+\sin^2 t)\cos t.$$

$$\therefore \quad \mathbf{i(t) = (1+\sin^2 t)\cos t.}$$

Example 19.17 *Find the current through a 0.1 H inductor at t = 2 sec if drop across L is* $\left(\dfrac{2}{t^2+4}\right)$ *volts for all t. Take* $i_L(-\infty) = 0$.

Solution. As $v_L = \dfrac{2}{t^2+4}$ volts for all *t* and $i_L(-\infty) = 0$.

$$\therefore \quad i(t) = \frac{1}{L}\int v_L\,dt = \frac{1}{0.1}\int_{-\infty}^{2}\frac{2}{t^2+4}\,dt$$

$$= \frac{2}{0.1}\int_{-\infty}^{2}\frac{dt}{t^2+4} = 20\left[\frac{1}{2}\tan^{-1}\frac{t}{2}\right]_{-\infty}^{2}$$

$$= 20\left[\frac{1}{2}\left\{\frac{\pi}{4} - \left(-\frac{\pi}{2}\right)\right\}\right]$$

or $$\mathbf{i(t) = 23.6\ A.}$$

Example 19.18 *Find i(t) in Fig. 19.13.*

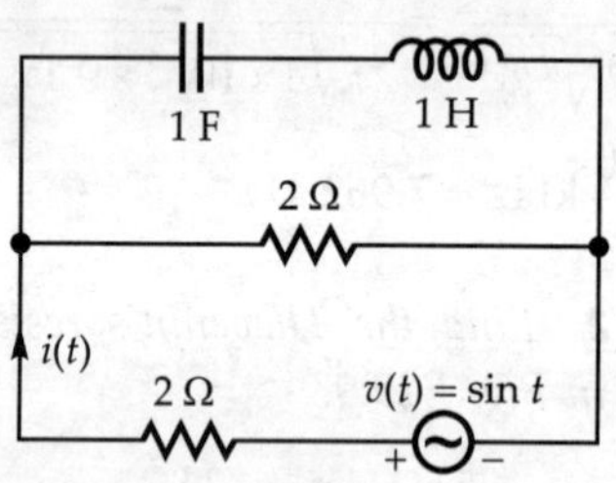

Fig. E19.13

Solution. $v(t) = \sin t \;\therefore\; \omega = 1$ rad/sec.

Thus $X_C = \dfrac{1}{\omega C} = 1\Omega$ (capacitive)

$X_L = \omega L = 1\Omega$ (inductive)

Since $X_C = X_L$, hence the circuit reduces to that as shown in Fig. 19.13(*a*).

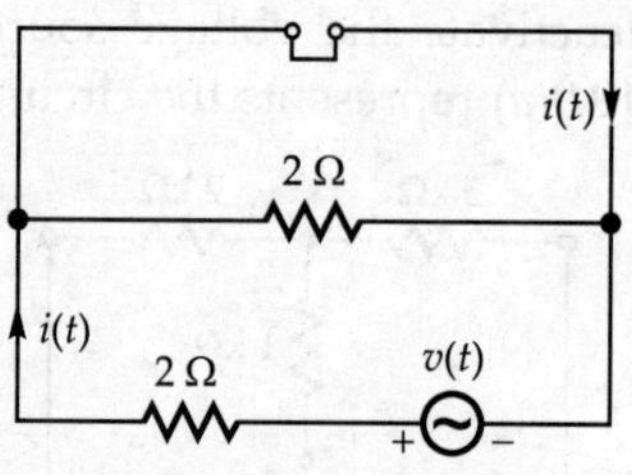

Fig. E19.13 (*a*)

$$\therefore \quad i(t) = \frac{v(t)}{2\Omega} = \mathbf{(0.5\sin t)\,A.}$$

Example 19.19 *Assume* $V = 5\cos t$ *and the complex power drawn by the load is* $P_{comp.} = \left(\dfrac{3}{2} + j2\right)$. *Find the values of R and L.*

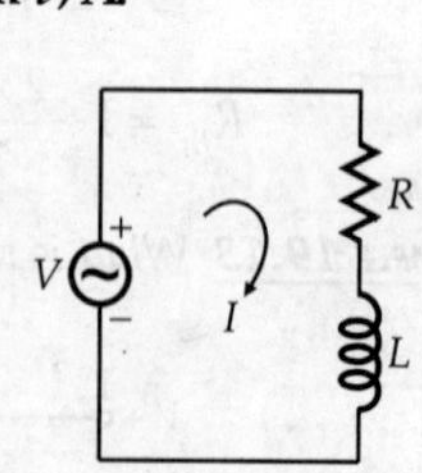

Fig. E19.14

Solution. $S = \left(\dfrac{3}{2} + j2\right) = P + jQ$

$$\therefore \quad \tan\theta = \frac{Q}{P} = \frac{4}{3}; \quad \cos\theta = \frac{3}{5}$$

$$P = VI\cos\theta = \frac{3}{2} \text{ (given)}$$

or, $\frac{5}{\sqrt{2}} \times I \times \frac{3}{5} = \frac{3}{2}$ $\left[\because V = \frac{5}{\sqrt{2}}\cos t\right]$

$\therefore$ $I = \left(\frac{1}{\sqrt{2}}\right)$ A

Also, $P = I^2 R = \frac{3}{2}$

or, $\left(\frac{1}{\sqrt{2}}\right)^2 R = \frac{3}{2}$

$\therefore$ $R = 3\Omega$

$\because$ $\tan\theta = \frac{\omega L}{R} = \frac{L}{R}$ [$\because$ from $V = 5\cos t, \omega = 1$]

$\therefore$ Here, $\frac{4}{3} = \frac{L}{R} = \frac{L}{3}$ giving $L = 4\text{H}$

Thus $\mathbf{R = 3\Omega,\ L = 4H}$.

EXAMPLE 19.20 *At what value of Z parallel resonance will occur in the given circuit at $f = 500$ Hz ?*

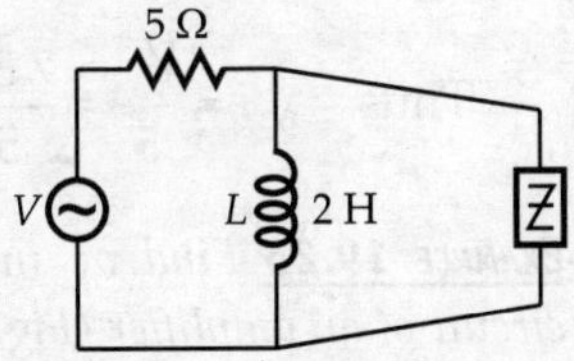

Fig. E19.15

SOLUTION. Resonance can only occur in the given circuit provided Z is capacitive.

In parallel resonance condition susceptance of the circuit should be zero.

i.e., $\frac{1}{j\omega_n L} + j\omega_n C = 0$ [ω_n = angular frequency of resonance]

or $1 - \omega_n^2 LC = 0$

or $\omega_n = \frac{1}{\sqrt{LC}}$

$$\therefore\ C = \frac{1}{\omega^2 L} = \frac{1}{4 \times \pi^2 \times 500^2 \times 2} = \mathbf{0.05\ F}.$$

Thus C = 0.05 F will provide parallel resonance.

EXAMPLE 19.21 *A 25 μF capacitor is connected to a 230 volts 50 Hz a.c. supply. Determine the steady state current, the maximum instantaneous charge and the maximum instantaneous energy stored in the capacitor.*

SOLUTION. X_C (Capacitive reactance)

$$= \frac{1}{2\pi f C} = \frac{1}{2\pi \times 50 \times 25 \times 10^{-6}} = 27.3 \text{ Ohms}$$

$$\therefore\ I_C = \frac{V}{X_C} = \frac{230}{27.3} = 8.425 \text{ Amps}$$

Max. Instantaneous charge (q)

$$= CV_{max} = 25 \times 10^{-6} \times 230 \times \sqrt{2}$$

$$= \mathbf{9.96\ mC};$$

and max. instantaneous energy

$$(W) = \frac{1}{2}CV_{max}^2 = \frac{1}{2} \times 25 \times 10^{-6} \times (230\sqrt{2})^2$$

$$= \mathbf{1.32\ J.}$$

$\therefore$ Steady state charging current being 8.425 Amps, max. instantaneous charge is **9.96 mC**, while max. instantaneous energy is **1.32 J.**

EXAMPLE 19.22 *Solve for i_1, i_2 and i_3 in the network of Fig. E19.16.*

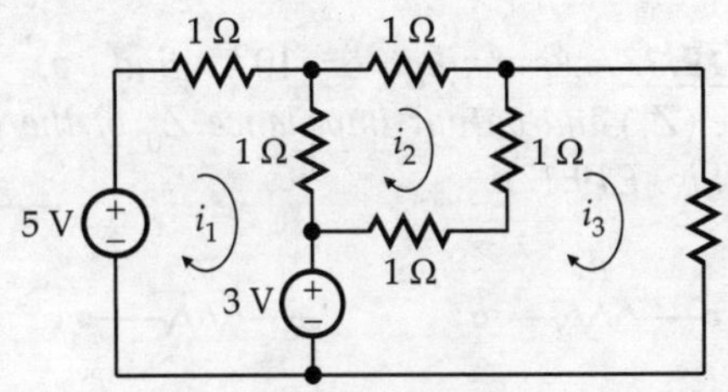

Fig. E19.16

SOLUTION. The loop equations can be written as follows :

$$-5 + 1 \times i_1 + (i_1 - i_2) \times 1 + 3 = 0$$

or $2i_1 - i_2 = 2$ ...(1)

$$1 \times i_2 + (i_2 - i_3) \times (1+1) + (i_2 - i_1) \times 1 = 0$$

or $-i_1 + 4i_2 - 2i_3 = 0$ ...(2)

Also, $-3 + (i_3 - i_2)(1+1) + i_3 \times 1 = 0$

or $0 \times i_1 - 2i_2 + 3i_3 = 3$ ...(3)

In matrix form these equations can be written as

$$\begin{bmatrix} 2 & -1 & 0 \\ -1 & 4 & -2 \\ 0 & -2 & 3 \end{bmatrix} \begin{bmatrix} i_1 \\ i_2 \\ i_3 \end{bmatrix} = \begin{bmatrix} 2 \\ 0 \\ 3 \end{bmatrix}$$

$$\therefore\ i_1 = \frac{\begin{vmatrix} 2 & -1 & 0 \\ 0 & 4 & -2 \\ 3 & -2 & 3 \end{vmatrix}}{\Delta} = \frac{2(12-4) + 3(2)}{13} = 1.69 \text{ A}$$

$$\left[\because \Delta = \begin{vmatrix} 2 & -1 & 0 \\ -1 & 4 & -2 \\ 0 & -2 & 3 \end{vmatrix} = 2(12-4) + (1)(-3) = 13\right]$$

$$i_2 = \frac{\begin{vmatrix} 2 & 2 & 0 \\ -1 & 0 & -2 \\ 0 & 3 & 3 \end{vmatrix}}{\Delta} = \frac{2 \times 6 + 1 \times 6}{13} = 1.39 \text{ A.}$$

$$i_3 = \frac{\begin{vmatrix} 2 & -1 & 2 \\ -1 & 4 & 0 \\ 0 & -2 & 3 \end{vmatrix}}{\Delta}$$

$$= \frac{2 \times 12 + 1(-3+4)}{13} = 1.92 \text{ A}$$

$\therefore$ $\mathbf{i_1 = 1.69\ A,\quad i_2 = 1.39\ A,\quad i_3 = 1.92\ A.}$

EXAMPLE 19.23 *Assuming $\alpha = 10^6$, find v, input impedance (Z_i) and output impedance Z_0 of the given network (Fig. E19.17).*

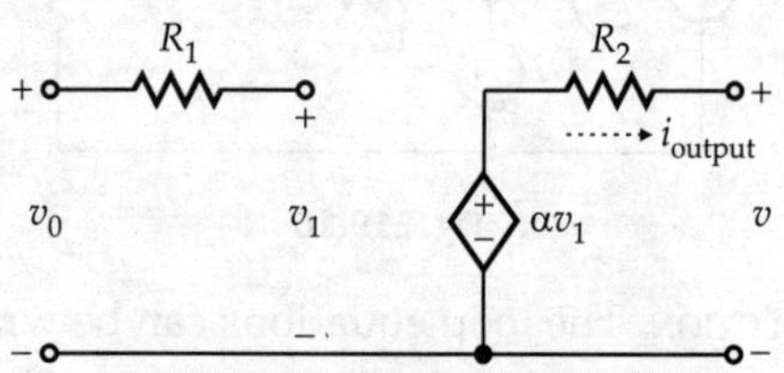

[$R_1 = 0.5$ MΩ, $R_2 = 10\ \Omega$, $v_1 = 5\ \mu$V]

Fig. E19.17

SOLUTION. Output voltage (v)

$$= \alpha v_1 = 10^6 \times 5 \mu\text{V} = \mathbf{5\ V}.$$

Input impedance (Z_i)

$$= \frac{v_1}{i_1} = \frac{v_1}{0} = \infty$$

Output impedance (Z_0)

$$= \frac{v}{i_{output}} = \frac{\alpha v_i}{i_{output}} = R_2 = \mathbf{10\ \Omega}.$$

EXAMPLE 19.24 *Find i in the network shown in Fig. E19.18.*

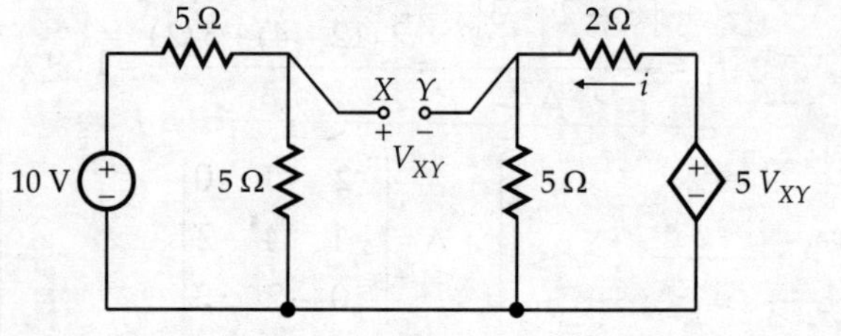

Fig. E19.18

SOLUTION. At node '*X*', we have

$$\frac{V_x}{5} + \frac{V_x - 10}{5} = 0,$$

or $$0.4\ V_x = 2$$

or $$V_x = 5 \text{ V}$$

At node '*Y*', we have

$$\frac{V_Y}{5} + \frac{V_Y - 5V_{XY}}{2} = 0$$

or $$0.7V_Y - 2.5V_{XY} = 0$$

or $$0.7V_Y - 2.5(V_X - V_Y) = 0$$

or $$-2.5V_X + 1.7V_Y = 0$$

or $$1.7V_Y = 12.5$$

$\therefore$ $$V_Y = \frac{12.5}{1.7} = 7.35 \text{ V}$$

Thus $$i = \frac{V_Y}{5} = \frac{7.35}{5} = \mathbf{1.47\ A.}$$

EXAMPLE 19.25 *Find v_L in the small signal equivalent circuit of an amplifier (Fig. E19.19).*

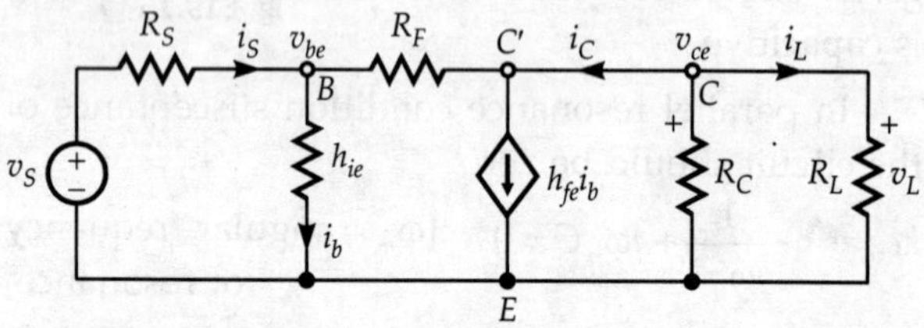

Fig. E19.19

SOLUTION. At node *B*,

$$i_s + i_C - i_b = 0$$

or $$\frac{v_s - v_{be}}{R_s} + \frac{V_{ce} - V_{be}}{R_F} - \frac{v_{be}}{h_{ie}} = 0 \quad \text{...(1)}$$

At node *C'*,

$$-h_{fe}i_b - \frac{v_{ce}}{\frac{R_C R_L}{R_C + R_L}} + \frac{v_{be} - v_{ce}}{R_F} = 0$$

or $$\frac{v_{be} - v_{ce}}{R_F} - h_{fe}i_b - \frac{R_C R_L}{R_C + R_L} \cdot v_{ce} = 0 \quad \text{...(2)}$$

Rearranging (1) and (2) and substituting $i_b = \dfrac{v_{be}}{h_{ie}}$, we find

$$\begin{bmatrix} \dfrac{1}{R_s}+\dfrac{1}{R_F}+\dfrac{1}{h_{ie}} & -\dfrac{1}{R_F} \\ \dfrac{h_{fe}}{h_{ie}}-\dfrac{1}{R_F} & \dfrac{1}{R_F}+\dfrac{R_C+R_L}{R_C R_L} \end{bmatrix} \begin{bmatrix} v_{be} \\ v_{ce} \end{bmatrix} = \begin{bmatrix} \dfrac{v_s}{R_s} \\ 0 \end{bmatrix}$$

Here the determinant Δ is given by

$$\Delta = \left(\frac{1}{R_s}+\frac{1}{R_F}+\frac{1}{h_{ie}}\right)\left(\frac{1}{R_F}+\frac{R_C+R_L}{R_C R_L}\right)+\frac{1}{R_F}\left(\frac{h_{fe}}{h_{ie}}-\frac{1}{R_F}\right)$$

$$\therefore \; v_L \; (= v_{ce}) = \frac{\left(\dfrac{1}{R_F}-\dfrac{h_{fe}}{h_{ie}}\right) v_s}{R_s \, \Delta},$$

using Cramer's Rule.

EXAMPLE 19.26 *A circuit with a dependent source is shown in Fig. E19.20. What is the equivalent capacitance of the input loop ?*

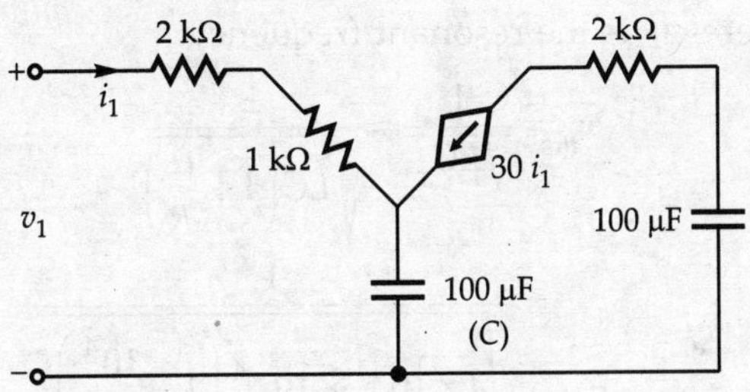

Fig. E19.20

Solution. Using KVL at the input loop,

$$-v_1 + 2\times10^3 i_1 + 1\times10^3 i_1 + (i_1 + 30 i_1)\frac{1}{j\omega C} = 0$$

$$\therefore \quad v_1 = 3\times10^3 i_1 + \frac{31}{j\omega C}\times i_1$$

$$\therefore \quad \frac{v_1}{i_1} = Z_{input} = \left(3\times10^3 + \frac{31}{j\omega C}\right)$$

$$= \left(3\times10^3 + \frac{31}{j\omega(C/31)}\right)\Omega$$

$$\text{Thus,} \quad C_{eq} = \frac{C}{31} = \frac{100}{31}\,\mu\text{F}$$

$$\therefore \quad C_{eq} = \frac{\mathbf{100}}{\mathbf{31}}\,\boldsymbol{\mu}\mathbf{F}$$

EXAMPLE 19.27 *In the circuit shown in Fig. E19.21, find* v_L.

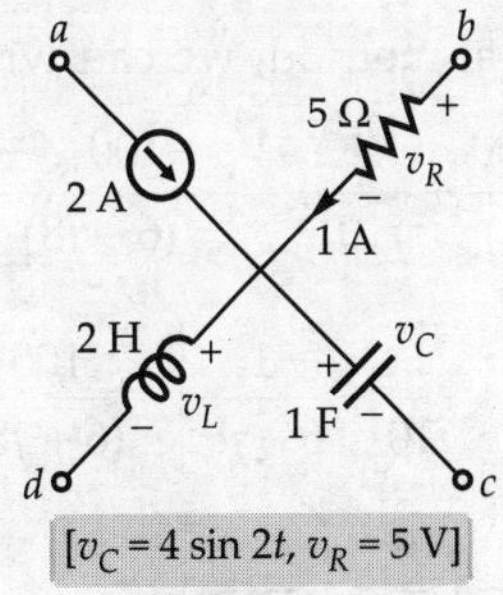

Fig. E19.21

SOLUTION. Let us apply KCL at node *n* in the redrawn circuit shown in Fig. E19.21(*a*)

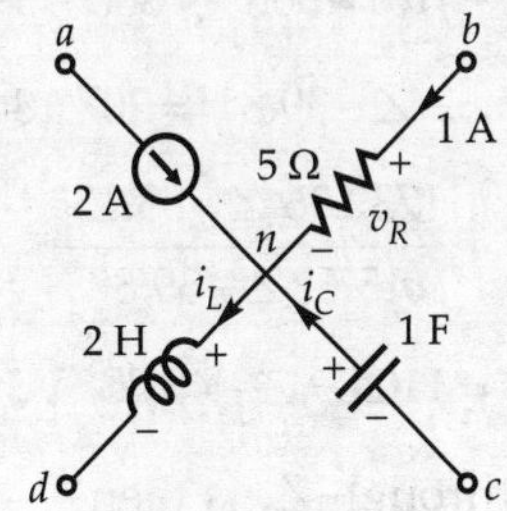

Fig. E19.21 (*a*)

At node '*n*',

$$i_L = i_C + 1 + 2 = i_C + 3$$

$$\text{But} \quad i_C = -C\frac{dv_c}{dt}$$

$$= -1.\frac{d}{dt}[4\sin 2t] = -8\cos 2t$$

$$\therefore \quad i_L = -8\cos 2t + 3$$

Voltage across the inductor is given by

$$v_L = L\frac{di_L}{dt} = 2\times\frac{d}{dt}[-8\cos 2t + 3]$$

$$= 32\sin 2t$$

$$\therefore \quad v_L = \mathbf{32\sin 2t \; Volts}$$

EXAMPLE 19.28 *In the network of Fig. E19.22, find the current* Z_3 *using nodal method. The values of voltages are given in the figure.*

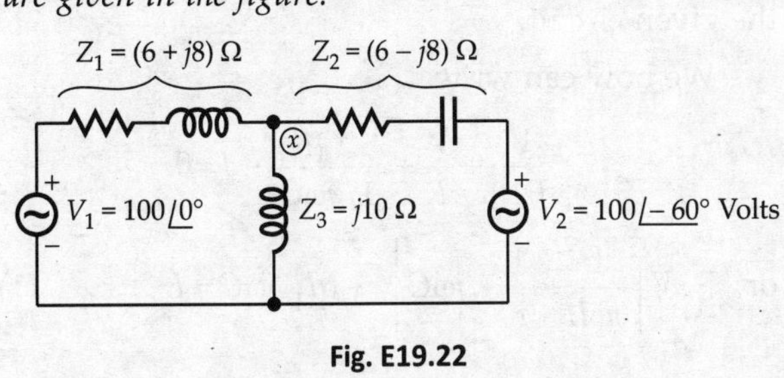

Fig. E19.22

Solution. Let us assume the node (x) voltage be V_x.

Using nodal method, we can write

$$\frac{V_x - 100}{(6+j8)} + \frac{V_x}{j10} + \frac{V_x - 100\angle -60°}{(6-j8)} = 0$$

or $$V_x\left[\frac{1}{6+j8} + \frac{1}{j10} + \frac{1}{6-j8}\right] = \frac{100}{(6+j8)} + \frac{100\angle 60°}{(6-j8)}$$

or $$V_x\left[\frac{6-j8}{100} - \frac{j10}{100} + \frac{6+j8}{100}\right]$$

$$= \frac{100\,(6-j8)}{100} + \frac{100\angle -60°}{100}.10\angle -53.13°$$

or $$V_x\,[12 - j10] = 600 - j\,800 - 392.82 - j919.60$$

or $$V_x\,[15.62\angle -39.8°] = 207.18 - j\,1719.60$$

or $$V_x = \frac{1732.06\angle -83.13°}{15.62\angle -39.8°}$$

$$= 110.89\angle -43.33°\ \text{V}$$

$\therefore$ Current through Z_3 is then

$$I = \frac{110.89\angle -43.33°}{10\angle 90°}$$

$$= \mathbf{11.09\angle -133.32°\ A.}$$

Example 19.29 *Obtain the value of the resonant frequency of the network shown in Fig. E19.23. Assume $\alpha = 10^4$.*

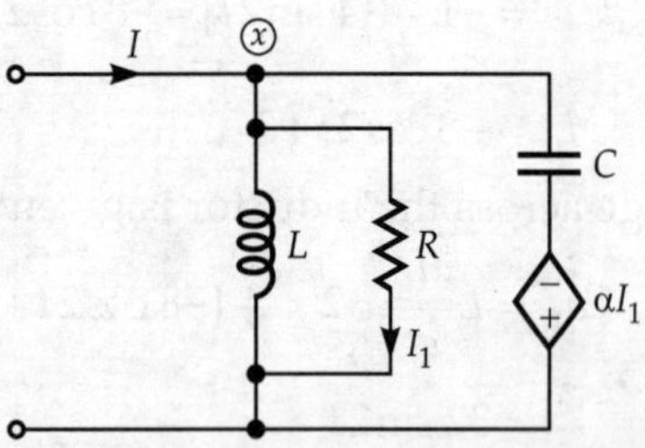

$[L = 4\times10^{-4}\ \text{H}; C = 100\ \mu\text{F}, R = 10\times10^3\ \text{ohm}]$

Fig. E19.23

Solution. Let V_x be the voltage at node (x) in the given circuit.

We now can write

$$\frac{V}{jX_L} + \frac{V}{R} + \frac{V + \alpha I_1}{1/j\omega C} - I = 0$$

or $$V\left[\frac{1}{j\omega L} + \frac{1}{R} + j\omega C\right] + \alpha I_1\ j\omega C = I \qquad ...(1)$$

But, $I_1 = \dfrac{V}{R}$; thus from (1)

$$V\left[\frac{1}{j\omega L} + \frac{1}{R} + j\omega C\right] + \alpha.\frac{V}{R}.j\omega C = I$$

or $$V\left[\frac{1}{R} + \frac{1}{j\omega L} + j\omega C + \frac{\alpha.j\omega C}{R}\right] = I$$

$$\therefore \quad \frac{I}{V} = Y_{input} = \frac{1}{R} + \frac{1}{j\omega L} + j\omega C\left(1 + \frac{\alpha}{R}\right)$$

where Y_{input} is the admittance of the network looking from the input terminals of the given network.

We then write

$$Y_{input} = \frac{1}{R} + j\left[\omega C_x - \frac{1}{\omega L}\right],$$

where $C_x = C\left(1 + \dfrac{\alpha}{R}\right)$.

At resonance, the imaginary term must be zero.

$$\therefore \quad \omega_n C_x = \frac{1}{\omega_n L}$$

where ω_n is the resonant frequency.

i.e., $$\omega_n = \frac{1}{\sqrt{LC_x}} = \frac{1}{\sqrt{LC\left(1+\dfrac{\alpha}{R}\right)}}$$

$$= \frac{1}{\sqrt{4\times10^{-4}\times10^{-4}\left(1 + \dfrac{10^4}{10^4}\right)}}$$

$$= \frac{1}{\sqrt{8\times10^{-8}}}$$

$$\therefore \quad \omega_n = \frac{10^4}{\sqrt{8}} = \mathbf{3535.53\ rad/sec.}$$

Example 19.30 *In Fig. E19.24 find the unknown voltage drops if $V_C = 3e^{-2\times10^4 t}$ volts. Find actual direction of drops and check whether the marked arbitrary directions are correct or not.*

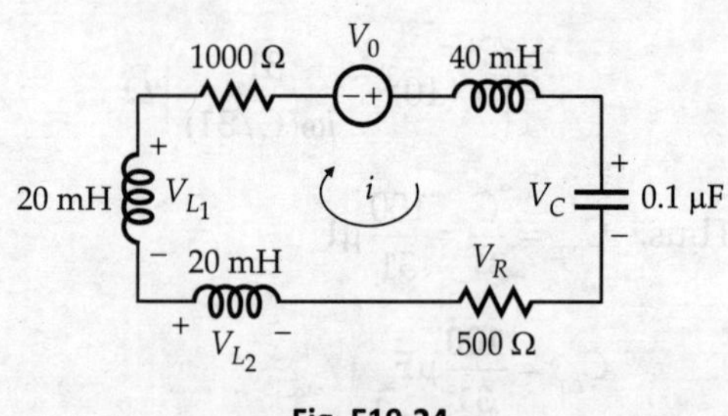

Fig. E19.24

Solution. In Fig. E19.24,

$$i = C\frac{dV_C}{dt} = C\frac{d}{dt}[3e^{-2\times10^4 t}]$$

or $$i = 0.1\times10^{-6}(-2\times10^4)\times 3e^{-2\times10^4 t}$$

$$= -6\,e^{-2\times10^4 t}\ \text{mA.}$$

∴ Actual direction of current is reverse (*i.e.*, $6\,e^{-2\times10^4 t}$).

∴ $$V_R = i\times 500 = [+6e^{-2\times10^4 t}\times10^{-3}]\,500$$

$$= \mathbf{+3e^{-2\times10^4\ t}}\ \textbf{volts.}$$

Actual direction of voltage is correct to that what is given.

Also, $$V_{L_2} = L\frac{di}{dt}$$

Here $$V_{L_2} = [20\times10^{-3}]\frac{d}{dt}[+6e^{-2\times10^4 t}\times10^{-3}]$$

i.e., $$V_{L_2} = 20\times10^{-3}\times(+6)(-2\times10^4)\,e^{-2\times10^4 t}\times10^{-3}$$

$$= -2.4\,e^{-2\times10^4 t}\ \text{Volts.}$$

The direction of V_{L_2} is thus the reverse to that what is given.

$$V_{L_1} = V_{L_2} = \mathbf{-2.4\,e^{-2\times10^4\ t}}\ \textbf{Volts.}$$

Voltage drop across 1000 Ω resistor would be twice the drop across 500 Ω resistor.

∴ $$V_{1000\Omega} = 2V_R = \mathbf{+6e^{-2\times10^4\ t}}\ \textbf{Volts.}$$

Also, drop across 40 mH inductor will be twice the drop of V_{L_1}.

∴ $$V_{40\,\text{mH}} = \mathbf{-4.8\,e^{-2\times10^4\ t}}\ \textbf{Volts.}$$

The actual figure of the network is shown in Fig. E19.24(*a*).

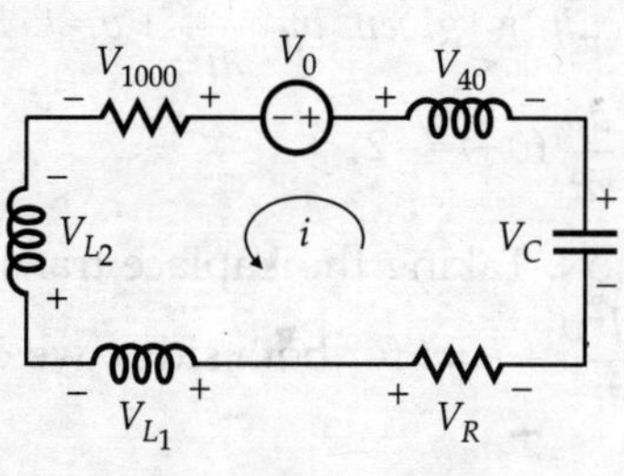

Fig. E19.24 (*a*)

∴ Considering the entire loop following KVL, we can write

$$V_0 + V_{1000} - V_{L_2} - V_{L_1} + V_R - V_C - V_{40} = 0$$

or $$V_0 = V_C + V_{L_1} + V_{L_2} + V_{40} - V_R - V_{1000}$$

$$= (3 + 2.4 + 2.4 + 4.8 - 3 - 6)\,e^{-2\times10^4 t}$$

$$= \mathbf{3.6\,e^{-2\times10^4\ t}}\ \textbf{Volts.}$$

Example 19.31 *Find I_2, I_3 and I in Fig. E19.25. Also find potential at x and y.*

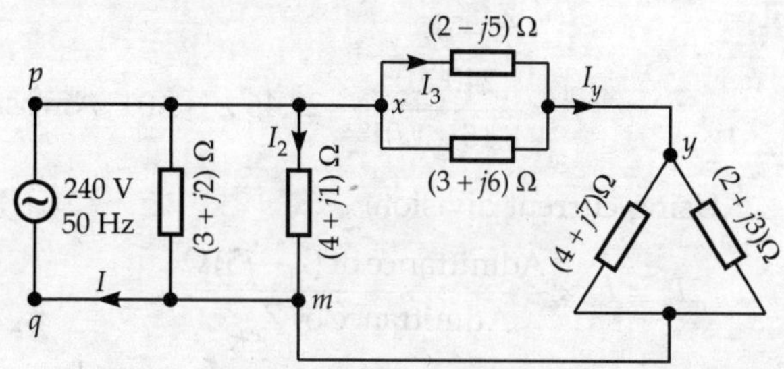

Fig. E19.25

Solution. $$I_2 = \frac{240\angle 0^\circ}{(4+j1)} = \frac{240\angle 0^\circ}{4.123\angle 14.04^\circ}$$

$$= 58.21\angle -14.04^\circ\ \text{Amps.}$$

Equivalent impedance of (3 + *j*2) Ω and (4 + *j*1) Ω gives

$$Z_{eq_1} = \frac{(3+j2)(4+j1)}{3+j2+4+j1} = 1.95\angle 24.54^\circ\,\Omega$$

Equivalent impedance of (2 – *j*5) and (3 + *j*6) Ω is given by

$$Z_{eq_2} = \frac{(2-j5)(3+j6)}{(2-j5)+(3+j6)} = 7.1\angle -16.05^\circ\,\Omega$$

and equivalent impedance of (4 + *j*7) and (2 + *j*3) Ω is

$$Z_{eq_3} = \frac{(4+j7)(2+j3)}{(4+j7)+(2+j3)} = 2.5\angle 57.55^\circ\,\Omega.$$

∴ Z_{x-m} (equivalent imp across *x*-*m* for Z_{eq_2} and Z_{eq_3})

$$= Z_{eq_2} + Z_{eq_3} = 7.1\angle -16.05^\circ + 2.5\angle 57.55^\circ$$

$$= 8.15\angle 1.01^\circ\,\Omega = (8.15 + j0.145)\,\Omega$$

CHAPTER 19

$\therefore$ Input impedance of the circuit (Z_{pq} *i.e.,* the impedance across *p-q*) is given by

$$Z_{pq} = \frac{Z_{eq_1} \times Z_{xm}}{Z_{eq_1} + Z_{xm}} = \frac{1.95 \angle 24.54° \times 8.15 \angle 1.01°}{1.95 \angle 24.54° + 8.15 \angle 1.01°}$$

$$= 1.6 \angle 20° \Omega.$$

$$\therefore \quad I = \frac{V}{Z_{pq}} = \frac{240 \angle 0°}{1.6 \angle 20°}$$

$$= 150.4 \angle -20° \text{ Amps.}$$

Also, $$I_y = \frac{V_{x-m}}{Z_{x-m}}$$

$$= \frac{240 \angle 0°}{8.15 \angle 1.01°} = 29.46 \angle -1.01° \text{ Amps.}$$

Using current division,

$$I_3 = I_y \times \frac{\text{Admittance of } (2 - j5)\Omega}{\text{Admittance of } Z_{eq_2}}$$

$$= 29.46 \angle -1.01° \times \frac{0.186 \angle +68.2°}{0.141 \angle +16.05°}$$

$$= 38.74 \angle 51.15° \text{ Amps.}$$

Thus $\mathbf{I = 150.4 \angle -20° \text{ A}}$

$\mathbf{I_2 = 58.21 \angle 14.04° \text{ A}}$

$\mathbf{I_3 = 38.74 \angle 51.15° \text{ A}}$

V_{x-m}, potential at

$x = \mathbf{240 \angle 0° \text{ Volts,}}$

V_{y-m}, potential at

$y = I_y \times Z_{eq_3} = 29.46 \times 2.5 = \mathbf{73.65 \text{ Volts.}}$

EXAMPLE 19.32 *Write down the state equation for the current I_1 in the circuit shown in Fig. E19.26 in terms of voltage V_0 and the independent source V.*

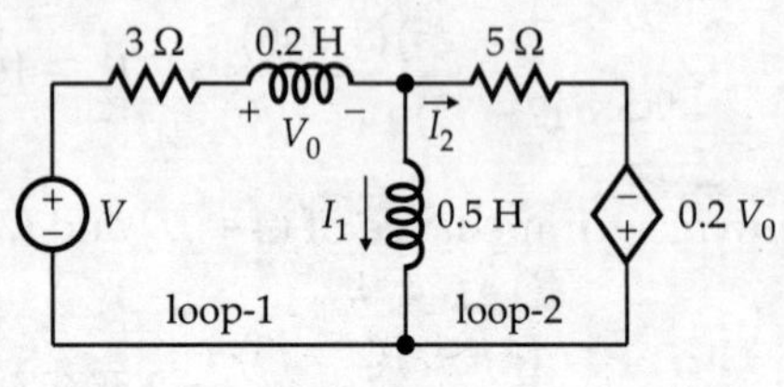

Fig. E19.26

Solution. In loop-1

$$-V + 3(I_1 + I_2) = V_0 + 0.5 \frac{dI_1}{dt} = 0$$

or $$V - 3I_1 - 3I_2 - V_0 - 0.5 \frac{dI_1}{dt} = 0 \qquad ...(1)$$

In loop-2

$$5I_2 - 0.2 V_0 - 0.5 \frac{dI_1}{dt} = 0$$

$$I_2 = 0.04 V_0 + 0.1 \frac{dt_1}{dt} \qquad ...(2)$$

Substituting the value of I_2 form equation (2) in equation (1) we get

$$V - 3I_1 - 3\left[0.04 V_0 + 0.1 \frac{dI_1}{dt}\right] - V_0 - 0.5 \frac{dI_1}{dt} = 0$$

or $$\frac{dI_1}{dt} = \left(-1.4 V_0 - 3.75 I_1 + \frac{5}{4} V\right)$$

Thus the required state equation is

$$\frac{dI_1}{dt} = \left(\mathbf{-1.4 V_0 - 3.75 I_1 + \frac{5}{4} V}\right).$$

EXAMPLE 19.33 *The voltage across a circuit is given by*

$$V(s) = \frac{(s+1)(s+3)}{s(s+2)(s+4)}.$$

Obtain the current in that circuit at t = 0.1 sec if the circuit impedance is $|Z| = 1\Omega$.

SOLUTION.

$$V(s) = \frac{(s+1)(s+3)}{s(s+2)(s+4)} = \frac{3}{8s} + \frac{1}{4}\frac{1}{s+2} + \frac{3}{8}\frac{1}{s+4}$$

or $$v(t) = £^{-1}\left[\frac{3}{8} \times \frac{1}{s} + \frac{1}{4} \times \frac{1}{4} \times \frac{1}{s+2} + \frac{3}{8} \times \frac{1}{s+4}\right]$$

$$= \frac{3}{8} + \frac{1}{4} e^{-2t} + \frac{3}{8} e^{-4t}$$

at $t = 0.1$ sec,

$$v(0.1) = \frac{3}{8} + \frac{1}{4} e^{-0.2} + \frac{3}{8} e^{-0.4}$$

i.e., $v(0.1) = 0.831$ Volts.

$$\therefore \quad i(0.1) = \frac{0.831}{|Z|} = \mathbf{0.831 \text{ Amp.}}$$

EXAMPLE 19.34 *The voltage across a passive element in an electric circuit is given by $\frac{d^2 v}{dt^2} + v = t$. Find $v(t)$ if $v(0+) = 1;\ \frac{dv}{dt}(0+) = -2.$*

SOLUTION. Taking the Laplace transform of the equation $\frac{d^2 v}{dt^2} + v = t$ for both sides, we can write

$$s^2 V(s) - sv(0+) - \dot{v}(0+) + V(s) = 1/s^2$$

or $\quad V(s)[(s^2+1)]-sv(0+)-\dot{v}(0+)=1/s^2$

or $\quad V(s)(s^2+1)-s+2=1/s^2$

$$\therefore \quad V(s)=\frac{1}{s^2(s^2+1)}-\frac{s}{s^2+1}-\frac{2}{s^2+1}$$

[using partial fraction]

$$=\frac{1}{s^2}-\frac{s}{s^2+1}-\frac{3}{s^2+1}$$

$$\therefore \quad v(t)=£^{-1}\left[\frac{1}{s^2}-\frac{s}{s^2+1}-\frac{3}{s^2+1}\right]$$

$$= \mathbf{t+\cos t-3\sin t.}$$

EXAMPLE 19.35 *For the following equation, what is the value of $x(t)$ at $t\to\infty$?*

$$\frac{d^2x}{dt^2}+3\frac{dx}{dt}+2x(t)=5$$

SOLUTION. Taking Laplace transform at both sides of the given equation,

$$s^2x(s)+3sx(s)+2x(s)=(5/s)$$

$$\therefore \quad x(s)=\frac{5}{s(s^2+3s+2)}$$

Using final value theorem,

$$\lim_{t\to\infty}x(t)=\lim_{s\to 0}x(s).s$$

$$=\lim_{s\to 0}s\frac{5}{s(s^2+3s+2)}=\frac{5}{2}$$

$\therefore$ **at $t\to\infty$, $x(t)=\frac{5}{2}$.**

EXAMPLE 19.36 *A system is represented by the following differential equation :*

$$\frac{d^2x}{dt^2}+6\frac{dx}{dt}+8x=0$$

Find its solution with initial conditions $x(0)=1;\left.\frac{dx}{dt}\right|_{t=0}=0$

SOLUTION. Given equation is

$$\frac{d^2x}{dt^2}+6\frac{dx}{dt}+8x=0$$

Using initial conditions with the Laplace transformation of the given equation we get

$$s^2x(s)-sx(0)-x(0)+6[sx(s)-x(0)]+8x(s)=0$$

or $\quad s^2x(s)-s(1)-0+6[sx(s)-1]+8x(s)=0$

$$x(s)[s^2+6x+8]-s-6=0$$

$$\therefore \quad x(s)=\frac{(s+6)}{(s^2+6s+8)}$$

Using partial fraction,

$$x(s)=\frac{2}{s+2}-\frac{1}{s+4}$$

$$\therefore \quad x(t)=[2e^{-2t}-e^{-4t}]$$

EXAMPLE 19.37 *A two port network has zero initial conditions. At $t=0$; an impulse voltage $\delta(t)$ is applied at the input producing a voltage $u(t)[e^{-2t}+e^{-3t}]$ volts at the output. Determine the input voltage if the output voltage is required to be $[te^{-2t}u(t)]$.*

SOLUTION. Let $V_{in}(t)$ be the input voltage while $V_{out}(t)$ be the output voltage.

For $\quad V_{in}(t)=\delta(t)$,

i.e., for $\quad v_{in}(s)=1$,

$$V_{out}(t)=(e^{-2t}+e^{-3t})u(t)$$

i.e., $\quad v_{out}(s)=\frac{1}{s+2}+\frac{1}{s+3}.$

$$\therefore \quad \frac{v_{out}(s)}{v_{in}(s)}=\frac{\frac{1}{s+2}+\frac{1}{s+3}}{1}$$

$$=\frac{2s+5}{(s+2)(s+3)}$$

= Transfer function $H(s)$.

Again, if

$$V_{out}(t)=te^{-2t}u(t),$$

$$v_{out}(s)=\frac{1}{(s+2)^2}$$

However,

$$H(s)=\frac{2s+5}{(s+2)(s+3)}=\frac{v_{out}(s)(\text{new})}{v_{in}(s)(\text{new})}$$

$$\therefore \quad v_{in}(s)(\text{new})=\frac{v_{out}(s)(\text{new})}{H(s)}$$

or $\quad v_{in}(s)(\text{new})=\frac{1}{(s+2)^2}\times\frac{(s+2)(s+3)}{(2s+5)}$

$$=\frac{1}{2}\left[\frac{2}{s+2}-\frac{1}{s+2.5}\right]$$

Taking inverse of Laplace,

$$V_{in}(t)(\text{new})=\left(e^{-2t}-\frac{1}{2}e^{-2.5t}\right)u(t)\ \textbf{Volts.}$$

CHAPTER 19

EXAMPLE 19.38 *For the network of Fig. E19.27, the switch K is changed from position a to b at t = 0. Assume steady state was established at position a. Find i_1 (t), i_2 (t) and i_3 (t) at t = 0+.*

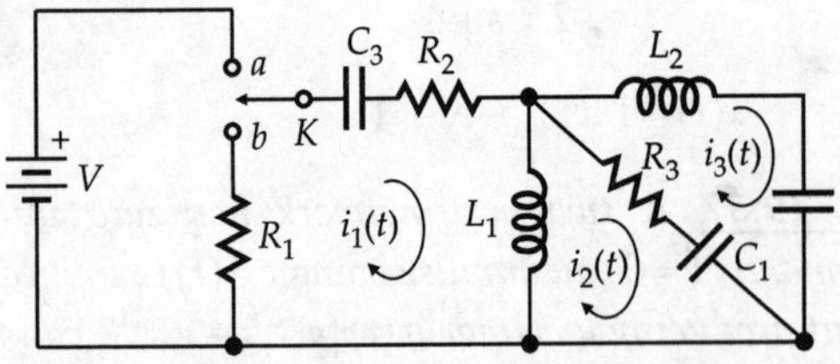

Fig. E19.27

SOLUTION. In the steady state condition the switch was at 'a' and C_1, C_2 and C_3 were obviously open-circuited. C_3 must have been charged at V, the battery voltage.

$\therefore$ at $t = 0-$, the current through L_2 being $i_3(t)$, $i_3(t) = 0$, C_2 being open-circuited ; also current through L_1 is $i_1(0-) - i_2(0-) = 0$

(Since C_1 and C_3 open-circuited).

i.e., $\quad i_1(0-) = i_2(0-)$.

At $t = 0$, K moves from a to b ; since current through L_1 and L_2 cannot change instantaneously, the current through L_1 and L_2 will remain zero.

i.e., $\quad i_3(t) = 0$ and $i_1(t) = i_2(t) \quad$ [at $t = 0+$]

To visualise the current flow at $t = 0+$, we refer to Fig. E19.27(*a*).

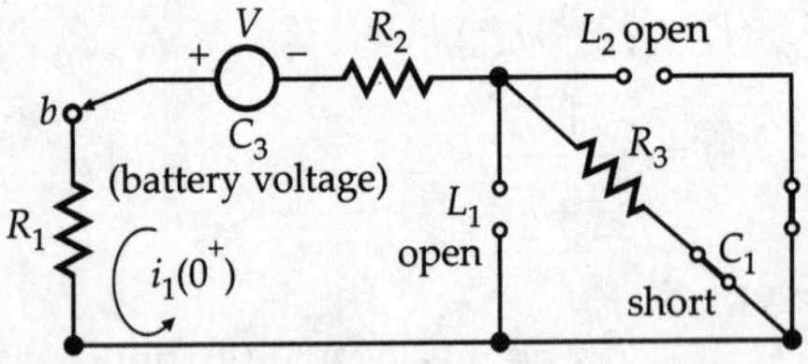

Fig. E19.27 (*a*)

Here $i_1(0+) = i_2(0+) = -\dfrac{V}{R_1 + R_2 + R_3}$ Amps.

$$\therefore \quad \mathbf{i_1(0+) = i_2(0+) = -\frac{V}{R_1 + R_2 + R_3}\ Amp}$$

and $\quad \mathbf{i_3(0+) = 0.}$

EXAMPLE 19.39 *An ideal capacitor C is charged to a voltage V_0 and connected at t = 0 across an ideal inductor L. If $\omega_0 = 1/\sqrt{LC}$, find the voltage across the capacitor at time t > 0.*

Solution. With reference to Fig. E19.28

$$i_c(t) = C\frac{dv_c(t)}{dt}$$

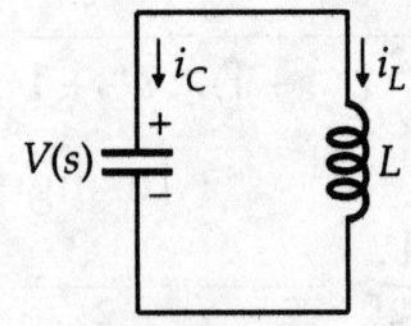

Fig. E19.28

Taking Laplace transform,

$$I_C(s) = CsV(s) - V(0)$$

[assuming $V(0)$ as initial voltage]

Also, $i_L(t) = \dfrac{1}{L}\int v_C(t)\,dt$

or $\quad I_L(s) = \dfrac{1}{L}\cdot\dfrac{V(s)}{s}$

As $t > 0$, $\quad I_C(s) + I_L(s) = 0$

or $\quad C_s V(s) - V(0) + \dfrac{1}{L}\dfrac{V(s)}{s} = 0$

or $\quad \left[s^2 + \dfrac{1}{LCs}\right]V(s) = V_0$

$\therefore \quad V(s) = \dfrac{V_0}{s^2 + \omega_0^2}\cdot V_0 \quad \left[\because \omega_0^2 = \dfrac{1}{LC}\right]$

i.e., $\quad \mathbf{v(t) = V_0 \cos \omega_0 t \ ; \ (t > 0)}$

EXAMPLE 19.40 *A voltage is given by $V(s) = \dfrac{1}{s(s+\alpha)}$. If $v(\infty) = 2$ volts, find v (1).*

SOLUTION. $\quad v(\infty) = \lim\limits_{s\to 0} s\,V(s)$

$$= \lim_{s\to 0} \frac{s}{s(s+a)} = \frac{1}{a}$$

It is given that $v(\infty) = 2$

$\therefore \quad 2 = \dfrac{1}{a} \quad \therefore \ a = 0.5.$

Thus $V(s) = \dfrac{1}{s(s+a)} = \dfrac{1}{s(s+0.5)}$

$$= 2\left(\frac{1}{s} + \frac{1}{s+0.5}\right)$$

$\therefore \quad v(t) = 2(1 - \varepsilon^{-0.5t})$

and hence $v(s) = 2(1 - \varepsilon^{-0.5})$

$$\mathbf{= 0.787\ Volts.}$$

EXAMPLE 19.41 *The current in a ac circuit is given by*

$$\frac{d^2i}{dt^2}+5\frac{di}{dt}+6i=e^{-t}$$

where e^{-t} is the source voltage. Obtain $I(s)$ if $i(0+)=\frac{di}{dt\,(0+)}=1$.

SOLUTION. We can write the given current equation in s-domain as

$$s^2I(s)-si(0+)-\frac{di}{dt}(0+)+5[sI(s)-i(0+)]+6I(s)=\frac{1}{s+1}$$

or $$I(s)[s^2+5s+6]=\frac{1}{s+1}+s+1+5$$

or $$I(s)=\frac{1}{(s+1)(s^2+5s+6)}+\frac{s+6}{s^2+5s+6}$$

$$=\frac{\mathbf{1}}{\mathbf{s^2+5s+6}}\left[\frac{\mathbf{1}}{\mathbf{s+1}}+\mathbf{s+6}\right].$$

EXAMPLE 19.42 *For the circuit shown in Fig. E19.29, find the current through the resistance R connected between points a and b by Thevenins theorem.*

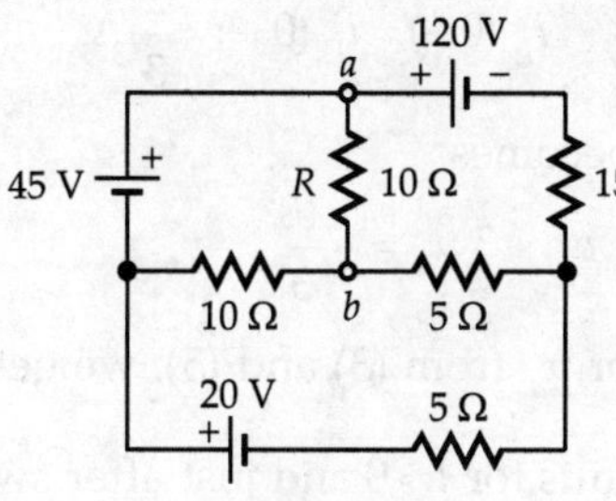

Fig. E19.29

SOLUTION. Let us first find the Thevenin's resistance (*i.e.*, the internal resistance) of the network across $a-b$ by removing R and making the active sources deactivated [Fig. E19.29(*a*)].

$$R_{AB}=10\,||\,(5+3.75)=4.67\,\Omega.$$

Thus the internal resistance across $ab=4.67\,\Omega$. Next we are to obtain $V_{o.c}$ across *a-b* [Refer to Fig. E19.29(*b*)]. Let the loop currents be i_1 and i_2. Hence we can write for first loop

$$-45+120+i_1\times 15+(i_1-i_2)5+(i_1-i_2)10=0$$

i.e., $$75+30\,i_1-15i_2=0 \quad ...(1)$$

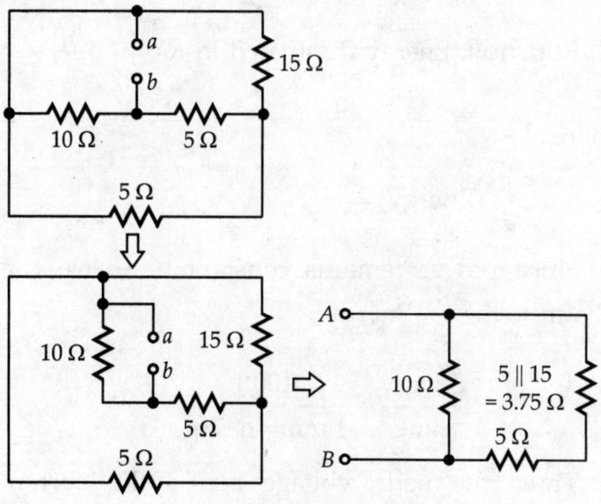

Fig. E19.29 (*a*)

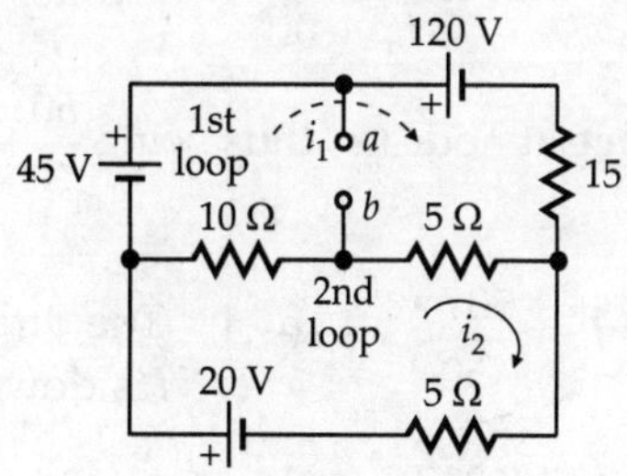

Fig. E19.29 (*b*)

and for the second loop,

$$-20+(i_2-i_1)10+(i_2-i_1)5+5i_2=0$$

or $$-20-15\,i_1+20\,i_2=0 \quad ...(2)$$

Solving (1) and (2)

$$i_1=-3.2\text{ A};\quad i_2=-1.4\text{ A}$$

$\therefore$ $V_{o.c}$ (across *a-b*)

$$=45-(i_1-i_2)\times 10$$
$$=45-(-3.2+1.4)10$$
$$=45-(-1.8)10=63\text{ Volts.}$$

$$\therefore\quad I_{Th}=\frac{V_{o.c}}{R_{ab}+R}=\frac{63}{4.67\times 10}=\mathbf{4.285\ A.}$$

EXAMPLE 19.43 *In the network of Fig. E19.30, $I_1=0.05$ A; $I_2=0.1$ A, $R=50\,\Omega$. The unknown current source has strength i. If 100 J of energy is delivered to I_2 in 1 min, find the magnitude of i.*

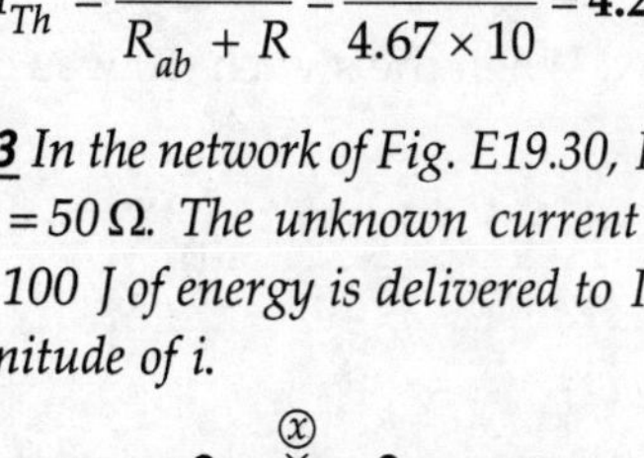

Fig. E19.30

CHAPTER 19

Solution. Energy dissipated in $R = \int_0^{\infty} p\, dt$

where $p = vi.$

$$\therefore \quad \frac{d}{dt}(\text{Energy}) = p = vi$$

Since power remains constant here, we can substitute for $\frac{d}{dt}$ (Energy),

$$\frac{\text{Energy}}{\text{time}} = \frac{100 \text{ J}}{1 \text{ min} \times 60 \text{ sec}} = \frac{5}{3} \text{ W}.$$

Thus, the node voltage across the current sources (I_2) is given by

$$v = \frac{P}{I_2} = \frac{5/3}{0.1} = \frac{50}{3} \text{ volts.}$$

The voltage at node (x), thus being $\frac{50}{3}$ volts, we can write,

$$-I_1 + I_2 + \frac{50/3}{50} + i = 0 \quad [\because \text{ The direction of } i \text{ is downwards}]$$

or $\quad -0.05 + 0.1 + 0.333 + i = 0$

or $\quad i = \mathbf{0.383 \text{ A.}}$

Example 19.44 *In the network of Fig. E19.31 steady state is reached with K open. At t = 0, K is closed. Find v_a (0 −) and v_a (0 +).*

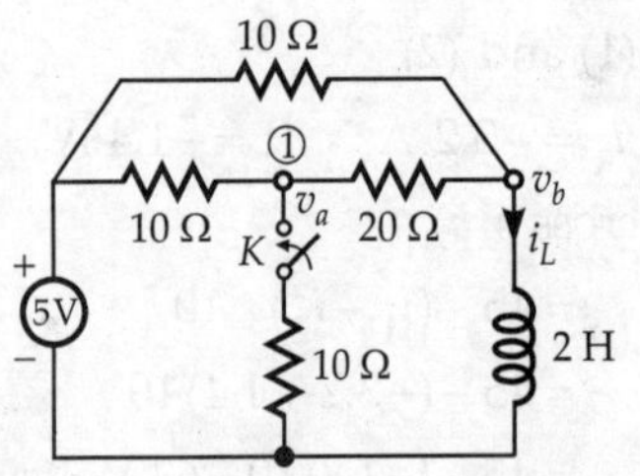

Fig. E19.31

Solution. When the switch (K) was open ($t < 0$). at node (1),

$$\frac{v_a - 5}{10} + \frac{v_a - v_b}{20} = 0 \qquad ...(1)$$

and at node (2),

$$\frac{v_b - v_a}{20} + \frac{v_b - 5}{10} + i_L = 0 \qquad ...(2)$$

However, at steady state the inductor acts as short circuit.

$$\therefore \quad v_b(0-) = 0. \qquad ...(2A)$$

Thus equation (1) becomes

$$\frac{v_a}{10} + \frac{v_a}{20} = \frac{5}{10},$$

or $\quad v_a(0-) = \mathbf{\frac{10}{3} \text{ Volts.}}$

With $v_a(0-) = 10/3$ Volts, using (2A) from (2),

$$\frac{0 - \frac{10}{3}}{20} + \frac{-5}{10} + i_L(0-) = 0$$

or $\quad i_L = \frac{2}{3}$ amps at $t = (0-)$.

Again with switching of K at $t = 0$, at node (1), for $t > 0$,

$$\frac{v_a - 5}{10} + \frac{v}{10} + \frac{v_a - v_b}{20} = 0$$

or $$5v_a - v_b = 10 \qquad ...(3)$$

and at node (2), for $t > 0$,

$$\frac{v_b - v_a}{20} + \frac{v_b - 5}{10} + i_L = 0. \qquad ...(4)$$

Since the current in an inductor can't change instantaneously,

$$i_L(0-) = i_L(0+) = \frac{2}{3} \text{ A.}$$

Thus (4) becomes

$$-v_a + 3v_b = -\frac{10}{3}. \qquad ...(5)$$

Solving for v_a from (3) and (5), we get

$$v_a = \mathbf{\frac{40}{21}} \textbf{ Volts} \text{ for } t > 0 \text{ and just after switching.}$$

Example 19.45 *In the network shown in Fig. E19.32 the switch S is closed at t = 0. With $i_L(0) = 0$; $v_C(0) = 0$, obtain the value of V_C at steady state.*

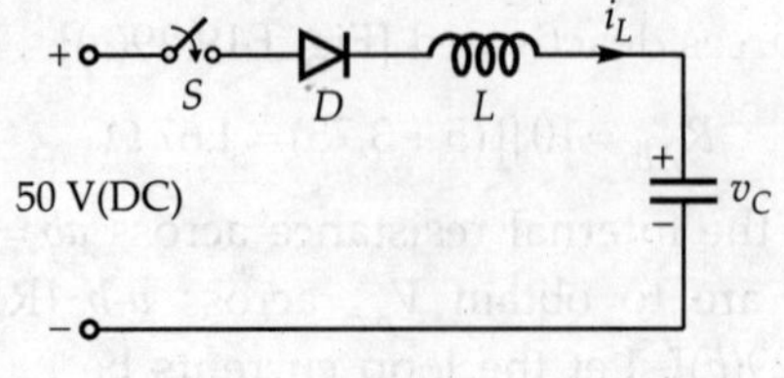

Fig. E19.32

Solution. Input impedance of the given circuit is

$$Z(s) = Ls + \frac{1}{Cs}$$

Given $V(s) = (50/s)$

$$I_L(s) = \frac{V(s)}{Z(s)} = \frac{50/s}{Ls + \dfrac{1}{Cs}}$$

$$= \frac{50C}{s^2 LC + 1} = \frac{50}{L\left(s^2 + \dfrac{1}{LC}\right)}$$

since $v_c(0) = 0$, hence

$$V_C(s) = \frac{I_L(s)}{Cs} = \frac{50}{LCs\left(s^2 + \dfrac{1}{LC}\right)}$$

$\therefore$ Steady state voltage across the capacitor is

$$\lim_{t\to\infty} V_C(t) = \lim_{s\to 0} s.V_c(s)$$

$$= \lim_{s\to 0} \frac{50}{LC\left(s^2 + \dfrac{1}{LC}\right)} = 50\text{ V}$$

$\therefore$ **$V_c(t)$ at steady state is 50 V.**

Example 19.46 *For the circuit shown in Fig. E19.33 find the transfer function $G_{12}(s) = V_2/V_1$.*

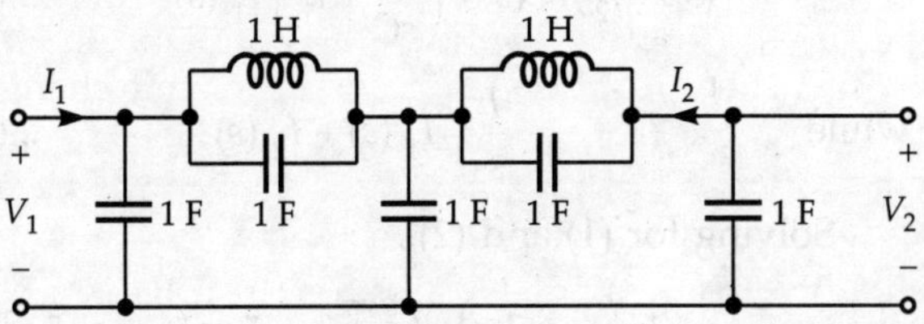

Fig. E19.33

Solution. The given network is redrawn in Fig. E19.33(*a*) in *s*-domain.

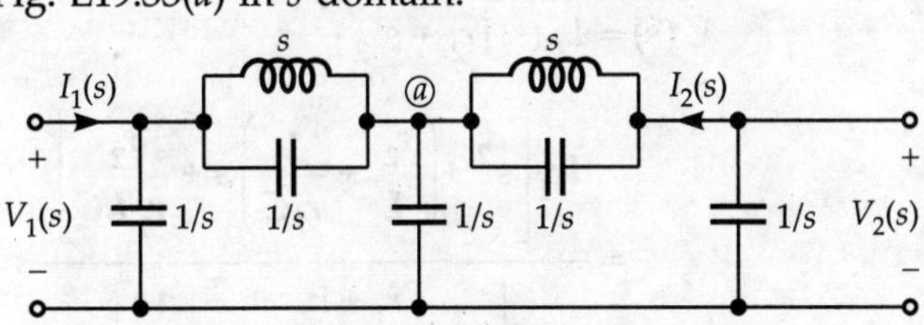

Fig. E19.33 (*a*)

Let the voltage at node (*a*) be $V_a(s)$.

The nodal equation at node (*a*) becomes

$$[V_a(s) - V_1(s)]\left(s + \frac{1}{s}\right) + \left(V_a(s)/\frac{1}{s}\right)$$

$$+ [V_a(s) - V_2(s)]\left(s + \frac{1}{s}\right) = 0$$

[$\because$ admittance of parallel combination of "s" and "$1/s$" is $\left(s + \dfrac{1}{s}\right)$]

On simplification,

$$V_1(s)\left[s + \frac{1}{s}\right] = V_a(s)\left[3s + \frac{2}{s}\right] - V_2(s)\left[s + \frac{1}{s}\right] \quad ...(1)$$

Similarly, at the output node, nodal equation gives

$$[V_2(s) - V_a(s)]\left[s + \frac{1}{s}\right] + \frac{V_2(s)}{1/s} = 0$$

or $$-V_a(s)\left[s + \frac{1}{s}\right] + V_2(s)\left[2s + \frac{1}{s}\right] = 0 \quad ...(2)$$

Eliminating $V_a(s)$ we obtain

$$\frac{V_2(s)}{V_1(s)} = G_{12}(s) = \frac{\left(s + \dfrac{1}{s}\right)^2}{5s^2 + 5 + \dfrac{1}{s^2}}$$

$$\therefore \quad \mathbf{G_{12}(s) = \frac{(s^2+1)^2}{5s^4 + 5s^2 + 1}}.$$

Example 19.47 *Find the steady state transfer function $H(j\omega)$ in the network (Fig. E19.34).*

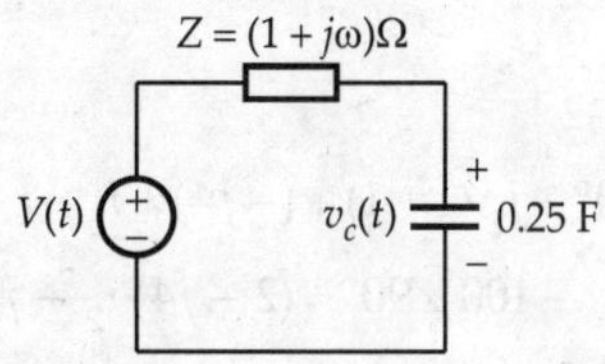

Fig. E19.34

Solution.

$$H(j\omega) = \frac{V_C(j\omega)}{V(j\omega)}$$

But

$$V_C(j\omega) = \frac{V(j\omega)\, Z_C(j\omega)}{Z_R(j\omega) + Z_L(j\omega) + Z_C(j\omega)}$$

$$\therefore \quad H(j\omega) = \frac{Z_C(j\omega)}{Z_R(j\omega) + Z_L(j\omega) + Z_C(j\omega)}$$

$$= \frac{\dfrac{1}{j\omega \times 0.25}}{1 + j\omega + \dfrac{1}{j\omega \times 0.25}} = \frac{(4/j\omega)}{1 + j\omega + \dfrac{4}{j\omega}}$$

$$= \frac{4}{(j\omega)^2 + (j\omega + 4)} = \frac{4}{4 - \omega^2 + j\omega}$$

$$\therefore \quad \mathbf{H(j\omega) = \frac{4}{(4 - \omega^2 + j\omega)}}.$$

EXAMPLE 19.48 *Find the current through any of the 1Ω resistors (Fig. E19.35).*

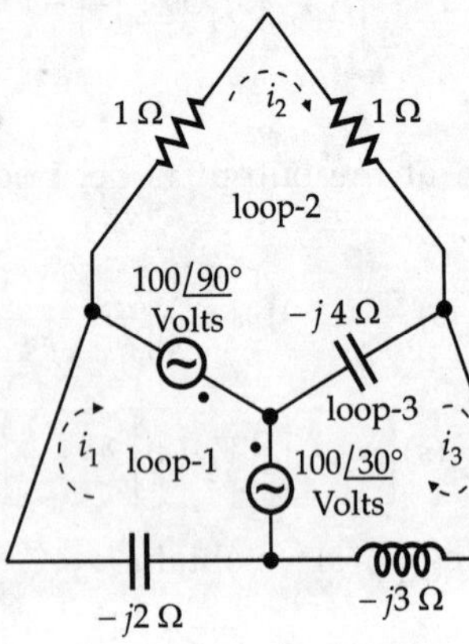

Fig. E19.35

SOLUTION. Let the assumed loop currents are designated by dotted arrows in Fig. E19.35.

Using KVL in loop-1, the loop equations are given by

$$-100\angle 90° + 100\angle 30° + i_1 \times (-j2) = 0$$

or $$100\angle 90° - 100\angle 30° = -j2 \times i_1 \quad ...(1)$$

In loop-2,

$$100\angle 90° + i_2(1+1) + (-j4)\times i_2 - (-j4)\times i_3 = 0$$

or $$-100\angle 90° = (2-j4)\,i_2 + j4 \times i_3 \quad ...(2)$$

and in loop-3,

$$-100\angle 30° + (-j4)\times i_3 - (-j4)\times i_2 + j3 \times i_3 = 0$$

or $$100\angle 30° = j4 \times i_2 + (j3 - j4)\,i_3$$

or $$100\angle 30° = j4 \times i_2 - j1 \times i_3 \quad ...(3)$$

Solving (1), (2) and (3),

$$i_2 = 29.65\angle -64.5° \text{ Amp.}$$

∴ Current through 1Ω resistor = **29.65 Amps.**

EXAMPLE 19.49 *A current is given by*

$$I(s) = \frac{(s+2)(s+4)}{(s+1)(s+3)\,s}.$$

Determine the initial and final values of the currents.

SOLUTION. Using initial value theorem,

$$i(0+) = \lim_{s\to\infty} sI(s) = \lim_{s\to\infty} \frac{(s+2)(s+4)}{(s+1)(s+3)} = \mathbf{1\ A.}$$

While using final value theorem,

$$i(\infty) = \lim_{s\to 0} sI(s) = \lim_{s\to 0} \frac{(s+2)(s+4)}{(s+1)(s+3)} = \frac{\mathbf{8}}{\mathbf{3}}\ \mathbf{A.}$$

EXAMPLE 19.50 *Determine the voltage at node (x) in Laplace domain when switch K is opened at t = 0. Assume zero initial condition.*

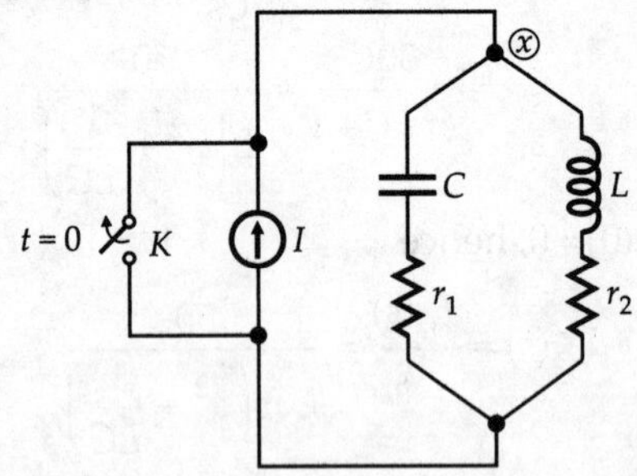

Fig. E19.36

SOLUTION. At steady state (t = 0 −) there was no current through r_1 or r_2. Let the current through r_1 be I_1 and that through r_2 be I_2 at t = 0 + (after switching) *i.e.*, when the current source is applied.

Then, in the loop containing r_1, C and r_2, L is governed by the equation

$$(sL + r_2)I_2(s) = \left(\frac{1}{sC} + r_1\right) I_1(s) \quad ...(1)$$

while $$\frac{I}{s} = I_1(s) + I_2(s) \quad ...(2)$$

Solving for (1) and (2),

$$I_2(s) = I\frac{r_1}{L}\left(s + \frac{1}{r_1 C}\right) \Big/ \left\{ s\left[s^2 + \frac{r_1 + r_2}{L}.s + \frac{1}{LC}\right]\right\}$$

∴ V (s), voltage at node (x) is given by

$$V(s) = I_2(s)[r_2 + sL_2]$$

$$= \frac{Ir_1\left[s^2 + \left(\frac{r_2}{L} + \frac{1}{r_1 C}\right)s + \frac{r_2}{r_1 LC}\right]}{s\left[s^2 + \frac{r_1 + r_2}{L}.s + \frac{1}{LC}\right]}.$$

EXAMPLE 19.51 *Obtain Thevenin's equivalent across AB (Fig. E19.37).*

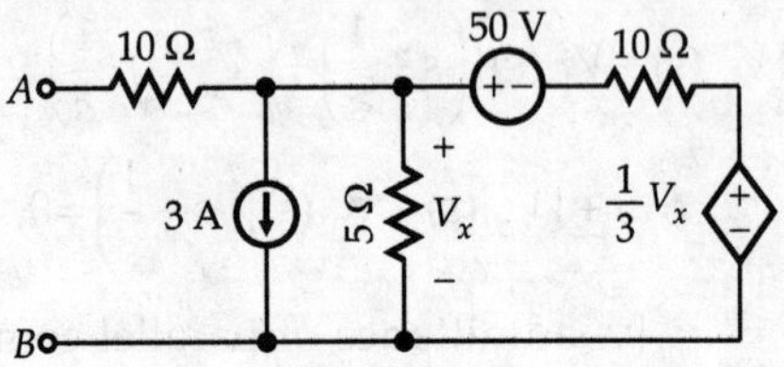

Fig. E19.37

SOLUTION. Let us redraw the circuit with AB open [Fig. E19.37(*a*)]. Obviously V_x is the open circuit voltage across A-B $[V_{o.c} = V_x = V_{AB}]$

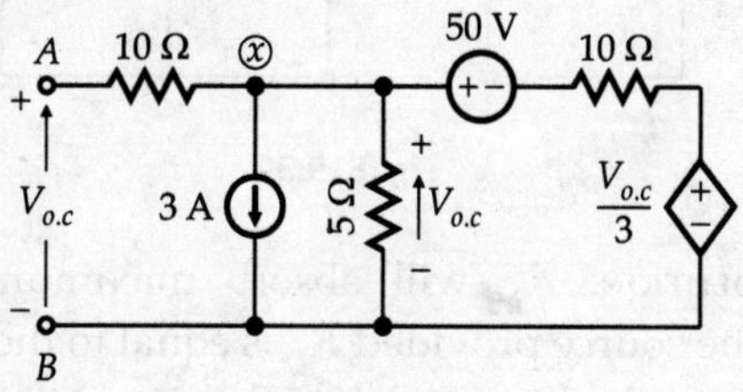

Fig. E19.37 (*a*)

At node (x),

$$3 + \frac{V_{o.c}}{5} + \frac{V_{o.c} - 50 - \frac{1}{3}V_{o.c}}{10} = 0$$

or $$V_{o.c}\left[\frac{1}{5} + \frac{1}{10} - \frac{1}{30}\right] = 2$$

or $$V_{o.c} = \frac{60}{8} = 7.5 \text{ Volts.}$$

Next, we short A-B terminal.

Then at node (x) [Fig. E19.37(*b*)],

$$\frac{V_x}{10} + 3 + \frac{V_x}{5} + \frac{V_x - 50 - \frac{1}{3}V_x}{10} = 0$$

$$V_x\left[\frac{1}{10} + \frac{1}{5} + \frac{1}{10} - \frac{1}{30}\right] = 2$$

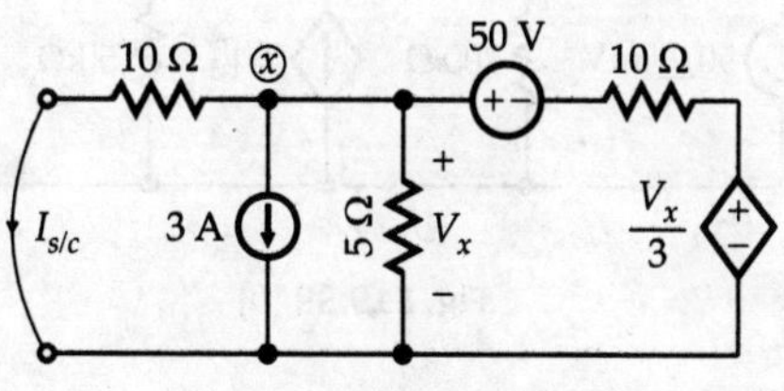

Fig. E19.37 (*b*)

$$\therefore \quad V_x = \frac{60}{11} \text{ Volts.}$$

$$\therefore \quad I_{s.c} = \frac{V_x}{10} = \frac{60}{11} \times \frac{1}{10} = \frac{6}{11} \text{ Amps.}$$

$$\therefore \quad R_{int} = \frac{V_{o.c}}{I_{s.c}} = \frac{7.5}{6/11} = \frac{82.5}{6} = 13.75\,\Omega$$

Then for the given network,

$\boldsymbol{V_{o.c} = 7.5}$ **Volts**

$\boldsymbol{R_{int} = 13.75\,\Omega}$.

EXAMPLE 19.52 *Using Thevenin's theorem calculate the current flowing through 6 Ω resistor in Fig. E19.38(a).*

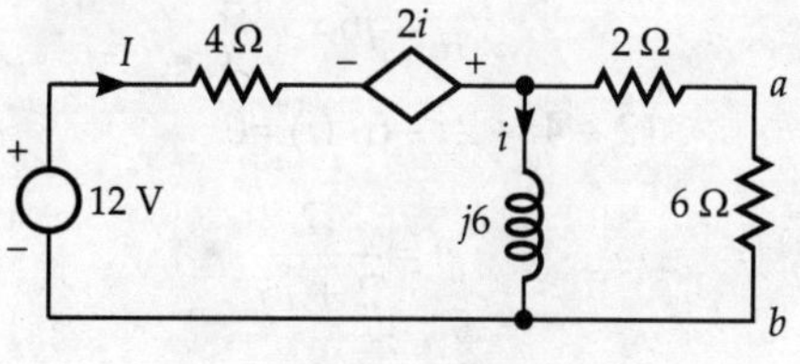

Fig. E19.38 (*a*)

SOLUTION. Let us first remove the load resistance (6 Ω) and apply short circuit across terminals (ab).

Let the short circuit current be I_{sc} [Fig. E19.38(*b*)]

$$\therefore \quad I = i + I_{sc}$$

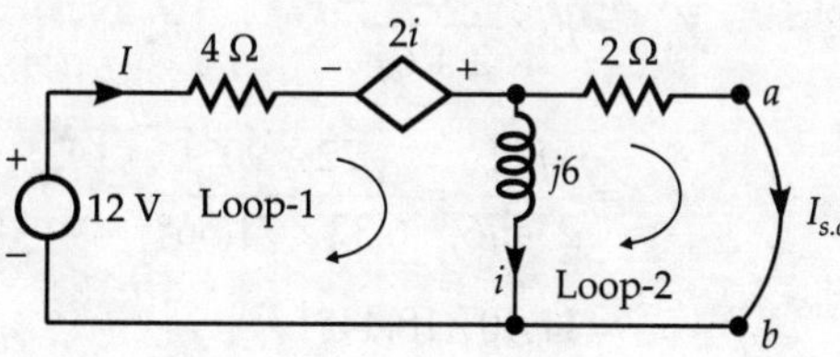

Fig. E19.38 (*b*)

In loop-1 we have

$$12 - 4I + 2i - 6ji = 0$$

$$12 - 4(i + I_{s.c}) + 2i - 6ji = 0$$

or $$12 = 4I_{s.c} + (2 + j6)\,i \quad ...(1)$$

In loop-2 we have

$$-2I_{s.c} + j6 \,.\, i = 0,$$

as, $$i = \frac{2I_{s.c}}{j6} = -j\frac{I_{s.c}}{3}$$

With the value of i in eqn. (1), we get

$$12 = 4\,I_{s.c} + (2 + j6)\left(-j\frac{I_{s.c}}{3}\right)$$

$$= I_{s.c}\left[\frac{12 - j2 + 6}{3}\right]$$

$$= \left[\frac{18 - j2}{3}\right] I_{s.c}$$

$$\therefore \quad I_{s.c} = \frac{36}{18 - 2j} = 1.98\angle 6.3° \text{ A}$$

Next we will have calculation to find V_{th}.

With reference to Fig. E19.38(c),

$$I_{s.c} = 0$$

$$\therefore \quad V_{Th} = j6 \times i$$

$$12 - 4i + 2i - 6j\,(i) = 0$$

or
$$i = \frac{12}{2 + j6}$$

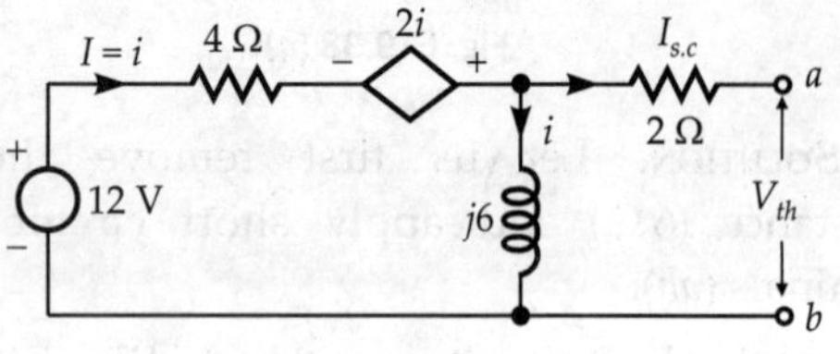

Fig. E19.38 (c)

$$\therefore \quad V_{Th} = j6 \times \frac{12}{2+6j}$$

$$= \frac{j72}{2 + j6} = \frac{72\angle 90°}{6.32\angle 71.56°}$$

$$= 11.40\angle 18.44°$$

$$\therefore \quad R_{Th} = \frac{V_{Th}}{I_{s.c}}$$

$$= \frac{11.40\angle 18.44°}{1.98\angle 6.4°} = 5.75\angle 12.04\,\Omega$$

∴ Thevenin equivalent circuit is obtained [Fig. E19.38(d)]

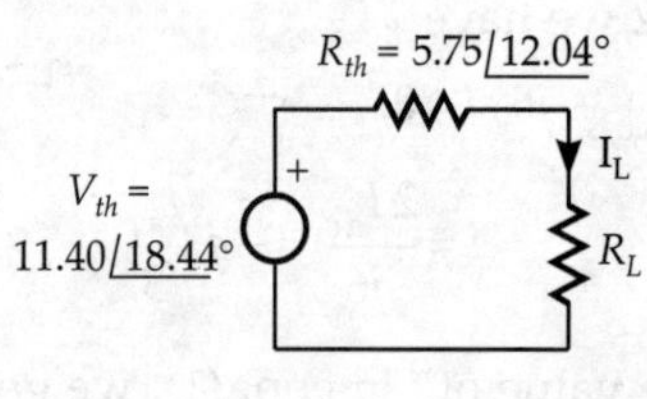

Fig. E19.38 (d)

$$\therefore \quad I_L = \frac{V_{Th}}{R_{Th} + R_L}$$

$$= \frac{11.40\angle 18.44°}{5.75\angle 12.04° + 6}\ \text{A}$$

$$\therefore \quad \mathbf{I_L \simeq 0.98 \angle 12.55°\ A.}$$

Example 19.53 *In Fig. E19.39, find the value of R_L such that R_L absorbs maximum power. Determine the value of maximum power.*

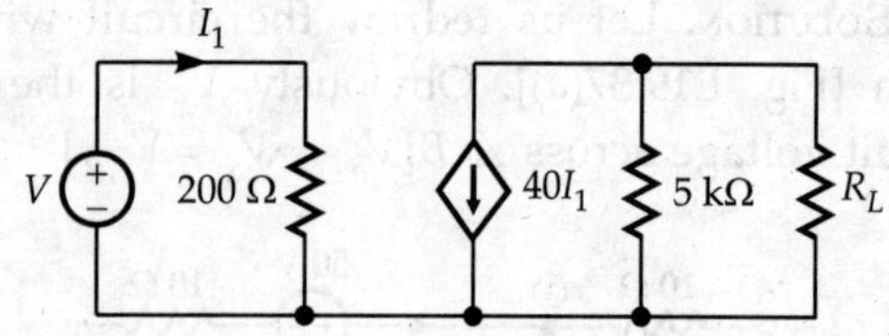

Fig. E19.39

Solution. R_L will absorb maximum power from the source provided R_L is equal to the internal impedance looking back into the circuit through the open-circuited terminals of R_L [Fig. E19.39(a)].

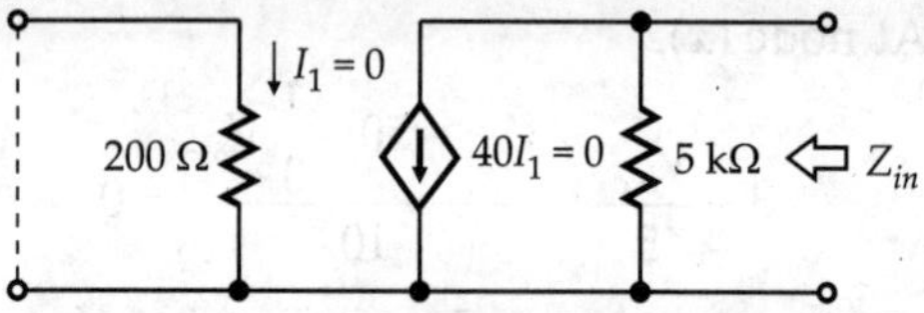

Fig. E19.39 (a)

Here $Z_{in} = 5\ \text{k}\Omega$ [∵ with replacement of V by short circuit, $I_1 \to 0$, giving $40\,I_1$ to be zero, equivalent to open circuit.]

Next we find $V_{o.c}$ [Fig. E19.39(b)] across R_L (replaced by open circuit).

$$I_1 = \frac{50 \times 10^{-3}\,\angle 0°}{200} = 0.25\,\angle 0°\ \text{mA}.$$

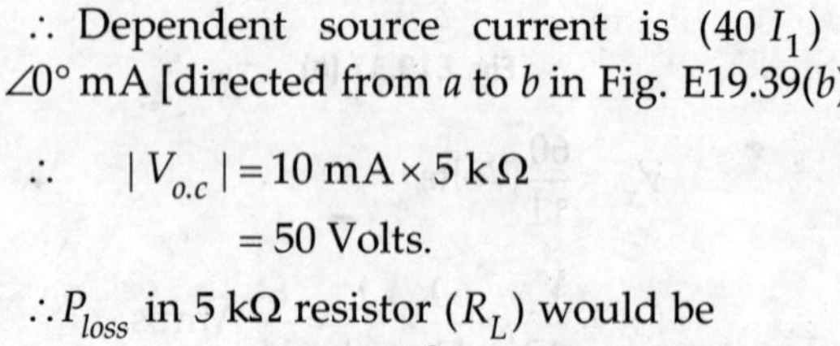

Fig. E19.39 (b)

∴ Dependent source current is $(40\,I_1)$ *i.e.*, $10\,\angle 0°$ mA [directed from a to b in Fig. E19.39(b)]

$$\therefore \quad |V_{o.c}| = 10\ \text{mA} \times 5\ \text{k}\Omega$$

$$= 50\ \text{Volts}.$$

∴ P_{loss} in 5 kΩ resistor (R_L) would be

$$P_L = \frac{(50/\sqrt{2})^2}{4 \times 5 \times 10^3} = \frac{2500}{40 \times 10^3} = 62.5\ \text{mW}.$$

[Since $|V_{o.c}| = 50$ Volts ∴ $|V_{o.c}|_{rms} = \frac{50}{\sqrt{2}}$ Volts.]

∴ $\mathbf{R_L = 5\ k\Omega}$ **for maximum power transfer and**

$P_{\max} = P_L = \mathbf{62.5\ mW.}$

EXAMPLE 19.54 *Find v_L in terms of v_B in Fig. E19.40.*

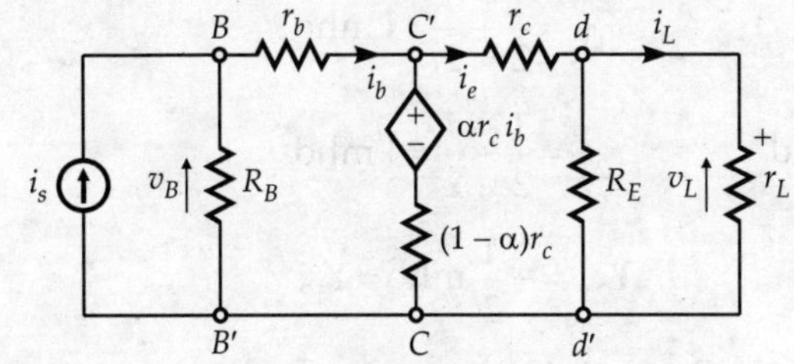

Fig. E19.40

SOLUTION. In loop $BC'CB'$,

$$-v_B + i_b r_b + i_b \alpha r_C + (1-\alpha) r_c\, (i_b - i_e) = 0$$

or $$v_B = (r_b + r_c)\, i_b - (1-\alpha)\, r_c i_e \qquad ...(1)$$

Again, in loop $C'dd'C$,

$$i_e r_e + \frac{R_E r_L}{R_E + r_L} . i_e - \alpha r_c i_b - (1-\alpha)\, r_c\, (i_b - i_e) = 0$$

or $$0 = -r_c i_b + \left[r_c + (1-\alpha)\, r_c + \frac{R_E r_L}{R_E + r_L} \right] i_e \qquad ...(2)$$

In matrix form,

$$\begin{bmatrix} v_B \\ 0 \end{bmatrix} = \begin{bmatrix} (r_b + r_c) & -(1-\alpha) r_C \\ -r_c & \left[r_c + (1-\alpha)\, r_c + \dfrac{R_E r_L}{R_E + r_L} \right] \end{bmatrix} \begin{bmatrix} i_b \\ i_e \end{bmatrix}$$

$$\therefore \Delta = r_b \left[r_c + (1-\alpha)\, r_c + \frac{R_E r_L}{R_E + r_L} \right] + r_c \left(r_c + \frac{R_E r_L}{R_E + r_L} \right)$$

But $v_L = i_e\, (R_E \,||\, r_L) = i_e \dfrac{R_E r_L}{R_E + r_L}$.

Since $i_e = \dfrac{\Delta_2}{\Delta}$, by Cramer's rule,

hence $$v_L = \frac{R_E r_L\, \Delta_2}{\Delta (R_E + r_L)}$$

From the above analysis, $\Delta_2 = r_c v_B$

$$\therefore v_L = \frac{R_E r_L r_c v_B}{(R_E + r_L) \left\{ r_b \left[r_c + (1-\alpha)\, r_c + \dfrac{R_E r_L}{R_E + r_L} \right] + r_c \left[r_c + \dfrac{R_E r_L}{R_E + r_L} \right] \right\}}.$$

EXAMPLE 19.55 *Find Z-matrix for the network shown in Fig. E19.41.*

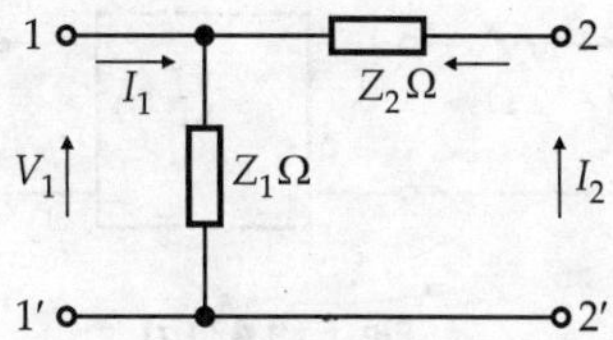

Fig. E19.41

SOLUTION. In the left loop,

$$V_1 = (I_1 + I_2) Z_1 = Z_1 I_1 + Z_1 I_2$$

In the right side loop,

$$-V_2 + I_2 Z_2 + (I_1 + I_2) Z_1 = 0$$

$$V_2 = Z_1 I_1 + (Z_1 + Z_2) I_2$$

$$\therefore \quad V_1 = Z_1 I_1 + Z_1 I_2$$

$$V_2 = Z_1 I_1 + (Z_1 + Z_2) I_2$$

$$\therefore \quad Z = \begin{bmatrix} Z_1 & Z_1 \\ Z_1 & Z_1 + Z_2 \end{bmatrix} \Omega$$

EXAMPLE 19.56 *M is a two port network represented by Z-parameter network. Obtain the Z parameters of the entire network when a resistor of 1Ω is connected in series with terminal and as shown in Fig. E19.42. Assume the input and output currents same in both the cases.*

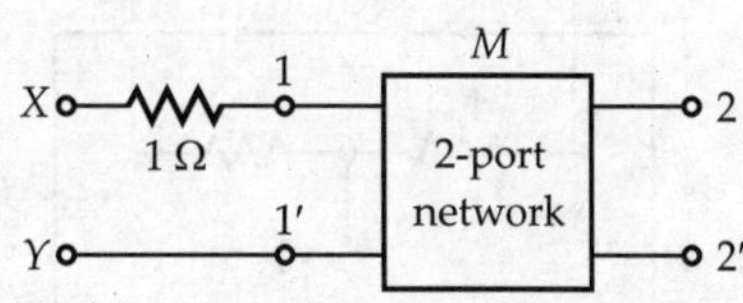

Fig. E19.42

SOLUTION. For *M*, without 1Ω resistor in series,

$$[Z] = \begin{bmatrix} Z_{11} & Z_{12} \\ Z_{21} & Z_{22} \end{bmatrix}$$

i.e., $$V_1 = Z_{11} I_1 + Z_{12} I_2$$

$$V_2 = Z_{21} I_1 + Z_{22} I_2$$

With 1Ω resistor connected in series with 1, the Z parameter equation can be written as

$$V_1' = Z_{11}' I_1' + Z_{12}' I_2'$$

$$V_2' = Z_{21}' I_1' + Z_{22}' I_2'$$

See Fig. E19.42(*a*).

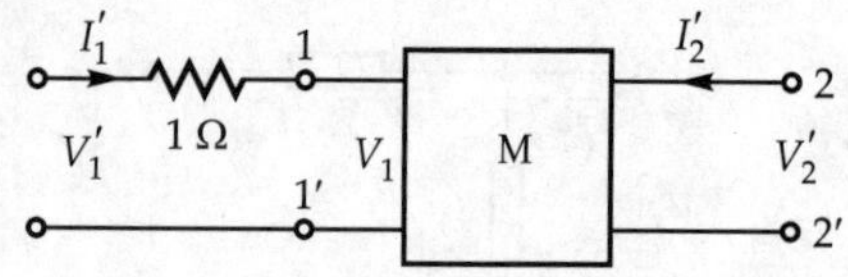

Fig. E19.42 (*a*)

As $\quad I_1' = I_1 \;;\; I_2' = I_2,$

with 1Ω resistor connected we can write

$$V_1' = V_1 + I_1' \times 1 = V_1 + I_1 = (Z_{11}I_1 + Z_{12}I_2) + I_1$$

$$= (Z_{11} + 1)I_1 + Z_{12}I_2$$

$\therefore$ Finally, $Z_{11}' = Z_{11} + 1 \,;\, Z_{12}' = Z_{12}$

Similarly, for output port,

$$V_1' = Z_{21}'I_1' + Z_{22}'I_2' = Z_{21}'I_1 + Z_{22}'I_2$$

i.e., $\quad Z_{21}' = Z_{21} \;;\; Z_{22}' = Z_{22}$

$$\therefore \quad [Z_{New}] = \begin{bmatrix} \mathbf{Z_{11}+1} & \mathbf{Z_{12}} \\ \mathbf{Z_{21}} & \mathbf{Z_{22}} \end{bmatrix} \textbf{Ohm}.$$

EXAMPLE 19.57 *Find Y parameters for the network shown in Fig. E19.43.*

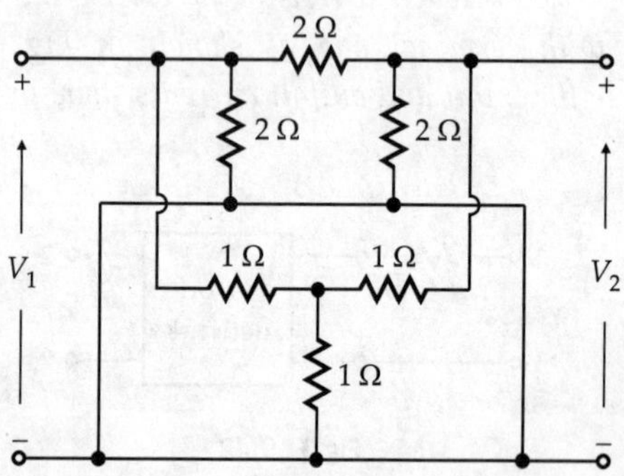

Fig. E19.43

SOLUTION. Observation reveals that two networks are in parallel [shown in Figs. E19.43(*a*) and (*b*)]

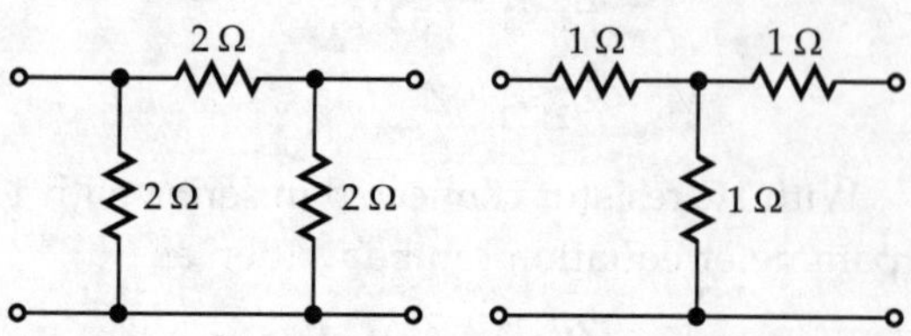

(*a*) (*b*)

Fig. E19.43

In Fig. E19.43(*a*),

$$Y_{11} = \frac{1}{2} + \frac{1}{2} = 1 \text{ mho}$$

and $$Y_{22} = \frac{1}{2} + \frac{1}{2} = 1 \text{ mho.}$$

$$Y_{21} = -\frac{1}{2} \text{ mho} = Y_{12}$$

In Fig. E19.43(*b*),

$$Z_{11} = 1 + 1 = 2\,\Omega,$$

$$Z_{12} = Z_{21} = 1\Omega.$$

$$Z_{22} = 1 + 1 = 2\,\Omega.$$

$$\therefore \Delta Z = (Z_{11}Z_{22}) - (Z_{12}\,Z_{21}) = 3.$$

Thus for Fig. E19.43(*b*),

$$Y_{11} = \frac{Z_{22}}{\Delta Z} = \frac{2}{3} \text{ mho} = Y_{22}$$

$$Y_{12} = -\frac{1}{3} \text{ mho} = Y_{21}$$

For the continued network of Fig. E19.43,

$$Y_{11} = 1 + \frac{2}{3} = \mathbf{\frac{5}{3}} \textbf{ mho}$$

$$Y_{12} = Y_{21} = -\frac{1}{2} - \frac{1}{3} = -\mathbf{\frac{5}{6}} \textbf{ mho}$$

$$Y_{22} = \frac{2}{3} + 1 = \mathbf{\frac{5}{3}} \textbf{ mho.}$$

[In S.I. units we write Siemens(s) instead of mho]

EXAMPLE 19.58 *Find $[I_2(s)/V_1(s)]$ in the circuit of Fig. E19.44.*

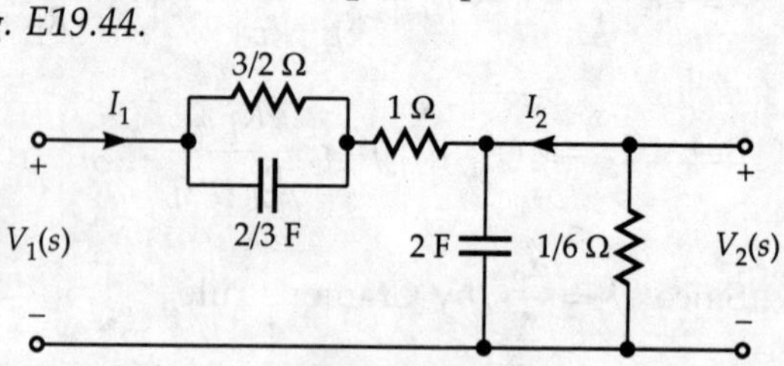

Fig. E19.44

SOLUTION. The given circuit is redrawn [Fig. E19.44(*a*)] in *s*-domain.

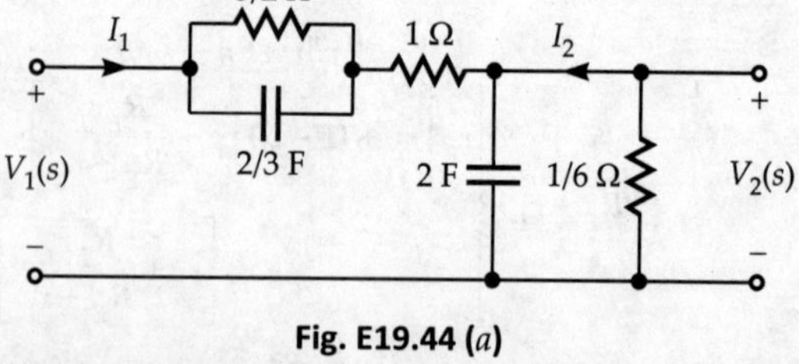

Fig. E19.44 (*a*)

Application of nodal equation at output node yields

$$\frac{V_2(s)}{1/6}+\frac{V_2(s)}{1/2s}+\left\{[V_2(s)-V_1(s)]\bigg/\left(1+\frac{\frac{3}{2}\times\frac{3}{2s}}{\frac{3}{2}+\frac{3}{2s}}\right)\right\}=0$$

or $$V_2\left[2s+6+\frac{1}{1+\frac{3}{2(s+1)}}\right]=V_1(s)\ \frac{1}{1+\frac{1}{\frac{2s}{3}+\frac{2}{3}}}\qquad ...(1)$$

Also, $I_2(s)=-6\,V_2(s)$ ...(2)

Eliminating $V_2(s)$, we find

$$\frac{2(s+1)\,V_1(s)}{2s+5}=-\frac{I_2(s)}{6}\left[2s+6+\frac{2(s+1)}{2s+5}\right]$$

or $$2(s+1)\,V_1=-\frac{I_2(s)}{6}[4s^2+24s+32]$$

$$\therefore\quad \frac{I_2(s)}{V_1(s)}=\frac{-12(s+1)}{4s^2+24s+32}=\frac{-3(s+1)}{s^2+6s+8}$$

$$=\mathbf{\frac{-3(s+1)}{(s+2)(s+4)}}.$$

EXAMPLE 19.59 *In the network shown in Fig. E19.45, the capacitor initially has a charge of 10 C. Find i(t) after one second of closing the switch S.*

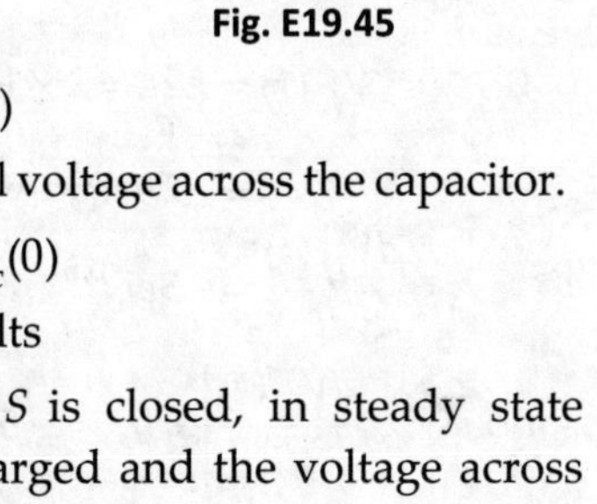

Fig. E19.45

SOLUTION.

$$Q=Cv_c(0)$$

where $v_c(0)$ is the initial voltage across the capacitor.

or $$10=0.5\,v_c(0)$$

$$\therefore\quad v_c(0)=20\text{ volts}$$

Once the switch S is closed, in steady state capacitor becomes charged and the voltage across the capacitor is given by

$$v(\infty)=100\text{ V}$$

At time (t), the transient response is

$$v_c(t)=v_c(\infty)+[v_c(0)-v_c(\infty)]e^{-t/RC}$$

$$=100+(20-100)e^{-t/2\times0.5}$$

$$=100-80e^{-t}$$

Current $i(t)$ is given by

$$i(t)=C\frac{dv_c(t)}{dt}=C.\frac{d}{dt}[100-80e^{-t}]$$

$$=0.5\times80e^{-t}=40e^{-t}$$

At $t=1$ sec,

$$i(t)=40\times e^{-1}=\mathbf{14.71\ A}$$

EXAMPLE 19.60 *In the circuit shown in Fig. E19.46, SW_1 is closed initially while SW_2 is open. The initial current through L is 10 A and the capacitor is charged to 10 V. At $t=0$, SW_2 is closed, while SW_1 is made open. Find the current through C and the voltage across L (at $t=0^+$).*

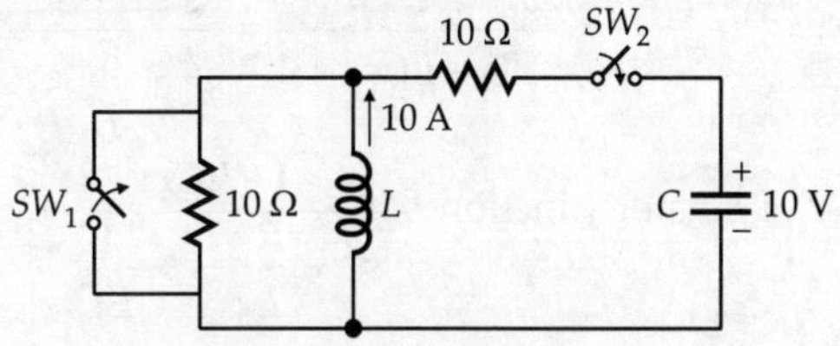

Fig. E19.46

Solution. At $t=0^+$, when SW_1 is opened and SW_2 is closed the inductor current and capacitor voltage do not change simultaneously.

$\therefore$ at $t=0(+)$,

$$v_c(0+)=v_c(0-)=10\text{ V};$$

$$i_L(0+)=i_L(0-)=10\text{ A}$$

Fig. E19.46(*a*) represents the equivalent circuit at $t=(0+)$.

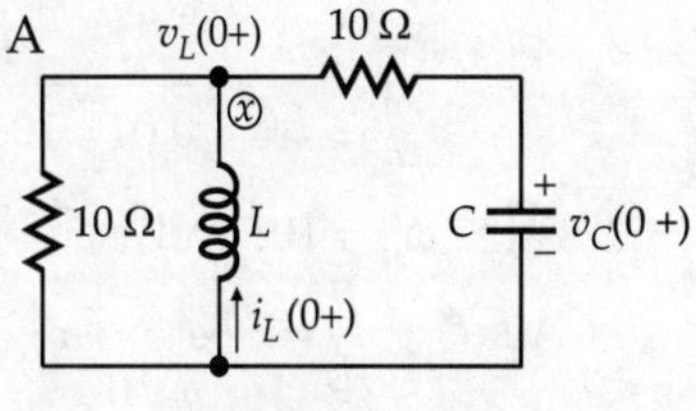

Fig. E19.46 (*a*)

At node x,

$$\frac{v_L(0+)}{10}+\frac{v_L(0+)-v_C(0+)}{10}-i_L(0+)=0$$

or $$\frac{v_L(0+)}{5}=1+10=11$$

$$\therefore\quad v_L(0+)=55\text{ V}$$

Hence current in capacitor (*c*) is given by

$$i_{C(0+)}=\frac{v_L(0+)-v_c(0+)}{10}=\frac{55-10}{10}=\mathbf{4.5\ A}$$

EXAMPLE 19.61 *What is the transfer function of the circuit shown in Fig. E19.47 ?*

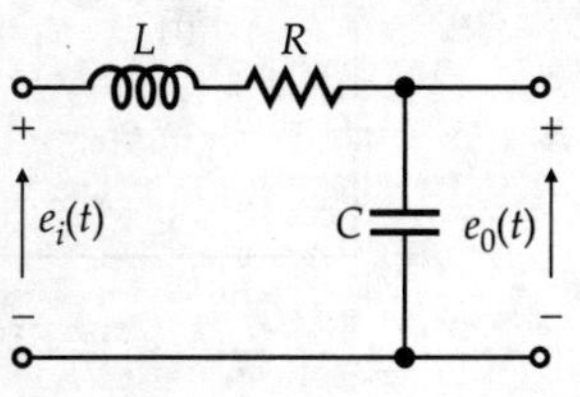

Fig. E19.47

SOLUTION. Transferring the time domain circuit to Laplace domain [Fig. E19.47(*a*)],

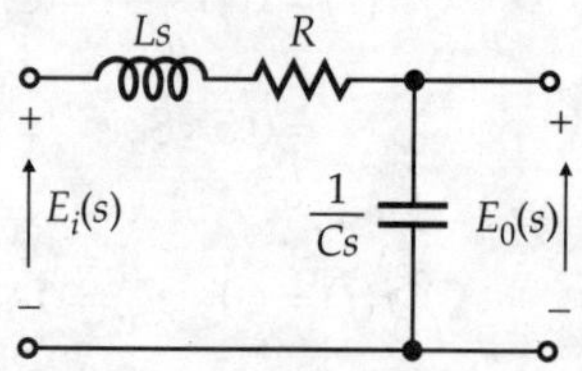

Fig. E19.47(*a*)

$$E_i(s) = I(s)\left[R + Ls + \frac{1}{Cs}\right]$$

$$E_0(s) = I(s) \times \frac{1}{Cs}$$

$$\therefore \quad \frac{E_0(s)}{E_i(s)} = \frac{1}{RCs + LCs^2 + 1} = \frac{1/LC}{s^2 + \frac{R}{L}.s + \frac{1}{LC}}$$

$$\therefore \text{ Transfer function} = \frac{\mathbf{1/(LC)}}{\mathbf{s^2 + \frac{R}{L}.s + \frac{1}{LC}}}.$$

EXAMPLE 19.62 *What is the Q-factor of a series RLC circuit shown in Fig. E19.48 ? Given $R = 10\,\Omega$, $L = 0.01$ H, $C = 100\,\mu$F.*

SOLUTION. We have just derived the transfer function of the *RLC* circuit as $\dfrac{1/(LC)}{s^2 + \frac{R}{L}.s + \frac{1}{LC}}$;

$$\therefore \quad \omega_n^2 = \frac{1}{LC} = \frac{1}{0.01 \times 100 \times 10^{-6}} = 10^6.$$

$$\therefore \quad \omega_n = 10^3 \text{ rad/sec.}$$

$$\text{Also,} \quad \frac{R}{L} = 2\,\delta\omega_n \quad \text{or} \quad 2\delta\omega_n = \frac{10}{0.01} = 1000$$

$$\therefore \quad 2\delta = \frac{1000}{\omega_n} = 1.$$

$$\therefore \text{ Q-factor} = \frac{1}{2\delta} = \frac{1}{1} = \mathbf{1.}$$

EXAMPLE 19.63 *Consider the circuit shown in Fig. E19.48. Determine $v_0(t)$ in terms of $i(t)$. Evaluate*

$$v_0(0+), \left.\frac{dv_0(t)}{dt}\right|_{t=0+} \text{ and } \left.\frac{dv_L(t)}{dt}\right|_{t=0+}$$

Assume the switch is closed at $t = 0$.

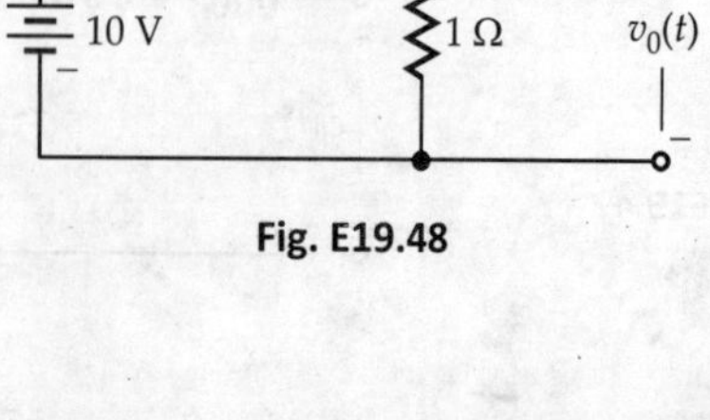

Fig. E19.48

SOLUTION. Let us first draw the equivalent circuit in *s*-domain [Fig. E19.48(*a*)]

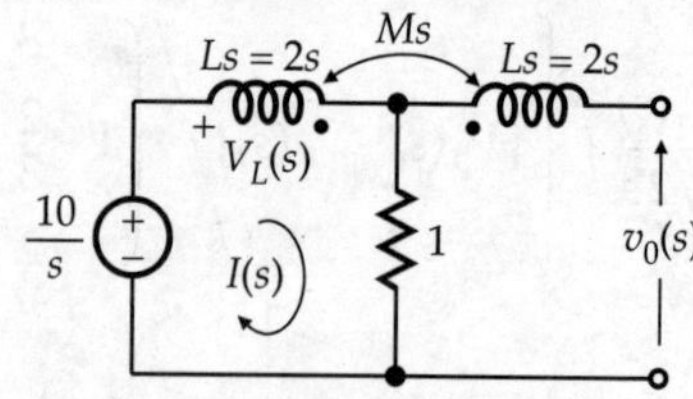

Fig. E19.48 (*a*)

In the left loop,

$$\frac{10}{s} = 2s\,.\,I(s) + 1 \times I(s)$$

$$\text{or} \qquad I(s) = \frac{10}{s(2s+1)} = 10\left[\frac{1}{s} - \frac{1}{s + 0.5}\right]$$

$i(t)$ at $t = 0+$ being the inverse of Laplace current $I(s)$,

$$i(t = 0+) = 10(1 - e^{-0.5t})$$

In the right loop, in time domain,

$$v_0(t) = M\frac{di}{dt} + i(t)$$

$$= 1 \times 10[-e^{-0.5t} \times (-0.5)] + 10[1 - e^{-0.5t}]$$

$$= 10[1 - 0.5\,e^{-0.5t}]$$

Thus we obtain $v_0(t)$ in terms of $i(t)$.

$\therefore$ At $t = 0+$, $\quad v_0(t) = 5$ Volts.

$$\text{Again,} \left.\frac{dv_0(t)}{dt}\right|_{t=0} = 2.5 \text{ Volts/sec.}$$

$$\left[\because \frac{dv_0(t)}{dt} = 10[-0.5 \times e^{-0.5t} \times (-0.5)]\right.$$

$$= 2.5\,e^{-0.5t}$$

Also,

$$V_L(t) = L\frac{di}{dt} = 2 \times 10 \times (-0.5)(-e^{-0.5t})$$

$$= 10\,e^{-0.5t} \text{ Volts.}$$

$$\therefore \quad \frac{dV_L(t)}{dt} = \mathbf{-5e^{-0.5t}\ Volts/sec}$$

$$\text{and} \quad \left.\frac{dV_L(t)}{dt}\right|_{t=0+} = \mathbf{-5\ Volts.}$$

EXAMPLE 19.64 *In the circuit shown in Fig. E19.49, V(0), the initial voltage in the capacitor is 2 V. Also, $I_0 = u(t)\cos t$. Find $v(t)$ for $t > 0$.*

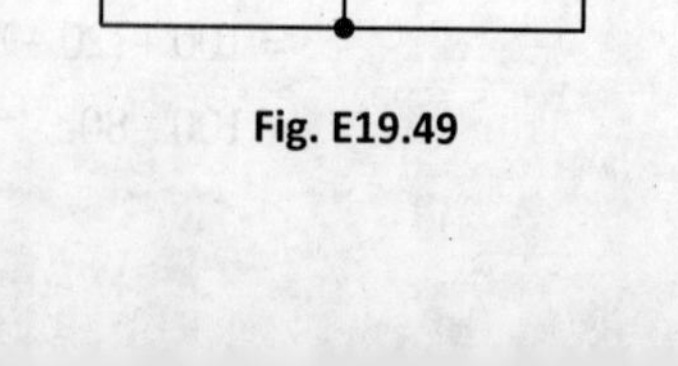

Fig. E19.49

SOLUTION. $Z_{input} = \dfrac{R}{1+j\omega RC} = \dfrac{1}{1+j}$

$$[\because\ R=1\Omega, C=1\text{F}, \omega=1\text{ rad/sec or } I_0 = u(t)\cos 1.t]$$

$$\therefore\quad V(t) = I_0 \frac{1}{1+j} \qquad [\because\ V(t) = I_0 \times Z_{input}]$$

But $\dfrac{1}{1+j} = \dfrac{1}{\sqrt{2}}\angle -45°$;

$$V(t) = \frac{1}{\sqrt{2}}\cos(t-45°) + Ke^{-\alpha t} \qquad ...(1)$$

As $t=0$, $V(t) = 2\text{ V} (= V(0))$

$\therefore$ Also, $\alpha = \dfrac{1}{RC} = 1$

Thus $K = \left(\dfrac{3}{2}\right)$.

[With $\alpha = 1$ and $t = 0$, from equation (1)]

Finally, $V(t) = \left(\dfrac{1}{\sqrt{2}}\cos(t-45°) + \dfrac{3}{2}e^{-t}\right)$ **V**

EXAMPLE 19.65 *If* $V_R = e^{-2t}(\sin t + \cos t)$ *find* $|V_L(t)|$. *(Fig. 19.50).*

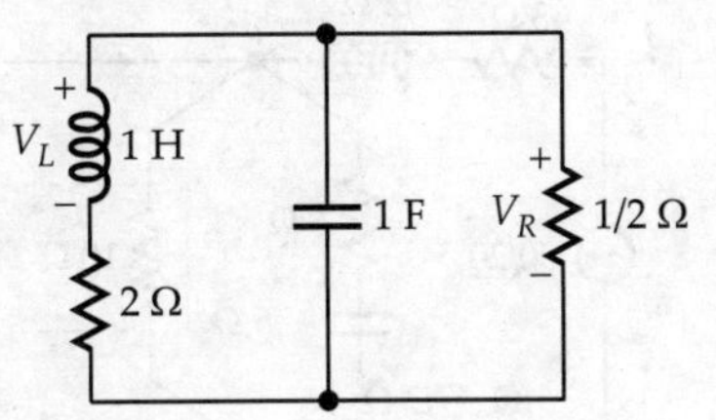

Fig. E19.50

SOLUTION. Nodal analysis is performed at node 'A' [Fig. E19.50(a)]

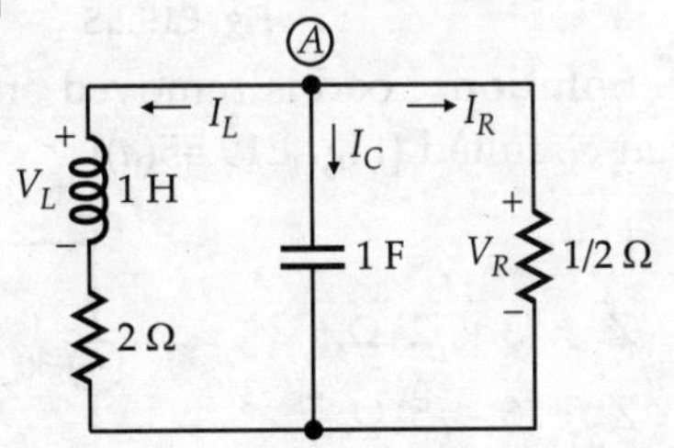

Fig. E19.50 (a)

$$I_C + I_R + I_L = 0$$

$$I_L + \frac{V_R}{1/2} + C\frac{dV_R}{dt} = 0$$

$$\text{or}\quad -I_L = \frac{e^{-2t}(\sin t + \cos t)}{1/2} + \frac{d}{dt}.e^{-2t}(\sin t + \cos t)$$

$$= e^{-2t}(\cos t - \sin t)$$

$$\therefore\quad |v_L(t)| = \left|L\frac{di}{dt}\right| = 1.\frac{d}{dt}e^{-2t}(\cos t - \sin t)$$

$$= e^{-2t}\sin t - 3e^{-2t}\cos t$$

Thus, $|v_L(t)| = \mathbf{(e^{-2t}\sin t - 3e^{-2t}\cos t)}$

EXAMPLE 19.66 *In Fig. E19.51, find* $v, \dfrac{dv}{dt}$ *and* $\dfrac{d^2v}{dt^2}$ *at* $t = 0^+$.

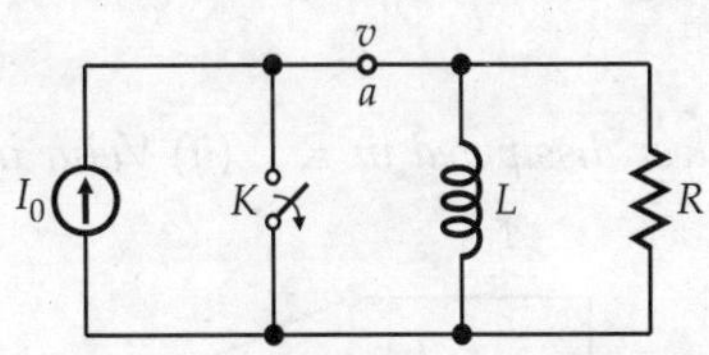

Fig. E19.51

SOLUTION. In steady state $(t<0)$, the switch K being closed, no current flows through R or L At $t=0$, K being opened, we can write, at node "a"

$$\frac{v}{R} + \frac{1}{L}\int v dt = I_0 \qquad ...(1)$$

Since inductor acts as open circuit at $t=0^+$,

$$\frac{1}{L}\int v\, dt = 0 \text{ at } t = 0^+.$$

$$\therefore\quad I_0 = \frac{v}{R} \quad\text{or}\quad v(0^+) = RI_0 = 100\times 1 = \mathbf{100\ Volts.}$$

From equation (1), by differentiation,

$$\frac{1}{R}\frac{dv}{dt} + \frac{v}{L} = 0, \qquad ...(2)$$

$$\text{or}\quad \frac{dv}{dt} = -\frac{R}{L}.v$$

$$\therefore\quad \frac{dv}{dt}(0^+) = -\frac{100}{1}\times 100 = \mathbf{-10^4\ Volts/sec.}$$

Differentiating equation (2),

$$\frac{1}{R}\frac{d^2v}{dt^2} + \frac{dv}{dt}\times\frac{1}{L} = 0$$

$$\text{or}\quad \frac{d^2v}{dt^2} = -\frac{R}{L}\frac{dv}{dt}$$

$$\therefore\quad \frac{d^2v}{dt^2}(0^+) = -\frac{100}{1}\times -10^4 = \mathbf{10^6\ Volts/sec^2.}$$

EXAMPLE 19.67 *Obtain the value of power delivered by the load assuming* $v_L(t) = v(t)$.

SOLUTION. Power delivered by the load $= V_L I^*$

$= 10\angle+150° \times 10\angle 60° = 100\angle 210°$ VA

$= (100\cos 210° + j100\sin 210°)$

$= \mathbf{(-86.6 - j50)\ VA}$

Since both the real and reactive power values are negative hence the load cannot deliver such power and on the other hand, the load absorbs both real and reactive power.

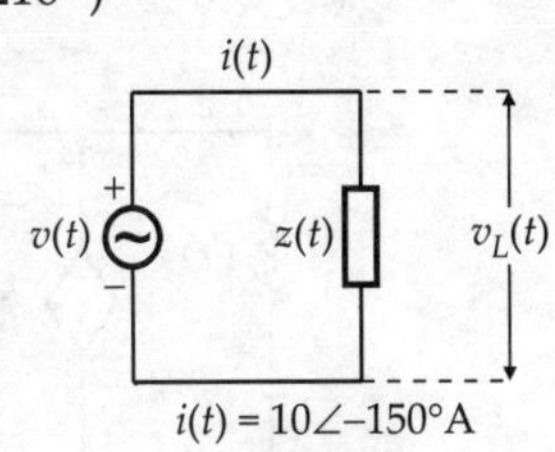

Fig. E19.52

EXAMPLE 19.68 *Assume* $I_1 = \sqrt{2}\angle{-45°}$ *A,*

$$I_0 = \sqrt{2}\angle{+45°}\ A.$$

Find

(*i*) *Power dissipated in R.* (*ii*) *Value of* I_2.

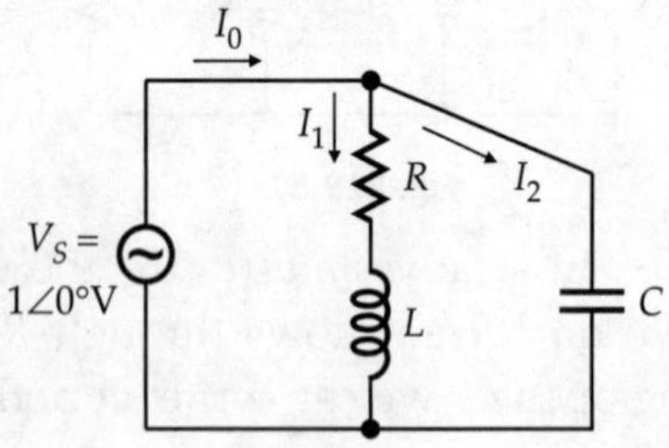

Fig. E19.53

SOLUTION. $P_{dissipated}$ = Power (*supplied*)
[as active power can be dissipated in resistor only and there is no resistor in the circuit except is R]

∴ We have

$$P_{dissipated} = V_S I_0 \cos 45° = 1 \times \sqrt{2} \times \frac{1}{\sqrt{2}} = 1\ \text{W}$$

Also, $\bar{I}_2 = \bar{I}_0 - \bar{I}_1 = \sqrt{2}\angle 45° - \sqrt{2}\angle{-45°}$

$= \sqrt{2}(\cos 45° + j \sin 45°) - \sqrt{2}(\cos 45° - j \sin 45°)$

$= 2\sqrt{2}\, j \sin 45° =$ **(*j*2) A.**

EXAMPLE 19.69 *Thevenise the circuit shown in Fig. E19.54 across x-y*

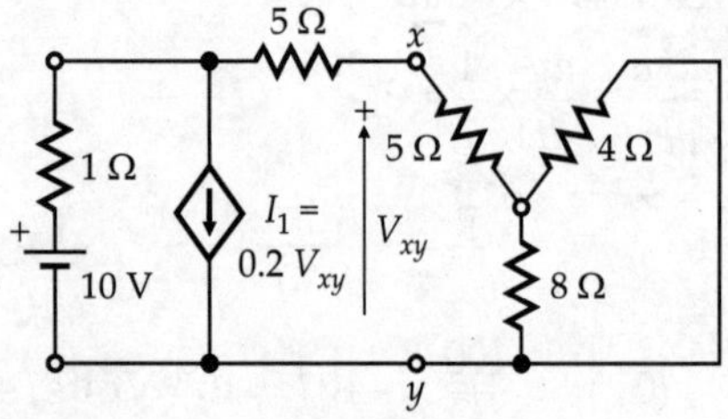

Fig. E19.54

SOLUTION. Make *x-y* open circuit [Fig. E19.54(*a*)], then V_{x-y} is the open circuit voltage V_0.

Here, $-10 + 0.2\ V_0 + V_0 = 0$

∴ $1.2\ V_0 = 10$ or $V_0 = 8.33$ Volts.

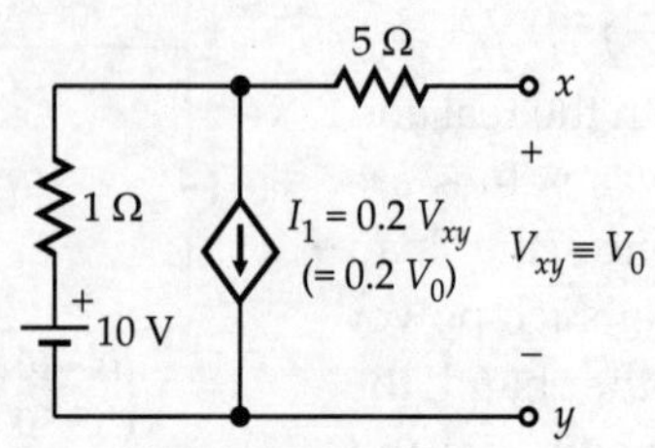

Fig. E19.54 (*a*)

Next, short circuit is applied across *x-y* [Fig. E19.54(*b*)].

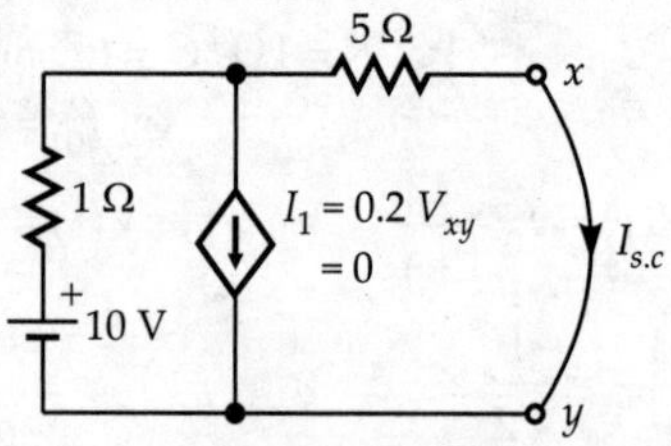

Fig. E19.54 (*b*)

Here, $I_{s.c} = \dfrac{10}{1+5} = 1.67$ Amps.

∴ Z_{int} (Thevenin's impedance)

$$= \frac{V_0}{I_{s.c}} = \frac{8.33}{1.67} = 4.99\ \Omega$$

Thus, $V_0 =$ **8.33 Volts**

$Z_{int} =$ **4.99 Ω.**

Example 19.70 *Find Thevenin's equivalent circuit across ab (Fig. E19.55) and find the load currents.*

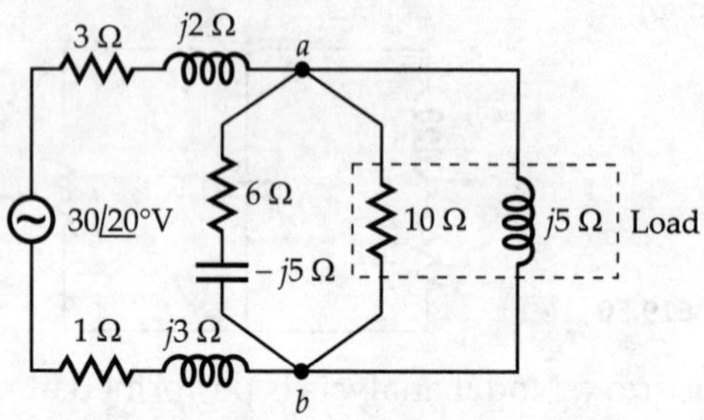

Fig. E19.55

Solution. Load is removed and terminal *a-b* is open-circuited [Fig. E19.55(*a*)].

Here

$Z_1 = (3 + j2)\,\Omega$,

$Z_2 = (6 - j5)\,\Omega$,

$Z_3 = (1 + j3)\,\Omega$.

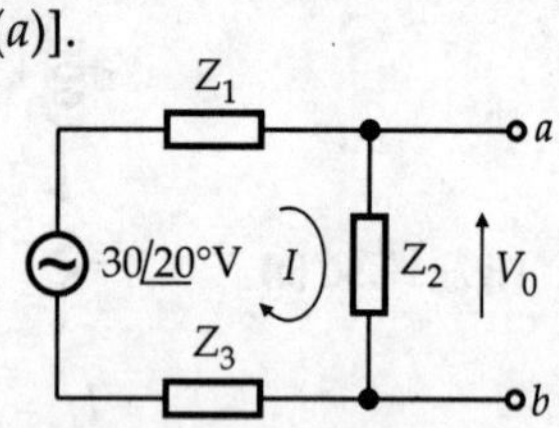

Fig. E19.55 (*a*)

Now, $I = \dfrac{30\angle 20°}{Z_1 + Z_2 + Z_3}$

and V_0 = drop across Z_2

$$= \frac{30\angle 20°}{Z_1 + Z_2 + Z_3} \times Z_2$$

$$= \frac{30\angle 20° \times (6 - j5)}{(3 + j2) + (6 - j5) + (1 + j3)}$$

= **23.42 ∠ – 19.80° Volts.**

Next, Z_{int} is obtained from Fig. E19.55(*b*), and is given by

$$Z_{int} = \frac{(Z_1 + Z_3)Z_2}{Z_1 + Z_2 + Z_3} = \frac{[(3 + j2) + (1 + j3)](6 - j5)}{3 + j2 + 1 + j3 + 6 - j5}$$

$$= 5 \angle 11.5° \,\Omega = \mathbf{(4.89 + j0.001)\,\Omega}$$

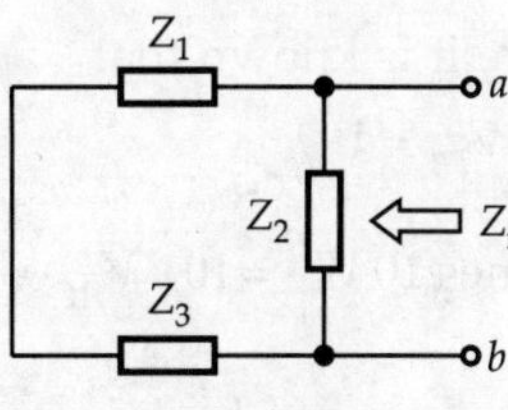

Fig. E19.55 (*b*)

Again,

$$Z_{load} = \frac{10 \times j5}{10 + j5} = \frac{50\angle 90°}{11.18 \angle 26.565°} = 4.47 \angle 63.44° \,\Omega$$

From Fig. E19.55(*c*), Thevenin equivalent circuit,

$$I_{Th} = \frac{V_0}{Z_{int} + Z_{load}}$$

$$= \frac{23.42 \angle -19.8°}{4.89 + j0.001} + 1.998 + j3.998$$

$$= \frac{23.42 \angle -19.8°}{7.965 \angle 30.14°}$$

$$= 2.94 \angle -49.94° \text{ Amp.}$$

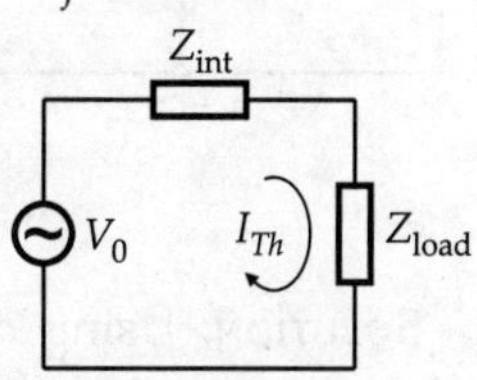

Fig. E19.55 (*c*)

Thus load current (net)

$$= 2.94 \angle -49.94° \text{ Amp}$$

While the component of the load current through 10 Ω is given by

$$I_{10\Omega} = 2.94 \angle -49.94° \times \frac{j5}{10 + j5}$$

$$= 1.32 \angle 13.495° \text{ Amp.}$$

and current through $j5\,\Omega$ induction is

$$I_{j5\Omega} = 2.94 \angle -49.94° \times \frac{10}{10 + j5}$$

$$= 2.63 \angle -76.5° \text{ Amp.}$$

$$\therefore \quad I_{load} = \mathbf{2.94 \angle -49.94° \ A}$$

while

$$I_{10\Omega} = \mathbf{1.32 \angle 13.495° \ A}$$

$$I_{j5\Omega} = \mathbf{2.63 \angle -76.5° \ A.}$$

EXAMPLE 19.71 *In the given circuit (Fig. E19.56), $I_1 = 1.667 \angle 0°$ A, $I_2 = 0.895 \angle 93.4°$ A. Find V_1 where V_1 and V_2 are the nodal voltage at nodes (1) and (2). Use nodal method.*

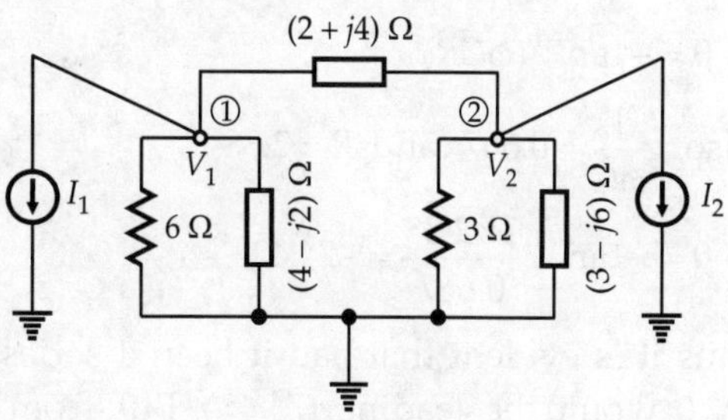

Fig. E19.56

SOLUTION. At node (1), the nodal equation is

$$-I_1 = \frac{V_1}{6} + \frac{V_1}{(4 - j2)} + \left[\frac{V_1}{2 + j4} - \frac{V_2}{(2 + j4)}\right]$$

$$\text{or} \quad -1.667 \angle 0° = V_1 \left[\frac{1}{6} + \frac{1}{(4 - j2)} + \frac{1}{(2 + j4)}\right] - V_2 \left[\frac{1}{(2 + j4)}\right] \quad ...(1)$$

At node (2), the second nodal equation is

$$-I_2 = \frac{V_2}{3} + \frac{V_2}{(3 - j6)} + \left[\frac{V_2}{(2 + j4)} - \frac{V_1}{(2 + j4)}\right]$$

$$\text{or} \quad -0.895 \angle 93.4° = -V_1 \left[\frac{1}{(2 + j4)}\right] + V_2 \left[\frac{1}{3} + \frac{1}{(2 + j4)} + \frac{1}{(3 - j6)}\right] \quad ...(2)$$

Simplifying equations (1) and (2), we find the following equations :

$$[-1.667 + j0] = [0.4667 - j0.1]\, V_1 + [-0.1 + j0.2]\, V_2 \quad ...1(a)$$

$$\text{and} \quad [0.0535 - j0.8925] = [-0.1 + j0.2]\, V_1 + [0.5 - j0.0667]\, V_2 \quad ...2(b)$$

Thus,

$$\begin{bmatrix} -1.667 + j0 \\ 0.535 - j0.8925 \end{bmatrix} = \begin{bmatrix} 0.4667 - j0.1 & -0.1 + j0.2 \\ -0.1 + j0.2 & 0.5 - j0.0667 \end{bmatrix} \begin{bmatrix} V_1 \\ V_2 \end{bmatrix}$$

Solution yields $V_1 = \mathbf{3.88 \angle 188.5°}$ **Volts.**

EXAMPLE 19.72 *An unknown series circuit is Thevenised and the end result is given by*

$$v_{o/c} = 3.5 \angle -20° \,;\; Z_{int} = (2.38 - j0.667)\Omega$$

at ω = 5 rad/sec. Identify the circuit components.

SOLUTION. Given :

$$Z_{int} = (2.38 - j0.667)\Omega$$

$$= (R - j/\omega C), \text{ assuming a series } RC \text{ circuit.}$$

C
H
A
P
T
E
R
19

$\therefore\ \theta = -\tan^{-1}(\omega CR)$

Also, $\dfrac{1}{\omega C} = 0.667$ and $R = 2.38\ \Omega$

$\therefore\ \theta = -\tan^{-1}\dfrac{1\times 2.38}{0.667} = -74.4°$

Thus it is evident that had it been a series RC circuit, θ would be leading (74.4°). But from the given data it is evident that $\theta = -20°$.

Hence, the given circuit is not pure RC circuit and as the lading angle has reduced for 74°4° to 20° hence this circuit must have an inductor too.

Hence the given circuit has R, L, C elements.

Example 19.73 *In Fig. E19.57, the source load line is $v + 2i = 100$. If a resistor of $2\ \Omega$ is connected across a-b output terminals, find the current through this $2\ \Omega$ resistor.*

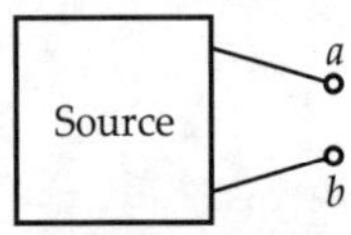

Fig. E19.57

Solution. If ab is open circuit, $v_{th} = 100$

$[\because\ i = 0 \text{ in } v + 2i = 100]$

When ab is shorted, $v = 0, 2i_{sc} = 100$

$$\therefore\quad i_{s/c} = 50\ \text{A}$$

$$\therefore\quad Z_{th} = \left(\frac{v_{th}}{i_{s/c}}\right) = \frac{100}{50} = 2\ \Omega$$

Thevenin circuit is drawn in Fig. E19.57(*a*)

Here i, current through $2\ \Omega$ resistor is

$$i = \frac{v_{th}}{Z_{th} + 2}$$

$$= \frac{100}{2+2} = \mathbf{25\ A}$$

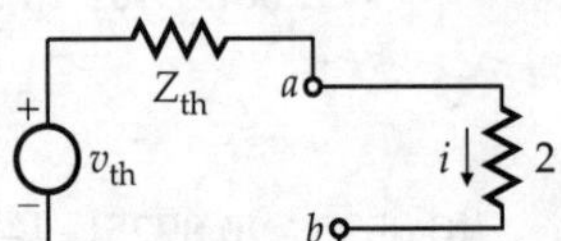

Fig. E19.57 (*a*)

Example 19.74

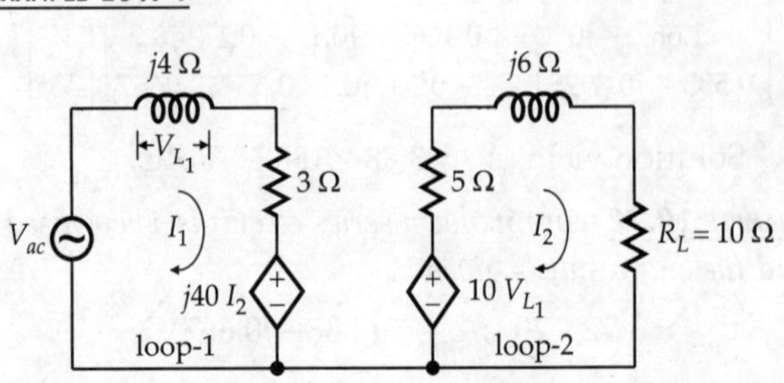

[Assume $V_{o/c} = 10\angle 30°$ V]

Fig. E19.58

Find $V_{o/c}$ across R_L. (Fig. E19.58)

Solution. Remove R_L ; this gives

$$I_2 = 0;\quad j40 I_2 = 0$$

i.e., the dependent source in loop-1 is shorted.

$$\therefore\ \text{in loop-1,}\quad V_{L_1} = V_{o/c} \times \frac{j4}{j4+3}$$

By inspection, it is known that

$$10V_{L_1} \equiv V_{Th} = V_{o/c}$$

$$\therefore\ V_{o/c} \text{ becomes } 10\,V_{L_1} = 10 \times V_{AC} \times \frac{j4}{j4+3}\ \text{V}$$

$$= 10 \times 10\angle 30° \times \frac{j4}{j4+3} = \mathbf{80\angle 66.66°\ V}$$

Example 19.75 *Find current gain (i_2 / i_1) in the given circuit (Fig. E19.59) and also determine interval resistance looking from input side.*

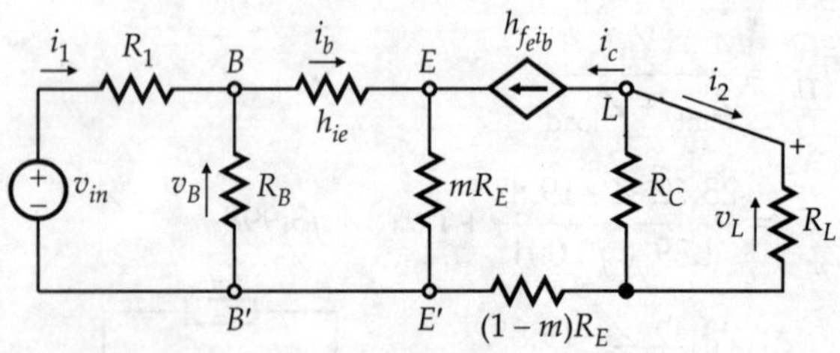

Fig. E19.59

Solution. Using current division formulae at node L,

$$i_2 = -i_C \frac{R_C}{R_C + R_L} = -\frac{h_{fe} i_b R_C}{R_C + R_L} \qquad \text{...(1)}$$

In loop $BEE'B'$, KVL yields

$$-v_B + i_b h_{ie} + (i_b + h_{fe} i_b)\, mR_E = 0$$

or

$$v_B = i_b h_{ie} + mR_E i_b\,(1 + h_{fe})$$

$$= i_b\,[h_{ie} + mR_E\,(1 + h_{fe})] \qquad \text{...(2)}$$

Again at node B,

$$-i_1 + \frac{v_B}{R_B} + i_b = 0.$$

or

$$i_1 = i_b + \frac{v_B}{R_B} \qquad \text{...(3)}$$

Using (2) in (3), we find

$$i_1 = i_b + \frac{i_b}{R_B}[h_{ie} + mR_E\,(1 + h_{fe})]$$

$$= i_b \left[\frac{R_B + h_{ie} + (1 + h_{fe})\, mR_E}{R_B}\right] \qquad \text{...(4)}$$

Substituting the value of i_b from (4) in (1)

$$i_2 = -\frac{h_{fe} R_C}{(R_C + R_L)} \frac{i_1}{\left[\frac{R_B + h_{ie} + (1+h_{fe}) mR_E}{R_B}\right]}$$

$$= -\frac{h_{fe} R_B R_C}{(R_C + R_L)[R_B + h_{ie} + (1+h_{fe}) mR_E} \cdot i_1$$

$\therefore$ Current gain

$$\frac{i_2}{i_1} = \frac{h_{fe} R_B R_C}{(R_C + R_L)[R_B + h_{ie} + (1+h_{fe}) mR_E])}$$

We can find R_{int} using equations (2) – (4).

$$R_{in} = \frac{v_B}{i_1} = \frac{R_B\,[h_{ie} + (h_{fe}+1)\, mR_E]}{R_B + h_{ie} + (1+h_{fe})\, mR_E}.$$

Example 19.76 *Obtain the Laplace transform of the waveform shown in Fig. E19.60.*

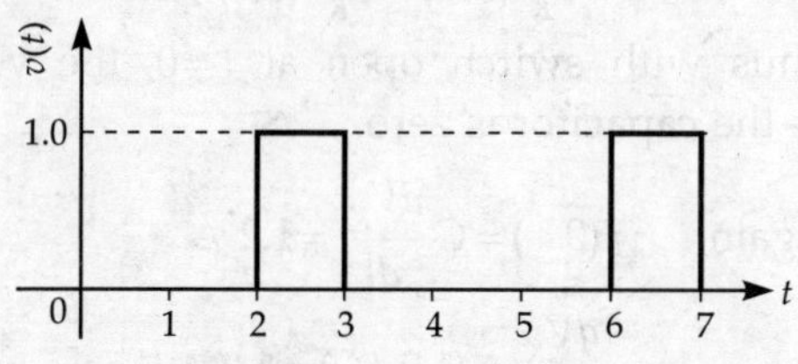

Fig. E19.60

Solution. Let us first express the two pulses as function of unit step voltages. Thus we write

$$v(t) = u(t-2) - u(t-3) + u(t-6) - u(t-7)$$

$\therefore V(s)$, the Laplace transform gives

$$V(s) = \frac{\varepsilon^{-2s} - \varepsilon^{-3s} + \varepsilon^{-6s} - \varepsilon^{-7s}}{s}.$$

$$= \frac{1}{s}[\varepsilon^{-2s} - \varepsilon^{-3s} + \varepsilon^{-6s} - \varepsilon^{-7s}].$$

Example 19.77 *A ramp is shown in Fig. E19.61. Find the Laplace transform.*

Solution. The equation of the ramp in form of $y = mx + c$ gives, in term of a step function

$$f(t) = \left(\frac{4}{2}.t + 4\right) u(t)$$

$$= 2(t+2)\, u(t)$$

$$\therefore \quad F(s) = \left(\frac{2}{s} + \frac{4}{s^2}\right).$$

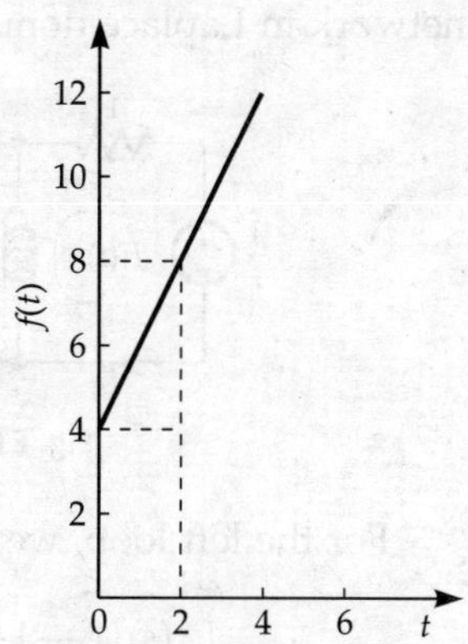

Fig. E19.61

Example 19.78 *Assuming V_0 to be a unit step function, find v (t) (Fig. E19.62).*

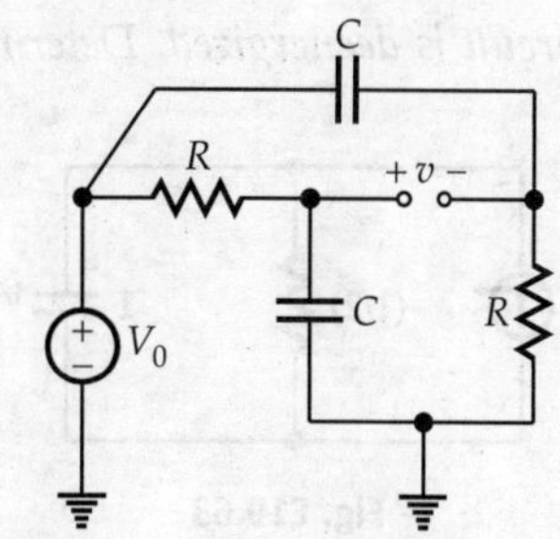

Fig. E19.62

Solution. The circuit is redrawn in Fig. E19.62(*a*).

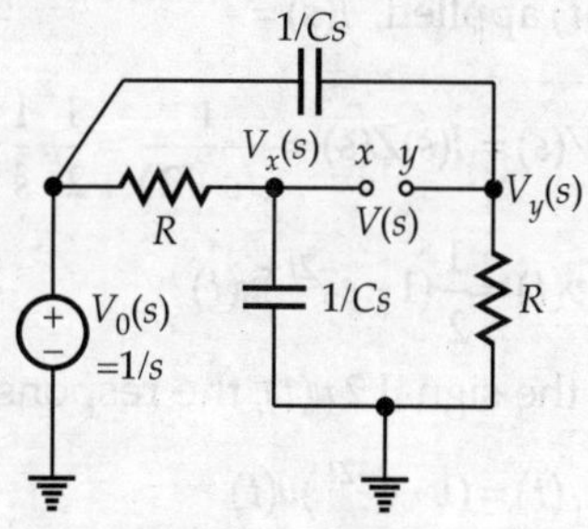

Fig. E19.62 (*a*)

$$V(s) = V_x(s) - V_y(s)$$

$$= \frac{V_0(s)\frac{1}{Cs}}{R + \frac{1}{Cs}} - \frac{V_0(s)\, R}{R + \frac{1}{Cs}} \qquad ...(1)$$

Since $\quad V_x(s) = \dfrac{V_0(s)}{R + 1/Cs} \times \dfrac{1}{Cs}$

and $\quad V_y(s) = \dfrac{V_0(s)}{R + \frac{1}{Cs}} . R$

Thus, from (1),

$$V(s) = V_0(s)\left[\frac{1}{1+RCs} - \frac{RCs}{1+RCs}\right]$$

$$= V_0(s)\left[\frac{1-RCs}{1+RCs}\right] = V_0(s) . \frac{(1/RC) - s}{(1/RC) + s}$$

$$= \frac{1}{s} . \frac{\frac{1}{RC} - s}{\frac{1}{RC} + s} = \frac{1}{s} . \frac{\alpha - s}{\alpha + s}$$

$$= \frac{1}{s} - \frac{2}{s+\alpha}. \qquad \left[\alpha = \frac{1}{RC}\right]$$

$$\therefore \quad v(t) = 1 - 2e^{-\alpha t} = \mathbf{1 - 2e^{-t/RC}} \textbf{ Volts.}$$

EXAMPLE 19.79 *The parallel RC circuit (Fig. E19.63) is excited by :* $I_0 = 2u(t) - 3u(t-1) + u(t-2)$

Initially the circuit is deenergized. Determine $V_C(t)$ *for* $t > 0$.

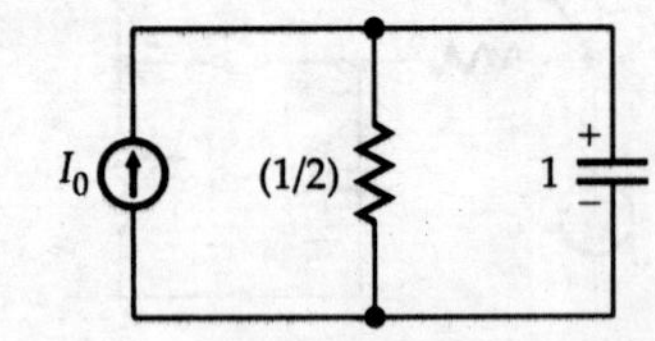

Fig. E19.63

SOLUTION. Here, $Z(s) = \dfrac{1}{s+2}$

With $u(t)$ applied, $I(s) = \dfrac{1}{s}$

$$V(s) = I(s)Z(s) = \frac{1}{s(s+2)} = \frac{1}{2}\cdot\frac{1}{s} - \frac{1}{2}\cdot\frac{1}{s+2}$$

$$\therefore \quad v(t) = \frac{1}{2}(1 - e^{-2t})u(t)$$

$\therefore$ For the signal $2u(t)$, the response is

$$v_1(t) = (1 - e^{-2t})u(t)$$

Also, for the signal $[-3u(t-1)]$,

$$v_2(t) = -\frac{3}{2}(1 - e^{-2(t-1)})u(t-1)$$

and for the signal $u(t-2)$,

$$v_3(t) = \frac{1}{2}(1 - e^{-2(t-2)})u(t-2)$$

$\therefore$ using the concept of superposition, for the excitation I_S, the response is

$$v(t) = v_1(t) + v_2(t) + v_3(t)$$

or
$$v(t) = (1 - e^{-2t})u(t) - \frac{3}{2}(1 - e^{-2(t-1)})u(t-1) + \frac{1}{2}(1 - e^{-2(t-2)})u(t-2)$$

EXAMPLE 19.80 *With switch K closed, the network is in steady state. At t = 0, the switch is opened. Obtain the voltage* (V_K) *across the switch and find* $\dfrac{dV_K}{dt}$ *at* $t = 0+$ *(Fig. E19.64).*

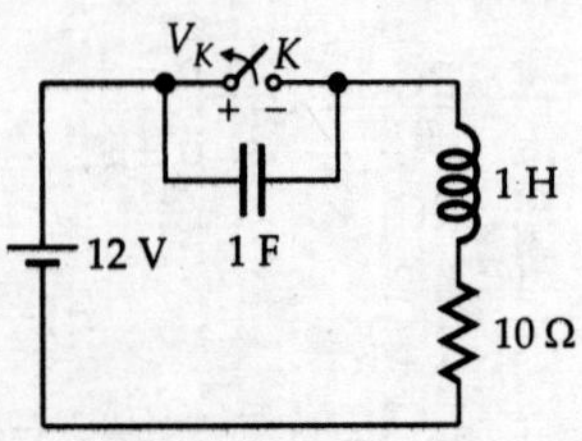

Fig. E19.64

SOLUTION. At $t < 0$, the switch is in closed position and the network is in steady state. Thus the capacitor is shorted and the network is a *RL* circuit having steady state current

$$I = \frac{V}{R} = \frac{12}{10} = 1.2 \text{ A.}$$

The switch opens at $t = 0$ and the capacitor gets connected in series with the *RL* circuit and the source. However, the current can not change through the inductor instantaneously and hence

$$i(0+) = i(0-) = 1.2 \text{ A} (= I).$$

The voltage across the switch is same as that across the capacitor.

At $t = 0-$, $\quad V_K(0-) = 0.$

Since the voltage across the capacitor also can not change instantaneously,

$$V_K(0+) = \mathbf{V_K(0-) = 0.}$$

Thus with switch open at $t = 0$, the voltage across the capacitor is zero.

Again, $\quad i(0+) = C\dfrac{dV_K}{dt} = 1.2 \text{ A.}$

$$\therefore \quad \frac{dV_K}{dt} = (1.2/C) = \mathbf{1.2\ A/sec.}$$

EXAMPLE 19.81 *Assuming initial conditions to be zero, find* $i_1(t)$ *and* $i_2(t)$ *in the network of Fig. E19.65.*

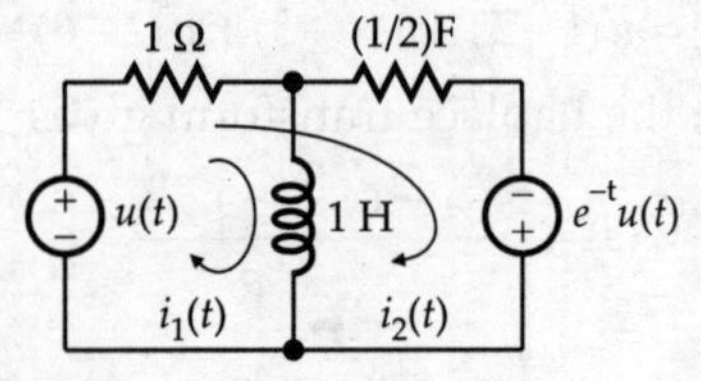

Fig. E19.65

SOLUTION. Figure E19.65(*a*) represents the given network in Laplace domain.

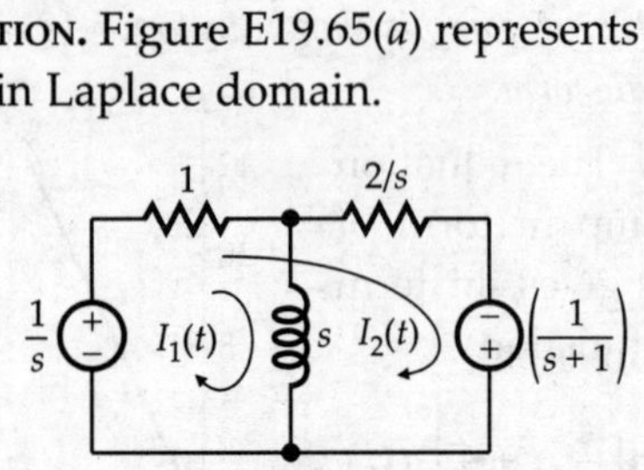

Fig. E19.65 (*a*)

For the left loop, we can write,

$$I_1(s)[1 + s] + I_2(s) \times 1 = \frac{1}{s} \qquad ...(1)$$

and for the entire (outer) loop,

$$I_1(s)\times 1+I_2(s)\left[1+\frac{2}{s}\right]=\frac{1}{s}+\frac{1}{s+1}$$

or $\quad I_2(s)[s+1][s+2]+[s(s+1)]I_1(s)=(2s+1)$ ...(2)

Solving (1) and (2),

$$I_2(s)=\frac{2s}{s^2+2s+2}=\frac{2}{(s+1+j)(s+1-j)}$$

$$=\frac{1-j}{s+1+j}+\frac{1+j}{s+1-j}$$

$$\therefore \quad i_2(t)=(1-j)\,e^{(-1-j)t}+(1+j)\,e^{-(1-j)t}$$

$$\text{and } I_1(s)=\frac{1}{s(s+1)}-\frac{2s}{(s+1)(s^2+2s+2)}$$

$$=\left(\frac{1}{s}+\frac{1}{s+1}\right)-\left(\frac{2}{s+1}+\frac{-1-j}{s+1+j}+\frac{-1+j}{s+1-j}\right)$$

$$\therefore \quad i_1(t)=(1-e^{-1t})-[2e^{-t}+(-1-j)\,e^{(-1-j)t}+(-1+j)\,e^{(-1+j)t}]$$

$$=(1-e^{-t})-[2e^{-t}-(1+j)\,e^{-(1+j)t}-(1-j)\,e^{(-1+j)t}]$$

We have thus obtained $i_1(t)$ and $i_2(t)$ as

$$\boldsymbol{i_1(t)=(1-e^{-t})-[2e^{-t}-(1+j)\,e^{-(1+j)t}-(1-j)e^{-(-1+j)t}]\ \mathrm{A}}$$

and $\boldsymbol{i_2(t)=(1-j)\,e^{(-1-j)t}+(1+j)\,e^{-(1-j)t}\ \mathrm{A}}$.

EXAMPLE 19.82 *Steady state is achieved for the circuit shown in Fig. E19.66 with switch (sw) at "a". At $t=0$, the switch is thrown at b. Find $i_L(t)$.*

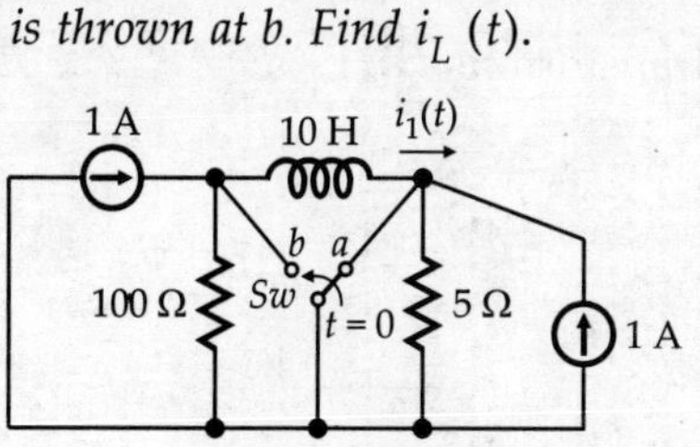

Fig. E19.66

SOLUTION. Fig. E19.66(*a*) represents the circuit configuration for $t=0^-$ (steady state). Inductor being behaving as short circuit in steady state, the current sources inject currents through the switch which is 2 A.

$\therefore \quad i_L(0-)=1\,\text{Amp}$

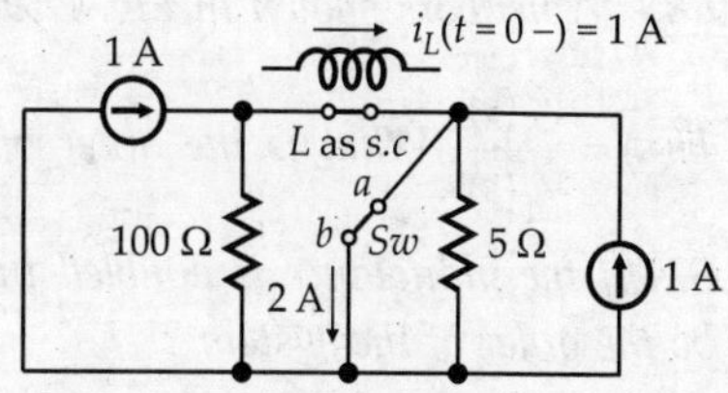

Fig. E19.66 (*a*)

Since inductor does not allow the current through it to change abruptly hence $i(0+)$ following switching from "*a*" to "*b*" will remain 1 A also [see Fig. E19.66(*b*)].

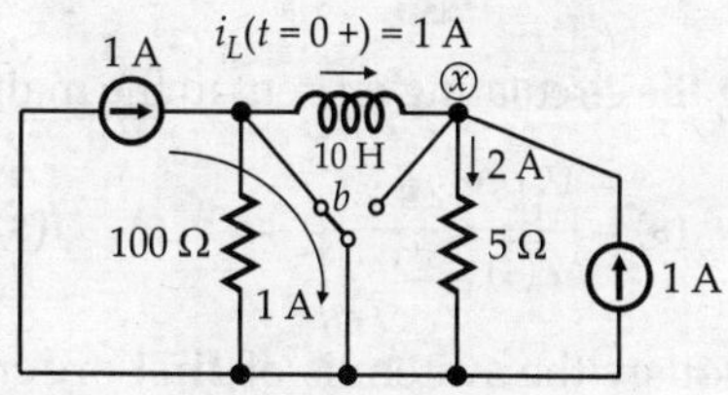

Fig. E19.66 (*b*)

Obviously, the inductor current being constant at $t=0+$, the left side source will inject current through the switch only and no current to the rest of the circuit. Now the current through 5 Ω resistor is 2 A (say i_0) and the drop across it is (5×2) *i.e.*, 10 volts. Thus, (*x*) node becomes +ve. Observation reveals that $i_L(t=0+)$ is directed opposite to + ve polarity of voltage at node (*x*). Thus we should take the inductor drop to be negative in the following equation :

$$i_L(t)=i_0+\frac{1}{L}\int_{t_0}^{t} v_L\,(dt)$$

$$\text{But } v_L(t)=10\,\varepsilon^{-R/L\,t}\,.\,u(t)\ \text{Volts}$$

$$=-10\,\varepsilon^{-5/10t}\,u(t)$$

[taking inductive drop –ve]

$$\therefore \quad i_L(t)=2+\frac{1}{10}\int_0^t -10\,\varepsilon^{-1/2t}\,dt$$

$$=2+\frac{-10(-2)}{10}\left[\varepsilon^{-\frac{1}{2}t}\right]_0^t u(t)$$

$$=2+2\,[\varepsilon^{-1/2t}-1]\,u(t)$$

$$\boldsymbol{=2+(2\varepsilon^{-1/2t}-2)\,u(t)\ \text{Amp.}}$$

EXAMPLE 19.83 *A network shown in Fig. E19.67,*

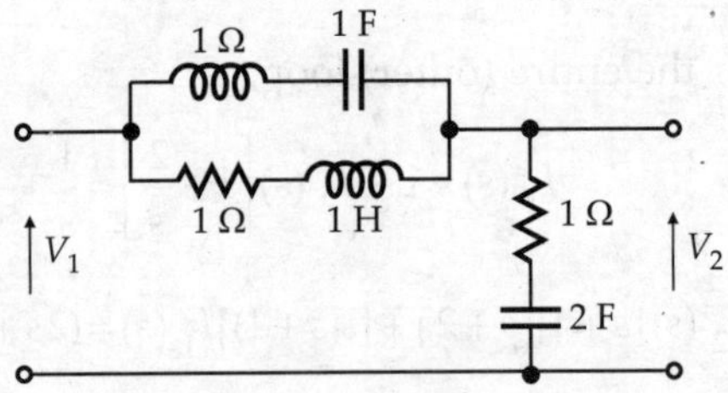

Fig. E19.67

Find $H(s)=\dfrac{V_2(s)}{V_1(s)}$. *What is the order of the system ?*

(Fig. E19.67) If the inductance is doubled in the next step what will be the order of the system ?

SOLUTION. Here input impedance ($Z(s)$) is given by

$$Z(s)=\left[\left(1+\frac{1}{s}\right)\middle\|(1+s)\right]+\left(1+\frac{1}{2s}\right)=\frac{\left(1+\frac{1}{s}\right)(1+s)}{\left(1+\frac{1}{s}\right)+(1+s)}+\frac{2s+1}{2s}=\frac{(s+1)^2}{(s+1)^2}+\frac{2s+1}{2s}=1+\frac{2s+1}{2s}=\frac{4s+1}{2s}$$

$$\therefore\quad V_2(s)=I(s)\times\left[1+\frac{1}{2s}\right],$$

assuming the circulating current in the main loop and passing through 1Ω resistor and 2 F capacitor to be $I(s)$.

or $\quad V_2(s)=\dfrac{V_1(s)}{Z(s)}\cdot\dfrac{2s+1}{2s}\quad$ or $\quad H(s)=\dfrac{V_2(s)}{V_1(s)}=\dfrac{2s+1}{2s}\times\dfrac{1}{2(s)}=\dfrac{2s+1}{2s}\times\dfrac{2s}{4s+1}=\left(\dfrac{\mathbf{2s+1}}{\mathbf{4s+1}}\right)$

Obviously the system is of **first** order. Next, we make $L=2$ H.

$$\therefore\quad Z(s)=\left[\left(1+\frac{1}{s}\right)\middle\|(1+2s)\right]+\left(1+\frac{1}{2s}\right)=\frac{\left(1+\frac{1}{s}\right)(1+2s)}{1+\frac{1}{s}+1+2s}+\left(1+\frac{1}{2s}\right)=\frac{(s+1)(2s+1)}{2s^2+2s+1}+\frac{2s+1}{2s}$$

$$\text{Hence,}\quad \frac{V_2(s)}{V_1(s)}=\frac{2s+1}{2s\times z(s)}=\frac{(2s+1)}{2s\left[\frac{(s+1)(2s+1)}{2s^2+2s+1}+\frac{2s+1}{2s}\right]}=\frac{1}{\frac{2s(s+1)}{2s^2+2s+1}+1}=\frac{2s^2+2s+1}{2s^2+2s+2s^2+2s+1}$$

$\therefore\quad H(s)=\dfrac{\mathbf{2s^2+2s+1}}{\mathbf{4s^2+4s+1}}$. It has now become a **second** order system.

EXAMPLE 19.84 *A 10 volt pulse of 5 μsec. duration is applied to a series RC circuit having R = 0.1 kΩ and C = 0.05 μF. Find* $i_C(t)$. *If the same pulse is applied to a series RL circuit where R = 2 Ω and L = 2 μH, find the series current* $i_L(t)$.

SOLUTION. The series *RC* circuit has impedance of $\left(R+\dfrac{1}{Cs}\right)$ *i.e.*, $100+\dfrac{1}{0.05\times10^{-6}.s}$ in Laplace domain.

The supply being an impulse of 10 volt for 5 μsec, its Laplace transform is $\dfrac{10}{s}(1-\varepsilon^{-5\times10^{-6}s})$.

$$\therefore\quad I_C(s)=\frac{\frac{10}{s}(1-\varepsilon^{-5\times10^{-6}s})}{100+\frac{1}{0.05\times10^{-6}s}}=\frac{10(1-\varepsilon^{-5\times10^{-6}s})}{100\left(s+\frac{10^6}{5}\right)}$$

$\therefore$ Inverse of $I_C(s)$ gives : $i_C(t)=0.1\,\varepsilon^{-t/5\times10^6}-0.1\,\varepsilon^{-(t-5\times10^{-6})/5\times10^{-6}}\times u(t-5\times10^{-6})$ Amp.

For the case of inductor circuit (*RL* series), series impedance in Laplace domain is

$(R+Ls)$ *i.e.*, $(2+2\times10^{-3}.s)$

$$\therefore\quad I_L(s)=\frac{10(1-\varepsilon^{-5\times10^{-6}s})}{s(2+2\times10^{-3}s)}=\frac{10}{2}(1-\varepsilon^{-5\times10^{-6}s})\left(\frac{1}{s}-\frac{1}{s+10^6}\right)$$

$$\therefore\quad i_L(t)=\mathbf{5\,(1-\varepsilon^{-2\times10^5 t})\,u(t)-5\,(1-\varepsilon^{-2\times10^5(t-5\times10^{-6})})\,u(t-5\times10^6)\ Amp.}$$

EXAMPLE 19.85 *A two terminal network consists of a coil of L and R is shunted by a capacitor C. (Fig. E19.68). The poles and zeros of the driving point function Z(s) of this network are pole at* $-\frac{3}{2} \pm j\frac{\sqrt{3}}{2}$, *zero at* $(-3+j0)$. *If* $Z(j0)=1$, *find the values of R, L and C.*

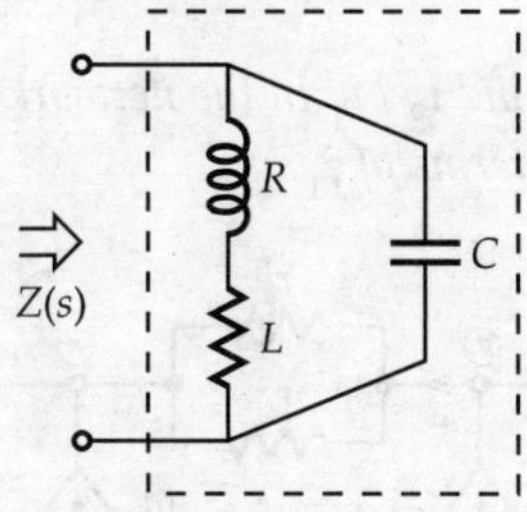

Fig. E19.68

Solution. Here,

$$Z(s) = \frac{K(s+3)}{\left(s+\frac{3}{2}+j\frac{\sqrt{3}}{2}\right)\left(s+\frac{3}{2}-j\frac{\sqrt{3}}{2}\right)} \quad ...(A)$$

$$= \frac{K(s+3)}{s^2+3s+3}$$

Also $$Z(s) = (R+Ls)\,||\,\frac{1}{Cs} = \frac{(R+Ls)\frac{1}{Cs}}{R+Ls+\frac{1}{Cs}}$$

$$= \frac{\left(s+\frac{R}{L}\right)}{C\left(s^2+\frac{Rs}{L}+\frac{1}{LC}\right)}$$

$$= \frac{\frac{1}{C}\left(s+\frac{R}{L}\right)}{s^2+\frac{R}{L}.s+\frac{1}{LC}} \quad ...(B)$$

Comparing equations (*A*) and (*B*), we have

$$K = \frac{1}{C}; \quad \frac{R}{L} = 3; \quad \frac{1}{LC} = 3$$

From equation (*A*), $Z(s=j\omega=j0) = \frac{K}{3}.3 = 1$

$\therefore \quad K = 1$

Hence C = 1 F.

Also, $\frac{1}{LC} = 3 \quad \therefore \quad L = \frac{1}{3C} = \frac{1}{3}\,\text{H}$

and $\frac{R}{L} = 3 \quad \therefore \quad R = 3L = 3 \times \frac{1}{3} = 1\,\Omega$

Then in the given circuit

$$\mathbf{R = 1\Omega, \quad L = \frac{1}{3}H, \quad C = 1F.}$$

EXAMPLE 19.86 *Assuming* Z_L *to be a parallel combination of R and C, find the optimum values of R and C such that maximum power transfer takes from source to load (Fig. E19.69),*

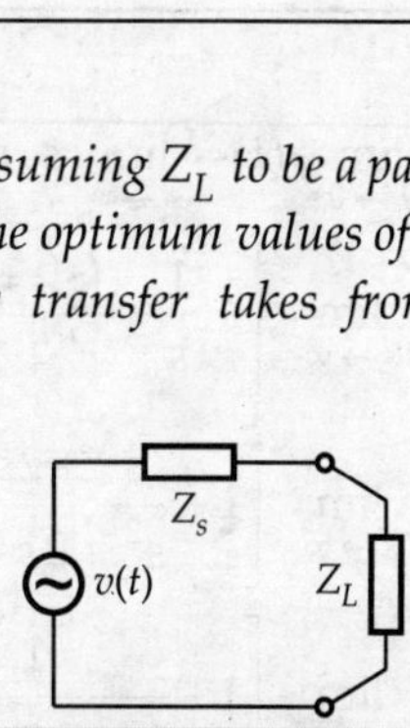

[$v(t)$ = 250 sin 500 *t* volts, $Z_s = (100 + j200)\Omega$]

Fig. E19.69

SOLUTION. As per the question, in the network of Fig. E19.69,

$$Z_L = R\,||\,(-jX_C)$$

i.e., $$Z_L = \frac{R(-jX_C)}{R-jX_C} = \frac{-jRX_C}{R-jX_C}.\frac{R+jX_C}{R+jX_C}$$

$$= \frac{RX_C^2}{R^2+X_C^2} - j\frac{R^2.X_C}{R^2+X_C^2} \quad ...(1)$$

For maximum power transfer $Z_L = Z_S^*$.

But $\quad Z_S = (100 + j200)\,\Omega$

$\therefore \quad Z_L = (100 - j200)\,\Omega \quad ...(2)$

Comparing (1) and (2)

$$\frac{RX_C^2}{R^2+X_C^2} = 100 \quad ...(3)$$

and $$\frac{R^2X_C}{R^2+X_C^2} = 200 \quad ...(4)$$

Solving for (3) and (4), $X_C = 250\,\Omega$

i.e., $$\text{C} = \frac{\mathbf{1}}{\mathbf{500\ X_C}} = \mathbf{8\ \mu F}$$

and $\quad R = \mathbf{500\,\Omega}$.

EXAMPLE 19.87 *Find the initial and final values of* $\phi(t) = 1 + e^{-t}(\sin t + \cos t)$.

SOLUTION. Since $\phi(t) = 1 + e^{-t}(\sin t + \cos t)$,

$$\phi(s) = \frac{1}{s} + \frac{1}{(s+1)^2+1} + \frac{s+1}{(s+1)^2+1}$$

$$= \frac{1}{s} + \frac{s^2+2s}{(s+1)^2+1}$$

$$= \frac{1}{s} + \frac{s^2+2s}{s^2+2s+2}$$

$$\therefore \quad \phi(0) = \lim_{t \to 0} \phi(t) = \lim_{s \to \infty} s \cdot \phi(s)$$

$$= \lim_{s \to \infty} \left[s \cdot \frac{1}{s} + \frac{(s^2 + 2s)\, s}{s^2 + 2s + 2} \right]$$

$$= \lim_{s \to \infty} \left[1 + \frac{s^3 + 2s^2}{s^2 + 2s + 2} \right]$$

$$= \lim_{s \to \infty} \left[1 + \frac{1 + 2/s}{1/s + 2/s^2 + 2/s^3} \right]$$

$$= 1 + 1 = \mathbf{2}$$

The initial value of $\phi(t)$ is 2

Again,

$$\phi(\infty) = \lim_{t \to \infty} \phi(t) = \lim_{s \to 0} s\, \phi(s)$$

$$= \lim_{s \to 0} \left[1 + \frac{s^3 + 2s^2}{s^2 + 2s + 2} \right] = 1 + 0 = \mathbf{1}$$

The final value of $\phi(t)$ is 1.

EXAMPLE 19.88 *N is a combination of linear passive bilateral network connected with a source V_s and load R (Fig. E19.70). Table 19.1 represents typical values of I for two combinations of V_s and R. Obtain the value of R such that maximum power transfer takes place between source and load.*

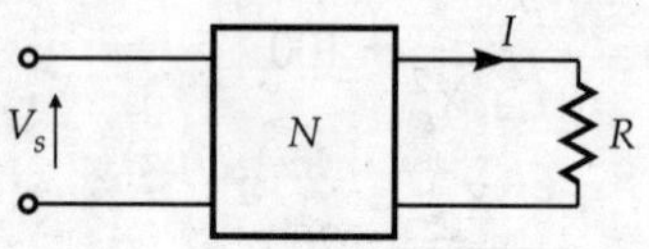

Fig. E19.70

Table 19.1

V_s (V)	R (Ω)	I (A)
10	1.5	2

SOLUTION. Let N has equivalent internal resistance of R_s, when looking back through output terminals with R removed. Let $V_{o.c}$ be the output voltage.

$$\therefore \quad V_{o.c} - IR_s = IR \qquad \text{...(1)}$$

For $R = 1.5\,\Omega$, $I = 2$ A, (1) becomes

$$V_{o.c} - 2R_s = 3 \qquad \text{...(2)}$$

Again, with $R = 4\,\Omega$, $I = 1$ A, thus (1) becomes

$$V_{o.c} - R_s = 4 \qquad \text{...(3)}$$

Solving for (2) and (3), we get

$$R_s = 1\,\Omega \quad \text{and} \quad V_{o.c} = 5 \text{ volts.}$$

Thus, R should be **1 Ω** to have maximum power transfer.

[Maximum power is $\dfrac{V_{o.c}^2}{4\,R_s} = \dfrac{5^2}{4 \times 1} = \mathbf{6.25\ W}$]

EXAMPLE 19.89 *Find i_2 / i_1 in the network of Fig. E19.71. Also find v_0 in terms of i_1.*

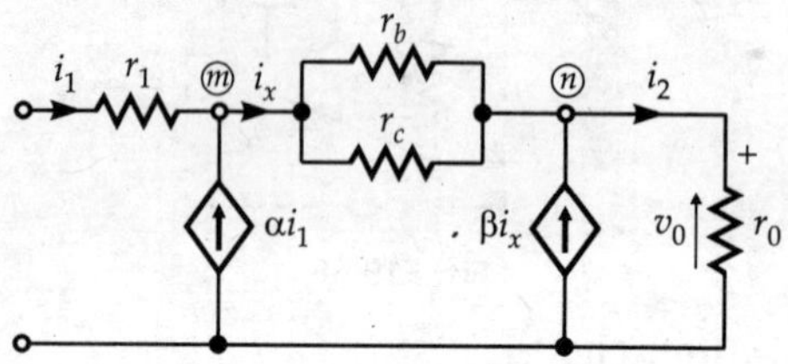

Fig. E19.71

SOLUTION. At node *m*,

$$i_x = i_1 + \alpha i_1 = i_1\,(1 + \alpha) \qquad \text{...(1)}$$

At node *n*,

$$i_2 = i_x + \beta i_x = i_x\,(1 + \beta) \qquad \text{...(2)}$$

From (2), using (1),

$$i_2 = i_1\,(1 + \alpha)(1 + \beta) \qquad \text{...(3)}$$

$$\therefore \quad \left(\frac{i_2}{i_1}\right) = \left(\frac{\mathbf{1 + \alpha}}{\mathbf{1 + \beta}}\right)$$

Since, $v_0 = i_2 r_0$, hence from (3),

$$v_0 = \boldsymbol{i_1 r_0\,(1 + \alpha)\,(1 + \beta)}.$$

EXAMPLE 19.90 *In Fig. E19.72,*

$$\begin{bmatrix} V_1 \\ I_1 \end{bmatrix} = \begin{bmatrix} 30 & 23 \\ 13 & 10 \end{bmatrix} \begin{bmatrix} V_2 \\ -I_2 \end{bmatrix}.$$

Find ABCD parameters of (N_0).

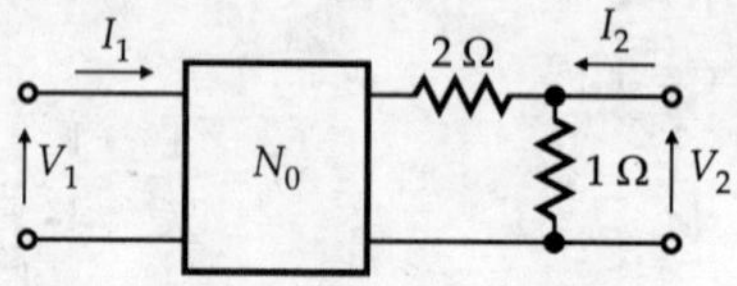

Fig. E19.72

SOLUTION. Let us represent the given network as shown in Fig. E19.72(*a*).

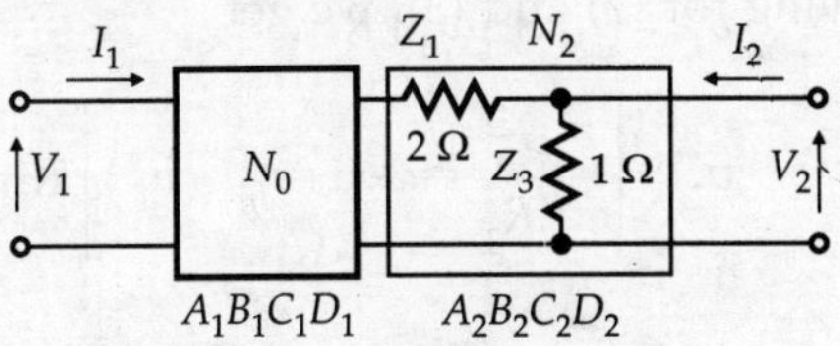

Fig. E19.72 (a)

In N_2 circuit [Fig. E19.72(a)]

$$Z_{11} = Z_1 + Z_3 = 2 + 1 = 3\,\Omega$$
$$Z_{12} = Z_3 = 1\,\Omega$$
$$Z_{21} = Z_3 = 1\,\Omega$$
$$Z_{22} = Z_2 + Z_3 = 0 + 1 = 1\,\Omega$$
$$\therefore \quad [Z] = \begin{bmatrix} 3 & 1 \\ 1 & 1 \end{bmatrix}$$

Now converting [Z] parameter circuit to *ABCD* parameters,

$$A = \frac{Z_{11}}{Z_{21}} = 3$$
$$B = \frac{\Delta Z}{Z_{21}} = 2 \quad [\Delta Z \text{ is the determinant of } Z]$$
$$C = \frac{1}{Z_{21}} = 1$$

and
$$D = \frac{Z_{22}}{Z_{21}} = 1.$$

$\therefore$ For N_2 network,

$$\begin{bmatrix} A & B \\ C & D \end{bmatrix} = \begin{bmatrix} 3 & 2 \\ 1 & 1 \end{bmatrix}$$

For the cascaded $N_0 - N_2$ network,

$$\begin{bmatrix} A & B \\ C & D \end{bmatrix} = \begin{bmatrix} A_1 & B_1 \\ C_1 & D_1 \end{bmatrix} \begin{bmatrix} A_2 & B_2 \\ C_2 & D_2 \end{bmatrix}$$

Also, $A_2 = 3,\ B_2 = 2,\ C_2 = 1,\ D_2 = 1.$

or,
$$A = A_1 A_2 + B_1 C_2 = 30$$
$$[\because A = 30, \text{ given}]$$

or,
$$3A_1 + B_1 = 30 \qquad \text{...(1)}$$

Again,
$$B = A_1 B_2 + B_1 D_1 = 23$$
$$[\because B = 23, \text{ given}]$$

or,
$$2A_1 + B_1 = 23 \qquad \text{...(2)}$$

and
$$C = A_2 C_1 + C_2 D_1 = 13$$

or
$$3C_1 + D_1 = 13 \qquad \text{...(3)}$$

Also,
$$D = B_2 C_1 + D_1 D_2 = 10$$

or
$$2C_1 + D_1 = 10 \qquad \text{...(4)}$$

Solving (1) and (2), $A_1 = 7,\ B_1 = 9.$

Solving (3) and (4), $C_1 = 3,\ D_1 = 4.$

Thus for N_0 network

$$\begin{bmatrix} A_1 & B_1 \\ C_1 & D_1 \end{bmatrix} = \begin{bmatrix} \mathbf{7} & \mathbf{9} \\ \mathbf{3} & \mathbf{4} \end{bmatrix}.$$

EXAMPLE 19.91 *Find the current in the capacitor using superposition theorem (Fig. E19.73).*

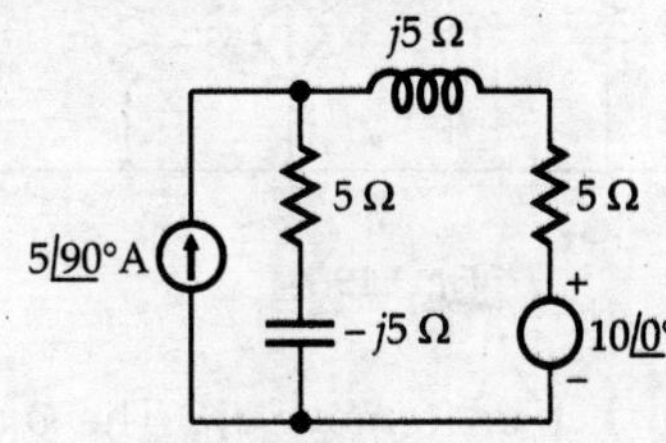

Fig. E19.73

SOLUTION. Let us take first the voltage source alone. Current source is deactivated [Fig. E19.73(a)].

$$I' = \frac{10\angle 0^\circ}{(5 + j5) + (5 - j5)} = 1\angle 0^\circ \text{ A} = 1 \text{ A}$$

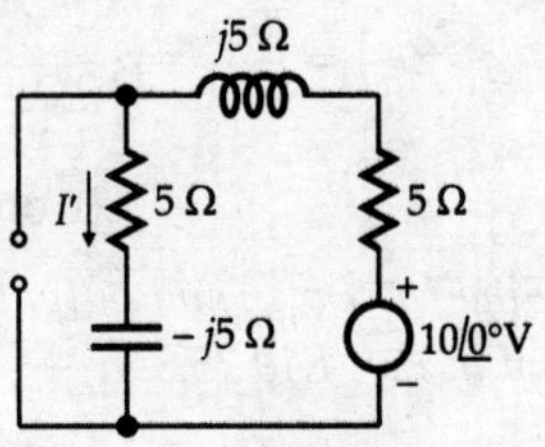

Fig. E19.73 (a)

Next, we take the current source alone deactivating the voltage source [Fig. E19.73(b)].

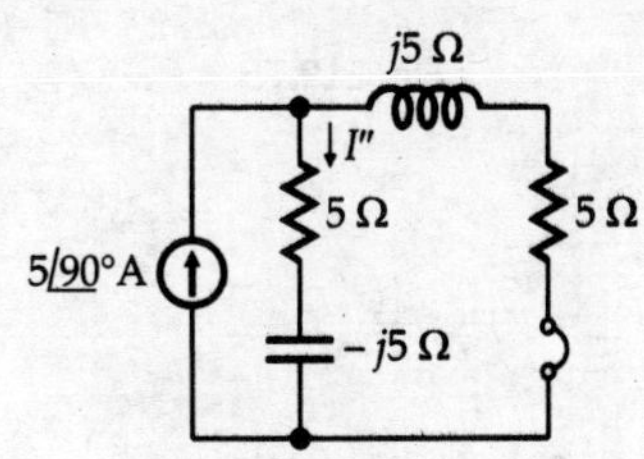

Fig. E19.73 (b)

Here, $I'' = 5\angle 90° \dfrac{5+j5}{(5+j5)+(5-j5)}$

$= 5\angle 90° (0.5 + j0.5)$

$= j5\,(0.5 + j5) = (-0.25 + j0.25)$ A.

∴ Total current through capacitor as per the principle of superposition is $I' + I''$ (= I).

∴ $I = 1 + (-0.25) + j0.25 = \mathbf{(0.75 + j0.25)\ A}$.

Example 19.92 *Determine internal impedance of the circuit (Fig. E19.74) looking back from the output.*

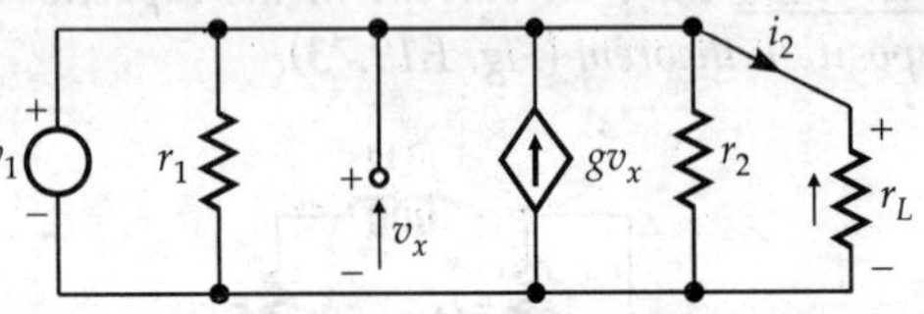

Fig. E19.74

Solution. Let us remove r_L. The *o.c* voltage being $v_{o.c}$ across the output, we can write

$$v_{o.c} = r_2\, g v_x \qquad ...(1)$$

Next, the output is shorted. Let the short circuit current at the output terminals be $i_{s.c}$, the direction being same as i_2 in Fig. E19.74.

Obviously, $i_{s.c} = g v_x$ ...(2)

∴ $$Z_{int} = \frac{v_{o.c}}{i_{s.c}} = \mathbf{r_2}$$

[from (1) and (2)]

Example 19.93 *Find (v_L / v_{in}) and output impedance of the circuit shown in Fig. E19.75.*

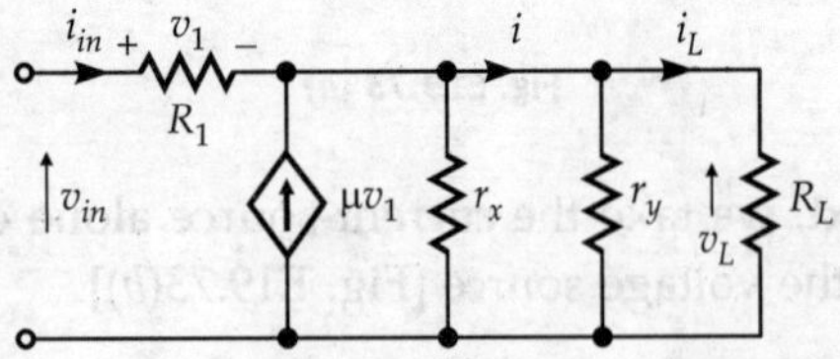

Fig. E19.75

Solution.

$$i_{in} = \frac{v_{in} - v_L}{R_1} \qquad ...(1)$$

and $$\frac{1}{R} = \frac{1}{r_x} + \frac{1}{r_y} + \frac{1}{R_L} \qquad ...(2)$$

Also, $v_L = (i_{in} + \mu v_1)\, R$ ...(3)

or $$v_L = \left[\frac{v_{in} - v_L}{R_1} + \mu\,(v_{in} - v_L)\right] R$$

since $v_1 = v_{in} - v_L$

$$= \frac{v_{in}}{R_1} \times R - \frac{v_L}{R_1}\,.\, R + \mu v_{in} R - \mu v_L R$$

or $$v_L \left(1 + \frac{R}{R_1} + \mu R\right) = v_{in} \left(\frac{R}{R_1} + \mu R\right)$$

∴ $$\frac{v_L}{v_{in}} = \frac{R(1+\mu R_1)}{R_1 + R + \mu R R_1} = \frac{R(1+\mu R_1)}{R_1 + R(1+\mu R_1)}$$

Let us now remove R_L and deactive v_{in} by shorting it. Next we apply a *d.c.* source v_{dc} at output open circuit terminal such that $v_{dc} = v_L$. [*see* Fig. E19.75(*a*)]

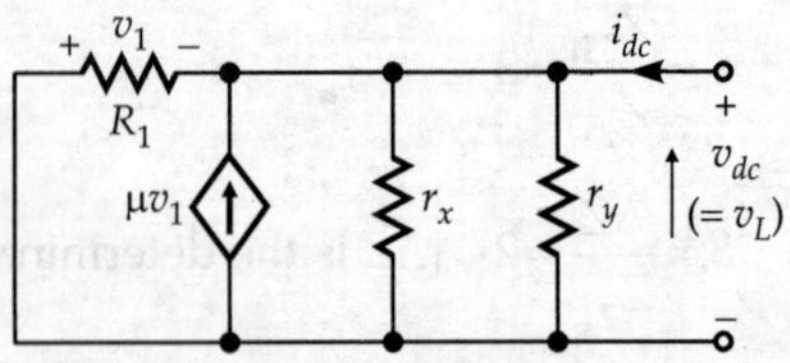

Fig. E19.75 (*a*)

Obviously, $v_1 = -v_{dc}$.

∴ Applying KCL at output node,

$$i_{dc} = v_{dc}\left(\frac{1}{r_x} + \frac{1}{r_y} + \frac{1}{R_1}\right) - \mu v_1$$

$$= v_{dc}\left(\frac{1}{r_x} + \frac{1}{r_y} + \frac{1}{R_1} + \mu\right)$$

[∵ $v_{dc} = -v_1$]

Thus, $$\frac{v_{dc}}{i_{dc}} = \mathbf{R_{int}} = \frac{\mathbf{1}}{\dfrac{\mathbf{1}}{r_x} + \dfrac{\mathbf{1}}{r_y} + \dfrac{\mathbf{1}}{R_1} + \mu}.$$

Example 19.94 *Figure E19.76 represents an unknown element getting charged by a voltage source V. If V = sin 100 t and I = cos 100 t, find whether the given element is an inductor or a capacitor (v is the voltage drop across the element, the direction of the drop being indicated by an arrow in the figure).*

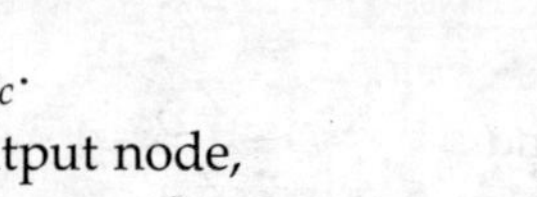

Fig. E19.76

Solution. If the element E is an inductor,

$$v = L\frac{dI}{dt} \qquad ...(1)$$

and if it be an capacitor,

$$I = C\frac{dV}{dt} \qquad ...(2)$$

From (1) $v = L\frac{d}{dt}(\cos 100\,t) = -100\,L\sin 100\,t$

so the drop across the unknown elements comes out as opposite to the drop shown. On the other hand, from (2)

$$I = C\frac{d}{dt}(\sin 100\,t) = 100\,C\cos 100\,t.$$

Since I turns out to be + ve, it is identical to the given direction of I. Thus the unknown element is a **capacitor.**

It may be noted that if the arrow in the Figure for v is given to be downwards instead of upwards, then the element would have been an inductor as the induced voltage becomes opposite to the applied voltage polarity and it follows from the obtained result of $v = -100\,L\sin 100\,t$.

Example 19.95 *The transient current in a series ac circuit is given by*

$$I(s) = \frac{s+1}{s^2+s+1}.$$

(a) What is the initial current ?

(b) What is the transient current in time domain ?

Solution. (a) $i(0^+) = \lim_{s\to\infty} sI(s)$

$$= \lim_{s\to\infty}\frac{s(s+1)}{(s^2+s+1)} = \mathbf{1\ Amp.}$$

(b) $i(t) = \pounds^{-1}\left(\frac{s+1}{s^2+s+1}\right)$

$$= \pounds^{-1}\left[\frac{s+\frac{1}{2}+\frac{1}{2}}{\left(s+\frac{1}{2}\right)^2+\frac{3}{4}}\right]$$

$$= \pounds^{-1}\left[\frac{s+\frac{1}{2}}{\left(s+\frac{1}{2}\right)^2+\frac{3}{4}}\right] + \frac{1}{\sqrt{3}}\pounds^{-1}\frac{\sqrt{3}/2}{\left(s+\frac{1}{2}\right)^2+\frac{3}{4}}$$

$$\therefore\ i(t) = \varepsilon^{-t/2}\cos\frac{\sqrt{3}}{2}t + \frac{1}{\sqrt{3}}\varepsilon^{-t/2}\sin\frac{\sqrt{3}}{2}t$$

$$= \varepsilon^{-t/2}\left(\mathbf{\cos\frac{\sqrt{3}}{2}t + \frac{1}{\sqrt{3}}\sin\frac{\sqrt{3}}{2}t}\right)\mathbf{Amp.}$$

[**Check :** at $t = 0$, $i(t) = 1$ A]

Example 19.96 *In the network of Fig. E19.77, K is closed at t = 0. At t = 0 –, all the capacitor voltages and inductor currents are zero. The three node datum voltages are identified as v_1, v_2 and v_3. Find v_3 and dv_3/dt at t = 0(+). Also obtain v_1, $\frac{dv_1}{dt}(t=0+)$ and v_2, $\frac{dv_2}{dt}(t=0+)$.*

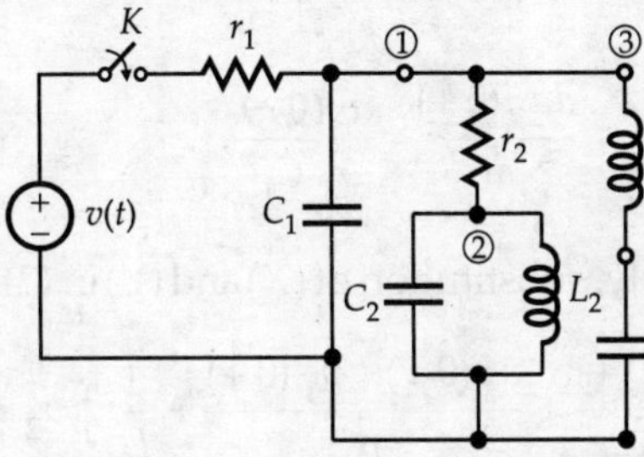

Fig. E19.77

Solution. Since at $t = 0(-)$, all the capacitor voltages and inductor currents were zero,

$$v_1(0-) = v_2(0-) = v_3(0-) = 0.$$

Switch being closed at $t = 0$, at $t > 0$, at node (1),

$$\frac{v_1 - v(t)}{r_1} + C_1\frac{dv_1}{dt} + \frac{v_1 - v_2}{r_2} + \frac{1}{L_1}\int(v_1 - v_2)\,dt = 0. \qquad ...(1)$$

At node (2),

$$C_2\frac{dv_2}{dt} + \frac{v_2 - v_1}{R_2} + \frac{1}{L_2}\int v_2\,dt = 0 \qquad ...(2)$$

And at node (3),

$$C_3\frac{dv_3}{dt} + \frac{1}{L_1}\int(v_3 - v_1)\,dt = 0 \qquad ...(3)$$

At $t = 0+$, the voltages across the capacitors being same as those at $t = 0(-)$,

$$v_1(0+)[= v_1(0-)] = \mathbf{0} \qquad ...(X)$$

Similarly, $v_2\ \mathbf{(0+) = 0}$ and $v_3\ \mathbf{(0+) = 0}$

Again, at $t=0+$, the currents through the inductor being constant and same to those values as $t=0-$,

$$\frac{1}{L_1}\int (v_1 - v_3)\,dt = 0 \qquad ...(Y)$$

$$\frac{1}{L_2}\int v_2\,dt = 0$$

Substitution of equations (X) and (Y) in (1) yields

$$\frac{v_1(0+) - v(0+)}{r_1} + C_1\frac{dv_1}{dt}(0+) + \frac{v_1(0+) - v_2(0-)}{r_2} + \left[\frac{1}{L_1}\int (v_1 - v_3)\,dt\right] = 0$$

or
$$\frac{dv_1(0+)}{dt} = \frac{\boldsymbol{v(0+)}}{\boldsymbol{r_1 C_1}}.$$

Similarly, substitution of (X) and (Y) in (2) yields

$$C_2\frac{dv_2(0+)}{dt} + \frac{v_2(0+) - v_1(0+)}{r_2} + \frac{1}{L_2}\int v_2\,dt = 0$$

i.e.,
$$\frac{\boldsymbol{dv_2(0+)}}{\boldsymbol{dt}} = \mathbf{0}$$

and substitution of (X) and (Y) in (3) yields

$$C_3\frac{dv_3}{dt}(0+) + \frac{1}{L_1}\int (v_3 - v_1)\,dt = 0$$

or $\quad$ **$[(dv_3)/(dt)] = 0$ at $t = 0+$.**

EXAMPLE 19.97 *In Fig. E19.78, a LR network is shown fed by a battery B (switch Sw being in position 1) in steady state and then switched over to position (2) at t = 0. If the current source has magnitude of 5u (t) Amp, find v and i for t > 0.*

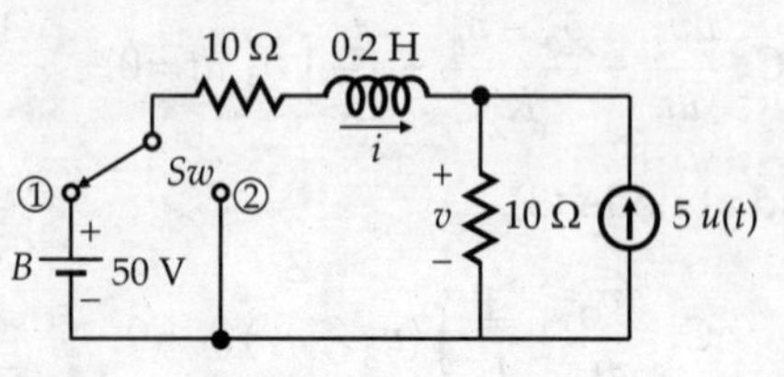

Fig. E19.78

SOLUTION. At $t<0$, inductor acts short-circuited while current source remains invalid. The steady state circuit configuration is then shown in Fig. E19.78(*a*).

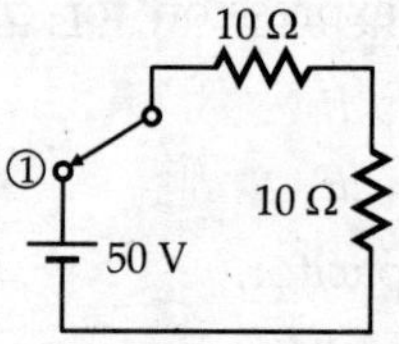

Fig. E19.78 (*a*)

Thus

$$i(0-) = \frac{50}{10+10} = 2.5\text{ A};\ v(0-) = 2.5 \times 10 = 25\text{ V}$$

At $t=0+$, *Sw* is moved from (1) to (2). Since current through inductor can not change instantaneously,

$$i(0+) = i(0-) = 2.5\text{ A}$$

At $t=0+$, $5u(t)$ source also appears [Fig. E19.78(*b*)]

$$\therefore \qquad v = (2.5 + 5)\,10 = 75\text{ Volts}$$

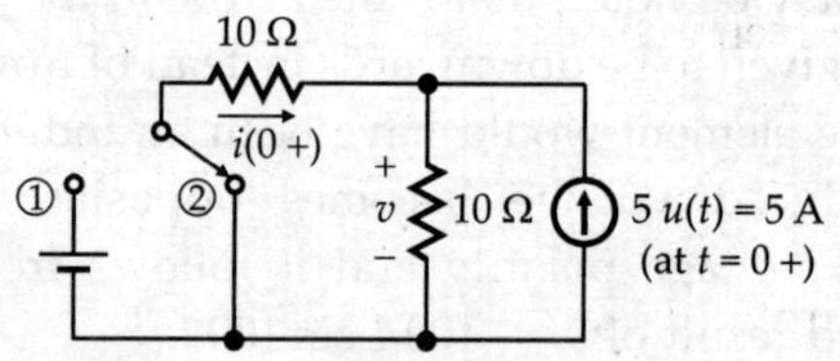

Fig. E19.78 (*b*)

$\therefore$ At $t=0+$, $\quad i(0+) = 2.5$ A

$$v(0+) = 75\text{ Volts.}$$

As $t \to \infty$, the transient current $i(0+)$ decays to zero and the inductor acts as short circuit [Fig. E19.78(*c*)].

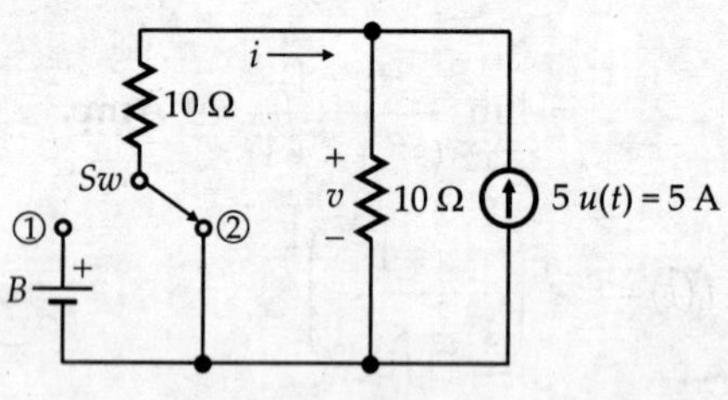

Fig. E19.78 (*c*)

Obviously 5 A current then gets divided along 10 resistance paths.

$$\therefore \qquad v = \frac{5}{2} \times 10 = 25\text{ Volts.}$$

$\therefore$ at $t \to \infty$, $\qquad$ **$i = -2.5$ A**

$$\boldsymbol{v = 25}\textbf{ Volts.}$$

The general expression for current at $t>0$ is given by

$$i=-2.5+(2.5+2.5)\,e^{-200t}$$

where $L/R=\dfrac{0.2}{10}=200$ sec.

i.e., $\mathbf{i=[-2.5+5e^{-200t}]\ Amps.}$

and $v=25+(75-25)\,e^{-200t}$

$=\mathbf{[25+50\,e^{-200t}]\ Volts.}$

EXAMPLE 19.98 *Find Thevenin's equivalent network across X-Y (Fig. E19.79).*

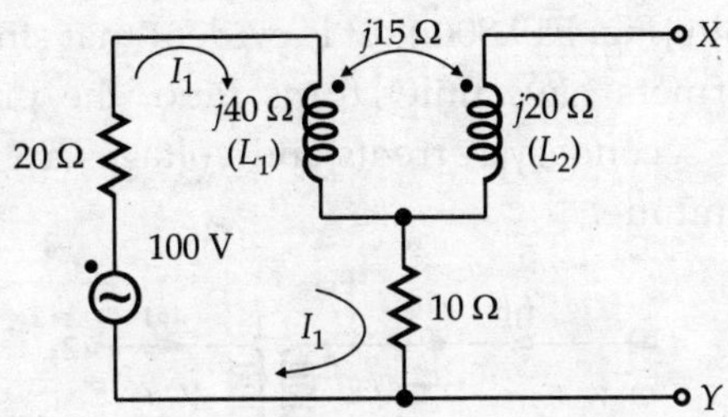

Fig. E19.79

SOLUTION. When the X-Y terminals are open, no current would flow through L_2 coil and hence there is no mutually induced emf appearing in coil L_1.

Assuming I_1 current flowing through the left loop of Fig. E19.79, we can write

$$100=I_1\,(20+j40+10)$$

$$\therefore\ I_1=\frac{100}{30+j40}=\frac{100}{50\,\angle 53.15^\circ}$$

$$=2\,\angle -53.15^\circ\ \text{A}$$

$$\therefore\ V_{X-Y}\,(o.c)=I_1\times 10$$

[i.e., drop across $10\,\Omega$ resistor]

$$=\mathbf{20\,\angle -53.15^\circ\ Volts.}$$

Let us now apply a 1 volt source across X-Y [Ref. Fig. E19.79(*a*)] and 100 V source is deactivated in order to find Z_{Th} looking back from X-Y.

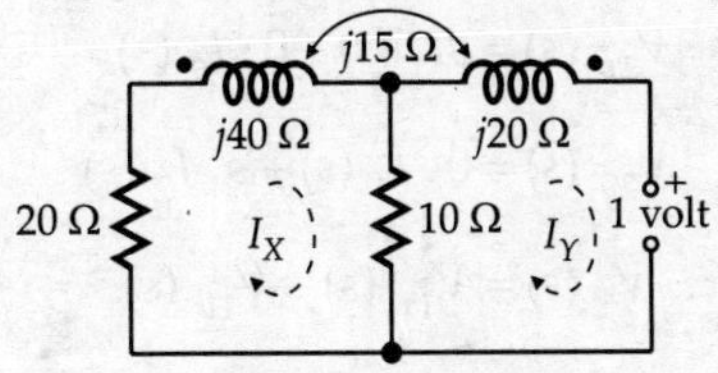

Fig. E19.79 (*a*)

Assuming I_X and I_Y to be the loop currents, in the leftmost loop of Fig. E19.79(*a*),

$$I_X\,(20+j40)+10\,(I_X-I_Y)-I_Y\times(j15)=0$$

or $$I_X\,(30+j40)+I_Y\,(-10-j15)=0 \quad ...(1)$$

In the right loop,

$$10\,(I_Y-I_X)+I_Y\,(j20)-I_1\,(j15)=1$$

or $$I_X\,(-10-j15)+I_Y\,(10+j20)=1 \quad ...(2)$$

Let us now arrange (1) and (2) as follows :

$$\begin{bmatrix} I_X \\ I_Y \end{bmatrix}\begin{bmatrix} (30+j40) & (-10-j15) \\ (-10-j15) & (10+j20) \end{bmatrix}=\begin{bmatrix} 0 \\ 1 \end{bmatrix}$$

$$\therefore\ \Delta=\begin{vmatrix} 30+j40 & -10-j15 \\ -10-j15 & 10+j20 \end{vmatrix}$$

$$=-375+j700=794.12\,\angle 118.18^\circ.$$

Using Cramer's rule,

$$I_2=\frac{\begin{vmatrix} 30+j40 & 0 \\ -10-j15 & 1 \end{vmatrix}}{\Delta}$$

$$=\frac{30+j40}{\Delta}=\frac{50\,\angle 53.14^\circ}{794.12\,\angle 118.18^\circ}$$

$$=0.063\,\angle -65^\circ\ \text{A}$$

$$\therefore\ Z_{Th}\,(x-y)=\frac{\text{Applied voltage}}{I_2}$$

$$=\frac{1}{0.063\,\angle -65^\circ}$$

$$=15.87\,\angle +65^\circ\,\Omega$$

i.e., $$Z_{Th}=15.87\,\angle 65^\circ$$

$$=\mathbf{(6.696+j14.39)\,\Omega.}$$

The Thevenin's equivalent circuit is drawn in Fig. E19.79(*b*).

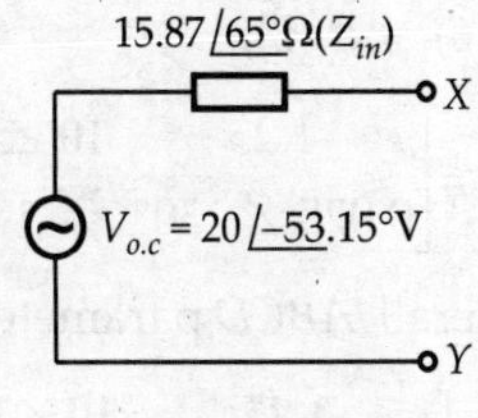

Fig. E19.79 (*b*)

CHAPTER 19

EXAMPLE 19.99 *Two transmission lines are connected in cascade whose ABCD parameters are*

$$\begin{bmatrix} A_1 & B_1 \\ C_1 & D_1 \end{bmatrix} = \begin{bmatrix} 1 & 10\angle 30^\circ \\ 0 & 1 \end{bmatrix} \text{ and}$$

$$\begin{bmatrix} A_2 & B_2 \\ C_2 & D_2 \end{bmatrix} = \begin{bmatrix} 1 & 0 \\ 0.025\angle -30^\circ & 1 \end{bmatrix} \text{ respectively.}$$

Find the resultant ABCD parameters.

SOLUTION. From the concepts of *ABCD* parameter network,

$$V_{S_1} = A_1 V_{R_1} + B_1 I_{R_1};$$

$$V_{S_2} = A_2 V_{R_2} + B_2 I_{R_2}$$

$$I_{S_1} = C_1 V_{R_1} + D_1 I_{R_1};$$

$$I_{S_2} = C_2 V_{R_2} + D_2 I_{R_2}$$

Since $A_1 = 1;\ B_1 = 10\angle 30^\circ;\ C_1 = 0;\ D_1 = 1$, we can write

$$V_{S_1} = V_{R_1} + 10\angle 30^\circ .\, I_{R_1} \qquad ...(1)$$

$$I_{S_1} = I_{R_1} \qquad ...(2)$$

Again, $A_2 = 1;\quad B_2 = 0;$

$C_2 = 0.025\angle -30^\circ$ and $D_2 = 1$

$$\therefore \quad V_{S_2} = V_{R_2} \qquad ...(3)$$

and $$I_{S_2} = 0.025\angle -30^\circ .\, V_{R_2} + I_{R_2} \qquad ...(4)$$

Since the two lines are connected in cascade,

$$V_{R_1} = V_{S_2} \text{ and } I_{R_1} = I_{S_2} \qquad ...(5)$$

Thus from (2) and (3), utilising (5),

$$I_{S_1} = I_{R_1} = I_{S_2} \text{ and } V_{S_2} = V_{R_2} = V_{R_1}$$

Thus from (1) and (4),

$$V_{S_1} = V_{R_2} + 10\angle 30^\circ\, I_{S_2} \qquad ...(6)$$

$$= V_{R_2} + 10\angle 30^\circ [0.025\angle -30^\circ .\, V_{R_2} + I_{R_2}]$$

$$= 1.25\, V_{R_2} + 10\angle 30^\circ\, I_{R_2}$$

and $$I_{S_1} = 0.025\angle -30^\circ\, V_{R_2} + I_{R_2} \qquad ...(7)$$

Thus from (6) and (7),

$$\begin{bmatrix} V_{S_1} \\ I_{S_1} \end{bmatrix} = \begin{bmatrix} 1.25 & 10\angle 30^\circ \\ 0.025\angle -30^\circ & 1 \end{bmatrix} \begin{bmatrix} V_{R_2} \\ I_{R_2} \end{bmatrix}$$

Thus the overall *ABCD* parameter is

$$\begin{bmatrix} A & B \\ C & D \end{bmatrix} = \begin{bmatrix} \mathbf{1.25} & \mathbf{10\angle 30^\circ} \\ \mathbf{0.025\angle -30^\circ} & \mathbf{1} \end{bmatrix}.$$

EXAMPLE 19.100 *In Fig. E19.80, using Z-parameter network, find whether the given circuit is reciprocal or symmetrical.*

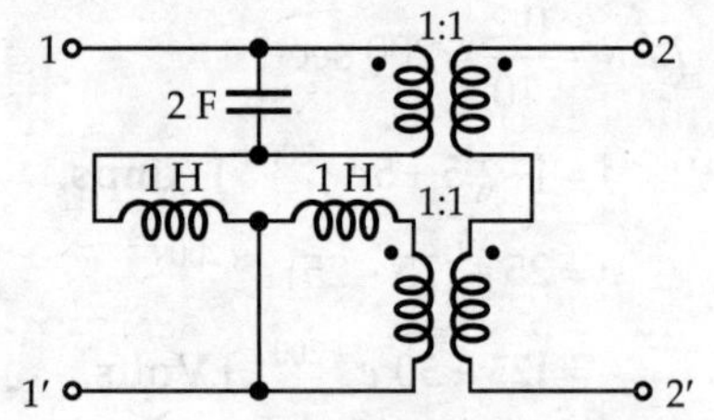

Fig. E19.80

SOLUTION. Let us redraw Fig. E19.80, in *s*-domain [Fig. E19.80(*a*)]. It is evident that since the transformers have unity turns ratio, the primary and the secondary currents and voltages are equal in magnitude.

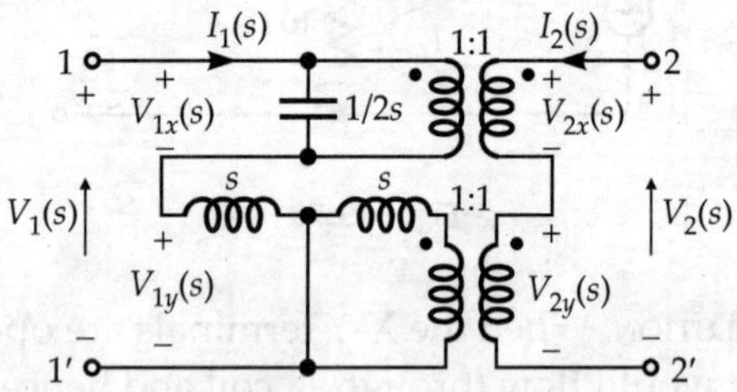

Fig. E19.80 (*a*)

The upper half of the network is named as *x* while the lower half is named as *y*.

In the *x*-portion of the network,

$$V_{1x}(s) = \frac{1}{2s}[I_1(s) + I_2(s)]$$

$$= \frac{1}{2s} \times I_1(s) + \frac{1}{2s} \times I_2(s) \qquad ...(1)$$

$$V_{2x}(s) = V_{1x}(s)$$

$$= \frac{1}{2s} .\, I_1(s) + \frac{1}{2s} .\, I_2(s) \qquad ...(2)$$

For *y*-portion of the network,

$$V_{1y}(s) = sI_1(s) + 0 .\, I_2(s)$$

$$V_{2y}(s) = 0 .\, I_1(s) + s .\, I_2(s)$$

Again $$V_1(s) = V_{1x}(s) + V_{1y}(s)$$

$$= I_1(s)\left[\frac{1}{2s} + s\right] + \frac{1}{2s} .\, I_2(s)$$

while $V_2(s) = V_{2x}(s) + V_{2y}(s)$

$$= \frac{1}{2s} \cdot I_1(s) + \frac{1}{2s} \cdot I_2(s) + sI_2(s)$$

$$= \frac{1}{2s} \cdot I_1(s) + \left(s + \frac{1}{2s}\right) I_2(s)$$

Comparing with Z-parameter equations,

$$Z_{11} = Z_{22} = s + \frac{1}{2s};$$

$$Z_{11} = Z_{21} = \frac{1}{2s}$$

Since $Z_{11} = Z_{22}$, the circuit is **symmetrical** and as $Z_{21} = Z_{12}$, the circuit is **reciprocal**.

EXAMPLE 19.101 *Obtain Thevenin's equivalent circuit across X-Y in Fig. E19.81. Assume $V = 20\angle 0°$ volts.*

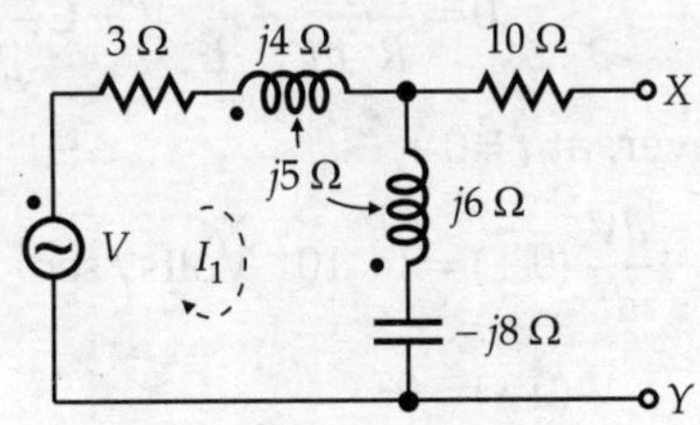

Fig. E19.81

SOLUTION. Let I_1 be the current flowing through the leftsided loop in Fig. E19.81. Applying KVL we can write

$$-V + (3 + j4 + j6 - j8 - j5 \times 2)\, I_1 = 0$$

or $$(3 - j8)\, I_1 = V = 20\angle 0°$$

$\therefore$ $$I_1 = 2.35\angle 69.45° \text{ A}$$

It may be noted here that M is –ve here as I_1 enters $j4\,\Omega$ coil through dotted end while leaves $j6\,\Omega$ coil through dotted end. This gives $j\omega M$ as –ve. Since I_1 links both the coils' mutual inductance hence $j\omega M$ must be multiplied by 2 in KVL equation.

$\therefore$ $V_{o.c}$ (voltage across $X - Y$) $= I_1\,(j6 - j8) - j5\, I_1$

[drop across mutual inductance opposes the drop across the self inductance component.]

i.e., $$V_{o.c} = -j7 \times I_1 = 2.35\angle 69.45° \times -j7$$

$$= 16.45\angle -20.55° \text{ Volts.}$$

Let us now consider a voltage source being applied across X-Y deactivating the original source V. This voltage source is having voltage $16.45\angle -20.55°$ volts [*see* Fig. E19.81(*a*)]. Loop currents are I_2 and I_3.

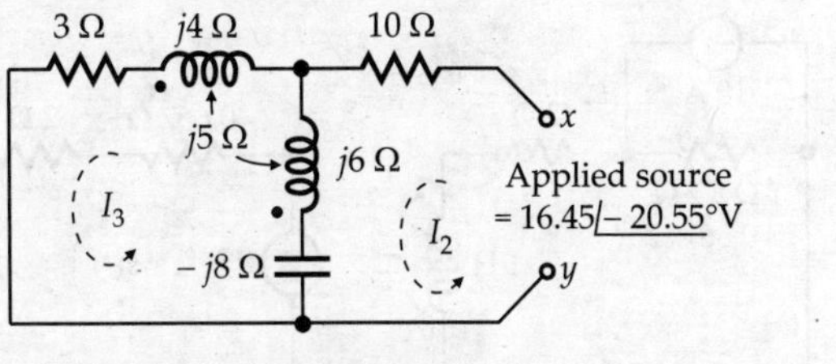

Fig. E19.81 (*a*)

In the rightmost loop,

$$-16.45\angle -20.55° + (10 - j8 + j6)\, I_2 - (-j8 + j6)\, I_3 - (-j5)\, I_3 = 0$$

or $$(10 - j2)\, I_2 + j7\, I_3 = 16.45\angle -20.56° \quad \text{...(A)}$$

In the leftmost loop,

$$(3 + j4 + j6 - j8 - j5 \times 2)\, I_3 - (-j8 + j6)\, I_2 - (-j5)\, I_2 = 0$$

or $$j7\, I_1 + (3 - j8)\, I_2 = 0 \quad \text{...(B)}$$

Solution of (A) and (B) gives

$$I_2 = 1.32\angle -36.25° \text{ A}$$

$\therefore Z_{input}$ from x-y is then given by

$$Z_{in} = \frac{V_{o.c}}{I_2} = \frac{16.45\angle -20.55°}{1.32\angle -36.25°}$$

$$= 12.462\angle -56.80°\,\Omega$$

Thus Thevenin's equivalent circuit becomes

$$\mathbf{V_{o.c} = 16.45\angle -20.55° \text{ Volts}}$$

and $$\mathbf{Z_{in} = 12.462\angle -56.83° \text{ Ohm}}.$$

EXAMPLE 19.102 *In Fig. E19.82, K is switched on at $t = 0$. If $I = 10$ A, find $i(t)$ for $t > 0$.*

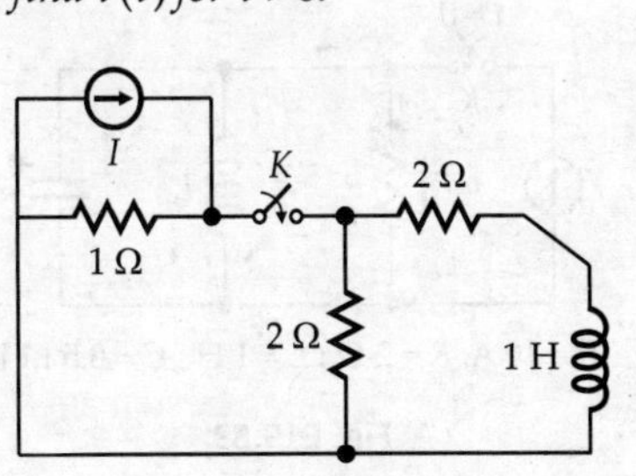

Fig. E19.82

SOLUTION. At $t = (0-)$, current through the inductor is zero. Since current through an inductor can't change instantaneously, $i(0+) = 0$.

For $t > 0$, let us simplify the given circuit as shown in Fig. E19.82(*a*). Here, current source is converted to equivalent voltage source.

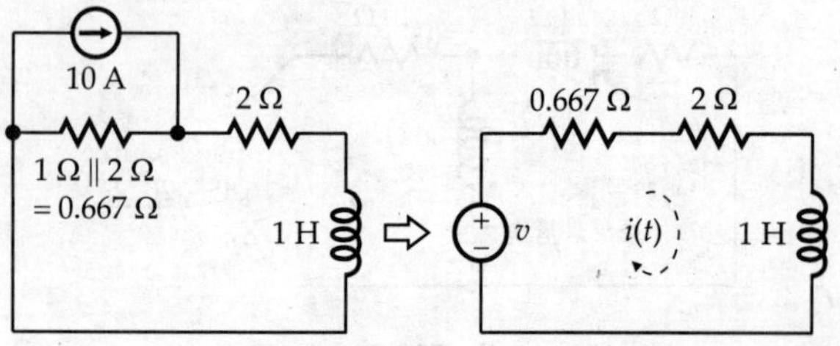

Fig. E19.82 (*a*) v is equivalent voltage source of I.

It is evident that

$$v = 10\text{ A} \times 0.667\,\Omega$$

$$= 6.67\text{ Volts.} \qquad [\theta \text{ is equivalent voltage source of } I]$$

$\therefore$ We can write,

$$-v + 2.667\, i(t) + 1 \times \frac{di(t)}{dt} = 0.$$

or
$$\frac{di(t)}{dt} + 2.67\, i(t) = 6.67$$

i.e.,
$$i(t) = (6.67/2.67) + Ae^{-2.67t}$$

$$= 2.5 + Ae^{-2.67t}$$

where A is a constant determined from initial condition.

At $t = 0$, $i(0) = 0$.

This gives $0 = (2.5 + A)$ giving $A = -2.5$

Finally, $i(t) = 2.5 - 2.5e^{-2.67t}$

$$= \mathbf{2.5\,(1 - e^{-2.67t})\text{ A.}}$$

EXAMPLE 19.103 *Assuming initial conditions to be zero, find* $\frac{dV}{dt}(0+)$ *and* $\frac{d^2V}{dt^2}(0+)$ *in the network of Fig. E19.83.*

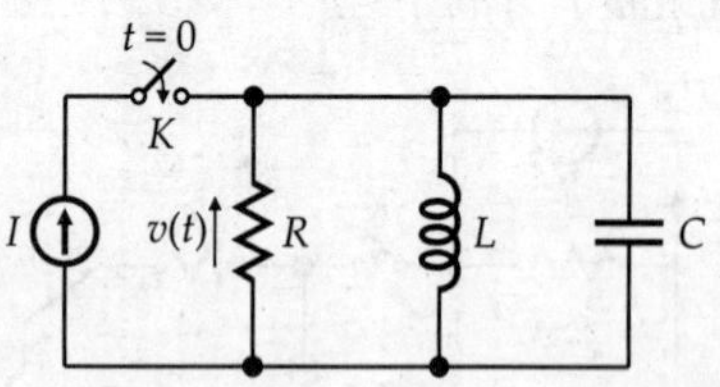

[$I = 10$ A, $R = 2\,\Omega$; $L = 1$ H; $C = 0.5\,\mu$F]

Fig. E19.83

SOLUTION. In the given circuit, nodal analysis reveals that

$$I = \frac{V}{R} + \frac{1}{L}\int_{-\infty}^{t} V\,dt + C\frac{dV}{dt} \qquad \text{...(1)}$$

or
$$10 = \frac{V}{2} + 1\int_{-\infty}^{t} V\,dt + 0.5 \times 10^{-6}\,\frac{dV}{dt} \qquad \text{...(1A)}$$

At $t = 0+$, (1A) becomes

$$10 = \frac{V(0+)}{2} + \int_{-\infty}^{t} V(0+)\,dt + 0.5 \times 10^{-6}\,\frac{dV(0+)}{dt} \qquad \text{...(2)}$$

But at $t = 0+$, L will act as short circuit.

$\therefore$ $V(0+) = 0.$

$\therefore$ From (2),

$$10 = 0.5 \times 10^{-6}\,\frac{dV(0+)}{dt}$$

$$\therefore \quad \frac{dV(0+)}{dt} = \mathbf{2 \times 10^7\text{ Volts/sec.}}$$

Now, differentiating (1),

$$0 = \frac{1}{R}\frac{dV}{dt} + \frac{1}{L}\,.\,V + C\frac{d^2V}{dt^2} \qquad \text{...(3)}$$

However, at $t = 0+$,

$$\frac{dV}{dt}(0+) = 2 \times 10^7\text{ Volts/sec}$$

and
$$V(0+) = 0.$$

$\therefore$ At $t = 0+$, from (3).

$$0 = \frac{1}{R} \times 2 \times 10^7 + \frac{1}{L} \times 0 + C\frac{d^2V}{dt^2}(0+) \qquad \text{...(3A)}$$

where $R = 2\,\Omega$, $C = 0.5 \times 10^{-6}$ F, from (3A),

$$\frac{d^2V}{dt^2}(0+) = \frac{-10^7}{0.5 \times 10^{-6}}$$

$$= \mathbf{-2 \times 10^{13}\text{ Volts/sec}^2.}$$

EXAMPLE 19.104 *In Fig. E19.84, find the voltage across C.*

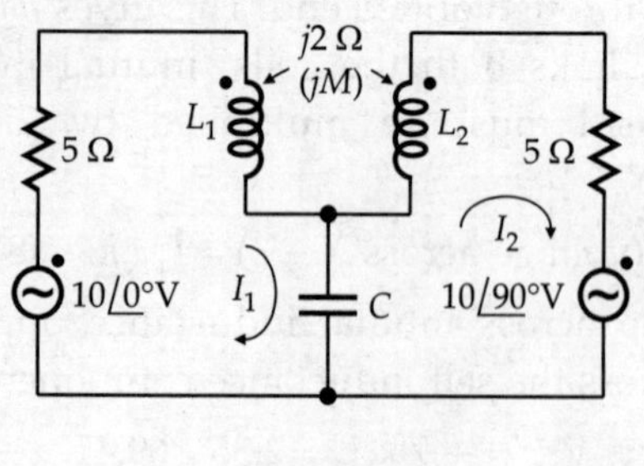

Fig. E19.84

SOLUTION. Let I_1 and I_2 be the loop currents shown in the given Fig. E19.84. As per this current direction, M is –ve since in the left loop I_1 enters L_1 through dotted terminal while in the right loop I_2 leaves the dotted terminal of L_2.

In the left loop KVL yields

$$I_1(5+j5)+(I_1-I_2)(-j10)-I_2(j2)=10\angle 0°$$

or $$I_1(5-j5)+I_2(j8)=10\angle 0° \quad ...(1)$$

In the right loop KVL yields

$$I_2(5+j5)+10\angle 90°+(I_2-I_1)(-j10)-I_1(j2)=0$$

or $$I_1(j8)+I_2(5-j5)=-10\angle 90° \quad ...(2)$$

∴ We can write

$$\begin{bmatrix} I_1 \\ I_2 \end{bmatrix}\begin{bmatrix} 5-j5 & j8 \\ j8 & 5-j5 \end{bmatrix}=\begin{bmatrix} 10\angle 0° \\ -10\angle 90° \end{bmatrix}$$

∴ $$\Delta=\begin{vmatrix} 5-j5 & j8 \\ j8 & 5-j5 \end{vmatrix}$$

$$=64-j50=81.22\angle -38°$$

and $$I_1=\frac{\begin{vmatrix} 10\angle 0° & j8 \\ -10\angle 90° & 5-j5 \end{vmatrix}}{\Delta}=\frac{58.31\angle -121°}{81.22\angle -38°}$$

$$=0.718\angle -83°\text{ A};$$

$$I_2=\frac{\begin{vmatrix} 5-j5 & 10\angle 0° \\ j8 & -10\angle 90° \end{vmatrix}}{\Delta}$$

$$=\frac{139.29\angle -111°}{81.22\angle -38°}$$

$$=1.715\angle -73°\text{ A}$$

Thus current though the capacitor C is

$$(I_1-I_2)=0.718\angle -83°-1.715\angle -73°$$

$$=1.015\angle 114°\text{ A}$$

∴ V_{drop} across the capacitor is given by

$$v_C=-j10\times 1.015\angle 114°$$

$$= \mathbf{10.148\angle -24°\ Volts.}$$

EXAMPLE 19.105 *In the network of Fig. E19.85, $V(t)=5\cos[t-\pi/4]$ volts. Find $i_L(t)$.*

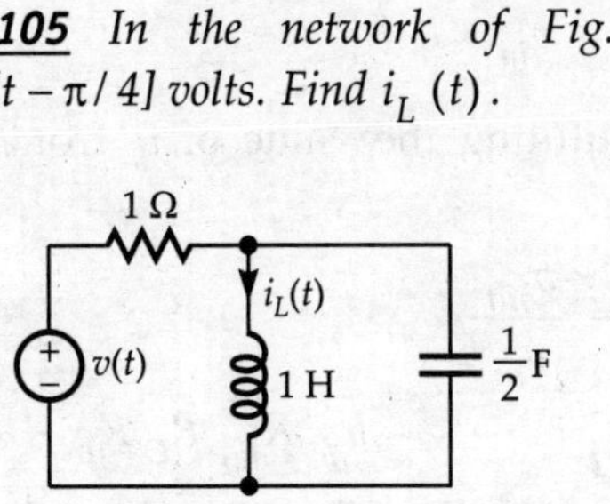

Fig. E19.85

SOLUTION. Observation reveals that since

$$V(t)=5\cos\left[t-\frac{\pi}{4}\right]\text{ Volts}$$

∴ $$\omega=1\text{ rad/sec}$$

and $$V(t)=5\angle -45°\text{ Volts.}$$

∴ $$Z_R=1\Omega$$

$$Z_L=j\omega L=j1\Omega=1\angle 90°\Omega$$

$$Z_C=\frac{1}{j\omega C}=-j2=2\angle -90°\Omega.$$

Z (equivalent) for the parallel L-C circuit can then be obtained as follows :

$$Z_{equiv.}=\frac{1\angle 90°\times 2\angle -90°}{-j1-j2}=\frac{2\angle 0°}{1\angle -90°}$$

$$=2\angle 90°=j2\,\Omega.$$

∴ Impedance across $V(t)$ is $(1+Z_{equiv.})$

i.e., $$Z=(1+j2)=\sqrt{5}\angle 63.44°\Omega.$$

∴ Source current I_S

$$=\frac{V}{Z}=\frac{5\angle -45°}{\sqrt{5}\angle 63.44°}$$

$$=\sqrt{5}\angle -108.44°\text{ A}$$

∴ Voltage drop across the parallel branches is given by

$$V_{drop}=I_S\times Z=\sqrt{5}\angle -108.44\times 2\angle 90°$$

$$=2\sqrt{5}\angle -18.44°\text{ Volt.}$$

∴ $$i_L(t)=\frac{V_{drop}}{Z_L}=\frac{2\sqrt{5}\angle -18.44°}{1\angle 90°}$$

$$=2\sqrt{5}\angle -108.44°\text{ A}$$

$$= \mathbf{2\sqrt{5}\cos(t-108.44°)\ Amp.}$$

EXAMPLE 19.106 *What is the pole-zero plot for $\frac{I_2(s)}{I_1(s)}$ in Fig. E19.86 ?*

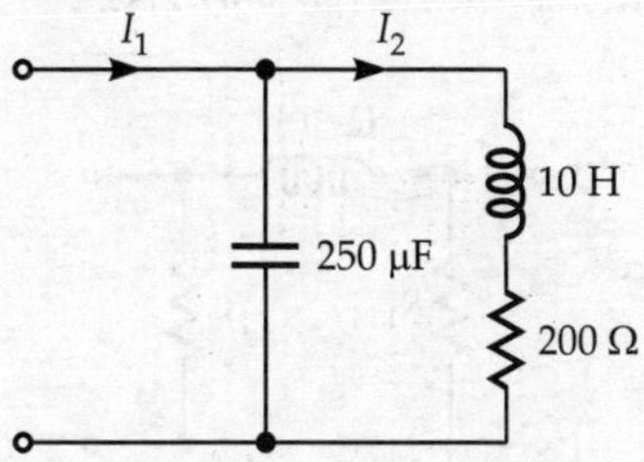

Fig. E19.86

Solution. Figure E19.86(a) represents the transformed network.

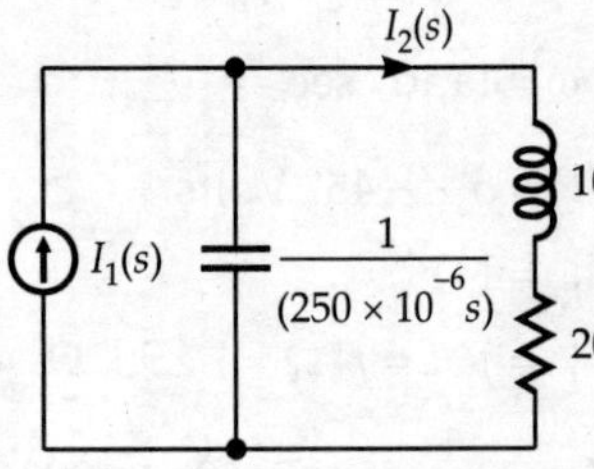

Fig. E19.86 (a)

$$I_2(s) = I_1(s) \times \frac{\dfrac{1}{250 \times 10^{-6}\,s}}{\dfrac{1}{250 + 10^{-6}\,s} + 10\,s + 200}$$

$$\therefore \quad \frac{I_2(s)}{I_1(s)} = \frac{400}{s^2 + 20s + 400}$$

$$= \frac{400}{(s + 10 + j10\sqrt{3})(s + 10 - j\,10\sqrt{3})}$$

The pole zero plot is shown in Fig. E19.86(b). It may be noted that the function $[I_2(s)/I_1(s)]$ has no zero and poles are at

$$S = -10 \pm j10\sqrt{3}.$$

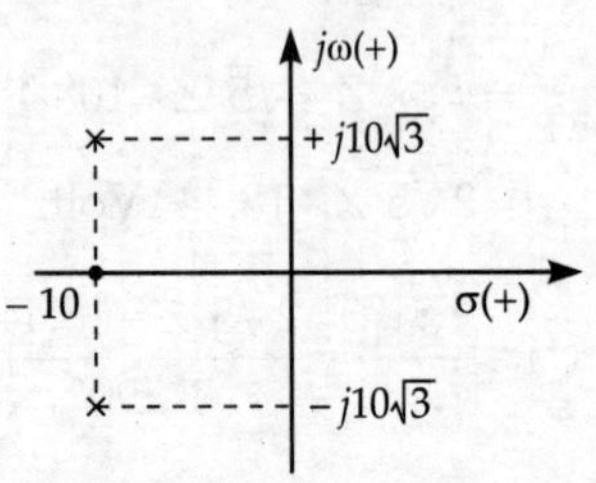

Fig. E19.86 (b)

Example 19.107 *At port 1-1′, the short circuit natural frequency is given by $s+2=0$ and open circuit natural frequency by $s+5=0$. Obtain the value of short circuit natural frequency (SCNF) at port 2-2′.*

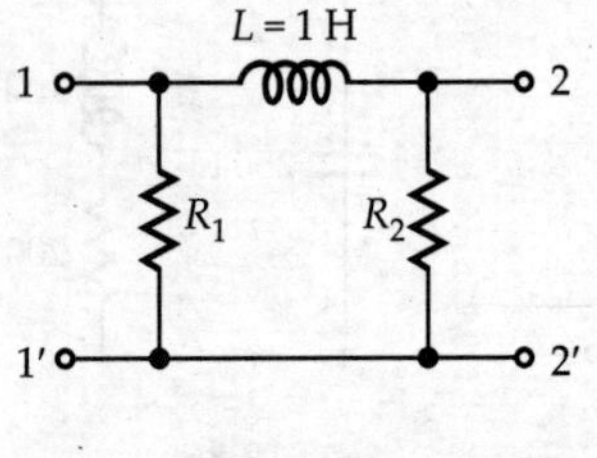

Fig. E19.87

Solution. Short circuit natural frequency (SCNF) at port 1-1′ is $(S+2)=0$

i.e., $S+2=0=SL+R_2=s+R_2$

$\therefore \quad R_2 = 2\,\Omega$

Open circuit natural frequency at port 1-1′ is $(S+5)=0$

i.e., $(s+5)=0=SL+R_{eq}=s+R_{eq}$

$\therefore \quad R_{eq} = 5\,\Omega$

But $\quad R_{eq} = R_1 + R_2$

$\therefore \quad R_1 = -R_2 + R_{eq} = 3\,\Omega$

Hence, SCNF at port 2-2′ is $(s+3)=\mathbf{0}$.

Example 19.108 *Find the gain in Fig. E19.88.*

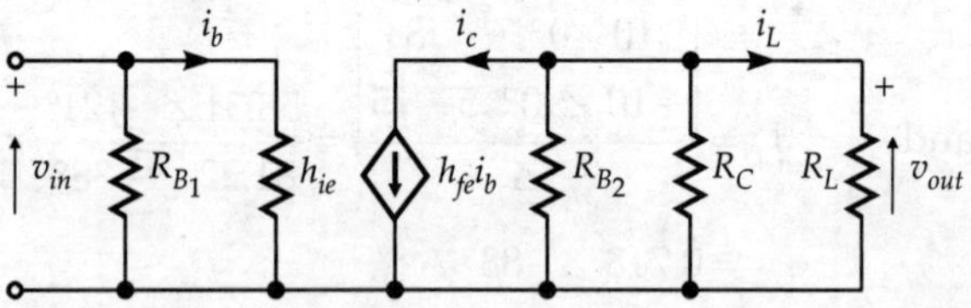

Fig. E19.88

Solution. Gain is v_{out}/v_{in} ; to relate v_{out} and v_{in} we proceed as follows :

At the right loop,

$$v_{out} = -\frac{h_{fe}\,i_b}{[R_{b_2} \,||\, R_C \,||\, R_L]}$$

$$= -\frac{h_{fe}\,i_b\,R_{B_2}\,R_C\,R_L}{R_{B_2}\,R_C + R_{B_2}\,R_L + R_C\,R_L} \qquad \text{...(1)}$$

However,

$$v_{in} = i_b\,h_{ie} \qquad \text{...(2)}$$

Substituting the value of i_b from (2) in (1) it yields

$$\textbf{gain} = \frac{v_{out}}{v_{in}}$$

$$= -\frac{h_{fe}\,R_{B_2}\,R_C\,R_L}{h_{ie}\,(R_{B_2}\,R_C + R_{B_2}\,R_L + R_C\,R_L)}.$$

EXAMPLE 19.109 *Find i_3 in terms of i_2 in Fig. E19.89. Also find v_L in terms of i_1 and α.*

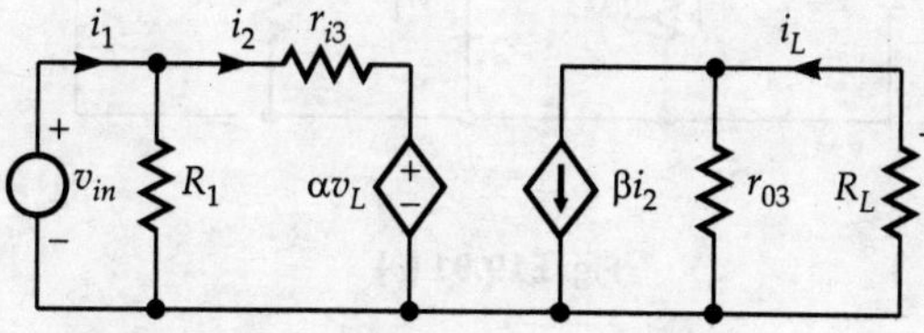

Fig. E19.89

SOLUTION. At the rightmost loop,

$$-\beta i_2\left(\frac{r_{03}\,R_L}{r_{03}+R_L}\right)=v_L \quad \text{...(1)}$$

Also, $$v_L=-i_3\,R_L \quad \text{...(2)}$$

Equating (1) and (2),

$$-i_3\,R_L=-\beta i_2\left(\frac{r_{03}\,R_L}{r_{03}+R_L}\right)$$

or $$i_3=i_2\,\frac{r_{03}\,\beta}{r_{03}+R_L}$$

$$=i_2\,\frac{\beta}{1+(R_L/r_{03})}$$

Also, $$i_2=i_1\,\frac{R_1}{R_1+r_{i_3}}$$

$\therefore$ $$i_3=i_1\,\frac{\beta R_1}{(R_1+r_{i_3})(1+(R_L/r_{0_3}))}$$

Again, $$-(i_1-i_2)\,R_1+i_2\,r_{i_3}+\alpha v_L=0$$

or $$-\left(i_1-i_1\,\frac{R_1}{R_1+r_{i_3}}\right)+i_1\,\frac{R_1}{R_1+r_{i_3}}\,.\,r_{i_3}+\alpha v_L=0$$

or $$-i_1\left(\frac{r_{i_3}}{R_1+R_{i_3}}\right)+i_1\,\frac{r_{i_3}}{R_1+r_{i_3}}\,.\,R_1+\alpha v_L=0$$

$\therefore$ $$v_L=i_1\left(\frac{r_{i_3}}{R_1+r_{i_3}}\right)[1-R_1]\times\frac{1}{\alpha}.$$

EXAMPLE 19.110 *Switch K is shifted from position 1 to 2 at $t=0$. Find V_R and V_L (Refer to Fig. E19.90).*

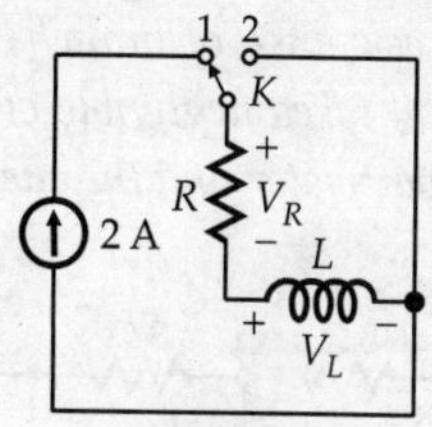

$R=100\ \Omega$
$L=2$ H

Fig. E19.90

SOLUTION. At $t<0$, the switch at 1 position and the network is at steady state with current 2 A flowing through R while L acts as short circuit.

At $t=0$, the switching is done and K is now connected at 2. Application of KVL yields,

$$Ri+L\frac{di}{dt}=0$$

or $$100i+2\,\frac{di}{dt}=0.$$

Taking Laplace transformation,

$$100\,I(s)+2\,[sI(s)-I_0]=0$$

or $$100\,I(s)+2\,[sI(s)-2]=0$$

$\therefore$ $$I(s)=\frac{2}{s+50}.$$

Taking inverse Laplace,

$$i(t)=\pounds^{-1}\,[I(s)]$$

$$=\pounds^{-1}\left[\frac{2}{s+50}\right]$$

$$=2e^{-50t}$$

$\therefore$ V_R (drop across R) $=i(t)\,R=200\,e^{-50t}$ Volts

and $$V_L=L\frac{di}{dt}$$

$$=2\,\frac{d}{dt}(2\times e^{-50t})$$

$$=-200\,e^{-50t}\text{ Volts.}$$

Thus,

voltage drop V_R across $R=200\,e^{-50t}$ Volts
while **voltage drop V_L across $L=-200\,e^{-50t}$ Volts.**

CHAPTER 19

EXAMPLE 19.111 *The current coil of a wattmeter is connected in series with 5 H inductance, and its pressure coil is connected across the 8 Ω resistance as shown in Fig. E19.91. The resistance of branch AB is negligible and the pressure coil takes negligible current. Calculate the reading of the wattmeter and the energy stored in the inductor.*

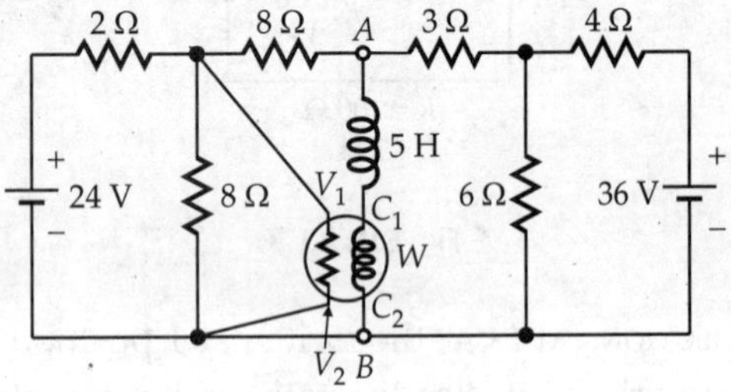

Fig. E19.91

SOLUTION. Let us apply the principle of superposition [Fig. E19.91(*a*)]

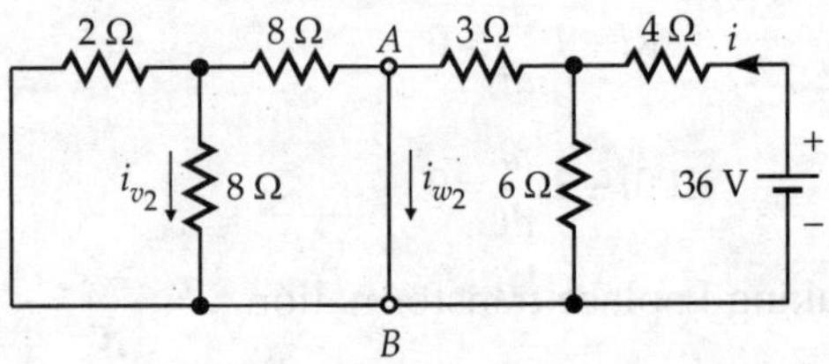

Fig. E19.91 (*a*)

Since branch *AB* has negligible resistance, *AB* can be assumed to be directly short and hence the right side of *AB* has got no role in draining current from the 24 V source in Fig. E19.91(*a*).

Thus R_{1eq}, the equivalent resistance across the 24 V source is given by

$$R_{eq_1} = (8||8) + 2 = 6\,\Omega$$

$$\therefore \qquad i = \frac{24}{6} = 4 \text{ A.}$$

This gives

$$i_{W_1} = 4 \times \frac{8}{8+8} = 2 \text{ A}$$

and $\qquad i_{V_1} = 4 - 2 = 2 \text{ A}$

Next we take 36 V source [Fig. E19.91(*b*)].

Here, the equivalent resistance R_{eq_2} across 36 V source is given by

$$R_{eq_2} = (3||6) + 4 = 6\,\Omega$$

and $\qquad i' = \frac{36}{6} = 6 \text{ A.}$

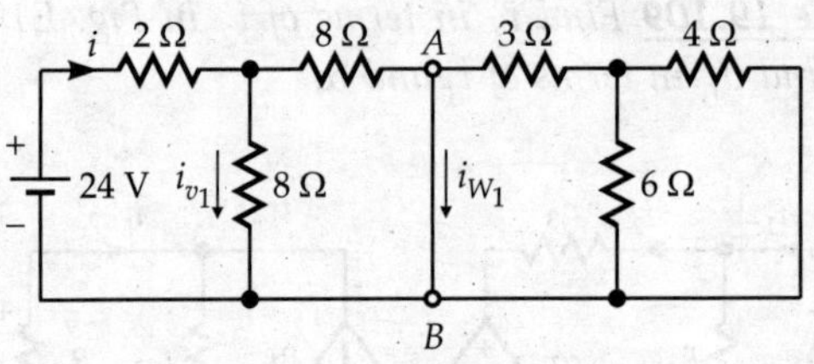

Fig. E19.91 (*b*)

$$\therefore \qquad i_{W_2} = 6 \times \frac{6}{6+3} = 4 \text{ A}$$

and $\qquad i_{V_2} = 0 \text{ A}$

∴ Using principle of superposition, we find the net current i_W is given by

$$i_W = i_{W_1} + i_{W_2}$$

$$= 2 + 4 = 6 \text{ A}$$

This current is flowing through the current coil of the wattmeter.

Again, the current in potential coil of the wattmeter being negligibly small, we calculate the potential drop across the potential coil to be equal to the drop across the 8 Ω resistor.

Obviously $\qquad i_V = i_{V_1} + i_{V_2} \qquad$ (principle of superposition)

$$= 2 + 0 = 2 \text{ A.}$$

∴ V_{drop} across 8 Ω

$$= 8 \times 2 = \mathbf{16\ Volts.}$$

Hence the wattmeter reading is given by

$$W = V_{drop} \times i_W$$

$$= 16 \times 6 = 96 \text{ W.}$$

Energy stored in inductor is

$$\text{Energy} = \frac{1}{2} L i_W^2$$

$$= \frac{1}{2} \times 5 \times 6^2$$

$$= \mathbf{90\ Joules.}$$

EXAMPLE 19.112 *In Fig. E19.92, obtain the value of Z_L such that maximum power transfer takes place from the sources to Z_L. Assume $jX_{L_1} = jX_{L_2} = j8\,\Omega$; $jM = j5\,\Omega$; $V_1 = 10\angle 0°$ volts and $V_2 = 10\angle 90°$ volts. What is the amount of power transfer ?*

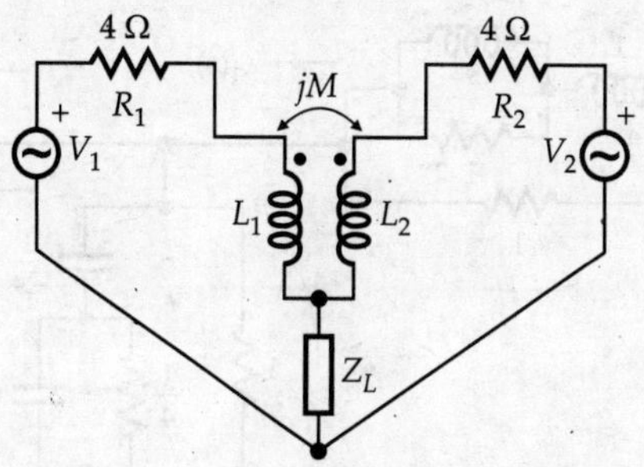

Fig. E19.92

Solution. Let us first find Thevenin's equivalent circuit across $m-n$ removing Z_L [Fig. E19.92(*a*)]. Let I_1 (shown by dotted line) be the circuit current. It may be noted here that I_1 enters L_1 through dotted end while leaves L_2 through dotted terminal. Thus M is –ve.

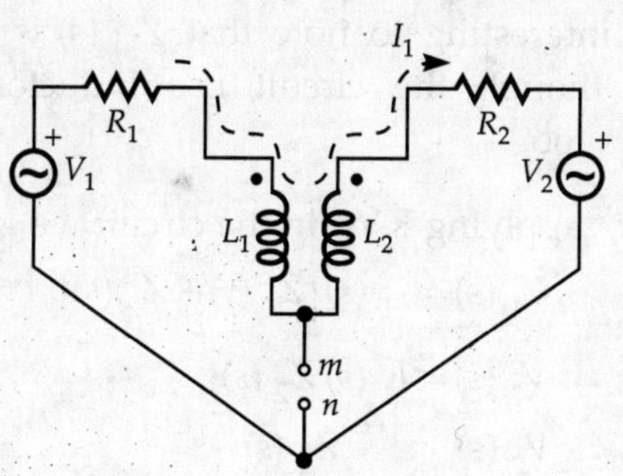

Fig. E19.92 (*a*)

Applying KVL in Fig. 19.92(*a*),

$$I_1[(4+j8)+(4+j8)-j5\times 2]+10\angle 90°-10\angle 0°=0.$$

Simplification yields

$$I_1=1.414\angle -81.9° \text{ A.}$$

$$\therefore\ V_{m-n}(o.c)=\text{potential at } m-\text{potential at } n$$

i.e., $$V_{m-n}(o.c)=10\angle 0°-I_1(4+j8-j5)$$

$$=10-(1.414\angle -81.9°)\times(5\angle 36.87°)$$

Simplifying,

$$V_{m-n}(o.c)=(5+j5)\text{ Volts}$$

$$=7.07\angle 45°\text{ Volts}$$

i.e., $$V_{o.c}=7.07\angle 45°\text{ Volts}$$

Next we deactivate the voltage sources and apply 1.0 volts at $m-n$ terminal [Fig. E19.92(*b*)].

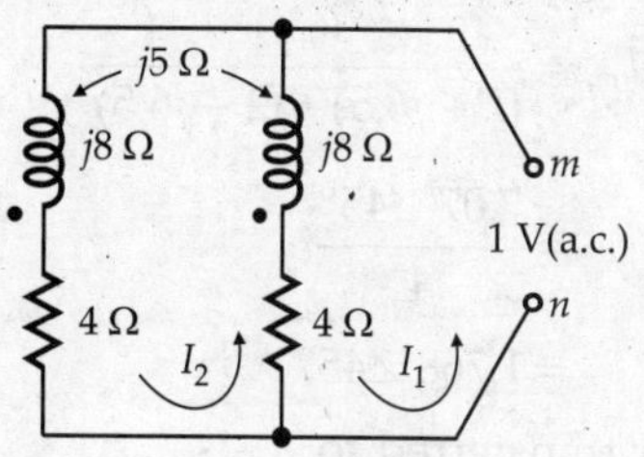

Fig. E19.92 (*b*)

Let I_1 and I_2 be the loop currents.

In the right sided loop,

$$(I_1-I_2)(4+j8)+j5\times I_2=1$$

or $$I_1(4+j8)+I_2(-4-j3)=1 \qquad ...(1)$$

In the left sided loop,

$$I_2(4+j8)+(I_2-I_1)(4+j8)$$
$$+(I_2-I_1)(j5)+I_2\times j5=0.$$

or $$I_1(-4-j13)+I_2(8+j26)=0 \qquad ...(2)$$

$$\therefore\ \begin{bmatrix}I_1\\I_2\end{bmatrix}\begin{bmatrix}(4+j8) & (-4-j3)\\(-4-j13) & (8+j26)\end{bmatrix}=\begin{bmatrix}1\\0\end{bmatrix}$$

$$\therefore\ \Delta=\begin{vmatrix}4+j8 & -4-j3\\-4-j13 & 8+j26\end{vmatrix}$$

$$=-153+j104=185\angle 145.8°$$

$$\therefore\ I_1=\frac{\begin{bmatrix}1 & -4-j13\\0 & 8+j26\end{bmatrix}}{\Delta}$$

$$=0.147\angle -73° \text{ A.}$$

Thus $$Z_{Th}=\frac{V_{o.c}}{I_1}=\frac{1}{0.147°\angle -73°\text{ A}}$$

$$=6.803\angle 73°\,\Omega\ \ [=(2+j6.5)\,\Omega].$$

$\therefore$ For maximum power transfer, the load Z_L should be complex conjugate of Z_{Th}

i.e., $$\mathbf{Z_L=(2-j6.5)\,\Omega.}$$

Thevenin's equivalent circuit is drawn now. [Fig. E19.92(*c*)]

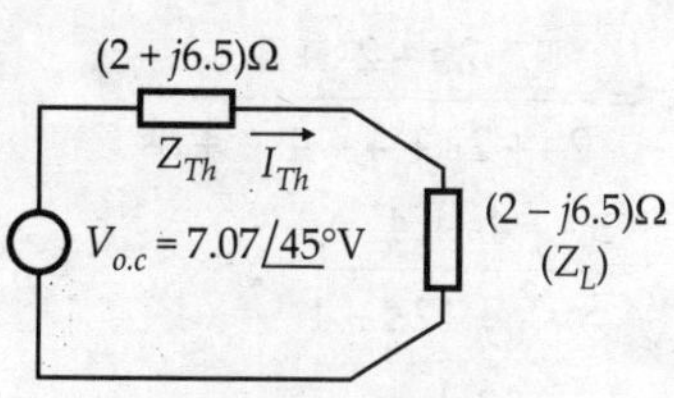

Fig. E19.92 (*c*)

CHAPTER 19

$$\text{Here} \quad I_{Th} = \frac{V_{o.c}}{(2 + j6.5) + (2 - j6.5)}$$

$$= \frac{7.07 \angle 45°}{4}$$

$$= 1.768 \angle 45° \text{ A.}$$

$\therefore$ Power transferred to Z_L is

$$(1.768)^2 \times R_L = 1.768^2 \times 2$$

$$= \mathbf{6.25\ Watts.}$$

EXAMPLE 19.113 *What is the input impedance of the network shown in Fig. E19.93 with 3 - 4 terminals open ? Find (V_2 / V_1) for the given network.*

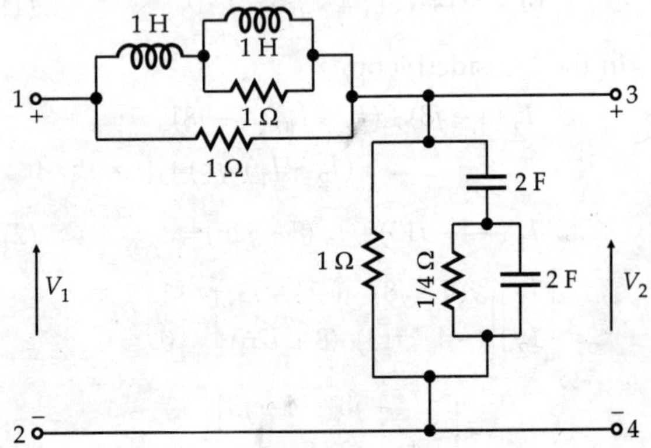

Fig. E19.93

SOLUTION. Let us transform the given network to Laplace domain [Fig. E19.93(*a*)]. With terminals 3-4 open, deactivating voltage sources,

$$Z_{in}(s) = Z_1(s) + Z_2(s)$$

$$\text{where } Z_1(s) = \frac{\left(s + \dfrac{s \times 1}{s+1}\right) \times 1}{\left(s + \dfrac{s \times 1}{s+1}\right) + 1} = \frac{s^2 + 2s}{s^2 + 3s + 1}$$

$$\text{and} \quad Z_2(s) = \left[\left(\frac{1/4 \times 1/2s}{1/4 + 1/2s}\right) + \frac{1}{2s}\right] \times 1 \Bigg/ \left[\left(\frac{1/4 \times 1/2s}{1/4 + 1/2s}\right) + \frac{1}{2s} + 1\right]$$

$$= \frac{2s + 2s + 4}{2s + 2s + 4 + 4s^2 + 8s}$$

$$= \frac{4s + 4}{4s^2 + 12s + 4}$$

$$= \frac{s + 1}{s^2 + 3s + 1}$$

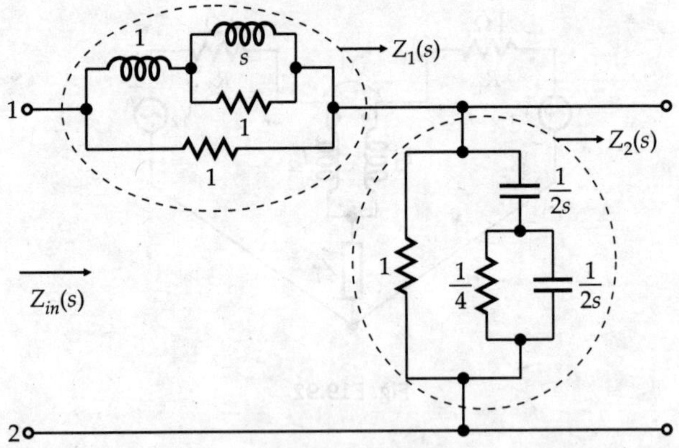

Fig. E19.93 (*a*)

$$\therefore \quad Z_{in}(s) = \frac{s^2 + 2s}{s^2 + 3s + 1} + \frac{s + 1}{s^2 + 3s + 1}$$

$$= \frac{s^2 + 3s + 1}{s^2 + 3s + 1} = \mathbf{1\Omega.}$$

It is interesting to note that $Z_{in}(s)$ is purely resistive though the circuit has inductors and capacitors too.

Now, applying KVL in the circuit we get,

$$V_1(s) = I_1(s)[Z_1(s) + Z_2(s)]$$

$$\text{Also,} \quad V_2(s) = I_1(s) Z_2(s)$$

$$\therefore \quad \frac{V_2(s)}{V_1(s)} = \frac{Z_2(s)}{Z_1(s) + Z_2(s)}$$

$$= \frac{Z_2(s)}{1}$$

$$= \mathbf{\frac{s+1}{s^2 + 3s + 1}}.$$

EXAMPLE 19.114 *The current in a circuit is given by*

$$I(s) = \frac{s^2}{(s^2 + 1)^2}.$$

At what instant does the current reach its maximum value ?

SOLUTION. $I(s) = \dfrac{s^2}{(s^2 + 1)^2}$

$$= \frac{s^2}{(s + j)^2 (s - j)^2}$$

$$= \frac{1}{4} \cdot \frac{1}{(s + j)^2} + \frac{j}{4} \cdot \frac{1}{s + j}$$

$$+ \frac{1}{4} \frac{1}{(s - j)^2} - \frac{j}{4} \cdot \frac{1}{s - j}$$

$$\therefore \quad i(t) = \frac{1}{4}(te^{-jt} + te^{+jt}) + \frac{j}{4}(e^{-jt} - e^{-jt})$$

$$= \frac{1}{2}t\cos t + \frac{1}{2}\sin t;$$

Again for $i(t)$ will be at maximum,

$$\frac{di}{dt} = 0.$$

i.e., $$\frac{d}{dt}\left[\frac{1}{2}t\cos t + \frac{1}{2}\sin t\right] = 0$$

or $$\cos t - t\sin t + \cos t = 0$$

i.e., $$\tan t = \frac{2}{t}.$$

Solving for t, $t = \mathbf{1.07}$ **sec.**

EXAMPLE 19.115 *A capacitor of 0.5 F is initially charged to 1.0 volt and is subjected to discharge at $t = 0$ across a LR series circuit where $L = 1$ H; $R = 2\,\Omega$. Find $i(t)$ for $t > 0$ (Fig. 19.94).*

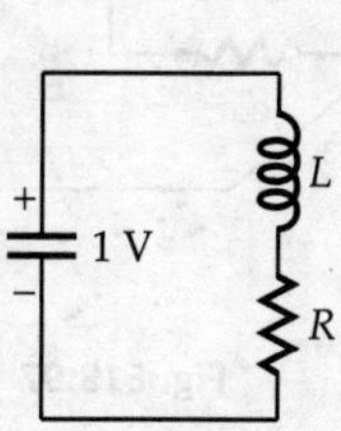

Fig. E19.94

SOLUTION. In this circuit,

$$\frac{di}{dt} + 2i + 2\int_{-\infty}^{t} i\,dt = 0.$$

or $$[sI(s) - i(0+)] + 2\,I(s) + \frac{2}{s}[I(s) + q(0+)] = 0;$$

since the capacitor is initially charged to 1 volt,

$$\frac{2q(0+)}{s} = -\frac{1}{s}.$$

$$\therefore \quad I(s) = \frac{1}{s^2 + 2s + 2}$$

$$= \frac{1}{(s+1)^2 + 1}$$

$$\therefore \quad i(t) = \mathbf{e^{-t}\sin t\,u(t)}\ \mathbf{A}.$$

EXAMPLE 19.116 *At $t = 0$, the switch K is closed in the network shown in Fig. E19.95. Find the initial values of v, $\frac{dv}{dt}$ and $\frac{d^2v}{dt^2}$ if $v_0 = V_0 \sin\left(\frac{1}{\sqrt{MC}}\right)t$ Volts.*

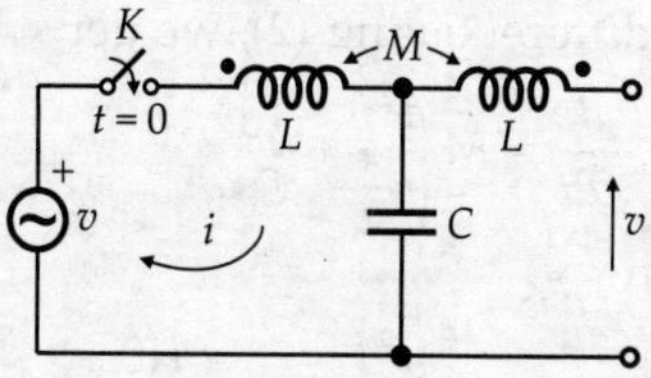

Fig. E19.95

SOLUTION. At $t = 0$, K is closed and L will behave as open circuit.

$$\therefore \quad i(0+) = i(0-) = 0.$$

Obviously in the right loop being having zero current, there will be not mutually induced emf in the left L coil due to second loop current.

In the left loop, in general

$$0 = -v_0 + L\frac{di}{dt} + \frac{1}{C}\int i\,dt \qquad ...(1)$$

[assuming a current i in the loop]

but at $t = 0+$ v_0 is zero and as no current flows,

$$1/C\int i\,dt = 0.$$

$\therefore$ We can write, at $t = 0+$, equation (1) becomes

$$\frac{di}{dt}(0+) = 0.$$

In the right loop,

$$-v + M\frac{di}{dt} + \frac{1}{C}\int i\,dt = 0$$

or $$v = M\frac{di}{dt} + \frac{1}{C}\int i\,dt \qquad ...(2)$$

At $t = 0+$, $\quad v = 0 + 0 = 0.$

Again, differentiation of (1) yields

$$\frac{1}{\sqrt{MC}}V_0\cos\left(\frac{1}{\sqrt{MC}}\right)t = L\frac{d^2i}{dt^2} + \frac{i}{C} \qquad ...(3)$$

at $t = 0+$,

$$\frac{V_0}{\sqrt{MC}} = L\frac{d^2i}{dt^2}(0+) + \frac{i(0+)}{C}$$

$$= L\frac{d^2i}{dt^2}(0+) + 0.$$

$$\therefore \quad \frac{d^2i}{dt^2}(0+) = \frac{V_0}{L\sqrt{MC}}.$$

Next, differentiating (2), we get

$$\frac{dv}{dt} = M\frac{d^2i}{dt^2} + \frac{i}{C} \quad ...(4)$$

At $t = 0+$,

$$\frac{dv}{dt}(0+) = M\frac{d^2i}{dt^2}(0+) + \frac{i(0+)}{C}$$

$$= M\frac{d^2i}{dt^2}(0+) + 0$$

$$= M\frac{V_0}{L\sqrt{MC}}$$

$$\therefore \frac{dv}{dt}(0+) = \frac{V_0}{L}\sqrt{\frac{M}{C}}.$$

Next, we differentiate (3) to get

$$-\frac{1}{\sqrt{MC}}.V_0 \sin\left(\frac{1}{\sqrt{MC}}\right)t = L\frac{d^3i}{dt^3} + \frac{1}{C}\frac{di}{dt}$$

At $t = 0+$,

$$0 = L\frac{d^3i}{dt^3}(0+) + \frac{1}{C}\frac{di}{dt}(0+)$$

$$= L\frac{d^3i}{dt^3}(0+) + 0$$

$$\therefore \frac{d^3i}{dt^3}(0+) = 0.$$

Again, differentiating (4),

$$\frac{d^2v}{dt^2} = M\frac{d^3i}{dt^3} + \frac{1}{C}\frac{di}{dt}$$

At $t = 0+$,

$$\frac{d^2v}{dt^2}(0+) = M(0) + \frac{1}{C}(0) = 0.$$

Thus $\quad \boldsymbol{v(0+) = 0}$

$$\boldsymbol{\frac{dv}{dt}(0+) = \frac{V_0}{L}\sqrt{\frac{M}{C}}}$$

and $\quad \boldsymbol{\dfrac{d^2v}{dt^2}(0+) = 0.}$

EXAMPLE 19.117 *A network is shown in Fig. E19.96. For this network, find $G_{12} = V_2/V_1$.*

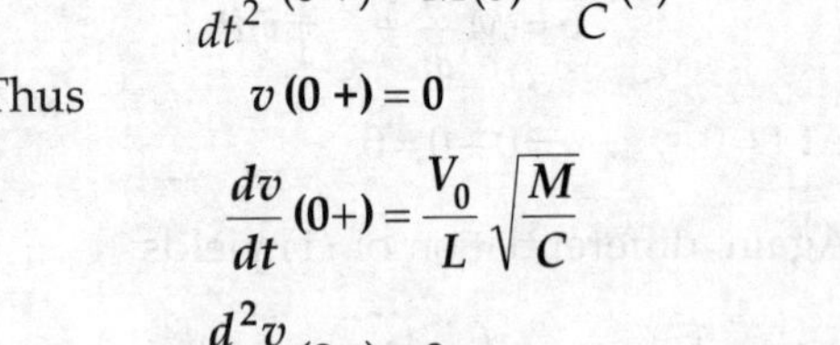

Fig. E19.96

SOLUTION. In loop *abcde*, KVL yields

$$V_1 = I_a + 3I_a + 2V_1 + 3I_a$$

or $\quad -V_1 = 7I_a \quad ...(1)$

Again in branch *c-d*,

$$V_2 = 3I_a \quad ...(2)$$

Using (1) and (2),

$$\frac{V_2}{V_1} = G_{12} = -\mathbf{(3/7)}.$$

EXAMPLE 19.118 *For the circuit shown in Fig. E19.97, find $V_0(s)/V_i(s)$.*

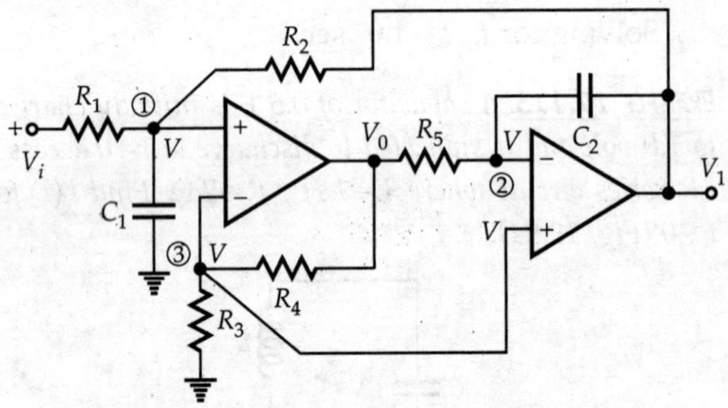

Fig. E19.97

SOLUTION. At node (1),

$$\frac{V - V_i}{R_1} + \frac{V - V_1}{R_2} + \frac{V}{(1/sC_1)} = 0$$

or $$-\frac{V_i}{R_1} + V\left[\frac{1}{R_1} + \frac{1}{R_2} + sC_1\right] - \frac{V_1}{R_2} = 0 \quad ...(1)$$

At node (2),

$$\frac{V - V_0}{R_5} + \frac{V - V_1}{(1/sC_2)} = 0$$

or $$V\left[\frac{1}{R_5} + sC_2\right] = \frac{V_0}{R_5} + sC_2 V_1 \quad ...(2)$$

At node (3),

$$\frac{V - V_0}{R_4} + \frac{V}{R_3} = 0$$

or $$V = \left(\frac{R_3}{R_3 + R_4}\right)V_0 \quad ...(3)$$

Using the value of V from (3) in (1) and (2),

$$-\frac{V_i}{R_1}+\left(\frac{R_3}{R_3+R_4}\right)V_0\left[\frac{1}{R_1}+\frac{1}{R_2}+sC_1\right]-\frac{V_1}{R_2}=0 \qquad ...(4)$$

and $$V_0\left[\frac{R_3}{R_3+R_4}\right]\left[\frac{1}{R_5}+sC_2\right]=\frac{V_0}{R_5}+sC_2V_1$$

i.e., $$V_1=V_0\left[\frac{sR_3R_5C_2-R_4}{sR_5C_2\,(R_3+R_4)}\right] \qquad ...(5)$$

Using (5) in (4) for V_1, simplification yields

$$V_0\left[\left(\frac{R_3}{R_3+R_4}\right)\left(\frac{R_1+R_2+sR_1R_2C_1}{R_1R_2}\right)-\frac{sR_3R_5C_2-R_4}{sR_2R_5C_2\,(R_3+R_4)}\right]=V_i/R_1$$

$$\therefore \frac{V_0(s)}{V_i(s)}=\left[\frac{1/R_1}{\left(\frac{R_3}{R_3+R_4}\right)\left(\frac{R_1+R_2+sR_1R_2C_1}{R_1R_2}\right)-\frac{sR_3R_5C_2-R_4}{sR_2R_5C_2\,(R_3+R_4)}}\right]$$

EXAMPLE 19.119 *A current in a circuit is given by*

$$I(s)=\frac{2s+8}{s^2+4s+12}.$$

If the current flows through a 5 Ω resistor, find power dissipated at t = 0.

SOLUTION. $$i(0+)=\lim_{s\to\infty} sI(s)$$

$$=\lim_{s\to\infty}\frac{s(2s+8)}{s^2+4s+12}=2\text{ A.}$$

$\therefore$ Power dissipated is $[i(0+)]^2\,5$ *i.e.,* **20 Watts.**

EXAMPLE 19.120 *The voltage across an element in a circuit is given by $V(s)=1/[s(s+\alpha)]$. If $v(\infty)=2$ volts, find $v(1)$.*

SOLUTION.

$$v(\infty)=\lim_{s\to 0} sV(s)$$

$$=\lim_{s\to 0}\frac{1}{s+\alpha}=\frac{1}{\alpha}.$$

Since $v(\infty)=2$ $\quad\therefore$ α becomes (1/2).

$$\therefore \quad V(s)=\frac{1}{s(s+1/2)}=2\left(\frac{1}{s}-\frac{1}{s+1/2}\right)$$

$$\therefore \quad v(t)=2\,(1-e^{-1/2.\,t})$$

or $$v(1)=2\,(1-e^{-1/2})=\mathbf{0.787\ Volts.}$$

EXAMPLE 19.121 *A voltage is given by*

$$V(s)=\frac{8s-17}{(s+1)(s-4)}.$$

Find $v(t)$ at $t\to\infty$.

SOLUTION. Using partial fraction,

$$V(s)=\frac{8s-17}{(s+1)(s-4)}=\frac{5}{s+1}+\frac{3}{s-4}$$

or $$v(t)=5e^{-t}+3e^{4t}\text{ Volts.}$$

At $t\to\infty$, $v(t)\to\infty$.

[This circuit is not physically realisable].

EXAMPLE 19.122 *In Laplace domain, the energy in a network is given by*

$$E(s)=\frac{(s+8)}{(s+1)(s+3)(s+5)}.$$

Find initial and final values of energy and power.

SOLUTION.

$$E(0)=\lim_{s\to\infty} sE(s)$$

$$=\lim_{s\to\infty}\frac{s(s+8)}{(s+1)(s+3)(s+5)}$$

= **0 (initial energy).**

$$E(\infty)=\lim_{s\to 0} sE(s)$$

$$=\lim_{s\to 0}\frac{s(s+8)}{(s+1)(s+3)(s+5)}$$

= **0 (final energy).**

Now $$P(t)=\frac{d\,(\text{Energy})}{dt}$$

$$\therefore \quad P(s)=sE(s)$$

[Assuming zero initial condition]

$$\therefore \quad P(0)=\lim_{s\to\infty} sP(s)$$

$$=\left.\frac{s^2(s+8)}{(s+1)(s+3)(s+5)}\right|_{s\to\infty}$$

= **1 (initial power).**

while $P(\infty) = \lim_{s\to 0} sP(s)$

$$= \lim_{s\to 0} \frac{s(s+8)}{(s+1)(s+3)(s+5)}$$

$$= \left.\frac{s^2(s+8)}{(s+1)(s+3)(s+5)}\right|_{s\to\infty}$$

= **0 (final power).**

EXAMPLE 19.123 *In Fig. E19.98 having a network of dependent and independent sources, find* (I_2 / I_1).

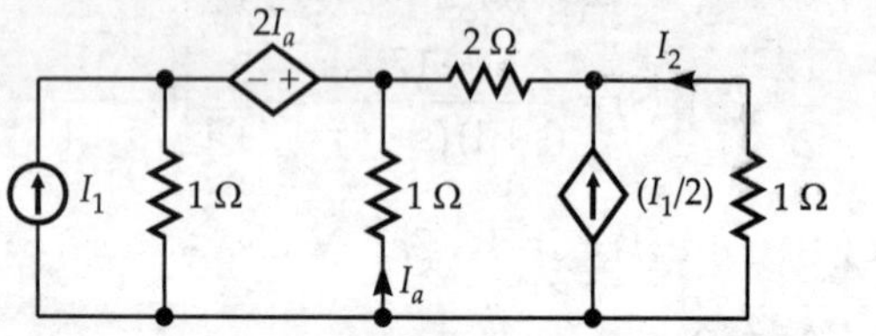

Fig. E19.98

SOLUTION. The given network is redrawn in Fig. E19.98(*a*) for convenience where current directions have been marked.

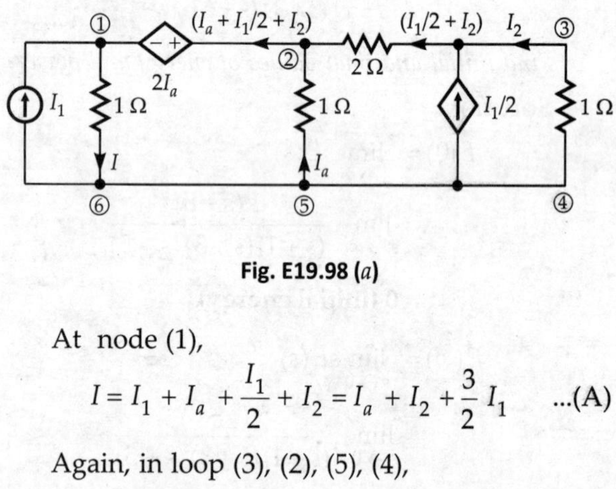

Fig. E19.98 (*a*)

At node (1),

$$I = I_1 + I_a + \frac{I_1}{2} + I_2 = I_a + I_2 + \frac{3}{2} I_1 \quad \text{...(A)}$$

Again, in loop (3), (2), (5), (4),

$$2\left(I_2 + \frac{I_1}{2}\right) - I_a \times 1 + I_2 \times 1 = 0$$

or $$3I_2 + I_1 = I_a \quad \text{...(B)}$$

Next, in loop (1), (2), (5), (6),

$$2I_a + I \times 1 + I_a \times 1 = 0 \quad \text{...(C)}$$

Using (A) in (C) we get

$$2I_a + \left(I_a + I_2 + \frac{3}{2} I_1\right) + I_a = 0$$

or $$4I_a + \frac{3}{2} I_1 + I_2 = 0 \quad \text{...(D)}$$

Using (B) in (D),

$$4(3I_2 + I_1) + \frac{3}{2} I_1 + I_2 = 0$$

or $$12I_2 + 4I_1 + \frac{3}{2} I_1 + I_2 = 0$$

or $$13I_2 = -\frac{11}{2} I_1$$

$$\therefore \quad \frac{I_2}{I_1} = -\frac{\mathbf{11}}{\mathbf{26}}.$$

EXAMPLE 19.124 *In the network of Fig. E19.99, N is a two port network. If I = 1 A, find* V_1 *and* V_2.

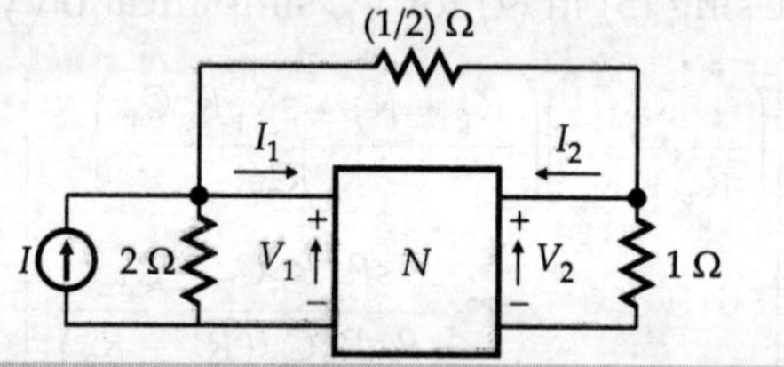

[Given $y_{11} = y_{22} = 2$ mho ; $y_{21} = 2$ mho ; $y_{12} = 1$ mho]

Fig. E19.99

SOLUTION. At the input node, using nodal analysis,

$$I = \frac{V_1}{2} + \frac{V_1 - V_2}{1/2} + I_1$$

or $$1 = \frac{5}{2} V_1 - 2V_2 + I_1 \quad \text{...(1)}$$

At the output node, nodal analysis gives

$$0 = \frac{V_2 - V_1}{1/2} + \frac{V_2}{1} + I_2$$

or $$0 = -2V_1 + 3V_2 + I_2 \quad \text{...(2)}$$

For the network N, the y parameters are

$$I_1 = y_{11} V_1 + y_{12} V_2 = 2V_1 + V_2$$

$[\because y_{11} = 2, y_{12} = 1]$

$$I_2 = y_{21} V_1 + y_{22} V_2 = 2V_1 + 2V_2$$

$[\because y_{21} = 2, y_{22} = 2]$

Substituting I_1 and I_2 in (1) and (2), we get

$$1 = \frac{5}{2} V_1 - 2V_2 + 2V_1 + V_2 = \frac{9}{2} V_1 - V_2 \quad \text{...(3)}$$

and $$0 = -2V_1 + 3V_2 + 2V_1 + 2V_2 = 5V_2$$

i.e., $V_2 = 0$ ...(4)

Using (4) in (3)

$$V_1 = \frac{2}{9}\ \textbf{Volts and obviously}\ \boldsymbol{V_2 = 0}.$$

EXAMPLE 19.125 *A network is shown in Fig. E19.100. Write down the KVL equation at t = 0+ when K is closed at t = 0. Convert this equation to Laplace domain and find $I_L(s)$ at t = 0+ if initially the circuit is deenergized.*

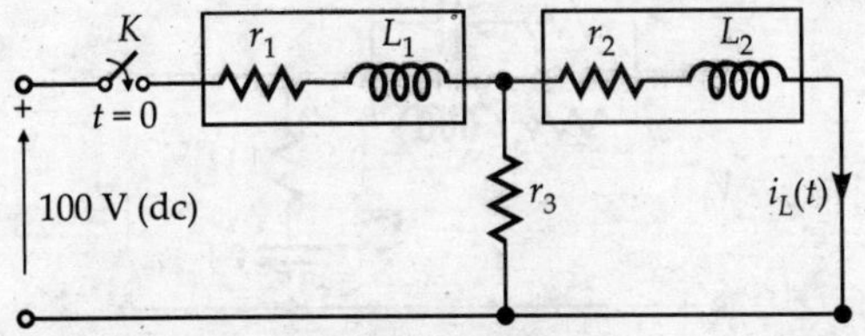

$[r_1 = r_2 = r_3 = 10\Omega\,;\, L_1 = L_2 = 1\,\text{H}\,]$

Fig. E19.100

SOLUTION. Let $i_1(t)$ be the left loop current while $i_2(t)$ be the right loop current, both being taken as clockwise. The differential equations using KVL are as follows :

For left loop at $t = 0+$

$$\frac{di_1(t)}{dt} + 20i_1(t) - 10i_2(t) = 100\,u(t)$$

and for right loop at $t = 0+$,

$$\frac{di_2(t)}{dt} + 20i_2(t) - 10i_1(t) = 0$$

[obviously $i_2(t) \equiv i_L(t)$]

The Laplace transform of these two equations yields

$$(s+20)\,I_1(s) - 10\,I_2(s) = \frac{100}{s}$$

for the left loop

and $\quad -10\,I_1(s) + (s+20)\,I_2(s) = 0$

for the right loop.

$$\therefore \quad I_2(s) \equiv I_L(s) = \frac{\begin{bmatrix} s+20 & 100/s \\ -10 & 0 \end{bmatrix}}{\begin{bmatrix} s+20 & -10 \\ -10 & s+20 \end{bmatrix}}$$

$$= \frac{\mathbf{10^3}}{\mathbf{s\,(s^2+40s+300)}}.$$

[If we convert it to time domain, at $t = 0+$,

$i_2(t) = i_L(t) = 3.33 - 5e^{-10t} + 1.67e^{-30t}$]

EXAMPLE 19.126 *Find $V, \dfrac{dV}{dt}, \dfrac{d^2V}{dt^2}$ at t = 0+ after opening switch K at t = 0 (Fig. E19.101).*

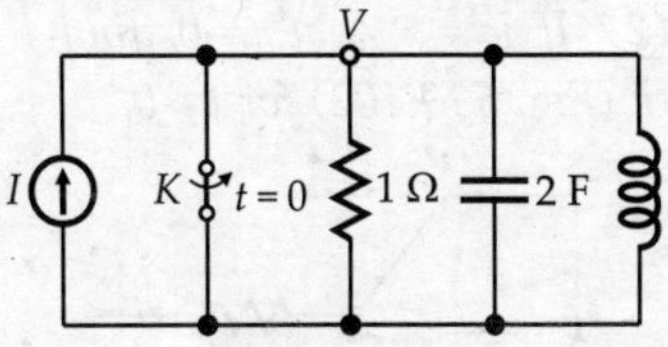

[I = 5 A]

Fig. E19.101

SOLUTION. Once the switch is opened at $t = 0$, the circuit of Fig. E19.101 is drawn for $t = 0+$ in Fig. E19.101(*a*). *L* will act as open circuit while *C* will

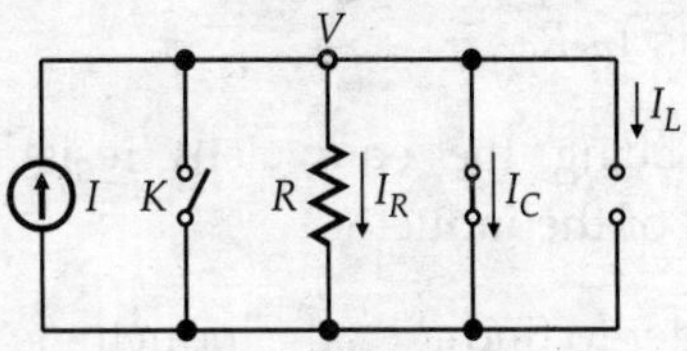

$(t = 0+)$

Fig. E19.101 (*a*)

act as short circuit. Then *I* will flow through *R* only making $I_C \equiv I$. Obviously $V = 0$ (since no current passes through *R*).

$$\therefore \qquad I = I_R + I_C + I_L = 0 + 2\frac{dV}{dt} + 0$$

$$\therefore \quad \frac{dV}{dt}(0+) = \frac{I}{2} = \mathbf{2.5\ Volts/sec.}$$

To find $\dfrac{d^2V}{dt}(0+)$, let us write the general form of node equation again.

$$I = I_R + I_L + I_C$$

$$= \frac{V}{R} + \frac{1}{L}\int V\,dt + C\frac{dV}{dt} \qquad \text{...}(x)$$

Differentiating equation (*x*),

$$0 = \frac{dV}{dt} + V + 2\frac{d^2V}{dt^2}$$

$[\because\ R = 1\Omega,\ L = 1\,\text{H},\ C = 2\,\text{F}]$

at $t = 0+$, $\qquad 0 = \dfrac{dV}{dt}(0+) + 2\dfrac{d^2V}{dt^2}(0+)$

$$\therefore \quad \frac{d^2V}{dt^2}(0+) = -\frac{1}{2}\frac{dV}{dt}(0+)$$

$$= \mathbf{-1.25\ Volts/sec^2}.$$

EXAMPLE 19.127 *If $i_L = 5$ A at $t = 0$, find $i_L(t)$ for the given network (Fig. E19.102) for $t > 0$.*

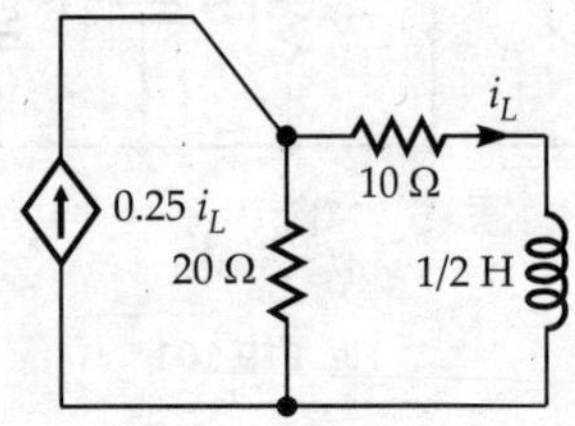

Fig. E19.102

SOLUTION. $i_L(t) = i_L(0)\, e^{-t/T}$, where T, the time constant is L/R_{net}.

R_{net} being the equivalent resistance at the terminals of the inductor.

In order to find R_{net}, the inductor is replaced by a 1.0 volt voltage source (v_0) and the input current

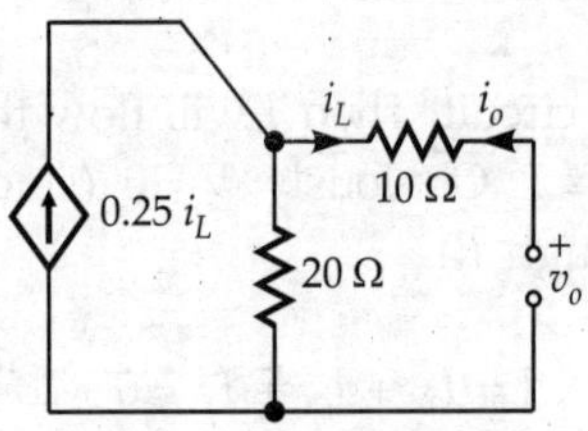

Fig. E19.102 (a)

to the network from this source is i_0 Amps [Fig. E19.102(*a*)]. Obviously $R_{eq} = (v_0/i_0)$. In this figure KVL yields

$$10 i_0 + 20\left(i_0 + \frac{i_L}{4}\right) = 1 \qquad \text{...(1)}$$

and $$i_0 = -i_L \qquad \text{...(2)}$$

From (1) and (2),

$$i_0 = (1/25) \text{ Amps.}$$

$$\therefore \quad R_{eq} = \frac{v_0}{i_0} = \frac{1}{1/25} = 25\,\Omega.$$

This gives $T = L/R_{eq} = (1/2)/25 = 1/50$ sec.

$$\therefore \quad i_L(t) = i_L(0)\, e^{-50t} = \mathbf{10\, e^{-50t}} \textbf{ Amps.}$$

EXAMPLE 19.128 *(a) Find the transfer function*

$$H(s) = \frac{V_2(s)}{V_1(s)}$$

for the network in Fig. E19.103.

(b) What is the order of the systems ?

(c) If the inductance value is changed to 2 H, what will be the order of the modified network ?

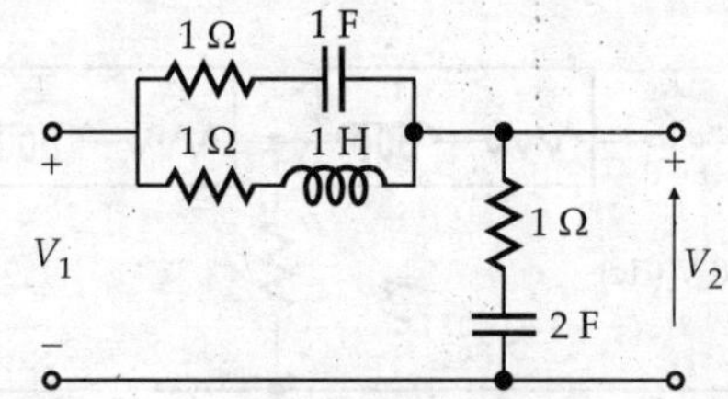

Fig. E19.103

SOLUTION. Let us first transfer the time domain circuit to Laplace domain [Fig. E19.103(*a*)].

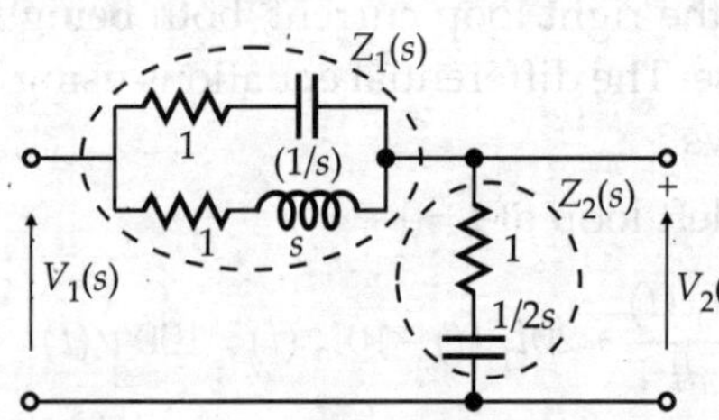

Fig. E19.103 (a)

Now,

$$Z_1(s) = \frac{\left(1 + \frac{1}{s}\right)(1+s)}{1 + \frac{1}{s} + 1 + s} = \frac{(s+1)^2}{s^2 + 2s + 1} = 1$$

and $$Z_2(s) = 1 + \frac{1}{2s}$$

$$\therefore \quad V_1(s) = I_1(s) \times Z_1(s) + V_2(s)$$

where $$V_2(s) = I_1(s) \times Z_2(s) = I_1(s) \times \left[1 + \frac{1}{2s}\right]$$

$$\therefore \quad V_1(s) = \frac{V_2(s)}{1 + \frac{1}{2s}} + V_2(s) \qquad [\because Z_1(s) = 1]$$

$$= V_2(s)\left[\frac{1}{\left(1 + \frac{1}{2s}\right)} + 1\right]$$

$$= V_2(s)\left[\frac{1 + 1 + \frac{1}{2s}}{1 + \frac{1}{2s}}\right] = V_2(s)\left[\frac{4s+1}{2s+1}\right]$$

$$\therefore \quad \frac{V_2(s)}{V_1(s)} = \frac{\mathbf{(2s+1)}}{\mathbf{(4s+1)}}.$$

If $L=2$,

$$Z_1(s)=\frac{\left(1+\frac{1}{s}\right)(1+2s)}{1+\frac{1}{s}+1+2s}=\frac{(s+1)(2s+1)}{2s^2+2s+1}$$

$$\therefore \quad V_1(s)=I_1(s)\,Z_1(s)+V_2(s)$$

$$=\frac{V_2(s)}{1+\frac{1}{2s}}\times\frac{(s+1)(2s+1)}{2s^2+2s+1}+V_2(s)$$

$$=V_2(s)\left[\frac{2s(s+1)(2s+1)}{(2s+1)(2s^2+2s+1)}+1\right]$$

$$=V_2(s)\left[\frac{2s(s+1)}{2s^2+2s+1}+1\right]$$

$$=V_2(s)\left[\frac{4s^2+4s+1}{2s^2+2s+1}\right]$$

$$\therefore \quad \frac{V_2(s)}{V_1(s)}=\mathbf{\frac{2s^2+2s+1}{4s^2+4s+1}}.$$

Thus it is evident that if $L=1$,

$\frac{V_2(s)}{V_1(s)}$ is a **1st order system** $\left[\frac{V_2(s)}{V_1(s)}=\frac{2s+1}{4s+1}\right]$

while for $L=2$,

$\frac{V_2(s)}{V_1(s)}$ is a **2nd order system**.

EXAMPLE 19.129 *In Fig. E19.104, calculate*

(a) the power delivered by each source.

(b) the power dissipated in each resistor.

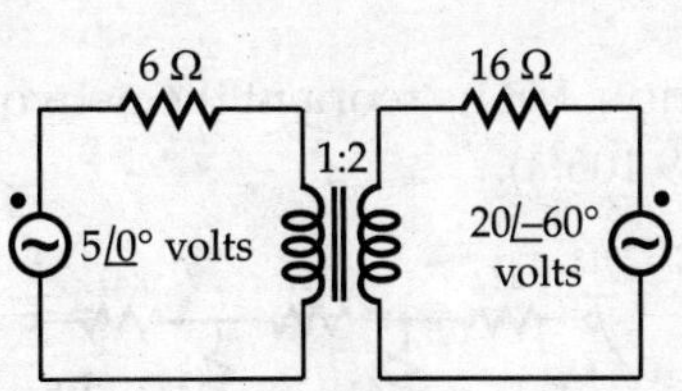

Fig. E19.104

SOLUTION. If we refer the secondary resistance to primary, from the theory of transformer primary resistance $R_1=6+\frac{16}{2^2}=10\,\Omega$ and the secondary voltage $20\angle-60°$ volts when reference to primary becomes $10\angle-60°$ volts.

The given circuit is now redrawn (referred to primary) [Fig. E19.104(*a*)].

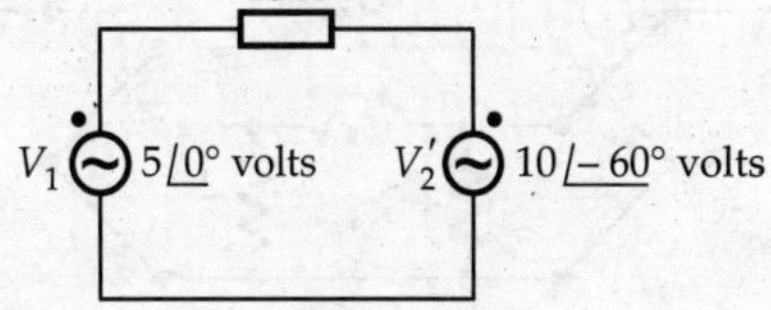

Fig. E19.104 (*a*)

Applying superposition theorem, taking V_1 first,

$$i_1=\frac{V_1}{10}=\frac{5\angle 0°}{10}=0.5\angle 0°\text{ A};$$

then taking V'_2,

$$i'_2=\frac{V'_2}{10}=\frac{10\angle-60°}{10}=1\angle-60°\text{ A}$$

$\therefore \quad i=-i_1+i'_2$, applying superposition.

or $\quad i=-0.5+j0+0.5-j0.866$

$$=-j0.866\text{ A}$$

[*i.e.*, current is flowing opposite to i_2]

Since the current does not have any real component, hence power dissipated in each resistor would be zero.

If we now calculate the power supplied by each source, we proceed as follows :

for source : V_1,

$$\text{Power}=|V_1|\times|I_1|=5\times 0.5=\mathbf{2.5\ W}$$

for source : V_2,

$$\text{Power}=|V_2||I_2'|=10\times 1=\mathbf{10\ W}.$$

Also $V_1I_1^*=5\angle 0°\times(0.5-j0)$

$=(2.5+j0)\text{ VA}=2.5\text{ W}$

$V_2I_2^*=10\angle-60°\times(0.5+j0.866)$

$=10(0.5-j0.866)\times(0.5+j0.866)$

$=10(0.5^2+0.866^2)$

$=2.5+7.5=10\text{ VA}=\mathbf{10\ W}.$

EXAMPLE 19.130 *The overall network in Fig. E19.105 is a parallel combination of two resistive networks – one T network and one π network. Determine Y-parameters.*

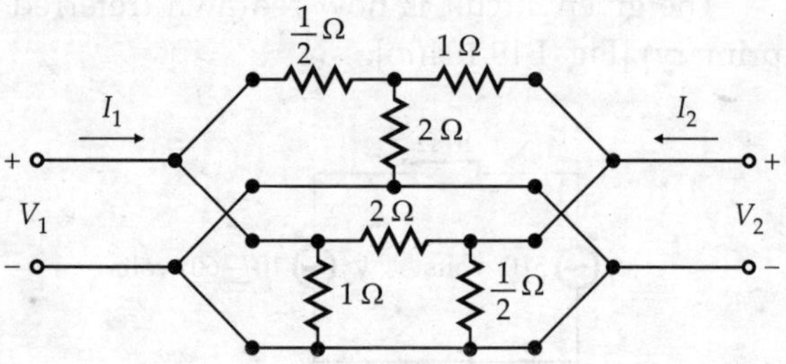

Fig. E19.105

Solution. The combined network is segregated in T and π components and shown below [Figs. E19.105(*a*) and (*b*)] :

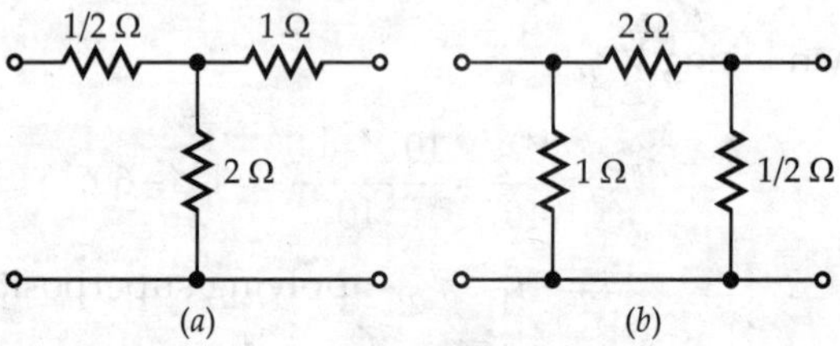

Fig. E19.105

Let us first convert the T network into an equivalent π network as shown in Fig. E19.105(*c*).

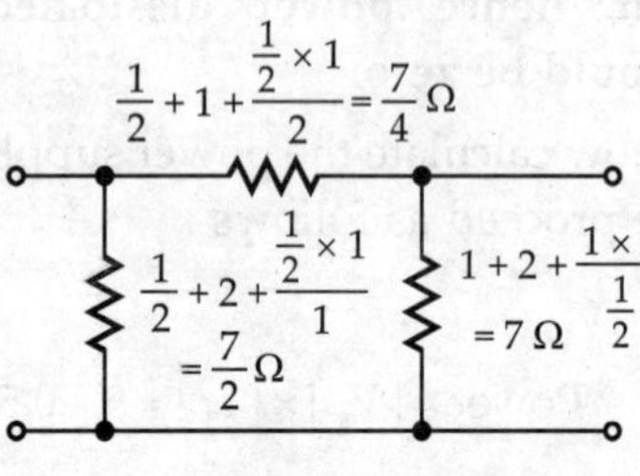

Fig. E19.105 (*c*)

Next we convert these two π networks of resistance into π networks of conductances.

In Fig. E19.105(*d*),

$$Y_{11a}=\frac{2}{7}+\frac{4}{7}=\frac{6}{7}\text{ mho};$$

$$Y_{12a}=-\frac{4}{7}\text{ mho}$$

$$Y_{21a}=-\frac{4}{7}\text{ mho};$$

$$Y_{22a}=\frac{1}{7}+\frac{4}{7}=\frac{5}{7}\text{ mho}$$

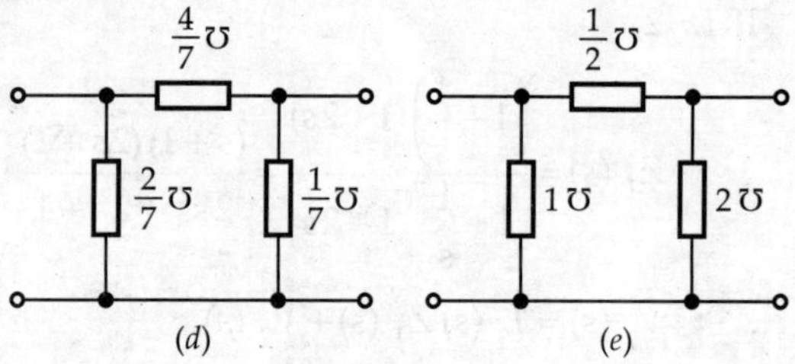

Fig. E19.105

In Fig. E19.105(*e*),

$$Y_{11b}=1+\frac{1}{2}=\frac{3}{2}\text{ mho};\quad Y_{12b}=-\frac{1}{2}\text{ mho}$$

$$Y_{21b}=-\frac{1}{2}\text{ mho};\quad Y_{22b}=2+\frac{1}{2}=\frac{5}{2}\text{ mho.}$$

$\therefore$ Overall Y-parameter is

$$\mathbf{Y_{11}=Y_{11a}+Y_{11b}=\frac{33}{14}\text{ mho};}$$

$$\mathbf{Y_{12}=Y_{12a}+Y_{12b}=-\frac{15}{14}\text{ mho};}$$

$$\mathbf{Y_{21}=Y_{21a}+Y_{21b}=-\frac{15}{14}\text{ mho};}$$

$$\mathbf{Y_{22}=Y_{22a}+Y_{22b}=\frac{45}{14}\text{ mho.}}$$

Example 19.131 *Obtain Y parameter for the network shown in Fig. E19.106.*

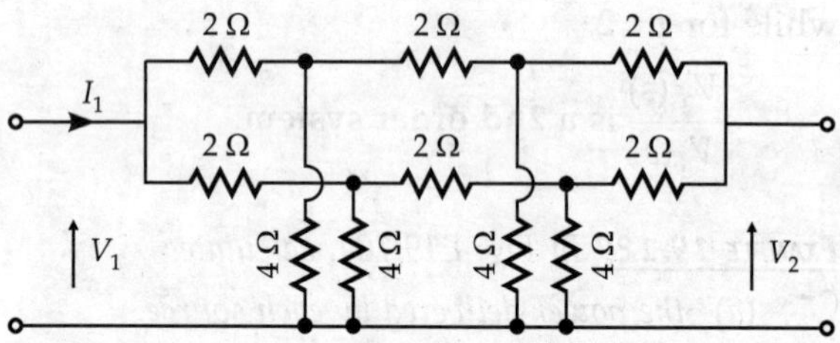

Fig. E19.106

Solution. Let us reorient the network as shown in Fig. E19.106(*a*).

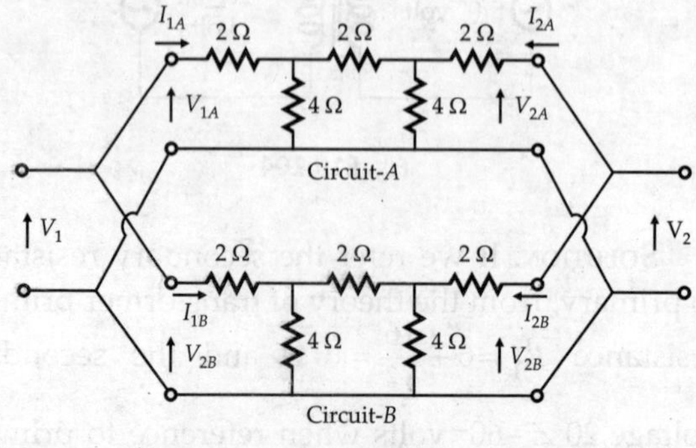

Fig. E19.106 (*a*)

Circuit A is then separated and redrawn as shown in Fig. E19.106(b).

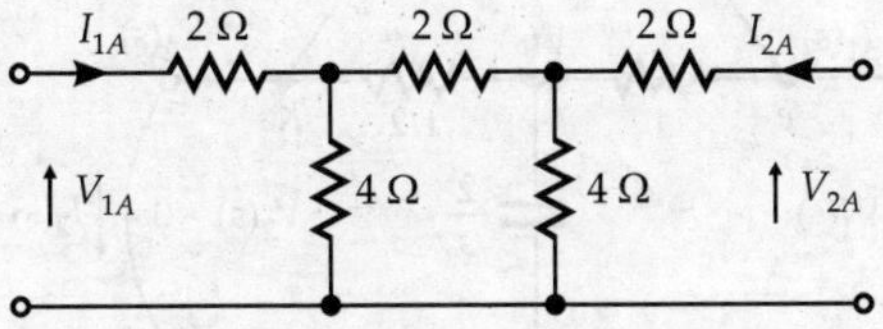

Fig. E19.106 (b)

Keeping the secondary short circuited, we get $V_{2A} = 0$ [Fig. E19.106(c)]

$$V_{1A} = I_{1A}\left[\left\{\frac{4\times 2}{4+2}+2\right\}\|4\right]+2I_{1A}$$

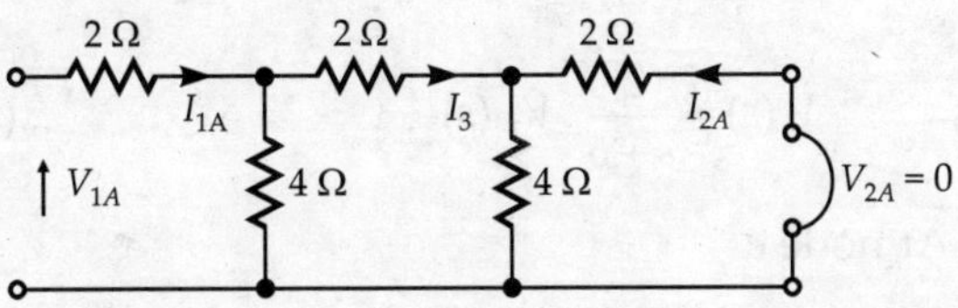

Fig. E19.106 (c)

This gives

$$V_{1A} = 3.818\, I_{1A}$$

$$\therefore \quad Y_{11A} = V_{1A}/I_{1A} = 3.818.$$

Also, $$I_3 = I_{1A}\times\frac{4}{4+2+\dfrac{4\times 2}{4+2}} = \frac{12}{22}I_{1A}$$

$$-I_{2A} = I_3\frac{4}{2+4} = \frac{4}{11}I_{1A}$$

$$\therefore \quad Y_{21A} = \frac{I_{2A}}{V_{1A}} = \frac{-(4/11)\,I_{1A}}{3.818\, I_{1A}} = -0.095$$

Next we apply short circuit at the input of the circuit shown in Fig. E19.106(b) [see Fig. E19.106(d)].

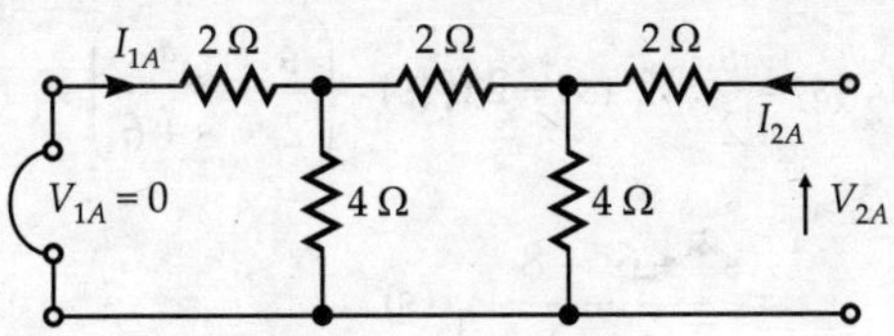

Fig. E19.106 (d)

Here,

$$V_{2A} = 2I_{2A} + I_{2A}\left[2+\left(\frac{2\times 4}{2+4}\right)\right]\|4$$

$$= (42/11)\, I_{2A}$$

$$\therefore \quad Y_{22A} = \frac{I_{2A}}{V_{2A}} = \frac{11}{42} = 0.262.$$

Since the given circuit is a symmetrical circuit, we can write

$$Y_{21A} = Y_{12A} = -0.095.$$

$\therefore$ We have

$$\begin{bmatrix} Y_{11A} & Y_{12A} \\ Y_{21A} & Y_{22A}\end{bmatrix} = \begin{bmatrix} 3.818 & -0.095 \\ -0.095 & 0.262\end{bmatrix}$$

We observe that network B is identical to network A; hence for network B we can write,

$$\begin{bmatrix} Y_{11B} & Y_{12B} \\ Y_{21B} & Y_{22B}\end{bmatrix} = \begin{bmatrix} 3.818 & -0.095 \\ -0.095 & 0.262\end{bmatrix}$$

Since both the networks A and B are in parallel, the final Y parameters will be

$$\begin{bmatrix} Y_{11} & Y_{12} \\ Y_{21} & Y_{22}\end{bmatrix} = \begin{bmatrix} Y_{11A}+Y_{11B} & Y_{12A}+Y_{12B} \\ Y_{21B}+Y_{21B} & Y_{22A}+Y_{22B}\end{bmatrix}$$

$$= \begin{bmatrix} 7.636 & -0.190 \\ -0.19 & 0.524\end{bmatrix}$$

Hence for the network of Fig. E19.106(a), the Y parameters are obtained as

$$\begin{bmatrix} \mathbf{7.636} & \mathbf{-0.19} \\ \mathbf{-0.19} & \mathbf{0.524}\end{bmatrix}\ \textbf{mho.}$$

EXAMPLE 19.132 *In Fig. E19.107, determine ABCD parameters.*

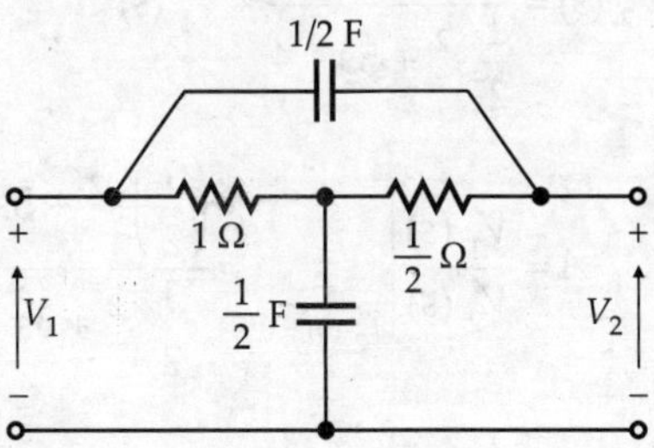

Fig. E19.107

SOLUTION. Let us redraw the given circuit in Laplace domain [Fig. E19.107(a)] when the output of the given circuit is open.

In mesh *aefgb*, KVL yields

$$[I_1(s) - I(s)]\times 1 + I_1(s)\times\frac{2}{s} = V_1(s)$$

or $$V_1(s) = I_1(s)\left[1+\frac{2}{s}\right] - I(s) \qquad ...(1)$$

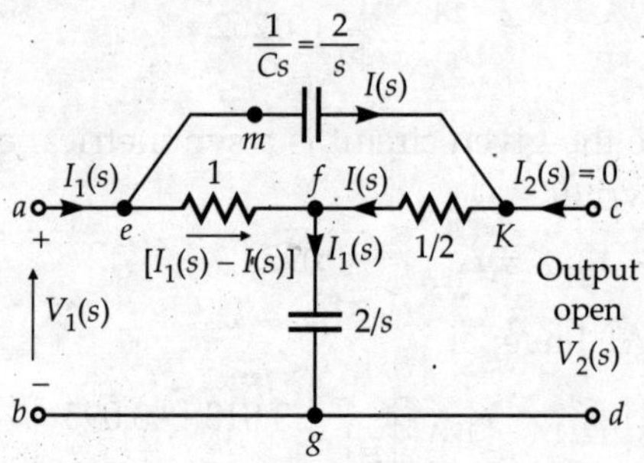

Fig. E19.107 (*a*)

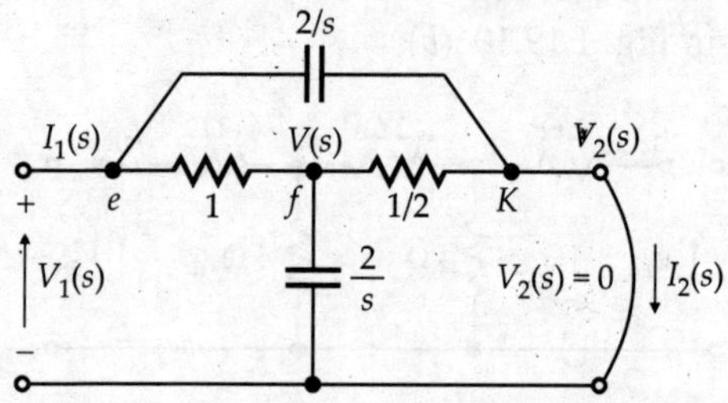

Fig. E19.107 (*b*)

In mesh *emkf*, KVL yields

$$0 = I(s)\left[\frac{2}{s}+\frac{1}{2}\right]+[I(s)-I_1(s)]\times 1$$

or
$$0 = -I(s)+\left[\frac{3}{2}+\frac{2}{s}\right]I(s) \qquad ...(2)$$

Solving (1) and (2), we find

$$I_1(s) = \frac{s\left(\frac{3}{2}s+2\right)}{0.5s^2+\frac{1}{2}s+4}\times V_1(s) \qquad ...(3)$$

Again from Fig. E19.107(*a*) it is evident that

$$V_2(s) = I(s)\times\frac{1}{2}+I_1(s)\times\frac{2}{s} \qquad ...(4)$$

Using (3) in (4),

$$V_2(s) = \frac{\frac{1}{2}s^2+3s+4}{\frac{1}{2}s^2+5s+4}\times V_1(s)$$

$$\therefore \quad A = \left.\frac{V_1(s)}{V_2(s)}\right|_{I_2(s)=0} = \frac{\left(\frac{1}{2}\right)s^2+5s+4}{\frac{1}{2}s^2+3s+4}$$

and
$$C = \left.\frac{I_1(s)}{V_2(s)}\right|_{I_2(s)=0}$$

$$= \frac{s\left(\frac{3}{2}s+2\right)}{\frac{1}{2}s^2+3s+4} \text{ mho.}$$

Next, we make output of the given network shorted, *i.e.*, $V_2(s)=0$ and $I_2(s)$ is directed outwards. [Fig. E19.107(*b*)]

At node *f*,

$$\frac{V(s)-V_1(s)}{1}+\frac{V(s)}{2/s}+\frac{V(s)-V_2(s)}{1/2}=0$$

or
$$V(s) = \frac{2}{s+6}\cdot V_1(s) \qquad ...(5)$$

At node *e*,

$$-I_1(s)+\frac{V_1(s)-0}{2/s}+\frac{V_1(s)-V(s)}{1}=0$$

or
$$-I_1(s)+\frac{V_1(s).s}{2}+V_1(s)-V(s)=0$$

or
$$I_1(s) = \left[\frac{s}{2}+1-\frac{2}{s+6}\right]V_1(s)$$

$$= \frac{s^2+8s+8}{2(s+6)}\cdot V_1(s) \qquad ...(6)$$

At node *K*, $I_2(s)+\dfrac{0-V(s)}{1/2}+\dfrac{0-V_1(s)}{\frac{2}{s}}=0$

or
$$I_2(s)-2V(s)-\frac{s}{2}\cdot V_1(s)=0$$

$$\therefore\ I_2(s) = \frac{s}{2}\cdot V_1(s)+2V(s) = \left(\frac{s}{2}+\frac{4}{s+6}\right)V_1(s)$$

$$= \frac{s^2+6s+8}{2(s+6)}V_1(s) \qquad ...(7)$$

$$\therefore \quad B = \left.\frac{V_1(s)}{-I_2(s)}\right|_{V_2(s)=0} = \frac{-2(s+6)}{s^2+6s+8}\,\Omega$$

and
$$D = \left.\frac{I_1(s)}{-I_2(s)}\right|_{V_2(s)=0} = \frac{-(s^2+8s+8)}{s^2+6s+8}$$

$$\therefore \quad A = \frac{\frac{1}{2}s^2 + 5s + 4}{\frac{1}{2}s^2 + 3s + 4}; \quad B = \frac{-2\,(s+6)}{s^2 + 6s + 8}$$

$$C = \frac{s\left(\frac{3}{2}s + 2\right)}{\frac{1}{2}s^2 + 3s + 4}; \quad D = \frac{-(s^2 + 8s + 8)}{s^2 + 6s + 8}.$$

EXAMPLE 19.133 *In Fig. E19.108, two 2-port networks are in parallel – one 2-port network contains only a gyrator while the other is a resistive network having a controlled source. Determine Y-parameters for the combined networks.*

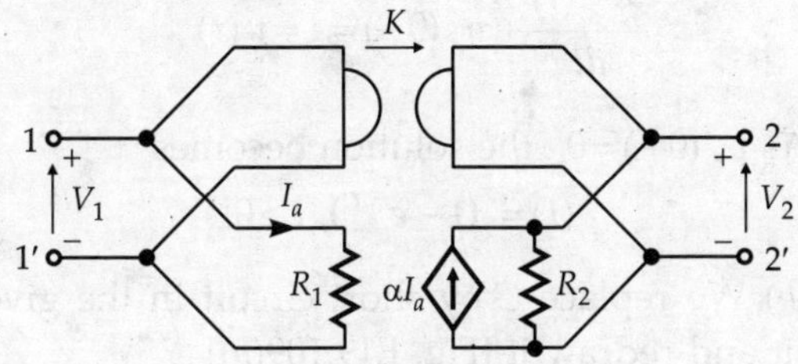

Fig. E19.108

SOLUTION. Let us redraw the given circuit with assumed current directions [Fig. E19.108(*a*)].

where I = gyrator primary current

I' = gyrator secondary current

I'_a = input current from terminal-2 to the controlled source

I_1 = input current from terminal-1

I_2 = input current from terminal-2

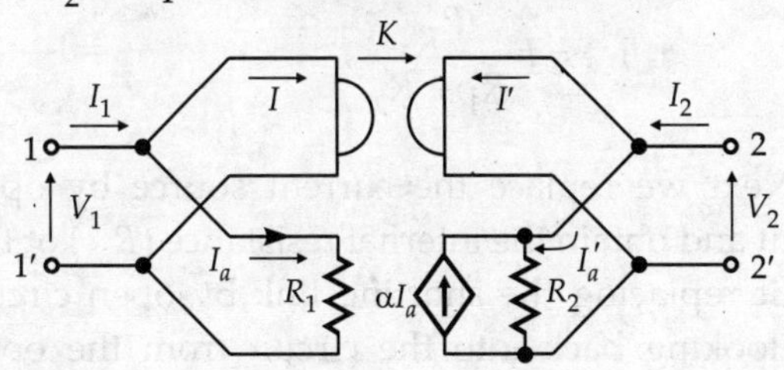

Fig. E19.108(*a*)

Since the gyrator is characterised by

$$V_1 = -KI' \text{ and } V_2 = KI,$$

the nodal equations in the gyrator part can be expressed as

$$I = 0.V_1 + I = 0.V_1 + \frac{V_2}{K} \qquad ...(1)$$

and
$$I' = I' + 0.V_2 = -\frac{V_1}{K} + 0.V_2 \qquad ...(2)$$

However for *y*-port representation,

$$I = Y_{11}V_1 + Y_{12}V_2\,;$$

$$I' = Y_{21}V_1 + Y_{22}V_2$$

Comparing these *Y*-parameter equations with (1) and (2),

$$Y_{11} = 0\,; \; Y_{12} = \frac{1}{K}\,; \; Y_{21} = -\frac{1}{K}\,; \; Y_{22} = 0.$$

Thus, for the gyrator part

$$[Y]_G = \begin{bmatrix} 0 & 1/K \\ -\frac{1}{K} & 0 \end{bmatrix}$$

Again, for the lower part of the network,

$$V_1 = I_a R_1$$

i.e.,
$$I_a = \frac{V_1}{R_1} + 0.V_2 \qquad ...(3)$$

and
$$V_2 = (\alpha I_a + I'_a).R_2$$

or
$$V_2 = \alpha.\frac{V_1}{R_1}.R_2 + I'_a R_2$$

$$= R_2\left[\frac{\alpha V_1}{R_1} + I'_a\right]$$

or
$$I'_a + \frac{\alpha V_1}{R_1} = \frac{V_2}{R_2}$$

or
$$I'_a = -\frac{\alpha V_1}{R_1} + \frac{V_2}{R_2} \qquad ...(4)$$

Again, comparing (3) and (4) with *Y*-parameter representations given by

$$I_a = Y_{11}V_1 + Y_{12}V_2$$

$$I'_a = Y_{21}V_1 + Y_{22}V_2$$

we can write

$$Y_{11} = \frac{1}{R_1}\,; \; Y_{12} = 0\,; \; Y_{21} = -\frac{\alpha}{R_1}\,; \; Y_{22} = \frac{1}{R_2}$$

Thus, for the non-gyrator part,

$$[Y]_{NG} = \begin{bmatrix} \frac{1}{R_1} & 0 \\ -\frac{\alpha}{R_1} & \frac{1}{R_2} \end{bmatrix}$$

Since both the circuits in the network are in parallel,

$$Y = \begin{bmatrix} \left(0+\frac{1}{R_1}\right) & \left(\frac{1}{K}+0\right) \\ \left(-\frac{1}{K}-\frac{\alpha}{R_1}\right) & \left(0+\frac{1}{R_2}\right) \end{bmatrix}$$

$$= \begin{bmatrix} \left(\frac{\mathbf{1}}{\mathbf{R_1}}\right) & \left(\frac{\mathbf{1}}{\mathbf{K}}\right) \\ -\left(\frac{\mathbf{1}}{\mathbf{K}}+\frac{\alpha}{\mathbf{R_1}}\right) & \left(\frac{\mathbf{1}}{\mathbf{R_2}}\right) \end{bmatrix}.$$

EXAMPLE 19.134 *A delta circuit is suddenly energized by switching action as shown in Fig. E19.109(a).*

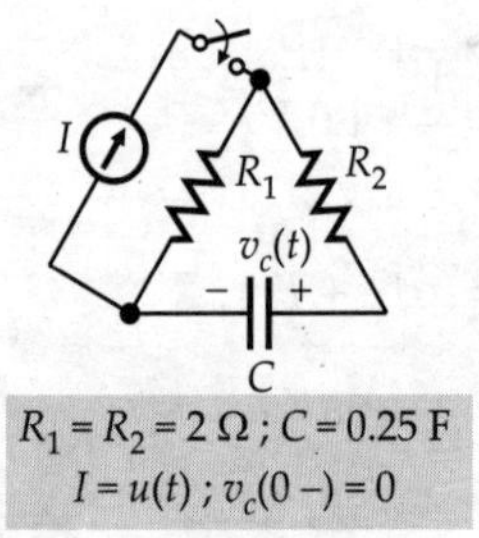

Fig. E19.109(a)

(a) Obtain $v_c(t)$ for $t > 0$.

(b) Use Norton's theorem to obtain the differential equation of the circuit assuming C the load.

SOLUTION. (a) In the given delta circuit, R_2 is in series with C. Let v_{R_1} be the voltage across R_1.

$\because$ Voltage across R_1 = Voltage across R_2 and C,

$$\therefore \qquad v_{R_1} = R_2 C \frac{dv_c(t)}{dt} + v_c(0-)$$

[where $v_c(0-)$ is initial capacitor voltage before switching]

The differential equation of the given circuit is given by

$$I = \frac{v_{R_1}}{R_1} + C\frac{dv_c(t)}{dt} \qquad [\because \text{ current through the capacitor at } t = 0+ \text{ is } C.\frac{dv_c(t)}{dt}]$$

or
$$I = \frac{1}{R_1}\left[R_2 C\frac{dv_c(t)}{dt} + v_c(0-)\right] + C\frac{dv_c(t)}{dt}$$

or
$$I = C\left[\frac{R_2}{R_1}+1\right]\frac{dv_c(t)}{dt} + \frac{1}{R_1}.v_c(0-)$$

or
$$I.R_1 = C(R_1+R_2)\frac{dv_c(t)}{dt} + v_c(0-)$$

or
$$\frac{dv_c(t)}{dt} + Av_c(0-) = I\frac{R_1}{C(R_1+R_2)} \qquad ...(1)$$

where $A = \dfrac{1}{C(R_1+R_2)}$.

Substituting the values of R_1, R_2, C and I we get the final form of equation (1) for the given problem as

$$\frac{dv_c(t)}{dt} + v_c(0-) = I = u(t)$$

As $v_c(0-) = 0$, the solution becomes

$$v_c(t) = \mathbf{(1-e^{-t}),\ t > 0.}$$

(b) We replace C by short circuit in the given circuit and redraw it [Fig. E19.109(b)]

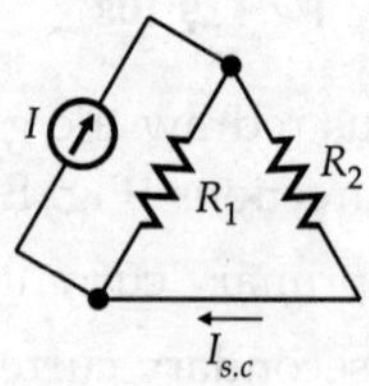

Fig. E19.109(b)

The Norton's equivalent current ($I_{s.c}$) is given by

$$I_{s.c} = I\frac{R_K}{R_1+R_2}$$

Next we replace the current source by open circuit and obtain the internal resistance (R_N) of the circuit replacing the shorting link by open circuit and looking back into the circuit from the open circuit.

$$R_N = R_1 + R_2$$

The Norton's equivalent circuit is drawn next [Fig. E19.109(c)].

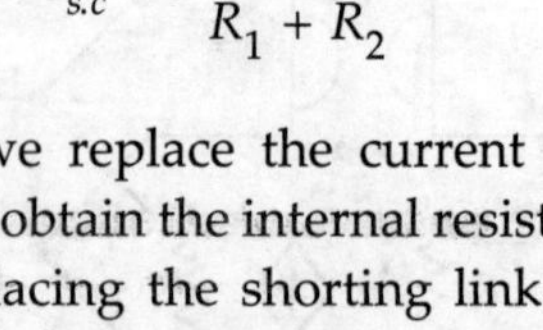

Fig. E19.109(c)

Here, $I_{s.c} = (I_N) = \dfrac{v_c(0-)}{R_N} + C\dfrac{dv_c(t)}{dt}$

[at $t = 0+$] ...(2)

However,

$$I_{s.c} = I\frac{R_1}{R_1 + R_2}$$

and $R_N = R_1 + R_2$

Using these values in equation (2), we get

$$I\frac{R_1}{R_1 + R_2} = \frac{v_c(0-)}{R_1 + R_2} + C\frac{dv_c(t)}{dt}$$

or $$\frac{dv_c(t)}{dt} + \frac{1}{C(R_1 + R_2)} \cdot v_c(0-) = I\frac{R_1}{C(R_1 + R_2)}$$

or $$\frac{dv_c(t)}{dt} + Av_c(0-) = I\frac{R_1}{C(R_1 + R_2)} \qquad ...(3)$$

Equation (3) represents the differential equation using Norton theorem for the given circuit. It may be observed that equations (1) and (3) an identical.

EXAMPLE 19.135 *In a RLC parallel circuit, the inductor L is carrying a current i_L (= I) while the capacitor is charged at a voltage v_0 at the moment of switching on at $t = (0+)$. Obtain the expressions for $i_L(t)$ and $v_L(t)$ at $t > 0$. [assume underdamped condition in the circuit]*

SOLUTION. Figure E19.110 represents the circuit configuration just during the moment of switching. Obviously the voltage across all the elements

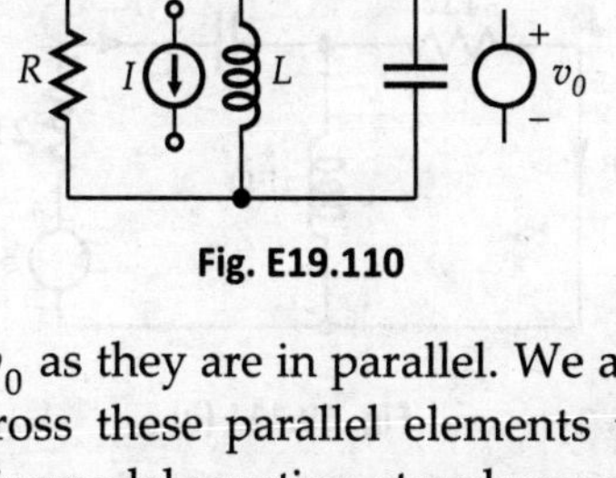

Fig. E19.110

would be v_0 as they are in parallel. We assume the voltage across these parallel elements to be v at $t = (0+)$. Using nodal equation, at node x we can write:

$$\frac{v}{R} + C\frac{dv}{dt} + i_L = 0 \qquad ...(1)$$

[∵ the current through the inductor at $t = 0+$ is i_L and the current through the capacitor is $\left(C\dfrac{dv}{dt}\right)$]

Also, $$v = L\frac{di_L}{dt} \qquad ...(2)$$

Differentiating (1) and using (2), we get

$$C\frac{d^2v}{dt^2} + \frac{1}{R}\frac{dv}{dt} + \frac{1}{L} \cdot v = 0$$

or $$\frac{d^2v}{dt^2} + \frac{1}{RC}\frac{dv}{dt} + \frac{1}{LC} \cdot v = 0 \qquad ...(3)$$

Also from (3) using (2) we can write

$$\frac{d^2i_L}{dt^2} + \frac{1}{RC}\frac{di_L}{dt} + \frac{1}{LC}i_L = 0 \qquad ...(4)$$

Both (3) and (4) can be expressed in the following form (as explained in Art 5.2)

$$\frac{d^2y}{dt^2} + 2\alpha\frac{dy}{dt} + \omega_0^2 y = 0 \qquad ...(5)$$

Here $2\alpha = \dfrac{1}{RC}$; $\omega_0^2 = \dfrac{1}{LC}$

If $\alpha < \omega_0$ [underdamped condition], the natural response is given by

$$y_n = e^{-\alpha t}(K_1 \cos\omega_d t + K_2 \sin\omega_2 t) \qquad ...(6)$$

The constants K_1 and K_2 can be evaluated from initial conditions.

At $t = (0+)$, $v(t = 0+) = V_0$

[since capacitor voltage cannot change abruptly from its value at $t = (0-)$]

Also, $C.\dfrac{dv}{dt}$ at $t = (0+)$ is given by

$$C\frac{dv}{dt} = -\left(\frac{V_0}{R} + I\right)$$

[using equation (1) with initial condition]

∴ From (6) at $t = (0+)$, we find

$$v(0+) \equiv V_0 = K_1$$

Differentiating equation (6) and using $\dfrac{dv}{dt} = -\dfrac{1}{C}\left(\dfrac{V_0}{R} + I\right)$ at $t = 0+$, we finally obtain

$$-\alpha K_1 + \omega_d K_2 = -\frac{1}{C}\left(\frac{V_0}{R} + I\right)$$

∴ $$B = -\frac{1}{\omega_d}\left(\alpha V_0 + \frac{I}{C}\right) \quad \left[\because 2\alpha = \frac{1}{RC}\right]$$

$$\therefore v(t) = v_L(t) = e^{-\alpha t}\left[V_0 \cos \omega_d t - \frac{\alpha}{\omega_d} . V_0 \sin \omega_d t - \frac{I}{\omega_d C} \sin \omega_d t\right], \text{ for } t > 0.$$

In order to find the solution for current, we use equation (4) in the form of equation (5) when equation (6) represents the solution.

Here also, at $t = (0+)$,

$$i_L(0+) = I$$

and $$L\frac{di_L}{dt}(0+) = v(0+) = V_0$$

This gives $$K_1 = I$$

and $$-\alpha K_1 + \omega_d K_2 = (V_0 / L)$$

Obtaining the values of K_1 and K_2 as done in the previous case, we get

$$i_L(t) = e^{-\alpha t}\left(I \cos \omega_d t + \frac{\alpha}{\omega_d} . I \sin \omega_d t + \frac{V_0}{L . \omega_d} \sin \omega_d . t\right), \text{ for } t > 0.$$

EXAMPLE 19.136 *Determine the value of K such that the roots of the characteristic equation given below lie to the left of line s = – 1.*

$$s^3 + 10s^2 + 18s + k = 0.$$

SOLUTION. With $s = (s_1 - 1)$, we can write from the given equation

$$(s_1 - 1)2^3 + 10(s_1 - 1)^2 + 18(s_1 - 1) + k = 0$$

or $$s_1^3 + 7s_1^2 + s_1 + (k - 9) = 0$$

The Routh's tabulation is given below :

s_1^3	1
s_1^2	7
s_1^1	$\frac{7-(k-q)}{7}$
s_1^0	$k-9$

To have stability, from Routh's table we observe

$$9 < k < 16$$

Then it is evident that *K* can have any value between 9 and 16 for the given characteristic equation to have stability.

EXAMPLE 19.137 *Verify Reciprocity Theorem for the network shown in Fig. E19.111(a).*

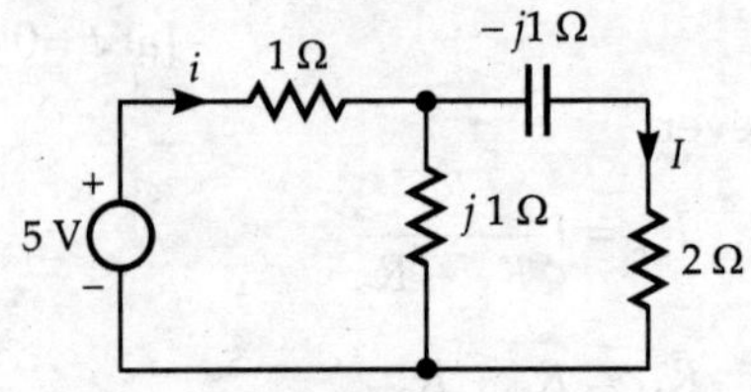

Fig. 19.111 (a)

SOLUTION. Step 1. Net impedance across the SV source is

$$Z = [(2 - j1)\, j1] + 1$$

$$= \left[\frac{(2 - j1)j1}{2 - j1 + j1}\right] + 1$$

$$= \frac{j2 + 1}{2} + 1 = \left(\frac{3 + j2}{2}\right)\Omega$$

The total current from the 5 V is obtained as

$$i = \frac{5}{Z} = \frac{5.2}{3 + j2} = \frac{10}{3 + j2} \text{ A}$$

Therefore

$$I = i_1 . \frac{j1}{j1 + (2 - j1)} = \frac{j5}{3 + j2} \text{ A}$$

Step 2. From Fig. E19.111(*b*), net impedance is

$$Z = (1 \| j1) - j1 + 2 = \frac{j1}{1 + j1} - j1 + 2$$

$$= j0.5 + 0.5 - j1 + 2 = 2.5 - j0.5 = 0.5(5 - j)\Omega$$

So $$i' = \frac{5}{Z} = \frac{5}{0.5(5 - j)}$$

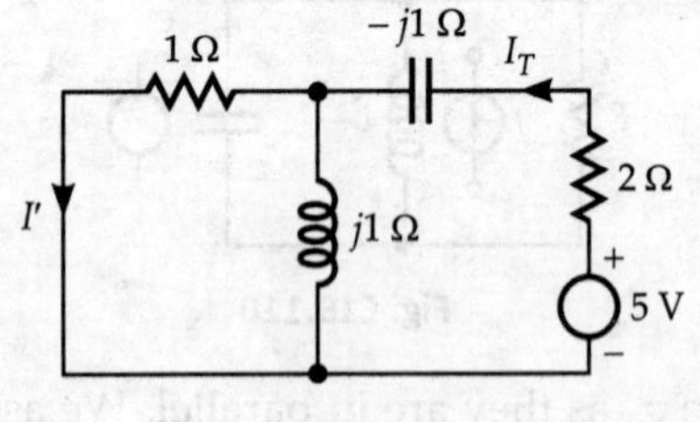

Fig. 19.111 (*b*)

Therefore $$I' = \frac{j1}{j1 + 1} . i' = \frac{j5}{0.5(5 - j)(j1 + 1)}$$

$$= \frac{j5}{0.5[j5 + 5 + 1 - j]} = \frac{j5}{3 + j2}$$

Since $I = I'$

Hence, reciprocity theorem is verified.

EXAMPLE 19.138 *Using Millman's theorem, find the current in the load impedance $Z = (2 + j4)\,\Omega$ for the circuit shown in Fig. E19.112.*

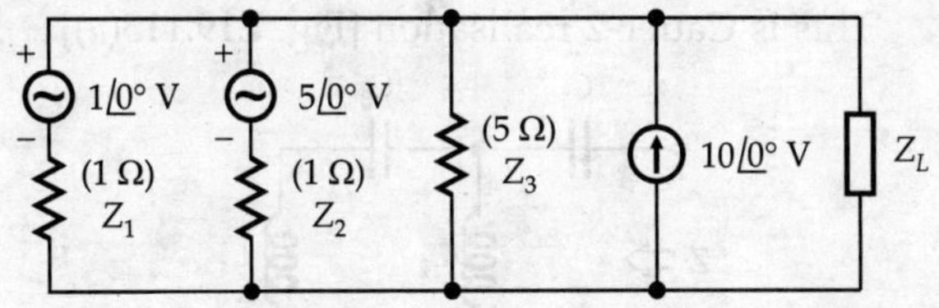

Fig. 19.112

SOLUTION. Converting current source into a equivalent voltage source as [Fig. E19.112(*a*)], we get

$$E_1 = 1\angle 0° = 1 \text{ Volt}$$

$$E_2 = 5\angle 0° = 5 \text{ V}$$

$$E_3 = 50\angle 0° = 50 \text{ V}$$

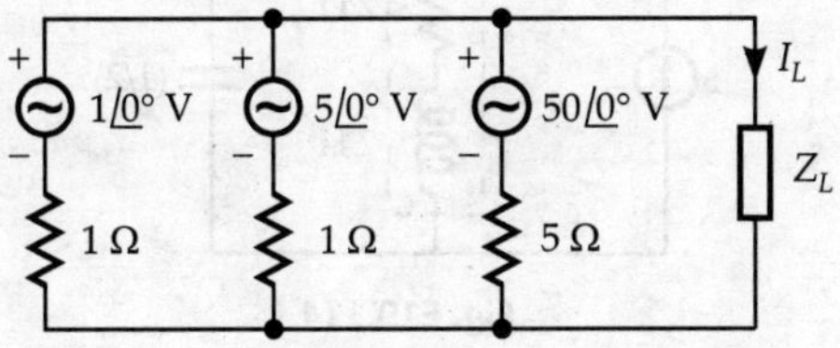

Fig. 19.112 (*a*)

Also

$$Y_1 = \frac{1}{Z_1} = \frac{1}{1} = 1 = 1 \text{ mho}$$

$$Y_2 = \frac{1}{Z_2} = \frac{1}{1} = 1 \text{ mho}$$

$$Y_3 = \frac{1}{Z_3} = \frac{1}{5} = 0.2 \text{ mho}$$

Applying Millman's theorem,

$$V_m = \frac{\sum_{i=1}^{3} V_i Y_i}{\sum_{i=1}^{3} Y_i}$$

$$= \frac{1\times 1 + 5\times 1 + 50\times 0.2}{1+1+0.2} = \frac{1+5+10}{2.2} = 7.272$$

$$Z_m = \frac{1}{\sum_{i=1}^{3} Y_i} = \frac{1}{2.2} = 0.4545\,\Omega$$

The equivalent circuit is given as in Fig. E19.112(*b*).

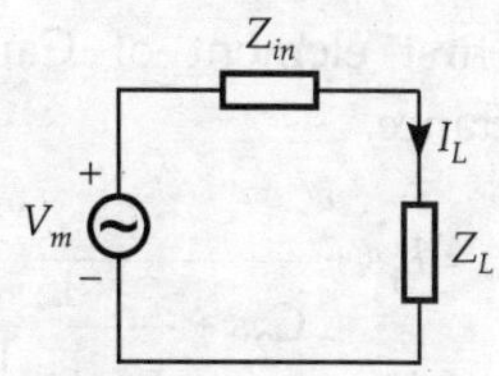

Fig. 19.112 (*b*)

$$I_L = \frac{V_m}{Z_m + Z_L}$$

$$= \frac{7.272}{0.4545 + 2 + j4} = \frac{7.272}{2.4545 + j4}$$

$$= \frac{7.272}{4.69\angle 58.46°} = \mathbf{1.56\angle -58.50°\ A.}$$

EXAMPLE 19.139 *The driving point impedance of a reactive network is given by*

$$Z(s) = \frac{2(s^2+1)(s^2+3)}{s(s^2+2)}.$$

Develop Cauer types of network.

SOLUTION.

$$Z(s) = \frac{2(s^2+1)(s^2+3)}{s(s^2+2)} = \frac{2s^4+8s^2+6}{s^3+2s}$$

Now we proceed for Cauer-1 network by continued fraction

$$s^3 + 2s)\ 2s^4 + 8s^2 + 6\ (2s$$
$$\underline{2s^4 + 4s^2}$$
$$4s^2 + 6)\ s^3 + 2s\ (1/4s$$
$$\underline{s^3 + \tfrac{3}{2}s}$$
$$\tfrac{1}{2}s)\ 4s^2 + 6\ (8s$$
$$\underline{4s^2}$$
$$6)\ s/2\ (s/12$$
$$\underline{s/2}$$
$$\times$$

$$\therefore \quad Z(s) = 2s + \cfrac{1}{\cfrac{1}{4}s + \cfrac{1}{8s + \cfrac{1}{s/12}}} \qquad ...(1)$$

Observation reveals that the degree of polynomial in numerator is greater than that of denominator by unity *i.e.*, $n > m$. Also, $Z(s) \to \infty$ with $s \to \infty$.

Thus the first element of Cauer-1 network becomes inductance.

i.e.,
$$Z(s) = L_1 s + \cfrac{1}{C_2 s + \cfrac{1}{L_3 s + \cfrac{1}{C_4 s}}} \qquad ...(2)$$

the network being shown in Fig. E19.113.

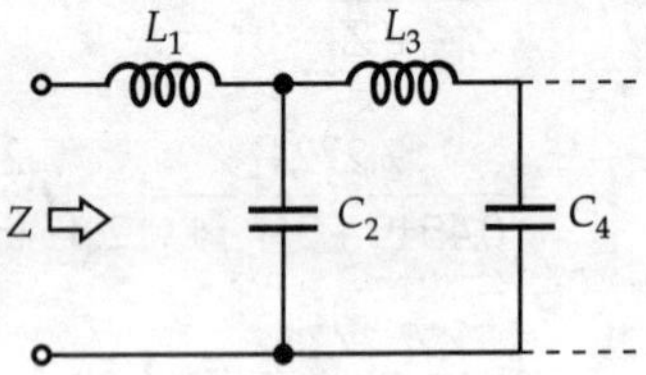

Fig. E19.113

Comparison of (1) and (2) reveals

$$L_1 = 2\text{ H},\quad C_2 = \frac{1}{4}\text{ F},\quad L_3 = 8\text{ H},\quad C_4 = \frac{1}{12}\text{ F}.$$

Next we proceed for Cauer-2 network realisation. We write $Z(s)$ as follows :

$$Z(s) = \frac{6 + 8s^2 + 2s^4}{2s + s^3}$$

We now perform continued fraction ;

$2s + s^3)\ 6 + 8s^2 + 2s^4\ (3/s$
$6 + 3s^2$
$5s^2 + 2s^4)\ 2s + s^3\ (2/5s$
$2s + \frac{4}{5}s^3$
$\frac{1}{5}s^3)\ 5s^2 + 2s^4\ (25/s$
$5s^2$
$2s^4)\ 1/5s^3\ (1/10s$
$1/5s^3$
$\times$

$$\therefore \quad Z(s) = \frac{3}{s} + \cfrac{1}{\cfrac{2}{5s} + \cfrac{1}{\cfrac{25}{s} + \cfrac{1}{s/10s}}} \qquad ...(3)$$

Since the degree of the polynomial is higher in numerator and since $Z(s) \to \infty$ with $s \to 0$, we can write for the Cauer-2 realisation [Fig. E19.113(*a*)],

$$Z(s) = \frac{1}{C_1 s} + \cfrac{1}{\cfrac{1}{L_2 s} + \cfrac{1}{\cfrac{1}{C_3 s} + \cfrac{1}{L_4 s} + \ldots\ldots}} \qquad ...(4)$$

Comparing (3) and (4),

$$C_1 = \frac{1}{3}\text{ F};\quad L_2 = \frac{5}{2}\text{ H};\quad C_3 = \frac{1}{25}\text{ F},\quad L_4 = 10\text{ H}.$$

This is Cauer-2 realisation [Fig. E19.113(*a*)].

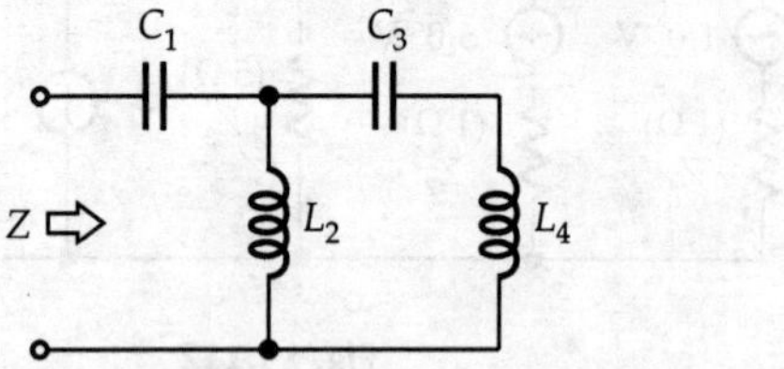

Fig. E19.113 (*a*)

Example 19.140 *At steady state SW is open (Fig. 19.114). SW is closed at $t = 0$. If $i_L(t)$ is the current in the inductor, at $t = 0$, find $\frac{d}{dt}(i_L)$.*

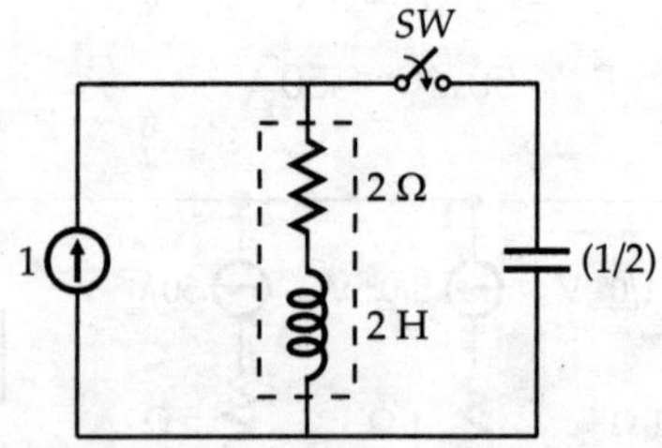

Fig. E19.114

Solution. At $t = 0(+)$ we have the circuit as shown in Fig. 19.114(*a*).

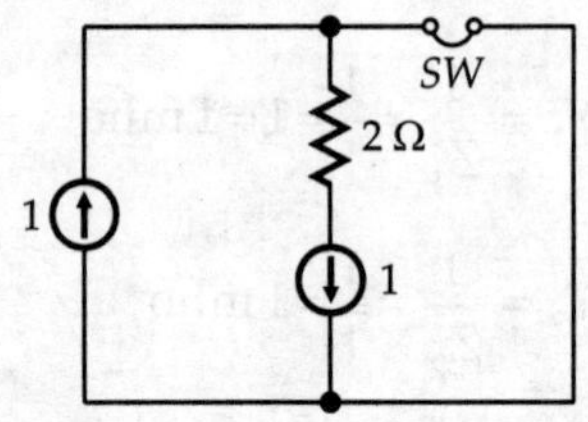

Fig. E19.114 (*a*)

It may be noted that as at $t = (0-)$, the current was 1 A at the inductor hence at $t = 0(+)$, same 1 A current will flow through the inductor.

At $t = 0$, C acts as short circuit.

At $t = (0+)$;

$$V_R(\text{drop across } R) + V_L(\text{drop across } L) = 0$$

But $\quad V_R = 2 \times 1 = 2$ V.

$\therefore \quad V_L = -2$ V

Since $\quad V_L = L\frac{di_L}{dt}$,

hence $\quad \frac{di_L}{dt} = \frac{V_L}{L} = -\frac{2}{2} = \mathbf{-1\ A/s.}$

CHAPTER

20

Multiple Choice Questions

M20.1 *For the circuit shown in Fig. 20.1, R_{eq} is obtained as*

(a) $\frac{2}{3}R$ (b) $\frac{1}{3}R$

(c) $3R$ (d) $6R$

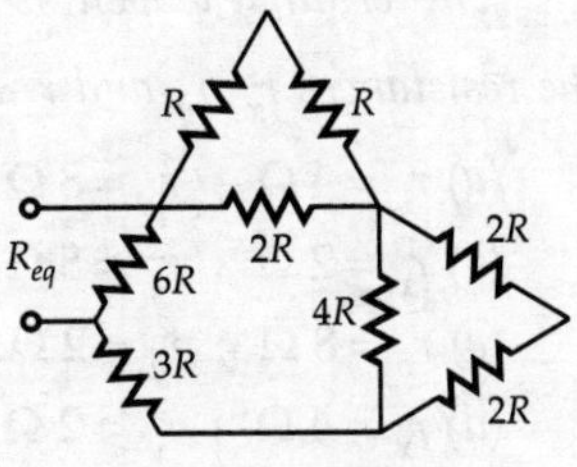

Fig. 20.1

Solution. The given circuit is simplified as shown in Fig. 20.2

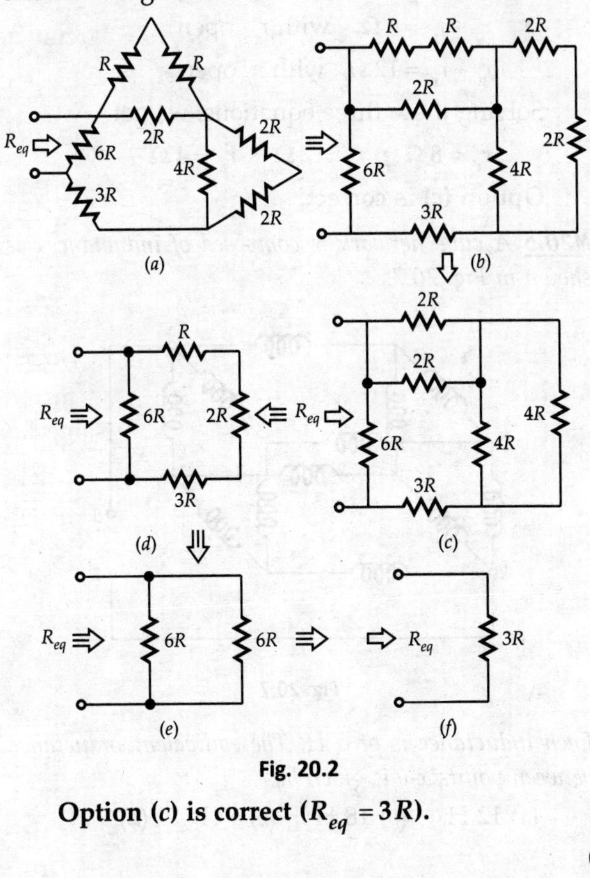

Fig. 20.2

Option (c) is correct ($R_{eq} = 3R$).

M20.2 *The current i (in ampere) in the load R_L (Fig. 20.3) is given by*

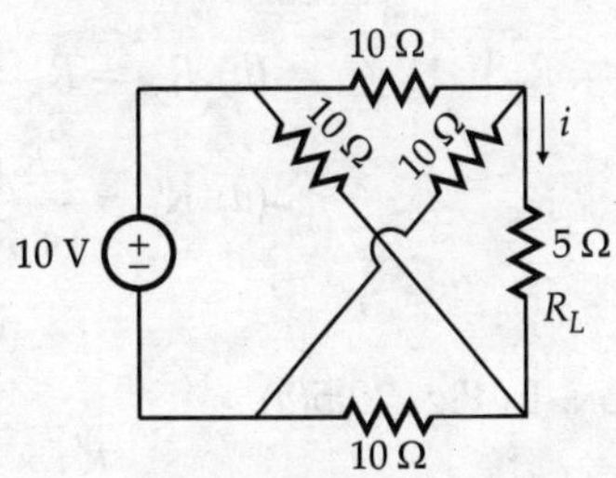

Fig. 20.3

(a) 0 (b) 0.5 A

(c) 1 A (d) 2.5 A

Solution. The given circuit be redrawn as follows (Fig. 20.4) :

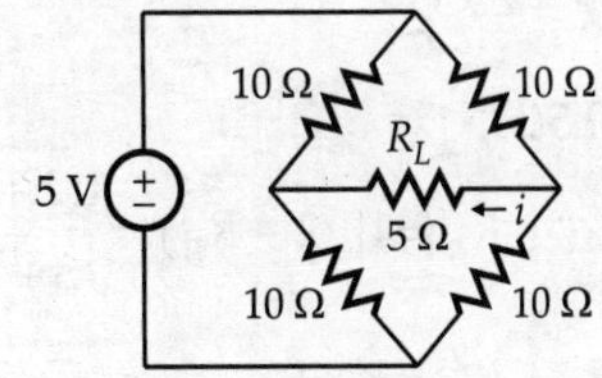

Fig. 20.4

It is evident that the given circuit is basically a Wheatstone bridge.

Since it is a balanced bridge hence no current will flow through R_L.

$$\therefore \quad i = 0$$

Option (a) is correct.

M20.3 *R_A and R_B are the input resistances of the circuits as shown in Fig. 20.5(a) and Fig. 20.5(b). The circuits extend infinitely in the direction shown. Which of the following statements is TRUE ?*

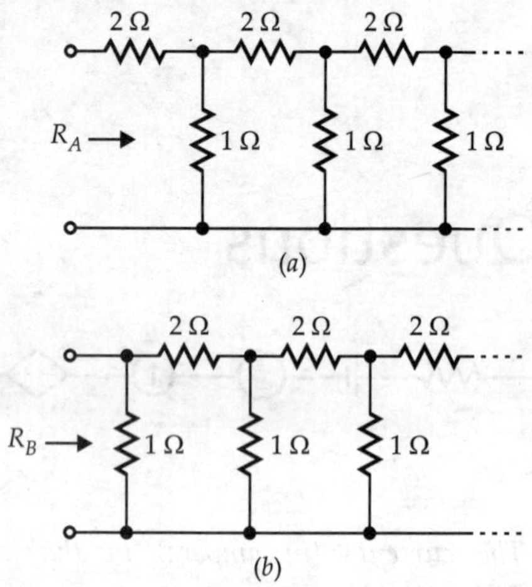

Fig. 20.5

(*a*) $R_A = R_B$ (*b*) $R_A = R_B = 0$

(*c*) $R_A < R_B$ (*d*) $R_B = \dfrac{R_A}{1+R_A}$

[GATE 2016]

Solution. In Fig. 20.5(*a*),

$$R_A = 2 + R_A || 1 = 2 + \frac{R_A \times 1}{R_A + 1}$$

or, $$R_A^2 + R_A = 2R_A + 2 + R_A$$

or, $$R_A^2 - 2R_A - 2 = 0$$

$\therefore$ $R_A =$ either 2.73 Ω or − 0.73 Ω.

Since negative value of resistance can be neglected, $R_A = 2.73\ \Omega$.

In Fig. 20.5(*b*),

$$R_B = 1||(2+R_B) = \frac{1(2+R_B)}{3+R_B}$$

$\therefore$ $$3R_B + R_B^2 = 2 + R_B$$

or, $$R_B^2 + 2R_B - 2 = 0$$

i.e., $R_B =$ either 0.73 Ω or − 2.73 Ω.

Neglecting the negative resistance, $R_B = 0.73\ \Omega$

$\therefore$ $R_A > R_B$

$$\left[R_B = \frac{R_A}{1+R_A} \text{ is correct as } \frac{2.73}{1+2.73} = 0.73\Omega \right]$$

Option (*d*) is correct.

M20.4 *A network of resistances is shown in Fig. 20.6. Observe the following statements :*

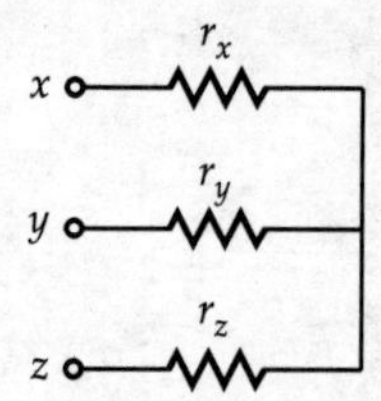

Fig. 20.6

(*i*) *The resistance between terminals x and y, with terminal z open, is 10 ohm.*

(*ii*) *The resistance between terminals y and z, with terminal x open, is 6 ohm.*

(*iii*) *The resistance between terminals x and z, with terminal y open, is 12 ohm.*

The resistances r_x, r_y and r_z are obtained as

(*a*) $r_x = 4\ \Omega$; $r_y = 8\ \Omega$; $r_z = 2\ \Omega$;

(*b*) $r_x = 2\ \Omega$; $r_y = 8\ \Omega$; $r_z = 6\ \Omega$;

(*c*) $r_x = 8\ \Omega$; $r_y = 2\ \Omega$; $r_z = 4\ \Omega$;

(*d*) $r_x = 4\ \Omega$; $r_y = 2\ \Omega$; $r_z = 8\ \Omega$;

Solution. As per question,

$r_x + r_y = 10\ \Omega$, with r_z open

$r_y + r_z = 6\ \Omega$, with r_x open

$r_z + r_x = 12\ \Omega$, with r_y open

Solving these three equations, we get

$$r_x = 8\ \Omega \ ; \ r_y = 2\ \Omega \ ; \ r_z = 4\ \Omega$$

Option (*c*) is correct.

M20.5 *A cube network is composed of inductances as shown in Fig. 20.7.*

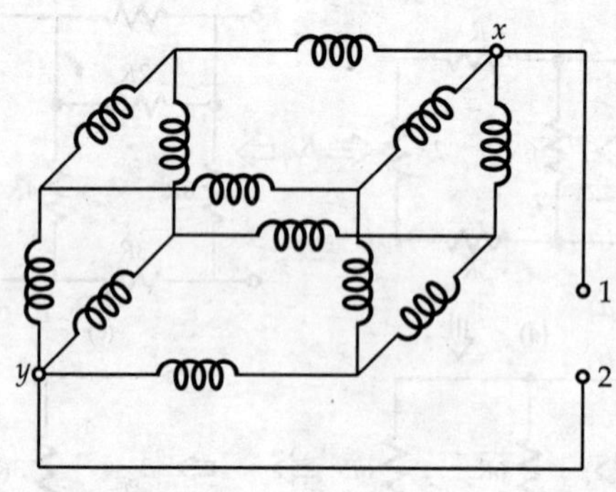

Fig. 20.7

Each inductance is of 6 H. The equivalent inductance between points x-y is given by

(*a*) 12 H (*b*) 18 H (*c*) 5 H (*d*) 9 H

Solution. Let a voltage V be applied at terminals 1-2 so that current I enters terminal x and gets divided to $\frac{I}{3}$ in each of the edge inductances as shown in Fig. 20.8.

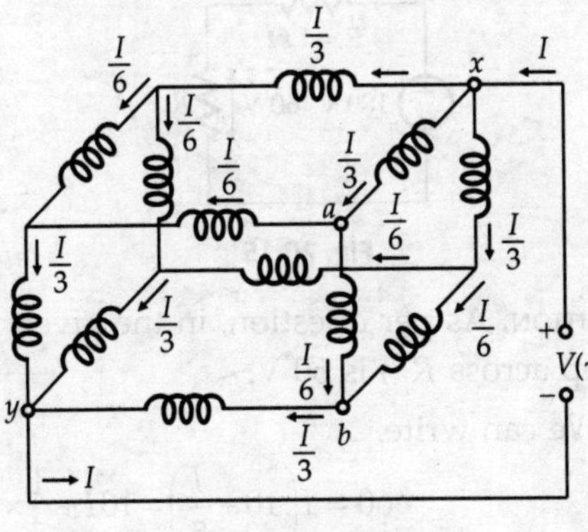

Fig. 20.8

$\frac{I}{3}$ gets further divided to $\frac{I}{6}$ to subsequent edge inductances. Following the distribution of currents, the current $\frac{I}{3}$ meets from each edge at point y and the exit current becomes I.

Observing symmetry of the network, application of KVL in path $xaby$ yields

$$-V+(j\omega\times 6)\frac{I}{3}+(j\omega\times 6)\frac{I}{6}+(j\omega\times 6)\frac{I}{3}=0$$

or,
$$V=j\omega\times 2I+j\omega I+j\omega\times 2I$$
$$=5(j\omega I)=(j\omega\times 5)I=j\omega L_{eq}\times I$$

$\therefore$ $\mathbf{L_{eq}=5\ H}$

Option (c) is correct.

M20.6 *A cube structure of capacitances has been shown in Fig. 20.9. Each edge of the cube has capacitance of 1 F. A current I enters terminal (x) and exits vertex (y) at voltage V with polarities marked. The equivalent capacitance between vertices x-y is*

(*a*) 2.5 F
(*b*) 1.2 F
(*c*) 3 F
(*d*) 1 F

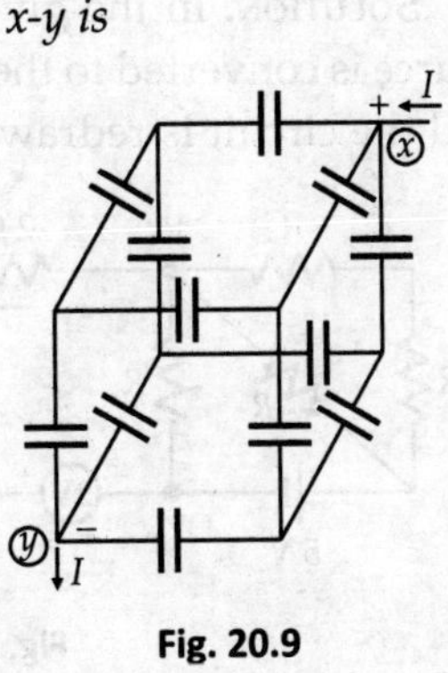

Fig. 20.9

Solution. The given figure is redrawn with current distribution diagram marked on Fig. 20.10.

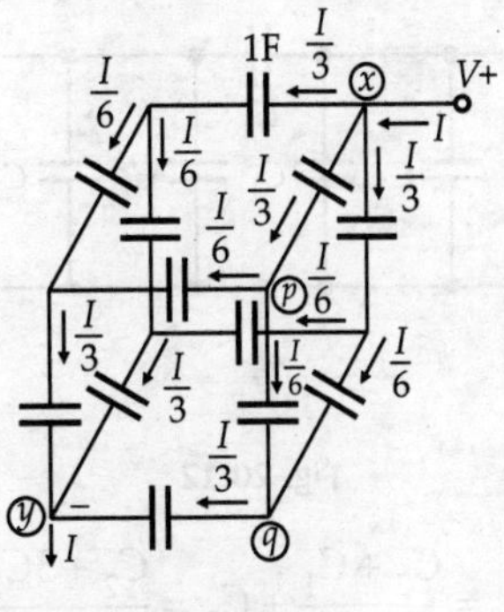

Fig. 20.10

In path x-p-q-y, KVL yields,

$$-V+\frac{I}{3}\times\frac{1}{j\omega\times 1}+\frac{I}{6}\times\frac{1}{j\omega\times 1}+\frac{I}{3}\times\frac{1}{j\omega\times 1}=0$$

$$\therefore \quad V=\frac{I}{j\omega}\left[\frac{1}{3}+\frac{1}{6}+\frac{1}{3}\right]=I\times\frac{1}{j\omega}\times\frac{5}{6}$$

$$=\frac{I}{j\omega\times\frac{6}{5}}=\frac{I}{j\omega\times C_{eq}}$$

$$\therefore \quad C_{eq}=\frac{6}{5}\text{F}=\mathbf{1.2\ F}$$

Option (*b*) is correct.

M20.7 *In Fig. 20.11, equivalent capacitance C_{eq} between terminals (1) and (3) is*

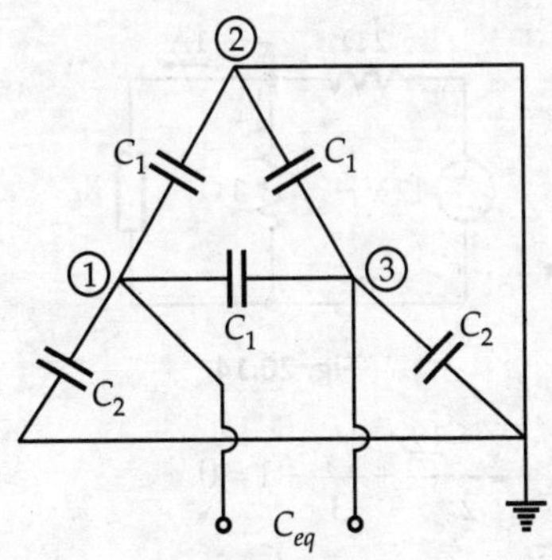

Fig. 20.11

(*a*) $\frac{1}{2}(3C_1+C_2)$ (*b*) $\left(\frac{C_1C_2}{C_1+C_2}\right)$

(*c*) $\left(C_2+\frac{C_1}{2}\right)$ (*d*) $\left(\frac{C_1+C_2}{2}\right)$

Solution. The given circuit is redrawn as shown in Fig. 20.12.

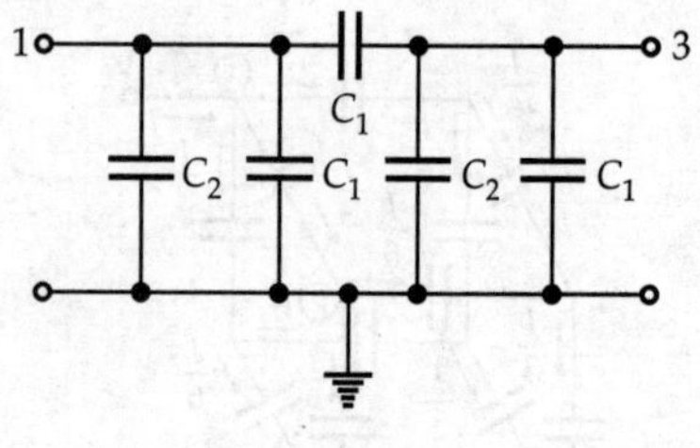

Fig. 20.12

Here, $C_{eq} = \dfrac{C_2 + C_1}{2} + C_1 = \dfrac{C_2 + 3C_1}{2}$

$= \dfrac{1}{2}(3C_1 + C_2)$

Option (*a*) is correct.

M20.8 *R_L is a pure resistive load (Fig. 20.13).*

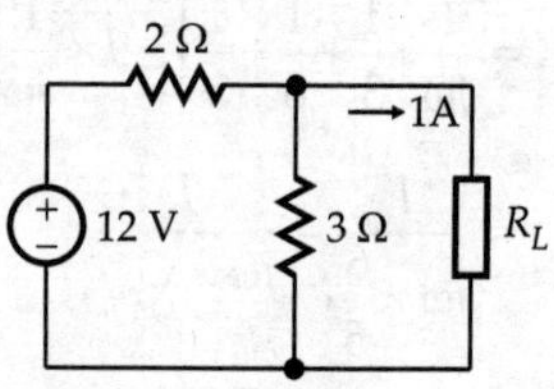

Fig. 20.13

The value of R_L is

(*a*) 6 Ω (*b*) 9 Ω (*c*) 4.5 Ω (*d*) 5 Ω

Solution. In Fig. 20.14, let V_x be the node voltage at node *x*.

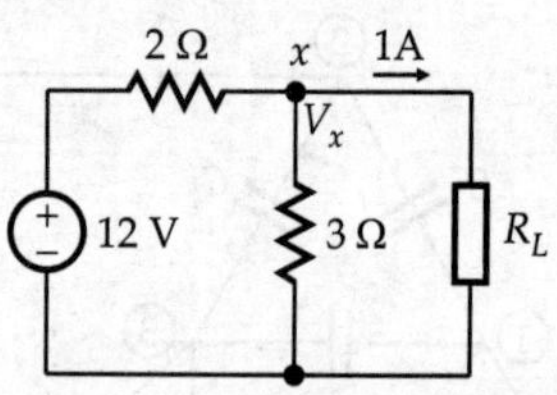

Fig. 20.14

Here, $\dfrac{V_x - 12}{2} + \dfrac{V_x}{3} + 1 = 0.$

or, $\dfrac{5}{6} V_x = 5 \qquad \therefore \quad V_x = 6 \text{ V}$

We can now write,

$\dfrac{V_x}{R_L} = 1 \text{ A}$

$\therefore \quad R_L = \dfrac{V_x}{1} = 6\ \Omega.$

Option (*a*) is correct.

M20.9 *The voltage source in Fig. 20.15 being ideal, the value of V_1 is _____ volts when R_L is the load resistance and is given by $R_L = \left(10 + \dfrac{I}{5}\right)\Omega$.*

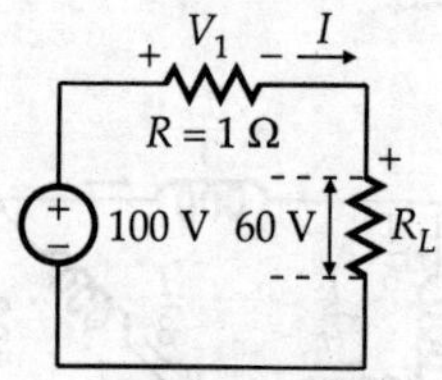

Fig. 20.15

Solution. As per question, in the given figure, V_{R_L} (drop across R_L) is 60 V.

$\therefore$ We can write,

$$60 = I\left(10 + \frac{I}{5}\right) = 10I + \frac{1}{5} \times I^2$$

or, $\dfrac{1}{5} I^2 + 10I - 60 = 0$

$\therefore \quad I =$ either -55.415 A or 5.415 A

Considering the direction of current in the given circuit to be from source to load, the feasible value is $I = 5.415$ A.

$\therefore \quad V_1 = I \times R = 5.415 \times 1 =$ **5.415 Volts.**

M20.10

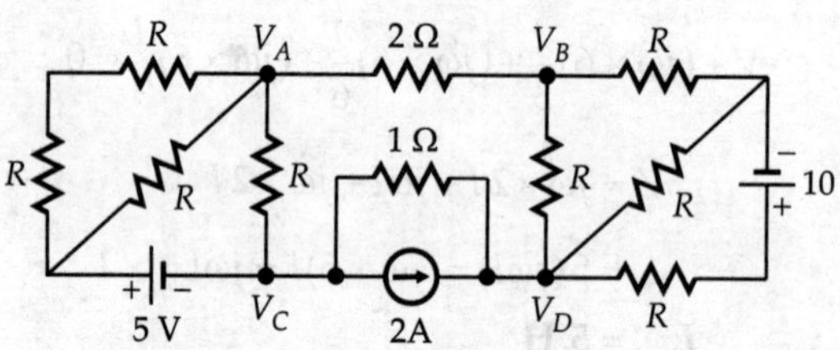

Fig. 20.16

If $(V_A - V_B) = 6$ V (Fig. 20.16), then $(V_C - V_D)$ is

(*a*) −5 V (*b*) 2 V (*c*) 3 V (*d*) 6 V

[GATE 2012]

Solution. In the given circuit, the 2 A current source is converted to the equivalent voltage source and the circuit is redrawn accordingly (Fig. 20.17).

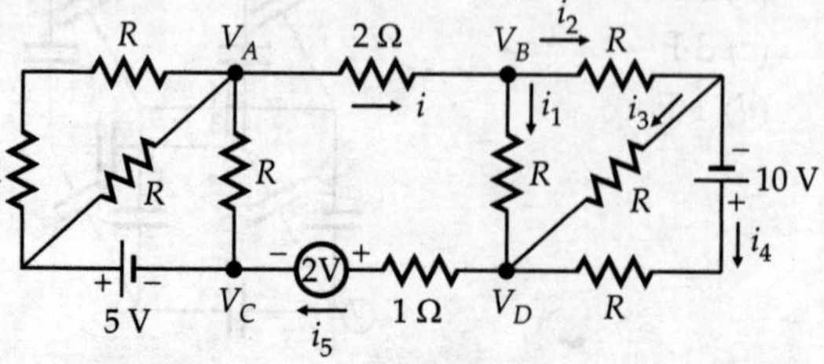

Fig. 20.17

In Fig. 20.17, $\frac{V_A - V_B}{2} = i = \frac{6}{2} = 3\text{ A}$

Also, $i = i_1 + i_2 = i_1 + i_3 + i_4 = i_5 = 3\text{ A}$

$\therefore\ V_C - V_D = -2 + 1 \times (-3) = \mathbf{-5\ V}$.

Option (*a*) is correct.

M20.11 *The value of node voltage V_x at node x in the circuit shown in Fig. 20.18 is*

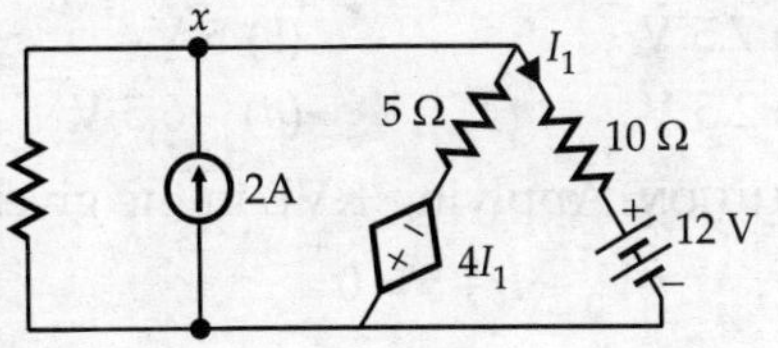

Fig. 20.18

(*a*) 8 V (*b*) 3.2 V (*c*) 9.45 V (*d*) 4.727 V

Solution. At node *x*, with node voltage V_x, nodal analysis yields

$$\frac{V_x}{2} - 2 + \frac{V_x - (-4I_1)}{5} + \frac{V_x - 12}{10} = 0$$

or, $$\frac{4}{5}V_x + \frac{4}{5}I_1 = 3.2 \qquad ...(1)$$

However, $$I_1 = \frac{V_x - 12}{10} \qquad ...(2)$$

Using (2) in (1), we get

$$\frac{4}{5}V_x + \frac{4}{5} \times \frac{V_x - 12}{10} = 3.2$$

or, $$\frac{4}{5}V_x + \frac{2}{25}V_x - \frac{24}{25} = 3.2$$

or, $$\frac{22}{25}V_x = 4.16$$

$\therefore\ V_x = \mathbf{4.727\ V}$

Option (*d*) is correct.

M20.12 *In the circuit shown in Fig. 20.19, the current source $I = 1$ A, voltage source $V = 5$ volts, $R_1 = R_2 = R_3 = 1\Omega$; $L_1 = L_2 = L_3 = 1$ H and $C_1 = C_2 = 1$ F. The value of current (in A) through R_3, and current through voltage source V (in A) respectively will be under steady state*

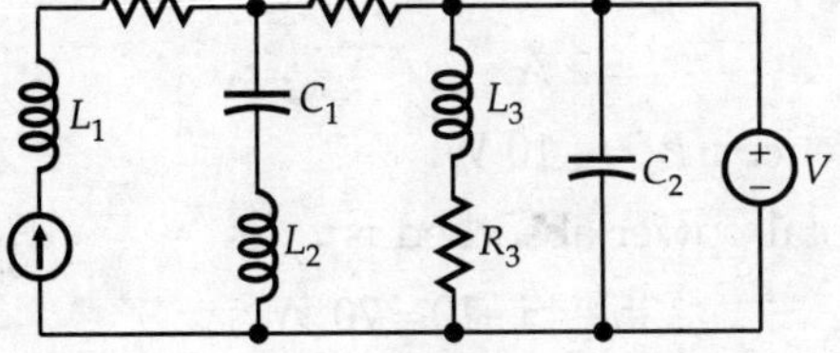

Fig. 20.19

(*a*) 1, 4 (*b*) 5, 1 (*c*) 5, 2 (*d*) 5, 4

Solution. Figure 20.20 represents the given circuit under steady state condition. The current through R_3 under steady state condition is

$$I_Y = I_{R_3} = \frac{5}{1} = 5\text{ A}$$

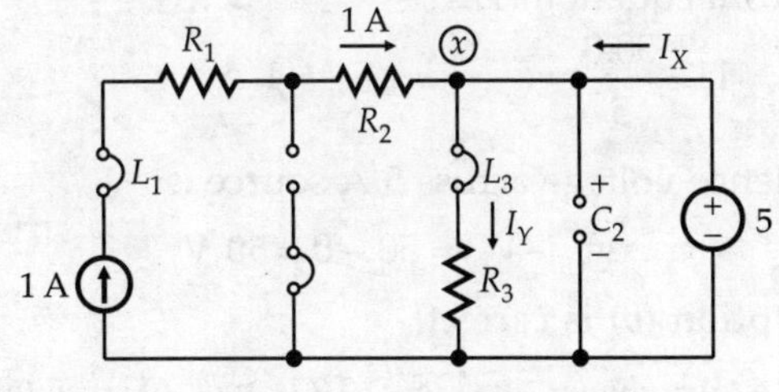

Fig. 20.20

Also, applying KCL at node (*x*), we have

$$1 + I_X = I_Y$$

or, $1 + I_X = 5 \qquad \therefore\ I_X = 4\text{ A}$

$\therefore$ Current through R_3 is **5 A** and current from voltage source is **4 A**.

Option (*d*) is correct.

M20.13 *In Fig. 20.21, what is the value of voltage (V_{bc}) across 5 A source ?*

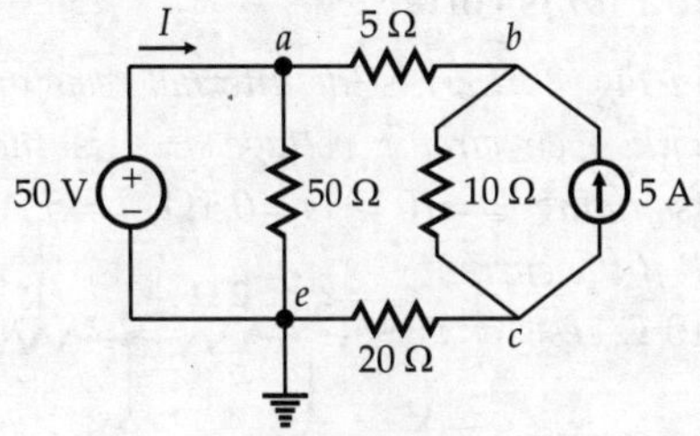

Fig. 20.21

(*a*) 12 V (*b*) 50 V

(*c*) – 62.5 V (*d*) – 6.5 V

Solution.

At node *a*, $$-I + \frac{50}{50} + \frac{50 - V_b}{5} = 0$$

or, $$I = 11 - \frac{V_b}{5} \qquad ...(1)$$

At node *b*, $$\frac{V_b - 50}{5} + \frac{V_b - V_c}{10} - 5 = 0$$

or, $$\frac{3V_b}{10} - \frac{V_c}{10} = 15 \qquad ...(2)$$

At node c, $5+\frac{V_c-V_b}{10}+\frac{V_c-V_e}{20}=0$

or, $\frac{3V_c}{20}-\frac{V_b}{10}=-5$ ...(3)

[$\because V_e=0$ due to earthed node e]

Solving for equations (2) and (3),

$V_b=50\text{ V}$; $V_c=0\text{ V}$

From equation (1),

$11-\frac{50.0}{5}=I$ i.e., $I=1$ A

Hence voltage across 5 A source is

$(V_b-V_c)=50-0=\mathbf{50\text{ V}}$

Option (*b*) is correct.

M20.14 *As shown in Fig. 20.22, a 1 Ω resistor is connected across a source that has load line $(V+i)=100$. The current through the resistance is*

(*a*) 25 A
(*b*) 50 A
(*c*) 100 A
(*d*) 200 A **[GATE 2010]**

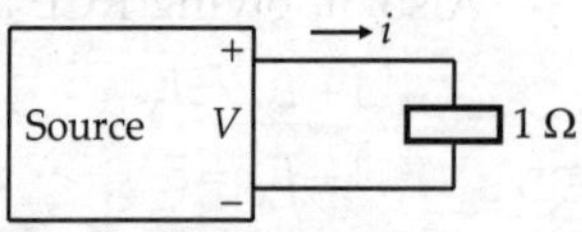

Fig. 20.22

Solution. Here $i\times1=V$ i.e., $V=i$

Since load line is $V+i=100$, we can write

$i+i=100$ i.e., $\mathbf{i=50\text{ A}}$.

Option (*b*) is correct.

M20.15 *In Fig. 20.23, r is the internal resistance of the battery with open circuit voltage E. I is the current source. Assuming $E=10\text{ V}$, $r=0.5\Omega$, $I=5$ A, find the value of R if the current through 10 Ω resistor is 2 A.*

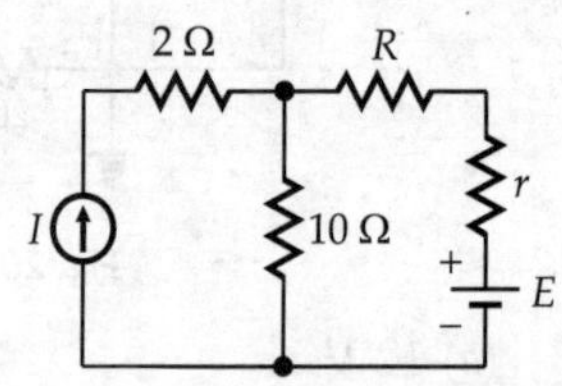

Fig. 20.23

(*a*) 6.329 Ω
(*b*) 3.532 Ω
(*c*) 1.972 Ω
(*d*) 2.833 Ω

Solution. Applying KVL in the rightmost loop,

$-10-3\times R+2\times10-3\times r=0$ [See Fig. 20.24]

or, $10-3\times0.5=3R$

i.e., $\mathbf{R=2.833\ \Omega}$

Option (*d*) is correct.

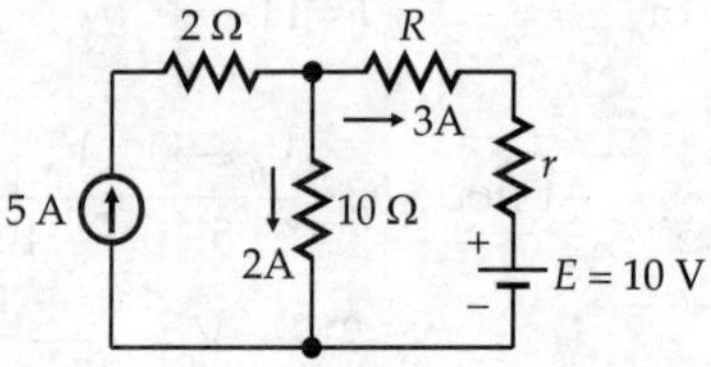

Fig. 20.24

M20.16 *In Fig. 20.25, the voltage (V_0) across the current source is given by*

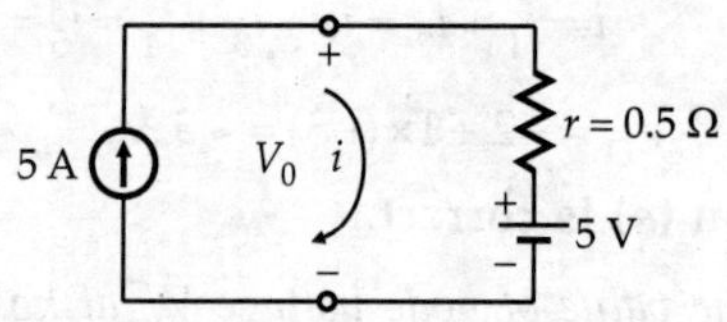

Fig. 20.25

(*a*) 7.5 V (*b*) 5 V
(*c*) 2.5 V (*d*) – 6.5 V

Solution. Applying KVL in the given circuit,

$-V_0+Ir+5=0$

or, $V_0=5+Ir=5+5\times0.5=\mathbf{7.5\text{ V}}$

Option (*a*) is correct.

M20.17 *The voltage sources shown in Fig. 20.26 are ideal and they are the part of a network. The total power absorbed by the three sources is*

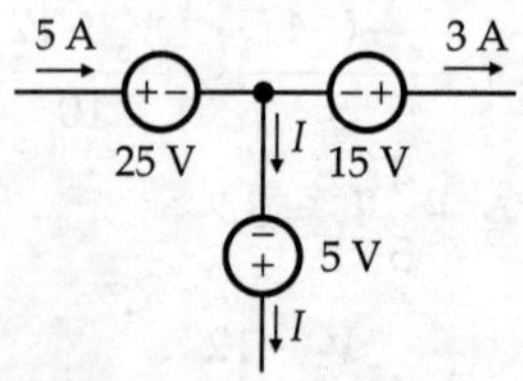

Fig. 20.26

(*a*) – 40 W (*b*) 25 W
(*c*) 70 W (*d*) – 50 W

Solution. Observation reveals that power is absorbed by 25 V source while power is delivered by 15 V and 5 V sources.

Power absorbed by 25 V source is

$P_{25}=5\times25=125\text{ W}$

Power absorbed by 15 V source is

$P_{15}=-3\times15=-45\text{ W}$

Power absorbed by 5 V source is

$P_5=(-I\times5)\text{ W}$

However using KCL in the junction of the three sources,

$I=2$ A

Hence $P_5=-10$ W.

Total power absorbed is

$125-45-10=\mathbf{70\text{ W}}$.

Option (*c*) is correct.

M20.18 *Assuming voltage and current sources to be ideal, the voltage (V_0) across the current source (Fig. 20.27) is given by*

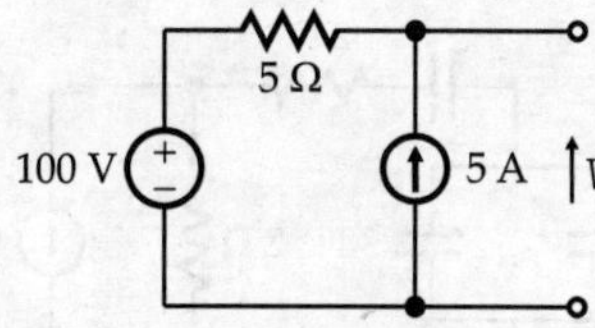

Fig. 20.27

(*a*) 75 V (*b*) 0 V (*c*) 100 V (*d*) 125 V

SOLUTION. In the given circuit,

$$\frac{V_0 - 100}{5} = 5 \quad \text{[Using KCL at output node]}$$

or, $\mathbf{V_0 = 125\ V.}$

Option (*d*) is correct.

M20.19 *The power dissipated in the circuit shown in Fig. 20.28 is*

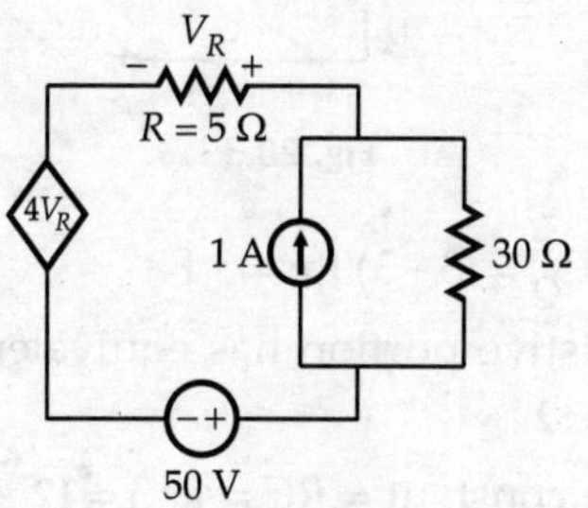

Fig. 20.28

(*a*) 1045 W (*b*) 110.58 W
(*c*) 704.48 W (*d*) 350 W

SOLUTION. The given circuit is redrawn in Fig. 20.29.

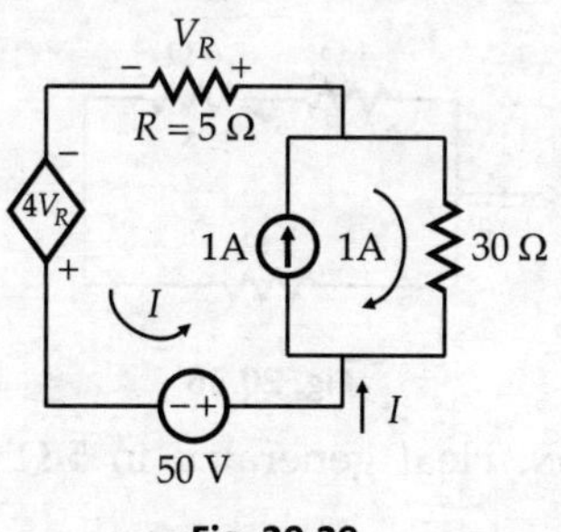

Fig. 20.29

Since the voltage across 5 Ω resistor is V_R hence,

$$V_R = 5I. \qquad ...(1)$$

The loop equation becomes

$$-4V_R - 50 + (I-1)30 + V_R = 0$$

or, $$-3V_R + 30I = 80 \qquad ...(2)$$

Using equation (1) in (2),

$$-15I + 30I = 80$$

$\therefore$ $$I = 5.333\ \text{A}$$

Hence total power loss in the given circuit is

$$P = I^2R + (I-1)^2 \times 30$$
$$= (5.33)^2 \times 5 + (4.33)^2 \times 30 = 704.48\ \text{W}$$

$\therefore$ $\mathbf{P = 704.48\ Watt}$

Option (*c*) is correct.

M20.20 *In the circuit shown in Fig. 20.30, the power rating of the resistance r is 63 W. The voltage drop across r is 21 V.*

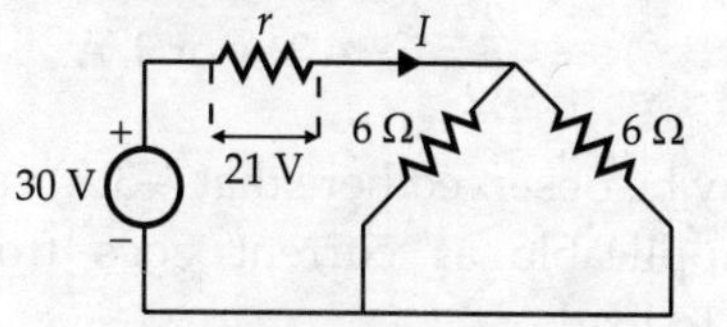

Fig. 20.30

The value of r is

(*a*) 3.5 Ω (*b*) 7 Ω (*c*) 10 Ω (*d*) 19 Ω

SOLUTION. Net resistance of the given circuit across the voltage source is

$$r + \frac{6 \times 6}{6+6} = (r+3)\ \Omega$$

Also, $$P_r = V_{drop(r)} \times I$$

or, $$63 = 21 \times I$$

$\therefore$ $$I = 3\ \text{A}.$$

Since input voltage is 30 V

$\therefore$ $$\frac{30}{I} = (r+3)\ \Omega$$

With $I = 3$ A, $\mathbf{r = 7\ \Omega}$

[Also $V = IR$ *i.e.*, 21 = 3 × R giving $R = 7\ \Omega$]

Option (*b*) is correct.

M20.21 *A 3 V dc supply with an internal resistance of 2 Ω supplies a passive non-linear resistance characterized by the relation $V_{NL} = I_{NL}^2$. The power dissipated in the non-linear resistance is ______ .*

(*a*) 1.0 W
(*b*) 1.5 W
(*c*) 2.5 W
(*d*) 3.0 W

[GATE 2007]

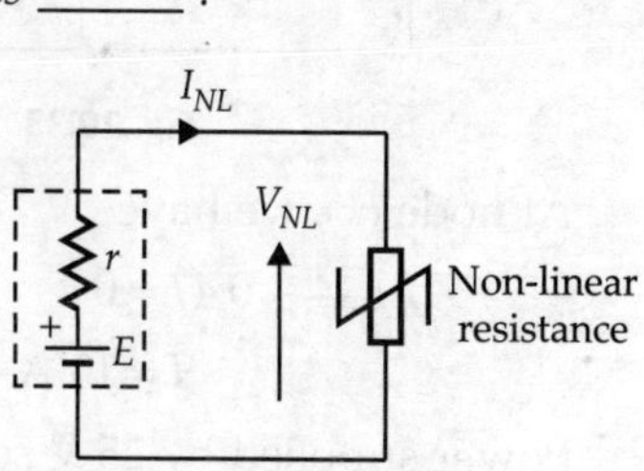

Fig. 20.31

Solution. In the given figure,

$$V_{NL} = E - I_{NL} \cdot r \quad ...(i)$$

Here $r = 2\,\Omega$; $E = 3$ V

Also, $V_{NL} = I_{NL}^2$

$\therefore$ From (*i*), we can write

$$I_{NL}^2 = 3 - I_{NL} \times 2$$

i.e., $$I_{NL}^2 + 2I_{NL} - 3 = 0 \quad ...(ii)$$

Solving for I_{NL},

$$I_{NL} = \frac{-2 \pm \sqrt{4 + 4\times 3}}{2}$$

$$= \frac{-2 \pm 4}{2} = -3 \text{ A or } 1 \text{ A}$$

It may be observed here that (–3 A) value of I_{NL} is not applicable as current goes from source (battery) to load.

$\therefore \quad I_{NL} = 1$ A

Power dissipated in the non-linear resistor is then

$$V_{NL} \times I_{NL} = I_{NL}^2 \times I_{NL} = I_{NL}^3 = 1^3 = \mathbf{1\ W}.$$

Option (*a*) is correct.

M20.22 *The power supplied by the 25 V source in Fig. 20.32 is _____ W.* **[GATE 2017]**

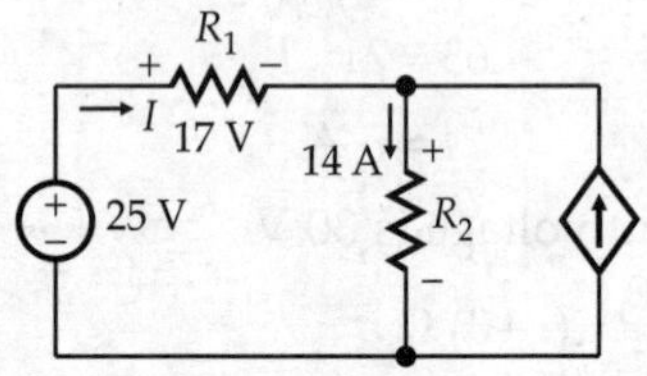

Fig. 20.32

Solution. The given figure is redrawn in Fig. 20.33.

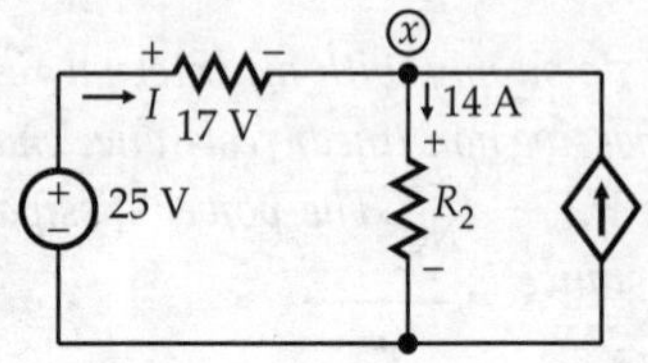

Fig. 20.33

At node (x), we have

$$-I + 14 - 0.4I = 0$$

$$\therefore \quad I = 10 \text{ A}$$

Power supplied by 25 V source is thus

$$(25 \times 10) = \mathbf{250\ W}.$$

M20.23 *A RC circuit is shown in Fig. 20.34, which is energized by A 5 A current source. The time constant of the circuit is given by*

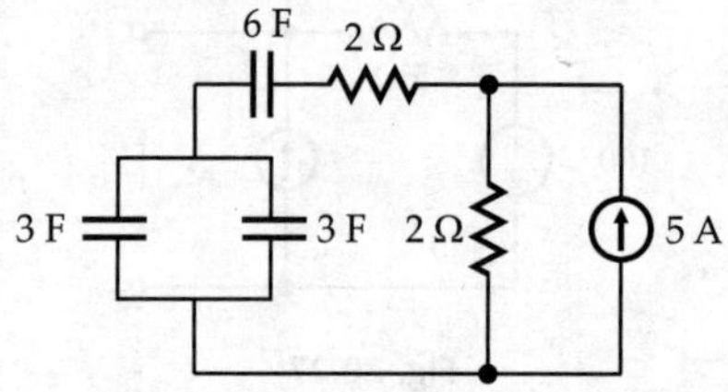

Fig. 20.34

(*a*) 3 s (*b*) 30 s (*c*) 9 s (*d*) 12 s

Solution. Figure 20.35 represents the capacitance portion of the given circuit.

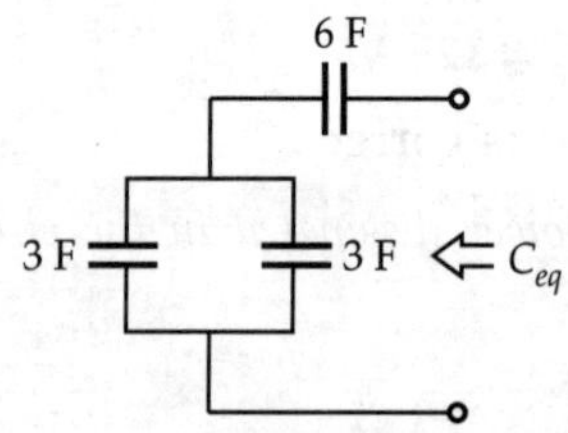

Fig. 20.35

Here, $C_Q = (3+3) \,||\, 6 = 3$ F.

The resistive portion has equivalent resistance of $(2+2) = 4\,\Omega$.

$\therefore$ Time constant $= RC = 4 \times 3 = \mathbf{12\ s}.$

Option (*d*) is correct.

M20.24 *In the portion of the circuit shown (Fig. 20.36), if the heat generated in 5 Ω resistance is 10 calories per second then heat generated by the 4 Ω resistance, in calories per second is _____ .* **[GATE 2016]**

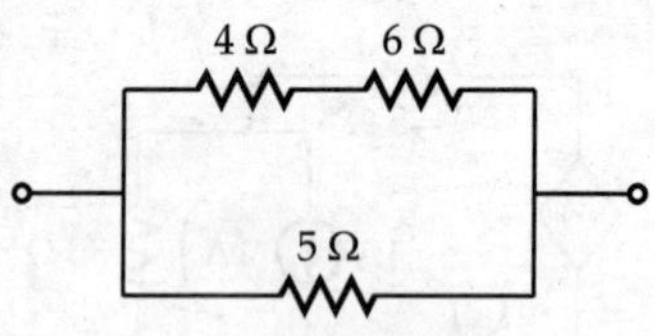

Fig. 20.36

Solution. Heat generated in 5 Ω resistance is 10 cal/sec ;

We then can write

$$H_{5\Omega} = 10 \times 4.2 \text{ J/sec} = 42 \text{ J/sec}$$

i.e., $$I_{5\Omega}^2 R = 42$$

$$\therefore \quad I_{5\Omega} = \sqrt{\frac{42}{R}} = \sqrt{\frac{42}{5}} = 2.9 \text{ A}$$

Hence current through 4 Ω resistance is

$$I_{4\Omega} = 2.9 \times \frac{5}{4+6} = 1.45 \text{ A}$$

Heat generated in 4 Ω resistance

$$H_{4\Omega} = 1.45^2 \times 4 = 8.4 \text{ J/sec}$$

$$= \frac{8.4}{4.2} \text{ cal/sec} = \mathbf{2\ cal/sec.}$$

M20.25 *In the figure shown in Fig. 20.37, 1 A current flows through R. Power consumption is 10 W. R absorbs same power for another magnitude of current i. The value of i is ______ A.*

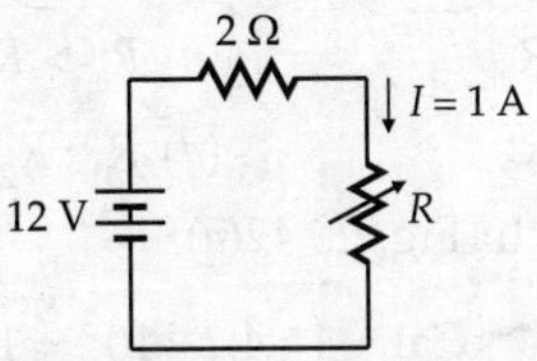

[R is the variable resistance]

Fig. 20.37

SOLUTION. With new circulating current i, we can write

Power consumption in R

= Power delivered by 12 V source

– Power consumption in 2 Ω resistance.

or, $$10 = 12i - i^2 \times 2$$

or, $$2i^2 - 12i + 10 = 0$$

∴ $$i = 5 \text{ A or } 1 \text{ A}.$$

Hence another current of **5 A** will make R to absorb same magnitude of power.

$[P_R = 12 \times 5 - 5^2 \times 2 = 10 \text{ W}]$

M20.26 *When a resistor R is connected to a current source, it consumes power of 18 W. When the same R is connected to a voltage source having the same magnitude as the current source, the power absorbed by R is 4.5 W. The magnitude of the current source and the value of R are :*

(*a*) $\sqrt{18}$ A *and* 1 Ω (*b*) 3 A *and* 2 Ω

(*c*) 1 A *and* 18 Ω (*d*) 6 A *and* 0.5 Ω

[GATE 1999]

SOLUTION. Case A. Resistor is connected across current source [Fig. 20.38]

$$P = I^2 R = 18 \text{ W}$$

∴ $$R = \frac{18}{I^2} \quad \text{...(1)}$$

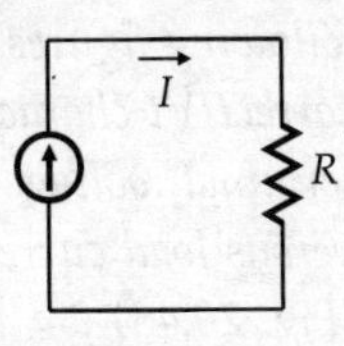

Fig. 20.38

Case B. Resistor is connected across voltage source (Fig. 20.39)

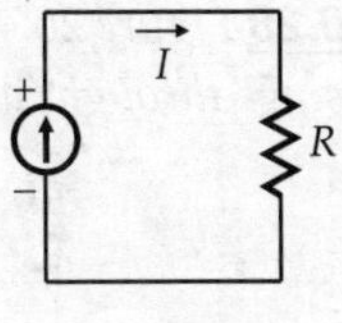

Fig. 20.39

$$P = \frac{V^2}{R} = 4.5 \text{ W}$$

∴ $$R = \frac{V^2}{4.5} \quad \text{...(2)}$$

As per the given question, $|V| = |I|$

Hence equations (1) and (2) can be written as

$$R = \frac{18}{I^2} = \frac{I^2}{4.5} \text{ i.e., } I^4 = 81.$$

∴ $$I = \mathbf{3\ A}$$

From (1), $$R = \frac{18}{3^2} = \mathbf{2\ A.}$$

Option (*b*) is correct.

M20.27 *In the circuit shown in Fig. 20.40, the potential difference between points X and Y (V_{xy}) is*

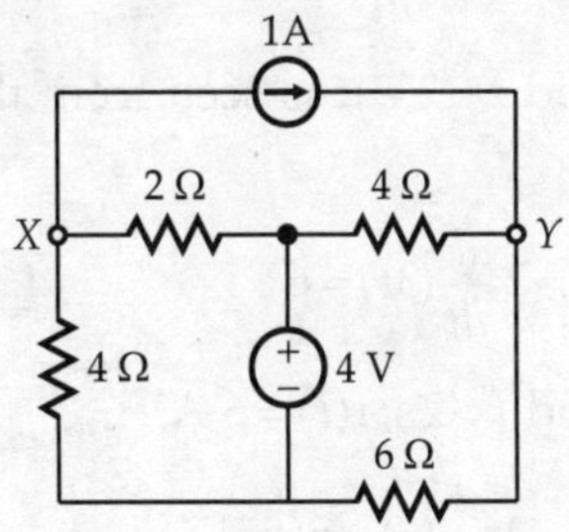

Fig. 20.40

(*a*) – 7.2 V (*b*) 8.533 V

(*c*) – 3.47 V (*d*) 2.583 V

SOLUTION. At node x, using nodal analysis, we have

$$\frac{V_x - 4}{2} + \frac{V_x}{4} + 1 = 0$$

$$\frac{3}{4} V_x = 1$$

∴ $$V_x = \left(\frac{4}{3}\right) V = 1.333 \text{ V}$$

At node y, using nodal method, we get

$$\frac{V_y - 4}{4} + \frac{V_y}{6} - 1 = 0$$

or, $$\frac{5}{12} V_y = 2$$

∴ $$V_y = \frac{24}{5} V = 4.8 \text{ V}$$

∴ $$V_{xy} = V_x - V_y = 1.333 - 4.8 = \mathbf{-3.47\ V}$$

Option (*c*) is correct.

M20.28 *Figure 20.41 shows the waveform of current $i(t)$ passing through an inductor of resistance $1\,\Omega$ and*

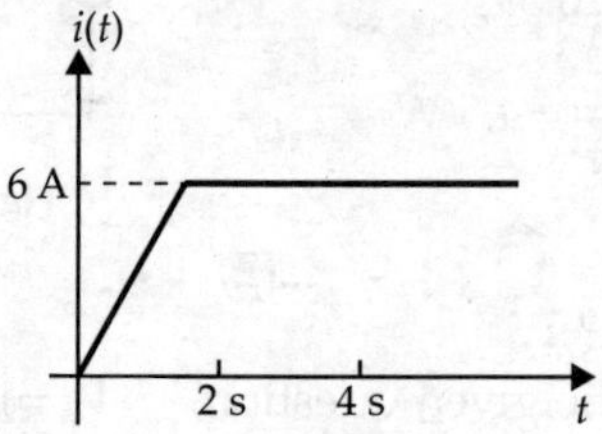

Fig. 20.41

inductance 2 H. The energy absorbed by the inductor in the first four seconds is

(*a*) 144 J (*b*) 98 J (*c*) 132 J (*d*) 168 J

[GATE 2003]

Solution. Let current passing through the inductor be $i(t)$ and the voltage drop across it be $v_L(t)$.

$$v_L(t) = L\frac{di(t)}{dt}$$

For period $t < 2\text{s}$, it is seen from the waveform that $i(t) = 3t$

$$\therefore \quad v_L(t) = 2\frac{d}{dt}(3t) = 6 \qquad [\text{For } t < 2s]$$

For period $t > 2\text{s}$, $i(t) = 6$ A.

$$\therefore \quad v_L(t) = 2\frac{d}{dt}(6) = 0 \qquad [\text{For } t > 2s]$$

Net energy absorbed by the inductor (coil) = energy stored in inductor + energy dissipated in resistor.

$$= \int_0^2 v_L(t)i(t)\,dt + \int_2^4 v_L(t)i(t)\,dt + \int_0^2 i^2(t)R\,dt + \int_2^4 i^2(t)R\,dt$$

$$= \int_0^2 (6\times 3t)\,dt + \int_2^4 (0\times 3t)\,dt + \int_0^2 (3t)^2\times 1\times dt + \int_2^4 (6)^2\times 1\times dt$$

$$= 9t^2\Big|_0^2 + 0 + 3t^2\Big|_0^2 + 36t\Big|_2^4$$

$= 132$ **J.**

Option (*c*) is correct.

M20.29

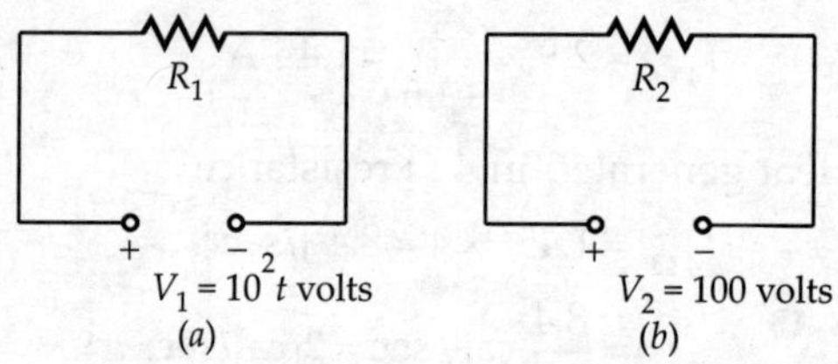

Fig. 20.42

Each of both the heating elements R_1 and R_2 generate heat of 4 kCal in 30 sec. When supplied by voltage sources V_1 and V_2 [Figs. 20.42(a) and (b)], which of the following relations is true ?

(*a*) $R_1 = R_2$ (*b*) $R_1 > R_2$

(*c*) $R_1 < R_2$ (*d*) $R_1 : R_2 = 1:10$

Solution. In Fig. 20.42(*a*),

$$W_1 = 4\text{ kCal} = 4\times 4.2\times 10^3 = 16800\text{ J}$$

$$\text{Also,} \quad W_1 = \int_0^{30}\frac{(100t)^2}{R}\,dt = \frac{10^4}{R_1}\cdot\frac{t^3}{3}\Bigg|_0^{30}$$

$$\text{or,} \quad 16800 = \frac{10^4\times 30^3}{3R_1}$$

$$\therefore \quad R_1 = \frac{10^4\times 30^3}{16800} \quad \text{i.e., } R_1 = 1.6\times 10^4\,\Omega$$

In Fig. 20.42(*b*),

$$W_2 = 4\text{ kCal} = 16800\text{ J}$$

$$\text{or,} \quad 16800 = \int_0^{30}\frac{100^2}{R_2}.dt = \frac{10^4}{R_2}.t\Bigg|_0^{30} = \frac{30\times 10^4}{R_2}$$

$$\therefore \quad R_2 = \frac{30\times 10^4}{16800} = 0.00179\times 10^4\,\Omega$$

$$\therefore \quad R_1 > R_2.$$

Option (*b*) is correct.

M20.30 *Open circuit voltage of the source is 36 V. With load current of 20 A and internal resistance of 0.2 ohm, which of the following figures denote the correct VI characteristics of terminal voltage V at a-b versus load current I (Fig. 20.43) ?*

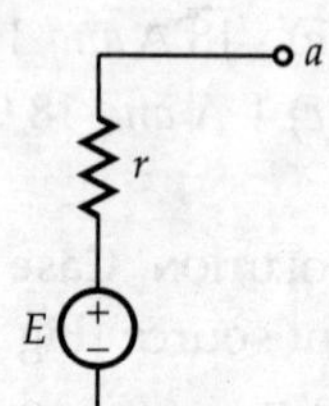

Fig. 20.43

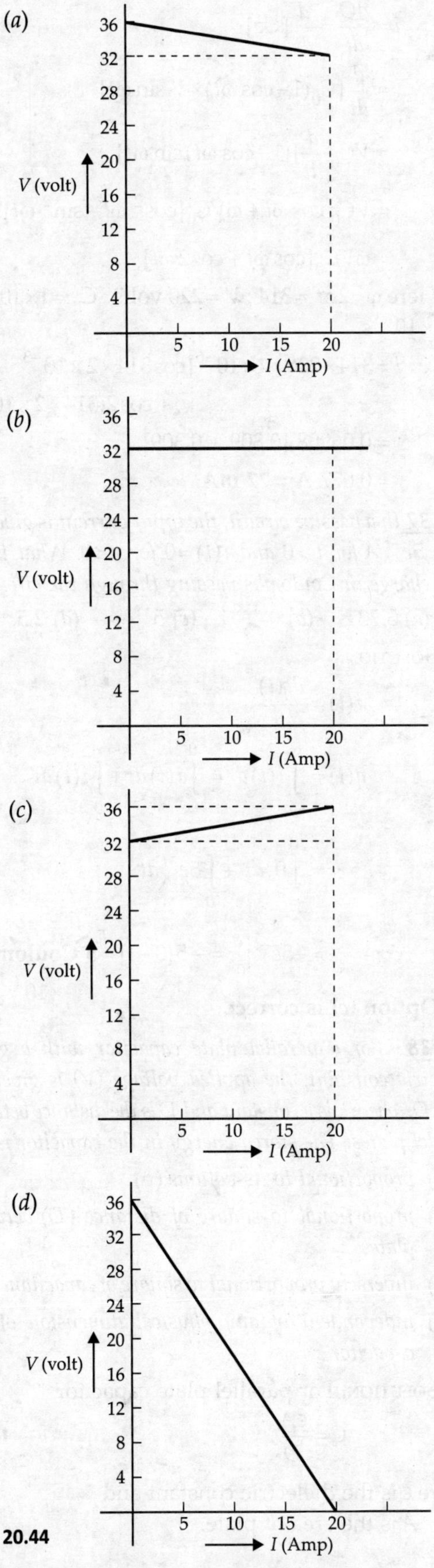

Fig. 20.44

Solution. In Fig. 20.44, with $I = 0$, $V = E = 36$ V (open circuit voltage).

With $I = 20$ A, using the relation $V = E - Ir$,

$$V = 36 - 20 \times 0.2 = 32 \text{ V}$$

$\therefore$ *VI* characteristic is a straight line following equation $V = E - Ir$ with open circuit voltage $E = \mathbf{36\ V}$ and terminal voltage $V = \mathbf{32\ V}$ with $I = 20$ A.

Option (*a*) [Fig. 20.44(*a*)] is correct.

M20.31 *A constant current source I_0 is applied to a time variable inductor having inductance $L = \sin t$ for $0 \le t \le \pi$. The magnitude of the induced voltage across the inductor is given by*

(*a*) $I_0 \cos 2t$ (*b*) $\frac{1}{I_0} \sin t \cos t$

(*c*) $\sin t$ (*d*) $I_0 \cos t$

Solution.

$$|v| = \left|\frac{d\psi}{dt}\right| = \frac{d}{dt}(Li) = I_0 \frac{d}{dt}(L)$$

$$= I_0 \frac{d}{dt} \sin t = \mathbf{I_0 \cos t} \text{ for } 0 \le t \le \pi$$

Option (*d*) is correct.

M20.32 *A current given by $i = \sin t$ for $0 \le t \le \pi$ is applied across a capacitor of $\left(\frac{1}{2}\right)$ F. The voltage across the capacitor is given by*

(*a*) $(2 - \sin t)$ (*b*) $2 \sin t$

(*c*) $2(1 - \cos t)$ (*d*) $2t$

Solution.

$$v_c = \frac{1}{c}\int_0^t i\,dt = 2\int_0^t \sin t\,dt$$

$$= -2[\cos t]_0^t = -2[\cos t - 1]$$

i.e., $v_c = \mathbf{2(1 - \cos t)}$

Option (*c*) is correct.

M20.33 *The rise of current in a 1 H pure inductance is 1A/sec. from $t = 0$. The quantity of charge in micro Coulomb passed through the inductor after 50 ms is obtained as*

(*a*) 1500 (*b*) 1.25

(*c*) 1250 (*d*) 850

Solution.

$$q = \int_0^t i\,dt = i\left.\frac{t^2}{2}\right|_0^t = \frac{it^2}{2}$$

Here $i = 1\,\text{A}$ at any interval of time of 1 sec and $t = 50\,\text{ms} = 50 \times 10^{-3}\,\text{s}$.

$$\therefore\ q(50\,\text{ms}) = \frac{1 \times (50 \times 10^{-6})^2}{2} = \mathbf{1250\ \mu C}$$

Option (*c*) is correct.

M20.34 *A current of 2 A passes through a (1/2 F) capacitor for t = 1 to t sec. Voltage developed across the capacitor is*

(*a*) $4(t-1)$ (*b*) $4t$

(*c*) $2t^2$ (*d*) $(t-1)$

Solution.

$$v_c = \frac{1}{c}\int_1^t i\,dt = 2\int_1^t 2\,dt = 4[t]_1^t = 4t - 4$$

or, $\quad v_c = \mathbf{4\,(t-1)}$

Option (*a*) is correct.

M20.35 *The charge (Q) and voltage (V) in a certain non-linear capacitor are related by the equation $Q = k\sqrt{V}$, k being a constant. The energy stored in this capacitor is obtained as*

(*a*) kQ (*b*) $\dfrac{Q^3}{3k^2}$

(*c*) $\dfrac{Q}{3k}$ (*d*) $2Qk^2$

Solution.

$$Q = k\sqrt{V} = kV^{1/2}$$

$$\therefore\quad V = \frac{Q^2}{k^2}$$

Energy stored in the capacitor is given by

$$W_C = \int_{-\infty}^{t} VI\,dt = \int_{-\infty}^{t} V\frac{dQ}{dt}\,dt$$

$$= \int_0^Q V\,dQ = \int_0^Q \frac{Q^2}{k^2}\,dQ$$

$$= \frac{1}{k^2}\frac{Q^3}{3} = \frac{Q^3}{3k^2}$$

Option (*b*) is correct.

M20.36 *A 50 Hz sinusoidal voltage $v = V\sin\omega t$ is applied across a time varying capacitor having $C = C_0(1 - \cos\omega t)$. Assuming $V = 220\,V$ and $C = 1\,\mu F$, the current through the capacitor at t = 2 ms is given by ______ mA.*

Solution. $v = V\sin\omega t\,;\ C = C_0(1-\cos\omega t)$

$$i = \frac{dQ}{dt} = \frac{d}{dt}[Cv]$$

$$= \frac{d}{dt}[C_0(1-\cos\omega t) \times V\sin\omega t]$$

$$= VC_0\frac{d}{dt}[(1-\cos\omega t)\sin\omega t]$$

$$= VC_0\cos\omega t + \omega VC_0[\cos^2\omega t - \sin^2\omega t]$$

$$= \omega VC_0[\cos\omega t + \cos 2\omega t]$$

Here $\omega = 2\pi f = 314\,;\ V = 220$ volts$\,;\ C_0 = 1 \times 10^{-6}\,\text{F}$; $t = 2 \times 10^{-3}\,\text{s}$.

$$\therefore\quad i = 314 \times 220 \times 1 \times 10^{-6}[\cos 314 \times 2 \times 10^{-3} + \cos 2(314 \times 2 \times 10^{-3})]$$

$$= 0.06908\ [0.809 + 0.309]$$

$$= 0.077\ \text{A} = \mathbf{77\ mA}.$$

M20.37 *In a passive circuit, the input current is given by $i(t) = 5e^{-t}$ A for $t > 0$ and $i(t) = 0$ for $t < 0$. What is the total charge in Coulombs passing through the circuit ?*

(*a*) 3.73 (*b*) 0 (*c*) 5 (*d*) 2.5

Solution.

$$i(t) = \frac{dq(t)}{dt}$$

$$\therefore\quad q(t) = \int_{-\infty}^{\infty} i(t)\,dt = \int_{-\infty}^{0} i(t)\,dt + \int_0^{\infty} i(t)\,dt$$

$$= \int_{-\infty}^{0} 0.dt + \int_0^{\infty} 5e^{-t}\,dt$$

$$= -5e^{-t}\Big|_0^{\infty} = -5[0-1] = \mathbf{5\ Coulombs}.$$

Option (*c*) is correct.

M20.38 *For a parallel plate capacitor with a given dielectric constant, the applied voltage (V) is given by V = kD, where k is a constant and D is the distance between parallel plates. The stored energy in the capacitor is*

(*a*) *proportional to its volume (v)*

(*b*) *proportional to square of distance (D) between plates*

(*c*) *inversely proportional to square of capacitance (c)*

(*d*) *independent of any physical dimension of the capacitor*

Solution. For parallel plate capacitor

$$C = \frac{\epsilon A}{D},$$

where ϵ is the dielectric constant and A is the area of plate.

Stored energy

$$W_C = \frac{1}{2}CV^2 = \frac{1}{2}\frac{\epsilon A}{D}.(k^2D^2)$$

$$= \frac{1}{2}A.D.\epsilon k^2 = \frac{1}{2}A.D.k_1,$$

where k_1 is another constant.

$$W_C = \left(\frac{1}{2}\times k_1\right)AD = \left(\frac{1}{2}k_1\right)v,$$

v being the volume of the capacitor ($v = A\times D$)

$$\therefore \quad W_c \propto v$$

Option (*a*) is correct.

M20.39 *The rms value of the voltage $u(t) = 3 + 4\cos(3t)$ is*

(*a*) $\sqrt{17}$ V (*b*) 5 V
(*c*) 7 V (*d*) $(3+2\sqrt{2})$ V

[GATE 2005]

Solution. The voltage $u(t) = 3 + 4\cos(3t)$ has both dc value 3 V and ac value $4\cos(3t)$.

RMS value of dc voltage $[V_{dcrms}] = 3$ V

RMS value of ac voltage $(V_{acrms}) = \frac{4}{\sqrt{2}}$ V

$$\therefore \text{ RMS of } u(t) = \sqrt{3^2 + \left(\frac{4}{\sqrt{2}}\right)^2} = \mathbf{\sqrt{17}\ V}$$

Option (*a*) is correct.

M20.40 *Currents I_1, I_2, I_3 meet at a junction (node) in a circuit. All currents are marked as entering the node. If $I_1 = -6\sin(\omega t)$ mA and $I_2 = 8\cos(\omega t)$ mA, then I_3 will be*

(*a*) $10\cos(\omega t + 36.87°)$ mA
(*b*) $14\cos(\omega t + 36.87°)$ mA
(*c*) $-14\sin(\omega t + 36.87°)$ mA
(*d*) $-10\cos(\omega t + 36.87°)$ mA **[GATE 1999]**

Solution.

$$I_1 + I_2 + I_3 = 0 \text{ (as per kCL)}$$

$$\therefore I_3 = -I_1 - I_2 = -[-6\sin(\omega t)] - 8\cos(\omega t)$$

$$= 10\left[\frac{6}{10}\sin(\omega t) - \frac{8}{10}\cos(\omega t)\right]$$

$$= 10[0.6\sin(\omega t) - 0.8\cos(\omega t)]$$

$$= -10[\cos(36.87°)\cos\omega t - \sin(36.87°)\sin\omega t]$$

$$= \mathbf{-10\cos(\omega t + 36.87°)\ mA}$$

Option (*d*) is correct.

M20.41 *25 V DC is applied at terminals $a-a'$ in the given circuit (Fig. 20.45). At steady state the input current I will be*

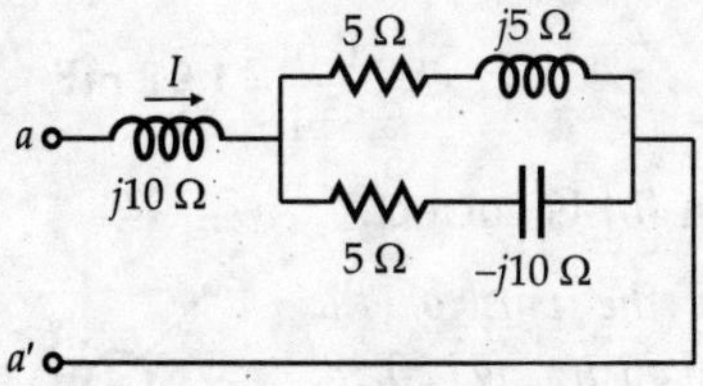

Fig. 20.45

(*a*) 1.025 A (*b*) 10 A
(*c*) 5 A (*d*) 3.75 A

Solution. At study state, the capacitor acts as open circuit while the inductor acts as short-circuit for the input dc voltage. Figure 20.46 represents the circuit at steady state.

$$I = \frac{25}{5} = \mathbf{5\ A}$$

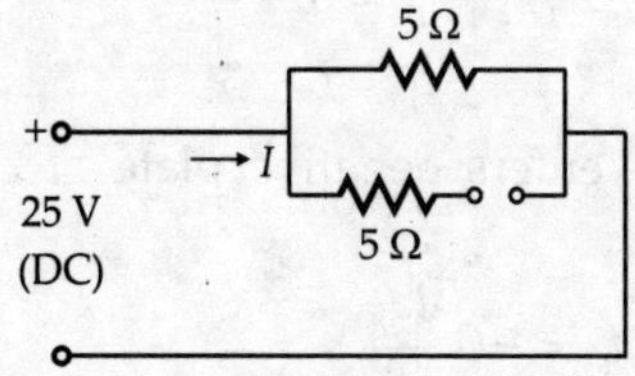

Fig. 20.46

Option (*c*) is correct.

M20.42 *A capacitor 'C' is connected across a series RL circuit having $R = 6\ \Omega$ and $|X_L| = 8\ \Omega$. The supply voltage is 240 V, 50 Hz AC. In order to have unity power factor for the overall circuit, the value of C would be*

(*a*) 0.62 mF (*b*) 1.91 mF
(*c*) 191 μF (*d*) 10 μF

Solution. Let z be the net impedance of the given circuit (Fig. 20.47).

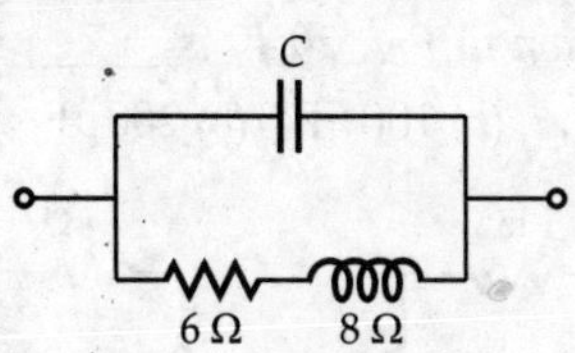

Fig. 20.47

$$\frac{1}{z} = \frac{1}{6+j8} + j\omega C = \frac{6-j8}{10} + j314C$$

$$= 0.6 - j\,0.6 + j314C$$

or,

$$\frac{1}{z} = 0.6 + j(314C - 0.6)$$

To have u.p.f. for the overall circuit, the imaginary part of Z must be zero.

i.e., $314C - 0.6 = 0$

$$\therefore \quad C = \frac{0.6}{314} = \mathbf{1.91\ mF}$$

Option (*b*) is correct.

M20.43 *In the part of the network shown in Fig. 20.48, $v_c = 6 \sin 2t$ volt. Voltage v_L is given by*

(*a*) 0.24 *sin* 2*t*
(*b*) 12 *cos*2*t*
(*c*) (6 *sin*2*t* + 3)
(*d*) 3 *cos*2*t*

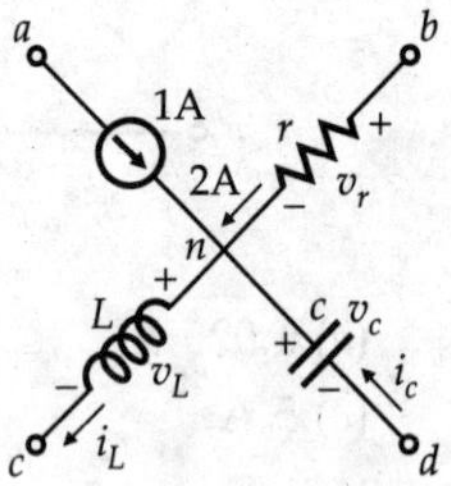

$r = 2\,\Omega$; $C = 1$ F
$L = 10$ mH

Fig. 20.48

Solution. Applying KCL at junction n of the given circuit, it yields

$$-1 - 2 + i_L - i_C = 0$$

$$\therefore \quad i_L = i_C + 3 \qquad ...(1)$$

Since i_C enters negative plate of capacitor C, hence

$$i_C = -C\frac{dv_c}{dt}$$

$$\therefore \quad i_L = -C\frac{dv_c}{dt} + 3 = 3 - 1 \times \frac{d}{dt}(6\sin 2t)$$

$$= 3 - 12\cos 2t \qquad ...(2)$$

$$v_L = L\frac{di_L}{dt} = 10 \times 10^{-3}\frac{d}{dt}[3 - 12\cos 2t]$$

$$= 0.01[24 \sin 2t]$$

or, $\quad v_L = \mathbf{0.24\ sin\ 2}\boldsymbol{t}\ \mathbf{Volts}$

Option (*a*) is correct.

M20.44 *The equivalent capacitance of the input loop of the circuit shown in Fig. 20.49 is ______.*

(*a*) 2 μF (*b*) 100 μF (*c*) 200 μF (*d*) 4 μF

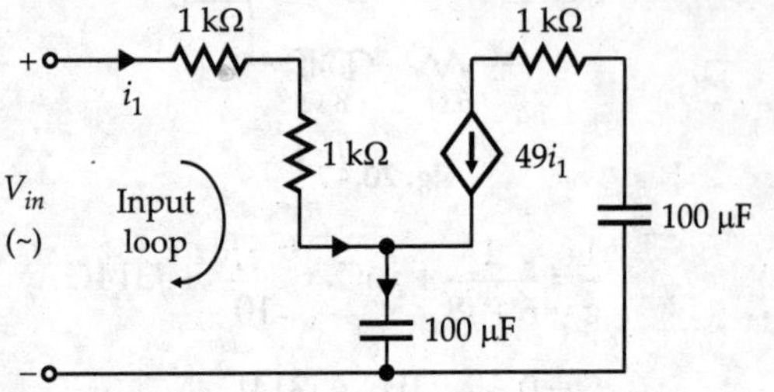

Fig. 20.49

[GATE 2009]

Solution. Applying kVL in the input loop,

$$-V_{in} + i_1(1+1)\times 10^3 + (i_1 + 49i_1)(-jX_C) = 0$$

$$\therefore \quad V_{in} = i_1[2 \times 10^3 - j(50)X_C]$$

$\therefore$ The capacitive part is $[-j(X_C)50]$

i.e., $\quad |X_{eq}| = 50\,X_C$

$$\text{or,} \quad \frac{1}{\omega C_{eq}} = \frac{50}{\omega C} = \frac{50}{\omega \times 100 \times 10^{-6}} = \frac{1}{\omega \times 2 \times 10^{-6}}$$

Hence $C_{eq} = (2 \times 10^{-6})\text{F} = \mathbf{2\,\mu F}$

Option (*a*) is correct.

M20.45 *A capacitor draws 1 A at 220 V, 50 Hz AC source. The instantaneous voltage drop (in volt) across the capacitor is expressed as*

(*a*) 220 *cos* ω*t* (*b*) – 311.08 *sin*90°
(*c*) 220 *sin*(ω*t* + 90°) (*d*) (–311.08 *cos* ω*t*)

Solution.

$$I_m = \sqrt{2} \times 1 = 1.414 \text{ A}$$

$$\omega = 2\pi f = 314 \text{ rad/s}$$

$$\therefore \quad i = (1.414 \sin 314t)A$$

$$V_{in} = \sqrt{2} \times 220 = 311.08 \text{ V}$$

Since the capacitive current leads the voltage by 90°, hence in the capacitive circuit,

$$v = 311.08 \sin(\omega t - 90°)$$

or, $\quad \boldsymbol{v} = \mathbf{-311.08\ cos\ \omega t\ volt}$

Option (*d*) is correct.

M20.46 *In the circuit shown in Fig. 20.50, the current through the inductor is*

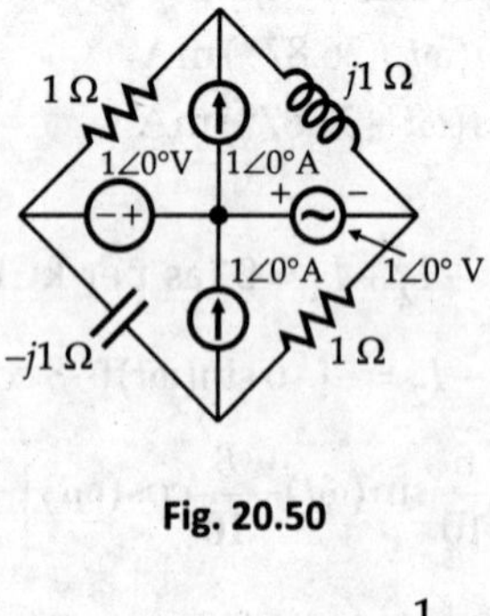

Fig. 20.50

(*a*) $\frac{2}{1+j}A$ (*b*) $-\frac{1}{1+j}A$

(*c*) $\frac{1}{1+j}A$ (*d*) 0 *A*

[GATE 2012]

SOLUTION. Let us redraw the given circuit as shown in Fig. 20.51.

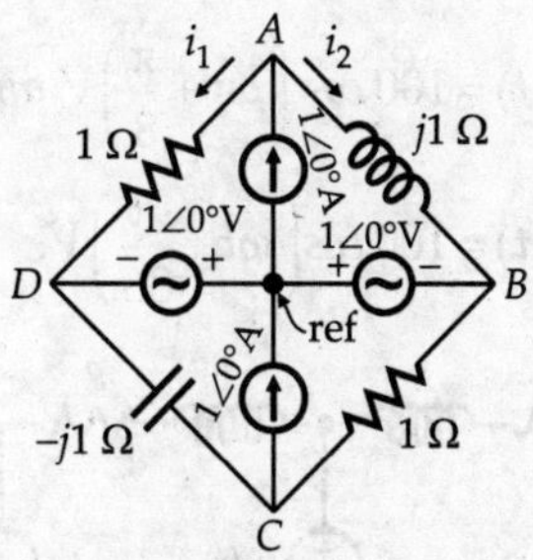

Fig. 20.51

Let V_A, V_B, V_C and V_D be node voltages at nodes *A*, *B*, *C* and *D* respectively.

i_1 and i_2 are the branch currents as shown.

Applying nodal equation at node *A*,

$$\frac{V_A-(-1\angle 0°)}{1}+\frac{V_A-(-1\angle 0°)}{j1}-1\angle 0°=0$$

or,
$$\frac{V_A+1}{1}+\frac{V_A+1}{j1}=1$$

$$\therefore \qquad V_A=-\left(\frac{1}{1+j}\right)\text{Volt}$$

i_2 (current through the inductor)

$$=\frac{V_A+1}{j1}=\frac{\left(\frac{-1}{1+j}\right)+1}{j1}$$

$$=\frac{-1+1+j}{j\times 1(1+j)}=\frac{1}{1+j}A$$

The inductor current then is $\left(\frac{1}{1+j}\right)A$.

Option (c) is correct.

M20.47 *An ac voltage $v=V_m\sin\omega t$ is applied across a resistor r. The dc voltage that must be connected across the same resistor r such that the power dissipated is the same as average power is*

(a) V_m (b) $\left(\frac{V_m}{\sqrt{2}}\right)$ (c) $(\sqrt{2}V_m)$ (d) $\frac{\sqrt{3}}{2}V_m$

SOLUTION. Here,

$$P\text{ (instantaneous power)}=\frac{V_m^2}{R}\sin^2\omega t$$

$$=\frac{V_m^2}{2R}(1-\cos 2\omega t)$$

$$\therefore \qquad P_{av}=\frac{V_m^2}{2R}$$

$$P_{dc}=\frac{V_{dc}^2}{R}$$

Since as per question

$P_{dc}=P_{av}$, hence we can write

$$\frac{V_{dc}^2}{R}=\frac{V_m^2}{2R} \quad i.e., \quad V_{dc}=\frac{V_m}{\sqrt{2}}$$

∴ **Option (*b*) is correct.**

M20.48 *The voltage and current for a circuit element (X); as shown in Fig. 20.52 are $v=12\cos(314t-70°)V$; $i=6\cos(314t+10°)A$.*

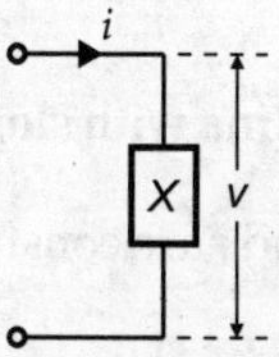

Fig. 20.52

The unknown element is a ______ and its value is ______.

SOLUTION. By observation it is seen that *i* is leading the voltage by an angle [10–(–70)] *i.e.*, 80°.

Hence the unknown element is a **capacitor**

$$X_C=\frac{V_m}{I_m}=\frac{12}{6}=2\,\Omega$$

$$=\frac{1}{\omega C}=\frac{1}{314C}$$

i.e., $C=\frac{1}{2\times 314}=$ **1.59 mF.**

M20.49 *A battery has open circuit terminal voltage E volt and internal resistance r. With a load connected across the battery, a current i flows through the load. Assuming V to be the terminal voltage of the battery, identify which of the following statements is correct.*

(*a*) *The equation of i is a straight line with slope $-\frac{1}{r}$.*

(*b*) *The equation of i is a circle with $\frac{1}{r}$ as its radius.*

(*c*) *The profile of i is shown in Fig. 20.53.*

(*d*) *i is constant and independent of r and V.*

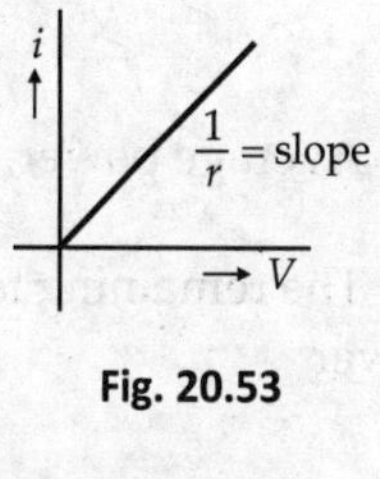

Fig. 20.53

Solution. Here, in Fig. 20.54,

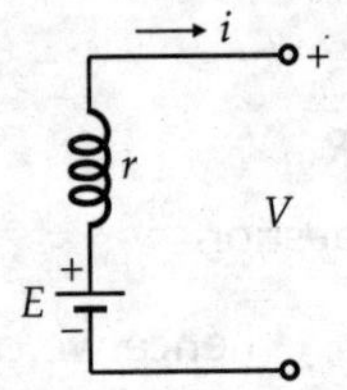

Fig. 20.54

$$-E + ir + V = 0$$

$$\therefore \quad i = \frac{E - V}{r}$$

or, $$i = -\frac{1}{r}V + \frac{E}{r}$$

$\therefore$ ***i* is a straight line with slope** $\left(-\frac{1}{r}\right)$; *i* and *V* are variables while *E* and *r* are constants. See Fig. 20.55.

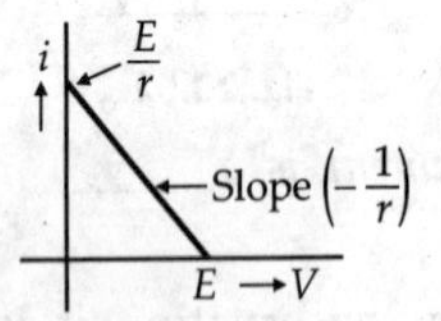

Fig. 20.55

Option (*a*) is correct.

M20.50 *The voltage (V) and current (A) across a load are as follows :* **[GATE 2016]**

$$v(t) = 100\, sin(\omega t) \; ;$$

$$i(t) = 10\, sin(\omega t - 60°) + 2\, sin(3\omega t) + 5\, sin(5\omega t)$$

The average power consumed by the load is ______ .

Solution. Let the instantaneous power be *p*.

$$p = (100 \sin \omega t)[10 \sin(\omega t - 60°) + 2 \sin 3\omega t + 5 \sin 5\omega t]$$

$$= \frac{1}{2} \times 1000[\cos 60° + \cos(2\omega t - 60°)] + \frac{1}{2} \times 200[\cos 2\omega t + \cos 4\omega t] + \frac{1}{2} \times 500[\cos 4\omega t + \cos 6\omega t]$$

Average power, $P_{av} = \frac{1}{2} \times 1000 \times \cos 60° = \mathbf{250\ W}$.

The remaining terms contribute to zero average power.

M20.51 *In Fig. 20.56, the voltages are*

$$v_1(t) = 100 \cos(\omega t)\, V,$$

$$v_2(t) = 100 \cos\left(\omega t + \frac{\pi}{8}\right) V \text{ and}$$

$$v_3(t) = 100 \cos\left(\omega t + \frac{\pi}{36}\right) V.$$

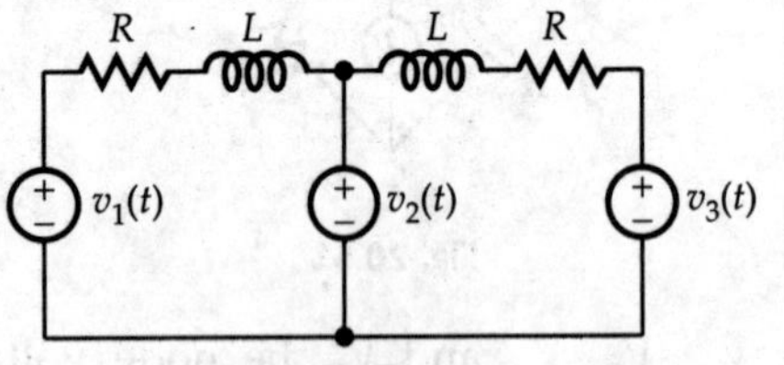

Fig. 20.56

The circuit is in sinusoidal steady state, and $R << (L\omega)$. P_1, P_2 *and* P_3 *are the average power outputs. Which one of the following statements is true ?*

(*a*) $P_1 = P_2 = P_3 = 0$

(*b*) $P_1 < 0,\ P_2 > 0,\ P_3 > 0$

(*c*) $P_1 < 0,\ P_2 > 0,\ P_3 < 0$

(*d*) $P_1 > 0,\ P_2 < 0,\ P_3 > 0$ **[GATE 2018]**

Solution. The three voltage phasors $v_1(t), v_2(t)$ and $v_3(t)$ are drawn in Fig. 20.57.

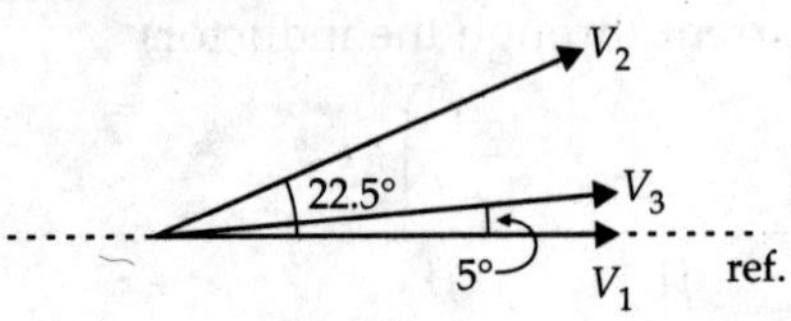

Fig. 20.57

V_1 is reference,

V_2 leads V_1 by $\frac{\pi}{8}$ (=22.5°).

V_3 leads V_1 by $\frac{\pi}{36}$ (=5°)

It is evident that since V_2 leads both V_1 and V_3 hence this voltage V_2 is the primary source.

$\therefore$ $P_2 > 0$. However, V_3 and V_1 lag V_2 and hence they absorb power from V_2.

$\therefore$ $P_1 < 0$; $P_3 < 0$

Hence, $\mathbf{P_1 < 0\ ;\ P_2 > 0\ ;\ P_3 < 0}$.

Option (*c*) is correct.

M20.52

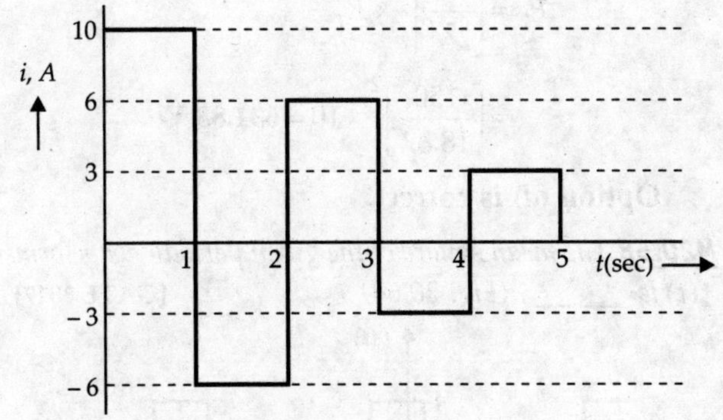

Fig. 20.58

The rms value of the current waveform shown in Fig. 20.58 is _______ A.

SOLUTION.

$$I_{rms} = \sqrt{\frac{(10)^2 \times 1 + (-6)^2 \times 1 + (6)^2 \times 1 + (-3)^2 \times 1 + (3)^2 \times 1}{5}}$$

$$= \sqrt{\frac{100+36+36+9+9}{5}}$$

$= \mathbf{6.164\ A}$

M20.53

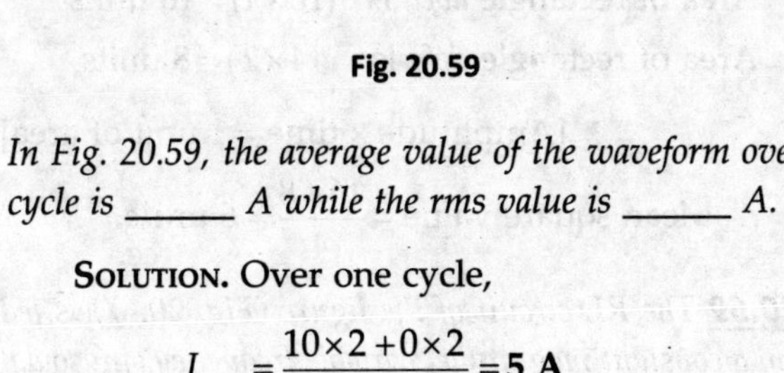

Fig. 20.59

In Fig. 20.59, the average value of the waveform over a cycle is _______ A while the rms value is _______ A.

SOLUTION. Over one cycle,

$$I_{avg} = \frac{10 \times 2 + 0 \times 2}{4} = \mathbf{5\ A}$$

$$I_{rms} = \sqrt{\frac{10^2 \times 2 + 0^2 \times 2}{4}}$$

$$= \sqrt{50} = \mathbf{7.07\ A}$$

M20.54

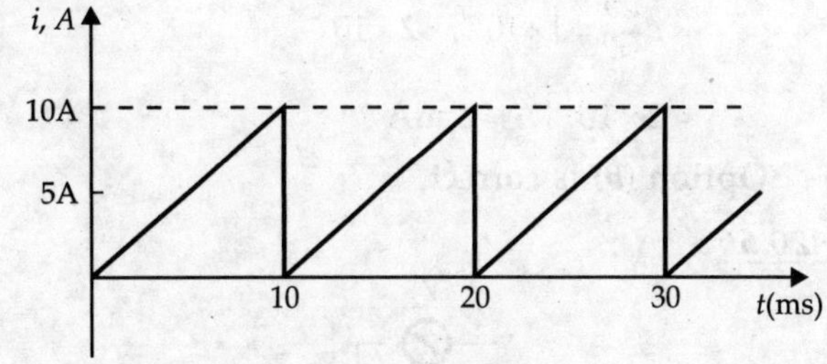

Fig. 20.60

The average value and rms value of the current shown in Fig. 20.60 is _______ and _______ A.

SOLUTION.

$$I_{avg} = \frac{1}{2}\left[\frac{10 \times 10 \times 10^{-3}}{10 \times 10^{-3}}\right] = \mathbf{5\ A}$$

$$I_{rms} = \sqrt{\frac{1}{T}\int_0^T i^2 dt}$$

$$= \sqrt{\frac{1}{10 \times 10^{-3}} \int_0^{10 \times 10^{-3}} (10^3 t)^2 dt}$$

$$\left[\because i = \frac{10}{10 \times 10^{-3}} . t = 10^3 t\right]$$

$$\therefore \quad I_{rms} = \sqrt{\frac{10^6}{10 \times 10^{-3}} \left[\frac{t^3}{3}\right]^{10 \times 10^{-3}}}$$

$$= \sqrt{10^8 \left[\frac{10^3 \times 10^{-9}}{3}\right]} = \mathbf{5.78\ A}$$

M20.55 *A saw tooth voltage waveform (Fig. 20.61) is applied across a capacitor of 1 μF. The charging current flowing through the capacitor is*

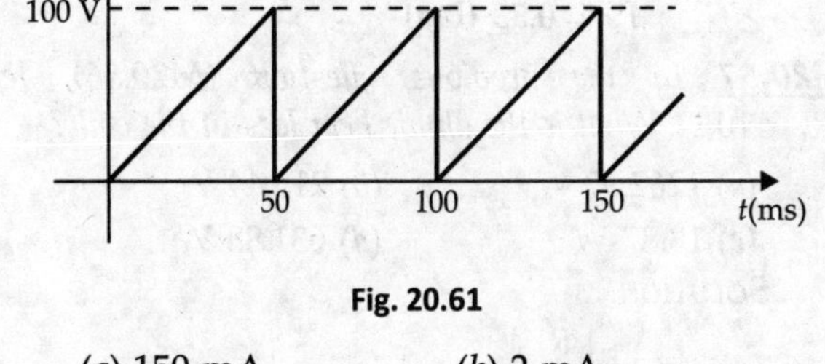

Fig. 20.61

(*a*) 150 mA (*b*) 2 mA
(*c*) 0.2 A (*d*) 1 mA

SOLUTION. $\frac{dv}{dt} = \frac{100}{50 \times 10^{-3}} = 2 \times 10^3 \text{ V/s}$

$\therefore$ i_c (charging current in the capacitor)

$$= c\frac{dv}{dt} = 1\times10^{-6}\times2\times10^{3}$$

$$= 2\times10^{-3}\text{ A} = \mathbf{2\ mA}$$

Option (*b*) is correct.

M20.56

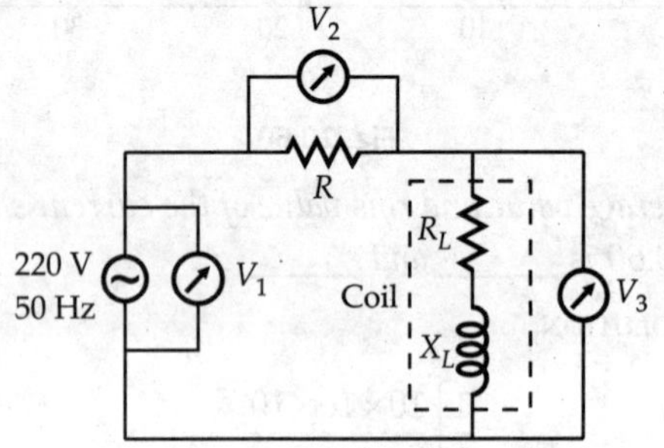

Fig. 20.62

R represents a heater (pure resistance) in series with a choke coil ($R_1 + jX_L$) (Fig. 20.62). The supply is 220 V, 50 Hz AC. Three voltmeters are connected as shown in the figure. The voltmeter readings are V_1 = 220 V ; V_2 = 100 V ; V_3 = 150 V. The power factor of the overall circuit (Fig. 20.62) is ______ .

Solution. V_2 being the resistive drop, it is taken as reference phasor in Fig. 20.63.

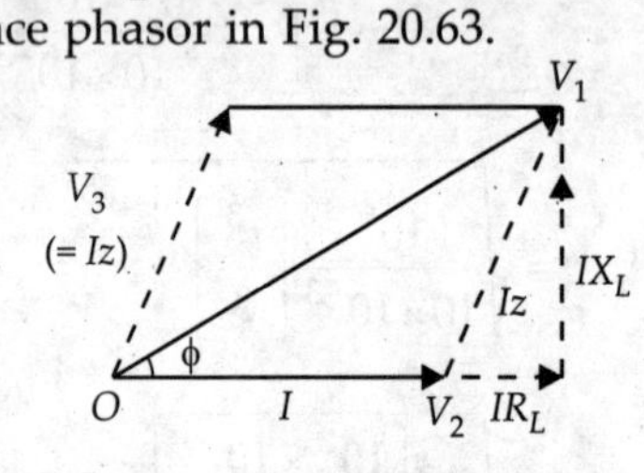

Fig. 20.63

We have,

$$V_1^2 = V_2^2 + V_3^2 + 2V_2V_3\cos\phi$$

or, $\quad 220^2 = 100^2 + 150^2 + 2\times100\times150\cos\phi$

or, $\quad 15900 = 30{,}000\cos\phi$

$\therefore \quad \cos\phi = 0.53$

$PF = \mathbf{0.53\ (lag)}$

M20.57 *In the previous question (M20.56), let $R_L = 10\ \Omega$. What is the ohmic heat loss in the coil ?*

(*a*) 1262.97 W (*b*) 215.44 W

(*c*) 18.87 W (*d*) 631.88 W

Solution.

$$\cos\phi = \left|\frac{R_L}{Z}\right|$$

$$\therefore \quad |Z| = \frac{R_L}{\cos\phi} = \frac{10}{0.53} = 18.87\ \Omega$$

Power consumed by the coil

$$P_L = \left[\frac{V_3}{|Z|}\right]^2 \times R_L$$

$$= \left[\frac{150}{18.87}\right]^2 \times 10 = \mathbf{631.88\ W}$$

Option (*d*) is correct.

M20.58 *The mean square of the given periodic waveform $f(t)$ is ______ . (Fig. 20.64)* **[GATE 2017]**

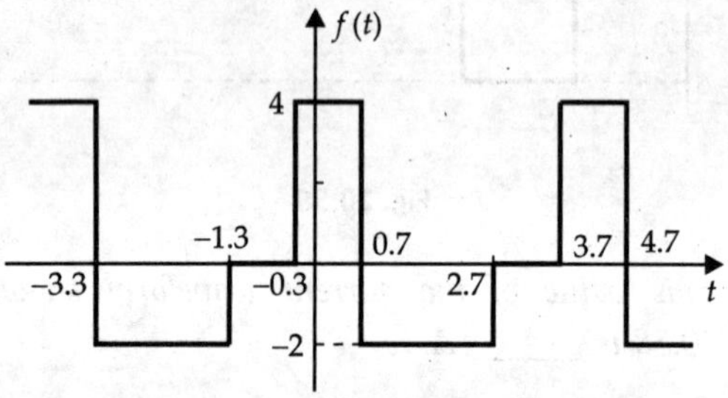

Fig. 20.64

Solution. Let us take one time period, from (–0.3) s to (3.7) s. The time interval of this period is then 4 s (see Fig. 20.65). To calculate the mean square value first we need to find $f^2(t)$. Figure 20.66 represents $f^2(t)$.

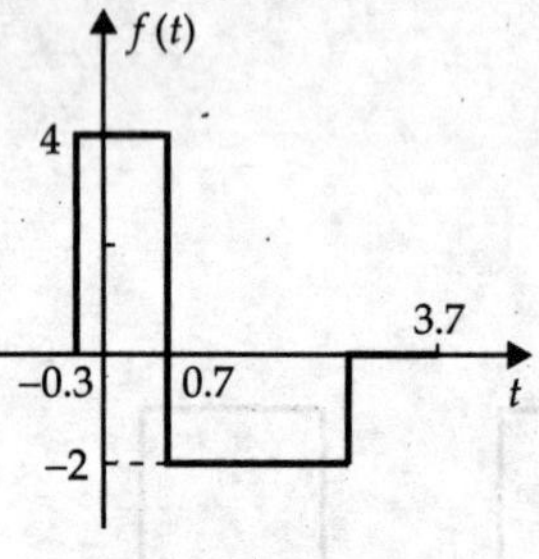

Fig. 20.65

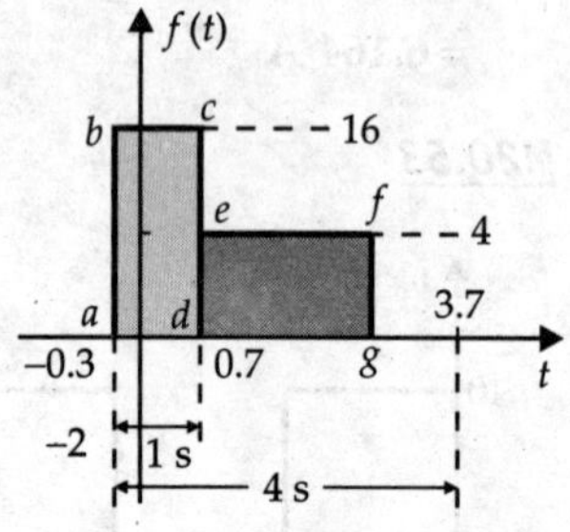

Fig. 20.66
(*not as per scale*)

Area of rectangle *abcd* is $(16\times1) = 16$ units

Area of rectangle *defg* is $(4\times2) = 8$ units

[Amplitude × time = 1 unit of area]

$$\therefore \text{ Mean square value} = \frac{16+8}{4} = \mathbf{6\ units.}$$

M20.59 *The RL circuit of the figure (Fig. 20.67) is fed from a constant magnitude, variable frequency sinusoidal voltage source V_{IN}. At 100 Hz, the R and L elements each have a voltage drop U_{RMS}. If the frequency of the source is changed to 50 Hz, then new voltage drop across R is*

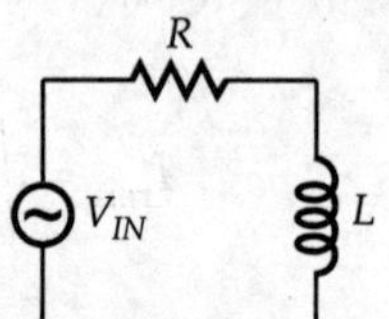

Fig. 20.67

(a) $\sqrt{\frac{5}{8}}U_{rms}$ (b) $\sqrt{\frac{2}{3}}U_{rms}$

(c) $\sqrt{\frac{8}{5}}U_{rms}$ (d) $\sqrt{\frac{3}{2}}U_{rms}$ **[GATE 2005]**

Solution.

$$f = 100 \text{ Hz}, \ |V_R| = |V_L|$$

As R and L are connected in series (Fig. 20.67), current through R and L is same.

$$\therefore \quad IR = IX_L = I\omega L$$
$$R = X_L = \omega L$$

Also, $$I = \frac{V_{IN}}{\sqrt{R^2 + X_L^2}} = \frac{V_{IN}}{\sqrt{R^2 + R^2}} = \frac{V_{IN}}{\sqrt{2}R}$$

$$\therefore \quad V_R = U_{rms} = IR$$
$$= \left(\frac{V_{IN}}{\sqrt{2}R}\right)R = \frac{V_{IN}}{\sqrt{2}}$$

i.e., $$V_{IN} = \sqrt{2}U_{rms}$$

We know $X_L \propto f$

Here at 50 Hz,

$$X'_L = X_L \times \frac{50}{100} = \frac{X_L}{2} = \frac{R}{2}$$

$$I' = \frac{V_{IN}}{\sqrt{R^2 + (X'_L)^2}} = \frac{V_{IN}}{\sqrt{R^2 + (R/2)^2}}$$
$$= \frac{2}{\sqrt{5}} \cdot \frac{V_{IN}}{R}.$$

$$V'_R = I'R = \left[\frac{2V_{IN}}{\sqrt{5}R}\right]R = \frac{2}{\sqrt{5}} \cdot V_{IN}$$

$\because$ $V_{IN} = \sqrt{2}\,U_{rms}$, hence,

$$V'_R = \frac{2}{\sqrt{5}} \times \sqrt{2}\,U_{rms}$$
$$= \frac{2\sqrt{2}}{\sqrt{5}}U_{rms} = \sqrt{\frac{8}{5}}\,\boldsymbol{U_{rms}}$$

$\therefore$ **Option (c) is correct.**

M20.60 *In a RC circuit switching is done at $t = 0$. The supply voltage is $v = (10e^{-t} \sin 314t)\,V$ for a 50 Hz source. The transient current at $t = (0+)$ is given by*

$$i = [(\cos 314t - \sin 314t) - e^{-10t}]\,A$$

The power loss across the $1\,\Omega$ resistor at $t = 0.2$ s is given by

(a) 0.2 mW (b) 1.135 mW

(c) 153.6 mW (d) 10 mW

Solution.

$$v = (10e^{-t} \sin 314t)\text{ V}$$

and $$i = [(\cos 314t - \sin 314t) - e^{-10^3 t}]\text{ A}$$

At $t = 0.2$ s,

$$i = [(\cos(314 \times 0.2) - (\sin 314 \times 0.2)) - e^{-10 \times 0.2}]\text{ A}$$
$$= [(\cos 62.8 - \sin 62.8) - e^{-2}]\text{ A}$$
$$= [(\cos 3600° - \sin 3600°) - e^{-2}]\text{ A}$$
$$\left[\because 62.8 \text{ rad} = \frac{62.8 \times 180}{3.14} = 3600°\right]$$

$$\therefore \ i = [(0-1) - 0.135] = -1.135 \text{ A}$$

Power loss in $1\,\Omega$ resistor

$$= i^2 R = (-1.135)^2 \times 1 = 0.1536 = \mathbf{153.6\ mW}$$

Option (c) is correct.

M20.61 *In the circuit shown below (Fig. 20.68); the supply voltage is $10 \sin(1000t)$ volts. The peak value of the steady state current through the $1\,\Omega$ resistor, in amperes, is _____.* **[GATE 2016]**

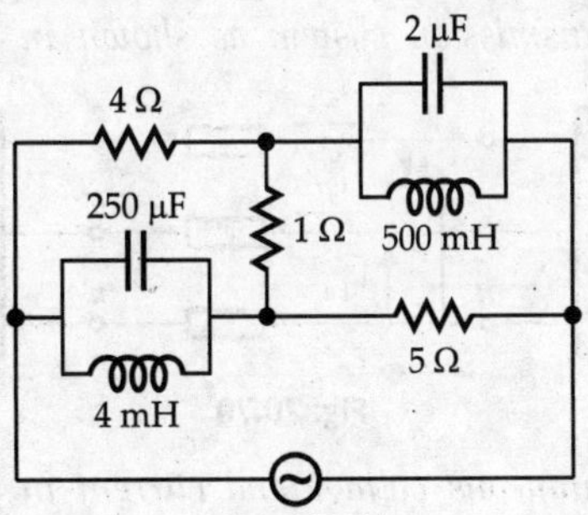

Fig. 20.68

Solution. Here $\omega = 1000$ rad/sec, the supply voltage frequency.

$\therefore$ X_{C_1} (of 2 μF capacitor)

$$= \frac{-j}{\omega C} = -\frac{j}{1000 \times 2 \times 10^{-6}} = -j500\ \Omega$$

X_{C_2} (of 250 μF capacitor)

$$= \frac{-j}{1000 \times 250 \times 10^{-6}} = -j4\ \Omega$$

X_{L_1} (of 500 mH inductor)

$$= j\omega L$$
$$= j \times 1000 \times 500 \times 10^{-3}$$
$$= j500\,\Omega$$

X_{L_2} (of 4 mH inductor)

$$= j \times 1000 \times 4 \times 10^{-3} = j4\ \Omega.$$

CHAPTER 20

Since $X_{C_1} = X_{L_1}$; $X_{C_2} = X_{L_2}$, hence the impedance of two circuits of parallel combination of 2 μF and 500 mH as well as 250 μF with parallel combination of 4 mH are infinite. They may be treated as open circuit. (Fig. 20.69)

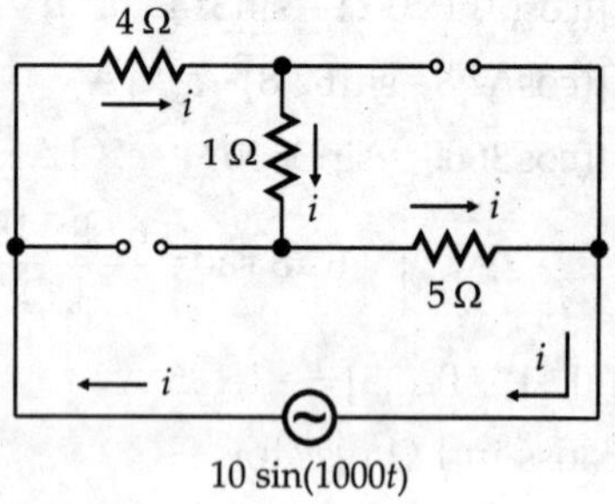

Fig. 20.69

$$\therefore \quad i = \frac{10 \sin 1000t}{4+1+5} = \sin 1000t$$

∴ Peak value of this ($\sin 1000t$) current is **1 A**.

M20.62 *A source is supplying a load through a 2-phase 3 wire transmission system as shown in Fig. 20.70.*

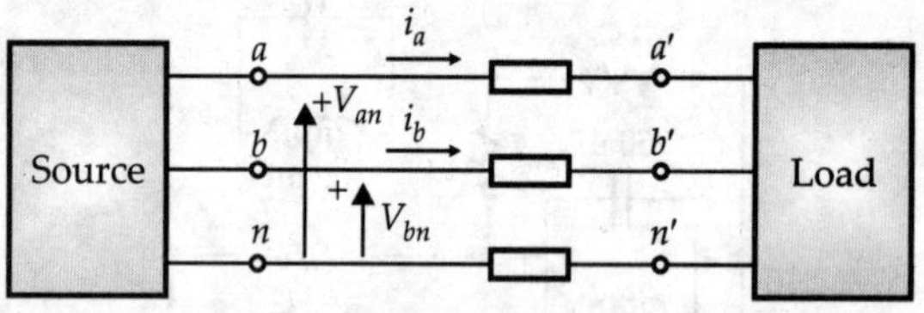

Fig. 20.70

The instantaneous voltage and current in phase-a are $v_{an} = 220 \sin(100\pi t)\, V$ *and* $i_a = 10 \sin(100\pi t)\, A$ *respectively. Similarly, for phase-b the instantaneous voltage and current are* $v_{bn} = 220 \cos(100\pi t)\, V$ *and* $i_b = 10 \cos(100\pi t)\, A$ *respectively.*

The total instantaneous power flowing from the source to the load is

(*a*) 2200 W (*b*) 2200 $\sin^2(100\pi t)$ W

(*c*) 4400 W

(*d*) 2200 $\sin(100\pi t)\cos(100\pi t)$ W **[GATE 2017]**

Solution. Since instantaneous power, hence

$$P = v(t) \times i(t)$$

here, $$P = v_{an} i_a + v_{bn} i_b$$

$$= 220 \sin(100\,\pi t) \times 10 \sin(100\,\pi t) + 220 \cos(100\,\pi t) \times 10 \cos(100\,\pi t)$$

$$= 2200\,[\sin^2(100\pi t) + \cos^2(100\pi t)]$$

$$= \mathbf{2200\ W}$$

∴ **Option (*a*) is correct.**

M20.63 *An energy meter connected to an immersion heater (resistive) operating on an AC 230 V, 50 Hz, AC single phase source reads 2.3 units (kWh) in 1 hour.*

The heater is removed from the supply and now connected to a 400 V peak to peak square wave source of 150 Hz. The power in kW dissipated by the heater will be

(*a*) 3.478 (*b*) 1.739

(*c*) 1.540 (*d*) 0.870 **[GATE 2006]**

Solution.

Case 1. Heater is connected to 230 V, 50 Hz source.

$$P_1 = \frac{\text{Energy}}{\text{Time period}} = \frac{2.3\ \text{kWh}}{60\ \text{min}}$$

[∵ 2.3 units of energy is equivalent to 2.3 units]

$$t = 1\ \text{hr} = 60\ \text{min}$$

$$\therefore \quad P_1 = 2.3\ \text{kW}$$

Also, $$P_1 = \frac{V^2_{ac(rms)}}{R} = \frac{230^2}{R} = 2.3 \times 10^3$$

$$\therefore \quad R = \frac{230^2}{2.3 \times 10^3} = 23\ \Omega$$

Case 2. Heater is connected to 400 V (peak to peak) square wave source with $f = 150$ Hz.

$$V_{rms(sq.\,wave)} = \left[\frac{1}{T}\int_0^T V^2 dt\right]^{1/2}$$

$$= \left[\frac{1}{T}\left\{\int_0^{T/2} 200^2\, dt + \int_{T/2}^{T} (-200)^2\, dt\right\}\right]^{1/2}$$

i.e., $$V_{rms} = 200\ \text{V}$$

$$\therefore \quad P_2 = \frac{200^2}{R} = \frac{200^2}{23}$$

i.e., $$P_2 = \mathbf{1.739\ kW}$$

Option (*b*) is correct.

M20.64 *A 0.1 μF capacitor charged to 100 V is discharged through a 1 kΩ resistor. The time in ms (round to two decimals) required for the voltage across the capacitor to drop to 1 V is ______.* **[GATE 2019]**

Solution.

For the discharging capacitor (Fig. 20.71),

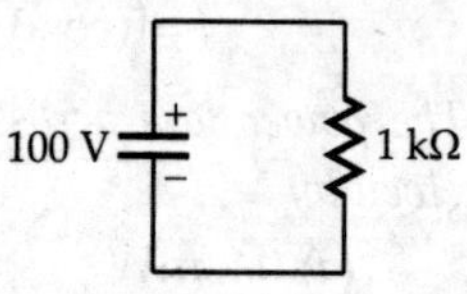

Fig. 20.71

$$v_c(t) = V_0 e^{-t/\tau}$$

Here, $V_0 = 100$ V ;

$$RC = \tau = 10^3 \times 10^{-7} = 10^{-4}\text{s}.$$

$$\therefore \quad v_c(t) = 100e^{-t/10^{-4}} = 100e^{-10^4 t} \text{ V}.$$

Let the time required to drop the voltage to +1 V across the capacitor be t_1.

$$\therefore \quad v_c(t_1) = 100e^{-10^4 t_1}$$

Here, $\quad v_c(t_1) = 1$ volt

$$\therefore \quad 1 = 100e^{-10^4 t_1}$$

or, $$0.01 = e^{-10^4 t_1}$$

or, $$-10^4 t_1 \log e = \log 0.01$$

or, $$-10^4 \times t_1 \times 0.434 = -2$$

$$\therefore \quad t_1 = \frac{2}{0.434 \times 10^4} = \mathbf{46\ ms.}$$

M20.65 *In Fig. 20.72, if $X_C = -j100\ \Omega$, the value of I_0 is*

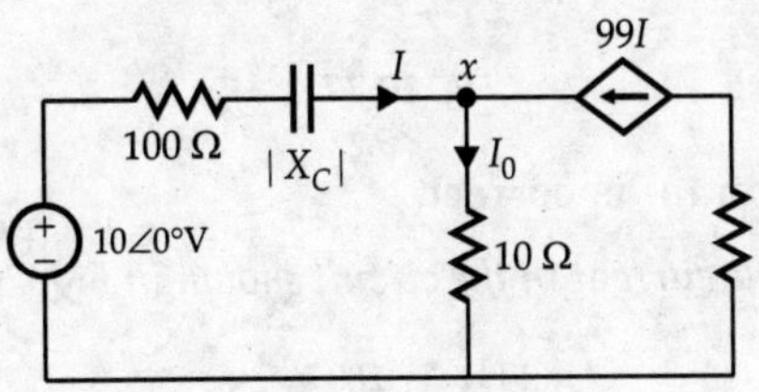

Fig. 20.72

(*a*) 10 ∠–9.29° A (*b*) 0.9057 ∠5.194° A

(*c*) 1.295 ∠–30° A (*d*) 0.5072 ∠6.297° A

Solution.

$$I_0 = I + 99I = 100I$$

$$= 100\left[\frac{10\angle 0° - V}{100 - j100}\right],$$

assuming V to be the node voltage at node x, marked on the given figure

Also, $V = 10I_0$

$$\therefore \quad I_0 = 100\left[\frac{10 - 10I_0}{100 - j100}\right] = \frac{10 - 10I_0}{1 - j1}$$

or, $$I_0(1 - j1) = 10 - 10I_0$$

or, $$I_0 - jI_0 + 10I_0 = 10$$

or, $$I_0(11 - j1) = 10$$

$$\therefore \quad I_0 = \frac{10}{11 - j1.0} = \frac{110 + j10}{122}$$

$$= 0.902 + j\,0.082$$

i.e., $\quad I_0 = \mathbf{0.9057\angle 5.194°\ A}$

Option (*b*) is correct.

M20.66 *A sinusoidal source of voltage V and frequency f is connected to a series circuit of variable resistance R and a fixed reactance X. The locus of the tip of the current phasor I as R is varied from 0 to ∞ is*

(*a*) *a semicircle with a diameter of* $\dfrac{V}{X}$

(*b*) *a straight line with a slope of* $\dfrac{R}{X}$

(*c*) *an ellipse with* $\dfrac{V}{R}$ *as major axis*

(*d*) *a circle of radius* $\dfrac{R}{X}$ *and origin* $\left(0, \dfrac{V}{2}\right)$.

[GATE 1998]

Solution.

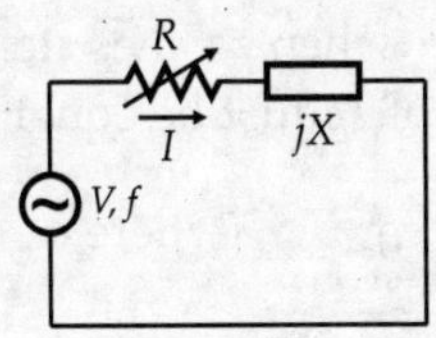

Fig. 20.73

In Fig. 20.73,

$$I = \frac{V}{(R + jX)} = \frac{V}{\sqrt{R^2 + X^2}} \angle -\tan^{-1}\frac{X}{R}$$

For $R = 0$; $I = \dfrac{V}{X}\angle -90°$

$R = X$; $I = \dfrac{V}{\sqrt{2}X}\angle -45°$

For $R = \infty$; $I = 0\angle 0°$

Figure 20.74 is a plot of I, as per the three points just obtained. **The locus of I is a semicircle, diameter $= \dfrac{V}{X}$.**

Option (*a*) is correct.

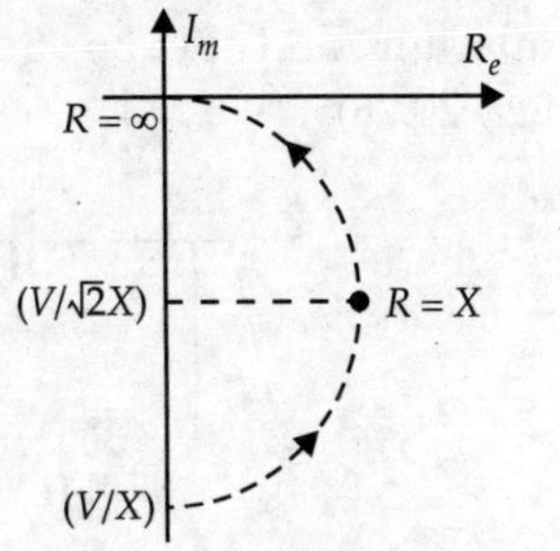

Fig. 20.74

M20.67 *The following circuit shown in Fig. 20.75 resonates at :*

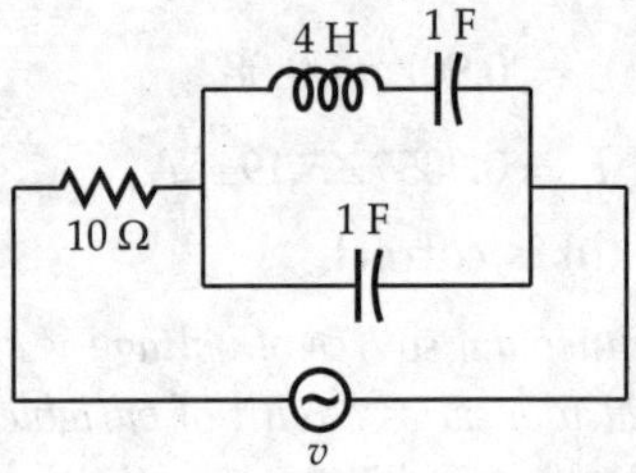

Fig. 20.75

(*a*) *all frequencies* (*b*) 0.5 rad/s
(*c*) 5 rad/s (*d*) 1 rad/s **[GATE 1993]**

Solution. The circuit impedance is given by

$$z = 10 + \left[\left(j4\omega - \frac{j}{\omega}\right) \middle\| \left(-\frac{j}{\omega}\right)\right]$$

$$= 10 - j\left[\frac{4 - \dfrac{1}{\omega^2}}{4\omega - \dfrac{2}{\omega}}\right]$$

The circuit when comes to resonance, the imaginary part of *z* must be equal to zero.

$\therefore \quad 4 - \frac{1}{\omega_n^2} = 0$ [where ω_n is the frequency of resonance]

i.e., ω_n = **0.5 rad/s**

Option (*b*) is correct.

M20.68 *A fixed capacitor of reactance* $(-j0.02\Omega)$ *is connected in parallel across a series combination of a fixed inductor of reactance* $j0.01\ \Omega$ *and a variable resistance R. R is varied from zero to infinity, the locus diagram of the admittance of this RLC circuit will be*

(*a*) *a semicircle of diameter j*100 *and centre at zero.*
(*b*) *a semicircle of diameter j*50 *and centre at zero.*
(*c*) *a straight line inclined at an angle.*
(*d*) *a straight line parallel to the x-axis.*

[GATE 1999]

Solution. Let Y_1 be the admittance of the capacitor and Y_2 be that of series *RL* circuit (Fig. 20.76)

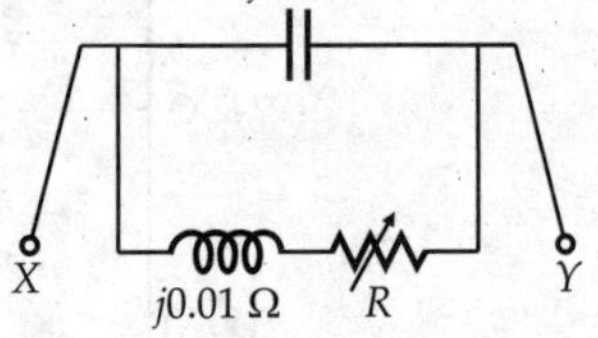

Fig. 20.76

$$Y_1 = \frac{1}{-j0.02}\ ; \quad Y_2 = \frac{1}{R + j0.01}$$

$$\therefore \quad Y_{XY} = Y_1 + Y_2 = \frac{1}{-j0.02} + \frac{1}{R + j0.01}$$

For $R \to 0, \quad Y_{XY} = -50j = 50\angle -90°\text{S}$

For $R \to 0.01, \ Y_{XY} = 50\,\text{S}$

For $R \to \infty, \quad Y_{XY} = 50j = 50\angle 90°\text{S}$

[*S* stands for Siemens]

∴ **Locus of Y_{AB} is a semicircle of diameter (*j*100) and centre at zero (Fig. 20.77).**

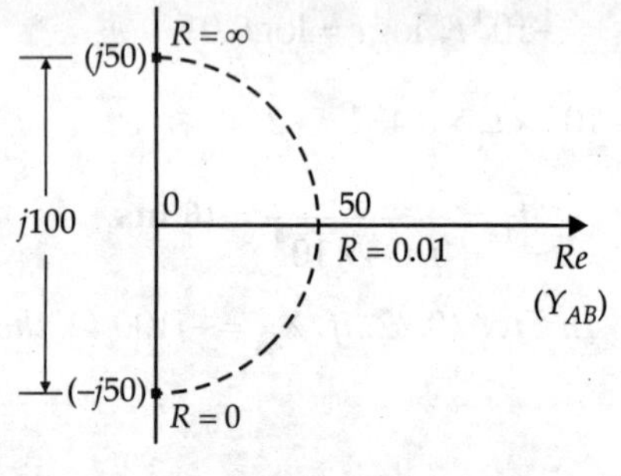

Fig. 20.77

Option (*a*) is correct.

M20.69 *The current in the circuit shown in Fig. 20.78 is*

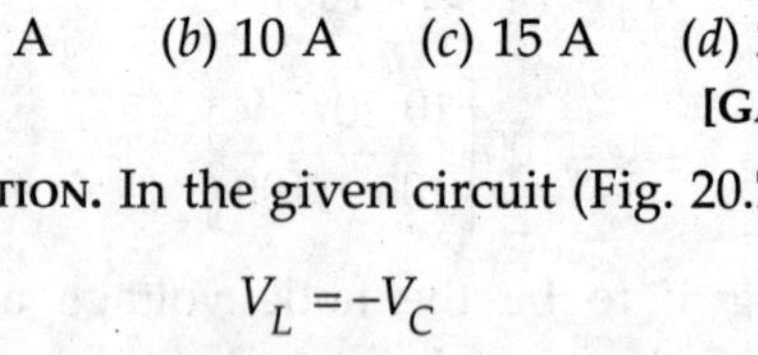

Fig. 20.78

(*a*) 5 A (*b*) 10 A (*c*) 15 A (*d*) 25 A

[GATE 1999]

Solution. In the given circuit (Fig. 20.78),

$$V_L = -V_C$$

Hence the given circuit is at series resonance.

Hence, $I = \frac{V}{R} = \frac{100}{20} = \mathbf{5\ A}$

∴ **Option (*a*) is correct.**

M20.70 *In a series RLC circuit at resonance, the magnitude of voltage developed across the capacitor.*

(*a*) *is always zero*
(*b*) *can be greater than the input voltage, however it is 90° out of phase with the input voltage.*

(*c*) *can never be greater than the input voltage.*

(*d*) *can be greater than the input voltage, and in phase with the input voltage.* **[GATE 2001]**

Solution. In a series *RLC* circuit, at resonance,

$$V_L = j\omega L \cdot I = j\omega L \cdot \frac{V_S}{R};$$

V_S is the source voltage.

$$= j\frac{\omega L}{R} \cdot V_S = jQV_S \quad ...(1)$$

$$V_C = -j\frac{1}{\omega C} \cdot I = -j\frac{1}{\omega cR} \cdot V_S = -jQV_S \quad ...(2)$$

If $Q > 1$, from (2) it is evident $|V_C| > |V_S|$.

$\therefore$ **Option (*b*) is correct.**

M20.71 *In the circuit shown in Fig. 20.79, the magnitudes of V_L and V_C are twice that of V_R. Given that $f = 50$ Hz, the inductance of the coil is*

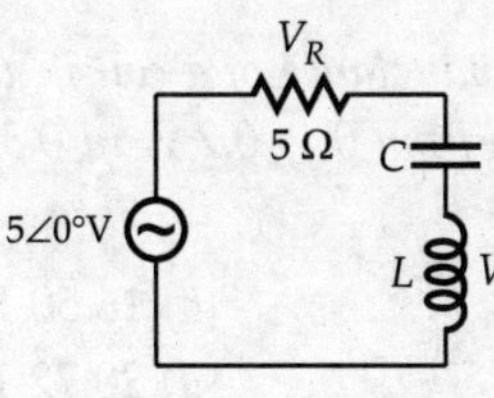

Fig. 20.79

(*a*) 2.14 mH (*b*) 5.30 H

(*c*) 31.8 mH (*d*) 1.32 H **[GATE 2003]**

Solution. Let V be the supply voltage $V = 5\angle 0°$ V.

Here, in the given circuit,

$$V = V_R + j(V_L - V_C) \quad ...(1)$$

Also, as per the given question,

$$|V_L| = |V_C|\ ; \quad |V_L| = 2|V_R|$$

$$Q \text{ factor} = \frac{V_L}{V} = \frac{2V}{V} = 2$$

$$\left[\text{from (1), } V = V_R \ \therefore V_L = V_C \ \textit{i.e., } V = \frac{|V_L|}{2}\right]$$

$$\text{Also,} \quad Q = \frac{\omega L}{R} = \frac{2\pi f . L}{R} = \frac{2 \times 3.14 \times 50 \times L}{5}$$

$$\text{or,} \quad 2 = \frac{314L}{5}$$

$$\therefore \quad L = 0.0318 \text{ H} = \mathbf{31.8\ mH}$$

Option (*c*) is correct.

M20.72 *The value of Z (in Fig. 20.80) which is most appropriate to cause parallel resonance at 500 Hz is*

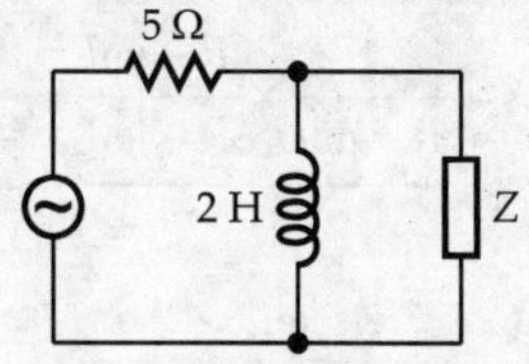

Fig. 20.80

(*a*) 125.00 mH (*b*) 304.20 mH

(*c*) 2.00 μF (*d*) 0.05 μF **[GATE 2004]**

Solution. $Y = Y_1 + Y_2 = \dfrac{1}{j\omega L} + \dfrac{1}{\dfrac{1}{j\omega C}}$

It may be noted in this context that to have parallel resonance, the supply p.f. should be unity. This is only possible if Z is capacitive. This simply means that branch Y_2 is purely capacitive.

Y is thus purely imaginary and for parallel resonance condition,

$$I_m(Y) = 0$$

$$\textit{i.e.,} \quad \frac{1}{j\omega L} + \frac{1}{\dfrac{1}{j\omega C}} = 0$$

$$\text{or,} \quad \frac{1}{j\omega L} + j\omega C = 0$$

$$\text{or,} \quad \frac{1}{\omega L} - \omega C = 0$$

$$\therefore \quad C = \frac{1}{\omega^2 L} = \frac{1}{(2\pi \times 50)^2 \times 2} = \mathbf{0.05\ \mu F}$$

Option (*d*) is correct.

M20.73 *At resonance, the given parallel circuit (Fig. 20.81) constituted by an iron-cored coil and a capacitor behaves like*

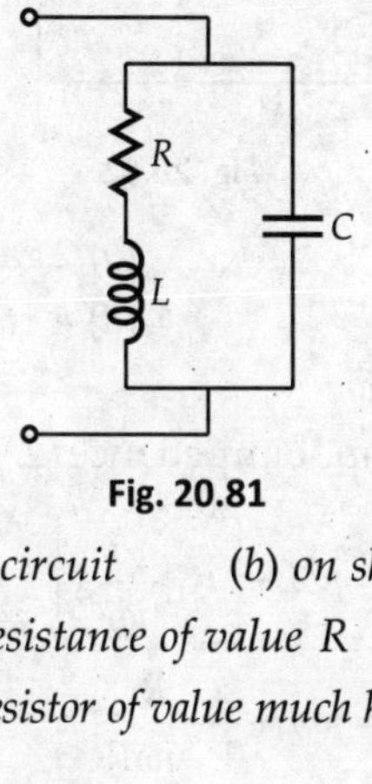

Fig. 20.81

(*a*) *on open circuit* (*b*) *on short-circuit*

(*c*) *a pure resistance of value R*

(*d*) *a pure resistor of value much higher than R.* **[GATE 1990]**

CHAPTER 20

Solution. The admittance of the given parallel circuit can be calculated as

$$Y = \underbrace{\frac{1}{R+j\omega L} \times \frac{R-j\omega L}{R-j\omega L}}_{Y_1} + \underbrace{\frac{1}{-jX_C}}_{Y_2}$$

$$= \frac{R-j\omega L}{R^2+(\omega L)^2} + \frac{j}{X_C} \qquad ...(1)$$

[Y_1 is the admittance of series R-L branch $Y_1 = \frac{1}{R+j\omega L}$; Y_2 = admittance of parallel branch (having C). $Y_2 = \frac{1}{-jX_C}$]

[At resonance, imaginary parts are equal to zero.

i.e., $$\frac{-j\omega L}{R^2+(\omega L)^2} + \frac{j}{X_C} = 0$$

or, $$\frac{\omega L}{R^2+(\omega L)^2} = \omega C \;]$$

At resonance, since the imaginary parts are zero hence only real parts of Eq. (1) will be retained.

$$\therefore \quad Y = \frac{R}{R^2+(\omega_0^2 L^2)}$$

$$\therefore \quad Z = \frac{1}{Y} = \frac{R^2+(\omega_0^2 L^2)}{R}$$

i.e., **Z >> R**

Option (*d*) is correct.

M20.74 *The resonant frequency for the given circuit (Fig. 20.82) will be*

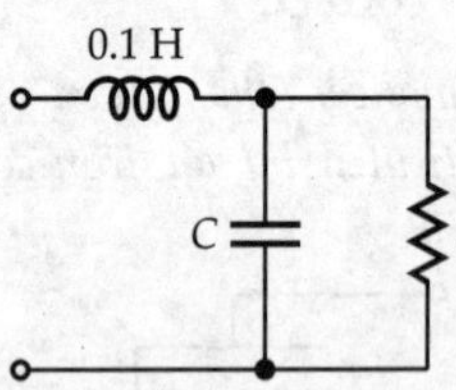

Fig. 20.82

(*a*) 1 rad/s (*b*) 2 rad/s
(*c*) 3 rad/s (*d*) 4 rad/s

[GATE 2008]

Solution. Input impedance (Z_{in}) is obtained as

$$Z_{in} = j\omega L + \left[R \,||\, \frac{1}{j\omega C}\right]$$

$$= j\omega L + \frac{R}{1+j\omega RC}$$

i.e., $$Z_{in} = j0.1\omega + \frac{1}{1+j\omega \times 1 \times 1}$$

$$= j0.1\omega + \frac{1}{1+j\omega} \times \frac{1-j\omega}{1-j\omega}$$

$$= j0.1\omega + \frac{1-j\omega}{1+\omega^2}$$

$$= \frac{1}{1+\omega^2} + j\left[0.1\omega - \frac{\omega}{1+\omega^2}\right]$$

At resonance, $I_m(Z_{in}) = 0$

$$\therefore \quad \left[0.1\omega - \frac{\omega}{1+\omega^2}\right] = 0$$

or, $$0.1 = \frac{1}{1+\omega^2}$$

i.e., ω = **3 rad/s**

Option (*c*) is correct.

M20.75 *(i) The inductance of a coil in which a current increases linearly from 0 to 0.2 A in 0.3 s, producing a voltage of 25 V is*

(*a*) 37.88 H (*b*) 16.50 H
(*c*) 83.33 H (*d*) 20.72 H

(ii) When a dc voltage is applied to a capacitor, the voltage across its terminals builds up in accordance with $v_c = 100(1-10e^{-100t})$*. After the time interval of 0.01 s, the current becomes 5 mA. The value of capacitance 'C' is*

(*a*) 2.36 μF (*b*) 0.987 μF
(*c*) 13.44 μF (*d*) 1.36 μF

Solution. (*i*) Current in one second $= \frac{0.2}{0.3} = 0.66$ A

$\therefore$ Rate of change of current is 0.66 A/s.

$$|v| = L\left|\frac{di}{dt}\right|$$

i.e., $$L = \frac{|v|}{\left|\frac{di}{dt}\right|} = \frac{25}{0.66} = \mathbf{37.88\ H.}$$

Option (*a*) is correct.

(*ii*) $$i = C\frac{dv_c}{dt} = C\frac{d}{dt}[100(1-10e^{-100t})]$$

$$= C \times 100 \times 100 \times e^{-100t} = 10^4 C \times e^{-100t} \text{ A}$$

At $t = 0.01$ s, $i = 5$ mA

$$\therefore \; C = \frac{5\times10^{-3}}{10^4 \times e^{-100\times0.01}} = \frac{5\times10^{-3}}{3678.79} = \mathbf{1.36\ \mu F.}$$

Option (*d*) is correct.

M20.76 *The voltage $v(t)$ across the terminals a and b shown in Fig. 20.83 is a sinusoidal voltage having a frequency $\omega = 100$ rad / s. When the inductor current $i(t)$ is in phase with the voltage $v(t)$, the magnitude of the impedance Z(in Ω) seen between the terminals a and b is ______ (upto 2 decimal places).* **[GATE 2018]**

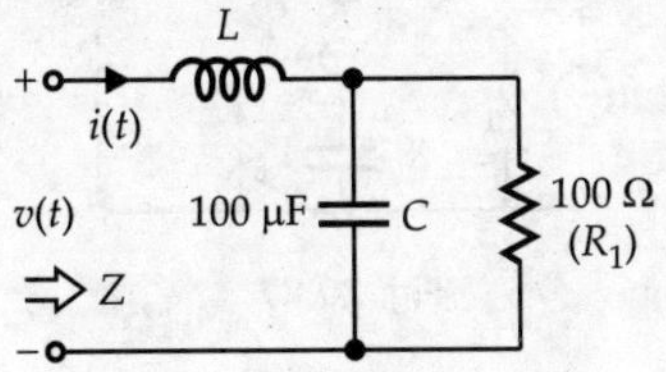

Fig. 20.83

SOLUTION. $Z(\text{imag.}) \to 0$ at resonance

$[\because\ i(t)$ is in same phase with $v(t)]$

$$Z(\text{real}) = \frac{R_1 X_C^2}{R_1^2 + X_C^2}$$

where $R_1 = 100\ \Omega$.

$$|X_C| = \frac{1}{\omega C}$$

$$= \frac{1}{1000 \times 100 \times 10^{-6}} = 100\ \Omega$$

$$\therefore\quad Z(\text{real}) = \frac{100 \times 100^2}{100^2 + 100^2} = 50\ \Omega$$

Hence, $Z(\text{input}) = \mathbf{50\ \Omega}$.

M20.77 *The average power delivered in an impedance $(4 - j3)\ \Omega$ by a current $5\cos(100\pi t + 100)$ A is*

(*a*) 44.2 W (*b*) 50 W

(*c*) 62.5 W (*d*) 125 W **[GATE 2012]**

SOLUTION.

$$i = 5\cos(100\pi t + 100)\text{ A}$$

$$\therefore\quad I_{\max} = 5\text{ A};\ I_{rms} = \frac{5}{\sqrt{2}}\text{ A}$$

$$P_{av} = I_{rms}^2 \times R = \left(\frac{5}{\sqrt{2}}\right)^2 \times 4 = \mathbf{50\ W}$$

Option (*b*) is correct.

M20.78 *The voltage across the circuit in the figure (Fig. 20.84) and the current through it, are given by the following expressions :*

$$v(t) = 5 - 10\cos(\omega t + 60°)\ V$$

$$i(t) = 5 + X\cos(\omega t) A$$

where, $\omega = 100\pi$ radians/s. If the average power delivered to the circuit is zero, then the value of X(in ampere) is ______ upto 2 decimal places). **[GATE 2018]**

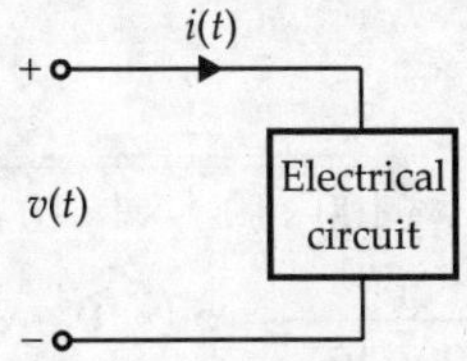

Fig. 20.84

SOLUTION. Given :

$$v(t) = 5 - 10\cos(\omega t + 60°)\text{ V}$$

$$i(t) = 5 + X\cos(\omega t)\text{ A} = 5 + X\cos(\omega t - 0)$$

Since average power = 0

$$\therefore\quad 0 = 5 \times 5 + \tfrac{1}{2}[\{-(10)\}\{(X)\cos 60°\}]$$

$$\left[\because \text{ Average power} = \frac{1}{2} V_m I_m \cos\phi \right.$$

$$\text{Here } |V_m| = |10|\ ;\ I_m = |X|$$

$$\left. \text{and } \cos\phi = \cos 60° \right]$$

$$\therefore\quad -25 = \frac{1}{2}[(-10)X\cos 60°]$$

i.e., $\quad X = \mathbf{10.}$

M20.79 *A series RLC circuit, when excited by a 10 V sinusoidal voltage source of variable frequency, exhibits resonance at 100 Hz and has a 3 dB bandwidth of 5 Hz. The voltage across the inductor L at resonance is*

(*a*) 10 V (*b*) $10\sqrt{2}$ V

(*c*) $\dfrac{10}{\sqrt{2}\text{ V}}$ (*d*) 200 V

[GATE 1999]

SOLUTION.

$$Q = \frac{\omega_0}{dB}\ ;\ \omega_0 = \text{resonant frequency}$$

$$dB = \text{Bandwidth}$$

$$= \frac{f_0}{\Delta f} = \frac{100}{5} = 20$$

$\because$ At resonance,

$$|V_L| = |V_C| = Q.|V_S|$$

where V_S is the source voltage.

$$\therefore\quad |V_L| = 20 \times 10 = \mathbf{200\ V}$$

Option (*d*) is correct.

M20.80 *A series RLC circuit has $R = 50\ \Omega$; $L = 100\,\mu H$ and $C = 1\,\mu F$. The lower half power frequency of the circuit is*

(*a*) 30.55 kHz (*b*) 3.065 kHz

(*c*) 51.92 kHz (*d*) 1.92 kHz

[GATE 2002]

Solution.

$$\omega_0 = \frac{1}{\sqrt{LC}} = \frac{1}{\sqrt{100\times10^{-6}\times1\times10^{-6}}} = 10^5\ \text{rad/s}$$

$$\Delta\omega = \frac{R}{L} = \frac{50}{100\times10^{-6}} = 50\times10^4\ \text{rad/s}$$

$$\omega_{lower} = \left[\sqrt{\omega_0^2+\left(\frac{\Delta\omega}{2}\right)^2} - \frac{\Delta\omega}{2}\right]$$

$$= \left[\sqrt{(10^5)^2+\left(\frac{5\times10^5}{2}\right)^2} - \frac{5\times10^5}{2}\right]$$

$$= 10^5[\sqrt{1+6.25} - 2.5] = 0.1925\times10^5\ \text{rad/s}$$

Hence, $f_{lower} = \dfrac{\omega_{lower}}{2\pi}$

$$= \frac{0.1925\times10^5}{2\times3.14} = \mathbf{3.065\ kHz.}$$

$\therefore$ **Option (*b*) is correct.**

M20.81 *The circuit shown in Fig. 20.85 is energized by a sinusoidal voltage source V_1 at a frequency which causes resonance with a current I.*

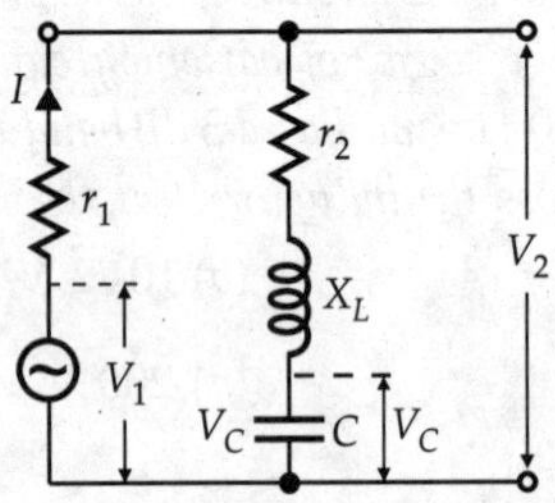

Fig. 20.85

The power diagram which is applicable to the circuit is

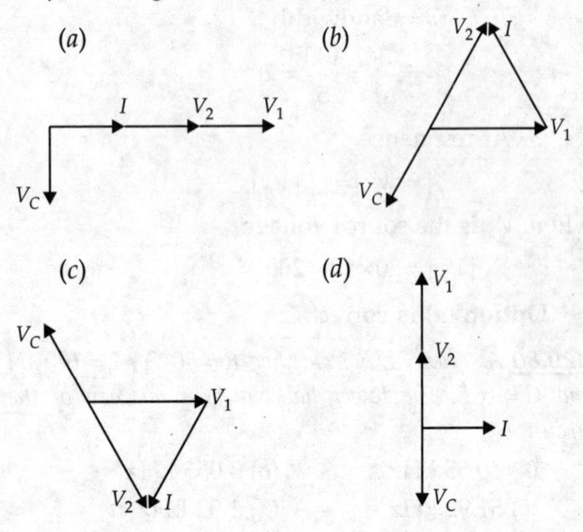

Fig. 20.86

Solution. Let us redraw the figure (Fig. 20.85) as shown in Fig. 20.87.

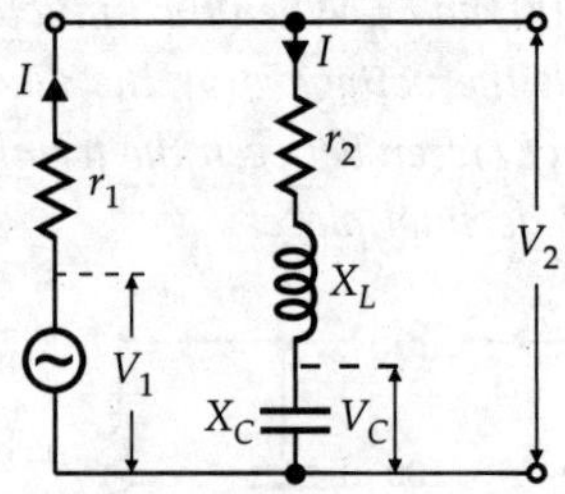

Fig. 20.87

Here, $Z = r_1 + r_2 + j(X_L - X_C)$

At resonance, $|X_L| = |X_C|$

$\therefore\ Z = r_1 + r_2$

Hence *Z*, the input impedance, is purely resistive.

Since *Z* is purely resistive, the input voltage and output current are in phase ; *i.e.*, V_1 and *I* are in phase.

Also, $V_2 = \dfrac{V_1}{r_1+r_2+j(X_L-X_C)}\times[r_2+j(X_L-X_C)]$

With $|X_L| = |X_C|$, $V_2 = \dfrac{V_1}{r_1+r_2}\times r_2$

$\therefore$ V_2 is also in phase with V_1 and also, $V_2 < V_1$.

In addition to this,

$$V_C = IX_C = I\frac{1}{j\omega C}$$

$$\therefore\quad V_C = \frac{1}{\omega C}\angle-90°$$

i.e., V_C lags the current by 90°.

Hence phasor diagram **(*a*)** is correct.

Option (*a*) is correct.

M20.82 *In the circuit shown in Fig. 20.88, what value of C will cause a unity power factor at the ac source ?*

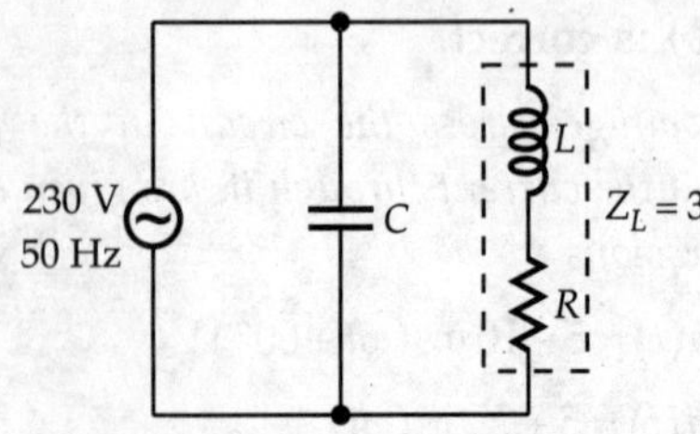

Fig. 20.88

(*a*) 68.1 μF (*b*) 165 μF

(*c*) 0.681 μF (*d*) 6.81 μF **[GATE 2002]**

Solution. For the given circuit, let Y_1 be the admittance of the branch containing C while Y_2 be the admittance of the branch containing L and R.

$\therefore$ Total admittance (Y) of the circuit is given by

$$Y = Y_1 + Y_2 = j\omega C + \frac{1}{Z_L} = j\omega C + \frac{1}{30\angle 40°}$$

$$= j\omega C + 0.0255 - j0.0214$$

$$= 0.0255 + j(\omega C - 0.0214)$$

$$= \text{Real part of } Y + \text{Imaginary part of } Y$$

The power factor at the ac source will be unity only when imaginary part of $Y = 0$.

i.e., $j(\omega C - 0.0214) = 0$

$\therefore$ $\omega C = 0.0214$

or, $C = \frac{0.0214}{\omega} = \frac{0.0214}{2\pi f}$

$= \frac{0.0214}{100\pi} = \mathbf{68.1\ \mu F}$

Option (*a*) is correct.

M20.83 *If the input real power at terminal XY be $10^3 W$, find power consumption in r_1 and r_2. (Fig. 20.89)*

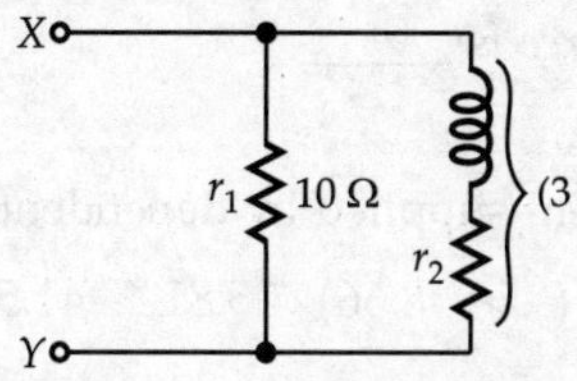

Fig. 20.89

(*a*) 545.46 W ; 454.53 W

(*b*) 375.25 W ; 624.75 W

(*c*) 454.53 W ; 545.46 W

(*d*) 500 W ; 500 W

Solution. Let us redraw the circuit as shown in Fig. 20.90.

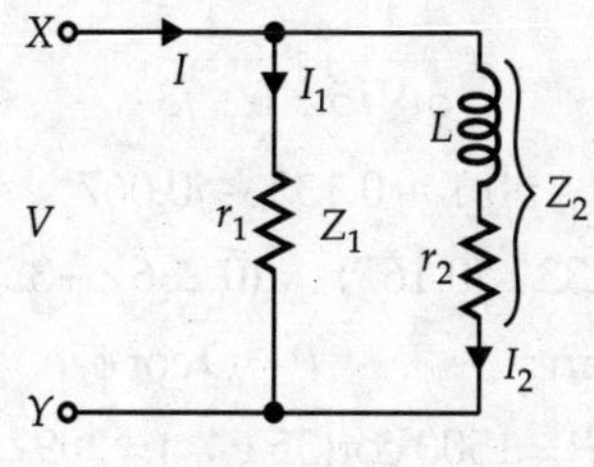

Fig. 20.90

$$V = I_1 Z_1 = I_2 Z_2$$

$\therefore$ $$\frac{|I_1|}{|I_2|} = \frac{|Z_2|}{|Z_1|}$$

Here, $$\frac{|I_1|}{|I_2|} = \frac{\sqrt{3^2+4^2}}{10} = \frac{1}{2}$$

$\therefore$ $$\frac{P_1}{P_2} = \frac{|I_1|^2 R_1}{|I_2|^2 R_2} = \left(\frac{1}{2}\right)^2 \times \frac{10}{3} = 0.8333 \quad ...(1)$$

Also $P_1 + P_2 = 1000$ W

or, $(0.8333 P_2) + P_2 = 1000$ W

$\therefore$ $$P_2 = \frac{1000}{1.8333} = 545.46 \text{ W}$$

$$P_1 = 1000 - 545.46 = 454.53 \text{ W}$$

Thus,

P_1, power consumption in r_1 = **454.53 W**

P_2, power consumption in r_2 = **545.46 W**

Option (*c*) is correct.

M20.84 *A series RLC circuit is observed at two frequencies. At $\omega_1 = 1 k\ rad/s$, we note that source voltage $V_1 = 100\angle 0° V$ results in a current $I_1 = 0.03\angle 31° A$. At $\omega_2 = 2\ k\ rad/s$, the source voltage $V_2 = 100\angle 0° V$ results in a current $I_2 = 2\angle 0° A$. The closest values for R, L, C out of the following options are :*

(*a*) $R = 50\ \Omega$; $L = 25$ mH ; $C = 10\ \mu F$

(*b*) $R = 50\ \Omega$; $L = 10$ mH ; $C = 25\ \mu F$

(*c*) $R = 50\ \Omega$; $L = 50$ mH ; $C = 5\ \mu F$

(*d*) $R = 50\ \Omega$; $L = 5$ mH ; $C = 50\ \mu F$ **[GATE 2014]**

Solution. It may be observed that at $\omega_2 = 2$ krad/s, the circuit current I_2 is $2\angle 0°$ A for the source voltage of $V_2 = 100\angle 0°$ V. Thus the circuit acts as a resistive circuit.

$$R = \frac{V_2}{I_2} = \frac{100\angle 0°}{2\angle 0°} = \mathbf{50\ \Omega}$$

This is possible provided the series circuit is at resonance and $X_L = X_C$. With this

$$\omega_0 (= \omega_2) = 2 \times 10^3 \text{ rad/s} = \frac{1}{\sqrt{LC}}$$

However, at $\omega_1 = 1 \times 10^3$ rad/s,

Z (impedance of the series circuit) $= \frac{V_1}{I_1}$

or, $$Z = \frac{100\angle 0°}{0.03\angle 31°} = 3333.3\angle -31°$$

i.e., $$R + j\omega_1 L + \frac{1}{j\omega_1 C} = 3333.3\angle -31°$$

$$\therefore \quad \tan^{-1}\left[\frac{\omega_1 L - 1/\omega_1 C}{R}\right] = -31°$$

or, $$\omega_1 L - \frac{1}{\omega_1 C} = R[\tan(-31°)]$$

$$\therefore \quad \omega_1 L - \frac{1}{\omega_1 C} = -30 \qquad [\because R = 50\Omega]$$

Substituting $L = \frac{1}{\omega_2^2 C}$, we have

$$\omega_1 \times \frac{1}{\omega_2^2 C} - \frac{1}{\omega_1 C} = -30$$

$$10^3\left[\frac{1}{(2\times 10^3)^2 C}\right] - \frac{1}{10^3 . C} = -30$$

$\therefore$ $C = \mathbf{25\,\mu F}$ and $L = \frac{1}{\omega_2^2 C} = \mathbf{10\ mH}$

Option (*b*) is correct.

M20.85

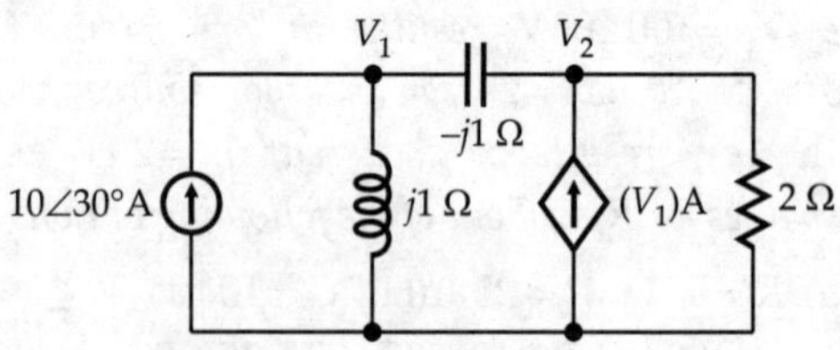

Fig. 20.91

The complex power supplied by the current source (Fig. 20.91) is

(*a*) 129.4∠0° VA (*b*) 12.94∠−66.08° VA
(*c*) 158.10∠11.56° VA (*d*) 120∠90° VA

Solution. Let us name the node as x_1 where voltage is V_1 and x_2 when voltage is V_2

$\therefore$ At node x_1,

$$-10\angle 30° + \frac{V_1}{j1} + \frac{V_1 - V_2}{-j1} = 0$$

or, $$\frac{V_1}{j1} + \frac{V_1 - V_2}{-j1} = 10\angle 30° = 8.66 + j5$$

or, $$-jV_1 + jV_1 - jV_2 = 8.66 + j5$$

or, $$V_2 = \frac{8.66 + j5}{-j} = j8.66 - 5$$

i.e., $$V_2 = (-5 + j8.66)\text{ Volts}$$

At node x_2, we can write

$$\left[\frac{V_2 - V_1}{-j1}\right] - V_1 + \frac{V_2}{2} = 0$$

or, $$jV_2 - jV_1 - V_1 + 0.5V_2 = 0$$

$$V_1(1+j) = (0.5+j)V_2$$
$$= (0.5+j)(-5+j8.66)$$
$$= -2.5 + j4.33 - j5 - 8.66$$
$$= (-11.16 - j0.67)$$

$$\therefore \quad V_1 = \frac{-11.16 - j0.67}{1+j}$$
$$= \frac{(1-j)(-11.16 - j0.67)}{2}$$
$$= \frac{-11.16 - j0.67 + j11.16 - 0.67}{2}$$
$$= (-11.83 - j10.49)\text{V}$$
$$= 15.81\angle -41.56°\text{ V}$$

$$\therefore \quad S\text{ (complex power)} = V_1 I^*$$
$$= 15.81\angle 41.56° \times 10\angle -30°$$
$$= \mathbf{158.10\angle 11.56°\ VA}$$

Option (*c*) is correct.

M20.86 *In Q. No. 20.85, the complex power supplied by the dependent source is ______ VA.*

Solution.

$$S = V_2 \times (\text{Current supplied by dependent source})^*$$
$$= V_2 \times V_1^* = [(-5 + j8.66) \times 15.81\angle -41.56°]$$
$$= [10\angle -60° \times 15.81\angle -41.56°]$$
$$= \mathbf{158.1\angle -101.56°\ VA.}$$

M20.87 *An impedance* $(5 + j5)\ \Omega$ *is connected in parallel to another impedance of* $10(6 + j3)\Omega$. *If the input reactive power is 1500 VAR (lagging), the total active power is given by*

(*a*) 1500 W (*b*) 2092.34 W
(*c*) 1680.34 W (*d*) 2802.39 W

Solution.

$$Y = Y_1 + Y_2 = \frac{1}{5 + j5} + \frac{1}{6 + j3}$$
$$= 0.1 - j\,0.1 + 0.133 - j0.067$$
$$= (0.233 - j0.167)s = (0.286\angle -35.64°)s$$

$$Q = P\tan\phi \qquad \therefore \quad P = Q\cot\phi$$

Hence $P = 1500\cot(35.64°) = \mathbf{2092.34\ W}$

Option (*b*) is correct.

M20.88 *Two magnetically coupled inductive coils have Q factor q_1 and q_2 at the chosen operating frequency. Their respective resistances are R_1 and R_2. While connected in series, their effective Q factor at the same operating frequency is*

(*a*) $q_1 + q_2$ (*b*) $\frac{1}{q_1} + \frac{1}{q_2}$

(*c*) $\left(\frac{q_1 R_1 + q_2 R_2}{R_1 + R_2}\right)$ (*d*) $\frac{q_1 R_2 + q_2 R_1}{R_1 + R_2}$

[GATE 2013]

SOLUTION. $q_1 = \frac{\omega L_1}{R_1}$; $L_1 = \frac{q_1 R_1}{\omega}$

Similarly, $L_2 = \frac{q_2 R_2}{\omega}$

$\therefore \quad L_1 + L_2 = \frac{q_1 R_1}{\omega} + \frac{q_2 R_2}{\omega}$

or, $\omega(L_1 + L_2) = q_1 R_1 + q_2 R_2$ ...(1)

Also, $Q = \frac{\omega(L_1 + L_2)}{(R_1 + R_2)}$ $\left[\text{When in series, } Q = \frac{\omega L}{R} = \frac{\omega(L_1 + L_2)}{R_1 + R_2}\right]$

or, $Q = \frac{\boldsymbol{q_1 R_1 + q_2 R_2}}{\boldsymbol{(R_1 + R_2)}}$ [From (1)]

Option (*d*) is correct.

M20.89 *An inductor is connected in parallel with a capacitor as shown in the figure (Fig. 20.92). As the frequency of current i is increased, the impedance (Z) of the network varies as shown in Figs. 20.93(a), (b), (c) and (d). Pick up the correct answer.* **[GATE 2016]**

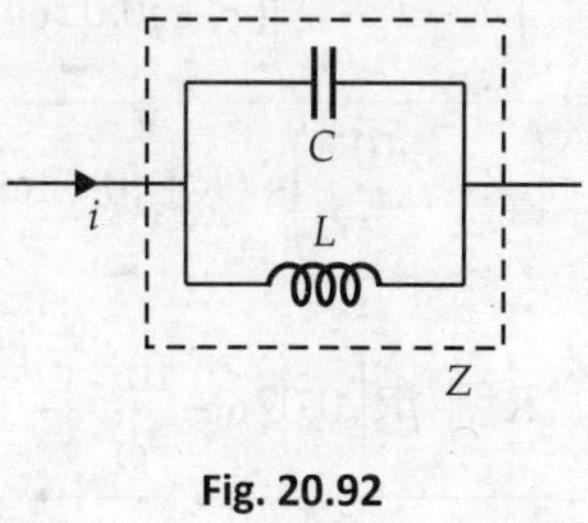

Fig. 20.92

(*a*)

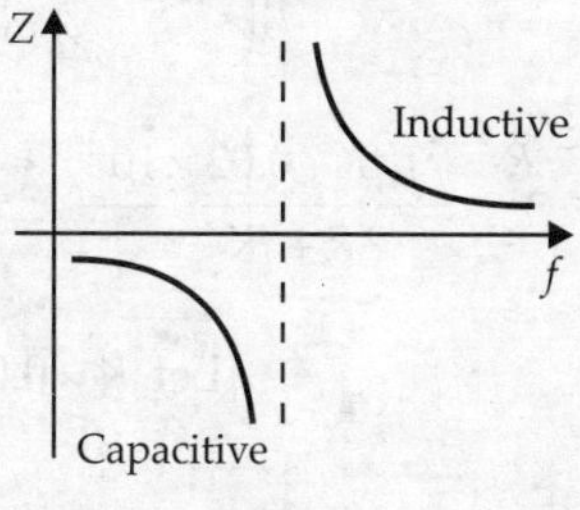

(*b*)

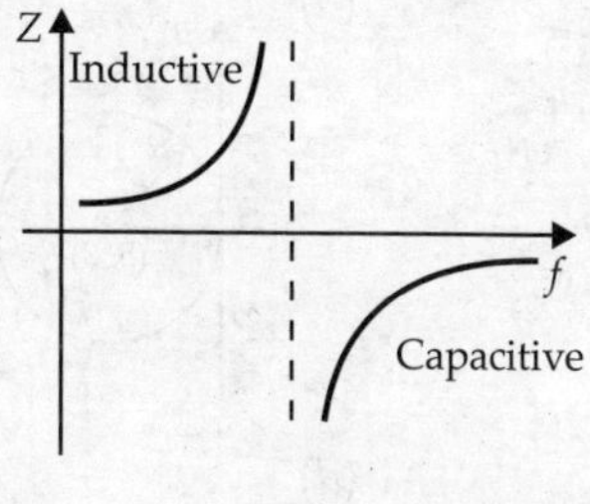

(*c*)

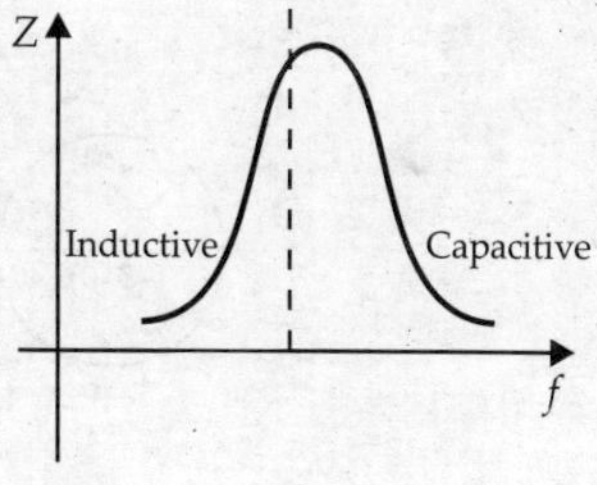

(*d*)

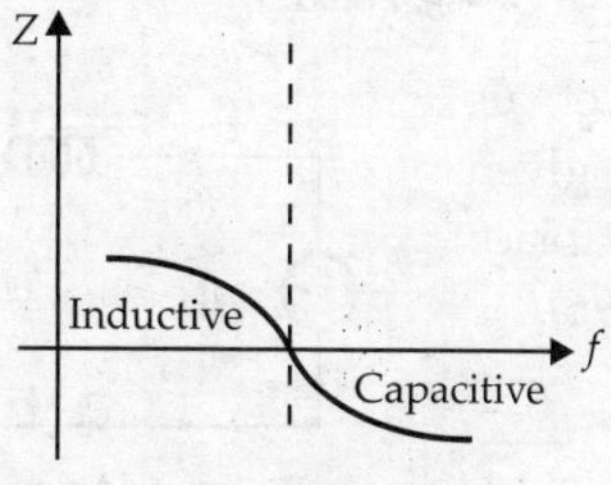

Fig. 20.93

SOLUTION.

$$Z = \frac{j\omega L\left(\frac{1}{j\omega C}\right)}{j\omega L + \frac{1}{j\omega C}} = \frac{j\omega L}{1 - \omega^2 LC}$$

if $1 - \omega^2 LC > 0$, Z is inductive

if $1 - \omega^2 LC < 0$, Z is capacitive

if $1 - \omega^2 LC = 0$, Z is infinity and $\omega = \frac{1}{\sqrt{LC}}$.

Hence for lesser value of f, $(1 - \omega^2 LC)$ *i.e.*, Z is +ve and for higher value of f, it is –ve. Then option (*a*) is not possible. Also, with f increasing, Z (inductive) increases. Thus option (*d*) is also not possible. With higher values of f, Z (capacitive) becomes –ve and hence option (*c*) is not possible.

The only option that is possible is option (*b*).

M20.90 *A dc voltage source is connected to a series L-C circuit by turning on the switch S at time t = 0 as shown in the figure (Fig. 20.94). Assume i(0) = 0 ; V(0) = 0. Which of the following circular loci represent the plot of i(t) versus v(t) (Fig. 20.95) ?* **[GATE 18]**

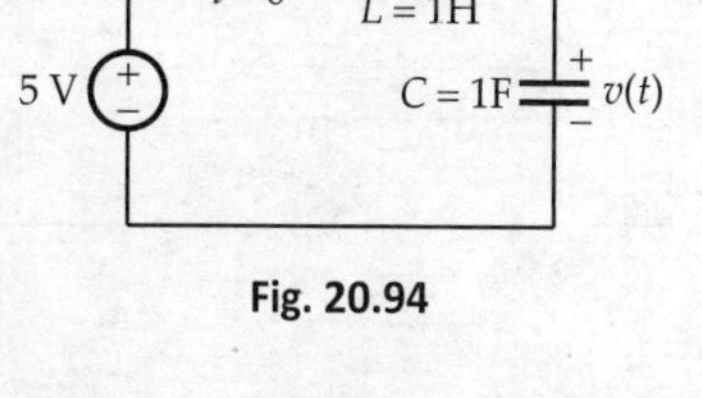

Fig. 20.94

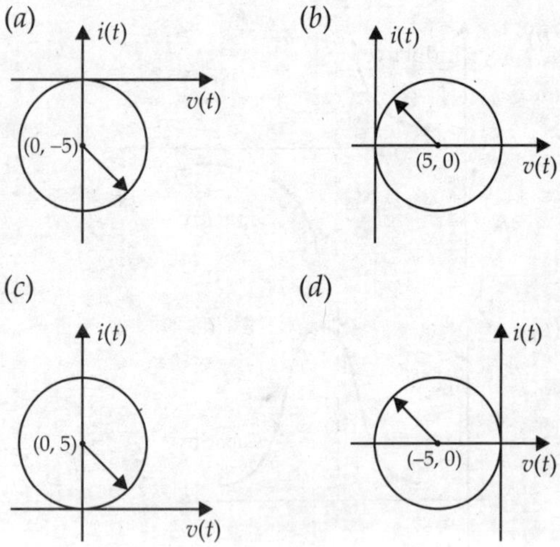

Fig. 20.95

Solution. Let us first transfer the given circuit to Laplace domain (Fig. 20.96).

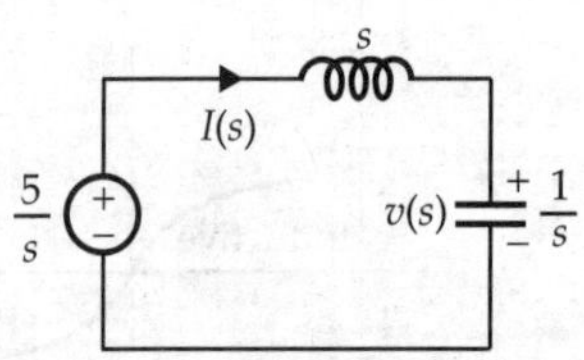

Fig. 20.96

$$I(s) = \frac{5/s}{s+\frac{1}{s}} = \frac{5}{s^2+1}$$

$$\therefore \qquad i(t) = 5\sin t$$

$$v(t) = \frac{1}{C}\int_0^t i(t)\,dt = \int_0^t 5\sin t\,dt$$

$$= 5[-\cos t]_0^t = 5[-\cos t + 1]$$

i.e., $\qquad v(t) = 5 - 5\cos t$

Let us now plot $i(t)$ and $v(t)$ for different values of t (Table 20.1).

Table 20.1

t	$i(t)$	$v(t)$
0	0	0
$\frac{T}{4}$	$5\sin t = 5\sin\frac{2\pi}{4} = 5$	$5-5\cos t$ $= 5-5\cos\frac{2\pi}{4} = 5$
$\frac{T}{2}$	$5\sin t = 5\sin\frac{2\pi}{2} = 0$	$5-5\cos t$ $= 5-5\cos\frac{2\pi}{2} = 10$
$\frac{3T}{4}$	$5\sin t = 5\sin\frac{3\times 2\pi}{4} = -5$	$5-5\cos t$ $= 5-5\cos\frac{3\times 2\pi}{4} = 5$
T	$5\sin t = 5\sin 2\pi = 0$	$5-5\cos t$ $= 5-5\cos 2\pi = 0$

Let us now plot the graph (20.97)

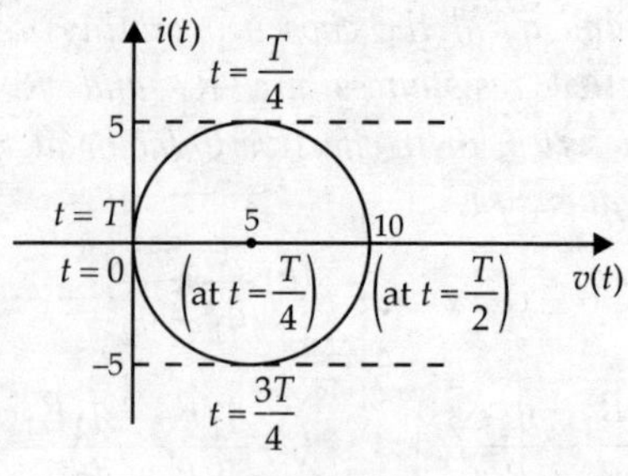

Fig. 20.97

Option (b) is correct.

M20.91 *The circuit shown below (Fig. 20.98) is excited by a sinusoidal source. The value of R, in Ω, for which the admittance of the circuit becomes a pure conductance at all frequencies is ______ .* **[GATE 2016]**

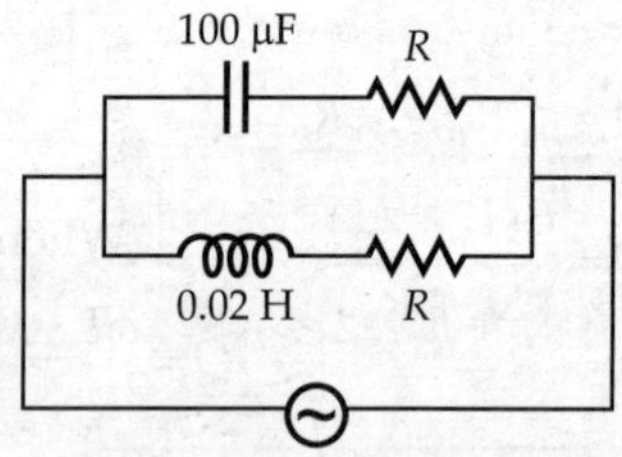

Fig. 20.98

Solution. In Fig. 20.98,

$$X_C = \frac{-j}{\omega C} = \frac{-j}{100\times 10^{-6}\,\omega} = \frac{-j\times 10^4}{\omega}$$

$$X_L = j\omega L = j0.02\,\omega$$

$$\therefore \qquad Z_{eq} = \frac{\left(R - j\frac{10^4}{\omega}\right)(R + j0.02\,\omega)}{\left(R - j\frac{10^4}{\omega}\right) + (R + j0.02\,\omega)}$$

$$= \frac{R^2 + jR\left(0.02\,\omega - \frac{10^4}{\omega}\right) + 0.02\times 10^4}{2R + j\left(0.02\,\omega - \frac{10^4}{\omega}\right)}$$

$$= \frac{R^2 + jRK + 0.02\times 10^4}{2R + jK}$$

$$\left[\text{Let } K = 0.02\,\omega - \frac{10^4}{\omega}\right]$$

$$= \frac{(R^2 + jRK + 200)(2R - jK)}{(2R + jK)(2R - jK)}$$

$$= \frac{(2R^3 + K^2R + 400R) + j(KR^2 - K.20)}{4R^2 + K^2}$$

$$\therefore \quad Y_{eq} = \frac{4R^2 + K^2}{(2R^3 + K^2R + 400R) + j(KR^2 - 200K)}$$

Y_{eq} to become a pure conductance, imaginary part must be zero.

i.e., $\quad KR^2 - 200K = 0$

i.e., $\quad R = \sqrt{200} = \mathbf{14.14\ \Omega}.$

M20.92 *The line A to neutral voltage is $10\angle 15°$ V for a balanced three phase star connected load with phase sequence ABC. The voltage of the line B with respect to line A is given by* **[GATE 2014]**

(*a*) $10\sqrt{3}\angle 105°$ V (*b*) $10\angle 105°$ V

(c) $10\sqrt{3}\angle -75°$ V (*d*) $-10\sqrt{3}\angle 90°$ V

Solution.

$$V_{AN} = 10\angle 15° \text{ V (given)}$$

$$\therefore \quad V_{BN} = 10\angle -120° + 15° = 10\angle -105° \text{ V}$$

$$V_{CN} = 10\angle -240° + 15°$$

$$= 10\angle -225° \text{ V}$$

In a balanced three phase star connected system, the line voltage always leads the corresponding phase voltage by 30°.

$\therefore$ V_{BA} will lead V_{BN} by 30°

Then $V_{BA} = \sqrt{3}V_{BN}\angle -105° + 30°$

$$= \mathbf{10\sqrt{3}\angle -75° \text{ V}}$$

Option (*c*) is correct.

M20.93 *In Fig. 20.99,*

$Z_{10} = (5 + j5)\ \Omega$ *and* $Z_{30} = (10 - j5)\ \Omega$.

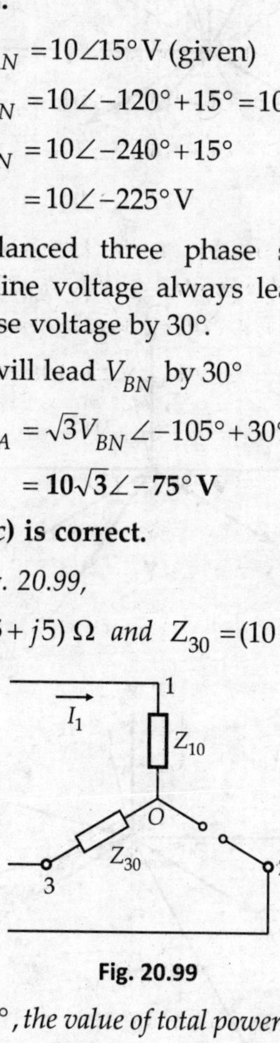

Fig. 20.99

If $V_{13} = 225\angle 0°$, *the value of total power consumption in kW, for the given circuit is*

(*a*) 5.29 kW (*b*) 22.51 kW

(*c*) 5.845 kW (*d*) 10.124 kW

Solution. Here, with phase 2 open, the circuit no longer behaves as 3-phase circuit.

$$\therefore \quad I_1 = \frac{V_{13}}{Z_{10} + Z_{30}} = \frac{225\angle 0°}{5 + j5 + 10 - j5}$$

$$= 15\angle 0° \text{ A}$$

$$\therefore \quad p.f.(\cos\phi) = \text{unity}$$

$$P_{3\phi} = \sqrt{3}V_L I_L \cos\phi$$

$$= \sqrt{3} \times 225 \times 15 \times 1$$

$$= \mathbf{5.845\ kW}$$

Option (*c*) is correct.

M20.94 *Each phase of a balanced star connected load has three impedances in parallel : 100 Ω, –j100 Ω and (50 + j50) Ω. If this load be supplied from a balanced three phase 400 V supply, the total power absorbed by the load is*

(*a*) 0 kW (*b*) 3.199 kW

(*c*) 1.067 kW (*d*) 2.327 kW

Solution. Let $V_{ab} = 400\angle 0°$ V;

$V_{bc} = 400\angle -120°$ V; $V_{ca} = 400\angle -240°$ V

$$\therefore \quad V_{an} = \frac{400}{\sqrt{3}}\angle -30° \text{ V} = 231\angle -30° \text{ V}$$

[as in a balanced three phase system, with star connection, line voltage leads the phase voltage by 30°]

$$V_{bn} = 231\angle -150° \text{ V}$$

$$V_{cn} = 231\angle -270° \text{ V}$$

In each phase,

$$Z = 100 \| (-j100) \| (50 + j50) = 50\Omega$$

$$\therefore \quad I_a = \frac{231}{50}\angle -30° = 4.618\angle -30° \text{ A}$$

Power absorbed by each phase is

$$P = V_{ph} I_{ph} \cos\phi$$

$$= 231 \times 4.618 \times \cos(-30° + 30°)$$

$$[\because V_{an} = 231\angle -30°;\ I_a = 4.618\angle -30°$$

$$\because \phi = \angle -30° - (-30°) = \angle -30° + 30°]$$

i.e., $\quad P = 1.067$ kW

$\therefore$ Total power absorbed by the load

$$= 3 \times P = \mathbf{3.199\ kW}.$$

Option (*b*) is correct.

M20.95

Two delta connected loads are connected from a balanced three phase 50 Hz system (Fig. 20.100). Load 1 draws apparent power of 40 kVA at 0.8 p.f. (lag) while load

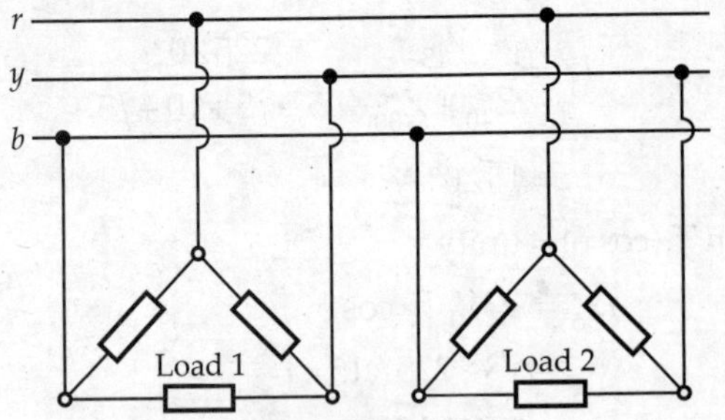

Fig. 20.100

2 draws real power of 24 kW at 0.9 p.f. (lead). Assuming $V_{ry} = 440\angle -30°$ *V, the line current in phase r is given by*

(*a*) $50.50\angle 48.98°$ A (*b*) $62.30\angle 27.30°$ A

(*c*) $75.24\angle -12.46°$ A (*d*) $87.47\angle -12.46°$ A

Solution. Load 1 draws apparent power of $\frac{40}{3} = 13.33$ kVA per phase at p.f. 0.8 (lag)

$$\therefore\ I_{r(\text{load 1})} = \frac{13.33\times 10^3 \angle -\cos^{-1} 0.8}{440\angle -30°}$$

$$= 30.30\angle -6.87°\text{ A} = I_{r_1}.$$

Load 2 draws $\frac{1}{3}\cdot\frac{24}{0.9} = 8.89$ kVA per phase at p.f. of 0.9 (lead)

$$\therefore\ I_{r(\text{load 2})} = \frac{8.89\times 10^3 \angle \cos^{-1} 0.9}{440\angle -30°}$$

$$= 20.20\angle 55.85°\text{ A} = I_{r_2}$$

$$\therefore\ I_r = [(I_{r_1} + I_{r_2})\sqrt{3}]\angle -30°$$

[$\because$ line current lags phase current by 30° in delta connection]

$$= (75.24\angle 17.54°)\angle -30° = \mathbf{75.24\angle -12.46°\ A}$$

Option (*c*) is correct.

M20.96 *The line current of a lightly loaded three phase induction motor, operating from a 400 V, 3-phase, 50 Hz source, is 25 A. The power factor (p.f.) of the motor is 0.25 (lag). Two watt-meter method is used to measure the three phase power input to the motor. The readings of* W_1 *and* W_2 *are*

(*a*) $W_1 = -2.676$ kW, $W_2 = 5.273$ kW

(*b*) $W_1 = -2.676$ kW, $W_2 = 7.006$ kW

(*c*) $W_1 = 2.676$ kW, $W_2 = -7.006$ kW

(*d*) $W_1 = 7.00$ kW, $W_2 = 3.00$ kW

Solution.

Here, $\theta = \cos^{-1}(0.25) = 75.52°$

$$W_1 = V_L I_L \cos(\theta + 30°)$$
$$= 400\times 25\times \cos(75.52° + 30°)$$
$$= -2.676\text{ kW}$$
$$W_2 = V_L I_L \cos(\theta - 30°)$$
$$= 400\times 25\times \cos(75.52° - 30°)$$
$$= \mathbf{7.006\ kW}$$

Option (*b*) is correct.

M20.97 *A two wattmeter method is used to measure three phase active power to a three phase balanced lagging load. Which of the following phasor diagrams (Fig. 20.101) is correct ?*

(*a*)

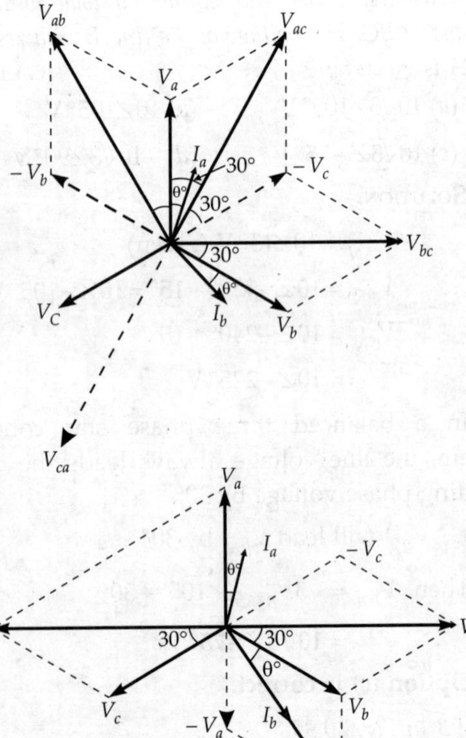

(*b*)

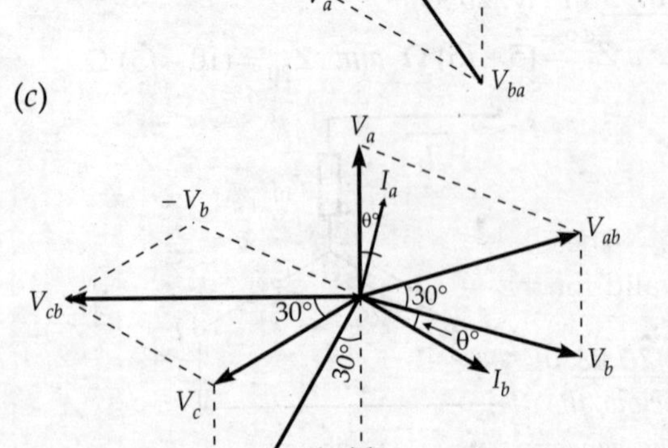

(*c*)

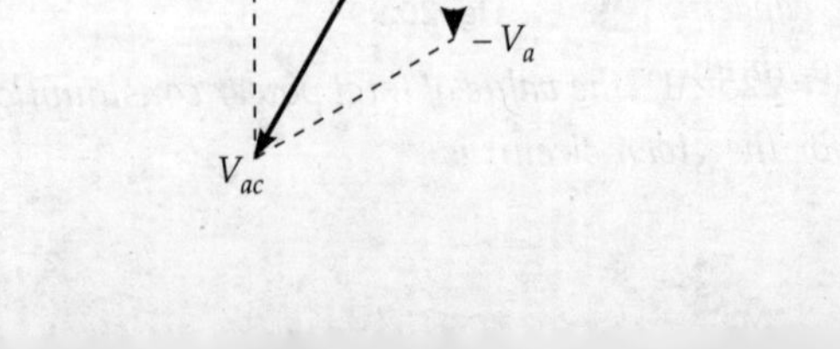

(*d*)

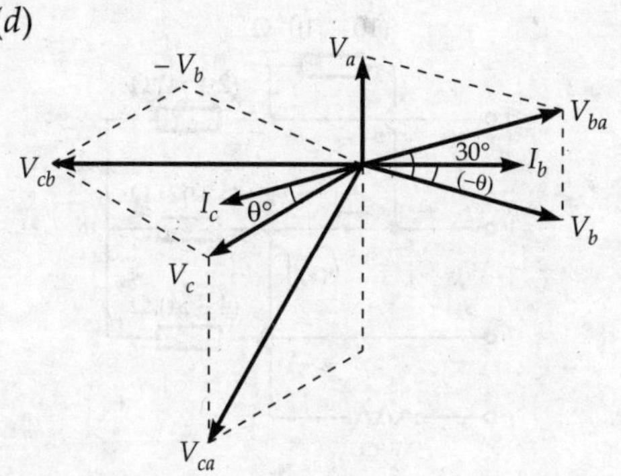

Fig. 20.101

SOLUTION. Option (*a*) correct.

[In a two wattmeter method (Fig. 20.102), current through W_1 is I_a ; voltage across W_1 is $V_{ac} = V_a - V_c$ (phasor difference).

$$W_1 = V_{ac} I_a \cos(30° - \theta);\ V_{ac} \text{ lags } I_a \text{ by } (30° - \theta)°$$

$$W_2 = V_{bc} I_b \cos(30° + \theta);\ V_{bc} \text{ leads } I_b \text{ by } (30° + \theta)°$$

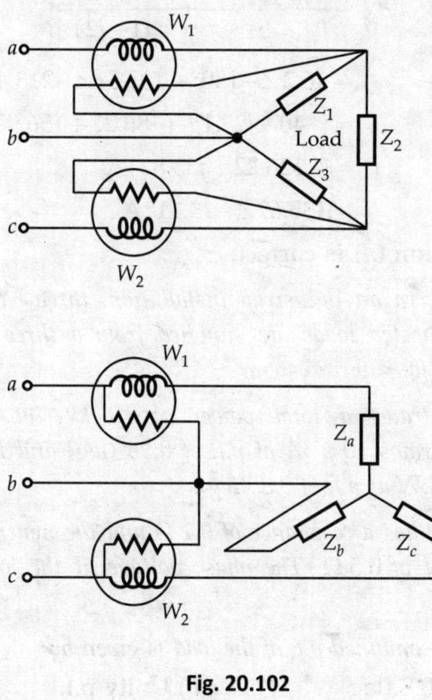

Fig. 20.102

These equations and interpretations are only valid for the phasor diagram in Fig. 20.101(*a*).]

M20.98 *In the balanced 3 phase, 50 Hz, circuit shown below, the value of inductance (L) is 10 mH. The value of the capacitance (C) for which all the line currents are zero, in millifarads, is ______ .*

[GATE 2011]

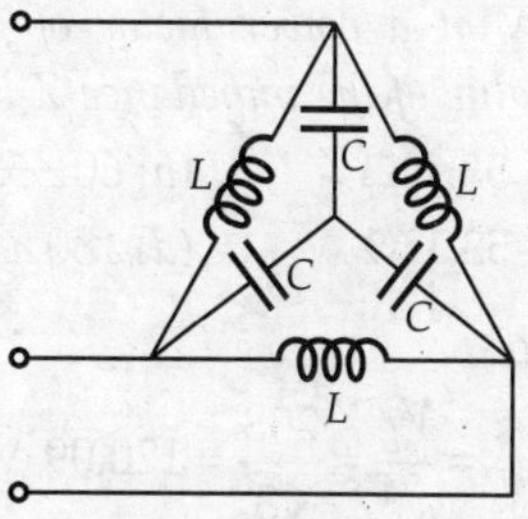

Fig. 20.103

SOLUTION. The given circuit can be redrawn as shown in Fig. 20.104. When the inner star connection is converted to equivalent delta.

$$C_\Delta = \frac{1}{3} C_\lambda$$

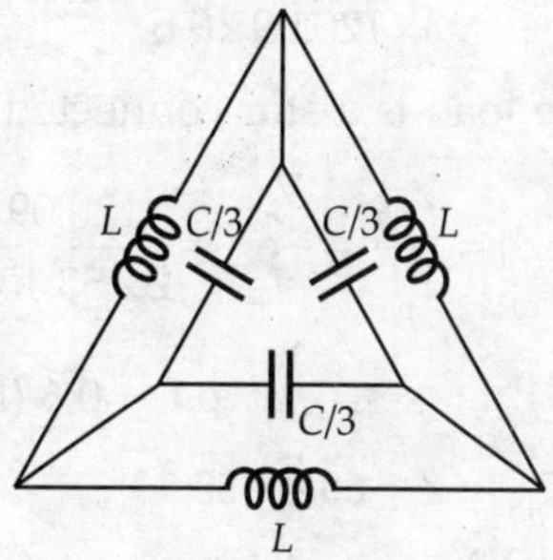

Fig. 20.104

For all the line currents to be zero, the phase currents are also zero and this requires that the impedance of each phase is infinite. This is possible provided in the parallel LC circuit of each phase, $X_L = X_C$.

i.e., $$\omega L = \frac{1}{\omega C/3}$$

i.e., $$C = \frac{3}{\omega^2 L} = \frac{3}{(2\pi \times 50)^2 \times 10 \times 10^{-3}}$$

$$= 3.03 \times 10^{-3}\,\text{F } \textit{i.e., } \mathbf{3.03\ mF.}$$

M20.99 *For the balanced Y - Y connected 3-phase circuit shown in the figure below (Fig. 20.105), the line–line voltage is 208 V rms and the total power absorbed by the*

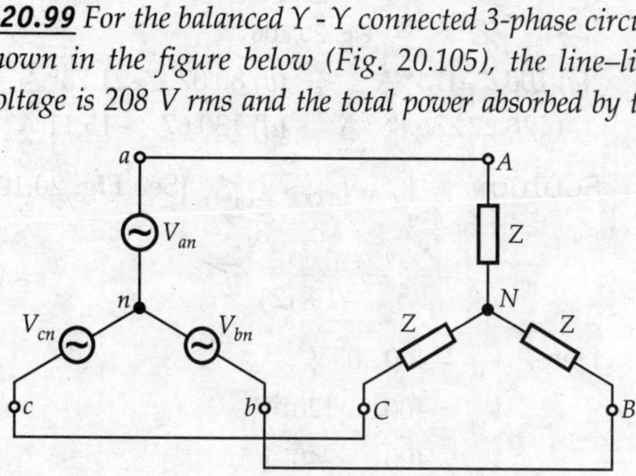

Fig. 20.105

load is 432 W at a power factor of 0.6 leading. The approximate value of the impedance Z is **[GATE 2017]**

(*a*) $33\angle -53.1°\Omega$ (*b*) $60\angle 53.1°\Omega$

(*c*) $60\angle -53.1°\Omega$ (*d*) $180\angle -53.1°\Omega$

SOLUTION.

$$V_{ph} = \frac{V_L}{\sqrt{3}} = \frac{208}{\sqrt{3}} = 120.09 \text{ V};$$

p.f. $= 0.6$ (leading)

$$\text{Power } (P) = 3V_{ph} \cdot I_{ph} \cos\phi$$

$$\therefore \quad I_{ph} = \frac{P}{3V_{ph}\cos\phi}$$

$$= \frac{432}{3 \times 120.09 \times 0.6} = 2 \text{ A}$$

Since the load is a star connected circuit

$$\therefore Z_{ph}(=Z) = \frac{V_{ph}}{I_{ph}} = \frac{V_{ph}}{I_L} = \frac{120.09}{2\angle 53.13°}$$

$[\because$ p.f. $= 0.6$ (lead) $= 53.13°]$

i.e., $Z_{ph} \equiv Z = \mathbf{60\angle -53.13°}$.

Option (*c*) is correct.

M20.100 *In the circuit shown in Fig. 20.106, the value of I_X is*

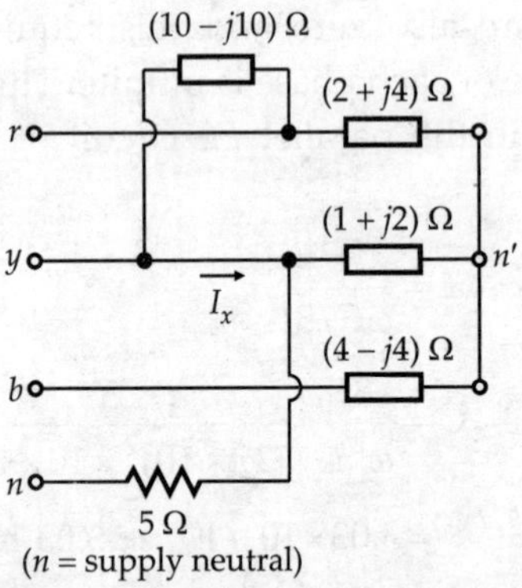

Fig. 20.106

(*a*) $100\angle -173°$ A (*b*) $80.02\angle -21.73°$ A

(*c*) $126.22\angle 36.86°$ A (*d*) $130.67\angle -15.11°$A

SOLUTION. $I_X = I_{5\Omega} + I_{xn'}$ [See Fig. 20.107]

$$\therefore \quad I_X = \frac{V_{yn}}{5} + \frac{V_{yn'}}{(1+j2)} \quad \text{...(1)}$$

Here, $V_{ry} = 400\angle 0°$ V

$V_{yb} = 400\angle -120°$ V

$V_{br} = 400\angle -240°$ V

$= 400\angle +120°$ V

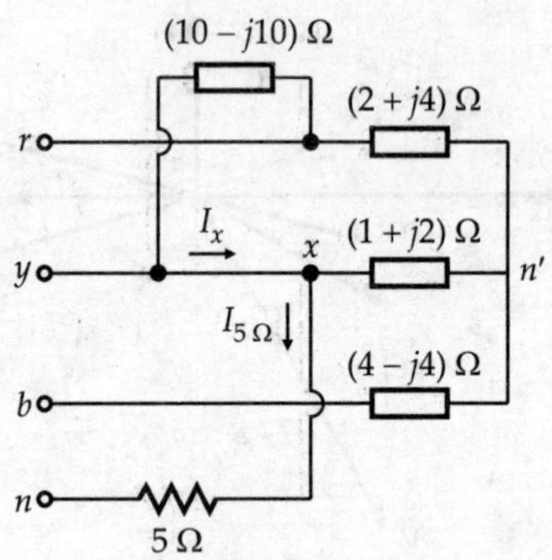

Fig. 20.107

Since the line voltage in a 3-phase balanced system leads 30° the respective phase voltage in star connection,

$$\therefore \quad V_{yn'} = \frac{400}{\sqrt{3}}\angle -120° - 30°$$

$$= 231\angle -150° = V_{yn}.$$

[n is the supply neutral and n' is load neutral]

$$I_X = \frac{231\angle -150°}{5} + \frac{231\angle -150°}{(1+j2)}$$

$$= 46.2\angle -150° + 103.31\angle -213.43°$$

$$= (-40 - j23.1) + (-86.22 + j56.92)$$

$$I_x = (-126.22 + j33.82) \text{ A}$$

$$= \mathbf{130.67\angle -15.11° \text{ A}}$$

Option (*d*) is correct.

M20.101 *In an industrial installation, three balanced star connected loads are supplied from a three phase balanced four wire system.*

Load-1 draws a total power of 10 kW at u.p.f., Load-2 draws 10 kVA at p.f. of 0.96 (lag) and Load-3 draws 7 kW at p.f. of 0.85(lag).

Each line has a resistance of 0.1 Ω and the neutral has resistance of 0.5 Ω. The phase voltage at the loads is 200 V.

(*i*) *The combined p.f. of the load is given by*

(*a*) 0.8 (lag) (*b*) Unity p.f.

(*c*) 0.965 (lead) (*d*) 0.965 (lag)

(*ii*) *The power loss in four lines is given by*

(*a*) 410.39 W (*b*) 210.78 W

(*c*) 632.34 W (*d*) 1 kW

(*iii*) *The source voltage magnitude is given by*

(*a*) 346.42 V (*b*) 204.59 V

(*c*) 200 V (*d*) 354.35 V

(iv) The source power factor is given by

(*a*) 0.96 (lag) (*b*) 0.85 (lag)
(*c*) upf (*d*) 0.85 (lead)

Solution. (*i*) Complex power drawn by the load is

$$\left[10\angle 0° + 10\angle \cos^{-1} 0.96 + \frac{7}{0.85}\angle \cos^{-1} 0.85°\right] \text{kVA}$$

i.e., $[10 + j0 + 9.6 + j2.8 + 7 + j4.338]$ kVA

$= (26.6 + j7.188) = 27.55\angle 15.11°$

Combined load p.f. $= \cos 15.11° = 0.965$ (lag)

Option (*d*) is correct.

(*ii*) At the loads,

$$|V_{ph}| = 200 \text{ V}$$

In each phase, the complex power demand is

$$\frac{27.55}{3}\angle 15.11° = 9.183\angle 15.11° \text{ kVA}$$

∴ Line current is

$$I_l = \left[\frac{9.183 \times 10^3\angle 15.11°}{200\angle 0°}\right]^*$$

$= 45.91\angle -15.11°$ A

Loss in each line is $(45.91)^2 \times 0.1 = 210.78$ W

Total loss = summation of loss in all the three lines + loss in neutral

Since the loads are balanced, there is no neutral current.

∴ Total loss $= 3 \times 210.78 = 632.34$ W

Option (*c*) is correct.

(*iii*) The source voltage magnitude is given by

$$(200 + 0.1 \times I_l) = 200 + 0.1 \times 45.91 = 204.59 \text{ W}$$

Option (*b*) is correct.

(*iv*) The total impedance across the source is :

$$0.1 + \frac{200}{45.91\angle -15.11°} = 0.1 + 4.356\angle 15.11°$$

$= (0.1 + 4.205 + j1.135)\ \Omega$

i.e., $(4.305 + j1.135)\ \Omega = 19.64\angle 14.57°\ \Omega$

∴ Source operates at a p.f. of

$\cos(-14.57°)$ *i.e.*, **0.96 (lag)**

Option (*a*) is correct.

M20.102 *The given circuit in Fig. 20.108 is supplied by a 415 V, 50 Hz, 3 phase source.*

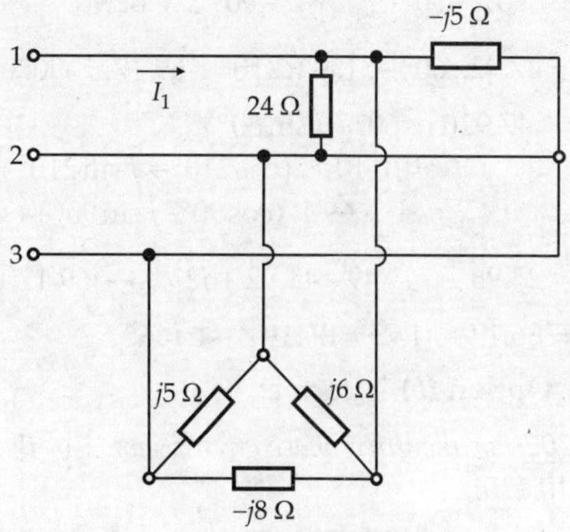

Fig. 20.108

The value of I_1 is

(*a*) $40\angle -20.79°$ A (*b*) $86.19\angle -1.146°$ A
(*c*) $27.96\angle -10°$ A (*d*) $100\angle 20.39°$ A

Solution. Let us redraw the given circuit with respective current components of I_1 (Fig. 20.109).

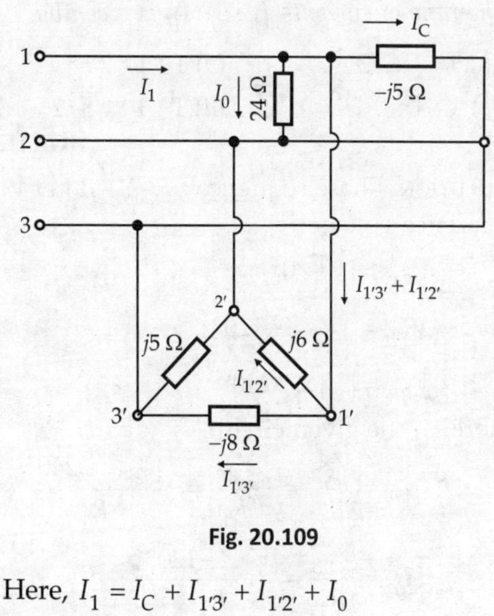

Fig. 20.109

Here, $I_1 = I_C + I_{1'3'} + I_{1'2'} + I_0$

or, $$\frac{V_{1n}}{-j5} + \frac{V_{13}}{-j8} + \frac{V_{12}}{j6} + \frac{V_{12}}{24} = I_1$$

Here, $$|V_{1n}| = \frac{|V_L|}{\sqrt{3}} = \frac{|V_{12}|}{\sqrt{3}} = \frac{415}{\sqrt{3}} \text{ V}$$

Angle of $V_{1n} = -30°$ as V_{12} is reference.

$V_{1n} = 239.6\angle -30°$ V

$V_{13} = -V_{31} = -415\angle +120°$ V

$V_{12} = 415\angle 0°$ V

CHAPTER 20

Hence

$$I_1 = \frac{239.6\angle -30^\circ}{5\angle -90^\circ} + \frac{-415\angle 120^\circ}{8\angle -90^\circ} + \frac{415\angle 0^\circ}{6\angle 90^\circ} + \frac{415\angle 0^\circ}{24}$$

$$= 47.92\angle 60^\circ - 51.87\angle 210^\circ + 69.17\angle -90^\circ + 17.29$$

$$= 47.92(\cos 60^\circ + j\sin 60^\circ) - 51.87(\cos 210^\circ + j\sin 210^\circ) + 69.17(\cos 90^\circ - j\sin 90^\circ) + 17.29$$

$$= 23.96 + j41.49 + 44.92 + j25.93 - j69.17 + 17.29$$

$$= 86.17 - j1.75 = \mathbf{86.19\angle -1.146^\circ\ A}$$

$\therefore$ **Option (*b*) is correct.**

M20.103 *For the three-phase circuit shown in the figure (Fig. 20.110),*

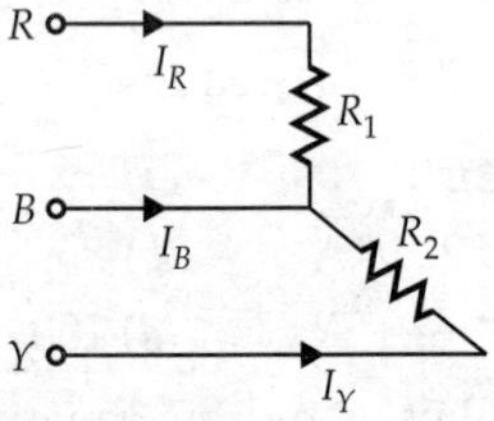

Fig. 20.110

The ratio of currents $I_R : I_Y : I_B$ is given by

(*a*) $1 : 1 : \sqrt{3}$ (*b*) $1 : 1 : 2$

(*c*) $1 : 1 : 0$ (*d*) $1 : 1 : \sqrt{3/2}$

[GATE 2005]

Solution. Phase sequence : *R*-*Y*-*B*. Let V_{RY} be the reference voltage.

$$\therefore \quad V_{RY} = |V|\angle 0^\circ\ ;$$

$$V_{YB} = |V|\angle -120^\circ;$$

$$V_{BR} = |V|\angle -240^\circ$$

Here, in the given circuit,

$$I_R = \frac{V_{RB}}{R_1} = -\frac{V_{BR}}{R_1} = -\frac{|V|\angle -240^\circ}{R_1}$$

$$I_Y = \frac{V_{YB}}{R_1} = \frac{|V|\angle -120^\circ}{R_1}$$

Also, $I_R + I_Y + I_B = 0$

i.e., $$-\frac{|V|\angle -240^\circ}{R_1} + \frac{|V|\angle -120^\circ}{R_1} + I_B = 0$$

$$\therefore \quad I_B = \frac{|V|\angle -240^\circ}{R_1} - \frac{|V|\angle -120^\circ}{R_1}$$

$$= \frac{|V|}{R_1}[\cos 240^\circ - j\sin 240^\circ - \cos 120^\circ + j\sin 120^\circ]$$

$$= \frac{|V|}{R_1}[-0.5 + j0.866 + 0.5 + j0.866]$$

$$= \frac{|V|}{R_1}(j1.732) = \frac{\sqrt{3}|V|}{R_1}\angle 90^\circ$$

$$\therefore \quad |\boldsymbol{I_R}| : |\boldsymbol{I_Y}| : |\boldsymbol{I_B}| = \mathbf{1 : 1 : \sqrt{3}}$$

Option (*a*) is correct.

M20.104 *A two phase load draws the following phase currents : $i_1(t) = I_m \sin(\omega t - \phi_1)$; $i_2(t) = I_m \cos(\omega t - \phi_2)$ these currents are balanced if ϕ_1 is equal to :*

(*a*) $-\phi_2$ (*b*) ϕ_2

(*c*) $\left(\frac{\pi}{2} - \phi_2\right)$ (*d*) $\left(\frac{\pi}{2} + \phi_2\right)$

[GATE 2012]

Solution.

$$i_1(t) = I_m \sin(\omega t - \phi_1)$$

$$i_2(t) = I_m \cos(\omega t - \phi_2) = I_m \sin(\omega t - \phi_2 + 90^\circ)$$

$\therefore$ The phase difference between the two is $\frac{\pi}{2}$.

i.e., $$(\omega t - \phi_1) - (\omega t - \phi_2 + 90^\circ) = 90^\circ$$

$$-\phi_1 + \phi_2 = 0$$

$$\therefore \quad \phi_1 = \phi_2$$

Option (*b*) is correct.

M20.105 *A set of 3 equal resistors, each of value R_x, connected in star across RYB of given figure consumes the same power as the unbalanced delta connected load shown. The value of R_x is ______ Ω.* **[GATE 1994]**

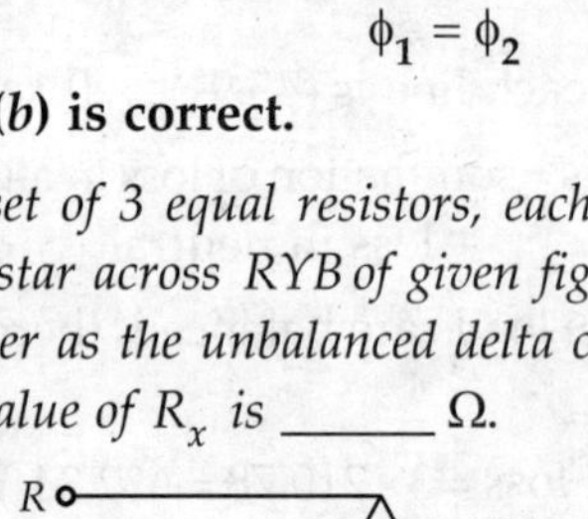

Fig. 20.111

Solution. Power consumed in unbalanced delta connected load

$$= \frac{V_{ph}^2}{R} = \frac{V_{L-L}^2}{R}$$

$$= \frac{400^2}{100} = 1600\ \text{W}$$

Power consumed in a balanced star connected load having equal resistors in all three phases is given by

$$3.\frac{V_{Ph}^2}{R_x} = \frac{V_{L-L}^2}{R_x} = \frac{400^2}{R_x}$$

It is stated in the question that both the delta and star circuits consume same power

$$\therefore \quad \frac{400^2}{R_x} = 1600$$

$$\therefore \quad R_x = \mathbf{100\ \Omega.}$$

M20.106 *A three phase 100 kW load operating at 0.6 p.f. lagging is fed from a 240 V, 50 Hz three phase ac source. The operating p.f. needs to be increased from 0.6 lag to 0.95 lag using either delta or star connected capacitor banks in parallel to the load. If C_1 be the value of the capacitance per phase for star connected bank and C_2 be the capacitance per phase for the delta connected load, the ratio (C_1 / C_2) is given by*

(*a*) 1.732 (*b*) 3.018 (*c*) $\frac{1}{2}$ (*d*) 0.577

Solution. Initial power factor angle

$$\theta_0 = \cos^{-1} 0.6 = 53.13°.$$

Desired power factor angle

$$\theta_f = \cos^{-1} 0.95 = 18.19°.$$

Initial KVAR

$$= \theta_0 = P \tan\theta_0 = 100 \tan 53.13°$$

$$= 133.33 \text{ KVAR}$$

Desired KVAR

$$= Q_f = P \tan\theta_f$$

$$= 100 \tan 18.19° = 32.86 \text{ KVAR}$$

$\therefore$ KVAR of capacitor bank (Q_c)

$$= 133.33 - 32.86 = 100.47 \text{ KVAR}$$

$$Q_c \text{ per phase} = \frac{100.47}{3} = 33.49 \text{ KVAR}$$

$$\text{Also,} \quad Q_C = \frac{V_{ph}^2}{X_C}$$

$$\therefore \quad X_C = \frac{V_{ph}^2}{Q_C} = \frac{(240/\sqrt{3})^2}{33.49 \times 10^3} = 0.57\ \Omega/\text{ph.}$$

$$\text{Since} \quad X_C = \frac{1}{2\pi f C_1}$$

$$\therefore \quad 0.57 = \frac{1}{2 \times \pi \times 50 \times C_1}; \quad \text{or} \quad C_1 = 5.59 \text{ mF/ph}$$

Here we assumed the capacitor bank was connected in star.

If we connect the bank in delta, we have

$$\frac{Q_c}{3} = \frac{V_c^2}{X_C} \quad \textit{i.e.,} \quad \frac{100.47}{3} = \frac{240^2}{X_C}$$

$$\textit{i.e.,} \quad X_C = 1.72\ \Omega/\text{ph} = \frac{1}{2\pi f C_2}$$

$$\therefore \quad C_2 = \frac{1}{X_C \times 2 \times \pi \times 50} = 1.852 \text{ mF}$$

$$\text{Hence,} \quad \frac{C_1}{C_2} = \frac{5.59}{1.852} = \mathbf{3.018}$$

Option (*b*) is correct.

M20.107 *The line currents of a three phase four wire systems are square waves with amplitudes of 100 A. The three currents are phase shifted by 120° with respect to each other. The rms value of neutral current is*

(*a*) 300 A (*b*) 0 A (*c*) 100 A (*d*) $\frac{100}{\sqrt{3}}$ A

[GATE 2019]

Solution. The three line currents are drawn in Fig. 20.112.

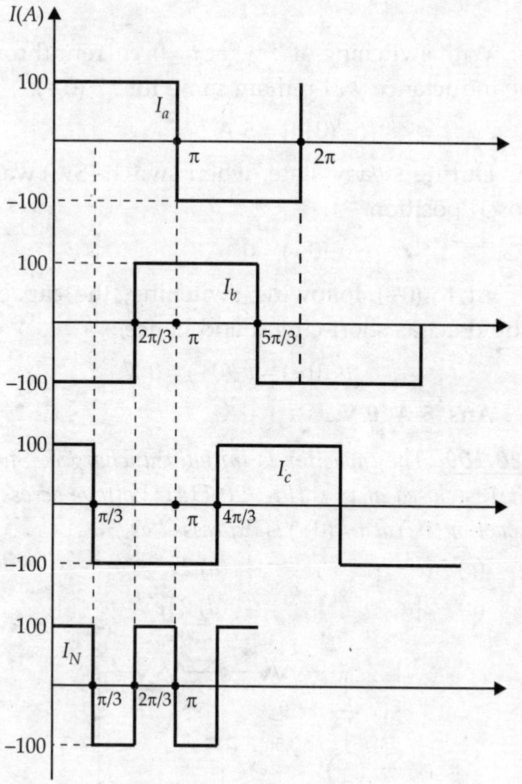

Fig. 20.112

I_b is shifted from I_a by $120° \left(= \frac{2\pi}{3}\right)$ and I_C is shifted from I_a by $240° \left(\frac{4\pi}{3}\right)$ in the x-axis.

From the graph (Fig. 20.112), it is evident that

$$I_{rms(\text{neutral})} = I_A + I_B + I_C$$

$$= \mathbf{100\ A}, \text{ since it is a square wave.}$$

Option (*c*) is correct.

M20.108 *In Fig. 20.113, a coil is in series with a capacitor. The switch is closed at steady state. At t = 0, the switch is opened. The current through the inductor at t = 0 + is ______ A, while the voltage across the capacitor at t = 0 + is ______ V.*

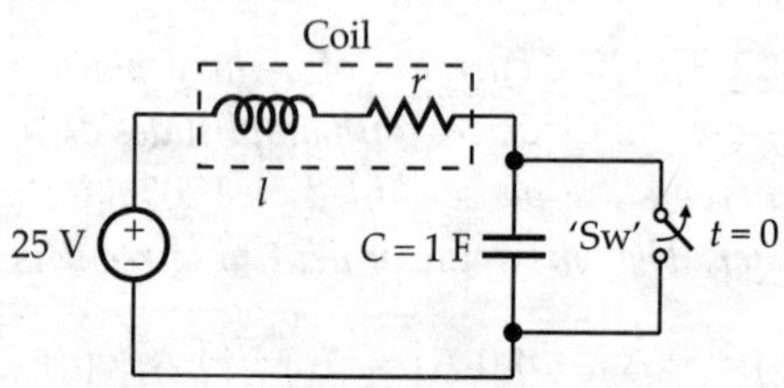

[$r = 5\ \Omega$; $l = 1$ H]

Fig. 20.113

Solution. At steady state,

$$i_L[t = (0-)] = \frac{V}{r} = \frac{25}{5} = 5\ \text{A}$$

With switching of 'Sw' at $t = 0$, current through the inductance will remain same for $t = (0+)$.

$$\therefore \quad i_L[t = (0+)] = \mathbf{5\ A}$$

During steady state, when switch (Sw) was in closed position,

$$v_c(0-) = 0$$

At $t = (0+)$, following switching, the capacitor would act as short-circuit and hence,

$$v_c(0-) = v_c(0+) = \mathbf{0\ V}$$

Ans. 5 A, 0 V.

M20.109 *The capacitor is initially uncharged. Switch (Sw) is closed at t = 0 (Fig. 20.114). Voltage across the capacitor (v_c) at t = (0+) is expressed as*

(*a*) $2(e^{-t} + e^{-2t})$ (*b*) $2e^{-2t}$

(*c*) $-2[e^{t} - e^{-2t}]$ (*d*) $2[e^{-t} - e^{-3t}]$

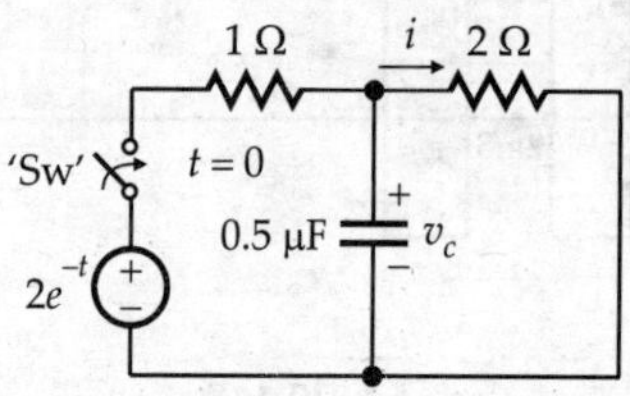

Fig. 20.114

Solution. At $t = (0+)$, following switching, in the given figure,

$$\frac{v_c}{2} + c\frac{dv_c}{dt} = \frac{2e^{-t} - v_c}{1}$$

or, $$\frac{v_c}{2} + 0.5\frac{dv_c}{dt} = 2e^{-t} - v_c$$

or, $$\frac{dv_c}{dt} + 3v_c = 4e^{-t}$$

$$\therefore \quad v_c = Ae^{-3t} + 2e^{-t} \quad \text{...(1)}$$

At $t = (0+)$, capacitor will act short-circuit and hence

$$v_c = 0 \text{ at } t = (0+)$$

Then from (1), $A = -2$

$$\therefore \quad v_c = \mathbf{2[-e^{-3t} + e^{-t}]}$$

Option (*d*) is correct.

M20.110 *The time constant for the given circuit (Fig. 20.115) will be* **[GATE 2018]**

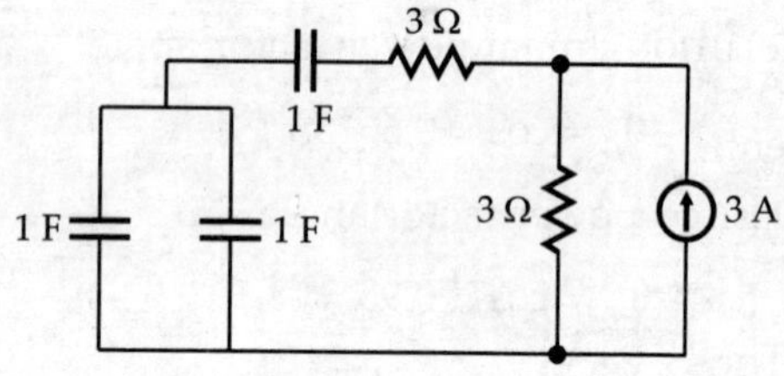

Fig. 20.115

(*a*) $\frac{1}{9}$ s (*b*) $\frac{1}{4}$ s (*c*) 4 s (*d*) 9 s

Solution. Let us remove the current source from the given circuit. Figure 20.116 represents the circuit without the current source.

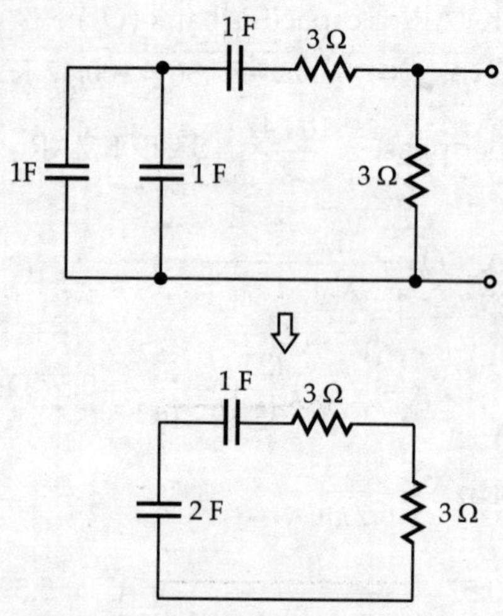

Fig. 20.116

Here $C_{eq} = \frac{2\times 1}{2+1} = \frac{2}{3}$ F

$R_{eq} = 6\ \Omega$

$\therefore$ Time constant (R_C) is $R_{eq}C_{eq} = 6\times\frac{2}{3} = \mathbf{4\ s}$

Option (*c*) is correct.

M20.111 *In the circuit shown in the figure (Fig. 20.117), it is desired to have a constant direct current $i(t)$ through the ideal inductor L. The nature of the voltage source must be*

(*a*) *constant voltage*
(*b*) *linearly increasing voltage*
(*c*) *an ideal impulse voltage*
(*d*) *exponentially increasing voltage* **[GATE 1998]**

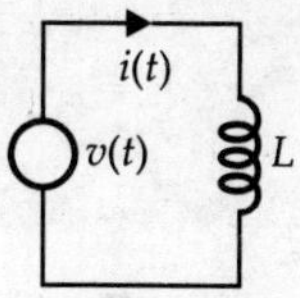

Fig. 20.117

Solution. For the current flow of $i(t)$ through the inductor *L*, the voltage developed in the inductor is

$$V = L\frac{di(t)}{dt}$$

As per question, $i(t) = I\,u(t)$, the constant direct current.

$$\therefore \quad V = L\frac{d}{dt}I\,u(t) = LI\,\delta(t)$$

Thus voltage source becomes an ideal impulse voltage.

Option (*c*) is correct.

M20.112 *In Fig. 20.118, the inductive coil has 2 Ω resistance and 1 H inductance. Steady state is reached*

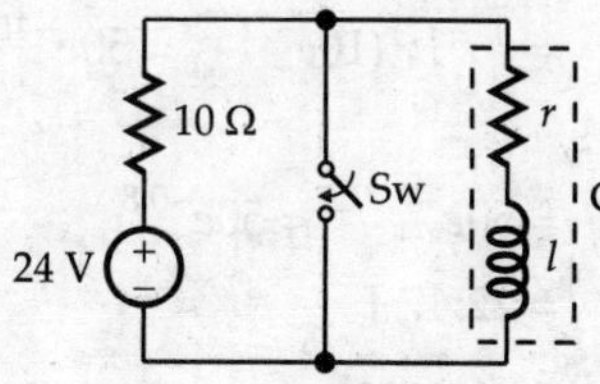

Fig. 20.118

with switch in open position. At t = 0, the switch is closed. The flux linkage with the inductive coil at t = 0.1 s is

(*a*) 2.212 Wb (*b*) 1.638 Wb
(*c*) 2 Wb (*d*) 0.2 Wb

Solution. In the given circuit, at steady state $[t=(0-)]$

$$I_0 = \frac{24}{10+2} = 2\text{ A.}$$

Figure 20.119 represents the circuit following switching at $t=0$. Here, $L = 1$ H, $R = 2\ \Omega$

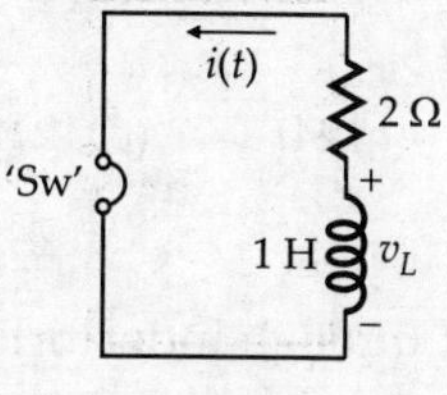

Fig. 20.119

$$\therefore \quad \tau = \frac{L}{R} = \frac{1}{2}$$

$$i(t) = I_0 e^{-\frac{t}{\tau}} = 2e^{-2t}\text{ A}$$

Flux linkage

$$\lambda = L.i(t) = 1\times 2e^{-2t}$$

At $t = 0.1$ s,

$$\lambda = 2e^{-2\times 0.1} = 2e^{-0.2}$$

$$= \mathbf{1.638\ Wb.}$$

Option (*b*) is correct.

M20.113 *Consider the circuit shown in the figure (Fig. 20.120). If the frequency of the source is 50 Hz,*

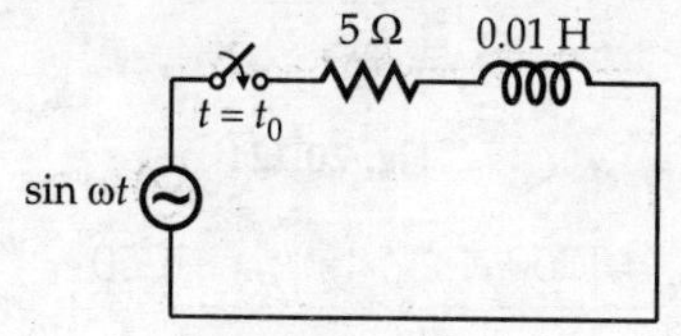

Fig. 20.120

then a value of t_0 which results in a transient free response is

[GATE 2002]

(*a*) 0 ms (*b*) 1.78 ms
(*c*) 2.71 ms (*d*) 2.91 ms

Solution. Let t_0 be the time for transient free response.

$$(\omega t_0) = \tan^{-1}\left(\frac{\omega L}{R}\right),$$

at transient free response period.

$$\text{or,}\quad 2\pi\times t_0\times 50 = \tan^{-1}\left(\frac{2\pi\times 50\times 0.01}{5}\right)$$

$$= 32.14 = 0.561\text{ rad}$$

$$\therefore \quad t_0 = \frac{0.561}{100\pi} = \mathbf{1.786\ ms}$$

Option (*b*) is correct.

M20.114 *A voltage waveform $v(t) = 12t^2$ is applied across a 1 H inductor for $t \geq 0$, with initial current through it being zero. The current through the inductor for $t \geq 0$ is given by* **[GATE 2000]**

(*a*) $12t$ (*b*) $24t$ (*c*) $12t^3$ (*d*) $4t^3$

Solution.

$$I_L \text{ (current through inductor)} = \frac{1}{L}\int_{-\infty}^{t} v(t)\,dt$$

or,
$$I_L = \frac{1}{1}\int_{-\infty}^{t} 12t^2 dt, \text{ for } t \geq 0$$

$$\therefore \quad I_L = \mathbf{4t^3\,A}$$

Option (*d*) is correct.

M20.115 *In the circuit shown in Fig. 20.121 the current at $t = (0-)$ through the inductor is 5 A. At $t = 0$, switching is done. What are the values of power in 50 Ω resistor and 1 H inductance at $t = (0+)$?*

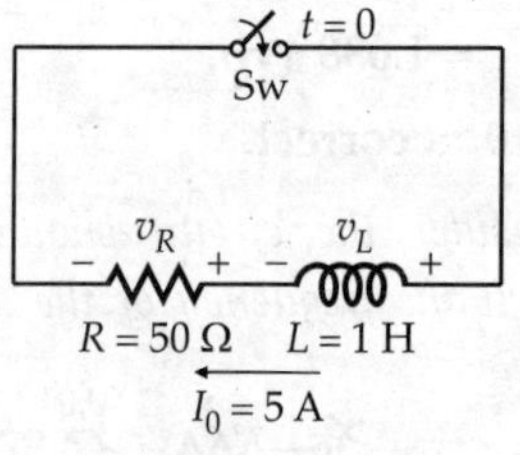

Fig. 20.121

(*a*) $p_R = 1250\,e^{-5t}$; $p_L = -1250\,e^{-5t}$

(*b*) $p_R = 1250\,e^{-10t}$; $p_L = 1250\,e^{-10t}$

(*c*) $p_R = 1250\,e^{-10t}$; $p_L = -1250\,e^{-10t}$

(*d*) $p_R = 1250\,e^{-10t}$; $p_L = -1250\,e^{-5t}$

Solution. At $t = (0+)$ inductor will start discharging through 50 Ω resistor following switching at $t = 0$.

The discharge current (i) is given by

$$i = I_0 e^{-tR/L} = 5e^{-(5/1)t} = (5e^{-5t})\,\text{A}$$

$$v_R = iR = (5e^{-5t})50 = (250e^{-5t})\,\text{V}$$

In the source free given circuit,

$$v_R + v_L = 0$$

i.e.,
$$v_R = -v_L$$

$$\therefore \quad v_L = (-250e^{-5t})\,\text{V}$$

Hence, p_R(= Power at 50 Ω resistor)

$$= v_R \times i = 250e^{-5t} \times 5e^{-5t}$$

$$= \mathbf{(1250e^{-10t})\,W}.$$

p_L(= Power at 1 H resistor) $= v_L \times i$

$$= (-250e^{-5t})(5e^{-5t})$$

$$= \mathbf{(-1250e^{-5t})\,W}$$

Option (*d*) is correct.

M20.116 *Steady state is reached with 'Sw' in position 'a'. At $t = 0$, the switch is moved to position 'b'. How much energy is stored in the inductor given in the circuit (Fig. 20.122) at $t = 0.2$s ?*

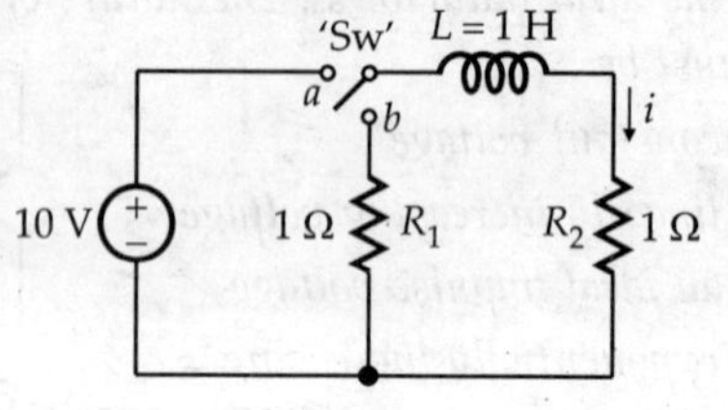

Fig. 20.122

(*a*) 50 J (*b*) 10.67 J
(*c*) 12.47 J (*d*) 22.47 J

Solution. At $t = (0-)$, $i = \frac{10}{1} = 10$ A (L acts as short-circuit)

Hence, initial current (I_0) through the inductor is 10 A.

At $t = t_0 = (0+)$, following movement of switch '*Sw*' from position '*a*' to '*b*', the discharge operation starts. Discharge current

$$i_d(t) = I_0 e^{-t(R/L)} = 10e^{-(R_1+R_2)/L \times t}$$

$$= 10e^{-(2/1)t} = (10e^{-2t})\,\text{A}$$

Energy stored in inductor,

$$W_L = \frac{1}{2}L[i_d(t)]^2$$

$$= \frac{1}{2} \times 1 \times (10e^{-2t})^2 = 50e^{-4t}$$

At $t = 0.2$ s,

$$W_L = 50e^{-4 \times 0.2} = 50e^{-0.8}$$

$$= \mathbf{22.47\,J}$$

Option (*d*) is correct.

M20.117 *In Fig. 20.123, Sw is moved from position a to b at $t = 0$. The value of i_2 at $t = 25$ ms is*

(*a*) 2.68 A

(*b*) 16.05 A

(*c*) 1.78 A

(*d*) 5.35 A

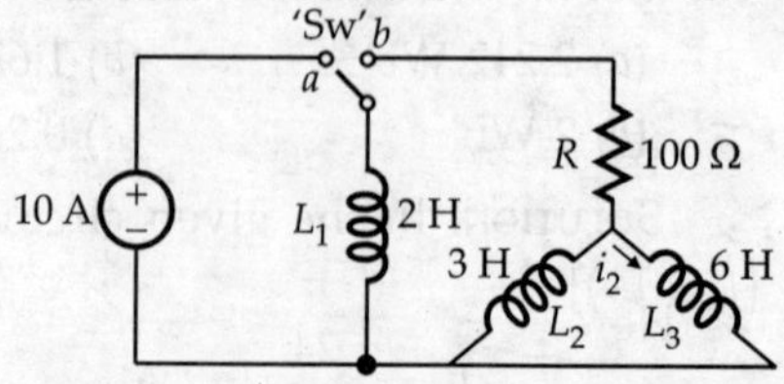

Fig. 20.123

Solution. Figure 20.124 represents the given circuit at $t = (0+)$

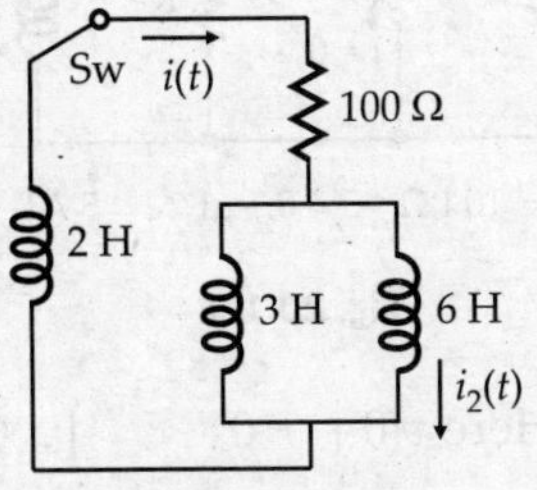

Fig. 20.124

$$L_{eq} = 2 + \frac{3\times 6}{3+6} = 4 \text{ H}$$

$$R = 100\ \Omega$$

$$\therefore \quad \tau = \frac{L}{R} = \frac{4}{100} = 0.04 \text{ sec}$$

$$i(0+) = I_0 e^{-t/\tau}$$

$$= 10e^{-t/0.04} = 10e^{-25t}$$

At $t = 25$ ms,

$$i(25\text{ ms}) = 10e^{-25\times 25\times 10^{-3}}$$

$$= 5.35 \text{ A}$$

$$\therefore \quad i_2(25\text{ ms}) = 5.35 \times \frac{3}{3+6} = \mathbf{1.78\ A}$$

Option (*c*) is correct.

M20.118 *An 11 kV pulse of 10 μs duration is applied to the circuit shown in Fig. 20.125. Assuming that the capacitor is completely discharged prior to applying the pulse, the peak value of the capacitor voltage is*

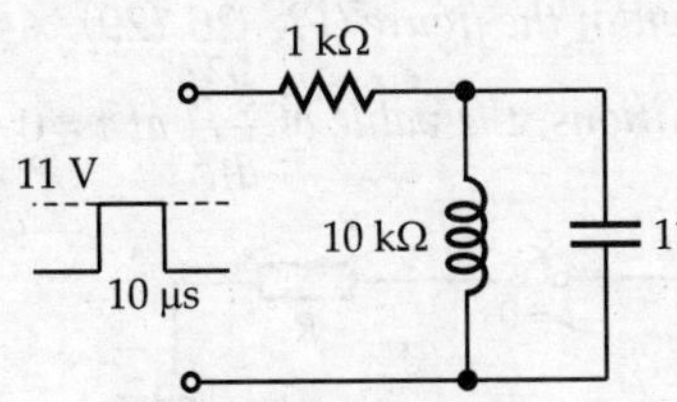

Fig. 20.125

(*a*) 11 V (*b*) 5.50 V

(*c*) 6.32 V (*d*) 0.96 V

[GATE 2002]

Solution.

$$V_C(t) = V_C(\infty) - [V_C(\infty) - V_C(0)]e^{-t/RC} \quad ...(1)$$

Here, $R = 10\text{ k}\Omega \,||\, 1\text{ k}\Omega = \frac{10}{11}\text{ k}\Omega$

$C = 11$ nF

$$\therefore \quad \tau = RC = \left(\frac{10}{11}\times 10^3 \times 11\times 10^{-9}\right) \text{s}$$

$$V_C(0) = 0 \text{ (given)} \; ; \; t = 10\,\mu\text{s} = 10\times 10^{-6}\text{ s}$$

$$V_C(t) = V_C \text{ (peak)}$$

[Here $V(\infty)$ is the final steady state voltage across the capacitor *i.e.*, the drop across 10 kΩ resistance

$$\therefore \quad V(\infty) = V_{\text{drop}(10\text{ k}\Omega)} = \frac{11\text{ V}}{11\text{ k}\Omega}\times 10\text{ k}\Omega = 10 \text{ V}]$$

From eqn. (1) we can now write

$$V_C(\text{peak}) = 10 - [10 - 0]e^{-\frac{10\times 10^{-6}}{\frac{10}{11}\times 10^3\times 11\times 10^{-9}}}$$

$$= 10(1 - e^{-1}) = \mathbf{6.32\ V}$$

Option (*c*) is correct.

M20.119 *A rectangular voltage pulse of magnitude V and duration T is applied to a series combination of resistance R and capacitance C (Fig. 20.126). The maximum voltage developed across the capacitor is*

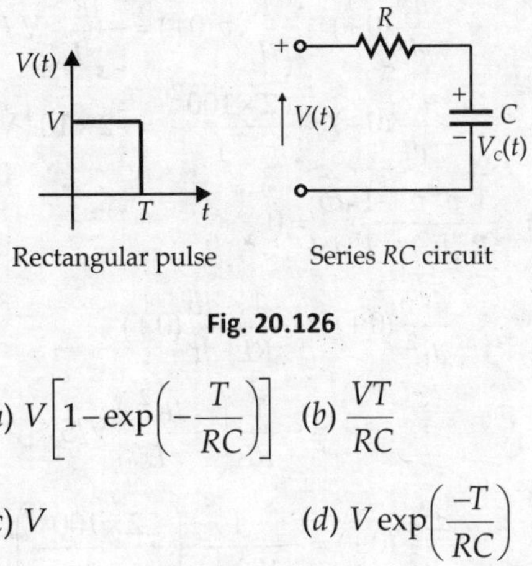

Rectangular pulse Series RC circuit

Fig. 20.126

(*a*) $V\left[1 - \exp\left(-\frac{T}{RC}\right)\right]$ (*b*) $\frac{VT}{RC}$

(*c*) V (*d*) $V\exp\left(\frac{-T}{RC}\right)$

[GATE 1999]

Solution.

$$V(t) = V[u(t) - u(t-T)]$$

$$V_C(t) = V(t)[1 - e^{-t/RC}]$$

$$= V[u(t) - u(t-T)][1 - e^{-t/RC}]$$

Capacitor is charged till $t = T$ and then discharges.

At $t = T$, the voltage across the capacitor is

$$V_C(t) = \mathbf{V[1 - e^{-T/RC}]}$$

Option (*a*) is correct.

M20.120 *In the circuit shown in Fig. 20.127, the value of* $\frac{dv}{dt}(0+)$ *and* $\frac{d^2v}{dt^2}(0+)$ *are*

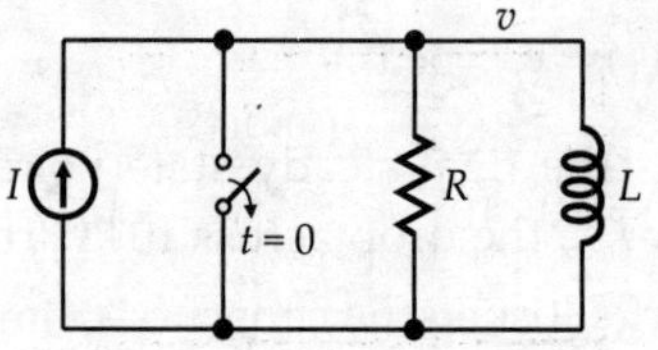

Fig. 20.127

(*a*) -2×10^4 V/S; 2×10^2 V/S^2
(*b*) 2×10^2 V/S; -2×10^4 V/S^2
(*c*) -2×10^{-2} V/S; -2×10^4 V/S^2
(*d*) 2 V/S; -2×10^2 V/S^2

Solution. $v(0+) = IR$ [∵ as L behaves as open circuit at $t = (0+)$]

$$\frac{v}{R}+\frac{1}{L}\int v\,dt = I$$

$$\therefore \quad \frac{1}{R}\frac{dv}{dt}+\frac{v}{L}=0$$

or, $$\frac{dv}{dt}(0+) = -\frac{R}{L}.v(0+) = -\frac{IR^2}{L}\text{ V/S}$$

i.e., $$\frac{dv}{dt}(0+) = -\frac{2\times100^2}{1} = -2\times10^4\text{ V/S}$$

Also, $$\frac{1}{R}\frac{d^2v}{dt^2}+\frac{1}{L}\frac{dv}{dt}=0$$

$$\therefore \quad \frac{d^2v}{dt^2}(0+) = -\frac{1}{RL}.\frac{dv}{dt}(0+)$$

$$= -\frac{1}{RL}\left(-\frac{IR^2}{L}\right)\text{V/S}$$

i.e., $$\frac{d^2v}{dt^2}(0+) = -\frac{1}{100\times1}\left(-\frac{2\times100^2}{1}\right)$$

$$= 2\times10^2\text{ V/S}^2$$

Thus, $$\frac{dv}{dt}(0+) = -2\times10^4\text{ V/S}$$

$$\frac{d^2v}{dt^2}(0+) = \mathbf{2\times10^2\ V/S^2}$$

Option (*a*) is correct.

M20.121 *In the circuit of Fig. 20.128,* $\frac{d^2v}{dt^2}(0+)$ *is given by*

(*a*) 50×10^6 V/S (*b*) -10^3 V/S^2
(*c*) 10^2 V/S^2 (*d*) -10^4 V/S^2

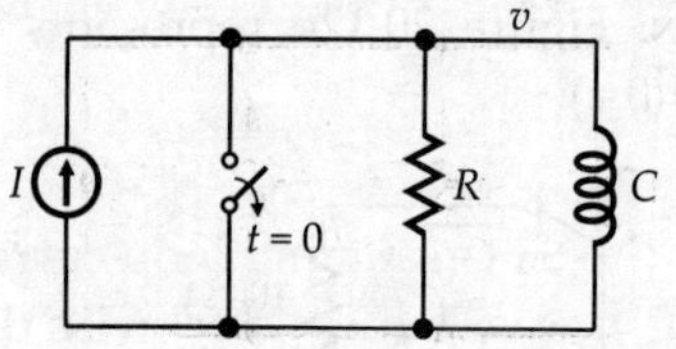

[R = 10 kΩ ; C = 0.1 μF ; I = 5 A]

Fig. 20.128

Solution. Here $v(0+) = 0$ [∵ C behaves as short-circuit at $t = (0+)$]

Also, $$C\frac{dv}{dt}+\frac{v}{R}=I$$

or, $$\frac{dv}{dt}(0+) = \frac{I}{C}\text{ V/S} = \frac{5}{0.1\times10^{-6}}$$

$$= 50\times10^6\text{ V/S}$$

Here, $$C\frac{d^2v}{dt^2}+\frac{1}{R}\frac{dv}{dt}=0$$

$$\therefore \quad \frac{d^2v}{dt^2}(0+) = -\frac{1}{RC}\frac{dv}{dt}(0+)$$

$$= -\frac{1}{RC}.\frac{T}{C} = -\frac{1}{RC^2}\text{ V/S}^2$$

i.e., $$\frac{d^2v}{dt^2}(0+) = -\frac{1}{10\times10^3\times0.1\times10^{-6}}$$

$$= \mathbf{-10^3\ V/S^2}$$

Option (*b*) is correct.

M20.122 *A series RL circuit is excited at t = 0 by closing a switch as shown in the figure (Fig. 20.129). Assuming zero initial conditions, the value of* $\frac{d^2i}{dt^2}$ *at t = 0+ is*

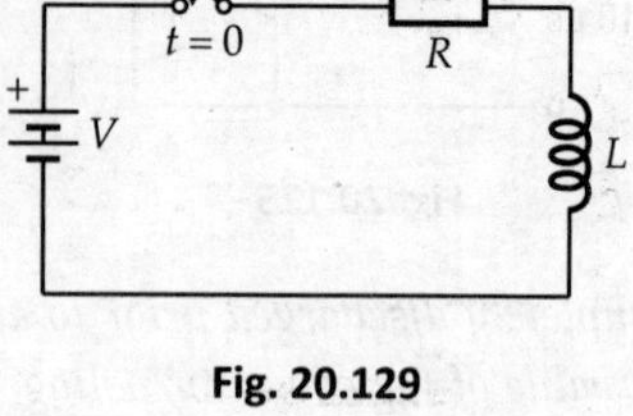

Fig. 20.129

(*a*) $\frac{V}{L}$ (*b*) $-\frac{V}{R}$

(*c*) 0 (*d*) $-\frac{R_V}{L^2}$

[GATE 2015]

Solution. The switch is closed at $t = 0$.

Hence $i(0+) = 0$, due to presence of L in the circuit.

In the given circuit, at $t = (0+)$, we have

$$L\frac{di}{dt} - V + iR = 0$$

[Assuming loop current to be i in the clockwise direction]

i.e., $$L\frac{di}{dt}(0+) + i(0+)R = V$$

Since $i(0+) = 0$, hence we get

$$\frac{di}{dt} = \frac{V}{L}\ \text{A/s}$$

Also we can write

$$\frac{d}{dt}\left[L\frac{di}{dt}\right] - \frac{d}{dt}V + \frac{di}{dt}R = 0$$

or, $$L\cdot\frac{d^2i}{dt^2} + \frac{di}{dt}\cdot R = 0 \qquad [\because V \text{ is constant}]$$

$$\therefore \quad \frac{d^2i}{dt^2}(0+) = -\frac{R}{L}\cdot\frac{di}{dt}(0+)$$

$$= -\frac{RV}{L^2}\ \text{A}^2/\text{s}^2$$

Option (*d*) is correct.

M20.123 *In the circuit shown in Fig. 20.130, the initial capacitor voltage is 4 V, switch S_1 is closed at t = 0. The charge (in μC) lost by the capacitor from t = 25 μsec to t = 100 μsec, is ______ .* **[GATE 2016]**

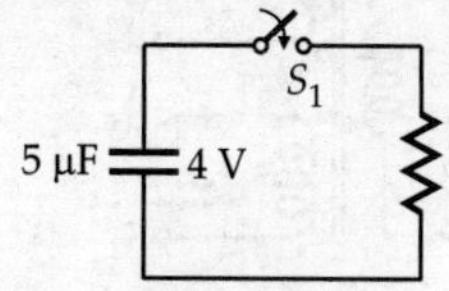

Fig. 20.130

Solution. The time constant of the circuit is given by

$$\tau = RC = 5 \times 5 = 25\,\mu\text{s} = 25 \times 10^{-6}\,\text{s}.$$

At $t = 0$, the switch S_1 is closed but as there is no source in the circuit, the circuit would have only natural response.

$\therefore$ $V_C(t)$, the voltage across the capacitor is given by

$$V_C(t) = V_C(0)e^{-t/\tau}$$

where $V_C(0) = 4$ V.

Charge across the capacitor $q(t) = CV_C(t)$

$$= 20 \times 10^{-6} e^{-t/\tau}$$

$$= 20 \times 10^{-6} e^{-t/25\times10^{-6}}$$

At $t = 25\,\mu$ sec,

$$q(t) = 20 \times 10^{-6} e^{-\frac{25\times10^{-6}}{25\times10^{-6}}} = 7.36\,\mu\text{C}$$

At $t = 100\,\mu$ sec,

$$q(t) = 20 \times 10^{-6} e^{-\frac{100\times10^{-6}}{25\times10^{-6}}} = 0.37\,\mu\text{C}.$$

$\therefore$ The charge lost by the capacitor from $t = 25\,\mu$s to $t = 100\,\mu$s, is (7.36 – 0.37) *i.e.,* **6.99 μC.**

M20.124 *The initial charge in the 1 F capacitor present in the circuit shown (Fig. 20.131) is zero. The energy in joules transferred from the DC source until steady state is reached equals ______ . (Give the answer upto one decimal place.)* **[GATE 2017]**

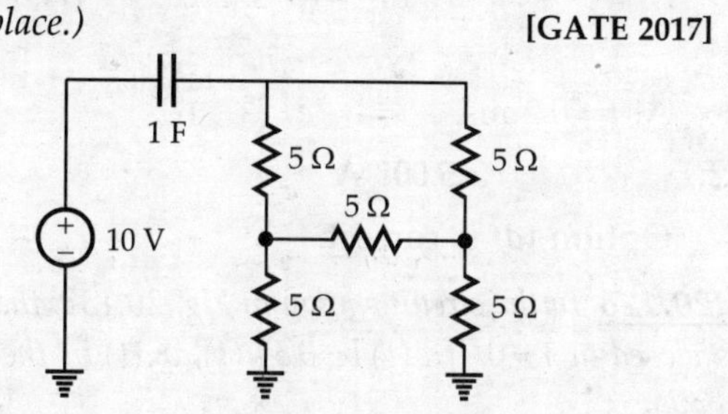

Fig. 20.131

Solution. The resistive portion of the circuit is like a balanced bridge containing resistances of 5Ω each.

$$\tau = RC, \text{ the time constant}$$

$$= 5 \times 1 = 5\,\text{s}.$$

Also, $$i(0+) = \frac{10}{5} = 2\,\text{A}.$$

$$I(t) = I_0 e^{-t/RC} = i(0+)e^{-t/RC}$$

$$= 2e^{-t/5}\,\text{A}.$$

Energy transferred until steady state reached is given by

$$E = \int_0^\infty VI(t)\,dt = \int_0^\infty 10 \times 2e^{-t/5}\,dt$$

$$= -10 \times 2 \times 5 \times e^{-t/5}\Big|_0^\infty = \mathbf{100\ J}.$$

M20.125 *Find i at t = 0.2 ms following switching at t = 0. (Fig. 20.132)*

(*a*) 6 A
(*b*) 1 A
(*c*) 3.005 A
(*d*) 5.008 A

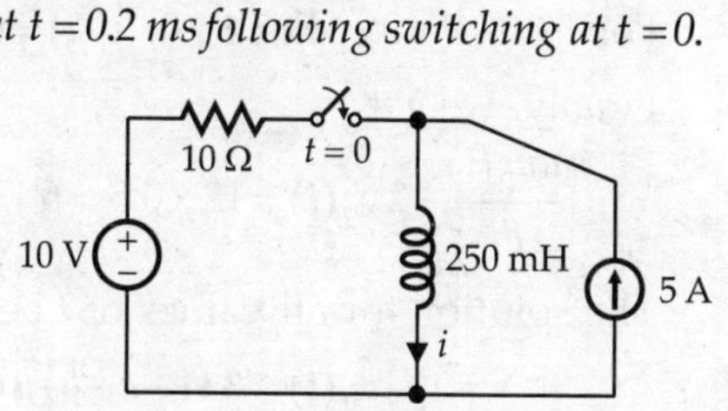

Fig. 20.132

Solution. Due to presence of 5 A current source, $i(0+) = 5\text{ A}$; τ (time constant) $= \frac{L}{R} = 25\text{ ms}$.

Forced response i_f (the inductor current at steady state due to presence of 10 V source and 5 A source) is summation of the currents in the inductor due to both the sources.

i.e., $$i_f = \frac{10\text{ V}}{10\Omega} + 5\text{ A} = 6\text{ A}.$$

Natural response,

$$i_n = (5-6)e^{-t/\tau} = -e^{-\frac{t}{25\times10^{-3}}}$$

$$\therefore \quad i = i_f + i_n = (6 - e^{-t/25\times10^{-3}})\text{ A}$$

At $t = 0.2$ ms, $\quad i = 6 - e^{-\frac{0.2}{25}\times10^3\times10^{-3}}$

i.e., $\quad i = \mathbf{5.008\ A}$

Option (*d*) is correct.

M20.126 *In the circuit shown in Fig. 20.133, the switch is closed at $t=0$. If $v(t)$ be $0.5\,u(t)$, $v_2(t)$ in the circuit shown is*

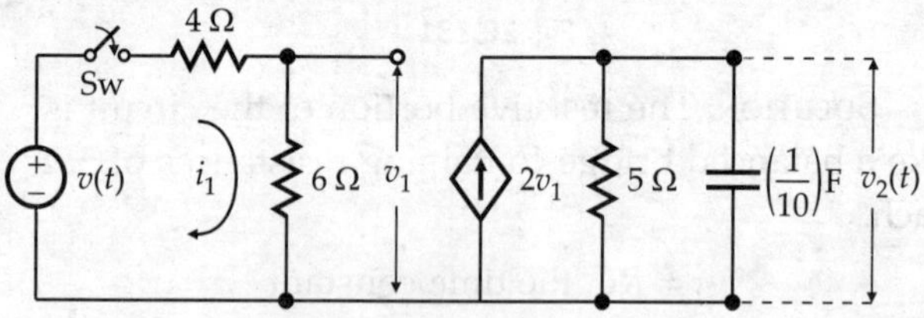

Fig. 20.133

(*a*) $0.3(1-2e^{-t})u(t)$ (*b*) $3(1-e^{-2t})u(t)$

(*c*) $5e^{-2t}u(t)$ (*d*) $e^{-t}\,u(t)$

Solution. Following switching action, nodal analysis in the given circuit at $t = (0+)$ yields

$$-2v_1 + \frac{v_2(t)}{5} + \frac{1}{10}\cdot\frac{dv_2(t)}{dt} = 0$$

However, $v_1 = 6i_1$ and $i_1 = \frac{v(t)}{10}$

$$\therefore \quad \frac{v_2(t)}{5} + \frac{1}{10}\frac{dv_2(t)}{dt} = 12i_1 = 12\frac{v(t)}{10} = 1.2\,v(t)$$

For $t<0$, $v=0$. For $t>0$, $v(t) = 0.5$.

Finally, we get

$$\frac{dv_2(t)}{dt} + 2v_2(t) = 12\times0.5 = 6$$

The solution for all values of t becomes

$$v_2(t) = \mathbf{3\,(1-e^{-2t})\,u(t)}$$

Option (*b*) is correct.

M20.127 *In the Fig. 20.134, the transformer T_1 has two secondaries, all three windings having the same number of turns and with polarities as indicated. One secondary*

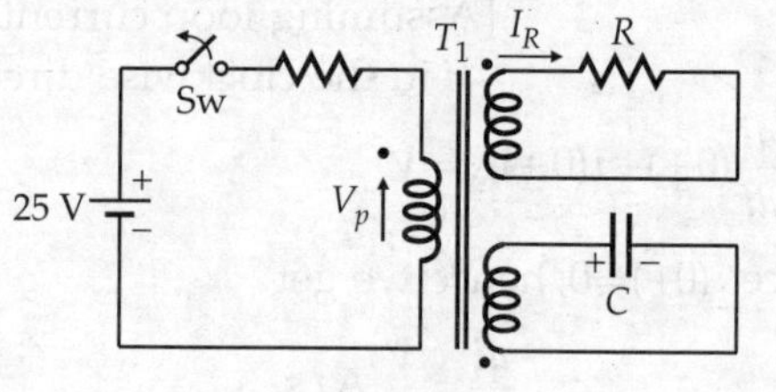

Fig. 20.134

is shorted by a 10Ω resistor R, and the other by a 15 mF capacitor. The switch Sw is opened ($t=0$) when the capacitor is charged to 5 V with the left plate as positive. At ($t=0+$) the voltage V_P and current I_R are

(*a*) – 25 V, 0.0 A

(*b*) *Very large voltage, very large current*

(*c*) 5.0 V, 0.5 A

(*d*) – 5 V, – 0.5 A **[GATE 2007]**

Solution. The dot convention in the given circuit indicates that P_1 and S_4 have same polarity and P_1 and S_1 are having same polarity (Fig. 20.135) at $t = (0+)$. It is evident from the given question that at $t = 0+$, S_3 is +ve as the capacitor connected with S_3 is having +ve polarity at the S_3 end (left plate).

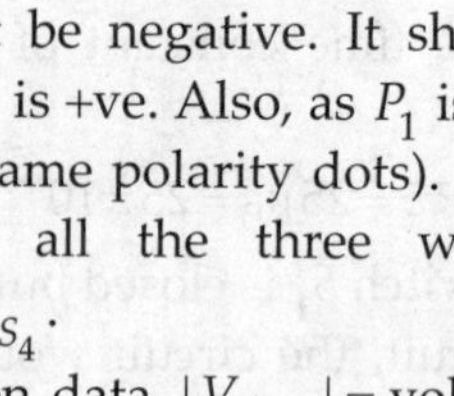

Fig. 20.135

Hence S_4 must be negative. It shows P_1 is also negative and P_2 is +ve. Also, as P_1 is negative, S_1 is also negative (same polarity dots). As twins ratios are equal for all the three windings hence $V_P = V_{S_1S_2} = V_{S_3S_4}$.

As per given data, $|V_{S_3S_4}|$ = voltage across the capacitor = 5 V.

Thus $V_{S_3S_4} = +5$ V with S_4 having –ve potential. This gives $V_P = \mathbf{-5\ V}$, with P_1 as –ve terminal. Also, $V_{S_1S_2} = -5$ V, with S_1 negative terminal.

$$I_R = (V_{S_1S_2}/R) = -\frac{5}{10} = -\frac{1}{2}\text{ A}.$$

Hence, we get $V_P = -5$ V ; $I_R = \mathbf{-0.5\ A}$.

Option (*d*) is correct.

M20.128 *A resistor and a capacitor are connected in series to a 10 dc supply through a switch (Fig. 20.136). The switch is closed at $t = 0$ and the capacitor voltage is found to cross 0 V at $t = 0.4\tau$, where τ is the circuit time constant. The absolute value of percentage change required in the initial capacitor voltage if the zero crossing has to happen at $t = 0.2\tau$ is ______ . (rounded off to 2 decimal places)* **[GATE 2020]**

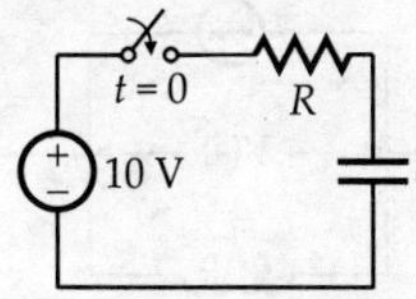

Fig. 20.136

Solution. It may be observed from the given problem that the capacitor voltage crosses the zero crossing and this can happen only if the capacitor had been charged initially with opposite polarity of applied voltage.

$$V_C(t) = [\text{Initial value} - \text{Final value}]e^{-t/\tau} + \text{Final Value}$$

$$= [-V_0 - 10]e^{-t/\tau} + 10$$

At zero crossing, for $t = 0.4\,\tau$,

$$0 = [-V_0 - 10]e^{-0.4\tau/\tau} + 10$$

or, $$-10 = (V_0 + 10)e^{-0.4}$$

$\therefore$ $$V_0 = 4.92 \text{ V}$$

In the second case of zero crossing at $t = 0.2\,\tau$,

$$0 = [-V_0' - 10]e^{-0.2} + 10$$

$\therefore$ $$V_0' = 2.214,$$

Percentage change in voltage (ΔV)

$$= \frac{V_0 - V_0'}{V_0} = \frac{4.92 - 2.214}{4.92}$$

$= 54.99\% \simeq$ **55%.**

M20.129 *Switch (Sw) is opened at $t = 0$ and the circuit starts discharging through the diode (D) (Fig. 20.137). Assuming the diode having negligible resistance,*

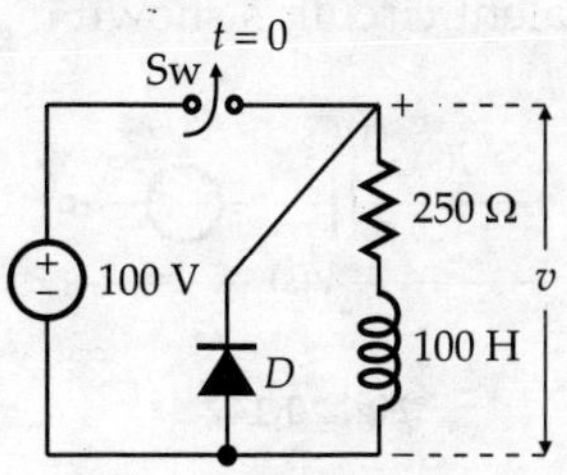

Fig. 20.137

(i) The current through 100 H inductance after 1.0 sec is

(a) 0.033 A (b) 0.4 A

(c) 0.011 A (d) 0 A

(ii) Voltage 'v' across the R-L circuit at $t = (0-)$ and at $t = (0+)$ are

(a) $v(0-) = e^t$ V; $v(0+) = e^t$ V

(b) $v(0-) = 0$ V; $v(0+) = 100$ V

(c) $v(0-) = 100$ V; $v(0+) = 0$ V

(d) $[v_C(0-)] = -100$ V; $v_c(0+) = 100$ V

(iii) The instantaneous power in the circuit is

(a) 0.87 W (b) 0 W

(c) 0.27 W (d) 5.25 W

(iv) The energy dissipated in the resistor in 1 sec is ______ mJ.

Solution. Due to presence of the inductance, the inductor current i_L at $t = (0-)$ will be same as inductor current i_L at $t = (0+)$.

i.e., $$i_L(0-) = i_L(0+) = \frac{100 \text{ V}}{250\ \Omega} = 0.4 \text{ A}.$$

However, no current will flow through D as it is reverse biased when the switch was closed.

Figure 20.138 represents the circuit at $t = (0+)$.

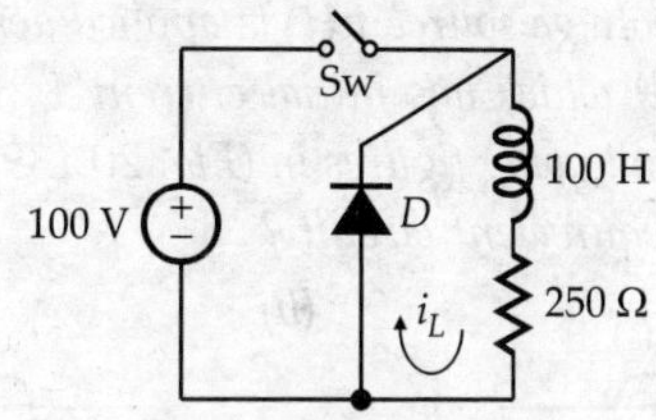

Fig. 20.138

Here, $$L\frac{di_L}{dt} + 250 i_L = 0$$

$\therefore$ $$i_L = Ae^{-t/\tau} \quad ...(1)$$

Equation (1) becomes

$$i_L(t) = Ae^{-2.50t} \quad ...(2)$$

At $t = (0+)$, $i_L(t) = 0.4$ A $\quad [\because i_L(0+) = 0.4 \text{ A}]$

$\therefore$ $$A (= I_0, \text{say}) = 0.4 \text{ A}$$

Equation (2) becomes

$$i_L(t) = I_0 e^{-2.5t} = 0.4e^{-2.5t} \text{ A}$$

(i) At $t = 1$ sec,

$$i_L(t = 1 \text{ sec}) = 0.4e^{-2.5\times 1} = \mathbf{0.033\ A}$$

Option (a) is correct.

(*ii*) At $t = (0-)$ the voltage across *RL*-circuit was the battery voltage only.

$$\therefore \quad v[t = (0-)] = 100 \text{ V}.$$

At $t = (0+)$, the voltage across *R-L* circuit is the drop across the diode. Since the diode has negligible resistance, hence the drop across the diode is zero.

$$v[t = (0+)] = v_d = 0.$$

$$\therefore \quad v[t = (0-)] = \mathbf{100\ V}$$

$$v[t = 0(+)] = \mathbf{0\ V}$$

Option (*c*) is correct.

(*iii*) Instantaneous power

$$P = i^2 R = (0.4e^{-2.5t})^2 \times 250$$
$$= 40\, e^{-5t}$$

At $t = 1$ s, $P = 40e^{-5} = \mathbf{0.27\ W}$

Option (*c*) is correct.

(*iv*) Energy dissipated in the resistor of the circuit is (for $t = 0$ to 1 sec.)

$$E = \int_0^1 (i^2 R)\, dt = 0.16 \int_0^1 e^{-5t}\, dt$$

$$= \mathbf{21.44\ mJ}.$$

M20.130 *A voltage source $v(t)$ is applied across a pure inductance (L) which has initial current I_0 through it. Which of the following figures in (Fig. 20.139) represent the s-domain equivalent circuit ?*

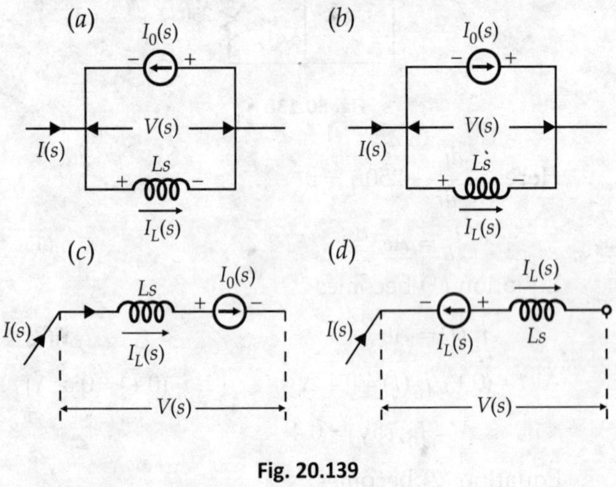

Fig. 20.139

Solution. The current through the inductor being $i(t)$, we can write

$$i(t) = \frac{1}{L} \int_0^t v(t)\, dt + i(0+)$$

In *s*-domain, we get

$$I(s) = \frac{1}{L} \frac{v(s)}{s} + \frac{i(0+)}{s}$$

$$= I_L(s) + I_0(s) \qquad \left[\because \frac{i(0+)}{s} = I_0(s)\right]$$

Figure 20.140 represents the equivalent circuit.

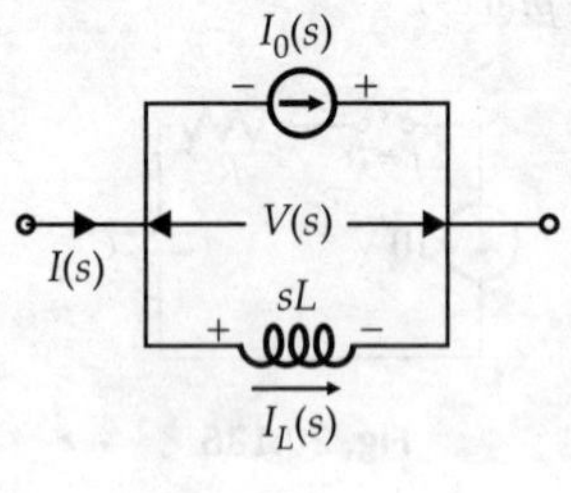

Fig. 20.140

Option (*b*) is correct.

M20.131 *A voltage $v(t)$ is applied to a capacitance C which has initial voltage $(-V_0)$. If the charging current be $i(t)$, which of the following figures in (Fig. 20.141) represents the equivalent circuit in s-domain ?*

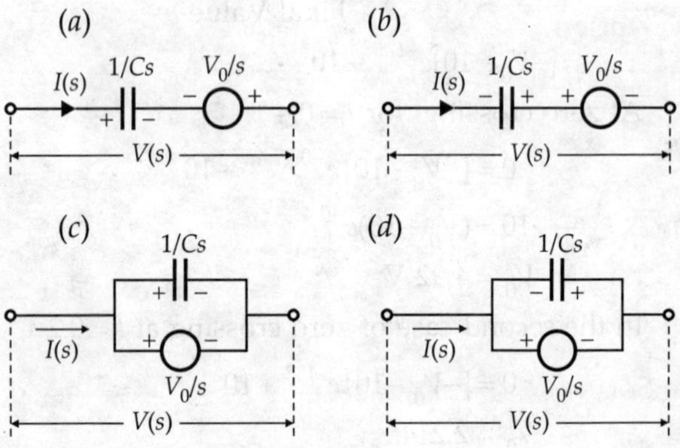

Fig. 20.141

Solution. $v(t) = -V_0 + \frac{1}{C} \int_0^t i(t)dt$

In *s*-domain,

$$V(s) = -\frac{V_0}{s} + \frac{I(s)}{Cs}$$

The equivalent circuit is shown in Fig. 20.142.

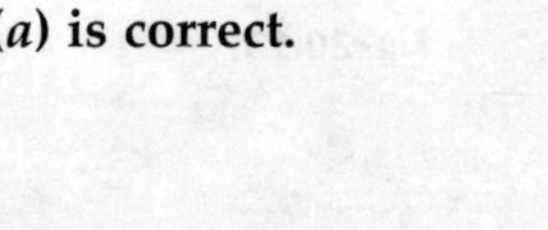

Fig. 20.142

Option (*a*) is correct.

M20.132 *In a series LC circuit, $L = 1\,H$; $C = 1\,F$. The supply voltage is $v = 2e^{-4t}$ volt. Assuming the capacitor is discharged initially, obtain the charge in the capacitor for $t > 0$.*

(*a*) $0.118\,(e^{-4t} - \cos t + 4\cos t)$

(*b*) $0.118\,(\sin t - \cos t)$

(*c*) $2\,(e^{-4t} + \cos t)$

(*d*) $2\,(e^{-4t} + \sin t - \cos t)$

Solution. In the LC circuit, at $t = (0+)$, the governing equation is

$$\frac{d^2q}{dt^2} + q = 2e^{-4t}$$

[q is the charge of the capacitor]

$$\therefore \quad Q(s)[s^2+1] = \frac{2s}{s+4}$$

or, $$Q(s) = \frac{2s}{(s^2+1)(s+4)}$$

$$\therefore \quad q(t) = \mathbf{0.118\,(e^{-4t} - \cos t + 4\cos t)}$$

Option (*a*) is correct.

M20.133 *In a circuit, the voltage at a node is given by*

$$v(s) = \frac{1}{s(s+\alpha)}$$

If $v(t)$, for $t = \infty$ is 10 V, find $v(t)$ at $t = 1$ s.

(*a*) 0 V (*b*) 0.952 V

(*c*) 10 V (*d*) 0.1 V

Solution. $v(\infty) = \lim_{s\to 0} s.\dfrac{1}{s(s+\alpha)} = \dfrac{1}{\alpha} = 10$

$$\therefore \quad \alpha = 0.1$$

$$V(s) = \frac{1}{s(s+0.1)} = 10\left[\frac{1}{s} - \frac{1}{s+0.1}\right]$$

$$\therefore \quad v(t) = 10(1 - e^{-0.1t})$$

$v(t)$ at $t = 1$ sec is

$$v(1) = 10(1 - e^{-0.1\times 1})$$

$$= \mathbf{0.952\ Volts}$$

Option (*b*) is correct.

M20.134 *Switch S is at position (1) at steady state. At $t = (0-)$ it is moved to position (2). The expression of $i(t)$, the current through R, at $t = (0+)$ is obtained in Fig. 20.143 as*

(*a*) $(2e^{-50t})$ A (*b*) $(2 + e^{50t})$ A

(*c*) $(2 - e^{-50t})$ A (*d*) $(-2 + e^{50t})$ A

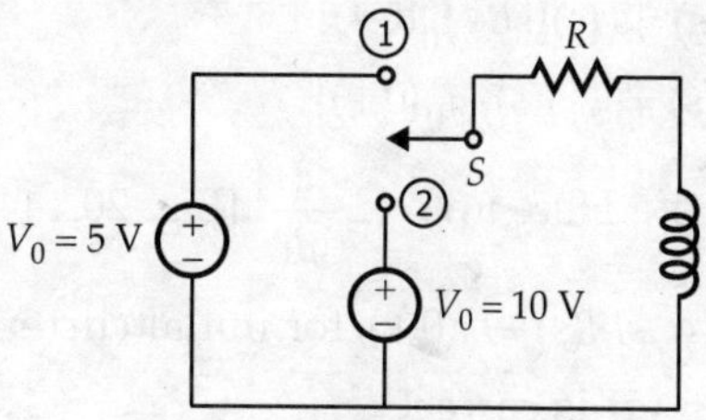

$R = 5\,\Omega,\ L = 1\times 10^{-1}$ H

Fig. 20.143

Solution. When the switch is at position (1), i at $t = (0-)$ is given by $i(0-) = \frac{5}{5} = 1$ A; at steady state, L acts as short-circuit.

When the switch is shifted to (2), the loop equation becomes

$$5i(t) + 0.1\frac{di(t)}{dt} = 10$$

or, $$5I(s) + 0.1[sI(s) - i(0+)] = \frac{10}{s}$$

In L-R circuit $i(0+) = i(0-)$

$\therefore$ We have,

$$5I(s) + 0.1[sI(s) - 1] = \frac{10}{s}$$

or, $$I(s)[5 + 0.1s] - 0.1 = \frac{10}{s}$$

or, $$I(s) = \frac{10/s + 0.1}{5 + 0.1s} = \frac{10 + 0.1\,s}{s(0.1\,s + 5)} = \frac{s+100}{s(s+50)}$$

However, $$\frac{s+100}{(s+50)s} = \frac{A}{s} + \frac{B}{s+50}$$

Using partial fraction method,

$$A = \left.\frac{s+100}{s+50}\right|_{s=0} = 2$$

$$B = \left.\frac{s+100}{s}\right|_{s=-50} = -1$$

$$\therefore \quad I(s) = \frac{2}{s} + \frac{(-1)}{s+50} = \frac{2}{s} - \frac{1}{s+50}$$

$$\therefore \quad i(t) = \mathbf{(2 - e^{-50t})\,A.}$$

Option (*c*) is correct.

M20.135 *If the initial current through inductance (L) is $(-i_0)$ (Fig. 20.144), the voltage equation in s-domain at $t = (0+)$ is given by*

(*a*) $v(s) = [sLI(s) - Li(0+)]$

(*b*) $v(s) = sLI(s) - sLi_0(0+)$

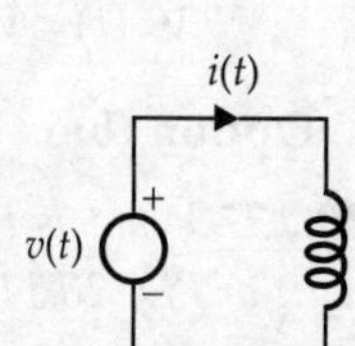

Fig. 20.144

CHAPTER 20

(c) $v(s) = I(s)[sL + i_0(0+)]$

(d) $v(s) = sL[I(s) - i_0(0+)]$

Solution. Here $v(t) = L\dfrac{di(t)}{dt}$ [Fig. 20.144]

$\therefore V(s) = sLI(s) - Li(0+)$, for initial current $(-i_0)$.

Option (a) is correct.

M20.136 *An ideal capacitor is charged to a voltage V_0 and connected at $t = 0$ across an ideal inductor L. (The circuit now consists of a capacitor and inductor alone). If $\omega_0 = \dfrac{1}{\sqrt{LC}}$, the voltage across the capacitor at time $t > 0$ is given by* **[GATE 2006]**

(a) V_0 (b) $V_0 \cos(\omega_0 t)$

(c) $V_0 \sin(\omega_0 t)$ (d) $V_0 e^{-\omega_0 t} \cos(\omega_0 t)$

Solution. Figure 20.145 represents the circuit at $t > 0$. Let V_C be the voltage across the capacitor at $t > 0$.

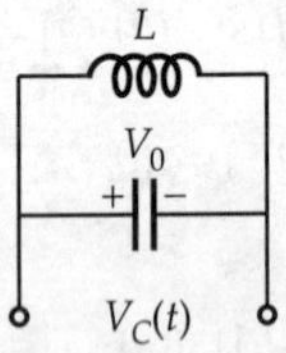

Fig. 20.145

In Fig. 20.145, we can write

$$C\frac{dV_C(t)}{dt} + \frac{1}{L}\int_{-\infty}^{t} V_C(t)\,dt = 0$$

Transforming this equation to Laplace domain,

$$C[sV_C(s) - V_C(0+)] + \frac{V_C(s)}{Ls} = 0$$

or, $$CsV_C(s) - CV_C(0+) + \frac{V_C(s)}{Ls} = 0$$

or, $$V_C(s)\left[s^2 + \frac{1}{LC}\right] = sV_C(0+)$$

$$\therefore \quad V_C(s) = V_0\left[\frac{s}{s^2 + \omega_0^2}\right]$$

i.e., $$V_C(t) = \mathbf{V_0 \cos(\omega_0 t)}$$

Option (b) is correct.

M20.137 *What is the value of $i_L(t)$ at $t = 0.5$ ms in the circuit of Fig. 20.145 following switching at $t = 0$?*

(a) 0.5 mA (b) –3 A

(c) 2.998 mA (d) 0 A

Solution. In s-domain circuit of the given figure following switching, the governing equation is

$$I(s)[(4 + 2s)] = \frac{12}{s}$$

$$\therefore \quad I(s) = \frac{12}{s(4+2s)} = \frac{K_1}{s} + \frac{K_2}{4+2s}$$

$$= \frac{K_1(4+2s) + K_2 s}{s(4+2s)}$$

$$= \frac{s(2K_1 + K_2) + 4K_1}{s(4+2s)}$$

Substituting $(2K_1 + K_2) = 0$; $4K_1 = 12$, we get

$$K_1 = 3 \ ; \ K_2 = -6$$

$$\therefore \quad I(s) = \frac{3}{s} - \frac{6}{4+2s} = \frac{3}{s} - \frac{3}{2+s}$$

$$= 3\left[\frac{1}{s} - \frac{1}{2+s}\right]$$

$\therefore i(t)$ at $t = (0+)$ is

$$i(t) = 3(1 - e^{-2t})\,\text{A}$$

At 0.5×10^{-3} s,

$$i(t) = 3(1 - e^{-2\times 0.5\times 10^{-3}}) = \mathbf{2.998\ mA}$$

Option (c) is correct.

M20.138 *In the following figure (Fig. 20.146), C_1 and C_2 are ideal capacitors. C_1 has been charged to 12 V before the ideal switch is closed at $t = 0$.*

The current $i(t)$ for all t is

(a) *zero*

(b) *a step function*

(c) *an exponentially decaying function*

(d) *an impulse function*

[GATE 2012]

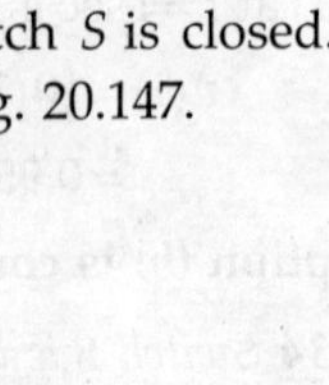

Fig. 20.146

Solution. At $t = 0$, the switch S is closed. The s-domain circuit is drawn in Fig. 20.147.

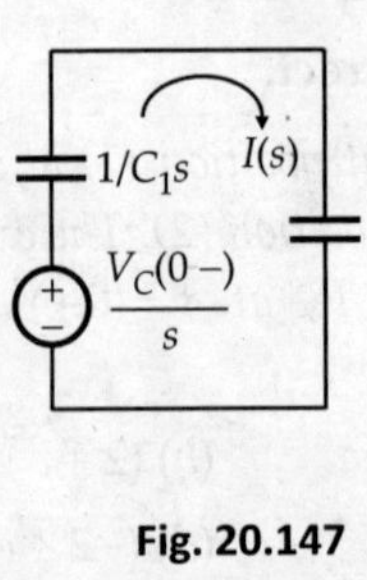

Fig. 20.147

Here, $-\frac{V_C(0-)}{s}+\frac{1}{C_1 s}.I(s)+\frac{1}{C_2 s}.I(s)=0$

$$\therefore \quad I(s)=\frac{V_C(0-)/s}{\frac{1}{C_1 s}+\frac{1}{C_2 s}}$$

With $V_C(0-)=12$ V, we get

$$I(s)=\frac{V_C(0-)}{\frac{1}{C_1}+\frac{1}{C_2}}=\frac{12}{\frac{C_1+C_2}{C_1 C_2}}$$

$$=\frac{12(C_1 C_2)}{C_1+C_2}=12C_{eq}.$$

$\therefore$ $i(t)=\mathbf{12}C_{eq}\,\delta(t)$**, an impulse function for all** t.

Option (*d*) is correct.

M20.139 *In the figure given below (Fig. 20.148), the initial capacitor voltage is zero. The switch is closed at* $t=0$.

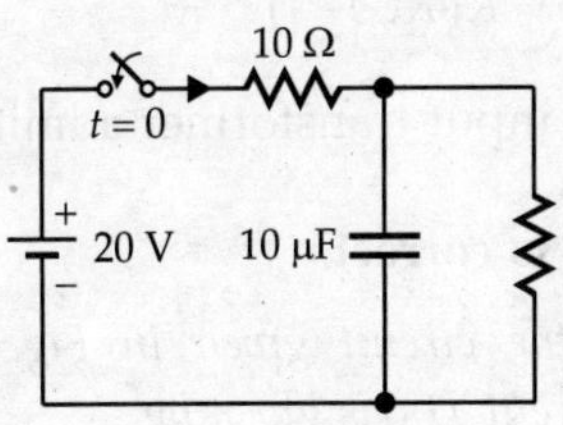

Fig. 20.148

The final steady state voltage across the capacitor is

(*a*) 20 V (*b*) 10 V (*c*) 5 V (*d*) 0 V **[GATE 2005]**

Solution. Let $V_C(\infty)$ be the steady state voltage across the capacitor. At $t=\infty$, after the switch is closed, the capacitor will be charged and act as open circuit (Fig. 20.149).

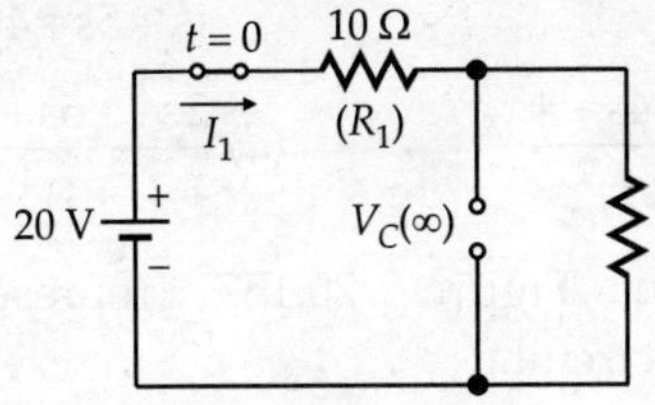

Fig. 20.149

Here, $I=\frac{20}{10+10}=1$ A

$\therefore$ $V_C(\infty)=$ Voltage drop across R_2

$=1\text{A}\times 10\ \Omega=\mathbf{10\ V}$

Option (*b*) is correct.

M20.140 *In the circuit shown in Fig. 20.150, the coil has impedance* $(4+j2)\Omega$. *The circuit is at steady state with switch open. At* $t=0$, *switch K is closed. The current*

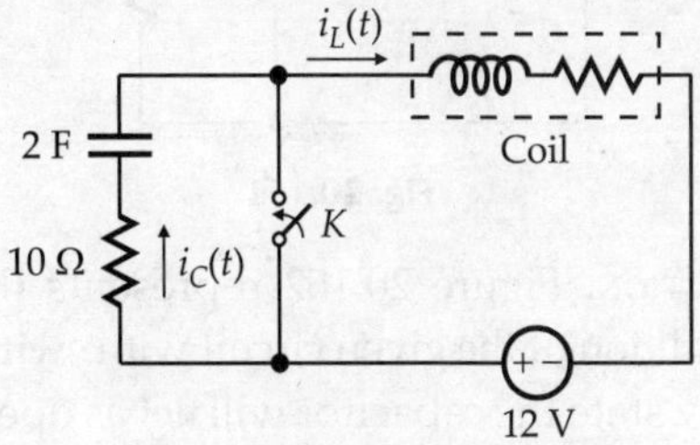

Fig. 20.150

through the inductor and voltage across the capacitor at $t=(0-)$ *and* $t=(0+)$ *are given by*

(*a*) 0, 12 V (*b*) 12 A, 0 V

(*c*) 0.85 A, 12 V (*d*) 6 A, 12 V

Solution. At $t(0-)$, $i_L(0-)=0$.

Inductor can not suddenly change the current

$\therefore$ $i_L(0-)=i_L(0+)=0$

At steady state capacitor voltage is 12 V.

i.e., $v_c(0+)=v_c(0-)=\mathbf{12\ V}$.

Option (*a*) is correct.

M20.141 *In an inductive circuit, in s-domain the current through the inductor is given by*

$$I(s)=-\frac{10}{(s+3)^2}$$

How much energy is stored in the inductor in mJ at $t=1s$? *Assume* $L=1H$.

(*a*) 248 (*b*) 124 (*c*) 498 (*d*) 10

Solution. $I(s)=-\frac{10}{(s+3)^2}$

$\therefore$ $i_L(t)=-10te^{-3t}$

i.e., $i_L(1)=-10\times 1\times e^{-3}=-0.498$ A

$\therefore$ $W_L(t)$, at $(t=1\text{s})$ is $\frac{1}{2}L[i_L(1)]^2$

i.e., $W_L(t)=\frac{1}{2}\times 1\times(-0.498)^2$

$=$ **124 mJ**

Option (*b*) is correct.

M20.142 *The switch in circuit (Fig. 20.151) has been closed for a long time. It is opened at* $t=0$. *At* $t=(0+)$, *the current through* $1\mu F$ *capacitor is*

(*a*) 0 A (*b*) 1 A

(*c*) 1.25 A (*d*) 5 A **[GATE 2010]**

CHAPTER 20

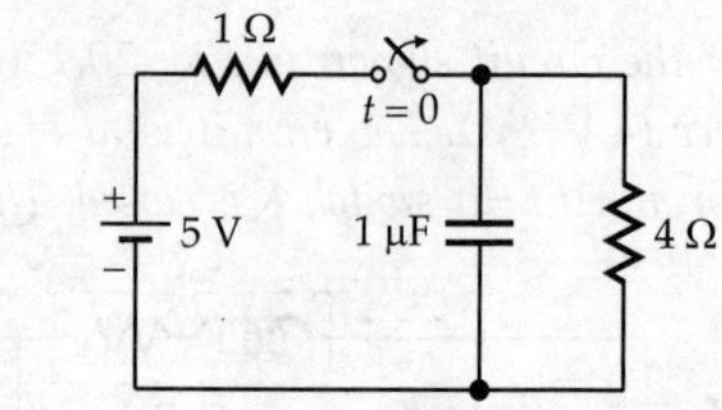

Fig. 20.151

Solution. Figure 20.152 represents the steady state condition of the given circuit with switch closed. At steady state the capacitor will act as open circuit.

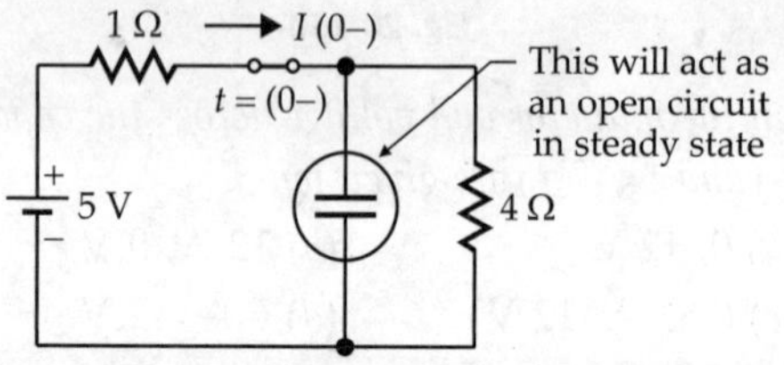

Fig. 20.152

$\therefore$ V_C (0 –), the voltage across the capacitor at $t = (0–)$ is the drop across the 4Ω resistor.

Assuming $I(0–)$ to be the current for the battery (5 V source),

$$V_{4\Omega} = \frac{5}{1+4} \times 4 = 4 \text{ V} = V_C\,(0–)$$

At $t = 0$, the switch is opened (Fig. 20.153).

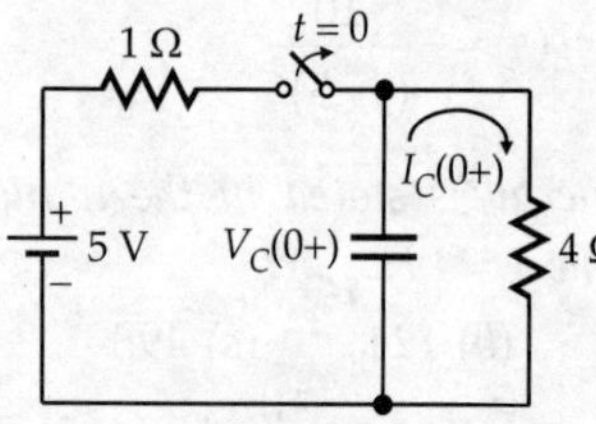

Fig. 20.153

Obviously $V_C\,(0+) = V_C\,(0–) = 4$ V.

$$\therefore \quad I_C\,(0+) = \frac{4}{4} = \mathbf{1\ A}$$

Option (*b*) is correct.

M20.143 *With $R_1 = R_2 = R$ and $L = R^2C$, for the network shown in Fig. 20.154, the transformer input admittance $Y(s)$ is given by*

(*a*) *LC*

(*b*) $\dfrac{1}{RC}$

(*c*) $\dfrac{1}{R}$

(*d*) *R*

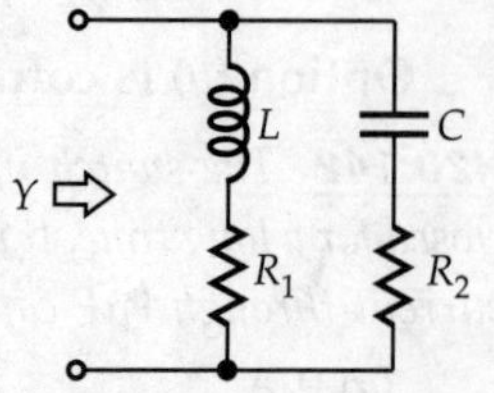

Fig. 20.154

Solution. Let us first transform the given circuit to *s*-domain circuit (Fig. 20.155).

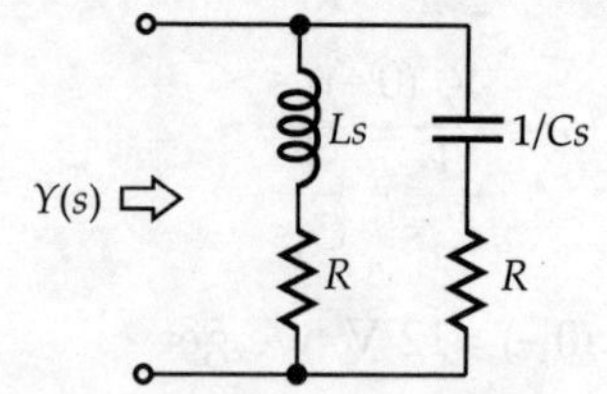

Fig. 20.155

$$Y(s) = \frac{1}{R + Ls} + \frac{1}{R + \dfrac{1}{sC}}$$

With $L = R^2C$,

$$Y(s) = \frac{1}{R + R^2Cs} + \frac{1}{R + \dfrac{1}{sC}}$$

$$= \frac{1}{R(1 + RCs)} + \frac{sC}{(RCs + 1)}$$

$$= \frac{sCR + 1}{R(RCs + 1)} = \frac{1}{R}$$

$\therefore$ $Y(s)$, the input transformer admittance $= \dfrac{\mathbf{1}}{\boldsymbol{R}}$.

Option (*c*) is correct.

M20.144 *In the circuit given in Fig. 20.156, the transformer current $I(s)$ is given by*

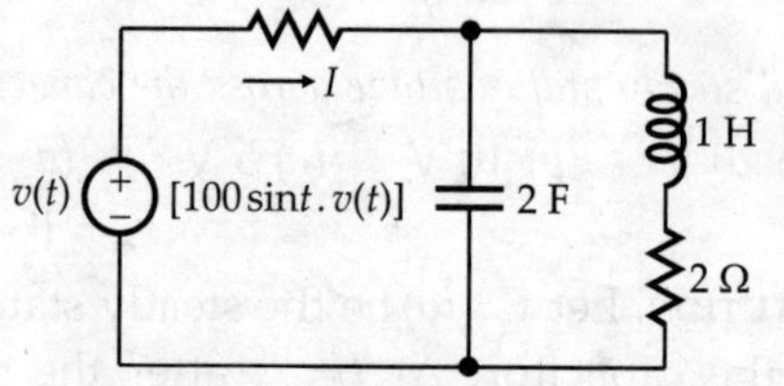

Fig. 20.156

(*a*) $(s+1)^2\,(s^2 + 5s + 1)$ (*b*) $\dfrac{(s+1)^2}{s^2 + 5s + 4}$

(*c*) $\dfrac{s^2 + 4s + 4}{(s+1)^2}$ (*d*) $\dfrac{2s^2 + 5s + 4}{(s+1)^2}$

Solution. Figure 20.157 represents the transformed circuit.

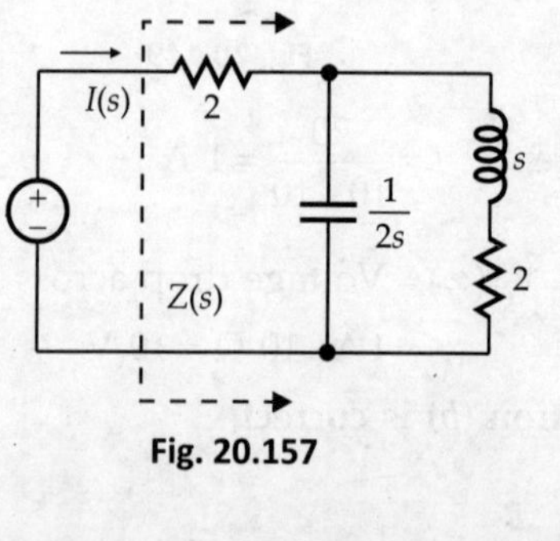

Fig. 20.157

$$Z(s) = 2 + \frac{1}{\left(s + \frac{1}{s+2}\right)}$$

$$= 2 + \frac{s+2}{s(s+2)+1}$$

$$= \frac{2s^2+4s+2+s+2}{s^2+2s+1}$$

$$= \mathbf{\frac{2s^2+5s+4}{s^2+2s+1}}$$

Option (*d*) is correct.

M20.145 *In the circuit shown in Fig. 20.158, the value of $I(s)$ is given by*

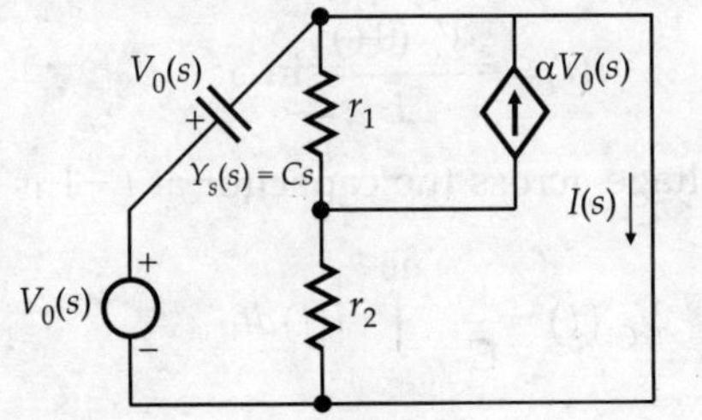

$[r_1 = 5\ \Omega, r_2 = 10\ \Omega, V_0(s) = \frac{10}{s}, C = 1\text{ F}, \alpha = 0.6]$

Fig. 20.158

(*a*) $\frac{1}{s}(3+5s)$ (*b*) $(3s+5s)\frac{1}{s}$

(*c*) $(5s+2)$ (*d*) $\frac{2}{s}[1+5s]$

Solution. The given circuit is redrawn (Fig. 20.159) with respective currents.

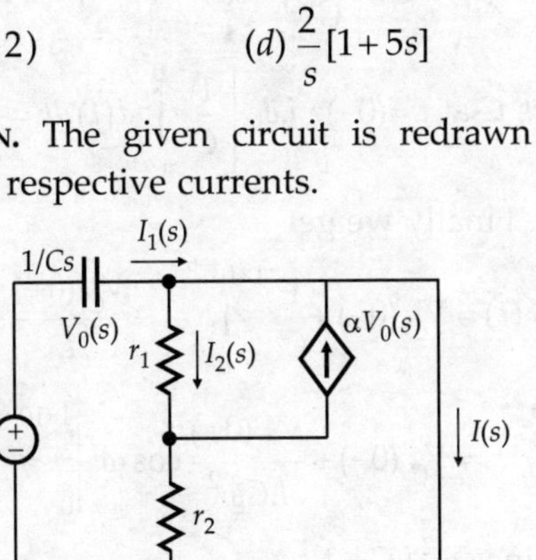

Fig. 20.159

$$I_1(s) = V_0(s)Cs$$

$$I_2(s) = V_0(s)Cs \times \frac{r_2}{r_1+r_2}$$

Current through r_2 due to $\alpha V_0(s)$ is

$$\alpha V_0(s) \times \frac{r_1}{r_1+r_2}$$

Current through r_2 due to $V_0(s)$ is

$$V_0(s)Cs \times \frac{r_1}{r_1+r_2}$$

$I(s)$ = current through r_1 + current through r_2

$$= V_0(s)Cs\frac{r_2}{r_1+r_2} + V_0(s)Cs\frac{r_1}{r_1+r_2} + \alpha V_0(s)\frac{r_1}{r_1+r_2}$$

$$= \frac{V_0(s)Cs}{r_1+r_2} + [r_2+r_1] + \alpha V_0(s)\frac{r_1}{r_1+r_2}$$

$$= V_0(s)Cs + \alpha V_0(s)\frac{r_1}{r_1+r_2}$$

$$= \frac{10}{s} \times 1 \times s + 0.6 \times \frac{10}{s} \times \frac{5}{15}$$

$$= 10 + \frac{2}{s} = \mathbf{\frac{2}{s}[1+5s]}$$

Option (*d*) is correct.

M20.146 *The current $i(t)$ sketched in Fig. 20.160 flows through an initially uncharged 0.3 nF capacitor.*

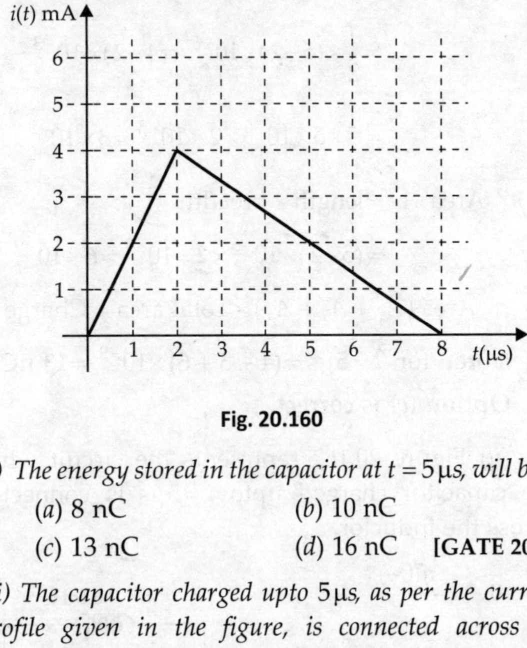

Fig. 20.160

(*i*) *The energy stored in the capacitor at $t = 5\ \mu s$, will be*

(*a*) 8 nC (*b*) 10 nC

(*c*) 13 nC (*d*) 16 nC **[GATE 2008]**

(*ii*) *The capacitor charged upto 5 μs, as per the current profile given in the figure, is connected across an inductor of 0.6 mH. Then the value of voltage across the capacitor after 1 μs will approximately be*

(*a*) 18.8 V (*b*) 23.5 V

(*c*) – 23.5 V (*d*) – 30.6 V

[GATE 2008]

Solution.

(*i*) Charge stored in the capacitor for $t = 5\ \mu s$ is the summation of charge stored in $t = 2\ \mu s$ and the charge stored for $t = 2\ \mu s$ to $t = 5\ \mu s$. Let us shade the areas representing the charge stored in the capacitor for different time intervals in Fig. 20.161.

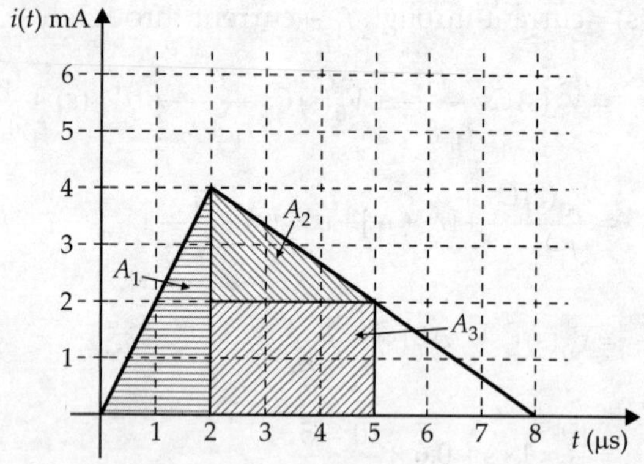

Fig. 20.161

Here,

$$\text{Area } A_1 = \frac{1}{2}\text{base}\times\text{ altitude}$$

$$= \frac{1}{2}\times 2\times 10^{-6}\times 4\times 10^{-3} = 4\times 10^{-9}$$

$$A_2 = \frac{1}{2}\times(5-2)\times 10^{-6}\times(4-2)\times 10^{-3}$$

$$= \frac{1}{2}\times 3\times 10^{-6}\times 2\times 10^{-3} = 3\times 10^{-9}$$

$$\text{Area } A_3 = \text{length}\times\text{breadth}$$

$$= (5-2)\times 10^{-6}\times 2\times 10^{-3} = 6\times 10^{-9}$$

$\therefore$ Area $(A_1 + A_2 + A_3)$ = Total area = Charge stored for $t = 5\,\mu s = (4+3+6)\times 10^{-9}$ = **13 nC**

Option (*c*) is correct.

(*ii*) Figure 20.162 represents the circuit when the capacitor charged upto $t = 5\,\mu s$ is connected across the inductor.

$$V_C(0-) = \frac{q(0-)}{C}$$

$$= \frac{13\times 10^{-9}}{0.3\times 10^{-9}}$$

$$= 43.33 \text{ V}$$

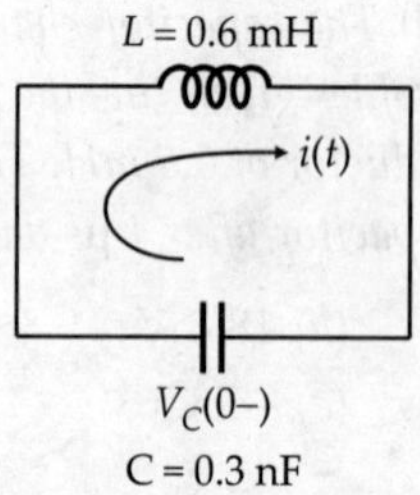

Fig. 20.162

Also it is to be noted that

$$V_C(0-) = V_C(0+)$$

We can write,

$$L\frac{di(t)}{dt} + \frac{1}{C}\int_{-\infty}^{t} i(t)\,dt = 0 \qquad ...(i)$$

Transforming this circuit to Laplace domain, equation (*i*) becomes

$$L[sI(s) - i(0+)] + \frac{V_C(0+)}{s} + \frac{1}{C}\frac{I(s)}{s} = 0$$

$$\therefore \quad I(s) = -\frac{V_C(0+)}{L}\left[\frac{1}{s^2 + \left(\frac{1}{\sqrt{LC}}\right)^2}\right] \qquad ...(2)$$

$\because \omega = \dfrac{1}{\sqrt{LC}}$, equation (2) may be written as

$$I(s) = -\frac{V_C(0+)}{L}\left[\frac{\omega}{\omega(s^2+\omega^2)}\right]$$

$$\therefore \quad i(t) = -\frac{V_C(0+)}{L}\sin\omega t \qquad ...(3)$$

Voltage across the capacitor at $t = 1\,\mu s$ is

$$V_C(t) = \frac{1}{C}\int_{-\infty}^{1\times 10^{-6}} i(t)\,dt$$

$$= \frac{1}{C}\int_{-\infty}^{0} i(t)\,dt + \frac{1}{C}\int_{-\infty}^{1\times 10^{-6}} i(t)\,dt$$

However, $\left[\dfrac{1}{C}\displaystyle\int_{-\infty}^{0} i(t)\,dt\right]$ represents the drop across C at $t = (0-)$; *i.e.*, $\left[\dfrac{1}{C}\displaystyle\int_{-\infty}^{0} i(t)\,dt = V_C(0-)\right]$.

$\therefore$ Finally we get

$$V_C(t) = V_C(0-) + \frac{1}{C}\int_{0}^{1\times 10^{-6}}\left(-\frac{V_C(0+)}{L}\sin\omega t\right)dt$$

$$= V_C(0-) + \frac{V_C(0+)}{LC\omega^2}\cos\omega t\Big|_0^{1\times 10^{-6}}$$

Since $\omega^2 LC = 1$,

$$V_C(t) = V_C(0-) + V_C(0+)\cos\omega t\Big|_0^{1\times 10^{-6}}$$

$$= V_C(0+)[1 + \cos 135° - 1] \qquad ...(4)$$

$$\left[\text{ since } \quad \omega = \frac{1}{\sqrt{LC}} = \frac{1}{\sqrt{0.6\times 10^{-3}\times 0.3\times 10^{-9}}}\right.$$

$$= 2.36\times 10^{6} \text{ rad/sec}$$

$\therefore \quad \omega t = 2.36\times 10^{6}\times 10^{-6} = 2.36$ rad, for $t = 1\,\mu s$

i.e., $\omega t = 135°$]

Hence, $V_C(t) = 43.33\cos 135° = -$ **30.6 V**.

Option (*d*) is correct.

M20.147 *Find the transformer ratios 'a' and 'b' such that the impedance (Z_{in}) is resistive and equals to 2.5 Ω when the network (Fig. 20.163) is excited with a sine wave voltage of angular frequency of 5000 rad/s.*

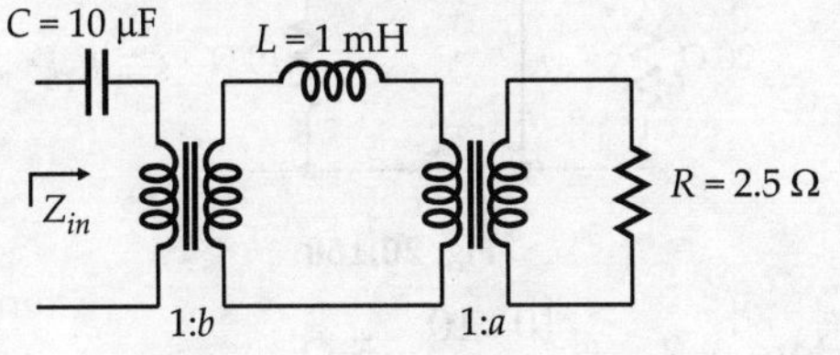

Fig. 20.163

(*a*) $a = 0.5, b = 2.0$ (*b*) $a = 2.0, b = 0.5$
(*c*) $a = 1.0, b = 1.0$ (*d*) $a = 4.0, b = 0.5$

[GATE 2015]

Solution. For any transformer, the impedance Z_L at the secondary side can be referred to the primary side impedance (Z'_L) with the following relation,

$$Z'_L = Z_L \times \frac{1}{n^2},$$

where n is off nominal the turns ratio

$$\left(N_1 / N_2 = \frac{1}{N_2 / N_1} = \frac{1}{n} \right)$$

Thus $R = 2.5\ \Omega$ can be referred to unity side of the transformer having turns ratio 1 : a as $R' = \frac{2.5}{a^2}$.

It can be further referred to the unity side of the transformer having turns ratio, 1 : b as $R'' = \frac{2.5}{a^2 b^2}$.

Similarly, the inductance 1 mH, which is equivalent to X_L of $j \times 5000 \times 1 \times 10^{-3}$ *i.e.*, $j5\Omega$, may be referred to unity side of transformer having turns ratio 1 : b as

$$X'_L = \frac{j5}{b^2}$$

Also, the X_C of the capacitance of 10 μF is given by

$$X_C = \frac{1}{j \times 5000 \times 10 \times 10^{-6}} = -j20\ \Omega$$

Hence,

$$Z_{in} = -j20 + j\frac{5}{b^2} + \frac{2.5}{a^2 b^2}$$

As per question, $Z_{in} = 2.5\ \Omega$.

$$\therefore \quad 2.5 = -j20 + j\frac{5}{b^2} + \frac{2.5}{a^2 b^2}$$

Separating the real and imaginary parts,

$$-j20 + j\frac{5}{b^2} = 0, \text{ i.e., } b = 0.5 \text{ and } \frac{2.5}{a^2 b^2} = 2.5$$

It gives $a = +2$

$\therefore$ **$a = 2, b = 0.5$**

Option (*b*) is correct.

M20.148 *The voltage across the capacitor, as shown in the figure (Fig. 20.164) is expressed as*

$$v_c(t) = A_1 \sin(\omega_1 t - \theta_1) + A_2 \sin(\omega_2 t - \theta_2)$$

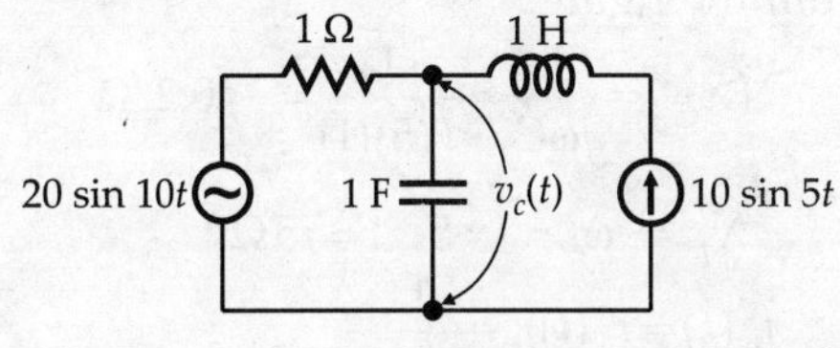

Fig. 20.164

The values of A_1 and A_2 respectively, are

(*a*) 2.0 and 1.98 (*b*) 2.0 and 4.20
(*c*) 2.5 and 3.50 (*d*) 5.0 and 6.40

[GATE 2014]

Solution. **For the source 20 sin 10 *t* acting alone (Fig. 20.165) :**

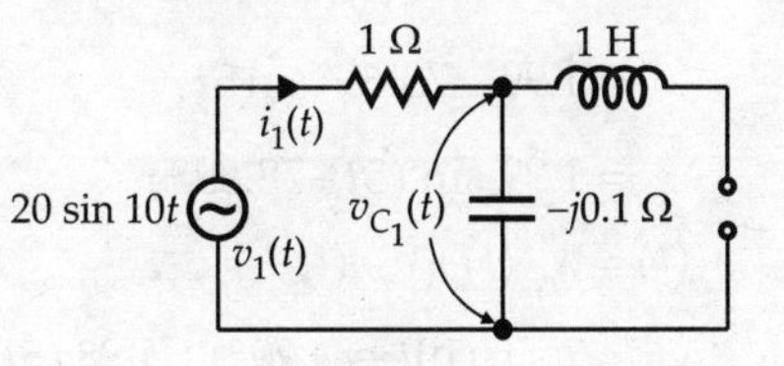

Fig. 20.165

The capacitive reactance

$$(X_C) = \frac{1}{j\omega C} = \frac{1}{j10.1} = -j0.1\ \Omega$$

$$i_1(t) = \frac{v_1(t)}{1 - j0.1} \text{ (see Fig. 2.165)}$$

$$\therefore \quad v_{c_1}(t) = i_1(t) \cdot (-j0.1)$$

$$= \frac{v_1(t)}{1 - j0.1} \times (-j0.1)$$

$$= \frac{20 \sin 10t}{1 - j0.1} \times (-j0.1)$$

$$= (2 \angle -84.29°) \sin 10t$$

$$= 2 \sin(10t - 84.29°)$$

[It may be observed here, in Fig. 20.165, that no current flows through the inductor as deactivating the current source means it is open circuited.]

For the current source 10 sin 5*t* acting alone (Fig. 20.166)

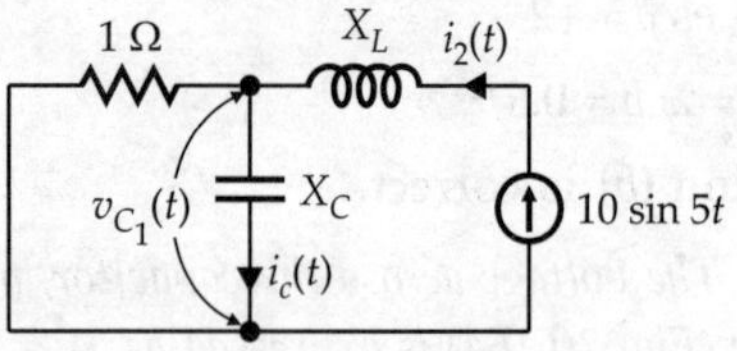

Fig. 20.166

From the figure,

$$(X_C) = \frac{1}{j\omega C} = \frac{1}{j(5)(1)} = -j0.2\ \Omega$$

$$X_L = j\omega L = j\times 5\times 1 = j5\Omega$$

$$i_c(t) = i_2(t)\times\frac{1}{1-j0.2}$$

$$\therefore\quad v_c(t) = i_c(t)\times X_C$$

$$= (10\sin 5t)\frac{1}{1-j0.2}\times(-j0.2)$$

$$= \frac{10\sin 5t(1+j0.2)(-j0.2)}{1^2+0.2^2}$$

$$= 9.8\sin 5(t)[0.04-j0.2]$$

$$= 1.99\angle 78.69°\sin 5t$$

$$= 1.99\sin(5t-78.69°)$$

$$\therefore\quad v_c(t) = v_{c_1}(t)+v_{c_2}(t)$$

$$= 2\sin(10t-84.29°)+1.98(5t-78.69°)$$

Comparing with the given expression in the question, $A_1 = 2$; $A_2 = 1.98$.

Option (*a*) is correct.

M20.149 *In the given figure (Fig. 20.167), the Thevenin's equivalent pair (voltage, impedance), as seen at the terminal P-Q is given by*

(*a*) (2 V, 5Ω)
(*b*) (2 V, 7.5 Ω)
(*c*) (4 V, 5 Ω)
(*d*) (4 V, 7.5 Ω)

[GATE 2005]

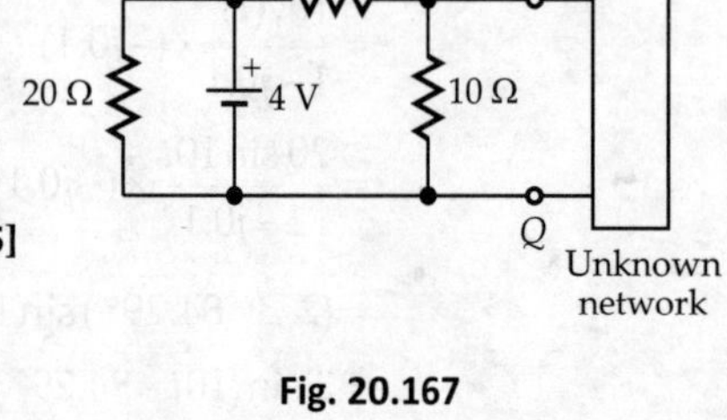

Fig. 20.167

Solution. In order to find R_{Th}, the voltage source is shorted and the unknown network is removed (Fig. 20.168).

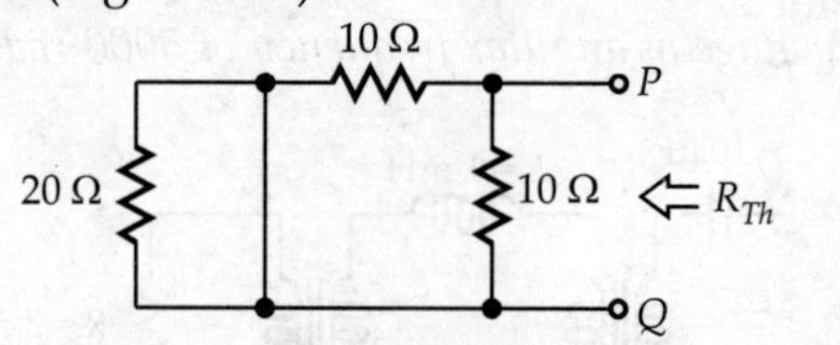

Fig. 20.168

Here, $R_{Th} = \frac{10\times 10}{10+10} = 5\ \Omega$

Let $V_{o/c}$ $(=V_{Th})$ be the open circuit voltage at terminals *P-Q*.

$$\therefore\quad V_{o/c} = \frac{4}{10+10}\times 10 = 2\text{ V.}$$

[See Fig. 20.167 with *P-Q* open circuit]

Hence Thevenin's pair (voltage, impedance) is (2 V, 5 Ω).

Option (*a*) is correct.

M20.150 *In figure (Fig. 20.169), the current source is* $1\angle 0°$ *A.* $R = 1\ \Omega$, *the impedances are* $Z_C = (-j)\Omega$ *and* $Z_L = (2)j\Omega$. *The Thevenin's equivalent looking into the circuit across X-Y is*

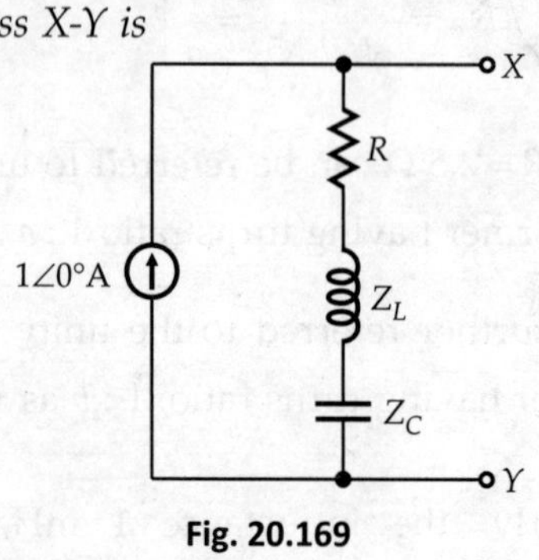

Fig. 20.169

(*a*) $5\sqrt{2}\angle 0°$ V, $(1+j2)\Omega$
(*b*) $2\angle 45°$ V, $(1-j2)\Omega$
(*c*) $2\angle 45°$ V, $(1+j)\Omega$
(*d*) $\sqrt{2}\angle 45°$ V, $(1+j)\Omega$ **[GATE 2006]**

Solution. The current source is removed by open circuit (Fig. 20.170).

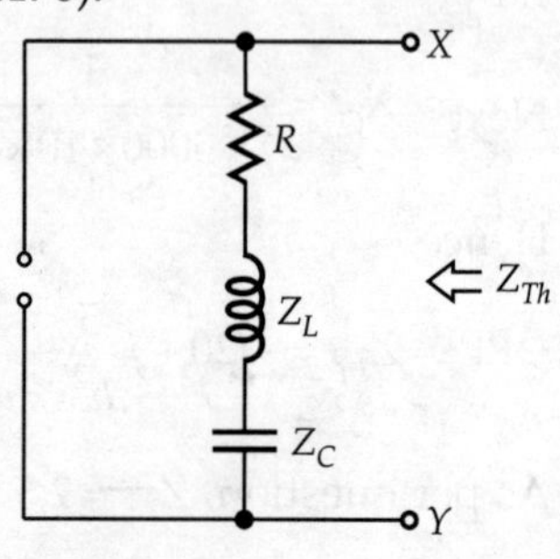

Fig. 20.170

$$Z_{Th} = R + Z_L + Z_C$$
$$= 1 + j2 - j = (1 + j)\Omega$$

Since $I = 1\angle 0°$ A, the open circuit voltage across *X-Y* is $I \times Z_{Th}$.

$$\therefore \; V_{XY(o/c)} = 1\angle 0° \times Z_{Th}$$
$$= 1(1 + j) = (1 + j)\text{V}$$
$$= \sqrt{2}\angle 45°\text{ V}$$

Hence, $V_{o/c}$ (across *X-Y*) $= \sqrt{2}\angle 45°$ V

When $Z_{Th} = \mathbf{(1 + j)\ \Omega}$.

Option (*d*) is correct.

M20.151 *The circuit shown in the figure (20.171) has two sources connected in series. The instantaneous voltage of the AC source (in volts) is given by $v(t) = 12 \sin t$. If the circuit is in steady state, then the rms value of the current (in Amperes) flowing in the circuit is ____.* **[GATE 2015]**

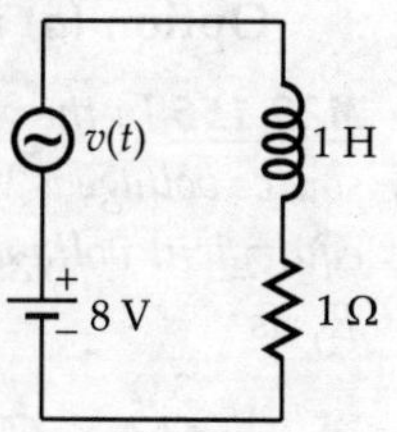

Fig. 20.171

Solution. In this given figure, the two sources are having two separate frequencies. One source is AC while the other is DC. It is most convenient to apply the superposition theorem in the circuit to find the circuit current. Let us first take the AC source (Fig. 20.172).

$$I_1 = \frac{12 \sin t}{1 + j(1)} = \frac{12 \cos(t - 90°)}{\sqrt{2}\angle 45°}$$
$$= \frac{12\angle -90°}{\sqrt{2}\angle 45°} = 6\sqrt{2}\angle -135°\text{ A}$$

$$\therefore \quad i_1(t) = 6\sqrt{2}\cos(t - 135°)\text{ A}$$

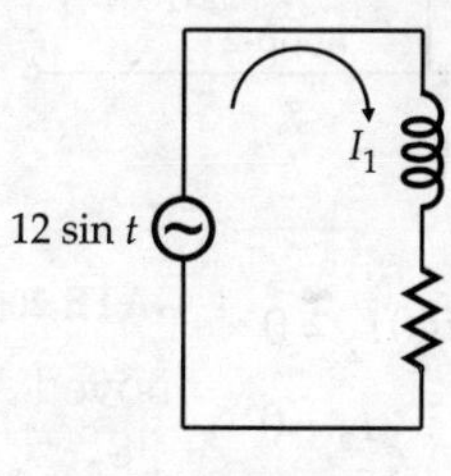

Fig. 20.172

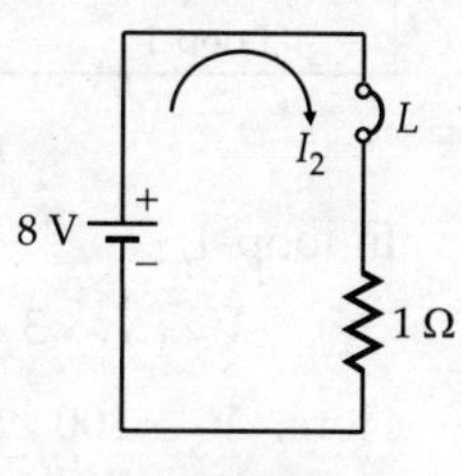

Fig. 20.173

Next we take the DC source (Fig. 20.173),

$$I_2 = \frac{8}{1} = 8\text{ A}$$ [The inductor at steady state acts as short-circuit]

Applying the principle of superposition,

$$i(t) = i_1(t) + I_2 = (6\sqrt{2}\cos(t - 135°) + 8)\text{A}$$
$$= \mathbf{8 + 6\sqrt{2}\cos(t - 135°)\ A.}$$

M20.152 *The Thevenin's equivalent of a circuit operating at $\omega = 5$ rad/s, has $V_{o/c} = 3.71\angle -15°$ V and $Z_0 = (2.38 - j0.667)\Omega$. At this frequency, the minimal realization of the Thevenin's impedance will have a*

(*a*) *resistor, a capacitor and an inductor*
(*b*) *resistor and a capacitor*
(*c*) *resistor and inductor*
(*d*) *capacitor and inductor* **[GATE 2008]**

Solution. $Z_0 = (2.38 - j0.667)\ \Omega$

Since the real part of Z_0 is 2.38, it must have the resistor. Also, img.$[Z_0] = -j0.667$. Hence, Z_0 will have either a capacitor or having a capacitor and inductor both but $(-jX_C)$ should be predominant than (jX_L) so that img.$[Z_0]$ becomes –ve.

Here, $-jX_C = \dfrac{-j}{\omega C} = \dfrac{-j}{5.C} = \dfrac{-j0.2}{C}$

and $\quad j\omega L = j.5.L$

However, for canonical realization *i.e.*, to have img.$[Z_0]$ with minimum circuit elements, img.$[Z_0]$ must be capacitor only. Hence, Z_0 contains the resistance and capacitance only.

Option (*b*) is correct.

M20.153 *Thevenin's equivalent voltage and impedance across terminals a – b in the network shown in Fig. 20.174 are*

(*a*) 0 V, 5 Ω (*b*) 35 V, 5 Ω
(*c*) 15 V, 15 Ω (*d*) 25 V, 5 Ω

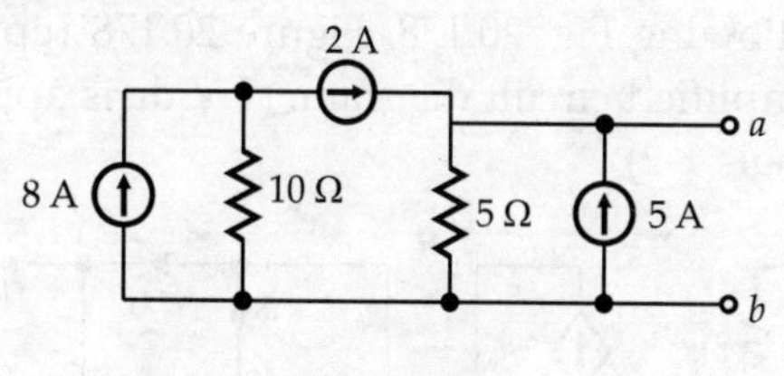

Fig. 20.174

Solution. Let us redraw the circuit as shown in Fig. 20.175.

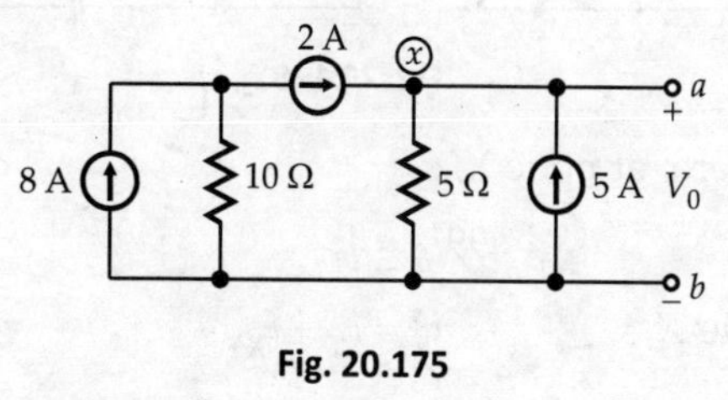

Fig. 20.175

At node (*x*),

$$\frac{V_0}{5} = 5 + 2 = 7\text{ A}$$

$\therefore \quad V_0 = 35$ V

i.e., $\quad V_{Th} = 35$ V

Next we deactivate current sources to get Z_{Th}.

In Fig. 20.176, $\quad Z_{Th} = 5\ \Omega$.

$\therefore \quad \boldsymbol{V_{Th} = 35}$ **V ;** $\boldsymbol{Z_{Th} = 5\ \Omega}$.

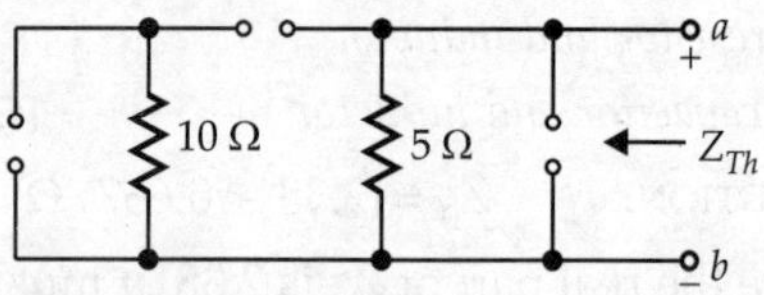

Fig. 20.176

Option (*b*) is correct.

M20.154 *The impedance looking into nodes 1 and 2 in the given circuit (Fig. 20.177) is* **[GATE 2012]**

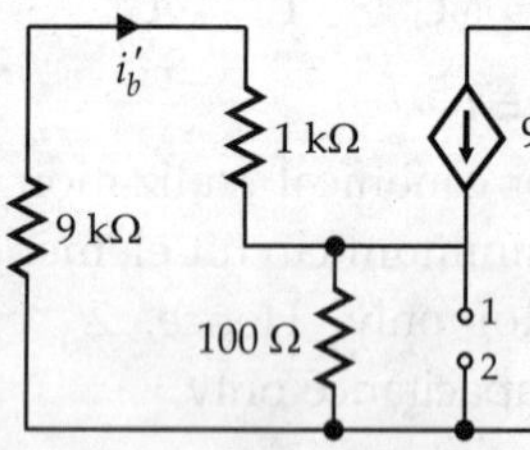

Fig. 20.177

(*a*) 50 Ω (*b*) 100 Ω

(*c*) 5 kΩ (*d*) 10.1 kΩ

Solution. To find Z_{Th} across nodes 1 and 2, we need to connect 1 V dc source across 1-2 as shown in the following Fig. 20.178. Figure 20.178 represents the simplified circuit diagram. (1 V dc is applied at terminals 1-2)

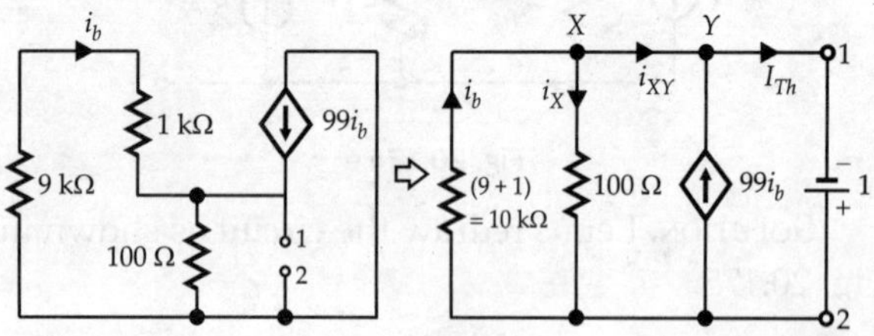

Fig. 20.178

Here, at node *Y*,

$$i_{XY} + 99i_b = I_{Th} \qquad ...(1)$$

at node *X*,

$$i_b = i_X + i_{XY} \qquad ...(2)$$

Substituting for i_{XY} from (1) in (2)

$$i_b = i_X + (I_{Th} - 99i_b)$$

i.e.,

$$100i_b - i_X = I_{Th} \qquad ...(3)$$

Next, we apply KVL in the outer loop $10 \times 10^3\, i_b = 1$.

$$\therefore \quad i_b = 10^{-4}\ \text{A}$$

Also, $\quad 10 \times 10^3\, i_b = -100 i_X$

$$\therefore \quad i_X = -100 i_b \qquad ...(4)$$

From equation (3), substituting the value of i_X from (4)

$$100\, i_b - (-100 i_b) = I_{Th}$$

i.e., $\quad I_{Th} = 200 i_b = 200 \times 10^{-4} = 0.02$ A.

Hence, $\quad Z_{Th} = \dfrac{1\ \text{V}}{I_{Th}} = \dfrac{1}{0.02} = \mathbf{50\ \Omega}$

Option (*a*) is correct.

M20.155 *In the circuit shown below (Fig. 20.179), if the source voltage is* $V_S = 100\ \angle 53.13°$ *V then the Thevenin's equivalent voltage in volts as seen by the load resistance* R_L *is*

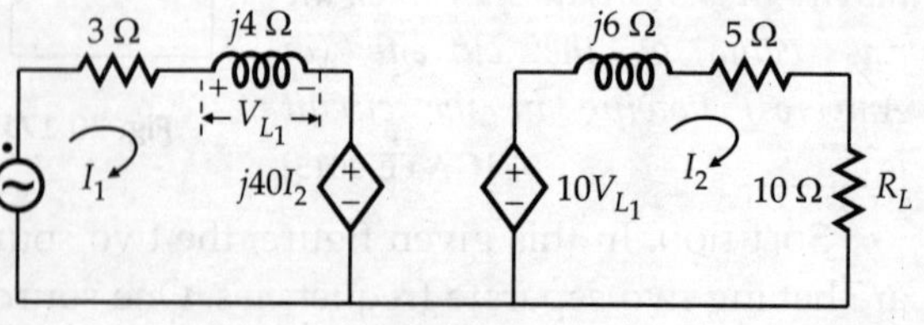

Fig. 20.179

(*a*) 100 ∠90° (*b*) 800 ∠0°

(*c*) 800 ∠90° (*d*) 100 ∠60° **[GATE 2013]**

Solution. To determine Thevenin's voltage, we are to remove R_L [see figure (Fig. 20.180) below]

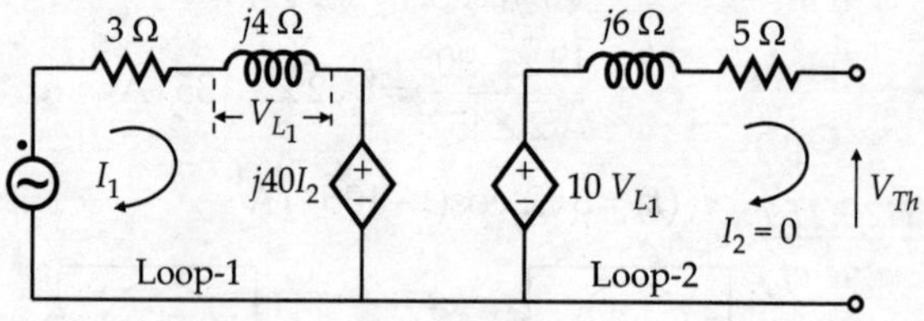

Fig. 20.180

In loop-1,

$$-V_S + I_1 \times 3 + jI_1 4 + j40 I_2 = 0$$

Here, $\quad V_S = 100\ \angle 53.13°$ V ; $\quad I_2 = 0$

$$\therefore \quad 100 \angle 53.13° = I_1(3 + j4) + j40(0)$$

i.e.,

$$I_1 = \frac{100 \angle 53.13°}{(3 + j4)} = 20\ \text{A}$$

$$V_{L_1} = j4.\, I_1 = j4(20) = j80\ \text{V}$$

$$\therefore \quad V_{Th} = 10 V_{L_1} = 10(j80) = j800\ \text{V}$$

$$= \mathbf{800\ \angle 90°\ V}.$$

Option (c) is correct.

M20.156 *Assuming an ideal transformer (Fig. 20.181), the Thevenin's equivalent voltage and impedance as seen from the terminal X-Y for the circuit in Fig. 20.181 are :*

(*a*) $2 sin(\omega t), 4\ \Omega$ (*b*) $1 sin(\omega t), 1\ \Omega$

(*c*) $1 sin(\omega t), 2\ \Omega$ (*d*) $2\ sin(\omega t), 0.5\ \Omega$

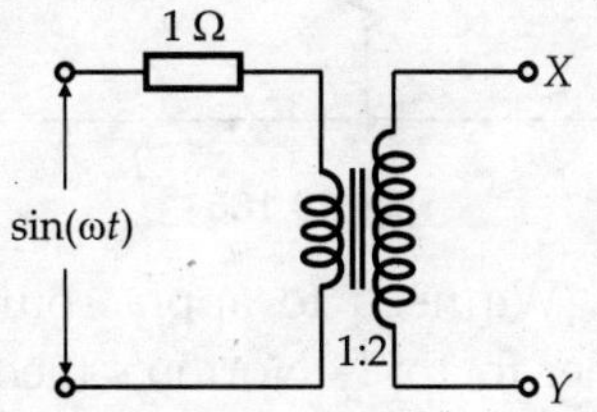

Fig. 20.181

[GATE 2014]

Solution. $Z_{XY} = \left(\frac{1}{N^2}\right) R_p$, where N is the turn ratio and R_p is the primary resistance.

i.e., $Z_{XY} = 2^2 \times 1 \quad \left[\because \frac{N_1}{N_2} = N = \frac{1}{2}\right]$

$= 4\ \Omega.$

Let $V_1 = \sin \omega t$

$\because$ For the transformer, $\frac{V_1}{V_2} = \frac{N_1}{N_2}$

$\therefore \quad V_2 = \frac{N_2}{N_1} \times V_1 = 2V_1 = 2\sin(\omega t).$

Here, $V_2 \equiv V_{XY}$

Hence, $\mathbf{Z_{XY} = 4\ \Omega\ ;\ V_{XY} = 2\sin(\omega t)}$

Option (*a*) is correct.

M20.157 *In the circuit shown below (Fig. 20.182), the value of capacitor C required for maximum power to be transferred to the load is*

(*a*) 1 nF (*b*) 1 μF

(*c*) 1 mF (*d*) 10 mF **[GATE 2017]**

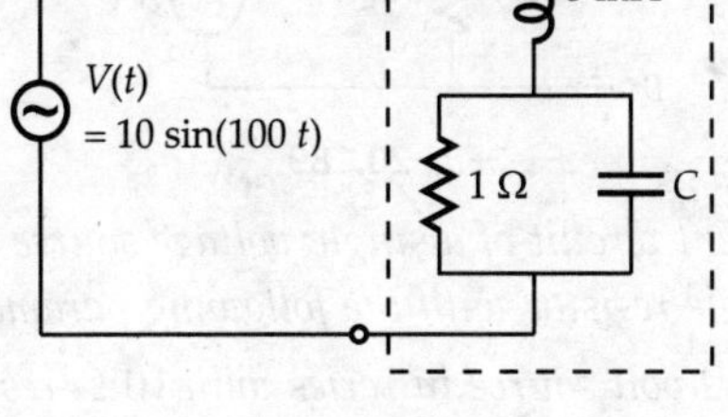

Fig. 20.182

Solution. In the given circuit,

$$L = 5\ \text{mH}$$

$$X_L = 2\pi f L = \omega L = 100 \times 5 \times 10^{-3} = 0.5\ \Omega = j\,(0.5\ \Omega)$$

$$X_C = \frac{1}{j\omega C} = \frac{1}{j100C}\ \Omega$$

$\therefore$ Across *X-Y* terminal, in Fig. 20.183,

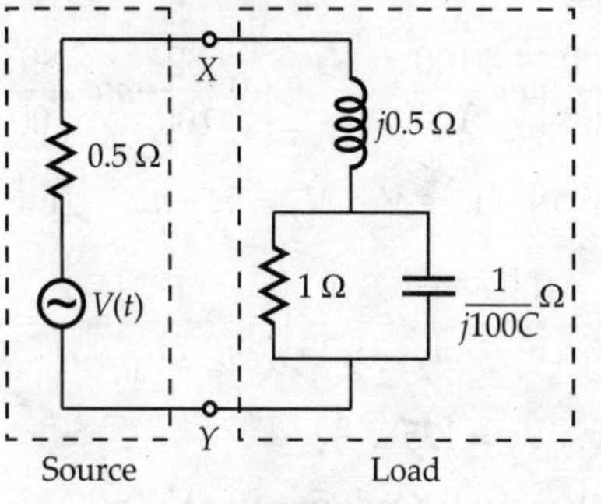

Fig. 20.183

$$Z_{XY} = j0.5 + \left[\frac{1 \times 1/j100C}{1 + 1/j100C}\right]$$

or, $$Z_{XY} = \frac{1}{1 + 10^4 C^2} + j\left[\frac{0.5 + 5000C - 100C}{1 + 10^4 C^2}\right]$$

For maximum power transfer in AC circuits,

$\text{Re}[Z_{XY}] = R_S$, the source resistance

and $\text{Im}[Z_{XY}] =$ complex conjugate of $\text{Im}[Z_S]$,

where Z_S is the imaginary part of source impedance.

Here, $\text{Im}(Z_S) = 0.$

$\therefore \quad \text{Re}[Z_{XY}] = R_S$

and with this we can write

$$\frac{1}{1 + 10^4 C^2} = 0.5$$

i.e., $C = 0.01\ \text{F} = \mathbf{10\ mF}.$

Option (*d*) is correct.

M20.158 *The following arrangement (Fig. 20.184) consists of an ideal transformer and an attenuator which attenuates by a factor 0.8. An ac voltage $V_{WX_1} = 100$ V is applied across WX to get an open circuit voltage V_{YZ_1} across YZ. Next, an ac voltage $V_{YZ_2} = 100$ V is applied across YZ to get an open circuit voltage V_{WX_2} across WX. Then, $\left[\frac{V_{YZ_1}}{V_{WX_1}}\right], \left[\frac{V_{WX_2}}{V_{YZ_2}}\right]$ are respectively.*

[GATE 2013]

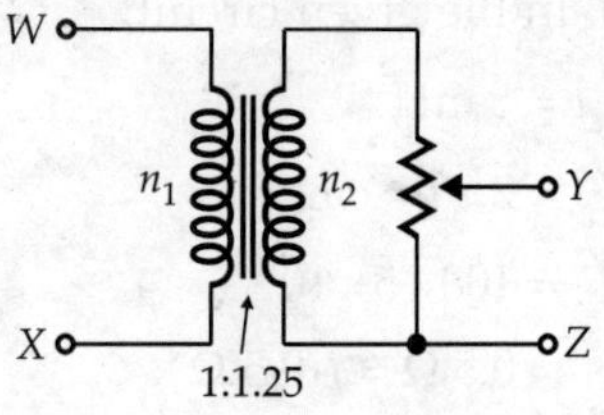

Fig. 20.184

(a) $\frac{125}{100}$ *and* $\frac{80}{100}$ (b) $\frac{100}{100}$ *and* $\frac{80}{100}$

(c) $\frac{100}{100}$ *and* $\frac{100}{100}$ (d) $\frac{80}{100}$ *and* $\frac{80}{100}$

Solution. Here $V_1 : V_2 = n_1 : n_2$ [Fig. 20.185]

$$\frac{V_{WX_1}}{V_2} = \frac{100}{V_2} = \frac{n_1}{n_2} = \frac{1}{1.25}\left(= \frac{1}{n_2/n_1} = \frac{1}{n} = \frac{1}{1.25}\right)$$

$$\therefore \quad V_2 = 125 \text{ V}$$

$$V_{YZ_1} = 0.8 \times 125 = 100 \text{ V}$$

$$\therefore \quad \frac{V_{YZ_1}}{V_{WX_1}} = \frac{100}{100} \qquad \text{...(1)}$$

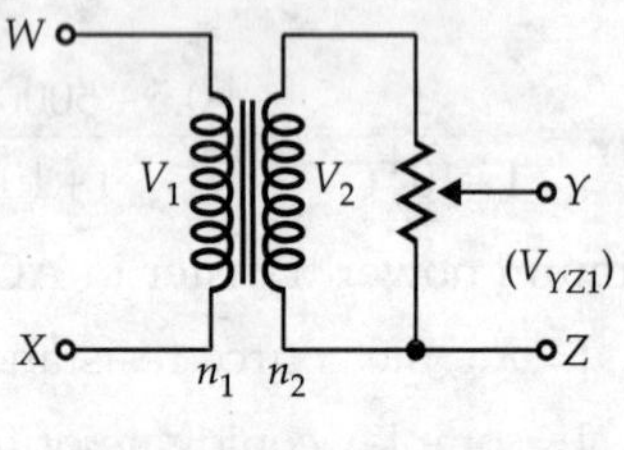

Fig. 20.185

Next, we apply V_{YZ_2} = 100 V. This voltage appears across the transformer winding.

i.e., $$V_{YZ_2} = V_2$$

However, $$\frac{V_1}{V_2} = \frac{1}{1.25}$$

$$\therefore \quad V_1 = \left(\frac{V_2}{1.25}\right) = \frac{100}{1.25} = 80 \text{ V}$$

i.e., $$V_{WX_2} = 80 \text{ V}$$

Hence,

$$\frac{V_{WX_2}}{V_{YZ_2}} = \left(\frac{80}{100}\right) \qquad \text{...(2)}$$

Observing (1) and (2) it can be inferred that **option (b) is correct.**

M20.159 *For the circuit shown in Fig. 20.186, Norton equivalent source current value is _____ A and its resistance is ______ ohms.* **[GATE 1997]**

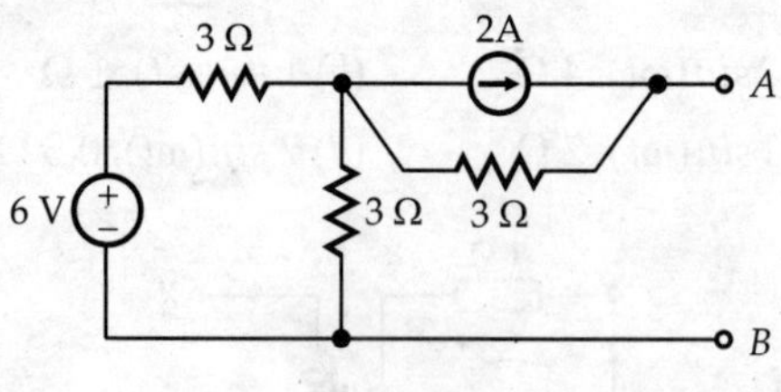

Fig. 20.186

Solution. We need to apply source transformation in order to apply Norton's theorem.

Figures 20.187 and 20.188 represent the transformed source equivalent circuit.

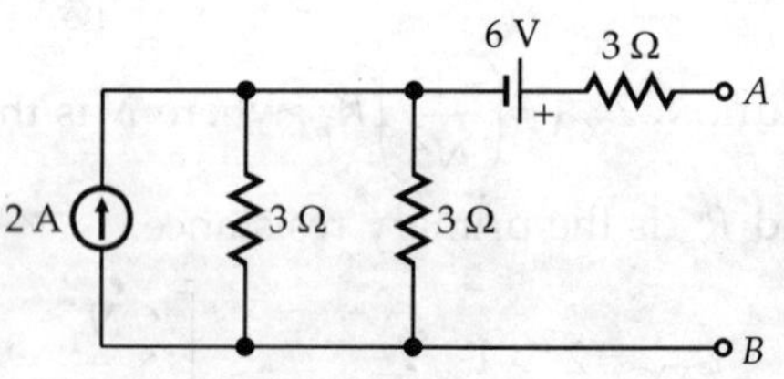

Fig. 20.187

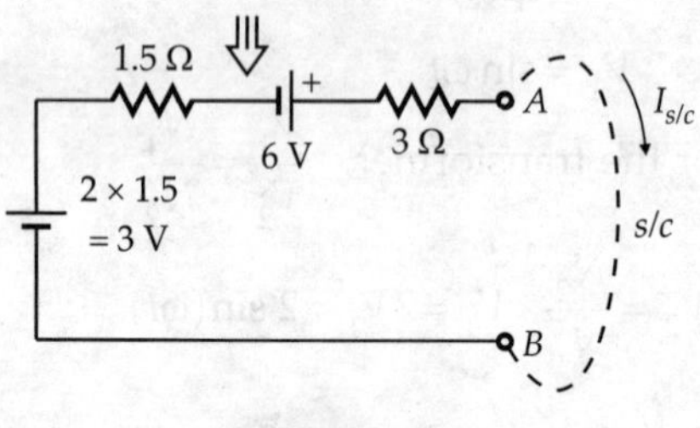

Fig. 20.188

Let us now apply short-circuit across terminal *A–B*.

$$\therefore \quad I_{s/c} = \frac{3+6}{1.5+3} = \mathbf{2\ A}\ ; \quad R_{in} = 1.5 + 3 = \mathbf{4.5\ \Omega}$$

M20.160 *Viewed from the terminals A and B, the following circuit shown in Fig. 20.189 can be reduced to*

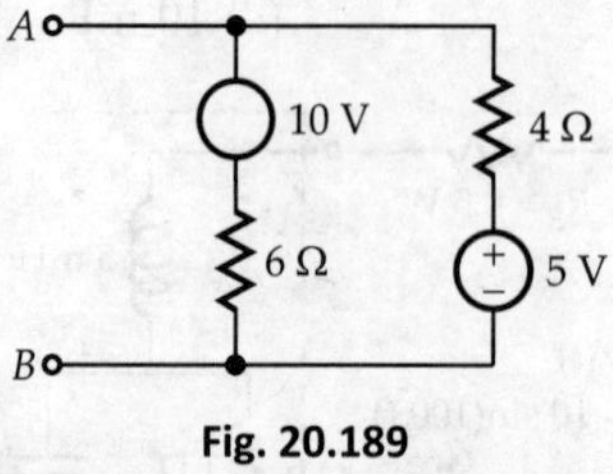

Fig. 20.189

an equivalent circuit of a single voltage source in series with a single resistor with the following parameters :

(a) *10 volt source in series with 10 Ω resistor*

(b) *7 volt source in series with 2.4 Ω resistor*

(*c*) 15 *volt source in series with* 2.4 Ω *resistor*

(*d*) 1 *volt source in series with* 10Ω *resistor.*

[GATE 1998]

Solution. Since voltage sources with series resistances are in parallel hence we can use Millman's theorem the reduce the given network to a single voltage source in series with a single resistor.

$$V = \frac{V_1Y_1 + V_2Y_2}{Y_1 + Y_2} = \frac{10\times\frac{1}{6}+5\times\frac{1}{4}}{\frac{1}{6}+\frac{1}{4}} = 7 \text{ volt}$$

$$R = \frac{1}{Y_1 + Y_2} = \frac{1}{\frac{1}{6}+\frac{1}{4}} = \mathbf{2.4\ \Omega}$$

Option (*b*) is correct.

M20.161 *A source $v_s(t) = V\cos 100\pi t$ has an internal impedance of $(4 + j3)\Omega$. If a purely resistive load connected to this source has to extract the maximum power out of the source, its value in Ω should be*

[GATE 2013]

(*a*) 3 (*b*) 4 (*c*) 5 (*d*) 7

Solution. The equivalent circuit of the given problem is drawn in Fig. 20.190.

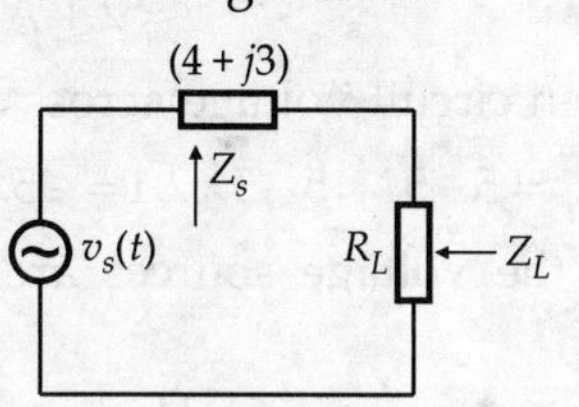

Fig. 20.190

If Z_s is complex and Z_L is resistive, then for maximum power transfer,

$$R_L = |Z_s| = \sqrt{R_s^2 + X_s^2} = \sqrt{4^2 + 3^2} = \mathbf{5\ \Omega}$$

Option (*c*) is correct.

M20.162 *The Norton's equivalent source in ampere as seen into the terminals X and Y (Fig. 20.191) is ______.*

[GATE 2014]

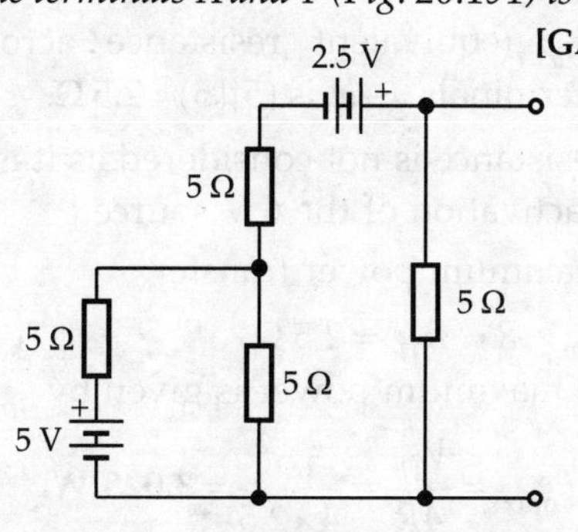

Fig. 20.191

Solution. The given circuit is redrawn as shown in Fig. 20.192.

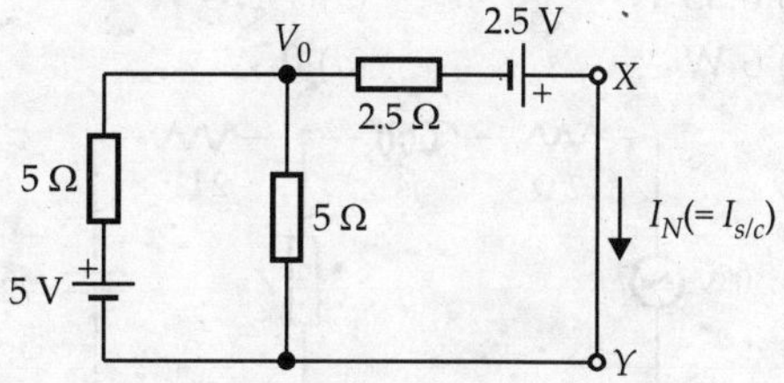

Fig. 20.192

Here, $\frac{V_0 - 5}{5} + \frac{V_0}{5} + \frac{V_0 + 2.5}{2.5} = 0$

∴ $V_A = 0$

Also, $I_{s/c}(= I_N) = \frac{V_0 + 2.5}{2.5} = \mathbf{1\ A}.$

M20.163 *In the circuit given below (Fig. 20.193), the value of R required for the transfer of maximum power to the load having a resistance of* 3 Ω *is*

(*a*) *Zero* (*b*) 3 Ω

(*c*) 6 Ω (*d*) *infinity* **[GATE 2011]**

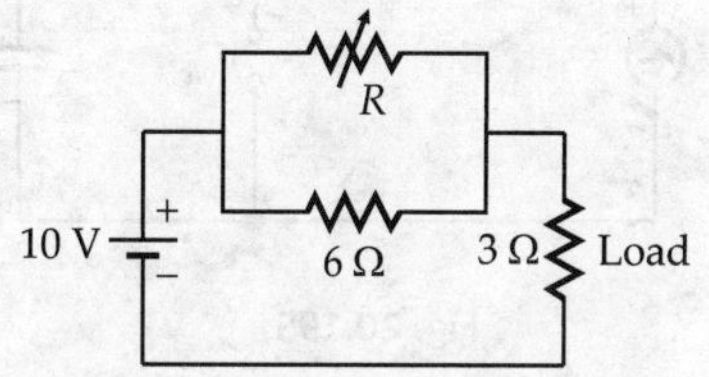

Fig. 20.193

Solution. In the given circuit, the net resistance across the voltage source is

$$R_{eq} = 3 + \frac{6\times R}{6 + R}$$

$$\therefore \quad I = \frac{10}{R_{eq}} = \frac{10}{3 + \frac{6R}{6+R}} \quad \text{...(1)}$$

For maximum power transfer, the current is also to be maximum. Observing eqn. (1) it is evident that for I to be maximum, the denominator in the right hand side expression of eqn. (1) is to be minimum.

i.e., $\left(3 + \frac{6R}{6+R}\right)$ is to be minimum.

This is possible if $R = \mathbf{0}$.

Hence the answer is that maximum power transfer is possible provided $R = 0$.

Option (*a*) is correct.

M20.164 *For the circuit shown in Fig. 20.194, the maximum power transferred to the load Z_L is obtained as*

(*a*) 8.33 W (*b*) 1.178 W
(*c*) 6 W (*d*) 0 W

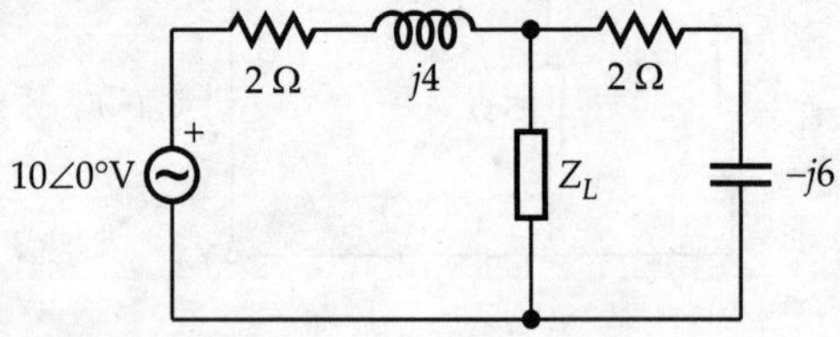

Fig. 20.194

Solution. Let us remove Z_L (Fig. 20.195)

$$V_{o/c} = 10\angle 0^\circ \frac{(2-j6)}{4-j2}$$

[Using voltage division formula]

$$= 10 \times \frac{6.32\angle -71.56^\circ}{4.47\angle -26.56^\circ}$$

$$= 14.14\angle -45^\circ \text{ Volt}$$

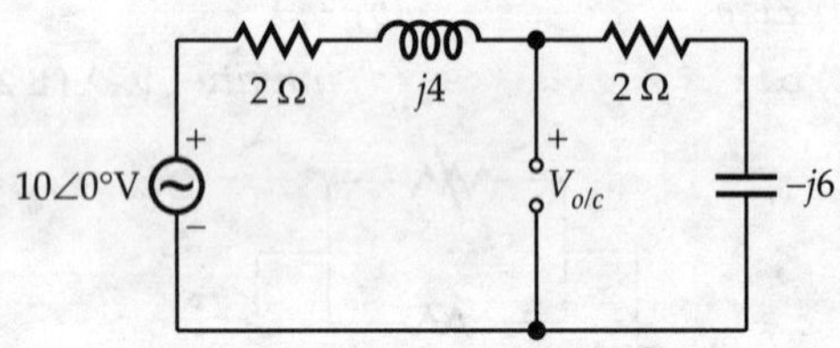

Fig. 20.195

The internal impedance of the circuit is obtained as

$$Z_{int} = \frac{(2+j4)(2-j6)}{4-j2}$$

$$= \frac{4.47\angle 63.43^\circ \times 6.32\angle -71.56^\circ}{4.47\angle -26.56^\circ}$$

$$= 6.32\angle 18.43^\circ = (6+j2)\Omega$$

$$\therefore \quad Z_L = Z_{Th}^* = (6-j2)\Omega$$

[for maximum power transfer]

$$I_{Th} = \frac{V_{o/c}}{Z_{int}+Z_L} = \frac{14.14\angle -45^\circ}{(6+j2)+(6-j2)}$$

$$= 1.178\angle -45^\circ$$

$$\therefore \quad P_{max} = (I_{Th})^2 \times 6 = \mathbf{8.33\ W.}$$

Option (*a*) is correct.

M20.165 *In the circuit (Fig. 20.196) shown below, the maximum power transferred to the resistor R is ______ W.* **[GATE 2017]**

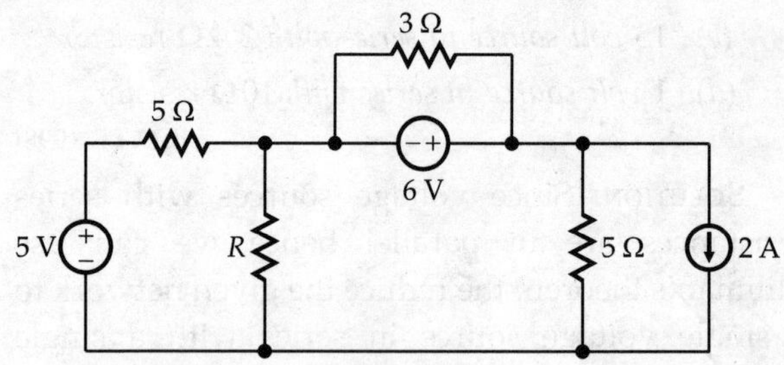

Fig. 20.196

Solution. Here the current source of 2 A alongwith the parallel resistance of 5 Ω has been converted into equivalent voltage source of 10 V with series resistance of 5 Ω, as shown in Fig. 20.197.

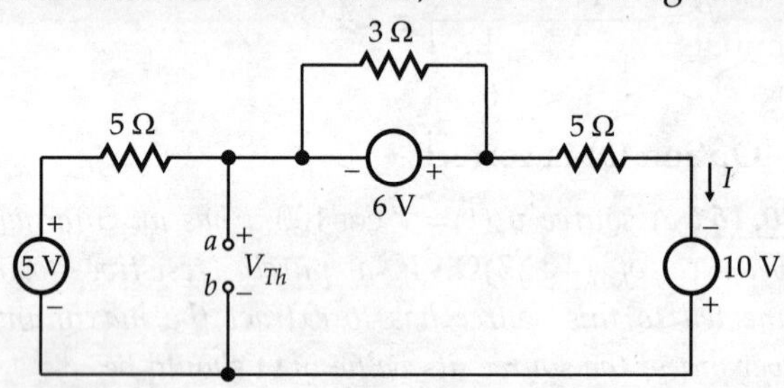

Fig. 20.197

Using KVL,

$$-5 + I \times 5 - 6 + I \times 5 - 10 = 0$$

$$\therefore \quad I = 2.1 \text{ A}$$

$\therefore V_{th}$ (open circuit voltage across $a-b$) is

$$V_{Th} = 5 - 5I = 5 - 5 \times 2.1 = -5.5 \text{ V.}$$

Next, all the voltage sources are deactivated (Fig. 20.198)

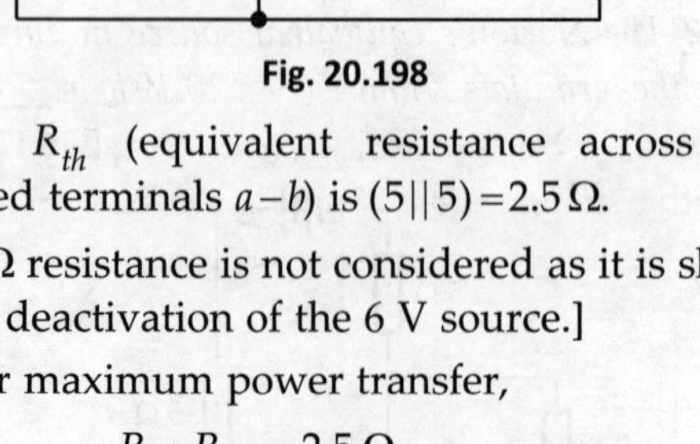

Fig. 20.198

$\therefore R_{th}$ (equivalent resistance across open circuited terminals $a-b$) is $(5||5) = 2.5\,\Omega$.

[3Ω resistance is not considered as it is shorted due to deactivation of the 6 V source.]

For maximum power transfer,

$$R = R_{Th} = 2.5\,\Omega$$

$\therefore$ The maximum power is given by

$$P_{max} = \frac{V_{Th}^2}{4R} = \frac{5.5^2}{4 \times 2.5} = \mathbf{3.025\ W.}$$

M20.166 *In the circuit of Fig. 20.199, short-circuit is applied at terminals x-y. Find Norton equivalent current through short-circuit link x-y.*

(*a*) 12 A (*b*) 5 A (*c*) 15 A (*d*) 17 A

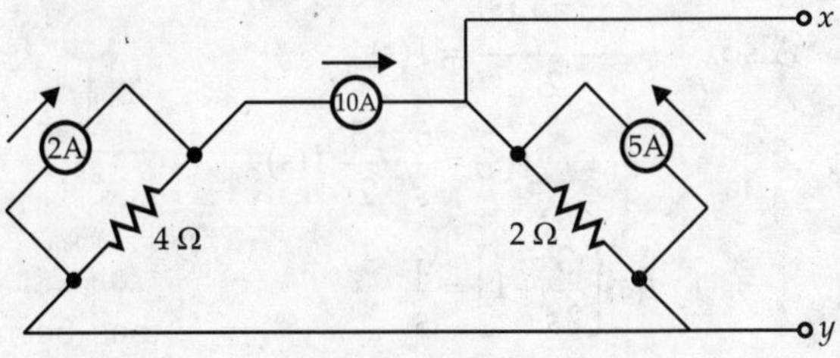

Fig. 20.199

Solution. Let us redraw the circuit shorting terminals *x-y* (Fig. 20.200)

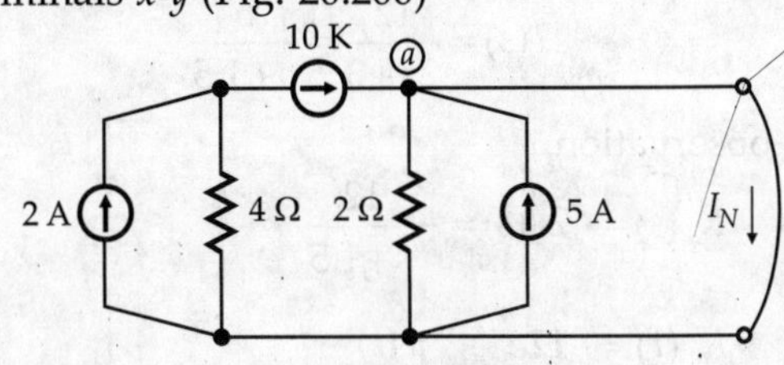

Fig. 20.200

At node (*a*),

$$-10-5+I_N=0 \quad \therefore \; I_N = \mathbf{15\ A}$$

Option (*c*) is correct.

M20.167 *The internal impedance Z_{Th} looking from x-y terminal of the circuit shown in Fig. 20.201 is*

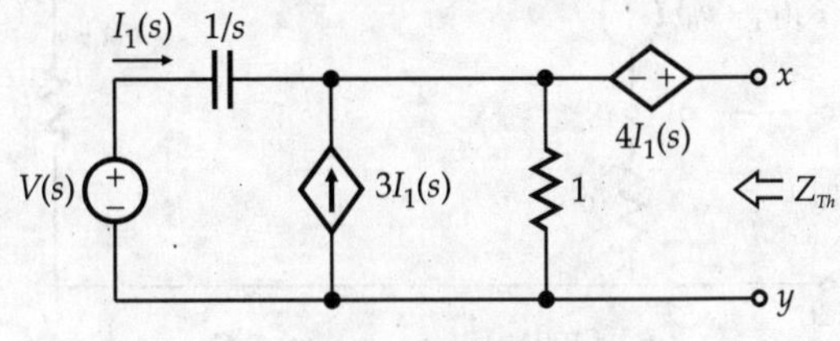

Fig. 20.201

(*a*) $\left(1+\frac{1}{s}\right)(1+3s)$ (*b*) $\frac{s+1}{1-4s}$

(*c*) $\frac{1-4s}{1+4s}$ (*d*) $\frac{1}{(4s+1)(3s+1)}$

Solution. Let us deactivate source $V(s)$ and redraw the given circuit (Fig. 20.202)

$$-I_1(s)\times\frac{1}{s}=V(s) \quad \therefore \; I_1(s)=-sV(s)$$

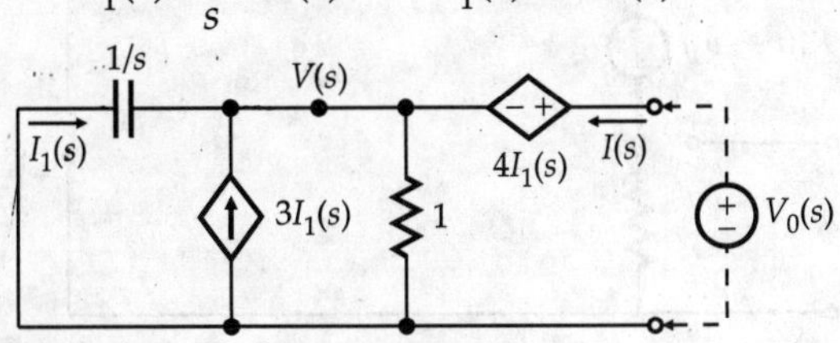

Fig. 20.202

Also, $V_0(s)=4I_1(s)+V(s)=4[-sV(s)]+V(s)$

$$=V(s)[1-4s]$$

$$I(s)=\frac{V(s)}{1}-4I_1(s)=V(s)-4[-sV(s)]$$

$$=V(s)[1+4s]$$

$$\therefore \quad Z_{Th}(s)=\frac{V_0(s)}{I(s)}=\frac{\mathbf{1-4s}}{\mathbf{1+4s}}$$

Option (*c*) is correct.

M20.168 *What is the value of $Z_{in}(s)$ looking from terminal x-y in the circuit of Fig. 20.203 ?*

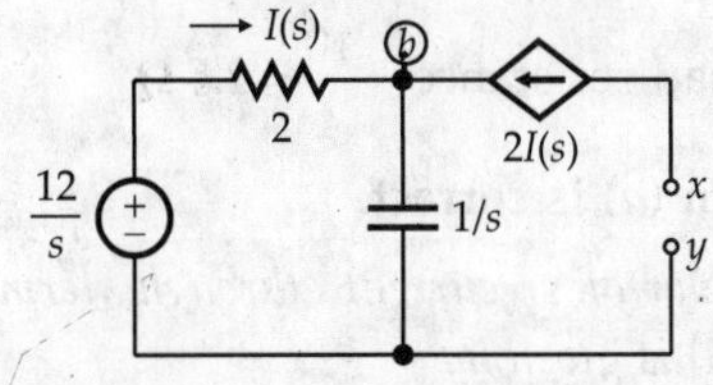

Fig. 20.203

(*a*) $\frac{1}{2s}$ (*b*) s (*c*) 0 (*d*) ∞

Solution. We need to remove the $(12/s)$ source by short circuit across it and connect a $V_0(s)$ voltage source across *x-y* (Fig. 20.204).

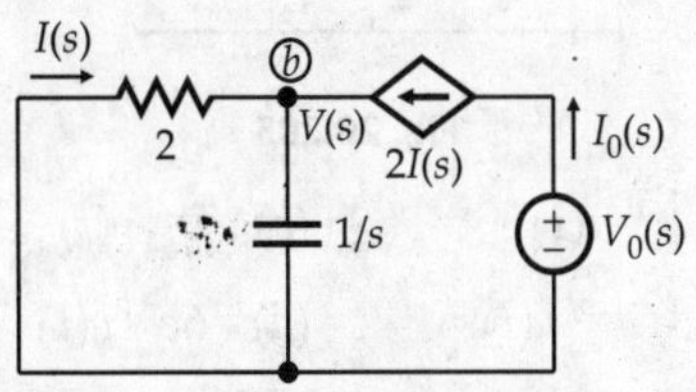

Fig. 20.204

At node '*b*',

$$-I(s)-2I(s)+\frac{V(s)}{1/s}=0$$

or, $$-3I(s)+sV(s)=0$$

or, $$3.\frac{V(s)}{2}+sV(s)=0$$

i.e., $$V(s)=0$$

$$\therefore \quad I(s)=0$$

i.e., $$I_0(s)=0$$

$$\therefore \quad Z_{in}(s)=\frac{V_0(s)}{I_0(s)}=\frac{V_0(s)}{0}=\infty$$

Option (*d*) is correct.

M20.169 *A bench top dc power supply acts as an ideal 4 A current source as long as its terminal voltage is below 10 V. Beyond this point, it begins to behave as an ideal 10 V voltage source for all load currents going down to 0 A. When connected to an ideal rheostat, find the load, resistance value at which maximum power is transferred, and the corresponding load voltage and current.* **[GATE 2020]**

(*a*) 2.5 Ω, 4 A, 10 V (*b*) 2.5 Ω, 4 A, 5 V

(*c*) Open, 4 A, 0 V (*d*) Short, ∞ A, 10 V

Solution. It is evident from the given problem that current maximum is 4 A while the voltage maximum is 10 V.

$\therefore$ Load resistance $= \frac{10}{4} = \mathbf{2.5\ \Omega}$

Option (*a*) is correct.

M20.170 *Norton's current through terminals x-y (Fig. 20.205) is given by*

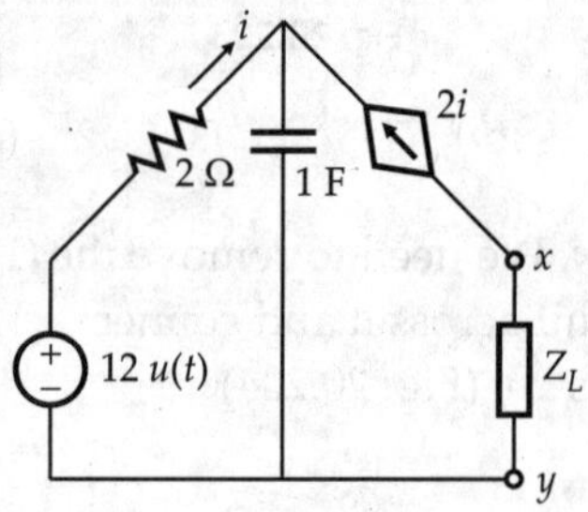

Fig. 20.205

(*a*) $2e^{-1.5t}u(t)$ (*b*) $e^{-12t}u(t)$

(*c*) $-12e^{-1.5t}u(t)$ (*d*) $-6e^{-t}u(t)$

Solution. Figure 20.206 represents the s-domain circuit, and *x-y* is short-circuited.

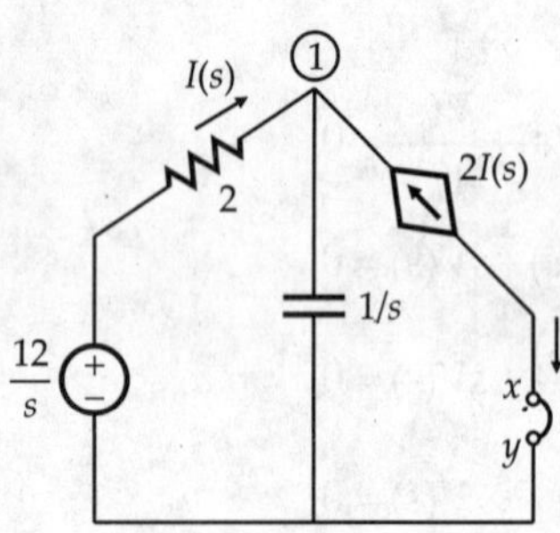

Fig. 20.206

At node (1),

$$-2\,I(s) + \frac{V(s)}{1/s} - I(s) = 0$$

[Assuming voltage at node '1' to be $V(s)$]

$$\therefore \quad 3I(s) = sV(s)$$

or, $$V(s) = \frac{3}{s}\,I(s)$$

Also, $$\frac{\frac{12}{s} - V(s)}{2} = I(s)$$

or, $$I(s) = \frac{6}{s} - \frac{3}{2s}\,I(s)$$

$$\therefore \quad I(s)\left[\frac{3}{2s} + 1\right] = \frac{6}{s}$$

or, $$I(s)\left[\frac{3+2s}{2s}\right] = \frac{6}{s}$$

$$\therefore \quad I(s) = \frac{12}{2s+3} = \frac{6}{s+1.5}$$

By observation,

$$I_N(s) = -2\,I(s) = -\frac{12}{s+1.5}$$

$$\therefore \quad \mathbf{I_N(t) = -12e^{-1.5t}\,u(t)}$$

Option (*c*) is correct.

M20.171 *In the circuit, the Thevenin's voltage (V_{th}) across r_L (Fig. 20.207) is*

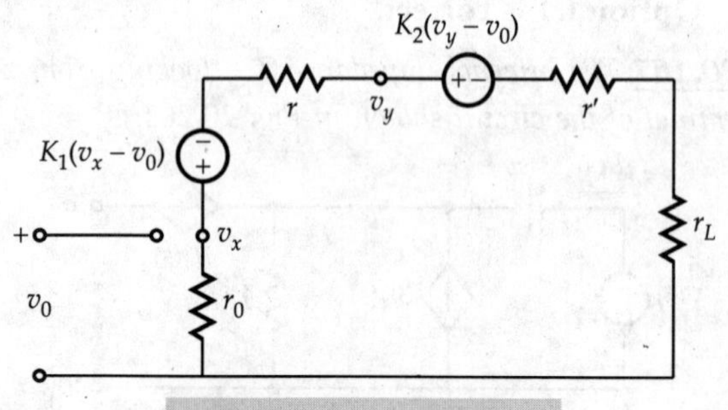

Fig. 20.207

(*a*) 100 mV (*b*) 76 mV

(*c*) 64 mV (*d*) 50 mV

Solution. Let us first remove r_L (Fig. 20.208)

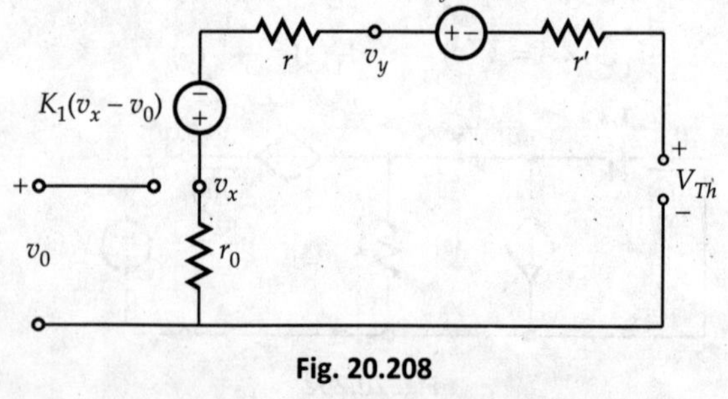

Fig. 20.208

Since there is no circuit current, drop across r_0 is zero and hence $v_x = 0$.

$$\therefore \quad v_y = -k(0-v_0) = kv_0$$

$$v_{Th} = -k_2(v_y - v_0) + v_y$$
$$= -k_2(k_1v_0 - v_0) + k_1v_0$$
$$= v_0[-k_1k_2 + k_2 + k_1]$$
$$= 100\times10^{-3}[-0.6\times0.4+0.6+0.4]$$
$$= 0.1[-0.24 + 1] = 0.076 \text{ V}$$
$$= \mathbf{76 \text{ mV}}.$$

Option (*b*) is correct.

M20.172 *In the circuit of Fig. 20.209, $R_1 = R_2 = R_3$ and $\frac{L}{C} = R_1^2$, $v_0(t)$ being an unit step function. What is the Thevenin's voltage (V_{Th}) across X – Y in s-domain ?*

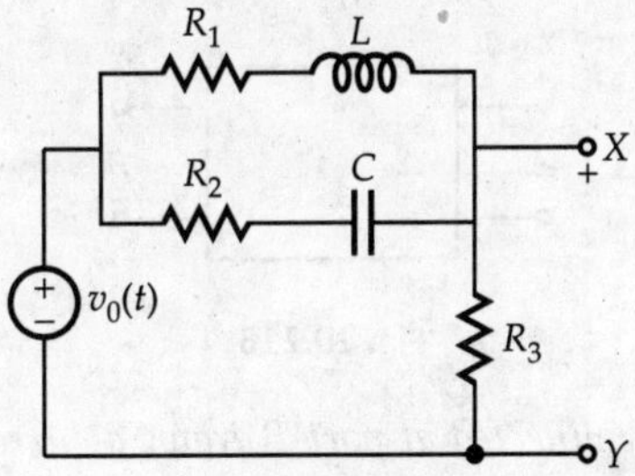

Fig. 20.209

(*a*) $\frac{s}{2}$ (*b*) $2s$ (*c*) $\frac{1}{2s}$ (*d*) $\frac{2s+1}{2}$

Solution. The parallel *R-L* and *RC* circuit admittance $Y(s)$ can be obtained by the *s*-domain transformed circuit as shown in Fig. 20.210.

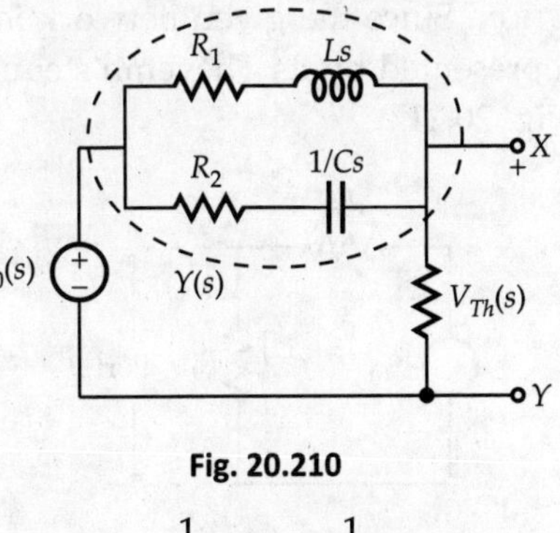

Fig. 20.210

$$Y(s) = \frac{1}{R_1 + Ls} + \frac{1}{R_2 + \frac{1}{Cs}}$$

With $R_1 = R_2$ and $\frac{L}{C} = R_1^2$

$$Y(s) = \frac{1}{R_1(R_1Cs+1)} + \frac{Cs}{CsR_1+1} = \frac{1}{R_1}$$

By using the concept of voltage division,

$$V_{Th}(s) = V_0(s)\frac{R_3}{R_1 + R_3}$$

$$\text{With } R_1 = R_3,\ V_{Th}(s) = \frac{1}{2}V_0(s) = \frac{\mathbf{1}}{\mathbf{2s}}$$

Option (*c*) is correct.

M20.173

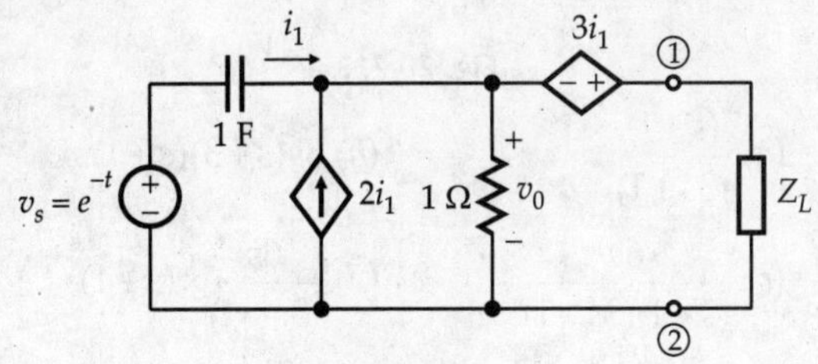

Fig. 20.211

What is Thevenin's impedance across terminal 1-2 in s-domain ?

(*a*) $\left(\frac{1-3s}{1+3s}\right)$ (*b*) $\left(\frac{2s+1}{3s-1}\right)$

(*c*) $\left(\frac{1-3s}{1-2s}\right)$ (*d*) $\frac{s}{(1-3s)(2s+1)}$

Solution. We first remove Z_L and apply voltage v_{dc} across (1) - (2) [Fig. 20.212] deactivating v_s. This figure is drawn in *s*-domain.

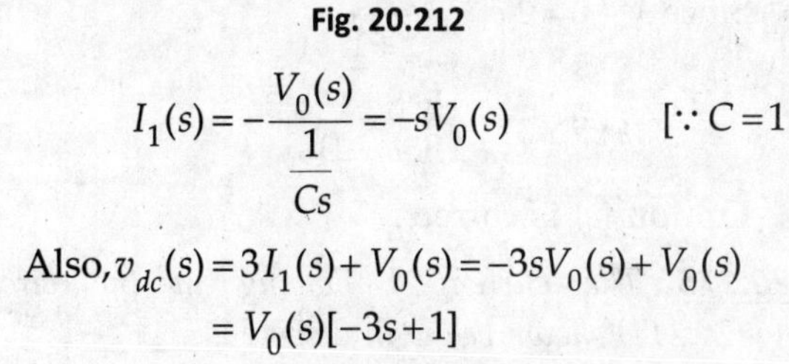

Fig. 20.212

$$I_1(s) = -\frac{V_0(s)}{\frac{1}{Cs}} = -sV_0(s) \qquad [\because C = 1\text{F}]$$

$$\text{Also, } v_{dc}(s) = 3I_1(s) + V_0(s) = -3sV_0(s) + V_0(s)$$
$$= V_0(s)[-3s+1]$$

$$I_{dc}(s) = \frac{V_0(s)}{1} - 3I_1(s) = V_0(s) + 3sV_0(s)$$
$$= V_0(s)[3s+1]$$

$$\therefore \quad Z_{Th}(s) = \frac{v_{dc}(s)}{I_{dc}(s)} = \left(\frac{\mathbf{1-3s}}{\mathbf{1+3s}}\right)$$

Option (*a*) is correct.

CHAPTER 20

M20.174 *In the circuit shown in Fig. 20.213, find $V_{Th}(s)$, the Thevenin's voltage across (1)-(2) in s-domain is*

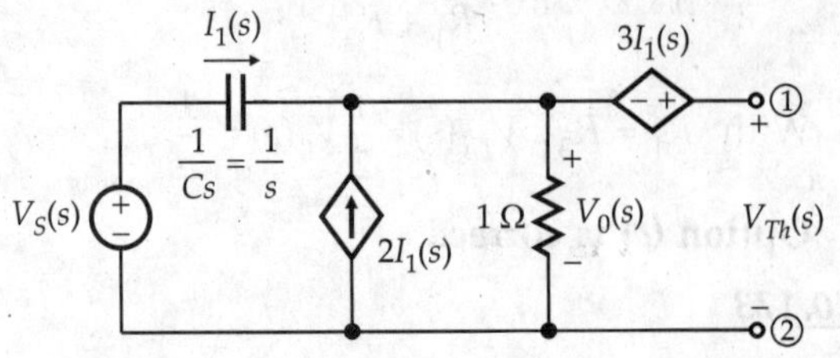

Fig. 20.213 $[V_s(t) = e^{-t}]$

(*a*) $\frac{(s+1)}{(3s+1)}$ (*b*) $6s(s+3)(s+1)$

(*c*) $\frac{6s}{(s+1)(3s+1)}$ (*d*) $\frac{6s}{(3s+1)} \times (s+1)$

Solution. Figure 20.213 represents the given circuit in s-domain replacing Z_L by open circuit.

$$V_0(s) = [2I_1(s) + I_1(s)] \times 1 = 3I_1(s)$$

$$I_1(s) = \frac{V_s(s) - V_0(s)}{\frac{1}{Cs}}$$

$$= [V_s(s) - 3I_1(s)]s \qquad [\because V_a(s) = 3I_1(s) \text{ and } C = 1]$$

or, $I_1(s)[1+3s] = sV_s(s)$

$$\therefore \quad I_1(s) = \frac{sV_s(s)}{1+3s}$$

However,

$$V_{Th}(s) = 3I_1(s) + V_0(s)$$

$$\therefore \quad V_{Th}(s) = 3\frac{sV_s(s)}{3s+1} + 3\frac{sV_s(s)}{(3s+1)} = 6\frac{sV_s(s)}{(3s+1)}$$

Since $V_s(s) = Le^{-t} = \frac{1}{s+1}$,

$$V_{Th}(s) = \frac{\mathbf{6s}}{\mathbf{(s+1)(3s+1)}}$$

Option (c) is correct.

M20.175 *The current I flowing in the circuit (Fig. 20.214) shown below in ampere is _____.*

[GATE 2019]

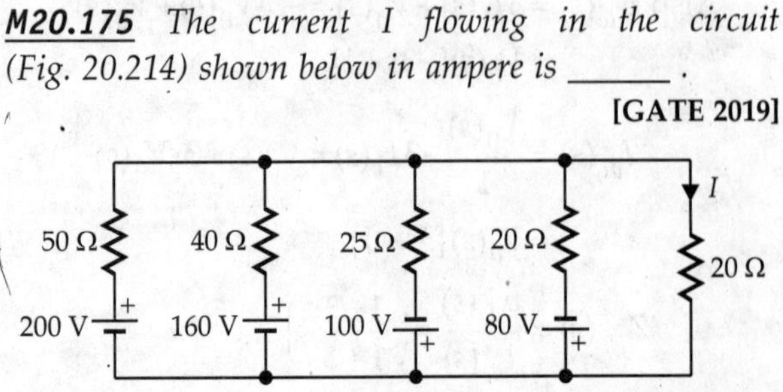

Fig. 20.214

Solution. Using Millman's theorem,

$$E = \frac{\frac{200}{50} + \frac{160}{40} - \frac{100}{25} - \frac{80}{20}}{\frac{1}{50} + \frac{1}{40} + \frac{1}{25} + \frac{1}{20}} = 0 \text{ V}$$

$$\frac{1}{R} = \frac{1}{50} + \frac{1}{40} + \frac{1}{25} + \frac{1}{20}$$

Equivalent circuit is shown in Fig. 20.215.

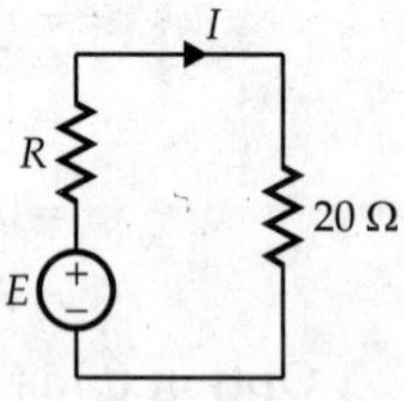

$$I = \frac{E}{R+20} = \mathbf{0\ A}$$

[as $E = 0$ V]

Fig. 20.215

M20.176 *With 10 V dc connected at port A in the linear non-reciprocal two port network shown below (Fig. 20.216), the following were observed :*

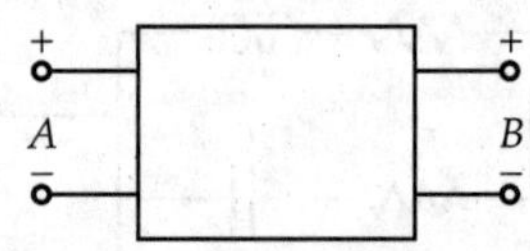

Fig. 20.216

(*i*) *1 Ω connected at port B draws a current of 3 A.*

(*ii*) *2.5 Ω connected at port B draws a current of 2 A.*

With 10 V dc connected at port A, the current drawn by 7Ω connected at port B is

(*a*) $\frac{3}{7}$ A (*b*) $\frac{5}{7}$ A (*c*) 1 A (*d*) $\frac{9}{7}$ A

[GATE 2012]

Solution. Since the given network is linear, it can be represented by its Thevenin's equivalent at port B. (Fig. 20.217)

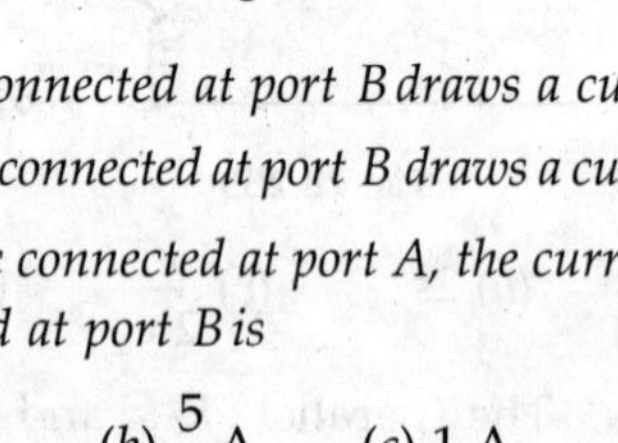

Fig. 20.217

For $R_L = 1\ \Omega$, $i = 3$ A

$$\therefore \quad 3 = \frac{V_{Th}}{R_{Th} + 1}$$

or $\qquad V_{Th} = 3(R_{Th} + 1) \qquad$ ...(1)

For $R_L = 2.5\ \Omega,\ i = 2\ \text{A}$

$$\therefore \quad 2 = \frac{V_{Th}}{R_{Th} + 2.5}$$

or, $$V_{Th} = 2(R_{Th} + 2.5) \qquad ...(2)$$

Solving for (1) and (2), we have

$$R_{Th} = 2\,\Omega\ ;\ V_{Th} = 9\text{ V}$$

$\therefore$ For $R_L = 7\Omega$,

$$i = \frac{V_{Th}}{R_{Th} + 7} = \frac{9}{2 + 7} = \mathbf{1\ A.}$$

Option (*c*) is correct.

M20.177 *For the same network, as shown in Fig. 20.216 with 6 V dc connected at port A, 1 Ω connected at port B, it draws $\frac{7}{3}$ A. If 8 V dc is connected to port A, the open circuit voltage at port B is*

(*a*) 6 V (*b*) 7 V (*c*) 8 V (*d*) 9 V

[GATE 2012]

Solution. With change in source voltage, in a linear network, the Thevenin's network resistance does not change.

When 6 V source is connected at port *A*, 1 Ω connected at port *B*, the current flow is $\frac{7}{3}$ *A*, as per the question.

$$\therefore \quad \frac{7}{3} = \frac{V_{Th}}{R_{Th} + 1}$$

or, $$V_{Th} = \frac{7}{3}(R_{Th} + 1) = \frac{7}{3}(2 + 1) = 7\text{ V}$$

From concept of *ABCD* parameter

$$V_S = AV_R - BI_R$$

Here with the given question,

$$10 = 3\text{ A} - 3\text{ B} \qquad ...(1)$$

$$[\because V_S = \text{supply voltage} = 10\text{ V}$$
$$V_R = i \times R_L = 3\text{ A} \times 1\,\Omega = 3\text{ V}]$$

Similarly, for the second given condition,

$$10 = 5\text{ A} - 2\text{ B} \qquad ...(2)$$

$$[\because V_S = 10\text{ V}\ ;\ V_R = 2.5\,\Omega \times 2\text{ A} = 5\text{ V}]$$

Solving (1) and (2),

$$B = \frac{-20}{9};\quad A = \frac{10}{9}$$

In this question, 8 V dc is applied at port *A*, open circuit voltage at port *B* is say $V_{o/c} (= V_R)$

$\therefore$ We can write

$$8 = AV_{o/c} - B.0 \qquad [\because \text{Open circuit at port } B, \text{ hence } I_R = I_L = 0]$$

$$\therefore \quad V_{o/c} = \frac{8}{A} = \frac{8}{\frac{10}{9}} = \mathbf{7.2\ V}$$

Option (*b*) is correct.

M20.178 *The Z matrix of a 2 port network is given by*

$$\begin{bmatrix} 0.9 & 0.2 \\ 0.2 & 0.6 \end{bmatrix}$$

The element Y_{22} of the corresponding Y matrix of the same network is given by **[GATE 2004]**

(*a*) 1.2 (*b*) 0.4 (*c*) – 0.4 (*d*) 1.8

Solution. From theory, $Y_{22} = \frac{Z_{11}}{\Delta Z}$;

Given that $Z_{11} = 0.9\,\Omega$;

$$\Delta Z = Z_{11}Z_{22} - Z_{12}Z_{21}$$
$$= 0.9 \times 0.6 - 0.2 \times 0.2 = \frac{1}{2}$$

$$\therefore \quad Y_{22} = \frac{Z_{11}}{\Delta Z} = \frac{0.9}{\frac{1}{2}} = \mathbf{1.8\ mho.}$$

Option (*d*) is correct.

M20.179 *Which of the relations is true for the following network shown in Fig. 20.218 ?*

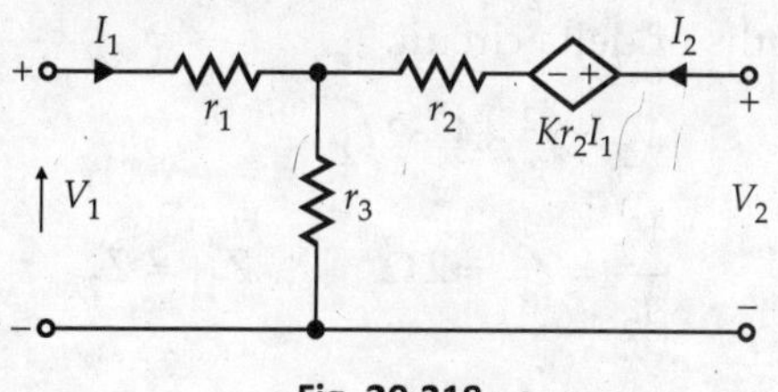

Fig. 20.218

(*a*) $Z_{11} = Z_{22}$ (*b*) $Z_{12} = Z_{21}$

(*c*) $Z_{12} \neq Z_{21}$ (*d*) $Z_{11} \times Z_{22} = Z_{21}$

Solution. In leftmost loop of the given figure, we have

$$-V_1 + I_1 r_1 + (I_1 + I_2) r_3 = 0$$

or, $$V_1 = I_1(r_1 + r_3) + I_2 r_3 \qquad ...(1)$$

In the rightside loop, we have

$$-V_2 + Kr_2 I_1 + I_2 r_2 + (I_1 + I_2) r_3 = 0$$

or, $$V_2 = I_1(r_3 + Kr_2) + I_2(r_2 + r_3) \qquad ...(2)$$

$$\therefore \quad Z_{11} = (r_1 + r_3)\ ;\ Z_{12} = r_3\ ;$$
$$Z_{21} = (r_3 + Kr_2)\ ;\ Z_{22} = (r_2 + r_3)$$

We find here $\mathbf{Z_{12} \neq Z_{21}}$ and hence **option (*c*) is correct.**

C H A P T E R 20

M20.180 *In the circuit shown in Fig. 20.219.*

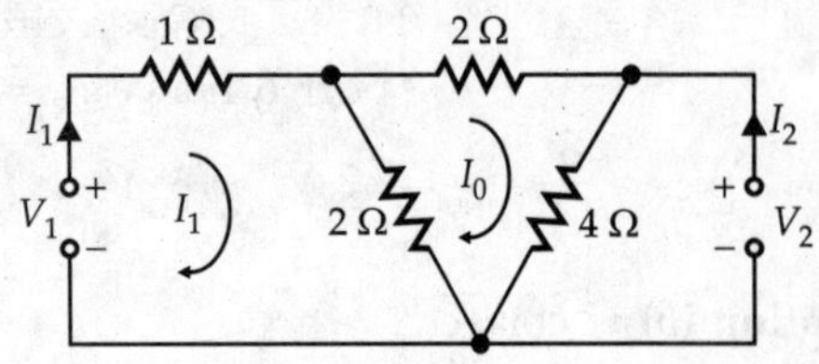

Fig. 20.219

(*a*) $Z_{11} \neq Z_{22}$ (*b*) $Z_{11} = Z_{22}$

(*c*) $Z_{12} \neq Z_{21}$

(*d*) $Z_{11} = Z_{22} = Z_{12} = Z_{21}$

Solution. With $I_2 = 0,\ V_2 = 4I_0$

and $(I_0 - I_1)2 + 2I_0 + 4I_0 = 0$

i.e., $2I_1 = I_0(2+2+4) = 8I_0 = 2V_2$

$$\therefore \quad \frac{V_2}{I_1} = Z_{21} = 1\Omega$$

Again, $V_1 = 1 \times I_1 + 2(I_1 - I_0)$

$$= I_1 + 2\left(I_1 - \frac{1}{4}I_1\right) = \frac{5}{2}I_1$$

$$\therefore \quad \frac{V_1}{I_1} = Z_{11} = \frac{5}{2}\Omega$$

With $I_1 = 0$, I_2 gets equally divided between two paths of delta circuit.

$$\therefore \quad V_2 = \frac{I_2}{2} \times 4 = 2I_2$$

$$\frac{V_2}{I_2} = Z_{22} = 2\Omega \quad \therefore\ Z_{11} \neq Z_{22}$$

Also, $V_1 = \frac{I_2}{2} \times 2 = I_2$

$$\therefore \quad \frac{V_1}{I_2} = Z_{12} = 1\,\Omega$$

$$\therefore \quad Z_{12} = Z_{21}$$

Option (*a*) is correct.

M20.181 *Two networks are connected in cascade as shown in Fig. 20.220. With the usual notation the equivalent A, B, C, D constants are obtained. Given that, $C = 0.025\angle 45°$, the value of Z_2 is* **[GATE 2005]**

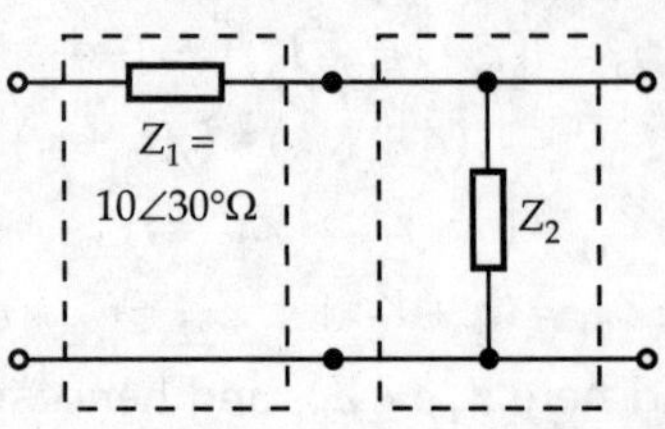

Fig. 20.220

(*a*) $10\angle 30°\Omega$ (*b*) $40\angle -45°\Omega$

(*c*) $1\ \Omega$ (*d*) $0\ \Omega$

Solution. The voltage and currents are marked on Fig. 20.221.

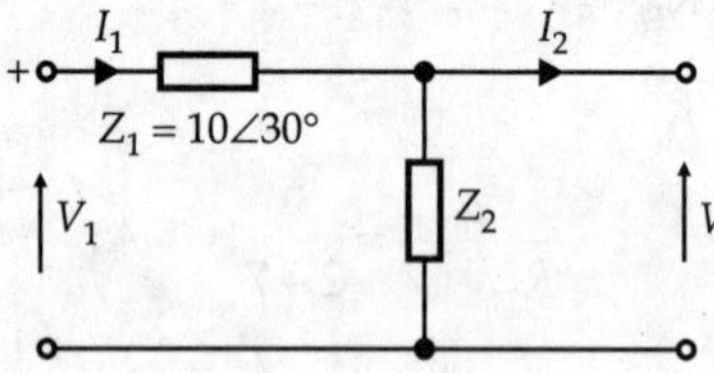

Fig. 20.221

Here, $V_1 = AV_2 - BI_2,\ I_1 = CV_2 - DI_2$

$$\therefore \quad C = \left.\frac{I_1}{V_2}\right|_{I_2=0} = \frac{I_1}{I_1 Z_2} = \frac{1}{Z_2}$$

or, $$Z_2 = \frac{1}{C} = \frac{1}{0.025\angle 45°} = \mathbf{40\angle -45°\,\Omega}$$

Option (*b*) is correct.

M20.182 *For the two port network shown in Fig. 20.222, the Z matrix is given by* **[GATE 2005]**

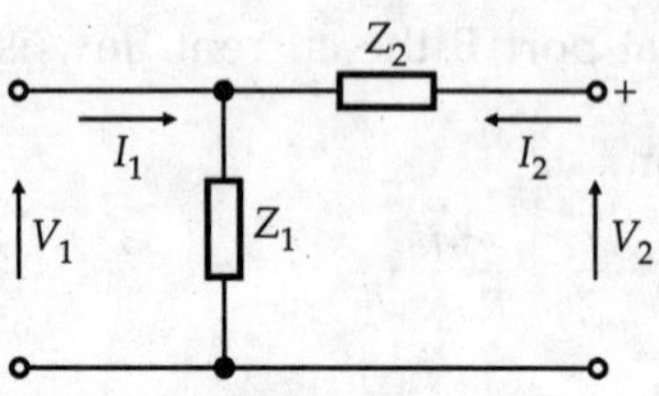

Fig. 20.222

(*a*) $\begin{bmatrix} Z_1 & Z_1 + Z_2 \\ Z_1 + Z_2 & Z_2 \end{bmatrix}$ (*b*) $\begin{bmatrix} Z_1 & Z_1 \\ Z_1 + Z_2 & Z_2 \end{bmatrix}$

(*c*) $\begin{bmatrix} Z_1 & Z_2 \\ Z_2 & Z_1 + Z_2 \end{bmatrix}$ (*d*) $\begin{bmatrix} Z_1 & Z_1 \\ Z_1 & Z_1 + Z_2 \end{bmatrix}$

Solution. Figure 20.222 is redrawn (Fig. 20.223) with currents and voltages marked.

Here $V_1 = Z_1(I_1 + I_2)$

$$= Z_1 I_1 + Z_1 I_2$$

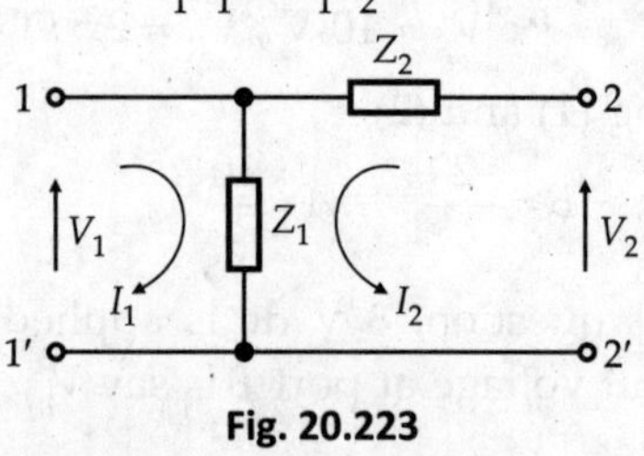

Fig. 20.223

Also, $V_2 = Z_1(I_1 + I_2) + I_2Z_2$

$$= Z_1I_1 + (Z_1 + Z_2)I_2$$

$$\therefore \quad \begin{bmatrix} V_1 \\ V_2 \end{bmatrix} = \begin{bmatrix} Z_1 & Z_1 \\ Z_1 & Z_1 + Z_2 \end{bmatrix}$$

Option (*d*) is correct.

M20.183 *The Z matrix of a 2-port network is given by* $\begin{bmatrix} 0.9 & 0.2 \\ 0.2 & 0.6 \end{bmatrix}$. *The element Y_{22} of the corresponding Y matrix of the same network is given by* **[GATE 2004]**

(*a*) 1.2 (*b*) 0.4 (*c*) – 0.4 (*d*) 1.8

Solution. From theory, $Y_{22} = \frac{Z_{11}}{\Delta Z}$;

Given that $Z_{11} = 0.9\ \Omega$;

$$\Delta Z = Z_{11}Z_{22} - Z_{12}Z_{21}$$

$$= 0.9 \times 0.6 - 0.2 \times 0.2 = \frac{1}{2}$$

$$\therefore \quad Y_{22} = \frac{Z_{11}}{\Delta Z} = \frac{0.9}{1/2} = \mathbf{1.8\ mho.}$$

Option (*d*) is correct.

M20.184 *The Z parameters of the two port network shown in Fig. 20.224 are $Z_{11} = 40\ \Omega$; $Z_{12} = 60\ \Omega$; Z_{21} = 80 Ω and $Z_{22} = 100\ \Omega$. The average power delivered to $R_L = 20\ \Omega$, in watts, is* ______. **[GATE 2016]**

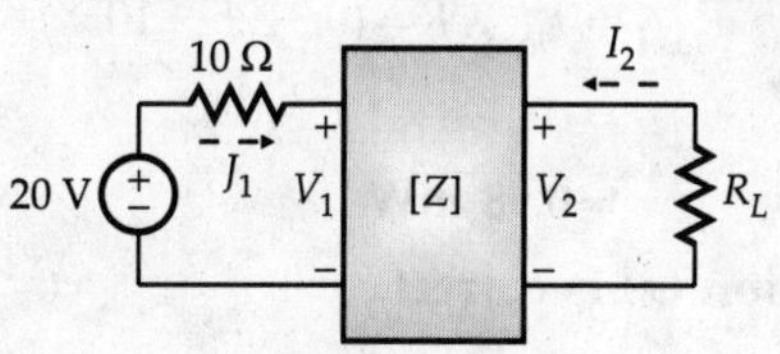

Fig. 20.224

Solution. The Z parameter equations are written as follows :

$$\begin{bmatrix} V_1 \\ V_2 \end{bmatrix} = \begin{bmatrix} Z_{11} & Z_{12} \\ Z_{21} & Z_{22} \end{bmatrix} \begin{bmatrix} I_1 \\ I_2 \end{bmatrix}$$

$$= \begin{bmatrix} 40 & 60 \\ 80 & 100 \end{bmatrix} \begin{bmatrix} I_1 \\ I_2 \end{bmatrix}$$

$$\therefore \quad V_1 = 40I_1 + 60I_2 \quad ...(1)$$

$$V_2 = 80I_1 + 100I_2 \quad ...(2)$$

However, for the given network,

$(20 - 10I_1) = V_1$ and $V_2 = -I_2 \times R_L = -I_2 \times 20$

Hence for (1) and (2), we get

$$20 - 10I_1 = 40I_1 + 60I_2 \text{ and}$$

$$-20I_2 = 80I_1 + 100I_2$$

i.e., $50I_1 + 60I_2 = 20$ and $80I_1 + 120I_2 = 0$

Solving we get, $I_1 = 2$ A ; $I_2 = \frac{-4}{3}$ A

$\therefore$ Average power delivered to load

$$P_{L(av)} = I_2^2 R_L = \frac{16}{9} \times 20 = \mathbf{35.55\ W}$$

M20.185 *For the given 2-port network, the value of transfer impedance Z_{21} in ohms is* ______.

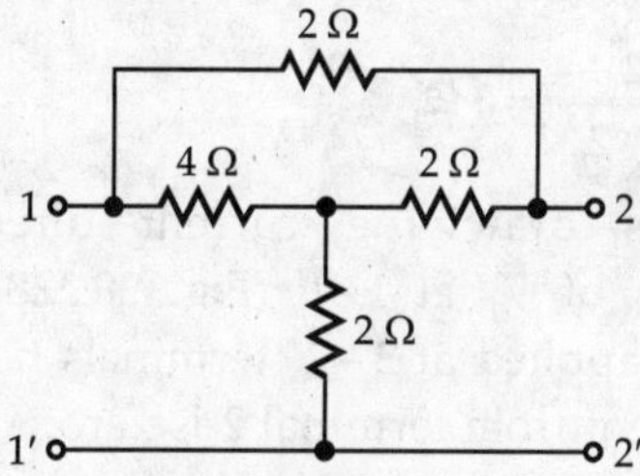

Fig. 20.225

Solution. Z_{21} (Transfer impedance) $= \left.\frac{V_2}{I_1}\right|_{I_2=0}$

With $I_2 = 0$, the current distribution is shown in Fig. 20.226.

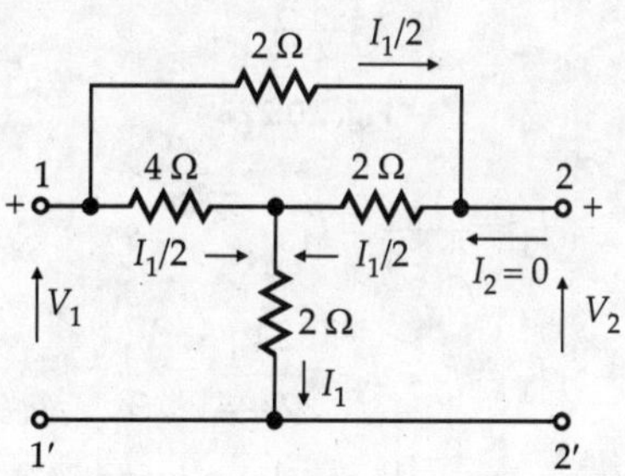

Fig. 20.226

Here $V_2 = \left(\frac{I_1}{2}\right) \times 2 + 2I_1 = 3I_1$

$$\therefore \quad Z_{21} = \left.\frac{3I_1}{I_1}\right|_{I_2=0} = \mathbf{3\ \Omega.}$$

M20.186 *Z-parameters of the given lattice network (Fig. 20.227) are given by*

(*a*) $[Z] = \begin{bmatrix} 6 & 6 \\ 6 & 6 \end{bmatrix} \Omega$ (*b*) $[Z] = \begin{bmatrix} 2 & 4 \\ 4 & 2 \end{bmatrix} \Omega$

CHAPTER 20

(c) $[Z]=\begin{bmatrix}3 & 4\\ 4 & 3\end{bmatrix}\Omega$ (d) $[Z]=\begin{bmatrix}3 & 1\\ 1 & 3\end{bmatrix}\Omega$

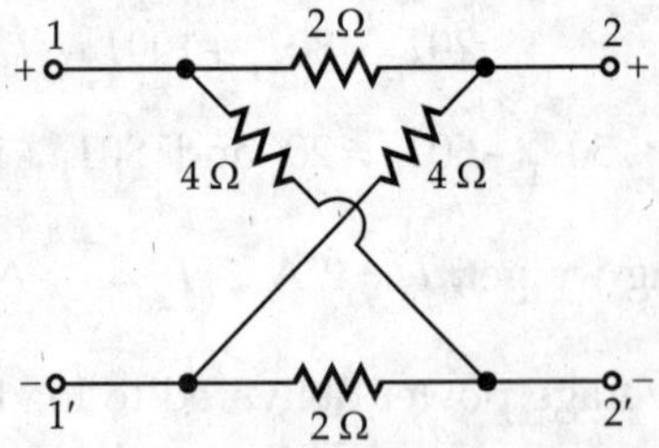

Fig. 20.227

Solution. By observation,

$Z_{11} = Z_{22}$

= resistances connected at 1–1′ or 2 –2′

$= \dfrac{2+4}{2} = 3\ \Omega.$

Let us draw the current direction with application of V_1 at 1–1′ (Fig. 20.228). Since no voltage is applied at 2 –2′ terminals hence I_2, the input current from terminal 2 is zero.

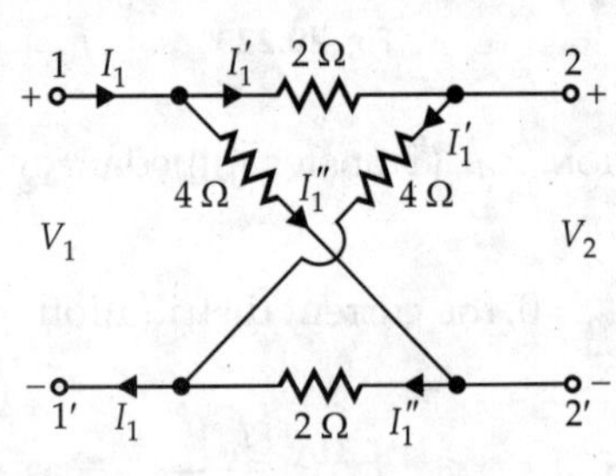

Fig. 20.228

$$I_1' = \frac{V_1}{2+4} = I_1''$$

$$I_1 = I_1' + I_1'' = \frac{2V_1}{2+4} = \frac{V_1}{3}.$$

Let V_2 be the voltage developed at 2 –2′

$$V_2 = I_1' \times 4 - \frac{V_1}{6}\times 2$$

$$= \frac{2}{3}V_1 - \frac{1}{3}.V_1 = \frac{V_1}{3}$$

$$\therefore \quad Z_{12} = Z_{21} = \frac{V_2}{I_1} = \frac{V_1/3}{V_1/3} = 1\ \Omega$$

$$[Z] = \begin{bmatrix} Z_{11} & Z_{12}\\ Z_{21} & Z_{22}\end{bmatrix} = \begin{bmatrix}\mathbf{3} & \mathbf{1}\\ \mathbf{1} & \mathbf{3}\end{bmatrix}$$

Option (*d*) is correct.

<u>**M20.187**</u> *Figure 20.229 represents the equivalent circuit of a two port network. Assume $y_{21} = -25\,\mu s$; $y_{22} = 300\,\mu s$; $y_{11} = 125\,\mu s$; $y_{12} = -25\,\mu s$; $V_1 = 50\,V$; find the power drawn by the load.*

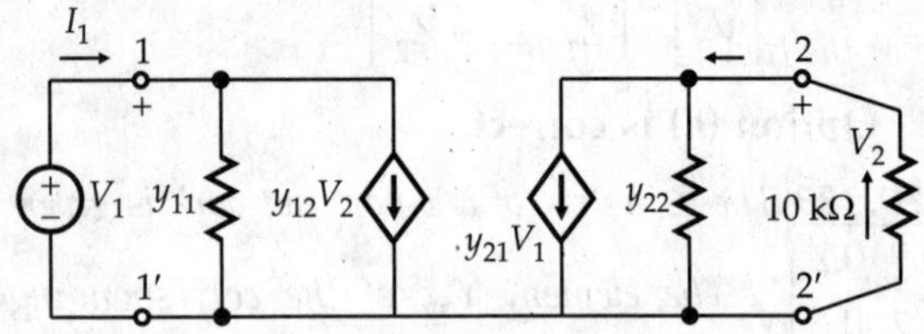

Fig. 20.229

(*a*) 0.98 mW (*b*) 5 mW

(*c*) 0.312 mW (*d*) 98 mW

Solution. Load admittance

$$= \frac{1}{10\times 10^3} = 100\,\mu s = y_l$$

In the output loop, at load terminal we have

$$Y_{21}V_1 + y_{22}V_2 + y_l V_2 = 0$$

or, $$-y_{21}V_1 = V_2[y_{22} + y_l]$$

or, $$25\times 10^{-6}\times 50 = [300\times 10^{-6} + 100\times 10^{-6}]\,V_2$$

$$\therefore \quad V_2 = \frac{25\times 50\times 10^{-6}}{400\times 10^{-6}} = 3.125\text{ V}$$

$$I_{load} = \frac{3.125}{10\times 10^3} = 0.3125\text{ mA}$$

Power drawn by the load is

$$P_{load} = I_{load}^2 . R = (0.3125\times 10^{-3})^2 .10\times 10^3$$

$$= (0.098\times 10^{-2})\text{W}$$

$$= \mathbf{0.98\ mW}$$

Option (*a*) is correct.

<u>**M20.188**</u> *Find the input current I_1 from the 50 V source in the problem 20.187.*

(*a*) 8.721 mA (*b*) 3.125 mA

(*c*) 6.172 mA (*d*) 4.72 mA

Solution. At node 1 in Fig. 20.229,

$$-I_1 + V_1 y_{11} + y_{12}V_2 = 0$$

$$\therefore \quad (I_1 - y_{12}V_2) = V_1 y_{11}$$

or, $$I_1 + 25\times 10^{-6}.V_2 = 125\times 10^{-6}.50$$

With $V_2 = 3.125$ V,

$$I_1 = 125\times 50\times 10^{-6} - 25\times 3.125\times 10^{-6}$$

$$= 6171.87\times 10^{-6}\text{ A} = \mathbf{6.172\ mA}$$

Option (*c*) is correct.

M20.189 *The h-parameters for a two port network are defined by*

$$\begin{bmatrix} E_1 \\ I_2 \end{bmatrix} = \begin{bmatrix} h_{11} & h_{12} \\ h_{21} & h_{22} \end{bmatrix} \begin{bmatrix} I_1 \\ E_2 \end{bmatrix}$$

For the two port network shown in Fig. 20.230, the value of h_{12} is given by **[GATE 2003]**

(*a*) 0.125 (*b*) 0.167

(*c*) 0.625 (*d*) 0.25

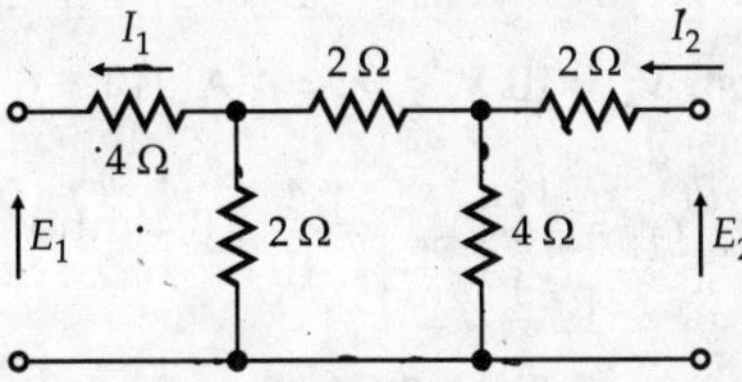

Fig. 20.230

Solution. The network shown in Fig. 20.230, is reduced as shown in Fig. 20.231.

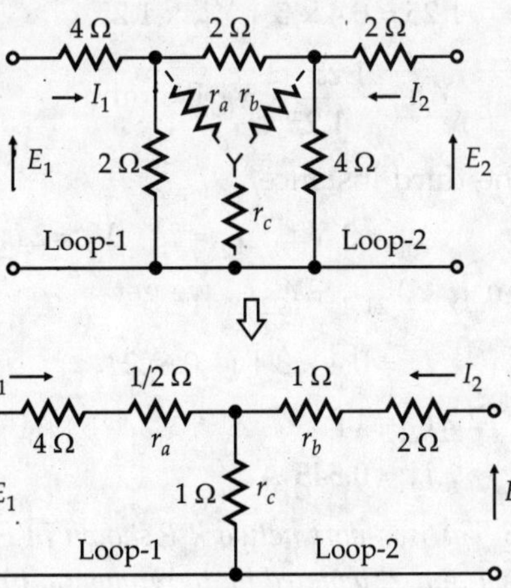

Fig. 20.231

Delta network with resistors 2 Ω, 2 Ω and 4 Ω is transformed to star network with equivalent resistances r_a, r_b and r_c.

$$r_a = \frac{2\times 2}{2+2+4} = \frac{1}{2}\ \Omega$$

$$r_b = \frac{2\times 4}{2+2+4} = 1\ \Omega$$

$$r_c = \frac{2\times 4}{2+2+4} = 1\ \Omega$$

In loop-1,

$$-E_1 + 4I_1 + \frac{1}{2}\times I_1 + (I_1 + I_2)\times 1 = 0$$

or, $$E_1 = 5.5 I_1 + I_2 \qquad \text{...(1)}$$

In loop-2,

$$-E_2 + 2I_2 + 1\times I_2 + (I_1 + I_2)\times 1 = 0$$

or, $$E_2 = I_1 + 4I_2 \qquad \text{...(2)}$$

From (1) and (2), $$h_{12} = \left.\frac{E_1}{E_2}\right|_{I_1=0} = \frac{I_2}{4I_2}$$

Here, $$h_{12} = \frac{1}{4} = \mathbf{0.25.}$$

Option (*d*) is correct.

M20.190 *Two passive two-port networks are connected in cascade as shown in Fig. 20.232. A voltage source is connected at port 1.*

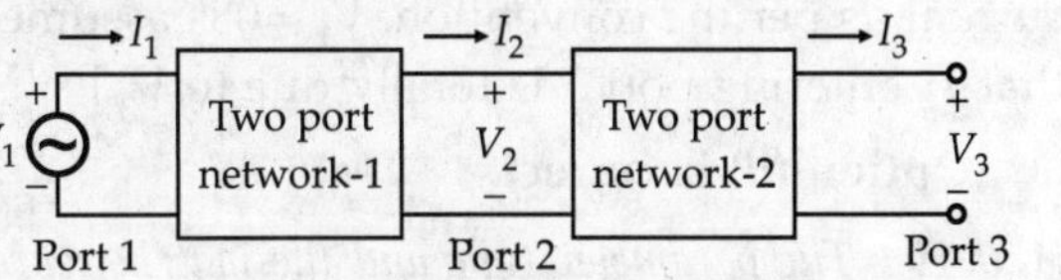

Fig. 20.232

Given, $V_1 = A_1V_2 + B_1I_2$; $I_1 = C_1V_2 + D_1I_2$

$V_2 = A_2V_3 + B_2I_3$; $I_2 = C_2V_3 + D_2I_3$

A_1, B_1, C_1, D_1, A_2, B_2, C_2 and D_2 are the generalized circuit constants. If the Thevenin equivalent circuit at port 3 consists of a voltage source V_T and impedance Z_T connected in series, then **[GATE 2017]**

(*a*) $V_T = \dfrac{V_1}{A_1A_2}$, $Z_T = \dfrac{A_1B_2 + B_1D_2}{A_1A_2 + B_1C_2}$

(*b*) $V_T = \dfrac{V_1}{A_1A_2 + B_1C_2}$, $Z_T = \dfrac{A_1B_2 + B_1D_2}{A_1A_2}$

(*c*) $V_T = \dfrac{V_1}{A_1 + A_2}$, $Z_T = \dfrac{A_1B_2 + B_1D_2}{A_1 + A_2}$

(*d*) $V_T = \dfrac{V_1}{A_1A_2 + B_1C_2}$, $Z_T = \dfrac{A_1B_2 - B_1D_2}{A_1A_2 + B_1C_2}$

Solution. In cascaded network, we can write

$$\begin{bmatrix} A & B \\ C & D \end{bmatrix} = \begin{bmatrix} A_1 & B_1 \\ C_1 & D_1 \end{bmatrix}\begin{bmatrix} A_2 & B_2 \\ C_2 & D_2 \end{bmatrix}$$

$$= \begin{bmatrix} A_1A_2 + B_1C_2 & A_2B_2 + B_1D_2 \\ C_1A_2 + D_1C_2 & C_1B_2 + D_1D_2 \end{bmatrix}$$

and $$\begin{bmatrix} V_1 \\ I_1 \end{bmatrix} = \begin{bmatrix} A & B \\ C & D \end{bmatrix}\begin{bmatrix} V_3 \\ I_3 \end{bmatrix}$$

$$= \begin{bmatrix} A_1A_2 + B_1C_2 & A_1B_2 + B_1D_2 \\ C_1A_2 + D_1C_2 & C_1B_2 + D_1D_2 \end{bmatrix}\begin{bmatrix} V_3 \\ I_3 \end{bmatrix}$$

$$\therefore\; V_1 = (A_1A_2 + B_1C_2)V_3 + (A_1B_2 + B_1D_2)I_3$$

$$I_1 = (C_1A_2 + D_1C_2)V_3 + (C_1B_2 + D_1D_2)I_3$$

Thevenin's voltage,

$$V_T = V_3\Big|_{I_1=0} = \frac{V_1}{A_1A_2 + B_1C_2}$$

where, V_T is the open circuit voltage at port-3.

Series impedance

$$Z_T = \frac{V_3}{-I_3}\Bigg|_{V_1=0} = \frac{A_1B_2 + B_1D_2}{A_1A_2 + B_1C_2}$$

[Current at port-3 is considered as a negative current as per the convention. $V_1 = 0$ is assumed so that I_3 entering port 3 is totally due to V_3.]

Option (*d*) is correct.

M20.191 *The parameter type and the matrix representation of the relevant two port parameters that describe the circuit shown in Fig. 20.233 are*

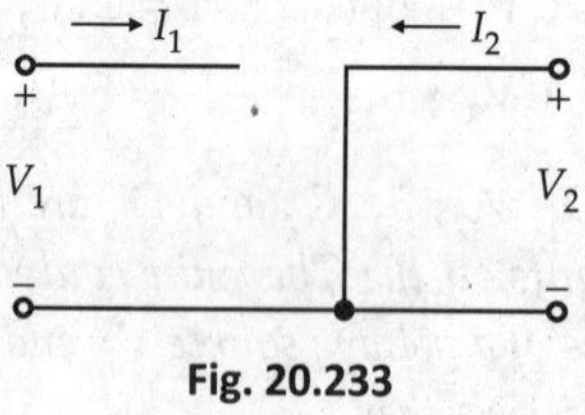

Fig. 20.233

(*a*) *Z parameter*, $\begin{bmatrix} 0 & 0 \\ 0 & 0 \end{bmatrix}$ (*b*) *h parameter*, $\begin{bmatrix} 1 & 0 \\ 0 & 1 \end{bmatrix}$

(*c*) *g parameter*, $\begin{bmatrix} 0 & 0 \\ 0 & 0 \end{bmatrix}$ (*d*) *y parameter*, $\begin{bmatrix} 1 & 0 \\ 0 & 1 \end{bmatrix}$

[GATE 2006]

Solution. Here, in the given circuit $I_1 = 0$, $V_2 = 0$.

The g parameter model has I_1 and V_2 as dependent variables expressed in terms of independent variable V_1 and I_2 as

$$I_1 = g_{11}V_1 + g_{12}I_2\;;\quad V_2 = g_{21}V_1 + g_{22}I_2$$

Here,

$$g_{11} = \frac{I_1}{V_1}\Bigg|_{I_2=0} = \frac{0}{V_1} = 0\;;\quad g_{12} = \frac{I_1}{I_2}\Bigg|_{V_1=0} = \frac{0}{I_2} = 0$$

$$g_{21} = \frac{V_2}{V_1}\Bigg|_{I_2=0} = \frac{0}{V_1} = 0\;;\quad g_{22} = \frac{V_2}{I_2}\Bigg|_{V_1=0} = \frac{0}{I_2} = 0$$

$$\therefore\; g = \begin{bmatrix} 0 & 0 \\ 0 & 0 \end{bmatrix}$$

Option (*c*) is correct.

M20.192 *In a linear 2-port network, when 10 V is applied to Port 1, a current of 4 A flows through Port 2 when it is short-circuited. When 5 V is applied to Port 1, a current of 1.25 A flows through a 1 Ω resistance connected across Port 2. When 3 V is applied to Port 1, the current (in Amperes) through a 2 Ω resistance connected across Port 2 is ______.* **[GATE 2015]**

Solution.

$$I_1 = Y_{11}V_1 + Y_{12}V_2\;;\; I_2 = Y_{21}V_1 + Y_{22}V_2$$

At first, $V_1 = 10$ V ; $I_2 = 4$ A ; $V_2 = 0$

$$\therefore\; Y_{21} = \frac{I_2}{V_1}\Bigg|_{V_2=0} = \frac{4}{10} = 0.4 \text{ mho}$$

Next, $V_1 = 5$, $I_2 = 1.25$ A,

$$V_2 = I_2R_L = 1.25 \times 1 = 1.25 \text{ V}$$

$\therefore$ From $I_2 = Y_{21}V_1 + Y_{22}V_2$, we get

$$1.25 = 0.4 \times 5 + Y_{22} \times 1.25$$

$$\therefore\; Y_{22} = \frac{1.25 - 2}{1.25} = -0.6 \text{ mho}$$

In the third instance,

$$V_1 = 3 \text{ V};\quad I_2 = ?\;;\; V_2 = 2I_2$$

From $I_2 = Y_{21}r_1 + Y_{22}r_2$, we get

$$I_2 = 0.4 \times 3 + (-0.6).2I_2$$

or, $$2.2I_2 = 1.2$$

$$\therefore\; \mathbf{I_2 = 0.545 \text{ A}}$$

M20.193 *The two-port network P shown in Fig. 20.234 has ports 1 and 2, denoted by terminals (a, b) and (c, d) respectively. It has an impedance matrix Z with*

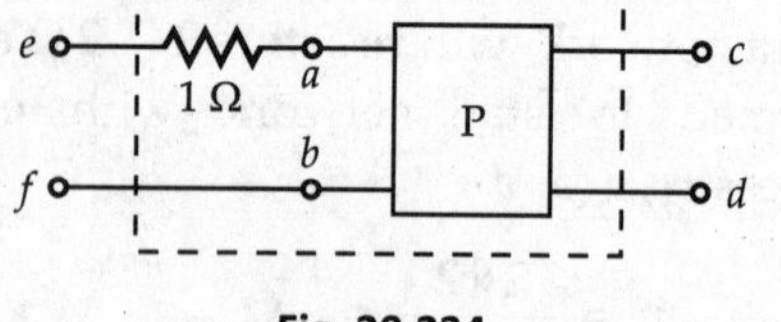

Fig. 20.234

parameters denoted by Z_{ij}. A 1 Ω resistor is connected in series with the network at port 1 as shown in the figure. The impedance matrix of the modified two port network (shown as a dashed box) is **[GATE 2010]**

(*a*) $\begin{bmatrix} Z_{11}+1 & Z_{12}+1 \\ Z_{21} & Z_{22}+1 \end{bmatrix}$ (*b*) $\begin{bmatrix} Z_{11}+1 & Z_{12} \\ Z_{21} & Z_{22}+1 \end{bmatrix}$

(*c*) $\begin{bmatrix} Z_{11}+1 & Z_{12} \\ Z_{21} & Z_{22} \end{bmatrix}$ (*d*) $\begin{bmatrix} Z_{11}+1 & Z_{12} \\ Z_{21+1} & Z_{22} \end{bmatrix}$

Solution. Figure 20.235 represents the 1 Ω resistor included in port-1 with the equivalent circuit of Z parameter model.

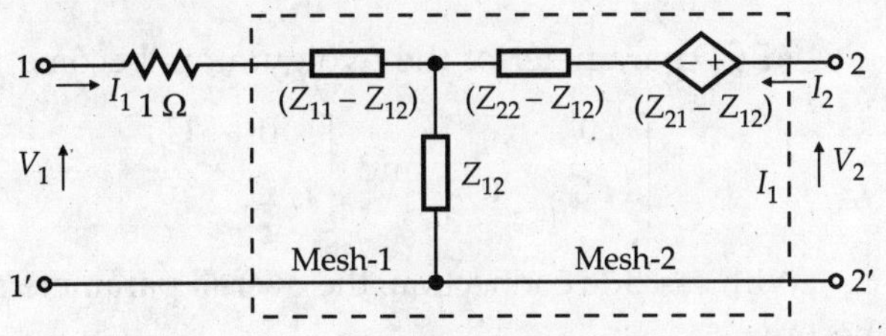

Fig. 20.235

For mesh 1 we have

$$V_1 = I_1 \times 1 + I_1(Z_{11} - Z_{12}) + Z_{12}I_1 + Z_{12}I_2$$

or, $V_1 = (Z_{11} + 1)I_1 + Z_{12}I_2$ ...(1)

and $V_2 = (Z_{21} - Z_{12})I_1 + (Z_{22} - Z_{12})I_2 + Z_{12}(I_1 + I_2)$

or, $V_2 = Z_{21}I_1 + Z_{22}I_2$ ...(2)

Thus the modified impedance matrix is given as

$$Z_{mod} = \begin{bmatrix} \mathbf{Z_{11} + 1} & \mathbf{Z_{12}} \\ \mathbf{Z_{21}} & \mathbf{Z_{22}} \end{bmatrix}$$

Option (*c*) is correct.

M20.194 *The parameters of the circuit shown in Fig. 20.236 are $R_1 = 1\ M\Omega$; $R_0 = 10\ \Omega$; $A = 10^6\ V/V$. If $V_1 = 1\ \mu V$, then output voltage, input impedance and output impedance respectively are* **[GATE 2006]**

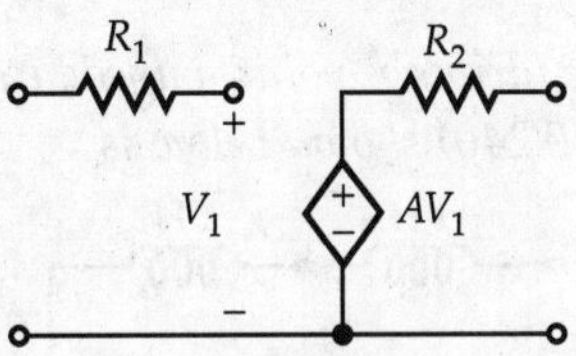

Fig. 20.236

(*a*) 1 V, ∞, ∞ (*b*) 1 V, 0, 10 Ω
(*c*) 1 V, 0, ∞ (*d*) 10 V, ∞, 10 Ω

Solution. Figure 20.237 represents the given circuit with currents and voltages marked.

A_v, the voltage gain $= \dfrac{V_2}{V_1}$

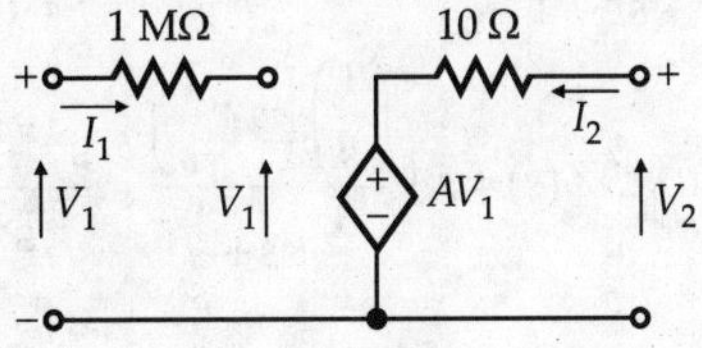

Fig. 20.237

Since $A_v = A$ (given)

$\therefore \quad V_2 = AV_1 = 10^6 \times 1 \times 10^{-6} = \mathbf{1\ V}$

$$Z_{input} \text{ (the input impedance)} = \frac{V_1}{I_1}$$

$$= \frac{1 \times 10^{-6}}{0} = \infty\ \Omega$$

$$Z_{output} \text{ (the output impedance)} = \left.\frac{V_2}{I_2}\right|_{V_1 = 0} = \mathbf{10\ \Omega}$$

[∵ With $V_1 = 0$, at the output loop,

$$V_2 = 10\,I_2 + AV_1 = 10I_2$$

$$\therefore \quad \frac{V_2}{I_2} = 10 \;]$$

∴ **Option (*b*) is correct.**

M20.195 *Figure 20.238 represents an ideal transformer. The ABCD parameter is given by*

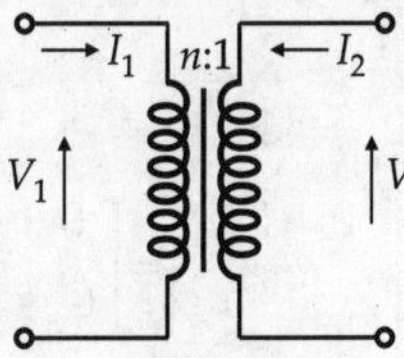

Fig. 20.238

(*a*) $\begin{bmatrix} 0 & 0 \\ n & n \end{bmatrix}$ (*b*) $\begin{bmatrix} 1/n & 0 \\ 0 & n \end{bmatrix}$

(*c*) $\begin{bmatrix} n & 0 \\ 0 & 1/n \end{bmatrix}$ (*d*) $\begin{bmatrix} -n & 0 \\ 0 & -1/n \end{bmatrix}$

Solution. For an ideal transformer,

$$\frac{V_1}{V_2} = \frac{n}{1} \qquad i.e.,\ V_1 = nV_2 \qquad ...(1)$$

$$\frac{I_1}{-I_2} = \frac{1}{n}, \qquad i.e.,\ I_1 = -\frac{1}{n}.I_2 \qquad ...(2)$$

ABCD parameter equations are :

$$V_1 = AV_2 + B(-I_2) \qquad ...(3)$$

$$I_1 = CV_2 + D(-I_2) \qquad ...(4)$$

Comparing equations (1) and (2) with equations (3) and (4)

$$\begin{bmatrix} A & B \\ C & D \end{bmatrix} = \begin{bmatrix} \mathbf{n} & \mathbf{0} \\ \mathbf{0} & \mathbf{1/n} \end{bmatrix}$$

Option (*c*) is correct.

M20.196 *A gyrator is a conceptual device which conserves power. An ideal gyrator is terminated with a pure capacitor load C.*

The input impedance is given by

(a) $G_t Cs$ (b) $\frac{G_t C}{s}$ (c) $\frac{G_t^2}{Cs}$ (d) $G_t^2 Cs$

Solution. Since gyrator conserves power, from Fig. 20.239.

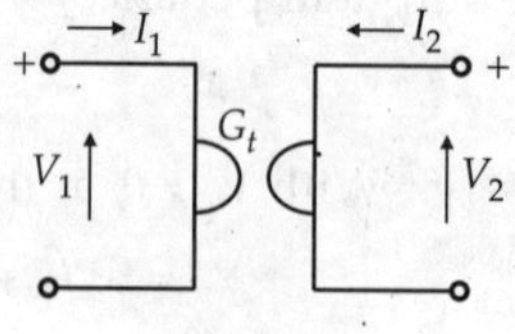

Fig. 20.239

$$V_1 I_1 + V_2 I_2 = 0$$

$$\therefore \quad \frac{V_2}{I_1} = -\frac{V_1}{I_2} = G_t \text{ (say)}$$

However, $\frac{V_2}{I_1} = Z_{21}$; $\frac{V_1}{I_2} = Z_{12}$

$\therefore$ We have $Z_{21} = -Z_{12}$

i.e., $$Z = \begin{bmatrix} 0 & Z_{12} \\ Z_{21} & 0 \end{bmatrix} = \begin{bmatrix} 0 & -G_t \\ G_t & 0 \end{bmatrix}$$

We further write, for capacitor termination,

$$V_1 = -G_t I_2 \text{ and } V_2 = G_t I_1,$$

for Z parameter representation.

Also, $V_2 = -I_2 \times \frac{1}{Cs}$, for capacitor termination.

Writing V_1 in terms of I_1, we have

$$V_1 = G_t (V_2) Cs = G_t (G_t I_1) Cs$$

$$\frac{V_1}{I_1} = Z_{in} = (G_t^2 C)s \; ;$$

i.e., $$Z_{in} = \mathbf{G_t^2 Cs}$$

Option (*d*) is correct.

M20.197 *An ideal gyrator is a device that conserves power. Cascade connection of two ideal gyrators become a ______.*

Solution. Since the gyrator conserves power, from Fig. 20.239,

$$V_1 I_1 + V_2 I_2 = 0$$

i.e., $$-\frac{V_1}{I_2} = +\frac{V_2}{I_1} = G_t \text{ (say)}$$

i.e., $$V_1 = -G_t I_2 \; ; \; V_2 = G_t I_1$$

ABCD parameter of the gyrator is thus given as

$$\begin{bmatrix} V_1 \\ I_1 \end{bmatrix} = \begin{bmatrix} 0 & G_t \\ 1/G_t & 0 \end{bmatrix} \begin{bmatrix} V_2 \\ -I_2 \end{bmatrix}$$

ABCD parameter of the two gyrators become

$$\begin{bmatrix} 0 & G_{t_1} \\ 1/G_{t_1} & 0 \end{bmatrix} \text{ and } \begin{bmatrix} 0 & G_{t_2} \\ 1/G_{t_2} & 0 \end{bmatrix}$$

With cascade connection, the overall parameters become,

$$\begin{bmatrix} 0 & G_{t_1} \\ 1/G_{t_1} & 0 \end{bmatrix} \times \begin{bmatrix} 0 & G_{t_2} \\ 1/G_{t_2} & 0 \end{bmatrix} = \begin{bmatrix} \frac{G_{t_1}}{G_{t_2}} & 0 \\ 0 & \frac{G_{t_2}}{G_{t_1}} \end{bmatrix}$$

Assuming the turns ratio of a transformer to be *n*, we can write

$$\begin{bmatrix} \frac{G_{t_1}}{G_{t_2}} & 0 \\ 0 & \frac{G_{t_2}}{G_{t_1}} \end{bmatrix} = \begin{bmatrix} n & 0 \\ 0 & 1/n \end{bmatrix}$$

where, $n = \frac{G_{t_1}}{G_{t_2}}$

Thus, cascade connection of two gyrators become an ideal **transformer.**

M20.198 *The driving point impedance Z(s) for the circuit (Fig. 20.240) shown below is*

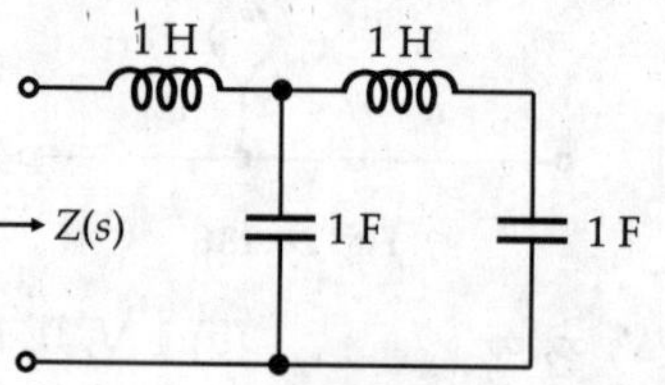

Fig. 20.240 **[GATE 2014]**

(a) $\frac{s^4 + 3s^2 + 1}{s^3 + 2s}$ (b) $\frac{s^4 + 2s^2 + 4}{s^2 + 2}$

(c) $\frac{s^2 + 1}{s^4 + s^2 + 1}$ (d) $\frac{s^3 + 1}{s^4 + s^2 + 1}$

Solution. $$Z(s) = s + \frac{\left(\frac{1}{s}\right)\left(s + \frac{1}{s}\right)}{\frac{1}{s} + s + \frac{1}{s}} = \mathbf{\frac{s^4 + 3s^2 + 1}{s^3 + 2s}}$$

Option (*a*) is correct.

M20.199 *The transfer function* $\dfrac{V_2(s)}{V_1(s)}$ *of the circuit shown below (Fig. 20.241) is*

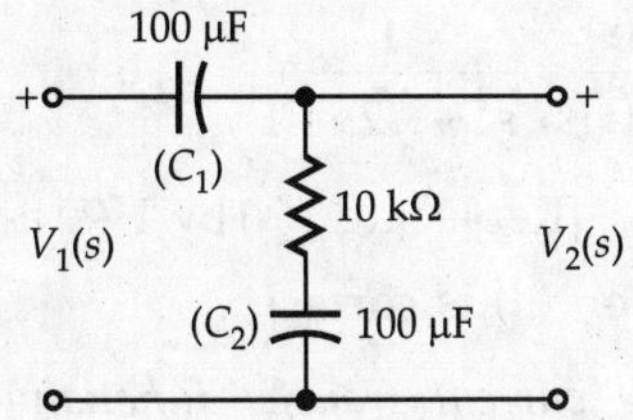

Fig. 20.241 **[GATE 2013]**

(*a*) $\dfrac{0.5s+1}{s+1}$ (*b*) $\dfrac{3s+6}{s+2}$

(*c*) $\dfrac{s+2}{s+1}$ (*d*) $\dfrac{s+1}{s+2}$

Solution.

$$\frac{V_2(s)}{V_1(s)} = \frac{R+\dfrac{1}{C_2 s}}{R+\dfrac{1}{C_1 s}+\dfrac{1}{C_2 s}}$$

$$= \frac{10^4+\dfrac{1}{10^{-4}s}}{10^4+\dfrac{1}{10^{-4}s}+\dfrac{1}{10^{-4}s}} = \mathbf{\frac{s+1}{s+2}}$$

Option (*d*) is correct.

M20.200 *The driving point input impedance seen from the source* V_s *of the circuit shown below (Fig. 20.242), in* Ω, *is* ______ **[GATE 2016]**

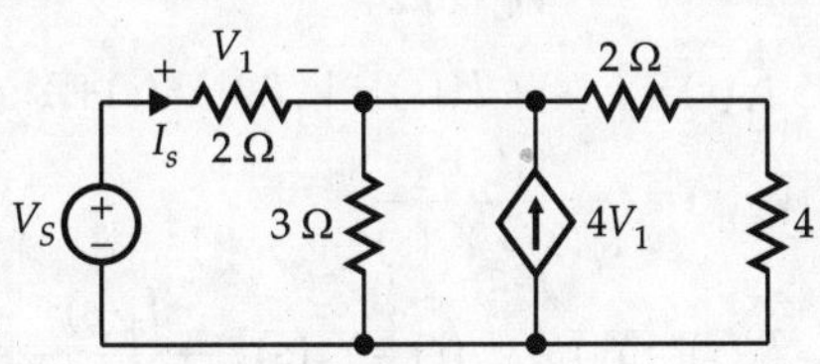

Fig. 20.242

Solution. The circuit is redrawn to identify the node voltage V_0, shown in Fig. 20.243.

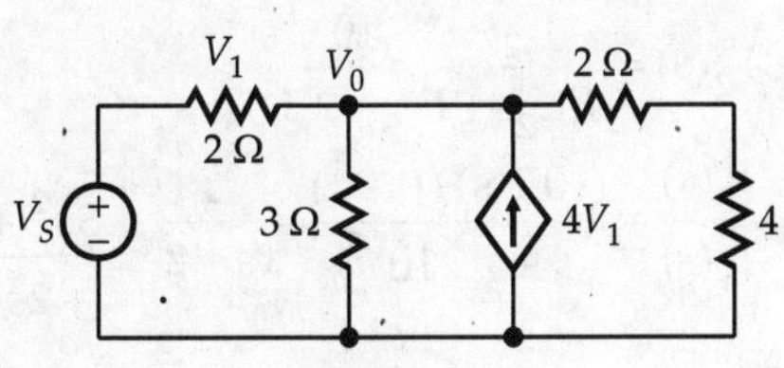

Fig. 20.243

Nodal analysis yields

$$\frac{V_0}{3}+\frac{V_0-V_s}{2}+\frac{V_0}{6}-4V_1=0$$

or, $$4V_1 = V_0-\frac{V_s}{2}$$

But $V_1 = 2I_s$

$\therefore$ $$8I_s = V_0-\frac{V_s}{2} \quad \text{...(1)}$$

Also, $$V_s-V_1 = V_0 \quad \text{...(2)}$$

$\therefore$ $$V_s-2I_s = V_0$$

$\therefore$ From (2), $$8I_s = (V_s-2I_s)-\frac{V_s}{2}$$

$$= \frac{V_s}{2}-2I_s$$

or, $$10I_s = \frac{V_s}{2}$$

$\therefore$ $$\frac{V_s}{I_s} = \mathbf{20\ \Omega}$$

M20.201

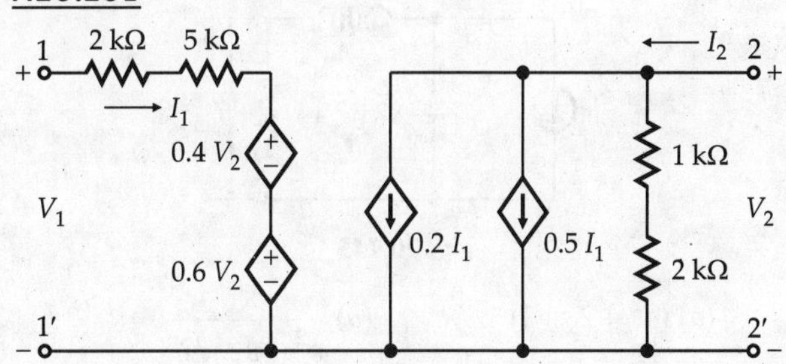

Fig. 20.244

The network shown in Fig. 20.244 is

(*a*) *Reciprocal and symmetrical*

(*b*) *Reciprocal but not symmetrical*

(*c*) *Symmetrical but not reciprocal*

(*d*) *Neither reciprocal nor symmetrical*

Solution. At input port loop,

$$V_1 = (2+5)\times 10^3 .\, I_1 + (0.4+0.6)V_2$$

or, $$V_1 = 7\times 10^3 I_1 + V_2 \quad \text{...(1)}$$

Also at the output port,

$$I_2 = (0.2+0.5)I_1 + \frac{V_2}{(1+2)10^3}$$

or, $$I_2 = 0.7I_1 + \frac{1}{3}V_2\times 10^{-3} \quad \text{...(2)}$$

Comparing with h-parameter network equations

$$V_1 = h_{11} I_1 + h_{12} V_2$$

$$I_2 = h_{21} I_1 + h_{22} V_2, \text{ we get}$$

$$h_{11} = 7 \times 10^3 \Omega \;;\; h_{12} = 1$$

$$h_{21} = 0.7 \;;\quad h_{22} = \frac{1}{3} \times 10^{-3} \text{ s}$$

We see, $h_{12} \neq h_{21}$

and hence the network is not reciprocal.

Also, $h_{11}h_{22} - h_{12}h_{21} = 7 \times 10^3 \times \frac{1}{3} \times 10^{-3} - 1 \times 0.7$

$$= \frac{7}{3} - 0.7 = 1.63$$

i.e., $h_{11}h_{22} - h_{12}h_{21} \neq 1$

∴ Circuit is not symmetrical.

Option (*d*) is correct.

M20.202 *In the circuit shown in Fig. 20.245, the transfer impedance* $[Z_t(s)]$ *is given by*

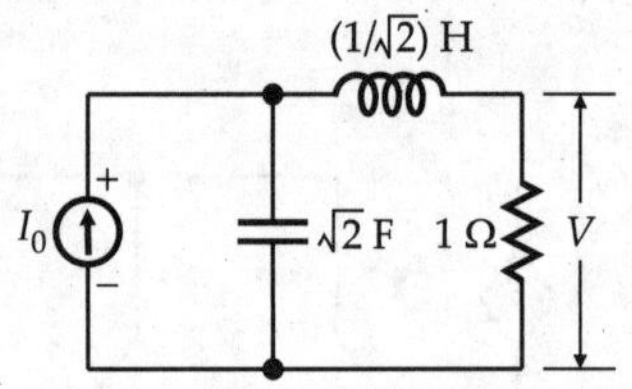

Fig. 20.245

(*a*) $(s^2 + 2s + 1)$ (*b*) $\frac{1}{s^2 + s + \sqrt{2}}$

(*c*) $(s^2 + \sqrt{2}s + \sqrt{2})$ (*d*) $\frac{1}{s^2 + \sqrt{2}s + 1}$

Solution. Let us transfer the given circuit in s-domain (Fig. 20.246).

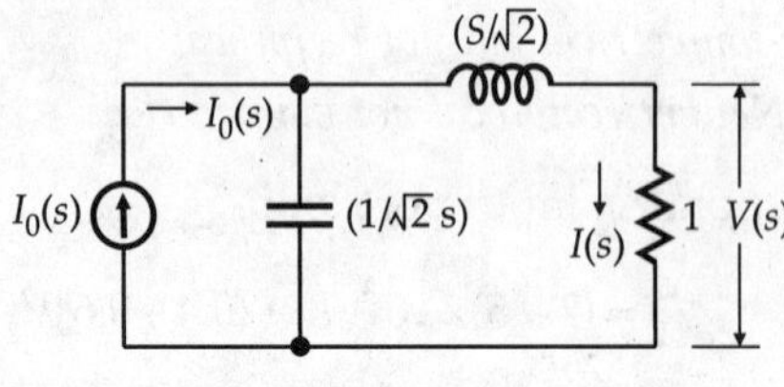

Fig. 20.246

Here, $V(s) = I(s) \times 1 = I(s)$

Also $I(s) = \dfrac{\frac{1}{\sqrt{2}s}}{\frac{1}{\sqrt{2}s} + \frac{s}{\sqrt{2}} + 1} \times I_0(s)$

[Using current division formulae]

$$\therefore \quad \frac{I(s)}{I_0(s)} = \frac{\frac{1}{\sqrt{2}s}}{\frac{1}{\sqrt{2}s} + \frac{s}{\sqrt{2}} + 1} = \frac{1}{1 + s^2 + \sqrt{2}s} \quad ...(i)$$

or, $$\frac{V(s)}{I_0(s)} = \frac{\mathbf{1}}{\mathbf{s^2 + \sqrt{2}s + 1}} = \mathbf{Z_t\,(s)}$$

[Replacing $I(s)$ by $V(s)$ as $V(s) = I(s)$]

∴ **Option (*d*) is correct.**

M20.203 *The current transfer function* $\frac{I_2(s)}{I_1(s)}$ *of the given network is given by*

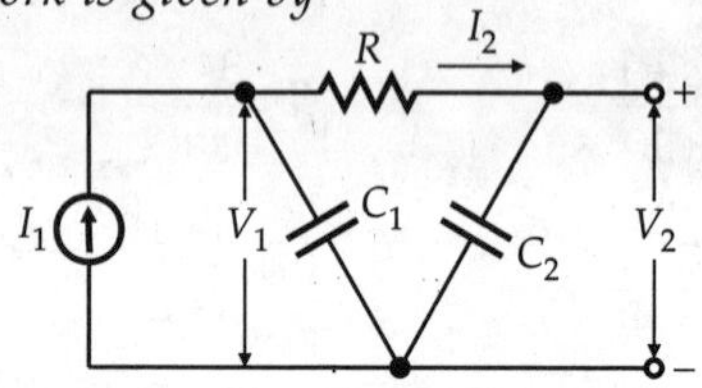

$R = 1\text{ k}\Omega \,;\, C_1 = C_2 = 1 \text{ mF}$

Fig. 20.247

(*a*) $\frac{1}{s^2 + s + 10^{-3}}$ (*b*) $\frac{1}{s+2}$

(*c*) $\frac{10^{-3}s}{10^{-3}s^2 + 10s + 10}$ (*d*) $(s^2 + s + 10^{-3})$

Solution. Let us redraw the circuit in s-domain

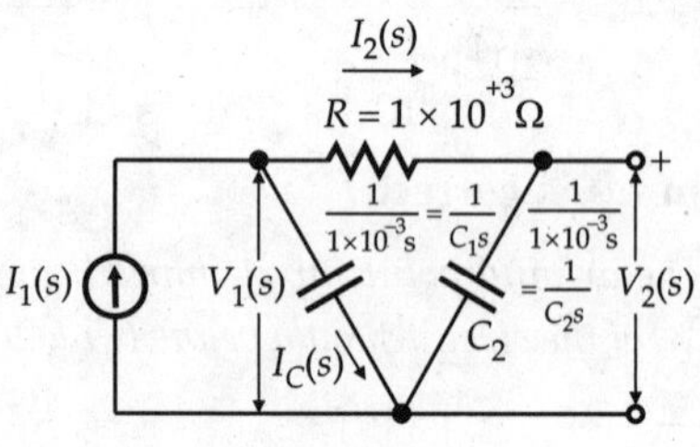

Fig. 20.248

$$I_1(s) = I_c(s) + I_2(s) = V_1(s)[Y_c(s) + Y_2(s)]$$

$$\therefore \quad V_1(s) = \frac{I_1(s)}{Y_c(s) + Y_2(s)}$$

Also, $I_2(s) = Y_2(s)\,V_1(s) = Y_2(s)\dfrac{I_1(s)}{Y_c(s) + Y_2(s)}$

$$\therefore \quad \frac{I_2(s)}{I_1(s)} = \frac{Y_2(s)}{Y_c(s) + Y_2(s)}$$

Here, $Y_c(s) = C_1 s = 1 \times 10^{-3}$ s

$$Y_2(s) = \frac{C_2 s}{RC_2 s + 1} = \frac{10^{-3}\text{s}}{\text{s}+1}$$

$$\therefore \quad \frac{I_2(s)}{I_1(s)} = \frac{(10^{-3}\text{s})/(\text{s}+1)}{10^{-3}\text{s} + \frac{10^{-3}\text{s}}{\text{s}+1}} = \frac{\mathbf{1}}{\mathbf{s+2}}$$

Option (*b*) in correct.

M20.204 *The elemental values of the circuit are shown in Fig. 20.249. The input impedance for s = j1 is given by*

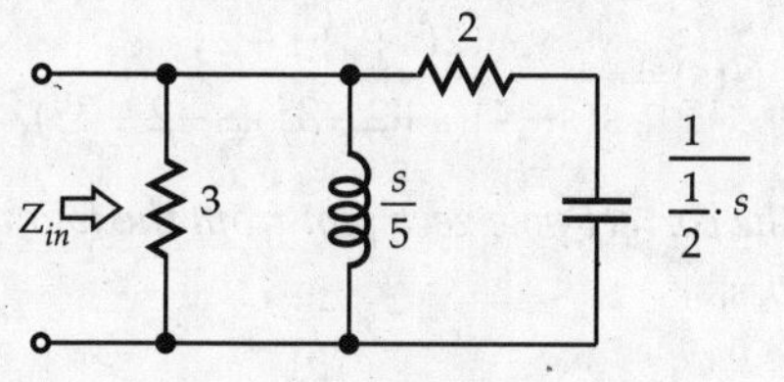

Fig. 20.249

(*a*) $\left(\dfrac{3(1-j)}{25-j30}\right)$ (*b*) $\left(\dfrac{j3+2}{-37+j32}\right)$

(*c*) $\left(\dfrac{6+j6)}{25+j32}\right)$ (*d*) $\left(\dfrac{3+j2}{25+j30}\right)$

SOLUTION. Let

$$Z_1(s)=\frac{3\times\frac{s}{5}}{3+\frac{s}{5}};\quad Z_2(s)=2;\quad Z_3(s)=\frac{2}{s}$$

$$\therefore\quad Z_{in}(s)=\frac{Z_1(s)[Z_2(s)+Z_3(s)]}{Z_1(s)+Z_2(s)+Z_3(s)}$$

$$=\frac{3s}{s+15}\cdot\frac{2+\frac{2}{s}}{\frac{3s}{s+15}+2+\frac{2}{s}}$$

$$=\frac{3(2s+2)}{5s^2+32s+30}$$

Since s = j1, hence we have

$$Z_{in}(s)=\frac{6(s+1)}{5\times(j1)^2+32\times j1+30}$$

$$=\frac{6+j6}{25+j32}$$

i.e., $$Z_{in}(s)=\frac{6+j6}{25+j32}$$

Option (*c*) is correct.

M20.205 *In the circuit shown in Fig. 20.250, the transfer function is given by*

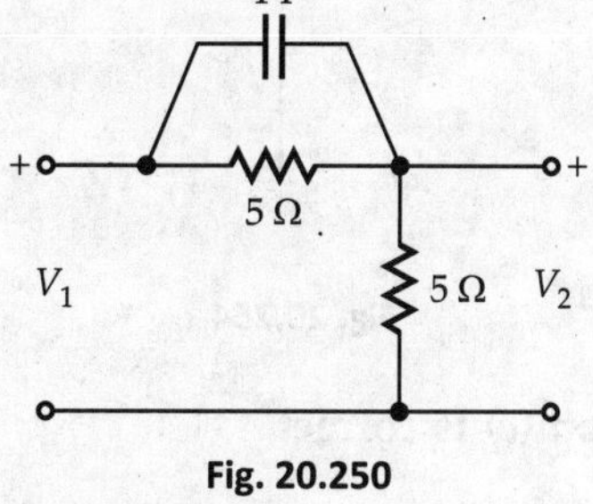

Fig. 20.250

(*a*) $(s+0.3)(s+0.4)$ (*b*) $(s+0.2)(s+0.3)$

(*c*) $\dfrac{s}{(s+0.2)(s+0.4)}$ (*d*) $\dfrac{s+0.2}{s+0.4}$

SOLUTION. Let us redraw the given circuit as shown in Fig. 20.251.

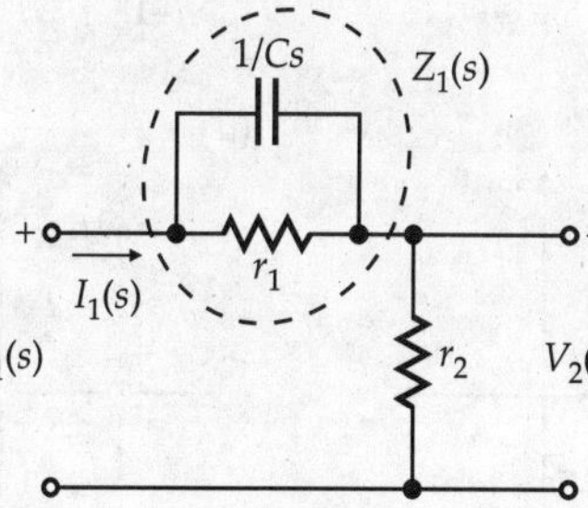

Fig. 20.251

$$Z_1(s)=\frac{1}{Cs+\frac{1}{r_1}}=\frac{r_1}{r_1Cs+1}$$

However, $$V_1(s)=I_1(s)[Z_1(s)+r_2]$$

and $$V_2(s)=I_1(s).r_2$$

$$\therefore\quad \frac{V_2(s)}{V_1(s)}=\frac{r_2}{Z_1(s)+r_2}=\frac{r_2}{\frac{r_1}{r_1Cs+1}+r_2}$$

$$=\frac{r_1r_2Cs+r_2}{r_1r_2Cs+r_1+r_2}$$

$$=\frac{5\times5\times1s+5}{5\times5\times1\times s+5+5}$$

$$=\frac{25s+5}{25s+10}=\frac{s+\left(\frac{1}{5}\right)}{s+0.4}=\frac{\mathbf{s+0.2}}{\mathbf{s+0.4}}$$

Option (*d*) is correct.

M20.206 *Which of the following pole-zero diagram of the driving point impedance on s-plane is applicable for the network shown in Fig. 20.252 ?*

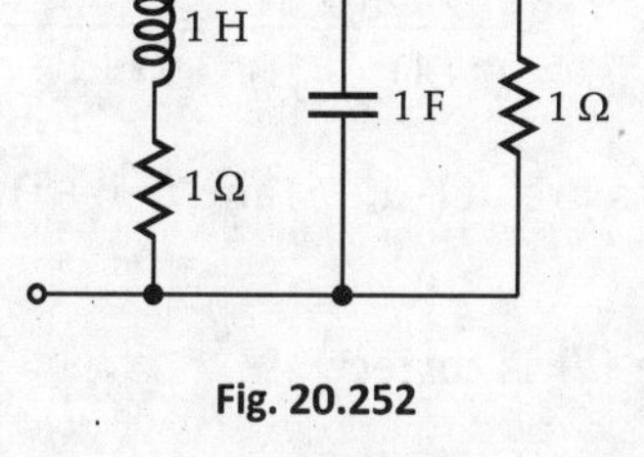

Fig. 20.252

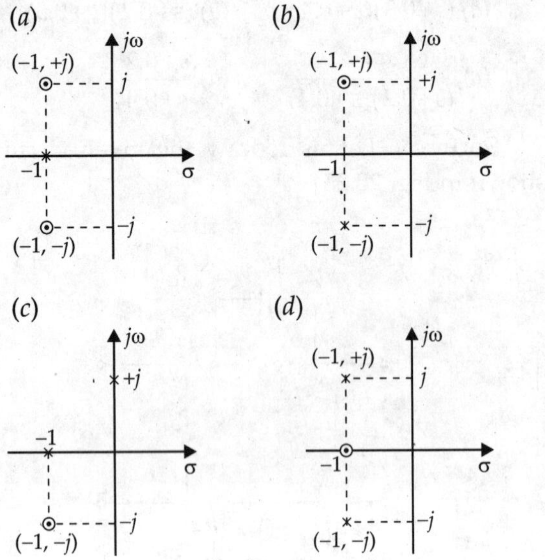

Solution. In the s-domain circuit of given diagram there are three parallel branches (Fig. 20.253)

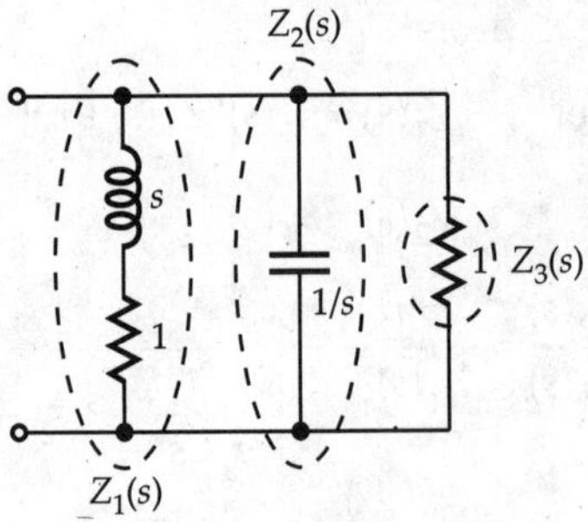

Fig. 20.253

Here $Z_1(s) = s+1$

$$Z_2(s) = \frac{1}{s}$$

$$Z_3(s) = 1$$

$$Y(s) = Y_1(s) + Y_2(s) + Y_3(s)$$

$$= \frac{1}{s+1} + s + 1 = \frac{s^2+2s+2}{s+1}$$

$$\therefore \quad Z(s) = \frac{1}{Y(s)} = \frac{s+1}{s^2+2s+2}$$

$$= \frac{s+1}{(s+1)^2 - (j1)^2} = \frac{s+1}{(s+1+j)(s+1-j)}$$

$\therefore$ Poles are at $(-1, -j)$ and $(-1, +j)$ while zero at –1.

Option (*d*) is correct.

M20.207 *A transfer function is given by the following expression :*

$$G(s) = \frac{2(s+1)(s+2)}{s(s+4)(s+2-3j)(s+2+3j)}$$

Identify the correct pole zero plot from the following four alternatives.

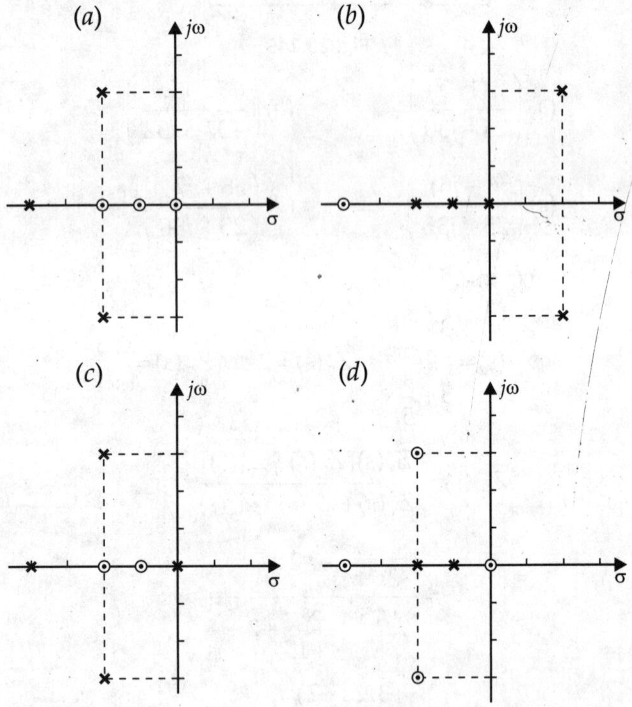

Solution. Gain factor = 2

Zeros : $s = -1, s = -2$

Poles : $s = 0, -4, (-2+j3), (-2-j3)$

The pole zero plot is shown in Fig. 20.254.

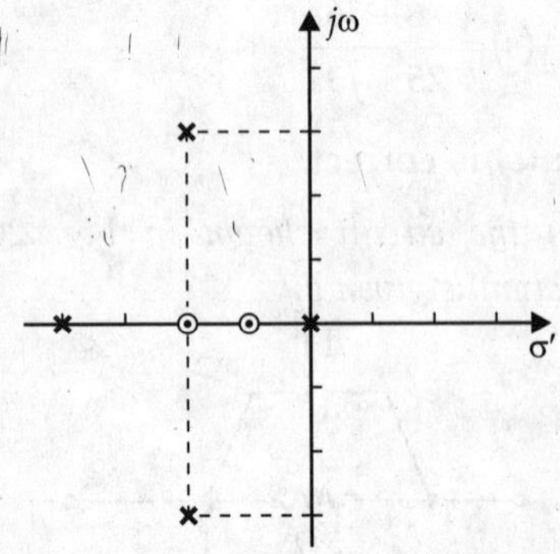

Fig. 20.254

$\therefore$ **Option (*c*) is correct.**

M20.208 *Three mutually inductive coils are connected in series on a common core and the dotted equivalent circuit is shown in Fig. 20.255 with the self and mutual inductive reactances marked in the figure. The equivalent inductive reactance is ______ Ω.*

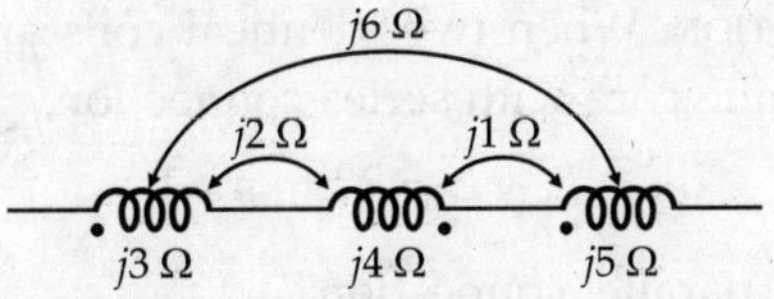

Fig. 20.255

Solution. Z_{eq} (equivalent inductive reactance)

$$X_{L_1}+X_{L_2}+X_{L_3}-2X_{M_{12}}+2X_{M_{13}}-2X_{M_{23}}$$
$$=j3+j4+j5-j2\times 2+j6\times 2-j1\times 2$$
$$=j12-j4+j12-j2=\mathbf{j18\ \Omega}.$$

M20.209 *In Fig. 20.256, T_1, T_2 and T_3 are number of turns of primary and secondary windings of an ideal transformer. If $I_2=10\angle 30°\ A$; $I_3=20\angle -60°\ A$, what is the value of I_1 ?*

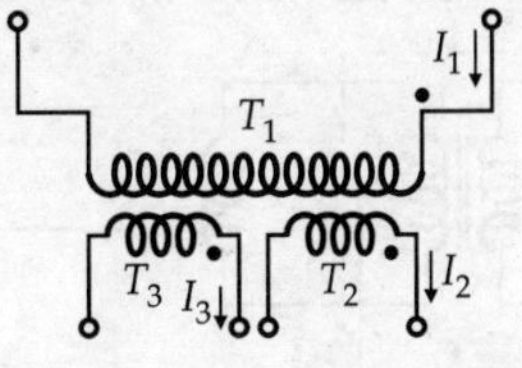

$[T_1=50;\ T_2=30;\ T_3=20]$

Fig. 20.256

Solution. A transformer balances the ampere turns.

$$\therefore \quad T_1I_1-T_2I_2-T_3I_3=0$$

or, $$50I_1=30\times 10\angle 30°+20\times 20\angle -60°$$
$$=300(\cos 30°+j\sin 30°)+400(\cos 60°-j\sin 60°)$$
$$=(300\times 0.866+j300\times 0.5)+(400\times 0.5-j400\times 0.866)$$
$$=259.8+j150+200-j346.4$$
$$=(459.8-j196.4)$$

$$\therefore \quad I_1=\mathbf{(9.196-j3.928)\ A.}$$

M20.210 *The effective inductance of the circuit across the terminals A, B in the figure shown below (Fig. 20.257) is*

(*a*) 9 H
(*b*) 21 H
(*c*) 11 H
(*d*) 6 H

[GATE 1998]

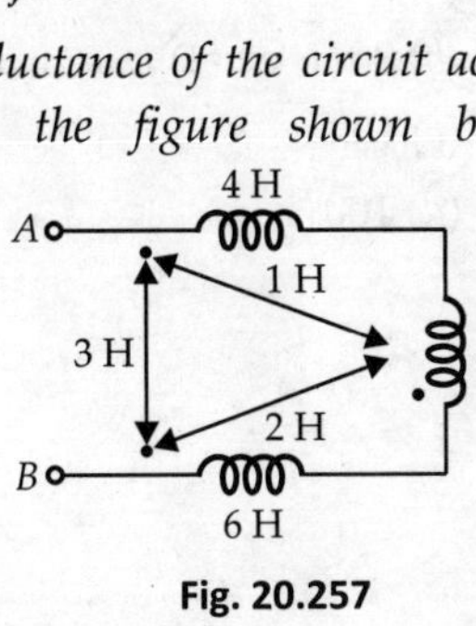

Fig. 20.257

Solution.

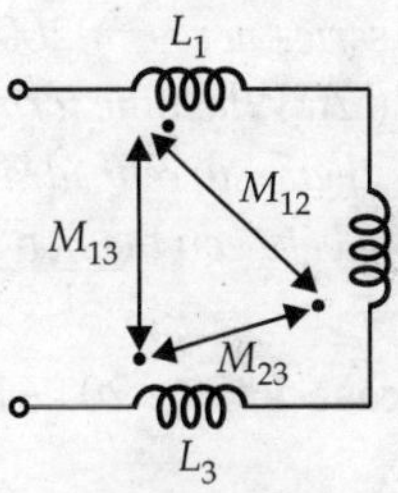

Fig. 20.258

$$L_{eq}=L_1+L_2+L_3-2M_{12}+2M_{23}-2M_{13}$$

(See Fig. 20.258)

$$=4+5+6-(2\times 1)+(2\times 2)-(2\times 3)=\mathbf{11\ H}$$

Option (*c*) is correct.

M20.211 *Given two coupled inductors L_1 and L_2, their mutual inductance M satisfies* **[GATE 2001]**

(*a*) $M=\sqrt{L_1^2+L_2^2}$ (*b*) $M>\frac{L_1+L_2}{2}$

(*c*) $M>\sqrt{L_1L_2}$ (*d*) $M\le\sqrt{L_1L_2}$

Solution. $M=K\sqrt{L_1L_2}$, K is coefficient of coupling

$$\therefore \quad M\le\sqrt{L_1L_2} \quad [\because\ 0<K<1]$$

Option (*d*) is correct.

M20.212 *The equivalent inductance seen at terminals A – B in Fig. 20.259 ______ H.* **[GATE 1992]**

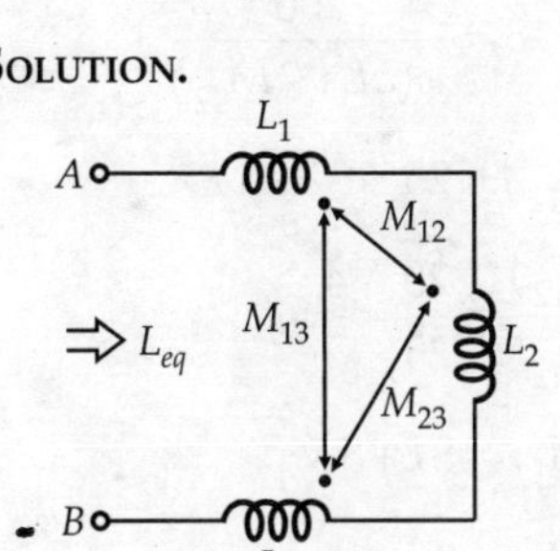

Fig. 20.259

Solution.

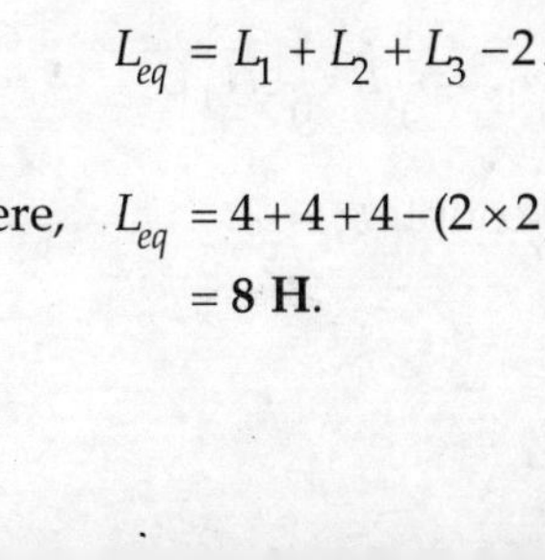

Fig. 20.260

$$L_{eq}=L_1+L_2+L_3-2M_{12}+2M_{23}-2M_{13}$$

(see Fig. 20.260)

Here, $$L_{eq}=4+4+4-(2\times 2)+(2\times 1)-(2\times 1)$$
$$=\mathbf{8\ H.}$$

CHAPTER 20

M20.213 *Two identical coils of negligible resistance when connected in series across a 200 V, 50 Hz source draws a current of 10 A. When the terminals of one of the coils are reversed, then current drawn is 8 A. The coefficient of coupling between the two coils is ______.*

[GATE 1997]

Solution. In **case-I** (Fig. 20.261), let the circuit current be I_1 amps.

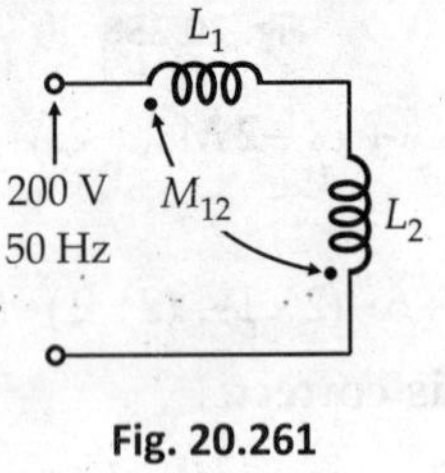

Fig. 20.261

$$|I_1| = \frac{V}{\omega(L_1 + L_2 - 2M_{12})}$$

or, $$10 = \frac{200}{\omega(2L - 2M_{12})} \qquad [\because L_1 = L_2 = L]$$

or, $$\omega(2L - 2M_{12}) = 20 \qquad ...(1)$$

In **case-II** (Fig. 20.262), let the circuit current be I_2 amps.

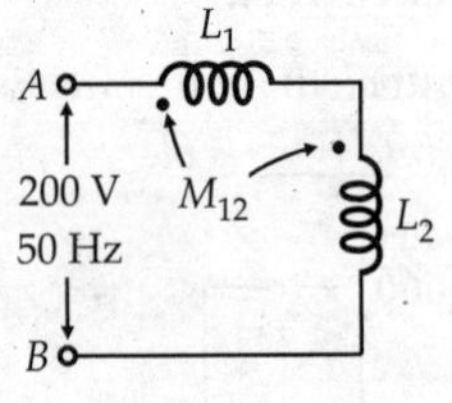

Fig. 20.262

$$|I_2| = \frac{V}{\omega(L_1 + L_2 + 2M_{12})}$$

or, $$8 = \frac{200}{\omega(2L + 2M_{12})}$$

$\therefore$ $$\omega(2L + 2M_{12}) = 25 \qquad ...(2)$$

$\therefore$ $$\frac{\omega(2L - 2M_{12})}{\omega(2L + 2M_{12})} = \frac{20}{25} = \frac{4}{5}$$

or, $$10L - 10M_{12} = 8L + 8M_{12}$$

or, $$18M_{12} = 2L$$

i.e., $$M_{12} = \frac{1}{9}L = \frac{1}{9}\sqrt{L_1 L_2}$$

$\therefore$ Coefficient of coupling $= \mathbf{\frac{1}{9}}$.

M20.214 *Two identical coils each having inductance L are placed together on the same core. If an overall inductance of (aL) is obtained by interconnecting these two coils, the minimum value of (a) is ______.*

[GATE 2015]

Solution. When two identical coils are placed on the same core with series connection,

$$L_{eq} = L_1 + L_2 = 2L; \quad a = 2.$$

With parallel connection,

$$L_{eq} = \frac{L_1 L_2}{L_1 + L_2} = \frac{L^2}{2L} = \frac{L}{2}; \quad a = 0.5.$$

Since L_1 and L_2 are of identical inductance values hence for differential connections,

$$L_{eq} = 0$$

Hence the minimum value of 'a' is **zero.**

M20.215 *If an ideal transformer has an inductive load element at port 2 as shown in the figure below (Fig. 20.263), the equivalent inductance at port 1 is*

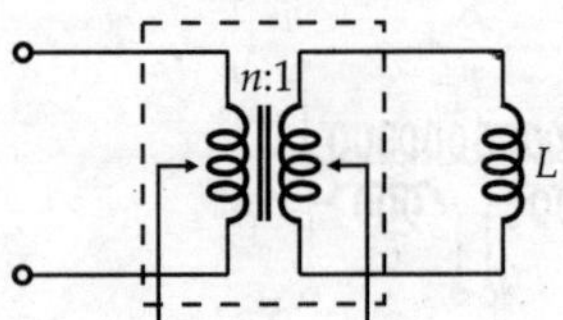

Fig. 20.263

(a) nL *(b)* n^2L *(c)* $\frac{n}{L}$ *(d)* $\frac{n^2}{L}$

[GATE 2016]

Solution. When L is transferred to primary,

$$L' = \mathbf{n^2 L}$$

Hence option (*b*) is correct.

M20.216 *A coupled coil is shown in Fig. 20.264, polarities marked. A voltage* $v_0(t) = 30 \sin t$ *is applied at the input side. The output is shorted. The short-circuit current is given by*

(a) $30 \sin t$

(b) $30(1 - \sin t)$

(c) $100 \cos t$

(d) $100(1 - \cos t)$

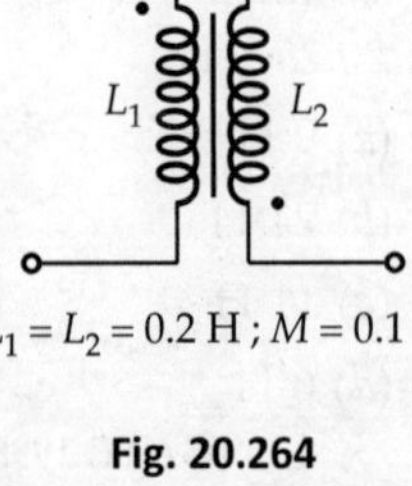

$[L_1 = L_2 = 0.2\text{ H}; M = 0.1\text{ H}]$

Fig. 20.264

Solution. Figure 20.265 represents the given network with voltage source applied at input terminal (1 – 1′) of the coupled coils and short-circuit applied at the output terminals (2 – 2′).

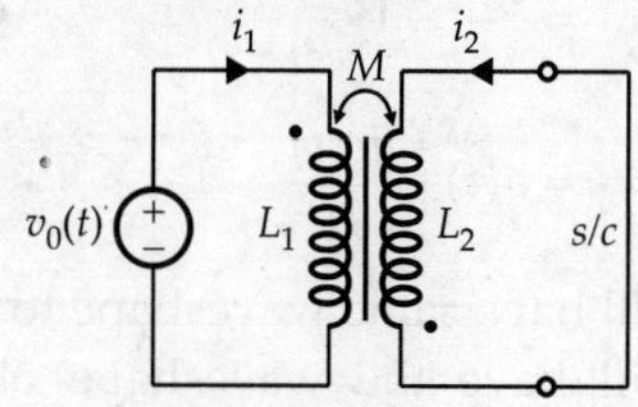

$[i_2 \equiv I_{s/c}]$

Fig. 20.265

The loop equations are :

$$V_0 = L_1 \frac{di_1}{dt} - M\frac{di_2}{dt} \qquad ...(1)$$

$$V_2(\text{output voltage}) = 0 = -M\frac{di_1}{dt} + L_2\frac{di_2}{dt} \qquad ...(2)$$

Substituting the values of respective quantities, for equations (1) and (2),

$$30 \sin t = 0.2\frac{di_1}{dt} - 0.1\frac{di_2}{dt} \qquad ...(1A)$$

$$0 = -0.1\frac{di_1}{dt} + 0.2\frac{di_2}{dt} \qquad ...(2A)$$

From equation (2A),

$$\frac{di_1}{dt} = 2\frac{di_2}{dt} \qquad ...(3)$$

Using equation (3) in (1A), we get

$$30 \sin t = 0.4\frac{di_2}{dt} - 0.1\frac{di_2}{dt}$$

$$\therefore \quad \frac{di_2}{dt} = 100 \sin t$$

or, $$\int_0^t \frac{di_2}{dt}.dt = \int_0^t 100 \sin t\, dt$$

or, $$i_2(t) = [-100 \cos t]_0^t$$

or, $$\mathbf{i_2(t) = 100\,(1 - \cos t)}$$

Option (*d*) is correct.

M20.217 *The supply to an ideal transformer is switched off so that the flux ϕ decreases following the relation*

$$\phi = 2e^{-t}\, Wb \text{ for } t > 0.$$

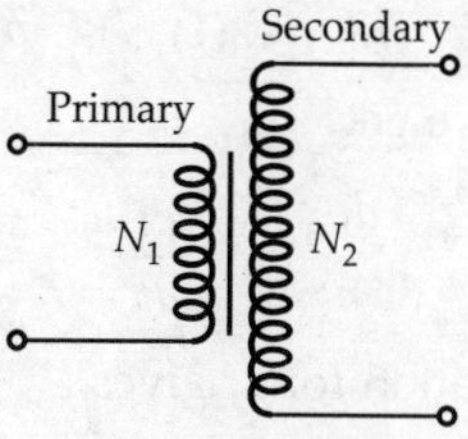

$[N_1 = 100\ ;\ N_2 = 200]$

Fig. 20.266

The voltage magnitude included (V_2) in the secondary (Fig. 20.266) is

(*a*) $100\, e^{-t}$ Volts (*b*) $400\, e^{-2t}$ Volts
(*c*) $400\, e^{-t}$ Volts (*d*) $800\, e^{-t/2}$ Volts

Solution. Let ψ_p and ψ_s be the flux linkages in primary and secondary of the ideal transformer.

$$\therefore \quad \psi_p = 100 \times 2e^{-t}\,\text{Wb turns} \quad [\because \psi = N_1\psi]$$

and $$\psi_s = 200 \times 2e^{-t}\,\text{Wb turns}$$

$$\therefore \quad |V_2| = \left| N_2 \frac{d\phi}{dt} \right| = 200 \times \frac{d}{dt}[2e^{-t}]$$

$$= \mathbf{400\, e^{-t}\ Volts}$$

Option (*c*) is correct.

M20.218 *Figure 20.267 represents a gyrator network which is described by the following equations :*

$$v = ri_0\ ;\ v_0 = -ri$$

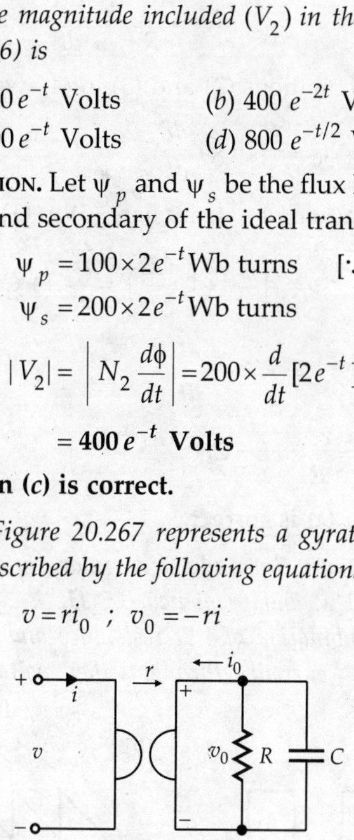

Fig. 20.267

Which of the following figures represent the two element equivalent network ?

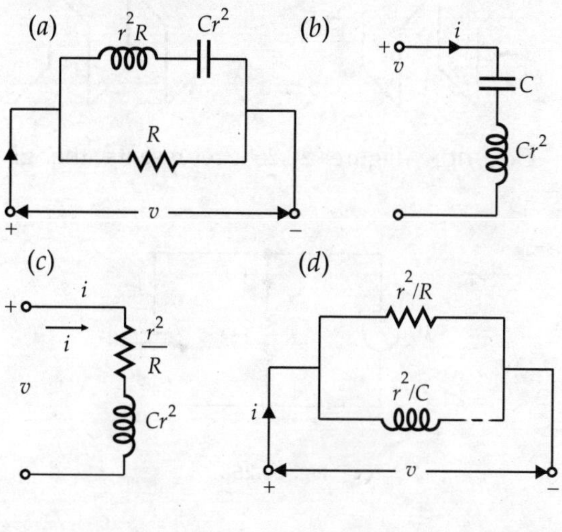

Solution. $v = ri_0$ ...(1) ; $v_0 = -ri$ ...(2)

From (2), we get

$$\frac{dv_0}{dt} = -r\frac{di}{dt} \quad ...(3)$$

Nodal equation for i_2 gives

$$i + \frac{v_0}{R} + C\frac{dv_0}{dt} = 0$$

or,
$$i = -\frac{v_0}{R} - C\frac{dv_0}{dt} \quad ...(4)$$

Using equations (2) and (3) in (4), we get

$$i_0 = \frac{r}{R}i + Cr\frac{di}{dt} \quad ...(5)$$

Substitution of i_0 from eqn. (5) in (1) yields

$$v = r\left[\frac{r}{R}i + Cr\frac{di}{dt}\right] = \frac{r^2}{R}.i + Cr^2\frac{di}{dt}$$

$$= R'i + L\frac{di}{dt},$$

where $R' = \frac{r^2}{R}$; $L = Cr^2$.

Option (c) is correct.

M20.219 *When a periodic triangular voltage of peak amplitude 1 V and frequency 0.5 Hz is applied to a parallel combination of 1 Ω resistance and 1 F capacitance, the current through the voltage source waveform is* **[GATE 1998]**

(*a*)

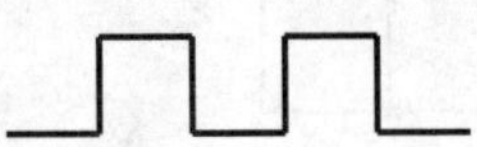

(*b*)

(*c*)

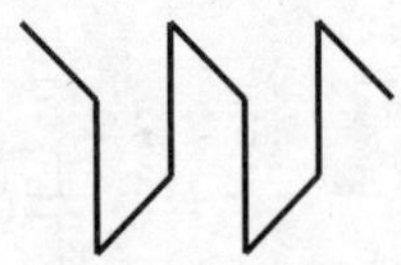

(*d*)

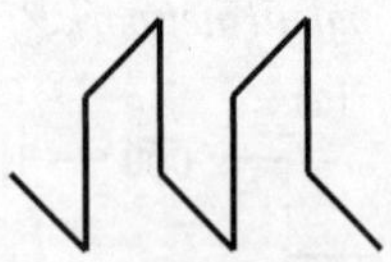

Solution. Figure 20.268 represents the given circuit.

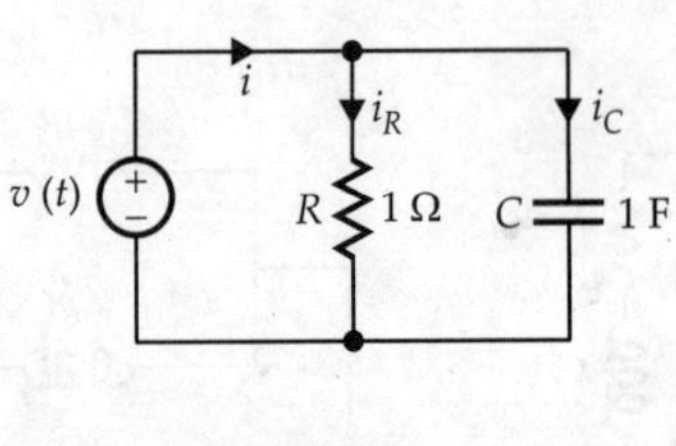

Fig. 20.268

Here, $i = i_R + i_C$

$$= \frac{v(t)}{R} + C\frac{dv(t)}{dt}$$

$$= \frac{v(t)}{1} + 1\frac{dv(t)}{dt}$$

$$= v(t) + \frac{dv(t)}{dt}$$

$\therefore$ i_R will have same waveshape to that of $v(t)$ while i_C will have the waveshape obtained by differentiation of $v(t)$ waveshape with respect to time. Since $v(t)$ is a triangular wave hence $\frac{dv(t)}{dt}$ *i.e.*, i_C will be a square symmetrical wave across the *x*-axis. Both the waves are drawn in Fig. 20.269.

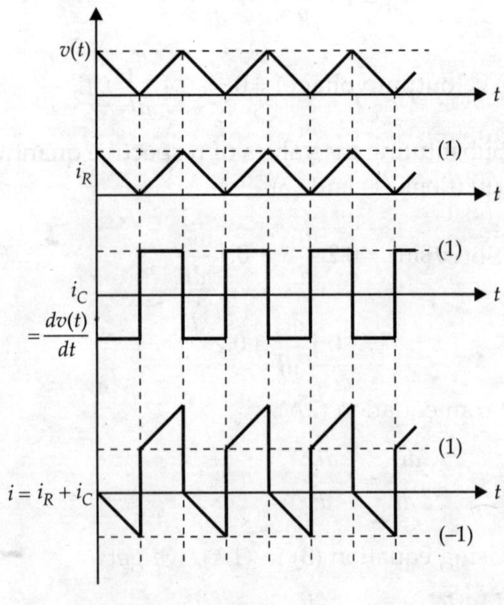

Fig. 20.269

Option (d) is correct.

M20.220 *The impedance seen by the source in the circuit in the figure (Fig. 20.270) is given by* **[GATE 2000]**

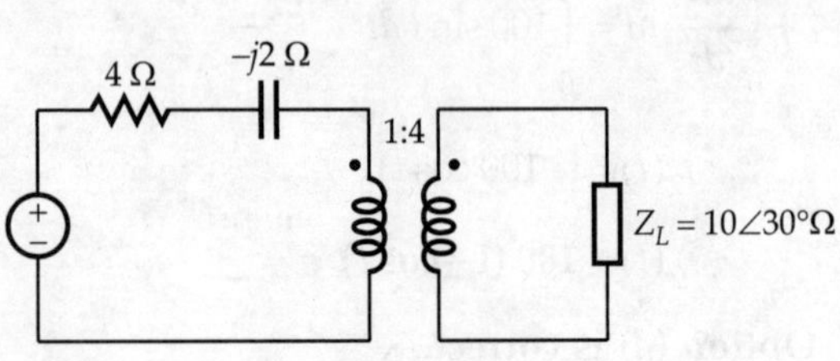

Fig. 20.270

(*a*) $(0.54 + j0.313)\ \Omega$ (*b*) $(4 - j2)\ \Omega$

(*c*) $(4.54 - j1.69)\ \Omega$ (*d*) $(4 + j2)\ \Omega$

Solution. Z_L is transferred to the primary side of the coupled coils.

$$Z'_L = \left(\frac{1}{4}\right)^2 Z_L = \frac{1}{16} \times 10 \angle 30°$$

$$= \frac{10}{16}(\cos 30° + j \sin 30°)$$

$$= (0.5412 + j0.3125)$$

$\therefore$ Z_{in}, the input impedance looking through primary is

$$Z = (4 - j2) + (0.5412 + j0.3125)$$

$$= 4.5412 - j1.6875$$

$$\simeq \mathbf{(4.54 - j1.69)\Omega}$$

Option (c) is correct.

M20.221 *Two coupled coils have self-inductances $L_1 = 50\, mH$ and $L_2 = 100\, mH$ and the coefficient of coupling $K = 0.5$. If i_1, the current in coil–1, be $i_1 = 10 \sin 314\, t\ A$, the induced voltage in coil–2 is*

(a) 11.11 *sin* 628 *t* (b) 11.11 *cos* 314 *t*

(c) 111 *sin* 314 *t* (d) 111 *cos* 314 *t*

Solution.

$$M = K\sqrt{L_1 L_2}$$

$$= 0.5\sqrt{50 \times 100} = 35.35 \text{ mH}$$

$$v_2 = M\frac{di_1}{dt}$$

$$= 35.35 \times 10^{-3}\frac{d}{dt}(10 \sin 314\, t)$$

$$= \mathbf{111 \cos 314\, t}$$

Option (a) is correct.

M20.222 *In a transformer, the primary current is I_1 ampere while the secondary current (I_2) is $10\angle -30°$ A (Fig. 20.271). The value of I_1 in Amp. is*

(a) $7.5 \angle -25°$ (b) $24.61 \angle 15.29°$

(c) $22.02 \angle -48.14°$ (d) $11.18 \angle 63.43°$

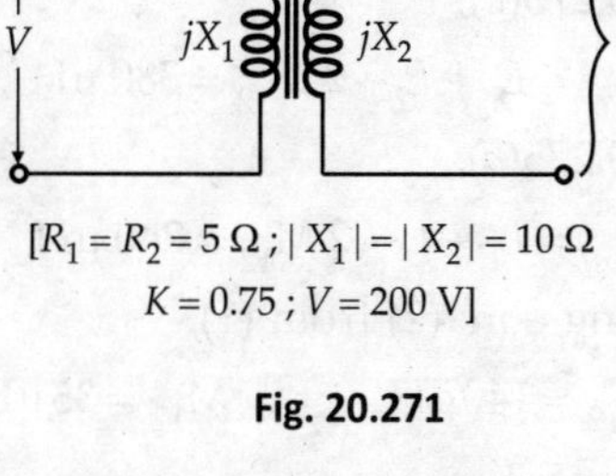

$[R_1 = R_2 = 5\,\Omega\,;\, |X_1| = |X_2| = 10\,\Omega$
$K = 0.75\,;\, V = 200$ V]

Fig. 20.271

Solution.

$$X_m = K\sqrt{X_1 X_2} = 0.75\sqrt{10 \times 10} = 7.5\,\Omega$$

In the primary loop,

$$(R + jX_1)I_1 - jX_m \cdot I_2 = V$$

or, $$(5 + j10)I_1 - j7.5 \times 10\angle -30° = 200 \angle 0°$$

or, $$I_1 = \frac{(200 + j0) + j75(\cos 30° - j \sin 30°)}{(5 + j10)}$$

$$= \frac{200 + j64.95 + 37.5}{11.18\angle 63.43°} = \frac{246.22\angle 15.29°}{11.18\angle 63.43°}$$

$$= \mathbf{22.02\angle -48.14°\ A}$$

Option (c) is correct.

M20.223 *In the circuit shown in the Fig. 20.272, it is found that the input ac voltage (v_i) and current (i) are in phase.*

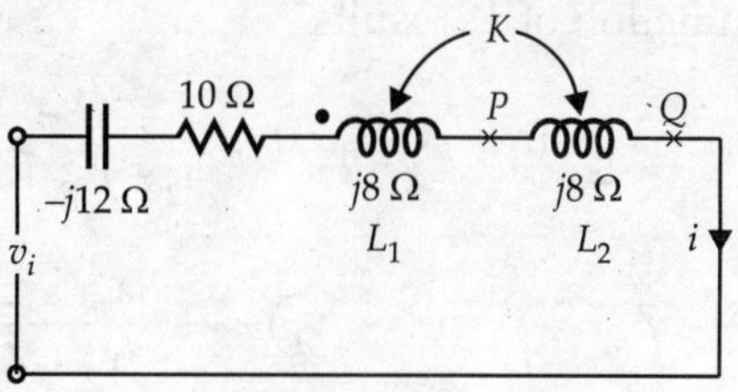

Fig. 20.272

The coupling coefficient is $K = \frac{M}{\sqrt{L_1 L_2}}$, where M is the mutual inductance between the two coils. The value of K and the dot polarity of the coil P-Q are :

[GATE 2002]

(a) *K* = 0.25 *and dot at P*

(b) *K* = 0.5 *and dot at P*

(c) *K* = 0.25 *and dot at Q*

(d) *K* = 0.5 *and dot at Q*

Solution. Input ac voltage (v_i) and current (i) will be in phase in a *LCR* circuit only when

$|X_C| = |X_L|$ *i.e.*, at resonance.

or, $$|-j12| = |j8 + j8 + 2K\sqrt{j8 \times j8}|$$

$$[\because \text{at } |X_L| = |X_C|\,;\ \underbrace{\omega . j8}_{j\omega L_1} + \underbrace{\omega . j8}_{j\omega L_2} + \underbrace{2K\sqrt{j8 \times j8}}_{j\omega M_{L_1 L_2}} = \underbrace{|-j\omega 12|}_{-j\omega C}\ ]$$

i.e., $$12 = 8 + 8 + 16K$$

i.e., $$K = -0.25$$

Since *K* is –ve, coupling will be opposite.

$\therefore$ Dot will be at *Q*. **Option (c) is correct.**

M20.224 *In the transformer circuit shown in Fig. 20.273, find the input impedance from primary side.*

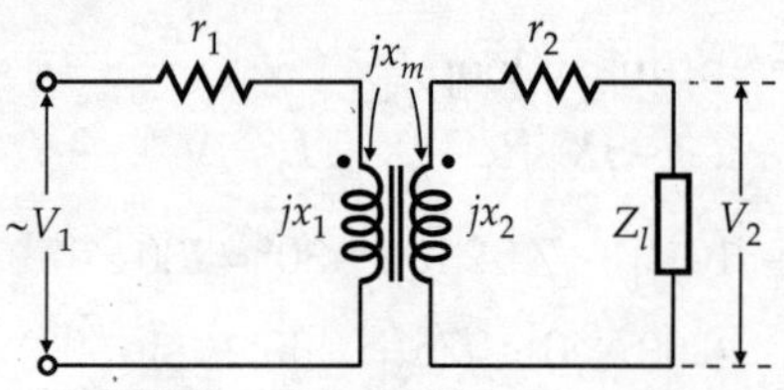

Fig. 20.273

Solution. The mesh equation for the left loop is given by

$$V_1 = (r_1 + jx_1)I_1 + jx_m I_2 \quad ...(1)$$

and that for the right side loop is

$$0 = (r_2 + jx_2 + Z_l)I_2 + jx_m I_1 \quad ...(2)$$

Elimination of I_2 results

$$V_1 = (r_1 + jx_1)I_1 + jx_m \frac{-jx_m}{r_2 + jx_2 + Z_l} . I_1$$

or, $$Z_{in} = \frac{V_1}{I_1} = (r_1 + jx_1) + \frac{x_m^2}{r_2 + jx_2 + Z_2}$$

The input impedance is thus given by

$$\boldsymbol{Z_{in} = (r_1 + jx_1) + \frac{x_m^2}{r_2 + jx_2 + Z_2}}.$$

M20.225 *The following arrangement (Fig. 20.274) consists of an ideal transformer and an attenuator which attenuates by a factor of 0.8. An ac voltage $V_{ab_1} = 10$ V is*

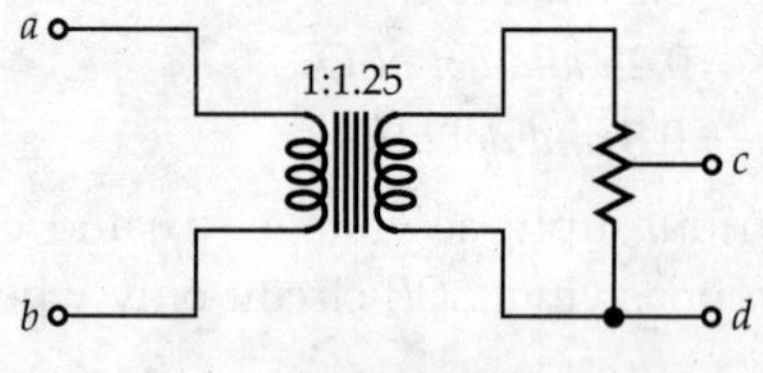

Fig. 20.274

applied across ab to get an open circuit voltage V_{cd_1} across cd. Next, an ac voltage $V_{cd_2} = 10$ V is applied across cd to get an open circuit voltage V_{ab_2} across ab. Then $\frac{V_{cd_1}}{V_{ab_1}}, \frac{V_{ab_2}}{V_{cd_2}}$ are respectively :

(a) $\frac{1.25}{10}$ and $\frac{8}{10}$ (b) $\frac{10}{10}$ and $\frac{8}{10}$

(c) $\frac{10}{10}$ and $\frac{10}{10}$ (d) $\frac{8}{10}$ and $\frac{8}{10}$

Solution.

$$V_{cd_1} = V_2 \times 0.8$$
$$= 10 \times 1.25 \times 0.8$$
$$= 10 \text{ V} \quad \left[\because \frac{V_1}{V_2} = \frac{N_1}{N_2}; \text{ Here, } \frac{V_{ab_1}}{V_2} = \frac{1}{1.25}; \quad \therefore V_2 = V_{ab_1} \times 1.25;\right.$$

We assume V_2 to be the voltage across the transformer secondary]

In second case, 10 V is applied across *cd*.

$$\therefore \quad V_2 = 10 \text{ V } (= V_{cd_2})$$

$$\because \quad \frac{V_2}{V_{ab_2}} = \frac{1.25}{1.00},$$

Here, $$V_{ab_2} = V_2 \times \frac{1}{1.25} = \frac{10}{1.25} = 8 \text{ V}$$

Hence, $$\frac{V_{ab_1}}{V_{cd_1}} = \frac{\mathbf{10}}{\mathbf{10}} \quad \therefore \quad \frac{V_{ab_2}}{V_{cd_2}} = \frac{\mathbf{8}}{\mathbf{10}}.$$

Option (*b*) is correct.

M20.226 *Two identical coupled inductors are connected in series. The measured inductances for the two possible series connections are 380 μH and 240 μH. Their mutual inductance in μH is ______ .* **[GATE 2014]**

Solution. There are two possible series connections as shown below [Fig. 20.275(*a*) and Fig. 20.275(*b*)]

Here, Fig. 20.275(*a*) represents additive connection while Fig. 20.275(*b*) represents subtractive connection.

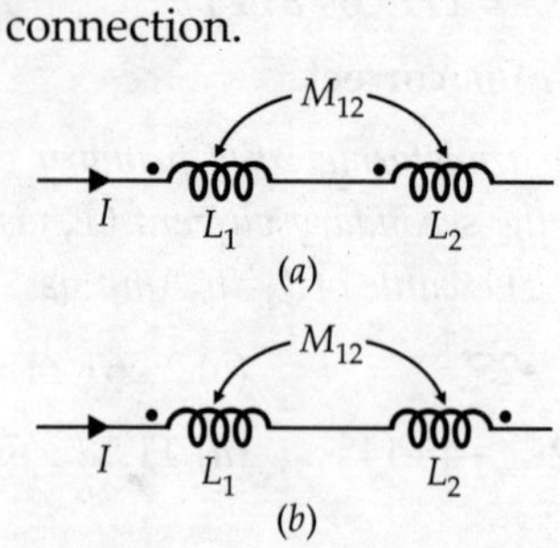

Fig. 20.275

In Fig. 20.275(*a*),

$$L_{eq} = L_1 + L_2 + 2M_{12} = 380 \text{ μH} \quad ...(1)$$

In Fig. 20.275(*b*),

$$L_{eq} = L_1 + L_2 - 2M_{12} = 240 \text{ μH} \quad ...(2)$$

Subtracting eqn. (2) from (1),

$$4M_{12} = 140 \text{ μH} \quad \therefore \quad M_{12} = \mathbf{35\,μH}$$

M20.227 *In the coupled coil circuit (Fig. 20.276); $V = 1V$ and the internal resistance $r = 1\ \Omega$, while load resistance $R_L = 1\ \Omega$.*

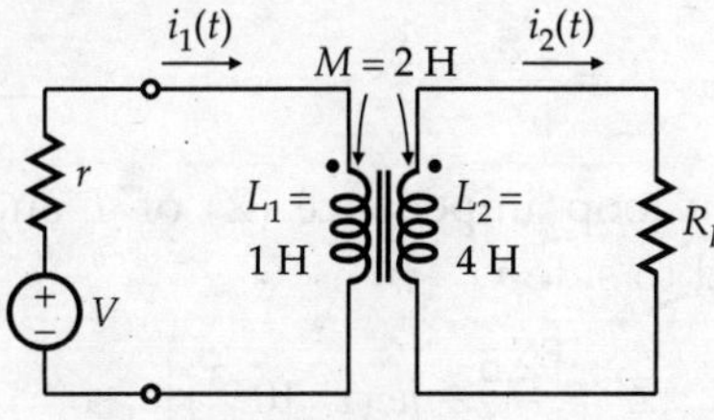

Fig. 20.276

Following switching of the circuit at $t = 0$, the value of $i_1(t)$ is obtained as

(*a*) $[1+0.5e^{2t}]$ (*b*) $[1-0.2e^{-0.2t}]$

(*c*) $[0.5e^{-0.2t}]$ (*d*) $[0.5-2e^{-0.2t}]$

Solution. Mesh equations at $t > 0$ are given as

$$I_1(s)[s+1]-2sI_2(s)=\frac{1}{s} \quad ...(1)$$

$$-I_1(s).2s+(4s+1)I_2(s)=0 \quad ...(2)$$

From (2), $I_2(s)=I_1(s)\dfrac{2s}{4s+1}$ ...(3)

Using (3) in (1),

$$I_1(s)(s+1)-2s\frac{2s}{4s+1}.I_1(s)=\frac{1}{s}$$

$$I_1(s)\times\left[s+1-\frac{4s^2}{4s+1}\right]=\frac{1}{s}$$

$$I_1(s)\left[\frac{(s+1)(4s+1)-4s^2}{4s+1}\right]=\frac{1}{s}$$

or, $$I_1(s)\left[\frac{5s+1}{4s+1}\right]=\frac{1}{s}$$

$\therefore$ $$I_1(s)=\frac{4s+1}{s(5s+1)}=\frac{1}{s}-\frac{0.2}{s+0.2}$$

i.e., $i_1(t) = \mathbf{(1-0.2e^{-0.2t})\ A}$

Option (*b*) correct.

M20.228 *What is $i_2(t)$ in Fig. 20.276 at $t = 0+$?*

(*a*) $0.4e^{-0.2t}$ (*b*) $-e^{0.4t}$

(*c*) $2e^{-0.2t}$ (*d*) $(1-e^{-0.2t})$

Solution. $I_2(s)=\dfrac{2}{5s+1}=\dfrac{0.4}{s+0.2}$

$$\left[\because I_2(s)=I_1(s)\frac{2s}{4s+1}=\frac{4s+1}{s(5s+1)}.\frac{2}{4s}=\frac{2}{5s+1}\right]$$

$\therefore$ $i_2(t) = \mathbf{0.4\ e^{-0.2t}}$

Option (*a*) is correct.

M20.229 *In Fig. 20.276, what is the voltage developed across L_2 at $t = 0.1$ s?*

(*a*) – 250 mV (*b*) 4 V

(*c*) – 0.2 V (*d*) – 3.14 V

Solution. $v_{L_2}=L\dfrac{di_2(t)}{dt}$; $i_2(t)=0.4\ e^{-0.2t}$

$\therefore$ $$v_{L_2}=4(0.4)(-0.2)e^{-0.2t}$$
$$=[-0.32e^{-0.2t}]\text{ volts}$$

At $t = 0.1$ s,

$$v_{L_2}(t)=-0.32\ e^{-0.2\times0.1}=-\mathbf{0.314\ Volt}$$

Option (*d*) is correct.

M20.230 *In the mutually coupled coil shown in Fig. 20.277, find mutual inductance L_m.*

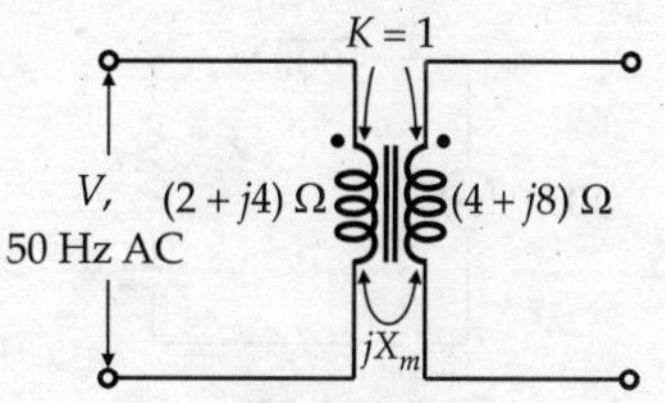

Fig. 20.277

(*a*) 10 mH (*b*) 20 mH

(*c*) 12 mH (*d*) 18 mH

Solution. $X_m = K\sqrt{X_1X_2} = 1\sqrt{4\times8} = 5.66\ \Omega$

Also, $X_m = 2\pi fL_m$

$\therefore$ $$L_m=\frac{X_m}{2\pi f}=\frac{5.66}{2\times3.14\times50}=\mathbf{18\ mH}$$

Option (*d*) is correct.

M20.231 *Two coils A and B are mutually inductive (Fig. 20.278). $I_1 = I_2 = (5 + j10)A$.*

If the input impedance is $(2 + j4)\Omega$, find the complex power drawn by the circuit if the supply voltage be $V_1(AC)$ 50 Hz.

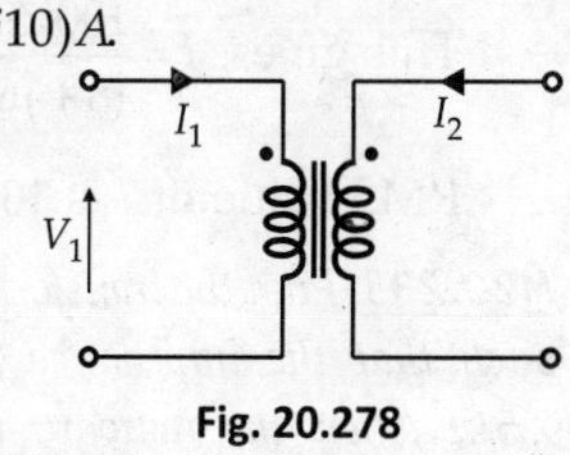

Fig. 20.278

Solution. $I_1 = I_2 = (5 + j10)$ A

$\therefore$ $$I_1^* = I_2^* = (5-j10) = 11.18\angle-\tan^{-1}2$$
$$= 11.18\ \angle-63.43°\text{ A}$$

$\therefore$ $$IZ = 11.18\angle-63.43°\times(2+j4)$$
$$= 11.18\times4.24\angle-63.43°+63.43°$$
$$= 47.4°\angle0°\text{ V}$$

Complex power $S = VI^*$

$$= 47.4\angle0°\times11.18\ \angle-63.43°$$
$$= \mathbf{(530\angle-63.43°)\ VA.}$$

M20.232 *The following Fig. 20.279 shows the connection of an ideal transformer with primary to secondary turns ratio 1 : 100. The applied primary voltage is 100 V(rms), 50 Hz, AC. The rms value of the current I, in ampere, is* **[GATE 2016]**

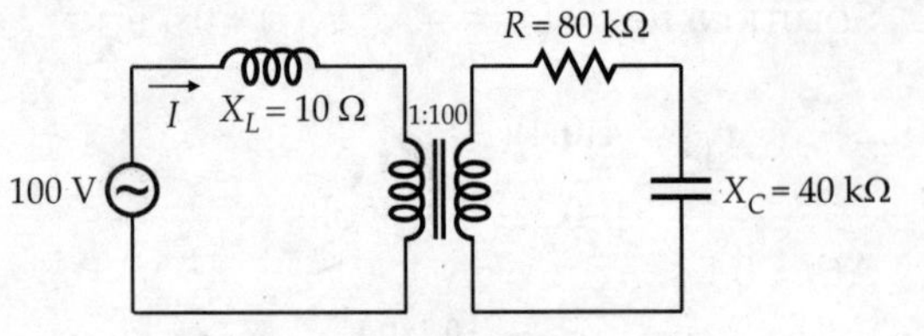

Fig. 20.279

Solution. Let us transfer secondary impedance elements to primary. Figure 20.280 represents the modified circuit.

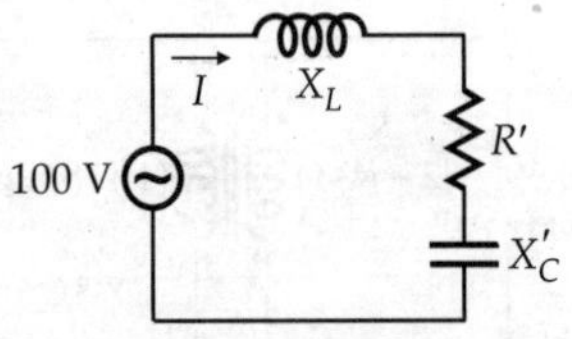

Fig. 20.280

$$|X_C'| = \frac{40\text{ k}\Omega}{100^2}$$

$$\therefore \quad X_C = -j\frac{40\times10^3}{100^2} = -j4\ \Omega$$

$$R' = \frac{80\times10^3}{100^2} = 8\ \Omega$$

∴ Impedance of the circuit

$$Z = 8 + j10 - j4 = (8 + j6)\ \Omega$$

This gives, $I = \dfrac{100\angle 0°}{(8+j6)}\text{ A} = 10\angle -36.86°\text{ A}$

RMS value of I is **10 A.**

M20.233 *Find the transformer ratios a and b (Fig. 20.281) such that the impedance (Z_{in}) is resistive and equals 2.5Ω when the network is excited with a sine wave voltage of angular frequency of 5000 rad/s.* **[GATE 2015]**

(a) $a = 0.5,\ b = 2.0$ (b) $a = 2.0,\ b = 0.5$

(c) $a = 1.0,\ b = 1.0$ (d) $a = 4.0,\ b = 0.5$

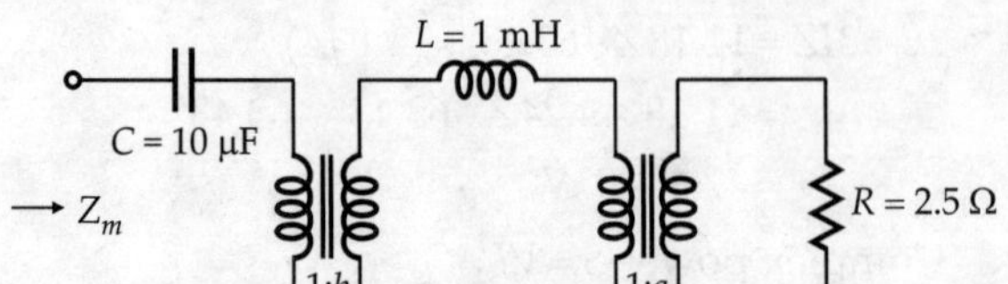

Fig. 20.281

Solution. Let the leftmost loop be x; the middle one be y and the rightmost loop be z.

When R is transferred to side y,

$$R' = \frac{2.5}{a^2}$$

Next y loop impedance (Z) of L and R' are transferred to side x.

$$Z' = \left[\frac{2.5}{a^2} + j\omega(1\times10^{-3})\right]$$

∴ Input impedance without considering C is given as

$$Z = \frac{Z'}{b^2} = \frac{1}{b^2}\left[\frac{2.5}{a^2} + j\omega(1\times10^{-3})\right]$$

$$= \left(\frac{2.5}{a^2b^2} + \frac{j\omega\times10^{-3}}{b^2}\right)$$

Considering the series connection of C with Z, the input impedance becomes

$$Z_{in} = \frac{2.5}{a^2b^2} + \frac{j\omega\times10^{-3}}{b^2} + \frac{1}{j\omega(10\times10^{-6})}$$

$$= \frac{2.5}{a^2b^2} + j\left[\frac{5000\times10^{-3}}{b^2} - \frac{1}{5000\times10\times10^{-6}}\right]$$

[∵ $\omega = 5000$ rad/s]

$$= \frac{2.5}{a^2b^2} + j\left[\frac{5}{b^2} - \frac{1}{5\times10^{-2}}\right]$$

From the given question,

$$Z_{in} = 2.5 \qquad \textit{i.e.,}\quad 2.5 = \frac{2.5}{a^2b^2},$$

equating real parts of the equation of Z_{in}

$$\therefore \quad a^2b^2 = 1$$

Also, for the imaginary part,

$$j\left[\frac{5}{b^2} - \frac{1}{5\times10^{-2}}\right] = 0$$

$$\therefore \quad \frac{5}{b^2} = \frac{1}{5\times10^{-2}}$$

i.e., $\quad b^2 = 0.25$

or, $\quad b = 0.5$

Substitution of b in equation $a^2b^2 = 1$,

$$a^2 = 4;\quad a = 2$$

$$\therefore \quad \mathbf{a = 2;\ \ b = 0.5}$$

Option (b) is correct.

M20.234 *In the circuit shown in Fig. 20.282, $i_1(t)$ is given by*

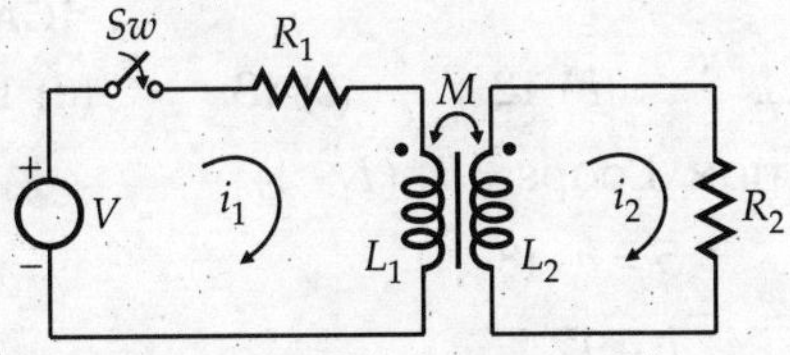

$R_1 = R_2 = 1\,\Omega\,;\, L_1 = 1\,\text{H}\,;\, L_2 = 4\,\text{H}$

$M = 2\,\text{H}\,;\, V = 1$ volt

Fig. 20.282

(*a*) $0.2 + 2e^{-0.2t}$ (*b*) $2 - e^{-0.2t}$

(*c*) $1 - 0.2\,e^{-0.2t}$ (*d*) $0.2\,e^{0.2t}$

Solution. The given circuit is transformed into *s*-domain circuit (Fig. 20.283) at $t = 0+$.

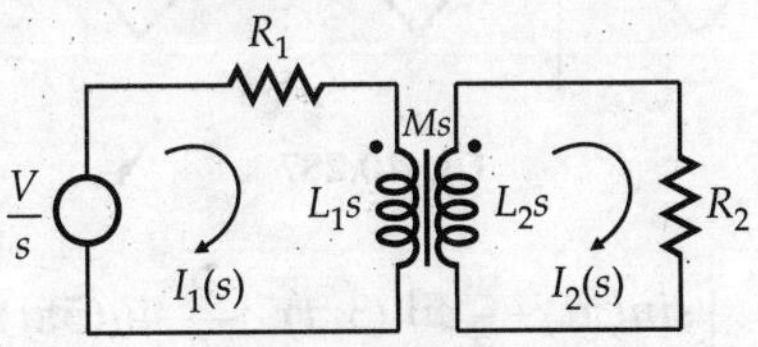

Fig. 20.283

Since $V = 1$ volt, therefore in left loop,

$$\frac{V}{s} = (R_1 + L_1 s)\, I_1(s) - 2s I_2(s)$$

or,
$$\frac{1}{s} = (1+s) I_1(s) - 2s.\, I_2(s) \qquad \ldots(1)$$

In the right loop,

$$0 = -2sI_1(s) + (4s+1) I_2(s)$$

$$\therefore \quad I_2(s) = \frac{2s}{4s+1} I_1(s)$$

Substitution of $I_2(s)$ in (1) simplification yields

$$I_1(s) = \frac{4s+1}{s(5s+1)} = \frac{4s+1}{5s(s+0.2)} = \frac{0.8s+0.2}{s(s+0.2)}$$

$$= \frac{1}{s} - \frac{0.2}{s+0.2}$$

$$\therefore \quad i_1(t) = \mathbf{1 - 0.2e^{-0.2t}}$$

Option (*c*) is correct.

[We can find $i_2(t)$ also

$$I_2(s) = \frac{2s}{4s+1} \times I_1(s) = \frac{2s}{4s+1} \times \frac{4s+1}{s(5s+1)}$$

$$= \frac{2}{(5s+1)} = \frac{0.4}{s+0.2}$$

$$\therefore \quad i_2(t) = 0.4\,e^{-0.2t}\,]$$

M20.235 *The graph of an electrical network has N nodes and B branches. The number of links L, with respect to the choice of a trees is given by* **[GATE 2002]**

(*a*) $B - N + 1$ (*b*) $B + N$

(*c*) $N - B + 1$ (*d*) $N - 2B - 1$

Solution. No. of links $= B - (N-1) = \mathbf{B - N + 1}$

Option (*a*) is correct.

M20.236 *The matrix A is given below is the node incidence matrix of a network. The columns correspond to branches of the network while the rows correspond to nodes. Let $V[v_1 v_2, \ldots, v_6]^T$ denote the vector of branch voltages while $I = [i_1 i_2, \ldots, i_6]^T$ that of branch currents. The vector $E = [e_1 e_2 e_3 e_4]^T$ denotes the vector of node voltages relative to a common ground.* **[GATE 2007]**

$$A = \begin{bmatrix} 1 & 1 & 1 & 0 & 0 & 0 \\ 0 & -1 & 0 & -1 & 1 & 0 \\ -1 & 0 & 0 & 0 & -1 & -1 \\ 0 & 0 & -1 & 1 & 0 & 1 \end{bmatrix}$$

Which of the following statements is true ?

(*a*) *The equations :*

$$V_1 - V_2 + V_3 = 0, \; V_3 + V_4 - V_5 = 0$$

are KVL equations for the network for some loops.

(*b*) *The equations :*

$$V_1 - V_3 - V_6 = 0, \; V_4 + V_5 - V_6 = 0$$

are KVL equations for the network for some loops.

(*c*) $E = AV$

(*d*) $AV = 0$ *are KVL equation for the network.*

Solution. When a branch leaves a node, the direction of graph is +ve(+1) while the branch enters the node signifies the direction to be –ve (–1).

The given node incidence matrix can be shown as :

Nodes \ Branches	b_1	b_2	b_3	b_4	b_5	b_6
N_1	1	1	1	0	0	0
N_2	0	–1	0	–1	1	0
N_3	–1	0	0	0	–1	–1
N_4	0	0	–1	1	0	1

The oriented graph is shown in Fig. 20.284.

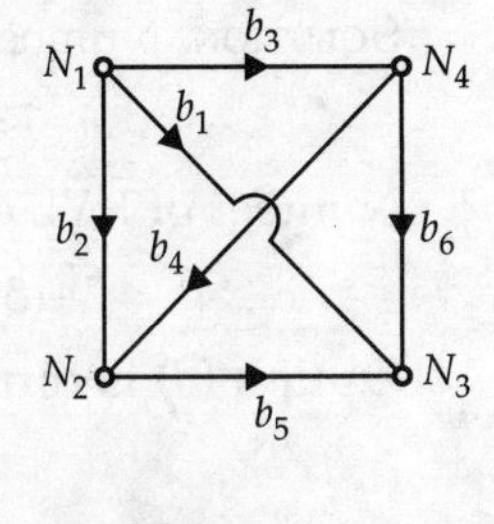

Fig. 20.284

CHAPTER 20

Using KVL in loop containing branches b_1, b_3 and b_6, we get

$$V_1 - V_6 - V_3 = 0$$

In loop containing branches,

b_4, b_5 and b_6, we get

$$V_4 + V_5 - V_6 = 0$$

Option (*b*) is correct.

M20.237 *The number of chords in the graph of the given circuit will be* **[GATE 2008]**

(*a*) 3 (*b*) 4 (*c*) 5 (*d*) 6

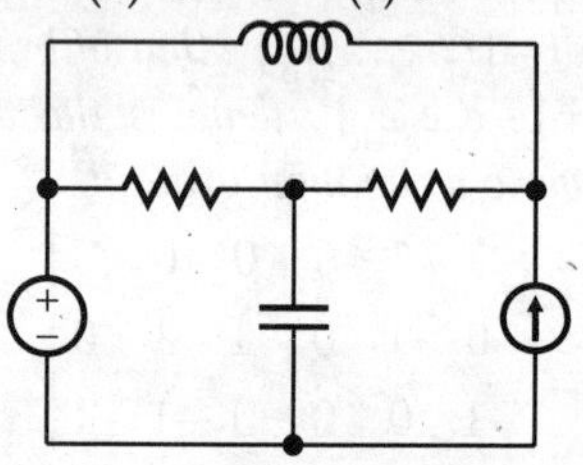

Fig. 20.285

SOLUTION. The network graph is drawn in Fig. 20.286.

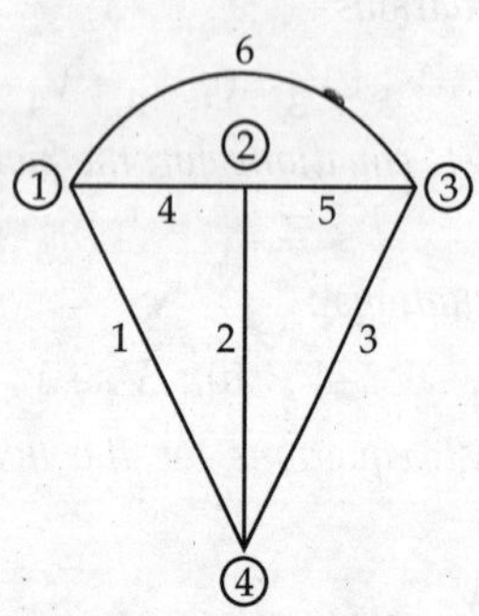

Fig. 20.286

Here, Number of branches $= b = 6$

Number of nodes $= n = 4$

Number of chords $= b-(n-1) = 6-(4-1) = \mathbf{3}$.

Option (*a*) is correct.

M20.238 *The graph associated with an electrical network has 7 branches and 5 nodes. The number of independent KCL equations and the number of independent KVL equations, respectively, are* **[GATE 2016]**

(*a*) 2 and 5 (*b*) 5 and 2

(*c*) 3 and 4 (*d*) 4 and 3

SOLUTION. Number of KCL equations

$$= n-1 = 5-1 = \mathbf{4}$$

Number of KVL equations $= b-(n-1)$

$$= 7-(5-1) = \mathbf{3}$$

Option (*d*) is correct.

M20.239 *The graph of a network has 8 nodes and 5 independent loops. The number of branches of the graph is* **[GATE 2018]**

(*a*) 11 (*b*) 12 (*c*) 13 (*d*) 14

SOLUTION. Loops $= b-(N-1)$

or, $5 = b-(8-1)$

$\therefore$ $b = \mathbf{12}$.

Option (*b*) is correct.

M20.240 *Fourier series for the waveform, $f(t)$ shown in Fig. 20.287 is* **[GATE 2002]**

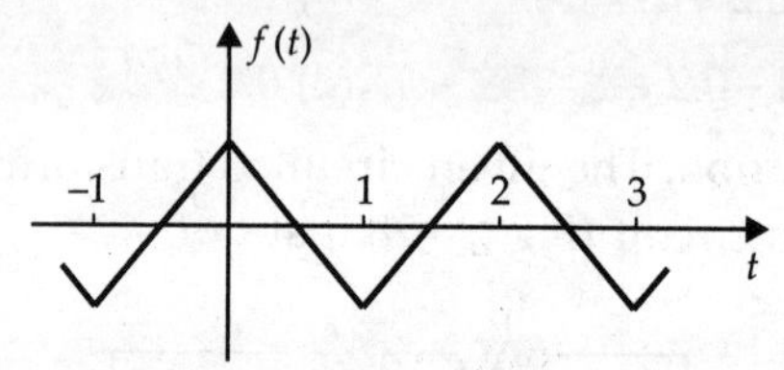

Fig. 20.287

(*a*) $\frac{8}{\pi^2}\left[sin(\pi t)+\frac{1}{9}sin(3\pi t)+\frac{1}{25}sin(5\pi t)+......\right]$

(*b*) $\frac{8}{\pi^2}\left[sin(\pi t)-\frac{1}{9}cos(3\pi t)+\frac{1}{25}sin(5\pi t)+......\right]$

(*c*) $\frac{8}{\pi^2}\left[cos(\pi t)+\frac{1}{9}cos(3\pi t)+\frac{1}{25}cos(5\pi t)+......\right]$

(*d*) $\frac{8}{\pi^2}\left[cos(\pi t)-\frac{1}{9}sin(3\pi t)+\frac{1}{25}sin(5\pi t)+......\right]$

SOLUTION. $f(t)$ is an even function with half wave symmetry. Thus the average value (the dc term) as well as all sine terms are individually zero. Since only cosine terms are present it means only odd harmonics are present.

$\therefore$ **Option (*c*) is correct.**

M20.241 *The rms value of the periodic waveform given in Fig. 20.288 is*

(*a*) $2\sqrt{6}$ A (*b*) $6\sqrt{2}$ A

(*c*) $\sqrt{4/3}$ (*d*) 1.5 A **[GATE 2004]**

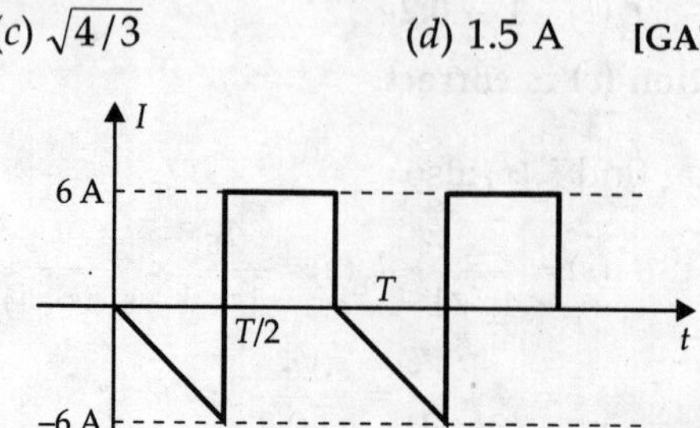

Fig. 20.288

SOLUTION.

$$I_{rms} = \left[\frac{1}{T}\int_0^T i^2(t)\right]^{1/2}$$

$$\therefore \quad I_{rms}^2 = \left[\frac{1}{T}\int_0^{T/2}\left(-\frac{12t}{T}\right)^2 dt + \int_{T/2}^{T} 6^2 dt\right]$$

[$\because$ Slope 'm' of the curve from $t=0$ to $T/2$ is $\frac{-6-0}{T/2-0} = -\frac{12}{T}$ giving $i = -\frac{12}{T}.t$ when $0 \le t \le \frac{T}{2}$. Also $i = 6$ A for $\frac{T}{2} \le t \le T$]

$$\therefore \quad I_{rms}^2 = \left[\frac{1}{T}\int_0^{T/2}\frac{144t^2}{T^2}dt + \frac{36}{T}\int_{T/2}^{T} dt\right]$$

$$= \frac{144}{T^3}\left[\frac{t^3}{3}\right]_0^{T/2} + \frac{36}{T}\left[\frac{T}{2}\right]$$

$$= \frac{144}{8\times 3} + \frac{36}{2} = 24$$

$$\therefore \quad I_{rms} = \mathbf{2\sqrt{6}\ A.}$$

Option (*a*) is correct.

M20.242 *The average power of a network having*

$$v = 4\cos(t+45°) + \cos(2t+45°) + \cos(3t-60°)\,V$$

and $i = 20\cos t + 10\cos(2t-60°)\,A$

is given by ______ W.

SOLUTION.

$$P = \tfrac{1}{2}(4\times 20)\cos 45° + \tfrac{1}{2}\times 1\times 10\cos(45-(-60))$$

$$= 40\times 0.707 + 5\cos 105°$$

$$= 28.28 - 1.294 = \mathbf{26.986\ W}.$$

[Average power in a network, having non-sinusoidal sources, is the sum of harmonic powers which are given by $\frac{1}{2}V_m I_m \cos\theta$.]

M20.243 *A periodic rectangular signal, $x(t)$ has the waveform as shown in Fig. 20.289. Frequency of the fifth harmonic of its spectrum is*

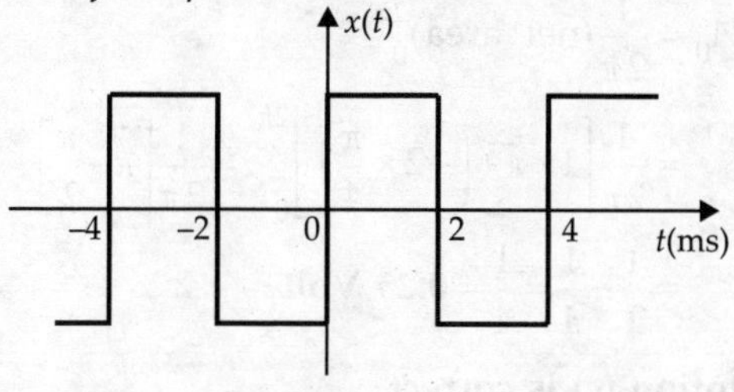

Fig. 20.289

(*a*) 40 Hz (*b*) 200 Hz
(*c*) 250 Hz (*d*) 1250 Hz **[GATE 1996]**

SOLUTION. By observation, time period

$$T = 4\text{ ms} = 4\times 10^{-3}\text{ s}$$

$$\therefore \quad f_0 = \frac{1}{T} = \frac{1}{4\times 10^{-3}}\text{ H,}$$

where f_0 is the fundamental frequency.

$\therefore$ Frequency of the 5th harmonic

$$f_5 = \frac{5}{4\times 10^{-3}} = \mathbf{1250\ Hz}$$

Option (*d*) is correct.

M20.244 *The Fourier series for the function*

$$f(x) = sin^2 x \text{ is}$$ **[GATE 2005]**

(*a*) $sin\,x + sin2x$ (*b*) $1 - cos2x$
(*c*) $sin2x + cos2x$ (*d*) $0.5 - 0.5\,cos\,2x$

SOLUTION.

$$f(x) = \sin^2 x = \tfrac{1}{2}.2\sin^2 x = \tfrac{1}{2}[1-\cos 2x]$$

$$\therefore \quad f(x) = \mathbf{0.5 - 0.5\cos 2x}$$

Option (*d*) is correct.

M20.245 *A voltage across a resistor (R) is given by*

$$v = 10 + 2sin(\omega t - 60°) + sin(2\omega t - 75°)\,V$$

If $R = 10\ \Omega$, find the power dissipated in R.

(*a*) 3.16 W (*b*) 5 W (*c*) 13 W (*d*) 10.25 W

SOLUTION.

$$V_{eff} = \sqrt{\tfrac{1}{2}\times 2^2 + \tfrac{1}{2}\times 1^2 + 10^2} = 10.124\text{ V}$$

$$\therefore \quad P_R = \frac{V_{eff}^2}{R} = \frac{10.124^2}{10} = \mathbf{10.25\ W}$$

Option (*d*) is correct.

M20.246 *A non-sinusoidal current*

$$i = (12\sin\omega t + 10\sin 3\omega t + 6\sin 5\omega t)\,A$$

is passing through a pure resistance of $R = 5\ \Omega$. What is the average power consumed in R?

(*a*) 700 W (*b*) 3.92 kW
(*c*) 600 W (*d*) 140 W

SOLUTION. Effective value of current is

$$I_{eff} = \sqrt{\tfrac{1}{2}(12)^2 + \tfrac{1}{2}(10)^2 + \tfrac{1}{2}(6)^2}$$

$$= 11.83\text{ A}$$

$$\therefore \quad P = I_{eff}^2 R = (11.83)^2 \times 5$$

$$= 699.87 \simeq \mathbf{700\ W.}$$

Option (*a*) is correct.

CHAPTER 20

M20.247 *The rms value of the resultant current in a wire which carries a dc current of 10 A and a sinusoidal alternating current of peak value 20 A is*

(*a*) 14.1 A (*b*) 17.3 A
(*c*) 22.4 A (*d*) 30.0 A **[GATE 2004]**

Solution. DC current = 10 A ;

$$\text{RMS value of AC current} = \frac{20}{\sqrt{2}}\text{ A}$$

$\therefore$ RMS value of the resultant current

$$= \sqrt{10^2 + \left(\frac{20}{\sqrt{2}}\right)^2} = \mathbf{17.32\ A}$$

Option (*b*) is correct.

M20.248 *A non-sinusoidal voltage waveform is given as :*

$V = 10\ V$ *for* 0 *to* $\pi/2$
$= 0\ V$ *for* $\pi/2$ *to* π
$= -5\ V$ *for* π *to* 2π

What is the average value ?

(*a*) 7.5 V (*b*) 10 V
(*c*) 0 (*d*) 5 V

Solution. Let us first draw the waveform (Fig. 20.290).

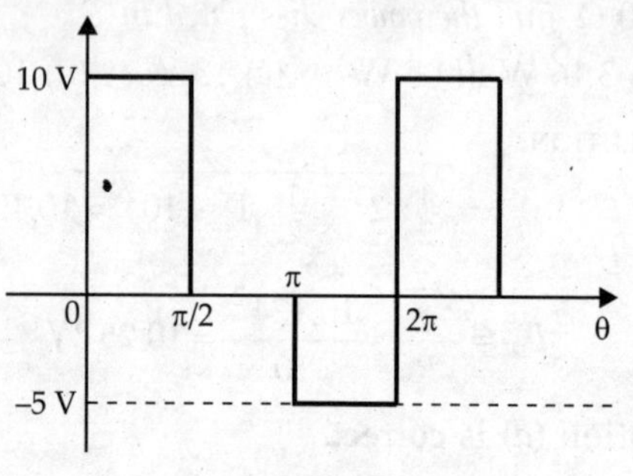

Fig. 20.290

$$A_0 = \frac{1}{2\pi} \times [(10 \times \pi/2) - 5 \times \pi]$$

$$= \frac{1}{2\pi}[5\pi - 5\pi] = \mathbf{0}$$

Option (*c*) is correct.

M20.249 *In the waveform given in Q. No. 20.248, obtain the value of coefficients of third harmonic.*

(*a*) $A_3 = 2.23$; $B_3 = 0$
(*b*) $A_3 = 0$; $B_3 = -1.06$
(*c*) $A_3 = -1.06$; $B_3 = 2.123$
(*d*) $A_3 = 2.123$; $B_3 = 1.06$

Solution.

$$A_3 = \frac{1}{\pi}\int_0^{\pi/2} 10\cos(3\theta)\,d\theta + \frac{1}{\pi}\int_\pi^{2\pi}(-5)\cos(3\theta)\,d\theta$$

$$= \frac{1}{\pi}\left[10\frac{\sin 3\theta}{3}\right]_0^{\pi/2} + \frac{1}{\pi}\left[-5\frac{\sin 3\theta}{3}\right]_\pi^{2\pi}$$

$$= \frac{10}{3\pi}.[\sin 3.\pi/2 - \sin 3.0] - \frac{5}{3\pi}[\sin 6\pi - \sin 3\pi]$$

$$= \frac{10}{3\pi}[-1] - \frac{5}{3\pi}[0 - 0] = -1.06$$

$$B_3 = \frac{1}{\pi}\int_0^{\pi/2} 10\sin(3\theta)\,d\theta + \frac{1}{\pi}\int_\pi^{2\pi} -5\sin(3\theta)\,d\theta$$

$$= \frac{10}{\pi}\left[-\frac{\cos 3\theta}{3}\right]_0^{\pi/2} - \frac{5}{\pi}\left[-\frac{\cos 3\theta}{3}\right]_\pi^{2\pi}$$

$$= \frac{10}{3\pi}[-\cos 3.\frac{\pi}{2} + \cos 3.0] - \frac{5}{3\pi}[-\cos 6\pi + \cos 3\pi]$$

$$= \frac{10}{3\pi}[0 + 1] - \frac{5}{3\pi}[-1 + (-1)]$$

$$= \frac{10}{3\pi} + \frac{5}{3\pi} + \frac{5}{3\pi} = 2.123$$

i.e., $A_3 = \mathbf{-1.06}$; $B_3 = \mathbf{2.123}$

Option (*c*) is correct.

M20.250 *A non-sinusoidal voltage wave is represented as shown in Fig. 20.291. The average value is given as*

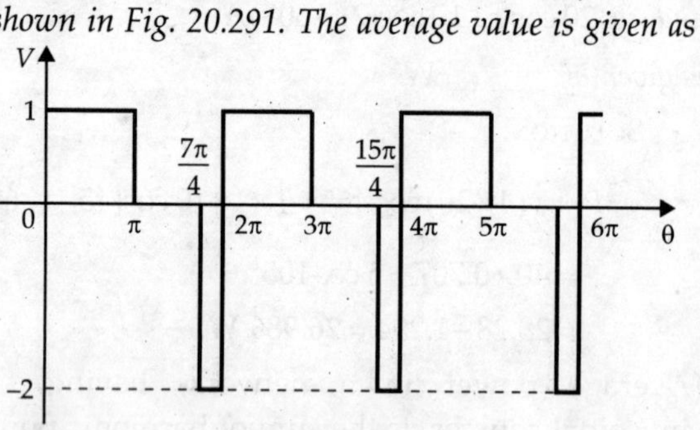

Fig. 20.291

(*a*) 0 V (*b*) 1 V
(*c*) 0.25 V (*d*) 0.64 V

Solution.

$$A_0 = \frac{1}{2\pi}(\text{net area})_0^{2\pi}$$

$$= \frac{1}{2\pi}\left[1 \times \pi + \left(-2 \times \frac{\pi}{4}\right)\right]_0^{2\pi} = \frac{1}{2\pi}\left[\pi - \frac{\pi}{2}\right]$$

$$= \frac{1}{2} - \frac{1}{4} = \frac{1}{4} = \mathbf{0.25\ Volt}$$

Option (*c*) is correct.

M20.251 *In the figure shown in Fig. 20.291, the amplitude of the wave is obtained as*

(*a*) 1.08 (*b*) 0.25

(*c*) 0.94 (*d*) – 0.45

Solution. We use Fourier coefficients to obtain the amplitude of the given wave.

$$\text{Amplitude} = \sqrt{A_1^2 + B_1^2}$$

where $A_1 = A_K$ for $K=1$; $B_1 = B_K$ for $K=1$

$$A_K = \frac{1}{\pi}\int_0^{2\pi} f(\theta)\cos(K\theta)\,d\theta$$

$$= \frac{1}{\pi}\int_0^{\pi} 1.\cos(K\theta)\,d\theta + \frac{1}{\pi}\int_{\pi}^{7\pi/4} 0.\cos(K\theta)\,d\theta + \frac{1}{\pi}\int_{7\pi/4}^{2\pi} (-2)\cos(K\theta)\,d\theta$$

$$= \frac{1}{\pi}\left[\frac{\sin(K\theta)}{K}\right]_0^{\pi} + 0 + \frac{1}{\pi}\left[\frac{(-2)\sin(K\theta)}{K}\right]_{7\pi/4}^{2\pi}$$

$$= \left(\frac{2}{K\pi}\sin\frac{7K\pi}{4}\right);$$

$$\therefore \quad A_1 = \frac{2}{\pi}\sin\frac{7\pi}{4} = -0.45.$$

$$B_K = \frac{1}{\pi}\int_0^{2\pi} f(\theta)\sin(K\theta)\,d\theta$$

$$= \frac{1}{\pi}\int_0^{\pi} 1.\sin(K\theta)\,d\theta + \frac{1}{\pi}\int_{\pi}^{7\pi/4} 0.\sin(K\theta)\,d\theta + \frac{1}{\pi}\int_{7\pi/4}^{2\pi} (-2)\sin(K\theta)\,d\theta$$

$$= \frac{1}{\pi}\left[\frac{(-\cos/\,K\theta)}{K}\right]_0^{\pi} + 0 - 2\left[\frac{-\cos(K\theta)}{K}\right]_{7\pi/4}^{2\pi}$$

$$= \frac{1}{K\pi}[-(\cos K\pi - 1) + 2(1 - \cos 7K\pi/4)]$$

$$\therefore \quad B_1 = \frac{1}{\pi}[-(\cos\pi - 1) + 2(1 - \cos 7\pi/4)]$$

$$= \frac{1}{\pi}[2 + 2 - 1.414] = 0.824$$

$$\text{Amplitude} = \sqrt{A_1^2 + B_1^2} = \mathbf{0.94}.$$

Option (*c*) is correct.

M20.252 *For the waveform shown in Fig. 20.292, the average value (A_0) is ______ and the (A) coefficient of third harmonic (A_3) is ______.*

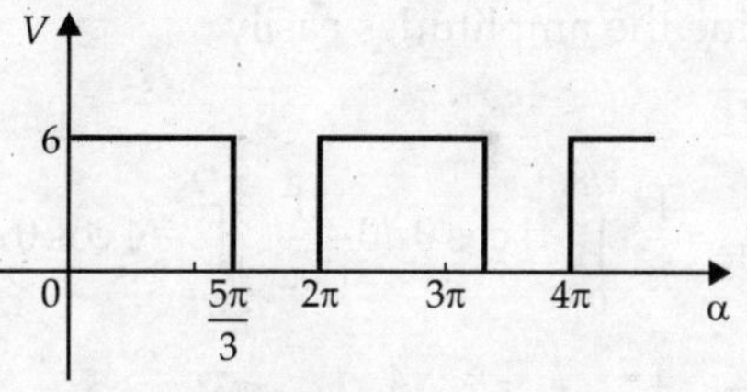

Fig. 20.292

Solution.

$$A_0 = \frac{1}{2\pi}(\text{net area})_0^{2\pi}$$

$$= \frac{1}{2\pi}[6 \times 5\pi/3] = 5\text{ V}$$

$$A_3 = \frac{1}{\pi}\int_0^{5\pi/3} 6\cos(3\alpha)\,d\alpha = \frac{6}{\pi}\left[\frac{\sin 3\alpha}{3}\right]_0^{5\pi/3}$$

$$= \frac{2}{\pi}[\sin 5\pi - \sin 0°] = 0$$

$$\therefore \ A_0 = \mathbf{5\ V}; \quad A_3 = \mathbf{0}$$

M20.253 *For the waveform drawn in Fig. 20.292, the value of B coefficient of the fourth harmonic is ______.*

Solution.

$$B_4 = \frac{1}{\pi}\int_0^{5\pi/3} 6\sin(4\alpha)\,d\alpha = \frac{6}{\pi}\left[-\frac{\cos 4\alpha}{4}\right]_0^{5\pi/3}$$

$$= -\frac{3}{2\pi}\left[\cos\frac{20\pi}{3} - \cos 0\right] = -\frac{3}{2\pi}[-0.5 - 1]$$

$$= 0.23 + 0.478 = \mathbf{0.708}$$

$\therefore$ B_4, coefficient of fourth harmonic is **0.708.**

M20.254 *A voltage wave is displayed in Fig. 20.293. Obtain its amplitude.*

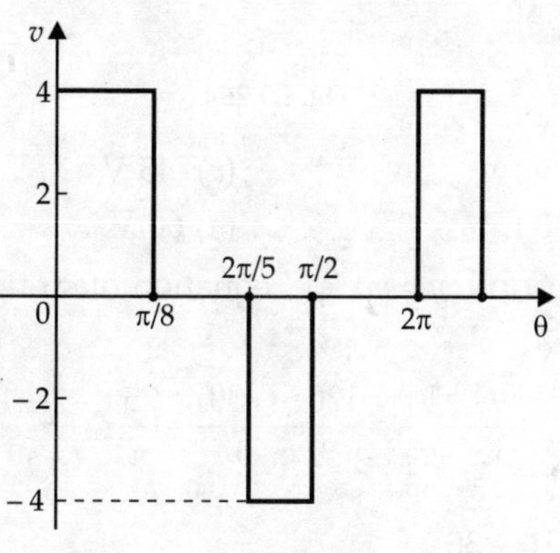

Fig. 20.293

CHAPTER 20

(*a*) 2 V (*b*) – 4 V
(*c*) 0.29 (*d*) 0.52 V

SOLUTION. Use of Fourier coefficients helps us to determine the amplitudes easily.

Here,

$$A_1 = \frac{1}{\pi}\int_0^{\pi/8} 4\cos\theta\, d\theta + \frac{1}{\pi}\int_{2\pi/5}^{\pi/2} -4\cos\theta\, d\theta$$

$$= \frac{4}{\pi}[\sin\theta]_0^{\pi/8} - \frac{4}{\pi}[\sin\theta]_{2\pi/5}^{\pi/2}$$

$$= \frac{4}{\pi}\times\sin\pi/8 - \frac{4}{\pi}[\sin\pi/2 - \sin 2\pi/5]$$

$$= 0.425$$

$$B_1 = \frac{1}{\pi}\int_0^{\pi/8} 4\sin\theta\, d\theta + \frac{1}{\pi}\int_{2\pi/5}^{\pi/2} -4\sin\theta\, d\theta$$

$$= \frac{4}{\pi}[-\cos\theta]_0^{\pi/8} - \frac{4}{\pi}[-\cos\theta]_{2\pi/5}^{\pi/2}$$

$$= \frac{4}{\pi}\left(-\cos\frac{\pi}{8} + \cos 0°\right) - \frac{4}{\pi}\left[-\cos\frac{\pi}{2} + \cos\frac{2\pi}{5}\right]$$

$$= -0.298$$

$$\therefore \text{ Amplitude} = \sqrt{A_1^2 + B_1^2} = \sqrt{(0.425)^2 + (-0.298)^2}$$

$$= \mathbf{0.52\ V}$$

Option (*d*) is correct.

M20.255 *For the waveform shown in Fig. 20.294, the average value is*

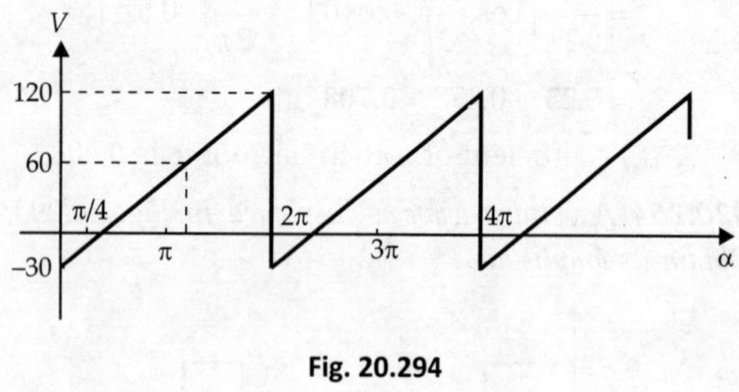

Fig. 20.294

(*a*) 90 V (*b*) 45 V
(*c*) 30 V (*d*) 60 V

SOLUTION. $y = mx + C$, equation of straight line.

Here,

$$m = \frac{y_2 - y_1}{x_2 - x_1} = \frac{120-(-30)}{2\pi - 0} = \frac{75}{\pi}$$

$$C = -30$$

$$\therefore \quad v = \left(\frac{75}{\pi}\alpha - 30\right)$$

$$A_0 = \frac{1}{2\pi}\int_0^{2\pi}\left(\frac{75}{\pi}\alpha - 30\right)d\alpha$$

$$= \frac{1}{2\pi}\left[\frac{75}{\pi}\cdot\frac{\alpha^2}{2} - 30\alpha\right]_0^{2\pi}$$

$$= \frac{1}{2\pi}\left[\frac{75}{\pi}\times\frac{4\pi^2}{2} - 0 - 30\times 2\pi + 0\right]$$

$$= 75 - 30 = \mathbf{45\ V}$$

Option (*b*) is correct.

M20.256 *In the waveform shown in Fig. 20.295, the average value is _____ V while the amplitude of first harmonic is _____ .*

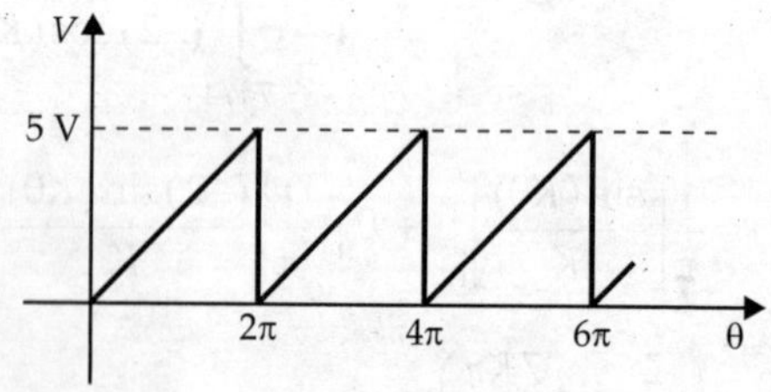

Fig. 20.295

SOLUTION.

$$A_0 = \frac{1}{2\pi}\times\text{net area}$$

$$= \frac{1}{2\pi}\left[\frac{1}{2}\times 2\pi\times 5\right] = 2.5\text{ V}$$

Also, $v = m\theta + C$

$$= m\theta = \frac{5-0}{2\pi - 0}.\theta = \frac{5}{2\pi}.\theta$$

$$\therefore \quad A_1 = \frac{1}{\pi}\int_0^{2\pi}\left(\frac{5}{2\pi}\theta\right)\cos\theta\, d\theta$$

$$= \frac{5}{2\pi^2}\left[\frac{1}{1^2}\cos\theta + \frac{\theta}{1}\sin\theta\right]_0^{2\pi}$$

$$= \frac{5}{2\pi^2} = 0.2536$$

$$\therefore \quad B_1 = \frac{1}{\pi}\int_0^{2\pi}\left(\frac{5}{2\pi}.\theta\right)\sin\theta\, d\theta$$

$$= \frac{5}{2\pi^2}\left[\frac{1}{1^2}\sin\theta - \frac{\theta}{1}\cos\theta\right]_0^{2\pi}$$

$$= -\frac{5}{2\pi^2}\times 2\pi\cos 2\pi = -1.59$$

$\therefore\ C_1$ (amplitude) $= B_1 + jA_1 = -1.59 + j0.2536$
$= 1.61\ \angle 170.94°$ V

$\therefore$ **Ans. 2.5 V ; 1.61 ∠170.94°.**

M20.257 *A periodic function $f(t)$, with a period of 2π, is represented as its Fourier series,*

if $f(t) = a_0 + \sum_{n=1}^{\infty} a_n \cos nt + \sum_{n=1}^{\infty} b_n \sin nt$

$$f(t) = \begin{cases} A\sin t, & 0 \le t \le \pi \\ 0, & \pi < t < 2\pi \end{cases}$$

The Fourier series coefficients a_1 and b_1 of $f(t)$ are :

(a) $a_1 = 0$; $b_1 = \frac{A}{\pi}$ (b) $a_1 = \frac{A}{\pi}$; $b_1 = 0$

(c) $a_1 = 0$; $b_1 = \frac{A}{2}$ (d) $a_1 = \frac{A}{2}$; $b_1 = 0$

[GATE 2019]

SOLUTION. $T_0 = 2\pi$; $\omega_0 = \frac{2\pi}{T_0} = 1$

Now, $a_1 = \frac{2}{T_0}\int_0^{T_0} f(t)\cos\omega_0 t\, dt$

$= \frac{2}{2\pi}\int_0^{2\pi} f(t)\cos t\, dt$

$= \frac{1}{\pi}\int_0^{\pi} A\sin t \cdot \cos t\, dt$

$\therefore\ a_1 = \frac{A}{2\pi}\int_0^{\pi} \sin 2t\, dt = 0$

i.e., $\boldsymbol{a_1 = 0}$

$b_1 = \frac{2}{T_0}\int_0^{T_0} f(t)\sin\omega_0 t\, dt$

$= \frac{2}{2\pi}\int_0^{2\pi} f(t)\sin t\, dt$ $[\because \omega_0 = 1]$

$= \frac{1}{\pi}\int_0^{\pi} A\sin t \cdot \sin t\, dt$

$= \frac{A}{2\pi}\int_0^{\pi} 2\sin^2 t\, dt$

$= \frac{A}{2\pi}\int_0^{\pi} [1 - \cos 2t]\, dt$

$= \frac{A}{2\pi}\left[t - \frac{\sin 2t}{2}\right]_0^{\pi}$

$= \frac{A}{2\pi}[(\pi - 0) - (0 - 0)] = \frac{A}{2}$

i.e., $\boldsymbol{b_1 = A/2}$

Option (c) is correct.

M20.258 *Let $f(x)$ be a real, periodic function satisfying $f(-x) = -f(x)$. The general form of its Fourier series representation would be*

(a) $f(x) = a_0 + \sum_{K=1}^{\infty} a_k \cos(Kx)$

(b) $f(x) = \sum_{K=1}^{\infty} b_k \sin(Kx)$

(c) $f(x) = a_0 + \sum_{K=1}^{\infty} a_{2k} \cos(Kx)$

(d) $f(x) = \sum_{K=0}^{\infty} a_{2k+1} \sin(2K+1)x$

[GATE 2016]

SOLUTION. It is given that

$$f(-x) = -f(x)$$

$\therefore$ The given function is an odd function. Hence the Fourier series will have sine terms only.

$\therefore\ f(x) = \sum_{K=1}^{\infty} b_k \sin(Kx)$

Option (b) is correct.

M20.259 *The Fourier expansion :*

$f(t) = a_0 + \sum_{n=1}^{\infty} a_0 \cos n\omega t + b_n \sin n\omega t$

of the periodic signal shown below (Fig. 20.296) will contain the following non-zero terms :

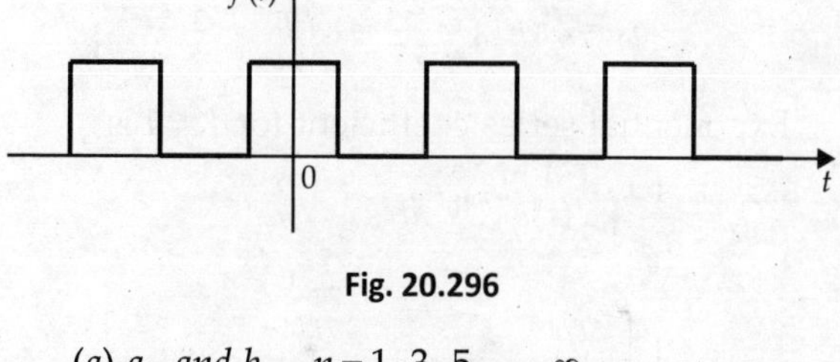

Fig. 20.296

(a) a_0 *and* b_n , $n = 1, 3, 5, \ldots, \infty$

(b) a_0 *and* a_n , $n = 1, 2, 3, \ldots, \infty$

CHAPTER 20

(*c*) a_0, a_n *and* b_n $n = 1, 2, 3, \ldots, \infty$

(*d*) a_0 *and* a_n , $n = 1, 3, 5, \ldots, \infty$

[GATE 2011]

Solution. The given function is an even function.

Hence, Fourier expansion of $f(t)$ is having dc term (average value) with odd harmonics.

Option (*d*) is correct.

M20.260 *A signal* $x(t)$ *is given by*

$$x(t) = \begin{cases} 1, & -T/4 < t \le 3T/4 \\ -1, & 3T/4 < t \le 7T/4 \\ -x(t+T) & \end{cases}$$

Which among the following gives the fundamental Fourier term of $x(t)$?

(*a*) $\frac{4}{\pi} \cos\left(\frac{\pi t}{T} - \frac{\pi}{4}\right)$ (*b*) $\frac{\pi}{4} \cos\left(\frac{\pi t}{2T} + \frac{\pi}{4}\right)$

(*c*) $\frac{4}{\pi} \sin\left(\frac{\pi t}{T} - \frac{\pi}{4}\right)$ (*d*) $\frac{\pi}{4} \sin\left(\frac{\pi t}{2T} + \frac{\pi}{4}\right)$

[GATE 2007]

Solution. As per question, the signal is drawn in Fig. 20.297.

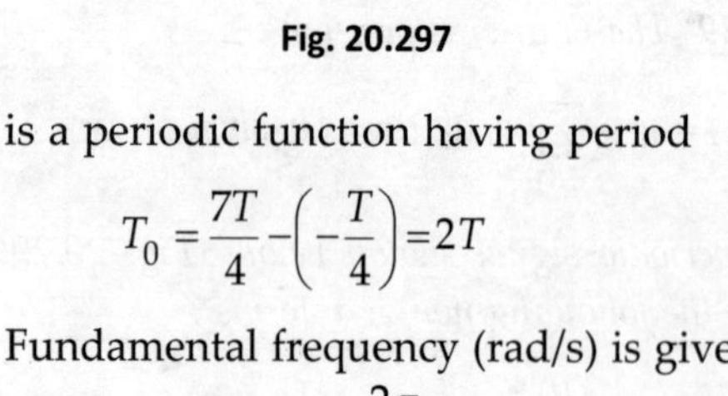

Fig. 20.297

It is a periodic function having period

$$T_0 = \frac{7T}{4} - \left(-\frac{T}{4}\right) = 2T$$

$\therefore$ Fundamental frequency (rad/s) is given by

$$\omega_0 = 2\pi / T_0 = \frac{2\pi}{2T} = \pi / T$$

Exponential series coefficient for $K = 1$ is

$$C_1 = \frac{1}{T_0} \int x(t) e^{-j\omega_0 t} dt$$

or, $$C_1 = \frac{1}{T_0}\left[\int_{-\pi/4}^{3T/4} e^{-j\omega_0 t} dt + \int_{3T/4}^{7T/4} -e^{-j\omega_0 t} dt\right]$$

$$= \frac{1}{j2\pi}[2e^{j\pi/4} + 2e^{j\pi/4}]$$

$$= \frac{2}{j\pi} e^{j\pi/4} = \frac{2}{\pi} e^{-j\pi/4}$$

$$= \frac{2}{\pi}\left[\frac{1}{\sqrt{2}} - j\frac{1}{\sqrt{2}}\right]$$

However, $C_1 = \frac{a_1}{2} - j\frac{b_1}{2}$

$\therefore$ Here $a_1 = \frac{4}{\sqrt{2}\pi}$; $b_1 = \frac{4}{\sqrt{2}\pi}$

$\therefore$ Fundamental Fourier term is

$a_1 \cos \omega_0 t + b_1 \sin \omega_0 t$

$$= \frac{4}{\sqrt{2}\pi} \cos\left(\frac{\pi}{T}.t\right) + \frac{4}{\sqrt{2}\pi} \sin\left(\frac{\pi}{T}.t\right)$$

$$= \frac{4}{\pi} \cos\left[\frac{\pi t}{T} - \frac{\pi}{4}\right]$$

Option (*a*) is correct.

M20.261 *The second harmonic component of the periodic waveform given in the figure has an amplitude of* **[GATE 2010]**

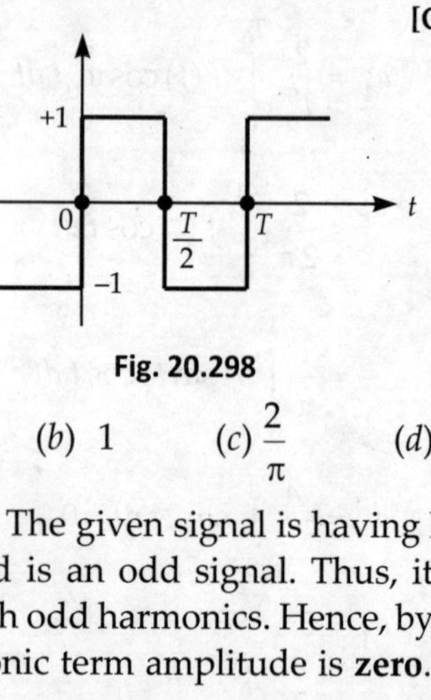

Fig. 20.298

(*a*) 0 (*b*) 1 (*c*) $\frac{2}{\pi}$ (*d*) $\sqrt{5}$

Solution. The given signal is having half wave symmetry and is an odd signal. Thus, it has only sine terms with odd harmonics. Hence, by logic, the second harmonic term amplitude is **zero**.

Option (*a*) is correct.

M20.262 *For a periodic signal*

$$v(t) = 30 \sin 100t + 10 \cos 300t + 6 \sin(500t + \pi/4)$$

The fundamental frequency in rad/s is

(*a*) 100 (*b*) 300 (*c*) 500 (*d*) 1500

[GATE 2013]

Solution. By inspection we see that the fundamental term in the signal is (30 sin 100t). It is in form of $V_m \sin \omega t$. Hence $\omega = 100$ is the fundamental frequency in rad/s.

Option (*a*) is correct.

M20.263 *Let $x(t)$ be a periodic signal with time period T, let $y(t)=x(t-t_0)+x(t+t_0)$ for some t_0.*

The Fourier series coefficients of $y(t)$ are denoted by b_k. If $b_k=0$ for all odd K, then t_0 can be equal to

(a) $\frac{T}{8}$ (b) $\frac{T}{4}$ (c) $\frac{T}{2}$ (d) $2T$

[GATE 2008]

SOLUTION. $y(t)=x(t-t_0)+x(t+t_0)$

Since $x(t)$ is a periodic function with period T hence $x(t-t_0)$ and $x(t+t_0)$ both will also be periodic with period T.

$$\therefore \quad b_k = a_k\, e^{-jK\omega_0 t_0} + a_k\, e^{jK\omega_0 t_0}$$

[a_k is the Fourier series coefficient of signal $x(t)$]

$$\therefore \quad b_k = a_k\,[e^{-jK\omega_0 t_0} + e^{jK\omega_0 t_0}]$$

$$= 2a_K \cos . K\omega_0 t_0$$

Since $b_K=0$ for odd values of K,

i.e., $K\omega_0 t_0 = K\frac{\pi}{2}$, where $K=\pm 1, \pm 3, \pm 5, \ldots$

or, $\omega_0 T_0 = \frac{\pi}{2}$

$$\therefore \quad t_0 = \frac{\pi/2}{\omega_0} = \frac{\pi}{2}\times\frac{T}{2\pi} = \boldsymbol{\frac{T}{4}}$$

Option (*b*) is correct.

M20.264 *$x(t)$ is a real valued function of a real variable with period T. Its trigonometric Fourier series expansion contains no terms of frequency $\omega=2\pi(2K)/T$, $K=0, 1, 2, \ldots$ Also no sine terms are present, then $x(t)$ satisfied the equation*

(a) $x(t)=-x(t-T)$

(b) $x(t)=x(T-t)=-x(-t)$

(c) $x(t)=x(T-t)=-x(t-T/2)$

(d) $x(t)=x(t-T)=x(t-T/2)$ **[GATE 2006]**

SOLUTION. $x(t)$ will be an even signal as there is no sine term in the Fourier expansion but have only cosine terms.

$$\therefore \quad x(t)=x(-t)$$

$$\text{or,} \quad x(t-T)=x(-t+T) \qquad \ldots(i)$$

However, the signal is periodic with period T.

$$\therefore \quad x(t-T)=x(t)$$

$\therefore$ From (*i*), we get

$$x(t)=x(T-t) \qquad \ldots(ii)$$

It is also given that the signal contains only odd harmonics *i.e.,* no terms of frequency.

$$\omega = \frac{2\pi\times 2K}{T}, \quad K=0, 1, 2, 3, 4 \ldots$$

All even harmonics are absent.

This simply means that the signal has half wave symmetry and this implies that

$$x(t) = -x\left(t-\frac{T}{2}\right) \qquad \ldots(iii)$$

From (*ii*) and (*iii*),

$$x(t)=x(T-t)=-\boldsymbol{x}\left(\boldsymbol{t}-\frac{\boldsymbol{T}}{\boldsymbol{2}}\right)$$

Option (*c*) is correct.

M20.265 *For the triangular waveform shown in the figure (Fig. 20.299), the RMS value of the voltage is equal to*

(a) $\sqrt{\frac{1}{6}}$ V (b) $\sqrt{\frac{1}{3}}$ V

(c) $\frac{1}{3}$ V (d) $\sqrt{\frac{2}{3}}$ V **[GATE 2005]**

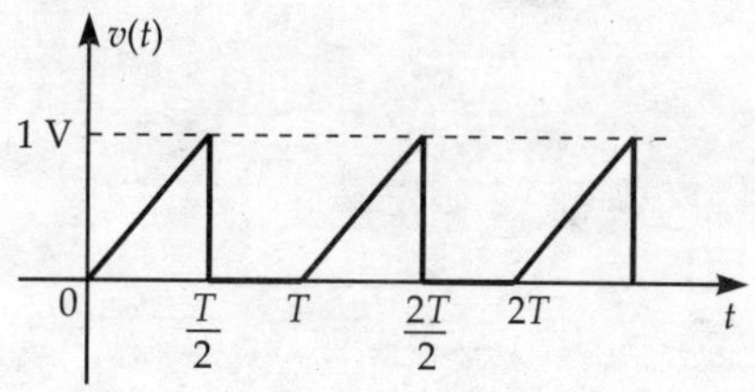

Fig. 20.299

SOLUTION.

$$V_{rms} = \left[\frac{1}{T}\int_0^{T/2}\left(\frac{2t}{T}\right)^2 dt + \int_{T/2}^{T} 0.dt\right]^{1/2}$$

$$\left[\because \text{ Slope of triangular waveform is } \frac{1-0}{T/2-0} = \frac{2}{T}\right]$$

for $0 \le t \le \frac{T}{2}$

$$\therefore \quad V_{rms}^2 = \frac{1}{T}\int_0^{T/2}\frac{4t^2}{T^2}dt$$

$$= \frac{4}{3T^3}\left[\frac{T^3}{8}\right] = \frac{1}{6}$$

$$\therefore \quad V_{rms} = \sqrt{\frac{\boldsymbol{1}}{\boldsymbol{6}}}\ \textbf{V}$$

Option (*a*) is correct.

CHAPTER 20

APPENDIX A

Operational Aspects of Complex Numbers

A.1 COMPLEX NUMBERS

A *complex number* Z can be represented in the form

$$Z = R + jX$$

where R and X are real numbers and the symbol j is used to denote $\sqrt{-1}$. The symbol j represents *imaginary number* (or imaginary or j operator). R is the real part while jX is the imaginary part of Z.

Obviously,

$$j = \sqrt{-1}\,; \quad j^2 = j \times j = -1\,;$$

$$j^3 = j^2 \times j = -j$$

$$j^4 = j^2 \times j^2 = (-1) \times (-1) = 1$$

$$j^{-1} \equiv \frac{1}{j} = \frac{j}{j \cdot j} = \frac{j}{(\sqrt{-1})^2} = -j$$

In electrical engineering the operation of complex quantities involves following representations :

(*i*) Rectangular or Cartesian Form

Here, the real part is plotted in x-axis (*real axis*) while the imaginary part in *y*-axis (*quadrature axis*). Fig. A.1 represents such a representation.

Here, $\quad Z = R + jX$

$$\therefore \quad |Z| = \sqrt{R^2 + X^2} \quad \text{while} \quad \theta = \tan^{-1}\frac{X}{R}$$

$$\text{Hence} \quad Z \equiv \sqrt{R^2 + X^2}\ \angle \tan^{-1}\frac{X}{R}.$$

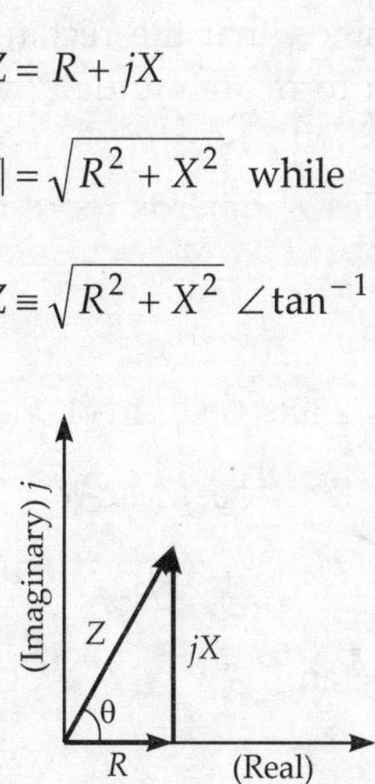

Fig. A.1 Rectangular form of representation.

(*ii*) Polar Form

The location of a point in a complex plane (a two dimensional plane containing a real axis and imaginary axis) can also be represented in terms of *polar* co-ordinates. Here, the radial distance *r* of the point from the origin, and the angle θ made between the radial line and the +ve real axis, measured anticlockwise, are specified.

In symbolic form,

$$Z = r\,\angle\theta.$$

In Fig. A.2, R, the real part of z is $r \cos \theta$ and X, the quadrature part of z is $r \sin \theta$.

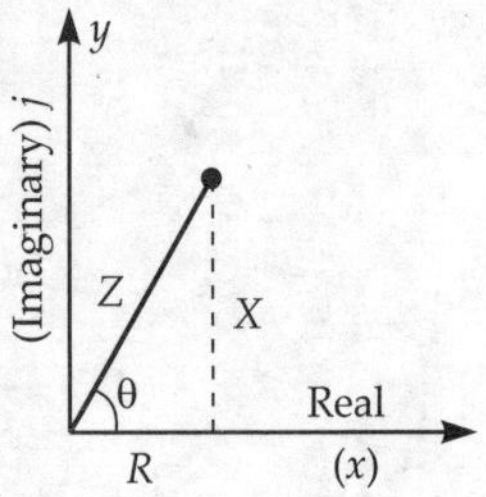

Fig. A.2 Polar representation.

Hence, $\sqrt{R^2 + X^2}$ becomes the magnitude of the rotating vector r.

and $$\tan \theta = \frac{X}{R}.$$

Assuming $r \equiv Z$, we then can write

$$Z = \sqrt{R^2 + X^2} \angle \tan^{-1} \frac{X}{R}.$$

It may be noted that the rectangular form as well as the polar form are mutually *interchangeable.* This is shown as follows :

Say a complex number is represented in polar form *i.e.*, $Z \angle \phi$.

We can then write

$$Z \angle \phi = Z(\cos \phi + j \sin \phi)$$
$$= Z \cos \phi + jZ \sin \phi$$
$$= R + jX \text{ (say)}$$

while $$\phi = \tan^{-1} \frac{X}{R}.$$

Then we represented $Z \angle \phi$ as $R + jX$ while $\phi = \angle \tan^{-1} \frac{X}{R}$. Again, when a vector is given in form of rectangular form, it can be converted to polar form

$$R + jX = \sqrt{R^2 + X^2} \angle \tan^{-1} \frac{X}{R}$$
$$= Z \angle \phi \text{ [polar form]}.$$

It may be noted that if X be negative,

$$R - jX = \sqrt{R^2 + X^2} \angle \tan^{-1} \left(-\frac{X}{R}\right)$$
$$= Z \angle -\phi$$

(*iii*) Exponential Form

$$Z = R + jX = r \cos \theta + jr \sin \theta$$
$$= r(\cos \theta + j \sin \theta)$$

From Euler's Formulae,

$$\cos \theta + j \sin = \varepsilon^{j\theta}$$
$$\therefore \quad Z = r\varepsilon^{j\theta}$$

Thus to convert the *exponential form* to *rectangular form*, let us assume

$$a = r\varepsilon^{j\phi}$$

where a is a complex number.

Now, $$r\varepsilon^{j\phi} = r(\cos \phi + j \sin \phi)$$
$$= r \cos \phi + jr \sin \phi = c + jd \text{ (say)}$$

Thus $a = c + jd$ (rectangular form)

A.2 OPERATION OF COMPLEX NUMBERS

Sum and difference of two complex numbers are performed through rectangular type of repre sentations.

Say we are to add $(a + jb)$ to $(c + jd)$.

Then $(a + jb) + (c + jd) = (a + c) + j(b + d)$
$= x + jy$ (say)

Similarly, $(a + jb) - (c + jd) = (a - c) + j(b - d)$
$= x' + jy'$ (say)

and $(a - jb) - (c - jd) = (a - c) - j(b + d)$
$= x' - jy''$ (say)

Once the answer of sum and difference of two or more complex members is obtained in rectangular form, it can be converted either to polar or exponential form, if desired.

Multiplication of complex numbers can be obtained in different representations as follows :

(*a*) in rectangular form

$$(a + jb)(c + jd) = ac + jad + jbc + j^2 bd$$
$$= (ac - bd) + j(ad + bc)$$

(*b*) in polar form*

$$r_1 \angle \theta_1 \times r_2 \angle \theta_2 = r_1 r_2 \angle (\theta_1 + \theta_2),$$

[if $r_1 \angle \theta_1$ is multiplied to $r_2 \angle -\theta_2$, the answer would be

$$r_1 r_2 \angle \theta_1 + (-\theta_2) \quad \text{or,} \quad r_1 r_2 \angle \theta_1 - \theta_2 \;]$$

(*c*) in exponential form

$$a\varepsilon^{j\theta} \times b\varepsilon^{j\phi} = ab\varepsilon^{j(\theta + \phi)}$$

Division of complex numbers can be obtained in different representations as follows :

(*a*) in rectangular form

$$\frac{a+jb}{c+jd} = \frac{(a+jb)(c-jd)}{(c+jd)(c-jd)}$$

$$= \frac{ac+bd+j\,(bc-ad)}{c^2+d^2}$$

$$= \frac{ac+bd}{(c^2+d^2)} + j\,\frac{bc-ad}{(c^2+d^2)}.$$

(*b*) in polar form

$$\frac{r_1\angle\theta}{r_2\angle\phi} = \frac{r_1\angle\theta r_2\angle-\phi}{r_2\angle\phi r_2\angle-\phi}$$

$$= \frac{r_1 r_2}{r_2 r_2}\angle\theta-\phi = \frac{r_1}{r_2}\angle\theta-\phi.$$

Similarly, $\dfrac{r_1\angle\theta}{r_2\angle-\phi} = \dfrac{r_1}{r_2}\angle\theta+\phi$

(*c*) in exponential form

$$\frac{r_1\,\varepsilon^{j\theta_1}}{r_2\varepsilon^{j\theta_2}} = \frac{r_1}{r_2}\,\varepsilon^{j(\theta_1-\theta_2)}.$$

Conjugate of a Complex Number

The conjugate of a complex number $Z = x + jy$ is the complex number $Z^* = x - jy$.

Thus, $\text{real}\,(Z) = \dfrac{Z+Z^*}{2}$

$\text{Imaginary}\,(Z) = \dfrac{Z-Z^*}{2j}$ and $|Z| = \sqrt{ZZ^*}$

[In the complex plane, Z and Z^* are the mirror images in the axis of reals] .

* Also, $r_1\angle\theta_1 \times r_2\angle\theta_2$

$= r_1(\cos\theta_1 + j\sin\theta_1)\, r_2(\cos\theta_2 + j\sin\theta_2)$

$= r_1 r_2\,[(\cos\theta_1\cos\theta_2 - \sin\theta_1\sin\theta_2)$
$+ j(\sin\theta_1\cos\theta_2 + \sin\theta_2\cos\theta_1)]$

$= r_1 r_2\,[\cos(\theta_1+\theta_2) + j\sin(\theta_1+\theta_2)]$

** In trigonometric form,

$$\frac{r_1(\cos\theta + j\sin\theta)}{r_2(\cos\phi + j\sin\phi)} = \frac{r_1(\cos\theta + j\sin\theta)(\cos\phi - j\sin\phi)}{r_2(\cos\phi + j\sin\phi)(\cos\phi - j\sin\phi)}$$

$$= \frac{r_1}{r_2}\cdot\frac{\cos(\theta-\phi) + j\sin(\theta-\phi)}{\cos^2\phi + \sin^2\phi}$$

$$= \frac{r_1}{r_2}[\cos(\theta-\phi) + j\sin(\theta-\phi)].$$

Also $(Z^*)^* = Z,\ (Z_1 \pm Z_2)^* = Z_1^* \pm Z_2^*$

$$\left(\frac{Z_1}{Z_2}\right)^* = \frac{Z_1^*}{Z_2^*}$$

$$(Z_1 Z_2)^* = Z_1^* Z_2^*.$$

Also, if $Z = r\varepsilon^{j\theta}, Z^* = r\varepsilon^{-j\theta}$

(in exponential form)

$Z = r\angle\theta, Z^*$

$= r\angle-\theta$ (in polar form)

$Z = r(\cos\theta + j\sin\theta),\ Z^*$

$= r(\cos\theta - j\sin\theta)$

(in trigonometric form)

In electrical engineering we express complex power in a.c. circuit(s) as $S = VI^*$. The reason is as below :

$S = P + jQ\,[P = \text{real power};\ Q = \text{reactive power}]$

$= S\angle\phi$

$= S\cos\phi + jS\sin\phi = (VI)\cos\phi + j\,(VI)\sin\phi$

$= VI(\cos\phi + j\sin\phi)$

$\therefore\quad S = VI\varepsilon^{j\phi} \qquad = VI\angle\phi.$

[*exponential form*] [*polar form*]

Since, $I = I\angle\theta \quad \therefore\ I^* = I\angle-\theta$ [Fig. A.3]

$\therefore\quad VI^* = (V\angle\phi+\theta)(I\angle-\theta) = VI\angle\phi = S$

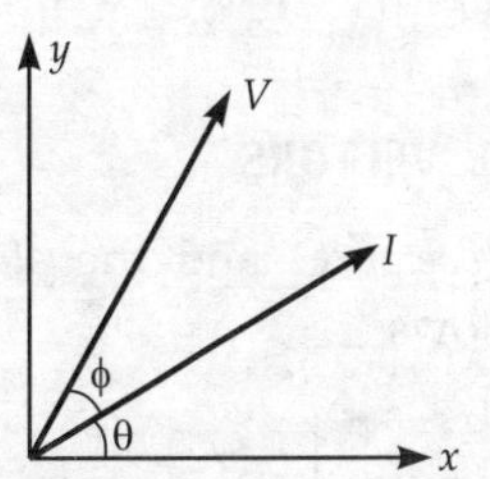

Fig. A.3 Current-voltage representation in phasor form.

Thus, $S = VI^*$

where $Re[VI^*] = VI\cos\phi = I^2 R$

and $Im[VI^*] = VI\sin\phi = I^2 X.$

APPENDIX

B

Introduction to Vector and Matrix Algebra

B.1 VECTORS

A vector $\overline{X}$ is defined as an ordered set of numbers (real or complex), *i.e.*,

$$\overline{X} \triangleq \begin{bmatrix} x_1 \\ x_2 \\ \vdots \\ \vdots \\ x_n \end{bmatrix} \qquad \text{...(B-1.1)}$$

where $x_1, x_2, \ldots\ldots, x_n$ are known as components of the vector $\overline{X}$. It is a n-dimensional column vector. The *transposed form* of it is given by

$$\overline{X}^T \triangleq [x_1, x_2 \ldots\ldots, x_n] \qquad \text{...(B-1.2)}$$

B.2 SPECIAL VECTORS

The *null vector* $\overline{O}$ and the *sum vector* $\overline{1}$ are defined as follows :

$$\overline{O} \triangleq \begin{bmatrix} 0 \\ 0 \\ \vdots \\ \vdots \\ 0 \end{bmatrix} \qquad \text{...(B-1.3)}$$

$$\overline{O} \triangleq \begin{bmatrix} 0 \\ 0 \\ \vdots \\ \vdots \\ 0 \end{bmatrix} \qquad \text{...(B-1.4)}$$

The *unit vector* $\overline{e}_j$ is defined as the vector whose jth component is unity and the rest of the components are zero.

$$\overline{e}_j \triangleq \begin{bmatrix} 0 \\ \vdots \\ \vdots \\ 0 \\ 1 \\ 0 \\ \vdots \\ \vdots \\ 0 \end{bmatrix} \qquad \text{...(B-1.5)}$$

B.3 SOME ELEMENTARY VECTOR OPERATIONS

Vector $\overline{X}$ and $\overline{Y}$ are said to be equal if $x_i = y_i$ for $i = 1, 2, \ldots n$.

Then we may write

$$\overline{X} = \overline{Y} \qquad \text{...(B-1.6)}$$

The product of a vector $\overline{X}$ with a scalar γ result into a new vector $\gamma\overline{X}$, each component being multiplied by same scalar ; *i.e.*,

$$\gamma\overline{X} = \overline{X}\gamma \triangleq \begin{bmatrix} x_1 \\ x_2 \\ \vdots \\ \vdots \\ x_n \end{bmatrix} = \begin{bmatrix} \gamma x_1 \\ \gamma x_2 \\ \vdots \\ \vdots \\ \gamma x_n \end{bmatrix} \qquad \text{...(B-1.7)}$$

Addition and subtraction of vectors $\overline{X}$ and $\overline{Y}$ of same dimensions resulting to two vectors *viz.*,

$$\overline{X} \pm \overline{Y} \overset{\Delta}{=} \begin{bmatrix} x_1 \pm y_1 \\ x_2 \pm y_2 \\ \vdots \\ \vdots \\ x_n \pm y_n \end{bmatrix} \quad \text{...(B-1.8)}$$

The following vector operations are also feasible,

$$\begin{gathered} \overline{X} + \overline{Y} = \overline{Y} + \overline{X} \\ \overline{X} + (\overline{Y} + \overline{Z}) = (\overline{X} + \overline{Y}) + \overline{Z} \\ \gamma_1 (\gamma_2 \overline{X}) = (\gamma_1 \gamma_2) \overline{X} \\ (\gamma_1 + \gamma_2) \overline{X} = \gamma_1 \overline{X} + \gamma_2 \overline{X} \\ \gamma (\overline{X} + \overline{Y}) = \gamma \overline{X} + \gamma \overline{Y} \\ \gamma (\overline{X} + \overline{Y} + \overline{Z}) = \gamma \overline{X} + \gamma \overline{Y} + \gamma \overline{Z} \\ O\overline{X} = \overline{0} \end{gathered} \quad \text{...(B-1.9)}$$

B.4 INNER VECTOR PRODUCT

The multiplication of two vectors $\overline{X}$ and $\overline{Y}$ of equal dimensions gives a very useful product and is called a *scalar or inner product.*

$$\overline{X}^T \overline{Y} \overset{\Delta}{=} \sum_{j=1}^{n} x_j y_j \overset{\Delta}{=} \overline{Y}^T \overline{X} \quad \text{...(B-1.10)}$$

Considering the two vectors $\overline{X}$ and $\overline{Y}$ defined by

$$\overline{X} = \begin{bmatrix} x_1 \\ x_2 \end{bmatrix} \overset{\Delta}{=} \begin{bmatrix} |\overline{X}| \cos \alpha \\ |\overline{X}| \sin \alpha \end{bmatrix};$$

$$\overline{Y} = \begin{bmatrix} y_1 \\ y_2 \end{bmatrix} \overset{\Delta}{=} \begin{bmatrix} |\overline{Y}| \cos \beta \\ |\overline{Y}| \sin \beta \end{bmatrix}$$

$$\begin{aligned} \overline{X}^T \overline{Y} &= x_1 y_1 + x_2 y_2 \\ &= |\overline{X}||\overline{Y}| (\cos \alpha \cos \beta + \sin \alpha \sin \beta) \\ &= |\overline{X}||\overline{Y}| \cos (\alpha - \beta) \\ &= |\overline{X}||\overline{Y}| \cos \phi \end{aligned} \quad \text{..(B-1.11)}$$

where $\phi(\alpha - \beta)$.

$$\therefore \quad \cos \phi = \frac{\overline{X}^T \overline{Y}}{|\overline{X}||\overline{Y}|} \quad \text{...(B.11(a))}$$

If $\overline{X} = \overline{Y}$, then $\alpha = \beta$ and $x_j = y_j$

$$\therefore \quad \overline{X}^T \overline{X} = x_1 x_2 + x_1 x_2 = |\overline{X}|^2 \quad \text{...(B-1.12)}$$

Two non-zero vectors are said to be *orthogonal* when $\phi = 90°$

i.e., $\quad \overline{X}^T \overline{Y} = 0 \quad$ ...(B-1.13)

B.5 MATRICES AND DETERMINANTS

B.5.1 Matrix

A *matrix* is a rectangular array of scalars arranged in rows and columns, each scalar being called an element or entry, of the matrix. The scalars involved may be *real* or *complex* numbers, *functions* of time, functions of frequency, derivative operators, etc.

The rectangular array

$$A = [a_{ij}]_{m,n} = \begin{bmatrix} a_{11} & a_{12} & \dots a_{1n} \\ a_{21} & a_{22} & \dots a_{2n} \\ a_{31} & a_{32} & \dots a_{3n} \\ \vdots & \vdots & \vdots \\ \vdots & \vdots & \vdots \\ a_{m1} & a_{m2} & a_{m3} \end{bmatrix}$$

is called a matrix of m rows and n columns. The scalar a_{ij} is called the ith row and the jth column element or the ijth element of the matrix. We shall use capital bold face letters, such as **A**, to denote matrices and the corresponding lower case letters with subscripts, such as a_{ij}, to denote its elements.

A matrix with m rows and n columns is known as the matrix of *order* $m \times n$ (read as m by n matrix). If for a matrix $m = n$ then the matrix is known as a *square matrix* or order n. A matrix with one row and n columns is known as a *row vector* and a matrix with m rows and one column is known as a *column vector*.

B.5.2 Use of Matrix

In analysis of problems in the fields of science and engineering there arise systems of linear equations, either algebraic or differential. If the systems contain many individual equations, the mere process of writing and visualizing them all becomes cumbersome. Matrix notation is a convenient method for writing such equations. Also, matrix notation simplifies the operations to be performed on the equations and their solutions. Just as one learns to think of a space vector with three components as a single entity, so also one can think of a system of equations as one matrix equation.

B.5.3 Basic Operations

Equality. Two matrices $\mathbf{A}=[a_{ij}]$ and $\mathbf{B}=[b_{ij}]$ are said to be equal if they are of the same order and if corresponding elements of the two matrices are identical.

$\therefore$ if A and B are both $(m\times n)$ matrices and $a_{ij}=b_{ij}$ for $i=1,2,\ldots,m, m=1,2,\ldots,n$

$$[A]=[B].$$

Multiplication by a Scalar. If a matrix A is multiplied by a scalar K (for example, a real or a complex number), then KA will be the matrix obtained by multiplying each element of one row or one column $[a_{ij}]$ of the matrix by K such that $K\mathbf{A}=[Ka_{ij}]$.

Addition of Matrices. Addition of two matrices is only possible if both the matrices are of the same order. If the two matrices are $A=[a_{ij}]$ and $B=[b_{ij}]$ then $A+B=[a_{ij}+b_{ij}]$.

Also (*i*) addition is commutative, that is

$$A+B=B+A$$

(*ii*) addition is associative, that is

$$A+(B+C)=(A+B)+C.$$

Subtraction of Matrices. Subtraction is addition with a negative sign. Hence the rule is the same as for addition.

Multiplication of Matrices. If $A=[a_{ij}]_{m,n}$ and $B=[b_{ij}]_{n,p}$ then the product of A and B is defined as $AB=C=[c_{ij}]_{m,p}$ where the elements of the product c_{ij} are given by

$$C_{ij}=\sum_{K=1}^{n} a_{ik}\, b_{kj}$$

$$=a_{i1}\, b_{1j}+a_{i2}\, b_{2j}+\ldots+a_{in}\, b_{nj}$$

That is, the (i, j)th element of the product is obtained by multiplying the elements of the ith row of the first matrix by the corresponding elements of the jth column of the second matrix, then adding these products. *This means that multiplication is valid only when number of columns in the first matrix is equal to the number of rows in the second matrix.* The product matrix has the same number of rows as the first matrix and the same number of columns as the second matrix.

Hence $AB\neq BA$.

Multiplication is associative if

$$(AB)\,C=A\,(BC)=ABC$$

and is distributive if

$$A\,(B+C)=AB+BC$$

EXAMPLE *Multiply matrix A by B where*

$$A=\begin{bmatrix} a_{11} & a_{12} & a_{13} \\ a_{21} & A_{22} & a_{23} \end{bmatrix}_{2,3}$$

$$B=\begin{bmatrix} b_{11} & b_{12} \\ b_{21} & b_{22} \\ b_{31} & b_{32} \end{bmatrix}_{3,2}$$

SOLUTION. Here A has 3 columns and B has 3 rows. Hence matrix multiplication is possible.

$$\therefore \quad AB=C=\begin{bmatrix} (a_{11}b_{11}+a_{12}b_{21}+a_{13}\,b_{31}) & (a_{11}b_{12}+a_{12}b_{22}+a_{13}\,b_{32}) \\ (a_{21}b_{11}+a_{22}b_{21}+a_{23}\,b_{31}) & (a_{21}b_{12}+a_{23}b_{22}+a_{23}\,b_{32}) \end{bmatrix}_{2,2}$$

B.5.4 Diagonal Matrix

If A is a square matrix, then the elements of the form a_{ij} are called the *diagonal elements*. A matrix in which all elements except the diagonal elements are zero is called a *diagonal matrix* ($a_{ij}=0$ for $i\neq j$). If A and B are $n\times n$ diagonal matrices, then $AB=BA$.

B.5.5 Identity of Unit Matrix

If in a diagonal matrix A, $a_{ij}=1$ for all i, then the matrix is known as *identity* or *unit matrix.* If an unit matrix is multiplied by a constant, the resulting matrix is a diagonal matrix with all diagonal elements equal to that constant. This matrix is called a *scalar matrix.*

B.5.6 Zero Matrix

If in a matrix A, $a_{ij}=0$ for all i and all j, then the matrix is known as *zero matrix.*

B.5.7 Trace

The trace of a square matrix A is a number denoted by $tr\,A$ and is defined as

$$tr\,A=\sum_{i=1}^{n} a_{ij}$$

where n is the *order* of the matrix A. Hence $tr\,A$ is the sum of the main diagonal elements of matrix A.

B.5.8 Transpose

Transposing is the operation of interchanging the rows and columns of a matrix. If the matrix $A=[a_{ij}]_{m,n}$ then the transpose of matrix A denoted by $A^T=[b_{ij}]_{n,m}$ where $b_{ij}=a_{ij}$. The transpose of a row matrix is a column matrix and *vice versa*. The transpose of the product of two matrices **A** and **B** is equal to the product of the transposes A^T and B^T but in opposite order, *i.e.*, $(AB)^T = B^T A^T$

If $$A=\begin{bmatrix} a_{11} & a_{12} & a_{13} \\ a_{21} & a_{22} & a_{23} \end{bmatrix}$$

then $$A^T=\begin{bmatrix} a_{11} & a_{21} \\ a_{12} & a_{22} \\ a_{13} & a_{23} \end{bmatrix}; \text{ Also } (A^T)^T = A.$$

A square matrix is *symmetric*, if it is equal to its transpose, *i.e.*, $A^T = A$; A being a symmetric matrix.

B.5.9 Determinants

Determinant associated with a square matrix **A** is denoted by det. A or $|A|$. Note that a matrix and its determinant area altogether two different things. If two matrices have equal determinants, this does not imply that the matrices are equal; the two matrices may even by of different orders.

B.5.10 Minor

The determinant associated with the sub-matrix of A obtained by deleting its ith row and jth column is called the *minor* of the element a_{ij} and is denoted by M_{ij}.

B.5.11 Cofactor

The cofactor A_{ij} of the element a_{ij} is defined by the relation, $A_{ij}=(-1)^{i+j}M_{ij}$.

B.5.12 Evaluation of a Determinant

Let A be an $n\times n$ matrix with $n>2$, then

$$\det A=\sum_{i=1}^{n} a_{ij}A_{ij} \quad \text{for any } j=1,2,\ldots\ldots,n.$$

This formula is called as expansion of det A along the ith column.

Also $$\det A=\sum_{j=1}^{n} a_{ij}A_{ij}$$

for any $i=1,2,\ldots\ldots,n$.

This formula is called as expansion of det A along the ith row.

Example *Expand det. A along the row and also along the column.*

$$A=[a_{ij}]_{3,3}=\begin{bmatrix} a_{11} & a_{12} & a_{13} \\ a_{21} & a_{22} & a_{23} \\ a_{31} & a_{32} & a_{33} \end{bmatrix}$$

Solution. $\det A=\sum_{j=1}^{3} a_{ij}A_{ij}$ for any $i=1,2,3$

expansion along rows

$$=a_{11}A_{11}+a_{12}A_{12}+a_{13}A_{13}$$

for expansion along 1st row

$$=a_{11}M_{11}+a_{12}(-M_{12})+a_{13}M_{13}$$
$$=a_{11}M_{11}-a_{12}M_{12}+a_{13}M_{13}$$
$$=a_{11}\begin{vmatrix} a_{22} & a_{23} \\ a_{32} & a_{33} \end{vmatrix}-a_{12}\begin{vmatrix} a_{21} & a_{23} \\ a_{31} & a_{33} \end{vmatrix}+a_{13}\begin{vmatrix} a_{21} & a_{22} \\ a_{31} & a_{32} \end{vmatrix}$$

$$=a_{11}(a_{22}a_{33}-a_{23}a_{32})-a_{12}(a_{21}a_{33}-a_{23}a_{31})+a_{13}(a_{21}a_{33}-a_{23}a_{31})$$

Also $\det A=\sum_{i=1}^{3} a_{ij}A_{ij}$ for any $j=1,2,3$

expansion along columns

$$=a_{11}A_{11}+a_{21}A_{21}+a_{31}A_{31}$$

for expansion along 1st column

$$=a_{11}M_{11}+a_{21}M_{21}+a_{31}M_{31}$$
$$=a_{11}\begin{vmatrix} a_{22} & a_{23} \\ a_{32} & a_{33} \end{vmatrix}-a_{21}\begin{vmatrix} a_{12} & a_{13} \\ a_{32} & a_{33} \end{vmatrix}+a_{31}\begin{vmatrix} a_{12} & a_{13} \\ a_{22} & a_{23} \end{vmatrix}$$

$$=a_{11}(a_{22}a_{33}-a_{23}a_{32})-a_{21}(a_{12}a_{33}-a_{13}a_{32})+a_{31}(a_{12}a_{23}-a_{13}a_{22}).$$

B.5.13 Singular Matrix

A matrix whose determinant is zero is known as a singular matrix.

B.5.14 Non-singular Matrix

A matrix whose determinant is not zero is known as *Non-singular matrix.*

B.5.15 Rank of a Matrix

Consider a rectangular matrix **A** with m rows and n columns. Any matrix obtained from A by deleting some rows and/or some columns is called a submatrix of A. The number r is called the rank of A

is (*i*) all $l \times l$ submatrices with $l > r$ have a determinant which is equal to zero, and if (*ii*) at least one $r \times r$ submatrix has a determinant which is different from zero.

B.5.16 Inverse of a Matrix

For a given square matrix A if there exists another matrix B such that $\mathbf{AB} = \mathbf{BA} = U$ then B is called as the inverse of A, where U is the *unit or identity matrix* (which is defined as a square matrix of any order having elements on the main diagonal as I and all other elements as zero).

Such a B may not exist, but if it exists then we write $B = A^{-1}$ or $A = B^{-1}$ and B is given as

$$B = [b_{ij}], \quad \text{where } b_{ij} = \frac{A_{ij}}{\det \mathbf{A}}$$

In other words, to form the inverse of A replace all elements of A by its cofactor, take the transpose and finally divide by the determinant of A.

Also

$$A^{-1}A = AA^{-1} = I\ ;\ (AB)^{-1} = B^{-1}A^{-1};\ (A^{-1})^T = (A^T)^{-1};\ (A^T)^{-1} = A$$

B.5.17 Adjoint Matrix

The adjoint of matrix A is defined as a matrix whose elements in the ith row are the cofactors of the elements of the ith column of matrix A and is denoted as

$$\text{adj } A = [A_{ij}]^T = \begin{bmatrix} A_{11} & A_{21} & A_{31} \\ A_{12} & A_{22} & A_{32} \\ A_{13} & A_{23} & A_{33} \end{bmatrix}$$

Hence the inverse of a matrix A may be written as $A^{-1} = \dfrac{1}{\det A}$ adj A

EXAMPLE *Find the inverse of the matrix A*

$$A = \begin{bmatrix} 1 & 2 & 3 \\ 4 & 5 & 6 \\ 7 & 8 & 9 \end{bmatrix}$$

SOLUTION.

$$\det A = 1(445 - 48) - 2(36 - 42) + 3(42 - 35)$$
$$= -3 + 12 - 9 = 0$$

Hence matrix A does not have inverse.

EXAMPLE *Find the adjoint of matrix A.*

$$A = \begin{bmatrix} 1 & 2 & 3 \\ 4 & 5 & 6 \\ 7 & 8 & 1 \end{bmatrix}$$

and hence find the inverse matrix A^{-1}.

SOLUTION.

$$A = \begin{bmatrix} (5-6\times 8) & -(4-6\times 7), & (4\times 8-7\times 5) \\ -(2-3\times 8) & (1-7\times 3), & -(8-7\times 2) \\ (2\times 6-5\times 3) & -(6-4\times 3), & (5-4\times 2) \end{bmatrix}$$

$$= \begin{bmatrix} -43 & 38 & -3 \\ 22 & -20 & 6 \\ -3 & 6 & -3 \end{bmatrix}^T = \begin{bmatrix} -43 & 22 & -3 \\ 38 & -20 & 6 \\ -0 & 6 & -3 \end{bmatrix}$$

$$A^{-1} = \frac{1}{\det. A} \text{adj } A$$

$$\det A = 1(5-6\times 8) - 2(4\times 1 - 7\times 6) + 3(4\times 8 - 7\times 5)$$
$$= -43 + 76 - 9$$
$$= -52 + 76 = 24$$

$$\therefore \quad sA^{-1} = \frac{1}{24}\begin{bmatrix} -43 & 22 & -3 \\ 38 & -20 & 6 \\ -3 & 6 & -3 \end{bmatrix}$$

$$= \begin{bmatrix} \frac{43}{24} & \frac{11}{12} & \frac{1}{8} \\ 38 & -20 & 6 \\ -3 & 6 & -3 \end{bmatrix}$$

B.5.18 Some Important Properties of Determinants

1. If *A, B* are $(n \times n)$ square matrices, then
   (*a*) $\det \mathbf{A} = \det \mathbf{A}^T$.
   (*b*) $\det(AB) = \det A . \det B$.
2. Let p be an integer with $1 \le p \le n$. If all the elements of the pth row or of the pth column of the matrix A are zero, then $\det A = 0$.
3. If every element of any row or any column of a determinant is multiplied by a scalar K, the determinant is multiplied by K.
4. Interchanging any two rows or columns of determinant changes the sign of the determinant.
5. If any two rows or columns are identical then the determinant is zero.
6. The determinant is unchanged if to each element of any row of column is added a scalar multiple of the corresponding element of any other row or column.

Example *Show that the two matrices* **A** *and* **B** *have equal determinants though the matrices are not equal.*

$$A=\begin{bmatrix}1&2&3\\4&5&6\\7&8&9\end{bmatrix} \text{ and } B=\begin{bmatrix}2&4&6\\4&5&6\\7&8&9\end{bmatrix}$$

Solution.

$$\det A = 1(5\times 9-8\times 6)-2(4\times 9-7\times 6) +3(4\times 8-7\times 5) = -3+12-9=0$$

$$\det B = 2(5\times 9-8\times 6)-4(4\times 9-7\times 6) +6(4\times 8-7\times 5) = -6+24-18=0$$

Hence the determinants of matrices *A* and *B* are equal but the elements of the matrices are not identical.

B.6 SOLUTION OF LINEAR EQUATIONS BY DETERMINANTS. CRAMER'S RULE

Consider the system of three linear equations in three unknowns x_1, x_2, x_3

$$a_{11}x_1 + a_{12}x_2 + a_{13}x_3 = k_1$$
$$a_{21}x_1 + a_{22}x_2 + a_{23}x_3 = k_2$$
$$a_{31}x_1 + a_{32}x_2 + a_{33}x_3 = k_3$$

These equations may be written in matrix form as

$$\begin{bmatrix}a_{11}&a_{12}&a_{13}\\a_{21}&a_{22}&a_{23}\\a_{31}&a_{32}&a_{33}\end{bmatrix}\begin{bmatrix}x_1\\x_2\\x_3\end{bmatrix}=\begin{bmatrix}k_1\\k_2\\k_3\end{bmatrix}$$

The numerical value of the coefficient determinant, Δ_a, is multiplied by x_1 if each element of the first column is multiplied by x_1

$$\Delta_a = \begin{vmatrix}a_{11}&a_{12}&a_{13}\\a_{21}&a_{22}&a_{23}\\a_{31}&a_{32}&a_{33}\end{vmatrix} \text{ and}$$

$$x_1\,\Delta_a = \begin{vmatrix}a_{11}x_1&a_{12}&a_{13}\\a_{21}x_1&a_{22}&a_{23}\\a_{31}x_1&a_{32}&a_{33}\end{vmatrix}$$

If to each element of the first column of the last determinant we now add x_2 times the corresponding element of the second column and x_3 times the corresponding element of the third column, we get

$$x_1\Delta_a = \begin{vmatrix}(a_{11}x_1+a_{12}x_2+a_{13}x_3)&a_{12}&a_{13}\\(a_{21}x_1+a_{22}x_2+a_{23}x_3)&a_{22}&a_{23}\\(a_{31}x_1+a_{32}x_2+a_{33}x_3)&a_{32}&a_{33}\end{vmatrix}$$

$$= \begin{vmatrix}k_1&a_{12}&a_{13}\\k_2&a_{22}&a_{23}\\k_3&a_{32}&a_{33}\end{vmatrix}$$

or $$x_1 = \frac{\begin{vmatrix}k_1&a_{12}&a_{13}\\k_2&a_{22}&a_{23}\\k_3&a_{32}&a_{33}\end{vmatrix}}{\Delta_a} \text{ provided } \Delta_a \neq 0$$

Similarly, or $$x_2 = \frac{\begin{vmatrix}a_{11}&k_1&a_{13}\\a_{21}&k_2&a_{23}\\a_{31}&k_3&a_{33}\end{vmatrix}}{\Delta_a}$$ and

$$x_3 = \frac{\begin{vmatrix}a_{11}&a_{12}&k_1\\a_{21}&a_{22}&k_2\\a_{31}&a_{32}&k_3\end{vmatrix}}{\Delta_a}$$

This method of solution, called Cramer's Rule, can be applied to any system of *n* linear equations in *n* unknowns *provided* the coefficients determinant is not zero.

Example *Solve*

$$2x_1 - x^2 + 2x_3 = 2$$
$$x_1 + 10x_2 3x_3 = 5$$
$$-x_1 + x_2 + x_3 = -3$$

Solution. The determinant of the system is

$$\Delta = \begin{bmatrix}2&-1&2\\1&10&-3\\-1&1&1\end{bmatrix} = 46$$

According to Cramer's Rule

$$x_1 = \frac{D_1}{\Delta},\quad x_2 = \frac{D_2}{\Delta},\quad \ldots\quad x_n = \frac{D_n}{\Delta}$$

where D_n is the determinant obtained from Δ by replacing in Δ the *p*th column by the column with the elements $k_1, \ldots\ldots, k_n$.

Here we have

$$D_1 = \begin{bmatrix} 2 & -1 & 2 \\ 5 & 10 & -3 \\ -3 & 1 & 1 \end{bmatrix} = 92\,;$$

$$D_2 = \begin{bmatrix} 2 & -2 & 2 \\ 1 & 5 & -3 \\ -1 & -3 & 1 \end{bmatrix} = 0$$

$$D_3 = \begin{bmatrix} 2 & -1 & 2 \\ 1 & 10 & 5 \\ -1 & 1 & -3 \end{bmatrix} = -46$$

Therefore, $x_1 = 2,\ x_2 = 0$ and $x_3 = -1$

Alternatively, using the method of matrices

Let $\begin{bmatrix} 2 & -1 & 2 \\ 1 & 10 & -3 \\ -1 & 1 & 1 \end{bmatrix} = \begin{bmatrix} a_1 & b_1 & c_1 \\ a_2 & b_2 & c_2 \\ a_3 & b_3 & c_3 \end{bmatrix} = [A]$ (say)

Then $\Delta = \begin{vmatrix} a_1 & b_1 & c_1 \\ a_2 & b_2 & c_2 \\ a_3 & b_3 & c_3 \end{vmatrix}$

$$= \begin{bmatrix} 2 & -1 & 2 \\ 1 & 10 & -3 \\ -1 & 1 & 1 \end{bmatrix}$$

$$= 2 \times 13 - 1 \times 2 + 2 \times 11$$

$$= 46 \text{ (as found before)}$$

Co-factors are

$$A_1 = \begin{vmatrix} 10 & -3 \\ 1 & 1 \end{vmatrix} = 13,$$

$$B_1 = (-)\begin{vmatrix} 1 & -3 \\ -1 & 1 \end{vmatrix} = 2,$$

$$C_1 = \begin{vmatrix} 1 & 10 \\ -1 & 1 \end{vmatrix} = 11$$

$$A_2 = (-)\begin{vmatrix} -1 & 2 \\ 1 & 1 \end{vmatrix} = 13, \quad B_2 = \begin{vmatrix} 2 & 2 \\ -1 & 1 \end{vmatrix} = 4,$$

$$C_2 = (-)\begin{vmatrix} 2 & -1 \\ -1 & 1 \end{vmatrix} = -1$$

$$A_3 = \begin{vmatrix} -1 & 2 \\ 10 & -3 \end{vmatrix} = -17, \quad B_3 = (-)\begin{vmatrix} 2 & 2 \\ 1 & -3 \end{vmatrix} = 4,$$

$$C_3 = \begin{vmatrix} 2 & -1 \\ 1 & 10 \end{vmatrix} = 21$$

$$\text{adj}[A] = \begin{vmatrix} A_1 & A_2 & A_3 \\ B_1 & B_2 & B_3 \\ C_1 & C_2 & C_3 \end{vmatrix} = \begin{bmatrix} 13 & 3 & -17 \\ 2 & 4 & 8 \\ 11 & -1 & 21 \end{bmatrix}$$

and $[A]^{-1} = \text{adj}.[A]/\Delta$

$$= \frac{1}{46}\begin{bmatrix} 13 & 3 & -17 \\ 2 & 4 & 8 \\ 11 & -1 & 21 \end{bmatrix}$$

If we put $\begin{bmatrix} 2 \\ 5 \\ -3 \end{bmatrix} = [E]$

we may write the given set of equation as

$$[A]\,[x] = [E]$$

Pre-multiplying both sides by $[A]^{-1}$ we get

$$[x] = [A]^{-1}\,[E]$$

or $x = \begin{bmatrix} x_1 \\ x_2 \\ x_3 \end{bmatrix} = [A]^{-1}\begin{bmatrix} 2 \\ 5 \\ -3 \end{bmatrix}$

$$= \frac{1}{46}\begin{bmatrix} 13 & 3 & -17 \\ 2 & 4 & 8 \\ 11 & -1 & 21 \end{bmatrix}\begin{bmatrix} 2 \\ 5 \\ -3 \end{bmatrix}$$

$$= \frac{1}{46}\begin{bmatrix} 26 + 15 + 51 \\ 4 + 20 - 24 \\ 22 - 5 - 63 \end{bmatrix}$$

$$= \frac{1}{46}\begin{bmatrix} 92 \\ 0 \\ -46 \end{bmatrix} = \begin{bmatrix} 2 \\ 0 \\ -1 \end{bmatrix}$$

So that $x_1 = 2, x_2 = 0$ and $x_3 = -1$ (as before).

APPENDIX

C

The Fourier Integral and Transform

Let us consider a rectangular pulse train, shown in Fig. C0, which can be mathematically represented as

$$f(t) = V_0, \text{ for } -\frac{a}{2} < t < \frac{a}{2}$$

$$= 0, \quad \text{for } -\frac{T}{2} < t < -\frac{a}{2}, \ \frac{a}{2} < t < \frac{T}{2}.$$

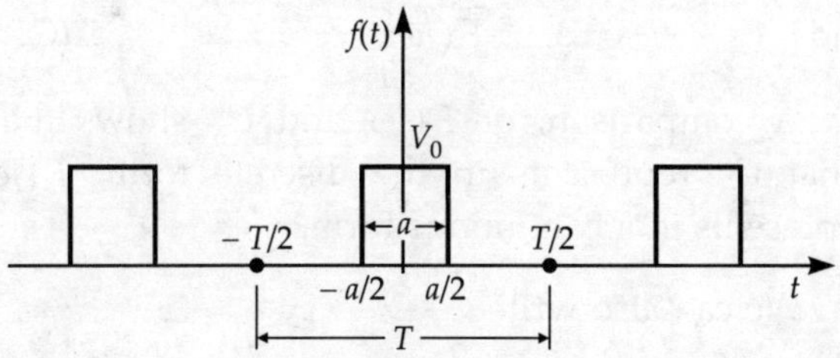

Fig. C0 Rectangular Pulse train.

The ratio (*a*/*T*) or pulse duration to time period, is important and is defined as the *duty factor*. The *n*th Fourier coefficient of $f(t)$ is given by

$$c_n = \frac{1}{T} \int_{-a/2}^{a/2} V_0 \, e^{-jn\omega_0 t} \, dt = \frac{V_0}{T} \left[-\frac{e^{-jn\omega_0 t}}{jn\omega_0} \right]_{-a/2}^{a/2}$$

For $T = 2\pi/\omega_0$.

$$C_n = \frac{V_0}{n\pi} \left[\frac{e^{jn\omega_0 a/2} - e^{-jn\omega_0 a/2}}{2j} \right]$$

$$= V_0 \frac{\omega_0 a}{2\pi} \left[\frac{\sin(n\omega_0 a/2)}{n\omega_0 a/2} \right]$$

or, $$C_n = V_0 \frac{a}{T} \left[\frac{\sin(n\omega_0 a/2)}{\pi\omega_0 a/2} \right] \qquad \text{...(C1)}$$

The expression of C_n is seen to be of the form of a sampling function, $k(\sin x / x)$, shown in Fig. C1; here *k*, in the expression, is a constant.

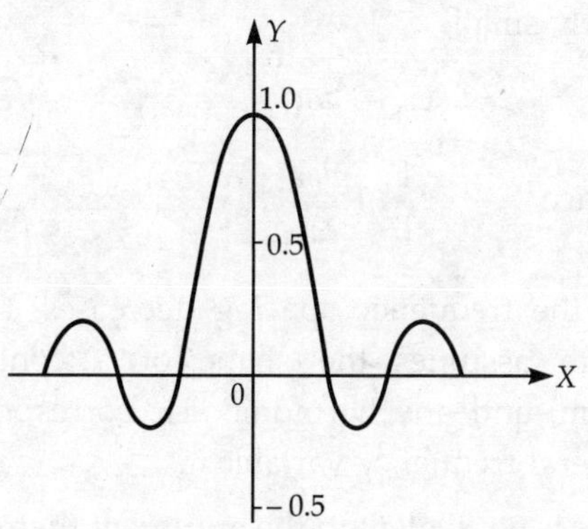

Fig. C1 The sampling function $\frac{\sin x}{x}$.

Equation (C1) has only discrete frequencies $n\omega_0$, so that the line spectrum may be plotted for C_n. However, we can also draw a continuous envelope of c_n by replacing $n\omega_0$ by ω in the equation. The effect of duty factor on the amplitude of spectra, is shown in Fig. C2.

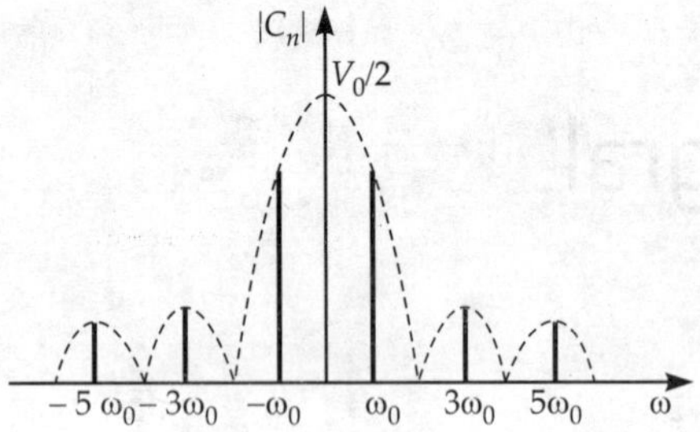

Fig. C2 Line spectra of periodic pulse trains for $\frac{T}{a} = 2$.

As (a/T) decreases, the number of lines in a specified interval would become large; the separation, between lines, would become small, while the amplitudes of the spectral lines would also decrease.

The general case for any waveform can be studied by starting with the exponential representation :

$$f(t) = \sum_{n=-\infty}^{\infty} C_n\, e^{jn\omega_0 t} \qquad \text{...(C2)}$$

where $$C_n = \frac{1}{T}\int_{-T/2}^{T/2} f(t)\, e^{-jn\omega_0 t}\, dt \qquad \text{...(C3)}$$

Let $T \to \infty$ [for non periodic waveforms]

This would make the value of $\omega_0 = \frac{2\pi}{T}$ extremely small,

i.e., $$\omega_0 \to d\omega \qquad \text{...(C4)}$$

Hence $$\frac{1}{T} \to \frac{d\omega}{2\pi} \qquad \text{...(C5)}$$

As the frequency spacing decreases, the line spectrum assumes the shape of a continuous spectrum; and any harmonic $n\omega_0$ corresponds to the general frequency variable ω.

This is equivalent to the argument that while n tends to infinity, ω_0 approaches zero, such that their product is finite, *i.e.,* $n\omega_0 \to \omega$

Substituting the limiting operations ($T \to \infty$), we find that, the amplitudes of C_n approach zero. In order to avoid this situation, we obtain the result for

$$C_n\, T \to \int_{-\infty}^{\infty} f(t)\, e^{-f\omega t}\, dt \qquad \text{...(C6)}$$

which is finite. The right hand integral is called the *Fourier Integral* $F(j\omega)$ and is a function of ω.

Hence $$F(j\omega) \triangleq \int_{-\infty}^{\infty} f(t)\, e^{-j\omega t}\, dt. \qquad \text{...(C7)}$$

Now $f(t)$ can be written as

$$f(t) = \sum_{n=-\infty}^{\infty} C_n\, T e^{jn\omega_0 t}\, \frac{1}{T}.$$

Using Eq. (C5), (C6) and (C7) under the limiting case, the summation becomes integration, so that

$$f(t) = \frac{1}{2\pi}\int_{-\infty}^{\infty} F(j\omega)\, e^{j\omega t}\, d\omega \qquad \text{...(C8)}$$

Eqs. (C7) and (C8) form the *Fourier Transform pair*. Here $F(j\omega)$ is the *Fourier transform* of $f(t)$, while $f(t)$ is the *Fourier inverse* of $F(j\omega)$,

$$F(j\omega) = \Im\, f(t) \qquad \text{...(C9)}$$

and $$f(t) = \Im^{-1}\, F(j\omega). \qquad \text{...(C10)}$$

A comparison, of $F(j\omega)$ and C_n shows that, what C_n represents in the discrete form, $F(j\omega)$ represents in a continuous form.

We can also write :

$$F(j\omega) = |F(j\omega)|\, e^{j\phi(\omega)} \qquad \text{...(C11)}$$

where $|F(j\omega)|$ is the *continuous amplitude spectrum* and $\phi(\omega)$ is the *continuous phase spectrum.*

The variation of $F(j\omega)$ with $\phi(\omega)$, does not indicate the magnitude of voltage at a given frequency (this being zero !). In fact, it can be defined that the voltage present, in an incremental frequency gap, $\Delta\omega$, is $F(j\omega)\,\Delta\omega$

Some important Fourier transforms are given in Table C1 on next page.

Table C1 *Fourier Transform Operation*

Function	*Fourier Transform*
$f(t)$	$F(f) = \Im f(t)$
$a\, f_1(t) + bf_2(t)$	$a\, F_1(f) + b\, F_2(f)$
$\dfrac{a^n f(t)}{dt^n}$	$(j\omega)^n F(f)$
$\int_{-\infty}^{t} f(T)\, dT$	$\dfrac{F(f)}{j\omega}$
$f(f - a)$	$e^{-j\omega a} F(f)$
$e^{j2\pi f_0 t}$	$F(f - f_0)$
$f(at)$	$\dfrac{1}{a} F(f/a)$
$\int_{-\infty}^{+\infty} f_1(T)\, f_2(t - T)\, dT$	$F_1(t)\, F_2(t)$
$f_1(t)\, f_2(T)$	$\int_{-\infty}^{+\infty} F_1(\bar{f})\, F_2(f - (\bar{f})\, d\bar{f}$

Dirichlet's Condition

All periodic functions satisfy Dirichlet's condition and then they can be expressed by a trigonometric series given by

$$f(x) = a_0 + \sum_{n=1}^{\infty} (a_n \cos nx + b_n \sin nx).$$

[a_0, a_n and b_n are constants].

A function $f(x)$ is said to satisfy the Dirichlet's condition when, during the interval of t_1 and t_2,

(*a*) it is uniformly bounded, *i.e.*, $|f(x)| \leq K$ where $t_1 < K < t_2$ and K is a constant;

(*b*) it has finite number of points of discontinuity and at each discontinuity, the function has finite limit both on left and right;

(*c*) it has finite number of points of maximum and minimum. Thus the function following Dirichlet's condition are single valued, finite and have a finite number of maxima and minima with finite number of discontinuities.

APPENDIX

D

Complex Frequency

It is a generalised frequency whose real part σ describes growth or decay of the amplitudes of signals and whose imaginary part $j\omega$ is the angular frequency. This complex frequency is applicable for cisoidal signals where

$$r(t) = Ae^{j\omega t} \quad \text{[Fig. D1]}$$

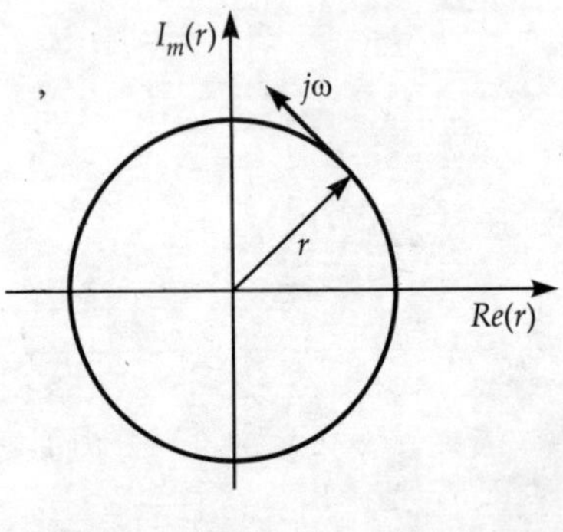

Fig. D1

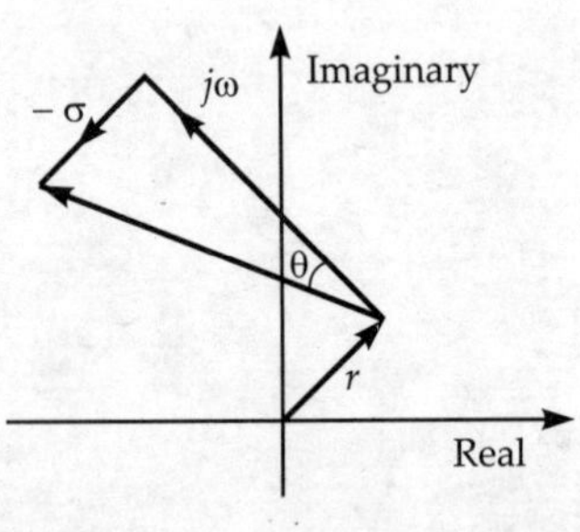

Fig. D2

The angular frequency ω can be taken as a velocity at the end of the phasor $r(t)$ [since the velocity is also at right angles to the phasor.]

Next, let us consider a general case when the velocity (symbolised as 's') is inclined with an angle θ [Fig. D2].

Here $\quad s = -\sigma + j\omega$

[s is composed of a component ω at right angles to r and another component $-\sigma$ parallel to r. $-\sigma$ component reduces magnitude of r as it rotates counter clockwise towards origin]

$$\therefore \qquad Re[r(t)] = Ae^{-\sigma t} \cos \omega t$$

$$I_m [r(t)] = Ae^{-\sigma t} \sin \omega t$$

[ref. Fig. D3]

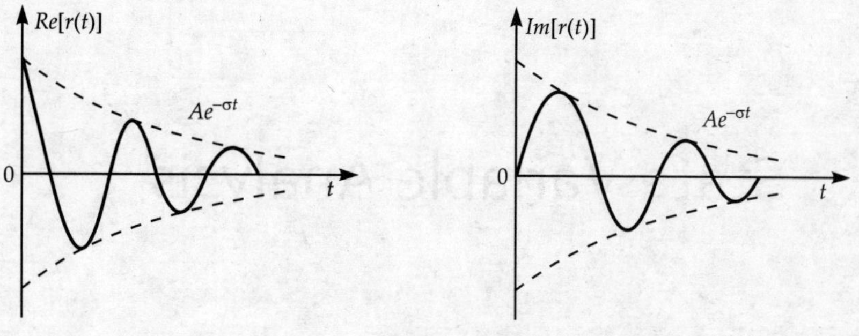

Fig. D3

On the other hand, if $s = \sigma + j\omega$ [Fig. D4], the phasor increases exponentially in magnitude.

Then, in general, for a cisoidal signal,

$$r(t) = Ae^{st} = Ae^{(\sigma + j\omega)t}$$

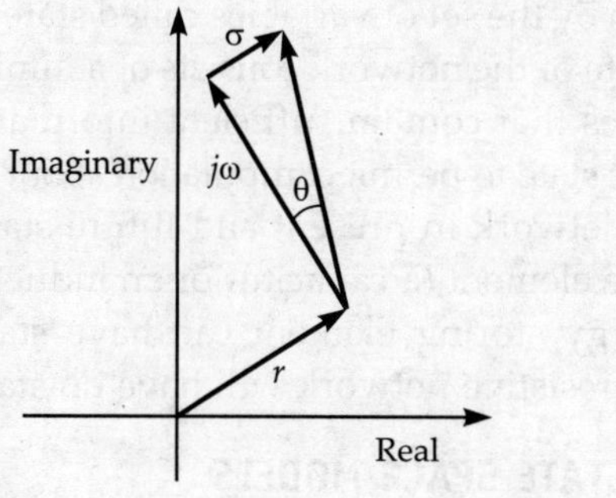

Fig. D4

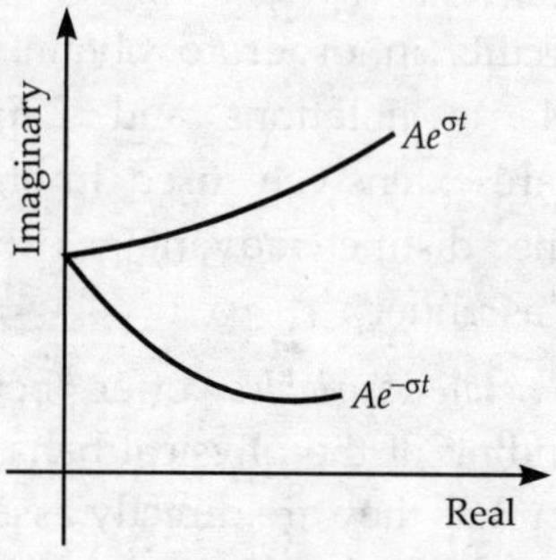

Fig. D5

If σ is +ve, signal amplitude increases,

σ is zero, sinusoid is undamped,

σ is –ve, sinusoid is damped,

$j\omega$ is zero, signal is exponential,

$j\omega = 0 = \sigma$, signal is constant.

APPENDIX

E

State Variable Analysis

E.1 INTRODUCTION

State variable analysis is a way of analysing the dynamic circuits in order to obtain its transfer function. Matrix notations and Laplace transformations are extensively used in state variable analysis. The distinct advantages of such an analysis are as under :

(*a*) the *state variables* offer better understanding of the physical behaviour of the circuit as they are directly associated with energy storage,

(*b*) formation of *state equations* may be easier in most of the cases than conventional mesh or node equations,

(*c*) for multiple input-output circuits, state equations represent the most compact form of representation,

(*d*) it is very convenient to solve state equations using Laplace transformation,

(*e*) transformed state equations can be combined with output equations to obtain transfer functions relating all inputs to outputs,

(*f*) using computer simulation techniques, it is convenient to solve state equations numerically in the time domain,

(*g*) for non-linear circuits, it is possible to represent the circuit behaviour using state equations.

The concept of *state* is important in state variable analysis. The state of a network at any time is given by the set of variables called state variables. The state of the network consists of a minimal set of variables that contain sufficient information about the past state to permit computation about behaviour of the network in present and future state. Only a reactive element (a capacitor or an inductor) acting as energy storing element can have states and a purely resistive network will have no state at all.

E.2 STATE SPACE MODELS

The linear, time invariant circuit analysis does not provide a complete solution to the task of analysing and controlling the circuit dynamics. This is basically due to the fact that some circuits can exhibit instability wherein the system variables alternate between low and high values from cycle to cycle. A model based on the assumption that variables change slowly may not be suitable in analysing this instability. Moreover, circuit models are sometimes inappropriate for describing the controllers used to regulate the circuit.

State space models provide a much more general and powerful basis for dynamic modelling. They are particularly important in analysing, simulating and controlling both steady state behaviour and perturbations away from it. State space models also provide a uniform and convenient starting point for the tasks of steady state computation, linearisation, stability evaluation, transient analysis and simulation.

E.3 STATE VARIABLES, INPUTS AND OUTPUTS

The key variables in a state-space model are the *state variables,* whose values together define the state of the system.

State variables may be defined by the smallest set of variables such that the knowledge of these variables at $t = t_0$ as well as the knowledge of the input for $t \geq t_0$ completely determines the behaviour of the system for any time $t \geq t_0$.

State variables summarise those aspects of the past that are relevant to the future; *i.e.*, they are the variables whose initial values are needed to determine future system behaviour. Natural state variables in electrical circuits are the currents or flux linkages in inductors and the voltage or charges on capacitors.

In addition to state variables, other variables of importance are *inputs* and *outputs* of the system. The inputs to the system are external signals, such as the waveforms of voltage or current sources. On the other hand, the outputs of the system are either measured quantities or those whose values are of interest. In electrical circuits, the typical outputs may be voltages, currents or power dissipation.

E.4 CONTINUOUS-TIME MODELS

Let us take a model system with n state variables x_i, $i = 1$ to n, and with m inputs u_j, $j = 1$ to m. A continuous state space model of the system then takes the form of a set of coupled, non-linear, time varying, first order differential equations :

$$\frac{dx_1}{dt} = \dot{x}_1(t) = f_1(x_1(t), x_2(t), \ldots, x_n(t), u_1(t), \ldots, u_m(t), t)$$

$$\frac{dx_2}{dt} = \dot{x}_2(t) = f_2(x_1(t), x_2(t), \ldots, x_n(t), u_1(t), \ldots, u_m(t), t)$$

....

$$\frac{dx_n}{dt} = \dot{x}_n(t) = f_n(x_1(t), x_2(t), \ldots, x_n(t), u_1(t), \ldots, u_m(t), t) \quad \text{...(E.1)}$$

The above equations represent the instantaneous rates of change of each of the n state variables as functions of the indicated arguments, namely, the instantaneous values of all the state variables and inputs and the time argument t itself. The model is of nth order involving n state variables.

E.5 STATE-SPACE MODELS APPLICABLE FOR ELECTRIC CIRCUITS

We know that, if the current through an inductor L is i_L, the inductor voltage is $\left[\frac{d(Li_L)}{dt}\right]$; and if the voltage across a capacitor C be v_C, the capacitor current is $\left[\frac{d(Cv_C)}{dt}\right]$.

These relationships suggest a simple way to express the state variable derivatives in the required form. Let us take a *RLC* series circuit to illustrate the formation of state variables. Let the current at time $t = 0$ be $i_L(0)$ and the capacitor voltage at time $t = 0$ be $v_C(0)$. Thus, the state of the network at $t = 0$ is specified by the inductor current and capacitor voltage.

Here, initial state being defined by $[i_L(0), v_C(0)]$, $[i_L(t), v_C(t)]$ define the state of the network at time t. The variables $i_L(t)$ and $v_C(t)$ are called *state variables* of the network.

The governing equations of this *RLC* series circuit may be represented by

$$Ri_L + L\frac{di_L}{dt} + v_C = 0 \quad \text{...(E.2)}$$

$$i_C = i_L = C\frac{dv_C}{dt} \quad \text{...(E.3)}$$

Rearranging these two equations,

$$\frac{di_L}{dt} = \left(-\frac{R}{L}\right)i_L + \left(-\frac{1}{L}\right)v_C \quad \text{...(E.4)}$$

$$\frac{dv_C}{dt} = \left(\frac{1}{C}\right).i_L \quad \text{...(E.5)}$$

Equations (E.4) and (E.5) are called *state equations*. In such equations all the variables present are state variables.

Any state equation represents the dynamical behaviour of the given network. State equations usually follow a specific 'format' while being represented. On the left side of each state equation, the derivative of only one variable is used (refer to equations E.4 and E.5). On the right hand side a mathematical function is represented involving any or all the state variables and the sources. Derivatives do not appear on the right-hand side.

Equations (E.4) and (E.5) can be represented in matrix form as

$$\begin{bmatrix} \dfrac{di_L}{dt} \\ \dfrac{dv_C}{dt} \end{bmatrix} = \begin{bmatrix} -\dfrac{R}{L} & -\dfrac{1}{L} \\ \dfrac{1}{C} & 0 \end{bmatrix} \begin{bmatrix} i_L \\ v_C \end{bmatrix} \quad \text{...(E.6)}$$

or

$$\frac{d}{dt}\begin{bmatrix} i_L \\ v_C \end{bmatrix} = \begin{bmatrix} -\dfrac{R}{L} & -\dfrac{1}{L} \\ \dfrac{1}{C} & 0 \end{bmatrix} \begin{bmatrix} i_L \\ v_C \end{bmatrix} \quad \text{...(E.6(a))}$$

Defining above matrix form as

$$x(t) \triangleq \begin{bmatrix} i_L \\ v_C \end{bmatrix}; \quad A = \begin{bmatrix} -\dfrac{R}{L} & -\dfrac{1}{L} \\ \dfrac{1}{C} & 0 \end{bmatrix},$$

equation (E.6(*a*)) can be represented as

$$\frac{d}{dt}x(t) = A\,x(t) \text{ i.e., } \dot{x}(t) = A\,x(t) \quad \text{...(E.7)}$$

Here, elements of $x(t)$, the column matrix are state variables i_L and v_C and hence $x(t)$ is known as *state vector*. $x(0)$ is termed as *initial state vector*.

The state variable analysis exhibits relationship between the state variable and the inputs. A circuit may have several inputs of voltage and current sources. Usually we represent the inputs as $u_1(t)$, $u_2(t), \ldots\ldots, u_k(t)$. The state variables may also be a mix of voltages and currents and we can denote them by $x_1(t)$, $x_2(t), \ldots\ldots, x_n(t)$ while their derivatives are $\dot{x}_1(t)$, $\dot{x}_2(t), \ldots\ldots, \dot{x}_n(t)$.

In state variable analysis, the state incorporates the required informations about the past needed to calculate the present values and to predict future behaviour. For this purpose a minimal set of mutually independent variables may be selected as state variables for any particular circuit. *The number of state variables never exceeds the number of energy storing elements in the circuit.* The number of state variables equals the number of independent energy-storage elements. Also, as the state variables provide circuit behaviour in dynamic state, the role of the derivatives of the state variable is also important. Thus, as a consequence of this property, it is possible to write the state equation as a set of coupled first order differential equations relating the state variables and the inputs.

Thus for the circuit with n independent energy storage elements is described by n state variables and since the circuit is assumed to have k inputs, we can write in matrix form

$$\begin{bmatrix} \dot{x}_1(t) \\ \dot{x}_2(t) \\ \vdots \\ \dot{x}_n(t) \end{bmatrix} = \begin{bmatrix} A_{11} & A_{12} & \cdots & A_{1n} \\ A_{21} & A_{22} & \cdots & A_{2n} \\ \vdots & \vdots & \cdots & \vdots \\ A_{n1} & A_{n2} & \cdots & A_{nn} \end{bmatrix} \begin{bmatrix} x_1(t) \\ x_2(t) \\ \vdots \\ x_n(t) \end{bmatrix} + \begin{bmatrix} B_{11} & B_{12} & \cdots & B_{1k} \\ B_{21} & B_{22} & \cdots & B_{2k} \\ \vdots & \vdots & \cdots & \vdots \\ B_{n1} & B_{n2} & \cdots & B_{nk} \end{bmatrix} \begin{bmatrix} u_1(t) \\ u_2(t) \\ \vdots \\ u_k(t) \end{bmatrix} \quad \text{...(E.8)}$$

This matrix equation [equation (E.8)] can be represented as

$$[\dot{x}(t)] = [A][x(t)] + [B][u(t)] \quad \text{...(E.9)}$$

where

$$[A] \triangleq \begin{bmatrix} A_{11} & A_{12} & \cdots & A_{1n} \\ A_{21} & A_{22} & \cdots & A_{2n} \\ \vdots & \vdots & \cdots & \vdots \\ A_{n1} & A_{n2} & \cdots & A_{nn} \end{bmatrix}_{n\times n}$$

and

$$[B] \triangleq \begin{bmatrix} B_{11} & B_{12} & \cdots & B_{1k} \\ B_{21} & B_{22} & \cdots & B_{2k} \\ \vdots & \vdots & \cdots & \vdots \\ B_{n1} & B_{n2} & \cdots & B_{nk} \end{bmatrix}_{n\times k}$$

$[A]$ and $[B]$ are called *coefficient matrices.* $[A]$ may also be termed as *state matrix* while $[B]$ as *input coefficient matrix*. $x(t)$ is termed as *state vector* while $u(t)$ as *input vector*.

The state equations follow a specific form of representation. On the left hand side of the state equation the term involved is the derivative of one and only one of the state variables. On the right hand side is the mathematical function involving any or all the state variables and the sources (no derivative will appear on the right hand side). We will represent the state equation (E.9) in *standard form* as

$$\dot{x}(t) = A\,x(t) + B\,u(t) \qquad \text{...(E.10)}$$

The solution of the state equation for any circuit provides the behaviour of the state variables. However, we may also be concerned with the output voltages or currents (which are not state variables). All such types of responses are called *outputs* and usually denoted by $y_1(t)$, $y_2(t)$,.....

Thus, we can represent the *r* outputs (say) as a *r*-element output vector $[y(t)]$ where

$$[y(t)] = \begin{bmatrix} y_1(t) \\ y_2(t) \\ \vdots \\ y_n(t) \end{bmatrix}$$

In order to get the desired response, the output equation may then be written in the general form as

$$y(t) = Cx(t) + Du(t) \qquad \text{...(E.11)}$$

where C is $(r \times n)$ and D is $(r \times k)$ coefficient matrices. These matrices can be obtained from the analysis of the circuit under consideration. The process of finding the solution to the state equation is also termed as *state variable analysis*. It may be noted here that equation (E.9) or (E.10) is a vector differential state equation while equation (E.11) is the *output equation*. The matrices *A, B, C* and *D* have **no** relation with *ABCD* parameters of the two port network.

An Illustration

Let us take the following second order differential equation

$$\frac{dy^2}{dt^2} + 5\frac{dy}{dt} + 6y = u(t) \qquad \text{...(A)}$$

Our aim is to express the concept of state variable form in terms of state equations formed from the original second order differential equation.

Let us write as follows

$$\ddot{y} + 5\dot{y} + 6y = u(t) \qquad \text{...(B)}$$

Also let $\quad x_1(t) = y(t)\,;\; x_2(t) = \dot{x}(t) = \dot{y}(t)$

and $\quad \dot{x}_2(t) = \ddot{y}(t)$

Since from (B),

$$\ddot{y} = -5\dot{y} - 6y + u(t)$$

in terms of x_1 and x_2 the required equations are

$$\dot{x}_1 = x_2\,;\; \dot{x}_2 = -6x_1 - 5x_2 + u(t)$$

In matrix form,

$$\begin{bmatrix} \dot{x}_1 \\ \dot{x}_2 \end{bmatrix} = \begin{bmatrix} 0 & 1 \\ -6 & -5 \end{bmatrix}\begin{bmatrix} x_1 \\ x_2 \end{bmatrix} + \begin{bmatrix} 0 \\ 1 \end{bmatrix} u(t)$$

or $\quad [\dot{x}] = [A][x] + [B][u]$

i.e., $\quad \dot{x}$ (vector) $= A$ (vector) x (vector) $+ B$ (vector) u (vector)

$$\therefore \quad [A] = \begin{bmatrix} 0 & 1 \\ -6 & -5 \end{bmatrix};\; [B] = \begin{bmatrix} 0 \\ 1 \end{bmatrix};\; [x] = \begin{bmatrix} x_1 \\ x_2 \end{bmatrix}$$

Thus we have represented the original 2nd order differential equation in the state variable form.

Example E.1 *Form the state equations for the circuit exhibited in Fig. E-E.1.*

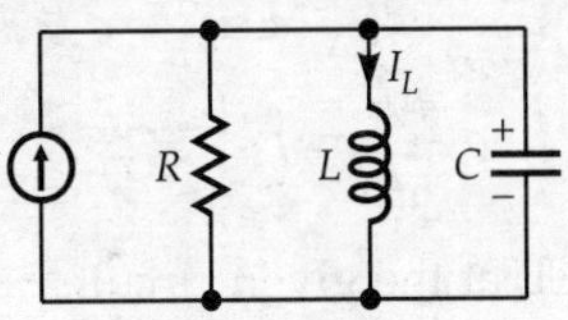

Fig. E-E.1

Solution. Taking i_L and v_C as variables, using KCL at the capacitor branch node of the given circuit, we can write,

$$C.\frac{dv_C}{dt} = I - \frac{v_C}{R} - i_L$$

or, $$\frac{dv_C}{dt} = -\frac{v_C}{RC} - \frac{i_L}{C} + \frac{I}{C} \qquad \text{....}(i)$$

Using KVL across *L*,

$$L\frac{di_L}{dt} = v_C$$

or, $$\frac{di_L}{dt} = \frac{1}{L}v_C \qquad \text{...}(ii)$$

In matrix form, equations (*i*) and (*ii*) give

$$\frac{d}{dt}\begin{bmatrix} v_C \\ i_L \end{bmatrix} = \begin{bmatrix} -\frac{1}{RC} & \frac{1}{C} \\ \frac{1}{L} & 0 \end{bmatrix}\begin{bmatrix} v_C \\ i_L \end{bmatrix} + \begin{bmatrix} 1/C \\ i_L \end{bmatrix}.\,I$$

as $$\frac{d}{dt}\begin{bmatrix} v_C \\ i_L \end{bmatrix} = A\begin{bmatrix} v_C \\ i_L \end{bmatrix} + B\,.\,I \qquad ...(iii)$$

or, $$\dot{x}(t) = Ax + Bu. \qquad ...[(iii)(a)]$$

Equations (*iii*) and [(*iii*) (*a*)] represent the required state equation of the given circuit.

EXAMPLE E.2 *For the given zero input circuit (Fig. E-E.2), write down the state equation.*

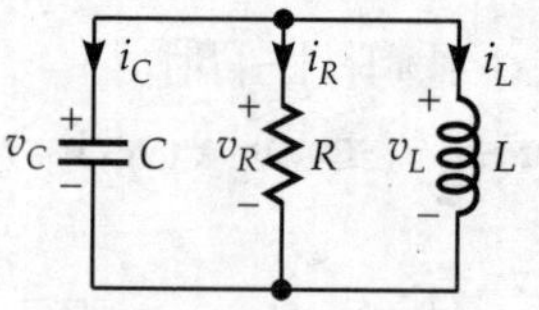

Fig. E-E.2

SOLUTION. Let the state variables be i_L and v_C.

In the given circuit,

$$\because \quad v_L = v_C,\ L\frac{di_L}{dt} = v_C$$

or, $$\frac{di_L}{dt} = \frac{1}{L}\,.\,v_C \qquad ...(i)$$

Also, $$C\frac{dV_C}{dt} = i_C \qquad ...(ii)$$

Using KCL at the given circuit,

$$i_R + i_L + i_C = 0$$

or, $$i_R + i_L = -C\frac{dv_C}{dt} \qquad \text{[using (ii)]}$$

i.e., $$\frac{dv_C}{dt} = -\frac{i_R}{C} - \frac{i_L}{C} \qquad ...(iii)$$

In this problem since i_C is not assumed to be a state variable, hence it is eliminated.

Thus, we finally obtain,

$$\frac{di_L}{dt} = \frac{1}{L}\,.\,v_C$$

$$\frac{dv_C}{dt} = -\frac{i_L}{C} - \frac{i_R}{C} = -\frac{i_L}{C} - \frac{v_C}{RC} \qquad \left[\because i_R = \frac{v_C}{R}\right]$$

In matrix form,

$$\begin{bmatrix} \dfrac{di_L}{dt} \\ \dfrac{dv_C}{dt} \end{bmatrix} = \begin{bmatrix} 0 & \dfrac{1}{L} \\ -\dfrac{1}{C} & -\dfrac{1}{RC} \end{bmatrix}\begin{bmatrix} i_L \\ v_C \end{bmatrix}$$

or $$\frac{d}{dt}\begin{bmatrix} i_L \\ v_C \end{bmatrix} = \begin{bmatrix} 0 & \dfrac{1}{L} \\ -\dfrac{1}{C} & -\dfrac{1}{RC} \end{bmatrix}\begin{bmatrix} i_L \\ v_C \end{bmatrix}$$

i.e., $$\frac{d}{dt}x(t) = A\,x(t)$$

or, $$\dot{x}(t) = A\,x(t) \qquad ...(iii)$$

Equation (*iii*) represents the state equation of the given circuit.

EXAMPLE E.3 *Form the state matrix equation for the network shown in Fig. E-E.3.*

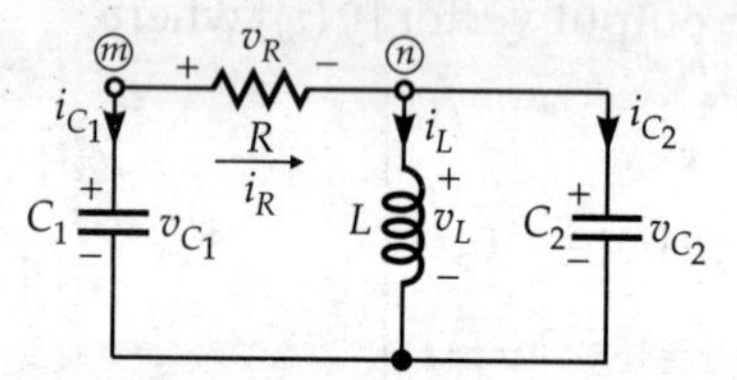

Fig. E-E.3

SOLUTION. By inspection,

$$v_{C_2} = v_L = L\frac{di_L}{dt}.$$

i.e., $$\frac{di_L}{dt} = \left(\frac{1}{L}\right).v_L = \frac{1}{L}.v_{C_2} \qquad ...(a)$$

Using KCL at *node m*,

$$i_{C_1} + i_R = 0 \quad \text{or,}\quad C_1\frac{dv_{C1}}{dt} = -\frac{v_R}{R}$$

$$\left[\because i_{C_1} = C_1\frac{dv_{C_1}}{dt};\ i_R = \frac{v_R}{R}\right]$$

or, $$C_1\frac{dv_{C_1}}{dt} = -\frac{v_{C1} - v_{C2}}{R} = -\frac{v_{C_1}}{R} + \frac{v_{C2}}{R}$$

$$\therefore \quad \frac{dv_{C1}}{dt} = -\frac{v_{C1}}{RC_1} + \frac{v_{C2}}{RC_1} \qquad ...(b)$$

Using KCL at *node (n)*, $i_{C_2} + i_L = i_R$

or $$i_{C_2} = i_R - i_L$$

or, $$C_2\frac{dv_{C_2}}{dt} = \frac{v_R}{R} - i_L = \frac{v_{C1} - v_{C2}}{R} - i_L$$

$$\therefore \quad \frac{dv_{C2}}{dt} = \frac{v_{C1} - v_{C2}}{RC_2} - \frac{i_L}{C_2}$$

$$= \frac{v_{C1}}{RC_2} - \frac{v_{C2}}{RC_2} - \frac{i_L}{C_2} \qquad ...(c)$$

Rewriting equations (*a*), (*b*) and (*c*),

$$\frac{d}{dt}(i_L) = 0 + 0 + \frac{1}{L}(v_{C_2})$$

$$\frac{d}{dt}(v_{C_1}) = 0 - \frac{1}{RC_1}(v_{C_1}) + \frac{1}{RC_1}(v_{C2})$$

and $\frac{d}{dt}(v_{C2}) = -\frac{i_L}{c_2} + \frac{1}{RC_2}(v_{C1}) - \frac{1}{RC_2}(v_{C_2})$.

In matrix form,

$$\frac{d}{dt}\begin{bmatrix} i_L \\ v_{C1} \\ v_{C2} \end{bmatrix} = \begin{bmatrix} 0 & 0 & \frac{1}{L} \\ 0 & -\frac{1}{RC_1} & \frac{1}{RC_1} \\ -\frac{1}{C_2} & \frac{1}{RC_2} & -\frac{1}{RC_2} \end{bmatrix} \begin{bmatrix} i_L \\ v_{C1} \\ v_{C2} \end{bmatrix}$$

or, $\dot{x}(t) = A\,x(t)$.

Thus, the state equation of the given network has been formed.

EXAMPLE E.4 *Obtain the state equation for the circuit shown in Fig. E-E.4.*

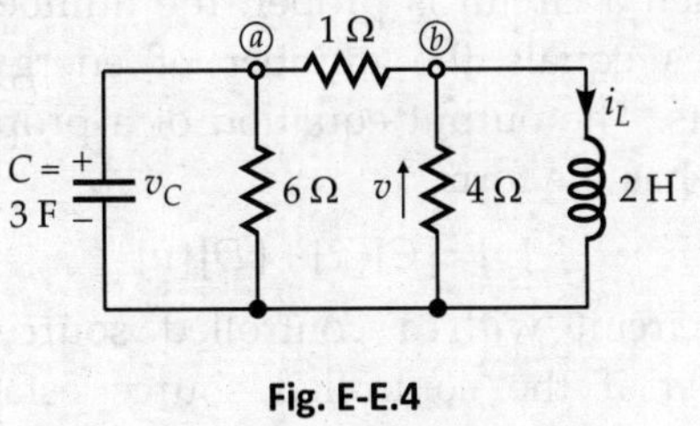

Fig. E-E.4

SOLUTION. Inspection reveals, at *node (a)*,

$$C\frac{dv_C}{dt} + \frac{v_C}{6} + \frac{v_C - v}{1} = 0$$

or, $$3\frac{dv_C}{dt} + \frac{v_C}{6} + \frac{v_C - v}{1} = 0$$

or, $$\frac{dv_C}{dt} = -\frac{v_C}{18} + \frac{v_C - v}{3}$$

$$= \frac{5}{18}v_C - \frac{v}{3} \quad ...(1)$$

At *node (b)*,

$$\frac{v_C - v}{1} = i_L + \frac{v}{4} \quad ...(2)$$

Also, $$2\frac{di_L}{dt} = v \quad ...(3)$$

From (2), $$\frac{v}{4} + v = v_C - i_L$$

or, $$\frac{5v}{4} = v_C - i_L$$

or, $$v = \frac{4}{5}v_C - \frac{4}{5}i_L \quad ...(4)$$

Using (4) in (3),

$$\frac{di_L}{dt} = \frac{v}{2} = \frac{4}{10}v_C - \frac{4}{10}i_L \quad ...(5)$$

Also, from (1), using (4), we get

$$\frac{dv_C}{dt} = \frac{5}{18}v_C - \frac{1}{3}\left(\frac{4}{10}v_C - \frac{4}{10}i_L\right)$$

$$= \frac{5}{18}v_C - \frac{4}{30}v_C + \frac{4}{30}i_L$$

$$= \frac{13}{90}v_C + \frac{4}{30}i_L \quad ...(6)$$

Thus, representing equations (5) and (6) in matrix form,

$$\begin{bmatrix} \frac{di_L}{dt} \\ \frac{dv_C}{dt} \end{bmatrix} = \begin{bmatrix} -\frac{4}{10} & \frac{4}{10} \\ \frac{4}{30} & \frac{13}{90} \end{bmatrix} \begin{bmatrix} i_L \\ v_C \end{bmatrix}$$

or, $$\frac{d}{dt}\begin{bmatrix} i_L \\ v_C \end{bmatrix} = \begin{bmatrix} -\frac{4}{10} & \frac{4}{10} \\ \frac{4}{30} & \frac{13}{90} \end{bmatrix} \begin{bmatrix} i_L \\ v_C \end{bmatrix}$$

or, $\dot{x}(t) = A\,x(t)$. ...(7)

Equation (7) represents the necessary state variable equation.

EXAMPLE E.5 *Obtain the state equation for the circuit shown in Fig. E-E.5.*

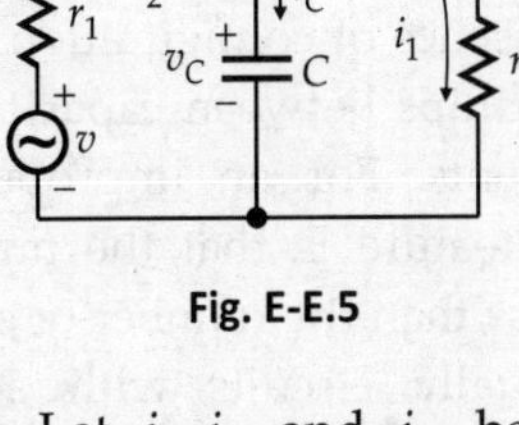

Fig. E-E.5

SOLUTION. Let i_1, i_2 and i_C be the currents coming out of *node (1)* in Fig. E-E.5.

Using nodal analysis at *node (1)*,

$$i_1 + i_2 + i_C = 0$$

or, $i_C = -i_1 - i_2$

or, $$\frac{dv_C}{dt} = -\frac{i_1}{C} - \frac{i_2}{C} \quad ...(a)$$

Using KVL in the *left loop*,

$$-v_C + L_1\frac{di_2}{dt} + i_2 r_1 + v = 0$$

or, $$L_1\frac{di_2}{dt} = v_C - i_2 r_1 - v$$

$$\therefore \quad \frac{di_2}{dt} = \frac{v_C}{L_1} + 0 - \frac{r_1}{L_1}i_2 - \frac{v}{L_1} \quad ...(b)$$

Again, using KVL in the *right loop*,

$$-v_C + L_2\frac{di_1}{dt} + i_1 r_2 = 0$$

or, $$L_2\frac{di_1}{dt} = v_C - i_1 r_2$$

or, $$\frac{di_1}{dt} = +\frac{v_C}{L_2} - \frac{r_2}{L_2}i_1 \quad ...(c)$$

Representing equations (*a*), (*b*) and (*c*) in matrix form,

$$\frac{d}{dt}\begin{bmatrix} v_c \\ i_2 \\ i_1 \end{bmatrix} = \begin{bmatrix} 0 & -\frac{1}{C} & -\frac{1}{C} \\ \frac{1}{L_1} & -\frac{r_1}{L_1} & 0 \\ \frac{1}{L_2} & 0 & -\frac{r_2}{L_2} \end{bmatrix}\begin{bmatrix} v_c \\ i_2 \\ i_1 \end{bmatrix} + \begin{bmatrix} 0 \\ -\frac{v}{L_1} \\ 0 \end{bmatrix} 1.$$

E.6 CLASSIFICATION OF CIRCUITS IN STATE VARIABLE ANALYSIS

The nature of circuit is important in state variable analysis. Two types of circuits usually designate the model for state variable analysis – the *proper* and *improper* circuit. A circuit is said to be proper when the energy storage elements in the circuit (capacitors or inductors) act independently, *i.e.*, there is absence of configuration that produces direct relationships between capacitor voltages or inductor currents. For an improper circuit, the characteristic feature is that the number of state variables is less than the number of energy storage elements. Usually circuits with a closed path consisting *only* capacitors or capacitors and voltage sources and a node whose currents consist *only* of inductive currents or inductive currents and source currents are improper circuits (Figs. E.1 and E.2). In

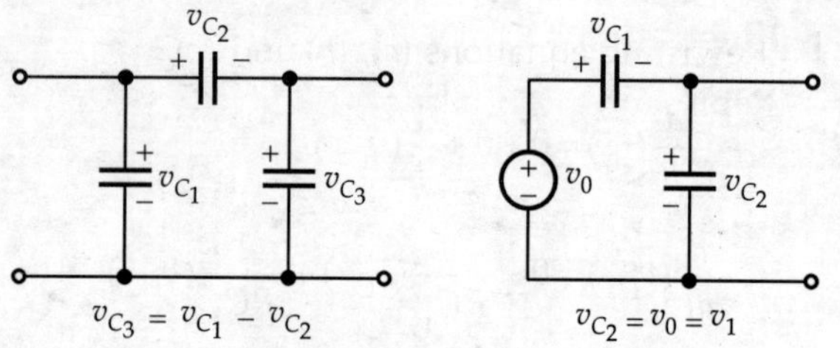

Fig. E.1 Improper capacitor loops.

Fig. E.1, from KVL it follows that one of the capacitor voltages equals an algebraic sum of the other loop voltages while in Fig. E.2, it follows from KCL that one of the inductor currents is equal to the algebraic sum of the other branch currents. Hence in both of these cases, the energy stored in one capacitor or in one inductor cannot be independent of the others.

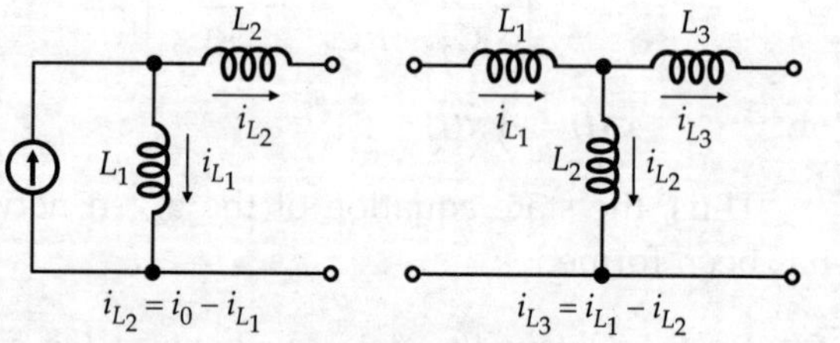

Fig. E.2 Improper inductor circuits.

When a circuit is proper, the number of state variables equals the number of energy storage elements. The output equation of a proper circuit always has the form

$$[y] = [C][x] + [D][u].$$

A circuit with a controlled source will be improper if the controlled source establishes a direct relationship between energy storage elements. Since any variable in a proper circuit depends only on the values of the capacitor voltages, inductor currents and the input sources, at any instant of time, it is usual in some state variable analysis to represent the capacitor as a voltage source of value v_C and the inductor as a current source i_L [Figs. E.3(*a*) and (*b*)]

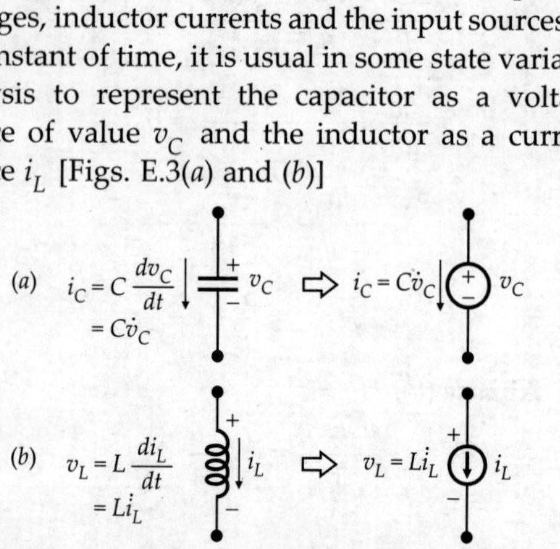

Fig. E.3 Source equivalencing.

An Illustration

Represent the capacitor voltage and inductor current of Fig. E.4 as fictitious sources.

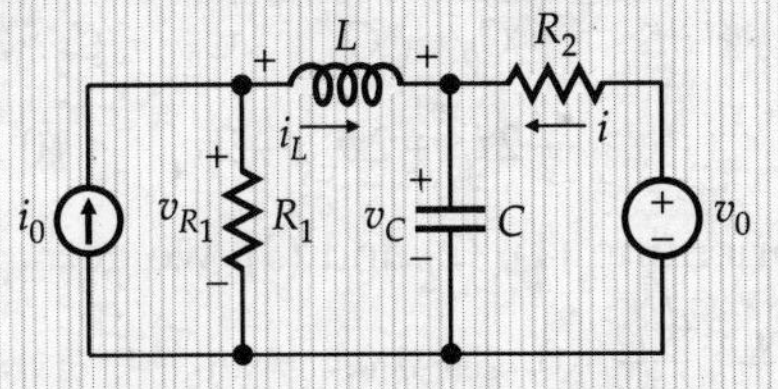

Fig. E.4 An illustrative circuit.

Figure E.5 represents the network with fictitious sources.

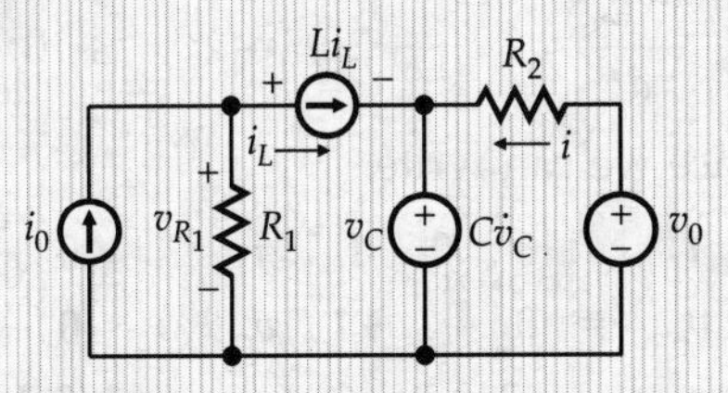

Fig. E.5 Fictitious source inclusion in the network of Fig. E.4.

E.7 STATE VARIABLE ANALYSIS OF A CIRCUIT WITH CONTROLLED SOURCES

When a circuit includes one or more *controlled* sources, it is difficult to assess by inspection whether it is a proper or an improper circuit. It is an usual practice to assume the circuit to be proper and apply the developed procedure to find the state equation. If the analysis yields valid matrix equations then the assumption of independent energy storage is confirmed.

An Illustration

Let us try to write the state equation of the circuit shown in Fig. E.6.

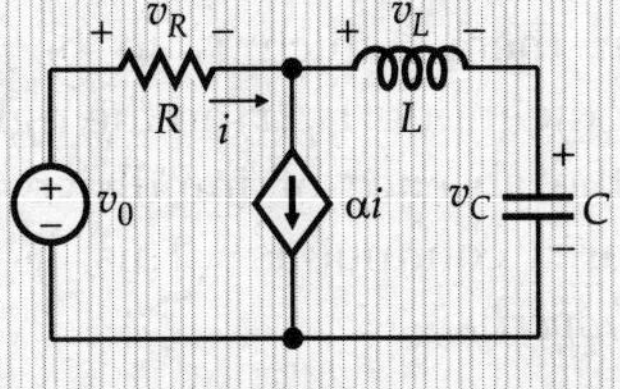

Fig. E.6 Controlled source network.

By inspection we can write

$$L\frac{di_L}{dt} = Ri + v_0 - v_c$$

or $$\dot{i}_L = \left(\frac{R}{L}\right)i - v_c + v_0 \quad ...(1)$$

Also, $$c\frac{dv_C}{dt} = i_L \quad ...(2)$$

Since $i = \alpha i + i_L$, we can write

$$i = \frac{1}{1-\alpha}\cdot i_L\,.$$

$\therefore$ Equation (1) can be written as

$$\dot{i}_L = \frac{R}{L}\cdot\left(\frac{1}{1-\alpha}\right)\cdot i_L + (-1)\,v_c + (1)\,v_0 \quad ...(3)$$

while equation (2) can be written as

$$\dot{v}_C = \frac{1}{C}\cdot i_L + 0\times v_C + 0\times v_0 \quad ...(4)$$

Equations (3) and (4) can be arranged as

$$\begin{bmatrix}\dot{i}_L\\ \dot{v}_C\end{bmatrix} = \begin{bmatrix}\frac{R}{L}\left(\frac{1}{1-\alpha}\right) & -1\\ \frac{1}{C} & 0\end{bmatrix}\begin{bmatrix}i_L\\ v_C\end{bmatrix} + \begin{bmatrix}1\\ 0\end{bmatrix}v_0 \quad ...(5)$$

Equation (5) represents the state equation.

EXAMPLE E.6 *Write the state equation for the circuit shown in Fig. E-E.6.*

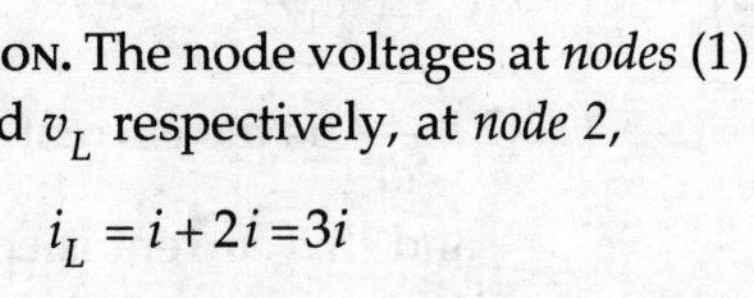

Fig. E-E.6

SOLUTION. The node voltages at *nodes* (1) and (2) being v and v_L respectively, at *node 2*,

$$i_L = i + 2i = 3i \quad ...(a)$$

Also,

$$-i = \frac{v}{1} = \frac{v_L + v_C}{1}$$

[$\because$ $v = v_L + v_C$ from Fig. E-E.6]

Again, $$v_L = L\frac{di_L}{dt} = \frac{di_L}{dt}$$

or, $$\frac{di_L}{dt} = v_L = -i - v_C = -\frac{1}{3}i_L - v_C \quad ...(b)$$

From the *right hand loop* of Fig. E-E.6,

$$i_L = C\frac{dv_C}{dt}$$

or, $$\frac{dv_C}{dt} = \frac{i_L}{C} = \frac{i_L}{1} = i_L \qquad ...(c)$$

Thus, from equations (*b*) and (*c*),

$$\begin{bmatrix} \frac{di_L}{dt} \\ \frac{dv_C}{dt} \end{bmatrix} = \begin{bmatrix} -\frac{1}{3} & -1 \\ 1 & 0 \end{bmatrix} \begin{bmatrix} i_L \\ v_C \end{bmatrix}$$

or, $$\frac{d}{dt}\begin{bmatrix} i_L \\ v_C \end{bmatrix} = \begin{bmatrix} -\frac{1}{3} & -1 \\ 1 & 0 \end{bmatrix} \begin{bmatrix} i_L \\ v_C \end{bmatrix}. \qquad ...(d)$$

Equation (*d*) represents the state equation of the given circuit.

EXAMPLE E.7 *Obtain the state equation for the circuit shown in Fig. E-E.7.*

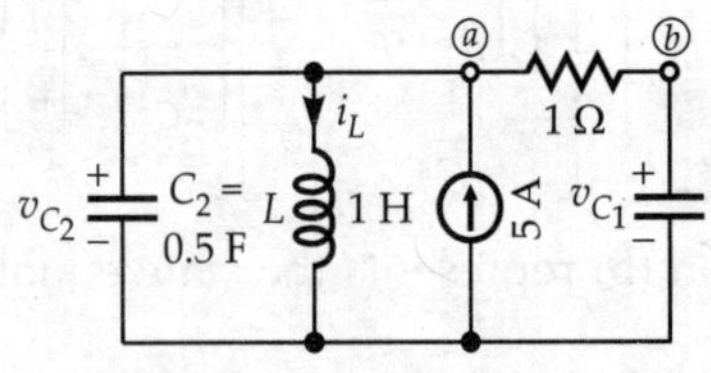

Fig. E-E.7

SOLUTION. By inspection,

$$L\frac{di_L}{dt} = v_{C_2}$$

or, $$\frac{di_L}{dt} = \frac{1}{L}v_{C_2} = v_{C_2} \qquad ...(1)$$

Also,

$$C_1\frac{dv_{C1}}{dt} = (v_{C_2} - v_{C_1})/1$$

[$\because C_1\frac{dv_{C1}}{dt}$ is the current through C_1 and this current is equal to p.d. between nodes (*a*) and (*b*) divided by circuit resistance between *a-b*.]

or, $$\frac{dv_{C_1}}{dt} = \frac{v_{C_2}}{C_1} - \frac{v_{C_1}}{c_1} = \frac{v_{C_2}}{1} - \frac{v_{C_1}}{1}$$

$$= v_{C_2} - v_{C_1} \qquad ...(2)$$

Again at *node (a)*,

$$C_2 \cdot \frac{dv_{C_2}}{dt} + i_L + \frac{v_{C_2} - v_{C_1}}{1} = 5$$

or, $$C_2 \cdot \frac{dv_{C_2}}{dt} = 5 - i_l - \frac{v_{C_2} - v_{C_1}}{1}$$

or, $$\frac{dv_{C_2}}{dt} = -\frac{i_L}{C_2} - \frac{v_{C_2}}{C_2} + \frac{v_{C_1}}{C_2} + \frac{5}{C_2}$$

$$= -2i_L + 2v_{C_1} - 2v_{C_2} + 10 \qquad ...(3)$$

Reorienting (1), (2) and (3), we get

$$\frac{di_L}{dt} = 0.i_L + 0.v_{C_1} + v_{C_2}$$

$$\frac{dv_{C_1}}{dt} = 0.i_L - v_{C_1} + v_{C_2}$$

$$\frac{dv_{C_2}}{dt} = -2i_L + 2v_{C1} - 2v_{C_2} + 10$$

Hence we can write,

$$\frac{d}{dt}\begin{bmatrix} i_L \\ v_{C1} \\ v_{C_2} \end{bmatrix} = \begin{bmatrix} 0 & 0 & 1 \\ 0 & -1 & +1 \\ -2 & +2 & -2 \end{bmatrix} \begin{bmatrix} i_L \\ v_{C_1} \\ v_{C_2} \end{bmatrix} + \begin{bmatrix} 0 \\ 0 \\ 1/0.2 \end{bmatrix} [5]$$

E.8 SOLUTION OF STATE EQUATION

Before going into the solution procedure let us explain first two aspects of solutions namely the *state property* and the *continuity property*.

State Property

The significance of state equations (refer to eqn. E.1) is that, knowing the values $x_i(t_0), i = 1$ to n, of all state variables at time t_0 and knowing the inputs $u_j(t)$ for t in some interval $t_0 \le t < t_f$, we can find $x_i(t)$ for t in the interval $t_0 < t \le t_f$. This property is referred to as *state property*.

Continuity Property

The state variables are continuous functions of time. If any state variable possesses discontinuity, the derivatives on the left hand side would have impulses in them, which is to be balanced by impulses in the inputs $u_j(t)$ on the right hand side. Hence, in the absence of impulsive inputs, state variables are continuous. This is called the *continuity property*.

In the classical methods of solution, Laplace transformation is extensively used in the solution of the state equations. In this method, let us first assume the state equation in the form of

$$\dot{x} = Ax + Bu$$

Taking the Laplace transform,

$$sX(s) - x(0-) = AX(s) + Bu(s)$$

or, $$(sI - A)X(s) = x(0-) + Bu(s) \qquad \text{...(E.12)}$$

where $X(s)$ is the Laplace transform of the unforced vector, $x(0-)$ represents initial condition and $(sI - A)$ represents the matrix function of s. Eliminating $(sI - A)$ from the left hand side of (E.12),

$$X(s) = (sI - A)^{-1}x(0-) + (sI - A)^{-1}Bu(s) \qquad \text{...(E.13)}$$

Taking the inverse of equation (E.13), the desired solution is obtained.

$$x(t) = \pounds^{-1}[(sI - A)^{-1}]\,x(0-) + \pounds^{-1}[sI - A)^{-1}Bu(s)]$$

$$x(t) = \pounds^{-1}\{[\phi(s)][x(0-)]\} + \pounds^{-1}\{[\phi(s)][B][u(s)]\} \qquad \text{...(E.14)}$$

The first term of r.h.s. of equation (E.14) is the *natural response* due to initial conditions. The second term of r.h.s. expression (or zero state) of the same equation represents the *state response* due to forcing function.

Also, from the matrix theory, we can write

$$(sI - A)^{-1} = \text{adjoint}\,[sI - A]/|[sI - A]|,$$

where, adj $[sI - A]$ is the adjoint matrix and $|[sI - A]|$ is the determinant.

However,

$$|[sI - A]| = s\begin{bmatrix} 1 & 0 & \cdots & 0 \\ 0 & 1 & \cdots & 0 \\ \vdots & \vdots & & \vdots \\ 0 & 0 & \cdots & 1 \end{bmatrix} - \begin{bmatrix} a_{11} & a_{12} & \cdots & a_{1n} \\ a_{21} & a_{22} & \cdots & a_{2n} \\ \vdots & \vdots & & \vdots \\ a_{n1} & a_{n2} & \cdots & a_{nn} \end{bmatrix}$$

$$= \begin{bmatrix} s - a_{11} & -a_{12} & \cdots & -a_{1n} \\ -a_{21} & s - a_{22} & \cdots & -a_{2n} \\ & \vdots & & \\ -a_{n1} & -a_{n2} & \cdots & s - a_{nn} \end{bmatrix}$$

Thus $|[sI - A]|$ becomes a polynomial in s.

Let $$P(s) \triangleq |[sI - A]|$$

$$\therefore\quad (sI - A)^{-1} = \frac{1}{P(s)}\,\text{adj}\,[sI - A] = \phi(s), \text{ say} \qquad \text{...[E.14}(a)]$$

The roots of $P(s)$ determine all the modes of the zero input response. $P(s)$ becomes the characteristic polynomial of the circuit. In state variable analysis thus the given circuit has only one characteristic polynomial.

Let us consider an arbitrary second order circuit. $[A]$ is (2×2) matrix and has the form

$$[A] = \begin{bmatrix} a_{11} & a_{12} \\ a_{21} & a_{22} \end{bmatrix}$$

while $$[sI - A] = \begin{bmatrix} s - a_{11} & -a_{12} \\ -a_{21} & s - a_{22} \end{bmatrix}$$

$$\therefore\quad (sI - A)^{-1} = \frac{1}{P(s)}\begin{bmatrix} s - a_{22} & a_{12} \\ a_{21} & s - a_{11} \end{bmatrix} \qquad \text{...[E.14}(b)]$$

with $$P(s) = |[sI - A]| = \begin{vmatrix} s - a_{11} & -a_{12} \\ -a_{21} & s - a_{22} \end{vmatrix}$$

$$= s^2 - (a_{11} + a_{22})s + (a_{11}a_{22} - a_{12}a_{21}).$$

Alternatively, a numerical solution may be carried out. This method involves using of some numerical integration routine. The numerical solution of state space models are of great importance.

Taking the starting time t_0 to be 0 and assuming that we know the initial values of state variables $x_i(0)$, $i = 1$ to n, as well as the inputs $u_j(t)$ for $t \geq 0$, in order to approximately evaluate $x_1(\Delta)$ in (E.1), for a small step Δ, we can use the expression

$$x_1(\Delta) \simeq x_1(0) + \Delta\frac{dx_1(0)}{dt} \qquad \text{...[E.14}(c)]$$

Equation [E.14(c)] is simply a Taylor series expansion truncated after the linear term. Here $\left[\dfrac{dx_1(0)}{dt}\right]$ stands for $\left[\dfrac{dx_1(t)}{dt}\right]$ evaluated at $t = 0$. The error in the approximation is of order Δ^2; so the smaller Δ is the better approximation.

The first expression in (E.1) shows that the derivative needed in [E.14(c)] can be attained by evaluating the function at $t = 0$ (for this purpose the values of the state variables and inputs at $t = 0$ must be known). Hence it is possible to find $x_1(\Delta)$ as accurately as desired by picking up a small value for Δ. The same procedure can be used to compute the approximate values of all the other state variables at time Δ, namely, $x_i(\Delta)$, $i = 2$ to n. Beginning with these approximate values of all the state variables at $t = \Delta$, and knowing the values of all the inputs at $t = \Delta$, we can similarly step forward in time once more to evaluate $x_i(2\Delta)$ approximately.

Interacting this process enables us to approximately solve the state equation forward in time. This solution procedure is referred to in the numerical analysis as the *forward Euler method**. More advanced methods like the popular *fourth order Runge-Kutta** algorithm yields an accumulated error of order Δ^4, a limitation of both of these methods is that the time step Δ has to be taken relatively small compound to smallest time constant in the solution.

The *backward Euler* method is another approach where the solution involves replacing $\frac{dx_1(0)}{dt}$ in eqn. [E.14(*c*)] by $\frac{dx_1(\Delta)}{dt}$ and similarly replacing the derivatives of other derivatives of the state variables.

E.9 FORMATION OF STATE EQUATIONS USING NETWORK GRAPH THEORY

The state equations can be written using the following step by step procedure :

1. Draw the graph of the network.
2. Select a tree that contains all independent voltage sources and the maximum possible number of capacitors. All inductors and current sources should be in the co-tree. The resistors may be in the tree or in the co-tree. The control voltages should be in the tree while the control currents should be in the co-tree.
3. Arbitrarily mark the polarities of the voltages across each capacitor and direction of current in each inductor. Then capacitor voltages and inductor currents are the state variables.
4. Form a nodal equation for each capacitor using KCL. Write a loop equation for each basic loop using KVL.
5. Eliminate all the non-state variables in the state equations obtained in step 4.

The resulting equations contain only the state variables and their derivatives. Then transforming the derivatives to the left hand side, the final state equation is obtained.

EXAMPLE E.8 *Apply the procedure of formation of state equations using network graph theory (Fig. E-E.8).*

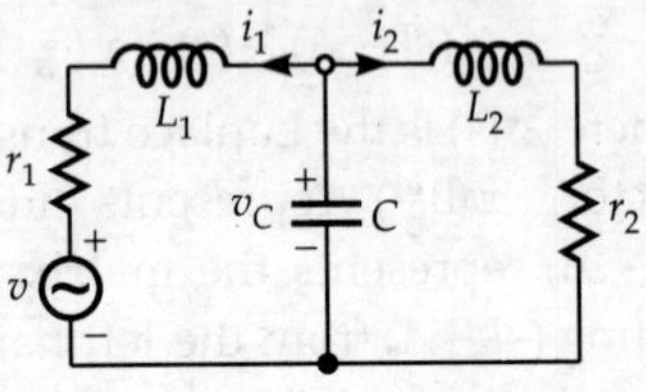

Fig. E-E.8

SOLUTION.

1. A tree is selected with all the capacitors only alongwith the voltage source (Fig. E-E.9).

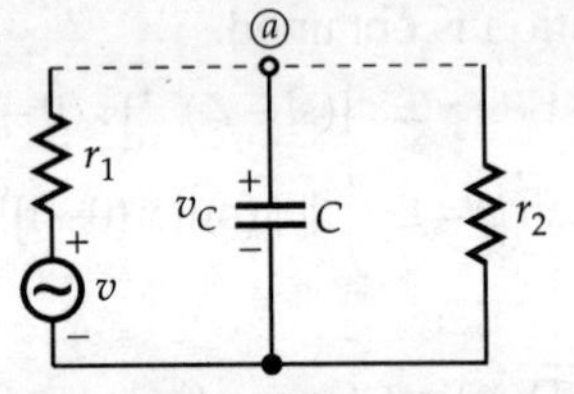

Fig. E-E.9

2. Select the tree-branch capacitor voltage v_C and the link inductor currents i_1 and i_2 as state variables. The reference directions have been arbitrarily selected.
3. Apply KCL at *node (a)*. This yields

$$C\frac{dv_C}{dt} + i_1 + i_2 = 0 \quad ...(1)$$

On the other hand, KVL for the basic loops yields

$$L_1\frac{di_1}{dt} + v_{r_1} + v - v_C = 0 \quad ...(2)$$

$$L_2\frac{di_2}{dt} + v_{r_2} - v_C = 0 \quad ...(3)$$

4. In (1), only state variables occur, no further simplification is needed except re-orientation of the terms. In (2) and (3), v_{r_1} and v_{r_2} are not state variables and hence they are to be eliminated.

Obviously, $v_{r_1} = r_i\, i_1\,; v_{r_2} = r_2\, i_2$.

5. Then (1), (2) and (3) become

$$\frac{dv_C}{dt} = 0 - \frac{1}{C}.i_1 - \frac{1}{C}.i_2 \quad ...(4)$$

$$\frac{di_1}{dt} = \frac{1}{L_1}v_c - \frac{r_1}{L_1}.i_1 + 0 - \frac{v}{L_1} \quad ...(5)$$

$$\frac{di_2}{dt} = \frac{1}{L_2}v_c + 0 - \frac{r_2}{L_2}.i_2 \quad ...(6)$$

* For details of these methods please refer to "Power System Analysis, Operation and Control" by A. Chakrabarti and S. Halder (3rd Edition, PHI).

In matrix form, (4), (5) and (6) give,

$$\begin{bmatrix} \frac{dv_C}{dt} \\ \frac{di_1}{dt} \\ \frac{di_2}{dt} \end{bmatrix} = \begin{bmatrix} 0 & -\frac{1}{C} & -\frac{1}{C} \\ \frac{1}{L_1} & -\frac{r_1}{L_1} & 0 \\ \frac{1}{L_2} & 0 & -\frac{r_2}{L_2} \end{bmatrix} \begin{bmatrix} v_C \\ i_1 \\ i_2 \end{bmatrix} + \begin{bmatrix} 0 \\ -\frac{v}{L_1} \\ 0 \end{bmatrix}$$

or, $\dot{x} = Ax + Bu.$

EXAMPLE E.9 *Obtain the state equation for the circuit shown in Fig. E-E.10.*

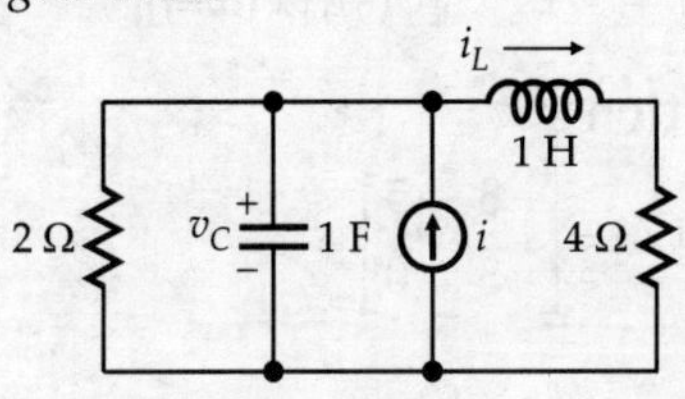

Fig. E-E.10

SOLUTION. The normal tree is shown in Fig. E-E.11.

The tree consists of the capacitor only. The co-tree is consisting of the current source and the inductor.

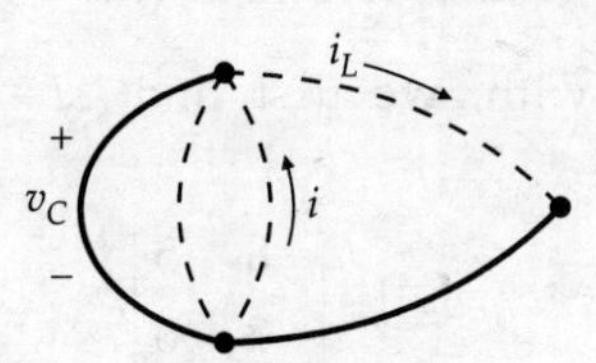

Fig. E-E.11

Using KVL in the *right loop*,

$$L\frac{di_L}{dt} + 4i_L - v_C = 0$$

or $$1.\frac{di_L}{dt} + 4i_L - v_C = 0$$

or $$\frac{di_L}{dt} + 4i_L - v_C = 0$$

or $$\frac{di_L}{dt} = -4i_L + v_C \quad \text{...(1)}$$

Using KCL at the positive polarity end of the capacitor,

$$C.\frac{dv_C}{dt} + i_L - i + \frac{v_C}{2} = 0$$

or, $$1\frac{dv_C}{dt} + i_L - i + \frac{v_C}{2} = 0.$$

or, $$\frac{dv_C}{dt} = -i_L + \frac{v_C}{2} + i \quad \text{...(2)}$$

Rewriting (1) and (2) in matrix form,

$$\begin{bmatrix} \frac{di_L}{dt} \\ \frac{dv_C}{dt} \end{bmatrix} = \begin{bmatrix} -4 & 1 \\ -1 & \frac{1}{2} \end{bmatrix} \begin{bmatrix} i_L \\ v_C \end{bmatrix} + \begin{bmatrix} 0 \\ i \end{bmatrix}$$

Above equation gives the **state equation** of the given network using network graph theory.

EXAMPLE E.10 *Obtain the state equation for the network shown in Fig. E-E.12.* $v_5 = 5e^{-2t}$.

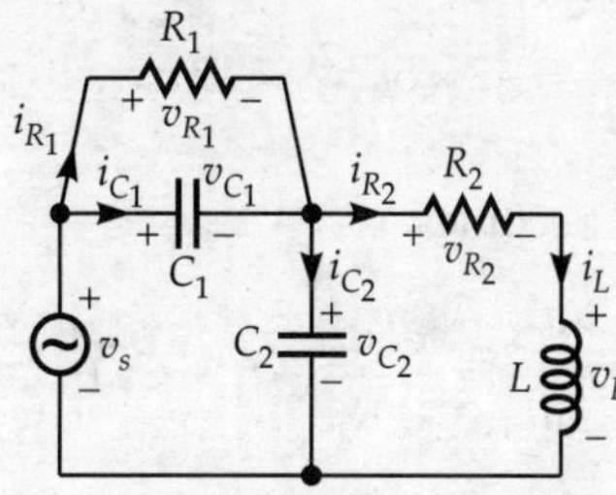

Fig. E-E.12

SOLUTION. The tree and co-tree are shown in Fig. E-E.13.

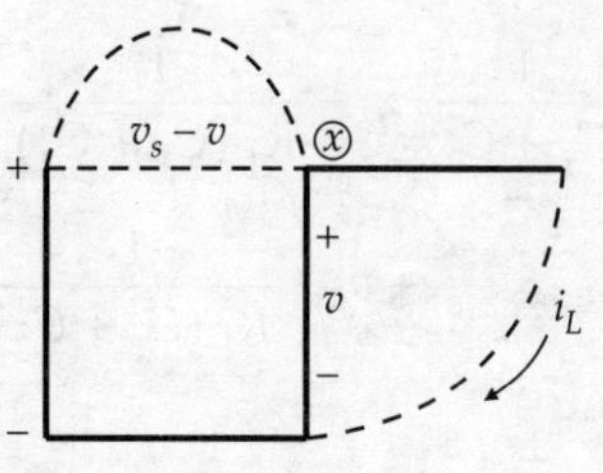

Fig. E-E.13

Using KVL at right hand loop,

$$L\frac{di_L}{dt} = -R_L\, i_L + v_{C_2}$$

or, $$\frac{di_L}{dt} = -\frac{R_2}{L}.i_L + \frac{1}{L}.v_{C_2} \quad \text{...(1)}$$

Using KCL at *node (x)*,

$$C_1\frac{dv_{C_1}}{dt} + \frac{v_{R_1}}{R_1} = C_2\frac{dV_{C_2}}{dt} + i_L \quad \text{...(2)}$$

Using KVL in the left hand loop,

$$v_S - v_{C_1} - v_{C_2} = 0$$

or, $$v_{C_1} = v_S - v_{C_2}$$

Also, $$v_{R_1} = v_{C_1}$$

Substituting these values in (2), we get

$$C_1 \frac{d}{dt}(v_S - v_{C_2}) + \frac{v_S - v_{C_2}}{R_1} = C_2 \frac{dv_{C_2}}{dt} + i_L$$

or, $$(C_1 + C_2)\frac{dv_{C_2}}{dt} = -\frac{v_{C_2}}{R_1} - i_L + C_1 \frac{dv_S}{dt} + \frac{v_S}{R_1} \qquad ...(3)$$

However,

$$v_S = 5\,e^{-2t},$$

$$\therefore \quad \frac{dv_S}{dt} = -2 \times 5e^{-2t} = -2v_S.$$

Thus, (3) becomes

$$(C_1 + C_2)\frac{dv_{C_2}}{dt} = -\frac{v_{C_2}}{R_1} - i_1 + C_1(-2v_S) + \frac{v_S}{R_1}$$

or, $$\frac{dv_{C_2}}{dt} = \frac{-i_L}{C_1 + C_2} - \frac{1}{R_1(C_1 + C_2)} v_{C_2} + \frac{C_1}{C_1 + C_2}(-2v_S) + \frac{v_S}{R_1(C_1 + C_2)}$$

or, $$\frac{dv_{C_2}}{dt} = -\frac{1}{C_1 + C_2}\,.\,i_L - \frac{1}{R_1(C_1 + C_2)} v_{C_2} + v_S\left(\frac{1}{R_1(C_1 + C_2)} - \frac{2C_1}{C_1 + C_2}\right)$$

$$= -\frac{1}{C_1 + C_2}\,.\,i_L - \frac{1}{R_1(C_1 + C_2)}\,.\,v_{C_2} + v_S\left[\frac{1 - 2R_1 C_1}{R_1(C_1 + C_2)}\right] \qquad ...(4)$$

Rewriting equations (1) and (4) in matrix form,

$$\begin{bmatrix} \frac{di_L}{dt} \\ \frac{dv_{C_2}}{dt} \end{bmatrix} = \begin{bmatrix} -\frac{R_2}{L} & \frac{1}{L} \\ -\frac{1}{C_1 + C_2} & -\frac{1}{R_1(C_1 + C_2)} \end{bmatrix} \begin{bmatrix} i_L \\ v_{C_2} \end{bmatrix} + \begin{bmatrix} 0 \\ \frac{1 - 2R_1 C_1}{R_1(C_1 + C_2)} \end{bmatrix} v_S \qquad ...(5)$$

Equation (5) represents the necessary state equation.

E.10 ZERO STATE RESPONSE OF THE STATE VECTOR

We have seen $\phi(s) \triangleq [sI - A]^{-1}$.

Laplace transform of the state vector for the zero input response is then

$$[X(s)] = [sI - A]^{-1}[x(0-)] = [\phi(s)][x(0-)]$$

In time domain,

$$[x(t)] = £^{-1}\{[X(s)]\}$$

$$= £^{-1}\{[\phi(s)][x(0-)]\} \qquad ...(E.15)$$

An Illustration

Let $$[A] = \begin{bmatrix} -8 & -5 \\ 3 & 0 \end{bmatrix}$$

$$[C] = \begin{bmatrix} 6 & 10 \\ 0 & -12 \end{bmatrix}$$

$$[x(0-)] = \begin{bmatrix} 2 \\ -4 \end{bmatrix}$$

We are to find $x_1(t)$ and $x_2(t)$.

To start with, we first find $[sI - A]$ and adj $[sI - A]$. Since

$$[A] = \begin{bmatrix} -8 & -5 \\ 3 & 0 \end{bmatrix},$$

$$[sI - A] = \begin{bmatrix} s+8 & 5 \\ -3 & s \end{bmatrix}$$

and $$\text{adj}\,[sI - A] = \begin{bmatrix} s & -5 \\ 3 & s+8 \end{bmatrix}$$

$$\therefore \quad P(s) = |[sI - A]| = s^2 + 8s + 15 = (s+3)(s+5)$$

Next we find $\phi(s)$.

$$\phi(s) = \frac{1}{P(s)}\text{adj}\,[sI - A]$$

Also, $X(s)$, the state vector is given by

$$[X(s)] = [\phi(s)][x(0-)]$$

$$= \frac{1}{P(s)}\begin{bmatrix} s & -5 \\ 3 & s+8 \end{bmatrix}\begin{bmatrix} 2 \\ -4 \end{bmatrix}$$

$$= \frac{1}{P(s)}\begin{bmatrix} 2s+20 \\ -4s-26 \end{bmatrix}$$

$$\therefore \quad X_1(s) = \frac{(2s+20)}{(s+3)(s+5)} = \frac{7}{s+3} + \frac{(-5)}{s+5}$$

and $$X_2(s) = \frac{(-7)}{s+3} + \frac{3}{s+5}$$

$$\therefore \quad x_1(t) = 7e^{-3t} - 5e^{-5t}$$

and $$x_2(t) = -7e^{-3t} + 3e^{-5t}$$

Output can be obtained from $[y] = [C][x]$.

Here,

$$[y] = \begin{bmatrix} 6 & 10 \\ 0 & -2 \end{bmatrix} \begin{bmatrix} x_1 \\ x_2 \end{bmatrix} = \begin{bmatrix} 6x_1 + 10x_2 \\ -2x_2 \end{bmatrix}$$

$$\therefore \quad y_1(t) = 6x_1(t) + 10x_2(t);\ y_2(t) = -2x_2(t)$$

E.11 COMPLETE RESPONSE OF THE STATE VECTOR

Since the state equation is given by

$$[\dot{x}] = [A][x] + [B][u],$$

while the input vector is

$$[u(s)] \overset{\Delta}{=} \{[u(t)]\} = \begin{bmatrix} u_1(s) \\ \vdots \\ u_n(s) \end{bmatrix}$$

Laplace transformation of the state equation yields

$$s[X(s)] - [x(0-)] = [A][X(s)] + [B][X(s)]$$

or $$[sI - A][X(s)] = [x(0-)] + [B][u(s)]$$

Multiplying both sides by $[\phi(s)]$ we can write

$$[sI - A][X(s)][sI - A]^{-1} = \{[x(0-)] + [B][u(s)]\}([sI - A])^{-1}$$

Since $$[\phi(s)] = [sI - A]^{-1}$$

This gives finally

$$[X(s)] = [\phi(s)][x(0-)] + [\phi(s)][B][u(s)] \quad \text{...(E.16)}$$

The inverse transform gives the complete response of the state vector $[x]$.

An Illustration

Let $$[B] = \begin{bmatrix} -8 & 0 \\ 3 & 1 \end{bmatrix};$$

$$[A] = \begin{bmatrix} -8 & -5 \\ 3 & 0 \end{bmatrix}$$

$$[u(s)] = \begin{bmatrix} 10/s^2 \\ 0 \end{bmatrix}$$

$$[x(0-)] = \begin{bmatrix} 2 \\ -4 \end{bmatrix}$$

The complete response is obtained from

$$[X(s)] = [\phi(s)][x(0-)] + [\phi(s)][B][u(s)]$$

$$= \frac{1}{P(s)} \operatorname{adj}[sI - A] \begin{bmatrix} 2 \\ -4 \end{bmatrix} + \frac{1}{P(s)} \operatorname{adj}[sI - A] \begin{bmatrix} -8 & 0 \\ 3 & 1 \end{bmatrix} \begin{bmatrix} 10/s^2 \\ 0 \end{bmatrix}$$

$$= \frac{1}{(s+3)(s+5)} \begin{bmatrix} s & -5 \\ 3 & s+8 \end{bmatrix} \left\{ \begin{bmatrix} 2 \\ -4 \end{bmatrix} + \begin{bmatrix} -8 & 0 \\ 3 & 1 \end{bmatrix} \begin{bmatrix} 10/s^2 \\ 0 \end{bmatrix} \right\}$$

$$= \frac{1}{(s+3)(s+5)} \begin{bmatrix} s & -5 \\ 3 & s+8 \end{bmatrix} \begin{bmatrix} 2 - 80/s^2 \\ -4 + 30/s^2 \end{bmatrix}$$

$$= \frac{1}{(s+3)(s+5)} \begin{bmatrix} (2s^3 + 20s^2 - 80s - 150)/s^2 \\ (-4s^2 - 26s + 30)/s \end{bmatrix}$$

$$\therefore \quad X_1(s) = \frac{2s^3 + 20s^2 - 80s - 150}{s^2(s+3)(s+5)}$$

and $$X_2(s) = \frac{-4s^2 - 26s + 30}{s(s+3)(s+5)}$$

E.12 ADDITIONAL EXAMPLES

EXAMPLE E.11 *Obtain the state equation for the circuit shown in Fig. E-E.14. Given L= 1H; C=0.25 F; R=5 Ω.*

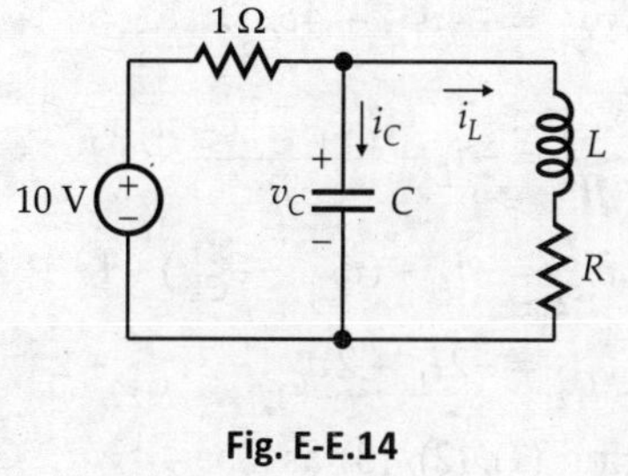

Fig. E-E.14

SOLUTION. From Fig. E-E.14.

$$C\frac{dv_C}{dt} = i_C = \frac{10 - v_C}{1} + (-i_L)$$

or $0.25\,\dot{v}_C = -i_L + (10 - v_C)$

or $\dot{v}_C = -4i_L - 4v_C + 4$ ...(1)

and $L\dfrac{di_L}{dt} = -5i_L + v_C$

or $\dot{i}_L = -5i_L + v_C$ ...(2)

Let us rewrite equations (2) and (1) as follows :

$$\dot{i}_L = -5i_L + v_C$$

and $\dot{v}_C = -4i_L - 4v_C + 4$

∴ The state equation can be formed now as

$$\begin{bmatrix} \dot{i}_L \\ \dot{v}_C \end{bmatrix} = \begin{bmatrix} -5 & 1 \\ -4 & -4 \end{bmatrix}\begin{bmatrix} i_L \\ v_C \end{bmatrix} + \begin{bmatrix} 0 \\ 4 \end{bmatrix} 1.$$

EXAMPLE E.12 *In the circuit of Fig. E-E.15, find the state equation.*

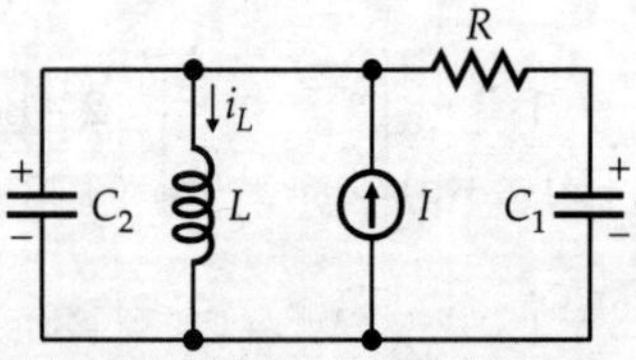

[$C_1 = 0.25$ F ; $C_2 = 0.5$ F ; $L = 0.2$ H ; $R = 1$ ohm ; $I = 1$ A]

Fig. E-E.15

SOLUTION. In Fig. E-E.15,

$$L\frac{di_L}{dt} = v_{C_2}$$

or $\dot{i}_L = 5v_{C_2}$ ...(1)

Also,

$$C_1\frac{dv_{C_1}}{dt} = \frac{v_{C_2} - v_{C_1}}{R}$$

or $\dot{v}_{C_1} = -4v_{C_1} + 4v_{C_2}$ ...(2)

and $C_2\dfrac{dv_{C_2}}{dt} = -i_L + \dfrac{v_{C_1} - v_{C_2}}{R} + I$

or $0.5\,\dot{v}_{C_2} = -i_L + (v_{C_1} - v_{C_2}) + 1$

or $\dot{v}_{C_2} = -2i_L + 2v_{C_1} - 2v_{C_2} + 2$ ...(3)

Rewriting (1), (2), (3) as

$$\dot{i}_L = 0 \times i_L + 0 \times v_{C_1} + 5v_{C_2}$$

$$\dot{v}_{C_1} = 0 \times i_L - 4v_{C_1} + 4v_{C_2}$$

$$\dot{v}_{C_2} = -2i_L + 2v_{C_1} - 2v_{C_2} + 2$$

∴ The state equation is

$$\begin{bmatrix} \dot{i}_L \\ \dot{v}_{C_1} \\ \dot{v}_{C_2} \end{bmatrix} = \begin{bmatrix} 0 & 0 & 5 \\ 0 & -4 & 4 \\ -2 & 2 & -2 \end{bmatrix}\begin{bmatrix} i_L \\ v_{C_1} \\ v_{C_2} \end{bmatrix} + \begin{bmatrix} 0 \\ 0 \\ 2 \end{bmatrix} 1.$$

EXAMPLE E.13 *Write the state equation and the output equation for the circuit shown in Fig. E-E.16.*

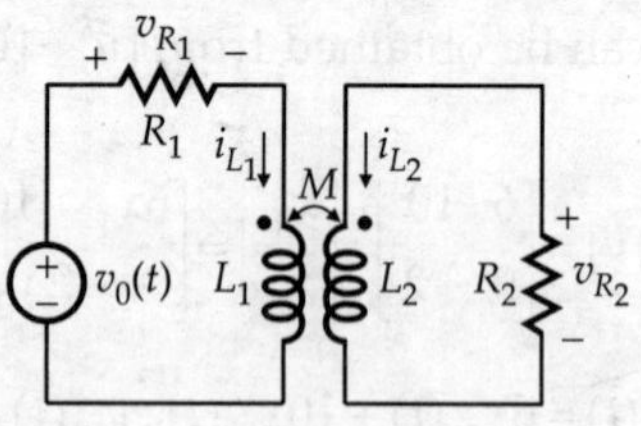

Fig. E-E.16

SOLUTION. From Fig. E-E.16,

$$R_1\, i_{L_1} + L_1\frac{di_{L_1}}{dt} + M\frac{di_{L_2}}{dt} = v_0(t)$$

$$R_2\, i_{L_2} + L_2\frac{di_{L_2}}{dt} + M\frac{di_{L_1}}{dt} = 0$$

These two equations can be solved and written in following form :

$$\frac{di_{L_1}}{dt} = -\frac{R_1 L_2}{L_1 L_2 - M^2}\, i_{L_1} + \frac{R_2 M}{L_1 L_2 - M^2}\, i_{L_2} + \frac{L_2}{L_1 L_2 - M^2} . v_0(t)$$

and

$$\frac{di_{L_2}}{dt} = \frac{R_2 M}{L_1 L_2 - M^2}\, i_{L_1} + \left(-\frac{R_2 L_1}{L_1 L_2 - M^2}\right) i_{L_2} + \left(-\frac{M}{L_1 L_2 - M^2}\right) v_0(t)$$

The state equation is then written as

$$\begin{bmatrix} \dot{i}_{L_1} \\ \dot{i}_{L_2} \end{bmatrix} = \begin{bmatrix} -\dfrac{R_1 L_2}{L_1 L_2 - M^2} & \dfrac{R_2 M}{L_1 L_2 - M^2} \\ \dfrac{R_2 M}{L_1 L_2 - M^2} & -\dfrac{R_2 L_1}{L_1 L_2 - M^2} \end{bmatrix}\begin{bmatrix} i_{L_1} \\ i_{L_2} \end{bmatrix} + \begin{bmatrix} \dfrac{L_2}{L_1 L_2 - M^2} \\ -\dfrac{M}{L_1 L_2 - M^2} \end{bmatrix}[v_0(t)]$$

The output equation is given by

$$v_0(t) = -R_2\, i_{L_2}$$

Example E.14 *Write the state equation for the network shown in Fig. E-E.17.*

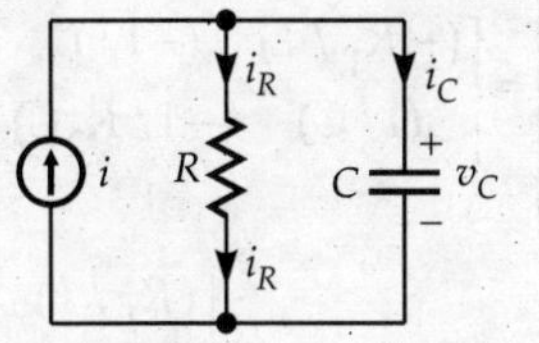

Fig. E-E.17

Solution. Obviously,

$$i_R = \frac{v_C}{R};\ i_C = C\frac{dv_C}{dt}.$$

Since $i = i_R + i_C$, we can write

$$i = \frac{v_C}{R} + C\,\dot{v}_C$$

$$\therefore \quad \dot{v}_C = -\frac{1}{RC}v_C + \frac{1}{C}i \qquad ...(1)$$

Equation (1) represents the state equation of the given circuit.

Example E.15 *Obtain the state equation of the series RLC circuit (Fig. E-E.18) in terms of charges and fluxes.*

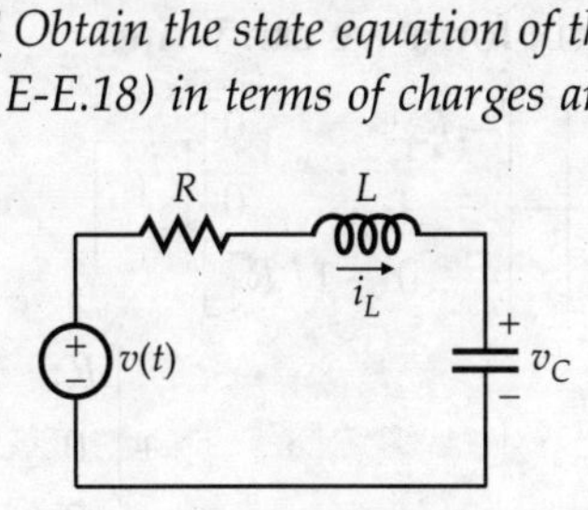

Fig. E-E.18

Solution.

$$v(t) = Ri_L + L\frac{di_L}{dt} + v_C \qquad ...(1)$$

Also, $$i_L = C\frac{dv_C}{dt} \qquad ...(2)$$

But $\quad q_C = C\,v_C(t)$ and $\phi = L\,i_L(t)$

$$\therefore \quad \dot{q}_C = C\,\dot{v}_C = i_L \qquad \text{[Using equation (2)]}$$

i.e., $$\dot{q}_C = \frac{\phi}{L} \qquad ...(3)$$

Again from (1)

$$\frac{di_L}{dt} = -\frac{R}{L}i_L - \frac{v_C}{L} + v(t)/L$$

or $$\frac{1}{L}\dot{\phi} = -\frac{R}{L}i_L - \frac{v_C}{L} + v(t)/L$$

$$= -\frac{R}{L}.i_L - \frac{q_C}{C}\times\frac{1}{L} + v(t)/L$$

$$= -\frac{R}{L}.\frac{\phi}{L} - \frac{1}{L}\times\frac{q_C}{C} + \frac{v(t)}{L}$$

$$\therefore \quad \dot{\phi} = -\frac{R}{L}.\phi - \frac{q_C}{C} + v(t)$$

We now arrange expressions of $\dot{q}_C$ and $\dot{\phi}$ as under

$$\dot{\phi} = -\frac{R}{L}\phi - \frac{1}{C}.q_C + 1\times v(t)$$

$$\dot{q}_C = \frac{1}{L}\phi + 0\times q_C + 0\times v(t)$$

The state equation is then represented as

$$\begin{bmatrix}\dot{\phi}\\ \dot{q}_C\end{bmatrix} = \begin{bmatrix}-\dfrac{R}{L} & -\dfrac{1}{C}\\ \dfrac{1}{L} & 0\end{bmatrix}\begin{bmatrix}\phi\\ q_C\end{bmatrix} + \begin{bmatrix}1\\ 0\end{bmatrix} v(t).$$

Example E.16 *Obtain the state equation and output equation for the circuit shown in Fig. E-E.19.*

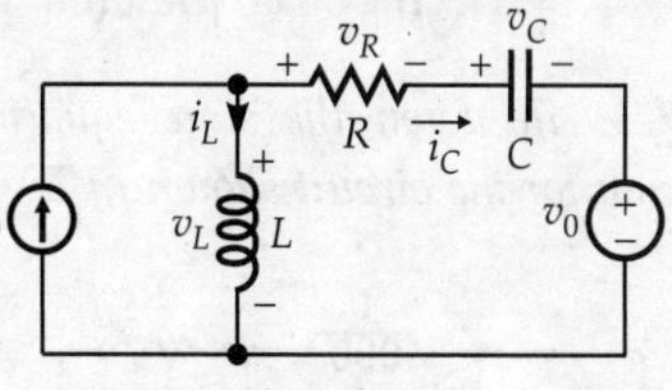

Fig. E-E.19

Solution. In Fig. E-E.19,

$$i_C = i_0 - i_L;\ v_R = i_C\times R = R(i_0 - i_L);$$

$$v_L = v_R + v_C - v_0 = Ri_0 - Ri_L + v_C - v_0$$

Also,

$$L\frac{di_L}{dt} = v_L = Ri_0 - Ri_L + v_C - v_0$$

and $$C\frac{dv_C}{dt} = i_C = i_0 - i_L$$

Combining these equations,

$$\frac{di_L}{dt} = \left(-\frac{R}{L}\right)i_L + \left(\frac{1}{L}\right)v_C + \left(\frac{R}{L}\right)i_0 + \left(-\frac{1}{L}\right)v_0$$

i.e., $$\dot{i}_L = -(R/L)i_L + (1/L)v_C + (R/L)i_0 + (-1/L)v_0 \qquad ...(1)$$

and $$\frac{dv_C}{dt} = \left(-\frac{1}{C}\right)i_L + 0\times v_C + \left(\frac{1}{C}\right)i_0 + 0\times v_0$$

or $$\dot{v}_C = (-1/C)\,i_L + 0\times v_C + (1/C)\,i_0 + 0\times v_0 \qquad ...(2)$$

Thus expressing (1) and (2) in matrix form, the state equation is formed where,

$$\begin{bmatrix} \dot{i}_L \\ \dot{v}_C \end{bmatrix} = [A]\begin{bmatrix} i_L \\ v_C \end{bmatrix} + [B]\begin{bmatrix} i_0 \\ v_0 \end{bmatrix};$$

here $[A] = \begin{bmatrix} -R/L & 1/L \\ -1/C & 0 \end{bmatrix}$

$[B] = \begin{bmatrix} R/L & -1/L \\ 1/C & 0 \end{bmatrix}$

The output equation is obtained from the following :

$$v_L = (-R)\, i_L + 1 \times v_C + R \times i_0 + (-1)\, v_0$$

$$v_R = (-R)\, i_L + 0 \times v_C + R \times i_0 + 0 \times v_0.$$

The output equation is then given by

$$\begin{bmatrix} v_L \\ v_R \end{bmatrix} = [\mathbf{C}]\begin{bmatrix} i_L \\ v_C \end{bmatrix} + [\mathbf{D}]\begin{bmatrix} i_0 \\ v_0 \end{bmatrix}$$

where $[\mathbf{C}] = \begin{bmatrix} -\mathbf{R} & \mathbf{1} \\ -\mathbf{R} & \mathbf{0} \end{bmatrix}; [\mathbf{D}] = \begin{bmatrix} \mathbf{R} & -\mathbf{1} \\ \mathbf{R} & \mathbf{0} \end{bmatrix}.$

EXAMPLE E.17 *Write down the state equation and the output equation for the circuit shown in Fig. E-E.20.*

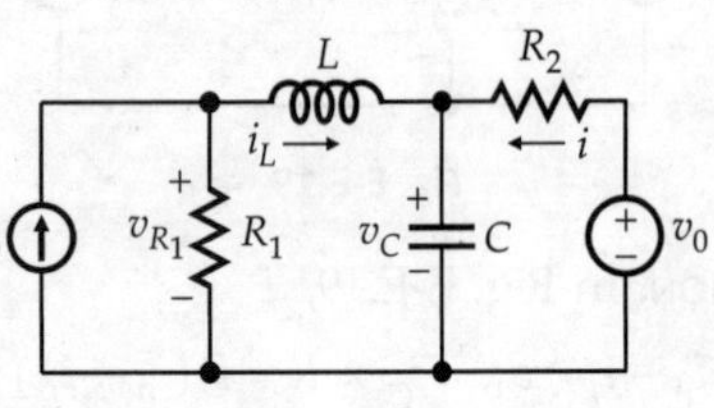

Fig. E-E.20

SOLUTION. Application of KVL yields

$$v_{R_1} = R_1\,(i_0 - i_L)$$

and $$L\frac{di_L}{dt} = v_{R_1} - v_C$$

while the application of KCL yields

$$i = (v_0 - v_C)/R_2$$

and $$C\frac{dv_C}{dt} = i_L + i$$

Combining these four equations we can write

$$\frac{di_L}{dt} = (-R_1/L)\, i_L + (-1/L)\, v_C + (R_1/L)\, i_0 + 0 \times v_0$$

and $$\frac{dv_C}{dt} = (1/C)\, i_L + (-1/R_2C)\, v_C + 0 \times i_0 + (1/R_2)\, v_0$$

∴ The matrix state equation is written as

$$\begin{bmatrix} \dfrac{di_L}{dt} \\ \dfrac{dv_C}{dt} \end{bmatrix} = \begin{bmatrix} (-R_1/L) & (-1/L) \\ (1/C) & (-1/R_2C) \end{bmatrix}\begin{bmatrix} i_L \\ v_C \end{bmatrix} + \begin{bmatrix} (R_1/L) & 0 \\ 0 & (1/R_2C) \end{bmatrix}\begin{bmatrix} i_0 \\ v_0 \end{bmatrix}$$

or $$\begin{bmatrix} \dot{i}_L \\ \dot{v}_C \end{bmatrix} = [A]\begin{bmatrix} i_L \\ v_C \end{bmatrix} + [B]\begin{bmatrix} i_0 \\ v_0 \end{bmatrix} \quad ...(1)$$

where coefficient matrices are $[A]$ and $[B]$, both 2×2 (here $n = 2$, $k = 2$ *i.e.*, two states and two inputs.) **Equation (1) is the required state equation.**

In order to find the output equation, we write

$$v_{R_1} = (-R_1)\, i_L + 0 \times v_C + R_1\, i_L + 0 \times v_0$$

$$i_L = 1 \times i_L + 0 \times v_C + 0 \times i_0 + 0 \times v_0$$

$$i = 0 \times i_L + (-1/R_2)\, v_C + 0 \times i_0 + (1/R_2)\, v_0$$

∴ In matrix form we can write

$$\begin{bmatrix} v_{R_1} \\ i_L \\ i \end{bmatrix} = \begin{bmatrix} -R_1 & 0 \\ 1 & 0 \\ 0 & -1/R_2 \end{bmatrix}\begin{bmatrix} i_L \\ v_C \end{bmatrix} + \begin{bmatrix} R_1 & 0 \\ 0 & 0 \\ 0 & 1/R_2 \end{bmatrix}\begin{bmatrix} i_0 \\ v_0 \end{bmatrix}$$

i.e., $$\begin{bmatrix} v_{R_1} \\ i_L \\ i \end{bmatrix} = [\mathbf{C}]\begin{bmatrix} i_L \\ v_C \end{bmatrix} + [\mathbf{B}]\begin{bmatrix} i_0 \\ v_0 \end{bmatrix}.$$

This equation is the output equation where both matrices $[C]$ and $[D]$ are (3×2) then there are three outputs ($r = 3$) and two states ($n = 2$).

EXAMPLE E.18 *For the network shown in Fig. E-E.21 write the state and output equations. Obtain A, B, C and D matrices.*

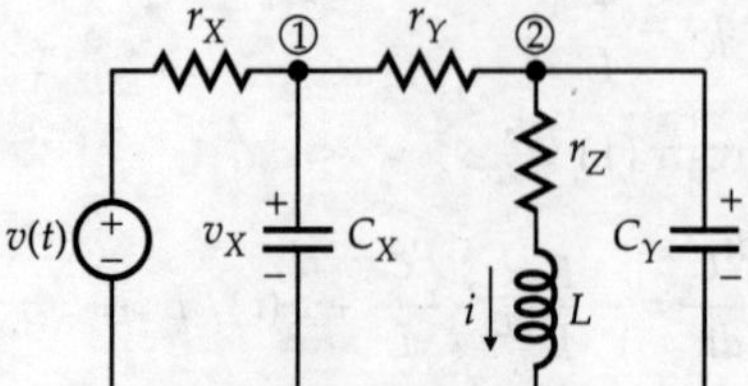

Fig. E-E.21

Solution. Let us mark the nodes in Fig. E-E.21 as (1) and (2).

At node (1),

$$C_X \frac{dv_X}{dt} = \frac{v - v_X}{r_X} + \frac{v_Y - v_X}{r_Y}$$

or
$$\frac{dv_X}{dt} = -\frac{1}{C_X}\left(\frac{1}{r_X} + \frac{1}{r_Y}\right) v_X + \frac{1}{C_X\, r_Y} + \frac{1}{C_X\, r_X} . v \quad ...(1)$$

At node (2)

$$C_Y \frac{dv_Y}{dt} = \frac{v_X - v_Y}{r_Y} - i$$

or
$$\frac{dv_Y}{dt} = \frac{1}{C_Y\, r_Y} v_X - \frac{1}{C_Y\, r_Y} v_Y - \frac{1}{C_Y} i \quad ...(2)$$

Also at the inductance,

$$L\frac{di}{dt} = v_Y - r_Z\, i$$

or
$$\frac{di}{dt} = \frac{1}{L} . v_Y - \frac{r_Z}{L} . i \quad ...(3)$$

∴ The state equation can be written from (1), (2) and (3) as

$$\begin{bmatrix} \frac{dv_X}{dt} \\ \frac{dv_Y}{dt} \\ \frac{di}{dt} \end{bmatrix} = \begin{bmatrix} -\frac{1}{C_X}\left(\frac{1}{r_X} + \frac{1}{r_Y}\right) & \frac{1}{C_X\, r_Y} & 0 \\ \frac{1}{C_Y\, r_Y} & -\frac{1}{C_Y\, r_Y} & -\frac{1}{C_Y} \\ 0 & \frac{1}{L} & -\frac{r_Z}{L} \end{bmatrix} \begin{bmatrix} v_X \\ v_Y \\ i \end{bmatrix} + \begin{bmatrix} \frac{1}{C_X\, r_X} \\ 0 \\ 0 \end{bmatrix} v$$

The output equation is given by

$$y = [v_Y] = [0\ 1\ 0] \begin{bmatrix} v_X \\ v_Y \\ i \end{bmatrix} + [0]\, v$$

The *A, B, C* and *D* matrices are given as

$$[A] = \begin{bmatrix} -\frac{1}{C_X}\left(\frac{1}{r_X} + \frac{1}{r_Y}\right) & \frac{1}{C_X\, r_Y} & 0 \\ \frac{1}{C_Y\, r_Y} & -\frac{1}{C_Y\, r_Y} & -\frac{1}{C_Y} \\ 0 & \frac{1}{L} & -\frac{r_Z}{L} \end{bmatrix};$$

$$[B] = \begin{bmatrix} 1/C_X\, r_X \\ 0 \\ 0 \end{bmatrix};$$

$$[C] = [0\ 1\ 0]; \quad [D] = [0].$$

Example E.19 *A system is described by* $\frac{d^3 y(t)}{dt^3} = u(t)$, *where,* $y(t)$ *is the observed output and* $u(t)$ *the input.*

Find the state and output equations of the system. Also find the state transition matrix.

Solution. Let $x_1(t) = y(t)$ giving

$$\frac{dx_1(t)}{dt} = x_2(t) \text{(say)}$$

and
$$\frac{dx_2(t)}{dt} = x_3(t), \text{(say)};$$

also we can write

$$\frac{dx_3(t)}{dt} = u(t)$$

since $\frac{d^3 y(t)}{dt^3} = u(t)$ can be written as

$$\frac{dx_3(t)}{dt} = u(t)$$

Thus the state equation can be written as

$$\begin{bmatrix} x_1(t) \\ x_2(t) \\ x_3(t) \end{bmatrix} = \begin{bmatrix} 0 & 1 & 0 \\ 0 & 0 & 1 \\ 0 & 0 & 0 \end{bmatrix} \begin{bmatrix} x_1(t) \\ x_2(t) \\ x_3(t) \end{bmatrix} + \begin{bmatrix} 0 \\ 0 \\ 1 \end{bmatrix} u(t)$$

while the output equation is

$$y(t) = [1\ 0\ 0] \begin{bmatrix} x_1(t) \\ x_2(t) \\ x_3(t) \end{bmatrix} + [0]\, u(t)$$

The state transition matrix is given by

$$\phi(s) = [(sI - A)]^{-1}$$

Here

$$(sI - A) = \begin{bmatrix} s & 0 & 0 \\ 0 & s & 0 \\ 0 & 0 & s \end{bmatrix} - \begin{bmatrix} 0 & 1 & 0 \\ 0 & 0 & 1 \\ 0 & 0 & 0 \end{bmatrix} = \begin{bmatrix} s & -1 & 0 \\ 0 & 0 & -1 \\ 0 & 0 & s \end{bmatrix}$$

$$\therefore \quad \phi(s) = [(sI - A)]^{-1} = \begin{bmatrix} 1/s & 1/s^2 & 1/s^3 \\ 0 & 1/s & 1/s^2 \\ 0 & 0 & 1/s \end{bmatrix}$$

In time domain the state transition matrix is $£^{-1}\,[(sI - A)]^{-1}$

$$= £^{-1} \begin{bmatrix} 1/s & 1/s^2 & 1/s^3 \\ 0 & 1/s & 1/s^2 \\ 0 & 0 & 1/s \end{bmatrix}$$

$$= \begin{bmatrix} \mathbf{1} & \mathbf{t} & \dfrac{\mathbf{t^2}}{\mathbf{2}} \\ \mathbf{0} & \mathbf{1} & \mathbf{t} \\ \mathbf{0} & \mathbf{0} & \mathbf{1} \end{bmatrix} \mathbf{u(t)}.$$

EXAMPLE E.20 *Draw the tree of the network shown in Fig. E-E.22 and write the state equations.*

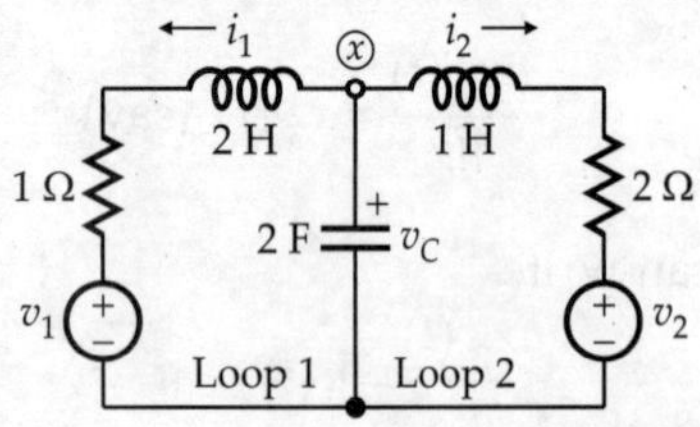

Fig. E-E.22

SOLUTION. The tree is drawn in Fig. E-E.23.

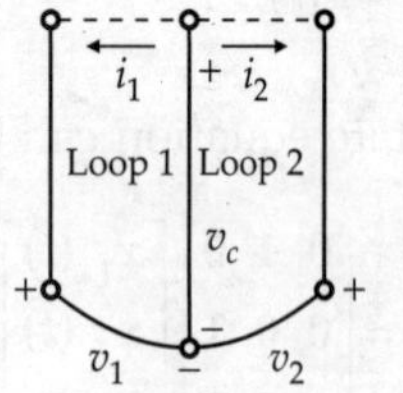

Fig. E-E.23

In loop 1 KVL yields

$$2\frac{di_1}{dt} + 1 \times i_1 + v_1 - v_C = 0$$

or
$$\frac{di_1}{dt} = -0.5 \times i_1 + 0 \times i_2 + 0.5\,v_C - 0.5 \times v_1 \quad ...(1)$$

In loop 2, KVL yields

$$1 \times \frac{di_2}{dt} + 2 \times i_2 + v_2 - v_C = 0$$

or
$$\frac{di_2}{dt} = 0 \times i_1 - 2 \times i_2 + v_C - v_2 \quad ...(2)$$

Also, at node (x), we can write

$$2 \times \frac{dv_C}{dt} + i_1 + i_2 = 0$$

or
$$\frac{dv_C}{dt} = -0.5 \times i_1 - 0.5 \times i_2 + 0 \times v_C \quad ...(3)$$

From (1), (2) and (3), the state equation can be written as

$$\begin{bmatrix} \dfrac{di_1}{dt} \\ \dfrac{di_2}{dt} \\ \dfrac{dv_C}{dt} \end{bmatrix} = \begin{bmatrix} -0.5 & 0 & 0.5 \\ 0 & -2 & 1 \\ -0.5 & -0.5 & 0 \end{bmatrix} \begin{bmatrix} i_1 \\ i_2 \\ v_C \end{bmatrix} + \begin{bmatrix} -0.5\,v_1 \\ -v_2 \\ 0 \end{bmatrix}$$

or
$$\begin{bmatrix} \dot{i}_1 \\ \dot{i}_2 \\ \dot{v}_C \end{bmatrix} = \begin{bmatrix} \mathbf{-0.5} & \mathbf{0} & \mathbf{0.5} \\ \mathbf{0} & \mathbf{-2} & \mathbf{1} \\ \mathbf{-0.5} & \mathbf{-0.5} & \mathbf{0} \end{bmatrix} \begin{bmatrix} \mathbf{i_1} \\ \mathbf{i_2} \\ \mathbf{v_C} \end{bmatrix} + \begin{bmatrix} \mathbf{-0.5\,v_1} \\ \mathbf{-v_2} \\ \mathbf{0} \end{bmatrix}.$$

EXAMPLE E.21 *Fig. E-E.24 represents an electrical network with time varying capacitance and inductance. Obtain the state equation.*

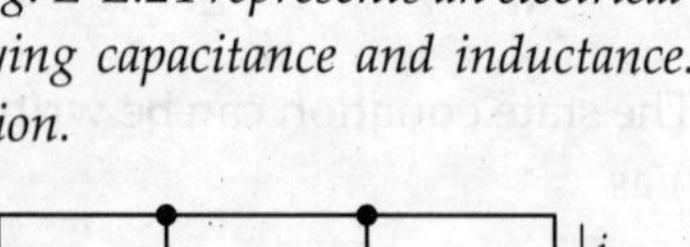

[C(t) = 2 + 0.5 sin 2t, L(t) = 4 + sin 2t]

Fig. E-E.24

SOLUTION. We can write for the given network

$$i = \frac{v_C}{R} + i_C + i_L \quad ...(1)$$

[where v_C is the voltage across the capacitor and i_L the current through the inductor]

However, $q_C = C\,v_C\,(t)$ giving $\dot{q}_C = i_C$

and $\phi_L = L\,i\,(t)$ giving $\dot{\phi}_L = v_L$;

Thus from (1) we can write

$$\dot{q}_C = -\frac{1}{RC(t)}\,q_C - \frac{1}{L(t)}\,\phi_L + i(t) \quad ...(2)$$

However, $v_C = v_L$ [v_L is the voltage drop across L]

But because $\dot{\phi}_L = v_L$ and $q_C = C v_C$,

$$\frac{1}{C(t)} q_C = \dot{\phi}_L \quad \text{...(3)}$$

Let us choose $\phi_L \equiv x_1$ and $q_C \equiv x_2$

∴ We can write equations (2) and (3) as

$$\dot{x}_1 = \frac{1}{C(t)} x_2 \quad \text{...(4)}$$

and
$$\dot{x}_2 = -\frac{1}{RC(t)} x_2 - \frac{1}{L(t)} x_1 + i(t) \quad \text{...(5)}$$

The state equation is obtained from (4) and (5) as

$$\begin{bmatrix} \dot{x}_1 \\ \dot{x}_2 \end{bmatrix} = \begin{bmatrix} 0 & \frac{1}{C(t)} \\ -\frac{1}{L(t)} & -\frac{1}{RC(t)} \end{bmatrix} \begin{bmatrix} x_1 \\ x_2 \end{bmatrix} + \begin{bmatrix} 0 \\ 1 \end{bmatrix} i(t)$$

or
$$\begin{bmatrix} \dot{x}_1 \\ \dot{x}_2 \end{bmatrix} = \begin{bmatrix} 0 & \frac{1}{2+0.5 \sin 2t} \\ -\frac{1}{4+\sin 2t} & -\frac{1}{(2+0.5 \sin 2t)5} \end{bmatrix} \begin{bmatrix} x_1 \\ x_2 \end{bmatrix} + \begin{bmatrix} 0 \\ 1 \end{bmatrix} i(t).$$

EXAMPLE E.22 *The state equation of a linear time invariant system is given by*

$$\begin{bmatrix} \dot{x}_1(t) \\ \dot{x}_2(t) \\ \dot{x}_3(x) \end{bmatrix} = \begin{bmatrix} 0 & 1 \\ -1 & -2 \end{bmatrix} \begin{bmatrix} x_1(t) \\ x_2(t) \end{bmatrix} + \begin{bmatrix} 0 \\ 1 \end{bmatrix} r(t)$$

(i) *Find the state transition matrix $\phi(t)$ and the characteristic equation of the system.*

(ii) *Determine the state vector $x(t)$ for $t \geq 0$ when $r(t) = u(t)$. Assume value of the initial state to be zero.*

SOLUTION. The state transition matrix is $(sI - A)^{-1}$.

Here,
$$(sI - A) = \begin{bmatrix} s & 0 \\ 0 & s \end{bmatrix} - \begin{bmatrix} 0 & 1 \\ -1 & -2 \end{bmatrix}$$

$$= \begin{bmatrix} s & -1 \\ 1 & s+2 \end{bmatrix}$$

∴
$$\phi(s) = (sI - A)^{-1}$$

$$= \frac{1}{P(s)} \text{adj}[sI - A]$$

where $P(s) = |(sI - A)| = (s^2 + 2s + 2) = (s+1)^2$

∴
$$\phi(s) = \frac{1}{(s+1)^2} \begin{bmatrix} s+2 & -1 \\ 1 & s \end{bmatrix}^{\bar{1}}$$

$$= \frac{1}{(s+1)^2} \begin{bmatrix} s+2 & 1 \\ -1 & s \end{bmatrix}$$

Expanding in partial fraction

$$\frac{s+2}{(s+1)^2} = \frac{K_1}{(s+1)^2} + \frac{K_2}{(s+1)}$$

when $K_1 = (s+2)\big|_{s=-1} = 1$; $K_2 = \frac{d}{ds}(s+2) = 1$

∴
$$\frac{s}{(s+1)^2} = \frac{1}{(s+1)^2} + \frac{1}{s+1};$$

Similarly,
$$\frac{s}{(s+1)^2} = \frac{-1}{(s+1)^2} + \frac{1}{s+1}$$

∴
$$\phi(s) = \begin{bmatrix} \frac{1}{(s+1)^2} + \frac{1}{s+1} & \frac{1}{(s+1)^2} \\ -\frac{1}{(s+1)^2} & -\frac{1}{(s+1)^2} + \frac{1}{(s+1)} \end{bmatrix}$$

In time domain

$$\phi(t) = \begin{bmatrix} te^{-t} + e^{t} & te^{-1} \\ -te^{-t} & -te^{-t} + e^{-t} \end{bmatrix} u(t)$$

The complete state vector can be obtained from

$$[X(s)] = [\phi(s)][x(0-)] + [\phi(s)][B][u(s)]$$

Here $x(0) = \begin{bmatrix} 0 \\ 0 \end{bmatrix}$, given

∴
$$[X(s)] = [(sI - A)^{-1}][B][u(s)]$$

$$= \frac{1}{(s+1)^2} \begin{bmatrix} s+2 & 1 \\ -1 & s \end{bmatrix} \begin{bmatrix} 0 \\ 1 \end{bmatrix} \cdot \frac{1}{s}$$

$$= \frac{1}{(s+1)^2} \begin{bmatrix} 1 \\ s \end{bmatrix} \frac{1}{s} = \begin{bmatrix} \frac{1}{s(s+1)^2} \\ \frac{1}{(s+1)^2} \end{bmatrix}$$

But $\quad \dfrac{1}{s(s+1)^2} = \dfrac{K_3}{s} + \dfrac{K_4}{(s+1)^2} + \dfrac{K_5}{s+1}$

when, $\quad K_3 = \dfrac{1}{(s+1)^2}\bigg|_{s=0} = 1;$

$$K_4 = \frac{1}{s}\bigg|_{s=-1} = -1$$

$$K_5 = \frac{d}{ds}\left[\frac{1}{s}\right]\bigg|_{s=1} = -\frac{1}{s^2}\bigg|_{s=-1} = -1$$

$$\therefore \quad \frac{1}{s(s+1)^2} = \frac{1}{s} - \frac{1}{(s+1)^2} - \frac{1}{s+1}.$$

$\therefore$ The state vector $x(t)$ is given by

$$x(t) = £^{-1}\,[X(s)]$$

$$= £^{-1}\begin{bmatrix} \dfrac{1}{s(s+1)^2} \\ \dfrac{1}{(s+1)^2} \end{bmatrix} = \begin{bmatrix} 1 - te^{-1} - e^{-t} \\ te^{-t} \end{bmatrix} u(t)$$

E.13 CONCLUSION

The state variable approach enables us to describe the nth order system by a set of n-first order simultaneous differential equations. This method of analysis is advantageous because the solution of first order differential equation is comparatively easier, particularly, using digital methods. The stability, controllability and observability of the network can also be determined easily. The state variable analysis is also applicable to time invariant and linear systems as well as time varying and non-linear systems.

EXERCISES

1. What do you mean by the 'state' ? What are state variables ? How would you form state equation ? What is output equation ?

2. Write the state equation of the network shown in Fig. E_P.1 if $R = 1\Omega$, $L = 0.2$ H and $\alpha = 0.5$.

   [Hint. See Art E.7]

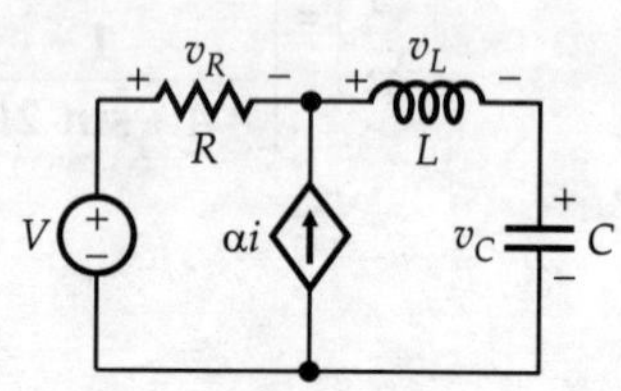

Fig. E_P.1

3. What is state transition matrix ? How will you find the zero state response of a state vector using the state transition matrix ?

4. Write the state equation for the series RC network shown in Fig. E-P.2.

   [Hint. $\quad v(t) = R\,i(t) + v_C(t)$

   Since $\quad i(t) = i_C(t) = C\dfrac{dv_C}{dt}$,

   We can write, $\quad v(t) = RC\dfrac{dv_C}{dt} + v_C(t)$

   i.e., $\quad \dfrac{dv_C}{dt} = \dfrac{1}{RC}v(t) - \dfrac{1}{RC}v_C(t)$

   i.e., $\quad \dot{v}_C = \dfrac{1}{RC}v(t) - \dfrac{1}{RC}v_C(t)]$

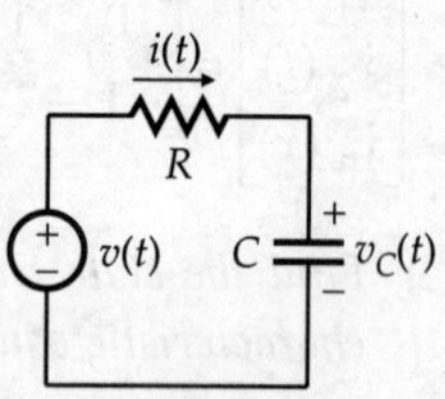

Fig. E-P.2

5. Using state variable analysis, obtain the complete response of the state vector.

6. Obtain the state equation and output equation for the circuit shown in Fig. E-P.3. $[R = 1\Omega\,;\, C = 1\,\text{F}\,;\, L = 1\,\text{H}]$

   [Hint. See Ex. E.16]

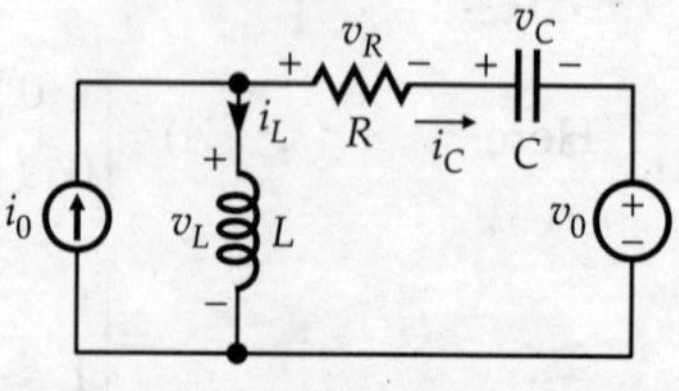

Fig. E-P.3

7. Obtain the state equation for the circuit shown in Fig. E-P.4.

[**Hint.** $3\frac{di_L}{dt} = -v_C + 10$;

$$2\frac{dv_C}{dt} = i_C + \frac{-v_C + 10}{4} - 5$$

∴ State equation is given by

$$\begin{bmatrix} \dot{i}_L \\ \dot{v}_C \end{bmatrix} = \begin{bmatrix} 0 & -1/3 \\ 1/2 & -1/8 \end{bmatrix} \begin{bmatrix} i_L \\ v_C \end{bmatrix} + \begin{bmatrix} 1/3 & 0 \\ 1/8 & -1/2 \end{bmatrix} \begin{bmatrix} 10 \\ 5 \end{bmatrix}$$

or $[\dot{y}] = [A][y] + [B][u]$

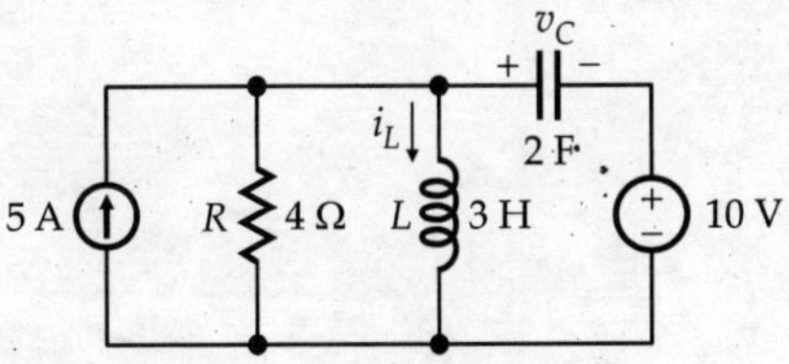

Fig. E-P.4

8. Draw the tree of the network shown in Fig. E-P.5 and find the state equation.

[**Hint.** The tree is drawn in Fig. E-P.5. From the concept of the graph theory it is evident that the two capacitors and the voltage source cannot be placed in a same tree. Using KVL,

$$0.2\frac{di}{dt} - v + 2i = 0 \quad \text{...(1)}$$

Using KCL at the node of interconnection of the capacitors,

$$0.3\frac{dv}{dt} + i - 0.2\frac{d}{dt}(v_s - v) - \frac{v_s - v}{3} = 0$$

However, $\dot{v}_s = -2v_s$

$$\therefore \quad \frac{dv}{dt} = -2i - \frac{2}{3}v - \frac{2}{15}v_s \quad \text{...(2)}$$

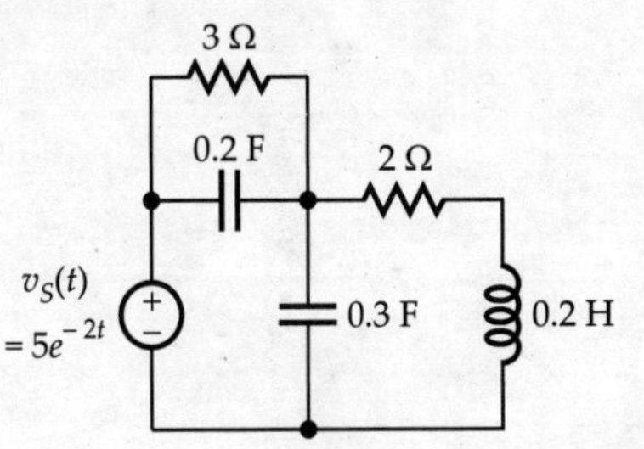

Fig. E-P.5

The state equation is formed from (1) and (2), $\begin{bmatrix} \dot{i} \\ \dot{v} \end{bmatrix} = \begin{bmatrix} -10 & 5 \\ -2 & -2/3 \end{bmatrix} \begin{bmatrix} i \\ v \end{bmatrix} + \begin{bmatrix} 0 \\ -2v_s/15 \end{bmatrix}$

INDEX

A

B

C

D

E

F

T

U

V

W

Y

Z